EDITED BY E. F. BOZMAN, M.A. (Cantab.)

EVERYMAN'S ENCYCLO-PAEDIA

**FIFTH EDITION
IN TWELVE VOLUMES**

VOLUME 8

LÖBAU–
MYXOMYCETES

LONDON: J. M. DENT & SONS LTD

PUBLISHER'S NOTE

The names of articles, which are printed first in bold type, have been abbreviated within each article itself to the initial letter or letters. For other abbreviations used throughout the work see ABBREVIATIONS; ABBREVIATIONS IN MUSIC; ELEMENTS; METROLOGY; PHYSICAL UNITS.

Photographs are grouped under related headings with cross references from individual articles where relevant.

An appendix will be found at the end of volume 12 which discusses the alphabetical arrangement used in the encyclopaedia.

L

Löbau, Ger. tn in the dist of Dresden (q.v.), 40 m. E. of Dresden. It has textile and sugar industries and manufs. pianos. Pop. 16,800.

Lobby, term applied to the entrance hall or corridor outside a legislative chamber. As a verb it means to accost members of a legislature in the lobby with a view to influencing their votes or (in the case of journalists) to obtain news.

L'Obel, Matthias de (*c.* 1538–1616), Fr. botanist, *b.* Lille, who gives his name to the lobelia genus. He was botanist and physician to James I and Lord Zouche placed him in charge of his garden at Hackney, N. London.

Lobelia, large and varied genus of annuals and perennials, some hardy, some tender, family Campanulaceae. *L. cardinalis,* or cardinal flower, is a tall perennial, nearly hardy, bearing flowers of a rich 'cardinal' crimson during the late summer and early autumn. *L. inflata,* or Indian tobacco, yields lobeline, an alkaloid used as an antidote to overdoses of narcotic drugs. *L. erinus,* a S. African species, has given rise to a large number of dwarf bedding varieties of various shades of blue, white and maroon. *L. fulgens,* like *L. cardinalis,* is a N. Amer. species, growing from 1 to 3 ft tall, flowering in May. Its varieties include white, rose, violet and blue colours. *L. syphilitica* is hardy and has given rise to numerous blue and white hybrids. Dwarf L.s thrive best in a light soil, but the taller species need abundant plant food and frequent watering.

Lobengula (1833–94) became king of the Matabele (q.v.) in 1870 on the death of his father and made Bulawayo (q.v.) his cap. In 1888 he signed a treaty with England admitting her suzerainty, but on the Brit. S. Africa Co. receiving permission to settle in Mashonaland in 1892, L. made repeated raids against the British and in 1893 his cap. was taken and he was forced to flee, dying not long afterwards.

Lobito Bay, fine harbour on W. coast of Africa, ter. of Benguela Railway. Pop.: Whites, 15,000; Africans, 64,600 (1960).

Lobo, Jeronimo (1593–1678), Jesuit missionary, *b.* Lisbon. In 1621 he went to India, but in 1625 left for Abyssinia, where he began his missionary labours, being superintendent of missions in Tigre for nearly 10 years. The Abbe Legrand pub. a Fr. trans. of L.'s Portuguese MS. account of his travels in Abyssinia, trans. again into English in an abridged form by Dr. Johnson.

Lobola, Nguni (q.v.) word for bridewealth (q.v.), the payment of cattle or other wealth that is transferred at marriage from the groom's family to that of the bride and which legitimises the union.

Lobositz, *see* LOVOSICE.

Lobsters are aquatic crustaceans of the macrurous or long-tailed type of the order Decapoda. Their long tail distinguishes them clearly from crabs, in which the segments of the tail are short and flattened and expanded laterally. The common lobster (*Homarus vulgaris*) frequents rocky coasts, varying slightly according to locality. The general colour is a dull pale reddish-yellow, spotted with bluish-black. The female carries the eggs attached to the false abdominal swimming feet, until they hatch into larvae, which lead an active existence in the open water and are much preyed upon. When mature the average weight of the common lobster is from 8 to 12 lb. Enormous catches of L. are made annually from Mar. to Aug., but the supply is augmented by imports of the large Amer. lobster and of the elegant Norway lobster. The common spiny lobster is of very anct origin and is found on the W. coast of England, often being taken in crab pots. The shell or carapace is thickly covered with spines of various sizes and a large spine occurs over each eye. It has the power of producing a loud noise by rubbing the antennae against the carapace. The size of L. is regulated by restrictions as to a minimum at Billingsgate and other fish markets, but in spite of the prolificity of the females the numbers are believed to be decreasing.

LOBSTER

Local Authorities, Audit of Accounts of, *see* LOCAL GOVERNMENT FINANCE.

Local Authorities, Officers and Employees of. Over 1 million people (including teachers, transport staff and building workers) are employed in local gov. Certain appointments, for instance, the clerk, the treasurer and the medical officer of health, are compulsory to almost all authorities and it has been provided that each London bor. and the City of London must have a bor. (or city) architect by not later than 1968. Apart from these appointments, councils are free to employ such staff as they think necessary. Choice of personnel is left, to a great extent, to the individual council; a few appointments of chief officers are subject to central confirmation, but the choice of the council is nearly always accepted. However, at the request of the Association of Municipal Corporations, the Co. Councils Association, the Rural and the Urb. Dist Councils Associations, a committee was appointed by the Minister of Housing and Local Gov. in Mar. 1964 to consider the existing methods of recruiting local gov. officers, their opportunities and their relationship to committees and councils, and what changes might help local authorities to get the best possible service and help their officers to give it.

It is against the law to appoint council members to the staff, or ex-council members for a period of at least 12 months after they have ceased to hold office; and the standing orders of local authorities usually provide that canvassing for appointment is forbidden and will lead to the immediate disqualification of the candidate. It is also usual to require candidates to disclose any relationship that may exist between themselves and any council member or senior officer.

Employees are of 3 kinds: (1) heads of depts; (2) a variety of subordinate officers employed in a professional, technical or clerical capacity; and (3) a large number of manual workers, who are employed to do the actual physical work for which the council may be responsible, such as road construction and maintenance, building, refuse collection and disposal and footpath clearing.

Most of the duties of heads of depts are of a managerial and administrative kind. Their functions may be clearly set out on approved lists drawn up by the employing council, and some of their duties can be discharged from day to day without any special reference to the committee or the council. The dividing line between questions of administration and management and those involving policy decisions is, however, not always easily drawn. Close and frequent contact between heads of depts and committees is necessary, both to give the officers the opportunity of submitting particular items for direction and to allow committee members to take advantage of the expert experience of the officer concerned. The councils (or committees) are the sole arbiters of policy, but it often falls to the head of a dept to suggest some adjustment to a proposed scheme or to initiate some project which his daily work leads him to believe should be put through for the general good.

Formal contacts between committee members and heads of depts are maintained by regular meetings, at which the officers submit their periodical reports. Urgent matters which may arise between meetings are generally dealt with in informal discussions between the head of a dept and the chairman of the committee, who may act as its representative on occasions of this kind.

Method of Appointment. As a rule, senior staff appointments are made at the instance of the committee or committees which are particularly concerned. The post may be filled either by the promotion or transfer of one of the existing staff, or after public advertisement in newspapers or jours. circulating primarily among persons who may be expected to possess the necessary qualifications for the job. When answers to the advertisements have been received, it is a common practice to appoint a group of committee members to interview the candidates and to make a selection which may later have to be confirmed by the council as a whole. Junior appointments are normally made by heads of depts, who are also responsible for engaging manual workers. Committees are informed of appointments and engagements of this kind, which are always made in conformity with an estab. laid down by the council.

Conditions of Employment. Rates of pay and conditions of service for local authority staff are within the jurisdiction of the employing council, except in the rare cases where the proposed salary of an officer requires ministerial approval.

Special arrangements are made for the staff of the G.L.C., whilst in par. councils pay and conditions are solely a matter of agreement between council and employee; elsewhere they are governed by recommendations of national joint councils consisting of representatives of the employers' side appointed by the local authority associations and representatives of the employees' side appointed by the trade unions and other officers' associations. The 2 largest of the councils are: the National Joint Council for Local Authorities' Administrative, Professional, Technical and Clerical Services; and the Industrial National Joint Council for Local Authorities' Non-trading Services (Manual Workers). For the great majority of local gov. officers the first-mentioned council is also concerned with such matters as the maintenance of agreed standards of entry to the service and the conduct of recognised qualifying examinations for promotion. Conditions of service and salary scales of chief officers are determined by separate joint negotiating committees. Contributory pension schemes for the superannuation of their permanent whole-time officers are made by all local authorities.

Movement of officers between one council and another occurs frequently. An officer in local gov. service does not have to wait until his superior officer is due to retire for change or promotion. As occasion offers he may apply for an improved position under any local authority in the country and is able to transfer to his new employment any accrued superannuation rights.

Ethical Code. All local gov. officers, of whatever standing, are expected to regulate their behaviour according to a code of ethics drawn up by the National Joint Council for Local Authorities' Administrative, Professional, Technical and Clerical Services. This code lays particular stress on the fact that the local gov. officer, as a public servant, 'must not only be honest in fact, but must be beyond the reach of suspicion of dishonesty', and states that 'he is not to subordinate his duty to his private interests, or to put himself in a position where his duty and private interests conflict. He should not make use of his official position to further those interests, but neither is he so to order his private affairs as to allow the suspicion to arise that a trust has been abused or a confidence betrayed'.

Local Debts, *see* PUBLIC DEBT.

Local Defence Volunteers, *see* HOME GUARD.

Local Education Authority (L.E.A.), *see* EDUCATION.

Local Government, that part of the administration of a state or nation which deals mainly with such matters as concern the inhab. of a particular place or dist, including those functions which the central gov. consider it desirable to be so administered. The bodies entrusted with these matters are known as local authorities and are, in the main, elective. A local authority means any body of persons empowered to spend money derived from the proceeds of a local rate. The term has a special meaning in particular Acts of Parliament. The Local Government Act, 1933, defines it as the council of a co., co. bor., co. dist or rural par. A par. meeting is not, therefore, a local authority for purposes of that Act. A co. dist includes a non-co. bor., an urb. dist or a rural dist.

There is no strict line of demarcation between the functions of the central and L. G.s so far as home affairs are concerned. Parliament decides the scope of L. G. and the local authorities' powers are defined by statute.

History. L. G. has its roots deep in the past. The present-day structure corresponds roughly with that of Saxon days when the freemen assembled in their moots—shire, hundred and township—similar to the co., dist and par. of today. The *burh,* or large fort. tn, may be compared with the co. bor. of our time. The shire moot maintained local usages and by-laws and, through the tythingman and frankpledge, kept the peace.

The sheriff (q.v.) became so powerful that Edward III appointed Justices in Eyre to tour the provs. to administer justice and Henry VIII appointed lord lieutenants to be the king's representative in the co. (*see* LORD-LIEUTENANT). At the Norman Conquest the Saxon moots were abolished and power concentrated in the lord of the manor and the co. court or court leet. The eccles. vestry meeting survived and constituted a basis for the administration of the growing functions of L. G., police, poor relief, highways, sanitation and rating. (*See* ABUTTALS; ALDERMAN; BEADLE; FREEMAN; MAYOR; MUNICIPALITY; TOWNSHIP). To obtain freedom from the lord of the manor and his courts, application was made to the king, frequently by a merchants' guild, for a charter of incorporation creating part of the manor a bor. free from the jurisdiction of the lord of the manor and with its own bailiffs and courts (*see* BAILIFF; BOROUGH; BURGESS; BY-LAW; CATCHPOLL; CHARTERS; CORPORATION).

Owing to the dissolution of the monasteries in 1536, provision had to be made for certain functions to be maintained locally—the care of pauper children, the sick, the aged, the destitute and vagrants. Thus the poor law developed at first on a parochial basis and the laws promulgated were consolidated in the Poor Relief Act, 1601. Under the Highway Act, 1555, the vestry elected waywardens who were the precursors of our modern surveyors of highways. Similarly the vestries became the unit for the administration of local matters, and the justices in their quarter sessions became burdened with numerous functions of L. G. over wider areas—roads, bridges, explosives, diseases of animals, weights and measures, fisheries and police.

Until the 19th cent. the growth of L. G. was slow and haphazard in its development. The industrial revolution altered the entire basis of the economic and social structure of the country and created many problems of L. G. The vastly growing pop. gathered around the newly developing industrial tns. Houses were built without any proper regard to public health requirements and existing houses became grossly overcrowded. Devastating infectious diseases carried off large numbers of the pop. in early life (*see* HOUSING). The bor. councils were unfit to deal with the problems created, and so public-spirited individuals obtained powers from Parliament to carry out the necessary services. Boards of guardians, highway boards, burial boards, local boards of health and many others were formed. Under this *ad hoc* system, L. G. became a chaos of areas, authorities and rates; and it became evident that more effective administration of these new bodies was needed. With the changes in parl. gov. inaugurated by the Reform Act, 1832, an era of reform in local administration followed. The Act of 1832 was followed closely by 2 royal commissions, one to inquire into the abuses of the poor law and the other into the administration of the notoriously corrupt bors. The former resulted in the passing of the Poor Law Amendment Act, 1834, which abolished the former parochial system and set up boards of guardians for unions of pars. The Municipal Corporations Act, 1835, brought about a measure of reform in the bors. Particularly, every bor. then was required to maintain a police force. A number of statutes followed to amalgamate and reform other bodies and to simplify 'this adhoccery', as Bentham called the former chaotic conditions. The first general Public Health Act, 1848, set up the General Board of Health as a controlling and co-ordinating central authority. In 1871 it became the Local Gov. Board and in 1919 the Ministry of Health, but in 1951 the work was divided between the Ministry of Health and the new Ministry of Housing and L. G.

The Local Government Act, 1888, transferred from the justices their L. G. functions to elected co. councils and newly created co. bors. The Local Government Act, 1894, co-ordinated the work of L. G. within the administrative cos. by distributing the work in urb. areas between bor. and urb. dist councils. In the rural areas an attempt was made to restore some of their anct glory to the pars. by the creation of par. councils and meetings, and so the Act is sometimes referred to as the 'peasants' charter'. In 1923 a Royal Commission on L. G. under the chairmanship of Lord Onslow was appointed. It arose out of the frequency of the changes brought about by the creation of new co. bors. and the enlargement of existing co. bors. It was recommended that new co. bors. should be created only by a private bill submitted to Parliament; that extensións should be similarly treated if there was any opposition; and that co. councils should regularly review generally the existing areas of co. dists and pars. *See* AREAS OF LOCAL GOVERNMENT.

In the early years of the 20th cent. a number of acts were passed empowering local authorities to provide school meals and a school medical service, to attend to maternity and child welfare and the care of the blind and mental deficients, and to make provision for dist hospitals. The Local Government Act, 1929, abolished the boards of guardians and transferred their poor law functions to the new public assistance authorities—the councils of cos. and co. bors. This, however, was a short-lived reform, for the National Assistance Act, 1948, ended the poor law and set up the National Assistance Board.

There has been a considerable growth of L. G. since the middle of the last cent. Public libraries were authorised in 1845; the first Housing Act was passed in 1851; school boards were set up in 1870; trading services were inaugurated by the Tramways Act, 1870, followed by markets and gas undertakings in 1875 and electric lighting in 1882. During the present cent. there has been a marked movement to transfer many major services from the minor authorities to the control of the large authorities—the councils of cos. and co. bors. Examples of this are education and midwifery (1902), libraries (1919) and tn and country planning (1947). Many services have been nationalised. Jails were transferred to the State in 1877. The State accepted responsibility for the able-bodied unemployed in 1934; the minister of transport took over financial responsibility for certain trunk roads in 1936; the veterinary service, including the control of milk production on farms, became the responsibility of the minister of agriculture in 1947; hospitals passed to the control of regional boards in 1946; central and regional boards took over electricity in 1947; the responsibility for the valuation of property for local rates was transferred to the board of inland revenue in 1948; and gas undertakings were transferred to gas boards in 1948.

Financial assistance to L. G. from the State may be considered to have started with grants for the building of schools in 1833, although voluntary bodies were undertaking the task at that time. Aid to many other services followed. *See* LOCAL GOVERNMENT FINANCE.

Local Government Reorganisation. The decision to undertake a comprehensive review of the existing local gov. structure was first taken at the end of the Second World War when the Local Gov. Boundary Commission was set up in 1945. At that time, movements of pop. and the spread of large industrial areas seemed to call for substantial adjustments in local authority areas. There was, moreover, the question of examining claims for the creation and extension of co. bors., which had been held up during the war, and a series of reviews of co. dists had become due. However, although the Boundary Commission carried out a thorough-going review, it was then found impracticable to adopt the far-reaching changes in local authority areas, status and functions that it recommended.

After the dissolution of the Boundary Commission in 1949, the question of local gov. reform was discussed at joint conferences of the various local authority associations. Subsequent discussions between the associations and the gov. led, in 1956 and 1957, to the pub. of 2 gov. White Papers (*Areas and Status of Local Authorities in England and Wales*, Cmd 9831; and *Functions of County Councils and County District Councils in England and Wales*, Cmd 161), the main proposals of which were embodied in the Local Gov. Act, 1958.

Local Government Commissions. The 2 Local Gov. Commissions (one for England and one for Wales) estab. by the Local Gov. Act, 1958, were charged with reviewing all local gov. (outside Greater London) in their respective countries to see whether a more effective and convenient structure could be achieved. Wales was treated as a single unit for the purpose but England was divided into areas of 2 types: special review areas covering the conurbations of Tyneside, W. Yorks, SE. Lancs, Merseyside and the W. Midlands and general review areas which are mixed urb. and rural areas covering the rest of the country.

By their terms of reference, the Local Gov. Commissions were empowered to recommend the alteration of the areas of existing cos. or their abolition, the constitution of new cos. or co. bors. into non-co. bors. In the special review areas the Eng. Commission was also given power to make proposals for changes in non-co. bors. and co. dists, to recommend the creation of a new type of local authority—'a continuous co.' (in effect, an urb. co. with no co. bors. within its boundaries)—and to suggest the way in which local authority functions should be distributed between the co. and the bor. and dist councils in such an area.

The Act provided that consultations must be held with local authorities and other local interests in the area, and their views taken into account throughout the review process. It also required that the final proposals submitted to the Minister of Housing and Local Gov. and accepted by him, with or without modification, should be presented to parliament.

The Welsh Commission's final proposals (which involved a reduction in the number of cos. in Wales from 13 to 7 by a process of div. and amalgamation) were pub. in Mar. 1963. They were not, however, accepted by the

Minister as providing a fully satisfactory basis for an effective local gov. structure and except for the co. bors. of Cardiff, Swansea and Newport, where boundary adjustments are proceeding according to the commission's recommendations, the pattern which might be appropriate to the circumstances of Wales is now being reconsidered by the Secretary of State for Wales.

County Council Reviews. The commissions' reviews are to be followed by reviews of the non-co. bors., co. dists and pars. which the Local Gov. Act, 1958, requires co. councils to carry out. The co. councils, like the commissions, must consult and confer with representatives of the bor. and dist councils in their co. and must submit to the Minister a report on their review, with proposals for such changes as appear to them to be desirable in the interests of effective and convenient local gov. The minister must consider these proposals together with any representations, and, if necessary, must hold a local inquiry into objections; any orders he may decide to make to give effect to the proposals must be presented to Parliament.

By June 1965 1 co. council had completed its review and a public inquiry into objections had been held by the minister. Others had begun work on their reviews and their reports were awaited.

Functions. It has already been shown how, for the purpose of L. G., certain areas have been created. The largest is the co., but the anct co. area is not used in every case. For example, Yorks is divided into 3 'ridings', each under a separate co. council (*see* COUNTY COUNCIL). Certain areas, being those of the larger tns and cities, have been taken out of the administrative co. to form almost entirely independent areas known as co. bors. These are 'all purposes' areas having all the functions of L. G. exercised by the co. bor. council. Apart from these areas, the co. is divided into urb. and rural areas chiefly for sanitary administration. The urb. areas are either non-co. bors. or urb. dists; the rural areas are further divided into rural pars. in which par. councils and meetings have certain functions to carry out (*see* AREAS OF LOCAL GOVERNMENT). There are 62 co. councils, 83 co. bors., 318 non-co. bors., 562 urb. dists, 474 rural dists, 7407 pars. with par. councils and 3771 pars. controlled only by par. meetings.

The functions administered by local authorities are of 2 main classes: certain national services undertaken as the agent of the central gov. and services provided for each area in a communal manner for itself and, in some cases, optionally. In the first class are, for example, civil defence, police, education and the prevention of diseases. In the second are those such as housing, tn and country planning, water supply, street lighting, highways, drainage, cleansing, baths and washhouses, parks and welfare services such as the care of children, the blind and the aged. Provision must be made for the maintenance of a local legislature with power to make by-laws (q.v.). For this purpose elections must be held and this necessitates the compilation of the Register of Electors in accordance with the Representation of the People Act, 1949; this register is used for both parl. and L. G. elections. Local authorities are empowered to sue and are liable to be sued in a court of law in a corporate capacity. All but the parochial authorities may promote or oppose bills in Parliament.

Certain judicial functions are undertaken by some bors. in addition to the financial responsibility of co. councils and some bors. for the administration of justice. Some bors. have their own local court of petty sessions and certain bor. courts of quarter sessions have existed since 1360. There still survive in some bors. local civil courts of record presided over by the recorder in some cases; but in others, under special Act of Parliament, by a presiding judge appointed for the purpose, e.g. Liverpool Court of Passage. In 1956 new crown courts were set up in Liverpool and Manchester analogous to the Old Bailey in London.

The following information shows how functions are allocated to the various local authorities:

I. RURAL AREAS

1. *Parish councils*: Maintenance of par. property; administration of lay charities; safeguarding sanitary conditions; maintenance and repair of footpaths; protection of boundaries; appointment of school managers; public improvements; burials; baths and washhouses; protection of rights of way and commons; provision of allotments; utilisation of local water resources; street lighting; recreation grounds; maintaining war memorials; facilitating extra postal services; assisting harbour authorities; libraries (prior to 1919).

2. *Rural district councils*: Rating; housing; sanitary services; markets; building by-laws; baths and washhouses; parks and open spaces; cemeteries and crematoria; protection of rights of way; licensing, e.g. pawnbrokers; harbour authorities' assistance; small dwellings advances; entertainments; extra postal facilities; water supplies; ferries; light railways; civic restaurants; control of fairs; advertising amenities; esplanades and piers; application for bor. charter.

3. *County councils*: Administration of justice costs; local health services; tn and country planning; children and young persons; residential accommodation provision; co. roads and bridges; private street works; registration of electors; public education; sea fisheries; welfare of handicapped persons; inebriates' retreats and reformatories; fabric misdescription prevention; registration and licensing, e.g. motor vehicles; betting and lotteries control; small holdings; libraries; Shops Act administration; Food and Drugs Act administration; open spaces; ferries; light railways; explosives control; weights and measures inspection; control of boundaries of internal authorities; fire services; appointing coroners.

II. Urban Areas

1. *Urban district councils*:
   (a) Same as for rural dist councils
   (b) Parochial services in rural dists:
   Appointment of school managers; provision of allotments; stopping or diverting highways; street lighting; libraries (prior to 1919).
   (c) Co. services in rural areas:
   Unclassified roads control; private street works; fabric misdescription prevention; war charities registration (15,000 pop.); Shops Act administration (20,000 pop.); Food and Drugs Act administration (40,000 pop.); education divisional executive (60,000 pop.).
   (d) Urb. powers:
   Offensive trades control; passenger transport

2. *Borough councils*:
   (a) As for urb. dist councils
   (b) Appointment of mayor and aldermen; appointment of bor. auditors; licensing inebriates' retreats; inebriates' reformatories; care of anct monuments; separate commission of the peace (possibly); court of quarter sessions (possibly); fish conservancy; explosives control; appointment of coroner (10,000 pop.); weights and measures (10,000 pop.).

3. *County borough councils*:
   All purposes authority.

Meetings. Local authorities must hold at least 4 meetings each year. Except for co. councils, monthly meetings are usual. At least 3 days' notice must be given of any meeting specifying the business to be transacted. The names of those attending must be recorded. The quorum is generally one-third of the total number except for a co. council when it is one-fourth. Minutes must be kept of the proceedings of every council and committee. The press must be admitted to every meeting of the council unless precluded temporarily by resolution. The public have no right to attend meetings except in the case of a par. council, but provision is usually made for attendance by arrangement. Local authorities usually draw up Standing Orders to regulate their proceedings. Much of the work of a local authority is done in the first instance in committee. Persons not members of the local authority may be co-opted on some committees providing the statutory limit is not exceeded. This limit is generally not more than one-third the number of members of the local authority, but recent Acts have extended this limit so that it is only necessary to have a majority of members of the local authority on the committee.

Control over the administration of local authorities is exercised by the central gov. in many ways. The work of control is carried out chiefly by the minister of housing and local gov., the minister of health, the Home Office, the minister of education and the minister of transport and civil aviation. Parliament itself controls the functions of local authorities through their statutes. Local authorities have no powers except those granted by statute and any function not authorised by the general law must be sought by the promotion of a special private bill. Some of the rating powers of local

authorities are limited by law, such as the amount which may be spent out of the rates on entertainments, which is limited to a rate of 6d. in the £. Through various Acts, Parliament has given wide powers to ministers to issue rules, regulations and orders, now known generally as statutory instruments, to control the operations of local authorities. Standards of administration are maintained by inspections, such as the Home Office inspections of police forces. Inquiries are held in relation to the exercise of various powers, such as the borrowing of money, and all borrowing has to be sanctioned by the minister of housing and local government or the minister of transport. Consent of the minister is required to enable local authorities to sell land. Control is exercised over the appointment of certain officers such as the education officer and the children's officer. Certain officers cannot be dismissed without the consent of the appropriate minister, such as the clerk to the co. council and the chief constable. Parliament authorises local authorities to make local by-laws such as those for the good gov. of their areas.

Where it appears to the minister of housing and local gov. that a local authority has defaulted in the exercise of statutory duties he may take action to remedy the default; and with the approval of the House of Commons, the minister may reduce the grant of a local authority for inefficiency or unreasonable or excessive expenditure.

See also Areas of Local Government; Franchise, Local Government; Local Authorities, Audit of Accounts of; Local Authorities, Officers of; Local Government Finance.

Bibliography. J. Redlich and F. W. Hirst, *Local Government in England*, 1903; S. and Beatrice Webb, *English Local Government* (9 vols.), 1906–29, and *English Poor Law History*, 1929; Faraday on *Rating* (4th ed.), 1934; Arnold's *Municipal Corporations* (7th ed.), 1935; H. J. Laski, W. A. Robson and W. I. Jennings, *A Century of Municipal Progress*, 1835–1935, 1935; Lumley's *Public Health Acts* (11th ed., 3 vols.), 1937–40; Sir R. S. Wright and H. Hobhouse, *Local Government of England and Wales* (8th ed.), 1937; Lord Macmillan, *Local Government Law and Administration in England and Wales* (17 vols.), 1937–42; K. Gibberd, *Citizenship through the Newspaper* (for children), 1939; E. Dixon Grubb, *Citizen's Choice*, 1943; K. B. Smellie, *A History of Local Government*, 1946; G. D. H. Cole, *Local and Regional Government*, 1947; W. M. Mackenzie, *The Scottish Burghs*, 1948; R. Warner, *The Principles of Public Administration*, 1948; E. L. Hasluck, *Local Government in England* (2nd ed.), 1948; E. C. R. Hadfield and J. E. Macoll, *British Local Government*, 1949; N. Tillett, *Town Hall and Shire Hall*, 1949; C. Wilson (ed.), *Essays on Local Government*, 1949; H. Finer, *English Local Government* (4th ed.), 1950; W. O. Hart, *Introduction to the Law of Local Government and Administration* (5th ed.), 1952; J. H. Warren, *The English Local Government System*

(3rd ed.), 1953, and *Municipal Administration* (2nd ed.), 1953; W. A. Robson, *The Development of Local Government* (3rd ed.), 1954; J. J. Clarke, *History of Local Government*, 1955, *Local Government of the United Kingdom* (15th ed.), 1956, and *Outlines of Local Government* (18th ed.), 1957.

Local Government Board, *see* HEALTH, MINISTRY OF.

Local Government Finance. Local authority current expenditure is financed from 3 sources: gov. grants (about two-fifths); local rates paid by the occupiers of land and buildings (about two-fifths); and rents from municipal houses, dividends and interest (about one-fifth). Capital investment is for the most part financed by borrowing.

Government Grants. Gov. grants occasionally take the form of capital grants, paid on approval of claims made by local authorities in respect of capital expenditure on specific services—principally roads and public lighting. More often, however, they are made on an ann. basis either as specific grants, i.e. for particular services, or as non-specific grants. The latter, which include the general grant and the rate deficiency grant (made to authorities whose rateable resources in relation to pop. are below the average for their class) now account in the U.K. as a whole for about four-fifths of all current grants. Specific grants are paid as 'unit' grants (a fixed ann. payment for each unit provided) for housing and as 'percentage' grants (a percentage of approved expenditure) for a small number of services—mainly school milk and meals, the police service and the construction and upkeep of roads.

The general grant is paid by the Ministry of Housing and Local Gov. to co., co. bor. and the London bor. councils on the basis of a formula that takes account not only of the size of the pop. but of such factors as the number of children of school age, the number of young children and old people, exceptionally high and exceptionally low densities of pop. and declining pop.—all of which reflect the expenditure needs of local authorities. The total amount of grant in any year is fixed in advance, after consultation between the minister and the local authority associations.

Generally speaking, current grants by the central gov. to local authorities have risen steadily during the past decade—reflecting the big increase in local authorities' expenditure, especially the increase in expenditure on education, which is due both to expansion of the service and to increasing costs. The revenue from rates—the other main source of local authorities' income—has also risen sharply.

Loans. Loans may be raised by local authorities for financing such capital expenditure as the acquisition of land, the erection of buildings and other permanent work, either under the general powers contained in the Local Gov. Act, 1933, or under powers conferred by local Acts of Parliament. The Greater London Council promotes an ann. Bill, to get parl. approval to its proposed capital expenditure.

An authority's general power to borrow can be exercised only if loan sanction is given by the appropriate gov. dept. All applications for loan sanctions must be for a specific purpose; most of them are dealt with by the Ministry of Housing and Local Gov., although for a few purposes other gov. depts may deal with them. The Treasury is the loan-sanctioning dept for the Greater London Council. A par. council must obtain the sanction of the co. council as well as of the appropriate minister.

Local authorities may borrow in a variety of ways. They may raise long term loans from the public by issuing stock on the Stock Exchange, or by bonds, or by mortgages. They may also raise a proportion of their long-term borrowing each year from the central gov. through the Public Works Loan Board. The quota for the financial year 1965–6 was fixed at 30 per cent of long-term borrowing, or £100,000, whichever was the greater. Authorities may also borrow from the board, as lender of last resort, if they cannot raise the balance of their requirements on the market. Authorities may borrow short term (up to 1 year) from the public, but they are on notice that by 31 Mar. 1968 their temporary debt must not exceed 20 per cent of their total outstanding debt.

Loans may be repaid in instalments (yearly or half-yearly) over the period of the loan, or in a lump sum at the end of the period, with interest only being paid yearly or half-yearly.

The rates of interest on loans from the Public Works Loan Board are fixed from time to time by the Treasury. For loans within the authorities' permitted quota, interest is normally based on the rate at which the gov. itself can borrow. The rate for other loans from the board is based on current market rates for local authority borrowing.

Financial Control. Control of finance is usually exercised internally on behalf of the council by a specially appointed finance committee, whose function it is to watch the activities of the spending committees from the standpoint of the council's financial policy. Such a committee is compulsory for every co. council and the London bor. councils; and although there is no statutory obligation upon any other type of council, it is customary for all except the smallest to make the appointment.

As a rule, control is exercised by the finance committees' examination of, and, if necessary, amendments to, draft estimates drawn up annually by the executive depts in informal consultations with the finance dept and presented through the appropriate committees. In this way the various claims and proposals can be balanced and adjusted before the final estimate is presented to the council as a whole. It is left to the council to accept or reject the estimate in its final form or to eliminate any figure that it may contain.

In England and Wales the accounts of the councils of cos., London bors., the G.L.C., the urb. dists, rural dists and pars. are all, by statute, subject to audit by a dist auditor. In addition, the accounts of a few co. bor. councils and just under half the total number of non-co. bor. councils are also (by decision of the councils) fully subject to dist audit. In the remaining co. and non-co. bors. the accounts relating to children, education and local health and welfare services (in the case of co. bors.) and rating and coast protection (in the case of both co. and non-co. bors.) are also subject to dist audit.

The other accounts of these councils are audited mostly by professional auditors who must be members of one of the prin. accounting bodies in England and Wales. A small number of councils still use elective audit—a system which provides for the appointment of 3 auditors, 2 of whom are elected by the local gov. electors and 1 appointed by the mayor.

The dist auditors are appointed by the Minister of Housing and Local Gov., but they are independent officers and, in the exercise of their powers and the performance of the duties conferred on them by statute, they are not subject to his direction or control. One auditor is assigned to each of the 15 dists into which England and Wales are divided for audit purposes to be responsible for the audit of the accounts of all the appropriate authorities in that dist. The work of the dist auditors is co-ordinated by the Chief Inspector of Audit who, together with his deputy, is on the staff of the Ministry of Housing and Local Gov.

Dist auditors are required to disallow every item of account which is contrary to the law (except for items sanctioned by the Minister of Housing and Local Gov.) and to surcharge the amount of any expenditure disallowed upon the person or persons responsible for incurring or authorising it. They must also surcharge upon the person responsible any item which has not been duly brought into account, or any item of loss or deficiency caused by negligence or misconduct.

Any person aggrieved by a disallowance or surcharge, or any local gov. elector aggrieved by a decision of a dist auditor on a matter in respect of which he made an objection at audit, may appeal to the High Court. If the amount is not in excess of £500 and he so prefers, he may appeal to the Minister of Housing and Local Gov., who may state a case for the opinion of the High Court on any point of law arising from his consideration of an appeal, but whose decision, otherwise, is final.

Professional auditors and elective auditors have no powers of disallowance or surcharge.

Rates and Valuation. Rates are a form of local tax paid by the occupiers of land and buildings (except agric. buildings) in a local authority area as contributions to the cost of local services. The amount paid by each occupier depends upon the rateable value of his property and upon the rate poundage fixed by the rating authority. The rateable value is equivalent to the net ann. value of the property, which in turn is based on the rent which it might reasonably be expected to command if let from year to year, with the tenant

bearing the rates and the cost of insurance and repairs. The rate poundage, which is the number of pence in the pound which occupiers have to pay on the rateable value of their property, is calculated by dividing the total sum to be raised by the estimated yield of a penny rate in the area of the rating authority. Thus, if expenditure to be met from the rates were to be £432,000, and the yield of a penny rate were £6000, the rate poundage would be 6s.

Rates in the co. bors. are levied by the co. bor. councils; in the administrative cos. they are levied by the non-co. bor. and co. dist councils; and in Greater London by the London bor. councils (under the London Gov. Act the Minister of Housing and Local Gov. is empowered to make a scheme for reducing disparities in the rates levied in different parts of Greater London) and the Common Council of the City Corporation. In non-co. bors. and co. dists the rate includes separate items for the expenses of the bor. or dist councils and of the co. council, which issues a precept to each rating authority within the administrative co. In Greater London, likewise, a proportion of the rates is earmarked for the purpose of the G.L.C. In rural dists the rate levied in each par. takes into account precepts issued by the par. council or par. meeting.

The valuation of property is undertaken by valuation officers of the Board of Inland Revenue, who are independent of the local authorities. A valuation officer (who may deal with sev. rating areas) is responsible for preparing a new valuation list every 5 years for each rating area; and for making proposals (a) to insert new properties in the list and (b) to change entries if he thinks the original value is wrong or if the property has been altered. In the latest valuation lists (1963) rateable values for all classes of property are based on current rental values.

Anyone may ask that an assessment in the valuation list should be altered. Disputes arising out of such requests (if they have not been settled previously by agreement between the valuation officers and the individuals and bodies concerned) are referred to local valuation courts, consisting of 3 members of a local valuation panel. The panels are constituted by co. and co. bor. councils (sometimes acting jointly) under schemes approved, or made, by the Ministry of Housing and Local Gov. They are independent bodies whose members are not appointed to represent any local body or interest, but are chosen for their capacity to carry out the work. They give their services voluntarily, but their expenses are borne by the Exchequer. Appeals against the decisions of the local valuation courts are heard by the Land Tribunal, an expert body appointed by the Lord Chancellor.

The Rating (Interim Relief) Act, 1964, provides that an Exchequer grant of £5 per person may be made to rating authorities in whose areas people of 65 years and over represent more than one-tenth of the pop. The Act also empowers councils to remit part of the rates for householders whose rates have risen steeply since the latest revaluation. Charities pay half the full rate on property they occupy for charitable purposes and may be given further relief by the rating authorities, who are also empowered to reduce or remit the rates for a wide range of non-profit-making bodies. The 1966 Rates Act (*see* RATES AND RATING) made it possible for certain sections of the pop. to receive rate relief and for rates to be paid monthly.

Local Government in Northern Ireland. As in England and Wales, the machinery of L. G. in N. I. is vested, with similar powers and duties, in the councils of cos., co. bors., bors., urb. dists and rural dists with their various committees. Tn commissioners have been constituted in 3 tns (Antrim, Aughnacloy and Gilford) under the Towns Improvement (Ireland) Act, 1854. The Act may be adopted by tns with over 1500 inhab. Their powers are very limited and relate mainly to the cleansing, lighting and paving of streets, prevention of fire, safeguarding the community from dangerous buildings, regulation of traffic and licensing of hackney carriages. Later Acts authorise the estab. and regulation of markets and the formulation of housing schemes. The council of the rural dist in which the tn is situated provides other necessary services. For their own services the commissioners may strike a rate of not more than 1*s*., but they have to pay the charges to meet the cost of services provided by the rural dist council.

Finance. As in the U.K., gov. grants are made, through the minister of housing and local gov., in aid of expenditure on various local services which have something more than a local characteristic and value. Percentage grants are made in respect of health and welfare services generally. With regard to the maintenance and improvement of roads and bridges the system of state assistance resembles that in the U.K. Grants for housing purposes which commenced in 1923 were discontinued from 31 March 1937, but were reintroduced by the Housing (Northern Ireland) Act, 1944. A general exchequer contribution is paid under the provisions of the Local Government (Finance) Act (Northern Ireland), 1948, and includes relief in respect of derating. After derating and highways, the largest grant-aided service is education.

Derating has been provided by the Local Government (Rating and Finance) Act (Northern Ireland), 1929, and the Local Government (Finance) Acts (Northern Ireland), 1936 and 1944. Agric. land has been entirely derated and industrial and freight transport hereditaments partly derated.

IMPORTANT LEGISLATION AFFECTING LOCAL GOVERNMENT IN IRELAND.

1. *Drainage.* The Drainage Act, 1925, constituted for the first time the co. councils of N. Ireland as drainage authorities within their areas and enabled them to formulate schemes for carrying out drainage works and charging the whole or a portion of the cost against the owners of the lands which are benefited thereby. Further developments were made in the Drainage Acts of 1929, 1931, 1933, 1935 and 1942. The Drainage Act of 1947 transferred most of the drainage functions of co. councils to the Ministry of Agriculture, which became the drainage authority for N. Ireland, and a drainage council was set up, on which co. councils are represented. Over a period of years the cost of works carried out under the Act is to be borne equally between the exchequer and contributions from rates. The drainage of main watercourses thus became the first time a gov. responsibility.

2. *Education.* The Education Act, 1923, estab. in N. Ireland for the first time the principle of establishing local authorities as education authorities, and charged them with the duty of ensuring adequate facilities for voluntary, secondary and technical education. The Education Acts (Northern Ireland), 1947–53, provided for a reorganisation and enlargement of the statutory system of education and contains similar provisions to the English Education Act, 1944, and its amendments.

3. *Health.* The Public Health and Local Government (Administration Provisions) Act (Northern Ireland), 1946, made provision for the establishing of a co. and co. bor. health service forming an integral part of the National Health Service subsequently estab. by the Health Services Act (Northern Ireland), 1948.

4. *Housing.* Between the wars, various Acts were passed to encourage local authorities and private builders to provide houses for the working classes, and in all about 50,000 houses were built in N. Ireland from 1919 to 1944, including over 4000 cottages provided under the Labourers' Acts. Legislation since 1944 has enabled subsidy to be paid on houses built by local authorities, the N. Ireland Housing Trust (a special body estab. by the Housing Act (Northern Ireland), 1945), housing associations and private enterprise builders providing houses for owner-occupation or letting. There has also been a scheme for the benefit of the agric. community, to enable farmers to build houses for themselves and their workers, and grants are available for the reconditioning of farmhouses and approved workers' houses. In all, by Dec. 1955, 58,409 new permanent houses had been built by the various agencies since 1944. The Housing (Northern Ireland) Act, 1948, consolidated the law relating to borrowing.

5. *Elections.* The Acts dealing with local gov. elections and representation, etc., passed since the establishing of the gov. of N. Ireland have been so numerous that it is impracticable to summarise even their main effects hereunder.

The most important Acts and regulations (which have the force of an Act of Parliament) made under them are as follows: Local Government Act (Northern Ireland), 1922; Parliamentary and Local Government Elections Act (Northern Ireland), 1930; the Elections and Franchise Acts (Northern Ireland), 1946–53, which now contain most of the general statute law on the subject; and various Electoral

Regulations, 1949–55, which contain the detailed statutory provision based upon the general enactments. In particular, the 1949 regulations as amended in 1953 and 1955 govern the actual conduct of local gov. elections.

6. *Motor traffic.* In 1926 an Act was passed which transformed the whole system in regard to motor traffic in N. Ireland. The Act abolished the old 20 m.p.h. speed limit; required applicants for motor licences to make declarations of physical fitness; imposed heavier penalties for the more serious offences of (*a*) dangerous driving and (*b*) drunkenness in charge of a car; reduced the penalties for technical and minor offences; and estab. a central system and scheme of licensing and regulation of public service vehicles and their drivers and conductors. Under this Act all operators of public service vehicles have to comply with certain conditions as to fares, routes and services, and have also to keep their vehicles in a fit state of repair. Acts of 1929, 1930, 1934 and 1935 made further new regulations.

The system of public transport by road and rail is operated by 2 public bodies, the Ulster Transport Authority constituted under the Transport Act (Northern Ireland), 1948, and the Great N. Railway Board, constituted jointly by the N. Ireland Gov. and the gov. of the Rep. of Ireland under the Great Northern Railway Act (Northern Ireland), 1953.

Roads and road development. Under the Roads Act (Northern Ireland), 1948, the roads constituting the main system of traffic routes in N. Ireland were designed as trunk roads and the Ministry of Commerce became the road authority for these roads. This Act also deals with the construction of new roads, the adoption of roads and the abandonment of roads. Matters concerning the improvement and safety of roads generally are also dealt with in the Act, which supplements and amends previous legislation passed by the Parliament of N. Ireland on the subject, namely the Local Government (Roads) Act (Northern Ireland), 1923, the Roads Improvement Act (Northern Ireland), 1928, and the Roads Act (Northern Ireland), 1937.

See also IRELAND, NORTHERN and ROYAL ULSTER CONSTABULARY.

Local Government in Scotland. Scotland was formerly divided into pars. for purposes of public assistance and education, and into burghs and cos. for all other purposes of local gov. The Local Government (Scotland) Act, 1894, like the Eng. Act of the same date, readjusted the boundaries and relations of the existing local bodies, and created new local bodies and a new central authority. The par. council superseded the parochial board and the Local Gov. Board (Scotland) the old Board of Supervision. In 'mixed' pars. (partly urb. and partly rural) a landward committee was appointed, composed of par. councillors elected for the rural wards. The functions of the urb. pars. were practically confined to the administration of the poor law, but rural par. councils and landward committees exercised many of the functions of a tn council.

Under the Local Government (Scotland) Act, 1929, the par. councils and dist. boards of control were abolished and their functions transferred to the co. councils. Under this Act administration was divided between cos. (33, but only 31 councils owing to amalgamations), burgh or tn councils (195), royal burghs (68), parl. burghs (14), police burghs (115) and dist. councils (199).

The Local Gov. (Scotland) Act, 1947, consolidated and codified local gov. law very much in the same manner as the 1933 Act did for England and Wales. The co. area for local gov. purposes is, generally speaking, the geographical co., excluding the royal and parl. burghs. Some smaller burghs are, however, included in their co. for certain purposes but are autonomous for others. Councillors are representatives of landward areas (areas not in a burgh) elected by the local gov. electors and of burghs elected by the tn council. The functions of co. councils are generally derived from the Local Government Act, 1889, under which they were created and took over the local gov. functions of the justices of the peace and superseded the old Commissioners of Supply for all purposes except the management of the police force, the control of capital expenditure and borrowing. These functions were enlarged by the Act of 1894 which enabled them to make orders for the purchase of land, adjust the boundaries of par. wards and entertain representations by par. councils as to leasing land for allotments, and as to lighting, scavenging streets and maintaining baths and washhouses. These have been further augmented by subsequent Acts. Commissioners of supply were entirely superseded by the Act of 1929. With approval of the secretary of state for Scotland co. councils may set up dist councils to act as agents. Except for the raising of money, most of the work is delegated to committees, in some cases by statute. Committees *must* be appointed for certain purposes, e.g. health. The tn council of any small burgh and any dist, council or any joint committee thereof may be appointed by co. councils to perform their functions as agents. Their powers over roads extend only over co. roads, but these include all roads in small burghs which are classified as co. roads. Some burghs have separate police forces and joint police committees may be set up. Cos. and large bors. are responsible for road improvements, construction of new roads, speed limit signs, pedestrian crossings and dealing with trunk roads as agents of the secretary of state for Scotland. Cos. and large bors. are also responsible for local health services, milk testing, prevention of damage by pests, the protection of historic buildings and anct monuments, tn and country planning, provision of residential accommodation for aged and infirm persons, employment of blind persons, care of children, registration of electors, probation of offenders and remand homes. Co. councils share with burghs road safety activities, closure of slaughterhouses, provision of gymnasia, baths, playing fields, etc., aiding the supply of water and a sewerage system to rural areas and the provision of housing accommodation. They are responsible outside the cos. of cities for public education.

The cos. of cities are Edinburgh, Glasgow, Aberdeen and Dundee. They are 'all purpose' authorities similar to co. bors. in England and Wales. They are presided over by their Lord Provost. In Edinburgh and Glasgow they are 'Right Hon.' In the large burghs the co. council is responsible for education and in some cases for police. The small burghs are similar to non-co. bors., urb. dists and rural dists in England and Wales.

Tn councils consist of a provost (mayor), bailies (aldermen) and councillors. The provost and bailies are elected by the councillors, hold office for 3 years and are the justices of the peace for the burgh. Fire brigades are the responsibility of joint committees representing cos., large burghs and the city of Glasgow. Dist. councils are composed of the members of the co. council for the dist., together with others directly elected for the dist. They hold office for 3 years. They act outside the burghs as the agents of the co. council, having delegated to them such functions as allotments, recreation grounds, control of rights of way and other minor matters. They receive their funds from the co. council. Royal burghs are those created by royal charter. Parl. burghs are those created by the Reform Act, 1832, having the right to send separate representatives to Parliament. As in England and Wales, the Poor Law has been abolished and public aid, as national assistance, is paid by the National Assistance Board.

Valuation. Responsibility for valuation in Scotland lies with independent assessors appointed by the Local Valuation Authority, i.e. the co. of cities and the cos. Under the Valuation Acts the assessor is required to value and enter in the valuation roll all lands and heritages within the area. In broad terms the valuation is the rent at which, in the assessors' professional judgment, a property might be expected to let from year to year in a balanced market. Complaints about valuations which cannot be settled between the assessor and the occupier may be referred to local Valuation Appeal Committees from which there is a further right of appeal to the Lands Valuation Appeal Court. The Valuation and Rating (Scotland) Act, 1956, provides for a Quinquennial Review of valuations, the first took place in 1961-2.

Rating. Rating authorities are the cos. of cities, cos. and burghs. Rates are the prin. source of local authority income and the level of rates is determined by the individual authorities after taking account of gov. grants and other income. Rates are paid by occupiers (owners or tenants) of property. The prin. exemptions from rating are churches and agric. lands and buildings. Industry is de-rated to the extent of 50 per cent. Charitable and similar organisations are eligible for rating relief. The Rating Act, 1966, which came into effect in Scotland on 16 May 1966, provides a rate rebate scheme for persons with low incomes and gives householders the right to pay rates by monthly instalments.

Local Government in the United States. There are about 11,000 units of local gov. in the U.S.A. For those not living in cities, the co., the township and, in New England, the tn are the most important types. Cos. are found throughout the U.S.A. and are responsible for law enforcement, highway construction and maintenance, tax collection and property assessment and welfare. The New England tn has a unique form of gov.—'the town meeting'—which has been called the 'cradle of democracy' because the voters assemble annually, or more often if necessary, and legislate on local affairs. The 3 main forms of local gov. are: (1) the mayor-council system—found in 54 per cent of the cities with over 5000 people—in which a mayor is elected to be responsible for the administration; (2) the city manager system, which is found in 38 per cent—1114—of the cities—in which the manager is a paid professional administrator who appoints the heads of the various depts and gives advice on policy; (3) the commission system, found in the remaining 261 cities, in which an elected commission of 3 or 5 men is responsible for the city's administration.

Local Option, or **Local Veto,** *see* LICENCES AND LICENSING LAWS; LIQUOR CONTROL.

Locarno, tn and health resort in the S. canton of Ticino, Switzerland, at the N. end of Lago Maggiore, 14 m. SW. of Bellinzona. It is situated on the St Gotthard route. The anct church of Madonna del Sasso is a place of pilgrimage. Pop. 10,100, chiefly It.-speaking Rom. Catholics.

Locarno Conference and Treaties (1925). The Locarno treaties represented an attempt to supplement the covenant of the League of Nations after the rejection of the protocol for the Pacific Settlement of International Disputes (1924). They purported to meet the Fr. demand for security, while at the same time involving Great Britain in only the most specifically limited obligations. The Locarno agreements comprised a treaty of mutual guarantee between Germany, Belgium, Great Britain, France and Italy, arbitration conventions between Germany and Belgium and Germany and France, and arbitration treaties between Germany and Poland and Germany and Czechoslovakia. At the time of their conclusion it was widely believed that the Locarno treaties were an effective instrument for peace in Europe, but the Locarno treaties themselves had no inherent efficacy in bringing about the requisite contacts between govs., any more than had the League of Nations. One fundamental weakness of the Locarno treaties lay in the E. compromise, for it should have been obvious that Germany would never accept, for all time, the Versailles territorial settlement interposing the Polish corridor between E. and W. Prussia, and in the event of a conflict over this question it was difficult to see how Britain could avoid being drawn into war. In 1935 the Brit. Gov. discussed strengthening the Locarno Pact so as to make it specifically applicable to air attacks, but Germany refused

(1936) to join in negotiations for such a pact, using the impending conclusion of the Franco-Soviet pact as a justification for denouncing the Locarno treaties and thereafter proceeded to assert her unrestricted sovereignty over the demilitarised zone of the Rhineland, in token whereof Ger. troops had already been drafted in large numbers into that dist.

Lochaber, wild, mountainous dist of S. Inverness-shire, Scotland, with beautiful glens and moors, near Lochs Linnhe, Leven and Eil. In 1926 was begun the L. hydro-electric power scheme. Two main dams contain the waters of Loch Treig and Loch Laggan, and it is conveyed by a 15-m. tunnel to a power plant at Fort William. The total catchment area is 300 sq. m. and the plant has a potential h.p. of 100,000. The power is used for the manuf. of aluminium in electric furnaces.

Loches, Fr. tn in the dept of Indre-et-Loire, on the Indre. It was known to the Romans as Leucae. There is a remarkable 15th-cent. royal château, within which is the 10th-cent. church of St Ours. Across the riv. is the vast 11th-cent. abbey church of Beaulieu, partly in ruins. De Vigny (q.v.) was *b*. here. Pop. 6200.

Lochgelly, police burgh in the pars. of Auchterderran and Ballingry, in central W. Fife, Scotland, 7 m. NE. of Dunfermline and 7 m. NW. of Kirkcaldy. There are coal-mines and brick works. Pop. 9108.

Lochleven, *see* LEVEN, LOCH.

Lochmaben, royal and police burgh of Dumfriesshire, Scotland, 8 m. NE. of Dumfries. In Castle Loch are the ruins of L. Castle, the traditional bp. of Robert Bruce. There is coarse fishing in three lochs. Pop. 1286.

Lochner, Stefan (fl. 15th cent.), Ger. painter, *b*. Meersburg, Lake of Constance, the leading master of the Cologne School. Prin. works in which his freshness of colour and charm of style can be appreciated are his altarpiece (*c*. 1426) in Cologne Cathedral, 'Madonna and Child in the Rose Garden' (Cologne) and 'Presentation in the Temple' (Darmstadt).

Lochy, Loch, lake (10 m. long and three-quarters m. wide) of Inverness-shire, Scotland, forming part of the Caledonian Canal system and linked to Loch Oich by Laggan Locks.

Lock, Matthew, *see* LOCKE.

Lock, *see* GUN.

Lock, short section of a canal, with sluiced gates at each end, separating stretches in which the water is at different levels and designed to enable boats to be raised or lowered from one level to the other. L.s are also often used at the entrances to docks to isolate them from the main seaway so that the water inside the docks may be kept at the same level irrespective of the state of the tide. *See* CANALS; DOCKS.

Lock-outs, *see* STRIKES AND LOCK-OUTS.

Locke, John (1632–1704), philosopher, *b*. Wrington in Somerset. L. was at Westminster School from 1646 to 1652, when he entered Christ Church, Oxford. After taking his M.A. in 1658 he became a tutor of Christ Church in Greek and philosophy. He early showed a dislike for the scholasticism of men such as John Owen, the Puritan dean of Christ Church, and, though inclined towards an eccles. career, became interested in experimental inquiries and for a time practised medicine in Oxford, though he never took his doctor's degree. During the summer of 1666 he met Lord Ashley, afterwards Earl of Shaftesbury, and later became his confidential secretary, remaining with him for 15 years.

While Shaftesbury was in power L. was appointed secretary of the board of trade (1672), but on Shaftesbury's fall in 1675 L. was deprived of office and of his Oxford studentship, and was obliged to find a retreat abroad. At Montpellier and Paris he devoted his time to study and writing. In 1679, Shaftesbury having been restored to power, L. returned to England, and, though he took no part in the political plots of the following years, he was under suspicion as the friend of that statesman. In 1683 he withdrew to Holland, which was then the refuge of many men who were not allowed freedom of thought in their own country. After the revolution of 1688 he returned to England, and was rewarded with a commissionership of appeals. L. now appeared, late in life, as an author, and won European fame. In 1689 his *Epistola de Tolerantia*, dedicated to Limborch (q.v.), the champion of Liberal theology in Holland, was trans. into English and was followed in 1690 by *Two Treatises of Government* and the *Essay concerning Human Understanding*. The *Letter on Toleration* had called forth an *Answer* from Jonas Proast and L. contributed to the controversy that ensured a *Second*, 1690, and a *Third Letter*, 1692. Meanwhile his health was failing and in 1691 he went to reside permanently at Oates in Essex, the country seat of Sir Francis Masham. In 1693 he pub. *Some Thoughts concerning Education*, which were collected from a series of letters he had written from Holland to Edward Clark of Chipley concerning the education of his son.

Two years later he pub. anonymously *The Reasonableness of Christianity*, endeavouring to separate fact from dogma. This treatise also evoked a controversy and L. defended himself in a *Vindication*, 1695, and a *Second Vindication*, 1697. During 1696–1700, when he was busy with his duties as a commissioner of trade and plantations, he pub. answers to his various critics, an *Examination* of Malebranche's philosophy, additions to and alterations of his *Essay*, and wrote his *Conduct of the Understanding* (first printed in *Posthumous Works*, 1706). In 1700 he retired from public office, and during the remaining 4 years of his life spent much time in meditation and in close study of the Bible. He was buried in the par. church of High Laver, about a mile distant from Oates.

The object of the *Essay* is to examine the character of thinking and the extent of our abilities in thought. L. took an empiricist and materialist standpoint, arguing that experience is the sole original source of knowledge. In his *Toleration* he urges that there should be no disability attached to religious belief. The individual's absolute freedom of religious thought, which is widely taken for granted today, has been achieved by means of L.'s advocacy. His political philosophy, contained in the *Two Treatises of Government* (ed. P. Laslett, 1960) is based upon the doctrine of the ultimate sovereignty of the governed, and had a profound effect upon the future course of political thought and upon the constitution of the U.S.A. His method of presenting his ideas is straightforward and vigorous, but his style is lacking in grace.

L. left his papers and correspondence to his cousin Peter King (afterwards 7th Baron King). In 1942 these MSS., almost intact, were eventually deposited by their subsequent owner, Lord Lovelace, in the Bodleian Library for which they were purchased through the Pilgrim Trust in 1948 (see *Summary Catalogue of the Papers of John Locke in the Bodleian Library*, ed. P. Long, 1959). The Lovelace collection was already partly known through the medium of Lord King's *Life and Letters of John Locke*, 1829. Exhaustive reports of selected papers, with a view to pub., have been made by Dr W. von Leyden of Durham Univ., who has so far ed. *Essays on the Law of Nature*, 1954. The Lovelace collection includes 10 jours. which form a record of L.'s life from 1675 until his death. Lord King printed long extracts from them, though only up to 1687. In addition to the jours. there are 28 of L.'s note-books, written in a shorthand to which Dr von Leyden found the key. It is from these note-books and from numerous loose papers in the collection that most new light can be thrown on L.'s writings. It was L.'s practice to enter in his note-books drafts of the treatises he wrote; thus while the *Essay concerning Human Understanding* was first pub. in 1690, the draft of it in L.'s note-books dates from 1670. Other treatises written by L. and as yet unpublished go to supplement the *Essay*, which deals but briefly with the ideas of pleasure and pain, their fuller treatment being reserved for a *Discourse on the Passions*, and that *Discourse* is now found in the collection though it may not have the final form which L. would have given it. Of still greater interest is his hitherto unknown treatise on the *Law of Nature*, written in 1660-4. In this brief treatise he wrote his views on morality and knowledge almost 30 years before his first book appeared, and its discovery explains the curious absence from his pub. work of any detailed discussion of that natural law which forms the basis of his whole system. There is, however, nothing that bears upon his work as an educational reformer and little to throw new light on the political thought contained in the *Treatises on Government* (see *The Times*, 12 Jan. 1948). *See also* INNATE IDEAS.

L.'s works were first collected in 1714 in 3 vols. The best ed. is that of Bishop Law (1777); and there are eds. of *The Philosophical Works*, ed. by J. A. St John, 1843 and 1854, and of *The Educational Writings*, ed. by J. W. Adamson, 1912 and 1922. The *Essay*, which has been trans.

into most European languages, has passed through numerous eds., of which the best is J. W. Yolton's (Everyman's Library), 1962. *See* J. Gibson, *Locke's Theory of Knowledge and its Historical Relations*, 1917; S. G. Hefelbower, *The Relation of John Locke to English Deism*, 1918; K. MacLean, *John Locke and English Literature of the Eighteenth Century*, 1936; J. W. Gough, *John Locke's Political Philosophy*, 1950; R. I. Aaron, *John Locke*, 1955; J. W. Yolton, *John Locke and the Way of Ideas*, 1956; M. Cranston, *John Locke: A Bibliography*, 1957; K. Dewhurst, *John Locke: Physician and Philosopher*, 1963. (*See Plate: Philosophy*.)

Locke, or **Lock**, **Matthew** (1622-77), composer, *b*. Exeter. He learnt music as a choir-boy at Exeter Cathedral under Edward Gibbons and may afterwards have been a pupil of Wm Lake there. He went to the Netherlands in 1648 and to London about 1650, and in 1653 collaborated with Christopher Gibbons in Shirley's masque *Cupid and Death* performed before the Portuguese ambas. In 1656 he was one of the composers who took part in the setting of Davenant's *Siege of Rhodes*. For Charles II's coronation in 1661 he wrote instrumental music for the procession and was appointed composer in ordinary to the king. He was a vigorous and acrimonious defender of 'modern music', writing in 1666 a pamphlet defending his church music and in 1672 opening a controversy with Thomas Salmon. In 1673 L. and Draghi wrote music for Shadwell's *Psyche*. Purcell wrote an elegy on his death. His works include anthems; Lat. hymns; consorts for viols in 3 and 4 parts (the latter in 6 suites); songs in 3 parts, duets; airs and songs for 1 voice with accompaniment, etc.

Locke, **William John** (1863-1930), novelist and playwright, *b*. Georgetown, Demerara, Guyana. Educ. in Trinidad and at Cambridge Univ., he was a master at Glenalmond School and later secretary to the Royal Institute of Brit. Architects. During the later part of his life he lived on the Riviera. His most popular novels include *At the Gate of Samaria*, 1895, *The Morals of Marcus Ordeyne*, 1905, later dramatised, *The Beloved Vagabond*, 1906, later dramatised, *Septimus*, 1909, *The Joyous Adventures of Aristide Pujol*, 1912, *Stella Maris*, 1913, *The Wonderful Year*, 1916, *The Rough Road*, 1918, *The Great Pandolfo*, 1925, *The Old Bridge*, 1926. In 1930 he pub. a vol. of short stories, *The Town of Tombarel*, and after his death appeared *The Shorn Lamb*, 1931. His chief play was *The Mun from the Sea*, 1910.

Locker-Lampson, **Frederick** (1821-95), poet *b*. Greenwich Hospital. He was a clerk at Somerset House and then at the Admiralty. In 1857 he pub. *London Lyrics*, a collection of charming light verse. He compiled *Lyra Elegantiarum*, 1867, an anthology of light verse, and *Patchwork*, 1879, a selection of prose passages. *My Confidences*, an informal autobiography, appeared posthumously (1896) with a preface by his son-in-law, Augustine Birrell. In 1886 he printed a catalogue of his famous library at

Rowfant. *See* A. Birrell, *Frederick Locker-Lampson: a Character Sketch*, 1920.

Lockerbie, burgh of Dumfriesshire, Scotland, 12 m. E. of Dumfries. The largest lamb fair in Scotland is held there annually in August. Pop. 2826.

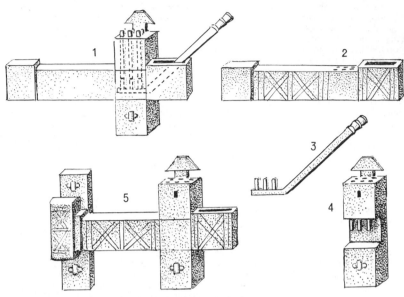

EARLY EGYPTIAN LOCK

1, diagram showing how the key raises the pins that hold the bolt; 2, bolt; 3, key; 4, lock with bolt out, showing the pins in dropped position; 5, complete lock and bolt.

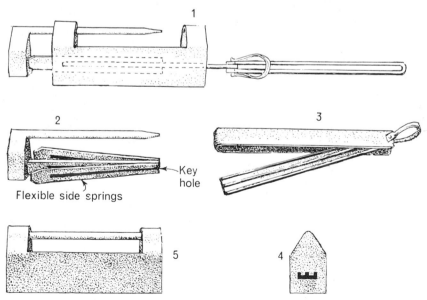

CHINESE LOCK

1, diagram to show how the channels on the key compress the springs of the bolt into line; 2, bolt with springs expanded; 3, key; 4, keyhole; 5, complete lock and bolt.

Lockhart, John Gibson (1794–1854), author and editor, *b.* Cambusnethan, Lanarkshire. Educ. at Glasgow Univ. and Oxford, he studied law and was called to the Scottish Bar in 1816. He was an early contributor to *Blackwood's Magazine* (founded 1817). In 1818 he met Walter Scott, and 2 years later married the novelist's eldest daughter, Sophia. He wrote many articles and novels, and in 1825 accepted the editorship of the *Quarterly Review*, and settled in London. He did not retire from the control of the *Quarterly* until 1853. In 1828 appeared his biography of Robert Burns; in the following year he pub. a *History of Napoleon Bonaparte*, and in 1832 his *History of the late War, including Sketches of Buonaparte, Nelson and Wellington—for Children*. His greatest work was the *Memoirs of the Life of Sir Walter Scott* (7 vols.), 1837–8, a biography which ranks second only to Boswell's *Johnson*. L. made over the profits of this book to the creditors of Sir Walter Scott. As a novelist L. was not particularly successful, but *Some Passages in the Life of Mr Adam Blair*, 1822, repays perusal. *See* S. Smiles, *A Publisher and his Friends*, 1891; A. Lang, *The Life and Letters of John Gibson Lockhart*, 1897; Marion C. Lochead, *John Gibson Lockhart*, 1954.

Lockhart, Sir Robert Hamilton Bruce, (1887–), journalist, *b.* Anstruther Fife. Educ. at Fettes and the univs. of Paris and Berlin, he was Brit. consul in Moscow, 1911–17, and later was on the staff of the *Evening Standard*. During the Second World War he was deputy under-secretary at the Foreign Office. His books, largely autobiographical, include *Memoirs of a British Agent*, 1932, *Retreat from Glory*, 1934, *Return to Malaya*, 1936, *My Scottish Youth*, 1937, *Comes the Reckoning*, 1947 and *My Europe*, 1952. K.C.M.G., 1943.

Lockjaw, *see* TETANUS; in horses *see under* HORSE (DISEASES).

Lockport, co. seat of Niagara co., New York, U.S.A., 22 m. ENE. of Buffalo, on the Erie Canal. There are textile and fibre factories and manufs. steel, paper products, auto parts, hardware, chemicals, radiators, canned goods and leather, wood and glass products. Pop. *c.* 25,000.

Locks and Keys. A lock is a fastening device which consists of a bolt held by one or more movable parts in a certain position, requiring a key which will manipulate these movable parts in the required way, before it can be opened. The most primitive forms of fastening were by means of knotted thongs or a wooden or metal bar placed across the inside of a door. A curved key, in shape somewhat like a sickle, was used to move the bar, and examples have been found in many parts of N. Europe. The earliest locks of all are probably the Chinese, of which some extant specimens are as secure as any made in Europe up to the 18th cent. Some Egyptian locks are known to be 4000 years old, and locks on the Egyptian plan may be found in many remote places in Europe. The Egyptians made the portion of the hole into which the retaining pegs were inserted hollow, and the key had pins upon it corresponding with these pegs. The key was inserted into the end of the bolt. The Romans based their locks on the same principle as the Egyptians, but the bolt was smaller and the dropping pins were pressed downwards by a spring.

The early Eng. and medieval keys were the forerunners of the modern keys from a mechanical point of view. In the locks of this period a pivoted tumbler is used instead of dropping pins. A number of impediments contained in the lock case were interposed between the key and the bolt; these are called wards, and the portion of the key which enters the lock is formed so as to escape them. Robert Barron improved the mechanism of locks in 1774 by placing 2 levers to guard the bolt, instead of only one; and he also made it necessary for the levers to be lifted up to the right height before the bolt could be turned. The Bramah lock of 1784, invented by Joseph

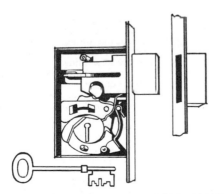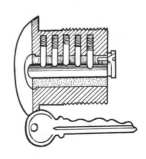

MODERN LOCKS

(Left) Mortise lock, in which the key raises a tumbler (kept in place by a spring) to free the bolt. (Right) Cylinder lock, closed by a number of two-part pins of different lengths; the insertion of the key brings the join in each pin into line with the cylinder, thus allowing it to turn.

Bramah (1749–1814), marks the next stage in the improvement of locks. A number (generally 6) of thin metal plates called sliders, the notches in which must be brought into certain positions before the key could be used, formed the distinguishing feature of the lock. The Chubb lock was patented in 1818, and since then has been many times altered and improved. It is a lever lock, and has more levers than usual with the addition of one called the detector. This is so placed that it moves and fixes the bolt if any of the levers be lifted a little too high. Notice is thus given of any attempt at picking the lock, even if unsuccessful, as the rightful key will not then open the lock until it has first been turned the reverse way. Both the Bramah and Chubb locks were erroneously thought to be 'unpickable'. The Yale lock was an Amer. invention of about 1860. It is a tumbler lock, but the small flat key and the keyway interlock throughout their length owing to their peculiar cross section. It is a modern adaptation of the old Egyptian lock, which had pins made of wood, whereas the modern pin-cylinder lock has metal pins.

In a master-keyed suite of locks the wards of each lock are different so that each key will fit only 1 lock, whilst the master key will have the bit filed off and so fit all the locks. This is open to the objection that any of the subordinate keys may be made into a master key by filing. The other method is to make all the levers of each lock alike save one; another 'gating' is cut in the differing levers so that the master key, which is specially cut, will fit all the locks. In safe deposits, unless a fresh lock were to be fitted every time a safe changed hands, which would be a troublesome and expensive proceeding, some invention by which the key of the out-going tenant of the safe might be rendered useless was necessary. Such an invention was patented by R. Newell in 1841, and introduced into Great Britain by A. C. Hobbs in 1851. There are now many good designs for change-key locks.

Locks in which the internal parts were arranged in their right position by the manipulation of external parts which were marked with letters, numbers or other devices have been common in China for cents., but the hist. of their invention remains obscure. Such locks are, of course, the predecessors of the combination locks which have been brought to such a degree of excellence in America. Blocks of metal corresponding to the different letters of the alphabet are introduced into the lock, and the person locking the door places these to spell any word or combination of letters he chooses. When the door is once locked, it cannot be opened without a knowledge of the codeword, even if the key is available. Combination locks are also made in which the mere fact of setting the dial, mounted on the spindle which passes through the door to work the wheels, in the right manner opens or closes the door, no key being required. Keyless locks are now usually made with number combinations, which give a greater number of 'differs' than are possible with letters. The application of time to locks, so that the period during which a door remains locked may be exactly predetermined, is very suitable for strongrooms, etc. The modern time lock is an extremely complicated arrangement, and once the time lock has been set it cannot be opened until the appointed hr.

Lockyer, Sir (Joseph) Norman (1836–1920), astronomer, b. Rugby. His early astronomical work was carried out while a scientific adviser to the gov., until in 1881 he became prof. in the Royal College of Science, and in 1885 director of the Solar Physics Observatory at S. Kensington, until its removal to Cambridge in 1913. In 1869 he was elected F.R.S., and became founding ed. of the scientific weekly jour. *Nature*. A pioneer of solar and stellar spectroscopy, he discovered in 1868, at the same time as Janssen (q.v.), the possibility of observing the sun's prominences without an eclipse. In 1869 he discovered the hitherto unknown element helium (q.v.) in the sun's spectrum. His theories on the evolution of stars in some respects anticipated modern ideas, in the div. into giant and dwarf stars. On retirement from S. Kensington in 1913, L. and Lady L. founded the Norman Lockyer Observatory in Sidmouth, Devon.

Locomotives. STEAM. (For hist. of steam L. *see* RAILWAYS.) The modern steam locomotive has a frame which consists of a pair of longitudinal side plates joined together by cross members called stretchers. The frame is supported on the coupled wheels by springs which bear on the axleboxes in which the axles run. Additional weight bearing axles may be provided in front of or behind the coupled wheels; to facilitate the negotiation of curves these axles are permitted a slight sideways movement or are mounted on separate bogies which pivot on the main frame. The boiler is attached to the smoke-box at the front and is supported on expansion brackets at the rear. Behind it is the footplate, covered by a cab to protect the driver and fireman. The smoke-box is bolted to the frames at the front of the engine, and contains the super-heater and steam pipes leading to the cylinders; also the blast pipe through which the exhaust steam escapes up the chimney, creating a powerful draught on the fire. The cylinders are mounted at the front of the frame, either outside the side plates or between them. The force exerted on the piston by the expanding steam is transmitted through the piston rod, crosshead and connecting rod to the crankpin on the driving wheel or axle. The pair of driving wheels is linked to one or more pairs of similar wheels by coupling rods. The steam supply to the cylinders is controlled by a regulator valve, operated by a lever in the cab, and the timing of admission and exhaust is governed by piston or slide valves which uncover ports in the cylinder walls. These valves are operated through either a Stephenson or a Walschaerts linkage (*see* STEAM ENGINES) controlled by a reversing screw in the cab. For stopping, cast-iron brake blocks are pressed against the treads of the wheels by a steam, air or vacuum cylinder (according to the braking system employed) operated by a driver's brake

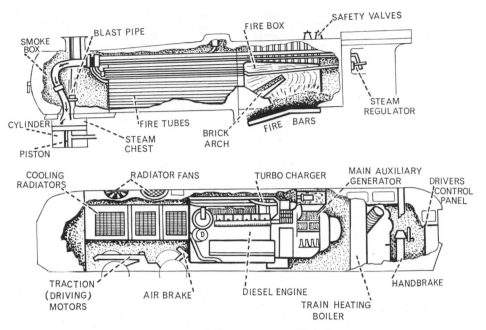

CROSS-SECTION OF STEAM (*above*) AND DIESEL (*below*) LOCOMOTIVES

valve in the cab. Coal and water are usually carried on a separate tender but in the case of small L. may be carried on the locomotive itself, the water in tanks on either side of the boiler and the coal in a bunker behind the cab. Condensing is rarely used on L., the theoretical increase in output not being obtained in practice, because a substitute for the blast pipe would have to be found; and, owing to space restrictions, a separate condenser vehicle would have to be provided and hauled; and both these would absorb power.

Locomotive boilers. For a railway locomotive the design must satisfy rigid limitations on height, breadth and weight and must be capable of providing full output for long periods without the need for maintenance. The coal is burnt in a firebox of rectangular cross-section which is attached to the rear of the boiler. The firebox consists of an inner and an outer shell, the space between forming a water jacket. The outer shell is made of steel; the inner shell may be of steel or copper and is held in position by stays attached to the outer shell. The floor of the firebox forms a grate with an ashpan underneath. The furnace gases are led forward from the upper part of the inner firebox through a large number of horizontal tubes, surrounded by water contained in a cylindrical steel barrel; this barrel is connected to the firebox outer shell, and is closed at the front by the smoke-box tube plate, through which the tubes discharge the gases to the smoke-box and chimney. The tubes are generally made of steel, though copper is

sometimes used, and form the main heating surface of the boiler. Modern L. are usually fitted with super-heaters (*see* Boilers); in this case a number of the fire-tubes are made of larger diameter, and each contains a double loop of seamless steel tube. The front ends of these elements are connected to the 2 chambers of a 'collector', placed in the smoke-box at the top of the smoke-box tube plate; the one chamber receives wet steam from the boiler, while the other collects the super-heated steam for the delivery to the cylinders. Locomotive boilers are nearly always hand fired, though very large machines are sometimes fitted with a mechanical stoker, by which coal, suitably crushed, is distributed over the grate by steam jets. The draught is provided by the exhaust steam from the cylinders. Locomotive boilers require frequent emptying and washing out, to remove the scale caused by different feed water, and the forcing of the boiler.

Diesel. The steam locomotive has sev. disadvantages. Because of the time required to raise steam it cannot be brought into service at short notice and it consumes coal during long periods when it is standing idle. Its efficiency is low, it is dirty, and its fuel is awkward to handle. The modern tendency is to use electric L. where the traffic justifies the capital cost of power lines and diesel L. elsewhere. Unlike the steam engine, which produces maximum torque when starting from rest, the diesel engine produces no torque at very low speeds and so cannot be coupled directly to the driving wheels. For diesel railcars and small shunting L. the transmission incorporates a hydraulic torque converter or a fluid flywheel and a gearbox. Railcars are usually powered by sev. small engines, similar to those used in heavy road vehicles and mounted under the floor so as to allow as much room as possible for passengers. They are operated in multiple units, some of the cars being powered and some not; all the engines are controlled from the cab of the front car.

In large diesel L. the engine is generally coupled to an electrical generator supplying traction motors which drive the wheels although in some cases hydraulic transmission is used. Four-stroke engines are more common than 2-stroke and are often turbocharged to provide a higher power to weight ratio. For shunting L. the 2-stroke engine has the advantage that it can be made reversible, so dispensing with the need for a separate means of reversing the drive. One example of the bigger L. engines, a turbocharged 4-stroke, has 16 cylinders arranged in vee formation and develops 2500 h.p. at a speed of 850 r.p.m.

The d.c. generator is coupled directly to the engine and is designed so that it can also be used as a motor, operated by batteries, for starting the engine. The traction motors are d.c. series motors. The output of the unit is regulated partly by varying the speed of the diesel engine and partly by varying the excitation of the generator. When powers greater than about 3000 h.p. are required, 2 L. are generally coupled together.

Electric. These L. are powered by electricity supplied from overhead wires or conductor rails along the track. Both a.c. and d.c. systems are widely used (*see* ELECTRIC TRACTION). High voltages are more economical to transmit than low, but cannot be applied directly to the traction motors. For this reason a.c. systems employ higher voltages (up to 25 kV) than d.c. systems (600–3000 volts) as the voltage can be reduced by a transformer on the locomotive. Driving motors are of the series wound type (*see* ELECTRIC MACHINES). A.c. commutator motors may be used where the supply is at low frequency (16⅔ to 25 cycles/sec) but are less satisfactory at the normal commercial frequencies of 50 and 60 cycles/sec and in a.c. systems the current is usually rectified to d.c. in the locomotive before being supplied to the motors. Obviously it is an advantage to use the commercial frequency as the current can then be taken directly from the national electricity supply. In 3000 V d.c. systems the motors are connected in pairs in series so that the voltage across each motor is 1500 volts. When there is one motor per driven axle it may be mounted on bearings through which the axle passes, and a 'nose' on the rear of the motor frame is spring-hung from the bogie frame. The motor may also be rigidly mounted on the main frame, the axle passing through a quill shaft which runs in bearings in an 'axleway' on the motor frame and is gear-driven from the armature. Spring-cups on the quill flanges transmit the power to the wheels. In the

'Buchli-link' (Brown Boveri) a spring pinion on the armature shaft drives a gear-wheel attached by springs to the wheel. Heavy freight or shunting L. sometimes have the driving-wheels coupled as in steam L. For smooth acceleration d.c. motors are started with a resistance in series, so that the voltage across the motor is reduced, the resistance being gradually cut out until full speed is attained. It is usual also to employ 'series-parallel connection': 2 motors, with their starting-resistances, are first connected in series, each taking only half the full voltage, and the resistances are gradually cut out; the motor connections are then changed to 'parallel', the resistances being at the same time reinserted and finally cut out again gradually. The whole process is carried out by a 'master controller' with a system of contactors closed and opened in correct sequences by turning a handle. In a.c. L. a stepwise increase of voltage on the motors, from the low starting-value to full voltage, is obtained by tappings on the secondary windings of the transformer or, in modern L., on the primary, where current values are less. These operations are also handled by controller and contactors.

When the train is running downhill, then the wheels drive the motors, and these act as generators which may be made to feed energy back to the supply wires if adequate field excitation is provided for raising the voltage slightly above the normal supply voltage. This 'regenerative braking' is often used on d.c. L. Vacuum or air brakes (q.v.) are always fitted. On d.c. L. a motor-generator set supplies lighting and power for operating controls, charging stand-by batteries, and sometimes electric heating of trains, or of boilers for hot-water heating and pantry. In a.c. L. supply for these auxiliaries is taken from transformer tappings. Connection to the pantograph (q.v.) is through a circuit breaker controlled by overload and no-current relays and also operated by pushbutton in the driver's cabin. The 3000 V d.c., 4000 h.p. locomotive of the Paulista (Brazil) Railway develops a maximum tractive effort of 67,300 lb. and maximum service speed is 90 m.p.h. A Swiss 15,000 V a.c., 11,400 h.p. locomotive has a tractive effort of 110,000 lb. at 68 m.p.h. A special type of electric locomotive is in use on the Great Northern Railway in NW. U.S.A. The 11,000 V, 25 cycles supply is stepped down in the locomotive transformer and a synchronous motor fed from the secondary drives a d.c. generator supplying the traction motors. Conversion of single-phase to 3-phase by motor-generator, and use of 3-phase induction motors for traction, are found in Hungary, and the use of rectifiers on L. for converting a.c. into d.c. has been tried in Germany. Electric and diesel electric L. are classified by representing groups of coupled driving axles by a letter (A = 1 axle, B = 2, C = 3, etc.); if the axles are uncoupled the letter is followed by a suffix 'O'. Axles which are solely weight carrying are denoted by a number, the absence of a number indicating that all the axles are driving axles (e.g. a Bo–Bo locomotive has 2 bogies each with 2 uncoupled driving axles).

Experimental L. using gas turbines together with electric transmission have been built in sev. countries and in the U.S.A. a number of 8500 h.p. units are in service hauling trains over the Rocky Mts.

See also ELECTRIC MACHINES; ELECTRIC TRACTION; INTERNAL COMBUSTION ENGINES; RAILWAY; STEAM ENGINES. *See* A. T. Dover, *Electric Traction*, 1931; B. Reed, *Diesel Locomotives and Railcars*, 1935; E. A. Phillipson, *Steam Locomotive Design*, 1936; W. A. Agnew, *Electric Trains, their Equipment and Operation*, 1937; Railway Publishing Co., *British Locomotive Types*, 1946; D. W. and M. Hinde, *Electric and Diesel-Electric Locomotives*, 1948; C. J. Allen, *Locomotive Practice and Performance in the Twentieth Century*, 1949; G. Dow, *British Steam Horses*, 1950. (*See plate: Railway*.)

Locomotor Ataxia, or **Tabes Dorsalis,** degeneration of the posterior nerve columns of the spinal cord caused by syphilis (q.v.), of which L. A. is a late manifestation. The chief symptoms are due to the lack of co-ordination of the muscular movements, from which the disease gets its name, but the eyes and other special senses are also disturbed. Severe paroxysms of pain in the abdomen and limbs, known as 'lightning pains', are also a feature of L. A. The disease may come on quite gradually and remain in any of its stages, but continued progress leads to paralysis. One of the earliest signs is the inability of the patient to stand upright with his feet together and his eyes closed; the pupil of the eye fails to contract in response to a bright light, and the knee-jerk reflex is diminished. The posterior (sensory) columns of the spinal cord are the sites particularly affected. Anti-syphilitic treatment arrests the progress of the disease but cannot restore the function of those nerves the tissues of which have suffered extensive damage. Treatment therefore should be started as early as possible and pursued rigorously.

Locri, people occupying 2 separate dists of anct Greece. One of these dists, also called E. Locris, was bounded N. by Malis, E. by the Euboean strait, S. by Boeotia, W. by Doris and Phocis. The N. part was inhabited by Epicnemidian L., called after their situation on the spurs of Mt Cnemis; the S. part by the Opuntian L., whose chief tn was Opus.

The other dist, W. Locris, was bounded N. by Doris, E. by Phocis, S. by the Corinthian gulf, W. by Aetolia. The inhab. were called Ozolian L. They were less civilised than their E. namesakes, and do not appear in hist. until the Peloponnesian war.

C. 683 BC colonists from E. Locris founded a city on Zephyrium, a promontory in the 'toe' of Italy, and were hence known as L. Epizephyrii. This was the 1st 'Gk settlement to receive a written code of laws, given by Zaleucus *c.* 664 BC.

Löcse, *see* LEVOČA.

Locus, in mathematics, the line or curve traversed or surface covered by a point limited in its motion by definitive conditions. The L. of a point moving subject to the condition of constant distance from another, but fixed, point is the surface of a sphere; if, on the other hand, it be restricted to motion in one plane only, the L. will be the circumference of a circle.

Locus Standi, literally, a place of standing: (1) In law means the right of audience in a lawsuit. No counsel has a right to say anything during the hearing of a case unless he has been 'briefed' or instructed by solicitors acting for one or other of the litigating parties. A counsel who holds a 'watching brief' for parties interested, but not actually on the record as parties to the suit, may, like any member of the public, hear the evidence, but, having no L. S., he may not speak. (2) In parl. practice a term used in regard to the right of petitioners to be heard against private bills in the House of Commons. Questions on the L. S. of the petitioners are heard by the Court of Referees, which consists of the Chairman of Ways and Means, the Deputy Chairman and the Council to Mr Speaker with not less than 7 other members of the House. The L. S. of petitioners against hybrid bills is decided by the committee to whom the bill is committed. (*See* COMMITTEES, PARLIAMENTARY.)

Locust, orthopterous (straight-winged) insect of the family Acrididae, closely allied to the grasshoppers (Tettigoniidae), characterised by long antennae and typified by the great green grasshopper (*Tettigonia viridissima*). The true L.s have short antennae, the head has 3 ocelli on the forehead, and the female lacks a projecting ovipositor. Perhaps their most remarkable physiological feature is the large apertures in the first segment of the abdomen containing organs which undoubtedly possess auditory functions. The 'chirping' is produced by working the hind legs so that the thighs, on which are minute teeth, pass over the wing-cases, A number of species are responsible for the terrible ravages which, since agriculture began, have made L.s its most feared enemies. The best-known European species is the migratory L. (*Locusta migratoria*), which is also widely distributed in other countries, and it may be said that L.s range from the W. of Europe to China, while the Amer. continents, including Canada, are not infrequently visited by devastating migrations. When a migration occurs, probably owing to increasing density of pop. in the solitary phase of the insect, whereby the gregarious phase arises, the insects will eat anything that is green and, if need be, will devour animal substances, including their own young. The young, which hatch from eggs laid by the female in a hole in the ground, are destructive from the first. They resemble the parents except that they lack wings, and advantage is taken of this in waging war on the pests. While wingless they cannot surmount smooth surfaces, and the line of march of the migratory horde is intercepted by canvas screens 4 ft high. When they try to pass round the obstacle they fall into deep pits where they rapidly collect, and the pits are covered with earth when nearly full. Poison bait consisting of bran mixed with arsenic or 'gammexane' is also used to destroy the 'hoppers', as these immature flightless forms are called. Attempts have been made to spray both hoppers and flying swarms with poison dust from aircraft. Biological control has also been tried, e.g. by the fungus *Empusa gryllae*, which parasitises the L. Elaborate systems of giving warnings of the approach of a migratory horde enable full precautions to be taken, and many well-farmed dists claim that the screen method of destruction has had extraordinary success, though it cannot check the aerial migrations of adults. Swarms in the air have been known to darken the sun.

The periodicity of the appearance of migratory L.s has been the subject of much speculation: it is governed by the rapid increase in their numbers, and some divide their visitation in multiples of 11; but with the spread of systematic agriculture and persecution of the pests any definite periodicity grows less likely. The activities of the anti-L. research centre at the Natural Hist. Museum in S. Kensington, in charge of B. P. Uvarov (1949), are largely directed to tracing the H.Q. of the solitary phase of the different species and so preventing migration; it is known, for instance, that the middle Niger is the breeding ground of *L. migratoria*. Similar work was initiated in the U.S.A. by C. V. Riley (q.v.), the state entomologist of Missouri. *See also* ENTOMOLOGY. *See* B. P. Uvarov, *Locusts and Grasshoppers*, 1928, and *Locust Outbreak in Africa and West Asia, 1925–31*, 1933; and fourth report of Commission on Locust Control, 1932 (Cmd. 4124).

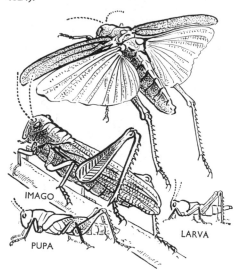

LOCUST
Stages of development.

Locust Tree, *see* ACACIA.
Lodes. Metals and metallic ores are usually found in cracks in the rocks of the earth's crust.

Lode is the miner's term for these veins, as distinguished from non-metalliferous veins. The thickness varies from a few inches to hundreds of feet. Veins may traverse every kind of rock. They seldom run parallel to the bedding, but more or less vertically, though the branching is very varied and irregular, as also is their persistence and thickness. There is no proof that the mineral deposits have intruded in a molten state from below; probably in most cases they are deposited from infiltrated solutions obtained from the surrounding strata, or from deeper sources by ore-bearing fluids which are concentrated from hot or molten rock-material rising from the lower parts of the crust. The material often shows aggregated layers due to successive stages of deposit. The richness of a lode is extremely variable, but in general the portions nearer the surface which have been subject to attrition and exposed to oxidation by the atmosphere, or to action of water, have waste matters (gangue) removed, the heavier minerals remaining collected together. They are, further, in the form of oxides and carbonates, and much more easily subject to extraction of the metal than the unoxidised sulphides, arsenides, etc., which are found deeper. The working of L. is very often rendered troublesome by the appearance of *faults* (q.v.) which displace pre-existing L. On the other hand, faults may serve as channels for ore-bearing fluids and may themselves be mineralised. Prospecting for such deposits is a matter of searching for the slightest and often very indirect indications, among which may be mentioned the stones washed down the beds of streams, mineral springs, the presence in soils of disintegrated and chemically transformed products, and the growth of plants feeding on such soils. Magnetic iron is indicated by the magnetic needle. *See* F. H. Hatch, *Study of Ore Deposits*, 1929; T. Cook, *Theory of Ore Deposits*, 1933; W. Lindgren, *Mineral Deposits*, 4th ed., 1933; Jones and D. Williams, *Minerals and Mineral Deposits*, 1948; geological works of Sir C. Lyell, Sir J. Prestwich and Sir A. Geikie. *See also* MAGNETISM.

Lodestone, *see* MAGNETITE.
Lodève (anct **Luteva,** later **Forum Neronis**), Fr. tn in the dept of Hérault, on the Lergues. Cardinal Fleury (q.v.) was *b.* here. Army clothing, woollens and wine are manuf. Pop. 7200.

Lodge, Henry Cabot (1850–1924), Amer. historian and senator; *b.* Boston, Massachusetts. He was Republican member of Congress, 1887–93, member of the House of Representatives, Massachusetts, 1880–1, and U.S. senator from 1893 until his death. During the First World War he was opposed to 'negotiated' peace; and it was he who, at the end of 1918, began the campaign that ended in America's rejection of the treaty of Versailles and the whole of President Wilson's foreign policy.

Lodge, Henry Cabot (1902–), Amer. politician, educ. at Harvard Univ. He entered journalism and first became a Republican senator in 1936. L. served in the Second World

War. He was Senator for Massachusetts, 1946–53; U.S. Representative to U.N., 1953–60. L. was U.S. Ambas. to S. Vietnam, 1963–4, and again from 1965. Generally regarded as a moderately progressive Republican.

Lodge, Sir Oliver Joseph (1851–1940), physicist, *b.* Penkhull, Staffs, educ. at Newport Grammar School, Salop and (part-time) Univ. College, London. Prof. of physics, Liverpool, 1881–1900, principal of Birmingham Univ. 1900–19, awarded Rumford medal of Royal Society 1898, elected F.R.S. 1902 and knighted in the same year. He pursued research on electromagnetic radiation with special reference to aether (q.v.), invented the 'coherer' and was a pioneer in radio telegraphy. He also studied electrolysis. His writings on psychical research attracted wide attention and include *The Survival of Man*, 1909, and *Raymond*, 1916, the latter claiming contact with the spirit of his son killed in 1915. He pub. many other books including *Pioneers of Science*, 1893, *The Ether of Space*, 1909, *Parent and Child*, 1910, *Atoms and Rays*, 1924, *Ether and Reality*, 1925, *Evolution and Creation*, 1927, *Beyond Physics*, 1930, and an autobiography, 1934.

Lodge, Thomas (c. 1558–1625), dramatist and poet, *b.* West Ham. Educ. at Merchant Taylors' and Trinity College, Oxford, he entered Lincoln's Inn in 1578, but soon abandoned himself to the lighter aspects of literature. From 1589 to 1591, seeking variety and change of life, L. took part in 2 sea expeditions against the Spaniards near the Azores and Canary Is. During the latter expedition he composed his prose tale of *Rosalynde*, which furnished Shakespeare with the story of *As You Like It*. He also pub. about the same time 2 romances, *Robert, Second Duke of Normandy* and *Euphues' Shadow, the Battaile of the Sences*. He excelled as a lyric poet, and *Glaucus and Scilla* appeared in 1589; his main vol. of verse, *Phillis*, a collection of amorous sonnets, was pub. in 1593 and *A Fig for Momus* in 1598. L. is likewise the author of 2 second-rate dramas entitled *The Wounds of Civile War* and, in collaboration with Robert Greene (q.v.), *A Looking-glass for London and England*, and he trans. the works of Seneca and Josephus. During the latter part of his life he practised as a doctor, having studied medicine at Avignon about 1595. His works were ed. by Sir E. Gosse (4 vols.) in 1884. *See* C. J. Sisson, *Thomas Lodge and Other Elizabethans*, 1933; *also* lives by N. B. Paradise, 1931 (with bibliography), and E. A. Tenney, 1935.

Lodgers and **Lodgings**, *see* LANDLORD AND TENANT.

Lodi, It. tn in Lombardy (q.v.), on the Adda, 18 m. SE. of Milan. It has a 12th cent. cathedral and a beautiful 15th cent. Renaissance church. Near by, Napoleon (q.v.) gained a victory over the Austrians in 1796. Near by, also, are the remains of the anct *Laus Pompeia*. Linen, silk, majolica and Parmesan cheese are manuf. Pop. 31,000.

Łódź: 1. Prov. (*województwo*) of central Poland. It is low-lying in the N., and has a hilly plateau in the S. The prin. rivs. are the Warta, Pilica and Prosna. Livestock is raised, and cereals and potatoes are grown. The prin. industry is textile milling. Area 6503 sq. m.; pop. 1,632,000.
2. City of Poland, 75 m. WSW. of Warsaw. It is the cap. of L. prov., but also itself ranks as an autonomous prov. It is the second largest city of the country. At the beginning of the 19th cent. it was still a small tn, but it grew rapidly as a textile centre after the importation of Ger. weavers by the gov. In the First World War it was the scene of a battle on 1–5 Dec. 1914, after which it fell to the Germans. During the Second World War the Germans expelled 250,000 Jews and 150,000 Poles from the city, and replaced them by 150,000 Ger. colonists. As well as being the centre of the Polish textile industry, the city has manufs. of machinery, chemicals, leather goods, paper, tobacco and foodstuffs. It has a univ. (1945) and an airport. Pop. 723,000.

Loeb, Jacques (1859–1924), Ger.-Amer. physiologist. In 1910 he became head of the div. of general physiology, Rockefeller Institute. His most striking book is *Tropisms and Animal Conduct*, 1918.

Loeb, James (1867–1933), Ger.-Amer. banker and antiquarian scholar, *b.* New York. On his retirement in 1901 he devoted himself to classical scholarship and archaeology. President of the Amer. School of Archaeology at Athens. He will be chiefly remembered for launching at his own expense the Loeb Classical Library, designed to cover all works of literary importance from the time of Homer to the fall of Constantinople. He trans. Paul Decharme's book on Euripides, Maurice Croiset's on Aristophanes and Couat's *Alexandrian Poetry under the First Three Ptolemies.*

Loeffler, Charles Martin (1861–1935), Alsatian-Amer. composer and violinist, *b.* Mulhouse; studied the violin under Joachim in Germany and composition under Guiraud in France. In 1881 he went to New York. From 1882 to 1903 he was a member of the Boston Symphony orchestra. He held a leading place among modern Amer. composers with his orchestral, choral and chamber compositions. His best-known works, both for orchestra with solo instruments, are *La Mort de Tintagiles* (after Maeterlinck) and *A Pagan Poem* (after Virgil).

Loeffler, Friedrich (1852–1915), Ger. bacteriologist, *b.* Frankfurt-on-Oder. He studied medicine at Würzburg and Berlin, graduated in 1874 and served for some years as a Prussian army surgeon. In 1879 he took charge of the health office in Berlin, where he made important bacteriological discoveries with R. Koch (q.v.) and G. Gaffky. He moved in 1888 to the chair of hygiene at Greifswald and in 1913 became director of the Koch Institute for Infectious Diseases, Berlin. Koch cultured the diphtheria bacillus (1884) recently discovered by Klebs and later called 'Klebs-Loeffler bacillus'; discovered the causal organism of glanders and swine erysipelas in 1886; isolated *Salmonella typhi-*

murium, an organism causing food poisoning; showed that foot-and-mouth disease is caused by a filterable virus (1897), the first recognition of such an organism as the cause of animal disease; and introduced a preventive vaccine against this disease (1899). He made important contributions to immunology and to microscopical technique and wrote a useful but unfinished hist. of bacteriology (1887).

Loeillet, Jean-Baptiste (1680–1730), Flem. composer, *b.* Ghent, the outstanding member of a family of musicians. He learnt the harpsichord, flute and oboe. By 1705 he was in London as a member of the Queen's Theatre in the Haymarket, retiring in 1710 but remaining as a teacher in London, where he *d.* He wrote numerous sets of chamber music, mainly for his own instruments.

Loëss, name given originally to a loamy deposit occurring in the basins of the Rhine and Danube. It consists mainly of clay particles deposited by the wind, and since somewhat solidified by its own weight and the action of percolating water. Extensive deposits have been recognised and studied in many regions, notably China, where thousands of sq. m. are covered to a depth of over 1000 ft, the black earth dists of Russia and the Mississippi basin. There has been much discussion as to its origin, leading to a general conclusion that it is wind-borne from desert or steppe land, desiccated lake basins, glacial moraine and the sediment left by vastly swollen rivs. of the glacial epoch. The distribution of L. may be summarised with some approximation to correctness as forming a fringe on the equatorial side of the limit of Pleistocene glaciation and on the great desert and steppe lands. Prof. von Richthofen studied the great deposit in China, and concluded that it was the wind-drifted fine dust from the central deserts of Asia, brought down by the moister air near the coast. Given sufficient rainfall L. is extremely fertile; it weathers into vertical cliffs and horizontal terraces; excavations in the former provide homes for large numbers in China. It gives colour and name to the Hoang Ho and Yellow Sea.

Loewe, Karl (1796–1869), Ger. composer, *b.* Löbejuen, near Halle, and studied at Halle. He settled in Stettin and produced an enormous quantity of compositions. His songs and ballads are particularly expressive, and in spite of their ingenuousness have remained favourites in Germany. The Scottish *Edward* and a setting of Goethe's *Erlkönig* are among his most characteristic ballads. His other compositions, which include oratorios, operas, overtures, choruses, symphonies and concertos, are now forgotten. *See* A. B. Bach, *The Art Ballad, Loewe and Schubert,* 1890; *also* lives by H. Bulthaupt, 1898; M. Runze, 1903; O. Altenburg, 1924.

Lofoten Islands, large group of is. lying off the NW. coast of Norway. The group is separated from the mainland by the Vestfjord, and is divided into 2 sections by the Raftsund, the L. I. proper lying to the W. and S. and the Vesteraalen Is. to the E. and N. The famous Maelström

lies between Mosbenaes and Mosken. The climate is not rigorous; there is good pasturage for cattle, and barley can be grown. The chief industry is cod-fishing, culminating in mid Mar., when as many as 30,000 fishermen and 9000 boats are engaged, and cod-liver oil and other fish products are manuf. Brit. commando raiders landed on the is. on 6 Mar. 1941, sank 18,000 tons of Ger. shipping, took 215 Ger. prisoners and destroyed an important fish-oil plant. Another raid was carried out on 29 Dec. In retribution the Germans burnt houses and took hostages. Area about 2812 sq. m.; pop. 60,000.

See under NAVAL OPERATIONS IN THE SECOND WORLD WAR. (*See Plate: Norway.*)

Lofting, Hugh (1886–1947), Amer. author and illustrator, *b.* Maidenhead, Berks. He settled in the U.S.A. in 1912 as a practising civil engineer. After military service in the First World War he turned to writing and illustrating children's books, the most successful being the 'Dr Dolittle' series. This series includes *The Voyages of Dr Dolittle,* 1912, *Dr Dolittle's Caravan,* 1926, and *Dr Dolittle's Return,* 1933. Other books are *Porridge Poetry,* 1924, and *Gub Gub Book,* 1932. In 1922 he was awarded the Newbery medal, an Amer. distinction given specially for children's books.

Loftus, urb. dist and par. of N. Riding, Yorks, England, 9 m. NE. of Guisborough. A manor of L. existed before the Conquest, and L. is mentioned in Domesday Book; though still partly agric., the dist has long been associated with the growth of the iron and steel industry. Alum, stone and iron are found, and there are steel works, joinery works and a small iron foundry. Pop. (civil par.) 4137; (urb. dist) 8112.

Log (word of uncertain origin) in a nautical sense is an apparatus for measuring the speed of a ship. There are 2 main varieties of L.: the common L. and the patent L. The origin of the former is obscure and no mention of it is found until 1577. There are 4 parts to a common L.: the L.-ship or L.-chip, the L.-reel, the L.-line and the L.-glass. The L.-ship is a wood quadrant about ½ in. thick, of a radius of 5 or 6 in. and having the circumference weighted with lead to keep it upright. There are 2 holes near the lower angles, through one of which the end of a short piece of thin line is passed and knotted; the other end of the line is spliced to a hard bone peg, which is inserted in the other hole. The L.-ship hangs square from this span of rope, to which the L.-line is secured. The first portion of the line (from 10 to 20 fathoms) is known as the stray line, and should be long enough to take the L.-ship out of the ship's wake. A piece of bunting marks the end of the stray line and from this the line is marked with 'knots' at regular intervals. A nautical mile is assumed to be 6080 ft, and the distance between knots bears the same relation to this distance as the number of seconds in the L.-glass bears to an hour. If the glass is a 28-sec. one the distance is 47 ft 3 in.; if, as is more rarely the case, it is a 30-sec. glass the distance is 50 ft 7 in. For speeds over 6 knots a 14-sec. glass is generally used, and the indicated speed doubled. To heave the log a man holds the L.-reel over his head, and an officer throws the L.-ship, with the peg in, clear to windward. The L.-glass is turned when the bunting reaches the officer's hand, and as soon as the glass has run out the progress of the line is stopped and the distance measured.

Hand logs are now obsolete, those in use today employing either a towed rotator, revolutions of which are recorded as distance run, or a rod projecting from the hull known as a 'bottom' log by means of which the speed is measured, either by recording the pressure of the water when forced through a small orifice on the fore side, or by means of a small impellor which is rotated by the forward motion of the ship. Improvements in the precision with which it is now possible to manuf. these instruments have greatly increased their accuracy.

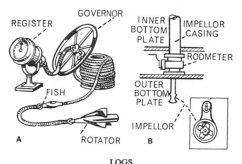

LOGS

A, Trident-type towed log; B, Chernikeel bottom log.

Log-book, book into which the contents of the log-board or rough L. are transcribed daily. The columns of the L. make provision for the nature and velocity of the wind, the state of the weather, the observed lat. and long., the course, progress, etc. Under the heading 'Remarks' are entered the employment of the crew, the times of passing prominent landmarks, any alteration of the course, signals made and exchanged, drills performed, etc., and in the case of sailing ships the making, shortening and trimming of sails. The deck L. is kept by the officer of the watch, is copied into the ship's L., which is the official L., by the navigating officer in charge and is then initialled by the officer on watch. In steam vessels rough and fair engine-room registers are kept, giving information as to the state of the engines, etc. All ships in the Brit. Mercantile Marine are compelled to keep an official L. in a form approved by the Board of Trade. Various L.s are used in aircraft, the pilot's L. being the most important.

Logan, John (1748–88), minister and poet, b. Soutra, Midlothian. In 1771 he was presented to the charge of S. Leith, and ordained 2 years later. Some local scandal having arisen in connection with his name, he resigned his charge in 1786, retaining part of his salary. He settled in London, where he contributed to the *English*

Review. His undisputed works include *View of Ancient History, 1788–93, A Review of the Principal Charges against Warren Hastings,* 1788, and 2 vols. of *Sermons,* 1790–1. His poems, especially the ballad *Braes of Yarrow,* are marked by passages of rare beauty, but the charges of plagiarism and of appropriating the verses of Michael Bruce (q.v.) led to a large amount of controversy, more especially in connection with the famous 'Ode to the Cuckoo'.

Logan, Sir William Edmund (1798–1875), geologist, b. Montreal. Graduated at Edinburgh, 1817. From 1842 to 1871 he was director of the Canadian Geological Survey. He discovered the Stigmaria under-clays and the *Eozoon canadense.* He was knighted in 1856. His *Geology of Canada* was pub. in 1863. *See* life by J. Harrington, 1883.

Logan, city and co. seat of Cache co., Utah, U.S.A., on the L. R., 35 m. N. of Ogden. It is the seat of the State Agric. College and the centre of a rich agric. and mining dist. Pop. 18,400.

Logan, Mount, in the SW. corner of the Yukon ter., Canada. It is the second highest known peak in N. America, and the highest in Canada, having an altitude of 19,850 ft.

Logan Stone, The (Cornwall), *see* ROCKING STONES.

Loganberry, cross between a raspberry and the Amer. blackberry (*Rubus ursinus vitifolius*), originally raised by Judge Logan in California. The fruit resembles the raspberry in character, but is larger, darker coloured and more prolific. Its core remains in the fruit when the stalk is removed, as in the blackberry. Its flavour is sharper and more acid than the raspberry. The cultivation of L.s has rapidly developed; the chief use of the fruit is for bottling and preserving. The plant is hardy and easily grown.

Logansport, city, cap. of Cass co., Indiana, U.S.A., on the Wabash R. in agric. area 68 m. NW. of Indianapolis. It manufs. fire apparatus, farm equipment, clothing, oxygen and acetylene gas, etc. Pop. *c.* 25,000.

Logarithm. The preface to Chambers's *Logarithmic Tables* gives the following explanation: 'A table of logarithms is a collection of auxiliary numbers so constructed that by it Multiplication of common numbers can be performed by *addition* of their logarithms; Division by their *subtraction*; Involution, or the raising of powers, by *multiplication*; and Evolution, or extraction of roots, by *division*.' The definition of a L. is then given as follows: 'These auxiliaries of logarithms are the exponents of powers to which an invariable number called the *base* has to be raised, in order to produce the number of which it is the logarithm.' Expressed mathematically, if x is the L. of a number N to the base b, then x is *defined* by the equation $N = b^x$. A convenient way of stating the fact that x is the L. of N to the base b is $x = \log_b N$. In this article we shall show the usefulness of L. by verifying the facts stated in the explanation and, finally, how the tables are constructed and how they are to be used. (i) *Multiplication of numbers.* Suppose M and N are

	0	1	2	3	4	5	6	7	8	9	1	2	3	4	5	6	7	8	9
10	0000	0043	0086	0128	0170						4	9	13	17	21	26	30	34	38
						0212	0253	0294	0334	0374	4	8	12	16	20	24	28	32	37
11	0414	0453	0492	0531	0569						4	8	12	15	19	23	27	31	35
						0607	0645	0682	0719	0755	4	7	11	15	19	22	26	30	33
12	0792	0828	0864	0899	0934	0969					3	7	11	14	18	21	25	28	32
							1004	1038	1072	1106	3	7	10	14	17	20	24	27	31
13	1139	1173	1206	1239	1271						3	7	10	13	16	20	23	26	30
						1303	1335	1367	1399	1430	3	7	10	12	16	19	22	25	29
14	1461	1492	1523	1553							3	6	9	12	15	18	21	24	28
					1584	1614	1644	1673	1703	1732	3	6	9	12	15	17	20	23	26
15	1761	1790	1818	1847	1875	1903					3	6	9	11	14	17	20	23	26
							1931	1959	1987	2014	3	5	8	11	14	16	19	22	25
16	2041	2068	2095	2122	2148						3	5	8	11	14	16	19	22	24
						2175	2201	2227	2253	2279	3	5	8	10	13	15	18	21	23
17	2304	2330	2355	2380	2405	2430					3	5	8	10	13	15	18	20	23
							2455	2480	2504	2529	2	5	7	10	12	15	17	19	22
18	2553	2577	2601	2625	2648						2	5	7	9	12	14	16	19	21
						2672	2695	2718	2742	2765	2	5	7	9	11	14	16	18	21
19	2788	2810	2833	2856	2878						2	4	7	9	11	13	16	18	20
						2900	2923	2945	2967	2989	2	4	6	8	11	13	15	17	19
20	3010	3032	3054	3075	3096	3118	3139	3160	3181	3201	2	4	6	8	11	13	15	17	19
21	3222	3243	3263	3284	3304	3324	3345	3365	3385	3404	2	4	6	8	10	12	14	16	18
22	3424	3444	3464	3483	3502	3522	3541	3560	3579	3598	2	4	6	8	10	12	14	15	17
23	3617	3636	3655	3674	3692	3711	3729	3747	3766	3784	2	4	6	7	9	11	13	15	17
24	3802	3820	3838	3856	3874	3892	3909	3927	3945	3962	2	4	5	7	9	11	12	14	16
25	3979	3997	4014	4031	4048	4065	4082	4099	4116	4133	2	3	5	7	9	10	12	14	15
26	4150	4166	4183	4200	4216	4232	4249	4265	4281	4298	2	3	5	7	8	10	11	13	15
27	4314	4330	4346	4362	4378	4393	4409	4425	4440	4456	2	3	5	6	8	9	11	13	14
28	4472	4487	4502	4518	4533	4548	4564	4579	4594	4609	2	3	5	6	8	9	11	12	14
29	4624	4639	4654	4669	4683	4698	4713	4728	4742	4757	1	3	4	6	7	9	10	12	13
30	4771	4786	4800	4814	4829	4843	4857	4871	4886	4900	1	3	4	6	7	9	10	11	13
31	4914	4928	4942	4955	4969	4983	4997	5011	5024	5038	1	3	4	6	7	8	10	11	12
32	5051	5065	5079	5092	5105	5119	5132	5145	5159	5172	1	3	4	5	7	8	9	11	12
33	5185	5198	5211	5224	5237	5250	5263	5276	5289	5302	1	3	4	5	6	8	9	10	12
34	5315	5328	5340	5353	5366	5378	5391	5403	5416	5428	1	3	4	5	6	8	9	10	11
35	5441	5453	5465	5478	5490	5502	5514	5527	5539	5551	1	2	4	5	6	7	9	10	11
36	5563	5575	5587	5599	5611	5623	5635	5647	5658	5670	1	2	4	5	6	7	8	10	11
37	5682	5694	5705	5717	5729	5740	5752	5763	5775	5786	1	2	3	5	6	7	8	9	10
38	5798	5809	5821	5832	5843	5855	5866	5877	5888	5899	1	2	3	5	6	7	8	9	10
39	5911	5922	5933	5944	5955	5966	5977	5988	5999	6010	1	2	3	4	5	7	8	9	10
40	6021	6031	6042	6053	6064	6075	6085	6096	6107	6117	1	2	3	4	5	6	8	9	10
41	6128	6138	6149	6160	6170	6180	6191	6201	6212	6222	1	2	3	4	5	6	7	8	9
42	6232	6243	6253	6263	6274	6284	6294	6304	6314	6325	1	2	3	4	5	6	7	8	9
43	6335	6345	6355	6365	6375	6385	6395	6405	6415	6425	1	2	3	4	5	6	7	8	9
44	6435	6444	6454	6464	6474	6484	6493	6503	6513	6522	1	2	3	4	5	6	7	8	9
45	6532	6542	6551	6561	6571	6580	6590	6599	6609	6618	1	2	3	4	5	6	7	8	9
46	6628	6637	6646	6656	6665	6675	6684	6693	6702	6712	1	2	3	4	5	6	7	7	8
47	6721	6730	6739	6749	6758	6767	6776	6785	6794	6803	1	2	3	4	5	5	6	7	8
48	6812	6821	6830	6839	6848	6857	6866	6875	6884	6893	1	2	3	4	4	5	6	7	8
49	6902	6911	6920	6928	6937	6946	6955	6964	6972	6981	1	2	3	4	4	5	6	7	8
50	6990	6998	7007	7016	7024	7033	7042	7050	7059	7067	1	2	3	3	4	5	6	7	8

Reproduced from the Ministry of Education's 'Four-figure Tables and Constants'

COMMON LOGARITHMS

	0	1	2	3	4	5	6	7	8	9	1	2	3	4	5	6	7	8	9
51	7076	7084	7093	7101	7110	7118	7126	7135	7143	7152	1	2	3	3	4	5	6	7	8
52	7160	7168	7177	7185	7193	7202	7210	7218	7226	7235	1	2	2	3	4	5	6	7	7
53	7243	7251	7259	7267	7275	7284	7292	7300	7308	7316	1	2	2	3	4	5	6	6	7
54	7324	7332	7340	7348	7356	7364	7372	7380	7388	7396	1	2	2	3	4	5	6	6	7
55	7404	7412	7419	7427	7435	7443	7451	7459	7466	7474	1	2	2	3	4	5	5	6	7
56	7482	7490	7497	7505	7513	7520	7528	7536	7543	7551	1	2	2	3	4	5	5	6	7
57	7559	7566	7574	7582	7589	7597	7604	7612	7619	7627	1	2	2	3	4	5	5	6	7
58	7634	7642	7649	7657	7664	7672	7679	7686	7694	7701	1	1	2	3	4	4	5	6	7
59	7709	7716	7723	7731	7738	7745	7752	7760	7767	7774	1	1	2	3	4	4	5	6	7
60	7782	7789	7796	7803	7810	7818	7825	7832	7839	7846	1	1	2	3	4	4	5	6	6
61	7853	7860	7868	7875	7882	7889	7896	7903	7910	7917	1	1	2	3	4	4	5	6	6
62	7924	7931	7938	7945	7952	7959	7966	7973	7980	7987	1	1	2	3	3	4	5	6	6
63	7993	8000	8007	8014	8021	8028	8035	8041	8048	8055	1	1	2	3	3	4	5	5	6
64	8062	8069	8075	8082	8089	8096	8102	8109	8116	8122	1	1	2	3	3	4	5	5	6
65	8129	8136	8142	8149	8156	8162	8169	8176	8182	8189	1	1	2	3	3	4	5	5	6
66	8195	8202	8209	8215	8222	8228	8235	8241	8248	8254	1	1	2	3	3	4	5	5	6
67	8261	8267	8274	8280	8287	8293	8299	8306	8312	8319	1	1	2	3	3	4	5	5	6
68	8325	8331	8338	8344	8351	8357	8363	8370	8376	8382	1	1	2	3	3	4	4	5	6
69	8388	8395	8401	8407	8414	8420	8426	8432	8439	8445	1	1	2	2	3	4	4	5	6
70	8451	8457	8463	8470	8476	8482	8488	8494	8500	8506	1	1	2	2	3	4	4	5	6
71	8513	8519	8525	8531	8537	8543	8549	8555	8561	8567	1	1	2	2	3	4	4	5	5
72	8573	8579	8585	8591	8597	8603	8609	8615	8621	8627	1	1	2	2	3	4	4	5	5
73	8633	8639	8645	8651	8657	8663	8669	8675	8681	8686	1	1	2	2	3	4	4	5	5
74	8692	8698	8704	8710	8716	8722	8727	8733	8739	8745	1	1	2	2	3	4	4	5	5
75	8751	8756	8762	8768	8774	8779	8785	8791	8797	8802	1	1	2	2	3	3	4	5	5
76	8808	8814	8820	8825	8831	8837	8842	8848	8854	8859	1	1	2	2	3	3	4	5	5
77	8865	8871	8876	8882	8887	8893	8899	8904	8910	8915	1	1	2	2	3	3	4	4	5
78	8921	8927	8932	8938	8943	8949	8954	8960	8965	8971	1	1	2	2	3	3	4	4	5
79	8976	8982	8987	8993	8998	9004	9009	9015	9020	9025	1	1	2	2	3	3	4	4	5
80	9031	9036	9042	9047	9053	9058	9063	9069	9074	9079	1	1	2	2	3	3	4	4	5
81	9085	9090	9096	9101	9106	9112	9117	9122	9128	9133	1	1	2	2	3	3	4	4	5
82	9138	9143	9149	9154	9159	9165	9170	9175	9180	9186	1	1	2	2	3	3	4	4	5
83	9191	9196	9201	9206	9212	9217	9222	9227	9232	9238	1	1	2	2	3	3	4	4	5
84	9243	9248	9253	9258	9263	9269	9274	9279	9284	9289	1	1	2	2	3	3	4	4	5
85	9294	9299	9304	9309	9315	9320	9325	9330	9335	9340	1	1	2	2	3	3	4	4	5
86	9345	9350	9355	9360	9365	9370	9375	9380	9385	9390	1	1	2	2	3	3	4	4	5
87	9395	9400	9405	9410	9415	9420	9425	9430	9435	9440	0	1	1	2	2	3	3	4	4
88	9445	9450	9455	9460	9465	9469	9474	9479	9484	9489	0	1	1	2	2	3	3	4	4
89	9494	9499	9504	9509	9513	9518	9523	9528	9533	9538	0	1	1	2	2	3	3	4	4
90	9542	9547	9552	9557	9562	9566	9571	9576	9581	9586	0	1	1	2	2	3	3	4	4
91	9590	9595	9600	9605	9609	9614	9619	9624	9628	9633	0	1	1	2	2	3	3	4	4
92	9638	9643	9647	9652	9657	9661	9666	9671	9675	9680	0	1	1	2	2	3	3	4	4
93	9685	9689	9694	9699	9703	9708	9713	9717	9722	9727	0	1	1	2	2	3	3	4	4
94	9731	9736	9741	9745	9750	9754	9759	9763	9768	9773	0	1	1	2	2	3	3	4	4
95	9777	9782	9786	9791	9795	9800	9805	9809	9814	9818	0	1	1	2	2	3	3	4	4
96	9823	9827	9832	9836	9841	9845	9850	9854	9859	9863	0	1	1	2	2	3	3	4	4
97	9868	9872	9877	9881	9886	9890	9894	9899	9903	9908	0	1	1	2	2	3	3	4	4
98	9912	9917	9921	9926	9930	9934	9939	9943	9948	9952	0	1	1	2	2	3	3	4	4
99	9956	9961	9965	9969	9974	9978	9983	9987	9991	9996	0	1	1	2	2	3	3	3	4

by permission of the Controller of Her Majesty's Stationery Office

COMMON LOGARITHMS

2 numbers and that $x = \log_b N$; $y = \log_b M$. From the above definition of L., $N = b^x$ and $M = b^y$. Hence $MN = b^{x+y}$, i.e. $\log_b MN = \log_b M + \log_b N$. In other words, $\log_b MN$ is found by *addition* of the L. of the 2 numbers; from the tables we then discover the required number.

Example. Using a table of L.s constructed to the base 10 multiply 26 by 47. We find $\log_{10} 26 = 1\cdot4150$; $\log_{10} 47 = 1\cdot6721$. Hence by our rule $\log_{10}(26 \times 47) = 1\cdot4150 + 1\cdot6721 = 3\cdot0871$. From the same tables we find that $\log_{10} 1222 = 3\cdot0871$; hence $26 \times 47 = 1222$. The above argument can be extended for the multiplication of any set of numbers. Thus $\log_b MNOP \ldots = \log_b M + \log_b N + \log_b O + \log_b P + \ldots$

(ii) *Division of numbers*. $\log_b \left(\dfrac{M}{N}\right) = \log_b M - \log_b N$, for if $x = \log_b N$ and $y = \log_b M$, then by definition $N = b^x$ and $M = b^y$. Hence $\dfrac{M}{N} = b^{y-x}$, whence $\log_b \left(\dfrac{M}{N}\right) = y - x$.

Example. Using tables to the base 10, divide 63 by 9. We find $\log_{10} 63 = 1\cdot7993$ and $\log_{10} 9 = 0\cdot9542$. Hence by our rule $\log_{10}\left(\dfrac{63}{9}\right) = 1\cdot7993 - 0\cdot9542 = 0\cdot8451$. From the same tables we find that $\log_{10} 7 = 0\cdot8451$; hence $\dfrac{63}{9} = 7$. This obvious answer has been used for simplicity. The reader may easily verify that $\log_b(N)^p = p \log_b N$, a rule that enables us to find $(N)^p$ by means of tables with a minimum of trouble. Further it is easily shown that $\log_b(N)^{\frac{1}{q}} = \dfrac{1}{q}\log_b N$, a rule that enables us to find $(N)^{\frac{1}{q}}$ at once by use of L. tables.

John Napier (q.v.) (1550–1617) invented L.s in order to aid astronomers in their trigonometrical calculations; his table of log sines for every minute of the quadrant was pub. in 1614. Before the invention of the decimal point (q.v.) multi-figure accuracy in tables of sines was obtained by using a high power of 10 for radius = sin 90°, and Napier's table of L.s was on the same basis: in terms of $r = 1$, the base of his system would be $(1/e)$. Briggs (q.v.) (1561–1631) wrote to Napier (1615) proposing a new table; in terms of $r = 1$, his proposed base was (1/10). When they met in Scotland, Napier said he had already been thinking along the same lines, but would prefer a system that would (in effect and for $r = 1$) make the base 10. Briggs agreed that this was preferable and immediately started to compile the first table of common logs: the first thousand were pub. in 1617 and his friend Gunter produced a table of log sines to the new base in 1620.

Logarithms to the base 10 *and their use*. In the first place since $10^1 = 10$, $\log_{10} 10 = 1$; $10^2 = 100$, $\log_{10} 100 = 2$; $10^3 = 1000$, $\log_{10} 1000 = 3$, etc. Again $10^0 = 1$, hence $\log_{10} 1 = 0$; $10^{-1} = \frac{1}{10}$, $\log_{10} 0\cdot1 = -1$;

$10^{-2} = \frac{1}{100}$, $\log_{10} 0\cdot01 = -2$, etc. From the first part of this statement it follows that the L. of any number greater than 1 and less than 10 will be greater than 0 and less than 1, i.e. a decimal without an integer. The L. of any number greater than 10 and less than 100 will be greater than 1 and less than 2, i.e. $1 +$ a decimal. In general the L. of a number consisting of n integral numbers is $(n - 1) +$ a decimal. The integral part of a L. is called its *characteristic* and the decimal part the *mantissa*.

Example. From tables we find that $\log_{10} 8 = 0\cdot9031$. Find $\log_{10} 80$. $\log_{10} 80 = \log_{10} 8 + \log_{10} 10 = 0\cdot9031 + 1 = 1\cdot9031$. Similarly $\log_{10} 800 = 2\cdot9031$. Thus the mantissa is the property of the number 8, the characteristic being determined by the position of the decimal point.

When we come to deal with the L. of proper fractions we see from the second part of the statement at the beginning of the paragraph that they are negative. Thus $\log_{10} 0\cdot8 = \log_{10}\frac{4}{5} = \log_{10} 4 - \log_{10} 5 = 0\cdot6021 - 0\cdot6990 = -0\cdot0969 = -1 + 0\cdot9031$. For the moment the simplicity of L.s seems to have disappeared as soon as we come to proper fractions. We might naturally inquire if the welcome property of the *mantissa* mentioned above can be retained for proper fractions as well. If we write $\log_{10} 0\cdot8 = \log_{10}\frac{8}{10} = \log_{10} 8 - \log_{10} 10 = 0\cdot9031 - 1$, or as it is usually written $\bar{1}\cdot9031$ or $9\cdot9031$ we get a L. in which only the characteristic is negative, and the mantissa is that belonging to the number 8 as before. Similarly we deduce $\log_{10} 0\cdot08 = \bar{2}\cdot9031$ or $8\cdot9031$. The results may be summed up then as follows: The *mantissa* of the L. to the base 10 is the same for all numbers consisting of the *same* digits arranged in the *same* order. The position of the decimal point only affects the characteristic. Hence if the number whose L. we require consists of one or more integral figures, the characteristic is always *one less* than the number of integral figures, and it is positive. If the number is wholly a decimal, its characteristic is the same as the number of the place from the decimal point occupied by its first significant figure. This simple method is only true of L.s to the base 10, because that base is the same as the radix of the scale of the natural numbers. Napier's base or radix was a number denoted by e, whose value is $2\cdot7182818.\ldots$ This number is defined by the mathematical series

$$e = 1 + 1 + \frac{1}{2!} + \frac{1}{3!} + \frac{1}{4!} + \ldots \textit{ad infinitum}.$$

Its importance is due to the fact that for all positive values of x less than 1,

$$\log_e(1 + x) = x - \frac{x^2}{2} + \frac{x^3}{3} - \frac{x^4}{4} +$$

$\ldots$ *ad infinitum*. Algebraical analysis enabled Napier to compute his L. to the base e by means of this expansion of $\log_e(1 + x)$ and L. to the base 10 are computed from an expression derived from the one above. It is shown in text-books on algebra that $\log_{10}(n + 1) - \log_{10} n = \dfrac{\mu}{n} - \dfrac{\mu}{2n^2} + \dfrac{\mu}{3n^3} - \ldots$ where $\mu = \log_{10} e =$

0·43429448 . . . Hence if the L. of one number to the base 10 is found, the L. of the next number can be computed. Repeated application of this formula results in the table of L. with which we are familiar.

The reverse process of finding, from the tables, the number when the L. is given is also done in 2 parts. The *mantissa* is considered first; from it the actual digits of the number are found; the whole-number part of the L., the characteristic, then gives the position of the decimal point. These results can also be obtained from antilogarithm tables, on which the L.s are arranged round the edge of the table and the numbers in the centre. *See also* MATHEMATICS; SLIDE RULE. *See* W. Chanin, *Logarithms in Commerce*, 1931; Sir C. V. Boys, *Natural Logarithm*, 1935; F. W. Chambers, *Arithmetic of Logarithms*, 1935; H. S. Hall and S. R. Knight, *Higher Algebra*, 1940. Good four-figure tables are those of Godfrey and Siddons, while *Chambers's Seven-figure Mathematical Tables* are invaluable for accurate work. (*See* tables on pp. 24–25.)

Logau, Friedrich, Freiherr von (1604–55), Ger. poet, *b.* Brockut, in Silesia. He studied law at Brieg and Frankfurt, and entered the legal service of the Duchy of Liegnitz as chancery councillor. He is chiefly famous as a writer of epigrams. Under the anagrammatic pseudonym 'Salomon von Golaw' he pub. a collection of epigrams, *Zweihundert teutscher Reimensprüche*, 1638, which are a shrewd satire of 17th cent. life. A selection from his *Sinngedichte* was made by Lessing and K. W. Ramler in 1759, and a complete ed. of his works by G. Eitner in 1876.

Loggan, David (1635–1700), Ger. engraver and designer, *b.* Danzig. He settled in London and pub. engravings of the colleges of Oxford and Cambridge—*Oxonia Illustrata*, 1675, and *Cantabrigia Illustrata*, 1676–90. At the court of Charles II he engraved sev. portraits of the king and of his courtiers.

Loggia (It.), covered gallery or room, usually adjoining or forming part of a larger building, with one or more of its sides open to the air, and colonnaded or arcaded.

Logging, *see* LUMBER AND LUMBERING.

Logia (Gk 'oracles'). Papias, a writer of the 2nd cent., who is said to have been a disciple of St John, wrote that 'Matthew composed the oracles (*logia*) of the Lord in the Hebrew tongue' (Eusebius, *Historia Ecclesiastica*, iii. 39). It was once believed that they were a collection of passages from the Heb. Bible such as were susceptible of a Messianic interpretation, or a collection of our Lord's sayings later incorporated in our 1st and 3rd Gospels. Today the prevailing opinion holds that the word is a description of the Gospel of St Matthew in its original Heb. form, as was clearly thought by Eusebius and Irenaeus. *See* G. D. Kilpatrick, *The Origins of the Gospel according to St Matthew*, 1946.

Logic may be most briefly defined as the study of the general conditions of valid inference. The three 'products of thought', the instruments employed by the logician, are the term, the proposition or premiss and the inference. (1) A term may be said to denote an individual or a group of individuals, or to connote an attribute or a group of attributes. (2) A proposition or premise asserts or denies one term or another as the result of comparison, e.g. 'All triangles are bounded by three sides'. Here the term 'bounded by three sides' (an attribute) is called the predicate, while the term 'all triangles' (a group of individuals) is called the subject; the connecting verb 'are' is the *copula*. Thus 'bounded by three sides' is said to be predicated of 'all triangles'. Propositions or premises may be subdivided (*a*) according to quality, i.e. affirmative or negative, or (*b*) according to quantity, i.e. universal ('All men are fools') or particular ('Some men are fools'). There is a further possible subdivision into universal-affirmative ('All X is Y'), universal-negative ('No X is Y'), particular-affirmative ('Some X is Y') and particular-negative ('Some X is not Y'). The most important part of L. deals with inference, i.e. the process of combining two propositions or premises so as to arrive at a proposition distinct from any that has preceded. Inferences are of two kinds: inductive (*see also* INDUCTION) and deductive. (i) *Induction*, or inference from the particular to the universal. *Analogy*, or inference from the particular to an adjacent particular, is a form of imperfect induction and, though justifying a more or less probable conclusion, never leads to certainty (e.g. War between A and B is wicked. War between A and B is similar to war between A and C. Therefore war between A and C is wicked). (ii) *Deduction* or syllogism (q.v.) is inference from the universal to the particular (e.g. All war is wicked. Armed conflict between A and B is war. Therefore armed conflict between A and B is wicked). Syllogisms may be combined in what is called a 'train of reasoning' and the complex or hypothetical syllogism may be employed in which one or more complex (or hypothetical) premises occur. A complex premise is a combination of two or more simple premises in one sentence, in such a manner that the truth or falsity of one premise or set of premises is made to depend on the truth or falsity of the other premise or set of premises; when dependent on the truth of the one premise or group of premises, the complex premise is termed conjunctive, when upon the falsity, disjunctive. A conjunctive syllogism is a syllogism one or both of whose premises are conjunctive premises; a disjunctive syllogism one whose premise is a disjunctive and the minor a simple proposition, the latter affirming or denying one of the alternatives stated in the former. A *dilemma* occurs when one premise of the complex syllogism is a conjunctive and the other a disjunctive premise (e.g. if A is B, C is D and E is F; but either C is not D or E is not F; therefore A is not B). *See* BARBARA.

Aristotle (q.v.) was the first to produce a definite and developed system of L. in the *Organon*. Among later schools of anct philosophy the Stoics, Epicureans, Sceptics and

Neoplatonists all contributed to the science of L. To Abelard (q.v.) is due in great measure the revival of L. in the 12th cent.; his disciple John of Salisbury shows acquaintance with the entire *Organon*. St Thomas Aquinas consolidated this advance in the 13th cent. Thereafter L. tended to become a lifeless classification or meaningless dialectic in the hands of Wm of Occam and the Nominalists until the Renaissance humanists revolted. Francis Bacon (q.v.) in his *Novum Organum* introduced his 'new' inductive L. to replace Aristotelian deductive L. Modern L. has developed along the lines of empiricism (Hobbes, Locke, Hume and J. S. Mill) and, in strong contrast, along those of Rationalism (Spinoza and Leibniz) and the transcendentalism of Kant. *See* J. S. Mill, *A System of Logic*, 1843; W. E. Johnson, *Logic*, 1921–4; A. Wolf, *Textbook of Logic*, 1930; L. S. Stebbing, *Thinking to Some Purpose*, 1939, and *Modern Introduction to Logic*, 1940; A. N. Prior, *Logic and the Basis of Ethics*, 1949; *W. C. Salmon, Logic*, 1963; J. D. Carney and R. K. Scheer, *Fundamentals of Logic*, 1964; I. Kant, *Introduction to Logic* (trans.), 1964.

Logical Positivism, *see* POSITIVISM, LOGICAL.

Logistics, term used for the military science of quartering, moving and maintaining men and equipment, mostly in the Amer. forces. *See* ARMY; COMMISSARIAT.

Logos (Gk 'word') as a theological term has no exact counterpart in any other language. *Verbum*, word, is perhaps the least satisfactory of sev. which have from time to time been adopted. In Gk philosophy, especially in Heraclitus of Ephesus and Anaxagoras and among the Stoics, L. is the divine reason immanent in the cosmic process. But their systems are forms of pantheism, recognising no transcendent god and teaching that this truth or reality (half hidden, half revealed in the visible world) can be found in the self.

In the Septuagint L. signifies the uttered word or wisdom of God expressed in creation, providence and revelation. Philo and the Alexandrian-Jewish school combined these two originally separate meanings. Philo's L. may be said to correspond to Plato's idea of the Good endowed with the creative activity or universal causality of the Stoics. Christian use applied the term to the Second Person of the Trinity. Heretical teaching in the early church tended to include Christ in the imaginary hierarchy of intermediary spirits or emanations between God and man. To this the L. doctrine of St John was an effective barrier. *See* J. Réville, *La Doctrine du Logos dans le quatrième évangile et dans les œuvres de Philon*, 1881; A. Harnack, *History of Dogma* (trans.), 1894–9; A. Aall, *Der Logos*, 1896–9; J. Lebreton, *Histoire du dogme de la Trinité*, 1928.

Logroño: 1. Sp. prov. in Castilla la Vieja (q.v.), lying S. of the Ebro. The Ebro basin is very fertile, producing cereals, olives, fruit and the red Rioja wines. Iron, silver, copper, lead and lignite are found. Area 1947 sq. m.; pop. 230,000.

2. (anct **Lucronius**), Sp. tn., cap of the prov. of L., on the Ebro. It is a well-built tn, with 3 old churches and a 12th-cent. bridge. It is a centre for the Rioja wines, and has a large agric. trade. Pop. 61,300.

Logwood, *see* DYE.

'Lohengrin', old High Ger. poem of the 13th cent. L. was the son of Parsifal and one of the knights of the Holy Grail. At King Arthur's command he was carried to Mainz in a car drawn by a swan to rescue Elsa, daughter of the Duke of Brabant. He overthrew her enemy, Telramund, and married Elsa. In spite of her promise not to question him, she insisted on demanding his origin. Twice he persuaded her not to question him, but on her asking a third time he told her, and immediately was carried away by the swan-drawn car to return to the Grail. L. is a continuation of Wolfram von Eschenbach's *Parzival*. Wagner founded his opera *Lohengrin*, 1848, on this legend.

Loidis, *see* LEEDS.

Loigny, Fr. vil. in the dept of Eure-et-Loir, the scene of a Fr. victory (Dec. 1870) during the Franco-Ger. war (q.v.). Pop. 400.

Loir, Fr. riv., rising in the dept of Eure-et-Loir and flowing SW. to join the Sarthe near Angers. Length 180 m.

Loir-et-Cher, dept of central France, formed of parts of the anct provs. of Touraine and Orléanais. It is drained by the Loir in the N., the Loire in the centre and the Cher in the S. A large part of the surface is forested, but there are also rich agric. dists in the riv. basins, and on the fertile plateau of lower Beauce (q.v.), which lies across the centre of the dept cereals, vines, fruit-trees and vegetables are cultivated, and sheep and turkeys are raised. There are foodstuff, chemical and pottery manufs. Stone, alabaster and flint are quarried. The prin. tns are Blois (the cap.), Romorantin and Vendôme (qq.v.). Area 2478 sq. m.; pop. 251,000.

Loire (anct **Liger**): 1. Longest riv. of France, which rises (4430 ft) near Mont Gerbier de Jonc in the Central Plateau, in the Cévennes (q.v.), flows in a wide curve to the N., bends W. at Orléans and enters the Bay of Biscay at St-Nazaire. Its chief tribs. are: on the r. b., the Nièvre, Maine, Erdre; and on the l. b., the Allier, Cher, Indre, Vienne and Sèvre Nantaise (qq.v.). The L. drains more than one-fifth of the area of France. In summer it is generally low, but it is subject to sudden floods (especially in L.-Atlantique, (q.v.)) and, except in its lower course, is only intermittently navigable. Dykes have been erected in many places between Orléans and Angers. The 'lateral canal of the L.' accompanies the riv. from Roanne to Briare, and thence proceeds to the Seine (q.v.). Large ships can ascend as far as Nantes (q.v.), through the 35-m.-long L. estuary. Many celebrated vineyards (Vouvray, Rochecorbon, Montlouis) lie on the banks of the L., and its valley is famous for its splendid châteaux (Blois, Chambord, Chaumont, Chenonceaux, Amboise). The prin. tns which the riv. passes are Roanne, Nevers, Gien, Orléans, Blois, Amboise, Tours, Saumur,

Angers, Nantes and St-Nazaire (qq.v.). Length 630 m.

2. Dept of central France formed from the old dist of Forez and parts of Beaujolais and Lyonnais; it is bounded on the N. by the dept of Saône-et-Loire, S. by Ardèche and Haute-Loire. It is drained in the N. by the L. and its tribs. and in the SE. by the tribs. of the Rhône. The dept is largely mountainous, but the plains of Forez and Roanne provide good agric. and pasture lands. The vine is grown in the valley of the Rhône. The basin of the St Étienne is one of the richest coal dists of France, and iron and lead are mined in large quantities. The chief manufs. are glass, ribbons, silk, cast steel, hardware, machinery and cutlery. The prin. tns are St Étienne (the cap.), Montbrison and Roanne (qq.v.). Area 1825 sq. m.; pop. 697,000.

Loire, Haute-, dept of SE. France, formed of parts of the anct provs. of Languedoc, Lyonnais and Auvergne. Situated on the central plateau of France, it is traversed by 4 mt ranges, running N.-S.: the Vivarais and its continuation, the Boutières; the Massif du Mégal; the Velay mts; and the Margeride mts. There are many signs of volcanic activity. The chief rivs. are the L., with its tribs. the Borne and the Lignon, and the Allier. The climate is cold. In the riv. valleys fruit trees and vines are cultivated. In the rest of the dept the prin. industries are the raising of stock and the exploitation of the forests. Coal and antimony are mined, and much lace is made. The prin. tns are Le Puy (the cap.), Brioude (qq.v.) and Yssingeaux. Area 1930 sq. m.; pop. 212,000.

Loire-Atlantique, maritime dept of W. France, formed from part of anct Brittany and the dist of Retz and lying between the Bay of Biscay on the W. and Main-et-Loire on the E. The surface is very flat, and is drained by the Loire, with its tribs. the Erdre and the Sèvre, and by the Isac, a trib. of the Vilaine. Horse- and cattle-breeding prospers, and cereals, vines, flax and fruit are cultivated. There are deposits of tin, lead and iron. There are foundries and shipbuilding yards at Nantes and St Nazaire. The chief manufs. are hemp, linen, paper, sugar, biscuits and soap. The prin. tns are Nantes (the cap.), Ancenis, Châteaubriant and St Nazaire (qq.v.). Area 2693 sq. m; pop. 803,000.

Loiret, dept of central France, formed of parts of the anct provs. of Orléanais, Berry and Île-de-France. It includes parts of Beauce and Gâtinais (qq.v.). The Loire valley in the S., in spite of the frequent floods, is famed for its agric. fertility and its vineyards. There is a vast forest around Orléans. The dept is mainly agric., grain, beet, vegetables and fruit being produced, but there are also rubber, iron, preserved foods and other manufs. The prin. tns are Orléans (the cap.), Montargis and Pithiviers (qq.v.). Area 2629 sq. m.; pop. 390,000.

Loisy, Alfred Firmin (1857–1940), Fr. modernist theologian, b. Ambrières, Marne; studied at the Catholic theological seminary, Châlons, and was ordained priest in 1879. He was prof. of Heb. and biblical literature at the

Institut Catholique, Paris, 1881–93, and lecturer at the École des Hautes. Études, Sorbonne, 1900–4. He was dismissed, and was excommunicated in 1908, but in 1909 he became prof. of church hist. at the Collège de France. The whole controversy arose out of his L'Évangile et l'Église, 1902, a Catholic's reply to Harnack's Wesen des Christentums. His excommunication came after the pub. of his most important work, Les Évangiles synoptiques, 1907–8. Other works are Les Actes des Apôtres, 1920, L'Apocalypse de Jean, 1923, Mémoires pour servir à l'histoire réligieuse de notre temps, 1930, and La Naissance du Christianisme, 1932. See studies by M. J. Lagrange, 1932, and Maud Petre, 1944.

Loitoine, see LUTON.

Loja: 1. Or Loxa, Sp. tn in the prov. of Granada, on the Genil. It was one of the last strongholds of the Moors. Salt is found near by, and textiles, paper and cakes (roscos) are manuf. Pop. 12,500.

2. Cap. of L. prov., S. Ecuador, bordering on Peru. There is a univ. Sub-tropical agriculture and stock-raising are carried on. L. has an airport and a radio station. Area of prov. 4438 sq. m. Pop. (prov.) 322,000; (tn) 26,000.

Lokeren, industrial tn in the prov. of E. Flanders, Belgium, 12 m. ENE. of Ghent, on the R. Durme. It has manufs. of linen, cotton, silk, wool, carpets, furs, ropes, chemicals and tobacco.

Loki, god of evil in Norse mythology. See BALDER; HEIMDALLR; HELL; HOENIR; JÖTUNS; TYR.

Lokoja, tn in N. Nigeria, W. Africa, at the confluence of the R.s Niger and Benue. The site of the first Brit. Consulate on the mainland of Nigeria (1859). L. is now a small market tn. Pop. about 8000.

Lolland (low land), Dan. is. to the S. of Zealand at the S. entrance to the Great Belt, with an area of 475 sq. m. It is difficult of access by reason of the surrounding shallows. The surface is very flat and the soil fertile. The S. coast of L. is protected by dykes from inundations of the Baltic Sea. Cap. Maribo. Produces corn, hops, apples, sugar, hemp, etc. Pop. 84,780.

Lollards, The (from the Middle Dutch lollen, to mutter), name applied at the end of the 14th cent. to the followers of Wycliffe (q.v.) and to many others who carried Wycliffe's theories far beyond what Wycliffe himself can have intended. The 'political' L. were the group of courtiers who used the movement as a counter to the political power of some of the bishops; but as time went by and persecution mounted the majority of L. were found among the very poor, chiefly in the Midlands, and the movement seems to have become quasi-social in character. The chief statute against the L. was the De Heretico Comburendo (1401), under which many were burned at the stake. After the execution of Oldcastle (1417) little is heard of the L. They were clearly dwindling fast in numbers by the turn of the 15th cent. and lost their intellectual leadership when Arundel and Courtenay suppressed Lollardry at Oxford Univ. Though some of Wycliffe's theories returned to England at the Reformation via individual Eng. Lutherans, there is no proof that the L. as a body survived long enough to provide the nucleus of 16th cent. Eng. Protestantism, as was once thought. On the contrary, areas in which the L. had been strongest (e.g. Oxford Univ. and the Midlands) often proved more stubbornly Catholic than average. *See* H. Rashdall, *Universities of Europe in the Middle Ages*, vol. ii, 1895; G. M. Trevelyan, *England in the Age of Wyclif*, 1899; H. B. Workman, *Wyclif*, 1926; H. Maynard Smith, *Pre-Reformation England*, 1938; K. B. McFarlane, *John Wycliffe and the Lollards*, 1950.

Lolos, *see* Yi.

Lombard, Lambert (1506–60), Flem. painter, engraver and architect, *b.* Liège. He visited Italy and was one of the 'Romanists' who departed from their native Flem. style.

Lombard, Peter (*c.* 1100–60), It. scholastic theologian and philosopher, *b.* Novara in Lombardy. Having studied at Bologna and Reims, he joined the Victorines at Paris where he was appointed prof. of theology *c.* 1140. In 1159 he became Bishop of Paris. L. is often referred to as 'magister Sententiarum' because of his famous *Sentences*, i.e. opinions. These are divided into 4 books, dealing with the Trinity, Creation, Incarnation and the Sacraments. L. divided each book into questions; later the questions were subdivided into distinctions and chapters, thus fixing the form of most later scholastic treatises. His aim was to unite the then received theology into a body giving weight both to scripture and reason. The 'Book of the Sentences' became after his death the accepted manual of theology until the *Summa Theologica* of St Thomas Aquinas (1225–74) gradually supplanted it. The *Libri IV Sententiarum* has been ed. by the Bonaventurans (2 vols), 1916. *See* E. F. Rogers, *Peter Lombard and the Sacramental System*, 1917.

Lombardia, *see* Lombardy.

Lombardic Architecture, *see* Architecture, 5.

Lombardo Toledano, Vicente (1894–   ), Mexican lawyer and administrator, *b.* Teziutlan, Puebla, and founder of the prin. trade union in Lat. America, the Mexican Workers' Confederation or C.R.O.M. He is also prominent in international affairs.

Lombards, The: 1. Teutonic tribe (*See* Longobards).

2. Class of It. merchants, brokers and bankers, not all, in fact, from Lombardy, who settled in England from the 13th to the 16th cent. In 1338 Edward III pledged his jewels to the L. in order to raise money for his Fr. wars, and Henry V did likewise in 1415. In that they were usurers and pawnbrokers they were unpopular, like the Jews, who, until their expulsion in 1290, had largely controlled those occupations. The L. first arrived in England in the reign of Henry III (1216–72), and were formally banished by Queen Elizabeth I. But even before her accession Eng. merchants had taken over most of their functions. It is said that Edward II handed over as much as £56,000 to the Frescobaldi in payment of his father's debts, whilst the wealthy firms of the Peruzzi and Bardi, the leading L. of the day, were actually ruined by Edward III, who was never able to redeem his pledges. Lombard Street, in the city of London, commemorates their former residence in the neighbourhood and is still a prominent banking centre.

Lombardy (It. **Lombardia**), region (*compartimento*) of N. Italy, comprising the provs. of Bergamo, Brescia, Como, Cremona, Mantua, Milan, Pavia, Sondrio and Varese (qq.v.). It is bounded N. by Switzerland, W. by Piedmont, S. by Emilia-Romagna and E. by Veneto and Trentino-Alto Adige (qq.v.). L. lies between the Alps and the R. Po, is very high in the N. (Pizzo Bernina, 11,253 ft) and is part of the great 'Plain of Lombardy' in the S. The dist was conquered by Rome (223 BC), by the Longobards (AD 568) and in 774 by Charlemagne (qq.v.). In 1167 the cities of the Plain of L. formed a 'Lombard League' against the Emperor Frederick I (q.v.). L. was subsequently in the hands of Spain, Austria, France (under Napoleon I, q.v.) and Austria again. In 1859 it became part of united Italy. The main products of L. are cereals, wine, rice, chestnuts, flax, mulberries (for silkworm breeding) and cheese. There is an important silk industry (Milan and Como), and there are engineering and chemical manufs. The chief tn is Milan. Area 9185 sq. m.; pop. 7,310,000.

Lombardy Poplar, *see* Poplar.

Lombok, is. situated eastward of Java, Indonesia. It is separated W. from Bali by L. Strait and E. from Sumbawa by the strait of Alas. The area is 1826 sq. m. Two mt chains extend along the N. and S. coasts, the former being volcanic. Between the ranges are well-watered fertile plains, where sugar, coffee, maize, indigo, cotton and tobacco are cultivated. The cap. is Mataram and the chief port Ampenan, situated on the W. coast. The is. was captured by the Japanese in Feb. 1942, but reverted to the Dutch in 1945. L. became part of Indonesia in 1950. Pop. 1,200,000.

Lombroso, Cesare (1836–1909), It. criminologist and prof. of forensic medicine, later prof. of criminal anthropology at Turin; *b.* Verona. His name is mainly associated with theories relative to the responsibility or irresponsibility of criminals and, as incidental thereto, with theories as to the physical and psychical characteristics that go to form the criminal type. For a general criticism of his theory of the evidence of a criminal type *see under* Criminology. Chief works: *L'Uomo delinquente*, 1876; *La Pellagra in Italia*, 1885; *L'Uomo di genio*, 1888; *La Donna Delinquente*, 1893 (Eng. trans. *The Female Offender*, 1959); *Delitti vecchi e delitti nuovi*, 1902; *Nuovi studi sul genio*, 1902.

Lommel, tn in the prov. of Limbourg, Belgium, 22 m. N. of Hasselt, near the Dutch border. It is one of the new industrial places of the Kempen (Campine) region. Chief manufs. are zinc, lead, tin and bottles. Pop. 18,000.

Lomond, Loch, largest loch in Scotland, situated in the cos. of Stirlingshire and Dunbartonshire. Its length is 23 m., and it varies in width from 5 m. to ½ m.; its area is 27 sq. m. It contains 30 is., of which the largest is Inchmurrin. Mts and valleys encircle the lake and from these numerous streams fall to its banks. Its S. shore near Balloch has been industrialised.

Lomonosov, Mikhail Vasil'yevich (1711–65), Russian scientist and poet, son of an Archangel fisherman. When 17 years old he ran away to Moscow, where he was educ. in a state school, and later studied on state scholarships in St Petersburg and abroad (Freiburg). After his return to Russia L. worked at the Academy of Sciences in St Petersburg, and contributed to many fields of scientific research. He enunciated the principle of the conservation of matter, and to some extent anticipated the atomic theory of the structure of matter later developed by Lavoisier and Dalton (qq.v.). He struggled constantly with the 'German party' in the Academy and worked for the spread of education in Russia; he was largely responsible for the foundation of Moscow Univ. in 1755. As a poet, L. belonged to the Classicist school.

Lomonosov Ridge, submarine mt range running from N. Greenland to Novosibirskiye Ostrova (New Siberian Is.) and dividing the Arctic Ocean into 2 basins. It was discovered by Soviet scientists, from their work during expeditions carried out at intervals since 1937 on floating sea ice, drifting according to wind and current over the polar basin.

Łomża, tn of Poland, in Białystok prov., on the Narew, 45 m. W. of Białystok (q.v.). It passed to Prussia in 1795, and was in Russian Poland, 1815–1921. There are manufs. of electrical goods, rolling-stock and food-stuffs. Pop. 21,000.

London, John Griffith (1876–1916), Amer. novelist who wrote as **Jack London,** b. San Francisco. In 1897 he took part in the Klondike gold rush, and from his experiences afterwards wrote *The Call of the Wild*, 1903. In 1907 he set out with his wife on a world cruise of which he wrote in *The Cruise of the Snark*, 1911. In 1912 he sailed round the Horn. At one time he was the most popular and best paid writer in America, but drink and extravagance caused his work to deteriorate, and he finally committed suicide. He is best remembered for his sensational novels. His books include *The God of his Fathers*, 1901, *The People of the Abyss*, 1903, *The Sea Wolf*, 1904, *White Fang*, 1905, *Before Adam*, 1906, *Smoke Bellew*, 1912, *John Barleycorn*, 1913, and *The Star Rover*, 1914. See Charmian London, *The Book of Jack London*, 1921, and I. Stone, *Sailor on Horseback*, 1938.

London, cap. of the U.K. and of the Brit. Commonwealth of Nations, situated 37 m. from the mouth of the R. Thames. (This article is divided into the following prin. aspects of the subject: *Area and Population*; *Archaeology*; *History*; *Local Government*; *Parliamentary Representation*; *Commerce and Industry*; *Education and Cultural Facilities*; *Transport and Communications*; *Parks and Open Spaces*; *Architecture*; *Reconstruction and planning.*)

Area and Population. The term L. is used in more than one sense, and it is necessary to define the more important of these meanings: (1) The city of L., the original nucleus, occupies only 677 ac., just a square mile, but the old walled city has been surrounded by younger suburbs which have grown up all round it. It continues to function as an administrative unit with a civic constitution mainly medieval in structure. The great financial and mercantile centre of the metropolis, its day pop. is approx. 500,000, but the residential pop. is barely 5000. (2) The Greater L. brought into being on 1 April 1965 (as a result of the L. Gov. Act of 1963) comprising the City of L., the 28 metropolitan bors. of the former Co. of L., the whole of the Co. of Middx, and a large number of bors. and urb. dist councils, making a Greater L. of 616 sq. m. (the Co. of L. was 117 sq. m.), with a pop. estimated in 1965 as 7,986,100. A new unit of local gov., the L. Borough, was created, most of them considerably larger than the former metropolitan bors. All these new units are listed below under *Local Government*. There are other definitions of this term, for instance, the areas covered by certain *ad hoc* authorities for special purposes, such as the Metropolitan Water Board, serving an area of 575·8 sq. m. and the Port of L. Authority with jurisdiction from Teddington, 67 m. inland, to the sea. The definitions could thus be extended still further, and none of the areas so defined would be found co-terminous with another.

Archaeology. It is a matter of conjecture whether there was a Celtic settlement. Some fine pieces of Celtic metal work, notably the Battersea shield, have been found in the Thames. Soon after the Rom. invasion (AD 43) a settlement grew up on the E. of the Walbrook. The Romans probably built the first bridge (possibly only a pontoon structure) at this the lowest fordable point on the riv. Nothing certain can be adduced from the Rom. name Londinium. It is perhaps derived from the Celtic word Londinos, which may be a personal or tribal name based on an adjective meaning wild or fierce. The first settlement was burned in AD 61 by Boudicca q.v. (Boadicea), which is mentioned by Tacitus in his *Annals* (AD 115–17). He states that it was then a considerable trading centre. The Romans built L., the area of settlement spreading up to Ludgate Hill, and a fort was estab. in the Cripplegate area. During the 3rd decade of the 2nd cent. a great wall was built round the city, with ditches to the N. and E. The wall ran from the SE. corner, where later the Tower of L. was built, up to a point near the Moorgate marsh, where it curved and ran towards the Fleet R., and then continued S. to the Thames. Some authorities consider that the wall continued along the bank of the riv. The area enclosed was 330 ac., just half the size to which the city eventually grew, and it was the fifth largest tn in the W. It soon became the financial centre of Rom. Britain, and the centre of the road system.

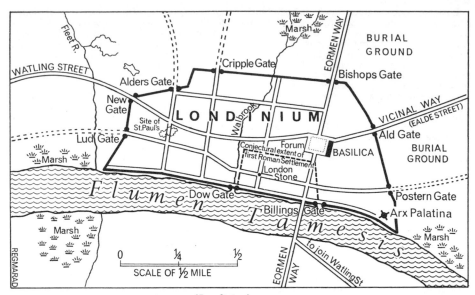

LONDON (*Londinium*) IN ROMAN TIMES

The great basilica, built about AD 80, where Leadenhall Market now stands, was 500 ft long and the largest building of its kind outside Rome. A temple of Mithras in Walbrook was built *c.* 200 and continued in use until the 4th cent. A mint was estab. *c.* 290–326, again during 383–8, and some time during the 4th cent., L. received the title of Augusta. In the same cent. it was apparently the seat of a bishopric. The only surviving remains are the mithraeum, part of the wall at Cripplegate, part of a heated building at the Coal Exchange and numerous pieces of sculpture, pottery, etc. in the London Guildhall and Brit. Museum. *See* G. Home, *Roman London*, 1948.

History. To understand the growth of L. it is necessary to appreciate the great importance of its geographical position. What is known as the L. Basin is a downfold in the chalk formation. At the point where L. began its existence were 2 small areas of riv. gravel covering and surrounding 2 small hills (Cornhill, Ludgate Hill), with marshland to the E. up to and beyond the R. Lea, and to the N. and NW. were more marshland and wooded clayland. On the S. bank of the riv. was another tract of gravel where Southwark now stands. To the W. was the R. Fleet. It was a naturally defensible point, at what was then the tidal limit of the Thames, which has been from prehistoric times the prin. entry into England from the continent of Europe.

By now, a half-cent. before the Norman Conquest, L. was already the most important tn in England. It was the prin. resort of traders, and its constitutional development had reached a stage far beyond any other tn in the kingdom. It was not a cap. city in the usual sense, for the centre of gov. was the king's court wherever he chose to hold it. But a patrician class had emerged; there was a folkmoot, an assembly of popular gov. which met in the open at the NE. of St Paul's; there was a husting (originally a Dan. word meaning 'house assembly'), which by the time of the Norman Conquest had assumed judicial functions presided over by aldermen sitting as lawyers. After the battle of Hastings, when William the Conqueror marched to secure L., the citizens put up a stout resistance, not being intimidated by the burning of Southwark, but William evaded further direct action from the S., crossed the Thames at Wallingford and threatened L. from the N., whereupon the city submitted to him. In a few years he granted a charter confirming existing rights, and built the Tower of L. and 2 other towers to dominate and to protect the city. At first the Tower was a royal residence and a fortress, but gradually the kings lived more and more at Westminster. A Benedictine abbey existed at Westminster in the late 9th cent. if not earlier, but it was Edward the Confessor's abbey which brought fame to the area, and there he also built a great royal palace on the site now occupied by the Houses of Parliament. The city of L. was now left more completely in the hands of its merchants, who asserted their privilege of freedom from the direct control of the Crown. To this day, though now it is only symbolic, when the sovereign enters the city she must be met by the lord mayor who hands her the keys of admission at Temple Bar. The city was ever watchful of its prerogatives, and after the Conquest was busy securing its rights against the encroachments of the autocratic kings. An important charter was granted by Henry I in 1132 whereby L. secured further privileges, electing its own justices and

TUDOR LONDON: AFTER THE MAP BY PIETER VANDEN KEERE

1, Clerkenwell; 2, St Jones; 3, Charterhouse; 4, St Andrewes; 5, Holbourn Conduct; 6, Temple Bar; 7, St Dunshous; 8, Olde Baylye; 9, S. Nic shambles; 10, St Paules; 11, S. Taphyns; 12, London Stone; 13, The Stockes; 14, The Exchange; 15. Leaden hall; 16, Fancshurche; 17, Bassings hall; 18, Alhallowes in the wall; 19, Aldermanburye; 20, Winchester House; 21, Battle bridge; 22, Bermondsoy streete.

collecting its own customs, and Middx (of which it secured the *ferm* for £300 annually) was placed under the control of a sheriff.

About this time we have the first records of the guilds that were to play so important a part in the life of L. in the Middle Ages. The Weavers were in existence in 1130, the Saddlers in 1154, and sev. others before the end of the cent. Gradually they secured control of economic activities and the nomination of the chief civic officials, and carried out social and religious functions. These, except for the Goldsmiths, were the merchant guilds. Soon after them there came into existence the craft guilds, societies of craftsmen, the skilled men in the trades— masters, journeymen, apprentices. It is possible that some artisans belonged to both kinds of guilds, but there was nevertheless a clear div. With increasing commercial and industrial prosperity there was an accompanying increase of craft guilds, especially so in the era of great industrial activity under Edward III. A certain amount of friction between the 2 kinds of guilds was inevitable, but it was the rise of the craft guilds, whose master craftsmen often became wealthy employers, and the play of economic forces, that led to the supersession of merchant by craft guild. In time the latter secured the majority of nominations to the common council. They attained their greatest power in the late 14th and during the 15th cents., and in the latter cent. were building their great halls, so magnificent a feature of the architecture of the city.

Another kind of organisation, the religious guilds, increased in number from the 13th cent. onwards. These were really private societies, some of them supporting schools, and maintaining bridges and roads, and in course of time took some part in municipal gov. Broadly speaking, in the Middle Ages L. was under the control of the merchant class; but it must be remembered that the kings were not always ready to keep the promises made in their charters. The theory of the municipal constitution does not always correspond closely with the facts. During the civil wars of Stephen's reign the Londoners were mainly on the side of the *de facto* king, though they received Matilda within their walls when she was too strong to be kept outside. When Richard I was on crusade his minister, Longchamp, whose H.Q. were in the Tower, tried to play the despot. The citizens were summoned by the assembly bell and heard Prince John and the nobles of his party depose the tyrant, and graciously grant the city the right to be governed by a commune, though in fact L. already possessed to a great extent the right of self-gov. It is from this time that the gov. took the form of a mayor and aldermen.

The city of L. played a considerable part in the agitation for Magna Carta, for it was at St Paul's Cathedral that the barons assembled on 25 Aug. 1213, when Langton, the Archbishop of Canterbury, appealed to them to maintain the liberties of the realm. A provision in Magna Carta granted L. all its anct liberties and free customs, and the mayor of L. (the only person not a peer) was among the 25 especially to see that the charter was carried out. When Henry III would not recognise the appointment of one Fitz-Thomas as mayor in 1261, the Londoners threw themselves on the side of the barons in their struggle against the king, and fought with them at the great battle of Lewes in 1264. It was the indiscretion of Prince Edward in chasing the Londoners too far from the field which lost his father the battle, and when Edward turned back to his father's assistance the king was a prisoner. However, generally speaking relations between the Crown and the city of L. were friendly, and it was certainly in the Crown's interest to maintain this amity, for it received considerable financial aid from the citizens and the guilds. Some of the richer merchants, e.g. Sir Wm Walworth and Sir Richard Whittington, both mayors, lent considerable sums to the Crown. Edward IV was a particular favourite with Londoners, because he generously granted or renewed charters, became a wool trader himself, and paid his debts punctually. He granted the famous Hanseatic League (q.v.) of foreign merchants almost complete independence within their guild house, the Steelyard, but this became unpopular, and the privileges were withdrawn under Elizabeth.

Something must be said of the social, intellectual and religious hist. of L. during the Middle Ages. It was a city too often beset with plague and fire. In 1136 a great fire swept from St Paul's to L. Bridge and Aldgate. Except for a few great nobles' houses, the city was then almost entirely built of wood. In 1189, under Richard I, a law was passed commanding that ground floors at least were to be built of stone, while the roofs were to be tiled or slated. L. Bridge (q.v.) was first built of stone 1176–1209. The streets were narrow and generally dirty; the Walbrook and Fleet streams and the City Ditch were indescribably filthy. Water was obtainable only from the Thames and some pumps until matters were taken in hand in 1236, when clean water was taken by pipes from the Tyburn to conduits at Cheapside and other centres in the city. It was not until the early 17th cent., with the New Riv. Scheme of Sir Hugh Middleton, that L. had an adequate water supply. In spite of such conditions the great commercial centre thrived. The craftsmen were among the very finest in Europe, and as a mart L. offered variety and the highest excellence. Special dists were given over to the use of particular trades, particularly in the area of the Cheap, the great market of L. which originated in A.-S. times (see CHEAPSIDE). The Church was the great force uniting the community in the medieval period, and in addition to a hundred or more par. churches there were, in or near L., about a dozen greater conventional churches, among them the abbey at Westminster, the Charterhouse, the Temple, St Bartholomew's Priory and the priories at Bermondsey and Southwark. As early as the Norman period there were 4 schools in the city: St Paul's, St Martin-le-Grand, St Mary-le-Bow and Holy Trinity; and the Inns of Court constituted the

legal univ. of the kingdom. In the earlier Norman period hardly any of L. lay beyond the city wall, but by the end of the period small suburbs had grown up at the various gates, chiefly at Ludgate, Cripplegate and Bishopsgate, the more important suburbs being made into wards of the city. By 1222 the city had grown into its modern boundaries. Fleet St (q.v.), then already in existence, led into the Strand (q.v.), at the end of which was the vil. of Charing, only a few hundred yards from Westminster. By the early 14th cent. L. with its wealth and commerce, and Westminster with its royal residence and centre of administration, were a unity that in effect was the cap. of the kingdom.

In Tudor times the power of the Crown increased at the expense of the power of the Church and the guilds, and industrial progress since the medieval period was increasing the power and wealth of the merchant and trading classes, with a corresponding influence on the hist. of the city. L. was prominent in the Reformation. The first step in the dissolution of the monasteries was taken when Henry VIII dissolved Trinity Priory, Aldgate. When eventually all the monasteries were dissolved the land was generally sold for development, but some houses became gov. offices and even storehouses, and some of the monastic wealth went towards paying for the Royal Navy. Under Edward VI the religious guilds were suppressed, and the revenues of craft guilds devoted to religious purposes reverted to the Crown. Under Mary I L. achieved notoriety with the burning of martyrs at Smithfield (q.v.). During Elizabeth's reign the aristocracy was abandoning its houses in the city for mansions in the Strand or Westminster and its neighbourhood, thus leaving the city a still greater stronghold of the merchant oligarchy. Both Tudor and Stuart monarchs tried in vain to arrest the outward growth of L. By the end of Elizabeth's reign L. and its suburbs had a pop. of about 200,000, but only a third or so of this number was inside the city. The 17th cent. witnessed the building of sev. L. squares, early essays in planning, the first being Covent Garden (q.v.). During the Civil war the city was a centre of non-conformity and sided with Parliament, a very large factor in the defeat of Charles I, and during the struggle the city train-bands (see TRAINED BANDS) played a notable part. However, L. changed sides when it was angered by the Rump parliament's actions toward the city, and was influenced also by Charles II's promise to renew its charter and to grant new privileges. Within a few years of the Restoration occurred the disasters of the Great Plague and the Fire of L. (see GREAT FIRE OF LONDON). The city, however, recovered its prosperity; in 1670 the Hudson's Bay Co. was formed, resulting in the estab. of a world-wide fur trade centring on L., and in 1694 the Bank of England was estab. The great genius of Wren was employed to rebuild 50 churches and other buildings, but his ideas for replanning L. were rejected.

During the 18th cent. certain new features of social and mercantile life in L. developed, and building rapidly extended towards the vils. and hamlets that surrounded it. With the development of coaches coaching inns became more numerous; so did coffee-houses, the resort of the *beau monde*, the *literati*, merchants, and others, and in Queen Anne's reign there were some 500 of them in L. alone. On the darker side, the extension of the docks (there were only 2 hitherto) and the consequent need for labour largely led to the development of slums E. of the city. When the first official census was taken (1801) the pop. of L. was 859,000, but in the next 40 years the pop. in the area that subsequently became the co. of L. increased by a million. This period, coinciding with the introduction and growth of railways, saw a further extension of the slums. The 19th cent. was an era when the local gov. of L. was reorganised and improved. The Metropolitan Police Force was instituted in 1829, and in 1848 the Metropolitan Board of Sewers was set up to replace 8 local sewer authorities. In 1855 some 300 local bodies were abolished and replaced by locally elected administrative vestries for the larger pars. and dist boards for groups of smaller pars.; over all these was set up the Metropolitan Board of Works, members of which were appointed by the vestries and boards. The Local Gov. Act of 1888 abolished the Board of Works, and created the co. of L. (117 sq. m.) and the L. Co. Council to administer much the same area as the body it replaced. This was followed in 1899 by the regrouping of pars. and dists (except the city of L.) into 28 metropolitan bors. By 1901 the pop. of the co. of L. reached the highest it has ever done—over $4\frac{1}{2}$ millions.

L. suffered very little damage in the First World War, but in the Second the devastation was immense, some areas (e.g. the city of L. and Poplar) losing a third of their buildings. Many of the great architectural features were severely damaged or destroyed, among them the House of Commons, the Guildhall and many of the city churches. Altogether about 30,000 persons were killed in the Greater L. area. *See* T. H. O'Brien, *Civil Defence*, 1955; B. Collier, *Defence of the United Kingdom*, 1957. *See also* AIR RAIDS; BRITAIN, BATTLE OF.

Local Government. L. has a distinct form of local gov. compared with the provs. There are 3 elected—the Greater L. Council, the 32 L. Bor. councils and the City of L. Corporation. It was the aim, as stated in the Report of the Royal Commission of Local Gov. in Greater L. (1957–60), that 'the bors. should be the primary units of local gov. and should perform all functions except those which can only effectively be performed over the wider area of Greater L.' The London Gov. Act of 1963 provided a two-tier structure of gov. for this new administrative area of 616 sq. m. (the City of L. remains a separate administrative unit governed by the Corporation of L., q.v.). The two-tier structure consists of the Greater L. Council (q.v.) and the L. Bor. councils, with a distribution of powers

that is complex, and was the inevitable result of the systems of local gov. obtaining in the area now comprised in Greater L.

The Bor. councils are the local authorities for the new L. Bors. created under the L. Gov. Act of 1963. The bors. in the inner ring, 12 in number, were formed out of the 28 metropolitan bors. of the administrative Co. of L., averaging about three times the area and pop. of the former bors. In the outer ring the area of each bor. is considerably larger than in the inner ring. The pop. varies from about 145,000 to 340,000, and the rateable value from £9,185,000 (Sutton) to £108,000,000 (City of Westminster). The new L. Bors., to which separate articles are assigned, are: BARKING; BARNET; BEXLEY; BRENT; BROMLEY; CAMDEN; CROYDON; EALING; ENFIELD; GREENWICH; HACKNEY; HAMMERSMITH; HARINGEY; HARROW; HAVERING; HILLINGDON; HOUNSLOW; ISLINGTON; KENSINGTON AND CHELSEA; KINGSTON-UPON-THAMES; LAMBETH; LEWISHAM; MERTON; NEWHAM; REDBRIDGE; RICHMOND-UPON-THAMES; SOUTHWARK; SUTTON; TOWER HAMLETS; WALTHAM FOREST; WANDSWORTH; WESTMINSTER, CITY OF.

The L. Bor. councils, being the local planning authorities, are obliged to produce bor. development plans in conformity with the strategic Greater L. Development Plan; and deal with planning applications other than those that affect the planning of Greater L. as a whole. They are responsible for the construction, maintenance and lighting of roads except main and trunk roads. Overall traffic control is reserved for the G.L.C., but bor. councils must provide traffic signs and signals, pedestrian crossings and subways and parking places with meters. They may provide on- and off-street car parks. Within their bors. they have full housing powers, including the supply of new houses, slum clearance and improvement schemes, and loans for house purchase. They have taken over nearly 340,000 homes from the authorities they have replaced; and are empowered to make and enforce Building Preservation Orders for buildings of historic and architectural interest. The 20 outer bor. councils have the control of building construction in their bors.; the inner bor. councils are more limited in this respect, having some control functions under powers delegated from the G.L.C. The bor. councils have power to provide parks and open spaces. They are responsible for sewerage, except main sewers and control drains. They can provide entertainment of all kinds, including concert halls, theatres, dance halls, etc.

For the services mentioned above they share responsibility with the G.L.C. The services for which they are solely responsible include the personal health services, welfare services and the Children's Service; and all other purely local services such as libraries, cemeteries and crematoria, swimming baths, etc. The need for co-operation between the former metropolitan bors., which found expression in the Metropolitan Bors'. Standing Joint Committee, finds its counterpart in the L. Bors.' Committee (set up in 1964), consisting of two representatives from each of the 32 bors. and the City of L. Its purpose is to protect and advance the privileges, rights and powers of those bodies, and to take action if such privileges, etc. are affected by legislation or threatened by proposed legislation.

In addition to those above it must be mentioned that there are 5 *ad hoc* authorities —the Metropolitan Water Board, the Port of L. Authority, the Thames Conservancy Board, the Lee Conservancy Catchment Board and L. Transport. The Inner and Middle Temples are administered by Benches of Masters.

The City of London Corporation. The City is controlled by the Court of Aldermen, the Court of Common Council and the Court of Common Hall. The Court of Aldermen consists of the lord mayor and aldermen who are all justices of the peace for life. It is the only extant example of a municipal second chamber. They make the final selection of the next lord mayor from 2 nominees from the Court of Common Hall. The Court of Common Council consists of 26 aldermen elected for life (including the lord mayor), and 206 common councillors (reduced to 159 in 1959). The City have their own separate police force. They act as the Port Health Authority for the port of L. They can amend their own constitution. The Court of Common Hall consists of the lord mayor, aldermen and liverymen of the City Livery Companies. They choose 2 aldermen each year who have served the office of sheriff for presentation to the Court of Aldermen for the office of lord mayor.

The metropolitan bor. councils consist of a mayor selected as in the provs., aldermen who number one-sixth of the councillors, and the councillors who all retire together. The councils are incorporated and not the inhab. as in the provs. Thier accounts are all audited by the dist auditor of the Ministry of Housing and Local Gov. The L. Gov. Act, 1939, did for L. almost the same as the Local Government Act, 1933, did for the provs. There is also a separate Public Health (London) Act, 1936.

The Metropolitan Water Board are constituted under the Metropolitan Water Board Act, 1902. The members are representatives elected by all the local gov. authorities in the area of the board. The board collects charges for water based on the rateable value of premises in their area.

Parliamentary representation. This remains as it did when the Co. of L. was in existence, i.e., the representation in the inner ring of 12 bors. follows the electoral division of the metropolitan bors., whereby parl. bors. were identical with metropolitan bors. except in the two cases where parts of contiguous bors. formed separate electorates. In the outer ring of 20 bors. the representation remains as before, with the consequent anomaly that parl. constituencies in 6 cases are straddled by the boundary of Greater L. No changes in electoral boundaries will be made before 1970 at the earliest, but if the proposals of the Boundary Commission are

accepted there will be fewer members representing the old L. bors.

Commerce and industry. L. is not an industrial city in the usual sense, but mainly a centre of distributors and middlemen, of import and export, of bankers and financiers. The city of L. (with part of Finsbury and Holborn) is the area of financial, banking and insurance activity. The city is the European centre for gold distribution, although 2 world wars have concentrated the chief gold reserves in other countries, but it holds the gold and dollar reserves of the sterling countries. It is from the great port of L., which has a vast *entrepôt* trade with all parts of the world, that L. derives its commercial prosperity. Of the grand total 4,110,000 tons were transhipment cargoes. The docks begin just below the Tower of L., and stretch to Tilbury, covering an area of over 4000 ac. (water area 722 ac.), with 45 m. of quayage. *See* PORT OF LONDON AUTHORITY.

Trade, manuf. and the professions have become largely localised as in many other tns. The industries, and there are only a few heavy industries, are found in the Port of L. in the riverside dists of Stepney, Poplar, Bermondsey, Deptford and Woolwich. The distributive trades, which employ over half a million persons, are, of course, found throughout the metropolis. Clothing is carried on in Stepney, cabinet-making in Shoreditch, St Pancras and Bethnal Green, with boot-making as well in the last-named. Bermondsey specialises in leather-tanning. In Mark Lane and Mincing Lane in the city are the chief markets for corn, tea, wine and colonial produce, and near by are Leadenhall Market (poultry, fish and miscellaneous, both wholesale and retail), and Billingsgate (q.v.), the prin. wholesale fish market. The central meat markets are at Smithfield, a little W. of which is Hatton Garden, the centre of the diamond trade. Clerkenwell is noted for watch-making and for optical and electrical instruments. The Inns of Court for the legal profession are all within a short distance of each other immediately to the W. of the city. In and off Fleet St is the centre of the newspaper industry, whereas publishers are located mainly in Bloomsbury and in the area to the W. of Covent Garden. Soho is noted for its foreign restaurateurs and distributors of foreign food and wines. Consulting physicians and surgeons are mostly in and around Harley St in Marylebone. Most theatres are in the W. End, the court, governmental and fashionable area of L., comprising the city of Westminster and parts of Kensington and St Marylebone; and in the W. End are some of the best shopping localities, such as Piccadilly, Bond St, Regent St and Oxford St. The centre of the cinema industry is in Wardour St, off Oxford St.

Education and cultural facilities. By the creation (under the L. Gov. Act of 1963) of the Inner London Education Authority (I.L.E.A.) a dual system of administration was introduced into Greater L. The I.L.E.A. provides the full range of educational services (including the youth employment service) formerly provided by the L.C.C. The area for which the I.L.E.A. is responsible is that of the former administrative Co. of L., i.e. the inner ring of 12 bors. Each of the 20 outer Bor. councils is its own education and youth employment authority. The Greater L. Council maintains or helps to maintain 30 nursery schools, 933 primary and 316 secondary schools, as well as 89 schools for handicapped children and 5 hospital schools. The Education Act of 1944 required local education authorities to prepare 2 separate development plans, 1 for primary and secondary and the other for further education. As a result there emerged the L. School Plan for primary and secondary education, which has been partly implemented by the experiment, since 1946, of building comprehensive schools, which aim to provide for all types of aptitude and ability, instead of localising these types at the secondary schools best suited to them. In further education the G.L.C. maintains or helps to maintain 90 evening institutes and over 60 technical colleges, polytechnics and colleges of commerce. L. Univ. (q.v.), the only univ. in the metropolis, but with 37 'schools of the univ.' attached to it, receives grants from the G.L.C. Although not a statutory authority under the Education Acts the Corporation of L. has been engaged in education for more than a cent. It maintains a public school for boys (City of L. School, q.v.) and one for girls (City of L. School for Girls), a school for the orphans of freemen (City of L. Freemen's School) and the Guildhall School of Music and Drama.

For specialised education there are various estabs. of the highest standing. These include the Imperial College of Science and Technology, the Imperial College of Tropical Agriculture, the L. School of Economics and Political Science, the Royal Academy of Music (qq.v.), the Royal College of Music, the Royal Academy Schools of Painting, Sculpture and Architecture (see ACADEMY, ROYAL), the Architectural Association School of Architecture, the Royal College of Art, S. Kensington, the Slade School of Fine Art at Univ. College, the City and Guilds of L. Art School and the Royal Academy of Dramatic Art. The City of L. aims to become a major centre for the arts, and by 1971 will be paying annually about £400,000 to the arts, double the amount spent in 1966. The teaching of law is in the hands of the Inns of Court (q.v.), and medicine can be studied at the 12 teaching hospitals (see HOSPITALS). In view of the scope and excellence of educational facilities offered, and in view also of the magnificence of its art galleries and museums covering all branches of knowledge, L. can fairly claim to be the greatest cultural centre in the world.

Transport and communications. The beginnings of modern transport in L. may be said to date from the first omnibus, horse-drawn, which ran in 1829 from Paddington Green to the Bank. Trams, also horse-drawn, did not appear until 1861, followed 2 years later by the first underground steam railway, running in a deep trench roofed over. The Tower Subway that followed in 1870 was the first tube railway in the world, but was still driven by steam. The first electric tube railway, the City and S. L., appeared in 1890. Shortly afterwards trams began to use electricity and buses to use petrol. With the increase of pop. transport facilities increased, until there was a multiplicity of operating companies, especially for buses. In 1933 the whole was taken over by the L. Passenger Transport Board, a public corporation replaced in 1948 by the L. Transport Executive. Unity of administration was gained, but it did not solve the prin. problem of congestion on the roads, which has long been the main recurring anxiety, owing to the difficulty of an adequate appreciation of coming changes. Road traffic has had to adapt itself as well as possible to haphazard methods of development and change; and with the 2 outstanding exceptions of the Victoria Embankment (1864–70) and the Kingsway-Aldwych improvement (completed 1905), the general policy for too long was one of patchwork and expediency. After the First World War came the first co-ordinated attempts to relate tn planning to traffic needs, which has culminated, under the Co. of L. Development Plan, in the provision for a series of ring roads round L. connected to the centre by radial roads. One aspect of the traffic problem was solved by the introduction in 1930 of controlling automatic lights at the prin. road crossings. The elimination of trams, completed in 1952, has also helped to ease the movement of traffic; and the latest attempt at traffic regulation is in the form of stricter police control over the parking of cars, which can only be parked at appointed places off the main highways, often on bombed sites, and in certain streets on alternate sides according to the odd and even days of the month. (For the administrative aspects see *Local Government*, above.)

The work of L. Transport is a vast undertaking, covering an area of nearly 2000 sq. m., extending in all directions from the centre of L. for some 25 m., in other words, the whole Greater L. area and well beyond. Over 300 Green Line coaches provide through services with limited stopping places, and coaches for sightseeing tours of L. and its environs. The electric underground trains that serve the L. area are of 2 kinds. First, there are the Metropolitan and Dist Railways which use tunnels and cuttings not far below ground level; and secondly there are the five 'tube' railway systems—the Central, Northern, Bakerloo, Victoria and Piccadilly lines—which operate much deeper though at varying levels, and have to be reached by electric escalators. Although all these are called 'underground' railways, in fact only about a quarter of their length is actually within tunnels, and that largely in the central areas. They do not serve the area S. of the riv. nearly as fully as in the N., but the electric trains of Brit. Railways provide a full suburban service. Altogether in the L. area there are 277 stations served by L. Transport, and over 300 served by Brit. Railways.

Other transport facilities in the L. region are provided by about 5500 taxi-cabs run by private companies or owner-drivers, and in summer water transport is provided by private companies which operate the 'water-bus' service between Greenwich and Putney and riv. steamers up to Hampton Court.

L. is the railway centre of the country. The great trunk railways converge on the metropolis, and their prin. termini, of which there are 13, are within easy reach of any part of the area. The first railway in L. was the line between L. Bridge and Deptford, officially opened in 1836, though passengers had been carried over part of the course in the previous year. The first trunk line was the L.–Birmingham Railway, completed in 1838, the greatest railway undertaking up to that time, which terminated first at Chalk Farm, later extended to Euston, where the first L. trunk line terminus was opened in 1838.

The first canal in L. was the Limehouse Cut linking the R. Lea with the Thames, completed in 1770, followed by the Surrey Canal (1803–7) connecting the Surrey Docks with Peckham and Camberwell. The Regent Canal (1812–20) joined the Grand Union Canal and thus connected L. by waterway with the industrial midlands. It is one of the paradoxes of L. hist. that only L. Bridge (q.v.) crossed the Thames until the construction of a timber bridge between Fulham and Putney in 1729, followed 10 years later by a start on Westminster Bridge (q.v.). Blackfriars Bridge (q.v.) was built 1760–9, and a wooden bridge at Battersea in 1772. Four were built between the years 1811 and 1827, and sev. more until the completion of Tower Bridge (q.v.) in 1894. Not counting railway bridges, 15 now span the riv. within the area of the co. of L. Although a scheme was mooted for a Thames tunnel as early as 1799, the first one, the Thames Tunnel from Wapping to Rotherhithe, was not completed until 1843. There are now 6 tunnels under the riv.

The main airport for L. is Heathrow Airport (q.v.). There are subsidiary airports at Gatwick in Surrey and Stansted in Essex. All parts of the U.K. and of the world are served by these airports. *See also* AIRFIELDS; AVIATION, CIVIL.

Parks and open spaces. There is a considerable amount of open space in L., partly owing to the survival of the royal parks and partly to the growing realisation of the need to preserve and extend such space in a vast area of concentrated urbanisation. Within the co. of L. there are nearly 8000 ac. of open space, of which the most famous and most central is Hyde Park (q.v.). In many of the parks there are facilities for boating, bathing and other recreations. The royal parks are administered by the Ministry of Works. The G.L.C. maintains a total of some 7000 ac., of which about two-thirds are outside the co. of L. (*see also* REGENT'S PARK).

Architecture. The only surviving remains of Rom. buildings in London comprise mosaic pavements, foundations of walls, etc., below the present street level. Of 'Saxon' or pre-Conquest Romanesque architecture, nothing survives

above ground except, possibly, the lower part of some of the monastic buildings of Westminster Abbey. Of 'Norman' or post-Conquest Romanesque architecture (1066 onwards) the chief examples are the 'White Tower' or keep of the Tower of London, built late in the 11th cent. but much altered since; the remarkable little vaulted chapel of St John within the 'White Tower'; the E. portion of the former Augustinian priory church of St Bartholomew the Great in Smithfield (1123–45), a fine example; and the crypt of the church of St Mary-le-Bow in Cheapside. From the late Romanesque or 'Transitional' style, when 'Norman' was evolving into 'Gothic', are the crypt of the priory church of St John of Jerusalem, Clerkenwell (*c.* 1140–80); and the circular aisled nave of the Temple Church (consecrated 1185, almost completely rebuilt during the 19th cent., and seriously damaged in the Second World War).

Gothic architecture prevailed in England *c.* AD 1200–1550. The greatest Gothic church in London was Old St Paul's, which, with its lofty spire 500 ft high (burnt in 1561), dominated the city until the whole building perished in the Great Fire of 1666. Westminster Abbey (q.v.) was built in stages between 1245 and 1420, Henry VII's Chapel being added in 1502–10. Of Southwark Cathedral, formerly the Augustinian priory of St Mary Overie, the E. part was built in the 13th–14th cents., but the nave was entirely rebuilt in 1890–7. Other surviving Gothic churches are the chancel of the Temple Church (1240); the chapel of Lambeth Palace (1245); parts of St Helen, Bishopsgate, and of St Etheldreda, Ely Place, Holborn, *c.* 1300; (the nave of the church of the Austin Friars, 1354, was destroyed in the Second World War); the Chapel of the Savoy; and the par. churches of St Margaret, Westminster, St Olave, Hart St and St Dunstan, Stepney. A late Gothic example is St Giles, Cripplegate (1545, gutted in the Second World War).

Of secular Gothic buildings (once very numerous), hardly any examples survive, owing to fires, bombing, or rebuilding. They include the upper parts and magnificent roof of Westminster Hall (1394–1402); the crypt of the Guildhall (begun 1411); the hall of Eltham Palace (1480); the Lollards' Tower (1435) and Morton's Tower (1490) at Lambeth Palace; St Stephen's Chapel and Cloister, formerly part of the Palace of Westminster and now incorporated in the Houses of Parliament. One reason why so many medieval houses and halls have been destroyed by fire is that they were built of wood.

A miraculous survival of both the Great Fire of 1666 and the Second World War is the half-timbered front of Staple Inn, Holborn; which, though built as late as 1581, is typical of L. dwellings of the late Gothic period.

Among examples of Elizabethan and Jacobean architecture (*c.* 1558–1625)—the 'Early Renaissance' period—are, or recently were, Holland House, Kensington (1605–7); and the halls, all with fine timbered roofs, of the Middle

Temple (1562–70), Staple Inn (1581), Gray's Inn (1555–60), and the Charterhouse (1565–1611); all these buildings were severely damaged in the Second World War. Others which escaped damage were Charlton House, Greenwich (1607–12); and No. 17 Fleet St, formerly the Inner Temple Gatehouse (c. 1611). The timbered front of Sir Paul Pindar's house in Bishopsgate (c. 1610), and a beautiful panelled room from the palace of Bromley-le-Bow (1606), are now both exhibited at the Victoria and Albert Museum. Portions of Crosby Hall, Bishopsgate (1466), were incorporated in Crosby Hall, Chelsea, 1909.

During the reign of James I a revolution was created in Eng. architecture by Inigo Jones (q.v.), whose 2 most remarkable works, displaying features of It. Renaissance design derived from Palladio (q.v.), are both situated in London: the Queen's House at Greenwich (1617–35) and the Banqueting House in Whitehall (1618–22)—its magnificent ceiling painted by Rubens was restored in 1964. The church of St Paul, Covent Garden, rebuilt 1795–8, is a copy of its predecessor designed by Inigo Jones in 1631, when he also laid out the surrounding streets. He designed the chapel of Marlborough House (1623–6), and, possibly, Lindsay House in Lincoln's Inn Fields (c. 1640); but there is no proof that he was the author of the following buildings often attributed to him: the chapel of Lincoln's Inn (1617); the Water Gate of York Stairs (1626); Ashburnham House, Westminster (c. 1640). During the disturbed period of the Civil war very little building took place.

Christopher Wren (q.v.) became a prof. of astronomy in L. in 1657, but turned his genius to architecture some 6 years later. He was consulted about the condition of Old St Paul's Cathedral before the Fire of London occurred in 1666; thereafter his enormous practice in London included the complete rebuilding of the cathedral and of 52 destroyed churches in the city; additions, some on a large scale, to the royal palaces of Kensington, St James's, Westminster and Whitehall; the military hospital at Chelsea and the naval hospital at Greenwich; Marlborough House; additions to Christ's Hospital (now demolished); buildings in the Middle Temple; the churches, outside the city, of St James, Piccadilly; St Clement Danes; and St Anne, Soho; but there is no proof that he made designs for rebuilding any of the City Livery Companies' halls—of which 44 perished in the Fire of 1666—though sev. were then rebuilt in his style, but few of these survived the air-raids of 1940–4. Wren also restored Westminster Abbey, and carried out a great deal of other building in L.

In the early 18th cent. a boom in church-building resulted from an Act of Parliament in 1708 authorising the erection of 50 new churches. In L. these included St Mary Woolnoth (1716–27), St Anne, Limehouse (1712–24), Christ Church, Spitalfields (1723–9), St George, Bloomsbury (1720–30), St Alphege, Greenwich (1712–14) and St George-in-the-East (1715–

1723)—all by N. Hawksmoor (q.v.); St Martin in the Fields (1722–6), St Mary-le-Strand (1714–17) and St Peter, Vere St (1723–4)—all by James Gibbs (q.v.); and St John the Evangelist, Westminster (1714–28), by T. Archer (q.v.).

Among secular buildings of the first half of the 18th cent. are part of St Bartholomew's Hospital (1730) by Gibbs; sundry work at Greenwich Hospital by Hawksmoor and by Sir J. Vanbrugh (q.v.), who also built 'Vanbrugh Castle' at Greenwich; and the Mansion House (1739–52) by G. Dance (q.v.). During this period, L. was spreading westwards. Lincoln's Inn Fields, Covent Garden, Leicester Square, and Bloomsbury Square had already been laid out between 1618 and 1665. They were followed by Grosvenor, Berkeley, Kensington, St James's, Red Lion, Golden, Hanover and Cavendish Squares between c. 1688 and c. 1717. Charming examples of early 18th cent. houses in brick are to be seen in Church Row, Hampstead, and elsewhere in L.

The second half of the cent. produced Somerset House (1776–86) by Sir Wm Chambers (q.v.). His chief rival, Robert Adam, laid out, in partnership with his brothers, the Adelphi estate near the Strand (1768–72), now partly demolished; and also Portland Place with its adjoining streets (1773 onwards). Other buildings by Adam include the magnificent houses of Kenwood near Hampstead (1767–9), 20 St James's Square (1772–4) and 20 Portman Square (1775–7). Bedford, Manchester and Fitzroy Squares were laid out between 1775 and 1790.

Architecture of the period c. 1800–37 is commonly called 'Regency' architecture, though in fact the Regency itself lasted only from 1820 to 1830. The prin. architect for the period in L. was John Nash (q.v.), who laid out not only 'The Regent's Park', with its surrounding terraces and crescents, but also a continuous street leading to it from the Regent's own mansion, Carlton House (since demolished), situated where Carlton House Terrace now stands. This street consists of Waterloo Place and Regent St, joining the already existing Portland Place at All Souls' Church (1822–5, by Nash). The buildings of Regent St, originally colonnaded, were all replaced early in the 20th cent.; but Park Crescent and the fine terraces around the park still stand, though mostly converted into gov. offices.

Other notable buildings of the period are the National Gallery (1834–8), Univ. College (1827–8) and St George's Hospital (1828–9) —all by W. Wilkins (q.v.); the Athenaeum Club (1827), Charing Cross Hospital (1831–4), the screen at Hyde Park Corner—all by D. Burton (q.v.); the Bank of England (1788–1823), by Sir J. Soane (q.v.); the Brit. Museum (1823–47) and the General Post Office (1823–9), both by Sir R. Smirke (q.v.); also St Pancras Church, in Gk style (1819–22), by H. W. Inwood. The dists of Belgravia and Pimlico were covered with stucco houses, c. 1825–30. All the above buildings were in classical style; but abreast of them appeared others in the 'Gothic Revival' style popularised

GREATER LONDON, 1966

by A. W. N. Pugin (q.v.) early in the 19th cent. His own chief work in L. is St George's Rom. Catholic Cathedral in Southwark (1841), destroyed by bombs in the Second World War and now being rebuilt. The best of the early 'Gothic Revival' churches is St Luke, Chelsea (1820–4). From that date onwards, throughout the Victorian era, most new churches were Gothic. Notable examples are: All Saints, Margaret St (1849), by Butterfield (q.v.); Catholic Apostolic Church, Gordon Square (1849), by Brandon; St Mary Abbots, Kensington (1869–72), by Sir G. G. Scott (q.v.); St Augustine, Kilburn (1871), by J. L. Pearson (q.v.); St Michael, Bedford Park (1878), by Norman Shaw (q.v.); Holy Trinity, Sloane Square (1890), by Sedding; Holy Trinity, Kensington (1902), by G. F. Bodley (q.v.).

In the second quarter of the 19th cent., Gothic came to be adopted for secular buildings: first in the new Houses of Parliament (1840–60), by Sir C. Barry (q.v.); later for St Pancras Station (1865), by Sir G. G. Scott (q.v.), and for the Law Courts (1866–8), by G. E. Street (q.v.). Some other public buildings, however, continued to follow the classical style, e.g. the Royal Exchange (1840), by Sir W. Tite (q.v.). The Natural Hist. Museum (1873–81), by A. Waterhouse (q.v.), is Romanesque rather than Gothic, as are his other important L. buildings. The Imperial Institute (1887–93), by T. E. Collcutt (q.v.), is notable for its fine tower.

During the early years of the 20th cent. most public buildings were designed in a somewhat grandiose 'Renaissance' or 'Free Classic' style. e.g. the L. Co. Hall (1908 onwards), by R. Knott (q.v.); the Central Hall at Westminster (1905), by Lanchester and Rickards (q.v.); the Port of L. Building (1912), by Sir E. Cooper (q.v.); while the Victoria and Albert Museum (1899–1909): by Sir A. Webb (q.v.), displays a medley of styles. The Rom. Catholic Cathedral at Westminster (begun in 1895), by J. F. Bentley (q.v.), was deliberately designed in Byzantine style to avoid rivalry with the Gothic of Westminster Abbey.

Sir H. Baker (q.v.) remodelled the Bank of England (1931) and built the Church House at Westminster (1939). In that year, Charles Holden (q.v.) completed the great Senate House of L. Univ. His firm also designed the remarkable H.Q. building of the underground railways at St James's Park Station. Especially since the Second World War, with its resultant damage, new buildings in L. have become much more functional and austere in appearance. Office buildings are of greatly increased height, and flats are rapidly replacing houses in the residential areas. Most of the buildings are architecturally mediocre, but a few are outstanding. Among these is the Royal Festival Hall (designed by R. Matthew and J. L. Martin), the only permanent survival of the 1951 exhibition on the S. Bank. Sir Basil Spence designed a highly original

Central Library for Hampstead, which was to form part of a new civic centre, but as a result of the change in local gov. it will form part of a development in the Bor. of Camden. Also original is the main building of the Commonwealth Institute in Kensington, which has the curious feature of a tent-like copper-covered roof. The building is placed diagonally, with the result that the office block joins it at an awkward angle. The Post Office Tower off Tottenham Court Road, 580 ft high, was built for the chief purpose of providing more long distance telephone circuits and television channels. A remarkable construction, it includes a revolving floor, but is aesthetically as unsatisfying as the nearby 350 ft Centrepoint building at St Giles's Circus, which was built without the aid of external scaffolding. The large commercial building which is part of the joint development at the corner of City Road and Old Street has its façade strongly accented by dark bands on the floor levels, between which are large decorative panels.

For the periods and styles of architecture mentioned above *see* ARCHITECTURE; *also* ENGLISH ARCHITECTURE.

Reconstruction and planning. Schemes for replanning L. were prepared by Wren and others immediately after the Great Fire of 1666, but none was carried out. The landlords of the great L. estates have since exercised some control over planning on their land; but the first really effective measure of civic control resulted from the Town and Country Planning Act of 1932, which gave increased powers to local authorites. The outbreak of war in 1939 interrupted the schemes of the L. Co. Council for replanning L.; but war damage created an urgent need for expediting action, and in 1944 Sir P. Abercrombie's masterly *County of London Plan* was pub., showing equal regard for social, practical and aesthetic considerations. In common with all other local authorities, the L. Co. Council was required, under the Town and Country Planning Act of 1947, to prepare a Development Plan, which appeared in 1951, and was designed to govern the development of L. for 20 years ahead. It made provision for open spaces, the grouping of houses in self-contained communities, the decentralisation of pop. and industry, the requirements of traffic, etc.

Owing to the Greater L. Council being the traffic authority, the highway authority, and the planning authority for Greater L., there is now for the first time a single authority entrusted with the planning and execution of these matters, thereby avoiding the overlapping, frustration and delay when such functions are distributed amongst sev. authorities.

Because of the shortage of labour, of materials, of the claims upon the building industry for dwellings and schools, and of financial stringency, planning proceeded only piecemeal for a considerable period after the Second World War. Beginnings were made in Poplar, Stepney, Southwark and other areas devastated by bombing. In the City of L., though much has been accomplished, much yet remains to be done. The devastated area beyond the E. end of St Paul's Cathedral has been rebuilt, and so has the Ludgate Hill approach to the cathedral. A start has been made on the large Barbican area of the city, so discussed and delayed. In central L., developments that have been completed or are in course of construction include the housing estate at Pimlico, the re-development (mainly office blocks) of Victoria St in Westminster, the Theobalds Rd blocks in Holborn, the Chelsea residential blocks, the riverside office blocks in Lambeth, the Elephant and Castle area of Southwark and the Marylebone housing centre. Piccadilly Circus is to be re-planned on a double-deck system, but so far the matter has got only as far as controversial discussion of Lord Holford's plans.

In the outer ring of bors., Croydon has a large development under way, and the bor. of Merton is planning a very large development of the centre of Wimbledon.

In the matter of road transport, the G.L.C. is involved on a threefold basis as the overall traffic authority, the highway authority and the planning authority responsible for the strategic Development Plan for Greater L., with particular emphasis on the planning of the future road system. For traffic management the Minister of Transport retains the reserve power to introduce, amend or abandon schemes over which there are serious differences of opinion. The G.L.C. is responsible for all means (one-way traffic schemes, clearways, traffic signals, etc.) to improve the flow of traffic and ensure safety. One of its latest schemes is the extension of the central London parking meter zone from 8 sq. m. in 1966 to 40 sq. m. in 1968, affecting the whole or parts of 11 bors.—an area stretching from Hammersmith to Bermondsey, and from Brixton to Camden Town.

Road improvement schemes must of severe necessity be speeded up. What may fairly be described as the largest single road improvement in central L. for 50 years occurred when the Hyde Park Corner, Park Lane and Marble Arch scheme was completed at a cost of over £5,000,000 in 1962. One of the prin. features of the scheme was the underpass between Hyde Park Corner and Knightsbridge, which, however, left unsolved the problem of congestion at the Knightsbridge end. However, a scheme will eventually be put in hand for the rebuilding of Knightsbridge. Other road improvements already completed include the Chiswick roundabout and flyover, the Hammersmith flyover, the widening of the Strand, the Strand underpass (between Waterloo Bridge and Kingsway), the Charing Cross road plan and the two-mile long viaduct at the E. end of the Chiswick–Langley section of the M4.

Bibliography (confined to a selection of the more important books). REFERENCE: H. B. Wheatley, *London Past and Present*, 1891; L. Co. Council and the Greater L. Council, *The Survey of London* (in progress, 30 vols. so far issued); H.

Harben, *A Dictionary of London*, 1918; W. Kent, *An Encyclopaedia of London*, 1951; E. Ekwall, *Street Names in the City of London*, 1954. HISTORY: J. Stow, *A Survey of London*, 1603 (ed. J. L. Kingsford, 1908; new ed. Everyman's Library, 1956); W. J. Loftie, *A History of London* (2nd ed.), 1884; Sir W. Besant, *London in the Time of the Stuarts*, 1903, and *London in the Time of the Tudors*, 1904; G. Home, *Medieval London*, 1927; Sir H. Llewelyn, *History of East London*, 1939; S. Rasmussen, *London: the Unique City*, 1948; J. T. Coppock and H. C. Prince (editors), *Greater London*, 1964; R. Merrifield, *The Roman City of London*, 1965; C. Trent, *Greater London: its growth and development*, 1965. ADMINISTRATION: Sir G. Gibbon and R. W. Bell, *History of the London County Council, 1889–1939*, 1939; W. A. Robson, *The Government and Misgovernment of London*, 1949; H. Morrison, *How London is Governed*, 1949; Anon., *The Corporation of London*, 1950. TOPOGRAPHY: H. Williams, *South London*, 1949; G. James, *London: the Western Reaches*, 1950; C. Golding, *London: the City*, 1951; R. Sinclair, *East London*, 1951; D. Newton, *London West of the Bars*, 1951; R. Colville, *London: the Northern Reaches*, 1951; H. P. Clunn, *The Face of London*, 1952; D. Piper, *Companion Guide to London*, 1964. ARCHITECTURE: Royal Commission on Historical Monuments, *Roman London*; *The City of London*; *East London*; *West London*; *Westminster Abbey*, 1924–30; J. Summerson, *Georgian London*, 1946; N. Pevsner, *London: except the Cities of London and Westminster*, 1952; *London: the Cities of London and Westminster*, 1957; E. and W. Young, *Old London Churches*, 1957. SOCIAL: P. Egan, *Life in London*, 1821; H. Mayhew, *London Labour and the London Poor*, 1861–2; J. Timbs, *Clubs and Club Life in London*, 1886; C. Booth, *Life and Labour of the People in London*, 1891–1903; M. D. George, *London Life in the 18th Century*, 1925; E. B. Chancellor, *The Pleasure Haunts of London during Four Centuries*, 1925; A. Crew, *London Prisons Today and Yesterday*, 1933; N. G. Brett-James, *The Growth of Stuart London*, 1935; H. and P. Massingham (editors), *The London Anthology*, 1950; B. Lillywhite, *London Coffee Houses*, 1963. (*See Plate.*)

London, cap. of Middlesex co., Ontario, Canada. Situated 115 m. SW. of Toronto and 125 m. W. of Niagara Falls, it is on the Canadian National and Canadian Pacific Railways' main lines; there is an airport near by, and it owns the civic lake, port and park at Port Stanley, on Lake Erie, 25 m. S. Founded originally in 1826 by Governor Simcoe as military H.Q. at the forks of R. Thames. Eng. L.'s names were given not only to Ontario L.'s streets, parks, bridges and churches, but also to adjoining vils. and townships. Here is the univ. of W. Ontario; there is also a fine technical and commercial high school, sev. collegiate institutes or senior high schools, many separate Rom. Catholic schools, a music college and a teachers' college. L. has 2 cathedrals, nearly 80 other churches and a splendid public library. There are 6 hospitals

and 6 large parks. There are very fine residential dists and L. is called 'Forest City' from the great number of trees in its shaded streets. Now an important manufacturing centre, its chief industrial plants are concerned with the manuf. of refrigerators, agric. implements, stores, clothing, shoes, small steel wares and cereals. The surrounding SW. Ontario region is rich in agriculture. Pop. 169,569.

London, Midland and Scottish Railway Company (L.M.S.), The, see RAILWAYS.

London, New, see CONNECTICUT.

London, Pact of, concluded Sept. 1914, between Great Britain, France and Russia. The signatories mutually engaged not to conclude peace separately or to demand terms of peace from the central empires without obtaining previous agreement of each of the other signatories. In Sept. 1915 Italy came into the pact, and in the following Oct. Japan also joined it.

London, Treaties of. A number of international conferences have been held in London since the 18th cent. and have resulted in sev. international treaties, including the following. (1) 1720: treaty under which the kingdom of Sardinia (q.v.) passed to the Dukes of Savoy. (2) 1827: treaty between Great Britain, France and Russia to secure the independence of Greece from Turkey; confirmed by a second treaty of London (1832), by which Greece became an independent kingdom (*see* GREECE, *History*). (3) 1839: treaty between the great powers in Europe confirming the creation of Belgium as an independent kingdom and declaring her perpetual neutrality (*see further under* QUINTUPLE TREATY (1839)). (4) 1840: treaty between Great Britain, Russia, Prussia and Austria agreeing to support Sultan Mahmoud II against Mehemet Ali (q.v.). (5) 1867: treaty between the great powers in Europe to secure the independence and neutrality of Luxemburg (q.v.). (6) 1871: treaty between Great Britain, France, Austria, Germany, Russia, Italy and Turkey, abrogating the provisions of the Declaration of Paris (q.v.) in respect of preserving the neutrality of the Black Sea. (7) 1913: *see* BALKAN WARS. (8) 1915: secret treaty between Italy and the Entente Powers, designed to secure the adherence of Italy to the cause of the Allies in the First World War. Under it Italy was to obtain, eventually, the Trentino, Trieste, S. Tyrol, Gorizia and Gradisca, Dalmatia, Istria and the various Austrian is. in the Adriatic, thereby fulfilling It. irredentist aspirations. (9) 1925: treaty of non-aggression between Great Britain, France and Belgium on the one hand and Germany on the other, concluded as part of the Locarno treaties (q.v.). (10) 1936: naval treaty signed by Britain, France and the U.S.A., providing for periodical exchanges of information about naval programmes, and with a view to limiting naval armaments. It lacked the adherence of Italy and Japan, signatories of previous naval treaties, and had little practical significance. *See also* LONDON AND PARIS AGREEMENTS. *See further under* AUSTRIA-HUNGARY; EUROPE; ITALY; WORLD WAR, FIRST.

London Airport, Heathrow, Middx, 15 m. from London, the chief airport for the metropolis, and the main air terminal for the U.K. Before the Second World War it was realised that the airports at Northolt, Heston, Hanworth and Hendon, all in the co. of Middlesex, were insufficient for the needs of civil aviation, and in 1937 the development of one at Heathrow was advised. Construction began in 1944, and it was first used by passengers in 1946. There are also subsidiary airports at Gatwick and Stansted. In 1963 there were over 200,000 flights from these 3 airports and some 8 million passengers were carried. *See also* AIRFIELDS; AVIATION, CIVIL.

London and North-Eastern Railway Company, The, *see* RAILWAYS.

London and Paris Agreements (1954). After the Fr. Assembly rejected the European Defence Community (q.v.) (30 Aug.) a conference was called in London on Brit. initiative of the former E.D.C. powers and Canada, Britain and the U.S.A. to evolve a formula to supersede the defensive arrangements which E.D.C. had been intended to cover. The conference met Sept./Oct. and agreement was reached on admitting the Federal Ger. Rep. and Italy to the Brussels Treaty organisation, and it was also decided that Germany should be admitted to N.A.T.O. There was to be an agency for the control of armaments and Britain pledged herself to maintain substantial defensive forces in Europe. Both these conditions were, from France's viewpoint, vital improvements on E.D.C. Subsequently, in Oct., the ministers of the N. Atlantic Council met in Paris, invited W. Germany to join N.A.T.O and approved a resolution strengthening the existing machinery for European defence. All the countries concerned had ratified the agreements by May 1955. *See also* EUROPE, *History.*

London Bridge crosses the R. Thames from the SE. corner of the city of London to the bor. of Southwark. It is possible that the Romans were the first builders of a bridge across the Thames, but nothing certain is known until we hear of the existence of a bridge in the late 10th cent. This was destroyed by a hurricane in 1091, was not rebuilt until 1120, and perished in a fire in 1136. A temporary structure followed. All these were timber constructions. The first stone structure, the L. B. famous in hist. and literature, was begun in 1176 by Peter de Colechurch, chaplain of St Mary's Church, and completed after his death (1205) in 1209. It spanned 900 ft, with 19 pointed arches, which resulted in dangerous rapids. A drawbridge allowed ships to pass. Before long the superstructure was crowded with dwellings, shops and a chapel. In spite of various vicissitudes the structure lasted for over 600 years, and was the only bridge in or near London until Westminster Bridge (q.v.) was built, 1739–52. In 1824 a new bridge, designed by John Rennie, was begun a little W. of the old structure, and completed in 1831. Old L. B. was demolished in 1831–2. The Corporation of the City of London has decided that the present bridge shall be demolished and replaced by a new structure in prestressed concrete by 1970. *See* Gordon Home, *Old London Bridge,* 1931.

London Clay, geological name applied to the Tertiary clay of the Lower Eocene age which outcrops below much of London. The L. C. underlies a great part of the London basin between Reading and the Essex coast and appears around the margins of the Hants basin. When fresh, L. C. is a stiff blue clay; it passes upward through passage beds into the Bagshot Sand (q.v.). The L. C. has played an important part in the economy of London; it provides an adequate foundation for large buildings, but is readily worked. Most of the tube railways pass through L. C.; stock bricks are made from L. C. The clay, which is up to 700 ft thick, forms an impermeable capping to the artesian basin below, from which water is obtained. Though not usually fossiliferous, the fauna of the L. C. indicates it was deposited in warm seas or estuaries where turtles, crocodiles and palms flourished. The Isle of Sheppey is the best locality for collecting L. C. fossils. *See also* EOCENE SYSTEM. *See* Sir C. Lyell, *Principles of Geology,* 1840; J. S. Bowerbank, *Fossils of the London Clay,* 1840; C. E. N. Bromehead, *Geology of North London,* 1925; R. L. Sherlock, *London and the Thames Valley,* 1935, 1947; Geologists' Association Guide No. 30, *The London Region,* 1958.

London County Council, former local authority for London when it was an administrative co. consisting of 28 metropolitan bors., but as a result of the London Gov. Act of 1963 it was replaced on 3 April 1965 by the Greater London Council (q.v.). The L.C.C. was estab. by the Local Gov. Act of 1888, and latterly consisted of 147 members, of whom 126 were councillors and 21 were aldermen. *See* Sir G. Gibbon and R. W. Bell, *History of the London County Council, 1889–1939,* 1939.

London Fire Brigade. The former Metropolitan Fire Brigade (founded 1866) was taken over by London Co. Council under the Local Gov. Act, 1888, and in 1904 the title 'London Fire Brigade' was adopted. It was considerably augmented during the 1939–45 war, when it was part of the National Fire Service (1941–March 31 1948). The L. F. B. set up on 1 April 1965, under the London Gov. Act, 1963, consists of the Brigades of the former co. of London and Middlesex (excluding the dists of Staines, Sunbury and Potters Bar), the former co. bors. of E. Ham, W. Ham and Croydon and of parts of Essex, Herts., Kent and Surrey. The Brigade is organised in 3 Commands (E., N. and S.) and 11 Divs. It has 121 land and 2 riv. stations. Whole time authorised estab.: 6533. There are 513 land appliances and 2 fire boats in commission. Fire calls (estimated) 60,000 per annum. H.Q. Albert Embankment, London, S.E.1.

'London Gazette', official organ of the Brit. Gov., claiming to be the oldest existing newspaper in the W. hemisphere. It first appeared as the *Oxford Gazette* on 16 Nov. 1665, when the court of Charles II was at Oxford to avoid the Great Plague, and became the *L. G.* with issue

No 24, 5 Feb. 1666. Now pub. by H.M.S.O. every Tuesday and Friday (including bank holidays), it has failed to appear only once, in Sept. 1666, when the Great Fire destroyed every printing press in the city of London. Early issues ran to 2 or 4 pages of proclamations, official announcements and a few news items copied from contemporary continental news-sheets. Nowadays each issue comprises 100–110 pages of official announcements and legal advertisements. There are regular supplements in which army and air force promotions, retirements, etc., are 'gazetted', and the new year and birthday honours lists are also pub. as supplements.

London Group, The, society of professional artists which was formed in 1913 by a number of painters associated with Walter Sickert (q.v.). The first president was Harold Gilman (q.v.) (1876–1919). The aim of the society was to break away from academic tradition and allow Brit. painting to nourish itself freely from the influence of Fr. Post-Impressionism. Under its auspices a number of modern painters who have since achieved fame were encouraged to develop in an individual and experimental style.

London Hospital, The, Whitechapel Road, London, E.1, founded in 1740. Formerly the largest voluntary hospital in England, it has expanded and modernised its facilities and equipment during the present cent., particularly during the chairmanship of Sydney Holland, Lord Knutsford. Under the National Health Service Act of 1946 it was designated an undergraduate teaching hospital. Its medical college is one of the medical schools of London Univ. and the hospital is approved as a training school for nurses, midwives, physiotherapists and radiographers. There are over 1000 beds in the main hospital in Whitechapel and its annexes, and there are over 720,000 out-patient attendances each year.

London Irish Rifles, *see* LONDON REGIMENT.

London Library, founded by Thomas Carlyle and opened on 3 May 1841. It is the largest private subscription library in the country and now contains about 750,000 vols. on all subjects except medical, legal and scientific. Books are sent to members in all parts of the Brit. Isles and in many countries overseas.

'London Magazine', once famous for contributions by Hazlitt, De Quincey, Keats and Stendhal, was revived in 1954 as a monthly review of literature. Non-political and cosmopolitan, it pubs. poetry, short stories, literary reminiscences, critical articles and book reviews.

London Military District was formed in 1905 by an army order of 6 Jan. which reorganised the various military dists, staffs and commands of the U.K. The London dist covers the co. of London, the Guards' depot at Caterham, Purfleet, Rainham rifle ranges, Warley and Pirbright for training, Windsor and Woolwich.

London Museum, Kensington Palace, London, devoted to the hist. and social life of London from the earliest times. It was first opened at Kensington Palace in 1912 and was transferred to Lancaster House, St James's, in

1913–14. After 1945 Lancaster House was put to other uses and in 1950 the museum was granted temporary accommodation at Kensington Palace by King George VI. London's hist. is illustrated by archaeological material (the prehistoric and medieval sections of which are outstanding), by topographical views and models (including a model of the Great Fire), by costumes and furniture and by the products of L. craftsmen. Special galleries are devoted to coronation robes and royal relics (such as Queen Victoria's dolls), the L. theatre and toys.

London Naval Conference (1930) was opened in the Royal Gallery of the House of Lords to finish the work begun at Washington in 1921. Whereas the earlier treaty had regulated capital ships and aircraft carriers, the L. N. C. dealt with cruisers and submarines. The outcome of the conference was the treaty of 22 April 1930, signed by 27 delegates of Great Britain, the dominions, U.S.A., Japan, France and Italy, but never ratified by the last 2 countries, owing chiefly to Fr. objection to Italy's insistence on parity with her. It provided that all construction on capital ships should be suspended for 6 years; that Great Britain, U.S.A. and Japan should reduce their capital ship quotas to 15, 15, 9; that the maximum tonnage of cruisers and destroyers should be 489,000 for Great Britain, 475,500 for the U.S.A. and 313,850 for Japan. Under the later naval treaty of 1936 between the same powers, capital ship gun calibre was reduced to 14 in., the tonnage of aircraft carriers to 23,000 (from 27,000), and a naval holiday declared from the construction of cruisers. Italy was unable to associate herself with this agreement, Japan left the conference and rising international tension stultified it.

See NAVY AND NAVIES; SEA POWER.

London Passenger Transport Board, *see* LONDON TRANSPORT EXECUTIVE.

London Pride, *Saxifraga umbrosa,* family Saxifragaceae, perennial herb with a rosette of fleshy leaves. Flowering stem is reddish, the flowers white. L. P. grows wild locally in Yorks and is common in rockeries.

London Regiment, The. The L. R. embraced all the infantry territorial army regiments entitled City of London Regiment and L. R. Each regiment within the L. R. corresponded in all respects to a battalion of other infantry regiments. In 1859 there was a great revival of volunteers, owing to a panic arising out of the supposed unfriendly attitude of Napoleon III of France towards England. Public feeling practically compelled the gov. of the day to authorise the formation of volunteer rifle corps under an Act of 1804, and many such corps were formed in the city and co. of London, Middlesex, etc. These corps bore titles indicating their place of origin, for example Middlesex Volunteer Rifle Corps, until 1908, when they came into the new territorial force scheme as part of the L. R., a new regiment formed for the purpose. Each separate regiment was numbered in seniority throughout the regiment. The 9th L. R. (Queen Victoria Rifles) claimed descent from a unit raised at the beginning of the 19th cent. When the volunteers of that period were disbanded this corps maintained its existence as a rifle club, and was officially recognised and placed in the army list in Sept. 1853 under the title of The Middlesex (The Victoria) Volunteer Rifle Corps. Of the territorial battalions of the L. R. the 5th was the London Rifle Brigade, the 13th the Kensingtons, the 14th the London Scottish, the 16th the Queen's Westminsters, the 18th the London Irish Rifles and the 28th the Artists' Rifles. The 7th City of London Regiment (Post Office Rifles) had the distinction of bearing honours for the earliest campaign in which volunteers participated, viz. Egypt, 1882. During the S. African war, 1899–1902, the volunteers of Middlesex and in and about London were permitted to participate either by providing service companies for regular regiments (*see* LONDON SCOTTISH) or by individuals joining the City Imperial Volunteers. Thousands of volunteers thus served in the war. In the First World War each regiment raised from 2 to 6 battalions, which served with considerable distinction on every front, sev. individual members gaining the Victoria Cross. The L. R. ceased to exist in 1937. The units which composed it were linked with the ordinary line regiments (for example, the linking of the London Scottish with The Gordon Highlanders). Some now form part of the Royal Regiment of Artillery and Royal Corps of Signals.

London Rifle Brigade, *see* LONDON REGIMENT.

London School of Economics and Political Science, *see* ECONOMICS AND POLITICAL SCIENCE, THE LONDON SCHOOL OF.

London Scottish, London territorial army infantry regiment. The L. S. was formed in 1859 during the general Brit. volunteer movement. Its first commanding officer was Lord Elcho (later Earl of Wemyss), who retained the appointment for 20 years. During the S. African war, 1899–1902, the regiment furnished a service company, which served with The Gordon Highlanders (its parent regular regiment), and a detachment for service with the City Imperial Volunteers. This service is commemorated on its colours. On 1 April 1908 it joined the newly formed territorial force (now territorial army), and took the title 14th (Co. of London) Batt., the London Reg., the L. S. In the First World War the L. S. was part of the original B.E.F. and was the first territorial infantry battalion to engage the enemy. It raised 3 battalions, which served in France, Flanders, Macedonia and Palestine. In 1937 it was linked with The Gordon Highlanders. In the Second World War there were 3 battalions, 2 of them infantry and the third a unit of heavy anti-aircraft artillery. The 1st and 3rd served overseas in many notable actions on the It. front. Its present H.Q., to which it moved in 1886, are at 59 Buckingham Gate, Westminster, London, S.W.

London Society, The, founded in 1912 by the Earl of Plymouth, its first president. The aim of the society is to stimulate interest in the historic buildings and amenities of London, to concern itself with their preservation and to give consideration to schemes for the future development of London. The society arranges lectures and provides facilities for its members to visit places of interest. It publishes a *Journal* 5 times a year. The offices of the society are at 3 Dean's Yard, London, S.W.1. The ann. subscription is 1 guinea and life membership 10 guineas.

London Stone, anct relic in Cannon Street, London. Originally on the S. side of the street, it stood for long within the S. wall of St Swithin's Church in Cannon Street. The church was gutted in 1940 and subsequently demolished, and the relic has been placed on the S. wall of an office building on the site of the church. Its age and original purpose are not known. Camden believed that it was the point from which the Romans measured distances, but it may be a Saxon ceremonial stone. The rebel Jack Cade (q.v.), according to Holinshed, struck his sword against it when proclaiming himself master of the city.

London Topographical Society, founded for the pub. of material illustrating the hist. and topography of the city and co. of London from the earliest times to the present day. It reproduces maps, views and plans and publishes documents and data of every description. Over 80 maps and plans—the earliest dating from 1550—have been produced, along with 22 vols. of the *London Topographical Record* and an indexed facsimile of Mills and Oliver's *Survey* (5 vols.) after the Great Fire of 1666. Hon. Secretary: 9 Rivercourt Road, London, W.6.

London Transport Board, public authority (with 4 full-time and 3 part-time members) responsible for the operation of all road and rail passenger transport services (except taxicabs and Brit. Rail, main and suburban lines) in the London Passenger Transport Area—an area of approximately 2000 sq. m. containing a pop. of *c.* 10 million.

In 1933 London's transport was first amalgamated into a single unit with the creation of the London Passenger Transport Board, which took over the operations of some 170 underground railway, bus, coach, tram and trolleybus undertakings. Under the Transport Act, 1947, the L.P.T.B. system became the responsibility of the Brit. Transport Commission (q.v.) on whose behalf it was managed by the London Transport Executive from 1 Jan. 1948 until the dissolution of the B.T.C. under the Transport Act, 1962, which created the L.T.B.

London Transport's Underground railway network (operating above ground in outer areas) is worked entirely by electric traction, while its road services are provided by a fleet of diesel-engined double- and single-deck buses and coaches (red for central area services and green for country area and Green Line coach operations). Trams and trolley buses are no longer operated.

London University, founded by royal charter in 1836. Its founders sought, in the words of Spring Rice, chancellor of the exchequer in 1835, 'an equality in all respects with the anct univs., freed from those exclusions and religious distinctions which abridge the usefulness of Oxford and of Cambridge'. Thomas Campbell, Lord Brougham and friends raised sufficient funds to buy a site in Gower Street and to start to build what became Univ. College, London, opened to students in 1828. In 1831 a rival, King's College, London, was opened, founded by supporters of the Church of England and the then Tory gov. Neither college was empowered to confer degrees and the compromise reached in 1836 was that the students from these 2 colleges should sit for examinations conducted by the univ. on the results of which degrees were awarded. Candidates were also accepted for these examinations from any institution recognised by the Privy Council for the purpose.

By 1858 the list of such institutions was long and far from homogeneous, and accordingly under the charter of that year the requirement of attendance at an approved institution was dropped. Thereafter the univ. admitted to its degree examinations any candidate who had passed the matriculation examination. The same charter gave the graduates of the univ. the right to assemble in convocation to discuss any matter relating to the univ. and to make nominations for filling a certain number of the places on the senate.

During the 19th cent. a succession of institutions of higher learning were founded in London, in addition to the existing medical schools some of which were already well estab. These new institutions included Bedford College for Women, the London School of Medicine for Women (now the Royal Free Hospital School of Medicine), the Royal College of Science, the Royal School of Mines, the City and Guilds College (amalgamated in 1907 to form the Imperial College of Science and Technology) and the London School of Economics and Political Science. In 1878 the univ. extended its degrees to women, being the first univ. in Great Britain to do so. There was a strong movement to make the univ. a teaching rather than a purely examining body, but the Gresham Commission, which reported in 1894, recommended that the univ. should be reconstructed so as to provide for teaching as well as for continuing the functions of an examining body for students both from Britain and from abroad. Under the University of London Act, 1898, and subsequent statutes a number of teaching institutions were admitted as 'schools of the univ.' and their students became 'internal students'. The teachers at these 'schools' recognised by the univ. were given the right to elect 16 of the 56 members of the senate. Students admitted to the examinations of the univ. who had not attended courses of instruction at these 'schools' were known as 'external students' unless they followed courses at certain institutions in London the teachers of which were 'recognised' by the univ.

The University of London Act, 1926, made 2 important changes. Heads of certain 'schools'

became *ex officio* members of the senate, and responsibility in financial matters was transferred to the court, which has the sole right of approaching public bodies for grants and for allocating the sums so received to the 'schools' and to the senate.

The following are the 'schools of the univ.': Bedford College, Birkbeck College, Imperial College of Science and Technology, King's College, London School of Economics and Political Science, Queen Elizabeth College, Queen Mary College, Royal Holloway College, Royal Veterinary College (qq.v.), School of Oriental and African Studies, School of Pharmacy, Univ. College, Westfield College, Wye College, the medical schools associated with the following hospitals: Charing Cross, Guy's (q.v.), King's College, London (q.v.), Middlesex, Royal Dental, Royal Free (q.v.), St Bartholomew's, St George's (q.v.), Westminster; the British Postgraduate Medical Federation (15 federated institutes), the London School of Hygiene and Tropical Medicine; the Lister Institute of Preventive Medicine; King's College Theological Dept, New College and Richmond College (all theological schools of the univ.).

The univ. maintains a number of institutes, some of which cater only for postgraduate students: Courtauld Institute of Art, Institute of Advanced Legal Studies, Institute of Archaeology, Institute of Classical Studies, Institute of Commonwealth Studies, Institute of Computer Science, Institute of Education, Institute of Germanic Studies, Institute of Historical Research, School of Slavonic and E. European Studies and Warburg Institute (q.v.).

There are also a number of institutions with recognised teachers and some internal students of the univ., including Battersea, Chelsea and Northampton Colleges of Technology, Northern and Woolwich Polytechnics, Royal Academy of Music (q.v.), Royal College of Music (q.v.), Trinity College of Music (q.v.), E. Malling Research Station and Rothamsted Experimental Station, and Goldsmiths' College.

There are faculties of theology, arts, laws, music, medicine (including dental surgery, pharmacy and veterinary medicine), science, engineering and economics. The number of full-time internal students in the 'schools' in the session 1962–3 was 23,338 of whom 4063 were postgraduate. About 20 per cent resided in colleges or halls of residence. Medical and dental students comprised one-third of the total. There were in Mar. 1964 1052 appointed teachers of whom 550 were profs. There were 26,688 registered external students, including 2900 at univ. colleges overseas in special relation to the Univ. of London. Considerable work is done in adult education under the council for Extra-Mural Studies in London, Middx, Surrey and parts of Essex and Herts. Thirty-five teachers' training colleges in London and SE. England are affiliated to the Institute of Education.

The administrative offices of the univ. were originally in Somerset House and later Marlborough House. In 1855 the univ. moved to

Burlington House. New buildings were erected in Burlington Gardens in 1870 and used until 1900 when the univ. moved to part of the Imperial Institute at S. Kensington. A site in Bloomsbury was purchased in 1927 and the present Senate House and Library (architect, Charles Holden) N. of the Brit. Museum were opened in 1936. The main buildings also house the Institute of Historical Research, Institute of Education and School of Slavonic and E. European Studies. In the group of buildings N. of these are the School of Oriental and African Studies, Birkbeck College, the Students' Union and the Warburg Institute.

The block recurrent grant to the univ. from the univ. grants committee was £15,910,000 in 1963-4. The L.C.C. made a grant of £250,000 and the home counties and co. bors. made grants totalling £175,000. The univ. grants committee made capital grants of £6,486,000. In 1962-3 the 'schools' obtained 73 per cent of their income from public grants and 7·1 per cent from fees.

The senate, 'the supreme governing and executive body of the univ. in all academic matters', consists of the chancellor, vice-chancellor, chairman of convocation, principal and 54 members, including 14 collegiate representatives, 18 elected by convocation and 18 by teachers in the faculties. The court, which controls the finances of the univ., comprises the chancellor, vice-chancellor, chairman of convocation and 14 other members, of whom 6 are appointed by the senate, 4 by Her Majesty in council and 3 by local authorities, 1 member being co-opted. Queen Elizabeth the Queen Mother was installed as chancellor in Nov. 1955 at a ceremony attended by representatives of over 130 univs. from all parts of the world. (*See Plate.*)

Londonderry, Charles Stewart Henry Vane-Tempest-Stewart, 7th Marquess of (1878–1949), statesman, eldest son of the 6th Marquess of L. Educ. at Eton and Sandhurst. From 1906 to 1915, when he succeeded to the title, he was Conservative M.P. for Maidstone. In the Coalition Gov. he was under-secretary for air and vice-president of the Air Council from 1920 to 1921. He gave up the post to join the gov. of N. Ireland, being appointed minister of education and leader of the senate. After the settlement of the boundary question he returned to England and in 1931 became secretary of state for air with a seat in the Cabinet. When Baldwin became Prime Minister in 1935 he removed L. from the Air Ministry and made him lord privy seal, but after the general election in Nov. 1935 he dropped L. altogether. Churchill later wrote that the great achievement of L.'s period of office was the designing and promotion of the Hurricane and Spitfire fighters, which were to prove vital in the Battle of Britain.

Londonderry, Robert Stewart, 2nd Marquess of, *see* CASTLEREAGH.

Londonderry, or Derry: 1. N. co. of Ireland, in the prov. of Ulster, bounded N. by the Atlantic. The surface varies, being composed of riv. valleys rising to tablelands and mts, of which the highest elevation is Mt Sawell (2236 ft). The most important rivs. are the Foyle, which forms the W. boundary of the co., and the Bann (q.v.), which bounds the E. The Roe cuts the co. in two and flows into Lough Foyle, which also receives the Faughan and the Foyle R.s. Further S. is the R. Moyola. Lough Neagh forms part of the E. co. boundary. Lough Foyle is an important naval base. The climate is suitable for agriculture; cattle and sheep are reared, and oats, turnips, barley, potatoes and flax are grown. In 1609 the estates of the O'Neills, who owned most of the co., were confiscated and made over to the citizens of London; the common council of London then inaugurated the Irish Society and retained the tns of L. and Coleraine, while the remainder was divided amongst the livery companies of the city of London. James I cancelled their charter, but it was restored by Cromwell and some of their rights are still retained. The prin. present-day industries are shirt, collar and pyjama production, light engineering and the manuf. of synthetic fibres and rubber. The Bann affords fine salmon and eel fisheries. The co. sends 1 member to the House of Commons for the L. constituency; also, a portion of the co. is in the mid-Ulster constituency. Five members are returned to the Northern Ireland parliament. Area 816 sq. m.; pop. 111,565.

2. Co. tn of the above, situated about 21 m. from the mouth of Lough Foyle on both banks of the R. Foyle. 'Derry' means 'oak grove', and its original appellation was *Derry-Calgaich*, the 'oak-wood of Calgaich' (fierce warrior), by which name it was known down to the 10th cent. L.'s hist. dates from the foundation of the monastery there by St Columba in 546, and it became a place of great importance. It was pillaged by the Danes on scv. occasions. In 1164 Abbot O'Brolchain, first Bishop of Derry, built the Teampall Mor or 'great church'. In 1311 the tn was granted to Richard de Burgo, Earl of Ulster, and a more or less uneventful period followed. But in 1566, on the rebellion of Shane O'Neill, Earl of Tyrone, there was a renewal of trouble; O'Neill suffered a great defeat at the hands of Edward Randolph, who commanded the Eng. forces, and was killed. Randolph's successor, Edward St Low, abandoned L. in 1568, after an accidental explosion by which the tn and fort were blown up, including the Teampall Mor or 'great church'. With the plantation of Ulster under James I a large tract of the prov. of Derry was distributed among the London companies or guilds. Subsequently, in order to avoid jealousy among the companies, the City of London Corporation retained the bors. of L. and Coleraine in its own hands and appointed the Irish Society from among its members to administer them. The Irish Society was created in 1610 and incorporated by royal charter in 1613; its court consists of a governor, a deputy governor and 24 assistants, in addition to the Recorder of London, and the society is trustee for the corporation of L. It was in connection with the association of Derry with

the corporation of London that the name of the city was changed to Londonderry. In 1688 occurred the great siege of Derry, which it sustained against the forces of James II under Tyrconnell and which has made the name of L. and of the Rev. George Walker, the governor, famous.

L. is still surrounded by the old city walls which extend for about a mile and include 7 gates and sev. bastions. The waterside, the part of the city on the r. b. of the Foyle, is connected to the old city by the Craigavon Bridge, opened in 1933, which carries a roadway 1200 ft long. There are some fine old buildings, including the Protestant cathedral of St Columb dating from 1633. The bells in the tower are the oldest peal in Ireland; in 1929 they were recast and increased from 8 to 13. The Rom. Catholic cathedral of St Eugene was completed in 1833. Educational institutions are Magee Univ. College (in affiliation with the Queen's Univ., Belfast), Foyle College for Protestants, St Columb's College for Rom. Catholics and the municipal technical college. Among the parks are Brooke Park in which is situated the municipal library, St Columb's Park and Meenan Park. The staple industry, the making of shirts and collars, is a cent. old, having begun as a handicraft in cottages; it is now carried on in large factories in all parts of the city. Subsidiary industries are motor and mechanical engineering, fancy-box making, snuff, mineral waters, light engineering, rayon spinning for tyre manuf., sound reproducers, activated carbon and bacon curing. Surrounded by a fertile agric. dist, the port has a large cattle-shipping and sheep and pig export trade. In the Second World War it was the main base in the battle of the Atlantic. L. is a co. bor. and returns 1 member to Parliament. Pop. 53,744. (*See Plate: Ireland, Northern.*)

'**Londonderry Air**', *see* LIMAVADY.

'**Lone Star State**', *see* TEXAS.

Long, Crawford Williamson (1815–78), Amer. physician, *b.* Danielsville, Georgia. He studied medicine at the univs. of Transylvania and Pennsylvania. After some experiments he decided to try ether inhalation as a method of preventing pain in surgical operations. There is no doubt that L. was the first successfully to use ether vapour as an anaesthetic; this was at Jefferson, Georgia, on 30 Mar. 1842. Unfortunately he did not publish his results until others, notably W. T. G. Morton (q.v.), had independently introduced ether and had claimed priority. *See* life by F. L. Taylor, 1928; F. K. Boland, *The First Anesthetic*, 1950.

Long, G. W. de, *see* DE LONG.

Long, Huey Pierce (1893–1935), Amer. lawyer and politician, *b.* Winnfield, Louisiana. Admitted to the Bar (1915), he practised in Winnfield for a few years in cases against public utility companies. In 1928 he was elected governor of Louisiana and he was U.S. senator 1931–5. His methods as a governor were those of an unbridled and unprincipled dictator who, having gained control of the state machinery of government, proceeded to abuse its functions.

He was assassinated in the State House at Baton Rouge. His brother Earl Kemp (*b.* 1895) was lieutenant-governor from 1936 to 1938 and became governor on the resignation of Governor Richard Leche (1939), but he was defeated at the election for governor in 1940 and then returned by a great majority, 1948–52.

Long, Loch, sea loch of Scotland, being a branch of the Firth of Clyde between Argyll and Dunbartonshire. It extends N. from Holy Loch to Arrochar for about 18 m. (width $\frac{1}{2}$–$1\frac{1}{2}$ m.).

Long-haired Dachshund, *see* DACHSHUND.

Long Beach, city, watering-place and summer resort of California, U.S.A., situated on San Pedro Bay. A harbour has been constructed with 10 sq. m. of anchorage; the system is one of the bases of the U.S. Pacific Fleet. There is an airport. L. B. manufs. aircraft, tyres and soap, and there are oil refining, automobile assembling and fish and fruit canning plants. An oilfield was discovered in 1921. Pop. 344,170.

Long Branch, coastal city of New Jersey, U.S.A., in Monmouth co., about 30 m. S. of New York. It developed into a watering-place and was chartered as a city in 1904. It manufs. silk and rubber goods, clothing and boats. It has a seafood industry and there are nursery products and truck farming. Pop. *c.* 25,000.

Long Day Plants. Many plants, though they may continue to produce healthy vegetative growth, will only produce flowers if they are subjected to a daily illumination of a definite duration suitable to the particular plant. Some plants, known 'L. D. P.', require a much longer period of illumination than do other 'short day' plants. If L. D. P. are artificially subjected to the right quantity of additional illumination in spring, they can be induced to flower early. Short day plants can similarly be induced to flower by shading daily for the appropriate length of time, e.g. tobacco flowers abnormally early if given only 5–8 hours illumination per day, and if given 18 hours it will probably never produce flowers. Most flowering plants of the tundra and other regions of high latitudes are short day plants; most tropical plants are L. D. P. Wheat is a long day plant, but the breeding of new, shorter day strains now makes it possible to grow wheat in higher latitudes than before.

Long Eaton, urb. dist of Derbyshire, England, midway between Derby and Nottingham in the valley of the R. Trent. Prin. industries are the manuf. of lace, upholstery, elastic web and braid, corsetry, metal tubing, stainless steel sinks, electric wire and cables, spring seating, piano actions and pencils. Pop. 30,464.

Long Island (Denmark), *see* LANGELAND.

Long Island, is. lying off the coast of Connecticut and New York States, U.S.A., and forming part of the latter. It is 118 m. long, from 12 to 20 m. wide and is separated from the mainland by L. I. Sound, which varies in width from 2 to 25 m. and is over 100 m. in length. L. I. covers 1401 sq. m. and has a pop. of over 6,000,000. On the N. the coast is much indented, and there are numerous bays, headlands and smaller is. In the Great S. Bay there are large oyster-beds, the famous Blue Points growing there. Market gardens flourish, and their potatoes and truck produce are an important source of supply for New York City. Brooklyn and Queens bors., which form part of New York City, lie at the W. end, Nassau and Suffolk forming the remaining cos. It is mainly a residential area, with farming in the E. La Guardia and Idlewild airports are on the is. and at Lake Success the U.N. General Assembly took up in 1946 its temporary H.Q. There are sev. recreational areas, including Coney and Fire Is. and Jones Beach. The earliest white settlement was in 1636. L. I. is entirely of glacial origin and consists of sands and clays marking the maximum extent of the Amer. ice-sheets.

Long Island City, formerly a city of Queens co., New York, U.S.A. Since 1898 it has been part of the bor. of Queens, New York City, at the W. end of Long Is. Over 1400 factories produce a variety of products. It has large railroad yards and is an express terminal.

Long Measure, see METROLOGY.

Long Parliament, name generally confined to the Eng. Parliament which met in Nov. 1640, sat almost continuously until 1653 and was revived 1659–60, Its first act was to secure the execution of the Earl of Strafford by a Bill of Attainder (1641), and it then proceeded to abolish the Star Chamber. A constitutional church and royalist party grew up under the leadership of Hyde and Falkland, when Pym and Hampden, the chief statesmen of the puritan party, showed by the 'Root and Branch Bill' and the 'Grand Remonstrance' that they intended to abolish the existing system of eccles. gov. and get the reins of gov. into their own hands. In 1642 Charles I made a futile attempt to seize Pym, Hampden, Holles, Hazlerig and Strode, his chief enemies in the House. From 1644 parl. power passed into the hands of the Independents. Laud was executed and the New Model Ordinance enforced, whereby a single parliamentarian army was created, the officers of which had all to subscribe to the Covenant (1645). In 1648 Cromwell got rid of the Moderate and Presbyterian members by the high-handed action immortalised as 'Pride's Purge'. The 'Rump', as the remnant was called, was submissive to its master, and obediently voted the execution of Charles and the institution of the Commonwealth (1649). In 1653 it was dismissed, Cromwell having no further use for it. It was restored in 1659, and finally passed an Act declaring itself dissolved in Mar. 1660.

Long Range Desert Group. This unit was estab. in the Second World War, in June 1940, in the vast interior of Libya. Its sphere of activities ranged over about 600 m. inland from the Mediterranean coast and about 1700 m. westwards from the Nile. All ranks were selected volunteers. Its role began as one of reconnaissance, but its mobility, training and knowledge of the desert fitted it admirably for harassing the enemy offensively. Among many successful raids in which the group participated were those against enemy outposts in the Fezzan (1200 m.

from base across entirely unmapped country) in the autumn of 1940, and against the garrisons of Benghazi, Barce and Tobruk in Sept. 1942. It also surveyed the routes used by the Eighth Army in their outflanking movements against the El Agheila and Mareth positions.

The basic unit of the group in the desert was the ·patrol, which normally consisted of 5 unarmoured vehicles and 20 men. Each patrol was commanded by an officer and contained an expert navigator, R.E.M.E. fitter, Royal Signals wireless operator and a R.A.M.C. orderly. For most of the desert campaign the group was based either in the oases of Siwa or Kufra, where its own 2 aircraft were maintained for all evacuation of casualties, communication and dropping of minor necessities to patrols on operations. At the conclusion of the desert campaign in early 1943 the group returned to the Delta and later to the Lebanon. It was reorganised to operate in Italy and the Balkans on foot, on skis and with animal transport, and to reach its target by parachute or by sea. In Sept. 1943 the unit was sent to the Dodecanese where it became involved in the ill-fated operations on the is. of Cos and Leros. In early 1944 the unit moved to Italy to operate under F.-M. Alexander. Its primary roles were to obtain information on enemy movements, to harass the enemy lines of communications, to support partisan movements and to provide watches on the movement of enemy shipping in the Adriatic. Patrols operated continuously in Greece, Albania, Yugoslavia and Italy, carrying out more than 100 successful operations.

Long Range Navigation or **Loran,** see RADIO BEACONS.

Long Service and Good Conduct Medal, award instituted in the Brit. Army and Navy by William IV in 1830 and 1831 respectively. The military medal is awarded to warrant officers, non-commissioned officers and other ranks after 18 years' service, during which character and conduct have been irreproachable. The medal carries on the obverse a bust of the sovereign in military uniform and on the reverse the words 'For long service and good conduct'. The ribbon is crimson with white edges. The naval medal is awarded to petty officers and other ratings of the Royal Navy and to non-commissioned officers and men of the Royal Marines after 15 years' service with 'very good' certificate of character continuously earned. Hung on a straight clasp, the medal has on the obverse a bust of the sovereign in naval uniform and on the reverse a design of a frigate-of-the-line with the appropriate words. A medal with similar qualifications as obtain in the army is awarded in the R.A.F. It has a bust of the sovereign on the obverse and eagle and crown on the reverse. The ribbon is dark blue and crimson with white edges. L. S. medals are also awarded in certain colonial regiments associated with the Brit. Army, and in the various naval reserve forces. The Board of Trade issues a L. S. medal to rocket apparatus volunteers.

Long-xuyen, cap. of prov. of same name in S.

Vietnam on the R. Bassac, 90 m. WSW. of Saigon (q.v.). Communication is maintained between the tn and the Gulf of Siam by the Rach-gia Canal. Rice is the main crop of this prov., secondary crops being sugar, ground-nuts and tobacco. Pop. of prov. 300,000; tn 23,300.

Longbenton, urb. dist. of Northumberland, England, 5 m. NNE. of Newcastle upon Tyne, with coal-mines. In the dist are Weetslade, Forest Hall and Benton. Pop. 44,633.

Longbow. Introduced into England from Wales, the L. was first used on a large scale by Edward I. Until the development of firearms it was the most effective weapon known. About 6 ft in length, made of ash or yew, its arrows could penetrate 4 in. of oak. Its supremacy was shown, amongst other instances, at Agincourt, where a Fr. cavalry charge was reduced to complete confusion by a barrage of arrows.

Longchamp, racecourse near Paris, on the SW. side of the Bois de Boulogne. Here the race for the Grand Prix is run. There are remains of an anct abbey.

Longchamps, William de (d. 1197), chancellor of England, a Norman of humble origin, whom Richard I made Bishop of Ely in 1189, and afterwards, when he went on the crusade (1190), joint-justiciar with Hugh de Puiset, Bishop of Durham. By becoming papal legate in 1190 L. united supremacy in Church and State. Though loyal to Richard, his scorn of everything English and his burdensome taxation aroused such a storm of popular dislike that it was not difficult for John to arrest and imprison him. He escaped and joined Richard in Germany. He d. at Poitiers.

Longépée, William de, see SALISBURY, WILLIAM LONGSWORD, 3rd EARL OF.

Longepierre, Hilaire-Bernard de Requeleyne, Baron de (1659–1721), Fr. writer, b. Dijon. His works include poems (*Idylles*, 1683, *Idylles nouvelles*, 1690), tragedies (including *Médée*, 1694, *Électre*, 1702) and a *Discours sur les anciens*, 1687.

Longevity, scientifically, refers to the length of life of any organism. In the case of lower forms of life very little has been determined, but the range is probably large; L. of a few hours is common. Higher plants are classed as annuals, biennials, perennials, etc., the range extending from a month to thousands of years. De Candolle gives figures as follows in years: elm, 335; ivy, 450; palms, 600–700; lime, 1076–1147; oak, 810–1500; yew, 2880; baobab, 5000. In the animal kingdom the range is considerably less, complexity of organism giving rise to greater chance of death. In general, for any one species, life is longer at lower temps. Certain infusoria live less than 48 hrs. Coldblooded animals are comparatively long lived: pike and carp, 150; tortoises, 100. Birds also are long lived: eagles and crows, 100; peacocks, 20; but many smaller birds only 5 or 6. Among mammals the elephant ranks highest, over 100; camel, 50–80; horse, up to 40; deer, 30; ox, 15–20; dogs, pigs, 15–20. Although it has been suggested that in certain cases the complete term of life would appear to

bear some relation to the period of gestation or the age of maturity, no laws have been formulated. Amongst the human race the biblical 3 score and 10 still gives a healthy average, though it is not uncommon for the cent. to be passed. In 1945 there *d.* at Serowe (Bechuanaland) a native named Ramonotowane Seran, who was claimed to be 130 years old; but some doubt has been cast on the validity of the claim, though according to the Johannesburg *Star* 'there could hardly be a shadow of doubt that he was 130 years old' (see *The Times*, 31 Aug. and 5 Sept. 1945).

During the 20th cent. attempts based on knowledge of the endocrine system have been made to prolong the life of animals. Voronoff in particular applied the process of grafting genital glands of apes into young men suffering from abnormalities of the endocrine organs, and into men approaching senescence. As the rationale of the treatment is scientifically extremely controversial and the effects are only partial and transient and not free from objections the operation has largely fallen into disrepute. Moreover the gland of the ape atrophies in man. The life of sheep and rats has been prolonged by transplanting glands from young animals of the same species into animals approaching senescence. Wigglesworth has recently prolonged and extended the larval life and size of insects by brain implantations.

See also GERIATRICS.

See Voronoff, *Old Age and Rejuvenescence* and *The Conquest of Life*, 1920; B. Sokoloff, *The Battle for Youth*, 1922; R T. Gould, *Enigmas*, 1929; A. Guéniot, *Pour Vivre 100 ans*, 1931.

Longfellow, Henry Wadsworth (1807–82), poet, b. Portland, Maine, son of a lawyer. In 1822 he was sent to Bowdoin College, of which his father was a trustee, and after graduating was appointed to a new Chair of Modern Languages. Returning from a 3-year trip to Europe in 1829 he commenced his professional duties, writing in the *North American Review*. In 1831 he married Mary Potter and in 1833 he pub. his first books, a trans. from the Spanish, followed by the first part of *Outre-Mer: A Pilgrimage Beyond the Sea*, 1835, giving an account of his travels. At the end of the year L. was invited to become Professor of Modern Languages at Harvard. He paid a second visit to Europe accompanied by his wife, who, however, *d.* at Amsterdam. He returned to his duties in 1836, and in 1838 appeared *Voices of the Night*, containing the 'Psalm of Life' and 'Excelsior', which has extraordinary popularity and gave him a place in the affections of his countrymen which he held until his death. The same year saw the pub. of *Hyperion*. His next work was *Ballads and other Poems*, 1842, containing 'The Wreck of the Hesperus' and 'The Village Blacksmith'.

In 1843 he married his second wife, Frances Appleton, and in the same year appeared *The Spanish Student*, a drama. The *Belfry of Bruges* and *Evangeline*, 1847, generally considered his masterpiece, followed. In 1849 he published *Kavanagh*, a novel which added nothing to his reputation, and in 1851 *Seaside and Fireside*, and

The Golden Legend. Having now a sufficient and secure income from his writings, he resigned his professorship and devoted himself entirely to literature. *Hiawatha* appeared in 1855 and *The Courtship of Miles Standish* in 1858. In 1861 his wife was accidentally burned to death, a tragedy which told heavily upon him. Later works were a trans. of Dante's *Divina Commedia*, 1865–7, *Tales of a Wayside Inn*, 1863, *The New England Tragedies*, 1868, and the *Divine Tragedy*, the last 2 of which he combined with the *Golden Legend* into a trilogy, which he named *Christus*, 1872. In 1868 he paid a last visit to England, where he was received with the highest honour. Among his last works were *Three Books of Song*, 1872, *Aftermath*, 1873, and *Ultima Thule*, 1880–2. L. lacked the intensity of feeling and power of imagination to make him a great poet; but though he never soars to the heights of deep feeling, he touches the heart by appealing to universal and deepseated affections. *See* O. Smeaton, *Longfellow and his Poetry*, 1919; E. Goggio, *Longfellow and Dante*, 1924; C. L. Johnson, *Professor Longfellow of Harvard*, 1945. (*See Plate: American Literature*.)

Longford, 7th Earl of, Francis Aungler Pakenham (1905–), banker and politician, educ. at Eton and New College, Oxford. He left the Conservatives to join the Labour Party and was made Baron Pakenham, 1945. Succeeded to the L. title, 1961. L. was chancellor of the duchy of Lancaster 1948–51, minister of civil aviation 1948–51 and first lord of the admiralty 1951. From 1955–63 he was chairman of the National Bank Ltd. In 1964 he became leader of the House of Lords and Lord Privy Seal; colonial secretary, 1965–6. His wife Elizabeth is a writer whose books have included biographies of Dr Jameson and Queen Victoria. Pubs: *Peace by Ordeal*, 1935; *The Idea of Punishment*, 1961; *Five Lives*, 1964.

Longford: 1. Co. of Rep. of Ireland, bounded NW. by Leitrim, NE. by Cavan, E. and S. by Westmeath and W. by Lough Ree and Roscommon. The surface is generally hilly and there are areas of marsh and bog. The chief rivs. are the Camlin, flowing into the Shannon, and the Inny, flowing into Lough Ree. Marble has been found in the co., also iron and lead. The pasturage is good and cattle and sheep are reared; oats and potatoes are the chief crops. L. has literary associations with Goldsmith and Maria Edgeworth. The co. sends 2 members to the Dáil. Area 421 sq. m.; pop. 9555.
2. Co. tn of above. It has one of the finest churches in Ireland, St Mels Rom. Catholic cathedral for the diocese of Ardagh, and 2 textile factories. Pop. 3858.

Longhena, Baldassare (1595–1682), Italian baroque architect, *b*. Venice, started as a mason, then studied architecture under Scamozzi. He designed the famous church of S. Maria della Salute, 1631–82; the Rezzonico Palace, 1680; and the Pesaro Palace, 1679 onwards, all in Venice.

Longhi (Falca), Pietro (1702–1785), It. painter of the Venetian School, son of Alessandro Falca,

a goldsmith. He painted *genre* pictures of Venetian life which have some points of resemblance with Hogarth's London scenes. His son, Alessandro L. (1733–1815), was a portrait painter and engraver who reproduced some of his father's paintings.

Longhorn Breed, *see* CATTLE.

Longicorns, *see* CERAMBYCIDAE.

Longinus, Cassius (*c*. AD 213–73), Gk rhetorician, *b*. Emesa in Syria. After visiting Alexandria and Rome he taught at Athens for about 30 years and was a strong opponent of Neoplatonism. Meeting Zenobia, Queen of Palmyra, while travelling in the E., L. was engaged to teach her Greek and was soon appointed a member of her council, in which his influence was paramount. Acting on his advice, Zenobia rebelled against Rome, and after the capture of Palmyra L. was executed by order of Aurelian. Only fragments of his numerous works remain. Scholars are now agreed that he was not the author of a treatise *On the Sublime* once attributed to him. *See* PSEUDO-LONGINUS.

Longitude, *see* LATITUDE AND LONGITUDE.

Longleat, one of the great historic houses of England, seat of the Marquess of Bath, situated in Wilts, midway between Warminster and Frome, near the Somerset border. L. was built for Sir John Thynne between 1566 and 1580 on the site of the monastery of St Radegund. Since then the gardens and grounds have been replanned and a chain of lakes made by Lancelot Brown (q.v.) in the late eighteenth cent. About 1800 Sir Jeffrey Wyattville made a number of alterations to the house and added a large quadrangle of stables, and in the mid 19th cent. heavy ornate ceilings and marble door surrounds were added by It. workmen in the prin. rooms. L. therefore shows the influence of many fluctuations of taste; yet in the lofty hall and in the second-floor library, in which latter from 1691 to 1711 Bishop Ken (q.v.) lived and worked, something of the original house remains, while the S., E. and W. façades are almost as they were in 1580. Much of the interest of L. lies in its contents, which are of many periods: a large ormolu table which belonged to Talleyrand, a library rich in MSS, and printed books, including a beautiful 12th cent. psalter and the Book of Bath (1428, a miscellany of verse and prose originally belonging to the monastery of Bath), some MSS. of Matthew Prior, Caxton's *Historyes of Troye, c*. 1475, and 4 folios of Shakespeare. Among the portraits at L. are examples of Lely and most of the other noted 17th cent. portrait painters. Other portraits are those of Lord Thurlow by Reynolds, of the first Lord Bath by Sir Thomas Lawrence and of the 4th Lady Bath by G. F. Watts; while paintings by foreign masters include a head by Raphael and a small Holy Family by Titian. There is also a series of huge sporting paintings by John Wootton (*c*. 1678–1765), the most important being a number of hunting scenes which reveal Wootton's decorative power when painting on a large scale. Open to the public, L. is a 'show-place' of wide appeal, the lake of

Shearwater being among the most beautiful stretches of private property in Europe. (*See Plate; Wiltshire.*)

Longman, Thomas (1699–1755), publisher. He took over in 1724 the business of Wm Taylor (the publisher of *Robinson Crusoe*) at the signs of the Ship and the Black Swan in Paternoster Row. Until the fire of Dec. 1940 the present firm, Longmans Green & Co. Ltd, occupied premises on the original site. They now have their H.Q. at 48 Grosvenor Street, W.1., a warehouse and more offices at Harlow, Essex, and branches and offices all over the world. Longmans are one of the oldest publishing houses in Great Britain. Many famous names on the Eng. literary scene have appeared on the Longmans List and the firm is known throughout the world for the great variety of its publishing activities, both educational and general.

Longo, Luigi (1900–), It. politician, joined the Communist party while a student. He was imprisoned for political activities 1923–4 and later left Italy. From 1932–4 L. was in Moscow; he was inspector-general of the International Brigade in Spain, 1936–9, and then settled in France. He was imprisoned there, 1939–41, and then returned to Italy to work with the Communist resistance groups. In 1945 he became deputy secretary-general of the It. Communist party and entered Parliament, 1946. He succeeded Togliatti (q.v.) as the party Secretary-General, 1964.

Longobards, Langobardi or **Lombards,** E. Ger. (Suevic) tribe, first mentioned in connection with their defeat in AD 5 by the Romans under Tiberius (later emperor). They were then dwelling on the lower Elbe, but during the 4th or 5th cent. they settled on the banks of the Danube, and were successful in destroying the Heruli, while about the middle of the 6th cent. they lived in Pannonia, and here they were victorious over the Gepidae. In 568, after crossing the Julian Alps under their king Alboin (q.v.), they subjugated N. Italy, and the name Lombardy (q.v.) derives from them. They settled in the region permanently, making it their kingdom, under the somewhat nominal sovereignty of various elected kings, for about 2 cents. The L. had been Arians since the 5th cent. but were converted to orthodox Catholicism about 600. They were, however, a constant threat to the papacy, particularly under Liutprand (712–43), who estab. a definite control over the Longobard dukes. After his death Pepin, son of Charles Martel, in answer to the appeal of Gregory III, began a conquest of the L., completed by his son Charlemagne in 774.

Longridge, eccles, par. and tn of Lancs, England, 6 m. NE. of Preston. There are large stone quarries in the neighbourhood, and the industries include cotton and rayon weaving, iron founding, building, civil engineering and cheese-making. The Preston water reservoirs are at L. Pop. 4677.

Longstreet, James (1821–1904), Amer. Confederate general, *b.* S. Carolina. He was wounded in the Mexican war, and was made a confederate brigadier-general at the outbreak of the civil war. He took part in the battles of Bull Run, Fredericksburg, Gettysburg and Chickamauga (1863), being chiefly responsible for the victory at the last-named. His accidental wound by his own men at a turning point of the battle of the Wilderness (1869) checked the Confederates' assault at a critical moment. After the war L. became a Republican. He was minister to Turkey under Grant, and commissioner for railways to McKinley and Roosevelt. He pub. *From Manassas to Appomattox,* 1896, and his defence of his action at Gettysburg appeared after his death. See H. J. Eckenrode and B. Conrad, *James Longstreet, Lee's War Horse,* 1936; D. B. Sanger and T. R. Hay, *James Longstreet,* 1952.

Longsword, William, see SALISBURY, WILLIAM LONGSWORD, 3rd EARL OF.

Longton, formerly bor. and tn of Staffs, England, since 1910 part of the city and co. bor. of Stoke-on-Trent (q.v.). It is a pottery dist of considerable size, the manuf. of bone china being concentrated there. There are coal-mines in the vicinity.

Longton Hall (Staffs), 1750–60, a factory producing soft-paste porcelain (q.v.), the earliest in Staffs., under Wm Littler. See B. Watney, *Longton Hall Porcelain,* 1957.

Longueuil, Barony of, see LE MOYNE.

Longueville, Anne Geneviève, Duchesse de (1619–79), Fr. princess, daughter of the Duke of Condé, *b.* Vincennes. The great Condé was her brother. She married the Duke of Longueville, but the marriage was unhappy and she became the mistress of La Rochefoucauld (q.v.). She took a prominent part in the second Fronde rising. Later La Rochefoucauld discarded her, and after her husband's death she retired to a convent. She was a supporter of Jansenism.

Longus (3rd or 4th cent. AD), Gk author of the pastoral novel *Daphnis and Chloë.* There is an ed. by J. M. Edmonds (1924) and a trans. by George Moore (1924).

Longview: 1. Tn of Texas, U.S.A., situated in Gregg co., 60 m. W. of Shreveport. The chief industry is the refining of oil from the E. Texas oilfield. It has foundries and plough works, saw-mills and office furniture factories, as well as a shipping trade in lumber, cotton, hides, fruit, etc. Pop. *c.* 30,000.

2. Co. seat of Cowlitz co., Washington, U.S.A. It is one of the world's largest timber centres, and its cantilever bridge across the Columbia is one of the largest of its type in America. Pop. *c.* 22,000.

Longwood, see ST HELENA.

Longwy, Fr. tn in the dept of Meurthe-Moselle, an anct fortress. It is in an iron-mining dist, and has metallurgical and pottery industries. Pop. 22,000.

Lonicera, or **Honeysuckle,** family Caprifoliaceae; genus of 180 bush or climbing shrubs, deciduous or evergreen, found in the N. hemisphere. Now divided into 3 groups: (1) Periclymenum or Caprifolium Climbers, of which *L. periclymenum,* the native Woodbine, *L.*

sempervirens, Trumpet Honeysuckle, and *L. tragophylla*, Chinese Honeysuckle, are typical; (2) Chamaecerasus or Xylosteum Bush Honeysuckles, represented by *L. nitida*, hedging Honeysyckle, *L. standishii*, winter-flowering Honeysuckle, and *L. xylosteum*, Fly Honeysuckle; (3) Nintova, climbers, usually evergreen, with flowers which are in pairs, as in *L. japonica.*

Lonk Breed, *see* SHEEP.

Lönnrot, Elias (1802–84), Finnish scholar, *b.* Sammatti in Nyland. He became a country doctor, but was greatly interested in Finnish philology and folklore, and he travelled widely in Finland and Russian Karelia, collecting songs and legends. *Kanteletar,* 1829–31, was a collection of folk-songs. In 1835 he pub. a first ed. of the *Kalevala*, which was a collection of legendary poems and songs, from which L. evolved a reasonably connected epic of about 12,000 lines; it deals with the fortunes of 3 brothers, sons of Kalewa, whose origin dates from mythological times. An enlarged ed. was pub. by L. in 1849, and a still more complete text in 1887 by A. V. Forsman. Longfellow adopted the *Hiawatha* metre from it. L. was prof. of Finnish literature and languages at Helsingfors Univ. from 1854 to 1862. To establish a literary Finnish language, for use instead of Swedish, he compiled a notable Finnish-Swedish dictionary (1866–80). He also ed. *Sananlaskuja,* 1842, *Arwoituksia,* 1844, and pub. amongst other works *Flora Fennica,* 1860, *Suomen kansan muinaisia loitsurunoja,* 1880. and *Valiaikainen Suomalainen Virsikirja,* 1883. *See* A. E. Ahlqvist, *Elias Lönnrot,* 1885; J. F. Perret, *La Littérature finlandaise,* 1936.

Lonsdale, Earl of, Eng. title borne by the family of Lowther. In 1696 Sir John Lowther, a wealthy baronet of Cumberland, was given a viscounty, but the title became extinct in 1750 and his estates descended to Sir James Lowther who, in 1784, was made Earl of L. This title too became extinct when he *d.* in 1802. In 1807 Sir Wm Lowther was made Earl of L. and from him the 5th earl, Hugh Cecil Lowther (1857–1944), was descended. He won a great reputation as a sportsman, notably in boxing (he was the donor of the L. belts) and horse-racing. The present (7th) earl was *b.* in 1922 and succeeded his grandfather in 1953.

Lonsdale, Frederick, originally **Frederick Leonard** (1881–1954), dramatist, *b* Jersey, son of a tobacconist. Before becoming a prominent playwright he served as a private in the Army and worked as a clerk for the London and SW. Railway, Jersey, and as a ship's steward. In 1908 he had 2 plays produced: *The Early Worm, The King of Cadonia,* and *The Best People* in 1909. Later he wrote many witty comedies, including *Aren't We All?,* 1923, *The Street Singer,* 1924, *Spring Cleaning,* 1925, *The Last of Mrs Cheyney,* 1925, *On Approval,* 1927, *Canaries Sometimes Sing,* 1929, *Once is Enough,* 1938, *Another Love Story,* 1943, and *The Way Things Go,* 1950. He also collaborated in sev. musical comedies, of which *The Maid of the Mountains,* 1917, was the most successful. *See* life by his daughter Frances Donaldson, 1957.

Lons-le-Saunier, Fr. tn, cap. of the dept of Jura, on the Vallière. It is a tourist centre, and has been known as a spa since the 4th cent. There are some fine old buildings. Rouget de Lisle (q.v.) was *b.* here. Wines and salt are produced, and there is a trade in cheese, horses and cattle. Pop. 16,000.

Loo (formerly called **Lanterloo**), round game of cards played by any number of persons. Three cards are dealt to each player, and an extra hand called 'miss', and the top of the undealt cards is turned up for trumps. The dealer puts a stake into the pool. A player can 'pass', or exchange for 'miss'. If the leader holds ace of trumps he must play it, or the king if the ace is turned up, or if he has two trumps he must lead one. Subsequent players must follow suit, and must head the trick if able. If not able to follow suit, but able to trump, they must do so. The winner of each trick must lead a trump if able. When the hand has been played out, the winners get one-third of the amount for each trick. If each declared player wins at least one trick, it is a 'single', and a fresh pool is made as before; but if any of the declared players fails to make a trick he is looed by paying a stake into the next pool, adding to the contribution put in by the dealer.

Loo Castle, *see* APELDOORN.

Loo Choo Islands, *see* RYUKYU.

Looe, seaport and urb. dist of Cornwall, England, on L. Bay, 16 m. W. of Plymouth. The urb. dist comprises W. and E. L., joined by a bridge across the riv. L. It was once a smuggler's resort. Fishing and shipping are carried on; the L.s were once flourishing seaports. Pop. 3670.

Loofah, or **Vegetable Sponge,** fibrous skeleton of a gourd (*Luffa cylindrica*). After the pulp in which the seeds are embedded has been removed, the fibre is used as a bath sponge.

Lookout Mountain, ridge in NW. Georgia and adjacent parts of Tennessee and Alabama, U.S.A., rising to 2000 ft above the Tennessee R. It was stormed by Gen. Hooker in 1863.

Loom, *see* COTTON.

Loon, Hendrik Willem van (1882–1944), Dutch historian and writer, *b.* Rotterdam. He went to America at the age of 20, took a hist. degree at Cornell Univ., spent a year at Harvard and became a journalist. He then studied hist. at Munich, and taught in sev. Amer. univs. In the First World War he was a reporter in Europe. His first book, *The Story of Mankind,* pub. in 1921, achieved great success as a popular, picturesque, universal hist. Other pubs. include *The Fall of the Dutch Republic,* 1913, *A Short History of Discovery,* 1918, *The Story of the Bible,* 1923, *Van Loon's Geography,* 1932, *The Arts,* 1937, and *The Story of the Pacific,* 1940.

Loon, tn on the is. of Bohol, Philippine Is. It possesses a sheltered harbour and grows coconuts, mango and rice. Pop. *c.* 30,000.

Loon, or **Great Northern Diver,** *Colymbus immer*, bird, principally known as a winter visitor to Britain, when it is seen on most of the coasts and occasionally on inland waters. It also breeds in Iceland, S. Greenland and across the whole of N. America. The head, neck and upper tail-coverts are glossed with deep purplish green on a black ground; short transverse bar on the throat collar or middle of the neck; upper plumage black, marked with white spots; under plumage white. Total length 28 in. On account of the extreme watchfulness of this bird, and its wonderful powers of diving, specimens are by no means easily obtained by a person who has not had considerable experience of its habits. In smooth water a boat and its moving shadow can be seen from beneath the surface of the water for a considerable distance, and hence the bird is most frequently dogged and shot during a breeze. The instant it perceives itself threatened with danger it either sinks the body low in the water or entirely disappears, seldom emerging before it has traversed a distance of 100 yds, or perhaps even 500 yds.

LOON

Loos, Anita (1893–), Amer. novelist, *b.* Sisson, California. In 1919 she married John Emerson, and they wrote sev. films for Douglas Fairbanks. Her first novel, *Gentlemen Prefer Blondes*, 1925, a satirical account of a hard-boiled gold-digger, was a popular success; its sequel, *But Gentlemen Marry Brunettes*, 1928, was less successful.

Loos, Battle of, name given to the Brit. share in the Anglo-Fr. offensive in Artois between 25 Sept. and 8 Oct. 1915. Operations, which centred round the vil. of Loos, were conducted by the First Army (Gen. Sir Douglas Haig), the initial attack at 6.30 a.m. on 25 Sept. being by 6 Brit. Divs. forming the I and IV Corps. They were opposed by 2 Ger. divs. (with 2 others in close support) in a well-entrenched position protected by barbed wire and an unusually large number of machine-guns. The operation was notable as being the first in which the British used gas and the first in which divs. of the New ('Kitchener's') Armies took part. Owing to the vagaries of the wind the gas on some parts of the front did more damage to the attackers than to the defenders. Nevertheless, except on the extreme left, the attack met with considerable success on the first day; but this was not exploited quickly enough owing to the 2 Brit. reserve divs. being located too far back. They did not reach the battlefield until the morning of the 26th, by which time the Germans had recovered. Subsequent operations of a limited kind centred round the dominating feature Hill 70, and were hampered by bad weather. Preparations for a further attack were interrupted by a Ger. counter-attack on 8 Oct.—which eventually proved unsuccessful—and on that day the offensive was brought to an end.

Brit. casualties were 48,267, the total Fr. losses 191,767 and the Ger. estimated at about 178,000. Although the British had captured some 8000 yards of a well-organised Ger. defence system, the operation rates as a limited and indecisive success. *See* FRANCE AND FLANDERS, FIRST WORLD WAR CAMPAIGNS—1915.

Loosestrife. The purple L. is *Lythrum salicaria*, a herbaceous perennial, native to Britain with many varieties, family Lythraceae. Yellow L. is *Lysimachia vulgaris*, perennial herb, native to Britain, family Primulaceae. Both are water-side plants.

Lop Nor, *see* LOB NOR.

Lope de Rueda, *see* RUEDA.

Lope (Felix) de Vega Carpio, *see* VEGA.

López, Carlos Antonio (1790–1862), nephew of José Gaspar Rodriguez de Francia (q.v.) whom he succeeded as President of Paraguay on the latter's death in 1840, and father of Francisco Solano Lopez (q.v.) to whom he handed over the Presidency on his death in 1862. During his relatively enlightened but despotic rule he became the country's biggest landowner and amassed a huge fortune. However, his administration was dynamic and much was done to improve the country's economy particularly in terms of transport (he started the Central Paraguayan Railway) and education.

López, Francisco Solano (*c.* 1827–70), Paraguayan soldier and statesman, *b.* Asunción. He was the son of Carlos L., by whose will he assumed the executive in 1862, and became president and effective dictator for 8 years. It has been said that his acts of cruelty and torture bordered on insanity. He became involved in the disastrous War of the Triple Alliance (1865–70) against Brazil, Argentina and Uruguay in which Paraguay's pop. was reduced from 525,000 to 221,000, of which only 28,700 were men. He was killed in battle near Cerro Corá in 1870. Today he is Paraguay's greatest national hero. *See* G. F. Masterman, *Seven Eventful Years in Paraguay*, 1869; R. B. Cunninghame Graham, *Portrait of a Dictator*, 1933.

López de Ayala, *see* AYALA, PERO.

Lopez y Portaña, Vicente (1772–1850), Sp. painter, *b.* Valencia, follower of Goya (q.v.) whom he succeeded as court painter to Ferdinand VII. His portrait of the aged Goya is in the Prado. *See* life by M. Gonsalez Marti, 1928.

Lophiidae, or **Angler Fishes,** family of fishes with a very large mouth and teeth hinged so as to bend over towards the throat. They have a depressed body and live on the sea bottom, often at great depth. The angler fish (*Lophius piscatorius*) is a Brit. species (*see* ANGLERS). The first few dorsal fin rays are long and flexible and terminate in expansions over the snout which lure small fish within reach of the great mouth.

Lophiodonts, group of Eocene tapirs, odd-toed ungulate mammals.

Lopokova, Lydia (Lady Keynes) (1891–), danseuse and actress, *b.* in Russia, married the 1st Baron Keynes (q.v.), 1925. She was educ. at the Imperial Ballet School, St Petersburg, graduating in 1909. She joined the Diaghilev Ballet in 1910, dancing with them intermittently until 1926. Among her creations were the role of Mariuccia in *Les Femmes de bonne humeur*, and the female cancan dancer in *La Boutique fantasque*. She played a leading part in the Camargo Society and danced as guest artist with the Vic-Wells Ballet in 1931 and 1933. She has also appeared as an actress. her stage roles including Olivia in *Twelfth Night*, 1933; Nora Helmer in *A Doll's House*, 1934; Hilda Wangel in *The Master Builder*, 1936; and Célimène in *Le Misanthrope*, 1937. She is a member of the Arts Council of Great Britain.

Lorain, lake-port and city of Ohio, U.S.A., on Lake Erie, 25 m. SW. of Cleveland. There is a good harbour. Various steel goods are produced and it has shipbuilding yards and a fishing industry. Pop. 71,300.

Lorca, Federico Garcia (1899–1936), Sp. poet and playwright, *b.* Fuentevaqueros. *Libros de Poemas*, 1921, was followed by *Canciones* in 1927, *Romancerogitano* in 1928 and *Poema del cante jondo* in 1931. His plays include *El Maleficio de la Mariposa*, *Bodas de Sangre*, *Yerma* and *La Casa de Bernarda Alba*. Among his best poems is his lament for the toreador Sánchez Mejías. He was killed by the Falangists. His creative versatility and many-sided genius have made L. the most popular contemporary poet in Spain as well as on the Continent. His works have been trans. into many European languages. *See* A. Barea, *Lorca, the Poet and his People*, 1944; J. B. Trend, *Lorca*, 1952; R. Campbell, *Lorca*, 1952.

Lorca (Moorish **Lurka**), Sp. tn in the prov. of Murcia. It has anct walls, a Moorish castle, sev. Baroque churches and fine mansions. It stands in a very fertile dist, has chemical, textile and porcelain manufs., and there are iron, silver and sulphur mines near by. Pop. 21,000.

Lorch, *see* ENNS.

Lord, a term with a variety of usages, derived from O.E. *hlaford*, provider of food (*hlaf*, loaf; *ward*, keeper). Historically its use has been largely determined by its equivalence to the Lat. *dominus*; it has had particular reference to rulers, heads of households and owners of land. In feudal times it was the common term for a feudal superior, hence 'L. of the manor', and the king was often referred to as 'the L. king'. It is the prefix of many official titles, e.g. L. high steward, L. chamberlain, L. high chancellor (qq.v.). Where a board has taken the place of an office of state, the members of that board are termed L.s commissioners, or, more commonly, L.s of the particular office, e.g. L.s of the admiralty. The chief modern use of the term is in connection with the peerage. Except in the case of dukes, the less formal designation of peers is by reference to them as, e.g., L. Salisbury instead of the Marquess of Salisbury. In the case of

barons, however, they are nearly always referred to as L.s, the term baron being used for foreign holders of that rank. The eldest sons of dukes, marquesses and earls assume, by courtesy, an inferior title of the peerage and by common use are referred to as L.s. Younger sons of dukes and marquesses have L. prefixed to their Christian names and surnames, e.g. L. John Russell. Bishops, whether members of the House of L.s or not, are addressed as 'My L. bishop', or 'The L. Bishop of——'. All judges of the high court are addressed throughout the U.K. as 'My L.' when acting in their official capacity. Mayors of certain large tns are entitled to the prefix L.

Lord Chamberlain, *see* CENSORSHIP OF THE DRAMA and CHAMBERLAIN.

Lord Chief Justice, name given to the judge who presides over the queen's bench div. of the high court of justice. He ranks, in the legal hierarchy, next to the lord chancellor and usually he is created a peer on appointment (*see also* CRIMINAL APPEAL, COURT OF). The former court of common pleas of from 4 to 9 judges was presided over in the time of Edward I by a *capitalis justiciarius*; later, from the earlier half of the 17th cent., the 4 judges of the court were presided over by a L. C. J. The third co-ordinate court of common law, the old court of exchequer, was presided over by a chief baron of the exchequer first appointed in 1312. *See also* COMMON PLEAS, COURT OF; QUEEN'S BENCH DIVISION; EXCHEQUER COURT.

'Lord Haw Haw', *see* JOYCE, WILLIAM.

Lord High Chancellor, *see* CHANCELLOR.

Lord High Steward, *see* HIGH STEWARD.

Lord Howe Island, situated in the Pacific Ocean midway between Norfolk Is. and Sydney, about 520 m. ENE. of Sydney. It is a dependency of New S. Wales, some 3200 ac. in area, and is of great natural beauty, rich in bird life and rare plants. The is. is of volcanic formation and has coral reefs. Discovered in 1788, it was first settled in 1853 by a party of Maoris from New Zealand and other settlers from Sydney followed them. None but the descendants of these early settlers may now establish themselves permanently in the is. It is the home of the handsome and hardy Kentia palm, the export of the seed of the plant being the staple industry. The is., which is a favoured tourist resort, is linked with Sydney by air. Pop. 210. L. H. is also the name given to Mopiha Is. of the Society Group, and to Ongtong, Java, of the Brit. Solomon Is., the latter being an atoll (q.v.). The Santa Cruz or La Pérouse Is. in the Pacific are also known as the L. H. Is.

Lord-Lieutenant, The (of a co.), is nominated by the sovereign by patent under the great seal. He stands as the permanent local representative of the Crown, and as such takes precedence in the co., even in the area of a co. bor. He is responsible for the maintenance of public order. This title was first created in the reign of Henry VIII, and entailed many responsibilities. The L.-L. had to maintain the efficiency of the militia of the co., and had the right of appointing his own officers. These rights were withdrawn in

1871 and revested in the Crown. The chief duties imposed on the L.-L. at present consist in the recommendation for the appointment of magistrates for the co. bench, the appointment of deputy lieutenants and the raising of the militia, if need be, in times of riot or invasion. He is head of the Commission of the Peace for the co. and of the territorial army. The prefix 'Lord' is colloquial only. Officially, he is the Queen's Lieutenant in the co.

Lord-Lieutenant of Ireland, see IRELAND.

Lord Mayor, title given to the mayor of London and also of certain other large cities. The first recorded mayor of London was Henry FitzEylwin, who held the office for about 25 years until his death in 1212. The right to elect their mayor ann. was granted to the citizens in 1215 by King John. The term L. M. was used intermittently during the 13th–mid 16th cents., first occurring in a description of events taking place 'coram domino maiori'; but after 1545 it became the regular title. In 1966 the Queen conferred the title of L. M. on the mayor of Westminster.

Lord Mayor of London, see CORPORATION OF LONDON; LORD MAYOR.

Lord of Misrule was the 'master of mirth and fun' appointed in the king's court for the feast of Christmas. His nomination took place on All Hallows' Eve (q.v.) and he remained in office till the feast of Purification (q.v.). According to Stubbs these mock dignitaries had from 20 to 60 officers under them and were furnished with hobby-horses, dragons and musicians. In Scotland they received the title of 'Abbot of Unreason'.

Lord of the Isles, see ISLES, LORD OF THE.

Lord President of the Council, see PRESIDENT OF THE COUNCIL, LORD.

Lord Privy Seal, see SEAL, LORD PRIVY.

Lord Provost, see PROVOST.

Lord Steward, see HIGH STEWARD.

Lords, House of, see HOUSE OF LORDS.

Lords and Ladies, see ARUM.

Lords Appellant, see APPELLANTS.

Lord's Brethren, The, frequently mentioned in the N.T.; cf. Matt. xiii. 55: 'Is not this the carpenter's son? is not his mother called Mary? and his brethren, James, and Joseph, and Simon, and Judas? And his sisters, are they not all with us?'

There have been 3 theories to explain their relationship with Jesus Christ: (a) the theory of Helvidius (c. 380), that they were the children of Joseph and Mary born after Jesus; (b) the theory of St Jerome, that they were cousins of Jesus, loosely called brothers and sisters; (c) the theory of Epiphanius, that they were the children of St Joseph by a former wife, Joseph being a widower when he married Mary, and at least middle-aged. This accords with the disappearance of St Joseph (by death) before Christ's public ministry. Of these the Helvidian theory runs counter to Christian tradition and teaching that Mary remained a virgin after the birth of Christ. It was supported by an erroneous exegesis of Matt. i. 25 and Luke ii. 7, as implying that our Lord was only the first of many children born to Mary. Matt. i. 25 merely says that Joseph and Mary did not come together as man and wife before the birth of Jesus, without implying anything about afterwards. It merely asserts the fact of the virgin birth. Luke ii. 7 no more implies that there were other children after the first-born than do Coloss. i. 15, and Heb. i. 6, in describing Christ's relation to His Heavenly Father. Moreover the attitude of Christ's brethren towards Him in the Gospels is not that of younger, but of older, protective and sceptical brothers towards a younger member of the family. Jerome's theory was condemned as novel and false by synods in Rome, Capua and Illyria. We have no evidence of it before him, and he was concerned with maintaining the virginity not only of Mary, but also of Joseph. It identifies, in John xix. 25, Mary, the wife of Cleophas, with the sister of the Blessed Virgin, mentioned just before (the Peshitto separates them with 'and'), and also with the wife of Alphaeus. Whether Alphaeus and Cleophas can represent a single Aramaic original is queried by many scholars. It is also strange to find 2 sisters bearing the same name, Mary. It is noteworthy too, that in every reference in the Gospels to the L. B., except John vii. 3, it is expressly said the L. B. were with (the Virgin) Mary. The theory also demands an extension of the meaning of 'brethren' to include cousins. This is of course found in the O.T., but it is contrary to Gk usage, at any rate. But it fits in well with St John's guardianship of Mary. It is strange, if He had step-brothers, that Christ should commend His mother to the care of someone else at His death. The Epiphanian view, which makes the brethren Christ's half-brothers and sisters, is found quite early, e.g. in the apocryphal gospel of Peter and the Protevangel of James. Hegesippus, a Palestinian Christian Jew of the 1st cent. (Eusebius, *Historia Ecclesiastica*, ii. 23; iii. 20), mentions James as the Lord's brother, but explicitly distinguishes him from the Lord's cousin, and describes Jude as 'called His (the Lord's) *brother according to the Flesh*' which suggests, and seems to have suggested to Eusebius (*Historia Ecclesiastica* i. 1), reputed or step-brotherhood. It was the view of Clement of Alexandria, Origen, Ambrose, Hilary, Ambrosiaster and remains that of the Oriental Churches. The Rom. Catholic Church, however, has generally followed the view of Jerome, accepting the perpetual virginity of Joseph. The brethren of the Lord known to us outside the Gospels are James, the first Bishop of Jerusalem (identified with James, the son of Alphaeus, or James the Little), Simon the Zealot and Jude. *See* J. Hastings, *Dictionary of Christ and the Gospels*, 1906–8; C. Gore, etc., *A New Commentary on Holy Scripture* (Epistle of James), 1928; J. B. Orchard, etc., *A Catholic Commentary on Holy Scripture*, 1953.

Lord's Day, see SABBATH.

Lord's Day Observance Society, founded in 1831. It aims to promote the religious observance of Sunday as the Christian Sabbath in accordance with the fourth commandment, and 'to resist all sports and amusements which would tend to assimilate the traditional quiet British Sunday to the continental Sunday'. Its methods consist of sermons in churches, talks in schools, youth meetings and circulation of scriptural pamphlets and books. Where 'Sunday' laws are infringed, it draws attention of transgressor and authorities to the fact. It also influences Parliament regarding 'Sunday' legislation. The society's watchword is 'For our Lord and His Day'. H.Q.: 55 Fleet St, London, E.C.4.

Lord's Prayer, see OUR FATHER.

Lord's Seat, commanding viewpoint, over 2000 ft high, of Edale, Cumberland, England (National Trust).

Lord's Supper, see EUCHARIST.

Lorelei, or **Lurlei,** precipitous rock in the Rhine, near the tn of St Goar in the *Land* of Rhineland-Palatinate (q.v.), Germany. It is 427 ft high, and has a remarkable echo. There are many legends associated with the L.: one runs that a maiden sits on the rock combing her beautiful hair and tempting boatmen to death by the sweetness of her song, which makes them approach the rock too closely; in another the rock is a scaly monster; and in another it is the hiding-place of the Nibelungen treasure. The legends are celebrated in poems, songs and stories; Heine's famous poem about the L., *Ich weiss nicht, was soll es bedeuten,* was set to music by F. Silchen (1789–1860).

Lorentz, Hendrik Antoon (1852–1928), Dutch physicist, *b.* Arnhem. He was educ. at Leyden Univ., where he was subsequently prof. of mathematical physics. His researches in electro-dynamics won for him and his pupil, Zeeman, the Nobel prize for physics in 1902. L. related atomic theories to the electro-magnetic wave theory of Maxwell, and explained the interaction of magnetism and light known as the Zeeman effect (q.v.). His researches paved the way for the famous theory of relativity of another of his pupils, Einstein. He also advanced research work in the theory of gases, radiation and thermodynamics. In 1919 he was chairman of the Committee of Intellectual Co-operation of the League of Nations. Pubs.: *Text-book of Differential and Integral Calculus,* 1882, *Text-book of Physics,* 1888–90, *Clerk-Maxwell's Electro-magnetic Theory,* 1892, *Theory of Electrical and Optical Phenomena in Moving Bodies,* 1895, *Treatise on Theoretical Physics,* 1907, *Les Théories statistiques et thermodynamiques,* 1916, *Theory of Electrons and its Applications to the Phenomena of Light and Radiant Heat* (2nd ed.), 1916, and numerous other contributions to the periodicals of various learned and scientific societies.

Lorenzetti, Pietro (fl. *c.* 1306–45), It. painter, *b.* Siena. He may be the Petruccio Lorenzo who is known to have painted in Siena in 1306. Authenticated works are an altar-piece (1320) in the Pieve at Arezzo, and 'The Nativity of the Virgin' in the Siena Museum. His brother, called *Ambrogio L.* or *Ambrogio di Lorenzo,* active 1319–47, was also a painter. In 1337–9 he

executed in the Palazzo Pubblico some frescoes representing saints worshipping. 'The Presentation' (Uffizi) is another authentic work. *See* G. Sinibaldi, *I Lorenzetti,* 1933.

Lorenzo de' Medici, see MEDICI.

Lorenzo Monaco, Don (*c.* 1370–*c.* 1422), It. painter of the Florentine School, the 'monk' as he is known, was Piero di Giovanni, who came from Siena and took his vows and the name of Lorenzo in Florence. He produced illuminated MS., altar pieces and frescoes. His 'Annunciation' (Florence Accademia) foreshadows the style of Fra Angelico (q.v.).

Loreto: 1. Dept of E. Peru, situated in the basin of the Amazon. The cap. is Iquitos (pop. 58,000). The area is densely covered with forest and jungle, making transport other than by riv. and air impracticable. Most tropical products are produced including rubber, balata, ivory, nuts, tobacco, hardwood, skins. Petroleum is produced (about 5 per cent of Peru's total production), the main oil-field being at Ganza Azul. The oil is shipped to Iquitos where it is refined. The area of L. is regarded of great economic potential but development is greatly hampered by the physical inaccessibility of the place.

2. Or **Loretto,** It. tn in the Marches (q.v.), 15 m. SSE. of Ancona. It is famous as a place of pilgrimage because of the *Santa Casa,* or Holy House, which is reputed to be the home of the Virgin Mary at Nazareth miraculously transported here in the 13th cent. A magnificent church, begun in the 15th cent., has been built around the shrine; it contains work by Bramante, Sansovino, Signorelli, Giuliano Sangallo and Antonio Sangallo the Younger (qq.v.). The name 'L. nuns' is given in Ireland to sisters of the Institute of Mary, a congregation devoted to the education of girls, founded by Mary Ward in 1609. L. has a trade in silk and livestock. Pop. (tn) 3100; (com.) 4400.

Loretto School, Scottish public school for boys at Musselburgh, Midlothian, founded in 1827. There are some 250 pupils.

Lorient, Fr. seaport in the dept of Morbihan, on an inlet of the Bay of Biscay (q.v.), formed by the estuaries of the R.s Scorff and Blavet, 57 m. SE. of Brest. It was founded in 1664 by the Fr. E. India Co., came into the hands of the Fr. Gov. in 1782, and by 1815 was the prin. naval shipyard in France. Three-quarters of the tn was destroyed during the Second World War and had to be rebuilt. L. is a port of importance, with fishing and shipbuilding industries. Pop. 60,500.

L. was an important submarine base during the Ger. occupation, with protected pens capable of berthing 30 U-boats, and was frequently bombed by the Brit. and Amer. air forces. By the end of 1943 most of the tn had been razed to the ground and the civilian pop. had to leave. L. was one of the last tns in Brittany to be yielded up by the Germans after the allied break-through in Normandy.

Lorimer, Sir Robert Stodart (1864–1929), architect, *b.* Edinburgh; started practice in Edinburgh, 1892. He restored, extended or built many large country houses in Scotland; and restored Dunblane Cathedral and Paisley Abbey. His other work included the Chapel of the Thistle in St Giles's Cathedral, Edinburgh, 1909–11, and the Scottish National War Memorial, Edinburgh Castle, 1918–27. He designed many war cemeteries after the First World War. He was knighted in 1911.

Loris, name given to certain types of lemurs, of which the 2 best known are the Grey Slow L. and the Slender L. They are nocturnal in habit and are found in W. Africa, India and China.

Loris-Melikov, Count Mikhail Tarielovich (1825–88), Russian statesman of Armenian origin. After a series of attempts on Alexander II's life by the Populist (*see* POPULISM) terrorists, a Supreme Commission was appointed under L. to examine the causes of terrorism and suppress it. The Commission was given dictatorial powers over all gov. authorities; L. used these powers to placate liberal opinion in the country and the period of his rule became known as 'the dictatorship of the heart'. After 6 months the Commission was abolished and L. became minister of the interior. He drew up a plan for the introduction of a representative assembly with consultative functions and a system of cabinet gov., but after the assassination of Alexander II in 1881 Pobedonostsev (q.v.) prevailed upon Alexander III to reject it, and L. resigned. *See also* GREAT REFORMS.

Lörrach, Ger. tn in the *Land* of Baden-Württemberg (q.v.), near the Fr. and Swiss frontiers, 5 m. NE. of Basel. It has a ruined castle, and has textile manufs. Pop. 30,500.

Lorraine, Claude of, *see* CLAUDE.

Lorraine, Mary of, *see* MARY OF GUISE.

Lorraine (Ger. **Lothringen**), anct prov. of the NE. of France which was originally that portion of the empire of Charlemagne which fell to Lothaire I (q.v.) by the treaty of Verdun in 843, and was called Lotharingia. The name was originally given to 2 ters. between the Saône and the Rhine, the N. portion between the Moselle and the Rhine bearing the name Upper L. and the S. portion Lower L. The latter soon became known as Brabant, and the name L. became confined to the Moselle country. It was an area of constant dispute between France and Germany. In 1736 the French obtained the duchy for the ex-king of Poland, Stanislas, whose daughter had been married to Louis XV. In 1766 the death of Stanislas was followed by the incorporation of L. with France, until 1871, when it was annexed by Germany, forming one of the 3 dists of Elsass-Lothringen. It is now comprised in the depts of Vosges, Moselle, Meurthe-et-Moselle and Meuse (qq.v.). *See* ALSACE-LORRAINE.

Lorraine, Cross of, red cross, with 2 horizontal cross-pieces. It was the emblem carried by Joan of Arc, and was adopted by de Gaulle (q.v.) in 1940 as an emblem of resistance to the Ger. occupation and again in 1958.

Lorris, Guillaume de (fl. *c.* 1235), Fr. poet of the Orléanais who wrote the first 4058 lines of *Le Roman de la Rose* which, completed some 40 years later by Jean de Meung (q.v.), is one of the

CROSS OF LORRAINE

most influential and representative works of Fr. medieval literature. It presents allegorically the practical and psychological dangers besetting the courtly wooer in his quest of love (the Rose), the aristocratic delicacy of L.'s treatment standing in sharp contrast to Jean de Meung's cynicism.

Lortzing, Albert (1801–51), Ger. singer, actor and composer, *b.* Berlin. He came of a theatrical family and, without much systematic musical education, picked up experience as a theatre conductor and light operatic tenor. Of his 14 comic and romantic operas, all set to his own librettos, *Zar und Zimmermann, Der Wildschütz, Undine* and *Der Waffenschmied,* are still popular in Germany.

Lory (*Lorius* or *Eclectus*), genus of brilliantly coloured parrots. They are honey eaters, and the bill is but slightly curved, and the tongue long and protrusible. Also a S. African name (Louri is the native name) for the white-crested plantain eater (*Corythaix musophaga*). It is about 19 in. long, its general colour is green, and the feathers of its beautiful crest are tipped with white; the wing feathers are brilliant carmine.

Los Alamos, settlement in the New Mexican desert, U.S.A., 24 m. NW. of Santa Fé. The first atom bomb was made in the atomic-energy laboratories here and tested at Alamogordo in desert region W. of Sierra Oscura, 16 July 1945. Pop. 10,000.

Los Andes, or **Santa Rosa de los Andes,** tn of Chile, 65 m. NE. of Valparaiso, at the foot of the Uspallata Pass (q.v.), on the Transandine railway. Standing on the Aconcagua R., it is the cap. of dept of A., and a tourist resort. Centre of rich agric. area also producing fruit and wine and tobacco. Pop. 33,000.

Los Angeles: 1. Largest city of California, U.S.A., co. seat of L. A. co., 350 m. SE. of San Francisco. The Spaniards settled it in 1781. Alternately with Monterey it was the cap. of Mexican California. Acquired by U.S.A. in 1848, when it was already a thriving place, it is now the largest city in area (452 sq. m.) and the 2nd in pop. in the U.S.A. In size and pop. it has now far outstripped the rival city of San Francisco, and is one of the chief commercial ports of California. L. A. is an aviation centre, with aircraft factories and sev. airports, notably at Burbank and Culver City. It is a terminus of 3 continental rail lines and the commercial, distribution, marketing and financial centre of S. California. There are automobile assembly plants, and the manuf. of rubber products, furniture and clothing; food processing, and the canning, packaging and packing of fruits, meats and fish; the manuf. of machinery, electrical machinery and equipment, household appliances, glassware, pottery, tiles, building materials, glass products, chemicals, pharmaceuticals, soap and paints; also steel fabricating, shipbuilding, printing and publishing, brewing, flour milling, coffee roasting and spice grinding. Educational institutions include the Univ. of California, the Univ. of S. California, the Occidental College, the Loyola Univ. of L. A., Chapman College, Pepperdine College, Mt St Mary's College, Immaculate Heart College, the Southwestern Univ., the Bible Institute of L. A., art schools, junior colleges, theological seminaries and professional and technical schools. Hollywood (part of L. A.) is the centre of the Amer. film industry. The 1960 pop. was 2,479,000, but this is an artificial figure for the legal limits of the city itself. The real L. A. is an urb. complex of linked tns with a pop. of the order of 6 millions.

One of the chief features of L. A.'s recent growth has been the construction of an immense system of urb. motorways which has almost destroyed the commercial centre of the old L. A. See H. Carr, *Los Angeles, City of Dreams*, 1935; C. Landery, *Hollywood is the Place*, 1940; and Amer. Guide Series, *Los Angeles; a Guide to the City and Its Environs*, 1941.

2. Cap. of the prov. of Bíobío, central Chile, connected by rail to Concepcion. The prin. occupations are connected with cereals and lumbering. Pop. 79,000.

Los Islands, small group of is. off the coast of Guinea, W. Africa, near the port of Conakry. The is. have rich deposits of bauxite, which have been mined systematically since 1950.

Los Ríos, prov. of Ecuador, partly on the W. slope of the Andes and partly in the coastal zone. The prin. occupations are stock-raising in the E., and tropical agriculture, particularly cacao, in the W. Cap. Babahoyo. Area 2295 sq. m.; pop. 232,000.

Löss, *see* LOËSS.

Loss Angle. If a perfect insulating material is used as dielectric in a capacitor on a.c. supply, the power factor is zero, the current leading by 90°. In most materials the phase angle is slightly less, power is 'lost' in the dielectric and the deviation from 90° is the L. A., usually dependent on frequency and temperature. *See* DIELECTRIC, *Dielectric Loss.*

Lossiemouth, seaport of Morayshire, Scotland, stands at the mouth of the R. Lossie on the Moray Firth, and has a very fine harbour. Bp. of James Ramsay MacDonald, the first Labour Prime Minister of Great Britain. Pop. 5975.

Lossky, Nikolai Onufrievich (1870–1965), Russian philosopher, one of the founders of modern Intuitivism and Personalism. In 1916 he became a prof. at Petrograd Univ., and in 1922 was expelled from Russia by the Communist gov. He at first lived in Czechoslovakia, but now

lives in the U.S.A. His works include *The Intuitive Basis of Knowledge*, 1919, *The World as an Organic Whole*, 1928, *Freedom of Will*, 1932, *Value and Existence*, 1935, and *History of Russian Philosophy*, 1951.

Lost Property. If anything is lost the owner can claim it any time from anyone he sees in possession of it; the one who finds the article is entitled to it next after the owner provided he comes upon it in a public place. But should the finder keep the property when he knows the owner, he is guilty of theft. So too is the man who discovers a valuable brooch while digging in another man's garden and fails to give it up; for the owner of private land is entitled to all found on it. But the mere keeping of a lost article, in hope of getting a reward for giving it up, though the owner be known, does not amount to theft, and there is no obligation on the finder of L. P. to incur expense in advertising for the owner. *See* TREASURE TROVE.

Lostwithiel, municipal bor. and mrkt tn of Cornwall, England, on the Fowey, 21 m. NE. of Truro; it contains the ruins of Restormel Castle, built in the time of Henry III. Pop. 1954.

Lot, son of Haran, brother of Abraham (Gen. xi. 27), went with his uncle from their fatherland and chose for himself the prosperous Jordan valley near Sodom and Gomorrah. When these cities were destroyed, he and his family escaped. L.'s wife, turning back to look, became a pillar of salt. It has been suggested that she was overcome with fumes and her body encrusted with salt. Wisdom x. 7, however (borne out by Josephus, *Antiquities*, I, xi. 4), refers to a pillar of rock-salt, still standing cents. later, and one about 40 ft high did in fact exist till recently on the hill of Usdun, SW. of the Dead Sea (W. F. Lynch, *Expedition to Jordan and the Dead Sea*, 1849). This may have given rise to a legend, recorded in scripture for the moral it contains, to which attention is drawn by Christ in Luke xvii. 28–32. This does not prove that Christ regarded the event as historical. L. took refuge in the mts near Zoar, and became the father of Moab and Ammon by his 2 daughters.

Lot, Ferdinand (1866–1952), Fr. historian and philologist, *b*. Plessis-Piquet; a prof. at the Sorbonne. Among his many important works on the early hist. of Europe, and of France in particular, are *Les derniers carolingiens*, 1891, *Études sur le règne de Hugues Capet et la fin du Xᵉ siècle*, 1903, *Le règne de Charles le Chauve*, 1909 (with L. Halphen), *La fin du monde antique et le début du moyen-âge*, 1921, *Les invasions germaniques*, 1935, *Les invasions barbares et le peuplement de l'Europe*, 1937, *La Gaule*, 1947. On mediaeval literature he wrote *Étude sur le Lancelot en prose*, 1918, and various articles.

Lot, Fr. riv., the anct **Oltis**. It rises in the Lozère Mts, flows through the depts of Lozère, Aveyron, L. and L.-et-Garonne, and joins the Garonne NW. of Agen. Length 300 m.

Lot, dept of SW. France, formed from the dist of Quercy. The surface, which is varied, is crossed from E. to W. by the L. and is highest in the NE. Wheat is the chief cereal, but maize, oats and barley are also cultivated. Wine is the prin. product, the most valued being that of Cahors, grown in the valley of the L. Large quantities of chestnuts come from the NE., and the dept also produces potatoes, tobacco and hemp. The chief minerals are coal, iron and zinc; cloth-making, tanning, brewing and the making of agric. instruments are among the industries. The prin. tns are Cahors (the cap.), Figeac and Gourdon (qq.v.). Area 2020 sq. m.; pop. 150,000.

Lot-et-Garonne, dept of SW. France formed from parts of Guienne and Gascony. Its surface, which consists mainly of wide plains, is traversed by the Garonne from SE. to NW., and by the Lot from E. to W. The valleys of these rivs. are exceedingly fertile, and the slopes of the low hills are covered with orchards and vineyards; coal forests occur. The soil is highly cultivated, wheat being the chief cereal, then maize and barley. Iron is found. The prin. tns are Agen (the cap.), Marmande, Nérac and Villeneuve (qq.v.). Area 2079 sq. m.; pop. 275,000.

Lotario de' Conti, see INNOCENT (popes), *Innocent III.*

Lothaire I (795–855), Holy Rom. emperor, eldest son of the Emperor Louis I, who divided the empire among his sons in 817. He undertook the gov. of Italy in 822, and was crowned emperor at Rome in 823. He claimed the whole of the empire on his father's death, but was defeated by his brothers at Fontenoy (841); and by the treaty of Verdun (843) received Italy and the imperial title, together with some land in the valleys of the Rhine and Rhône. This state was called Lotharingia, and the modern Lorraine (q.v.) is derived from it. He renounced the throne in 855 just before his death.

Lothaire II (*c.* 1060–1137), called 'The Saxon', Holy Rom. emperor, succeeded to his father's lands in Saxony in 1075, and became Duke of Saxony in 1106. He was elected King of Germany in 1125, succeeding Henry V, and was crowned emperor at Rome by Pope Innocent II in 1133.

Lothian, Philip Henry Kerr, 11th Marquess of (1883–1941), statesman and ambas., educ. at the Oratory School and New College, Oxford. In 1916 he became secretary to Lloyd George, and played an important part in the peace conference at Versailles. Later he was appointed secretary of the Rhodes trust. On accession to the peerage in 1930 he sat in the Lords as a Liberal and, in 1931, became chancellor of the duchy of Lancaster in Ramsay MacDonald's National Gov. In 1939 he became ambas. to the U.S.A. He became a popular figure with the Amer. people, doing much to foster Anglo-Amer. friendship in the most critical days of the Second World War.

Lothians, The, dist on the S. side of the Firth of Forth, which includes the cos. of Haddington, Edinburgh and Linlithgow, which are called respectively E. Lothian, Midlothian and W. Lothian (qq.v.). The city of Edinburgh is an administrative co. apart from Midlothian, within which it is geographically situated. It

formerly embraced the E. part of the Lowlands from the Forth to the Cheviots, i.e. all the Eng. part of Scotland in the 11th cent.

Lothringen, see LORRAINE.

Loti, Pierre, pseudonym of **Louis Marie Julien Viaud** (1850–1923), Fr. novelist, *b.* Rochefort. He was a captain in the Fr. Navy, and his travels in the Near and Far E. form the background to many of his novels, marked by colourful descriptions of exotic landscapes. As an author his works marked a revival of the spirit of romanticism in Fr. literature. Pubs. include *Le Mariage de Loti,* 1880, set in Tahiti; *Mon Frère Yves,* 1883, describing the life of a Fr. bluejacket; *Pêcheur d'Islande,* 1886, describing life among the Breton fisherfolk; *Madame Chrysanthème,* 1887; *Ramuntcho,* 1897; *L'Inde sans les Anglais,* 1903; *Pélerin d'Angkor,* 1912. See R. Lefèvre, *La Vie inquiète de Pierre Loti,* 1934; P. Flottes, *Le Drame intérieur de Loti,* 1937.

Lotions, liquid washes used as remedies for bruises, sores and enlarged joints. They are usually solutions of various salts, and differ from embrocations or ointments in that oils or fats are absent. The chlorides of ammonia, soda and lime are common washes. Sal ammoniac with vinegar or spirit is used for application when there is no open wound; chloride of lime or soda for ulcerated mouth and throat or tumours. Calomel in lime water, known as *black wash,* is a more efficient lotion for obstinate ulcers.

Lotophagi, see LOTUS-EATERS.

Lots, Casting, system of divination common among primitive and civilised peoples alike. A common method is by pieces of wood or straw, which are marked and covered up, one or more being then drawn out at random. Tacitus speaks of this method being used by the anct Teutons. The Romans also made use of the famous *Sortes Vergilianae* (q.v.). See DIVINATION.

Lötschberg, or **Lötschenpass,** pass in the Swiss Alps (8842 ft), linking Kandersteg in the Bernese Oberland with the Lötschental, a side valley of the Rhône in the canton of Valais. The railway between Bern and Brig passes beneath the L. in the L. tunnel (9 m. long, built 1906–12).

Lotta, see CRABTREE, CHARLOTTE.

Lotteries are not easy to define with precision, but generally are schemes for distributing prizes by lot or by chance. In their simplest form L. consist of the sale of tickets bearing different numbers, duplicate numbers being placed in a receptacle, such as a hat or a drum, from which numbers are drawn to establish the prize winners, being those holding the tickets with those corresponding numbers.

The presence of some degree of skill in securing a prize avoids the activity being a lottery, but participating in a lottery may in fact involve gaming (q.v.), if those purchasing tickets in the lottery play some part in establishing the winning numbers, for instance by tossing a ball into numbered holes on a board, the prize winners being those holding the ticket with corresponding numbers.

Gambling (q.v.) in the form of L. dates from earliest times and there are records of organised

L., particularly in Italy, in the 16th cent. Certainly by the 17th cent. L. were estab. in England and were promoted by the state or by individuals under licence from the state. State L. were abolished by the L. Act, 1823.

From time to time, however, exceptions were made by statute to provide for L. to be conducted on behalf of charitable institutions or societies not connected with gambling.

The statutory provisions regulating L. are now to be found in the Betting, Gaming and L. Act, 1963. With the exceptions mentioned below all L. are unlawful and penalties of up to £750 and 1 year's imprisonment are provided for certain specific offences, such as printing, selling and distributing tickets, and printing, publishing and distributing advertisements.

Although participating in a lottery may involve gaming, and some gaming may involve a lottery, providing the gaming is conducted lawfully under the provisions of the Act of 1963, no offence is committed. The offences in connection with L. moreover do not apply to the provision of amusements with prizes at certain functions of a non-commercial nature, such as bazaars, sales of work, fêtes, dinners, dances and sporting events, or at certain commercial entertainments, such as fairs and amusement arcades licensed by local authorities, or to the distribution of prizes by innocuous gaming machines.

The L. which are allowed by law are small L. incidental to entertainments, private L. conducted among members of societies, small L. for charitable purposes promoted by societies registered with local authorities, and L. promoted by voluntary associations known as Art Unions, for allotting or distributing works of art.

A lottery promoted as an incident of a bazaar, sale of work, fête, dinner, dance, sporting or athletic event, or other entertainment of a similar character, is not unlawful provided the whole of the proceeds of the entertainment (and the lottery) after deducting certain expenses are devoted to purposes other than private gain. No prizes may be money prizes and the promoters may not appropriate more than £10 towards the purchase of prizes. Tickets must be sold and the result of the lottery declared on the premises where the entertainment takes place during the progress of the entertainment. The facilities afforded for participating in I , or to take part in gaming, or the opportunity to win prizes at amusements with prizes, must not be the only or a substantial inducement to persons to attend the entertainment.

A private lottery is one which is promoted in Great Britain and the sale of tickets confined to members of one society estab. and conducted for purposes not connected with gaming, betting or L., or to persons all of whom work or reside on the same premises. The whole of the proceeds, after deducting only expenses incurred for printing and stationery, must be devoted to the provisions of prizes, or in the case of a lottery promoted for the members of a society, either to the provision of prizes or to the purposes of the society. No restriction is placed on the value of the prizes or the cost of tickets, which must all be the same price. Tickets may not be sent through the post and advertising is restricted to the announcements on the ticket itself and to notices exhibited on the premises of the society concerned, or on the premises on which the persons for whom the lottery is promoted work or reside.

Small L. may be promoted on behalf of certain societies, clubs, institutions or organisations registered by a local authority in order to raise money for the purposes of the society. The society must be one estab. and conducted wholly or mainly for charitable purposes, for playing or supporting athletic sports or games or cultural activities, or for other purposes not for private gain or for a commercial undertaking. No more than one-half of the proceeds may be distributed as prizes and no prize may exceed £100. The price of all tickets must be the same and must be stated on the ticket, which must not cost more than 1s. The total value of tickets sold must not exceed £750. Limits are placed on the expenses of the lottery and advertising. Tickets may be sold to persons who are not members of the society, but tickets may not be sent through the post.

L. are promoted in some countries under the supervision of the state to raise money for the gov. or charitable institutions. The sweepstakes promoted on behalf of the Irish Hospitals enjoyed considerable popularity in G. Britain until the restrictions placed upon the distribution of tickets and lists of prizewinners in 1934, which restrictions are re-enacted in the Betting, Gaming and L. Act, 1963. *See* J. T. Chenery, *The Law and Practice of Bookmaking, Betting, Gaming and Lotteries*, 2nd ed., 1963; *see also* BETTING.

Lotto, Lorenzo (*c.* 1480–1556), It. religious painter, *b.* Venice. His most celebrated altarpieces are to be seen in the churches of the Carmine and SS. Giovanni e Paolo, Venice, the cathedral of Asola and at Monte San Giusto, near Ancona, where the church possesses a Crucifixion containing 23 life-size figures. L. also painted some fine portraits. *See* life by B. Berenson, 1895.

Lotus, genus of 60 perennials (family Leguminosae). Some of them are low and prostrate and others of shrubby habit. *L. betholetii*, Coral Gem, a valuable plant for hanging baskets in the greenhouse, bears large red pea shaped blooms and silvery foliage. A number of species are British; the bird's-foot trefoil (*L. corniculatus*) is abundant in pastures, and is sometimes grown in the rock garden. Two small species occur rarely on the S. coast. The sacred L. (*Nelumbium speciosum*) is believed to have been the Egyptian L. of anct hist., though it does not now occur in Egypt (*see* NELUMBO).

Lotus Club, *see* CLUB.

Lotus-eaters (Gk *Lotophagi*), a legendary people who lived on the fruit of the lotus, which Homer said was so delicious that anyone who ate it lost all desire to return to his native land. In historical times the Greeks came across people who ate the lotus on the N. coast of Africa (perhaps on the large is. of Meninx or Lotophagitis, adjacent to that coast) and called them L. They traded with Egypt and the interior of Africa by caravan routes that still exist.

Lotze, Rudolf Hermann (1817–81), Ger. philosopher and physiologist, b. Bautzen. His first essay was *De futurae biologiae principibus philosophicis*, with which he gained his M.D. in 1838. He laid the foundation of his philosophical system in *Metaphysik*, 1841, and *Logik*, 1843; but these books went unnoticed, and he first became known as a physiologist combating the then accepted doctrine of vitalism, his physiological works being *Allgemeine Pathologie und Therapie als mechanische Naturwissenschaften*, 1842 and 1848, *Allgemeine Physiologie des körperlichen Lebens*, 1851, and *Medizinische Psychologie oder Psychologie der Seele*, 1852. His great work, however, was his *Mikrokosmos*, 1856–64 (trans. 1890), which expounds his views on nature and man, and shows him to be essentially the philosopher of the transition from the exaggerated idealism of the first half of the cent. to the most recent modifications of materialism. Other notable works are *Geschichte der Aesthetik in Deutschland*, 1868, *System der Philosophie*, 1874–9, *Logik*, 1874, 1880 (trans. 1884) and *Metaphysik*, 1879 (trans. 1884). L. was prof. of philosophy at Leipzig in 1842, and from 1845–80 held the chair of speculative philosophy at Göttingen. *See* H. Jones, *Critical Account of the Philosophy of Lotze*, 1895.

Loubet, Emile François (1838–1929), Fr. politician, President of the Fr. Rep. from 1899 to 1906, b. Marsanne, Drôme. He entered politics in 1876, and supported the Gambetta and Ferry ministries. In 1885 he became a senator, and 2 years later was appointed minister of public works. In 1892 he became minister of the interior, and in 1895 president of the Senate. He succeeded Faure (q.v.) as president. During his presidency the Dreyfus case was settled, and the Fr. ambas. was recalled from the Vatican, the separation of Church and State being voted in the Chamber of Deputies.

Loudon, Loudun or **Laudon, Gideon Ernst, Baron von** (1717–90), Austrian soldier, b. Tootzen, Livonia, of Scottish extraction. He left the Russian Army to join the Austrian service, and, in the Seven Years War, twice defeated Frederick the Great. He was made a field marshal, and commanded during the War of the Bavarian Succession and the Turkish war (1788–9), when he gained sev. victories and captured Belgrade. *See* life by G. B. Malleson, 1894.

Loudon, John Claudius (1783–1843), Scottish horticult. writer and landscape gardener, apprenticed at 14 to nurserymen and landscape gardeners. At 20 L. went to London, where he pub. an article, *Observations on Laying out Public Squares of London*, 1803, and advocated 'breathing zones' around London. In 1809 he opened an agric. school at Tew Park, Oxon. In

1812 and later he travelled on the continent, studying farming and gardening methods, which led to the pub. of his *Encyclopaedia of Gardening*, 1822, *Greenhouse Companion*, 1823, *Encyclopaedia of Agriculture*, 1825, and *Encyclopaedia of Plants*, 1829. In 1826 he brought out the monthly *Gardener's Magazine*, and in 1828 the *Magazine of Natural History*. In the same year he designed the Birmingham Botanic Garden. In 1832 he pub. *Encyclopaedia of Cottage, Farm and Villa Architecture*, and in 1834 founded the *Architectural Magazine*. Their success led to the pub. of *Arboretum et Fruticetum Britannicum*, his most valuable book, but greatest financial failure. L. spent his remaining years in repaying his debts, laying out the Arboretum at Derby, 1839, and cemeteries at Southampton and Bath. He helped to develop Great Tew vil. (q.v.); is commemorated by a genus *Loudonia* described by Lindley, and an oil-painting by Linnell, presented by subscription to the Linnaean Society.

Loudspeaker, instrument for the conversion of electric energy into sound at a level which can be heard by one or more persons. It is used in communications equipment, domestic wireless receivers and public address systems. In its early form the L. was derived from the telephone receiver earpieces fitted with a horn to concentrate sound. This sound was produced by a thin metal diaphragm, caused to vibrate by an electro-magnet placed close to it, and whose coils carried the audio-frequency current from an amplifier. The efficiency was very low, the response to notes of different frequencies uneven, and marked resonances rendered the reproduced speech or music unpleasant. The diaphragm was replaced by a steel reed joined to a paper or parchment cone which had the vibrations imparted to it axially. This was known as the 'moving-iron' L., and was widely used in domestic wireless receivers. The condenser L. depended for its action on the electrostatic forces between a diaphragm and a fixed surface when an audio voltage was applied between them, while the crystal L. relied on the piezo-electric effect present when an electric voltage is applied to a crystal of Rochelle salt or similar substance. These were soon superseded by the moving-coil L., which in its various forms fulfils almost all requirements. It consists of a small coil of wire suspended in an annular gap between the poles of either a permanent or an electro-magnet. This coil is joined to the apex of a light paper, parchment or metal-foil cone, and the assembly is free to move within limits along its axis so that any movement of the coil is imparted to the cone, and thence to the air in front and behind it. The audio-frequency current is passed to the coil, whose movement, induced electromagnetically, faithfully follows its variations. As the impedance of the coil is low it is usually coupled to the output valve by means of a step-down transformer, the latter often being incorporated with the L. The recent advances in high-flux-density permanent magnets have resulted in a L. which is both compact and efficient, and which is employed in all modern domestic wireless receivers. When in a suitable cabinet or on a baffle board this type is capable of a high degree of fidelity.

A field of application in which L. design has become largely specialised is that of public address where it is required to project sound at a high power level in given directions. The cone is only 3 or 4 in. in diameter, and made of spun aluminium foil. The speaker unit feeds into a large horn which provides the requisite air loading and directivity. The high-power units can handle power of the order of 10 W. and upwards, and can project sound over considerable distances. A public address installation may employ very large numbers of L.s with horns designed to give the directivity and sound distribution required. Speakers are usually divided into groups so that the sound level may be adjusted for each one independently to obtain an even distribution of sound over the area. Considerable skill is required in the placing and choice of L.s to obtain optimum results. L.s are also used from aircraft to broadcast propaganda in such countries as Malaysia and Viet Nam.

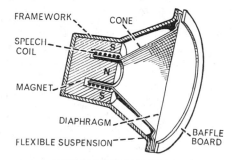

MOVING COIL LOUDSPEAKER

Loughborough, Baron, see WEDDERBURN, ALEXANDER.

Loughborough, industrial and mrkt tn, and municipal bor. of Leics, England, 11½ m. NNW. of Leicester. Prin. industries include hosiery, electrical and general engineering, pharmaceutical products, bell founding, lifting, transport and hosiery machinery, brick-making and vehicle body-building. There is a college of technology, a teachers' training college and a college of further education. The grammar school was founded in 1495. Pop. 38,621.

Loughrea, mrkt tn of co. Galway, Rep. of Ireland, 10 m. SE. of Athenry. It is the seat of the Rom. Catholic Bishop of Clonfert and has a cathedral, built 1897–1905, with interesting stained glass. Pop. 2834.

Loughton, see CHIGWELL.

Louis, or **Ludwig** (**Lewis**), name of a number of Holy Rom. emperors from the 8th cent. onwards:

Louis I ('the Fair' or 'the Pious') (778–840), son of Charlemagne, succeeded him as Rom. emperor and king of the Franks (814).

Louis II (*c.* 822–75), son of Lothaire I, associated in the gov. from 844, sole emperor from 855.

Louis III (880–928), grandson of above, succeeded his father under his mother's regency (887), and was nominal emperor from 901 to 905, being deposed and blinded by Berengar of Friuli.

Louis IV ('the Bavarian') (1282–1347), elected Holy Rom. emperor with the help of the Ghibellines (1314). He was excommunicated (*c.* 1324) by Pope John XXII, and later opposed by Clement VI.

Louis I–V, see FRANCE, *History*.

Louis VI (surnamed 'Le Gros') (1078–1137), King of France, son of Philip I, with whom he ruled jointly from 1100, succeeding him in 1108. He made Suger, abbot of St Denis, his chief minister. L. tried to check the power of the feudal lords of the Île de France by increasing the authority of the tns, and continually sought to add lands to the royal domains. His wars with Henry I of England for the possession of Normandy were unsuccessful, however, and in 1113 he had to surrender Brittany and Maine to Henry. *See* A. Luchaire, *Louis VI, le Gros*, 1889.

Louis VII, VIII, see FRANCE, *History*.

Louis IX (1214–70), King of France, commonly called St L., *b.* Poissy. He succeeded his father, L. VIII, at the age of 11, and the days of the regency of his mother, Blanche of Castile, were a period of feudal reaction on the part of the nobility. Having taken over the gov. himself, he defeated an invading Eng. army, forcing Henry III to acknowledge the overlordship of France in Guienne. In 1248 he embarked on his first crusade, but his army was overwhelmed and defeated in Egypt and he himself was captured and held to ransom. On his release he went to Acre, but achieved no lasting success, and returned to France in 1254. In 1270 he went on his second crusade, which was, however, owing to the influence of Charles of Naples, his brother, diverted to N. Africa, and in this same year L. d. of the plague at Tunis. His personal piety was already legendary in his lifetime, and he was canonised in 1297. He made considerable legal and constitutional reforms, and encouraged education. His contemporary, Joinville (q.v.), gives a detailed account of many of L.'s actions in his *Vie de St Louis*. *See also* lives by H. Wallon, 1893; F. Perry, 1901; M. R. Toynbee, 1930. *See also* E. J. Davies, *The Invasion of Egypt by Louis IX*, 1898.

Louis X, see FRANCE, *History*.

Louis XI (1423–83), King of France, the eldest son of Charles VII, *b.* Bourges. Owing to his attempts on his father's throne, he was forced into exile in Burgundy, and remained there until his accession in 1461. His crushing taxes and his attempts to increase the power of the Crown led to a revolt of his feudal vassals, 1464–5; after this was put down, L. granted the nobility certain of their demands, but in general he tried to raise the position of the lower classes, to counter the power of the barons. His greatest opponent was Charles the Bold of Burgundy (q.v.); although a better soldier than L. Charles lacked L.'s diplomatic guile, and after Charles's death L. obtained Burgundy and Artois. He also talked his way out of a war with England (1473). A vivid picture of L.'s personality and reign is given in the *Mémoires* of Comines (q.v.). *See also* lives by C. Hare, 1907, and P. Champion, 1927.

Louis XII (1462–1515), King of France, son of Charles of Orléans and successor of Charles VIII, *b*. Blois. His benevolence gained for him the title of the 'father' of his people. Much of his time was spent in campaigns in Italy, where he was successful in overrunning Milan and in helping in the Sp. conquest of Naples. In 1512 he controlled nearly the whole of Italy; in 1513, however, he was finally driven out of the country, and in the same year suffered defeat at the hands of the emperor and Henry VIII at the battle of the Spurs. By his second marriage to Anne of Brittany, widow of Charles VIII (q.v.), he ensured that Brittany remained attached to the Fr. crown. He married, thirdly, Mary, the sister of Henry VIII of England, but *d*. 3 months later. *See* P. Lacroix, *Louis XII et Anne de Bretagne*, 1882, and A. R. de Maulde, *Histoire de Louis XII*, 1889–93.

Louis XIII (1601–43), King of France, *b*. Fontainebleau, son of Henry IV, on whose assassination he succeeded to the throne at the age of 9. His mother, Marie de' Medici, acted as regent, and L. was brought up in an atmosphere of court intrigue and general insecurity. A Protestant rising in 1619 was suppressed 2 years later, and after the rise to power of Richelieu (q.v.) in 1624, the gov. became considerably more stable. L. was soon completely under Richelieu's influence. By the capture of La Rochelle (1628) the military power of the Huguenots was finally crushed, and Richelieu pursued a general policy of consolidation of the central authority at home, and of Fr. aggrandisement abroad in which L., as king, gained immensely in prestige. *See* M. Topin, *Louis XIII et Richelieu*, 1876; R. de Beauchamp, *Louis XIII d'après sa correspondance avec Richelieu*, 1902; K. A. Patmore, *Court of Louis XIII*, 1909; L. Balas, *Scènes et tableaux du règne de Louis XIII*, 1935.

Louis XIV (1638–1715), King of France, *b*. St Germain-en-Laye, the son of L. XIII, whom he succeeded in 1643. His mother, Anne of Austria (q.v.), became regent, but the chief power lay in the hands of her minister, Mazarin (q.v.). The policy of the exclusion of the nobility from the chief posts in the gov. led to the rising known as the Fronde (q.v.), which led, indirectly, to a war with Spain which ended in 1659. In the following year L. married the Infanta Maria Theresa, and in 1661, on the death of Mazarin, L. began his long period of personal gov. The keynote of the whole of his reign was despotism, and his motto, 'L'État, c'est moi', typifies the whole of his policy. Under Colbert (q.v.) the finances of the kingdom were reformed, trade was increased and a strong colonial policy pursued. Under his war minister, Louvois (q.v.), the armies were

re-formed, and under his generals, Turenne (q.v.) and Condé (q.v.), the Fr. Army became the finest fighting machine in Europe. The war of Devolution began on the death of Philip IV of Spain, L.'s father-in-law. In right of his wife, L. claimed part of the Netherlands. He made himself master of Flanders and the Franche-Comté. The alliance of England, Holland and Sweden prevented his power from expanding, and in 1668 the treaty of Aix-la-Chapelle led to the surrender of the Franche-Comté. He again entered the Netherlands in 1672, his armies being led by Turenne and Condé. He overran many of the cities of Alsace and also continued the conquest of the Netherlands. In 1678 the treaty of Nijmegen left him in possession of the Franche-Comté and of many of the fortresses of the Sp. Netherlands. By means of the law courts he succeeded in obtaining many cities on the borders of Germany, amongst them being Strasbourg and Metz. At home his power was absolute. The courts were entirely under his control, and the *lettres de cachet* were a weapon of great efficacy. L. had had a large number of mistresses, and many illegitimate children, but in 1684, after his wife's death, he married Mme de Maintenon (q.v.), who was much influenced by the Jesuits and who was probably influential in persuading L. to revoke the Edict of Nantes (q.v.) in 1685. This in reality marked the beginning of the fall of L.'s greatness. In 1688 France invaded the Palatinate and left William of Orange free to invade England. The war of the League of Augsburg which followed was terminated by the treaty of Ryswick, which was in reality merely a truce and caused L. to give up all conquests which he had made since 1678. In 1700 Charles II of Spain *d*., leaving the crown of Spain to Philip of Anjou, the second grandson of L. L., in spite of the Second Partition Treaty, accepted the will of the Sp. king. This led to the War of the Sp. Succession, Eng. participation against France being encouraged by L.'s recognition of the Old Pretender as James III. The war terminated in the treaty of Utrecht in 1713, and gave Spain to L.'s grandson, but the victories of Marlborough (q.v.) had left France a ruined country.

L.'s reign is supreme in the age of Fr. literature, and was productive of such men as Corneille, Racine, Molière and Boileau, whilst religion was represented by men of the type of Bossuet and Fénelon. *See* Voltaire, *Siècle de Louis Quatorze*, 1751; A. Hassal, *Life of Louis XIV*, 1895; St Simon, *Mémoires* (Eng. trans.), 1899; Lord Acton, *The Age of Louis XIV*, 1902; Sir C. Petrie, *Louis XIV* (new ed.), 1940; M. Ashley, *Louis XIV and the Greatness of France*, 1946; V. Cronin, *Louis XIV*, 1964.

Louis XV (1710–74), King of France, *b*. Versailles. He was the great-grandson of Louis XIV, and became heir to the throne in 1712. L. was just over 5 years of age when he succeeded, and the country was administered by the king's uncle, Orleans. The age of Orleans was noted for its profligacy and its financial chaos. In 1725 L. married the daughter of Stanislas, the deposed

London

Above: Aerial view of Buckingham Palace: the wing in the foreground contains the state apartments and picture gallery; that facing the Victoria Memorial, the state visitors' suites.
Aerofilms Ltd
Below: Part of the lake in St James's Park.
Central Press Photos Ltd

London

Old houses in Cheyne
Walk, Chelsea.
G.L.C.

Highgate Pond,
Hampstead Heath.
G.L.C.

Part of the London docks,
which stretch from the
Tower of London to
Tilbury.

London

Above: The heart of London: the Houses of Parliament and Westminster Bridge, from the south bank of the Thames.
British Travel Association
Below left: Part of Regent Street, one of London's central shopping streets, originally planned by John Nash (although none of his architecture survives).
C.O.I.: Crown copyright
Below right: Tower Bridge, with the Tower of London in the background.
British Travel Association

London

Henry VII's Chapel in Westminster Abbey was begun in 1503 and replaced the Lady Chapel of 1220.

London University

Above: The Senate House in Bloomsbury was opened in 1936.
University of London
Below: The portico of University College, designed by William Wilkins (who also designed the National Gallery) and completed in 1827.
University College

Above: REMARKABLE ROUNDHOUSE—This is an aerial view of the giant geodesic dome which the Union Tank Car Company built near Baton Rouge, Louisiana.
U.S. Information Service
Below: Salt Mining, Louisiana—This photo, taken deep within the famous Avery Island salt dome that pushes up from the marshes of Southern Louisiana, shows the mine storage area.
U.S. Information Service

Louisiana

Above: A French Colonial mansion in the Garden District, an older section of New Orleans.
Right: About 50 per cent of the land is devoted to forestry.
Below: A Spanish musk-rat trapper in the marshlands of the Mississippi delta.
Photos: U.S. Information Service

Luxembourg

The Corniche, Luxembourg, separates the upper town from the lower.

Far left: A scene at Alzette, in the important mining district.

Near left: The Benedictine abbey at Clervaux in the Ardennes (restored after war damage in 1944).

The village of Ehnen on the Moselle, in the heart of the vineyard country.
Photos: Luxembourg National Tourist Office

King of Poland. After the death of Orléans his chief minister was Fleury. In the War of the Polish Succession France succeeded in establishing the claims of L.'s father-in-law to the Polish throne. During the War of the Austrian Succession the French supported the claim of the elector of Bavaria to the throne of Austria in lieu of Maria Theresa. They were repeatedly successful on land, but their trade and navy were ruined by the English. The great duel in India and America between England and France was fought out during this reign. The financial state of France, however, was chaotic, though L. lavished money extravagantly on his mistresses, especially on Mme de Pompadour (q.v.) and, later, on Mme du Barry (q.v.). The country was overtaxed, and was further humiliated by the practical conquest of all the Fr. possessions in India and America during the Seven Years War. The peace of Paris (1763) definitely deprived France of the nucleus of her colonial empire. On L.'s death France was bankrupt and ready for revolution; the attitude towards state affairs of the king himself (who was not without intelligence or latent ability) is characterised by the expression attributed to him: 'Après moi, la déluge'. His reign was, however, notable for its culture and artistry. Art, literature and philosophy flourished, owing much to court patronage. *See* P. Gaxotte, *Louis XV and his Times*, 1934; A. Leroy, *Louis XV*, 1938 (Eng. trans. 1939); S. P. Gooch, *Louis XV*, 1956.

Louis XVI (1754–93), King of France, the grandson of Louis XV, *b.* Versailles. In 1770 L. married the daughter of Maria Theresa, Marie Antoinette (q.v.). L. succeeded to a bankrupt kingdom (*see* LOUIS XV). The king agreed to many minor reforms, but was prevented by the nobility from accepting the more sweeping reforms urged by Turgot (q.v.). Necker succeeded in reforming the finances of the country to a certain extent, but again a proposal to tax the classes who were excluded by privilege led to such violent opposition that Necker resigned. Finally (1789) it became apparent that the States-General, which had not met since 1614, would have to be called. The Third Estate speedily took upon themselves the rectifying of grievances and formed themselves into a National Assembly. Proclaiming a new constitution they gained for themselves the title of the Constituent Assembly and the revolution had begun. The king refused to accede to their demands for *liberté, égalité, fraternité*, and retaliated by dismissing Necker and calling out the troops, but to little effect. In Oct. Versailles was attacked, and L. and his family were forced to take up residence in Paris. The next 2 years were spent by the assembly in experimenting with constitutions, and the king and his family, in 1791, escaped to Varennes, only to be brought back as prisoners to Paris, where L. was forced to swear to rule constitutionally.

In 1792 the king's hand was forced, and he was compelled to declare war against Austria. Hostility in Europe was aroused by the republican fervour of the left-wing of the assembly: in

Sept. 1792 the rep. was proclaimed as a reply to Prussian invasion. In Dec. 1792 the king was brought to trial for treason against the rep., was sentenced to death, and executed on 21 Jan. He was guillotined in 'La Place de la Révolution'. Marie Antoinette soon shared the same fate. L.'s own standards of morality formed a considerable contrast to those of his predecessors, and he was conscientious and well intentioned. He lacked personality and initiative, however, and suffered from the reflected unpopularity of his wife. He was the victim of events largely not of his making, which would have defeated a far more capable ruler. *See* J. M. Thompson, *The French Revolution*, 1929, and L. Madelin, *Louis et Marie Antoinette*, 1936; *also* life by M. de la Fuye, 1943.

Louis XVII (1785–?95), titular King of France, *b.* Versailles, the second son of L. XVI, became dauphin on the death of his elder brother in 1789. He was imprisoned in the Temple, at first with his father and mother. After his father's execution (Jan. 1793) he was nominally king; but nothing definite is known of him after this date and his death was announced in June 1795. It is now generally accepted that he *d.* or was put to death on or before this date. There are, however, stories of his alleged escape, and until recent times claims of descent from him were made by a number of people. Immediately after the Bourbon restoration he was impersonated by a Prussian named Karl Wilhelm Naundorff, whose resemblance to the Bourbons was striking. This pretender made his way to France in 1833, but was later expelled. *See* lives by G. Lenôtre (Eng. trans.), 1922, and H. R. Madol (Eng. trans.), 1930.

Louis XVIII (Stanislas Xavier) (1755–1824), King of France, *b.* Versailles, the younger brother of L. XVI. He claimed the title of King of France after the assumed death of L. XVII in 1795. He lived in exile, mainly in England, until Napoleon's first abdication (1814), when he crossed to Calais and ascended the throne of France. L. and his family fled to Ghent during the Hundred Days, and remained there until after Waterloo. For a time he attempted a liberal form of gov., under the influence of Decazes, but Royalist extremism gained the upper hand after the murder of the Duc de Berry in 1820. *See* J. Lucas-Dubreton, *The Restoration and the July Monarchy* (trans.), 1925, and J. François-Primo, *La Vie privée de Louis XVIII*, 1938. He was succeeded by his brother Charles X (q.v.).

Louis I, or **Ludwig (Karl August)** (1786–1860), King of Bavaria. He succeeded in 1825, and the early part of his reign was successful. He initiated many liberal reforms, but gradually became increasingly reactionary. In 1848 he was forced to abdicate in favour of his son Maximilian.

Louis, or **Ludwig II (Otto Friedrich Wilhelm)** (1845–86), King of Bavaria, grandson of L. I of Bavaria, and son of Maximilian II. He succeeded his father in 1864. During the Austro-Prussian war he fought with the Austrians, but went ultimately over to the side of Prussia. He spent large sums of money carrying out theatrical ideas proposed by Wagner, whose patron he was. His mind became increasingly deranged and he was declared incapable of ruling in 1886. Shortly afterwards he was drowned in the lake at Starnberg. *See* life by D. Chapman-Huston, 1955.

Louis, Joe (real name **Joseph Louis Barrow**) (1914–), Amer. Negro boxer, *b.* near Lafayette, Alabama. As a professional boxer his first fights were against Hans Birkie and Lee Ramage, whom he beat. After beating Ramage for the second time the papers nicknamed him 'Brown Bomber'. A New York promoter then arranged a fight with ex-heavyweight champion Primo Carnera, whom he defeated in the 7th round, and for which he received £60,000 (June 1935). After the Carnera fight he knocked out (1935) Max Baer, but in June 1936 he was defeated by Max Schmeling in the 12th round. In Aug. he knocked out Jack Sharkey in the 3rd round, and in Sept. Al Ettore in the 5th round. On 22 June 1937 he knocked out Jimmy Braddock (8th round), thereby winning the world's heavyweight championship. Then came the return match with Schmeling, whom he knocked out in the opening round. He held the title until 1948, when he retired undefeated.

Louis, Pierre Charles Alexandre (1787–1872), Fr. physician, *b.* Aï, Champagne. He studied medicine at Rheims and Paris, graduating at the latter univ. in 1813. After a few years in Russia he returned to Paris and worked at the Charité for 7 years, devoting all his time to the collection and analysis of facts—his 'numerical method', which became an invaluable instrument of research in his hands. By the introduction of this method, Louis became the founder of medical, as distinct from vital, statistics, and estab. medicine as an exact science. This is well shown in his *Recherches sur les effets de la saignée*, 1835. In 1825 he pub. *Recherches anatomico-pathologiques sur la phthisie*, a valuable study of nearly 2000 cases of tuberculosis. His next great work was *Recherches anatomiques, pathologiques et thérapeutiques sur la maladie connue sous les noms de fièvre putride*, etc., 1829, in which he studied 138 cases of typhoid, estab. the pathology of the condition and gave to it its present name. *See* life by E. J. Woillez, 1873.

Louis Bonaparte, King of Holland, *see* BONAPARTE, *Louis Bonaparte*.

Louis de la Trinité, Father, *see* D'ARGENLIEU, GEORGE THIERRY.

Louis-d'Or, Fr. gold coin first issued by Louis XIII in 1640, and discontinued in 1795.

Louis Napoleon, *see* NAPOLEON III.

Louis Philippe (1773–1850), king of the French, *b.* Paris. He was the eldest son of the Duke of Orleans, together with whom, at the time of the Fr. Revolution, he gave up his title and assumed the name of Égalité. During the early revolutionary campaigns he fought for the rep., but after his father's execution fell under suspicion, fled to Austria and did not enter France again until the Restoration. He was a teacher in Switzerland, visited the U.S.A. and

finally settled at Twickenham. He married, in 1809, the daughter of Ferdinand, King of the Two Sicilies, and returned to France in 1814. Louis XVIII disliked and distrusted him, and he soon left France again, living in England until 1827. He became exceedingly popular in Paris, and after the revolution of 1830 was invited to be king, having first taken the title of lieutenant-governor. L. P. had to contend on the one hand against a rising tide of radical republicanism, and on the other against the antagonism of the Bonapartists, who protested that the national honour was being degraded by his pacific foreign policy. Twice Louis Napoleon entered France as pretender, but with no success. Eventually, discontent with his illiberal home policy, combined with the scandal caused by France's ill-timed intervention in Spain, precipitated the revolution of 1848. The Paris mob rose and, helped by the army and the police, forced the king to abdicate, although he promised redress and dismissed his Prime Minister, Guizot, who was the prin. target of popular dislike. L. P. fled to England, where 2 years later he *d.* at Claremont, Surrey. *See* lives by P. de la Gorce, 1931; J. Lucas-Dubreton, 1938; *also* Agnes de Stoeckl, *King of the French*, 1957.

Louisa Augusta Wilhelmina Amelia (1776–1810) Queen of Prussia, a daughter of Charles, Duke of Mecklenburg-Strelitz, *b.* Hanover. In 1793 she married the prince-royal of Prussia, later Frederick Wm III, becoming the mother of Frederick Wm IV and Wm I, afterwards emperor. She endeared herself to her people by her spirit and energy, and particularly distinguished herself during the Napoleonic campaign by her efforts to obtain concessions at Tilsit from Napoleon. The Prussian order of Louise was instituted in her honour, and also the Louise foundation for the education of girls. *See* lives by Mary Moffat, 1906, and G. Aretz, 1927.

Louisbourg, tn in Cape Breton Is., Canada, off the Atlantic coast, commanding the entrance to the Gulf of St Lawrence, 27 m. SE. of Sydney. It is now little more than a fishing vil., but under France had a large export trade in cod, and was the strongest fortress in N. America. Taken in 1745 by the troops of Massachusetts under Pepperell and a Brit. squadron under Warren. The fort is now a national historic park. L. was restored to France in 1748 by the treaty of Aix-la-Chapelle. It was again taken by Amherst in 1758. It possesses a very fine harbour. Pop. 1417. *See* J. S. McLennan, *Louisbourg, from its foundation to its fall, 1713–1758*, 1918.

Louisiade Archipelago, group of is. at the SE. extremity of Papua, Brit. New Guinea. They are all mountainous and covered with vegetation, the inhab. partaking of both Malayan and Papuan characteristics. The is. were discovered in 1606, and taken by the Brit. in 1888. Alluvial gold has been found. Area *c.* 600 sq. m.; pop. *c.* 3000.

Louisiana, known as the Pelican state, one of the S. central states of the U.S.A., bordering the Gulf of Mexico, bounded on the N. by Arkansas and Mississippi, on the E. by Mississippi, Gulf of Mexico on the S. and Texas on the W., covering an area of 48,523 sq. m., including 3346 sq. m. of inland water. It was admitted to the Amer. Union in 1812. The surface of the state consists chiefly of the broad marshy valley of the Mississippi and Red R.s. About a third of the area of the state is occupied by the Mississippi delta. In many places, notably at New Orleans, the riv. is at a considerably higher level than the surrounding land (*see* MISSISSIPPI). Marshlands extend W. all along the coast and are the home of musk-rat, opossum, skunk, fox and other fur-bearing animals. Timber is also produced on these marshes, L. being U.S.A.'s third lumber producer. The state has a large number of rivs., creeks, bayous and lakes, giving it over 4000 m. of navigable waterways. The prin. riv., after the Mississippi, is its great trib., the Red R.; the Sabine forms L.'s W. boundary, the Pearl bounds it on the SE. The geological formations belong to the Tertiary and Quaternary periods and contain oil and sulphur. The climate is semi-tropical and unhealthy in the lowlands, but the soil is exceedingly fertile, except in the extreme N. The chief manufacturing industries of the state are those of petroleum, lumber, rice, cotton-seed, sugar and molasses. Sugar is the most important agric. product; others are rice, cotton, corn, fruit, especially strawberries, and tobacco. There are valuable fisheries. The chief mineral products are rock-salt (the state has 3 of the largest salt-mines in the world), sulphur, clay beds, petroleum and natural gas. The cap. is Baton Rouge (pop. 152,420); other important tns are New Orleans (627,530), the largest city and one of the chief Amer. seaports, Shreveport (164,370) and Monroe (52,220). L. State Univ. is at Baton Rouge and other univs. are at New Orleans. L. sends 2 senators and 8 representatives to Congress. The 4 years' (1931–5) governorship of Huey Pierce Long was a landmark in L. politics. After his assassination (1935) there followed a reactionary period of 12 years in which L. political life reverted to something more normal—the conflict between New Orleans, predominantly Catholic, and the poor and largely Protestant countryside; and the parsimony which replaced Huey Long's enormous expenditure on roads, hospitals and education. But in the 1948 election, by a huge majority, L. chose Earl Long, brother of Huey, as governor (*see* LONG, H. P.). His programme, if less flamboyantly presented than his brother's doctrine of 'share the wealth', rested on the same assumptions but he was defeated in 1952. Pop. 3,257,020, of whom 1,039,200 are Negro.

The old Fr. prov. of L., named by La Salle in honour of Louis XIV, stretched from Manitoba and the Great Lakes to the Gulf of Mexico, and from the Brit. colonies in the E. to the Sp. colonies in the W. When France lost Canada L. passed to England and Spain, the Mississippi being the boundary. In 1800 it passed again into Fr. possession, to be sold to the U.S.A. 3 years later for £3,000,000. *See also* U.S.A., *History*. *See* Johnson, *Highways and Byways of the Mississippi Valley*, 1906; L. Saxon, *Old Louisiana*, 1929; Federal Writers' Project, *Louisiana*: *A Guide to the Pelican State*, 1941. (*See Plate*.)

Louisville, city in Jefferson co., Kentucky, U.S.A., on the l. b. of the Ohio, 90 m. SW. of Cincinnati at the L. Falls which interrupted navigation until passed by a canal. It is connected with New Albany and Jeffersonville by bridges, and is an important riv. port. It is the largest city of the state, and a prin. commercial, financial, industrial and distribution centre of the S. L. is a rail junction with repair shops, and also an important tobacco-marketing and processing centre. Its distilleries produce a large part of the U.S. supply of bourbon. It has stockyards, meat-packing and woodworking plants, foundries, machine shops, flour-mills and plants processing petroleum and metals. It manufs. farm equipment, clothing, textiles, builders' and plumbers' supplies, leather and electrical goods, rubber, chemicals, synthetics, gases and cement products. Its Bluegrass hinterland produces livestock, burley, tobacco, grain, vegetables, phosphate, limestone and clay. Here are the univ. of L., L. Presbyterian Theological Seminary, the S. Baptist Theological Seminary, the Jefferson School of Law and other colleges. L. is the site of Churchill Downs race-track, scene of the ann. Kentucky Derby. Pop. 390,640.

Louping Ill, Sheep Staggers or **Trembles,** virus disease principally of sheep and cattle, but horse, pigs and man are susceptible. It is an encephalomyelitis giving rise to fever, with twitchings of the skin and limbs. Affected sheep carry the head high and take short jumpy steps; finally they become paralysed and die. The causal virus is transmitted by the bites of the blood-sucking tick, *Ixodes ricinus* (castor bean tick), which is to be found in large numbers on rough grazings where coarse herbage—such as bracken, heather and gorse bushes—abounds. No treatment can be recommended apart from careful nursing, but the disease may be controlled by vaccination. Preventive measures to control tick infestation, such as dipping of sheep and improvements to grazings aimed at the elimination of herbage which harbours the ticks, are also advisable.

Lourdes, Fr. tn in the dept of Hautes-Pyrénées, on the gave du Pau, at the foot of the central Pyrenees, 11 m. SSW. of Tarbes (q.v.). Until the second half of the 19th cent. it was a large vil. dominated by the 13th–17th cents. Château Fort (now a museum). In 1858, in a grotto in the vil., the Blessed Virgin is believed to have made 18 appearances, between 11 Feb. and 16 July, to a young peasant girl, Bernadette Soubirous, who was canonised as St Bernadette in 1933. In 1862 the church authorities declared the facts to be authentic, and since then L. has become the greatest Christian place of pilgrimage in the modern world. Some 1 million pilgrims travel there each year, including many invalids who go there to wash in the waters of a spring which first made its appearance during the period of the apparitions. There have been numerous cures of bodily ailments, of which some have been pronounced miraculous, after

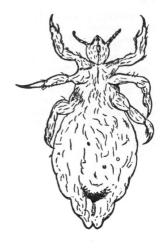

LICE

(Diameter enlarged fourteen times)

1, head-louse (*Pediculus capitis*); 2, pubic louse (*P. pubis*); 3, body-louse (*P. corporis*).

From 'Clinical Methods' (Hutchinson and Rainy), by courtesy of Cassell & Co. Ltd.

inquiry, by the eccles. authorities. A medical bureau, the Bureau des Constatations Médicales, examines persons who claim to have been cured; it consists of a permanent president and a panel of other doctors (of any nationality or religious persuasion) who happen to be in L. and who have registered their names with the bureau. A neo-Gothic basilica was erected in 1876, and below it, opening on to the vast Esplanade des Processions, is a church in Byzantine style, the Church of the Rosary, built in 1889. A new underground basilica, oval in shape and accommodating 20,000 pilgrims, was consecrated in Mar. 1958; it is dedicated to St Pius X (q.v.). L. is in a marble- and slate-quarrying dist. Pop. 16,000. *See* R. Cranston, *The Mystery of Lourdes*, 1956; F. Leuret and H. Bon, *Modern Miraculous Cures*, 1956; R. Laurentin, *Meaning of Lourdes*, 1960. (*See Plate: France.*)

Lourenço Marques: 1. Dist in Mozambique. It is traversed by the R.s Lunde and Limpopo, and is divided into 5 sub-dists.

2. Cap. of the L. M. dist, Portuguese E. African ter. of Mozambique, in the NW. of Delagoa Bay. It is linked by rail and road with the S. African system and is the nearest port to Johannesburg (395 m.), and the industrialised Rand. L. M., founded by the Portuguese in 1544, is a modern tn with one of the finest harbours in Africa. With a healthy climate and many other attractions L. M. has become a popular holiday resort for S. Africans and Rhodesians. Pop. Whites, 62,000; Africans, 183,798 (1960).

Louse, parasitic insect without wings, including the Aptera, with the exception of the flea. Among the distinct groups are human lice (*Pediculidae*), true lice (*Haemetopinus*), bird lice (*Mallophaga*) and epidermis eaters (*Trichodectes*). Three kinds of human L. are common in England. There is the head-L., which makes the scalp its home and pasture-ground; the crab-L., which chiefly occupies the hairy part of the

pubes; and the body-L., which lives in the clothing and visits the body only for nourishment. Head-lice and crab-lice lay their eggs on the hairs of their respective hunting grounds. The body-L. deposits its eggs not only on the small hairs of the skin, but also on the clothes. The nits are firmly stuck to the hairs or clothing by a sort of cement, and are usually not very easy to detach. Nits take about a week to hatch, and the young reach maturity in about a fortnight after birth.

The presence of lice is generally made known by the intense irritation of the skin which they provoke. As a result of the consequent scratching, surface infection is common, and neighbouring lymphatic glands may become swollen and tender. Fortunately pediculosis, as an L.-infested condition is called, is amenable to treatment if it be carried out persistently and with assiduity. In the case of the head-L. and the pubic (crab) L., the first thing is to cut as short as possible the hairs of the affected region. Twice daily, until all trace of these nauseous insects has disappeared, the shortened hair should be thoroughly combed with a fine-toothed comb. After combing the parts should be vigorously scrubbed with warm water and Derbac soap, or, if this is difficult to obtain, coal-tar soap. The skin having been dried by thorough rubbing with a towel, a little perchloride of mercury lotion, of a strength 1 in 2000, should be well rubbed in. Lastly ammoniated mercury ointment may usefully be applied. The whole of these procedures should be carried out systematically, twice daily, until not a L. or nit can be found. The body-L. presents a somewhat more complex problem. To begin with all bed-clothing and all linen that has been in contact with the skin should be baked in a disinfecting apparatus or be boiled in water. Twice a day the whole surface of the body should be vigorously washed with coal-tar soap and warm water containing a generous allowance of washing soda. Before the washing it is a good plan to rub into the skin—at any rate of those parts notably affected—an equal mixture of olive oil and common lamp paraffin, the warm water and soap being used some 10 min. later. Half-hearted or irregularly applied treatment is useless whereas regular and persistent treatment is invariably successful—though a measure of patience may be called for. Infestation with lice is likely to occur in conditions of overcrowding and where washing facilities are deficient. The insecticide D.D.T. dusted into clothing and on the bodies of those exposed to infestation is a most valuable preventive measure. Its efficacy was proved among the troops in the Second World War.

Louth: 1. Mrkt tn of Lincs, England, 15 m. SE. of Grimsby, and 'cap.' of the Wolds. Industries include plastics, malting in a modern factory unique in Europe, making of agric. implements and packing materials. The 15th cent. par. church of St James has a beautiful spire, and there are ruins of a Cistercian abbey at L. Park. Pop. 11,556.

2. Maritime co. of Rep. of Ireland in the prov. of Leinster, bounded E. by the Irish Sea. The surface generally is low and undulating, with a high mt range in the NE., bordering Carlingford Lough (q.v.). On the coast are the watering-places of Carlingford and Greenore, with Dundalk (qq.v.), the co. tn, facing the bay of that name. The chief rivs. are the Fane, Lagan, Glyde and Dee, with the Boyne (q.v.) forming part of the S. boundary. Agriculture is the chief occupation, but there are also linen factories, and deep-sea and salmon fisheries. L. is rich in anct buildings and remains. Area 317 sq. m.; pop. 69,194.

3. Anct vil. of co. L., 8 m. SW. of Dundalk, formerly of such importance that it gave its name to the co. It contains some fine ruins.

Louvain (Flem. **Leuven;** Ger. **Löwen**), city in the prov. of Brabant, Belgium, 15 m. E. by N, of Brussels, on the R. Dyle. Among its numerous historical buildings are the tn hall (1448–59), one of the finest examples of the Gothic style in NW. Europe, and the church of St Peter (1425–97), damaged in 1914 and bombed in 1944, but restored again. The tn was a prosperous cloth-making centre in the 13th cent., and became the cap of the Duchy of Brabant in the 14th cent., before the rise of Brussels. The univ. of L. was founded in 1426 and was designed as the Catholic Univ. in 1835. The beginning of the First World War was the most tragic episode in L.'s hist. It was sacked by the Germans on 25 Aug. 1914. After the fall of Liège the prin. line of the Belgian defence was centred at L., and after L. fell the Belgians were driven back on Antwerp and Malines. The greater part of the city of L., including the church of St Peter, the law courts, the theatre, the Academy for Fine Arts and the anct halls, with the famous univ. library, was then razed by the Germans on the pretext that the civilian pop. had joined in an attack on the Ger. occupying troops. This vandalism, how-

ever, reacted severely on Ger. prestige, and by the treaty of Versailles Germany undertook to deliver MSS. and prints equivalent in value to those destroyed at L. In 1940 the library, rebuilt with the help of the Amer. people in 1928, and containing over 900,000 vols., was again destroyed by the Germans. L. is an important market-place and road and railway junction. It has foodstuff, metal and electrical industries.

Louvière, La, see LA LOUVIÈRE.

Louviers, Fr. tn in the dept of Eure, on the R. Eure. The church, partly 12th cent., has a remarkable flamboyant porch. L. has been a textile (particularly woollen) centre for many cents. Pop. 13,100.

Louvois, François Michel Le Tellier, Marquis de (1641–91), Fr. statesman and war minister under Louis XIV, b. Paris. Turenne noted his talents in the war of Devolution, and after the peace of Aix-la-Chapelle he was set to reorganise the Fr. Army. He founded the military orders of merit, the Hôtel des Invalides and the Fr. standing army. The efficiency of his instrument was demonstrated in the war of 1672. Until 1690 L. was a chief statesman of France. *See* C. Rousset, *Histoire de Louvois*, 1872, and L. André, *Michel Le Tellier et Louvois*, 1942.

Louvre, The, greatest of the modern palaces of Paris, forming a square of 576 ft by 538 ft, was connected with the palace of the Tuileries by a great picture gallery overlooking the Seine and 1456 ft long. Between the 2 palaces lay the Place du Carrousel, and Napoleon III further connected the 2 palaces on the N. side, making them into one vast palace. The L. is erected on the site of an old 13th cent. château; the first part of the modern structure, the SW. wing, was built, after the designs of Pierre Lescot, in 1541, while the main portion of the square was built by Louis XIV, after the design of Claude Perrault, though the building was not completed until the 19th cent. After the building of the Tuileries the L. proper became a series of great galleries filled with pictures, sculptures, Egyptian, Gk and Rom. antiquities. The fire originated by the Communards in 1871, which destroyed the Tuileries, burnt only that corner of the L. which contained the library.

The L. is the largest national gallery in the world and very comprehensive, though numerically strongest in Fr. painting. The 'Grande Galerie' of the L., redecorated and rehung, was officially opened again on 6 Oct. 1947. It had been closed and empty since the outbreak of war. The 'Grande Galerie' contains the Renaissance painters and their successors down to the 18th cent. Venetians. Near the end of the gallery are the paintings of the Sp. school: Velazquez, Murillo and Goya. As before the war, the centre of the gallery is reserved for the special masterpieces: 'Joan of Aragon' and 'Baltasar Castiglione' by Raphael, 'Francis I' by Titian and Leonardo's 'Mona Lisa'. Cimabue's 'Virgin with the Angels' first meets the visitor at the top of the stairs. In the 'Seven Metres Hall' are the It. primitives and the artists of the early Renaissance, including Botticelli and Ghirlandaio.

Among the notable It. pictures are the following: Leonardo, 'The Virgin of the Rocks', 'John the Baptist in the Wilderness', and the world-famous 'Mona (Monna) Lisa'; Raphael, 'Holy Family' and 'The Madonna', known as 'La Belle Jardinière'; Sebastiano del Piombo, 'Holy Family'; Titian, 'Vierge au lapin', 'Entombment', 'Antiope', 'L'Homme au Gant'—one of the glories of the L.; Correggio, 'Mystical Marriage of St Catherine'; Giorgione, 'Concert champêtre'; Tintoretto, 'Susanna in the Bath'; and Paul Veronese, 'Feast in the House of Simon'. Dutch and Flemish pictures include Rembrandt, 'Venus and Cupid', 'Tobit' and 'Pilgrims at Emmaus'—one of the great treasures of the L.; Van Eyck, 'Vierge au Donateur'; Frans Hals, 'Bohémienne'; Jordaens, 'Christ expelling the Moneychangers'; Vermeer, 'La Dentellière'; Ter Borch, 'Concert'; and Rubens, landscapes. The Fr. pictures in the L. range from eccles. paintings of the 15th cent. and the great classical painters of the 18th cent.—notably Poussin and Claude—to the Chauchard, Schlichting, Thomy-Thierret, Moreau-Nélaton and Camondo collections. Among the glories of the L. are Nicolas Poussin's 'Inspiration of a Poet', 'The Shepherds of Arcady' and 'The Funeral of Phocion'. Masterpieces by Claude include his 'Village Dance' and 'Cleopatra landing at Tarsus'. In the Chauchard collection are Corot's 'Le Moulin', Millet's 'La Tricoteuse' and 'La Bergère'. Boucher's brilliant 'Odalisque' is in the Schlichting collection. In the Thomy-Thierret collection Corots are in abundance. In the Moreau-Nélaton collection are other Corots; Manet's famous 'Picnic'; and, in the Camondo collection, works of the Impressionist school. This collection well represents Degas, notably by his 'Absinthe Drinkers', and Cézanne by his 'Maison du Pendu'. A reorganisation of the national museums in Paris was called for by the reappraisal of 19 cent. art and its relation with the 20th cent. (which in Britain has made great post-war changes at the Tate Gallery) and necessitated the overhaul of the old Luxembourg collection. The Jeu de Paume Gallery in Paris is now that branch of the L. devoted to the great Impressionists, where Manet, Monet, Renoir, Degas and others are richly represented. The Musée Nationale d'Art Moderne separately represents the modern art of which Paris has been the mainspring. The Eng. collection in the L. if not large is at least representative and includes Reynolds, Romney, Raeburn, Lawrence, Hoppner, Bonington, Constable, Turner and Wilson. *See* PARIS. *See also* C. Aulanier, *Histoire du Palais et du Musée du Louvre* and R. Huyghe, *Art Treasures of the Louvre,* 1952.

Louvre, in architecture, a ventilator or foul-air outlet, its sides formed of inclined strips of wood or metal. L.s were fixed on the roof ridges of medieval halls to remove smoke from a fire on a central hearth (*see* CHIMNEY). Miniature glass L.s can be fixed in window-panes.

Lovat, Simon Fraser, 11th **Baron** (*c.* 1675–1747), Scottish Jacobite, educ. Aberdeen.

LOUVRE

A, on the ridge of a roof; B, in a gable.

Though professing loyalty to the Stuarts, one of his first acts on leaving college was to raise 300 men from his clan to form part of a regiment in the service of William and Mary. In 1690 he was declared guilty of treason and fled to France. In 1702 he was at the court of St Germain, and one of his first steps towards gaining influence in France was to announce his conversion to the Catholic faith. In 1714, at the request of his clan, he returned to England. He hid in London (1715) but escaped surveillance and returned to Scotland, appearing to support the gov. In the rebellion of 1745 he made false profession of fidelity to the gov., and after the battle of Culloden was forced to flee to the W. highlands. He was finally arrested on an is. in Loch Morar, and was tried at Westminster Hall and executed on Tower Hill, April 1747. One of his greatest private outrages was the forced marriage of the widow of the 10th Lord L., his cousin, with the view of securing his own succession to the estates. See *Memoirs of Lord Lovat,* 1797, purporting to be authentic, and M. McLaren, *Lord Lovat of the '45,* 1957.

Lovat, Simon Joseph Fraser (1871–1933), 16th **Baron,** succeeded to the barony in 1887. He served in S. Africa in the Boer War, and raised a corps, designated 'L.'s Scouts', with himself in command. On returning from Africa he raised 2 yeomanry regiments, which formed part of the Highland Mounted Brigade. L.'s Scouts also fought in both world wars. L. served in France and Gallipoli during the First World War.

Love. In its most common use the term denotes a sentiment centred upon one particular person, most commonly the affection existing between parent and child, and that affection between 2 persons of opposite sex, which forms the normal basis of marriage. It manifests itself in a desire for the welfare of the beloved object, in a longing for his presence and delight in his approval, and sorrow at parting. The term is usually restricted to a sentiment in which tender emotion predominates, so distinguishing it from mere passion. Although the term 'animal passion' is often used, careful observation does not confirm the popular view that among sub-human animals the sex relations are without tenderness. Socrates distinguished between heavenly and vulgar L., and utterly condemned the latter, and Plato followed in his steps. Platonic L. is the affection between 2 persons that is free from sexual desire, that is a striving after the infinite and a lowly adoration of perfect beauty. Aristotle, searching after the psychological basis of the emotions, found in L. not a metaphysical principle, an aspiration after perfect beauty, but a natural physical bond between the sexes designed for the procreation of children. The Christian ideal makes L. to man, or charity, the unvarying method of manifesting L. to God. In the words of the beloved disciple God is L. (1 John iv. 8). *See* A. Bain, *The Emotions and the Will*, 1859; C. Darwin, *Descent of Man*, 1871; A. Shand, *Foundations of Character*, 1914; O. Pfister, *Love in Children*, 1924; I. D. Suttie, *Origin of Love and Hate*, 1935; K. Z. Lorenz, *King Solomon's Ring*, 1952.

Love Apple, *see* TOMATO.

Love Bird, popular name of various small parrots of the genus *Agapornis* (separated from *Psittacula* by Jardine and others) of the family Psittacidae. They are so named from the affection the male displays towards the female whether caged or wild. The African short-tailed rosy-faced L. B., which is about 6½ in. long, is a favourite cage-bird and among the hardiest of the genus. Other varieties are the Melanesian pygmy parrots and *Melopsittacus undulatus*, a long-tailed grass-parrot once much used for fortune-telling, and known as the Australian budgerigar (q.v.).

Love-in-a-Mist, popular name of a genus (*Nigella*) of flowering plants, family Ranunculaceae, bearing blue or white blossoms surrounded by feathery leafy bracts. The most popular species are *N. damascena*, bearing dark blue flowers, *N. d. Miss Jekyll* (pale blue or white flowers), and *N. hispanica* (dark blue).

Love-in-Idleness, *see* PANSY.

Love-Lies-Bleeding, *see* AMARANTHUS.

Lovedu, Bantu speaking tribe of the Transvaal, S. Africa. They are famed for their queen, who is celebrated as a rain maker throughout S. Africa. They number about 40,000. *See* E. J. and J. D. Krige, *The Realm of a Rain-Queen*, 1943.

Lovelace, Richard (1618–58), poet, *b.* Woolwich, Kent. Educ. at Charterhouse and Oxford, he spent his fortune in support of the royal cause, and though he could have shone at court, preferred warfare. In 1645 he took up arms on the king's behalf, fought for France against Spain, and on returning to England in 1648 was imprisoned till the king's death, thus obtaining leisure for verse-making. During his imprisonment he wrote the lyric by which he is best

LOVE-IN-A-MIST
A, seed pod; B, under-side of flower.

remembered 'To Althea from Prison', and collected and revised for the press a vol. of occasional poems. In 1649 they were pub. under the title *Lucasta*. He also wrote, when quite a young man, a comedy and a tragedy, entitled respectively *The Scholar* and *The Soldier*. The last 10 years of his life were passed in obscurity. His poems were pub. after his death, and ed. in 1930 by C. H. Wilkinson. *See* C. H. Hartmann, *The Cavalier Spirit, and its Influence on the Life and Work of Richard Lovelace*, 1925.

Lovell, Sir (Alfred Charles) Bernard (1913–), radio astronomer, *b.* Glos. During 1936–9 he worked on cosmic rays at Manchester Univ. and during 1939–45 on radar development. Returning to Manchester he estab. the Jodrell Bank experimental station (q.v.), where sev. very large radio telescopes were constructed, including one of 250 ft diameter. He became prof. of Radio Astronomy in 1951, F.R.S. in 1955, knighted, 1961. He gave the B.B.C. Reith lectures in 1958, pub. as *The Individual and the Universe*; and in addition to many technical papers has pub. sev. popular books, including (with R. Hanbury Brown) *The Exploration of Space by Radio*, 1957; *The Exploration of Outer Space*, 1961; *Discovering the Universe*, 1963.

Lover, Samuel (1797–1868), novelist and song-writer, *b.* Dublin. He wrote a number of songs, of which 'Molly Bawn' and 'The Low-backed Car' had great popularity. He also wrote sev. novels, of which *Rory O'More*, 1837, which was in its first form a ballad, and *Handy Andy*, 1842, are the best known; also short Irish sketches which, with his songs, he combined into a popular entertainment called *Irish Nights*. *See* lives by W. B. Bernard, 1874, and A. J. Symington, 1880.

Low, Archibald Montgomery (1888–1956), physicist, educ. at St Paul's School; Skerry's College, Glasgow; and the Imperial College of Science and Technology, London. He was honorary assistant prof. of physics at the R.A. college, 1919–22. His numerous inventions include a system of radio signalling, a television system (1914), electrical rocket control (1917), a coal fuel engine, radio torpedo control gear, vibrometer and audiometer. President of the British Institute of Engineering Technology and of the Institute of Patentees; his numerous scientific pubs. include over 50 works on inventions and experimentation.

Low, Sir David (1891–1963), caricaturist, *b.* Dunedin, New Zealand. He worked for various New Zealand papers till 1911, when he joined the staff of *Bulletin*, Sydney, New S. Wales. He came to London, 1919, at the invitation of the *Star*, on the suggestion, it is said, of the late Arnold Bennett, and became as celebrated for his portraits of Lloyd George as was Sir F. C. Gould for his pictures of Joseph Chamberlain. He left the *Star* for the *Evening Standard* in 1927, and moved to the *Daily Herald* in 1950; in 1953 he became political cartoonist of the *Manchester Guardian*, now the *Guardian*, where he remained until his death. L.'s work is remarkably free from the conventional devices of the professional cartoonist, and in drawings of celebrities in various walks of life, appearing in the *New Statesman*, showed a great gift for genially humorous portraiture. His most noted stock character, Col. Blimp, pungently satirised a type. His appeals to national sentiment were founded on an understanding of the prin. political figures of 1932–45, from Churchill, Baldwin and Chamberlain to Mussolini, Hitler and Goering, who were portrayed with rare genius. He was knighted in 1962. He pub. collections of his cartoons, including *The New Rake's Progress*, 1934, *Years of Wrath*, 1949, and *The Fearful Fifties*, 1960. See also *Ye Madde Designer*, 1935.

Low, Sir Sidney James Mark (1857–1932), historical writer and journalist, *b.* Blackheath and educ. at King's College School and Balliol College, Oxford. Editor of *St James's Gazette*, 1888–97, he was called to the Bar, Inner Temple, 1892. Subsequently L. became a lecturer on imperial and colonial hist. at King's College, London. Pubs. include *The Governance of England*, 1904 (revised 1914), *Political History of the Reign of Queen Victoria*, 1907, *De Quincey*, 1911, *Egypt in Transition*, 1914, *The British Constitution*, 1928, and *Indian States and Princes*, 1929. He was knighted in 1918.

Low Church, *see* EVANGELICAL.

Low Countries, region of NW. Europe, comprising Belgium, the Netherlands and the grand duchy of Luxembourg (*see* individual countries).

Low Latin, properly the Latin of the Middle Ages, but more often used in a general sense for the Latin spoken and written after the fall of the Rom. Empire. Great changes in the form of the language had begun even in Cicero's day, and in the course of time the different divs. of the empire formed distinct varieties, greatly influenced by Gallic and Germanic tongues, which finally developed into the modern Romance languages (q.v.).

Low Sunday, first Sunday after Easter, so called because it ends the octave of the Easter festival, some parts of the solemnity of which great feast were repeated on this day, thus celebrating it as a festival itself, though of a lesser order than that of Easter-tide. Probably 'Low' is a medieval corruption of 'Laudes', the first words of the sequence of the day in the rites of Sarum and Hereford being 'Laudes Salvatori', thus naturally 'Laudes Sunday', corrupted into 'L. S.' It is also known as *Quasimodo* (q.v.) and *Antipasch*.

Lowe, Sir Hudson (1769–1844), general, *b.* Galway. He entered the army in 1787, and in 1793, after the outbreak of the war with France, saw active service in Corsica, Gibraltar, Minorca and Egypt. In 1812 he returned to England, and 3 years later was appointed custodian of Napoleon and governor of St Helena, a post which he retained till Napoleon's death in 1821. From 1825 to 1830 he commanded the forces in Ceylon. *See* W. Forsyth, *History of the Captivity of Napoleon at St Helena*, 1853; Lord Rosebery, *Napoleon, the Last Phase*, 1900; R. C. Seaton, *Napoleon's Captivity in Relation to Sir Hudson Lowe*, 1903; Dormer Creston, *In Search of Two Characters*, 1945.

Lowe, Peter (?1550–1612), surgeon, was *b.* in Scotland but studied in France and practised there and in Flanders for many years, gaining a considerable knowledge of surgery. In 1596 he pub. *A Discourse of the Whole Art of Chyrurgerie*, one of the best works of the period on this subject. About 1598 he returned to Scotland and practised in Glasgow. As a result of a report by L. to the Privy Council on quacks, he was appointed to examine those wishing to practise surgery. He founded the Faculty of Physicians and Surgeons of Glasgow in 1599. *See* J. Finlayson, *Life and Works of Maister Peter Lowe*, 1889.

Lowe, Robert, *see* SHERBROOKE.

Lowell, Abbott Lawrence (1857–1943), Amer. historian, *b.* Boston, a brother of Amy L. (q.v.). He was educ. at Harvard and in Germany. From 1880 to 1897 he practised as a barrister. In 1896 his *Government and Parties in Continental Europe* attracted wide notice. In 1897 he was appointed lecturer, and in 1900 prof. of the science of gov., at Harvard; in 1909 he became president. He had an enormous influence on educational methods at Harvard. Other pubs. include *The Government of England*, 1908, *Public Opinion and Popular Government*, 1913, and *What a College President has Learned*, 1938.

Lowell, Amy (1874–1925), Amer. poetess and critic, *b.* Brookline, Massachusetts. Collateral descendant of James Russell L. (q.v.), she studied in private schools and then travelled abroad. An intense student of Fr. poetry, after 1902 she devoted herself almost continuously to the writing of verse. She was the real leader of the Imagist school of poetry, and was one of those who fought in America the battle for free verse. Her best book of poetry is probably *Sword Blades and Poppy Seeds*, which appeared in 1914. She also wrote an illuminating series of essays on some of the Fr. poets, illustrated by her own versions of their verse, a book on the life and work of John Keats, 1925, and *Tendencies in Modern American Poetry*, 1917. Her *Selected Poems*, ed. J. L. Lowes, was pub. in 1928. *See* S. F. Damon, *Amy Lowell; a Chronicle, with Extracts from her Correspondence*, 1935.

Lowell, James Russell (1819–91), Amer. poet, essayist and diplomat, *b.* Cambridge, Massachusetts. He was admitted to the Bar, but took little interest in his profession, and frequently contributed poems and prose articles to various magazines. He was attracted to the steady pursuit of literature largely through the influence of Maria White, a poetess of delicate power, to whom he became betrothed in 1840. The outcome of this was a vol. of poems entitled *A Year's Life*. Three years later he pub. a collection of his poems and *Conversations on some of the Old Poets*. He married in 1844, and went to Philadelphia for a time, where he became editor of the *Pennsylvania Freeman*, a fortnightly jour. devoted to the anti-slavery cause. In 1848 he pub. a further ed. of his poems with some new ones added, including 'To the Dandelion', 'The Changeling', 'A Fable for Critics', 'The Vision of Sir Launfal', a romantic story suggested by the Arthurian legends and one of his best-known poems, and 'The Biglow Papers', a reprint of dialect poems furnished to the newspapers of the day, satires of an effective nature, which attracted a great deal of attention.

In 1851 L. sailed for Europe with his wife, whose health was failing, and spent a year, chiefly in Italy, in study and travel. Mrs L. *d.* in 1853. Two years later L. became prof. of modern languages and literature at Harvard in succession to Longfellow, and spent a couple of years in Europe to prepare himself more fully. In 1857 he married Frances Dunlap. From this time till 1862 he was editor of the *Atlantic Monthly*. He was Amer. minister in London from 1880 to 1885. His essays are marked by great literary refinement. *Fireside Travels, My Study Windows* and *Among My Books* all have descriptive and critical articles of permanent value and charm. *Latest Literary Essays* appeared in 1892. *See* lives by H. E. Scudder, 1901; F. Greenslet, 1905; L. S. Livingstone (with bibliography), 1914; R. C. Beatty, 1942. *See also* W. H. Hudson, *Lowell and his Poetry*, 1912; J. J. Reilly, *Lowell as a Critic*, 1915; *New Letters*, ed. M. A. de W. Howe, 1934.

Lowell, Percival (1855–1916), Amer. astronomer, *b.* Boston, Massachusetts. Graduating at Harvard he lived for some time in Japan; in 1902 was appointed non-resident prof. of astronomy at the Massachusetts Institute of Technology. He wrote sev. popular books and encouraged amateur astronomers. His chief interest was observation of the planets, especially Mars, and for this purpose he founded an observatory at Flagstaff, Arizona, at a height of 7000 ft. Important spectroscopic investigations of the planets were made at the L. Observatory. L. advocated the now discredited theory that the faint markings of Mars are artificial 'canals'. He initiated the search programme that led to the discovery of Pluto in 1930.

Lowell, Robert (1917–), Amer. poet, *b.* Boston, great-grandson of James Russell L. (q.v.). Educ. at Kenyon College, Louisiana State Univ. and Harvard, he was converted to Rom. Catholicism. In 1947–8 he was consultant in poetry to the Library of Congress and at the same time was awarded the Pulitzer Prize for poetry. Vols. of his verse are *Land of Unlikeness*, 1944, *Lord Weary's Castle*, 1946, and *The Mills of Kavanaughs*, 1952. His sombre but powerful work has been said to mark him as one of the leading Amer. poets of his time. *See* H. B. Staples, *Robert Lowell; The First Twenty Years*, 1962.

Lowell, city of Massachusetts, U.S.A., on the Merrimack R., 24 m. NNW. of Boston. The riv. falls afford great hydraulic power. There are a number of cotton and woollen factories and manufs. of leather, paper and iron goods. It has large machine shops, munition factories and carpet factories. The chief institutions are a public library, L. textile school and a state teachers' college. Pop. 97,250.

Löwen, *see* LOUVAIN.

Lowenheld, *see* LEOVIGILD.

Lowenstjern, Johann Kunkel von, *see* KUNKEL.

Lower, Richard (1631–91), physician, *b* Bodmin, Cornwall. He was educ. at Oxford Univ., where he became assistant to Thomas Willis (q.v.). In 1665 he transfused blood from one animal to another, one of the earliest of such experiments; 2 years later he performed the first successful transfusion on a man in England. In 1666 he qualified in medicine and soon afterwards moved to London, where he built up a large practice. He became a distinguished fellow of the Royal Society. His *Tractatus de Corde*, one of the classics of medicine, appeared in 1669. It contained a full and accurate description of the anatomy and physiology of the heart and of the blood flow. L. became involved in politics and eventually lost much of his practice and reputation. *See* F. Gotch, *Two Oxford Physiologists*, 1908.

Lower Austria, *see* AUSTRIA, LOWER.

Lower Hutt, city of N. Is., New Zealand. It is situated in Hutt valley, 9 m. NE. of the cap. city of Wellington. There is a fine civic centre. Pop. 54,900.

Lower Merion, town in Montgomery co., Pennsylvania, U.S.A., and a suburb of Philadelphia. Pop. 59,420.

Lower Saxony (Ger. **Niedersachsen**), *Land* of NW. Germany, in the Federal Rep., bounded on the N. by the N. Sea and Schleswig-Holstein, on the E. by the dists of Halle and Magdeburg (in the Ger. Democratic Rep.); on the S. by Hessen and N. Rhine-Westphalia; and on the W. by The Netherlands. It comprises the former Prussian prov. of Hanover, and the former *Länder* of Brunswick, Oldenburg and Schaumburg-Lippe. The *Land* of Bremen forms 2 enclaves in L.S., and the *Land* of Hamburg forms an enclave on the border between L. S. and Schleswig-Holstein. The *Land* lies mainly in the sandy N. Ger. plain, and includes Lüneburg Heath. In the SE. are the Harz Mts. There are 8 areas, 76 urb.

and rural dists, and 4267 coms. There is a univ. at Göttingen. The pop. is mainly Protestant. Agriculture is the chief occupation. Cap. Hanover. Area 18,262 sq. m.; pop. 6,642,000. *See* SAXONY.

Lowes, John Livingston (1867–1945), Amer. scholar, *b.* Decatur, Indiana. Educ. at Leipzig and Berlin univs. and Harvard, he was prof. of English successively at Swarthmore, Washington univ. and Harvard. His best-known works are *Convention and Revolt in Poetry*, 1919, *The Road to Xanadu*, 1927, *Of Reading Books and Other Essays*, 1930, and *The Art of Geoffrey Chaucer*, 1931.

Lowestoft, seaport and municipal bor. of Suffolk, England, 113 m. NE. of London. The harbour was formed by linking Lake Lothing, now known as the Inner Harbour, with the sea in 1831. The construction of the Trawl Basin in 1846, the Waveney Basin in 1883 and the Hamilton Dock in 1906 greatly extended the quay space for trawl and herring fishing. Mutford Lock at the W. end of the Inner Harbour gives access to Oulton Broad and the 200 m. of inland waterways of Suffolk and Norfolk. The name L. appears in Domesday Book as *Lothu Wistoft*, from Hloover's Toft, a dwelling belonging to Hloover (an Old Norse name).

The older part of L. is built on the cliff overlooking the sea, the later development after the opening of the railway in 1847 being further S. where are to be found 2 piers, hotels and holiday amenities. Large coast protection schemes have been carried out to the N. and S. of the harbour and provide fine esplanades. As a fishing port L. is the fifth largest in the country, and is specially noted for prime sole, cod, turbot and plaice, and in the autumn season for herring. As a holiday resort L. is famous for its bracing air, which is particularly suitable for convalescents. In the First World War the tn was bombarded by Ger. warships, 25 April 1916, and it suffered severely during the Second World War from 'hit and run' raids. Its role as a large naval base and the H.Q. of the minesweeping service is marked by the Royal Naval Patrol Service Memorial in Belle Vue Park, unveiled on 7 Oct. 1953.

The tn has good modern schools, a recently opened College of Further Education, a large general hospital and a variety of industrial undertakings, including shipbuilding, canning, engineering, coachbuilding, television, radar and electrical products and activities ancillary to the fishing industry. L. china was made here from 1757 to 1802. Kirkley was incorporated in L. in 1854 and Oulton Broad in 1921. Pop. 48,140.

Lowestoft (Suffolk), 1757–1802, small factory producing soft-paste porcelain (q.v.) with a bone ash content.

Loweswater, lake of Cumberland, England, 1 m. long, ¼ m. broad, 429 ft above sea level and 60 ft deep, with trout, pike and perch. The vil. of the same name is on the Park Beck, which drains the lake into Crummock Water. St Ringan's

(Ninian's) Well is in Fang's Brow. The lake is owned by the National Trust.

Lowlands of Scotland, *see* SCOTLAND.

Lowndes, Marie, *see* BELLOC LOWNDES.

Lowndes, William Thomas (1789–1843), Eng. bookseller and bibliographer. Compiled *The Bibliographer's Manual of English Literature*, 2nd ed., 1857–64, and *The British Librarian*, 1839, the former's unfinished supplement. The *Manual* was the first systematic work of its kind.

Lowth, Robert (1710–87), theologian and orientalist, *b.* Winchester and educ. there and at Oxford. In 1741 he became prof. of poetry at Oxford and in 1750 was appointed to the archdeaconry of Winchester. He pub. his *Life of William Wykeham* in 1758 and *A Short Introduction to English Grammar* in 1762. He was consecrated Bishop of St Davids in 1766, soon afterwards being transferred to Oxford, and in 1777 becoming Bishop of London. L. was one of the first to treat the Bible poetry as literature, and in 1778 wrote a new trans. of Isaiah. *See* memoir by W. Bent, 1787.

Loxa, *see* LOJA.

Loxia, *see* CROSSBILL.

Loxodromic Curve, *see* GREAT CIRCLE; MAPS.

Loyal Regiment (North Lancashire), The, formerly 47th and 81st Regiments, linked in 1881 to form the present regiment. The 47th was raised in 1740, and its first service was in Scotland in the 1745 rebellion. It then took part in Wolfe's campaign against Quebec, and later served in America under Gen. Burgoyne. In 1782 it received the title 'The Lancashire Regiment'. In 1813 it joined Wellington's army in the Peninsula, later serving in the Burmese war (1825–6) and the Crimea. The 81st was raised in 1793 as the Loyal Lincoln Volunteers. It served in the 1800 Kaffir war, then at Maida (1806). A battalion was with Moore during the retreat to Corunna, and with Wellington in the Peninsula and at Waterloo. It was in India and Afghanistan in 1878–9. During the First World War it raised 21 battalions, which served in France, Flanders, Macedonia, Gallipoli, Egypt, Palestine, Mesopotamia and E. Africa. In the Second World War the Loyals fought in NW. Europe, N. Africa, Italy and Malaya.

Loyalists, or **Tories,** name applied to those who remained loyal to the Brit. Gov. at the time of the revolutionary war in America. Many migrated to Canada after the U.S.A. had secured independence, and originally formed the greater part of the pop. of Ontario and New Brunswick, which they founded. *See* C. Van Tyne, *The Loyalists in the American Revolution*, 1929.

Loyalty Islands, group of is. in the SW. Pacific, 60 m. E. of New Caledonia, consisting of Lifu, Maré and Urea and sev. smaller is., having a total area of about 800 sq. m. They are an administrative dependency of New Caledonia. The chief export is copra. The climate is healthy. Pop. about 12,000.

Loyang, city in Honan, China, situated on the Lo R., a trib. of the Yellow R. Under the E. Chou, Later Han, N. Wei and other dynasties it was the cap. of China for nearly 8 cents. Strategically important, the city has been ruined sev. times during civil wars. The famous Lungmen Gorge of the Yellow R., with thousands of Buddhist statues, is 7 m. N. of the city. L.'s power station and tractor plant were built in 1955 and the city in now regaining importance. Pop. (1958) 500,000.

Loyola, Ignatius of, St, see IGNATIUS OF LOYOLA.

Loyson, Charles, see HYACINTHE, PÈRE.

Lozère, dept of France, formerly part of the old prov. of Languedoc. It is mountainous and is traversed by the Cévennes and other ranges. On the mt slopes, looking towards the Rhône valley, cattle and sheep are reared, and the olive, vine and mulberry are cultivated. The rearing of silkworms and the manuf. of cheese are important industries. The mineral wealth consists of lead, silver, copper and antimony. Marble, granite and slate are quarried. The prin. tns are Mende (the cap.) and Florac. Area 1996 sq. m.; pop. 82,000.

Lozi, the ruling tribe of Barotseland, in the NW. of Zambia. They provide the rulers of a large cluster of peoples, which are formed into a single polity by the L. kingship. The king has under him a number of chiefs and stewards who are given parts of the total ter. to rule and who form the king's body of councillors. The L. are probably related to the neighbouring peoples of the S. Congo.

See M. Gluckman, *Seven Tribes of British Central Africa*, 1951.

L.P.G. (Liquefied Petroleum Gases), see BUTANE.

Luanda, São Paulo de, seaport on the W. coast of Africa, cap. of the Portuguese colony of Angola, situated between the mouths of the Bango and Kwanga, and protected from the sea by a narrow, sandy is. 18 m. long. It affords good harbourage. Pop. 20,170 whites and 141,013 Africans.

Luang Prabang, cap. of the kingdom of Laos (q.v.), and site of the royal palace, on l. b. of the R. Mekong. Formerly the cap, only of the N. provs. of Laos, it is now the seat of the king. L. P. is situated in a forest of palm trees and surrounded by mts. Pop. 10,000.

Luanshya, tn of Zambia, adjoining Roan Antelope copper-mine, L. is the terminus of a branch line from Ndola, 20 m. Pop. (Europeans) 6500; (Africans) 60,000.

Lubań (Ger. **Lauban**), tn of Poland, in Wrocław prov., on the Kwisa, 75 m. W. of Wrocław. It was in lower Silesia. Pop. 15,500.

Lubao, tn of Luzon, Philippine Is., 9 m. SW. of San Fernando, situated in a sugar-producing dist. Pop. *c.* 37,000.

Lubbock, Sir John, see AVEBURY.

Lübeck, Ger. seaport in the *Land* of Schleswig-Holstein, on the Trave, 15 m. from the Baltic, 38 m. SE. of St. of Kiel. It is joined to the Elbe by canal. The tn was founded in 1143. It became one of the great cities of the Hanseatic League (q.v.), and (with a strip of ter. along the Trave, and some other dists, total area 115 sq.

m.) a free state. In the 14th cent. it had a pop. of 30,000. With the decline of the Hanseatic League the fortunes of L. declined also, although it became known as a centre of the wine trade. After the incorporation of Schleswig-Holstein into Prussia, L. joined the N. Ger. Confederation (q.v.). In 1937 it relinquished its 7-cents.-old status as a free city on becoming part of Schleswig-Holstein. The older part of the city stands on an is. formed by the Trave and its tribs. The is. is served by 8 bridges. From the main street, *Breite Strasse*, streets of beautiful old houses lead to the perimeter of the is.; most of these, and most of the anct public buildings, are built of the brick and tile for which L. is known. The city hall dates from the 13th–15th cent; near it is the splendid 13th cent. *Marienkirche*. There are 2 remarkable medieval gateways: the Burgtor (1444) and the Holstentor (1466–78). L. has a large passenger and commercial trade with Scandinavia and Finland, and has shipyards, iron industries and manufs. of machinery and food-stuffs. Pop. 234,800.

Lüber, Thomas, see ERASTUS (*See Plate; Germany.*)

Lubitsch, Ernst, see CINEMATOGRAPH (HISTORY).

Lübke, Heinrich (1894–), Ger. politician, educ. at the Univs. of Bonn, Berlin and Münster. He was a member of the Prussian *Landtag*, 1931–1933, but was stripped of all offices and imprisoned 1933–5. He entered post-war politics as a member of the Christian Democratic Union, 1946. From 1953–9 he was minister of food and agriculture in the Federal Gov., and became president of the Ger. Federal Rep. in Sept. 1959.

Lublin: 1. Prov. (*województwo*) of SE. Poland, separated on the E. from the U.S.S.R. by the Bug. The Vistula forms part of its W. boundary. It is low-lying and, in places, marshy in the N., but is hilly in the S. Livestock is raised, and cereals, potatoes, flax and hemp are grown. There are phosphate deposits, and there are metal, food-stuff and electrical industries. Area 10,525 sq. m.; pop. 1,843,000.

2. City of Poland, cap. of L. prov., on the Bystrzyca, 105 m. SE. of Warsaw. At a diet held in the city in 1569 Poland and Lithuania were united. In 1795 the city went to Austria, and in 1815 it was included in Russian Poland. There is a 16th cent. cathedral, and a univ. (1918, refounded 1944). Machinery, aircraft and foodstuffs are manuf. Pop. 188,500.

Lubricants and Lubricators. Lubricants are media introduced between moving surfaces to reduce friction between them and to prevent them becoming hot. There are 2 main types of lubrication: hydrodynamic or fluid film lubrication and boundary lubrication. The former is the condition where the surfaces are separated by a relatively thick film of lubricant and the latter where the surfaces are separated by a film of lubricant only a few molecules thick. The co-efficient of friction will, of course, in the second case be higher than that in the case of hydrodynamic lubrication and where boundary conditions exist more or less permanently, special properties will be required of the lubricant in use.

Lubricants may be of the solid, semi-solid or fluid type. The first variety, such as graphite or molybdenum disulphide, act as rollers or skids, and serve to fill the roughness of the surfaces in contact, thus coating them in a soft, slippery material. They are used either dry or as a fluid in the form of a colloid or semi-colloid for bearings working in an extremely high temp., or where boundary conditions are liable to occur for more than momentary periods.

Semi-solid lubricants consist essentially of soap-thickened mineral oils to form greases, the most common soaps being calcium, sodium and lithium. More recently greases have been produced by gelling mineral oil with other materials, the most common of which is bentonite clay. The advantages of these greases are that they do not have a melting point, as do the soap-thickened types and are not affected by most acids, alkalis or water.

The primary object of greases is to keep a lubricant in a bearing, the soap acting in much the same way as a sponge, thus often permitting periods between application of lubricant to be extended; in fact many bearings on small electric motors are packed with grease and sealed for life. Another advantage of greases is that they form a protective seal against the ingress of dirt and moisture. Greases are made in varying consistencies, from semi-fluids to blocks of the consistence of cold butter.

The fluid type of lubricants are used generally where hydrodynamic lubrication can be obtained, so a copious supply of lubricant is required between the surfaces which are moving relative to one another at moderately high speeds. The film between the surfaces, due to the movement between them, depends solely on the viscosity of the type of lubricant. Thus it is possible to lubricate extremely high-speed spindles by means of air or any other gas at high pressure. A lubricant should have a viscosity such that it is low enough for the fluid film to be maintained. Generally speaking, the higher the speed of the moving surfaces, the less viscous or thinner the lubricant required. The lubricant must not, however, be volatile or decompose under heat or congeal with cold. It should have resistance to oxidation by exposure to air or acid, and have no adverse effect on bearing metals, nor must it be easily inflammable, but should be able to carry away heat produced by the inevitable amount of friction. This being the case, mineral oils have numerous advantages over other fluids, e.g., resistance to chemical change. Mineral oils may also be enhanced or fortified by means of chemical additives, producing improved resistance to oxidation, foam suppression, improved load-carrying capabilities, lower pour points, corrosion prevention, detergency, etc.

A typical example of fluid lubrication may be obtained from a simple journal bearing. When the shaft is at rest it is only separated from the bearing surface by a molecule or so of oil. As soon as the rotation of the shaft commences, it immediately starts to drag oil down between itself and the bearing wall, with the result that a wedge of high-pressure oil is built up between the shaft and the bearing, thus keeping the 2 surfaces apart. This wedge may be in the order of only a thousandth of an in., but thick when compared with the original boundary conditions at rest with only a molecule or so separating the shaft from the bearing.

Lubricators are mechanical devices for introducing lubricants to the rubbing surfaces, and provide 3 basic lubrication systems: (1) total loss systems; (2) circulating systems and (3) bath and splash systems.

With total loss systems a comparatively small amount of lubricant is delivered either continuously or intermittently to the bearing surfaces, the used oil from these working surfaces eventually running from the bearing to waste and is not recirculated. Fresh lubricant may be applied by a number of ways, using methods ranging from hand application, with oil can or grease gun, to relatively complicated centralised pressure systems. Typical examples of wick or syphon feeds consist essentially of an oil cup with a wick from the cup, up and over the edge, to the bearing. The oil feeds through the wick by capillary action from the cup to the bearing. These are generally found on older types of machinery. Drip feeds consist of an oil cup with an adjustable outlet from which oil issues drop by drop to the bearing. A window or sight glass is provided so that the oil drips may be seen and the flow regulated. These 2 types of lubricators, however, have the disadvantage that they must be turned off and on each time the machine is stopped and started, otherwise oil is wasted. Mechanical lubricators, however, operate only when the machine is running, and deliver a measured amount of lubricant at given intervals by means of pipes to the various lubrication points. These systems are used both for oil and grease. This method is used in large machines with numerous lubrication points, such as marine engines, paper mills, etc.

With circulatory systems a relatively large supply of oil is kept in circulation and is delivered under pressure to the bearings. From a reservoir oil is fed by means of a pump or by gravity to the working surfaces through pipes or passages. From there the lubricant returns to the reservoir by gravity or pump to be circulated again. Typical examples are petrol engines, high-speed diesels and turbines. A most important function of this method of lubrication is as a coolant, and also to remove dirt and extraneous matter from the working surfaces.

Bath or splash systems usually consist of the working surfaces immersed, or partially immersed, in a bath of oil, e.g. a gearbox. The pinions are partially immersed in oil, and during rotation splash lubricant to bearing and other moving parts. Variations of these are journals from which a loosely-hanging ring or chain dips into a bath of oil. As the shaft rotates, so does the ring or chain, which in turn carries the lubricant to the bearing, from whence it returns to the bath.

Lubsko (Ger. **Sommerfeld**), tn of Poland in Zielona Góra prov., 28 m. WSW. of Zielona Góra. It was formerly in Brandenburg, and has a 13th cent. church and a castle. Pop. 11,200.

Luc, Jean André de (1727–1817), geologist and meteorologist, who invented a new form of hygrometer and pub. the first correct rules for measuring heights by the barometer. His *Recherches sur les modifications de l'atmosphère*, 1772, contains many important facts relating to heat and moisture.

Luca, *see* LUCCA.

Luca della Robbia, *see* ROBBIA.

Lucan, *see* LUCANUS, M. ANNAEUS.

Lucan, vil. 9 m. W. of Dublin, Rep. of Ireland, formerly famous for the L. spas. Pop. 2656.

Lucania, anct div. of S. Italy, between the Tyrrhenian Sea and the Gulf of Tarentum, separated from Campania by the R. Silarus (N.) and from Bruttii (q.v.) by the R. Laus (S.). The Lucanians sided with Pyrrhus in 218, but were finally subdued by the Romans in 272 BC. Sybaris, Heraclea, Thurii and Paestum were among the chief cities. Together with Bruttii L. formed the 3rd Augustan *regio* (*see* ITALIA). In modern times the compartiménto of Basilicata (prov. of Potenza and Matera, represents L.

Lucanus, Marcus Annaeus, called in English **Lucan** (AD 39–65), Lat. epic poet, *b.* Corduba, in Spain, a nephew of L. Annaeus Seneca the Stoic philosopher. Brought up at Rome, he was introduced to the court of Nero. There he incurred the jealous hatred of the Emperor, who believed himself a poet without peer; and having joined the conspiracy of Piso, he was obliged to commit suicide. L. is the author of *Bellum Civile*, afterwards known as *Pharsalia*. Its 10 books (the last incomplete) deal with the civil war, 49–48 BC. *See* text ed. by A. E. Housman, 1926; trans. by Robert Graves, new ed., 1961.

Lucaris, Cyril (*c.* 1572–1638), theologian, *b.* Crete. He became a priest and studied at Venice, Padua and Geneva, where he conceived a strong liking for Calvinism. He became patriarch of Alexandria (1602) and of Constantinople (1621), and attempted to Calvinise the Orthodox Church, sending young theologians to study in Europe and to Oxford. Deposed no less than 6 times, through the intrigues of his Orthodox opponents and of his bitter enemies the Jesuits and by the venal interventions of the sultan, in 1637 he was recalled from exile in Rhodes and restored for the last time. In 1638 he was arrested, and was strangled by the sultan's Janissaries when supposedly on his way to an is. prison. His body was thrown into the harbour. His *Confession*, a conflation of Orthodoxy and Calvinism, was pub. in 1629. It was he who gave Britain the *Codex Alexandrinus*, now in the Brit. Museum. *See* J. Aymon, *Lettres anecdotiques de Cyrille Lucar*, 1718; G. Hofmann's study of C. L., 1929; C. Emereau, 'Cyrille Lucar', in *Dictionnaire de Théologie Catholique*, ed. by A. Vacant and E. Mangenot, 1926–50.

Lucarne (Fr.), a dormer window (q.v.).

Lucas, Edward Verrall (1868–1938), author and editor, *b.* Eltham, Kent. In 1902 he joined the staff of *Punch*, and achieved success with skits written in collaboration with C. L. Graves. He also wrote many travel books, and became chairman of the publishing house of Methuen. His other works include a biography of Lamb, 1905, and *The Letters of Charles Lamb*, 1935, *A Book of Verses for Children*, 1897, *The Open Road*, 1899, *Highways and Byways in Sussex*, 1904, *A Wanderer in Holland*, 1905, *Fireside and Sunshine*, 1906, *Listener's Lure*, 1906, *A Wanderer in Florence*, 1912, and *Vermeer the Magical*, 1929. His memoirs, *Reading, Writing, and Remembering*, appeared in 1932, in which year he was made a companion of honour.

Lucas, Frank Laurence (1894–), scholar and poet, *b.* Hipperholme, Yorks. Educ. at Rugby and Cambridge, he was in 1920 elected a fellow of King's College, and later became reader in English. His critical works include *Seneca and Elizabethan Tragedy*, 1922, *Euripides and his Influence*, 1923, *Authors Dead and Living*, 1926, *Eight Victorian Poets*, 1930, *Studies French and English*, 1934, *The Decline and Fall of the Romantic Ideal*, 1936, *The Greatest Problem*, 1960. He also pub. many trans. from the Greek including the popular selections *Greek Poetry for Everyman*, 1951, and *Greek Drama for Everyman*, 1954. His original works include the books of verse *Time and Memory*, 1929, *Marionettes*, 1930, and *Ariadne*, 1932; the plays *The Bear Dances*, 1932, and *Land's End*, 1938; and sev. novels. In 1946 he was awarded the O.B.E.

Lucas van Leyden (*c.* 1489–1533), Dutch painter, *b.* Leyden. He studied under Cornelis Egelbrechtz, and was a celebrated engraver early in life. In 1514 he settled in Antwerp, and was elected a member of the guild of St Luke. He painted many religious subjects and is eminent as an engraver for his skill in grouping figures. *See* studies by R. Kahn, 1918, and L. Baldass, 1923; F. W. H. Hollstein, *Graphic Art of Lucas van Leyden*, 1954.

Lucayos Islands, *see* BAHAMAS.

Lucca: 1. Prov. of Italy, in NE. Tuscany (q.v.). It borders on the Ligurian Sea, and is generally mountainous but has a broad plain in the S. The mts in the N. are bisected by the valley of the Serchio. Silk, oil, wine and chestnuts are produced. The prin. tns include L., Bagni di L., and Viareggio. Area 694 sq. m.; pop. 370,000.

2. (anct **Luca**) It tn, cap of the prov. of L., on the Serchio, 36 m. WNW. of Florence. It is first mentioned in 218 BC. In 177 BC the Romans colonised it, and it was a municipium by 90 BC. In 53 BC it was the scene of a conference between Julius Caesar, Crassus and Pompey, at which Caesar's command in Gaul was prolonged for 5 years. Napoleon made it into a principality for his sister, Marianne Élise (*see* BONAPARTE). L. has a magnificent 11th–15th cent. cathedral. There are also fine palaces and 16th–17th cent. ramparts, now converted into a promenade. The Rom. remains in the tn include an amphitheatre.

There is a trade in silk, oil, fruit, wines and tobacco. Pop. 86,000. See J. Ross and N. Erichson, The Story of Lucca, 1912; E. Lazzareschi, Lucca, 1931.

Luce, Clare Boothe (1903–), Amer. playwright and journalist, b. New York city. She married Henry L. (q.v.) in 1935. In 1930 she joined the staff of Vogue, and from 1931 to 1934 was on that of Vanity Fair. She was a member of the U.S. House of Representatives from 1943 to 1947. Her plays The Woman, 1937, and Kiss the Boys Good-bye, 1938, are maliciously witty satires on the foibles and deceptions of women. Stuffed Shirts, 1933, Margin for Error, 1939, and Europe in the Spring, 1940, are among her other pubs., the last-named being a description of the Ger. invasion of France and the Low Countries in 1940. She has also written articles on travel. She was U.S. ambas. to Italy from Feb. 1953 to Nov. 1956, when she resigned for health reasons.

Luce, Henry Robinson (1898–), American publisher and editor, b. Shantung, China. A graduate of Yale Univ., he studied at Oxford. On his return from England he and some Yale friends, in 1923, founded and pub. Time, the great success of which magazine encouraged the foundation in 1930 of Fortune, which 'sold' the romance and glamour of Amer. business far more effectively than the conventional and uncritical business magazines had done. In 1936 L. bought the title of the derelict comic periodical, Life (q.v.), and estab. a new and lavish pictorial weekly, which was as successful as his previous ventures. In recent years L.'s pubs. have been notable for their right-wing Republicanism. See D. Brogan, U.S.A., 1941.

Luce Bay, inlet of the Irish Sea, extending 20 m. into Wigtownshire, Scotland, some 19 m. wide at its mouth. At its head is the vil. of Glenluce.

Lucena, Sp. tn in the prov. of Cordoba. It has textile manufs., and is well known for its wine and horses. Pop. 19,400.

Lucense, see LUGO.

Lucentum, see ALICANTE.

Lucera, Duke of, see GALLAS, M. VON.

Lucera, It. tn in Apulia, 11 m. WNW. of Foggia. It has a 14th cent. cathedral, a ruined 13th cent. castle and a fine episcopal palace. Pop. 24,800.

Lucerne, see LUZERN.

Lucerne, see ALFALFA.

Luchu Islands, see RYUKYU ISLANDS.

Lucian (c, AD 125–after 180), Gk writer. After practising for some time as an advocate at Antioch he set up as a sophistic rhetorician and travelled in Asia Minor, Greece, Italy and Gaul. About 165 he settled at Athens, where he remained for some 20 years before accepting an official post in Egypt. The 65 genuine works of L. include rhetorical declamations, literary criticism, biography, romance and satirical dialogues. Among the most interesting or entertaining (for L. was one of the world's greatest wits) are Dialogues of the Gods, Dialogues of the Dead, Zeus Confounded, Zeus Tragedian, Sale of Lives, The Incredulous,

Symposium, Charon, Menippus, Demonax, Twice Accused, The Fisherman and Timon. His True History inspired Rabelais's Voyage of Pantagruel, Swift's Gulliver's Travels and Cyrano de Bergerac's Journey to the Moon. The best ed. of L.'s works is that by C. Jacobitz. 1905. There is a text with trans. by K. Kilburn in the Loeb Library. See M. Caster, Lucien et la pensée religieuse dans son temps, 1938.

Lucian, St (c. AD. 240–312), martyr, b. Samosata. A priest of Antioch and a celebrated biblical scholar, he prepared a revised ed. of the Septuagint from the Hebrew. L. was tortured to death by order of the emperor Maximinus.

Lucientes, Goya y, Francisco José de, see GOYA Y LUCIENTES.

Lucifer: 'Light-bearer', Lat. trans. of Gk phosphoros: 1. In Gk mythology, the morning star (Venus), son of Astraeus, or Cephalus, by Eos (Dawn), and brother of Hesperus, the evening star, whose identity with the other was unknown to the early poets.
2. In the A. V. of Isaiah the word is used with reference to the glory of the King of Babylon, but the Church fathers attached the name to Satan, thinking that the passage, 'How art thou fallen from heaven, O Lucifer, son of the morning', contained a reference to the Prince of Darkness, no doubt connecting this (perhaps rightly) with Luke x. 18. Thus the word L. has come to be used to denote the fallen archangel. See A. Müller, Die Gestalt Lucifers in der Dichtung vom Barock bis zur Romantik, 1940. See also DEVIL.

Lucilius, Gaius (c. 180–c. 102 BC), Rom. satirist, b. Suessa Aurunca, Campania. He was the first to mould Rom. satire into the form later developed by Horace, Persius and Juvenal (qq.v.) L. was a personal friend of Scipio, whom he accompanied on the expedition against Numantia. He wrote 30 books of miscellaneous verse (saturae), but only 1300 lines remain. See C. Lucilii Carminum Reliquiae, ed. F. Marx (2 vols.), 1904–5; G. C. Fiske, Lucilius and Horace, 1920; J. Wight Duff, Roman Satire, 1936.

Lucina, Rom. goddess of light, corresponding to the Gk Ilithyia. When invoked by women in labour she brought children to light. L. was a surname of both Juno and Diana, who presided over childbirth.

Luck, see LUTSK.

Lucknow, city of India, cap. of Uttar Pradesh state, pop. 595,000. The city stands on the r. b. of the Gumti, 43 m. NE. of Cawnpore by rail. L. probably dates back to the 13th cent. and became a centre of importance in the 16th cent. As it is today, it mainly represents the Nawabs of Oudh (1732–1847), who erected the outstanding buildings. The most notable buildings are the Imambara, the mausoleum of Asaf-un-Daulá, the palaces of Chhattar Manzil, the Residency and the Lawrence Memorial. It is of especial interest to Englishmen for the historic defence of the Residency during the Indian Mutiny (May–Nov. 1857). The Canning College, founded in 1864, the univ. (1920) and La Martinière College for soldiers' sons are the prin. educational estabs. *See* J. J. McLeod Innes, *Lucknow and Oude in the Mutiny*, 1895.

Luçon, Fr. tn in the dept of Vendée, connected to the sea by the 8-m.-long L. canal. It is the seat of a bishopric once held by Richelieu, and has a cathedral, partly 13th cent. There are small metal industries, and liqueurs and clogs are manuf. Pop. 7600.

Lucretia, in Rom. legend, wife of L. Tarquinius Collatinus (q.v.).

Lucretius Carus, Titus (*c*. 99–55 BC), Rom. poet, about whose life authentic information is entirely lacking. His *De Rerum Natura* is a didactic poem in 6 books on Epicurean philosophy, and is addressed to C. Memmius Gemellus, who was praetor in 58 BC. The chief aim of the poem is to free men from superstition, to accustom them to the idea of complete annihilation at death and to rid them of the idea of divine interference in human affairs. Gods there are, beings a little higher than mortals, but to them too death and corruption come, bringing total eclipse; of mortal concerns they live in supreme contempt. Throughout the universe the atom alone is eternal and incorruptible. These theories are expounded by L. with a passionate eloquence, fervour and power that are quite unparalleled in Lat. literature. The definitive ed. (with trans., commentary, *apparatus criticus* and prolegomena) is that of C. Bailey (3 vols.), 1947. *See* E. E. Sikes, *Lucretius*, 1936.

Lucronius, *see* LOGRONO.

Lucullus, Lucius Licinius (*c*. 110–57 BC), Rom. general. As consul in 74 he was given command of the third Mithradatic war (*see* MITHRADATES) and remained in Asia for 9 years. During the campaigns of 74–72 he relieved Cotta, who had been besieged in Chalcedon, destroyed the enemy's fleet off Lemnos, entered Bithynia and forced Mithradates to take refuge at the court of his father-in-law, Tigranes, King of Armenia. L. pursued him across the Euphrates, and took Tigranocerta, cap. of Armenia. In 66 he was superseded by Pompey. On his return to Rome L. retired from public life and became notorious as a *bon viveur*. He had a famous villa on the promontory of Misenum, which afterwards became the property of Tiberius. He wrote a hist. of the Marsian war in Greek, and is said to have been the first to introduce cherries into Italy, which he had brought from Cerasus (q.v.) in Pontus.

Lucus Augusti, *see* LUGO.

Lucy, St (281–304), virgin and martyr, *b*. and *d*. at Syracuse. She was betrothed to a rich pagan who, irritated at her refusal to marry him, denounced her as a Christian to Paschasius, the governor, who beheaded her. She is the patron of the blind, and her feast is 13 Dec.

Lucy, Sir Henry William (1845–1924), journalist, *b*. Crosby, near Liverpool. In 1873 he became parl. writer for the *Daily News*, of which he was editor in 1886–7. In 1811 he succeeded Shirley Brooks on *Punch* as the writer of 'The Essence of Parliament', for which he created the characters of 'Toby, M.P.' and the 'Member for

Sark'. He wrote *Men and Manners in Parliament*, 1875, *Faces and Places*, 1895, *Mr Gladstone: a Study from Life*, 1896, *Memories of Eight Parliaments*, 1908, *Sixty Years in the Wilderness*, 1909 (second series, 1912), *Nearing Jordan*, 1916, *The Diary of a Journalist*, 1920–3, and *Lords and Commoners*, 1921. He was knighted in 1909.

Ludd, or **Nudd**, deity of the Brit. Celts confused later with a legendary Brit. king of the same name. Tradition says that his temple stood on Ludgate Hill, London, and that he was worshipped chiefly at Lydney, Glos., where another temple of his has been found with inscriptions naming him. His Irish equivalent is Nuada Argetlam (L. of the Silver Hand).

Luddite Rioters, or **Luddites**, organised bands of workmen who gave voice to the popular distress caused by the introduction of industrial machinery and the consequent scarcity in the demand for manual labour. From 1811 to 1812 the Luddites destroyed stocking frames, steam power looms and shearing machines throughout Notts., Derbyshire, Leics. and Yorks., and their rioting broke out again in 1816. They derived their name from Ned Ludd, a Leicestershire imbecile, who, it is said, unable to catch someone who had been tormenting him, destroyed some stocking frames in a fit of temper (1779). Charlotte Brontë's *Shirley* includes an account of the attack on Rawfolds Mill at Liversedge.

Ludendorff, Erich von (1865–1938), Ger. soldier, *b*. Kruszewina, near Posen, entered the Cadet Corps in 1877 and the 57th Infantry Regiment in 1882; he gained rapid promotion, and at the beginning of the First World War was a brigade commander at Strasburg. He joined von Emmich's staff for the siege of Liège. In these operations he showed much initiative in organising and leading a Ger. brigade which penetrated the outer line of forts, for which service he received the order *Pour le Mérite*. On 22 Aug. 1914 he was appointed chief of staff of the Eighth Army in E. Prussia, the command of which was given to von Hindenburg (q.v.). Here L. was instrumental in winning one of the most brilliant battles in the hist. of warfare (*see* TANNENBERG, BATTLE OF). Following this he was appointed chief of staff to the S. army in E. Prussia, but shortly afterwards went farther S. to work in conjunction with the Austro-Hungarian Army in its operations against Przemysl (q.v.).

On 29 Aug. 1916 L. was appointed 'first quartermaster-general' to von Hindenburg and was largely responsible for the subsequent military action of the Central Powers during the war. He staked practically his last throw on victory in Mar. 1918, when peace with Bolshevik Russia enabled him to withdraw vast numbers of trained troops from the E. front and put them into action in the W. before the Americans could give the Allies anything approaching numerical superiority. When the Brit. and Fr. troops withstood his onslaughts he lost heart and insisted that an armistice should be sought.

He resigned his post on 26 Oct. 1918, and fled

in disguise to Sweden. Later he returned to Germany, settling in Munich. He played an inglorious part in one of the 'putsches', whose object was to overthrow the Ger. rep., but after the success of the Nazi revolution emerged again, and gained prominence for his violently nationalist and anti-Christian utterances. Later he became an extreme pacifist and withdrew his support from Hitler. L.'s *War Memoirs* were pub. in 1919, and he also wrote *The General Staff and its Problems*, 1920, and *Warfare and Politics*, 1922.

Lüdenscheid, Ger. tn in the *Land* of N. Rhine-Westphalia, 36 m. E. of Düsseldorf. It once belonged to the Hanseatic League (q.v.), and its iron industries date from the Middle Ages. Pop. 58,300.

Lüderitz (SW. Africa), *see* ANGRA PEQUEÑA. L. is a small port and a few m. away Bartholomew Dias made his first landing in southern Africa. He planted a stone cross near L. to record the event. The original cross was destroyed but a replica has been erected at the same spot. In the First World War, L. Bay was occupied by S. African forces in Sept. 1914. *see* AFRICA, SOUTH-WEST, *First World War Campaign.*

Ludger, St (*d.* 809), Frisian by birth, educ. under Gregory of Utrecht and Alcuin at York. He became a missionary in Westphalia, and played a great part in converting the Saxons to Christianity. He founded Münster and was its first bishop.

Ludhiana, tn of E. Punjab state, India, 73 m. SE. of Amritsar. It is a famous market for grain, and a centre for hosiery and silk goods. There was much important fighting at L. and to the W. during the first Sikh war.

Ludi Megalenses, Rom. games in honour of the Great Mother of the Gods (q.v.), instituted 204 BC. From 191 BC they were celebrated annually on 5 April, but from the reign of Claudius (AD 41–54) they lasted from 4 to 10 April.

Ludlow, Edmund (*c.* 1617–92), parliamentarian and regicide, *b.* Maiden Bradley, Wilts, and educ. at Trinity College, Oxford. On the outbreak of the Civil war he joined Essex and fought at Worcester and Edgehill (1642). He was elected to Parliament in 1646 and was one of the promoters of Pride's Purge (1648). He signed the death warrant of Charles I (1649). In 1651 L. was sent to Ireland as lieutenant-general of horse, and on the death of Ireton took over the chief command. But when Cromwell was declared Protector he refused to acknowledge his authority, and retired from public affairs until 1659, when he was returned to Parliament as member for Hindon. At the Restoration (1660) he fled to Vevey in Switzerland, where he *d.* His memoirs were pub. in 1698–9, and ed. by C. H. Firth, 1894. They are valuable for their insight into the republican opposition to Cromwell.

Ludlow, Washington L. (?–1916), inventor, in conjunction with W. A. Reade (1867–1930), of the Ludlow system of type-setting (*see* TYPE-CASTING AND TYPE-SETTING MACHINES). The

first L. machine was installed in the office of Chicago's *Evening Post*, 1913. A Brit. company was formed, 1912, by M. J. Slattery.

Ludlow, tn of Salop, England, 28 m. S. of Shrewsbury, at the junction of the Corve and the Teme. It was an old Rom. settlement, and contains a castle of the 11th cent. Here, in 1634, Milton's masque *Comus* was presented before the Earl of Bridgewater. The grammar school was founded in 1282. Industries include manuf. of clothing, light engineering (agric. machinery, electrical instruments and light castings) and there are cabinet works and corn-mills. Pop. 6774. (*See Plate: Fortification*.)

Ludolfus, Job (the Latinised name of **Hiob Leutholf**) (1624–1704), Ger. orientalist, *b.* Erfurt. He studied philology at Erfurt and Leyden, where, and on his travels, he is said to have acquired a knowledge of 25 languages. In 1649 he was sent by the Swedish Court to Rome to examine some documents, and he used this occasion to study Ethiopic with the Abyssinian prelate Gregorius, then in Rome. Later L. persuaded Duke Ernest of Saxony to invite Gregorius to his dominions, and was thus able to collect copious historical and linguistic material. For many years, 1652–78, he served the Duke of Saxe-Gotha and in 1690 was appointed president of the Collegium Imperiale Historicum at Frankfurt. His works include *Historia aethiopica*, 1681, and *Grammatica amharica et lexicon amhariconum*, 1691. He supplied the material for the pub. by his pupil, J. M. Wansleben, of a *Grammatica aethiopica et lexicon aethiopico-latinum*, 1661, followed by the celebrated *Confessio fidei Claudii regis Aethiopae*.

Ludovisi, Alessandro, *see* GREGORY (popes), *Gregory XV.*

Ludwig (Ger. emperors), *see* LOUIS.

Ludwig, Emil (1881–1948), Ger. Author, *b.* Breslau, son of a celebrated prof. of ophthalmology of Jewish race. He was educ. at various Ger. univs. and at Lausanne; he wrote 2 verse dramas at the age of 21. Eloping with Elga Wolff, he went to Locarno, where he wrote a play on Napoleon. During the First World War he was a gov. journalist in various European caps. He made his reputation with a 'psychological' study of Bismarck, his first attempt in that method of biography which was soon to achieve such an enormous vogue. In 1920 he produced his first full-length biography, the 2-vol. work *Goethe: Geschichte eines Menschen*, which was followed in 1924 by *Napoleon*. In 1925 he wrote a drama on Bismarck and his biography, *Bismarck: Geschichte eines Kämpfers*, in 1926, both highly successful. L. was a prolific and facile writer and among his next works were a life of Wilhelm II, 1926 (whose faults of character he attributed to the psychological inheritance of a withered arm); a life of Christ, *Der Menschensohn*, 1928; *Talks with Mussolini*, 1932; *Hindenburg*, 1935; *The Nile in Egypt*, 1937; *Roosevelt*, 1938. L. adopted Swiss nationality in 1932 but went to California, where he lived until 1945. He *d.* in Switzerland. The fashion of romanticising biography, which he so effectively developed, led him, especially in *Der Menschensohn*, to subordinate intellectual power to dramatic interest. His last works, written while living in America and in Switzerland, were *Stalin*, 1942, *The Germans*, 1942, and *Beethoven; Life of a Conqueror*, 1945. *See* critical biography by N. Hansen, 1930.

Ludwig, Karl Friedrich Wilhelm (1816–95), Ger. physiologist, *b*. Witzenhausen, near Kassel. In 1849 he was appointed prof. of anatomy and physiology at Zürich, and of physiology at Vienna (1855–65) and at Leipzig (1865–95). His *Lehrbuch der Physiologie des Menschen* appeared in 1852–6. He was one of the founders of the Leipzig Physiological Institute for original scientific research, and invented sev. instruments used in physiological research.

Ludwig, Otto (1813–65), Ger. novelist and playwright, *b*. Eisfeld in Thuringia. He studied music under Mendelssohn Bartholdy, but later adopted a literary career, and made his first success with a drama, *Der Erbförster*, 1850, followed by *Die Makkabäer*, 1852. His extraordinary power of psychological analysis is seen in his pictures of Thuringian life, *Die Heiterkeit und ihr Widerspiel*, 1851, and *Zwischen Himmel und Erde*, 1855. His *Shakespearestudien*, pub. posthumously by A. Stern, 1891, shows a fine discriminating taste. Unfortunately his créative powers were crippled by illness, and by excessive self-criticism. His *Gesammelte Schriften* were pub. in 1891–2 and in 1900. *See* studies by A. Stern, 1891; E. Tyrhoff, 1931; H. Schönweg, 1941; and the *Otto Ludwig Kalender*, 1929–41.

Ludwigsburg, Ger, tn in the *Land* of Baden-Württemberg, 8 m. N. of Stuttgart. It was formerly the second royal residence of Württemberg, and is a tn with fine parks and avenues. There are 3 castles, one of which, the former *Residenzschloss* (1704–33), is an enormous baroque structure containing some 450 rooms in 18 buildings. The prin. manufs. are textiles, machinery and toys. Pop. 73,500.

Ludwigshafen, Ger. industrial tn in the *Land* of Rhineland-Palatinate, 37 m. S. by E. of Mainz. It is on the l. b. of the Rhine, opposite Mannheim (qq.v.), and has important chemical industries. Machinery and textiles also are manuf. Its riv. port is busy. L. was heavily bombed by the allied forces during the Second World War. Pop. 166,000.

Ludwigskanal, *see* MAIN.

Luffa, *see* LOOFAH.

Luftwaffe, Ger. Air Force of Second World War, was created in contravention of the treaty of Versailles before Hitler's advent to power and had its roots in the gliding and flying clubs of Germany and in the air transport genius of the old pre-war Deutsche Lufthansa. Among the chief aircraft designers and constructors were Junkers, Focke, Klemm, Messerschmitt, Dornier and Heinkel. While the Allies were still flying obsolete biplanes of wood and fabric, Germany was already producing all-metal monoplanes. Hitler's decision to use the L. as a political weapon influenced its development. The L. was intended to produce quick results

and therefore became a largely tactical force, and heavy bombers were not favoured.

The Nazis prepared for a series of 'lightning' campaigns. The combined achievements of the L. and *panzer* divs. in Poland, the Low Countries and France suggested that Goering and his coadjutors had created a war-winning machine, but when the RAF first checked the L. at Dunkirk, and then defeated it in the battle of Britain, doubts arose. Subsequent events proved that Germany was in no way invincible in the air, and the initial successes of the L. were due mainly to the element of surprise and the unpreparedness of other nations. The Anglo-Amer. bomber offensive turned the L. more and more into a home defence force, and aircraft production in Germany was largely concentrated on fighter aircraft and pilotless missiles in 1944–5. The modern L. was formed in 1956, after the accession in May 1955 of the Ger. Federal Rep. to NATO. For details *see* GERMAN FEDERAL REPUBLIC. *See also* BOMBER COMMAND; BRITAIN, BATTLE OF; WORLD WAR, SECOND, *Aerial Warfare: British Policy of Strategic Bombing*. *See* A. M. Pamphlet 248, *The Rise and Fall of the Luftwaffe*, 1948; A. Galland, *The First and the Last*, 1955; B. Collier, *Defence of the United Kingdom*, 1957; Sir C. Webster and N. Frankland, *The Strategic Air Offensive against Germany*, 1961; L. F. Ellis, *Victory in the West*, vols. i and ii, 19.

Lug-worm, **Fishing-worm**, or **Lob-worm** (*Arenicola*), marine polychaet worm common on the Brit. coasts, burrowing in the sand and mud, and indicating its whereabouts by spiral rolls of excrement. The worms are sought after by ground-feeding fish, and are therefore used in considerable quantities as bait by fishermen. L.s grow up to 10 in. long, and are formed of numerous segments, 13 of which have branchial tufts.

Lugano, tn in the S. canton of Ticino, Switzerland, on Lake L., 50 m. NNW. of Milan. It is a much frequented resort, situated on the main St Gotthard railway line. The prin. church, San Lorenzo, in part dates back to the 13th cent. To the S. is Monte Salvatore (3004 ft), on the SE. (across the lake) Monte Generoso (5590 ft) and to the E. Monte Brè (3061 ft), all 3 mts being accessible by cog railways. A famous cattle fair, held in Oct., dates from 1513. Pop. 19,800. chiefly It.-speaking.

Lugano, Lake, in Switzerland and N. Italy, between Lakes Maggiore and Como, covers an area of 19 sq. m., and is noted for its beautiful scenery. Its altitude is 890 ft and its greatest depth is 945 ft. (*See Plate: Switzerland*.)

Lugansk: 1. (until 1958 **Voroshilovgrad**) Oblast in E. Ukraine, comprising the central part of the Donets Basin (q.v.) and a ravined area on the l. b. of the Severskiy Donets, in the black earth steppe belt. It has large coal deposits (40 per cent of all the reserves of the Donbas; half anthracite). There are iron and steel engineering, coke, chemical, food and light industries; wheat, maize and sunflowers and sugar are grown, market gardening is practised, and cattle and hogs are raised. The prin. tns are L. Kadiyevka, Kommunarsk, Krasnyy Luch. The area was unpopulated until annexed by Russia and colonised after 1753 (*see* NEW RUSSIA). The first colonists were Serbian immigrants. Industrial development dates from the late 18th cent. The Stakhanov Movement (q.v.) originated here. During the Ger. occupation (1941–3) the underground youth organisation the 'Young Guard' (q.v.) in Krasnodon performed heroic deeds. Area 10,300 sq. m.; pop. (1965) 2,732,000 (84 per cent urb.) Russians and Ukrainians.

2. (1935–58 **Voroshilovgrad**) Cap., economic and cultural centre of the above, the oldest industrial centre of the Donets Basin, with large engineering and metallurgical industries (locomotives—formerly steam, now diesel—mining equipment, machine tools, automobile parts, building industry equipment, pipes). Known since the mid-18th cent., it became a tn in 1882, and prov. cap. in 1938. A cannon foundry was built in 1796 (the first experiments in Russia in the smelting of iron with coke took place in 1797); a large locomotive plant was built in 1900, and further rapid industrial development took place in the 1930s. Pop. (1965) 330,000 (1917, 60,000; 1939, 213,000).

Lugar, vil. of Ayrshire, Scotland on L. Water 1½ m. NE. of Cumnock. The disused ironworks are now occupied by the E. Ayr Area Offices of the National Coal Board, and barytes mines are near by. Here in 1754 was *b.* Wm Murdoch, inventor of gas lighting.

Lugard, Frederick John Dealtry Lugard, 1st **Baron** (1858–1945), Brit. soldier and colonial administrator, *b.* Madras, and educ. at Rossall and Sandhurst. He joined the Norfolk Regiment in 1878 and served in the Afghan war, 1879–80, in the Sudan campaign for the relief of Gordon, 1884–5, and in the operations in Burma after the fall of King Thebaw, in 1886–7. His later campaigns were directed mainly against the slave trade and native misrule in Africa. The 3 outstanding achievements in his career were his success in winning and in securing the retention of Uganda for Britain in 1893, his initiation of the policy of 'indirect rule' (rule through native chiefs and bodies) during his governorship of Nigeria, and the pub. of his great book, *The Dual Mandate in British Tropical Africa*, 1922.

His earliest efforts against the slave trade were in Nyasaland, where in 1888 he commanded an expedition from Blantyre against Arab slave-raiders which defeated the slavers, L. being badly wounded. This was followed by his expedition to Uganda, on whose chief ruler, the *kabaka* of Buganda, the notorious Carl Peters had imposed a Ger. treaty. But the Anglo-Ger. agreement of 1890 assigned the Uganda to Great Britain, and L. and his small band of soldiers marched with remarkable rapidity to the cap. of Buganda, where he eventually obtained the treaty he sought and brought order to the country.

In 1894 L. was sent by the Royal Niger Co. to Borgu, where he forestalled the French and Germans in obtaining treaties with the chiefs, by which they acknowledged the sovereignty of the Brit. company. After a settlement had been reached with France, and the Royal Niger Co. had surrendered its charter, L. was appointed high commissioner of N. Nigeria. By 1906, when he resigned his post, all Nigeria was being peacefully administered under the supervision of Brit. residents. In 1906 L. resigned his commissionership to take up the governorship of Hong Kong. In 1912 he was sent back to the protectorate of Nigeria, which now included S. as well as N. Nigeria, and also the colony of Lagos. In 1914 he amalgamated the 2 Nigerias into 1 administration known as the colony and protectorate of Nigeria, which, with the personal title of governor-general, he administered with conspicuous ability. K.C.M.G., 1901, and G.C.M.G., 1911. Retiring from the colonial service in 1919, he became P.C. in 1920, and was raised to the peerage in 1928. Member of the Permanent Mandates Commission of the League of Nations, 1922–36. *See* M. Perham, *Lugard*, 1956.

Lugdunum, *see* LYON.

Lugger, small 2- or 3-masted vessel with a running bowsprit and lug-sails, i.e. sails having a gaff but no boom, and generally 2 or 3 jibs.

Lugo: 1. Sp. prov, in Galicia, with a coastline on the Bay of Biscay. It is watered by the Miño and its trib. the Sil, the basins of which are very fertile. Area 3815 sq. m.; pop. 480,000.

2. (Rom. **Lucus Augusti** or **Lucense**) Sp. tn, cap. of the prov. of L., on the Miño. It is surrounded by massive Rom. walls, now promenades, and has a beautiful cathedral, partly 12th cent. There are hot sulphur springs near by, used since Rom. times. Pop. 50,000.

3. It. tn in Emilia-Romagna, 16 m. W. of Ravenna. Pop. 13,800.

Lugoj, tn in the Banat, Rumania, 35 m. E. of Timisoara. It trades chiefly in wine and fruit, and is a main railway junction. Pop. 31,800.

Lu Hsün (Chou Shu-jen) (1881–1936), Chinese thinker and writer, known as the father of modern Chinese literature, *b.* Shaoshing, Chekiang, of a scholar's family. He studied medicine in Japan, but later changed to literature on the grounds that the soul was more important than the body. In 1909 he returned to China and taught school in Shaoshing until joining the ministry of education in 1912, when he moved to Peking; he stayed with the ministry until 1925, but lectured also at Peking Univ. from 1917 onwards. He left Peking to avoid arrest as an agitator in 1926, and went first to Amoy Univ., then on to Sun Yat-sen Univ. in Canton in 1927. Before long he resigned in protest against repressive measures taken against students and went to live in Shanghai where he lived off his writings until his death. L. S. did not make a mark with his early efforts written in the literary language, but fame came to him overnight with his first story in the vernacular called *Diary of a Madman*, pub. in the *New Youth* magazine in May 1918. This was followed over the next 4 years by further stories eventually collected under the title *Battle Cries*; a second collection of stories written 1924–5 was called *Wandering*. These stories, unemotional in tone yet unmistakably deeply felt, not only held up a mirror to the Chinese but also vindicated the vernacular as a medium for self-respecting literature: as a stylist L. S. is still unsurpassed. The best known of his stories is *The True Story of Ah Q*, in which the eponymous hero manifests the common weaknesses of the Chinese character. In L. S.'s collected works topical essays far exceed fiction in vol., which reflects his involvement in the polemics of the 20's and early 30's; but the essays are in turn outweighed by trans. of Western literature and learned works, all part of the effort to introduce new ways of thought to replace the outlook that had made China weak and contemptible. Having been given Mao Tse-tung's special seal of approval his work is now beyond criticism in China. *See Selected Works of Lu Hsün* (4 vols.), trans. H. Y. and G. Yang, 1959.

Luigi (or **Aloigi**), **Andrea di** (commonly called **Andrea d'Assisi** and nicknamed 'L'Ingegno') (*c.* 1470–*c.* 1516), It. painter, *b.* Assisi. He studied under Pietro Perugino, and in his youth was regarded as the rival of Raphael (q.v.). Vasari assigned him work in the hall of Cambio, and the Sistine Chapel at Rome, but none of his works has been identified. When L. became blind at an early age Pope Sixtus IV allowed him a pension. A 'Holy Family' attributed to him is in the Louvre, and a 'Virgin and Child' in the National Gallery.

Luigi Amadeo Giuseppe Maria Ferdinando Francesco di Savoia-Aosta, *see* ABRUZZI, DUCA DI.

Luik, *see* LIÈGE.

Luines Charles d'Albert, *see* LUYNES.

Luini, **Bernardino** (*c.* 1470–1532), It. painter of the Milanese school. He was *b.* Luino, on Lake Maggiore, and was a follower, some think also a pupil, of da Vinci. His finest frescoes are in the church of the Madonna at Saronno, and he is represented by an oil-painting, 'Christ disputing with the Doctors', in the National Gallery.

Luis de Granada, *see* GRANADA.

Luise, **Auguste Wilhelmine Amalie**, Queen of Prussia, *see* LOUISA.

Luke, **St**, Gk physician of Antioch, who joined St Paul in his missionary work. He is author of the third Gospel and of the Acts of the Apostles. His feast is on 18 Oct. *See* LUKE, THE GOSPEL ACCORDING TO ST.

Luke, **The Gospel according to St.** By a continuous tradition, traceable to the beginning of the 2nd cent. and accepted by most critics, including Harnack, the third Gospel and the Acts are universally ascribed to one compiler, St L. It was written before Acts (as the prologue to Acts shows) and the conclusion of Acts seems to indicate *c.* AD 63 for that work, though many critics place it later than the fall of Jerusalem in AD 70. There is, however, no sign in it or in Acts of a hostile attitude to Christianity among the Rom. authorities such as started in AD 64. The author does not claim to be an eye-witness

narrating from his own recollections, but a compiler intending to give a more accurate compilation than those already in circulation. One of his sources was St Mark's gospel. For the relation of L. to Matthew *see* MATTHEW and SYNOPTIC PROBLEM. L.'s gospel is addressed to the pagan world, as one might expect from one who was a Gentile convert himself and a companion of St Paul. It is a highly polished and sensitive work of art, greatly interested in all that shows the universal scope of Christ's work, His mercy to sinners, His concern for sinners and His practice of prayer. *See* commentaries by L. Ragg, 1922; J. M. Creed, 1930; H. Balmforth, 1930; *also* J. Chapman, *Matthew, Mark and Luke*, 1937; and B. C. Butler, *The Originality of Matthew*, 1951.

Lukuga, or **Lukuja**, *see* TANGANYIKA, LAKE.

Luleå: 1. Seaport and the cap. of the co. of Norrbotten, Sweden, at the mouth of L. R. on the NW. coast of the Gulf of Bothnia. It exports ore from the iron mines of Gällivare. Fish, skins and forest products are also exported. The harbour is closed by ice from Nov. to June. Pop. 30,600.
2. Riv. in the N. of Sweden, flows through the co. of Norrbotten into the Gulf of Bothnia, entering the sea at L. after a course of 255 m.

Lull, **Ramón**, or **Lully**, **Raymond** (*c.* 1235–1315), Sp. mystic and poet, known as the 'enlightened doctor'. He was *b.* at Palma in Majorca, and led a wild, dissolute life till 1266, when he was converted. After sev. years spent in solitude and meditation, he began a great missionary enterprise, preaching throughout Italy and in France, Armenia and Africa. In 1314 he sailed on a crusade against Mohammedanism to Bugia (modern Bougie) in Africa, where he was stoned and *d.* of his wounds. L.'s philosophy, as set forth in *Libri XII Principiorum Philosophorum contra Averroistas*, was condemned by a papal Bull (1376), and is now of interest only for its breaking away from the scholastic system. His novel *Blanquerna*, 1283, in some ways anticipates More's *Utopia*. His poems *El Desconort*, 1295, and *Lo Cant de Ramon*, 1299, are of great beauty. *See* E. Allison Peers, *Ramón Lull*, 1929; F. Sureda Blanes, *El beato Ramón Lull*, 1934; J. Xirau-Palau, *Vida y Obra de Ramón Lull*, 1946.

Lully, **Jean-Baptiste** (**Giovanni Battista Lulli**) (1632–87), Fr. composer of It. origin, *b.* Florence. He went to Paris, where he joined the band of Louis XIV, who made him director of the Académie Royale de Musique (the Opéra) in 1672. He introduced lively ballets into the Fr. opera, and in conjunction with Benserade, Molière, Quinault, Thomas Corneille and others, composed 63 works for the stage, the chief of which are *Alceste*, 1674, *Thésée*, 1675, *Atys*, 1676, *Isis*, 1677, *Psyché*, 1678, *Bellérophon*, 1679, *Proserpine*, 1680, *Persée*, 1682, *Phaéton*, 1683, and *Armide et Renaud*, 1686. *See* lives by H. Prunières, 1929, and E. Borrel, 1949.

Lulworth Cove, *see* WEST AND EAST LULWORTH.

Lumbago, medical term for pain in the lumbar

region of the back. Typically, L. is sudden in onset and an acute pain fixes the patient during some movement of the back which is often of quite a normal kind. In some cases the onset of pain is gradual and becomes increasingly severe. While an attack of L. is at its height any attempted movement of the lumbar spine causes agonising pain and the sufferer is fearful of any change of position. The lumbar muscles are set in spasmodic contraction. It used to be thought that L. was due to muscular rheumatism brought on by damp, cold or exposure. It is now widely held that it is caused by a displacement of a spinal disk (see SPINE), the displaced disk pressing upon the sensitive spinal cord. Patients stricken with L. frequently report that a click in the back occurred simultaneously with onset of the pain and in these cases it is the displaced, or 'slipped', disk which causes the sensation. Sometimes a disk is displaced sideways, in which case pressure is exerted on the roots of the spinal nerves and sciatica (q.v.) may result. While it is probable that the majority of cases of true L. are due to some form of displacement of a lumbar spinal disk, there are other kinds of backache that cannot properly be classed as L. (but often are), nor can they be attributed to a slipped disk. Straining of the lumbar muscles, muscular rheumatism, arthritis of the spine (q.v.) and certain internal disorders may all cause lumbar pain. *Treatment* of L. consists primarily in rest, the patient lying flat in the most comfortable position. In most cases the disk goes back into place of its own accord. Analgesics and local heat, apart from providing much-needed relief, induce muscle relaxation, which in turn assists in the natural replacement of the disk. Spinal manipulation by a skilled operator sometimes effects an immediate cure, and this should certainly be done in persistent cases. Chronic L. occurs when the disk remains permanently dislocated, and in these cases a surgical operation may be necessary. Prevention of L. is more important than treatment, and all those engaged in heavy work, and all who in the natural course of events have occasionally to lift some heavy article, should observe the correct technique of weight-lifting. So far as possible the article to be lifted should be straddled by the legs, the knees should then be bent and then straightened in the act of lifting. In this way the centre of gravity is in the vertical plane and the strain is distributed evenly. Bending over and lifting the weight by straightening the spine should be avoided whenever possible. Not only does this place the centre of gravity in front of the body, thus throwing a tremendous strain on the supporting structures of the spine, but also in a flexed spine the vertebral bodies are separated posteriorly, thus creating a gap through which the intervertebral disk is more easily displaced. *See* James Cyriax, *Osteopathy and Manipulation*, 1950.

Lumbar Puncture, insertion of a hollow needle through the dural membrane of the spinal cord below the third lumbar vertebra for the withdrawal of cerebro-spinal fluid (C.S.F.). The C.S.F. circulates in and about the central nervous system and a sample taken from the lumbar region will indicate fairly accurately the conditions throughout the pathways of its circulation. Since the C.S.F. is so closely related to the nervous system its composition reflects disease changes in nervous tissue and its adjacent meninges and blood vessels. consideration of its pressure, cell content and chemical composition often enables a diagnosis to be made or confirmed which would not be achieved by other means. Withdrawing C.S.F. by L. P. is also carried out as a therapeutic measure to relieve increased intracranial pressure. L. P. was first performed by Corning of New York in 1885, and soon afterwards Quincke in Germany and Wynter in England improved upon Corning's method for the relief of raised intracranial pressure. In adults the spinal cord ends at the lower border of the first lumbar vertebra and the arachnoid membrane continues down to the level of the second sacral vertebra. There is therefore a cavity in the lower lumbar vertebral canal containing C.S.F. and spinal nerve roots. It is into this sac or cavity that the needle is inserted in L. P. The needle is inserted posteriorly. The patient lies on his left side with the knees and hips flexed to their greatest extent and the neck likewise flexed, so that the chin rests on the chest in close apposition to the knees. This curled up position opens the interspinous spaces of the spinal column as widely as possible and allows free passage for the needle. The operation must be performed under strictly aseptic conditions. In addition to drawing off C.S.F. for pathological examination and tests, L. P. may be used to introduce antibiotics and other drugs for therapeutic purposes, opaque fluids for diagnostic X-ray purposes and anaesthetic drugs for the purposes of spinal anaesthesia.

Lumber and Lumbering (cf. Swedish *lomra*, to roar, a frequentative of *ljumma*, to make a noise). Formerly the word lumber was applied to a pawnbroker's shop, being a variant of 'Lombard', which was equivalent in meaning to pawnbroker, someone who accumulated discarded furniture, etc. The word, with its twofold meaning of rubbish and timber, is probably associated with both these sources. Lumber and lumbering are Amer. terms for converted or converting wood and for felled trees prepared for the sawmill. Lumber is timber split, sawn or machine planed for use in industry or for building etc. Hence a lumber mill is a sawmill. Lumbering is a very large and important industry in the U.S.A., Canada, Newfoundland, Sweden, Finland, the Soviet Union and other countries possessing large forest resources. *See* CANADA, *Forestry and Lumbering*; FORESTRY; TIMBER; TREE. (*See Plate; Finland.*)

Lumbricus, *see* EARTHWORMS.

Lumbumbashi, *see* ELISABETHVILLE.

Lumière, Auguste (1862–1954) and **Louis** (1864–1948), Fr. pioneers of cinematography. Their father, Antoine L., was a manufacturer of photographic materials, and the L. brothers had made a number of improvements in photographic technique before the arrival in France of the first Edison Kinetoscopes turned their attention to motion pictures. They recognised the desirability of projecting the moving pictures Edison had achieved, and of an intermittent movement of the film—conditions fulfilled in their cinématographe, an instrument of great ingenuity and elegance, combining camera, printer and projector, which was perfected in 1894 and publicly exhibited in Paris, 28 Dec. 1895, and London, 20 Feb. 1896. The L. claw-motion intermittent movement was abandoned after a short time, owing to the strain it imposed on the film. The L. brothers continued to interest themselves in photographic and film technique throughout their lives, and conducted some of the earliest successful experiments in large screen, stereoscopic and colour cinematograph systems.

Luminal, *see* PHENOBARBITONE.

Luminescence, property of emitting light without the simultaneous manifestation of heat. Any substance which exhibits L. is called a *phosphor*. It is convenient to distinguish between *fluorescence*, for which the emission of light ceases within 10^{-8} sec. of the removal of the excitation, and *phosphorescence*, for which the emission is delayed by more than 10^{-8} sec. This period is the lifetime of an excited state of an atom for a normal allowed transition. The most familiar instances are those of phosphorescence in decaying fish, the glow-worm, fire-flies and the 'phosphorescence' of the sea. Chemical action accounts for it in the case of phosphorus itself, oxidation taking place in air at ordinary temps. In the case of radium and electric discharges, disintegration of substances largely accounts for it (*see* X-RAYS). In the case of quinine sulphate solutions fluorescence is due to emission of previously absorbed light; other substances exhibiting L. are the sulphides of calcium, barium and strontium, used in the manuf. of luminous paints. These possess the power of storing up light rays of higher refrangibility. Some crystals exhibit L. on being warmed slightly, e.g. diamond, or as a result of friction due to rubbing or crushing, e.g. sugar. *See* FLUORESCENCE; PHOSPHORESCENCE.

Luminosity, state of emitting light. Intrinsic L. or brightness is the comparative light-emitting power of a shining body per unit area. Bodies may be self-luminous or luminous by reflected light; in the former case *incandescence* is usually due to a state of heat. The whole question concerns the effect of light rays on the retina of the eye, and a rough classification may be made into glowing or dull red, bright red, yellow and white, but the eye fails completely to make any approximation to scientific comparison, judging, for example, a surface ascertained by photometry to be 100 times as bright as another to be only 5 times as bright. The eye, unable to estimate difference of L., can recognise equal L. It can be shown that the intensity of illumination at any point of a surface held normally to the light from a point source varies inversely as the square of the distance. By so adjusting distances

of 2 luminous objects that they give equal illumination on a surface, we arrive at their comparative L.s. There are, however, many attendant difficulties, for example colour and standard (but *see* PHOTOMETRY).

As a rule L.s of gases or vapours are low, even with intense heat, high L. being due to incandescent solids. Bright flames owe their intensity to small particles of solid in an incandescent state, for example coal gas owes its luminous powers to carbon particles liberated chemically; if air be mixed as in the bunsen flame, though the heat is more intense, the brightness is altogether lost: the solid incandescent mantle, however, becomes intensely luminous in the flame.

Luminous Paint. Substances with the power of luminescence have been incorporated in paint. Such paints do not give off enough light to illuminate their surroundings, but serve to render the object coated with them visible in the dark by the phosphorescent glow. The luminous substances mainly employed are the sulphides of barium, calcium and strontium. The earliest L. P. was 'Bologna phosphorus', the sulphide of barium; Balmain's L. P. is another mixed sulphide preparation. The essential point about these substances is that they lose the property unless exposed periodically to sunlight or other actinic rays. The energy is stored, and when the source of light has been removed is slowly emitted. L. P. can also be excited by radiations of higher frequency such as ultra-violet or X-rays. By mixing ordinary L. P.s with radioactive substances such as mesothorium, a L. P. can be made which is self-exciting and does not need to be exposed to light in order to function. Such paints are used for illuminating instruments in aircraft, clocks, watches, etc. although it would now seem to be advisable to discontinue the use of radioactive substances on watches in view of the cumulative effect of radiation on the human body. There is a clear distinction between L. P.s and fluorescent paints. The latter contain substances which, when irradiated with ultra-violet rays, even at a low level of intensity, exhibit great luminosity, far more so than is possible by simple reflection of light from a coloured surface. However, unlike L. P.s, as soon as the source of excitation is removed the luminous effect ceases. The nature of the fluorescent compositions is becoming very complex and fluorescent dye-stuffs, metallic tungstates, borates and silicates are among those used.

Lump-sucker, *see* CYCLOPTERIDAE.

Lumumba, Patrice (1926–61), Congolese politician. He was a gov. clerk, who became leader of the *Mouvement National Congolais*, and premier of the Congo (Leopoldville) Rep. in June 1960. A fluent and demagogic speaker, L. proved incapable of holding together the various separatist elements in Congolese politics. Chaos ensued and in Sept. L. was arrested after an army *coup*. In Feb. 1961 he was kidnapped and murdered by Katangese tribesmen. After his death L. was hailed as an African nationalist martyr, and memorials and institutions were named for him in both African and Communist countries. *See* CONGO (LEOPOLDVILLE KINSHASHA), *History*.

Lumumbashi, *see* ELISABETHVILLE.

Lunacharsky, Anatolii Vasil'evich (1873–1933), Russian politician and literary critic. From his early youth he belonged to Marxist circles, later joining the Social Democratic party and its Bolshevik faction. In 1904–5 he supported Lenin against the Bolshevik Central Committee (*see* LENIN). In 1909 he broke with Lenin and, together with Bogdanov and Gorky (q.v.), formed the left-wing Bolshevik sub-faction 'Forward'. During the First World War he was an internationalist. After the Feb. revolution (q.v.) in 1917 he returned to Russia from emigration and soon rejoined the Bolshevik party. From the Oct. revolution (q.v.) till 1929 he was people's commissar for education in the Russian Federal Rep. In 1933 he was appointed ambas. to Spain, but *d.* in Paris on the way there. Himself a Bogdanovist, L. was largely responsible for the flourishing of Bogdanovism (*see* BOGDANOV) in the 1920s. His removal from the Ministry of Education put an end to modernistic experimentation in schools. In recent years more liberal Soviet literary critics have often referred to L.'s views to support their pressure for a liberalisation of the Party's cultural policy.

Lunacy, *see* MENTAL DISORDER.

Lund, tn in the co. of Malmöhus, and 12 m. NE. of Malmö, Sweden, was the cap. of Denmark in the 12th cent., and reunited with Sweden, 1658. It contains a fine 11th cent. cathedral, observatory, zoological museum, botanical gardens and a univ. founded in 1668. The industries are sugar refining, woollen manufs. and tanning. Pop. 40,000.

Lundy, Benjamin (1789–1839), American abolitionist, *b.* Handwick, New Jersey, of Quaker parentage. He was the first to establish anti-slavery periodicals, which included the *Genius of Universal Emancipation* and the *National Engineer*, later to become the *Pennsylvania Freeman*.

Lundy Island, in the Bristol Channel, England, 12 m. NW. of Hartland Point; area 1051 ac., most of which is pasture land. N. and S. there are 2 modern lighthouses; there are remains of an anct castle and round towers, and L. Is. is a Royal Naval signal station with telephone connection with Barnstaple. It was a stronghold of smugglers. Botanically L. Is. is most interesting, with a profusion of wild and rare flowers. Puffins and other birds are also found. Pop. *c.* 20. *See* monograph by J. R. Chanter, 1877, and P. T. Etherton and V. Barlow, *Tempestuous Isle*, 1949.

Lüneburg, Ger. tn in the *Land* of Lower Saxony, on the Ilmenau, 66 m. NNE. of Hanover. It stands at the edge of L. Heath (q.v.), once belonged to the Hanseatic League (q.v.) and was the cap. of a duchy. It has sev. fine old churches, a Gothic tn hall and Gothic, Renaissance and baroque houses. There are chemical, paper and iron industries. Pop. 59,600.

Lüneburg Heath (Ger. **Lüneburger Heide**), low, sandy dist in the *Land* of Lower Saxony, Germany, lying S. of the Elbe and SE. of Hamburg. It has typical heath vegetation, and the chief tn on it is called Lüneburg. It was at F.–M. Montgomery's H.Q. on L. H. that the Germans surrendered all their forces in Holland, NW. Germany and Denmark, in May 1945. *See* WESTERN FRONT IN SECOND WORLD WAR.

Lünen, Ger. tn in the *Land* of N. Rhine-Westphalia, on the Lippe, 43 m. NE. of Düsseldorf. It has coal-mines and aluminium and iron industries. Pop. 72,200.

Lunenburg, seaport tn, cap. of L. co., Nova Scotia, Canada, 45 m. SW. of Halifax. A fishing centre, with processing plants and factories for marine equipment and supplies, it has shipyards and was the home of *Bluenose*, undefeated champion schooner of the N. Atlantic fishing fleet. Pop. 3056.

Lunette (Fr. *lune*, moon), in architecture, a crescent-shaped or semicircular aperture, to admit light. The word is also applied to a semicircular panel, filled sometimes with decorative carving.

Lunéville, Fr. tn in the dept of Meurthe-et-Moselle, on the Meurthe. The peace of L. was signed here between Napoleon and Austria in 1801 (*see under* FRANCE, *History*). The château of the Dukes of Lorraine is now a museum. There are textile and pottery industries, and railway carriages are made. Pop. 24,600.

Lungchow, *see* LUNGTSIN.

Lungkow, part of China, in the Laichow Bight on the coast immediately opposite the mouth of the Hwang-Ho. It was made a treaty port in 1915.

Lungs, greyish, spongy, irregularly pyramidal or conical elastic organs of respiration, occupying the greater portion of the thorax, the remaining central portion of this cavity being termed the *mediastinum*, and containing the heart, great vessels, roots of L., etc. Each organ has a apex extending into the root of the neck just above the first rib, and a concave base resting on the diaphragm. The outer surface is smooth and convex, and the inner is concave and in part adapted to the pericardium. The posterior border fitting into the deep concavity on either side of the spinal column is broad and rounded, while the anterior edge is thin and overlaps the front of the pericardium. Each lung is enclosed in its serous membrane, the *pleura*, a double bag, the inner closely covering the lung and the outer forming a lining to the cavity of the chest. Between the 2 surfaces of the pleura there is a small amount of lubricatory fluid as in the case of the pericardium. The bronchus (q.v.) and the great vessels join the lung at its *root*, which is situated upon the inner surface, somewhat above the middle of the lung and towards its posterior border. Within the lung the arterial trunks run behind the bronchial branches, and the venous trunks are situated in front.

Dimensions, etc. The right lung is a little thicker and heavier than the left, but is almost an inch shorter owing to the curvature of the diaphragm in accommodation of the liver. The organs vary in weight and size according to the amount of blood they may happen to contain. In general the right lung weighs about 22 oz. (623 gr.) in the adult male, and the left weighs about 20 oz. (566 gr.). The totals are less in the case of the female, both absolutely and also relatively, for the lung weight is about $\frac{1}{37}$ of the body weight in the male and about $\frac{1}{42}$ in the female.

Properties and structure. The mass of the organ is of a light, porous, spongy texture, and when healthy is buoyant in water, hence the popular name of 'lights' applied to the L. When fully distended the sp. gr. of the organ is only 0·126, but rises to 1·056 on being entirely deprived of air (Krause). The pulmonary tissue is endowed with great elasticity, in consequence of which the L. collapse to about one-third of their bulk when the thorax is opened. The right lung is divided into 3 lobes, one of which is less distinct; the left is divided into 2 lobes. The surface of each lung is marked out into polygonal spaces, which are the bases of the lobules; the substance of the organs is made up of lobules united by connective tissue (*interlobular septa*), which is continuous with the sub-pleural and peribronchial connective tissues. Each lobule is a complete system in itself, consisting of (*a*) a small bronchial branch; (*b*) artery, capillaries and vein; (*c*) nerves; (*d*) lymphatics.

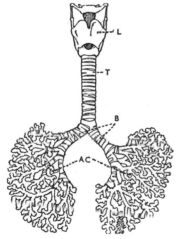

LUNGS: THE AIR PASSAGES

L, larynx; T, trachea; B, bronchi; AC, air cells.

Air circulation. The L. may be regarded as a many-chambered elastic bag placed in the air-tight thorax and having a communication with the exterior only by means of the trachea (windpipe). Atmospheric pressure acting down the trachea keeps the L. so far stretched that the 2 pleural layers are always in apposition, and together with the heart and great blood-vessels

they completely fill the thorax. The air passes on into and through the bronchi (q.v.), which somewhat resemble the trachea in structure; the current then continues through the various subdivisions of bronchia, bronchioles and bronchial tubes, which, diverging in all directions, never anastomose, but terminate separately. After a certain stage of subdivision (diameter about 1 mm.) the walls of the bronchial tubes become beset with blind, cup-shaped pouches termed *air-cells* or *alveoli*, the walls of which consist of a thin membrane of areolar and elastic tissue lined by thin, transparent, flat cells. The cells are about $\frac{1}{70}$ in. in diameter, and are said to number upwards of 700,000,000 and to present a very great surface to the air. It is from the air in these cells that the blood obtains a fresh supply of oxygen and gives up its carbon dioxide, for between adjacent alveoli there is a layer of thin-walled capillaries, the vessels twisting first to one side and then to the other of the septa between the alveoli.

Blood-vessels. The branches of the pulmonary artery accompany the bronchial tubes, but in their remote ramifications they subdivide more frequently. They are independent of one another, though the corresponding veins frequently anastomose. The terminal arterial branches are about $\frac{1}{1000}$ in. in diameter, and from them arise the capillaries $\frac{1}{3000}$ in. in diameter, so closely meshed that their interspaces are even narrower than the vessels. The radicles of the pulmonary veins arise from the capillary network of the alveoli and from that of the smaller bronchial tubes; the fusion of these and other venous vessels gives rise to the pulmonary veins, which leave the roots of the L. and return the blood to the left auricle of the heart (q.v.). The pulmonary vessels differ from the systemic in regard to their contents; the arteries in the former circulation carry dark red deoxygenated blood, while the veins carry bright red oxygenated blood. The pulmonary veins have no valves, nor are they more capacious than their corresponding arteries. Apart from the circulation mentioned above, there are also smaller bronchial arteries springing from the aorta which nourish the bronchi, lymphatic glands and connective tissue of the L., while bronchial veins return much of this blood to the systemic circulation, though some small amount of it is returned by the pulmonary veins.

Lymphatics. Part of the numerous lymphatics of the L. takes origin from lymphatic capillaries in the interalveolar septa, others near the surface of the L. come into connection with the sub-pleural lymphatic plexus. Both sets emerge at the roots of the L., where they enter the bronchial glands, passing thence from the left lung into the thoracic duct, and from the right lung into the right lymphatic trunk. Foreign particles caught by the mucus in the bronchial passages often find their way through the epithelium into the lymphatics, and may finally reach the bronchial glands. Particles of carbon are frequently found embedded in the lymphatic glands of coalminers.

Nerves. The nerves of the L. come from the anterior and posterior plexuses, which are formed chiefly by branches from the pneumogastric or vagus nerve, joined by others from the sympathetic system. They enter the L. and follow the distribution of the vessels and bronchi, small ganglia being situated in the walls of the latter. In the lower vertebrates (frog, newt) the nerves are chiefly distributed to a layer of plain muscular tissue, which is everywhere found taking part in the composition of the relatively simple pulmonary wall (Stirling), but in mammals their exact mode of termination is not clear. Impulses pass from the L. along the pneumogastric and along other nerves to a respiratory centre in the medulla, and from this centre efferent impulses proceed along various nerves, bringing about respiratory movements.

Condition in the foetus and change after birth. In the foetus the L. contain no air, and consequently sink in water. After birth they undergo rapid and remarkable changes consequent on the commencement of respiration. The chief changes are given below. In a still-born child or in a full-period foetus the L. lie packed at the back of the thorax; subsequent respiration in the latter case causes the L. to fill the pleural portions of the thoracic cavity. The introduction of air and of an increased quantity of blood converts their tissue from a compact, heavy, yellow-pink substance into a loose, light, rosy-pink, spongy material, resembling blood froth. These changes occur first at the anterior borders, and in the right lung rather earlier than in the left. The absolute weight, which has been increasing gradually during the intra-uterine period, undergoes a marked increase at birth, amounting to more than one-third of its previous weight owing to the increased amount of blood. The relative weight usually increases from about $\frac{1}{70}$ of the previous body weight to $\frac{1}{36}$; a proportion which suffers no material change during later life. The sp. gr. is, as might be expected, materially reduced on the commencement of breathing.

Diseases, etc. The L. are particularly subject to disease. Pneumonia (q.v.) which may attack 1 lung or both, frequently arises as a secondary complication in association with other diseases. It is due to inflammation of the lung tissue, and is generally accompanied by pleurisy or inflammation of the pleura. Wounds of the thorax caused by piercing implements, or even by the fractured ends of broken ribs, may allow air to enter between the pleurae. This is termed *pneumothorax.* The natural elasticity of the L., coupled with the atmospheric pressure acting on their exterior, leads to their contraction and to a consequent difficulty of inspiration. Artificial pneumothorax is used as a method of collapsing the L. in the treatment of pulmonary tuberculosis (q.v.). *Empyema* is the presence of an abscess in the pleural space between the L. and the chest, and is usually caused by the micro-organisms of pneumonia (q.v.). An opening of the chest space and draining away of the contained fluid is the usual surgical treatment.

Other disorders may require the removal of portions of the lung tissue itself. *Bronchiectasis* is a condition following chronic bronchitis or pneumonia; the bronchioles become expanded here and there into large cavities filled with infected mucus. It has been estab. that cigarette-smoking and air pollution have a connection with lung cancer. *See also* ARTIFICIAL RESPIRATION; For methods of ventilation of mammal and other vertebrate L. *see* RESPIRATION. *See also* Hughes, *Vertebrate Respiration*, 1963.

Lungtsin, or **Lungchow,** tn in the prov. of Kwangsi, China, near the borders of Indo-China. It is on one of the main trade routes, but its trade is of no great importance today owing to the diversion of the Laiping-Hunankuan railroad, which is 35 m. E. of L.

Lungworm, *see* HUSK; ROUNDWORMS.

Lungwort, lichen growing on tree trunks in damp subalpine regions. Sometimes prescribed in pulmonary diseases, like Iceland moss. Also the name of a boraginaceous perennial herb, the narrow-leaved L. or Jerusalem cowslip (*Pulmonaria officinalis*), with lance-shaped leaves and pink funnel-shaped flowers.

Luo, or **Lwoo,** Nilotic people of W. Kenya. living in the Kavirondo country near the Lake Victoria port of Kisumu. They are the most southerly of all the Nilotic tribes, most of whom live in the Sudan. The L. are agriculturists, with a strong clan system and without centralised political authority. The name L. is also applied to all the Nilotic peoples of E. Africa.

Lupercalia, yearly Rom. festival of purification, celebrated on 15 Feb., in honour of Lycaean Pan (or Faunus), or, as some think, in honour of the wolf that suckled Romulus and Remus. It was held at the foot of the Palatine Hill, near the cave of Lupercus in which was a bronze statue of a wolf. The officiating priests, the *Luperci,* sacrificed goats and dogs, with whose blood they touched the foreheads of 2 youths. The blood was wiped off with wool dipped in milk, the youths being obliged to smile during the whole process. The skins of the victims were then cut into long lashes, called *februa* (Lat. *februare*, to purify); with these the priests ran along the walls of the city, slashing anyone they met as a purificatory rite. Women were eager to receive a cut, to remove barrenness. In AD 494 Pope Gelasius I replaced the L. by the festival of purification of the Blessed Virgin Mary, celebrated on 2 Feb.

Lupescu, Magda, *see* CAROL II.

Lupiae, *see* LECCE.

Lupino, family of actors and acrobats which includes George (1853–1932), *b.* London of It. parentage; his sons Barry (1882–1962) and Stanley (1895–1922), and the latter's daughter Ida (1916–), whose career has been mainly in films. Henry George L. (1892–1959) took the name of his great-aunt Sara Lane, manageress of the famous Britannia Theatre, and was known as Lupino Lane. He made a great success in 1937 in *Me and My Girl*, in which he created 'The Lambeth Walk'.

Lupinus, or **Lupin** (family Leguminosae), genus of 300 species of ann., perennial herbs, or shrubs. *L. arboreus*, the Californian Tree L., crossed with *L. polyphyllus* gave rise to the perennial Russell L.s now so popular in gardens. *L. hartwegii* is the ann. L. from Mexico; the S. European ann. *L. luteus* is often used to improve sandy soils, ploughed in as green manure.

Lupus, 'The Wolf', anct but inconspicuous S. constellation between Centaurus and Scorpius.

Lupus, *L. vulgaris*, chronic tuberculosis of the skin, characterised by raised, reddish nodules arranged singly or in groups and commonest on the face. Scarring may occur from destruction of the tissues, and the consequent disfigurement gives rise to its name L. (wolf). *L. vulgaris* is not now a common disease, and modern treatments for tuberculosis (q.v.) are effective. *L. erythematosus* is chronic toxic erythema affecting mostly the skin of the face, but also the hands and fingers, where it may be mistaken for chilblains (q.v.) It is not tuberculous, and is caused by toxic substances in the blood such as drugs or bacterial toxins. Usually in chronic form, it may be acute and disseminated, involving large areas of skin and sometimes causing inflammation of the kidneys and heart.

Luray Caverns, in Page co., Virginia, U.S.A., has one of the finest displays of stalactites and stalagmites in the world. Its sev. chambers are covered with formations of various colours and fantastic shapes.

Lurçat, Jean (1892–1966), Fr. painter and decorative designer, *b*. Bruyères, Vosges. Influenced by Cézanne and Picasso, he painted barren landscapes in Spain and the Sahara in the 1920's but is best known for his tapestry designs which have stimulated a Fr. revival of tapestry as an art.

Lurcher, cross between a collie and a greyhound (qq.v.), used by poachers on account of its speed and sagacity. It is very swift and silent.

Lurgan, bor. of co. Armagh, N. Ireland, 21 m. SW. of Belfast. It is the centre of an agric. dist and of the co. linen industry, with important manufs. of handkerchiefs, lawn, cambric and damask, optical components and furniture. Pop. 17,873.

Luria, Isaac Ben Solomon (1534–72), Jewish mystic, one of the 'Five Sages' of the 16th cent., *b*. Jerusalem. He began life as a spice merchant in Alexandria, but was so much influenced by the *Zohar* of Moses de Leon, that he became a visionary, and propagated his mystic doctrines among a large company of disciples at Safed. His teaching as recorded by his biographer, Hayim Vital, had a lasting influence on Jewish mysticism.

Luristan, mountainous district of Persia, bounded on the N. by Kermanshah, on the E. by Borujerd and Malayer, on the W. by Iraq, and on the S. by Khuzistan. It is inhabited by numerous tribes, chiefly Lurs. Area 15,060 sq. m. Between 1929 and 1932 important archaeological finds were made in L. These included vessels and ornaments covering the period 2600 BC to AD 800. Pop. about 270,000.

Lurka, *see* LORCA.

Lurlei, *see* LORELEI.

Lusaka, tn in Zambia, of which it is the cap., the centre of an important agric. dist and on main rail and road routes to N. and S. L. is rapidly expanding. The main road to Salisbury, Rhodesia, crosses the Zambezi at Chizundu Pop. (1964) Europeans, 11,800; Africans, 120,500.

Lusatia (Ger. **Lausitz**), name given to a dist of Germany which lay on the borders of Brandenburg, Saxony, Silesia and Bohemia. In the 14th cent. it was possessed by Bohemia, but in 1469 it fell into the hands of Matthias Corvinus of Hungary. In 1490 it was regained by Bohemia, which ceded it to Saxony by the treaty of Prague (1635). In 1815 most of it was transferred to Prussia with the exception of Bautzen and 900 sq. m. of Upper L., which were retained by Saxony. The chief tns of Upper L. were Bautzen Zittau and Löbau, and of Lower L. Guben (Gubin), Kottbus and Forst. L. is now part of the dists of Dresden and Kottbus (in the Ger. Democratic Rep.), with the exception of a portion which lies E. of the R. Neisse and has belonged to Poland since 1946.

Lü-Shih Ch'un-chiu, *see* CHINESE LITERATURE.

Lu-shun Kow, *see* PORT ARTHUR.

Lusiadas, or **Lusiads**, patriotic poem written by Luís de Camoens (q.v.) in 1572. It takes its name from Lusus, the mythical first settler in Portugal.

Lusignan, Fr. tn in the dept of Vienne, 15 m. SW. of Poitiers. It has a beautiful church (11th–15th cents.). The castle of L. was founded, according to legend, by the fairy Melusina (q.v.), who was also the protectoress of the great feudal family of L., one branch of which ruled Cyprus and Jerusalem, 1192–1489. Pop. 2100.

Lusitania, one of the 3 provs. into which Augustus reorganised the div. of Hispania, anct Spain, the 2 others being Tarraconensis and Baetica. L. was called after the tribe Lusitani (who had submitted to Rome in 139 BC), and in extent corresponded very closely to modern Portugal. The Rom. seat of gov. was Augusta Emerita (Mérida, q.v.). *See* T. Mommsen, *Provinces of the Roman Empire* (Eng. trans.), 1886.

'Lusitania', Cunard liner, sunk without warning by a Ger. submarine on 7 May 1915 off the Old Head of Kinsale. She sank within 45 min. and of 1255 passengers and 651 crew, 1198, including 124 Americans, were drowned or killed. The action caused anti-Ger. riots in London's E. End, and the greatest indignation in America, but Germany, in a note to her embassy at Washington, dated 10 May 1915, gave various unsatisfactory explanations and even struck a medal to commemorate the sinking incident. This elicited a strong reply from President Wilson, who condemned the action in the most emphatic language. The sinking of the *L*. had a great influence upon America's decision to enter the First World War on the allied side.

Lussac, Joseph Louis Gay-, *see* GAY-LUSSAC.

Lustre (for technique and hist. of early period

see HISPANO-MORESQUE WARE). In the late 18th cent. and the first half of the 19th cent. a distinct new process was introduced by Wedgwood (q.v.) and others by which platinum salts were reduced to give a 'silver' surface to earthenware. Gold was used to give a pink or purple L.; a mother-of-pearl L. was made by these means at Belleek, N. Ireland. *See* W. Bosanko, *Collecting Old Lustreware*, 1916; J. R. Hodgdon, *Collecting Old English Lustre*, 1937.

Lustrum (Lat. *luere*, to purify), sacrifice for purification and expiation by the censors (q.v.) at the end of the quinquennial census of the Rom. people; a 5-year period thus became known as a L. The sacrificial boar, sheep and bull were carried round the people assembled in the Campus Martius, and so it was also called the Ambilustrium. *See* LUPERCALIA.

Lute (Arabic *al-ûd*), stringed instrument of music, widely used in the 16th and 17th cents. The primitive type of L. is the 2-stringed *tanbur* of Persia. It came into Europe through the Arabian *al-ûd*, which consists of a convex sound-body in the shape of half a pear, stringed with silk and played upon by a shell or quill plectrum. The anct L. seems to have had 4 pairs of catgut strings, but later types had 6 or more pairs, called courses. The *theorbo* (q.v.) or *archlute* is a double-necked L.; it has extra brass strings outside the fingerboard, and the necessity of retuning these at an alteration of key led to the custom of using only 1 key for the movements of a suite; the *chitarrone* has a very long neck. The Sp. *vihuela* was a special type of L. The instrument was particularly suited to song accompaniment. It is extinct as far as composition is concerned, but is still cultivated by a few specialists for the performance of old music.

LUTE

Lutetium (Lutecium), symbol Lu, atomic number 71, atomic weight 175·0, an element discovered independently by A. von Welsbach (1905) and G. Urbain (1907). The former named it Cassiopëium, and the latter adopted Lu, which is now the accepted name. It was separated from ytterbium proper (called neo-ytterbium for a time) in the so-called 'ytterbium', which was really a mixture of the 2 elements. This was achieved by fractionation of the nitrates. Lu is a rare-earth element, with the typical valency of 3. It forms colourless salts such as the chloride and sulphate. Pure lutecia, Lu_2O_3, was isolated in 1913. *See* RARE EARTHS.

Luteva, *see* LODÈVE.

Luther, Martin (1483–1546), Ger. reformer and translator of the Bible, the 'Founder of Protestant Civilisation', *b.* Eisleben, in Saxony, of peasant parents. His father, Hans L., a slate-cutter, moved after his birth to Mansfeld. L. was sent to school at Magdeburg; and went in 1498 to Eisenach. At 18 L. entered the univ. of Erfurt, where he took a degree in 1503 and a doctorate in philosophy in 1504. He then began lecturing on the physics and ethics of Aristotle, and within a year, against the will of his father, who meant him to be a lawyer, he entered an Augustinian monastery at Erfurt. He passed through severe mental conflicts, and found much comfort in reading the works of St Augustine. He was ordained priest in 1507, and in 1508 became prof. of philosophy in the new univ. of Wittenberg. Abandoning the methods of a decayed scholasticism and the guidance of traditional authorities, he was much attracted by the works of Wm of Occam, the Eng. Nominalist and advocate on reform. In 1510 L. visited Rome on business for his monastic order, and was shocked at the irreligion and corruption there. On his return to Wittenberg in 1512 he became a doctor of divinity and began to preach at the desire of Staupitz, the vicar-general of his order, drawing great crowds by his eloquence.

His first public demand for eccles. reform was his pub. in Lat. of 95 propositions against the sale of indulgences by the Dominican Johann Tetzel, which he nailed to the church door at Wittenberg Castle on 31 Oct. 1517. A trans. spread rapidly throughout Germany. The original propositions were burnt as heretical, but L. refused to recant, and even to obey a papal summons to Rome, though he asserted that he did not contemplate abandoning the Church. In the same year (1517) he pub. his first work, an *Exposition of the Seven Penitential Psalms*, which was soon followed by an *Exposition of the Ten Commandments* and *Of the Lord's Prayer*. At a general meeting of his order in 1518 he attacked outworn scholastic methods in theology, and in the same year had a controversy with Dr Eck. He also pub. his *Resolutions*, which emphasised his objection to the sale of indulgences. Though refusing to go to Rome, he met Cardinal Cajetan at Augsburg, but no agreement was reached.

In 1520 L. pub. 3 of his most important works, namely *On the Liberty of a Christian Man, An Address to the Nobility of the German Nation*, and *On the Babylonian Captivity of the Church of God*. In these he attacked the supremacy of the Pope and the doctrines of the Church. He argued for tolerance and the practical need of the individual to approach God by his own prayer, without any priestly mediator. He now realised that his separation from the Church was inevitable. The Pope replied to his attack in a Bull of 41 theses. This L. publicly burnt at the Elster Gate of Wittenberg before a large crowd of students and sympathisers. That same year Charles of Spain was crowned emperor at Aachen, and to his first Ger. diet, held in Jan. 1521, L. was summoned. L. went to Worms and, called upon to retract his writings, made his own confession of faith. He was placed under the ban of the empire, but received practical help from some of the princes of the empire. Rumours that he had been assassinated by papal emissaries put Germany in a ferment. It became known later, however, that L. had been safely conducted to the castle of the Wartburg by his friend, the Elector of Saxony. There he was detained until the excitement subsided. He spent this time in study and in translating the Bible into German.

Meanwhile Lutheran opinions were spreading fast among the Ger. populace, restive under both social and eccles. grievances. Germany, in consequence, was threatened with disorders, and even with revolution. The trouble was worst at Wittenberg, excited by the teaching of the Zwickau prophets. L. left his retreat, and by reinstating order estab. his own position as leader. He did his utmost to prevent the Peasants' war of 1525, but, though previously opposed to the tyranny of the ruling classes, he was no democrat, and urged them to suppress the insurgents in every way in order to procure peace. This lost him much popular sympathy and helped to give the Lutheran Church an oligarchic and Erastian form. In this year too he fell out with Erasmus, to whose treatise *De Libero Arbitrio* he replied hotly in *De Servo Arbitrio*. About the same time he married Catherine von Bora, a Cistercian nun, who with 8 others had left her convent under the influence of his teaching.

At the diet of Speyer in 1526 it was resolved that both parties, Catholic and Protestant, should preach according to their conscience, but 3 years later the diet abolished this clause, and added another to the effect that no religious body might be deprived of its eccles. revenues, i.e. that the Church retained her medieval revenues. The princes, who had changed their religion and seized Church endowments, protested against this edict and were therefore called Protestants. But the Protestants were divided among themselves on political questions as well as on the doctrine of the Lord's Supper. Zwingli and L. met at Marburg in this year to discuss their views. To the diet of 1530 three separate Protestant confessions were sent, namely that of Zwingli, the *Confessio Tetrapolitana* and the famous *Augsburg Confession*. L., still in disgrace, did not appear in person, and his place as leader was taken by Melanchthon (q.v.). Charles V was determined to suppress the Reformation. Finding compromise impossible he enforced the edict of Worms against L. and his followers. The Protestant princes united to oppose the decisions of the diet and formed the Schmalkald League. The Reformation now became more political, and L. gradually retired from the leadership. In fact, after the drawing up of the *Augsburg Confession*, he lived in comparative privacy, but continued to do much to organise

the new church and to suggest its form of worship. The Lutheran Church, unlike the Reformed Church, retained most of the medieval ceremonies and vestments, but the whole service (singing, reading of the scriptures and preaching of the sermon) was conducted in German.

L.'s doctrine was never developed into a logical system. He maintained that scripture freely interpreted was the only rule of faith. Though he retained the Apostles', the Nicene and the Athanasian creeds. he regarded them as being historical records of what had been believed, rather than as possessing binding authority. The result is that there is a wide diversity of opinion among his followers, from the orthodoxy of those who cling to the old confessions to the liberalism of those who deny even the authority of scripture. L. firmly held the doctrine of the Real Presence (q.v.) as plainly taught in scripture, but rejected Trans-substantiation in favour of Con-substantiation (q.v.) as the expression of the truth about it. He insisted on the use of the vernacular in worship, and on communion in both kinds. But the basic tenet upon which all his teaching depends, and which he called 'the article of the standing and falling church', was that of justification by faith alone (*sola fide*) without works, which he derived from St Paul's Epistle to the Romans.

L.'s writings were voluminous. The most interesting of those not already mentioned are the *Table Talk* and his *Letters*. He also wrote commentaries on the Bible, and many of the sermons are still read. The chief eds. of his works are those of Wittenberg (12 vols.), 1539–58; Halle (24 vols.), 1740–53; Erlangen and Frankfurt (67 vols.), 1826–73; reissue Weimar, 1883; people's ed., 1892; *see also* H. Wace's trans. of his primary works, 1896. His life was written by Melanchthon, *Historia de vita et actis Lutheris*, 1545. *See* V. H. H. Green, *Luther and the Reformation*, 1964; J. M. Todd, *Martin Luther*, 1964. There is an interesting if unorthodox interpretation of L. in John Osborne's play: *Luther*, 1960. (*See Plate: Church History*.)

Luthuli, Albert (1899–), S. African nationalist leader, educ. at Adams College and an Amer. mission college, Natal. He taught for sev. years and was appointed chief at Groutville by the S. African gov., 1935, being deprived of this position in 1952. In 1946 L. became a member of the African National Congress, and its president from 1952. The movement was banned, 1960: L. was arrested on a treason charge and detained till 1958. In 1959 he was banished and banned from all meetings for 5 years, and was detained under emergency regulations, 1960. An advocate of non-violence, L. was awarded the Nobel Peace Prize, 1960, and elected rector of Glasgow Univ., 1962, but was not allowed to come to Britain for his installation. He wrote: *Let My People Go*, 1962.

Luton, called by the Saxons **Lygetune,** and in the Domesday Book **Loitoine,** is an industrial and mrkt tn of Beds, England, 19 m. S. of Bedford and 30 m. N. of London. The tn was incorporated as a municipal bor. in 1876, and became a co. bor. on 1 April 1964, with extended boundaries and a pop. of 145,000.

L. has sev. fine buildings, the most modern of which is the tn hall, opened by the Duke of Kent in 1936. Its tall clocktower contains a clock which was a bequest of a former mayor of the tn. The anct par. church of St Mary is, however, the chief building of traditional interest. Dating from Norman times, it is a cruciform building largely in the Decorated and Perpendicular styles, and is among the largest of the par. churches of England. The interior of the church is full of interest, one of the most striking features being the unique canopied baptistery of the Decorated period. On the outskirts of L., at L. Hoo, is the famous Wernher collection of china, glass, pictures and other *objets d'art*.

L. is an anct tn, but until the founding of the straw-hat industry in the early 19th cent. it was of little importance. From then onwards L. has progressed. The straw-hat trade was gradually replaced by ladies' felt-hat making and today it is still a centre of this trade. Other industries were attracted to the tn by the offer of good sites, transport and abundant skilled labour. L. is the Brit. H.Q. of General Motors, manufacturing Vauxhall cars and Bedford trucks. Commer commercial vehicles are also produced here, and there are other industries connected with the motor industry. A municipal airport was estab. in 1936, and attracted aircraft industry. The airport has recently been further developed with concrete runways, and is now the H.Q. of sev. charter companies. Other manufs. include ball-bearings, refrigerators, vacuum cleaners and other light engineering products. The M1 motorway passes through L. near the W. boundary. Pop. 131,505. *See* W. Austin, *History of Luton and its Hamlets*, 1928; J. G. Dony, *History of the Straw-hat Industry*, 1942; F. Grundy and R. M. Titmuss, *Report on Luton*, 1945. (*See Plate: Bedfordshire*.)

Lutsk (Ukrainian **Luts'ke**; Polish **Luck**), tn in the W. Ukraine, cap., econ. and cultural centre of the Volhynia (q.v.) oblast. Known since 1085, L. belonged to Volhynia, became Lithuanian in 1336, Polish in 1569, Russian in 1791 and again Polish in 1919–39. It was the scene of much fighting in 1916. Pop. (1965) 75,000 (1931, 36,000).

Lutterworth, mrkt tn and dist of Leics, England, 6½ m. NNE. of Rugby. St Mary's Church contains the pulpit and various alleged relics of John Wycliffe, who held the living from 1374 until his death in 1384. This dist is mainly agric., but there have been recent developments in engineering, aircraft and textile works. Pop. (rural dist), 13,044.

Lüttich, *see* LIÈGE.

Luttrell Psalter, one of the most outstanding illuminated MSS. of the 14th cent. E. Anglian School. Its date is about 1340. Its text, comprising the usual church offices, is embellished with exquisitely drawn illustrations of contemporary life, and include a picture of Geoffrey Luttrell (or Louterell) on a charger, with his wife and

daughter. The MS. passed into the possession of the Weld family of Lulworth Castle, Dorset. Since 1929 it has belonged to the nation, having been purchased for £31,500. (*See Plate; Crusades*.)

Lutyens, Sir Edwin Landseer (1869–1944), architect, *b*. London, son of a painter. After a very brief training in the office of Sir Ernest George (q.v.), he actually began practice at the age of 19, his first commission being a country cottage for Miss Gertrude Jekyll, the landscape gardener, who greatly influenced his earlier work. For many years this consisted almost entirely of country houses, picturesque in design and showing sympathetic understanding of traditional materials. Typical examples are The Deanery, Sonning, 1900, and Marsh Court, Stockbridge, 1901. His later designs displayed a more formal Georgian or 'Queen Anne' style, a particularly formal example being Heathcote, Ilkley, 1906. In 1907–9 he designed sev. buildings, including 2 churches, in the Hampstead Garden Suburb. His Cenotaph in Whitehall has acquired a sentimental fame, but is also a fine design intrinsically. From 1910 onwards he carried out many public and a few commercial buildings. Among these were the Brit. Pavilion at the Rome Exhibition, 1910 (now housing the Brit. School at Rome); the Art Gallery at Johannesburg, 1911; Britannic House, 1926 and (in collaboration with J. A. Gotch), the Midland Bank—both in the City of London; the Brit Embassy at Washington, 1926; the Viceroy's House at New Delhi, completed 1930; Campion Hall, Oxford, 1934. His plans for a new Rom. Catholic Cathedral at Liverpool (q.v.) were abandoned after the Second World War, when only the crypt had been completed. L. was president of the Royal Academy from 1938 to 1944, and was awarded the R.I.B.A. Royal Gold Medal in 1921.

Lutynia (Ger. **Leuthen**), vil. of Poland, in Wrocław prov., 11 m. W. of Wrocław. It is famous for the great victory of Frederick the Great (*see* FREDERICK II) over the Austrians here in 1757. *See* J. Kutzen, *Die Schlacht bei Leuthen*, 1901.

Lützen, Ger. tn in the dist of Leipzig, 13 m. WSW. of Leipzig. Two famous battles took place in its neighbourhood: (1) The victory of the Swedes (numbering 18,000) over the Imperialists (numbering 30,000) led by Wallenstein, on 16 Nov. 1632, during the Thirty Years War. Gustavus Adolphus (*see* GUSTAVUS II) was killed in the battle. (2) The victory of Napoleon I in May 1813, over the Prussians and Russians at Grossgörschen, 4 m. SE. L. has an anct castle and a sugar industry. Pop. 6000.

Lützow, Franz Heinrich Hieronymus, Count (1849–1916), Bohemian historian, *b*. Hamburg, son of Franz, Count L. English on his mother's side, he spent much time in England. He was Ilchester lecturer on Slavonic subjects at Oxford in 1904, and lectured in Amer. univs., 1912. His pubs. include *Bohemia, an Historical Sketch*, 1896, *History of Bohemian Literature*, 1899, a trans. of Comenius's *Labyrinth of the World*,

1901, *The Life and Times of Master John Hus*, 1909, and *The Hussite Wars*, 1914.

Lützow, Ludwig Adolf Wilhelm, Freiherr von (1782–1834), Prussian soldier, *b.* Berlin. He entered the army in 1795, and was at the battle of Auerstadt and the siege of Colberg. At the outbreak of the war of Liberation (1813) he raised a volunteer corps of infantry and cavalry which was called the 'Black Rifles'. The corps was dissolved in 1814, becoming the 25th Regiment. L. led a gallant charge of the 6th Uhlans at Ligny (1815).

Luwian Language, *see* INDO-EUROPEAN LANGUAGES.

Luxation, *see* DISLOCATION.

Luxembourg, François Henri de Montmorency-Bouteville, Duc de (1628–95), marshal of France, cousin of the great Condé, *b.* Paris. He shared Condé's fortunes in the wars of the Fronde, was pardoned by Louis XIV on his return to France (1659) and subsequently was created a peer of the realm (1661). He served in the Netherlands (1667), and defeated William of Orange at Woerden (1672). His retreat from Utrecht (1673), in the face of tremendous odds, was a masterly exploit. In 1690 he defeated the allied troops at Fleurus, and put his old enemy, now William III of England, to rout at Steinkirk (1692) and Neerwinden (1693). *See* J. de Beaurain, *Histoire militaire du Duc de Luxembourg*, 1756, and life by Comte de Ségur, 1907.

Luxembourg: 1. (Luxembourg; Letzeburg), independent grand-duchy of Europe, bounded on the E. by the Ger. Federal Rep., S. by France, W. and N. by Belgium. Area 998 sq. m. The S. part belongs to the plateau of Lorraine, and the N., which is still higher, consists of the forest of Ardennes. The country is watered by the Sûre and affluents of the Moselle, which forms part of its E. border. About a quarter of the pop. is engaged in agriculture, the chief crops being wheat, oats, rye, barley and beet. Much wine is produced. L.'s iron and steel industries are important; the country has large iron ore deposits, and obtains the necessary coal from the Ruhr. L. also has textile and leather manufs. In 1948, L. joined with Belgium and the Netherlands in the Benelux (q.v.) customs union.

The reigning grand-duke is Jean (q.v.). The legislative power is vested in a Chamber of Deputies numbering 56, who are elected for 5 years on a basis of universal suffrage. The sovereign nominates the ministers as well as an advisory council of state. Education is compulsory between the ages of 6 and 15, and military service has been obligatory since 1944. The chief tns are L., the cap., Esch-sur-l'Alzette, a mining centre, Differdange, Dudelange and Petange. Pop. 326,000, nearly all Roman Catholics.

The counts of L., who first achieved prominence in the 11th cent., took their name from the castle of Lucelin-burhuc. In 1308 Count Henry became Henry VII, Emperor of Germany. Henry's grandson, Charles IV, raised L. to the rank of a duchy in 1354. In 1443 it was united with Burgundy, and in 1596 became Spanish. By the treaty of Utrecht (1713) it was ceded to Austria, but was annexed to France at the peace of Campo-Formio (1797). At the congress of Vienna (1815) it was created a grand duchy, the king of the Netherlands being grand duke, and part of the Ger. confederation, and by the treaty of London (1867) it was declared a neutral independent state. When William III of the Netherlands *d.* in 1890, L. passed to the Duke of Nassau. In 1914 it was overrun by the Germans and was occupied by them until 1918. In 1919, by the treaty of Versailles, it was declared free of all Ger. ties. In 1921 a Bill was passed for the economic union of L. with Belgium and the use of Belgian currency. In 1948 a customs union (Benelux) of Belgium, the Netherlands and L. came into being. In April and May 1948 constitutional changes were decided upon, the most important of which was the abandonment of unarmed neutrality, imposed upon the grand-duchy in 1867. L. is a member of NATO and of the European Economic Community and its subsidiary bodies. In 1964 the Grand Duchess Charlotte abdicated, and was succeeded by her son, Jean (q.v.).

On 10 May 1940 L. was again invaded by Ger. troops and the grand duchess went to England. The Germans appointed a gauleiter with the intention of absorbing L. in the Reich as Gau Moselland. Early in Sept. 1944 the Amer. First Army advanced rapidly across Belgium and L. on a 65-m. front and the city of L. was liberated on the 11th. The Allies then crossed the frontier N. of L. on 14 Sept. But on 16 Dec. Rundstedt's army drove sev. m. into L. in the battle of the Ardennes. The Allies again advanced in N. L., Amer. forces launching N.-eastward from the Arlon-L. area and driving the Germans out again. *See further* WESTERN FRONT IN SECOND WORLD WAR, *Marshal von Rundstedt's Counter-Offensive. See* P. Weber, *Geschichte Luxembourgs im zweiten Weltkrieg*, 1947, and *Histoire du Grand-Duché de Luxembourg*, 1949, J. Petit, *Luxembourg Yesterday and Today*, 1953.

Language and Literature. The L. language, based upon old Teutonic roots, has borrowed extensively from the Celtic, Roman and French. Throughout the cents. Ger. and Fr. roots have been phonetically altered and the language is still spoken in Ger., Belgian and Fr. border regions which in the course of hist. were separated from the grand duchy proper. There is an extensive literature in the L. language. In spite of the Luxembourger's affection for his mother tongue, which is exclusively used by every class of the pop., French has been for over 400 years the official legislative, administrative and judicial language. The second official language is German.

2. Cap. of the grand duchy of L., situated on the Alzette, 42 m. N. of Metz. It consists of 2 parts; the upper tn stands on a rocky cliff and is connected with the lower tn, lying in a ravine, by flights of steps. The chief buildings are the Gothic cathedral of Notre Dame, the Grand Ducal Palais (1580) and the tn hall. Steel and

iron works, tanning and brewing comprise the main industries. Pop. 74,500. *See* T. H. Passmore, *In Further Ardenne*, 1905; R. Putnam, *Luxembourg and her Neighbours*, 1918; Muirhead and Monmarché (editors), *Belgium and Luxembourg*, 1929; *The Luxembourg Grey Book* (preface by J. Bech), 1942; J. Petit, *Luxembourg Yesterday and Today*, 1953.

3. Prov. in the SE. of Belgium, bounded on its E. side by the grand-duchy of L. and to the S. by France. It is the region of the Ardennes and is watered by tribs. of the Meuse and of the Moselle. There are large areas of forest and poor mt pastures. Agriculture is mainly carried on in the fertile valleys. In its S. part, which forms an extension of the Lorraine iron-field of France, iron ore is found and worked. The prov. produces mainly timber, slate, iron, leather and tobacco. The breeding of horses, cattle and pigs is carried on. Chief tns are Arlon (the cap.), Bastogne, Marche, St Hubert and Virton. Area 1705 sq. m.; pop. 216,900. (*See Plate*.)

Luxembourg Palace, in Paris, on the S. side of the Seine, was erected by Marie de' Medici, and in 1879 became the meeting-place of the Senate. Attached to it is a gallery, the role of which in the past has been to represent contemporary European art, though the modern reorganisation of Paris galleries (*see* LOUVRE) has rendered it obsolete. *See* PARIS.

Luxemburg, Rosa (1870–1919), Ger. revolutionary of Polish descent. She acquired Ger. nationality by marriage to a Ger. workman. Having devoted her energies to the Socialist papers *Arbeiterzeitung* and *Leipziger Volkszeitung* she went to Russia, and there took part in the uprising of 1905. During the First World War she was imprisoned, but after the revolution of 1918 she joined Liebknecht (q.v.) as co-editor of the Communist *Rote Fahne*. Together they were arrested, and charged with complicity in the Berlin disturbances of Jan. 1919, but were attacked on their way to jail and murdered. *See* life by J. P. Nettl, 1966.

Luxeuil-les-Bains (anct **Lixovium**), Fr. spa in the dept of Haute-Saône, 27 m. NW. of Belfort. It was known to the Romans. St Columban founded a celebrated abbey here in 590. There are metal, textile and wood manufs. Pop. 8200.

Luxor, *see* THEBES.

Luxulian, tn of Cornwall, England, 6 m. SW. of Bodmin (q.v.). It has important granite quarries and gives its name, Luxulianite, to a porphyritic rock found in the neighbourhood. Here is L. valley and the Treffry viaduct. Pop. 861.

Luynes, or **Luines, Charles d'Albert, Duc de** (1578–1621), courtier and soldier of Louis XIII of France, son of Honoré d'Albert (*d.* 1592), Governor of Beaucaire, *b.* Pont St Esprit, Gard. He instigated the assassination of the Marshal d'Ancre (q.v.), 1617, and suppressed a Huguenot rebellion. In 1621 he was made constable of France, but *d.* soon afterwards, while heading another army against the Protestants.

Luzán, Ignacio de (1702–54), Sp. writer, *b.* Saragossa. His literary reputation is based on his *Poética*, 1737, which influenced Sp. poetry in a classical direction.

Luzern (Fr. **Lucerne**): 1. Canton in N. central Switzerland. The surface in the N. is mountainous, but the soil is generally fertile. Its area is about 580 sq. m., and about four-fifths consists of pasture land. Grain, flax, hemp and potatoes are produced, and the manuf. of cheese and condensed milk is important. The spoken language is Swiss-German. Pop. 253,500.

2. Cap. of the canton, and one of the most popular tourist centres in Switzerland. It is situated picturesquely on the banks of the Reuss as it issues from the lake, and is 24 m. SSW. of Zürich. To the S. of the city towers Mt Pilatus (7000 ft above sea level), while on the E. rises the famous Rigi. Amongst the numerous features of interest are the celebrated rock, the 'Lion of L.', carved by Thorwaldsen as a memorial to the Swiss guards who fell in Paris (1792), the Hofkirche of Leodegar, glacier garden and the tn hall dating from the 17th cent. The Reuss is crossed by the old covered wooden bridge called the Kapellbrücke. Pop. 67,500.

Luzern, Lake of (Vierwaldstättersee, lake of the Four Forest Cantons), one of the most lovely of European lakes, situated in the N. central part of Switzerland. It has 4 main basins, connected only by narrow channels. Parts of the lake are in the cantons of Luzern, Uri, Schwyz and Unterwalden. The lake is subject to sudden and violent storms. Most of the vils. on the shores are summer resorts. Altitude 1435 ft; greatest depth 700 ft.

Luzon, or **Luçon,** largest and most northerly of the Philippine Is., with an area of 40,420 sq. m. L. was Sp. from the 16th cent. until it was ceded to America in 1898. It became part of the new Philippine Rep. in 1946. The coastline is much indented, the prin. inlets being the Gulf of Lingayen and Manila Bay on the W., Tayabas and Ragay Bays on the S. and the bays of Lagonoy, San Miguel and Lamón on the E. The is. is very mountainous. The highest peak is the volcano Mayón (7926 ft). There are 6 chief rivs., Rio Grande de Cagayán, Agno Grande, Rio Grande de la Pampanga, Vicol and Pasig, besides many streams and lakes. The vegetation is tropical and luxuriant. The chief products are silk, tobacco, ivory carvings and mats. Iron, copper and coal are mined; a very large chrome deposit has been found; gold is produced in N. and S. L. The pop. of 7,374,798 is of mixed race.

Japan began hostilities against the U.S.A. on 7 Dec. 1941, and among other places raided the Clark airfield in N. L., killing 200 men. Soon afterwards Jap. forces landed on the is. Manila, the cap., was raided by bombers on 13 Dec. and captured on 1 Jan 1942. Though greatly outnumbered the Americans and Filipinos under Gen. MacArthur put up a remarkable defence on the Bataan peninsula until April, the garrison at Corregidor holding out for nearly a month longer. The Americans returned within 3 years, when very large forces of troops landed on

L. on 9 Jan. 1945. On the next day the Americans controlled all beaches in Lingayen Gulf and captured the Lingayen airfield. The Jap. armies were split in two by the Amer. advance of 20 Jan., and on 25 Jan. the Japanese lost the main air base. The Americans entered Manila on 3 Feb. Bataan and Corregidor were in their possession by 21 Feb. See PACIFIC, NAVAL OPERATIONS AND CAMPAIGNS IN.

L'vov, Prince Georgy Evgen'evich (1861–1925), Russian politician, Constitutional Democrat. He was active in the Zemstvo movement (see ZEMSTVO) and was chairman of the All-Russian Union of Zemstvos. Upon the abdication of Nicholas II in Feb. 1917 the Provisional Committee of the State Duma authorised L. to form a provisional gov.; he was prime minister until July, when he was replaced by Kerensky. After the Bolsheviks came to power he lived in emigration in France.

L'vov (Ukrainian L'viv; Polish Lwów; Ger. Lemberg): 1. Oblast (prov.) in Galicia (W. Ukraine) adjacent to the Polish frontier, on the N. slopes of the Carpathian mts and the Volhynia-Podolia upland, traversed by the upper W. Bug. It is on the edge of the forest and wooded-steppe belts; 28 per cent of the area is covered with forest, partly oak. Deposits of oil, natural gas (see DASHAVA), ozokerite, coal and salt are worked, and there are engineering, chemical, woodworking and diverse light and food industries. Grain and potatoes are grown, cattle and pigs raised. In the 1960's the industries of L. have been re-organised on commercial lines—the first time this has been attempted on a regional basis rather than in individual factories. Area 8400 sq. m.; pop. (1965) 2,336,000 (45 per cent urb.), chiefly Ukrainians, before the war many Poles and Jews. For history, see GALICIA.

2. Cap. of the above, the main economic and cultural centre of W. Ukraine. There are large metal-working (engineering, electro-technical), food and textile industries. It is an important railway transportation centre (9 railway lines, airport). It has a branch of the Ukrainian Academy of Sciences (founded in 1073 as the Shevchenko Society); a univ. (1661; before 1862 Latin and German, then Polish and partly Ukrainian, now Ukrainian); polytechnic (1844), veterinary (1897) and other institutes; and a conservatoire (1904). There are many architectural monuments of the 13th–18th cents. L. was founded c. 1250, and soon became cap. of Galicia (q.v.); it became Polish in 1340, and received Magdeburg Law in 1356. It was an important centre of crafts and commerce (Armenian, later also Jewish, merchants) and of the Russian (Ukrainian) Orthodox religions and cultural movement. From 1848 it was the main centre of the Ukrainian national movement. Much fighting took place here in 1914–15, 1920 (Soviet-Polish war) and 1944. Pop. (1964) 496,000 (1931, 316,000), mostly Ukrainians (pre-war mostly Poles and Jews).

Lwoo, see LUO.

LXX, abbreviation for Septuagint (q.v.), the Gk version of the O.T. (see BIBLE).

Lyakhov Islands, see NOVOSIBIRSKIYE.

Lyall, Edna, pseudonym of Ada Ellen Bayly (1857–1903), novelist, b. Brighton. Her 3-vol. novel Donovan, 1882, was admired by Gladstone, but it was the sequel to it, We Two, 1884, which estab. her reputation. Others are In the Golden Days, 1885, and The Autobiography of a Slander, 1887. See life by J. M. Escreet, 1904.

Lyautey, Louis Gonzalve Hubert (1854–1934), Fr. administrator and soldier, b. Nancy and educ. at St Cyr. Sent to Indo-China in 1894, he later became chief of staff to Galliéni, whom he accompanied to Madagascar in 1897. L. brought order to the S. part of the previously unsubdued is. Brigadier-general in 1903, in 1906 he became chief of the div. of Oran. Put by Poincaré at the head of the new Fr. protectorate of Morocco in 1912, L. proved himself a superb colonial administrator, and it was largely owing to his firm but enlightened policy that Morocco remained loyal to France during the First World War. L. was elected to the Academy in 1914; for a few months in 1916–17 he was minister for war; in 1921 he was made marshal. He resigned his position in Morocco in 1925. See life by A. Maurois (Eng. trans. 1931).

Lycanthropy (Gk lukos, wolf; anthropos, man), the power attributed to certain mortals of changing themselves into wolves. It is also used in a broader sense, and applied to the metamorphosis into any animal, i.e. tiger, dog, bear, fox, etc. Herodotus relates that the Neuri turned to wolves for a few days every year, and in Virgil's eighth Eclogue we read how Moeris makes himself a wolf by means of poisonous herbs. In the Scandinavian sagas, too, there are 'werewolf' warriors of peculiar ferocity, and the belief was long current in Denmark that a werewolf could be recognised by its eyebrows meeting. The word is used in pathology to denote a mental disease in which the patient imagines he is an animal. See R. Eisler, Man into Wolf, 1951.

Lycaon, in Gk legend, a king of Arcadia, who, when visited by Zeus, served the god with a dish of human flesh. He and all but one of his sons were thereupon killed with a flash of lightning or, according to another version, changed into wolves. L. was the traditional founder of Lycosura (q.v.). See R. P. Eccles, Greek Wolf-lore, 1937.

Lycaonia, anct ter. of Asia Minor. Its boundaries varied, but at its greatest extent it was bordered N. by Galatia, E. by Cappadocia, S. by the Taurus range, W. by Pisidia and Phrygia. Though affording good pasture for sheep and wild asses, it suffered from lack of water and a salty soil; the inhab. lived largely by plunder. L. remained virtually independent of Persia, but was included in the dominions of Alexander the Great. After his death it belonged to the Seleucids until the defeat of Antiochus III (190 BC) by the Romans, who gave it to Eumenes II of Pergamum (q.v.). The prin. tns in the time of St Paul were Iconium, Lystra and Derbe (Acts xiv; xvi).

Lyceum, The, a gymnasium and garden with

covered walks at Athens (q.v.), near the temple of Apollo Lyceus. Aristotle (q.v.) taught here, whence his school (*see* PERIPATETICS) was sometimes called the L.

Lyceum Theatre, London, from 1871 to 1902 the home of Sir Henry Irving's company, and the scene of his and Ellen Terry's greatest triumphs. There was a theatre on this site from 1772 onwards, and part of Irving's theatre, which opened in 1834, is still standing, though it was extensively altered in 1904. It then became the home of melodrama under the Melville brothers, who owned it from 1909 to 1939. It was scheduled for demolition, and closed after 6 performances of *Hamlet* by Sir John Gielgud. Owing to the Second World War it remained standing and is now a dance hall.

Lych-gate, *see* LICHGATE.

Lychnis, genus of perennial herbs, family Caryophyllaceae, about 24 species of N. temperate regions; *L. flos-cuculi* is the Cuckoo flower or Ragged Robin, native to Britain and Europe.

Lych-wake, *see* WAKE.

Lycia, anct coastal dist of SW. Asia Minor, between Caria and Pamphylia. The Lycians are shown in the *Iliad* as allies of Troy, under their leaders Sarpedon and Glaucus L. received Gk colonies at an early date; various sites have yielded fine specimens of both Gk and native art, many of which are in the Brit. Museum. L. was never subdued by Lydia; it belonged to Persia 546–*c.* 468, and from 387 BC until the conquests of Alexander. It continued however, through those periods, as well as under the Seleucids, to enjoy a large measure of independence, which was hardly affected even by Rom. supremacy until Claudius (AD 41–54) annexed it to the empire and united it with Pamphylia (q.v.). The prin. tns were Xanthus, Myra and Patara.

Lycian Language, *see* INDO-EUROPEAN LANGUAGES.

Lycomedes, legendary king of Scyros (q.v.), to whose court Achilles was sent, disguised as a girl, by his mother who vainly sought to prevent his going to the Trojan war. Here Achilles begat Neoptolemus (q.v.) by Deidameia, daughter of L. *See also* THESEUS.

Lycopene, red carotenoid pigment found in tomatoes, rose hips and many berries. It is the parent substance of all the natural carotenoids (so called from carotene, the pigment in carrots).

Lycoperdon, genus of about 100 cosmopolitan fungi, order Lycoperdales; common Puff-balls, with a double peridium, the outer being warted, spiny, scaly, etc.; usually growing on the ground; edible when young. *L. perlatum* (synonym *gemmatum*) is the common Puff-ball of Britain; *L. pyriforme* grows on dead wood; *L. hiemale* often forms rings in grass.

Lycophron, Gk poet and scholar, *b.* Chalcis in Euboea. He was commissioned by Ptolemy Philadelphus to arrange the works of the comic poets in the museum library, and while thus engaged he wrote a substantial work on comedy. This has been lost, as have all his tragedies

except the *Cassandra*, a learned but poetically futile piece. *See* text with trans. by A. W. Mair in *Callimachus, Lycophron and Azatus* (Loeb Library), 1921.

Lycopodiales, Pteridophytes, group of spore-bearing plants which grew as large trees in Carboniferous forests. *Lepidodendron* had numerous small leaves spirally arranged on the stem; in *Sigillaria* the leaf-bases formed vertical lines on the ribbed trunk. Tree stumps and roots are called *Stigmaria*.

Lycopodium, family Lycopodiaceae, genus of plants known as Club Mosses. They form dense masses of verdure. *L. clavatum* is the Brit. Club Moss, and *selago* the Fir Club Moss.

Lycosura, anct city of Arcadia, traditionally founded by Lycaon (q.v.). The temple of Despoina (Persephone) housed a colossal group by Damophon of Messene, showing Despoina and Demeter seated, with Artemis and the Titan Anytus in attendance. Remains of both temple and sculptures were excavated in 1889.

Lycurgus, traditional legislator of Sparta. Many scholars find no evidence that he ever existed; they suppose him to have been a pre-hellenic Arcadian deity whose cult was adopted at Sparta, where indeed sacrifices were offered to him in historical times.

Lycurgus (*c.* 390–324 BC), one of the Ten Attic orators. He was one of the prin. supporters of Demosthenes (q.v.). He administered the finances of Athens from 338 to 326, during which time he increased its revenue, beautified the city, and served the cause of literature by establishing state texts of the tragic drama, to which actors were obliged to adhere. Most of his speeches were for the prosecution in criminal cases; only one is extant, *Against Leocrates* (330). *See* ed. by O. Navarre, 1932; *also* J. F. Dobson, *The Greek Orators*, 1919.

Lydd, bor. of Kent, a corporate member of the Cinque Ports and a limb of New Romney (3 m. to the SSW.). Lyddite (Picric acid, q.v.), a powerful explosive, was first tried out on the artillery ranges attached to the military camp at L. L. Ferryfield Airport, operated by private enterprise, which opened in July 1954, provides a 20-min. cross-Channel car ferry and passenger service. Pop. 2685.

Lydda (Gk *Ludda*; Heb. *Lōd*), city of Israel, situated in the plain of Sharon, 3 m. SE. of Tel-Aviv, 11 m. SE. of Joppa. It was renamed Diospolis in the 2nd cent. AD, and is referred to in both the O.T. and N.T. St George is said to have been born and buried here, and in the 4th cent. a bishopric was instituted under his patronage. The church erected over his tomb has been repeatedly destroyed and rebuilt. L. airport is the most important in the country and there is also a railway junction. It was captured by the Israeli army in July 1948. The Arab pop. fled and the tn was repopulated by Jewish immigrants. Pop. 22,000.

Lyddite, *see* PICRIC ACID.

Lydenburg, *see* LEYDENBURG.

Lydford, vil. and par. in Devon, England, 11½ m. E. of Launceston. It was a walled tn before the Conquest, and Judge Jeffreys held his assizes at the castle. For many years it was the cap. of Devonshire 'stannary', owing to its important position on the edge of the great tin dist of Dartmoor (q.v.). The par. includes the whole of Dartmoor. Pop. (of vil.) 300; (of par.) 2000.

Lydgate, John (*c.* 1370–*c.* 1451), poet, *b.* Lydgate, Suffolk. He was educ. at the Benedictine monastery of Bury St Edmunds, where he became a monk at the age of 16; a great part of his life was spent there, whence he is often styled the Monk of Bury. He is said to have studied at Oxford, Paris and Padua, was for a time a court poet, and was patronised by Humphrey, Duke of Gloucester. He wrote copiously and with tiresome prolixity a great variety of poems— moral tales, legends of the saints and histories. His total output runs to 130,000 lines. His chief works are *Troy Book*, 1412–20, written at the request of Henry V when Prince of Wales, *The Falls of Princes*, 1430–8, and *The Story of Thebes*, 1420–2, the last being represented as a new Canterbury Tale in tribute to Chaucer, of whom L. was an avowed admirer, though he largely follows the Fr. romanticists previous to him. *See* E. P. Hammond, *Chaucer and Lydgate*, 1912; W. F. Schirmer, *John Lydgate*, 1952.

Lydia, anct dist of varying boundaries in Asia Minor. The original ter. seems to have consisted of the upper Hermus region and the plain of Sardis; but 2 of its monarchs, Alyattes and Croesus (qq.v.), gradually extended their dominions to form a commercial empire which included all Asia Minor W. of the R. Halys (excepting Lycia, q.v.), with Sardis as Cap. In 546 BC this empire became subject to Persia, from which it passed to Alexander the Great and then to the Seleucids. After the defeat of Antiochus III (190 BC) the Romans gave L. to Eumenes II of Pergamum (q.v.), whose son Attalus III bequeathed his kingdom to Rome. L. was thus included in the prov. of Asia, bounded N. by Mysia, E. by Phrygia, S. by Caria, W. by the Aegean.

The Lydians are said to have been the first people to coin money (*c.* 700 BC). They were celebrated also for their music and their system of physical training. Highly civilised at an early date, they undoubtedly exercised a profound influence on the culture of the Ionian city-states which lay between them and the sea.

Lydian Language, *see* INDO-EUROPEAN LANGUAGES.

Lydian Mode, one of the 3 modes of anct Gk music, a minor scale suited to soft pathos. Hence the phrase L. M., meaning of effeminate, plaintive character. Cf. Milton, *L'Allegro*:

'Ever against eating cares,
Lap me in soft Lydian airs';

and Dryden, *Alexander's Feast*:

'Softly sweet, in Lydian measures,
Soon he sooth'd his soul to pleasures'.

Lye, par. of Worcs, England, part of the municipal bor. of Stourbridge (q.v.), with manufs. of galvanised and enamelled hollow-ware, fire-bricks, scholastic equipment and heavy and light forgings. There are public open spaces.

Lye. Caustic L.s are solutions of potassium and sodium hydroxides; mild L.s, of their carbonates.

Lyell, Sir Charles, 1st **Baronet** (1797–1875), geologist, *b.* near Kirriemuir in Forfarshire. He studied at Exeter College, Oxford, where he was attracted to geology by the lectures of Dr Buckland, and in 1819 joined the Geological and the Linnean Societies of London, being secretary of the former from 1823 to 1826. He was elected F.R.S. in 1826, and in 1830 pub. the first vol. of his *Principles of Geology*, the summary of which is given in the continuation of the title, 'being an attempt to explain the former changes of the earth's surface, by reference to causes now in action'. The second and third vols. appeared in 1832 and 1833 respectively, and the whole work was reprinted in 4 smaller vols. in 1834. The book won acceptance from the first and finally discredited the catastrophic view of geology and estab. the doctrine of uniformitarianism (*see* GEOLOGY). It is one of the classics of geology, 12 eds. being pub. in L.'s lifetime. Besides this great work he pub. *Elements of Geology* as a supplement to the *Principles*, 1838, *Travels in North America, with Geological Observations*, 1845, *A Second Visit to the United States of North America*, 1849, *The Antiquity of Man*, 1863, and *The Student's Elements of Geology*, 1871. He was prof. of geology at King's College, London, 1831–3, and president of the Geological Society, 1835–7 and 1849–51. He was knighted in 1848, and created a baronet in 1864. His *Life, Letters and Journals* appeared in 1881.

Lygetune, *see* LUTON.

Lykewake, *see* WAKE.

Lyly, John (*c.* 1554–1606), dramatist and novelist, *b.* Kent. He took his degree of B.A. at Magdalen College, Oxford, in 1573, and his M.A. in 1575, but he also studied at Cambridge, and was incorporated M.A. at that univ. in 1579. The same year he first part of his novel, *Euphues, the Anatomy of Wit*, appeared and he at once became famous. This was followed by *Euphues and his England* in 1580, which brought him under the notice of Lord Burghley, who gave him some employment. After this he wrote light plays to be performed at court by the children's acting companies of the Chapel Royal at St Paul's, London, among which were *Campaspe*, 1584, *Sapho and Phao*, 1584, *Endymion*, 1591, and *Midas*, 1592. In 1589 he championed the cause of the bishops in the Martin Marprelate controversy (q.v.), and pub. a tract entitled *Pappe with an Hatchet*. In 1589 he entered Parliament for Hinton, being subsequently elected for Aylesbury in 1593, for Appleby in 1597 and again for Aylesbury in 1601.

L.'s chief work was his *Euphues*, which, although a very tedious story, is remarkable for its prose style, which is chiefly characterised by a continuous straining after antithesis and epigram. The novelty of this style gave it the name of 'euphuism' (q.v.). L. also enjoyed some reputation as a writer of comedies, and is described as 'eloquent and witty'; but his plots are loosely fashioned, and his language artificial, the most attractive feature of his plays being the lyrics. See R. W. Bond (editor), *Complete Works, with Life and Notes*, 1902; also C. G. Child, *John Lyly and Euphuism*, 1894; V. Jeffery, *John Lyly and the Italian Renaissance*, 1929; and studies by J. D. Wilson, 1905; A. Feuillerat, 1910; S. A. Tannenbaum, 1940; G. K. Hunter, 1962.

Lyme Regis, seaport and holiday resort of Dorset, England, standing on the Lym near its entrance to the Eng. Channel. Edward I gave L. R. its charter, and Elizabeth I incorporated it. Monmouth landed here in 1685. The Lias rocks in the vicinity have yielded remains of the Ichthyosaurus and Plesiosaurus. The locality is geologically interesting. The Cobb, now a massive stone pier joined to the tn, was first mentioned in mid 13th cent., when it formed an artificial harbour. Shipping is no longer a prin. occupation but fishing is carried out, and the Cobb harbour is a centre for sailing enthusiasts. Pop. 3533.

Lymington, municipal bor. and small port of Hants, England, on L. R., 12 m. SW. of Southampton, and incorporating Milford-on-Sea (4 m.), New Milton (7 m.) and Barton-on-Sea (which gives its name to Barton Clay). L. is an old-world tn with engineering and yachting industries; New Milton is a modern residential and holiday resort. Pop. 28,642.

Lymm, urb. dist of Cheshire, England, 5 m. E. of Warrington, Lancs. Pop. 7500.

Lymph and Lymphatics. Lymph (Lat. *lympha*, water), slightly yellow, waterish, somewhat salt, alkaline fluid pervading all the tissues of the body, and originating as an exudation of blood plasma from the capillaries. It is a medium acting between the cells and the blood, and performs a double function: conveying waste matter from the tissues to the blood and conveying new substances for the formation of blood. Chemically lymph shows little difference from blood itself except in the red matter; it contains less protein, more chlorides and in it are corpuscles not distinguishable from the colour-less blood corpuscles. Lymphatics are the vessels which carry the lymph throughout the body. Waste products diffuse through the fluid to the blood capillaries, which reabsorb some of the exuded fluid. The surplus fluid is carried away by the lymphatic vessels. The L. vessels of the intestine are different in that they are carrying fats absorbed from the food the latter to renew the blood and tissue. The lymphatics of the small intestine are known as *lacteals* and convey *chyle*. The structure of lymphatics resembles that of veins. The capillaries enter larger vessels, or the nodes themselves, and form 2 sets; the superficial lymphatics lying immediately beneath the skin at the surface of the body, and the deep lymphatics in the interior of the body lying in the areolar tissue; the former com-municate with the latter, which are larger. The

final vessel of the lymphatic system is the *thoracic duct*, which enters the system of circulation at the junction of the subclavian and jugular veins on the left. Another much smaller duct, the right lymphatic, enters the right subclavian and conveys L. from the right side of the body from the chest upwards. The lymphatic nodes are small, solid, kidney-shaped bodies, usually compared in size to variation from hempseed to the almond; there are again 2 sets, (1) in the thorax and abdomen, the deep set, (2) the superficial set distributed in the groin, behind the knee, the armpits, at the elbow and in the neck. The lymphatics thus form a circulatory system regulated by valves. The lymph nodes filter the lymph and act as barriers to protect the body from invasion by bacteria from a septic focus. L. nodes also impede the progress of malignant cells migrating from a primary cancer and themselves become the site of secondary cancer. Lymphangitis, or inflamma-tion of the lymphatics, may occur with the invasion of infective bacteria, and when lymphangitis occurs in the superficial lymph it may be recognised by the scarlet lines of the inflamed vessels beneath the skin. Suppuration of a lymphatic gland may occur from infection with pyogenic organisms. A highly malignant form of cancer, known as lymphosarcoma, may have its primary site in a lymphatic node. *See* BUBO; CANCER; TONSILS; TUBERCULOSIS.

LYMPHATIC NODE
Showing lymph vessels entering
and leaving.

Lympne, vil. of Kent, England, 2½ m. W. of Hythe. An air station estab. here in 1915 was used for military purposes during the First World War. It was then converted into a station on the route between the Continent and London, but became a fighter station in the Second World War. In 1949 it was being maintained as an airport by a charter company. L. was once a Rom. port, though not now on the sea. Pop. 700.

Lynas Point, *see* LINAS or LYNAS POINT.

Lynceus, legendary son of Aegyptus and husband of Hypermestra. *See* DANAUS.

Lynch Law, mob vengeance without form of law on a person suspected of having committed a crime. For many years the term has been associated mainly with the killing of Negroes in the U.S.A. for supposed assaults on white women, though actually sex offences account for less than one-fourth of all lynchings. The origin of the term is variously ascribed to the name of Col. Lynch, who illegally whipped Tory conspirators in 1780, and to James Lynch Fitz-Stevens, mayor of Galway, who, in 1493, acting on the classic precept of Brutus, tried his son for murder and, when prevented from publicly executing him, hanged him from the window of his own house. In Amer. law all present and consenting at a person's death by lynching are guilty of murder in the first degree, unless the act were committed in sudden anger. Lynching was strongly condemned in the report of the S. Commission on the Study of Lynching (Atlanta, Georgia, 1931). Ignorance, low economic status and bigotry are assumed as factors responsible for lynching. Of all the lynchings in the previous 40 years nearly 80 per cent were for non-sexual offences, real or alleged, and sometimes men were lynched for political offences. The commission also found that L. L. was not necessary for the protection of white women. Mob leaders have rarely been proceeded against owing to public indifference and the fact that the Negro had no vote where most lynchings occurred. Three anti-lynching bills have been introduced in Congress, but all failed of enactment.

Lynchburg, city of Virginia, U.S.A., stands on the James R., 124 m. W. by S. of Richmond. Transportation, highway and distribution centre of the W. Piedmont (tobacco, fruit, dairy products and grain); an important dark-tobacco market and manufacturing centre: shoes, textiles, clothing, paper, drugs, tanning extracts, farm equipment, foundry products and food products. Randolph-Macon Woman's College, Virginia Theological Seminary and College and L. College are here. Pop. 54,790.

Lynd, Robert (1879–1949), essayist and critic, *b.* Belfast. He took his B.A. at Queen's College, Belfast, and from 1908 produced a series of books, chiefly essays, among which may be mentioned *Home Life in Ireland,* 1909, *The Art of Letters,* 1921, *The Peal of Bells,* 1924, *It's a Fine World,* 1930, *I Tremble to Think,* 1936, and *Life's Little Oddities,* 1941. L. was literary editor of the *News Chronicle.*

Lyndhurst, John Singleton Copley, 1st Baron (1772–1863), lord chancellor, *b.* Boston, Massachusetts. He was brought to England at an early age, and studied at Trinity College, Cambridge. In 1804 he was called to the Bar and joined the Midland circuit, and in 1812 became popular at Nottingham by defending a Luddite rioter, John Ingham. In 1819 he became chief justice of Chester, solicitor-general and was knighted. He was attorney-general in 1824–6 and became master of the rolls in 1826. As Baron L. he was lord chancellor under 3 administrations.

Lyndhurst, vil. of Hants, England, the beautifully situated cap. of the New Forest, 8 m. WSW. of Southampton; it contains the Queen's House, now the Crown Office of the Forestry Commission, where the Verderer's Court is held. Pop. 3000.

Lyndsay, Sir David, *see* LINDSAY.

Lyndsay of Pitscottie, *see* LINDSAY, ROBERT, OF PITSCOTTIE.

Lyne, Rev. Joseph Leycester, *see* IGNATIUS, FATHER.

Lynedoch, Thomas Graham, 1st Baron (1748–1843), Brit. general. In 1793 he joined Hood's fleet in the Mediterranean as a volunteer, and on returning home he raised a battalion known as the 'Perthshire Volunteers'. He became brevet-colonel in 1796, and was appointed Brit. military commissioner with the Austrian Army in Italy, 1798. Later he accompanied Sir John Moore to Sweden and Spain as aide-de-camp, being present in the Corunna retreat. His most memorable victory was the defeat of the French at Barossa, Mar. 1811; during the rest of the Peninsular war he acted as second in command to Wellington, and was created Baron L. of Balgowan, 1814. *See* C. F. Aspinall-Oglander, *Freshly Remembered,* 1956.

Lynmouth and **Lynton,** 2 picturesque vils. of N. Devon, England, standing on the Bristol Channel, 12 m. E. of Ilfracombe, within the Exmoor National Park. Lynmouth is on the shore, at the base of a lofty cliff, and Lynton lies on the hillside, 428 ft above. A cliff railway connects the vils. Between 1934 and 1946 the National Trust acquired some 390 ac., mostly wooded, on both sides of the R. Lyn. Lynmouth has been completely reconstructed since the floods of 1952. Pop. (urb. dist of Lynton) 1918.

Lynn, seaport of Essex co., Massachusetts, U.S.A., stands on Massachusetts Bay, 9 m. NE. of Boston. L. manufs. boots and shoes, machinery, wire goods, electrical machinery, clothing and bakery products. Pop. 94,500.

Lynn Regis, *see* KING'S LYNN.

Lynx, general name for a widely distributed genus of fierce, bloodthirsty Felidae. Of the 2 European L.s, the N. L. ranges throughout Scandinavia and N. Russia, but is very scarce. The S. or small spotted L. is common in the less frequented parts of S. Europe. The African L., or Caracal (q.v.), occurs throughout the African continent, and there are 4 species in the New World. L.s are larger than the true wild cats, and have long limbs, the tail is short, the ears are tipped with a tuft of hair, and the cheeks are bearded. The soft, valuable fur is light brown or grey with darker spots varying according to species.

Lynx, inconspicuous N. constellation between the Great Bear and Auriga. L. contains no bright stars, and was so named by Hevelius because those would examine the constellation ought to be lynx-eyed. *See illus. overleaf.*

Lyon, Emma, *see* HAMILTON, EMMA.

Lyon (often anglicised **Lyons**; anct **Lugdunum**), Fr. city, cap. of the dept of Rhône, at the

LYNX

confluence of the Saône and the Rhône, 240 m. SSE. of Paris. It is the third city of France. The Romans founded a colony here in 43 BC, and it gave its name to Lugdunensis, one of the 4 provs. of Gallia in the time of Augustus. It was here that Christianity was introduced into Gallia in the 2nd cent. In 197 the tn was razed by Septimius Severus against whom it had revolted. It was ruled by its archbishops until the beginning of the 14th cent., when Philip IV incorporated it in the kingdom of France. Two important church councils were held in the tn in 1245 and 1274. A Stock Exchange, the first in France, was estab. in the tn in 1506. In 1793 L., which was controlled by Royalists and Moderates, was taken and partly destroyed by the forces of the Convention. During the Second World War the tn was a very important centre of the Resistance Movement. The city proper lies on the long tongue of land between the 2 rivs.; on the W. bank of the Saône is the old tn, and E. of the Rhône is the new tn. Among the buildings of interest in the main part of the city are the fine 17th cent. hôtel-de-ville, the Palais des Arts (1667–1879), and the churches of St-Martin d'Ainay (11th cent.) and St-Nizier (15th cent.). Here also are the silk dists of La Croix-Rousse and Terreaux. The Fourvière hill, above the old tn, is crowned by the richly decorated basilica of Notre-Dame de Fourvière (1872–96); its site has been a place of pilgrimage since 1643. At the foot of the hill is the archiepiscopal cathedral of St Jean (12th–14th cents.) which, although badly damaged by the Huguenots in the 16th cent., retains some notable examples of Gothic sculpture. The Archbishop of L. bears the title of 'Primate of All the Gauls'. The new tn has the fine suburb of Les Brotteaux, bounded on the N. by the park of the Tête-d'Or, and industrial suburbs, of which the prin. is Villeurbanne. There is a univ. (1808). The city has an interior funicular railway, is an important centre of railway communications (linking Paris with Switzerland, Italy and the S. of France), and is

a busy riv. port. It is also a financial centre (H.Q. of Crédit Lyonnais). A well-known international fair is held annually. The textile industry of L. for which the city is famous, began with the introduction of a silk industry by Italians in the 15th cent. In 1802 this industry was given added impetus by the invention of the Jacquard loom. In recent times the city has turned more and more to the production of rayon and other artificial fibre fabrics. There are also chemical, metallurgical, electrical, distilling and food-stuff industries. The Emperors Claudius and Caracalla, and Ampère, Delorme, Puvis de Chavannes and the De Jussieu family were natives. Pop. 528,600.

Lyon Court, see LYON KING OF ARMS.

Lyon King of Arms, The Lord, permanent officer of state and prin. herald of Scotland. The office incorporates that of royal sennachie or bardic historian of the Celtic Scottish kings, of whom he was official inaugurator. The office and its duties are very anct, for, according to Sir James Balfour Paul, the L. K. of A. and his heralds and pursuivants certainly attended at the coronation of Robert II in 1371. Originally the functions of the office were mainly ministerial, e.g. 'denouncing' war, proclaiming peace and carrying public messages. The L. K.'s existing jurisdiction in regard to the inspection of arms and ensigns-armorial of the Scottish nobility and gentry was conferred by Acts passed in 1592 and 1672, and was expressly reserved by the treaty of Union. Formerly a Scots privy councillor, the lord L. is one of the monarch's lieutenants in Scotland; has management of all state and public ceremonial; is official adviser to the secretary of state for Scotland on these and heraldic matters; and has precedence of all knights. He administers the law of name and change of name in Scotland; is sole king of arms in Scotland, his armorial jurisdiction being both at common law and by statute; is president of the court of the lord L., dealing with matters of heraldry and genealogy, in which he has both civil and criminal jurisdiction. From this court appeal lies through the court of session to the House of Lords. The court of the lord L. is situated in H.M. Register House, Edinburgh.

Lyonesse, scene of Arthurian romances, was a legendary country off the coast of Cornwall. It is described in early Eng. chronicles as flourishing until its sudden disappearance beneath the sea. It was the scene of the 'last great battle of the West', and of the final conflict between Arthur and Sir Modred. In an archaeological sense, L. is a submerged level off the coast of Wessex, dating from the Early Bronze Age.

Lyonnaise, anct prov. of France, corresponding to the present depts of Rhône, Loire and parts of Haute-Loire and Puy-de-Dôme. It was joined to the crown in 1312. The cap. was Lyon (q.v.).

Lyons, Edmund, Lord (1790–1858), Eng. admiral. He distinguished himself in operations against the Dutch off Java. In 1835 he was appointed minister and plenipotentiary at the court of Athens. He took a prominent part in the attack on Sebastopol, and during the latter part of the Crimean war held the position of commander-in-chief of the fleet.

Lyons, Joseph Aloysius (1879–1939), Australian statesman, *b.* Stanley, Tasmania, of Irish descent. A teacher, he joined the Labour party in Tasmania, and in 1909 entered the Tasmanian Parliament, becoming Premier of Tasmania in 1923. Returned as a Labour member to the Commonwealth Parliament in 1929, he joined the Scullin Gov. as postmaster general and minister for works and railways. In 1931 he resigned owing to disagreement with the gov.'s financial policy, and formed the United Australia party. In conference with the gov. he drew up, at the gov.'s request, the terms of a conversion loan which was accepted and which proved highly successful. When in the same year the gov. was defeated, L. became Prime Minister of a Coalition Gov. with the Country party. He was successful also in the elections of 1934 and 1937, being the first Australian Prime Minister to survive 3 successive appeals to the electorate.

Lyons, *see* LYON.

Lyons, Gulf of, *see* LION, GOLFE DU.

Lyot, Bernard (1897–1952), Fr. astronomer, who developed new techniques for the observation of sun and planets. His most striking achievement, in 1931, was the observation of the sun's corona, in full daylight; for this he used a special *coronagraph* telescope, which he carried to the summit of the Pic du Midi (9400 ft) in the Pyrenees. He developed also the *L. filter* for observing the sun's disc in the light of a single spectral line of hydrogen. He continued solar and planetary observations at the Pic du Midi observatory, and *d.* suddenly in Egypt shortly after observing the total solar eclipse of 1952.

Lyra, 'The Lyre', compact N. constellation, lying between Cygnus and Hercules. From its shape, known from anct times as the lyre, the fabled instrument invented by Hermes and transferred by Apollo to Orpheus; α Lyrae or Vega (q.v.) is the fourth brightest star in the heavens; ε Lyrae is a remarkable eclipsing binary star (*see* STAR); and ζ Lyrae is the well-known 'double-double' star. The constellation contains also the 'ring nebula', a planetary nebula (*see* NEBULAE) that is a striking object in large telescopes.

Lyre, most anct of the stringed instruments of music. Though associated for us with the anct Greeks it is probably of Asiatic origin. It was perhaps the instrument (*kinnor*) played by David and by the exiles in Babylon. The Greeks attributed its invention to their Hermes, who struck sounds from the dried cartilages of a tortoise-shell he picked up on the banks of the Nile. The L. consists of a hollow sound-chest surmounted by 2 branching horns joined by a cross-bar to which the cords were attached. A *plectrum* of ivory or polished wood was used to touch the cords, which were of gut. The Greeks used tortoise-shells from India for their sound-chests, whence the name *chelys* (tortoise); the framework of the Egyptian L. was of wood.

Lyre-birds, members of the passerine family

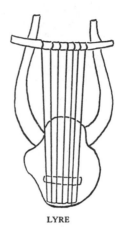

LYRE

Menuridae, which inhabit the forests and bush dists of SE. Australia. They are large birds with very stout beaks and short, rounded wings; the tail has 16 feathers, and in the males of some species the exterior pair of feathers are curved in the shape of a lyre; the tail of the female is long, broad and normal in shape. L. live in the thick undergrowth, or sandy gullies of forests, and feed upon insects, worms and molluscs; they rarely fly, but run or strut with the tail spread horizontally. *Menura novaehollandiae* is 33 in. long, and of a brownish colour, with blue tinges; *M. alberti* is of a warmer, reddish colour. *See* A. C. Chisholm, *Birds and Green Places*, 1929.

LYRE-BIRD

Lyric (Gk *lura*, lyre, a musical instrument with 7 strings). Lyrical poetry among the ancients was so called because it was sung or recited to the accompaniment of music. L. poetry may perhaps be best described as that class of poetry which expresses emotion directly, and in this sense includes the ode, the sonnet, the elegy, the psalm, the hymn and the song. 'In lyric poetry the poet gives vent to his personal emotions or experiences—his joy, sorrows, cares, complaints, aspirations, despair—or reproduces in words the impressions which nature or hist. has made upon him' (S. R. Driver, *Introduction to the Literature of the Old Testament*, 1891). Examples of L. poetry occur in the Vedantic hymns of India and in the Heb. psalms, but in Europe the art reached its zenith in Greece with the love songs of Alcaeus and Sappho, the choral hymns of Pindar and Bacchylides and the dramatic choruses of Aeschylus, Sophocles, Euripides and Aristophanes. If it be true that in succeeding ages the field of L. poetry widened in scope and variety of expression, it remains certain that no poets have surpassed the Greeks in sublimity of thought or passion of utterance. The most noteworthy of Lat. lyrists are Catullus, Horace, Tibullus and Propertius, all of whom followed Gk models. The triumph of Christianity tended to dry up the sources of inspiration, though during the 'Dark Ages' a wealth of religious hymns was produced. During the Middle Ages the chivalric love L. was perfected by the troubadours and by the minnesinger of Germany. Chief among the latter is Walther von der Vogelweide (1170–1228), the author of *Frauenminne* and the glorious ode *Unter den Linden*. A cent. later Petrarch (1304–74) in Italy pub. his *Canzoni* which moulded the whole L. poetry of the Renaissance.

The poets of the Renaissance not only revived the external qualities of the classical tradition, but also returned to the anct wells of inspiration. The odes of Ronsard (1550) follow closely the models of Pindar and Horace, while the sonnets of Shakespeare rank among the greatest of the world's literature. The 17th cent. witnessed a great outpouring of religious poetry, notably in England, where the chief names are John Milton, George Herbert, Henry Vaughan and Richard Crashaw. In the 18th cent. the most famous lyrists are both German: Schiller (1759–1805), whose magnificent 'Ode to Joy' was set to music by Beethoven, and Goethe (1749–1832), who wrote some fine L.s during his stay at Strasburg (*c*. 1770–2). During the next cent. there was a wonderful flowering of L. poetry all over Europe. In England Keats's 'Ode to the Nightingale', Shelley's 'Ode to the West Wind' and the love songs of Robert Burns are among the most splendid achievements of the human mind. Representative of the best Fr. work are V. Hugo's *Feuilles d'automne*, 1831, and *Légende des siècles*, 1856; the impressionist Verlaine's *Sagesse*, 1881, and *Jadis et naguère*, 1885; and Baudelaire's *Les Fleurs du mal*, 1857. Of the Germans in this period may be mentioned F. Rückert's *Liebesfrühling* and *Kindertotenlieder*; E. Mörike's *Gedichte*; and the *Nachts* and *Waldesgespräch* of J. von Eichendorff, the greatest lyrist of the Ger. romantics. There is a preference in modern poetry for the shorter L. presenting brief emphasised impressions, generally of everyday life. The effect is produced by

clever and apt imagery, a whole technique in itself, which seems to give intuitive, if fleeting, visions of transient experiences, moods, or passions. Such are the L.s of Robert Bridges and Thomas Hardy.

At the end of the 19th cent. Ernest Dowson, Lionel Johnson and A. E. Housman were leaders of a group of poets who strove to capture the spirit of the dying romanticism in L.s which excluded the problems of morality and philosophy in favour of brief poignant lines imaging their own moods or moments of experience. But if they were often concerned largely with symbols they could express profound emotions with striking brevity. More open to criticism are the 'Georgian poets', and particularly Rupert Brooke, whose poetry is often said to lack profundity; but much of the revolt against the Georgians sprang from the belief that poetry in the modern world must discover a new manner, and even some writers who began with lyrical and melodious verse abandoned it for an expression nearer to the temper of modern life.

Shortly before the First World War there was developed the movement known as Imagism, a revolt against the vagueness and over-luxuriance of the Romantics. Its chief exponents, Ezra Pound (1885–) and Amy Lowell (1874–1925), were Americans, and most of the Imagist writers gradually abandoned their original creed and developed along divergent lines. An important result of the movement was the popularising of free verse, which came to be accepted as a regular medium for L. In 1918 the pub. of the poems of Gerard Manley Hopkins (1844–89) gave a stimulus to the use of novel rhythmical effects. About the same time war experiences inspired the realist poetry of Siegfried Sassoon (1886–) and Robert Graves (1895–). Afterwards, in 1922, T. S. Eliot's *Waste Land* expressed the feeling of frustration and disillusionment which followed what was regarded as the betrayal of ideals. During the period between the wars there arose a group of followers of Eliot, chief of whom were W. H. Auden (1907–), L. MacNeice (1907–) and S. Spender (1909–); in ironical and satirical vein they wrote more on political and social than on personal themes. But from 1940 onwards there was a reaction towards the more personal utterance characteristic of L., typified in the poems of Dylan Thomas (1914–53) and the so-called 'neo-romantic' group.

Meanwhile there had been a great efflorescence of L. poetry in the U.S.A. There the realist revolt took the form of a reaction against the 'genteelism' of Longfellow, Lowell and others who followed Eng. or European traditions. Outstanding pioneers of the movement for a distinctively Amer. L. were Edgar Lee Masters (1869–1950) and Carl Sandburg (1878–), both of whom drew inspiration from the Middle W. About 1913 Robert Frost (1874–), an Easterner by adoption though not by birth, started publishing his restrained but distinctive verse. Among the finest of Amer. lyrists of this period were the women writers Sara Teasdale

(1884–1933), Elinor Wylie (1885–1928) and Edna St Vincent Millay (1892–1950). The effort to be original as well as distinctively American was carried further by E. E. Cummings (1894–1962), who used typographical eccentricities to enhance the effect of jazz rhythms and a slang dialect and is one of the few ultra-modern poets whose experiments have met with success. Another unconventional L. poet is Marianne Moore (1887–), who writes free verse with irregular but effective rhythm patterns. America's output of L. verse is at the present day at least as important as that of England, and the compliment paid to Brit. culture by T. S. Eliot when he became a Brit. citizen has been returned by W. H. Auden and others who have adopted Amer. nationality. *See also* BALLAD; EPIC; HYMNS; ODE; POETRY; and the articles on the authors mentioned.

Among the best L. anthologies are *The Golden Treasury*, ed. F. T. Palgrave, 1861; *Early English Lyrics*, ed. E. K. Chambers, 1907; *An Anthology of Modern Verse*, ed. Sir A. Methuen, 1921; the *Faber Book of Modern Verse*, ed. Michael Roberts, 1936. *See also* F. Brunetière, *L'Évolution de la poésie lyrique au XIXe siècle*, 1894; E. Rhys, *Lyric Poetry*, 1913; J. Drinkwater, *The Lyric*, 1916; J. P. Postgate, *Prosodia Latina*, 1923; J. M. Gibbon, *Melody and the Lyric*, 1930; C. M. Bowra, *Greek Lyric Poetry*, 1936; A. Closs, *The Genius of German Lyric*, 1938; C. M. Ing, *Elizabethan Lyrics*, 1951.

Lyric Theatre, Hammersmith, London, opened under the management of Cordingley, 1870, had varying success. Having been closed for some time it was taken over (1918) by Nigel Playfair (q.v.), whose most successful venture was Gay's *The Beggar's Opera*. In 1944 the theatre was reopened by Baxter Somerville with a highly successful series of plays presented by Tennent Productions Ltd, including the John Gielgud season of revivals (*The Way of the World, Venice Preserv'd* and *Richard II*), Peggy Ashcroft in *Hedda Gabler*, and Dorothy Tutin in *The Lark*.

Lyric Theatre, Shaftesbury Avenue, London, opened 1888 with *Dorothy*. Some of its greatest successes have been Wilson Barrett's production of *The Sign of the Cross*, 1896; Leslie Stuart's *Floradora*, 1899, and, more recently, *Lilac Time* and *The Winslow Boy*.

Lys, riv. of France and Belgium, which rises near Fruges in the Pas-de-Calais and flows past Aire, Armentières and Courtrai, to join the Scheldt at Ghent. Length 133 m.

Battle of the Lys. The second phase of the final Ger. offensive in the First World War (9–29 April 1918), the first phase being the second battle of the Somme, begun on 21 Mar. Both phases are called the battle of Picardy in Fr. official documents, the names L. and Somme being those adopted by the Battles Nomenclature Committee of the Brit. War Office. The L. battle, so far as the Brit. armies were concerned, began with a gigantic Ger. effort between Arras and Ypres, with the object of separating the armies of Gens. Horne and Plumer, and the

severest fighting took place near Hazebrouck, Kemmell Hill, Passchendaele and Messines. *See* WESTERN FRONT IN FIRST WORLD WAR.

Lysander, Spartan general and statesman during the last few years of the Peloponnesian war. Appointed in 407 BC to command the Spartan fleet on the W. coast of Asia Minor, he enlisted the aid of Cyrus the Younger (q.v.), who supplied him with large sums of money. This flood of Persian gold, at a time when the Athenian treasury was almost exhausted, enabled L. to win the crowning victory of Aegospotami (405) and so to conclude the war. In 404 he entered Athens and obliged the Ecclesia (q.v.) to vote for an oligarchy (*see* THIRTY TYRANTS). It was through the influence of L. that the Spartan king Agesilaus II succeeded his half-brother Agis II, excluding the latter's son Leotychides, in 401 BC. L. accompanied Agesilaus on the expedition against Persia (396); but the king thwarted his designs, and on his return L. planned to alter the constitution by abolishing hereditary kingship and making the throne elective. But before he could do so he was killed in action beneath the walls of Haliartus in Boeotia, 395 BC.

Lysenko, Trofim (1898–), Russian biologist and agriculturist who until 1954 was president of the Lenin academy of agric. sciences; *b.* Karlovka, Ukraine. He continued the work of his fellow countryman Michurin in practical plant breeding, and denies the validity of the results in genetics obtained by Gregor Mendel, T. H. Morgan and the Neo-Mendelians, i.e. the chromosome theory of heredity, which most biologists consider to rest on a sound basis of fact. L. maintains that heritable changes can be brought about in plants by environmental influences, such as subjecting wheat to extremes of temp., and by grafting (the scion being supposed to influence the stock and vice versa). This is, of course, the argument of nature versus nurture; L., in accordance with the general ideas of Marxism and Communism, believes that nurture is all-important, and that acquired characters can be inherited—a theory which biologists have not yet disproved, though few subscribe to it. L.'s experimental methods and the purity of his breeding stock have been criticised, and likewise his failure to make statistical analysis of his results. Although L.'s earlier attempts to inspire the peasant farmers were successful, in 1953 he was criticised publicly by Khrushchev, and in 1955 demoted. It remains to be seen whether 'classical' genetical work will again be carried out in the Soviet Union. See *Agrobiology—Essays on Problems of general Plant Breeding and Seed Growing* by L., trans. by E. A. Ashby, 1954, and literature quoted by J. S. Huxley in *Nature*, June 1949. *See also* BREEDING; GENETICS; HEREDITY; LAMARCKISM; MENDELISM.

Lysias (*c.* 458–*c.* 380 BC), one of the Ten Attic Orators, *b.* Athens, son of Cephalus, a native of Syracuse. In 443 he sailed with the colonists (among them was Herodotus) who went to found Thurii; but he returned to Athens in 413. During the rule of the Thirty Tyrants (q.v.) in 404 he was imprisoned, but escaped and joined Thrasybulus (q.v.), to whom he rendered useful service. The speeches of L. are remarkable for their unadorned simplicity of style. About 30 have survived; *see* ed. with trans. by W. R. M. Lamb in the Loeb Library, 1950. L. is the earliest writer known to have composed *erōtikoi*, and it is not impossible that the *erōtikos* attributed to him in Plato's *Phaedrus* is genuine.

Lysimachus (360–281 BC), Macedonian general under Alexander. After the latter's death, Thrace and the neighbouring countries as far as the Danube were assigned to L., who extended his kingdom still further and founded the city of Lysimachia on the Hellespont. In conjunction with Seleucus he defeated the combined armies of Antigonus and Demetrius at Ipsus (301 BC). He obtained possession of Macedonia (286 BC), and retained it until his death in battle against Seleucus on the plain of Corus.

Lysippus (*c.* 336–270 BC) of Sicyon, the 'greatest figure in the sculpture of the second half of the fourth century', was originally a workman in bronze, and most of his statues were executed in that medium. He was the first to introduce portrait sculpture, and made many representations of Alexander the Great. Many statues seem to be copies of his, notably the Apoxyomenus of the Vatican. *See* study by F. Johnson, 1928.

Lysozyme, *see* FLEMING, SIR A.

Lyte, Henry Francis (1793–1847), hymn-writer, *b.* Ednam, near Kelso, of an anct Somerset family. He took holy orders, and held sev. curacies; afterwards he had charge of Lower Brixham for 25 years. His health compelled him to reside abroad, and he *d.* at Nice, and is buried there in the Eng. cemetery. L. is the author of 'Abide with Me', 'Praise, my Soul, the King of Heaven', and other well-known hymns.

Lytham St Annes, municipal bor. of Lancs, England, 7 m. SSE. of Blackpool, incorporating 2 tns, on the estuary of the R. Ribble. It is a seaside resort with golf-courses. Pop. 36,222.

Lyttelton, Alfred (1857–1913), politician and athlete, educ. at Eton and Trinity College, Cambridge. In 1895 he became a Liberal-Unionist M.P. From 1903 to 1905 he was secretary of state for the colonies, and was much criticised for his conduct of S. African affairs. He was a famous athlete in his day, playing cricket and football for England. He was also amateur champion of real tennis (q.v.) (1882–95).

Lyttelton, Humphrey (1921–), trumpeter, *b.* Windsor, Berks. Educ. Eton (1934–40), served in Second World War in Grenadier Guards. He learned the trumpet at school and started playing jazz and worked with George Webb's Dixielanders (1947), formed own group 1948. Member of Brit. band representing Great Britain at the International Jazz Festival in Nice in 1948. Accompanied and recorded with Sidney Bechet (1949). L. worked as a cartoonist and writer for the *Daily Mail* during amateur

musical period. Became leader of New Orleans Revival movement; recorded in 1951 with Australian Graeme Bell and octet and later introduced W. Indian influences in the Paseo band. L. gradually remoulded his group to cover broader musical scope and to present more up-to-date interpretations of jazz. His own trumpet style is modelled on Louis Armstrong and Buck Clayton. L. toured Great Britain with Jimmy Rushing (1958), Buck Clayton (1963), Joe Turner (1963) and played U.S. tour in 1959. Resident compère of B.B.C. TV show 'Jazz 625' (1964) and regular radio broadcaster. He has pub. *I play as I please*, 1954, and *Second Chorus*, 1958.

Lyttelton, Oliver, *see* CHANDOS.

Lyttelton, port and bor. of S. Is., New Zealand, 5 m. SE. by E. of Christchurch. The entrance to the harbour is more than 2 m. wide and is protected by 2 breakwaters. There is a lighthouse at Godley Head, on the NW. Pop. 3,380.

Lytton, Edward George Earle Lytton Bulwer, 1st **Baron Lytton** (1803–73), novelist, playwright and statesman, *b.* London. He was educ. at a private school and afterwards at Trinity College, Cambridge, where he greatly distinguished himself. Finding it necessary after his marriage in 1827 to augment his income, he turned to novel writing. *Falkland* appeared in 1827 and in the following year he pub. *Pelham*, an excellent and amusing book, and *The Disowned. Eugene Aram* was pub. in 1832, *The Last Days of Pompeii* in 1834 and *Rienzi* in 1835. In 1838 *The Lady of Lyons* was produced at Covent Garden and his other successful plays were *Richelieu*, 1839, and *Money*, 1840. His popular historical novel, *The Last of the Barons*, came out in 1843 and 5 years later was followed by *Harold*. L. had been in Parliament since 1831 and became (1858–9) secretary of state for the colonies. He was raised to the peerage in 1866. Of his other books the best were *The Caxtons*, 1850, in which the influence of Sterne is very clearly to be seen, *A Strange Story*, 1862, *The Coming Race*, 1871, *Kenelm Chillingly*, 1873, and *The Parisians*, 1873, unfortunately incomplete. L. had a keen sense of character, a sufficiency of historical lore, a knowledge of life and society and all these qualities he pressed into his service. *See* L.'s *Life, Letters and Literary Remains*, by his son, 1833; memoir by his grandson, 1913; life by T. H. Escott, 1910; also *Letters to His Wife*, 1884; M. Sadleir, *A Panorama*, 1931.

Lytton, Edward Robert Bulwer, 1st **Earl of Lytton** (1831–91), statesman and poet, son of Bulwer L., 1st Baron L. (q.v.). Educ. at Harrow and Bonn, he entered public life as private secretary to his uncle, Lord Dalling, at Washington and Florence. He was subsequently attaché at The Hague and Vienna, at which last city in 1862 he was second secretary of the legation. He served at Copenhagen (1863), Athens (1864), Lisbon (1865) and at Madrid and Vienna (1868–72), becoming in the last year secretary to the Paris embassy. He succeeded to his father's barony in 1873 and went out to India as viceroy (1876–80), when in 1877 he proclaimed Queen Victoria as empress. On his return he was raised to the earldom. From 1887 to 1891 was ambas. at Paris. Like all the L.s he had a love of literature and in 1855, under the pseudonym of 'Owen Meredith', he pub. *Clytemnestra and other Poems*; *The Wanderer* followed in 1857 and *Lucile* 3 years later. *Chronicles and Characters* appeared in 1868 and *Orval, or The Fool of Time* in 1869. His poetry was much admired, and he had a lyrical gift, though some of his longer pieces are somewhat dull. *King Poppy* (pub. posthumously, 1892) is usually regarded as his masterpiece. His *Letters* were ed. in 1906 by his daughter, Lady Betty Balfour.

Lytton, Sir Henry (1867–1936), actor, the 'Savoyard' who for 40 years delighted audiences with his appearances in Gilbert and Sullivan operas. Making his début in *Princess Ida* at the age of 17, in 3 years he was promoted to the Savoy Co., proceeding thence to the D'Oyly Carte Co., with which he remained for many years. He was especially notable in the role of Jack Point. *See* his *Secrets of a Savoyard*, 1922, and *A Wandering Minstrel*, 1933.

Lytton, Victor Alexander George Robert Bulwer, 2nd **Earl of Lytton** (1876–1947), administrator, statesman and author; *b.* Simla, son of 1st Earl of L., whom he succeeded, 1891, and educ. at Eton and Trinity College, Cambridge. He began his public career in 1901 as private secretary to George Wyndham, chief secretary for Ireland; was civil lord of the Admiralty, 1916 and 1919; Brit. commissioner for propaganda, France, 1918; parl. undersecretary of state for India under Edwin Montagu, 1920; he was appointed to an India Office committee on the political claims of Burma and earned a reputation for sympathy with Indian aspirations. He was governor of Bengal, 1922–6; for 4 months in 1925 he acted as Governor-General, being proclaimed viceroy on the 49th anniversary of his father's assumption of office. L. will, however, best be remembered for his sustained labours for international goodwill and understanding through the agency, after the First World War, of the League of Nations and, after the Second World War, of the U.N. In addition to a biography of his grandfather, the novelist (1913) and Indian reminiscences (1942) he wrote *New Treasures*, 1934, *The Web of Life*, 1938, and *Love Incarnate*, a harmony of the Gospels, 1946.

Lyubertsy, tn in the U.S.S.R., in the Moscow 'green belt', an industrial suburb on the railway to Kazan; about 10 m. SE. of Moscow. It has an important agric. engineering industry. Pop. (1965) 111,000.

M

M, thirteenth letter in the alphabets of W. Europe. It also was the thirteenth letter in the N. Semitic alphabets, but it is the twelfth in the Gk, the eleventh in the Etruscan, the twelfth in the Lat. and the fourteenth letter in the early Slavonic alphabets. In the N. Semitic alphabets, as well as in the early Gk, Etruscan and Lat. alphabets, which were written from right to left, it was written ᵂ|. In early Crete, Chalcis and its colonies it was drawn with 5 strokes, so /Ⅵ. In the cursive Rom. writing of the 1st cent. AD, as we meet it in the wall inscriptions and in the waxed tablets of Pompeii, the vertical (slightly oblique) 4-stroke M (/ᴵᴵ/) was preferred. In the Rom. uncial script, which appears from the 3rd cent. AD onwards, it has the typical rounded shape (*m*), which is the main feature of the uncial hand. Roughly at the same time the cursive minuscule assumes a form similar to the modern small *m*. Like *b*, to which it is closely related, it is pronounced with both lips (bi-labial). Curiously enough, *b* is sometimes slipped in after *m*, as in the Gk *Mesēmbria*, noon and the Fr. *nombre* (from Lat. *numerus*, number). Unlike *b*, however, *m* is nasal. *See* ALPHABET.

M, used by the Romans for the numeral 1000. Their word for thousand was *mille* and the initial letter is commonly considered as having become a symbol for the number.

Maas, or **Maes, Nicolaes,** *see* MAES.

Maas, *see* MEUSE.

Maaseyck (Maaseik), tn in the prov. of Limbourg, Belgium, on the R. Meuse, 22 m. NE. of Hasselt. The brothers Van Eyck were *b.* here. Pop. 8100.

Maasin, port at the mouth of the M., on the SW. of the is. of Leyte in the Philippine Is., which exports hemp, copra and rice. Pop. *c.* 32,000.

Maastricht, or **Maestricht** (anct Trajectus Superior, upper ford), cap. of the prov. of Limburg, Netherlands. It lies 19 m. NNE. of Liège by rail and is situated on the l. b. of the R. Maas. There are glass, pottery and metal works and manufs. of wine, beer, earthenware, paper and cigars. Originally a Rom. fort, it became the residence of the Frankish kings and later of the dukes of Brabant. It was besieged by the Spaniards in 1579 and by the French in 1673, 1748 and 1794, when it was made the Fr. cap. of the Lower Meuse dept. In 1815 M. was reunited to the kingdom of the Netherlands. The failure to blow up 2 bridges over the Albert Canal, a result of fifth-column work, was the beginning of the gap in the allied line which led to disaster, in May 1940. Pop. 93,400.

Maat, Egyptian goddess, the personification of right and truth, represented bearing on her head an ostrich feather, her symbol. She was daughter of Ra, because Ra the sun god ruled the universe by the principles which she personi-

fied and she therefore regularly stood on the prow of his boat.

Mab, Queen, queen of the fairies and Oberon's wife, according to the *Nymphidia* of Drayton and the *Hesperides* of Herrick. Shakespeare, in *A Midsummer Night's Dream*, gives the honour to Titania.

Mabille de Poncheville, André (1886–), Fr. writer, *b.* Valenciennes. His works include *L'Hymne aux Américains* (poetry), 1917, *Nord et Midi* (poetry), 1925, *Le Chemin de Rome*, 1927, *Le Chemin de Saint Jacques*, 1930, *Le Chemin de Jérusalem*, 1939, and books on Verhaeren, Péguy, Pierre de Nolhac, Louis Le Cardonnel, Watteau, Lamartine, etc.

Mabillon, Jean (1632–1707), Fr. historian, entered the Benedictine order in 1653 and from 1664 onwards was engaged in editing a colossal number of MSS. at the abbey of St-Germain des Prés in Paris. The result of his research was his *Acta Sanctorum ordinis S. Benedicti* (1668–1702), a monumental hist. of the order. His monograph entitled *De Re Diplomatica*, 1681, is an important contribution to Lat. palaeography. *See* J. U. Bergkamp, *Mabillon and the Benedictine Historical School*, 1928.

Mabinogion, The, title of a collection of 11 medieval Welsh prose tales found in *The White Book of Rhydderch* (c. 1300–25), *The Red Book of Hergest* (c. 1375–1425) and other MSS. The title, originally a scribal error for *mabinogi* (meaning 'youth', 'tale of youth', 'tale') is meaningless, but has been made convenient by usage. The 11 tales are (1) 'The Four Branches of the *Mabinogi*', consisting of 'Pwyll Prince of Dyfed', 'Branwen daughter of Llŷr', 'Manawydan son of Llŷr' and 'Math son of Mathonwy'; (2) 'Culhwch and Olwen' and 'The Dream of Rhonabwy', native Arthurian tales; (3) 'The Dream of Macsen Wledig' and 'The Adventure of Lludd and Llefelys', both influenced by Geoffrey of Monmouth's *Historia Regum Britanniae*; (4) the 2 Arthurian romances 'Owain and Luned' (or 'The Lady of the Fountain'), 'Geraint and Enid' and 'Peredur son of Efrawg'. These 3 tales, in which Fr. influence is obvious in mode and matter, correspond to Chrétien de Troyes's 'Yvain', 'Erec' and 'Perceval', but the exact nature of the relationship between the Welsh and the Fr. texts is still a subject of debate. All 11 tales, which range in date from the second half of the 11th cent. to the close of the 13th cent., are conscious literary compositions largely based on earlier oral traditions which were, in turn, a medley of mythology in decline, folklore and heroic and aetiological material. In her trans., Lady Charlotte Guest included another story, 'The Tale of Taliesin', which is found only in MSS. dating from the 16th cent. but which represents a late form of an earlier tale which is known to have existed as early as the 9th cent. *See* G. and T. Jones (translators), *The Mabinogion*, 1949 (Everyman's Library), where a bibliography of texts, trans. and discussions is given. (*See Plate; Wales.*)

Mablethorpe and Sutton, urb. dist and seaside resort of Lincs, England, 15 m. E. of Louth, characterised by its sand dunes and fine sandy beach. The sea front was almost entirely reconstructed after the E. coast floods in Jan. 1953. Pop. 5389.

Mabuse, Jean (1472–1536), Flem. painter, really **Jan Gossaert**, *b.* Utrecht, called Mabuse because his family came from Maubeuge. His 'Adoration of the Magi' in the National Gallery, London and 'The Upright Judges' in Antwerp, are fine works in his early and purely Flem. style, but his triptych of 'Adam and Eve' (1516) in the Berlin Gallery shows the influence of his sojourn n Italy. He afterwards worked at Antwerp. *See also* FLEMISH ART. *See* monograph by A. Ségard, 1923.

Mac, Gaelic prefix signifying 'son of', like the Norman 'Fitz' in Fitzmaurice, the Irish 'O' in O'Grady and the Welsh 'Map' or 'Ap' in ApRichard ('Pritchard). MacGregor and Mac-Lean are common examples. A confusion with *magnus* probably accounts for the meaning of 'great' which 'Mac' sometimes seems to bear.

Mac Liammóir, Micheál (1899–), theatrical director, actor, writer and stage designer, *b.* Cork. In 1928, with Hilton Edwards, he founded the Gate Theatre as the first permanent international theatre in Dublin. He has written sev. full-length plays (in English and Irish). *See* his autobiography, *All for Hecuba*, 1946.

Macadam, Elizabeth (1871–1948), Scottish social worker and writer. Served her apprenticeship in the Women's Univ. Settlement in Southwark, where she trained many generations of social workers. She wrote *The Equipment of the Social Worker*, 1925, *The New Philanthropy*, 1934, and *The Social Servant in the Making*, 1945.

McAdam, John Loudon (1756–1836), Scottish inventor, has given his name to the surfacing of roads with granite or other durable stone broken small enough to make a hard, smooth surface, suitable for traffic. In 1816 he successfully 'macadamised' the Bristol roads. He was appointed surveyor-general of metropolitan roads in 1827 and granted £10,000. *See* life by R. Devereux, 1936.

McAdoo, William Gibbs (1863–1941), Amer. politician, *b.* Georgia, a prominent figure in the Democratic party. He was secretary to the Treasury from 1913 to 1919. He was responsible for far-reaching financial reforms, such as the Federal Reserve Banking Act and, during the war, the introduction of the Liberty Loan system, by which he raised over 18,000 million dollars, to provide for the huge Amer. war expenditure. From 1933 to 1939 he was senator from California. *See* his autobiography, *Crowded Years*, 1931.

MacAlpin, Kenneth, *see* KENNETH I.

Macao (Chinese Aomen), Portuguese dependency in China, at present held in virtue of a treaty with China of 1 Dec. 1887. The tn lies on a peninsula flanking the W. side of the mouth of the Canton R., 35 m. WSW. of Hongkong. Practically all the inhab. are Chinese. The main industries and exports are dried fish, matchboxes and fire crackers, but tourism, gold and opium traffic produce more revenue. With Timor it is the see of a Rom. Catholic bishop. The façade of the former cathedral church of St Paul is all that remains of a baroque church burnt 100 years ago in a typhoon. Portuguese factors settled here as early as 1557. Area 6 sq. m. Pop. *c.* 180,000 (including 3000 Portuguese).

Macaque, group of monkeys of the genus *Macaca*, family Cercopithecidae. *M. cynomolgus*, the common M. of the Malayan archipelago, is representative of the long-tailed section of the genus, *M. inuus*, or the Barbary ape, is a species which is found in N. Africa and on the rock of Gibraltar. *M. silenus* is the wanderoo of India. All species are of stout build, the body large in proportion to the limbs, the shoulders abnormally developed, longish muzzle and cheek pouches, large callosities on the buttocks, tail long or short or absent. They live in troops in the forests and are most active. Good-tempered when young, they become savage and brutal as they grow older.

Macaroni (It. *maccaroni*, perhaps from obsolete *maccare*, to bruise), form of wheat paste whose manuf. was for a long time exclusively confined to Italy, where it is an important article of diet. A particular variety of wheat is required for this purpose, viz. *durum*, a hard type, containing a large percentage of protein. At one time M. was made by hand but this practice has been superseded by machinery. The wheat is ground to make *semolina* or coarse meal (*see* FLOUR-FILLING), from which the bran is removed; this is worked into a dough with water and afterwards extruded through a cylinder, generally into tube shapes, but also into sheets, etc. Vermicelli differs from M. only in thickness and shape. Spaghetti is made of the same paste as M., but pressed out into a solid, cord-like form.

Macaronic Verse, species of burlesque, the humour of which depends partly on tagging Lat. suffixes on to all the words so as to suggest the dignity of Lat. poems, and thus turn the rhyme into a mock-heroic. Two lines from *Polemo-Middinia*, 1684, which is attributed to Drummond of Hawthornden, are quoted:

'Maggaeam, magis doctam milkare cowaeas,
Et doctam sweepare flooras, et sternere beddas.'

The *Liber Macaronicus* of Teofilo Folengo (q.v.), who first popularised this device, appeared in 1517. The author was a dissolute Benedictine monk, who explains that his doggerel, like the native macaroni, is nothing but a rude hotch-potch. The Fr. classic writer of such verse is Antonius de Arena (*d.* 1544). A further illustration is J. R. Lowell's 'Kettelopoto-machia' in *The Biglow Papers* (second series).

The term is also used more generally of verse in which 2 different languages are employed. The following example is taken from verses attributed to Prof. Porson at the time when Napoleon was theatening to invade Britain:

'Such tempora numquam videbant majores,
For then their opponents had different
    mores;
But we will soon prove to the Corsican
    vaunter,
Though times may be changed, Britons never
    mutantur!'

Macaronies, group of London dandies, who flourished about 1772 and were known by the extravagance of their dress and more especially by their amazing wigs.

Macaroon, dry pastry made of eggs, sugar and paste almonds. The name (Fr. *macaron*) is perhaps derived, like 'macaroni', from the obsolete It. *maccare*, to bruise.

Macarsca, *see* MAKARSKA.

MacArt, Cormac, *see* CORMAC.

MacArthur, Douglas (1880–1964), Amer. general, *b.* Little Rock, Arkansas, son of Arthur M., Amer. lieutenant-general. He spent his childhood at various military posts, attended military school in Texas and graduated from W. Point in 1903 with a distinguished record. He served in the Philippines and Japan and entered the First World War as chief of staff of the 42nd Div.; he was made brigadier-general in 1918. From 1919–22 he was superintendent of W. Point. He was commander in the Philippines, 1922–5 and returned to the U.S.A. to be chief of the general staff, 1930–5. As head of the Amer. military mission to the Philippines in 1935 he set up training and defence plans. In 1939 he retired from the army, but was recalled in 1941 as commander of U.S. forces in the Far. E. After the Jap. attack on Pearl Harbor, 7 Dec. 1941, he became head of the defence of the Philippines, but was sent by President Roosevelt (Mar. 1942) to command the allied forces in the SW. Pacific. In 1944–5 he led in the liberation of the Philippines, becoming a 5-star general in Dec. 1944. He was appointed supreme commander for the allied powers in Japan following the Jap. surrender and was head of the allied occupation of Japan. In 1950 he became commander of the U.N. forces in Korea. Disagreement with President Truman on Far E. policy led to his being removed from his posts and caused nation-wide controversy. In 1952 he became chairman of Remington Rand Incorporated and retained his position when that firm merged with Sperry to form Sperry-Rand in 1955. His *Reminiscences* were pub. in 1964. *See* J. Gunther, *The Riddle of MacArthur*, 1951; C. Lee and R. Henschel, *Douglas MacArthur*, 1952; F. Hunt, *The Untold Story of Douglas MacArthur*, 1954; C. Whitney, *MacArthur, His Rendezvous with History*, 1956; C. A. Willoughby and J. Chamberlain, *MacArthur, 1941–1951: Victory in the Pacific*, 1956.

Macarthur, John (1767–1834), Australian pioneer, *b.* near Plymouth, Devon. M. went to Australia in 1790 as lieutenant in the New S. Wales Army Corps. In 1793 he received his first grant of land and shortly afterwards began experiments in breeding for fine wool, importing merinos from S. Africa and England. Sent to England in 1801 for court martial, he succeeded in interesting the Brit. Gov. in the possibilities of wool production in Australia. He was allowed to return in 1805 and was encouraged by a further grant of land, to continue his work in founding the wool industry in Australia. See *Early Records of the Macarthurs of Camden*, ed. S. M. Onslow, 1914; M. H. Ellis, *John Macarthur*, 1955.

MacArthur (formerly **Ormoc**), city of Leyte, Philippine Is., on the W. coast, 32 m. SW. of Tacloban. Sugar milling is carried on and rice and sugar are exported. It was used by the Japanese as a supply port during the Second World War (up to 1944). In 1950 its name was changed to MacArthur. Pop. 72,730.

Macartney, George, 1st **Earl Macartney** (1737–1806), diplomat and administrator, educ. at Trinity College, Dublin. He was chief secretary for Ireland from 1769 to 1772 and sat in the Irish Parliament. For 2 successive periods of 5 years (1775–85) he was governor of Grenada and Madras respectively. In 1792 he was sent as first Brit. ambas. to China and from 1796–8 he was governor of Cape Colony. *See* H. M. Robbins, *Our First Ambassador to China*, 1908.

Macassar, *see* MAKASSAR.

Macaulay, Dame Rose (1881–1958), novelist and poetess, *b.* Cambridge. Her childhood and early youth were spent mainly in Italy. Her first novel, *The Valley Captives*, 1911, appeared while she was still an undergraduate at Oxford. Her novels reflect the contemporary scene with wit and a shrewd understanding. She first came into prominence with the satirical *Potterism*, 1920. *Dangerous Ages*, 1921, was awarded the Femina-Vie Heureuse Prize and years later her *Towers of Trebizond*, 1956, was awarded the Tait Black Memorial Prize. Others of her novels are *Told By an Idiot*, 1923, *Orphan Island*, 1924, *Crew Train*, 1926, *Keeping Up Appearances*, 1928, *Staying with Relations*, 1930, *They Were Defeated*, 1932, *Going Abroad*, 1934, *I Would Be Private*, 1937, *And No Man's Wit*, 1940, and *The World My Wilderness*, 1950. *They Went to Portugal*, 1948, and *The Fabled Shore*, 1950, are books of travel. She also pub. 3 vols. of verse, *The Two Blind Countries*, 1914, *Three Days*, 1919, and *Poems*, 1927, as well as critical studies of Milton, 1934, and E. M. Forster, 1938. *A Casual Commentary*, 1925, is a book of essays. D.B.E., 1958. *Letters to a Friend* was pub. posthumously, 1961.

Macaulay, Thomas Babington, 1st **Baron Macaulay** (1800–59), historian and statesman, *b.* Rothley Temple, Leics, the son of Zachary M., the philanthropist. He was educ. privately and at Trinity College, Cambridge. In 1825 he began to contribute to the *Edinburgh Review*, when his essay on Milton appeared. He entered Parliament in 1830 and 2 years later was appointed a commissioner, and a year later secretary of the Board of Control. In 1834, tempted by the large salary that would enable him to save enough to support himself for the rest of his life, he accepted an appointment as a member of the Supreme Council of India, and he stayed there for 5 years. During this time he assisted in preparing a criminal code for India, which did not, however, become law until the year after his death. On his return to England he was returned to Parliament as member for Edinburgh and in 1839 became secretary of war, which office he held for 2 years. He lost his seat in 1847, but regained it in 1852.

M. pub. *Lays of Ancient Rome* in 1842 and in the following years revised some of his *Edinburgh Review* articles for pub. in book form. Since 1839 he had been at work on his *History of England*, which was to deal with the period from the revolution to the death of George III; but it was not until 1848 that the first 2 vols. appeared, vols. iii and iv being pub. 7 years later and the fifth posthumously (1861). The *History* was received with a chorus of praise. Its sale was enormous and its vivid style made it eminently readable and induced the reader to overlook the Whig bias that everywhere dominated it. His work is now read rather for its literary style than for its historical value; his search for effect and his prejudices militate against accuracy. As a narrative writer he is of the first rank, as in his description of England in 1685. M. was raised to the peerage in 1857 and was buried in Westminster Abbey 2 years later. *See* his collected works, 1866; Sir G. O. Trevelyan (editor), *Life and Letters of Lord Macaulay*, 1876; C. Firth, *A Commentary on Macaulay's History of England*, 1938; *also* lives by J. C. Morrison, 1882; A. S. Canning, 1913; A. Bryant, 1932.

Macaw, general name for large brilliant coloured parrots of the genus *Ara*, natives of S. America. Their cry is unpleasantly harsh and they are less docile than the true parrots. M.s may live to a great age. *See* ARA. (*See Plate: History*.)

Macaw-tree, S. Amer. palm, *Acrocomia sclerocarpa*, known as 'gru-gru' or 'mucaja'. It attains a height of 40 ft and has a prickly trunk, with a spreading head of large pinnate leaves divided into slender leaflets, which when young are eaten as a vegetable. The tree yields fruits which possess both pulp and kernel oil. The pulp contains about 63 per cent of a yellow oil which bears a considerable resemblance to palm oil. As a rule it is used locally. The kernel contains 55–65 per cent of oil bearing a close resemblance to palm kernel oil but having a softer consistency.

Macbeth (*d.* 1057), King of Scotland, son of Findlaech and hereditary ruler of Moray and Ross. In 1040 he killed Duncan, the successor of Malcolm and became King of Scotland, basing his claim to the throne through his wife Gruach. According to St Berchan, his reign was prosperous; he made a pilgrimage to Rome in 1050. In 1054 he was defeated by Siward at Dunsinane

MACAW

(Perthshire) and in 1057 defeated and slain by Malcolm, the son of Duncan, at Lumphanan in Aberdeenshire. Shakespeare's tragedy of *Macbeth* is based on his life as given in Holinshed. *See* study by S. R. J. Erskine, 1930.

Macbride, Ernest William (1866–1940), zoologist, *b.* Belfast, N. Ireland. Educ. at Queen's College, Belfast, St John's College, Cambridge and at London Univ. Strathcona prof. of zoology, McGill Univ., Montreal, 1897–1909; prof. of zoology, Imperial College of Science, S. Kensington, 1913–34. Author of *Text-book of Invertebrate Embryology*, 1914, *Introduction to the Study of Heredity*, 1924, *Evolution*, 1927, *Embryology*, 1929, and *Huxley*, 1934.

MacBride, Sean (1904–), Irish lawyer and politician, son of Maj. John M., who was executed after the 'Easter Rising' of 1916 (*see* SINN FEIN). He was educ. in Paris and in Ireland, took part at an early age in the Sinn Fein movement and was a junior member of the Irish delegation which went to London in 1921 to negotiate a settlement. He supported the Republicans who rejected the Anglo-Irish Treaty of 1921, but in the 1930's found himself in conflict with De Valera (q.v.). In 1937 he was called to the Irish Bar and he was admitted to the Inner Bar in 1943; he became known for his conduct of the defence in sev. much-discussed capital cases. A new political party, *Clann na Poblachta* (q.v.), was founded by M. in 1946 and he became minister for external affairs in the coalition gov. of 1948–51 (*see* COSTELLO, JOHN, FINE GAEL). M. was vice-president of O.E.E.C., 1948–51. Pub.: *Civil Liberty*, 1948, *Our People—Our Money*, 1951.

Maccabees, The, *see* ASMONEANS.

Maccabees, The Books of the, certain writings of which only the first 2 are biblical and important. These 2 books, as forming part of the LXX, are recognised by Rom. Catholics as canonical; by the Church of England they are placed in the canonical apocrypha. 1 M. begins with a sketch of the conquests of Alexander the Great and the oppression which the Jews suffered from Antiochus Epiphanes. It then continues with a hist. of the Jewish struggle for independence from the first revolt under Mattathias until the death of Simon (135 BC). The work concludes with a note telling of the accession of John Hyrcanus and referring to 'the chronicles of his priesthood'. 1 M. was originally written in Hebrew (probably c. 130 BC, if not a little earlier), but only Gk versions are extant. The author was a patriotic Jew of unknown name. 2 M., a late composition of inferior historical quality, being written to edify, begins with 2 letters addressed by the Jews of Jerusalem to those in Egypt. It then gives an account of the wars of the M. from about 176 to 161 BC, covering the same ground as the first 7 chapters of 1 M. The author does not claim great accuracy and speaks of his work as the epitome of a larger work by a certain Jason of Cyrene. 3 M. and 4 M. are not strictly historical, though Josephus in *Contra Apionem* to some extent confirms 3 M. The former deals with the period of Ptolemy Philopator and the latter is better described by its subtitle, 'The Sovereignty of Reason'. Neither book is in any sense scriptural. See W. O. E. Oesterley, *An Introduction to the Books of the Apocrypha*, 1935; M. Hadas (editor), *The Third and Fourth Books of Maccabees*, 1953; J. C. Dancy, *A Commentary on 1 Maccabees*, 1954.

McCarrison, Sir Robert (1878–1960), physician, b. Portadown, N. Ireland and educ. at Belfast and Dublin, qualifying in medicine in 1900. He entered the Indian Medical Service in 1901 and later made important investigations into goitre and nutritional deficiency diseases. He was knighted in 1933. His pubs. include *Aetiology of Endemic Goitre*, 1913, and *Studies in Deficiency Disease*, 1921.

MacCarthy, Denis Florence (1817–82), poet, b. Dublin. His earlier verses appeared in the *Dublin Satirist* and by 1843 he was a regular contributor to the *Nation*. He received a medal from the Royal Sp. Academy for translating Calderón's dramas; he had previously been granted a Civil List pension. Among his works may be mentioned *Ballads, Poems and Lyrics*, 1850, a very popular work; *The Bellfounder*, 1857; *Under-Glimpses*, 1857; and *Shelley's Early Life*, 1871.

MacCarthy, Sir Desmond (1877–1952); author and literary critic, b. Plymouth. He was educ. at Eton and Trinity College, Cambridge and Leipzig Univ. Entering journalism he gained editorial experience with the *New Quarterly* and the *New Witness*. In 1913 he became a regular contributor to the *New Statesman*, of which in 1920 he was literary editor and later dramatic critic. During the intervening war years he served with the Red Cross, being attached to the Fr. Army. In 1928 he took over the editorship of *Life and Letters* and in later years contributed a weekly literary article to the *Sunday Times*. Clarity of thought, wide reading and a discerning knowledge of the literary figures of his time are among his characteristics as a critic and essayist. His writings over a

number of years have been collected under the following titles: *Portraits*, 1931, *Criticism*, 1932, *Experience*, 1935, and *Drama*, 1940. He was knighted in 1951 and held honorary doctorates of Oxford and Aberdeen.

McCarthy, Joseph Raymond (1909–57), Amer. politician, b. near Appleton, Wisconsin. He graduated from Marquette Univ. in 1935 and practised law in Wisconsin, becoming circuit judge in 1939. M. enlisted in U.S. marines, 1942 and left the service in 1945. He was elected to the Senate as a Republican in 1946. M. was member of sev. committees, but was best known for his work in investigating persons presumed to be Communists or subversives, in which he used means that caused nation-wide disagreement. When the Republicans lost control of the Senate M.'s already declining power disappeared. A vote of censure against him was passed by the Senate in Dec. 1954, on grounds of abuse of the Senate Elections Sub-committee in 1952 and more recent attacks on the Censure Session. See life by R. H. Rovere, 1960.

McCarthy, Justin (1830–1912), historian, novelist, journalist and politician, b. Cork. He began his working life as a journalist, but from 1879 devoted himself increasingly to politics. He was Home Rule member at different periods for Longford co., N. Longford and Londonderry. He was chairman of the Home Rule party from Parnell's fall in 1890 until 1896. His chief historical works are *Epoch of Reform*, 1874, *A History of Our Own Times*, 1882–97 and 1905, *A History of the Four Georges and William IV*, 1884–1901, and *Rome in Ireland*, 1904. *Reminiscences*, 1899, and *Irish Recollections*, 1911, are autobiographical.

Macchiavelli, *see* MACHIAVELLI.

McClellan, George Brinton (1826–85), Amer. soldier, b. Philadelphia and graduated from W. Point in 1846. He served with distinction in the war with Mexico, was an instructor afterwards at W. Point and in 1885 was sent to Europe to study military affairs. He resigned from the army in 1857 and became president of a railway company. In 1861 the people of the W. section of Virginia, opposing secession, founded a new state, W. Virginia. M. was called upon by Lincoln to take charge of the troops whose task it was to drive out the secessionists. This he did and Lincoln then gave him command of the army of the Potomac. In a few months M. made of it a superbly trained and disciplined force, which was to retain its spirit throughout the war. In the winter of 1861 M. was made commander-in-chief of the Union Armies. He soon came into conflict with both the administration and public opinion. Lincoln wanted a direct advance on Richmond which would preclude any Confederate advance on Washington, but M. preferred to move upon the Confederate cap. from the peninsula formed by the James and York R.s. He was allowed to have his way, but was removed from supreme command of the armies, only having charge of the army of the Potomac. He fought a series of battles, among them the victory of Malvern Hill. By Sept. 1862, when the Union armies were suffering reverses, Lincoln asked him to resume command. He did so and his new campaign resulted in the bloody battle of Antietam. The administration expected M. to cross the Potomac at once in pursuit of Lee, but he delayed 5 weeks. In Nov. he was relieved of his command. This ended his military career. His friends attributed his dismissal to political machinations; Lee later said the best commander who ever opposed him was M. The Democrats named M. for President in 1864, but he was defeated by Lincoln. *See* lives by W. S. Myers, 1934; C. E. Macartney, 1940; H. J. Eckenrode, 1941.

Macclesfield, municipal bor. and mrkt tn of Cheshire, England, 17 m. SSE. of Manchester. It is the chief silk manufacturing centre of England, producing all kinds of ribbons, small-wear, silk, rayon, nylon and terylene fabrics. Other prin. industries are manuf. of textiles, pharmaceuticals and photographic equipment and light engineering. Pop. 37,380.

McClintock, Sir Francis Leopold (1819–1907), Brit. explorer and admiral,, *b*. Dundalk in Ireland, entered the navy in 1831. He first went to the Arctic regions in 1848 with Sir James Ross; his most famous achievement was ascertaining the fate of Sir John Franklin on his expedition with the *Fox* in 1857. He describèd his expedition in *The Voyage of the 'Fox'*, pub. 1859. *See* life by Sir C. R. Markham, 1909.

McClure, Sir Robert John le Mesurier (1807–73), vice-admiral and Brit. explorer, was a native of Wexford, Ireland. In 1824 he joined the navy and in 1836 went on Capt. Back's expedition to the Arctic regions. In 1848 he accompanied Ross to the Arctic and in 1850 went on his third expedition as commander of the *Investigator*. During this expedition he was successful in journeying through the NW. passage. *See* S. Osborn (editor), *The Discovery of the NW. Passage by H.M.S. 'Investigator'*, *Capt. R. M'Clure*, 1856.

MacColl, Dugald Sutherland (1859–1948), artist, art critic and author, son of a well-known Glasgow preacher of the same names. He was educ. at Univ. College School, London Univ. and at Lincoln College, Oxford, where he won the Newdigate prize for a poem on 'The Fall of Carthage'.

After visits to the important European galleries he became art critic to the *Spectator* (1890–5) and pugnaciously supported the Fr. impressionists, Whistler and such younger contemporaries as Steer, Sickert, Conder, Beardsley and Augustus John. He ed. the *Architectural Review*, 1901–5 and lectured at the Slade School on the hist. of art. As a trustee of the Tate Gallery he secured reforms in the administration of the Chantrey Bequest and in 1903 helped to promote the National Art Collections Fund. In 1906 he was appointed keeper of the Tate and Wallace collections. His writings include *Nineteenth Century Art*; *Confessions of a Keeper and other Papers*, 1931, a selection from his critical writings; and *Life, Work and Setting of Philip*

Wilson Steer, 1945. He was a delicate water-colourist.

McColvin, Lionel Roy (1896–), Eng. librarian. Successively chief at Ipswich, Hampstead and Westminster (1938) public libraries. In 1938 M. became the Honorary Secretary of the Library Association (q.v.) and in 1942 pub. his famous *Report on the Public Library System of Great Britain*. He was President of the L.A. in 1952 and served in 1958 on the Roberts committee which led to the Public Libraries and Museums Act, 1964. He was best known as an international publicist for libraries and was especially enthusiastic for children's libraries. His many books are still authoritative and include *Music libraries* (with E. Reeves), 1937–8, *Reference library stock*, 1950, *Public libraries in Australia*, 1947, *The chance to read*, 1956, *Libraries in Britain*, 1961 and *Libraries for children*, 1961. He was vice-president of the International Federation of Library Associations and retired in 1961.

MacCormac, Sir William (1836–1901), surgeon, *b*. Belfast and educ. there and at Berlin. He qualified M.D. Belfast, 1857. During the Franco-Prussian war of 1870–1 M. volunteered for surgical service with the Anglo-Amer. Association. In 1871 he was appointed assistant surgeon to St Thomas's Hospital; 2 years later he became full surgeon and lecturer in surgery, retiring in 1893 to become consulting surgeon. During the S. African war he was gov. consulting surgeon to the field force, 1899–1900. He was knighted in 1881 and was created baronet in 1897. He was president of the Royal College of Surgeons, 1896–1900 and was appointed sergeant-surgeon to King Edward VII in 1901. His writings include *Notes and Recollections of an Ambulance Surgeon*, 1870, and *Surgical Operations* (2 vols.), 1885–9.

McCormack, John (1884–1945), Irish tenor, *b*. Athlone. He won the gold medal at Feis Ceoil, Dublin, in 1903. In 1905 he received instruction at Milan from Sabbatini and in 1907 he sang at ballad concerts in London and made his début in opera at Covent Garden as Turiddu in *Cavalleria Rusticana*. A greater opportunity awaited him in the same season, when he was cast for the part of Don Ottavio in *Don Giovanni*, his singing of the 2 big arias of the part creating the highest impression of his powers. Later he appeared with great success in subsequent seasons at Covent Garden, especially with Tetrazzini in *La Traviata* and in *Lucia di Lammermoor* and *Rigoletto*. He was also the ideal partner to Melba's Mimi in *La Bohème* in the seasons up to 1914. From 1910 to 1911 M. was with the Boston Opera Co. and he visited Australia in 1911. After a year with the Chicago Opera Co. he visited Australia again. In 1917 he became an Amer. citizen. Later he sang mostly at concerts and also in the popular film *Song of my Heart*. He became chevalier of the Legion of Honour in 1924, was made a papal count in 1928 and knight commander of Malta in 1932. He gave his farewell concert at Dublin in Oct. 1938. *See* life by L. A. G. Strong, 1941, 1949.

McCormick, Robert Rutherford, see 'CHICAGO TRIBUNE'.

McCrae, John (1872–1918), Canadian doctor and poet, *b.* Guelph, Ontario. He studied medicine at Toronto Univ., served in the Boer War and the First World War and is remembered for 'In Flanders Fields', one of the great war poems.

McCreery, Sir Richard Loudon (1898–), soldier, educ. at Eton and Sandhurst. Entered the 12th Lancers, 1915 and, in the First World War, served in France. Served in France, 1940. Chief of staff, Middle E., 1942; Tunisia, 1943. In Italy, under Alexander, he led the Eighth Army (q.v.) against Kesselring's Ger. armies, launching the offensive of May (1944) which resulted in the storming of Cassino (*see* CASSINO, BATTLE OF), the destruction of the Gustav line, S. of the Apennines and the fall of Rome (4 June) and, soon afterwards, the occupation of Florence (22 Aug.). In the 1945 campaigns his army, in co-operation with the Fifth Amer. Army, destroyed the Gothic line and so brought about the final surrender of the Ger. armies (April). G.O.C.-in-C., Brit. Forces of Occupation in Austria and Brit. representative on the Allied Commission for Austria, 1945–6. G.O.C.-in-C. of the Brit. Army of Occupation of the Rhine, 1946–8. Brit. Army representative, military staff committee, from 1948. General, 1948. Brit. Military Adviser to U.N., 1948–9.

McCudden, James Byford (*d.* 1918), Brit. air ace of the First World War. He joined the R.F.C. in 1913 and served in the corps for 5 years. Awarded the V.C. M. brought down over 50 enemy machines during his service on the W. front.

MacCulinan, Cormac, see CORMAC.

MacCulloch, John (1773–1835), geologist, *b.* Guernsey. He qualified as a surgeon and was afterwards employed in research work on the geology of Scotland. He wrote *A Description of the Western Isles of Scotland*, 1819, and *A System of Geology*, 1831.

MacCunn, Hamish (1868–1916), Scottish composer, *b.* Greenock. Studied under Parry and Stanford at the Royal College of Music. He was conductor to the Carl Rosa and other opera companies and prof. of composition at the Guildhall School of Music. His concert overtures, *The Land of the Mountain and the Flood*, 1887, *The Dowie Dens o' Yarrow*, 1888, and *The Ship o' the Fiend*, 1888, are his best works. Others include *Bonny Kilmeny* and *The Lay of the Last Minstrel* (cantatas), 1888, *Jeanie Deans* (opera), 1894, and *The Golden Girl* (musical comedy), 1905.

McDiarmid, Hugh, see GRIEVE, C. M.

MacDonagh, Thomas (1878–1916), Irish poet, *b.* Cloughjordan, co. Tipperary. Both his parents were teachers and he became assistant prof. of English at the National Univ., Dublin. Vols. of his verse, which has been compared to Crashaw's, are *Through the Ivory Gate*, 1902, *April and May*, 1903, *The Golden Toy*, 1906, *Songs of Myself*, 1910, and *Lyrical Poems*, 1913. Joining the Irish Republican forces, he was shot as a rebel by the English after the Easter Rising of 1916.

MacDonald, Betty (1908–58), American humorous writer, *b.* Boulder, Colorado. Educ. at Washington Univ., she married Robert E. Heskett in 1927 and they started a chicken farm, of which she wrote in *The Egg and I*, 1942, which sold over a million copies. Later books are *The Plague and I*, 1948, telling of her months in a sanatorium, and *Anybody Can Do Anything*, 1950, on the problems of job-hunting.

Macdonald, Sir Claude Maxwell (1852–1915), soldier and diplomat, educ. at Uppingham and Sandhurst. He served in 1882 in the Egyptian campaign and in the Suakin expedition of 1884. He was minister at Peking, 1896–1900 and during the Boxer siege there had command of the legation quarters. He was transferred to Tokyo in 1900 and in 1905 became first Brit. ambas. to Japan, retiring in 1912.

Macdonald, Étienne Jacques Joseph Alexandre (1765–1840), Duke of Taranto, marshal of France, *b.* Sedan of Scottish Jacobite descent. He entered the army in 1785, rapidly rising to high rank. After withstanding Suvórov in Italy he was defeated by him on the Trebia, but was again successful in 1800 by his march across the Splügen. In 1809 he defeated the Austrians at Wagram, being rewarded by the title of marshal. He was in command in Spain in 1810 and was completely defeated by Blücher at Katzbach in 1813. He deserted to the Bourbons in 1814. *See* M. C. Rousset (editor), *Recollections of Marshal Macdonald*, 1892.

Macdonald, Flora (1722–90), Scottish Jacobite, rescuer of Charles Stuart, *b.* Milton, S. Uist, Hebrides. After the battle of Culloden (1746), she was successful in helping the Pretender to land in Skye, having disguised him as 'Betty Burke', her maid. Because of this she was arrested and imprisoned, but was released in 1747 and 3 years later she married Macdonald of Kingsburgh. They emigrated to America and Flora, who returned alone to Scotland in 1779, was joined later by her husband.

MacDonald, George (1824–1905), poet and novelist, *b.* Huntly, Aberdeenshire. Educ. at the Univ. of Aberdeen, he became a Congregationalist minister, but later turned to literature. In 1857 he pub. *Poems* and in 1858 *Phantastes, a Faerie Romance*. Among his numerous novels are *David Elginbrod*, 1862, *Alec Forbes*, 1865, *Robert Falconer*, 1868, *The Marquis of Lossie*, 1877, and *Sir Gibbie*, 1879. He also wrote children's books of great charm and originality including *At the Back of the North Wind*, 1871, and *The Princess and the Goblin*, 1872. *See* life by J. Johnson, 1906; *also* G. MacDonald, *George MacDonald and his Wife*, 1924.

Macdonald, Sir Hector Archibald (1852–1903), soldier, known as 'Fighting Mac', *b.* Muir of Allan-Grange, Ross-shire, Scotland. At 18 he enlisted in the Gordon Highlanders. Taken prisoner at Majuba in the first Boer war (1881), Joubert returned him his sword on account of his bravery. He took part in the Nile expedition (1885) under Sir Evelyn Wood. He distinguished himself in the Dongola expedition (1896) and gained a brilliant success in the battle of Omdurman (1898), where he routed the Mahdi's troops. In the Transvaal war of 1899 he commanded the Highland Brigade during the Paardeberg, Bloemfontein and Pretoria campaign under Roberts and was made K.C.B. in 1901.

MacDonald, James Ramsay (1866–1937), statesman, *b.* Lossiemouth. He was educ. at a Moray board school, where, after work on a farm, he was a pupil teacher. In London he worked as a clerk and attended evening classes, obtaining work in a chemical laboratory. In 1888 he became private secretary to Thomas Lough, M.P. He earned his living, after leaving Lough, mainly by writing for Liberal papers. He joined the Independent Labour party soon after its formation and stood unsuccessfully as its candidate at Southampton in 1895.

In 1906 M. was elected for Leicester, which he had already contested in 1900. He was on the London Co. Council, 1901–4 and chairman of the I.L.P., 1906–9. In 1911 he became leader of the Labour party. In 1914 he attacked Great Britain's entry into the First World War and later appeared sympathetic to the Russian Communists, with the result that he was heavily defeated at W. Leicester in Dec. 1918 and again, in E. Woolwich, in Mar. 1921. But on his return to Parliament in 1922, he was placed at the head of a Labour party which had become the official opposition. At the general election of Dec. 1923 the Labour party and the Liberal party secured the balance and M. formed the first Brit. Labour gov., which lasted from 22 Jan. till 4 Nov. 1924. M. was his own foreign secretary. He was prominent in the discussions in the Assembly of the League of Nations in 1924 on the treaties of mutual assistance, delivering an important address in Sept. 1924 on the great task of trying to solve the related problems of security, disarmament and arbitration in one document which became the Geneva Protocol (q.v.) of 1924. His gov. was deserted by the Liberals on the matter of the Campbell prosecution and fell. In the succeeding general election great use was made, by anti-Socialists, of the Zinoviev letter; and the Conservatives came back triumphant. When the general election of May 1929 left Labour in the position of the largest party in the Commons, M. took office a second time, now representing the Seaham div. of Durham Co. In Aug. 1931, when the Labour gov., in the face of a crisis over the nation's financial situation, resigned, M. accepted office as Prime Minister of a 'National Gov.' (*see* NATIONAL GOVERNMENT).

The formation of the National Gov. meant the final break between M. and the party which he had helped to found and of which he had been so long leader. With Snowden and other supporters he formed the 'National Labour party', the Labour party expelling him and all the members of the new party. The election which followed endorsed his action and though his personal following was small in the new

House of Commons, all but 60 seats were captured by candidates who supported the gov. After 4 years he decided to retire from the premiership and in 1935 was succeeded by Baldwin, he himself retaining the post of Lord President of the Council. In the election of Nov. 1935, which followed Baldwin's assumption of office, he was heavily defeated in his old constituency of Seaham Harbour, but in Feb. 1936 was returned as a member for the Scottish univs. He *d.* at sea when going to S. America for the benefit of his health, which had been failing for some time. Malcolm M. (q.v.) is his son. *See* life by Lord Elton, 1939. (*See Plate: Parliament.*)

Macdonald, Sir John Alexander (1815–91), Canadian statesman, *b.* Glasgow, Scotland. His family moved to Upper Canada in 1820. M. was educ. at the Royal Grammar School, Kingston. Called to the Bar in 1836, he became Q.C. in 1846. He was elected to the Legislative Assembly, 1844, for Kingston, which he represented until 1878, continuing its member in the new Dominion Parliament. In 1854 he became attorney-general in a coalition gov. In 1857 became Premier and, with one brief interval, he continued so till 1862. In 1864 he became attorney-general in Taché's cabinet. The defeat of the Tachénald administration of 1864 and the consequent paralysis of gov., brought about the formation—largely through M.'s efforts—of the 'Great Coalition' and so led to the confederation of the Brit. N. Amer. provs. M. was chosen to be the first Prime Minister of the new Dominion of Canada and he filled that office from 1867 till 1873 and then again from 1878 to his death.

His gov. fell in 1873 on account of its members being detected receiving campaign funds from a railway concessionaire—the so-called 'Pacific Scandal'. M.'s reputation survived this catastrophe and in 1878 he returned to office on the 'National Policy' of high protection; and in the succeeding general elections, 1882, 1886 and 1891, he carried all before him. M. had not a lofty conception of political morality, but if he was an opportunist, he was also a politician of strong views and was outstanding in the art of managing men. On the continuance of the Brit. connection and the maintenance of law and order he was uncompromising. It was due to M.'s initiative that Brit. Columbia and the NW. ters. were included in the dominion and the project of the Canadian Pacific Railway was also due to him; and in some ways therefore the Dominion of Canada may be regarded as the product of his statesmanship. *See* D. Creighton, *Sir John A. Macdonald* (2 vols.), 1952–5.

Macdonald, Sir John Hay Athole, *see* KINGSBURGH.

MacDonald, Malcolm John (1901–), administrator, son of J. Ramsay M., (q.v.), educ. at Bedales School and Queen's College, Oxford. He was an M.P., 1929–45, entering Parliament as a Labour M.P., but sitting as National Labour, 1931–5, and National Gov., 1936–45. He held a number of junior posts in pre-war govs. but is best known as an administrator.

From 1941 to 1946 he was Brit. High Commissioner in Canada; from 1946 to 1948, Governor-General of Malaya and Brit. Borneo; and from 1948 to 1955 Commissioner-General for the U.K. in SE. Asia. From 1955–60 M. was Brit. High Commissioner in India; since 1963 he has been Governor-General, and subsequently High Commissioner, in Kenya, and in 1965 was given a roving commission in E. Africa. Pubs. include: *Borneo People*, 1956; *Angkor*, 1958; *Birds in the Sun*, 1962.

Macdonald of Gwaenysgor, Gordon, 1st Baron (1888–1965), politician and administrator, *b.* Prestatyn, Flintshire. He went to an elementary school in Ashton-in-Makerfield and began work at 13 in a coal-mine. Later he studied at Ruskin College, Oxford. He was Labour M.P. for Ince, 1929–42. In 1946 he was made governor of Newfoundland, being one of the most popular governors in the hist. of the is. His term ended when the is. joined the confederation with the rest of Canada (1949). He was paymaster-general, 1949–51, and Governor of the B.B.C. for Wales, 1952–60. He was raised to the peerage in 1949.

MacDonell, Archibald Gordon (1895–1941), novelist, *b.* Aberdeen. Educ. at Winchester, he served in the First World War with the Royal Field Artillery, and from 1922 to 1927 was on the H.Q. staff of the League of Nations Union. In 1933 he pub. a hilarious satire on Eng. country life, *England, their England*; other satirical novels are *Lords and Masters*, 1936, and *The Autobiography of a Cad*, 1939. He also wrote detective stories under the name Neil Gordon, 2 of them being *The New Gun Runners*, 1928, and *The Shakespeare Murders*, 1933. He was killed in an air-raid.

Macdonnell, Randal, see ANTRIM, RANDAL MACDONNELL, 1ST MARQUESS OF.

Macdonnell Ranges, mt ranges in the N. ter. of Australia running E. and W. for a distance of 400 m. in parallel ridges along the tropic of Capricorn and rising in places to over 4000 ft. The colours of the rocks and the spectacular chasms, accessible from Alice Springs (q.v.), are attracting many tourists to the area. The Arltunga gold-field is at the E. end. Alice Springs, the second largest tn in the ter., is located in the centre of the M. R. The Hermannsburg Aboriginal Mission (pop. 450), operated by the Finke Tiver (Lutheran) Mission, lies in the S. portion of the ranges. It is a lease of 1524 sq. m. of cattle country and is the oldest of the mission stations, having been estab. in 1877. The water-colour work of the Arunta artists, the most famous of whom was Albert Namatjira, began here under the guidance of the Australian artist, Rex Battarbee.

Macdonough, Thomas (1783–1825), Amer. naval commander, was *b.* in the state of Delaware, and entered the navy in 1800. When the war with England broke out M., in 1812, had charge of the small fleet of fresh-water boats on Lake Champlain, and taking full advantage of the fact that the Brit. authorities had neglected the defence of the lakes, he defeated Sir George

Prevost's projected attack on the ter. adjacent to Lower Canada at the Battle of Platsburgh. He later served as commandant of the Portsmouth (N.H.) navy yard and in 1824 was commander of the Mediterranean squadron.

McDougall, William (1871–1938), psychologist, *b.* Chadderton, Lancs. He graduated at Cambridge in 1892 and then studied medicine at St Thomas's Hospital, London. After qualification he became Wilde reader in mental philosophy at Oxford. During the First World War he served in the R.A.M.C., and from 1920 to 1927 taught psychology at Harvard Univ. From 1927 to his death he was prof. of psychology at Duke Univ., N. Carolina. He was particularly interested in psychical research and founded a dept at Duke to study parapsychology. M. had a great influence on social psychology in the Eng.-speaking world. His main contribution to psychology lay in the study of instinct and emotion, which in his classification were interrelated, each instinctive impulse being accompanied by its own quality of emotional experience. His teaching, which was a powerful counterbalance to the mechanistic view of human behaviour, is contained in a remarkable series of books: *An Introduction to Social Psychology*, 1908; *The Group Mind*, 1920; *An Outline of Psychology*, 1923; *An Outline of Abnormal Psychology*, 1926; *Modern Materialism and Emergent Evolution*, 1929; *Religion and the Sciences of Life*, 1934; *The Frontiers of Psychology*, 1935; and *Psycho-Analysis and Social Psychology*, 1936. He also wrote a number of other books which had a more direct bearing on the problems of the day, principally on ethics, nationalism, which he considered 'essentially a mental condition', and the problem of racial degeneration.

MacDowell, Edward (1861–1908), Amer. composer and pianist, *b.* New York. He was the first Amer. musician to receive the recognition of European composers and executants. In 1876–8 he studied at the Paris Conservatoire, then went to Germany, where he studied the piano under Louis Ehlert and composition under Raff, the latter exercising a great influence on his development. Raff introduced him to Liszt in 1882 and through Liszt's influence M. was given the opportunity of playing his first piano suite at the nineteenth ann. festival of the *Allgemeine Deutsche Musikverein* held in Zürich. Remaining in Germany till 1888, he devoted himself chiefly to composition, writing piano concertos and tone poems for the orchestra. In 1888 he returned to America, and settled in Boston, his first public appearance in America being in 1888. In 1896 he took charge of the newly organised dept of music at Columbia Univ. This restricted his activity as a piano virtuoso and recitalist, but the next 5 or 6 years saw the production of his best piano compositions. *See* L. Gilman, *E. MacDowell: a Study*, 1909; E. F. Page, *MacDowell, his Work and Ideals*, 1910; J. F. Porte, *E. MacDowell*, annotated catalogue, 1922; A. F. Brown, *The Boyhood of Edward MacDowell*, 1924.

Macduff, burgh and port of Banffshire, Scotland; it is a popular seaside resort on account of the bathing facilities and bracing air. White fishing and boat-building are the chief industries. Pop. 3495.

Mace, spice consisting of the ground seed covering (aril) of the nutmeg, *Myristica fragrans.*

Mace, originally a heavy club, an offensive weapon with the head made of metal and sometimes spiked. Bishop Odo, William's brother, used a M. at Hastings. The name M. is now given to a staff of office symbolising authority; the head is often elaborately worked in precious metal, or bejewelled. Such M.s are used in Parliament, etc., and on ceremonial occasions. In the House of Commons the M. lies on the table before the Speaker when the House is in session and is carried before him by the serjeant at arms whenever he enters or leaves the Chamber.

CEREMONIAL MACE

Mace of the Nutmeg, blood-red lacerated membrane which contains a very fragrant oil. If expressed the oil serves as a liniment, and if distilled it possesses the fragrance of mace.

Macedonia: 1. Ter. in Europe in the Balkan peninsula, lying roughly between the present S. frontier of Bulgaria and the Gulf of Salonika. A small portion of it is now in Bulgaria, but it is mainly divided between Yugoslavia (*see* 2, below) and Greece.

The kingdom of M. is said to have been founded *c.* 700 BC by one Perdiccas, and to have been called originally Emathia. Little is known of it until the reign of Amyntas I (*c.* 540–498 BC), who made an alliance with the Peisistratids. Philip II (q.v.) enlarged its boundaries and eventually conquered the whole of Greece. The kingdom survived until subdued by Rome in 168 BC (*see* PERSEUS). M. then became Rom. ter.; it was formed into a prov. 20 years later. It was settled by Slavs (q.v.) in the 6th cent., was under Bulgarian domination from the 9th to the 11th cents., and was later ruled by Serbia. From the 15th to the 20th cents. it was in Turkish hands (*see* TURKEY, *History*). In 1893, when the reforms in the Turkish Gov. promised in the Treaty of Berlin (q.v.) were not forthcoming, an 'Internal Macedonian Revolutionary Organisation' was formed by the Bulgarian inhab., the aim of which was stated to be 'M. for the Macedonians'. After the Balkan war (q.v.) in 1912–13, the ownership of M. was a source of contention between the members of the Balkan League. Eventually it was divided between Greece and Serbia. During the First World War M. was the scene of much fighting (*see* MACEDONIAN FRONT, OPERATIONS ON), and at the end of the war the treaty of Neuilly confirmed its div. between Greece and the new kingdom of the Serbs, Croats and Slovenes— later Yugoslavia. After the Second World War there was much Communist activity in M. during the Gk civil war period. In anct times M. was celebrated for its gold and silver mines, and for its wine and oil. Its cap. was first Edessa (q.v.) and later Pella (q.v.). Other important tns were Philippi (q.v.) and Thessalonika (*see* SALONICA).

2. Constituent rep. of Yugoslavia, the N. part of the old ter. of M. It is bordered on the N. by Serbia, E. by Bulgaria, S. by Greece and W. by Albania. It is mountainous, many peaks being over 8000 ft, with an irregular massif of volcanic origin in the E. The mts of the W. are thickly wooded and have good pastures. The country is bisected NW.–SE. by the Vardar (q.v.), the valley of which is very fertile. On the SW. border are 2 great lakes, Ohrid and Prespa. The climate is severe on the mts but Mediterranean in the riv. valleys. The chief occupations are agriculture, stock raising and tobacco growing. The prin. tns are Skopje (the cap.) and Bitola. Area 10,230 sq. m.; pop. 1,405,000.

Macedonian Front, Operations on. The Allies landed an expeditionary force at Salonica on 5 Oct. 1915, in a general attempt to dominate the Near E. By 1916, reinforced by Fr. and Serbian troops, it numbered over 600,000 men under Sarrail. These forces occupied a broad front N. of Salonica, the left flank resting on the Serbian frontier to the S. of Monastir, the centre occupying the valley of the Vardar to Doiran, and the right flank resting on the Struma R. The immediate purpose of the offensive launched in Aug. 1916 by Sarrail was to force the Bulgarians to defend their gains in Serbia rather than march against Rumania, and, at the same time, to induce Rumania to enter the war on the side of the Allies. The Rumanians were soon advancing into Bukovina, but thereafter they were routed. The Rumanian breakdown was largely due to Sarrail's failure to press the offensive in Macedonia, and he was indeed driven back from Florina, and the Bulgar forces captured Koritza and Kastoria, the railway through Demir Hissar and, later, the Gk port of Kavala. In 1917 Sarrail was superseded by Guillaumat; but decisive operations were not begun until the following year, when Franchet d'Espérey (q.v.) succeeded Guillaumat. The 2 decisive allied victories were those of the Vardar (15–25 Sept.) and Doiran (18–19 Sept.). Brit. and Gk troops operated in the region of Lake Doiran, on the right front; Franco-Serb troops in the centre, along the Vardar; and It. troops on the left in Albania. Then came the capture of Prilep, the Babuna Pass, Ishtip and finally of the Bulgarian tn, Strumnitza. Bulgaria then asked for an armistice, which was signed 29 Sept. 1918.

Macedonian Language and Literature, *see* YUGOSLAVIA, *Yugoslav Languages* and *Macedonian Literature.*

Macedonians, early Christian sect who taught that the Holy Ghost was inferior to the Father and the Son; so called from Macedonius, Bishop

4615

of Constantinople in the 4th cent.

Macedonski, Alexandru (1854–1920), Rumanian writer, *b.* Bucharest. He pub. his first vol. of verse, *Prima verba*, in 1872, at the age of 18. Later vols. are *Poezii*, 1882, *Excelsior*, 1895, *Flori sacre*, 1912, *Poema rondelurilor* (posthumous), 1927; other well-known poems were his 11 *Nopți* ('Nights') pub. between 1880 and 1902. He also wrote a number of short plays in Rumanian and some works in French, including a novel, *Le calvaire de feu*, 1906, and a play, *Le fou*, 1910.

Maceió, city of NE. Brazil, cap. of the state of Alagoas, Jaraguá, its port, exports sugar, rum and cotton; and its main industries cover cotton textiles, sugar-refining, tanning, tobacco, sawmills and distilleries. It is the terminus of a railway line which after running through the interior arrives at Bahia to the S. and also of a line to Recife on the coast to the N. Pop. 153,000.

Macerata: 1. Prov. of Italy, in the central Marches. It is mainly mountainous and has some high ridges of the Apennines, but has fertile riv. valleys and an undulating coastal plain in the E. on the Adriatic. The chief rivs. are the Potenza and the Chienti. The prin. tns include M. and Recanati. Area 1070 sq. m.; pop. 299,000.

2. It. tn, cap. of the prov. of M., 22 m. S. of Ancona. It stands on a hill, and has a cathedral, some fine Renaissance buildings, a small univ. (1290) and an important library (1773). There is a trade in agric. produce and manufs. of chemicals, glass and musical instruments. Pop. 23,000.

Maceration, process by which some of the constituents of plants are extracted by steeping the seeds, leaves, roots, etc., in a suitable solvent; there may be also a certain amount of breaking up of the fibres by mechanical means. The operation is adopted in the preparation of liqueurs and perfumes.

McEvoy, Ambrose (1878–1927), painter, *b.* in W. of England, studied at the Slade school. He began as a painter of restful interiors and poetic landscapes, and then sprang into fame as a fashionable portrait painter. 'The Ear-ring' (1911) in the Tate Gallery, is a characteristic figure painting. A.R.A., 1924.

McEwen, Sir John (1868–1948), Scottish composer, *b.* Hawick and educ. at Glasgow Univ. He came to London, 1891, and studied music at the Royal Academy of Music. In 1895 he returned to Scotland and settled at Greenock as church choirmaster and pianoforte teacher, but in 1898 he was invited to join the Royal Academy of Music as prof. of harmony and composition. In 1924 he became principal, and he remained there until 1936. Knighted 1931. His work became well known through the success of *Grey Galloway*, a border ballad for orchestra, and his symphony in C sharp minor, entitled *Solway*, is outstanding. He was at his very best in his 17 remarkable string quartets, and he wrote other admirable chamber music.

Macewen, Sir William (1848–1924), surgeon, *b.* Rothesay, Scotland, and educ. at Glasgow Univ., where he qualified M.B., 1869 (M.D., 1872). From 1892 until his death M. was Regius prof. of surgery at Glasgow. He was the first to operate for brain abscess (1876), and successfully removed a tumour of the brain in 1878; he was also the first to perform complete removal of a lung for tuberculosis (1895; the patient still living in 1940). He made important studies on bone growth and was a pioneer in bone surgery; he introduced and perfected the method of operation in cases of mastoid disease. He was a strong supporter of Lister's antiseptic method. He contributed many papers to medical jours.; his books include *Osteotomy*, 1880, *Pyogenic Infective Diseases of the Brain and Spinal Cord*, 1893, and *The Growth of Bone*, 1912. He was knighted in 1902.

See A. K. Bowman, *Life and Teaching of Sir William Macewen*, 1942.

Macfarren, Sir George (1813–87), composer and writer on musical theory, *b.* London. He became prof. of the Royal Academy of Music in 1834 and principal in 1875. His musical productions include operas, cantatas, chamber music and vocal and instrumental items, but he is now best known for his theoretical pubs. *Rudiments of Harmony*, 1860, six *Lectures on Harmony*, 1867, *Counterpoint*, 1879, and *A Musical History*, 1885.

McGill, James (1744–1813), philanthropist, *b.* Glasgow. He emigrated to Canada and settled down in Montreal as a fur merchant. He became a member of the Lower Canadian Assembly and amongst many other philanthropic enterprises he presented valuable lands to McGill Univ. (q.v.).

McGill University, college in Montreal, Canada, which was endowed by James M. with property then valued at £4000. The year of foundation was 1821. Since then it has had other benefactors, among them Lord Strathcona. Under the direction of Sir Wm Dawson (who retired in 1895, and *d.* 1899) it made rapid progress. The univ. has an imposing range of buildings on Mt Royal, with facilities in the shape of laboratories, libraries, etc., for every branch of study. There are residential halls and sev. theological and other colleges are affiliated to it. It is coeducational. A short hist. of the univ. is given in the *Commonwealth Universities Yearbook*, 1929.

Macgillicuddy's Reeks, mt range in the co. of Kerry, Rep. of Ireland, lying to the W. of Killarney (q.v.). It has sev. high peaks, including Carntual (Carrantuohill, q.v.), which attains 3414 ft. In the basin between them and the Mangerton (2756 ft) group are the lakes of Killarney (q.v.).

Macgillivray, James Pittendreigh (1856–1938), sculptor, *b.* Port Elphinstone in Aberdeenshire. His sculptures include the Burns statue, the national memorial to Gladstone and the John Knox Memorial.

McGinley, Phyllis (1905–), Amer. poetess, *b.* Ontario, Oregon. Educ. at the univs. of Utah and California, she was a teacher for a time, then entered journalism. A Rom. Catholic, she married Charles Hayden in 1937. As a writer of humorous verse she has been compared with Ogden Nash (q.v.). Her pubs. include *On the Contrary*, 1934, *One More Manhattan*, 1937, *Pocketful of Wry*, 1940, *Husbands Are Difficult*, 1941, *Stones from a Glass House*, 1946, *The Love Letters of Phyllis McGinley*, 1955, *Times Three*, 1961, essays, and a number of children's books.

McGonagall, William (1830–*c*. 1902), poetaster, *b*. Edinburgh. After some schooling in Glasgow he became a weaver in Dundee, but his heart was in the crude but sincere verses which he wrote on topical subjects and would recite in public houses, afterwards taking a collection. The unconscious humour of his work has won it immortality, and two vols. of selections were pub. after his death, *Poetic Gems*, 1954, and *More Poetic Gems*, 1962.

MacGregor, Robert, *see* ROB ROY.

Mach, Ernst (1838–1916), Austrian physicist and philosopher, *b*. Turas, Moravia. After studying at Vienna he was appointed prof. of mathematics at Graz in 1864 and 2 years later prof. of physics. In 1867 he became prof. of physics at Prague, where he remained till 1895, when he went to Vienna as prof. of philosophy. His work in physics included research on supersonic projectiles and jets, and in a paper in 1887 with the title 'Photography of Projectile Phenomena in Air', he described the 'Mach angle'. M. was a positivist in his philosophy and in accordance with his outlook advocated that physical science should be interpreted entirely in terms of actual observation—a philosophical position known as phenomenalism. *See* MACH NUMBER. *See* N. A. V. Piercy, *Elementary Aerodynamics*, 1944.

Mach Number, ratio of the airspeed of a projectile or an aeroplane to the speed of sound (about 750 m.p.h.) at sea level. When this ratio is 1 the critical M. N. has been reached. Mach angle is the angle between the axis of a projectile and the envelope of the pressure waves which it produces. If $V\rho$ is the velocity of the projectile, V_s the velocity of sound, the mach angle (a) is given by $\sin a = V_s/V\rho$. *See* SOUND.

Machado y Ruiz, Antonio (1875–1939), Sp. poet, *b*. Seville. Among his books are *Soledades*, 1903, and *Campos de Castilla*, 1912.

Machado y Ruiz, Manuel (1874–1947), Sp. writer, *b*. Seville, brother of the above. He arranged plays by Lope de Vega, produced poetic dramas in collaboration with his brother, and wrote poetry depicting Andalusian life and reminiscences of Spain's past, the most notable being *Alma*, 1900, *Muses y los Cantares*, 1907, *Canto hondo*, 1912, and *Sevilla y otros poemas*, 1921. *See* M. Pérez Ferrers. *Vida de Antonio Machado y Manuel Machado*, 1947.

Machaerodonts, or **Sabre-Toothed Tigers,** extinct Pleistocene carnivores (e.g. *Smilodon*), as large as a lion, with extraordinarily developed sabre-shaped upper canine teeth.

MacHale, John (1791–1881), Irish ecclesiastic, *b*. Tobbernavine, Co. Mayo; educ. at Maynooth College and, after ordination, appoin-

MACHAERODONT
(*Smilodon*)

ted lecturer in theology there. In 1820 appeared the first of series of letters signed 'Hierophilos' directed against the co-education of the Rom. Catholics and Protestants. He was consecrated bishop in 1825 and, despite opposition, was made archbishop of Tuam in 1834, and continued to express his views against mixed schools and colleges even in face of the acquiescence of 3 archbishops and 15 bishops in the scheme for creating national schools. This confirmed his popularity, which was further enhanced by his uncompromising aversion from everything Eng. When Newman came to Ireland M. openly opposed him on the ground that an Englishman was not wanted in a univ. in Dublin, and he quarrelled with Archbishop Cullen (q.v.) over the Catholic Univ., but his eccles. influence gradually waned as that of Cullen grew. M. trans. the Pentateuch into Irish, as part of an *Irish Translation of the Holy Bible*, Dublin, 1861. In 1841 he pub. an Irish trans. of sev. of Moore's *Irish Melodies* (later ed., 1871). He also trans. the *Iliad* into Irish verse in 8 books, 1844–71. In 1854 he pub. in Irish *The Way of the Cross* by St Alphonsus Liguori (q.v.).

Machar, Josef Svatopluk (1864–1942), Czech poet, *b*. Kolin. In his early work in verse the influence of Musset and Heine was evident, and later he wrote objective poems on social subjects. But his chief work is a large series called collectively *The Consciousness of the Centuries*, 1905–26, including *Golgotha, In the Rays of the Hellenic Sun, The Poison of Judea, The Barbarians, Pagan Flames* and *The Apostles*. He has also written 2 other books of verse: *They*, dealing with the Fr. revolution, and *He*, dealing with Napoleon. In his great cycle, written mainly in blank verse, one of his main themes is that life found its apogee in the Rom. Empire which was ruined by Christian morality. *See* life by V. Martinek, 1912.

Machaut, Guillaume de (*c*. 1300–77), Fr. priest and composer, *see* FRENCH MUSIC.

Machen, Arthur Llewellyn Jones (1862–1947), novelist, *b*. Caerleon-on-Usk. He was educ. at Hereford Grammar School. In this countryside, the abiding traditions of old religions strongly influenced him, and when he went to London as a young man he had the task of cataloguing a library of occult books. In his own prose, measured and musical, he wrote of strange beliefs, of mystics who walked on lonely hills in Wales or in sinister streets in Holborn. His earliest works, apart from trans., were *The Chronicle of Clemendy*, 1884, and *The Anatomy of Tobacco*, 1888, in imitation of Rabelais and Burton respectively. His best early work includes *The Great God Pan*, 1894, *The Inmost Light*, 1894, *The Three Impostors*, 1895, *Hieroglyphics*, 1902, and *The Hill of Dreams*, 1907. Popularity eluded him until he wrote *The Great God Pan*. This made his reputation, though *Hieroglyphics* is highly regarded by critics; in it he proclaimed his literary creed and view of art as 'the presentment in temporal earthly symbols of an eternal unchanging mystery'. From 1910 to 1921 he was on the staff of the *Evening News*, which paper pub. his fantasy 'The Bowmen'. From that the legend of the Angels of Mons was born. The best remembered of his later books are *The Hill of Dreams*, 1922, and *The Secret Glory*, 1922. In recognition of his work he was granted a Civil List pension in 1932. His last books were *The Children of the Pool*, 1936, and *Holy Terrors*, 1947. *Far-Off Things*, 1922, and *Things Near and Far*, 1923, are autobiographical. *See* study by V. Starrett, 1918, bibliography by H. Danielson, 1923, life by A. Reynolds and W. Charlton, 1963.

Machiavelli, Niccolò (1469–1527), It. statesman and author, *b.* Florence. In 1488 he was made secretary of 'The Ten', a board which had the management of foreign affairs. In 1502 he was sent on a mission to the formidable Cesare Borgia to make professions of friendship on the part of the Florentines. In 1507 he was sent to the Emperor Maximilian, and on his return wrote sev. reports. In 1509 he was sent to the camp before Pisa, which was besieged by the Florentines, and in 1510 to France a third time where he consolidated the alliance of Florence with France. When in 1512 the Medici possessed themselves of Florence, M. was banished, imprisoned and put to the torture on suspicion of being implicated in a conspiracy against the Medici, but was released by the intervention of Leo X. He then withdrew from public life and wrote his *Discorsi sopra la prima deca di Tito Livio* and *Dell'arte e della guerra*, 1519–21, and his *Principe*—not pub. until 5 years after M.'s death—which may be described as a guide for the perfect autocrat, and is a really great attempt to strike a new path. M. almost alone in his period saw that the world (or Italy) would never be a perfect place until things were looked at unveiled. Men of his time had no other alternatives to the prevailing systems, but M. wished to get at the fundamental issues of life, and would have liked mankind to do likewise. Every one and everything were to be subordinated to the ends of the State. M.'s work may be said to have called an end to the unsystemised state of medieval times. The *Legazioni*, or letters

of the political missions of M., which are the key to his *Principe*, were not made public till the middle of the 19th cent. The chief works of M. not mentioned above are the comedies *La Mandragola*, 1513, *La Clizia*, 1515, and *Storie Fiorentine*, 1521–5. *See* lives by P. Villari, 1877–82 (trans., 1878); V. Turri, 1902; J. H. Whitfield, 1947; R. Ridolfi, 1954. *See also* L. Dyer, *Machiavelli and the Modern State*, 1904; F. Ercole, *La Politica di Machiavelli*, 1926; E. Grillo, *Machiavelli and Modern Political Science*, 1928; D. E. Muir, *Machiavelli and his Times*, 1936; H. Butterfield, *The Statecraft of Machiavelli*, 1940. (*See Plate: Literature.*)

Machicolation (Fr. *mèche*, match, combustible matter, and O.F. *coulis*, flowing), architectural term for the openings between the corbels supporting a projecting parapet; or in the vault of a portal; through which combustibles were dropped on the heads of assailants. Also a projecting structure containing a range of such openings.

Machine Drawing, *see* ENGINEERING DRAWING.

Machine-gun, weapon rated as 'small-arms' and capable of providing rapid and sustained fire. Although detailed statistics are not available it is probable that M.-g.s have caused more casualties than any other weapons of war.

Attempts to make such a weapon began in the 16th cent., but it was not until 1884 that Sir Hiram Stevens Maxim demonstrated the first M.-g. to be used effectively in battle. The 'Maxim-gun' was used by the British in the S. African War (1899–1902). In the First World War it had been succeeded by the improved 'Vickers', both being water-cooled and of very similar design.

The static conditions of trench warfare in 1914–18 were ideal for the employment of M.-g.s, which came to be classified in 3 groups—heavy (used mainly by the Germans), medium (such as the Brit. Vickers) and light (a new air-cooled type such as the Brit. Lewis). Heavy and medium M.-g.s fired at a rate of some 500 rounds per min. and had a maximum effective range of about 1500 yards; the light considerably less in both rate of fire and effective range. Protected by concrete and earth the heavy and medium types were the main defensive weapons of all belligerents; the light being designed for mobile operations. Modified types were introduced for use in the early makes of military aircraft. The Second World War saw little alteration in the basic principles connected with M.-g.s, although the much more mobile nature of operations resulted in changes of detail. In the Brit. Army the more efficient Bren superseded the Lewis and became the normal infantry weapon, the Vickers being concentrated in special M.-g. battalions. In the Ger. Army the Spandau was the chief weapon. The Second World War saw the use of M.-g.s in tanks and armoured cars and against low-flying aircraft. At the same time the advent of tanks in large numbers greatly reduced the M.-g.'s effectiveness in terrain suitable for tanks. Another

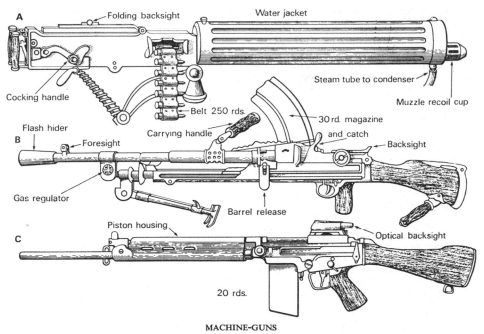

MACHINE-GUNS

A, Vickers ·303: probably the most reliable machine-gun ever produced and the main Brit. defensive weapon in the First World War. B, Bren light automatic machine-gun: a light gun, easily carried and operated by one man; used extensively in the Brit. Army in the Second World War. C, F. N. (Fabrique Nationale) Automatic Rifle: in the mid-1960s the standard weapon of the Brit. Army, being light and capable of firing single shots like a rifle, or short bursts of automatic fire.

development was the sub-M.-g. (or 'Tommy gun'), a form of small quick-firing rifle, usually fired from the hip.

In recent years the Brit. Army has progressively replaced its old magazine loading rifles with the Belgian made F. N. automatic rifle, capable of firing single shots or short bursts of fire. Most other modern armies have adopted similar weapons. Air M.-g.s are usually of 20- or 30-mm. (1965) and are sometimes known as cannon because they can fire small shells. See FIREARMS. See Capt. M. M. Johnson, *Automatic Weapons of the World*, 1945; Lieut.-Col. G. M. Chinn, *The Machine Gun*, 1951; Maj. W. G. B. Allen, *Pistols, Rifles and Machine Guns*, 1953.

Machine-made Lace, *see* LACE.

Machine Tools, *see* TOOLS, MACHINE.

Machinery, Agricultural, *see* AGRICULTURAL MACHINERY.

Machines, Automatic, *see* AUTOMATION.

Machpelah, 'before' (i.e. E. of) Mamre (the place by the oaks where Abraham pitched his tent—Gen. xiii. 18), name of a dist in Hebron, kingdom of Jordan, containing a cave. Abraham bought the cave from the Hittite Ephron for a burial-place and buried Sarah there. In this cave he himself was also buried, as were Isaac, Rebekah, Leah and finally Jacob (Gen. xxv. 9, xlix. 30, and l. 13). Tradition identifies this cave

with that under the great mosque at Hebron. It lies on the E. edge of the modern city, on the SW. slope of the mt, but of the cave no recent reliable account is available.

Machu Picchu, anct city of Peru, in the Andes, discovered in 1911 by Hiram Bingham, the Amer. explorer. It is thought that M. P. may have been 'Tampu-tocco', traditional cradle of Inca (q.v.) civilisation, and that it was built as a refuge when invaders occupied the Cuzco valley about AD 800, enjoying a high degree of inaccessibility in its situation above the deep valley of the Urabamba R. Overcrowding led to its abandonment for a new Cuzco, eventually the centre of the Inca empire. When the Spaniards arrived in the 16th cent., the advantages of M. P. led the Incas to rebuild the city. The profusion of feminine ornaments has led to the theory that M. P. became the final home of the priestesses of the Inca sun god, the Virgins of the Sun. The remains of the city are of great beauty. *See* H. Bingham, *Inca Land*, 1922; C. Sandeman, *A Wanderer in Inca Land*, 1948.

Machynlleth, tn and par. of Montgomeryshire, Wales, near the R. Dovey, 10½ m. from Dolgelley. Owen Glendower summoned a parliament here in 1402. Agriculture and forestry are the prin. local occupations, and there are slate quarries in the vicinity. Pop. 1903.

McIndoe, Sir Archibald Hector (1900–60), plastic surgeon, *b.* Dunedin, New Zealand. Educ. at Otago Boys' High School and Univ. of Otago. Mayo Foundation and Univ. Minnesota, 1927, M.S., 1929; F.R.C.S. England, 1932; F.A.C.S., 1934. Foundation Fellow and Assistant Surgeon Mayo Clinic, Rochester, Minnesota, 1924–30; Chief Assistant Plastic Surgery Unit, St Bartholomew's Hospital, London, 1930–4. Plastic Surgeon St Bartholomew's Hospital; Consultant Plastic Surgeon, RAF; Surgeon in charge, Maxillo-Facial Unit, Queen Victoria Hospital, E. Grinstead, Sussex. His mentor in plastic surgery was his cousin and fellow-countryman, Sir Harold Gillies (q.v.), whose chief assistant he became at St Bartholomew's Hospital. M. is best known for his work as consultant in plastic surgery to the RAF during the Second World War. Hundreds of badly burned and maimed patients, most of them flying men, passed through his hands at the Queen Victoria Hospital. It was to help with their rehabilitation and future welfare that he founded the famous Guinea-pig Club. His skill won him international fame and the lasting gratitude of those whose ruined features he refashioned to as near normality as was possible. He was appointed C.B.E. in 1944 and knighted in 1947. He also held numerous foreign orders and decorations awarded for his services to men in allied armed Forces. *See* L. Mosley, *Faces from the Fire*, 1962.

McIntire, Samuel, *see* FURNITURE.

Macintosh, Charles (1766–1843), Scottish chemist and inventor of waterproof materials. He introduced the manuf. of sugar of lead from Holland (1786), started the first alum works in Scotland (1797) and obtained a patent (1825) for converting malleable iron into steel, helping Neilson to bring his 'hot-blast' process into use (1828). He took out a patent for his 'mackintosh' cloth in 1823. See *Memoir* by G. Macintosh.

Macintyre, Duncan, *see* SCOTTISH GAELIC LANGUAGE AND LITERATURE.

Mackail, Denis George (1892–   ), novelist and biographer, *b.* Kensington. Educ. at St Paul's and Balliol College, Oxford, he was for a time a stage designer, and later worked in the Print Room of the Brit. Museum. He wrote a large number of light novels which were extremely popular, and also many short stories for magazines. Among his best-known books are *Bill the Bachelor*, 1922, *Summertime*, 1924, *Greenery Street*, 1925, *The Fortunes of Hugo*, 1926, *Another Part of the Wood*, 1929, *Having Fun*, 1933, *London Lovers*, 1938, *Life with Topsy*, 1942, *Tales for a Godchild*, 1944, *We're Here*, 1947, *By Auction*, 1949, and *It Makes the World Go Round*, 1950. He also wrote *The Story of J. M. B.*, 1941, which is the standard life of Barrie (q.v.) of whom he was a close friend. He is a fellow of the Royal Society of Literature.

Mackail, John William (1859–1945), Scottish classical scholar, *b.* Bute; educ. at Ayr Academy, Edinburgh Univ. and Balliol College, Oxford. He won the Newdigate prize, and was elected to a fellowship at Balliol, but in 1884 he entered the

education dept, in the offices of whose successor, the Board of Education, he remained until his retirement in 1919. His years as a civil servant were marked by a copious stream of scholarly works, including a prose trans. of the *Eclogues* and *Georgics*, *Select Epigrams from the Greek Anthology*, 1890, and *Latin Literature*, a survey of the whole literature of anct Rome, 1895. In 1899 he pub. a life of Wm Morris. In 1906 M. was appointed prof. of poetry at Oxford, and the 3 vols of his lectures, *The Springs of Helicon*, 1909, *Lectures on Greek Poetry*, 1910, and *Lectures on Poetry*, 1911, deal not only with Gk and Lat. literature, but also with the Eng. poets from Chaucer to Keats. *The Approach to Shakespeare*, a vol. of criticism, was pub. in 1930. Many honours came to him, including honorary degrees of Edinburgh, St Andrews, Adelaide, Oxford and Cambridge Univs., while Balliol made him an honorary fellow in 1922. In 1924 he was appointed to the professorship of anct literature by the Royal Academy. Fellow of the Brit. Academy, 1914, he became president in 1932, and received the O.M. in 1935. Later works include *Studies in Humanism*, 1938, and *The Sayings of Christ*, 1938.

Mackay, Charles (1814–89), poet and journalist, *b.* Perth. He was editor of the *Glasgow Argus* (1844–7) and the *Illustrated London News* (1852–9). As special correspondent at New York to *The Times* during the Amer. Civil War (1862–5), he revealed the Fenian conspiracy. His works include *The Salamandrine*, 1842, *Voices from the Crowd*, 1846, *Egeria*, 1850, *Under Green Leaves*, 1857, various prose works, and many popular songs, such as 'There's a Good Time Coming' and 'Cheer, Boys, Cheer', pub. in *Collected Songs*, 1859. Marie Corelli (q.v.) was his daughter. *See* his *Through the Long Day*, 1887.

Mackay, Hugh (*c.* 1640–92), Scottish general, fought for Charles II after the Restoration (1660), and then for France against Holland. He later attached himself to William of Orange (1689), accompanying him to England. Sent against Claverhouse, M. was defeated at Killiecrankie. He served in Ireland (1691), and fell fighting in Flanders at Steinkerk.

Mackay, John William (1831–1902), Amer. capitalist, called the 'Silver King'. He emigrated from Ireland to New York (1840), moved to California in 1851, and to Nevada in 1858. He bought many shares (1873) in the Bonanza mines of the Comstock lode, and became very rich. With Flood and other partners he estab. the Bank of Nevada in San Francisco. In 1884–6, with J. G. Bennett, he formed the Commercial Cable Co. and the Postal Telegraph Cable Co., to fight Jay Gould and the W. Union.

Mackay, city and seaport of Queensland, Australia, 598 m. by rail N. of Brisbane, centre of a sugar region. It also produces butter, timber and tobacco, and is a tourist centre of the Great Barrier Reef (q.v.). Pop. 16,809.

Macke, August (1887–1914), Ger. painter, *b.* Meschede, Rhineland. He was one of the 'Blue Rider' group at Munich (1909) with Kandinsky and Marc. He became noted for his paintings of park and street scenes but was killed in action in the First World War.

McKee's Rocks, suburb of Pittsburgh, on the Ohio R. in Allegheny co., Pennsylvania, U.S.A. It has railway, iron and steel and glass industries. Pop. 13,180.

McKeesport, tn of Allegheny co., Pennsylvania, U.S.A., close to the iron centre of Pittsburgh, with iron and steel works of its own. Coal and iron are produced and steel tubes, pipes and sheet steel. On the Monongabela R., the bor. began its growth at the end of the 18th cent. as a 'fitting-out' centre for the migrants moving down the Ohio. Pop. 45,490.

McKell, Sir William John (1891–), Australian politician, educ. at a state school in Sydney. He became a prominent member of the Labour party, entering the federal parliament in 1917. From 1941 to 1947 he was premier of New South Wales, and from 1947 to 1953 governor-general of Australia.

McKenna, Reginald (1863–1943), financier, b. London. He was M.P, for N. Monmouthshire, 1895–1918. In 1915 he succeeded Lloyd George as chancellor of the exchequer, raised nearly £600,000,000 by a 4½ per cent loan, and, as part of war taxation, along with an excess profits tax, introduced the McKenna Duties (q.v.) on a large range of imports. He also inaugurated the issue of war savings certificates. In 1916 he imposed new duties on amusements, railway tickets, matches and mineral waters. He left office when Lloyd George became Prime Minister, 1916. In 1919 he became chairman of the London City and Midland Bank—now the Midland Bank—retaining the post up to the time of his death. As a member of the Macmillan Committee on Finance and Industry he signed the report which appeared in 1931 just before the abandonment of the gold standard. *See* S. McKenna, *Reginald McKenna, a Memoir*, 1948.

McKenna Duties, duties imposed on imports of motor cars, cinema films and musical instruments by R. McKenna (q.v.) in 1915. Their initial object was to curtail unnecessary imports for the duration of the war; but they were retained, becoming the basis of later Brit. policies of protection (q.v.).

Mackennal, Sir Bertram (1863–1931), Australian sculptor, b. Melbourne, studied art in France. His work soon won him public recognition and he was chosen to carve sev. statues of Queen Victoria, for Australia, Lahore and Blackburn, and, later, to design the coinage issued on the accession of George V. In 1889–91 he was engaged on the decoration of Gov. House, Melbourne. His other works included the national memorial to Gainsborough, memorials to Edward VII in St George's Chapel, Windsor, and elsewhere, the quadriga at Australia House, and much small decorative sculpture. A.R.A., 1909; R.A., 1922.

Mackensen, Anton Ludwig Friedrich August von (1849–1945), Ger. field-marshal; b. Haus Leipnitz, near Wittenberg. In 1869 he entered the army and served in France 1870–1. In 1898

he accompanied William II to Palestine, and in 1899 was ennobled. At the opening of the First World War on the E. front he commanded the Ninth Army, repulsing the Russians at Kutno, Lodz and Lowicz. In April 1915 he led the forces in W. Galicia, assisting in the break-through at Gorlice. On 26 June 1915 he was made field-marshal, and in Aug. and Sept. again repulsed the Russians at Brest-Litovsk and Pinsk. In Oct. and Nov. he commanded the army that overran Serbia. In 1916 he completed the conquest of Rumania by subduing the Dobrudja dist. After the armistice he surrendered at Budapest, Dec. 1918. *See* his *Geschichte der Leibhusaren-regiment*, 1892; and essays on army and war hist. in the *Militär Zeitschrift. See* study by M. Luyken, 1920.

His third son, **Everhard von M.** (1889–), was an army commander in the Second World War.

Mackenzie, Agnes Mure (d. 1955), historian, b. Stornoway, Lewis, educ. at Aberdeen Univ. She is best known for her 6-vol. *History of Scotland*, pub. 1934–41. She was made C.B.E. in 1945.

Mackenzie, Sir Alexander (c. 1755–1820), Canadian explorer, b. Stornoway, Isle of Lewis. He emigrated to Canada, and for 8 years (1781–9) traded in fur with the Indians at Lake Athabasca. His famous expedition of June–July 1789, consisting of 3 canoes with Indians, crossed Great Slave Lake and paddled down the riv. which now bears his name. He thought that the riv. which Cook had found flowing into Cook's Inlet might be connected with that which flowed N. from Lake Athabasca. Finding that it flowed into the Arctic, and not into the Pacific, he named it R. Disappointment, but went on to its mouth and on 12 July he reached the ocean. By 12 Sept. he was back at the Hudson's Bay Co.'s post of Fort Chipewyan, having travelled 3000 m. in 102 days, and having put on the map one of the continent's greatest rivs. One more possibility of a route to the Pacific still lay open, the Peace R., as it is now called, and M. resolved to explore it. His small party, starting from a post on the Peace R., got to the headwaters of the Fraser R., and he then decided to do the rest of the journey overland. Starting afresh up the Blackwater valley his party got down to the Bella Coola R., and after 15 days reached the salt water of an inlet. Three days' paddling took him still farther towards the open sea into Dean's Channel, where hostile Indians forced him to turn back, but before doing so he had determined his position. The journey had taken 72 days, and in 33 more M. was back at his post on the Peace R. The real significance of his journey is that he was the first explorer to penetrate the Rocky Mt barrier, and his historic exploit was, in fact, a forecast of the expansion of Brit. N. America from sea to sea. On his return to England in 1801 he pub. *Voyages from Montreal to the Frozen and Pacific Oceans*. He was knighted in 1802. *See* F. R. de Chateaubriand, *Voyages en Amérique*, 1828, and G. W. Brown, *Building the Canadian Nation*, 1942.

Mackenzie, Alexander (1822–92), Canadian

statesman, b. Dunkeld, Perthshire, Scotland. He emigrated to Canada in 1842 and settled at Kingston, Ontario, where he became a builder and contractor. In 1867, on the union of Canada, he was elected to the Dominion Parliament, and a year later became leader of the opposition. He became Prime Minister, on Sir John A. Macdonald's defeat through the 'Pacific Scandal', in 1873. A self-educ. stonemason, M. was a man of severe probity, in sharp contrast to his predecessor. But he lacked Macdonald's vision and boldness; the great Canadian Pacific project languished and Brit. Columbia was nearly lost. One of the cabinet ministers, Edward Blake, indeed invited Brit. Columbia to go its own way. M. was forced by the severe depression of 1873 to forswear his strong Cobdenite principles of free trade and to raise the tariff. The depression persisted almost until M.'s defeat in 1878. His was an honest but uninspired administration.

Mackenzie, Sir Alexander (1847–1935), Scottish composer, teacher of music, and violinist, b. Edinburgh. His forbears for many generations were professional musicians, his father being leader of the orchestra of the Theatre Royal, Edinburgh, and a writer of many successful songs. M. studied music in Germany and in London, under Sainton and Charles Lucas. He became (1888) principal of the Royal Academy of Music on the death of Sir George Macfarren, the institution making remarkable progress under his control. He was also conductor of the Philharmonic Society from 1892 to 1899. As a composer he had his first successes in Germany. His early works of importance include The Bride, a cantata, 1881; Jason, dramatic cantata, 1882; an opera Colomba, 1883. After he had become principal of the Royal Academy of Music, he did not give up his work of composition, producing, at this later period, among many other things, a Concerto and 2 suites for violin and orchestra, the Britannia overture, 1894, and the Scottish pianoforte Concerto, 1897. His other compositions include incidental music to Coriolanus and The Little Minister, 3 Scottish Rhapsodies, 2 oratorios, The Rose of Sharon, 1884, and Bethlehem, 1894, part-songs, Coronation March, 1902, and anthems, etc. Two later operas, The Cricket on the Hearth, after Dickens, 1914, and The Eve of St John, 1924, had some success.

Mackenzie, Sir Compton (1883–), novelist, b. W. Hartlepool, of a literary and theatrical family; the son of Edward Compton, his name originally being Edward Montague Compton. He was educ. at St Paul's School and Magdalen College, Oxford, and studied for the Bar. Forsaking law, he wrote a play, The Gentleman in Grey, produced in Edinburgh in 1907, but his career was decided by the outstanding success of his first 3 novels: The Passionate Elopement, 1911, Carnival, 1912, and Sinister Street (2 vols.), 1913–14. The last named in particular estab. a vogue for the realistic biographical novel, a genre to which he returned in 1922 with The Altar Steps. His carefully wrought love story

of the Eng. country before the war of 1914, Guy and Pauline, was pub. in 1915, being written at Capri in that year in which M. was invalided out of the Royal Marines after service in Gallipoli. During the latter years of the war he was military control officer in Athens, and in 1917 director of the Aegean Intelligence Service. His experiences at that time became the subject of 3 books: Gallipoli Memories, 1929, Athenian Memories, 1931, and Aegean Memories, 1940. The latter first appeared as Greek Memories in 1932, but was banned under the Official Secrets Act. As a writer he possesses remarkable insight into the contemporary scene, power of description and, on the whole, a stronger grasp of events than of character, his romantic conception of character contrasting with the realism of his background. He has written over 30 novels, including the notable series, 'The Four Winds of Love' the East Wind, 1937, The South Wind of Love, 1937, The West Wind of Love, 1940, West to North, 1940. Whisky Galore, 1947, and Rockets Galore, 1957, have both been successfully adapted for the screen. Among his later novels is Thin Ice, 1956. In 1923 he founded a magazine, The Gramophone, which he has since ed. Chevalier of the Legion of Honour; Lord Rector of Glasgow Univ., 1913; knighted, 1952. His autobiography, My Life and Times, is being pub. in a series of 'octaves'.

Mackenzie, Sir George (1636–91), lawyer, author and politician, b. Dundee. He became king's advocate in 1677. In spite of his professional work he found time for literature, and pub. a number of books. As criminal prosecutor in the days of the Covenanters, he earned the nickname of 'bluidy Mackenzie'. See A. Lang, Sir George Mackenzie, King's Advocate, his Life and Times, 1909, and life by T. Ruddiman, prefixed to his Collected Works, 1716–22.

Mackenzie, Henry (1745–1831), novelist and essayist, b. Edinburgh. He was by profession a lawyer, becoming crown attorney for Scotland and, in 1804, comptroller of taxes for Scotland. It is, however, as a writer that he is best remembered. In the late sixties he began to compose his best-known work, The Man of Feeling, which was pub. anonymously in 1771 and attracted much attention. Two years later, designed as a contrast to the earlier work, appeared The Man of the World, which was at once prolix and dull, and in 1777 appeared his Julia de Roubigné, written in a strain of high-wrought sentimentalism. His work shows strongly the influence of Sterne. His Anecdotes and Egotisms, first pub. in 1927, is an entertaining work of his old age. See H. W. Thompson, A Scottish Man of Feeling, 1931.

Mackenzie, Sir James (1853–1925), physician, b. Scone, Perthshire. He was apprenticed to a chemist until the age of 21, when he began the study of medicine at Edinburgh, qualifying in 1878. Soon afterwards he settled in general practice in Burnley. He saw many patients with irregularities of the pulse, some of whom d. of heart failure while others were unaffected. In 1883 he embarked on a careful study of his cardiac patients which lasted for 20 years and culminated in the pub. of his classical *Study of the Pulse*, 1902. He invented a polygraph, with which he was able simultaneously to make tracings of the pulse, apex beat, etc., and to distinguish and classify for the first time most of the irregularities of the heart with which we are today so familiar. His *Diseases of the Heart*, 1908, confirmed his reputation as one of the world's greatest cardiologists. Another classic, *Angina Pectoris*, appeared in 1923. M. left Burnley in 1907 to practise as a consultant in London; in 1910 he was appointed lecturer in cardiac research at the London Hospital, was in charge of the cardiac Department there 3 years later, and became consulting physician in 1918. He believed that every general practitioner should be a research worker, checking his findings in the midst of an active population. He therefore left London in 1918 to found the Institute of Clinical Research at St Andrews, designed to further the prevention of common diseases by investigation and assessment of symptoms before structural changes had taken place. Elected a fellow of the Royal College of Physicians in 1913, he was knighted in 1915, and was appointed physician to the king in Scotland in 1920. *See* R. M. Wilson, *The Beloved Physician*, 1926.

Mackenzie, Sir Morell (1837–92), physician, *b.* Leytonstone, Essex, and educ. professionally at the London Hospital Medical College, Paris and Budapest. At the London Hospital he held successively the posts of medical officer, assistant physician, and physician from 1860 till 1874, when he resigned. The London Throat Hospital was founded by him in 1863, and his skill as a laryngologist led to his attending the Emperor Frederick III of Germany in his fatal illness. His most important pubs. are *The Use of the Laryngoscope*, 1865, *Essay on Growths in the Larynx*, 1871, *Diseases of the Throat and Nose* (2 vols.), 1880–4, *The Fatal Illness of Frederick the Noble*, 1888, etc. *See* lives by H. R. Haweis, 1893, and R. S. Stevenson, 1946.

Mackenzie, William Lyon (1795–1861), leader of the Canadian rebellion of 1837–8, *b.* Dundee, Scotland. He emigrated to Canada in 1820 and settled in Queenstown, where he became a journalist and ed. a newspaper entitled the *Colonial Advocate*, in which he took an extreme stand against the gov. and violently attacked the Family Compact, or system by which, in each colony, power lay in the hands of a small minority of wealth and influential people. He was elected to the legislature, but was expelled for alleged libel on the ministry. He visited the U.S.A. in 1829, and was sent to England in 1832 as the delegate of his party, to appeal against certain abuses. In 1834 he became mayor of Toronto and founded the Canadian Alliance Society. In 1837 he led the rebels in the insurrection of Upper Canada. They were, however, utterly defeated, and M. escaped to the U.S.A. till 1849, when the Canadian Gov. granted an amnesty to all who had taken part in the rebellion, enabling him to return to Toronto.

Wm Lyon M. King (q.v.) was a grandson of M. *See* life by C. Lindsay, 1862.

Mackenzie: 1. Former ter. of N. Canada, now a dist of the NW. Ters. (q.v.).

2. Riv. of NW. Canada, originates as the Athabasca in Brit. Columbia and flows over 600 m. to Lake Athabasca, whence it issues as the Slave R., and after a course of 240 m. enters the Great Slave Lake. As the M. R., it leaves the W. end of the lake and flows into the Arctic Ocean, its final course being estimated at more than 1080 m. Its most important tribs. are the Liard, or Mountain R., Peel R. and Bear R., from Great Bear Lake; near its mouth it forms an intricate delta. This great waterway was first discovered by Sir Alexander Mackenzie (q.v.) in 1789. Little of the basin is settled, but there are mining camps (e.g. working uranium-rich minerals) and the upper basin contains an enormous reserve of oil in the form of tar-sands, as yet unworked. The tiny settlement of Aklavik is at the mouth of the M. (*See Plate: Canada.*)

Mackenzie Highway, road built to open up the rich mineral deposits and agric. areas in N. Alberta and the NW. Ters. of Canada. Begun in 1938, it was held up by the Second World War but was completed in 1949. It runs for 385 m. from Hay Riv. on Great Slave Lake to Grimshaw in Alberta, whence a railway connects with Edmonton.

Mackenzie King, William Lyon, *see* KING.

Mackerel, popular name given to members of the genus *Scomber*. They are fusiform fishes, covered with small scales, or occasionally with a naked skin surface; the eyes are lateral; the teeth well developed; there are 2 dorsal fins and generally finlets; the pseudo-branchiae are well developed. The M. are widely distributed and are greatly valued as food. The back is marked by alternate bands of black and green, and the sides are brilliantly iridescent. In habit these fishes are generally pelagic and spawn in the open sea; they travel at considerable speed. *Scomber scombrus*, the common M., found in the N. Atlantic, has no air-bladder; *Scomber colias* has an air-bladder. The tunnies also belong to the M. family, Scombridae, *Thunnus thynnus*, the largest species, reaching a length of 12 ft; other species of this genus are provided with long pectoral fins and are called by sailors albacores. Allied genera include *Cybium*, *Acanthocybium* and *Rhachicentron*. Fossil forms of Scombridae are found in the Eocene and Miocene strata.

McKim, Charles Follen (1847–1909), Amer. architect; *b.* Isabelle Furnace, Pennsylvania, U.S.A.; educ. Harvard Univ., then École des Beaux Arts, Paris. Returned to U.S.A., 1870, worked under H. H. Richardson (q.v.) and began practice in 1877, at first in partnership with W. R. Mead. In 1879 they were joined by Stanford White (*d.* 1906). Their prin. buildings, mainly monumental and classical in style, were the Boston public library, 1887–95; agric. pavilion at the World's Fair, Chicago, 1893; the following in New York: Tiffany Building, Herald Square Building, Univ. Club, Pierpont

Morgan Library, Pennsylvania station, Columbia Univ., Madison Square Garden; also the Amer. Academy at Rome, Rhode Island State House, restoration of the univ. of Virginia and of the White House, Washington. M. was awarded the R.I.B.A. Royal Gold Medal in 1903.

Mackinac Island, U.S.A., 3 m. long, 2 m. wide, in the straits of M. between Lake Michigan and Lake Huron which separate the upper and the lower peninsulas of Michigan. First visited by Jean Nicolet in 1634–5, it became the chief fur-trading centre of a vast region. Under British rule from 1761 onwards, it passed to the U.S.A. in 1783. Since the decline of the fur trade about 1840 it has become a summer and health resort. On it is the small city of M. It is connected by ferry with Mackinaw City on the lower peninsula and St Ignace on the upper. A bridge connecting the peninsulas, 5 m. long with a 4-lane roadway, was constructed 1954–7.

Mackinder, Sir Halford John (1861–1947), geographer, educ. at Epsom College and Christ Church, Oxford. A paper of his on *The Scope and Methods of Geography* so much impressed the council of the Royal Geographical Society that it agreed to subsidise univ. lectures in the subject, and M. was appointed to Oxford, he being the second reader in geography to lecture at Oxford since Richard Hakluyt. In an address to the Brit. Association in 1895 M. proposed a scheme for a Univ. Institute of Geography where physical and human teaching might be collated, and a few years later his plan was realised as the Oxford School of Geography. In 1899 he led an expedition to Mt Kenya and climbed the summit of the peak Batian (17,000 ft). The following year he became reader and later prof. of geography at London Univ. He succeeded W. A. S. Hewins (q.v.) as director of the London School of Economics and Political Science, while continuing as reader at Oxford. His pub. lectures include *Britain and the British Seas*, 1902, 1930, *The Rhine, its Valley and History*, 1908, and *Eight Lectures on India*, 1910. In 1910 M. was elected as Unionist member for the Camlachie div. of Glasgow and kept his seat till 1922. He will be chiefly remembered for his theories of geopolitics (q.v.). He put to the practical test in his political career the main idea of his science, namely the influence of geographical environment upon political development, and the value of geography as a factor in social reconstruction. *See* especially his *Democratic Ideals and Reality*, 1919. He was sent to Russia on a mission as Brit. high commissioner for S. Russia, being knighted on his return. He became privy councillor in 1926 and was chairman of the Imperial Shipping Committee from 1920 to 1945.

McKinley, William (1843–1901), 25th president of the U.S.A., *b.* Niles, Ohio. When the civil war broke out he enlisted as a private in the Ohio volunteer infantry and finished as a major. At the end of the war he returned home to study law. He identified himself with the Republican party, and rapidly became known as an able speaker. In 1876 he was elected to Congress. In 1889 he was Republican leader in the House of Representatives and chairman of the committee of Ways and Means; as such he introduced and carried the great measure of 1890 known as the M. tariff, which raised the tariff by 50 per cent on the average. In 1891 he became governor of Ohio, and was re-elected in 1893. In 1896 he was elected president of the rep., and again in 1900. The Sp.-Amer. war was the chief event of his first term of office. He visited the city of Buffalo (New York) to deliver a public address, was shot by an anarchist at a reception there, and *d.* from his wounds a few days later. M. was undoubtedly one of the most popular of Amer. presidents, although not politically outstanding. *See* lives by C. S. Olcott, 1916, and C. V. Gordon, 1942.

McKinley, Mount, situated in S. central Alaska, N. America, and the highest point on that continent. It rises to a height of 20,270 ft, with glaciers on every side. Dr Cook laid claim (later disallowed) to having ascended the mt in 1906 (*see* COOK, FREDERICK AUGUSTUS), and in June 1913 a party led by Archdeacon Hudson Stuck accomplished the feat. (*See Plate: Alaska.*)

Mackinnon, Sir William (1823–93), *b.* in Argyll, founder of the Brit. E. Africa Co., and co-founder, with Robert Mackenzie, of the Brit. India Steam Navigation Co., which, under his inspiration, created a huge trade around the coasts of India and E. Africa. In 1878, through a series of negotiations with the Sultan of Zanzibar, M. secured, by lease, large strips of the E. African coast for Great Britain. The Imperial E. Africa Co. was instrumental in opening up trade in E. Africa and in suppressing the slave trade.

Mackintosh, Charles Rennie (1869–1928), architect and decorative designer; *b.* Glasgow, was educ. there and also travelled in Italy. In 1894 he won the competition for the Glasgow School of Art, but the building was not completed till 1906. It was a most remarkable design for its period, and had a great influence upon the trend of architecture abroad. M. also decorated Cranston's tea-rooms in Glasgow, 1897–1904; and designed the Scottish pavilion at the Turin exhibition, 1902, and Queen's Cross Church, Glasgow. *See* life by T. Howarth, 1952.

Mackintosh, Elizabeth (1897–1952), playwright and novelist, *b,* Inverness. Educ. at the Royal Academy there and at Anstey Physical Training College in Birmingham. Her mystery stories under the name Josephine Tey include *The Man in the Queue*, 1929, *Miss Pym Disposes*, 1947, *Brat Farrar*, 1949, and *The Singing Sand*, 1952. Even more successful were her plays, written under the name Gordon Daviot. *Richard of Bordeaux* was followed by *Queen of Scots*, 1934, and *The Stars Bow Down*, 1949. She also wrote a biography of Claverhouse, 1937.

Mackintosh, Sir James (1765–1832), philosopher, *b.* Aldowrie; educ. at Aberdeen and at Edinburgh Univ., where he studied medicine. He wrote *Vindiciae Gallicae*, a reply to Burke's

Reflections on the Revolution in France; a *History of England*, 1830–2, a *History of the Revolution in England in 1688*, 1834, and philosophical writings. *See* R. J. Mackintosh, *Memoirs of Sir James Mackintosh*, 1836.

Macklin (M'Laughlin), Charles (*c.* 1700–97), Irish actor, best remembered for his portrayal of Shylock at Drury Lane in 1741, which drew from Alexander Pope the couplet 'This is the Jew, That Shakespeare drew'. The part had for long been played by a low comedian, and M. raised it again to a dignified and tragic status. He joined a company of strolling players in 1716, and in 1730 was engaged for Lincoln's Inn Fields. He was an excellent actor, but a quarrelsome person, and moved constantly from one company to another. He was at his best in such parts as Scrub and Peachum, and as Sir Pertinax Mac-Sycophant in his own play, *The Man of the World* (1781). He remained on the stage until 1789, making his last appearance as Shylock, which he was unable to finish, on 7 May.

Maclaren, Ian, *see* WATSON, JOHN.

Maclaurin, Colin (1689–1746), mathematician, *b.* Kilmodan, Argyllshire. He was educ. at Glasgow Univ. and in 1717 was appointed prof. of mathematics at Marischal College, Aberdeen, then assistant to the professor of mathematics at Edinburgh Univ. in 1725 and finally to the professorship there. He was instrumental in preparing the defences at Edinburgh against the Pretender in 1745. In 1740 he shared with Euler (q.v.) and Daniel Bernouilli (q.v.) the prize offered by the Fr. Academy of Science for an essay on the flux and reflux of the sea. This essay was subsequently revised by M. and included in his *Treatise on Fluxions*. M.'s purpose in this treatise was to found the doctrine of fluxions on geometrical demonstration and he thus laid down the fluxional method, regarding fluxions as velocities, after Newton; but the most valuable part of the work is his essay on tides. In this he investigated the attraction of an ellipsoid of revolution, and demonstrated that a homogeneous fluid mass revolving uniformly round an axis under the action of gravity must assume the form of an ellipsoid of revolution. The significance of his investigation in relation to the theory of the tides, the shape of the earth and kindred questions has always caused it to be regarded as one of the cardinal problems of mathematical physics. Among his writings are *Geometrica organica*, 1719, *A Treatise on Fluxions*, 1742, and *An Account of Sir Isaac Newton's Philosophical Discoveries* and *Algebra*, both pub. in 1748.

Macle, in crystallography, a term used for the phenomenon otherwise known as twinning. This occurs when 2 crystals have a common face and are so disposed that one may be brought into the position of the other by rotation about an axis called the twin-axis. The mineral known as chiastolite, consisting of aluminium silicate with magnesium and iron, is also called M. It is used for making beads for rosaries.

Maclean, Donald Duart, *see* BURGESS AND MACLEAN CASE.

McLean, Norman (1865–1947), orientalist, *b.* Lanark, son of the Rev. Daniel M. of Jamaica. He was educ. at the high school and univ. of Edinburgh and at Christ's College, Cambridge, where he remained for the rest of his life, becoming Master of the College in 1927; Heb. lecturer at Christ's College, and later univ. lecturer in Aramaic. He collaborated with A. E. Brooke in the preparation of the larger Cambridge ed. of the Septuagint, of which the 2 vols. from Genesis to the second Book of Chronicles appeared between 1906 and 1935. To the *Encyclopaedia Biblica* M. contributed, in co-operation with Sir Arthur Shipley and others, a series of articles on the flora and fauna of the Bible. But his most valuable work was on Syriac, where his name will always be associated with that of Wm Wright, whose pupil he was. He wrote numerous articles for the 11th ed. of the *Ency. Brit.* on Syriac literature. His prin. pubs. are *The Book of Judges in Greek*, etc. (with A. E. Brooke), 1897; *Eusebius Pamphili* (with W. Wright and A. Merx), 1898; *The Old Testament in Greek*, etc. (with A. E. Brooke), 2 vols., 1906–35.

Maclean, Somhairle, *see* SCOTTISH GAELIC LANGUAGE AND LITERATURE.

MacLeish, Archibald (1892–), Amer. poet, *b.* Glencoe, Illinois. He was educ. at Yale and Harvard. His early verse, *Tower of Ivory*, 1917, embodies his subjective experiences as a soldier in the First World War and there is a return to this individualistic mood in *The Hamlet of A. MacLeish*, 1928. This latter work and the interim vols. of verse, *The Happy Marriage*, 1924, *The Pot of Earth*, 1925, and *Streets in the Moon*, 1926, reveal the influence of T. S. Eliot and Ezra Pound. His *Conquistador*, 1932, was awarded the Pulitzer prize. It is an epic in verse based on the eye-witness account of Bernal Diaz del Castillo entitled *The True History of the Conquest of Mexico*, 1632. In *Public Speech*, 1936, M. begins to show his growing preoccupation with collectivist social theory, and in similar vein is his *America Was Promises*, 1939—a call to save democracy. After the First World War he practised law for a time and then became assistant editor of *Fortune* and afterwards director of the Harvard School of Journalism. In 1939 he was appointed librarian of Congress, in 1944 he became an assistant secretary of state, and in 1949 was appointed prof. of rhetoric at Harvard. His other works include *Panic*, 1935, a verse drama; *The Fall of the City*, 1937, a radio verse play illustrating the hollowness of totalitarian dictatorship; *The Irresponsibles*, 1940, a rebuke to contemporary indifference towards democracy; *The Trojan Horse*, 1952; *J. B.*, 1958, another play; and *Poetry and Experience*, 1961. His *Collected Poems, 1917–1952*, appeared in 1952.

Macleod, Fiona, *see* SHARP, WILLIAM.

MacLeod, George (1895–), Scottish minister, educ. at Winchester and at Oxford and Edinburgh Univs. He served with distinction in the First World War. M. became a Presbyterian minister and since 1938 has been leader of the

Iona Community, which has become a centre of Christian unity. He was moderator of the General Assembly of the Church of Scotland 1957–8, and is known for his pacifist views. M. succeeded to a baronetcy in 1944, but does not use his title. Pubs. include: *We Shall Rebuild*, 1944; *Only One Way Left*, 1956.

Macleod, Iain Norman (1913–), Brit. politician, educ. at Fettes and Caius College, Cambridge. He served in the Second World War and entered Parliament as a Conservative in 1950. He was minister of health, 1952–5, and minister of labour, 1955–9. M. proved an outstanding and markedly progressive colonial secretary, 1959–61, and from 1961 until 1963 was chancellor of the duchy of Lancaster and leader of the House of Commons. He declined to take office under Sir Alec Douglas-Home, 1963, and was editor of the *Spectator*, 1963–5. After the 1964 general election M. again became prominent in Conservative affairs, and was Conservative spokesman on steel and subsequently on economic affairs. Pubs. include a life of Neville Chamberlain, 1961.

Macleod, John James Rickard (1876–1935), physiologist, *b.* Cluny, near Dunkeld, Scotland. He studied medicine at Aberdeen, Leipzig and Cambridge. He was prof. of physiology, W. Reserve Univ., Cleveland, Ohio, 1903–18, at Toronto, 1919–28, and at Aberdeen, 1928 until his death. He was president of the Amer. Physiological Society, 1922, F.R.S., 1923. His pubs. include works on general physiology, on metabolism of carbohydrates, etc. While at Toronto he was associated with F. G. Banting (q.v.) and C. H. Best in their isolation of insulin (1921), one of the most beneficial discoveries in medicine. With Banting he shared the Nobel prize for medicine, 1923.

MacLiammóir, *see* MAC LIAMMÓIR.

Maclise, Daniel (1806–70), painter, *b.* Cork, settled in London in 1827, and acquired fame as a hist. and portrait painter. He was elected R.A. in 1840. In the late fifties he painted 2 fine frescoes in the Royal Gallery of the House of Lords, but these were more coldly received than his other works. He is, perhaps, most popularly known for the long series of portrait drawings of notable folk which he contributed to *Fraser's Magazine*, 1830–8, collected under the title of *The Maclise Portrait Gallery*, 1874, 1882.

McLoughlin, John (1784–1857), fur trader, a founder of Brit. Columbia and of Oregon, *b.* at Rivière du Loup. He studied medicine, and joined the N. W. Co. (which had not then amalgamated with the Hudson's Bay Co.) about 1803, to try his fortune as a young physician, and acted as surgeon at Kaministiquia. In 1808 he nearly gave up the fur trade, but by 1814 he had become a partner in the N. W. Co., being in charge of the Rainy Lake Dist. Seven years later he accepted a commission in the Hudson's Bay Co. as chief factor, and in 1823 was put in charge of the Columbia dept, and later built Fort Vancouver. He occupied an almost independent position and over a period of 25 years did much to lay the foundations of commerce along the

Brit. Columbian coast. He sent out expeditions which built strategic points along the sea and far into the interior. One of them chose the site of Victoria; and Fort Vancouver became not only a fur-trading centre but also a prosperous agric. community. *See* R. G. Montgomery, *The Whiteheaded Eagle*: *John McLoughlin, Builder of an Empire*, 1935; R. C. Johnston, *John McLoughlin, Patriarch of the North-West*, 1935; E. E. Rich (Ed.) (Champlain Society), *McLoughlin's Fort Vancouver Letters* (3 series: 1825–38, 1839–44 and 1844–6), 1942–5.

MacMahon, Marie Edmé Patrice Maurice de (1808–93), Duke of Magenta, marshal of France and second president of the third rep., *b.* Sully, Seine-et-Loire, France, of Irish descent. He graduated at the military school of St Cyr and served in the Algiers campaign of 1830. In 1853 he went to the Crimea and took part in the operations against Sebastopol, successfully assaulting Malakov. On the outbreak of the war with Austria in 1859 he distinguished himself at the battle of Magenta, and again at the battle of Solferino. In 1870 he was defeated at Weissenberg and at Worth. In 1871 he was called to recover Paris from the Commune, and on Thiers's resignation in 1873 he was elected president of France, resigning 6 years later. Extremely conservative in attitude, he was popularly suspected of favouring a restoration of the empire. *See* J. Bertaut, *Paris sous MacMahon*, 1930.

McMath, Robert Raynolds (1891–1962) Amer. astronomer and engineer, *b.* Detroit. With Judge Henry S. Hulbert he estab. in 1930 at Lake Angelus, Michigan, the McMath-Hulbert observatory, which became a major centre of research in solar physics. He was for many years a prof. in the Univ. of Michigan, and advised the U.S. Gov. on scientific policy, especially through the National Science Foundation.

Macmillan, Daniel (1813–57), publisher of Scottish birth, and senior partner of a business founded in 1843 and carried on successfully after Daniel's death by his younger brother Alexander (1818–96). Daniel M. was apprenticed and employed as a bookseller in Irvine and Glasgow before coming to work in London and then in Cambridge. Cambridge was the H.Q. of the brothers' own business until in 1863 Alexander moved it to London, where he had opened a branch in 1858. Alexander was a publisher of the 'old school', whose letters contributed greatly to the growth of the firm. In 1869 a branch was opened in New York which subsequently, 1951, became an independently incorporated firm (The Macmillan Co., New York) of general and textbook publishers. At the same time this firm became wholly Amer. owned. *See* C. Morgan, *The House of Macmillan*, 1943.

Macmillan, (Maurice) Harold (1894–), Brit. statesman, educ. at Eton and Balliol College, Oxford. He served with distinction in the First World War and first entered Parliament as a Conservative in 1924. Except for 2 intervals, 1929–31 and a few months in 1945, M. was from then until 1965 an M.P. representing Bromley from 1945 until his final retirement from politics in 1965. In the inter-war years M. was one of the severest critics of his party leaders' foreign policy, and in 1936, after voting against the National Gov.'s decision to abandon a policy of sanctions towards Italy, he refused the party whip for more than a year. M. was also interested in social reform, his views being generally in advance of his party at the time, and pub. a number of books on social questions.

From 1940 to 1942 M. was parl. under-secretary at the Ministry of Supply; in 1942 he was parl. under-secretary for the colonies. Later that year he was made minister resident at allied H.Q. in NW. Africa, a position he held with great success until 1945, when he was for a short time secretary for air.

M. became a conspicuous member of the Conservative opposition, 1945–51; when the Conservatives returned to power he was appointed minister of housing and local gov., and under his direction the housing programme was outstandingly successful. From 1954 to 1955 he was minister of defence, and in 1955 became foreign secretary. He held this post only until Dec., when he was appointed chancellor of the exchequer in succession to R. A. Butler (q.v.). His budget of 1956 was intended to remedy the unstable economic situation then prevailing but was popularly most remembered for the intro-duction of premium bonds. In Jan. 1957 Eden (q.v.) resigned the premiership and M. was appointed his successor in preference to Butler, a decision which caused considerable public comment. He was subsequently made leader of the Conservative party. (*See Plate: Parliament*.)

When M. became premier the country and his own party were divided on the Suez issue, and inflationary pressures added to domestic dis-content. Between taking office and the general election of 1959, M. made a highly successful Commonwealth tour and also visited Moscow and Washington, becoming an influential figure in world politics: while tax reductions and industrial expansion at home pushed inflation into the background. M fought the 1959 election on the theme of belief in an affluent society ('you've never had it so good'), and actually increased the Conservative majority. Subse-quently, his gov. suffered a series of reverses. The 'wages pause' in 1961 caused bitterness but failed to halt inflation: early in 1963 Britain's failure to enter E.E.C., to which M. had tied his plans, left the gov. virtually in a policy vacuum. The Profumo (q.v.) scandal which broke in June 1963 almost brought the gov. down. In Oct. M. resigned the premiership for health reasons, being succeeded by Lord Home (Sir A. Doug-las-Home, q.v.). He remained in the Commons until the general election of Oct. 1964, when he announced his retirement from politics.

In his political prime M. was a brilliant and highly successful figure. Cool, resourceful and a superb political tactician, he brought his party and his country through a series of national and international crises. Abroad, he consolidated the Anglo-Amer. alliance, attempted to take Britain into Europe, strove for a *modus vivendi* with Communism, and imbued his party with a much more progressive spirit in colonial and commonwealth affairs, typified in his famous 'wind of change' speech, made in Africa in 1958. His domestic policies have been criticised for their concession of principle to expediency: under M. the Brit. standard of living rose unprecedently, but basic economic problems tended to be shelved. P.C., 1942; Chancellor of Oxford Univ., 1960. Pubs. include: *Planning for Employment*, 1935; *The Middle Way*, 1938; *Economic Aspects of Defence*, 1939.

McMillan, Margaret (1860–1931), pioneer social worker and educationist, *b*. Westchester, New York State, of Scottish parents; she was educ. in Scotland and Switzerland. In 1893 she arrived in Bradford and joined the newly formed Independent Labour Party, the following year she was elected to the local school board and was largely responsible for estab. the first recorded medical inspection of school children in 1899. In 1902 she joined her sister Rachel in London. Together they opened a children's clinic at Bow (1908) and a new one in Deptford (1910) which was immediately successful. It received grants from the L.C.C. for dental treatment (1911) and eye and ear treatment (1912). It was linked with a nursery school for infants and a camp for boys and girls. During the First World War the estab. of an open air nursery school for children under 5 attracted much attention. In 1917 M. M. was awarded the C.B.E. In 1923 she became the first president of the Nursery School Association. At this time she turned her attention to teacher training. From the nursery school to which she attracted students grew the Rachel M. College which was opened in 1930. It is now a constituent college of the Univ. of London, Institute of Education. Students now take a 5-year course of training in preparation for Nursery/Infant or Infant or Junior school teaching. The course provides a wide back-ground of general education, opportunities to specialise in a selected field and a variety of practical experiences in associated schools. In 1936 the college extended its activities by setting up a holiday house for Deptford nursery school children at Wrotham. Today college students spend part of their course at M. M. House, Wrotham which is now a residential nursery for deprived children.

M. was appointed C.H. in 1930. Her pioneer-ing work in social welfare of children, the education of young children and teacher education had a profound influence in each of these aspects of the educational system. Pubs.: *Early Childhood*, 1900; *Education Through the Imagination* (new ed.) 1923; *Labour and Child-hood*, 1906; *The Child and the State*, 1911; *The Camp School*, 1917; *The Nursery School* (rev. ed.) 1930; *The Life of Rachel McMillan*, 1927. See A. Mansbridge, *Margaret McMillan, Prophet and Pioneer*, 1932; D'A. Cresswell, *Margaret McMillan, a Memoir*, 1949; G. A. N. Lowndes, *Margaret McMillan: 'The Children's Champion'*, 1960. See also COLLEGES OF EDU-

CATION; INFANT SCHOOLS; NURSERY SCHOOL. (*See Plate: Education.*)

McMillan, Rachel (1859–1917), elder sister of Margaret McMillan (q.v.). Together they devoted their lives to social welfare of children, the estab. of humane teaching methods and a teacher training college for intending teachers of young children. She was associated with her sister in their work in Bradford, Deptford and Kent. The R. M. Training College was named after her. *See* M. McMillan, *The Life of Rachel McMillan*, 1927.

McMullan, C. W. K., *see* MUNRO, C. K.

McNamara, Robert Strange (1916–), Amer. businessman and gov. official, educ. at the Univs. of California and Harvard. He joined Ford Motors in 1946, was its Vice-President 1955–60, and President 1960–1. Kennedy appointed him defence secretary, a position he continued in under Johnson, and in which he has made considerable world impact.

M'Naughten, Daniel, Brit. assassin. On 20 Jan. 1843 he shot and killed Edward Drummond, secretary to Sir Robert Peel. Tried for murder, he was acquitted on the ground of insanity. This verdict gave rise to a debate in the House of Lords as to the nature and degree of mental instability which would excuse the commission of a crime. (*See* M'Naughten RULES.)

M'Naughten Rules, formerly governing the law of England as to the nature and degree of insanity as a defence in criminal cases, were propounded by the judges in answer to 5 questions submitted by the House of Lords after a debate following the trial of Daniel M'Naughten (q.v.) in 1843. It was laid down that to establish a defence on the ground of insanity it must be clearly proved that, at the time of the committing of the act, the party accused was labouring under such a defect of reason, from disease of the mind, as not to know the nature and quality of the act he was doing, or, if he did know it, that he did not know he was doing what was wrong. (*See* CRIMINAL LAW.) *See also* MENTAL DISORDER.

McNaughton, Hon. Andrew George Latta (1887–1966), Canadian soldier, engineer and administrator, *b.* Moosomin, Saskatchewan; educ. at Bishop's College School, Lennoxville, and McGill Univ. He entered the army in 1910 and served throughout the First World War; D.S.O., 1917. He became chief of staff, 1929–35, with the rank of major-general. On the outbreak of war in 1939 he was chosen to command the 1st Div., Canadian Overseas Force. He was promoted lieutenant-general in 1940, and commanded the Canadian Corps, 1940–2, being then appointed commander-in-chief, a post which he held until his retirement in 1944 with the rank of general. He was minister of defence, 1945, during the crisis over the voluntary system for overseas service. Permanent Canadian delegate to the U.N. President, Canadian Atomic Energy Control Board, 1946–8. Chairman, Canadian section, International Joint Commission, 1950–62.

MacNiece, Louis (1907–63), poet, *b.* Belfast. He was educ. at Marlborough School and Merton College, Oxford. For some years he lectured in classics, first at Birmingham Univ. and later at Bedford College for Women, and in 1940 was in the U.S.A. as lecturer in English at Cornell Univ. Returning to England for war service, he joined the B.B.C. and was feature writer and producer from 1941 to 1963. *The Dark Tower*, 1947, is a collection of plays for radio. His first vol. of poems, *Blind Fireworks*, was pub. in 1929, and was followed by others, including *Autumn Journal*, 1939, *The Last Ditch*, 1940, *Plant and Phantom*, 1941, *Spring Board*, 1944, *Holes in the Sky*, 1948, *Ten Burnt Offerings*, 1952, *Autumn Sequel*, 1954, *Visitations*, 1957, *Eighty-Five Poems*, 1959, and *Solstices*, 1961. *The Sixpence that Rolled Away*, 1956, is a children's book. His ability in reflecting the spirit of his times in his own emotional experience has earned him an appreciative public. The Group Theatre produced his verse trans. of Aeschylus' *Agamemnon* in 1936, and his play, *Out of the Picture*, in 1937. His study of the poetry of W. B. Yeats was pub. in 1941. C.B.E. 1958. *See* his autobiography, *The Strings are False*, 1966; J. Press, *Louis MacNiece*, 1966.

McNeile, Herman Cyril (1888–1937), author, who wrote under the pseudonym of 'Sapper', *b.* Bodmin, Cornwall. He was educ. at Cheltenham and the Royal Military Academy, Woolwich, passing out into the Royal Engineers in 1907 and retiring in 1919 with the rank of lieutenant-colonel. He wrote numerous novels and short stories of 'thriller' type which enjoyed wide popularity, their outstanding character being 'Bulldog Drummond'.

MacNeill, John Gordon Swift (1849–1926), Irish politician, *b.* Dublin; educ. at Trinity College, Dublin, and Christ Church, Oxford. He was prof. of constitutional and criminal law at King's Inn, Dublin, 1882–8, and he represented S. Donegal in Parliament as a Nationalist, 1887–1918. He took silk in 1893. It was M. who secured the abolition of flogging in the navy. M. also succeeded in obtaining recognition of the principle that a minister of the Crown must not be a director of a public company. He pub. *The Irish Parliament, what it was and what it did*, 1885, *The Constitutional and Parliamentary History of Ireland till the Union*, 1917, *Phases of Irish History*, 1919, and *Studies in the Constitution of the Irish Free State*, 1925.

Mâcon (anct **Matisco**), Fr. tn, cap. of the dept of Saône-et-Loire, on the Saône. Lamartine (q.v.) was *b.* here. A busy riv. port, M. has a trade in Burgundy wines and brandy, and manufs. textiles, vats, agric. machinery and motor-cycles. Pop. 25,800.

Macon, co. seat of Bibb co., Georgia, U.S.A., and head of navigation on the Ocmulgee R., 75 m. SE. of Atlanta, and a great railway centre. It possesses a Wesleyan college and Mercer (Baptist) Univ. It manufs. clothing, yarn, tyre fabrics, paper products, lumber, furniture, prefabricated houses, brick, tile and concrete

Maine

Above: A fishing village on the coast of Maine, a state famous for its lobsters and other sea foods.

Left: Lumbering is a major industry, with saw-mills and paper-mills throughout the state.

Below left: A potato-storage warehouse in the fertile Aroostook valley; the state is the largest producer of potatoes in the U.S.A.
Photos: U.S. Information Service

Malagasy Republic

General view of Tananarive, the capital.

A worker in a paddy-field ripe for harvest; rice is one of the island's chief crops.

Scene in the harbour of Tamatave, the port of Madagascar.
Photos: Information Service, Madagascar

Malawi

Mlanje Peak, 9,843 ft, the highest point in the country.

The Ministry of Natural Resources and Local Government in Zomba, the capital.

M.v. *Ilala*, commercial steamship of the Malawi Railways, in Monkey Bay on Lake Malawi. *All photos: Malawi High Commission*

Malawi

Tobacco plays an important part in the economy.

Women cleaning cotton in the village of Phalu, about fifty miles north of Blantyre.

This blanket factory at Cholo is an example of Malawi's developing textile industry.
All photos: Malawi High Commission

Malaya

Part of the extensive waterfront of Singapore, the most important port in South-East Asia.
Singapore Information Office

A Malay family group: Malays form the largest racial group in the country.
Federal Information Services, Malaysia

Education, like everything in Malaya, is on a multi-racial basis: here, Chinese and Indian boys work together in their classroom.
Federal Information Services, Malaysia

Malaysia

The railway station, Kuala Lumpur.
Federal Information Services, Malaysia

Penang's hill railway, built by a Swiss engineer, takes passengers from the warm plains to the cool atmosphere of 2,400 ft in half an hour.
Federal Information Services, Malaysia

Corner of the communal hall in a longhouse in Sabah (N. Borneo).

Malaysia

Above left: Collecting latex in a rubber plantation, rubber being one of Malaysia's main products.
Federal Information Services, Malaysia

Above right: A farmer in Sarawak weeding paddy-fields.
Federal Department of Information, Sarawak

Left: The Malay peninsula is one of the world's chief sources of tin; this tin dredge floats on a lake which it excavates for itself as it moves.
Federal Information Services, Malaysia

Left: The new oil refinery at Port Dickson, with a capacity of one million tons a year.
Shell Photograph

Malta

Above: The harbour of Valletta, the capital.

Left: Breastplate in the Malta Museum, a relic of the Knights of St John, who occupied the island from 1530 to 1798.

Below: The prehistoric temples at Tarxien date from *c.* 1500 BC.
All photos: Malta Government Tourist Board

products, and is the centre of a peach- and cotton-growing dist. Pop. 69,760.

MacOrlan, Pierre (1883–), pseudonym of **Pierre Dumarchey**, Fr. writer, *b.* Péronne. He has pub. vols. of tales, e.g. *La Bête conquérante*, 1914, poems, collected in his *Œuvres poétiques*, 1946, numerous novels, *Le Chant de l'équipage*, 1918, *La Cavalière Elsa*, 1921, *La Vénus internationale*, 1923, *Malice*, 1923, *Sous la lumière froide*, 1926, *Le Quai des brumes*, 1927, *La Tradition de minuit*, 1930, etc., and various other works. *See* P. Berger, *Pierre MacOrlan*, 1951.

Macpherson, James (1736–96), author, *b.* Ruthven, Inverness-shire. He studied for the ministry, but became a teacher. He began to write poetry at an early age. In 1762–3 he pub. 2 poems, *Fingal* and *Temora*, which he stated were trans. from the Gaelic of Ossian, a 3rd cent. poet. The works attracted much attention and had a considerable effect on European literature, but presently the critics cast doubts upon the source, and a prolonged controversy took place. It is now believed that the trans. were based on traditional Gaelic poems, but embellished with a great many passages of M.'s own. M., in 1775, ed. *Original Papers containing the Secret History of Great Britain from the Restoration to the Accession of George I. See* Boswell's *Johnson*; M.'s life and letters by T. B. Saunders, 1895; J. S. Smart, *James Macpherson: an Episode in literature*, 1905. *See* OSSIAN.

Macquarie, Lachlan (1761–1824), governor of New S. Wales, 1810–21; *b.* Ulva, Hebrides Is. M. had distinguished himself as a first-rate officer and administrator in the army before his appointment as governor of New S. Wales. During his term of office New S. Wales changed from little more than a penal settlement to a flourishing infant colony. M. believed that ex-convicts should be given the chance to redeem themselves, and he encouraged them to become small settlers and appointed some to official positions, a policy which was resented by many of the free settlers and eventually led to his resignation. *See* M. H. Ellis, *Lachlan Macquarie: his Life, Adventures, and Times*, 1947.

Macquarie: 1. Bay of Tasmania, on the W. coast; forms an important harbour.

2. Riv. of New S. Wales formed by the junction of the Fish and Campbell streams, and after a course of 590 m. joining the Darling R.

Macready, William Charles (1793–1873), actor, one of the finest tragedians of the Eng. stage. Son of an unsuccessful theatre manager, he left school to assist his father, appeared at Birmingham in 1810 as Romeo. In 1816 he appeared at Covent Garden and then at Drury Lane, both of which he became manager in later life. He was good in a wide variety of parts, but outstanding as Lear, Hamlet and Macbeth. His rivalry with Edwin Forrest (q.v.) culminated in a riot in Astor Place, New York, in 1849, when sev. people were killed. He disliked his profession, but did a great deal for it, insisting on rehearsals, restoring the texts of Shakespeare and working to free the London stage from the monopoly of the patent theatres. He retired in

1851, after appearing at Drury Lane as Macbeth on 26 Feb. *See* J. C. Trewin, *Mr M., a tragedian and his Theatre*, 1955.

Macrinus, M. Opilius Severus, Rom. emperor (AD 217–8), *b.* Caesarea, Mauritania, AD 164, of humble parentage. At the instigation of his patron, Plantianus, he was admitted to the service of the Emperor Septimius Severus, and, after holding sev. dignities, eventually became praetorian prefect under Caracalla. On the latter's death he was proclaimed emperor by the troops, but was murdered in the following year by the generals of Elagabalus, who succeeded him.

Mac-Robertson Land, Australian Antarctic ter., *see* ANTARCTIC.

Macrobius, Ambrosius Aurelius Theodosius (fl. *c.* AD 400), Rom. grammarian. Only a comparatively small number of his works are extant, among which are a commentary on Cicero's *Dream of Scipio* and a collection of essays, *Saturnaliorum conviviorum libri septem*, the latter incomplete. *See* T. Whittaker, *Macrobius*, 1923.

Macrocollon, *see* MANUSCRIPTS.

Macrocosm, *see* MICROCOSM AND MACROCOSM.

Macroom, tn in co. Cork, Rep. of Ireland, important market centre and Irish-speaking dist. It has an anct castle, modernised and inhabited. Pop. 2169.

Macropodians, or **Macropodidae**, family of marsupials or pouched animals with large powerful hind feet, comprising all the kangaroos. The name is also given to sea spiders and spider crabs, a family of Oxyrhynchi.

Macrozamia, genus of tall evergreen perennials (family Cycadaceae) with long, leathery, graceful palm-like leaves and bearing scaly ovoid cones. *M. peroffskyana* and *M. spiralis* grow well but slowly in a greenhouse, needing liberal watering.

Macrura, or **Macroura**, group of decapod crustaceans, characterised by long broad-swimming tails, and including the lobsters, crayfish, prawns and shrimps.

McTaggart, John McTaggart Ellis (1866–1925), Scottish philosopher; educ. at Clifton College and Trinity College, Cambridge. Fellow of Trinity, 1891; lecturer at Cambridge Univ. 1897–1923. His theories were basically those of Hegel (q.v.) on whom he pub. *Studies in the Hegelian Dialectic* in 1896 and *Studies in Hegelian Cosmology* in 1901. *See also The Nature of Existence* (unfinished), the first vol. of which appeared in 1921. *See* memoir by G. Lowes Dickinson, 1931.

Mactán, prov. of the Philippines, consists of a small coral is. off the E. coast of Cebú. Magellan (q.v.) was killed here in 1521.

Mačva, see ŠABAC.

MacWhirter, John (1839–1911), painter, *b.* Slatford, near Edinburgh, studied art in Edinburgh under Lander. In 1879 he was elected an A.R.A. and in 1894 an R.A. The most characteristic of his works are highland landscapes. Perhaps his best-known picture is 'June in the

Austrian Tyrol' in the Tate Gallery.

Madách, Imre (1823–64), Hungarian poet and dramatist, *b.* Alsósztregova. In 1845 he married Erzsebét Fráter, who left him in 1852 during his political imprisonment. In 1854 he retired to his estate to devote himself to literature. His chief work is *The Tragedy of Man*, a philosophical drama owing something to *Faust*, and *Cain*. Eng. versions are by W. N. Loew, 1909, C. P. Sanger, 1933, and C. H. Meltzer and P. Vajda, 1933. *See* A. Hevesi, *Madách and 'The Tragedy of Man'*, in the Slavonic Review, vol. ix, 1931–2.

Madagascar, *see* MALAGASY REPUBLIC.

Madagascar Cat, *see* MEERKAT.

Madariaga, Salvador de (1886–), Sp. diplomatist and author, *b.* Corunna. He was educ. at Paris, and writes Spanish, English and French with equal facility. For a time he was connected with the permanent bureaux of the League of Nations, and later was prof. in Sp. studies at Oxford. When the Sp. rep. was proclaimed, M. was sent as Sp. minister to the U.S.A. He was ambas. to France, 1932–4, chief Sp. delegate to the League of Nations, 1931–6, and minister of education in 1934. His works include *Shelley and Calderón and other Essays*, 1920, *Spanish Folksongs*, 1922, *The Genius of Spain* (on modern Sp. writers), 1923, *Don Quixote, an introductory essay*, 1934; *The World's Design*, 1938, *Christopher Columbus*, 1939, *Hernán Cortés*, 1941, *The Heart of Jade* (a novel), 1944, *The Fall of the Spanish-American Empire*, 1947; *The Rise of the Spanish-American Empire*, 1947, *Bolivar*, 1952, *Essays with a Purpose*, 1954, *Democracy versus Liberty*, 1958, *Latin America between the Eagle and the Bear*, 1962, and 2 novels, *A Bunch of Errors*, 1954, and *War in the Blood*, 1957. He also wrote verse: *Romances de ciego*, 1922, *La fuente serena*, 1927, *Rosa de cieno y ceniza*, 1941. *See* J. Pemartín, *La obra de S. de Madariaga* in *Arbor*, 1953.

Maddaloni, It. tn, in Campania (q.v.), 15 m. NNE. of Naples. It is supposed to occupy the site of the anct Suessula. There is a splendid aqueduct near by built in the 17th cent. to convey water to the cascades in the gardens at Caserta (q.v.). Pop. 27,200.

Madden, Sir Charles Edward (1862–1935), Eng. admiral. He took a prominent part in naval design under Lord Fisher when the *Dreadnought* was laid down. During the period 1912–4 as a rear-admiral he commanded successively the 1st Battle and 2nd and 3rd Cruiser squadrons. On the outbreak of the First World War he was appointed chief of staff to Admiral Jellicoe, and was present at the battle of Jutland. Was second in command, Grand Fleet, under Beatty (q.v.), 1916–8. Became commander-in-chief, Atlantic Fleet, after the war till 1922. In 1927 he succeeded Admiral Beatty in the post of First Sea Lord, retiring in 1930. K.C.M.G., 1916; baronet, 1919; O.M., 1931.

Madder, name given to sev. species of genus *Rubia*. Dyers's M. (*R. tinctorum*) is a trailing or climbing annual; its root from early times has been extensively used for the production of a wide range of dyes, notably Turkey-red, all of

which are very stable. Synthetic dyes have now almost entirely superseded it.

MADDER

Madeira, Portuguese is. in the Atlantic, off the NW. coast of Africa, about 600 m. SW. of Lisbon. It is the most important is. of a volcanic archipelago, 'the M.s', which forms an administrative dist of Portugal (*see* FUNCHAL); the rest of the archipelago consists of the is. of Porto Santo and 2 uninhabited is. groups, Desertas and Selvagens. The is. were known to the Romans, and were rediscovered in 1418–20 by João Gonçalves Zarco and Tristão Vaz Teixeira, who were captains of Henry the Navigator (q.v.). M. was in Brit. occupation 1807–14. In April–May 1931 there was a rebellion which collapsed after a demonstration by warships. M. is a mass of basalt, rising with a steep ascent from S. and N. towards the interior, the highest point being the Pico Ruivo (6100 ft). The declivities of the mt masses are furrowed by deep and generally narrow valleys and depressions, traversed by streams of clear water. The coastline is bold and rocky, with good natural harbours. The is. is thickly covered with vegetation: coniferous and deciduous trees are found at the higher elevations, and there are also palms, bamboos, camphor and eucalyptus trees and ferns. Every piece of practicable ground in the ravines is terraced for cultivation and irrigated by means of stone or cement water conduits (levadas). The chief product is the famous M. wine (q.v.). Sugar-cane, cereals, sweet potatoes, vegetables and fruit (oranges, bananas, mangoes, guavas, pears) are grown. Much butter is produced, and fishing is important. The embroidery and wicker-work of the is. are well known. The climate is remarkably mild (ann. extremes 50° F.–85° F.), and for this reason the is. is much resorted to by consumptive invalids. The inhab. are of Portuguese, Moorish, It. and Negro blood. The cap. is Funchal. Length 35 m.; greatest width 13 m. Area 286 sq. m.; pop. 264,000. (*See Plate: Portugal.*)

Madeira River (Rio Madeira), riv. of Brazil,

and the main r. b. trib. of the Amazon. Formed primarily by a union of the Mamoré and the Beni which flows E. from Bolivia, it flows through the state of Amazonas to join the Amazon below the city of Manaus. It is navigable for a distance of 715 m. by ocean steamers. *See also* MAMORÉ.

Madeira Wine, in the Regency period the most popular wine in England, is a fortified wine with 4 main types called after the grapes from which they are made: Bual, Malmsey, Sercial and Verdelho. Sercial is a dry wine which may be drunk before meals. Both Verdelho and Bual are dessert wines of moderate sweetness, and Malmsey, made from Malvasia grapes grown near the seashore (the other vineyards being on terraces on the side of the steep cliffs), is the sweetest and most magnificent of all M.s. Madeira is made on the Solera system of Sherry (q.v.) and is stored in hot chambers—*estufas*—for sev. months. This process gives Madeira its special character, which becomes more and more remarkable with age in bottle, and makes it the hardiest and longest-lived of wines. The vines were destroyed by *oidium* in the 1940s and by *phylloxera* after replantation, but they are again today producing good wine. *See* A. L. Simon and E. Craig, *Madeira*, 1933; A. J. B. Rutherford in *Wine* (ed. A. Muir), 1953; A. Croft-Cooke, *Madeira*, 1961; H. Warner Allen, *The Wines of Portugal*, 1962. *See also* WINE.

Madeleine, La, Fr. tn in the dept of Nord, a suburb of Lille. It has chemical and textile manufs. Pop. 23,400.

Madeley, par. now part of the bor. of Wenlock (q.v.), Shropshire, England.

Maderno, Carlo (1556–1629), It. Baroque architect, trained under D. Fontana and G. della Porta. His prin. works—all in Rome—are the façade of St Peter's, 1612; façade of S. Susanna; Palazzo Mattei; S. Maria della Vittoria; and the great Palazzo Barberini, begun 1624 but completed by Borromini (q.v.).

Madhuca (synonym, **Bassia**), genus of tall trees with milky juice, natives of India and SE. Asia, family Sapotaceae. *M. butyracea,* Indian Butter Tree, gives seeds yielding a fatty substance used in soap-making; *M. latifolia,* Mahwah, Mahua or Moa, has edible flowers, and yields a valuable hardwood; *M. longifolia,* the Indian Oil Tree, gives fruits yielding an oil for burning and soap-making, and good hardwood.

Madhya Pradesh, the central state of the Indian Union, with Maharashtra and Rajasthan to the W., Uttar Pradesh to the N., Bihar and Orissa to the E., and Maharashtra and Andhra Pradesh to the S. It consists largely of highlands and mts furrowed by the riv. valleys of the Narmada (Narbada), the Son and the Tapti. It includes the Malwa Plateau, the plateaus of Rewa, the Bundelkhand highlands and Vindhya and Satpura ranges.

Climatically the region varies from the fairly dry areas of the W. to the much more humid conditions found in Bundelkhand, Rewa and elsewhere. Temps. vary with altitude. Much of the state is heavily forested.

History. The present state came into being on 1 Nov. 1956 with the merger of the states of Madhya Bharat and Vindhya Pradesh with most of the old Central Provinces (renamed M. P. after independence) after excluding the Maratha-speaking dists of the latter. It includes many places famous in Indian hist. such as Indore, Bhopal and Gwalior (qq.v.).

Development. Rice, wheat, millets and cotton are the staple crops. Composed of areas with differing degrees of industrialisation, the state has not a high general level of development. Gwalior (Lashkar) is the centre of textile, pottery, leather, tobacco and engineering industries as well as a flying-boat station. Jabalpur and Indore have textile mills, and so has Ujjain (the traditional cap. of Malwa). Better communications are needed if the state is to be developed fully. It is rich in iron and manganese in the E. The Narmada valley project and the Bhilai steelworks, when completed, should help industrialisation.

Culture. Hindi is the language of the state. With 4 million aboriginals, it has a larger tribal element than probably any other state. Ujjain was the prime meridian of Sanskrit geographers and the reputed cap. of the great King Vikramaditya. Sagar is the H.Q. of a univ. estab. in 1949. Educational levels vary, some of the former small princely states having lagged behind the rest of India. There are 8 univs.

Government. The governor acts through ministers responsible to an elected assembly of 288. There is also an upper chamber of 72 members (legislative council). In the Indian Parliament, M. P. has 16 and 36 seats in the upper and lower houses respectively.

The cap. is Bhopal (pop. 185,000). Other big tns are Indore (pop. 395,000); Jabalpur, or Jubbulpore (pop. 295,000); Gwalior, or Lashkar (pop. 300,000), built below a 'stranded rock of Gibraltar', highly fortified; and Ujjain (pop. 144,000). Area 171,200 sq. m. (the second largest state of India); pop. 32·3 million. *See also* BHOPAL; GWALIOR; INDORE.

Madison, James (1751–1836), 4th president of the U.S.A., *b.* Port Conway, Virginia, graduated at Princeton (1771), and afterwards studied law. He was appointed a member of the Virginia Convention (1776) and of the Continental Congress (1780), and thenceforth devoted himself to politics. From 1784 to 1786 he served in the Virginia Legislature, and became a zealous advocate of religious freedom. M. was also a member of the Constitutional Convention at Philadelphia in 1787, which drew up the U.S. Constitution, his work bringing him the title of 'Father of the Constitution'. It was he who drew up the plan whereby the gov. was to be composed of 3 divs.—legislative, executive and judicial. He collaborated with Hamilton and John Jay in *The Federalist Papers*, 1788. He was elected to the Lower House in the first National Congress of 1789. He became a leader of the Republican party, and held the post of secretary of state during Jefferson's presidency. Mainly through the influence of Jefferson, his lifelong friend, he was elected president in 1809, and his period of office was a stormy one, its chief event being the war with England (1812–14). He was elected to a second term as president in 1812. In 1814, when Brit. troops captured Washington and burned the White House, M.'s wife, the famous and charming Dolly M., saved Stuart's celebrated painting of George Washington and also the original draft of the Declaration of Independence. In 1817 he retired to his seat at Montpelier, Virginia, where he remained until his death. See G. Hunt, *The Life of James Madison*, 1902, and (ed.) *The Writings of J. Madison*, 1900–10; I. Brant, *James Madison*, 1941–50.

Madison: 1. City, cap. of Wisconsin, U.S.A., on an isthmus between lakes Mendota and Monona of the Four Lakes group, in a dairying area 75 m. W. of Milwaukee. It manufs. machinery, electrical supplies and furniture. In addition to the state capitol it has the Univ. of Wisconsin (some 20,000 students), the U.S. Forest Products Laboratory, the Wisconsin Union, with permanent art collection, the State Historical Society of Wisconsin, with museum and large library, the Wisconsin State Library, the Wisconsin Legislative Reference Library, the Univ. of Wisconsin Library and a 1200-ac. arboretum. Pop. 126,700.

Madison River, one of the headstreams of the Missouri, rises in the Rocky Mts., Wyoming, flows through Montana, and has a course of 183 m.

Madley, vil. of Herefordshire, England, 6½ m. from Hereford, with a church (partly Norman but mostly dating from the 13th and 14th cents.) which has the last crypt built in medieval England beneath its 14th cent. chancel apse. Pop. 1067.

Madness, see INSANITY.

Madoc, or **Madog** (fl. 1170), Welsh prince, a son of Owen Gwynedd. According to Welsh legend, he is said to have discovered America about 1170, at which time he was forced to fly from Wales on account of a rebellion against his dynasty. A 15th cent. poem gives the first reference to him, and his discovery of America was not suggested until considerably later, and has no historical foundation whatsoever. His story forms the subject of a poem by R. Southey, entitled *Madoc*, 1805.

Madonna, the usual title in Lat. countries for Mary, the mother of Jesus, and widely used for pictures and statues of her, particularly when represented with her Son. There is no authentic likeness. The earliest representation is that in the catacombs of S. Priscilla (early 2nd cent.). The Byzantine pictures attributed formerly to St Luke are not earlier than the 6th cent. *See* Anna Jameson, *Legends of the Madonna*, 1872, 1902. *See also* MARY, BLESSED VIRGIN.

Madras: 1. State of S. India, embracing most of the Tamil-speaking areas, bounded on the N. by Mysore and Andhra Pradesh, on the E. and S. by the Bay of Bengal and the Indian Ocean. It consists of 2 main types of country—coastal

plains S. of Madras City including the Cauvery delta, and the hilly hinterland which includes the pleasant Nilgiri Hills and extensions of the W. Ghats almost to the tip of the peninsula. The region gets its rain mainly from the NE. monsoon (Oct.–Dec.) and generally has a scanty fall.

History. For cents. from the start of the Christian era, and even earlier, this part of India, as yet untouched by the Aryan invasion, was ruled by powerful dynasties—the Cholas, Pallavas, Pandyas and Cheras. Its people even then sailed for distant lands and carried Indian culture and religion to Ceylon, Indo-China, Malaya, Java and Bali, just as in recent times Tamils have been the most numerous among the Indian communities settled in Malaya, S. Africa, W. Indies, though drawn from the ranks of unskilled labour in recent decades. The Vijayanagar empire included all of modern M. in the 14th–16th cents., after which petty chiefs, including the Maratha Nayaks and the Tanjore Rajas, set up their own kingdoms, and later a Muslim overlord, the Nawab of the Carnatic, became master of most of what is now M. The Brit. trading post at M. (Fort St George) was their most important factory before the conquest of Bengal. The 18th cent. wars between the British and the French and their respective Indian allies led to the British becoming overlords of the Carnatic, pensioning the Nawab and also the Tanjore Raja, and of much of Tipu Sultan's Mysore, by 1801. The presidency of M., including much of what is now Kerala and Andhra Pradesh, made a good start towards self-gov. thanks largely to the leadership of C. Rajagopalachari, chief minister, 1937–9 (later Governor-General of India). Demands for linguistic provs. and for more convenient units led to the reduction of the state to its present size to include primarily the Tamilnad (land of the Tamils). After the reorganisation of the constituent states of the Indian union in 1956, and a smaller reshuffle in 1960, parts of M. state were lost to Kerala and Mysore, but parts of the former state of Travenchore-Cochin were gained.

Development. M. is relatively unindustrialised, a semi-urban state of medium and large villages bunched in concentrated groups. Rice and millet take up most of the sown area; also grown are pulses, sugarcane, potatoes, tapioca, ground-nuts, cotton, gingelly, tobacco, coconuts and pepper. Tea and coffee are grown in the hills. Big hydro-electric projects in operation are the Mettur, Papanasam, Pykara and Moyar schemes. The last two are in the Nilgiris. A number of other major projects are scheduled for the third Five Year Plan. The main factories are textile (cotton) mills at Madras, Coimbatore, Madurai, Tiruchirapalli and Tirunelveli. The state has 12 sugar factories, 5 cement plants, a big film industry, cycle works, motor manuf. plants, tobacco factories. Mines in S. Arcot dist yield 2500 tons of lignite yearly. Salem dist has deposits of bauxite, magnesite and iron ore. The state forests have valuable teak, rosewood and ebony. M. City is the H.Q. of the S. Railway of the Indian system.

Culture. Tamil is the language of all but 5 million of the nearly 34 million people of M. M. is a stronghold of Hindu orthodoxy and of anct Hindu art and culture at its best—e.g. the temples of Madurai, the dance art (Bharata Natyam (q.v.)), Vedic scholarship—as it was of reactionary aspects like untouchability. M. Univ., estab. 1857, is one of the biggest in India with 106 colleges. Annamalai Univ. is a unitary teaching univ. Most of the children of school age are at school and literacy is above Indian average.

Government. The governor acts through 8 ministers responsible to an elected 2-house legislature of 270 members. The state has 18 representatives in the Upper and 41 in the Lower House of India's Parliament.

The cap. is M. (pop. 1,729,841). Other big tns are Madurai (pop. 424,810). Tiruchirapalli or Trichinopoly (pop. 249,862), Salem (pop. 249,145) and Coimbatore (286,305). Area 50,331 sq. m.; pop. 33,687,000.

2. Cap. of M. state, and 4th largest city in India. The city largely owes its existence to the estab. of a small fort, Fort St George, and a trading settlement by the British in 1644. It was the scene of fighting with the French between 1746 and 1758, and changed hands. It is of particular interest to Englishmen—displaying much of the atmosphere and conditions which the early Brit. settlers created. It covers a considerable area, stretching 9 m. along the coast, and has many large and gracious bungalows set in spacious compounds, providing coolness in the hot weather. Inside the fort, which now accommodates the gov. secretariat, is St Mary's Church, the first Eng. church built in India (1678–80), where there are many interesting monuments and records. There is a fine esplanade; the Marina and Mount Road is a wide thoroughfare traversing the main residential quarter N. and S. The port was an artificial harbour built out into the sea, to afford protection from the cyclonic storms which cross the coast every winter. The main business quarter, Georgetown, lies behind the port. There are many large public buildings of no particular architectural interest. There are many legends associating St Thomas with M., particularly with St Thomas's Mount, 8 m. S. of M., but their authority is questionable. M. is a centre of scientific and industrial research and is the seat of the Univ. of M. Pop. (with suburbs) 2,000,000.

Madras, University of, founded in 1857 and like Calcutta Univ. (q.v.) was a purely examining body until the early part of the 20th cent. Its research and teaching functions were given impetus by the M. Univ. Act of 1923. It is a federal univ. exercising control over the work of constituent and affiliated colleges. There are some 30 teaching and research depts comprising almost all the faculties. There are about 60,000 students and some 180 univ. teaching and research staff.

Madre de Dios: 1. Riv. rising in Peru, flowing through N. Bolivia, and joining the Beni near its junction with the Mamoré at Riberalta on the Brazilian border. The total length is about 850 m., most of which is navigable and is used for transport in the upper reaches.

2. Dept. of SE. Peru, bordered on the E. by Bolivia, on the N. by Brazil, on the W. by the dept of Cuzco and on the S. by the dept of Puno. The M. de D. riv. flows E. through the dept, which lies at the S. extremity of the Amazon forest region called the Montaña and produces rubber and other tropical products. The cap. is Puerto Maldonado on the M. de D. R. Area 58,842 sq. m.; pop. 33,289.

Madrid: 1. Sp. prov., in Castilla la Nueva (q.v.). The Sierra de Guadarrama (q.v.) is on its NW. boundary and the Tagus (q.v.) on its SE. boundary. It is arid plateau country, cut up by sev. rivs. of which the chief is the Jarama, a trib. of the Tagus. Fruit and vegetables are grown in the S., and the forests of the NE. provide good timber. There are granite and gypsum quarries in the mts. Area 3090 sq. m.; pop. 2,607,000.

2. (anct **Magerit** or **Majrit**) Sp. city, cap. of the country and of the prov. of M. It is built on the l. b. of the Manzanares (q.v.), on rising ground which merges into the tableland of Castilla la Nueva. It was originally a Moorish fortress, which came permanently into the hands of the Christians in 1083. Although occasionally a royal residence, M. remained a tn of small importance until Philip II, on account of its position in the centre of the peninsula, made it his cap. in 1561. From this time the city developed rapidly. In May 1808, during the Napoleonic Wars, the citizens rose against the French, and the tragic scenes in the cap. have been recorded by Goya. During the civil war of 1936–9, M. sustained a siege of two and a half years' duration; the republican forces in the city finally surrendered to the insurgents on 28 March 1939. M. is the largest city in Spain, the seat of the gov., the meeting-place of the Cortes and, formerly, the chief residence of the king. It is also the seat of an archbishop and has a univ. (1590). It is a spacious and beautiful city, though less distinctively Spanish than many tns of smaller importance. The riv., on the W. side of the city, is overlooked by the grandiose royal palace (now a museum), which occupies the site of the original Moorish alcázar; the palace armoury contains a notable collection of historic arms. S. of the palace is the new cathedral (begun 1881), and to the E. lies the Plaza Mayor, a square originally constructed as a place for royal entertainments. From here 2 great streets, the Calle de Alcalá and the Calle de Atocha, run, respectively, NE. and SE. Some distance along the former is La Puerta del Sol (once the E. gate), a square which is the hub of M. life. The Calle de Alcalá and the Calle de Atocha are joined at their E. ends by the Paseo del Prado, a magnificent boulevard lined with public buildings, one of which, the Museo del Prado (q.v.), is one of the world's richest art galleries. Behind the Prado is the Retiro, M.'s chief public park.

M. has a great library (Biblioteca Nacional), containing over 1 million vols. and 2000 incunabula, a supreme court, numerous museums and literary and scientific institutions. The city is served by an underground railway, and it has an airport. There are numerous manufs., including chemicals, glass, tobacco and leather goods. Pop. 2,260,000. See E. Epton, *Madrid*, 1964.

Madrigal, originally a short poem generally on the subject of love. Pietro Casella, a contemporary of Dante, is the first composer who is known to have written M.s under that name. After the 14th cent. the word seems to have denoted pastoral or idyllic lyrical poems designed for musical settings. The word, after being displaced by the (sacred) *Landi Spirituali* and the (secular) *Frottole*, became fixed in its musical sense in the 16th cent., when Flem. composers who had settled in Italy as church musicians and It. composers wrote unaccompanied vocal compositions under that style. The literary M. proper consists of 3 verses or strophes, generally bound together by rhymes; but the name is sometimes applied to love-poems of any form. Among the Italians the best writers of M.s are Petrarch and Tasso (qq.v.) and, in modern times, Carducci and D' Annunzio; among the Fr., Montreuil (the 13th cent. *trouvère*), Marot (according to Warton 'the reviver of the madrigal'), Lainez and Moncrif; among the Germans, Ziegler Voss, Goethe and A. W. Schlegel; and among the English, the poets of the Elizabethan and Caroline ages, such as Lodge, Wither, Carew and Suckling. The musical M. is a setting of a poem of the kind described in contrapuntal style for sev. voices (sometimes performed by 1 voice with instruments contributing the polyphony). The now familiar musical form which originated with the Flemings about the middle of the 16th cent. went out of fashion in the course of the 17th cent. It. composers of M.s include Marenzio, A. Gabrieli, Ruffo, Palestrina, Gesualdo and Monteverdi. The Eng. madrigalists are equally famous, and include Bennet, Orlando Gibbons, Morley, Weelkes, Bateson, Tomkins and Wilbye. See E. H. Fellowes, *The English Madrigal Composers*, 1921, 1948; A. Einstein, *The Italian Madrigal*, 1949; J. Kerman, *The Elizabethan Madrigal*, 1962.

Madroño Tree, or *Arbutus menziesii*, Californian evergreen (family Ericaceae). The smooth trunk and branches are brilliant maroon, the large leaves are dark green, and the flowers, which are borne in masses, are wax-white; they are followed by loose clusters of scarlet berries. The tree is slow-growing, but attains a height of about 100 ft. The wood yields a fine charcoal.

Madura, is. of Indonesia, in the Java Sea; separated from Java by the Surabaja Strait. It is mountainous and not particularly fertile, but possesses salt-mines and large tracts of timber. The only navigable riv. is the Maringan, and the prin. ports are Bangkalan, Sumenep and Pamekasan. Area 1762 sq. m.; pop., including that of the numerous small is. adjacent, 2,000,000.

Madurai, city of Madras state, India. M. is a great centre of Hinduism in S. India and the temple is one of the most famous in India. It is in fact a twin temple to the goddess Minakshi and the god Sundareswar (Siva), which has outstanding carving both outside and inside. Another famous building is the palace of Tiromala Nayak (1623–60), who built much of the temple as it now is. Pop. 425,000.

Madvig, Johan Nicolai (1804–86), Dan. philosopher, statesman and classical scholar, chiefly known for his eds. of Cicero, Livy and Lucretius, and for his Gk and Lat. grammar books for schools. He was appointed prof. of Lat. language and literature at Copenhagen in 1829. As a politician M. was minister of education (1848), director of public instruction (1852) and later president of the Dan. Parliament. He was also a distinguished palaeographist.

Maeander, riv. of Asia Minor, proverbial for its winding course, rising in the S. of Phrygia, close to the source of the Marsyas (q.v.), flowing between Lydia and Caria, of which it forms the boundary, falling into the Icarian Sea between Myus and Priene.

Maebashi, city of Gunmaken, in central Honshu, Japan, 70 m. N.W. of Tokyo. It is noted for its silk trade, furniture and flour mills. Pop. 188,000.

Maecenas, Gaius (c. 69–8 BC). Rom. statesman and patron of literature, b. probably at Arretium in Etruria. Proud of his anct lineage on both sides, he was long a close friend and chief minister of Augustus. In later years, for some unknown reason, their relations grew less cordial, and M. retired from public life; but he left his great fortune to the emperor, from whose liberality it was in large part derived. M.'s title to immortality is his patronage of Horace, Virgil and Propertius (qq.v.).

Maecianus, Lucius Volusius, Rom. jurist. He held many offices under Antoninus Pius, and also under Marcus Aurelius whose law tutor he had been. A list of those offices was found at Ostia in 1930. Last of them was the governorship of Alexandria, in which capacity he took part in the rebellion of Avidius Cassius (AD 175) and was murdered by the troops. None of M.'s legal works have survived; but we have part of his *Distributio*, a treatise on numerical divs., weights and measures. See the ed. by H. Hultsch in *Metrologicorum scriptorum reliquiae*, vol. ii, 1866.

Maeides Stana, see MAIDSTONE.

Maelstrom (Dan. *malström,* a great whirlpool in the sea), usually associated with the celebrated whirlpool arising occasionally in a strong current off the is. of Moskoe on the W. coast of Norway. It is very dangerous in winter, especially when the NW. wind interferes with the set of the tide. Formerly, and erroneously, it was supposed to be dangerous enough to engulf ships at any time.

Maenades, see BACCHAE.

Maerlant, Jacob van (1225–91), Flem. poet, b. Brugse Vrije. Founder of the didactic school of poetry in the Netherlands, he has been called the 'father of Flemish poetry'. He began by writing romances of chivalry on the Fr. models. His prin. work is the *Mirror of History*, left uncompleted; he also wrote *The Secrets of Secrets*, 1824, *Flowers of Nature*, and a poem, *The Lands over the Sea*, a summons to the crusades. *See* J. van Mierlo, *J. van Maerlant*, 1946.

Maes, or **Maas**, **Nicolaes** (1632–93), Dutch *genre* and portrait painter, *b.* Dordrecht; a pupil of Rembrandt (q.v.). He worked mainly in Antwerp. His early pictures are extremely rare, but the National Gallery (London) has some of the best: 'The Idle Servant', 'The Dutch Housewife', 'The Cradle' and 'Portrait of a Girl'. If popularity is a guide to merit, the picture curiously entitled 'The Never-ending Prayer' in the Rijksmuseum, Amsterdam, was one of his most popular works. Also in the Rijksmuseum is the 'Old Woman at the Spinning Wheel', also a popular favourite. Other works in various galleries are 'Old Woman Saying Grace' (Louvre), 'Interior' (Wallace Collection) and some portraits in the Old Pinakothek, Munich. The change in style of his later pictures is so marked as to raise a doubt whether they were his work or perhaps that of another pupil of Rembrandt.

Maesteg, tn in Glamorganshire, Wales, 8 m. SE. of Neath. Chiefly engaged in coal-mining and light industries. Pop. 21,652.

Maestricht, *see* MAASTRICHT.

Maestro, wind blowing from the NW. around the Adriatic Sea, usually in the summer, foretelling fine weather.

Maeterlinck, Maurice Polydore Marie Bernard (1862–1949), Belgian dramatist, poet and essayist, *b.* Ghent. He went to Paris at the age of 25, and came into touch with the Fr. and Belgian symbolists—Villiers de l'Isle Adam, Le Roy, Verhaeren and Rodenbach—whose ideals won his sympathy and support. His wealth permitted him to take up literature as his life-work. The vol. of verse entitled *Serres chaudes* appeared in 1889; the play, *La Princesse Maleine*, later the same year. His works include the following plays: *L'Intruse*, *Les Aveugles*, 1890; *Les Sept Princesses*, 1891; *Pelléas et Mélisande*, 1892; the famous 'marionette' plays *Alladine et Palomides*, *Intérieur* and *La Mort de Tintagiles*, 1894; *Monna Vanna*, 1902; *Joyzelle*, 1903; *L'Oiseau bleu*, 1909. Other pubs. are a trans. from Ruysbroeck, 1891; a study of Novalis and *Annabella*, a trans. of Ford's *'Tis Pity She's a Whore*, 1895; *Le Trésor des humbles*, 1896; *La Sagesse et la destinée*, 1898; *La Vie des abeilles*, 1901; *Le Temple enseveli*, 1902; *La Mort*, 1913; *Les Sentiers dans la montagne*, 1919, *La Vie des termites*, 1927; *La Vie des fourmis*, 1930; *L'Araignée de verre*, 1932; *La Grande Loi*, 1933; *Avant le grand silence*, 1934; *L'Ombre des ailes*, 1936; *Devant Dieu*, 1937. His essays show the influence chiefly of Emerson and Novalis, but his plays suggest a fatalistic turn of mind. Studies in the psychology of terror, despair and other emotional phenomena, they are devoid of action and of dramatic commonplace; they are not pre-eminently suited for the stage, although they have often met with a good reception. *Pelléas et Mélisande* was made into an opera by Debussy, 1902. M.'s later plays and essays revealed a freer acceptance of modern life, but little real deepening of vision or more capacity to create human character. He has been called a mystic man of the world and this, perhaps, aptly defines his qualities and defects. *See* J. Bithell, *Life and Writings of Maurice Maeterlinck*, 1913; M. Lecat, *Maurice Maeterlinck et son œuvre*, 1950; W. D. Halls, *Maurice Maeterlinck*, 1960. (*See Plate: Belgium*.)

Mafeking, tn in the N. of Cape Prov., S. Africa. Pop. Whites, 7103; Coloureds, 1528; Bantus, 55,017. The tn was laid out in 1885 by Sir Charles Warren. M. is particularly remembered in connection with the 217 days' siege it underwent during the Boer War of 1899–1902. It was gallantly defended by Baden-Powell, to whose resource and courage was due the fact that it was able to hold out against the investors for 7 months, until it was relieved by Col. (later F.-M. Lord) Plumer. The investment was followed with the closest interest in England, and on the receipt of the news of the relief London gave itself up to rejoicing of unaccustomed spontaneity—whence the word 'mafficking'. Cattle farming in the dist has developed considerably. M. owes much of its present development to its importance as a railway centre, and to its railway workshops. In these workshops during the siege were manuf. a look-out tower, ammunition, a searchlight and even a gun—improvised out of drain-pipes (called 'The Wolf' and now to be seen at the Royal United Service Institution). *See* F. D. Baillie, *Mafeking, a Diary of the Siege*, 1900, and J. A. Hamilton, *The Siege of Mafeking*, 1900.

Maffei, Scipione (1675–1755), It. dramatist and archaeologist, *b.* Verona. His tragedy *Merope*, 1713, was highly esteemed. In 1731–2 appeared his prin. work, *Verona illustrata* (2 vols.), treating of the origin, hist. and literature of Verona. He also founded, together with Zeno and Vallisnieri, the *Giornale dei letterati*, 1710.

Mafia, or **Maffia**, secret society of Sicily. Historically the M. is said to be a result of the long period of bad foreign govs. before Italy became united in the mid 19th cent. The M. dominated Sicilian social life during the 19th cent., embracing all classes and always holding itself out as the supporter of the particular gov. in power. It issued decrees, fixed land rents and practised extortion on a wide scale. Resistance to its 'decrees' was met with murders and vendettas. It was temporarily crushed under the Fascist regime, although there was a resurgence of the M. in Sicily and S. Italy, and the M. also has close connections with aspects of crime in New York.

Mafra, tn of Portugal, in Lisboa dist, near the Atlantic coast, 18 m. NNW. of Lisbon. It possesses a great, white marble convent built by John V in 1717–31, in imitation of the Escorial (q.v.). Pop. 3100.

Magadan: 1. Oblast (prov.), formed 1953, in

the N. of the Russian Far E., stretching from the Sea of Okhotsk to the Bering Straits. The area is largely mountainous, with coniferous forests in the SW. and tundra in the NE. Most of M. is affected by permanent frost. There are rich deposits of gold, tin and rare metals. Occupations include gold and tin mining, fishing and reindeer raising; food and consumer goods are almost all imported. From the 1930s to the mid 1950s it was one of the most notorious areas of forced labour camps (see KOLYMA and DAL'STROV). The mining industry relied entirely on forced labour; the release of most prisoners and the departure of many of them in the 1950s resulted in a serious labour shortage, and attempts are being made to fill the gap by attracting volunteers and by semi-compulsory colonisation. Area 460,000 sq. m.; pop. (1965) 309,000 (86 per cent urb.), mostly Russian with some Chukchi (q.v.).
2. Cap., economic and cultural centre of the above, port on the Sea of Okhotsk, and starting-point of a highway to the gold-mining area on Upper Kolyma. Founded in 1933, it reached the status of a tn in 1939, and has absorbed the fishing vil. of Nagayevo. There is some industry (ship repairing, mining equipment). Pop. (1965) 79,000 (1939, 27,000; 1956, 55,000; 1958, 24,000).

Magadha, name of an anct kingdom of India, the cap. of which, Palibothra (Sanskrit, Pataliputra), was situated on the Ganges, where Patna now stands. The Gk knowledge of this kingdom was probably derived from the expedition of Seleucus against Sandracottus Chandragupta (q.v.), King of M.

Magalhães, Fernão de, see MAGELLAN, F.

Magallanes, southernmost prov. of Chile extending from 49° S. to Cape Horn. It includes the W. half of the is. of Tierra del Fuego; the E. half belonging to Argentina. The total area is about 66,000 sq. m. with a pop. of 75,000 the vast majority of whom live in the S. Sheep raising and its auxiliary industries form the basis of the economy. There are important oil fields on the is. of Tierra del Fuego.

Magazines. This term is usually applied to periodical pubs. dealing with general or particular subjects, literary, artistic, social, professional, scientific, etc. The earliest scientific periodicals were the transactions of learned societies. The *Journal des Savants*, Paris, and the *Philosophical Transactions* of the Royal Society both appeared in 1665 and survive. The first memorable figure in periodical literature was Daniel Defoe, who in 1704 launched the thrice-weekly *Review*. Richard Steele pub. the short-lived *Tatler* in 1709, and with Addison the *Spectator*, 1711–12, while in 1731 Edward Care pub. the *Gentleman's Magazine* (ceased 1907). This was followed by the *Scots Magazine*, 1739–1817, *Monthly Review*, 1749–1845, Samuel Johnson's *Rambler*, 1750–2, and later the famous though short-lived *London Magazine*, 1820–9. *Blackwood's Magazine* appeared in 1817, having a great influence owing to its topical criticisms. An *Edinburgh Monthly*

Review was pub. 1819–23. *Fraser's Magazine* 1830, which became *Longman's Magazine* in 1882, numbered Carlyle and Thackeray among its contributors. The first magazine pub. at one shilling was *Tait's Edinburgh Magazine*, 1832. Among other M. pub. under these conditions was *Temple Bar*, 1860–1906, and the *Cornhill*, 1860, the latter ed. by Thackeray. The price was reduced to sixpence with *Longman's Magazine*, 1882–1905, *Review of Reviews*, pub. in 1890, and the *Strand Magazine*, 1891–1950.
The 20th cent. has seen the issue of innumerable M. designed for every taste. Of the near-6000 jours. in Britain and Ireland that were in print in Jan. 1965, 2006 were general magazines, 2058 trade and technical jours., 642 were house M. and 1061 included directories and year books. In the field of general M., the Amer. *Reader's Digest* and the London *World Digest*, 1939, were designed to cater for a public demand for short stories and 'instant' knowledge. Political and financial weeklies include the *New Statesman*, 1913, the *Spectator*, 1828, the *Economist*, 1843, and *Tribune*, 1937. The inclusion of advertisements in the periodical press had a marked effect on women's M. The divs. and sub-divs. of M. for women are almost endless. *The Lady*, 1885, is of the old school, while the *Queen*, 1861, under the recent control of Jocelyn Stevens, has become one of the most up-to-date of women's M. Mass circulation M. for women include *Woman* and *Woman's Own* which are circulated to sev. million readers. A modern addition to the ranks of women's M. is *Nova* which caters, from fashion to fiction, for the 'thinking' emancipated woman. Teenagers and younger women are catered for by *Honey* and *Woman's Mirror*. The *Illustrated London News*, 1842, was the first periodical to use photography, and photography is also a feature of the new *London Life* (formerly *Tatler and Bystander*) and *Town*, a magazine for men. Among M. devoted to the countryside are *The Field*, 1853, and *Country Life*, 1897. M. for juveniles include the *Boys' Own Paper*, 1879, and the *Scout*, 1908, while the advent of 'pop' music and singing groups recently brought sev. new M. on to the market to cater for this taste, including *Fabulous*. The weekly *Punch* holds a unique position among humorous periodicals, while the present *Private Eye* is symptomatic of a demand for satirical M. Many of the major Brit. M. are controlled by the International Publishing Corporation (see NEWSPAPERS) which in 1961, as Daily Mirror Newspapers, perpetrated a £37,000,000 take-over bid for Odhams Press 'to secure advantages by the closer co-operation of the two groups' magazines interests'. At that time it emerged that Fleetway Publications (controlled by the Mirror) embraced over 100 magazines, periodicals, trade and technical jours., while Odhams had 135 pubs. and George Newnes (controlled by Odhams) another 57 jours.
In the U.S.A., where vast distances preclude a national press, periodicals have a nation-wide circulation. Among the more prominent Amer.

M. are (or were) the *Saturday Evening Post*, 1728, *Harper's Magazine*, 1850, *Scribner's Magazine*, 1870–1939, and *Ladies' Home Journal*, 1883. H. R. Luce founded *Time*, 1923, a weekly news commentary now enjoying a worldwide circulation, *Life*, 1936, and *Fortune*, 1930. The *New Yorker*, 1925, is a weekly satirical and humorous magazine. The earliest Canadian M. were the *Canadian Magazine*, pub. in Quebec in the 1820's, the *Nova Scotia Magazine*, the *Quebec Magazine*, the first bilingual pub. (1791–3) and *Maclean's Magazine*, 1911.

In France the *Revue des Deux Mondes*, 1829, *L'Illustration*, 1843, *Mercure de France*, 1890, *Revue de Paris*, 1894, and *Paris Match* have had international success. The French women's M., *Elle*, has an equally enviable reputation. The *Sydney University Magazine*, begun in 1855, was the first of the Australian M. of repute, and it is noteworthy that the tone of dominion univ. M. is uniformly high.

During the present cent. the number of scientific and technical M. has grown to vast proportions; the *World's List of Scientific Periodicals* lists over 50,000, and it is estimated that in medicine alone there are about 5000 current periodicals. This has led to the appearance of another type of jour., devoted entirely to abstracts of articles in the national or international periodical press, and covering wide fields such as biology or chemistry, or restricted to specialities such as anaesthesia or economic geology. *See* H. W. Peet, *Bibliography of Journalism*, 1915; W. Graham, *The Beginnings of English Literary Periodicals*, 1926, and *English Literary Periodicals*, 1930; F. L. Mott, *History of American Magazines* (3 vols.), 1930–8; D. Whitelaw, *A Bonfire of Leaves*, 1937; L. S. Turner, *Boys will be Boys* (a hist. of juvenile magazines), 1948; *World List of Scientific Periodicals*, 1952; *Union List of Serials in Libraries of the United States and Canada*, 1943 (supplements, 1945–); *Willing's Press Guide* (ann.); *Writers' and Artists' Year Book* (ann.).

Magdala, hill fortress of Ethiopia, stood on the plateau of Talanta at an altitude of 9110 ft; it was the stronghold of Theodore, and in 1868 was taken and destroyed by the British under Sir Robert Napier, afterwards Lord Napier of M.

Magdalen College, Oxford, founded in 1448 and enlarged and moved to its present site in 1458 by Wm of Waynflete, Bishop of Winchester (1447–86) and Lord Chancellor of England. Its original buildings (1467–1505) have been preserved with little external change. Of later additions the most admired are the New Buildings (begun 1733), part of a vast scheme which, if carried out, would have involved the destruction of the medieval cloisters. The beautiful great tower dominates the E. entrance to the old city; from its top a Lat. hymn is sung at sunrise on May Day. The Grove with its deer and Addison's Walk by the Cherwell are also famous. The fellows gained great credit by their resistance to James II. Cardinals Wolsey and Pole, John Lyly, Hampden, Addison, Gibbon, Edmund Cartwright, J. A. Symonds, Wilde and

Edward VIII were members of M. C. There are some 300 undergraduates and 100 postgraduate students. *See* H. A. Wilson, *Magdalen College*, 1899. (*See Plate: Oxford University*.)

Magdalen College School, Oxford, public school for boys, founded about 1478 by Wm of Waynflete as part of M. College, the choristers of which are now amongst its pupils. There are 64 boarders and about 400 dayboys.

Magdalen Hall, *see* HERTFORD COLLEGE.

Magdalena: 1. Chief riv. of Colombia, rising in the Central Cordillera and uniting with the R. Cauca, 130 m. from the Caribbean Sea, which it reaches at the port of Barranquilla. The M. is about 1000 m. long and used to be the backbone of the transportation system of the country. However, the development of road, rail and air transport is diminishing the riv.'s importance. It is navigable by stern-wheeled steamers up to the Honda rapids.

2. Dept of NE. Colombia with a coastline on the Caribbean Sea. Although most of the dept consists of tropical lowland, well-watered by the R. M., there is in the NE. corner a group of mts, the Sierra Nevada de Santa Marta. At their foot are Colombia's great banana plantations and coffee is grown in the foothills. Other important crops are sugar-cane, cotton and tobacco. Cattle-raising is of importance. Santa Marta is the cap. and an important port. Area 20,819 sq. m.; pop. 520,000.

Magdalene, or **Magdalen, Mary, St,** woman mentioned in the Gospels as a devoted follower of Jesus (Luke viii. 2). It is recorded that 7 demons were cast out of her. She apparently came from Magdala or Magadan (mod. El-Mejdel), near Tiberias. She witnessed the crucifixion of Christ, followed Him to burial and prepared sweet spices for the sepulchre. The account in John xx tells how she found the tomb empty and was the first to behold the risen Jesus (*see also* Mark xvi. 9). From confusion with the woman who anointed Christ's feet in Simon's house (Luke vii. 37), the popular conception of her has been that of one fallen from chastity who later repented of her sins. Hence the name M. asylums was adopted for homes for penitent women, and the word maudlin (weeping-eyed) is derived from this same unfounded idea. There are many famous pictures of the M. by Correggio, Titian, Paul Veronese and others. She has also been confused with Mary of Bethany, sister of Lazarus (John xi), and with the daughter of the Syrophoenician woman (Mark vii). The legend of her residence in France is quite fictitious. Her feast is on 22 July.

Magdalene College, Cambridge, founded by Lord Audley in 1542; the right of presentation to the mastership is by statute vested in the Lord Braybrooke for the time being as representing the founder's family. The oldest buildings are those of an earlier Benedictine foundation dating from the time of Henry VI. Samuel Pepys was at M. C. and bequeathed to it his remarkable library (including the MS. of the *Diary*). The college has among its recent alumni Marshal of the R.A.F. Lord Tedder and the

Archbishop of Canterbury, the Most Rev. A. M. Ramsey. There are some 250 undergraduates and 50 postgraduate students.

Magdeburg: 1. Dist (*Bezirk*) of the Ger. Democratic Rep. (E. Germany), bounded on the N. by Schleswig-Holstein and Schwerin, on the E. by Potsdam, on the S. by Halle and on the W. by Lower Saxony (qq.v.). Area 4510 sq. m.; pop. 1,374,000.

2. Ger. city, cap. of the dist of M., on the Elbe, 80 m. WSW. of Berlin. It was first mentioned in 805. It became an important member of the Hanseatic League (q.v.), and had a famous local judicial system, the *Magdeburger Recht*. It joined the League of Schmalkald (*see* SCHMALK-ALDEN) in 1531, and, although taken by the emperor's (*see* CHARLES V) supporters in 1551, became a staunch supporter of the Reformation on the conversion of the archbishops to Protestantism. The tn was sacked by Tilly in 1631. Under the treaty of Westphalia (q.v.) its secularised archbishopric passed to Brandenburg (q.v.). During the Second World War the city was very severely damaged by bombing, and much of the old city was destroyed. The fine Gothic cathedral of M. dates from the beginning of the 13th cent. There is an airport, and there are textile, paper, engineering, chemical and oil industries. The region grows sugar-beet, and there are lignite and potash mines near by. Pop. 261,700.

Magdeburg Hemispheres, *see* HYDROSTATICS.

Magellan, Ferdinand (Portuguese **Fernão de Magalhães**) (1480–1521), Portuguese navigator, *b.* Vila de Sabrosa. He served under Albuquerque in the E. Indies for sev. years, taking part in the capture of Malacca (1511). Considering that his services were not properly recompensed, he renounced allegiance to Portugal and went over to Spain, where Charles V gave him command of a fleet of 5 vessels, with which he set out in 1519 to discover a W. route to the E. Indies. He was the first navigator of the Pacific Ocean, so called by him, and on his voyage also discovered the strait which bears his name, and the Ladrones (so named by M. from the thieving habits of the inhabitants.). He also discovered the Philippine Is. where he became the ally of the prince of Cebu, one of the smaller is., against the prince of Mactán, another little is. of the group. Here he was killed in 1521. The only ship to return to Spain was the *Vittoria*, which was thus the first to circumnavigate the globe. *See* lives by F. H. Guillemard, 1890; E. F. Benson, 1929; S. Zweig, 1938; C. McKew Parr, *So Noble a Captain*, 1955.

Magellan, Strait of, between S. America and Tierra del Fuego, 360 m. in length, varying in width from $2\frac{1}{2}$ to 17 m. and joining Atlantic to Pacific Ocean. It was discovered by the Portuguese explorer Magellan in 1520. The Strait provides a safer route than that round Cape Horn. Although belonging to Chile it is demilitarised by Argentine-Chile consent and is open to all ships of all nationalities. *See also* TERRA AUSTRALIS INCOGNITA. *See* M. H. Mason, *Where Tempests Blow*, 1933.

Magellanic Clouds (Nebeculae Major and Minor), the 2 galaxies nearest to our own, appearing as nebulous patches in the S. sky, and named after the navigator Magellan. The Large M. C., 6° in diameter, lies in the constellation Dorado and Mensa; the Small M. C., 3° in diameter, is in Tucana. Being separate galaxies but still much closer (180,000 light years) than external galaxies such as that in Andromeda (2,000,000 light-years), the Clouds occupy a strategic position in astrophysics. They contain many interesting objects: variable stars, novae, star clusters and gaseous nebulae. (*See Plate*: *Astronomy*.)

Magendie, François (1783–1855), physiologist and physician, *b.* Bordeaux and educ. at Paris. His *Précis élémentaire de physiologie* appeared in 1816. In 1821 he became a member of the Academy of Sciences and 10 years later prof. of anatomy and medicine in the Collège de France, where he became noted for his experiments on the physiology of the nerves. Among his works are (Fr. titles trans.) *Lectures on the Physical Phenomena of Life*, 1839, and *Lectures on the Functions and Diseases of the Nervous System*, 1839. He founded the *Journal de physiologie expérimentale*. *See* lives by P. M. Dawson, 1908, and J. M. D. Olmsted, 1944.

Magenta, It. tn in Lombardy (q.v.) 15 m. W. of Milan. Near by the French and Sardinians defeated the Austrians in 1859 and compelled them to withdraw from Lombardy (*see* ITALY, *History*). The tn has a silk industry, and gives its name to a colour (*see* FUCHSIN). Pop. 16,600.

Magenta, *see* FUCHSIN.

Magerit, *see* MADRID.

Mageröy Island, near the coast of Finnmark, Norway, in the Arctic Ocean. It is irregular in outline and terminates on the N. in N. Cape (q.v.), the most northerly point of Europe.

Magersfontein, notable as the scene of a Brit. defeat by Boer forces in 1899. In the third week in Nov. Lord Methuen set out to relieve the beleaguered tn of Kimberley. After some initial success, and when within 20 m. of his objective, he encountered a strong force of Boers near M. He attempted to capture their position by means of a night march followed by an attack at dawn; but this failed with heavy losses and, for the time being, the advance was held up.

Maggiore, Lake (anct **Lacus Verbanus**), European lake, largely in Italy where it is bounded on the W. by Piedmont (q.v.) and on the E. by Lombardy (q.v.). Its N. end is in the Swiss canton of Ticino (q.v.). It is 39 m. long, and, at its widest, 7 m. broad. The R. Ticino (q.v.) flows through it, and the Borromean Is. (q.v.) are in its SW. extension. The lake is enclosed on the N. and W. by high mts, and on the S. and E. by vine-covered slopes. Tourist resorts on its shores include Arona, Stresa, Intra, Pallanza and Locarno (qq.v.).

Maggot, grub or larva of a fly or other insect hatching from an egg deposited in its food supply. The term, which is unscientific, is usually applied to legless larvae, such as those of the blue-bottle and green-bottle flies; one of the latter is the well-known sheep M. The M.s of fruit include a large number of insect types. The M.s found in plant galls are those of the gall wasps.

Maghera, par. and mrkt tn of co. Londonderry, N. Ireland, 14½ m. N. of Cookstown. There are manufs. of sewn muslins and linens, and a gov. school of machine embroidery. Pop. 1730.

Magherafelt, mrkt tn of co. Londonderry, N. Ireland, 8 m. SE. of Maghera. Shirts and linen are manuf. Pop. 2460.

Magi, tribe of the Medes set aside for the management of sacred rites and the preservation of traditional lore. The M. found their way, under Cyrus, into Persia. They were also diviners, seers, augurs and astrologers, and no transaction of importance took place without or against their advice.

Magic, word of sacerdotal origin, being derived from the Magi, whose earlier functions were divinatory or prophetic but later, in the Persian court, sank to the level of mere occultism. M. is a process that attempts to influence the course of nature or the activities of men by the operation of a formula or by the manipulation of magical objects, medicines or charms. It effects a desired end by mechanical or automatic means, and Frazer compared it therefore to science and contrasted it with religion, which is concerned rather with influencing personal forces of nature. Frazer, following Tylor, saw that the principles upon which magical processes are founded are those of association, and he divided M. into positive M., consisting of homoeopathic M. (working by the principle of similarity, like producing like), contagious M. (working by the principle of contact) and negative M. or taboo (q.v.). Black M., or the black art, or M. proper, is that branch of M. which is practised with evil intentions by such persons as witches or sorcerers; they are persons who try to influence nature or other people, especially the health or success of those of whom they feel envy. White M., on the other hand, connotes the altruistic practice of M., often to counter black M. White M. is that practised by witch doctors (*see* WITCH DOCTOR), who may also use it to effect medical cures. *See* A. Lang, *Magic and Religion*, 1901; L. Thorndyke, *The Place of Magic in the Intellectual History of Europe*, 1905; J. G. Frazer, *The Golden Bough*, 1911; R. R. Marett, *The Threshold of Religion*, 1914; E. B. Tylor, *Primitive Culture*, 1924; L. Levy-Bruhl, *How Natives Think*, 1926; E. E. Evans-Pritchard, *Witchcraft, Oracles and Magic among the Azande*, 1937; B. Malinowski, *Magic, Science and Religion*, 1948.

Magic Circle, founded 1905, to promote the art of M. or conjuring (q.v.). Its objects are the advancement of magical invention, and the development of magical technique. The M. C. organises entertainments, lectures, displays, exhibitions and conferences. It publishes monthly *The Magic Circular*. The library of over 2600 vols. is one of the most comprehensive collections of works on magic now extant.

Magic Lantern, or **Optical Lantern,** apparatus for projecting upon a white screen enlarged representations of diagrams, pictures, etc., drawn or photographed on glass slides. The instrument is said to have been invented by Athanasius Kircher, who described it in 1646. It was at first used as an amusing toy, but in its later developments is a means of representing small pictures and objects to large audiences. The cinematograph is essentially an optical lantern. The instrument consists of a lantern body to contain the source of light and the reflectors, an optical system and a slot to accommodate the slide-frame. The light source used to be limelight or an open arc but tungsten filament, tungsten-iodide or enclosed xenon-arc lamps are now used. The optical system in the ordinary type consists of a 'condensing' lens, which transmits the rays from the light to the object, and an 'objective', which receives the rays from the object and transmits them to the screen.

Magic Squares, sets of numbers arranged in the form of a square in such a manner that the sum of the numbers in each vertical and horizontal column and in each diagonal is constant. The following may serve as examples:

2	1	5	3	4
3	4	2	1	5
1	5	3	4	2
4	2	1	5	3
5	3	4	2	1

FIG. 1

15	5	0	20	10
0	20	10	15	5
10	15	5	0	20
5	0	20	10	15
20	10	15	5	0

FIG. 2

In Fig. 1 the numbers 1 to 5 are arranged in any order in the first row; the second commences with the number in the fourth cell of the first row and proceeds in the same relative order. The third row commences with the number in the fourth cell of the second row, and proceeds in order, and so on. Fig. 2 consists of the numbers 0 to 4 multiplied by 5, and each row starts with the number in the third cell of the row above. If now the numbers in the cells of Fig. 1 be added to those in the corresponding cells of Fig. 2 the result is a magic square as in Fig. 3.

17	6	5	23	14
3	24	12	16	10
11	20	8	4	22
9	2	21	15	18
25	13	19	7	1

FIG. 3

By altering the order of the numbers in the top row and making corresponding changes in the other rows, a large number of such M. S. can be obtained by successive additions. The simplest of all M. S. is formed by the 9 digits, with 5 in the centre and the even numbers at the corners.

Maginot, André (1877–1932), Fr. soldier, b. Paris, originator of the famous fortifications which became known as the Maginot line. He enlisted as an infantryman in the First World War and was at Verdun. In 1917 he became minister of colonies. In 1922, and again in 1929, he was minister of war. Together with Painlevé, the Fr. president, he worked out the scheme for the Maginot line. The original scheme was completed in 1934, 2 years after M.'s death. The line stretched from the Belgian frontier to the Swiss frontier. It cost more than £30,000,000 to construct and was subsequently augmented in strength. The Maginot line was outflanked by the Germans in 1940, and in June of that year they crossed the Rhine and broke through the line. The overrating of the Maginot line and the passive strategy resulting from it are regarded as one of the contributory causes of the Fr. collapse. As early as 1927 the Maginot line was described by Maj.-Gen. Fuller, the Brit. mechanised war expert, as 'the tombstone of France'. *See also* WESTERN FRONT IN SECOND WORLD WAR. *See* P. Belperon, *Maginot of the Line,* 1940. (*See Plate*: *Fortification*.)

Magistrate, one in whom is vested jurisdiction or executive authority in affairs of civil gov.; in other words, an administrator of the law. In this sense the king is the first M. in a monarchical state, while in a rep. the president is the chief M. The word is now more usually applied to subordinate officers to whom a part of executive judicial power is delegated. In England it means, specifically, a minor judicial officer, such as a justice of the peace, or a stipendiary M.; in Scotland, a provost or bailie of a burgh. Prior to the Local Government Act, 1888, the administrative work of the co. fell to the lot of the justices or magistracy, but the Act, while leaving them their judicial functions, took away the bulk of their administrative functions. *See also* JUSTICE OF THE PEACE. *See* Stone's *Justices' Manual* (annually). *See also* L. Page, *Justice of the Peace* (3rd ed.), 1947; E. J. Hayward and H. Wright, *Office of Magistrate* (7th ed.), 1948; F. T. Giles, *The Magistrates' Court,* 1949; W. Shaw, *Evidence and Procedure in Magistrates' Courts,* 1953; J. P. Eddy, *Justices' Handbook* (3rd ed.), 1953.

Magliabecchi, Antonio da Marco (1633–1714), It. librarian and bibliophile, b. Florence. Was in turn greengrocer's servant, goldsmith and then librarian in 1673 to Duke Cosimo III of Tuscany. M. was famous for his self-taught and vast learning. His library was left to the city, which housed it with the Uffizi gallery.

Magma (geological) is a molten rock material formed within the interior of the earth, which on consolidation gives rise to igneous rock (q.v.). Partially consolidated M. may contain crystals of minerals but remain sufficiently fluid to move and to be forced into spaces within the earth to form intrusive or plutonic rocks or to reach the surface to form extrusive or volcanic rocks. Magmatic melts consist principally of oxygen, silicon, alumina, iron, magnesia, lime, potash and soda, together with smaller quantities of minor and trace elements. The nature of the igneous rock formed depends on the proportions in which the major elements are present in the M. Acid M.s rich in silica and poor in the bases, iron, magnesia and lime, consolidate to give the acid rocks of which granite is the most abundant. Basic M.s rich in these 3 bases give rise to the basic rocks, gabbro, dolerite and basalt. The lava of volcanoes represents M. which has reached the surface of the earth and from which much of the included gases may have escaped into the atmosphere. The violence of some types of volcanic eruptions is the result of the escape of magmatic gases under decreasing pressure as the M. approaches the surface of the earth.

Magna Carta, or **The Great Charter,** document granted by King John at Runnymede, on the R. Thames, to the barons in 1215, was viewed in after times as the basis of Eng. liberties, though it is now recognised that its compilers were little concerned with the liberties of the common people and were simply trying to maintain their own rights. Some historians have gone as far as to call M. C. a reactionary document. The supreme importance of M. C. lies in the legal interpretations made of it in succeeding cents., based on its underlying

King John's revenge: barons of Magna Carta face 'treason trial'

By Patrick Sawer

THEY have long been credited with helping to lay the foundations of the British state as we know it today – the rule of law, the right to a fair trial and the protection of private property.

But this summer the barons and bishops who forced King John to agree to the Magna Carta are to be tried for treason, 800 years after the historic sealing of the document at Runnymede, Surrey, on June 15, 1215.

Senior lawyers, including the president of the UK Supreme Court, will sit in judgment on the nobles and clergymen who defied King John while advocates from across the Commonwealth will make the cases for the prosecution and the defence when the mock-trial is staged on July 31 at Westminster Hall, central London.

The sealing of the Magna Carta, drafted by the Archbishop of Canterbury to make peace between the unpopular King and a group of rebel barons, was designed to ensure the protection of church rights, protection for the barons from illegal imprisonment, access to swift justice, and limitations on feudal payments to the Crown.

Sir Robert Worcester, chairman of the Magna Carta 800th Anniversary Commemoration Committee which is staging the event, said: "The evidence being examined by these eminent judges will help explore some timeless questions of legal and constitutional importance.

"Is the King above the law? Is there ever a defence for breaking a solemn promise?"

Lord Judge, the former Lord Chief Justice, who will play the role of William Marshall, Earl of Pembroke – described as "the greatest knight that ever lived" – at the mock trial, said: "While the weight of modern scholarship certainly suggests the barons' and bishops' resistance was the right thing to do, this, the 800th anniversary of Magna Carta is a chance to test whether a court of law would say that their ends justified their means."

July's mock-trial will be judged by Lord Neuberger, president of the UK Supreme Court; Dame Sian Elias, chief justice of New Zealand, and The Hon Stephen Breyer, associate justice of the US Supreme Court.

"King John" will appear as a witness for the prosecution.

Among the witnesses for the defence will be Sir Robert Rogers, now Lord Lisvane, who was until last August the Clerk to the House of Commons. He is expected to argue that Parliamentary democracy might not exist today where it not for the actions of the barons at Runnymede.

Around half of the 800 seats at the two-hour mock-trial at Westminster Hall will be open to members of the public via a ballot to be held at the end of June.

Sir Robert Worcester said: "I hope people from across the country, of all ages and backgrounds, enter the draw for tickets to come and witness what I am sure will be one of the highlights of this year of commemorations."

For more information on the trial, go to www.magnacarta800th.com

...gees resorted to stabbing each other for food

the dead, would the judiciary have made the same decision?"

Giovanna Di Benedetto, a spokesman for Save the Children, said it was "absolutely essential" for the bodies to be recovered so that "families can pray next to graves and grieve for the dead".

Mr Salvi claimed it was not the responsibility of the judiciary to recover the bodies, despite prosecutors – who have opened a manslaughter investigation into the tragedy – asking

the navy to locate the boat. After another migrant vessel sank in October 2013, the judicial authorities in Agrigento, 93 miles west of Catania, recovered 350 bodies from the seabed so they could be identified.

Mr Salvi said: "Recovering the bodies] is not necessary for us. If the government want to do it for humanitarian reasons then that's fine, but we cannot cope with the costs and the delays to the investigation that it

would entail. It's not a decision for the judicial authorities." Only 28 people survived the disaster on the former fishing boat, which was found at a depth of 1,230ft. The navy said raising the wreck to the surface was possible, but it was up to prosecutors to decide whether to proceed.

Matteo Renzi, the Italian prime minister, previously said that the boat should be raised so that the victims could be given proper funerals.

---

between seven and 100 people died during the ethnic-based violence among the migrants, all from Burma and Bangladesh.

Mahmud Rafiq, 21, a Rohingya man from Burma, blamed the Bengalis, saying they refused to give the remaining food to women and children and "started hitting us. They beat us and attacked us with knives."

Mohammad Abdur Rahim,

Rohingyas. "Burma people do not give us any food, any water, they are torturing [us] every day," he said.

The violence erupted on a boat carrying about 700 people which was reportedly turned away by the Indonesian navy and escorted to Malaysian waters, where it was rejected by the Malaysian navy. It ended up in Indonesian waters, where passengers were rescued by fishermen.

A police chief said: "They

ing people overboard." Iqbal Foriza, a doctor treating the refugees, added: "They were oppressed Rohingya Muslims on the sea for four months, no food, no clean water, no bedding, that made them dehydrated and caused trauma."

The horrific accounts came as countries in the region turned away migrants in what has been described as a "human ping pong".

The UN has urged South-east Asian nations to accept the thousands of migrants

from Burma and Bangladesh stranded on boats. Many are from Burma, described by the UN as one of the world's most persecuted peoples.

Malaysia, the favoured destination for many, has urged Burma and Bangladesh to halt the flow but regional efforts to solve the crisis have so far been unsuccessful, with Burma saying it will not attend a regional summit in Thailand on May 29 "if 'Rohingya' is mentioned on the invitation" principle that the king must keep the law. John's arbitrary actions had aroused the barons to take up arms to redress their grievances, their demands being based on the charter granted by Henry I. In addition it contained 63 clauses embodying provisions for the protection of the 'ghts of feudal proprietors and against the abuse of the royal prerogative. Its prin. provisions were the redress of a number of grievances connected with feudal tenures; provisions regarding the relief of heirs, wards and marriage of the widows of tenants-in-chief; the inviolability of the liberties of the city of London and other ports and tns; freedom of commerce to foreign merchants; the strict administration of justice; the permanent abode of the court of common pleas at Westminster; the holding of assizes in the different cos., and the estab. of assizes; the abolition of extraordinary taxation; the protection of life, liberty and property; one standard of weights and measures; no banishment or imprisonment save by judgment of peers. It may be noted that the word 'outlawed' in M. C. is out of date and meaningless, but a standing committee of the House of Commons, when discussing the Administration of Justice (Miscellaneous Provisions) Bill which, *inter alia*, proposed to repeal the word from M. C., decided for sentimental reasons to leave the anct statute as it was on the Statute Book. See W. S. McKechnie, *Magna Carta*, 1905; A. J. Collins, *Documents of the Great Charter of* 1215, 1952, and J. C. Holt, *Magna Carta*, 1965.

Magna Carta (Charta) Island, 2 m. NW. of Staines, in the Thames, Bucks, England. It is reputed that King John landed here before crossing to Runnymede to seal Magna Carta in 1215.

Magna Graecia, Lat. trans. of Gk *Hē megale Hellas* (Great Hellas), collective name first given in the 6th cent. BC to the Gk city-states on the E. coast of what the Romans later called Bruttii (q.v.), i.e. the 'toe' of Italy. It was gradually extended to include those on the W. coast and even Sicily. The inhab. were known as Italiotes.

Magnalium Alloys, *see under* MAGNESIUM.

Magnani, Anna (1910–), It. actress, *b.* Alexandria, Egypt. She began on the stage and made her motion picture début in *The Blind Woman of Sorrento*, 1934; other films include *Open City, The Miracle, Volcano, Wild Women* and *Mamma Roma*. For *The Rose Tattoo*, made in Hollywood, she won the Academy Award for the best actress of 1955.

Magnasco, Alessandro (1681–1747), It. painter, *b.* Genoa, son of a painter, Stefano M. He worked in Milan, Genoa and Florence and was admired in his own time for his brilliant, febrile style of painting, and for his pictures of social life in which there was a fantastic and perhaps satiric element. Market scenes, gypsy encampments, Jewish synagogues and monks at prayer are among his subjects. Long neglected, he has regained esteem in the course of the last half century.

Magnes, Judah Leon (1877–1948), Jewish rabbi and Zionist, *b.* San Francisco. He was

educ. at Cincinnati Univ. and Heb. Union College, and later, at Berlin and Heidelberg. Appointed instructor and librarian at the Heb. Union College in 1903, he became rabbi of Temple Israel, Brooklyn, 1904. His early years were spent in the Jewish ministry. He was secretary of the Amer. Zionists, 1905–8, but had no sympathy with political Zionism. He settled in Palestine in 1922. His prin. work was in connection with the Heb. Univ., on Mt Scopus, the site of which he chose in 1912. When in 1925 it took shape he became chancellor. In 1935, when its constitution was remodelled, M. became president.

Magnesia: 1. Name of 2 anct cities of Asia Minor. (a) *M. ad Maeandrum,* in Ionia on a small trib. of the Maeander. The fact that it was not a member of the Ionian League supports the tradition that it was founded by colonists from Thessaly (*see* 2 below) and Crete. Its political hist. follows that of Ionia (q.v.); commercially it enjoyed great prosperity until Rom. imperial times, when it disappears from the records. Themistocles (q.v.) *d.* here *c.* 460 BC. (b) *M. ad Sipylum* (modern Manisa, q.v.) 40 m. NE. of Smyrna, famous for the battle in which Antiochus III was defeated by a Rom. army under L. Cornelius Scipio, 190 BC. In the neighbourhood was a rock-hewn figure of 'Niobe', probably intended to represent the Great Mother of the Gods (q.v.).

2. Dist of E. Thessaly, between the Vale of Tempe and the Pagasaean Gulf.

3. Dept of W. Greece, in Thessaly. Its cap. is Vólos. Area 995 sq. m.; pop. 662,300.

Magnesia, *see* MAGNESIUM.

Magnesia, Sulphate of, *see* EPSOMITE.

Magnesian Limestone. Geological name of the group of limestones and dolomites which make up much of the Permian rocks of NE. England. They are deposits of the desiccated Zechstein sea and are interbedded with valuable deposits formed by evaporation, such as anhydrite and potassium salts. The term M. L. as a rock-name is used for limestone carrying dolomite, a mineral consisting of calcium and magnesium carbonate.

Magnesite, mineral consisting of magnesium carbonate ($MgCO_3$). It is isomorphous with calcite, and is met with in 3 forms: crystalline, massive and earthy. The crystals occur in rhombohedra, and have a hardness of 4 and a sp. gr. of 3. The other forms are white in colour and are often mixed with meerschaum or other magnesium salts. The mineral is mined in Euboea, Madras and California, and is used for the manuf. of fire-bricks, as a source of magnesium salts and as a pigment.

Magnesium, symbol Mg; atomic number 12; atomic weight 24·32, a metallic bivalent element. First known in the form of the sulphate, or Epsom salts; in the 18th cent. the oxide, or magnesia alba, was prepared and was at first thought to be chemically identical with lime. In 1808 Davy demonstrated that magnesia was the oxide of a metal; the metal was obtained in a fairly pure state by Bussy in 1829. Mg occurs in the form of carbonate in magnesite, dolomite and magnesian limestone; as sulphate in sea water and some mineral waters, as at Epsom in Surrey and Seidlitz in Bohemia, also as the mineral kieserite; it occurs as chloride in the mineral carnallite at Stassfurt; it also enters into the composition of many silicates, as hornblende, talc, olivine, asbestos and meerschaum. Metallic Mg is commonly prepared from the mineral carnallite, which is fused with fluorspar in the presence of metallic sodium. The impure metal thus obtained is then sublimed and the product pressed into the form of ribbon. It is usually prepared from fused carnallite by electrolysis. The operation is performed in an iron pot which acts as the cathode, whilst carbon rods form the anode. The whole apparatus is closed inside an electric furnace so that the temp. may be so maintained that the resulting Mg shall remain molten. A current of coal gas and hydrogen serves to prevent the access of oxygen which would cause oxidation. Chlorine, a gaseous product of the electrolysis, is led off by a side pipe. Mg is a lustrous white metal of sp. gr. 1·75 and m.p. 649° C. It is malleable and ductile. When heated in air it burns with great brilliancy, forming the oxide MgO, a white powder slightly soluble in water and very infusible (used as a refractory lining for furnaces); at the same time a little Mg nitride is usually formed, Mg_3N_2. When the metal burns in chlorine, the chloride $MgCl_2$ is formed. It may also be prepared by the action of hydrochloric acid on magnesia or Mg carbonate. The bromide and iodide resemble the chloride; they are soluble in water and occur in sea water.

The sulphate formerly obtained from the springs at Epsom is now obtained from the mineral kieserite; the salt is fairly soluble in water. Mg is used in photography for producing a brilliant light rich in chemical rays; it is used for a similar purpose in pyrotechny. The salts are useful purgatives. The sulphate, or Epsom salts, is most commonly employed, and acts by virtue of abstracting water from the tissues into the bowel; the stronger the solution, the more water is thus abstracted. Fluid magnesia is an aperient prepared by dissolving the carbonate in water impregnated with carbon dioxide. Citrate of magnesia, a popular effervescent aperient, consists of a mixture of bicarbonate of soda with tartaric and citric acids with a small proportion of Epsom salts. Mg finds a ready use in chem., since it is a powerful reducing agent. It is very valuable in organic chem. in the form of Mg alkyl and aryl compounds, used in numerous syntheses. The magnalium alloys contain Mg and aluminium in various proportions. A common one contains 10 per cent Mg, is of a silvery colour and can be soldered. One containing 25 per cent Mg is very like bronze. The magnalium alloys possess the advantage of being lighter, bulk for bulk, than aluminium, and they are used for castings. They do not corrode easily, and have considerable tensile strength. An aircraft, called the Planet Satellite, has been constructed largely of Mg. *See* E. V.

Pennell, *Magnesium, its Production and Use* (2nd ed.), 1948.
Magnet, *see* MAGNETISM.
Magnetic Belts, *see* ELECTRO-THERAPY.
Magnetic Circuit in an electric machine, the path of the magnetic flux through the field core, air gap, armature and back through air gap to the core of the S.-pole. A law similar to Ohm's law (q.v.) for the electric circuit holds: magnet − motive force (amp. turns per cm.) = reluctance × flux, the reluctance being the length divided by permeability × cross-section area.
Magnetic Pole, *see* MAGNETISM.
Magnetic Shell, *see* CURRENT ELECTRICITY, *Magnetic Effects of a Current.*
Magnetic Susceptibility, *see* INDUCTION, MAGNETIC.
Magnetism. The familiar property of a magnet, viz. its power of attracting iron, has been known since the time of Thales of Miletus (640–546 BC). The name magnet is derived from the tn Magnesia (now Manisa), in Asia Minor, in whose neighbourhood natural magnets were found. This mineral, known as magnetite (q.v.) or lodestone, contains considerable quantities of the oxides of iron, FeO and Fe_2O_3. It was used as a crude compass (hence the name lodestone; lode = A.-S. *lād* = way) before artificial magnets were employed for that purpose. Artificial magnets can be made by stroking iron with a magnet as shown in Fig. 1, by the method of single touch, or by the method of double touch as shown in Fig. 2. The relation between the poles should be noticed.

In 1819 Oersted discovered the phenomenon of electro-magnetism, and since that time powerful magnets are made as follows. A solenoid consisting of a narrow tube of any non-magnetisable substance is closely wound with a large number of turns of insulated wire. The bar to be magnetised is then placed inside the solenoid and a current is passed through the wire. Iron, nickel and cobalt are highly magnetisable, but the best substances for making permanent magnets that will retain their M. if treated with care are steel alloys containing small quantities of tungsten, cobalt, aluminium, etc. The residual power of soft iron is very small, although it is highly magnetic. It is therefore used for the cores of electromagnets. All steel magnets lose their M. if they are heated in a bright red heat; they lose some of their M. if subjected to shocks or hammering, and they are best kept by storing together in pairs, opposite poles (*see* below) being connected by short pieces of soft iron.

Properties of a magnet. If a bar magnet is dipped into iron filings, the latter cling to the ends of the bar and very few to the middle of the bar. The regions near the ends are called the poles of the magnet, and there appears to be no difference between them as regards their power of attraction of the filings; this fact can be confirmed by quantitative experiments. Such a magnet, if pivoted so that it can rotate about a vertical axis in a neighbourhood free from iron

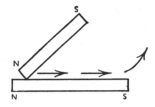

FIG. 1

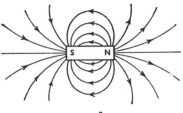

FIG. 3

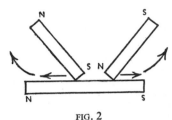

FIG. 2

and electrical machinery, will come to rest in a line approximately N. and S. (*see* below). The pole of the magnet that seeks the N. is called the N. pole, the other is called the S. pole. Experiment shows that like poles repel and unlike poles attract each other. This fact accounts for the behaviour of the compass; the earth itself is a magnet, with a magnetic S. pole in the Arctic regions and a magnetic N. pole in the Antarctic regions. It also explains why a magnet attracts iron; the iron becomes magnetised, and is then attracted by the magnet. These familiar properties of a magnet, and the fact that the earth is a magnet, were discovered by Wm Gilbert (q.v.), 'the father of magnetic philosophy'.

Quantitative magnetism. The quantitative law of the force of attraction and repulsion between magnetic poles was determined by Coulomb (1736–1806) and verified more exactly by Gauss (1777–1855). Coulomb defined unit magnetic pole as one that repels a similar pole placed one centimetre away *in vacuo* with a force of one dyne, and his experiments led to the conclusion that a pole of strength m repels a pole of strength m' at a distance of r cm. *in vacuo* with a force of $\frac{mm'}{r^2}$ dynes. For mathematical computations it is convenient to designate N. poles as positive poles and S. poles as negative poles, and it can be shown that every magnet can be regarded for quantitative calculations as consisting of 2 poles of strengths: $+ m$ and $- m$. The line joining the poles is called the *magnetic axis*. The pole strength of a good small steel magnet is of the order of 200 units.

The region of magnetic attractions and repulsions round a magnet is known as a magnetic field. The character of a magnetic field was investigated by Faraday (1791–1867), to whom the idea of 'action at a distance' was repugnant. Instead of magnetic poles attracting

or repelling each other without the intervention of a medium, Faraday imagined the medium traversed by lines of magnetic force that gave the direction of the magnetic force at any point. Fig. 3 shows the lines of magnetic force in the neighbourhood of bar magnets. Faraday imagined these lines to spread in all directions, beginning on N. poles and ending on S. poles, and this physical theory was mathematically interpreted at a later date by Maxwell with great success. A magnetic 'map' can be surveyed by means of a small compass or, alternatively, by means of iron filings sprinkled on a piece of thin glass or perspex placed above the magnet or magnets. The filings become magnetised by induction and act as a myriad of small compasses that set themselves along the lines of force. The quantitative character of a magnetic field is determined by defining the magnetic force at a point in the field. The unit of magnetic field is 1 oersted, defined as the strength of the field at a point where a unit pole is repelled with a mechanical force of 1 dyne. Thus the magnetic force at a point is H oersteds if a pole of strength m placed there is repelled with a mechanical force of mH dynes. The strongest magnetic fields are those between the poles of the most powerful electro-magnets; they can have strengths up to 70,000 oersteds over small vols. For short times much stronger fields can be produced. The strength of the earth's magnetic field in London at the present time is about 0·45 oersted; the horizontal component is about 0·18 oersted.

Quantitative measurements in magnetism involve the use of a magnetometer which can be used to test the inverse square law as follows. Suppose a magnetic needle, AB, is placed at O, at which point there is a magnetic field, F (Fig. 4), in an E. and W. direction. Let NS be the magnetic meridian at O, and H the horizontal component of the earth's field at O. Let θ be the angle which AB makes with NS. If m is the strength of each pole, the horizontal force on each due to the earth is Hm, and if $2l$ be the distance between the poles, the couple due to the earth is $2ml$H $\sin \theta$. Similarly, the couple due to F is $2ml$F $\cos \theta$. Thus we get that H $\tan \theta = $ F, the basic equation of the magnetometer. $2ml$ is called the *moment*, M, of the *magnet*, and is of more fundamental significance than the concept of a magnetic pole. Single, isolated poles have not yet been found in nature, and location of a pole within a magnet is somewhat arbitrary. All magnetic phenomena can be accounted for in

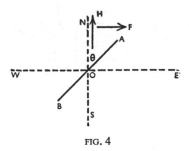

FIG. 4

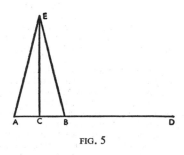

FIG. 5

terms of magnetic dipoles, although it is sometimes easier to derive a formula by considering magnetic poles. Thus, assume, for the time being, the inverse square law. Let AB (Fig. 5) be a small magnet, of length $2l$ and pole strength m. Consider the magnetic field F_1 at a point D in AB produced at a distance r from C, the centre of AB.

$$F_1 = \frac{m}{(r-l)^2} - \frac{m}{(r+l^2)} = \frac{m[(r+l)^2 - (r-l)^2]}{(r-l)^2(r+l)^2}.$$

Neglecting terms involving l^2 this becomes

$$F_1 = \frac{2M}{r^3} \text{ (where } M = 2ml, \text{ the magnetic}$$

moment of AB). Now consider the field at E a point on the normal to AB at C, such that CE = r. The forces due to the poles act along AE and EB respectively. The resultant acts through E parallel to AB. The value of the field is

$$F_2 = \frac{2m}{(AE)^2} \cdot \frac{AC}{AE} = \frac{2m}{r^2+l^2} \cdot (r^2+l^2)^{-\frac{1}{2}} = \frac{M}{r^3}$$

$$\text{neglecting terms in } \frac{l^2}{r^2}.$$

If we had assumed that the field varied inversely as the nth power of the distance, we should have had $F_1 = \frac{nM}{r^{(n+1)}}$ and $F_2 = \frac{M}{r^{(n+1)}}$, i.e. $F_1 = nF_2$. On testing the fields at D and E with a magnetometer, it is found that $F_1 = 2F_2$, and therefore the inverse square law holds. This proof is due to Gauss. The magnetometer can also be used in conjunction with a vibration experiment to measure the horizontal component of the earth's field. We know that a bar magnet produces a field of intensity $\frac{2M}{r^3}$ at a point end-on to it, and at a distance r. Thus a

compass needle will be deflected through an angle θ, where $\frac{2M}{r^3} = H \tan \theta$, if placed at the point. Thus we have one relation between H and M. If now the bar magnet is suspended so as to be in a horizontal position and it is allowed to oscillate, its period can be proved to be

$2\pi \sqrt{\dfrac{I}{MH}}$ (where I is the moment of inertia of

the magnet). Thus we have a second relation between M and H, if the period is accurately determined. Hence we can find M and H. If the dip is known, it is easy to determine the vertical component of the earth's field and the total intensity F (say). For $F = \dfrac{H}{\cos i}$ (where i is the dip) and $V = F \sin i = H \tan i$.

Theories of magnetism. All substances are magnetic to a slight degree, and their feeble magnetic properties may be observed when they are placed in an intense magnetic field. Most substances are paramagnetic, i.e. they become magnetised with their magnetic axes (the line joining the S. pole to the N. pole) parallel to the magnetising force; a few, notably bismuth, are diamagnetic; these substances become magnetised with their axes making an angle of 180° with the magnetising force. The ferromagnetic substances, iron, nickel, cobalt and some of their alloys, are all paramagnetic, but the extent to which they are magnetised depends not only on the magnetising force, but also on their previous magnetic hist. Furthermore, if the magnetising force is increased, a stage is reached when the magnet becomes saturated, i.e. its pole strength reaches a maximum value (*see* INDUCTION, MAGNETIC). Now, when a magnet is broken in two, we do not obtain 2 halves, one with a N. pole, the other with a S. pole. Two new poles appear at the point of fracture: however often this process is repeated the same result is obtained; every magnet has 2 poles. Weber suggested that every magnet was really composed of magnetic particles or magnetised domains that are now believed to be of molecular dimensions. Ewing developed his theory and suggested that, since the act of magnetisation did not change the chemical character nor the weight of the specimen, but simply endowed it with magnetic properties, magnetisable substances consisted of molecular magnets. According to this theory, an ordinary piece of iron is made up of molecular magnets arranged in haphazard fashion, so that they neutralise each other's effects on external bodies. This disorder disappears when the iron is placed in a magnetic field and the molecular magnets are set with their axes parallel to the field: free poles appear at the ends of the magnet, while the central portions exhibit only feeble magnetic powers because equal and opposite poles neutralise each other's effects. This theory accounts for the appearance of new poles wherever the magnet is broken, and the state of saturation is reached when all the molecular magnets have been arranged in order. Subsequent loss of M. is explained by the partial return to disordered array.

Early in the present cent. Weiss suggested the existence of the magneton or elementary magnet, an analogue of the electron (q.v.), the elementary charge of electricity. This idea has been developed by physicists, notably Einstein, de Haas and Bohr. An electric current flowing round a circular coil has a magnetic field similar to that of a magnet whose axis coincides with that of the coil: the electrical theory of matter attempts to ascribe the magnetic properties of bodies to the orbital motions of the electrons in the atom. The quantum theory of the atom developed by Bohr supported the magneton theory, and subsequently direct experimental evidence of the existence of the magnetic moment associated with electron orbits was obtained by Gerlach and Stern in 1921.

Terrestrial magnetism. The importance of the magnetic properties of the earth was realised by navigators, and it is to sailors and those connected with nautical matters that most of the investigations and records of terrestrial magnetic phenomena are due. By a series of observations at different points of the earth's surface it has been possible to chart the magnetic elements peculiar to a locality, and thus enable mariners to correct their compasses to the true geographical meridian. The magnetic elements at any point on the earth's surface are (i) the horizontal component of the earth's magnetic force; (ii) the declination (or magnetic variation), the angle between the magnetic meridian and the geographical meridian; (iii) the angle of dip (q.v.) (or inclination), the angle between the direction of the earth's resultant magnetic force and the horizontal at that point. The magnetic elements are by no means constant; they are subject to secular changes, to diurnal variations and to irregular changes known as magnetic storms that are especially violent in the Arctic and Antarctic regions. The declination in London, for example, was 11° 15′ E. in 1580; in 1657 it was nil; in 1800 it was 24° 0′ W., and in 1930 it was 8° 07′ W., and decreasing annually by about 7′. The magnetic poles of the earth are at present situated in lat. 74°, long. 100° W. (N. pole), and lat. 67°, long. 142° E. (S. pole).

The daily variation of the declination in London takes place from E. to W. in the morning, and then returns, the extent of the variation being 11′ in summer and 3·3′ in winter. As the variation is also greater during the day than at night, it is evident that the cause is connected with solar radiation. The intensity of the magnetic storms is found to bear some relation to the frequency of sun-spots, and often to displays of aurora borealis. The actual cause of the earth's M. and its secular changes is obscure. The obvious suggestion that the former is due to the lodestone present in the earth does not nearly account for the magnitude of the magnetic effects or for the secular changes; other tentative explanations have similar grave defects.

The variation of the earth's magnetic force from one locality to another requires the constant attention of mariners during a voyage. The modern gyro-compass that is used as a master compass on all large vessels is not a magnetic compass (*see* GYROSCOPE AND GYROSTAT), and it is set so that it always indicates the true geographical meridian. It is interesting to note that a magnetic compass, freely suspended, will come to rest in a vertical position at the earth's magnetic poles (*see* GEOMAGNETISM).

Magnetic observatory. The prin. observatory in Great Britain is at Eskdalemuir in Scotland, on a site far removed from the presence of iron and electrical machinery. Formerly the H.Q. of the gov. survey were at Kew, but the advent of the trams and the electrification of the S. Railway at Richmond, about 1 m. away, caused irregular variations of the magnetic field, so that reliable survey became impossible. The authorities received compensation for this magnetic interference and removed to the present site. For other articles on M. *see* COMPASS, MAGNETIC; INDUCTION, MAGNETIC; ISOCLINIC AND ISOGONIC; POTENTIAL, MAGNETIC. *See also* PHYSICAL CONSTANTS.

See (elementary), W. C. Badcock and E. J. Holmyard, *Electricity and Magnetism for Beginners*, 1931; (advanced), J. Clerk-Maxwell, *Electricity and Magnetism*, 1873; J. J. Thomson, *Elements of the Mathematical Theory of Electricity and Magnetism*, 1895; Sir J. Jeans, *Mathematical Theory of Electricity and Magnetism*, 1908, 1941; F. B. Pidduck, *A Treatise on Electricity*, 1925; E. C. Stoner, *Magnetism and Atomic Structure*, 1926, and *Magnetism and Matter*, 1934; S. Chapman, *The Earth's Magnetism*, 1936; N. F. Mott and others, *Magnetism*, 1938; L. F. Bates, *Modern Magnetism*, 1939; J. A. Fleming (Ed.), *Terrestrial Magnetism and Electricity*, 1939; S. Chapman and J. Bartils, *Geomagnetism*, 1940; D. Schoenberg, *Magnetism*, 1949; B. I. Bleaney and B. Bleaney, *Electricity and Magnetism*, 1957.

Magnetite, mineral consisting mainly of black oxide of iron, Fe_3O_4. It is identical with lodestone, and is famous under that name for its magnetic qualities (A.-S. *lād*, way). It occurs as crystals in the cubic system, having a hardness of 6 and a sp. gr. of 5; it is black and opaque, and has a metallic lustre. It is widely distributed, entering into the composition of many volcanic rocks, and is valuable as an iron ore.

Magneto Ignition, *see* MOTOR CARS; MOTOR CYCLES.

Magnetograph, instrument automatically recording the daily variations of either the horizontal or vertical components of the earth's magnetic field, or the declination (*see* MAGNETISM, *Terrestrial Magnetism*) at a given magnetic observatory. M.s are essentially sensitive magnetometers (q.v.) in which the movements of the magnetic needle are magnified by focusing a beam of light reflected from a small thin mirror, attached to it, on a strip of sensitised paper. The paper is wrapped round a drum that slowly revolves by clockwork.

Magnetometer, *see* MAGNETISM, *Quantitative measurements in magnetism.*

Magnificat, song of thanksgiving of the Blessed Virgin Mary (Luke i. 46–55). It may be compared with the Song of Hannah (1 Sam. ii), which was evidently well known to its inspired utterer. This canticle forms the climax of the Rom. Catholic office of Vespers, its place here dating back to about the 6th cent., and was thence included in the Anglican Evening Prayer (which combines elements of Vespers and Compline).

Magnifying-glass, *see* LENS.

Magnitogorsk, city in the Urals, on the R. Ural in the Chelyabinsk oblast, one of the biggest industrial centres of Russia. It has a vast iron and steel plant (largest in Russia) based originally on local ore deposits (Mt Magnitnaya, worked since 18th cent.) but now, as these become exhausted, changing to the use of poorer ores from Rudnyy (q.v.) in NW. Kazakhstan. Coal is brought by rail from the Kuznetsk Basin and from Karaganda, oil by pipe from Shkapovo in Bashkiria and natural gas by pipe from Gazli, near Bukhara in Central Asia. Subsidiary industries include chemicals and engineering; M. is also an important railway junction (4 lines) and a local cultural centre. It was founded in 1929 to provide accommodation for the builders and workers of the giant plant which was built 1929–33 by forced labourers and Communist enthusiasts, and has been constantly expanded since. Pop. (1965) 348,000 (1939, 146,000). *See* M. Gardner Clark, 'Magnitogorsk: A Soviet Iron and Steel Plant in the Southern Urals', in R. S. Thoman and D. J. Patton (Ed.), *Focus on Geographic Activity*, 1964.

Magnitude, in astronomy, a measure of the brightness of a star. The term dates back to the time of Hipparchus (q.v.) who divided the stars into 6 classes, those of 1st M. being the brightest in the sky, while those of 6th M. were only just visible. Hipparchus' classification was perpetuated by Ptolemy in his *Almagest* (q.v.); apart from decimal sub-div. the system was not advanced until the time of Sir John Herschel (q.v.), who concluded that a given *difference* of magnitudes was equivalent to a certain *ratio* of apparent brightness. Pogson of Oxford proposed that a magnitude difference of 1 should be *defined* as a brightness ratio of $2 \cdot 512 \ldots$ or $10^{0 \cdot 4}$, so that e.g., a star of M. $1 \cdot 00$ is *exactly* 100 times brighter than a star of M. $6 \cdot 00$. This made it possible to assign unambiguous M.s to stars by means of devices that measured the intensity of the star's light: visually, photographically, photoelectrically.

To make a M. precise, the colour of the light that is measured must be specified. Thus we have photographic M.s (blue light), visual M.s (yellow light) and other systems.

The M. system can be extended to the brightest stars, having negative M.s, and to stars much fainter than 6th M., invisible to the naked eye. On the visual scale, the M. of Sirius, the brightest star, is $-1 \cdot 44$, while that of Procyon is $0 \cdot 36$; the M. difference of $1 \cdot 80$ implies that

Procyon is $5 \cdot 25$ times fainter than Sirius. The faintest stars measurable with the 200-in. Palomar telescope, of about 23rd M., are nearly 10,000,000,000 times fainter than Sirius. *See also* ABSOLUTE MAGNITUDE; STAR.

Magnolia, large genus of hardy and half-hardy deciduous and evergreen shrubs and trees, family Magnoliaceae, with fragrant solitary flowers. *M. grandiflora* is a fine evergreen tree attaining a height of 70 ft in America, known as the Amer. bull bay. From its seeds the free-flowering Exmouth variety, *Lanceolata*, was propagated. The Chinese yulan, *M. denudata*, has a purplish, double flowered variety. The yulan bears large, water-lily-like, very fragrant flowers on leafless twigs in Mar. *M. stellata* is a small shrub with an abundance of white star-shaped blooms, which appear in April. *M. × soulangiana* and varieties *alba superba* and *Lennei* make shapely bushes, flowering April to June. Both the Jap. *M. sieboldii* (*parviflora*) and its Chinese cousins *M. sprengeri*, *M. wilsonii* and *M. sinensis* are good strong garden plants, though liable to be damaged by late spring frosts. They tend to form small bushy trees, very symmetrical when well grown. These M.s flower over a long season; *M. sieboldii*, in particular, is seldom without flowers from June to Aug. A rich open soil is necessary for the M. and the addition of ample manure is also desirable. The M. should, when possible, be grown in sheltered positions. Some species are tender and suitable only for very mild dists.

MAGNOLIA

'Magnolia State', *see* MISSISSIPPI.

Magnoliaceae, family of dicotyledons, in 10 genera of shrubs and trees, found in Asia and America. Leaves alternate, flowers perfect and showy, with 3 sepals normally, 6 or more petals, many stamens and carpels, one-celled ovary. Typical genera are *Drimys, Illicium, Liriodendron, Magnolia* and *Michelia.*

Magnus, name of sev. kings of Norway, among whom may be mentioned:

Magnus the Good (d. 1048), accepted as king in 1035, who became King of Denmark also in 1042, was a son of St Olaf.

Magnus the Barefooted (1073–1103), became king in 1098. He subdued the Orkneys and the

Hebrides, but was killed while on an expedition to Ireland.

Magnus the Lawgiver (1238–80), son of Haakon IV, reigned from 1263. He constituted himself a reformer of the laws of his country, compiled laws for Iceland and made the crown hereditary.

Magnus Eriksson (1316–74), King of Norway and Sweden in 1319. In 1343 Norway was given to his son Haakon, and in 1365 he was forced to give up the Swedish throne to Albert of Mecklenburg.

Mago (*d*. 203 BC), Carthaginian general, youngest son of Hamilcar Barca and brother of Hannibal. He took part in Hannibal's great campaign in Italy (218–216 BC), and then joined his elder brother Hasdrubal in Spain. Here he was defeated by M. Junius Silanus (207), and again (this time together with Hasdrubal) by Scipio Africanus at Silpia (206). The Carthaginian Gov. forthwith ordered him to invade Gallia Cisalpina, 205; but he was defeated and recalled to Carthage, dying of wounds on the homeward voyage.

Magog, *see* GOG AND MAGOG.

Magog, city in Quebec, Canadà, 16 m. SW. of Sherbrooke. The prin. industries are textiles, cotton yarn and thread. Pop. 13,139.

Magpie, familiar name of sev. species of *Pica*, a genus of passeriform birds belonging to the family Corvidae. *P. pica*, the commonest species, is known all over Europe, and extends through the Palaearctic region; it can easily be tamed. *P. nuttalli*, a native of California, is distinguished by a bright yellow bill and a naked blue spot behind the eye.

COMMON MAGPIE

Magritte, René (1898–), Belgian painter, *b*. Lessines. Influenced by Chirico (q.v.), he began to produce a new kind of pictorial imagery inspired by Surrealism (q.v.) and was associated with a Surrealist group of painters and poets in Brussels. He is represented in the Museum of Modern Art, New York, and in the Tate Gallery.

Magsaysay, Ramón (1907–57), president of the Rep. of the Philippines. Educ. at the univ. of the Philippines and José Rizal College, he served as guerrilla leader against the Japanese in the Second World War. He was elected to the presidency in Nov. 1953.

Magwe: 1. Div. of Upper Burma, comprising the Irrawaddy valley from the delta to the confluence of the Chindwin. Area 17,575 sq. m.; pop. 1,905,900.

2. Dist. of Upper Burma in the M. div. The Irrawaddy forms its W. boundary. The soil is fertile, and oilseeds, rice, cotton, maize, etc., are grown and there are oilfields. Area 3313 sq. m.; pop. 160,000.

3. Cap. of above dist, and port of the Irrawaddy R., 70 m. S. of Pagan. It has an Intermediate College. Pop. 7,500.

Magyar Népköztársaság, *see* HUNGARY.

Magyarorszag, *see* HUNGARY.

Magyars, or **Hungarians,** nowadays the main pop. of Hungary (q.v.), were originally nomadic tribes living in the region between the Volga and the Urals. Generally speaking the M. nowadays are a uniform people speaking one language; but there are still small groups having distinct characteristics which go back to the original different tribes: they are the Sárköz (in the prov. of Tolna), the Ormánság (SW. Baranya), the Csököly (near Kaposvár), the Göcsej and the Hetés (to the W. of Balaton), the Palócz (in the N. provs.) and the Matyo (in the dist of Mezökövesd). The Magyar (or Hungarian) language belongs to the Ugrian group of the Ugro-Finnish linguistic family. The earliest document written wholly in Magyaric belongs to 1295 and contains 300 words, but from the 10th cent. onwards Hungarian words appear in Gk-Byzantine works and in Gk and Lat. documents found in Hungary. At the end of the 9th cent. the M. descended into the Moravian realm, under the leadership of Arpad, and caused great devastation and pillage, until they were defeated in the 10th cent. After this they settled down and embraced Christianity about the year 1000.

Mah Jong, game of anct Chinese origin, popular in the U.S.A. and Britain in the early 20th cent. The 4 players, called after the 4 winds, use ivory or bone pieces, or tiles, on a principle similar to that of playing cards. These are divided into suits: Bamboos (four of each number up to 9); Circles (four of each number up to 9); Characters (four of each number up to 9); Honours, or Dragons (four red, four green and four white); Winds (four e., four W., four N., four S.); and (extra tiles often not used) 4 Seasons and 4 Flowers. The basis of the game, io that players, by picking up and discarding from their hands, try to collect 1 pair and 4 triplets of tiles belonging to the same suit and denomination, or the same suit with a sequence of numbers.

Mahabad, formerly called Sauj Bulagh, dist and tn of the Persian prov. of Azerbaijan. The tn is 65 m. SSE. of Reza'iyeh. The pop. of M. is mainly Kurdish. Pop. of tn, 20,300.

Mahableshwar, chief hill station of Bombay state, on the E. slope of the W. Ghats, founded as a sanatorium in 1828. It is situated on a ridge about 4500 ft high, 74 m. S. of Poona. Near the foot of the hill is the reputed source of the R. Krishna, marked by an anct temple which is the resort of Hindu pilgrims.

Mahábhárata, sacred book of the Hindus, and

one of the 2 great epics of anct India, the other being *Rámáyana*. It is probably the longest epic in the world, being about 8 times as long as the *Iliad* and *Odyssey* together. The authorship has been ascribed to Vyása, but that is probably a generic name; it bears all the marks of being a compilation, for its contents are heterogeneous in the extreme. The leading story relates the contest between the Kurus, representing the spirit of evil, and the Pandus, representing the spirit of good. The temporary triumph of evil is shown by the adversities of the Pandus, while their ultimate renunciation of an earthly for a heavenly kingdom signifies the final victory of good. The text was first printed in 1834–9 in Calcutta. A new critical ed., in which scholars in all parts of the world are assisting, has been under preparation at Poona for some years. *See* R. C. Dutt, *Mahábhárata*, 1899 (Everyman's Library, 1910), and E. W. Hopkins, *The Great Epic of India, its Character and Origin*, 1901, 1921. *See also* E. P. Rice, *The Mahábhárata* (analysis and index), 1934.

Mahadeva, *see* SIVA.

Mahan, Alfred Thayer (1840–1914), Amer. rear-admiral and naval historian, *b.* New York. His books on the influence of sea power on hist. struck a new note and soon attained the position of classics on the subject. The grip of the Brit. Navy during the First World War fully substantiated M.'s theories; while in the Second World War the combined power of the Brit. and Amer. navies supplied still further confirmation subject to the modifications caused by the development of air power. *See* C. C. Taylor, *The Life of Admiral Mahan*, 1920; G. K. Kirkham, *The Books and Articles of R. Adm. A. T. Mahan*, 1929.

Mahanadi, riv. in India, rises in the Rajpur dist, Madhya Pradesh state, and flows first NE., then SE. and finally through Orissa to the Bay of Bengal, which it enters by numerous arms. It is connected with sev. canals and is used for irrigation purposes. Its length is 520 m.

Maharajah, *see* RAJAH.

Maharashtra. State of the Indian Union, situated on the W. coast, bounded on the N. by Gujarat and Madhya Pradesh, on the E. by Madhya Pradesh and Andhra Pradesh, on the S. by Mysore and on the W. by the Arabian Sea. It was founded on 1 May 1960 from the southern and mainly Mahratta speaking dists of the Old Bombay States. For its previous hist. *see under* BOMBAY. It is divided by the W. Ghats into a coastal strip and the Deccan uplands. The former receive the full force of the SW. monsoon with rainfall up to 250 in. Between June and Sept. the climate in the Deccan uplands is agreeable.

Development. The prin. crops grown are cotton, jouvar, rice and groundnuts. The great industry of the area is textiles, employing a quarter of a million workers daily. But industry generally is diversifying and expanding. The prin. cities are Bombay (4,152,000), Nagpur (644,000), Poona (597,000), Sholapur (337,000) and Kolhapur (187,000).

Culture. M. is predominantly Mahratta speaking. Out of a total pop. of 39,550,000 (1961) 32,000,000 are Hindus, virtually all Mahratta speaking, 3,000,000 are Muslims and 2,750,000 Buddhists. There are 5 univs., at Bombay, Poona, Nagpur, Aurangabad and Kolhapur, and a women's univ. with constituent colleges at Bombay and Poona.

Government. The governor is assisted by a council of ministers consisting of the chief minister and 14 other ministers. The legislature is bi-cameral. The Legislative Council contains 78 members. The Legislative Assembly contains 264 elected members and 1 nominated member (Anglo-Indian).

Mahatma, Sanskrit word meaning 'great soul'. The name was conferred, as a kind of title, on Gandhi by those who looked upon him as a saint, on account of his sincerity, asceticism and simple eloquence. It has been given by Theosophists to a great brotherhood of persons who are believed to have attained to a higher state of evolution than that of average humanity and to possess the 'secret wisdom of theosophy'. They 'work ever for the service of their race with a perfect and selfless devotion' (Annie Besant). The M. is said by W. theosophists to be endowed with preternatural powers acquired by ascetic or astral means. *See also* THEOSOPHY.

Mahâvamsa, title of a celebrated historical work in 2 books, written in Páli, and recording the hist. of Ceylon from its earliest period to the reign of Mahâsena, who *d. c.* AD 302.

Mahávíra was the twenty-fourth and last deified saint of the Jains, and his name signifies 'great hero'. His story is told in the *Kalpa-Sútra* and the *Mahávíra-Charitra*, 2 works held in great authority by the Jains. M. appears to have been a contemporary of Buddha.

Mahaweli-Ganga, prin. riv. in Ceylon, rises in the centre of the is., flows N. past Kandy and enters the Indian Ocean to the S. of Trincomalee.

Mahāyāna, *see* BUDDHA AND BUDDHISM.

Mahdi (Arabic passive participle, 'guided', then 'under the peculiar guidance of God'). In the 1st cent. of Islam some hoped for the coming of one 'who will fill the earth with righteousness as it is now full of iniquity'; the Shiites seized on the idea and made it an essential part of their faith. Before the end of the world the hidden imam will return to earth and destroy evil; in this aspect of his being he is the M. Authoritative leaders of the Sunnites do not countenance this idea; they say that before the end Jesus will come down to earth, slay al-Dajjal (the equivalent of Antichrist) and restore the true religion. But among the masses the hope for the M. was always alive (Jesus will be under his orders) and anyone who claimed to be the M. could get a following. The founder (*d.* 934) of the Fatimid dynasty in Egypt, the founder (*d.* 1128 or 1130) of the Almohades in Morocco, and the M. Mohammed Ahmad (*d.* 1885) who conquered the Sudan shared and exploited this belief. *See* D. S. Margoliouth, 'On Mahdis and Mahdiism', *Proceedings of the Brit. Academy*, vol. vii, and F.

Wingate, *Mahdiism and the Egyptian Soudan*, 1891. *See* A. Höllriegel, *The Mahdi of Allah* (trans.), 1931.

Mahé, largest is. of the Seychelles, in the Indian Ocean, 17 m. long and covered with high granite mts. The chief tn is Port Victoria. M. is 970 m. E. of Mombasa, and 934 m. ENE. of Mauritius. Area 55½ sq. m.; pop. (1960) 33,478.

Mahler, Gustav (1869–1911), Austrian composer and conductor, *b.* Kalist, Bohemia. He studied at the Vienna Conservatory under Epstein, Fuchs and Krenn. His first completed work was *Das klagende Lied* (pub. 1899), a cantata, the poem of which was written by him in 1878. He composed his first vol. of songs in 1882, and his first symphony was finished in 1888. M. held the posts of director of Royal Opera in Budapest, 1888–91, Hamburg, 1891–7, and of the Vienna Court Opera in 1897—the greatest period of the Vienna Opera House—where he remained till 1907. He went to America for the first time in 1907. His works include 10 symphonies (the last unfinished), *Das Lied von der Erde* (on Chinese poems), for contralto, tenor and orchestra, and sev. sets of songs (42 songs in all), many from the anthology *Des Knaben Wunderhorn. See* Alma Mahler, *Memories and Letters*, 1946; Paul Stefan, *Gustav Mahler: a Study*, 1931; G. Engel, *Gustav Mahler: Song-Symphonist*, 1933; H. Redlich, *Bruckner and Mahler*, 1966; D. Mitchell, *Gustav Mahler: the Early Years*, 1958.

Mahmud I (1696–1754), Sultan of Turkey, son of Mustafa II. He ascended the throne in 1730 after the deposition of his uncle, Ahmed III, and continued the war against Nadir, Shah of Persia, but with little success, making peace in 1736. He then entered upon a war with Russia and lost Ochakov in 1737. The Austrians, the allies of Russia, met with a serious defeat at Krotzka, and peace was made at Belgrade in 1740.

Mahmud II (1785–1839), Sultan of Turkey, son of Abd-ul-Hamid I and successor of his brother Mustafa IV in 1808. The war with Russia was concluded 4 years after his accession by the treaty of Bucharest. In 1821 the war of Gk Independence broke out and Gk sailors of the Turkish Navy mutinied. After the battle of Navarino Russia declared war (1827) and forced M. to sign the Peace of Adrianople (1829). In order to suppress his upstart vassal, Mehemet Ali, the pasha of Egypt, he secured a Russian alliance in 1833, and ordered the invasion of Syria in 1839, dying before the news of defeat reached him.

Mahmud of Ghazna (998–1030), ruler of Khorasan and Ghazna. His father, Sabuktegin, was nominally a vassal of the Samanids (q.v.); he *d.* in 997, and left his throne to a younger son, Isma'il. M., who was governor of Nishapur, hastened to Ghazna, deposed his brother, seized the throne and repudiated the overlordship of the Samanids. He made 12 inroads into India between 1001 and 1024, and carried away much booty. He extended his kingdom as far as Samarkand on the N. and Isfahan on the W.

Mahobá, tn of Uttar Pradesh state, India, 87 m. SSW. of Cawnpore. It is a tn of very great antiquity and contains many architectural remains: Hindu, Buddhist, Jain and Muslim. It is not now of any other importance.

Mahogany, one of the best-known and most widely used hardwoods in the world. The original Sp. M. (*Swietenia mahagoni*), introduced into Britain in the 16th cent. from Cuba and Central America, is now rare. Its place has been taken by another species, Central Amer. M. (*S. macrophylla*), and by African M., which is of another genus (*Khaya*). The standard name 'Amer. M.' covers all species of *Swietenia*. Trade names, indicating individual species or timber from a particular part or locality, may be used as alternatives to the standard name, e.g. Honduras M. African M. is the standard name for all species of *Khaya*, and large quantities are imported from Nigeria and Ghana. From the 18th cent. to the present day M. has been one of the most popular woods for furniture, reaching its peak in Victorian times. Sp. M. is very close grained, with a fine, silky texture; it may be beautifully figured, and is heavier than the Central Amer. and African M. which have largely displaced it. These are lighter in colour and slightly coarser in texture, although they are available in larger sizes. All the M.s are stable timbers, fairly durable, and strong for their weight. African M. weighs about 34 lb. per cu. ft when seasoned. In addition to furniture M. is used for all types of high-class joinery, shipbuilding and boatbuilding, panelling and in the form of veneers. A number of woods which have some resemblance to the colour, grain and texture of M. have been given the name M. Strictly speaking only woods of the true M., or *Meliaceae*, family are entitled to the name. *See* TIMBER.

Mahomedanism, *see* ISLAM.

Mahomet, *see* MOHAMMAD.

Mahón (Eng. **Port Mahon**), Sp. seaport, cap. of the is. of Minorca (q.v.). It is situated on an inlet at the E. end of the is., and the tn itself overlooks the harbour, which was once considered the best in the Mediterranean. M., which was in Brit. hands for most of the 18th cent., has the appearance of a garrison tn and is today a Sp. naval base. Pop. 16,600.

Mahonia, or **Ash-barberry,** genus of the Berberidaceae family and closely allied to the barberry; consisting of elegant evergreen shrubs, with pinnate leaves and yellow flowers. There are over 90 species, 58 Asiatic, others of N. and Central America. Those cultivated in gardens for their ornamental foliage and flowers include *M. aquifolium, M. bealei, M. japonica, M. fortunei* and *M. toluacensis.*

Mahony, Francis Sylvester, known as Father Prout (1804–66), humorist, *b.* Cork. He was admitted into the Society of Jesus, but was expelled after a few years. He was ordained priest at Rome in 1832 and returned to Ireland. He became a contributor to *Fraser's Magazine*, and his best work, contributed originally to that periodical, is the *Reliques of Father Prout*, 1836. His poem 'The Bells of Shandon' is a tribute to his native city. His works were ed. with a memoir by C. Kent, 1881.

Mahrattas, or **Marathas,** term commonly applied to a mixed people, mainly of Hindu origin, inhabiting central India, largely in the former states of Baroda, Indore and Gwalior (*see also* INDIAN PRINCELY STATES), but now used to designate all Marathi-speaking Hindus in India. They are first heard of as such in the 17th cent. as rebels, who rose against the Mogul emperor at Delhi under the leadership of Sivaji, a determined and successful fighter who proclaimed himself the chief. He was succeeded by his son, Sambaji (1680), who endeavoured to carry out his father's policy, but 9 years later he fell into the hands of his enemy, Aurangzeb, who put him to death. For over a cent. the M. waged incessant war against the Mogul dynasty with varying success, but at length they sustained a heavy defeat at Panipat in 1761 at the hands of Ahmed Shah Abdalli, the Amir of Afghanistan. Their power was eventually broken by the British in 1843. The M. are an active and hardy people, and devout Hindus. Their literature is abundant.

Mähren, *see* MORAVIA.

Mährisch-Schönberg, *see* ŠUMPERK.

Maia, in Gk mythology, daughter of Atlas and Pleione. She was the eldest and most beautiful of the Pleiades (q.v.). In a grotto on Mt Cyllene (Arcadia) M. bore to Zeus Hermes (q.v.). She was identified by the Romans with an anct It. divinity of spring, also called M., or Maiesta.

Maid of Norway, *see* FAIR MAID OF NORWAY.

Maida Vale, residential suburb in the NW. of London, adjoining Kilburn, in the dist of Paddington, named in honour of the victory over the French at Maida, Calabria, in 1806.

Maiden, early form of guillotine (q.v.). An axe was fixed in a frame about 10 ft high, so that it could move upwards in grooves. When the axe had reached the topmost groove, it was suddenly released and fell on the victim's neck. It was first used at the execution of the minor agents employed to murder Rizzio (1561). It was last used in 1710 and is displayed in the museum of the Society of Antiquaries of Scotland, in Edinburgh.

Maiden Castle, great earthwork on a hill-top 2 m. SW. of Dorchester (q.v.), Dorset, England, some 115 ac. in extent and systematically excavated, 1934–7, by Sir R. E. M. Wheeler (q.v.). The site was first occupied *c.* 2500–1800 BC; in the late Neolithic period there was a settlement on the hill, and when the settlement was deserted a great Neolithic bank-burrow over 500 ft long was built across the ridge. There is evidence of occupation by late Neolithic and Beaker peoples, but it was not until *c.* 350 BC, i.e. in the Early Iron Age, that the site was extensively developed, an enclosure being built at the E. end of the camp to encompass a small vil. The Iron Age vil. was later extended W. to cover some 45 ac., and the E and W. entrances to the camp were given additional protection in the form of projecting earthworks. Early in the 1st

cent. BC a band of the tribe of the Veneti had settled at M. C. and considerably amplified the defences. In AD 43 or 44 Vespasian (q.v.), advancing with the Second Augustan Legion, reached M. C. and, attacking probably at the E. end, reduced the tn after a fierce battle which appears to have ended in a massacre of men and women alike. Excavation revealed a 'war cemetery' beside the gates of M. C. where the Brit. inhab. hastily buried their dead. The defences of M. C. were slighted by the Rom. invaders, and by about AD 70 the remnants of the pop. were moving to the new Rom. tn of Dorchester (q.v.). About 380 a small Romano-Brit. temple was built on the site of M. C. and its excavated foundations may be seen. *See* R. E. M. Wheeler, *Maiden Castle, Dorset,* 1943. (*See Plate: Archaeology.*)

Maidenhair Fern, or *Adiantum capillus-veneris,* pretty Brit. fern found in moist, warm situations. It bears its fructification (sporangia containing spores) in short marginal patches on the edges of the sub-div. of the fronds, which are in turn to protect it. It grows well in pots where frost is excluded. Maidenhair spleenwort is *Asplenium adiantum-nigrum.*

MAIDENHAIR FERN

A, part of frond, showing sporangia.

Maidenhair Tree, *see* GINKGO.

Maidenhead, anct municipal bor. and riverside resort in Berks, England, situated 26 m. W. of London. Two fine bridges cross the R. Thames, a seven-arched road bridge completed in 1777, and a railway bridge designed by Brunel which has two of the widest spans ever constructed in brick. The tn is bounded on the W. by M. Thicket, once part of Windsor Forest and now preserved by the National Trust. Its situation on a beautiful stretch of the Thames has made M. a tourist centre. Since the Second World War a number of light industries have been estab., and the tn is prosperous and expanding. Pop. 35,374.

Maidens, vil. of Ayrshire, Scotland, 15 m. from Ayr, on the sea coast, a centre for sea fishing and tourist attraction, particularly for caravanners. Nearby are Culzean Castle (seat of the Marquess of Ailsa) and Thomaston Castle, now in ruins. Pop. 700.

Maids of Honour, *see* HOUSEHOLD, ROYAL.

Maidstone (*maeides stana* is given in the *Textus Roffensis, c.* 975 AD. and 'maiden's stone' as the probable meaning in the *Oxford English Place Names*), co. tn of Kent, 41 m. SE. of London by railway and 34 m. by road. A municipal bor., assize and mrkt tn possessing its own court of quarter sessions. It contains among numerous public buildings a tn hall, co. hall, co. mental hospital, co. ophthalmic hospital, W. Kent General Hospital and a museum of Kent antiquities. There is a grammar school, founded in the 16th cent. On the banks of the R. Medway is a group of noteworthy anct buildings, including the par. church of All Saints, the college of priests, the archbishop's palace and the archbishop's stables. The latter building houses a unique collection of anct carriages; the tn possesses sev. parks, including the picturesque Mote Park of over 500 ac. Industries including paper-making, brewing, agric. and electrical engineering, fruit canning, printing and confectionery. Around the tn are extensive fruit orchards and hop gardens. Some 337 properties were destroyed or severely damaged and 6384 were damaged as a result of enemy action during the Second World War. The tn was shelled by long-range guns in France, but only minor damage was caused. Pop. 59,761.

Maidu, name of a group of 3 Indian tribes—the valley or Nisinan M., the foothill M. and the mt M.—once occupying the NE. of California, U.S.A. A few are still found in this region, while about 800 live on the Round Valley reservation. Their chief occupation is basket weaving.

See Laura Bride, *Tribes of California*, 1877; R. B. Dixon, *The Northern Maidu*, Amer. Museum of Natural Hist. (vol. xvii), 1905; R. L. Beals, *Ethnology of the Niseman*, 1933.

Maidu Language, *see* NORTH AMERICAN NATIVE LANGUAGES, *Pacific Areas*.

Maiidae, or **Maians**, spider crabs with the first pair of feet much larger than the second pair. The carapace is much longer than it is wide.

Maikop, *see* MAYKOP.

Mail Armour, fabric of interlinked metal rings used as a flexible defence against weapons, sometimes vulgarly called 'chain mail'. The origin of mail is unknown, but one finds it on Rom. sites, and it is represented on sev. Rom. monuments. It probably reached the Romans from outside the empire. In the course of the Dark Ages mail superseded the plate armour of classical times, and in the 12th and 13th cents. the feudal horseman was covered in mail from head to foot, with a mail hood (coif) for the head and neck, a sleeved hauberk or shirt of mail for the body and arms, and mail leggings. In the course of the 14th cent. there was a return to plate armour, this time of steel, but mail continued to have its uses (*see* ARMOUR). Some of the mail of the finest texture dates from the 16th cent. In oriental mail the links are often not riveted as in European mail, but the ends of each link are merely butted together. Mail constructed in this way could more easily be torn apart.

Mail was much worn in Turkey, Persia, India and, up to modern times, in the Sudan.

Mail Coaches, *see* COACH AND COACHING.

Maillol, Aristide Joseph Bonaventure (1861–1944), Fr. sculptor, *b*. Banyuls-sur-Mer in Roussillon, son of a cloth merchant and vineyard owner. Educ. at the École des Beaux Arts, he began as a painter and then took up tapestry work. In 1900 he taught himself sculpture. With his ceramics he attracted a Paris dealer, Vollard, who cast them in bronze; these sold well and M. began to exhibit in 1902. Attention abroad was attracted to him by his large figures in stone and bronze. Between 1910 and 1914 he was engaged in producing studies for the memorial to Cézanne at Aix-en-Provence. He owed much to Count Harry Kessler, for whose Cranach Press he executed wood engravings. After the First World War his large works included the war memorial for his native Banyuls. He pursued classic structure, and in that sense belonged to a period that is past; but by his own quality of workmanship he had become part of the hierarchy of sculptors whose reputation will endure. He was the first to revolt against the cloying idealism that mars Rodin's pursuit of the naturalistic. His terracottas have the directness and grace of Tanagra figurines, and the rustic beauty of the S. countryside where he spent most of his days. Among his best works are 'La Douleur', a monument to the dead, at Céret, and the great series of illustrations of Virgil's *Eclogues* which he executed for Kessler. *See* studies by O. Mirbeau, 1921; M. Denis, 1925; J. Rewald, 1939; M. Bouvier, 1945.

Maim. By the old law of England he that maimed any man, whereby he lost any part of his body, was sentenced to lose the like part of his own body. This relic of the *lex talionis* (q.v.) for long survived in Sweden, but has now disappeared from the criminal codes of all civilised nations. In common law (q.v.) it was only the loss of those limbs or members which might be useful to a man in fight that amounted to maiming, or mayhem, as it was called. It is a felony, punishable by imprisonment even to the extent of life, to wound, shoot at or cause grievous bodily harm to a person with intent to M. him. To kill, M. or wound cattle is a felony. To M. or wound any dog, bird or beast, not being cattle, is punishable summarily.

Maimacheng, vil. of Outer Mongolia situated on the Russian frontier, opposite Kiakhta, an *entrepôt* of Chinese trade with Russia.

Maimana, dist and tn in Afghanistan, Asia, 2860 ft above sea level. The tn is large, but has no important industries, its only manufs. being carpets. The pop. of 25,000 is mixed, the largest proportion being Uzbek.

Maimon, Salomon (1754–1800), Ger. philosopher, *b*. of Jewish parentage near Mir, in Polish Lithuania. He was trained in the study of the Talmud for the rabbinate, but went to Berlin to study medicine, where he was attracted by the philosophy of Maimonides (q.v.). In 1770 he pub. a commentary on that philosopher's *Moreh*

Nebuhim (or *Nebuchim*). His *Versuch über die Transzendentalphilosophie*, pub. in 1790, estab. his reputation and secured his friendship with such men as Moses Mendelssohn and Kant. His philosophy is based on that of Kant, but he owes a large debt to Hume. His *Autobiography* was pub. in 1792 (Eng. trans. by J. C. Murray, 1888). *See* S. Atlas, *From Critical to Speculative Idealism:The Philosophy of Solomon Maimon*, 1964.

Maimonides, or more properly **Moses Ben Maimon** ('the light of Israel') (1135–1204), one of the most celebrated of the Jewish rabbis, a theologian, philosopher and physician, *b.* Córdova in Spain. Owing to persecution of the Jews he removed to Fez in 1160, but afterwards travelled to Jerusalem, ultimately settling near Cairo, where he became physician to the sultan and superintendent to the Jewish communions. He won such fame as a physician that the ruler of Palestine, the lieutenant of Saladin, made him physician of his court and of Saladin's family. He even received an invitation to become the physician of Richard Cœur de Lion during his crusade, but declined as he had grown weary of wandering. His 2 great works are the *Mishneh Torah*, 1180, and the *Moreh Nebuchim*. His Thirteen Dogmas soon became, and have remained, the most popular definition of orthodox Judaism. Until his time the laws of the rabbis had never been scientifically arranged by subjects. The work of co-ordinating the laws was accomplished by M. in the *Mishneh Torah*, literally 'Repetition of the Law', which, despite criticism, has remained the most distinguished code of Jewish law. The best ed. is that printed at Amsterdam (1702, 4 vols.). His crowning achievement was his philosophical work *Moreh Nebuchim* or 'Teacher of the Perplexed', originally written in Arabic, trans. into Hebrew by his disciple, Samuel Ibn Tibbon, and into Latin by Justinian, Bishop of Nebio (Paris, 1520), and by the younger Buxtorf (Basel, 1629). *See* J. S. Minkin, *World of Moses Maimonides*, 1958. (*see Plate: Hebrew Language and Literature.*)

Main, riv. of Germany, which rises in 2 headstreams, the White M. (in the Fichtelgebirge, q.v.) and the Red M. (6 m. S. of Bayreuth, q.v.), and flows in a very winding course, generally E., to join the Rhine at Mainz). The prin. tns on its banks are Würzburg, Aschaffenburg and Frankfurt (qq.v.). It is navigable for 220 m., and is linked with the Danube, between Bamberg and Kelheim, by the Ludwigskanal. Length 310 m.

Maine, Sir Henry James Sumner (1822–88), jurist and legal historian, *b.* India. Educ. at Christ's Hospital and Pembroke College, Cambridge, in 1847 he was made regius prof. of civil law at Cambridge, and in 1852 reader in Rom. law and jurisprudence for the Inns of Court; called to the Bar in 1850. He went to India as legal member of the Indian Council, which post he held with distinction for 7 years. Appointed in 1869 Corpus prof. of jurisprudence at Oxford; became a bencher of the Middle Temple in 1881. His best-known work is

Ancient Law, 1861, new ed. by Sir E. Pollock, 1930. *See* J. Hutchinson, *Notable Middle Templars*, 1902, and W. S. Holdsworth, *Some Makers of English Law*, 1938.

Maine, most N.-easterly state of the U.S.A., known as the Pine Tree state, bounded N. and E. by the Canadian prov. of New Brunswick, W. by New Hampshire and the Canadian prov. of Quebec, and S. by the Atlantic Ocean. So greatly is the coast indented that though only some 250 m. by direct distance its windings make the actual length 2380 m. There are over 1000 wooded is., among them Grand Manon Is. containing Acadia National Park. M. was at one time overrun by the Laurentian glacier, and as a result there are innumerable lakes affording excellent fishing. The N. part of the state is hilly, the highest peak being Mt Katahdin (5268 ft). The prin. rivs. are the St John, Kennebec, Androscoggin, Penobscot, St Croix and Saco; their waters are utilised as a source of power. Moose, caribou and deer abound, so that there are good hunting and shooting. A considerable part of the state is unfit for cultivation, but in the valleys the soil is good, and farming, especially dairy and poultry farming, and market gardening are carried on. M. has the largest potato output in the U.S.A.; oats, hay, corn, buckwheat, barley and apples are also grown. Seventy-five per cent of U.S. blueberries are grown in M. Horses, cattle, sheep and pigs are reared. Granite, limestone, feldspar and slate are quarried. Fishing and the canning of fish and lumber are important industries, wood-pulp and paper-mills being the chief manufacturing products; 110,000 ac. of standing timber were destroyed by fire in 1947. M. still has 17,000,000 ac. of valuable forest land. Other manufs. are cotton and woollen goods and boots and shoes. The chief tns are Portland, the main port, pop. 72,570; Lewiston, 40,800; Bangor, 38,900; Auburn, 24,500; S. Portland, 22,800; Augusta, the cap., 21,680; Biddeford, 19,250; Waterville, 18,690. The state is governed by a Senate of 33 members and a House of Representatives of 151 members, both elected for 2 years; it sends 2 senators and 3 representatives to Congress. There is a state univ. at Orono, Bowdoin College at Brunswick, Bates College at Lewiston and Colby College at Waterville. Communications are good, there being excellent roads, some 2750 m. of railway, steam and electric, which connect with Canadian lines, and many airports.

Sir Ferdinando Gorges, regarded as the founder of M., was granted land S. of the Kennebec R. in 1622. During the Eng. Commonwealth, however, Massachusetts took possession of the dist and retained it until 1820, when M. was admitted to the Union as a separate state. The boundary was long a cause of dispute, first between Britain and France, then between Britain and the U.S.A. It was finally settled in 1842 by the Webster-Ashburton Treaty. Area 33,215 sq. m. (including 2175 of inland waters); pop. 969,270.

See Maine Historical Society's Collections

and Baxter MSS., 46 vols. (Portland), 1865–1916; L. C. Hatch, *Maine: a History*, 1919; G. Starkie, *Maine, its History, Resources and Government*, 1930; Federal Writers' Project, *Maine: a Guide 'Down East'*, 1937. (*See Plate*.)

Maine, former prov. of W. France. It formed, with Perche, a military gov. during the 16th cent. Since 1790 its ter. has been comprised in the depts of Mayenne and Sarthe and parts of Orne and Eure-et-Loir (qq.v.). Its cap. was Le Mans (q.v.). The first hereditary Count of M. was Roger (*c*. 892–*c*. 898). In 1110 M. formed part of Anjou (q.v.), but in 1154 it became an Eng. possession under Henry Plantagenet (*see* HENRY II). In 1204 it again passed into the hands of the French, and in 1246 was given to the Count of Provence. In 1328 it once more passed to the crown of France, but was given to Louis, the second son of King John II, in 1356. In 1425 it was taken by the English and lost again in 1448, returning permanently to the crown of France in 1481.

Maine de Biran (real name **Maine François Pierre Gonthier de Biran**) (1766–1824), Fr. philosopher, *b*. Bergerac, son of a physician. He early devoted himself to the study of psychology, leading a secluded life during the revolution on his patrimonial estate at Bergerac. But after the Reign of Terror he took part in political affairs, becoming in 1797 a member of the Council of Five Hundred. He was subsequently excluded from that body as a suspected royalist. In 1816 he became councillor of state. His philosophical works include the essay *Influence de l'habitude*, 1802, *L'Aperception immédiate*, 1807, and *Examen des leçons de philosophie de Laromiguière*, 1817. The first named revealed the influence of Locke and Condillac's sensualist philosophy, but M. subsequently concluded that Condillac's notion of passive receptivity in the formation of habits as the sole source of conscious experience was erroneous in both fact and method. He developed the genetic method and method and concentrated on the psychological aspect of experience, progressing from intellectualist to mystical theosophist. His chief works, which showed both metaphysical subtlety and great originality, were not pub. in his lifetime, but an incomplete collection, by Victor Cousin, appeared in 1834 and 1841, new ed. by P. Tisserand, 1920 ff. *See* A. Lang, *Maine de Biran und die neuere Philosophie*, 1901.

Maine-et-Loire, dept in France, consisting of part of the old prov. of Anjou, and named from its 2 prin. rivs. the Maine and the Loire. It is bounded N. by the depts of Mayenne and Sarthe, E. by Indre-et-Loire, S. by Vienne, Deux-Sèvres, and Vendée and W. by Loire-Atlantique, Cholet, Saumur and Segré. The hilly parts of the dept are mostly vine-growing (Saumur wines are well known), and the plains are very fertile and produce cereals, hemp and beet. The dept is renowned for its horticulture. Coal is mined near Chalonnes. The Loire crosses the dept from E. to W., and forms in its course sev. beautiful islands, The N. dists are drained by the Mayenne and its feeder the Oudon and by the Sarthe and the Authion. The Mayenne and the Sarthe unite above Angers and form the Maine, which, after a course of about 5 m. falls into the Loire S. by W. of Angers, the cap. Area 2810 sq. m.; pop. 557,000.

Mainland, sometimes called **Pomona**, largest of the Orkney Is., off the N. of Scotland, divided by Kirkwall Bay and Scapa Flow into 2 main parts (E. and W.). The name Pomona is the result of G. Buchanan's misapprehension of a Lat. text, and is never applied to the is. by Orcadians. The surface is mountainous, but has fertile tracts, and lochs abounding in trout. Stromness Harbour (W.) is the best in N. Scotland, situated N. of Hoy Sound. Between the tns of Kirkwall and Stromness are the Standing Stones of Stenness (Stennis) and Maes Howe with runic inscriptions on the wall (*see* Scott's *Pirate*). The Pictish vil. of Skara Brae is on the Bay of Skaill, 8 m. from Stromness. The chief occupations are agriculture and fishing. The climate is mild. Scapa Flow, the H.Q. of the Brit. fleet during the First World War, lies between Hoy and S. Ronaldshay, and here the surrendered part of the Ger. fleet was scuttled by von Reuter's orders, 21 June 1919. Area 150 sq. m.; pop. 14,500.

Mainotes, The, inhab. of Maina or Mani, the central peninsula of the S. Peloponnese in Greece. They claim to be pure Spartans; but there are signs of Slavonic influence in M. It is a remote area, lacking roads, rivs. and springs, and remained virtually independent under the Turks. The M. under their local chiefs, the Mavromichali, fought well in the War of Independence but their loyalties were tribal, not national. They practised the blood feud as a religious duty and were responsible for the murder of President Capodistrias in 1831. Their folklore and dialect are of great interest.

Maintenance, in criminal law, the officious intermeddling in a civil lawsuit that in no way concerns one, by *maintaining* or assisting either party with money or other material aid to prosecute or defend it. Champerty (q.v.) is a species of M. M. is a misdemeanour punishable by fine and imprisonment. *See* CHAMPERTY.

Maintenance, Cap of, in heraldry, a cap of crimson velvet turned up with ermine, which is carried before a Brit. sovereign at his or her coronation, and on other state occasions, by the hereditary bearer, the marquess of Winchester.

Maintenon, Françoise d'Aubigné, Marquise de (1635–1719), Queen of France, daughter of Constant d'Aubigné and of Jeanne de Cardillac, and granddaughter of Théodore Agrippa d'Aubigné. Françoise was *b*. in the prison of Niort, where her father, a Huguenot, was then confined. On obtaining his release, he went (1639) with his wife and daughter to Martinique, where he *d*. in 1645. Françoise and her mother then returned to France, and on her mother's death, her father's sisters placed her in a convent, where, at the age of 14, she was reluctantly converted to Rom. Catholicism. When she was 16 she met the poet Scarron, whom she married. He *d.* in 1660, and a few years afterwards she was entrusted with the education of the 2 sons whom Mme de Montespan had borne to Louis XIV. M. soon acquired an extraordinary ascendancy over the king. He made her a marquise in 1678. In 1684, after the death of the queen, Louis privately married her, and she had much influence in the selection of his ministers and generals, and probably influenced his religious policy considerably; for her Catholicism became increasingly rigid and fanatical as she grew older. When he *d.* in 1715, she retired to St Cyr, and here she *d. See* lives by C. C. Dyson, 1909; Mme Saint-René Taillandier, 1920; H. C. Barnard, 1934; *also* M. Danieliou, *Madame de Maintenon, éducatrice,* 1946.

Maintenon, Fr. tn in the dept of Eure-et-Loir, on the Eure. There is a magnificent, unfinished 17th cent. aqueduct, and the château of Mme de Maintenon (q.v.). Pop. 2100.

Mainz (Fr. **Mayence,** anct **Moguntiacum**), city of West Germany, cap. of the *Land* of Rhineland-Palatinate (q.v.). It is situated on the l. b. of the Rhine, just below the influx of the Main (qq.v.), and is a riv. port and a centre of the wine trade. It was by origin a Celtic settlement, on the site of which Drusus (q.v.) estab. a Rom. camp in 13 BC. Conrad II (q.v.) was crowned king in the cathedral in 1021, and subsequent emperors held Diets in the city. In the 13th cent. M. was the head of a confederacy of Rhenish cities, and in the 15th cent. it was the city in which Gutenberg (q.v.) set up his printing press. The small size of the type of the *Mainz Indulgence* is the first evidence of the use of metal matrices and hand moulds for casting type. During the Thirty Years War the city was in the hands of the Swedes 1631–5, and it was occupied by the Fr. in 1792, 1797–1814 and 1918–30. In 1816 it was assigned to Hessen (q.v.). Its univ. (1477–1816) was re-estab. in 1946. The splendid cathedral of M., the *Martinsdom,* was begun in 975; originally Romanesque, it has now also Gothic, Renaissance and baroque features. There are other notable churches, a palace and fine old houses. Much of the oldest part of the city was destroyed in the Second World War. Pop. 134,400.

Maiolica, name properly applied to a species of It. ware in which the earthenware body is coated with a tin-glaze, on which is laid and fired a painted decoration. The name is also used to denote similar wares made in other countries in imitation of the It. ware.

History. The name was first applied by the Italians to the lustred Sp. earthenware (*see* HISPANO-MORESQUE WARE) imported by way of Majorca. Later it was used to describe their own imitations, first made at Orvieto, of the imported ware. By about 1460 close copies were made in Tuscany, particularly at Florence and in Faenza. Large dishes painted with figure scenes were made in this imperishable medium, and the highest standard of excellence was attained in the 20 years 1505 to 1525, though M. has been made continuously up to the present day. *See*

B. Rackham, *Italian Maiolica,* 1952. *See* EARTHENWARE, *European,* and TILE.

Mair, John, *see* MAJOR, JOHN.

Mais, Stuart Petre Brodie (1885–), journalist and critic, *b.* Matlock, son of a clergyman. Educ. at Denstone College and Oxford, he was games master at various schools from 1909 to 1920, then worked as a literary critic in Fleet Street. His books of criticism include *From Shakespeare to O. Henry,* 1917, *Books and their Writers,* 1919, *Some Modern Authors,* 1923, *Books I Like* (2 series), 1932, 1934, and *The Writing of English,* 1935. He also pub. novels and a number of travel books, e.g. *Mediterranean Cruise Holiday. All the Days of My Life,* 1937, and *Buffets and Rewards,* 1952, are autobiographical.

Maisonneuve, Paul de Chomedey, Sieur de (*d.* 1676), Fr. colonial missionary and first governor of Montreal. A veteran warrior, he was chosen to be the leader of a body of devout Fr. men and women whose mission in the Iroquois country led to the founding of Montreal. With a party of only 40 men and 4 women, M. left Quebec on 8 May 1642, in a pinnace, a barge and 2 row-boats, and 10 days later reached the is. of Montreal, where he preached a sermon and raised an altar. He was governor of the settlement of Montreal for 22 years and proved a tower of strength. The tn of M., named after the sieur de M., is a manufacturing centre adjoining the city of Montreal.

Maisons-Alfort, Fr. tn in the dept of Seine, a SE. suburb of Paris. It has a veterinary school founded by Bourgelat (q.v.) in 1766. Pop. 51,200.

Maisons-Laffitte, Fr. tn in the dept of Seine-et-Oise, on the Seine. It has a racecourse and a fine château built by F. Mansard (q.v.). Pop. 19,200. (*See Plate: House.*)

Maistre, Joseph Marie, Comte de (1754–1821), Fr. publicist and philosopher, *b.* Chambéry. In 1793, on the approach of the republican armies, he fled with his prince, the King of Sardinia, but a year later he returned to Chambéry. Forced to leave Savoy, he settled at Lausanne, where he pub. his *Lettres d'un royaliste savoisien à ses compatriotes* and the *Adresse de quelques parents des militaires savoisiens à la nation française.* In 1797 he made a worldwide reputation with his book, *Considérations sur la France.* In 1803 the King of Sardinia sent him as minister-plenipotentiary to St Petersburg. Here he pub. a number of works, notably *Examen de la philosophie de Bacon,* 1817, *Du Pape,* 1819, *De l'église gallicane,* 1821, and *Soirées de St Petersbourg,* 1821. The founder of ultramontanism and an inveterate enemy of revolutionary ideas, he scourged without mercy or discrimination the 'irreligious doctrines of the 18th cent.' *See* G. Goyau, *La Pensée religieuse de Joseph de Maistre,* 1921, and F. Bayle, *Les Idées politiques de Joseph de Maistre,* 1945.

Maistre, Xavier de (1763–1852), Fr. soldier and writer, brother of the above, *b.* Chambéry. He served in the Piedmontese Army, but on the annexation of Savoy by the Fr. soldiers he took a commission in the Russian Army, in which he rose to the rank of general. He served in the Austro-Russian campaign and fought in the Caucasus. Finally he settled in St Petersburg, where he *d.* He wrote a very pleasant fantasy called *Voyage autour de ma chambre* in 1794. His subsequent works include *Le Lépreux de la cité d'Aoste*, 1811, *Les Prisonniers du Caucase*, 1825, *La Jeune Sibérienne*, 1825, *L'Expédition nocturne*, 1825, *See* A. Berthier, *Xavier de Maistre*, 1920; H. Bordeaux, *Amours de Xavier de Maistre*, 1931.

Maitland, Sir Frederic William (1850–1906), jurist and legal historian; educ. at Eton College and Trinity College, Cambridge. Called to the Bar, 1876, and practised for 8 years. Appointed reader in Eng. law at Cambridge, 1884; Downing prof. there from 1888 till his death. Founded the Selden Society for the study of Eng. law and ed. the vols. of the society (1887). His merits as a legal historian were shown in his first important work, *Bracton's Note-Book*, 1887. The work on which his reputation chiefly rests is the *History of English Law before the time of Edward I*, written in collaboration with Sir F. Pollock (2 vols.), 1895, the standard authority on the subject. Other works include *Doomsday Book and Beyond*, 1897, *Roman Canon Law in the Church of England*, 1898. *Year Books of Edward II for 1307–10* (text and trans.) (pub. in 1903–5). His lectures (1887) on the *Constitutional History of England from Edward I to the Present Time* were pub. posthumously (1908). His collected papers were ed. by H A. L. Fisher in 1911. *See* W. S. Holdsworth, *Some Makers of English Law*, 1938.

Maitland, John (and **Duke of**), *see* LAUDERDALE, EARL.

Maitland, Sir Richard (1496–1586), of Lethington, poet, lawyer and historian. He studied at St Andrews and in France, and on his return to Scotland was successively employed by James V, the Regent Arran and Mary of Lorraine. About 1551–2 he received the honour of knighthood, became a lord of the court of session in 1561 (before which, however, he had the misfortune to lose his sight) and Lord Privy Seal in 1562. All his own verses were written after his sixtieth year, and show what things he had most deeply at heart. For the most part they consist of lamentations for the distracted state of his native country, the feuds of the nobles and the discontents of the common people. A complete ed. of M.'s original poems was first pub. in 1830 (one 4to vol.) by the Maitland Club, a society of literary antiquaries formed in his honour. His collection of early Scottish poetry consists of 2 MS. vols. now in the Pepysian Library, Magdalene College, Cambridge. M.'s prin. historical performance is the *Historie and Cronicle of the Hous and Surename of Seytoun. See* W. A. Craigie (ed.), *The Maitland Folio Manuscript*, 1919.

Maitland, William (1528–73), Scottish statesman, son of Sir Richard M., Lord Lethington, known as 'Secretary Lethington'. He was educ. at St Andrews. He became secretary of state to the queen regent of Scotland in 1558, but joined the Lords of Congregation, then in arms against her. In 1560 he acted as speaker in the Convention of Estates and was sent on a mission to the Eng. court as the representative of Protestant interests in Scotland. He was secretary of state, 1561–6, being responsible for the foreign policy of Mary Queen of Scots, whom he and Moray supported in opposition to the more extreme proposals of Knox. He showed a conciliatory attitude towards England at this time and worked for the union of the 2 crowns. At first he seems to have favoured Bothwell and probably participated in the murder of Darnley, but on Bothwell's marriage with Mary he sided with the insurgents against Mary's forces at Langside. After Mary's flight to England he became the leader of her cause and formed a party of her adherents and, together with Kirkcaldy, held out in Edinburgh castle till 1573, when he surrendered. He *d.* in prison at Leith.

Maitland, tn of New S. Wales, Australia, 120 m. N. of Sydney. It is both an agric. and an industrial centre; the productivity of the alluvial lands has been much increased by irrigation plants, and various agric. products are to be found in the dist, including oranges and other citrus fruits from the Paterson R. area. There are textile mills, manufs. of bricks, tiles and pottery, engineering and locomotive workshops, etc., whilst to the S. are the world's richest coal seams. Pop. 22,917.

Maître de Moulins, *see* MASTER OF MOULINS.

Maiwand, tn in Afghanistan, situated 35 m. NW. of Kandahar, was the scene of a Brit. defeat by Ayub Khan, 27 July 1880.

Maize, or **Indian Corn** (*Zea Mays*), cereal grass with broad leaves and stout succulent stems indigenous to the Amer. continent. When ripe the valuable grains are arranged in compact rows on a rachis; they are white, yellow, red or purple in colour, very firm, and flattened at the apex. The crop is of great economic importance in the warmer parts of America, S. Europe, India and Australia. The plant is frequently grown in gardens for its ornamental effect and for the green unripened cobs which are used as the vegetable called sweet or sugar corn. It is also grown as a fodder crop. The ripe grains are fermented in S. America to produce M. beer. A meal flour known as corn meal is widely used in the U.S.A. for making corn bread which is served hot. Hominy, which is ground M. boiled in water and milk, is also widely used in the U.S.A. *See also under* AGRICULTURE IN THE U.S.A.
See over.

Majesty (Fr. *majesté*; Lat. *majestas*, grandeur, greatness, from the root *mag-*, as in *magnus*, great, *major*, greater, etc.), dignity, greatness, a term used especially to express the dignity and power of a sovereign. This application is to be traced to the use of *majestas* in Latin, to express the supreme sovereign dignity of the Rom. state, the *majestas reipublicae* or *populi Romani*: hence *majestatem laedere*, or *minuere*, was to commit high treason, *crimen majestatis*. Mommsen

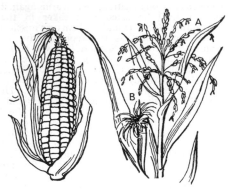

MAIZE, SHOWING COB (*left*) AND FLOWERING
SHOOT

A, male flower; B, female flower.

conjectures that the crime of *crimen majestatis* or *lèse-majesté* in earlier times related exclusively to violation of the rights of the plebs, and only later of popular rights generally. (*See* LEZE-MAJESTY.) There is, however, little evidence in support of this conjecture. In its more precise use, *crimen majestatis* was distinguished from *perduellio*, which connoted essentially acts hostile to the State, as treason and desertion, whereas *crimen majestatis* meant rather some act involving an attack on the respect due to the dignity or sovereignty whether of the people or their representative the king. Later usage, however, made no distinction between *lèse-majesté* and *perduellio*, except to assign a much lighter punishment to the former. The term M. was strictly confined in the Middle Ages to successors of the Rom. emperors in the W. Later the word was used of kings also. In England its first use is generally assigned to the reign of Henry VIII. The fullest form in Eng. use is 'Her Most Gracious M.'.

Majolica, *see* MAIOLICA.

Major, or **Mair, John** (*c.* 1469–1550), Scottish historian, *b.* near N. Berwick, studied at Cambridge and Paris, and was the teacher of John Knox and George Buchanan. In 1505 he began lecturing at the Sorbonne and in 1519 became prof. of divinity at St Andrews. He wrote in Latin treatises on divinity and morals and a *History of Greater Britain,* in which the separate hists. of England and Scotland (*Historia de Gestis Scotorum*) were brought together (pub. 1521). In his writings, while upholding the doctrinal teaching of Rome, he was outspoken in condemning the corruption of the clergy. There is a trans. of M.'s *History,* with a life of the author, by A. J. G. Mackay, 1892.

Major, commissioned army rank, between those of captain and lieutenant-colonel, and the lowest in field rank. In the Brit. and most other armies a M. acts as second-in-command to any unit commanded by a lieutenant-colonel, and also normally commands squadrons of the Royal Armoured Corps, batteries of Artillery, Infantry companies and equivalent sub-units. General Staff Officers 2nd Grade (G.S.O.2) usually hold the rank of M.

Major, in music, greater. A M. third consists of 4 semitones, e.g. C–E, a minor third of 3, e.g. C–E♭. A M. tone has the ratio 8 : 9, e.g. in the scale of C M. the interval C–D. A minor tone has the ratio 9 : 10, e.g. in the same scale the interval D–E. A M. scale consists of the following sequence of intervals (T = tone, S = semitone): T T S T T T S. On the piano the scale of C M. is played on the white keys, starting on C. All other M. scales are successions of whole tones and semitones in the same order.

Major-General, *see* GENERAL.

Majorca (Sp. **Mallorca**), largest of the Balearic Isles (q.v.), lies 107 m. SE. of the mouth of the Ebro, the nearest point of the Sp. coast, and 171 m. N. of Algiers. Its greatest length (from E. to W.) is 64 m., and its breadth (from N. to S.) 48 m. The NE. half of the is. is mountainous. The climate is healthful, the sea breeze preserving a nearly equable temp. over the whole is. The inhab., who much resemble the Catalans in their appearance and manners, are mostly employed in agriculture. The chief products of the is. are marble, coal, iron, slate, plaster, some semi-precious stones, cereals and legumes, oranges, silk, lemons, oil, wine of excellent quality, olives, figs and aromatic herbs. M. is one of the most popular tourist resorts of the Mediterranean. The chief tn is Palma (q.v.). Chopin and George Sand (qq.v.) spent Dec. to Feb. 1838–9 at the deserted Carthusian monastery of Valdemosa, near Palma. In the Sp. civil war of 1936–9 M. was held by the insurgents. Area 1310 sq. m.; pop. 400,000.

Majorian (Julius Valerius Majorianus), Rom. soldier, one of the transient emperors in the W. (457–61) appointed by Ricimer (q.v.). After a victory over the Vandals on the coast of Campania, 458, he defeated and then concluded an alliance with Theodoric the Visigoth in 460, and crossed the Pyrenees to join forces with the fleet he had concentrated at Carthagena. But the Vandal king, by corrupting some of M.'s officers, succeeded in destroying this fleet. His defeat so prejudiced his military reputation that Ricimer, with as little compunction as he had shown when he deposed Avitus (q.v.) in 456, forced M. to abdicate (461). M. committed suicide a few days later.

Majority, the age at which a person becomes legally old enough to manage his own affairs; in Eng. law 21.

Majrit, *see* MADRID.

Majsa, *see* KISKUNMAJSA.

Majuba Hill, in Natal (properly **Amajuba,** Zulu for 'hill of doves'), mt in N. Natal, part of the Drakensberg range, rising about 7000 ft above the sea, and over 2000 ft above the level of the surrounding country. It overlooks the pass through the Drakensberg known as Laingsnek, and is 8 m. S. of the Transvaal border and 18 m. N. of the tn of Newcastle. The railway from Durban to Johannesburg skirts the base of the mts. The Boers defeated the British here in 1881.

Makalla, Baggära Arabs of Semitic origin, so called from an Arabic word denoting that they are great cattle owners and breeders. They occupy the country W. of the White Nile between the Shilluk ter. and Dar Nuba, being found principally in Kordofan (q.v.) They are true nomad Arabs. having intermarried little with the Nuba (q.v.) and having preserved most of their national characteristics.

Makalla, or **Mokalla,** port of Arabia, 300 m. NE. of Aden, the prin. port of Hadhramaut. M., together with Shihr and dependencies, is under one sultan, who is in treaty relations with Britain, his tribesmen being part of the Aden protectorate. Pop. 18,000.

Makalu, Himilayan mt in E. Nepal, 12 m. SE. of Everest; height 27,790 ft. It is the world's fifth highest mt. In 1955 it was climbed by a Fr. expedition led by Jean Franco, and for the first time in the hist. of high Himalayan climbing all 8 members reached the summit.

Makarios III Mouskou, Archbishop of Nova Justiniana and All Cyprus (1913–), *b.* in a vil. in W. Cyprus. As a deacon he spent 5 years in Greece and 3 at Kykko monastery in Cyprus. After being ordained priest he studied at Boston Univ., U.S.A., for 2 years. In 1948 he became Metropolitan of Kition (Citium) in Cyprus, and in 1950 succeeded Makarios II as archbishop. He was an uncompromising partisan of *enosis*, the union of Cyprus with Greece, and in 1954 visited Britain, the U.S.A. and Greece to agitate for this cause. In 1956 he was accused by the Brit. of collaborating with EOKA, and deported to the Seychelles. He was freed in 1957, and after the Zürich and London agreements of 1959 (*see* CYPRUS, *History*) he was elected president of the independent republic of Cyprus, receiving twice as many votes as his left-wing opponent. M.'s suggestion that Cyprus might unilaterally abrogate the 1959 agreements touched off a new conflict between Gks and Turks in Cyprus, Dec. 1963, which led eventually to U.N. intervention. *See* S. Mayes, *Cyprus and Makarios*, 1960.

Makart, Hans (1840–84), Austrian painter, *b.* Salzburg, son of an inspector of the imperial castle. He became a fashionable decorative painter in Vienna but in a florid style borrowed from Veronese and others which is now little esteemed.

Makassar, or **Macassar,** tn of S. Sulawesi, Indonesia; exports coffee, teak and vegetable oils. M. has an airport and is the terminus of submarine cables to Java and Borneo. Pop. 384,000.

Makassar, Strait of, separates the is. of Sulawesi and Borneo. It was the scene of prolonged naval operations in 1942. *See* NAVAL OPERATIONS IN THE SECOND WORLD WAR.

Make-up, *see* COSMETICS.

Make-Up, Theatrical. Stage M. can, broadly speaking, be divided into straight M. and character M. The first is designed to enhance the actor's natural features, and to counteract the effect of stage lighting. Some form of straight M. was no doubt in use from earliest times, except

where masks were used, as in the Gk and Rom. theatre and in the comic roles of the *commedia dell' arte* (q.v.), and the normal beauty aids of the fashionable lady would serve to strengthen the appeal of actresses and the boy-players of Elizabethan times. It was the introduction of gas, and later electric, lighting that intensified the use of such aids, which were basically in powder form mixed with water or some kind of grease. Modern M. dates from the invention by Ludwig Leichner, a Wagneran opera-singer, in about 1865 of the round sticks of numbered and coloured paints with a grease base which are in general use today. There has been some change since the abolition of the footlights and the prevalence of arena theatre with overhead lighting, but basically a straight M. continues to add to or subtract from an actor's looks without altering his features, though grease paints are now being replaced by pancake M. applied with a sponge.

Character M. is, on the contrary, a disguise, and includes materials for altering the shape of a nose, blacking out teeth, rounding out cheeks, simulating wrinkles or scars, adding false hair for beards and moustaches, and colouring to simulate Negro or Far Eastern pigmentation. Character M. is an art which must be learned by trial and error (though there are some books on the subject) and some actors excel at it. In the theatre actors usually do their own M. but the requirements of film and television M. are so specialised, and alter so rapidly, that a M. expert is employed who often shows a high degree of skill. *See* N. E. B. Wolters, *Modern Make-Up for Stage and Screen*, 1935; R. Carson, *Stage Make-Up*, 1961.

Makerere College, *see* EAST AFRICA, THE UNIVERSITY COLLEGE OF.

Makeyevka (until early 1930s **Dmitriyevsk**), city in the Donets basin (q.v.), in the Donetsk oblast (prov.) of the Ukraine. It is situated 8 m. E. of Donetsk, forming a part of Donetsk conurbation, and is one of the most important industrial centres of the Donets basin. It has large iron and steel, chemical and coal-mining industries. M. was founded in 1899 to provide accommodation for the builders and workers of the iron and steel plant which was built in 1898–1900, and has been constantly expanded since, except for the periods of the Russian Civil War, the Ger. occupation (1941–3) and the subsequent periods of restoration. M.'s rapid growth in the 1930's was partly due to the absorption of neighbouring settlements. Pop. (1965) 399,000 (1926, 51,000; 1939, 240,000).

Makhachkala (until 1921 **Petrovsk-Port**), tn in the Caucasus, cap., economic and cultural centre of Daghestan (q.v.) Autonomous Rep., and a Caspian Sea port. It has engineering (aircraft), oil-refining (pipeline from Groznyy), textile and fish-canning industries. M. was founded as a Russian fort in 1844, and became a tn in 1857. It was made cap. of Daghestan in 1921. Pop. (1965) 152,000 (1926, 34,000; 1939, 87,000), mostly Russians and Kumyks (q.v.).

Makhno, Nestor Ivanovich (1889–1935),

Ukrainian Anarchist leader. Imprisoned for terrorism in 1907, he was released after the February Revolution (q.v.) of 1917. During the civil war (q.v.) he organised a band of followers in S. Ukraine which attracted many peasants who were against both the Red and the White sides. M.'s raids were invariably accompanied by great violence and, despite his condemnation of anti-Semitism, pogroms. In 1919 and 1920 he allied himself for a time with the Red Army and his movement were legalised on Soviet Ter. But a new conflict soon broke out between the Red Army and M.'s band, and he was defeated. He then emigrated. *See* D. Footman, *Nestor Makhno*, St Antony's Papers, No. 6, Soviet Affairs, No. 2, 1959.

Makó, tn of Hungary, in Csongrád co., on the Maros (q.v.), 18 m. SE. of Hódmezövásárhely (q.v.). It is in an agric. dist and is famous for its onions. Pop. 29,900.

Makran, dist in the S. of the Persian prov. of Baluchistan, bounded S. by the Sea of Oman.

Makronisi, Gk islet in the Aegean Sea, between Ceos and Attica.

Makrygiannēs, *see* GREEK LITERATURE, *Modern.*

Malabar, name generally, and somewhat inaccurately, applied to the whole SW. coast of India S. of Mangalore. It should more strictly cover the area where the Malayalam language is spoken. The term Kerala is taking its place.

Malabar Christians, *see* NESTORIUS.

Malabon, tn of Luzon, Philippines. It produces fruit, rice and sugar, and also mills sugar. Pop. *c.* 50,000.

Malaca, *see* MÁLAGA.

Malacca: 1. A state of the Federation of Malaysia, formerly one of the Straits Settlements and subsequently part of Malaya. From 1511 until modern times it continued to be a possession of one or other of the European powers (*see further under* MALAYA, *History*). The word (Malay *Melaka*) is the name of a species of jungle fruit, and it also gives name to the strait which divides the Malay Peninsula from Sumatra. The chief products are rubber and tin. Area 640 sq. m.; pop. 355,000.

2. Cap. of above, a seaport on a small like-named riv., on the r. b. of which the old Dutch tn stands, connected with the business quarter òn the other side by a bridge. In anct times M. was important as a port, but it is now used only by small craft. There is a training college for women teachers. Pop. 45,000.

Malachi, last of the minor prophets, about whom nothing more is known. The actual existence of a prophet of that name seems doubtful. The Septuagint has in 1.i. 'by the hand of his messenger'; the Targum has 'by the hand of Malachi (or, "of my messenger"), whose name is Ezra the scribe'. The prophecy belongs to the age of Ezra and Nehemiah, when Judah was a Persian prov. and after the rebuilding of the temple. A comparison of the book with Ezra and Nehemiah shows much similarity of subject-matter, especially in the strong condemnations of intermarriage with the heathen

and laxity in the payment of the priestly dues. M. further prophesies the purification of the priesthood by the Messiah. *See* W. E. Barnes, *Haggai, Zechariah and Malachi*, 1917; E. A. Annett, *The Hidden Centuries: Malachi to Matthew*, 1926.

Malachite, mineral consisting of basic cupric carbonate $CuCO_3$. $Cu(OH)_2$. It has a fine green colour; it generally occurs massive, with a mammillated, reniform or botryoidal surface. It is occasionally found as dark green monoclinic crystals, and when associated with limonite in compact fibrous or earthy masses (hardness $3\frac{1}{2}$, sp. gr. 3·9–4·0). It is found in great quantity in Siberia, and the finer quality is used for making ornaments, mosaic, etc., as it takes a fair polish. It also occurs in Russia, Australia, Arizona, etc., and is smelted with other minerals.

Malachite Green, brilliant green dye derived from coal-tar. It is a double salt, consisting of the chlorides of zinc and tetramethyldiaminotriphenyl carbinol. M. G. Dyes silk and wool without any previous preparation of the material, but cotton requires to be mordanted with tannin and tartar emetic. It is not very fast to light, and much more valuable green dyes are now known (*see* DYE).

Malachy, St, or **Malachy O'Morgair** (1094–1148), Irish prelate, *b.* Armagh. At an early age he placed himself under the tutelage of a recluse named Imac, whose cell became the nucleus of a monastery. Ordained priest at the age of 25, he preached among the poor, and having learnt the anct rule of Celtic monasticism from Malchi, Bishop of Lismore, he was elected abbot of Bangor. He was later bishop of Connor, but on the ruin of that tn by the King of Ulster he returned to Armagh, of which he was elected archbishop in 1127. Resigning in 1135 he re-estab. the see of Connor, and then went to live in Down, where he founded a new diocese. In 1148 he set out for Rome to confer with Pope Eugenius III on the needs of the Irish Church, but *d.* at Clairvaux in the arms of St Bernard (q.v.), who wrote his life.

Malacology (from Gk *malakos*, soft; *logos*, discourse), science which is concerned with soft-bodied invertebrates and particularly molluscs.

Malacopterygii, Cuvier's name for an order of fishes in which the rays of the fins are soft and cartilaginous and not pointed at the extremities. The Salmonidae (salmon and trout family) are examples.

Malacostraca, that div. of the Crustacea which includes the higher forms such as crabs, lobsters, shrimps, woodlice and sand-hoppers. The remaining species are placed in the div. Entomostraca, and include the barnacles, water 'fleas', etc.

Málaga: 1. Sp. prov., in Andalucia (q.v.), with a coastline on the Mediterranean. It is mountainous, reaching 7000 ft in some places. The lowlands, and particularly the coastal plain, are very fertile and have a temperate climate, They produce oranges, sugarcane, melons, pomegranates, cotton and M. wine (q.v.). Area 2813 sq. m.; pop. 775,300.

2. (anct **Malaca**) Sp. tn, cap of the prov. of M., on the Mediterranean, at the mouth of the Guadalmedina. It was founded by the Phoenicians (*see* PHOENICIA), and under the Moors was a great seaport and for a time the cap. of a kingdom dependent on Granada (q.v.). Ferdinand II (q.v.) and Isabella took it in 1487. In 1656 it was attacked by the English, and in 1810 it was sacked by the French. M. has a 16th cent. Renaissance cathedral and a beautiful 15th cent. Gothic church, the Sagrario. Tobacco, textiles, pottery and sugar are manuf., and there is a trade in wine, fruits and raisins. Pop. 301,000.

Málaga Wine, grown in the Axarquia dist of the prov. of Granada from the Pedro Ximenez grape (called **P.X.** at Jerez where its wine is used for the sweetening of the finest sherries), is a very sweet and delicate dessert wine. Its colour and flavour are a small dose of *vino tierno* or *maestro*, i.e. wine slightly boiled down. The *lagrima* of Malaga is a quintessence of the grapelike Tokay (q.v.) essence, being fermented from the 'tears' (as its name denotes) which drip unpressed from ripe bunches of muscatel grapes. *See* P. Morton Shand, *A Book of Wine*, 1921; H. Warner Allen, *A History of Wine*, 1961.

Malagasy, indigenous inhab. of the is. of Madagascar (q.v.). They are mainly of Malay origin, although in the NW. there are sev. tribes of Negro stock, mostly immigrants from the Comoro Is. The M. are divided into many distinct tribes. Before Fr. occupation, the most powerful tribe of the central plateau was the Hova, ruled over by their queen. Other important M. tribes are the Antaisaka, Antandroy, Bara, Betsileo, Manja, Merina and Tanala. *See* J. Faublee, *L'Ethnographie de Madagascar*, 1946; O. Mannoni, *Prospero and Caliban*, 1956.

Malagasy Republic, formerly **Madagascar** and a Fr. colony which became independent within the Fr. community on 4 April 1960. The fifth largest is. in the world lying 250 m. off the coast of Mozambique, E. Africa, from which it is separated by the Mozambique Channel. The interior is traversed by a mt range (rising in some places to over 10,000 ft) which lies parallel to the E. coast, making the descent to the sea very abrupt. On the W. and SW. are wide grassy plains. Numerous rivs. flow E. and W., none of them of much use for navigation. Extinct volcanoes and hot springs are found in various parts of the is., the highest peak being Ankaraba (over 9000 ft) in the NE. The coast is remarkably unindented, and the chief harbours are Tamatave, Majunga, Tulear and Diego Suarez which is an important Fr. naval base. M. contains some magnificent scenery.

Vegetation is luxuriant, and the is. is ringed round the coast with dense forests which supply valuable timber, such as ebony, palms, gums and rubber trees. Many rare varieties of orchids and ferns are found, and a peculiar feature is the traveller's tree (*Ravenala madagascariensis*). Fruits abound, and include mangoes, tamarinds, bananas, lemons, bread-fruit and ground-nuts; and coffee, cocoa, sugar-cane,

hemp and vanilla are cultivated to a considerable extent. The climate is salubrious for about half the year in the central plateau where lies the cap., but during the rainy season it is unhealthy for Europeans. The E. and N. coasts are very wet, the S. and W. of the is. very dry. The highest mean temp. (80°) occurs at Diego-Suarez, and the average rainfall is about 28 in., but it may exceed 40 in., while in the S. are waterless deserts. Hurricanes and thunderstorms are prevalent and severe. There are many minerals, including gold, but they are not greatly exploited. Minerals which figure prominently in the exports are graphite, mica and uranothorianite. Other exports, in order of importance, are coffee, sugar, sisal, vanilla, rice, tobacco, cloves, ground-nuts and raffia.

Cattle do well but do not yet figure prominently as an export. Total exports (1964): Frs. FMG 22,653,500,000. Total imports: Frs. FMG 33,451,600,000.

Communications. There are 10,000 m. of all-weather roads and 6000 which are not usually in use during the rainy season. Public motor services are extensive. In addition there are 4 railways linking Tananarive with Tamatave, 229 m., another Fianarantoa with the E. coast, 101 m., and Tananarive to Antsirabe, 99 m. A line goes to Lake Alaotra, 105 m., branching off between Tananarive and Tamatave.

Fauna. This includes many curious animals, such as the aye-aye and lemur, but is devoid of the larger carnivora. There are over 240 species of birds, many of brilliant plumage, and also sev. varieties of chameleons. Fossils of extinct animals, birds and reptiles have been found, including the Aepyornis, Mullerornis, hippopotami and a gigantic dinosaur.

Population. In 1962 the pop. was estimated at 5,670,000 of whom some 74,000 were French or other European origin. There are sev. distinctive tribes including the Sihhanakas, Ibaras, Betsileos and the Sakalavas. There is no certainty as to where they originated, but fossil remains prove that M. was at one time a part of Africa. There are others like the Hova, who number 900,000, whose language is a *lingua franca* and who, through their language and customs, are definitely identified with the Malayan and Oceanic people. To Alfred Grandidier (1836–1921) most of our knowledge of M. is due. He explored it thoroughly, 1865–70, and his great treatise *Histoire physique, naturelle et politique de Madagascar* (1875–1930) remains the standard work on the is.

History. M. was known to Ptolemy under the name of Menuthias, and traces of an Arab occupation are evident today in the Malagasy language. Marco Polo mentioned M., but the first known European to land on its shores was Diaz, the Portuguese, who visited the is. in 1500. Later the Dutch and then the French estab. small ports in different parts of the country, which was ultimately brought under Fr. control in 1896, when it was known as Madagascar. Some unsuccessfully conceived attempts were made by Brit. expeditions to settle in the is.

during the seventeenth cent. King Rainilaiari-vony wanted to prevent annexation by the French, and with the aid of Brit. officers armed and trained a body of native levies. But these efforts proved abortive, and the Fr. protector-ate, first estab. in 1885, became perpetual. Queen Ranavalona III, last sovereign of Mada-gascar, was deposed and exiled to Algeria, where she *d.* in 1917. She had reigned since 1883. The is. was occupied by the Brit. to forestall Vichy collaboration with the Gers., May–Sept. 1942, but the Fr. resumed the administration after the Second World War. In 1947 there was a nationalist uprising against the Fr., which caused widespread damage and loss of life. In 1958 Madagascar became a member of the Fr. Community, and in 1960 an independent republic, adopting the name of M.

M. is divided into 5 provs., and each is under a prov. administrator-in-chief. It is represented in the National Assembly by 5 deputies, by 5 senators in the Council of the Rep., and by 7 councillors in the Assembly of the Fr. Union. Natives are employed in minor posts in both military and civil gov. Education is now compulsory between the ages of 8 and 14.

See A. and C. Grandidier, *Histoire physique, naturelle et politique de Madagascar* (24 vols.), 1875–1930; *Collection des ouvrages anciens concernant Madagascar*, pub. under the direc-tion of A. Grandidier, C. Roux, C. Delhorbe and others (9 vols., the first seven of which contain the works of or citations from Fr., Portuguese, Brit., etc., writers or travellers, and the eighth and ninth Flacourt's hist. of the is. and the narrative of François Martin (1665–8), 1920; A. Dandouan, *Géographie de Madagas-car*, 1922; J. Sibree, *Fifty Years in Madagascar*, 1924; H. Paulin, *Madagascar*, 1925; H. Rusillon, *Un Petit Continent, Madagascar*, 1933; Sir J. Fraser (ed. by R. A. Downie), *Native Races of Africa and Madagascar*, 1938; Olive Chapman, *Across Madagascar*, 1943; *Mada-gascar Encyclopédie*, 2 vols., 1947; H. Des-champs, *Histoire de Madagascar*, 1960. (*See* Plate.)

Malahide, coastal tn 12 m. NE. of Dublin (q.v.), Rep. of Ireland. It is a beauty spot, with a fine view of the Dublin and Wicklow Mts across the Fingal Plain. It has 2 golf-links, 9 and 18 holes. Pop. 2534.

Malaita, is. of the Brit. Solomon Is. protec-torate, lying SE. of the large is. Ysabel, being crossed in the centre by lat. 9° S. and long. 161° E. Area 2396 sq. m. It was named Ramos by the Spaniards, whose explorer, Mendana, visited the Solomons in 1595. Cape Astrolabe at the N. end of the is. is named after one of 2 Fr. frigates under the command of the ill-fated La Pérouse, who came to the is. 20 years after Mendana and was wrecked off Vanikoro Is. M. is the most densely populated of all the Solomons (pop. estimated at 50,000, mainly Melanesians). The people fall into 2 classes. The 'salt-water men' live on the coast, where they fish and grow food crops; many live on coral islets and in 2 lagoons; artificial islets have been built on the reefs. The 'bush-men' live in the interior where they cultivate gardens skilfully cleared from the jungle. Most of the plantation labour force in the protectorate comes from M. The M. dist of the Brit. Solomon Is. Protectorate has its H.Q. at Auki, and comprises the is. of M. and Small M. with adjacent islets. *See* SOLOMON ISLANDS.

Malakand, pass lying N. of Peshawar in W. Pakistan. It extends from the valley of Kabul to that of the Swat R. Dargai is at the mouth of the pass. In 1897 the Swats attacked the Brit. frontier post here and this led to the M. expedition of that year. A large hydro-electric plant has now been installed.

Malakoff, Fr. tn in the dept of Seine, a SW. suburb of Paris. It has an important institute for electrical research, and manufs. textiles and chemicals. Pop. 33,600.

Malalas, or **Malelas, Johannes,** Byzantine chronicler of the 6th cent., was probably of Syrian origin, but little is known of his life. He wrote a universal hist., from the creation to the reign of Justinian, which was trans. into Latin by Edmund Chilmead (*d.* 1653) and first pub., ed. by Hody, in 1691. *See* R. C. Jebb, *Bentley* (Eng. Men of Letters), 1882.

Malan, Daniel François (1874–1959), S. African statesman, *b.* Riebeek West, Cape Prov.; educ. at Victoria College, Stellenbosch, and at Utrecht Univ. Dutch Reformed minister; then elected member for Calvinia in Hertzog's National party gov., in which he became minister of the interior, health and education, 1924–33. He later led the National party which stood for an independent S. African rep. Opposed the Union's entry into the Second World War, and joined forces with Hertzog (q.v.) in Jan. 1940 to combat Smuts's policy of imperial co-operation in war. At this time his party held only 28 seats (out of 150) in the House of Assembly. His advent to power in 1948 was somewhat unexpected; but a significant devel-opment before that election was a party pact between M. as leader of the Nationalist party and Havenga as leader of the Afrikaner party. The general election of May resulted in the defeat of Smuts, who even lost his own seat, and M. on 3 June formed a new cabinet, which included the Afrikaner party leader. Under M., despite his early statements, S. Africa remained within the Commonwealth. He was a staunch supporter of *apartheid*, and on his accession to power his gov. took steps to place the Cape coloured (mixed blood) voters on a separate electors' roll. M. resigned the premiership in Nov. 1954 and was followed by Strijdom (q.v.), and in 1955 retired from politics.

Malapropism, ludicrous misuse of a word, especially in mistake for one resembling it. The term derives from Mrs Malaprop, a character in Sheridan's play *The Rivals* who prided herself on 'a nice derangement of epitaphs' (meaning 'arrangement of epithets'). Her name in turn was taken from the Fr. *mal à propos* ('out of place'). Sheridan was not the first to use this mannerism in a comic character; Dogberry, in Shake-speare's *Much Ado About Nothing*, declares that 'comparisons are odorous' and that his men 'have comprehended two aspicious persons'. M. may sometimes be used jokingly, as when a girl speaks of her fiancé as 'my fiasco', or says that her aunt is in 'a home for indignant gentlewomen'. But they may also arise from involuntary confusion or ignorance; words like 'complacent' and 'complaisant', 'deprecate' and 'depreciate', 'luxuriant' and 'luxurious' are often so confused.

Malapterurus, genus of fish typified by *M. electricus*, the electric catfish, found in the fresh water of tropical Africa. The electric organ lies beneath the skin and is thickest on the abdomen but extends over the whole body.

Malaria (from It. *mala*, bad; *aria*, air), infectious disease caused by specific protozoa which are transmitted by the bite of mosquitoes of the genus *Anopheles*, and characterised by periodic fever, enlargement of the spleen and the presence of the protozoa in the blood. The names remittent, intermittent, tertian, quartan fever, etc., are given to forms characterised by particular kinds of periodicity. The paroxysms comprise cold, hot and sweating stages, which recur in that order. If there is an interval of normal conditions between the paroxysms, the fever is known as *intermittent*; if the symptoms are merely ameliorated for a time, the fever is called *remittent*. If the paroxysms recur daily the fever is designated *quotidian*; if on alternate days, *tertian*; if 2 days elapse between paroxysms, *quartan*. If 2 paroxysms occur in a day, the fever is called *double quotidian*. The quotidian form usually occurs in the morning, the tertian at noon, the quartan in the afternoon. There are 4 recognised species of human M. parasite: *Plasmodium vivax*, the parasite of benign tertian M.; *P. falciparum*, the parasite of malignant tertian M.; *P. ovale*, the parasite causing a very mild form of tertian M.; and *P. malariae*, the parasite of quartan M. *P. vivax* has the most extensive distribution. *P. falciparum* is common in most tropical and subtropical countries, and is associated with the great regional epidemics which occur from time to time in India, Ceylon and elsewhere. *P. malariae* occurs in most regions, and *P. ovale* has the most restricted distribution of all. It was in 1894 that Sir Patrick Manson put forward the 'mosquito-M.' theory. He suggested that flagellating bodies were set free in the stomach of a mosquito and that these gained access to water through the insects drowning in it and that man acquired infection by imbibition of water. A vital discovery was made in 1897 by Sir Ronald Ross (q.v.), who found pigmented bodies (oöcysts) in the stomach wall of 'dapple-winged' mosquitoes bred from larvae; and in 1898–9 Koch and Pfeiffer confirmed Ross's findings in birds as applicable to human M. Continued research since Manson's and Ross's epochmaking discoveries has estab. that the reproductive cycle of the M. parasite occurs in 2 phases: (1) the endogenous or asexual cycle, which takes place in man, and (2) the exogenous or sexual cycle, which takes place in the mosquito. The endoge-

nous cycle starts with the inoculation of sporozoites into a human being from an infected mosquito. The sporozoites disappear from the bloodstream of the host a few minutes after inoculation and go through an exo-erythrocytic (i.e. outside the red blood corpuscles) stage of development in the tissues. After about 7 days parasites appear in the red blood corpuscles. Here the asexual forms (trophozoites) increase in size and take on an amoeboid-like form. The trophozoite then divides within itself into 2 or 4 or more portions and is then known as the schizont. The mature schizont consists of a variable number of young forms (generally 8 to 16) known as merozoites. The merozoites escape into the plasma and invade other red blood corpuscles, restarting the cycle over again. It is during the stage of the escape of the merozoites that the M. symptoms are most acute. In addition to the asexual reproduction of merozoites by schizogony, certain sexual forms known as gametocytes are also liable to appear in the blood corpuscles following a bout of M. fever. When a human whose blood corpuscles are infected with gametocytes is bitten by a mosquito, the insect sucks in and swallows some of the blood cells. In due course these rupture in the insect's body and liberate the gametocytes. The exogenous, or sexual, reproductive cycle of the parasite then begins. First the male gametocytes produce flagella (microgametes) which break off and penetrate the female gametocytes (macrogametes). The resulting body, known as a zygote, penetrates the stomach wall and forms what is called an oöcyst within the body cavity of the mosquito. The oöcyst, which becomes packed with sickle-shaped sporozoites, subsequently ruptures and the sporozoites escape and make their way to the mosquito's salivary glands. From thence they are transferred to a human host and the chain of events is completed. The exogenous, sexual cycle takes about 8 to 20 days. As may be imagined, the facts of the life hist. of the M. parasite, set out here in a few lines, took years of patient research by doctors and entomologists, and their discovery, from Manson onwards, represents one of science's greatest gifts to mankind. It was only recently that the exo-erythrocytic stage of the endogenous cycles was proved, although long suspected. Application of the knowledge of the life cycle of the parasite is all important in treatment, which aims at bringing drugs lethal to the organism into contact with it at a time when they will be most effective.

After the cause of M. and the life-hist. of the organism were known, the quantitative investigation of M. as an epidemic disease was first attempted in the Punjab by S. R. Christophers in 1908. Results of this show that as an epidemic disease M. may be localised or regional. Mild localised epidemics may be due to seasonal recurrence of M.; severe ones may occur amongst non-immune forces or labour gangs in foreign countries. The so-called 'pandemics' of M. are best regarded as regional epidemics, for they were probably due to seasonal recrudescence of the disease, and what appeared to be the diffusibility characteristic of pandemics was due to the recrudescence beginning at different times in different individuals.

There are 3 recognised zones of malarial distribution: temperate, i.e. between 40° and 60° N., where the benign tertian is the prevailing form (in the corresponding zone in the S. hemisphere M. is uncommon); subtropical (between 40° N. and 40° S.), where subtertian and benign tertian are both common, the former being epidemic in autumn; and tropical, where subtertian predominates.

The prevention of M. was first concerned with the extinction of the mosquito. Mosquito-nets are useful as a means of defence if the meshes be sufficiently fine, but permanently healthy conditions can be estab. only by preventing the reproduction of the mosquito responsible for the infection. The life-hist. of the mosquito comprises stages as ovum, larva, pupa and insect. The ova are deposited on the surface of still or slowly moving water, the larvae and pupae also float about on the water, and the complete insect may be developed within 30 days of the deposition of the ova. The partial or complete extinction of the insect was attempted by throughly draining off all stagnant surface waters, and by stocking water with fish and other carnivorous animals that will devour the larvae. A thin film of oil was spread on the water to suffocate larvae and pupae, for neither can breathe under water. Even if the insect is suppressed only for a time, the cycle of existence of the parasite may be broken and the mosquito itself is thus rendered comparatively harmless. *Anopheles maculipennis*, or the speckled-wing mosquito, still flourishes in England, and at the outbreak of the First World War was not acting as a carrier of M. organisms, although it was associated with the disease in other parts of Europe and in America. After the return of infected soldiers to England, these species of *Anopheles* carried infection from man to man, and there is always the possibility of M. being spread in this way by insects previously uninfected. But early attempts to eradicate M. by destruction of larvae were, with a few notable exceptions, disappointing. For one thing they involved too much recurring work. Later on better results were obtained by 'species control', that is by studying the individual and peculiar habits of the different anophelines. In this way it often proved possible to devise a simple but effective measure which could be applied without having recourse to the more expensive and laborious blunderbuss methods. The most important advances, however, have been made in the materials used for the destruction of larvae. D.D.T. dissolved in oil (1 gallon will treat the same area of water as 10 to 20 gallons of plain oil) is now applied by hand-sprayer or, on a large scale, by aircraft. D.D.T. sprayed on the walls and roofs of dwellings has also proved effective in the destruction of adult mosquitoes. By attacking both larvae and adults with these modern methods it has been possible in places to exterminate the entire mosquito pop.

'Many drugs have been employed in the treatment of malarial disease, and many drugs have some influence on it; all sink into insignificance in comparison with quinine.' These words of Manson's, written in 1900, remained unchallenged for many years. Quinine still holds its own as a schizonticide, but it was found to be unsuccessful as a prophylactic and had little effect in countering massive infections. This was found to be particularly so during the M. outbreak in Macedonia during the First World War. It failed to produce radical cure in benign tertian (*vivax*) M., and it did not destroy the gametocytes of *P. falciparum*. In the last 35 years a number of new, synthetic, antimalarial drugs have been discovered which have a wider range of action than quinine. Pamaquin, mepacrine, chloroquine, paludrine and proguanil all have their uses and advantages. Mepacrine is outstanding in the prevention of M. and is able to suppress massive infecting doses of sporozoites. Its regular administration to troops in the S.-W. Pacific campaign in the Second World War had a vital influence, as M. infections were negligible. Proguanil and paludrine are also effective suppressants, but unfortunately there are indications that long administration of proguanil for prophylactic purposes may lead to the emergence of strains of falciparum infection resistant to the drug. J. S. K. Boyd has written: 'It may now be claimed that ways and means have been discovered by which mosquitoes, and hence malaria, can be eradicated; by which infection can be suppressed when eradication is impossible or impracticable; and by which attacks of malaria can be cured when suppression has been faulty or when suppressive drugs are withdrawn. The major problems of malaria are now administrative rather than medical.' Nevertheless M. remains the most important of tropical diseases and there is no room for any relaxation in the continued and intensive measures for its eradication. It may well be that resistant strains of protozoa will become more numerous, and there are already signs that the mosquito is becoming resistant to D.D.T. If this is estab., a search for new and better insecticides will have to be made. In 1955 the World Health Organisation constituted a World Fund for M. eradication to receive contributions from govs. and private sources for research and to provide equipment, supplies and services for M. control and eradication. By 1963 half the pop. of India had been freed from M., and similar progress had been made in the Middle E. and Pacific Areas. *See also* BACTERIA; ENTOMOLOGY; EPIDEMIOLOGY.

See Sir R. Ross, *Memoirs*, 1923, and *Studies on Malaria*, 1928; L. W. Hackett, *Malaria in Europe*, 1937; W. Herms and H. Gray, *Mosquito Control* (2nd ed.), 1944; W. N. Bispham, *Malaria: its Diagnosis, Treatment and Prophylaxis*, 1944; J. F. Marshall, *Report on the Proceedings of the Hayling Mosquito Control*; Survey of Expert Committee on Malaria, W.H.O., 1947; J. S. K. Boyd, article on tropical medicine in *Fifty Years of Medicine* (ed. H. Clegg), 1950; Manson's *Tropical Diseases* (14th ed.), 1954.

Malaspina Glacier, Alaska, N. America, is one of the world's largest ice sheets; it lies W. of Yakutat Bay and is part of the St Elias Mts glacier system.

Malatesta, It. family who ruled Rimini with intermissions from the 13th to the 16th cent. Rimini, defeated by Cesena, took the desperate course of granting citizenship to 2 members of the powerful M. tribe, Giovanni and Malatesta, in order to secure their military aid. The M. family thereupon settled in Rimini, Giovanni being made *podestà* (1237), the initial step to the sovereign power afterwards consolidated by his descendants. During the struggles of the Guelphs and Ghibellines the M. succeeded in becoming masters and tyrants of Rimini. Giovanni *d*. in 1247 and was succeeded by his son M., surnamed M. da Verruchio (1212–1312), who consolidated the position of his house. He was a determined foe of the Ghibellines, and led the Guelphs back in triumph to Rimini. The Pope (Boniface VIII), while conscious of the threatened rights of the holy see, preferred to maintain good relations with a *condottiere* who had restored the Guelphs in the Romagna, and in 1299 conferred high honours on M. This tyrant had 4 sons: Malatestino, Giovanni the Lame, Paolo the Handsome and Pandolfo, but only the eldest and youngest survived him. Giovanni the Lame, in return for his military help to Giovanni da Polenta of Ravenna, was given the hand of the latter's daughter, known to hist. and poetry as Francesca da Rimini (q.v.). Malatestino succeeded his father as lord of Rimini, and on his death (1317) power devolved on Pandolfo, who *d*. in 1326, leaving 2 heirs: M. and Galeotti. M. tried to aggrandise his small principality by force of arms and treachery, but it was devastated at the instance of Pope Innocent VI, and thereafter M. ruled in subordination to the papal see. He was then granted Pesaro, which later devolved on his descendants: Carlo and Galeazzo. Sigismondo M. (*c*. 1417–68) received the state of Rimini by bequest of his brother, Galeotto (1411–32), an ascetic who *d*. early. Sigismondo is the splendid and tragic personage to whom Rimini owes its renown during the Renaissance. A patron of art and letters and a soldier, he was excommunicated (1460) for waging war on the Pope, Pius II. Sigismondo was eventually defeated by the papal forces, and deprived of all his possessions save Rimini; but, his power having been broken, the sentence of excommunication was withdrawn. His descendant, Pandolfo (called Pandolfaccio in allusion to his evil character), sold his rights in Rimini to Venice (1503), an arrangement of which Pope Julius II so strongly disapproved that he marched against and crushed the Venetians (1509) and became master of Rimini. Pandolfo made sev. attempts to regain his city from him but in vain, for his former subjects preferred the papal regime and Pandolfo *d*. in poverty (1534). From that time the M. became citizens of Venice.

Malatesta, Enrico (1853–1932), It. anarchist and revolutionary, *b*. Santa Maria Catua Vetere. He was a friend and pupil of Bakunin (q.v.) and in 1872 joined the International Socialists. M. founded the reviews *Volunta* and *La Révolte* and the London Anarchist Club was named after him.

Malatya, or **Malatieh,** tn of Asiatic Turkey, in the il of the same name, 100 m. NE. of Marash, near the Euphrates. It is noted for its orchards and vineyards, and there are copper-mines in the il. In 1895 M. was the scene of a massacre of Christians. Pop. il, 394,162; tn, 83,692.

Malaviya, Pandit Madan Mohan (1861–1946), Hindu Nationalist politician, *b*. Allahabad, studied at the gov. high school there and the Muir Central College. He was associated with the Indian National Congress almost from its inception, being a delegate to the second session held in Calcutta in 1886. Became editor of the weekly paper, *Hindustan*, and also ed. the *India Union*. Some years later he started a weekly Hindu paper, the *Abhyudaya*, and, many years later still, collaborated in founding the Nationalist daily paper, the *Leader*, at Allahabad. In 1902 he became a member of the United Provs. Legislative Council. In 1910, on the introduction of the Morley-Minto reforms (*see* INDIAN SUBCONTINENT, *History*), he was elected to the Imperial Legislative Council and remained a member until 1921.

M. was the originator and for long the president of the militant Hindu Mahasabha, the founder and for many years the vice-chancellor of the Benares Hindu Univ., and thrice president of the Indian National Congress. For nearly 50 years he was a constitutional if vehement advocate of Indian political advancement, but in 1930 took a prominent part in the civil disobedience movement. Notwithstanding his constant political activities his deepest attachments were to Hinduism, and his outstanding contribution to neo-Hinduism was his creation of the Hindu Univ. at Benares out of the nucleus of the Central Hindu College.

Malawi, formerly **Nyasaland,** country about 320 m. in length and varying from 50 to 100 m. in width, lying approx. between lat. 9° 45′ and 17° 16′ S., and long. 33° and 36° E. Area is 47,949 sq. m. (land area 37,374 sq. m.). There has been a variation in pop. figs. in recent years but in 1962 there were 9400 Whites, 2,960,000 Africans and 14,200 Asiatics. M. comprises the W. shore of Lake M. with the table lands separating it from the basin of the Loangwa R. and the region lying between the watershed of the Zambezi and Shire R.s on the W. and the lakes Chiuta and Chilwa and the Ruo R. (an affluent of the Shire) on the E., including the mt system of the Shiré highlands and Mlanje. M. is bounded on the N. by Tanzania and on the S. and E. by Mozambique and on the W. by Zambia.

Climate and Health. The climate of M. in its essential features is similar to the rest of SE. Africa within the tropics. The cool months are from May to Aug. when the temp. which is normally between 90° to 98° F. falls to as low as 40° F. The rains fall between Nov. and April and are heavy in Jan. and Feb. Malaria is still widespread. Gov. hospitals are maintained at Zomba, Blantyre and Lilongwe and gov. medical officers at sev. other tns. Smaller gov., as well as mission hospitals, are situated throughout the country.

Education. School enrolments exceeded 300,000 in 1962. Higher education is provided in the univ. at Salisbury, Rhodesia, and students are also accepted at Bantu univ. colleges in S. Africa.

Industry and Commerce. The economy of M. is essentially based on agriculture. The main products are tobacco, (43,888,185 lb. in 1963 valued at £3,989,414); tea, record export in 1960, 24,731,000 lb.; cotton, 13,566 short tons in 1960. Groundnuts and tung oil are also grown for export, 20,000 short tons and 1000 long tons respectively in 1960. Rice and maize are grown for local consumption but barely meet M.'s requirements. Coffee is produced but not in large quantities. In areas free from the tse-tse fly, cattle and sheep do well. An intensive search for minerals has been made and many occurrences have been reported of a large variety, but unfortunately not apparently in exploitable quantities. There is a small local production of soap, cigarettes, confectionery, biscuits, fishing nets, blankets and clothing. Timber could become an important industry and over 7000 sq. m. equal to 19 per cent of the country is forest. In the past M. was no doubt mostly forest. The Dept of Forestry is actively engaged in reafforestation. Good prospects are held out for the commercial production of a local species of mahogany and cedar.

Communications. M. is linked by the Central African Airways and E. African Airways with Salisbury, Nairobi, Dar-es-Salaam and other important tns in neighbouring countries. Air M. operates internally. Bus services run to the remotest areas and in dry weather 5900 m. of road are open. This total may be cut down to 2000 during the wet seasons. A railway system connects M. with Beira in Mozambique through which port most of M.'s imports and exports must pass. The M. railway also runs a motor goods and passenger service where there is no railway.

Constitution and Administration. Following its withdrawal from the Federation of Rhodesia and Nyasaland, M. achieved independence from 6 July 1964 and became a rep. within the Commonwealth with Banda as President, July 1966. The full text of the Constitution is embodied in the Nyasaland (Constitution) Order in Council, 1963. Certain matters are reserved to the Governor but such powers may well become theoretical, otherwise the Governor acts on the advice of the Prime Minister. The Cabinet, presided over by the Prime Minister, is composed of 9 elected Ministers and the Financial Secretary, *ex officio.* The Legislative Assembly has 29 members; 20 elected on a ᵀ ower Franchise and 8 on a Higher Franchise,

and the Financial Secretary, *ex officio.* One-party gov. prevails. Owing to the paucity of industry in M. there are always a large number of M. males in remunerative employment in Rhodesia, Zambia and S. Africa.

Ethnology. The pop. of M. consists of sev. Bantu-speaking peoples, the more important including the Nyanja, Cewa, Yao and Ngoni. Today traditional tribal boundaries have been largely effaced and there is much inter-tribal mixture. Most of the pop. are Christian (adhering especially to the Church of Scotland) or Muslim.

History. Livingstone (q.v.) reached the S. shore of Lake Nyasa in 1859. As a result, various missions were founded in the area. These were followed in 1883 by the formation of the African Lakes Corporation, and 2 years later the first Brit. consul was sent out. In 1884 the Brit. S. Africa Co. applied for a charter to trade in the country. An expedition under Serpa Pinto was sent to explore the Upper Zambezi and Lower Loangwa, and Sir H. H. Johnston arrived as consul with the special task of composing differences with the Arabs of the interior. Treaties were concluded with the Makolo chiefs and with the Yaos around Blantyre, and in 1889 the Brit. gov. proclaimed a Brit. protectorate over the Shiré dists. Johnston induced the sultan of Kota Kota to put his country under Brit. protection and arranged similar treaties with Mlosi and other Arab and Wahenga chiefs. Johnston's work was ratified in 1891 by an Anglo-Portuguese convention, and soon afterwards a Brit. protectorate over the countries adjoining Nyasa was proclaimed. The protectorate of Nyasaland was confined to the Shiré and Lake Nyasa dist, the rest of the ter. under Brit. influence being placed under the Brit. S. Africa Co. Within the next few years slavery and the slave trade in the protectorate were suppressed. In 1893 the protectorate's name was changed to the 'Brit. Central Africa Protectorate', but it reverted to Nyasaland in 1907.

In 1953 Nyasaland was joined to the Federation of Rhodesia and Nyasaland despite African opposition. The Africans were suspicious of a federation which they considered to be dominated by a European gov. in Salisbury, and under Hastings Banda (q.v.) continued to agitate against it. There was serious rioting in 1959 and Banda was arrested. The Brit. Colonial Secretary alleged that a plot to massacre pro-federation elements had been formulated by Banda's Nyasaland African Congress party. But in 1960 Banda was released, and in Aug. 1962 his party, now renamed the M. Congress Party, won control of the Nyasaland Legislative Assembly. A constitutional conference held in London in Nov. 1962 resulted in agreement that Nyasaland should be self-governing from Feb. 1963. A month later the Brit. gov. acknowledged Nyasaland's right in principle to secede from the federation, which was in fact dissolved with effect from 31 Dec. 1963.

In July 1964 Nyasaland, under Banda's leadership, became an independent member of the Commonwealth, under the name of M. Banda soon had to deal with serious divisions within his gov. and before the end of 1964 had crushed an attempt by some of his own ministers to reorientate M. policy on more left-wing and pan-African lines. The rebel politicians fled the country. Since then Banda's position has remained supreme: though authoritarian, his gov. has overwhelming mass support. It has based its attitude towards Portuguese Africa, S. Africa, Rhodesia, etc., on economic realism rather than African nationalism, and has, since independence, proved a moderating force in Central African politics.

See F. Debenham, *Nyasaland, Land of the Lake*, 1955; Lord Hailey, *African Survey*, 1957; G. Jones, *Britain and Nyasaland*, 1964. (*See Plate*.)

Malawi, Lake, formerly **Nyasa** or **Nyanja**, large lake in Malawi in Central Africa, discovered by Livingstone in 1859. Its greatest length is 350 m., and its breadth from 15 to 45 m. with a total area of 14,000 sq. m. It lies 1650 ft above sea level. The lake has abundance of fish, and is drained by the Shiré into the Zambezi. Transport on the lake is by native craft and also by modern steamships.

Malay Archipelago, see MALAYA and EAST INDIES.

Malaya, the largest component of the Federation of Malaysia, comprising the 11 states of Perlis, Kedah, Penang, Perak, Selangor, Negri Sembilan, Malacca, Johore, Pahang, Trengannu and Kelantan (qq.v.). The ters. which make up M. occupy the Malay Peninsula, which extends SSW. from the narrow Kra Isthmus to Singapore (q.v.), which is not part of M. M. has a narrow frontier with Thailand on the N. and is separated from the Indonesian is. of Sumatra by the narrow Straits of Malacca. Sabah and Sarawak, the other 2 constituent parts of the Malaysian Federation are in the large is. of Borneo, separated from M. by the S. China Sea. The area of M. is 50,690 sq. m. and the pop. 7,500,000, of whom 49 per cent are Malay, 36 per cent Chinese and 10 per cent Indians or Pakistanis. The cap. is Kuala Lumpur (q.v.), which is also the federal cap. of Malaysia; other large tns are Penang, Malacca, Taiping, Port Swettenham (qq.v.), Ipoh and Seremban.

Physical features and climate. M. lies close to the equator between lat. 1° and 7° N. and long. 100° and 105° E., and is open to maritime influences from the Indian Ocean and the S. China Sea. The year is commonly divided into SW. and NE. monsoon seasons corresponding in time with summer and winter in the N. hemisphere. The months between the 2 monsoons are generally the wettest, though on the E. coast the NE. monsoon brings the heaviest rain. Rainfall averages between 65 in. in Negri Sembilan and 198 in. in Perak annually. The average daily temp. on the plains varies between 70° and 90° F., but is considerably lower on the hill stations. At Cameron Highlands for example, the extreme temps. recorded are 79° and 36° F. Humidity is generally high.

M. consists of an E. and W. coastal plain between which the central mt ranges run roughly N. and S. Gunong Tahan (7186 ft) is the highest peak. From this central ridge run many streams, the largest being the Perak which flows into the Straits of Malacca and the Pahang flowing into the S. China Sea.

Vegetation and fauna. In spite of progressive industrialisation along the W. seaboard, fourfifths of M. is primeval forest, forming on the plains an almost unbroken canopy 100 ft or so above the ground, but in the mts it tends to thin out, allowing for a tremendous variety of flora. The most famous flower is the Bunga Raya, a cultivated hibiscus, which has become the national flower of Malaysia. Indigenous fruits include the durian, banana, paw-paw, rambutan, mangosteen, cherry, lime and passion fruit. Pineapples and coconuts are commercial crops.

The fauna includes elephants, wild oxen, tigers, tapirs, bears, deer, leopards, panthers, monkeys, gibbons, civets and mouse-deer. There are many reptiles, and in the S. China Sea is found the leather-back turtle, largest species in existence.

Economy. The chief crop and the country's major source of prosperity is natural rubber, of which M. supplies over 30 per cent of the world's requirements. More than 3·5 million ac. are planted with the high-quality species *Hevea brasiliensis*, and the industry employs over half the country's labour force. Ann. production is around 570,000 tons and exports amount to approximately M$ 1400 million, or 55 per cent of M.'s export earnings. The crop is chiefly grown in the W. states, especially Kedah, Perak, Negri Sembilan, Malacca and Johore. The latex is processed locally and sent abroad mainly in the form of ribbed smoke sheet.

Tin is the second major industry and rich deposits extend from the state of Perlis in the N., through part of Kedah, S. into the Kinta valley of Perak, and thence to Selangor, Negri Sembilan, Malacca and Johore. E. of the main mt range tin fields are not widespread, though E. Pahang has one of the largest lode mines in the world. Smelting is carried out at Penang and Butterworth, using not only locally produced concentrates but also those from Thailand and elsewhere. Before Indonesia adopted her hostile policy, ore from that country was also processed. Other minerals produced in smaller quantities and in many cases not fully exploited include iron-ore, coal, bauxite, gold, tungsten, titanium and china-clay.

Oil-palms are cultivated, yielding over 90,000 tons of oil and over 27,000 tons of palm kernels annually. Copra is another important export, though it is mainly a smallholder crop, less than 20 per cent of the 500,000 ac. under coconut palm being in estate form. Over 90,000 tons of coconut oil per annum are produced, exports of which bring in about M$ 28 million; copra brings in about M$ 19 million.

Pineapples for canning are grown in Johore, Selangor and Perak, and rice is a subsistence crop, occupying more than 950,000 ac. Other crops for internal consumption are sweet potatoes, tapioca, yams, green vegetables, water-melons, spices, citrus fruit, maize, groundnuts and soya-beans. Coffee, cocoa and some tea are grown, the former having been a major crop before the ascendancy of rubber.

There are 13,356 sq. m. of reserved forests, and production of round timber is about 80,000 solid cub. ft. per annum, only about 20 per cent of which is exported.

By Asian standards manufacturing industry in M. is well advanced, and is expanding owing to pop. increase and the necessity of becoming less dependent on the world price of rubber. Engineering, especially motor vehicles, public works equipment, boat-building and foundry work, has now become a major industry. Local crafts such as jewellery, gold and silver work, ivory and wood carving, sarong weaving, etc. are however still widespread.

The chief harbours for handling the import and export trade are Penang and Port Swettenham, the rapidly developing port for the cap. Kuala Lumpur, both on the W. coast. Malacca, the famous spice port of biblical times is now only used by small craft. The E. coast has no major ports. Some of M.'s trade is still handled by the port of Singapore.

Communications. M. has the best system of communications in SE. Asia, the Railway Administration having 1028 m. of track, with up-to-date rolling stock, including air-conditioned Pullman cars and diesel locomotives. The main line from Singapore via Kuala Lumpur and Prai, opposite Penang Is. connects up with the long distance Thailand trains. Branch lines connect the main line with Port Dickson, Port Swettenham, Teluk Anson and Port Weld, and a line to the E. coast forks off at Gemasin Negri Sembilan and runs N. to reach the coast at Tumpat in Kelantan, from whence there is a connection into Thailand. There are now 7657 m. of public roads of which 5368 m. have a metalled surface. Air transport has made rapid strides since 1955 and there are 8 airports operating scheduled flights and 27 other minor airfields and landing strips.

Education and social services. Malayan social services are of high quality and schools, hospitals and mobile dispensaries are up to date, though since independence there has been a shortage of doctors, which has had to be made up by recruiting overseas on short-term contracts. The gov. maintains (1962) 65 general and dist hospitals with nearly 14,000 beds as well as sev. specialised hospitals and institutions and spends over M$ 80 million annually on health services. Malaria, tuberculosis and epidemic diseases, once a scourge, have been greatly reduced.

The main problem in education is posed by the language diversity. Malay and (for the time being) English are compulsory subjects; other languages will be allowed in the gov. schools to the extent of preventing them from dying out. In 1963 the expenditure on education was M$ 230 million, nearly a quarter of the national budget expenditure. 1,408,800 children attended gov., gov. aided and private schools of all types in 1963. The Univ. of M. was estab. in 1949 as the result of a merger between Raffles College and the King Edward VII College of Medicine, and was then situated at Singapore. In 1957, the year of independence, a new div. of the univ. was estab. at Kuala Lumpur, and in 1962 the 2 divs. became autonomous. That at Kuala Lumpur is now the Univ. of M., with 1736 full-time students and a staff of 121. Kuala Lumpur also has a technical college, and training colleges for secondary, specialist and technical teachers, while primary training colleges exist in Penang, Perak, Malacca (for women) and Kota Bharu.

Labour organisations. Trade unions were illegal in M. before the Second World War and there was much exploitation by employers, but after the war Brit. advisers estab. a system of unions and there are now 296 registered trade unions with a membership of over 265,000, the largest being the Union of Plantation Workers. There is a Malayan Trade Union Congress and labour relations are generally good.

Defence. Before the Second World War M. looked to the U.K. for her system of defence, and on achieving autonomy entered into an agreement which still left her to a large extent dependent on Britain for defence. This agreement was extended in 1963 to cover the rest of the new Malaysian Federation. M. now has conscription for national service and a regular army, navy and air force, estab. during the post-war emergency created by communist rebels. The nucleus of this already existed in the Malay Regiment founded in 1933. There is also a Territorial force, and a military college at Sungei Besi near Kuala Lumpur, founded in 1953. The small navy consists of 1 frigate, 8 minesweepers and a number of fast patrol boats. It is used primarily for fishery protection and the suppression of piracy. The air force is intended for a supporting role and consists chiefly of transport planes. There are navy and air force volunteer reserves.

Constitution. A paramount ruler is elected every 5 years from among themselves by the sultans of the 9 states which were formerly Brit. protectorates, i.e. excepting Penang and Malacca, which are under governors. He is known as Yang di-Pertuan Agong, meaning Supreme Head of State, and he heads a parliament consisting of a Senate of 38 members holding office for 6 years and a House of Representatives of 104 members with a maximum life of 5 years. The Yang di-Pertuan Agong is also head of the Malaysian Federation. *See* MALAYSIA, FEDERATION OF.

History. Before the Majapahit conquest. There is archaeological evidence of human occupation at least 5000 years ago, and it is clear that the peninsula was one of the routes by which the prehistoric pops. of Indonesia, Melanesia and Australia travelled on their way S. to their ultimate homes, and that successive waves of people left some of their number in the N. part of the Malay Peninsula.

The earliest known inhab. had physical characteristics which suggest an affinity to present-day Melanesians and Papuans; they lived in caves, made rough stone tools and were probably in undisturbed possession until a little before 2000 BC, when a people with Neolithic culture arrived from the N., possibly from SW. China. These were farmers, kept domestic animals and were skilled in pottery-making and in selecting and working stone to make tools and ornaments.

Evidence of a Bronze Age culture, dating from about 250 BC, has been found in 2 widely separated places in M., at Klang and on the Tembeling R. in Pahang. This is known as the Dongson culture. Two bronze gongs and 3 large bronze bells are the most important articles of this period which have so far been discovered. They were almost certainly brought into the country from Sumatra or Indo-China.

Archaeological discoveries belonging to the Iron Age period can be divided into 2 categories, those probably representing the indigenous pop. and those brought in by settlers. The earliest and most mysterious of these is the collection of beads found by Dr G. B. Gardner at Kota Tinggi, in Johore, about 20 per cent of which have been identified as of Rom. origin and dating from the first two or three cents. AD. This probably indicates a foreign settlement on the Johore R. at a very early date. The most important settlements of foreigners on the W. coast during this early period were near Kedah Peak, where colonies of S. Indians lived from the 4th to the 12th cent. AD.

At Kuala Selinsing, in N. Perak, considerable quantities of wheel-made pottery, gold ornaments, cornelian and glass beads and shell ornaments have been found, alongside skeletons of proto-Malay types, which point to the conclusion that this was an important indigenous settlement probably flourishing about AD 800. The only other material evidences of indigenous settlements during the proto-historic period, are slab graves and iron implements found in Perak, Selangor and Pahang, dating probably from the 10th cent. AD.

From early in the Christian era there were merchant ships plying between India and China, some of which put in at riv. mouths in the Malay Peninsula. The reports which these traders carried back to their native lands are the main source of historical information about this early period.

Though in the centre and S. of M. there are few traces of continuous occupation except by primitive tribes before the 15th cent., there is ample evidence of Malay settlements in the N., notably in Kedah, Singgora and Ligor from a very early date. At one period they formed part of the anct Buddhist kingdom of Lankasuka. Kelantan, Trengganu and Pahang can also be identified from ealy Chinese records as Malay settlements of some importance, reaching a high standard of culture and wealth.

But the main source of Malay power seems to have stemmed from Sumatra (see MALAYS). Here a very powerful Malay kingdom, with its cap. at Palembang, finds a place in Chinese records as early as AD 600. This was a Hindu state and is best known by its Sanskrit title of Sri Vijaya. This kingdom conquered Lankasuka, Kedah, Kelantan, Trengganu and Pahang some time before AD 800, and its ruler became the overlord of the Malay Peninsula as well as of a substantial part of E. Sumatra.

At the same time, also based on E. Sumatra, was another Malay kingdom, which was later known as the kingdom of Menangkabo, but which was originally referred to as 'Malayu'. Though this kingdom never controlled any part of the Malay Peninsula, it was probably the first Malay kingdom to adopt Islam as its religion, and in 1281 envoys from Malayu to China had Muslim names.

Colonists from Palembang founded a separate is. kingdom of Tumasik (Sanskrit, *Singapura*) some time between 1200 and 1300, but this, together with Palembang, Malayu, parts of Borneo, and the whole of the occupied portions of the Malay Peninsula, was overrun and destroyed by the Javanese Majapahit kingdom between 1360 and 1365. The Majapahit king made no attempt to occupy the Malay Peninsula after his conquest, but traces of Majapahit influence are still to be found in Kelantan and Patani.

The Malacca sultanate. The destruction of Singapore by Majapahit led to the rise of Malacca. At first a fishing vil., occupied by 'sea gypsies' (aboriginal *orang-laut*), it attracted fugitives from Tumasik, among them its dispossessed ruler, Parameswara. The new Malay state he founded was beset with enemies, chief among whom were the Siamese. Appeals to the Chinese emperor for protection resulted in the raising of the title of the Malay ruler to that of King of Malacca in 1405, and freed him from any dependence on the Siamese. During the 15th cent. this kingdom flourished. Its trade developed: its influence extended as far N. as Patani and even over the coastal regions of W. Sumatra. The main conversion of the Malays to Islam also began in this cent. Parameswara was a Hindu when he came to Malacca; the conversion to Islam was gradual, probably beginning under Parameswara's successor, and was not completed until the 17th cent. when Iskandar Muda, Sultan of Acheh, took a leading part in spreading Islam to the Malay Peninsula itself.

In 1511 a Portuguese fleet under Alfonso D'Albuquerque conquered the kingdom of Malacca. Its ruler, Sultan Mahmud, fled to Johore and there estab. the kingdom of Riau Johore. The Portuguese held Malacca for over a cent. Though they attempted, largely unsuccessfully, to convert the people they had conquered to Christianity, their prin. concern was trade, and they allowed the Asian communities in Malacca a fairly wide measure of self-gov. within prescribed limits. In 1641 the Portuguese were defeated by the Dutch, who were also principally interested in trade and who held Malacca until 1795. In 1795, during the Napoleonic wars, the British took possession of Malacca. This was later returned to the Dutch, but the Anglo-Dutch treaty of 1824 recognised the Malay Peninsula as being within the Brit. sphere of influence, and in 1825 the Dutch exchanged Malacca for Benkoelen, on the W. coast of Sumatra.

The kingdom of Riau Johore. This kingdom, founded by the fugitive Sultan of Malacca, loosely took in all parts of M. over which the Portuguese did not have effective control. Weak and poor, it was chronically unstable. The murder of its sultan in 1699, marking the extinction of the royal stock of Malacca, and the periodic invasions of the Bugis from the Celebes, began the disintegration of the Riau Johore kingdom. The Bugis estab. themselves in Selangor, and in 1722 became *de facto* rulers of the Johore kingdom. During the 18th cent. the Malay Peninsula lost all semblance of cohesive gov. and was split up into a number of weak and mutually hostile states. A Menangkabo migration to M. from Sumatra had begun in the 16th cent., and in 1773, when, threatened by Bugis domination, they united under a Sumatran prince of Menangkabo descent. This state should have become extremely powerful, since she could produce more tin than any other state in the peninsula, but 18th cent. Bugis interference and 19th cent. Siamese invasion, coupled with internal dissension, kept her in a condition of constant weakness.

The British in Malaya. The efforts of Francis Light brought Penang under the control of the E. India Co. in 1786. Penang had hitherto formed part of Kedah, and the sultan hoped that its cession would bring him Brit. aid in the event of any attack on Kedah by the Bugis of Selangor or the Siamese. In 1821, however, the Siamese invaded and conquered Kedah, though the sultan was reinstated in 1842. In 1826 the E. India Co. concluded an agreement with Siam, the essential clause of which provided for non-interference by Siam in Perak, Selangor, Kelantan and Trengganu. But the threat of Siamese encroachment in N. M. was not finally removed until the Anglo-Siamese treaty of 1909, in which Siam transferred to Britain all her rights in the N. states.

In 1824, as the result of an earlier agreement between Stamford Raffles (q.v.), the Temenggong of Johore and Sultan Hussein, Singapore was ceded in perpetuity to Britain. This treaty was destined to convert a mangrove swamp into one of the world's greatest ports, and to change Johore from forest and jungle into a prosperous state. Raffles's 'Malta of the East' rapidly justified his hopes. A year after its cession the pop. numbered 10,000, and by 1823 imports and exports in this free trade port exceeded 13 million Malay dollars in value. The is. of Pangkor and the Sembilan is. were ceded to Britain by Perak in 1826, and this cession was confirmed in 1874, when the strip of ter. on the mainland opposite, known as the Dindings, also became British. In Feb. 1935 the Dindings ter. was retroceded to the state of Perak.

In 1805 Penang was made a separate presidency, of equal rank with Madras and Bombay. It was reduced to a lieutenant-governorship subordinate to Bengal in 1830. In 1825 Singapore and Malacca were incorporated with it under one governor, Penang still remaining the seat of gov. In 1836 the seat of gov. of the Straits Settlements was transferred to Singapore. From the founding of Penang in 1785 down to 1858, the constitutional hist. of the Straits Settlements is part of the hist. of the E. India Co., and in M. were reflected the evils and disadvantages apparent in the administration of India by a trading company, so that in so remote a peninsula, despite the work of Raffles, many reforms were bound to be belated. But in 1858 the E. India Co. was abolished, though at least its occasional firmness in foreign policy had saved most of the Malay Peninsula from subjugation by Siam. With the abolition of the E. India Co. the Straits Settlements fell automatically under the India Office for a brief spell. Then, in 1867, the Brit. Gov., bowing to local agitation, approved their transfer to the Colonial Office.

Raffles had strongly favoured Brit. expansion in the Malay archipelago. With his disappearance from the scene, his policy became largely dormant until it was awakened in the last quarter of the 19th cent. by the rivalries of the great European powers and by the demands of Brit. and Chinese capital seeking fresh fields for expansion, coupled with the discovery of rich mineral resources in the hinterland. But though the 5 decades after 1824 have been described as 'half a century of inactivity', this is true only in so far as Brit. policy towards the Malay states was concerned, for here a policy of non-intervention was strictly enforced. Singapore, however, grew with remarkable rapidity, Penang developed at a modest pace, and only Malacca stagnated. Meanwhile, in the Malay states of the W. coast, the rulers' authority became increasingly weakened, and to the troubles caused by court factions was added the disturbance caused by Chinese immigration in the tin-mining areas.

In the seventies of the 19th cent., after the opening of the Suez Canal, Brit. policy became more active. The period 1874–1914 is marked by the gradual institution by treaties of the Brit. protectorate over the Malay states. With the transfer of the 3 settlements of Singapore, Malacca and Penang to the Colonial Office in 1867, the governor and leading citizens in the Straits Settlements were able to represent the deplorable conditions in the W. Malay states more effectively, and to press for a new policy of intervention. Civil war was causing loss of trade in the Settlements, and piracy was rife in the Straits of Malacca. Serious faction fights occurred among Chinese miners in Perak, and there were rival claimants to the sultanate. The sheer anarchy compelled the Brit. Gov. to intervene. In Nov. 1873 Sir Andrew Clarke came to Singapore with the task of reporting what steps should be taken by the colonial gov. (Straits Settlements) to promote the restoration of peace and order, and especially to examine the question of appointing a Brit. officer to reside in any of the states. Perak's situation demanded and received priority. In Jan. 1874 Clarke temporarily settled the succession by the Pangkor engagement and secured the agreement of Sultan Abdullah to the appointment of a Brit. resident who was to advise on the collection and control of all revenues and on the general administration of the state. The heads of the Chinese factions were present and they signed a bond to disarm completely and to keep the peace. Before the end of 1874 residents had also been appointed in Selangor and Sungei Ujong, the most prosperous member of the Menangkabo confederation, and a measure of peace and order had been restored. Brit. advice was later extended to the rest of Negri Sembilan, and to Pahang in 1887, and the 4 states were united in a federation in 1896, with its cap. in Kuala Lumpur.

In the development of the residential system the wisdom, skill and sympathetic understanding of Sir Hugh Low in Perak and Sir Frank Swettenham in Selangor and Perak Perak (and later as the first Resident-General) did much to establish sound administration and to reconcile the Malay ruling class to the new regime. Both the Federated Malay States and the states of Kedah, Perlis, Kelantan, Trengganu and Johore, which remained outside the Federation, continued under a separate form of administration from the Straits Settlements and were never declared Brit. ter. Relations with Johore were regulated by a treaty in 1914. All these treaties were substantially similar: (a) the Malay states agreed to accept Brit. protection and to have no dealings with foreign powers except through Britain; (b) Britain guaranteed the states protection against attack by foreign powers; (c) the agreements provided for the appointment of a Brit. officer in each state whose advice had to be taken except in matters concerning Malay custom and religion.

The opening of the Suez Canal in 1869, which enabled the sea journey from England to be completed in 42 days instead of 116, soon led to a notable increased in trade, which stimulated economic enterprise on the mainland; and construction of a railway, followed by the first rubber boom of 1906, brought a degree of prosperity to the W. states which was hitherto unknown. The pop. increased rapidly. Chinese miners had been encouraged to enter the tin-mining areas by earlier Malay rulers and chiefs, but now they poured in of their own accord, and by the middle of the 20th cent. were to be almost as numerous as the Malays themselves. S. Indian labour was recruited by rubber estate owners, and by 1920 M. was exporting 196,000 tons of rubber each year.

In the Federated Malay States a federal council had been created by Sir John Anderson in 1906. The High Commissioner presided over the council, which consisted of the 4 rulers, the Resident-General, the 4 Brit. residents, and 4 unofficial members nominated by the High Commissioner. The membership remained unchanged until 1927, when the rulers withdrew, the officials were increased to 13 and the unofficials to 11. The proceedings of the council then began to adopt something of the modern Brit. aspect of gov. and opposition. There was no further constitutional change until the Jap occupation of M. (1942–5) ended; gov. remained extremely decentralised, each state had considerable autonomy, but Brit. control was paramount, and already some Malays were demanding a greater voice in the affairs of their country.

For events in M. during the Second World War *see* MALAYA, BRITISH, JAPANESE INVASION OF (1941–2).

Malaya since 1945. On the eve of a campaign for the liberation of M. the Japanese surrendered unconditionally, and in Sept. 1945 a Brit. military administration was estab. under the Supreme Allied Commander, SE. Asia, whose H.Q. were in Singapore. This was followed by the pub. in Jan. 1946 of a White Paper setting out proposals for a Malayan Union, which would unite the whole of the peninsula (except Singapore, which was to become a separate colony) under a governor and a strong central gov., and which considerably curtailed the authority of the rulers and the states.

These proposals were strongly resisted by the Malays, who rapidly formed a political organisation, the United Malay National Organisation, with branches all over the country. Their attitude was supported by a group of retired Malayan civil servants in England, including the nonagenarian Sir Frank Swettenham, and the scheme for a Malayan Union was abandoned. In its place the Federation of M. Agreement was signed in Kuala Lumpur on 21 Jan. 1948, and came into force on 1 Feb. of that year. This agreement provided for a High Commissioner and a federal legislative council containing 75 members, 50 of whom were unofficial. A considerable degree of authority was restored to the rulers, acting in consultation with their state executive councils, and a form of common citizenship was created for all who acknowledged M. as their permanent home and the object of their undivided loyalty. Within this framework the settlements of Penang and Malacca remained Brit. ter.; Singapore was a separate colony under its own governor.

The year in which the Federation was inaugurated saw the outbreak of a serious Communist revolt. The Communists had hoped to gain control of the country in Sept. 1945, but they were forestalled by the arrival of the Brit. military administration. During the next 2 years they made increasingly determined efforts to paralyse the economic recovery of the country, and finally launched a campaign of violence and murder in which the prin. targets were Brit. rubber planters and tin-miners, and those Chinese who actively opposed them. A state of emergency was declared in June 1948. Captured documents have shown that the Communists had hoped to declare a Communist Rep. on 3 Aug. 1948.

The number of active Communist terrorists probably never exceeded 7000, the majority of them Chinese, but they proved an elusive enemy. In spite of increasingly effective measures, a Communist hard core was still in armed revolt in July 1955, when a general election was held to elect 52 unofficial members to the federal legislative council. All except one of those elected were members of the Alliance party under the leadership of Tunku Abdul Rahman, who then became chief minister.

On 9 Sept. 1955 Tunku Abdul Rahman's gov. declared an amnesty for the Communists, thereby fulfilling an election promise, but this was withdrawn in Feb. 1956 after rejection by the Communists and some fruitless attempts at negotiation. The number of active terrorists dwindled until in 1960 the state of emergency was declared at an end. Their remarkable decline since 1948 was undoubtedly due to the effective action of the security forces and, after 1955, to the counter-attraction which Tunku Abdul Rahman's administration had for the great majority of M.'s people, including those of Chinese origin.

The Alliance party was pledged to press for immediate Malayan independence. In Jan. 1956 the chief minister led a 'Merdeka' mission to London where (Feb.) agreement was reached with the colonial secretary bringing self-gov. into effect and envisaging full independence for the Federation within the Commonwealth by 31 Aug. 1957. Early in Mar. 1956 an independent commission was appointed to make recommendations for a form of constitution for a fully independent and self-governing M. In May 1957 the chief minister again took to London a delegation in order to reach final agreement on independence for the Federation.

M. became an independent state on 31 Aug. 1957 remaining a member of the Brit. Commonwealth. M.'s relations with Britain since independence have been extremely close and cordial; her political development has continued smoothly and her economy has flourished. In 1963 she became part of Malaysia (for subsequent events *see* MALAYSIA, FEDERATION OF).

See L. A. Mills, *British Malaya, 1824–67*, 1926, and *British Rule in Eastern Asia*, 1942; Sir F. Swettenham, *British Malaya*, 1939, 1949, and *Footprints in Malaya*, 1942; Sir R. Winstedt, *Britain and Malaya, 1786–1941*, 1944, *The Malays, a Cultural History*, 1950, and *Malaya and its History*, 1953; V. Purcell, *The Chinese in Malaya*, 1948; V. Bartlett, *Report from Malaya*, 1954; J. Kennedy, *A History of Malaya*, 1962; Oci Jin Bee, *Land, People and Economy in Malaya*, 1963.

Malaya (1941–2), **Japanese Invasion of British,** part of the Jap. plan to seize all Amer., Brit. and Dutch possessions in SE. Asia and the Pacific. The main object of this particular operation was to capture the Brit. naval base on Singapore Is. The base had been heavily fortified during the years between the wars; the defences were designed primarily to meet an attack from the sea, it being considered that a landing on the Malayan mainland would involve negotiating jungle country too difficult for large scale military operations. Shortly before the war this view was revised and increasing attention was given to a possible Jap. landing on the mainland, but preoccupation with the war against Germany and Italy made it impracticable to change the fixed defences to meet such an eventuality.

The Jap. assault was entrusted to the Twenty-fifth Army (Lieut.-Gen. Yamashita), comprising the Imperial Guard, 5th and 18th Divs., supported by the 3rd Air Div. The plan was to land in Southern Siam and Northern Malaya, and advance rapidly S. to attack Singapore.

The overall commander of all Brit. Commonwealth Forces in the Far. E. was Air Chief Marshal Sir Robert Brooke-Popham. The Land Forces in Malaya and Singapore were under Lieut.-Gen. A. E. Percival and consisted of III Corps (9th and 11th Indian Divs.) located in N. and Central Malaya and the 8th Australian Div. in Southern Malaya. Most of the personnel were war-enlisted men, not very highly trained and short of many items of equipment. They were supported by 158 aircraft, many of which were obsolete.

The Japanese began landing in N. Malaya, near Kota Bharu, in the early hours of 8 December 1941 (the day after the attack on Pearl Harbor), making simultaneous landings in S. Siam at Singora and Patani. Their troops acted vigorously and the Brit. position deteriorated very rapidly. On the 10th they captured Kota Bharu airfield and on the same day the two Brit. cap. ships H.M.S. *Prince of Wales* and *Repulse*, were sunk by Jap. air action off the E. coast. Within 48 hrs of the start of hostilities the Brit. air forces had been virtually destroyed by bombing on their airfields, and for the rest of the campaign the troops were without air support.

Throughout Dec. the situation worsened, the excellently trained and well equipped Jap. troops advancing steadily towards Singapore. An attempt by the III Corps to make a stand on the Slim R. was defeated by Jap. landings along the W. coast in rear of the position. On 8 Jan. it was decided to abandon central Malaya and organise a defensive position in Johore State in the S. Meanwhile the 18th Brit. Div. had arrived in Singapore from the U.K. and began preparations to defend the is. Following further Jap. successes on the mainland the decision was made to withdraw all troops to Singapore Is. on the night of 30/31 Jan.

Commonwealth Forces were no more successful in defending the is. than they had been on the mainland. After 2 days' heavy bombardment the Japanese, on the night of 8/9 Feb., launched an assault across the narrow dividing channel. The Brit. defences were overrun and on 12 Feb. the MacRitchie Reservoir—Singapore City's main source of water—was captured. This was decisive and at 8.30 p.m. on 15 Feb. 1942 all fighting ceased and the Commonwealth troops laid down their arms in surrender. Singapore had fallen in 70 days. The loss in fighting men was 138,708, of whom more than 130,000 were prisoners of war.

See Lieut.-Gen. A. E. Percival, *The War in Malaya*, 1949; Maj.-Gen. S. Wooburn Kirby (H.M.S.O.), *The War Against Japan*, vol. i, *The Loss of Singapore*, 1957. (*See Plate*.)

Malays, name given, in a restricted sense, to the largest single racial group of the Malay Peninsula and Archipelago. It is also used in a wide sense to denote the racial type which forms the majority of the pop. of the modern Indonesia, and which is also found, in varying strengths, in Borneo, the Celebes, the Philippines and Madagascar. The M. are a Mongoloid people, black-haired and olive-complexioned, with high cheekbones. They are generally slight in build, with small wrists and ankles.

The M. are essentially islanders, and have the daring and enterprise so often associated with maritime peoples. Their early hist. and origins are very obscure. There is evidence that some Malay tribes were living in the N. of the Malay Peninsula very early in the Christian era. But the main centre of Malay power appears to have been Sumatra; here a powerful Malay kingdom known by its Sanskrit name of Sri Vijaya grew up, with its cap. at Palembang. Its people had some admixture of Indian blood, were considerably influenced by Indian culture, and were Hindu in religion. Its ruler became overlord of the Malay Peninsula some time before AD 800. Colonists from Palembang founded the separate is. kingdom of Tumasik (later, from Sanskrit, Singapore) during the 13th cent. In the 14th cent. Sri Vijaya and Tumasik were conquered by a Javanese empire, and the dispossessed ruler of Tumasik then founded a Malay kingdom in Malacca. When in the 16th cent. the Portuguese conquered Malacca the fugitive Malay Sultan fled to the Malay Peninsula and founded the kingdom of Riau Johore.

The conversion of the main body of the M. to Islam began in the 15th cent. But there is evidence which suggests that another early Malay kingdom in Sumatra, known contemporaneously as Malayu, but later as Menangkabo, was Muslim as early as the 13th cent. (Though this kingdom never extended to the Malay Peninsula, the association of its original name and that of the race as a whole is interesting.) The conversion to Islam was not completed until the 17th cent.; even today, a few primitive Malay tribes probably remain animist, and there are a number of Malay Christians.

Since the 'golden age' of Malay hist. (c. 9th–14th cents.) the M. have shown little signs of political cohesion until the present day. In 1957 the Federation of Malaya became a self-governing dominion of the Brit. Commonwealth; and Indonesia achieved political independence from the Netherlands shortly after the Second World War, but has since shown much internal instability.

The Malay language belongs to the Austro-

Asiatic linguistic family. Of its numerous dialects, Javanese is the most refined, having been much enriched by Sanskrit influences. *See* INDONESIA; MALAYA; SINGAPORE. *See* L. R. Wheeler, *The Modern Malay*, 1928; Sir R. Winstedt, *Malaya and its History* (3rd. ed.), 1951; Joanna Moore, *The Land and People of Malaya and Singapore*, 1958.

Malaysia, Federation of, a federation formed on 16 Sept. 1963 from peninsular Malaya, Singapore, Brit. N. Borneo (renamed Sabah) and Sarawak (qq.v.). Britain had already renounced her sovereignty over Malaya in 1957 and she now did the same in the case of N. Borneo, Sarawak and Singapore. The new federation automatically became a member of the Brit. Commonwealth. On 9 Aug. 1965 Singapore seceded from the federation and became an independent state but retained military ties with M. who kept control of military bases on the is.

Area and population. M. covers an area of approximately 130,000 sq. m., occupying the Malay peninsula (except for Singapore) and the NW. coastal belt of Borneo, 400 m. E. across the S. China Sea. The pop. is about 9 million, of which approximately 50 per cent are indigenous and 34 per cent Chinese, the remainder comprising Indians, Pakistanis, Indonesians and others. Over 80 per cent of the pop. live in Malaya. The federal cap. is Kuala Lumpur and the official language is Malay.

Constitution. Under the new constitution of M. a Supreme Head of the Confederation, officially known as the Yang di-Pertuan Agong, is elected from among themselves by the sultans of the states of Malaya, and holds office for 5 years. As originally constituted, Parliament had a Senate of 60 members and a House of Representatives with 159 members, 104 from Malaya, 15 from Singapore, 11 from Sabah and 24 from Sarawak, but the Singapore contingent was withdrawn after secession. In the 1964 elections the Alliance Party held a majority with 89 seats, its nearest rival being the Pan-Malayan Islamic Party with 9.

Armed Forces. When in Sept. 1963 M. joined with Singapore, N. Borneo and Sarawak to form the Federation of M. some reorganisation of the army took place. In 1964 the army comprised about 19,000 officers and men, organised into 8 infantry battalions and 1 reconnaissance battalion with artillery, engineer and administrative units. In 1963–4 sev. units served in Borneo, together with Brit. units, against raiding forces from Indonesia. Later the strength of the army is to be increased to 20 battalions to form 5 mobile brigade groups, 2 of which will be stationed in Borneo. It is also planned to increase the Territorial Army to 27,000. The 1964 strength of the para-military field police was 23,000 (24 companies). All persons between 21 and 29 are liable for conscriptions into the armed forces or for civil defence work. The Royal Malayan Navy formed in 1958 under the Malayan Defence agreement with the U.K., provided for the transfer of 2 coastal and 4 inshore minesweepers from the RN and in 1963 after the granting of independence, it was agreed to strengthen the new Malayan Navy by the addition of a frigate and 10 fast patrol craft, making, with local vessels, a force of 23 ships. There is (1965) a small force of tactical transport aircraft, mostly Pioneers, Heralds and Alouette helicopters.

History. By 1960 the Federation of Malaya had achieved independence and elected a House of Representatives; the newly elected gov. of Singapore, now independent, was in favour of merging with Malaya, and of the states in NW. Borneo, Brunei had achieved autonomy, while Sarawak and Sabah were well-advanced on the road to independence.

In 1961 Tunku Abdul Rahman, Prime Minister of Malaya, took the initiative and suggested that a plan should be devised whereby Singapore, N. Borneo, Brunei and Sarawak would be brought closer together with Malaya in political and economic co-operation. The proposal was on the whole well received. Trade benefits would accrue from the creation of a larger economic unit and resources could be pooled. There would also be political advantages. For Malaya the upsetting of the balance of power which would result from amalgamation with Singapore with its preponderance of Chinese would be offset by the largely indigenous pop. of the Bornese states; for Singapore it was a means of ending colonial status and for Sarawak, Brunei and N. Borneo it would advance the date of independence. There was also the advantage that the existing central gov. at Kuala Lumpur was already federal in structure. Britain was also favourable to the proposal. In 1962 a joint Malayan and Brit. commission under Lord Cobbold concluded, after testing public opinion, that most people in Sarawak and N. Borneo were in favour of federation; and a referendum in Singapore showed a considerable majority for the merger, despite frantic efforts by the Communists to turn the people against it.

In Brunei, however, political power passed in the elections of Sept. 1962 to the People's Party, which maintained that before the move towards M. was made there should be a unification of the 3 Borneo ters. under the Sultan of Brunei as constitutional ruler. A revolt within the party tried to bring about this state by force, but it was speedily repressed. Nevertheless Brunei ultimately decided to remain outside the federation, possibly because with her small pop. and large riches in the form of oil she was unwilling to share her prosperity. Also, the Sultan of Brunei's precedence was called into question, and this matter carried considerable political weight against joining.

Eventually the agreement between the 4 ters and Britain was signed in July 1963. Singapore, despite its small size was second to Malaya in pop., having 1·7 million people, among whom Chinese outnumbered Malays, and there was a strong Communist element. In these circumstances the existence of a political faction hostile to the central gov. is not surprising, especially

when the situation was worsened by the activities of Indonesian agitators bent on formenting riots and on splitting up the new federation. Ultimately the political situation in Singapore got so out of hand that Tunku Abdul Rahman, now Prime Minister of Malaysia, had no alternative, short of taking repressive measures, but to suggest that Singapore became a separate state. Accordingly, as from 9 Aug. 1965, Singapore withdrew from the Malaysian Federation by agreement amid widespread disappointment in M. and among the more responsible elements in Singapore itself, but to the accompaniment of considerable gloating from Indonesia, who since the autumn of 1964 had been pursuing a policy of what President Sukarno called 'confrontation', aimed at breaking up the federation, which was considered to be an organisation for maintaining Brit. imperialism in the E. Implementation of the policy took the form of constant attempts to infiltrate armed patrols into Malaya by sea and air and into Sabah and Sarawak across the border of Indonesian Borneo. Though singularly unsuccessful and fraught with economic repercussions disastrous to Indonesia herself, this policy continued to be pursued until talks in Bangkok ended the 'confrontation' in Aug. 1966. (*See Plate.*)

Malbork (Ger. **Marienburg**), tn of Poland, in Gdańsk prov., on the Nogat, 25 m. SE. of Gdańsk (q.v.). It was formerly in E. Prussia (q.v.). As Marienburg it was famous as the seat of the Grand Master of the Teutonic Knights (q.v.), in succession to Venice. In 1466 the tn became the cap. of Polish W. Prussia, it passed to Prussia in 1772. It remained in Ger. hands after a plebiscite in 1920, and was then, until 1939, a Ger. frontier post on the border of the Polish Corridor (q.v.). The *Marienburger Schloss* was regarded as the largest and strongest fortress in medieval Europe, with walls 10–15 ft thick and quarters for a garrison of 10,000 men. It was restored at the beginning of the 19th cent., but suffered much damage from Russian bombardment in 1945. The tn has sugar and timber industries, and it also has a power station. Pop. 26,000.

(*See Plate: Poland.*)

Malchin, Ger. tn in the dist of Neubrandenburg, 24 m. NW. by W. of Neubrandenburg (q.v.). It lies on the Peene R., between 2 lakes. It has a 14th cent. church, an agric. market and sugar and timber industries. Pop. 7000.

Malcolm I (Macdonald) (*d.* 954), King of Scotland, succeeded to the crown in 943. He made a treaty with Edmund of England in 945, and renewed it with his successor, Eadred, but in 950 he allowed his followers to ravage Northumbria.

Malcolm II (Mackenneth) (*d.* 1034), King of Scotland, son of Kenneth II, succeeded in 1005 by defeating and killing Kenneth III. In 1018 he won a great victory over Eadulf Cudel at Carham on the Tweed, which resulted in N. Northumbria becoming part of the Scottish kingdom.

Malcolm III (called **Canmore**) (*d*. 1093), King of Scotland, succeeded his father, Duncan I, in 1057 after defeating and killing Macbeth at Lumphanan. He married Margaret, sister of Edgar Atheling, and is said to have done homage to the Eng. kings in 1072 and 1091. He was treacherously slain while invading Northumberland.

Malcolm IV (**the Maiden**) (1141–65), King of Scotland, succeeded his grandfather, David I, in 1153. He surrendered Northumberland and Cumberland to Henry II in 1156, and received in return Huntingdon. He served with the Eng. forces in the expedition against Toulouse (1159), and on his return encountered rebellions in Scotland (1160–4) which he crushed with vigour.

Malcolm, Sir John (1769–1833), Indian administrator and diplomat, *b*. Burnfoot in Scotland. In 1798 he was appointed by Lord Wellesley assistant to the resident at Hyderabad. He was envoy to Persia (1800, 1807, 1810); private secretary to Wellesley (1801–2); political agent to Wellesley during the Mahratta war (1803–4); governor of Bombay (1826–30); and M.P. for Launceston (1831–2). He wrote *Political History of India*, 1811, *History of Persia*, 1818, *Administration of India*, 1833, and *Life of Clive* (pub. 1836).

Malcomia, a genus of crucifers, of which the best-known species is *M. maritima* (Virginian stock), a valuable ann. garden plant with numerous varieties of various colours, giving a lengthy succession of bloom.

Malczewski, Antoni (1793–1826), Polish poet. During the Napoleonic wars he served as a lieutenant of engineers in the Polish contingents of Napoleon's army. He took part in the heroic defence of Modlin against the Russians. In 1818 he was one of the first to accomplish the ascent of Mt Blanc. He subsequently returned to Poland, where he managed an estate in the country, but devoted most of his time to his literary work, which took the shape of a long narrative poem, *Maria*, 1825. As a poet M. links Polish literature with the romanticism of the W. of Europe, particularly, with that of England. In many ways his great poem was inspired by Byron. The descriptions of a battle between Poles and Tartars, the vast loneliness of the steppes, the wild gaiety of a carnival, are all famous in Poland.

Maldegem, tn in the prov. of E. Flanders, Belgium, 17 m. NW. of Ghent, engaged in horticulture and manufs. of lace, baskets and leather. Pop. 13,000.

Malden: 1. Malden and Coombe, municipal bor. in NE. Surrey, England, mainly residential. Merton College, afterwards removed to Oxford, was founded here in 1264 and still owns property in the dist. Pop. 46,587.
2. City of Middlesex co., Massachusetts, U.S.A., on the R. M., 5 m. N. of Boston of which it is a part though under separate administration. It is noted for the manuf. of rubber boots and shoes; soap, chemicals, paint, leather goods, radio equipment and canned foods are also produced.

3. Is. in the S. Pacific which has an active trade in guano. It was taken possession of by Britain in 1864. As dist H.Q. of the Line Is. it forms part of the Gilbert and Ellice Is. and comes under the authority of the high commissioner for the W. Pacific. Area 35 sq. m.; pop. (estimated 1963) 477.

Maldive Islands, group of 12 coral is. in the Indian Ocean, 400 m. SW. of Ceylon. The people are expert navigators and keen traders. They are Muslims. Mali, or King's Is., is the cap. of the group. The sultanate, estab. under the constitution of 1932, was abolished in 1952 when the ter. became a rep. Amir Amin Didi became president. That gov. was overthrown in Sept. 1953, and the sultanate restored in Feb. 1954. Formerly under Brit. protection, the is. were granted independence in 1965, but Britain retained the right to keep her bases there for a further 20 years. There is an R.A.F. Staging Post on Gan Is.

Maldon, municipal bor., mrkt tn and port of Essex, England, at the head of the Blackwater estuary, 44 m. ENE. of London. Industries are flour-milling, timber-milling, iron-working, engineering, crystallised salt manuf., brewing, oyster fishing, barge and yacht building and sail making. Pop. 10.507.

Maldon, The Battle of, took place in 993, according to the *Anglo-Saxon Chronicle*, and was a contest between a band of raiding Northmen under Anlaf and the earldorman Byrhtnoth, which resulted in the death of Byrhtnoth. It is described in a contemporary epic poem of which about 700 lines still exist, but no one of the enemy is mentioned by name, as it was written immediately after the battle, before the poet had time to find out any information about the opponents. There is an annotated ed. by W. J. Sedgefield 1904.

Maldenado: 1. Dept of SE. Uruguay on the sea coast. Agriculture and cattle raising are the chief occupations. The dept has sev. splendid resorts, such as Punta del Este. Area 1824 sq. m. Pop. 76,500.
2. Cap. of the above dept, seaport and commercial centre, 70 m. E. of Montevideo. It exports cattle, hides and limestone to Montevideo. Good transport connections by road, rail and air with Montevideo. Pop. 10,000.

Male Fern (*Dryopteris filix-mas*), one of the commonest Brit. ferns. lightish-green, bipinnate fronds rise erectly from a stout rhizome like the feathers from a shuttlecock. The fern exhibits wide variation in type, and has been split up into 3 subspecies. The spore capsules are borne in circular sori or heaps on the back of the fronds, and at first are covered by kidney-shaped scales. The plant, and especially the rhizome, has anthelmintic properties, and oil of M. F. is used as a vermifuge.

Malebranche, Nicolas (1638–1715), Fr. philosopher, *b*. Paris. At the age of 22 he entered the congregation of the Oratory, and devoted himself to the study of Bible hist. and of the fathers of the church, till Descartes's treatise *De Homine* attracted him to philosophy. His

4673

famous work, *De la recherche de la vérité*, was pub. at Paris in 2 vols., 1674–5. It shows great depth and originality of thought, and had for its object the psychological investigation of the causes of the errors to which the human mind is liable, and of the nature of truth and the way of reaching it. He maintains that we see all things in God, that all beings and thoughts exist in God. His system is a kind of mystic idealism. It was immediately opposed by Antoine Arnauld, Bossuet and many others, and was subjected to a thorough and critical examination by Locke and Leibniz. Besides the work above mentioned M. wrote *Conversations chrétiennes*, 1677, *Traité de morale*, 1683, *Traité de l'amour de Dieu*, 1707, and other religious works. *See* H. Gouhier, *La Philosophie de Malebranche*, 1926.

Malekula, is. of the New Hebrides, W. Pacific, being the second largest is. of the group. A mt chain runs along the whole length of the E. coast and another inland parallel to the S. coast. Sharp Peak is 2765 ft high and Mt Penot 2925 ft. Copra, coffee and sandalwood are exported. The Brit. administrative H.Q. are at Bushman's Bay on the NE. coast, the Fr. at Port Sandwich on the SE. coast. The natives are Melanesians. The inhab. have been subject of much field work by anthropologists. Pop. 5000. *See* A. B. Deacon, *Malekula: a Vanishing People in the New Hebrides*, 1934, and J. Layard, *Stone Men of Malekula*, 1942.

Malenkov, Georgiy Maksimilianovich (1902–), Russian Communist. His early life is obscure, but he probably had a middle-class background. In 1919 he became political commissar in the Red Army, and in 1920 he joined the Communist party. From 1921 to 1925 he studied at a Moscow technical institute, then he worked in the apparatus of the Central Committee and in the Moscow committee of the party under Kaganovich. From 1934 to 1939 he was head of the Central Committee dept for leading party personnel, and in this capacity one of the chief perpetrators of the great purge (q.v.). In 1939 he became a member and secretary of the Central Committee and head of its administration of cadres. He became candidate member of the Politburo (q.v.) in 1941, and from 1941 to 1945 he was a member of the State Defence Committee (q.v.), responsible for the technical equipment of the army and air force, and a high-ranking political commissar on various fronts. In 1943 he was appointed chairman of the Committee for Rehabilitation in former occupied ters. After the war he was secretary of the Party Central Committee and deputy Prime Minister, and in 1946 he became a Politburo member. At the nineteenth Party Congress in 1952 M. presented the Central Committee report. After Stalin's death in 1953 M. became Prime Minister and the most prominent member of the 'collective leadership': for the first week he was also the leading Party secretary, before losing his secretaryship altogether. He took the lead in denouncing Beria (q.v.). He resigned as Prime Minister in 1955, making a humiliating statement about his 'lack of experience', and

became a deputy Prime Minister. During his premiership M. advocated the policy of an equal development of production goods and consumer goods industries; this policy was officially discarded at the time of his resignation. In 1957 he was expelled from the Party Central Committee and its Presidium, together with Molotov, Kaganovich (qq.v.) and Shepilov, for trying to oust Khrushchev by means of this 'anti-party group'. In 1964 it was stated by Suslov that M. had been expelled from the Party after the 22nd Party Congress in 1961. *See* M. Ebon, *Malenkov*, 1953.

Malesherbes, Chrétien Guillaume de Lamoignon (1721–94), Fr. statesman, *b.* Paris, associate of Turgot (q.v.) and the party that sought by moderate reforms to maintain the Fr. monarchy. Among numerous other offices he held those of president of the Cour des Aides and minister of the king's household. When Louis XVI was brought to trial, M. defended him, and was himself subsequently guillotined. The works of M., who was a member of the Fr. Academy and of the Academy of Belles Lettres and Inscriptions, are mostly on subjects of natural hist. and rural economy. *See* life by J. M. Allison, 1938.

Malet, Lucas, pseudonym of **Mary St Leger Harrison** (1852–1931), novelist, *b.* Eversley, daughter of Charles Kingsley (q.v.). In 1876 she married Wm Harrison, formerly rector of Clovelly, and in 1899 became a Rom. Catholic. Her most celebrated work was *History of Sir Richard Calmady*, 1901. Others include *Colonel Enderby's Wife*, 1885, *The Wages of Sin*, 1890, *The Far Horizon*, 1906, *Adrian Savage*, 1911, *The Survivors*, 1923, and *The Dogs of Want*, 1924.

Malevick, Kasimir (1878–1935), Russian painter and art theorist, *b.* Kief. Influenced by the modern Fr. paintings being collected in Moscow by wealthy merchants, before 1914 he passed through Fauve (q.v.), Cubist (*see* CUBISM) and Futurist (*see* FUTURISM) phases but in 1915 turned to the completely non-figurative art he called 'suprematism'. He vigorously propagated his ideas in the early years of the Bolshevik Revolution, but the return to conservatism in the U.S.S.R., *c.* 1930, marked the end of his influence there. In W. Europe he counts as an important pioneer of abstract art.

Malham, vil. in the W. Riding of Yorks, England, 6 m. E. of Settle (q.v.), on the R. Aire. The Craven Fault, a displacement of limestone, forms 2 amphitheatres of rock, M. Cove and Gordale Scar, 1 m. from the vil. The cliffs of M. Cove are nearly 300 ft high; the R. Aire rises at their foot. M. Tarn, N. of the cove, is an upland lake. Pop. 135.

Malherbe François de (1555–1628), Fr. poet *b.* Caen in Normandy. He accompanied Henri of Angoulême, son of Henri II, who went to Provence as governor in 1579, and remained attached to his household till that prince's death in 1585. He was patronised by Henri IV, on whose death his widow, Marie de' Medici, settled a pension upon him. M. has been styled by competent judges the restorer of the Fr.

language and poetry. His criticism of the Pléiade poets and their use of language helped to create the classical doctrine of perfection. *See* F. Brunot, *La Doctrine de Malherbe*, 1891, and R. Bray, *La Formation de la doctrine classique en France*, 1927.

Mali, a rep. of W. Africa, bounded on the N. by the Sahara desert, on the S. by the Rep. of Guinea, Ivory Coast and Upper Volta, on the E. by Niger, and on the W. by Mauritania and Senegal. Area 464,752 sq. m. The cap. is Bamako on the R. Niger; other principal towns are Kayes, Ségou, Mopti, Sikasso and Tombouctou.

Physical features and climate. In the N. is a large desert tract on the fringe of the Sahara; further S. the land is watered by the Niger and the upper Senegal and supports crops and animals. In the SW. M. reaches to the foothills of the Fouta Djalon. The climate is hot and dry, but the rainfall varies considerably from N. to S. The Saharan region has practically no rain, but in the S. there is a rainy season from July to Oct. during which humidity is generally high.

Population. The N. is sparsely populated by desert peoples including Touaregs and Moors; farther S. the chief tribes are the Bambara and Mandingo, but there are also Senoufos, Peuls and others. Many dialects are spoken, but French is the official language. Pop. *c.* 4,100,000, of whom about 60 per cent are Muslims, 5 per cent Christians and the remainder chiefly animists.

Economy. M. is almost exclusively agric. and future prosperity depends on the success of gov. development plans to increase production. Priority schemes include the damming of the Niger rapids and the installation of hydro-electric plants. Long-term plans involve the setting up of processing plants for the country's products, the construction of an oil refinery and the exploration of mineral resources. The most fertile area is in the extreme S., but the existing irrigated area fed by the Sansanding barrage on the upper Niger above Tombouctou produces rice, cotton and groundnuts. Food crops include millet, sorghum, maize, beans and yams. Only about 20 per cent of the land is productive. In the N. nomadic tribes, moving from pasture to pasture, breed cattle, sheep and camels. Fisheries on the Niger are important.

Education. In 1963–4 there were 108,000 children receiving primary education, 4000 secondary school pupils, and 900 students attending technical schools.

Communications. A railway runs from Koulikoro to the cap., from there to Kayes and on into the Rep. of Senegal, but the inter-state link ceased to function when the M. Federation broke up in 1960. It was re-opened in 1963. The Senegal riv. is navigable from Kayes, and small steamers runs services on the Niger. There is an international airport at Bamako.

Government. The constitution introduced after the attainment of independence in 1960 provides for a National Assembly of 70 members, elected by universal suffrage. The adminis-

tration is in the hands of a council of 12 ministers.

History. M. was originally Fr. Sudan, a colony formed in 1904 from the ters. of Senegambia and the Niger, less the Senegal Protectorate, which was returned to Senegal. Until 1920 it was known as Upper Senegal and Niger. In 1933 a part of the Upper Volta was added, and further minor changes to the frontiers were made in 1948 and 1954. In Nov. 1958 the colony became an autonomous rep. within the Fr. community and was renamed the Sudanese Rep. From Jan. 1959 to Sept. 1960 it joined with Senegal to form the M. Federation, which it left on attaining full independence. In Dec. 1960 M., Ghana and Guinea entered into an agreement to co-ordinate their economic and financial policies and their diplomatic representation. Another economic grouping was entered into in 1965, when the Senegal Riv. Committee was formed to co-ordinate development projects in M., Guinea, Mauritania and Senegal, all bordering the Senegal riv. *See* M. R. Delavignette, *Afrique occidentale française*, 1931; G. Spitz, *Soudan Français*, 1955.

Malibran, Maria Felicita (1808–36), Franco-Sp. operatic singer, *b.* Paris, a daughter of Manuel Garcia, Sp. tenor. She appeared at a very early age in Paris and made her London début in 1825 in *The Barber of Seville* at Covent Garden. She then went to America and later sang with great success in France and Italy. She married Bériot, the violinist, in 1836, but *d.* suddenly at Manchester the same year.

Malic Acid, or **Monohydroxysuccinic Acid** ($C_4H_6O_5$), an organic acid which occurs in the free state and in the form of its salts in many fruits, including apples, grapes and mountain-ash berries. It forms deliquescent crystals melting at 100° C.; it dissolves readily in water and alcohol. It may be prepared by boiling bromosuccinic acid with moist silver oxide or by treating aspartic acid with nitrous acid. It is usually obtained by squeezing the juice out of unripe mountain-ash berries; the juice is boiled with milk of lime, and the resulting precipitate is dissolved with hot nitric acid, crystals of calcium, hydrogen malate being formed. The salt is then decomposed with oxalic acid.

Malice, in popular language, means ill will or spite against a particular person or class of persons. In law it can also mean this, as in actions for malicious falsehood or improper motive as in defamation (q.v.). In criminal law in practically all cases it merely connotes that which is unlawful and is tantamount to criminal intent (*see* CRIMINAL LAW). M. when used in law in the non-technical sense is generally called express M., or M. in fact, in contradistinction to technical or implied M., i.e. the M. or criminal intention that is really nothing more than an inference of law resulting from doing the objectively criminal act, e.g. murder is generally defined as killing with 'M. aforethought', or *prepense*, while manslaughter (q.v.) is defined as killing another without M., either express or implied. In civil actions M., or indeed any other state of mind, is for the most part irrelevant, and it is now settled law (1) that a violation of a legal right committed knowingly gives a right to sue for damages, not on the ground of malicious intention, but simply because the interference with other people's contractual relations is wrongful if not justified; (2) if such violation or interference be unjustifiable, the presence or absence of M. is immaterial to the cause of action.

Malicious Prosecution. A person who has been criminally prosecuted 'without reasonable and probable cause' may sue his prosecutor for damages for M. P. He will not necessarily succeed merely because he has been acquitted of a criminal charge. If a crime has been committed and the circumstances were such that the prosecutor had reasonable cause for believing that the plaintiff (in the civil action) was probably the guilty person, he is justified in protecting his interests by prosecuting him. If the judge decides that there was no reasonable and probable cause, the plaintiff must prove to the satisfaction of the jury that the defendant (prosecutor) was actuated by malice or some indirect motive like personal spite or ill will against him; but if the judge decides on the facts that there was such cause, then malicious motives are immaterial, and there is no case to go to the jury. As a rule a claim for damages for M. P. is joined with a claim for false imprisonment (q.v.), for there cannot be a prosecution without at least technical imprisonment. The false imprisonment, however, is more or less merged in the M. P. where joined with such a claim.

Malignant Jaundice, see JAUNDICE.

Malignant Pustules, see ANTHRAX.

Malignants, name given by the Parliamentarians to the Royalists during the Great Rebellion in England. It first occurs in the Grand Remonstrance of 1641.

Maligne Lake forms part of the Jasper National Park (q.v.) on the slopes of the Rocky Mts, Alberta, Canada. The lake is about 17 m. in length; it is about 40 m. SE. of Jasper by road. The lake was named by Father De Smet from the Fr. *maline*, bad. (*See Plate: Alberta.*)

Maliki, see IMAM.

Malinidi, anct Arab seaport, 66 m. NE. of Mombasa, now used by dhows. Vasco da Gama visited it in 1498. M. is a holiday resort.

Malines, see MECHELEN.

Malingering, word of obscure derivation, which according to Cotgrave comes from the Fr. *malingre*, sickly, denoting deliberately feigned or exaggerated illness or disability for any purpose of gain. It differs aetiologically from somatic hysteria in that its motivation resides in consciousness. M. is probably most commonly met with in attempts to evade duties in the services in wartime, and it may be used with the purpose of obtaining a service pension or to sustain a claim in the civilian courts for compensation for personal injury. M. takes various forms, from simulating pyrexia by placing the thermometer in contact with a

hot-water bottle, to producing a derangement of cardiac action by swallowing tobacco juice, but the malingerer's lack of any real medical knowledge usually prevents the disease picture from being either complete or consistent and generally leads to speedy exposure. M. rarely succeeds in defeating a combination of skilled medical examination and careful supervision. M. *per se* is not an offence except in the case of service personnel or when it is used in an attempt to obtain money.

Malinovskiy, *see* BOGDANOV, ALEKSANDR ALEKSANDROVICH.

Malinovsky, Rodion Yakovlevich (1898–), Russian soldier, Marshal of the Soviet Union, and Soviet minister of defence since 1957. He took part in the Civil war, 1918–20 (*see* CIVIL WAR, RUSSIAN), joined the Communist party (*see* COMMUNIST PARTY OF THE SOVIET UNION) in 1926 and graduated from the M. V. Frunze Military Academy in 1930. During the Second World War he commanded an army in the Stalingrad offensive in 1942, the SW. army group in 1943 and the 2nd Ukrainian army group in 1944. Signed the Rumanian armistice at Moscow, Sept. 1944. (*See also* EASTERN FRONT IN SECOND WORLD WAR.) He was commander-in-chief of the Soviet forces in Manchuria, 1945–6, and subsequently commander of a military dist. He has made many belligerent speeches against the W. but is considered to have a very limited grasp of the problems of modern warfare. He became a candidate member of the Communist Party's Central Committee in 1952, a full member in 1956, and succeeded Marshal Zhukov as minister of defence in Oct. 1957.

Malinowski, Bronislaw Kaspar (1884–1942), Anglo-Polish social anthropologist, *b.* Cracow, Poland, and educ. at the Polish Univ. there. He accompanied the Robert Mond anthropological expedition to New Guinea and NW. Melanesia in 1914 and visited Australia in 1918 and Mexico in 1926. Reader in social anthropology (1924–7) and prof. (from 1927) in the univ. of London. Visiting prof. to Yale (1939). His work in London Univ. from 1927 made him world famous as one of the leading social anthropologists. He was the founder of modern anthropological field research methods, and most modern Brit. anthropologists were trained by him. His main works are *Argonauts of the Western Pacific*, 1922, *Sex and Repression in Savage Society*, 1928, *The Sexual Life of Savages in NW. Melanesia*, 1929, and *Coral Gardens and their Magic . . . in the Trobriand Islands* (2 vols.), 1935. *See* R. Firth (ed.), *Man and Culture: an Evaluation of the Work of Bronislaw Malinowski*, 1957.

Malipiero, Gian Francesco (1882–), It. composer, *b.* Venice, studied at Venice and Bologna under Bossi, became prof. of composition at the Parma Conservatory in 1921 and in 1939 director of the Liceo Marcello at Venice. He has written much music of all kinds in a modern idiom, but in the It. traditions preceding those of the 19th cent., which he regards as debased. His stage works, e.g. the *Orfeide* trilogy, 1918–22, another, *Il mistero di Venezia*, 1925–8, *Torneo notturno*, 1929, *Mondi celesti e infernali*, 1948–9, often explore new dramatic forms, and two, *Guilio Cesare*, 1935, and *Antonio e Cleopatra*, 1938, are based on Shakespeare. His output also includes large choral works, numerous symphonies and other orchestral works, music for solo instruments and orchestra, 7 string quartets, and other chamber music.

Mall, The: 1. London thoroughfare running along the N. side of St James's Park, between the Admiralty Arch near Trafalgar Square and the Queen Victoria memorial in front of Buckingham Palace. It was originally constructed for Charles II, who was fond of the game of pall-mall (*see* below). By the 18th cent. the M. was the fashionable evening lounge.
2. The original name of **Pall Mall**, London thoroughfare running from the S. end of St James's St to the S. end of Haymarket, and a centre of social clubs. It derives its name from the Fr. game of *paille maille* (from which croquet is believed to be derived), played here at least as early as 1635, when Pall M. was a part of St James's Park, but the game was discontinued during the Commonwealth when there was a considerable increase of building in the area. It was the first London street lighted by gas (1807). Among the famous inhab. of Pall M. were Nell Gwyn, the 1st Duke of Marlborough (*see* MARLBOROUGH HOUSE), Gibbon and Gainsborough.

Mallard, *Anas platyrhynchos*, subfamily Anatinae of the order Anseriformes. The common wild duck of Great Britain and the N. hemisphere, from which most domesticated breeds are derived. The sexes have distinctive colour patterns. The drake has a glossy green head, white collar and chestnut brown breast, while the duck has a mottled brown plumage. The drake, which reaches a total length of nearly 2 feet, is also larger than its mate, but both sexes carry on the wing a blue, white-edged speculum and have orange coloured legs. Of all freshwater ducks the M. is the commonest, and though it was more plentiful in former days there are still so many retired dists in Great Britain where it is encouraged to breed that it is extremely numerous in some places, and every winter there is a great accession of migrants from the Continent. At this season it quits its N. habitat and is absent from many of the N. dists of Scotland and its is. Like the tame duck the M. is almost omnivorous in its choice of food, many kinds of aquatic plants and weeds, as well as water insects, worms and slugs, forming its usual diet, though it will also eat grain and acorns.

Mallarmé, Stéphane (1842–98), Fr. poet and theorist, *b.* Paris. In 1876 he pub. his *L'Après-midi d'un faune*, and in 1887 *Poésies complètes*. His vol. *Vers et prose*, containing some of his most important work, appeared in 1893. He had previously pub. in 1888 a notable trans. of the poems of Edgar Allan Poe and some essays of literary criticism. His poems contain some verses of extraordinary beauty and grace, but are, for the most part, wrapped in mysticism and are not very intelligible. M. is an important figure in the development of Fr. literature of the Third Empire and his influence on Paul Valéry and other later writers is as great as that of Verlaine. M. expresses in his fragmentary pieces the spirit of a new kind of literature which dominates the whole period of the Third Empire. He was the first Fr. writer to formulate a definite theory of the function of poetry (*Vers et prose*). According to M. reality is not art; nothing that tells a tale is poetry; nothing that teaches a lesson is poetry; nothing that expresses feeling is poetry; drama is the least poetic of all forms of writing. Poetry must learn from music. Thus he condemns nearly all previous literature, save for some isolated exceptions. He proclaims that the true function of poetry is to restore the eternal, and its true subjects the failures of reality, as exemplified in Baudelaire's *Fleurs du mal*, 1857. M. wrote comparatively little, he was essentially a thinker and talker. He seems deliberately to make his verse incomprehensible to square with his theories—theories which impelled him to Symbolism, the strongest single influence in Fr. literature of the period. See G. Michaud, *Mallarmé, l'homme et l'œuvre*, 1953; W. Fowlie, *Mallarmé*, 1953.

Malleability, physical property of materials which determines the extent to which their shape can be altered by hammering without breaking. Most metals and metal alloys are malleable to some degree, gold being particularly malleable. Temp. may be an important factor in M.: some metals are only malleable at temps. below, and some at temps. above, their recrystallisation temp. The property is of especial importance in rolling, pressing and forging. *See* METALLURGY.

Malleco, inland prov. of central Chile, in the centre of which is a rich plain where agriculture is carried on. The chief industries are wheat-growing and cattle-raising. M. lies just to the S. of the R. Bío Bío. Angol is the cap. Area 5511 sq. m.; pop. 207,477.

Malle, the Australian name for *Eucalyptus dumosa* and *oleosa*, 2 dwarf species of the gum-tree, which are able to live under extremely adverse conditions, and form dense thickets over tracts of country called M. scrub. Much may be accomplished by irrigation schemes, in course of preparation, to relieve the constant threat of drought in these areas. The M. country is subject to dust-storms, which cover roads, gardens and fences and pile dust in drifts up to 6 ft in depth.

Malleson, George Bruce (1825–98), author, *b.* Wimbledon. Educ. at Winchester. For some time he was Indian correspondent of *The Times*. His first work to attract notice was the *Red Pamphlet* pub. at Calcutta during the mutiny (1857). Among his other works are *History of the French in India*, 1868, *History of Afghanistan*, 1878, *The Founders of the Indian Empire*, 1882, and *The Decisive Battles of India*, 1883. He also re-wrote the *History of the Indian Mutiny*, 1878–80, left uncompleted by Sir John Kaye.

Mallet (originally **Malloch**), **David** (*c.* 1705–65), poet and miscellaneous writer, *b.* Crieff, Perthshire. He was educ. there and at the univ. of Edinburgh, where he met Thomson. In 1723 appeared his ballad of 'William and Margaret', by which he is chiefly remembered, and which made him known to Pope, Young and others. His *Excursion*, an imitation of Thomson, was pub. in 1728. At the request of the Prince of Wales, whose secretary he had become, he wrote with Thomson a masque, *Alfred*, 1740, in which 'Rule, Britannia' first appeared, which, though he claimed the authorship, is now generally attributed to Thomson. On the accession of George III M. became a zealous supporter of Lord Bute, and was rewarded with a sinecure. M. wrote also some indifferent dramas, including *Eurydice*, 1731, *Mustapha*, 1739, and *Elvira*, 1763. He is included in Johnson's *Lives of the Poets*.

Malling, East and **West,** *see* EAST and WEST MALLING.

Malloch, David, *see* MALLET.

Mallophaga, *see* BIRD LICE.

Mallorca, *see* MAJORCA.

Mallory, G. Leigh-, *see* LEIGH-MALLORY.

Mallow, tn on the Blackwater R., 20 m. NW. of Cork, Rep. of Ireland, an important rail and distribution centre and fishing centre for the Blackwater and its tributaries. It has a large sugar beet factory (2 m.), and a regional hospital and racecourse. The remains of an anct McCarthy castle are on the riv. near the modern bridge. Pop. 5520.

Mallow, or **Malva,** genus of hardy annuals and perennials. The musk M. (*M. moschata*), with rose or white flowers, is grown in gardens.

Malmaison, Fr. château at Rueil-Malmaison (q.v.). It was a favourite retreat of Napoleon, and the residence of the Empress Joséphine (q.v.) after her divorce. It is now a museum.

Malmache, Tanguy (1875–1953), *see* BRETON LANGUAGE AND LITERATURE.

Malmédy, tn and dist of E. Belgium, was given to Prussia in 1814, together with the dist of Eupen (q.v.), but was returned to Belgium in 1919. In 1940 M. was again attached to Germany, but was liberated by Amer. troops in 1944. Pop. 6400.

Malmesbury, James Harris, 1st Earl of (1746–1820), diplomat, *b.* Salisbury and educ. at Winchester and Oxford. In 1767 he was appointed secretary at the Brit. embassy at Madrid. From 1777 to 1784 he was ambas. to St Petersburg. In 1788 he became minister at The Hague. For services while here he was raised to the peerage. In 1794 he was employed to negotiate the marriage between the Prince of Wales and Caroline, daughter of the Duke of Brunswick, and accompanied her to England. See *Diaries and Correspondence*, 1844, and *Lord Malmesbury and his Friends*, 1870, both ed. by his grandson, **James Howard Harris,** 3rd Earl of M. (1807–89), who succeeded in 1841 and in 1852 and 1858–9 was foreign secretary and later lord privy seal. *See* his *Memoirs of an Ex-Minister*, 1884.

Malmesbury: 1. Bor. and mrkt tn in Wilts, England, 19½ m. NNW. of Bath, picturesquely situated on the R. Avon. The par. church was

MALLOW

formerly the Saxon abbey where Athelstan was buried. In the market-place stands a beautiful Gothic cross of the time of Henry VII. Pop. of bor. 2600.

2. Municipality in Cape Prov. of S. Africa, 40 m. by road from Cape Tn, has salt pans and sulphur springs. Pop. White, 11,405; Coloureds, 28,646; Bantu, 3566.

Malmö, fort, tn of Sweden, on the Sound, cap. of co. of Malmöhus. It has a citadel and port with 3 harbours. It has a good trade in grain and whisky, and manufs. sugar, beer and textiles. There are also iron works and dockyards. Bothwell was imprisoned in its castle. Pop. 229,500.

Malmöhus, co. of Sweden, the S. part of the Scania peninsula, is a very fertile dist. Area 1872 sq. m.; pop. 626,000.

Malmsey, or **Malvoisie,** once famous as the Malvasia of Crete, is now a sweet fortified wine made in Madeira (q.v.), Cyprus and the Canaries from the Malvasia grape. *See also* MADEIRA WINE.

Malo-les-Bains, Fr. seaside resort in the dept of Nord, 1 m. from Dunkirk. It has a fine promenade and beach. Pop. 14,500.

Malolos, tn of Bulacan prov., Luzon, Philippines, 20 m. NW. of Manila. The chief crop is rice. Pop. *c.* 40,000.

Malone, Edmund (1741–1812), critic and editor, *b.* Dublin. He was educ. at Trinity College, Dublin, and called to the Irish Bar in the late sixties. He came to London in 1777, and 8 years later was elected to the Literary Club, with the most prominent members of which, Johnson, Burke, Reynolds and Boswell, he was on intimate terms. He devoted himself to the study of Shakespeare. In 1778 he pub. an *Attempt to ascertain the Order in which the Plays of Shakespeare were written*, and from 1783 worked at his ed. of *Shakespeare*, which appeared in 1790. In 1800 appeared his ed. of Dryden's works with a biographical introduction. M. was one of the first to express his disbelief in Chatterton's *Poems supposed to have been written by T. Rowley*, and in 1796 he denounced the forgeries of Samuel Ireland. *See* life by Sir J. Prior, 1864.

Malonic Acid, $CH_3(COOH)_2$, organic acid formed by the oxidation of malic acid. It forms colourless crystals melting at 132° C., and is readily soluble in water, alcohol and ether. When heated above its melting-point it decomposes into acetic acid and carbon dioxide.

Malory, Sir Thomas (*c.* 1400–70), translator, *b.* Newbold Revell, Warwickshire, son of the sheriff. He saw military service in France with the Earl of Warwick, and in 1445 sat in Parliament as knight of the shire. In 1451 he was arraigned on a long list of offences, including the attempted assassination of the Duke of Buckingham, and spent a great part of the rest of his life in prison, where he wrote his famous work, the *Morte d'Arthur*. It is a very fine prose rendering in 21 books of the Arthurian legends, made up from the Fr. versions with additions of his own. Completed in 1469, it was printed by Caxton in 1485. Details of M.'s life previously lacking were supplied in a MS. of his work discovered at Winchester in 1934. There is an ed. of his works by E. Vinaver, 1947. *See* studies by V. Scudder, 1921; E. Hicks, 1928; E. Vinaver, 1929; G. R. Stewart, 1935.

Malpighi, Marcello (1628–94), It. anatomist, *b.* Crevalcuore, near Milan. He held, at different periods of his life, the professorship of medicine at Bologna, Pisa and Messina. He is chiefly known for his discoveries in the anatomy of the skin, kidney and spleen; the Malpighian bodies or corpuscles of the kidney and the spleen still retain the name of their discoverer. He was also the first to examine the blood-vessels with the microscope, and thus discovered the capillaries (minute vessels connecting arteries to veins), the final link in the chain explaining Harvey's discovery of the circulation.

Malpighiaceae, dicotyledonous family of trees and shrubs, occurring mostly in the S. hemisphere, with glandular 5-parted calyx, 5 petals spurred at the base, and fruit a drupe, woody nut or samara.

Malplaquet, hamlet in dept of Nord, France, the site of the victory of Marlborough and Prince Eugene over the French, 11 Sept. 1709. It is 21 m. E. by S. of Valenciennes.

Malraux, André (1901–), Fr. writer and politician, *b.* Paris. Before the Second World War, M. sympathised with communism and was in China in 1925–7, during the civil war, and took part in the Spanish civil war on the side of the Republicans. He served in the Fr. resistance, came to reject communism, and was made Minister of Information in de Gaulle's gov. in 1945–6. After de Gaulle's return to power in 1958, M. again entered the gov. and has been Minister of State for Cultural Affairs since 1959. Episodes of his early career provide the background for many of his novels. An archaeological mission he undertook in Cambodia in 1923 furnished material for *La Voie royale*, 1930, dealing with just such an expedition. From his experiences in a revolutionary situation in China came *Les Conquérants*, 1928, and *La Condition humaine* (probably his greatest novel), 1933. *L'Espoir*, 1937, another fine novel, records vividly many episodes of the Sp. civil war. M.'s other novels are *Le Temps du mépris*, 1935, on the theme of a Czech communist in the hands of the Gestapo, and *Les Noyers de l'Altenburg*, 1943, which, though unsuccessful as a novel, is important for understanding the author's philosophy. (The MS. of *Les Noyers* was smuggled out of occupied France and first pub. in Switzerland; the MS. of a second vol. fell into the hands of the Gestapo and was destroyed, and will not, M. says, be re-written.) In his novels, M. frequently shows individuals placed in situations in which they are forced to examine the meaning of their own life. M. has also made an outstanding contribution to aesthetics with his *Psychologie de l'art*, 3 vols., 1947–9. Among his other works are *Lunes en papier*, 1921, *La Tentation de l'Occident*, 1926, *Royaume farfelu*, 1928, *Esquisse d'une psychologie du cinéma*, 1946, *Le Musée imaginaire de la sculpture mondiale*, 3 vols., 1952–5, and *La métamorphose des dieux*, 1957. *See* W. M. Frohock, *André Malraux and the Tragic Imagination*, 1953; C. D. Blend, *André Malraux, Tragic Humanist*, 1962; J. Hoffman, *L'Humanisme de Malraux*, 1963.

Malström, *see* MAELSTROM.

Malt, applied to grain which has been softened and prepared by germination. Barley is the chief cereal which is malted. It is soaked in water for about 2 days and then exposed to air either in a layer on a malting floor, or, in most recent installations, in a cylindrical drum or a large air-conditioned rectangular container. This treatment induces germination in the small germ which lies at one end of the grain. The shoot starts to grow along each corn and the rootlets protrude. With restricted light and moisture the growth of the germ is somewhat checked, but in the germ development proceeds in the enzymes which can attack and liberate for the use of the germ the food stores of the grain. During growth the grain is turned over by hand or mechanically to prevent the felting together of the rootlets. After 8 to 10 days' growth the M. is used directly if it is intended for the production of whisky, but M. for brewing or M. extract manufacture is usually dried by hot air to a low moisture content and the rootlets (M. culms) are removed. Such dried M. can then be transported or stored. When required for use, it is crushed in roller mills and mixed with hot water (mashed). Rapid action ensues in which the enzymes of the grain liberate the bulk of the contents as soluble compounds. The chief grain constituent is starch and this is rapidly split up by the enzyme diastase (or amylase) to yield simple sugars and more complicated dextrins and malto-dextrins. Similarly the proteins yield a range of soluble breakdown products. The insoluble residues —the spent grains—are used as cattle food.

The soluble products of the M. are fermented by yeast in the production of whisky or beer; in the production of M. extracts, they are concentrated to a syrup by evaporation at low pressures and temps. M.s intended for brewing are produced with a wide range of flavour and colour by varying the temp. and other conditions during drying, according to whether the M.s are intended for pale ales, brown ales or stouts. By control of the mashing conditions, M. extracts can be produced with high or low proportions of sugar or dextrins, or with high or negligible contents of enzymes. *See* BREWING.

Malta G.C. (anct **Melita**), prin. is. of a group of is. in the Mediterranean which together form the independent *State of M*. The group comprises M., Gozo (q.v.), Comino (lying between M. and Gozo; area 1·075 sq. m., pop. 70) and various small islets, including Cominotto. The total area of the group is 121·8 sq. m., and the total pop. 338,000.

M. lies about 60 m. S. of Sicily, and about half way between Gibraltar and Suez. It is oval in shape (17½ m. long, 8½ m. wide, area 94·9 sq. m.), and has a rocky, deeply-indented coast, with good harbours in the NE. and E. In the S. the cliffs reach a height of 400 ft. The action of the sea has hollowed out grottoes and caves in the cliffs, many of them very large. The surface of the land is uneven; parallel valleys run from SW. to NE., the largest being the valley called Mellcha. There are no rivs., but there are subterranean basins. The climate is equable, but in summer M. suffers from the sirocco (q.v.). Much of the is. has been terraced for farming. The soil is thin but productive, and wheat, barley, onions, beans, potatoes, tomatoes, citrus fruits and grapes are grown. There are traditional manufs. of lace and tobacco, and the gov. has encouraged the estab. of new industries, including light engineering and textile manufs. The former Brit. naval dockyard has been converted to commercial use. Tourism is an important source of revenue. M. is of great interest to archaeologists; megalithic monuments are found at Hagar Qim and Mnajdra in the S., and there are enormous troglodyte temples with prehistoric paintings at Tarxien, 2 m. S. of Valletta. The people of M. are of mixed race, but are believed to be largely Semitic in origin. Almost all of them are Rom. Catholic. The official languages are English and Maltese; the educ. classes also speak Italian. The Maltese language is akin to Arabic, with It. elements; some believe it to be derived from Phoenician. M. has a university at Valletta. About 20 per cent of the pop. is illiterate. The country has a cabinet system of gov., with a one-chamber legislature, the House of Representatives, which has 50 members. M. is a member of the Brit. Commonwealth.

History. It is thought by some that M. was the Hyperion or Ogygia of Homer, but there is little doubt that the Phoenicians (*see* PHOENICIA) colonised the is. at a very early date, probably in the 16th cent. BC. Before they were dispossessed by the Greeks in 736 BC, they had developed considerable commerce. The Greeks, who called the is. Melita, were driven out by the Carthaginians about 500 BC. As early as the first Punic war M. was plundered by the Romans, but did not come finally into their possession until 201 BC. St Paul's Is., or Selmunett, in St Paul's Bay on the NE. coast, is the traditional site of St

Paul's shipwreck (Acts xxvii), and the place is marked by a statue. During the 5th cent. AD M. fell successively under the Vandals and Goths, whose barbarism nearly annihilated its commerce. In 533 Belisarius (q.v.) restored M. to the Byzantine Empire, in nominal union with which it remained for more than 3 cents.; but its civilisation almost vanished amid constant local feuds. In 870 the Arabs destroyed the Gk power in M., and fortified the harbour as a station for their corsairs. Count Roger of Sicily (*see* ROGER I) drove out the Arabs in 1090, and estab. a popular council for the gov. of the is., composed of nobles, clergy and elected representatives of the people. This council in a modified form subsisted for 700 years. Under a marriage contract M. passed to the Ger. emperor, who constituted it a marquisate, but it had ceased to be a place of trade and was merely a garrison of more expense than value. Charles of Anjou (*see* CHARLES I of Naples), after overrunning Sicily, made himself master of M., which the French retained even after they had been expelled from Sicily, but after a time the houses of Aragon and Castile successively held the is. Subsequently the Emperor Charles V took possession of M., and in 1530 granted it, with Gozo and Tripoli, in perpetual sovereignty to the knights of the Order of St John of Jerusalem (*see* HOSPITALLERS, KNIGHTS), from whom the Turks had recently captured their great stronghold at Rhodes. The grand master of the knights defended the is. against the Turks in 1565, and founded Valletta. In 1571 they, with the Maltese, behaved most courageously at the battle of Lepanto (q.v.), where the Turks lost 30,000 men. Though waging perpetual war with the Mohammedans, the knights continued to possess M. until 1798, when, weakened by internal quarrels, the order surrendered its fortresses to the French. Britain then blockaded the is. and in 1802 the Maltese asked for Brit. protection. The is. was finally annexed to the Crown in 1814 by the treaty of Paris. Her importance as a coaling station on the Europe–Far E. trade routes began with the opening of the Suez Canal (q.v.), and in the first half of the 20th cent. M. became of vital importance to Britain as a naval and air base.

During the 19th cent. M., as a Brit. Crown Colony, was given a number of constitutions. After the First World War there was some political unrest in the is. However, a new constitution was given to M. in 1921, under which M. became in effect a self-governing colony, questions of defence and foreign policy remaining in the hands of the Brit. gov., but the constitution was subsequently suspended owing to agitation resulting from a dispute between the Brit. Gov. and the Rom. Catholic Church in the is., in which the Vatican became deeply involved (1929). The constitution was restored in 1932, only to be suspended again a year later. Under the constitution of 1921 English and Italian (which had been used in educ. circles and in the law courts for sev. cents.) were the official languages, but during the 20th cent. Maltese had gradually supplanted Italian. From 1934 Maltese was used in the courts and taught at the univ. In 1936 a new constitution was promulgated providing for crown colony gov. again. At the same time English and Maltese became the official languages of M., Maltese thus finally ousting Italian. The Maltese people as a whole were proud of their individual national character, and It. Fascist attempts to start a pro-It. 'irredentist' movement in M. between the world wars received little support from the islanders. Crown colony gov. was, however, hardly a striking advance in M.'s constitutional progress, and another constitution of a slightly more progressive character was promulgated in 1939.

The siege of Malta in the Second World War. The resistance of M. to attack from June 1940 to Nov. 1942 was a unique example of a combined operation in which the RN, Merchant Navy, Army, RAF and people of M. were all indispensable and inseparable; and to bear witness to their heroism George VI in 1942 conferred the George Cross upon the is. From the day after Italy's entry into the war until the winter during the siege of 1942, when siege-raising ships fought through to the is., M. fought a continuous battle against the Germans and Italians, against superior numbers, shortage of equipment, isolation, terror and hunger. From this long-drawn battle the is. emerged in 1943 to dominate the central Mediterranean as a striking base, a strong weapon in the armoury of the allied forces, more deadly than ever before in the long hist. of warfare in the Middle Sea. But M. suffered heavily from the air attacks. During its long ordeal the is. had 3343 alerts. By the end of 1942 over 14,000 tons of bombs had fallen upon the 122 sq. m. of M. and Gozo. The enemy lost over 1000 aircraft, and in the is.'s defence 568 Brit. aircraft were lost. Some of the most concentrated attacks were made in Jan. 1941, when the Germans strained every nerve to destroy the aircraft carrier *Illustrious* which had put in for repairs. By early 1942, air-raids having been incessant throughout the previous 2 years, the skyline of M. had become much changed. Church spires and belfries were missing. There was not a single building of the Knights of St John which had not been destroyed or damaged, though repair and restoration were carried out on a large scale when the war ended. In all about 35,000 buildings were destroyed or damaged, including three-quarters of the city of Valletta and from 80 to 85 per cent of the other tns. The number of civilians killed or *d.* of injuries was 1486. The casualties would have been heavier than they were but for the fact that a large proportion of the people slept in the rock caves, which are an interesting historical landmark of the is. (On the loss of monuments see *Works of Art in Malta. Losses and Survivals in the War* (H.M.S.O.), 1946.)

Malta after the Second World War. In 1947 a new constitution for M. came into force, granting her once more a large measure of self-gov. Women were for the first time given the vote. Reconstruction work proceeded apace and there were notable achievements in the field of social welfare. But the is.'s economy remained dependent on the U.K., while the uncertainty implicit in the ann. assessment of the Brit. financial grant to the is. made for bad feeling on both sides. The uncertain future of the service bases in M. added to unrest on the is., for in the early 1950s over 25 per cent of its labour force depended for work on projects connected with defence; and M.'s economic difficulties were emphasised by her relatively dense pop., fast increasing in total despite considerable emigration, which was encouraged by the authorities.

In 1955, despite the hostility of the Catholic Church, Dominic Mintoff (q.v.), the Maltese Labour leader, became Prime Minister of M. Mintoff suggested that M.'s problems would best be settled by 'integrating' M. in the U.K. A subsequent Brit. round-table conference approved his proposal as 'practicable and reasonable' (Dec. 1955). It suggested that M. should send 3 members of parliament to Westminster. On 11–12 Feb. 1956 a Maltese referendum on the integration of M. with Great Britain resulted in 67,607 votes in favour, 20,177 against, 2559 invalid.

In Britain, the recommendations had met with a generally warm welcome. In M. the main Opposition party, the Nationalists led by Borg Olivier (q.v.), opposed them bitterly, saying their implementation would lead eventually to the obliteration of M. as an individual entity. They suggested instead Dominion status for the is.

As time went by, the Rom. Catholic Church leaders in M. also expressed opposition to the proposals in their existing form, and the project gradually lost favour in both M. and Britain, and was eventually dropped altogether. Mintoff's relations with Britain deteriorated: Maltese fears over Britain's naval reorganisation, which was to affect M. drastically, caused ill-feeling between both countries. In April 1958 Mintoff resigned. There was rioting in M., a state of emergency was proclaimed and the governor took over the administration. Soon after this the 1947 constitution was revoked and an interim one introduced.

While new constitutional approaches were being examined, steps were taken to diversify the Maltese economy and end its dependence on the naval base. A Five Year Development Plan was launched, 1959: with Brit. financial assistance, the naval dockyard was converted into a commercial one, tourism made one of M.'s prin. industries and new factories estab. In 1961 a new constitution was introduced, and in elections held in Feb. 1962 the Nationalists won a majority, Mintoff's party suffering a severe setback owing to Church hostility. Borg Olivier became premier, and in Aug. 1962 formally asked Britain to grant M. independence within the Commonwealth. During the negotiations which followed, M.'s underlying fears regarding her financial and economic future caused some bitterness and delays. Eventually the differences were resolved, and on 21 Sept. 1964 M. became an independent state within the

Commonwealth. At the same time, the Catholic Church lifted its ban on Labour Party supporters. In Mar. 1966 Borg Olivier's Nationalists were returned at the General Election with an increased majority.

See F. W. Ryan, *The House of the Temple: Story of Malta and its Knights*, 1930, and *Prehistoric Malta*, 1930; A. Maurois, *Malte*, 1935; C. Willis Dixon, *The Colonial Administration of Sir Thomas Maitland*, 1939; I. Hay, *The Unconquered Isle: the Story of Malta, G.C.*, 1943; H.M.S.O., *Air Battle of Malta* and *East of Malta, West of Suez*, 1944; F. S. de Domenico, *An Island Beleaguered*, 1946; H. Smith, *Britain in Malta*, 1954; S. W. Roskill, *The War at Sea* (3 vols.), 1954–61; T. Balogh and D. Seers, *Interim Report on the Economic Problems of Malta*, 1955; Sir H. Luke, *Malta* (2nd ed.), 1962; E. Bradford, *The Great Siege: Malta 1565*, 1964. (*See Plate.*)

Malta, Knights of, *see* HOSPITALLERS, KNIGHTS.

Malta Fever (*Brucellosis*), **Undulant Fever,** or **Mediterranean Fever,** specific febrile affectation due to a group of micro-organisms discovered by Sir David Bruce and named after him *Brucellosis. Brucella melitensis*, the micro-organism prevalent around the Mediterranean, is transmitted with the raw milk of goats, as shown by Sir Themistocles Zammit; hence the disease was very prevalent in Malta where raw goat's milk was much in use, but it has now been much reduced and is being stamped out by having goat's milk boiled or pasteurised. The occurrence of rock fever in Gibraltar was traced to infection from the milk of goats imported from Malta. The diseases were found to be identical, and on the prohibition of Maltese goats the disease disappeared from Gibraltar. The disease has been found to be much more widely distributed than was formerly supposed. It is common in N. Africa, and is found also in S. Africa; it has also been reported from SW. Texas and other countries. In 1910 Sir David Bruce described its occurrence in Ankole, on the E. shore of Lake Albert Edward. The presence of *B. melitensis* was shown to be the cause in all cases, and infection was traced to the goats of the dists. A closely related micro-organism, *B. abortus*, is the cause of contagious abortion of cattle and of abortus fever in man in Britain, U.S.A. and other countries. Undulant fever due to *B. melitensis* is characterised by an incubation period of 1 to 3 weeks, an irregular and prolonged fever sometimes occurring in waves (hence the term undulant). The temp. may keep low (much more so in abortus fever) but may rise to 105° with toxaemia and even higher to 108° in fatal cases. The course of the disease used to be protracted from a few weeks to a year or more and arthritis and rheumatic pains were common complications, but the antibiotics aureomycin and chloromycetin have been found to be specific against the infections and a rapid cure can now be achieved.

Maltby, urb. dist of the W. Riding of Yorks, on the R. Ryton, 6 m. from Rotherham, on the

E. Region railway. It is a coal-mining centre. Pop. 13,693.

Malte-Brun, Conrad, or **Malte Conrad Bruun** (1755–1826), Dan.-Fr. geographer and publicist, banished from Denmark (*c.* 1796) for his violent political pamphlets upholding the principles of the Fr. Revolution. With Mentelle and Herbin he collaborated in *Géographie mathématique*, 1803–7. He founded the Geographical Society of Paris, and, with Eyriès, ed. the *Annales des voyages*, 1808. His *Précis de la géographie universelle*, 1810, was completed by Huot, 1829. His poems also were much admired. See B. de Saint-Vincent, *Notice biographique*, 1827, and J. Quérard, *La France littéraire*, 1827–64.

Maltese Dog, often, though wrongly, called Maltese terrier, the most anct lap-dog, its types and character having been preserved for over two thousand years. The coat reaches nearly to the ground, and is straight and silky and parted from head to tail; it is pure snowy white. The eyes are dark, the nose black, the drop ears long, the back and legs short and the feet small. The short tail is doubled into the coat on the back. Maximum height 10 in.; weight 4 to 9 lb.

Malthus, Thomas Robert (1766–1834), political economist, was a pupil of Richard Graves and Gilbert Wakefield, and afterwards went to Jesus College, Cambridge, where he distinguished himself in classics and mathematics. He entered the Church and in 1798 was curate at Albury in Surrey. He had already begun to write on economic subjects, and in 1798 wrote and pub. anonymously the famous *Essay on the Principle of Population as it affects the Future Improvement of Society*, 1798, 1926. Charles Darwin was led from a study of this essay to enunciate his theory of 'natural selection'. M.'s next most important work was *Principles of Political Economy with a view to their Practical Application*, 1820. *See also* CLASSICAL ECONOMISTS; ECONOMIC THOUGHT, HISTORY OF; POPULATION. See G. F. MacCleary, *The Malthusian Population Theory*, 1953 (*See Plate: Economic Thought, History of*).

Malton, mrkt tn in the N. Riding of Yorks, England, on the Derwent, 17½ m. NE. of York. Burnt in Stephen's reign, it was rebuilt as New M. The remains of the 12th cent. priory at Old M. include part of the priory church of St Mary's, the only remaining church of the Gilbertine Order in England in which services are still held. There is a site of a Rom. fortress on the Orchard Fields. Lime and whinstone are quarried near by. Agric. implements are manuf., and there is a brewery. Pop. 4450.

Maltose is a di-saccharide sugar consisting of 2 molecules of glucose coupled together and has the molecular formula $C_{12}H_{22}O_{11}$. It crystallises in the form of needles with one molecule of water of crystallisation. It is the main product of the action of the enzyme diastase (amylase) on starch, and consequently is the main sugar produced in the brewing (q.v.) process and present in malt extracts. It has about one-third of the sweetness of cane sugar.

Maluku, *see* MOLUCCAS.

Malus, Étienne Louis (1775–1812), Fr. physicist and engineer, *b.* Paris, noted for bridge building and fortifications, and for discoveries in optical polarisation.

Malus, formerly **Pyrus,** genus of deciduous shrubs and trees, family Rosaceae, which includes *M. pumila,* parent of orchard apples, and many species and varieties of crab apples, grown for their ornamental value.

Malvaceae, dicotyledonous family of herbs and shrubs, of tropical and temperate zones, with lobed leaves and 5-parted flowers. Sev. genera are of economic value, such as *Gossypium,* yielding cotton; others ornamental, such as *Abutilon, Hibiscus, Lavatera, Malva, Pavonia, Sidalcea,* etc.

Malvern of Rhodesia and Bexley, 1st **Viscount, Godfrey (Martin) Huggins** (1883–), surgeon and politician, educ. at Malvern College and St Thomas's Hospital, London. F.R.C.S., 1908. After being Medical Superintendent at the Hospital for Sick Children, Great Ormonde Street, M. went to Rhodesia in 1911. He served with the R.A.M.C. during the First World War. Later M. entered Rhodesian politics and was premier of S. Rhodesia 1933–53. He was the first premier of the short-lived Federation of Rhodesia and Nyasaland, 1953–6, its estab. owing much to his efforts. P.C., 1947; C.H., 1944; K.C.M.G., 1941. M. was created a viscount, 1955.

Malvern, health and holiday resort, educational and conference centre, in Worcs, England, near the R. Severn, on the slopes of the M. Hills, 8 m. from Worcester. M. is noted for its spring water of exceptional purity. The priory church was formerly part of an 11th cent. Benedictine monastery. Here are the Royal Radar Estab. and M. College and M. Girls' College (qq.v.). Pop. 24,375.

Malvern College, Eng. public school for boys, founded in 1862 and opened in 1865 at Malvern (q.v.), Worcs. It was incorporated in 1929. There are some 600 pupils.

Malvern Girls' College, independent boarding school, founded at Malvern (q.v.), Worcs, in 1893. There are 500 girls whose ages range from 12 to 18.

Malvern Hills, hill range on the borders of Worcs. and Herefordshire, England. They extend for 9 to 10 m. with abrupt heights, such as Worcs Beacon (1395 ft, highest point) and Herefordshire Beacon (1300 ft), an anct Brit. fortress. Some areas of the M. H. are protected or owned by the National Trust; all are administered by the M. H. Conservators, a statutory body. (*See Plate: Worcestershire.*)

Malvoisie, *see* MALMSEY.

Mameli, Goffredo (1827–49), It. poet and patriot, *b.* Genoa. He wrote the patriotic hymn, *Fratelli d'Italia,* and *d.* in defence of Rome.

Mameluke (Arabic *memalik,* a slave), former class of slaves in Egypt, who became and long remained the dominant people of that country. They had their origin in the importation into Egypt of a large number of Turkish slaves from the Caucasus and neighbouring regions by the sultan of Egypt in the middle of the 13th cent. They soon displayed insubordination, and finally, in 1254, appointed one of their own number Sultan of Egypt. From this time until the Ottoman conquest in 1517, Egypt and Syria were ruled exclusively by the Mameluke dynasty. In 1811, by a stratagem, a massacre of the Mamelukes was ordered by the pasha of Egypt, Mehemet Ali. The few survivors managed to escape to New Dongola, but were virtually exterminated in 1820. The M.s were famous for their courage and skill in horsemanship, and their military organisation was far in advance of their time. They were also patrons of art and literature.

Mamers, *see* MARS.

Mamertina, *see* MESSINA.

Mammals, or **Mammalia,** name given by Linnaeus to those vertebrates which suckle their young. M. differ from all other vertebrates not only in nourishing the young by means of mammary glands (q.v.) but also in being covered with hair which is associated with the very important fact that they are homeothermic (maintain a constant body temp.), the birds being the only other homeothermic group. This fact accounts to a large extent for M. success. Three characteristic internal features are 7 vertebrae in the neck, epiphyses to the centre of the vertebrae and a diaphragm which separates the thoracic from the abdominal cavity.

Until 1884 it was supposed that all M. were vivaparous, but it was then demonstrated that primitive forms of M. still exist which lay eggs. These comprise 3 species of a single order Monotremata. The best known of these interesting links with the reptiles is the duck-billed platypus (*Ornithorhynchus*), native of Australia and Tasmania. The others are the spiny anteaters (*Echidna*), also natives of the same continent. The female *Echidna* produces a temporary pocket for her young, which disappears when they are able to look after themselves, and in this respect exhibits some relationship to the marsupials which comprise a second order. This order is characterised by the possession of the marsupium, a permanent pocket in which the young are placed as soon as born. In these the period of gestation is short, and the young, helpless, are but little developed when born. They attach themselves to a teat and the milk is forced into their throats by muscular action on the mother's part. For a long time marsupials were believed not to form a placenta, but the occurrence of a peculiar form of this complex structure has been discovered in the bandicoots (*Paramelidae*). Except for the opossum of N. America and a few S. Amer. species, the marsupials are now confined to Australasia, although at one time their distribution was very extensive. They vary widely in their types and habits; some are herbivorous, some rodent and some carnivorous.

In all the members of the remaining orders (the placental mammals) the reproductive organs are highly developed, the period of gestation is relatively long and the young are born in an advanced state of development. These orders are: Insectivora, Chiroptera (bats), Primates, Dermoptera (flying lemurs), Edentata, Pholidota (pangolins), Lagomorpha (rabbits and hares), Rodentia, Cetacea (whales and dolphins), Carnivora, Tubulidentata (aardvark), Hyracoidea (coneys), Sirenia (sea-cows), Proboscidea (elephants), Perissodactyla and Artiodactyla. In certain of the Edentata and Cetacea the teeth tend to be suppressed, but in the other orders they are important features and of great assistance in classification. Generally speaking, M. are terrestrial in habit, but the Sirenia, Cetacea and sea Carnivora are important exceptions. The fact that they are air breathers, having no gills, or their equivalent, which would enable them to stay under water for more than a limited period, indicates that they are probably land animals which have adapted themselves to an aquatic life. The only M. with true powers of flight are the Chiroptera or bats. Other so-called flying animals have only a broad fold of skin on each side of the body which sustains them in the air for a limited time. The bat's wings are composed of a thin flexibile leathery membrane stretched between the bones of the fore- and hind-legs. All M. bear some hair at some period of their existence, even if only in the foetal stage, as in the Cetacea, where a layer of blubber under the skin displaces the hair. The Edentata, which include the sloths, anteaters and armadillos, are characterised by the absence of teeth in the front of the jaw. Many of these animals are arboreal and some are burrowing. Sirenia include only 2 genera of living animals; a third, Steller's Rhytina, became extinct early in the 19th cent. To this order belong the manatees and dugongs, characterised by a long, cylindrical body, flipper-like fore-limbs and the absence of hind-limbs. There are no ears, and the eyes are very small. The animals feed entirely on aquatic vegetation and occur on the coasts of both Africa and America. The ungulates (Perissodactyla and Artiodactyla) include all the hoofed M. The toes vary from 1 to 5 in number and never bear claws, but are usually provided with hoofs. The Rodentia are the gnawing M., and include a large number of some of the smallest forms, such as mice and rats and many S. American animals. Their incisor teeth are large and sharp, and consist usually of a pair in both jaws. They are kept sharp by the back surface, which has no enamel coat, wearing away faster than the front. They are mostly herbivorous, but some are practically omnivorous, and are serious enemies of man. The Carnivora include many of the most magnificent M. Though mainly flesh-eating the members of this order are somewhat artificially classified, for the bears are largely vegetable feeders. Carnivora are either fissipeds, the limbs being converted into appendages with separate clawed digits for terrestrial life, or pinniped, the limbs being converted into flippers for aquatic life. The fissipeds are subdivided into cats, dogs and bears; also included are the raccoon, stoat,

weasel, otter, badger, etc. The pinnipeds comprise the seals, sea-lion and walrus. The Insectivora, or insect-eaters, are placed high in the classification of M. on account of their relationship to lemurs, but their brain exhibits a rather low organisation, and they probably had a common origin with marsupials. The mole and the hedgehog are familiar examples of this order, which is unrepresented in S. America and Australasia. The Chiroptera or bats are specialised Insectivora, differing from other Insectivora essentially in powers of flight. They are widely distributed over the surface of the globe, but abound chiefly in the tropics. They are nocturnal in habit, and though the brain is not highly developed, the senses are all exceptionally acute. The Primates, or highest M., are divided into 3 suborders: the Lemuroidea, or lemurs; the Tarsioidea (tarsiers); and the Anthropoidea, which include all monkeys, apes and man. See also BIOLOGY and the separate articles on individual orders and species. See Sir W. Flower and R. Lydekker, *Introduction to the Study of Mammals*, 1891; F. E. Beddard, *Mammalia*, 1902; A. Thorburn, *British Mammals*, 1920; G. C. Shortridge, *Mammals of South West Africa*, 1934; E. G. Boulenger, *Apes and Monkeys*, 1936; W. J. Hamilton, *American Mammals*, 1940; L. H. Matthews, *British Mammals*, 1952; F. Bourliere, *The Natural History of Mammals*, 1955. (*See Plates: Mammals; Australia*.)

Mammary Gland, organ which secretes the milk with which mammals feed their young. It is thought to be a modified form of the apocrine sweat glands. The female breast in the human being is a compound racemose gland composed of from 15 to 20 lobes each representing a number of lobules. Lactiferous ducts lead from each lobule and unite into one main duct in each lobe, which leads to the nipple. Between the lobules and lobes there is a considerable amount of fatty areolar tissue. The nipple is surrounded by a circular patch called the areola, which is ordinarily pigmented. The pigmentation deepens to dark brown during pregnancy and lactation. The size of the M. G. increases from the age of puberty and reaches its greatest size towards the end of pregnancy and during lactation. In later life the breasts are apt to become pendulous.

In lactation the blood supply to the breast is greatly increased. Lactation is estab. by the action on the mammary glands of the lactogenic hormone, prolactin, secreted by the anterior pituitary gland working in conjunction with at least 3 other hormones (*see under* HORMONE) and coincides with the termination of labour and the beginning of the puerperium (*see under* PREGNANCY). Once estab. regular lactation is largely maintained by the stimulation of the infant's sucking, When this is removed the secretion of milk gets less and finally ceases. Inflammation of the breast leading to abscess formation is a complication of lactation. If the inflammation does not respond to antibiotic treatment the abscess which forms must be opened and drained by surgical operation. The breast is one of the common primary sites of cancer (q.v.) and any painless lump in this situation must be regarded as a matter for medical advice. Fortunately breast cancer is one of the types of this disease in which it is possible to make an early diagnosis, and with the prompt treatment which this allows the rate of cure is high.

Mammea americana, large tropical tree (family Guttiferae). Its showy flowers are distilled by the inhab. of tropical America to produce Eau de Creole, a strong perfumed liqueur, and the huge, double-rind, bitter fruits, known as mammee apples or Santo Domingo apricots, are eaten.

Mammillaria, large genus of succulents (family Cactaceae), with fleshy, leafless stems, rarely higher than 12 in. and often only a few inches, and round and flattened, or cylindrical, or branching from the base. Arranged in various designs over the surface are tubercles or nipples, which bear spiny leaves in tufts, rosettes or stars. The flowers spring from the axils of the upper tubercles, and though small and fugitive are showy and are followed by finely tinted berry-like fruits. A dry, warm greenhouse suits most M.s.

Mammon, or more correctly **Mamon** (representing the Aramaic *mamona*, 'wealth' or 'riches'). The derivation of the word is uncertain, but it was used by the Phoenicians for 'gain' or 'profit'. In the N.T. M. is personified, and set in opposition to God. being used in the Sermon on the Mt and the parable of the Unjust Steward (Matt. vi. 24; Luke xvi. 13). The 'mammon of unrighteousness' or 'unrighteous mammon' is a phrase which occurs in Enoch lxiii. 10.

Mammoth, best known of the extinct elephants (*Elephas primigenius*) common throughout the Pleistocene. Many perfectly preserved speciments have been found, principally in the ice of N. Sibcria. It was of great size, and differed mainly from the living members of the order Proboscidea by the thick, hairy covering and by the tusks, some 8 ft long, curved upwards, inwards towards the head, and out sideways in somewhat spiral fashion. The remains of the M. have been found in large numbers, not only in the neighbourhood of the Arctic Sea, but also throughout Europe and N. America as far S. as the Gulf of Mexico. There are sev. related species.

Mammoth Cave, great cavern formed in limestone as a series of vast chambers in Edmonson co., Kentucky, U.S.A., between Nashville and Louisville, first discovered by white men in 1799. It is 6 m. from Cave City. The diameter of the cavern's area is 9 to 10 m. 150 m. of its passages have been explored. In some of the grottoes there are branches of the subterranean R. Echo. Mammoth Dome is 540 ft long, by 200 ft wide, by 120 ft high. Blind fishes, crickets, crustacea and insects have been found in the caves. Bats abound in the outer galleries. The temp. ranges from 52° to 59° F. M. C. is famous for its stalactites, resulting from the action of water on the limestone formation, and is considered the finest cave in the world. *See*

MAMMOTHS, RECONSTRUCTED FROM REMAINS

H. C. Hovey, *Celebrated American Caverns*, 1897; J. W. Turner, *Wonders of the Great Mammoth Cave of Kentucky*, 1912.

Mammoth Hot Springs, group of thermal springs in the N. of Yellowstone National Park, Wyoming, U.S.A., about 1000 ac. in area. They are remarkable for their snow-white calcareous deposits. The waters are turquoise-blue in colour, the temps. varying from 60° to 160° F.

Mamoré, riv. of S. America, forming part of the boundary between Bolivia and Brazil, and joining with other rivs. to form the Madeira. It rises in the Cochabamba Mts., in Bolivia, and is called Rio Grande in part of its course.

Mâmûn, *see* AL-MAMUN.

Man, zoologically speaking, is a genus of the order Primates, or highest order of mammals. This order is usually divided into 3 groups: the Anthropoidea, including M., apes, monkeys and baboons; the Lemuroidea or lemurs; and the Tarsioidea (tarsiers). As far as mere physical characteristics go, M. must be considered as related to monkeys and apes; in common with those animals he possesses 5 fingers and 5 toes, armed with flat nails towards the extremities, has a similar array of teeth, which are normally preceded by milk-teeth, has a simple stomach and can live on a vegetarian diet. The young are brought forth usually one at a time and are quite helpless at the time of birth.

It is now generally conceded that, as far as physical characteristics are concerned, there is no reason to suppose that M. is other than a form of development with characteristics sufficiently in common with monkeys, apes, etc., to justify his being placed in the same order of mammals. M. does not differ from those animals in possessing structures fundamentally different, but only in possessing them either in a more generalised or more developed form. Some of the ways in which M.'s physical organism differs from that of the rest of the Primates may now be pointed out. The lower limbs are long and the upper limbs short in M. as compared with the apes. He maintains an erect posture, stands flat upon the soles of his feet, instead of on the outer edges, as most apes do. His backbone has a graceful sinuous curve which is entirely wanting in other members of the order. The neck is long and flexible, and the head is set normally to look ahead when the individual is in an erect posture. His skull shows a marked diversity of proportions to those of apes generally; the braincase is large and the jaws are not massively developed. The teeth are regular, although the different forms are distinct on examination, they make an even series without any break and without any individual teeth projecting markedly beyond the rest. The body is comparatively hairless, but in the beard and head hair may attain a length which is peculiar to the human genus. The thumb is long, and opposes itself easily to any of the other fingers; on the other hand, the big toe is not opposable at all, and the foot has little power of prehensile movement. Probably the most important difference between M. and other members of the same or any order is the higher physical development of the brain. Not only is the size greater in proportion to the rest of the body, but it presents a more elaborate series of folds, or convolutions. When it is understood that the physical processes corresponding to the highest mental activities are located in the cortex or rind of the brain, it is seen that the extent and number of the convolutions, by increasing the area of the cortex, must play a considerable part in determining the intellectual effectiveness of the animal.

It appears, therefore, that the physical differences between M. and his nearest kin in the animal world are of degree rather than of kind. It is difficult to point to any one characteristic which can be looked upon as an adequate cause for M.'s superiority over other animals. The truth probably is that many causes have contributed to that superiority. Among them, in addition to mere size of brain, may be quoted the adaptability of his hands to many uses, allowing a degree of manipulation impossible to other animals, the more exquisite differentiation of sense perception than is apparent in most animals, the voice capable of many various sounds and so lending itself to the formation of a language. When differences other than physical are considered, the superiority of M. is so great as to incline some to the opinion that M. is a separate creation on the ground of his mentality alone. However great this superiority is, it does not appear that M. possesses any faculty or fairly fundamental mental process which is not possessed in some degree by some lower animal or other, save that of purely abstract intellection. Memory, the powers of abstraction, and of reasoning are demonstrably possessed by certain animals, if only in rudimentary form. Present-day opinion strongly inclines to the theory that the processes of evolution as ordinarily understood are quite sufficient to account for the marked superiority of a single species.

Origin and antiquity of man. The ultimate origin of M. is a problem bound up with that of the origin of organic life as a whole, as the conception of a sudden creation of separate and permanent species has long been abandoned by scientists. It has, however, been the aim of many anthropologists to arrive at a form of animal which may reasonably be supposed to represent the common ancestor of M. and his nearest relatives in the animal world. At various times human or semi-human remains have been discovered which bear an ape-like appearance. The generalisations made as a result of the examinations of the Neanderthal (q.v.), Java and other skulls have had to be considerably modified owing to discoveries during the 20th cent. These include a skull, *Australopithecus*, discovered in 1924 at Taungs in Bechuanaland, which has aroused considerable discussion and dissension amongst anthropologists. The shape and proportions of the brain resemble those of primitive types of human beings, but the size and convolutions correspond to those of the apes. On this and other evidence it is regarded by some anthropologists as belonging to the same stock as the gorilla and chimpanzee, and by others as human. In either case it provides valuable evidence in support of the theory of the common origin of men and apes. Other interesting discoveries in Palestine show that Neanderthal man lived there, as in Europe. In both Europe and Palestine he was followed by Neanthropic man but the place of origin of the latter has long been problematic.

In May 1944 there was discovered in the Olorgasailie Mt in the Great Rift valley, not far from Nairobi, a site where there is clear evidence of occupation by prehistoric Acheulian M. Hitherto, however, no bones have been found which can be unhesitatingly attributed to Acheulian M., a term which in itself is misleading, as it describes not a variety of M., but a M. who made and used a certain sort of chipped stone instrument. But Africa is undoubtedly assuming more and more importance for M.'s prehistory. If men 'arose' (i.e. became differentiated from a non-human stock) in one single area of the world, then, until a short time ago, most anthropologists would have set that area in Asia, and more especially in SE. Asia. The balance of what evidence there is still favours an Asiatic home for the earliest men, but the balance is not so marked as it was. The most anct forms of men are still those of the Far E. sites, Java and China, but every day it is becoming clearer that Africa played a great part in M.'s early hist. Fossil material (Hominoidea) discovered recently at Sterkfontein and Kromdraai is believed to represent a link in the evolution of M. Prof. Le Gros Clark thinks that the skulls found here can be interpreted as slight modifications of the chimpanzee or gorilla, or as very closely related to M., coming near to what was popularly known as the 'missing link', and in an extraordinary number of details these specimens are said to show such typically human characteristics as to rule out parallelism.

At present no remains have been discovered older than the early Pleistocene period, and the antiquity of man is provisionally suggested as about 250,000–300,000 years, but new discoveries may modify the present conclusions with regard to M.'s origin and antiquity. It may be too early to assess the full significance of the recent S. African fossil discoveries. Since 1936, and notably in 1947, sev. skulls of adults of the same fossil group, together with jaws and limb bones, have been found 40 m. W. of Johannesburg. The common group to which all these S. African remains belong is now recognised as one subfamily, the Australopithecinae, and it is believed that they date either from the beginning of the Pleistocene age or from the later Pleiocene, which would date M.'s hist. as 1,000,000 years or more. These facts support the theory which includes the Taungs skull, mentioned above, as human. But the question still remains of their place in the classification of the higher Primates. They show much closer resemblances to M. than do any of the living or fossil apes known, but this leaves open the question whether they should be grouped with the Hominidae or with the anthropoid apes. If the absolute size of the brain is the most important criterion, the Australopithecinae are to be regarded as apes of a very advanced type, showing, in the details of their anatomy, a remarkable approximation to the Hominidae and no very close relationship to the modern anthropoid apes. But if more emphasis is laid on the criteria of the skull structure, dental anatomy and the details of the pelvis and limb bones, there is no doubt that they should be grouped with the human family or exceedingly primitive types of mankind. Further important discoveries were made in S. Africa in 1948 and 1949. At Swartkrans colony there was evidence of a large ape-man with a jaw far larger than that of any M. and yet with human teeth. His brain is 850–900 c.c. and therefore within human range. At Makapan Prof. Dart found another type, also with a large brain, and in some ways so human that it was difficult to decide whether to call it M. or not.

Future of man. It is sometimes maintained that M. has now arrived at a fairly permanent physical form, but it is difficult to reconcile the idea of a creative evolution having precisely this form as its limit. Through increasing knowledge M. is likely to take a greater and greater part in the estab. of his own environment, and may in a sense determine his own evolution. His discovery of the ways of releasing nuclear energy and the making of atomic bombs is the greatest threat to his civilisations—if such bombs should be used in war. It may be said that there are two tendencies perceptible as to the manner in which a different type may be reached; one is the tendency to differentiation of individuals and races, the other is the tendency to the movement of mankind as a whole. The first tendency can be seen in such conceptions as a chosen race, the authority of conscious superiority as in the superman, with its corollary of subject individuals or subject races, and the like. On the other hand we have the conception of solidarity implied in the idea of a common humanity with the widest possible notion of social obligations. This antithesis expressed itself in the rival ideologies of the Ger. *Herrenvolk* and the world democracies, and later of atheistic communism and W. thought. Still more speculative than the

probable results of human endeavour for M.'s uplifting are the problems of M.'s possible enemies and conquerors in the evolutionary struggle. Some writers see in the organisation and adaptability of some sections of the insect world the rudiments of a development which will surpass and conquer human development. Others see in the great diversity of animal forms below us, which have no consciousness of our existence, the possibility of a corresponding diversity of animal forms above us with which we have not yet come into contact or, consequently, conflict. Of more practical import are the efforts of bodies of men like the modern 'eugenists', who seek to improve the race in directions which will meet with the common approval. Their efforts are as yet restricted to the prevention of the propagation of tendencies we know to be harmful to the physical well-being of mankind. It appears likely too that M. will be called on to adapt himself to interplanetary space-travel. Further than that our ignorance of our common destiny makes it impossible to advance. This article deals with anthropological and biological M.; for M. considered as a spiritual being *see* CHRISTIANITY; CREATION; PHILOSOPHY; PSYCHOLOGY; RELIGION.

See also ANTHROPOLOGY; BIOLOGY; DARWINISM; EVOLUTION; HEREDITY; KEITH, SIR ARTHUR; RACE.

See C. Darwin, *Descent of Man*, 1871; G. Elliott Smith, *Essays on the Evolution of Man*, 1924; F. Wood Jones, *Man's Place among the Mammals*, 1929; W. E. Le Gros Clark, *Early Forerunners of Man*, 1934, *History of the Primates*, 1953, and *The Fossil Evidence for Human Evolution*, 1955; W. K. Gregory, *Man's Place among the Anthropoids*, 1934; E. A. Hooton, *Up from the Ape*, 1936, and *Man's Poor Relations*, 1942; J. Huxley, *Evolution: the Modern Synthesis*, 1942; M. Boule, *Les Hommes fossiles*, 1946; F. Weidenreich, *Apes, Giants and Men*, 1946; W. W. Howells, *Mankind so Far*, 1947; A. Keith, *A New Theory of Human Evolution*, 1948; G. G. Simpson, *The Meaning of Evolution*, 1950; L. S. B. Leakey, *Adam's Ancestors*, 1953.

Man, Isle of (anct **Monapia** or **Menavia**; Manx **Vannin** or **Mannin**, middle), small is. in the Irish Sea, almost equidistant (hence its name) from England and Ireland, about 16 m. from Burrow Head, Scotland. It is a self-governing dependency under the Brit. Crown. Its area is about 227 sq. m. A cable (32 m. long) runs between Port of Ayre and St Bees. A tiny islet known as the Calf of M., an important nature reserve, lies to the SW. A mt range stretches from NE. to SW. through the is., culminating near the centre in Snaefell (about 2030 ft). The climate is very equable, W. and SW. winds predominating, while fuchsias, myrtles and other exotics flourish all the year round. Lead, copper, iron and zinc are found, but no coal. The Laxey lead-mines yield quantities of silver. The is.'s small breed of horses is noted and its tailless cats. There are herring, mackerel and other fisheries. Granite, marble, limestone and greenstone are quarried. The is. is a favourite holiday resort, and has steamboat services to Liverpool, Fleetwood, Ardrossan, Dublin, Belfast and other ports. There are also air services to many ports in the U.K. A casino was opened May 1963. The chief tns are Douglas (cap.), Castletown, Peel and Ramsey (qq.v.). The inhabitants are Manx (Menaviae) of Celtic race. From the 6th to the 9th cent. they had Welsh kings. These were followed by a Scandinavian dynasty, who in turn yielded their rights to Alexander III of Scotland (1266). In 1406 the is. was granted to the Stanleys (earls of Derby), and was purchased by the Brit. Gov. after long negotiations (1765–1829) from the dukes of Atholl, who held it from 1735. The is. forms the bishopric of Sodor and M. It has its own lieutenant-governor, council and House of Keys (q.v.) (a representative assembly of 24 members chosen by adult suffrage). The is. is not bound by Acts of the Imperial Parliament unless specially mentioned in them. Pop. 48,150. *See* J. G. Cumming, *History of Man*, 1848; W. Harrison (ed.), *The Old Historians of the Isle of Man, Camden, Speed, etc.*, 1871; R. D. Farrant, *The Isle of Man*, 1937; E. H. Stenning, *Isle of Man*, 1950; R. H. Kinvig, *A History of the Isle of Man*, 1950; and the pubs. of the Manx Society, comprising monographs on the hist., antiquities, language, laws, etc. (1859–95). (*See Plate.*)

Man-made Fibres is the term used to describe all textile fibres other than those of natural origin such as wool, cotton, silk and flax. Either singly or in blends M. F. are widely used in all the staple textile industries. Rayon was first of M. F., its commercial production dating from about 1890, but in the years before and after the Second World War many other types were developed. They can be divided into 2 main groups—regenerated and strictly synthetic fibres. The former include regenerated cellulose, viscose, acetate and cuprammonium rayons, and fibres made from regenerated protein with wool-like qualities such as Ardil and Fibrolaine (qq.v.). The latter are classified according to their chemical composition—polyamides (nylon), polyvinyl (vinyon), acrilic fibres (orlon) and polyesters (terylene). All these fibres are produced either in the form of filament yarn (continuous thread) or staple fibre (uniform-length fibres to be spun in the same manner as cotton or wool). Special features of fabrics made from these fibres are their high strength and elasticity, resistance to abrasion, low water absorption and quick-drying properties. Nylon first became popular as hosiery material but now, like terylene, is widely used for clothing and industrial purposes. *See* ARDIL; CLOTH MANUFACTURE AND FINISHING; DYE; FIBROLAINE; NYLON; PLASTICS; RAYON; RUBBER; SYNTHETIC RESINS; TERYLENE. (*See Plate.*)

Man-of-war Bird, *see* FRIGATE BIRD.

Man-powered Flight, attempted since the earliest times. Various experimental models are on trial and monetary awards are offered for a figure-of-eight flight but so far (1966) only short flights of a few yards have been achieved. *See* AERONAUTICS; AEROPLANE.

Man-trap. Formerly M.s were set on land and in houses without let or hindrance. But the Offences against the Person Act, 1861, punishes with penal servitude the act of 'setting engines calcuated to destroy human life or inflict grievous bodily harm', and specifically mentions spring-guns and M.s among such offending devices. Homicide resulting from such traps is manslaughter. But the Act expressly saves the right of anyone to set a M., spring-gun or any other 'engine' in his dwelling-house between sunset and sunrise for the purpose of protecting the house.

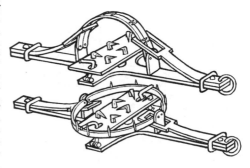

MAN-TRAP, SPRUNG (*above*) AND SET (*below*)

Manaar, or **Manar, Gulf of,** arm of the Indian Ocean between Ceylon and S. India, separated from Palk Strait by the is. of Rameswaram and M., and a reef, Adam's Bridge. It is about 150 m. wide at the entrance, and has pearl fisheries. M. Is. is situated W. of N. Ceylon, at the gulf's head, and is 18 m. long by 2½ m. broad.

Manacle Rocks, or **Point,** dangerous reef off the SE. coast of Cornwall, England, by St Keverne, 7 m. S. of Falmouth (q.v.).

Manacles, *see* HANDCUFFS.

Manacor, Sp. tn in the SE. of the is. of Majorca (q.v.), with a ruined palace. It produces shoes, handicraft souvenirs and artificial pearls. At Porto Cristo, near by, is the Cave of the Dragon (*Drach*) with stalactite formations and subterranean lakes. Pop. 20,000.

Management, Office, *see* INDUSTRIAL SOCIETY; OFFICE MANAGEMENT; SALES MANAGEMENT.

Managua: 1. Dept. of W. Nicaragua, bordering all but the N. edge of Lake M., and having a coastline on the Pacific. Although small in area, it is the most heavily populated of all Nicaragua's depts, and is also the most important economically. Coffee and cotton are the main crops, followed by fruit and vegetables. The climate is hot and humid with plentiful rain in the summer but little in winter. The cap. is M. Area 1332 sq. m. Pop. 317,641 (1963).

2. Cap. of above dept and also of Nicaragua. It is situated on the S. shore of Lake M. at an

altitude of 200 ft, lying 28 m. from the Pacific and 86 from the port of Corinto with which it is connected by rail. Created the cap. in 1855, it was largely destroyed by earthquake and fire in 1931, and the city has been rebuilt as a modern commercial city. By far the largest of Nicaragua's cities, it is the leading commercial and industrial city of the country and in it or near by is concentrated a substantial proportion of Nicaragua's industry. Pop. 234,793 (1963).

3. Lake in W. Nicaragua, whose Indian name was *Xolotlán*, is 38 m. long and 16 m. wide and is drained SE. by the R. Tipitapa into the even larger Lake Nicaragua. The lake, which has great scenic beauty, is used for transport purposes and tourism. (*See Plate: Nicaragua.*)

Manama, or **Manameh,** tn and the commercial cap. of the Bahrein (q.v.) Is., Persian Gulf. It has hospitals, schools and a wireless station, and is the official residence of the ruler. Pop. 61,837.

Manáos, *see* MANAUS.

Manapla, tn in the prov. of Negros Occidental, is. of Negros, Philippine Is., situated in the extreme N. of the prov. It mills sugar. Pop. *c.* 36,000.

Manasarowar, or **Tso-Mapham,** lake of Tibet, situated at the base of Mt Kailas, about 15,000 ft above the level of the sea. In Hindu legend it is a sacred lake, and is an object of pilgrimage both for natives and Hindus. Area 150 sq. m.

Manassas, co. seat of Prince William co., Virginia, U.S.A., 25 m. WSW. of Washington, D.C. Near here was the scene of the 2 battles known as the battles of Bull Run, fought in 1861 and 1862 during the Civil war.

Manasseh: 1. Eldest son of Joseph, *b.* Egypt, ancestor of the tribe which settled on both sides of Jordan. M. was deprived of the rights of primogeniture by Ephraim (Gen. xlviii).

2. King of Judah (694–642 BC), son of Hezekiah and Hephzibah, came to the throne at a time when Judah was a trib. of Assyria, and had Assyrian cults imposed on her; Baalism was also revived and in these M. participated, offering a human sacrifice of his son like his grandfather Ahaz (2 Kings xxi. 6). He is credited by Jewish tradition with the martyrdom of Isaiah. He is twice mentioned in the Assyrian tribute lists (*see* D. D. Luckenbill, *Ancient Records of Assyria and Babylonia,* 1926–7). About 652 he joined a revolt led by the King of Babylon, and was defeated and carried in fetters to Babylon, but Ashurbanipal released him. On his return M. repented and reformed (2 Chron. xxxiii. 11–19). The prayer of M., in the Anglican Apocrypha, is excluded from the Rom. Catholic Bible as uninspired.

Manasseh ben Israel (1604–1657), learned Jewish writer, *b.* La Rochelle; at 18 he was rabbi at Amsterdam. His greatest work, which took 29 years to write, was an effort to reconcile 472 apparently contradictory biblical passages. He strongly advocated the return of the Jews to England and negotiated with Cromwell to that end in 1655.

Manatee (*Trichechus*), marine mammal of the order Sirenia, which, though of ungainly appearance, is probably the origin of the mermaid legend. It ranges along the W. coast of Africa and the E. coast of tropical America, and ascends the rivs. where it browses on the aquatic vegetation. M.s are slow and inoffensive, but for their valuable oil and their skin and flesh they are hunted and their numbers are rapidly diminishing. They are from 8 to 12 ft long; their skin is like an elephant's, and the long body ends in a tail like a beaver's. The forepaw or flipper has small, flat nails, and its resemblance to the human hand is supposed to have given M. its name. The upper lip is cleft, and the parts diverge and clasp the food in eating.

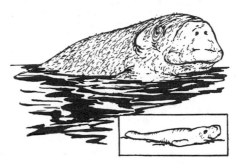

MANATEE, WITH INSET SHOWING
THE ANIMAL ON LAND

Manaus, cap. of the state of Amazonas, NW. Brazil, situated on the Rio Negro about 10 m. from its junction with the Amazon R. It is the trading and commercial centre of the state and its chief port, the only connection with the outside world being by riv. and air. Although 1000 m. from the sea, its altitude is only 100 ft above sea-level. The climate is hot (around 80° F. generally) and humid. The tn is a mixture of modern buildings and wooden shacks, and the port area with its many floating dwellings is reminiscent of Hong Kong. The tn was the centre of the fabulous rubber boom at the turn of the cent. Its chief exports are timber (particularly hardwoods), rubber, skins, brazil nuts, fibres, vegetable oils and a variety of other forest products. Its main industries are saw-mills, jute mills, rubber plants and a petrol refinery. Pop. 154,000.

Manche, maritime dept of NW. France on the Eng. Channel (La Manche), formed (1790) from the old prov. of Normandy. It consists in part of the peninsula of Cotentin, terminating NW. in Cape la Hague. Its prin. tns are St Lô (the cap.), Avranches, Cherbourg and Coutances. The chief products are grain, flax, hemp, beetroot and fruit (especially apples for ciders), and horses are reared. There are metal and textile industries. In the SW. is the Bay of St Michel, lying around the Tombelaine and Mont St Michel. M. was the scene of allied landings on 6 June 1944. Area about 2475 sq. m.; pop. 447,000.

Manchester, Edward Montagu, 2nd **Earl of** (1602–71), general and statesman. Created Baron Montagu of Kimbolton in 1626, he succeeded to his father's title in 1642. He identified himself with the opposition to Charles I, and was accused with the 'five members' of high treason, but exonerated by a Bill passed in both houses. He was in nominal command at Marston Moor and Newbury (second battle), but was charged with neglect and incompetence by Cromwell, 1644, and resigned his commission, 1645. He opposed the trial of Charles I and subsequently retired from public affairs. He welcomed the return of Charles II, 1660.

Manchester (Rom. *Mancunium*): 1. City, municipal, co. and parl bor. of Lancs, England, 189 m. NW. by N. of London. M. may be said to have grown up with the cotton industry, but cotton now employs less than 5 per cent of the regional working pop. and the prin. industries are engineering and chemicals. M. is an important centre for the application of the civil uses of atomic energy and for technical training in this subject. It is a modern city covering an area of 27,255 ac. (43 sq. m.). Five rivs. flow through the city: the Irwell, Mersey, Irk, Medlock and Tib, much of the latter two being built over; and the M. Ship Canal (q.v.) connects M. to the Mersey estuary at Eastham, making the city, though 35 m. from the sea, the third seaport in Great Britain. M., being a regional cap., is the home of gov. offices and of the N. presses of 5 popular national newspapers. The total of morning daily papers is 6, of which the *Guardian* (q.v.), the leading independent newspaper in the country, is pre-eminent. Prin. thoroughfares in the centre of the city are Market, Oxford, Cross and Corporation Streets, Piccadilly and Deansgate. There is a complex network of road and rail transport linking up the various suburbs and surrounding tns.

History. During the Civil war M. was besieged by the Royalists under Lord Strange, but the inhab. held out under the command of Colonel Rosworm, a Ger. soldier of fortune. In 1689 occurred the trial of those implicated in the 'Lancashire plot', which ended in the triumphant acquittal of the alleged Jacobites; but that there were in the dist many warm adherents of the Stuarts was shown in the rising of 1715, when the clergy sided with the Pretender, and again in the rebellion of 1745, when M. was occupied by Prince Charles Edward and the M. Regiment (q.v.) was raised to defend the Stuarts. In the retreat of the Stuart forces, however, the M. contingent was assigned the task of defending Carlisle, but surrendered to the Duke of Cumberland, and their officers were tried for treason and executed. In 1819 M. was the scene of what was known as the Peterloo massacre (q.v.). From that date the M. politicians took a prominent part in the reform agitation, which may be said to have its real impetus from this incident. Their economic position gave rise to the name 'Manchester school' for the extreme *laissez-faire* school.

Among famous Mancunians may be mentioned Humphrey Chetham (q.v.); John Owens (q.v.); Sir Robert Peel (father of the Prime Minister); John Dalton (q.v.), the great chemist who, though *b*. in Cumberland, lived and worked for many years in M.; James Nasmyth (q.v.); Daniel Adamson; James Brindley (q.v.); Rebecca Gaskell (mother of Clive of India); Sir Richard Arkwright (q.v.); Lt-Col. Worsley, the M.P. who, at Cromwell's order, 'took away that bauble' from the House of Commons; David Lloyd George; Richard Cobden; J. P. Joule (qq.v.); and the brothers Grant (merchants), the originals of Dickens's Cheeryble brothers.

M. has been a bishopric since 1847, but the cathedral is much older. It is the third church to stand on the site. The present Perpendicular building was begun early in the 15th cent. in the reign of Henry V, who gave the church collegiate status. The magnificent woodwork of the stalls and screens was put in at that time. The building was extensively damaged in the last war, but the restoration includes some notable examples of modern craftsmanship.

M. is the bp. of Nonconformity and is well endowed with churches of all denominations. There are also sev. Jewish synagogues, a Muslim mosque and an unusually fine Quaker meeting house.

One of the most interesting old buildings is Chetham's Hospital and Library, built in the early 15th cent. on the site of a former baronial hall. In Market Place stands the Old Wellington Inn, last of M.'s old inns. The tn hall (1877), designed by Albert Waterhouse, contains mural paintings by Ford Madox Brown and a very fine organ. The Lord Mayor uses the tn hall as his official residence during his term of office, being the only lord mayor outside London to do this. To meet the needs of local gov. an extension of the tn hall, designed by E. Vincent Harris, A.R.A., was opened by H.M. King George VI in 1938. Other fine buildings are the Art Gallery by Sir Charles Barry (q.v.); the Royal Exchange (1869); Ship Canal House, which houses the chamber of commerce; Midland Bank buildings; the Central Library, opened by King George V in 1934; John Rylands Library (q.v.); the M. Univ. and Museum; and the famous Free Trade Hall originally built to the design of Walter in 1865 and standing on the site of the Peterloo massacre (q.v.). Recent completed buildings (1963) include the Courts of Justice, Albert Bridge House, the Domestic and Trades College, Piccadilly Place, the Granada television studios, the College of Building, the Co-operative Insurance Society premises (400 ft high) and the terminal building at M. Airport.

Local government. Finds of coins and pottery and the preserved fragment of the Rom. wall show that M. has been inhabited since the Rom. invasion. It is supposed to have been the home of Ina, King of Wessex (689), and is mentioned in Domesday. The first charter was granted in 1301, but the tn remained under the feudal system of manorial gov. until incorporated in 1838, the manorial rights passing from the Greslys to the de la Warrs, Wests, Lacys and

Mosleys successively until purchased by the M. Corporation in 1846. After 1838 progress was rapid. In 1853 M. became a city. In 1889 co. bor. status was granted, and in 1893 the title of lord mayor was conferred on its chief citizen. Today the city is divided for local gov. purposes into 38 wards, and the city council is composed of 38 aldermen and 144 councillors. Municipal services include a water supply from Longdendale in Cheshire, and from Lakes Thirlmere and Haweswater in Westmorland; markets; libraries, art galleries and museums; parks and cemeteries; highways and transport. The last named service, inaugurated in 1901, is now operated by motor buses over 406 route m. The corporation owns 2 airports, M. Airport at Ringway and a small one at Barton. M. Airport is the largest municipally owned airport in the country and the most important outside London in terms of passengers and freight. Over 36,000 aircraft, 1,005,598 passengers and 16,375 short tons of freight were handled in 1962, and at May 1963 there were 9 direct services to New York each week, 4 to Toronto and Montreal, and a total of 43 services to Brussels, Zürich, Paris, Copenhagen, Frankfurt, Düsseldorf, Amsterdam and Barcelona, as well as 170 services within the Brit. Isles. M.'s rateable value is £27,339,456 (1963). In 1945 the corporation pub. *The City of Manchester Plan* by R. Nicholas, city surveyor and engineer, setting out his proposals for replanning the city during the next 50 years. The plan, which was designed to fit into a broad regional scheme covering an area of over 1000 sq. m., aims 'to enable every inhabitant of this city to enjoy real health of body and health of mind'. This plan, in a modified form, was the basis of the city's development plan which was approved by the Minister of Housing and Local Gov. in 1961. A typical redevelopment proposal concerns an area of 4 ac. in the neighbourhood of the cathedral and the Corn Exchange (which now includes all forms of groceries). The whole site will be covered by a four-deck development. The basement deck provides parking for 350 cars. At ground-floor level trucks and vans can make direct deliveries to the Corn Exchange, warehouses, refrigerator chambers and storerooms. The main entrances to office buildings, hotel and service flats will be from mezzanine floor level, and access will be provided for cars from street level. The upper deck for pedestrians contains larger shops and a courtyard and terrace overlooking the cathedral. Above will be multi-storey blocks of offices and flats, and a hotel. A big municipal enterprise is the 3000-ac. Wythenshawe Estate, now almost fully developed, which will house about 100,000 people and is intended as a satellite to M. with its own light industries and civic centre. M. is a leading municipality in tackling the problem of smoke pollution. In 1962, 9344 ac. of the city were subject to smoke control orders, either made or awaiting confirmation.

Trade and commerce. Early in its hist. M. became a flourishing manufacturing centre, and in 1538 was described by Leland as 'the fairest, best builded and most populous town in all Lancashire'. Today M. is still the marketing centre for the Lancs cotton trade although cotton is no longer its *raison d'être*. The manufacturing processes are almost entirely carried on in the many surrounding tns of Lancs, and the city is now the distributing centre not only for the cotton textile industry but also for manuf. goods of all kinds. M.'s industries are varied and extensive. Engineering and chemicals are the largest industries (in M. was built the empire's largest turbo-electric generator for the Battersea power station), but hats, clothing, waterproof and indiarubber goods, and electrical and electronic equipment are also produced in very large quantities. Research and development in the civil uses of atomic energy are of increasing importance. Owing to its situation near the Ship Canal and the docks, Trafford Park, once the estate of the de Traffords, has become a world famous industrial estate. M. has one of the most modern dock systems in the world, the estate covering 700 ac., of which 179 ac. are water, and containing 8 docks with accommodation for vessels up to 15,000 tons deadweight. (*See* MANCHESTER SHIP CANAL). The city is also the food distributing centre for one of the most densely populated areas in the world. To facilitate the handling of the vast quantities of goods for which M. is the entrepôt there are cotton, stock, coal, corn and produce and estate exchanges, and a chamber of commerce, dating from 1794, which now has about 4000 members. Banking and insurance also form an important section of the city's business life, the M. Bankers' Clearing House handling £565,151,216 in 1962 (the area covered being half a mile radius from the clearing house).

Education and culture. The 2 oldest educational institutions in M. are the M. Grammar School (*q.v.*) and Chetham's Hospital and Library, now also a grammar school, estab. under the will of Humphrey Chetham, a M. merchant and benefactor who *d.* in 1653. Chetham's Hospital (hospice) and Library still occupy their 15th cent. building in Victoria Street. Inaugurated in 1653, these twin institutions have been administered under the terms of the original foundation and have been maintained chiefly by the income from property left by their founder, the buildings being used almost unchanged in their medieval state. The hospital provides a number of foundation and exhibition places at the independent resident and day grammar school. The library, which was probably the first free public library in Europe, contains upwards of 100,000 vols. and valuable MSS. The univ. of M. is situated in Oxford Road (*see* MANCHESTER UNIVERSITY). The College of Science and Technology, the largest of its kind in Britain, was created from the M. College of Technology by a charter granted in 1956. Other colleges include the Royal College of Music, the Regional College of Art, the College of Building and the Domestic and Trades College.

M. is well endowed with libraries. There is the

John Rylands Library including Earl Spence's great Althorp Library and the famous Crawford collection of 1955 (the finest private collections ever brought together), and having a total of 400,000 printed books and some 12,000 MSS. The Portico Library and Newsroom, founded in 1806 as a social and literary institution, was, until the passing of the Public Libraries Act of 1850, the chief circulating library in M. It contains rare first eds., and though a private library is now open to visitors. Finally there is the municipal library service based on the Central Library in St Peter's Square. M. was the first in the country to take advantage of the powers granted by the Public Libraries Act of 1850; today the reference collections contain 549,086 vols.; the Henry Watson Music Library contains 103,984 vols. and 286,301 copies of sheet music, including 120,683 part-songs and 77,226 anthems; the 22 dist libraries and 4 travelling libraries have some 671,146 books (1963).

The city possesses more than 100 parks, recreation grounds, open spaces, etc., with a total area of 2482 ac.

The 2 largest are Heaton Park and Wythenshawe Park. Belle Vue zoological and amusement gardens are a noted addition to M.'s recreational and exhibition facilities. At Heaton Park there is a municipal golf-course. The prin. theatres are the Opera House, Palace and the Library Theatre in the Central Library. The Hallé concerts, first estab. by Sir Charles Hallé, still continue to be given by the Hallé orchestra and have been instrumental in making M. an important musical centre. The B.B.C. Northern Orchestra, resident in M., gives a season of midday promenade concerts, and there are Tuesday Midday Concerts, society and Chamber Music Society concerts. The B.B.C. N. Region H.Q. and television studios are in M., and so are the studios of 2 commercial television companies. There are 9 art galleries and museums in M. Apart from the city art gallery, perhaps the 2 most interesting ones are the Gallery of Eng. Costume in Platt Hall, Rusholme, and Heaton Hall in Heaton Park, a Georgian building by Wyatt, appropriately furnished.

The prin. industrial areas of M. are on the E. of the city, comprising Clayton, Gorton, Newton Heath and Openshaw, with large chemical and engineering plants. Just over the W. boundary of the city is the industrial estate of Trafford Park, adjoining the M. Ship Canal. The prin. residential areas are Didsbury, Withington, Chorlton-cum-Hardy and Wythenshawe on the S. side of the city, and Blackley and Moston on the N. Pop. 661,041.

Bibliography. S. Hibbert-Ware, *History of the Foundations, in Manchester, of Christ's College, Chetham's Hospital and the Free Grammar School,* 4 vols., 1828–48; J. Reilly, *History of Manchester,* 1861; W. E. A. Axon, *Annals of Manchester,* 1886; W. A. Shaw, *Manchester old and new,* 3 vols., 1894; F. A. Bruton, *A short history of Manchester and Salford,* 2nd ed., 1927;

A. Redford, *Manchester Merchants and Foreign Trade,* 2 vols., 1934, 1956; A. P. Simon, *Manchester made over,* 1936; Lady Shena Simon, *Manchester 1838–1938,* 1938; A. Redford, *History of Local Government in Manchester,* 3 vols., 1939–40; R. Nicholas, *City of Manchester Plan,* 1945; H. Cooke, *Manchester and the North West,* 1957; T. H. G. Stevens, *Manchester of Yesterday,* 1958; C. Stewart, *The stones of Manchester,* 1956; L. P. Green, *Provincial Metropolis,* 1959; *Manchester Corporation Development Plan,* 1961; C. F. Carter (ed.), *Manchester and its regions,* 1962; N. J. Frangopulo (ed.), *Rich inheritance,* 1963; *Official Handbook of the Manchester District,* annually. (*See Plate: Lancashire.*)

2. Tn in Hillsboro co., New Hampshire, U.S.A. The tn is situated on the l. b. of the Merrimac R., 18 m. SSE. of Concord and 59 m. NW. from Boston. It is built on a plain at the height of 90 ft above the riv., and is regularly laid out. The prin. street is wide, and is upwards of a mile in length, parallel to the riv. M. is the largest city and the industrial centre of New Hampshire; it manufs. shoes, textiles, mill machinery, electrical instruments, building materials, food products, clothing, luggage, metal and lumber products and cigars. It is the seat of St Anselm's College, and other features of the tn are the Historic Association Building, the art gallery, the institute of arts and sciences and the fine library. The Grenier Air Force Base was built in 1941. Amoskeag Falls furnish industrial power. Massabesic Lake is just E. M. was settled in 1722. Pop. 82,730.

3. Tn of Hartford co., Connecticut, U.S.A., 8 m. E. of Hartford. It manufs. textiles, paper products, machinery, tools, electrical appliances, soap, cleansers, cigars, sports equipment, clothing, leather and rubber products, dairy and nursery products. Pop. 34,100.

Manchester College, Oxford, founded at Manchester in 1786. It was settled in York (1803–40), Manchester again (1840–53), London (1853–88) and thereafter at Oxford. It is the essential aim of the college to impart theological learning without insisting on the adoption of particular doctrines. It is closely associated with the General Assembly of Unitarian and Free Christian Churches and most of its students are members of those churches and are trained for their ministry. There are some 60 students.

Manchester Grammar School, founded in 1515 by Hugh Oldham, Bishop of Exeter. Although sev. times rebuilt, the school remained on its original site in Long Millgate until 1913, when the demands of 20th cent. standards necessitated the erection of new buildings in Fallowfield. The school admits able boys from all walks of life, without barriers of cost, in the endeavour to fulfil the aim of the original statutes that 'there shall no scholar or infant of what county or shire so ever he be, being manchild, be refused'. There are some 1450 pupils.

'Manchester Guardian', *see* 'GUARDIAN, THE'.

Manchester Regiment, The. The 1st Battalion

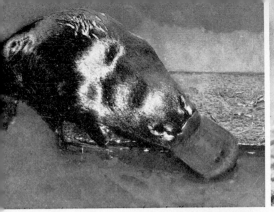

Mammals:

Monotremata

Top left: Duck-billed platypus.
Top right: Echidna, or spiny ant-eater.

Marsupialia (*see also under* Australia).

Above left: Brush-tail possum.
Above right: Tasmanian devil.
Left: Black-striped wallabies.
All photos: Harry and Claudy Frauca

Mammals: Placentalia

Insectivora

Above left: Common shrew.
John Markham
Above: Hedgehog.
Sdeuard C. Bisserôt
Left: Mole.
Jane Burton

Chiroptera

Below left: Noctule or great bat.
John Markham

Pholidota

Below: Ground pangolin or scaly ant-eater.
Des Bartlett, Armand Denis Productions

Mammals: Placentalia

Edentata

Above: Six-banded armadillo.
Right: Hoffman's sloth.
Both photos: Zoological Society of London

Primates

Left: Young galago (bush-baby).
Des Bartlett, Armand Denis Productions

Below left: Ape (gorilla).
Harry Miller

Below: Vervet monkey.
Des Bartlett, Armand Denis Productions

Mammals: Placentalia

Lagomorpha

Left: Young rabbit.
John Markham

Right: Brown hare.
Arne Schmitz

Rodentia

Below left: Harvest mouse.
John Markham

Below right: Grey squirrel.
John Markham

Bottom left: Porcupine.
Norman Lightfoot

Bottom right: Beaver.
Ed Park

Mammals: Placentalia

Carnivora

Top: Seal.
Tom Weir

Top: Hyaena.
Donald Paterson

Above: Dingo dog.
Zoological Society of London

Above: Lion.
C. Guggisberg

Left: Indian mongoose.
Jane Burton

Right: Common raccoon.
Norman Lightfoot

Mammals: Placentalia

Tubulidentata

Above: Aardvark.
Des Bartlett, Armand Denis Productions

Carnivora

Above right: Young polar bears.
Toni Angermayer

Right: Giant panda and young.
World Wildlife Fund

Cetacea

Left: Common dolphins.
Jane Burton

Below left: Beluga (white whale).
Russ Kinne

Hyracoidea

Below: Rock hyrax.
C. Guggisberg

Mammals: Placentalia

Perissodactyla

Above: Rhinoceros.
Donald Paterson

Artiodactyla

Below: Warthog and young.
Simon Trevor, Armand Denis Productions

Bottom: Hippopotamus.
Des Bartlett, Armand Denis Productions

Proboscides

Top: African elephant.
Donald Paterson

Perissodactyla

Above: Tapir.
Cesco Ciopanna

Below: Zebras.
Simon Trevor, Armand Denis Productions

Mammals: Placentalia

Artiodactyla

Left: Wild sheep (bighorn ram).
Ed Park

Right: Arabian camels.
V. K. Anthony

Left: Bison.
Ed Park

Right: Antelope (Thomson's gazelle).
C. Guggisberg

Left: Giraffe.
Donald Paterson

Right: Red deer.
John R. Brownlie

was originally the 63rd Foot formed in 1756 and the 2nd was the 96th Foot raised after the Napoleonic wars. One of the chief campaigns in the hist. of the regiment was in Egypt, whence their badge of the Sphinx; other campaigns were the Amer. War of Independence, the Crimean War and the S. African war, where they were prominent at Elands Laagte and at Ladysmith. The 2nd Battalion was with the original Brit. expeditionary force in the First World War and fought at Le Cateau. Many territorial units took part in the Gallipoli campaign, 1915, being in heavy fighting at Sari Bair and Achi Baba. In 1916, at the battle of the Somme, city and other service battalions fought at Montauban and Guillemont. The 1st Battalion was with the Kut relief force and took part in the severe fighting at the Hannah redoubt. In 1917 various units were in the Ypres battles, notably at Passchendaele, and at Neuville Vitasse in the battle of Arras, while in the final Ger. offensive of 1918 other units fought at Houthulst and Zonnebeke in Flanders. Altogether the regiment raised no less than 42 battalions in the First World War. In the Second World War units of the M. R. served in NW. Europe, Italy, Malta, Malaya and Burma. In 1958 the M. R. and the King's Regiment (q.v.) were amalgamated to form the King's Regiment (Manchester and Liverpool) in the Lancastrian Brigade. See Col. H. C. Wylly, *History of the Manchester Regiment* (2 vols.), 1923–5.

Manchester Ship Canal, opened for traffic on 1 Jan, 1894. Up to that time there had been barge navigation between Liverpool and Manchester along the R.s Mersey and Irwell, and via the Bridgewater Canal, the first and second sections of which were completed in July 1761. This canal was extended to the tn of Runcorn in 1767, and to the R. Mersey at Runcorn in 1773; early in the next cent. a junction with the Leeds and Liverpool Canal was made at Leigh. Between 1824 and 1882 various schemes were advanced for the construction of a canal to link Manchester with the sea. The plan finally accepted was that of Leader Williams, who favoured a scheme with sev. levels maintained by locks rather than a tidal canal, and it was decided to draft proposals for Parliament. A parl. Bill was prepared in 1882, but was rejected by the House of Lords. A second Bill was also rejected, on a second reading by the Commons; a third Bill was finally passed in Aug. 1885, and work was begun in Nov. 1887.

The length of the canal is 36 m.; it begins at Eastham on the Cheshire side of the Mersey and runs near or through the Mersey estuary to Runcorn. It then goes inland to Latchford, near Warrington, where tidal action ceases, and from there to Manchester it is fed by the waters of the Mersey and Irwell. Manchester port has 8 docks, the largest (the No. 9 dock, opened 1905) being 2700 ft by 250 ft. The dock estate covers an area of 700 ac., of which water space occupies 179 ac. The quays are 5⅝ m. long. Oil docks at Stanlow were opened in 1922 and 1933; the Queen Elizabeth II Dock at Eastham at the canal

entrance was opened in Jan. 1954 (it covers an area of 19 ac. and has its own entrance lock). There are 3 entrance locks to the canal which keep the water level nearly to mean high-water level. The depth of the canal is 30 ft between Eastham and Ince Oil Berth, and 28 ft from Ince to Manchester. The general constructed bottom width of the canal is 120 ft for most of its length, though the excavated width varies from 180 ft at the Weaver outfall to only 90 ft for about ¾ m. from Warburton Bridge. At Eastham locks the width is 315 ft.

The construction of the canal is a great engineering feat. At Barton the Bridgewater Canal crosses the R. Irwell on a swing aqueduct, the first of its kind constructed in England. This aqueduct is made of steel and worked by hydraulic power. The canal is crossed by 5 lines of railways, carried by high-level viaducts. There are also 7 swing bridges for main roads, while underneath the canal great siphons are constructed to enable the R. Gowy to continue its course uninterrupted. At intervals along the whole length of the canal are wharves and works of all kinds, as at Runcorn and Weston Point. The immense advantage the M. S. C. has been to trade throughout Lancs and the surrounding dist has more than justified the tremendous outlay, the canal being in direct communication with all the prin. railway systems and barge canals of the U.K. In 1963 the shipping using the canal amounted to 15,113,000 tons. See the M. S. C. Co.'s booklet *Resolution and Achievement*, 7th ed., 1965. (*See Plate: Cheshire.*)

Manchester Terrier. The earliest recognisable M. T. is portrayed in an illuminated MS. book of hrs of the 15th cent. Later they were known as Eng. terriers. It is generally accepted that the pure breed had its origin in and around Manchester. Dog shows have conduced to the refinement of the original breed, though it is still a useful rat catcher. The head should be long, flat, narrow and wedge-shaped; eyes, very small, sparkling and dark; nose, black; ears V shaped, hanging close to the head above the eyes; neck long and tapering from the shoulders to the head, with sloping shoulders; narrow and deep chest; legs quite straight; feet more inclined to be cat- than hare-footed; tail thick where it joins the body and tapering to a point; and smooth short and glossy coat. The coat should be jet black and rich mahogany tan on the head; the muzzle should be tanned to the nose, which, with the nasal bone, is jet black; forelegs should be half tanned and the hind legs tanned on the inside, but not on the outside. The usual weights are 16 to 20 lb.; height 15 to 16 in.

Manchester, Victoria University of, in Oxford Road, owes its existence principally to John Owens (q.v.), who provided in his will for the foundation of a college in which instruction would be given 'in such branches of learning and science as are usually taught in the Eng. univs.'. Owens College was opened in a house in Quay Street in 1851. Growth was rapid, and by 1873 the first of the present buildings, designed by Waterhouse, was in occupation. In 1880 a charter was granted for the institution of the Victoria Univ., with its seat in Manchester. Four years later the colleges of Liverpool (q.v.) and Leeds (q.v.) were admitted, and the Federal Univ. continued until 1903, when a new charter was granted and separate univs. were estab. in the 3 cities. Today the univ. contains 9 faculties, and the original Owens College is surrounded by additional buildings containing the Whitworth Hall, Christie Library, the Manchester Museum and the many depts of learning. There are over 8750 students.

Manchukuo, Jap. puppet state set up in Feb. 1932 in conquered Manchuria, with its cap. at Hsinching (the present Changchun). The 'chief executive' was Henry Pu Yi, ex-emperor of China. Pu Yi was promoted in Mar. 1934 to be 'emperor' of M. The Lytton Commission set up by the League of Nations pronounced the state apparatus a charade, but the sole result was that Japan resigned from the League. M. vanished with the defeat of the Japanese in 1945. *See* MANCHURIA.

Manchuria, old name of the 3 NE. provs. of the Chinese People's Rep. The N. half, before the 17th cent., was the land of the Manchus. It lies between outer Mongolia on the W. and Korea and Siberia on the E. and N. M. extends between 39° 40′ and 53° 50′ N. lat. and 115° 20′ and 135° 20′ E. long. The R. Amur forms the boundary on the N. Prior to 1930 M. was divided into 3 provs.: N. M., or Heilungkiang; central M., or Kirin; and S. M., or Liaoning. Great changes took place after the Jap. invasion (1931). Under the puppet 'Manchukuo' the original provs. were reorganised into 10 new administrative provs. (1935). After the Jap. surrender in 1945 the Nationalist Gov. divided the area into 9 provs. In 1953 the People's Gov. restored it to the original 3 provs. with Shenyang (Mukden) as the cap. of Liaoning, Changchun of Kirin and Harbin of Heilungkiang.

M. is a country of mts and plains. The Greater Khinghan Mts cover the W. of the prov., the Lesser Khingham run parallel to the Amur R., which forms the NE. boundary, while the Shangpai Mts, the highest, mark the frontier with Korea. Between these ranges unfold the plains of the Nun (Nonni), Sungari and Liao R.s. The Liao R. is shallow and silt-laden, and its port of Newchuang (Yingkow) is diminishing in importance. The Sungari R., which empties into the Amur R., is able to take larger vessels. The main ports for the region are the ice-free Dairen and Port Arthur on the Liaotung Pen. In general the climate of long hard winters and short hot summers allows only one crop a year. Soybeans, kaoliang, wheat, sugar beet, cotton and hemp are the main crops. A specially profitable local plant is the medicinal ginseng root, now cultivated in plantations. The mt areas of M. are China's main source of timber.

The M. plains beyond the Great Wall have been the 'reservoir' where various tribes in hist. have built up their strength prior to an invasion of N. China. The 'Manchus' themselves (they actually derived from outlying tribal followers of the Jurchid, and only acquired the name of Manchus when they founded the Ch'ing dynasty in China) came under the banner of Nurhachi at the beginning of the 17th cent.; when he *d.* in 1626 they had control of the 'Chinese Pale' outside the Great Wall. The Ch'ing dynasty was estab. under Nurhachi's descendants in 1644 as a result of their conquest of China and lasted until 1911. M. was closed against Chinese settlers until the latter half of the 19th cent.; by the end of the cent. the Chinese constituted 80 per cent of the pop. The Russian concession to build the Chinese Eastern Railway, granted 1896, started M. on the road to becoming China's main industrial region. The Russians were supplanted by the Japanese after their victory in the Russo-Jap. War in 1905; Jap. control was economic until their military occupation of the region in 1931-2. Development has been continuous since the Japanese began to invest in the region except for a setback in 1945 as a result of Russian spoliation. The Chinese Communist regime has directed very large numbers of people there to work on state farms and man the busy industries. Chief among these are coal (the main fields being at Fushun, Fuhsin, Penki and Haolikang) and steel (at Anshan, Penki and Tungpientao: production of steel at Anshan amounted to over 4 million tons in 1960). The biggest industrial city of M. is Shenyang (Mukden), cap. of Liaoning prov. (q.v.). Manuf. of farm machinery and generating equipment is concentrated in Harbin, of chemicals in Kirin and of motors in Changchun. The shipyards at Dairen build vessels of 20,000 tons. M. has over 8000 m. of railway track, far above the average concentration for China. It is also well supplied with hydro-electric power: dams at Supung (on the Yalu), Fengman (on the Sungari) and on the Mutankiang R. have a combined capacity of $1\frac{1}{2}$ million kW.; a fourth dam is being built at Kumotsin on the Nonni R.

Although M. was not the scene of any serious fighting in the Second World War, it suffered, in some ways, heavier damage than any other part of China. For the Russians took away much of the rolling stock, and stripped the factories and industrial plants of their heavy machinery; and between the departure of the Russians and the arrival of the Chinese Nationalist forces there was still further looting and destruction of property. This spoliation by the Russians as well as by the Chinese themselves dealt the industry of M. a severe blow, though it did not account altogether for the decline from the old-time prosperity. After the surrender of Japan in 1945 the Chinese Gov. regained the splendidly developed rail and road systems of M. together with numerous large airfields, the hydro-electric plant near Kirin, the Fushan coal-mines and thousands of modern buildings and other valuable properties, most of this being in effect a form of reparations, though they were built by the forced labour of the local Chinese. When Nationalist Gov. officials came to 'recover' M. in 1946, they labelled all industrial enterprises, including those owned by the local people, as 'enemy property', requisitioned them and quickly ruined them through mismanagement and corruption. This act of requisition was unanimously condemned by the local people as 'official robbery', and it accounted for the subsequent success of the Communists, to whom the rich and poor alike turned as their only alternative. In the ensuing years of civil war further damage to industry was done by the retreating Nationalist troops, who either dismantled or destroyed the machinery. The steel centre in Anshan, which in the early days under the Japanese had an ann. output of nearly half a millions tons, could produce after a year's repair work only 150,000 tons in 1949. Heavy industry in M. developed by the Japanese was geared to Japan's imperialist economic pattern. Since 1949 efforts have been made by the Peking Gov. to restore and expand it with Russian machinery and blue-prints. By 1956 most of China's 4,500,000 tons of steel was produced in M., together with nearly all her output of seamless tubes, rails and heavy machinery. In 1955–6 the prov. of Heilungkiang absorbed 270,000 peasants from overcrowded Shantung and Honan to reclaim the vast virgin ter. of N. M. Light industries such as paper, sugar, flour, food canning, tobacco and flax textiles are also being developed. Total area of the 3 provs. 307,107 sq. m. Pop. 41,732,529 (1954).

See A. Hosie, *Manchuria*, 1901; O. Lattimore, *Manchuria: Cradle of Conflict*, 1932, *The Mongols · of Manchuria*, 1935, and *Inner Asian Frontiers of China*, 1940; F. C. Jones, *Manchuria since 1931*, 1949; Chou En-lai, *Report on the Proposals for the Second Five-Year Plan*, 1956; Chao Kuo-chun, *NE. China (Manchuria) Today*, 1953; O. Edmund Clubb, *Chinese Communist Development Programmes in Manchuria*, 1954. (*See Plate: China*.)

Mancini, Pasquale Stanislao (1817–88), It. lawyer and statesman, *b.* near Ariano. He took part in the Neapolitan revolution of 1848 and subsequently went to Turin and practised as an advocate, being appointed prof. of international law at the univ. there. From 1881 to 1883 he was minister of foreign affairs.

Mancunium, *see* MANCHESTER.

Mandaeans ('knowers'), Mesopotamian religious sect (*see* MANICHAEISM), still surviving, about 2000 strong, in the neighbourhood of Basra and Kut, akin to the 2nd and 3rd cent. Gnostics. They worship *Mand d'hayye* ('Knowledge of Life') and regard the whole material universe as evil, the product of *Ur*, son of *Ruha*, the female demon of the primeval watery chaos. The whole material creation is doomed to destruction, swallowed by Leviathan; but the human soul, now imprisoned in the body, comes from *Hebel-Ziwa*, or 'Abel the Bright', son of *Mand d'hayye*, and is to be liberated and saved by *Anush-Utra*, or 'Enosh the Good Spirit', the true Christ, as opposed to Jesus 'the Byzantine', the false Christ worshipped by Christians. M. baptise frequently in running waters, which they call Jordans, whence they get the name Subba (Baptists), and were

identified by the Muslims with the Sabaeans. They call themselves Nazoraeans (which they take to mean 'true believers') and have been mistakenly called the Christians of St John Baptist, though they have no real connection with him or with Christianity, in spite of obvious and ignorant borrowings from the N.T. and the O.T. Their sacred books are written in a form of Aramaic. See S. A. Pallis, *Mandaean Studies*, 1926, and E. S. Drowser, *The Mandaeans of Irak and Iran*, 1937.

Mandalay, tn of Upper Burma, a riv. port, centre of communications and railway junction, with an airport, on the E. bank of the Irrawaddy above Amarapura and Ava, 386 m. N. of Rangoon. It was the last of the Burmese caps. and was founded in 1857 by King Mindon, who convened the 5th Buddhist synod there in 1870. Before the Second World War the walled city was the military cantonment of the British (Fort Dufferin). There are many temples, pagodas and monasteries, including the Shwesandaw Kyaung, a magnificent structure of carved wood, ruined during the war. Silk weaving is carried on extensively. The former Intermediate College was raised to univ. status in 1958 and has a new medical school; there is also a training college for teachers and a technical institute. M. is a seat of Buddhist learning. Pop. 213,000 (mostly Buddhists).

M. dist has an area of 2120 sq. m. and a pop. of 409,000. The land is fertile and, irrigated by canals, can produce 2 crops a year. M. div. has an area of 12,504 sq. m. and contains the dists of M., Kyaukse, Myingyan, Meiktila and Yamethin.

M. was devastated by Jap. bombing before its capture in 1942, and was again bombed heavily by the Allies in 1945. See BURMA, SECOND WORLD WAR, CAMPAIGNS IN. (*See Plate: Burma*.)

Mandamus, prerogative order made by the queen's bench div. commanding an inferior court or public authority to carry out a duty required by law which it has refused to perform (e.g. a magistrates' court which has declined to exercise its jurisdiction or a local authority which has failed to provide some obligatory service to the ratepayers).

Mandarin: 1. General name under the empire for a Chinese magistrate or public official, civil or military. The Civil M.s, chosen from the men of letters or scholars from every part of the country, were divided into 9 degrees, each consisting of 2 classes, the highest of which were ministers of state, counsellors of the emperor and presidents of the supreme court. Each order was distinguished by the button worn on the top of the cap, while the highest grade also wore a peacock's feather at the back of the cap, not as a sign of office or rank, but as a reward for peculiar merit. The buttons of the higher orders were made of coloured coral, the lower of glass, and the lowest of gilt metal.

2. Also, the name given to the language of these officials (in Chinese, *kuan-hua*); based on the language of Peking, it was in fact the most

widely spread dialogue as well as the lingua franca. The term is no longer used in China, having been replaced by *kuo-yu* ('national language'), or *pu-tung-hua* ('common language'). M. dialects are spoken in the lower Yangtze valley and in SW. China, as well as the N.

Mandarin Duck, or **Chinese Teal** (*Dendronessa*), very small ornamental waterfowl. The drake's head has a long, erectile crest, green, purple and chestnut in colour, and a curious fan or sail. The duck and drake are an extraordinarily devoted pair.

MANDARIN DUCK

Mandarin Orange, *Citrus nobilis,* variety *deliciosa. See* ORANGE.

Mandate System, system of gov. evolved under the treaty of Versailles after the First World War, for the expropriated Ger. colonies and outlying portions of the Turkish Empire. The principle of the M. S., which was embodied in the covenant of the League of Nations, was new in international law (q.v.). There is no essential difference in the mandate as it exists today under the UNO from what it was under the covenant (*see* COLONIAL TRUSTEESHIP). It places the mandated ter. under the tutelage of the mandatory, the hypothesis being that the inhab. of the mandated ter. are not sufficiently advanced to safeguard their own interests; the mandatory nation may not exploit the mandated ter. in its own interests, but exercises the mandate as a 'sacred trust' of civilisation on behalf of the U.N. Mandates were classified as A, B and C mandates, depending on the stage of development of the inhab., geographical position and economic conditions. Under the charter of the U.N. (International Trusteeship System) mandatories undertake to transmit information relating to the economic, social and educational conditions of the ters. for which they are responsible. Approval of the M. S. has not been unanimous. Allocation of mandates was exercised by the Allies of the First World War in favour of allied powers. But outright annexation was and is discountenanced, and the ultimate authority of the League was some guarantee of the equity of a system which is perpetuated in the trusteeship principle of the charter of the U.N. The major work of the Trusteeship Council of the U.N. (as was that of

the Permanent Mandates Commission of the League) is to focus attention on the problem of native welfare and economic development, to co-ordinate investigations and experiments towards its solution, and to see that mandated areas are administered in the interests of the natives and the world, thus setting examples for the administration of backward areas everywhere. *See* N. Bentwich, *The Mandates System,* 1930; M. Mortimer, *Trusteeship in Action,* 1951; U.N., *Autonomy in Trusteeship Lands,* 1954.

Mande-nga, *see* MANDINGOES.

Mander, Karel van (1584–1606), Dutch painter and writer on art, *b.* Meulebeke. He studied at Ghent and had a successful academy of painting at Haarlem. He is best known as the author of a biographical work on artists, pub. in 1604, a valuable source of information on Dutch and Flem. painting.

Mandeville, Bernard de (*c.* 1670–1733), Brit. philosopher and satirist, *b.* Dordrecht, Holland, where his father was a physician. He was educ. at the Erasmus School, Rotterdam, and at Leyden Univ. In 1691 he took his medical degree and came to England, but did not practise widely. His fame rests on his *Fable of the Bees, or Private Vices, Public Benefits,* which appeared first in 1705, and in later eds. 1714 and 1723. It was primarily written as a political satire on the state of England in 1705, when Marlborough's ministry was accused by the Tories of advocating the Fr. war for personal reasons. He also wrote *Free Thoughts on Religion, the Church and National Happiness,* 1720, *An Enquiry into the Origin of Honour,* 1732, and *The Planter's Charity,* 1704. *See* J. M. Robertson, *Pioneer Humanists,* 1907, F. B. Kaye, *The Writings of Bernard Mandeville,* 1921; P. B. Anderson, *Splendor out of Scandal,* 1936.

Mandeville, Sir John, ostensible author of a book of travels bearing his name, written about the middle of the 14th cent., giving an account of journeys in the E., including India and the Holy Land. It appears to have been compiled from the writings of Wm of Boldensele, Oderic of Pordenone and Vincent de Beauvais. The name M. was probably fictitious. Wynken de Worde's ed. of *Sir John Mandeville's Travels,* 1499, was remarkable for its illustrations, of which it contained a set 'not less wonderful than the adventures they portray'. *See* P. Hamelius, *Mandeville's Travels* (Early Eng. Text Society), 1919; H. Plomer, *Wynken de Worde and his Contemporaries* (London), 1925; M. Letts, *Sir John Mandeville: the man and his book,* 1949.

Mandible (Lat. *mandibulum,* the jaw), name applied in anatomy and zoology to the jawbone. In birds it signifies both upper and lower jaws, together with their horny integument, although the terms maxilla and mandibula are sometimes used to refer respectively to the upper and lower parts. In mammals the term applies only to the under jaw. In insects it applies to the anterior, upper or outer pairs of jaws.

Mandigoes, Mandingos, Mandingans, Mandenga or **Mandiña,** names of an important div. of Sudanese Negro peoples of W. Africa, especially in Senegambia, between the headwaters of the Niger and the Senegal. The majority represent a mixture of Negro, Berber and Arab elements. The Mandi speech is very widely diffused, and largely employed by translators. The empire of Melle (Mali) was founded by their ancestors under Musa (1311–31). They were conquered by the Songhai *c.* 1500. They are zealous Muslims estimated at over 10 million in number. *See* L. Binger, *Du Niger au golfe de Guinée*, 1892; F. Lugard, *A Tropical Dependency*, 1905; H. Johnston, *Liberia*, 1906; L. Marc, *Le Pays Mossi*, 1909.

Mandla, tn of Madhya Pradesh state, India. The tn, on the Narbadá 50 m. SE. of Jubbulpore, was the former cap. of the Gond kings, who built a great fort (*c.* 1670) of which little now remains.

Mandoline, stringed musical instrument of the lute family (treble member), but with greater convexity of back. It is of It. origin but is now used in most civilised lands. The 2 chief varieties are the Neapolitan (with 4 pairs of metallic strings) and the Milanese (with 5 pairs). It is played with a plectrum or quill of tortoiseshell, whalebone or some pliable substance, held in the right hand. The finger-board, or neck, has many frets across. *See* Grove's *Dictionary of Music*, vol. v, p. 547, 5th ed., 1954.

Mandrake, or **Mandragora**, small genus of perennial plants of the family Solanaceae. In anct legend the roots were once thought to be of human shape and to shriek when pulled from the ground. They are stemless plants, with thick tap roots and dark-green wrinkled leaves. *M. autumnalis* bears pale purple flowers in Sept., and *M. officinarum*, Devil's Apples, white or blue flowers in May, followed by yellow, globose fruit. Both have been supposed to be the M. of Genesis, and the plants were and still are credited with many miraculous properties.

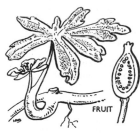

MANDRAKE

Mandrill (*Mandrillus sphinx*), large W. African baboon. Its immense canine teeth, large blood-red ischial callosities and huge, naked, gaudily striped cheeks render it one of the most hideous creatures in nature. It is insectivorous. Both the M. and the drill (q.v.) are largely arboreal, sleeping in the trees at night.

Manduria (formerly *Casalnuovo*), It. tn in Apulia (q.v.), 22 m. ESE. of Taranto. It is an anct tn, referred to by Pliny (q.v.). There is a trade in grain, wine, fruit and olives. Pop. 24,000.

Manes, in Rom. religion, spirits of the dead considered as divinities, to be distinguished from the *lemures* (q.v.), who were simply ghosts. The name was derived from old *manus*, 'good'. In course of time the *di manes* were identified with the deceased ancestors of a family, and even with the gods of the underworld; cf. the inscription D.M.S. (*dis manibus sacrum*) on many Rom. tombs.

Manesse: 1. Name of a Swiss knight of Zürich (Ruediger of M.) who, in the 13th cent., started collecting the songs of the Minnesingers (q.v.). The MSS., which contain verses by as many as 140 poets from the middle of the 12th until the first half of the 14th cent., are not the only source of the Ger. minnesongs, but are by far the most voluminous and most valuable. Adorned with 138 miniatures, they are now preserved at the univ. of Heidelberg.
2. Swiss publishing house, named after the above. It started publishing a series of 'World's Classics' (*Manesse Bibliothek der Weltliteratur*) in pocket size in 1944, which now numbers 150 titles, including a collection of the M. medieval songs, and ranging from Gk prose over the well-known European classics to Chinese and Jap. literature, trans. into German.

Manet, Édouard (1832–83), Fr. realistic *genre* and portrait painter, regarded as the founder of Impressionism. *B.* Paris, he sailed in a training ship to Rio de Janeiro (1848), but persisted in taking up an artist's career and became a pupil of Couture. He travelled widely in Europe and devoted much time to studying the Sp. masters in the Louvre. Velazquez and the realist Courbet both helped to form his outlook. His works were severely criticised and often rejected by the Salon. His 'Déjeuner sur l'herbe', 1863, caused a scandal and also made him a leader of young painters. His 'Olympia', 1865, was another storm-centre. Zola, Baudelaire and Mallarmé were his defenders against popular clamour. M. served in the National Guard, 1870; after the war he was much in contact with the Impressionist group, working in the open air with Claude Monet at Argenteuil, 1874. To paint contemporary life as vividly as possible was M.'s aim and such pictures as his 'Bon Bock', 1873, and 'Un Bar aux Folies Bergère', 1882, are modern masterpieces. His large 'Execution of Maximilian' survives in fragments (National Gallery). *See* lives by J. E. Blanche (Eng. trans.), 1925; A. Tabarant, 1931; Jamot and Wildenstein, 1932; *also* P. Courthion (ed.), *Manet raconté par lui-même et par ses amis*, 1945, trans. M. Ross, 1960; D. Cooper, *The Courtauld Collection*, 1954.

Manetho, native of Sebennytus in the Delta and probably high priest of Heliopolis, was Ptolemy I's Egyptian adviser in the introduction of the statue of Serapis (q.v.) to Alexandria. He is chiefly known for his hist. of Egypt written from Egyptian sources in Greek for the instruction of foreigners and in correction of Herodotus. Unfortunately his writings, which included also works on the religion of Egypt, are known only from fragmentary and often distorted quotations preserved chiefly by Josephus because of the historical connection of the Jews with Egypt, and by the Christian chronographers Africanus and Eusebius, in an epitomised form giving a list of 31 dynasties. This list is important as being the foundation for the generally accepted scheme by which the anct Egyptian historic period is divided into dynasties. *See* trans. of his hist. by W. G. Waddell, 1940 (Loeb Library).

Manfred (1231–66), King of Sicily and natural son of the Emperor Frederick II, on whose death he acted as regent in Italy during the minority of his nephew Conradin. In 1258, with Saracen help, he was proclaimed king of the Two Sicilies and crowned at Palermo. He was thereupon excommunicated by the Pope, but marched into the papal ter. and was acknowledged master of Tuscany. Later, however, Pope Urban IV re-excommunicated him and gave his kingdom to Charles I of Anjou, and finally he was defeated and killed at Benevento.

Manfredonia, It. seaport in Apulia (q.v.), 22 m. NE. of Foggia. It is on the Gulf of M., an inlet of the Adriatic, and was founded by Manfred (q.v.) of Sicily in 1263, 2 m. E. of the anct Sipontum (q.v.). It has a cathedral and an old castle. Pop. 33,800.

Mangalore, or **Mangalur,** tn and seaport of Madras state, India, on the Malabar coast, 125 m. NNW. of Calicut. M. has been a commercial centre for 500 years or more, and though there is no harbour is regularly visited by merchant shipping. The main exports are coffee and cashew nuts. It was captured by Tippu Sultan in 1784 after gallant and prolonged resistance, and was returned to Brit. control in 1799.

Mangan, James Clarence (1803–49), poet, *b.* Dublin. He wrote for the *Nation* (founded 1842) and contributed to many Irish newspapers under various pseudonyms. *Anthologia Germanica,* 1845, and *Romances and Ballads of Ireland,* 1850, were among his chief works. *See* D. J. O'Donoghue, *Life and Writings of Mangan,* 1897, and his eds. of *Poems,* 1903, and *Prose Writings,* 1904.

Manganese, symbol Mn, atomic number 25, atomic weight 54·95, suspected to be present by Scheele (1774) in pyrolusite, and isolated by Ghan. It occurs as the dioxide (MnO_2) in pyrolusite, as the sesquioxide (Mn_2O_3) in braunite, as the tetroxide (Mn_3O_4) in hausmannite, and as the carbonate ($MnCO_3$) in association with iron carbonates in iron ores. The metal is somewhat difficult to reduce; it is prepared by mixing the oxide or the carbonate with charcoal and subjecting the mixture to a high temp. or (*see* GOLDSCHMIT METHOD) by mixing manganese tetroxide with powdered aluminium in a resistant crucible, and starting the reaction by means of a magnesium wire fuse. The metal is silvery white when pure, but has a slightly red tinge when impure. It is not attacked by air or water unless it is impure, but evolves hydrogen rapidly from dilute acids. It has a sp. gr. of 7·4, melting-point 1242° C. It is used commercially for the production of the following alloys:

manganese bronze (up to 3·5 per cent Mn), Mn brass (with copper and zinc), Mn Ger. silver (with copper and zinc), manganin—a very useful alloy for electrical resistance (Cu 84, Ni 12, Mn 4), Heussler's alloy, a magnetic alloy (containing aluminium, Mn and copper), spiegel iron (20–32 per cent Mn), ferromanganese (70–80 per cent Mn) and Mn steel (as much as 12 per cent Mn). This steel is extremely hard, does not lose its temper and is used particularly in machinery for crushing rocks, manganese-nickel alloys for anchor bolts and boiler firebricks. The chief compounds are manganese oxide (MnO), a green powder obtained by igniting the higher oxides in a current of hydrogen; trimanganese tetroxide (Mn_3O_4), a reddish powder obtained by heating any oxide in the presence of air; manganese sesquioxide (Mn_2O_3), a dark brown powder obtained by heating MnO or MnO_2 to redness in air; manganese dioxide (MnO_2), a black solid found native as pyrolusite and prepared as a hydroxide by shaking up the manganous hydroxide, $Mn(OH)_2$, with chlorine water. It may be used as a source of oxygen when heated alone or with sulphuric acid. Mn heptoxide (Mn_2O_7), a red-brown liquid made by the action of a little ice-cold water on a solution of potassium permanganate in strong sulphuric acid. The manganates of the alkalis, formed by fusing manganese dioxide with the hydroxides of the alkalis; the permanganates of the alkalis, formed by treating the manganates with acids; manganous sulphide (MnS), formed by precipitation from alkaline solutions of manganese salts with soluble sulphides; manganese sulphate ($MnSO_4$), a pink crystalline solid, and manganese chloride ($MnCl_2$) are both formed by the action of the appropriate acid on manganese, its oxides, hydroxide or carbonate. Some of the salts of manganese are used in medicine for the treatment of anaemia and chlorosis. The manganates and permanganates of sodium and potassium are used in solution as disinfecting fluids, e.g. in Condy's fluid. *See also* FERROMANGANESE.

Mangbetu, a Sudanic people of the N. Belgian Congo, famed for their highly organised empire and kingship. They conquered many surrounding peoples, and during the last cent. were the most important tribe of the area. They are also famous for their magnificent carving, smithing and dancing, and for their custom of binding the heads of infants to produce a long pointed share to the skull. *See* G. Schweinfurth, *The Heart of Africa,* 1873; W. Junker, *Travels in Africa,* 1892.

Mange, parasitic disease of the skin caused by the presence of minute M.-mites. They are of 4 main kinds: (1) Sarcoptes, which burrow through the skin; (2) Psoroptes; (3) Symbiotes; and (4) Dermatodectes, which are more superficial in their operations. M. affects the horse, cow, sheep, pig, dog and cat, but man only rarely. M. in horses in compulsorily notifiable to the local authorities, as also is psoroptic M. in sheep, or sheep scab. Repeated application of greasy dressings destroys the parasites.

Mangel-wurzel, or **Mangold,** important root crop rich in cane-sugar and derived, like sugar-beet and garden beet, from *Beta maritima*, a weed (family Chenopodiaceae) found on the Eng. S. coast. The varieties of M. are of 3 types—long, tankard and globe; red, yellow or orange in colour. Many varieties are suited to special conditions, and the gold tankard is the most nutritious. The fruit is a rough integument containing 4 or 5 seeds, and is drilled in April in rows 20 to 30 in. apart, the young plants being subsequently singled out 10 to 14 in. apart in the rows. The crop, requiring a warm, dry climate, is grown chiefly in the S. of England, thriving best in richly manured, deep clay loams. The root is very sensitive to frost, and must be lifted in Oct., before it is ripe; it is kept in clamps till Jan. before feeding to stock.

Mangin, Charles Marie Emmanuel (1866–1925), Fr. general, *b.* Sarrebourg, Meurthe. Educ. at Toulon and Versailles lycées, at the college of St Francis Xavier, Lunéville, and at St Cyr, he began his army career as an infantry marine subaltern and saw service in the Sudan (1893–9), Tongking (1901–4) and Morocco (1912–3). In the First World War he commanded the 5th Div.; then the 11th Army Corps, the 9th Corps, the 6th Corps (1917), and in 1918 the Tenth Army. He rendered most distinguished service in the First World War, notably in 1916 in the great counterstroke at Verdun; the furious attack on the Meuse, N. of the famous fortress, nominally conducted under the general command of Nivelle, being actually conducted by M. The scheme of the counter-attack at the second battle of the Marne was drawn up by Pétain in consultation with M., Fayolle and Dégoutte; and M. and Dégoutte commanded the Franco-Amer. troops which attacked the Germans W. of Soissons near Château Thiérry on 18 July. He then assailed the Germans on the line from the Oise to the Aisne with equal success. Finally in Aug. his army broke the 'Hunding line' between the Oise, Serre and Aisne, and reached Mézières by 8 Nov. just before the armistice. Pubs.: *La Force noire*, 1910, crowned by the Academy; *Comment finit la guerre*, 1921; *Commentaires et portraits*, 1922; 'La Plus Grande France' and 'Histoire militaire et navale' (in *Histoire de la nation française*, ed. G. Hanotaux). *See* lives by G. Hanotaux, 1925; C. Bugnet, 1934; P. Noreau-Vauthier, 1936.

Mango, kidney-shaped fruit, yellow and red in colour, of the M.-tree (*Mangifera indica*), which is extensively cultivated both for the fruit and for its numerous medicinal and economic uses.

Mangold, *see* MANGEL-WURZEL.

Mangonel, *see* ARMOUR.

Mangosteen, brown orange-like fruit filled with a most deliciously flavoured sweet pulp, of an evergreen tropical tree (*Garcinia mangostana*) with red unisexual flowers (family Guttiferae).

Mangotsfield, urb. dist of Gloucestershire, England, 5 m. ENE. of Bristol. Pop. 24,092.

Mangrove, or *Rhizophora*, genus of tropical trees of great value in reclaiming coast land. The seeds germinate on the parent tree, sending

MANGO
A, cross-section of fruit.

down roots of considerable size, and forming as the trees grow a great network which retains vegetable matter and gradually converts swamps into solid ground. The fruit of *Rhizophora mangel* is edible.

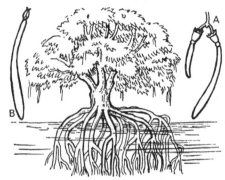

MANGROVE
A, seeds germinating on the tree; B, fallen seedling with long radicle and small pumule.

Mangyshlak Pen, on the E. coast of the Caspian Sea, in Kazakhstan, largely desert and semi-desert. It has manganese and phosphorite deposits, but since 1959 it has become prominent through the discovery and exploitation of oil deposits. The oil is viscous and can be piped only through heated pipelines. A railway was completed in June 1964 from Makat, on the Gur'yev-Orsk line, to the new tn of Shevchenko (until 1964, Aktau) on the S. of the pen. In 1964 natural gas was also discovered.

Manhattan Club, *see* CLUB.

Manhattan Island, situated at the mouth of the Hudson R., U.S.A. Its length is about 13 m. and its greatest width about 2¼ m. It contains the commercial and financial centre and bor. of Manhattan, which is the chief business part of New York City though there are also large residential and industrial areas. The rocks of which it is formed rise to a height of more than 240 ft in the N. of the is. Peter Minuit, the first Dutch governor-general, bought it from the Indians in 1624 for the equivalent of 25 dollars. The permanent H.Q. of UNO have been erected on M. *See also* NEW YORK CITY.

Mani, *see* MANICHAEISM.

Manic Depressive Psychosis, *see* INSANITY; PSYCHOSIS.

Manichaeism, religion professed and taught by a Persian named Mani (AD 216), a native of Ecbatana. He was well educ. by his father, and brought up in the sect of the Mandaeans (q.v.). At the time of his birth 2 great religions, utterly opposed to one another, were the accepted creeds of the world he knew. One was Mithraism, an Iranian creed, and the other was Christianity. Mani had studied both, and also the anct Persian Magism; and the new faith which he proclaimed combined many points from each. M. was a dual system of religion open to grave moral abuse, as St Augustine, once a Manichaean, witnesses. Good and evil reigned as equal powers; the first man was a product of Satan, though containing a spark of the light of God. Mani believed he was the last of the chosen prophets, preached that Noah and Abraham, and probably Zoroaster and Buddha, were also prophets; he also taught a curious, shadowy, spiritual belief in Jesus Christ. The Persian king Shapur I was certainly influenced by his teaching; Hormizd, his successor, was tolerant and interested in this faith; but Barham I, who succeeded Hormizd, was a believer in the power of the priestly caste of Magians, who, bitterly hostile to Mani and his creed, secured his deliverance into their hands. They crucified him and flayed him while still alive. The Manichaean belief existed, though modified by Christian influences, until the 13th cent., and its moral dualism is found continually at the base of various early and medieval heresies. *See* F. C. Burkitt, *The Religion of the Manichees*, 1925; C. Widengren, *The Great Vohu Manah and the Apostle of God*, 1943, and *Mani and Manichaeism*, 1963; D. Obolensky, *The Bogomils*, 1948.

Manicouagan, riv. of Quebec, Canada, flowing 300 m. S. from Mushalagan and M. lakes to Baie Comeau on the St Lawrence. Together with the Outardes riv. which enters the St Lawrence from the other side of a triangular peninsula lying E. of its mouth, the M. is the source of the most ambitious hydro-electric power complex in Canada, with a potential output of 6,000,000 kW.

Manifest (from Lat. *manifestus*, plain), document signed by the master of a vessel, and containing a list of all the packages or separate items of freight on board the vessel with their distinguishing marks, numbers, destination, description, etc. It is designed for the use and information of the custom-house officers.

Manifesto, formerly a public declaration of war by a prince, explaining his motives. It was pub. within his own ter. and communicated to other states through the channels of diplomacy.

The term is also used in politics as a statement of policy or political theory (e.g. Peel's 'Tamworth Manifesto', 1835, and Marx's and Engels' 'Communist Manifesto', 1848).

Manifold Valley, situated at the S. end of the Peak dist (q.v.) in NE. Staffordshire, a picturesque limestone gorge of the R. Manifold in which for about 1 m. the riv., like its trib., the Hamps, disappears in swallow-holes for part of the year.

Manila, former cap. and prin. port of the Philippine Is., stands on the W. coast of the is. of Luzon, at the mouth of the Pasig. It was founded in 1571 by Legaspi, who inaugurated Sp. rule, and, except for a brief Brit. occupation (1762–4), it remained Sp. until 1898, when it was captured by Amer. troops under Gen. Wesley Merritt. After the Philippines were ceded to the U.S.A. in 1899 many improvements were made both in and about the city. The old Sp. city, which was called Intramuros, remained substantially unaltered within the walls, which were restored by the Americans after they took possession in 1898, The walls are stout and about 25 ft high, with a circuit of 2½ m. They were begun in 1584 and completed by forced Filipino and Chinese labour. The small old city is in striking contrast to the city and suburbs outside it. There is a central square on which stood the cathedral, the chief gov. buildings and the old Sp. gov. library. There were numerous churches and convents, with hospitals and other Catholic institutions, and in all essentials Intramuros was a Sp. tn, though the Filipinos have not been slow to adopt Amer. ways. The observatory was founded in 1865 by the Jesuits, and up to the Second World War was still run by them, the official meteorological service for the Philippines being supervised there. Of the outstanding examples of 17th cent. Sp. architecture, only the church of San Augustin survived Jap. bombing in the Second World War. In 1955 plans were made to rebuild Intramuros.

Under Sp. rule the tn, surrounded by swamps and marshes, was malarial and unhealthy. Amer. engineers drained this land and on it were built healthy suburbs. Similarly what is now the promenade of Luneta was then beneath the sea. The Americans introduced a good system of electric lighting, a telephone service and an excellent water supply, and linked the city with neighbouring tns by fine motor roads. The railway service was extended and the small tramways were replaced by an Amer. street railway. But the greatest improvement was the construction of a deep and safe harbour with a range of new quays, unequalled in the Far E. and hardly surpassed in any seaport of the world; and M. Bay (q.v.), area 770 sq. m., is the finest harbour in the Far E. The quays were severely damaged in the Jap. attack in 1942, and the fact that the harbour was found in 1945 to be cluttered with sunken craft showed that during the Jap. occupation the port was used only to a limited extent. For the planning of M. the Amer. Gov. employed D. H. Burnham, the Chicago architect of the World's Fair in 1893 and later of

Selfridge's store. Burnham and his associates designed avenues and parks, commercial quarters and suburbs, and the steady growth of the city justified the magnificence of their scheme. The moat was filled in in 1905. M. before 1941 was the greatest hemp market in the world and a famous port for the export of sugar, copra, tobacco, coconut oil, embroideries, lumber and cordage, and for the import of food-stuffs, coal, cotton goods and manuf. articles. The Philippine mint is at M., and the city had more than 1000 factories, employing over 20,000 workers. There were tobacco and sugar factories, hemp works and mills for expressing oil. The temp. of M. rarely exceeds 100° even in the hot season, when the seat of gov. moves to Baguio. The Archbishop of M. is metropolitan of the eccles. prov. of the Philippines. Pop. 983,906.

The Japanese before the war were engaged in a systematic policy of infiltration, and were gradually making their way into various depts of business. The census statistics are significant: in 1925 the Japanese in M. were well under 2000 in number; by 1939 they numbered at least 30,000. The Amer. pop. was about 4000. Jap. bombers first raided M. on 7 Dec. 1941, the day on which they attacked Pearl Harbour. Jap. forces landed on Luzon on 9 Dec. There were repeated savage bombing attacks on the city throughout Dec., churches and other centres of Christian worship and culture being deliberately selected as targets. The beautiful old church of Santo Domingo, with its valuable art treasurers and venerated relics, was reduced to ruins. The great cathedral of the Immaculate Conception was attacked sev. times, as also was the college of San Juan Lateran, with its irreplaceable library of original MSS. Repeated attacks on successive days were made on the Santa Rosa and the Santa Catalina convents. The San Juan de Dios hospital was also singled out for attack. In the hope of saving the city from bombing its defender, Gen. MacArthur, declared M. an open city and its anti-aircraft guns were evacuated. Jap. troops entered M. on 2 Jan. 1942. Early in Jan. 1945 Amer. troops under Gen. MacArthur landed at Lingayen Gulf and advanced southwards towards M. Three weeks later other Amer. forces, having landed in Batangas Prov., menaced the cap. from the S. Two Amer. forces soon afterwards encircled the city and the first Amer. flying column entered it on 4 Feb. Gen. MacArthur was always in touch with the resistance movement in M., and communication with the city was maintained by numerous radio stations about the island and by submarine throughout the period of Jap. occupation. See also PACIFIC NAVAL OPERATIONS. See J. B. Arnold, The Philippines, 1912; N. Roosevelt, The Philippines, 1927; H. W. Krieger, Peoples of the Philippines, 1942; W. C. Forbes, The Philippines Islands (revised ed.), 1945.

Manila, or **Manilla, Hemp,** fibre obtained from Musa textilis, which grows and is cultivated in the Philippines. The coarser fibre is used for cordage and sailcloth, the finer for handkerchiefs and scarves.

Manila Bay, large bay on the W. of Luzon Is., Philippine Is. Its mouth is 11 m. wide, and it expands in the interior to a width of 35 m. and a length of 30 m. It is considered one of the finest harbours in the world.

Manilius, Gaius, Rom. tribune of the plebs in 66 BC, when he proposed the Lex Manilia which conferred on Pompey supreme command in the third Mithradatic war, and which is the subject of Cicero's oration, Pro lege Manilia.

Manilius, Rom. poet, lived probably in the reign of Augustus or Tiberius. His Astronomica, incomplete and probably never pub., is a work of great learning and considerable literary merit. The best ed. is that of A. E. Housman, 1932; see also text and trans. by H. W. Garrod, 1911.

Manilla, metal hoop in the shape of a small horseshoe made principally from copper, bronze and nickel. M.s were manuf. in Europe and exported to Africa (especially W. Africa) where they were used as ornaments and currency. This trade flourished during the 18th and 19th cents. M.s were demonetised during the periods of colonial rule, and have now passed out of circulation.

Manin, Daniel (1804–57), It. patriot, b. Venice. From 1831 he was a recognised leader of Liberal opinion in Venice; in 1847 he was thrown into prison for his political opinions. When revolution broke out in 1848 he was rescued from prison by the mob and elected president of the Venetian rep. He inspired the Venetians during the heroic defence of the city for 4 months against the besieging Austrian Army. On 24 Aug. Venice capitulated, but M., with 40 of the prin. citizens, being excluded from the amnesty, went into exile in Paris, where he d. See G. M. Trevelyan, Manin and the Venetian Revolution of 1848, 1923.

Maning, Frederick Edward (1812–83), by birth an Irishman, in 1833 went to New Zealand, settled at Onaki and was made a naturalised Maori. He took part in the wars of 1845 and 1861, and in 1865 was made a judge for the purpose of settling titles of land. He wrote Old New Zealand, 1863, and The History of the War in the North in 1845, 1876.

Manioc, or **Mandioc,** see CASSAVA.

Maniple, eucharistic vestment derived from the Mappula, a large handkerchief carried in the hand or across the arm by Rom. consuls and other magistrates. It was still carried in the hand by clergy in Rome and England until the 12th cent. It is now a strip of silk (to suit the chasuble, q.v.) looped over the left forearm. See A. Fortescue, The Ceremonies of the Roman Rite, 1917; G. Dix, The Shape of the Liturgy, 1945. See VESTMENTS.

Maniple, see LEGION.

Manipulative Surgery is the manual treatment without the use of instruments of affected joints. It thus includes massage (q.v.), but is more usually applied to special manipulation of the joints. It is often confused with osteopathy, which is a separate science of treatment. The medical profession as a whole at one time regarded M. S. with suspicion, partly because it had for many years been practised by people without medical qualifications. Although undoubtedly harm has been done in some cases, there are many in which good has resulted. Doctors have now put manipulative treatment on a scientific basis, and it is a recognised branch of orthopaedic surgery. Some affections that can be cured by skilful M. S. are adhesions of muscles and tendons to their sheaths; certain forms of dislocation; the wedging of synovial membrane between 2 bones. A tubercular joint should never be treated by manipulation, and any affection should be carefuly diagnosed, if necessary with the aid of a radiograph, before any manipulative treatment is applied. An anaesthetic is usually administered to ensure the complete relaxation of the muscles. In the treatment of adhesions the limb is grasped just above and below the joint, and, if extension be difficult, flexion is first performed, and then extension in such a way that the adhesions are separated. After the pain has subsided appropriate massage may be applied. Obviously if the operation be performed by anyone without adequate knowledge considerable harm may result. See H. J. Burrows and W. D. Coltart, *Manipulation* (2nd ed.), 1951, and J. Cyriax, *Textbook of Orthopaedic Medicine* (vol. ii): 'Treatment by Manipulation and Deep Massage' (6th ed.), 1959.

Manipur, a small, centrally administered state of India, lying between Assam and Burma. The state is very hilly but contains a large and beautiful valley in which is situated Imphal, cap. of M. During the Second World War the Japanese attempted to invade India through M., and reached Kohima on the road from Imphal to Dimapur, thus encircling Imphal. The allied troops were reinforced and supplied by air, and their successful resistance marked the end of the attempted Jap. invasion. See NAGAS.

Manis, see PANGOLIN.

Manisa, il and tn in Turkey. The tn is 30 m. NE. of Izmir and has various light industries. It is on the site of anct Magnesia (q.v.) and there are deposits of magnesium and zinc ore nearby. Pop. (il) 657,104; (tn) 59,675.

Manitoba, prov. of the dominion of Canada. Since its northward extension in 1912 to the 60th parallel, and N.-eastward to Hudson Bay, it has been a maritime prov.: its length is 1260 m. It has a S. frontier with N. Dakota and Minnesota (U.S.A.); to the E. lies Ontario, to the NE. is Hudson Bay, to the N. the NW. Ters. and to the W. Saskatchewan. It includes all Lake Manitoba (q.v.), Lakes Winnipeg and Winnipegosis, the Dauphin and Swan Lakes in the NW., the Pelican and White Water Lakes in the SW. and many smaller lakes; the total area under water in the prov. is 39,255 sq. m. The surface of the prov. is, on the whole, level, though there are some hilly tracts, such as the Turtle Mts in the SW. and the Riding Mts farther N., which are well wooded. In the E. is a continuation of the old crystalline rock formation which prevails in M., and some of the scenery is wild and rugged in character; NW. the first prairie steppe extends

through the prov., occupying one-half its area; on the W. and SW. lies the second prairie steppe, occupying one-quarter; the boundary between the 2 steppes is marked by a series of elevations—Pembina Mts, Riding Mts and Duck Mts in the prov. itself and the Porcupine Hills on the boundary between M. and Saskatchewan. The Turtle Mts stand in the SW. part of M. by themselves. The surface of the first steppe is generally flat prairie, that of the second is more rolling, but on the whole there is little difference. The prin. lakes lie within the first steppe, which has an elevation of about 800 ft above sea level. The surface in the NE. is very diversified, rough and broken, with frequent bogs and marsh land. All the lakes are very shallow, even Lake Winnipeg being nowhere more than 70 ft in depth. The explanation of this is that all were at one time the centre of a glacial lake, Lake Agassiz to geologists, which covered three-quarters of M. and extended into the U.S.A. in the S., into Ontario on the E. and as far W. as the E. boundary of the second steppe. When the waters declined the S. central area of M. was left under deposits of clay and silt now covered with black vegetable mould of great fertility. The prin. rivers are the Assiniboine, rising in Saskatchewan, and the Red R., which rises in the U.S.A. and after a course of 700 m. (500 of which are in the U.S.A.) flows into Lake Winnipeg. At the junction of the 2 rivs. is Winnipeg.

The climate is generally healthy and dry. The trees include elm, oak, aspen, spruce, tamarack, maple, poplar, etc. and many varieties of fruit are grown. There are 37,547,000 ac. of forest whose products in 1963 were valued at over 20 million dollars. M. is a great wheat prov. and Winnipeg the great market, and though the output of the crop dropped for a time through impoverishment by 1-crop farmers, it has now risen again owing to the introduction of scientific cropping methods and new varieties which enable the wheat-growing zone to be extended farther W. and N. In 1951 there were 17,730,393 ac. in occupied lands. In 1963 the wheat acreage in M. was 3,153,000. The figure for other crops was: barley, 584,000,000; oats, 1,620,000; flax seed, 820,000; rye, 107,000; mixed grains, 126,000; grasses and legumes, 56,500; potatoes, 21,000; hay and clover, 1,039,000; fodder corn, 40,800. Stock-raising has become an important activity and hog-raising, poultry-farming and bee-keeping are widely carried on. The livestock statistics in 1963 were: horses, 43,000; cattle, 1,065,000; swine, 385,000; sheep, 73,000; poultry, 6,775,000.

Whilst the S. areas of M. are fertile agric. land, the N. two-thirds of the prov. form part of the Laurentian Shield, the pre-Cambrian rocks of which hold promise of rich mineral deposits. In the Rice-Beresford Lakes dist gold is being mined, whilst N. M. has large deposits of zinc, copper, gold, silver, selenium, tellurium and cadmium. In the Snow Lake dist large new gold deposits are being developed, as are rich nickel-copper deposits in the Lynn Lake area

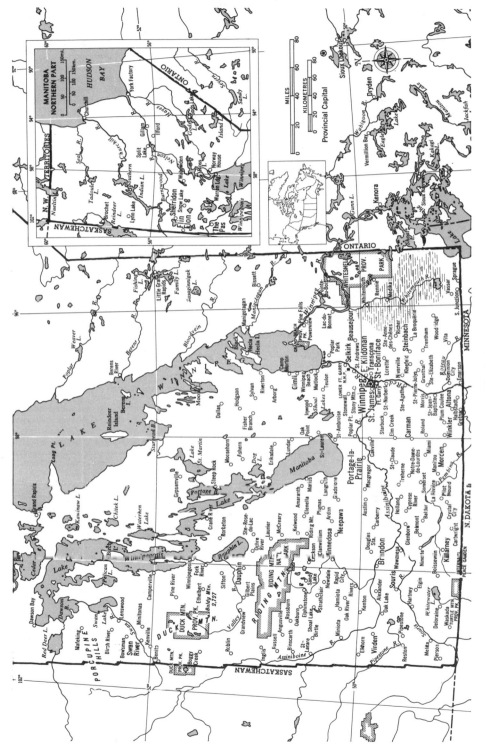

Manitoba

MANITOBA NORTHERN PART

HUDSON BAY

N.W. TERRITORIES

SASKATCHEWAN

ONTARIO

MILES
KILOMETRES

⊛ Provincial Capital

York Factory

Churchill

Seal R.

Tadoule L.

Nueltin L.

Brochet

Reindeer L.

Lynn Lake

Indian L.

Southern Indian L.

Sherridon

Flin Flon

The Pas

Snow L.

Sipiwesk L.

Thompson

Wabowden

Norway House

Warren Ldg.

Lake Winnipeg

Split Lake

Ilford

Gillam

Gods Lake

Oxford House

Island Lake

Sandy L.

Severn R.

Hayes R.

Nelson R.

Churchill R.

Heyes R.

Gods Post Lake

Grand Rapids

Red Deer L.

Dawson Bay

Mafeking

PORCUPINE HILLS

Swan River

Bowsman

Birch River

Lenswood

Minitonas

Benito

Swan L.

Pelican L.

Cedar Lake

Chitek L.

Waterhen Lake

Kawinaw L.

Long Pt.

LAKE WINNIPEG

Reindeer Island

Berens River

Berens R.

Poplar R.

Weaver L.

Family L.

Little Grand Rapids

Sasaginnigak L.

Fishing L.

BLOODVEIN

Pigeon R.

Sturgeon R.

Wanipigow R.

Grand Rapids

Camperville

Winnipegosis

Pine River

Gilbert Plains

Sifton

Ethelbert

Fork River

DUCK MTN. PROV. PK.

DUCK MTN.

Boggy Creek

DUCK MTN. PROV. PK.

Baldy Mtn. 2,727

Dauphin

Valley R.

Grandview

Roblin

Inglis

Russell

Binscarth

Angusville

Rossburn

St-Lazare

Oakburn

Birtle

Shoal Lake

Strathclair

Minnedosa

RIDING MTN. NAT'L PARK

Erickson

Clanwilliam

Sandy Lake

Elphinstone

Onanole

Rapid City

Hamiota

Miniota

Oak River

Newdale

Rivers

Kenton

Virden

Elkhorn

Alexander

Oak Lake

Brandon

Souris

Wawanesa

Nesbitt

Ninette

Hartney

Elgin

Deloraine

Melita

Pierson

Whitewater

Pipestone R.

Reston

Pipestone

PEACE GARDEN

Waskada

Boissevain

TURTLE MTN. PROV. PK.

INTERN'L

Killarney

Cartwright

Pilot Mound

Crystal City

Manitou

Morden

Winkler

Altona

Emerson

N. DAKOTA

MINNESOTA

SASKATCHEWAN

Lake Winnipegosis

Waterhen Lake

Lake St. Martin

Steep Rock

Gypsumville

Moosehorn

Ashern

Dog Lake

Eriksdale

St-Laurent

Lundar

Oak Point

Manitoba Lake

Ste-Rose-du-Lac

Laurier

McCreary

Kelwood

Riding Mt.

Glenella

Plumas

Arden

Neepawa

Gladstone

Amaranth

Langruth

Lang Lake

Portage-la-Prairie

Austin

MacGregor

Carberry

Douglas Sta.

Sidney

Treherne

Holland

Cypress River

Glenboro

Belmont

Baldur

La Rivière

Somerset

Notre-Dame-de-Lourdes

St-Claude

Miami

Roland

Carman

Elm Creek

Starbuck

Sperling

Plum Coulee

Gretna

Halbstadt

Rosenfeld

St-Jean-Baptiste

Morris

Ste-Agathe

St-Pierre-Jolys

Ste-Elizabeth

Rosenort

Dominion City

Vita

St-Norbert

Ste-Anne-des-Chênes

Lorette

Niverville

Otterburne

St-Adolphe

Winnipeg

Selkirk

E. Kildonan

St. James

St-Boniface

Transcona

Ft. Garry

Stonewall

Teulon

St-Andrews

Lower Ft. Garry N.H.P.

Stony Mtn.

Poplar Pt.

St-Ambroise

St. Martin

Ste-Rose

Dallas

Hodgson

Fisher Branch

Sylvan

Riverton

Arborg

Inwood

Shoal Lake

Gimli

Winnipeg Beach

Matlock

Camp Morton

Hecla I.

Hecla

Moose I.

Manigotagan

Manigotagan R.

Bissett

WHITESHELL PROV. PARK

Rennie

Whitemouth

Medika

Whitemouth R.

Vassar

Sprague

S. Junction

Sandilands

Woodridge

Vita

Ste-Elizabeth

La Broquerie

Richer

Steinbach

Ste-Anne

Giroux

Kleefeld

Grand Beach

Grand Marais

Pine Falls

Powerview

Great Falls

Lac-du-Bonnet

Pinawa

GRAND BEACH PROV. PK.

Victoria Beach

Beausejour

Garson

Tyndall

ONTARIO

Winnipeg R.

Nopiming

Bird R.

Sioux Lookout

Dryden

Vermillion Bay

Kenora

Lake of the Woods

Sioux Narrows

Gunn L.

Webiqoon Lake

Kakagi L.

Jackfish

Rainy Lake

and new copper-zinc deposits in the Flin Flon area. M.'s first lithium mine has been started.

Lignite has been found in the M. portion of the Turtle Mts, and good coal in the SE. In the NW. are salt springs; in the Star Lake belt tungsten and molybdenum are mined; large deposits of gypsum occur at Gypsumville, NE. of Lake M. Cement, bricks and limestone are also produced. The total value of mineral production in 1963 was $171,000,000, including oil valued at $9,000,000.

Large quantities of high-grade freshwater fish are caught from the numerous lakes, with a marketed value of $7,271,000 (1963). Forest reserves, including the Riding Mt National Park, cover 3,545,000 ac. The estimated value of raw furs taken in 1962 was $4,700,000. In 1963 water-power generated totalled 4,710,000,000 kWh. In 1963 the gross value of manuf. products was $875,000,000, produced by some 45,000 workers, the largest industry being slaughtering and meat packing.

Winnipeg is the cap. and centre of trade. Other cities include St Boniface, the seat of a Rom. Catholic archbishop, who is metropolitan of an eccles. prov. comprising all the Middle W.; St James; Brandon; and Portage la Prairie. The univ. of M., in Greater Winnipeg (Fort Garry Municipality), was founded in 1877 and has 6 affiliated colleges; the medical school is one of the best in Canada, as is the M. Agric. College. There were 205,816 pupils attending school in 1962-3. Religious denominations number approximately (1961): Rom. Catholics, 210,871; United Church, 269,975; Anglican, 127,487; Presbyterian, 29,661; Baptist, 17,247. In 1956 there were some 5591 m. of railway in M., and the prov. is traversed by the 2 transcontinental lines, joining at Winnipeg.

M. was known as the Red R. Settlement before it entered the dominion in 1870. During the 18th cent. its only inhab. were fur trappers, but a more settled colonisation began in the 19th cent. Until 1869 the administration of the area was in the hands of the Hudson's Bay Co. It was then purchased by the new dominion; in 1870 M. prov. was set up, enlarged in 1881, and again in 1912 by the addition of part of the NW. Ters. The prov. gov. is administered by a lieutenant-governor, appointed by a governor-general, and a Legislative Assembly of 57 members elected for 5 years. Six members represent M. in the Senate and 14 in the Canadian House of Commons.

The area of M. is 251,030 sq. m., comprising 211,775 of land and 39,255 of water. In 1871 the pop. was 25,228; in 1961 it was 921,686.

See M. McWilliams, *Manitoba Milestones*, 1928; F. H. Kitto, *Manitoba: its Development and Opportunities*, 1931; G. F. G. Stanley, *The Birth of Western Canada*, 1936; Morton and Fahrni, *Third Crossing*, 1946; W. L. Morton, *History of Manitoba*, 1956; T. R. Weir, *Economic Atlas of Manitoba*, 1960. (*See Plate.*)

Manitoba, Lake, fresh-water lake of M., Canada, 60 m. SW. of Lake Winnipeg. It has an area of 1817 sq. m. with a length of 120 m., a width of 25 m. and an elevation of 813 ft. Irregular in shape and tideless, the lake is drained by the Little Saskatchewan R. into Lake Winnipeg.

Manitou, presiding or protecting spirit in the religious beliefs of sev. Amer. Indian tribes. Their number is unlimited, each person having a M. The M. is in almost all cases connected with an animal chosen by the individual as the object of his veneration. The idea of a supreme being or Great M. (*Kittanit*) existed.

Manitowoc, port city, co. seat of M. co., Wisconsin, U.S.A., on Lake Michigan at base of Door Peninsula, 77 m. N. of Milwaukee, in dairying, stock-raising area. It builds ships and manufs. food products, aluminium ware, machinery and furniture. Pop. 32,280.

Manizales, cap. of Caldas dept, Colombia, 170 m. by road S. of Medellin. 7000 ft high, it is the centre of one of the most important coffee producing areas in the country. Its manufs. include textiles, leather goods, chemicals, hats, shoes, candles, matches and beer. Pop. 187,000.

Mankato, co. seat of Blue Earth co., Minnesota, U.S.A., on the Minnesota R., 65 m. SW. of St Paul, in grain, livestock and poultry area, with limestone quarries. It manufs. food products, agric. equipment, and cement, wood and paper products. It has a state teachers' college. Pop. *c.* 20,000.

Manley, Mary de la Rivière (1663-1724), authoress, *b.* Jersey. She wrote sev. plays, two of which, *The Lost Lover* and *The Royal Mischief*, were produced in 1696 at Drury Lane and Lincoln's Inn Fields respectively. She led an irregular life and pub. sev. scurrilous works; is best remembered for the *Secret Memoirs and Manners of Several Persons of Quality of both Sexes. From the New Atlantis*, 1709-10, in which she slandered many well-known people. *See* P. B. Anderson, *Mistress Delarivière Manley's Biography*, 1936.

Manlius, Marcus, consul 392 BC; took refuge in the capitol when Rome was taken by the Gauls in 390. The story went that when the barbarians tried to ascend the capitol M. was roused from sleep by the cackling of sacred geese. Hurriedly collecting a body of men, he succeeded in driving back the enemy, who had just reached the summit, and for this heroic deed he was surnamed Capitolinus. In 385 he defended the cause of the plebians who were suffering from harsh treatment by their patrician creditors. In the following year he was charged by the patricians with aspiring to kingly power, and, being condemned to death by the people, was hurled from the Tarpeian Rock. His house on the Capitol was razed, and the members of the Manlia *gens* resolved that none of them should ever again bear the *praenomen* Marcus.

Manly, seaside suburb of Sydney, New S. Wales, 8 m. NE. of city, bordering Sydney Harbour and Pacific Ocean. Noted for its surfing beach of same name. Pop. 36,049.

Mann, Heinrich (1871-1950), Ger. novelist, *b.* Lübeck of a rich merchant family, brother of

Thomas M. (q.v.). His youth was spent in France and Italy. Showing no taste for business of politics, he began his career as a writer at an early age. His first novel, *Im Schlaräffenland* (Eng. trans., *Berlin, the Land of Cockaigne*, 1925) was pub. in 1901. His nationalism, his merciless analysis based on sound documentation, have given him the name of the Ger. Zola, but side by side with the influence of Zola and de Maupassant has been that of D'Annunzio. M. is the acknowledged master of Wassermann and Feuchtwanger. His best works were suppressed by the censor until after the advent of the rep. His novels show us Germany as it was in its newly won vulgar prosperity from the end of the 19th cent. to the period just before the First World War. His next work was sensuous and romantic and with a fervid style from which the later Expressionist writers drew much of their inspiration. His 3 novels on the life of the Duchess of Assy, pub. in 1902–3 under the title of *Die Göttinnen*, were in this vein. In the main, however, M. made himself the novelist of the Ger. middle classes when he was not dealing with It. subjects. Perhaps his greatest work is the trilogy in which he seeks to paint a vast fresco of Ger. life as it existed under Kaiser Wilhelm II: *Die Armen*, 1917, portrays the proletariat; *Der Untertan*, 1918, the bourgeois; and *Der Kopf*, 1925, the governing class. His social criticism and psychological insight also found masterly expression in the novels *Professor Unrat*, 1904 (Eng. trans., *The Blue Angel*, 1932), which became widely known as a film; *Die kleine Stadt*, 1909, a romantic story of a band of actors visiting an It. tn; and *Zwischen den Rassen*, 1907. Under the Weimar rep. M. became president of the writers' section of the Prussian Academy of Arts, but was expelled by the Nazis in 1933. Thereafter he lived in exile in France until 1940, when he escaped to the U.S.A. By this time he had estab. an international position with such works as *Mutter Marie*, 1927, *Eugénie oder die Bürgerzeit*, 1928, and *Ein ernstes Leben*, 1932. He also wrote 2 long historical novels on the life of Henry of Navarre, *Die Jugend des Königs Henri Quatre*, 1935, and *Die Vollendung des Königs Henri Quatre*, 1938. These are ambitious studies of human greatness, but show a decline in artistic standards. M.'s miscellaneous writings include essays on Fr. literature and political writings against the Nazi regime. He also wrote his autobiography, which is an outstanding work, *Ein Zeitalter wird besichtigt*, 1945–6. See studies by W. Schröder, 1931, K. Lemke, 1946, and H. Thering, 1951.

Mann, Horace (1796–1859), Amer. educationist and statesman, *b.* Franklin, Massachusetts, of poor parents, but eventually went to Brown Univ., where he graduated with high honours. He practised law with considerable success from 1823 to 1837, when he took up educational work and public affairs. Elected to the legislature of Massachusetts in 1827, he served until 1837—in 1836–7 as president of the state senate. He was secretary of the board of education, 1837–48. In 1849–53 he was a

member of Congress, as the successor of ex-president John Quincy Adams, whose example he followed in energetic opposition to the extension of slavery. His able administration as secretary of the state board of education gave him a central position in the hist. and development of education in America. His prin. works are his educational reports and *Slavery, Letters, and Speeches*, 1851. See life by his wife (3 vols.), 1865–8; L. A. Cremin, *The Republic and the School*, 1957.

Mann, Sir Horace, *see* WALPOLE, HORACE.

Mann, Thomas (1875–1955), Ger. novelist and critic, *b.* Lübeck, the younger brother of Heinrich M. (q.v.). There is a striking contrast between the 2 brothers. In Thomas the Lat. strain inherited from his mother is more prominent. As an artist he is largely subjective, drawing his themes from his own life and inner thought. He is constantly preoccupied with the thought of death in the midst of life and with the position of the artist as an outcast from life. When he was 15 years old his father *d.* His mother moved to Munich, where, after a brief interlude in an insurance office, during which he pub. his first story, *Gefallen*, he registered at the univ. but did not follow a set course. During a long stay with his brother Heinrich in Palaestrina in N. Italy he began work on the novel which later appeared with the title *Buddenbrooks*. On his return to Munich he joined the staff of *Simplicissimus* as reader. Some of his stories were pub. in this jour. *Buddenbrooks* was pub. in 1900 (Eng. trans., 1924). It is a saga of the life of a merchant family of Lübeck, tracing through 4 generations the gradual growth of decay as culture slowly saps virility. The novel at once estab. M. as one who had an individual contribution to make to literature. It was followed by *Tristan*, 1903, a vol. of short stories, including 'Tonio Kröger', a story which exemplifies the conflict between the normal man and the artist, and *Fiorenza*, 1905, a dramatic dialogue. Of this story he wrote in the *Sketch of my Life* (Eng. trans., 1930), that in it he first 'grasped the idea of epic prose composition as a thought texture woven of different themes', a conception which he later put to greater use in *Der Zauberberg*. He married in 1905. *Königliche Hoheit* (Eng. trans., *Royal Highness*, 1916) appeared the following year. In 1912 a visit to his wife, who was undergoing a cure at Davos, laid the foundations for the great novel *Der Zauberberg*, which was not, however, completed until some years later. In the meantime he pub. *Der Tod in Venedig*, 1913 (Eng. trans., *Death in Venice*, 1925), and *Das Wunderkind*, 1914. His writings after the outbreak of war in 1914 were directed towards justifying the Ger. position, notably in an essay on Frederick the Great, *Friedrich der Grosse und die grosse Koalition*, 1915. His 'reflections of a non-political man', *Betrachtungen eines Unpolitischen*, of which he said 'the problem of the German nation there treated was beyond doubt my own—therein lay the national character of the book', was pub. in 1918. Other essays were collected in 2 vols. and pub. in 1922—*Rede und Antwort* and *Bemühungen*—also an essay on Goethe and Tolstoy, 1923. Part of his study of a swindler, Felix Krull, belongs to this period, and was later completed and pub. in 1938 as *Bekenntnisse des Hochstaplers Felix Krull. Der Zauberberg* was pub. in 1923 and was immediately trans. into most European languages (Eng. trans., *The Magic Mountain*, 1927). The novel, based on life in a sanatorium, treats not only of the process of disease in sick minds and bodies, but also of the sickness of Europe. It is a vast symbolical work probing the question of culture in relation to life. In 1929 M. was awarded the Nobel prize for literature. The following year he pub. *Mario und der Zauberer* (Eng. trans., *Mario and the Magician*, 1930). The coming of the Nazi regime led to a self-imposed exile and he went to Switzerland, where from 1937 he ed. a literary jour., *Mass und Wert*. He was deprived of his Ger. citizenship and also of the degree of 'Ehrendoktor' which he held at Bonn Univ. The letter from the dean of the univ. and M.'s reply were pub. together as *Ein Briefwechsel*, 1937 (Eng. trans., *An Exchange of Letters*, 1937). Meanwhile his greatest work was in course of pub., *Joseph und seine Brüder*, a long novel which appeared in 4 parts: *Die Geschichten Jakobs*, 1933, *Der junge Joseph*, 1934, *Joseph in Ägypten*, 1936, *Joseph der Ernährer*, 1944 (Eng. trans., *Joseph and his Brothers*, 1934, *Young Joseph*, 1935, *Joseph in Egypt*, 1938, and *Joseph the Provider*, 1944). In this work he attempts, in his own words, to construct 'by means of mythical psychology, a psychology of the myth', showing how the process of life, the duality of spirit and flesh, expresses itself through myth. The novel is notable not only for its philosophical questioning of the nature of man but also for its narrative power and characterisation. Throughout this period M. constantly wrote or lectured on political themes in support of anti Nazi movements. He stressed the indivisibility of his nature as artist and social critic, and the unity of the world of intellect. A number of his political essays and speeches have since been pub. in an Eng. trans. under the title *Order of the Day*, 1942. In 1938 M. went to the U.S.A. and became an Amer. citizen. He returned to Europe and settled near Zürich in 1934, where he d. Later works include *Lotte in Weimar*, 1939 (Eng. trans., *The Beloved Returns*, 1940), *Die vertauschten Köpfe*, 1940 (Eng. trans., *The Transposed Heads, a Legend of India*, 1941), and a contribution to *The Ten Commandments*, 1945, a collection of 10 short novels by different writers, each on the theme of one of the commandments. M.'s contribution was on the first commandment and is a story of the life of Moses. In 1949 he pub. *Dr Faustus: the Life of the German Composer Adrian Leverkuehn as told by a Friend*, the Faust legend brought up to date with a background of pre-war amd post-war Germany. He received an honorary doctorate of literature at Oxford Univ. in the same year. His last work, uncompleted, was *Bekenntnisse des Hochstaplers Felix Krull*, the confessions of a

confidence trickster. Pub. in 1954 it is widely considered to be the greatest comic novel in Ger. literature. *See* J. Cleugh, *Thomas Mann, a Study*, 1933; J. G. Brennan, *Thomas Mann's World*, 1942; V. Mann, *Wir waren fünf. Bildnis der Familie*, 1949; H. Hatfield, *Thomas Mann: an Introduction to his Fiction*, 1952; K. W. Jonas, *Fifty Years of Thomas Mann Studies: A Bibliography of Criticism*, 1955; R. H. Thomas, *Thomas Mann: The Mediation of Art*, 1956; also *Thomas Mann: Stories and Episodes* (a selection, Everyman's Library), 1955.

Mann, Tom (1856–1941), Labour leader, *b.* Foleshill, Warwickshire. He worked from 9 to 14 on farms and in the mines, served an apprenticeship in engineering for 7 years at Birmingham, settled in London in 1876, joined Amalgamated Society of Engineers in 1881 and became a Socialist in 1885. He was one of the leaders of the great dock strike (1889); president of the Dockers' Union (1890–3); president, International Ship, Dock and Riv. Workers (1892–6). He was secretary of the Independent Labour party (1894–6), and first secretary of the London Reform Union and of the National Democratic League; and thrice stood as parl. candidate. After residing (1902–8) in Australia, where he continued his Socialist propaganda and was imprisoned, he visited S. Africa and returned (1910) to England, where he became leader of the Syndicalist movement and was imprisoned for his connection with the 'Don't Shoot' manifesto to soldiers (1912). M. was general secretary of the Amalgamated Engineering Union (1919–21). Pub. his memoirs in 1923. (*See Plate: German Literature.*)

Manna, name given to a variety of natural products. Many people suppose the M. eaten by the Israelites in the wilderness to have been *Lecanora esculenta*, an edible lichen which is removed from rocks by wind and carried long distances. According to others it is the gummy saccharine secretion discharged by a tree, *Tamarix mannifera*, which punctured by a cochineal-like Coccus. The M. or flowering ash (*Fraxinus ornus*) exudes a sweet substance containing mannite (q.v.), commonly found in many forms of vegetable life.

Mannerheim, Baron Carl Gustaf Emil (1867–1951), Finnish soldier, *b.* Villnäs. He served in the Russo-Jap. war (1904–5) and in the First World War, becoming leader of the Russian cavalry in 1917. After the Bolshevik revolution he returned to Finland to lead the Finnish White Army, and, aided by Ger. forces, defeated the Russo-Finnish Red troops at Tammerfors and Viborg. Regent of Finland (Dec. 1918–July 1919), he was defeated in the Finnish presidential election by Staehlberg (1919). It was at his suggestion that the M. line, the former Finnish defence system on the Karelian Isthmus, was constructed. He commanded the Finns in the Russo-Finnish war of 1939 (*see* FINLAND). Marshal of Finland from 1942. President of Finnish Rep. (1944–6), when he retired from public life. He wrote *Across Asia from West to East in 1906–8*, 1940, and *Memoirs*, 1953. *See* also T. Borenius, *Marshal Mannerheim*, 1940, and Col. P. Rodzianko, *Mannerheim*, 1940.

Mannerism, in the hist. of art, a distinct phase of the 16th cent. between the Renaissance (q.v.) and Baroque (q.v.). Largely based on an admiration for Michelangelo, it is marked by exaggerations of the figure, violent gestures and crowded composition. It developed in Florence, Rome and Bologna, and is represented by such artists as Parmigianino, Daniele da Volterra, Salviati, Jacopo da Pontormo and others. A graceful form of M. was introduced into France by It. artists working for Francis I. *See* FONTAINEBLEAU, SCHOOL OF.

Mannheim, Ger. tn in the *Land* of Baden-Württemberg (q.v.) at the confluence of the Rhine and the Neckar, 58 m. NW. by N. of Stuttgart. On the opposite bank of the Rhine is Ludwigshafen (q.v.). There was a settlement on the site as early as the 8th cent., but the real hist. of M. dates from the building of a city here by the Elector Frederick IV in 1606. It rose to importance in 1720, when the seat of the Electors Palatine was transferred to it from Heidelberg. In 1798 the Electoral residence was moved to Munich and the fortunes of M. declined, only to revive in the 19th cent. after the building of a riv. port. The city was repeatedly bombed by the RAF during the Second World War. The older part of the city is laid out in a regular chessboard pattern: streets running parallel to the rivs. are lettered, and streets at right angles to the rivs. are numbered; each block of buildings is therefore identified by a letter and a number. There is a splendid castle (the largest baroque building in Germany) and a notable 18th cent. Jesuit church. M. has manufs. of electrical goods, chemicals, motor-cars, agric. machinery, iron goods, textiles and food-stuffs. Pop. 313,900.

Mannin, Ethel Edith (1900–), novelist and travel writer, *b.* London. Her first novel, *Martha*, 1922, was followed by many others, including *Sounding Brass*, 1925, *The Pure Flame*, 1936, *The Blossoming Bough*, 1943, *Late Have I Loved Thee*, 1948, and *The Blue-eyed Boy*, 1959. Among her travel books are *South to Samarkand*, 1936, *Jungle Journey*, 1950, and *Moroccan Music*, 1953. *Confessions and Impressions*, 1929, and *Privileged Spectator*, 1939, are autobiographical.

Mannin, *see* MAN, Isle of.

Manning, Ernest Charles (1908–), Canadian politician, premier of Alberta, *b.* Cardiff, Sasketchewan, and educ. at Rosetown. A follower of Wm Aberhart (q.v.), he was a founder-member of the Social Credit party, and in 1935 was elected to the prov. gov. On the death of Aberhart, M. became premier of Alberta (1943); he has also held concurrently the posts of prov. secretary (1944–55) and minister of mines and minerals (1952).

Manning, Frederic (1882–1935), Australian novelist, *b.* Sydney, son of its mayor. Coming to England he pub. *Scenes and Portraits*, 1909, *Poems*, 1910, and the novel *Her Privates We*, 1930, based on his experiences of the First World War, with its punning title borrowed from *Hamlet*.

Manning, Henry Edward (1808–92), cardinal, *b.* Totteridge, Herts, and educ. at Harrow and Oxford, where he became notable as an eloquent preacher and as one of the ablest of the Tractarian party. He was rector of Woollavington-cum-Graffham, 1833, and archdeacon of Chichester, 1840. In 1851 he entered the Church of Rome, in which he attached himself to the Ultramontane party. Becoming Archbishop of Westminster in 1865, he took a leading part in the debates of the first Vatican Council (1870) on papal infallibility. Afterwards he pub. *Petri privilegium*, 1871, and when this was attacked by Gladstone in *Vaticanism* M. wrote *The Vatican Decrees*, 1875, in which year he was created cardinal. His other writings consist of sermons. M.'s later life was devoted largely to social reform. He encouraged Gen. Booth's work in this direction, founded a Rom. Catholic total abstinence association, the League of the Cross, and took a prominent part in industrial pacification, especially in the London dock strike of 1889. More practical than Newman, he was an outstanding figure in the Rom. Catholic Church in England during the 19th cent. *See* life by Shane Leslie, 1921; *also* V. A. McClelland, *Cardinal Manning: His Public Life and Influence*, 1962.

Manning, or **Mannyng, Robert,** or **Robert of Brunne** (*c.* 1264–*c.* 1340), poet, *b.* Brunne, now Bourne, Lincs. He wrote *Handlyng Synne*, a trans. of the *Manuel des Pechiez* of Wm of Wadington, and *The Chronicle of England*, a new version in octosyllabic rhyme of Wace's *Brut d'Angleterre*, also a trans. of the Fr. rhyming chronicle of Peter Langtoft. M.'s work is of great linguistic importance, and did much to further the adoption of the Midland dialect as the acknowledged literary instrument. *See* life by Ruth Crosby, 1942.

Manning, Thomas (1772–1840), traveller and writer, *b.* Suffolk and educ. at Caius College, Cambridge, where he studied Chinese. He went to Canton in 1806 as a medical practitioner, and visited Lhasa in Tibet (1811–12), being the first Englishman to go there. He was a master of Chinese classical literature, and in his time was regarded as the first Chinese scholar in Europe. He also wrote on mathematics. *See* memoir by Sir C. R. Markham, 1876.

Manning, tn of Alberta, Canada, 56 m. N. of Grimshaw, named in honour of Alberta's premier, E. C. Manning (q.v.). The tn is one of the newest in the prov. The Grimshaw–Yellowknife Highway runs right through the centre of the tn, which is situated in the centre of an extensive wheat-growing dist. The present pop. is less than 1000.

Manningtree, mrkt tn and par. of Essex, England, on the R. Stour, about 8 m. from Colchester. Malt and agric products are manuf. near by. Pop. (including the neighbouring pars. of Mistley and Lawford) 4613.

Mannite, or **Manna Sugar,** $C_6H_8(OH)_6$, chief constituent of manna, an exudation from the manna ash-tree, *Fraxinus ornus*. M. occurs also in onions, brown seaweed and many other plants. It is a crystalline substance, readily soluble in water and alcohol. M. is obtained from manna by extraction with alcohol and subsequent crystallisation. It was formerly used as an aperient in Europe, and is still employed for this purpose in S. America.

Mannteufel, E. H. K., *see* MANTEUFFEL, EDWIN HANS KARL, FREIHERR VON.

Manoel I, King of Portugal, *see* EMANUEL I.

Manoel II, of Portugal, *see* MANUEL II.

Manometer, instrument for determining the pressure of fluids enclosed in a vessel. The simplest form consists of a long, straight tube, dipping into a box containing mercury. The pressure of the gas to be gauged is communicated through an opening in the box to the surface of the mercury, and the upper end of the tube is open to the atmosphere. If the pressure of the enclosed gas is greater than that of the atmosphere, the mercury is forced up the tube. A pressure of 2 atmospheres forces the mercury upwards to a distance of about 30 in. above the level of the mercury in the box, so that this form of M. cannot be used for great pressures. Another form used for small pressures consists of a bent tube open at both ends and containing a quantity of mercury in the bend. When the pressure of the enclosed gas is communicated to one surface of the mercury, the mercury in the other limb rises or falls as the pressure is greater or less than that of the atmosphere. If, for instance, the mercury sinks h in. in one limb, it will rise h in. in the other, and the difference of level will be $2h$. The pressure of the enclosed gas will therefore be equal to 1 atmosphere, plus the pressure produced by $2h$ in. of mercury. For greater pressures a U-tube closed at one end is employed. The open end communicates with the enclosed gas and the closed end is furnished with a scale. If the pressure of the enclosed gas is equal to that of the atmosphere, the mercury will be at the same level in both limbs. If the pressure rises above that of the atmosphere, the mercury in the open limb sinks, and that in the closed limb rises, thus compressing the air in the closed limb. Suppose H to represent the length of the air column at atmospheric pressure, and h the length at the pressure of the gas; then the pressure of the air column is $\frac{H}{h}$ atmospheres. The difference in height of the 2 mercury columns is $2(H-h)$, therefore the pressure of the enclosed gas must be equal to the pressure produced by a column of mercury whose length is $2(H-h) + \frac{H}{h}$ atmospheres.

Manor (Lat. *manerium*, from *maneo*, remain or dwell, the connotation being the *usual* residence of the owner). In Domesday Book each tract of land belonging to the king or some great feudal noble holding of the king is generally found to consist of sev. holdings called *maneri* or M.s, which for the most part are coterminous with the vills, tns or vils. A M. appears to have denoted such dist of a great personage as he kept in his own hands for the abode and use of his family, and hence this dist was also termed *demesne* (or *terrae dominicales*, from Lat. *domus*, home) lands, in contradistinction to the *tenemental* lands, which the lord distributed among his tenants. In the domain there was generally a mansion or M.-house, which was occupied by the owner of the *manerium* or by his bailiff (for a number of the greater barons held numerous M.s, and could not personally occupy them all), together with a certain quantity of arable and meadow land in scattered strips. (*See* as to common field system under LAND.) Quite early in the Eng. land-holding system the great barons granted out smaller M.s by way of sub-infeudation, to be held of themselves, the seignory of such lesser lords being termed an *honour*. These inferior lords in their turn carved out of their estates yet smaller estates, and the practice would doubtless have been followed out almost to infinity but for that provision in Magna Charta, designed in the interest of the greater barons, who found that they were being deprived of their feudal profits, which enforced on lesser barons the obligation to retain sufficient land to answer their overlords' demands. Later the statute of *Quia Emptores* (q.v.) forbade sub-infeudation altogether by the provision that the grantee should always hold not of the grantor but of the chief lord of the fee. All M.s existing in present times were, therefore, stereotyped from the time of that statute (Edward I). The reservation of mineral rights, exiguous quit rents from manorial freeholders, and fines on admission to copyhold estates were the prin. remaining benefits attaching to a M. up to recent times. What privileges or anachronisms of tenure survived, however, were abolished by the Law of Property Act, 1922, which Act, *inter alia*, enfranchised all copyhold land on terms which are laid down in Part V of the Act. *See* D. Jerrold, *Introduction to the History of England*, 1949; Sir P. Vinogradoff, *Growth of the Manor*, 1951.

Manorhamilton, tn of co. Leitrim, Rep. of Ireland, 30 m. N. of Carrick-on-Shannon, situated in the heart of the limestone mts of the dist. Pop. 888.

Manresa (Rom. **Munorisa**), Sp. tn in the prov. of Barcelona, on the Cardoner. It has a fine Gothic church, formerly collegiate, and there is a 17th cent. baroque church adjoining the cave in which St Ignatius of Loyola (q.v.) lived for some time after his conversion. M. has important cotton manufs. Pop. 40,000.

Manrique, Gomez (*c.* 1413–91), Sp. poet and dramatist, *b.* Amusco. He took a prominent part in politics. As a writer he was greatly esteemed in his own day and composed didactic verses and satires as well as dramas; indeed he appears to be the earliest Sp. dramatist. Among his works are *Representación del nascimiento de Nuestro Señor*, a play on the Passion, and 2 *momas*, or interludes.

Manrique, Jorge (*c.* 1440–79), Sp. poet and soldier, nephew of Gomez M. He owes his reputation as a poet to *Coplas por la muerte de su padre*, 1476, a sublime elegy on the death of his father.

Mans, Le, Fr. tn, cap. of the dept of Sarthe, 112 m. SW. of Paris. It has a cathedral, founded by St Julian, which contains the tomb of Berengaria, Queen of Richard Cœur de Lion. The *hôtel de ville* is built on the site of the former castle of the counts of Maine. Le M. is the seat of a bishopric dating from the 3rd cent. It is the scene of the Le M. Grand Prix motor race (24 hrs). Le M. has an agric. market and is an industrial centre. Manufs. are textiles, tobacco, metals and preserved foods. Henry II of England was born at Le M. Pop. 132,200.

Mansard, or **Mansart, François** (1598–1666), Fr. architect, *b.* Paris. The M. roof, though named after him, was earlier used by Lescot (q.v.). Among his buildings, the chief are the châteaux of Maisons-sur-Seine and Balleroy, and the churches of Sainte Marie-de-Chaillot, the Minimes, the Visitation de Sainte-Marie and Val-de-Grâce, all in Paris; the Orleans wing of the château at Blois; and the remodelling of the Carnavalet Museum in Paris.

Mansard, or **Mansart, Jules Hardouin** (1646–1708), Fr. architect, grand-nephew of François M., *b.* Paris. He superintended the construction of all the prin. buildings of Louis XIV, including the palace of Versailles, the Grand Trianon, the dome of the Hôtel des Invalides, the châteaux of Clagny, Marly and Dampierre; and laid out the Place des Victoires and the Place Vendôme in Paris.

Mansbridge, Albert (1876–1952), educationist, *b.* Gloucester and educ. at Battersea Grammar School. He was one of the pioneers of adult education (q.v.), founding the Workers' Educational Association in England in 1903 and in Australia in 1913. From 1903 to 1915 he acted as secretary of the association. He was a member of the Consultative Committee of the Board of Education, 1906–12, and again in 1924; also a member of the royal commission on the univs. of Oxford and Cambridge, 1919–22. In 1918 he founded the World Association for Adult Education, and was its first chairman and later became president. He founded the National Central Library, the Seafarers' Education Service and the Brit. Institute of Adult Education. He wrote many books and was created Companion of Honour in 1931. *See* ADULT EDUCATION.

Manse, name given in Scotland to the house of the minister of the Estab. Church and Free Church; also used by the Methodists. Every first minister of a rural par. is entitled to his M., or an allowance in lieu thereof; formerly, if one did not exist the landed proprietors in the par. were bound to build one. He was also entitled to a stable or barn as part of his dwelling-house, and his M., when built, had to be kept in repair by the heritors, but these could, after the M. was 'made sufficient', apply to the presbytery to declare it free, when the incumbent had to do the repairs. During the time occupied by rebuilding or repairs, the minister is entitled to an allowance

as M. rent. The building and upkeep of a M. are now the responsibility of the congregation.

Mansfeld, Peter Ernst II, Graf von (1580–1626), Ger. soldier, illegitimate son of Peter Ernst, and one of the greatest generals of the Thirty Years War, first fought under the Duke of Savoy against the Spaniards. Sent to help the Bohemian rebels, he took Pilsen and compelled Bucquoi to evacuate Bohemia, but afterwards induced the Bohemians to make Frederick, the elector palatine, their king. The latter being defeated by the imperial troops, M. for a long time held out at Pilsen and Thabor, but yielding to superior numbers he retreated to the Palatinate (1621). The following year he ravaged Alsace and, joining forces with Frederick, defied both the Bavarians and the Hessians. Entering Belgium and uniting with the Duke of Brunswick, he defeated the Spaniards at Fleurus and penetrated into Westphalia. In 1625, at the head of a motley army, he re-entered Germany, but being defeated by Wallenstein he retreated to Brandenburg. Giving up the command against Austria he decided to try his fortunes in Venice, but *d.* at Vranovitz. *See* C. V. Wedgwood, *The Thirty Years' War*, 1938.

Mansfield, Katherine (1888–1923), pen-name of Kathleen Mansfield Beauchamp, short story writer, *b.* Wellington, New Zealand, daughter of a banker. Her first story was pub. when she was 9, and later when at Queen's College, London, she ed. the college magazine, but her plans then were for a musical career. In 1909 she married George Bowden, but left him after a few days. In 1911 she met John Middleton Murry (q.v.), whom she married in 1918 when she obtained a divorce from her first husband. Ill-health due to lung trouble made her move about seeking a congenial climate, and she lived at different times in France and in Germany. In 1920 *Bliss and Other Stories* made her famous. Other collections were *The Garden Party*, 1922, *The Dove's Nest*, 1923, *Something Childish*, 1924, and *The Aloe*, 1930. In 1922 she went to Paris for special treatment and *d.* at Fontainebleau. In her mastery of the short story, depending on atmosphere rather than on incident, she has been compared with Chekhov. Her *Poems* were pub. in 1923 and her autobiographical *Journal*, 1927, *Letters*, 1928, and *Scrapbook*, 1940, were ed. by her husband. *See* Ruth E. Mantz, *The Critical Bibliography of Katherine Mansfield*, 1931; A. Sewell, *Katherine Mansfield: a Critical Essay*, 1936; life by Ruth E. Mantz and J. Middleton Murry, 1933; and studies by S. Berkman, 1951, and A. Alpers, 1954. (*See Plate: New Zealand.*)

Mansfield, William Murray, Earl of (1705–1793), judge, *b.* Scone, Perthshire. He was educ. at Westminster School and Christ Church, Oxford, and was called to the Bar in 1730. He was made king's counsel and solicitor-general to Lord Wilmington's gov., 1742, entering Parliament as member for Boroughbridge. In 1754 he became attorney-general to the Duke of Newcastle's administration, which he defended against the attacks of Pitt, and in 1756 was called to the degree of serjeant-at-law, sworn in as lord chief justice of the king's bench and created Baron M. in the co. of Nottingham. In 1767 he incurred hatred by discountenancing prosecutions under the penal law of 1700 which made celebration of Mass by a Rom. Catholic priest punishable by imprisonment for life, and further increased his unpopularity by his conduct in the case of Wilkes in 1768, and by his directions to the jury in 3 cases of seditious libel out of the pub. and sale of Junius's letter to the king in 1770. In 1776 he became Earl of M. His house was sacked and burnt during the Gordon riots, 1780, and he retired from office in 1788. He did much to improve mercantile law, the law of evidence and the procedure of courts, and as a parl. debater was second only to Chatham. *See* Lord Campbell, *Lives of the Chief Justices*, 1849–57; W. S. Holdsworth, *History of English Law*, vol. xii, 1923 ff.; Lord Birkenhead, *Fourteen English Judges*, 1926; C. H. S. Fifoot, *Lord Mansfield*, 1936.

Mansfield: 1. Municipal bor. in Notts, England, 14 m. N. of Nottingham, on the R. Maun; it is in the centre of the N. Notts coal-field and a large industrial area. The prin. industries include coal-mining, hosiery, cotton doubling, artificial silk, woollen goods, boots and shoes, leather goods, light engineering, iron and brass foundries, radio and aircraft components, stone quarrying, moulding sand and sand lime bricks, malting, the manuf. of decorated tin boxes and plastics. Sherwood Forest (q.v.) and the vale of Trent are in close proximity. Pop. 53,222.

2. City, co. seat of Richland co., Ohio, U.S.A., 66 m. SW. of Cleveland. It manufs. electrical appliances, steel products and machinery, and is the seat of Ohio State Reformatory. Pop. 47,500.

Mansfield College, Oxford, removed there from Birmingham in 1886. Originally intended to provide a theological college in Oxford for Congregational and other ministers from Britain and overseas and founded as a non-univ. college it became a permanent private hall of the univ. in 1955, admitting undergraduates to read for degrees in any subject. There are some 75 undergraduates in residence.

Mansfield Woodhouse, tn of Notts, England, 1½ m. N. of Mansfield. Two Rom. villas were discovered in the neighbourhood in 1786. Pop. 20,137.

Mansi (formerly Russian **Yugra,** then **Voguls**), Ugrian-speaking people of W. Siberia, living in the W. of the Khanty-Mansi National Okrug (Dist) of Tyumen' oblast (prov.) and numbering (1962) 7000 (1927, 6000). They are hunters, reindeer breeders and labourers, and are partly Russified. They have been known since the 11th cent., and stubbornly resisted Muscovite rule in the 15th–16th cents.

Mansion House, official residence of the lord mayor of London, opposite the Bank of England. It was built 1739–52 by George Dance the elder (q.v.) on the site of the old Stocks Market, and has a fine Corinthian portico.

Manslaughter is the killing of another (1) on a 'sudden affray', i.e. without premeditated design; or (2) through culpable negligence. The first class closely approximates to murder. If, for example, the slayer were carrying weapons, that fact of itself might well afford evidence of a deliberate intent to seek what might, *prima facie*, look like a sudden quarrel. The second class forms the bulk of charges of M. An endless variety of negligent acts causing death may amount to M.; e.g. a labourer engaged in house demolition, without in the least taking precautions, hurls debris down on to a highway and kills a passer-by; a 'peculiar' person, not believing in the efficacy of doctors, allows his child to die of disease when it might easily have been cured. But negligence, however gross, cannot be the basis of a charge of murder, though if the jury believe the facts show design and not negligence at all, the case will be otherwise. Frequently an indictment (q.v.) for murder contains an alternative count for M. where the prosecution are doubtful about the circumstances.

In Scots law the term M. is not used. The cardinal div. of criminal homicide is into *murder* and *culpable homicide*. The taking of another's life without intention of killing, but in circumstances which display such a complete and wicked recklessness as 'to imply a disposition depraved enough to be wholly regardless of consequences', is *murder*. Under 'culpable homicide' are included all types of homicide which are neither *casual* nor *justifiable*. *See* HOMICIDE; MURDER.

Manson, Ethel Gordon, *see* FENWICK.

Manson, Sir Patrick (1844–1922), 'father of tropical medicine', *b.* Oldmeldrum, Aberdeenshire. He studied medicine at Aberdeen and Edinburgh, graduating in 1865. Next year he was appointed medical officer in the Chinese Imperial Maritime Customs Service at Formosa and later went to Amoy. In 1877 he discovered that the parasite of filarial elephantiasis was transmitted by a mosquito—the first proof that infective diseases are spread by animal carriers. Returning to Scotland in 1889, he set up as a consultant in London the next year. By analogy with filaria he advanced the hypothesis (1894) that the malaria (q.v.) parasite also used the mosquito as transmitting agent. He inspired Ronald Ross (q.v.) to prove the transmission of malaria and identify the species of mosquito involved. He lectured on tropical diseases and in 1898 pub. his chief work, *Tropical Diseases*. He was appointed medical adviser to the colonial office, 1895. He reorganised the W. African medical service and in 1899 founded the London School of Hygiene. He was created K.C.M.G., 1903, and G.C.M.G., 1912. *See Life and Work*, by P. H. Manson-Bahr and A. Alcock, 1927.

Mansûra, or **Mansaurah,** cap. of the prov. of Daqahlia, Lower Egypt, on the r. b. of the Damietta branch of the Nile. M. marks the spot where the crusaders were finally overcome (Mansûra means 'the victorious'). M. manufs. sail cloth, cottons and linens. Pop. 101,965.

Mansur-al-Kamily was chief chemist at the

Cairo mint in the 13th cent. He wrote an excellent book on assaying and the purification of gold, and his chemical knowledge was far above the general contemporary level.

Mantazas: 1. Prov. of E. Cuba with an area of 3260 sq. m. and a pop. of 430,000. The terrain is undulating or low-lying and it is a fertile agric. area whose main products are sugarcane and cattle raising.

2. Cap. of above prov. and an important sugar exporting port on the N. coast. There is also a considerable amount of industry including textiles manuf. and chemical fertilisers. It is an attractive tn, 65 m. E. of Havana. Pop. 65,000.

Mantegna, Andrea (1431–1506), It. painter and engraver, *b*. Isola di Carturo, between Vicenza and Padua. He studied in the school of Squarcione, who entered him in the guild of painters before he was 11, but afterwards came under the influence of Jacopo Bellini (q.v.) whose daughter he married. His reputation was assured by his frescoes in the chapel of S. Cristoforo, in the church of S. Agostino degli Eremitani, Padua, mainly destroyed in the Second World War. In 1459 he went to Verona, and painted an altar-piece for the church of S. Zeno, and in 1460 took up his abode at Mantua at the invitation of the Marquis Lodovico Gonzaga. In Rome in 1488 he painted a series of frescoes in the chapel of the Belvedere in the Vatican, among which was the noted 'Baptism of Christ', but all were destroyed by Pius VI. He returned to Mantua in 1490 to continue the 'Triumph of Caesar', his masterpiece, a series of 9 pictures, each 9 ft square, painted in tempera, now in Hampton Court. Another notable picture of his later years was his 'Madonna della Vittoria' (1495), now in the Louvre. M. was also an engraver, and amongst other works engraved 'A Bacchanal Festival', 'Marine Gods', 'The Entombment' and 'The Resurrection'. His work is sculptural in character (resembling carving in low relief) and much influenced by classical antiquity.

Mantell, Gideon Algernon (1790–1852), geologist, *b*. Lewes, Sussex. His noted collection of fossils is in the Brit. Museum. Pub. many geological works, among which may be mentioned *The Wonders of Geology*, 1838. F.R.S., 1825.

Mantes (-**Gassicourt**, or -**La-Jolie**), Fr. tn, in the dept of Seine-et-Oise, on the Seine. It was burnt in 1087, in retaliation for a witticism of the Fr. King Philip I, by William the Conqueror, who was fatally wounded here. Paper. musical instruments and bricks are manuf. Pop. 18,900.

Manteuffel, or **Mannteufel, Edwin Hans Karl, Freiherr von** (1809–85), Prussian general and diplomat, *b*. Dresden. Appointed chief of the military cabinet in 1857, and adjutant-general of the King of Prussia in 1861. In 1864 he served in the Dan. war as a lieutenant-general, after which he was made civil and military governor of Schleswig. In 1866 he invaded Holstein on the plea that the Austrians, who then held it, had broken the convention of Gastein by appealing to the Germanic Confederation. On the latter

deciding against Prussia M., co-operating with Falkenstein, crossed the Elbe and invaded Hanover. Having humbled the Hanoverian army M. was placed in sole command against the united forces of S. Germany. After this he went as envoy to St Petersburg to advance Prussian interests in Germany. In the Franco-Ger. war (1870–1) he forced Bazaine to capitulate at Metz, defeated Farre at Amiens and forced Clenchant to retreat into Switzerland.

Manticore, mythical creature used as an heraldic device, having the head of a man, the body of a lion, a scorpion's sting and porcupine's quills.

Mantinea, city of Arcadia, founded soon after 479 BC by the merging of 5 vils. It was situated on the riv. Ophis, which, when the city was rebuilt in 370 BC, was diverted so as to encircle the place instead of flowing through it as before. The hist. of M. is largely one of intermittent conflict with its neighbour Tegea (q.v.). As a result of its treachery to the Achaean League (q.v.), Aratus (q.v.) put to death its leading citizens, sold the rest into slavery and called the city Antigonea in honour of the Macedonian king Antigonus Doson. The original name was restored by Hadrian in AD 133.

The neighbourhood of M. witnessed sev. historic battles, most notable of which are the victory of Epaminondas (q.v.) over the Spartans, 362 BC, and that of the Achaean League under Philopoemen over the Spartans, 207 BC.

Mantis, genus of the family of orthopterous insects Mantidea. The first pair of limbs are large, powerful and peculiarly modified, and are used to seize and maim insects for food. The praying M. (*M. religiosa*) occurs in S. Europe, and is called from the devotional attitude of the creature as it lies in wait for its prey. Many of the species have developed colour protection to a wonderful degree, so as to be hardly distinguishable from the leaves or flowers of the plant which they frequent. Their pugnacity and deadly armament have caused them to be kept and matched against one another like gamecocks.

PRAYING MANTIS
(*Mantis religiosa*)

Mantissa, *see* LOGARITHM.

Mantle of Earth, region of the interior of the earth which underlies the Crust and surrounds the Core. The upper surface of the mantle lies about 10 km deep in oceanic regions and between 25 and 75 km (usually c. 35 km) below the crust from which it is separated by the Mohorovicic discontinuity (q.v.). The transition from mantle to still denser core material occurs at about 2900 km depth.

Mantling, or **Lambrequin,** see HERALDRY, *The Helmet.*

Mantua (It. **Mantova**): 1. Prov. of Italy, in SE. Lombardy (q.v.). It is part of the fertile plain of Lombardy, and is watered in its S. part by the Po (q.v.) tribs. of which, including the Mincio (q.v.), cross the prov. NW.–SE. Area 904 sq. m.; pop. 440,000.

2. It. city, cap. of Milan. of M., on the Mincio, 78 m. SE. of Milan (q.v.). The riv. here forms a lagoon, surrounding the city on 3 sides. M. was originally an Etruscan tn (*see* ETRURIA). From 1328 to 1708 it was ruled by the family of Gonzaga (q.v.) under whom it became famous as a centre of learning. The tn is well built, with wide streets and squares and many historic buildings. The cathedral (10th–18th cents.) is one of the finest in Italy, and there is a castle (14th cent.), a vast ducal palace, the Renaissance house of Mantegna (q.v.), many beautiful old churches and mansions and the Palazzo del Te, which was built by Giulio Romano (q.v.) whose works are among the prin. glories of M. The chief industries are tanning, printing, brewing, sugar-refining and the manuf. of iron goods and ceramics. Virgil (q.v.) was *b.* at the anct *Andes,* now a suburb of M. Pop. 61,600.

Manu (Sanskrit, 'man'), or **Manu Vaivasvata** ('the sun-born'), the seventh of a class of 14 demiurgic beings, each of whom presides over a period of M. He is regarded as the progenitor of the present race, and was founder and first King of Ayodhya. To him are ascribed the so-called *Laws of Manu,* as well as a work on Vedic ritual.

Manuel I, see EMANUEL I.

Manuel II (1889–1932), King of Portugal, *b.* Belem, near Lisbon, second son of Carlos I. He succeeded to the throne on the assassination of his father and the crown prince in 1908. He was dethroned in Oct. 1910 on the estab. of the rep. and came to live in Twickenham, England. In 1913 he married Augusta Victoria of Hohenzollern.

Manuel, Francisco (1734 1819), *see* NASCI-MENTO, FRANCISCO MANOEL DO.

Manukau, harbour and co. of N. Is., New Zealand, on the W. coast of Auckland prov. dist. M. is ˙the W. coast harbour for the city of Auckland. It is separated from Waitemata Harbour on the E. coast by only a mile or two. M. harbour is a large inlet at the head of which is the port of Onehunga, 8 m. from Auckland. Pop. 36,000.

Manumission, in Rom. law, the act of freeing a slave. The usual form was *per vindictam,* in which the master turned the slave round with the words '*liber esto*' (be free), in presence of the praetor, that officer or his lictor (*see* LICTORS) at the same time striking the slave with his rod. M. might also be effected by adoption, by will or by registration in the census; but this last was

abandoned after the reign of Vespasian. All the foregoing were forms of *manumissio iusta* (valid M.). Less valid (*manumissio minus iusta*) were a variety of acts which had come to be regarded as signifying an intention to manumit, e.g. pronouncing a slave free in presence of 5 friends, asking him to dinner, etc. An edict of Constantine the Great gave freedom to any slave who had been abandoned by his master; and under the Christian emperors M. could be effected by declaration before a bishop on one of the great Church festivals.

Manures and/or **Fertilisers,** materials which maintain or increase the fertility of soils by supplying elements essential for plant growth, directly or indirectly. Some 14 of these nutrient elements are necessary; 7, known as major, in relatively large amounts—nitrogen, phosphorus, calcium, magnesium, potassium, sulphur and iron; others, known as trace elements, in relatively minute amounts—manganese, boron, copper, zinc, molybdenum and silicon, and possibly sodium and chlorine. Primarily, these elements are provided by the inorganic and organic particles of a soil; but soils vary in the amounts and proportions available to plants. Under cultivation soils lose some nutrient elements, chiefly the major ones of nitrogen, potassium, phosphorus, calcium and magnesium, much more readily than others. It is the purpose of M.s and/or F.s to replace or augment them. M.s, today, imply substances very rich in humus-forming organic matter, indispensable in ameliorating soil texture and structure, in improving aeration and moisture retention, and providing a base for biochemical activity by which soil fertility is released. They also contain useful amounts of nutrient elements. Farmyard M., a mixture of cow and animal dung with litter, is a variable product, and may contain 0·5 to 1·3 per cent nitrogen, 0·2 to 0·5 per cent phosphoric acid and 0·3 to 1·2 per cent potash, considered low in phosphates. The richer samples are of M. made and stored under cover, with ample litter to absorb the liquid part. Horse or stable M. is drier with slightly higher amounts of nutrient elements; sheep M. is richer still; but pig M. is moist and should be well mixed with litter. Poultry M. is more concentrated, with good percentages of nitrogen and phosphates, but low in potash. All M., when fresh, can be applied to vacant ground at 10 to 40 tons per ac., some time before cropping. Rotted M.s can be used in spring. Where animal M.s are not available, some alternative must be used: vegetable compost, the decomposed organic wastes of garden and house, is equivalent to farmyard M. Dried sewage, tn refuse compost, spent hops, seaweed, shoddy, green M.s, and fish guano are invaluable on the farm or in the garden. Organic M.s, however, usually need the supplement of F.s, which primarily supply plant nutrient elements in some concentration. F.s may be organic or inorganic (chemical) in nature. They are usually assessed on their content of nitrogen, phosphorus and potash (N.P.K.). Nitrogen promotes good stem and leaf growth and is the nutrient most easily lost from soils. The chief nitrogenous F.s are: organic—hoof and horn meal (12–14 per cent N), steady-acting; dried blood (12 per cent N), quick-acting; inorganic—sulphate of ammonia (20·6 per cent N), nitrate of soda (16 per cent N), nitro-chalk (15·5 per cent N, 48 per cent calcium carbonate), all relatively quick-acting; and urea (46 per cent N), a concentrated synthetic chemical. Phosphorus stimulates rooting and the maturing of fruits or seeds. The chief phosphatic F.s, in terms of Phosphoric acid content are: organic—bonemeal (20–24 per cent P_2O_5, 3–4 per cent N), relatively slow-acting; and steamed bone flour (27·5 per cent P_2O_5, 0·8 per cent N), quicker-acting; inorganic—basic slag (9–18 per cent P_2O_5, with high lime content), by-product of steel-making, slow-acting, excellent for grazing land, encouraging clovers; ground rock phosphate (27·5 per cent P_2O_5), slow-acting; superphosphate (17–18 per cent P_2O_5), quick-acting and most commonly used phosphatic F., also available as triple superphosphate (48 per cent P_2O_5) for farming. Potash is held to induce sturdiness and resistance to disease. The chief potassic F.s are inorganic: muriate of potash (50–60 per cent K_2O), steady-acting for winter use, with salt content and more useful on light than heavy soils; sulphate of potash (48–50 per cent K_2O), relatively quick-acting, and the most useful; wood-ashes (2·5 to 7 per cent K_2O) with high lime content, quick-acting. Some F.s provide more than one nutrient element. Meat-and-bone-meal, fish guano and dried poultry droppings usually contain nitrogen and phosphoric acid in varying amounts, but are often balanced with added potash and sold as proprietary compounds. Ammonium phosphate (11–16 per cent N, 31–48 per cent P_2O_5) may enter into liquid feeds. Chilean potash nitrate (15 per cent N, 9–11 per cent K_2O) is quick-acting and useful on light soils; potassium nitrate or saltpetre (12 per cent N, 40 per cent K_2O) is quick-acting but usually used in liquid feeds. In practice it is desirable that basic fertilisation should consists of F.s balanced in nitrogen, phosphorus and potash to suit the crop and the soil. These may be simple mixtures of the above chemicals; but manuf. compounds tend to become more sophisticated, being compounded not only to suit specific crops, but also in more easily handled granular form and more concentrated, so that less total weight is needed. The relative value of F.s is best determined by comparing the cost of a unit of nitrogen, phosphorus or potash, the unit being taken at 1 per cent of a ton. *See* H. V. Garner and others, *Profits from Fertilisers*, 2nd ed., 1954; H.M.S.O., *Manures and Fertilisers*, 1962; K. Paisley, *Fertilisers and Manures*, 1960. *See also* AGRICULTURE.

Manus, *see* HAND.

Manuscripts. This term, from Latin, meaning written by hand, indicates writings of any kind, on any material, although nowadays it is mainly used to indicate medieval writings on vellum or

modern writings on paper, as distinguished from printed matter. Man naturally makes use of those writing materials which are the most readily procured and the most suitable. Palm-leaves, bamboo-sticks, clay, stone, metals, ivory, bone, wood, bark, linen, wax, papyrus, leather and other materials were used, and still are used, for writing in various parts of the world. If something durable was wanted, metal, clay, or stone or other hard materials were employed: the writings thus produced are termed inscriptions (q.v.), and will not be considered in this article.

In various parts of India and other E. countries the leaves of palm-trees, especially the talipot palm-leaves, which are long and narrow, have been in use for cents., the local scribes employing an iron stylus to scratch the letters, and ink is rubbed over the surface of the leaf and fills up the scratches that form the letters. MSS. written on palm-leaf have been found in various E. countries which date back many hundreds of years. In Siam the material used was an indication of the social standing of the person for whom the written document was intended; the king's letters were engraved on sheets of gold when they were sent to princes, or on paper, either black or white, when written to lesser people. Sacred works were written on *Corypha* palm-leaves, their edges being gilded or painted with vermilion, and the leaves threaded on strings and folded like a fan; these MSS. are mainly preserved in the Siamese Buddhist monasteries. The MSS. of some Indonesian peoples consist of long strips of bamboo welded by beating one to the other, then folded together, accordion-like, between wooden covers, and bound together with a string of woven rushes. Instead of bamboo strips, sometimes long strips of thin bark of trees are used. The anct books of the Bataks (Sumatra) are written in brilliant ink on paper made of bark. The bark of trees, as writing material, is still used by many other primitive peoples in America, Africa and Asia, and its general use in anct Rome caused its name, *liber*, to be attached to the book, which was made from it. The Lat. word *liber* (book) passed to Fr. (*livre*), It. (*libro*), Sp. (*libro*), etc., also the Eng. words library, librarian, etc., have derived from it. The Eng. term book (q.v.) and the Ger. *Buch* have a similar etymology.

Linen cloth was employed by the anct Egyptians to receive writing, but it was also used by the Romans, many Lat. authors referring to it (*libri lintei*, *volumina lintea*, etc.), as well as by the Etruscans (the 'mummy' of Zagreb'; *see* ETRUSCAN LANGUAGE AND WRITING). More extensive was the anct Rom. (and Gk) use of wax, or rather wooden tablets coated with wax, termed in Greek *pinax*, *puxion*, *grammateion*, etc., and in Latin *cera*, *tabella*, *tabula* or *tabulae ceratae*. These tablets were used for school exercises, accounts, literary compositions, etc. A *candex* or *codex* contained 2 or more wooden tablets, coated with black wax and held together by rings; it was termed (according to the number of its tablets) *diptycha* or *duplices*, *triptycha* or *triplices*, etc., or *polyptycha, multiplices*.

The main vehicle, however, by which the Gk and Rom. literatures were preserved from the earliest times down to the early Middle Ages was the papyrus roll. The oldest books known are written on rolls of papyrus, and the earliest preserved written papyri go back to the 5th Egyptian dynasty (late 28th–early 27th cents. BC). The largest library in antiquity, that of Alexandria (q.v.) was said to comprise 700,000 vols. in the 1st cent. BC. The manuf. of papyrus appears to have ceased in Egypt about the middle of the 10th cent. AD.

The manuf. of papyrus (q.v.) had its H.Q. at Alexandria, and all matters relating to its size, quality and price were carefully regulated in Rom. times. It was made out of the pith of the stems of the papyrus plant (*Cyperus papyrus l.*), which then grew plentifully in the Nile, and it was termed *papuros, bublos, biblos*. The length of the early rolls was very considerable. We are told of some that were 150 ft long and would contain the whole *Iliad* or *Odyssey*; some were 30 or 40 ft long. The best quality of papyrus was about $9\frac{1}{2}$ in. wide, though there was a kind of 'large paper', *macrocollum*, as much as a cubit wide. Papyrus lingered on in Europe for ordinary documents, letters, etc., until the 11th cent. However, on account of climate papyri have been preserved mostly in upper Egypt. Very few have been found in Palestine and N. Mesopotamia; charred papyri have been discovered in Herculaneum, Italy, and in lower Egypt. Still, some 30,000 Gk papyri, and many others couched in Aramaic, Latin, Persian, Coptic, Arabic and Hebrew, are preserved in the prin. collections of Europe, U.S.A., Egypt, Palestine, etc.

In the 3rd cent. AD, while the papyrus roll was still the dominant form of book for pagan literature, most of the Christian literature was written in codices: the papyrus material was then combined with the codex form, as, for instance, in the famous Chester Beatty papyri, which are a group of papyrus codices of various books of the Bible, mostly of the 3rd cent., but at least one belonging to the first half of the 2nd cent. However, the codex did not become fashionable until perhaps the 4th cent. AD. It was the growth of the Christian community which brought it into prominence; and with the codex, the material best adapted to that form, namely parchment or vellum, also came into favour. It may be said that while the papyrus roll was the book of the pagan world, the vellum codex was the book of medieval Christianity.

The invention of vellum (*vitulinum*), a material prepared from the skins of calves, sheep and other animals, is commonly attributed to King Eumenes II of Pergamum (197–159 BC), in Asia Minor, who was ambitious of forming a library, but was unable to obtain papyrus because his rival, Ptolemy of Egypt, jealous for his own library at Alexandria, forbade papyrus to be exported. This story is told by Pliny (*Natural History*, xiii. 11) on the authority of Varro, but its historical value need not be believed.

However, there is no doubt that Pergamum (hence the name *pergamena*, which is the origin of our word *parchment*) was the chief centre of the vellum trade. Actually vellum was not 'invented' in the 2nd cent. BC; it was rather an extension of, or improvement upon, an old practice. Rolls of skin were used by the Egyptians in quite early times: the first mention of documents on skin goes back to the 4th dynasty (29th–28th cent. BC), although the earliest extant examples of such documents are a roll of leather of the 12th dynasty (*c*. 2000–1788 BC) and a mathematical text of the 17th cent. BC now in the British Museum. It is uncertain whether the Babylonians and Assyrians employed skin as writing material (no such documents have been recovered in Mesopotamia, because her soil was unsuitable to the conservation of such perishable stuff as leather or papyrus), but Ctesias reported that the Persian royal records were kept on skins of sheep or goats, and that the Avesta was said to have been written on skins of oxen. Herodotus, too, tells us that the Ionian Greeks wrote upon skins, and so also did many barbarians in his own time. The Jews probably employed skins throughout their hist. for the reception of their sacred books (a few fragments of these, apparently belonging to the 3rd or 4th cent. BC, have been discovered), as indeed they do at the present day. The Christian scribes, influenced no doubt by the practice of the Jews, chose parchment upon which to write their sacred books.

However, the papyrus roll continued to be predominant, and parchment was mainly used for note-books and cheap copies until the end of the 3rd cent. AD. Then its superior advantages seem to have been suddenly realised. It was more durable than the papyrus; it provided a beautiful surface for writing; arranged in sheets or pages, it could contain in a single vol. a far greater quantity of matter than the papyrus roll. Thus it became possible to have the whole of Homer or Virgil or of the Bible in a single vol. It was possible to use it more than once, for it could be written upon, then washed out, and another text written over it, known as *palimpsest*. Two other circumstances favoured the vellum codex: (1) From Pergamum the article made its way in great quantity to Rome, and once in Rome its diffusion over the whole civilised world was assured. (2) The Christians, having chosen it as their main writing material, soon extended its use, first to the reception of their theological literature and then to that of literature in general. It must also be borne in mind that the 4th cent. AD witnessed the victory of the vellum codex over the papyrus roll, just at the time when the Emperor Constantine accepted Christianity as the official religion of the Rom. Empire (*c*. AD 313–25), and one of his first acts was to instruct Eusebius to have 50 copies of the Gk Bible written on vellum for his cap., Constantinople. The earliest extant great codices belong to this cent.: *Codex Sinaiticus* (Brit. Museum), *Codex Vaticanus* (Vatican library). Others belong to the 5th or 6th cents.: *Codex Alexandrinus* (Brit.

Museum), *Codex Ambrosianus* (Milan), *Codex Ephraemi* (Paris), *Codex Sarravianus* (Leyden and Paris), *Codex Washington* (Washington), *Codex Argenteus* (the famous Gothic MS. preserved in Upsala), and so forth. From the 4th cent. AD the vellum codex definitely superseded the papyrus roll, and remained the chief writing material for MSS. until the general estab. of the use of paper in the 14th cent.

The use of paper as writing material was unknown in Europe before the 11th cent. AD, although the Chinese had known it already for about 1000 years. It was invented in China about AD 105. In the 8th cent. the Arabs learned paper-making from the Chinese, and in the 9th cent. they brought it to Spain and Sicily. By Europeans paper was first made in the 12th cent. in Spain and Italy. The art of paper-making spread from Spain to France in 1248, from Italy to Germany and Switzerland in the 13th cent., and later to England, where the first important paper-mill was set up in Hertford by John Tate in the second half of the 15th cent. However, in the second half of the 14th cent. paper was in fairly general use throughout Europe, and began to rival parchment as writing material for books. In the course of the 15th cent. it gradually superseded it. At that time, however, printing superseded handwriting in the manuf. of books.

The Mexican pre-Columbian MSS., known as Aztec codices, are painted in colours, on coarse cloth made from the fibre of the *Agave americana*, or on a long sheet of *amatl* paper, of an average width of 6 or 7 in., but of different length. The sheet was folded up screen fashion to form the leaves, and was fastened to what may be called the binding of the codex, which was of fine, thin wood covered with brilliant varnish: it had no 'back".

For the lettering of MSS. *see* ALPHABET; PALAEOGRAPHY; WRITING; and the single letters A, B, C, D, and so on. *See also* BOOK; ILLUMINATION OF MANUSCRIPTS; PALIMPSEST; PAPYRUS; PARCHMENT.

Bibliography. E. A. Bond, E. M. Thompson and C. F. Warner, *Facsimiles of MSS. and Inscriptions* (2nd series), 1884–94; F. Madan, *Books in Manuscript*, 1893; G. H. Putnam, *Books and their Makers during the Middle Ages*, 1896; G. F. Warner, *Illuminated Manuscripts in the British Museum*, 1899–1903; A. Maire, *Materials used to Write before the Invention of Printing*, 1904; E. M. Thompson, *Greek and Latin Palaeography*, 1912; M. R. James, 'Books and Writing' in L. Whibley's *Companion to Greek Studies*, 1916, and J. E. Sandy's *Companion to Latin Studies*, 1925; F. G. Kenyon, *Ancient Books and Modern Discoveries*, 1927, *Books and Readers in Ancient Greece and Rome*, 1932, *The Story of the Bible*, 1936, and *The Text of the Greek Bible*, 1937; A. C. Moorhouse, *Writing and the Alphabet*, 1946; D. Diringer, *The Alphabet* (4th impression), 1953 (with bibliography), and its sequels, *The Hand-Produced Book*, 1953, and *The Illuminated Book*, 1958.

Manutius, Aldus, *see* ALDUS MANUTIUS.

Manx-cat, variety of the domestic cat distinguished by having no tail, or only a rudimentary one. A native of the Isle of Man, it may be of Jap. origin. It is now almost extinct.

Manx Language, member of the Gaelic branch of the Celtic languages (q.v.). It is closer to Scottish Gaelic than to Irish. The earliest known text is Bishop Phillips's trans. of the Book of Common Prayer (1610, but not pub. till 1894). The earliest printed book was Bishop Wilson's *Principles and Duties of Christianity* (1707). There also exist trans. of the Bible and other religious works. There is little original literature apart from some religious poems and a few ballads. A private census made by Henry Jenner in 1875 (by asking each par. priest to estimate the number of Manx-speakers in his par.) revealed that at that time there were probably some 12,000 speakers of the language. The numbers of speakers have since declined rapidly. When Prof. K. H. Jackson pub. his *Contribution to the Study of Manx Phonology*, 1955, there were only 6 left and the language may now be deemed extinct. The language was however preserved for posterity by means of tape-recording of the last surviving speakers made by *Yn Cheshaght Ghailckagh* (The Manx Language Society). *See* J. J. Kneen, *Grammar of the Manx Language*, 1931.

Manych, *see* KUMA-MAYNCH DEPRESSION.

Manzanares: 1. Sp. tn in the prov. of Ciudad Real. It has a castle, once the property of the Marqués de Santillana (q.v.), and produces wine, textiles and saffron. Pop. 17,800.

2. Sp. riv. which rises in the Sierra de Guadarrama (q.v.) and flows past Madrid to the Jarama, a trib. of the Tagus (q.v.). Length 50 m.

Manzanilla, *see* SHERRY.

Manzanillo: 1. Port in Oriente prov., Cuba (q.v.), on the Gulf of M., in the SE. of the is., 550 m. E. by rail from Havana and 80 m. from Santiago. M. produces sugar, molasses and rice, and processes fish and forest products. It has an airfield. Pop. 48,000.

2. Port and tn on the Pacific coast of Mexico in the state of Colima. Since being linked by rail with Guadalajara and Mexico City it has become Mexico's chief port on the Pacific. Main locally produced exports are coconut oil, maize, timber, fruit and fish. Industry is confined to processing the local products apart from the exploitation of salt in Lake Cuyutlau which is close to the tn. Itself a tourist resort, there are various other small ones along the coast. Pop. 21,000.

Manzanita, *see* ARCTOSTAPHYLOS.

Manzoni, Alessandro (1785–1873), It. poet and novelist, *b.* Milan. In 1805 he went to Paris, where the philologist Claude Fauriel introduced him to Shakespeare's works and the new romantic tendencies. His *Inni Sacri*, 1812–22, were widely admired. In 1822 he pub. his ode to Napoleon, *Il cinque maggio*. The work by which M. attained to European fame is his historical novel *I Promessi Sposi*, 1825–6, a Milanese story of the 17th cent. It is remarkable for its clear and dignified style, its masterly characterisation and its skilful dialogue. M. has been regarded as the head of the romantic movement, but he remained a classic in his serenity, harmony and respect for the 'true'. Among his other works are *Osservazione sulla morale cattolica*, 1819, and the tragedies *Il Conte di Carmagnola*, 1820, and *Adelchi*, 1822. *See* B. Croce, *Alessandro Manzoni*, 1930; J. F. De Simone, *Alessandro Manzoni: Esthetics and Literary Criticism*, 1946; Archibald Colquhoun, *Manzoni and his Times*, 1954.

Mao Tse-tung (1893–), Chinese Communist leader, was *b*. of a well-to-do farmer's family in Shaoshan vil, Hsiang-t'an, Hunan. He had an elementary classical education in his youth, but specialised in modern subjects at Changsha First Normal School. A brief period was spent in Peking, 1918–19, working in the univ. library under the wing of Li Ta-chao, who did much to introduce Marxism into China. Back in Changsha, M. married Yang K'ai-hui, daughter of a former teacher, in 1920 (she was executed 10 years later). He attended the founding meeting of the Chinese Communist Party in Shanghai in July 1921, then returned to Hunan where he worked for the party until 1927. He was elected to the Central Committee in June 1923, and also to the Central Executive Committee of the Kuomintang (KMT) in Jan. 1924. As early as Mar. 1927, when Chinese Communism as a whole was concentrating its attention on the urb. workers, M. wrote a report analysing from a Marxist standpoint the Chinese social structure and emphasising the important role the Chinese peasants could play in a future Communist revolution; but his opinions were largely ignored. After Chiang Kai-shek (q.v.) had launched his grand purge in 1927, the Communist (CCP) leadership vainly attempted to answer it with such orthodox tactics as the organising of workers' uprisings in big cities; M., however, organised a peasant uprising in Hunan, and when it failed led the remnants to Chingkangshan, Kiangsi, where he was joined by Chu Teh's army from Nanchang in April 1928. M. became chairman of the Council of the People's Commissars in 1931. Hard pressed by Chiang Kai-shek's fifth campaign of 'Extermination of Bandits', M. led the Long March from Kiangsi to Shensi in 1934–5. It was not until he was elected chairman of the CCP at the Tsunyi (in Kweichou) conference in Jan. 1935 that his authority in the party was firmly estab. His policy of opposing rigid dogmatism and acclimatising Marxism to the special conditions in China soon won him the unanimous support of the CCP as well as of many intellectuals outside the party. In the Communist cap. Yenan he reversed the previous 'closed door' policy of the party leadership and thereby rallied to it a great number of middle-class intellectuals who could no longer see any hope for China's regeneration under the KMT regime. In Dec. 1936 he helped to bring about a united front with the KMT. In Jan. 1940 he pub. his treatise, *On New Democracy*, in which he described in great detail plans for economic, cultural and political reconstruction for a new and Communist China

after the war. After the Communists had driven Chiang Kai-shek out of China and taken over the gov. of the country M. was elected chairman of the rep. by the first People's Political Consultative Conference in 1949, and was re-elected by the first National People's Congress in 1954. He was succeeded as head of state in 1959 by Liu Shao-ch'i (q.v.).

As the head of a national party which had nearly destroyed itself by following Russian directives in the 20's and the ruler of a nation that was determined to regain its greatness, M. was unlikely to recognise Russia's hegemony for very long. With Stalin dead he could with some justice be regarded as the *eminence grise* of world communism. Personal ambitions aside, there was a basic contradiction between the middle-aged Russian and dynamic new Chinese revolutions which led to a rift opening between the 2 parties around 1959, since when it has progressively widened. Now keeping in the background, his only post being honorary chairman of the People's Political Consultative Conference, M. is still the venerated leader of the nation, and presumably fully behind the 'permanent revolution' in his country. *See* CHINA, *History*. *See also Selected Works of Mao Tse-tung* (vols. i–iv), 1953–6; E. Snow, *Red Star Over China*, 1937; B. Schwartz, *Chinese Communism and the Rise of Mao*, 1951; S. Schran, *The Political Thought of Mao Tse-tung*, 1963; H. Boorman, *Mao Tse-tung: the Lacquered Image*, Chinese Quarterly No. 16; J. Chen, *Mao and the Chinese Revolution*, 1965. (*See Plate: China*.)

Maoris, or **Maui** (New Zealand word signifying *native* or *indigenous*), the name given to themselves by the inhab. of New Zealand. The M., in common with the natives generally of Polynesia, belong to the Caucasoid race or family of mankind. Though calling themselves indigenous, the M. have a tradition that their ancestors migrated to the present seat of the nation from the is. of Hawaiki about 500 years ago. This is. has been identified with Hawaii and Savaii in the Pacific Ocean. On their arrival in New Zealand the M. found inhab. on the E. coast of the N. Is. of similar racial origins to themselves. Known to the M. as Morioris, 'inferior people'. this race was driven to the S. Is. and to the Chatham Is. Through absorption by the dominant M. the Morioris finally became extinct in 1933. Of their hist. nothing definite is known and even their origin remains a mystery. The M. mainly confined themselves to the warmer N. Is., and, when discovered by Europeans, were in a high state of Neolithic civilisation, with marked superiority in the arts of wood-carving and military engineering. Their prin. social unit was the family group and from combinations of the numerous groups were formed sub-tribes and tribes, which possessed highly developed social and ritual customs. Inter-tribal warfare was common and indeed the M. have never been united as a nation, tribes fighting against tribes to the death. As individuals they show exceptional courage and intelligence.

Maori society had 3 grades, each one having sev. degrees of position or influence. The first class was that of the 'Rangatira', or chieftain; the second, the 'Waro', or commoner; the third, the 'Pononga', or slave. The 'Ariki', or priest, was generally found in the person of the chief. A chief is believed to possess or to be associated with a divine spiritual power, known as *mana*. This makes him both sacred and also dangerous to ordinary people, a condition known as *tapu* (from which comes our word 'taboo').

The M. were fierce warriors, and fought much among themselves and against the Whites, in the wars between 1843–69. They are skilled artists, especially in wood-carving, and formerly tattooed their faces and skins with elaborate patterns, known as *moko*. They declined in numbers to about 40,000; there are many M. with White (*Pakeha*) ancestry; they are literate and Christian, although with great pride in their ancestry and traditions.

Of the great number of Maori legends, those relating to the hero Maui are most widely known. This hero was skilled in magic; it was Maui who snared the sun, and in his preparations for the feat he invented a rope made from flax. It was Maui who fished up the is. of New Zealand with a hook made of the enchanted jaw-bone of an ancestress, and this jawbone in Maori belief now forms the curve in the S. extremity of Hawke's Bay. The numerous adventures of Maui have given rise to a set of proverbs, and reference to these in speeches or ordinary conversation lends a subtlety to the language of the learned which eludes those not acquainted with Maori mythology. Another hero of Maori myth is Ngatoro, whose name is associated with Mt Tongariri, the volcano in the middle of N. Is. Ngatoro climbed this mt, first enjoining on his brothers not to touch food during his absence; they disobeyed with the result that Ngatoro, in his wrath, felt faint, and calling on the gods to send fire to him the mt became a volcano, so that the hero was revived by the heat and descended to the plains below. The route by which the fire came became, in the Maori belief, the famous thermal dist around Rotorua and Taupo. The primal being of Maori myth was Io, the supreme god, who in some manner caused the earth and sky to exist, and these are personified in Rangi, the Sky Parent, and Papa, the Earth Mother. Fairies figure prominently in Maori legends, with many stories of monsters known as 'taniwhas' who lived in sea caves or in swamps, stories which probably had their foundation in the schools of seals and porpoises seen off the coast.

Dancing has always been a favourite recreation of the M., in which, as in their other arts, there is a well-defined constructive scheme so that the progression of movements adequately expresses the passions or the development of a dramatic idea. Of the latter type the 'poi' dance, or famous canoe dance, which is perhaps the favourite among the M., exhibits considerable interpretative skill. Maori carving is a most characteristic, if dying, art. Dists, tribes and even families specialised in some particular form of art expression, and were jealous to preserve their secrets. Carved figures, interiors of houses, such as carved pillars, and, above all, the embellishments of the war canoes afford some of the most striking examples of Maori carving.

More than five-sixths of the M. are now converted to Christianity. Since the native wars, which lasted from 1843 to 1869, the M. have enjoyed complete peace, but they steadily declined in numbers from about 100,000 to 40,000 in 1901. During the last 60 years, however, they have increased, and their number may now be put at about 100,000. Much may depend on the creation of a native land settlement scheme, for there is very little land held by 'customary' tenure—i.e. land which has never been the subject of a Crown grant, and is held by natives under the customs and usages of the Maori people, as recognised and guaranteed by the treaty of Waitangi. Nor, again, is there any large area of 'native freehold' land. It seems, however, that the M. have no future as a distinct race, for even though the downward trend in pop. has long been arrested, there is a continuous infusion of Maori blood in the New Zealand pop. Two Maori members may be appointed to the Legislative Council by the governor-general (since 1927). There are 4 Maori members in the House of Representatives, elected for 3 years, and every adult Maori living in any of the 4 Maori electoral dists is entitled to vote (Act of 11 Dec. 1937). Maori children may attend public schools, but there are also native vil. schools provided for their primary education. There are also a few mission schools remaining from the pre-Maori war system estab. with the help of gov. subsidies.

See A. W. Shrimpton, *Maori and Pakeha: a History of New Zealand*, 1921; R. Firthi, *Primitive Economics of the New Zealand Maori*, 1929; J. Cowan, *The Maori, Yesterday and To-day*, 1930; H. Grieve, *Sketches for Maoriland*, 1939; I. L. G. Sutherland (ed.), *The Maori People to-day* (tribal organisation, arts and crafts, religious influences, customs, social welfare and education), 1941; R. Duff, *Moahunter Period of Maori Culture*, 1950; A. Alpers, *Maori Myth and Legends*, 1964. (*See Plates: New Zealand; British Commonwealth; Race.*)

Map, or **Mapes, Walter** (*c.* 1127–*c.* 1209), Eng. author and wit, probably a native of Herefordshire. He studied under Girard la Pucelle at Paris, and on his return to England was made clerk of the royal household, being frequently employed as a justice itinerant. He was with Henry II at Limoges in 1173, and in Anjou in 1183, and in 1179 was sent to the Lateran Council at Rome. In 1176 he received the prebend of Mapesbury at St Paul's, becoming before 1186 chancellor of Lincoln, and in 1197 he was made archdeacon of Oxford. He wrote *De nugis curialium*, a collection of legends and anecdotes from his native country. This book gives some information of the Templars and Hospitallers, and also contains a sketch of the Eng. court and kings from the reign of

William II to his own time. Besides this, it gives an account of M.'s life. *See* the ed. of M. R. James, 1914, (trans., 1923).

Map, *see* MAPS.

Map-making, *see* MAPS and ORDNANCE SURVEY.

Map Reading. Whereas formerly a map indicated more or less inaccurately a number of places and their supposed relative positions, a modern map, carefully selected and studied, can be a mine of compressed authentic information. The maps generally referred to in this article will be those of the official Brit. Ordnance Survey, on which all privately pub. maps (e.g. Bartholomew's) are based.

In 'reading' a map the first thing to do is to study carefully the conventional signs employed. These vary somewhat according to the scale and the date of pub. Ordnance Survey maps being now subjected to a process of continuous revision and improvement, those of latest date will, in general, be the most accurate and informative. These maps show both natural physical features and man-made constructions; the special character of the ground surfaces; areas, distances, levels and boundaries; also archaeological features. Printed on the margin of the map sheet, these conventional signs can also be obtained on a separate card. The most generally useful map for all purposes is the inch-to-a-mile (coloured).

Roads are readily distinguishable according to their categories, from good main roads down to narrow, bad, unfenced roads, footpaths and bridle paths. Railways, whether single or double tracks, with embankments, cuttings, tunnels, viaducts, stations, level crossings, bridges (over or under), mineral lines and tramways are also shown. Public Rights of Way are shown on the sheets for England and Wales. Waterways comprise rivs., lakes, tarns, reservoirs, all coloured blue, streams and tribs. in meandering blue lines, canals with straight banks, ditches, generally in fine blue straight lines. Boundaries of various kinds include co., bor., par., etc., shown by various combinations of black dots and dashes. Electric transmission lines are represented by fine black lines with pylons spaced conventionally.

Many conventional signs (more numerous on the large-scale plans) indicate the character of the ground surface, e.g. slopes, broken slopes, cliffs, mud-banks, flat rock, boulders, shingle, sand, sand-pits, gravel-pits, pasture, orchards, etc.; also abbreviations or signs for artificial objects like letter-box, police call-box, well, trough, post office, youth hostel, windmill, lighthouse, church, etc. Sites of antiquities have a conventional sign, with distinctive lettering to indicate either prehistoric, Rom. or medieval remains.

Contour lines, usually drawn in brown or red ink, are an invaluable modern invention and display relief without obscuring other features. Widely spaced contour lines indicate gentle slopes, generally devoted to agriculture, and closely packed lines steep or precipitous slopes.

Aerial photographs may reveal features not otherwise discernible. *See* J. W. Cameron, *Map Reading*, 1920; G. T. McCaw, *The Basis of Map-making*, 1938; F. F. Crossley, *Map Reading*, 1943; B. Lockey, *The Interpretation of Ordnance Survey Maps—Geographical Pictures* (4th ed.), 1946; D. Sylvester, *Map and Landscape*, 1952; T. Pickles, *Map Reading* (new ed.), 1955.

Maple, or *Acer*, genus of deciduous trees of the family Aceraceae, with opposite, stalked, palmately veined leaves of great decorative value, and racemes of green flowers followed by samaras. The common or small-leaved M. (*A. campestre*) has the racemes erect, and is the only Brit. species, but the greater M., or sycamore (*A. pseudo-platanus*, with pendulous racemes, is now perfectly naturalised. Of the numerous N. Amer. species, the sugar M. (*A. saccharum*) is one of the most valuable. M. wood has many uses. The M. leaf is the national emblem of Canada. *See* FORESTRY; LUMBER; TIMBER.

MAPLE
Acer saccharum, the sugar maple.
A, winged seed.

Maps are representations on a plane, and on a reduced scale, of part or the whole of the earth's surface. They are either topographical, cadastral, general or atlas. Topographical M. are based on accurate survey, and show the natural features of the country, hills and rivs., forests and swamps; also such artificial features as tns and vils., buildings, roads, railways, canals, bridges and telegraphs. They serve as guides for travel on business or pleasure, or for the operations of war. The 'one-inch' map (scale 1 in. to 1 m.) is the standard topographical map of the Brit. Isles. Cadastral M. are on a larger scale, as required for local administration, taxation, management of estates, legal documents, etc. These M. in other countries are often in MS. and deposited with the local authority. The Brit. map of the scale (q.v.) of 25 in. to 1 m., commonly called the 25-in. plan, shows hedges and fences, etc., but is not strictly a cadastral map, though commonly called so, because the real boundary of properties may frequently be some feet beyond the hedge. Moreover a cadastral map proper records the co-ordinates of boundary stones, corners, etc., referred to in the general framework of the survey. This registration of co-ordinates is more important in a country such as Egypt, which has no permanent hedges or boundary walls and where the ann. inundation of the Nile may obliterate the very vague boundaries of cultivated lands. General or atlas M. are on a small scale, in which the topographical details are necessarily suppressed, for these M. aim at the representation of a large tract of country, a continent or even the world. (An international world map, to a uniform scale of 1/1,000,000, is described later.)

M. of the sea-coast, and to some extent of the sea bottom, are generally known as charts (q.v.). They give information of buoys, lights, soundings, etc., all referred to low water as datum, instead of to mean sea level, with information on tides or currents. It is to be noted that charts which were good enough in the old days of sail and low-powered steamships are not now satisfactory for the requirements of the fast, deep-draught vessels of today. The hydrographic dept of the Brit. Admiralty, since the Second World War, is engaged in the great task of recharting the oceans of the world. Particular attention is given to the location of wrecks, which is effected by means of an echo-sounder, which records electric impulses 'bounced' off the sea bed. In shallow coastal water dual cameras on aircraft, using panchromatic film, will locate wrecks to within 3 ft of their depth. (*See* H.M.S.O., *Charting the Seas in Peace and War*, 1949.)

The oldest extant map in the world is said to be a sketch of roads to the gold-mines found on an Egyptian papyrus about 1300 BC. The anct Egyptians were skilled mathematicians, and were producing scientifically constructed cadastral M. as early as Rameses II (1330–1300 BC). From such M. Eratosthenes (276–*c*. 194 BC) may have measured the distance from Syene to Alexandria, from which he estimated the size of the earth, though the good result may have been accidental. The estimate of Eratosthenes was not improved upon till the determinations of Picard in 1671. The *Mappa Mundi* at Hereford Cathedral was made about 1290.

PROJECTIONS. A spherical surface, unlike a cylindrical, cannot be unrolled into a plane surface. Hence it follows that it is impossible to give an absolutely true representation of the earth on a plane map, but only on a globe. To represent it at all the sphere must be *projected* on

to the plane. It is usual to define position by reference to lat. and long. lines, and any representation of these lines upon a plane is called a 'map projection'. Though projections in actual use are not strictly projections in the geometrical sense, they approximate to them. The perfect map would show uniform and correct shape, and correct angles (bearings). In settling the particular kind of projection to be adopted in showing parts of the earth's surface on a plane map surface, consideration must be given to the area of the survey, the purpose for which it is required and the degree of accuracy desired. Some of the qualities desirable in a theoretically correct map must therefore be sacrificed, and the main purpose of the map will be the deciding factor. The system of meridians and parallels forming, as it were, the general framework construction of any map is known as the graticule, and every 'hole' in it is known as a mesh. It is only possible here to give a brief account of the more important projections.

Rectangular projection. In this the meridians are all straight, vertical, parallel lines and the parallels of lat. are horizontal parallel lines perpendicular to the meridians. The map is started by drawing a central meridian and marking off degrees of lat. thereon, as given in geodetic tables, through which parallels of lat. are drawn as straight lines at right angles to the central meridian. Degrees of long. are marked off in a similar way on the middle parallel and meridians drawn through these points parallel to the central meridian. This method should not be used for sheets containing a larger area than 100 sq. m. The detailed plotting of topographical details may be done by polar or rectangular co-ordinates.

Trapezoidal projection. This may be used for M. containing an area of not more than 25 m. square, i.e. 625 sq. m., in which the meridians and parallels are all straight lines, but the meridians are drawn to converge. It is started by drawing a central vertical meridian and dividing it for lats. all as before. Two parallels of lat. are then plotted, one about quarter the height of the sheet up from the bottom and the other about quarter the height down from the top. These are then divided into degrees and minutes at their respective lats., as given in geodetic tables. The meridians are then drawn as straight converging lines through the points of div. on these 2 parallels. The longs. indicated on the map will be correct, and the lats. nearly so.

Cylindrical. Let us imagine a plane surface wrapped round the globe in the form of a

---

In simple conical projections, the meridians are projected on to a cone which touches the earth along a parallel through the origin (marked x); the spacing of the meridians along the standard parallel (radius, R cot ϕ) will be at their true-to-scale separation of $\dfrac{2\pi \, R \, \cos\phi}{360}$ for each degree. *In the oblique Mercator's projection*, the cone of the conical projection is elongated until it becomes a cylinder touching the earth along the equator. *Oblique zenithal projection*: the apex angle of the cone in the conical projection is widened to 180°; the cone becomes a plane touching the sphere at x, resulting in a zenithal projection (it need not be centred on the pole). *Aitoff's* is a zenithal equal-area projection of a hemisphere.

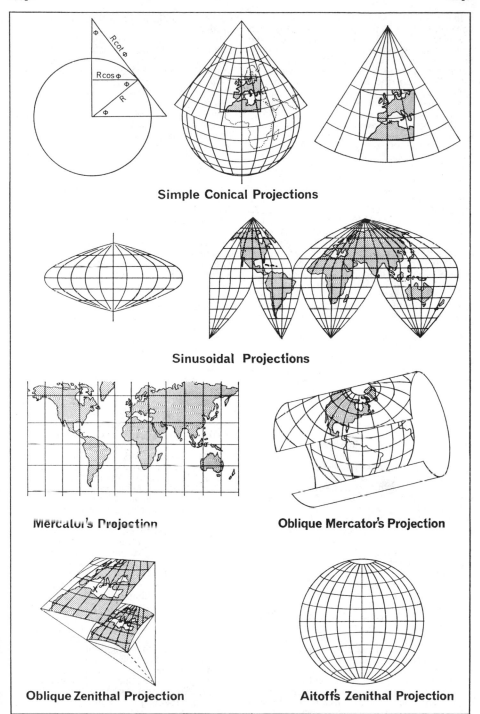

Simple Conical Projections

Sinusoidal Projections

Mercator's Projection

Oblique Mercator's Projection

Oblique Zenithal Projection

Aitoff's Zenithal Projection

MAPS: VARIOUS PROJECTIONS (*see opposite*)

cylinder of the same height, touching the equator. Further let us suppose the plane of each meridian and parallel produced to touch the cylinder, so that, on unfolding, the former would be represented by vertical straight lines, and the latter by horizontal. Such a projection would be much distorted in the region of the poles, though approximately true in equatorial regions. Its merit is that in spite of distortion in shape, equal areas on the globe are represented by equal areas on the map. Hence it is called an equal area cylindrical projection. Another cylindrical projection, almost universally used for navigation, is Mercator's. Its approximate form can be visualised by supposing a light at the centre of the globe to cast a shadow of the meridians and parallels on a cylinder of infinite length enclosing it. Here, as the polar shadows are at infinity, there is obviously tremendous distortion in size at extreme lats., but within 30° N. or S. lat. of the equator the representation is good. This projection retains the characteristic property of orthomorphic or stereographic projection, viz. similarity of representation of small parts of the surface (*see* next paragraph). Its importance is due to the fact that the loxodromic curve, i.e. a line on the sphere cutting all the meridians at the same angle, becomes a straight line on the map. In effect this means that bearings read from the map are true bearings.

Stereographic. Here the point of vision is supposed to be on the sphere's surface, and the plane of projection is the tangent plane at the other end of the diameter through the point of vision. In this projection the scale varies, but is orthomorphic, i.e. a small area of any particular shape on the globe is represented on the map by an area of the same shape.

Central or gnomonic projection. Here the point of vision is supposed to be at the centre of the sphere, and all great circles are accordingly represented by straight lines. The plane of projection may be either parallel to the plane of the equator, or parallel to the plane of some meridian, or inclined to the axis of the sphere at any angle. These 3 variations are known as polar, meridional, or horizontal.

Conical. Many modifications of the conical projections are in use. They are (1) the simple conic with one selected parallel; (2) De L'Isle's projection with two standard parallels and with rectified meridians; and (3) Bonne's projection, in which all the parallels are properly divided. This was largely used by the French but abandoned in 1917. It was used for the 1-in. Ordnance Survey (O.S.) map of Scotland. The most important is that with 2 standard parallels. A mental picture approximating to it can be formed by supposing the plane of the map to be folded into a cone cutting the sphere's surface at any 2 selected parallels. When the map is unfolded again these 2 parallels will be represented by concentric arcs of correct length; other parallels will be concentric arcs not quite true to length; and the meridians will be radii, also untrue to length. Provided the portion of the sphere represented on the map is not too great,

no very significant distortion of any kind is produced.

Sinusoidal equal-area projection. This is a particular case of Bonne's projection, the selected parallel being the equator. It is a projection very suitable for the map of Africa.

Polyconic projection. In the foregoing simple conic projections only 1 tangent or intersecting cone is used, but for very large areas it is better to make each parallel of lat. the development of the base of a cone tangent to the sphere at that lat. This polyconic projection is employed for the M. of the U.S. Coast and Geodetic Survey.

Some special purpose projections. (1) Globular; (2) Elliptical (equal area); (3) Zenithal, in which some point on the earth is selected for a central point of the map, great circles radiating from this point being represented by straight lines; (4) the Two-point Equidistant—having chosen 2 points on the sphere, the distances on the map from these 2 points to all other points are true to scale; (5) a map based on a modified oblique Mercator projection, by A. R. Hinks, was used in connection with the preparatory International Conference on Trade and Employment, London, in Feb. 1946 (pub. in *World Affairs*, June 1947).

A comprehensive disquisition on sphere and map projections, with finely drawn steel engravings, will be found in P. Nicholson's *Popular Course of Pure and Mixed Mathematics*, 1825.

THE GREAT INTERNATIONAL MAP OF THE WORLD. This was first proposed by Prof. Penck at the International Geographical Congress at Bern in 1891. It is to the scale of one-millionth (1/1,000,000 or 1/M), and a kilometre of distance is therefore represented on the map by 1 millimetre. It is officially known as the *Carte du monde au millionième.* Since this original proposal a series of conferences has been held at various times from 1891 to 1928 at London, Geneva, Rome, Paris and London, and a comprehensive convention on points of detail was gradually and unanimously built up. Greenwich was adopted for the prime meridian, a colour scheme (*gamme*) for the representation of altitudes was agreed, and after much discussion a metric system for units, contours, and for the 'grid' was accepted. A central office for the world map was estab. at the H.Q. of the Brit. O.S. Dept at Southampton (since removed to Chessington, Surrey), and sheets could be consulted at the Royal Geographical Society; but no definite arrangements were made for a centralised publishing and selling agency. The projection of this international world map is a slightly modified form of the simply polyconic projection proposed by one of the Fr. delegates, M. Lallemand. It has all the properties necessary for such a map—that neighbouring sheets shall fit along their edges; that the representation of distances and bearings within the sheet shall be sensibly perfect; and that it shall be constructed with ease. Each sheet comprises 4° of lat. by 6° of long., each being plotted independently. The upper and lower parallels have the radius V cot. lat., where V in each case is the normal terminated by the minor axis. Instead of the central meridian (which is a straight line) being exactly to scale the meridians 2° to the E. and W. of it are true to scale, the object of this device being to reduce the maximum error. The meridians themselves are divided equally and the inner parallels join the appropriate points on the meridian. The normal vertical interval of contours is 100 metres. The international world map is generally referred to by the symbol 1/M—but the system of numbering and lettering the sheets is complicated. On this map Great Britain falls on no less than 7 sheets. To avoid this inconvenience the Brit. O.S. decided to produce a special ed. in 2 sheets, each 26¼ in. by 26¼ in., and in this form one is better able to appreciate the real merit of the international map. The system of layer colouring brings out the relief with great clearness. Communications are very well delineated, prin. roads being shown by strong red lines and secondary roads by fine red lines. Railways are shown in black, double and single lines and narrow gauge and light railways being distinguished. The international co-operative effort involved in the preparation of the 1/M international world map was interrupted by the two world wars—and its progress since 1919 has been disappointing. The 30 or 40 publishing estabs. concerned have not always been consistent in conforming strictly to the conventions agreed; but the map is beginning to be very useful as it becomes more complete and its merits better recognised, especially in relation to peace conferences, to UNESCO and to other international organisations. The former offices of the Central Bureau, with their contents, including the whole of the collection of the international 1/M map series, were destroyed during the Second World War. In 1952 the Central Bureau was transferred to the Cartographic Office of the Dept of Social Affairs, U.N., New York.

REPRESENTATION OF HILL FEATURES. A difficulty in cartography is to show hill features on a flat surface. The earlier M. either did not attempt to do so, or represented them by 'mole-hills' drawn on the map. These showed approximate positions, but little else. The idea of contours was introduced by M. S. Cruqius in 1728. They may be considered as successive coastlines at equal vertical intervals, if the landscape were to sink into the sea. It is possible to obtain an accurate mental picture from a contour map, as well as to deduce mathematically exact information; but it may involve detailed study and requires previous education in map-reading. To render hill features visible at a glance and without special training 'hachures' were devised by L. C. Müller in 1788. They are lines crossing the contours at right angles, their thickness varying with the slope. The disadvantage in the older M. was that, in hilly country, the black hachures concealed other features and names. Hachures belonged to the days of delicate and expensive engraving upon copper and are rapidly becoming obsolete. Excellent examples of the system, however, are to be seen in the old engraved sheets of the 1-in. O.S. M. of the U.K., and it survives on a few modern colour-printed M., but hill shading is more generally used. J. G. Bartholomew (of the celebrated firm of cartographers, Messrs John Bartholomew & Son) was responsible for the now universally recognised way of portraying the relief of the earth's surface: the introduction into Britain of hypsometric (or contour) colouring.

LAYER MAPS' Layer M., in which the spaces between different contours are tinted in different colours, were first constructed by Carl Ritter in 1806. Contour M. immediately became easy to visualise. Improvements in the mechanical processes of colour printing, and the use of transparent colours, have led to a great development of layer M. The system of using colours in the order of the spectrum, now almost universal, was introduced by E. G. Ravenstein in his map of Ben Nevis. In some of the finest examples of modern cartography the layer system is supplemented by hill shading in transparent colours, giving the effect of a relief map. The main drawback to such M. is the cost of printing. The specimen plate attached to the report of the International Map Conference of 1913 was printed at the Brit. War Office. It is a masterpiece of layer printing.

MAPS OF THE ORDNANCE SURVEY. For the hist. and functions of this institution in Great Britain see ORDNANCE SURVEY. For convenience in production the M. pub. by the O.S. are classified as (1) small scale—up to 1 in. to 1 m.; (2) medium scale—2½ in. and 6 in. to 1 m.; and (3) large scale, about 25 in. and 50 in. to 1 m. Normally the line between 'maps' and 'plans' is drawn just below the 6 in., everything smaller in scale being known as a map. The ¼-in. map has been for many years the standard map for motoring. The usefulness of these has been greatly increased by a rearrangement of the sheet lines, by showing the Ministry of Transport road numbers and classification, and adding the national grid (q.v.). Separate administrative M. for each co. are pub. for England and Wales. One-in. M. are the original standard M. of the O.S., and are valuable not only to the student of geography, but also are well suited for the needs of walkers, cyclists and motorists, and those who wish to understand and appreciate the details of the countryside. Footpaths, roads, rivers, streams, woods, high- and low-water marks are all delineated, and altitudes above mean sea level are shown along main roads, etc., while contours are drawn at 50-ft intervals, and the grid lines are 1 kilometre apart. Among the new features shown on the seventh series are National Trust areas, youth hostels, wireless masts and electricity transmission lines and telephone call-boxes in open country.

The new O.S. map, to a scale of 1/25,000, or about 2½ in. to 1 m., was produced as a result of the recommendations of the departmental committee set up in 1935, it having been considered that there was too wide a gap between the 1-in. and the 6-in. series. More than

2000 sheets had been pub. by 1966. The new map has been produced on National Grid sheet lines and is based on the old 6-in. map to which certain revision material has been added. It is obtainable in 2 styles, the fully coloured and the outline.

Special Ordnance Survey maps. In former days the main function of a map was to provide a guide for travellers, showing them where different places were, and how to get there by road, rail, or by ship. Today these functions have been enormously extended, and M. are now produced (in the Brit. Isles at least) to provide special visual information on a variety of matters other than communications, e.g. historic, political and economic, and administrative, of special interest to 'planners' of all kinds. First may be mentioned 4 'period' M.: (1) Rom. Britain, (2) Britain in the Dark Ages (AD 410–871), (3) Anct Britain and (4) Monastic Britain. These are on the 1/M scale, or 15·782 m. to 1 in., except Monastic Britain, which is on the 1/625,000 scale, and with the map can be obtained an explanatory pamphlet giving a list of reliable books on the period, a chronological table of important events and an index of names.

Among the remaining M. constituting the special 'Planning' Series, but to a scale of 1/625,000 or about 10 m. to the inch on the transverse Mercator projection and carrying the new National Grid lines at 10-kilometre intervals, are the following, sponsored by many gov. depts and by independent research organisations for planning purposes: base M., administrative areas, land classification, land utilisation, types of farming, grasslands, pop. density, pop. of urb. areas, geological, topographical, coalfields, iron-mines and quarries, iron and steel works, roads, railways (including underground), electrical statutory supply areas (both power companies and joint boards, etc.), gas supply, pop. changes and migrations. Other special M., to varying scales, include the Channel Is., the Scilly Isles, the Royal Botanic Gardens at Kew and the 1¼ Million of Great Britain (on one sheet).

Relief maps. These are models produced by sev. methods from contoured M. In the peg method heights above sea level are represented by pegs of appropriate length set up along the contours; a suitable medium is packed between them so as to create a smooth surface. In the layer method contours are drawn on separate cardboard sheets and cut out; these are placed above each other and clay or plasticine used to make an even surface. In the section method vertical, parallel sections are drawn on cardboard, profiles cut out, thickened with plasticine and arranged in order. The surface is smoothed, streams marked in, etc. From originals made by these methods moulds may be constructed from which cement or plaster casts can be taken. Geological features, strata, etc., may be shown by colour. Some vertical exaggeration as compared with the horizontal scale is usually necessary. The project for a 6-in. to 1-m. relief map of England and Wales, proposed in 1949 by

Sir Clive Morrison Bell, envisaged a model 100 yds long, showing all natural features, roads, etc., and divided by gangways for inspection.

AIR SURVEY MAPS. Among the recommendations contained in the final report (dated 3 Feb. 1938) of the departmental committee on the O.S. (commonly known as the Davidson Committee) was one to the effect that short-term contracts to civil firms, for aerial photographs, should not be continued as a permanent policy but that the gov. should consider the formation, as soon as possible, of a special air survey unit capable of satisfying the requirements of the O.S. This recommendation was accepted, and aerial photographs for the O.S. are now supplied either by the Ministry of Transport and Civil Aviation Flying unit, or by contract with air survey charter firms. Considerable work has been done in the aerial photography of central London streets and blitzed buildings, and in airphoto mosaics and obliques by commercial air photographers. *See also* CHART; CONTOUR; NATIONAL GRID; ORDNANCE SURVEY; PHOTOGRAPHY; SCALE.

Bibliography. Brig. H. S. L. Winterbotham, *A Key to Maps*, 1936; W. W. Jervis, *The World in Maps* (2700 BC to the present day), 1936; A. R. Hinks, *Map Projection*, 1936, and *Maps and Survey*, 1942; T. Pickles, *Map Reading*, 1937, 1948; Col. Sir Charles Close, *Text-book of Topographical Surveying*, 1905; T. W. Birch, *Maps: Topographical and Statistical*, 1949; The Royal Geographical Society's *Journals*; a paper by A. E. Young, *Some Investigations into the Theory of Map Projection* (pub. by the Royal Geographical Society); the O.S. booklets on various map scales and Phoenix House (pub.), *An Air Photo Atlas of London. (See Plate.)*

Maqrizi, Taqi al-din Ahmad ibn Ali (1364–1442), Arabic historian and geographer, *b.* Cairo. His most important work is a description of Egypt, including the natural features of the land, customs and beliefs of the inhab., accounts of the mosques, colleges and churches in Cairo, and an outline political hist. He also wrote a hist. of the Fatimid caliphs, another of the Mameluke sultans, and various pamphlets, including one on weights and measures.

Maquis, *see* GUERRILLAS.

Mar, Earl of, *see* COCHRANE, ROBERT.

Mar, John Erskine, 11th **Earl of** (1675–1752), Jacobite leader, famed as the leader of the 1715 rebellion. He continually changed sides politically, being in turn Whig and Tory as it was advantageous to him, this practice earning him the name of 'Bobbing John'. As a Whig he assisted in the union of Scotland and England. After the union, and on the overthrow of the Whig gov., he again became a Tory, and was made secretary of state for Scotland. Later, on the accession of George I, he again tried to keep his position by changing sides, but failing on this occasion to obtain favour he lost his office. He returned to Scotland in disgrace, started the rebellion at Braemar and soon had a large and enthusiastic following. However, his long delay in the highlands enabled the Duke of Argyll to check him when he finally advanced at the battle of Stirling. He escaped with the Pretender to France. He was deprived of the earldom of M. for his part in the rising, the Pretender, however, creating him Duke of M.

Mar, name of an old Scottish dist and forest in the S. of the co. of Aberdeen. It lies between the R.s Don and Dee, and is divided into Cromar, Braemar and Midmar. W. of Braemar vil., at the head of the Dee valley, stretches the forest of M., originally a royal hunting ground in the 12th cent. The forest has been considerably thinned, but Glen Tilt and Glen Dee still afford scenery of great beauty and grandeur.

Mar del Plata, tn and major tourist resort in Argentina, on the coast near Cape Corrientes and 230 m. SE. of Buenos Aires. Agric. products are processed, there are sev. fish-canning factories, and there is good coastal fishing. Pop. 150,000.

Mar Saba, deep canyon on the E. side of the plateau of Judaea, Kingdom of Jordan, where it abruptly slopes to the Lower Jordan and the Dead Sea. The Arabs use the natural caves in the *wadis* for camps for their families. Between Bethlehem and the Dead Sea at the head of the canyon lies the orthodox monastery of St Sabbas (or M. S.), an anct settlement of ascetics estab. in the 5th cent. Women are not admitted to the monastery, which stands precipitously on the side of the canyon, but are able to overlook it from a medieval tower outside the porch.

Marabou, large W. African stork (*Leptoptilos crumeniferus*). Its feathers and those of the related adjutant (q.v.) are used chiefly for trimming feminine headgear.

Marabouts, class of religious saints or holy men among the Berbers (q.v.) of N. Africa, held in high esteem. They held Spain and Morocco for a considerable period. The Almohads put an end to their temporal dominion, but they continued to exercise spiritual superiority over the Muslim Negroes of Barbary.

Maracaibo, port of Venezuela, on NW. shore of Lake M. M. is cap. of the state of Zulia. It is a handsome tn with a hot but healthy, though humid, climate. M. owes its present importance to the oilfields centred in and around Lake M., but it also exports sugar, coffee, cocoa. It is the second city in Venezuela and has a univ. It has good air connections with most Venezuelan tns. M. is now connected with the rest of Venezuela by a 6-m.-long bridge across the neck of the Lake. Dredging of the sand bars in this neck has enabled M. to develop rapidly as a seagoing port during the past decade. Pop. 433,000.

Maracaibo, Lake and Gulf. The lake of M., in the N. of Venezuela, is about 130 m. in length and 70 m. in breadth. It is connected with the gulf of the same name by a strait 34 m. in length and from 5 to 10 m. in breadth which is now bridged for road traffic. The gulf is a wide inlet of the Caribbean Sea, 150 m. from E. to W., and about 75 m. from N. to S. The oilfields in and around Lake M. produce about 70 per cent of Venezuela's oil production.

Maracay, cap of Aragua state, Venezuela, near the NE. shore of Lake Valencia. M. is mainly important as a centre of military institutions and is sometimes called 'the Aldershot of Venezuela'. It has 2 military airfields. Main industry is textiles. Pop. 135,000.

Maragha, dist and tn of Azarbaijan, Persia. The tn is 50 m. S. of Tabriz. An observatory was founded on an adjacent hill by the Mongol, Hulagu Khan. M. is noted for its fine marble. Grain, rice, cotton, sugar-beet, vines and fruit are produced in the dist. Pop. of tn 36,600.

Maraka, see NEW DONGOLA.

Maramures, see under CRISANA.

Maranhão, maritime state of NE. Brazil, bordered in the N. by the Atlantic, M. forms a transitional area between the semi-arid NE. region and the Amazon basin with its tropical climate and vegetation. In the S. and SW. it is mountainous or hilly upland with scrub forest and dry climate; here stockraising is the main economic activity. Towards the N. the land surface becomes lower and flatter and the rainfall greater; here stock-raising is supported by cultivated crops; on the coastal belt the land is flat with thick forest and tropical rainfall. Cotton, sugar, rice, vegetable oils, maize and mandioca are the main crops. M. is distinguished by its proliferation of babacu palms from which a high-grade vegetable oil is produced. Gold, bauxite and other minerals are produced. Numerous rivs. flow S.–N. through the State, many of them flowing into the Bays of São Marcos and São José which are separated by an is. on which is São Luís, the cap. of the state. Area: 128,278 sq. m. Pop. 2,492,139.

Marañón, see AMAZON.

Maranta, genus of perennials of tropical America (family Marantaceae), with tuberous or creeping rhizomes, and ornamental leaves, green above and grey, purple or rose below. *M. arundinacea* is the source of W. Indian arrowroot.

Maraş or **Marash,** tn of Asiatic Turkey, the chief tn of the il of M., E. of the Jihun R., at the foot of Mt Taurus. There is a large trade in carpets and embroideries. The name Marasi is found in Assyrian inscriptions, and the tn, under the name of Germanicia-Marasion, played an important part in Byzantine hist. Pop. (il) 389,857 (tn) 54,447 (1960).

Maraschino, see LIQUEUR.

Marat, Jean Paul (1743–93), Fr. revolutionary, b. Boudry, Neuchâtel. In 1759 M. went to Bordeaux for 2 years to study medicine. From Bordeaux he went to Paris, from there to Holland and finally to London, where he went into practice. In 1773 he wrote his *Philosophical Essay on Man*, and in 1774 he pub. *The Chains of Slavery*. In 1775 he was made an M.D. of St Andrews. He was now famous as a doctor and in 1777 he became brevet physician to the Comte d'Artois's guards. In 1789 he pub. his first jour., *L'Ami du Peuple*, and soon abandoned his profession for a political career. He was imprisoned sev. times for his revolutionary principles, and while hiding in the Paris sewers from his pursuers contracted a painful skin disease. He took a leading part in the struggle between the Jacobins and the Girondists. After the rep. was declared he began to edit *Le Journal de la République française*. He was one of those who were implacable towards the king, and demanded his death for the good of the people. The skin disease from which he suffered was so painful that only by lying in warm baths could he obtain relief. While sitting in his bath writing his jour. he was stabbed to death by Charlotte Corday (q.v.), a Girondist. His works were ed. by A. Vermorel in 1869, and *Correspondance* by C. Villay in 1908. *See* E. Defrance, *Charlotte Corday et la mort de Marat* (2nd ed.), 1909; *also* lives by E. B. Bax, 1900, and P. Compton, 1935.

Marathas, *see* MAHRATTAS.

Marathi Language, *see* INDO-EUROPEAN LANGUAGES.

Marathon, tn of anct Greece, in Attica, on a plain between the mts and the sea-coast, about 20 m. NE. of Athens. It is famous in mythology for the killing of a monstrous bull by Theseus (q.v.), and in hist. for the victory of the Athenians over the Persians. The date generally given is 490 BC; but the *Cambridge Ancient History*, iv, 245, has 'probably the 21st September, 491 BC'.

Marathon Race, road-race included in the Olympic Games (q.v.) at Athens in 1896, at the suggestion of Prof. Michel Bréal of the Sorbonne, to commemorate the legendary exploit of Pheidippides (q.v.), who was said to have run to Athens after the battle of Marathon in 490 BC to bring the news of victory over the Persian army. In fact, early accounts of the battle mention a courier, Pheidippides, who ran from Athens to Sparta (*c.* 140 m.) in 2 days requesting reinforcements, while later authors credit Thersippus or Eucles with the run from Marathon to Athens (about 24 m.) after the battle had been won.

The M. R. has always been an important feature of the Olympic Games, and has become accepted as a standard event in international athletics. At first the distance varied between 24 and 26 m., but it was eventually standardised at 26 m. 385 yds—an odd measurement chosen because this was the exact distance covered in the Olympic race in 1908. Much of the glamour surrounding the M. R. arises from dramatic incidents which have attracted much publicity over the years since the inaugural race, which was won by a Gk shepherd, Spiridon Loues. There was the sensational finish to the 1908 Olympic race, Dorando Pietri of Italy being assisted over the finishing line by officials after collapsing twice in the last few hundred yards; inevitably he was disqualified. In 1954 there was a similar incident at the Empire Games in Vancouver, involving Jim Peters of England, who collapsed sev. times in the final stages, to be carried eventually from the track, semiconscious, only 200 yds from the finish. On a happier note, there was the victory of Émil Zátopek in the Olympic marathon of 1952, his debut at this event and his third Olympic title

within 8 days. In 1960 and 1964 the Olympic champion was Abebe Bikila of Ethiopia—the only man ever to win the Olympic title twice. *See* ATHLETICS; OLYMPIC GAMES.

Maratta, or **Maratti, Carlo** (1625–1713), It. painter and engraver, *b.* Camerano. His Madonnas were particularly numerous and admired. He was entrusted by Clement XI with the charge and restoration of the frescoes of Raphael (whom he admired and copied) in the Vatican, and was commissioned by Louis XIV to paint his celebrated picture of 'Daphne'.

Maravedi, old Sp. coin in use until the end of the 18th cent. Originally the name was used for Moorish coins, both silver and gold, but after 1494 it was only used for a small copper coin, in value about 7 centimes ($\frac{3}{4}d.$), and a silver coin ($1\frac{1}{2}d.$).

Marazion, or **Market Jew,** fishing tn of Cornwall, England, on Mount's Bay, 3 m. E. of Penzance. At low tide it is united to St Michael's Mount (q.v.) by a causeway of boulders. It was burnt by the French in 1513, and again in 1549 during the Arundel rebellion in the reign of Edward VI. Horticulture is the chief occupation. Pop. 1300.

Marbeck, or **Merbecke, John** (*c.* 1510–85), church musician and author. He composed the first book of chants for use in the Anglican Church, *Booke of Common Praier Noted*, 1550. He compiled the first concordance of the Eng. Bible, 1550.

Marbella, Sp. tn in the prov. of Málaga, on the Mediterranean, a popular tourist resort. There are iron-mines near by. The port has a trade in oranges, fish and wine. Pop. 5300.

Marble, crystalline form of limestone. The term is usually applied to those forms of limestone or dolomite which are sufficiently compact to take a high polish. A characteristic M. consists of calcite granules of uniform size closely packed together. When broken the fracture presents a multitude of glistening facets, owing to the granules breaking along their rhombohedral cleavage planes. The colour is usually white, but markings of many hues and patterns are produced by the presence of impurities. All M.s are probably metamorphosed limestones. The metamorphosis has been brought about by great heat and pressure below the surface of the earth. Much crushing, folding and twisting have often taken place, so that streaks or bands of impurities in the original limestone frequently take on peculiar shapes. The economic importance of M.s is derived from the adaptability of the finer forms to uses in statuary, and of the other forms to more or less ornamental architecture. Many fine M.s were known to the ancients, of which Pentelic and Parian M.s are the most famous. The former was obtained from Mt Pentelicus in Attica, and served as the material for the Elgin M.s, now lodged in the Brit. Museum. Parian M. was quarried in the Isle of Paros; the Venus de Medici was carved in stone from this source. The M. used by medieval and modern sculptors is that found in the neighbourhood of Carrara in

Italy. Architectural M.s are quarried from the Devonian system in Devon. In the U.S.A. M. is quarried in Tennessee, New York, Massachusetts and California.

Marble Arch, London landmark by the NE. corner of Hyde Park. It was designed by John Nash (q.v.) in 1828, in the style of the Arch of Constantine, as the gateway to Buckingham Palace at the order of George IV, and moved to its present position near the site of the old Tyburn (q.v.) gallows in 1851.

Marbles, known in Scotland as 'bools', are small balls of clay, glass or marble, used for a variety of children's playground games. M. as toys seem to date back to anct Greece and Rome, and marble games were played by adults in and around Eng. public-houses during the 18th cent. Some technicians roll their M., others place a marble on the forefinger and flick it off with the thumb; a third method is: catch the tip of your right thumb with your middle finger, place the marble just above the first thumb-joint, hold it in place with the forefinger and let fly.

There are a large number of marble games. The simplest is as follows: One player rolls his marble, and when it rests the other tries to strike with his own. If he succeeds he pockets his opponent's marble; if he fails his opponent rolls at him. An alternative type of game is played like this: A chalk circle is drawn and each player puts in a marble. Players shoot in rotation to knock a marble out of base. Anyone who succeeds pockets it or a substitute provided by its owner, according to the rules. Each player's first shot is from a starting-line, the second from wherever his shooting marble comes to rest, unless that is in the base, in which case it stays there as an additional target. When the base is emptied, players aim at shooting one another's M. Other types of game involve shooting at holes in the ground or at arches in a board.

Marbling, imitation in paint—on wood, stone, metal, plaster, canvas or even paper—of the natural veining and colour of marble. The practice is very anct. *See* BOOKBINDING.

Marburg: 1. Tn in Slovenia, Yugoslavia, *see* MARIBOR.

2. Ger. tn in the *Land* of Hessen, on the Lahn, 56 m. NNE. of Wiesbaden. The 13th cent. Elisabethkirche was built to contain the tomb of St Elizabeth (q.v.) of Hungary, whose remains, however, are no longer in M.; Frederick the Great (q.v.) was also once buried in the church, which is now the resting place of Hindenburg (q.v., *and see* TANNENBERG). The univ. dates from 1527. There is an 11th cent. castle, the scene in 1529 of a conference between Luther and Zwingli (qq.v.). Pottery, photographic goods and tobacco are manuf. Pop. 44,900.

Marc, Franz (1880–1916), Ger. painter, *b.* Munich, associated with the 'Blue Rider' group (q.v.). He studied at Munich and was influenced by Fr. post-Impressionist painting. He is noted for his paintings of horses in which he used brilliant colour. He *d.* in action in the First World War.

Marcabru, or **Marcabrun,** one of the earliest of the troubadours (q.v.), fl. *c.* 1130–50. He was a Gascon of humble origins (tradition has it that he was a foundling). Many of his poems are in a satirical, moralising and realist vein that contrasts sharply with the conventional treatment of courtly love that is characteristic of many later troubadours. One of his best known poems deals with the crusade against the Moors in Spain. *See* J. M. L. Dejeanne's ed. of M.'s poems, 1909, and S. Errante, *Marcabru e le fonti sacre dell'antica lirica romanza,* 1948.

Marcantonio, or **Marcantonio Raimondi** (*d.* 1534), It. engraver, *b.* Bologna. Until 1510 he worked as a goldsmith and engraver at Bologna, under Francia. He was also influenced by Dürer, whose engravings he copied. From 1510 until the taking of Rome by the Spaniards (1527) he lived there, engraving many works by Raphael and his pupils. M. was the first and perhaps the most eminent of reproductive engravers, but he may be called an original artist inasmuch as he elaborated and interpreted Raphael's drawings, Raphael encouraging his independent skill.

Marcasite, mineral consisting of iron disulphide (FeS_2). It is chemically indentical with iron pyrites and was formerly looked upon as a variety of pyrites. M. is yellowish-brown and has a brilliant lustre. It is mined at Littmitz near Carlsbad.

Marceau, François Séverin Desgraviers (1769–1796), Fr. general, *b.* Chartres. He took part in the attack on the Bastille (1791), in the defence of Verdun (1792) and in the wars of the Vendée, and commanded at Fleurus (1794). He was in command of the 1st Div. of the Army of the Rhine, and fought at Lahn and at Altenkirchen where he was killed.

Marcel, Gabriel (1889–), Fr. dramatist and idealist philosopher. His philosophy, which has been described as the Christian expression of existentialism (q.v.), owes much to Bergson, Nietzsche and Dostoyevsky. M. differs from Sartre and other atheist existentialists in that despair and anguish at the absurdity of life are no part of his attitude. For him as for other Catholic existentialists despair is no more than a transient temptation; hope is the texture of his life, and is its essential condition. Among his plays are *La Chapelle ardente,* 1925, *Un Homme de Dieu,* 1929, *Le Fanal,* 1936, *Le Dard,* 1936, *Rome n'est plus dans Rome,* 1951, *Les Coeurs avides,* 1953, and *Croissez et multipliez,* 1955. His philosophical works include *Être et avoir,* 1935, *Le Mystère de L'Être,* 1951–2, *Présence et Immortalité,* 1959.

Marcello, Benedetto (1686–1739), It. composer and author, *b.* Venice. While holding various official positions he devoted himself to music and poetry. His masterpiece is the *Estro poetico-armonico,* 1724–6, a musical setting of the first 50 psalms as paraphrased into Italian by Girolamo Giustiniani. He also wrote *canzoni* in the madrigal style, instrumental concertos, an oratorio and an opera. His pamphlet, *Il Teatro alla moda,* 1720, was a brillant satire on contemporary opera. *See* monographs by L. Busi, 1884, and A. d'Angeli, 1940; *also* E. Fondi,

La vita e l'opera letteraria del musicista Benedetto Marcello, 1909.

Marcellus, Marcus Claudius: 1. Rom. general (*c.* 268–208 BC), 5 times consul. In his 1st consulship (222) he killed in battle with his own hand Britomartus or Viridomarus, king of the Insubrian Gauls, whose spoils (*see* SPOLIA OPIMA) he dedicated in the temple of Jupiter Feretrius on the Capitoline, the 3rd and last time in Rom. hist. that this offering was made. During the 2nd Punic war (211 BC) M. captured Syracuse after a 2-year siege (*see* ARCHIMEDES). He fell in battle against Hannibal near Venusia.

2. Son of Claudius M. (consul 50 BC) and Octavia, sister of Augustus. In 25 BC he was adopted by the emperor and married the latter's daughter, Julia. In 23 BC M. *d.* suddenly at Baiae, supposedly poisoned by Livia. He is the subject of a famous passage in Virgil, *Aeneid*, vi. 860–86.

Marcellus, name of 2 popes:

Marcellus I, St, succeeded Marcellinus probably in May 308. He imposed such severe penances upon all Christians who had apostatised under persecution that he was banished by popular demand in 309, dying the same year.

Marcellus II, succeeded Julius III in 1555, but *d.* the same year. As Cardinal Cervini he presided over the Council of Trent. Palestrina composed a famous mass for his coronation, but he was never crowned.

March, Auziàs (*c.* 1395–*c.* 1460), Catalan poet, *b.* Valencia. His poems show the influence of the troubadours as well as of Dante and Petrarch. His chief works are *Cants d'amor* and *Cants de mort.*

March, Earl of, *see* MORTIMER, ROGER.

March, tn in the isle of Ely, Cambs, with a bi-weekly market. It is situated on the R. Nene, 81 m. N. of London. It manufs. a considerable variety of farm tools and has engineering works. There are extensive marshalling yards, and the tn is an important railway junction. Pop. 13,119.

March, boundary, used more particularly of the Welsh M.s and Scottish M.s, the border countries between England and Wales and Scotland respectively. The Earl of March took his title from the Welsh M.s, and in the Middle Ages the governors of the border dists were known as wardens of the M.s The name is allied to the Ger. *Mark* (q.v.). *See also* BOUNDS, BEATING THE.

March, first month of the Rom. year, and the third according to our present calendar, consists of 31 days. It was considered as the first month of the year in England until the change of style in 1752, and the legal year was reckoned from 25th M., as the fiscal year still is. The A.-S. called it *Hlyd monath,* stormy month, and *Hraed monath,* rugged month. There is a proverb which represents M. as borrowing 3 days from April (*see* BORROWING DAYS). *See also* CALENDAR.

March, in music, is, as its name indicates, a musical composition intended to regulate the step of marching troops. M.s are either slow or quick; funeral M.s come into the former category. M.s also appear in operas, cantatas,

instrumental suites and other works in sev. movements (e.g. Mozart's cassations).

Marchand, Jean Baptiste (1863–1934), Fr. soldier, *b.* Thoissey, Ain. He was commissioned in 1886 and saw active service in Senegal (1888–91). In the course of numerous explorations in the African interior, he estab. the post of Fashoda (q.v.) on the White Nile (1898). His refusal to withdraw on a demand made by the British led to an international crisis. He was called home to report, and Fashoda was evacuated in his absence. He commanded colonial troops in the First World War, becoming a general of div. in 1917.

Marche, former prov. of central France, now comprised in the depts of Creuse and Haute-Vienne (qq.v.). It was originally a border dist of the duchy of Aquitaine (q.v.), and was united to the Fr. crown in 1527. Cap. Guéret (q.v.).

Marche, Le, *see* MARCHES, THE.

Marchena, Sp. tn in the prov. of Sevilla. It has a palace and a 15th cent. church. There are sulphur springs. Pop. 17,000.

Marches, The (It. **Le Marche**), region (*compartimento*) of central Italy, comprising the provs. of Pesaro-Urbino, Ancona, Macerata and Ascoli Piceno (qq.v.). It is bounded N. by Emilia-Romagna, W. by Umbria, S. by Abruzzi e Molise, and E. by the Adriatic (qq.v.). The region is largely occupied by ranges of the central Apennines (q.v.), was once a border dist (*mark*, q.v.) of the empire of the Carlovingians (q.v.), and later part of the States of the Church (q.v.). Limestone, sulphur, wine, silk and cereals are produced. The chief tn is Ancona. Area 3742 sq. m.; pop. 1,347,300.

Marches, Riding the, *see* BOUNDS, BEATING THE.

Marchfeld, plain in Austria, NE. of Vienna, the scene of the defeat of Ottakar II of Bohemia (*see* BOHEMIA, *History*) by Rudolf I (q.v.) in 1278, and of the battles of Aspern and Wagram (q.v.).

Marchienne-au-Pont, tn in the prov. of Hainaut, Belgium, 2 m. W. of Charleroi, on the R. Sambre. It is one of the most important iron and steel producing tns of Belgium. Pop. 21,000.

Marcianus, or **Marcian** (*c.* AD 391–457), emperor of the E., *b.* Thrace. He entered the army at an early age and served under Aspar, whom he accompanied to Africa on a campaign against the Vandals, in 431, and under Ardaburius. On the death of the Emperor Theodosius the Younger (450), his widow, Pulcheria, offered M. her hand in marriage, and he was crowned the same year (*see* CORONATION). During his reign he repelled attacks upon Syria and Egypt (452), and quelled disturbances on the Armenian frontier (456); he also refused payment of tribute to Attila, reformed the finances and repeopled the devastated dists.

Marcinelle, tn in the prov. of Hainaut, Belgium, 2 m. SW. of Charleroi. It has coalmines and blast furnaces, and manufs. steel goods and chemicals. Pop. 25,000.

Marcion, founder of the Marcionites, an ascetic Gnostic sect, was the son of a bishop of

Sinope on the Black Sea. The gospel of Christ, according to him, consisted in free love of the Good; the Mosaic system, with its motives of reward and punishments, was mere legality (*see* GNOSTICS). M. entirely rejected the O.T., and of the N.T. all but a few epistles and part of the gospel of St Luke. He is mentioned by Irenaeus in *Adversus Haereses* (*c.* 180), but our chief source of information is Tertullian's *Adversus Marcionem* (207). *See* E. Walder, *Marcion and the Roman Church*, 1929.

Marco Polo, *see* POLO, MARCO.

Marcomanni, 'men of the border', a Germanic tribe of the Suebic race, first mentioned by Caesar as dwelling between the Danube and the Rhine. Attacked by the Cimbri and Teutones, they moved (*c.* 100 BC) to the upper and middle Main. After an attack in 9 BC by the elder Drusus (q.v.), they emigrated to Bohemia and parts of Bavaria, where, under their prince Maroboduus, they estab. a powerful kingdom. Later, with the Quadi and other tribes, they were at war with Rome (*see* MARCUS AURELIUS) until Commodus purchased peace in AD 180. *See also* SUEVI.

Marconi, Guglielmo, Marchese (1874–1937), It. inventor of radio telegraphy, *b.* Bologna, son of Giuseppe M. and Annie Jameson, an Irish woman. Educ. at Bologna Univ. where he started his research before migrating to England. He estab. radio communication between France and England in 1899, and from Poldhu (Cornwall) to St John's (Newfoundland), over 2000 m., in 1901. The development of numerous other links followed soon after. In 1909 he shared the Nobel prize for physics. At the Peace Conference of the 1914–8 war he was It. plenipotentiary, and in 1929 was made Marchese and an It. Senator. He became president of the It. royal academy in 1930, and a member of the council of the Fascist party. *See* J. de Boinod, *Marconi, Master of Space*, 1936; lives by B. L. Jacob and D. M. Collier, 1937; S. Epstein and B. Williams, 1943.

Marcq-en-Barœul, Fr. tn in the dept of Nord, on the Marcq. It has metallurgical, textile and food-stuff manufs. Pop. 30,000.

Marcus Antoninus, *see* COMMODUS.

Marcus Aurelius (his full name after 139 was **Marcus Aelius Aurelius Antoninus**), Rom. emperor (AD 161–180), *b.* Rome in AD 121. His father, Annius Verus, who was of Sp. extraction, had been elevated to patrician rank by Vespasian. In 138 Hadrian adopted as his heir Antoninus Pius (q.v.) on condition that he in turn adopted Marcus and Lucius Ceionius Commodus (better known as Lucius Aelius Verus). M. A. married Pius's daughter Faustina, received the title of Caesar in 139 and was consul in the following year. Educ. privately by the rhetoricians Herodes Atticus and Marcus Cornelius Fronto, he abandoned the study of literature (*c.* 146) for that of philosophy and law under the Stoics Rusticus and Maecianus respectively. Stoicism, in fact, tempered by a naturally gentle disposition, remained the dominant influence of his life.

M. A. succeeded Antoninus Pius in 161 and admitted Verus as his partner in the empire. His entire reign was a struggle to protect the Rom. frontiers. From 162 to 165 Verus had nominal charge of the war against Vologeses III of Parthia, and his troops brought back a plague which spread throughout the empire. During the year 167–8 M. A. and Verus were engaged in hostilities against the Marcomanni in Noricum and Pannonia. In 169 Verus *d.*; the Marcomanni resumed hostilities, and were not driven from Pannonia until 172. During these 3 years M. A. had his H.Q. at Carnuntum, and in 174 he won the victory of 'the thundering legion' over the Quadi (*see* Gibbon, xvi). Next year M. A. received news that Avidius Cassius (who held the real command in the Parthian war) had revolted. He started for the E., but soon learned of the rebel's assassination. Meanwhile Faustina *d.* M. A. returned to Italy by way of Athens, where he did much to foster the intellectual life of the city, and celebrated a triumph at Rome in 176. It is uncertain what part, if any, M. A. himself played in the persecution of Christians which occurred in 177. In this latter year he once more took the field against the Germans. His efforts were on the whole successful, but he *d.* before achieving final victory. Notwithstanding his constant activity, M. A. found time to write his immortal *Meditations*, which embody the ideals of his philosophy (*see* the ed. by A. S. L. Farquharson (2 vols.), 1946). *See also* H. D. Sedgwick, *Marcus Aurelius*, 1921.

Marcy, William Learned (1786–1857), Amer. politician, *b.* Southbridge, Massachusetts, U.S.A. Educ. at Brown Univ., he practised law at Troy, New York. He came to the front as a Democratic politician and became one of the 'Albany regency' which was reputed to decide the policy of the party in New York state. He was a U.S. senator in 1831–2 and during his term uttered the famous phrase: 'To the victor belong the spoils of the enemy' (*see* Parton's *Life of Jackson*, vol. iii, 1860). He was governor of New York from 1833 to 1839; secretary of war under Polk, 1845–9, and secretary of state under Pierce, 1853–7.

Marcy, Mount, *see under* ADIRONDACK MOUNTAINS.

Mardi Gras ('fat' or 'meat' Tuesday), Fr. name for Shrove Tuesday (q.v.), the last day of fat living before Ash Wednesday and Lent (q.v.). Carnivals often take place on this day on the Continent, one of the best known being that held at Nice (q.v.).

Mardin, tn in the il of M., Anatolia, 54 m. SE. of Diarbekir. It has a picturesque position on the side of a hill, and is the transit point between E. Turkey and Iraq. Pop. (il) 353,411; (tn) 24,000 (1955).

Mardonius, Persian general, son-in-law of Darius I. He was sent by Darius in 492 BC to complete the settlement of Ionia, and to punish Eretria and Athens for their share in the Ionian revolt, but lost his fleet off Mt Athos while his land forces were partly annihilated on the march by Thracian tribes. On the succession of Xerxes in 485, however, he was again in favour, and was one of the chief instigators of the expedition against Greece. After the defeat of Salamis (480) he was left by Xerxes to conquer Greece, but was defeated and slain at the battle of Plataea (479).

Marduk (Merodach), god of Babylonia and Assyria, the Merodach of the O.T. and Bêl of the Apocrypha. He rose into prominence under Hammurabi (c. 1750 BC), who brought the upper and lower states of the Euphrates valley under one dominion and set up Babylon as his cap. Bêl of Babylon was invested with all the divine attributes of Enlil, the old Bêl of Nippur. He was lord and light of heaven and earth, in whose hands were the decrees of fate, and from early times had been a god of the morning light and of the spring sun. The Babylonian new year's feast commemorated his victory over the primeval being and rebel Tiamat and the monsters of her creation, and his marriage with Sarpanitum, the Succoth-Benoth of 2 Kings xvii. 30. M. was worshipped as a god of battle by the Babylonian kings, and some scholars identify him with Nimrod; others, however, identify the latter with Gilgamesh (q.v.). He was the son of Ea, the third of the great Babylonian triad of gods, the others being Anu and Enlil, and he partook of his father's powers; he acted as intermediary between mankind and the latter, and like Ea was a god of the exorcist cult. He himself was the father of Nabu, or Nebo of the O.T., and was identified with the planet Jupiter. The creation legend ends with a hymn of praise to this god, on whom innumerable titles of honour are bestowed. *See* A. Heidel, *The Babylonian Genesis*, 1951, and S. H. Hooke, *The Religion of Assyria and Babylonia*, 1953.

Maré, *see* LOYALTY ISLANDS.

Mare Caspium, or **Hyrcanium**, *see* CASPIAN SEA.

Mare Internum, *see* MEDITERRANEAN SEA.

Maree, Loch, Ross and Cromarty, Scotland, a large and beautiful lake, $13\frac{1}{2}$ m. long by $\frac{1}{2}$ to 2 m. broad. It is surrounded by magnificent mt scenery and studded with is. It is drained by the R. Ewe into Loch Ewe.

Marek (formerly **Dupnitza**), tn of Bulgaria, in Sofia prov., on the Dzherman at the foot of the Rila Mts, 32 m. SSW. of Sofia (q.v.). It has a trade in agric. produce, wine and tobacco. Pop. 19,000.

Maremma, marshy region of central Italy, in the S. part of Tuscany and the N. part of Lazio (qq.v.), extending along the coast of the Tyrrhenian Sea (q.v.). It was once extremely unhealthy, but has been extensively drained and settled. Area about 1000 sq. m.

Marengo: 1. Vil. of Piedmont, Italy, situated about 2 m. SE. of Alessandria. It was the scene of Napoleon's victory over the Austrians in 1800.
2. Tn of Algeria, 38 m. WSW. of Algiers. Pop. (com.) 8000.

Marenzio, Luca (1553–99), It. composer, *b.* Coccaglio, near Brescia. He occupied the position of *maestro* to Cardinal d'Este in 1579–86, after which he was at Venice and Florence, and in 1595 went to Poland and was employed by Sigismund III. About the year

1599, however, he returned to Rome and became organist at the pontifical chapel. His most important works are his madrigals, of which there are 9 vols. He is the most important of the It. madrigalists.

Mareotis, Lake, *see* BIRKET-EL-MARIUT.

Mare's-tail, or *Hippuris*, genus of glabrous aquatic herbs (family Hippuridaceae). The only Brit. species, *H. vulgaris*, occurs in ditches and stagnant water. M.s are sometimes planted beside ornamental waters.

Marettimo, *see* AEGADIAN ISLANDS.

Mareuil, Arnaut de, *see* ARNAUT DE MAREUIL.

Margai, Sir Milton (Augustine Strieby) (1895–1964), African politician, educ. at the Univ. College of Freetown and at Durham Univ. He was gov. medical officer in Sierra Leone 1928–50, being knighted in 1950. In 1953 he became Minister of Health in Sierra Leone, and from 1954 was first minister. From 1960 until his death he was Prime Minister: he led Sierra Leone's peaceful progress to dominion status in 1961, and was a moderating influence on his contemporaries in other African states. His brother Albert became Premier on his death.

Margam, *see* PORT TALBOT.

Margaret, St (*d.* 1093), Scottish saint and queen, sister of Edgar Atheling. On the accession of William the Conqueror to the Eng. throne Edgar Atheling, his mother, and his sisters M. and Christina, took refuge in Scotland, and M. married Malcolm III of Scotland in 1070. M. was deeply religious and influenced her husband to reform abuses in the Church. She when she heard the news of her husband's death and was formally canonised in 1250. *See* Lucy Menzies, *St Margaret, Queen of Scotland*, 1925.

Margaret (1353–1412), Queen of Denmark, Norway and Sweden, and daughter of Valdemar IV of Denmark. At the age of 10 she was married to King Haakon VI of Norway, and on his death in 1380 the whole of Norway was placed in her hands. Her son Olaf, whose election as King of Denmark she had procured, *d.* 7 years later, thus enabling her to secure this throne too for herself. Shortly afterwards she defeated Albert, the Swedish king, and obtained possession of the throne of Sweden. She combined Denmark, Sweden and Norway into one kingdom (effected formally by the Union of Kalmar, 1397), and was called the Semiramis of the N. *See* M. Hill, *Margaret of Denmark*, 1898.

Margaret, Duchess of Burgundy (1446–1503), sister of Edward IV of England. In 1468 she married Charles of Burgundy and was influential in obtaining financial help from her husband for Edward in 1470. After Henry VII's accession the Burgundian court became a refuge for discontented Yorkist exiles, M. using every opportunity to plot against Henry, even encouraging the pretenders Perkin Warbeck and Lambert Simnel.

Margaret, the 'Maid of Norway', *see* FAIR MAID OF NORWAY.

Margaret of Anjou (1430–82), Queen of England, daughter of René the Good of Anjou. She married Henry VI in 1445. M. of A. acted on behalf of her husband during his fits of insanity, and was the real leader of the Lancastrians in the Wars of the Roses (q.v.). She fled to France after the second battle of St Albans, 1461, but after allying with Warwick (1470) she returned to England. In 1471 she was decisively defeated at Tewkesbury, her son being killed. She was imprisoned until 1476, when she was banished to France, where she *d.* in poverty. M. of A. was a woman of strong character, ambition and determination; but she lacked any sense of diplomacy and many of her enemies were of her own making. See life by J. J. Bagley, 1949.

Margaret of Carinthia, called **Margaret Maultasch** ('sack-mouth') (1318–69), elder daughter of Count Henry of Tyrol and Duke of Carinthia (1310–35), son of Meinhard II, Count of Tyrol. Louis IV, Ger. king and Rom. emperor (1314–47), secured the mastery of Tyrol by separating her from her husband, son of John, King of Bohemia, and making her (1342) the wife of his own son, Louis (Duke of Bavaria) to whom, in 1322, he had granted the march of Brandenburg. The son of M. and Louis, Meinhard III, who succeeded on his father's death in 1361, *d.* 2 years later. M. of C. herself was forced to abdicate (1363) and thereupon assigned all her possessions to the house of Hapsburg, and from that time Tyrol formed part of the hereditary dominions of the arch-dukes of Austria. She is the subject of L. Feuchtwanger's novel, *Die hässliche Herzogin* ('The Ugly Duchess'), 1926.

Margaret of Navarre (1492–1549) (also known as **Margaret of Angoulême**), sister of Francis I of France, married to the Duke of Alençon in 1509 and to Henry d'Albret, titular king of Navarre, in 1527. She never reigned in Navarre, but kept a court at Nérac. She afforded protection to the Protestant reformers, and was a patroness of art and literature. Besides being an enthusiastic patron of such men of letters as Rabelais, Clément Marot and others, she was an accomplished writer herself. Her poetry is a curious mixture of gallantry and mysticism. In the *Chansons spirituelles*, which reveal the spirit of the Reformation, she shows genuine feeling. She also composed humorous epistles in the manner of Marot, and *dizains* on the model of Petrarch. She had already pub. *Le Miroir de l'âme pécheresse*, 1531, and *Marguerites*, 1547, when she planned a series of tales on the lines of Boccaccio's *Decameron*. Her death prevented the completion of more than 7 of the intended 10 sections of the work. These 7 were first printed in 1558, under the title of *Histoires des amans fortunez*; the second ed., which appeared in the following year, was edited by Claude Gruget, who gave it the title of *Heptaméron*. See P. Jourda, *Marguerite d'Angoulême* (2 vols., 2nd ed.), 1941.

Margaret of Parma (1522–86), illegitimate daughter of the Emperor Charles V, first married to Alexander, Duke of Florence (1533), and then to Ottavio Farnese, Duke of Parma (1542). From 1559 to 1567 she was regent of the Netherlands, ruling capably and intelligently;

but when revolution broke out she was forced to retire to Italy.

Margaret (Margot) of Valois (1553–1615), daughter of Henry II of France and Catherine de' Medici, married in 1572 to Henry of Navarre (later Henry IV of France). On the massacre of St Bartholomew, Henry fled from court and was not rejoined by his wife for 6 years. Later she again abandoned him, and was finally divorced in 1599. M. of V. had sev. lovers, but was a patron of the arts, beautiful and highly talented. Her poems and memoirs were trans. into English by Violet Fane, 1892.

Margaret (Rose) (1930–), princess, second child of George VI, younger sister of Elizabeth II (q.v.), *b.* Glamis Castle, Scotland, 21 Aug. She was educ. privately. She visited S. Africa and S. Rhodesia with her parents and sister in 1947. In recent years she has paid many visits abroad, both official and private, including tours of the W. Indies, visits to sev. European countries and to the U.S.A., and parts of Africa. She married on 6 May 1960, Antony Charles Robert Armstrong-Jones. He was created Earl of Snowdon on 3 Oct. 1961, and their son David Viscount Linley was *b.* 3 Nov. 1961, and a daughter, Lady Sarah Armstrong-Jones, in 1964.

Margaret Tudor (1489–1541), Queen of Scotland, daughter of Henry VII and wife of James IV of Scotland, whom she married at Edinburgh in 1503, the whole of her subsequent life being a series of political intrigues of one kind or another. In 1514 she married Douglas, Earl of Angus, and after divorcing him married thirdly Henry Stewart, Lord Methuen. Her son by James became James V of Scotland; a daughter, Margaret, by Douglas, was to be the mother of Lord Darnley and grandmother of James VI of Scotland, who succeeded Elizabeth as James I of England.

Margaric Acid, an acid, $C_{16}H_{33}\cdot COOH$, which was supposed to result from the saponification of certain fats, melting point 60° C. but now known to be a eutectic mixture of stearic and palmitic acids. M. A. is obtained by the hydrolysis of cetyl cyanide by caustic potash. It is said to occur in certain dead tissues.

Margarine, butter substitute, invented and first produced by Mège Mouriès in a small factory at Poissy near Paris in 1869, following research inaugurated by Napoleon III. No Patent Law operated in Holland at that time and during the 1870's and 1880's many butter merchants or creameries started making the new fat, prominent among them being the Jurgens and Van den Bergh families. Originally the fat used in M. was 'oleo', the softer part of beef tallow, obtained by pressing the crystallised purified tallow. Vegetable fats were also used but, since most vegetable oils and fats are liquid at room temp., only a small proportion of the vast quantities available could be used. In 1910 a hydrogenation process was perfected by which, with the aid of a catalyst, hydrogen could be combined with the oils and fats to 'harden' them, and this enabled the M. manufacturers to use a wide range of plentiful raw materials, e.g. palm, coconut, groundnut, cotton, soya bean, sunflower and whale oils (see HYDROGENATION). In the manuf. of M., fat-free milk powder is mixed with water in a s.s. tank and pasteurised; lactic acid cultures are added to control souring, and the liquid is gently stirred for about 18 hrs to mature. The pasteurised milk and refined oils, in exact proportions, with concentrates of vitamins A and D, are churned together to form an emulsion, which is then chilled by a spray of ice water or brine at a temp. of 57° C., or by spreading in a thin layer on a large drum kept at a very low temp. by means of a refrigeration plant. The solidified emulsion, M., is allowed to return to normal temp., kneaded by passing through rollers, and blended under partial vacuum in order to remove air from the M. and so avoid risk of oxidation. It is then extruded, cut and wrapped. In the latest continuous process the cooling, kneading, blending and extrusion are carried out in a totally enclosed rotator. M. was first vitaminised in 1927 and in Feb. 1940 the Brit. Gov. directed that all M. produced for domestic use should be vitaminised. The vitamin A and D content was later fixed by law. M. is used in the home for spreading, baking and cooking, and special types are made to suit large-scale production of cakes, pastries, buns and biscuits.

Margarita Island, in the Caribbean Sea, 15 m. off the NE. coast of Venezuela, to which it belongs, and constituting the greater part of Nueva Esparta state (area 444 sq. m.); 43 m. long and from 5 to 20 m. broad. It consists of 2 islands joined by a sand-bar. The W. portion is mountainous, rising to about 4800 ft; the E. portion is fertile, and sugar-cane, cotton, tobacco and other crops are raised. Magnesite is found in the NE. Pearl and deep-sea fishing are carried on. The is. was discovered by Columbus in 1498. La Asunción is the cap.; Porlamar is the chief port and commercial centre. Pop. about 62,400.

Margaritone (or **Margarito**) **d'Arezzo** (fl. 1262), It. painter, sculptor and architect, b. Arezzo. The best known of his paintings is his 'Madonna, with Scenes from the Lives of the Saints', now in the National Gallery. His work belongs to the strictly conventional Byzantine tradition.

Margate, seaport and municipal bor., in the Isle of Thanet, Kent, England, a few miles from the N. Foreland, and one of the most popular seaside resorts of England, 74 m. E. by S. of London. It has bracing air, excellent sands, bathing and entertainment facilities, and a fine pier and jetty. Some damage was done in air-raids in World War II, notably to the Winter Gardens and near the jetty. Pop. (including Birchington) 45,708.

Margaux, Fr. vil. in the dept of Gironde, on the Gironde and in the Médoc (q.v.). The first-growth claret, Château-M., is produced here. Pop. 1500.

Margay (Felis tigrina), species of tiger-cat about the same size as the domestic cat, native of the forests of Brazil and Guiana.

Margelan, or **Marghilan**, tn in the Fergana oblast (prov.) of the Uzbek S.S.R., 160 m. SE. of Tashkent. It is in a healthy position, surrounded by gardens. Its chief industries are silkworm culture and the manuf. of silk, woollen and camel-wool clothes. Pop. 68,000 (1959).

Marggraf, Andreas Sigismund (1709–82), Ger. chemist, b. Berlin, studied chem. at Berlin and Strasburg, and medicine at Halle. In 1738 he was elected to the Berlin Academy of Sciences, in 1760 being appointed director of the physics class. He is noted for his discovery of sugar in beetroot. His papers were collected into 2 vols. of Chymische Schriften, 1761–7.

Marghera, Porto, see VENICE.

Margin: 1. In business generally, (a) In a transaction in which money is advanced on security, the difference between the amount advanced on the security and the market value of such security. As regards trustees mortgaging the property of their beneficiaries, the effect of the Trustee Act, 1893, is that a trustee must not lend more than two-thirds of the surveyor's valuation even if the surveyor advises that a greater proportion may be advanced. If he does he will be liable for any resulting loss; but this statutory precaution relates not to the nature, but apparently only to the value, of the security, and hence a trustee who lends on property of a speculative or wasting character (e.g. factory or other trade property) will probably be liable for loss irrespective of the proportion to value advanced. (b) In banking practice the M. depends on the nature of the thing charged or pledged, but may be said to fluctuate from 10 up to 25 per cent. (c) In 'cover' transactions (see COVER), or speculation upon M.s through outside stockbrokers, the speculator deposits a certain M. or sum to cover prospective differences in price, which cover is said to run off if the difference turns out to be greater than he anticipated.

2. In economics. In the Ricardian theory of rent that land which will just pay for cultivation if it be let at a nominal rent is said to be the M. of cultivation, and in the absence of exceptional circumstances land below that M. cannot be cultivated with profit. The term is however now widely used in economics to denote the last unit of anything that is added (or subtracted) from a total quantity. Thus marginal revenue is the increase in revenue resulting from the sale of one more unit of product and marginal product the increase in output resulting from the employment of one more unit of a factor of production (q.v.). One of the most important propositions of elementary economic theory is that a profit-maximising firm will increase output up to the point where marginal revenue is equal to marginal cost (i.e. the increase in cost resulting from raising output by one more unit). Marginal utility theory is often applied to money so that economists used to argue that the more money one had the less satisfaction one received from an additional unit of income (the law of the diminishing marginal utility of money). Diffi-

culties however emerged in the utility analysis of consumers' demands and it is now generally replaced by revealed preference theory and indifference analysis (q.v.). *See* G. J. Stigler, *The Theory of Price*, 1953; J. A. Schumpeter, *A History of Economic Analysis*, 1954; T. Majumdar, *The Measurement of Utility*, 1958.

Margrave (Ger. *Markgraf*, count of the mark), formerly a governor entrusted with the care of a 'mark', or frontier (margravate), who stood immediately under the king or emperor. Margravates existed as early as the time of Charlemagne. In the 12th cent. they became hereditary, and later a M. held the same rank as a prince of the empire.

Marguerite, general term for a number of daisy-like flowers in the section Tubiflorae of the family Compositae. The common ox-eye daisy (*Chrysanthemum leucanthemum*) and the grand ox-eye (*C. uliginosum*) are often so called; but the name specially applies to *C. frutescens*, the Paris daisy, with fine white or yellow flowers. The blue M. is *Felicia amelloides*.

Marguerite de Valois, *see* MARGARET OF VALOIS.

Marguerite of Navarre, *see* MARGARET OF NAVARRE.

Mari (formerly known as **Cheremises**), people in Russia belonging to the Finnish family (*see* FINNS) who live in the Mari Autonomous Rep. (q.v.) and adjacent areas. They numbered 530,000 in 1962. Mostly peasants, now collectivised, they have been Orthodox Christians since the 16th cent. Since the 8th cent. the M. have lived under foreign rule (Khazar in the 8th cent., Volga-Bulgarian during 9th to 13th cents., Tartar from 1236 to 1552 and finally Russian). *See* W. Kolarz, *Russia and her Colonies*, 1952.

Mari Autonomous Republic, European Russia, lying on the l. b. of the Volga between Gor'ky and Kazan'. Largely lowland, it is more than half covered with mixed forests. The industries are timber, wood processing, metalworking and food; wheat, rye and flax are grown and there is dairy farming. The cap. is Yoshkar-Ola. Area 8950 sq. m.; pop. (1965) 656,000 (36 per cent urb.), mostly Mari Russians (since the 16th cent.).

Maria Christina (1806–78), regent of Spain, daughter of Francis I of Naples and fourth wife of Ferdinand VII of Spain. On his death she became regent for their daughter Isabella II. In 1840 she was forced to abdicate as a result of Carlist disturbances, and fled to France.

Maria Theresa (1717–80), ruler of the Holy Rom. Empire, daughter of the Emperor Charles VI, was *b*. Vienna. By the Pragmatic Sanction (q.v.) her father appointed her heir to his hereditary thrones. In 1736 she married Francis of Lorraine, Grand Duke of Tuscany, to whom she gave an equal share in the gov. when they became Queen of Hungary and Bohemia and Archduchess of Austria, on the death of her father, 1740. Prussia, Bavaria, Saxony, Naples and Sardinia, stirred up by France, put forward claims to portions of her dominions, chiefly founded on the extinction of the male line of the

house of Hapsburg, and Charles Albert of Bavaria was actually crowned emperor as Charles VII (q.v.). The War of the Austrian Succession, after lasting more than 7 years, was terminated by the Peace of Aix-la-Chapelle in 1748. M. T. lost Silesia and Glatz, and the duchies of Parma, Piacenza and Guastalla, but on the other hand her husband was elected emperor. This was a peace relatively favourable to the empire, which had at one time seemed in danger of complete disintegration; but revenge on Frederick the Great and the recovery of Silesia remained M. T.'s prime ambitions to the end of her life, and was responsible for acts of foreign policy fundamentally opposed to basic imperial interests. During times of peace she made sev. internal reforms. She found in Kaunitz (q.v.) a minister possessed of the wisdom and energy requisite for the conduct of affairs. But in the Seven Years War (q.v.) she joined the anti-Prussian coalition; but the war ended with her ters. impoverished and Frederick still in possession of Silesia. Later M. T. joined with Russia and Prussia in the partition of Poland (1772). Galicia and Bukovina were added to her dominions between 1772 and 1777. Her conduct in the Polish affair has been criticised as hypocritical; but since 1765 her son Joseph had governed with her, and the responsibility for the decision is certainly primarily his. Marie Antoinette (q.v.) was another of M. T.'s children. *See* lives by M. Goldsmith, 1936; C. L. Morris, 1938.

Maria-Theresiopol, *see* SUBOTICA.

Mariana, Juan de (1535–1623), Sp. historian, *b*. Talavera. He entered the Society of Jesus, was ordained priest in 1561, and subsequently held professorships of theology at Rome, at Loreto, in Sicily and in Paris. He became famous after the pub. of his *Historiae de Rebus Hispaniae* (trans. into English as *General History of Spain*) which appeared 1592–1605. His treatise, *De Rege et Regis Institutione*, 1599, was held to favour the doctrine of tyrannicide; *De ponderibus et mensuris*, 1599, aimed at the malversations of the Duke of Lerma, resulted in his imprisonment. *See* J. Laures, *The Political Economy of Juan de Mariana*, 1928.

Marianas, *see* LADRONES.

Marianne Islands, *see* LADRONES.

Mariánské Lázně (Ger. **Marienbad**), Czechoslovak tn in Západolaský. It is set amid forest-clad hills, has mineral springs and is a celebrated health resort. Antimony is mined. Pop. 12,600. (*See Plate: Czechoslovakia.*)

Marianus Scotus (1028–82), Irish chronicler. In 1058 he became a Benedictine at the abbey of St Martin at Cologne, passing his later life at the abbeys of Fulda and Mainz. He left a *Chronicon Universale*, first printed at Basel in 1559.

Mariazell, Austrian tn in the prov. of Styria. The shrine of the Blessed Virgin, in the triple-towered Gothic and baroque church, is the object of a famous pilgrimage. The tn is also a popular health resort and sports centre. Pop. 2300.

Maribo, co. of SE. Denmark, which includes

the is. of Lolland and Falster. Area 700 sq. m.; pop. 131,700. The cap. of the same name is on Lolland. Pop. 5300.

Maribor (Ger. **Marburg**), tn in Slovenia, Yugoslavia, on the Drava; the old tn stands on the l. b., and the modern tn is on the r. b. M. has a 14th cent. citadel and a Gothic cathedral. Pop. 82,400.

Marie Alexandra Victoria, Dowager Queen of Rumania (1875–1938), grand-daughter of Queen Victoria by her father, the Duke of Edinburgh, who married the Grand Duchess Marie, only daughter of Tsar Alexander the Second. She married in 1893 Ferdinand von Hohenzollern, King of Rumania 1914–27. Between the death of her husband and the return of King Carol II, she (with the 3 regents of the country) ruled Rumania. The most ambitious of her books was *The Story of my Life* (3 vols.), 1934–5. In *My Country*, 1916, and again in *The Country that I Love*, 1925, she described Rumania as seen through the eyes of an artist and a poet. Her first child, Charles (Carol, q.v.), was *b.* in 1893. There were 5 other children.

Marie Antoinette, Josephe Jeanne (1755–93), wife of Louis XVI of France. She was the fourth daughter of Maria Theresa and of the Emperor Francis I, and was *b.* Vienna. She married the Dauphin of France, afterwards Louis XVI (q.v.), in 1770, but her unconventional behaviour and her extravagance made her very unpopular, though her husband was devoted to her. On the accession of her husband to the throne (1774), her Austrian sympathies and her opposition to the demands of the popular party increased her unpopularity. At the outbreak of the revolution she showed extreme stubbornness and indomitable courage. Her personal hatred of moderates such as Mirabeau (q.v.) thwarted their attempts to prevent the destruction of the monarchy by reforming it, and makes her at least partially responsible for its violent downfall. She was guillotined on 16 Oct. 1793, after a trial in which her dignity and courage had impressed even her judges. *See* lives by E. and J. de Goncourt, 1858; H. Belloc, 1909; S. Zweig (Eng. trans.), 1933; A. Leroy, 1946; A. Castelot (Eng. trans. by D. Folliot), 1957.

Marie Byrd Land, *see* BYRD LAND.

'Marie Celeste', *see* MARY CELESTE.

Marie de France, earliest known Fr. poetess, writing, apparently in England, in the late 12th cent., and plausibly identified with an Abbess of Shaftesbury. Her surviving works, all in octo-syllabic verse, are: 12 Breton *lais* or short tales of sentimental adventure (before 1189); 103 fables, trans. from Eng. and dedicated to a certain Count Wm; the *Espurgatoire S. Patrice* (after 1189), faithfully following a Lat. account of a knight's visit to St Patrick's Purgatory in Ireland. The *lais* show particular technical skill, and M. emerges as an attractive personality interested in the world about her and especially in the problems of the human heart. *See* ed. by K. Warnke (*Lais*, 3rd ed., 1925; *Fables*, 1898, *Espurgatoire*, 1938); A. Ewart (*Lais*, 1944, selected *Fables* with R. C. Johnston, 1942); some

lais trans. by E. Rickert, 1901, and in *Lays of Marie de France* (Everyman's Library), 1954; monograph by E. Hoepffner, *Les Lais de Marie de France*, 1935.

Marie de' Medici (1573–1642), daughter of Francis of Tuscany and queen-consort of France, *b.* Florence. In 1600 she was married to Henry IV of France, and her eldest son, later Louis XIII, was *b.* in the following year. After Henry's assassination in 1610 she became regent, and was entirely under the influence of her It. favourites, Leonora Galigai and her husband, Concini, who was created Marquis d'Ancre. In 1617, however, Louis XIII asserted his authority, ordered the assassination of the Concinis and exiled the queen to Blois. In 1619 she escaped and headed a revolt, but was reconciled to her son through the mediation of Richelieu, who then gained royal favour. Her attempts to displace Richelieu led to her exile to Compiègne in 1630, whence she escaped to Brussels in 1631, and later to Cologne, where she *d.*

Marie Galante, is. in the W. Indies, a dependency of Guadeloupe (q.v.). Area 58 sq. m. Pop. 20,000.

Marie Louise (1791–1847), empress of the French, daughter of Francis II, Holy Rom. Emperor (Francis I, emperor of Austria) and second wife of Napoleon I, whom she married in 1810 on his divorce from Josephine. She bore him one son, called the King of Rome (1811). M L. returned to Austria on Napoleon's abdication, refusing to share his exile with him, and was appointed ruler of the duchies of Parma, Piacenza and Guastalla by the Allies in 1814. She became the mistress of Count von Neipperg, marrying him in 1822, and having sev. children by him. Her prin. desire after 1814 seems to have been to forget her marriage with Napoleon, and from 1814 she paid no attention to her son by him until he was dying (1832). A vol. of her *Correspondance* was pub. in 1887. *See* her *Diaries*, ed. by F. Masson, 1922. *See also* life by A. de Stoeckl, 1962.

Marienbad, *see* MARIÁNSKÉ LÁZNĚ.

Marienburg, *see* MALBORK.

Marienwerder, *see* KWIDZYŃ.

Marietta: 1. City, co. seat of Washington co., Ohio, U.S.A., on the Ohio R., 50 m. SE. of Zanesville. It has a ferro-alloy plant and manufs. chemicals and oil-well supplies. M. College is here. Pop. 16,850.

2. Co. seat of Cobb co., Georgia, U.S.A., 16 m. NW. of Atlanta. It manufs. hosiery, furniture, prefabricated houses, marble products, castings and pottery. Pop. 25,570.

Mariette, Auguste Ferdinand François (1821–81), Fr. Egyptologist, *b.* Boulogne. In 1850 he went to Egypt in search of Coptic MSS., and discovered the Serapeum, the catacombs of the Apis bulls at Memphis. In 1858 he became keeper of the Egyptian monuments—the virtual beginning of the Egyptian Antiquities Service —and devoted himself to archaeological exploration of the Nile valley, making many finds which became the nucleus of the Cairo Museum.

Marignano, see MELEGNANO.

Marigold, name for sev. flowering plants. The Fr., African and Mexican M.s (*Tagetes*) are valuable half-hardy garden plants. Seeds are usually sown under glass in Mar. and planted out at the end of May. Their colours vary from pale lemon to brown, and they bloom all the summer if faded flowers are removed. See BIDENS; CALENDULA; MARSH MARIGOLD.

Marigot, Le, see CAPESTERRE.

Marihuana, see MARIJUANA.

Mariinskiy Waterway, see VOLGA–BALTIC WATERWAY.

Marijuana, intoxicating, excitating narcotic extracted from the topmost leaves and flowers of the Indian hemp, *Cannabis sativa*. It releases inhibitions and impairs judgment, and it is illegal to use it as an ingredient in cigarettes. See HEMP; BHANG; HASHISH.

Marikina, tn of Luzon Is., Philippines, 8 m. NE. of Manila, on a trib. of the Pasig R. Shoes are made here; there is a rubber plant, and a hydro-electric project has been started. Pop. c. 25,000.

Marin, John (1870–1953), Amer. painter, b. Rutherford, New Jersey. He began his career as an architect but studied painting in Philadelphia and New York and became noted for water colours in a modern style. Many were inspired by the coast of Maine and the streets of New York.

Marín, Sp. port in the prov. of Pontevedra, on the Pontevedra estuary. It is a picturesque fishing tn, with a busy harbour and good beaches. Pop. 7300.

Marina di Carrara, see CARRARA.

Marina di Massa, see MASSA.

Marinduque, is. of the Philippines, S. of Luzon, NE. of Mindoro. Boac (NW.) is the chief tn. The port Marlanga is on the SE. Rice, hemp and coco-nuts are produced and gold and iron mined. Pop. c. 60,000.

Marine Biology is that branch of biology concerned with organisms living in the sea. M. B. is concerned with the nature and development of marine organisms, and also with the environment influencing their development. The effect of water on light, the pressure of water, the variability of its depth, air content and salinity are all factors affecting marine organisms and determining their distribution. Consequently M. B. is closely associated with oceanography, hydrography and biochemistry. (*See* articles on these topics.) The early development of M. B. has been slow and diffuse, and in many countries was directly or indirectly due to the fishing industry. Probably on account of the economic value of certain fishes, molluscs and crustacea, general interest in marine zoology was aroused before interest was extended to the much wider subject of M. B., which was not really developed until the 19th cent. One of the pioneers of M. B. was Karl August Mobius (1825–1908), who investigated Kiel Bay, and described its plants and animals and their ecology. Victor Hensen (1825–1924), also at Kiel, investigated marine plankton, the mass of organisms floating on the

surface of the water, and invented a statistical method to advance the study of fishes used as food. The first *Challenger* expedition (1872–5) did much to stimulate Brit. interest in M. B. The Marine Biological Association of the U.K. was founded in 1884, and 4 years later a laboratory was completed at Plymouth, primarily to facilitate research on food fishes and molluscs, and to improve the industries dependent on these. Its secondary aim was to increase the knowledge of marine life in general. The work of the Plymouth station has been concerned mainly with life in Plymouth Sound and in the Eng. Channel. Shortly before this station was opened a Scottish marine station was estab. at Granton. One large boat, the *Ark*, was used as a floating laboratory and aquarium; another, the *Medusa*, for sounding and dredging. In 1885 the Liverpool M. B. committee was formed to investigate the fauna and flora of the Irish Sea, and did much to advance knowledge of life and condition in this area. The work of the committee has, since 1920, been continued by the Dept of Oceanography of Liverpool Univ.

In 1925 the Falkland Is. Dependencies initiated a series of voyages, first in Capt. Scott's old vessel, *Discovery*, and later in the better equipped *Discovery II*, whereby many new facts were elucidated and new species discovered. In 1933 Dr Wm Beebe (q.v.) of the New York Zoological Society descended to the previously unexplored depth of ½ m., and described the habits of animals which had previously been known from dead specimens only. The Swedish research ship, *Albatross*, in 1948 collected specimens at over 25,000 ft (a depth nearly equal to the height of Mt Everest), and collected samples of the sea bed from 30,000 ft. In Sept. 1953 Prof. A. Piccard (q.v.) descended 10,335 ft into the Mediterranean in his bathyscaphe, while in Feb. 1954 two Fr. naval officers went down 13,287 ft (over 2½ m.) to the Atlantic sea bed 120 m. off Dakar, Fr, W. Africa; descents to such depths open up new possibilities of research into M. B.

Marine biological stations are now estab. on the coasts of most countries of the world, and contributions have been made to every branch of biological science. Amongst the interesting facts discovered is a distribution of plants and animals in the sea analogous to their distribution at different altitudes on land. Much of this knowledge is of extensive use to fisheries. In deep seas, as the depth of water increases, its temp. decreases, and plants and animals found near or at the surfaces of polar seas are found at some depth in the warmer seas. In this way some Arctic species spread continuously from pole to pole. Nitrogen-fixing bacteria flourish in colder seas, and consequently more plants are found in these than in warm ones. Another factor influencing plant distribution is the intensity of light. Blue-green and green algae are found on the surface and in shallow water, brown algae in slightly greater depths, and red algae at lower levels. From depths where sufficient light cannot penetrate, plants and the animals dependent on them are absent. Moreover, since these animals live in darkness, they are either blind or provided with luminescent organs. (*See* FISH.) In contributing its quota of new species of plants and animals, M. B. has helped to elucidate some of the problems of evolution. There is still considerable scope for research in this branch of biology. Among the most recent advances has been the use of skin diving techniques by professional biologists to study underwater ecology, behaviour and physiology. *See* BIOLOGY. *See also* ABYSSAL FAUNA; CEPHALOPODA; COELACANTHS; FISHERIES; LATIMERIA; SEASHORE. See *The Cambridge Natural History*, 1909; F. S. Russell, *The Seas*, 1936; L. R. Brightwell, *Neptune's Gardens*, 1937; N. B. Eales, *Littoral Fauna of Great Britain*, 1939; M. Duncan, *Wonders of Neptune's Kingdom*, 1948; F. D. Ommaney, *The Ocean*, 1949; N. B. Marshall, *Aspects of Deep Sea Biology*, 1954.

Marine Corps, United States, *see* UNITED STATES MARINE CORPS.

Marine Engine, *see* MOTOR BOATS; MOTOR SHIPS; STEAM ENGINES; STEAMSHIPS.

Marine Insurance, *see* INSURANCE.

Marines, Royal. The R. M. are essentially sea-soldiers. They may serve at sea, on land or in the air, but they have their own traditions and mode of life. In rank they correspond with the army, and the corps is commanded by a general. But they are an integral part of the naval service, their organisation being the function of the Navy Board. Every cruiser and heavier type of ship carries a detachment of the corps, and since 1956 they have been borne in certain frigates oversea. On board they are trained to seamen's duties, they man part of the ship's armament, provide guards and sentries, and are ready to land, whenever required, as a military unit, to assist the navy in keeping the peace. On shore they work frequently with the army and provide men for the commandos (q.v.) which specialise in landings and general water-borne assault. The uniform is blue, with red facings and white belts. On their colours the men bear the word 'Gibraltar', because they captured the Rock in 1704 under Adm. Rooke. R. M. were first estab. as a nursery from which to obtain seamen to man the fleet by order in council of 16 Oct. 1664. In the First World War their strength was about 40,000, and they proved valuable in such enterprises as Zeebrugge and Gallipoli, besides serving with the general forces elsewhere. (*See* E. Fraser and L. G. Carr-Laughton, *The Royal Marine Artillery, 1804–1923*, 1931.) In the Second World War the M. fought in Norway (notably at Narvik), Holland, France, Crete, Singapore, on the Irawadi and at Dunkirk, besides carrying out their sea-going duties of supplying a part of the armament of the ships in which they serve. The R. M. were the first sea-borne troops to land as spearhead of the allied invasion in Sicily, and among the first to land in Italy. In Crete, of the 2200 R. M. who landed with the mobile naval base only 1000 returned. In Iceland it was the R. M. who surprised the Ger. consul-general at Reykjavik,

and seized his confidential books and papers. On the Irawadi a force of R. M. formed a flotilla (Force Viper) which assisted in demolitions and fought a desperate battle with the Japanese at Padaung. Of the original force of 107 here only 48 eventually made their way to Calcutta. Madagascar was another of the scenes of successful operations of the R. M. Finally, the R. M. also took part in the amphibious operation of launching the invasion of Normandy in June 1944, and subsequently in the operations to cross the Rhine in 1945. The strength of the corps increased in the Second World War from 12,000 to 74,000. *See* H.M.S.O., *The Royal Marines: the Admiralty Account of their Achievements, 1939–43*, 1944, and Sir R. Bruce Lockhart, *The Marines Were There*, 1950.

Marinetti, Emilio Filippo Tommaso (1876–1944), It. poet, *b*. Alexandria, Egypt. He wrote in both French and Italian. He founded the jour. *Poesia*, 1905, and later created the Futurist movement with various manifestos and a novel (written in French), *Mafarka le futuriste*, 1910. He was one of the earliest supporters of Fascism. His literary works include poetry (*La Conquête des étoiles*, 1903, *La Ville charnelle*, 1908, *Otto anime in una bomba*, 1919, etc.), prose (*Le futurisme*, 1910, *Guerra, sola igiene del Mondo*, 1915, etc.), plays (*Le Roi Bombance*, 1905, *Il Tamburo di fuoco*, 1923, etc.).

Marinha Grande, tn of Portugal, in Leiria dist, 7 m. W. of Leiria (q.v.), in a pine forest. Its glass industry dates from the 18th cent. Pop. 4700.

Marini, or **Marino, Giovanni Battista** (1569–1625). It. poet, *b*. Naples, a friend of Tasso (q.v.). His works were much admired by contemporaries throughout Europe. If, however, he achieved an enviable reputation as a writer of verse—mainly of a rather flamboyant nature—he earned an equally unenviable one for the dissipation of his life. His excesses were eventually the cause of his being obliged to leave Italy and retire to Paris, where he lived under the patronage of Marie de' Medici. In 1623 he returned to Italy rich and famous. His aim was to produce surprise by the use of startling metaphors, hyperboles, antitheses, etc. The term 'Marinism' connotes the influence of his ornate and affected style on early 17th cent. poetry, Italian, French and English. His works include *La Strage degli Innocenti*, 1610; *Rime*, 1602, later eds. called *La Lira*; *Dicerie sacre*, 1614; *Epitalami*, 1616; *Il Rapimento d'Europa*, 1618; *La Sampogna*, 1620; *Adone*, 1623. See B. Croce, *Poesie varie*, 1913; R. Basalmo (ed.), *Le più belle pagine di Giambattista Marini*, 1925. *See also* A. Borzelli, *Storia della vita e delle opere di G. B. Marini*, 1927.

Marini, Marino (1901–), It. sculptor, *b*. Pistoia. He studied painting and sculpture at Florence and was later prof. of sculpture at Milan. His sculptures since 1936, especially of horses and horsemen in an archaic yet modern style, have made him one of the most highly esteemed It. artists of the period.

Marino, It. tn in Lazio (q.v.), on the Alban

Hills, 13 m. SE. of Rome. It was once a stronghold of the Orsini and Colonna (q.v.) families. M. produces well-known wines and has a wine festival each Oct. Pop. 16,400.

Mario (Giovanni), Cavaliere di Candia (1810–83), It. singer, the greatest operatic tenor of his time. Of noble birth, he appeared under his first Christian name alone. For a short time he studied under Ponchard, Michet and Bordogni, making his début at the Paris Opéra (1838), and appearing in London in 1839. He toured in Russia (1845–50) and in America (1854). M. sang for many years with Giulia Grisi (q.v.), whom he married (c. 1844). He retired in 1867. See G. Pearse and F. Hird, *The Romance of a Great Singer*, 1910.

Mariolatry, see MARY, THE BLESSED VIRGIN.

Marion, Francis (1732–95), Amer. soldier, b. near Georgetown, S. Carolina. He served in 1759 as a lieutenant in Governor Lyttleton's expedition against the Cherokees, and in 1761 as a captain in that of Col. Grant. Appointed brigadier-general in 1780, the scene of his activities was the country between the Pedee and the Santee from Camden to the coast, and he gained many victories over the Brit. troops. In 1781 he was joined by Lee's legion, and took part in the battle of Eutaw. After the war he was returned to the State Senate, and in 1790 was a member of the State Constitutional Convention.

Marion: 1. City, co. seat of Grant co., Indiana, U.S.A., 57 m. NNE. of Indianapolis in an agric. area with gas- and oil-fields. M. manufs. glass, paper, machinery, railway equipment, etc. Pop. c. 35,000.

2. City, co. seat of M. co., Ohio, U.S.A., 45 m. N. of Columbus. It is a railway centre, manufs. farm and road construction machinery and has limestone quarries. It was the home of President Harding. Pop. 37,520.

Marionettes, see PUPPETS.

Mariotte, Edmé (c. 1620–84), Fr. mathematician and physicist, of whose life little is known. He was b. in Burgundy, was a priest by profession, and resided in early life at Dijon. He was one of the earliest Fr. experimental philosophers and a member of the Académie des Sciences (founded 1666). His chief work, *De la nature de l'air*, 1676, contains a statement of Boyle's law (q.v.) known in France as M.'s law because of M.'s independent discovery of it. He discovered that air existed in liquids. He investigated sap pressure in plants, the recoil of guns, the nature of colour and other subjects, and in 1666 he discovered the blind spot in the eye. See his *Collected Works*, 1717 and 1740; Condorcet, *Éloges des Académiciens*, 1779.

Mariotte's Law, see BOYLE's LAW.

Mariposa (Sp. 'butterfly'), co. of central California, U.S.A., containing the Yosemite valley and the Mammoth Tree Grove with its famous sequoias (*S. gigantea*). The Sierra Nevada borders it on the NE. Much gold is produced. Cap. Mariposa, 137 m. from San Francisco. Area 1455 sq. m.; pop. 5145.

Mariposa Lily, see CALOCHORTUS.

Maris, name of a family of Dutch painters of

the 19th cent. Of the 3 brothers, *Matthijs* (1835–1917), *Jakob* (1837–99) and *Willem* (1843–1910), Jakob is perhaps the most famous. Matthijs's works are remarkable for tender colouring and poetic feeling. Jakob is especially noted as a landscape painter of water, clouds and misty skies. (*See* J. Veth in *Onze Kunst*, 1902; T. de Bock, *Leben*, 1904.) Willem preferred the bright, cheerful aspects of nature. He painted peaceful sunlit meadows. Influenced by the Barbizon school, the M. in their turn had an influence in Britain, especially on the Glasgow school. See M. Rooses, *Dutch Painters of the Nineteenth Century*, 1899; R. H. Wilenski, *Introduction to Dutch Art*, 1927; life of Matthijs by E. D. Friedländer, 1921.

Marischal, Earl, title created by James II of Scotland (c. 1458) and bestowed on Sir Wm Keith. The Keith family since the time of David I had possessed part of Keith in E. Lothian. From the early 14th cent. the office of Great M. became hereditary in this family, being conferred as an honour by Bruce for their services from Bannockburn (1314) onwards. *George, 5th Earl* (c. 1445–1623), founded M. College, Aberdeen (1593). *William, 7th Earl* (c. 1617–61), became head of the N. Covenanters. He supported Charles II (1650), but was taken prisoner at Alyth (1651). On the Restoration (1660) he became keeper of the privy seal of Scotland. *George, 10th Earl* (c. 1693–1778), fought for the Pretender at Sheriffmuir (1715), and was in consequence attainted, while the office of M. fell into abeyance (1716). He escaped to the Continent, and finally served under Frederick the Great.

Marist, member of the Rom. Catholic Society of Mary, a religious order of priests devoted to the work of foreign missions and to teaching. The M. Society was founded in the diocese of Belley, France, in 1816 by Jean Colin. The M. fathers and associate lay brothers maintain schools all over the world, and sev. missions in New Zealand and Polynesia.

Maritain, Jacques (1882–), Fr. writer, b. Paris. Educ. as a Protestant, he became a Rom. Catholic in 1906. Prof. at the Institut Catholique, Paris (1914–40), he was regarded as the leading neo Thomist of the times. After the collapse of France he joined the Institute of Medieval Studies, Toronto, and was visiting prof. at Princeton and Columbia univs. From 1945 to 1948 he was Fr. ambas. to the Holy See. His *Art et Scolastique*, 1920, is a classic of erudition and subtlety. He is rather philosopher and historian than a man of letters in the strict sense. His other works, many of them trans. into English, include *La philosophie bergsonienne*, 1914, *Primauté du spirituel*, 1927, *Religion et culture*, 1930, *Humanisme int gral*, 1947, *Art et scolastique*, 1959, *Réflexions sur l'Amérique*, 1959, and *La philosophie morale*, 1960.

Maritime Alps, div. of the W. Alps on the frontiers of France and Italy, extending from the Col di Tenda (W. of the Gulf of Genoa) NW. to the Col de l'Argentière and alps of Dauphiné. E. and NE. come the Cottian and Ligurian Alps.

Among the chief peaks are Punta dell' Argentera (10,794 ft), Cima dei Gelas (10,286 ft), Monte Matto (10,128 ft), Mont Pelat (10,107 ft). The chief passes include the Passo del Pagarin (Vésubie valley to Valdieri), Col della Ciriegia, Col de Pourriac (Tinée valley to Argentera), Col della Lombarda (Tinée valley to Vinadio), Col de la Cayolle (Var valley to Barcelonnette, carriage road), Col del Sabbione (Tenda to Valdieri). For the dept of France see ALPES-MARITIMES.

Maritime (Russian **Primorskiy) Kray**, in the S. of the Russian Far E., lies between the Manchurian frontier and Japan, comprising the Ussuri lowland in the W. and the Sikhote-Alin' mts (highest point 6100 ft) in the E. The area has a monsoon climate and is about ⅔ forested (coniferous in the N. and on the higher mt slopes, deciduous elsewhere in the S.). There are rich deposits of coal, tin, lead, zinc and gold. The main industries are non-ferrous metallurgy, fishing and lumbering. Wheat, oats, rice, fodder crops, soya beans and potatoes are grown along the Ussuri lowland, the rice under irrigation, and there is dairy farming. The pop. is heavily concentrated in the lowland, especially along the Trans-Siberian railway, and on the S. coast. Prin. tns are Vladivostock, Ussuriysk, Nakhodka. The area belonged to China until ceded to Russia in 1858. Area 64,900 sq. m.; pop. (1956) 1,305,000, mostly Russians and Ukrainians (since the mid 19th cent.), but before the 1930's there were also Koreans and Chinese. See W. Kolarz, *The Peoples of the Soviet Far East*, 1954.

Maritime Laws, see OLERON, JUDGMENTS OF, and SEA LAWS.

Maritime Museum, see NATIONAL MARITIME MUSEUM.

Maritza (Bulgarian **Marica**; Turkish **Meric**; Gk **Eyros**; Lat. **Hebrus**), riv. of SE. Europe, rising in the Rila Mts in W. Bulgaria and flowing across Bulgaria in an easterly direction for 170 m. It then turns S. and SW. to its delta on the Aegean Sea, N. of Enos. In the final 115 m. of its course it forms the boundary between Greece and Turkey. There are coal-mines in its vicinity. Length 300 m.

Mariuccia, see MAROZIA.

Mariupol', see ZHDANOV.

Marius, Gaius (157–86 BC), Rom. general and statesman, *b*. Arpinum. He served under Scipio Africanus at Numantia (134), was tribune of the plebs in 119 and later married Julia, aunt of Julius Caesar. By this time he had estab. himself as a leader of the popular party at Rome. In 107 he was consul and received command of the war against Jugurtha (q.v.). The brilliance of his quaestor Sulla (q.v.), to whom Jugurtha surrendered in 106, marked the beginning of that rivalry between the 2 men which led to civil war. M.'s next task was military reform (see ROMAN ARMY). Meanwhile Italy was threatened by the Cimbri and Teutones (qq.v.), and M. was elected consul a 2nd time for 104. The menace was postponed, but he was consul a 3rd and 4th time in 103 and 102. In the latter year he defeated

the Teutones and their allies at Aquae Sextiae, and in 101, with his colleague A. Lutatius Catulus, the Cimbri at Campi Raudii near Vercellae. In order to secure the consulship a 6th time, he associated himself with 2 demagogues, Saturninus and Glaucia, whose insurrection he put down as consul in 100. In 88, anxious for command in the Mithradatic war (see MITHRA-DATES), M. obtained a vote of the people conferring on him the command already bestowed on Sulla by the senate. Sulla joined his legions in Campania and marched on Rome; M. fled and eventually reached Africa. In 87, however, he returned to Italy, where the popular party under the consul L. Cornelius Cinna were making a new bid for power. Cinna had been driven from Rome, but he now re-entered the city together with M. Their guards stabbed everyone whom M. did not salute, and many of the noblest families perished. Without an election M. and Cinna nominated themselves consuls for the next year; but on the 18th day of his 7th consulship M. *d*. of pleurisy.

Marivaux, Pierre Carlet de Chamblain de (1688–1763), Fr. playwright and novelist, *b*. Paris. He turned to literature seriously when the loss of his fortune obliged him to earn his living. His plays such as *La Surprise de l'amour*, 1722, *Le Jeu de l'amour et du hasard*, 1730, *Le Triomphe de l'amour*, 1732, and *Les Fausses confidences*, 1737, deal, as the titles indicate, primarily with love. The dialogue is brilliant, full of veiled avowals and subtle indications, which has given rise to the name *marivaudage*. He wrote also 2 novels: *La Vie de Marianne*, 1731–41, a study of a young girl, written with great delicacy and psychological insight, and *Le Paysan parvenu*, 1735–6, which gives a broader picture of Fr. society. Both novels were left incomplete. See G. Deschamps, *Marivaux* (2nd ed.), 1907; R. K. Jamieson, *Marivaux, a Study in Sensibility*, 1941; M. Arland, *Marivaux*, 1950.

Marjoram, see ORIGANUM.

Mark, or **John Mark**, author of the second gospel, is mentioned many times in the N.T., though nowhere by name in the Gospels. Col. iv. 10 describes him as the cousin of Barnabas. His mother Mary (Acts xii. 12) was a woman of some position, whose house was a frequent resort of the Christians of Jerusalem and may have been the scene of the Last Supper. It has been, with some likelihood, suggested that the youth so oddly mentioned in Mark xiv. 51 f. was M. himself who had stolen from bed to follow Christ and the Twelve when they left the house. He accompanied Paul and Barnabas on their return from Judaea to Antioch (Acts xii. 25), and later set out with them on the first missionary journey. On their arrival at Perga in Pamphylia he left them for some unexplained reason, and this defection later caused a sharp dispute between Paul and Barnabas which led to their taking different roads (Acts xiii. 13; xv. 38 f.). We next read of M. as reconciled to Paul and with him at Rome (Col. iv. 10; Phil. 24). He was known to antiquity, however, chiefly as the disciple and interpreter of St Peter, whom he assisted at Rome, according to Papias (*see* Eusebius, *Historia Ecclesiastica* III, xxxix. 15), on whose catechetical instructions and preaching the Gospel is in some sense dependent. Later he seems to have visited Asia (2 Tim. iv. 11). Tradition makes him the founder of the Church in Alexandria where the Copts claim to possess his relics, but so does Venice where he was martyred (according to the Rom. Martyrology) in the eighth year of Nero. His symbol is the Lion, second of the 4 beasts of Apocalypse iv. 7. His feast day is 25 April. *See* C. H. Turner, 'Introduction to St Mark' in C. Gore's *New Commentary on Holy Scripture*, 1928.

Mark, originally, a silver coin of Germany containing 100 pfennigs. It began as a measure of weight (chiefly for gold and silver) used throughout W. Europe, and equal to about 8 oz. In 1194, after the Conquest, a M. represented in England 160*d*. (20*d*. to 1 oz.), or 13*s*. 4*d*., two-thirds of £1. In Scotland it had only one-twelfth of the Eng. value. M.s were first issued in Germany about 1875. They are used in both W. and E. Germany: a 5 M. is the largest coin, but there are notes of up to 1000 M.s. *See also* METROLOGY.

Mark, The Gospel according to St, second book of the N.T., widely regarded by critics as the first of the Gospels to be consigned to writing. The unanimous testimony of antiquity and of all our MSS. is that St M. was its author, the earliest explicit assertion of this being that of Papias (2nd cent.), who says that St M. was the 'interpreter' of St Peter, and that he wrote his gospel at Rome from information derived from the apostle. The truth of this tradition has been denied by many critics in the past, but is now widely conceded. *See* SYNOPTIC PROBLEM for the generally accepted view of most critics. This view is strongly contested, however, by Rom. Catholic critics (*see* MATTHEW). St M.'s Gospel was used by St Luke and the author of the first gospel. Harnack dates it between AD 65 and 70, so that the date offers no difficulty to accepting the traditional authorship, strengthened as its claim is by internal evidence. St M.'s Gospel is characterised by great vividness of narrative and a wealth of incidental detail. There is no attempt at a literary style, effect being gained mainly by the repetition of words and ideas. *See* commentaries by H. B. Sweete, 1902; J. Lagrange, 1920; A. W. Blunt, 1929; B. H. Branscomb, 1937; J. Chapman, *Matthew, Mark, and Luke*, 1937; B. C. Butler, *The Originality of St Matthew*, 1951.

Mark Antony, *see* ANTONIUS, MARCUS.

Mark System, the agrarian polity, common to all anct Teutonic races, by which the whole arable land of the community was annually or triennially allotted among the freemen, to be held till the time came for it to lie fallow, while the pasture land was both held and used in common. The M. S. as described in Tacitus is evidently a sign of the transition between the nomadic and agric. conditions of tribes, or between a genuine community of land tenure and an inchoate system of private ownership. In England, at any rate, the M. S. never took root.

Mark Twain, *see* CLEMENS, SAMUEL.

Markelius, Sven Gottfrid (1889–), Swedish architect, *b.* Stockholm, member of the Advisory Committees for U.N. H.Q. in New York and UNESCO H.Q. in Paris. He has designed many important buildings in Sweden.

Market (from Lat. *mercatus*, trade). This word is used either of the fixed place to which purchasers and retail merchants resort for purpose of buying and selling (such as, in London, Covent Garden M. for fruit and flowers, Leadenhall M. for meat and poultry) or of a body of people met together for commercial transactions, such as the sale of provisions, livestock, etc., exposed in public, often at a fixed time and place. From early times the right to establish a M. anywhere belonged to the Crown; M. rights became very valuable, and their illegal assumption was checked by Edward I's 'Quo Warranto' inquiries. The word was not commonly used in England before the 12th cent. In the Middle Ages the term included weekly and semi-weekly M.s, and the ann. mart or 'fair'. Until comparatively recent times the Duke of Norfolk owned the M.s in Sheffield, and the Duke of Bedford owned Covent Garden M. Today nearly all the M.s are owned and controlled by the city or bor. councils; while the great London M.s are controlled by the City Corporation or the G.L.C. Many tns, e.g. Nottingham and Peterborough, had a large open square or M. place in which the M. was held, traders setting up their stalls there. Some of them (e.g. the one at Norwich) remain. Cattle M.s are still held in uncovered places, but these are now generally distinct from ordinary M.s. Owing to modern communication there is little variation in the price of a given commodity at different places (*see also* FAIR).

M. is also used to describe the whole range of transactions in a particular commodity, such as cotton or wool, or the dealings in credit instruments which form the money M. The London Stock Exchange with its numerous subdivs. (consols, foreign stock, mining, etc.) is an example of a highly organised M. In economics the M. system is opposed to other methods of allocating goods to consumers. (*See* CAPITALISM; PLANNING, ECONOMIC.) In a M., producer's plans and consumer's plans are brought into equilibrium (q.v.) by the mechanism of price (q.v.). The organisation of M.s depends on the laws and other institutions in which the M. operates (*see* LABOUR LEGISLATION; MONOPOLY; RESALE PRICE MAINTENANCE). The conditions under which a M. may be described as theoretically 'perfect' are given under competition. *See* BLACK MARKET. *See* W. Addison, *English Fairs and Markets*, 1953.

Market Bosworth, *see* BOSWORTH.

Market Deeping, par. of Lincs, England, on the Welland, 7 m. E. by N. of Stamford. Pop. 1600.

Market Drayton, or **Drayton-in-Hales,** mrkt tn of Shropshire, England, 19 m. NE. of Shrewsbury, on the Shropshire Union Canal. It is an old tn and is in the centre of an agric. dist.

Agric. implements are made. There is a 16th cent. grammar school, and near by is Blore Heath, scene of a battle in the Wars of the Roses. Pop. 5853.

Market Gardening, *see* GARDENING.

Market Harborough, mrkt tn in S. Leics, England, 16 m. SE. of Leicester, in the rich grasslands of the R. Welland. Its lovely Gothic par. church has a fine crocketed broach spire, and stands next to the Grammar School, 1614. M. H. has light industry and manufs. of corsetry, patent foods, rubber goods and brushes. It is a centre for the production of meat. Pop. 11,556.

Market Jew, *see* MARAZION.

Market Overt, legal term used in reference to the acquisition of a good title by the purchaser of goods where the seller's title was defective. The general rule is that the owner or his agent alone can sell so as to confer ownership, but among the various exceptions to this rule is the statutory provision that where goods are sold in M. O., according to the usage of the particular market, the buyer acquires a good title to the goods provided he buys in good faith and without notice of any defect or want of title on the part of the seller.

Market Rasen, mrkt tn and urb. dist of Lincs, England, on the little Rase R., 13 m. NE. of Lincoln. Pop. 2257.

Market Research, the branch of business management which obtains and interprets information needed by a manufacturer to decide what products to make and how to sell them. The use of M. R. has grown as manufacturers have recognised the value of making such decisions according to the customers' needs and requirements rather than according to ease of manuf. Thus M. R. is called upon to provide information on customers' opinions about existing and new products; on levels of demand for particular products currently and in the future; on methods of distribution of products; on the effects of selling policies, etc. Much of this information is obtained by means of carefully planned interviews with the public or with buyers, but M. R. also uses statistics from sources such as shop sales records, gov. censuses, etc. Some manufacturers have their own M. R. depts, while others rely on agencies specialising in M. R. of various kinds within the Code of Standards laid down by the M. R. Society. *See* MARKETING; SALES MANAGEMENT.

Marketing, the profitable matching of total company resources against market requirements and opportunities. Production requirements are dependent upon the solution given to this commercial equation; i.e. a company should make what can be profitably sold. When a product is made there is no certainty that it will yield a profit. In the past, the business function has been more concerned with matching total company resources against production requirements, i.e. the company has attempted to sell what it wanted to make. The task of M. management is to identify, assess and realise market opportunities and potentials.

M. management is responsible for creating

customers by persuading them through advertising and personal salesmanship that the company's products or services match their indicated needs and preferences more closely than competitors' offerings, by developing products and services through technical and market research which appear to offer profitable sales opportunities, and by making these products or services available in a form and at a price, time and place that customers want.

The M. process starts with knowledge of the customer and his needs and ends with a customer purchase and the satisfaction of those needs. Through technical product and customer research, generalised needs are translated into specific product sales opportunities. Product planning identifies and specifies the particular product-price-package combinations to exploit these opportunities. Products are engineered or formulated (a number of variations of a single prototype may be made up), screened and tested with customers for overall acceptance and performance. Final decisions have to be taken on packaging design, pricing and trade terms. Assuming that one product stands out as eminently suitable in all *major* respects, the next step is to prepare a M. plan, in writing, setting down all the relevant facts about the product, the market and the competition, the company's M. objectives and sales goals and the means by which they are to be achieved. There must be liaison with production to determine product requirements and scheduling; ample stocks of the product must be available at the times required by the sales organisation. The advertising and promotional programme must be worked out in detail—the amount of money to be spent, the media to be used, the kind of advertising to be run. What is to be the basis of the advertising appeal, to reach what kind of audience with what degree of frequency and impact? Are there to be any introductory consumer offers, coupons, premiums or competitions? On the sales side, distribution and product sales targets must be set, by sales ter. and by individual sales representatives. Physical distribution facilities have to be organised, delivery schedules worked out and so on. The financial people have to provide costings and profit estimates based on proposed expenditures and forecasted sales volumes. Every part of the M. plan has to be costed out and budgets prepared.

The next stage is the implementation of the paper plan through the co-ordination and integration of the physical field selling and distribution effort and the company's advertising and promotional activities. The functions of the former are to see to it that the company's distribution and sales targets are met, that wholesale, retail and direct customers are efficiently serviced and at all times carry adequate stock to meet their anticipated requirements, and that customer information is fed back regularly to sales management in the form of daily, weekly or monthly reports.

Advertising and sales promotion activities run

DEVELOPMENT OF CO-OPERATIVE MARKETING IN ENGLAND, 1939–61

	No. of Soc.	Members 1939	No. of Soc.	Members 1949	No. of Soc.	Members 1959	No. of Soc.	Members 1961
Eggs and Poultry	25	19,984	20	24,200	27	56,396	27	64,547
Dairies	15	1,036	7	886	8	4,154	6	5,772
Livestock and Bacon	12	5,762	6	4,886	8	14,099	8	13,885
Wool	5	4,433	4	3,723	5	6,554	5	7,747
Growers	16	2,564	15	5,044	25	8,722	22	7,718
Total:	73	33,778	52	38,739	72	99,925	68	99,669

Source: G. Hallett and G. James, *Farming for Consumers*, 1963

parallel with the physical selling and distribution operations, and include advertising and display material aimed directly at the consumer or user; trade and technical press advertising to distributors, trade buyers, professional groups, etc.; direct mail, trade receptions and planned sales presentations to trade buyers, committees or associations; consumer and trade incentive schemes, such as special offers, bonuses, competitions, premiums, etc. *See also* ADVERTISING; SALES MANAGEMENT. *See* L. Rodgers, *Marketing in Competitive Economy*, 1965 (from which the above extract was taken).

See F. Knight, *The Ethics of Competition*, 1935; R. S. Edwards and H. Townshend, *Business Enterprise*, 1958; C. McIvor, *Marketing*, 1958; Christina Fulop, *Competition for Consumers*, 1964. *See also* MARKET RESEARCH; SALES MANAGEMENT.

Marketing, Agricultural. In the 1920s farmers attempted to organise co-operative M. arrangements. They aimed to strengthen their individual bargaining position *vis à vis* distributors and consumers, to offer wholesalers more regular supplies and to raise prices by withholding supplies from the market during times of surplus. the table above shows the growth of agric. co-operatives since 1939.

Since price is governed by both demand and supply, and producers can at best only regulate the latter, co-operative marketing cannot guarantee farmers' profits.

After the depression farmers believed that their difficulties in marketing had been due to the inadequacy of these arrangements, though it was truer to say that they had resulted from the general economic distress caused by the depression. They nonetheless began to urge that the special circumstances of their industry could be alleviated only by permitting them monopoly control over the selling of their products. In consequence the A. M. Acts of 1931 and 1933 estab. marketing boards for agric. produce while allowing production to be organised by independent farmers. By 1938 schemes had been introduced covering hops, potatoes, pigs and milk. The A. M. Act, 1949, introduced measures to safeguard consumers' interests.

Marketing boards may be empowered to buy all produce from farmers and there are such trading boards for wool, hops, milk and eggs. Alternatively they may be non-trading boards as

with potatoes, tomatoes and cucumbers. Farmers tend to assume that their marketing boards will automatically raise prices, but it is not so often realised that this is possible only if supply is also restricted, and even then will not be effective unless imports are controlled in some way.

Most economists now regard these special monopoly arrangements as undesirable, especially since they have been combined with guaranteed prices and production grants so that the whole net income of the farming community is now financed by exchequer subsidies which were more than £360 million in 1962 (*see* PRICE; SUBSIDIES). The system prevents supply responding to demand by obscuring from farmers the effect of fluctuating prices and tends to protect individual producers. It thus prevents adaptation and change. It is not without interest that the one agric. product which has not exhibited the general phenomenon of a price increase since 1950 is chicken, for which there is no marketing board and no guaranteed price. *See* P. Self and H. Storing, *The State and the Farmer*, 1962; G. Hallett and G. James, *Farming for Consumers*, 1963; E. F. Nash, *Agricultural Policy in Britain* (ed. by G. McCrone and E. A. Attwood), 1964. *See* AGRICULTURE; AGRICULTURAL CREDIT; SUBSIDIES.

Markham, Mrs, pseudonym of **Elizabeth Penrose** (1780–1837), daughter of Edmund Cartwright (q.v.), inventor of the power-loom. She married the Rev. John Penrose in 1804. She is noted as a writer of hist. and other books for the young. The best known are *Mrs Markham's History of England*, 1823, and *Mrs Markham's History of France*, 1828. Other works include *Amusements of Westernheath, or, Moral Stories for Children*, 1824, *A Visit to the Zoological Gardens*, 1829, and *Sermons for Children*, 1837. *See* S. Smiles, *A Publisher and his Friends*, 1891.

Markham, Sir Clements Robert (1830–1916), traveller and geographer, *b.* Stillingfleet, Yorks. Educ. at Cheam and Westminster, he was in the navy, 1844–52, and served in the Arctic expedition of 1850–1. He introduced quinine-yielding cinchona-trees from Peru to Brit. India, 1859–62, and also the *Hevea braziliensis*, or rubber-bearing tree, into Malaya. M. was geographer to the Abyssinian expedition; assistant-secretary to the India Office, 1867–77; secretary to the Royal Geographical Society,

1863–88; secretary, 1858–87, and president, 1893–1905, of the Hakluyt Society. Among his works are lives of Columbus, John Davis and Hakluyt; also *Travels in Peru and India*, 1862, *Memoir of the Indian Surveys*, 1871, *Quichua Dictionary*, 1908, and *The Incas of Peru*, 1910.

Markham, Edwin (1852–1940), Amer. poet, *b*. Oregon City, son of a farmer. Brought up in California, he was for a time a school teacher. In 1899 he wrote a poem, 'The Man with the Hoe', inspired by Millet's famous picture of that name; it made his name a household word, and he took to writing and lecturing. His second most famous poem is 'Lincoln', pub. in 1901. Later books of verse are *The Shoes of Happiness*, 1915, *Gates of Paradise*, 1920, *The Star of Araby*, 1937, and *Collected Poems*, 1940.

Markham, Gervase, or **Jervis** (1568–1637), poet, translator and writer on animals, *b*. Cottam, Notts. He served as a soldier in the Low Countries and Ireland, but retired into civil life about 1593. He displayed great industry as a translator, compiler and original writer. Among his works are a poem on the last fight of Sir Richard Grenville's ship, the *Revenge*, a continuation of Sidney's *Arcadia*, *The Discourse of Horsemanshippe*, 1593, *Cavelarice, or the English Horseman* (7 vols.), 1607, *Country Contentments*, 1611, *A Way to Get Wealth*, 1631, various books on agriculture, and some plays and poems. See D. F. Markham, *History of the Markham Family*, 1854, and Sir C. R. Markham, *Markham Memorials*, 1913.

Markievicz, Constance Georgine, Countess (1868–1927), Irish politician. She was the daughter of Sir Henry Gore-Booth, and in 1900 married the Polish Count Casimir Markievicz. Active first in the Labour movement and then in the Sinn Féin (q.v.) movement, she was sentenced to death for her part in the 'Easter Rising' in Dublin in 1916, the sentence being commuted to one of life imprisonment. She was released in 1917, and was the first woman to be elected to the Brit. House of Commons, being returned for St Patrick's, Dublin, in Dec. 1918; she did not take her seat.

Markinch, burgh in the co. of Fife, Scotland, 11 m. SW. of Cupar. The chief industries are whisky blending and paper manuf. Pop. 2440.

Marking Ink, *see* INK.

Markirch, *see* STE-MARIE-AUX-MINES.

Markneukirchen, Ger. tn in the dist of Karl-Marx-Stadt, in the Erzgebirge (q.v.), on the Czechoslovak frontier, 44 m. SW. by S. of Karl-Marx-Stadt (q.v.). It manufs. musical instruments. Pop. 10,000.

Markova, Alicia (Alicia Marks) (1910–), ballerina. She joined Diaghilev's Russian ballet in 1925, dancing the *adagio* of *The Swan Lake* in the same year. After Diaghilev's death she danced with the Ballet Club and the Camargo Society. She was prin. ballerina of the Vic-Wells Ballet (1933–5), the Markova-Dolin Ballet (1935–8), Ballet Russe de Monte Carlo (1938–41), Ballet Theatre (1941–5), Original Ballet Russe (1946–7), Festival Ballet (1950–2, 1954–5), guest artist with Sadler's Wells Ballet

(1948, 1953). M. was considered to be one of the finest contemporary exponents of the role of Giselle. In physique and temperament she was a classical dancer in the direct line of Pavlova and Spessivtseva. She occupies a unique position in contemporary ballet and has played a major part in the hist. of the art in England. D.B.E., 1963. (*See Plate: Ballet.*)

Marks of Broughton, 1st Baron, Simon Marks (1888–1964), businessman, educ. at Manchester Grammar School. He was the son of a Polish-Jewish immigrant, Michael Marks (*d*. 1907), who, with a Yorkshire textile salesman, Thomas Spencer (*d*. 1905), opened a haberdashery stall in Leeds market in the 1880's. In 1907 the company owned 70 penny bazaars: under M., who became chairman in 1916, these were expanded into one of Britain's most flourishing chain of stores, which did much to revolutionise the sale of mass-produced clothing in Britain. M. was a convinced Zionist, and gave generously to Jewish and British charities. He was knighted, 1944, and created a baron, 1961.

Marl, sedimentary deposit composed of clay and carbonate of lime. Shell M. is a soft white, crumbling deposit formed on the bottom of lakes and ponds by the accumulation of the remains of mollusca, entomostraca, and partly of fresh-water algae. Cricket pitches are treated with M. in order to bind and improve the turf.

Marlborough, John Churchill, 1st Duke of (1650–1722), soldier, educ. at St Paul's School, and for a while page to James, Duke of York. He entered the army in 1667 as ensign in the foot guards, and, after serving at Tangiers, was promoted captain (1672). In 1678 he became colonel, and in the same year married Sarah Jennings (1660–1744), maid of honour to Princess Anne, over whom she had great influence. He was created Baron Churchill in 1682, and 3 years later took an active part in suppressing Monmouth's insurrection. For this service he was made major-general. He vowed fidelity to James II, and at the same time promised William of Orange to support him. When William landed, Churchill joined him. He was given an earldom in 1689, and, after serving in Flanders, was in 1690 appointed commander-in-chief. On the accession of Anne he was made captain general of the forces and master-general of the ordnance; and, on the declaration of war against France, commanded the forces in Holland. After the successful campaign of 1702 he was created duke. One of England's greatest soldiers, a brilliant exponent of the use of mobility and fire-power, among his great victories were Blenheim (1704), Ramillies (1706), Oudenarde (1708) and Malplaquet (1709).

In the meantime his influence at home was steadily waning, partly owing to changes in the political atmosphere, partly to the imperious behaviour of the Duchess of M. towards the queen, who in 1710 dismissed her from her service, and partly to Harley's intrigues. Peace was declared by the Tories in 1711, and M., returning to England, was accused of malversation and dismissed from all his offices. The charges of peculation were, however, not proceeded with. He went abroad the following year, and took an active part in securing the Hanoverian succession. After the accession of George I he was reinstated as captain-general and master of the ordnance, which offices he held until his health gave way in 1716. He was hardly a scrupulous statesman, but due account must be taken of the times in which he lived. The most serious charges against him are that he betrayed James II and William III in turn; but such charge should be consistently made against all the great nobles who supported the revolution of 1688. Again, it is true that M., in common with Danby, Shrewsbury and most of William's ministers, conducted a correspondence with the Jacobites of St Germains. Macaulay's more serious charge that M. communicated to the enemy the Eng. Gov.'s intention to attack Brest in 1694 has been convincingly refuted in Sir Winston Churchill's *Marlborough* (4 vols., 1933–8; 2 vols., 1947). His letters and dispatches were pub. by Sir G. Murray, 1845–6. *See* lives by Sir J. Fortescue, 1932, M. Ashley, 1939, and M. Foot, 1957, and accounts of his campaigns by F. W. O. Maycock, 1913, F. Taylor, 1921, and H. Belloc, 1933. (*See Plate*: *British Army*.)

Marlborough: 1. Tn of Wilts, England, on the R. Kennet, 26 m. NE. of Salisbury. It is an old tn with interesting buildings and a college for boys (*see* MARLBOROUGH COLLEGE). It was here Henry III held the Parliament which enacted the 'Statutes of M.' in 1267. Pop. 4843.

2. Prov. dist and statistical area of S. Is., New Zealand, area of 4220 sq. m.; pop. 28,800. It is largely engaged in sheep farming, but there is also a tourist industry.

Marlborough College, public school for boys, founded in 1843 for sons of the clergy, being opened to laymen's sons 10 years later, situated at Marlborough, Wilts. Now has 800 boys.

Marlborough House, mansion in Pall Mall, London, built by Wren for the great Duke of Marlborough in 1709–10, and since much altered. It became crown property in 1817 and was used as a residence by Edward VII when Prince of Wales, by Queen Alexandra and Queen Mary. In 1959 the Queen gave the house as a Commonwealth centre for gov. conferences, and it was first used as such in 1962.

Marline-spike, or **Marlinspike** (from *marline*, a small line of 2 strands for seizings, etc.), pointed hardwood or iron spike used on board ship for unravelling the strands of a rope and as a lever in tying knots, etc.

Marlow, or **Great Marlow,** tn in Buckinghamshire, England, on the Thames, 5 m. NW. of Maidenhead. The riv. is crossed here by an iron suspension bridge. There are extensive beech woods, attractive scenery. Pop. 8724.

Marlowe, Christopher (1564–93), dramatist and poet, *b.* Canterbury, son of a shoemaker. He was educ. at King's School, Canterbury, and Corpus Christi College, Cambridge. Presently he joined the Earl of Nottingham's theatrical company, by which most of his plays were produced. He wrote *c.* 1587 the great blank verse tragedy, *Tamburlaine,* and followed this with *The Troublesome Reigne and Lamentable Death of Edward the Second, King of England,* 1594, and *The Tragedy of Dido Queene of Carthage* (in collaboration with Nash), 1594. After his death appeared *The Massacre at Paris* (*c.* 1600), *The Tragicall History of Dr Faustus,* 1604, and *The Famous Tragedy of the Rich Jew of Malta,* 1633. A number of other plays have also been wholly or partially ascribed to M., and it has been asserted by some critics that he was part author of Shakespeare's *Titus Andronicus,* of the second and third parts of *Henry VI* and of *Edward III.* As a poet he is best known as the author of 'Come live with me and be my love' (pub. in *The Passionate Pilgrim,* 1599). It was declared that M. was an atheist, and in 1593 the Privy Council issued a warrant for him to be brought before them. Before it was served M. was killed in a drunken brawl at Deptford. M. raised both the themes and treatment of the drama to a higher level by taking for dramatisation large serious subjects that appealed to popular imagination, and by converting the old stiff blank verse into a medium of delicate and plastic beauty. His plays show no outstanding power of characterisation or even of constructive skill, but they carry the reader away by the force and beauty of their language and by the heroic visions they conjure up.

Tamburlaine, his earliest, crudest creation, enters on the stage driving a team of kings before his chariot; M. found the raw material for his play *Tamburlaine* in such books as Pedro Maxia's *Life of Timur* (pub. at Seville in 1543 and trans. into English in 1571) and the *Vita Magni Tamerlanis* of Petrus Perondinus. But the thunderbolts of invective were his own, and it is the dramatist who makes the Scythian peasant and mass murderer into a poet. *Tamburlaine* is no doubt an expression of the overmastering prodigality of youth, but in the play M. lit the fires of Eng. heroic drama. By contrast his poem *Hero and Leander* reveals him in a gentle mood of sweet sensuousness in the vein of Spenser. Barabas in *The Jew of Malta* rules the world by the power of gold; Faustus sells his soul for the powers of a magician; each is impelled by a lust of power and the tragedy consistently follows its appointed course from vaulting triumph to a tremendous fall. In technique M.'s highest achievement is his *Edward II,* but in poetry and psychological interest it falls below *Doctor Faustus,* which latter became the accepted model of the finest philosophical drama of modern times, Goethe's *Faust. Doctor Faustus* is a great symbolic tragedy on a theme which, besides reflecting M.'s inner experience, exploits that pride of intellect which was the very spirit of the Renaissance. The story is of the Middle Ages but M., by giving it a Renaissance setting, thereby transformed the anxious alchemist into an ardent idealist, besides softening the crude horrors of the medieval version. M. not only saw that the romantic drama was admirably suited to the spiritual requirements of the needs of the

nation as expressing its full and strenuous life;
but also that for the romantic drama to achieve
beauty as well as force the medium of blank
verse must be used. M. no doubt shows the
defects of the temperament of his age—excess of
imagination, a lack of restraint, and at times an
extravagance approaching the ridiculous, but no
criticism can hide the fact that M. found the
drama crude and formless and left it a mighty
force in Eng. literature. His *Works* have been ed.
by A. H. Bullen, 1885, Havelock Ellis, 1887,
C. F. T. Brooke, 1910, and R. H. Case, 1930–3.
See J. H. Ingram, *Marlowe and his Associates*,
1904; C. F. T. Brooke, *The Marlowe Canon*,
1922; L. Hotson, *The Death of C. Marlowe*,
1925; J. Bakeless, *The Tragical History of
Christopher Marlowe*, 1942; P. H. Kocher,
Christopher Marlowe, 1947; C. Norman, *The
Muses' Darling*, 1948; F. P. Wilson, *Marlowe
and the Early Shakespeare*, 1953; J. B. Steane,
Marlowe: A Critical Study, 1964; A. L. Rowse,
Christopher Marlowe, 1964.

Marmalade, *see* JAM.

Marmande, Fr. tn in the dept of Lotonne, on
the Garonne. It is a centre for market garden
produce, and manufs. textiles and brandy. Pop.
10,200.

Marmion, Shackerley (1603–39), dramatist, *b.*
Aynho, Northants. Educ. at Wadham College,
Oxford, he was for a time a soldier in the Low
Countries. His writings include *Cupid and
Psyche*, an allegory in heroic verse, and 3
comedies in the manner of Ben Jonson,
Holland's Leaguer, 1632, *A Fair Companion*,
1633, and *The Antiquary*, 1634. His dramatic
works were ed. by J. Maidment and W. H.
Logan, 1875.

Marmolada, or **Marmolata**, It. mt 20 m. W. of
Bolzano (q.v.). It is the highest peak in the
Dolomites (q.v.). Height 10,972 ft.

**Marmont, Auguste Frédéric Louis Viesse de,
Duke of Ragusa** (1774–1854), marshal of France,
b. Châtillon-sur-Seine. He served as brigadier-
general in Egypt, returned with Bonaparte to
France, supported him in the revolution of the
18th Brumaire and afterwards continued in
active military service. Having defended the
Ragusan ter. against the Russians and Montenegrins, he was made Duke of Ragusa. He
joined the Grand Army in 1809, the day before
the battle of Wagram, won the battle of Znaym
and was made a marshal. He was thereafter for
18 months governor of the Illyrian provs. M.
succeeded Masséna in Spain in May 1811. On
the news of Soult's defeat by Beresford at
Albuera (16 May) he moved rapidly southward,
forcing Wellington to give up his siege of
Badajoz. Deadlock ensued for 2 months, and in
fact the offensive spirit of the French was gone.
In 1812 Wellington went over to the offensive,
captured Ciudad Rodrigo and Badajoz, and
advanced into Leon. M. retired behind the
Douro to await reinforcements. In July he took
the offensive, manœuvred Wellington from his
positions and threatened his communications
with Portugal. Both armies then moved on
parallel lines, M. attempting, but failing, to cut

his opponent's retreat. At Salamanca (22 July)
M. made the fatal mistake of over-extending his
line. The latter seized his opportunity and
attacked. M. was completely defeated and beat a
precipitate retreat; with the loss of nearly 15,000
men. In 1813 he commanded a *corps d'armée* and
fought at Lützen, Bautzen and Dresden. It was
not until further resistance was hopeless that he
concluded a truce with Barclay de Tolly, on
which Napoleon found himself compelled to
abdicate. On the return of Napoleon from Elba
he was obliged to flee. On the outbreak of the
revolution in 1830, at the head of a body of
troops, he endeavoured to reduce Paris to
submission, and finally retreating with 6000
Swiss and a few battalions that had continued
faithful to Charles X, conducted him across the
frontier. From that time he resided chiefly in
Vienna. In 1852 he engaged in an effort for the
fusion of the Fr. Legitimists and Orleanists, but
d. at Venice that year. His memoirs were pub.
1857–8.

Marmontel, Jean-François (1723–99), Fr.
writer, *b.* Bort in the Limousin. His works
include a number of tragedies (*Denys le Tyran*,
1748, *Aristomène*, 1749, etc.), a pastoral comedy,
La Bergère des Alpes, 1766, light operas (e.g.
Silvain, 1770, *Zémire et Azor*, 1771, both to
music by Grétry), 2 historical romances, *Béli-
saire*, 1767, and *Les Incas*, 1777, some vols. of
Contes moraux, posthumous *Mémoires d'un
père*, etc. His articles on literature for the great
Encyclopédie, 1751 onwards, were collected and
repub. as *Eléments de littérature*, 1787.

Marmora, A. F. La, *see* LA MARMORA.

Marmora, Sea of (anct **Propontis**), between
Europe and Asia, connected with the Aegean
Sea by the strait of the Dardanelles, and with the
Black Sea by the Bosphorus. Its length is 175 m.
and its greatest breadth about 50 m., while in
some parts it is over 4000 ft deep. Among the is.
in this sea is that of M., celebrated for its marble
quarries.

Marmora Arundelliana, *see* ARUNDEL
MARBLES.

Marmosets, or **Ouistitis (Hapalidae),** family of
S. Amer. monkeys, sometimes called bear-
monkeys (Arctopithecini) from their somewhat
bear-like extremities, the feet having paws and
claws which are necessary for the M.'s mainly
insectivorous habits. The face is short, and the
32 teeth include only 2 molars on each side. The
tail is not prehensile. M. are all arboreal in habit,
climbing and jumping with great activity. They
are not very intelligent, but their gentleness and
pretty appearance make them interesting pets.
The common M. (*Hapale jacchus*) is about the
size of a squirrel, with darkish brown fur and
long bushy tail marked with alternate rings of
black and grey. The side of the head bears a long
tuft of whitish hair over the ears.

Marmot (*Marmota*), genus of rodents,
resembling squirrels in their dentition, although
in their form and habits they more resemble rats
and mice. They have 2 incisors and 2 praemolars
in each jaw, 4 molars on each side above, and 3
below. The common M., or alpine M. (*M.*

MARMOSET

marmota), is a native of the Alps, the Pyrenees and the more N. mts of Europe, up to the limits of perpetual snow. It is not a native of Britain. It is about the size of a rabbit, greyish-yellow, brown towards the head. It feeds on roots, leaves, insects, etc., and is gregarious, often living in large societies. It digs large burrows with sev. chambers and 2 entrances, generally on the slopes of the mts. It spends the winter in its burrow, in one chamber of which is a store of dried grass, but the greater part of the winter is passed in torpidity. The alpine M. is easily tamed. The Quebec M., found in Canada in woody dists, is a burrowing but not a gregarious animal. M.s are classified in the squirrel family (Sciuridae). *See* Fur.

Marne: 1. (anct **Matrona**) Riv. of France, which rises on the Plateau de Langres, S. of Langres (q.v.), and flows NW. and W. past Chaumont, St-Dizier, Châlons, Épernay, Château-Thierry and Meaux, to join the Seine at Charenton-le-Pont, just SE. of Paris (qq.v.). It is navigable to St-Dizier, is joined to the Rhine, Rhône and Aisne (qq.v.) by canal, and has a lateral canal from Vitry-le-François to Épernay. It crosses Champagne (q.v.) and also the rich country of the Île de-France (q.v.). It was the scene of great battles during the First World War (*see* below). Length 328 m.

2. Inland dept in the NE. of France, formed out of the old prov. of Champagne, is traversed by the R. Marne and extends southward from the frontier dept of Ardennes. The soil is very fertile in the S., but chalky and arid in the N. The surface is undulating in the centre of the dept, the remainder being level. It is in the dry and chalky soil of the N. of this dept that the best varieties of the Champagne wines (q.v.) are grown. Other industries include tanning, iron and copper founding, brewing and pottery manuf. The rearing of a Sp. breed of sheep is a chief branch of industry, and woollen manufs. are largely carried on. The prin. tns are Châlons-sur-Marne (the cap.), Épernay, Rheims, Sainte-Menehould and Vitry-le-François (qq.v.). Area 3167 sq. m.; pop. 442,400.

Marne, Battles of the (1914; 1918). The first battle of the M. (fought 6–9 Sept. 1914) was one of the decisive battles of the First World War, and had a direct bearing on Germany's ultimate defeat. The victorious sweep of the Ger. right wing under von Kluck (q.v.) pressed back the Allies' left flank, first in a SW. direction, changing to S., then SSE., in an endeavour to envelop it and bring about a hasty collapse, in accordance with the approved Ger. plan. The Brit. Expeditionary Force was on the left of the Allies' line for a time, but in retreating to S. of the M., Joffre (q.v.), the commander-in-chief, formed a new army under Gen. Maunoury on the Brit. left. He formed another new army under Gen. Foch, which took up a position in the centre of the left section of the Allies' line which faced N., 'holding the debouches to the south of the marshes of Saint-Gond and posting a part of its forces on the plateau to the north of Sézanne'. When Kluck changed direction, he exposed his own right flank to Paris, and Gen Galliéni (q.v.), the governor, communicated with Joffre as soon as this movement became discernible. Joffre thereupon made arrangements to fall upon Kluck as soon as he was deeply committed to the new direction. He allowed him to advance over the M. and the Grand Morin. On 4 Sept. Joffre issued orders for an attack to be launched on 6 Sept. Great pressure was brought against the Allies' line towards the E. of the marshes of Saint-Gond on 8 Sept. Maunoury, on the extreme left, however, now began to attack Kluck, who, realising that he had exposed his right flank, at once faced W. to meet the danger. This sudden move caused a gap to appear on Kluck's left and von Bülow's right, where the British struck with great effectiveness and drove the Germans back beyond the Grand Morin and Petit Morin. This disorganised the entire Ger. front on this flank, and at 11 a.m. on 9 Sept. Kluck received the order to retire. This exposed Bülow's right still more, and gave Foch the opportunity for which he had been waiting. Foch struck hard at Bülow's centre, right and left. Maunoury had also driven the Germans from the Ourcq and the British then crossed the M. at Château-Thierry (q.v.). The Ger. right was now in full but orderly retreat (*see map overleaf*).

The second battle of the M. arose out of the final Ger. offensive. This offensive was launched in Mar. 1918, and the initial result was the creation of a large salient in the Allies' line in the direction of Amiens. In May a great effort was made by the Germans between Soissons and Rheims to break through to Paris. On this occasion the M. was reached about Château-Thierry. On 15 July the Germans launched a further offensive in this area and crossed the M. between Château-Thierry and Rueil (E. of Rheims), thus creating another and dangerous salient. Against the W. face of this bulge Foch launched a Franco-Amer. force on 15 July, the Americans capturing Courchamps, Torcy and Belleau. The fighting was very stubborn, and 16,000 prisoners and 50 guns fell to the Allies.

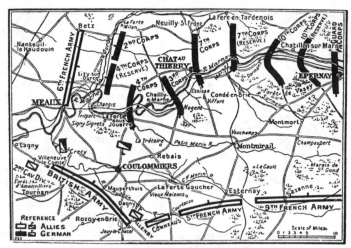

THE FIRST BATTLE OF THE MARNE, 1914

This victory showed the weakness of the Ger. position on the M., and they gradually withdrew. They recrossed to the N. bank by 20 July, under pressure, but without undue loss. Château-Thierry was abandoned the next day, and the withdrawal continued daily, but the retiring forces clung desperately to Buzancy (q.v.), which was not taken until 29 July. On the 31st the Americans defeated the Germans at Seringes, thus wiping out the salient altogether. *See also* FRANCE AND FLANDERS, FIRST WORLD WAR, CAMPAIGN IN, and WAR, THE FIRST WORLD.

Marne, Haute-, dept of NE. France, formed from the SE. part of Champagne, with parts of Burgundy, Lorraine and Franche-Comté. The centre of the dept consists of the plateau of Langres, the highest point being Haut-du-Sec (1695 ft) in the SW. To the NE. are the Monts Faucilles. The low country forming the remainder of the dept is called the Bassigny. The dist contains the upper basins of the Marne, Ourcq and Aube, tribs. of the Seine, the Meuse and some small tribs. of the Rhône. There is considerable forest land. The soil is mostly poor, but cereals and vines are produced in parts. There are iron-mines and mineral springs. The prin. tns are Chaumont (the cap.), Langres and St-Dizier (qq.v.). Area 2430 sq. m.; pop. 208,800.

Marnix, Philip van, Sainte Aldegonde, *see* SAINTE ALDEGONDE.

Maroc, or **Marocco,** *see* MOROCCO.

Marochetti, Carlo, Baron (1805–68), It. sculptor, *b.* Turin, settled in Paris after 1827 and was a pupil of Baron Bosio. His works include a relief on the Arc de Triomphe at Paris; equestrian statues of Emmanuel Philibert and the Duke of Orleans; and, in Great Britain, an equestrian statue of Richard Cœur de Lion, 1851, now at Westminster. He removed to London in 1848 and lived there mainly until his death. Statues of Queen Victoria (1854) and Wellington at Glasgow, and the Inkerman monument at St Paul's, are by him.

Maroni, *see* FRENCH GUIANA.

Maronites, oriental Church founded by the Syrian St Maro (fl. before 423). Their homeland is Mt Lebanon, the Anti-Lebanon and Hermon, and near Antioch. Originally Monothelites, prominent in the Monothelite controversy in 713, they united with the Lat. Church, *c.* 1182, and since 1216 have been steadfast Catholics. Their head, the Maronite patriarch of Antioch, lives in the monastery of Kanobin on Mt Lebanon. In 1584 a Maronite college was founded at Rome to train their clergy. *See* Schnurrer, *De ecclesia Maronitica,* 1810; F. J. Bliss, *Palestine Exploration Fund Quarterly Statement,* 1892; P. Dils, *Étude sur la liturgie maronite,* 1919.

Maroons, or **Nègres Marrons** (Amer.-Sp. *marrón;* Fr. *marron,* fugitive), name applied in Jamaica and Dutch Guiana to runaway Negro slaves. The term was first used of the Negroes of Jamaica who fled from their defeated Sp. masters to the mt fastnesses in the W. Indies after the Brit. occupation of Jamaica (1655). They long resisted the Brit. colonists and, although treaties were made with them from time to time, they were not finally pacified until 1796, when, following a rebellion and the Maroon war (the cost of which was £350,000), many of them were transported to Nova Scotia and thence to Sierra Leone. In the same period the M. of St Lucia also gave trouble to the Brit. Gov. and the is. was designated by the Fr. Convention 'the Faithful' on account of the support which its inhab. gave to Fr. revolutionary principles (*see* ST LUCIA). Maroon Tn, once called Trelawny Tn, in Jamaica, where the M. made their last stand against the gov. in 1795, has practically disappeared, and Accompong, still a Maroon settlement, is also in the wild and romantic Cockpit country, a dist about 150 sq. m. in area in the W. central part of the is.

Maros River, *see* MURES RIVER.

Maros-Vásárhely, *see* TIRGU MURES.

Marot, Clément (*c.* 1496–1544), Fr. poet, *b.* Cahors, son of Jean des Mares, surnamed Marot—one of the *rhétoriqueurs*—through whose influence he was introduced to court circles and entered (1518) the service of Margaret d'Alençon, afterwards Queen of Navarre. He made enemies by his witty satires against the Sorbonne (q.v.) and, suspected of sympathies with Protestantism, had to flee to the court of Queen Margaret and later to that of the Duchess of Ferrara. He returned to France in 1536 on condition of a formal recantation, but once more he was forced to leave France, his trans. of the Psalms (i to l) (1543) having been condemned by the Sorbonne (this work was subsequently completed by Beza). M. went to Geneva, but the austerity demanded of the true Calvinist was beyond him and he went on to Turin, where he *d.* The works of M. consist of trans. and allegories such as the trans. of the *Metamorphoses* (books i and ii), his *Temple de Cupidon*, 1515, his *Adolescence Clémentine*, 1532–3, and his allegorical satire *L'Enfer*; of *chants royaux, rondeaux, ballades* and *epigrams*; of occasional pieces such as *étrennes* and *blasons*; and of his trans. of the Psalms (1541). In poetic inspiration and education M. belongs to the preceding cent. and his learning is that of the Middle Ages. M. changed very little in the traditional medieval verse-forms. His great service to Fr. poetry is that he restored naturalness and simplicity and replaced artificial excess of ornament and allegory by native grace. His rondeaux, epigrams, epistles and ballades are examples of his best poetry. In epigram he has rarely been surpassed, and La Fontaine and others imitated the *style marotique*. *See* P. Villey, *Marot et Rubelais*, 1923; J. Plattard, *Marot*, 1938; C. E. Kinch, *La Poésie satirique de Clément Marot*, 1940; P. Jourda, *Marot*, 1950.

Marozia, or **Mariuccia** (*d. c.* 928), It. princess of the 10th cent., daughter of Theodora, noted for her beauty and profligacy. She married successively Alberic I of Spoleto, Guido of Tuscany and Hugo, King of Italy, and was possibly mistress of Pope Sergius III. She had Pope John X deposed and murdered (*c.* 928), and was instrumental in raising her sons John XI, John XII and Leo VII to the papal throne. She had thus entire control of Rome for some years, but was imprisoned by her son, Alberic II (932).

Marple, urb. dist and par. in the co. of Cheshire, England, 10 m. SE. of Manchester, a primarily residential area. Pop. 16,812.

Marples, Ernest (1907–), politician, educ. at Stretford Grammar School. He entered Parliament as a Conservative in 1945. After holding junior office he became postmaster-general, 1957–9, and minister of transport, 1959–64, and gained a reputation for his innovations. Pub.: *The Road to Prosperity*, 1947.

Marprelate Controversy, Puritan attack, in pamphlet form, on the episcopal structure of the Church of England. From 1587 to 1589 a series of anonymous, ribald and outspoken tracts, under the pseudonym of 'Martin Marprelate' were issued from a secret press, violently attacking the episcopate. The tracts were answered by equally outspoken pamphlets by Thomas Nashe, John Lyly and others. The identity of 'Martin Marprelate' has never been definitely proved, but Job Throckmorton and John Penry were clearly deeply involved in the affair. Eventually the secret press was discovered (1589); Penry escaped to Scotland, but later returned to England and was executed, but Job Throckmorton was allowed to go free. The episode is notable for the energy with which Whitgift acted to repress the pamphleteers. *See* W. Pierce, *The Marprelate Tracts*, 1909.

Marquand, John Phillips (1893–1960), Amer. novelist, *b.* Wilmington, Delaware. Educ. at Harvard, he became a reporter on the Boston *Transcript*. Chiefly known for his satires on the upper classes of New England and their out-of-date pretensions, as in *The Unspeakable Gentleman*, 1922, and *Wickford Point*, 1939, he was awarded the Pulitzer Prize for *The Late George Apley*, 1937, satirising the life of a Boston Brahmin. Others of his novels are *Four of a Kind*, 1923, *Black Cargo*, 1925, *Ming Yellow*, 1935, *H. M. Pulham, Esquire*, 1941, *So Little Time*, 1943, *Polly Fulton*, 1946, *Point of No Return*, 1949, *Sincerely, Willis Wayde*, 1955, and *Stopover Tokio*, 1957. Detective stories with a Jap. sleuth are *Thank You, Mr Moto*, 1936, and other Mr Moto exploits. *See* study by P. Hamburger, 1953.

Marque, Letter of, *see* LETTER OF MARQUE.

Marquesas, group of 11 high volcanic is., about 740 m. NE. of Tahiti, total area of 385 sq. m. The pop., which in 1797 numbered some 16,000, in 1963 was 3250 the result of decimation by European-introduced diseases. First discovered by the Sp. navigator Mendana in 1594, rediscovered by Capt. Cook in 1774. In 1813 Capt. David Porter raised the Amer. flag there. Thirty years later France took possession of the group, which is now administered as part of Fr. Polynesia (q.v.). The chief is. is Nukuhiva, containing 127 sq. m. The other is. of the NW. (Washington) group are: Hatutu, Eiao, Motuiti, Ua-Huka and Ua-Pou. The SE. (Mendana) group consists of Fatuhuku, Hiva-oa, Tahuata, Motane and Fatuhiva.

Marquet, Pierre Albert (1876–1947), Fr. landscape painter. He studied at the École des Beaux Arts and was one of the first Fauves (q.v.) with Matisse. He is noted for paintings of tns, harbours and rivs. which combine great simplicity of execution with truth of effect.

Marquetry (Fr. *marqueter*, to variegate, inlay), name of a kind of inlaid work similar to mosaic work, especially used for the decoration of furniture. It consists of veneering or inlaying plain white wood with costly woods of varied tints, or with other materials such as tortoise-shell, ivory, metal, mother-of-pearl. Shaped pieces are so combined as to form beautiful designs. M. is a later development of intarsia; the pieces are affixed to a matrix by glue. The art was known from the earliest times to the Egyptians and Greeks and other E. peoples, and was introduced from Persia to Venice in the 14th cent. The Dutch and Fr. *marqueteurs* (P. Gole, Vordt, Jean Macé and A. C. Boule) are some of the most noted. Roentgen, Reisner and Oeben were famous Ger. *ébénistes* of the 18th cent. *See* F. H. Jackson, *Intarsia and Marquetry*, 1903; P. A. Wells, *Veneering, Marquetry, and Inlay*, 1904; Edward Kitson, *Marquetry and Veneers*, 1952.

Marquette, port and co. seat of M. co., Michigan, U.S.A., on Lake Superior, 150 m. W. of Sault Sainte Marie. It is a shipping point and commercial centre for an iron-ore, lumbering, farming, resort area. It manufs. foundry and wood products and chemicals, and is the seat of the N. Michigan College of Education. Pop. *c.* 20,000.

Marquis, Donald Robert Perry (1878–1937), Amer. Journalist and poet, *b.* Walnut, Illinois. He spent a year at Knox College, and also studied art. After he had tried working as teacher, clerk, reporter and actor, Joel Chandler Harris (q.v.) made him assistant editor of *Uncle Remus's Magazine*. Later he was a columnist on the New York *Sun* and then on the *Herald Tribune*. His last years were spent in illness and poverty. He is best remembered by his comic poems in *archy and mehitabel*, 1927, and its sequels, supposed to be composed by archy, a cockroach, who types by butting the keys with his head and cannot use capitals; mehitabel, a cat, is his friend, and together they express M.'s views on life. *The Old Soak*, 1921, is a kind of comic autobiography.

Marquis, Frederick James, *see* WOOLTON, 1st EARL.

Marquis, or **Marquess** (at first an adjective, march count, O.F. *marchis*, from Romance *marca*, boundary). Originally in European countries this was the title of the rulers of certain frontier lands or marches (lords-marchers of Great Britain, margraves (*Markgrafen*) of the Continent). The title eventually came to indicate a certain degree of the peerage in England, ranking below a duke and above a count or earl. Robert de Vere, 9th Earl of Oxford, was the first M. in this sense, created 1385. He was created M. of Dublin by Richard II, to the great offence of the earls, who had to yield him precedence. The first marquessate in the peerage of England was that of Dorset, conferred in 1397 upon John Beaufort, Earl of Somerset. The oldest surviving is that of Winchester (1551). In Scotland the first 2 M.s were those of Huntly and Hamilton (1599).

Marquise (Fr.), in architecture, a flat canopy, usually of metal and glass, sheltering the entrance to an hotel, theatre or other building.

Marr, Nikolai Yakovlevich (1865–1934), Russian linguist, *b.* Kutais (Transcaucasia) of a Scottish father and a Georgian mother. Having first worked on the Armenian and Caucasian languages, he later turned his attention to more general problems and propounded a fantastic theory—his so-called 'Japhetic' theory—according to which all the languages of the world derived from an original set of 4 monosyllables, *sal, ber, yon* and *rosh*. He also taught that language was liable to 'revolutionary leaps' corresponding to changes in the structure of society. M.'s views exercised considerable influence on Soviet linguistics until they were condemned by Stalin in 1950. *See* L. L. Thomas, *The linguistic theories of J. N. Marr*, 1957.

Marradi, Giovanni (1852–1922), It. poet, *b.* Leghorn. His chief works are *Canzoni moderne*, 1879, *Fantasie marine*, 1881, *Ricordi lirici*, 1884, 1893, *Poesie*, 1887, 1902, *Rapsodie Garibaldine*, 1899–1907, and *Prose*, 1923. As a poet he is noted for his elegant style, his charming descriptions and his love of nature.

Marrakesh, or **Morocco**, second largest tn in Morocco and one of its 4 national caps. M. was the old cap. of the Moorish Empire and is situated on the N. side of the Great Atlas range, 90 m. from the Atlantic coast, 250 m. SW. of Fez (q.v.) and 158 m. from Casablanca (q.v.). It has manufs. of carpets and leather, is the trade centre of S. Morocco, and has an important airport. The city was founded in 1062, and in the 14th cent. had a pop. of 700,000, which has since dwindled to 264,300 (1964). In Jan. 1956 the Grand Kaïd Glaoui *d.* He had been a strong supporter of the French, and following his death many of his adherents were murdered. Kaïd Glaoui was said to own 'half of M.' and had 4 magnificent palaces.

Marram Grass, perennial grass, *Ammophila arenaria*, with a creeping rhizomatous rootstock, often used to bind sands near the sea.

Marriage and Marriage Law. REQUIREMENTS OF A VALIDLY CELEBRATED MARRIAGE.—*The religious ceremony*. In Rom. times consent was of the very essence of a valid marriage and religious ceremony a merely accessorial matter designed to bring the wife under the authority of the husband and initiate her in the *sacra* of her new family. Later, mere dissent would suffice to dissolve the marriage state. England, prior to the decrees of the Council of Trent in 1563, followed the general European law that a mere agreement to marry, supplemented by cohabitation, was enough to constitute marriage, and that no formal secular or eccles. ceremony was necessary. The Church, however, through the eccles. courts, could compel the parties to make an informal arrangement to celebrate and register the marriage in due form. But the validity of those informal marriages was directly destroyed after 1540 by an Act which provided that a subsequent *formal* marriage with another person constituted a valid marriage; and some 20 years later the decrees of the Council of Trent made a religious ceremony practically a *sine qua non* for all Catholic countries—decrees which after the Reformation had, of course, no civil force in Great Britain. The *Codex Juris Canonici* (*see* CANON LAW) forbids marriage between a Rom. Catholic and a non-Rom. Catholic except by dispensation from the Holy See, which entails a prior undertaking by the non-Rom. Catholic party that all children of the marriage will be baptised brought up and educ. as Rom. Catholics. Where either or both parties are Rom. Catholics, the Church does not recognise the validity of any form of marriage other than that prescribed by herself. In countries where the law of the land requires a civil marriage, this may be gone through before or after the religious ceremony; but consummation is not permitted before the latter has taken place. (*See also* SACRAMENTS.) It was only in 1753 that an Act was passed (Lord Hardwicke's Act) with the object of making a formal ceremony essential to an Eng. marriage. This Act was superseded by the Marriage Act of 1823, though the question of validity of informal as opposed to irregular marriages (e.g. marriages by 'Fleet parsons', *see* below) was left open; and again, informal marriages are valid to this day in Scotland (*see also* HABIT AND REPUTE). Since the decision of the House of Lords in the case of *Regina* v. *Millis* in 1843, it is generally agreed that *all* secular forms of marriage other than those allowed by statute, e.g. marriages before a registrar, are invalid. Jews and Quakers, however, enjoy certain privileges. The indirect effect of this decision was to foster the action of breach of promise, for the power of the eccles. courts to compel parties to marry who had contracted to do so informally was abolished. One anomaly follows from the sanctity of the religious ceremony: a girl of 12 and a boy of 14 can be married by the Church of England, though they would be incapable of contracting civilly. See, however, below.

English statutory provisions. The Marriage Act of 1823 covers the chief points of the law relative to marriage in Great Britain. In the case where the parties contracting the marriage reside in different pars., the banns of marriage must be pub. in both pars. The law prescribes the audible pub. according to the rubric, after the second lesson, on 3 Sundays preceding the ceremony. If 3 months elapse between the time of pub. and the proposed date of the marriage, the banns become void, and the parties must obtain a licence or agree to a republication of banns. A marriage may be performed in church on the authority of the superintendent registrar's certificate subject to the incumbent's consent. There are 2 kinds of marriage licence: (1) That granted by the Archbishop of Canterbury and bishops, through their surrogates, for marriage in a church or chapel licensed for marriage; (2) the special licence granted by the Archbishop of Canterbury for marriage at any time or in any place on good reason being shown. The marriage may be solemnised at any time between 8 a.m. and 6 p.m. and with open doors. It is a felony for any clergyman to conduct a marriage where the banns have not been pub. or a licence obtained. The officiating clergyman must see to it that there are at least 2 witnesses present, and that the entries in the register books are witnessed by 2 persons. Marriage with a deceased wife's sister was legalised in 1907 and marriage with deceased brother's widow in 1921.

By an Act of 1931 marriage with various other persons (formerly within the prohibited degrees of relationship) was legalised as a civil contract; with the deceased wife's brother's (or sister's) daughter; with the father's (or mother's) deceased brother's widow; with the deceased wife's father's (or mother's) sister; and with the brother's (or sister's) deceased son's widow. A person under 21 must obtain consent to marry, which must be given by both parents if living together, or, if divorced or separated, by the parent having custody of the infant. Where one parent is dead the consent of the survivor is necessary, and if the deceased parent had appointed a guardian, that guardian must also consent. By the Age of Marriage Act, 1929, marriage under 16 years of age is forbidden. Marriages may be conducted in a dist register office or in a Nonconformist building registered for marriages by certificate or by licence. Notice must be given personally to the superintendent registrar, a registrar of births and deaths, a registrar of marriages, or to the deputy registrar. A marriage at a register office must take place in the presence of the registrar of marriages and the superintendent registrar. If both parties reside in the same registration dist, the duration of such residence must have been at least 7 days before the notice of marriage can be given. If the parties reside in different registration dists, notice by each must be given to a registration officer, such notice being valid only after a 7 days' residence in one of the dists. In the case of marriage by licence, one notice is necessary whether the parties live in the same or in different registration dists. Where both live in the same dist, one of them must have lived there for 15 days before the notice can be accepted. If they live in different dists, notice may be given in either of the dists, provided the residential qualification has been fulfilled. Where this qualification has been fulfilled by one of the parties, the other must have been resident in England or Wales at the time of such notice. The Marriage Act, 1939, gives certain facilities in the case of one party residing in Scotland and the other in England; but the provisions as regards a marriage in Scotland apply only to a 'regular marriage', whereas no such distinction is necessary where the marriage is to be solemnised in England. A certificate of marriage (without licence) may be issued by the superintendent registrar after the lapse of 21 clear days from the date of entry of the notice in the notice-book, provided no impediment is shown. The marriage may then take place within 3 calendar months from the date of entry of the notice. A certificate and licence for marriage may be issued by the superintendent registrar, provided no impediment is shown, after the lapse of 1 weekday (Christmas Day and Good Friday excepted). The marriage may then take place within 3 calendar months from the date of entry of the notice.

Foreign marriages, or marriages abroad of British subjects, and marriages between persons one at least of whom is not domiciled in Britain.

The Foreign Marriage Act of 1892 provides that Brit. subjects may contract a valid marriage in a foreign country provided they conform to the provisions of the Act. It is sufficient that one of the contracting parties be a Brit. subject. The marriage officer must satisfy himself, where a marriage according to local law is valid by Brit. law, that: (a) both parties are Brit. subjects; or (b) when only one is a Brit. subject the other is not a subject or citizen of the country; (c) when only one is a Brit. subject, and the other is a subject or citizen of the country, proper facilities do not exist for the solemnisation of the marriage in the foreign country in accordance with the law of that country; or (d) when the man is a Brit. subject and the woman a subject or citizen of the country, no objection will be taken by the authorities of the country to the solemnisation of the marriage under the Act. In the case of any marriage under the Act where the woman is a Brit. subject and the man a foreigner, the marriage officer must be satisfied that: (a) the marriage will be recognised by the law of the country to which the foreigner belongs; or (b) some other marriage ceremony in addition to that under this Act has taken place, or is about to take place, between the parties, and that such other ceremony is recognised by the law of the country to which the foreigner belongs; or (c) the leave of the secretary of state has been obtained. By the Marriage with Foreigners Act, 1906, notice of an intended foreign marriage must be given by the Brit. party to a registrar in Britain, and a certificate showing that such notice has been given must be sent by the registrar to the marriage officer. There is also provision in the Act for reciprocal action by foreign countries whose inhab. desire to marry in Britain.

Marriage in the U.S.A. The law regulating marriage is not uniform throughout the U.S.A. The question is left to the law-making bodies of each individual state. The marriageable age varies widely. With parental consent, the age for males ranges from 14 to 21 and for females from 12 up to 18. Without the consent of parents, the age for males ranges from 14 up to 21, but in most states the latter age is required. Without consent of parents the age for females ranges from 12 to 21, but in the majority 18 is the age required. In some states a child can be disinherited by law for marrying below the legal age without parental consent. A marriage licence of some kind is required in every state of the union, usually obtainable from the co. clerk's office. Throughout the U.S.A. marriage is now on the civil contract basis, but religious ceremonies are authorised in all states, provided a marriage licence has been obtained. In many states there is no delay in issuing the licence or in marrying as soon as the necessary papers have been secured. In New York state a marriage certificate must be filed within 7 days, and all under 21 who wish to marry must present a birth certificate or other proof of age. In a considerable number of states a delay of 5 days is required before a marriage licence is issued. In some parts of the S. marriage

between Whites and Negroes is unlawful, and in sev. S. states there is a similar prohibition of marriage between Whites and Indians. Many states also require proof that both the man and the woman are free from venereal infection. Common law marriages of a year's duration or more without either licence or ceremony are now validated by the courts in most states upon proper proof and particularly where children or property are involved. In most Amer. states weddings can be performed at any time and place that suits the contracting couple.

MARRIAGE CUSTOMS, ANCIENT AND MODERN: *Britons.* Among the anct Britons a daughter was obliged to marry whomsoever her father selected for her husband. Courtship was of short duration, and the marriage was celebrated at a cromlech in the open air, while sacrifices were offered.

Romans. The oldest Rom. form of marriage was called *confarreatio*, the name and ceremony being derived from the time-honoured association of marriage with the cultivation of corn. The conferreate form of marriage was competent only to those patricians who had the privileges of the *jus sacrum*, and hence patricians and plebeians could not at one time intermarry. The plebeians had no analogous ceremony, and the wife only fell under the authority (*manus*) of the husband either by a process of fictitious sale called *coemptio* or by implication from remaining with the husband for 1 year; but *confarreatio* necessarily involved marital authority. The civil form of *usus* was not introduced out of grace to the plebeians, but rather for the express purpose of preserving the patriciate; for otherwise the *sacra* would have had to be extended to the plebeians. The union of mere slaves was called *contubernium*, and was never regarded as more than a promiscuous relationship. The peculiarity of these old Rom. forms of marriage was that they did not in themselves constitute the tie; they merely decided the position of the wife so far as the question of subjection to her husband's authority was concerned. The tie itself was apparently constituted by the mere consent given on both sides, and the nuptials or rites and ceremonies of initiation into the husband's *sacra* were looked upon as merely accessorial to such facts as evidenced the consent, e.g. the reception into the husband's home. The bar against patricians intermarrying with plebeians was removed 4 years after the decemviral revolution, viz. by the Cornelian Law (444 BC). In AD 9, after the extension of citizenship by the celebrated *Lex Papia Poppaea*, Romans were permitted freely to intermarry with foreigners and freedmen. By the time of Justinian, marriage was a purely commutal relationship subsisting only so long as the parties mutually consented to live with each other.

Greeks. With the anct Greeks the nuptial ceremony was a symbolic representation of the forcible carrying away of the bride, by way of allusion, it seems, to the Gk tradition that a bridegroom should only be entitled to his bride by performing some heroic feat or subtle stratagem; e.g. the mythical hero Theseus is famous for the traditional abduction of Helena, daughter of Leda. On the wedding day the betrothed pair, having laved themselves in water drawn from a special fountain, went to the temple, followed by friends singing paeans of praise. Sacrifices were made at the altar, and the bride, at least if of the wealthier classes, was conducted to her new home in the evening in a chariot drawn by oxen or mules.

Egyptians. In Egypt *mahr*, or bridewealth (q.v.), is indispensable to union with a chosen female. The compact of marriage is settled by the woman's *wekeel* (deputy). Among the upper classes the man has next to no chance of seeing the woman's face before marriage, and has to satisfy himself with the description of her by professional *khát'behs* or women whose vocation is to give men information about eligible girls. The marriage contract is witnessed by 2 Moslems, and all present recite the Fát'heh or opening chapter of the Koran, the various phases of this ceremony being performed or controlled by a *fikee* (schoolmaster). Marriage is no bar to the right of having concubines, who are, however, inferior in status to the legal wife.

Chinese. According to the traditional Chinese belief marriage goes by destiny, from the fact that the Buddhist teaching is to the effect that those connected in a previous existence become united in this. Once Yuelaou, the deity of the moon, has united all pre-destined couples with a silken cord, nothing can prevent their ultimate marriage. Courtship and marriage among the wealthy Chinese are matters settled exclusively by the parents, who fix the time of the nuptials and consult, therefore, the calendar for a propitious day. The solemnisation of marriage is always preceded by 3 days' 'mourning', during which time all the relatives abstain from every kind of amusement, since the Chinese regard the marriage of their offspring as a presage of their own deaths.

French. In France a prov. marriage requires both a civil and religious ceremony for its completion, all the pomp and parade being reserved for the latter occasion. The civil marriage is performed at the mayor's office before a registrar, who, having made the necessary entries, reads passages from the Code Napoléon relative to the law of marriage. Prior to the church ceremony the parties have to produce their tickets of recent confession.

Hebrew customs. According to scripture the custom of acquiring brides by transfer of wealth prevailed among the descendants of Abraham. The alternative for a poor man was to obtain a bride by servitude. Espousals began at a very early age, and males at the age of 13 and females at 12 were competent to marry. The ceremony itself was performed, as a rule, at the house of the bride's father, and usually the latter acted as the 'celebrator'; if not, the rabbi or *hazzan* of the synagogue performed the duties of that office, which consisted in covering the head of the bride with the extremity of the bridegroom's *tallith*

and consecrating a cup of wine. After the ceremony there was usually a procession with dancing and music by torchlight to the groom's house, the pair walking or being borne along under a canopy.

Scottish customs: Gretna Green marriages. Gretna Green is celebrated in hist. as having been the first convenient halting-place for fugitive couples from England. The rule of law being that a marriage was valid if contracted according to the law of the place where the parties entered into the contract, the couple being in Scotland had but to make a mutual declaration of marriage before a witness—the work of a moment—and such ceremony obviated all difficulties of age, consent of parents or guardians, banns and so forth (*see* R. Elliott, *The Gretna Green Memoirs*, 1842). The efficacy of Gretna Green marriages was destroyed by the provision in the Marriage Act, 1856, which requires residence for 3 weeks in Scotland of at least one of the parties (*see also* GRETNA GREEN). 'Handfasting' was an old customary form of marriage, which for long prevailed in Eskdale and neighbourhood. Couples chose each other at a fair and, after a year of cohabitation, they continued together for life if such probationary period proved mutually satisfactory. If not they separated, and the disaffected one was saddled with the issue. If each was disaffected it seems the husband had the issue. Later such marriages were looked upon as perfect only when subsequently confirmed by a priest. Betrothal by hands clasped across a brook in which the pair had been previously washed is celebrated as the ceremony that took place between Burns and 'Highland Mary'. In many rural dists the name of 'penny weddings' was popularly given to those weddings which were characterised by the observance of the anct custom of levying a penny from all who were going to be present at the celebrations. During the 17th cent. these weddings degenerated into scenes of disorder, and in 1645 they were condemned by the General Assembly.

Welsh customs. The old custom of giving 'bidding letters' intimating an intended marriage, its date, and the intent of the parties to make a bidding at an inn to ask for the pleasure of the company and support of the parties to whom the letters were sent, was formerly almost universal. There was also an old Brit. custom called 'purse and girdle', by which the bride's goods, comprising generally an oak chest and feather bed, were taken on the day before the marriage to the bridegroom's house, while the groom in the evening received his friends' gifts.

Fleet marriages. These were clandestine marriages that generally took place at the Fleet prison without pub. of banns, in the presence of real or pretended clergymen known to posterity and the readers of Tom Brown's works as Fleet parsons. Formerly these marriages took place at Duke's Place and Holy Trinity, Minories, until checked by the State, after which they were continued in unabated vigour at or in the vicinity of the Fleet by parsons, real or bogus, who were generally prisoners in the Fleet with neither money nor credit to lose by any proceedings which the bishop might see fit to institute against them. The Fleet weddings came to an end in 1754 when, after years of abortive legislation, Hardwicke's Marriage Act of that year came into operation.

Marriage in primitive societies is of many types, depending largely on the way of tracing descent and regulating inheritance and succession, whether through males only (patriliny), through females only (matriliny) or in other ways. In most patrilineal societies, especially in Africa, marriage is marked by the transfer of bridewealth (q.v.) (in cattle, spears, money or other goods) from the groom's family to that of the bride. Bridewealth ensures that the children of the union shall be legitimate and affiliated to the husband's clan or family. It is not payable in any large amount in matrilineal societies, since there, children belong to the wife's clan in any case and so rights in them need not be acquired by the husband. Bridewealth is not, of course, purchase of a woman but a means of legitimising the marriage. Polygyny (q.v.) is frequently the ideal—although perhaps only a small minority of men in any community actually have more than 1 wife. Polyandry (q.v.) is rare, being found in only a few societies with special forms of organisation. Polygyny is found in societies with both patrilineal and matrilineal descent, and in some systems with strong patriliny the necessity to ensure legitimate male offspring for all adult men leads to ghost marriage (q.v.) and other unusual forms. In societies in which clans and other descent groups form the basic units of the social system, the stable family is essential for the orderly perpetuation of these groups. The family in most primitive societies is not the simple conjugal family but rather a wider grouping of the joint or extended family (q.v.). Marriage is thus not merely a union between 2 persons but also between 2 groups, which are placed in an official relationship which may last for sev. generations. The immediate union is not necessarily dissolved at the death of one of the spouses, as the institutions of the levirate and sororate (qq.v.) show. Today in many parts of the world the indigenous forms of marriage are breaking down as a result of the change in the structure of primitive societies subsequent to European contact and industrialisation, and marriage is approximating more to W. forms. For descriptions of marriage in particular societies *see* B. Malinowski, *The Sexual Life of Savages*, 1929; I. Schapera, *Married Life in an African Tribe*, 1940; Margaret Mead, *Male and Female*, 1950; A. R. Radcliffe-Brown, *African Systems of Kinship and Marriage*, 1950; E. E. Evans-Pritchard, *Kinship and Marriage among the Nuer*, 1951. For marriage in general *see* S. C. Banerjee, *Hindu Law of Marriage and Stridhana* (first pub. 1879); J. Ashton, *The Fleet: its River, Prison and Marriages*, 1888; E. A. Westermarck, *The History of Human Marriage*, 1901; G. E. Howard, *History of Matrimonial Institu-*

tions, 1904; P. E. Corbett, *The Roman Law of Marriage*, 1930; R. E. Baber, *Marriage and the Family*, 1939; Margaret Cole, *Marriage Past and Present*, 1939; and references given under FAMILY.

Marriages, Registration of, *see* REGISTRATION OF BIRTHS, MARRIAGES AND DEATHS.

Marrickville, inner suburb of Sydney, Australia, $3\frac{1}{2}$ m. SW. of city proper. Industrial and residential area. Pop. 75,348.

Married Women's Property, *see* HUSBAND AND WIFE.

Marriott, Sir John Arthur Ransome (1859–1945), historian. He was educ. at Repton and New College, Oxford. In 1914 he was elected to a fellowship at Worcester College. He was Conservative M.P. for Oxford City from 1917 to 1922, and for York, 1923–8. He is remembered for his research on constitutional and imperial subjects, modern diplomacy in relation to the E. question (q.v.), and European hist. from Waterloo to the Versailles Treaty of 1920. He wrote also on economics and finance. His works include *The Eastern Question*, 1917, *a History of Europe from 1815 to 1923*, 1931, *The Evolution of the British Empire*, 1939, *A Short History of France*, 1942, *Anglo-Russian Relations*, 1944, and *Memoirs of Fourscore Years*, 1948.

Marrow, substance filling the central cavities of long bones and the cancellous tissue of other bones. It consists of fatty tissue, loose connective tissue and a network of intercommunicating, thin-walled, but comparatively large blood vessels. M. is the blood cell forming organ of the body. Active M. in the adult is estimated to be from 3 to 6 per cent of the body weight and its volume at about 4000 millilitres. The parent cells of the M. can produce many times their own volume of mature blood cells in a relatively short time. The stimulus for blood cell production is probably anoxaemia (lack of oxygen in the blood), but some think that there may also be some hormone (q.v.) stimulus as well, perhaps derived from the spleen (q.v.). M. which is actively engaged in producing blood cells is red in colour, while inactive M. is yellow and with a greater amount of fat. For the first 3 or 4 years of life (in man) all the bones in the body contain active red M. At about the age of 7 the M. in the long bones becomes less active and pale red in colour, and droplets of fat begin to appear. From the age of 10 to 14 an area of fatty M. appears at the lower ends of the shafts of the long bones and spreads upwards until, at the age of 20, the entire red M. of the long bones has been replaced by yellow M. In the adult the red M. is contained in the bones of the skull, the ribs, sternum, scapulae, clavicles, vertebrae and os innominatum. Red bone M. is extremely cellular, the cells consisting of red and white blood corpuscles in various stages of development from the parent cells. The parent cells of the white corpuscles are known as leucoblasts, and those of the red corpuscles as erythroblasts. Between these and the mature cells are cells of various intermediate kinds. Histological examination of the M. in various diseases of the blood system, such as the leukaemias (q.v.) and pernicious anaemia (q.v.), show abnormalities in the number and character of these cells.

Marrow, Vegetable, kind of gourd (q.v.).

Marrow Controversy. In 1718 an old Eng. puritanic book called *The Marrow of Modern Divinity*, first pub. in 1646, was repub. by some Scottish divines, including Thomas Boston of Ettrick in Selkirk. Its extreme Calvinism caused the General Assembly to condemn it as antinomian in 1720. This caused a great religious struggle in Scotland, at its fiercest from 1718 to 1722. This controversy eventually led the General Assembly to depose the Rev. Ebenezer Erskine and 3 others. They anticipated this decision by seceding and forming an 'Associate Presbytery' in 1733. Differences among the seceders themselves eventually led to the formation of 'burghers' and 'antiburghers'.

Marrucinian Dialect, *see* LATIN LANGUAGE AND LITERATURE.

Marryat, Frederick (1792–1848), captain and novelist, *b.* Westminster, son of Joseph M., who was at one time M.P. for Sandwich. He received a private education and joined the *Impérieuse*, under Lord Cochrane, in 1806. He formed a lasting friendship with Sir Charles Napier and Houston Stewart. In 1812 he was promoted to the rank of lieutenant. He married, in 1819, Catherine, second daughter of Sir Stephen Shairp, of Houston, Linlithgow. He took command of the *Beaver* sloop in 1820, and was employed on the St Helena station until the death of Napoleon. Serving in the Burma war of 1824 it was on his suggestion that the *Diana* was used, the first employment of a steamship on active service. He succeeded to sev. other appointments, but finally gave up the sea, after being nominated C.B., in 1830. He was elected a fellow of the Royal Society in 1819, through adapting Sir Hume Popham's system of signalling to a code for the mercantile marine. In 1833 the King of France decorated him with the Legion of Honour.

After his retirement from the navy he devoted himself to novel writing. Included in his works are *The Naval Officer, or Scenes and Adventures in the Life of Frank Mildmay*, 1829, *Peter Simple*, 1834, *Mr Midshipman Easy*, 1836, *The Phantom Ship*, 1839, *Masterman Ready*, 1841, *Percival Keene*, 1842, *The Settlers in Canada*, 1844, and *The Children of the New Forest*, 1847. He wrote a pamphlet, *Suggestions for the Abolition of the Present System of Impressment in the Naval Service*, 1822, which created a profound impression in naval circles at the time. He pub. sev. caricatures of a political and social nature. His stories, taken from personal experience, are full of life, humour and stirring narrative. See *Life and Letters of Captain Marryat* by his daughter Florence (herself a novelist), 1872; *also* a life by D. Hannay, 1889. *See also* M. McGrath, *A Century of Marryat*, 1929; C. Lloyd, *Captain Marryat and the Old Navy*, 1939; O. Warner, *Captain Marryat*, 1953.

Mars, Mavors or **Mamers,** together with Jupiter and Quirinus (qq.v.), one of the 3 great tutelary gods of Rome. He had his *flamen* (q.v.). As god of war, with the title *Gradivus*, he gave his name to a place set apart for military exercises (Campus Martius) and was identified with the Gk Ares (q.v.). *See also* SALII. But he was also a god of agriculture, and was regarded as protector of cattle. The wolf and the woodpecker were sacred to him, and he was the source of an oracle (q.v.).

Mars, fourth planet from the sun, its orbit lying between those of the earth and Jupiter. M. has been known from antiquity, its red colour suggesting the identification with the god of war. At closest approach, every 780 days, M. may come as close as 34,000,000 m. from the earth; it is then twice as bright as Sirius. M. revolves at a mean distance of 142,000,000 m. from the sun. its diameter is 4225 m., just over half that of the earth; its mass is 0·11 of the earth's, giving a mean density of 3·97, somewhat less than that of the earth. M.'s rotation period is 24 hrs 37 min. 23 secs. M. has 2 very small satellites (whose existence was remarkably foretold by Swift in *Gulliver's Travels*); they were discovered in 1877, and from their brightness cannot be more than 10 m. in diameter. M.'s companions Phobos (fear) and Deimos (panic) revolve respectively 5800 m. and 14,600 m. from the centre of the planet; Phobos revolves in only 7 hrs 39 min., thus rising in the W. and setting in the E.

Under good conditions the surface of M. shows much detail in the telescope. Three-fifths of the surface is reddish in colour, probably due to iron oxide; there are dark markings showing seasonal changes, and white polar caps that shrink in the Martian summers. The polar caps consist of ordinary ice, but are very thin. M.'s atmosphere is hazy, with occasional clearings; the pressure is about one-sixtieth of the earth's. The atmosphere probably consists chiefly of nitrogen; carbon dioxide is twice as abundant as in the earth's atmosphere, but very little free oxygen or water vapour are present. The average surface temperature is only −5° C. The *canali* or narrow dark lines reported by Schiaparelli in 1877, and later misinterpreted as 'canals' constructed by intelligent beings, have probably no real existence. The first close-up photographs, televised by the American 'Mariner 4' spacecraft in July 1965, revealed craters remarkably like those of the moon, but no trace of canals. *See* G. de Vaucouleurs, *Physics of the Planet Mars*, 1954; G. P. Kuiper and B. M. Middlehurst (eds), *Planets and Satellites*, 1961; E. C. Slipher, *The Photographic Story of Mars*, 1962; F. L. Whipple, *Earth, Moon and Plants*, 1963. (*See Plate: Space Travel.*)

Marsala (anct Lilybaeum), seaport in Sicily, in Mediterranean, 12 m. SSE. of Trapani. Originally a Carthaginian (*see* CARTHAGE) stronghold, founded in 397 BC, it long resisted siege by Pyrrhus (q.v.) and the Romans, but eventually surrendered to Rome in 241 BC. Under the Romans, and later the Saracens (q.v.), it was an important port. It was taken by the Normans in the 11th cent. In 1860 Garibaldi (q.v.) and his 'thousand' landed here. M. has a baroque cathedral (dedicated to St Thomas Becket) and an anct citadel. M. wine (*see* next article) is famous, and there is also a trade in agric. produce and olive oil. Pop. 39,300.

Marsala, fortified dessert wine from grapes grown in Sicily between Palermo and Messina. Woodhouse and Ingham are Eng. names long connected with the M. trade. The former supplied M. to Nelson's fleet at Malta in 1800 to eke out the rum ration.

Marschner, Heinrich (1795–1861), Ger. composer, *b.* Zittau. He became conductor at the Dresden Opera under Weber in 1823; in 1827 he took a similar post at Leipzig, and in 1831 became court *Kapellmeister* at Hanover, where he *d.* He is remembered exclusively as a composer of operas, which contributed to the romantic development, and of which the most important were *Der Vampyr*, 1828, *Der Templer und die Jüdin* (from Scott's *Ivanhoe*), 1829, and *Hans Heiling*, 1833.

Marsden, *see* COLNE VALLEY.

Marseillaise, La, Fr. national anthem, written and composed at Strasbourg in 1792 by Rouget de Lisle, an army officer. Its original title was *Le Chant de guerre de l'armée du Rhin*. It was an instant success and became known far and wide before it appeared in print on 7 July 1792, in *Affiches de Strasbourg* (or *Strassburgisches Wochenblatt*). It was sung by the volunteers of Marseilles (hence its present name) as they entered Paris (July), and at the storming of the Tuileries (Aug.).

Marseilles (Fr. **Marseille**; Gk. **Massalia**; Lat. **Massilia**), Fr. seaport on the Golfe du Lion (q.v.), cap. of the dept of Bouches-du-Rhône, 25 m. E. of the mouth of the Rhône and 400 m. SSE. of Paris. It is the second city and the prin. commercial port of the country. It was founded as a colony from Phocaea (q.v.) in Asia Minor about 600 BC, and itself later planted colonies along the N. Mediterranean shore. In 49 BC it was taken by Caesar from the supporters of Pompeius (qq.v.). In the 9th cent. it was razed by the Arabs. Charles of Anjou took it in 1252, and it was united with the kingdom of France in 1486. Many of the privileges it enjoyed as a free port were retained until 1660. A great plague, in 1720–1, killed nearly half the pop. The citizens of M. were enthusiastic supporters of the Revolution, and the arrival in Paris of the volunteers from M., singing Rouget de Lisle's battle song, earned for this the title of the 'Marseillaise' (q.v.). The modern prosperity of the city dates from the Fr. conquest of Algeria and the opening of the Suez Canal (q.v.). As a Mediterranean port M.'s only rival is Genoa (q.v.). During the Second World War the city and its port were damaged by allied bombardment and later by the Gers. as they withdrew from M. M. lies at the centre of an arc of bare limestone hills, and is itself built on slopes overlooking the famous Vieux-Port (old harbour), from which the modern harbour extends for 5 m. to the N., where, at l'Estaque, the Rhône–M. canal enters the Rove tunnel. The modern harbour consists of interconnecting docks (Joliette, Lazaret,

National, Mirabeau, etc.), with some 16 m. of quays and railway sidings. A breakwater 6 m. long, parallel with the coast, shelters the port installations on the seaward side. Just SSW. of the port are the is. of Ratonneau and Pomègues (quarantine stations), and between them and the mainland is the is. of If (q.v.). Despite its great antiquity, M. has few anct monuments. The new cathedral (1852–93), built in Byzantine style, stands above the Joliette basin. Near it is the old cathedral, a Romanesque church with some fine chapels. On a hill to the S. of the Vieux-Port, in the middle of a 17th cent. fort, is the basilica of Notre Dame de la Garde (1864), which rises to a height of 502 ft above sea level. The church of St Victor (13th–14th cents.) has crypts dating back to the 5th cent. The *hôtel de ville*, a baroque building, dates from 1672. A modern, and controversial, addition to the buildings of the city is the Cité Radieuse, the 'vertical community' of Le Corbusier (q.v.). The celebrated Canebière, the main thoroughfare of the city, runs E. from the head of the Vieux-Port; in it is the Bourse (1860), outside which King Alexander of Yougoslavia and M. Barthou (qq.v.) were assassinated in 1934. M. has the faculties of medicine and science of the univ. of Aix-M., and has also schools of art and music, observatories and museums. The inhab. of the city are renowned for their reputed individuality and for their habits of speech. There is a large trade with Africa and the Orient. Among the prin. exports are wines, liqueurs, olive oil, soap and foodstuffs, and among the prin. imports are fruit, spices, hides, oil-seeds and N. African wines. There are soap, shipbuilding, chemical, oil, textile and metallurgical industries. Pop. 778,000. *See* R. Busquet, *Histoire de Marseille*, 1945, and 'Le Corbusier', *The Marseilles Block* (Eng. trans.), 1953.

Marsh, Sir Edward Howard 1872–1953), Brit. man of letters, educ. Westminster School and Trinity College, Cambridge. He was private secretary to Asquith (1915–16) and Churchill (1917–22). From 1937–44 he was a Trustee of the Tate Gallery. His pubs. include *Georgian Poetry*, 1912–21, *Memoir of Rupert Brooke*, 1918, *Odes of Horace*, 1941, and *Minima*, 1947. His trans. of Horace and La Fontaine are outstanding.

Marsh, Ngaio Edith (1899–), New Zealand novelist, *b.* Christchurch, of partly Maori descent. After studying art for 5 years she became a touring actress. Her first novel was *A Man Lay Dead*, 1934. Her other detective stories, which are among the best of their kind, include *Death in Ecstasy*, 1937, *Overture to Death*, 1939, *Died in the Wool*, 1945, *Opening Night*, 1951, *Singing in the Shrouds*, 1959, and *Dead Water*, 1964. In 1948 she was awarded the O.B.E. and the D.B.E. in 1966.

Marsh, Othniel Charles (1831–99), A.mer palaeontologist, *b.* Lockport, New York, prof. at Yale (1866), noted for his discoveries of many new species of extinct vertebrates, largely from the Rocky Mts. His chief works are *Odontornithes: a Monograph on the Extinct Toothed Birds of North America*, 1880, *Dinocerata: a Mono-*

graph on an Extinct Order of Gigantic Mammals 1884, Sauropoda, 1888, and *The Dinosaurs of North America*, 1896. *See* C. Schuchert and C. M. LeVere, *O. C. Marsh, Pioneer in Paleontology*, 1940.

Marsh, Richard William (1928–), politician, educ. at Jennings School, Swindon, Woolwich Polytechnic and Ruskin College, Oxford. He became a Labour M.P. in 1959, and after holding junior office, 1964–6, became minister of power, April 1966.

Marsh Frog, *Rana ridibunda*. This frog is also called the Hungarian frog, but M. F. is its popular name—not unsuitable seeing that the frog is firmly estab. on Romney Marsh in Kent. The M. F. is said to have been first introduced to Romney in 1935, and there are now probably tens of thousands over the area from Hythe to Rye, and around Tenterden. The ground colour of the M. F. is like weathered cement and, in pattern, the most obscrvable peculiarity is a series of square dark brown spots on the legs which remain through all colour changes. When basking in the sun on a bank it assumes a striking grass-green hue. In size the M. F. much exceeds all other Brit. frogs or toads. In general, the M. F., like the edible frog, is very aquatic, and never seems to be more than a distance of one leap from the water. A six-foot leap is not beyond the powers of a full-grown specimen. Despite the scientific name, it is difficult to detect anything resembling laughter in its croaking.

MARSH FROG

Marsh Gas, *see* METHANE.

Marsh Mallow, or *Althaea*, genus of biennials or perennials (family Malvaceae). The common M. M. (*A. officinalis*) is a downy plant occurring in marshes near the sea and bearing cymes of rose-pink flowers. A demulcent is prepared from the root. The rare hispid M. M. (*A. hirsuta*) is the only other Brit. species.

Marsh Marigold, or *Caltha palustris*, handsome plant with large kidney-shaped, glossy leaves and golden-yellow sepals, the petals being absent. It is common in watery places.

Marshal, William, 1st **Earl of Pembroke and Strigeuil** of the Marshal line (*c.* 1146–1219), nobleman and soldier, trusted knight of Henry II, and tutor to his son, Prince Henry. He became marshal of England under Richard I. On Richard's death M. supported John's claim to the throne (1199), and held office under him. On John's death (1216) he became regent of England for Henry III during his minority. See

Histoire de Guillaume le Maréchal, c. 1225, a long Fr. poem dealing with M.'s exploits.

Marshal (Fr. *maréchal*, from Low Lat. *mariscalcus*, a farrier), word which originally meant a man who took care of horses. The importance of the persons appointed to take charge of the royal horses gradually increased, until the word M. signified one of the highest officers of the court. The word now in England usually means the officer who regulates questions of precedence, etc., at official functions. In U.S.A. a M. is an executive or administrative officer for the U.S. Supreme Court, appointed by the president. With various additions M. represents various ranks, etc., as in field-M., air M., M. of the hall, etc. *See* AIR-MARSHAL; FIELD-MARSHAL; MARSHAL OF THE R.A.F.

Marshal of the R.A.F., highest R.A.F. rank, equivalent to Admiral of the Fleet and Field-Marshal. *See* RANK.

Marshall, Alfred (1842–1924), political economist, *b.* London, was educ. at Merchant Taylors' School and St John's College, Oxford, Lecturer in moral science at Cambridge, 1865, and prof. of political economy there, 1885–1908, he became principal of Univ. College, Bristol, 1877, and in 1883 fellow and lecturer at Balliol College, Oxford. He was prof. of political economy at Cambridge, 1885–1908, and a member of the royal commission on labour, 1891. The leading Brit. economist for 30 years from about 1890, he continued the tradition of the Classical Economists (q.v.). Pubs. include *Economics of Industry*, 1879 (with his wife), *Principles of Economics*, 1890–1, *Industry and Trade*, 1919, and *Money, Credit, and Commerce*, 1923. *See* A. C. Pigou, *Alfred Marshall and Current Thought*, 1953.

Marshall, Benjamin (*c.* 1767–1835), painter of animals and sporting subjects, a follower of George Stubbs (q.v.). He painted a number of portraits of racehorses and their owners, exhibited at the Royal Academy.

Marshall, David Saul (1908–), Singapore politician of Jewish descent, educ. at Raffles Institution and London Univ. After the Second World War, as leader of the Labour front, he campaigned for radical constitutional reform in Singapore. In 1955 M. became Chief Minister, and visited London to confer on proposed changes in Singapore's constitutional status. In 1956 the London conference ended without agreement and M. resigned, being succeeded by Lim Yew Hock (q.v.). M. subsequently formed a new left-wing group in Singapore. *See also* SINGAPORE.

Marshall, George Catlett (1880–1959), Amer. soldier and statesman, *b.* Uniontown, Pennsylvania, rose from private to be the head of the Amer. Army. He attended Virginia Military Institute, entering the First World War as a captain, and was, in France, temporarily promoted to a colonelcy. A brilliant student of tactical problems and a soldier of great administrative skill, his work as an operations officer for America's 1st Div. during the Fr. attack at Cantigny in May 1918 won him the Croix de

Guerre. Later, as operations chief to the first Army in France, before the Meuse-Argonne offensive, he moved nearly 500,000 troops and 2700 guns up to the front in under a fortnight. He helped to refashion the Amer. Army after the war from horse-gun fixed-front tactics to those of the modern mechanised army. But he did not become a brigadier-general until 1936, and was made a general and chief of the U.S. Army General Staff on the day that the Germans invaded Poland, 1939. M. took a standing army of 200,000 and converted it into the vast and mobile machine of the Second World War. He served for some time in China, where he endeavoured, unsuccessfully, to mediate between the National gov. forces under Chiang Kai-shek and the Communists. (*See further* CHINA, *History*). He succeeded Byrnes as secretary of state to the U.S. Gov. in Jan. 1947, and produced the 'Marshall Plan' for the financial and economic rehabilitation of war-shattered Europe. He resigned because of ill health in 1949. *See* K. T. Marshall, *Together*, 1947. *See also* ORGANISATION FOR EUROPEAN ECONOMIC CO-OPERATION.

Marshall, John (1755–1835), Amer. Jurist. With George Washington and James Madison he was a powerful factor in bringing Virginia to adopt the U.S. constitution. President John Adams appointed him to his Cabinet as secretary of state and, in 1801, chief justice of the supreme court, a position he held for 34 years. It was his decisions which gave the U.S. Supreme Court the great power it now possesses, for it was M. who decided that the court had power to pass judgment on the validity of national and state law. In fact, M. was responsible for the whole trend of judicial decisions calling upon the powers inherent in the Federal constitution. M. wrote a *Life of George Washington*, 1804–7. *See* lives by A. J. Beveridge, 1916–19, Lord Craigmyle, 1933, and D. G. Loth, 1949.

Marshall, William (1748–1833), Scottish violinist and composer. He wrote strathspeys and similar pieces, of which collections were pub. in 1781, 1822 and 1847. His tunes were adapted by Burns in at least 2 of his best-known songs.

Marshall, co. seat of Harrison co., E. Texas, U.S.A., 40 m. from Shreveport, Louisiana. It has railway shops and is a minor trade centre. Pop. 32,850.

Marshall Hall, Sir Edward (1858–1927), lawyer, *b.* Brighton. Called to the Bar at the Inner Temple, 1888, he practised in London and on the SW. circuit. He was Conservative M.P. for the Southport div. of Lancs, 1900–6, and for E. Toxteth div. of Liverpool, 1910–16. As a criminal advocate, especially for the defence in murder trials, he was unrivalled. Among the most notable of his forensic triumphs were the Wood, the Peasenhall, the Greenwood, the Seddon and the Thompson-Bywater cases, all murder trials. *See* life by E. Marjoribanks, 1929.

Marshall Islands, group of coral formation in Micronesia, Pacific Ocean, NE. of the Ladrone Is. There are 2 groups, Ratak (E.) and Ralik (W.), both ranging SE. to NW. The whole archipelago is composed of some 33 atolls, 158 sq. m. in area. Copra and phosphate are exported. Pop. 10,500. The is. were annexed to Germany, 1885, and administered by the Jaluit Co. of Hamburg till 1906, when administration was taken over by the Ger. colonial authorities, the is. forming a dist under the New Guinea Gov. They were captured by Japan in Sept. 1914, and administered under the mandate of the League of Nations. The M. I. were captured by U.S. forces, 1944; included in U.S. Ter. of Pacific Is. under U.N. trusteeship, 1947. They were the site (at Bikini) of atom bomb tests in 1946.

Marshall Plan, *see* EUROPE, *History*.

Marshalltown, city, co. seat of Marshall co., Iowa, U.S.A., on the Iowa R., 48 m. NE. of Des Moines in agric. area with limestone quarries. It has railway shops, valve plants, foundries and makes power lawn-mowers. Pop. 22,520.

Marshalsea, prison formerly in Southwark, London, and existing as early as Edward III's reign. It was connected with the M. Court, held by the steward and marshal of the king's household, becoming later a prison for crimes committed on the high seas. From Elizabeth I's time it was used mainly for debtors, and was united with the King's Bench and the Fleet (qq.v.) prisons in 1842. It figures prominently in Dickens's *Little Dorrit*.

Marsh's Test, *see* ARSENIC.

Marsi, a people of central Italy; their prin. tn was Marruvium on the E. shore of L. Fucinus. At the SW. corner of the lake was the temple of Angitia, a local goddess of healing; and her worshippers, who professed acquaintance with medicinal herbs, earned their country the reputation as a home of witchcraft. The M. became allies of Rome in 304, and instigated the Social War (q.v.) in 90 BC.

Marsico Nuovo, It. tn in Basilicata (q.v.), 16 m. SSW. of Potenza (q.v.). Pop. 6000.

Marsillac, Prince de, *see* LA ROCHEFOUCAULD, FRANÇOIS.

Marsipobranchii, *see* CYCLOSTOMATA.

Marske-by-the-Sea, *see* SALTBURN.

Marsman, Hendrik (1899–1940), Dutch lawyer, poet and essayist, *b.* Zeist. He began to write poetry when he was 20, and he pub. his first vol. of poems, *Verzen*, in 1923. As editor of the *Vrije Bladen* he was the leader of the expressionistic-vitalist movement. His critical writings were of great influence. In June 1940 he tried to cross to England, but his ship was torpedoed and he was drowned. His collected works were pub. in 1938, and his last great poem, *Tempel en Kruis* (trans. *Temple and Cross*), in 1939. *See* A. Lehring, *Die vriend van mijn jeugd*, 1957.

Marsonia, *see* SLAVONSKI BROD.

Marston, Baron, *see* BOYLE, JOHN.

Marston, John (1576–1634), dramatist, satiric poet and clergyman, *b.* probably Coventry. Educ. at Brasenose College, Oxford, he studied law at the Middle Temple. As early as 1601 he was satirised under the name of Demetrius in Ben Jonson's *Poetaster*. However, in 1604, M. dedicated to Jonson, with expressions of affec-

Isle of Man

Top left: The sea front at Douglas, the capital and popular holiday resort.

Top right: Cashtyl-yn-Ard, megalithic burial place near Plort Cornaa.

Above left: Looking from the Calf of Man nature reserve towards the main island.

Above right: Scene during the annual Tourist Trophy motor-cycle races.
All photos: Isle of Man Tourist Board

Man-made Fibres

Above left: At the start of nylon spinning, polymer is poured from a travelling hopper into the process bins attached to the spinning units beneath.

Above: A stage in the production of Terylene staple fibre: individual tows of Terylene are brought together before entering the drawing and crimping machine.

Left: A warp being prepared from nylon yarn.
Photos: ICI Fibres Ltd

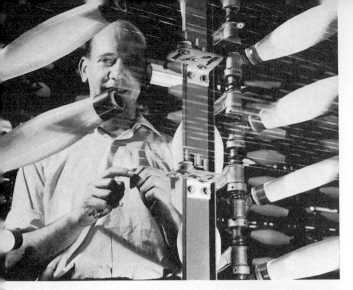

Man-made Fibres

'Tying in a new end' of nylon yarn on the beaming-machine magazine in the warping area.

An operative is testing newly spun cakes of nylon yarn for denier uniformity.

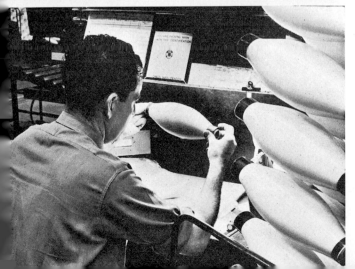

Final visual inspection of the yarn before it is packed for dispatch.
Photos: ICI Fibres Ltd

Manitoba

Top: Manitoba's Legislative Building, Winnipeg.
Manitoba Travel and Publicity Bureau

Above left: Harvesting in progress near Portage la Prairie.
National Film Board of Canada

Above right: The Cathedral of St Boniface, seat of a Roman Catholic archbishop;
the city has a large French-speaking population.
National Film Board of Canada

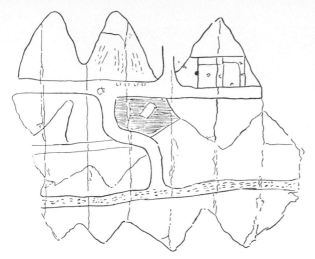

Maps

Egyptian map of a mining region in the eastern desert; roads from the gold mines lead to the sea past mountains where gold is washed, seen in childish perspective.
Reproduced from History of Ancient Geography by J. Oliver Thomson, Cambridge University Press

Below right: The *Mappa Mundi* in Hereford Cathedral, made *c.* 1290 and probably the earliest map of its kind in existence.
W. H. Bustin & Son

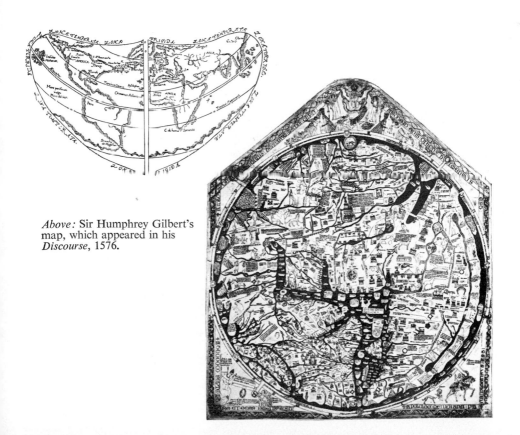

Above: Sir Humphrey Gilbert's map, which appeared in his *Discourse,* 1576.

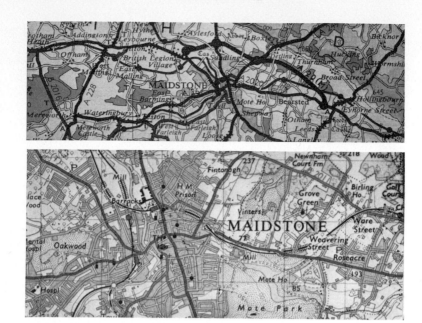

Maps

Top: Quarter inch to one mile: scale 1/250,000.

Above: One inch to one mile: scale 1/63,360.

Below: About two and a half inches to one mile: scale 1/25,000
Reproduced by permission of the Controller of H.M.S.O. and the Director-General of the Ordnance Survey

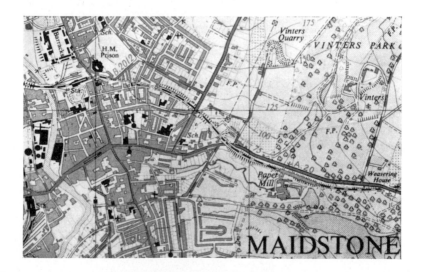

Maryland

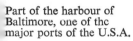

Gilman Hall, which houses the libraries of Johns Hopkins University, opened in 1876.

Part of the harbour of Baltimore, one of the major ports of the U.S.A.

Below: About a third of the land area of Maryland is devoted to farms.
Photos: U.S. Information Service

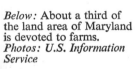

Massachusetts

Top: The kitchen of a Colonial house (built 1686) in Nantucket, which was one of the earliest settlements in N. America.

Above: Fishermen surf-casting for striped bass off Cape Cod.

Left: A computer laboratory at Harvard, the oldest American university (founded 1636).
Photos: U.S. Information Service

tion and esteem, *The Malcontent*. In the next year he was associated with Jonson and Chapman in the composition of *Eastward Ho*. For some reflections against the Scots in this comedy the authors were imprisoned. Shortly after this M., in his preface to his *Sophonisba*, hints at the plagiarisms from Rom. authors in Jonson's *Catiline* and *Sejanus*. M. and Jonson were the protagonists in the 'stage war' which then agitated London. With little of the imitative and inventive genius of the dramatist, M. had much of the spirited vigour and pungent wit of the satirist. In *The Scourge of Villanie*, 1598, he is lofty and intrepid in his censure of vice, but is often carried by his vehement invective to the verge of coarseness. In 1607 he abandoned writing, took holy orders, and was for 15 years rector of Christchurch, Hants. His works include *The Metamorphosis of Pigmalions Image*, a satire, 1598 *The History of Antonio and Mellida*, a tragedy, 1602, *The Dutch Courtezan*, a comedy, 1605, *Parasitaster, or the Fawne*, a comedy, 1606, *What You Will*, a comedy, 1607, and *The Insatiate Countesse*, a tragedy, 1613. There are eds. of his works by J. O. Halliwell-Phillipps, 1856, A. H. Bullen, 1887, and H. H. Wood, 1934. *See* J. H. Peniman, *The War of the Theatres*, 1897; M. S. Allen, *The Satire of John Marston*, 1920; Una M. Ellis-Fermor, *The Jacobean Drama*, 1936.

Marston Moor (Yorks), **Battle of,** fought on 2 July 1644 between the Royalists, under Prince Rupert, the Earl of Newcastle and Goring, and the Parliamentarians, commanded by Lord Fairfax and the Earl of Manchester, Cromwell commanding some cavalry on the left. The Royalists were completely routed after a bitter struggle.

Marsupials (from Lat. *marsupium*, pouch), also called Didelphia or Metatheria, form an important order of mammals, lying between the Monotremata and the placental mammals (*see* MAMMALS). The name Marsupialia (introduced by Tyson *c.* 1698) is derived from the characteristic ventral pouch of skin supported by 2 epipubic bones in which the young, born very imperfectly developed after a short period of gestation, are carried and nourished by the females. Existing M. are mainly restricted to the Australian and Austro-Malayan regions. The 2 main divs. are (1) Polyprotodontia (America and Australasia), including the Didelphyidae (Amer. opossums), dasyures, the thylacine or Tasmanian wolf, marsupial moles (*Notoryctes typhlops*) and bandicoots. They are mostly carnivorous and insectivorous and the pouch is often absent. (2) diprotodontia (Australasian, and a few in E. Austro-Malayan Is.), including the wombat, koala 'bear', cuscus, kangaroo (Macropodidae family), wallaby and phalanger. These are herbivorous, and represent the most highly evolved forms of the M. Fossil species of this group are found in the Trias of Europe and the Jurassic of N. America. *See* GEOGRAPHICAL DISTRIBUTION; MAMMALS. (*See Plate: Mammals.*)

Marsyas, in Gk legend, a Phrygian satyr who found the flute discarded by Athena because the playing of it distorted her face. He thereupon challenged Apollo to a musical contest, on condition that the victor should do what he pleased with the vanquished. The Muses decided in favour of Apollo, who bound M. to a tree and flayed him alive. His blood was the source of the R. M. *See* Ovid, *Metam.* vi. 382–99, and Sir J. G. Frazer, *Adonis, Attis and Osiris* (ch. vi), 1906.

Martaban, vil. of Lower Burma, on the Salween R., 10 m. NW. of Moulmein. Formerly the cap. of Pegu and a place of importance. There is a ferry at M. across the Salween to Moulmein.

Martel, Charles, *see* CHARLES MARTEL.

Martel de Janville, *see* GYP.

Martello, or Martelli, Pier Jacopo (1665–1727), It. dramatist, *b.* Bologna. He wrote a religious poem entitled *Gli Occhi di Gèsu*, and sev. tragedies, comedies and farces. In most of his tragedies he employed the Fr. Alexandrine, which was called after him 'Martellian' verse.

Martello Towers, round towers formerly used in Eng. coast defence. The name is derived from Mortella Point in Corsica. In 1794 an Eng. fleet under Lord Hood supported the Corsican insurgents, and a small round tower on the point withstood their fierce cannonade. The strong resistance shown by this tower led to towers of a similar nature being erected along the coasts of Kent, Sussex, Essex and Suffolk against Napoleon's threatened invasion. They are about 40 ft high.

MARTEN

Marten (*Martes*), name given to a number of animals of the weasel family, but applying specially to the pine M (*M. martes*) and the beech or stone M. (*M. foina*). The pine M. still occurs in the N. of England and Scotland. In shape it resembles a stoat, but its body is much longer, the tail alone being often a foot long, the legs are short, and the paws have sharp, clawed digits. The fur is a beautiful dark brown with a large yellow patch on the breast. The beech M. or stone M. of the S. of Europe (with a white patch) supplies the fur trade with stone or baum M. skins. Other species include the pekan (q.v.), or fisher M. (*Martes pennanti*), and the sable (q.v.). The foul M., or foumart, is the polecat (q.v.). All the M.s are terrestrial and arboreal, frequenting coniferous woods, where a nest of leaves or moss is made, and feeding on small animals and birds. If taken young M.s are easily tamed, and the beech M. was kept in Athens and Rome to catch mice.

Martens, Conrad (1801–78), Australian artist, *b*. London, studied art under Copley Fielding. For 2 years M. was official topographer on the *Beagle*. He settled in Sydney, and was one of the first to win a reputation as an Australian artist. His most successful paintings are his studies and sketches of Sydney Harbour.

Martensen, Hans Larsen (1808–84), Dan. theologian, *b*. Flensburg. Became prof. of theology at Copenhagen and court preacher. Among his works—which often diverged in some degree from strict Lutheran orthodoxy and inclined to mysticism—were treatises on Christian dogmatics and ethics, moral philosophy and, especially, a life of Jacob Boehme (q.v.). In a new ed. of this work by Stephen Hobhouse (1949) is told the strange story of the discovery in 1934 by Dr Werner Buccecke of Göttingen of the original MS. of Boehme's *Aurora*—in which the mystic sets down his apocalyptic visions—and many Boehme letters, which had been handed down as heirlooms within a secret fellowship of admirers of Boehme for some 250 years.

M. was appointed Bishop of Zealand in 1884. An 'official' panegyric of his on Bishop Mynster on his death in 1854 brought a fierce invective of Kierkegaard with the text 'a witness of the truth'.

Martensite, constituent responsible for the hardness of quenched steels, consisting of needle-shaped crystals interlaced at 60°. The structure is caused by the incipient precipitation of carbide from the original austenite grains, and the more carbon there is in the steel the greater is the hardness of M.

Martha, St, sister of Mary and Lazarus (Luke x. 38, John xi. 2), the patron saint of good housewives, represented in art in homely garb, with a bunch of keys in her girdle and a pot in her hand. Festival, 29 July.

Martha's Vineyard, is. in the Atlantic Ocean, 15 m. off SE. Massachusetts, U.S.A., 20 m. long and 10 m. wide. It forms the greater part of Dukes co., and was so named by the Gosnold expedition in 1602 on account of the abundant growth of vines. It is chiefly a summer resort area. Pop. approx. 5600.

Martial, *see* MARTIALIS, M. VALERIUS.

Martial d'Auvergne (*c*. 1430–1508), Fr. poet, *b*. Paris, author of *Arrêts d'amour*, 1460–5 (prose), *Vigilles de Charles VII*, etc.

Martial Law. This expression is used by writers on constitutional law in a three-fold sense: (1) The suspension of the ordinary or municipal law of a country in favour of the temporary gov. of the country or parts of it by military tribunals. In the Code Napoléon of France there is express provision for the proclamation of 'a state of siege' in certain circumstances of civil disorder, the effect of which is that military tribunals are empowered to try civilians by military law. The absence of precedent for such course of proceeding since the Petition of Right, 1628—which, *inter alia*, complained of the enforcement of M. L. against private individuals—led many writers to assume

4756

that it is unknown in England. But the decision of the Privy Council in the case of *Marais* v. *General Officer Commanding*, in 1902, on the appeal of a civilian, Mr Marais, against his detention under military arrest during the S. African War, is that there never was any doubt that in time of crisis the ordinary courts have no jurisdiction over the action of military authorities, the difficulty being to establish when in fact a state of rebellion or insurrection could be said to have existed. This can only be effected by an *ex post facto* decision of the civil courts, with whom, therefore, the last word remains as to the legality of the actions of the military authorities. An Act of Indemnity may of course be passed to protect these latter from actions brought as a result of the application of M. L. (2) The term is sometimes erroneously used to denote the *common law* right and duty of the Crown, its servants and all citizens to repel force by force in the case of any violent resistance to the law, whether by invaders or rioters. (3) As a synonym for military law, or the law administered either (*a*) by the long-abeyant Court of Chivalry of the earl marshal and lord high constable in affairs of honour, and generally in 'matters of arms and deeds of war', or (*b*) by courts-martial at the present day in matters of military discipline. *See* Sir C. G. Robertson, *Select Statutes, Cases and Documents illustrating English Constitutional History, 1660–1832* (7th ed.), 1936; S. T. Banning, *Military Law* (24th ed.), 1942.

Martialis, Marcus Valerius, called in Eng. **Martial** (*c*. AD 40–*c*. 104), Lat. poet, *b*. Bilbilis in Spain. Coming to Rome in 64, he enjoyed the patronage of Titus and Domitian, and returned to Spain in 98. Of his works the following survive: 33 poems from the *Liber Spectaculorum* (pub. AD 80 to commemorate the opening of the Colosseum); 2 collections of short mottoes entitled *Xenia* and *Apophoreta* (pub. 84–5); and 12 books of epigrams (pub. 86–102). All these are included by modern editors in 14 books under the general appellation *Epigrams*. M.'s fertility of imagination, ready wit, felicity of language and genuine affection for his friends are undeniable; but many of his poems are grossly obscene both in thought and expression, as well as servile in flattery of the Emperor Domitian.

M. throws much valuable light on Rom. social life in the 1st cent. AD. There are eds. by L. Friedländer, 1886, M. Lindsay, 1903, and W. Gilbert, 1912. *See also* the text with trans. by W. C. A. Ker (2 vols., Loeb Library), 1919–20, and A. G. Carrington, *Aspects of Martial's Epigrams*, 1960.

Martianus Capella (5th cent. AD), Rom. encyclopaedist, author of *De nuptiis Mercurii et Philologiae*, which is based on the lost *Disciplinae* of Varro (q.v.). There is an ed. by A. Dick (1925), and Johannes Sertus's commentary has been ed. by C. E. Lutz (1939).

Martigny, 3 united hamlets in the canton of Valais, Switzerland, 16 m. SW. of Sion. It is the starting-point of routes over the Great St Bernard and the Col de la Forclaz, and is on the

Simplon Railway, 24 m. SE of Lake Geneva. It has interesting Rom. remains. Its altitude is 1560 ft.

Martigues, Fr. fishing tn in the dept of Bouches-du-Rhône, on the Étang de Berre at its outlet to the Mediterranean, 18 m. WNW. of Marseilles. There are salt and vegetable-oil industries. Pop. 14,700.

Martin, St (*c.* 316–397), Bishop of Tours, *b.* Pannonia (now Hungary). He served in the army, first under Constantine and afterwards under Julian the Apostate. The virtues of his life as a soldier are the theme of more than one interesting legend. On obtaining his discharge from military service, M. became a disciple of St Hilary, Bishop of Poitiers. On his return to Gaul, about 360, he founded a monastery near Poitiers; but in 371 he was drawn by force from his retreat and consecrated Bishop of Tours. The only extant literary relic of M. is a short *Confession of Faith in the Holy Trinity*. His feast is on 11 Nov. (*see* MARTINMAS). M. was the greatest pioneer of W. monasticism before St Benedict. *See* monographs by C. Babut, 1912, and P. Ladoué, 1930.

Martin, name of 5 popes:

Martin I, St (649–53), *b.* Todi, in Umbria, taken captive to Constantinople in 653 and then banished to the Chersonese by the Emperor Constans II for his opposition to the Monothelites. He *d.* in 655. He is in the Orthodox calendar of saints.

Martin II, or improperly named *Marinus I* (82–4), had been sent by Adrian II as legate to Constantinople to preside over the eighth general council 869–70), concerning the controversy excited by Photius, whose excommunication he subsequently renewed.

Martin III, or *Marinus II* (942–46), was merely a puppet of Alberic (*d.* 954), a prince and senator of the Romans.

Martin IV (1281–5), a Frenchman named Simon de Brie, supported Charles of Sicily against Peter of Aragon and excommunicated Michael Palaeologus.

Martin V (1417–31), whose name was Otto Colonna, *b.* Gennazano, was chosen Pope by the Council of Constance, thus ending the Great Schism. He left Avignon for Rome (1418), and made separate concordats with Germany, France, Spain and England. *See* F. Hayward, *History of the Popes*, 1931.

Martin, (Basil) Kingsley (1897–), writer and journalist, educ. at Mill Hill School and Magdalene College, Cambridge. He was assistant lecturer at the London School of Economics, 1923–7, and on the editorial staff of the *Manchester Guardian*, 1927–31. From 1931–60 he was editor of the *New Statesman* (q.v.): editorial director, 1961–2, and since then editorial consultant. Pubs. include: *The Triumph of Palmerston*, 1924; *The Magic of Monarchy*, 1937; *The Crown and the Establishment*, 1962, and his autobiography (Vol. 1), 1966.

Martin, Frank (1890–), Swiss composer, was *b.* Geneva, studied there, lived at Zürich, Rome and Paris in 1918–26, and taught at Geneva from 1928. He married a Dutchwoman and in 1946 settled at Amsterdam, where he remained even after his appointment as prof. of composition at the Cologne Conservatory. M. is among the most distinguished composers of his generation. He uses note-series in his later works, but is not strictly a 12-note composer. His works include 3 ballets, incidental music (Sophocles, Shakespeare, etc.), the oratorios *Le Vin herbé* (after Joseph Bédier) and *Golgotha*, other choral music, a symphony, etc., for orchestra, concertos for piano, violin and harpsichord, chamber music, intrumental sonatas, ballades, etc.

Martin, Gregory (*d.* 1582), Eng. biblical translator, native of Mansfield, Notts. He organised the Eng. College at Rome (1577), and moved with it to Rheims, where he remained for the rest of his life. He trans. the Bible into English from the Lat. Vulgate, the first ed. appearing at Rheims; it was reprinted at Antwerp in 1660; revised by Bishop Challoner (1749–50), and reprinted by George Leo Haydock in 1812, and by Frederick Charles Husenbeth in 1850.

Martin, John (1789–1854), painter, *b.* near Hexham, in Northumberland. In 1806 he went to London, and 6 years later his 'Sadak in Search of the Waters of Oblivion' was hung in the Royal Academy, attracting considerable attention. His paintings give the impression that they were inspired by dreams. Massive perspectives, gigantic crags and towering battlements have the unreal quality of nightmare. Doomed cities were his main theme. He also illustrated *Paradise Lost. See* T. Balston, *John Martin, 1789–1854: his Life and Works*, 1948.

Martin, Sir Theodore (1816–1909), author, *b.* Edinburgh, son of a solicitor. Educ. at Edinburgh Univ., he followed his father's profession. In 1846 he set up as a parl. agent, and soon acquired a large practice and amassed considerable wealth. In 1851 he married Helena Faucit, the actress (q.v.). He was early attracted to letters, and with Aytoun wrote the *Bon Gau tier Ballads*, 1845, a series of parodies after the style of *Rejected Addresses*, but inferior to that collection. In 1866 he was invited to write the official *Life of the Prince Consort*. The work was pub. in 5 vols., 1875–80. He also wrote a biography of Lord Lyndhurst. 1883, and trans. the *Odes of Horace*, Dante's *Vita Nuova* and Goethe's *Faust*. In 1880 he was made a K.C.B., and in the following year Lord Rector of St Andrews.

Martin, Violet Florence, *see* ROSS, MARTIN.

Martin, William (*c.* 1767–1810), naturalist, *b.* Mansfield, Notts. He is famed for his works on Brit. fossils: *Petrificata derbiensia; or, Figures and Descriptions of Petrifactions collected in Derbyshire*, 1804, and *Outlines of Extraneous Fossils on Scientific Principles*, 1809.

Martin, name for some members of the swallow family, but usually implying the house martin (*Delichon urbica*), which builds a mud nest under the eaves of houses. It is 5½ in. long. The plumage of the upper parts is black with violet reflections, and of the lower pure white. It differs from the swallow chiefly in having a white band across the lower back. Other M.s include the sand M. (q.v.), the Amer. purple M. and the fairy M.

Martin de Porres, Saint (1579–1639), S. Amer. half-caste and patron of social justice, b. Lima, Peru. His father was Don Juan de Porres, a Sp. knight; his mother, Anna Velazquez, a coloured woman from Panama. As a boy he picked up the medical knowledge of his time, and in 1603 was admitted to the Dominican order. Thereafter his wonderful powers of healing and his saintly personal life, especially among the poor and outcast, estab. him as a pioneer social worker and friend of coloured people. He was beatified by Gregory XVI in 1837; canonised by John XXIII in 1962. See Claire Huchet Bishop, *Martin de Porres, Hero*, 1954.

Martin du Gard, Roger (1881–1958), Fr. novelist, b. Neuilly-sur-Seine. His archaeological thesis, *Étude archéologique des ruines de Jumièges*, was pub. in 1909, the same year as his first novel *Devenir*. His second novel, *Jean Barois*, 1913, was a more capable work and revealed M. as a penetrating social historian. He became interested in the formation of the theatrical group, the 'Vieux Colombier', for which he wrote 2 farces *Le Testament du père Leleu* and *Le Gonfle*. In his novels he follows the tradition of the Fr. realists of the 19th cent., and brings to his subject a capacity for scientific observation and objective research. He has a lucid, detailed and restrained style and places his narrative against a background of the events of the time. His ample construction allows a variety of incident and a careful building up of character. Such are the characteristics of his long series of novels which under the general title of *Les Thibault* (1922–40) carry the story of 2 families, one Catholic and one Protestant, through 8 books. M. was awarded the Nobel prize for literature, 1937. See R. Lalou, *Roger Martin du Gard*, 1937.

Martin-Harvey, Sir John (1863–1944), actor, b. Wyvenhoe, Essex. He was educ. at King's College School, London, and studied elocution under John Ryder. He made his first appearance at the Old Court Theatre under John Clayton in 1881, and then joined Sir Henry Irving, with whom he remained for many years. Early in his career he married Angelita Helena de Silva (1869–1949), daughter of Don Ramon de Silva Ferro, a capable and charming actress, who was his leading lady through most of his stage life. The choice of the part of Sydney Carton as that best suited to his talents was due to her suggestion, as also was the writing of the play, *The Only Way*, from Dickens' *A Tale of Two Cities*, by the dramatist Freeman Wills. This play, first seen in 1899, estab. him in his position as a leading actor-manager, and he revived it frequently. He was also successful in *The Breed of the Treshams*, *A Cigarette-Maker's Romance*, *The Bells*, *The Lyons Mail*, and others of Irving's successes, and as Everyman, Hamlet, Richard III and Henry V. Among his most striking

performances was his Pelléas to Mrs Patrick Campbell's Mélisande in Maeterlinck's play, while his impressive production of *Oedipus Rex* afforded scope for the stagecraft of Max Reinhardt (q.v.). During his career he managed the Lyceum, the Prince of Wales's, the Court, the Royalty and the Apollo theatres, and Covent Garden Opera House. See his *Autobiography*, 1933, and M. W. Disher, *The Last Romantic*, 1947.

Martín y Soler, Vicente (1754–1806), Sp. composer. He began as an organist at Alicante, but turned to opera, producing his first at Naples. In Vienna from 1785, he secured Lorenzo da Ponte as librettist and had a great success especially with *Una cosa rara*, an air from which Mozart quoted in the second-act finale of *Don Giovanni*. In 1788–94 M. was at the court of Catherine II in St Petersburg, returning there c. 1798 after a visit to London, where he produced 2 more works with da Ponte, who was then attached to the King's Theatre. M. d. in St. Petersburg.

Martina-Franca, It. tn, in Apulia (q.v.), 17 m. NNE. of Taranto. It has a fine 17th cent. ducal palace. Pop. 25,900.

Martineau, Harriet (1802–76), novelist and political economist, b. Norwich, of Huguenot descent. Without any intention of devoting herself to literature, she wrote, at the suggestion of her younger brother, a short paper 'Female Writers on Practical Divinity' which was reprinted in the *Monthly Repository* (1821). This encouraged her, and she composed some verses, short stories and a theological novel. *Devotional Exercises* appeared in 1823, *Traditions of Palestine* in 1830. Between 1832 and 1834 she brought out in 9 vols. *Illustrations of Political Economy*, and followed this with *Poor Law and Paupers Illustrated*, 1833–4, and *Illustrations of Taxation*, 1834. She wrote a *History of England during the Thirty Years' Peace*, 1849–50, and a work on *Household Education*, 1849. She issued books on mesmerism, 1845, and the *British Rule in India*, 1857, with equal facility and unbounded confidence. She pub. sev. novels, and some books for children, of which the best is *Feats on the Fiord* 1844. Her autobiography was pub. in 1877. See lives by Mrs Fenwick Miller, 1884; N. E. Ruenberg, 1933; also R. K. Webb, *Harriet Martineau, a Radical Victorian*, 1960.

Martineau, James (1805–1900), Unitarian theologian younger brother of the preceding, b. Norwich. Possessed of considerable inventive and mathematical talents, he was originally intended for engineering, but studied for the Unitarian ministry, to which he was ordained in 1828. In 1840 he became prof. of mental and moral philosophy in the Manchester New College (subsequently removed to London), and principal in 1869–85. Among his writings, which were very influential, are *Rationale of Religious Inquiry*, 1836, *Ideal Substitutes for God*, 1879, *Study of Spinoza*, 1882, *Types of Ethical Theory*, 1885, *Study of Religion*, 1888, *Seat of Authority in Religion*, 1890, and religious poems and hymns. See J. Estlin Carpenter, *James Mar-*

tineau, Theologian and Teacher, 1905.

Martinez de la Rosa, Francisco de Paula (1787–1862), Sp. statesman and writer, *b.* Granada. In 1812 he was elected deputy to represent Granada in the Cortes, and by his liberalism aroused the hostility of Ferdinand VII, who exiled him. In 1820 he was again elected, and again had to resign. He then resided in France. In 1833 he was recalled to Spain and held various political offices until 1861—twice being chief minister. One of his ministries is famous for the treaty with Lord Clarendon, abolishing the slave trade. Some of his works are *La Viuda de Padilla*, 1814, *Lo que puede un empleo* and other comedies, and *Ab n Humeya*, 1830 (both dramas), *Zaragoza*, 1811 (a poem), *El Espíritu del Siglo* (Spirit of the Age), 1835-1851.

Martínez Ruiz, José (1874–), Sp. writer, who uses the pseudonym of **Azorín**, *b.* Monóvar, Alicante. Two autobiographical novels, *La Voluntad* and *Antonio Azorín*, appeared in 1902 and 1903. Together they constitute a witness for the unrest of spirit amongst intellectual youth of his time, for the many conflicts between reason and sentiment, energy and inaction, tradition and progress, which beset them. The feeling for atmosphere and for time finds its centre in Castilian landscape and hist., in works such as *Los Pueblos*, 1905, and *Castilla*, 1912. In all his work, criticism, essays, drama and novels, is an intensely personal tone. His influence in the first 2 decades of the cent. was very powerful. His literary criticism is exemplified in *Lecturas españoles*, 1912, *Clásicos y modernos*, 1913, *Las valores literarias*, 1913, and *Al margen de los clásicos*, 1915. There is a vein of pure poetry in works such as *Don Juan*, 1922, *Doña Inés*, 1925, and *Félix Vargas*, 1928. See L. Villaronga, *Azorín*, 1931.

Martínez Sierra, Gregorio, *see* SIERRA.

Martini, Frederic (1832–97), Swiss engineer, Hungarian by birth and Swiss by adoption. After serving in the Austrian Army in the war of 1859, he estab. machine works at Frauenfeld in Switzerland. Here in 1871 he invented the breech-loading mechanism of the rifle which bears his name—the M.-Henry. Henry was the name of the inventor of the rifling system used in the barrel.

Martini, Giovanni Battista or **Giambattista** (1706–84), It. priest, composer and teacher, *b.* Bologna. Entering the Franciscan monastery at Lago he was ordained in 1722. In 1725 he returned to Bologna, became chapel master at the church of San Francisco and continued his musical studies under Perti. He collected a vast musical and scientific library, devoting himself to mathematics as well as to music. He became the most famous musical theorist and teacher of his time, Mozart being amongst his many famous pupils. A hist. of music, *Storia della musica*, 1757–81, and a treatise on counterpoint, *Saggio di contrappunto*, 1774–5, are among his works. His musical compositions include masses, Requiem, motets and other church music, as well as oratorios, songs, keyboard pieces, arias, etc. See L. Busi, *Il padre Martini*, 1891.

Martini, Simone, *see* MEMMI, SIMONE.

Martinique, is. in the Windward group, W. Indies, a Fr. possession with an area of 425 sq. m. Colonised by the French in 1635, occupied by the English sev. times until it finally became French again in 1814. The is. has a variety of terrain. The main mt range culminates in Mont Pelée (4700 ft). There are many rivs. but none is navigable. Pop. 300,000. The prin. industry is agriculture; main crops are sugar, pineapples and bananas. Coffee and cocoa are also grown. Industries based on sugar are the most important in the is. but under a Pioneer Industries scheme the gov. is encouraging the production of consumer goods. Exports (1963) 175,856 m. Nf., mainly to Metropolitan France. Imports 334,450 m. Nf. bananas, sugar and rum are the main exports. A network of roads joins the main tns of the is. Main airport, at Lamentin near Fort de France, handles international traffic; a number of small airfields cater for internal traffic. The coastline is indented with many small bays providing natural harbours. The cap. and prin. port is Fort de France. Free, compulsory education is provided in some 200 elementary schools and 2 *lycées*. There are also 2 private *lycées*. There is an agric. college and a public technical school. Private estabs. provide commercial and industrial education. M. became an overseas dept of France in Mar. 1946. The Prefect is the Representative of the gov. The local assembly (General Council) comprises 36 members elected on the basis of universal adult suffrage, for a period of 6 years.

Martins Bank, estab. as the Bank of Liverpool by deed of settlement in 1831; registered as limited, 1882. Name changed to Bank of Liverpool and Martins Ltd in Dec. 1918, and to its present title in Jan. 1928. Head office, Water St, Liverpool; prin. London city office, 68 Lombard St, E.C.3.

Martinsburg, tn of W. Virginia, U.S.A., co. seat of Berkeley co., 74 m. NW. of Washington. It is the centre of an agric. area (fruit, grain, dairy products, livestock). It manufs. textiles, hosiery, furniture and wood products, bricks, tiles, cement and food products. Pop. 15,180.

Martinů, Bohuslav (1890–1959), Czech composer, *b.* Polička, was a pupil of Suk at Prague and of Roussel in Paris. In 1928 he attracted attention as a composer at the Siena festival. In 1940 he fled from Paris with his Fr. wife, and he remained in the U.S.A. until 1945, when he became prof. of composition at the Prague Conservatory. His work includes operas, ballet music, radio operas and a great variety of symphonic pieces, concertos, chamber music, piano pieces, songs, etc. His output was enormous and unequal in quality, at its best full of invention and vitality.

Martius, Karl Friedrich Philipp von (1794–1868), Ger. naturalist and traveller, director of the botanic garden (1820) and prof. of botany (1826) at Munich. Among his works are *Historia Naturalis Palmarum*, 1823–53, *Nova Genera et*

Species Plantarum, 1824–32, and *Icones Plantarum Cryptogamicarum*, 1828–34.

Martos, Sp. tn in the prov. of Jaén, overlooked by an anct castle. It has textile manufs. and a trade in wine and fruit. Pop. 16,900.

Martov (real name **Tsederbaum**), **Yuly Osipovich** (1873–1923), Russian Social Democrat (from 1892) and leader of the Mensheviks (q.v.). He co-operated with Lenin in the Iskra (q.v.) organisation, but broke with him in 1903. After the Feb. revolution (q.v.) in 1917 he was in opposition to the majority of Mensheviks, maintaining an internationalist position against their 'revolutionary defencism', After the Oct. revolution (q.v.) he became official leader of the Menshevik party. M. left Russia in 1920 as head of a Menshevik delegation and remained in Berlin, where he ed. the monthly *Socialist, Courier*. *See* L. H. Haimson, *The Russian Marxists and the Origins of Bolshevism*, Cambridge, Mass., 1955.

Martyr (Gk. 'a witness'), one who bears witness to Christ by sacrificing his life for the Christian faith. The first recorded M. is St Stephen (q.v.), an account of whose death is given in Acts vi. and vii; and the proto-M. of Britain is St Alban of Verulam (q.v.). The use of a *Martyrology*, a list or catalogue of M.s or saints, arranged in the order of their anniversaries, is common to both the Rom. and the Gk Church (although in the latter it goes under a different name, i.e. menology), and is intended as a guide to the faithful in their devotions. The most important anct martyrology is the Hieronymian, falsely said to have been compiled by St Jerome; next to this come the Lesser Rom. and Bede's martyrology, the last of which has come down to us in that of Florus of Lyons; Rhabanus Maurus (*c.* 845); Ado of Vienne (*c.* 875); Usuard of Paris (*c.* 875), the most famous, on which the Rom. martyrology is based; Notker (896); and St Gall (912). The official 'Roman martyrology', designed for the entire Church, was pub. under Gregory XIII in 1584, and 2 years later Baronius pub. an annotated ed. It was revised under Benedict XV (1922). The best known list of the Greek Church, or 'menology', is that compiled by order of the Emperor Basil the Macedonian in the 9th cent. This was ed. in 1727 by Cardinal Urbini. In 1866 Thomas Wright (1810–77), in the *Journal of Sacred Literature*, pub. a Syriac martyrology which had been written about 412. Protestant M.s of the 16th cent. are celebrated in Jean Crespin's *Histoire des Martyrs*, and the chief Eng. work on the same subject is John Foxe's *Book of Martyrs*. *See* G. Ricciotti, *The Age of Martyrs* (trans.)), 1960.

Martyrology, *see* MARTYR.

Marugame, seaport and industria city of Kagawaken, Japan, 80 m. WSW. of K 'be, on the is. of Shikoku. Though noted for its 1 anuf. of traditional folding fans, it also prouuces cotton textiles and chemicals. The population is 64,000.

Maruts, Vedic storm and wind gods, companions of Indra. In anct mythology the sons of Rudra and Prisni, in later the sons of Kasyapa and Aditi.

Marvel, Ik, *see* MITCHELL D. G.

Marvell, Andrew (1621–78), poet and satirist, *b.* Winestead in Holderness Yorks, where his father was rector. Educ. at Hull Grammar School and Cambridge, thereafter travelled for a time on the Continent. He sat in Parliament for Hull, proving himself an assiduous and incorruptible member, with strong republican leanings. In spite of this he was a favourite of Charles II. In his own day he was best known as a powerful and fearless political writer, and for some time from 1657 was assistant to Milton in the Lat. or Foreign Secretaryship to the Council of State. After the Restoration he wrote against the gov., his chief work in this kind being his *Account of Growth of Popery and Arbitrary Government in England*, 1677. He also pub. *The Rehearsal Transpos'd*, 1673, which condemns religious intolerance. His controversial style was lively and vigorous, but sometimes coarse and vituperative. His fame now rests on his poems which, though few, have many of the highest poetical qualities. Among the best known are the *Song of the Emigrants in Bermuda*, the *Horatian Ode Upon Cromwell's Return from Ireland* and *Thoughts in a Garden*. Of the last Palgrave says that 'it may be regarded as a test of any reader's insight into the most poetical aspects of poetry'. The tn of Hull voted M. a monument, which was, however, forbidden by the Court. *See* Life by M. C. Bradbrook and M. G. Lloyd Thomas, 1940.

Marwar, *see* JODHPUR.

Marx, Heinrich Karl (1818–83), founder of revolutionary socialism, a Ger. subject of Jewish extraction, *b.* Trier. After starting the soon-suppressed *Rheinische Zeitung* at Cologne he was, from 1843 to 1845, in Paris, where he was converted to socialism by reading Proudhon. Here also he met Engels, his lifelong partner and friend. From France M. was expelled for contributing to another jour., the *Vorwärts*, and went to Brussels, Cologne and ultimately London, which last he made his permanent home. With Engels he pub. the *Communist Manifesto* in 1848. Thereafter he devoted himself almost exclusively to the development of his economic ideas, for although he was virtual leader of the International Working Men's Association, he never held high office in it. His works include the famous *Kapital*, the first vol. of which appeared in 1856 (the second and third, ed. by F. Engels from his papers after his death, were pub. in 1885 and 1894 respectively); also *The Poverty of Philosophy*, 1847, *The 18th Brumaire of Louis Bonaparte*, 1852, *Critique of Political Economy*, 1859, *The Civil War In France*, 1871, *The Class Struggle in France*, 1895. For an examination of his principles, *see under* CAPITAL and CAPITALISM.

See also: ANARCHISM; COMMUNISM; INTERNATIONAL, THE; SOCIALISM. *See* E. H. Carr, *Karl Marx*, 1938; I. Berlin, *Karl Marx*, 1939; L. Schwarzschild, *The Red Prussian*, 1948; L. Trotsky, *Marx*, 1948; R. L. Heilbroner, *The*

Great Economists, 1955; J. Lewis, *The Life and Teaching of Karl Marx*, 1965. (*See Plate: Economic Thought, History of*.)

Marx Brothers, Jewish-Amer. family of film comedians: Arthur (Harpo) (1893–1964); Julius (Groucho), *b.* 1895; and Leonard (Chico), *b.* 1891; Herbert (Zeppo), *b.* 1901, retired from the troupe after 1934. They estab. a distinctive style of clowning and achieved very great popularity. Among their film successes are *A Night at the Opera*, 1936, *A Day at the Races*, 1937, *The Big Store*, 1941, and *A Night in Casablanca*, 1946.

Mary, The Blessed Virgin, Mother of Jesus. The only authentic sources for her life are the Gospels (q.v.). In St Luke we learn of the announcement to her by the angel that she should conceive a son by the overshadowing of the Holy Ghost; of her being espoused to Joseph, a carpenter belonging to the house of David; of the events connected with the birth of Jesus, and of the presentation in the temple. Of the flight into Egypt we learn in Matt. ii, and of the finding of the child Jesus 12 years later, after he had disappeared from the caravan returning from Jerusalem, in Luke ii; of her presence and action at Cana in John ii, of her presence when Jesus was preaching in Mark iii. 31, and of her presence at the foot of the cross and the word of Our Lord consigning her to the care of the apostle St John in John xix. 26. Finally her presence among the apostles after the Ascension is mentioned in Acts i. 14. Nothing is told us of her death. The apocryphal gospels give many untrustworthy details of her early life. According to tradition she was the daughter of Joachim and Anne; it is an article of Rom. Catholic faith that after death she was taken up bodily into heaven, an event celebrated by the E. and Rom. Catholic Churches in the feast of the Assumption, 15 Aug. Other feasts commemorating events in the life of M. are her Nativity (8 Sept), the Presentation of M. in the temple (21 Nov.), the Annunciation or Lady Day commemorating the visit of the archangel Gabriel, Luke i. 26, 27 (25 Mar.), the Visitation, or Visit made to her cousin Elizabeth, Luke i. 39, 40 (2 July), the Purification or churching after the birth of Christ, popularly known as Candlemas, Luke ii. 25 (2 Feb.), and the Immaculate Conception (8 Dec.). This last, instituted by Pius IX in 1854, has nothing to so with the Virgin Birth or birth of Christ without the agency of man, but commemorates the complete freedom of M. from all taint of sin, i.e. she was conceived immaculate or unstained. The title of Mother of God (*Theotokos*) was formally conferred upon M. by the Council of Ephesus in 431, after the Nestorian controversy. M. has been the object of profound popular devotion in both the E. and W. Church, for by her motherhood of Christ she is deemed the supreme intercessor with her Son, as well as the mother of His mystical body, the Church. The countless statues and paintings of M. with her Child (*see* MADONNA) are all inspired by the thought that through the Virgin Mother of God the human touched the divine. The most striking phenomenon in modern times

in devotion to Our Lady is the apparition claimed for her at Lourdes (q.v.) in S. France on 18 occasions in 1858. This has received official recognition by the Rom. Catholic Church, and numerous miracles are claimed. Vast numbers of pilgrims go there every year from all parts of the world, estimated at sev. million for the centenary year, 1958, alone. In 1917 a similar apparition occurred at Fatima (q.v.) in Portugal. *See also* LEGION OF MARY. *See* W. B. Ullathorne, *The Immaculate Conception of the Mother of God*, 1855; J. Northcote, *Mary in the Gospels*, 1885; B. W. Randolph, *The Virgin Birth of Our Lord*, 1903; A. Schaefer and F. Brossart, *The Mother of Jesus in Holy Scripture*, 1913; O. R. Vassall-Phillips, *Mary, Mother of God*, 1927; Fr. Canice, O.S.F.S., *Mary*, 1936; E. Schillebeeckx, *Mary, Mother of the Redemption*, 1964.

Mary I (1516–58), Queen of England, elder daughter of Henry VIII by his first wife, Catherine of Aragon, *b.* Greenwich. Intelligent and courageous, she showed at the beginning of her reign that she possessed some at least of the traditional Tudor skill in statecraft. During the early years of her life she held an honoured position at court and marriages for her were suggested with the son of Francis I, and, later, with Charles V. But after Henry's divorce from Catherine in 1532 M. was deprived of her rank and precedence, declared illegitimate, separated from her mother and kept under virtual house-arrest. M.'s strong faith in the Catholic religion and in the justice of her mother's cause never wavered, and her personal tribulations only strengthened her desire to reunite the Eng. Church with Rome and to re-establish the political connection of England and Spain which the divorce had shattered. After Anne Boleyn's execution M.'s status was partially restored, and she actually acknowledged her father's position as supreme head of the Church in England, and during Edward VI's reign she lived in retirement in the country. On his death M. acted with characteristic Tudor resolution in the face of Northumberland's attempt to put Lady Jane Grey (q.v.) on the throne. She gathered a small force in E. Anglia and rode quickly to London, rallying the mass of the people to her. On 19 July 1553 she was proclaimed queen.

Her early actions were characterised by restraint and leniency. Northumberland was executed, but Lady Jane and her husband spared; the submission to Rome was carried through (in the face of some parl. opposition although there seems to have been little open opposition in the country as a whole), but there was little religious persecution. Then M. announced her intention of marrying Philip of Spain, against the wishes of many of her advisers. The proposed marriage was extremely unpopular, and a rebellion broke out under Sir Thomas Wyatt. This was rigorously put down: and in July 1554 M. married Philip at Winchester. After Wyatt's rebellion M. had Lady Jane Grey and her husband executed, and in 1555 a systematic persecution of the Protestants began. There is no doubt that M. underestimated the hidden strength that Protestantism had acquired during her brother's reign; there is also little doubt that the persecutions, with their biggest impact in London, only served to strengthen it further. M. *d.*, lonely and embittered, in 1558. Her marriage had been unhappy and childless, and her reign ended with the loss of Calais, England's last remaining Fr. possession, sacrificed in a Sp. war in which England had really no interest. The state of the country at her death probably made a future settlement on some Protestant basis virtually inevitable. *See* lives by J. M. Stone, 1901, and B. White, 1935; *see also* H. F. M. Prescott, *Spanish Tudor*, 1940.

Mary II (1662–94), Queen of England, elder daughter of James II by his first marriage to Anne Hyde, daughter of Clarendon the lord chancellor. She was *b.* in London, brought up a staunch Protestant and married to her cousin, William of Orange, stadtholder of Holland, in 1677. Eleven years later she ascended the throne of England, as joint-sovereign with her husband, after the revolution of 1688. Though William has been charged with neglecting her, M. seems to have been devoted to her husband, and he trusted her with the gov. of the country during his absences on the Continent. She was extremely popular in England; and whatever his past conduct, her husband never fully recovered from the shock of her premature death. She *d.* childless in 1694 of smallpox. *See* N. M. Waterson, *Mary II*, 1928; M. Bowen, *The Third Mary Stuart*, 1929; H. Chapman, *Mary II*, 1953.

Mary (Victoria Mary Augusta Louise Olga Pauline Claudine Agnes) (1867–1953), Queen of Great Britain, wife of George V, *b*, Kensington Palace, only daughter of the Duke of Teck. Her mother was the younger daughter of Adolphus Frederick, 1st Duke of Cambridge. Her childhood home was White Lodge, Richmond, where she studied music under Tosti. From 1883 till 1886 she lived with her parents in Italy, and, until her marriage, was popularly known as Princess May. She became engaged to Prince Albert Victor, Duke of Clarence, then second in succession to the throne in Dec. 1891, but he *d.* in Jan. 1892. She married the duke's younger brother—then Duke of York—in the Chapel Royal at St James's Palace on 6 July 1893. She bore him 5 sons and 1 daughter. During the First World War she was active in voluntary work for the war effort, and in 1917 visited military hospitals in France. During the Second World War, though age increasingly limited her outside activities, she again undertook much voluntary work; and after the war made her personal contribution to the 'dollar drive' by embroidering in *gros point* (her skill as a needlewoman is almost legendary) a carpet which was subsequently exhibited in Canada and the U.S.A. She became a popular figure with all classes of the people, conquering her fundamental shyness and charming all those she met by her dignity, sincerity and genuine interest in their problems. *See* lives by C. Cavendish, 1930; Sir G. Arthur, 1935; L. Wulff, 1949.

Mary (Victoria Alexandra Alice Mary), Prin-cess Royal (1897–1965), given that title in 1932. The only daughter of George V and Queen Mary, she was *b.* at York Cottage, Sandringham. In 1922 she married Viscount Lascelles, later 6th Earl of Harewood (*see* LASCELLES). Two sons were *b.* of this marriage: George Henry Herbert, 7th Earl of Harewood, in 1923 (*see* LASCELLES), and the Hon. Gerald David Lascelles, 1924. The Princess Royal was keenly interested in women's organisations, and always showed especial interest in local affairs in Yorks.

Mary (formerly known as **Merv**). A tn and railway junction in the Turkmen S.S.R. of the Soviet Union situated in the delta of the Murgab. R. on the Karakum canal. It has cotton ginning and wool washing works. Pop. 54,000 (1962). The anct city of Merv or Margiana was 18 m. E. of the modern tn. It was founded by Alexander. Later it was one of the imperial cities of Khorasan (Persia) but was captured by the Uzbeks in 1786. Taken by the Russians in 1884, it was developed on the modern site, the anct site being now called Bayram Ali.

Mary, Legion of, *see* LEGION.

Mary-bud, *see* CALENDULA.

'Mary Celeste', Amer. brig. of 282 tons which sailed from New York on 7 Nov. 1872 with a cargo of crude alcohol, bound for Genoa. Her crew comprised the Master, B. S. Briggs (who was accompanied by his wife and child) and 7 seamen. The vessel was found abandoned but intact on 5 Dec., 600 m. W. of Gibraltar by the brigantine *Dei Gratia*, and brought to port. Despite the most searching inquiry, the fate of all those on board the M. C. remains one of the unsolved mysteries of the sea. *See* R. Furneaux, *What Happened to the Mary Celeste*, 1964.

Mary Datchelor Girls' School, The, estab. at Camberwell, London, in 1877 (and named after Mary Datchelor, *d.* 1725) and reorganised under the management of the Worshipful Company of Clothworkers in 1895. It is now governed by a body appointed by the Clothworkers' Company and the G.L.C. There are some 650 pupils.

Mary Magdalene, *see* MAGDALENE, MARY.

Mary of Guise, called also **Mary of Lorraine** (1515–60), Queen and Regent of Scotland, daughter of the Duke of Guise, *b.* Bar-le-Duc. She married, in 1534, the Duke of Lorraine, who, however, *d.* in 1537. She next married James V of Scotland, to whom she bore a daughter, afterwards Mary Queen of Scots. After her husband's death at Solway Moss (1542) she played a leading role in Scottish politics, becoming regent for her daughter in 1554. She sought for close union with France, and tried to suppress the Protestants. Her rule was unpopular, and she was declared deposed in Oct. 1559.

Mary Queen of Scots (1542–87), Queen of Scotland and Queen-consort of France, daughter of James V of Scotland by his second wife Mary of Guise, *b.* Linlithgow. She was *b.* immediately after the disastrous defeat at Solway Moss (1542), and was a queen before she was a week old. Her father on his deathbed made the famous prophecy about his kingdom: 'It cam' wi' a lass, it will gang wi' a lass'. She was promised to Edward VI as wife, but finally after the battle of Pinkie married the dauphin of France, son of Henry II. She was sent to France at an early age, and educ. there. She conveyed by the marriage treaty the crown of Scotland to the King of France in the event of her dying childless, and also passed on by the same treaty her right of succession to the Eng. crown. In 1559 her husband became King of France, but he d. in the following year. In 1561 M. arrived in Scotland and found that the country was dominated by John Knox (q.v.) and that the Reformation had received parl. sanction. M. made no attempt to halt the progress of the Reformed Church, but stipulated for a private use of her own faith. Her chief minister and half-brother, Murray, succeeded in crushing an insurrection of the Catholics under the Earl of Huntly in the N., and for a time M. reigned not only in peace but also with the approbation of her subjects. She was, however, soon absorbed in plans for a second marriage. Failing in her attempt to bring about a marriage with Don Carlos of Spain she suddenly surprised everybody by marrying her cousin Darnley, the nearest heir after her to the throne of England and Scotland.

Darnley was weak in character and insolent in manner; immediately after his marriage he was given the title of king, but was granted but few privileges to accompany the title. He soon disgusted M. by his frequent love intrigues, and he in turn, failing in his attempt to gain his desires and ambitions towards the Scottish crown, began to intrigue in order to bring about these ends. He was jealous of Rizzio, the It. favourite, and conspired with Murray, Ruthven and Morton to murder him. This was done in Holyrood Palace in M.'s presence on the evening of 9 Mar. 1566. M., however, won Darnley from the conspirators, whom he betrayed, and for a time their relations were friendlier. Finally, after the birth of James, their son, afterwards James VI of Scotland and I of England, the rupture became complete, and on 10 Feb. 1567 the house in which Darnley lay ill was blown up and his body was afterwards found in the garden of the house. The queen could not be directly accused of complicity, but there were many who believed she was not altogether guiltless, especially as the chief instigator of the murder had been her new favourite Bothwell. M.'s real part in Darnley's murder has never been solved: the most incriminating evidence against her is contained in the Casket Letters (q.v.). Bothwell was tried and acquitted, and immediately after this he seized the queen and took her to Dunbar, nominally a prisoner. Protestant Scotland, however, had no doubt of the complicity of M. in the murder and the abduction when she publicly pardoned Bothwell and after he had obtained a divorce married him according to Protestant rites. An insurrection immediately broke out, and, deserted by almost all her nobles, M. was defeated at Carberry, forced to abdicate in favour of her very young son, and imprisoned in Loch Leven

Castle. From here, in 1568, she escaped, raised a small army, but was again defeated, at Langside. She fled this time, and placed herself under the protection of Elizabeth I of England.

Elizabeth's position was difficult; whilst she could not approve of rebellion against the queen, she equally could not allow M. to escape from her now, since M. was her greatest rival. M., therefore, found herself a prisoner for life. During the next 19 years she passed from prison to prison in England. As the Catholic heir to the Eng. throne, she had many supporters in England, and one long conspiracy was kept up during her imprisonment. It is certain that Elizabeth's position was unsafe as long as M. lived. Finally, in 1586, the conspiracy of Anthony Babington was discovered, and M. was accused of complicity. M. denied this, as she denied the jurisdiction of the court which tried her. But she was found guilty and sentenced to death, and in Feb. 1587 Elizabeth finally signed the death warrant. She was executed on 8 Feb. at Fotheringhay (q.v.), and d. in the eyes of her followers a martyr, protesting her innocence and strong in the faith of the Catholic Church. She was buried in Peterborough Cathedral, but her body was in 1612 removed to Westminster Abbey by her son James I. M. was a renowned beauty; she was also a woman of intense personal charm, intelligence and courage. She lacked her cousin Elizabeth's cool statesmanship and powers of leadership and compromise, and too often negatived political actions of real ability by giving way to her own passionate nature. See also CASKET LETTERS. See lives by D. Hay Fleming, 1897; E. Linklater, 1933; M. Bowen, 1934; S. Zweig (Eng. trans.), 1935; M. P. Willcocks, 1939; also T. F. Henderson, Casket Letters and Mary Queen of Scots, 1889; A. Lang, The Mystery of Mary Stuart, 1901, 1904; A. F. Stuart (ed.), Trial, 1923; M. Baring, In My End is My Beginning, 1931; Sir E. A. Parry, The Persecution of Mary Stuart: a Study in Criminology, 1931; A. F. Steuart (ed.), The Trial of Mary, Queen of Scots (2nd ed.), 1951. (See Plate: Scotland.)

Maryborough: 1. Tn in the Rep. of Ireland, see PORTLAOISE.

2. City of Queensland, Australia, on the Mary R., 160 m. N. of Brisbane. It is a port for agric. and forest products of the back country besides being an important manufacturing city—shipbuilding, construction of heavy machinery and locomotives. Pop. 18,210.

3. Tn of Victoria, 110 m. NW. of Melbourne, Australia. Once a gold-mining area but now an industrial tn, with knitting-mills, flour-mills, small-tool and twist-drill factory, butter factory and furniture and joinery factory. The tn is an important railway junction for 4 main lines and is surrounded by a dist devoted to mixed farming. Pop. 7235.

Maryland, maritime state of the U.S.A., bounded on the N. by Pennsylvania, W. and S. by W. Virginia, Dist of Columbia and Virginia, E. by Delaware and the Atlantic. It covers a total area of 10,577 sq. m., of which over 690 sq. m.

are water. M. consists chiefly of fertile coastal lowlands, but has a long narrow extension W. to the Appalachian mts. The most important riv. is the Potomac, which drains the W. portion of the state and forms its S. boundary. Other rivs. are the Susquehanna, Patapsco and Winconico, all except the Susquehanna, of which the mouth alone is in the state, being small and comparatively unimportant. The climate is moderated by coastal location: the normal winter is mild and summer hot. The state contains clay, sand, talc and lime. On the whole the soil is well adapted for agriculture and under good cultivation. About a third of M. is in farms. It is particularly fertile in the E. coastal cos., which are in market garden cultivation. The chief crops are wheat, maize, hay, potatoes and other vegetables, tobacco and fruit. Horses, cattle, sheep and pigs are reared. The fisheries, especially of oysters, are extensive. Steel manuf. and copper smelting and refining are among its chief industries; textiles and clothing have long been important, and there are many newer light engineering industries. The chief tn is Baltimore (pop. 939,020), but Annapolis (pop. 22,390) is the seat of gov. Cumberland, Hagerstown and Frederick are other important cities. M. is administered by a senate of 29 members and a house of delegates of 123, both elected for 4 years, and is represented in Congress by 2 senators and 7 representatives. There is a number of higher educational institutions, the most important being the Johns Hopkins Univ. (q.v.). The univ. of M. is at Baltimore, and the U.S. Naval Academy at Annapolis. Communication by water and land is excellent; there are good roads and over 2000 m. of railway, diesel and electric. Chesapeake Bay Bridge (1952) connects the E. Shore (hitherto isolated) with the W. Shore. There are 39 airports. Baltimore, which is one of the best ports on the coast, has a large trade. Total state pop. 3,100,690, of whom about 17 per cent are Negro.

M. was named after Henrietta Maria, queen consort of Charles I of England. It was first explored by Capt. John Smith in 1608. A charter granted by Charles I to Lord Baltimore to found a colony for Rom. Catholic recusants gave him practically royal power over the region. In 1638 the people were conceded the right to initiate legislation. The assembly passed the famous Act of Toleration in 1649 by which freedom of worship was granted to all Christians. This, however, provoked the Puritans to rebellion and in 1652 the colony was seized by the commissioners of Parliament, but was restored to Lord Baltimore in 1657. M. was one of the 13 original states. *See* M. P. Andrews, *History of Maryland Province and State*, 1919, and *The Founding of Maryland*, 1934; P. Wilstach, *Tidewater Maryland*, 1931; Federal Writers' Project, *Maryland: A Guide to the Old Line State*, 1940; and D. Cunz, *The Maryland Germans: A History*, 1949. (*See Plate*.)

Marylebone, *see* ST MARYLEBONE.
Marylebone Cricket Club, *see* CLUB and CRICKET.

Maryport, urb. dist and coastal tn of Cumberland, England, on the Solway Firth, 28 m. SW. of Carlisle. On the SW. of the tn are the factories of the Solway Estate. M. is the point of separation between industrial W. Cumberland and the scenic beauties of the co. Pop. 12,334.

Masaccio ('shiftless') (1401–*c*. 1428), nickname of **Tommaso di Giovanni di Guidi,** a Florentine painter, *b.* in the Arno valley. He is sometimes called the father of modern art, partly from his ability to suggest the mass and volume of objects in the round (later developed by Michelangelo), and is celebrated for his frescoes in the Brancacci chapel in the Carmine and in Santa Maria Novella at Florence. He also painted sev. pictures now in the Berlin Museum, and his 'Madonna and Child with Angels' is in the National Gallery, London. *See* M. Salmi, *Masaccio*, 1948.

Masai, people of Nilo-Hamitic (q.v.) stock. Up to the early years of this cent. they occupied a considerable part of the large plains which extend from about 1° N. lat. to 6° S. lat., in both Kenya and Tanganyika. Most of their ter. in Kenya was taken for European farms. They are a nomad people, practising cattle-raising, and regarding cattle as their true source of wealth. *see* A. C. Hollis, *The Masai, Their Language and Folklore*, 1905, and G. W. B. Huntingford, *The Southern Nilo-Hamites*, 1953. See NILO-HAMITES. (*See Plate: Kenya*.)

Masampo, *see* MASAN.
Masan (Masampo), Korea, former free port of commerce on the SE. coast, 180 m. SE. of Seoul. Pop. 157,500.

Masaniello, *see* ANIELLO, TOMMASO.
Masaryk, Jan Garrigue (1886–1948), Czech statesman, *b.* Prague, son of Thomas Garrigue M., and educ. at Prague. He emigrated to the U.S.A. in 1907, but when the Czech rep. was formed in 1918 he entered the ministry of foreign affairs there. Between 1919 and 1922 he was in the diplomatic service in Washington and London, returning to Prague in 1922 as secretary to the foreign ministry. From 1925 to 1938 he was Czech minister to Great Britain. He then lectured in America, returning to London in 1939, where he introduced the first news bulletin in the Czech language to be broadcast from the B.B.C. His national programme was a free Czechoslovakia in a free Europe, and he proved much the most popular and influential broadcaster his country had ever known. In July 1940 he was appointed minister of foreign affairs in the Czechoslovak provisional gov. and in 1941 Deputy Prime Minister. He was uncompromising in his view that the Sudeten Germans should leave Czechoslovakia, and unwilling to yield to Poland in the long-standing dispute over Teschen. Late in 1946 he was nominated, against Rom. Catholic opposition, as head of the Czechoslovak delegation to the U.N. Assembly. Though by upbringing and inclination he leant more to the W. than to the E. he strove, after the liberation of his country, to get each side to understand the point of view of the other. Disillusioned, in Mar. 1948 he committed

suicide by jumping from the window of his apartment in the Foreign Office, Prague, so dying a victim of communism.

Masaryk, Thomas Garrigue (1850–1937), first president and 'liberator' of Czechoslovakia, b. Hodonin in Moravia. At an early age he was apprenticed to a blacksmith, but, largely owing to his mother's determination, he was able to continue his education at school and at the univ. with a view to becoming a teacher. In 1878 he married Charlotte Garrigue, an American, whose name he added to his own, and, until her death in 1923, she was his ardent helper in all his work. He had been a teacher for some time when, in 1879, he was elected *privatdozent* or unsalaried lecturer in philosophy at the univ. of Vienna. In 1882 he became a prof. at the new Bohemian univ. of Prague. In 1891 he entered Parliament in Vienna, but resigned in 1893. In 1907 he returned to Parliament as a representative of the Realist party. He was an outspoken opponent of Germany's encroachment upon Austria, and more especially of Austria's encroachment upon the Balkans and the policy of amassing ter. in Bosnia. In 1914, after the outbreak of the First World War, he fled to Italy, and from there and in Switzerland, France and England carried on a ceaseless propaganda on behalf of the national aspirations of the Czechs and the Slovaks. In London he became a prof. at King's College. Two years later, in 1917, he went to Russia, and then to the U.S.A., where he secured recognition of the Czech National Council, of which he was president. On 14 Nov. 1918 he was elected president of the newly formed rep. of Czechoslovakia, being re-elected in 1920 for 7 years, and again in 1927 for a further period. On his eighty-first birthday his enthusiastic fellow-countrymen presented him with the sum of 20,000,000 crowns (£122,000), which M. allocated to humanitarian and educational institutions. (*See* CZECHOSLOVAKIA.) In addition to being one of the most respected statesmen in Europe, M. was a scholar and a renowned realistic philosopher. His works available in Eng. are *The Theory of Probability and Hume's Scepticism*, 1882; *The Czech Question*, 1896; *The Philosophy of History and Religion in Russia*, 1913; *The New Europe*, 1918; *The Making of a State*, 1927. *See* lives by V. Cohen, 1941; P. Selver, 1941; E. P. Newman, 1961; *also* K. Čapek, *President Masaryk tells his Story*, 1933. (*See Plate: Czechoslovakia.*)

Masaya, tn of Nicaragua and cap. of the dept of the same name. Situated between the Lakes of Managua and Nicaragua, it is on the road and railway connecting the cities of Managua and Granada. It is the commercial centre of a rich agric. area producing cotton, coffee and tobacco. Pop. 24,000.

Masbate, one of the Philippine Is., S. of Luzon and W. of Samar. Length 60 m., breadth 20 m., and it covers an area of 1262 sq. m. Gold is mined, and it is very fertile, yielding coco-nuts, corn, hemp and rice. Cattle are raised. The chief tn is M. Pop. *c.* 100,000.

Mascagni, Pietro (1863–1945), It. operatic composer, b. Leghorn, son of a baker, was educ. at Leghorn and at the Conservatory of Milan. But academic study was not to his taste and he threw it up for the job of conductor of a small touring operatic company. Later he settled in Apulia, where he gave pianoforte lessons and conducted the local band. Conditions could scarcely have been less promising for a young musician, but he had written *Guglielmo Ratcliff*, an opera on a gloomy subject of Heine's, and *Cavalleria Rusticana*. The latter was chosen in a competition organised by the Italian music publisher Sonzogno. The opera was produced on 17 May 1890 at the Costanzi Theatre, Rome, and, being crudely effective, was an instant success. Sev. other operas followed, but he never again approached this initial success. *L'Amico Fritz*, 1891, now neglected, deserved a better fate, for there is much in it which is charming. *Guglielmo Ratcliff* was first performed, revised, in 1895. His other operas include *Il Rantzau*, 1892, *Silvano*, 1895, *Zanetto*, 1896, *Iris*, 1898, *Le Maschere*, 1901, *Amica*, 1905, *Isabeau*, 1911, *Parisina*, 1913, *Lodoletta*, 1917, *Si* (operetta), 1919, *Il piccolo Marat*, 1921, *Pinotta*, 1932, and *Nerone*, 1935. Besides operas, he wrote some occasional works, cantatas, and the incidental music for Hall Caine's *The Eternal City*, produced in London in 1902. He became a member of the It. Academy in 1929. *See* lives by E. Mascagni, 1936; A. Jersi, 1945.

Mascara, tn of Algeria, 50 m. SE. of Oran. The former H.Q. of Abd-el-Kader, it was destroyed by the French in 1835, and occupied by them in 1841. It trades in cereals, wine and oil. Oriental rugs and agric. machinery are manuf. Pop. 39,830.

Mas-d'Azil, Le, Fr. tn in the dept of Ariège, on the Arize. It has prehistoric remains. Pop. 1600.

Masefield, John Edward (1878–), poet, playwright and novelist, b. Ledbury, Herefordshire. He was educ. at King's School, Warwick, and H.M.S. *Conway*, which trains cadets for the merchant service. At the age of 15 he went to sea as an apprentice on a wind-jammer and made the voyage round Cape Horn, whence his admirable sea scenes in some of his poems. Thereafter he lived for 3 years in New York, working successively in a bakery, a livery stable, a saloon and a carpet factory. In 1897 he returned to London and started writing for various periodicals. He became literary editor of the *Speaker*, and inaugurated the famous Miscellany column of the *Manchester Guardian*. Later he settled in Bloomsbury, forming a warm friendship with J. M. Synge (q.v.). Between 1901 and 1911 he wrote poems, plays, novels, short stories, essays and criticism, all with moderate success, and was an estab. writer by the time 'The Everlasting Mercy' appeared in the *English Review*, 1911. This long narrative poem in octosyllabic couplets, representing the spiritual conversion of a prodigal 'tokened to the devil', evoked much enthusiasm among the critics. M. was, in fact, a pioneer in the revival of the long narrative poem in England. Other such poems are *The Widow in the Bye Street*, 1912, *The*

Daffodil Fields, 1913, and *Dauber*, 1913, all somewhat marred by the artificiality of manuf. rhymes and effort at ultra-realism as expressed in the crude language and occasional blasphemous sentiments in the mouths of characters who, in ordinary life, would no doubt express themselves in that manner. *Dauber*, however, is relieved by some magnificent passages of sea verse. *Reynard the Fox*, 1919, also a narrative poem, the record of a fox hunt, is notable for its truly Chaucerian vignettes of human character. M.'s sea experiences have been a great source of inspiration to him, from his first vol. *Salt-Water Ballads*, 1902, onwards. His versatility is shown in his felicitous lyrics and other short poems, in *Ballads*, 1903, *Lollingdon Downs*, 1917, *Sonnets of Good Cheer*, 1926, and in his dramas and novels. *The Tragedy of Nan* was produced in 1909. Opinion is divided on its merits, but at the lowest estimate it is one of the few 20th cent. plays that approach true tragedy. But after 1919, apart from a few experimental performances in London, M.'s new plays got little farther than the private theatre in his home at Boar's Hill, Oxford. In *Good Friday*, 1916, and *The Trial of Jesus*, 1925, alternative versions of the same gospel incidents, he cramped himself in the effort to adhere to the scriptural record. There is a real element of dramatic and psychological interest in his portrayal of Pilate and Herod and others, but these religious plays would seem to suffer from the handicap of a static central figure. Among his energetic and thrilling novels are *Jim Davis*, 1911, *Sard Harker*, 1924, *Odtaa*, 1926, *The Bird of Dawning* (a swift-moving story of the tea-clippers), 1933, *The Taking of the Gry*, 1934, *The Country Scene*, 1937, and *Badon Parchments*, 1947. His miscellaneous works include studies of *Shakespeare*, 1911, *Synge*, 1915, *and Ruskin*, 1920; the well-known war books *Gallipoli*, 1916, *The Old Front Line*, 1917, and *Nine Days' Wonder*, 1941 (about Dunkirk); and a standard work on *Sea Life in Nelson's Time*, 1905. M. succeeded Bridges in 1930 as poet laureate, and was awarded the O.M. in 1935. His autobiography *So Long to Learn* appeared in 1952. *See* studies by W. H. Hamilton, 1922; G. O. Thomas, 1932; L. A. G. Strong, 1952; Muriel Spark, 1953. (*See Plate*: *English Literature*.)

Maseru, dist of Lesotho. Chief tn and settlement of the dist is M., 100 m. NNE. of Aliwal N. It links with the Bloemfontein–Natal railway at Marseilles. There is an air service 3 times a week to Ladysmith. Pop. Whites, 590; all other races, 5540.

Mashal, *see* PROVERBS, BOOK OF.

Masham, Abigail (*d.* 1734), royal favourite, was the daughter of Francis Hill, a London merchant who married the sister of Mr Jennings, the father of the Duchess of Marlborough. Her cousin, then Lady Churchill, procured her the place of waiting-maid to Princess Anne. She retained her situation after the princess ascended the throne and acquired great influence over her. Miss Hill married Samuel M. (son of Sir Francis M., of Otes in Essex) in 1707. Through her

influence with the queen Harley, afterwards Earl of Oxford, intrigued against his colleagues. In 1711 Samuel M. was raised to the peerage. He and his wife appear to have engaged in intrigues in favour of the exiled Stuarts, and after Anne's death M. went into retirement.

Masham, mrkt tn of Yorks, England, 10 m. NW. of Ripon, on the R. Ure. The church dates from Norman times, and M. has a 1000-year-old cross and the grave of Julius Caesar Ibbetson (q.v.). Main industries are brewing, cheesemaking and agriculture. Pop. 1586.

Mashhad, dist and tn of the prov. of Khorasan. NE. Persia. The tn, which is the cap. of the prov., is situated in a fertile plain, and is famous for the magnificent mausoleum of the Imam Riza, which is visited annually by thousands of Shi'ite pilgrims. A branch of the Trans-Iranian railway links M. with Tehran. M. is the main trading centre of E. Persia; it has a considerable trade in carpets, and has sugar, leather and spinning factories. Pop. of dist about 528,400; of tn, about 300,000. Also spelt Meshed, Meshad.

Mashona, *see* SHONA.

Mashonaland, region of Rhodesia, came under Brit. rule in 1890. The Mashona are the descendants of the inhab. of the famed medieval kingdom of Zimbabwe (q.v.), ruled by the Monowatapa. They are divided into sev. distinct tribes, of which the main are the Karanga, Korekore, Manyika, Ndau, Tawara and Zezura. They are industrious farmers, although much of their traditional land has been taken for White settlement. *See also* LOBENGULA; RHODESIA.

Masinissa or **Massinissa** (*c.* 238–148 BC), king of the Massyli, the easternmost tribe of Numidia (q.v.). On the outbreak of the 2nd Punic war (218) he supported Carthage, but later transferred his allegiance to Rome. He resisted attacks by the Carthaginians and by his neighbour Syphax until the arrival in Africa of Scipio, 204. In 203 he went over to the offensive, reduced Cirta and took Syphax prisoner (*see* SOPHONISBA). In 202 M. commanded the cavalry of the Rom. right wing at Zama, and after the war received most of Syphax's ter. Except for a dispute with Carthage, which led to the 3rd Punic war, he spent the rest of his life in peace, dying at the age of 90. M. was the grandfather of Jugurtha (q.v.).

Mask, name given to artificial covering for the face for the purpose of disguising or protecting the wearer. The making of M.s representing human, animal or grotesque faces dates back to prehistoric times, and the use of the M. in ceremonial dances, incantation ceremonies or other ritual occasions is found among primitive peoples at the present day. The M. is often believed to have a daemonic power which transfers to the wearer the attributes of the character represented, its purpose being either to create an illusion in the beholders or to give courage to the wearer, frightening evil spirits and enabling him to conquer his enemies or to propitiate his gods. Knowledge of the M. in Europe begins with its use in the theatre of the anct Greeks. It doubtless had its origin in the early mystery cults, but in the Gk and later the Rom. theatre it survived as a representational convention. In China, Japan and the Far E. the theatrical M.s had the same uses but retained more of their magical qualities. In the Middle Ages in Europe M.s were made with a Christian significance but not primarily to be worn. In the 16th cent. the M. gained a new vitality through the Commedia dell' Arte, and from this developed the Venetian social M., simply a covering for the eyes and nose, leaving the mouth free. It signified licence from social restraint and to that extent retained some of its primitive magical character. The M. is also a means of preserving a likeness of the features of a person once living, and in this connection, too, it has a long hist. The anct Egyptians made death M.s of thin gold plate. The Romans used wax. Later methods are to apply oil or grease to the face, and then coat the features with plaster of Paris, which hardens and can be removed to form a mould from which the M. can be cast. M.s are also used in modern industry as a protection to the face, necessary in various processes such as, for instance, oxyacetylene welding. The use of poison gas as a weapon in the First World War resulted in the invention of the gas M. or respirator.

Mask, Lough, Rep. of Ireland, 10 m. long by 4 m. broad, between cos. Mayo and Galway. It is connected with Lough Corrib (q.v.) by an underground riv.

Maskelyne, John Nevil (1839–1917), Illusionist, b. Cheltenham; apprenticed to a watchmaker. In 1873 he moved to London, where he founded and toured with an illusionist show. He rebuilt and opened St George's Hall (London) in 1904 for illusionist displays and was founder and first president of the Magic Circle (q.v.). Shortly after that time M. and Devant had become the most famous illusionist showmen in the world. John N. M.'s son, *Nevil* (1871–1926), introduced new disappearing and other illusions, and, during the First World War, carried out experiments in photographing and timing artillery shells in flight, and put at the Admiralty's disposal a fire-resisting formula which was later used by naval gunners. He also supplied illusionists who performed 'magic' for Lawrence of Arabia before Arab chieftains. His son *Jasper* (b. 1903) carried on the business. See CONJURING.

Maskelyne, Nevil (1732–1811), astronomer, b. London, graduated at Trinity College, Cambridge, in 1754. In 1755 he took orders. He was elected F.R.S. in 1758, and in 1761 he went to St Helena to observe the transit of Venus and to detect, if possible, the parallax of the fixed stars. In 1764 he acquired that knowledge of nautical astronomy which led to the formation, in 1767, of the *Nautical Almanac*. In 1765 he was appointed Astronomer Royal. In 1774 he measured the earth's mean density by determining the deflection of a plumb line on Mt Schiehallion, a quartzite cone in Perthshire.

Maskinongy, see PIKE.

Masnavi, see MATHNAVI.

Masochism, see SACHER-MASOCH, LEOPOLD VON.

MASKS

1, mask for Japanese Nō theatre; 2, ritual mask from the Congo; 3, Chinese, from the 'Funeral of the Old Year' ceremony; 4, Roman, from Pompeii; 5, German medieval devil mask.

Masolino (c. 1383–1447), It. painter of the Florentine School, first trained as a goldsmith.

He executed some of the frescoes in the Brancacci Chapel in the Carmine, Florence, 1424–7, the remainder being by Masaccio (q.v.), and though otherwise more Gothic in style seems to have endeavoured to match Masaccio's realism of style.

Mason, Alfred Edward Woodley (1865–1948), novelist, b. Dulwich. He was educ. at Dulwich College and Trinity College, Oxford, where he was president of the union and took honours in classics. Joining Sir Frank Benson's company, he appeared in Shaw's *Arms and the Man*, but soon gave up the stage. He became a Conservative political agent and also occupied himself with church work. He produced his first novel, *A Romance of Wastdale* (which he afterwards suppressed), in 1895, and in 1896 was very successful with his second, *The Courtship of Morrice Buckler*. In 1902 came his best-known novel, *The Four Feathers*, written in a vein of heroic adventure in a contemporary setting. Meanwhile M. stood for Parliament in the Liberal interest and was elected (1906) for Coventry; but, though he seems to have made a good impression with his first speech, he did not stand again. His novel *The Turnstile*, 1912, describes the effect of the House of Commons on those who become members. Among other novels of his earlier years were *Running Water*, 1907, which appeals to all mountaineers by virtue of its description of the famous Brenva ice arête on Mont Blanc, *The Broken Road*, 1907, and *At the Villa Rose*, 1910, the first novels in which appeared his highly popular character Inspector Hanaud of the Paris Sûreté. He served in the First World War in the Royal Marine Light Infantry and as a naval intelligence officer. Among the many novels he wrote in the next 30 years are *The Summons*, 1920, *The Winding Stair*, 1923, *The House of the Arrow*, 1924, and *The Prisoner of the Opal*, 1929, in all of which Hanaud appears; *No Other Tiger*, 1927; *The Dean's Elbow*, 1930; *Fire over England*, 1936 (a story of Armada days, stirring and spectacular); *Königsmark*, 1938; *Musk and Amber*, 1942; *The House in Lordship Lane*, 1946 (a Hanaud novel). M. dramatised sev. of his novels; his comedy, *Colonel Smith*, was produced in 1909. *See* life by R. L. Green, 1952.

Mason, James Murray (1798–1871), Amer. political leader, b. Georgetown, D.C. He was a member of the National House of Representatives, 1837–9, and the U.S. Senate, 1847–61, when he resigned with other S. senators. Appointed confederate commissioner to Great Britain, he was seized with John Slidell on board the Brit. ship *Trent* by Capt. Wilkes of the *San Jacinto*. Great Britain demanded his release, and war was imminent, but Lincoln recognised that the *Trent* was a neutral ship, and released the commissioners. M. was not officially recognised in Great Britain. He lived at Paris and in Canada, returning to the Unites States in 1869.

Mason, John (1586–1635), governor of Newfoundland, 1615–21. In 1622 he obtained grants in Mariana (now N. Massachusetts) and the prov. of Maine, and in 1629 in New Hampshire and Laconia.

Mason, William (c. 1724–97), poet, b. Hull. He was educ. at St John's College, Cambridge. From 1754 he held various livings in the Church. He was a profound admirer of Gray, who praised his classical tragedy *Caractacus*, 1759, but pointed out also his plagiarisms and his grammatical and other blunders. M. ed. the *Life and Letters of Gray*, 1774. *See* J. Mitford (ed.), *The Correspondence of Thomas Gray and William Mason: a Study in 18th Century Culture*, 1924.

Mason City, cap. of Cerro Gordo co., Iowa, U.S.A., 115 m. NNE. of Des Moines, with limestone quarries, clay deposits, meat-packing plants, beet-sugar refinery, creameries and machine shops. It manufs. building and foundry products and there is also printing. Pop. 30,640.

Mason-Dixon Line, boundary line (lat. 39° 43′ 26·3″ N.) separating Maryland from Pennsylvania. Charles Mason and Jeremiah Dixon were 2 Eng. astronomers who surveyed it between 1763 and 1767, and thus put an end to the disputes between the Calverts and Penns, the respective proprietors of the 2 colonies. This line was part of the boundary between free and slave (N. and S.) states. The term is still popularly used to distinguish N. from S.

Masonry, art of building in stone in a similar manner to building in brick; the fundamental difference between M. and brickwork (q.v.) being that in the former the stones are often of irregular and heterogeneous shape and size, as opposed to the uniform mass of bricks. This renders it difficult to obtain a bond in the work, as well as causing the walls to be thicker than brick walls. M., however, from these features, is better suited to imposing and beautiful structures, as work of greater projection can be included than is possible with brickwork. The art of M. is of great antiquity, the pyramids of Egypt being perhaps the most noteworthy examples in the world of M. without mortar. Today it is more common for natural stone to be used as a facing material over load-bearing brickwork or concrete.

The tools which a mason uses include squares, hammers of various shapes, 'boasters', chisels, saws, axes, picks, wedges, trammel heads for setting off distances, nippers for lifting the stones, etc. Building stone (q.v.) after being quarried is left exposed to the air for a period to season. The manner in which stones are treated either before or after building is described in various technical terms. Scrabbing is taking off the salient angular projections of the stone; when the stone is used in this condition the work is called rustic work. Hammer-dressing and half-sawing are terms which explain themselves. Half-plain work is the term applied to stone which has been roughly levelled, whilst plain work has been more accurately smoothed. Combed work has been treated by a steel scraper or comb; boasted or droned work has parallel chisel marks, which do not extend quite across the surface, as in tooled work. Sunk work is below the level of the surrounding stone, moulded work is work formed with a change of curvature, whilst chisel-draughted margins are smooth narrow spaces enclosing combed, boasted or plain work. Rubbed work is rubbed with another stone and with sand, water, etc., whilst polished work is brought to a high polish generally by machinery. Most building stones are composed of layers or laminations, and it is of the utmost importance when using them that they be correctly bedded. In the case of stones resisting heavy compressive forces, the laminae must be at right angles to the thrust, otherwise there is a tendency for the surface to peel off. All joints in M. must be at right-angles to the pressure which they have to bear. Joints between 2 blocks of stone are formed by dowels, cramps and various types of joggles. Great care must be taken to prevent the formation of rust when using iron for securing joints, because the consequent expansion is capable of splitting the stone.

Stone walls may be divided into 3 main classes, according to the manner in which the stones are set up: rubble, block in course and ashlar. The first category includes a great variety of methods, of which the chief are known as flint; random rubble set dry; random rubble set in mortar; Kentish rag; random rubble built in courses; uncoursed; squared or 'snecked' rubble built up to courses; and regular coursed rubble. 'Rubble' as a generic term means thinly bedded stone, generally taken as less than 9 in. in depth. When it is of irregular shape it is 'random', and when squared into shape it is said to be coursed. The various kinds of rubble walls thus explain their composition by their names. In random rubble set in mortar the bond is obtained by using one bond stone in every superficial yard in the face. In flint-work, windows and door dressings and groins are set with brick or squared stone for strength and appearance. 'Kentish rag' is built of a kind of unstratified sandstone which is found in Kent, and the blocks of which are usually roughly dressed to a polygonal form. 'Snecks' are small stones which are inserted where required in snecked rubble to prevent long vertical joints. Block in course work is made of stones larger than those used for coursed rubble, with hammer-dressed faces, squared and brought to a good joint; it resembles good coursed rubble or ashlar, and is very strong and durable. Ashlar is the name given to carefully worked stones of more than 12 in.; owing to its heavy cost ashlar is backed either by brickwork or by rubble. The backing should be built in cement mortar and brought to a level at every bed-joint of the ashlar. The facing of the ashlar may be plain, rebated or chamfered. *See also* BUILDING STONE. *See* E. G. Warland, *Constructional Masonry*, 1947, and *Modern Practical Masonry* (2nd ed.), 1953.

Masons, Free, *see* FREEMASONRY.

Masons' Marks, as used in medieval buildings, were devices cut in the stones to identify the responsible mason or master-mason. Their origin, however, may conceivably be traced to early Rom. times. A study of eccles. architecture in Britain shows that some master-masons identified themselves with their work, as, for example, by a symbolical device representing their names.

Masovia, *see* MAZOWSZE.

Maspero, Sir Gaston Camille Charles (1846–1916), Fr. Egyptologist; *b.* Paris, entered the École Normale Supérieure of Paris in 1865, and became lecturer on Egyptian archaeology at the École des Hautes Études in 1869. For many years he was a prof. at the Collège de France. He discovered many royal sarcophagi at Deir-el-Bahri and made further discoveries in clearing the temple of Karnak. His most valuable pub. is *Histoire ancienne des peuples de l'Orient classique*, 1894–1900.

Masque was a species of dramatic entertainment which reached its highest popularity in the reign of James I, but was also a favourite diversion at the courts of Henry VIII and Elizabeth. Many scholars look to Italy for the origin of the M., but it seems at least as likely that it grew out of the 'mummings' which are heard of in England as early as 1377. The growth of opera accounts for the speedy waning of the M.; in the latter, pageantry and spectacular display were of supreme importance, whilst in the former these were rightly subordinated first of all to music and then also to character-drawing and plot. M.s were played commonly before royalty and in the homes of nobility. Thus Daniel's *Vision of the Twelve Goddesses* was produced at Hampton Court in 1604, shortly after James's accession—when, be it noted, Queen Anne and her ladies were the masquers—and *The Masque of Queens* of Ben Jonson was presented at Whitehall in 1609. The *Hymenaei*, also by Jonson, was performed in 1606 to celebrate the marriage of Essex to Frances Howard, whilst his *Pleasure Reconciled to Vertue* was played at court on Twelfth Night in 1618. It was this libretto of Jonson, the great master of the literary M., which inspired Milton's *Comus*, a composition better described as a pastoral than a M., as there is no dancing or disguise. Inigo Jones often designed the scenery, dresses and mechanical contrivances for M.s; such composers as Lanier and Ferrabosco contributed the music, and the dances were specially arranged by profs. of the art. Money, time and thought were freely lavished, the sole aim of the inventor being to multiply his gorgeous effects and to make the spectacle as full and varied as he could. *See* H. A. Evans (ed.), *English Masques*, 1897; W. W. Greg, *List of Masques, Pageants, etc.*, 1902; E. K. Chambers, *The Elizabethan Stage*, 1923; M. S. Steele, *Plays and Masques at Court, 1558–1641*, 1926; E. Welsford, *The Court Masque*, 1927; A. Nicoll, *Masques, Mimes and Miracles*, 1931; *Stuart Masques and the Renaissance Stage*, 1937; A. H. Gilbert, *The Symbolic Persons in the Masques of Ben Jonson*, 1948.

Masquerade, festive gathering, the participators in which all assume some disguise. The name suggests that when M.s first came into vogue the mask was a necessary part of the disguise. Weekley suggests an origin (Arabic *maschara*, laughing-stock) different from that of mask, masque. M.s first appeared in England in the reign of Henry VIII; they were introduced into France by Catherine de' Medici. Fancy-dress balls are, it would seem, their modern development.

Mass, term used in physics and defined by Newton to denote the measure of the quantity of matter in a body. It is measured by the product of the vol. of the body and its density relative to that of water. A distinction is sometimes recognised between *inertial mass* and *gravitational mass*. The former is the ratio of the force acting on a body to the acceleration produced in that body, and its preference is claimed to rest on the 'direct awareness' of force compared with our inability to sense M. Gravitational or attractive M. is introduced by defining the attractive force between 2 bodies as proportional to the product of their masses divided by the square of their distance apart. Newton investigated, by means of the hollow pendulum, the ratio of gravitational and inertial M. and found it to be constant, i.e. a proper choice of units makes them experimentally indistinguishable. Later, Eötvös confirmed this result to an accuracy of 1 in 10^a.

Mass (Lat. *missa*), the eucharistic service of the Rom. Catholic Church in the W. The name, which corresponds to the term 'liturgy' in the E., originated in the words *Ite missa est* (Go, it is ended) with which the rite concluded, the word *missa* coming to mean dismissal and finally becoming the name of the rite itself. Originally the Eucharist was performed everywhere in Greek, but Latin prevailed in the W. from the 3rd cent. onwards. In the first ages there was no doubt considerable variety of detail in the order of the service. Universal, however, was the eucharistic anaphora or prayer by which the bread and wine were changed into the body and blood of Christ, and in which Christ was offered up to the Trinity as a victim in renewal of the sacrifice on Calvary. This prayer or canon was preceded by prayers, psalms and readings from sacred scripture, forming almost a separate service and modelled on that of the synagogue. The first part came to be called the M. of the Catechumens, as the non-baptised were present at it; then they withdrew, and there followed the M. of the Faithful or Eucharist proper. The main rites were the bringing up of the bread and wine by the faithful to the celebrant, the consecration of these elements, and the communion of the faithful. Of the early fathers Justin Martyr (*Apol. i.* 65, 66) gives the fullest account of these rites. After the peace of Constantine the era of church building began and greater freedom for the Church. Solemn chants were then introduced, the introit (q.v.) for the processional entry, the *Kyrie eleison* (q.v.) or litany of supplication (still in Greek) at the beginning, the hymn *Gloria in excelsis*, and a good deal later the singing of the Nicene creed. Chants were devised to cover the time spent in bringing up the offerings (offertory) and in communicating (communion). The *Sanctus* chant marked the beginning of the canon, and the *Agnus Dei* (about AD 700) filled the time taken up in breaking the bread before communion. Today the old form of the rite is best seen when performed pontifically, i.e. by a bishop or abbot. In a High Mass, which is always sung (*see* PLAINSONG), the celebrant is assisted by a deacon and sub-deacon, whose special functions are the chanting of the gospel and epistle respectively. A *missa cantata* is a M. sung by one priest unassisted by deacon and sub-deacon. The Low M. is one in which the priest recites the whole text, being answered only by a server; in a variety of this known as the dialogue M. the whole congregation recites the responses. In 1964 and 1965 the vernacular was introduced at Low M. throughout the world. Later ages introduced polyphonic music, Palestrina's *Missa Papae Marcelli* being particularly famous. The introduction of instrumental music and the development of solo singing in Italy and elsewhere marked a deterioration in the style of the M. as a religious service, and the M.s of the 18th and early 19th cents. Catholic composers (e.g. Haydn, Mozart, Weber and Schubert), though musically effective, have not the devotional qualities of the earlier chant. In recent years the Catholic Church has tried to exclude ornate and instrumental music and to revert for devotional reasons to Gregorian chant and the simpler forms of polyphonic music. Another recent development has been the widespread permissions for and attendances at midday, evening and midnight M.s. *See* P. Parsch, *The Liturgy of the Mass*, 1958; J. A. Jungmann, *The Mass of the Roman Rite*, revised ed. (trans.), 1959; A. Croegart, *The Mass: a liturgical Commentary* (trans.), 2 vols., 1958–9; F. Amiot, *History of the Mass* (trans.), 1959; H. A. Reinhold, *Bringing the Mass to the People*, 1961; G. Jenkins, *The Byzantine Mass*, 1961.

Mass Education, term used to describe any scheme of education provided for the whole pop.; used more particularly to describe such programmes in technologically underdeveloped countries and to include courses not only for young children but also for adults. By contrast, in technologically developed countries we speak of universal and, often, compulsory education. Historically, universal education developed in 19th cent. Europe, N. America, parts of the European empires and later in Japan. The emphasis in the elementary, or people's, schools was on the acquisition of the 3 R.s. European education was carried to all parts of the world by various agencies. Missionaries, traders and the military and colonial govs. set up schools for the education of the people in the area and for their own children. Commercial and administrative needs created a greater demand for educ. personnel. Thus the growth of M. E. was stimulated, but it tended to be in the European pattern, with an emphasis on literary skills. A great many adult literacy campaigns have been conducted throughout the world. Criticisms of them have been that they have been divorced from the real interests and needs of the indigenous pops. Particularly since the Second World War attempts have been made to move away from the basically literary education. The name Fundamental Education (q.v.) has tended to replace M. E.

Illustrations of 20th cent. M. E. movements are to be found in sev. countries. Perhaps those in Russia, Turkey and China are best known. In China M. E. received its impetus from Sun Yat-sen (q.v.) and has been carried on with success despite great difficulties and years of strife culminating in the war with Japan. National consciousness was to be developed through education. This involved a democratisation of it and attempts to unify the language (*see* ILLITERACY). The Chinese Rep. set M. E. in the forefront of its policy with the object of establishing a system of universal schooling—elementary, secondary and higher—on W. lines. To develop this national programme the Nationalist gov. introduced a highly centralised system of administration. A uniform curriculum was set up throughout the country, text-books were selected and approved by the ministry or prov. authorities. Adult education was given high priority. Whatever ideological and political differences divide the Koumintang and Communist groups it is unlikely that their educational policies will be radically different. The problem of literacy is likely to receive high priority, and attempts will be made to associate it with rural economics, agriculture, health measures, citizenship training and recreation.

Kemal Atatürk (q.v.), who *d.* in 1938, laid down the pattern for the Rep. of Turkey. Since 1923 M. E. has been assigned a crucial role in the life and development of the nation. One important reform was the official adoption of the Rom. alphabet—previously an Arabic script had been used. This change effectively cut the link of modern Turkey with her Islamic and imperial past. M. E. took 2 forms. Public schools were developed, and among adults the learning of the new alphabet was facilitated by setting up centres where adults attended lectures in language, hist., literature and so on, and where there were opportunities for sports and dramatics. Even after more than a quarter of a cent., however, only 80 per cent. of town children and some 55 per cent of rural children are enrolled in primary schools. Nevertheless the aims of M. E. in Turkey are to eradicate illiteracy and give to those who complete primary school a technical training suited to the needs of the nation, of society and of the individual.

Changes in Russian educational policy have, perhaps, been determined as much by circumstances as by ideology. Tsarist Russia had an old and well-developed educational system. It made no provision for a very large proportion of the pop., particularly those living in remote rural dists. Communist policy has been directed towards a complete revision of the educational system. Over the years details of policy have changed, but there have been constant efforts to extend educational opportunities throughout the vast area. M. E. has been closely allied to the economic objective of industrialising the country. This has involved an emphasis on literacy and technical training. Generally a policy of allowing linguistic minorities to have schools where the medium of instruction is the mother tongue has been followed. In many areas of the Far N. and in the NE. of the European part of the U.S.S.R. many tribes were nomadic or semi-nomadic, had no schools and no written language. Attempts have been made to provide schools, give instruction in their native language and encourage the learning of Russian. In addition to building up 7-year schools in these areas, holiday camps, walking tours, excursions and sports camps have supplemented the work of the schools. There are boarding schools for children of members of groups like the reindeer breeding collective farms who live far away from populated centres. Young workers and farmers are encouraged to go to schools provided for them. There is a definite attempt in Russia to link M. E., whether of children, adolescents or adults, with the local environment. A good deal of M. E. is done in association with trade unions, and in the country dists cottage reading-rooms, people's houses and 'red corners' supply books, papers, radio and sometimes travelling cinemas and theatres.

Many methods of M. E. have been tried since the Second World War (*see* FUNDAMENTAL EDUCATION). The Rep. of India, basing her educational reform on the Sargent Plan and Mahatma Gandhi's scheme for primary education centred on village or cottage industries, has made great efforts to improve social conditions through education. The aim is to provide education for all children between the ages of 6 and 14. This will be Basic Education: its goals are little more than the acquisition of literacy. This plan closely follows other community development schemes. One of these is that organised at the Jeanes School for Community Development in Kenya. Residential courses are offered to the adult citizen, the farmer, the shopkeeper, the housewife and so on. Instruction in methods of improving agriculture and animal husbandry is regarded as fundamental. Homecrafts, cultural activities and courses in citizenship are also provided. The Jeanes type of school had its origin in a bequest by Anna T. Jeanes for the training of visiting teachers for Negro schools in the S. states of America. There the Negroes have been at a disadvantage as far as educational facilities are concerned since their emancipation in the 19th cent. Since the Second World War these facilities have been improving steadily. In 1956 a Supreme Court decision made segregated schools illegal. The Negroes might expect further improvement in educational opportunities. *See Mass Education in African Society*, Col. No. 186, H.M.S.O., 1944 (reprinted 1946), and *The Year Book of Education*, 1954.

Mass Number, whole number nearest to the mass of a nucleus (q.v.) expressed in atomic mass units, on which scale the mass of the carbon atom is 12 units. It equals the number of protons, i.e. the atomic number, plus the number of neutrons in the nucleus. *See* ATOM and ISOTOPE.

Mass Production, *see* AUTOMATION.

Mass Psychology, study of the collective mind and emotional unity characteristic of a crowd of people responding to the same stimuli. Physical contiguity is an essential element, thus differentiating the crowd from the 'public', but M. P. has often been extended to cover the behaviour of any society as a whole, especially when acting under any widely shared emotion, whether in times of stress or general rejoicing. The psychology of the individual taking part in crowd activities is modified as the result of the weakening of individual intellectual effort. The psychology of a crowd is therefore different from the average psychology of its individual members. Cruder impulses come into play and inhibitions to which the individual is normally subject are liable to be loosened or removed. Thus the crowd is more fickle, credulous or courageous than would be any average member of it acting separately, and is liable to outbursts of hysteria, brutality or bravery. The individual becomes in effect assimilated with a new combination of impulses and reactions, and is thus part of a collective personality capable of a unified response to a common stimulus. The conscious application of stimulus in order to produce a desired reaction among large numbers of people whose individual psychology is merged in that of the crowd is known as mass suggestion. Speculations on crowd psychology became popular under the influence of the Fr. writer Gustav LeBon. The tendency to generalise the findings of crowd psychology to that of groups of any character has done much to discredit LeBon's work, of which little account is taken in modern social psychology. *See* L. S. Penrose, *On the Objective Study of Crowd Behaviour*, 1952, and W. J. H. Sprott, *Social Psychology*, 1952.

Mass Radiography, method of examining a number of people in quick succession to detect latent chest disease, particularly tuberculosis. An X-ray apparatus, producing an image of the chest on a fluorescent screen, is integrated with a camera that simultaneously photographs this image on a miniature film which, in enlarged projection, enables a trained observer to tell whether or not the chest is normal and so to sift out any person with an abnormality calling for further investigation by estab. diagnostic methods. M. R. for the civil pop. began in Great Britain in 1943. Both stationary and mobile units are operated by regional hospital boards. There are now some 75 such units in operation in England and Wales and many million examinations have been made since the introduction of M. R. *See* R. R. Trail, *Miniature Mass Radiography*, 1943.

Mass Spectrograph derives its name from the fact that its mode of operation bears certain similarities to that of the optical spectroscope;

moreover, the result of its action may be to produce on a photographic plate a pattern that is very similar to the one given by its optical analogue. Just as a spectroscope separates out light of a particular wave-length, so the M. S. can be used to separate from a mixture of charged atoms or groups of atoms those whose mass bears a fixed ratio to their charge. If an electric discharge is passed through a mixture of gases at low pressure, many of the atoms of the gas acquire a charge and become accelerated to high speeds. A stream of such high-speed atoms and groups of atoms can be allowed to escape through suitably placed slits into another vessel in which the pressure is so low that collisions between the gaseous atoms are relatively rare, and where they form a well-defined beam. This beam can be deviated by the use of electric and magnetic fields, the amount of the deflections being determined not only by the strength and extent of the fields, but also by the charges, masses and velocities of the particles. By a suitable choice of the strength and disposition of the fields it can be arranged that particles of the same ratio of mass to charge are caused to arrive along a particular line on a photographic plate, while particles having other ratios are concentrated along other lines. A spectrum is thus formed whose lines correspond to particles having definite ratios of mass to charge. Since the charges of the particles, however, can only be integral multiples of the charge of an electron, and are normally equivalent to that of either 1 or 2 electrons, the masses of the particles are readily inferred, and can be compared with high precision after measurement of the distances apart of the lines on the plate. The M. S. was developed by F. W. Aston, following Sir J. J. Thomson, and has proved a powerful weapon for determining the presence of isotopes (q.v.) and for measurement of their masses. Modern high-powered M. S.s have an important industrial application. A few isotopes such as the rare species of hydrogen, oxygen, nitrogen and carbon were first detected by optical spectroscopy since the presence of an isotope produces a shift in the positions of certain lines in the band spectra of mols. The faint doubling of spectral lines, showing the presence of isotopes, has been confirmed by the M. S. Since modern forms of the M. S. have been used to measure the relative masses of isotopes with great accuracy, a revision of atomic weights has been possible and has solved the difficulty of the apparent inversion of certain pairs of elements in the Periodic Table. The separation of U235 from U238 can be achieved by a modified M. S. Modifications are necessary to improve the economy of the process and to intensify the beams of charged atoms.

Mass Stipends, monetary offerings made to Rom. Catholic priests for their services in celebrating mass for the donors' intentions. In England, from the reign of Edward VI onward, bequests for masses were held by the courts to be void for superstition. This view was negatived in 1919 by the House of Lords on an appeal in the case of *Bourne v. Keane*, and a judgment delivered in the chancery div. 15 years later (*In re Caus*) decided that funds to be applied as M. S. could form the material of a charitable trust.

Massa (di Carrara), or **Massa Ducale**, It. city, cap. of the prov. of Massa e Carrara (q.v.), at the foot of the Apennines, 56 m. NW. of Florence (q.v.). It has a 16th cent. cathedral and a fine 16th–17th cent. ducal palace. Marina di M., 3 m. SW. on the Ligurian Sea, is its port and is a holiday resort. M. is a centre of the Carrara (q.v.) marble industry. Pop. 55,800.

Massa e Carrara, prov. of Italy, in NW. Tuscany. The greater part of the prov. is in the Apennines, but it has a coastal plain on the Ligurian Sea in the S., and a central plain around the valley of the Magra R. The prin. tns include Massa, Carrara and Pontremoli (qq.v.). Area 445 sq. m.; pop. 205,000.

Massa Marittima, It. tn in Tuscany (q.v.), 22 m. NNW. of Grosseto. It has a fine cathedral (partly 13th cent.) and a Romanesque tn hall. The tn is a mining centre (ferrous metal). Pop. 5700.

Massachusetts, one of the 13 original states of U.S.A., often called the Bay State, Bean State or Old Colony State. It is in the NE. in New England, and has an area of 8257 sq. m., including 350 sq. m. of inland water. It is bordered on the S. by Rhode Is. and Connecticut, W. by New York, N. by Vermont and New Hampshire. M. has a fine coast indented by many bays between rocky headlands and half-drowned offshore drumlins, with long spits (of which the largest is Cape Cod) composed of glacial debris re-worked by currents. The many harbours explain M.'s early growth in fishing and trading. From the glacial lowlands of the S. and E. the land rises to the Berkshire Hills, and in the N. to the higher White Mts. Glaciation has left many lakes (important for the summer tourist trade they attract) and ungraded rivs. which provided at their falls the first power for the early industries. The chief rivs. are the Merrimack, Housatonic and Connecticut. The climate is temperate, but winters are cool, with mean temps. falling to 25°–30° F., and the beauty of the autumn in M. is notable. Farmland comprises over 2,000,000 ac., hay, maize, potatoes, tobacco and onions being grown, and fruit farms, which produce chiefly apples and cranberries. Dairy farming is the most widespread branch of agriculture. There are 3,300,000 ac. classified as forest land. Today M. is essentially a manufacturing state, the textile and boot and shoe industries being the old but now declining industries. Of growing importance are printing, publishing, metal and machine products, chemicals, rubber goods, electrical equipment goods, food processing and ship building. Boston (pop. 697,200), a great seaport and the oldest in America, is the cap. Other tns are Worcester, Springfield, Lowell (centre of cotton industry) and Fall R., a large seaport on Mt Hope Bay, 50 m. from Boston. M. leads the New England states in an ann. fish catch, landed at many small ports.

The Puritan ancestry had a marked effect on the inhab. of this state, but waned because of the large influx of Irish, It. and Fr.-Canadian settlers. In its early days it was remarkable for its extreme religious intolerance, and later the great Unitarian movement made its H.Q. in Boston. There are over 2000 m. of railway in the state; the New York, New Haven and Hartford Railroad, follows the coastline and connects with the New York railway station systems. The Boston S. station is one of the largest in the world. There are airport facilities throughout the state. The educational system includes Harvard, Northeastern and Boston Univs., the M. Institute of Technology (founded in 1861) and Radcliffe College at Cambridge, and Wellesley college for women students at Wellesley, near Boston. Other educational institutions are Boston College at Chestnut Hill; Tufts College at Medford; Smith College at Northampton; Holybross College at Worcester; Williams College at Williamstown; and Amherst College and the Univ. of M., at Amherst.

Its legislative body, the General Court of M., consists of a Senate of 40 members, elected biennially, and a House of Representatives of 240. Two senators and 14 representatives are sent to Congress. Pop. 5,148,580. M. derives its name from an Indian tribe. The first permanent settlement was made by the Pilgrims from Holland (but of Eng. stock) at Plymouth in Dec. 1620. In 1626 a few settlers at Salem were joined by John Endicott and some colonists, and a charter was granted by Charles I. The charter was taken away in 1684, but a new one was granted in 1691, which united, under the name of M. Bay, New Plymouth, Maine, Acadia, or Nova Scotia and M. Bay; in 1783 Nova Scotia remained in the possession of the Eng. M. took a leading part in the War of Independence. *See* L. A. Frothingham, *Brief History of Constitution and Government of Massachusetts*, 1925; A. B. Hart, *Commonwealth History of Massachusetts*, 1928; Federal Writers' Project, *Massachusetts: a Guide to Its Places and People*, 1937. (*See Plate.*)

Massacre of St Bartholomew, *see* BARTHOLOMEW.

Massada (Heb. 'a fortress'), sheer-sided mountain, forming a natural fortress of barren, many-coloured rock, on the W. shore of the Dead Sea, about 1400 ft in height. Herod the Great fortified the place, supplied it with granaries and cisterns and built a fine palace just below the summit at the N. end. After the destruction of Jerusalem by Titus in AD 70, a remnant of the Jewish diehards retired there and held out for 3 years against siege by Rom. forces under Silva. With slave labour the attackers constructed a ramp of beaten earth, up which they brought siege engines. The garrison, 960 in number, chose death rather than defeat, and *d.* by their own hands. The story is fully recounted by Josephus in his *Wars of the Jews*. In the winters of 1963 and 1964 an archaeological expedition led by Prof. Yigal Yadin, and sponsored by prominent Jews and the London

Observer, conducted a thorough examination of the flat summit area, which is boat-shaped and some 1900 ft from N. to S. and 650 ft wide. A striking feature of the enterprise was the great number of overseas volunteers who came at their own expense from 28 countries for the honour of working under so distinguished a leader. The task occupied 12 months in all. In addition to laying bare the relics of the palace of Herod, with its bath, pavilion and colonnade, decorated plaster walls and mosaics, the expedition also unearthed hundreds of coins, remnants of food, human bones, shards, arrows, scales of armour plating and, greatest prize of all, a collection of biblical and other parchment scrolls, automatically dated by their positions from before the fall of the temple in AD 70. The M. Expedition, like the discovery of the Dead Sea Scrolls (q.v.) in the Qumran Caves, has undoubtedly added much to the world's knowledge of biblical source material and of a period of outstanding historical importance.

Massage is a scientific manipulative treatment applied to the softer body tissues in certain diseases and convalescence, when the usual innumerable movements of the body exciting tissue metabolism are in abeyance or impossible. The operator (masseur, masseuse), placing the patient in suitable positions, proceeds to aid movements of the limbs and joints; to stroke, pinch, press, knead the muscles. By this means the small muscles, cell tissue of all kinds, capillaries, etc., are agitated, and normal waste and repair of the healthy body promoted. A modern extension is the application of vibration, especially to joints in cases of rheumatoid affections, by mechanical or electric vibrators. The treatment has become usual in nervous ailments such as sciatica, neuritis, neuralgia, in insomnia, and after fracture of a limb. The other forms of M. in general use are effleurage, stroking, petrissage, frictions and tapotement.

Effleurage is a form of stroking performed so that the motion is always directed towards the heart. Superficial effleurage relieves pain; deep effleurage is stimulating, promotes circulation and tissue nutrition and counteracts inflammation.

Stroking is applied in the opposite direction, and by different movements from effleurage, and should have a soothing effect.

Petrissage consists of kneading, wringing and picking up tissues. The last operation is used to reduce obesity, and the 2 former ones in the treatment of muscles of the limbs. In addition to beneficial effects similar to those of effleurage, petrissage aids the elimination of waste matter from the muscles.

Frictions are circular movements used especially to remove thickenings and adhesions, to reduce inflammation, and to help fat absorption.

Tapotement, sometimes called percussion, consists of hacking, clapping, beating and pounding the tissues. It aids muscular contraction and metabolism, and stimulates the skin. Hacking is beneficial in nervous affections.

Vibrations, performed manually or by vibratory mechanisms, are used in the treatment of painful nervous diseases, such as neuritis and neuralgia.

In addition to sprains, muscular weakness, obesity, contusions and other ailments commonly treated by M., constipation, indigestion, gastritis and other disorders of the alimentary canal may similarly be relieved. The cause of the disorder, however, must be considered; when it has arisen as a result of irregular habits M. may be particularly helpful. M. has always been used by athletes, and was in regular use among the Greeks. Recently it has been employed in conjunction with carefully regulated series of exercises performed by the patient, as a means of rehabilitation, e.g. after war injuries. Certified masseurs undergo a long training at schools of M., usually connected with some large hospital. Diplomas are granted by the Chartered Society of Physiotherapy (q.v.). In physiology, anatomy and pathology the masseur's training is similar to that of a medical student; in addition he is taught the technique of M., including the science of remedial exercises. The Physiotherapists Board of the Council of Professions Supplementary to Medicine (set up under the Professions Supplementary to Medicine Act, 1960) keeps a register of qualified practitioners. See B. M. G. Copestake, *Theory and Practice of Massage* (7th ed.), 1949, and M. V. Lace, *Massage and Medical Gymnastics* (4th ed.), 1951.

Massalia, *see* MARSEILLES.

Massawua, fortified seaport, in former It. colony of Eritrea (now a prov. of Ethiopia), on a small sterile coral is. in the Red Sea, 1 m. in circumference and 200 yds from the mainland. It is connected with the shore by an embankment containing the water conduit. There is a good harbour between the is. and the mainland, and an active trade is carried on with Arabia, Suez, India, etc. Chief exports through M. are those of Ethiopia, i.e. skins and hides, oil seeds, coffee and live cattle. In all, 413 ships, totalling 780,964 tons, entered M., 1953–4, unloading 90,965 tons, and loading 149,761 tons. M. is very hot and unhealthy. It was occupied by Brit. forces on 12 April 1941. Pop. (1939) 17,000 (6000 Italians). *See* ITALIAN EAST AFRICA, CAMPAIGN IN.

Masséna, André, Duc de Rivoli, Prince d'Essling (1756–1817), Fr. marshal, was a wine merchant's son, *b.* Levens, near Nice. In 1775 he joined the Royal-Italien regiment. He became a general in 1793. In 1795 he captured Oneglio and drove the Piedmontese from the heights of Saorgio. The following year he enabled Schérer to win the battle of Loano against the Austrians and Sardinians. So brilliant were his successes during the campaign of 1796–7 that Napoleon called him 'l'enfant gâté de la victoire'. From that time onward, till he was repulsed by Wellington in Spain (1810–1), his career was one long, triumphal progress. In 1805 he received his marshal's baton. Having assured to Joseph Bonaparte the possession of the Neapolitan Crown (1806), he was put in command of the left wing of the 'Grande Armée' in Poland, and was accorded the title of Duc de Rivoli for the services he rendered against the Russians. His title of Prince d'Essling was given in recognition of his brilliant generalship at Eckmühl, Essling and Wagram. After his Sp. campaign (1811), the failure of which he attributed with some justice to the insubordination of Ney, Junot and others of his lieutenants, M. was never again entrusted with any responsible command. Wellington repulsed him at Busaco, and fell back to the lines of Torres Vedras. M. was completely halted, and his lines of communication cut. He retreated in Mar. 1811 into Spain, and an attempted resumption of the offensive was defeated at Fuentes de Oñoro on 5 May. *See* P. Sabor, *Masséna et sa famille*, 1926.

Massenet, Jules (1842–1912), Fr. composer, *b.* Montaud, near Saint-Étienne. Studied harmony at the Paris Conservatoire under Bazin and Reber, and composition under Ambroise Thomas, and won the Prix de Rome in 1863. He met with some difficulties in obtaining recognition, but the success of *Marie-Magdeleine*, a sacred drama or oratorio (1873), opened all doors to him. His originality was never very striking; yet he created for himself a style which certainly had its imitators. He delighted in the facile lyrical melodies which won such success with his public, but his very voluptuous music too often lacks dignity. A number of his orchestral compositions were frequently performed, including, especially, those of a series of 5 suites called *Scènes*, composed during travels in Germany and Hungary. He gradually made progress as an operatic composer, producing *Le Roi de Lahore* in Lahore, 1877; *Hérodiade* in 1881; *Manon* in 1884, his most popular work; *Le Cid* in 1885; *Werther* in 1892; *Thaïs* in 1894; *Le Jongleur de Notre-Dame* in 1902. Of their class *Manon* and *Werther*, with their love-duets, lyrical tunes and effectively dramatic scenes, are masterpieces of their kind. Mention may aso be made of his *Don Quichotte*, 1910, which was popularised by Shaliapin's singing of the title part. Among his song books are *Poème d'avril* and *Poème d'un soir*. He also composed some overtures, a piano concerto, incidental music to plays and many songs. *See* lives by A. Pougin, 1914; R. Brancour (5th ed.), 1930; *also* J. d'Udine, *L'Art du lied et mélos de Massenet*, 1931.

Massey, Gerald (1828–1907), poet and mystic, *b.* near Tring, Herts. As a boy he worked in a silk factory, but in 1843 he came to London, where he was taken up by Maurice and Kingsley. His first book was pub. in 1851, and this was followed by 4 others; a selection from these was pub. in 1889, entitled *My Lyrical Life*. Later he wrote and lectured on spiritualism, and produced prose works on the origin of myths and mysteries in *The Book of Beginnings*, 1881, *The Natural Genesis*, 1883, and *Ancient Egypt: the Light of the World*, 1907. He also wrote a book on the sonnets of Shakespeare.

Massey, Vincent (1887–), Canadian statesman, educ. at St Andrew's College, Toronto, Toronto Univ. and Balliol College, Oxford.

Lecturer in modern hist. in Toronto Univ., and dean of residence, Victoria College, 1913–5. He was appointed minister without portfolio in the dominion Cabinet after the First World War. He was honorary Canadian minister to U.S.A., 1926–30; president of the National Liberal Federation of Canada, 1932–5; and High Commissioner for Canada in the U.K., 1935–46. In his last year of office he was made Companion of Honour. From 1947 to 1950 he was chancellor of the univ. of Toronto, and in 1952 was appointed governor-general, the first Canadian to hold the post. Pubs.: *Good Neighbourhood and other Addresses*, 1931; *The Sword of Lionheart and other Wartime Speeches*, 1943; *On Being Canadian*, 1949; *What's Past is Prologue*, 1963.

Massey, William Ferguson (1856–1925), New Zealand statesman, *b.* Limavady, Co. Derry, Ireland. He migrated to New Zealand in 1870 and settled as a farmer near Auckland. Entering Parliament in 1894 he was opposition (Conservative) whip from 1895 to 1903, and in 1903 became leader of the Conservative opposition and so galvanised it that he became Prime Minister in 1912, being also minister of lands and labour. In 1913 he had to deal with a formidable waterfront strike. When war broke out in 1914 M. warmly supported Britain. He invited the co-operation of the Liberal party in a National gov. which was formed in Aug. 1915. He represented New Zealand at the Paris Peace Conference in 1919, when a rift developed between him and Ward, the Liberal leader, on various matters of policy including the settlement of returned soldiers. M.'s Reform party was returned to office in the election of 1919 with 44 seats and the largest majority he ever had, and Ward lost his seat. Economic difficulties lessened the party's appeal and in the election of 1922 the Reform party lost its overall majority. Under the growing strain of office M.'s health failed and he *d.* on 10 May 1925. *See* G. H. Scholefield, *W. F. Massey, A Personal Biography*, 1925.

Massicot, yellow oxide of lead, the monoxide, PbO, sp. gr. 9·3, occurs native, but is generally prepared by heating lead or white lead in air up to about 600° C. It is mostly used in the manuf. of red lead, the dioxide, and as a pigment.

Massilia, *see* MARSEILLES.

Massillon, Jean-Baptiste (1663–1742), Fr. preacher, *b.* Hyères. He was a popular preacher at the court of Versailles and is remembered especially for a course of Advent sermons, 1699, 2 courses of Lenten sermons (the *Grand Carême*, 1701, and the *Petit Carême*, 1718) and his funeral oration on Louis XIV, 1715. His sermons are moralising and philosophical, not dogmatic. He became bishop of Clermont in 1717.

Massillon, city in Ohio, U.S.A., 8 m. W. of Canton, in coal region. There are steel, aluminium, rubber and paper products. Pop. 30,000.

Massine, Leonide (1894–), Russian-born dancer and choreographer, *b.* Moscow. He was trained at the Imperial Ballet School, Moscow, and later taught by Enrico Cecchetti; he was choreographer and principal dancer with the

Diaghilev Ballet from 1914 to 1920 and from 1924 to 1928. He began his career as a soloist in 1914, and as a choreographer in 1915, dominating the stage in both capacities and establishing himself as one of the outstanding figures in the whole hist. of ballet. He succeeded Nijinsky in the Diaghilev Ballet, making his début in the title-role of Richard Strauss's *La Légende de Joseph*, and from the outset he showed exceptional ability and industry. Diaghilev entrusted his protégé's early artistic education to Lartonov, a leading Russian modernist painter. With his first important ballet, *Les Femmes de bonne humeur*, M. realised his full potentialities. The most distinguished of the ballets he produced for Diaghilev were *La Boutique fantasque* and *Le Tricorne* (both 1919). In the 1930's, working for the Ballet Russe de Monte Carlo, he broke new ground by arranging a series of ballets to well-known symphonies, *Les Présages*, 1933, to Tchaikovsky's fifth, *Choreartium*, 1933, to Brahm's fourth, and Berlioz's *Symphonie fantastique* being the most important. Another considerable success of M. was his *Le Beau Danube*, a one-act ballet to the music of Johann Strauss, first produced in 1933. From 1942 to 1945 he worked with Ballet Theatre in America. More recently he has staged sev. ballets for the Sadler's Wells Ballet; revivals of *La Boutique fantasque*, *Le Tricorne* and *Mam'zelle Angot* (all 1947), *Clock Symphony*, 1948, and *Donald of the Burthens*, 1951.

Massinger, Philip (1583–1640), dramatist, *b.* Salisbury, said to have been connected in some way with the 'noble family of the Herberts'. In 1602 he went to St Alban Hall, Oxford, but applied himself to poetry and romance to the exclusion of the subjects associated with an academic course, and came down without a degree. He came to London about 1606, but fell into debt and appealed to Henslowe for assistance. He speaks of his 'trod-down poverty' and his life would appear to have been a constant struggle. But he soon acquired fame as a playwright. In his earlier days, from 1613, he wrote in collaboration with John Fletcher until the death of the latter 12 years later, and one of their most successful efforts was *The Two Noble Kinsmen* (printed in 1634 as being by Fletcher and Shakespeare). The date of this play is, however, uncertain, and there is argument about the Fletcher-M. authorship. The plays written by M. alone, with the dates of first performance, include *The Duke of Milan* and *The Unnatural Combat*, before 1623; *The Bondman*, 1623; *The Renegado*, 1624; *The Parliament of Love*, 1624; *A New Way to Pay Old Debts*, probably his masterpiece, the character of Sir Giles Overreach being familiar in hist. of dramatic literature, and *The Roman Actor*, before 1626; *The Emperor of the East*, 1631; *Believe as you List*, 1631; *The City Madam*, 1632; *The Guardian*, 1633; *A Very Woman*, 1634; *The Bashful Lover*, possibly in collaboration with Dekker, 1636. With Nathaniel Field M. wrote *The Fatal Dowry*, 1632; with Middleton and W. Rowley, *The Old Law*, 1656. With Fletcher he collabo-

rated in writing *Sir John van Olden Barnavelt*, 1619, and half a dozen other plays. *The Virgin Martyr*, 1620, is also ascribed to him. Of his extant tragedies *The Fatal Dowry* and *The Duke of Milan* are perhaps the best. The latter in its plot is superficially reminiscent of *Othello* and is an impressive play. *The Virgin Martyr*, which suggests a miracle play, is also one of M.'s best plays, with its beautiful character St Dorothy. His best comedy, as implied above, is *A New Way to Pay Old Debts*. Other good comedies are *The Guardian* (notable for the character of Durazzo) and *The City Madam*. Above all he excelled in romantic comedy. He shared much of the versatility of Middleton and also something of Ben Jonson's power of exhibiting human nature as diseased, but he is a more severe satirist than Jonson. M.'s knowledge of the technique of the drama was great but his characters are often lifeless. His plays were ed. by F. Cunningham in 1868. *See* lives by A. C. Swinburne, 1889; W. von Wurzbach, 1900; A. H. Cruikshank, 1920; M. Eccles, 1931. *See also* J. G. McManaway, *Philip Massinger and the Restoration Drama*, 1934.

Massingham, Harold John (1888–1952), journalist and nature writer, *b.* London, son of Henry Wm M., editor of the *Nation*, 1907–23. Educ. at Westminster School and Queen's College, Oxford, he was on the staff of the *Morning Leader* and, from 1912 to 1914, that of the *Athenaeum*, becoming a regular weekly contributor to the *Nation and Athenaeum* from 1916 to 1924. He is especially noted for his studies of bird and animal life, folklore and the Eng. countryside. His works include *Some Birds of the Countryside*, 1921, *Untrodden Ways*, 1923, *In Praise of England*, 1924, *Downland Man*, 1926, *The Heritage of Man*, 1929, *Country*, 1934, *Genius of England*, 1937, *The Fall of the Year*, 1941, and *An Englishman's Year*, 1948; also *Remembrance*, an autobiography, 1942.

Massinissa, *see* MASINISSA.

Masson, André (1896–), Fr. painter, *b.* at Balagny, in the Oise dept. His early work was in a diluted post-cubist manner, resembling that of Gris, but an essential romanticism came to the fore and he joined the surrealist movement soon after its inception in 1924. With Yves Tanguy and Salvador Dali, M. introduced surrealism to America. His work includes *décor* for the ballet, and book decorations. *See* M. Leiris and G. Limbour, *André Masson and his Universe*, 1948.

Masson, Antoine (1636–1700), Fr. engraver and painter, *b.* near Orleans. He became engraver-in-ordinary to the king. His original portraits are of considerable merit.

Masson, David (1822–1907), biographer and historian, *b.* Aberdeen. He was educated at Marischal College, and at Edinburgh, where he studied theology under Chalmers. He began his literary career in 1844 with an article in *Fraser's Magazine*. In 1853 he was appointed prof. of Eng. literature at Univ. College, London, and in 1865 he went to Edinburgh Univ. to occupy the corresponding chair. From 1859 for 18 years he ed. *Macmillan's Magazine*. During many years he was engaged upon a monumental *Life of Milton*, narrated in connection with the political, eccles. and literary hist. of his time, the 6 vols. of which appeared between 1859 and 1880. In 1874 he ed. the poetical works of Milton, and he ed. also the works of Goldsmith (1869) and De Quincey (1889–90). In 1893 he was appointed historiographer-royal for Scotland. Other works include *Essays, Biographical and Critical*, 1856, *British Novelists*, 1859, 1874, *Drummond of Hawthornden*, 1873, *De Quincey*, 1878, and *Carlyle Personally and in his Writings*, 1885. See his autobiographical *Memories of London in the Forties*, 1908.

Massorah, a marginal critical textual comment on the Heb. O.T. It was the work of trained scholars, the Massoretes, and consists of 3 parts, the *M. parva*, written at the sides of the roll of scripture, the *M. magna* (a fuller comment), written at the top and bottom of the roll, and the *M. finalis*, written at the end of the roll. The *M. finalis* gave the number of verses in the book or part of a book, and notes on peculiar words and expressions in it. The Massoretic text, which is represented by all our Heb. MSS., has for its object the preservation of the traditional consonantal text and the fixing of its pronunciation by the most scrupulously careful system of vowel-points and accents. From the 6th to the 9th cent. the M. is anonymous, but in the 10th cent. it is connected with the names of Ben Asher of Tiberias and Ben Naphthali. See J. ben Hayyim, *Bomberg Bible*, 1524; E. Levita, *Massoreth ha-Massoreth* (both trans. and ed. by C. D. Ginsburg); 1867; C. D. Ginsburg's ed. of the M. (4 vols.), 1880–1906; the Massoretic ed. of the Heb. Bible, 1894, and the introduction to this, 1897; *also* P. Kahle, *Der masoretische Text des alten Testaments nach der Überlieferung der babylonischen Juden*, 1902; *Massoreten des Westens*, 1927–30.

Massys, Quentin, *see* MATSYS.

Mastaba, in anct Egypt, a tomb with battered sides. From this type were evolved the Pyramids (q.v.).

Master: 1. Chief or president of a society, guild, corporation or association, as the M. of Trinity College, the M. of a masonic lodge (*see* FREEMASONRY), the M. of the Stationers' Company, and the Grand M. of Malta.

2. The title given to the officer in charge of the navigation of a sailing vessel, in the days when soldiers were embarked to do the fighting. In time the military commander or captain took complete command and the M. became his navigating officer, with the status of warrant officer. In 1843 the title was changed to navigating lieutenant. In commercial navigation, the captain of the ship (skipper is used in the Merchant Shipping Act for the captain of a fishing vessel) or person entrusted with the care and navigation of the ship and cargo is designated the M. He must be a properly qualified person, and upon him is the responsibility of having a proper crew and equipment. He enjoys very wide powers, e.g. he may hypothecate, sell, tranship or jettison the cargo

when circumstances warrant any such course or courses being taken (*see* BOTTOMRY; HYPOTHEC; RESPONDENTIA). He has the same rights as an ordinary seaman, e.g. a maritime lien, to recover his wages and disbursements made within his authority. *See* MERCHANT SHIPPING ACTS.

Master and Servant, *see* CONTRACT; TORT; TRUCK ACTS.

Master Mariners, Honourable Company of, Livery Company of the city of London founded in 1926. Membership is open to mariners who have held a foreign-going master's certificate for 5 years, and numbers 600. In addition there may be 200 Liverymen of the Company. There is an apprentice scheme which enables young merchant navy men to begin a connection with the Company early in their careers; entrants must be of first-class character, and be approved by the Company's apprenticeship committee. The *Wellington*, a converted sloop, has been moored off the Victoria Embankment as the H.Q. of the Company since 1948.

Master of Arts, *see* DEGREES IN ARTS AND SCIENCE.

Master of Flémalle, description of an anonymous Flem. painter of the early 15th cent. who has been identified with Robert Campin, who there is reason to think was the master of Rogier van der Weyden (q.v.). Paintings attributed to this artist are the 'Were Altar' (Prado) and the 'Virgin and Child before a Fire-screen' (National Gallery).

Master of Moulins (maître de Moulins) (active 1480–1500), Fr. painter working at the court of the Bourbons at Moulins, whose most important work is the triptych (*c.* 1498–1500) in the cathedral there. His eleven known works are widely distributed in Europe and the U.S.A. Some Flem. influence appears in his work though it is distinctively Fr. in general character.

Master of Sacred Theology, post-graduate degree in divinity conferred by certain foreign univs., e.g. Gregorian and Angelicum Univs. in Rome. It ranks above D.D. (Doctor of Divinity). *See* DEGREES IN ARTS AND SCIENCE.

Master of Science, *see* DEGREES IN ARTS AND SCIENCE.

Master of the Ceremonies, *see* CEREMONIES.

Master of the Queen's Musick, official who, from the time of Charles I onwards (Nicholas Lanier was first appointed 'Master of the Music'), presided over the court band, which in Charles II's time became 'the King's 24 Violins'. The band played to the monarch at meals, performed on state occasions and combined with the men and children of the Chapel Royal (q.v.) in performing birthday and welcome odes. These ceased in the reign of William IV, and the band had undergone various changes in the Georgian era. By the accession of Queen Victoria it had shrunk to a small body of wind instruments, but in 1840 Prince Albert developed it into a small orchestra. After that the court music became a mere adjunct to various functions and no longer required the direct supervision of the M. of the Q. M., who, however, continues to attend royalty on musical occasions, organises the music for coronations and other state occasions, and is still expected, though not actually commanded, to write new music for them. Elgar (q.v.) was master at the time of his death (1934), being succeeded by Sir Walford Davies, Sir Arnold Bax and Sir Arthur Bliss (qq.v.).

Master of the Rolls, see PUBLIC RECORD OFFICE and ROLLS, MASTER OF THE.

Master-singers, see MEISTERSINGER.

Masters, Edgar Lee (1869–1950), Amer. poet, *b.* Garnett, Kansas. Educ. at Knox College, he became a lawyer, then turned to writing. In imitation of epigrams in the anct Gk anthology he composed the *Spoon River Anthology*, 1915, purporting to be a collection of epitaphs from an Illinois cemetery, and followed this in 1924 with *The New Spoon River*. He also wrote studies of Lincoln, 1931, Vachel Lindsay, 1935, Whitman, 1937, Mark Twain, 1938, and an autobiography, *Across Spoon River*, 1937.

Masterton, bor. of N. Is., New Zealand, 67 m. NE. of Wellington. It is the centre of one of the richest farming areas in New Zealand, with good trout fishing and wild game shooting. Pop. 16,000.

Mastic, jointing or sealing material that is plastic when applied and should remain yielding throughout its life. This property is important in 'movement joints' in buildings and other structures, where it is desired to accommodate slight movement due to temp. or moisture changes without cracking or other type of failure. Most M.s consist of bitumen, tar, resin, rubber or oil, with some inert fibrous or powdered filler. If the joint is to remain watertight, the M., besides yielding to movement, must adhere strongly to the sides of the joint. Modern M.s are butyl based and are developed for specific purposes, i.e. withstanding constant vibration and violent changes in temp. Butyl M.s do not lose their properties in excessive cold.

Mastiff, typically Brit. dog bred to its present type for sporting purposes, but now kept only as a guard or for showing. It is very powerful. The head is large and square, the muzzle deep, square and blunt, the ears small and the eyes wide apart. The forelegs are straight and strong and the hind-quarters broad and wide. The tail is carried low and the coat is short and close. The M. is fawn in colour, with black mask or black brindle. Dogs are usually larger than bitches, and an adult dog may stand as high as 34 in. at the shoulder with a girth of 50 in., and weigh up to 16 stone.

The M. appears in Babylonian and Assyrian art, and the breed was known in anct Egypt, Greece and Malta. It is not known how the M. reached Britain, but at the Rom. occupation M.s were noted by the invaders. The Mogul emperors of the 12th cent. kept M.s for lion-hunting; by the reign of Edward III a law had been passed stating that a certain number of M.s were to be kept in every Eng. vil. Later, M.s were used for the baiting of bears and bulls, though they also enjoyed the status of household pets. On the prohibition of bear- and bull-baiting in England (by Act of Parliament, 1835), the M. was again employed purely as a watchdog or guard, and this is its present function.

The bull-mastiff is a separate breed, similar to a small M. in appearance, powerful, but less massive. Height 25 to 27 in.; weight 70 to 100 lb.

Mastodons, fossil primitive elephants, abundant in Tertiary and Pleistocene times. The name (Gk *mastos*, breast, and *odous*, tooth) was given by Cuvier on account of the nipple-shaped tuberculations on the teeth. M. have been found in many parts of the world and probably persisted in N. America until a few thousand years ago. The earlier types (*Tetrabelodon*) have 2 pairs of tusks, the lower jaw being prolonged to support the upper pair.

Masurenland, see MASURIA.

Masuria (Ger. **Masurenland**), region of N. Poland, formerly the S. part of E. Prussia (q.v.). Originally inhabited by people of Mazowsze (q.v.), the land passed to the Teutonic Knights (q.v.) and thence to Prussia. In 1921 the pop. voted for Ger. nationality. M. was returned to Poland after the Second World War, and is now incorporated mainly in Olsztyn prov. (q.v.). The region is hilly, with many woods and lakes. Its climate is severe.

Masurian Lakes, Battle of, see TANNENBERG, BATTLE OF.

Masurium, see TECHNETIUM.

Matabele, properly **Ndebele,** an offshoot of the Zulu in S. Africa. They moved N. into what is now Rhodesia under their leader Mzilikazi; later, under King Lobengula, their military power was broken in 1893 by the British, and after a short rebellion in 1896 they ceased warfare and raiding and settled down as peaceful farmers.

Matabeleland, portion of Rhodesia which, together with Mashonaland, now constitutes S. Rhodesia. Much of the surface consists of rich plains traversed from SW. to NE. by the Motopo and Izimunte Mts, and watered by tribs. of the Zambesi, Lundi and Limpopo R.s. There is much mineral wealth, especially gold. Cereals, cotton, sugar and citrus fruits are grown, and there are large tracts of forest. Cattle and sheep are bred in the dists free from the tsetse fly. The chief tn is Bulawayo. Area 70,800 sq. m.

See RHODESIA.

Matadi, chief riv. port of Congo (Leopoldville/Kinshasha), 90 m. from mouth of R. Congo. It is the cap. of a dist and the starting place of the Congo railway.

Matador, *see* BULL-FIGHT.

Matanzas: 1. Prov. of W. Cuba, bounded by Havana, Santa Clara and Florida Strait. Largely mountainous, especially in the N., it is watered by the Yumurí, San Juan, Palma and Sagua R.s, and the N. coast has fine bays. In the S. is the great swamp, Gran Ciénaga Occidental de Zapata. Sugar, cereals, fruit, cotton and tobacco are grown. Area 3260 sq. m.; pop. 395,780.

2. Free port and cap. of above prov., on M. Bay, 50 m. E. of Havana. It has large sugar factories, and exports sugar and other produce.

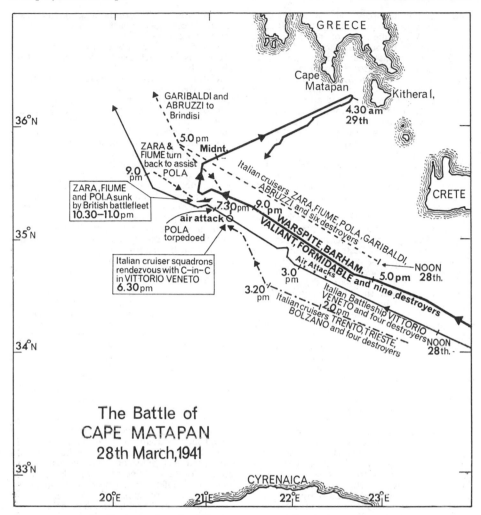

The Battle of
CAPE MATAPAN
28th March,1941

M. is a flourishing tourist area, noted for the nearby Bellamar Caves (crystalline 'Gothic' formation), and the hermitage of Monserrate with its views of the Yumurí valley. Pop. 82,000.

Matapan, Battle of Cape (28 Mar. 1941), one of the most successful naval actions of the Second World War, fought between the Brit. Mediterranean fleet under Adm. Cunningham and the It. main fleet under Adm. Iachino. The victory was without precedent in that it was won without any Brit. casualties, or even the slightest material damage to the Brit. ships, though 1 naval aircraft was lost. The forces opposed were British: 3 battleships, 1 aircraft carrier, 4 cruisers and a number of destroyers; Italian: 1 battleship, 8 cruisers and 14 destroyers. The Italians lost the heavy cruisers *Zara*, *Pola* and *Fiume*, the large destroyers *Vincenzo Gioberti* and *Maestrale* were both sunk and another destroyer was

seriously damaged. The battleship *Vittorio Veneto* was hit by a torpedo which reduced her speed to 19 knots. The battle was the first in hist. in which skilful co-ordination of naval operations with attacks launched by naval aircraft resulted in enemy ships' speeds being so reduced as to force them to action.

At noon on the previous day RAF Sunderland planes spotted the It. fleet putting to sea. Adm. Cunningham and the main fleet were then at Alexandria. Concluding that the It. ships intended to attack convoys carrying supplies from Egypt to Greece, the Brit. admiral ordered Vice-Adm. Pridham-Whippell, commanding the light-cruiser force, to sail to a position S. of Crete, from which he could intercept ships interfering with convoys. The commander-in-chief in his flagship *Warspite* with the battleships *Barham* and *Valiant*, and the carrier

Formidable, in company with a screen of 9 destroyers, sailed on the evening of the 27th and steamed NW. in the hope of intercepting the enemy. Shortly before 8 a.m. on the following day Brit. reconnaissance aircraft reported an enemy cruiser and destroyer force some 35 m. S. of Gavdo Is. (about 25 m. S. of Crete). This force was soon afterwards joined by 2 more cruisers and 2 more destroyers. The situation remained obscure during the forenoon with varying reports coming in of the number of enemy battleships in the area, but by noon it appeared that only one of the Littorio class was present. At 12.30 p.m. the vice-admiral, who had been under long range fire from the battleship, joined the commander-in-chief and the whole fleet continued in pursuit of the now retiring enemy. At about 3.15 p.m. torpedo aircraft from the *Formidable* scored a hit on the enemy battleship, reducing her speed, but not by as much as was hoped. Adm. Cunningham therefore ordered a third air striking force to attack. At 6.30 p.m. the distance between the 2 fleets was 55 m., and the chances of catching the enemy seemed poor. However, the *Formidable's* aircraft, although failing to score further hits on the battleship, managed to torpedo the 8 in. gun cruiser *Pola*, which stopped. Adm. Iachino then detached the cruisers *Zara* and *Fiume* with a div. of destroyers to stand by her, believing the Brit. fleet to be still well to the E. of him. Meanwhile Adm. Cunningham, informed of the success of the last air strike, decided on night action. Soon after 9.00 p.m. one of the battleships detected a stopped ship (the *Pola*) on her radar some 8 m. away to the S. As soon as he received this information, Adm. Cunningham altered course to the SW. to close the target, while maintaining a speed of 20 knots. During the run in, the steady stream of radar range and bearings being received was of great assistance to him in selecting the moment to open fire. He was about to give the order to do so, when 2 darkened ships were sighted crossing from starboard to port. Turning his ships to starboard to bring all their guns to bear, he enabled the battleships to open fire at almost point-blank range on the new and unsuspecting targets. These were the 8 in. cruisers *Zara* and *Fiume*, which were instantly reduced to a shambles by the devastating fire of their opponents' 15-in. guns. Two enemy destroyers were sunk by Brit. destroyers and the *Pola* was dispatched at 4.00 a.m. the next morning also by destroyers. On the 29th Adm. Cunningham resumed his search for the damaged enemy battleship which, however, succeeded in reaching port safely. Although he was disappointed that the main prize had eluded him, the victory made a substantial contribution to the success of the subsequent difficult operations of evacuating Brit. and Commonwealth forces from Greece and Crete. *See* A. Hurd, *The Battle of the Seas*, 1941; C. King, *Rule, Britannia*, 1941; H. G. Thursfield, *Action Stations*, 1942; *Official History of the Second World War: The War at Sea*, 1956; S. W. C. Pack, *The Battle of Matapan*, 1961.

Mataram, cap. of Lombok (q.v.), Indonesia, situated near the W. coast. It is the trade centre for an agric. area.

Matariyeh, vil. of lower Egypt, 5 m. NE. of Cairo. It is built on the site of the anct tn of On or Heliopolis.

Mataró, Sp. seaport in the prov. of Barcelona, on the Mediterranean. It has boatbuilding and fishing industries and manufs. hats. Pop. 41,200.

Matches. *Manufacture.* Matchsticks are peeled from a log as veneer which is subsequently chopped to the requisite size. They are then fed to an integrated production unit known as a 'Complete' machine, where they are inserted in holes in a conveyor belt, first to be dipped in paraffin wax and later in the mixture for the head. After further transport for a drying period they are ejected into boxes in predetermined numbers, and the boxes closed for transport to the wrapping and packing stations. In the most modern process a complete machine is supplied with inner and outer boxes made from a single piece of cardboard from plant operating as part of the complex.

Industry. Wood M. predominate in Europe and other areas following European traditions of manuf. Wax M. with sticks of paper or cotton are popular in Lat. countries, while N. America largely distributes cardboard book matches. Machinery is manuf. in Sweden and Germany, more recently in England, London being H.Q. of the industry for the Commonwealth and some foreign countries; other areas are dominated from Sweden and U.S.S.R. Cardboard book-match equipment comes mostly from the U.S.A. Although centres of manuf. were previously dependent on natural timber availability, modern forestry schemes, the increasing use of cardboard components and the shipment of matchsticks as a finished commodity, lend force to factories adjacent to sales areas.

Active Ingredients. Strike-Anywhere M. contain sesquisulphide of phosphorus, potassium chlorate and zinc oxide with binders and regulators. Safety match heads contain potassium chlorate, manganese dioxide and sulphur with binders and regulators; box paint is red phosphorus and antimony in binding agent. Sticks contain mineral wax and afterglow retardant.

History. Spills of vegetable fibres, paper or wood were originally used to transmit flame, with combustible substances like resin, sulphur, or oils added as an improvement. Yellow phosphorus in which to dip spills was used by 1786 giving immediate spontaneous combustion in air, but was toxic and likely to cause fires if the container was accidentally opened. An alternative approach by Chancel of Paris in 1805 involved tipping spills with potassium chlorate, sugar and gum; ignition was obtained by dipping head in sulphuric acid. This culminated in 'Promethean Match' invented 1828 by Samuel Jones of London, in which acid was contained in glass bulb on tip and ignition obtained by fracture.

Attempts to refine 2-part ignition system into

single entity was initiated by friction successfully by 1810. They were first based on phosphorus mixtures as patented by Dérosne of Paris in 1816 but were hazardous and unpredictable. Other suppliers progressed by making potassium chlorate spills originally developed for Chancel principle more sensitive to friction, and a sale was recorded of this type in England by John Walker of Stockton-on-Tees in 1827, commercial production following from Samuel Jones by 1829. Manuf. was widespread in many countries by 1830. In 1831 Dr Sauria of France discovered a workable yellow phosphorus formula, superior to chlorate friction mixtures, but the invention was not patented, which resulted in widespread change to this chemical by 1835.

Strike-Anywhere M. based on yellow phosphorus continued until the beginning of the First World War, but these caused 'phosphorus necrosis' amongst some of the workers and started many fires. As a result they were banned by sev. countries 1900–10. An alternative to phosphorus sesquisulphide was introduced by Cahen and Savene of France in 1898, but it was unable to give shelf life and resistance to climatic conditions until further developed.

Safety M. incorporating separation of ingredients, one part in the head and the other part painted on the box, were put forward in 1844. Less active red phosphorus was discovered in 1845 and both were successfully combined by Lundström of Sweden in 1855. They enjoyed increased sales in areas which ultimately banned Strike-Anywhere M. because of the use of yellow phosphorus and they later competed elsewhere on equal terms with phosphorus sesquisulphide Strike-Anywhere M.

Development. Manufacturers concentrate on raising quality of the conventional product and improving methods of manuf. Innovations such as double headed match, 2-colour heads, etc., have gradually been abandoned due to small sales. Patents for everlasting match are now in public domain as result of hazards in manuf. and use, also high cost per light.

Matchlock, *see* FIREARMS; GUN.

Mate. The name originally given to the men detailed as assistants to the warrant officers in a warship, of which Boatswain's M. is the only one which survives today. Subsequently it was used to designate ratings selected for promotion to commissioned rank, but this was discontinued in 1931. In the Merchant Navy officers junior to the master (q.v.) are designated M.'s, thus the chief officer is known as the 1st M. Most merchant ships carry at least three M.'s and larger ones sev. more.

Maté, or **Paraguay Tea**, dried leaves of the Brazilian holly (*Ilex paraguayensis*), an evergreen shrub, grown in 'yerbales' in Paraguay and Brazil. The best quality of M. (*caacuys*) is made from the unexpanded buds; the second (*caa-miri*) from leaves from which the midrib has been removed; and the third (*caa-gazu*, or *yerva dos polos*) from the whole leaf. The leaves are infused in water and sugar, and either milk or lemon is added to the liquid, which is rather bitter in taste, but has restorative qualities.

Matera: 1. Prov. of Italy, in E. Basilicata. It has a broad coastal plain on the Gulf of Taranto in the E.; in the W. are mt groups of the Apennines, broken up by long, fertile riv. valleys, running NW.–SE. The chief rivs. are the Bradano, Basento and Cavone. The prin. tns include M. and Ferrandina. Area 1330 sq. m.; pop. 195,000.

2. It. city, cap. of the prov. of M., built above a steep ravine, 42 m. E. of Potenza. It has a 13th cent. archiepiscopal cathedral. There are quarries in the neighbourhood, and troglodyte caves still used as dwelling places. Pop. 38,300.

Materia Medica, branch of medical science dealing in as complete a manner as possible with the hist., preparation, properties, uses and action upon the body, of the drugs used in medical prescriptions.

Anct Egyptian, Chinese and Jap. writings included extensive M. M. In the 1st cent. AD Dioscorides wrote on medicinal herbs, and some of his writings were trans. and incorporated in Arabian M. M. Nearly 800 medical plants were mentioned in a M. M. of India, written about the 5th cent. AD. In most countries there are official pubs., e.g. *British Pharmacopoeia*, by the General Medical Council. This has been rendered necessary to combat medieval superstitious remedies as well as those of modern quacks, and indirectly is supported by law. The *London Pharmacopoeia* was first pub. in 1618, and prescribed foxes' lungs as a cure for asthma. Two other eds. pub. during the 17th cent. included such remedies as 'moss from the skull of a victim of violent death' and Irish whiskey. An official list of drugs contains only those which have passed the test of experience, and of which the knowledge is sufficient to believe them to be safe for use. In 1962 the drug thalidomide, which had passed all the tests then considered sufficient, was proved to be the cause of malformations in babies born to women who had taken the drug early in pregnancy. This led to a reconsideration of what tests new drugs should be subjected to before being made generally available. M. M. is very extensive, and includes widely different topics, Its most important branch deals with the preparation of drugs in the pure state, and the recognition of adulterations; this comes under the head of *Pharmacy*. *Pharmacology*, another branch, deals with the physiological action of drugs on the living body, in large and small doses, in health and disease, and of the chemical form, solution, etc., in which best administered for assimilation by the body. *Toxicology* confines itself to drugs of toxic or poisonous action, and ascertains particularly the range of 'safe doses'. All these branches merge into *Therapeutics*, which is the concern of the medical practitioner. Classification of drugs is very varied and overlapping; chiefly there is the ordinary chemical classification, e.g. alkaloids, salts, infusions; and classification according to therapeutic action, e.g. tonics, sedatives, stimulants. *See also* PHARMACOGNOSY. See A. H. Douthwaite, *A. H. Hale-White's Materia*

Medica, Pharmacy, Pharmacology and Therapeutics (31st ed.), 1959; R. H. Micks, *The Essentials of Materia Medica, Pharmacology and Therapeutics* (8th ed.), 1961; and *British Pharmacopoeia*, 1958 ed.

Materialism, form of monism (q.v.), is the philosophy of the material as opposed to the idealistic. It denies the existence of non-material or spiritual being, and regards all phenomena, real and abstract, as explicable by physical science. It regards matter as the one ultimate fact, 'uncreatable as it is indestructible' (Vogt), and mind as a product of matter. M. is to be found in all philosop! ical systems, from anct Buddhism and Gk Epicureanism and scepticism down to Gassendi, Hobbes, Locke, Hume, Comte, Helvétius and Mill; and later Huxley, Spencer and Haeckel. M. flourished in Europe during the 18th cent. under De la Mettrie and Holbach as a reaction against Christian mysticidealism, and during the 19th cent. under Moleschott and Büchner as a reaction against the idealism of Kant and Hegel. The obvious objections are (1) that the recognition of the existence of matter presupposes the existence of mind as the medium of such recognition; and (2) that, taking, for example, imagination as one particular aspect of consciousness, the mind can originate an idea when wholly abstracted from matter, while matter cannot originate an idea when abstracted wholly from mind. Recent research in physiology, while seeming to confirm the materialistic hypothesis of the relation between neurosis and psychosis, and so giving an enhanced value to sensuous perception as the fundamental source of cognition, yet offers no justification for the belief of the 18th cent. Fr. school of sceptic encyclopaedists, that mental experience, faculty, idea and function are merely transformed sense experience. During the 19th cent. scientific thought supported M. and especially was this support found among the profs. of physics, astronomy and philosophy. They discussed M., particularly in relation to evolution. Whatever the view held as to the cause and purpose of evolution, there was general agreement that it was a purely material process.

The conclusions of investigators who examine the constituency of matter down to the analysis of the atom itself disprove the solidarity of material things. Even the dogma that material effects flow from material causes is regarded with scepticism, especially since the theories of Einstein have proved the accepted findings of Newton to be in error. Biologists assert that the conduct of a material thing is merely a form of reply to an external stimulus, but that in living creatures such instincts as the preservation of life can be explained by no such creed, that in a dead body all the material parts are present and the departed power to function, the will, comes within no laws governing matter. In the region of physics modern discoveries show that the material universe can no longer be regarded as tangible, occupying any defined position, and that the laws which direct it are as yet unfamiliar

and involved in mystery. The solidarity of matter is found to be merely a form of energy. Space eludes the limitations imposed upon it by Euclid, when considered by Relativists, and emerges from their studies with a fourth dimension involving the significance of time —that is, a body's position in space according to time, since its position changes with time. Psychologists add their evidence, especially in the study of memory, and Bergson has shown that the theory that the brain has any material connection with thought is fallible, since his own observations prove that living beings can continue to experience sensations hitherto claimed to emanate from a certain part of the brain after that portion has been removed by operation. Thus the present trend of opinion leads to the conclusion that M. will eventually claim significance merely as a curiosity of philosophical hist.

Dialectical M., a phrase coined by Karl Marx who, though neither a trained philosopher nor a natural scientist, convinced himself that he understood the philosophical implications of the scientific discoveries of his day, and that these implications constituted the general philosophy, which, deriving from the Hegelian dialectic, he called 'dialectical M.' Marxists assume that, unless the student has a proper idea of this philosophy, he cannot understand the objectives of Communism; but it would seem doubtful whether this obscure philosophy has any logical connection with the social theory professed by Communists. *Historical M.*, on the other hand, if not free from obscurities, is, on the whole, intelligible. It is clearly and vigorously stated by Marx in the *Communist Manifesto*, 1848, and in the preface to his *Critique of Political Economy*, 1859, and the gist of the theory is that to every system of production there is an appropriate system of property; that while the system, of production changes continuously, the system of property before the Socialist society has come into existence, will necessarily resist this change; and that there is, consequently, in every society prior to the Socialist one, an inherent contradiction giving rise to a conflict of classes, each of which will evolve an ideology adapted to its own interests.

See J. S. Haldane, *Materialism*, 1932; G. Sainsbury, *Dictatorship of Things*, 1933; G. V. Plekhanov, *In Defence of Materialism*, 1948; M. Cornforth, *Dialectical Materialism*, 3 vols., 1954–6; G. A. Wetter, *Dialectical Materialism* (trans.), 1958.

Materials, Strength of, subject which deals with the study of the distribution and effect of internal forces produced in M. of construction subjected to straining actions. It is not an exact science, like the mathematical theory of elasticity (q.v.), which is concerned mainly with problems of a physical rather than an engineering interest, but is founded partly on the result of experiment, and partly on conclusions drawn therefrom by the application of the principles of mathematics and mechanics. Within practical limits is enables formulae to be estab. which allow the strength of a given part to be assessed, and in this way suitable material and dimensions may be chosen.

Stress. The application of load causes internal stress in the material. Such stress is the force transmitted from a part of the material to the portion with which it is in contact, or it may be regarded as the force which the internal structure of the material exerts to oppose the tendency to alter its size and shape. The constituent forces, and therefore the stress, are distributed across the imaginary surface where interaction takes place, and the *intensity of stress* at a surface, generally referred to as *stress*, is estimated by the force transmitted per unit of area. However complex the loading, the states of stress existing within a body may be reduced to the following: tensile stress, compressive stress and shear stress.

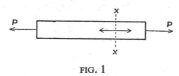

FIG. 1

Fig. 1 shows a bar of uniform cross-sectional area of A sq in., subjected to an axial pull of P pounds. At any plane xx perpendicular to the axis of the bar, the material is under a tensile stress, the intensity of which is $p = \dfrac{P}{A}$ lb. per sq. in. In Fig. 2 the direction of the force is reversed, and the material is being crushed. The stress at any section xx is a compressive stress, and its intensity $p = \dfrac{P}{A}$ lb. per sq. in. Shear stress exists in a body when the action of the load tends to cause one layer of material to slide over an adjacent layer. This is illustrated by Fig. 3, where the material of the rivet is under a shear stress across the section xx, the average intensity of which is $q = \dfrac{P}{A}$ lb. per sq. in., where A is the area of cross-section of the rivet.

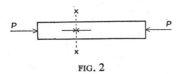

FIG. 2

Strain is the alteration of shape or dimensions resulting from the stress. Thus a tensile strain is the stretch in the direction of the tensile stress, and a compressive strain is a shortening. If a length of l units is stretched to $l + \delta l$, then the tensile strain per unit length, called the fractional strain, is equal to $\dfrac{\delta l}{l}$. The compressive strain is computed in a similar manner. The shear strain is slightly more complicated to

visualise, and is generally reckoned as an angular displacement measured in radians. *See* ELASTICITY.

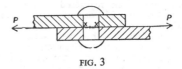

FIG. 3

The most commonly applied test of metals used in construction is the tensile test, which consists of stretching a specially shaped specimen by a gradually applied, uniformly increasing load until it fractures. From this test, by plotting stress and strain, the elastic limit and ultimate strength may be found. The ultimate strength is the ratio

$$\frac{\text{Maximum load}}{\text{Cross-sectional area of Specimen}}.$$

Material which is subjected to frequently repeated fluctuating stresses will fracture at stress much lower than its ultimate statical strength. Stresses of this type may vary in intensity from zero to a maximum, or they may alternate from tensile to compressive. In such circumstances the material is said to have become fatigued.

See J. A. Cormack and E. R. Andrew, *Properties and Strength of Materials*, 1939; F. V. Warnock, *Strength of Materials*, 1945; P. G. Lawson and W. J. Cox, *Mechanics of Materials* (3rd ed.), 1954; A. Morley, *Strength of Materials* (11th ed.), 1954; R. H. Trathen, *Statics and Strength of Materials*, 1954.

Maternity and Child Welfare. Public interest was not directed towards the welfare of infants and of women during maternity until the 20th cent. The Notification of Births Act was passed in 1907, and in 1915 this was extended to give local authorities the right to levy rates for infant welfare work. The first welfare centre was opened in 1906 by Dr Eric Pritchard in the bor. of St Marylebone. The next to be opened was in St Pancras, and came to be known as the 'School for Mothers' from the fact that class instruction was given to mothers in the care of infants, sewing, cooking, etc. By 1910 90 M. and C. W. centres were in existence, but the majority of these, especially the lying-in hospitals, depended on voluntary work and subscriptions. By 1939 there were 2300 centres in England and Wales, nearly 75 per cent of which were maintained by local authorities, while the remainder were provided by voluntary associations. From 1910 to 1914 the Board of Education and the Local Gov. Board (now part of the Ministry of Health) helped to finance the M. and C. W. centres and institutions. In 1918 the Maternity and Child Welfare Act was passed, empowering co. and local authorities to give assistance, subject to the approval of the minister of health, to expectant and nursing mothers and children below the age of 5. Provisions were also made towards a grant in aid of M. and C. W. centres, both voluntary and municipal.

The standard of midwifery was raised after the passing of the Midwives Act of 1902. Maternity homes have to be registered, and maternity benefit (40s.) was allowed under the National Health Insurance Act of 1911, this provision being repeated in subsequent acts. In 1966 benefits were: (a) a maternity grant of £22, and additional grants if more than one child is born (b) a maternity allowance of £4 weekly for 18 weeks, beginning 11 weeks before the expected date of confinement, payable (in addition to (a)) to a woman who normally goes out to work and pays full National Insurance contributions. Similar schemes operate in other countries, e.g. in New Zealand (introduced in 1938), in some provs. of Canada, in Sweden, etc.

Under the National Health Service Act (1946) fresh provision was made for M. and C. W. as follows:

(1) *Maternity medical services.* The expectant mother who is having her baby at home can obtain, without charge, maternity medical care from her own doctor or from a general practitioner obstetrician; this includes antenatal and post-natal examinations and attendance at confinement if necessary.

(2) *Local Health Authority services.* Responsibility for the local M. and C. W. services is now vested in co. and co. bor. councils, who provide the maternal and child welfare centres in which antenatal, post-natal and child-welfare clinics are held, as well as services for immunisation, vaccination, etc. Dental treatment is provided free for expectant mothers, mothers with a child under the age of 1 year and for young children.

(3) *Hospital and specialist services.* Maternity homes and hospitals, and medical staff, are provided without charge. When, for medical reasons or social needs, a confinement is booked in a hospital, the mother's antenatal and post-natal care is also given in a clinic at the hospital. About 4 out of every 6 mothers are confined in hospital.

Provision of a health visiting service is a duty of local health authorities, who also administer the welfare foods service, to provide mother and child with extra milk and vitamin supplements at reduced cost or gratis. The unmarried mother and her child have the same right to the M. and C. W. services as other mothers; in addition, special provision is made for their particular needs. The Act also provides for day nurseries and child minding, a home help service and a home nursing service.

Local authorities have no power to establish birth-control clinics as such, but information regarding birth control may be given at M. and C. W. centres or at special clinics for women suffering from gynaecological disorders; it is given only where further pregnancy would be detrimental to health. The National Association for Maternal and Child Welfare is at B.M.A. House, Tavistock Square, London, WC.1. The birth rate in England and Wales in 1938 was 15·1 per 1000 persons and the infant mortality under

one year was 53 per 1000. In 1960 the figures were respectively 17·2 and 21·8. Maternal mortality in 1938 was 2·7 per 1000 births, the corresponding figure in 1960 being 0·39.

A survey of the social and economic aspects of pregnancy and childbirth in Britain was undertaken by a joint committee of the Royal College of Obstetricians and Gynaecologists and the Population Investigation Committee. Through the co-operation of 424 M. and C. W. authorities in Great Britain, it was possible for health visitors to interview some 14,000 women who had had their confinements during a week in Mar. 1946. The findings of the committee were to some extent disquieting and disappointing in view of the large sums expended on the health services. The outstanding fact was the social class inequalities of the maternity services in Britain. Those women who belonged to the registrar-general's Social Class I were much better off not only in material wealth, but also in the kind of attention they received when pregnant compared with the poorer women in Social Class V. Most of them had doctors in attendance at the time of confinement, so that they were sure of being given more analgesic drugs during labour. Furthermore they ceased work much earlier in pregnancy and arranged for antenatal supervision sooner than those women who had to work, and who already had children. Finally the favoured group tended to have their confinements in hospitals or in private maternity homes. In the U.S.A. there is now some, but no unified, system of compulsory registration of births throughout the country. The rate of maternal mortality is higher in the U.S.A. than in many of the prin. countries of the world. But M. and C. W. work has done much to reduce both that and infant mortality, and the Amer. system of maternity hospitals is without equal. In other countries the work has progressed, especially in Belgium and Holland, which were 2 pioneer countries, and M. and C. W. has been the subject of many recent conventions, the most important being the Geneva Declaration (1924). The Save the Children Fund is an international organisation which is devoted to M. and C. W. work. Practically world-wide laws exist to prevent women working immediately after confinement, and in some countries before. The women of Soviet Russia receive particular help, being allowed by the state full pay during 2 or 3 months before and after childbirth if they are employed, or a grant if their husbands only are employed. The League of Nations, through the International Labour Office, directed attention towards the need of protection of women both before and after childbirth, and a draft convention relating to this was adopted at the International Labour Conference, held at Washington in 1919. *See* Janet Campbell, *Maternal Mortality*, 1924; H. H. Gregory, *Infant Welfare*, 1926; E. Fuller (ed.), *The International Handbook of Child Care and Protection*, 1928; G. F. McCleary, *The Early History of the Infant Welfare Movement*, 1933; *Maternity in Great*

Britain (a survey by a joint committee of the Royal College of Obstetricians and Gynaecologists and the Pop. Investigation Committee), 1949. *See* PUBLIC HEALTH.

Matfre, Ermengau (*c.* 1250–1322), Provençal writer, *b.* Béziers, spent the latter part of his life in the monastery of Béziers. His great work, the *Breviari d'Amor*, was begun in 1288.

Mathematical Instruments, *see* CALCULATING MACHINES; COMPASSES; ELECTRONIC COMPUTATION; PLANIMETER; SLIDE RULE.

Mathematics (Gk *mathēmatikē*, from *manthanein*, to learn; *technē*, art) is the science of space and number, and is the basis of all other sciences. The attempts to create a philosophical basis for M. are beset with many difficulties. For practical purposes M. is divided into pure M., of which the prin. branches are arithmetic, algebra, geometry, trigonometry and calculus, and applied M., which includes mechanics, kinetics, thermodynamics, the theories of light and electricity, astronomy, statistics, relativity, quantum theory and indeed every branch of physics. There is no hard and fast dividing line, but broadly speaking pure M. is abstract and can be developed and studied without reference to physical laws, whereas applied M. is frequently based on experimental discovery, and is designed to elucidate it, but is also often the precursor of new advances in natural science.

The reader will find separate articles devoted to most of the branches of M. named above; the purpose of the present article is to give an outline of the development of the subject. It is true that the Chinese and Hindus in the earliest times evolved crude methods of counting and measuring; that the Babylonians devised a system of numeration is clear from their cuneiform writings, while 1 Kings vii. 23 shows that the existence of a relation between the diameter and the circumference of a circle had been noted, though lacking in accuracy, at that time. Nevertheless the hist. of M. properly begins with Thales of Miletus (640–546 BC), for to him we owe the first theorems in plane geometry and the logical proofs of the same. Pythagoras (6th cent. BC) did not merely make the valuable contributions to geometry with which we are familiar today; he estab. it as a dignified branch of learning among the Greeks, so that Hipparchus, Plato and Aristotle prepared the ground for the renowned school of geometers at Alexandria that produced Euclid, Archimedes and Apollonius. This school flourished between 300 and 30 BC, and the system of Euclid's geometry was the result of their work. The range of their research was so great that geometry made no further material advance until the 17th cent. AD. The Greeks were not only geometers. Hipparchus was the most famous astronomer of their civilisation, and his contributions to M. include the beginnings of trigonometry. Archimedes has the greatest reputation of them all, because he also began the study of mechanics with his principle of the lever, and his researches in hydrostatics or the mechanics of fluids at rest were the first contributions to that branch of M.

Arithmetic made very little progress at the hands of these Gk mathematicians, a fact that is not surprising when we reflect that they handicapped themselves by adopting the letters of the alphabet for their system of numbers. Ptolemy (2nd cent. AD) extended the work of Hipparchus and Diophantus (4th cent. AD) began the study of universal arithmetic or algebra, but he too was at a disadvantage because of the laborious arithmetic inherited from the Greeks. Rom. civilisation added nothing of note to M., although Boethius became acquainted with a few of the theorems of Euclid, and he gave to Europe a Lat. trans. of his scanty knowledge of geometry.

The revival of M. in Europe began in the 12th cent., when Adelard of Bath became acquainted with a Lat. trans. of Euclid's *Elements*. This book he obtained from the Arabs, who had made an extensive study of M. from the 8th cent. onwards. They resurrected the geometry of Euclid, and they adopted the arithmetic of the Hindus who had found in Brahmagupta (7th cent. AD) the source of inspiration of modern arithmetic. The Arabic system of arithmetic developed rapidly in Italy and in England, and the study of algebra was based on a trans. of Al-Khwarizmi's treatise. This was written about the middle of the 9th cent. AD. With the later invention of printing and the revival of learning generally during the Renaissance, arithmetic gradually became simplified by the evolution of the ordinary processes of addition, multiplication, etc., that we know today, while algebraic symbols and operations slowly approached their present form.

The story of modern M. begins at the end of that epoch, viz. the close of the 16th cent., and it is an uninterrupted account of brilliant achievements. Geometry had been marking time since the days of Euclid, waiting as it were for a simple algebra. It took on a new lease of life with the invention of algebraical geometry by Descartes in 1637. His system is well known: a point is represented by a pair of numbers (x, y) that specify its position with respect to 2 fixed axes of co-ordinates. On this system of plane geometry a straight line is represented by an equation of the form $lx + my + n = 0$, and the conic sections by an equation of the second degree $ax^2 + 2hxy + by^2 + 2gx + 2fy + c = 0$. The time was ripe for the greatest mathematical genius of all time, and during the 17th cent. Newton made ample amends for the dark ages of M. His book, the *Principia*, gives us an idea of the debt M. owes to him. He built up mechanics at an amazing rate, and his system is still intact. Algebra, astronomy, optics and other branches of physics bear the imprint of his genius; the honour of inventing the infinitesimal calculus he shares with Leibnitz. The infinitesimal calculus is undoubtedly the greatest of all mathematical discoveries, the key which has assisted scientists in unlocking the secrets of all the physical sciences. Its discovery marks the beginning of the modern period in M., which has contributed far more to mathematical knowledge than the previous 2000 years. The calculus provides a means of dealing in mathematical form with the concept of continuous variation, and the principle of continuity extended enormously the content of algebra and geometry, and led later to the theory of complex and imaginary numbers and the whole structure of projective geometry. During the 18th cent. the work of such men as Euler, Laplace, Lagrange and Gauss, and the estab. of Taylor's theorem of infinite series, provided the tools and the means of calculation required for the far-reaching technical developments in mechanics and electricity that were to come later. The 19th cent. saw the invention by Lobachevsky, Bolyai and Riemann of 'non-Euclidean' geometry, later to be used for Einstein's theory of relativity, and another revolution in mathematical calculation in Hamilton's discovery of quaternions and vector analysis, which simplified the operations of multiplication, division, etc., where both vector and scalar quantities are involved. In astronomy the foundations laid by Copernicus, Tycho Brahe, Kepler and Galileo were rapidly surpassed, and new methods and ways of thought led firstly to a much vaster and more exact astronomy, and later to the quasi-metaphysical theories of the nature of universal space which have been a feature of the 20th century. At the microcosmic end of the scale, the refinements of mathematical analysis led to those brilliant discoveries in the fields of wave-theory, X-ray, radio and atomic structure, which have greatly increased the powers, and with them the responsibilities, of civilised man.

It is interesting to note some of the practical aids to mathematical computations that have proved their worth. The earliest of these is the abacus (q.v.) that was used in various parts of the world for the processes of addition and multiplication (by repeated addition). Another early piece of apparatus for addition was a flat polished tablet covered with sand on which figures were made with a stylus. Arithmetical computations were greatly simplified by the invention of logarithms (q.v.) by Napier (q.v.) in 1614; the logarithmic tables now used are due to Briggs, who first pub. his tables in 1617. They are logarithms of the natural numbers to the base 10. Briggs is also credited with the improvement of the decimal notation first invented by Stevinus. Hipparchus constructed the first trigonometrical tables, and these were extended by Hindu mathematicians. The modern tables are based on those of Rheticus (16th cent.) and Briggs, the latter being the first to pub. tables of the logarithms of trigonometrical functions.

Mechanical aids to the ordinary processes of computation followed rapidly. Gunter designed his logarithmic line of numbers (*see* LOGARITHM) that was simply a straight line with the numbers 1 to 10 arranged on it; the intervals between 1 and another number were directly proportioned to the logarithm of that number to the base 10. Shortly afterwards, in 1630, Wingate invented the first slide rule of the straight edge pattern, which was really 2 logarithmic lines of numbers

placed side by side, one fixed and the other movable. The modern slide rule has descended from that of Mannheim, who in 1850 introduced the cursor, the travelling runner with its finely graduated line that enables the readings to be made across the scales with great accuracy. Hundreds of various patterns of slide rules have been patented since that time, and they are employed extensively in engineering and commerce. Recently calculating machines have been brought to a high pitch of perfection and flexibility. Mathematical models have also reached great perfection, both for elementary teaching and for the demonstration of advanced concepts; *see* COMPUTERS, ELECTRIC. *See also* separate subjects referred to in this article, and CALCULUS; INSURANCE; INVOLUTION; LOGARITHM; MAXIMA AND MINIMA; SLIDE RULE.

See H. Poincaré, *La Science et l'hypothèse*, 1903; A. N. Whitehead, *Introduction to Mathematics*, 1911; W. W. R. Ball, *A Short Account of the History of Mathematics*, 1912; B. Russell, *Introduction to Mathematical Philosophy*, 1917; F. Cajori, *History of Mathematics*, 1919; T. L. Heath, *History of Greek Mathematics*, 1921; D. Larrett, *Story of Mathematics*, 1926; T. E. Peet, *Mathematics in Ancient Egypt*, 1931; F. Gouseth, *Les Mathématiciens et la réalité*, 1936; L. Hogben, *Mathematics for the Million*, 1937; A. C. Aitken, *Statistical Mathematics*, 1942; T. H. Ward Hill, *Mathematics*, 1948; J. Degrazia, *Maths is Fun*, 1949; M. Kraitchik, *Mathematical Recreations*, 1949; D. R. Hartree, *Calculating Instruments and Machines*, 1949. (*See Plate*.)

Mather, Cotton (1663–1728), Amer. clergyman and writer, *b.* Boston, son of Increase M. He was ordained in 1684 and was a minister in Boston from that time till his death. He was a considerable linguist and a prolific writer. A firm believer in witchcraft, he entered vigorously into the persecutions of the day. His *Memorable Providences relating to Witchcraft* appeared in 1689. Twenty executions took place at Salem in 1692. His works include *Magnalia Christi Americana*, 1702, a collection of biographies and historical fragments dealing with New England church hist. *See* B. Wendall, *Cotton Mather: The Puritan Priest*, 1891; R. P. and L. Boas, *Cotton Mather, Keeper of the Puritan Conscience*, 1928, new ed. 1963.

Mather, Increase (1639–1723), Amer. nonconformist divine, *b.* Dorchester, Massachusetts, and educ. at Harvard. In 1657 he came to England, and graduated the next year at Trinity College, Dublin. He returned to America, and was ordained at Boston in 1664. In 1680 he presided at the Boston Synod, and in 1683 was instrumental in procuring the refusal to give up the Massachusetts Charter. From 1685 to 1701 he was president of Harvard College, and during that time came on sev. missions to England. He wrote some religious treatises. *See* K. B. Murdock, *Increase Mather*, 1925.

Mathew, Theobald (1790–1856), Irish priest and temperance reformer, *b.* near Cashel, joined the Capuchin Franciscans in Dublin, and took charge of a small chapel in Cork. In 1838 he signed the total abstinence pledge and advocated the policy all over Ireland, with remarkable results. In 1843 he came to London, and during 1849 and 1851 travelled in America. He worked energetically during the Irish famine. The Rom. Catholic total abstinence movement now has a membership of half a million total abstainers. *See also* TEMPERANCE.

Mathews, Charles James (1803–78), actor, *b.* London, educ. at Merchant Taylor's School, son of the actor and entertainer Charles M. (1776–1835), best known for the short sketches in which he played a number of different parts. He did not wish his son to go on the stage, so it was not until after his death that the younger M. appeared professionally. He married Madame Vestris (q.v.) and with her managed Covent Garden, where M. played Dazzle in the first production of *London Assurance*, and the Lyceum, where he went bankrupt, being improvident and extravagant. He was the most accomplished light comedian of his time, especially in adaptations of Fr. comedy. With his second wife, an Amer. actress named Lizzie Davenport, he appeared in an entertainment in his father's style, *Mr and Mrs M. at Home*. Both father and son pub. their reminiscences.

Mathnavi, or **Mathnawi**, in Persian a long narrative or didactic poem, of which the 2 hemistichs of each line rhyme, the rhyme changing from couplet to couplet. The most famous is the mystical M. of Jalal ud-Din Rumi (q.v.).

Matico (*Artanthe* or *Piper elongata*), shrub (family Piperaceae), the leaves of which yield a heavy pale green aromatic oil, and are used as a styptic.

Matilda, or **Maud** (1102–67), only daughter of Henry I of England. She married Henry V of Germany (1114). At his death in 1125 she returned to England and in 1128 married Geoffrey of Anjou. At the death of Henry I (1135) she carried on an unsuccessful civil war with Stephen till 1142; her son by Geoffrey ascended the Eng. throne as Henry II on Stephen's death.

Matilda, Caroline, *see* CAROLINE MATILDA, Queen of Denmark and Norway.

Matilda, Countess of Tuscany (1046–1115), daughter of Count Boniface III, came into vast estates at an early age. She was twice married: to Godfrey V of Lorraine and to Welf V of Bavaria. Her life was spent in support of the popes against the emperor of Germany in the struggle over investiture. In 1074 she helped the Pope against the Normans, and in 1077 Henry IV underwent his humiliating penance before Gregory VII at her castle of Canossa. She granted her estates to the Holy See in 1077, and the grant was renewed in 1102, as a result of which the papacy claimed them on her death. *See* life by N. Grimaldi, 1928.

Matins, Morning Prayer, *see* BREVIARY.

Matisco, *see* MÂCON.

Matisse, Henri (1869–1954), Fr. painter, *b.* Cateau-Cambrésis. He went as a young man to study law in Paris, but soon gave up the idea of a legal career to become a pupil of Gustave Moreau at the École des Beaux-Arts. Early attracted to the Impressionist movement, his work in 1898 was similar in technique to the *intimiste* paintings of Sickert and Bonnard. Thenceforward, however, he came under the influence of Gauguin, and was soon to become leader of the group known as 'les Fauves' (q.v.). 'La Danse' (Hermitage, Leningrad) shows an aggressiveness of red, blue and green which he later modified. After some years of travel he settled at Nice in 1917. His Mediterranean interiors and many figure studies had much in common with E. painting, and achieved the maximum of expression with an astonishing economy of means. M.'s work is known all over the world, the largest collections being in the Moscow Museum of W. Art and the Barnes Foundation, Pennsylvania. He was etcher, lithographer, wood-engraver and sculptor as well as painter, and illustrated Mallarmé's poems and Joyce's *Ulysses*. He designed and built a chapel for the Dominicans of Vence, consecrated in 1951. *See* studies by A. C. Barnes and V. de Mazia, 1933, P. Courthion, 1942, and J. Casson, 1948; *also* F. Carco, *L'Ami des peintres*, 1944; G. Diehl, *Matisse*, 1954; B. F. Schneider, *Matisse*, 1956.

Matlock, urb. dist. of Derbyshire, England, in the valley of the Derwent, 18 m. NW. of Derby, an inland resort set in beautiful scenery among gritstone and limestone hills. M. dist includes Bonsall, noted for its well-dressing ceremony and its anct lead-mines; Cromford, with its imposing Black Rocks and associations with Richard Arkwright (q.v.); M. Bath, famous for its caverns, petrifying well, thermal water and illuminations, dominated by the High Tor and Heights of Abraham; Tansley; and the Darleys. Pop. 18,486.

Mato Grosso, state of W. central Brazil which, together with the neighbouring state of Goiás to the E., forms one of the 5 geographical regions of Brazil which although covering 20 per cent of Brazil's total area contains only 4 per cent of her pop. M. G. is part of the great Brazilian plateau, varying in height between 2 and 3000 ft. The northern part of the state is drained S.-N. by sev. great tribs. of the Amazon whilst the SW. is drained by the R. Paraguay flowing S. and the SE. by the Paraná and its tribs. The climate is sub-tropical with marked wet and dry seasons, whilst the vegetation is mainly grassland with a heavy distribution of semi-deciduous trees. Cattle raising is the main economic basis of the state, together with subsistence farming. There are considerable mineral deposits, particularly manganese in the SW., but transport difficulties have left them so far unexploited. A railway from São Paulo runs across the southern portion of the state terminating at the tn of Corumbá on the R. Paraguay, but on the other side starts the Bolivian line to Santa Cruz. The cap. is Cuiabá (q.v.) and other tns are Campo Grande (pop. 65,000), Corumbá (40,000) and Ponta Porá (12,000). Area 487,480 sq. m.; pop. 910,000.

Mátra, mt dist of N. Hungary, containing offshoots of the W. Carpathians. The highest peaks reach 3000 ft, and the region is wooded and rich in minerals. There are many health and holiday resorts. The prin. tn is Gyöngyös.

Matriarchy, 'mother-rule' is gov. by the mother or mothers. Many early anthropologists, in particular Bachofen (1861) and Morgan (1877), assumed that M. was the earliest form of social organisation, later to be superseded by patriarchy, or rule by the father. No known societies present all the attributes postulated for M. and the entire hypothesis has now been discredited, since it rests on conjecture rather than on demonstration. It is, however, still accepted by Marxist writers, since it was advanced by Engels, who followed Morgan's work in his own. M. is often confused with Matriliny, in which descent is traced through women rather than through men, so that a man's property is inherited by his sister's son. But the two are quite distinct. There are many peoples today who trace matrilineal descent, but who show no attributes of M. See J. Bachofen, *Das Mutterricht,* 1861; L. H. Morgan, *Ancient Society,* 1877; L. T. Hobhouse, *Morals in Evolution,* 1906; R. Briffault, *The Mothers,* 1927; R. H. Lowie, *The History of Ethnological Theory,* 1937.

Matricaria, genus of composite plants with leaves much divided into narrow segments, and white ligulate ray florets in a single row. *M. maritima,* Scentless Mayweed, and *M. chamomilla,* the wild chamomile, are native to Britain.

Matriculation (Lat. *matricula,* a public roll or register) denotes entry or admission to membership of a body or society; now chiefly used to describe the formal admission into a univ. or college. In England and in many Eng.-speaking countries whose univs. followed the civic univ. pattern, the M. examination became not only an entrance qualification but marked the end of a stage of secondary education and was widely accepted as a qualification for clerical occupations. London and other univs. held M. examinations. That of London was best known, being taken annually by a large number of students both at home and overseas. It was held for the last time in 1951. In most Eng. univs. admission is now granted to candidates on the basis of their success in the General Certificate of Education conducted by approved Examining Boards. Certain faculty requirements have often to be fulfilled (*see* EXAMINATIONS). At Oxford and Cambridge admission to the univ. follows upon entrance to a college. Most colleges require candidates to pass their entrance examination in addition to passing the univ. requirements: at Oxford *Responsions,* at Cambridge the *Previous* examination. Various exemptions from these examinations are offered at both univs.

Matrimony, *see* MARRIAGE.

Matrona, *see* MARNE.

Matroneum (Lat. *matrona,* wife), portion of an early Christian church reserved for women, usually an upper gallery overlooking the presbytery or apse. There are examples in sev. of the greater basilican churches in Rome, e.g. S.

Maria Maggiore, S. Lorenzo, SS. Cosma e Damiano.

Matsuoka, Yosuke (1880–1946), Jap. statesman, *b.* Yamaguchiken. Graduating from the Oregon Univ. law school in 1900 he became secretary to the Jap. premier, 1919; secretary to the Jap. delegation to Versailles peace conference, 1919. He led the Jap. delegation to the League of Nations, 1929, and at the meeting of the League Assembly in Geneva, 1932, he conducted the case for the approval of Jap. policy in Manchuria (Manchukuo); though he lost the day and Japan left the League of Nations, he enhanced his prestige in his own country. He was foreign minister, 1940–1, and conducted the negotiations through which Japan joined the Axis (q.v.), and signed a pact of non-aggression with the Soviet Union. Arrested as a war criminal in 1946, he *d.* in hospital.

Matsys, or **Massys, Quinten** (1466–1530), Flem. painter, *b.* Louvain. In 1491 he became a member of the painters' guild of St Luke in Antwerp. He was a painter of transition between the great period of early Flem. art and that of It. influence. His most famous work is the triptych, 'Pieta', now in Antwerp Museum. His 'Crucifixion' is in the National Gallery. See life by M. J. Friedlander, 1929. (*See Plate: Flemish Art.*)

Mattagami, riv. of N. Ontario, Canada, flowing N. to join the Missinaibi to form the Moose riv. which reaches the sea at James Bay. It is one of Ontario's chief sources of hydroelectric power.

Mattawa, tn of Nipissing co., Ontario, Canada, at the confluence of the M. and Ottawa R.s. A trading post since 1615, it became a Hudson's Bay Company post in 1830 and a lumbering centre. Veneers are manuf. and there is a large hydro-electric project near by. Pop. 3314.

Matte, in metallurgy, an intermediate product in refining sulphide ores of copper, nickel and lead. It contains from 30 to 40 per cent of sulphur, which is subsequently removed. Alternatively known as regulus.

Matteotti, Giacomo (1885–1924), It. Socialist politician, *b.* Fratta Polesine, in Rovigo. After Mussolini gained power M. was an outspoken opponent of the Fascist regime, and was consequently brutally murdered in June 1924. *See also* ITALY, *History.*

Matter: 1. In philosophy, according to the scholastics following Aristotle, M. was classified as *materia prima* (first matter) and *materia secunda* (second matter). The former is that of which a thing is made and is determined by the substantial form. For example, according to a commonly received opinion, first matter in man (wrongly called the body) is determined by the rational soul. First matter is the subject of all corporeal change and the principle of extension and quantity. Substantial form determines it, places it in a determinate species, gives it its specification and actualisation; and only through its substantial form can it be known. Second matter is determined by an accidental form (e.g. roundness, redness, hardness, etc.), and is therefore an already constituted body. Metaphysicians today define M. as one of the ultimate principles or substances, in a dualist system, of which phenomena are appearance or manifestations or, in materialistic monism and materialism (q.v.), the sole substance in terms of which the universe is ultimately to be explained. In this sense M. is unknowable; it underlies the properties of all particular things in which those properties inhere or by which, regarded as impressions made on the senses, they are caused; and it is the substratum of such qualities supposed to be necessary to explain their constant co-existence as a group. The Eng. empiricists Locke, Berkeley and Hume minimised or denied the importance of the conception of substance itself; but Kant retained the notion of M. as signifying the permanent which is found throughout all change. Modern phenomenalists, in so far as they recognise the concept of substance, and consequently of M., at all, regard it as denoting the unknown existent upon which the physical properties somehow depend. See W. C. D. Whetham. *Matter and Change*, 1924; E. I. Watkin, *A Philosophy of Form*, 1935.

2. In physics, is the name given to that out of which all objects external to the mind are thought to be composed. The physicist is concerned with the investigation of the phenomena of nature, and the ultimate goal of his researches is an interpretation of the physical nature of M. that will be consistent with the laws of natural phenomena. The earliest theory of M. of any importance is that of Democritus and Lucretius, who supposed that M. consists of hard atoms (Gk *atomos*—uncuttable) that could neither be created nor destroyed nor altered in any way. Experimental evidence that supported such a theory, modified in some respects, was forthcoming at the beginning of the 19th cent. when Dalton's chemical researches led to the discovery of the law of multiple proportions. He discovered that, in chemical combinations, elements combine in certain definite proportions by weight. If a given element really consisted of identical atoms, and if *n* atoms of one element always combined with *m* atoms of another given element, then the macroscopic observation of Dalton would follow directly. This hypothesis has been very fruitful in explaining chemical phenomena, and it has had a similar success in the realm of physics. Thus the Kinetic theory of matter, by postulating the existence of atoms and groups of atoms, called molecules, has been able to account quantitatively for many of the phenomena of gases, liquids and solids by a statistical inquiry into the motions of these molecules. A quasi-philosophical interpretation of the atom was forthcoming when Kelvin imagined it to be a vortex rising in the ether that permeated all space. Electrical research initiated by J. J. Thomson in the last decade of the 19th cent. carried the investigations a step further. While the atom of Dalton was the 'ultimate particle' in chemical reactions, it proved to be 'cuttable' by electrical means, for the existence of the electron, a particle carrying a negative charge of electricity, whose mass was very much less than that of the lightest atom, the atom of hydrogen, was estab. Its mass and electrical charge were determined by Millikan, who began his work in 1908 and, in a series of experiments extending over about 10 years, achieved a high degree of accuracy in his oil drop experiment. Rutherford's researches in radioactivity, supported by the researches of Moseley and others, gradually estab. the electrical theory of M. According to this theory all M. is composed of elementary positive charges of electricity called protons, and negative charges called electrons. In 1913 Bohr suggested that the atom of hydrogen is an elementary solar system, with a proton for its sun and an electron as the sole planet. The quantitative success of this model, together with experimental evidence concerning the essentially similar nature of other atoms, too complex to yield a mathematical solution of their solar systems, seemed to lead to the conclusion that M. had at last been reduced to its simplest term. The problem is, however, more complicated today. The theory of relativity (q.v.) correctly predicted the possible interconversion of mass and energy, and the production and annihilation of the positron (q.v.) yield clear examples of such processes. Nuclear processes yielding large amounts of energy (see NUCLEAR POWER) are other examples and the sun alone is losing about 250,000,000 tons a min., in the form of photons or light corpuscles. The discrete particles of which all matter was supposed to consist are now known to exhibit wavelike properties (see WAVE MECHANICS), and a series of families of 'fundamental' or 'elementary' particles (q.v.) as photons, leptons, mesons (q.v.) and baryons have been discovered. The properties of matter in its most fundamental forms are now interpreted in terms of 4 identified interactions (gravitational, electromagnetic, strong nuclear and weak nuclear) and a number of conservation laws (energy-mass, linear momentum, angular momentum, electric charge, lepton number, baryon number, isotopic spin, strangeness or hypercharge, parity and G parity) which in turn are related to or thought to be related to various symmetries in our experience or concepts. See also ATOM AND ATOMIC THEORY; HYPERONS; MESONS; NUCLEUS.

See F. Hoyle, *The Nature of the Universe*, 1953; V. Weisskopf, *Knowledge and Wonder*, 1962; C. E. Swartz, *The Fundamental Particles*, 1965.

Matterhorn (Fr. Mont Cervin), peak of the Pennine Alps, in the central zone of the Middle Alps, on the borders of Valais, Switzerland, and Piedmont, Italy, 6 m. SW. of Zermatt. Altitude 14,690 ft. Its appearance is most striking owing to its isolation and unusual steepness. The ascent by the NE. or Zermatt ridge was first made in 1865 by Whymper, Lord Douglas, Hudson and others, 4 of whom lost their lives. Subsequently it was climbed by the It. ridge, the Zmutt ridge and the N. face, and ultimately by all 4 ridges and faces. *See* E. Whymper, *The Valley of Zermatt and the Matterhorn*, 1901; G. Rey, *The Matterhorn*, 1946; R. W. Clarke, *The Day the Rope Broke*, 1965. (*See Plate: Mountaineering*.)

Matthay, Tobias (1858–1945), pianoforte teacher, *b*. London, a prof. of piano at the Royal Academy of Music. His book *The Art of Touch*, 1903, set out his own musical system. Harriet Cohen, Myra Hess, Irene Scharrer and York Bowen were among his pupils.

Matthew, St, or **Levi**, a tax-gatherer of Capernaum, chosen by Jesus as one of His 12 Apostles. He is the author of the first Gospel. There is no trustworthy account of his later career or of his death. His feast is on 21 Sept. *See* MATTHEW, THE GOSPEL ACCORDING TO ST.

Matthew, Basarab (1580–1654), hospodar of Wallachia from 1633. He ruled with wisdom, defending the country against frequent attacks by Basil the Wolf, of Moldavia. Among his reforms were the estab. of a printing press (1652), the codification of the law, and the trans. of the Bible into Rumanian.

Matthew, The Gospel according to St, first book of the N.T. There is no trace of any other title for the first Gospel than 'according to Matthew', nor was his authorship ever questioned in antiquity. The earliest explicit testimony to it is that of Papias (2nd cent.) quoted by Eusebius (*Historia Ecclesiastica*, iii. 39), 'Matthew composed the oracles (*Logia*, q.v.) of the Lord in the Hebrew tongue and each interpreted them as he was able'. This is borne out by St Irenaeus (before the end of the 2nd cent.) and by Origen (*c*. AD 233), who was severely critical about authorship. Equally unanimous and early is the testimony that the first Gospel was originally written substantially in the Heb. (Aramaic) tongue (cf. Papias, Irenaeus, Origen, Eusebius, Jerome). Scholars have, however, contested this, mainly because of the verbal identity of M. with Mark in over-lapping passages, and the prevailing critical theory is that M. is a conflation of Mark with other documents (*see* SYNOPTIC PROBLEM). This has led to the suggestion that Papias by *Logia* does not mean the Gospel, but a collection of the sayings of Christ or of O.T. proof texts, which were incorporated in the Gospel. It is certain, however, that Eusebius did not quote Papias in that sense, but as referring to our first Gospel, and the same is true of Irenaeus. 'This interpretation seems the most satisfactory one, especially as we know that the first Gospel was used by Ignatius some twenty years before Papias wrote' (G. D. Kilpatrick, *The Origins of the Gospel According to St Matthew*, 1946). This, of course, has a considerable bearing on the synoptic problem, and runs counter to the dominant critical hypothesis of the dependence of M. on Mark. Traditionally M. was the first Gospel to be written and this has been powerfully argued, against the critical orthodoxy of the priority of Mark, by Dom J. Chapman (*Matthew, Mark and Luke*, 1937), and still more urgently by Dom B. C. Butler (*The Originality of St Matthew*, 1951), who argues that M. wrote his

original Aramaic text in the forties, the Gk Gospel was produced before AD 51 and used by Mark, who in turn was used by Luke. The orthodox critics, on the contrary, place M. late in the 1st cent., e.g. Harnack (AD 70–5). The Gospel is characterised first by the number of its quotations from the O.T., emphasising the Messianic character of Christ's work; secondly by its strong Jewish flavour; and thirdly by its arrangement of the subject-matter in groups. Thus we have a collection of discourses in chs. v–vii, of miracles in ch. xiii. A much fuller account is given of Our Lord's discourses than in the Marcan narrative. *See also* commentaries by W. C. Allen, 1907; A. H. McNeile, 1915; F W. Green, 1936; A. Farrer, *St Matthew and St Mark*, 1954; R. V. G. Tasker, 1961.

Matthew of Paris, *see* PARIS, MATTHEW.

Matthew of Westminster, legendary 15th cent. Benedictine monk and chronicler, to whom the *Flores historiarum* was formerly assigned. This MS. was probably compiled by various writers at St Albans and Westminster.

Matthews, Albert Edward (1869–1960), actor, son of a Christy minstrel and nephew of the clown Tom M., who was Grimaldi's pupil. He had a long and successful career, making his first appearance in 1886 and continuing to act until shortly before his death. He excelled in farce, from Pinero and Wilde in his early days to the works of W. Douglas Home in the 1950's–60's, and in 1953 pub. his autobiography *Matty*.

Matthews, James Brander (1852–1929), Amer. author, *b*. New Orleans. He was educ. at Columbia College, New York. A founder of the Amer. Copyright League, the Dunlap Society and the Simplified Spelling Board, he became president of the Modern Language Association of America in 1910. His pub. works, comprising fiction, criticism and drama, include *French Dramatists of the Nineteenth Century*, 1882, *Vignettes of Manhattan*, 1894, *Introduction to the Study of American Literature*, 1896, *Aspects of Fiction*, 1896, 1902, *Tales of Fantasy and Fact*, 1896, *Molière, his Life and his Works*, 1910, *A Book About the Theatre*, 1916, *The Principles of Playmaking*, 1919, and *Playwrights on Playmaking*, 1923.

Matthews, Sir Stanley (1915–), Eng. professional footballer, *b*. Hanley, Notts. He played in his first football league match in 1931, and first played for England in 1934. He subsequently played in 55 internationals. He was knighted in 1965. *See* his autobiography, 1960.

Matthews, Walter Robert (1881–), Brit. cleric, educ. at Wilson's Grammar School, Camberwell and King's College, London. He was successively curate at St Mary Abbots, Kensington, and at St Peter, Regent Square, London; lecturer in philosophy, King's College, London, 1908–18, and in dogmatic theology, 1909–18; dean, 1918–32; vicar of Christ Church, Crouch End, London, 1916–18; canon theologian, Liverpool Cathedral, 1930; chaplain to the king, 1923–31; Boyle lecturer, 1920–2; Warburton lecturer, 1938; dean of Exeter, 1932–4; and of St Paul's, in succession to Dr

Inge, 1934. His pubs. include *Studies in Christian Philosophy*, 1921 (2nd ed. 1928), *God in Christian Thought and Experience*, 1930 (6th ed., 1942), *The Adventures of Gabriel in his Search for Mr Shaw*, 1933, *The Purpose of God*, 1935, *Hope of Immortality*, 1937, *Signposts to God*, 1938, *Moral Issues of the War*, 1940, *The Foundations of Peace*, 1942, *Strangers and Pilgrims*, 1945, *Some Christian Words*, 1956, *The Thirty-Nine Articles*, 1961. C.H., 1962.

Matthias Corvinus (1443–90), King of Hungary, *b*. Klausenburg (Cluj), the son of John Hunyadi; elected king in 1458. He was not crowned till 1464, after a long struggle against the Turks, the Bohemians, Emperor Frederick III and hostile factions at home. His reign was marked by a series of wars. In 1468 he conquered Moldavia and Wallachia, and in 1478 concluded a peace with Bohemia, by which he gained Moravia, Silesia and Lusatia. In 1485, during a war with Frederick III, he captured Vienna and made himself master of much of Austria. He was a great military tactician and a liberal patron of learning, and founded the univ. of Budapest and a fine library. (*See Plate: Hungary*.)

Matthiessen, Francis Otto (1902–50), Amer. critic, *b*. Pasadena, California. Educ. at Yale, in 1923 he went as a Rhodes Scholar to Oxford. After 2 years as an instructor at Yale he went to Harvard, where he was associate prof. of hist. and literature from 1934 to 1942. His greatest work was *American Renaissance: Art and Expression in the Age of Emerson and Whitman*, 1941. Others of his books are *Sarah Orne Jewett*, 1929, *The Achievement of T. S. Eliot*, 1935, *Henry James: the Major Phase*, 1944, *From the Heart of Europe*, 1948, and *Theodore Dreiser*, 1951.

Matthiola, family Cruciferae, genus of 30 herbs or sub-shrubs. *M. incana* (parent of 10-week, Brompton and garden Stocks), and *M. bicornis*, Night-scented Stock, are valuable garden plants. *M. sinuata* is a native biennial.

Matthisson, Friedrich von (1761–1831), Ger. poet, *b*. Hohendodeleben, near Magdeburg. From 1781 to 1784 he was prof. of economics at Dessau. In 1787 he pub. his *Gedichte*, which were praised by Schiller and Wieland. His *Adelaide* was set to music by Beethoven. A collected ed. of his writings was pub. in Zürich (1825–9, 8 vols.). *See* lives by H. Döring, 1833; W. Krebs, 1912; A. Heers, 1913.

Mattioli, Count, *see* IRON MASK.

Mattoon, city in Illinois, U.S.A., in an agric. area, 39 m. SE. of Decatur, with manufs. of shoes, brooms, diesel engines. Pop. 17,500.

Maturin, Charles Robert (1782–1824), novelist and dramatist, *b*. Dublin. He wrote sev. plays, one of which, a tragedy, *Bertram*, was produced by Kean at Drury Lane in 1816. He is best remembered for his 'horror' novels *Montario*, 1807, and *The Milesian Chief*, 1812, both of which won praise from Scott, and especially *Melmoth the Wanderer*, 1820, which was his masterpiece. *See* his letters to Lady Ewan-Smith, ed. J. Brumforth, 1927, and life by N. Idman, 1924.

Maturín, cap. of the state of Monagas, NE. Venezuela. It is an important commercial centre, and the prin. occupations are centred on agriculture and petroleum. M. has an international airport and is of rapidly increasing importance. Pop. 54,000.

Matyó, *see* MEZÖKÖVESD.

Mau Mau, name given to anti-European revolt among the Kikuyu of Kenya, starting in 1952. The leaders administered oaths, often by force, upon tribesmen who were then obliged to kill or harm Europeans and loyal Kikuyu if so ordered. Often seen as a reversion to savagery, it was a desperate attempt to regain power and land, put into ritual terms. One of the leaders was said to be Kenyatta (q.v.), who was imprisoned for his part in the movement but released, 1961. The movement had been crushed by 1957. *See* L. S. B. Leakey, *Mau Mau and the Kikuyu*, 1952; F. D. Corfield, *Historical Survey of the Origins and Growth of Mau Mau*, 1960.

Maubeuge, Fr. tn in the dept of Nord, on the Sambre. It is an anct fort. tn and has a fortress by Vauban. It was besieged by the Germans in 1814 (*see* FRANCO-PRUSSIAN WAR), and was the scene of heavy fighting in both world wars. It has steelworks, and engineering works, and manufs. mirrors. Pop. 20,300.

Mauchline, par. and tn of Ayrshire, Scotland, on the R. Ayr, 8 m. SE. of Kilmarnock, in the heart of the Burns country. Poosie Nancy's Inn is at M., and Burns lived at Mossgiel Farm. Agric. implements, optical lenses and curling stones are manuf. Pop. (par. and tn) 4454.

Mauclair, Camille (1872–1945), (pseudonym of Camille Faust) Fr. writer, *b*. Paris. He wrote poetry (*Sonatines d'automne*, 1895, *Le Sang parle*, 1904), a novel, *Le Soleil des morts*, 1898, and memoirs, *Servitude et grandeur littéraires*, 1922. His many works on literature and the arts include *Flausis*, 1894, *L'Impressionisme*, 1904, *Princes de l'esprit*, 1920, *Histoire de la musique européenne, 1850–1914*, 1914, *Les États de la peinture française de 1850 à 1920*, 1921, *Un siècle de peinture française, 1820–1920*, 1930, and books on Schumann, Watteau, Paul Adam, Rodin, Leonardo da Vinci, Greuze, Baudelaire, Heine, El Greco, etc.

Maude, Cyril Francis (1862–1951), actor, *b*. London, eldest son of Capt. Charles H. M., educ. at Charterhouse. He first appeared on the stage in Colorado in 1883 in *East Lynne*; and in 1884 returned to England, appearing at the Criterion Theatre, London, in 1886. He played in *The Great Divorce Case* and in the first performance of *The Second Mrs Tanqueray*, 1893. He was co-manager with Frederick Harrison at the Haymarket, London, 1896–1905, and in 1907 took over the managership of the Playhouse, Northumberland Avenue. His first wife was Winifred Emery, with whom he was long associated on the stage. His reminiscences were pub. in 1927. He was one of the best light comedians of his time.

Maude, Sir (Frederick) Stanley (1864–1917), general, *b*. Gibraltar. Educ. at Eton and Sandhurst. He joined the Coldstream Guards in

1884, and served in the Sudan, 1885; in the S. African war, 1899–1901. Early in the First World War he commanded the 14th Infantry Brigade. He commanded the 13th Infantry Div. in France, the Dardanelles, Egypt and, in Aug. 1916, Mesopotamia. He was made lieutenant-general in 1917. He marched from Basra up the Hai R. to Kut, and defeated the Turks at Shumran, entering Bagdad 11 Mar. See life by Sir C. E. Callwell, 1920.

Maudling, Reginald (1917–), politician, educ. at Merchant Taylors' and Merton College, Oxford. Called to the Bar, 1940. He was elected a Conservative M.P., 1950. After holding junior office he became minister of supply, 1955–7. He was paymaster-general, 1957–9; president of the board of trade, 1959–61; colonial secretary, 1961–2, and chancellor of the exchequer, 1962–4. In 1965 M. was a candidate for the leadership of the Conservative party, but was defeated by Heath (q.v.). Subsequently he became deputy leader of the party.

Maudsley, Henry (1835–1918), physician, b. Settle, Yorks, graduated as M.D. from Univ. College, London, in 1857. He was medical superintendent of Manchester Royal Lunatic Hospital, 1859–62; physician at the W. London Hospital, 1864–74; prof. of medical jurisprudence at Univ. College, London, 1869–79. He specialised in mental disorders and was editor of the *Journal of Mental Science*, 1862–78. Impressed with the need for research into the heredity and pathology of mental disease, he gave a large sum for the creation of a psychiatric hospital. The Maudsley Hospital, London, was the result, though M. did not live to see its completion. His numerous works include *Responsibility in Mental Disease*, 1874, *Physiology of Mind*, 1876, *Pathology of Mind*, 1879, *Body and Will*, 1883, *Natural Causes and Supernatural Seemings*, 1886, *Life in Mind and Conduct*, 1902, and *Heredity, Variation and Genius*, 1908.

Maufe, Sir Edward (1882–), architect, b. Ilkley; was trained in London. Prin. buildings: Kelling Hall, Norfolk; St Saviour's Church, Acton; work at Trinity College and St John's College, Cambridge, and St John's College, Oxford; Guildford Cathedral (won in competition, 1936); the Playhouse, Oxford, and the Festival Theatre, Cambridge; rebuilding of St Columba's Church, Pont Street, London, 1950; reconstruction of Gray's Inn, 1947, and of the Middle Temple, 1948; the Runnymede Memorial, 1953; also cemeteries and memorials for the Imperial War Graves Commission. Awarded the R.I.B.A. Royal Gold Medal, 1944.

Maugham, William Somerset (1874–1965), novelist and playwright, b. Paris. Educ. at the King's School, Canterbury, and Heidelberg Univ., he studied medicine, but in 1897 pub. his first novel, *Liza of Lambeth*, and the success of that novel and of *Mrs Cradock*, 1902, finally won him over to literature, though something of his hospital experience is reflected in the first of his masterpieces, *Of Human Bondage*, 1915. With the pub. of *The Moon and Sixpence*, partly based on Gauguin's life (1919), his reputation as a novelist was assured. His success as a playwright developed at the same time, and at one time Bernard Shaw alone had more plays running in London. One of his most successful plays was *Our Betters*, 1923, a social satire performed both in New York and in London. He also wrote sev. vols. of short stories, those with a Malayan or S. Pacific background being particularly well known. His autobiography, notable for its self-revelations, *The Summing Up*, was pub. in 1938 and *A Writer's Notebook* in 1949. His other plays include *Loaves and Fishes*, 1911, *Caesar's Wife*, 1919, *The Unknown*, 1920, *The Circle*, 1921, *East of Suez*, 1922, *The Sacred Flame*, 1929, and *For Services Rendered*, 1932. Other novels include *The Making of a Saint*, 1898, *The Bishop's Apron*, 1906, *The Painted Veil*, 1925, *Ashenden*, 1928, *Cakes and Ale*, 1930, *Theatre*, 1937, *The Razor's Edge*, 1944, and *Catalina*, 1948. *Ten Novels and Their Authors* was pub. 1954. In 1954 he was made a Companion of Honour. See life by R. Cordell, 1961, and B. Nichols, *A Case of Human Bondage*, 1966.

Maui (natives), see MAORIS.

Maui, one of the Hawaiian group of is., situated about 70 m. from Honolulu. It consists of 2 peninsulas divided by an isthmus of sand, the E. one containing the volcano of Haleakala, over 10,000 ft high and with a crater 19 m. in circumference. The chief tns are Lahaina, Wailuku and Kahului. Area 728 sq. m. Pop. 35,720.

Maule: 1. Maritime prov. of central Chile. Stock-raising and agriculture are carried on. Wine and wheat are the chief products, but M. is economically backward. The cap. is Cauquenes. Area 2172 sq. m.; pop. 93,942.

2. Riv. rising in Lake M. (7000 ft) in Talca prov., Chile, and flowing into the Pacific Ocean near Constitucion; length about 140 m.

Maumbury Rings, circular earthwork, situated ¼ m. S. of Dorchester, Dorset, England. Excavations carried out between 1908 and 1913 disclosed that the original work was an earthen circle, with an interior ditch, dating from the late Neolithic or Early Bronze Age (c. 1800 BC). In Rom. times the work was converted into an amphitheatre for the tn of Durnovaria (Dorchester). See also DORCHESTER; EARTHWORK; HILL-FORTS.

Mauna Kea, extinct volcano on the is. of Hawaii, 13,825 ft high. It is the highest mt of the Hawaiian Is., and is snow-clad for the greater part of the year.

Mauna Loa, active volcano of Hawaii, and the greatest in the world, erupting frequently. It lies S. of Mauna Kea and is 13,675 ft high.

Maundy Thursday, fifth day of Holy Week (q.v.). In the Rom. Catholic Church the holy oils are consecrated on this day, and a host consecrated at the mass (now celebrated in the evening in memory of the Last Supper) is carried in procession to the 'altar of repose' before which the faithful watch and pray in memory of Gethsemane. The word Maundy is derived from *Mandatum novum* ('a new commandment'), the first words chanted at a ceremony during which the celebrant washes the feet of 12 poor men on that day, in accordance with John xiii. 1–34. In England before the Reformation this rite was performed by the sovereign. James II was the last monarch to do so in person; thereafter the task was delegated to the Lord High Almoner, but was not performed after 1750. In the medieval Church the ceremony was accompanied by a distribution of 'doles' which used to be given in small baskets called 'maunds'. This part of the M. T. rites has survived in the Church of England. In 1833, however, the dole was replaced by a money payment ('Maundy money') distributed by the sovereign in person or through a royal almoner. The number of recipients varies according to the age of the sovereign. Specially minted silver coins (1*d*., 2*d*., 3*d*. and 4*d*.), introduced by Charles II, are still distributed.

Maupassant, Guy de (1850–93), Fr. novelist and writer of short stories, *b.* at the Château de Miromesnil, Seine-Inférieure. He early came under the influence of Flaubert, who assisted him with encouragement and advice. After about 1886 he gradually broke down in health and reason, and, after attempting suicide in 1892, *d.* in painful circumstances in Paris. As a novelist he was the last of the naturalists, and, though marked by considerable limitations in thought and imagination, he was a master in the vivid and accurate reproduction of life which he himself had observed with a wonderful intensity. His style is simple but most effective. As a writer of *contes*, of which he wrote some 260, he began, in 1880, with a masterpiece, *Boule de Suif*, contributed to *Soirées de Médan*, a collection by Zola, Huysmans and others. His best collections of short stories are *La Maison Tellier*, 1881, *Mademoiselle Fifi*, 1882, *Contes de la Bécasse*, 1883, *Miss Harriet*, 1884, *Contes du jour et de la nuit*, 1885, *Toine*, 1886, *La Petite Rogue*, 1886, *Le Horla*, 1887. His novels are *Une Vie*, 1883, *Bel-Ami*, 1885, *Mont-Oriol*, 1887, *Pierre et Jean*, 1888, *Fort comme la mort*, 1889, *Notre Cœur*, 1890.

Maupertuis, Pierre Louis Moreau de (1698–1759), Fr. mathematician, *b.* St Malo, educ. in Paris, and served for some time in the army. In 1723 he was elected to the Academy of Sciences, and in 1728 his ardent support of the theories of Newton led to his becoming F.R.S., London. In 1736 he was the head of a party of academicians, including Clairaut and Lemonnier, who were sent to Lapland to measure a degree of the meridian and succeeded in exposing the error in the previous measurement of Dominic and Cassini. He pub. *Sur la figure de la terre* in 1738. He formulated the principle of least (better stationary) action (*see* ACTION, STATIONARY, PRINCIPLE OF). His theory of pessimism, in *Essai de philosophie morale*, 1749, was later developed by Schopenhauer, Hartmann and others. *See* life by P. Brunet, 1930; *also* A. Le Sueur, *Maupertuis et ses correspondants*, 1897.

Maurepas, Jean Frédéric Phélippeaux, Comte

de (1701–81), Fr. statesman, *b.* Versailles. He succeeded his father as secretary of state of the king's household, and in 1724 became superintendent of the Marine. In 1749 he offended Mme de Pompadour by an epigram, and was banished from court. In 1774, on the accession of Louis XVI, he was recalled and made first minister. He remodelled the Marine dept, and was a liberal patron of art and science, but both Turgot and Necker were sacrificed to his jealousy and ambition.

Mauretania, in anct geography, region of NW. Africa, bounded by the Mediterranean, the Atlas and the Atlantic. The lower slopes of Atlas were well timbered and produced the ornamental wood called *citrum*, which was highly valued at Rome for tables.

The Romans first became acquainted with M. during the war against Jugurtha (q.v.), 110–106 BC, when it was ruled by Bocchus (q.v.). Half a cent. later it consisted of 2 kingdoms separated by the R. Mulucha. Both supported Caesar in the civil war, but were given as a whole to Juba II (q.v.) of Numidia by Augustus in 25 BC. Claudius formed it into 2 provs., M. Tingitana and M. Caesariensis. Diocletian included the former for administrative purposes in the diocese of Hispania.

'Mauretania', The, *see* CUNARD STEAMSHIP COMPANY.

Mauriac, François (1885–), Fr. novelist and critic, *b.* Bordeaux. His novels are studies, from a Rom. Catholic standpoint, of the psychological and moral problems of the members of the Catholic and prov. middle class and are usually set in M.'s own region, around Bordeaux and the Landes. They include *Le Baiser au lépreux*, 1922, *Génitrix*, 1923, *Le Désert de l'amour*, 1925, *Thérèse Desqueyroux*, 1927, *Le Nœud de vipères*, 1932, *Le Mystère Frontenac*, 1933, *La Fin de la nuit*, 1935, *La Pharisienne*, 1941, *Le Sagouin*, 1950. He has also written plays (*Asmodée*, 1938, *Les Mals Aimés*, 1945, *Le Passage du malin*, 1948) and poetry (including *Les Mains jointes*, 1909, and *Orages*, 1925). His critical and other writings include *Proust*, 1926, *La Vie de Jean Racine*, 1928, *La Vie de Jésus*, 1936, *Trois grands hommes devant Dieu* (a study of Molière, Rousseau and Flaubert), 1947, *Mémoires intérieurs*, 1959, *Ce que je crois*, 1962, *De Gaulle*, 1964, and sev. vols. of his *Journal*.

Mauriac, Fr. tn in the dept of Cantal, on the Dordogne. It has an agric. market. Pop. 3900.

Maurice, Sir Frederick Barton (1871–1951), major-general. Entering the army in 1892 he served in Tirah, 1897–8, and the S. African war, 1899–1900. He was director of military operations at the War Office, 1915–18, and major-general, 1916. K.C.M.G. early in 1918. In May 1918 he publicly denied the accuracy of certain ministerial statements as to army matters, and was retired for this breach of discipline. For the remainder of the war period he was a military correspondent. Principal of the Working Men's College, Camden Town, 1922–33, he became prof. of military studies at London Univ., 1927. Pubs. include *Forty Days in 1914*, 1919, *Robert*

E. Lee the Soldier, 1925, *History of the Scots Guards*, 1934, *Life of Lord Haldane* (2 vols.), 1937–8, and *Adventures of Edward Wogan*, 1945.

Maurice, Frederick Denison (1805–72), cleric, *b.* Normanstown, Suffolk; went to Cambridge Univ. Chaplain to Guy's Hospital, 1836–40, in the latter year he became prof. of Eng. literature at King's College, London, in 1845 Boyle lecturer and Warburton lecturer, and in 1846 prof. of theology; but in 1853, at the request of the council, resigned both chairs after the pub. of his *Theological Essays*, in which he had denied the doctrine of eternal punishment. He allied himself with the Christian Socialists and Charles Kingsley. In 1854 he took an active part in the foundation of the Working Men's College, of which he was appointed the first principal. The starting-point of his theology is God's redemption of man. His pubs. include *The Claims of the Bible and of Science*, 1863, and *Moral and Metaphysical Philosophy*, 1871–2. *See* lives by his son, 1884, and C. F. G. Masterman, 1907; *also* A. Vidler, *The Theology of F. D. Maurice*, 1949; A. M. Ramsey, *F. D. Maurice and the Conflicts of Modern Theology*, 1951.

Maurice, Prince of Orange and Count of Nassau (1567–1625), son of William the Silent (q.v.). On his father's assassination (1584), he became stadtholder of Holland and Zealand provs. and of the 7 United Provs. (1587). He was a brilliant general, capturing Breda, Zutphen and Nijmegen (1590–1), and expelling the Spaniards, who were compelled to acknowledge the United Provs. as a free rep. and to conclude a 12 years' truce (1609). The struggle was renewed (1621), and while negotiating an alliance with England and France M. *d.* He is also remembered for his quarrel with Barneveldt, his former friend, resulting in the latter's judicial murder.

Maurice of Saxony (1521–53), duke and elector of Saxony, *b.* Freiberg. He inherited the Duchy of Saxony in 1541, having become a Lutheran in 1539. His religious scruples, however, did not prevent him from joining the Emperor Charles (q.v.) against the Protestant Schmalkaldic League (1546) in return for Charles's help against the then elector of Saxony, John Frederick. M. defeated John Frederick at Mühlberg (1547), thereby obtaining the electoral title. He then joined the Protestants (1551) and, in 1552, allied with the King of France. He *d.* of wounds received at the battle of Sievershausen. M.'s policy was wholly directed by the desire first to obtain the electorate of Saxony, and then to increase its power, and his services to Protestantism were incidental to these aims.

Maurier, Daphne, George, and **Sir Gerald du,** *see* DU MAURIER.

Maurists, members of a Fr. congregation of reformed Benedictines estab. in 1621 and soon including most of the Fr. Benedictine houses other than those belonging to Cluny. The prin. monastery was Saint-Germain-des-Prés, Paris, The aim of the congregation was a return to strict Benedictine observance, with which, generally speaking, the great critical and his-

torical achievements of the M. never interfered. Among the most celebrated members of the congregation were Tarisse, 1st superior-general, Mabillon, Montfaucon, Ruinart, Martène, Bouquet and Chardon. It was dissolved by the Fr. Revolution in 1792.

Mauritania, republic in W. Africa between Senegal to the S. and Sp. Sahara to the N. Area 416,216 sq. m. M. is a poor country, having a large area of desert and a shortage of water. M. was occupied by the French during the early 20th cent., became a colony in 1920 and gained its independence in 1960. The constitution provides for a council of 8 ministers and a National Assembly of 34 elected members. The chief products are cattle, gum, salt and dates. The cap. is Nouakchott and the main harbour is at Port Etienne. The future of the country depends very largely on the results achieved from the exploitation of its iron and copper resources. Pop. 770,000.

Mauritia, genus of tall S. Amer. palms with fan-shaped leaves.

Mauritius (formerly **Île-de-France,** is. of the Indian Ocean, independent nation within the Commonwealth, lies in lat. 19° 59′ to 20° 33′ S., and long. E. from Greenwich 57° 17′ to 57° 46′. It is 39 m. from N. to S. and 28 m. from E. to W., having an area of 720 sq. m.

Physical Features. The surface is of varied formation, a great portion being volcanic, while its coast is fringed by extensive coral reefs pierced in sev. places by the estuaries of small streams. Its mts, although of no great height, are marked by the usual irregularities observed in volcanic formations. The most celebrated is the Peter Botte, situated in the rear of the tn of Port Louis, and forming a remarkable cone sustaining on its apex a gigantic piece of rock which has the appearance of being poised on its summit.

Climate. The climate is tropical and very moist, especially at sea level, and European residents live mostly in the hill dists, especially at Curepipe (1800 ft).

Towns. The prin. tns are Port Louis (90,375) the cap., and Mahébourg, in the dist of Grand Port, the S. port, the latter difficult of access for shipping and much encumbered by coral reefs. Port Louis has a spacious harbour.

Industry. M.'s greatest industry is sugar, and most of its accessible surface is covered with sugar plantations. To diversify their economy Mauritians have planted alternative crops, including tea, aloes, tobacco and coconuts.

Population. The pop. at the end of 1963 was estimated at 713,831, of which the general pop. (of European, African and mixed descent) made up some 30 per cent, Indo-Mauritians 67 per cent and Chinese 3 per cent.

Government. The gov. is vested in a Governor with a council of Ministers and a Legislative Assembly with 40 elected members and up to 15 nominated members. The Chief Secretary sits in the Assembly *ex officio*, and a Speaker presides. The Council of Ministers comprises the Premier, the Chief Secretary, and up to 13 Ministers, being Members of the House of Assembly appointed by the Governor after consultation with the Premier. At a conference held in London in 1965 it was decided that following the introduction of, and elections held under, a modified electoral system, M. should become an independent nation within the Commonwealth.

Trade. Exports in 1962 were worth 290,656,000 rupees (1 rupee = 1*s*. 6*d*.), the great bulk being shipped to Britain. Sugar and sugar derivatives accounted for over 90 per cent of their value, all being marketed by the M. Sugar Syndicate.

Communications. The international airport at Plaisance is served by 5 airlines. There are 525 m. of main and some 311 m. of secondary roads; the railway, with 68 m. of track, has now been closed. At the end of 1962 there were 257 primary and 105 secondary schools; the total enrolment in schools of all types was 165,000. The M. Broadcasting Corporation operates television and sound radio services.

History. M. was discovered in the year 1505 by the Portuguese commander, Don Pedro Mascarenhas. Later it was colonised by the Dutch, who named it M. after their stadtholder, Count Maurice. In 1710 the Dutch abandoned the is., which was then taken over by the Fr. India Co., and named Île-de-France. About this time the Fr. also colonised the is. of Réunion, then called Bourbon. In 1735 they sent to M. its most famous governor, Mahé de Labourdonnais, and the is. owed its later prosperity largely to his energy and foresight. He founded Port Louis, built roads and forts, cleared forests and encouraged and developed the cultivation of sugarcane, introduced into M. by the Dutch. In 1767 the is. passed to the Fr. Crown and, in the Napoleonic wars, was used as a base against Brit. shipping. Accordingly the British sent out an expedition from India, which captured the is. in 1810. By the treaty of Paris the Île-de France was ceded to Britain, and its original name, M., was restored. The Fr. laws and customs, however, together with the language and Rom. Catholic church, were not disturbed, and M. remains largely Fr. in character to this day. There are various scattered is. dependencies, including Rodrigues, with a pop. of 19,000, and Agelaga. M. has suffered much from hurricanes, notably in 1892, 1931, 1945 and 1960. The is. was the sole home of the dodo (q.v.) which became extinct during the Dutch occupation. *See* G. Hitié, *Histoire de Maurice*, 1897; R. Philogine, *The Island of Mauritius*, 1928; W. H. Ingrams, *Short History of Mauritius*, 1931; M. Malieu, *Island of the Swan*, 1952; also ann. Colonial Report.

Maurois, André (1885–), (pseudonym of **Émile Herzog**), Fr. writer of Jewish parentage, *b*. Elbeuf. He studied philosophy; during the First World War he was attached to Brit. troops as liaison officer. M. became known to Eng. readers through *Les Silences du Colonel Bramble*, 1918. Other works of his, many of them also on Eng. themes, are *Ni ange, ni bête*, 1919, *General Bramble*, 1921, *Les Discours du Docteur O'Grady*, 1922, *Ariel, ou la vie de*

Shelley, 1923, *Bernard Quesnay* (novel), 1926, *Meïpe, ou la délivrance*, 1926, *Études Anglaises*, 1927, *La Vie de Disraeli*, 1927, *Les Derniers Jours de Pompei* (study of Bulwer Lytton and his wife), 1928, *Aspects de la biographie*, 1928, *Byron*, 1930, *Marshal Lyautey*, 1931, *Voltaire*, 1932, *Dickens*, 1934, *Chateaubriand*, 1938, *Tragedy in France*, 1940, *Seven Faces of Love*, 1948, *Lélia, ou la vie de George Sand*, 1952, *Olympia, ou la vie de Victor Hugo*, 1953, *Les Roses de septembre* (novel), 1956, and *Les Trois Dumas*, 1957. His autobiographical *I Remember, I Remember* was pub. in 1942, and *Call No Man Happy* in 1943. *See* M. Droit, *André Maurois*, 1953.

Maurolico, or **Marullo, Francesco** (1494–1575), It. mathematician, *b*. Messina, was of Gk origin. He became a monk and taught mathematics at Messina. In that he used letters in arithmetical calculations, he may be said to have paved the way for algebra; in trigonometry he introduced secants; and in his *Treatise on Conics* he attempted to deduce the curves from the fact that they are arcs of circles in perspective. His *Cosmographia* appeared in 1543.

Maurras, Charles Marie Photius (1868–1952), Fr. writer, *b*. Martigues. He was the moving spirit of Action Française (q.v.). In 1945 he was sentenced to solitary confinement for life as a collaborator during the Ger. occupation of France. His writings include criticism, prose tales and poetry: *Jean Moréas*, 1891, *Chateaus briand*, *Michelet*, *Sainte-Beuve*, 1898, *Le Amants de Venise, George Sand et Musset*, 1902, *L'Avenir de l'intelligence*, 1905, *La Musique intérieure* (poems), 1925, *Au signe de Flore* (autobiography), 1931, *Dictionnaire politique et critique*, 1931–4. *Louis XIV et la France*, 1935, *Mes idées politiques*, 1937, *De la colère à la justice*, 1942. His collected writings about the First World War were pub. as *Les Conditions de la victoire*, 1916–18. *See* A. Thibaudet, *Les Idées de Maurras*, 1920; H. Massis, *Maurras et notre temps* (2 vols.), 1951.

Maury, Jean Siffrein (1746–1817), Fr. cardinal and orator, *b*. Valréas, Vaucluse, was a cobbler's son. In 1771 he wrote a much-admired *éloge* on Fénelon, and in the following year his *Panégyrique de Saint Louis* met with a most cordial reception. In 1785 he was elected to the Fr. Academy. On the outbreak of the Fr. Revolution he defended the Church and the *ancien régime* in the National Assembly from 1789 to 1792 with bravery and with a lively wit which succeeded in disarming his opponents. Pope Pius VI welcomed him on his emigration (1792), and in 1794 made him a cardinal. The acceptance on his part of the archbishopric of Paris from Napoleon (1810) was the cause of subsequent disgrace and imprisonment. His *Essai sur l'éloquence de la chaire*, 1777, has become a classic. *See* life by G. Bonet, 1892.

Maury, Matthew Fontaine (1806–73), Amer. naval officer, oceanographer. In 1825 he was appointed midshipman in the U.S. Navy, and in 1836 he was made lieutenant, but being lamed in 1839 by an accident he was appointed to the

MAUSOLEUM

The famous mausoleum at Halicarnassus in Asia Minor, one of the 'Seven Wonders of the World', built by King Mausolus (4th cent. BC). Based on the restoration by J. J. Stevenson in the British Museum, London.

Hydrographical Office at Washington in 1842. While there he issued his *Wind and Current Chart of the North Atlantic* and wrote his *Physical Geography of the Seas*, 1855, and his works on the ocean currents and great circle sailing. In 1858 he was made commander, and later pub. other works. *See* life by J. W. Wayland, *The Pathfinder of the Seas*.

Maurya, name of a great dynasty which was supreme over N. India for 137 years. In 321 BC Chandragupta M. captured the throne of Magadha (or Behar), and estab. an empire stretching from the Arabian Sea to the Bay of Bengal. The greatest of the M. kings was Asoka (q.v.), the founder's grandson: the last was Brihadratha. *See* R. Thapar, *Asoka and the Decline of the Mauryas*, 1961.

Mausoleum, essentially a large and imposing sepulchral monument. The word is derived from Mausolus, King of Caria, to whose memory Artemisia, his widow, raised in 353 BC a splendid tomb at Halicarnassus (q.v.). The remains of the colossal group which once crowned the 2 colonnaded tiers are in the Brit. Museum. Four

sculptors are said to have worked on the building, Bryaxis, Leochares, Skopas and Timotheus, each taking one side, though the apportionment of what remains is uncertain. The most ambitious mausolea are the Taj Mahal in India, those of Augustus and Hadrian (the castle of Sant' Angelo) at Rome; those of Frederick William III and Queen Louisa at Charlottenburg near Berlin; of Napoleon III at Farnborough; and that of Lenin at Moscow.

Mauve, Anton (1838–88), Dutch landscape painter, *b.* Zaandam, was a friend of Israels and Maris (qq.v.) and uncle of Vincent van Gogh who was his pupil for a short time at The Hague. He painted grey, rainy country scenes and his pictures are attractive for their subdued harmonies of tone.

Mauve (Lat. *malva*, mallow), first successful synthetic dye. Discovered by W. H. Perkin in 1856, it was patented and produced commercially in 1858. It was produced by the oxidation of aniline, which at that time was not available in a pure state, with potassium dichromate and sulphuric acid. Pure aniline does not give M. by this treatment, but the insoluble black dye Aniline Black. M. is the salt of the base Mauveine ($C_{26}H_{24}N_4$). *See* DYE.

Mayor, Osborne Henry, *see* BRIDIE, JAMES.

Mayors, *see* MARS.

Mavrogordato, Mavrocordato, or **Mavrocordatos,** name of a distinguished family of Phanariot Greeks.

Alexander Mavrogordato (*c*. 1636–1709), doctor of philosophy and medicine who was influential at the court of Mustapha II. He arranged the peace of Carlowitz.

Nicholas Mavrogordato (1670–1730), Alexander's son. He was prince (hospodar) of Wallachia, and ruled the Danubian principalities for the sultan, angering the Rumanians by his Hellenising efforts.

Prince Alexander Mavrogordato (1791–1865), descendant of Nicholas. He defended Missolonghi during the Gk War of Independence. In 1832 he was chosen vice-president of the Gk national assembly at Argos, and the following year he became first minister to King Otto. He was Gk ambas. at Berlin, London, and Constantinople and in 1853 was recalled to office to re-establish friendly relations with Turkey during a period of crisis.

Mawchi, *see* KAYAH STATE.

Mawla, *see* Mollah.

Mawson, Sir Douglas (1882–1958), Eng. explorer and geologist, *b.* Bradford, Yorks, and educ. at Sydney Univ. He was appointed to the scientific staff of Shackleton's expedition, 1907–9, during which he was a member of the first parties to climb Mt Erebus and to reach the S. magnetic pole. He organised and commanded the Australasian expedition, 1911–14, which discovered and explored George V Land and Queen Mary Land. A full account of this expedition is contained in M.'s work, *The Home of the Blizzard*, 1915. In 1929–31 he led the Brit., Australian, New Zealand Antarctic Research Expedition which discovered Mac-Robertson Land. Prof. of Geology Univ. of Adelaide, 1920–52. Knighted, 1914. Prof. of Geology Univ. of Adelaide, 1920–52. *See* C. E. Laseron, *South with Mawson*, 1948; J. K. Davis, *With the 'Aurora' in the Antarctic*, 1919; P. Mawson, *Mawson of the Antarctic*, 1964.

Max, Adolphe Eugène Jean (1869–1939), burgomaster of Brussels, his bp. He was educ. at the Athénées of Brussels and Ixelles, and at Brussels Univ. He joined the newspaper, *La Liberté*, with Paul Hymans. In Dec. 1909 he became burgomaster of Brussels. When the Germans occupied Brussels in the First World War M. tried to keep up the courage of his compatriots by issuing posters contradicting the demoralising ones pub. by the Germans, and by protesting incessantly against the violation of the citizens' rights. Finally the Ger. governor, von Bissing, stopped the distribution of food rations in order to extort an additional tax of 30,000,000 francs, whereupon M. warned all banks that the city no longer guaranteed its bonds. He was arrested and imprisoned in Germany. He escaped and returned to Brussels in Nov. 1918, was reinstated as burgomaster and held the position for the rest of his life.

Max Müller, Friedrich, *see* MÜLLER, F. M.

Maxence, St, *see* MAIXENT.

Maxentius, Marcus Aurelius Valerius, Rom. emperor (AD 306–312), son of Maximian (q.v.). He was passed over in the div. of the empire, following the abdication of his father and Diocletian (q.v.) in 305; but he seized Rome and was proclaimed emperor in 306. After the death of Galerius (311), Constantine the Great (q.v.) marched on Rome and defeated M. at Saxa Rubra (312). M. tried to escape into the city over the Milvian bridge, but was drowned.

Maxillaria, genus of terrestrial orchids with thick fleshy flowers, occurring mainly in Central America.

Maxim, Sir Hiram Stevens (1840–1916), Amer. civil, mechanical and electrical engineer, *b.* Sangersville, Maine, U.S.A. He first made experiments and improved steam engines, and invented an automatic gas engine. He then studied electricity, invented an incandescent electric lamp, and the method of using carbons in electric lighting. His great work, however, was the automatic system of firearms, and he was at one time connected with the firm of Vickers, Sons, & M. He became a naturalised Brit. subject, and was knighted in 1901. *See* his *My Life*, 1915. *See also* MACHINE-GUNS.

Maxim, Hudson (1853–1927), Amer. inventor of explosives; younger brother of Sir Hiram M. In 1890 he built a manufactory of dynamite and smokeless powder at M., New Jersey, a tn named after him. He invented the high explosive called Maximite. During the First World War he was chairman of the ordnance and explosive committee of the naval consulting board. Pubs.: *The Science of Poetry and the Philosophy of Language*, 1910; *Defenseless America*, 1915; *Dynamite Stories*, 1916.

Maxima and Minima. Many mathematical problems are comprised under this head. For example, a line of given length may be made to enclose various shaped and sized figures; what is the greatest space it can be made to enclose? A number is the sum of two other numbers: of all the pairs that can be selected, which pair will show the greatest product? Many such problems were stated and solved by the anct Greeks. Euclid has many propositions of this nature solved by geometrical methods. Such problems are of great practical value in the useful arts; e.g. given a certain amount of metal, what dimensions for a cylindrical cistern will provide the greatest capacity? Or again, given a log of wood, what dimensions on cutting to a rectangular beam will give the greatest strength? In each problem a maximum or minimum has to be found. The study of curves, the conditions of their formation by a moving point, has led to greater complications; there are 3 phases to be determined: rise, fall and turning. A curve attains a maximum height at the moment it ceases rising and commences to fall, a minimum at the moment it ceases to fall and commences to rise. Or, in algebraic language, when any value y

of a function is greater than the immediately neighbouring values, both before and after, it is called a maximum value of the function; when any value y of a function is less than the immediately neighbouring values, both before and after, it is called a minimum value of the function. There may be many maxima and many minima, and a maximum value according to the definition above is not necessarily the greatest value the function may have. Considering an irregular wavy curve, each maximum or minimum is the highest or lowest point occurring in any phase, and a minimum may have a higher value than a maximum. Bernoulli in 1696 propounded and solved problems by methods which became known as 'isopermetrico'. This was extended by Euler, and led to the invention by Lagrange of the calculus of variations. Practically speaking, the subject is now investigated by the differential calculus (q.v.). A curve is represented by $y(x)$. At the M. and M. of the curve the rate of change of y with respect to x is momentarily zero, i.e. $\frac{dy}{dx} = 0$. The solutions of this equation give the turning points of the curve, which, in addition to the M. and M., include the points of inflection. The tangent to the curve at these points is parallel to the x-axis (*see* Figure). To distinguish between these 3 cases we consider $\frac{d^2y}{dx^2}$, evaluated at the point of interest. For a maximum $\frac{d^2y}{dx^2} \langle 0$; for a minimum $\frac{d^2y}{dx^2} \rangle 0$; and for a point of inflection $\frac{d^2y}{dx^2} = 0$. On the figure the point x_1 is a maximum, x_2 is a minimum, and x_3 is a point of inflection.

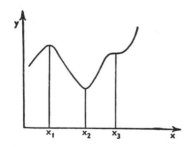

Maximian (M. Aurelius Valerius Maximianus), Rom. emperor (AD 286–305), originally a Pannonian soldier, was made by Diocletian his colleague in the empire, but was compelled to abdicate when the latter did so voluntarily, and went into retirement. When his son, Maxentius (q.v.), assumed the imperial title in the following year (306), he returned to Rome; but being expelled from the city by Maxentius, he took refuge in Gaul with Constantine, who had married his daughter, Fausta. It is generally believed that he was compelled by Constantine to put an end to his own life at Marseilles in 310.

Maximilian I (1459–1519), Holy Roman emperor, the son and successor of Frederick III, was *b*. Neustadt, near Vienna. He married Mary, the heiress of Charles the Bold, Duke of Burgundy and was soon involved in war with Louis XI of France, who attempted to seize some of her possessions. M. was finally compelled to betroth his daughter Margaret, then 4 years old, to the Dauphin, afterwards Charles VIII, and to give Artois, Flanders and the Duchy of Burgundy as her dowry. In 1486 he was elected king of the Romans. Insurrections in the Netherlands, encouraged and supported by France, again involved him in war with Louis XI. He afterwards repelled the Hungarians and the Turks. He again took up arms against France when Charles VIII repudiated Margaret and married Anne of Brittany. A peace was, however, made at Senlis in 1493, M. receiving back the provs. which he had given with his daughter. On the death of his father in 1493 he became emperor, and he subsequently married Bianca Sforza, daughter of the Duke of Milan. He tried to stop Fr. conquests in Italy, and was at first successful, but ultimately he had to give up Milan to France and Verona to the Venetians, and in 1499 the Swiss won their independence from the empire. The marriage of his son Philip with the Infanta Juana, and of his daughter Margaret with the Infant Juan of Spain, led to the subsequent union of Spain with Austria, whilst the marriage of two of his grandchildren with the son and daughter of Ladislaus, King of Hungary and Bohemia, brought both these kingdoms to the Austrian monarchy. *See* life by I. R. W. Seton-Watson, 1902. (*See Plate: Germany*.)

Maximilian II (Joseph) (1811–64), King of Bavaria, son of Louis I, *b*. Munich. He became king in 1848 on his father's abdication, and adopted a liberal policy.

Maximilian Ferdinand Joseph, Archduke (1832–67), Emperor of Mexico, a son of the Archduke Francis Charles of Austria and son-in-law of Leopold I, King of the Belgians, whose daughter Charlotte he married in 1857. He was *b*. Schönbrunn, Vienna, and was made governor of Lombardo-Venetia in 1857, where his rule was liberal and enlightened. Meanwhile Fr. troops invaded Mexico, and on the capture of Puebla in 1863, with the co-operation of the Mexican clerical party, they proclaimed M. Emperor of Mexico. Renouncing his Austrian rights, M. accepted the throne and arrived in Mexico in 1864. He never had more than limited support there. Civil war followed, and in 1866 the Fr. troops were withdrawn. M. was captured and shot at Queretaro, probably by order of Juarez. *See* M. Hyde, *Mexican Empire*, 1945; Bertita Harding, *Phantom Crown*, 2nd ed., 1961.

Maximinus, Gaius Julius Verus (Maximinus Thrax), Rom. emperor (AD 235–8), was originally a Thracian shepherd. He was of gigantic size and enormous physical strength. Alexander Severus (q.v.) gave him the command of a new legion raised in Pannonia, at the head of which he followed the emperor in his campaign against the Germans on the Rhine. There he induced some of his companions to murder Alexander and his mother, Mammaea. He was proclaimed emperor; but his cruelty and rapacity, which were the accompaniment of undeniable ability, aroused enemies against him in various parts of the empire. He was killed by his own soldiers while besieging Aquileia.

Maximinus, Galerius Valerius, Rom. emperor (AD 308–14). Originally an Illyrian shepherd, his real name was Daia, and he is often called **M. Daia**. Becoming a soldier, he was raised by his uncle Galerius (q.v.) to the rank of Caesar, and made governor of Syria and Egypt in 305. In 308 he assumed the title of Augustus, and on the death of Galerius (311) succeeded to the provs. of Asia, and entered into a secret alliance with Maxentius (q.v.). Having invaded Thrace in the absence of Licinius, he suffered a crushing defeat near Heraclea, and fled. He d. at Tarsus.

Maximinus of Trèves (d. c. 349), b. near Poitiers. He became Bishop of Trèves in 332, and was a staunch defender of the exiled St Athanasius. At the Councils of Milan, Sardica and Cologne he was an outstanding opponent of Arianism.

Maximus, Magnus Clemens, Rom. emperor (AD 383–8), a native of Spain. He accompanied Theodosius on sev. expeditions, and spent some years as a general in Britain. Here he was proclaimed emperor by the troops in 383, and immediately crossed to Gaul to attack Gratian. The latter was defeated and slain, and Gaul, Spain and Britain acknowledged M. In 387 he crossed the Alps, defeated Valentinian and estab. himself in Milan, but was defeated by Theodosius at Sixia, on the Saône and again at Poetovio on the Danube, being subsequently captured and put to death at Aquileia.

Maximus, Petronius Anicius, Rom. emperor (AD 455). At the age of 19 he was admitted to the council of Honorius, and in 420 held the office of city prefect, becoming consul in 433, and again in 443. He was friendly with Valentinian III until the emperor seduced his (M.'s) wife, after which M. murdered him in 455. M. was chosen to succeed him, and married the widowed Empress Eudoxia. She, on learning the truth of her former husband's death, secured the help of Genseric the Vandal, who sacked Rome. M. was slain.

Maximus Tyrius (of Tyre) Gk rhetorician and Platonic philosopher of the late 2nd cent. AD. There are extant 41 of his dissertations on various aspects of Platonism, written in an easy and pleasing style, but more commendable for their form than for their content. The following examples will give some idea of their subject matter: 'On Plato's Opinion respecting the Deity', 'Whether we ought to return Injuries done to us', 'Whether Prayers should be addressed to the Deity', etc. There is a Fr. trans. by Dounais, 1910. See K. Meiser, *Studien zu Maximus Tyrios*, 1909.

Maxton, James (1885–1946), politician, b. Glasgow, educ. at Grahamston School, Barrhead, Hutcheson's Grammar School, Glasgow

and Glasgow Univ. He became a school-teacher, and a prominent member of the Independent Labour Party. During the First World War M. was a pacifist and conscientious objector. In 1916 he was sentenced to 12 months' imprisonment for inciting munition workers to mutiny, in a public speech. In 1926 he became chairman of the I.L.P. and remained its real leader until his death. For 24 years he was M.P. for Bridgeton, Glasgow. An uncompromising revolutionary and advocate of 'direct action' he was none the less a man of great humanity, respected by all parties, and one of the most popular members of the House of Commons. See life by J. McNair, 1955. He pub. a study of Lenin, 1932.

Maxwell, James Clerk (1831–79), physicist, b. Edinburgh; educ. at the Edinburgh Academy and the univs. of Edinburgh and Cambridge. At the early age of 15 he sent to the Royal Society of Edinburgh a paper on the 'Description of Oval Curves', and during the next 3 years followed it up by 'On the Theory of Rolling Curves' and 'On the Equilibrium of Elastic Solids'. In 1856 he became prof. of natural philosophy at Marischal College, Aberdeen, and from 1860 to 1865 held the same post in King's College, London. He was a fellow of the Royal Societies of London and Edinburgh. On the endowment by the Duke of Devonshire of Cambridge Univ. with a model laboratory of experimental physics (the Cavendish Laboratory), M. was unanimously elected as the first prof. of experimental physics in that univ. M.'s final presentation of his theory was given in the treatise on electricity and magnetism in 1873. The theory at first had few adherents, one reason being that M.'s presentation of his theory was in some features exceedingly obscure. The two definite statements about electricity made by M. were: that wherever there is electric force there is electric displacement, and that electricity behaves like an incompressible fluid. M.'s electro-magnetic theory related the known laws of electricity and magnetism and showed that electromagnetic waves (q.v.) should be found with a velocity equal to that of light. This and other considerations indicated that light is electromagnetic in character. It was not until 10 years after M.'s death that direct experimental evidence of the existence of electrical waves was obtained by Hertz. M. also investigated the molecular constitution of matter, the kinetic theory of gases, and geometrical optics, and wrote, *inter alia*, treatises on the dynamical theory of gases (1859), heat (1871), and matter and motion (1873). See lives by L. Campbell and W. Garnett, 1882; R. T. Glazebrook, 1896; R. L. Smith-Rose, 1948; also C. Domb (editor), *Clerk Maxwell and Modern Science*, 1963. (See *Plate: Physics*).

Maxwell, Mrs John, *see* BRADDON, MARY ELIZABETH.

Maxwell, Sir John, *see* HERRIES.

Maxwell, Robert, Lord (d. 1546), Scottish statesman, member of the royal council under James V, a warden of the W. marches, and a lord provost of Edinburgh. He was also an extraordinary lord of session in 1533, and one of the regents in 1536. He was taken prisoner by the English at the rout of Solway Moss in 1542.

Maxwell, Lady Stirling-, *see* NORTON, CAROLINE ELIZABETH SARAH.

Maxwell, William Babington (1866–1938), Brit. author, son of John M., publisher, and his wife, Mary Braddon (q.v.). After a brief spell as an art student he turned to fiction. He pub. *The Countess of Maybury* in 1900, and produced a novel each year thereafter till 1913. His novels include *The Guarded Flame*, 1906, *The Devil's Garden*, 1913, *The Mirror and the Lamp*, 1918, *Tudor Green*, 1935, *The Emotional Journey*, 1936, and *Everslade*, 1937—the last 3 being a trilogy which appeared under the general title *Men and Women*. His autobiography, *Time Gathered*, appeared in 1938.

Maxwell Fyfe, Sir David, *see* KILMUIR, 1st VISCOUNT.

Maxwell-Boltzmann Statistics, *see* BOLTZMANN STATISTICS.

Maxwell's Equations, *see* ELECTRO-MAGNETIC WAVES.

Maxwelltown, *see* DUMFRIES.

May, Peter Barker Howard (1929–), Eng. cricketer, educ. Charterhouse School and Pembroke College, Cambridge. A double blue (cricket and football), he soon stepped into the front rank as a batsman. He first captained England in 1956, Surrey in 1957.

May, Philip William (1864–1903), humorous artist, *b.* Leeds, and known as Phil May. He pub. *Annuals* from 1892, and contributed sketches of low life to numerous papers. His 'Guttersnipes', 1896, shows all his appreciation of cockney character. In 1896 he became a member of the staff of *Punch*. He was one of the greatest black-and-white artists, and a lineal descendant of Leech and Keene. *See* life by J. Thorpe, 1932. *See Plate: Caricature.*)

May, Thomas (1595–1650), writer, *b.* Sussex. He graduated at Sidney Sussex College, Cambridge. He was admitted to Gray's Inn in 1615, but being prevented by a speech defect from practising the law, devoted himself to literature. He first produced a comedy entitled *The Heire*, 1622, which was much praised by Thomas Carew, and followed this by another comedy and 3 classical tragedies, but none of these met with success. In 1627 appeared his trans. of Lucan's *Pharsalia*, which met with unstinted praise from Ben Jonson, and gained him the favour of Charles I. In 1628 he pub. a version of Virgil's *Georgics*, and the following year Martial's *Epigrams*. In 1633 he was commissioned by the king to write 2 narrative poems, one on *Henry II*, the other on *Edward III*. His reputation as a prose writer rests upon his *History of the Long Parliament*, 1647, which is described by Chatham as being 'a much honester and more instructive book than Clarendon's'. *See* A. G. Chester, *Thomas May*, 1932.

May, Sir Thomas Erskine, 1st Baron Farnborough (1815–86), constitutional jurist, *b.* London. He was assistant librarian of the House of Commons in 1831, and a barrister at the Middle Temple in 1838. In 1844 he pub. *A Treatise on the Law, Privileges, Proceedings and Usage of Parliament*, a work which has been trans. into sev. languages. He was clerk of the House of Commons, 1871–86; created Baron Farnborough, 1886. He also pub. *The Constitutional History of England since the Accession of George III, 1760–1860*, 1861–3, and *Democracy in Europe: a History*, 1877.

May, fifth month of the year, and the last of spring. It was the third month in the Rom. calendar, and was called M. probably after Maia, the mother of Mercury, to whom the Romans used to sacrifice on the first day of this month.

May, Isle of, in the Firth of Forth, Fife co., Scotland, 5½ m. SE. of Crail. On the highest point of the is. is a lighthouse, and there are ruins of a 12th cent. priory.

May-apple, *see* PODOPHYLLUM.

May Day, 1 May, was formerly celebrated throughout Great Britain, and to a lesser extent in France and Germany, with festivities, which now survive only in a few rural dists. They are the direct descendants of the anct Rom. Floralia, and of the Druidic feasts in honour of the god Bel. In Tudor England the custom was for people to go into the woods in the night, gather branches of trees and flowers, and return with them at sunrise to decorate their houses. Then there was the crowning of the M. queen, who held sway for one day over her court, consisting of morris dancers, Robin Hood and members of his band, as well as of the villagers and townspeople, who danced round a maypole decorated with flowers and ribbons. The maypole was generally made of birch, and was set up on 30 April, except in London, where permanent maypoles stood in the streets. The M. revels were much censured by the Puritans, and in 1644 maypoles were forbidden to be erected by the Roundhead Parliament. They were, however, sanctioned at the Restoration, and in 1661 a cedar pole, 134 ft high, was erected in the Strand. It was taken down *c.* 1717, and used by Sir Isaac Newton as a support for the great telescope which had been presented to the Royal Society by a Fr. astronomer. M. D. is now observed as Labour Day (q.v.).

Maya, race of Amer. Indians, the aborigines of Yucatan. The old Mayan empire flourished between the 2nd and 8th cents. AD. Near the end of the 10th cent. a new empire was estab. which survived until the coming of the Spaniards in the early part of the 16th cent. There was an organisation of city states, though without one single ruler. The M.s had a written language, and have left numerous examples of MSS. and picture-writing. In religion they had much in common with the Aztecs; they were polytheistic, and worshipped a sky god, who was the creator, and gods of the moon, rain, death, etc. In their sculptures the 2 most frequently depicted are the rain god and the god of arts and crafts. Religious festivals were frequent: gifts of crops and animal sacrifices were made, and human sacrifices, though at first rare, became common later. The M.s subsisted chiefly on agriculture, the prin.

food being maize. They made many ornaments of gold, greenstone, jade and copper, but they were especially skilful in architecture and in carving in stone. They erected buildings of vast size, decorated in wonderful manner, and their massive character and lavish wealth of carvings attest a civilisation far superior to that of many civilised peoples in the old world. A form of picture-writing was used, and an arithmetical system of counting in twenties, which made possible considerable progress in mathematical and astronomical science. Numerous examples of Mayan pottery have also been found; also spear-heads, incense-burners, jadeite ear ornaments and greenish stone axes. The M.s of today, in Yucatan, have small, sturdy, agile figures, and the strange curve of the nostril and the nose, and the mouth with straight upper lip, that arc found represented in the early Mayan paintings. The women wear the traditional smock, called the *upil*, with embroidered flowers round hem and shoulders, and a white underskirt showing below. The love of the M.s for pageantry, which is evident in the old friezes, is maintained in the Christian tableaux in the churches, and in the wealth of decoration adopted from Spain. Round the churches the Mayan houses are still built like the models carved on the temple walls of Uxmal, being oval in shape and very primitive. So little have the people changed that their anct feud with the Aztecs is not forgotten, and even today the Yucatani hates to be called Mexican. The Mayan language is still spoken, but it has ceased to be written. *See* A. Joyce, *Maya and Mexican Art*, 1927; S. C. Morley, *The Ancient Maya*, 1946; V. W. von Hagen, *Maya Explorer: John Lloyd Stephens and the Lost Cities of Central America and Yucatan*, 1947; E. S. Thompson, *The Rise and Fall of Maya Civilisation*, 1956; H. J. Spinden, *Maya Art and Civilisation*, 1958. (*See Plate: Mexico.*)

Maya, or **Mahamaya,** mother of Gautama Buddha. According to tradition she and her sister, Prajapati, were the prin. wives of Suddhodana of the Kshattriya caste, a wealthy landowner of a small kingdom called Kapilavastu, near the boundary of Oudh and Nepal. At the age of 45 M. bore Gautama, *c.* 560–550 BC, in a wayside grove, which was visited 3 centuries later by Asoka (q.v.), whose commemorative pillar there was discovered in 1895. *See* BUDDHA AND BUDDHISM.

Maya-Quiché, collective name for all the pops. among the Amer. Indians who speak various forms of a common language, is derived from the 2 most important members of the group, the Mayas (q.v.) of the Yucatan plains and the Quichés (q.v.) of the Guatemalan plateaus. They inhabit Mexico, Yucatan, Guatemala and Honduras, and represented the most cultured inhab. of central America at the time of the Spanish conquest. (*See Plate: Guatemala.*)

Mayagüez, city on the coast of the is. of Porto Rico, 70 m. WSW. of San Juan. It is a shipping, processing and trading centre in an agric. area

(sugar, coffee, fruit, vegetables, tobacco, honey). It manufs. beer, alcohol, rum, candy, tiles and soap, and is a rail and road centre and a port of entry. Pop. 83,850.

Mayakovsky, Vladimir Vladimirovich (1893–1930), Russian poet, the most outstanding representative in Russia of the Futurist school. *B.* Transcaucasia, he joined the Bolshevik faction of the Russian Social Democratic Labour Party (q.v.) in 1908. His first poems were pub. in 1912 in the Futurist collection *A Slap in the Face of Public Taste*. After the seizure of power by the Bolsheviks (*see* OCTOBER REVOLUTION) M. deliberately put his talent at the service of the Communist Party (*see* COMMUNIST PARTY OF THE SOVIET UNION), taking an active part in its propaganda campaigns. However, his political poems (*Left March*, 1919, *150,000,000*, 1920, *V. I. Lenin*, 1924, *Good!*, 1927, *Verses about a Soviet Passport*, 1930) and plays (*Mystery-Buff*, 1918, *The Bedbug*, 1929, *The Bathhouse*, 1930) were always distinguished by a fresh approach to, and presentation of, the standard themes. The same is true of his lyrical poetry. Disillusionment with the Party and unhappy love drove him to suicide. M.'s poetic innovations influenced much contemporary and subsequent Russian poetry. In 1935 Stalin called M. 'the best, most talented poet of the Soviet epoch', and since then he has been held up in the U.S.S.R. as a model of Socialist Realism (q.v.). *See* C. M. Bowra, *The Creative Experiment*, 1949; *The Bedbug and Selected Poetry*, trans. M. Hayward and G. Reavey, 1961; *Mayakovsky*, trans. and ed. H. Marshall, 1965.

Maybole, par. and police burgh in Ayrshire, Scotland, 8 m. S. of Ayr, possesses an old castle. Crossraguel Abbey (in ruins), and Culzen Castle (seat of the Marquess of Ailsa) with its tropical gardens are nearby. The chief industries arc the manufs. of shoes and agric. implements. Pop. (par.) 1962; (tn) 4677.

Mayebashi, *see* MAEBASHI.

Mayen, Ger. tn in the *Land* of Rhineland-Palatinate, 50 m. WNW. of Mainz. It is the largest tn in the Eifel, and dates from Rom. times. It has an anct fortress (now a museum) and a notable church. There are textile, brewing and tanning industries. Pop. 17,400.

Mayence, *see* MAINZ.

Mayenne, dept of W. France, formed from parts of the old prov. of Maine and Anjou. M., which is included almost entirely within the basin of the Loire, has a mild climate. It has extensive sandy heaths in many places. The chief industry is the breeding of cattle, horses and pigs, and the keeping of bees, while iron-mines and marble and slate quarries are worked. The linen, hemp and paper manufs. and cider making are of some importance. The prin. tns are Laval (the cap.), Mayenne and Château-Gontier. Area 1986 sq. m.; pop. 250,000.

Mayer, Johann Tobias (1723–62), Ger. astronomer, *b.* Marbach. A self-taught mathematician, he became prof. of economy and mathematics at Göttingen in 1751, and director of the observatory in 1754. His prin. achievement was an improved set of tables of the moon's position for use in navigation.

Mayer, Julius Robert Von (1814–78), Ger. physicist, *b.* Heilbronn. He studied at Tübingen, Munich and Paris, and subsequently settled as a physician in his native tn. In 1842 and 1845 he pub. 2 treatises on the conservation and transformation of energy, but unfortunately M. received very little recognition during his life for his work. *See* E. Dühring, *Robert von Meyer, der Galilei des neunzehnten Jahrhunderts,* 1895; H. E. Timmerding, *Robert von Meyer und die Entdeckung des Energiesatzes,* 1925.

Mayfair, situated N. of Piccadilly, at one time the most fashionable quarter of London, but since the First World War largely given over to higher class commercial offices. M. derives its name from a fair held here in May from Charles II's time until 1809, and part of the site is now occupied by Shepherd Market, which was built *c.* 1735. M. was notorious for a time for the unofficial marriages solemnised by the Rev. Alexander Keith from 1730 until 1743, when he was imprisoned.

Mayfield, vil. of Sussex, England, 9 m. S. of Tunbridge Wells. It was a mrkt tn in the Middle Ages. The old palace (14th cent.) is now a convent school (*see* ST LEONARDS-MAYFIELD SCHOOL). St Dunstan's church (13th–15th cents.) has grave-slabs of Sussex ironwork. Pop. 3344.

'Mayflower': 1. *See* PILGRIM FATHERS.
2. *Mayflower II,* replica of the Pilgrim Fathers' ship. She sailed from Plymouth, Devon, on 20 April 1957, bound for Cape Cod, Massachusetts, the landfall of the original 'M.' party in 1620, in connection with the 350th anniversary of the founding of the first permanent Eng. settlement in America at Jamestown, Virginia, in 1607. She reached Cape Cod on 12 June, having taken the southerly route across the Atlantic. *See* W. Charlton, *Voyage of Mayflower II,* 1957.

Mayfly, *see* EPHEMEROPTERA.

Mayhem, *see* MAIM.

Mayhew, Henry (1812–87), author, founder and co-editor of *Punch* (q.v.), *b.* London. With Gilbert à Beckett he pub. the periodical, *Figaro in London,* 1831; he followed this by *The Thief* in 1832. His prin. book, *London Labour and the London Poor,* 1851, was later ed. by P. Quennell, 1949. His farce, *The Wandering Minstrel,* was produced in 1841. He collaborated with his brother Augustus in *The Good Genius,* 1847, *The Plague of Life,* 1847, *The Image of his Father,* 1851.

Maykop, cap. (since 1936) of the Adyge Autonomous Oblast (*see* CIRCASSIANS) in the Krasnodar Kray of S. Russia. It has woodworking and food industries, and important oilfields. There is a famous Bronze Age barrow. Pop. (1956) 77,000, mostly Russians. Founded, 1857. It was occupied by the Germans, 1942–3.

Mayne, Ethel Colburn (*d.* 1941), Irish novelist. In 1895 she contributed to the *Yellow Book.* Besides sev. vols. of short stories she wrote the novels *Jessie Vandeleur,* 1902, *The Fourth Ship,*

1908, *Gold Lace,* 1913, and *One of Our Grandmothers,* 1916. She also pub. an excellent 2-vol. study of Byron, 1912, and a book on Browning's heroines, 1913.

Mayne Reid, Thomas, *see* REID, MAYNE.

Maynooth, tn of co. Kildare, Rep. of Ireland, 15 m. W. of Dublin. Its chief interest is its Rom. Catholic college, which was estab. during the ministry of Pitt in the year 1795, by an Act of the Irish Parliament. In the year 1846 Sir Robert Peel carried a Bill for an increased and permanent endowment, no longer dependent on a vote of Parliament. An endowment of £369,000 from public funds was granted in 1871. The college, a Gothic building, receives students destined for the priesthood. A new chapel was erected in 1890. Pop. 950.

Mayo, Charles Horace (1865–1939), Amer. surgeon, *b.* Rochester, Minnesota. As surgeon at St Mary's Hospital and at the M. Clinic in Rochester he had much success in operations for goitre and cancer. He pub. works on goitre and cancer. He and his brother Wm James M. (q.v.) were chief consultants for all Amer. medical services in the First World War and between 1915 and 1934 gave $2,800,000 to establish and maintain the M. Foundation for Medical Education and Research. *See* H. Clapesattle, *The Doctors Mayo,* 1941.

Mayo, Katherine (1868–1940), Amer. journalist, *b.* Ridgeway, Pennsylvania. She wrote *Justice to All,* 1917, a critical study of the Amer. police system; *That Damn Y,* 1921, about the Y.M.C.A.; *Isles of Fear,* 1925, a criticism of Amer. rule in the Philippines; *Mother India,* 1927, vol. ii, 1931, exposing the iniquities of the Indian child-bride system; *The Face of Mother India,* 1935; *General Washington's Dilemma,* 1938.

Mayo, Richard Southwell Bourke, 6th Earl of, *see* BOURKE.

Mayo, William James (1861–1939), Amer. surgeon, *b.* Le Sueur, Minnesota. He specialised in cancer, gallstone and intestine cases. With his father, Wm Worrall M., and his younger brother, Charles Horace M. (q.v.), he founded the M. Clinic (1889) at Rochester, Minnesota, in connection with their work at St Mary's Hospital there.

Mayo, maritime co. of the prov. of Connaught, Rep. of Ireland, is bounded N. and W. by the Atlantic Ocean. The coastline of M. is about 250 m. and is much indented by bays, chief of which are Killala Bay, Clew Bay, Westport Bay, Newport Bay, Achill Sound, Blacksod Bay. The surface is irregular, the interior being part of the great plain of Ireland, bordered by 2 ranges of mts, separated from each other at the sea by Clew Bay. Of these ranges the highest points are Muilrea (2680 ft), Nephin (2646 ft), and Croagh Patrick (2510 ft) (q.v.). The soil of the central plain is fertile. Rearing of cattle is general, but tillage has increased of late years. Ironstone abounds in some dists but is not worked. An excellent marble is found in the NW. dist. The chief tns are Castlebar, Westport, Ballina, Ballinrobe (qq.v.)., and the prin. rivs. are the Moy, the Robe and the Owenmore. Loughs Cullen, Conn, Castlebar, Carramore, Carra and Mask lie within the co. A valuable salmon-fishery exists in the R. Moy, and the small lake of Lough Mask is the habitation of the well-known 'gillaroo' trout. The antiquities of M. are chiefly eccles. Four round towers are still in existence, and there are at Cong (q.v.) remains of a splendid 12th cent. abbey. The celebrated 'Cross of Cong' is now in the National Museum of Ireland, Dublin. Area 2156 sq. m.; pop. 146,000.

Mayon, volcano in the prov. of Albay, Luzon Is., Philippine Isles. Its cone, which is perfect, rises to a height of 7926 ft, and the mt is frequently in eruption.

Mayor, originally an overseer, or steward, or kind of bailiff, if the derivation from Norman *maeur, mair,* be correct, and the word is really cognate with Armoric *mear,* i.e. one that looks after, tends, or guards, e.g. *mear y biswal,* a land steward. Others, however, derive the word from Lat. *major,* greater, superior, *majores,* ancestors, a derivation which at once invites the assumption that it always, or very early, had its present connotation of chief magistrate (*magister* through *magnus*), whereas in Eng. hist. the mayorality is a comparatively late development of the bor. organisation. Everywhere the M., whatever his particular functions, appears to have risen to eminence, but none to so great a degree as the 'M. of the palace', or first officer of the royal household of the Merovingian kings. Holders of this office were successively chief officer of state, minister of the palace and king; for the last of them, Pepin, after deposing Childeric IV, founded the Carlovingian dynasty (AD 750). The M. at the present day as the head of a municipal corporation is in a prominent and responsible position (for term of office, qualifications, etc., *see* BOROUGH; COUNTY SESSIONS; LOCAL GOVERNMENT; MUNICIPALITIES). In times of riot or civil disorders he has power, and indeed is compelled, to call in the aid of troops, the exercise of which in certain circumstances may place him in a very unenviable position (*see* Regina v. Pinney, 1866), for technically at least he may be liable to criminal proceedings if he acts without justification and to an information for neglect if he omits to act. In other words, he must 'hit the precise line of his duty'. *See also* LORD MAYOR; MAYOR'S COURT; LOCAL GOVERNMENT; LONDON; PROVOST.

Mayor's Court, anct court of record, held before the lord mayor and aldermen of the city of London at the Guildhall. Some authorities trace its origin to the anct customary jurisdiction of the portreeve of London in the old hustings court of AD 675, from which the predecessor of the present M. C. became a distinct and separate tribunal in the reign of Henry III. The lord mayor and all the aldermen are the judges, but the recorder by custom sits as the sole judge, or, in his absence, the common serjeant, who in his turn, if unavoidably absent, may be represented by a barrister of 7 years' standing. There is much of antiquarian interest in the M. C., both as to

the names of its officials (e.g. the duties of a sheriff are carried out by the serjeant-at-mace and the deputy serjeant-at-mace) and as to the formalities of pleading. *See* L. E. Glyn and F. G. Jackson, *Jurisdiction and Practice of the Mayor's Court,* 1910.

Mayow, John (1640–79), chemist and physiologist, *b.* London, educ. at Wadham College, Oxford, and practised as a physician in Bath. He pub. *Tractatus quinque medicophysici,* 1674, containing 'De salnitro et spiritu nitro-aereo', which develops a theory of combustion, and important discoveries in pneumatic chem.

Maypole, *see* MAY DAY.

Mayreau Island, *see* GRENADINES.

Mayweed (*Matricaria maritima*), ann. or biennial plant of the order Compositae. It has a branching growth, with narrow finely divided leaves and daisy-like scentless flowers with yellow centres. The stinking M. (*Anthernis cotula*) has a malodorous juice which causes skin irritation when handled.

Maywood, residential suburb in Illinois, U.S.A., on the Des Plaines R., about 10 m. W. of Chicago. M. has minor industries and is the seat of Chicago Lutheran Theological Seminary. Pop. *c.* 30,000.

Mazagan, seaport tn of Morocco, 115 m. N. of Marrakesh. It is the port of Marrakesh and its roadstead affords facilities for a safe anchorage. The chief exports are grain, almonds, hides and wool. Pop. 34,781.

Mazandaran, prov. in the N. of Persia, lying between the Elburz Mts and the Caspian Sea, and bounded on the E. by Gorgan and on the W. by Gilan. It consists of a low coastal plain rising very rapidly to lofty mts. The rivs. are short and swift. The climate is unhealthy and malarious in the lowlands, where the ground is somewhat swampy, but fertile. The chief products are rice, citrus fruits and tea. Forests on the N. slopes of the Elburz are important. Silk textiles are manuf. at Chalus. Babol (pop. 36,200), is the largest tn, but Sari (pop. 26,200), 20 m. to the E., is the cap. Pop. about 528,000.

Mazara del Vallo, tn in Sicily, on the W. coast, at the mouth of the Mazara R., 26 m. S. of Trapani. The chief exports are corn and olive oil. Pop. 37,700.

Mazarin, Jules (properly **Giulio Mazarini**) (1602–61), cardinal and statesman of France, son of Pietro Mazarini, was *b.* at Piscina in the Abruzzi. His father was the intendant of the household of the Colonna family. He was educ. in Italy and Spain, and took minor orders, eventually entering the service of the Pope. While engaged on a diplomatic mission on behalf of the papacy, M. attracted the attention of Richelieu. He soon went to Paris at Richelieu's invitation, through whose influence he was made a cardinal (1641). On the death of his patron (1642), he succeeded to his position and influence with Louis XIII, who shortly before his death nominated M. to the council of regency, presided over by the queen mother, Anne of Austria. She made him prime minister, and soon entrusted him with absolute authority, and it has been suggested that she and M. were secretly married. The first years of his ministry were marked by the victories of the French over the Spaniards at Rocroi and Sens, which produced the peace of Westphalia, and by the outbreak of the civil war of the Fronde (q.v.). M. was twice compelled to quit France, but at length, as much by cunning as by force, he secured victory in the struggle. In 1659 M. concluded the peace of the Pyrenees, which put an end to the wars between France and Spain, and cemented it by a marriage between Louis XIV and the Infanta. He had also in the past made alliances with Cromwell. A brilliant administrator, though more tortuous in his methods than Richelieu, M. was little regretted when he *d*. Yet he was a generous patron of the arts, and worked consistently if not selflessly for the growth of Fr. power and the consolidation of the central authority. His letters were collected and reprinted at Amsterdam in 2 vols. under the title of *Négociations secrètes des Pyrénées*, 1745. The Abbé Allainval afterwards arranged these letters in chronological order, and, together with 50 unpublished letters, brought them out under the title of *Lettres du Cardinal Mazarin, où l'on voit le secret de la négociation de la paix des Pyrénées*, Paris (2 vols.), 1745. *See* A. Hassall, *Mazarin*, 1903; *also* lives by K. Federn, 1922; H. Tribout, 1933.

Mazatlán, tn and port in the state of Sinloa, it is Mexico's biggest port on the Pacific coast and lies 138 m. SE. of the state cap. Culiacán by rail. It is a port of call by international shipping lines and handles a considerable export-import trade. Its industries include cotton textile spinning and weaving, and sugar refining. The climate is hot and rather humid with little seasonal variation, but the tn is popular as a tourist resort partly due to the beauty of the local coastline with its many off-shore is. Pop. 75,000.

Mazdaism, *see* ORMAZD; PARSEES; ZOROAS-TRIANISM.

Mazdak, leader of a religious reform movement during the reign of Qubad, king of Persia (488–531). The movement spread among the lower classes and assumed the characteristics of a social reform, which is alleged to have had communistic tendencies. Qubad was won over, but was deposed by a palace revolution (497) provoked by the Zoroastrian hierarchy. In 498 or 499 he regained his throne and returned to Zoroastrian orthodoxy. In 528 or 529 the Mazdakites rebelled, but were massacred. On the death of Qubad in 531 his son Ka'us attempted with Mazdakite support to overthrow his brother, Khusraw, who had been declared Qubad's successor. From then onwards the Mazdakites existed only as a secret sect. *See* A. Christensen, *L'Iran sous les Sassanides*, 1936.

Mazepa, Ivan Stepanovych (1645–1709), Ukrainian hetman (q.v.), in his youth a page at the court of John Casimir of Poland, later in the service of the hetmans in the Ukraine. He was elected hetman in 1687. He built many churches, and endeavoured to strengthen the position of the privileged upper stratum of the Cossacks

(q.v.), thus causing dissatisfaction among the peasant and Cossack masses. In 1705 he entered into negotiations with the Polish King Stanislaw Leszczynski, later with Charles XII of Sweden, with the aim of throwing off the sovereignty of the Russian tsar. However, Peter the Great had complete confidence in him and did not believe the information about his treasonable activities. When Charles XII invaded the Ukraine in 1708 M., supported by the Zaporozh'ye Cossacks (*see* SICH), openly joined him, but both were beaten in the battle of Poltava in 1709 and fled to Turkey, where M. *d*.

Mazer, Brit. drinking-bowl, generally of maple wood, with a deep silver rim and a silver boss or print in the interior. It was formerly much used into Tudor times.

Mazo, Juan Bautista Martinez del (1610–67), Sp. painter, *b*. (probably) Cuenca, was the pupil and also son-in-law of Velazquez. They worked together and M. acquired many characteristics of his father-in-law's style, succeeding him in 1660 as court painter.

Mazo de la Roche, *see* DE LA ROCHE.

Mazowsze (Masovia), name given to a dist of central Poland, which is crossed by the Vistula, and includes Warsaw and Plock. It was a duchy from 1138 to 1526, when it was incorporated with the Polish kingdom.

Mazurka, old Polish folk dance in moderate 3/4 time, originating in the prov. of Masovia (Mazowsze), and favoured by the Polish gentry of the later 18th cent. In Napoleon's time the Ulans (Huzzars) popularised the dance in the tns of Poland, especially in Warsaw, thus giving it its traditionally military style. Skilful dancers introduced improvised steps of great variety, the basic step being a smooth run, with an accent on the second beat, corresponding with the music. It became fashionable in society throughout Europe, and was sometimes introduced into other dances of the period—as the polka M., the waltz M., or in the form of a quadrille. Chopin's piano works include 51 M.s. *See* POLAND, *Music*.

Mazzard, or **Gean** (*Prunus avium*), species of cherry tree, which is found throughout Britain, but is probably native only in the S. It reaches a height of over 50 ft, with a trunk 7 ft in girth and a spreading, loosely branched crown. The bark is a dull red, peeling in broad rings and marked with transverse stripes. It has long oval leaves, sharply toothed and somewhat drooping. Its large white flowers are borne in clusters. The fruits are dark red, with juice which stains. The M. is one of the parents of cultivated cherries. It also yields a fine timber, which has some resemblance to mahogany when polished and stained, and is used in cabinet-making, and also for pipes. *See* CHERRY.

Mazzini, Giuseppe (1805–72), It. patriot and republican, *b*. Genoa. He studied at Genoa univ. and became a lawyer. About 1830 M. joined the secret society of the Carbonari (q.v.) and 6 months later was betrayed and banished from Italy. The organisation of a new Liberal league, 'Young Italy', was M.'s next work while staying at Marseilles. The first fruits of Young Italy was the revolutionary expedition of Savoy, organised by M. at Geneva, but which was defeated by the royal troops. Sentence of death, *per contumace*, was recorded against M. in the Sardinian courts for his participation in the affair, but he soon recommenced his revolutionary operations from Switzerland.

In 1837 M. left Switzerland for London working unceasingly for the cause of It. unity in a complete and republican form. The determined opponent of partial union and monarchical leadership at Milan, M. retired to Switzerland on the capitulation of Milan to the Austrians, to reappear in Florence on the rising of Tuscany, and finally at Rome, where he was elected triumvir of the Rom. rep., 1849. But the rep. was suppressed, and M. fled to Switzerland. He subsequently returned to London, and at his instigation unsuccessful risings in Milan (1853) and in Piedmont (1857) were attempted. The Sicilian expedition of 1860 owed much to the inspiration of M. But he was a bitter opponent of the new It. monarchy, and continued to plot against it. This led to his arrest in 1870. He was subsequently released, but refused the king's offer of an amnesty and *d.* at Pisa, which he was visiting under an assumed name.

M.'s contribution to the unification of Italy was, in its early stages, of great value. He unified and vitalised the struggling aspirations of the Italians by his idealism. But his solution, a rep., to be achieved without any foreign help, was not in accordance with political realities, and the practical future lay with the Piedmontese monarchy and its greatest statesman, Cavour (q.v.).

His best work is *Il Dovere dell' Uomo*, 1858 (*The Duties of Man*, trans. 1862). See his *Letters*, trans. into English and ed. by Bolton King, 1929, and *Select Writings*, ed. by N. Ganguloo, 1945 See also lives by Bolton King, 1902; A. Reedman, 1922; I. Silone, 1948. (*See Plate: Italy.*)

Mazzoth, unleavened bread, see AZYMES.

Mazzoth, religious festival, see PASSOVER.

Mazzuchelli, Giovanni Maria (1707–68), It. man of letters. His ambitious dictionary of It. literature entitled *Scrittori d'Italia*, 1753–63, did not advance beyond the letter B, though the MS. of much of the rest remains.

Mbabane, tn and administrative H.Q. of Swaziland. Tin-mining is carried on in the vicinity, and iron ore exists in quantity. White pop. 2350 (1960). (*See Plate: Swaziland.*)

Mdina, tn of Malta, adjoining Rabat, 6 m, W. of Valletta. It dates from Rom. times and was the cap. of the is. until superseded by Valletta in 1570. The cathedral of St Paul was founded by the Normans in the 12th cent.; it was rebuilt in baroque style after being ruined in an earthquake in 1693. There is a Carmelite church of the 16th–17th cents., and sev. other churches of the same period. Perhaps the most important monuments of the tn are the numerous palaces, small stone buildings with their first floors lit by 2-light windows of early-Gothic form, dating from the end of the 15th cent. Pop. 1500.

Mead, Richard (1673–1754), physician, *b.* Stepney, London, and educ. at Utrecht, Leyden, and Padua, was appointed medical adviser to George II (1727). He held the post of physician at St Thomas's Hospital, London, from 1703 to 1722. He wrote numerous treatises, including *Mechanical Account of Poisons*, 1702, an account of snake venoms, and advocated quarantine and disinfection for plague, and inoculation for smallpox.

Mead, fermented liquor made by dissolving honey at the rate of 4 lb. to a gallon of water and boiling it with spices. On cooling 1 oz. of brewer's yeast per gallon is added, and after standing for about 8 hrs it is poured into a barrel to ferment. When fermentation ceases a small quantity of isinglass is added to clear the liquid. After bottling it is stored for 6 months or more, when it is ready for use as a dry table wine. A liquor licence for its sale is necessary. Sack M. and sack metheglin are varieties of M.

Meade, Elizabeth, *see* CHILDREN'S BOOKS.

Meade, George Gordon (1815–72), Amer. general. He first won distinction in the Mexican war, and fought in the civil war as brigadier-general of volunteers. Lincoln placed M. in chief command of the Army of the Potomac in place of Hooker. In July 1863 he defeated the Confederates under Lee at Gettysburg, though his own casualties were great. When Grant was made commander-in-chief of the Union armies he retained M. as his right-hand man in all the subsequent campaigns in Virginia.

Meadow Grass, genus *Poa*, and specially *P. Trivialis* and *P. pratensis*; hay and pasture grasses, with flat pale-green leaves and pyramidal panicles of flowers. *P. nemoralis* is the wood M. G.

Meadow Rue (*Thalictrum flavum*), perennial herb, family Ranunculaceae, with a creeping root-stock and tall furrowed stems. It has small yellow flowers clustered in a pyramid. See RUE.

Meadow Saffron, *see* COLCHICUM.

Meadow Sweet, or **Queen-of-the-Meadows** (*Filipendula ulmaria*), tall plant (family Rosaceae), with compound cymes of fragrant, creamy-white flowers and pinnate leaves. It is common in wet places.

Meagher, Thomas Francis (1823–67), Irish politician, *b.* Waterford. He joined the Young Ireland (q.v.) party, and in 1848 was condemned to death for his revolutionary propaganda. The sentence was commuted to transportation to Van Diemen's Land. From here he escaped (1852) to America, where, on the outbreak of civil war (1861), he organised the Irish brigade for the Federals, and was for a time governor of Montana.

Meal Tub Plot, fictitious plot invented by Thomas Dangerfield (q.v.) in 1679. Originally described as a Presbyterian conspiracy, Dangerfield later claimed that it was a popish plot. The plot took its name from a meal-tub in the house of a Mrs Cellier, a servant of the Countess of Powys, where Dangerfield alleged that incriminating documents were hidden. Mrs Cellier and

Lady Powys were subsequently tried but acquitted.

Meal-worm, larva of a common beetle (*Tenebrio molitor*), frequenting mills, granaries and bakehouses. It is thin and round, about 1 in. long, and tawny in colour, with bright rusty bands. The beetle is $\frac{1}{2}$ in. long, with stout legs and 11-jointed antennae, and black and red in colour.

Meall a' Bhùiridh (3636 ft), mt of Argyll, Scotland, summit of the Clachlet range in the Blackmount group, 3 m. S. of Kingshouse, and prin. Scottish ski centre, equipped with a modern ski-tow.

Mealy Bug, homopterous insect, which does considerable harm to plants in greenhouses by sucking the sap and by choking the pores of the leaves. The insects are minute and red in colour, but a covering of white mealy powder disguises them. The males have wings, but the females are wingless. The pest is destroyed, with difficulty, by spraying with insecticide; fumigation with tobacco smoke or cyanide of potassium is more effective. *Pseudococcus citri* is a serious pest of orange trees in the S. states of America.

Mean: 1., in philosophy, a term used in Aristotelian ethics. According to Aristotle, virtue consists in finding the M. (*to meson* or *mesotēs*) between every pair of extremes, because all desire tends to excess. *See* Aristotle, *Nicomachean Ethics*, books i–iii, and Sir W. D. Ross, *Aristotle*, 1923.

2., in mathematics. The arithmetic M. is the middle term of 3 quantities in arithmetic progression, but the word is extended to the average value of any number of quantities whether they are in arithmetic progression or not (*see* AVERAGE). The most common M.s are the arithmetic M., the geometric M. and the harmonic M. The geometric M. of 2 quantities is the square root of their product, and of any number n of values it is the nth root of the product of the values. The harmonic M. between 2 numbers is obtained by finding the arithmetic M. between their reciprocals and then taking the reciprocal of the result. Thus, if we require the harmonic M. between 4 and 6, the arithmetic M. between $\frac{1}{4}$ and $\frac{1}{6}$, that is, $\frac{5}{24}$, is determined, and the harmonic M. is $\frac{24}{5}$. *See* ARITHMETIC; AVERAGE; GEOMETRIC and HARMONICAL PROGRESSION.

Mean Sea Level. There is no absolute invariable figure which indicates M. S. L. as the sea level varies from place to place, owing to the gravitational attraction of the land. In the Brit. Isles a local datum for M. S. L. has been obtained by computing data obtained on the sea level at Newlyn in Cornwall by hourly measurements over a period of 6 years. The new datum is shown on maps pub. since 1929. Previously a datum at Liverpool was used.

Meander, *see* MAEANDER.

Meander, geographical and geological term applied to the loop in the course of a riv. flowing along a winding path across a very gently falling terrain. Name derived from the R. Maeander (q.v.) of the ancients. M.s form on gently inclined reaches of rivs., particularly when the underlying rocks are soft and easily eroded. For this reason many M.s are carved out of flood plain deposits. A M. forms when a bend in a riv. becomes progressively accentuated by erosion along the outer bank coupled with deposition along the inner bank. The loop formed in this way may ultimately be bypassed by the stream, if it cuts through the peninsula developed at the inner side of the bend. In this way a cut-off M. or ox-bow lake may develop.

Means Test, in connection with applications for transitional unemployment benefit, connotes the statutory test of the applicant's means in order to arrive at the amount of assistance for which he is eligible. It was introduced in 1931. In 1932 the Labour party complained bitterly of the retention of the M. T., but the gov. retained the test in principle, though in its Bill of 1933 it proposed that the test of need should be the income of the household. This proposal found expression in the regulations made under the Unemployment Assistance Act, 1934, which provided that the amount of allowance granted should be determined by reference to the applicant's needs, and for this purpose the resources of all members of his household are required to be known. The M. T. was replaced by the provisions of the National Insurance Act (1946) (q.v.). Aid under the present organisation of the Welfare State (q.v.) is for the most part allocated on a universal basis with services being provided 'free' (i.e. from tax revenue) by the state to all comers. Such a system avoids a M. T. and has other advantages in lack of discrimination. A serious criticism is that aid is not directed at those in most need of help since it is given to all. *See* B. Abel-Smith, *Freedom in the Welfare State*, 1964; R. Harris and A. Seldon, *Choice in Welfare*, 1965.

Meare, vil. of Somerset, England, $3\frac{1}{2}$ m. NW. of Glastonbury. Here are the remains of an Iron Age lake vil.; also the 14th cent. Fish House and Manor of the abbots of Glastonbury. Pop. 910.

Mearns, The, *see* KINCARDINESHIRE.

Measham, par. and vil. of Leics, England, 4 m. SW. of Ashby-de-la-Zouch. Red bricks and terra-cotta are manuf., and there are coal-mines in the vicinity. Pop. 2729.

Measles, acute infectious disease, characterised by reddish eruptions on the body and catarrh of the mucous membranes of the air passages, conjunctiva, etc. It is due to a virus. It is one of the commonest infectious diseases in England, occurring in scattered cases at all times, and in rapidly spreading periodic epidemics occurring most often in the early spring and continuing into early summer. It attacks children for the most part, and is usually disseminated by the congregation of children in school. The rate of mortality is low, but there are certain dangers arising from possible complications which render it desirable to prevent the frequent epidemics. An attack of true M. (*Rubeola* or *Morbilli*) confers immunity from subsequent attacks to the end of life. The early symptoms are so indefinite that contagion often spreads before the disease is recognised. After from 7 to 14 days' incubation, catarrh of the mucous membranes sets in. The eyes become red and watery, there is a watery discharge from the nose, a dry cough, sore throat, thirst, restlessness, and a high temp. After 3 or 4 days small dark-red spots appear on the face and neck, and the face becomes swollen; they are sometimes preceded by a rash inside the mouth ('Koplik's Spots'). The eruption extends downwards until the whole body is involved. The rash fades away in the same order as it attacked the body. The red spots become yellowish, and the skin crumbles off in a powder resembling bran. The duration of the eruption from first to last is about a week, and during that time the febrile conditions increase until the temp. is about 104° or 105° F. (40–40·6° C). At the height of the eruption the temp. usually falls, and convalescence proceeds rapidly. Infants under 6 months of age have a degree of inherited immunity to M. and rarely contract it. Those under 1 year of age have the disease only mildly. Children of from 2 to 4 years of age are apt to have severe forms of attack. Pneumonia, bronchitis and otitis media (q.v.), due to secondary infection with bacteria other than the M. virus, are the commonest complications. Chronic tonsil sepsis is a frequent sequela. Chemotherapy is ineffectual against the virus of M. but is effective against secondary infections. Passive immunity may be given, however, by the injection of serum from a person who has had M., and therefore containing appropriate antibodies. The immunity conferred by this method is short-lived and it is not a suitable method for general use. It is nevertheless a valuable way of protecting those children in contact with the infection who, because of their age or from reasons of poor health, might be expected to develop the complaint in a severe form. Convalescent serum, as it is called, is usually given therefore only to children suffering from some other illness, and to whom the added strain of an attack of M. might be serious, and to children between the ages of 2 and 4 years. In 1961 the first trials were made of a measles vaccine prepared by Enders in America. It was shown to be capable of conferring active immunity, and it has since been developed as an effective prophylactic. But M. vaccine is apt to cause a sharp reaction, and until this has been obviated, and a vaccine found which will give a higher degree of immunity than existing vaccines, it is likely that immunisation against M. will not become a universal procedure. *German measles* (*Rubella* or *Roseola*), infectious disease similar to M. but in a milder form. The rash is finer, paler and fades rapidly; there is little fever and few symptoms. Enlargement of the lymphatic glands of the neck is invariably present and is a valuable diagnostic sign. Adults suffering from Ger. M. sometimes develop a mild arthritis of the smaller joints which, although fleeting, may be painful. One attack of Ger. M. does not always grant permanent immunity. Temporary immunity may be conferred by the injection of gamma globulin, but as the disease is so mild this is a procedure which is seldom worth while considering except in women in the early stages of pregnancy who have been in contact with a case of Ger. M., and therefore likely to develop an attack themselves. There is evidence that if a woman suffers from Ger. M. during the first 4 months of pregnancy the foetus may suffer some arrest of development and be *b*. with a congenital defect. Because of this risk women should avoid contact with the disease in the early months of their pregnancy. The causative virus of Ger. M. was isolated in 1962.

Measures, *see* METROLOGY.

Meat, flesh from different animals which has been slaughtered for human consumption. With the widespread use of freezing, it has been possible for the large M. producing countries of the world to supply sufficient high grade carcases to satisfy the needs of those countries whose production of M. is inadequate to meet their requirements, and out of season demands. In general, the cuts from the forequarter are cheaper than those from the hind-quarter. There is more of the tougher connective tissue built up here, and long slow cooking in liquid is required to break down and tenderise these cuts, but this, combined with the slightly higher proportion of fat attached to them, results in an excellent flavour. The hind-quarter cuts which contain little fat and gristle are suitable for dry heat methods of cookery—roasting, grilling and frying.

Beef. Good quality beef is firm to the touch, and well finished with a layer of cream to yellow coloured fat on the outside. The lean M. should be marbled throughout with small flecks of fat, which melt during the cooking to baste the M. continually, thus ensuring moistness and tenderness. It should be bright red in colour, with a slight sheen on the surface; A very dark colour and dry appearance will usually indicate that it is not from a top quality animal, or that it has been cut and exposed to the air for some time.

Lamb is now available all the year round. Australian lamb reaches the Brit. market just before Christmas, the New Zealand lamb is on sale from mid-Jan. and home produced lamb from Easter or shortly afterwards. A well finished carcase should carry a reasonable proportion of fat to lean. This fat should be white or pale cream in colour. The M. from a young animal will be pale pink. Mutton is much darker, is little in demand these days and is generally available only in country dists.

Pork is fresh or unprocessed pig M. The size of a carcase used as fresh pork varies in different areas, heavier carcases being more common in the N. The lean, which contains more intramuscular fat and is more tender than some beef or mutton, is light pink in young animals and a deeper rose colour in older and heavier animals. Cuts and joints from a pork carcase may be cooked in a number of ways, the large pieces being normally roasted and the smaller cuts, such as chops, grilled or fried. Pork from heavy pigs and sows is processed to produce an infinite variety of manuf. products, such as fresh, cured or smoked sausage, pies, etc.

Veal is the M. from young calves. It is expensive and not widely available, the majority being imported from the Netherlands. Because of the early age of slaughtering, there is little development of natural fat, and therefore the M. tends to be flavourless, but is very tender. The flesh should be soft, moist and pink and any fat should be firm. Due to immaturity, the bones are soft, containing a large proportion of gelatinous tissue. When boiled, these bones make excellent jellied stock. Veal does not keep well, and should be cooked immediately.

Venison is a game M. from deer. Unless the carcase is well hung, and the M. cooked carefully, it may tend to be rather tough and dry. It is advisable to marinade the M. in a mixture of oil and wine, well seasoned with herbs, to offset this tendency. It is usually available from the larger food stores.

See Natalie R. Fitch and Charlotte A. Francis, *Foods and Principles of Cookery*, U.S.A., 1948; Good Housekeeping pubs. *The Roast Joint*.

Meath, maritime co. in the prov. of Leinster, Rep. of Ireland, bounded E. by the Irish Sea, S. by Kildare, N. by Monaghan, SW. by Offaly, NW. by Cavan, W. by Westmeath.

The surface is mainly flat, rising towards the W., and the coast is low and sandy. The chief riv. is the Boyne, into which flows the Blackwater. Agriculture flourishes, oats being the prin. grain crop; cattle and sheep are reared in considerable numbers. There are some woollen manufs., and linen is woven by handlooms. There are some fine old ruins at Duleek, Bective Abbey (q.v.), and Clonard, and a castle at Trim, the co. tn. Tara, the supposed site of the old Irish cap., with its palace, and St Columban's (q.v.) College, are in the co. Three members are returned to the Dail by M. Area 904 sq. m.; pop. 65,122.

Meaux, Fr. tn in the dept of Seine-et-Marne, on the Marne. There is a 13th–14th cent. cathedral. Bossuet (q.v.) was bishop of M. The tn has metal and chemical manufs. Pop. 22,300. *See also* BRIE.

Mecca (*Umm al-qura,* mother of cities), now the cap. of Hejaz, Saudi Arabia; it has always been the religious centre of Islam because the Kaaba (q.v.) is the house of God and every believer should make the pilgrimage (*see* HADJ) at least once in his lifetime. No unbeliever may enter M. or fly over it. It is about 50 m. E. of Jiddah in a narrow valley surrounded by barren hills with no agriculture near. The only water supply is from the well Zemzem in the mosque, and sev. persons at various times have acquired merit by bringing water in conduits from a distance. Before the advent of Islam, M. owed its importance to its being a stage on the N.–S. trade route and, in addition, a sanctuary; it was a place of pilgrimage for neighbouring tribes and sev. markets were held near by during an ann. 'truce of God'. Mohammad was *b.* there and one suspects that he made the pilgrimage a part of

Islam to ensure to M. the profits of this religious-cum-trade festival and so reconcile the inhab. to the new faith. The mosque is unique, being an open space, about 530 ft by 350 ft, round the Kaaba. This court is surrounded by arcades and a few small buildings stand in it. There are 7 minarets and a host of officials and servants. In the 18th cent. the servants were eunuchs. The door-keepers of the Kaaba are the descendants of those who held that office before the birth of Mohammad. As the mosque stands in the middle of the valley it is occasionally flooded. The inhab. of M. make money by letting accommodation to the pilgrims, acting as guides through the ceremonies and as agents in any capacity. Many have agents in other lands who secure clients for them. Pop. 200,000 or more. M. is the seat of the Consultative Legislative Assembly, since Islamic religious law is the common law throughout Saudi Arabia. *See* A. Wavell, *A Modern Pilgrim in Mecca*, 1912; E. Rutter, *The Holy Cities of Arabia*, 1928; E. Esin, *Mecca the Blessed, Madinah the Radiant*, 1963. (*See Plate: Arabia*.)

Mecca Stones, *see* MOCHA STONES.

Mechanical Accounting, *see* ACCOUNTING MACHINES; CALCULATING MACHINES; COMPUTER, ELECTRIC.

Mechanical Engineering, *see* ENGINEERING.

Mechanical Handling, *see* CONVEYORS.

Mechanics, science which considers the laws involved when bodies are acted on by forces. M. is arbitrarily subdivided into statics (including hydrostatics) and dynamics (including aerodynamics and hydrodynamics) (qq.v.), the former branch treating of forces in equilibrium, and the latter dealing with forces acting so as to produce motion. Not only does M. deal with the direct action of forces on bodies, but it also studies the nature and action of forces when they act on bodies by the agency of machinery. This gives the origin of the word M., and as a matter of fact M. was in its early stages the science of making machines. A machine in M. means any contrivance in which a force applied at one point is made to raise a weight or overcome a resisting force acting at another point. All machines can be resolved into 3 primary machines, viz. the lever, inclined plane and pulley; and 3 secondary, derived from these, viz. the wheel and axle, the wedge and the screw, for the properties of each of which see the articles dealing with them. These 6 machines are sometimes known as the mechanical powers. M. is of the utmost importance in structural engineering and is essentially an experimental science; all its laws are based on intuitive deductions from experimental observations. This is true, for example, of the 3 great laws of M. enunciated by Newton. M. has its origin in the mechanical powers that were employed long before any formal principles governing their action were discovered. Archimedes (q.v.), by his investigations of the principle of the lever and the property of the centre of gravity, estab. M. as a science. After Archimedes little progress was made until the time of Stevinus (1548–1620), who investigated the principle of the inclined plane. The golden age of M. began when Galileo (q.v.) made his first systematic inquiries into problems of motion. Aristotle had taught that the speed with which a body falls is directly proportional to its weight, but Galileo proved this to be false, and subsequently deduced the solution to the problems of falling bodies, re-examining the previous knowledge of M. Newton (q.v.) took up the subject after Galileo, and his contributions to it were so great that his 3 laws remain the fundamental laws of non-relativistic M. today (see RELATIVITY). His theory of universal gravitation enabled him to account for the motions of the members of the solar system as well as the motion of bodies on the earth. Lagrange and Laplace developed the subject in the 18th cent.

The formulation of the theory of relativity by Einstein has led to a complete revision of the fundamentals of M. When the bodies considered in a problem in M. have velocities (relative to a frame which is moving with a uniform or zero velocity with respect to the fixed stars) which are small compared with that of light, the old Newtonian or non-relativistic M. still holds. But for larger velocities important differences are predicted by relativity theory, and many have been confirmed by experiments.

See E. Mach, *Science of Mechanics*, 1902; H. Lamb, *Dynamics*, 1926, and *Statics*, 1928; A. S. Ramsey, *Dynamics* Part 1, 1933, Part 2, 1944; E. T. Whitaker, *A Treatise on the Analytical Dynamics of Particles and Rigid Bodies*, 1937; D. E. Rutherford, *Classical Mechanics*, 1951; S. L. Loney, *Elements of Statics and Dynamics*, Parts 1 and 2, 1953.

See also DYNAMICS; ENERGY; FORCE; HYDRODYNAMICS; HYDROSTATICS; KINEMATICS; KINETICS; RELATIVITY; STATICS; WAVE MECHANICS.

Mechanicsville, Battle of, 26 June, 1862, start of the 'Seven Days' Battle' of the Amer. Civil War, sometimes known as the battle of Beaver Dam Creek.

Mechanisation, see AUTOMATION.

Mechanisation and Motorisation, Military. These terms are often used synonymously, but properly speaking mechanisation means the employment of arms which depend for their functioning entirely on mechanical means (e.g. tanks, some forms of engineer equipment and A.-A. gear), whereas motorisation means the transport and supply by motor vehicles of men, arms and equipment which are also capable of being moved and maintained by other means.

Both are costly processes, and the mechanisation of the forces of a great power depends closely upon the peacetime industrial development (especially metallurgical) of that power. Motorisation again depends on the size and efficiency of its automobile industry. No power could afford to purchase the whole, or even a considerable part, of its mechanised and motorised equipment from abroad. Thus, though lacking specialised equipment such as tanks and anti-tank guns in 1939, the Brit. Army was at that time completely motorised, though the home forces were equipped largely with impressed civilian vehicles, while even at the height of its efficiency the first-line transport of the bulk of the Ger. armies depended on horse traction, in spite of the fact that the Ger. motor industry had been coerced in the years immediately before the war into adopting a standardised programme of production of vehicles (such as the *Volkswagen*) which could be immediately adapted to military use: the strategic moves of the Ger. Army, from the Russian to the W. front, were carried out by rail. By 1945 the 2 powers most conspicuous for mass production and mass employment of tanks were precisely those whose peacetime industries had the highest output of heavy agric. tractors: the U.S.A. and the U.S.S.R. Tanks and motorised troops played a relatively small part in the great successes of the Jap. Army, who fought their war in a style consistent with an economy whose forte was light industry and shipping. The armies of Poland, Hungary and the Balkan states hardly knew mechanisation or motorisation up to 1939.

The experience gained by the Brit. Army in the campaigns of the First World War waged in defence of the Suez Canal and the constant preoccupation of the imperial general staff with the security of the Middle E., would alone have been sufficient to account for the almost complete elimination of cavalry, horse artillery and animal transport from the Brit. Army before 1938. See ARMOURED CARS; ARTILLERY; ENGINEERING, MILITARY; INFANTRY; TANKS; TRANSPORT, MILITARY; MILITARY VEHICLES.

Mechelen (Fr. Malines), city in Belgium, 14 m. S. of Antwerp, on the R. Dyle. It is the see of an archbishop, primate of Belgium. The cathedral of St Rombaut contains a fine altar-piece by Van Dyck, and has an unfinished steeple of 318 ft with a famous chime of 45 bells. Some of the other churches in M. contain pictures by Rubens. Of these the finest is 'The Adoration of the Magi' in the church of St John. The Cloth Hall was built in 1320, and the old palace of the Grand Council of the Netherlands in 1374. M. was formerly known for its lace manufs. At present there are very important furniture manufs. M. also produces textiles, tapestry and tinned vegetables, and has a large workshop of the Belgian Railway Co. The surrounding dist is famous for the cultivation of early vegetables of which M. is an international market. Pop. 64,800.

Mechitarists, Rom. Catholic religious order professing the Benedictine rule, founded by the Armenian monk Mechitar (1676–1749). Originally a monk of an Orthodox monastery near Sebaste in Lesser Armenia, Mechitar developed as a young man a great enthusiasm for W. culture and a desire to introduce it among his fellow-countrymen. With this end in view, having been ordained priest of the Orthodox Church in 1699, he came to Constantinople and began to advocate reunion with Rome. To escape persecution for this unpopular cause, he withdrew to Venetian ter. at Modon, where he built in 1701 a church and monastery, and thus laid the foundation of the Mechitarist order, which received papal approval in 1712. Subsequently he settled his community at Venice on the is. of San Lazzaro, and this settlement still remains the mother-house of the order. Other houses are to be found at Vienna, Paris and Padua, and in Persia and Turkey. The monks work as missionaries, scholars and educationists. They are printers of Armenian books, and aim at the spread of Rom. Catholic culture and religion among their fellow-countrymen. Their activities have led to a marked revival of Armenian studies throughout the learned world.

Mechlin Lace, *see* LACE.

Mechnikov, Iliya, *see* METCHNIKOV.

Meckenen, Mekenen, or **Mecheln, Israel von** (*d.* 1503), engraver and goldsmith, is usually identified with the Ger. painter, Meister Israel, 18 of whose works hang in the Pinakothek of Munich. They are religious in subject, and belong clearly to the school of Van Eyck.

Mecklenburg, former (1934–45) state of NE. Germany, consisting of the anct Grand Duchies of M.-Schwerin (area 5080 sq. m.; capital Schwerin, and M.-Strelitz (area 1130 sq. m.; cap. a Neustrelitz). Since 1952 it has been divided into the administrative dists (*Bezirke*) of Schwerin, Rostock and Neubrandenburg in the Ger. Democratic Rep. (E. Germany). M. was bounded on the N. by the Baltic Sea, on the E. by Pomerania, on the S. by Lower Saxony and on the W. by Schleswig-Holstein. The country is low-lying, has numerous lakes, and is mainly agric. The inhab. of M. were Slavonic by origin. In 1701 the ter. was divided between 2 branches of the ruling house, and between 1815 and 1907 these 2 Grand Duchies were practically absolute monarchies; a form of constitutional gov. was then granted.

Meconopsis, genus of herbaceous plants, family Papaveraceae, about 45 species; *M. cambrica* is found wild in Britain; other species are largely Asian.

Medallions, large medals struck for a particular occasion. In architecture round or oval panels and tablets, often decorated with designs of figures in relief, are called M., from their shape. *See* MEDALS.

Medals. Numismatists have usually given the name of medal or medallion to those coin-like pieces that have been struck or cast for particular purposes commemorating victories, treaties, coronations and other important events, or in honour of remarkable persons, in contradistinction to coins, which have been issued for circulation as money. The art of engraving dies is of very anct origin (*see* NUMISMATICS). In some parts of the Gk world, especially in Sicily, coins struck for currency sometimes bore what may be called commemorative types, and so served one of the purposes of M., but true M. or medallions are rare; the only examples known before the Hellenistic age come from Syracuse, Acragas and Athens, the 2 latter being represented by 1 issue each. The later Syracusan series was associated with games, a

usage which recurs in Egypt under the Ptolemies. Under the Rom. Empire the art of the medallion reached a high degree of skill and beauty of imperial portraiture. These large pieces, of bronze, silver, or sometimes gold, were produced at the order of successive emperors for distribution on special occasions to friends, court officials, army officers and foreign rulers and envoys: many of them were provided with a loop for suspension.

In the early medieval period the It. term *medaglia*, first applied to large bronze Rom. coins or medallions, finally came to denote any subsequently made piece of similar bold size and elaborately finished style; and the It. Renaissance saw medallic art nobly developed by Pisano ('Pisanello') (*c.* 1390–1455) and Matteo de' Pasti, his younger contemporary, from both of whom the great It. school derived. One of the earliest pieces is a gold medal of the Council of Florence (1439). Papal M. begin with Paul II (1464); those of earlier Popes were issued by their successors. A second school of medallists began in Germany in 1453, and Ger. M. came to display much originality and strength in treatment, though they were inferior to the It. in not observing the limitations imposed upon the art by a circular shape. Sicilian M. appear as early as 1501, Sp. in 1503, and Dan. in 1516. Early Dutch M. (after 1566) are notable for their elaborate engravings of views, maps and plans. Fr. M., which began in 1451 and developed under Dupré (1576–1643) and Warin (1600–72), were remarkably transformed by the reign of Louis XIV (1643–1715), the events of which were mirrored in a long and splendid series of realistic design. The medallic hist. of the Napoleonic period is comparatively undistinguished through its addiction (with the *littérateurs*) to a false classicism. The series of Eng. M. is one of the most perfect, though more notable for its representations of contemporary events than for its artistic quality. The earliest example is a gold medal of Henry VIII. (Supremacy of the Church, 1545.) Edward VI's reign supplies the first of a long series of coronation M. Among the best-known die-engravers of Eng. M. are the Frenchmen Briot, active under Charles I; Thomas Simon, his near-contemporary and successor; the Italian Benedetto Pistrucci, designer of the Waterloo medallion; and later in the 19th cent. Wm Wyon, R.A. There are signs that in many countries the art of the medal is again claiming a place above that to which it sank in the late 19th cent. The work of Theodore Spicer-Simson between 1910 and 1930 attained a fine distinction. Since the invention of the 'reducing machine' the medal has come to belong to the sculptor rather than the die-engraver. But even in this new form the art is still alive. The striking of M. for the learned societies and (since 1849) for the services forms one of the regular functions of the Royal Mint in London. *See* L. Forrer, *Biographical Dictionary of Medallists,* 1904–30; G. F. Hill, *A Guide to the Exhibition of Historical Medals in the British Museum,* 1924, and *A Corpus of the*

Italian Renaissance Medals, 1930; J. Babelon, *La Médaille et les médailleurs*, 1927; H. Taprell Dorling, *Ribbons and Medals*, 1947.

MEDAL STRUCK TO COMMEMORATE THE APPOINT-
MENT OF JAMES (THE FUTURE JAMES II) AS ADMIRAL
OF THE FLEET

Medals, First and Second World Wars, (British), *see* DECORATIONS FOR WAR SERVICE; DEFENCE MEDAL; STARS, MILITARY; VICTORIA CROSS; VICTORY MEDAL; WAR MEDAL, BRITISH. *See also* Capt. H. Taprell Dorling, *Ribbons and Medals—Naval, Military, Air Force and Civil,* 1956.

Medan, tn of N. Sumatra, Indonesia, situated about 10 m. from the W. coast on the R. Deli. It is a trade centre for forestry and an agric. area, and has a tobacco research station. The port of Belawan is 15 m. N. Pop. 479,000.

Medawar, Peter Brian (1915–), Brit. biologist, *b.* Brazil and educ. at Marlborough and Oxford Univ. He was prof. of zoology, Univ. of Birmingham, 1947–51, and Jodrell prof. of zoology and comparative anatomy, Univ. College, London, 1951–61. He became Director of the National Institute for Medical Research (M.R.C.) in 1962. F.R.S. 1949 (Croonian lecturer, 1958; Royal Medal, 1959); Reith Lecturer, 1959. M. has pub. scientific papers on growth, ageing, immunity and cellular transformations. He shared a Nobel prize with Sir Frank Macfarlane Burnet (q.v.) in 1960 for work on acquired immunological tolerance. C.B.E. 1958.

Medea, *see* JASON AND MEDEA.

Medea (anct **Lamida**), tn of Algeria, situated 40 m. SW. of Algiers. M. lies 3000 ft above sea level, and produces fine grapes and orchard fruits. Pop. 7638.

Medellín, cap. of the dept of Antioquia, central Colombia, and third largest city of the country. After Bogota, the cap., it is the leading industrial city of the country. Textile manuf. is the leading industry and M. produces about ¾ of Colombia's total textile production. Other important industries include cement, steel, glass, pottery, chocolate and tobacco. M. is the prin. Colombian centre for coffee production and mining, particularly gold and silver. Its altitude

is 5046 ft and despite being surrounded by high mts has good road and rail links with the rest of the country. A railway and road run to the port of Buenaventura on the Pacific; a road to the port of Cartegena on the Caribbean; and a railway to the River Magdalena with its river traffic. There are 4 universities. The population is 775,000.

Medes, or **Medians,** *see* MEDIA.

Medford: 1. City and residential suburb of Massachusetts, U.S.A., in Middlesex co., situated on the Mystic R. and lakes, 5 m. NNW. of Boston. The manufs. include woollen goods, food products, machinery, chemicals, paper boxes, beds, soap, floor polish; printing is carried on. Pop. 64,970.

2. City of Oregon, U.S.A., cap. of Jackson co., 4 m. NE. of Jacksonville. It is a resort and a trade and shipping centre for a fruit-, dairy- and truck-farming area; it has fruit-canning and lumber-milling and is a U.S. Air Force base. Pop. 26,530.

Media, in anct times, name of the NW. part of Iran, corresponding to the present provs. of Azerbaijan, Ghilan, Mazanderan, Irak-Ajemi and the E. portion of Kurdistan. The Medians were in language, religion and manners very closely allied to the Persians. After they had shaken off the yoke of the Assyrians, their tribes, according to the common account, united about 708 BC, chose Deioces (Kai-Kobad) for their chief, and made Ecbatana their cap. His son, Phraortes, or Arphaxad, subdued the Persians. Cyaxares (Kai-Kaous), the son of Phraortes, in alliance with Nabopolassar, King of Babylon, overthrew the Assyrian cap. in 612 BC, and vanquished the brigand hordes of Scythia. He was succeeded by his son Astyages (Asdchak), who was deposed (560 BC) by his own grandson, Cyrus (Kai-Khûsru), King of Persia, and from this time the 2 nations are spoken of as one people. Ecbatana, the cap. of M., became the summer residence of the Persian kings. With the overthrow of the Persians by Alexander the Great after the battle of Arbela (331 BC) M. became part of Alexander's realm. After his death (323 BC) the NW. portion (*Atropatene*) of M. became a separate kingdom, and existed till the time of Augustus, the other portion, under the name of Great M., forming a part of the Syrian monarchy. M. was on sev. occasions separated from Persia. In 152 BC Mithridates I took Great M. from the Syrians and annexed it to the Parthian empire, and *c.* 36 BC it had a king of its own, named Artavasdes, against whom Mark Antony made war. Under the Sassanian dynasty the whole of M. was united to Persia. It became, during the 14th and 15th cents., the stronghold of Turkoman tribes. In early times the Medes were a warlike race, and distinguished for their skill with the bow. They were also celebrated for their horsemanship, and it was from them that the Persians adopted this and other favourite exercises. *See* J. von Prášek, *Geschichte der Meder und Perser*, 1906–10; H. H. Rowley, *Darius the Median*, 1935; G. G. Cameron, *History of Early Iran*, 1936.

Medial Section, see EXTREME AND MEAN RATIO.

Medias (Hungarian **Medgyes**), Saxon tn of Rumania in Transylvania, situated on the Tîrnava Mare, 25 m. NNE. of Sibiu. Pop. 38,400.

Mediation, Act of, Swiss constitution, the work of Napoleon, was drawn up in 1803, and was abolished, 1813. There were to be 19 cantons; the Diet was to meet in turn at the 6 large tns, and France was to guarantee Swiss neutrality.

Mediatisation (German *Mediatisterung*) is derived from Lat. *mediatus*, middle, and was coined to describe the process by which the title of certain Ger. princes was subordinated to that of other sovereigns, instead of being held directly from the emperor. Many minor houses were mediatised in 1806, and again in 1815 at the Congress of Vienna.

Medicago, genus of ann. or perennial herbs, family Leguminosae, about 50 species; of which *M. sativa* is Alfalfa or Lucerne, grown for fodder; *M. arborea* is the Moon Trefoil; and *M. echinus,* Calvary Clover. *M. falcata, M. lupulina, M. minima, M. hispida* and *M. arabica* are found wild in Britain, and known as Medick.

Medical Association, British, see BRITISH MEDICAL ASSOCIATION.

Medical Corps, Royal Army, see ROYAL ARMY MEDICAL CORPS.

Medical Council, General, a statutory body set up under the Medical Act of 1858 to maintain a register of qualified medical practitioners in the U.K. (pub. annually as the *Medical Register*), and to supervise and regulate the standards of medical education and qualifying examinations. The G. M. C. may remove from the *Register* any medical practitioners it finds guilty of infamous conduct in a professional respect, and may restore a name which it has erased. It is composed of representatives appointed by the Crown, by the univs. having medical faculties, by the medical corporations (e.g. the Royal College of Physicians) and directly by members of the profession as a whole. The Medical Act of 1950 provided for a new body, the Medical Disciplinary Committee, to be set up within the G. M. C. to take over its disciplinary powers. Another provision of this Act is that practitioners found guilty of professional misconduct and ordered to be struck off the *Register* may within 28 days appeal to the Privy Council; such an appeal was not previously allowed. The G. M. C. is also responsible for the pub. of the *British Pharmacopoeia.* Its H.Q. are at 44 Hallam Street, London, W.1, and there are branch offices at 8 Queen Street, Edinburgh, and 68 Fitzwilliam Square, Dublin.

Medical Education, special training in one or more branches of medicine, but since medicine itself is founded upon biology, physics and chem., M. E. includes instruction in these sciences. M. E. has developed very differently in different countries. Amongst the earliest records of definite surgical training are those of Hindus in about the 5th cent. BC. The Hindu student practised incisions and punctures in the veins and hollow stems of plants; he bandaged models; and in preparation for operations on cysts and ulcers in the human body, he tapped juicy fruits. The works of Hippocrates and Galen formed the foundations of most education in clinical practice and surgery until after the Renaissance, and some 'Hippocratic principles' are incorporated in modern professional etiquette. Except in anatomy M. E. was mainly didactic until the 18th cent., partly because of the difficulty in procuring specimens and partly because of the complete acceptance of the Gk writings. In Edinburgh all anatomical demonstrations were shown on a single body, and operations were practised on dogs. This difficulty led to the estab. of museums of anatomical and pathological specimens. Many Brit. students completed their M. E. at Padua, Montpellier, Leyden, Berlin, or Paris.

In Great Britain, Oxford, Cambridge, London, Edinburgh and Dublin and all prov. univs. (but not the univ. colleges), have a faculty of medicine. The student must first qualify for entrance to the univ. The medical examinations proper comprise the first M.B. in biology, physics and chem., taken either externally or after 1 year's study; the second M.B. in anatomy and physiology after a further 2 years; the third M.B. in clinical subjects after 3 years spent in hospital practice. After qualification the student must do 1 year's practical clinical work as a house officer in a recognised hospital before being registered as a fully registered medical practitioner (q.v.) by the General Medical Council. The requirement for this year of pre-registration work was laid down in the Medical Act, 1950. Before the latter half of the 19th cent. medical specialists were comparatively few, but with the growth of knowledge it became impossible for the general practitioner to learn how to deal adequately with all types and manifestations of diseases. Consequently some doctors and surgeons have specialised in special branches of medicine and surgery, gynaecology and obstetrics, and, after education in the elements of general medicine, it is necessary for the specialist to undergo a course of training for a higher degree or diploma in the particular branch of medicine he wishes to follow. The Brit. Postgraduate Medical Federation arranges postgraduate education in the univ. of London at a number of special institutes, and all univs. provide facilities for postgraduate study. One of the problems of M. E. today is how to contain the ever-swelling tide of new knowledge within the confines of the curriculum. It is clear that some reorientation is necessary and the line which it should take is receiving current attention from univs. and medical schools. The World Medical Association (q.v.) held an international conference on M. E. in London in 1953 and another on postgraduate M. E. in Chicago, 1959.

Since 1948 all the medical schools of London Univ. have followed the lead of the prov. univs. in admitting women on equal terms with men; in practice about one-fifth of the students are women. The first college of medicine for women was estab. in Philadelphia (1850), and in 1874 the London School of Medicine was opened, and training given in the Royal Free Hospital for Women. The cost of a M. E. varies somewhat in the different medical schools. The fees for tuition are in the region of £50 per annum, to which must be added considerable items for examination fees, purchase of books and instruments, and expenses of maintenance. Various scholarships are, however, available. The 2 important pubs. named below should be consulted by those seeking further information. The proposal in the *Goodenough Report* for a compulsory pre-registration, or 'intern year' in a hospital appointment after the third M.B. examination, before the student shall be legally entitled to practise his profession was, as already mentioned, embodied in the Medical Act of 1950. See *Inter-departmental Committee on Medical Schools* (the *Goodenough Report*), 1944; *The Training of a Doctor* (Report of the Brit. Medical Association), 1948; *Medicine, a Lifelong Study* (Proceedings of W. M. A. Conference, 1959), 1961.

Medical Jurisprudence, or **Forensic Medicine,** application of medical science to questions of common law. A large body of scientific facts has been built up, having for its purpose the elucidation of points, as far as medical knowledge can throw any light upon the matter, concerning the civil rights of individuals and the nature, extent, causation, etc. of personal injuries. So important has this legal aspect of medicine become that M. J. is included as a subject of study in the training course of every medical practitioner. Among the subjects dealt with are evidences of age, personal identity, pregnancy, insanity, paternity, etc., as far as they are likely to have any bearing on the responsibility of an individual or his capacity for certain rights; and evidences of rape, abortion, death by poison, drowning, or hanging, possibility of live-birth in trials for infanticide, the identification of bloodstains, etc. *See* A. S. Taylor, *Elements of Medical Jurisprudence,* 1836, and *Principles and Practice of Medical Jurisprudence* (12th ed.), 1962; J. Collie, *Fraud in Medico-Legal Jurisprudence,* 1932; K. Simpson, *Forensic Medicine,* 4th ed., 1961.

Medical Officer of Health, *see* LOCAL AUTHORITIES, OFFICERS OF.

Medical Officers of Health, Society of, the professional association of M. O. of H. It was founded in 1873 as the direct successor to the Metropolitan Association of M.O. of H., which was founded in 1856. The purpose of the society was 'to promote the advancement of public health in every branch, not only by intercourse among the members, but by practical and theoretical study of all questions connected therewith'. The Public Health Act of 1875 was followed by a large and rapid increase in the number of medical officers of health in the country and prov. branches of the society were founded. The society has attracted to its

membership doctors who work in many branches of local authority health work, such as school medical officers, maternity and child welfare officers, tuberculosis officers, etc., together with many profs. and lecturers in public health and hygiene. The membership is now so comprehensive that consideration is being given to a new title more nearly representing its scope. The S. has an agreement with the Brit. Medical Association (q.v.) that the 2 associations should work together in medico-political matters and that neither should pursue a divergent policy without previous consultation. The official jour. of the society is *Public Health,* which is pub. monthly. *See also* PUBLIC HEALTH.

Medical Practitioner, in Britain, one whose name is inscribed on the medical register of the General Medical Council in the U.K. The General Medical Council was estab. by the Medical Act of 1858 to regulate the conditions under which persons entered the medical profession, and a register was instituted to contain the names of qualified individuals. The amended Act of 1886 defined the general scope of the qualifying examination, and gave the council some measure of control over the corporate bodies licensed to grant diplomas. The general requirements do not vary to a great extent among the diploma-granting bodies of the U.K. Before being enrolled on the 'student's register', an intending practitioner has to produce one of many specified certificates relating to the subjects of general education. A period of study of 6 years' duration is then entered upon. In the first year of the course, the student is examined in physics, chem. and elementary biology. The course then becomes more purely medical, and includes anatomy, physiology, *materia medica* and pharmacy and pathology. After the second medical examination is passed, the student enters the clinical depts of a teaching hospital and is taught clinical medicine in all its branches, including medicine, surgery and obstetrics and gynaecology. The final examination is then taken. Since the Medical Act of 1950 the student is required on qualification to do a further year's work as a house officer in a hospital. This is known as the 'intern' or 'pre-registration' year. Having completed this year to the satisfaction of his supervisors the student may apply for full registration with the General Medical Council. The right of the General Medical Council to strike a practitioner's name off the medical register, either for a criminal conviction or for 'infamous conduct in any professional respect', is a statutory right, but under the Medical Act of 1950 a doctor who is struck off the register has the right of appeal to the high court. The use by unregistered persons of any title implying registration, or that they are recognised by law, is made an offence by the Medical Act, 1858. No unregistered person can give a valid certificate required by law, or hold an appointment at a hospital, or in a ship, etc., or practise under the National Health Acts, or obtain dangerous drugs, or treat venereal disease.

The laws governing medical practice vary with

different countries. In some there is little or no regulation and no registration of practitioners as there is in Great Britain. Broadly speaking the regulation of medical practice in the countries belonging to the Brit. Commonwealth of Nations is on similar lines to that in the U.K. There is no federal law regarding the practice of medicine in the U.S.A., this being left to the jurisdiction of each of the self-governing states. State medical boards can insist that a would-be practitioner have a diploma from some recognised medical school. In general any graduate of a medical school anywhere can set up in practice after having estab. his credentials and, in some cases, having passed certain tests. The standard of the medical schools has been raised through the efforts of the Amer. Medical Association and the local state associations, and now, in most schools, the student must have had an academic education and must attend sessions and lectures for 4 years before receiving his diploma. The distribution of doctors is uneven. In 1962 the Medical Register contained, for England, Wales and Scotland, 68,797 names, but not all of these were in active medical practice, some being retired, others being engaged in teaching and scientific research, and others working as administrators.

Medical Research, fundamentally concerned with the cause of disease, and thus its prevention and cure. To this end it is essential that the symptoms and nature of the disease should be known and experiments made to determine its reaction to various methods of treatment. Consequently the methods of M. R. are observational and experimental. The earliest M. R. must have been very haphazard and mainly experimental, but the anct civilisations and many savage tribes had herbal remedies for various affections, and the Chinese and Babylonians attempted to account for their remedies by formulating theories of disease. These theories were purely speculative, and it was not until the time of Hippocrates that the observational method was systematically employed. Arabian physicians made extensive use of this method, but Hippocrates is usually regarded as its founder. It is essential in clinical practice and leads to correct diagnosis. The experimental method was systematised by Galen, and in his investigation of the nervous system he laid the foundation of experimental physiology.

While the observational method could discover a connection between *Anopheles* and malaria (*see* MALARIA), experimental work was necessary to trace the life-hist. of the malaria parasite and its phases in man and mosquito. Semmelweiss (1857), as a result of clinical observations, showed that infection could be spread by living and by dead bodies; Pasteur and Koch, in the laboratory, were able to isolate infective organisms and to investigate their reactions. The development of this pioneer experimental work in bacteriology is seen in the growth of immunotherapy during recent years (*see* BACTERIA; MEDICINE).

Experimental M. R. is so wide a field that it

involves all branches of science. The behaviour of organisms and of tissues in culture may be very different from their behaviour in a patient. The reactions of rats, dogs and rabbits may be very different from the reactions of human beings. A healthy animal, infected in the laboratory with a disease, may not be affected in the same way as an unhealthy one or as an animal living a normal life. So long, however, as the research worker fully realises these and similar possibilities, they do not vitiate his results, but rather enable him to apply them with greater reserve and in a more critical manner. Obviously the best conduct of M. R. is in the co-ordination of the observational and experimental methods, and nowadays the clinician and the laboratory worker are closely allied. The experimental method receives severe criticism from some for its use of animals. The choice of the subject of the experiment must always fall either on the human being or on a different animal, and it is doubtful whether there will ever be unanimous agreement on this vexed question. That man has undoubtedly benefited by such experiments is shown by the use of insulin in *Diabetes mellitus*, of liver for pernicious anaemia, the efficacy of the antirachitic vitamin and the determination of its presence in various food substances. Man has also benefited by experiments on his fellows, as in the case of the voluntary infection of Sir Patrick Manson and others with the malaria parasite to forward the research on malaria. Opponents of vivisection should bear in mind that without it substantial progress in M. R. at the present day would be impossible. Such experiments in living animals are very carefully regulated by the Home Office (*see* ANTI-VIVISECTION).

Statistics are essential in M. R., and non-mathematical research workers need to co-operate with skilled statisticians in order to get as complete an interpretation as possible of their results. Recent research on these lines has led to the prediction and probable course of certain epidemics (*see* EPIDEMIOLOGY). Much work has been done on the best method of obtaining reliable statistics, and the best type of statistics for especial purposes. The research worker, in addition to skilled technique, needs patience, perseverance, ability to review his results critically and readiness to discard preconceived ideas or working hypotheses when there is insufficient experimental evidence to support them.

The first half of the 20th cent. was phenomenal for the strides made in M. R. Infant mortality—a reliable index of a nation's health—was at the rate of 138 per 1000 live births in the period 1901–5. In 1960 it was 21·8. In 50 years the death rate from infectious and contagious diseases fell by 94 per cent and the tuberculosis mortality by 74 per cent. The expectation of life has almost doubled. For these achievements, improved social conditions were partly responsible, but the major credit must go to M. R. The work that Pasteur and Koch had begun was followed up until the causative organisms of most infections became known. The most striking practical application of advances in bacteriology has been seen in diphtheria immunisation (*see* DIPHTHERIA) and B.C.G. vaccination against tuberculosis (*see* TUBERCULOSIS). The many problems of vaccination against virus infections are gradually being overcome and vaccines against acute anterior poliomyelitis, measles and influenza are in use.

The discovery of the bacterial causation of diseases led many to suppose that eventually a similar cause would be found for the majority of diseases. At the turn of the cent., however, a perception of disease as being a disorder of normal function, accompanied by related structural changes and brought about by many agencies, some specific, others predisposing, others precipitating and others perpetuating, began to take shape. To follow up this concept needed combination in research of the whole forces of medicine—the clinician to observe at the bedside and at the operating table, the morbid anatomist and the histologist to observe structural changes of tissue, the bacteriologist to observe and differentiate invading organisms, the biochemist to observe the chemical changes of living tissue, the haematologist to observe the function and changes of the blood as an essential organ of the body, the statistician to observe trends and interpret results, the pharmacologist to find specific remedies for specific diseases, the sociologist to observe the predisposing causes of disease in social environment, the psychologist to interpret the effect of mind on body and vice versa and the physicist to invent physical methods of investigation and treatment. Out of this combined operation there evolved, and is still evolving, a clearer understanding of living tissues and of the part played by the different organs in the functioning of the whole body in health and disease. Knowledge gained of the role of the ductless glands and their secretions (hormones), and their challenge to the primacy of the nervous system as the master controller of bodily function, shed a new light on the nature of some diseases and their treament. Myxoedema, diabetes, pernicious anaemia and Addison's disease, previously fatal conditions, may now be successfully treated by replacing the missing hormone. The discovery that allergic reactions are largely due to the release of histamine from sensitive cells by the action of the allergen has made possible a new approach to the treatment of these intractable states with synthetic antihistamine drugs. Rickets, scurvy, beri-beri and other nutritional deficiency diseases are almost things of the past in civilised countries since the discovery of vitamins. Tropical diseases are yielding before the scientist's revelation of their causes.

It was in 1935 that news first came of the effectiveness of the red chemical dye 'prontosil' against streptococcal infections. There followed sulphanilamide and the whole range of sulpha drugs with their specific actions against various infective organisms. Hardly were they in their stride when the Second World War gave the impetus needed to develop the product of the mould *Penicillium notatum*, to be known as penicillin. Alexander Fleming noted in 1928 the destructive action of penicillin (q.v.) on certain bacteria, but the possibilities of large scale production of it for therapeutic purposes seemed remote at that time. Indeed it is doubtful whether the commercial risk and expenditure necessary would have been taken had it not been for the urgent needs of war. That it was taken has resulted in an as yet unstemmed flow of related antibiotics, with an influence on the treatment of infections more far-reaching than anything in the hist. of therapeutic research.

The science of physics has been responsible for the refinements of the X-ray machine, so that radiology has become an exact science in treatment and diagnosis. The electrocardiograph and electroencephalograph have been further contributions to the diagnostic art. And now there are the radio-active isotopes. The scope of surgical treatment has advanced partly as a result of improved technique, but mainly because the biochemist, the physiologist and the pharmacologist have made prolonged anaesthesia possible. Relaxant drugs such as curare now enable the anaesthetist to reduce anaesthesia to the level just necessary for unconsciousness. In this way the minimal amount of poison is absorbed and the surgeon has time to undertake complicated procedures with little risk to the patient. Likewise many cases that would previously have been considered too ill may now be anaesthetised without undue harm. The introduction of hypothermia, in which the patient's temp. is gradually lowered before operation until a state of artificial hibernation is reached, with consequently a greatly diminished need for oxygen by the tissues, has allowed the surgeon to interrupt the circulation long enough to operate within the heart itself. Deprivation of oxygen for more than 3 min. at normal body temp. causes irreversible damage to the brain. Under hypothermic conditions the circulation, and hence the oxygen supply, has been cut off for up to 12 min. during brain operations without ill effect. The advantage to the surgeon is considerable. Hypothermia has also been used to reduce temporarily the metabolic needs of the brain during the critical period following an injury to it. A dramatic example of its use in this manner was provided in 1956 when a woman in the early stages of pregnancy was kept in a state of hypothermia and thus tided over the first critical week of unconsciousness following a severe head injury. Mother and baby both survived. A product of M. R. is the 'heart-lung machine' which has made possible a revolutionary advance in heart surgery. The patient's circulation is temporarily exteriorised through the machine, by-passing the heart which is left empty and idle, enabling the surgeon to work deliberately by direct vision without risk of severe haemorrhage. The heart-lung machine, besides artificially circulating and oxygenating the patient's blood, can also cool it if hypothermia is necessary. Another recent product of M. R. is the artificial kidney (see KIDNEY). A record of all the recent achievements of M. R. would need a book in itself, and the foregoing mentions a few signposts only. Research is never static, and each discovery points the way to another. The riddle of cancer is unsolved, and here the success of M. R. has created its own problems by lengthening the expectation of life and thus increasing the number of people within the cancer age. The viruses, the causative agent of so many infections, are, unlike most bacterial infections, unsusceptible to chemotherapy and antibiotics, and present a vast field for future research. Perhaps Interferon (q.v.) will prove to be a practical therapeutic agent against viruses. Another field for research, and one which should yield good fruit, is that of mental illness. Man will never conquer man's ills in their entirety, but nearer and nearer are we getting to the realisation of the dictum that life is not living, but living in health. See B. Dawson, *The History of Medicine: a Short Synopsis*, 1927; J. A. Delmege, *Towards National Health*, 1931; D. Riesman, *Medicine in Modern Society*, 1938; G. F. McCleary, *The March of Medicine*, 1941; G. W. Gray, *The Advancing Front of Medicine*, 1941; M. Silverman, *War against Disease*, 1942; Brit. Medical Association (ed. H. A. Clegg), *Fifty Years of Medicine*, 1950; J. G. Thwaites, *Modern Medical Discoveries*, 1957.

Medical Research Council, The, estab. under Royal Charter in 1920, administers the funds provided by Parliament for the promotion of work over the whole field of M. R. The Council maintains the National Institute for M. R. and a number of research units, mostly located within univs. and hospitals; it also awards grants to individual research institutes through a scheme of block grants, and provides post-graduate training awards.

Medical Service in the Armed Forces. *Army.* Medical service in the Brit. Army is provided by the Royal Army Medical Corps, the Royal Army Dental Corps and Queen Alexandra's Royal Army Nursing Corps (q.v.). Before the Crimean War the service was on no permanent basis, and was carried on in a haphazard manner. There existed expert advisers to the army, officers of high rank, but there was no unified corps of officers and other ranks as we know it today. In the early campaigns, and through the Peninsular and Waterloo, attention in the way of non-medical comforts was provided by the wives of soldiers, who were permitted to follow their husbands on active service. Florence Nightingale (q.v.) set the pattern for the present Army nursing service by volunteering to take 38 nurses to the Crimea in 1854, where they did much to relieve the suffering of the sick and wounded. During the Crimean War a corps of men only (no officers) was formed 'for the better care of sick and wounded', entitled Medical Staff Corps. In 1857 it became the Army Hospital Corps. In 1884 the doctors were formed into the Medical Staff, but

the final welding of officers and men did not take place until 1898, when the R.A.M.C. (q.v.) was formed. The opening of the Herbert Hospital at Woolwich in 1861 marked an important stage in the development of the A. M. S., and other hospitals followed at Netley, Aldershot, Millbank and elsewhere. The estab. of a corps for the medical service advanced the provision of medical units for subsequent expeditions; and the members of such units often distinguished themselves, many winning the Victoria Cross. During the First World War the estab. of the A. M. S. expanded from 9000 other ranks in Aug. 1914, to 133,000 in the last year of the war. A total of 9,000,000 casualties was dealt with, 2,000,000 being on the W. front. The R.A.M.C. was, of course, assisted by the Nursing Services, Red Cross and other similar organisations. A beautiful window in Westminster Abbey perpetuates the memory of countless acts of bravery performed by the A. M. S. The varied fronts on which fighting took place during the First World War were a test of the efficiency and organisation of the A. M. S. Every means of conveyance, modern, obsolete and improvised, was brought into use, and all sorts of buildings were converted into hospitals. Ingenuity contributed largely to the comfort of the sick and wounded. Protection of casualties from aerial attacks was a new feature of the First World War and, in the shell-fire zone, protection was of paramount importance. The range of modern weapons brought the activities of the A. M. S. well within the danger zone. Shells blew up aid posts and dressing stations or wiped out bearer-parties, and some 6873 members of the A. M. S. were killed and many thousands were wounded. Many Amer. doctors joined the Brit. A. M. S., and were granted officers' commissions in the R.A.M.C. When the Amer. Army came to Europe they were permitted to join the Amer. Army. For a full story of the A. M. S. during the First World War see Maj.-Gen. Sir W. G. Macpherson, *Official History of the Medical Service*, 1921–4.

Army Medical Service in the Second World War. The A. M. S. made great strides in the Second World War, as exemplified in operations performed in the battle zone. Thus in the N. Africa battle area first aid was administered on the field; then, by way of an advance dressing station, the wounded man arrived at a casualty clearing station. This was the most advanced medical post where operations could be properly performed. A mobile electric unit supplied power for X-ray and lighting. In fact, the casualty clearing station was completely mobile, carrying tentage for operating theatres and wards. Expert surgeons and eminent doctors were employed in these advanced stations. These stations, which in N. Africa were generally about 20–30 m. behind the front lines, were expert at moving, and from positions over 100 m. away could reach their new destination by evening, and be ready to receive patients the following morning. Each station had its team of specialists: physician, surgeon, anaesthetist,

X-ray specialists and dental officer, together with 8 sisters, R.A.M.C. nursing orderlies and cooks. From the casualty clearing station the patients were sent to a general hospital at the base, often by motor ambulance to an aerodrome and thence by ambulance plane. General hospitals were all equipped in the same manner as the casualty clearing station, and many of them had special sections for various types of casualties. They had from 40 to 80 trained sisters and many R.A.M.C. men for the other tasks necessary in a modern hospital. These hospitals were divided into 2 main divs., medical and surgical. Plaster fixation and sulphonamide drugs enabled the surgeon at the front to prepare his patients so well that even long journeys by road and rail did no harm. No doubt it would have been ideal if all patients could have been evacuated by air, but that was not possible, though in the Burma theatre it was largely achieved. See F. A. E. Crew, *Medical History of the Second World War, The Army Medical Services* (H.M.S.O.), 1953–9.

Army Medical Service of the U.S.A. The normal or peacetime strength of the medical corps of the U.S. Army is about 6400 officers and men. There are small hospitals connected with every army garrison, but there are also large general hospitals at Hot Springs, Arkansas, Denver, Colorado, El Paso, Texas and the presidio of San Francisco, and a general army medical centre, including Walter Reed Hospital, in Washington, D.C. In the colonial possessions the army has hospitals at Manila in the Philippines (lost to the Japanese in 1942), and at Honolulu in the Hawaiian Is. There is also an aviation hospital at San Antonio, Texas. Here has been developed a complete airborne emergency hospital, carried in one plane. The 100-bed field unit can be carried in 9 aircraft.

During the First World War there were, at front or at the base hospitals, more than 20,000 medical officers, and about 20,000 nurses attending over 350,000 beds.

During the Second World War there were at the front or at the base hospitals more than 14,000 medical officers and 4 times that number of other ranks with more than 10,000 nurses attending a total of over 120,000 beds.

Royal Air Force. The R.A.F. has its own medical branch, hospitals and nursing service, known as Princess Mary's R.A.F. Nursing Service.

Royal Navy. Entry into the Naval Medical Service is in the first instance on a short service basis of 3 or 5 years. Entrants must be qualified medical practitioners or dental surgeons. After 1 year's service application may be made for a permanent commission. (*See Plate: Army.*)

Medical Social Worker. In Oct. 1964 the Institute of Almoners changed its name to the Institute of M. S. W., because the new title was considered more appropriate to describe the work of M. S. W.s today. No longer primarily concerned with finance, they deal with all aspects of the patient's social problems linking the hospital services with those of the local authorities and voluntary bodies. Their activities include the aftercare, rehabilitation and resettlement of patients, and they are increasingly employed in public health and welfare depts. The Institute of M. S. W.s, 42 Bedford Square, London, W.C.1, is concerned with professional matters affecting its members, with training and with certification, and at present has 2000 M. S. W.s on its register. See L. F. Beck, *The Almoner*, 1948, and *Ten Patients and an Almoner*, 1956.

Medici, name of a famous Florentine family. *Cosimo de' M.* (1389–1464), called 'pater patriae' by his grateful fellow citizens, was the son of Giovanni (c. 1360–1429), who founded the wealth of the family. In 1433 Cosimo was banished from Florence and had to seek refuge in Venice as the result of a revolution in his native city. The following year, however, he was recalled, and until his death, though theoretically only an ordinary citizen, he directed the fortunes of Florence, saving her from the ravages of war by his prudent alliances and skilful foreign policy, and using his enormous riches for the generous and enlightened patronage of art and literature. He instituted an academy for the study of Platonic philosophy, collected a number of priceless classical and oriental MSS., which formed a splendid nucleus to the Laurentian library, gathered about him some of the foremost painters, sculptors and scholars of the day, and gave liberally to charity. His grandson, *Lorenzo the Magnificent* (1448–92), was also a victim of the family feuds which characterised Renaissance Italy, and narrowly escaped assassination at the hands of the influential and jealous Pazzi (1478). His wealth gave him great influence in Florence; his political policy was to strengthen Milan in order to weaken Venice. He was even more lavish in his patronage of learning than his grandfather. The academy which he founded did much to help the rapid dissemination over Europe of Gk and Lat. literature, as well as making Florence pre-eminent in the field of Renaissance culture. It was he who seized at once on the vital importance of printing, and it was he who procured, through John Lascaris, 200 MSS from the monastery of Mt Athos, which were destined to embellish the Laurentian library already referred to. This unique collection, together with the equally unique collection of anct sculptures and vases, etc., was broken up and in part destroyed when the French sacked the city, which was under the rule of Piero (1471–1503), the incompetent son of Lorenzo. The astute politician Giulio (1478–1534), who rose to be Clement VII, was an illegitimate son of Giuliano, Lorenzo's ill-fated brother who was assassinated in 1478. A second son of Lorenzo, Giovanni (1475–1521), succeeded to the papal chair as Leo X. Lorenzo II (1492–1519), grandson of Lorenzo the Magnificent, was an incompetent degenerate, and his faults were fully passed on to his natural son, Alessandro (1510–37), who governed Florence as duke from 1530, the year of her tragic surrender to the

Emperor Charles V. Cosimo I (1519–74), who was created Grand-Duke of Tuscany in 1569, and Ferdinand I (1549–1609) were descended from Lorenzo (1395–1440), a younger brother of the great Cosimo. The male line of the M. became extinct with Giovanni Gastone (1671–1737), the 7th grand-duke. *See* CATHERINE DE' MEDICI and MARIE DE' MEDICI for the alliance of this house with the royalty of France. *See* Janet Ross, *Lives of the Early Medicis*, 1910; C. Booth, *Cosimo I, Duke of Florence*, 1921; G. Maguire, *The Women of the Medici*, 1927; D. G. Loth, *Lorenzo the Magnificent*, 1930; H. Acton, *The Last Medici*, revised ed., 1958. (*See Plate: Italy*.)

Medici, Catherine de', *see* CATHERINE.

Medici, Giovanni de', *see* LEO (popes), *Leo X*.

Medici, Marie de', *see* MARIE.

Medici Chapel, one of the monumental works on which Michelangelo (q.v.) was employed in the years 1520–34, and intended to be the burial-place and monument of the Medici (q.v.) in their family church of San Lorenzo, in Florence. It was not built by Michelangelo, but the commission for its decoration, and for the monuments, was given to him by the Medici Popes, Leo X and Clement VII. For various reasons it was never completed, the execution of the commission being interrupted by the demands of earlier commissions, straitened papal finances, and the conflict between the papacy and the Florentines in which Michelangelo himself was deeply involved as engineer of the fortifications of Florence. The architectural decoration of the chapel, the 4 allegorical figures of Dawn and Evening, Night and Day, on the 2 sepulchres, and the seated figures of the dukes Lorenzo and Giuliano above them, are almost complete; but of the still more elaborate double sepulchre on the entrance wall only the group of the Virgin and Child, which was to have occupied the centre, was completed. The whole leaves an overwhelming impression and, although unfinished, it illustrates Michelangelo's power, in his prime, of achieving a unity which resolves discords and conflicts. *See* C. de Tolnay, *Michelangelo: the Medici Chapel*, 1949.

'Medici' Porcelain, *see* PORCELAIN, *Soft-paste*.

Medicinal Herbs. In medieval times few plants were without their supposed medicinal value, but the progress of medicine has limited them to a very small number. With a special state dept's aid, considerable attention is devoted to the culture of M. H. in the U.S.A., but in Britain, where in the E. cos. a cent. ago their culture was an important industry, they are little grown now and considerable importations are received from India and other countries. Some plants, such as foxglove, hemlock, belladonna, peppermint, valerian and henbane, can be grown in Britain better than elsewhere. Foxglove and hemlock need to have their juice expressed immediately after cutting.

Medicine, science of the treatment of disease; any substance administered with the object of curing a diseased condition. The term is used sometimes to indicate that branch of the healing art which deals with internal administrations as opposed to surgery or operative treatment. In its widest sense, however, M. includes all varieties of curative treatment, as well as discussion of the causation and prevention of disease, and kindred subjects. According to modern conceptions, the study of M. involves first of all the study of anatomy, or the structure and form of the body, physiology, or the study of function, and biochemistry, or the chem. of living tissues. Medical practitioners are called upon to deal with diseased conditions, hence pathology (q.v.) becomes part of the general subject. The treatment of diseased conditions is studied under the name of therapeutics, which, as far as it is concerned with drugs, involves a study of pharmacology (q.v.). Operative treatment of surgery (q.v.) has sev. subdivisions of which dentistry is an important example. Sev. branches of medical practice have been dealt with separately, of which obstetrics, or midwifery (q.v.), is of importance; it is closely allied to gynaecology, or diseases of women (q.v.). A special aspect of the application of medical knowledge is indicated in the term medical jurisprudence (q.v.).

The development and classification of medical science have proceeded by gradual steps from very early times. Among the more primitive peoples medical practice was an adjunct of the sacerdotal function, and relied more upon the influence of the deity than upon any intrinsic efficacy in the methods adopted. Even the priests of Asclepius, the Gk god of healing, relied upon purely religious exercises to effect a cure. The medical school of Cnidos was estab. between 700 and 600 BC, and was mainly concerned with the description of symptoms as symptoms, dissociated from the patient. In this respect it differed from the Coan school, founded later by Hippocrates (q.v.).

The rise of purely rational curative methods is associated with the name of this Gk physician (*c.* 460 BC), who was an outstanding member of a profession which had already taken a distinct place in Hellenic life. The great feature of the work of Hippocrates is the recognition of disease as the result of natural causes, and he and his followers bequeathed to the medical world the principles of minute observation of symptoms and the consideration of these in relation to the patient and environment. These principles have grown into the method of clinical M. The general theory of the Hippocratic school postulated 4 humours in the human body. These were blood, phlegm, yellow bile and black bile, and an improper proportion of the constituents was understood to be the cause of disease. Careful observation was necessary to diagnose the state of the body with regard to these elementary humours, and patient application of the available means of cure was combined with assiduous observation of their effects. When the victories of Alexander had disseminated Grecian knowledge throughout the known world, a school of physicians sprang up at Alexandria which founded what has been called the empirical school. The members of this school

Mathematics

Above left: The Greek geometrician, Euclid (*c.* 330–*c.* 275 BC).
Radio Times Hulton Picture Library
Above centre: John Napier (1550–1617), inventor of logarithms.
Above right: Sir Isaac Newton (1642–1727), who left his mark on many branches of physics. (Painting of 1702 by Sir Godfrey Kneller.)
National Portrait Gallery
Below left: Leonhard Euler (1707–83) made noted contributions to pure and applied mathematics.
Radio Times Hulton Picture Library
Below centre: The French astronomer, the Marquis de Laplace (1749–1827).
Radio Times Hulton Picture Library

Above: Karl Gauss (1777–1855), mathematician and physicist.
Radio Times Hulton Picture Library

Left: Programmer working with an Elliott 503 computer, which can perform 100,000 operations in one second.
Courtesy of Elliott Automation Computers Ltd

Medicine

Far left: The Greek physician Hippocrates (*c.* 460–*c.* 375 BC) originated the principles of clinical medicine.
Courtesy of the Wellcome Trustees

Left: Galen (*c.* AD 130–201), Greek physician living in Rome, laid the foundation of anatomy and experimental physiology.
Courtesy of the Wellcome Trustees

Far left: William Harvey's greatest discovery was that of the circulation of the blood.
National Portrait Gallery

Left: Edward Jenner (1749–1823), the originator of vaccination. (Painting of 1803 by J. Northcote.)
National Portrait Gallery

Far left: Louis Pasteur (1822–1895), pioneer of vaccination and inoculation.
Courtesy of the Wellcome Trustees

Left: Lord Lister (1827–1912), founder of the antiseptic principle.
British Medical Journal

Far left: Sir Alexander Fleming (1881–1955), Scottish bacteriologist, discoverer of penicillin.
Barratt's Photo Press Ltd

Left: The American Dr Jonas Salk, who gave his name to the first successful poliomyelitis vaccine.
U.S. Information Service

Melanesia

Fiji: view of the capital, Suva, with the wharf in the foreground.
Rob Wright

Below left: Solomon Islanders performing a traditional dance with pan-pipes.
Melanesian Mission

Below: The Western Pacific High Commission secretariat building at Honiara on Guadalcanal in the Solomon Islands.
C.O.I.: Crown copyright

Melanesia

Above left: A large leaf provides an effective sunshade for this mother and baby from the New Hebrides.
Above right: The papaya flourishes throughout Melanesia, and all parts of the tree have their economic uses.
Below: The thatched dwellings of this coastal village in the Solomon Islands are typical of the whole area.
Photos: Melanesian Mission

Melanesia

Above left: A New Hebridean medical assistant helps to care for the health of the islanders.
Melanesian Mission

Above: A Highland warrior from New Guinea; the beautiful feathers of birds of paradise have contributed to the making of his head-dress.
New Guinea Mission

Left: A European nurse working in infant welfare in the Solomons.
Melanesian Mission

Below: The traditional canoe now often carries an outboard motor.
Melanesian Mission

Mercantile Marine

Top: The fast cargo mail-ship *Southampton Castle*, 13,152 gross tons (Union-Castle Line).
Union-Castle Line
Centre: The fruit-carrier *Drakenstein*, 10,220 dw tons (British & Commonwealth Shipping Co.).
South African Marine Corporation Ltd
Above: The bulk carrier *Graigwerdd*, 18,618 gross tons, 28,370 dw (Graig Shipping
Co. Ltd).
Scotts' Shipbuilding & Engineering Co. Ltd

Mercantile Marine

Above: The cargo ship *Saxonia*, 5586 gross tons, 7300 dw (Cunard Line).

Below: The engine control room of the *Clan Ramsay*, 10,500 gross tons (British & Commonwealth Shipping Co.).
British & Commonwealth Shipping Co. Ltd

Mercantile Marine

The purser's cabin in the passenger liner *Canberra* is typical of officers' accommodation today.

The leading hands' cabin in the passenger liner *Oriana*.

The wardroom of *Canberra*.
All photos: P. & O.-Orient Lines

observed effects instead of inquiring after causes, and built up a body of clinical experience which appears to have led to considerable success in practice. Rome produced the school of 'methodics', which assigned all morbid conditions to the too great constriction or too great relaxation of the pores separating the atoms of the body. The general treatment, therefore, involved increasing or decreasing the amount of constriction to the required extent by the use of drugs and by carefully adjusted dieting. All the medical knowledge of the ancients was co-ordinated and the results recorded by Galen, who lived in Rome in the 2nd cent. AD. He was the first to try seriously to investigate the function of the body, and it was he who laid the foundation of experimental physiology. He also recognised the importance of anatomy. Galen was a voluminous writer and his works were copied and his precepts followed down to the Middle Ages. In so far as his facts were wrong so his mistakes were perpetuated for a like period. The revival of learning helped to clear away some of the masses of superstition which had been superposed on the work of Galen. Good trans. were made by Linacre and others, and the study of anatomy, botany and pharmacology proceeded apace. Scientific method, much as it helped forward the branches of knowledge which were ultimately to cause great developments in medical theory, did not, however, immediately have a great effect on medical practice. Success was more likely to attend the efforts of the empiricists who constantly sprang up, and overlaid with superstition as their theories were, nevertheless their knowledge of drugs and their skill in manipulation served them and their patients far better than somewhat dangerous dogma. In 1628 Wm Harvey pub. his discovery of the circulation of the blood, but it was some time before the importance of this phenomenon was adequately recognised. Progress was constant though gradual until the appreciation of the truths of biology as demonstrated by Darwin led to the development of theories with far-reaching effects. In Germany Schönlein commenced a new era by his discovery of a parasite as the cause of the skin disease called favus. Bacteriological research led, in the hands of Pasteur (q.v.) and others, to the conceptions of toxins produced in the blood by bacteria, and of the anti-toxins which are evolved as a result of the intoxication.

On the work of Pasteur and his contemporaries, Koch (q.v.) and Klebs, the modern treatment of infectious diseases is based. Pasteur did pioneer work in vaccination and inoculation; Koch worked out the life-hist. of certain infective organisms, showing their relation to disease. Klebs discovered bacteria causing typhoid fever and diphtheria, and showed that some bacteria could be removed from a medium by filtration. He thus began the important work on filterable and non-filterable micro-organisms. The results obtained by these 3 pioneers gave a stimulus to research on bacteriology and parasitology, and numerous infective bacteria and other parasites have been described since the middle of the 19th cent. As a result, most infectious diseases, even those of epidemic character, are comparatively well under control. (*See* BACTERIA; EPIDEMIOLOGY; PATHOLOGY.)

Pasteur's results helped to direct Lister's quest for a preventive of wound infections, and surgery, general healing and hospital sanitation were inestimably advanced by the introduction of antiseptics (*see* LISTER). Tropical M., which became of interest and importance as a result of exploration and colonisation, benefited by the impetus given to the study of bacteriology and parasitology. The first organised attempt to study tropical M. was made in 1864 by the Indian Medical Service of the Brit. Army. Sir Patrick Manson (q.v.) started the school of tropical M. in Hong Kong, 1866, and the London school in 1898. Subsequently similar schools have been opened in many busy ports, and much has been done to prevent, alleviate and cure diseases caused by bacteria and by plants and animals parasitic on human beings in tropical countries.

During the 19th cent. considerable progress was made in public hygiene, particularly in connection with water supplies, sanitation and the improvement of conditions in factories (*see* HYGIENE). The introduction by Ehrlich (q.v.) of salvarsan in 1910 for the treatment of syphilis paved the way for the discovery of prontosil, which was followed in turn by the manuf. of still more efficient bactericides such as sulphanilamide and sulphapyridine; these have proved to. great value in the treatment of pneumonia, puerperal fever, gonorrhoea and other diseases. The discovery of penicillin by Fleming in 1928, and its use on a large scale during and subsequent to the Second World War, are described in the article PENICILLIN. Streptomycin is helping in the battle against tuberculosis (q.v.), and other anti-bacterial extracts from fungi, as for instance, chloromycetin and aureomycin, are effective against other bacteria. The First World War stimulated research in most branches of M. New methods of surgery were necessitated by the large numbers of cases needing immediate attention, and quick methods of blood transfusion were introduced (*see* BLOOD TRANSFUSION). Important advances were made in physiotherapy, leading to the more extensive use of massage, diathermy, electrotherapy and radiotherapy (*see* sections on these subjects). Inoculation against influenza, cholera, typhoid and para-typhoid fevers, and other infectious and epidemic diseases was in general use in the army, and military hygiene was vastly improved. New antiseptics were introduced, and special investigations were made of diseases such as trench fever, gas gangrene and shell shock, peculiar to warfare. Psychological methods of treatment were increasingly used by doctors, and the field of psychology has widened considerably. Shortage of food supplies led to extensive research on diet and nutrition, and this research was helped to a great extent by the discovery by Sir Frederick Gowland Hopkins, in 1906, that in addition to protein, carbohydrates and fat, 'accessory food factors' are necessary for the maintenance of life. This led to the discovery of the vitamins (*see* HOPKINS, SIR F. GOWLAND, and VITAMINS). The Second World War led, amongst other improvements in M., to the large-scale production and use of penicillin (q.v.) as an anti-bacterial agent. Other noteworthy advances during the 20th cent. are mainly of social importance, and tend by preventive measures to raise the national standard of health. The institution of medical inspection of school children, the estab. of dental clinics, and also of welfare centres where advice may be obtained relating to pre- and post-natal care of the child, have done much to improve the health of school children, and to reduce infant mortality. The mortality of mothers during childbirth has also been reduced by improvements in obstetric practice, and new analgesic drugs such as pethidine and trilene have helped towards painless childbirth. The discovery by Landsteiner and Wiener of the rhesus blood factor in 1940 has enabled notable advances to be made in the treatment of haemolytic disease of the newborn, and has made the study of blood transfusion a science in its own right (*see* OBSTETRICS).

Arising out of the estab. by Mendel of heredity as a quantitative science, various methods of improving the race have been suggested (*see* EUGENICS; HEREDITY; MENDEL), while M. is also concerned with methods of contraception and their effect on the individual.

Endocrinology has developed into a specialised branch of M., a branch tending to connect it more closely with biochem. and to the recognition of the role of the tissue function. The effects of abnormal functioning of the ductless glands are seen in *Diabetes mellitus*, associated with the failure of the pancreas to secret insulin; cretinism and Graves' disease, associated respectively with too little or too much secretion of the thyroid gland; Addison's disease, with the suprarenal bodies; and acromegaly, with the pituitary gland. Much experimental work remains to be done in connection with the endocrine system. Cortisone (compound E), recently extracted from the cortex of the suprarenal bodies, has been used in the treatment of rheumatoid arthritis and in restoring the electrolyte balance of the tissues in conditions of stress.

The modern tendency in M. is to do far more experimental work. Micro-biology is a developing science which, with the aid of modern techniques of tissue culture and microscopy (e.g. electron microscopy), is enabling intracellular chemistry to be studied, and a new concept of cellular rather than bodily disease is emerging.

See D. Guthrie, *The History of Medicine*, 1945; G. Scott Williamson, *Physician Heal Thyself*, 1945; R. H. Shryock, *The Development of Modern Medicine*, 1948; H. L. Tidy, *Synopsis of Medicine* (10th ed.), 1954; *British Encyclopaedia of Medical Practice*, 1950; N. Compston

and D. Baron, *Recent Advances in Medicine* (14th ed.), 1962; Sir J. Conybeare, *Textbook of Medicine* (13th ed.), 1961; F. W. Price, *Textbook of the Practice of Medicine* (9th ed.), 1956. (*See* Plate.)

Medicine, Forensic, *see* MEDICAL JURISPRUDENCE.

Medicine, Patent, *see* PROPRIETARY MEDICINE.

Medicine Hat ('the town that was born lucky'—Kipling), city of Alberta, Canada, 180 m. ESE. of Calgary, on the Canadian Pacific Railway trans-continental main line and the Trans-Canada Highway, incorporated as a tn in 1899 and made a city in 1907. M. H. is reputedly named after the traditional head-dress of an Indian medicine man who lost his hat in the riv. It is the centre of a large farming and ranching area. The making of clay products and pottery is a major industry; milling plants and glassware factories are at nearby Redcliffe. In addition, there are extensive greenhouses which send fresh fruit, vegetables and flowers as far E. as Fort William and as far W. as Vancouver. Pop. 24,484.

Medicine Man, *see* WITCH-DOCTOR.

Medick, the genus *Medicago*, perennial leguminous herb, growing to a height of 2 ft in England, chiefly on waste land and gravelly or sandy soil, and also found in Europe generally, W. Asiatic countries and N. Africa. Brit. species include *M. falcata* or sickle M., and *M. lupulina* or black M. *M. lupulina*, the Hop-trefoil, sometimes called Shamrock and in Norfolk Non-such, is occasionally cultivated with other clovers. It is a trailing biennial with yellow flowers and smooth, kidney-shaped pods. *M. sativa*, with blue or violet flowers, also known as lucerne, is a Mediterranean plant, cultivated as a green fodder plant. *See* ALFALFA.

Medieval Period, *see* MIDDLE AGES.

Medina, or **Madina** (Arabic, short for *Madinat al-rasul*, 'the city of the apostle'), formerly **Yathrib**, a sacred city of Hejaz, about 250 m. N. of Mecca. It is situated in a relatively fertile oasis with groves of palms and fruit trees and is noted for its daks. Many of the peasants belong to the Shi'a sect (*see* SHIITES). The old tn is surrounded by a stone wall which is almost complete and a suburb has a mud wall, the ends of which meet the city wall. The whole is an oval a mile long from E. to W., and half a mile from N. to S. In the early Christian cents. M. was a Jewish centre; but these people may have been Arab converts, for nothing but their religion distinguished them from the tribes around them. Mohammad was invited to M. when Mecca grew too dangerous, so that M. became the cap. of the Muslim state and remained so till the first Umayyad caliph removed the gov. to Damascus in AD 661. After that M. became a centre of religious learning and, with Mecca, a playground for the wealthy. The tomb of Mohammad is in the main mosque, which stands on the site of the house of his favourite wife and the first place of worship. The present building dates from the 15th cent. with later additions. It is an imposing edifice, the walls

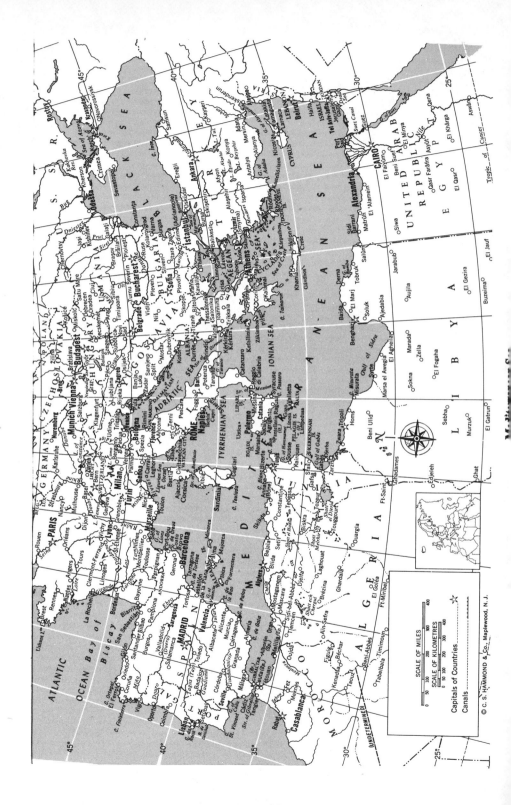

Mediterranean Sea

SCALE OF MILES
0   50   100   200   300   400
SCALE OF KILOMETRES
0 50 100   200   300   400

Capitals of Countries .... ☆
Canals ....

© C. S. HAMMOND & Co., Maplewood, N.J.

faced with marble or coloured tiles; the tombs of Mohammad and his first 2 successors are behind elaborate iron grilles, and the mosque also contains the library of Shaikh al-Islam Arif Hikmat. A visit to M. and the tomb of Mohammad is praiseworthy and is often combined with the pilgrimage, but is not part of it. Pop. 50,000. For the hist. *see* ARABIA and SA'UD, IBN; and for a description of the tn *see* H. St J. B. Philby, *A Pilgrim in Arabia*, 1946; *also* E. Esin, *Mecca the Blessed, Madinah the Radiant*, 1961. (*See Plates: Islam, Arabia*.)

Medina del Campo, Sp. tn in the prov. of Valladolid. It has an anct castle, the seat of the Castilian court during the 15th cent., and curious medieval streets. It is an important agric. centre. Pop. 14,300.

Medina Sidonia, Sp. tn in the prov. of Cadiz. It stands on a hill, and has a Gothic church, and the ruined palace of the dukes of M. S. Pop. 8700.

Medinat el Faiyum, city of Egypt, cap. of Faiyum prov., situated on the Bahr Yusuf. It is an important trade centre of a rich agric. dist. The tn stands close to the site of the anct city of Crocodilopolis (Arsinoë), where the Egyptians worshipped the sacred crocodiles kept in Lake Moeris. Hawara, with its labyrinth, is to the SE. Pop. (1965) 73,000.

Mediolanum, Italy, *see* MILAN.

Mediolanum, France, *see* SAINTES.

Meditation, or **Mental Prayer,** *see* PRAYER.

Mediterranean Fever, *see* MALTA FEVER.

Mediterranean Sea (anct **Mare Internum**), great inland sea, bounded on the N. by Europe, on the E. by Asia and on the S. by Africa, and communicating with the Atlantic by the Strait of Gibraltar, with the Black Sea by the Dardanelles, sea of Marmora and Bosphorus, and with the Red Sea by the Suez Canal. It has an area of about 1,008,000 sq. m., including its chief subdivisions, the Tyrrhenian, Ionian, Adriatic and Aegean Seas, and its extreme length is 2300 m., with a breadth varying from 86 to 600 m. It has a drainage area of about 3,000,000 sq. m., the prin. rivs. being the Ebro, Rhône, Po, Arno, Tiber and Nile. Italy, Sicily and the shallows of the Adventure Bank, stretching from Sicily to Cape Bon on the African coast, divide the sea into an E. and a W. basin, of which the former has an extreme depth of 2187 fathoms and the latter of 2406 fathoms, while the mean depth of the whole area has been estimated at 780 fathoms. The rivs. bring but a small supply of water compared with the size of the sea, and owing to this and the great amount of evaporation in such a lat. the water is saltier than in the great oceans. Its temp., too, at equal depths near the surface is on an average sev. degrees (Fahrenheit) higher than that of the Atlantic. At depths of less than 100 fathoms the water varies in temp. according to season and depth, but at great depths there is an almost constant and uniform temp. of about 55° F. In some places, under particular conditions, the tide rises as much as 5 ft, but taking the sea all over it may be said to be nearly tideless. The climate is warm

and equable, the mean daily temp. being above 50° F. for at least 8 months in the year, but the M. peninsulas have a marked deficiency of rain, the middle of summer being remarkable for its drought. Among local winds are the *sirocco*, a violent, dry, hot, parching and dust-laden southerly wind, prevalent chiefly in Malta and Sicily, but occasionally as far N. as Rome; the *leveche*, a similar wind experienced on the SE. of Spain; the *solano*, a moist E. wind visiting the same regions; the *mistral* and *bara*, cold, dry, northerly winds, the former of which prevails from the mouth of the Ebro to Genoa, especially round Marseilles, the latter along the coast of Dalmatia; and the *etesian* winds, which blow in the E. parts of the sea, chiefly in late summer and autumn. The prin. is. are Sicily, which divides the M. into an E. and W. portion, Cyprus, Crete, Malta and the Ionian Is. in the E., and Sardinia, Corsica and the Balearic Is. in the W. The most important gulfs are Taranto in Italy, Lepanto in Greece, Syrtis and Cabes in Barbary, in the E. portion; and Valencia in Spain, Lyons in France, Genoa in Italy and Tunis in Africa in the W. The M. is frequently subject to earthquakes and Vesuvius, Stromboli and Etna are among the most famous of its active volcanoes. The scenery of its shores is varied, mt ranges and high table-lands predominating. The fauna of the M. is similar in character to that of the neighbouring parts of the Atlantic Ocean, but a marked feature is the scarcity of life in the deeper parts. Fish are abundant, especially tunny, anchovies, pilchards and mackerel, and the finest coral, sponge and ambergris are procured. Since the opening of the Suez Canal, the pearl oyster and various other molluscs have come in from the Red Sea.

The M. is 'the Great Sea' of the Hebrews, but the Phoenicians were the chief agents in promoting the communion of peoples, and their flag flew in every part of the waters of the 'Internal Sea'. After them came the Greeks, who did much for trade, and even when Carthage had been destroyed and the Romans were all powerful, they still possessed the largest share of the commerce of the M., for the Romans despised all trade. In the Middle Ages the Venetians monopolised its commerce.

From the 18th cent. Great Britain exercised the main influence by the possession of Gibraltar and Malta, an influence which was contested by Italy during the Italo-Ethiopian war (1935–6). During the Sp. Civil War tension in the M. became acute when the Sp. insurgents claimed the right to blockade Sp. ports. In the second World War Great Britain and France controlled the M. up to the summer of 1940; but the whole position was changed by the collapse of France and the entry of Italy on the side of Germany. The position would have been still further compromised by the Vichy Gov., but for the prompt action of Churchill in securing the immobilisation of the Fr. fleet at Alexandria and the destruction of other units at Oran (July 1940). The balance of power in the M. swung in favour of Britain with the victory of Taranto when half the It. battle fleet was torpedoed by Brit. aircraft (Nov. 1940). This action confined the It. fleet to harbour besides virtually severing contact between Italy and Libya, and the complete opening of the M. to Brit. convoys to Libya seemed to be in sight at the end of the year. But early in 1941 the arrival of Ger. air squadrons in the airfields of Sicily destroyed this prospect, besides endangering Brit. naval operations, though these were not stopped, as was shown by the bombardment of Genoa and the naval victory off Cape Matapan (q.v.) (Mar. 1941). But with the combined Ger. and It. air bombardments of Malta, and the check of Brit. military operations in Egypt and Libya, Britain for a time lost the command of the M., and her supply ships had to take the 12,000-m. route round the Cape. The turning-point came with the victory of El Alamein (Oct. 1942), the landing of Amer. and Brit. forces in N. Africa (Nov. 1942) and the allied capture of Bizerta and Tunis, for these events, besides liberating Malta, foreshadowed the immediate invasion of Italy. After the war other factors entered into the adjustment of the balance of power. The Brit. mandate in Palestine ended in May 1948 and the U.K. recognised the State of Israel in Jan. 1949; Britain and Egypt reached agreement on the evacuation of Brit. troops from the Suez Canal Zone (1954). The adherence of Greece and Turkey to NATO, the signing of the Bagdad Pact (later renamed CENTO), the seizure of the Suez Canal by Egypt in 1955, the granting of independence to Tunisia and Algeria in 1961, the relinquishing of Malta as a naval base and the presence of an American fleet in M. waters are new factors affecting the future of this important area. *See also* NAVAL OPERATIONS IN SECOND WORLD WAR; AFRICA, NORTH, SECOND WORLD WAR, CAMPAIGNS IN. *See* E. C. Semple, *Geography of the Mediterranean Regions*, 1931; E. Muspratt, *Greek Seas*, 1933; J. Holland Rose, *The Mediterranean in the Ancient World*, 1934; C. A. Petrie, *Lords of the Inland Sea*, 1937; F. Saxl and R. Wittkower, *British Art and the Mediterranean*, 1948; A. Siegfried, *The Mediterranean*, 1948; B. Newman, *Mediterranean Background*, 1949; L. G. Pine, *The Middle Sea*, 1950.

Medium, paper size, *see* PAPER.

Mediumship, *see* PSYCHICAL RESEARCH.

Medlar, or *Mespilus germanica*, family Rosaceae, a branching tree to 10 ft high, with ornamental white flowers giving place to small rounded fruits, crowned by the calyx; they are gathered dry and laid, fruit-eye down, on a shelf for a few weeks to soften or blet. If its peculiar flavour is appreciated, the fruit may be eaten raw or used for preserves.

Medmenham, vil. of Buckinghamshire, England, 3 m. SW. of Marlow, famous for its abbey, which was founded by Cistercian monks at the beginning of the 13th cent. The vil. is prettily situated near the banks of the Thames. Pop. 1241. *See also* DASHWOOD, SIR FRANCIS.

Médoc, dist of France, in the dept of Gironde, extending for about 50 m. along the l. b. of the R.

Gironde. It is celebrated for its clarets.

Medomsley, *see* CONSETT.

Medtner, Nikolai Karlovich (1880–1951), Russian composer, *b.* Moscow. He studied the pianoforte under Safonov at the Moscow Conservatory, gained there the Rubinstein prize, and toured Europe as a pianist in 1901–2, becoming prof. at the conservatory for a year on his return, but then retiring to devote himself to composition. After the revolution he went on another tour in the W. in 1922, but found himself unable to return. He settled in Paris for a time and later in London, where he *d.* M.'s music is almost wholly confined to piano works (including 3 concertos and 12 sonatas) and to songs, but there are 3 sonatas and 3 *Nocturnes* for violin and piano, and at the end of his life he produced a Quintet for strings and piano. As a keyboard composer he is important and in his way as characteristic as Chopin or Schumann. The idiom is no more advanced than that of Brahms, but quite different and distinguished particularly for many new rhythmic ingenuities. Characteristic titles are *Improvisations*, *Dithyrambs*, *Fairy Tales* and *Novels*. His very numerous songs are deeply felt and tasteful, with piano parts quite as important as those for the voice. For their words he relied largely upon Russian and Ger. poets, including Pushkin, Tuchev, Goethe, Heine.

Medulla Oblongata, *see* BRAIN.

Medullary Rays, radial transverse bands of soft-celled tissue in woody stems and roots. M. R. serve to maintain continuity between the living cells of the pith and living tissues external to the wood. They often contain food reserves.

Medusa, *see* GORGON.

Medusae, *see* JELLY-FISH.

Medway, riv. of England, 70 m. in length. Its source is in Sussex, and it flows through Kent to Rochester, from which tn it forms an estuary, joining the R. Thames at Sheerness (q.v.). The prin. tns on its banks are Tonbridge, Maidstone (to which tn it is navigable), Rochester, Chatham and Gillingham (qq.v.).

Medwig-ston, *see* MAIDSTONE.

Mee, Arthur (1875–1943), editor and author, *b.* Stapleford, near Nottingham. In 1906 he produced the *Harmsworth Self-Educator*, and various other works followed, notably *The Children's Encyclopaedia*, which he ed. from 1908 to 1933, and *The Harmsworth History of the World*, 1907. He also founded and ed. the *Children's Newspaper*. In many productions he was associated with Sir John Hammerton (q.v.). He wrote *Joseph Chamberlain*, 1900, *Arthur Mee's Golden Year*, 1922, *The Children's Shakespeare*, 1926, *The Rainbow Books*, 1939, and *The King's England*, a survey of Eng. tns and vils. *See* Sir J. Hammerton, *Child of Wonder*, 1947.

Meegeren, Han van, *see* FORGERY, *Forgery in Art*, and VAN MEEGEREN.

Meenen, *see* MENIN.

Meer, Jan van der, name of 2 Dutch painters of Haarlem, who were father (1628–91) and son (1656–1705). Both painted landscapes with cattle. The father excelled also in sea-pieces and battle scenes, whilst the son, who had studied under Nicolas Berchem and was a charming etcher, was famous for his studies of sheep.

Meer, Jan van der (1632–75), Dutch painter, *see* VERMEER, JAN.

Meerane, Ger. tn in the dist of Karl-Marx-Stadt, 20 m. W. of Karl-Marx-Stadt (q.v.). It has textile and engineering industries. Pop. 24,500.

Meerkat, or **Suricate** (*Suricata tetradactyla*), mammal, with soft and long grey fur, which is found in Cape Prov. and belongs to the mongoose family. A third of its length (14 in.) is occupied by the tail. The M. feeds on succulent bulbs, is sociable and partial to sun baths. The Madagascar cat and the *Cynictis penicellata* are also termed M.s.

Meerschaum ($Mg_2Si_3O_8$)$2H_2O$, white or yellowish amorphous mineral which floats, composed of hydrous silicate of magnesia. It literally means 'foam of the sea'. Many 19th cent. specimens were elaborately carved. All, when smoked, produce a rich, dark colouring which is the main reason for their popularity. Hardness, 2 to 2·5. It decomposes in hydrochloric acid with gelatinisation, and gives off water when heated. It occurs in beds and in irregular masses in alluvial deposits at Lamos and Negropont, in Asia Minor, Morocco and in Spain, where it is used as a building stone. It is used for making pipes and pipe bowls, being admirably adapted by reason of its lightness and porosity. It is first soaked in tallow and in wax, and then polished.

Meerut, tn of Uttar Pradesh state, India, situated 40 m. NE. of Delhi. To the N. of the city is a cantonment, and it is the site of a military station. M. was the place at which the Indian Mutiny first broke out in 1857.

Mees, Charles Edward Kenneth (1882–1960), leading photographic chemist and physicist, *b.* Wellingborough. With S. E. Sheppard he continued at Univ. College, London, the fundamental work on the photographic process that had been started by Hurter and Driffield. Entering the commercial production of photographic plates, he introduced dyes giving improved colour sensitivity, of great value in spectroscopy and astronomy. He founded in 1912 the Kodak Research Laboratory at Rochester, New York, and developed it into one of the world's greatest industrial research laboratories. M. was in charge of research until 1955, when the staff had grown to 750. He was elected F.R.S. in 1939. His numerous works on many aspects of photographic science include *The Theory of the Photographic Process*, 1954.

Megaera, *see* ERINYES.

Megalith Culture (Gk *megas*, great; *lithos*, stone) is named from a development of Neolithic and early Bronze Age times characterised by the erection of menhirs, alignments, tombs and circles of large stones. Since the middle of the 19th cent. the term M. has come to mean either a large stone used in the construction or the construction itself as a whole. The M. tomb was essentially derived from the rock-cut tombs of the W. region of the Mediterranean, and the

fashion spread along the Atlantic seaboard of Europe, through Spain, France and the Low Countries, as far N. as the Baltic. The M.s postulate a most powerful religious practice based on the ritual significance of fertility and directed to the worship of the earth mother. M. C. included mixed farming, rearing of stock, and the development of potting and weaving of cloth. There are sev. varieties of graves, passage graves (Bryn Celli Dhu), gallery graves (especially in the Severn and Clyde areas) and long barrows. Many notable examples of standing stones and circles, such as Long Meg and her daughter, can be seen in Britain. The tomb is sometimes, when free standing, called a dolmen, a roofed burial chamber of stones, but it is merely the chamber of a long barrow from which the earth or stone mound has been denuded. Kit's Coty in Kent and the Devil's Den near Marlborough are well-known examples. Stonehenge, Avebury and Arbor Low, Derbyshire, are well preserved examples. *See* O. G. S. Crawford, *The Long Barrows of the Cotswolds*, 1925; G. E. Daniel, 'The . . . Passage Graves of the British Isles', *Proceedings of the Prehistoric Society*, 1949; *Prehistoric Chamber Tombs of England and Wales*, 1950. For distribution see the Ordnance Survey Period Map of Anct Britain, and J. Hawkes, *Guide to Prehistoric and Roman Monuments in England and Wales*, 1951. *See also* ARCHAEOLOGY; BARROWS; CROMLECH; DOLMEN; MENHIRS; MONOLITH; PREHISTORY; SOUTERRAINS; STANDING STONES; STONE CIRCLES. (*See Plates: Isle of Man; Burial Customs.*

Megalopolis, most recent but the most important of the cities of Arcadia, was founded on the advice of Epaminondas after the battle of Leuctra (371 BC), and was formed out of the inhab. of 38 vils. It was situated in the dist Maenalia, near the frontiers of Messenia, on the R. Helisson, which flowed through the city. It became afterwards one of the chief cities of the Achaean league. Philopoemen and the historian Polybius were natives of M.

Megalosaurus, large bipedal carnivorous dinosaur (q.v.) belonging to the Theropod group of the order Saurischia. Fragmentary fossil remains occur in European Jurassic deposits.

Megaphone (from Gk *megas*, great; *phōnē*, sound), instrument, invented by Edison, for facilitating the conveyance of sound for a distance of some miles and consisting of 2 large and tapering funnels. In a simpler (and older) form it is just a speaking trumpet.

Megapodiidae, *see* MOUND BIRDS.

Megara, *see* HYBLA and MELILLI.

Megara, anct Gk city-state between Attica and Corinth, bounded N. and S. by the Corinthian and Saronic Gulfs respectively. On the 1st of these was the port of Pegae, on the 2nd that of Nisaea. With such facilities M. soon attained commercial propriety and estab. numerous colonies of which the most famous was Byzantium (q.v.). Her commercial preeminence, however, gradually yielded to competition from Athens, Corinth and Corcyra. In

459 BC M. received an Athenian garrison, which was massacred in 445 by the citizens. Athens retaliated with an embargo on Megarian trade throughout her empire. After the Peloponnesian War M. regained some of her former prosperity and was eventually admitted to the Achaean League (q.v.). M. is celebrated as the seat of a philosophical school, usually called the Megarian, which was founded 398 BC by Euclid, a native of the city. It was also known for its white shell marble and for a white clay, of which pottery was made. The modern tn of M. has a pop. of 15,500. See E. L. Highbarger, The History and Civilization of Ancient Megara, 1927.

Megasthenes (3rd cent. BC), Gk historian and geographer. As ambas. of Seleucus I to the Indian king Sandrocottus at Magadha he wrote Indika, of which large fragments survive and which was used by Diodorus and Arrian.

Megatherium, gigantic extinct herbivorous ground-sloth of the order Edentata which lived in N. and S. America in Pleistocene times. It had a massive body about 20 ft long, and was the largest of the ground-sloths.

Megerle, Ulrich, see ABRAHAM A SANCTA CLARA.

Meghna, estuary of the Ganges and the Brahmaputra, where they enter the sea by 4 mouths.

Megiddo, Israel, old fortified city of Palestine, commanding the best pass from the Mediterranean to the valley of Esdraelon and onwards N. to Galilee and Damascus. It was always a point of great strategic importance; the great Pharaoh Thothmes III (middle 15th cent. BC) defeated here the Canaanites, and the Judaean King Josiah (2 Kings xxiii. 29 f.) was defeated and mortally wounded by Necho (609 BC); finally, in 1918, Allenby defeated here a Turkish army.

A Ger. expedition excavated this site in 1903–5, and a large-scale systematic excavation, by the Oriental Institute of the univ. of Chicago (1925–1939) produced extremely interesting results. The debris of occupation reaches about 70 ft of depth, the lowest level going back to the beginning of the fourth millennium BC or earlier. The most interesting results are the extensive stables of the Israelite kings, which were first built in the time of Solomon (970–931 BC), and the astonishing hoard of more than 200 carved and incised ivories from the 12th cent. BC. The M. stables covered a considerable portion of the site, and, according to the easily recognisable lay-out, provided room for 450 to 480 horses and 150 to 160 chariots. The stables were exceedingly well built; each unit consisted of a central passage (about 10 ft wide) flanked by 2 rows of stone pillars which served simultaneously as tie-posts and as supporters for the roof. Beyond were 2 aisles for the horses (each 10 ft wide), each unit accommodating over 30 horses. See J. Finegan, Light from the Ancient Past (3rd ed.), 1947; F. Thieberger, King Solomon, 1947; W. F. Albright, The Archaeology of Palestine, 1949.

Megrim, see MIGRAINE.

Megrims (vertigo or staggers in horses), temporary loss of voluntary power and movement. The symptoms frequently occur when a horse is going uphill with a stiff load and tight collar and is due to congestion of the blood vessels in the brain; the horse falls down and its pulse is very feeble. General attention to the animal's condition, the provision of a more comfortable collar and less heavy loads check its recurrence. This condition was common when coach and draught horses were numerous. Staggering and giddiness in horses may occur in the course of a variety of diseases, e.g. heart disorders and brain tumours.

Mehadia, mrkt tn of Banat, Rumania, 15 m. N. of Orsova. It was on this site that the Rom. tn of Ad Mediam was built, and the Hercules baths known in Rom. times are near here. Pop. 2500.

Mehemet Ali, or **Mohammed** (1769–1849), Pasha of Egypt, probably b. Albania. In Egypt, he co-operated with the British in driving out the French, and afterwards, having made an alliance with the Mamelukes against the Turkish sultan's regent Khosrew, became viceroy of the Mamelukes. Mainly through bribery he was made Pasha of Cairo by the sultan in 1806, and in 1811, turning against his former allies, the Mamelukes (q.v.), tried to exterminate them, and did indeed cause large numbers of them to be assassinated, thereby securing undisputed sway over upper Egypt. He now sought to suppress the fanatic Wahabis in a war which lasted for sev. years, during which his son, Ismail Pasha, conquered Dongola, Kordofan, Sennaar and other provs. Another son, Ibrahim, was sent in command of a large fleet to Morea to co-operate with the Turks against the Greeks in the latter's struggle for independence; but it was completely destroyed at Navarino (1827). The sultan, however, in return for his aid against the Greeks surrendered Crete to M. in 1830, and was promptly met with a demand for the cession of Syria. This having been rejected, M. invaded and conquered that prov., and, after inflicting a crushing defeat on the Turks at the battle of Konieh, marched on Constantinople, but was baulked by the intervention of the European powers. He succeeded, however, in acquiring Syria and Adana under a treaty signed at Kutaia. In 1839 Sultan Mahmoud II sought to regain Syria, but, being heavily defeated by M., apealed to the European powers for assistance. The outcome of European aid was that M. was defeated near Beirut, and, Alexandria being blockaded, gave up further claim on Syria, but secured for his family recognition as hereditary pashas of Egypt. In 1848 he resigned in favour of his son Ibrahim, who was soon afterwards succeeded by Abbas, M.'s grandson. See H. Dodwell, The Founder of Modern Egypt: a Study of Muhammad Ali, 1931.

Mehkemas, or **Mehkemehs**, courts of the Cadis which formerly gave judgments in Egypt on all matters concerned with the status of persons (marriage, inheritance, guardianship, etc.), abolished by decree in Sept. 1955 (effective from Jan. 1956). Their judgments were based on the code of laws derived from the Koran. The grand cadi (who had to be of the *Hanifis* sect) was assisted by a council of learned men or *Ulema*; the cadis were chosen from those studying at El Azhar Univ.

Mehlis, see ZELLA-MEHLIS.

Mehta, Sir Firozshāh Mehrvānji (1845–1915), leader of the moderate Congress party in W. India; *b.* Bombay, son of a Parsi merchant. He was the first Indian to be called to the Eng. Bar (Lincoln's Inn, 1868). He was one of the founders of the National Congress, becoming its president in 1890; K.C.I.E., 1904.

Méhul, Étienne Nicolas (1763–1817), Fr. composer, *b.* Givet, Mézières, had some lessons at home and became an organist, but in 1778 went to Paris, where he studied under J. F. Edelmann and taught. In 1779 he received advice from Gluck, under whose influence he found his true vocation of writing for the stage. He wrote 4 operas before *Euphrosine* was produced in 1790 and *Cora* in 1791. The former was comic, the latter serious, and he was soon to excel in both species. He had a genuine dramatic gift, great enterprise in orchestration that was not without its influence on Berlioz, and in his most serious work a nobility that impressed itself on Beethoven. Outside opera he produced patriotic works typical of the revolution period as well as, later on, a mass for the coronation of Napoleon I. He wrote 42 operas (11 unperformed), among which the best are *Le Jeune Henri* (with a famous overture, *La Chasse du jeune Henri*), 1797, *Les Deux Aveugles de Tolède*, 1806, *Uthal* (from Ossian, scored without violins), 1806, and especially *Joseph*, 1807, which held the stage longest and was known in England as *Joseph and his Brethren*.

Meighen, Arthur (1874–1960), Canadian Conservative statesman, *b.* Anderson Post Office, Perth co., Ontario. He studied at the univ. of Toronto. He went W. to Portage la Prairie to practise law in 1903, entered politics and was elected M.P. for Portage in 1908. From 1913 he successively held the posts of solicitor-general, secretary of state and minister of the interior in the Borden gov. In the conscription crisis of 1917, he earned the hatred of Quebec for his part in the Military Service Act, which was strongly opposed by that prov. In 1918 he attended the Imperial Conference, and in 1920 succeeded Sir Robert Borden as Conservative leader and Prime Minister. M. lost the general election of 1921 to Mackenzie King and the Liberals, and also lost his seat. He made a strong recovery in 1925, but Mackenzie King formed a coalition with the Progressives which lasted until June 1926. M. then inadvisedly accepted a commission from the governor-general to form a gov., and this developed into the constitutional crisis of 1926 and led to M.'s defeat and ruin. Bennett succeeded him as Conservative leader in 1927. In 1942 M. resigned his senatorship to resume the leadership of the Conservative party, after the failure of Manion, but failed to win a seat.

Meijo Tenno, see MUTSUHITO.

Meiktila, dist and tn in the Mandalay div. of Burma. The dist consists chiefly of a level plain, and large numbers of cattle are reared. The chief products are rice, cotton, millet and sesamum. The tn of M. stands on a lake. It has a training institute for teachers. Area (dist) 2183 sq. m.; pop. (dist) 344,000; (tn) 25,000. *See also* BURMA, SECOND WORLD WAR, CAMPAIGNS IN, *Battle for the Burma Oilfields.*

Meilhan, Gabriel Sénac de, see SÉNAC DE MEILHAN.

Meillet, Antoine (1866–1936), *b.* Moulins, prof. at the Collège de France (q.v.) (1906) and founder of the Paris *Institut d'études slaves*. The author of numerous important works on historical and general linguistics, including *Introduction à l'étude comparative des langues indo-européennes*, 1903, *Les Dialectes indo-européens*, 1908, *Altarmenisches Elementarbuch*, 1913, *Aperçu d'une histoire de la langue grecque*, 1913, *Caractères généraux de la langue germaniques*, 1917, *Les Langues dans l'Europe nouvelle*, 1918, *Linguistique historique et linguistique générale*, 1921, *Traité de grammaire comparée des langues classiques* (with J. Vendryes, q.v.), 1924, *Le Slave commun*, 1924, *La Méthode comparative en linguistique historique*, 1925, *Esquisse d'une histoire de la langue latine*, 1928, co-ed. (with M. Cohen) of *Les Langues du monde*, 1924 (revised ed., 1952).

'Mein Kampf' ('My Struggle'), title of a 2-vol. work written by Adolf Hitler (q.v.), setting forth his political programme. It has been called the 'Bible' of National Socialism. The first vol. was written in the fortress of Landsberg-am-Lech, Bavaria, where Hitler was undergoing a term of imprisonment after his abortive *putsch* of 1923. The second vol. was written in the years 1925–7 after he had reconstructed his party. The book is crudely written and turgid in style, but its influence in Germany was enormous, sales running into many millions. A full Eng. trans. appeared in 1939.

Meiningen, Ger. tn in the dist of Suhl, on the Werra, 14 m. W. of Suhl (q.v.). It was the cap. of the duchy of Saxe-M. (q.v.), 1680–1918. There is a palace (16th–18th cents.), and there are engineering, textile and timber industries. Pop. 23,700.

Meiosis: 1. Means (Gk *meion*, less) literally 'lessening' and is sometimes used of the process of belittling an opponent's arguments; but more commonly it is used of understatement in the same sense as litotes (q.v.) with which it is generally identified. *See also* FIGURE OF SPEECH.

2. In biology, process of nuclear division whereby the chromosome number is halved. *See* HEREDITY; MITOSIS.

Meissen, Heinrich von, see HEINRICH.

Meissen, Ger. tn in the dist of Dresden, on the Elbe, 14 m. NW. of Dresden. It became the seat of a margravate in the 10th cent., and was merged in the kingdom of Saxony (q.v.) about 1423. It has a 13th–14th-cent. cathedral, and a 15th-cent. castle where 'Dresden china' was manuf. from 1710 to 1863. after J. F. Böttger's discovery of a method of copying Chinese porcelain (*see* the following article). There are ceramic and engineering industries, and there are kaolin deposits near by. Pop. 48,200. *See* O. E. Schmidt, *Das tausendjährige Meissen*, 1928.

Meissen (1710–present day), the first hard-paste porcelain factory to be estab. in Europe, near Dresden in Saxony, Germany (*see* PORCE-LAIN, *Hard-paste* and TILE). *See* W. B. Honey, *Dresden China*, 1946. (*See Plate: Porcelain*.)

Meissonier, Jean Louis Ernest (1815–91), Fr. painter, *b*. Lyons, was a pupil of J. Potier and L. Cogniet at Paris. His most characteristic work depicts civil and military life of the 17th and 18th cents., or scenes of 'society' life, painted on small panels, and remarkable for finish and detail. The Wallace Collection (Hertford House, London) has good examples of his 'miniatures in oils', including 'Soldiers Gambling' and 'A Charge of Cavalry'. *See* works by J. Claretie, 1881; J. Mollett, 1882; J. Laurens, 1892; G. Larroumet, 1893; M. O. Gérard, 1897; E. Fromentin. 1901; *also* A. Alexandre, *Histoire de la peinture militaire en France*, 1891.

Meistersinger (master-singers), name given to the Ger. lyric poets of the 14th, 15th and 16th cents., who banded themselves into guilds for the revival of the national minstrelsy. Many schools for M. were formed in all parts of Germany, especially the S., perhaps the most famous being that of Nuremberg while under Hans Sachs. Each guild was divided into various classes, from beginners or *Schüler* up to *Meister* or poets, who could invent a new melody in addition to fitting new words to old tunes. Meetings were held weekly in the tn hall or the church, and there were special competitions and festivals at Easter, Whitsuntide and Christmas. The members of the guild regarded poetry and music too much in the light of *crafts*, in which excellence was attained by following certain rules, to produce any very great achievements, but their general effect was good rather than bad. After the 16th cent. the M. gradually died out. Wagner's opera has immortalised their tradition. *See* GERMAN (AND AUSTRIAN) MUSIC. *See* A. Taylor, *The Literary History of Meistergesang*, 1937; B. Nagel, *Der deutsche Meistergesang*, 1952.

Meitner, Lise, *b*. Vienna. Prof. of physics in Berlin (1926–33). In 1939 she was the first to propose, in conjunction with O. R. Frisch, that the explanation of certain radiochemical phenomena could be found in the fission of uranium nuclei into two roughly equal fragments with the liberation of relatively large amounts of energy. Since 1939 she has conducted research at the univ. of Stockholm. *See* NUCLEAR POWER.

Mejerda River, *see* BAGRADAS.

Mekenen, Israel von, *see* MECKENEN.

Mekinez (in Morocco), *see* MEKNÈS.

Meknès, Mekinez, or **Mequinez**, tn of Fr. Morocco, situated 35 m. W. by S. of Fez, on a mt. slope. It is one of Morocco's 4 caps., the summer residence of the sultan and the site of the Mulai Ismael mosque. Its chief manufs. are earthenware and leather. Pop. 140,380.

Mekong, major riv. of SE. Asia, about 2800 m. long. Its exact source is unknown, but it rises in Tibet, whence it flows through the Chinese prov. of Yunnan, the Shan country, Laos and Cambodia, entering the China Sea through sev. mouths in Cochin-China. For part of its length it forms the boundary between Thailand and Laos. There are rapids below Chienhoang and at Kratie. It is unsuitable for navigation except by small, shallow-draught ships. The branch from the Tonle Sap (Great Lake) joins the main riv. at Phnom Penh.

Melancholia, disorder of affect characterised by persistent depression. *See* INSANITY.

Melanchthon, Philip (1497–1560), Luther's assistant in the Reformation, *b*. Bretten, Baden, originally named Schwarzerd. The young Schwarzerd (Eng. 'black earth') took the more melodious Gk name of M., by which he is now known. He was educ. at Heidelberg, and in 1512 went to Tübingen, where he became student and teacher, till on Reuchlin's recommendation he was appointed prof. of Greek at Wittenberg (1518), where he met Luther.

In 1521 he pub. his *Loci communes rerum theologicarum*, the first great Protestant work on dogmatic theology, which passed through 50 eds. during his life. In 1530 he made a most important contribution to the cause of Protestantism in the Augsburg Confession (q.v.). His consent, conditionally given, to the introduction of the Augsburg Interim (q.v.) (*c*. 1547) led to painful controversies. Among his most notable works are *Summa doctrinae Lutheri*, 1524, *Libellus visitatorius*, 1527, and *Examen ordinandorum*, 1552. His numerous works, theological treatises, commentaries on sev. of the Gk and Lat. classics, Lat. poems and historical and philosophical writings, were pub. in 5 vols. at Basel in 1544 and in 4 vols. at Wittenberg in 1564, 1580 and 1601. The most complete ed. of his works is that by C. G. Bretschneider in his *Corpus reformatorum* (28 vols.), 1834–60 (supplements ed. by O. Clemen, 1910 ff.). *See also* Peucer's ed. of his works, 1562–4. M.'s life was written by his friend, Camerarius (q.v.), 1566. *See also* F. Hildebrandt, *Melanchthon, Alien or Ally*, 1946.

Melanesia (Gk *melas*, black; *nēsos*, is.), name given to a large group of is. of W.-central Oceania, between Micronesia (q.v.) in the N. and Polynesia (q.v.) in the S., inhabited mainly by people of Papuan origin. The term ₀M. embraces all the is. from the Bismarck Archipelago in the NW. to the Fiji Is. in the SE., and includes part of New Guinea, the Solomon Is., Santa Cruz, Banks Is., New Hebrides, D'Entrecasteaux, New Caledonia, Loyalty and Admiralty Is. The is. are either of volcanic or coral formation abounding in reefs and lagoons, with luxurious vegetation. The inhab. are (with some exceptions, notably in Fiji) little advanced and are ethnically affiliated to the Papuans of New Guinea. They are short in stature, with tight-curled hair and negroid features, denoting the intrusion of a Polynesian element into the aboriginal stock. Some tie their hair into small bunches with fibre, causing it to stick out all round the head. They speak anct forms of the Malayo-Polynesian language, and their religion is animism combined with spirit worship. The is. are devoid of the larger carnivora, but rats, opossums, bats, mosquitoes and reptiles abound. As M. stretches from 145° E. and 1° S. in a SE. direction to the Tropic of Capricorn at 180° E., the is. vary in their flora and fauna to a very great extent, as also in their manners and customs.

Anthropologically the different is. groups present many features that would appear to be common to Melanesian society generally, but in some cases there are marked divergencies. In the Banks Is. a noteworthy custom is that of initiation into the *sukwe*, a complicated organisation which may be compared to a man's club. A div. of the *sukwe* is the *tamate* or ghost society which meets in the bush. In most vils. in these is. there is a building called the *gamal*, which is the eating and sleeping house of the members of the *sukwe* as well as their general meeting-place in the vil. The process of initiation into the various ranks of the *sukwe* is an important element in the social life of the Banks islanders. Each of the *tamate* societies is entered by a ceremony of initiation which varies greatly in complexity and duration for the different societies. Most of the *tamate* societies possess objects worn as hats or as masks, or carried in the hand, and these often bear the shape of the animal or other object from which the society takes its name. The object of the *tamate* is partly disguise, and partly to produce fear among the uninitiated, and to enhance the mystery of the societies. A study of the *sukwe* and *tamate* societies is necessary to an understanding of their bearing on the general life of the people of the Banks Is., and especially on the determination of social rank and importance, the distribution of wealth and the protection of property. Though there are many points of similarity between the cultures of the Banks and Torres Is., notably in connection with relationship, the social organisation of the 2 groups of is. differs considerably. The main social divs. of both groups, however, are exogamous. In the New Hebrides the social structure is that frequently met with in Melanesian is., namely that of the dual exogamous organisation with matrilineal descent. Both sexual communism and communism in property were once practised in M. It is probable that the 2 kinds of communism were closely associated. Secret organisations, however, sprang up, which introduced the very widespread custom of taboo, an important feature of which was the protection of individual property.

Perhaps the most instructive is. for Melanesian sociology is New Guinea, the largest of all the M. is. 'The inhab. of this is. present extraordinary differences in physical characteristics and culture, and the contrast between the relatively tall, dark-skinned, frizzly-haired natives of Torres Strait, the Fly R. and the neighbouring parts of New Guinea on the one hand, and the smaller, lighter-coloured peoples of that part of the coastline stretching from the E. of Cape Possession to the archipelagos of the E. extremity, is so striking that the 2 peoples must be recognised as racially distinct' (Seligmann). Hence the term Papuan is really unsuitable to denote all the inhab. of the whole of New Guinea, and it is better to follow Professor Seligmann, who uses the term 'Papuasian' to denote all the inhab. of New Guinea and its archipelagos, and limits the term 'Papuan' to the geographically more W. Papuasians, a congerie of frizzly-haired and often mop-headed peoples, whose skin colour is some shade of brownish black. The E. Papuasians, or the generally smaller, lighter-coloured, frizzly-haired races of the E. peninsula of New Guinea and its archipelagos, may be called Papuo-Melanesians (or Massim). Many of these latter speak languages with a common Melanesian grammar. These languages are divisible into groups, the constituent languages of each containing many common words, all akin to the stock language of Oceania. But the vocabulary of the Papuan languages shows a number of evidently unrelated stock languages, and their grammar has no Melanesian characteristics. The inhab. of the N. is. of the Massim, like the inhab. of the Louisiades, are skilled in the craft of building the *waga*, large sea-going canoes, that figure so prominently in the life of the dist. It is in these is. too that the decorative art, characteristic of the whole of the Massim dist, has attained its peak in the carving of ornaments for the bows of the *waga*, and in the decorative patterns of the trobriand lime gourds. The most characteristic cultural feature of the Massim is the existence of a peculiar form of totemism with matrilineal descent. The members of each clan have as totems a series of associated animals belonging to different classes of the organic kingdom. Exogamy is strictly observed. Totem birds, snakes and fishes are commonly represented upon houses and canoes' bows and upon lime spatulae and indeed on most of the wooden utensils and ornaments of the Massim. For further details of the various groups of is. in M. *see* the separate articles NEW GUINEA; PAPUA; etc. *See* R. H. Codrington, *The Melanesians*, 1891; C. S. Belshaw, *Changing Melanesia*, 1954; W. H. R. Rivers, *The History of Melanesian Society* (2 vols.), 1914 (a survey of kinship and marriage); S. H. Ray, *Comparative Studies in the Melanesian Languages*, 1926; B. A. L. Cranstone, *Melanesia: A Short Ethnography*, 1961. (*See Plate*.)

Melanians, family of fresh-water snails, abounding in most tropical and sub-tropical countries and numbering about 1000 species. The shells are spiral and turreted, and are mostly of dark colours.

Melanorrhoea, genus of tall evergreen trees (family Anacardiaceae). *M. usitata* is the varnish tree of Burma. On tapping the tree the varnish is obtained as a thick, white juice which turns black on exposure to the air; it has anthelmintic properties. The wood is tough and very valuable.

Melanterite, *see* COPPERAS.

Melba, Nellie (Mrs Helen Porter Armstrong, *née* Mitchell), Dame (1861–1931), Australian soprano, *b.* Burnley, near Melbourne, of Scottish origin. Her first public appearance was on 17 May 1884 in Melbourne, and in 1886 she went to London. But Sullivan rejected her for the Savoy Opera Co., Randegger would not receive her as a pupil, and Carl Rosa did not keep a promised appointment open for her. She then went to Paris, where she became the pupil of Mathilde Marchesi. Soon she appeared in one of Marchesi's matinées as 'Mme Melba', the name being derived from Melbourne. Her début in opera was at the Théâtre de la Monnaie, Brussels, 1887, as Gilda in *Rigoletto*. Her success was immediate, and later she appeared in *La Traviata*, *Lucia*, Delibes's *Lakmé*, Thomas's *Hamlet*, and in London, at Covent Garden (24 May 1888), as Lucia in *Lucia di Lammermoor*. In 1889 she returned to Paris to make her first appearance at the Opéra, and after that her record was one of constantly growing popularity. She toured Europe and America with equal success. During the First World War she raised over £100,000 for the soldiers and was made D.B.E. In 1924 she made her farewell to the Australian operatic stage, taking the part of Mimi in *La Bohème*. Her last appearance at Covent Garden was in 1926, in the parts of Mimi, Desdemona and Juliet. M. had a voice of great range and of perfect purity and of absolutely even quality, yet left many unmoved by a certain coldness. Although essentially a coloratura singer, she made one or two attempts at parts such as Elsa in *Lohengrin* and Elizabeth in *Tannhäuser*, but her success was less in proportion as the music and dramatic force increased in profundity of meaning; and, after taking the part of Brunhildea in *Siegfried*, in 1896, with no success, she abandoned any further idea of being a Wagnerian singer. She married Charles Armstrong, son of a Queensland squatter, 1882. She was the first person to broadcast in a musical programme, from Marconi's station at Chelmsford (15 June 1920). She wrote an autobiography, *Melodies and Memories*, 1925. *See* lives by Agnes G. Murphy, 1909 and P. Colson, 1932. (*See Plate: Australia.*)

Melbourne, William Lamb, 2nd Viscount (1779–1848), statesman, *b.* London, educ. at Eton and Trinity College, Cambridge. He entered the House of Commons for Leominster in 1806, and joined the Whig opposition under the leadership of Fox. He accepted the chief secretaryship of Ireland in Canning's gov., and this partial alienation from the Whigs was increased when he not only took office under Goderich, but also remained for a short time in the gov. of the Duke of Wellington. In 1829 he succeeded to the viscounty. In 1830, having rejoined the Whigs, he was home secretary in the gov. of Earl Grey. In 1834 Grey retired, and William IV sent for M., who became Prime Minister. On the accession of Queen Victoria in 1837 it became the duty of M. to instruct the young sovereign and he came to have great influence over her. In 1841 his gov. was

succeeded by that of Sir Robert Peel. His wife, best known as Lady Caroline Lamb (1785–1828), whom he married in 1805, is remembered for her infatuation for Lord Byron. She and her husband formally separated, 1825. *See* Lord D. Cecil, *The Young Melbourne*, 1939, and *Lord M.*, 1954; and D. B. Wyndham Lewis, *Four Favourites*, 1948. (*See Plate: Parliament.*)

Melbourne: 1. Cap. of Victoria, Australia, founded in 1835 and named after Lord Melbourne, then Prime Minister of England; it lies on the Yarra R. at the head of an extensive sheet of water called Hobson's Bay, 2½ m. from the anchorage. It is the second largest city of Australia; the area of metropolitan M. is 212¼ sq. m. It is prettily situated overlooking the bay, with wide streets, modern, regularly planned, and richly endowed with parklands. Victoria's magnificent Shrine of Remembrance, erected in 1933, of Grecian classical architecture, is situated on the summit of a low hill off St Kilda Road, and is a landmark which may be distinguished from almost any part of the city. The city was designed by Robert Russell, a pupil of John Nash, the designer of much of Regent Street, London. The architectural beauty of its many impressive buildings is outstanding.

The first settlement was founded in 1835 by John Batman, a sheep farmer of Tasmania, who, with John Pascoe Fawkner, purchased 700,000 ac. from natives, and began to farm on ground that is now covered by the city. Batman's purchase was, however, repudiated by Governor Bourke as a trespass on crown lands, but eventually reasonable conditions were imposed on the settlers. Batman, in fact, founded a free city, and it was kept free. The name of the founder has been preserved in remembrance in Batman Avenue, on N. bank of the Yarra R. and Batman ward of the city. M. was created a city by letters patent of Queen Victoria dated 25 June 1847, and issued when M. was made the see of a bishop of the Church of England. development was greatly accelerated by the discovery of gold at Ballarat and Bendigo in the early fifties. The main thoroughfare is Collins Street and the chief shopping streets are Bourke Street, Swanston Street, Elizabeth Street and the 'Block' in Collins Street, where are the clubs and cafés.

More than one-fourth of M.'s total area of 7740 ac. is occupied by gardens and public parks. Within a few minutes' walk of the crowded business thoroughfares are the Botanic, Alexandria and Queen Victoria Gardens in the S., Royal Park and the Exhibition Gardens in the N., the Treasury and Fitzroy Gardens in the E., and the Flagstaff Gardens in the W. The splendid botanic gardens, occupying 130 ac. and containing 10,000 species of plants, representing 2000 genera, owe much to the direction of Baron von Muller, who estab. relations with similar institutions all over the world, and founded a national herbarium, which is now the most complete extant collection of Australian dried plants. 'The Separation Tree', an old red-gum, stands in the gardens. It was a well-developed tree when the first white settlers arrived in Victoria, and the citizens of M. gathered round it on 1 July 1851, to celebrate the separation of the colony from New S. Wales. Among the industries are engineering, brewing, tanning, printing, flour-milling, bacon curing and brick-making, while cheese, pottery, cigarettes, woollen goods and leather are manuf.

With its tall spires rising against the background of commercial M., St Paul's (Church of England) Cathedral, dominating the city, casts its shadow over the city's busiest intersection. Sandstone from the Barrabool Hills near Geelong, and limestone from Waurn Ponds, were the main materials used in its construction. Some of the interior granite columns were imported from England, but most of them were of Australian granite. St Patrick's (Rom. Catholic) Cathedral is erected on an area of land on E. Hill granted by the gov. to the Rom. Catholic Church in 1849. The present cathedral, the third building on the site, was designed by W. W. Wardell, an eminent architect who had studied under Pugin (q.v.). The dignity of the building externally is enhanced by its triple spires, the central spire rising to a height of 340 ft, and the carving and grouping at the E. end. An Act of the Imperial Parliament passed in the year 1850 decreed 'that the district of Port Phillip should be separated from the colony of New S. Wales, and should be named and designed as the colony of Victoria', having a separate Legislative Council. But not until 1855, when the daily discoveries of gold and the rapid progress of the state were exalting public ideas, was a start made on the erection of Houses of Parliament. On 25 Nov. 1856 the first session of the first Parliament of Victoria was inaugurated. The present Parliament House was built during the great boom in the eighties on a site in front of the former House. Visitors to M.'s art gallery are met on every side with the words 'Purchased in the terms of the Felton Bequest'. In this sentence is written much of the hist. of the M. gallery. After his arrival in Australia in 1852, when 21 years of age, Alfred Felton estab. himself as a druggist and general merchant. He amassed a fortune and bequeathed his estate of £378,000 for these purposes when he d. in 1904.

The M. mint is a branch of the Brit. royal mint, and was estab. by order of the council on 10 Aug. 1869, and opened on 12 Jan. 1872 to meet the problems created by the large discoveries of gold in Australia, and to reduce as far as possible its export. Today the mint does not produce gold coins, but anyone can sell gold there, and, if necessary, have it melted down and the fine gold extracted and weighed in his presence. Since the closing down of the Sydney mint in 1926 the royal M. has become the mint of the Commonwealth and the sole contractor for the production of Commonwealth coinage. Some of the original minting machinery is preserved within the building.

The univ. of M. was founded in 1853 and has an enrolment of between 8000 and 9000 students. It owes is origin largely to Hugh Culling Eardley Childers, a graduate of Trinity College, Cambridge, who was appointed inspector of schools in 1851 when only 23 years of age. One of his first efforts was to move for the estab. of a univ., and he recommended that £10,000 be provided for the purpose. In 1853 100 ac. of the present site were granted by the Crown, and the foundation-stone of the univ. was laid by the governor the following year. A permanent conservatorium of music arose in 1910, when Dame (then Madame) Nellie Melba laid the foundation-stone of Melba Hall, towards the cost of which she was a substantial contributor. A second univ., Monash Univ., was founded in 1958 and a third, Latrobe Univ., is to be opened in 1967.

M. has a large shipping trade; its port, called port M., is $2\frac{1}{2}$ m. away. The main airport is at Essendon and from there internal services are operated to all parts of Australia and external services to most parts of the world by the major airlines. (*See Plate: Victoria.*) Pop. 2,003,100.

2. Small tn of Derbyshire, England, 7 m. from Derby. It is a market gardening centre and shoes and warp-knitted piece goods in pure silk, rayon and other materials are manuf. Thomas Cook (q.v.) was b. in M. Pop. 4000.

'**Melbourne Herald**', estab. 1840, prints *The Sun News Pictorial* and *The Melbourne Herald.* It also has interests in periodicals, radio and television stations.

Melchett, Alfred Moritz Mond, 1st Viscount (1868–1931), politician and industrialist, *b.* Farnworth, son of the chemist Ludwig Mond (q.v.), and educ. at Cheltenham College, St John's College, Cambridge, and Edinburgh Univ. He became eventually chairman or director of a large number of industrial companies such as Brunner Mond & Co., the Imperial Chemical Industries and the Mond Nickel Co. He became a Liberal M.P. in 1906, but joined the Conservative party in 1926. Two years later he was created a peer, having been created a baronet in 1910.

Melchites, Melkites (Semitic *melek*, king), Christians of Syria, Palestine and Egypt who resisted the nationalist Monophysitism of their countries and remained orthodox, accepting the Council of Chalcedon and the Emperor. They adopted the Byzantine Liturgy (c. 1200); but by this time the laity and lower clergy were all Arabic-speaking, while the prelates were all Greek, which caused increasing tension and a tendency to look W. to Rome. In 1724 the Latinisers elected as bishop Seraphim Tanas, who at once submitted to the Pope and was created Lat. patriarch of Antioch, as Cyril VI. The term Melchite is now generally reserved for the subjects of this patriarchate, Syrian, Palestinian and Egyptian Uniats. The patriarch resides at Damascus.

Melchizedek ('King of Righteousness'), Canaanite King of Salem (Jerusalem) in the time of Abraham (Gen. xiv. 18) and called 'Priest of the Most High God'. Abraham acknowledged his priesthood by his offerings. His significance as a prophetic type of Christ is drawn out in Heb. vii. His gifts of bread and wine have always been taken as figures of the Christian eucharist (cf. Cyprian, *Epistles*, 63 n. 4). A sect of Gnostics asserted M. to be an earlier incarnation of the Second Person of the Trinity, superior to Jesus Christ. See V. Burch, *The Epistle to the Hebrews*, 1936.

Melcombe Regis, see WEYMOUTH.

Meleager. Oeneus, legendary king of Calydon, incurred the wrath of Artemis, who sent a huge boar to ravage the kingdom. His son M., who was also one of the Argonauts (q.v.), assembled a band of hunters and slew the boar. A quarrel over distribution of the spoils led to war, during which M. killed his uncles, brothers of his mother Althaea, but lived uneventfully thereafter until his death. Such is Homer's account. According to a later version, when M. was 7 days old his mother heard the Fates declare that the boy would live so long as a log then burning on the hearth remained unconsumed. Althaea extinguished the log and hid it in a chest; but to avenge her brothers she threw it back into the fire and M. died. Althaea then committed suicide and her daughters were changed by Artemis into guinea-fowl (*meleagrides*).

Meleager of Gadara (late 2nd-early 1st cent. BC), Gk poet, *b.* Gadara in the Decapolis; educ. at Tyre, but spent the remainder of his life in the is. of Cos. He compiled an anthology (q.v.), *The Garland*, which formed the original nucleus of the *Gk Anthology*.

See F. A. Wright, *Meleager's Complete Poems* (trans.), 1924.

Meleda (Yugoslav **Mliet**), is. in the Adriatic Sea, lying off the coast of Dalmatia. It is 23 m. by 4 m., of volcanic formation, and has been identified as the anct Melita. Pop. 1500.

Melegnano (formerly **Marignano**), It. tn in Lombardy (q.v.), 10 m. SE. of Milan. In 1515 Francis I of France defeated the Swiss allies of Milan here (see ITALY, *History*). Textiles are manuf. Pop. 9000.

Melek, see MOLECH.

Meléndez Valdés, Juan (1754–1817), Sp. poet, *b.* Ribera del Fresno (Badajoz). He was a pastoral and lyric poet, and was influenced by the ideas of the Fr. philosophical school. He collaborated with the Fr. invaders of his country, and was accordingly exiled in 1813. His poems include a number of odes and delicate and melodious elegies, which make him the greatest Sp. lyricist of the 18th cent.

Meletianism, 4th–5th-cent. schism at Alexandria, due to a dispute between Meletius, Bishop of Lycopolis in Egypt, and Bishop Peter of Alexandria; but the grounds of the quarrel are obscure. There is evidence that Meletius had conferred holy orders outside his own diocese; but St Athanasius merely states that Meletius was condemned (*c.* 305), having sacrificed to idols and slandered the bishops of Alexandria. Epiphanius says the dispute was over the treatment of *lapsi*, i.e. Christians who had failed under persecution but afterwards repented. Meletius is said to have refused them absolution like the Novatians in Rome and the Donatists in Africa, while the other Egyptian bishops were more lenient. The Council of Nicaea forbade Meletius to ordain any more, and those who had been ordained by him were to rank below those ordained by Peter and his successors.

See A. P. Stanley, *Lectures on the History of the Eastern Church*, 1884; C. J. Hefele, *A History of the Christian Councils* (translation), 1894.

Melfi, It. tn in Basilicata, at the foot of Mt Vulture, 26 m. NNW. of Potenza. It was founded *c.* 304, becoming the cap. of Apulia in 1044. It has a cathedral (partly 12th cent.) and a castle. Pop. 19,200.

Melford, Long, par. in the co. of Suffolk, England, situated 3 m. N. of Sudbury. It has a fine Perpendicular Church. Pop. 3700.

Meli, Giovanni (1740-1815), Sicilian poet, *b.* Palermo. He was prof. of chem. at Palermo Univ. His *canzonette*, odes and epigrams are mostly in the Sicilian dialect. His pastorals are exquisite specimens of their kind. In virtue of his *Favuli murali* he may be called a Sicilian La Fontaine. See *Opere poetiche* (ed. Alfano), 1909, and A. di Giovanni, *La vita e l'opera di Giovanni Meli*, 1934.

Melianthus, or **Honey Flower,** genus of evergreen shrubs of the family Sapindaceae, with graceful pinnate leaves and racemes of fragrant flowers which in some species yield much honey. *M. major*, S. Africa, grows outdoors in Cornwall.

Melilotus, genus of leguminous plants with trifoliate leaves and small yellow or white flowers. *M. alba*, white melilot, or Bokhara clover, is grown as a fodder crop but has a bitter taste and rapidly becomes hard and woody.

Méline, Félix Jules (1838–1925), Fr. statesman and economist, *b.* Remiremont. M. became Premier in April 1896 and held office till June 1898, and was a convinced anti-Dreyfusard.

Melinite: 1. Yellow clayey material, looking like yellow ochre. It has a sp. gr. of 2·24, is lamellar in structure, shining in streak and is found at Amberg, in Bavaria.

2. The Fr. army name for picric acid (q.v.), a high explosive commonly called lyddite in England and shinosite in Japan.

Meliotism, see OPTIMISM.

Meliphagidae, see HONEY-EATERS.

Melissic Acid, fatty acid which occurs in beeswax and carnauba wax. It is prepared by heating melissyl alcohol with caustic potash and forms a crystalline solid soluble in water.

Melita: 1. Anct name of Malta (q.v.).

2. See MELEDA.

Melitopol: tn in Tauria (q.v.) in the Zaporozh'ye oblast of S. Ukraine, 65 m. S. of Zaporozh'ye. It has varied engineering (since 1912) and food industries, and is a local cultural centre. It is the centre of a rich fruit growing area (cherries, apricots). Founded as a vil., M. has been a tn since 1841. Much fighting took place here in 1943. Pop. (1965) 112,000 (1926, 25,000).

Melittis, *melissophyllum*, or **Bastard Balm,** handsome Brit. perennial of the family Labiatae with long ovate leaves and conspicuous flowers, creamy white and blotched or spotted with pink or purple. It occurs, rarely, in woods in the SW.

Melk (Rom. **Namare**), Austrian tn in the prov. of Lower Austria, on the Danube. It is in the Wachau (q.v.). On a cliff, 170 ft above the tn, is a vast Benedictine abbey, one of the most magnificent baroque buildings in the world. Pop. 3100.

Melksham, tn of Wilts, England, on the R. Avon, between Trowbridge and Chippenham. Mentioned in Domesday Book, M. was formerly a royal demesne, and is now an agric. centre and a growing industrial tn. It manufs. rope and coco-nut matting, rubber goods, tyres, flour, dairy products, cattle food-stuffs, metal conveying equipment and wood trellis. Feathers are washed and purified here. Pop. 8279.

Mellanby, Sir Edward (1884–1955), physiologist and biochemist, *b*. W. Hartlepool. Educ. at Cambridge and St Thomas's Hospital (M.B., 1910; M.D., 1915). He was demonstrator of physiology at St Thomas's from 1909 to 1911 and lecturer (later prof.) of physiology at King's College for Women, 1913–20. He was then appointed prof. of pharmacology at Sheffield Univ. He was a member of the Medical Research Council from 1931 to 1933, and in the following year became secretary of that body, relinquishing his chair at Sheffield. He retired from the Council in 1949. At Cambridge M. was attracted to experiments in nutrition, a subject in which he retained an interest for the rest of his life. In 1918 he proved rickets to be a deficiency disease and soon afterwards produced it experimentally; his work on vitamins A and D was especially valuable. He was the driving force behind the movement for international standardisation of biological products. During the Second World War he played an important part, as member of the Scientific Food Policy Committee of the Cabinet, in the shaping of food policy. He drew attention to the possible dangers of chemical additives in food and, due to his observations, the use of agene to 'improve' flour was discontinued in 1955. M. contributed numerous papers to medical and scientific jours.; his books include *Nutrition and Disease*, 1934, and *A Study of Nutritional Research*, 1950. He was created K.C.B., 1937, and G.B.E., 1948. *See* memoir in *British Medical Journal*, 5 Feb. 1955.

Melleray Mount, Cistercian monastery of the Trappist observance in co. Waterford, Rep. of Ireland. It was estab. in 1830 by monks from the abbey of La Melleray in France, who settled at Cappoquin (q.v.) and called the new foundation after their original home. There is now a large community which conducts a school and cultivates extensive lands. M. M. is the motherhouse of sev. Cistercian abbeys, the most notable of which are Mount St Joseph, Roscrea, co. Tipperary, and Mount St Bernard, near Leicester, in England.

Mellifont Abbey, first Cistercian foundation in Ireland, founded in 1142 by St Malachy (1094–1148), 4 m. NW. of Drogheda (q.v.) in co. Louth. Its ruins were excavated in 1884–5.

Mellite, or **Honeystone,** hydrated salt of alumina and mellitic acid found in brown coal deposits. M. occurs in octahedrons with octahedral cleavage, or in granular nodules. Hardness 2–2·5; colour, honey-yellow; sp. gr. 1·65. It dissolves in nitric acid and is decomposed by boiling water.

Mellitus, St (*d*. 624), Rom. Benedictine abbot, was sent by Gregory the Great to England in 601 at the head of a group of missionary monks to carry on the work of St Augustine (q.v.). The first Bishop of London, he was exiled (616) for refusing communion to the apostate sons of King Sabert, but in 619 was recalled to Kent and became Archbishop of Canterbury.

Mellon, Andrew William (1855–1937), Amer. banker and politician, *b*. Pittsburgh, Pennsylvania. He entered the family banking house. Industrial development added to the prosperity of his chain of banks and he also became the largest producer of aluminium in the U.S.A., and so became one of the 3 or 4 wealthiest men in the world. In 1921 he was appointed secretary of the treasury, and later came to London as Amer. ambas. He presented to America an art collection estimated to be worth $50 million, and the $15 million National Gallery of Art to hold it. In 1911 he founded the M. Institute at Pittsburgh.

Mělník, Czechoslovak tn in the region of Prague (q.v.) at the confluence of the Labe (*see* ELBE) and the Vltava. It is noted for wine and apricots. Pop. 13,100.

Melo, tn of Uruguay, cap. of Cerro Largo dept on the R. Tacuari, 200 m. NW. of Montevideo. Commercial centre for wool, hides, cattle, grain. Pop. 23,000.

Melocactus, old genus of Cactaceae, of which the species have been reclassed to various other genera. *See* CACTUS.

Melodeon, *see* CONCERTINA.

Melodrama, originally a musical drama, or a drama interspersed with vocal or instrumental music. Now it is generally a non-operatic play of a semi-tragic or serious character, characterised by rapid action, sensational situations and violently expressed emotions, with marked contrast between hero and villain. The 2 earliest plays of this type in the Eng. language are *Deaf and Dumb*, 1801, by Thomas Holcroft (adapted from the Fr. *Mélodrame* by Bouilly), and *A Tale of Mystery*, 1802. The elements of M. had, however, existed long before this time, and were present in some of the Elizabethan tragedies as well as in late 18th-cent. romantic drama. More modern examples are Henry Irving's productions of *The Lyons Mail* and *The Bells*, and among famous Victorian M.s were *Sweeney Todd, the Demon Barber of Fleet Street*, and *Maria Marten, or the Murder in the Red Barn*. In music, *Melodrama* in German and *mélodrame* in French have a different connotation: the term stands for a musical accompaniment to spoken words, a whole play (such as Benda's *Ariadne*, 1775), short, spoken passages in an opera (as in Beethoven's *Fidelio* or Weber's *Freischütz*), passages of poetry or prose occurring in a concert work like Bliss's *Morning Heroes* or Honegger's *Jeanne d'Arc au bûcher*, the recitation of *Enoch Arden* with piano accompaniment by Richard Strauss, etc. *See* M. W. Disher, *Blood and Thunder*, 1949.

Melodunum, *see* MELUN.

Melody, succession of single musical sounds so arranged as to have a pleasing effect on the ear. It differs from harmony in being the production of only 1 voice or instrument, whereas harmony is the result of the blending of different voices or sounds. Rhythm is a most important element in M., whether it be the free rhythm of plainsong or the equal-measured rhythm of music of the classical period or that of the most modern composers. Much subtle elaboration of M. is to be found (e.g.) in Beethoven's sonata subjects. His M.s are often clearly harmonic in their structure and, similarly, in Bach's music harmony is a basis of M.

Meloidae, *see* CANTHARIDAE.

Melon, fruit of *Cucumis melo* (family Cucurbitaceae (q.v.)), tropical plant which has been cultivated for many cents. In Britain it is grown in pits or hot-houses, in frames and under cloches. The colour of the flesh may be green, scarlet or white. The size of the fruit, generally globular, varies from that of an olive to that of a giant gourd. *See also* WATER MELON.

MELON

A, section through fruit.

Meloria, It. islet in the Ligurian Sea, 4 m. from Leghorn (q.v.) harbour. The Genoese here defeated the Pisans at sea in 1284.

Melos (modern Gk **Mílos**), is. in the Aegean Sea, belonging to Greece, one of the Cyclades group. It is about 11 m. long and 5½ m. broad, and covers an area of 62 sq. m. It is of volcanic formation and has sev. mt peaks over 1000 ft high, Mt Prophet Elias rising to 2464 ft. M. was occupied in the 8th cent. BC by Dorians from Laconia; but there is evidence of Bronze Age settlements at Phylakopi, which have yielded pottery and painting. Melian ships fought at Salamis (480 BC); but M. did not join the Delian League (q.v.), and professed neutrality during the Peloponnesian war. In 416, however, it was attacked by an Athenian force: all adult males

were killed, the women and children reduced to slavery, and 500 Athenian colonists settled there. M. was important for certain natural products: Melian earth (used in the manuf. of pigments), and especially obsidian, of which M. was the prin. source for the whole Aegean area. In 1566 the is. was annexed by the Turks. The famous statue, the Venus de Milo, now in the Louvre, Paris, was discovered near Castro, the cap., by a peasant in 1820. Much damage was done in M. during the Second World War. Pop. 6000. *See* Evans, Hogarth and others, *Excavations of Phylakopi*, 1904.

Melpomene, muse of tragedy, *see* MUSES.

Melrose (Celtic *mao ros*, bare moor), police burgh of Roxburghshire, Scotland, on the Tweed, at the foot of the triple Eildon Hills, 37 m. SE. of Edinburgh. The famous Cistercian abbey was founded (*c.* 1136) by David I, and is celebrated by Scott as 'Kennaquhair'. Partly destroyed by Edward II (1322) and Richard II (1385) it was wrecked during Lord Hereford's expedition (1545). The Perpendicular style predominates and the beautiful traceried windows are famous. It contains the tombs of Alexander II and of the wizard Michael Scott (1175–1234), and is the reputed resting-place of the heart of Robert Bruce. Old M., 2½ m. E., is the site of a still more anct Columban monastery, estab. about 640 by St Aidan and deserted by 1075. There is an old border peel (fort) at Darnick. *Trimontium*, the site of a rom. camp erected AD 79, is 1½ m. E. at Newstead (q.v.). About 3 m. from M. is Abbotsford (q.v.), home of Sir Walter Scott. Pop. 2215. (*See Plate: Scottish Architecture.*)

Meltham, urb. dist. of the W. Riding of Yorks, England, 5 m. SW. of Huddersfield. Part of the area is moorland and falls within the Peak Dist. National Park. There are silk and woollen mills, and silica fire-bricks and tractors are made. Pop. 5425.

Melting, change of physical state when a solid is converted into a liquid by the application of heat. This change takes place at a definite point in the case of pure substances which do not decompose chemically under the action of heat. The presence of impurities depresses the M.-point and this furnishes a method of determining the purity of a substance and an important method of determining molecular weights. As an illustration of the fact that the presence of impurity lowers the M.-point, it may be noted that salt is used to remove ice from roads. In the case of the determination of molecular weights, it is found that the freezing-point of a *dilute* solution of a given substance is depressed below that of the pure solvent by an amount proportional to its concentration, i.e. the mass of dissolved substance per 1000 gm. of the solvent. Freezing mixtures also depend on the fact that the presence of impurity depresses the M.-point. Some solid substances contract in volume when melted while others expand. This can be shown more clearly by considering the reverse operation, i.e. solidification; thus a substance which contracts on M. will expand on solidifying. Taking water as an instance we find that when water freezes its volume increases. This explains the bursting of pipes in winter and also the fact that ice floats in water, since, because of this expansion, volume for volume, it is lighter. On the other hand, solid paraffin wax sinks in liquid wax, showing that liquid paraffin wax contracts on solidification.

Increase of pressure has little effect on the M.-point, unless the increase be large. Then it tends to depress or elevate the M.-point according to the substance. This increase of pressure lowers the M.-point of ice. The making of a snowball illustrates this point. The snow is pressed together, causing some of the snow to melt, and when the pressure is removed this melted snow freezes again, forming the ball into a compact mass. M. is employed commercially to separate bodies of different M.-points, and to take copies of objects as illustrated in an iron foundry. In the latter case bodies which expand on cooling are used so that every corner of the mould may be filled.

Melting-point. The determination of the M.-point of a substance is very important in the methods of organic chem. and affords a ready method for the detection of the presence of a substance. Many methods are employed to determine the M.-point, the most common of all being to draw a glass tube out to a very fine tube and seal one end. Very small pieces of the substance are introduced into the tube, which is then tied to the bulb of a mercury thermometer. Both are immersed in a bath of water or some other liquid, which is heated until the substance melts. The substance may then be allowed to cool and the temp. at which solidification commences can be obtained. The substance is again melted and the M.-point read off on the thermometer. Three or four readings may be taken in this manner, the M.-point being the mean of the readings. Some M.-points are (°C.) mercury, −38·3; tin, 232; zinc, 419; brass, 900; tungsten, 3390. *See also* METALLURGY (METALLURGICAL FURNACES).

Melton, par. and vil. of Suffolk, England, on the Deben, 9 m. ENE. of Ipswich. Pop. 2400.

Melton Mowbray, mrkt tn of Leics, England, on the Eye, near its confluence with the Wreake, 15 m. NE. of Leicester, noted for pork pies and Stilton cheese. There are iron-ore quarries and smelting and blasting furnaces. Dog foods are processed here. It is also noted as a hunting centre (Quorn (q.v.), Belvoir and Cottesmore hounds). The tn estate of M. M., an independent body founded 400 years ago, still owns the street market tolls and the corn exchange. The cattle market is leased by them to the urb. dist. council. Similarly its anct educational functions are now vested in the co. council, to whom it leases the land on which stands the tn's technical college. Apart from that, the tn estate maintains 2 parks, a sports ground and other recreational amenities. The estate is vested in 12 feoffees, elected for life or so long as they reside in the par., and is managed by 2 tn wardens, elected annually. Pop. 15,914.

Melun (anct **Melodunum**), Fr. tn, cap. of the dept of Seine-et-Marne. It is on the outskirts of the forest of Fontainebleau and grew up on and around an is. in the Seine. The tn was taken by Henry V of England in 1420, but was recovered by the French in 1430. There are many anct buildings, including a church dating from 1020. Amyot (q.v.) was *b*. in the tn. M. is an agric. centre, and manufs. glass, pottery and sugar. Pop. 26,900.

Melun et de Vaux, Vicomte de, *see* FOUQUET, NICOLAS.

Melusina, or **Mélusine,** in Fr. folklore, a water fairy, half woman and half fish; the daughter of Elinas, King of Albania. She married Count Raymond on the condition that he would never seek her on Saturdays, when she was accustomed to shut herself up alone because on that day she became a serpent from waist to feet. When they were married she built him a castle called Lusignan Castle. Raymond broke his promise, so she changed into a serpent and escaped from the castle by a window. After her escape she was supposed to have visited the castle, uttering cries a little time before the death of the lords of Lusignan. Hence the expression 'Cris de Mélusine', which is still heard in some provs. in France. *See also* FAIRIES. *See* J. Dunlop, *History of Fiction*, 1888, and S. Baring Gould, *Curious Myths of the Middle Ages*, 1897.

Melville, Melvill, or **Melvine, Andrew** (1545–1622), scholar and religious reformer, *b*. Baldovie, Angus. After leaving St Andrews he went to the Continent (1564), becoming regent of St Marceon College at Poitiers (1566). Leaving for Geneva owing to political troubles (1568), through Beza's influence he was appointed prof. of humanity at Geneva Academy (1568–74). On returning to Scotland, he became principal of Glasgow Univ. (1574–80). He was principal of St Mary's College, St Andrews (1580–97). A staunch champion of Presbyterianism, he helped to bring about the fall of episcopacy in Scotland and to draft the *Second Book of Discipline* (*c.* 1581). His extreme views frequently brought him into disfavour. He was forced to flee to England (1584–5), but then returned and was made rector of St Andrews (1590–7). Summoned with other ministers to London (1606) to confer with James I, he was imprisoned in the Tower till 1611. James refused his petition to return to Scotland and he accepted the chair of biblical theology at Sedan, where he *d.*

Melville, George John Whyte-, *see* WHYTE-MELVILLE.

Melville, Herman (1819–91), Amer. novelist and poet, *b*. New York City, of Scottish descent. At the age of 15 he left Albany Academy and earned his living variously as clerk, farm hand and teacher. In 1839 he began his long connection with the sea by shipping as cabin-boy in the *Highlander* on a voyage to Liverpool; his experiences on that occasion were later the basis of his book *Redburn*, 1849. His next voyage was from Fairhaven to the Pacific in 1841 in a whaler, the *Acushnet*, which gave him much of the material for his famous *Moby Dick, or The*

White Whale, 1851. He deserted the ship when it reached the Marquesas Is., was captured by cannibals, with whom he lived for some weeks, and wrote about them eventually in *Typee: a Peep at Polynesian Life*, 1846, his first pub. Escaping in an Australian whaler, the *Lucy Ann*, he was put ashore at Tahiti as one of a mutinous crew and later made the Society Is. the subject of his second book, *Omoo, a Narrative of Adventure in the South Seas*, 1847. Sailing from there to Honolulu, he came home as a seaman in the frigate *United States*, of which he wrote in *White-Jacket*, 1850. In 1847 he married and settled in New York, and in addition to the above books pub. *Mardi*, 1849, a satirical allegory which was not a success. In 1850 he bought a farm near Pittsfield, Massachusetts, and formed a friendship with Nathaniel Hawthorne (q.v.).

It was under Hawthorne's influence that he wrote *Moby Dick*, which is not merely a vivid and stirring account of a whaling voyage but also a cosmic allegory whose underlying theme is the enormity of evil, so that the book was declared by its author to have been 'broiled in hell-fire'. Misunderstood and only partly appreciated at first, it has come to be regarded as one of the great novels of Amer. literature. M. further developed the vein of symbolical fiction with *Pierre: or the Ambiguities*, 1852, which was ignored by readers who preferred his exotic romances. *The Piazza Tales*, 1856, is a fine collection of short stories, but his only later prose works were *The Confidence Man*, 1857, an unsuccessful satire, and a brilliant novelette, *Billy Budd*, written just before his death but not pub. till 1924, which was made into an opera by Benjamin Britten in 1950. During the last 35 years of his life M. worked in the New York customs house, and produced only some books of verse, *Battle Pieces*, 1866, *Clarel*, 1876, *John Marr and Other Sailors*, 1888, and *Timoleon*, 1891. For many years after his death his work was neglected, though in England especially he was always admired as a pioneer in the literature of the S. Seas; but about the time of his birth centenary there was a remarkable revival of interest in his books and he is now reckoned one of the greatest of Amer. authors, and an admirable prose stylist. His letters were pub. in 1960. *See* lives and studies by R. M. Weaver, 1921; L. Mumford, 1929, 1963; W. Brasswell, 1936; R. Anderson, 1939; W. E. Sedgwick, 1944; N. Arvin, 1950; L. Howard, 1952; A. R. Humphreys, 1962. (*See Plate: American Literature*.)

Melville, or Melvil, Sir James, of Halhill, Fife (*c.* 1535–1617), Scottish soldier, historical writer and diplomat. He was page and, later, privy councillor to Mary Queen of Scots, and accomplished various missions for her. His *Memoirs of my own Life*, first pub. by G. Scott, 1683, throw much light on the diplomatic hist. of the period.

Melville, James (1556–1614), Scottish reformer, *b.* near Montrose, a nephew of Andrew M. (q.v.), becoming under him tutor in Glasgow

Univ. (*c.* 1575) and prof. of oriental languages at St Andrews (1580). From 1586 he took an active part in Church controversy, and was moderator of the General Assembly (1589). Summoned to London with his uncle (1606) on the latter's imprisonment, he was forbidden to return N. beyond Newcastle. *See* his diary, pub. 1829.

Melville, Viscount, *see* DUNDAS, HENRY.

Melville: 1. Is. off the coast of N. Australia, separated by Clarence Strait from the mainland. It is 70 m. long and 30 m. broad.

2. One of the Queen Elizabeth Is. in the Canadian Arctic Archipelago, separated (W.) by Fitzwilliam Strait from Prince Patrick Is., by Viscount M. Sound (S. and SE.) from Victoria Island and Prince of Wales Island. It was discovered by Sir W. Parry (q.v.) in 1819.

3. Peninsula in NE. Canada, bounded W. by Boothia Gulf, N. by Fury and Hecla Strait (separating it from Baffin Land), E. by Fox Channel. Length 250 m.; average breadth 100 m.

4. Tn of Saskatchewan, Canada, 100 m. NE. of Regina. A railway and distributing centre for an agric. area, it has produce plants, flour-mills, a box factory and a cement block plant. Pop. 5191.

5. Viscount M. Sound, communicating with the Arctic Ocean and Baffin Bay, SE. of M. Is.

Melvine, Andrew, *see* MELVILLE.

Melzi, Francesco de' (*c.* 1491–1568), It. amateur painter, of a noble Milanese family, friend and pupil of Leonardo da Vinci. The 'Vertumnus and Pomona' at Berlin is often ascribed to him. To him is due the preservation of Leonardo's writings, which, with other belongings, were bequeathed to him.

Membrane, in anatomy, indicates the tissues of the animal body which, arranged as laminae, cover organs, line the interiors of cavities and take part in the formation of the walls of canals and tubes. For mucous M. *see* DIGESTION and EPITHELIUM; for deciduous M.s which enclose the foetus *see* PLACENTA. *See also* CELL; SEROUS MEMBRANES.

Memel: 1. *See* KLAIPEDA.

2. Riv., *see* NIEMEN.

Memelland, or **Memel Territory,** between the two World Wars, part of Lithuania until ceded to Germany Mar. 1939. Now incorporated in Lithuania (q.v.).

Memlinc, Memling, or **Hemling, Hans** (*c.* 1430–94). Flem. painter, *b.* Seligenstadt, near Frankfurt-on-Main, possibly a pupil of Rogier van der Weyden (q.v.). He settled at Bruges, where he mainly worked, producing religious paintings of great beauty and also portraits of reticent dignity. Among his notable works are the 'Triptych of Sir John Donne' (Chatsworth) and the 'Mystic Marriage of St Catherine' (Bruges, St John's Hospital). *See also* W. H. J. Weale, *Hans Memlinc*, 1901; Sir Martin Conway, *The Van Eycks and their Followers*, 1921; L. Baldass, *Hans Memling*, 1942. *See* FLEMISH ART (*See Plate: Flemish Art*.)

Memluk, *see* MAMELUKE.

Memmi, Lippo, di Filippuccio (*d.* 1356), It. painter, brother-in-law of the Sienese master,

Simone Martini, with whom he often worked. Most of his work was done between 1332 and 1351. The fresco over the door of the convent of the Servites at Siena and a small Madonna acquired for the Berlin Museum are the finest of the works attributed to him.

'Memmi', Simone, Simone Martini, or **Simon of Siena** (*c.* 1283–1344), It. painter, pupil of Duccio. He was a friend of Petrarch, and painted portraits of Laura and Petrarch, while the poet dedicated 2 sonnets to him. An illustrious painter, he shared the 'Gothic' ideals of the Pisani, his influence on the Sienese school of painting being evident for the 2 following cents. The frescoes in the church of Santa Maria Novella at Florence, 'The Annunciation' in the Uffizi and the triptych in Antwerp Gallery are his work. He *d.* at Avignon where he had worked in the papal court for some years.

Memmingen, Ger. tn in the *Land* of Bavaria (q.v.), 66 m. W. by S. of Munich. It was once a free city of the empire, and is a picturesque tn with anct walls and fine old buildings. Pop. 29,800.

Memnon, in Gk legend, son of Eos (dawn) and Tithonus, King of the Ethiopians. He fought for his uncle, Priam of Troy, against the Greeks, but was slain by Achilles. M. has been identified with Amenhotep (Amenophis III) whose colossal statue near Thebes is still standing. It was supposed to give forth musical sounds at dawn when touched by the sun's rays. See Quintus Smyrnaeus, *Posthomerica,* ii; G. Rawlinson on *Herodotus,* iii. 254; J. Frazer on *Pausanias,* i. 42; J. E. B. Mayor on *Juvenal,* xv. 5.

Memoirs, form of literature common to all nations in all periods. They may be described as a narrative of events happening or purporting to happen in the lifetime of the author, and relating to his entire life or to some portion of hist. with which he has been intimately connected or for which he has had access to particular sources of information. M. include not only such productions as bear that title, but also such as are styled confessions, reminiscences, souvenirs, diaries and the like. They differ from hist. in that they do not purport to cover all or even the significant events of a period, and frequently ignore a strict chronological order. Among the earliest examples of M. we may class the *Anabasis* and *Memorabilia* of Xenophon, Julius Caesar's *Commentaries,* the Gospels and the Acts of the Apostles, and the *Confessions* of St Augustine. Fr. literature is especially wealthy in M., probably because, as Chateaubriand remarks in his *Génie du Christianisme,* their form and the scope which they afford to the author's personal pride and prejudices are peculiarly suited to the Fr. temperament. M. are found covering the whole of Fr. hist. and every facet of Fr. life from those of Froissart and Joinville to the *Confessions* of Rousseau and, later, F. R. de Chateaubriand's celebrated *Mémoires d'outre tombe,* 1848 and F. P. G. Guizot's *Mémoires pour servir à l'histoire de mon temps,* 1858–67. One cannot say that elsewhere in Europe M. have a proportionate value as historical sources,

though mention must be made of the immortal diaries of Samuel Pepys and John Evelyn, and of Goethe's M. M. are especially adapted to reveal in great detail the social and cultural life of short periods of hist.; and among recent works of this kind are Oliver Gogarty's *As I was Going down Sackville Street,* 1937, Sir Osbert Sitwell's series of M., 1944–50, Lady Diana Cooper's *The Rainbow Comes and Goes,* 1958, and Sir Compton Mackenzie's *My Life and Times,* 1963 ff. See also BIOGRAPHY.

Memorial Day, *see* DECORATION DAY.

Memory is the name given to the capacity for remembering, that is, for reviving or utilising past perceptions, activities or other experiences. A little reflection convinces us that these activities of remembering are of many different kinds. Thus a man picturing in his own mind a past perception is said to be remembering it, or when he is giving an account in words of the activities of the past day. When we see that a dog avoids a place where he has been hurt, we attribute this to his M. of his past experience, though we know nothing of his thought but only observe that his past experience is affecting his present behaviour. Recognition is also regarded as evidence of M., as when we recognise the face of an acquaintance, although we could neither have pictured his face to ourselves nor have described it. M. thus stands for no single kind of mental activity, but is a name given to a number of different types of mental process which have in common the practical end of co-ordinating present behaviour with past experience. A particularly important distinction is that between habit or mechanical M., found most purely in the activity of learning dates or tables by heart, and logical memory, which is the much more important activity of learning material in such a way that its meaning is understood and can be reproduced in our own words. Mechanical learning has some place in the early stages of education but it is out of place in later school activities such as hist., science, mathematics, where what is required is not literal reproduction but understanding. Neglect of this distinction led to the trivialities of the associationist psychology in which learning by heart was regarded as the typical process of M. and the processes of thought were regarded as due to the linking together of ideas by the laws of association (q.v.). These laws are no doubt of importance in the relatively unimportant field of habit M. They explain, however, only that part of M. which is the formation of mental habits. Logical M. required more complex conceptions of the organisation of experiences into units in accordance with the principles of Gestalt psychology. We can remember a mathematical principle when we see it as a whole, organised in relation to the rest of our knowledge. The essential step towards remembering is insight or understanding, not the linking together of ideas by association. There is no experimental evidence in support of the common notion that different individuals differ in the effectiveness of their M. as a whole or that children have better

M.s than adults. Different individuals certainly differ in particular directions of M. ability. For example, some can perform what appear miraculous feats of mechanical remembering through the possession of a particularly stable and accurate form of mental imagery known as eidetic imagery. Children generally do better than adults at tasks involving merely mechanical M., but adults of not too advanced age are generally better at tasks requiring logical remembering. At a great age inability to remember new things may be the result of general loss of efficiency in the senile brain. Amongst adults of young to middle age the differences in capacity for logical remembering are almost entirely due to differences in general intelligence. There is no reason for believing that M. can be improved by exercise, although remembering can be improved by the use of improved methods of learning or by the use of mnemonics (q.v.). The most common cause of forgetting is oblivescence or fading through lapse of time and the incidence of new experiences. Freud has also drawn attention to a kind of forgetting which is important in the causation of mental disorder, the active banishment of unpleasant M.s from the mind which he calls repression. It has been argued that this form of forgetting is found too amongst normal people as well as amongst those suffering from neurotic disorders. See MENTAL TESTS. H. Ebbinghaus, *Über das Gedächtnis*, 1885; H. J. Watt, *The Economy and Training of Memory*, 1909; H. Bergson, *Matter and Memory* (trans.), 1911; S. Freud, *Psychopathology of Everyday Life* (trans.), 1914; T. H. Pear, *Remembering and Forgetting*, 1922; F. C. Bartlett, *Remembering*, 1932; C. A. Mace, *Psychology of Study*, 1932; E. J. Furlong, *A Study in Memory*, 1952.

Memphis: 1. First cap. of anct Egypt, now represented by mounds at Bedrashein on the W. bank of Nile, 14 m. S. of Cairo; traditionally founded in about 3100 BC by Menes (q.v.) who united Egypt and made it his cap. M. was the chief seat of the worship of Ptah. Two huge statues of Rameses II (one now in Cairo) are the prin. remains of M. Its name derives from *Men-nefer*, the name of the pyramid of Pepy I, who resided there *c.* 2400 BC. It was the Moph (Hos. ix. 6) and Noph (Isa. xix. 13, Jer. ii. 16, Ezek. xxx. 13, 16) of the O.T., and the largest city in Egypt, except in the New Kingdom, when it was surpassed by Thebes, regaining its position up to the conquest of Alexander, when it still remained the second city in Egypt after Alexandria, with a mixed pop. Eventually replaced by Arab Fostat. Petrie has pub. results of sev. years' exploration of M.

2. Co. seat of Shelby co., Tennessee, U.S.A., on the Mississippi 235 m. S. of St Louis, Missouri. It is a port of entry and the most important tn on the riv. between St Louis and New Orleans. It is the commercial centre for the rich cotton-lands of the Mississippi valley and fruit dists on the valley slopes. Other products are lumber, oil, grain, machinery and shoes. An iron railway bridge (completed 1892) spans the

riv. The area is subject to floods and the U.S. Army flood control is organised from M. It contains M. College, M. State College, the College of Optometry, the medical divs. of the Univ. of Tennessee, Le Moyne College, Siena College and the Christian Brothers College. M. owed its early importance to its trade as a riv. port, and the Mississippi still carries large cargoes of oil and coal. Pop. 497,524.

Mena, Juan de (*c.* 1411–56), Sp. poet, *b.* Córdoba, was secretary and historiographer to John II of Castile. He joined the Italianate school of Santillana (q.v.), and Dante's influence is evident in the ideas though not in the form of his poems. His chief work, *El Laberinto de Fortuna* or *Las Trescientas*, 1444, is a didactic allegory, visualising past and present. *See* study by M. Rosa Lida de Malkiel, 1950.

Ménage, Gilles (1613–92), Fr. scholar and writer, *b.* Angers. For some time he lived in the household of Cardinal de Retz, but soon quarrelled with his patron and founded a *salon* known as the Mercuriales. This, although gaining him European fame, also made him many enemies, amongst others, Boileau and Molière, who caricatured him in the role of pedant Vadius (*Femmes savantes*). His pubs. include *Origines de la langue française*, 1650. See *Menagiana* (a collection of his oral opinions) pub. in 1693.

Menagerie, small collection of wild animals kept in close captivity for display. Kings of early times used to bring back wild animals from abroad for public exhibition. Private collections later became common, and until the early 19th cent. such a one was maintained at the Tower of London. It is mentioned by Pepys. From these collections developed the great zoological gardens, the travelling M.s of Bostock and Wombwell (1864) and the present-day circuses of performing beasts.

Menai Bridge, urb. dist and seaside resort of Anglesey, on Menai Straits (q.v.), a developing residential dist. The council is the harbour authority. Pop. 2337.

Menai Straits, channel separating Anglesey from Caernarvonshire, N. Wales. Its maximum length is 13 m., and breadth 2 m., and it is famous for its 2 bridges. The suspension bridge (1710 ft), first built by Telford in 1819–25, was reconstructed to the original design in 1940, and freed from tolls. The tubular railway bridge (1380 ft), constructed by Robert Stephenson in 1850, is known as the Britannia Bridge. (*See Plate: Wales.*)

Menam, or **Chao Phraya,** chief riv. of Thailand, rising in the mts of N. Thailand, near the Burmese frontier, and flowing mainly in a southerly direction for a course of about 900 m., finally falling into the Gulf of Thailand. It is navigable for small boats to Chieng-Mai, 75 m. above Mutka, and for riv. steamers to Paknam Po, but its mouth is obstructed by sand-banks. Its chief trib. is the Ping, which forms one of the headstreams. The M. is valued for irrigation and transport.

Menander (342–292 BC), Athenian poet of the

New Comedy, drowned while swimming in the harbour of Peiraeus. He is said to have written more than 100 plays; most of what is extant was discovered at Oxyrhynchus (q.v.), 1900–10, before which time he was known almost exclusively through Lat. adaptations (*see* J. V. Powell and E. A. Barber, *New Chapters in Greek Literature*, 1st and 2nd series, 1921, 1929). In 1958, however, the complete text of *Dyskolos* was discovered by V. Martin among Egyptian papyri in the library of Martin Bodmer at Colgny, near Geneva. *See* ed. with commentary by E. W. Handley, 1965. M. is the fountainhead of the whole mod. comedy of manners. Through his Rom. disciples he transmitted an influence that can be traced in Shakespeare and Ben Jonson; it is strong in the Restoration dramatists and the Comédie Française, and is apparent in the school of Goldsmith and Sheridan. *See* T. B. L. Webster, *Studies in Menander*, 1950.

Ménard, Louis (1822–1901), Fr. poet, *b.* Paris, one of the Parnassians (q.v.). His works include the epic poem *Prométhée délivré*, 1844, *Prologue d'une révolution* (based on his experiences in the 1848 revolution), 1849, *Poèmes*, 1855, *Rêveries d'un païen mystique* (prose and verse), 1876.

Menavia, *see* MAN, ISLE OF.

Mencius (the latinised form of Mengtzǔ, or **Ment-tseu**, 372–289 BC), Chinese sage, *b.* Shantung, ranking next to Confucius as a moral teacher, author of one of the 'Four Books' which constitute the Chinese Scriptures. He was brought up by his mother, who is venerated in China as the pattern of all mothers. When about 40 he travelled with his disciples to the various princely courts then existing in China, preaching and teaching. His main teaching is that human nature is originally good and evil enters from without. The four instinctive feelings in human nature are: the feeling of pity and compassion that produces the virtue of love for others; the feeling of reverence with its converse, shame, that produces the virtue of righteousness; the feeling of modesty that produces the virtue of social propriety; the feeling of discrimination that produces the virtue of wisdom. One needs only to develop these innate feelings to be perfectly virtuous. On this ethical basis he expounds the political philosophy that the people's opinion is more important than the ruler's listening to the people. His dialogues and exhortations were pub. by his disciples as the *Book of Meng-tseu. See* CHINESE LITERATURE. There is an Eng. trans. of the *Book of Meng-tseu* by L. A. Lyall, 1932. *See also* J. Legge, *Chinese Classics*, ii, 1862, 1875; H. Giles, *History of Chinese Literature*, 1901; I. A. Richards, *Mencius on the Mind*, 1932; A. D. Waley, *Three Ways of Thought in Ancient China*, 1939, 1946. *See also* CHINESE LITERATURE.

Mencken, Henry Louis (1880–1956), Amer. critic, *b.* Baltimore, Maryland. He began work on Baltimore newspapers, and then joined the staff of the magazine *Smart Set* as its literary critic. For some years he was joint editor of this pub. with George Jean Nathan. Together with Nathan he founded the *American Mercury* in 1924. M. gained a wide reputation in the U.S.A. as a critic for the sophisticated. Most of his best essays have been reproduced in book form in a series under the general title of *Prejudices*, 1919–27. In *Americana*, 1925, his purpose was to show up the average man from the small tns. Other pubs. include criticisms of G. B. Shaw's plays, the philosophy of Nietzsche and the works of Ibsen, Brieux and other playwrights. Some later works include *The American Language*, 1919, with 2 *Supplements*, 1945, 1948; the autobiographical *Happy Days, 1880–1892*, 1940, *Newspaper Days*, 1941, and *Heathen Days*, 1943. He was editor of *A New Dictionary of Quotations on Historical Principles*, 1942. *See* B. De Casseres, *Mencken and Shaw*, 1930.

Mende, Erich (1916–), Ger. politician, educ. at Cologne and Bonn univs. After serving in the Second World War he was a co-founder of the Free Democratic Party, 1945, and has been its chairman since 1960. He was elected to the Bundestag in 1949. His party joined the gov. coalition in 1963, when M. became minister for all-Ger. affairs and deputy chancellor.

Mende, Fr. tn, cap. of the dept of Lozère, on the Lot. It is a curious old tn, is a bishopric and has a cathedral, begun in 1369 by Pope Urban V (q.v.), who was *b.* here. It has a textile industry and a market. Pop. 8400.

Mendel, Johann Gregor (1822–84), Austrian biologist, *b.* Heinzendorf, of peasant stock. Having taken a degree at the univ. of Vienna he joined the Augustinian order at Brünn (Brno), where he taught natural physics in the monastery school and eventually became abbot. It was here too that M. made those observations upon which was based his famous theory propounded in 1866 and known today as Mendelism (q.v.).

Mendeléev, Dmitri Ivanovich (1834–1907), Russian chemist, *b.* Tobolsk, Siberia, was educ. at St Petersburg, and was a pupil of Wurtz in Paris. After lecturing at Simferopol, Odessa and St Petersburg, he became prof. of chem. at the univ. there (1866–90). M. discovered and enunciated the periodic law of atomic weights (1869), which was partly foreshadowed by others but brought to its highest perfection by him (*see* ATOMIC THEORY). His prediction of new elements such as eka-boron, eka-silicon and dvi-manganese was subsequently realised in the discovery of scandium, germanium and rhenium respectively. He made a careful study of the chemical properties of petroleum in the mines of Pennsylvania and Caucasia, and performed valuable work on the subject of the liquefaction of gases (1884). In 1893 he became director of the Bureau of Weights. His chief work is *The Principles of Chemistry*, 1868–70 (Eng. trans. 1892). *See* T. E. Thorpe, *Essays in Historical Chemistry*, 1911.

Mendelism, biological theory of heredity first propounded by the Abbé J. G. Mendel (q.v.). At Mendel's death his immensely valuable contribution to the science of heredity had received no recognition; and it was principally owing to the trans. of his monograph by Prof. Wm Bateson in 1902 that its scientific possibilities were realised and developed. Mendel was evidently well informed in many branches of contemporary biology. In his little garden he spent much time cultivating the edible and the sweet pea and kept exact records of various features of about 10,000 plants which he had grown. The possibility grew upon him that there must be some natural law of inheritance. He found that where the parents showed a marked difference in special characters, e.g. tallness and dwarfness, the hybrid offspring in the first generation was always tall. This prepotency, as Darwin and others had called it, he termed a dominant characteristic and the other recessive. In the next generation, produced either by self-fertilisation, or by breeding hybrid with hybrid, he found that a form resulted in which the dominant characteristic occurred pure, while there was also one in which the recessive character was pure. These 2 occurred approximately as 2 in 4, the other 2, though exhibiting the dominant character, having the recessive one latent, as evidently was the case with the first filial generation (see HEREDITY, Fig. 2). That is to say, breeders have only to ascertain which characters that they wish to preserve are dominant and which recessive to be able to fix them permanently. Naturally the breeding operations are hardly ever so simple, as other characters may assert themselves and may have to be bred out. But where formerly breeders were compelled to work almost in the dark, Mendel's law gives them at any rate a sense of direction, and there can be no doubt that the law ranks among the greatest of scientific discoveries.

Mendel's success in obtaining results enabling him to formulate laws of heredity was due to his recognition of the necessity for quantitative experiments with very large numbers of plants, and for experiments with easily recognisable characteristics. After dealing with single pairs of characteristics such as tallness and dwarfness, yellow seeds and green seeds, round peas and wrinkled peas, he formulated his 'first law', or the 'law of the purity of the gametes', which states that any gamete, i.e. reproductive cell, male or female, can carry the determinant (gene) of only one of a pair of alternative characteristics (see HEREDITY). Mendel next experimented with the inheritance of 2 pairs of characteristics, crossing, for example, a tall yellow-seeded plant with a dwarf green-seeded one. As a result, he discovered his second law, the law of free assortment. According to this, characteristics were assorted independently, and thus tallness or dwarfness might be associated with either green or yellow seeds. The result in the F_2 (second filial generation) would be tall yellow, dwarf yellow, tall green, dwarf green, in the ratio 9 : 3 : 3 : 1. More recent workers have found numerous exceptions to this second law, and have proved the transmission of certain characteristics in groups, such 'linked' characteristics rarely being separable. In the pea there are 7 such groups (corresponding to 7 pairs of chromosomes) and Mendel unwittingly selected for experiment characteristics of different groups, so arriving at the conclusion that free assortment always occurred. We now know that this is possible only when the characteristics concerned are in different groups (i.e. when their respective 'genes' are situated in different pairs of chromosomes). Examples of 'sex linkage' are known, as described in HEREDITY. In Mendel's material the characteristics under observation were definitely dominant or recessive, but dominance is not essential to Mendelian inheritance. Red flowers of the Jap. 'four o'clock' (Mirabilus jalapa) crossed with white ones produce pink-flowered plants. These, intercrossed, yield plants with red, pink and white flowers in the Mendelian ratio 1 : 2 : 1. Other disturbances of the Mendelian ratio are caused by lethal factors inhibiting the development of characteristics, and by the interchange, or 'crossing over', of determinants of different groups (see HEREDITY). Knowledge of Mendelian inheritance has been of great economic importance in both plant and animal breeding. Animals immune to certain forms of disease, birds with increased egg-laying capacity, good milk cows, wheats immune to rusts, grain with good food reserves, are amongst the results due to selective breeding according to Mendelian laws. See R. C. Punnett, Mendelism, 1905; J. Wilson, A Manual of Mendelism, 1929; bibliography under BIOLOGY.

Mendelssohn, Erich (1887–1953), Ger.-Amer. architect, b. Allenstein, trained in Munich and Vienna, started practice 1911. He was a designer of great originality. He worked in England 1933–4, was in Palestine 1934–8, then settled in America. Prin. buildings: in Germany—the Observatory or 'Einstein Tower' at Potsdam; factory at Luckenwalde; the Columbushaus, Berlin; Universum Cinema, Berlin; Schocken Stores at Nuremberg, Stuttgart and Chemnitz; in England—De la Warr Pavilion, Bexhill (with S. Chermayeff, competition, 1934); in Israel —hospital and power station at Haifa; univ. at Jerusalem; in U.S.A.—Maimonides Health Center, San Francisco. See biography by A. Whittick, 1940 (2nd ed. 1956).

Mendelssohn, Felix (1809–47), Ger. composer, b. Hamburg, grandson of Moses M. (q.v.). He was baptised and educ. as a Christian, his father adding the surname Bartholdy to the family name. His youth was spent in the refined surroundings of a family of very considerable wealth, culture and brilliant social connection.

He benefited by the tuition and advice of Berger, Zelter, Weber, Cherubini and Moscheles, and by the time he was 20 had already produced his famous Octet, 3 piano quartets, 2 sonatas, 2 symphonies and the Midsummer Night's Dream overture, besides a host of songs, an opera and many short pieces. The next few years were passed in visiting London, Munich, Vienna and Rome, and in incidental tours in Scotland, Italy and Switzerland (1829–31); he achieved a wide fame as pianist, composer and conductor. The first of his 10 visits to England took place in 1829. The Hebrides (Fingal's Cave) overture was composed in 1830 (revised 1832).

In 1835 he became conductor of the celebrated Leipzig Gewandhaus orchestra, and 2 years later married Cécile Jeanrenaud at Frankfurt. He conducted his oratorio *St Paul* at Düsseldorf in 1836 and *Elijah* at Birmingham in 1846.

Persistent overwork and an excess of activities undermined his health: he *d.* in Leipzig. His reputation, extravagantly high in his lifetime, is now sustained mainly by his violin Concerto, 1844, the incidental music to *A Midsummer Night's Dream* (particularly the overture), the *Scottish* and *Italian* symphonies and the *Hebrides* overture. *Elijah* is still popular with choral societies, but the chamber music and piano works (examples of impeccable craftsmanship, like all M.'s music) appeal to a more limited circle. *See* lives by P. Radcliffe, 1954, and E. Werner, 1963. (*See Plate: German Music*.)

Mendelssohn, Moses (1729–86), Ger. philanthropist and eclectic philosopher of Jewish descent, grandfather of the musician, was *b.* Dessau on the Elbe. He endured great poverty in early life and was largely self-educ. In 1750 he entered the service of I. Bernhard, a wealthy silk merchant, becoming his book-keeper and finally his partner. He worked as a critic for Nicolai's (q.v.) *Bibliothek* which he helped to found. In 1754 he was introduced to Lessing, whose intimate friend he became, collaborating with him in the satire *Pope ein Metaphysiker*, 1755. He also wrote for Lessing's and Nicolai's *Briefe, die neueste Literatur betreffend*. Lessing pub. M.'s *Philosophische Gespräche* anonymously (1755), and made M. the hero of his *Nathan*. From *c.* 1767 M. turned his attention to the moral and political elevation of his race, becoming the foremost champion of Jewish emancipation in the 18th cent. He made a Ger. trans. of the Pentateuch and other parts of the Bible (1783), pub. a Ger. version of Manasseh ben Israel's *Vindiciae judaeorum* as *Jerusalem*, 1783 (Eng. trans. 1838, 1852), a plea for freedom of conscience and a demand for the total separation of Church and State. Other works were *Über die Evidenz in den metaphysischen Wissenschaften*, 1764 (Berlin Academy prize); *Phädon*, in support of immortality of the soul, 1767 (Eng. trans. 1789); *Morgenstunden*, in refutation of Pantheism and Spinozism and in defence of Lessing, 1785–6. *See* J. Pinto, *The Story of Moses Mendelssohn*, 1960.

Mendès, Catulle (1841–1909), Fr. poet, novelist and playwright, *b.* Bordeaux, was one of the group of 'Parnassians'. He founded *La Revue fantaisiste*, 1861, in which his *Roman d'une nuit* (for which he was fined and imprisoned) was pub. 1861. His poems include *Philoméla*, 1863; *Poésies*, 1876, 1885, 1892; *Hespérus*, 1872; *La Grive des vignes*, 1895. He wrote plays, novels and criticisms also, such as *Richard Wagner*, 1886, *L'Art au théâtre*, 1897–1900, *Le Mouvement poétique français de 1867 à 1900*, 1903; plays: *Medée*, 1898, *Glatigny*, 1906, and the novels *Méphistophéla*, 1890, and *La Maison de la vieille*, 1894.

Mendès-France, Pierre (1907–), Fr. politician, entered politics as a Radical-Socialist deputy in 1932. He served with the Free French Air Force during the Second World War and subsequently was noted for his knowledge of economic and financial problems. From June 1954 to Feb. 1955 he was premier and foreign minister, but his financial and Algerian policies soon alienated many of his early supporters, and eventually resulted in a split in his own party, from which he resigned in May 1957. He pub. his autobiography, *The Pursuit of Freedom* (Eng. trans.), 1955. *See also* A. Werth, *The Strange History of Pierre Mendès-France and the Great Conflict over French N. Africa*, 1957.

Mendicancy. In law M. is synonymous with begging. Begging *per se* is no more illegal than betting; what the law punishes is not so much begging as the habit of M., or begging in a certain way, or in a public place. Under the Vagrancy Act, 1824, the law punishes as a rogue and vagabond anyone who (1) *habitually* goes about as a collector of alms, (2) endeavours by fraudulent pretences to procure charitable contributions or (3) stands in a public street in order to beg alms. Obtaining money by sending a lying begging letter is punishable under the Larceny Act, 1861. *See* F. Gray, *The Tramp*, 1931.

Mendicant Orders (Lat. *mendicare*, to beg), name given collectively to religious orders which laid special stress on the vow of poverty and subsisted mainly upon alms. *See* CARMELITES; DOMINICANS; FRANCISCANS; FRIAR. *See also* Fr. Cuthbert, *The Friars and how they came to England*, 1903; M. D. Knowles, *The Religious Orders in England*, vol. ii, 1955.

Mendip Hills, range in Somerset, England, extending from near Wells and Shepton Mallet (qq.v.) towards the Bristol Channel, in the direction of Weston-super-Mare (q.v.), for a distance of about 18 m. The highest point is Blackdown, 1067 ft, and the range includes Cheddar (q.v.) Gorge and caves, Burrington Combe and Wookey Hole (qq.v.) caves. The hills are mainly composed of carboniferous limestone, with eruptive rocks at intervals. *See* A. W. Coysh, E. J. Mason and V. White, *The Mendips*, 1954.

Mendoza, Diego, *see* HURTADO.

Mendoza, Iñigo, *see* SANTILLANA.

Mendoza, Pedro González de (1428–95), Sp. cardinal and statesman. He rose to great power under Henry IV of Castile, by whose influence he was made a cardinal, and subsequently exercised equal influence over Isabella, whose right to the succession he favoured. He became Archbishop of Seville and Toledo (1481) and was sometimes called the third King of Spain. His influence was exerted in favour of the Jews and of the projects of Columbus. He took a vigorous part in the prosecution of the wars against the Moors. The college of Santa Cruz at Valladolid was founded by him.

Mendoza: 1. Andine prov. of Argentina adjoining Chile in the W. Apart from the SE. region, the prov. is mountainous and has within its borders the highest peak of the Andes— Aconcagua (23,000 ft), Tuptmgato (22,000),

Mercedario (22,000) and sev. others over 17,000 ft. The climate is arid, and without the artificial irrigation made possible by the sev. rivs. fed by the snow and glaciers of the Andes cultivation would not be possible. As it is, the valleys are extremely fertile and have gained for the prov. the title 'Garden of the Andes'. Viniculture is the leading economic activity and a great variety of other fruits is grown—peaches, apples, plums, pears, cherries, apricots and olives. M. is the chief wine producer of Argentina. Cattle raising is also important. The country's 2nd most productive oilfields are located in M. Other minerals are mined but have not been exploited on a large scale with the exception of sulphur. M. is a prosperous prov. doing a considerable trade with Chile. Cap. is M. Area 52,230 sq. m.; pop. 826,000.

2. Cap. of M. prov., Argentina. An attractive tn, 2300 ft high, set in beautiful surroundings. Founded in 1561 by the Spaniards then based in Chile, it was completely destroyed by earthquakes in 1861 and so it is today essentially a modern city. It is the commercial and industrial centre of the prov. basing itself on wine and petroleum. It is the port at which the Argentine and Chilean railway systems link, being the point of departure for the Transandine railway to Chile. The Univ. of Cuyo is located in M. Pop. 135,000.

Menelaus, in Gk legend, King of Sparta, brother of Agamemnon (*see* ATREIDS), husband of Helen (q.v.) and father of Hermione. After the Trojan war, in which he played an undistinguished part, M. returned with Helen to Sparta, where they lived peacefully until trans. by Zeus to Elysium (q.v.). In historical times their tombs were shown at Therapnae in Laconia, where they received divine honours jointly with the Dioscuri.

Menelik, or **Menelek, II** (*c.* 1842–1913), Emperor of Ethiopia, was the son of Haila Malakot, King of Shoa. In 1856 he *m.* Bafana, daughter of Theodore, the reigning emperor, and 10 years later became King of Shoa. On the assassination of Theodore in 1889 he declared himself emperor. Having inflicted an ignominious defeat on the Italians at Adowa in 1896, he was able to replace the treaty of Uchali (1889) by the peace of Addis Ababa (1896), whereby his independence was fully recognised.

Menéndez Pidal, Ramón (1869–), Sp. philologist and literary historian, *b.* La Coruña. Amongst his many works on the Sp. language, medieval literature, etc., are *Manual de gramática histórica española*, 1904 (later revised), *Cantar de mio Cid* (text, grammar and vocabulary), 3 vols., 1908–11, *Orígenes del español*, 1926, *Flora nueva de romances viejos*, 1928, *La España del Cid*, 1929, *La Epopeya castellana a traves de la literatura española*, 1945, *Los Españoles en la Historia*, 1947, *España eslabón entre la Cristiandad y el Islam*, 1953, *La Chanson de Roland y el neotradicionalismo*, 1959, *El dialecto leonés*, 1962.

Menéndez y Pelayo, Marcelino (1856–1912), Sp. writer and critic, *b.* Santander. His ortho-

doxy and ultramontanism are revealed in his popular essays *La ciencia española*, 1878, and in his *Historia de los heterodoxos españoles*, 1880–6, whilst his *Calderón y su teatro*, 1881, and his *Historia de las ideas estéticas en España*, 1883–91, 1903–12, are true monuments of literary criticism. He also wrote many other books and prepared the standard ed. of Lope de Vega (1890–1902).

Menes, Gk form of Mena, was the traditional first King of Egypt. He was probably Narmer, who united Upper and Lower Egypt, or possibly his successor Hor-Aha. Herodotus ascribes to him the building of Memphis.

Meng-ka, *see* BANGKA.

Menger, Karl (1840–1921), Austrian economist; prof. at Vienna, 1873–1903. Rejecting the historical method in economics he is remembered as a co-founder of the school of 'marginal utility' (the utility or importance to the buyer of the last or 'marginal' part of his consumption of a commodity), in opposition to the conventional explanations of values in form of costs without relation to the choices and preferences of consumers.

Mengo, dist of Uganda. It contains the prin. residence of the *kabaka* (or king) of Uganda, and is the seat of the native gov. of Buganda, as well as the H.Q. of the prov. administration (Kampala). The parliament is called the *Lukiko* and the meeting place or Parliament House, the *Bulange*, and both are in M. Area 9376 sq. m. (land and swamp 5781 sq. m.; open water 3595 sq. m.).

Mengs, Anton Raphael (1728–79), Bohemian painter, *b.* Aussig. He went early to Rome where he mainly worked and became a rival to Baloni as a fashionable portrait painter. A friend of Winckelmann, he shared in the neo-classic revival, though compositions such as the 'Parnassus' (Villa Albani) have been thought of small merit. He executed various paintings for Charles III of Spain, decorating the royal palaces of Spain. *See* K. Gerstenberg, *Winckelmann und Anton Raphael Mengs*, 1929. (*See Plate: German Art.*)

Mengtse, former treaty port in the SE. of Yunnan, China, opened to trade with Tongking in 1886. Zinc, lead, tin and tea are exported. Since 1957 M. has been the cap. of the Hung-ho Hani-Yi Autonomous *Chou* (pop. 640,000).

Menharden, Hardhead, or **Moss-banker** (*Brevoortia tyrannus*), important fish allied to the shads, common on the Atlantic coast of N. America. It is employed as a bait, but is chiefly valuable for its rich oil and for the manurial value of the residue.

Menhirs (Breton, *men*, stone; *hir*, long) are single, tall, upright standing stones, often known simply as monoliths. Some are of natural origin (Buck Stone, Staunton); many mark the sites of prehistoric burials; while others are boundary marks, meeting-places or sacred sites. They are of various ages, are distributed geographically in Europe, Asia and Africa, and in general give no indication whatever of their purpose. Most probably they belong to the late Neolithic or

Early Bronze Age, and certainly to a megalithic culture. The M. at Carnac in Brittany (Early Bronze Age) are especially well known; one is about 30 ft high. In the Morbihan are pieces of a menhir which was nearly 70 ft high. Occasionally M. bear rough engravings of conventional human and animal forms; some are of obvious phallic significance. *See* MEGALITHIC CULTURE; STANDING STONES.

Ménière's Disease, condition of middle age, in which vertigo, nausea, headache, deafness and *tinnitus* (i.e. ringing in the ears) are associated in sudden attacks. It is due to a disturbance of function of the labyrinth or internal ear, but the exact pathology is not known. While the vertigo may pass away, or at least become reduced, permanent deafness may result. Though the disease was first described 50 years ago, there is as yet no satisfactory treatment, though relief may be obtained by bromide, phenobarbitone and hyoscine. Sometimes the vestibular nerve has to be cut before relief is obtained. *See* EAR.

Menin (Flem. **Meenen**), tn in the prov. of W. Flanders, Belgium, 7 m. SW. of Courtrai, situated on the R. Lys, close to the Fr. border. It manufs. tobacco, chicory and soap. There are also textile and engineering industries. Pop. 24,500.

Menin Gate, *see* WAR GRAVES.

Meningitis, inflammation of the meninges (*see* BRAIN). M. may be due to one of many organisms, including *M. tuberculosis*, the meningococcus, *H. influenza*, *B. coli*, *B. proteus*, *B. typhosus* and the pneumococcus, staphylococcus and streptococcus. M. may occur as a result of direct infection from a head wound or injury, or from a spread of infection from a mastoid or middle ear abscess or abscess in a sinus. The commonest forms of M. are those due to tuberculosis and the meningococcus (*Diplococcus intracellularis*). The latter infection is known as cerebro-spinal fever, epidemic cerebro-spinal M. or spotted fever. M. is seen most frequently in children.

The symptoms of M. may come on suddenly or gradually according to the nature of the infection. There is always a period of general ill health, however, before the specific symptoms are apparent. Fever is usually present. Squints, photophobia, twitching, tremors and neck stiffness are symptoms in the later stages. At lumbar puncture the cerebro-spinal fluid pressure is raised. If not treated the disease progresses to delirium, coma, convulsions and death. *Tuberculous M.* is rare under the age of 6 months, is commonest in the second and third years, but may occur at any age. The source of infection is more frequently human than bovine (*see* TUBERCULOSIS), but infected milk has been identified as the cause in many cases. Tuberculous M. may be one aspect of a general miliary infection, it may occur as a spread of infection from a focus already present elsewhere in the body, or it may be the site of primary infection. The source of primary infection is as a rule another person in the house who is suffering from active tuberculosis. Once a fatal disease, at

least 30 per cent of cases of tuberculous M. may now expect cure with streptomycin treatment. Convalescence is slow, as in any form of tuberculosis. The earlier the treatment is started the better the prognosis. *Cerebro-spinal M.* is an epidemic infectious disease. It is apt to occur in communities such as schools and barracks. Infection may be spread by carriers who although healthy themselves carry the meningococcus in their noses and throats. The onset is more sudden and the symptoms develop more rapidly than in tuberculous M. At one time almost always a fatal disease, cerebro-spinal M. responds to sulphonamides and to a lesser degree to penicillin, and if treatment is started early enough there is every hope of recovery. The death rate from this disease is still disturbingly high, however, despite chemotherapy, and out of an average of about 1500 cases notified annually some 20 per cent end fatally. Chemotherapy is largely effective against M. due to other types of organism.

Meningocele, protrusion of the meninges through their bony covering. The meninges are the membranes covering the brain and spinal cord, and if there be any defect in the skull or vertebral column, the meninges may protrude, forming a cyst filled with cerebro-spinal fluid.

Meninsky, Bernard (1891–1950), painter, *b.* Russia. He studied at the Slade School, London, and also in Liverpool and Paris, gaining inspiration from post-impressionist art. The Tate Gallery has his 'Portrait of a Boy' and the Dublin Art Gallery his 'Mother and Child'.

Menippus (3rd cent. BC), Gk cynic philosopher and satirist, *b.* Gadara in Coele-Syria. His satires, written in a mixture of verse and prose, served as a model for those of M. Terentius Varro (q.v.), who called them *saturae menippeae*. Nothing of M.'s own work survives.

Meninx, *see* JERBA.

Menken, Adah Isaacs (1835–68), Amer. actress and poetess, *b.* New Orleans, daughter of a Sp. Jew. Her original name is variously given as Adelaide McCord and Dolores Adios Fuertes. In 1856 she married John Isaacs M., a Jew, and changed her name Adios to Adah. She is said to have been married at least 4 times, one of her husbands being R. H. Newell ('Orpheus C. Kerr'), and another Heenan (the 'Benicia Boy'). She had great success in 1864 in London as Mazeppa, to which her handsome physique largely contributed. Among her friends were Gautier, Dumas the elder, Dickens, to whom she dedicated her *Infelicia*, 1868, Charles Reade and Swinburne, whose poem *Dolores*, 1864, was inspired by her.

Mennonites, Protestant sect, successors to the Anabaptists (q.v.). They refuse to bear arms or to take oaths. They acknowledge only the authority of the Bible, postpone baptism until after a confession of faith and dislike all forms of eccles. hierarchy. Their principles were adopted and preached by the Dutchman Menno Simons (1492–1559), whose name they bear. It was he who rebuked the Westphalian Anabaptists for their fanatical excesses, which were responsible for the carnage and other horrors in Münster (1534), and it was largely owing to his influence that the sect spread to Germany and the Netherlands. For many years the M. were victims of persecution. In 1786 sev. colonies of Ger. M. found asylum in S. Russia, where Catherine II allowed them to practise their religion undisturbed. Today the sect numbers some 250,000 members, a third of these being in the U.S.A. Dutch refugees founded a Mennonite community at Germantown in Pennsylvania as early as 1683, and since 1871 there have been large Mennonite settlements in Kansas and Minnesota. See J. S. Hartzler and D. Kauffman, *Mennonite Church History*, 1905; C. Crahn, *Menno Simons*, 1936; C. H. Smith, *The Mennonites*, 1941; the *Mennonite Quarterly Review*.

Menologies, *see* HAGIOLOGY.

Menominee ('wild rice men'), Algonquian tribe of Amer. Indians living in Wisconsin, numbering about 2500.

Menopause (Gk *man*, month, *pausis*, cessation), the natural cessation of menstruation (q.v.): also known as the climacteric, and popularly referred to as the 'change of life'. The M. generally occurs between the ages of 45 and 55 and it results from a physiological decrease in the secretion of female sex hormones. Since this decrease is a gradual one, the term M. is commonly applied to a varying length of time in years preceding the complete cessation of menstruation during which the menstrual flow as a rule becomes irregular in amount and periodicity and there are accompanying symptoms such as fits of depression or over-anxiety and hot flushes. When distressing enough to affect the general health these may be helped by medical treatment or advice; otherwise they can be regarded as no more than a perfectly normal albeit bothersome temporary disturbance. *Artificial M.* before the age of physiological M. is sometimes brought about for therapeutic purposes in cases of menstrual disorder or occurs as a result of surgical operations in which both ovaries are removed. In these cases symptoms of the climacteric are controlled by hormone treatment.

Menopome (*Cryptobranchus alleghaniensis*), **Mud Devil**, or **Hellbender**, voracious 4-legged tailed amphibian found in some of the rivs. of N. America. It is slate-coloured and about 2 ft long; the body is short and thick, and the head large, flat and broad, with wide, fleshy lips. The neck has a single gill cleft on either side.

Menorca, *see* MINORCA.

Menorrhagia, *see* MENSTRUATION.

Menotti, Gian Carlo (1911–), It. composer, *b.* Cadigliano, was very precocious, went to Philadelphia in 1928, studied with Rosario Scalero there, settled in U.S.A. but retained his It. nationality. His first opera, *Amelia goes to the Ball*, composed at 23, was produced in 1937. His first great success came with *The Medium*, 1946, a crudely but effectively sensational one-act opera, followed by the one-act comedy *The Telephone*, 1947; but most striking of all, if musically no more refined, was the full-length

The Consul, produced in New York in 1950 and brought to London in 1951. Later operas include *Amahl and the Night Visitors* (written for television), 1951, *The Saint of Bleecker Street*, 1954, and *Maria Golorin*, 1958. M. has also written 2 ballets, a piano Concerto and smaller works.

Mensa, one of Lacaille's S. constellations, so named by him in 1752 after the Mons Mensae (Table Mt) at the Cape of Good Hope. It lies between Dorado and the S. pole, and contains no star of a brighter magnitude than 5·3.

Mensheviks (from Russian *men'she*, fewer), Russian political party, formed Aug. 1917 at a unification congress of sev. more or less organised groups of Social Democrats. Before 1917 the name M. was applied to the non-Leninist faction of the Russian Social Democratic Workers' party (q.v.). After the latter's split in 1903 the M., consisting of the 'soft' Iskraists (*see* ISKRA) and Economists (*see* ECONOMISM), had all the recognised party leaders except Lenin and soon gained control of the party's newspaper and the majority of the local committees. They advocated a broad proletarian party and co-operation with liberals against autocracy and for a democratic constitution. During the revolution of 1905 M. co-operated locally with Bolsheviks and in 1906 they formally reunited with them. In fact, relations between the factions remained tense, as the Bolsheviks by every means continued their efforts to control the party, although it was predominantly Menshevik. The situation was further complicated by the appearance among the M. of sev. trends: the 'liquidationists' (so called by their opponents), led by Potresov (q.v.), who felt that under the constitution a conspiratorial underground was unnecessary; the 'party-minded M.', led by Plekhanov (q.v.), who advocated the opposite; the centre, led by Martov (q.v.) and Akselrod, who tried to preserve the unity of the faction; and the followers of Trotskiy (q.v.), who wanted to unify all Social Democrats. The First World War brought about a regrouping into internationalists under Martov and Trotskiy, and defencists under Potresov, with whom Plekhanov was now reconciled. After the Feb. revolution (q.v.) in 1917 there were sev. organised groups of M., the main one, led by F. Dan, adhering to the policy of revolutionary defencism, i.e. defence of the new revolutionary Russia. The M. had a majority in most Soviets (q.v.) and supported and later participated in the Provisional Gov. (q.v.). After the Bolshevik seizure of power (*see* OCTOBER REVOLUTION) the official Menshevik party, led by Martov, tried unsuccessfully to adopt tactics of legal opposition to the Bolsheviks. The party was suppressed in Russia in 1922, although many former M. continued to work in Soviet institutions. A show trial of M. was held in Moscow in 1930, though in fact only one of the accused was a Menshevik. A delegation of M. left Russia in 1920 and still exists in emigration, though much depleted. Until 1965 it pub. in New York an exceptionally well-informed monthly,

Socialist Courier, with such regular contributors as B. I. Nicolaevsky, R. A. Abramovich and S. M. Schwarz.

Menshikov, Aleksandr Danilovich (1663–1729), Russian statesman and field marshal, *b.* Moscow. He began life by selling meat pies in the streets of Moscow, but owing to François Lefort, the tsar's favourite, he became popular with Peter the Great by 1697. As a soldier he distinguished himself at the siege of Azov (1696) and the battles of Kalisz and Poltava (1706, 1709). As a civil administrator he executed Peter's reforms with remarkable promptitude and success, and on his death assumed the reins of gov. during the brief rule of Catherine and the minority of Peter II. Ousted from power by the Dolgorukiys, he was banished and *d.* an exile in Siberia.

Menshikov, Aleksandr Sergeyevich (1787–1869), Russian general and admiral, great-grandson of A. D. M. (q.v.). During the Crimean War (1854–6) he unsuccessfully commanded the Russian forces at Alma, Inkerman and around Sevastopol'.

Menstruation (Lat. *menstruus,* monthly, from *mensis*), also known as **Catamenia**, discharge of blood, usually from 4 to 6 oz., which issues every 28 days from the uterus of a woman, so long as she is capable of procreation. M. begins at the age of puberty, which among Teutonic races varies from 12 to 16, and is a sign of the change from childhood to womanhood. The flow ceases between the ages of 45 and 55, this being a climacteric period popularly referred to as 'the change of life'. M. lasts as a rule from 3 to 4 days, and often occurs more or less frequently than once a month; during pregnancy and lactation it stops entirely, and its cessation, therefore, is an early indication of conception. M. comprises the discharge of the uterine lining, or endometrium, which has become thickened and vascular in preparation for the reception of a fertilised egg; it is thus part of the menstrual (oestrous) cycle.

The menstrual process is sometimes accompanied by disorders, which are broadly classified as amenorrhoea, dysmenorrhoea, menorrhagia and metrorrhagia. (1) Amenorrhoea implies absence or deficiency of catamenia. This may arise from such a physiological cause as pregnancy; from constitutional causes such as anaemia, malnutrition or emotional disturbance. Perhaps one of the commonest causes is a dysfunction of the endocrine system (*see* HORMONE). Amenorrhoea may also occur from local causes such as the absence, malformation or disease of the ovaries or uterus, or of both. Surgery will sometimes remove local causes, whilst anaemia and other constitutional causes may often be remedied by better nutrition, healthier surroundings, change of air or mental occupation. The appropriate hormone therapy will help those cases due to endocrine imbalance. (2) In dysmenorrhoea M. is attended by pain: with some women this is always so, whilst there are others to whom it brings no appreciable discomfort. The pelvis is the seat of the pain, but it is felt also in the groins, thighs and sacrum.

Other symptoms are headache, backache and general lassitude. As far as possible dysmenorrhoea should be disregarded, but when it is severe medical advice should be sought. (3) Menorrhagia is flooding, or excessive flow. Frequent causes are subinvolution of the uterus, fibroid tumour, polypus, cancer and ulceration of the cervix, and endocrine dysfunction. (4) Metrorrhagia is escape of blood from the uterus, independent of M.; it is usually occasioned by disease of the uterus or its appendages. Bleeding after the change of life is always a matter for medical advice.

Mensuration, section of geometry which investigates lengths, areas and volumes. The lengths of ordinary straight lines are measured by mechanical means, but the measurement of irregular lines forms a part of the integral calculus termed rectification. *The areas of plane figures,* such as the square, rectangle, etc., may be tabulated as follows: square = (side)^2; rectangle = length × breadth; parallelogram = base × perpendicular height; trapezium = $\frac{1}{2}h(a + b)$, where a and b are the lengths of the parallel sides, and h is the perpendicular distance between them. Various formulae are true for the area of the triangle: (1) half the base multiplied by the height, or (2)

$$\sqrt{s(s-a)(s-b)(s-c)},$$

where s = half the sum of the sides a, b, and c (*see* HERO (HERON) OF ALEXANDRIA). For quadrilaterals, and the various types of polygons, it is usual to divide them up into triangles, find the area of each triangle, and sum up the results. The area of the circle = πr^2, where π = 3·14159 . . ., and r = radius. The area of a sector of a circle = $\frac{1}{2}r^2\theta$, where θ is the angle expressed in circular measure, subtended by the arc at the centre. That of the ellipse = πab, where a and b are the semi-axes. Various other formulae for the triangle and polygons are known in terms of trigonometrical notation. The areas of the less familiar figures are determined by means of the integral calculus.

With regard to solids, the volumes and surface areas of the most common are as follows: *Volumes.* Prism = area of base × height. Cone = $\frac{1}{3}$ area of base × height. Pyramid = $\frac{1}{3}$ area of base × height. Cylinder = area of base × height. Sphere = $\frac{4}{3}\pi a^3$, where a = radius of the sphere. *Surface areas.* Prism, cone, pyramid and cylinder = area of ends + area of sides. The area of the base of a cone and of each end of a cylinder is πa^2, a being the radius of the end. The area of the side of a cylinder is $2\pi al$, where l is its length, and of the side of a cone it is πal. The surface area of the sphere = $4\pi a^2$, where a = radius. Various rules have been formulated for finding areas and volumes, such as Simpson's rule (q.v.), Pappus's theorems (q.v.). Amongst mechanical appliances. the planimeter (q.v.) is an instrument for measuring the area of an irregular plane surface.

Mental Deficiency Acts, *see* MENTAL DISORDER.

Mental Disorder (formerly **Lunacy**), (*a*)

Generally. This article deals with a person's liability to be legally detained on account of M. D. and the provisions for his discharge etc. and with the management of his property and affairs during mental incapacity and certain other related aspects of civil relations. (For the pathological side of the subject *see* INSANITY.)

Before 1 November 1960. The terms 'lunatic' derived from *luna*, the moon (from the supposed influence of the moon in causing mental disorder) an.! 'idiot' are now obsolete from the medical or legal point of view. Prior to the coming into operation of the Mental Health Act, 1959, the treatment and care of mentally disordered persons fell under 2 separate and distinct legal codes: the Lunacy and Mental Treatment Acts, 1890 to 1930, dealing with *persons of unsound mind* (until the Mental Treatment Act, 1930, referred to as 'lunatics') and defectives who were dealt with under the Mental Deficiency Acts, 1913 to 1938. For general purposes it is broadly sufficient to say that after the Mental Deficiency system came into operation, under the 1913 Act, persons who became mentally afflicted after maturity were dealt with as 'lunatics' and after 1930 as 'persons of unsound mind', under the Lunacy and Mental Treatment Acts, whereas persons in whose case there existed mental defectiveness, meaning a condition of arrested or incomplete development of mind existing before the age of 18 years and whether arising from inherent causes or induced by disease or injury, were dealt with as 'defectives' under the Mental Deficiency Acts. Provision existed for limited sideways transfers but the 2 separate systems were found to be inappropriate for the developing ideas as to the cause and treatment of mental ailments.

The Royal Commission, 1954–57. The whole subject was exhaustively examined by the Royal Commission on the Law Relating to Mental Illness and Mental Deficiency, 1954–7, which made its report to Parliament in May 1957 (Cmnd 169). There was general deprecation of the process and term of 'certification'; the view was advanced that, in any event, compulsory detention was often unnecessary on grounds of expediency and bad on medical grounds, and that, wherever possible, a person needing mental treatment should be admitted to hospital for treatment with absence of formality and that, normally, compulsory detention should, save in certain criminal proceedings, no longer be secured by Magistrate's Order but upon a simple application to a hospital supported by 2 medical recommendations.

The Mental Health Act, 1959. This Act, giving effect to most of the recommendations of the Royal Commission, became fully operative on 1 Nov. 1960. It introduced a completely new code and system for the care, treatment and detention of persons suffering from 'mental disorder'. This is the new generic statutory term, embracing all forms of mental disability previously dealt with under the 2 systems referred to above and including some forms of psychopathic disorder which hardly fell within either.

Section 4 of the 1959 Act defines 'mental disorder' to mean mental illness, arrested or incomplete development of mind, psychopathic disorder, and any other disorder or disability of mind; and 'mentally disordered' is construed accordingly. There are 4 classifications of mental disorder which have special significance when considering whether or not a person is liable to be dealt with compulsorily under the Act. They are mental illness, severe subnormality, subnormality and psychopathic disorder.

Mental illness is not defined but section 4 defines 'severe subnormality' to mean a state of arrested or incomplete development of mind which includes subnormality of intelligence and is of such a nature or degree that the patient is incapable of living an independent life or o guarding himself against serious exploitation, or will be so incapable when of an age to do so; 'subnormality' means a state of arrested or incomplete development of mind (not amounting to severe subnormality) which includes subnormality of intelligence and is of a nature or degree which requires or is susceptible to medical treatment or other special care or training of the patient and 'psychopathic disorder' means a persistent disorder or disability of mind (whether or not including subnormality of intelligence) which results in abnormally aggressive or seriously irresponsible conduct on the part of the patient, and requires or is susceptible to medical treatment; but no person may be dealt with under the Act by reason *only* of promiscuity or other immoral conduct.

Section 5 of the Act sets statutory seal upon the principle of informal admission for treatment for mental disorder, this being complementary to the strong view of the Committee and contemporary psychiatric opinion that, so far as possible, a mentally disordered person should be treated as one of the general community, who goes to hospital for treatment in the same way as for any other malady.

The previous central authority, the Board of Control, for whom the Minister of Health was the responsible Minister, was dissolved and its duties and functions are now performed by the Ministry of Health, the local health authorities and the Mental Health Review Tribunals.

(b) Reception, Detention and Discharge: Compulsory Admission. The normal way is by application, duly supported by medical evidence, to the manager of the hospital concerned, including certain mental nursing homes (*see* sections 14 and 15); the application itself, duly documented, is the authority for detention (*see* sections 26, 28 and 31). As regards a person over 21, the form of mental disorder relied upon must be mental illness or severe subnormality, but as regards a person under 21 (or a person in respect of whom an emergency application is made under section 29) the form of mental disorder may be mental illness, severe subnormality, subnormality or psychopathic disorder. In any case the disorder must be of a nature or degree which warrants detention for treatment and it is necessary in the interests of the patient's health

or safety or for the protection of others.

An application for observation or treatment may be made either by the nearest relative or by a mental welfare officer, but when admission is for treatment (as distinct from an emergency application), the mental welfare officer must, where practicable, consult with the person appearing to be the *nearest* relative and may not proceed if he objects (section 27): but an emergency application may be made by *any* relative *or* a mental welfare officer (section 29). Two medical recommendations are required to support the application, one by an approved mental specialist and the other by (preferably) the patient's medical practitioner (section 28), but in the case of an emergency application one is sufficient in the first instance (section 29 (3)).

Guardianship. A patient may be placed under the guardianship of a local health authority, or some other person, but guardianship is not available where the form of mental order relied upon is subnormality or psychopathic disorder, unless the patient is under 21. What is said above as to applicants and medical evidence in relation to compulsory admission applies to an application for guardianship, and it must be shown that the nature or degree of the disorder warrants guardianship and that it is necessary in the interests of the patient or for the protection of others. Guardianship enables a patient to live in the community yet be under control and supervision (*see* report, para. 399). A guardian has such powers as would be exercisable by him in relation to the patient if he were father of the patient and the patient were under 14 (section 34 (1)).

Duration of Detention or Guardianship. The initial period is for 1 year but may, upon prescribed medical report, be renewed for a further year and thereafter for successive periods of 2 years (section 43). As regards a psychopathic or subnormal patient compulsory detention or guardianship will terminate completely on his attaining 25, unless specially extended under the provisions of section 44.

Discharge. Wide powers to discharge patients are conferred upon the hospital, medical and health authorities and the nearest relative has the power to order discharge (section 47) provided that the patient, if discharged, would not be likely to act in a manner dangerous to himself or others.

Nearest Relative. The rules governing the ascertaining of the nearest relative are contained in sections 49 to 51 and in view of the importance of the functions of the nearest relative, e.g. to apply for admission or order discharge, the Co. Court has jurisdiction to order the transfer of such functions to another person (section 52) and to discharge and vary such order (section 53).

Mental Health Review Tribunals. In accordance with recommendations in the Report, a Mental Health Review Tribunal, comprising legal, medical and lay members under the chairmanship of a lawyer, is constituted for each Regional Hospital Board Area in England and Wales (section 3). The function of such a tribunal is to provide the patient, and in some instances relatives, with an independent body to review any case in which it is contended that the patient should not be liable to be detained or subject to guardianship, but questions of legality, as distinct from necessity, are matters for the Courts and not the Tribunals.

Detention in Criminal Proceedings. Part V of the Act confers wide powers on the Courts to make orders for detention or guardianship in respect of offenders suffering from mental disorders and such an order may be made notwithstanding that the offender may be a psychopathic or subnormal person under 21. Further, a court of assize or quarter sessions may make an order restricting discharge, so that the power of discharge can only be exercised with the consent of the Home Secretary (sections 65 and 66).

Consequentials. The Act includes (*inter alia*) provision as to transfer of patients within and to and from England and Wales (sections 72 to 96), prosecutions and penalties for offences (sections 125 to 131), correspondence of patients (section 134), custody, conveyance and detention and recapture (sections 139 and 140) and protection for acts done in pursuance of the act (section 141).

(c) *Management of Patient's Estate: The Court of Protection.* The protection and management of the property and affairs of mental patients fall to the Court of Protection, situated at 25 Store Street, London, W.C.1. The Court has a Master, Deputy Master and 4 Assistant Masters who exercise the jurisdiction under Part VIII of the Act. Some matters are dealt with by the judge (a judge of the Chancery Div. of the High Court nominated under section 100(1)). Appeals lie to the judge, from him to the Court of Appeal and thence to the House of Lords.

Prior to the 1959 Act, the jurisdiction of the Court of Protection ('In L.') was in part statutory and in part inherent under the Royal Prerogative. Part VIII of the new Act confers a plenary and completely statutory jurisdiction which is exercisable (a) for the maintenance or other benefit of the patient, (b) for the maintenance or other benefit of members of the patient's family, (c) for making provision for other persons or purposes for whom or which the patient might be expected to provide if he were not mentally disordered or (d) otherwise for administering the patient's affairs (section 102): without prejudice to the generality of the above provisions, section 103 sets out what would appear to be an exhaustive list of specific matters, e.g. control and management, sale, etc. of property, settlement or gifts of property, carrying on of a business, carrying out of contracts and exercise of any powers vested in a patient, whether beneficially or as guardian or trustee. The anct procedure of inquisition has been abolished.

Incapacity to Manage Affairs. The powers of the Court are exercisable where, after considering medical evidence, the Court is satisfied that a person is incapable by reason of M. D. of managing and administering his property and affairs (section 101), whether or not the patient is compulsorily detained or under guardianship and whether residing in his own home or elsewhere. No longer is a person automatically rendered incapable of managing his own affairs by lawful detention. In each case there is the test of mental capacity. Any person so incapable is not in a position to give any power of attorney or other authority to any person to manage his property and any such power of attorney or authority becomes inoperative by reason of supervening incapacity. Any person continuing to act under such a power of attorney or authority, or a bank or other person who, knowing of this incapacity, continues to deal or permit dealings with a patient's property incurs considerable risk.

Appointment of a Receiver. The proper course in such a case is to apply to the Court of Protection for the appointment of a receiver, though in very minor cases the Court may be prepared to deal with the matter without making a full receivership order. In cases of substance it is usual to instruct a solicitor, but there is a Personal Application Branch. Proceedings are commenced by way of originating application, supported by evidence of kindred and fortune and medical evidence to satisfy section 101. It is usual for a relative or near friend to be appointed, though a professional man, e.g. an accountant, may be appointed and allowed remuneration.

Powers and Duties of a Receiver. His powers are limited and defined in the order appointing him, but additional power will be conferred as may be required: he has no power to deal with capital in the absence of specific authorisation. The first general order, in addition to the appointment, will be directed to securing the control and safe custody of the patient's estate and rendering the same available for his maintenance and benefit. It is to be noted that the maintenance of a patient may take priority over his creditors but that of his wife and family will not. A receiver is usually required to give security (fidelity guarantee) and to account to the Court annually. A percentage fee is levied at the rate of 5 per cent on the clear ann. income at the patient's disposal, subject to certain exceptions and powers of remission.

It is the duty of the receiver to bring to the notice of the Court matters affecting the welfare of the patient or his estate. He is the statutory agent of the patient.

Death or Recovery of Patient. The powers of a receiver are determined automatically by the death of the patient, but upon recovery an order, made upon medical evidence, is required to restore the patient to the management of his property and affairs.

Lord Chancellor's Visitors. The Lord Chancellor's Visitors, comprising a barrister and 3 psychiatrists, in accordance with the directions of the Court, visit patients and report as to their mental capacity and generally as to their welfare.

Not infrequently they may be directed to report as to a patient's testamentary capacity. Their reports may not be disclosed except with the leave of the Court.

(*d*) *Related matters: Testamentary capacity.* A mentally disordered person is not necessarily unable to make a will: it will depend on whether he has testamentary capacity, i.e. capacity to understand the nature of the document being executed, the extent of the property to be disposed of and the claims of those to be benefited or excluded. It is desirable that the will should be witnessed by the testator's legal adviser and medical attendant and that, where the patient is the subject of a Court of Protection order, the Court should be communicated with first.

Contracts. A contract entered into by a mentally disordered person is binding upon him, unless on his behalf it can be proved that the other party knew he was incapable of understanding its terms or forming a rational judgment as to its effect, in which event it is not void but voidable at the option of the person under disability: to establish such knowledge of the other party something more than general reputation in the neighbourhood is requisite. A patient is liable on a contract entered into during a lucid interval but it is for the other party to prove the existence of this lucid interval. A patient is liable for necessaries supplied, notwithstanding that the other party knew of his incapacity. He will also be liable for necessaries supplied to his wife by anyone who was ignorant of his state of mind and to whom the patient when of sound mind had held out his wife as his agent. Contracts whether under hand or under seal (deeds) entered into by a patient personally after the Court has taken control of his estate by the appointment of a receiver, are void *ab initio* and not merely voidable.

Torts. It has been held that a mentally disordered person is liable in tort (civil wrongs apart from breach of contract) if at the time he committed the tort (in the case in question, assault and battery) he knew the nature and quality of his act, although he did not know that it was wrong. The view has also been advanced that a mentally disordered person is liable in tort to the same extent as any other person since intention and state of mind are hardly germane to questions of tortious liability, but as Pollock points out a 'lunatic would hardly be held liable in damages for incoherent words of vituperation'.

See Heywood and Massey, *Court of Protection Practice* (8th ed., 1961, and *Supplement*, 1964) by D. G. Hunt and M. E. Reed; Sir H. S. Theobald, *The Law Relating to Lunacy*, 1924.

Mental Disorders (Medical). There are varying degrees of mental disorder. Among the more common are cretinism, idiocy and imbecility.

Cretinism is a congenital disease, causing idiocy or arrested mental development, together with bodily deformity, always associated with absence or atrophy of the thyroid gland. The connection between goitre (q.v.), myxoedema (q.v.) and C. is close. Myxoedema, however, comes on in adult life, and is associated with a destructive change in the thyroid gland, although the removal of the gland will bring on a similar condition. C. is really a congenital myxoedema. It is found largely in the lower valleys of the Alps and Pyrenees, and other mountainous parts of Europe, and is probably associated with a lack of iodine in the soil and therefore in the drinking water. It is rarely met with in altitudes above 3000 ft. Cretins are usually dirty, obscene and shameless, and have large open mouths with protruding, large tongues. They have receding foreheads, large hands and feet and rickety limbs, while they usually have a dwarfish body, with thick, dry, loose skin and a protuberant abdomen. The treatment consists in the administration of thyroid. See GOITRE and MYXOEDEMA.

Idiocy is a congenital mental deficiency of severe degree. Little is known of the pathology of I. and, except in such cases as hydrocephalus (q.v.), no gross lesion of the brain can be found. I. is a hereditary disease due to the emergence of a recessive gene. It is commonly associated with other congenital defects, notably congenital heart disease. There is no direct evidence to show that shock or injury to the mother during pregnancy can cause I. in the foetus. It is interesting to note, however, that a greater number than average of children were *b.* with congenital malformation (but no idiocy) during the height of the aerial attacks in SE. England in 1941–2. Idiots are susceptible to infections and this, together with the allied heart disease when it exists, makes their expectancy of life about 14 years. *Mongolian I.* is a form of I. characterised by mongolian type of features, i.e. oblique eyes, thick protruding tongue and short, broad fingers. It is now known that mongols have an extra chromosome (47 instead of 46) in the nuclei of their cells, an abnormality known as trisomy. *See also* INSANITY; PSYCHIATRY; PSYCHOANALYSIS; PSYCHOLOGY; PUBLIC HEALTH.

Mental Health Services, *see* PUBLIC HEALTH.

Mental Hospitals, *see* HOSPITALS; MENTAL DISORDER; NATIONAL HEALTH SERVICE.

Mental Tests. Modern psychologists use tests of intelligence, of educational attainments, of aptitudes (mechanical, musical, etc.), of the senses and of personality and interests in studying children and adults. Such abilities or qualities are usually judged, in daily life, from casual observations of a person's behaviour when confronted with intellectual, mechanical or other tests. But a scientifically constructed test shows the following characteristics: (1) The problems or tasks are carefully chosen and graded and have usually been proved to measure the quality in question. (2) They often include a wide range of problems in order to cover the ground systematically and to allow scope for those who are highest and lowest in the quality. (3) They are given in a standard manner, often with a time limit, and should only be applied by testers who are trained both to get the co-

operation of the people tested and to follow the exact procedure and interpret the results correctly. (4) Accurate records are made of the responses. Problems are set in such a way that there is only one correct answer to each; hence the marking is objective and unaffected by the tester's personal judgment. (5) Scores may be based on numbers of correct responses or the time taken, etc. and these are evaluated by comparison with the *norms* or standards of performance for children of the same age, or for groups of similar adults. For example, a dull child of 10 years may only do as well on an intelligence or an arithmetic test as an average 8-year-old. He is then said to have a mental age or arithmetic age of 8, and his *Intelligence Quotient* or I.Q. is 8/10 × 100 = 80. The average I.Q. is 100; very bright children range from about 130 to 180, feeble-minded ones from about 70 down to less than 20. Adult test results are more often expressed by *percentiles*. Thus an army recruit would be regarded as high in mechanical ability if his score was better than that of 90 per cent of recruits.

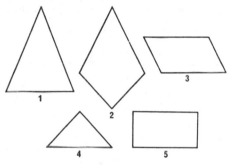

MENTAL TESTS

An example of one type of question encountered in perceptual tests of intelligence:

Question: Which figure differs from all the others?

Answer: 3, the only one which has no central axis of symmetry.

The earliest tests, devised by 19th-cent. physiologists and psychologists, including Fechner, Galton, Helmholtz, Cattell and others, were mostly for measuring the senses, for example, colour vision, auditory acuity and sense of pitch and touch. Quickness of response or *reaction time* to light and sound, as measured by electrically operated chronometers, was found to differ widely in different individuals. Sir Francis Galton conceived the idea of measuring higher mental abilities, and studied different types of mental imagery. But the first intelligence tests were Ebbinghaus's completion test (1897) and Binet and Simon's scale (1905). The latter consisted of groups of short tasks appropriate for children of different ages. It has been trans., revised and expanded in many countries, for example by Burt in England. The best-known versions are the Standford-Binet

(1916) and the Terman-Merrill scales. These are generally regarded as giving the most reliable measurement of a child's intelligence, e.g. for deciding what type of school (grammar, modern or special) is suitable for him. Cattell's Scale III is more suitable among adults, and scales based mainly on play material such as the Merrill-Palmer are used with pre-school children. For deaf or other verbally handicapped children, practical or *performance tests* are available. These mostly involve fitting pictures or coloured blocks together, or putting shapes into holes.

Tests for measuring scholastic attainments in reading, spelling, arithmetic, handwriting, etc., were prepared by Thorndike and other Amer. psychologists early in this cent. Valuable series of educational tests, which are especially useful in studying and coaching backward children, have been pub. by Sir Cyril Burt (*Mental and Scholastic Tests*, 1921) and F. J. Schonell (*Backwardness in the Basic Subjects*, 1942). This type of standardised examination was soon extended to the measurement of intelligence, and group tests consisting of series of printed problems were devised for Amer. recruits in 1917. Nearly 2,000,000 men took the army alpha (verbal) or army beta (non-verbal) tests. Many hundreds of tests along the same lines have been pub. since in Britain and America for measuring the intelligence or attainments of primary and secondary school pupils, ordinary adults and univ. students. Tests of intelligence, Eng. and arithmetic are prepared yearly by Moray House, Edinburgh and the National Foundation for Educational Research, and have been used by many education authorities for selecting children at 11 years for grammar schools. Since 1942 all recruits to the navy, army and RAF have taken intelligence, educational and other group tests, and the results have been shown to be useful in allocation to specialist training, in selecting officers, etc. Though group tests are quicker and easier to give and score than individual ones, they vary considerably in merit, and are often less trustworthy.

Testing of occupational aptitudes has been fostered in Britain by the Industrial Health Research Board and the National Institute of Industrial Psychology. Mechanical tests based on pieces of apparatus or pictures and diagrams, and clerical tests, play a useful part in advising school-leavers about suitable vocations and in classifying recruits. In selecting workers for a particular job more specialised tests are constructed after a careful analysis of the job requirements. Interests in different types of work can be measured by questionnaire tests, but personal qualities such as leadership, dependability and emotional stability are much more difficult to measure than abilities. They can be assessed only very inaccurately by questionnaires or in the ordinary interview. Ratings or judgments by acquaintances, and the extended practical exercises developed by the War Office and civil service selection boards, are of some value. So-called *projection tests*, where the person reveals his qualities indirectly

through his responses to ink-blots, pictures or verbal stimuli (free association), are often used by trained psychologists. *See* PSYCHOLOGY; MEMORY; EDUCATIONAL PSYCHOLOGY.

See Sir F. Galton, *Inquiries into Human Faculty and its Development*, 1883; O. Buros, *Mental Measurements Year Book*, 1933–6, 1938, 1940, 1948; R. B. Cattell, *A Guide to Mental Testing*, 1936; L. M. Terman and M. A. Merrill, *Measuring Intelligence*, 1937; P. E. Vernon, *The Measurement of Abilities*, 1940; J. E. Bell, *Projective Techniques*, 1947; H. J. Eysenck, *Dimensions of Personality*, 1947; P. E. Vernon and J. B. Parry, *Personnel Selection in the British Forces*, 1949.

Mentana, It. vil. in Lazio, 12 m. NE. of Rome, where in 1867 the Fr. and papal forces defeated Garibaldi (q.v.). Pop. 4200.

Menteith, Lake of, loch ($1\frac{1}{2}$ m. long, 1 m. broad) and dist of SW. Perthshire, Scotland. The loch contains 3 small picturesque is., among them Inchmahome (q.v.). The dist extends from the Teith to the Forth (q.v.), and formerly was an independent stewartry. The earldom of M. is long extinct.

Mentha, name applied to a genus of labiate plants, otherwise known as the mints; also to the volatile oil contained by the different species. The more important species are *M. viridis*, or spearmint, which is used for culinary purposes, and contains an oil used as an aromatic stimulant; *M. piperita*, or peppermint, used to relieve nausea, flatulence and pains in the stomach and intestines; and *M. sylvestris*, or horse mint, an uncultivated variety, used for the same purposes as spearmint and peppermint.

Menthol ($C_{10}H_{19}$·OH), alcohol derivative of menthone, one of the constituents of oil of peppermint. It also occurs in a free state in peppermint and is mainly responsible for the characteristic odour of the plant. It is also prepared synthetically. M. crystallises in prisms which melt at 43° C. and boil at 212° C. It is reduced by hydriodic acid to hexahydrocymene. The M. of pharmacy is commonly derived from *Mentha arvensis purpurescens*, a Jap. variety of mint. In this form it usually contains other ingredients, and is made up as a soft crystalline solid resembling camphor. In fact, it is often known ... .ut camphor. It volatilises readily on being rubbed on the skin, but has a stimulating effect if evaporation is prevented. It is used as an anodyne in neuralgia and in many irritating affections of the skin.

Menthu, *see* MONT.

Mentmore, vil. in Bucks, England, 4 m. from Leighton Buzzard (q.v.). Here is the seat of the Earl of Rosebery, once the property of the Rothschild family. Pop. 210.

Menton (It. **Mentone**), Fr. tn in the dept of Alpes-Maritimes, on the Riviera (q.v.) coast, 13 m. ENE. of Nice. It is on the It. border. Until 1848, in which year it was taken by Sardinia, it was part of Monaco (q.v.); in 1860 it was ceded to France after a plebiscite. It is backed by mts, and its vegetation is almost tropical. Cap Martin forms the SW. boundary of its bay. The mildness of its winter climate makes it a popular winter and health resort. Fruit and flowers are grown. Pop. 19,900.

Mentzelia, genus of half-hardy annuals or perennials (family Loasaceae) with large white, yellow or orange flowers. Sev. species are hardy in sunny borders. *M. lindleyi* is a popular annual.

Menuf, tn 35 m. NNW. of Cairo, situated in the Nile delta at the junction of 2 branches in Lower Egypt. It is an important market for agric. produce.

Menufia, or **Menufiyeh**, prov., 607 sq. m. in area, in the Nile delta, Lower Egypt. It stretches from the fork of the main arms along the Rosetta branch. Pop. 1,165,000.

Menuhin, Yehudi (1916–), Amer. violinist of Jewish descent. He began his musical studies at the age of 4 under Sigmund Anker and Louis Persinger in San Francisco, and later was a pupil of Georges Enesco at Paris. At the age of 11, having already made numerous public appearances, he performed the astonishing feat of playing the Beethoven concerto with the New York Symphony Orchestra under Fritz Busch. He made his Berlin and London débuts in 1929, and has since then played in all the prin. cities of the world. Appointed K.B.E., 1965.

Menura, see LYRE-BIRDS.

Menyanthes, see BUCK-BEAN.

Menzel, Adolph Friedrich Erdmann von (1815–1905), Ger. painter and engraver, b. Breslau. He lost both his parents before he was 8, and had later to support his family. Having illustrated Goethe's *Kunstlers Erdenwallen* and other works with pen-and-ink drawings, he revived the art of wood engraving, and made a name by his illustrations of Kugler's *Geschichte Friedrichs des Grossen*, and of the actual works of Frederick the Great (1843–9). *See* J. Meier-Graefe, *Der junge Menzel*, 1906; and lives by J. von Kurenberg, 1935, and E. Waldmann, 1941.

Menzies, Sir Robert Gordon (1894–), Australian statesman and lawyer, b. Jeparit, Australia. Educ. at state schools, Graneville College, Ballarat, Wesley College, Melbourne, and Melbourne Univ., he was called to the Bar, 1918, and entered the Victorian Parliament in 1928. Attorney-general, minister of railways and deputy premier of Victoria, 1932–4, and attorney-general of Australia, 1935–9, M. was elected leader of the United Australia party in April 1939, being Prime Minister and member of the advisory war council, 1939–41. Throughout his tenure of office during this period there was marked want of political stability in Australia, although all parties were agreed on the country's general war policy. Labour refused to join any coalition, and M. had to resign when Curtin rejected his proposal to form an all-party gov. M. again became Prime Minister of Australia in Dec. 1949 after the defeat of the Labour Gov. He pursued a policy of vigorous economic expansion, and though financial measures to curb inflation led to a fall in his gov.'s popularity, M. was again returned to power in the general election of 1954, but with a reduced majority. On

30 Nov. 1954 M. beat the record for long service as Australian Prime Minister previously held by Hughes (q.v.). The Petrov revelations (*see* PETROV AFFAIR) and the ensuing controversy led to sev. public exchanges between M. and Evatt (q.v.), marked by extreme personal bitterness. In Dec. 1955 the general election results appeared a vindication of M.'s policies, for his gov. was returned with an increased majority. It was re-elected in 1958 and 1961. M. has always been a staunch supporter of the Commonwealth connection. M. was knighted (K.T.) in 1963, and made Lord Warden of the Cinque Ports, in succession to Sir Winston Churchill, in 1965. He retired from the Australian premiership in Jan. 1966, being succeeded by Holt (q.v.). (*See Plate: Australia*.)

Menzies, tn in the gold-mining dist of W. Australia. It lies S. of Lake Ballard and is connected by rail with Malcolm, Albany and Perth. Pop. 536.

Menzini, Benedetto (1646–1704). It. poet, b. Florence. He enjoyed the patronage of Christina of Sweden, and was in some measure inspired by Francesco Redi. His original verse, which includes 12 pungent satires, some mediocre odes and a few dainty anacreontics, is more readable today than his somewhat antiquated essay in criticism entitled *Arte Poetica*, 1690.

Mepacrin (quinacrine, atabrine), a synthetic antimalarial drug, first made in 1930 by I. G. Farbenindustrie. *See also* CINCHONA BARK ALKALOIDS.

Mephistopheles is the evil spirit in the Faust legend, by whom Faust is persuaded to sign away his soul. M. receives very different treatment at the hands of Marlowe and Goethe in their versions of the Faust legend. Both, however, identify him with Lucifer (q.v.), the fallen archangel, with the medieval devil and also with the humorous kobold of Ger. folklore.

Meppel, tn in the prov. of Drenthe, Netherlands, 17 m NNE. by rail of Zwolle. It is a railway and canal junction, and an agric. market. Pop. 18,700.

Mequinez, see MEKNÈS.

Mer de Glace, glacier near Chamonix, in France, running northwards from Mont Blanc (q.v.) between the magnificent precipices of the Chamonix Aiguilles on one side and the Drus and the Verte on the other. It is the subject of a painting by Turner.

Merano, It. tn in Trentino-Alto Adige, on the Passirio, a trib. of the Adige. It is at the foot of the Ötztal Alps, and is a health and holiday resort. It has a 15th-cent. castle and a 14th-cent. Gothic church. Pop. 36,100.

Mérat, Albert (1840–1909), Fr. poet, one of the Parnassians (q.v.). His vols. of poetry include *Les Chimères*, 1866, *Les Villes de marbre*, 1874, *Au Fil de l'eau*, 1877, *Poèmes de Paris*, 1880, *Vers le soir*, 1900.

Merbecke, John, see MARBECK.

Mercadante, Saverio (1795–1870), It. composer, b. Altamura, near Bari. He studied under Zingarelli at Naples and in 1818 wrote 3 ballets and a cantata, producing his first opera at the

San Carlo theatre there the next year. He was director of the Naples Conservatory from 1840 till his death, in spite of losing his sight in 1862. He wrote 60 operas, some containing serious and advanced music not without its influence on Verdi. The most famous were *Il giuramento*, 1837, and *La Vestale*, 1840.

Mercantile Law. There is no part of Eng. law which is specifically called M. L. except in text-books, where the phrase usually covers topics connected with commerce, e.g. contract, partnership, insurance, negotiable instruments (q.v.), bankruptcy, companies.

Mercantile Marine. From A.-S. days the merchant seamen of Britain have made a vital contribution to national defence and commercial prosperity. The naval tradition has been for cents. a crucial factor in the life of the nation, though it developed slowly and irregularly. For seamen there was no contract lasting longer than a ship's commission and no security of re-employment until the middle of the 19th cent. But seamen congregated in dockyard tns and lived by and manned the navy. It was only during the reign of Henry V that the Eng. navy, as distinct from the merchant service, was estab., and it was only in that of Henry VIII that the king estab. dockyards at Woolwich, Deptford and Portsmouth, appointed a Board of Admiralty, placed the naval service on a separate footing and estab. Trinity House to encourage navigation. The dockyard tns were estab. to control the Channel approaches and to defend the mouth of the Thames. They were important military fortresses before the king developed his power upon the sea. The dockyards and the royal ships were, however, only one element of the king's marine forces; for over all vessels he possessed that indirect remote control which medieval theory gave, and for cents. certain tns could be called upon to furnish their due quota of ships in times of stress. Hence there was always the closest contact between the royal and merchant navies. The navigators of royal ships came from merchant vessels and returned to them. There is hardly an industry in the country that does not rely upon the Merchant Navy, and hardly a person whose prosperity and general wellbeing are not bound up in this vast and complicated organisation. The M. M. in Great Britain is controlled by the Ministry of Transport, which administers the Merchant Shipping Acts and other regulations dealing with it.

The Ministry issues a notice (No. M. 117) and there are two books pub. by Her Majesty's Stationery Office (Nos. 72 and 73) in their choice of careers series for the guidance of those who wish to go to sea in the Merchant Navy as officers or ratings. High standards of physical fitness are required, and those interested in service on deck should make sure that they can pass the Ministry's sight tests. Before a prospective navigating officer can sit for the Ministry's examination for a certificate of competency as second mate, he must be not less than 20 and have served 4 years at sea in foreign-going ships

or 6 in home-trade ships. The necessary experience at sea may be obtained either by apprenticeship to a shipping company at the age of 16, or by service as a deck rating. Alternatively, courses in certain training estabs. are accepted as counting towards experience at sea. Navigating officers must also hold the Ministry's Radar Observers' Certificate. The Merchant Navy Training Board was set up in 1935 to promote a uniform training scheme for navigating apprentices, and full particulars can be obtained from the Secretary, City Chambers, 65a Fenchurch Street, London, E.C.3. Prospective engineer officers must serve an apprenticeship of 4 years (in some cases 5) in a suitable engineering works, but particulars of an alternative scheme are given in Notice M. 117 (embracing a 2-year course for an ordinary national diploma in mechanical engineering, 18 months' service at sea and 12 months' training in a shipyard or suitable engineering works). The examination regulations, for both deck and engineer officers' certificates, are pub. by H.M.S.O. A radio officer must possess a certificate of proficiency issued or accepted by the Postmaster-General, and a list of schools providing suitable instruction can be obtained from the Inspector of Wireless Telegraphy, Wireless Telegraph Section, H.Q. Building, G.P.O., London, E.C.1. Standard rates of wages for the Merchant Navy are fixed by the National Maritime Board.

A record of all the certificates of competency issued or withdrawn is kept by the Registrar General of Shipping and Seamen, Cardiff. It is this body which, originally set up in 1835, maintains a complete copy of the register of every Brit. ship (including those on Commonwealth registers). The facts and figures so collected are pub. in the *Mercantile Navy List* (H.M.S.O.). The Registrar General's Central Register of Seamen (which excludes Asiatic seamen signed on in Asia) showed that on 31 July 1964 the strength of the Brit. Merchant Navy was 124,849, made up as follows:

Masters and deck officers (cert.)	13,510
Masters and deck officers (uncert.)	1,433
Apprentices and cadets	4,651
Engineer officers (cert.)	6,647
Engineer officers (uncert.)	18,110
Engineer apprentices and cadets	1,207
Radio officers	3,385
Deck ratings	26,318
Engine-room ratings	12,053
Catering (including Pursers and Writers)	35,005
Miscellaneous (including Surgeons)	2,530
Total	124,849

The Merchant Shipping Acts contain specific regulations for the manning of Brit. ships. A foreign-going ship (one which goes farther afield than continental ports between the R. Elbe and Brest) must carry a certificated master; if she is of 100 tons net or more she must also carry a certificated mate, and if a first and second mate are carried both must be certificated. The home-trade passenger ship (one which will not sail farther than the continental ports between the R. Elbe and Brest) must carry a certificated master and mate, unless she is of less than 100 tons net, when only the master need be certificated. The officers of home-trade cargo ships (which include the bulk of our coastal ships) need not be certificated. Most foreign-going ships must carry 2 certificated engineers; foreign-going ships with engines not over 100 nominal horse-power, and home-trade passenger ships, must carry one.

In order to meet the manning needs of the shipping industry during the war, the Merchant Navy Reserve Pool was started in 1941; its object was to provide a reserve of trained men and to avoid delays to convoys through crew shortage. When the war-time arrangements came to an end in 1947, the scheme was reorganised on an industrial footing as the Merchant Navy Estab. Service Scheme, with the object of affording the maximum regularity of employment for seafarers. It provides for the 'estab.' of a high proportion of officers and seamen, either with individual companies or with the central body of shipowners represented by the Shipping Federation. An 'estab.' man works on a contract which runs irrespective of whether he is actually at sea or not. In return for the continuity of service thus offered, he must serve in the ship to which he is sent, though every effort is made to find the man the ship he wants and the master the man he wants.

Officers and men of the Merchant Navy made great sacrifices to duty in the Second as in the First World War, and on 5 Nov. 1955 Queen Elizabeth II unveiled a memorial recording the names of 24,000 officers and men of the Merchant Navy and Fishing Fleets who lost their lives between 1939 and 1945 and have no grave but the sea. The memorial adjoins that erected for the First World War, which records the names of 12,600 officers and men of the earlier generation. The deaths due directly or indirectly to the Second World War were officially estimated as 32,952. (*See* 'Merchant Shipping and the Demands of War', by C. B. A. Behrens, in *History of the Second World War*, 1955.)

Brit. merchant ships (excluding fishing vessels) lost by enemy action during the Second World War totalled 2426, with a gross tonnage of 11,331,933. Of these 1332 (7,595,645 gross tonnage) were destroyed by U-boats; 296 (816,255 gross tonnage) by mines; 209 (969,087 gross tonnage) by surface craft; 383 (1,575,230 gross tonnage) by aircraft; and 206 (375,716 gross tonnage) by other or unknown causes. The heaviest losses were in 1941, when 717 ships (2,824,056 gross tonnage) were sunk: 291 by U-boats, 172 by aircraft, 76 by mines, 70 by surface craft and 108 by other or unknown causes. In the Second World War allied forces destroyed an average of $11\frac{1}{2}$ U-boats a month; in the First World War the losses of Ger. submarines were estimated at $3\frac{1}{2}$ a month.

In the period since the Second World War

there has in general been a shortage of man-power for the Merchant Navy. This has been due to the greater opportunities available ashore as compared with pre-war days, and to the attraction of home life for a married man. In particular, engineer and radio officers have been in short supply. They are of course well qualified to take up positions ashore after gaining experience at sea.

Ministry of Transport

BRITISH MERCHANT NAVY BADGE

In order to attract men, shipowners have gone to great lengths to provide comfortable accommodation in ships built since the war. The result has been to bring about marked changes in this field. Before the war, accommodation in ships, though adequate, was not always comfortable. Seamen were housed in cabins accommodating from 4 men upwards, and living space generally was often limited.

In post-war ships the general standard of accommodation is remarkably high. The task of ship designers in providing this better accommodation has been made easier by two factors. In the first place, general improvements in design technique have made it easier to devote more space to accommodation. In the second place, ships have generally become larger. The size of the crew does not increase proportionately to the size of the ship, and so the modern ship tends to have more space available. In passenger ships, where large crews have to be carried, space for crew accommodation is still limited. But in cargo ships, and even more so in large tankers, ample room is available. In these ships it is not uncommon for every man of the crew to have a cabin to himself, while senior officers will have a suite of rooms comprising day cabin, night cabin and bathroom.

A national strike, organised by the National Union of Seamen in 1966, lasted sev. weeks and virtually paralysed Brit. merchant shipping. It was caused primarily by a dispute relating to pay and hours, but underlying it was longstanding resentment of some of the requirements of the Merchant Shipping Acts. A gov. inquiry was estab. to examine these and other matters raised

Year	Entered			Cleared		
	With Cargo	In Ballast	Total	With Cargo	In Ballast	Total
1938	68,372	23,508	91,880	58,881	32,284	92,165
1948	50,562	12,833	63,396	35,762	28,629	64,391
1953	69,435	17,896	87,331	50,173	37,448	87,621
1958	79,865	20,859	100,724	51,392	49,662	101,054
1959	84,779	22,301	107,081	53,952	54,268	108,221
1960	91,625	22,600	114,226	54,806	60,478	115,284
1961	91,706	22,180	113,886	53,677	61,442	115,292
1962	95,434	25,080	120,514	56,318	64,438	120,756
1963	98,089	25,337	123,426	58,409	65,265	123,674

during the strike, and future changes were envisaged.

Statistics. The following table, covering vessels of 100 tons gross and over, excluding sail and barges, analyses the constitution of the Brit. Commonwealth fleet as at 1 July 1939 and 31 July 1964 (figures in thousands of tons gross):

	1 July 1939	31 July 1964
Tankers:		
U.K. register only	2,954	8,002
Commonwealth register only	360	437
Vessels other than tankers:		
U.K. register only	14,937	13,498
Commonwealth register only	2,751	5,618

The 13 leading merchant ship fleets are listed below, from which it will be seen that that of Great Britain is the largest because much of the U.S. tonnage is laid up. In the last 7 years the tonnage registered under the Liberian flag, now second in the world, has doubled, while there have been lesser additions to that under the Panamanian flag. Both these fleets are largely owned and operated by nationals of other countries, who register their ships under these flags in order to benefit from lower taxation. The position of Norway with the third largest fleet is notable for a country with such a small pop. Altogether the N. European nations (Great Britain, Norway, W. Germany, France, Netherlands, Sweden and Denmark) own and operate 38 per cent of the total world tonnage. During the last 5 years Russia has moved up from 11th to 6th place on the list.

Merchant fleets over 4 million tons gross

(Source: 1965 Statistical Tables of Lloyd's Register of Shipping)

Flag	'000 tons
Great Britain and N. Ireland	21,530
Liberia	17,539
Norway	15,641
Japan	11,971
U.S.A.	10,000*
Russia	8,238
Greece	7,137
Italy	5,701
Germany (West)	5,279
France	5,198
Netherlands	4,891
Panama	4,465
Sweden	4,290

* The total tonnage of the U.S. Merchant fleet is 21,527,349 tons gross, but of this some 11½ millions is gov. owned, most of which is in reserve.

The total net tonnage of shipping entering U.K. ports with cargo has increased steadily since 1945 and in 1963 was 32 per cent greater than in 1938. Clearances with cargo, however, have not yet reached the pre-war level. In 1951, 1954 and 1961 there was a slight reversal of the upward trend in these last figures, but they have shown a marked advance during the last 2 years. The above table shows the foreign trade entrances and clearances at U.K. ports for the years 1938, 1948, 1953 and from 1958 to 1963, in thousands of tons net. (*See Plates: Mercantile Marine; Ships and Shipbuilding.*)

Mercantile Pound, see METROLOGY.

Mercantile System, or **Commercial System,** policy of estimating the wealth of a country by the amount of gold and silver it contained, and, inferentially, of placing artificial restraints on commerce to prevent money (*see* CURRENCY and MONEY) from going out of the country. Towards the end of the 18th cent., when the policy obtained in England, heavy duties were put on the importation of Fr. wines and silks and other commodities, and generally importation was discouraged, while everything was done by bounties and otherwise to foster exports. Adam Smith (q.v.), in countering the M. S., as it was officially expounded in Thomas Mun's book, *England's Treasure by Forraign Trade,* the title of which at that time had become a fundamental maxim in the political economy of all commercial countries (*see* book iv of *The Wealth of Nations*), shows how deeply rooted was this theory of Eng. statesmen, by reference to the theory of its then foremost philosopher, Locke, that the great object of a nation's political economy ought to be the multiplication of the precious metals as 'the most solid and substantial part of its movable wealth'.

From Adam Smith we learn that there were some 6 prin. means by which the M. S. proposed to increase the aggregate amount of gold and silver in any country by turning the balance of trade in its favour. Two were restraints upon importation, and they were imposed either by high duties or by absolute prohibition: (1) Restraints upon the importation of such foreign goods for home consumption as could be produced at home. The Navigation Act, primarily aimed against the Dutch, was an especially gratuitous barrier to the economic supply of fish from a people who were not only the prin. fishers in Europe, but by reason of their proximity could supply Britain at a low cost of transportation. But even Adam Smith had to concede that the Navigation Act was eminently favourable to the development of Brit. shipping, whatever its effect on foreign commerce. (2) Restraints upon the importation of goods of almost all kinds from those particular countries with which the balance of trade was supposed to be disadvantageous. Adam Smith's lengthy argument against this restraint was that the balance of produce and consumption may be constantly in favour of a nation, though the balance of trade (the supposed loss from foreign trade through the amount of gold and silver exported, as measured by that part of the imports which had to be paid for in gold and silver) be against it, because though its circulating coin may be fast going out of the country or replaced by paper money, its *real wealth*, the ann. produce of its lands and labour, may be increasing in much greater proportion than its debts. Exportation was encouraged (*a*) by drawbacks (*see* CUSTOMS DUTIES) in favour of (1) home manufs. subject to duties on exportation, and (2) foreign dutiable goods imported for immediate re-exportation; (*b*) by bounties to foster new or developing manufs., such as were supposed to be especially meritorious; (*c*) by commercial treaties; (*d*) by the estab. of colonies in distant countries from the supposed advantage of compelling them to buy Brit. commodities in exchange for their own. The only exceptions to the M. S. were those required by the system itself. The materials and instruments of production were the subjects of a converse policy, designed to enable manufacturers to obtain them as cheaply as possible so as to stimulate exports.

From a wider view the M. S., in that it aimed to expand Brit. shipping and production, may be regarded as the economic concomitant of nationalism. The reaction against a system which tried to restrict colonies to the provision of raw materials and the absorption of Brit. manufs. was one element in the Amer. revolt. The question of a favourable balance of trade has again risen to great prominence since the end of the Second World War, especially in regard to the excess of imports over exports, which has added greatly to Britain's economic problems. *See further under* BALANCE OF TRADE; BULLIONISM; CURRENCY; MONEY; PROTECTION; TRADE AND COMMERCE. *See* E. F. Heckscher, *Mercantilism* (Eng. trans.), 2 vols., 2nd revised edition, 1956; E. Heimann, *History of Economic Doctrines*, 1964.

Mercaptans, substituted alcohols, such as methyl or ethyl, the oxygen in the hydroxyl group being replaced by sulphur, e.g. C_2H_5SH, ethyl M.

Mercator, Gerardus (whose real name was **Gerhard Kremer**) (1512–94), mathematician, *b.* Rupelmonde in E. Flanders, but of Ger. extraction. He was early fascinated by geography, and, after enjoying the patronage of the Emperor Charles V, became in 1559 cosmographer to the Duke of Jülich and Cleves. He was the first to develop the projection called after him, on which constant bearings are represented by straight lines. This was the world chart *Nova et aucta orbis terrae descriptio ad usum navigantium*. Other works are *Atlas sive cosmographicae meditationes*, 1595, and an ed. of Ptolemy's *Geography*.

Mercator, Nicholas (whose real name was **Nicholas Kauffmann**) (1620–87), Dan. mathematician, *b.* Holstein. He discovered an arithmetical means of determining the area of spaces between the hyperbola and its asymptote, and availed himself of this discovery to draw up logarithmic tables. His treatise, *Logarithmotechnia*, was pub. in 1668.

Mercator's Projection, *see* MAPS.

Merced, riv. of California, U.S.A., a trib. of the San Joaquin, having a length of 150 m. It traverses the Yosemite valley, has 2 falls, 600 ft and 350 ft respectively, and flows through Exchequer Reservoir, which is impounded by Exchequer Dam for power and irrigation.

Mercedes, cap. and health resort of the agric. and stock-raising prov. of Soriano, Uruguay, on the Rio Negro, 20 m. E. of Fray Bentos (q.v.). Pop. 40,000.

Mercenaries (Lat. *mercenarius*, from *merces*, gain) are soldiers who offer their services for money to the army of any country which is willing to employ them. Greece found it necessary to use M. (*peltasts*) in the 5th cent. BC, though for a long time the citizen hoplites remained the flower of the army. The famous Ten Thousand was composed of M., whom captains of reputation had collected at the bidding of the younger Cyrus. In Norman times M. were employed by the king, and the bulk of a medieval army often consisted of professional soldiers who were paid by a scutage tax levied on the peasantry. In addition to the mercenary cavalry, Brabançon pikemen and It. crossbowmen were employed as M. The Swiss, by such victories as those of Granson, Morat, Nancy, etc., showed themselves the finest soldiers in Europe, and devoted themselves for a long time to professional soldiering, particularly in the employ of France. The *Landsknechts*, who fought generally in imperial armies, were a fine type of mercenary, and contributed more to the modern army in customs, etc., than even the Swiss. Throughout the 18th cent. Hessian regiments were employed for temporary purposes by the Brit. Gov., and Germans, Swiss and Italians were enrolled during the Crimean War. The employment of mercenary soldiers led to such things as the 'right of sack', etc., and also to such developments as the *condottieri* (q.v.). True

M.s, in the 'free lance' sense, no longer exist. Their nearest equivalents in modern times have been the Fr. Foreign Legion, the Gurkhas (from Nepal) in the Indian and Brit. Armies and the small bands of 'white M.s' who operated in the Congo in 1963–4. *See* ARMY; FOREIGN LEGION.

Mercer, John (1791–1866), industrialist and 'father' of textile chem. *B*. Blackburn, Lancs, he began work at the age of 9 as a bobbin winder at the Oakenshaw print works. With the most meagre education M. invented a new method of textile printing and reorganised the Oakenshaw works. In 1844 he investigated the action of caustic soda on cotton, and his discoveries were the foundation of Lowe's invention of mercerised cotton. This discovery that cellulose is soluble in a solution of copper oxide in ammonia later made possible the Bemberg process of manufacturing rayon. In 1850 M. was elected to a fellowship of the Royal Society.

Mercerised Cotton, fabric resembling silk in appearance, obtained from ordinary cotton by the action of strong caustic alkalis. The process of mercerisation was patented by John Mercer (q.v.) in 1850. Hanks of cotton yarn are stretched between revolving rollers and passed through vats of caustic soda maintained at constant temp. and density, and warm and cold water, and afterwards dried. The cellulose fibres of the cotton thereby become semi-translucent, tensile and untwist to a cylindrical form. Cellulose hydrate probably results from the action of water on a cellulose-caustic soda compound first produced. *See* RAYON.

Mercerised Lisle, yarn processed exactly as lisle (q.v.), except that the cotton is chemically treated. While under tension in a solution of caustic soda, the fibres are stretched, and, swelling out, they regain their original tubular shape, this enabling the light to be reflected more readily, resulting in an appearance of lustre. This process is called mercerising after its inventor, John Mercer (q.v.). M. L. is now largely used for reinforcing the heels and toes of stockings so as to give extra strength at these points of wear; formerly stockings themselves were manuf. on a large scale from M. L.

Mercers' Company, first of the 12 great livery companies of the city of London. Mercers were originally dealers in small wares; later they traded in silks, velvets and other rich fabrics. In the Middle Ages homelier cloths tended to be left to the drapers. A London M. Gild existed in 1172; the M. C. was first chartered in 1393. The hall (destroyed by enemy action in 1941, reopened in May 1958) in Ironmonger Lane, off Cheapside, and the adjacent chapel are on the site of a hospital commemorating the bp. of Thomas Becket. The company governs St Paul's School, Hammersmith, and St Paul's Girls' School.

Merchandise Marks. At the present time (April 1966) the law relating to marks on merchandise is contained in the Merchandise Marks Acts, 1887 and 1953, and covers marks on goods whether imported into the U.K. or sold, or offered for sale, in the U.K. At the time of the dissolution of Parliament on 10 Mar. 1966 the Protection of Consumers (Trade Descriptions) Bill was about to start its Committee stage in the House of Lords. It was expected that the same, or a similar, Bill would be submitted to that House during the new Parliament.

The purpose of the Merchandise Marks Acts is to enable criminal proceedings to be taken against manufacturers and traders who forge trade marks (q.v.) or apply false, or misleading, *trade descriptions* to goods, or falsely apply to their goods marks that are the same as or similar to genuine trade marks (Section 2, 1887 Act).

Section 3 of the 1887 Act and Section 1 of the Merchandise Marks Act, 1953, taken together, define *trade description* as any description, statement or other indication, direct or indirect, (*a*) as to the number, quantity, measure, gauge or weight of any goods, or (*aa*) as to the standard of quality of any goods, according to a classification commonly used or recognised in the trade, or (*ab*) as to the fitness for purpose, strength, performance or behaviour of any goods or (*b*) as to the place or country in which any goods were made or produced, or (*c*) as to the mode of manufacturing or producing any goods, or (*d*) as to the material of which any goods are composed, or (*e*) as to any goods being the subject of an existing patent, privilege or copyright.

The definition of *false trade description* in Section 3 of the 1887 Act (the words in italics are amendments made by the 1953 Act) is as follows: 'The expression "false trade description" means a trade description which is false, *or misleading*, in a material respect as regards the goods to which it is applied, and includes every alteration of a trade description, whether by way of addition, effacement, or otherwise, where that alteration makes the description false, *or misleading*, in a material respect, and the fact that a trade description is a trade mark, or part of a trade mark, shall not prevent such trade description being a false trade description within the meaning of this Act'. Section 16 of the 1887 Act prohibits the importation into the U.K. of any goods to which a forged or false trade mark or a false trade description has been applied. It also prohibits the importation of goods of foreign manufacture that bear or purport to bear, the name or trade mark of any manufacturer, dealer or trader in the U.K. *unless* the goods bear an indication of origin. Section 1 of the Merchandise Marks Act 1926 extends the provisions of Section 16 of the 1887 Act to goods sold or exposed for sale in the U.K., though the Board of Trade has power to exempt goods from the operation of this particular provision.

In 1959 the Committee on Consumer Protection was appointed by the then Gov. 'to review the working of the existing legislation relating to M. M. and certification trade marks and to consider and report what changes, if any, in the law and what other measures, if any, are desirable for the further protection of the consuming public'. That Committee under the chairmanship of J. T. Molony, Q.C., pub. its final report in July 1962 and the Protection of Consumers (Trade Descriptions) Bill, referred to above, gives effect to a number of recommendations made in the Committee's Report (Cmnd 1781). The Bill is also designed to replace, consolidate and *extend* the existing legislation relating to M. M. *See* F. Moulton, *The Law of Merchandise Marks*, 1954; copies of the Bill are obtainable from H.M.S.O. Any further inquiries may be directed to the Institute of Trade Mark Agents, 69 Cannon Street, London, E.C.4.

Merchant Adventurers' Company was founded in 1296 by the Duke of Brabant. In England it did not begin its activities until the reign of Edward III, and it was not incorporated till 1553. Sebastian Cabot (1476–1557) was governor, and it was under his auspices that Chancellor reached Moscow via the White Sea and thus opened up a trade route between England and Russia. In 1564 a monopoly of trade with Germany and the Netherlands was acquired, and under James I the company's yearly commerce with the Dutch and Germans amounted to £1,000,000. The M. A. became known as the Hamburg Co. when Hamburg became their chief port of traffic (1578). The company was dissolved in 1808. *See* W. E. Lengelbach, *The Merchant Adventurers of England, their Laws and Ordinances*, 1902, and G. Unwin, *The Gilds and Companies of London*, 1908.

Merchant Banks, see ACCEPTING HOUSES.

Merchant Navy, see MERCANTILE MARINE.

Merchant Shipping Act. The M. S. A., 1854, which consolidated earlier enactments, led to the Act of 1894 which remains the principal Act, to which additions and amendments have been made from time to time.

The Act is mainly concerned with matters of safety, registry, certification of ship's officers, limitation of liability, wreck and salvage procedure, pilotage, protection of seamen, etc., and affects Brit.-owned vessels. A ship is not deemed to be Brit.-owned unless wholly owned by Brit. subjects, or by companies estab. under and subject to Brit. law having their prin. place of business within the Brit. Commonwealth. All owners of Brit. ships are required to have their vessels registered, and without such registration are not entitled to the privileges available under Brit. law. *See* MERCANTILE MARINE.

Merchant Taylors' Company, one of the 12 great livery companies of the City of London. Originating as a religious fraternity, the guild had developed into a powerful association of citizens, whose functions included the exclusive control of the tailoring craft, by 1327, when Edward III granted them their first royal charter as the Gild of Taylors and Linen Armourers (the latter made the padded suits worn under armour). In 1503 their extended influence was recognised when by the charter of Henry VII they were reconstituted under their present style of the Gild of Merchant Taylors of the Fraternity of St John the Baptist in the City of London.

Today the company, whose connection with the tailoring trade virtually ceased in the 17th cent., continue to exercise from M. T. Hall, which they have occupied since 1347, their traditional functions of charity and education, a notable product of which is M. T. School (q.v.), founded in 1561. Formerly the M. T. and the Skinners were bitter rivals for precedence, but since 1484, observing the wise edict of Mayor Billesden, they have ranked sixth and seventh in alternate years and have regularly entertained each other in their Halls.

Merchant Taylors' School: 1. Public day school for boys, located since 1933 at Sandy Lodge, Northwood, Middx. Founded in 1561 in the City of London by the Merchant Taylors' Company (q.v.), which is still the governing body. There are about 600 pupils, including 60 boarders. Famous old pupils include Edmund Spenser; Lancelot Andrewes, Bishop of Winchester; J. Walter, founder of *The Times*; Robert Clive; Gilbert Murray; and Sir James Jeans. *See* F. W. M. Draper, *Four Centuries of Merchant Taylors' School*, 1962.

2. Public school for boys at Great Crosby, Liverpool, founded in 1620 by John Harrison, citizen and Merchant Taylor of London. It was controlled by the M. T. Co. until 1910. The school, which receives a direct grant from the Ministry of Education, now has a governing body including among others representatives of the univs., the Old Boys' Association and local councils. There are some 700 pupils.

Merchants, Statutes of, *see* ACTON BURNELL.

Mercia, central kingdom of A.-S. England. The name refers to the march or borderland beyond which dwelt the hostile Welshmen. In the 7th cent. it extended from the Humber to the Thames, with the exception of E. Anglia. There were independent sovereigns of M. at least from 615 to 874, when the Danes overran the E. portion. The greatest kings were Penda (q.v.) and Offa (q.v.). *See* Sir F. M. Stenton, *Anglo-Saxon England*, 1943.

Mercier, Désiré Joseph (1851–1926), Belgian cardinal, *b.* Braine-l'Alleud, Brabant. Educ. at Malines, college of St Rombaud, Petit Séminaire and Grand Séminaire, he was ordained priest in 1874, when at Louvain Univ. In 1877 he was recalled to teach at Malines, and in 1882 attached to the faculty of theology at Louvain. After visiting Leo XIII at Rome he was placed at the head of an institute of Thomistic philosophy, endowed by that pope. He wrote some textbooks in this connection and became a leader of the modern Thomistic revival. In Feb. 1906 he succeeded Cardinal Goossens as Archbishop of Malines and Primate of Belgium. Made cardinal (1907), during the Ger. occupation of Belgium during the First World War he urged Belgians to be loyal only to the Belgian Gov., and provoked the wrath of the Ger. authorities, who ineffectually tried to prevent his visiting Rome, Jan. 1916. In the autumn of 1919 he made a tour of the U.S.A. and Canada. Later he pub. an *Appeal to all Christian People* which led to the 'Malines conversations' with representatives of the Anglican Church, 1923–4. *See* lives by A. Lavellie, 1926; C. Verwoort, 1928; J. A. Gade, 1934.

Mercier, Louis-Sébastien (1740–1814), Fr. writer, *b.* Paris. He wrote dramas (*Le Déserteur*, 1770, *La Brouette du vinaigrier*, 1775, *Le Campagnard*, 1779, *Le Vieillard et ses trois filles*, 1792, etc.), critical works (*Du théâtre, ou Nouvel essai sur l'art dramatique*, 1773, *De la littérature et des littérateurs*, 1778), a *Néologie ou vocabulaire des mots nouveaux*, 1801, and books on Paris, *Tableau de Paris*, 1781, and *Le Nouveau Paris*, 6 vols., 1798.

'**Mercure de France**': 1. Fr. monthly literary jour. founded in 1890 under the direction of Alfred Valette. Under the influence of R. de Gourmont it became the rallying point of the Symbolists and the centre of the new verse. It survived until June 1940, appeared again in Dec. 1946, and since then has devoted much space to contributions from young writers.

2. Fr. publishing house of Paris, noted for its eds. of Nietzsche (trans. by H. Albert) and the works of André Gide, Paul Claudel, Georges Duhamel and G. Apollinaire; also the above review.

Mercuric Chloride, see CORROSIVE SUBLIMATE.

Mercurius (Eng. **Mercury**), Rom. god of commerce and gain, his name coming from Lat. *merx*, merchandise. A temple near the Circus Maximus was dedicated to him. His festival was celebrated on 25 May by the *mercuriales*, members of a college regulating the corn trade. M. was often identified with the Gk Hermes (q.v.), to whom, however, he bore only the slightest resemblance. A fine 21-in. bronze M., 2nd cent. A.D., has been recovered at Colchester from an exceptionally large Rom. temple (no remains now visible) some 2 m. SW. of the tn.

Mercury, smallest of the planets, and closest to the sun. M.'s diameter is about 3000 m., or three-eighths of the earth's; its mass is 0·055 of the earth's, corresponding to a similar mean density. M. is only 40 per cent larger than the moon, but is 4 times as massive. It revolves round the sun in 87·97 days at a mean distance of 36,000,000 m. The orbit is eccentric and the temp. on the sunlit side varies between 550° F. and 800° F., so that M. can retain no significant atmosphere. Like Venus, M. can appear as a 'morning star' or as an 'evening star'; its angular distance from the sun never exceeds 28°, so that it is difficult to observe, although at times brighter than Arcturus. The disk varies from 5 to 13 sec. of arc. Indistinct markings are seen and most observers have hitherto agreed that the planet rotates in 88 days, thus constantly turning the same face to the sun, but radar observations have suggested faster rotation. M. crosses the sun's disk at intervals, the next occurrences being in 1970 and 1973. *See* W. Sandner, *The Planet Mercury*, 1963.

Mercury, Rom. god, *see* MERCURIUS.

Mercury, or **Quicksilver**. Symbol Hg; atomic number 80; atomic weight 200·61. A metal, a liquid at ordinary temps. It occurs to a small extent in an uncombined state as small globules, but its chief ore is *cinnabar*, HgS, mercuric sulphide. The metal is obtained from the ore by roasting it, when the sulphur is oxidised to sulphur dioxide, and the Hg is set free from combination. During this reaction the Hg becomes vaporised. The vapour is passed through a series of cooling chambers where it is condensed. The mines occur in a very few places; chief amongst them may be mentioned Almaden, Istria and California. The metal possesses some remarkable properties, in that at ordinary temps. it is a bright silvery liquid. At − 38·9° C. it assumes a solid form, which is crystalline, ductile, malleable and very soft. It boils at 357° C., giving off a colourless vapour. Owing to this large range of temp. between the limits of which it assumes the liquid state Hg is commonly used in thermometers, but its usefulness is restricted in the lower direction, since it freezes so easily. At 0° C. its density is 13·595 gm. per c.c., and its coefficient of expansion is 0·000182 between 0° C. and 100° C. It is a good conductor of heat and electricity. It dissolves certain metals to form *amalgams*. These amalgams are used for sev. practical purposes; zinc amalgam is used to cover the zinc plates of batteries owing to the fact that it is very slowly acted upon by dilute sulphuric acid; tin amalgam is used for the construction of mirrors; and gold and other amalgam are used by dentists for filling teeth. These amalgams can also be made by the electrolysis of salt solutions, using an Hg cathode, and by attacking a solution of a salt with sodium amalgam. The so-called ammonium amalgam (q.v.) is of special interest. Hg is employed very largely in scientific work for the construction of thermometers, barometers, vacuum pumps and on the large scale for the extraction of gold and silver (q.v.). For scientific work it must be clean and must not foul the surface of the containing vessel. Dirty Hg can be cleaned by filtering through muslin (or filter paper with a small hole punctured at the apex) to remove suspended dirt and then allowed to fall slowly down a burette filled with dilute nitric acid to remove other impurities. Hg forms 2 independent series of salts—the mercurous and mercuric. Mercuric oxide, a reddish crystalline powder, is obtained by heating Hg in contact with the air. This oxide is decomposed at a higher temp. into its constituent elements. In this connection the work of Priestley and Lavoisier should be recalled (*see* AIR and OXYGEN).

The mercuric salts are obtained from this oxide by dissolving it in the various acids. Mercuric chloride (corrosive sublimate) is prepared by heating together a mixture of mercuric sulphate and common salt. It is a violent poison, the best antidote being the white of an egg. It is largely used as an antiseptic. Mercuric iodide is prepared from a soluble mercuric salt and a soluble iodide. It is red and insoluble, but soluble in potassium iodide to form potassium mercuri-iodide. An alkaline (caustic soda) solution of the latter gives Nessler's solution, which is used for detecting certain nitrogenous compounds, e.g. ammonia and alkaloids. Mercuric sulphide is obtained by rubbing vigorously together Hg and sulphur. When sublimed it assumes a red crystalline form known commercially as the pigment *vermilion*. *Calomel*, or mercurous chloride, is the most important of the mercurous salts. It is generally prepared by heating a mixture of mercuric chloride and Hg. The mercurous chloride sublimes as a white fibrous cake. It is insoluble in water and is tasteless. Hg is used largely in medicine, in the form of chlorides or iodides. Hg compounds, especially if they are soluble, are very poisonous, and even as medicinal preparations should not be persisted in for long periods.

Mercuric fulminate is made by adding a solution of mercuric oxide in nitric acid to 90 per cent alcohol, warmed to about 54° C. After a brisk action white crystals of the fulminate appear, and after washing free from any acid they are spread out and vacuum dried. A very large number of organic derivatives of Hg, some with useful physiological properties, are known. Mercuric fulminate is used as a detonator (*see* EXPLOSIVES) since it is very susceptible to shock, under the influence of which it decomposes with explosive violence.

Mercury's Wand, *see* DIVINING ROD.

Méré, Paul Louis Courier de, *see* COURIER.

Mere, Maori weapon made of stone, flat and spatulate, and with a short handle.

Meredith, George (1828–1909), novelist and poet, *b*. Portsmouth, educ. there and at Neuwied in Germany. Owing to the neglect of a trustee, what means he had inherited were lost, and he was in his early days very poor. Articled to a lawyer in London, he had no taste for law, which he soon exchanged for journalism, and at 21 he was writing poetry for magazines, his first printed work, a poem on the Battle of Chillianwallah, appearing in *Chambers' Journal*. Two years later he pub. *Poems*, 1851, containing 'Love in the Valley'. Meantime he had been editing a small provincial newspaper, and in 1866 was war correspondent in Italy for the *Morning Post*; he also acted for many years as literary adviser to a publisher. By this time, however, he had produced sev. of his novels, and had become acquainted with Swinburne, the Pre-Raphaelites and other eminent writers. *The Shaving of Shagpat* had appeared in 1856, *Farina*, 1857, *The Ordeal of Richard Feverel*, 1859, *Evan Harrington*, 1861, *Emilia in England* (subsequently renamed *Sandra Belloni*), 1864, *Vittoria*, 1866, and *Rhoda Fleming*, 1865. In poetry he had produced *Modern Love and Poems of the English Roadside*, 1862, generally regarded as his best poetical work. These were followed by the *Adventures of Harry Richmond*, 1871, *Beauchamp's Career*, 1875, *The Egoist*, 1879, which marks the beginning in a change of style characterised by an even greater fastidiousness in the choice of words, phrases and condensation of thought than its predecessors, *The Tragic Comedians*, 1880, and *Diana of the Crossways*, the first of the author's novels to attain anything approaching general popularity. The same period yielded in poetry, *Poems and Lyrics of the*

Joy of Earth, 1883, *Ballads and Poems of Tragic Life*, 1887, and *A Reading of Earth*, 1888. His later novels, *One of our Conquerors*, 1891, *Lord Ormont and his Aminta*, 1894, and *The Amazing Marriage*, 1895, exhibit the tortuous and difficult style which denied general popularity to all his works, and they did little to add to his reputation. In 1897 he pub. his lecture on *The Idea of Comedy and the Uses of Comic Spirit*. In 1905 he received the Order of Merit. He was twice married, his first wife, with whom he was not happy, *d*. in 1860. She was a daughter of Thomas Love Peacock (q.v.). His second wife was Marie Vulliamy, who *d*. 1885.

Though the writings of M. never were and probably never will be generally popular, his genius was, from the very first, recognised by the best judges. Few writers have striven to charge sentences and even words so heavily with meaning, or to attain so great a degree of condensation, with the result that links in the chain of thought are often omitted and left for the careful reader to supply; hence Wilde's description of him as 'a prose Browning'. There is also a tendency to adopt unusual words and forms of expression where plainness and simplicity would have served as well, and these features taken together give reason for the charges of obscurity and affectation so often made. Moreover, the discussion of motive and feeling is often out of proportion to the narrative of events. But to compensate for these defects he offers humour, often, indeed, whimsical, but keen and sparkling, close observation of and exquisite feeling for nature, a marvellous power of word-painting, the most delicate and penetrating analysis of character and an invincible optimism.

See C. B. Petter, *Meredith and his German Critics*, 1939; L. Stevenson, *The Ordeal of George Meredith*, 1954; N. Kelvin, *A Troubled Eden: Nature and Society in the Works of George Meredith*, 1961.

Meredith, Owen, *see* LYTTON, EDWARD ROBERT BULWER.

Merendera, family Lilaceae, a Mediterranean genus of hardy bulbous plants, closely related to *Colchicum*, of which *M. bulbocodium* and *M. filifolia* are grown in gardens for their autumn flowers.

Meres, Francis (1565–1647), clergyman and critic, *b*. Lincs. Educ. at Cambridge and Oxford, he became rector of Wing in Rutland. In 1598 he pub. *Palladis Tamia, Wit's Treasury*, a review of Eng. writers from Chaucer to his own day, containing valuable references to Shakespeare's early works.

Merezhkovsky, Dmitry Sergeyevich (1865–1941), Russian writer and literary critic, a leader of the older Symbolists, played an important part in the religious revival among Russian intellectuals at the beginning of the cent. His first poems (1888) and his essay *On the Causes of the Decline of Contemporary Russian Literature*, 1892–3, heralded the advent of Symbolism in Russia and the rejection of the traditional sociological school of literary criticism. Among his works are the trilogy *Christ and Antichrist*, 1893–1902, his essay *Tolstoy and Dostoyevsky*, 1901, and his anti-Collectivist treatise *The Coming Hamite*, 1906. During 1906–12 and after the October Revolution he lived in emigration in France. *See December the Fourteenth*, trans. N. Duddington, 1923.

Merganser (*Mergus*), genus of sea ducks characterised by a very long slender beak. *M. merganser*, sometimes called the goosander or jackdaw, is a handsome Brit. bird. The male's plumage is variegated with black, greenish-black, pink and white. The red-breasted M. (*M. serrator*) breeds in the N. of Britain; the drake has a crested glossy green head, white neck, red breast and black upper surface with white margins. *M. australis* is a rare species found only in the Auckland Is.

Mergenthaler, Ottmar (1854–99), inventor of the principle of mechanical type-setting. He was *b.* at Hachtel in W. Germany, and emigrated to the U.S.A. in 1872, as a watchmaker. He became the first person to evolve the independently circulating matrix. This invention revolutionised newspaper printing. *See also* TYPE-CASTING AND TYPE-SETTING MACHINES.

Mergui, dist and seaport of Lower Burma. Forests of teak, etc., cover almost all the 9789 sq. m. of the dist which lies in the Tenasserim div. It has rich tin and wolfram mines and also produces rubber. The tn is a pearling station, and exports rice, timber, rattans, dried fish, etc. Pop.: (dist) 181,000; (tn) 34,000.

Mergui Archipelago, group of hilly is. off the Burma coast in the Bay of Bengal. Most of the is. have few inhab., who are mainly Selungs. The chief products are edible birds' nests and *bêches-de-mer*. M. is. itself has important pearl-beds near by.

Merian, Matthew (1593–1650), Swiss engraver, *b.* Basel; he settled in Frankfurt where he carried on his father-in-law's (J. T. de Bry) book and print business. He is noted mainly for engraved views of towns and as master of Wenceslaus Hollar (q.v.).

Mérida: 1. (Rom. **Augusta Emerita**) Sp. tn in the prov. of Badajoz, on the Guadiana. Founded by the Romans in 25 BC, it soon became one of the finest cities in the Empire and cap. of Lusitania (q.v.). The river was spanned during the reign of Trajan (AD 98–117) by a granite bridge of 81 arches, 2575 ft in length. Other Rom. remains include part of the city wall, a triumphal arch (Trajan), an aqueduct and a theatre. There are also Moorish remains, including an Alcázar and a 13th cent. church. Pop. 34,300.

2. Cap. of M. state, Venezuela, 336 m. SW. by W. of Caracas. It is the religious and academic centre of the region and the seat of an archbishop. M. has the univ. of Los Andes with nearly 2000 students. It is the centre of the main coffee growing area of Venezuela. Cottons, woollens and candied fruits are manuf. Pop. of state, 270,668; of tn, 40,000.

3. Cap. of Yucatán, Mexico, 23 m. S. of its port, Progreso, on the Gulf of Mexico. The fifth city in size of Mexico, it is situated in flat agric. country, almost entirely devoted to henequén (sisal fibre). Founded by the Spaniards in 1542 on the site of an anct Mayan city, it has a beautiful cathedral, large hospital, massive buildings and well-paved streets. Its dominant industry is based on sisal, and its chief exports are sisal, chicle, hides and agric. produce. There are important Maya ruins nearby. The tn contains the Univ. of Yucatán, an important archaeological and historical museum and a number of other cultural institutes. Pop. 170,513 (1960).

Meriden, tn 17 m. N. of New Haven, Connecticut, U.S.A. It manufs. plated ware and cutlery, tools, ball-bearings, machinery, automobile parts and electrical equipment, china, glassware and wood, rubber and plastic products. Pop. 54,700.

Meridian, co. seat of Lauderdale co., Mississippi, U.S.A., 89 m. from Jackson. It is an important cotton market and has cotton ginning and lumber-mills. Pop. 49,370.

Meridian (from Lat. *meridies*, noon), both a terrestrial and a celestial great circle. The terrestrial M. of any given place is the line running through that place and through both the N. and S. poles. Each terrestrial M. has a corresponding celestial M., which passes through the N. and S. celestial poles, and also through the zenith and nadir of any place on that terrestrial M. When the sun passes the M. of Greenwich, it is not only apparent noon at Greenwich, but also at all places situated on the same half of that M. The same applies to other M.s.

Meridian, Magnetic. When a magnet is mounted on a pivot so that it is free to rotate in a horizontal plane it comes to rest in a definite direction at a given locality. The vertical plane passing through the axis of the magnet, i.e. the line joining its 2 poles, is called the M. M. at that place. *See* COMPASS, MAGNETIC; ISOCLINIC AND ISOGONIC; MAGNETISM, *Terrestrial magnetism*.

Meridian Circle, *see* TRANSIT INSTRUMENT.

Mérignac, Fr. tn in the dept of Gironde, a suburb of Bordeaux. It has an aerodrome and a trade in fine wines. Pop. 40,000.

Mérimée, Prosper (1803–70), Fr. man of letters, *b.* Paris, the son of an artist. He became inspector-general of historical monuments. He began his literary career with some dramatic pieces professing to be from the Spanish of an imaginary Clara Gazul (*Théâtre de Clara Gazul*, 1825), and followed this with a collection of pretended Illyrian folk-songs, signed with an anagram of the previous name, 'La Guzla'. Up to that time his work was romantic in subject and form, but subsequently turned to the writing of the stories on which his enduring fame depends. Though still romantic in their predilection for strange and less civilised countries and the interest revealed in foreign literature (he travelled much in Spain and was fond of writing on Sp. themes), they are essentially realistic in their local background and atmosphere and in the truth of their historic archaeological and artistic descriptions.

His love of dwelling on the tragic, grim and eerie elements in life is emphasised in his powerful short stories, *La Vénus d'Ille* and *Lokis*, and in his vivid romance, *La Jacquerie*; and his fund of Rabelaisian humour is conspicuous in his letters to Panizzi. He recalled the Florentine scholars of the Renaissance in the diversity of his interests, a diversity which enabled him to write so valuable an archaeological essay as *Description des peintures de Saint-Savin*, the *Chronique du règne de Charles IX*, 1829 (a historical novel), and the *Histoire de Don Pèdre I*, 1848, a literary *supercherie* like *La Guzla*, 1827, and *nouvelles* like the Corsican tale *Colomba*, 1840. His chief writings, besides those already mentioned, are *Mateo Falcone*, 1829, *L'Enlèvement de la redoubte*, 1829, and *Carmen*, 1846, which inspired the libretto of Bizet's opera. He also wrote other historical works and books on his travels in various parts of France. *See* S. Lyon, *The Life and Times of Prosper Mérimée*, 1948.

Merioneth, Earl of, *see* PHILIP, PRINCE OF THE REALM, DUKE OF EDINBURGH.

Merioneth, maritime co. of N. Wales, bounded on the W. by Cardigan Bay (q.v.). Two-thirds of the co. forms part of the Snowdonia (q.v.) National Park. M. is mountainous, the chief peaks being Arran Mawddwy (2972 ft) and Cader Idris (2927 ft) (q.v.). There are sev. beautiful valleys, the Dovey (Dyfi) (q.v.), Mawddach and Maentwrog being among the loveliest. The R. Dee (Dyfrdwy) drains Bala Lake (5 m.), the largest in Wales, and flows towards Corwen, receiving sev. tribs. on the way; there are over 50 lakes among the mts and sev. waterfalls. Slate is quarried at Ffestiniog and near Dolgellau (qq.v.), the co. tn; gold is found, while lead, copper and manganese have been worked. Milk production is increasingly carried on, and the co. is noted for its hardy mt sheep, rams and Welsh black cattle. Barmouth (q.v.), Dolgellau and Harlech (q.v.) and other places in the co. are much visited by tourists. Area 422,372 ac.; pop. 39,007.

Meristem, generating tissue, that part of a plant where growth is active. It consists of cells of nearly uniform size capable of dividing to form new cells. These enlarge and after certain modifications form the permanent tissue. Primary M.s are at the apex of each stem and root; secondary M.s, or cambia (q.v.), are responsible for growth in girth and for the formation of corky layers.

Merit, Order of, Brit. order instituted in 1902, limited in number to 24 men and women of eminent distinction. It confers no precedence or knighthood. Membership is either military or civil, the badge of the former having crossed swords and the latter oak-leaves. Membership is designated by the suffix O.M., which follows the first class of the Order of the Bath precedes the letters designating membership of the inferior classes of the Bath and all classes of the remaining Orders of Knighthood. Ribbon, blue and crimson. An Indian O. of M. was instituted in 1837 for Indian officers and men.

Meritorious Service Medal, instituted in 1845 for the Brit. Army and extended to the Royal Marines in 1849 and to the R.N. in 1919. In the army it was originally granted to specially selected warrant officers and sergeants, but during the First World War all warrant officers, N.C.O.s and men were eligible as a reward for meritorious conduct in the performance of military duty. It is now restricted to warrant officers and N.C.O.s of the army above the rank of corporal. The grant carries with it an annuity not exceeding £20, save in the case of the special First World War awards mentioned above. The ribbon is crimson with white edges and centre. The effigy of the reigning sovereign is on the obverse of the medal and 'For Meritorious Service' on the reverse.

Merleau-Ponty, Maurice (1908–61), French philosopher, *b.* Rochefort-sur-Mer. He was prof. of psychology and paedagogy at the Sorbonne, 1949–52, and prof. of philosophy at the Collège de France, 1952–61. His works include *La Structure du Comportement*, 1945, *La Phénoménologie de la perception*, 1945, *Éloge de la philosophie*, 1953, *Les Aventures de la dialectique*, the posthumous *Le Visible et l'invisible*, 1964, and collected volumes of articles, *Sens et non-sens, Humanisme et Terreur* and *Signes*. He was for a time associated with Sartre and Simone de Beauvoir (qq.v.) with whom he founded in 1945 the periodical *Les Temps modernes*. *See* A. Robinet, *Merleau-Ponty*, 1963.

Merlin, in the Arthurian legend, wizard who worked many wonders at King Arthur's court. He sprang from the intercourse of a Welsh maiden with a demon, but was saved from evil by baptism, although, throughout life, he retained his father's gift, the power of magic and divination. It was he who had the care of the infant Arthur and later disclosed to him his royal parentage.

Merlin, or *Falco aesalon*, small Brit. falcon found breeding in the N. of England and Scotland; also in N. Europe, Asia and N. America. It is essentially a falcon of the rocks and moors. On the moors the nest is generally built on a slope among the heather, and in other localities on the ledge of a rock, and in it 3 to 5 bluish-white eggs, blotched with brown markings, are laid. Adult males are blue-grey on the head, back and wing coverts; the under parts are rufous; the tail is bluish-grey with dark bands and white tips. The young resemble the female, which is brown. It is an easy bird to tame and used to be trained to fly at larks in the autumn, while a female M. will take snipe and starlings.

Merlino Coccajo, *see* FOLENGO, TEOFILO.

Merlon, one of the solid or tooth-like portions of a battlement (q.v.), between the embrasures.

Mermaid Tavern. This tavern, mentioned in *Expenses of Sir J. Howard*, 1464, stood in Cheapside, with side entrances in Friday St and Bread St, and was destroyed by the Great Fire of London. Raleigh is the reputed founder of the famous Mermaid Club (*c.* 1603. *See* Gifford's ed. of Ben Jonson). Jonson, Beaumont, Fletcher, Donne, Shakespeare, Carew, Cotton and Selden were possibly members of this club, which was noted for its Canary wine and the sparkling wit of its frequenters. It is sometimes called the Friday St or Bread St Club.

Mermaid Theatre, London, *see* MILES, BERNARD.

Mermaids and Mermen (O.E. *mere*, lake; *maegd*, maid), in folklore a class of semi-human beings, whose true home is in riv. or sea. The origin of the legend may be the manatee (q.v.). M. were capable of living on land and of entering into social relationships with ordinary mortals, and the typical mermaid is represented as a woman of great beauty down to the waist, the figure ending in a fish's tail and body with scales and fins. The connection of these beings with mortals generally brought disaster in its train. The Phoenician Dagon and the Chaldaeo-Babylonian Oannes or Hea (fish-gods) were usually represented as half fish, half human. *See* J. L. Grimm, *Deutsche Mythologie*, 1835; S. Baring-Gould, *Curious Myths of the Middle Ages*, 1866–8; M. Yearsley, *The Folklore of Fairy Tales*, 1924; Jean Lang, *Book of Myths*, 1934.

Mermaid's Purse, purse-shaped egg case of the skates and dog-fish.

Merodach-Baladan, or **Marduk-apaliddina II** (*c*. 722–702 BC), King of Babylon. Under this powerful Chaldean prince the Babylonians, aided by the Elamite court, reasserted their independence. There was a long struggle with Sargon II, King of Assyria, who finally captured and destroyed Babylon (710). On Sargon's assassination, his successor, Sennacherib, drove M. from the Babylonian throne (705). *See* 2 Kings xx. 6.

Meroë, Isle of, the area between the R. Atbara (anct Astaboras) and the Blue Nile in S. Nubia, now the N. Sudan, so named after M., the cap. of the kingdom of Cush from 6th cent. BC–4th cent. AD, and successor of Napata, near modern Merowé (q.v.). The ruins of M. (tn, temples, pyramids and cemetries) lie on the E. bank of the Nile near the vil. of Begrawiya, 3 m. N. of Kabushia, the railway station N. of Shendi. The tn and temples were partly excavated (and very incompletely pub.) by Garstang, 1909–14, and the pyramids by Reisner, 1920–3. M. was in existence as the S. sub-cap. of the kingdom of Cush when that kingdom ruled Egypt as its 25th dynasty, and became the cap. after Napata was sacked, *c*. 591 BC, by an expedition of which the spearhead was Gk and Carian mercenaries armed with iron weapons, sent by Psamtik II to forestall a possible attempt by Cush to recover control of Egypt. After that, M. also became a centre of iron-working, from which the knowledge of iron must have been diffused into central and W. Africa. Its thousand-year hist. is one of gradual degeneration, until its final destruction by its trade rival Axum, *c*. AD 350, but its influence, with the religion of the divine king inherited from Egypt and the working of iron, lived on in a number of small kingdoms stretching westward across Africa. There are ruins mostly dating from the 2nd or 3rd cent. AD scattered over the I. of M., of which the most

important are at Nagaa and Musawwarat. They include numerous reservoirs (*hafirs*) sometimes associated with small temples, which show how the kingdom endeavoured to cope with the desiccation which was then becoming increasingly severe, no doubt contributing to the downfall of the kingdom. *See* J. Garstang, A. H. Sayce and F. Ll. Griffith, *Meroë, 1909–10*, 1911; A. J. Arkell, *A History of the Sudan*, 1955. *See also* MEROWÉ.

Merom, Waters of, *see* HULEH.

Meropidae, *see* BEE-EATER.

Merovingians, or **Merwings,** name of the first dynasty of Frankish kings in Gaul, who ruled after the fall of the Rom. Empire. The name is taken from Merwig or Merovech, King of the Salian (W.) Franks, who united a few tribes under his rule (*c*. 448–57). His grandson, Clovis (481–511), extended the power of the dynasty, which flourished until 639 and finally gave place to the Carlovingians (751). *See* F. Lot, *La Fin du monde antique et le début du moyen âge*, 1927.

Merowé (anct **Napata**), cap. of the kingdom of Cush (or Ethiopia, q.v.), which ruled Egypt cr 725–660 BC, providing its 25th dynasty. It owes its name to an outcrop of quartz pebbles (Arabic *mirwi*) on the right bank, leading to its wrongful identification by Caillaud in 1821 as Meroë (q.v.). The temple, cemetery, etc. near the modern tn were excavated by F. Ll. Griffith and the pyramid fields of Kurru, Nuri and Barkal in the vicinity by G. Reisner (*see* D. Dunham, *Royal Cemeteries of Kush* (Boston), vols. i and ii, 1950, 1955). In M. is a temporary museum housing statues, a fine sarcophagus, stelae, etc. from these excavations, pending the construction of a national museum at Khartoum. M. was once the H.Q. of the old Dongola (q.v.) prov. and is now H.Q. of an administrative sub-dist. It lies near the railhead of Kareima, below the 4th cataract, whence riv. steamers run to Dongola just above the 3rd cataract. The tn (pop. 15,000) has decreased in size with its decline in administrative importance. The dist. is fertile, its agriculture depending entirely on irrigation by pump and waterwheel. It produces excellent citrus fruit and dates, as well as Amer. cotton and cereals.

Merriam, John Campbell (1869–1945), Amer. palaeontologist, *b*. Hopkinton, Iowa. He taught palaeontology at the univ. of California and was head of the Carnegie Institute at Washington, D.C. He wrote many vols. on prehistoric animals. His *Published Papers and Addresses* appeared in 1938.

Merrick, Leonard (1864–1939), author, *b*. Hampstead. Educ. at Brighton College, he became especially noteworthy for his short stories representative of Bohemian life in Paris. His books include *Cynthia*, 1897, *One Man's View*, 1897, *When Love flies out of the Window*, 1902, *Conrad in Quest of his Youth*, 1903, *The House of Lynch*, 1907, *A Chair on the Boulevard*, 1908, *The Man who Understood Women, and Other Stories*, 1908, *The Position of Peggy Harper*, 1911, *The Quaint Companions*, 1918, and *While Paris Laughed*, 1918. A collected ed.

of his works was pub. in 1918.

Merrill, Stuart (1863–1915), Fr. poet, *b.* near New York. His infancy was passed in Paris, but he returned to the U.S.A. to study law. While still in the U.S.A. he pub. *Pastels in Prose*, 1890, consisting of trans. from some 13 Fr. writers. Returning finally to France in 1890 he became well known as a master of the intricacies of Fr. symbolist poetry. In 1897 he pub. *Poèmes, 1887–1897*; followed by *Les Quatre Saisons*, 1900, *Une Voix dans la foule*, 1909, *Prose et vers*, 1925. *See* M. L. Henry, *S. Merrill, sa vie, son œuvre*, 1929.

Merrimac, *see* HAMPTON ROADS.

Merrimack, riv. of S. New Hampshire, U.S.A., rising in the White Mts, flowing S. and ENE. through N. of Massachusetts to the Atlantic. Its many falls and rapids supply water-power for manufacturing cities. It passes Concord, Manchester, Nashua, New Hampshire, then Lowell, Laurence and Haverhill, Massachusetts. Length 110 m.

Merriman, Henry Seton, pen-name of **Hugh Stowell Scott** (1862–1903), novelist, *b.* Newcastle upon Tyne. Educ. at Loretto and Wiesbaden, he was for some time an underwriter at Lloyd's, then adopted a literary career (1889), winning success with his Russian story *The Sowers*, 1896. Among his best-known works are *In Kedar's Tents*, 1897, *Roden's Corner*, 1898, *The Isle of Unrest*, 1899, *The Velvet Glove*, 1901, *The Vultures*, 1902, *Barlasch of the Guard*, 1903, and *The Last Hope*, 1904.

Merry Andrew, jester, buffoon or quack doctor's assistant at fairs. Thomas Hearne (1678–1735) derives the name from Andrew Borde (*b.* 1549), physician to Henry VIII, who combined immense learning with marked eccentricity. Andrew, however, is a common name in old plays for a manservant, as Abigail is for a waiting-woman.

Mersalyl, mercurial diuretic given by hypodermic injection, particularly in cases of dropsy due to cardiac failure. *See* DIURETICS.

Merse, or **March,** strictly a fertile dist of SE. Berwickshire, Scotland, all the land being under 500 ft. Formerly it denoted all the country between the Cheviots and Lammermuir Hills (qq.v.).

Mersea, West, urb. dist, comprising a well-wooded is. of Essex, England, between the Colne and Blackwater estuaries, protected by a sea-wall. It is some 5 m. long and 2 m. wide. A causeway connects it with the mainland. It is noted for oysters. Pop. 3140.

Merseburg, Ger. tn in the dist of Halle, on the Saxonian Saale, 9 m. S. of Halle. It was a favourite residence of Henry I and Otho I (qq.v.), and was the cap. of the duchy of Saxe-M. (1656–1738). It passed to Prussia in 1815. There is a cathedral (11th–16th cents.). Manufs. include machinery and paper, and there are lignite-mines in the dist. Pop. 47,200.

Mers-el-Kebir (Sp. *mazalquivir*, great port), fortified seaport of Algeria, NW. coast, 3 m. NW. of Oran, taken by the Spanish in 1505 and by the French in 1830. Pop. 4332.

Mersenne, Marin (1588–1648), Fr. philosopher, theologian and mathematician; studied at the college of La Flèche, where he met Descartes, whose views, as expounded in the *M ditationes*, he championed throughout his life. Entering the Minim order of friars in 1611 he taught philosophy at the convent at Nevers. His chief works are the *Quaestiones celeberrimae in Genesim*, 1623 (a commentary on ch. vi of Genesis and an attack on atheism); a philosophical and theological refutation of the deists, 1624; miscellaneous dissertations on theology, physics and mathematics, 1634, wherein M. discusses the possibility of flying, the velocity of light, etc.; *Les Méchaniques de Galilée*, 1634; *L'Harmonie universelle*, 1636.

Mersey, riv. of England, formed by the confluence of the Goyt and Tame at Stockport, the Goyt being joined by the R. Etherow at Marple. These rivs. rise in the Pennine range. The M. flows westwards between Cheshire and Lancashire passing Warrington, Widnes and Runcorn to Birkenhead and Liverpool, and out into the Liverpool Bay. Its length is about 70 m. and its estuary is some 16 m. long. At Eastham on the estuary is the entrance to the Manchester Ship Canal (q.v.). Its chief trib. is the R. Irwell which joins it by way of the Manchester Ship Canal. In spite of sandbanks the riv. is second only to the Thames in commercial importance. Beneath the riv. runs the M. Tunnel, for road traffic between Liverpool and Birkenhead, opened in 1934, total length 2⅝ m. and capable of taking 4 lines of traffic. The railway tunnel was opened in 1886. *See* J. E. Allison, *The Mersey Estuary*, 1949.

Mers-les-Bains, *see* TRÉPORT, LE.

Merthyr Tydfil, or **Tydvil,** co. and parl. bor. and mrkt tn of Glamorganshire, S. Wales, on the R. Taff, 24 m. NNW. of Cardiff. It was formerly the centre of the iron and steel industry in S. Wales, but now has a variety of factories whose products range from nylon stockings to toys and washing machines. The eccles. par. of Dowlais (q.v.) forms part of the bor. M. T. returns one member to the House of Commons. It was made a co. bor. in 1907. Pop. 59,008.

Merton, Walter de (*d.* 1277), prelate, in all probability *b.* Merton, Surrey. In 1261 he was made lord chancellor, and founded M. College, Oxford (1264), when he became Bishop of Rochester.

Merton, London Bor. of, created on 1 April 1965 as a result of the London Gov. Act of 1963. It comprises the former municipal bors. of Mitcham and Wimbledon and the urb. dist of Merton and Morden. Rateable value £10,835,000; pop. 189,900.

Merton College, Oxford, founded in 1264 by Walter de Merton (q.v.). The buildings are among the oldest and most interesting in Oxford; the choir of the chapel dates from 1294 and the small treasury (? 1290) is among the earlier parts of the college. The large chapel was once used as a par. church and contains some fine stained glass. The 14th cent. library is one of the most anct extant medieval libraries in

England. The old city wall partly encloses the college and the garden. There are some well-designed new buildings. The warden is its head and its scholars are known as 'postmasters'. Past members include Wycliffe, Bodley, Carew, Antony Wood, Richard Steele, Harvey, Hartley Coleridge, Sir Max Beerbohm and T. S. Eliot. There are some 200 undergraduate and 60 postgraduate students. *See* hists. of the college by B. W. Henderson and J. H. White; P. S. Allen and H. W. Garrod, *Merton Muniments*, 1928; J. R. L. Highfield, *The Early Rolls of Merton College*, 1964.

Méru, in Tanzania, lying 40 m. WSW. of Kilimanjaro. It has an altitude of 14,979 ft and a surface crater.

Meru, in Hindu mythology, a fabulous mt, the abode of Vishnu. It is the most sacred of all mythical mts, is supposed to stand at the centre of the world and to be 80,000 leagues high.

Merulius, family Polyporaceae, genus of fungi. *M. Lacrymans* is the destructive fungus which causes dry rot of timber. Its control and prevention call for special treatment.

Merv, *see* MARY.

Merwede, *see* MEUSE.

Merxem, *see* MERKSEM.

Méryon, Charles (1821–68), Fr. etcher, *b.* Paris. He produced the wonderful etchings of Paris (1850–4) that remain classic. They include the famous 'Le Pont du Change', 'Abside de Notre Dame', 'La Vieille Morgue' and 'Stryge'. *See* M. C. Salaman, *Charles Méryon*, 1927.

Mesa, flat-topped hill made up of roughly horizontal strata. The top of the hill is generally made up of a hard stratum which is resistant to erosion and thus protects the rocks below it. Table Mt, near Cape Tn, is a typical M.

Mesabi Range, low hills in Itasca and St Louis cos., Minnesota, U.S.A., about 80 m. long. One of the largest iron-producing dists of the world, it has an ann. output of over 45,000,000 tons, now largely taconite.

Mesdag, Hendrik Wilhelm (1831–1905), Dutch marine painter, *b.* Groningen. He was a banker till 1867, when he took up art and studied under Alma Tadema. Represented the expanse and movement of water successfully in such works as 'Fishing Boats at Scheveningen' and 'Morning on the Scheld'. His work can be studied at The Hague.

Mesembryanthemum, or **Fig Marigold,** genus of S. African succulent plants with thick fleshy leaves and brilliant flowers. Some species are half-hardy in dry, sunny positions. *M. crystallinum*, or ice plant, is a trailing annual bearing white flowers in summer, and frosted leaves and stems. A number of species of herbaceous and shrubby habits are grown in the greenhouse.

Meschëra, lowland area in central Russia between the Oka and its tribs., the Moskva and the Klyaz'ma, in the Moscow, Ryazan' and Vladimir oblasts. There are many lakes and peat marshes, pine and spruce forests, rich alluvial grazing lands and phosphorite deposits. M. is now included in the Virgin and Idle Land Campaign. In the Middle Ages it was inhabited

Mesembryanthemum Crystallinum

by the Finnish tribe, M., assimilated by the Russians by the 16th cent.

Meshed, Meshhed, *see* MASHHAD.

Meshed Ali, Najaf, or **Nejef,** walled tn of Iraq, near Bagdad. It contains the tomb of Ali and is a place of Shiite (q.v.) pilgrimage. Pop. 45,000.

Mesitylene (1 : 3 : 5, or symmetrical, trimethyl benzene, $C_6H_3(CH_3)_3$), an aromatic hydrocarbon found in small quantities in coal tar. It is also prepared by distilling acetone with sulphuric acid. M. is a colourless, mobile, pleasant-smelling liquid boiling at 164·5° C. Treated with concentrated nitric acid it yields mono- and dinitromesitylene, but with dilute nitric acid it yields acids by the successive oxidation of the methyl groups.

Mesmer, Franz Anton (1734–1815), founder of animal magnetism or mesmerism (*see* HYPNOTISM), *b.* near Constance, graduated M.D. at Vienna in 1766. His medical dissertation *De Planetarum Influxu* ('On the Influence of the Planets') was largely plagiarised from Richard Mead's *Discourse concerning the Action of the Sun and Moon on Animal Bodies*, 1704, and did not originate in the ideas of Paracelsus and other practitioners of occult or magnetic medicine, as has commonly been thought. In 1774 he began with Father Hell, the Viennese astronomer, to investigate the curative powers of the magnet and developed the doctrine, closely related to that of his dissertation, that there exists an invisible fluid, animal magnetism, which is in some ways similar to mineral magnetism. He thought that the only cause of disease was an abnormal distribution of this fluid, or obstructions to its circulation, in the body and that the only correct treatment was the application of animal magnetism, which emanated from M.'s body when he stroked the bodies of his patients and produced 'crises' in the form of convulsive and other bodily reactions. He migrated to Paris in 1778, where he obtained only one disciple in the Faculty of Medicine. The pop. of Paris was divided in its opinions, some considering him a charlatan with an unintelligible doctrine and others believing that he had made a new discovery. M. asked the Faculty of Medicine and other official bodies to investigate his work and a commission was appointed by Louis XVI in 1784. It reported that no such fluid existed and that the effects produced by M. were due to the patients' imagination, an explanation never accepted by M. Completely discredited, he lived in S. Germany and Switzerland from c. 1791. His prin. work was *Mémoire sur la découverte du magnétisme animal*, 1779 (Eng. trans., 1948). *See* life by R. Tischner, Munich, 1928; F. Podmore, *Mesmerism and Christian Science*, 1909; G. Frankau's introduction to the trans. of M.'s *Mémoire sur la découverte du magnétisme animal* (1779), 1948; F. A. Pattie in the *Journal of the History of Medicine*, vol. xi, No. 3, 1956.

Mesmerism, *see* HYPNOTISM.

Mesolithic, *see* STONE AGE.

Mesolonghi, *see* MISSOLONGHI.

Mesons are particles with masses between those of the electron and the proton. Observations dating from the early years of the present cent. showed that the earth's atmosphere is continuously bombarded from outside by a stream of radiation with a quite exceptional power to penetrate through considerable thicknesses of matter. This is called the cosmic radiation (q.v.). In recent years it has become apparent that the primary radiation that impinges on the upper atmosphere consists chiefly of protons, or nuclei of hydrogen atoms, travelling at enormous velocities, but accompanied also by nuclei of other types, in approximately the same proportions as the different chemical elements occur in the universe.

Atomic nuclei are positively charged, extremely minute structures of diameter about 10^{-12} cm., built up of protons and neutrons (*see* ATOM and NUCLEUS). In consequence of their like charges they repel one another as they approach, and, unless their speeds are very high, collisions between them do not cause disruption of their structures. If, however, their speeds are as great as those of the alpha particles emitted from radioactive materials, or produced artificially in such machines as the cyclotron (q.v.), collisions between nuclei may be violent enough to cause changes that transmute nuclei of one type into those of another element. The highest energies of the protons in cosmic rays, however, are much higher than any yet produced in the laboratory or by radioactive material, and as their collisions with other nuclei are correspondingly more violent, they produce changes of an entirely different type. Much remains to be understood about the forces that hold nuclei together and the study of high energy collisions of particles is therefore very important. Accelerators such as the synchrotron (q.v.) are the prin. tools, but cosmic rays (q.v.) still provide the highest possible energies.

In 1935 the Jap. physicist Yukawa suggested that the forces between protons and neutrons, which could help to hold nuclei together, could be explained in terms of an as yet undetected particle with a mass between that of the electron

and the proton. His calculations showed that it should have a positive or negative charge and a mass about 137 times that of the electron, and also that it should be unstable and decay into a positive or negative electron after an average life of about 10^{-6} sec. During the next 2 years, Anderson and Neddermeyer, and Street and Stevenson, in the U.S.A. discovered particles in the cosmic rays with masses about 200 times that of the electron, both positively and negatively charged, and decaying in the manner predicted. At first these were called *mesotrons* and were naturally identified with the Yukawa particles. A variety of reasons argue against the equivalence of the observed and the predicted particles, e.g. the mesotron was found not to react with nuclei. The situation was enlivened in 1947 when Powell and Occhialini discovered another particle of intermediate mass. They used nuclear emulsions (q.v.) as detectors and found that this new particle with a mass about 300 times that of the electron changed spontaneously into the mesotron already detected. The heavier particle could be positively or negatively charged and was termed a pi-meson (or π-meson) and the lighter one was renamed the mu-meson (or μ-meson). Since 1947 a

MESONS

Symbol	Mass (MeV)	Mean Life (sec.)	Principal Decay Modes
$\pi^{\pm}$	139·7	$2 \cdot 55 \times 10^{-8}$	$\mu^+ + \nu_\mu$
π^0	135·0	$1 \cdot 8 \times 10^{-16}$	$\gamma + \gamma$
$K^{\pm}$	493·9	$1 \cdot 23 \times 10^{-8}$ (K^+)	$K^+ \rightarrow$ $\mu^+ + \nu_\mu$ $\pi^+ + \pi^0$ $\pi^+ + \pi^+ + \pi^-$
K^0	497·8	50% as K_1 50% as K_2	
K_1	497·8	$0 \cdot 92 \times 10^{-10}$	$\pi^+ + \pi^-$ $\pi^0 + \pi^0$
K_2	497·8	$6 \cdot 2 \times 10^{-8}$	$\pi + e + \nu_e$ $\pi + \mu + \nu_\mu$ $\pi^0 + \pi^0 + \pi^0$ $\pi^+ + \pi^0 + \pi^-$
η	548	$\sim 10^{-17}$	$\pi^+ + \pi^- + \pi^0$

Notes: The superscript $\pm$ or ^{0} indicates the electric charge of the particle. The mass is given in energy equivalent for which the mass of the electron is 0·511 MeV (energy = mass $\times c^2$, where c is the velocity of light, *see* ELECTRON VOLT). In the decay products the symbol π refers to a pi-meson (*see* MESONS), and γ refers to a gamma ray photon.

neutral pi-meson has been found which decays after a very short time (about 10^{-15} sec.) into 2 gamma rays (q.v.). The negative pi-meson reacts readily with a nucleus and causes it to explode, but the positive pi-meson nearly always decays to a mu-meson and hence to an electron.

Following the discovery of the K-meson by Rochester and Butler in 1947, a variety of possible decay modes were found for the same K-particle. In the early 1960's a considerable number of 'particles' with lifetimes in the range 10^{-21}-10^{-23} sec., and known as 'resonances', were identified. They were divided into M.s and hyperons (q.v.) and classification schemes were proposed. The full picture has yet to be revealed.

The mu-meson (μ) is now referred to as a muon and has properties identical with the electron except for its mass and decay. It is classified as a 'lepton' together with the electron and the two types of neutrinos—the electron neutrino (ν_e) and the muon neutrino (ν_μ). The 4 classes of particles are thus, photon, lepton, M. and baryon. See C. F. Powell, P. H. Fowler and D. H. Perkins, *The Study of Elementary Particles*, 1964; C. E. Swartz, *The Fundamental Particles*, 1965.
See table on p. 363.

Mesopotamia (Gk 'between rivers'), name used in different senses: (1) the country drained by the 2 rivs. Euphrates and Tigris and enclosed by the Syrian desert, the Amanus Mts, the mts of Armenia and the Zagros range in Iran; (2) the land between the Euphrates and Tigris with the fringe outside them N. of a line from Ana to Tekrit, the Arabic and Turkish prov. of al-Jazira, 'the Island'.

Taking the name M. in the wider sense, the land of Sumer and Akkad (qq.v.) (S. Iraq) was *c.* 2500 BC the home of the Sumerians and the foundation of the civilisation of W. Asia. With no natural barriers M. was open to invaders, most of whom were Semites, which means that they spoke related languages and were different from the Sumerians, with whom, however, they amalgamated. Later invaders were quickly absorbed. The kingdoms of Sumer were small city states, but Lugal-zaggisi reached the Mediterranean and Sargon of Agade claims to have conquered Crete. Hillmen from the E. destroyed these states, but were driven out again and a Sumerian dynasty ruled in Ur (*c.* 2120–2010), though it was always in danger from the E. It went down before 2 invasions, Elamites from the E. and Amorites from the N.; the Amorites, so named because they were thought to have come from the W. (Amurru), brought with them the Akkadian language, and Sumerian died out or was banished to the extreme S., though it remained the language of religion and scholarship. In the N. some of the Amorites stayed nomads and elsewhere they formed city states, usually at war with each other. Two outstanding figures were Samsi-Adad I of Assyria, who controlled N. M. and the middle course of the 2 rivs. and his part-contemporary, Hammurabbi, the law-giver of Babylon (*c.* 1790–1750), who was a smaller figure in contemporary politics.

The capture of Babylon by the Hittites (*c.* 1600), and a general movement of peoples, put an end to the Old Babylonian period and made way in the S. for a dynasty of Kassites from the E. From the 15th to the 13th cents. the centre of politics was Syria with Egyptians, Hurrians, Hittites and later Assyrians as the chief actors. In the 19th cent. Assyrian merchants had been estab. in the E., and perhaps the centre, of Asia Minor till the Amorite invasion swept them away. When the Kassite kings weakened, Assyria (q.v.) came to the fore but suffered sev. ups and downs, though it sacked Babylon *c.* 1240. The kingdom of Mitanni, founded by Hurrians in the W. loop of the Euphrates, flourished from the 15th to the 13th cent., now an ally and now a rival of Egypt. At this time the Aramaeans were seeping into the land; one branch, the Chaldaeans (q.v.), settled round Babylon (q.v.), and Assyria had a hard fight to keep others at bay. Again the fortunes of Assyria fluctuated; at the height of its power it ruled Egypt for a short time, but it was threatened both from N. and E. and was often engaged in war with Babylon. Raids by Cimmerians and Scythians were dangerous and portended the movement of the Medes, who, in alliance with Babylon, captured Nineveh in 612, and destroyed the Assyrian empire. Persians captured Babylon in 539 and held it till Alexander came. On his death the house of Seleucus ruled in M. till *c.* 150, and from that date till the Muslim conquest AD 637, Persians, whether Arsacid or Sassanian, ruled, though Rome challenged their possession in the N. With the accession of the Abbasid caliphs and the foundation of Bagdad, M. became the centre of the Muslim world; but the power of the caliphs soon waned and Dailamites of the Shi'a faith ruling in Persia were supreme in M. in 945, though small states like Mosul came into being in the N. In 1055 Seljuk Turks, who were Sunnites, conquered Persia and M.; for a few months in 1059 homage was done in Bagdad to the Fatimid caliph of Egypt. Hulagu captured the cap. in 1258, putting an end to the caliphate. He and his descendants ruled till 1340 and were followed by another Mongol tribe, the Jalair, who ruled, except for an interlude due to Timur's capture of Bagdad, till 1411 when Black Sheep Turkmens displaced them. These were followed by White Sheep Turkmens in 1469. The Persians conquered M. in 1509, to be driven out in 1534 by the Ottoman Turks, who kept possession, except for 15 years during the reign of Shah Ismail, till 1918. For later hist. and other details *see* IRAQ.

See Cambridge Ancient History, vols. i–iv, 1923–6; Sidney Smith, *Early History of Assyria*, 1928; A. L. Oppenheim, *Ancient Mesopotamia*, 1964.

Mesosaurs, primitive aquatic group of fossil reptiles from the late Carboniferous or early Permian rocks of S. Africa and S. America. They had small slim bodies, powerful tails, numerous long teeth and were probably fish-eaters.

Mesosuchians, group of Jurassic and cretaceous crocodiles.

MESOZOIC PLANTS

1–6, Cycadophites; 7 and 8, conifers. 1, Stem of *Cycadoidea superba*, South Dakota; 2, Leaves of *Zamites feneonis*, France; 3, Leaves of *Otozamites bearri*, England; 4, Leaf of *Nielssonia polymorpha* (Triassic); 5, Leaf of *Zamites articus*, Greenland; 6, Cone of *Williamsonia gigas* (Liassic); 7, *Voltzia heterophyllas*; 8, *Araucaria microphylla* (Jurassic). After Wicland, Saporta, Nathorst, Heer and Schimper.

Mesotrons, obsolete synonym for Mesons (q.v.).

Mesozoic, subdiv. of geological time, between the Palaeozoic and the Cainozoic (*c.* 225 to 70 million years before present); it includes the Triassic, Jurassic and Cretaceous systems, which cover much of England, France, N. Germany, the Alps and the W. states of America. The M. ages differ from the Palaeozoic ages in their fauna and flora. Cycads and conifers represented the early M. flora, and later monocotyledons flourished. In the animal world great changes took place. Brachiopods diminished in number, as also did the Crinoids, while the Echinoderms, as represented by the Urchins, occupied a prominent position. The Ammonites were the typical M. cephalopoda, and the variety and abundance of reptilian life constitute a remarkable feature of the life of the period. The first mammals made their appearance in marsupial forms during the M. time, and the first species of bird, *Archaeopteryx lithographica*, has been found in the Jurassic rocks of Germany.

Mess (O.F. *mes*; modern *mets*, dish), in its original meaning, a portion of food, or provision of food for a party for one meal. It was especially applied in early times to more or less liquid food, such as porridge, soup or broth (cf. the biblical 'mess of pottage'). The term is now used of a company of persons who sit at meals together, especially of the members of an official or professional body. At one time the number in a M. was usually a small group of about 4, seated at one table and sharing the same dishes. In the Inns of Court parties of 4 benchers or 4 students are still common, but in the naval or military service the number in a M. is considerably larger, consisting of the parties into which a ship's company or a regiment is divided for meals. Most ships in the Brit. Navy have the officers' or ward-room M., the junior officers' M. and the warrant-officers' M. The admiral and the captain usually take their meals alone. Similarly in the army and R.A.F. there are officers' and sergeants' M.s, and separate M.s for the men. The M. is generally managed by a committee of officers and supported by the joint subscriptions of the members, supplemented by a small yearly allowance from the gov. There is often a small monthly subscription for newspapers, magazines and washing. Meals are served in the barracks; but married men are allowed to dine at home, and there are sometimes certain exemptions for others. The senior officer present is responsible for the discipline. Billiards, smoking and reading rooms are often attached to the M. house, as well as the 'common room' or dining-hall, kitchen and cellars.

Messager, André (1853–1929), Fr. composer, pupil of Saint-Saëns, was known by his operettas and comic operas, of which *La Béarnaise*, 1885, was his first marked success. Others were *La Basoche*, 1890, *Madame Chrysanthème*, 1893, *Mirette* (written for the Savoy Theatre, London), 1894, *Les P'tites Michu*, 1897, *Véronique*, 1898, *Fortunio*, 1907, *Monsieur Beaucaire* (in English), 1919, and *L'Amour masqué*, 1923. From 1901 to 1906 he was artistic director at Covent Garden in London and from 1907 to 1914 at the Opéra in Paris. Debussy dedicated his *Pelléas et Mélisande* to him. *See* H. Férrier, *André Messager*, 1948; M. Auge-Laribe, *Messager, musicien de théâtre*, 1951.

Messageries Maritimes, Compagnie des, Fr. shipowners with 47 ships totalling 383,338 gross tons, serving Black Sea, S. and E. Africa, Indian Ocean, India, Pakistan, Ceylon, Burma, Malaysia, Indonesia, Far E., Caribbean, S. Seas, Australia, New Zealand and S. America. H.Q.: 12 Blvd de la Madeleine, Paris; London Office: 72 Fenchurch street, E.C.3.

Messalina, Valeria, daughter of Marcus Valerius Messala Barbatus, 3rd wife of the emperor Claudius and mother of Britannicus. Renowned for her insatiable lust, she fell in love with Gaius Silius, a young patrician, and obliged him to bring ruin upon himself by 'marrying' her in a public ceremony. Rome could stand no more; the emperor's secretary, Narcissus, persuaded Claudius to destroy her, and she was dispatched in the gardens of Lucullus (AD 48) by a tribune of the praetorian guard. *See* Tacitus, *Ann.*, xi. 12, 26 ff, 33–7; Juvenal, vi. 115–32; x. 329–45.

Messana, *see* MESSINA.

Messapii, *see* APULIA and IAPYGIA.

Messel, Oliver (1905–), stage designer, *b.* London, educ. Eton. He is a grandson of Linley Sambourne, the famous *Punch* artist. He came into prominence for his designs for C. B. Cochran's revues at the London Pavilion after having attracted attention as a maker of masks. His work embraces all types of stage productions, revues, ballet, opera, musical plays, poetic plays and comedies, and he is as well known in New York as in London. He has a touch of fantasy in his work and a great gift for colour. Author of *Stage Designs and Costumes*, 1933.

Messene: 1. Cap. of Messenia (q.v.), founded by Epaminondas in 369 BC to check the power of Sparta. It lay at the foot of Mt Ithome, on top of which was the citadel. There are remains of the walls, theatre, stadium, council house and gateway of the agora. *See* Pausanias, *Itinerary of Greece*, bk iii, ed. Sir J. G. Frazer, 1898. The site is now occupied by the vil. of Mauromati.

2. *See* MESSINA.

Messengers, King's or **Queen's,** officers of the Brit. Gov. appointed to carry official dispatches at home and abroad. Employed under the secretaries of state.

Messenia, country of anct Greece in Peloponnesus, bounded E. by Laconica, N. by Elis and Arcadia and E. and W. surrounded by the sea. It was separated from Laconica by the mt chain of Taygetus, and from Elis and Arcadia by the R. Neda and the high land which runs

between the bed of the Neda and the sources of Pamisos. The W. part of M. is drained by the R. Pamisos, which rises in the mts, between Arcadia and M., and flows southward into the Messenian Bay (Gulf of Koroni). The basin of the Pamisos is divided into 2 distinct parts. The upper part, usually called the plain of Stenyclerus, is small and only moderately fertile; but the lower part S. of Ithome is an extensive plain, celebrated in anct times for its great fertility, whence it was often called Macaria, the 'Blessed'. The E. part of M. is diversified by hills and valleys, but contains no high mts. The chief tns on the W. coast were Pylos and Mothone, or Methone (Modon). The Bay of Pylos (Navarino), which is protected from the swell of the sea by the is. of Sphacteria (Sphagia), is the best harbour in Peloponnesus. The only tn inland of any importance was Messene (*see* MESSENE 1). The anct hist. of M. is mainly that of its struggle for independence against Sparta in the 3 'Messenian' wars. The details of the first 2 (743–724 and 685–666 BC) are for the most part legendary (*see* ARISTODEMUS; ARISTOMENES). From 666 the Messenians were mere helots (q.v.). In 464 BC, however, they and other helots, taking advantage of the havoc caused by an earthquake at Sparta, revolted. The 3rd war followed (463–456). The Messenians were again defeated; but they were allowed safe passage out of the country and were settled by Athens at Naupactus. After the overthrow of Sparta at Leuctra (371) and the foundation of Messene (369 BC) M. remained independent until 146 BC, when it was included in the Rom. prov. of Achaea (q.v.). M. (modern Messinía) is now a dept of Greece and is known for its fruit. Its cap. is Katamai (q.v.). Area 1250 sq. m.; pop. 212,000.

Messerschmitt, Wilhelm (1898–), Ger. aircraft designer and maker. He designed his first aeroplane in 1916 and estab. a manufacturing firm under his own name a few years after the First World War. He was chief engineer of the Bayerische Flugzeugwerke (Bavarian Aircraft Works) until it was absorbed in 1938 by the M. Co. M. received the Lilienthal prize for research in aviation, 1937. His Me. 109 emerged as a standard Ger. single-seat fighter of the 1940–5 period. His twin-engined fighter bombers were represented by the Me. 110, 210 and 410. The tailless, rocket-propelled fighter monoplane, Me. 163 (*see* AEROPLANE), was the first operational type capable of over 550 m.p.h.; the 262, a twin-engined fighter, was the best Ger. jet-propelled aircraft.

Messiaen, Olivier (1908–), Fr. organist and composer, *b.* Avignon, was mainly self-taught while the family lived at Grenoble and Nantes, but entered the Paris Conservatoire at the age of 11. In 1931 he was appointed organist at the Trinité. His music is often religious and sometimes mystical, not to say esoteric (e.g. the vast and most elaborately scored *Turangalila* Symphony), and includes sacred choral works, orchestral music (often with religious titles), chamber, piano and organ music, etc.

Messiah, from Gk *Messias*, Aramaic *Mēsh-īhā*, anointed = Gk *Christos*, see CHRIST. *See also* JEWS. *See* the article on M. in J. Hastings, *Dictionary of the Bible*, 1900–2; W. Manson, *Jesus the Messiah*, 1943; T. W. Manson, *The Servant-Messiah: the public ministry of Jesus*, 1953.

Messier, Charles (1730–1817), Fr. astronomer, *b.* Badouvillier, Lorraine. Employed in Paris as a draughtsman at the Collège de France, and later as a clerk at the Marine Observatory in the Hôtel de Cluny, he became a noted observer of comets, earning from Louis XV the nickname 'the comet ferret'. During this work he compiled a catalogue of nebulae and star clusters, first pub. in 1774; this catalogue, with a few additions by Méchain, a younger colleague of M., finally contained 109 objects. The numbering given by M. is still used for the brighter nebulae: for example, M.31 is the great nebula in Andromeda. Lalande named a constellation after M., but the name has fallen into disuse.

Messina, Antonello da, see ANTONELLO.

Messina: 1. Prov. of Italy, in NE. Sicily, with coastlines on the Tyrrhenian Sea and the Strait of M. It is mountainous, with long ranges of the Nebrodi and Peloritani Mts. There are numerous short riv. valleys, running S.–N. The prin. tns include M., Barcellona, Milazzo and Castroreale (qq.v.). Area 1253 sq. m.; pop. 682,000.

2. (Anct Gk Messēnē, formerly Zancle; Lat. Messana), seaport of Sicily, cap. of the prov. of M., at the foot of the Peloritani Mts on the Strait of M. Zancle ('sickle', from the shape of its harbour) was settled early in the 8th cent. BC by colonists from Cumae and Chalcis. About 494 BC some Samian and Milesian refugees, who had come to Rhegium (q.v.) after the capture of Miletus by the Persians, helped Anaxilas to obtain possession of Zancle, the name of which was changed to Messene because Anaxilas or his ancestors were natives of Messene in Peloponnesus. In 397 the city was captured and destroyed by the Carthaginians, but was quickly retaken and rebuilt by Dionysius I of Syracuse. Nevertheless it supported Carthage against Agathocles (q.v.), after whose death it was seized (288 BC) by Mamertines from S. Italy, who in 264 invoked the aid of Rome against an attack by Hieron II of Syracuse. Rome took this long-desired opportunity to secure a foothold in Sicily (q.v.), and thus the 'affair of the Mamertines' became the *casus belli* of the 1st Punic war (*see* PUNIC WARS), since Hieron was allied with Carthage. At the end of this war Messana, as the Romans called it, was made a free city in alliance with Rome. It came within the prov. of Sicily in 211; supported Sextus Pompeius against Octavian; was sacked by the latter's forces in 35 BC but continued under the empire to flourish as a commercial port. In the 9th cent. AD it was taken by the Saracens and in 1072 by the Normans (qq.v.). It was in the hands of Spain, 1282–1713, and was greatly damaged in 1848, when it was taken by Neapolitan troops after a siege of 5 days. It has been devastated twice (1783 and

1908) by earthquakes. The city, as it exists today, is modern; few anct buildings remain, though some have been restored, including the archiepiscopal cathedral (begun *c.* 1160). The univ. was founded in 1548. M. has a textile industry, and the port, which has one of the best harbours in Italy, has a trade in oranges, lemons, wine and olive oil. Pop. 251,500.

Messina, Strait of (anct **Fretum Siculum**), channel separating Sicily from the It. mainland, and joining the Tyrrhenian and Ionian Seas. It is 20 m. long, and varies in width from 11 m. in the S. to 2 m. in the N. Here are to be found the Scylla and Charybdis (q.v.) of Gk legend: the former a rock on the It. side at the tn of Scilla (q.v.); the latter a whirlpool on the Sicilian side by the harbour of M.

Messines Ridge, spur of rising ground 6 m. S. of Ypres, Belgium, captured by the Germans in the First World War after severe fighting in Nov. 1914, and the scene of further fighting in June 1917 and April 1918. *See* WESTERN FRONT IN THE FIRST WORLD WAR.

Messinia, see MESSENIA.

Mestre, It. tn in Veneto (q.v.), a NW. suburb of Venice. It dates from Rom. times, is a road and railway junction and has metallurgical, chemical and saw-milling industries. Pop. 73,500.

Meštrović, Ivan (1883–1961), Yugoslav sculptor, *b.* Vrpolje in N. Dalmatia. A peasant's son, he was taught wood-carving by his father, apprenticed to a marble-cutter at Split, studied sculpture at Vienna, and vigorously led a nationalist art movement. He designed the Serb national temple for Kossovo; 2 equestrian statues in bronze of Amer. Indians for Chicago; portraits of Masaryk, Hoover, Pius XI; and the memorial chapel to the unknown soldier on Avala Mt, Belgrade. There is a torso by him in the Victoria and Albert Museum, and the Tate Gallery has a fine relief 'The Deposition' and his bronze of Sir Thomas Beecham. M. went to the U.S.A., 1947, and became an Amer. citizen, 1954.

Meta, riv. of E. Colombia, which rises in the Sumapaz glacier, 40 m. S. of Bogotá. It flows NE. to join the R. Orinoco on the Venezuelan border, after a course of about 650 m. It flows through a dept of the same name which consists of tropical lowland and is very sparsely populated. The cap. of the dept is Villavicencio with a pop. of 44,000. The pop. of M. is 85,000 with an area of 32,895 sq. m.

Meta, trade name for metaldehyde, a polymer (q.v.) of acetaldehyde (q.v.). It is used as a solid fuel in spirit lamps and stoves and, mixed with bran, as a slug and snail destroyer.

Metabolism embraces all chemical changes within living organisms. These changes are of 2 kinds: (1) synthetic or anabolic; (2) destructive or katabolic. If anabolism exceed katabolism, growth will result; if katabolism proceed more rapidly than anabolism, reduction or 'wasting' will occur (*see* GROWTH).

Green plants synthesise proteins, fats and carbohydrates from carbon dioxide, water and mineral salts. They differ fundamentally from animals in that the latter cannot synthesise from such simple materials, but use the products of plant anabolism, digest and distribute them, and re-synthesise them in various parts of the body. The protein, fat and carbohydrate incorporated in the cell substance or organisms are not used in normal M. Some of this endogenous material may be used during starvation, but if the material be reduced beyond the minimum essential to the composition of a living cell, the cell will die. The materials used in normal M. are exogenous, i.e. stored in or around the tissues or carried in circulation. Animals and plants gain energy by the oxidation (respiration) of these materials, and carbon dioxide and water are 2 almost universal products of this katabolic process. The liver of mammals plays a great part in the M. of fats, carbohydrates and proteins. The pancreas is important as an organ of secretion, forming both pancreatic juice and insulin; if too little or too much insulin be secreted, the normal carbohydrate M. is disturbed, and *Diabetes mellitus* and hypoglycaemia, respectively, result. Mammals fed on protein, carbohydrate and the requisite vitamins can synthesise fat, so that fat is not an essential article of diet, though it is usually regarded as desirable, being particularly useful for the production of energy when it is oxidised. It is possible to measure the amount of heat produced by a man (after fasting for 15 hrs and at rest) per sq. metre of body surface per hour, and this heat production, or M., is known as *basal M*. The following table gives the average values in Calories, a Calorie being the amount of heat required to raise 1 kilogram of water 1° C.

Age	*Basal Metabolism* (*Calories per sq. metre per hour*)
Boys . 12–13	50
Men . 20–50	40
Women . 20–50	37

For example, the surface area of a normal man of about 30 years, height 5 ft 8 in. (1·7 metres), and weighing 11 stone (69·9 kg), is 1·8 sq. metres; and the basal M. is therefore 40 × 1·8 calories per hour, i.e. 72 Calories per hour. In 24 hrs he produces 1728 Calories, and this is the amount of heat produced basally, i.e. without food and at rest. Work will, of course, increase the M., and the source of the increase must either be his own tissues or his food. *See* E. F. Du Bois, *Basal Metabolism*, 1936; E. Holmes, *The Metabolism of Living Tissues*, 1937; A. B. Callow, *Food and Health*, 1938; V. A. Najjar, *Carbohydrate metabolism*, 1953.

Metacentre, *see* HYDROSTATICS.

Metal Testing. Tests of metals and alloys fall into 2 categories: (1) destructive and (2) non-destructive. In general the destructive tests give information on the mechanical properties of the material, whereas the non-destructive tests only indicate whether the material, or more often a fabricated article, is free from defects.

Destructive tests. Most destructive tests involve the use of a test-piece, either specially formed as an appendage to the article being produced, e.g. to a casting or forging, or taken from a representative sample of the raw material, or machined out of the article itself. Whichever is the source of the test-piece, the latter is always stressed until it breaks. The 2 standard tests most used in engineering are the tensile and the impact tests. To these may be added the hardness test, which is not, strictly speaking, destructive, though a small mark remains.

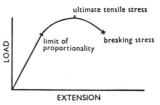

A NORMAL TENSILE TEST CURVE

The tensile test-piece is essentially a rod of circular cross-section (except when a flat strip is used as for sheet material) which is gripped at both ends and pulled apart by a machine which is capable of measuring the load applied. The centre portion is marked off by 2 small 'pop-holes' an accurately measured distance apart, and this distance is the gauge-length. At each end of the gauge-length the rod increases in diameter to ensure that the fracture takes place in the gauge-length. The test-piece may be of any size, but for comparable results between different sizes it has been found that the gauge-length must be 4 times the square root of the cross-sectional area. In the most popular size of test-bar the gauge-length is 2 in. and its diameter 0·564 in., so that the cross-sectional area is ¼ sq. in. If the load on the test-piece is increased in small increments of, say, half a ton and the corresponding stretch or extension measured and a load-extension graph plotted, it is found that there is first a straight line up to the 'limit of proportionality', then a curved portion which reaches a peak at the ultimate tensile stress (U.T.S.), after which there is a fall to the point at which fracture takes place, the breaking stress. After the bar has been broken the 2 halves are fitted together and the distance apart of the pop-holes measured; from this the elongation per cent can be calculated. Also it will be found that (if the metal is ductile) the fracture will have occurred in the middle of a well-marked waist which has appeared; measurement of the diameter at this point enables the reduction of area per cent to be calculated. While the ultimate tensile stress indicates the highest stress which the metal will stand, the elongation and reduction of area are measures of the ductility.

The impact test is a means of determining the ability of the metal to resist a sudden shock. The principle of the test is that a standard size of notch is machined in a round or square section bar to concentrate the stress. The bar is gripped vertically in a vice which holds it against the blow of a weight at the end of a pendulum. The energy in foot-pounds absorbed in breaking the bar is related to the distance which the bar swings after impact, and is quoted as the impact value. The Izod and Charpy tests are the best-known impact tests. There are sev. methods for determining the hardness of a metal, but the indentation test is the most universally accepted test in metallurgy and engineering. Examples are the Brinell, Vickers and Rockwell tests. In the Brinell test a heavy load forces a hard steel ball (3000 kg load and 10 mm diameter ball for steel testing) into the metal, and the diameter of the impression left is measured and trans. into hardness units. The standard Vickers test employs a pyramidal diamond, and the length of the diagonal of the diamond impression is converted into hardness units. The Rockwell test may use either a ball or diamond, but in each case the depth of penetration, after measuring an initial light load, is measured.

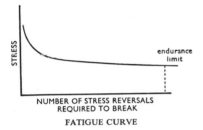

FATIGUE CURVE

The fatigue test: many mechanical components built from metal with a high tensile strength are found to have fractured in service when it is quite certain that the ultimate tensile strength has not been reached. It is nearly always found that stresses have been of a reciprocating nature, as in the case of an axle-shaft revolving under a bending stress, or a piston connecting rod which is alternately stretched and compressed once every stroke. Such failures under alternating stresses show a characteristic shiny fracture, and are known as fatigue failures. Common tests which give an evaluation of performance under fatigue conditions are the Wöhler, Haig and Schenk tests. The Wöhler test consists of a revolving bar of circular cross-section, gripped at one end by the revolving mechanism and having a weight hanging from a ball-race at the other, there being no further support between the 2. In the Haig and Schenk tests the bar is compressed and tensioned alternately thousands of times per min., plus and minus any desired load. Whichever test is used a graph can be plotted of load against the number of reversals of stress required to cause fracture. At low loads no fracture will occur after an infinite number of reversals, but as the load is increased the specimens begin to fail after decreasing numbers of reversals. The endurance

limit is the lowest load which will cause the test-piece to break within a stated number of stress reversals, e.g. 10,000,000.

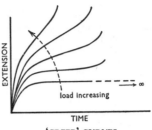

'CREEP' CURVES

The creep test is applied to alloys which spend most of their service life under stress at high temp., e.g. turbine blades. Such components slowly 'creep', i.e. extend over a period of hundreds of hours and then finally break under loads far lower than their normal short time strength at that temp. There are 3 stages of creep: the first is a rapid extension as the load is first applied; this merges into the second stage, where the rate of extension is much less than in stage 1, and may even be zero; then in the final stage the extension begins to proceed at an ever-increasing rate until it is terminated by fracture. Under low loads the third stage may never be reached even after thousands of hours, but with heavier loads the third stage appears, and as the loads are increased both the second and third stages become steeper and fracture follows after a comparatively few hours. The results of the test can be applied in 2 ways: either the highest load is determined which, at the required temp., will not cause fracture within the required lifetime of a component; or, it is first decided what is the maximum extension which can be tolerated and then determine the highest load which will give this extension during the required lifetime of the component without rupture.

Non-destructive tests. It is wasteful to saw up a casting, for instance, to look for shrinkage cavities or a welded component to investigate the soundness of the weld or a forging for internal tears. By the use of X-rays much of this is eliminated. To take an X-ray photograph, a special X-ray film in a light-tight *cassette* is placed at one side of the article to be radiographed, and a beam of X-rays directed at it from the other. The 'hardness' or penetrating power of the rays is controlled by the voltage across the generating tube, and this and the time of exposure are adjusted according to the thickness and density of the material being investigated. After development the film shows dense parts of the article in a light tone, while porosity, holes, etc., show up as dark areas. Internal flaws, etc., in bar stock or forgings can be revealed by the supersonic crack detector, by which a note of supersonic frequency is transmitted into the metal from a 'prod' containing a vibrating crystal. The 'echo' from a flaw is picked up by a receiving prod and its presence shown on an oscillograph screen. External cracks on magnetic material such as carbon steels can be revealed by the magnetic crack detector. The metal is first magnetised by passing a current through it or by placing a coil round it and then a suspension of fine iron powder in paraffin is poured over it. The 2 edges of a crack behave as opposite magnetic poles and the accumulation of iron powder between them shows up the otherwise invisible crack. Non-magnetic materials may be tested for cracks by fluorescence. A solution of a fluorescent substance such as anthracene in a volatile solvent is poured over the article being tested. The solution penetrates the cracks, so that when excess solution has been wiped away and the solvent evaporated, a deposit of anthracene is left in the cracks. This deposit fluoresces under ultra-violet light from a lamp and is visible in a darkened room. *See also* METALLURGY.

Metallic Corrosion, *see* CORROSION OF METALS.

Metallography, *see* METALLURGY.

Metallurgy can be defined as the theory and practice of metal treatment. The term embraces the extraction of the pure metal from its ores; alloying of the pure metal with other metals; and fabrication of the pure metal and its alloys into forms suitable for domestic and industrial use. This involves a study of the physical and chemical properties of the ores, of the pure metals and of the alloys. Much of M. is applied physical chem., while some branches are applied chem. and others applied physics.

EXTRACTION METALLURGY is the science of extracting the metal from its ores and refining it. The ore generally consists of the metal-bearing mineral, together with earthy material or 'gangue'. Before the extraction process can be carried out, as much as possible of the gangue must be removed from the ore, the process being known as ore dressing (*see* ORE AND ORE DRESSING). The metal may be extracted from the mineral after ore dressing by the application of high temps. (pyro-M.) or electric currents (electro-M.) or a combination of both. The former is the most widely used. The term pyro-M. covers calcining, roasting, sintering, smelting, converting and distilling. *Calcining* in kilns decomposes carbonates to oxides and drives off water from hydroxides. *Roasting* is generally intended to oxidise sulphides to oxides or sulphates, and is usually performed in a tall cylindrical furnace with a number of superimposed hearths fitted with mechanical rabbles which rake the charge as it falls from hearth to hearth down the furnace. *Sintering* causes finely ground material to cake, so that it can be charged into smelting furnaces without fear of clogging them with dust.

Smelting is the process in which the metallic compound is broken down to yield the metal. Two types of furnace are used: the reverberatory furnace and the blast furnace. In the reverberatory furnace the fuel (coal, coke, gas or oil) is burned in a separate chamber from the hearth where the concentrate lies. The products of combustion pass into the hearth and heat the charge to above its melting-point. The remaining gangue forms a slag which floats on top of either metal or matte. Matte is a mixture of sulphides, e.g. copper-iron matte in copper smelting, which is subsequently treated in a converter by blowing air through it. Some oxide is formed from the sulphides and then an oxide sulphide reaction takes place which yields copper and sulphur dioxide in this example, the iron reacting with silica to form an iron-silicate slag which floats on the copper. In blast-furnace smelting the metalliferous material and fuel in the form of coke are mixed together in the same chamber and air blown in from tuyères at the bottom. The coke serves 2 purposes: to be a source of heat and to provide carbon which reduces the oxide to metal, e.g. the iron blast furnace. Limestone is added to form a slag with the silica still remaining from the original gangue. In the case of certain metals, notably zinc, the temp. of dissociation of the compound is so high that the metal appears as a vapour. When this is so the coke for reduction and the metalliferous material are heated together in a retort by an external flame. As the metal vaporises it distils over into a condenser, where it is liquefied.

Electro-metallurgical extraction applies to the deposition of a metal from one of its salts by the passage of an electric current. In many cases an aqueous solution of the salt can be used, e.g. copper is deposited from copper sulphate solution, but for electro-chemical reasons other metals cannot be so treated; instead the salt is fused and the current passed through the molten bath, e.g. extraction of aluminium from bauxite. In electro-refining the principle is the same but the conditions are so adjusted that only the metal required is deposited, the contaminating metals being left in solution.

Hydro-metallurgy is closely connected with ore dressing. It is often possible to dissolve out the metallic compounds from an ore and leave the gangue behind. Sulphide ores may be rendered soluble by roasting to oxides and then converting to sulphates by the addition of sulphuric acid. The sulphates are 'leached' out with water. In the case of copper, electrolysis is a logical continuation; in gold extraction the metal is precipitated from a cyanide solution by zinc.

METALLURGICAL HEAT TREATMENT. In order to develop to the utmost the properties of an alloy it is almost always necessary to heat treat it. All alloys start life as castings, except those made by the method of powder M. Sometimes they are cast directly into the shape of the article required, but more often they are cast first into ingots which are rolled into bar or sheet for final forming. Whichever method is used the alloy first develops a structure which is typical of cast metals, e.g. large crystal size with the crystals often orientated in directions which give planes of weakness; non-uniform dispersal of constituents and unwanted phases present. In addition, cooling stresses will very likely be present. Therefore one of the most important heat treatments, *annealing*, is adopted, to remove this 'as cast' structure. Most engineering alloys are made up of a ductile solid solution, together with one or more relatively brittle phases. When alloys are heated to above a certain temp., which varies from one alloy to another, the brittle phase may be taken into solution in the first phase. As the temp. rises the crystals begin to run together and form larger ones; for this reason the temp. must not be any higher or the time any longer than necessary. During the rapid cooling that always follows casting there is not sufficient time for the diffusion processes, which enable the metals to sort themselves out into the various phases, to take place. Consequently there is sometimes more, sometimes less, of a particular phase present than there would be under conditions of slower cooling. By bringing the alloy to a single phase, holding at temp. for a while to enable rediffusion to take place and cooling very slowly in the furnace, the required proportion of the phases is brought about. Annealing is frequently used for another purpose. Metals and alloys become hard when cold worked, e.g. rolled, beaten or pressed, and if the cold-working is continued beyond a certain point tearing or cracking begins; an intermediate anneal between stages brings about recrystallisation and the metal is softened enough to permit further cold work.

Normalising is a term applied solely to steel. It is similar to annealing, except that the soaking time at temp. is shorter and cooling is in air. It confers a finer and therefore tougher structure to the steel.

The effect of quenching. When an alloy which contains 2 phases at room temp. is heated to a single phase condition and then cooled again, the second phase which has been dissolved reprecipitates, and the form which it assumes as it does so depends upon the rate of cooling. With very slow cooling in the furnace it usually has time to form a network in the boundaries of the grains of the first phase. With quicker cooling, say in air, it may not be able to do this, but instead precipitates as separate particles within the grains. Very often with fairly rapid cooling it deposits as plates in the crystallographic planes of the first phase. The condition of uniformly dispersed particles gives the best mechanical properties. When cooling is extremely rapid the precipitation of the second phase may be inhibited altogether so that at room temp. only one phase is present instead of two. This is extremely useful because it enables the alloy to be fabricated to the required shape. A second, lower temp., treatment then brings about the precipitation of the dissolved phase and the alloy hardens. The particles of a phase reprecipitated in this way are often exceedingly fine, sometimes sub-microscopic, but if the temp. is raised too high they coalesce and the hardness of the alloy falls. This is the basis of the 'solution heat treatment and ageing' of aluminium alloys and

the hardening and tempering of steels. In the latter, however, quenching does not prevent reprecipitation of the second phase and the condition of incipient precipitation makes the steel hard but brittle. Tempering takes the precipitation a stage further and the resultant fall in hardness is accompanied by a development of toughness.

Case-hardening is the treatment accorded to low carbon steels whereby a high carbon 'case' up to about $\frac{1}{16}$ in. thick is formed at the surface. The low carbon core is tough but soft, and the object of the high carbon case is to provide resistance to wear, only a hard brittle material being able to do this. The case can be applied in 3 ways: (*a*) by pack-hardening—the article is packed in charcoal containing an activating agent such as barium carbonate and the whole heated to 900–950° C. for sev. hours, followed by a grain-refining treatment; (*b*) by cyanide hardening—the article is this time immersed for $\frac{1}{2}$ to $1\frac{1}{2}$ hrs in molten sodium cyanide; (*c*) by heating at 900° C. in a suitable gas containing hydrocarbons. The above methods are alternatively called 'case-carburising' because the case is derived from absorbed carbon. Another kind of case is applied by 'nitriding'. The steel is heated to 450–500° C. in an atmosphere of ammonia gas. The steel combines with the nitrogen in the ammonia and forms iron nitride in the form of needles to the depth of 1 millimetre. Special steels have been developed for nitriding of which one, Nitralloy, covered by patent, is well known. These steels contain such alloying metals as chromium, vanadium, titanium, etc., with the object of reducing the brittleness of the nitrided case, and about 1 per cent of aluminium has been found to be beneficial. An initially higher carbon provides for loss during treatment.

Flame hardening and induction hardening are 2 methods of conferring a hard surface on steel purely by quench hardening the outer layers. A shallow depth of, say, $\frac{1}{4}$ in. of the steel is heated to hardening temp. by, in flame hardening, an oxy-acetylene flame, and in induction hardening by an electrical high-frequency induction coil. Heating is extremely rapid, and immediately the correct temp. is reached the source of heat is removed and a water spray turned on so as to shock-cool the steel. Fully automatic machines have been developed for production hardening of standard components by both flame and induction hardening. Gear-teeth hardening particularly lends itself to this, e.g. Shorterising.

METALLURGICAL FURNACES serve 2 main purposes:

(1) *Melting*, which may be (*a*) purely remelting of ingot and scrap, etc., (*b*) remelting with some degree of refining, or (*c*) part of an extraction process. Examples of (*a*) are the electric induction melting of steel and the crucible melting of brasses, bronzes, aluminium, lead, tin and zinc base alloys; of (*b*) the basic electric arc furnace for steel where impurities like sulphur and phosphorus are largely eliminated, the carbon and manganese adjusted to

any required value and alloy additions made; and of (c) the blast furnace for producing pig-iron and the reverberatory smelting of copper. Remelting furnaces find their widest application in the foundry and in plants where alloys are made up into 'notch bars' from their constituent pure metals to definite specifications. For non-ferrous alloys the crucible furnace is the most popular. Originally heated by coke fire, modern crucible furnaces are almost universally oil or gas fired. The crucible stands in a refractory-lined case closed by a lid. The oil or gas burner injects the flame tangentially into the bottom of the case, so that the flame spirals upward round the crucible and leaves at the top. The air supply to the burner is under compression from a blower. The furnace may be of the bale-out (metal baled out with a ladle), lift-out (crucible lifted out with tongs), or tilting type (furnace tilts on trunnions by means of either hand or power operation). For larger quantities of metal the Ajax-Wyatt low-frequency electric furnace or the rocking arc electric furnace may be used. In the former a V-shaped channel below and connected with the main chamber acts as the secondary coil of an electrical transformer. The low-frequency current induced in the channel heats the metal. The rocking arc furnace consists essentially of a spherical chamber with an electrode entering from each side on the horizontal axis and meeting at the centre to form a spark-gap. The furnace is mounted on trunnions and is rocked mechanically about the horizontal axis through an angle of about 90° during melting so that once in each cycle part of the lining is first heated directly by the radiation from the arc and then passes under the charge to which it imparts its heat. Rapid heating of the charge is thus ensured. For steel remelting the coke-fired pit crucible furnace is still used for tool steels, but for large melts the high-frequency electrical induction furnace is a more modern development. In this the metal is placed in a crucible in a tilting case. A water-cooled coil round the crucible carries a high-frequency current which induces eddy currents in the steel and melting results from the heat generated by the steel's resistance to these. Highly reactive metals which are easily contaminated by refractory materials and by air, e.g. titanium, are melted in an arc furnace containing an inert atmosphere of argon. The metal is melted by the arc in a water-cooled copper mould the bottom of which is gradually lowered as more metal is added, thus forming an ingot.

(2) *Heat-treatment furnaces* are either of the 'batch' type, which are loaded at the beginning of the treatment and unloaded again at the end, or of the 'continuous' type in which the work is continuously loaded at one door, and after moving slowly through the furnace are unloaded at another. The latter type may consist either of an annular hearth which rotates continually at predetermined speeds, the loading and unloading doors being side by side, so that the work completes one revolution during treatment; or it

may be a straight-through furnace with a loading door at one end and an unloading door at the other. The work is carried through either on a moving hearth working on the continuous belt principle or on rollers, in which latter case a ram pushes it from behind.' Heat-treatment furnaces in the majority of heat-treatment shops are either gas fired or electrically heated. Though special alloys, e.g. tool steels, require temps. above 1000° C., for the commoner industrial alloys furnaces capable of operating continuously at up to this temp. cover most needs. Gas-fired furnaces are mostly of the muffle type, and generally the flames from a row of burners down each side pass into the chamber, the burners being so designed that the flames follow the curve of the arch of the roof and escape to a chimney. Particularly in large high-temp. furnaces much heat which would otherwise be lost up the chimney is saved by incorporating a recuperative system. For smaller furnaces such as laboratory muffles, or wherever direct contact between the charge and flame is undesirable, a special muffle lining heated by gas flames on the outside holds the charge. For temps. over 1000° C. a fan-type blower provides a forced draught for combustion. Electrically heated furnaces of the muffle type have the heating elements of special alloy such as nichrome (80/20 nickel/chrome) disposed inside the chamber along the walls and roof, and under the heat-resisting alloy hearth plate. To avoid a lower temp. at the door end due to heat loss through the door, the door also is often fitted with rows of elements. The freedom from the necessity of providing burner inlets and exit flues makes electric furnaces ideal for inert atmosphere work. Such furnaces, e.g. the bell type, are used for 'bright annealing' steel and copper alloys, etc., wire, sheet and strip where the inert atmosphere preserves the original bright finish. Cracked ammonia is widely used for this purpose. For treatments when close limits are set to the temp. range it is essential to ensure that all parts of the furnace are at the same temp. Up to a temp. of about 750° C. the vertical air-circulating furnace fulfils these requirements. It is a vertical cylindrical furnace closed with a cover at the top. The heating elements are on the inside of the insulating outer case, but outside the metal basket which carries the charge. The basket has sheet-metal sides, a grid bottom and open top. A fan beneath the basket draws air over the elements, where it is heated and blows it up through the grid into the basket, from which it passes out at the top and is recirculated over the elements. Some alloys are heat treated in baths of molten salts heated by gas or electricity, e.g. the solution treatment of aluminium alloy sheet. Automatic temp. control can be provided on all furnaces by thermo-electric controllers operating motorised valves on gas furnaces and relay-operated contractors on electric furnaces. *See also* ELECTRO-METALLURGY.

POWDER METALLURGY is the study of a method of preparation of solid metal articles from powder. One of the earliest applications was in the manuf. of tungsten filaments for electric bulbs. Tungsten was available in powder form, but owing to its high melting-point of 3360° C. could not be melted and cast into bar for wire-drawing in the usual way. The difficulty was overcome by subjecting the powder to very high pressure in a steel die so that a small bar was formed which, though very weak and brittle, could be handled without falling to pieces. The bar was next placed in a tube containing hydrogen to keep the air from reaching the tungsten and oxidising it, and an electric current passed through it so that it became heated to a high temp. as a result of its own electrical resistance. This sintered the grains of powder together and the bar became strong enough to be hammered into a rod, and eventually drawn into fine wire. The same method, with improvements, is still used today. The stages of pressing and sintering are an essential part of powder M. Pressing locks the particles of powder together more or less mechanically, though it is possible that some superficial welding takes place, and the 'compact', as it is called, usually has very little strength, its density is much lower than that of the finished article, and the microscope reveals the presence of numerous cavities. Heating to a temp. near to but below the melting-point causes diffusion of the grains, so that the cavities disappear and the density rises. When an alloy compact is being made, as for instance bronze, the 2 constituent metals, copper and tin in powder form, are thoroughly mixed together, pressed and sintered. On completion of sintering, the tin and copper are found to have diffused together so thoroughly that instead of individual grains of reddish copper and grey tin being visible, the microscope shows only yellowish-red grains of the α-bronze phase. This is one of the reasons why the initial powders must be in an extremely fine state of subdiv., for then it takes a much shorter time for the various metals to diffuse into a homogeneous alloy. Sometimes incipient melting of one metal so that it can cement the grains of other higher melting-point constituents together is permitted, e.g. cobalt mixed with tungsten carbide for high-speed tool tips. It is possible for a compact to be hot-pressed, i.e. pressing and sintering combined in one operation. Hot-pressing is, however, more expensive than cold-pressing because of the difficulties of heating massive steel dies and because the die life is shorter. Another interesting application of powder M. is the manuf. of self-lubricating bearings. Copper and tin powder, together with a little graphite, are pressed and sintered, but the compact is deliberately left porous so that oil can be forced into the pores. So much oil is left in the bearing that it will run a lifetime without re-oiling. By suitably shaping the die the powders can be pressed into the final shape of the article required, in the same way that plastics can, and the surface finish and dimensional accuracy are very good. So far various considerations, such as the pressure required, have limited powder compacts to a few pounds in weight, but it has found numerous applications where the older methods of fabrication could not easily have been used.

FABRICATION OF METALS. This covers all the different ways in which the ingot metals from the smelters is rendered useful for engineering or decorative purposes. The actual manipulation of the metal is largely the business of the engineer or foundryman, but he has to work in close co-operation with the metallurgist, who will keep him informed of such matters as the effect the processes are having on the internal structure of the metal, e.g. grain size, growth and orientation; internal tears due to overstressing, heat treatments before and after manipulation, etc. The fabrication methods are briefly:

Rolling. This can serve 2 purposes: (1) to break down the coarse cast structure of the original ingot or slab, and (2) to give the required final shape and finish, e.g. square, round or hexagonal bar, rod for wire-drawing, or sheet of various gauges with or without a mirror finish. The final stages, where the reduction per pass is small, are often performed in the cold so that the metal is work-hardened in order to obtain greater strength (hard-rolled).

Forging embraces hammer-forging, drop-forging and press-forging. In hammer-forging a steam or pneumatically operated hammer reciprocates and beats the metal between itself and the anvil. It is useful for forging comparatively simple shapes and for breaking down the cast structure of ingots for further processing. In drop-forging the metal, initially in the form of a piece of rod or bar, is forced, under a blow, to fill the cavity in a mould or die and thereby reproduce its shape. The die is split into two and the top half is attached to a heavy 'tup', the bottom half being attached to the base of the machine. The tup is raised mechanically to some 10 ft above the base, and then allowed to fall under gravity so that it drops on to the bottom half-die, and the blow forces the bar into the cavity. A shallow trough round the die cavity receives excess metal or 'flash', which is later trimmed off. Where the shape is complicated sev. sets of preforming dies may be necessary to fashion the bar roughly to shape before the final operation. Press-forging employs a squeeze rather than a blow. Drop-stamping is very similar to drop-forging, but applies more particularly to the shaping of sheet metal into hollow-ware.

Extrusion is a process by which a cast billet is forced, by hydraulic pressure, through a hole in a die at the end of a cylindrical container in a comparable manner to tooth-paste being squeezed out of a tube. The hole in the die may be simple in shape, such as round or hexagonal, or it may be quite complicated, as in the shape of the Gk letter *psi* (ψ), which would be impossible by rolling. Brass and aluminium alloys and lead are commonly extruded.

Spinning is a process of forming hollow-ware of circular cross-section. A flat disk of the metal is revolved at high speed and by means of special tools is gradually spread over a wooden mandrel of the required shape. It is particularly applied to soft metal like pewter, aluminium and silver.

Wire-drawing consists of reducing rod to wire by drawing it on a special draw-bench through die-holes of tungsten carbide or diamond, using suitable lubricants.

Casting (q.v.) performed in the foundry consists of pouring molten metal into a mould. The mould is most commonly silica sand, bonded together with a small amount of clay material, water and sometimes a cereal binder such as dextrine. Metals with fairly low melting-points may, however, be die-cast, that is, cast into a metal die. In gravity die-casting the metal is caused to fill the mould by the force of gravity, as in sand casting; in pressure die-casting hydraulic pressure is employed to force the metal into the die. In centrifugal casting, centrifugal force helps the metal to fill all intricacies of the mould.

PHYSICAL METALLURGY attempts to define exactly what a metal is and to correlate its properties with both its fundamental atomic structure and also its crystal structure. In the case of alloys some properties are related to the micro-constituents, known as 'phases', present (*see* ALLOY). It studies the changes which take place during heat treatment and during deformation, the effect of dissolved gases, of traces of impurity and phenomena associated with solidification. The ideal to which the physical metallurgist looks is to be able to forecast which metals will alloy together and what will be the properties of the alloys so formed. Conversely should an alloy with given properties be required he aims eventually to be able to indicate what metals to use, in what proportion and what heat treatment will develop the properties most fully. Considerable progress has been made in recent years, but this ideal is still very far from fulfilment. The structures of alloys containing more than 3 or 4 metals are so difficult to represent, even in models, that the object may never be attained except for alloys of the simplest kind.

Solidification of a metal. A pure metal cooling from the liquid state begins to solidify as soon as the freezing-point is reached only if nuclei (not to be confused with atomic nuclei) such as specks of dust are present to 'touch off', so to speak, the process of crystallisation. If these nuclei are absent the liquid will 'undercool' well below its true solidification temp.; then suddenly something, perhaps a slight shock, will cause crystallisation to begin and rapidly go to completion, resulting in a mass of very fine crystals. The more nuclei there are present the more crystals there will be, and therefore the smaller they will be. A small number of nuclei and crystallisation at the freezing-point yields coarse crystals. Rapid cooling causes undercooling and therefore induces small crystals, while very slow cooling has the reverse effect. Hence the reason why die-castings in metal moulds are fine-grained and large sand-castings are coarse-grained. For most applications fine grains are preferred. The growth of a crystal

takes place in a special way. As soon as a nucleus has initiated the formation of a crystal a number of branches spread outwards; soon these begin to grow secondary branches and these in turn grow their own side-shoots until eventually all the space between the original 'dendrites' is filled in and the whole becomes a crystal, as seen under the microscope. Normally there are numerous small dendritic systems all growing at the same time, so that in due course these touch and no more liquid is left. In an alloy where there are often phases of different freezing-points and low freezing-point impurities the high freezing-point phases always crystallise first and the low freezing-point phases and impurities solidify last in the grain boundaries or between the dendrites.

Metallography. Although the arrangement of the atoms in a crystal of a metal or alloy and hence the system in which it crystallises can only be determined by the methods of X-ray crystallography, the various phases which are present in an alloy and the arrangement of the crystals can be identified by ordinary microscopy. To do this one face of a small piece of the alloy is ground flat on a grindstone or file and then taken down almost to a polish on successively finer grades of emery paper, e.g. coarse, 1M, 1F, O, OO, OOO. Finally a revolving wheel covered with velveteen such as Selvyt cloth, to which has been applied an aqueous suspension of very finely divided alumina, magnesia or chromic oxide, removes the last remaining scratches and leaves a mirror finish. Alternatively the final polish can be obtained, in many cases, electrolytically. The specimen is made the positive electrode in a suitable liquid through which a direct current is passed. Etching the polished surface with dilute acid or other reagent for a few seconds, washing first in water and then alcohol, and drying in a stream of air reveals the micro-structure. The etchant is always a reagent which attacks the constituents to varying degrees. For instance, one phase may appear dark, another light because it is untouched and a third coloured. Grain boundaries appear as dark lines. Unlike the biological microscope which transmits light through the transparent specimen, the metallurgical microscope reflects light from the face of the opaque specimen. In recent years the electron microscope, using plastic replicas of the etched metal surface, has revealed much new information about the very finest micro-structures. Other recent developments are the phase contrast microscope which emphasises minute differences in the depth of etching and the reflecting microscope, which employs mirrors instead of lenses and has a much greater working distance than the ordinary microscope, thus enabling phase changes at high temp. to be followed without risk of damage to the instrument.

See also ALLOY; ELECTRO-METALLURGY; METAL TESTING; ORE AND ORE DRESSING; REFRACTORIES; WELDING.

See W. Hume-Rothery, *The Metallic State* 1931; R. Greaves and H. Wrighton, *Practical*

Microscopic Metallography, 1933, D. M. Liddell and G. E. Doan, *The Principles of Metallurgy*, 1933; W. D. Jones, *Powder Metallurgy*, 1937; E. C. Rollason, *Metallurgy for Engineers*, 1939; A. G. Ward, *The Nature of Crystals*, 1939; F. Seitz, *The Physics of Metals*, 1943; G. V. Raynor, *Introduction to the Electron Theory of Metals*, 1947; J. E. Garside, *Process and Physical Metallurgy*, 1949; C. S. Barrett, *Structure of Metals* (2nd ed.), 1953; L. S. Darren and R. W. Gurry, *Physical Chemistry of Metals*, 1953.

Metals. By reason of certain properties which are common to a large number of the elements and more or less absent in others, the elements are divided into 2 classes—*metals* and *non-metals*. Gold, silver, copper, lead, tin, etc., are M.; sulphur, bromine, hydrogen, phosphorus, etc., non-M. From earliest days M. have been distinguished from all other substances by their peculiar properties and applied to useful purposes. In the earliest hist., we have records of the use of the 7 M., gold, silver, lead, copper, iron, tin and mercury. The M. are usually opaque; their smooth surfaces reflect light to a high degree, giving them the property known as metallic lustre; they are good conductors of heat and electricity. All M., except mercury, are solid at ordinary temps., and all of them will crystallise under suitable conditions. They are usually characterised by having high specific gravities relative to the non-M., but there are exceptions to this, notably lithium (0·534), sodium (0·98), potassium (0·86), beryllium (1·85) and calcium (1·54). The melting points of the M. range from 26° C. (caesium) to as much as 3270° C. (tungsten), excluding mercury which freezes at −38·9° C. Some M., like antimony, are quite brittle, while others, like iron, possess great tenacity, while malleability is very common. The non-M., on the other hand, may be either gases, liquids or solids, possessing little tenacity. They do not give the peculiar metallic lustre (graphite does, however, show a very definite lustre) and are bad heat and electricity conductors. Their sp. gr. is low, and hardness usually poor, whilst the solids are often very brittle. The 2 classes of M. and non-M. merge into one another, and certain elements are placed sometimes in one class and sometimes in the other, according as the distinction is based on physical or chemical properties. Arsenic, for example, possesses many of the physical properties of a metal, but in its chemical reactions it is more nearly allied to the non-M. Such elements as these are sometimes known as metalloids.

The chief chemical properties of M. include their strong affinity for certain non-metallic elements, e.g. sulphur, chlorine and oxygen, with which they form sulphides, chlorides and oxides. The metallic oxides are solid white or coloured bodies with an earthy appearance. Sometimes these oxides dissolve in water to give alkaline hydroxides (e.g. sodium, potassium, calcium). In any case there is always at least one oxide of a given metal which will function as a basic oxide by dissolving in acids to form salts,

together with water. This capacity for the production of basic oxides is a very distinctive one. At the same time it must be remembered that a few metallic hydroxides (such as those of aluminium and zinc) can behave as 'amphoteric electrolytes' by exhibiting both basic and acidic properties, under favourable conditions. M. will, when fused, enter into the forming of *alloys* (q.v.). Because of their strong affinity for other elements M. are generally found combined with other elements, and consequently they have to be extracted from their ores by processes described under METALLURGY. The halogen compounds of the metal are stable as a general rule and even in the cases where this is not so the decomposition of the halides by water is only of a partial nature. Thus sodium chloride is perfectly stable in contact with water, bismuth chloride is partially decomposed or hydrolysed by cold water, whilst the chloride of a non-M. like phosphorus is completely decomposed under like conditions. Again the M. have the power of entering into the formation of complex salts, e.g. iron in potassium ferrocyanide $K_4Fe(CN)_6$. The non-M. do not do this. The tendency of M. to combine with hydrogen is very small. They either do not form hydrides at all, or if they do the resulting compounds are of a very loose nature (*see* CALCIUM and SODIUM). This raises the question as to whether the element hydrogen is to be regarded as a metal or as a non-metal. The facts are conflicting. In appearance hydrogen is a gas, and physically a typical non-metal. It shows (unlike non-M. such as sulphur) little tendency to combine with M., but, on the other hand, the compounds formed are more like salt in appearance than a typical alloy of one metal with another. But hydrogen shares with the M. that all-important electro-positive character to an exceptionally high degree. It gives rise to the hydrogen ion (q.v.), which, like the metallic ions, carries a positive charge. No non-metal can do this. In the processes of electro-chemical deposition (*see* ELECTROLYSIS) M. act like hydrogen and are always set free at the cathode. Many of the M. can decompose water or steam with the production of hydrogen, whilst many more are capable of dissolving in acids to form salts, often with the production of hydrogen. The following schemes are essentially connected with M.:

Metal + acid = salt + hydrogen.
Metal oxide + acid = salt + water.
Metal hydroxide + acid = salt + water.
Metal carbonate + acid = salt + water + carbon dioxide.

Classification. Sev. schemes of classification of the M. have been suggested from time to time. One old method depended on the relative ease of decomposition of water and of acids by them. A modern scheme is based on measurements of the potential difference between a metal and a normal solution of one of its salts under standard conditions, taking the zero value as that of a platinum electrode saturated with

Metal	Symbol	Atomic Number	Atomic Weight	Melting Point, °C.	Specific Gravity	Specific Heat
Lithium . .	Li	3	6·94	186	0·534	0·94
Beryllium .	Be	4	9·02	1300	1·85	0·38
Sodium . .	Na	11	22·997	97·5	0·98	0·28
Magnesium .	Mg	12	24·32	650	1·74	0·25
Aluminium .	Al	13	26·97	658	2·7	0·218
Potassium .	K	19	39·096	62·5	0·86	0·166
Calcium . .	Ca	20	40·07	810	1·54	0·15
Scandium .	Sc	21	45·10	1200	2·5	
Titanium .	Ti	22	48·10	1665	4·5	0·113
Vanadium .	V	23	50·96	1720	6	0·12
Chromium .	Cr	24	52·01	1550	6·9	0·12
Manganese .	Mn	25	54·93	1260	7·2	0·107
Iron . .	Fe	26	55·84	1535	7·86	0·11
Cobalt . .	Co	27	58·94	1480	8	0·106
Nickel . .	Ni	28	58·69	1452	8·8	0·103
Copper . .	Cu	29	63·57	1083	8·95	0·092
Zinc . .	Zn	30	65·38	419·4	6·92	0·096
Gallium .	Ga	31	69·72	30	5·9	0·079
Germanium .	Ge	32	72·60	958	5·4	0·074
Arsenic .	As	33	74·96	Sublimes	5·73	0·08
Rubidium .	Rb	37	85·44	38	1·52	0·019
Strontium .	Sr	38	87·63	800	2·63	0·074
Yttrium .	Y	39	88·9	1490	5·5	
Zirconium .	Zr	40	91·0	1530	6·4	0·07
Columbium or ⎱ Niobium . ⎰	(Cb) ⎱ Nb ⎰	41	93·1	2478	12·7	0·071
Molybdenum .	Mo	42	96·0	2620	10·2	0·065
Ruthenium .	Ru	44	101·7	1900	12·1	0·061
Rhodium .	Rh	45	102·91	1910	12·1	0·058
Palladium .	Pd	46	106·7	1550	12	0·058
Silver . .	Ag	47	107·88	960	10·5	0·055
Cadmium .	Cd	48	112·41	320·9	8·65	0·057
Indium .	In	49	114·8	155	7·3	0·057
Tin (Tetragonal)	Sn	50	118·7	231·9	7·31	0·056
Antimony . .	Sb	51	121·77	630	6·68	0·051
Caesium .	Cs	55	132·81	26	1·9	0·048
Barium .	Ba	56	137·37	850	3·7	0·068
Lanthanum .	La	57	138·90	810	6·16	0·045
Cerium .	Ce	58	140·25	630	6·9	0·05
Praseodymium .	Pr	59	140·92	940	6·48	0·045
Neodymium .	Nd	60	144·27	840	6·96	
Samarium .	Sm	62	150·43	1300	7·8	
Europium .	Eu	63	152·0			
Gadolinium .	Gd	64	157·26			
Terbium .	Tb	65	159·2			
Dysprosium .	Dy	66	162·52			
Holmium .	Ho	67	163·4			
Erbium .	Er	68	167·7			
Thulium .	Tm	69	169·4	300	11·9	0·033
Ytterbium .	Yb	70	173·6			
Lutecium .	Lu	71	175·0			
Hafnium .	Hf	72	180·8	1700		
Tantalum .	Ta	73	181·5	2996		
Technetium .	Tc	43				
Tungsten .	W	74	184·0	3370	18·7	0·0358
Rhenium .	Re	75		3180		
Osmium .	Os	76	190·8	2600	24	0·0312
Iridium .	Ir	77	193·1	2290	22·4	0·032
Platinum .	Pt	78	195·23	1755	21·5	0·032
Gold . .	Au	79	197·2	1060	19·3	0·031
Mercury .	Hg	80	200·61	−38·9	13·595	0·033
Thallium .	Tl	81	204·39	304	11·85	0·033
Lead . .	Pb	82	207·20	327	11·35	0·031
Bismuth .	Bi	83	209·00	271	9·78	0·030
Radium .	Ra	88	225·95	? 700	? 5	
Thorium .	Th	90	232·15	1450	11·1	0·028
Uranium .	U	92	238·17	? 1850	18·7	0·028

hydrogen at 1 atmosphere pressure in contact with a solution normal in respect to hydrogen ions. Some of the results in volts are Li — 3·02; K — 2·92; Na — 2·72; Mg — 2·38; Al — 1·67; Zn — ·76; Fe — ·43; Ni — ·25; Sn — ·14; Pb — ·13 (H O); Sb + ·1; Bi + ·2; Cu + ·34; Hg + ·79; Ag + ·80; Au + 1·5. In this electromotive series, one metal will replace another lower down in the series thus:

$$Zn + CuSO_4 = ZnSO_4 + Cu.$$

The further they are away in the series the better the chance of the change taking place. The M. may be classified into (1) LIGHT METALS: (a) *alkali metals*, e.g. potassium; (b) *alkaline earth metals*, e.g. calcium; (c) *earthy metals*, e.g. aluminium; and (2) HEAVY METALS: (a) *metals whose oxides form weak bases*, e.g. iron; and (b) *noble metals*, e.g. gold. Another method of classification adopted more generally is to take them in their order as suggested by the periodic system (*see* CHEMISTRY). Thus:

I. (a) Lithium, sodium, potassium, rubidium, caesium, francium; (b) copper, silver, gold.

II. (a) Beryllium, magnesium, calcium, strontium, barium, radium; (b) zinc, cadmium, mercury.

III. (a) Scandium, yttrium; (b) aluminium, gallium, indium, thallium; (c) the rare earth metals.

IV. (a) Titanium, zirconium, thorium; (b) germanium, tin, lead.

V. (a) Vanadium, niobium, tantalum; (b) arsenic, antimony, bismuth.

VI. (a) Chromium, molybdenum, tungsten, uranium.

VII. Manganese.

VIII. Iron, cobalt, nickel, ruthenium, rhodium, palladium, osmium, iridium, platinum. *See* list of works cited under CHEMISTRY. *See also* ALLOY; ATOM AND ATOMIC THEORY; ELEMENTS. *See* Iliffe, *Metals and Alloys*, 1949.

Metalwork, art of shaping and joining metal either for decorative or utilitarian purposes, or for a combination of these. The many uses to which metals (q.v.) may be put are the result of their properties; they are malleable, ductile, fusible (*see* CASTING), and capable of being joined together by the application of heat (*see* SOLDER and WELDING). In the purely decorative uses of metal the precious metals take first place. They were probably the first metals known to man and have from the earliest times been used in the making of jewellery and articles of personal adornment (*see* GOLDSMITHS and SILVERSMITHS).

The working of metal precedes the Bronze Age (q.v.). Considerable skill was attained in early civilisations in working gold and copper before the discovery of bronze. Copper was known to the Mediterranean civilisation as early as 3500 BC and bronze about 2000 BC. In the second millenium also tin was being worked in Britain. Iron was known in China and India much earlier, and artistic work in iron was being carried out in Egypt before the first millenium.

With the coming of bronze, solid casting and then hollow casting were developed. Casting, hammering and riveting are the basic methods in M. Other techniques which developed later are inlaying, damascening (q.v.), niello work (q.v.), engraving, embossing (q.v.), repoussé (q.v.) and filigree (q.v.). Enamelling (q.v.) is another form of decorative M.

Examples of skilled M. survive from all early civilisations, including the Minoan, Sumerian, Egyptian, Indian and Chinese, and reveal that all methods of treating metal were known and practised. The precious metals, bronze and copper were preferred for decorative and artistic work until late Rom. times, iron finding its uses chiefly in the making of weapons and utensils. In the Middle Ages, however, wrought iron was put to decorative uses. Early Gothic work from the 11th to the 14th cents. is notable for its elaborate scrolls and flower designs, decorative hinges, locks and grilles. The dignitaries of the Church and the nobles turned their wealth into plate, thus giving ample opportunity to the smith. Later Gothic work was heavier, more geometrical and regular in design. Iron was treated cold, and the metalworker borrowed his style from the stonemason. The file, the saw and the drill took the place of the forge for artistic work. Pierced work became the fashion; that is, the riveting of decorative pieces to sheet metal, thus building up the decoration against a solid background. An excellent example is the screen made by John Tresilian, 15th cent. work in St George's Chapel, Windsor. Examples of oriental M. came to be known in Europe as a result of the Crusades and the commerce conducted by Venice. It. smiths were encouraged to perfect the art of engraving, gold and silver inlay and damascening. In Italy in the Renaissance the quatrefoil design prevailed in open-work wrought-iron grilles. During the early Renaissance M. was as a result of classical influences excluded from architecture as much as possible in the work of Palladio and others. By the end of the 16th cent., however, particularly in Venice, M. had come into use for railings, screens, balconies, staircases, lamp holders, etc. Mention must also be made of the Renaissance M. in Germany and Spain, principally in the service of the Church. The method of chiselling the required article from the solid iron came to be known as peculiarly French from the excellent work done in the 15th cent., but it later gave way to the It. style of working with thin strips of metal. In the baroque period of the later Renaissance, however, the Fr. smiths gave free play to elaborate designs in wrought iron, and during the 17th cent. the Fr. influence was predominant in Europe. The great châteaux of France show examples of wrought-iron gates, balustrades and staircases which are unsurpassed. One of the greatest of the Fr. smiths, Jean Tijou, came to England at the Invitation of William III and examples of his work are to be seen in Hampton Court Palace and St Paul's Cathedral. The 18th cent. was the great period of Eng. wrought-iron work, which only declined when cast iron came into general use. This was the result of using coal in smelting, first tried in England by Dud Dudley (q.v.). Wren used cast iron for the railings round St Paul's Cathedral. The use of M. in the service of architecture must not obscure its other uses as a means of artistic expression in the hands of the locksmith, the pewterer and coppersmith, the brassfounder (for church candlesticks, lecterns and memorial brasses) and the sculptor. Decorative work in lead is not common because of the nature of the material and is to be seen mainly on cisterns and waterpipe heads.

In recent times in Europe and the U.S.A. there has been an increasing use of M. in furniture and a revival of wrought iron in interior decoration. Greater opportunities have been allowed for original design, bringing new life to an art which suffered through the 19th cent. from the standardised production of decoration in cast iron and brass. *See also* BRONZE AGE; IRON AGE; IRONWORK. *See* C. J. ffoulkes, *Decorative Ironwork from the Eleventh to the Eighteenth centuries*, 1913; G. K. Geerlings, *Wrought Iron in Architecture*, 1929; D. Smith, *Metalwork*, 1948; H. Maryon, *Metalwork and Enamelling* (3rd revised edition), 1954; *also* the handbooks issued by the Victoria and Albert Museum.

Metamorphism, term used in geology to denote changes in chemical or mineral composition, taking place at some time after the original formation of the rocks. The term is most often applied to changes due to the action of temp. or pressure below the surface of the earth, and when these changes have greatly modified the original characteristics of the rocks, the products are referred to as metamorphic rocks. Metamorphic rocks may be derived from both igneous and sedimentary rocks. The process of M. may be subdivided according to which agent of M. predominates. Thermal M. is due principally to the action of heat and takes place around the edges of igneous intrusions, where the crust is locally heated by the intrusion of molten material, and new minerals are formed in response to the rise in temp. Tough, compact, structureless rocks known as hornfelses are formed by thermal M. Dynamic M. is caused largely by the effects of movements in the earth's crust. At shallow depths movements merely result in a crushing of the rocks, but at deeper levels the mechanical breakdown may be accompanied by the growth of new minerals. Rocks formed by dynamic M. include mylonites, which are very fine-grained and generally break readily into platy fragments, and some varieties of schist. In some parts of the earth, especially in anct mt chains where erosion has exposed rocks formed at considerable depths, great expanses of metamorphic rocks are found. These rocks are said to be the products of regional M. in which both heat and pressure have played a part. Schists, showing a clear crystalline structure and having a strong tendency to part along closely spaced parallel planes, and gneisses, which are coarser-grained than schists and less strongly foliated, are

common products of regional M. Their mineral content varies according to the composition of the parent rocks. *See* A. Harker, *Metamorphism*, 1939. *See also* GEOLOGY.

Metamorphosis, change in form which many animals undergo during their life hist. The larval existence is usually passed in an environment in which the animal can accumulate food supplies sufficient to enable differentiation to be completed during a resting stage. This may be passed in complete quiescence, as in the pupation of insects, or the 'rest' may be of a much more partial nature, as in the transformation of tadpole to frog. Some animals achieve their final adult form by a series of gradual changes, shown progressively at every moult, and are said to undergo incomplete M. Marked M. occurs in many aquatic animals, in Amphibia, Insecta and in many animal parasites. The larva of some Crustacea changes its form sev. times before reaching the adult stage. Work on Amphibian larvae has shown that their M. may be prevented by extirpation of the thyroid or of the pituitary gland. The M. of normal tadpoles may be accelerated by injecting appropriate extracts of either of these glands. The M. of Amphibia depends on the products of the endocrine system, and certain strains of axolotls apparently never metamorphose in nature, but do so if they are given thyroid preparations. By preventing frog or toad tadpoles from rising to the surface of the water, their M. may be retarded for a year or more; if the larvae are then allowed to come to the surface, they metamorphose in the usual way. In such typical examples as the M. of caterpillars into pupae and then butterflies and the maggot to puparium and then housefly, Wigglesworth has shown that insect M. is also controlled by hormones secreted by glandular portions of the brain. The adult portions arise from separate groups of cells which remain quiescent in larval life, due to the inhibiting action of a hormone which disappears before M. Some threadworms have a free-living larval form which assumes the adult form in a plant or animal host. Other threadworms, freshwater mussels and ichneumon flies are among the animals parasitic as larvae and free-living as adults. Parasites having a larval form in one host and becoming adult in a second or even a third host are not infrequent. Certain larval hookworms and tapeworms parasitise invertebrata and the adults live in vertebrata. *See* INSECTS; PARASITISM.

Metaphor (Gk *metapherein*, to transfer) is a similitude expressed without any indication of comparison. For example, instead of saying 'He fought like a lion', using a metaphor we would say 'He was a lion in the fight'. It can be described as a compressed simile (q.v.). This figure of speech is extremely common and has enriched the Eng. language more than any other. Everyday phrases like 'a ray of hope', 'a flight of fancy', 'the sunset of his years', are all metaphorical. Mixed M. occurs when the writer combines incongruous comparisons in the same sentence, as in Addison's lines:

'I bridle in my struggling muse with pain,
That longs to launch into a bolder strain.'

Mixed M. must not be confused with a legitimate succession of metaphors, as in Macbeth's speech on sleep:

'The death of each day's life, sore labour's bath,
Balm of hurt minds, great nature's second course.'

See also FIGURE OF SPEECH.

Metaphysics, name originally applied to those books of Aristotle which followed his *Physics*, and which his editors called the books 'after the physics' (*meta ta phusika*). As a philosophical term it is first used by Boethius (480–525). The medieval scholars held M. to be the science of Being as such, and divided it into general M. or ontology (q.v.), dealing with the immaterial concepts of essence, existence, causality, etc., and special M., comprising psychology and natural theology. The great debates of the Thomist and Scotist schools on the real distinction of essence and existence, as well as the disputes between the Arabian and Christian Aristotelian philosophers, were all fought on the battlefield of M.

In modern times the word has been variously applied, but is usually defined as the science which treats of the most fundamental problems of knowledge and reality. Knowledge is discussed in the article EPISTEMOLOGY, and M. is dealt with here only as touching upon the nature of reality transcending experience. The very possibility of a science beyond experience has been denied by numerous philosophers and many works called metaphysical should rather be termed inquiries into the possibility of M. Thus Kant's celebrated work, *Die Kritik der reinen Vernunft*, is a mere inquiry into the possibility of a theoretical science of things beyond experience, and concludes with a denial of such possibility. Hence some modern philosophers have considered Kant as no metaphysician, but as a critic of the mental faculties, whose labours were to be the precursors of a new system of speculation. Positivism (q.v.) likewise appears to deny the possibility of M. and certainly rejects its use.

Metaphysicians are concerned with 6 main problems in discussing the nature of reality: (1) The existence of anything permanent lying as it were behind and forming the basis of the constantly changing phenomena of experience. The early Ionian philosophers, the Eleatics, Plato, Aristotle and Spinoza all affirm such permanent reality against such opponents as Heraclitus, Bergson and W. James. (2) The unity or otherwise of reality. The attempt to answer this question has given rise to monism (q.v.) and pluralism (q.v.). The former has found its prin. adherents in Thales, Anaxagoras, the Eleatics, Plato and Spinoza, whilst pluralism is represented by such names as Democritus, Descartes and Leibniz. (3) Assuming that reality is not one but many, is it of one kind? Leibniz maintains that the monads which constitute the total of reality are of one spiritual kind, but differ in degree. Descartes, on the other hand, argues a plurality of substances, both material and mental, and God from whom both are distinct. (4) The number of fundamental attributes belonging to reality. The defenders of monism, such as Leibniz, the materialists, voluntarists (e.g. Schopenhauer, Nietzsche) and neutral monists (e.g. W. James, Bertrand Russell), all hold one such attribute. A multiplicity of irreducible attributes is defended by Spinoza and Descartes, and seems to be implicit in von Hartmann's 'philosophy of the unconscious'. (5) The relation between the various units or modes of reality. The mechanists and determinists affirm that each is absolutely determined by the others. The opposite view, allowing at least some measure of freedom of self-determination, is taught by creative evolution (Bergson), emergence (Lloyd Morgan, S. Alexander), teleology, libertarianism, necessitarianism and the extreme school of tychism. (6) Finally the existence of anything which can be called divine. Generally the atheists and materialists deny such a reality. Their opponents may be classed as theists, deists and pantheists. Theists include all the historical churches; deists many freethinkers of the 17th and 18th cents.; and pantheists spiritual monists, the stoics and Spinoza.

Besides the works of those mentioned above, *see* A. E. Taylor, *Elements of Metaphysics*, 1903; E. A. Burtt, *Metaphysics the Foundation of Modern Physical Science*, 1925; J. Mackenzie, *Outline of Metaphysics*, 1929; F. H. Bradley, *Appearance and Reality*, 1930; E. W. F. Tomlin, *Approach to Metaphysics*, 1947; J. K. Feibleman, *Ontology*, 1952; T. R. De George, *Classical and Contemporary Metaphysics*, 1962; T. Ando, *Metaphysics: A Critical Survey of Its Meaning*, 1963; W. H. Walsh, *Metaphysics*, 1963; D. A. Drennan (ed.), *A Modern Introduction to Metaphysics*, 1963; J. R. Benardete, *Infinity: An Essay in Metaphysics*, 1964; P. Bowes, *Is Metaphysics Possible?*, 1965.

Metaphysical Poets. The title M. P. was given by Dryden to that school of poetry of which Donne (q.v.) was the founder and greatest exponent. Original in thought and method, however, the fault of this school is the attempt to use lyric poetry as a vehicle for the expression of all manner of subjective or reflective ideas, and hence to subordinate to subtlety of thought and reasoning that appeal to the primary emotions which is the very *raison d'être* of lyric poetry. The use of philosophical *conclusions*, as exemplified by Francis Thompson's magnificent apostrophes to the sun, is perfectly legitimate; but the M. P. proved the futility of using the *processes* too. *See* studies by J. B. Leishman, 1934, and H. C. White, 1936; Sir H. Grierson, *Metaphysical Lyrics and Poems of the Seventeenth Century* (selected with an essay), 1950; Joan Bennett, *Four Metaphysical Poets* (2nd edition), 1953; Helen C. White, *The Metaphysical Poets*, 1962.

Metasequoia, genus of trees which is closely allied to the *Sequoia* (q.v.) or *Wellingtonia*. Up to 1945 it was known only from palaeobotanic specimens as a fossil age tree. But in that year were discovered 3 trees in NE. Szechuan, near the Hupeh border, which were subsequently identified as the same species known by the palaeobotanists. It was known that the species *M. glyptostroboides* was widely distributed, but it was on the verge of extinction. Expeditions to Szechuan in 1946–7 located in all only 100 trees. The largest was found to be more than 108 ft high and about $7\frac{1}{2}$ ft in girth and, like the *Larix* and *Taxodium*, it is deciduous. Many genera which existed during the Mesozoic or Triassic eras are known to us only through fossilised remains, although some examples exist, as in *Ginkgo biloba*, 'the maidenhair tree', of genera which have survived until the present day. *See also* FORESTRY and TIMBER.

Metastasio (originally **Trapassi**), **Pietro** (1698–1782), It. poet and librettist, b. Rome, of humble parents, but adopted by the famous scholar G. V. Gravina. In 1730 he succeeded Zeno as court poet in Vienna. Among the composers who availed themselves of his writings were Alessandro Scarlatti, Handel, J. C. Bach, Gluck and countless others. He also wrote some beautiful *canzonette*. His chief dramatic works were *Didone abbandonata*, *Catone in Utica*, *Olimpiade* and *La Clemenza di Tito*.

Metauro (anct **Metaurus**), riv. of Italy, in Le Marche which rises in 2 headstreams (Meta and Auro) in the Apennines and flows ENE. past Urbania and Fossombrone to the Adriatic, 2 m. SE. of Fano. Length 68 m. On its bank in 207 BC the Romans defeated and slew Hasdrubal (q.v.).

Metaxas, John (1871–1941), Gk general and statesman, b. Ithaca. He studied military science in Germany, and became prof. in the Gk military academy (1903) and, later, joined the general staff, serving with distinction in the Balkan wars of 1912–3, and becoming chief of staff. In 1935 he joined the gov. as minister without portfolio at the time of Venizelos's abortive military and naval coup, and later played an important part in the restoration of King George II. Becoming minister of war and then Prime Minister, he assumed the role of dictator, and projected drastic reforms in all branches of Gk life. When Italy invaded Greece in 1940 he led Greece in her resistance. *See* GREECE, *History*; GREECE, SECOND WORLD WAR CAMPAIGN IN.

Metayer System, system of land cultivation, in vogue principally in France and Italy, which has been evolved mainly by compulsion of circumstances as a result of the decay of feudal serfdom. Under this system the peasant landholder or cultivator pays no rent either in money or kind, but tills the soil for the landowner on condition of receiving half (hence the name, from Low Lat. *medietarius*, in its turn derived from *medius*, middle) its produce or some other proportion (in Italy usually two-thirds) thereof; while the landlord furnishes the whole or part of the stock, tools and implements of husbandry. A true peasant proprietor has the strongest of incentives to make his holding a success; but the quasi-partnership of metayage can, strictly speaking, be dissolved at will by the landowner, or, what amounts to the same thing, be rendered impracticable by a perfectly legal augmentation of demands on the part of the dormant partner. For an appreciation of the merits of the system *see* J. C. L. de Sismondi's *New Principles of Political Economy*, book iii, 1819, and J. S. Mill's *Principles of Political Economy*, ch. viii, 1848.

Metazoa. The animal kingdom is broadly divided into 2 main sections, the Protozoa and the M. The former are non-cellular, though they in many cases exist in colonies; M.s are multicellular, and include all the higher forms of animal life. The place of sponges in this classification is uncertain.

Metcalf, John (1717–1810), road and bridge builder, b. Knaresborough of poor parents and known as 'Blind Jack of Knaresborough', having lost his sight through smallpox at the age of 6. He was determined to conquer his disability and became a good horseman, swimmer and cock-fighter. In the '45 rebellion he was a recruiting sergeant on the King's side and fought at Falkirk and Culloden. Afterwards he operated a stage coach between York and Knaresborough and later constructed nearly 200 m. of turnpike road.

Metchnikov, Ilya (Elie) (1845–1916), Russian biologist, b. Ivanavka. Educ. at Kharkov, he graduated at 19, and went to Heligoland to study marine organisms. At Giessen he worked under Leuckart, with whom he went to Göttingen; at Munich under Siebold, and thence to Naples. Returning to Russia in 1867 he became Dozent in zoology at Odessa and St Petersburg, being appointed prof. of zoology and comparative anatomy at Odessa, 1873–82. With Kowalewsky he laid the foundations in 1866–86 of the cellular embryology of the invertebrates. In 1882 he removed to Messina, and pub. his *Intra-Cellular Digestion*, the first intimation of the function of the white corpuscles of the blood. He became director of the new bacteriological laboratory at Odessa, 1886. In 1888 he went to Paris, where a laboratory was provided for him by Pasteur at the École Normale. In 1892 he issued *The Comparative Pathology of Inflammation*, showing the curative nature of inflammatory process. In 1901 *Immunity from Infectious Diseases* attributed immunity to activity of phagocytes. He originated the theory of phagocytosis in 1884; he shared the Nobel prize for medicine, 1908. *The Nature of Man*, 1903, discussed among other things the cause of ageing, mainly poisonous matter formed in large intestine. Wrote also *Optimistic Essays*, 1907; *The Prolongation of Human Life*, 1910; and monographs on various invertebrates. *See* life by his second wife, 1920.

Metellus Scipio, Quintus Caecilius (1st cent. BC), Rom. senator, son of P. Scipio Nasica. He was adopted by Q. Caecilius Metellus (hence his compound name), member of a family distinguished for nearly 200 years in Rom. public life. Pompey, who had married M. S.'s daughter, had him elected as his colleague in the consulship (52 BC), and it was M. S. who in 50 BC proposed in

Mexico

The library of the new university outside Mexico City is decorated with brightly coloured mosaic.

A typical example of Spanish Colonial architecture in Puebla.
Photos: Eldon Studios

Mexico

A plantation of agave,
source of sisal hemp;
half the world's supply is
grown in the state of
Yucatán.

Although these men of
Hanitzio are fishing on
a small scale, fisheries are
of increasing importance
to the country's economy.
Photos: Eldon Studios

Mexico

Mexican Indians in the market-place of Ocotlán.

Part of the ruins of Chichén Itzá, city of the old Maya empire in Yucatán. Founded in the 6th cent., it developed most fully between the 11th and 13th cents.
Photos: Eldon Studios

Middlesex

Anne Boleyn's Gateway,
Hampton Court Palace.
The palace was begun in
1514 by Cardinal Wolsey.
*Ministry of Public
Building and Works*

London Airport, at
Heathrow, main air
terminal for the U.K. (the
picture shows a Super
VC 10 and a Boeing 707).
B.O.A.C.

Marble vestibule at Syon
House, seat of the dukes
of Northumberland since
1604.
G.L.C.

Mining

The copper deposit at Chuquicamata, Chile, is the largest in the world.
Anglo-Chilean Society

An open-cast copper mine at Mount Morgan in Queensland, Australia; the cut is 750 ft deep.
Australian News and Information Bureau

Asbestos mining at Thetford Mines in Quebec.
National Film Board of Canada

Mining

Automation in British coal-mining: R.O.L.F. (Remotely Operated Longwall Face), showing the shearer, cable-carrier and self-advancing powered supports.
National Coal Board

Scene below ground at the Giant Yellowknife gold mine in Canada.
Radio Times Hulton Picture Library

the senate that Caesar should disband his army or be declared a public enemy. On the outbreak of civil war (49 BC) he was appointed governor of Syria, and in 48 commanded the Pompeian centre at Pharsalus. From there he crossed to Africa, but was defeated by Caesar at Thapsus in 46 and committed suicide.

Metempsychosis, *see* TRANSMIGRATION.

Meteor, or **Shooting Star.** M.s are metallic or stony particles revolving in vast numbers around the sun, becoming briefly visible only when they plunge through the earth's atmosphere and produce luminous trails across the night sky. As the earth's orbital speed is 18 m. per sec., while M.s may reach 26 m. per sec. in nearly parabolic orbits, their relative speed may exceed 40 m. per sec. on entering the atmosphere. They begin to glow at a height of about 60 m., and are usually completely vaporised between 50 and 40 m. A M. as bright as 1st magnitude weighs only one-hundredth of an oz. 'Sporadic' M.s may be seen on any dark night at the rate of a few per hr, but on occasion a much more numerous 'shower' is seen, diverging from a point in the sky called the *radiant*. The orbits of M.s indicate that practically all of them belong to the solar system. Streams of M.s move around the sun, and a shower occurs when the earth meets such a M. stream. Well-known ann. showers are the Perseids (Aug.), the Orionids (Oct.) and the Geminids (Dec.). For dates *see Whitaker's Almanack*.

Some M. streams are associated with the orbits of comets (q.v.). The Perseids appear to be spread uniformly around the orbit of a comet that appeared in 1862. The Leonids swarm in a short section of the orbit of a comet of 1866; they produced spectacular displays in 1833 and 1866, but were thereafter deflected by Jupiter and Saturn, and now produce only scatted showers in Nov. The orbit of Halley's comet crosses the earth's path twice, producing the Eta Aquarid shower in May and the Orionid shower in Oct.

A M. produces in the upper atmosphere a short-lived column of hot, ionised gas, which strongly reflects radio waves and radar pulses. Thus radar enables M.s to be observed by the million, in daylight as well as in darkness; by this means Lovell (q.v.) and others at Jodrell Bank discovered important daytime M. streams. It is estimated that the total mass of meteoric material reaching the earth daily is about 10 tons; and that up to 1000 tons may be encountered in the form of tiny micrometeorites that drift slowly down through the atmosphere.

See J. G. Porter, *Comets and Meteor Streams*, 1952; A. C. B. Lovell, *Meteor Astronomy*, 1954; F. G. Watson, *Between the Planets*, 1956; G. S. Hawkins, *Meteors, Comets, and Meteorites*, 1964.

Meteorite, a meteor (q.v.) that is large enough to survive the passage through the earth's atmosphere and to reach the surface before being vaporised. The fall is preceded by the appearance of a large incandescent meteor or *fireball*, and is sometimes accompanied by explosive and roaring sounds. From the few

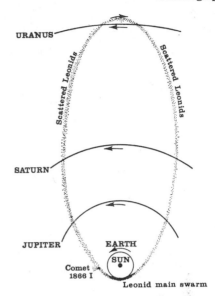

THE ORBIT OF THE LEONID METEORS

reliable observations of fireballs, it appears that they entered the atmosphere from orbits resembling those of some asteroids (q.v.); M.s are not associated with meteor showers. There is no record of serious injury having been caused by one. M.s often fall in groups, distributed over sev. miles. The largest M.s blast out craters; the giant M. crater in Arizona is 4200 ft across and 570 ft deep, and must have been caused by a prehistoric M. of more than a million tons. Large M.s fell in Siberia in 1908 and 1947. Most M.s have a thin, dark, vitrified crust. They are of 2 types: stony M.s or *aerolites*, and iron M.s or *siderites*. Of about 35 known individual M.s weighing more than 1 ton, the majority are of iron and nickel. The largest are the Hoba M. in SW. Africa, and the Ahnighito M. found in Greenland, weighing 34 tons. Stony M.s consist mostly of silicates; the largest known, weighing more than a ton, fell in Nebraska in 1948. It is estimated that sev. M.s large enough to be seen and found fall somewhere on earth every day, amounting to perhaps 200 tons per year. *See* H. H. Nininger, *Out of the Sky*, 1952; F. Heide, *Meteorites*, 1964; and references *under* METEOR.

Meteorograph, instrument which gives a continuous record of the fluctuations in the temp., pressure and humidity of the atmosphere. One type consists of a combined thermograph, barograph and hydrograph, and lines are plotted on a cylinder which, driven by clockwork, revolves once in about 8 hrs. Made of aluminium and enclosed in a cage, the whole apparatus weighs only about 30 to 40 oz., and is attached, for use, about 60 ft below a kite. The more usual light variety can be used with hydrogen-filled balloons rising to the stratosphere. Thus a continuous record of the meteorological conditions prevailing at various heights in the atmosphere is obtained. The development of radio-sonde (q.v.) is limiting the use of M.s.

Meteorological Office, estab. in 1855 under the Board of Trade and transferred in 1867 to the control of the Royal Society, the issue of forecasts and warnings being suspended until 1874, when it was resumed under pressure from the Board of Trade and the public. Since 1919 the M. O. has been administered by the Air Ministry (q.v.). The responsibility for the work of the Brit. Rainfall Organisation was transferred to the M. O. in 1919. The M. O. maintains numerous stations for daily telegraphic reports on which weather forecasts and warnings of gales are based, and also stations in various parts of the country for giving meteorological information to aircraft. It also collects and discusses meteorological observations from ocean and land areas all over the world, and maintains observatories for weather study and cognate subjects. It also carries out research in meteorology, in which it is advised by the Meteorological Research Committee. Pubs. of the M. O.: *Daily Weather Report, Daily Aerological Record, Weekly Weather Report, Monthly Weather Report, Meteorological Magazine, Marine Observer, British Rainfall, Observatories' Year Book, Scientific Papers, Geophysical Memoirs* and *Meteorological Glossary*; *also* handbooks, manuals, textbooks and tables of frequencies and averages.

Meteorological Society, Royal. The first Eng. society was founded in 1823 and was followed by the M. S. of London, which existed from 1836 to 1842. The Brit. M. S. was initiated in 1850 and assumed its present designation as R. M. S. in 1882. The Scottish M. S. amalgamated with the R. M. S. in 1921. Pubs. of the society: *Quarterly Journal, Weather, Bibliography of Meteorological Literature, Reports of the Council*, and *Proceedings. Meteorological Record*, which contained statistical data, is now superseded by pubs. of the Meteorological Office, such as the *Monthly Weather Report*. Offices: 49 Cromwell Road, London, S.W.7.

Meteorology is the science which deals with the study of atmospheric conditions and changes which mainly constitute the weather. Apart from some observations included by Aristotle in his book *Meteorologia*, very little was accomplished in the direction of making M. an exact science until the end of the 16th cent., when Galileo and the Florentine academicians constructed the first thermometer of any importance, and when Torricelli in 1643 discovered the principle of the barometer. The work of Boyle on gases, and that of his assistant, Hooke, on barometers, advanced the physical basis of M. Hooke actually constructed a barometer with the weather indications, a practice which is still followed. The invention of a superior mercury thermometer by Fahrenheit provided further means for the record of weather elements. In the early years of the 19th cent. a chain of meteorological stations was estab. in France, and weather maps were constructed from the data collected. The first weather map in England showing the trade winds and monsoon was made in 1688, and the first telegraphic weather report appeared on 31 Aug. 1848, in the *Daily News*, but was suspended after 3 months; after considerable demand the report was resumed on an improved basis in Mar. 1849. The first daily telegraphic weather map was prepared at the 1851 exhibition, but the Meteorological Office (q.v.) was not estab. in London until 1855. It was then founded as a dept of the Board of Trade under the direction of Adm. Fitzroy; since 1919 it has formed part of the Air Ministry. In 1860 Adm. Fitzroy began the first regular daily collections of weather observations by telegraph and with them produced the first Brit. daily weather report, the first daily printed maps appearing in 1868. The advance of M. since the inventions of the telegraph, telephone and wireless has been extremely rapid; for these made possible that rapid collection of data at H.Q., most essential in the production of a useful forecast.

With the growth of aviation and scientific planning M. has grown in importance. Meteorological services throughout the world have increased in both size and complexity. Observations are collected not only from thousands of land stations, but also from special weather ships, from aircraft, and from self-recording and automatic transmitting stations, such as the radio- or radar-sonde (q.v.). Radar (q.v.) is also used to 'map' a rain cloud, a thunderstorm, or even a tropical storm, on a small screen. Atmospherics, so annoying to the radio listener, have been traced to thundery activity, and specially equipped stations pick up bearings of these storms so that it is possible to plot all activity within a thousand miles or so. Weather knows no boundaries or frontiers. All countries unite in the World Meteorological Organisation (a specialised agency of the U.N.) of which the directors of the meteorological services of all countries from the supreme authority, the Congress, under whom, to make recommendations, are various commissions and sub-commissions of specialists for such subjects as agric. M., climatology, instruments and methods of observation, synoptic weather information, etc. There are also 6 regional commissions, one for each major continental region of the globe.

The atmosphere consists of a mixture of gases, of which oxygen and nitrogen account for about 99 per cent. together with small quantities of argon, carbon dioxide, helium, hydrogen, krypton, neon, ozone, radon and xenon; to these gases, which are in almost fixed proportions, are added very variable amounts of water vapour, water and ice drops, and smoke, dust and other particles which are so small that they are kept up in the air by turbulence. None of the gases can be seen, not even the water vapour, but smoke and dust particles are often visible as haze, and the water and ice drops can be seen as mist, fog, cloud, drizzle, rain, snow or hail. The nature of

M. is to describe, record, explain, and forecast the changes in the quantities of these elements, including also the changes in the physical state of the air.

OBSERVATIONS. Observing stations may be classified as follows:

Observatories, where reliable standard and absolute measurements are made as far as possible with autographic instruments, which are often duplicated for checking and research purposes. Some elements such as atmospheric electricity, solar radiation, etc., are measured only at observatories and other research estabs. Kew is the main meteorological observatory in Britain, but other observatories are at Eskdalemuir in the S. uplands of Scotland (where the earth's magnetism is the chief interest), Lerwick in the Shetlands (where the aurora is also studied) and Valentia in SW. Ireland.

Climatological reporting stations report the general daily weather conditions, and make observations at standard hours during the day so as to provide the cumulative data, such as average temp., maximum and minimum temps., rainfall, sunshine, mean pressure, days of fog, frost, snowfall, and of the extent'and persistence of snow-cover. After statistical analysis, climatic charts and tables are constructed containing the frequency of the different weather elements, such as gales, frost, etc. Climatic information from the hundreds of Brit. stations is pub. in the *Monthly Weather Report*, and periodically in tables of averages and frequencies.

Crop-weather stations make special observations for use in agric. M., where the elements of the weather need to be studied in very close detail, micrometeorology (q.v.) or microclimatology as it is called. Most agric. plants grow no higher than 4 ft, and it is necessary to know the temp., humidity and wind in great detail at heights less than this to be able first to study, and then to control, the plant diseases spread by the aphis or wind-borne virus. The details of frost hollows, wind breaks, and the sharpness of frost necessary to damage a plant must all be studied.

Rainfall stations, of which there are nearly 5000 in Great Britain alone, measure the amount of rain that falls. Most stations measure the daily amount, but some stations in out of the way moorland areas only measure the rainfall monthly. Their observations are pub. in an ann. vol., *British Rainfall*, a selection being pub. every month in the *Meteorological Magazine*.

Synoptic reporting stations, where observations are made simultaneously throughout the world, report in a mutually agreed form so that the observations at any one station can be compared directly with the observations at any other. These observations are mainly restricted to the elements considered essential for forecasting; they have to be brief and easily assimilated into code form suitable for rapid transmission to all parts. Reports are received at a national centre and a selection broadcast immediately for use by all other countries. Reports from more than 50 Brit. stations are broadcast regularly every 6 hrs, and almost as many every 3 hrs. Similarly large numbers of stations report at the same intervals from all other countries.

Meteorological observations, for whatever purpose, must be clear, precise and strictly comparable between one station and another. It is easy to decide whether it is fine or cloudy, or if there is a thunderstorm; the distinctions between rain, snow and hail are obvious; sleet is wet snow, melting snow or a mixture of rain and snow; soft hail is half way between snow and hail; and drizzle, which consists of very small drops, is half way between rain and cloud, the water drops being just large enough to fall to the ground. It is useful also to describe the rain as showery, intermittent or continuous, as light, moderate or heavy. More precise measurement of rain can be made with a rain-gauge (q.v.); this will give the total rainfall during a given period or with special types of gauge the rate of rainfall. Wind strength and direction can be measured in great detail by anemometers and wind vanes, (*see further* WIND). Clouds are closely related with the other weather conditions and careful observations of the amount and types of cloud are made (*see further* CLOUD). Fog (q.v.) may be thought of as cloud on the surface; it can indeed be cloud on the surface which drifts with the wind (as in sea and hill fogs); fog can also form on clear, quiet nights by the contact of the air with the cooling earth, the air then becoming saturated and condensing some of its water vapour into droplets. In M. an arbitrary distinction is made between fog and mist; objects being visible at more than 1 km. in mist, but not in fog.

Above any place the atmosphere extends vertically from some 200 m. or more, and, although some indication of the conditions of the air above can be deduced from cloud observations, actual measurements of the physical state of the atmosphere are made at as great a height as possible. The weight of the air above any point presses downwards, producing a force in all directions which is called the air pressure; it is measured by barometers and barographs, the unit of measurement being the millibar (mb.). With increase in height there is less air above and therefore pressure decreases with height. Providing the temp. of the air is known it is quite easy to calculate this decrease in pressure; near sea level it amounts to about 3 mb. in every 100 ft. Since it is useful to compare pressures between many stations at a constant level pressures are 'reduced to sea level', i.e. a suitable correction is added to or subtracted from the pressure as read by the barometer to find out what it would read if it were at sea level in the same place. To measure the temp. of the air is more difficult, for a thermometer gives the temp. of itself, not necessarily of its surroundings. In addition the temp. varies irregularly with heights, particularly in the first few feet above the earth's surface. On a hot, sunny afternoon the temp. at 4 ft may easily be 5° F. or 10° F. lower than the temp. near the surface, whereas on a following clear night the reverse usually occurs. On the other hand the temp. of air which rises 100 ft only cools about $\frac{1}{5}°$ F. by reason of its change of height and consequent expansion due to decrease in pressure. Therefore temps. are read at a standard height (usually 4 ft) above the surface, and not reduced to sea level. To make the thermometers the same temp. as the air they are sheltered in a Stevenson screen. The humidity of the air is found by comparing the temps. measured by the ordinary termometer and by one whose bulb is covered by moist muslin (*see further* HYGROMETER, where other methods of measuring humidity are also described). The temp. and humidity in the upper air are measured by attaching instruments to an aircraft, to a small balloon, or even to a rocket. With aircraft measurements have been made up to more than 50,000 ft, with balloons to 100,000 ft, and with rockets to more than 100 m. At first balloon-carrying instruments had to be recovered before any results were obtained; now, the radio-sonde (q.v.) balloon transmits the observations to earth. Balloons can also be used to measure the winds aloft, for, since they are carried by the wind, following their movement by theodolite, direction-finding radio or radar will enable their drift to be calculated, thus determining the winds at the different heights through which the balloon passes. Reports from ships follow exactly the same patterns as those from land stations, but also include the sea temp. and the state of the sea. Under international agreement, special ships are equipped to cruise at a fixed 'ocean weather station' making observations, including radio-sonde ascents at the standard intervals. These ocean weather ships are also used as navigational beacons for transoceanic aircraft, and provide rescue services if required. Transport and other aircraft also make reports. Special meteorological aircraft fly at a constant height, occasionally measure the sea-level pressure (by flying at a very small known height above the sea), and describe the weather as they fly along. Normally they make an ascent from near sea level to about 18,000 ft and, a little further on, a descent, thus obtaining the same data (to the limited height reached) as by 2 radio-sonde ascents. Before the estab. of ocean weather ships many meteorological flights used to cover large stretches of the Atlantic, but they are not so numerous there now. New routes are, however, being flown, one of which is from Alaska to the N. pole and back.

ANALYSIS OF OBSERVATIONS. The huge mass of synoptic data collected and disseminated for forecasting purposes is plotted on synoptic weather charts in a form suitable for rapid and easy assimilation. Modified copies of these charts are pub. daily by most meteorological services. The Brit. *Daily Weather Report* is divided into 3 sections, and contains a detailed map of the weather over the Brit. Isles, and also a less detailed map of the weather over the N. hemisphere, and the *Daily Aerological Record* contains full reports of the radio-sonde ascents made over the Brit. Isles, and from some of the ocean weather ships, together with maps of the

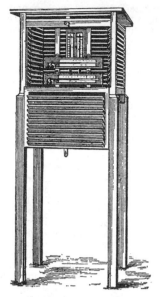

STEVENSON SCREEN
Front view with door open.

heights of the 700 mb., 500 mb. and 300 mb. pressure surfaces which give a picture of the winds at 10,000 ft, 18,000 ft and 30,000 ft; there is also a map of the height of the tropopause. Ships' reports are plotted on the same charts, using the same symbolic form. Data from radio-sondes and aircraft are plotted on upper air charts and on temp.-height diagrams, the diagram in use in Britain being the tephigram (q.v.). With the help of this diagram it is possible to predict the formation or otherwise of clouds, showers or thunderstorms, and sometimes to identify where the air comes from. (*See also* WEATHER FORECAST.)

In the early days of weather charts, when few stations were available, the features that seemed to stand out most clearly were the easily recognisable patterns made by isobars (lines joining places of equal pressure), forming regions of low pressure (depressions or cyclones), regions of high pressure (anticyclones) and the connecting patterns: ridges, troughs, cols and secondary depressions. It was soon noticed that the wind bore a definite relation to pressure which was enunciated by Prof. Buys Ballot of Utrecht in 1857 in the form 'that, in the N. hemisphere, if you stand with your back to the wind, pressure is lower on your left hand than on your right, while in the S. hemisphere the reverse is true'. This law was later confirmed by a dynamical formula based on physical principles which gave a theoretical speed and direction to the wind in the free atmosphere. known as the gradient wind. This wind blows along the isobars with low pressure on the left in

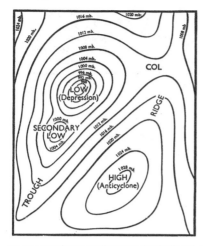

CHARACTERISTIC PRESSURE PATTERNS ON A
WEATHER CHART

the N. hemisphere with a speed proportional to the gradient of pressure between the isobars (the closer the isobars are together, the stronger the wind). It is increased by a smaller quantity for anticyclonic curvature, and decreased similarly for cyclonic curvature of the isobars. The effect of the curved isobars is normally small enough to neglect; then the theoretical wind is known as the geostrophic wind. However, both the gradient and geostrophic winds neglect change of pressure with time and vertical motion, as well as frictional forces. These terms are all generally small and the wind speed at about 2000 ft above the surface may be read off the synoptic chart by placing a scale appropriate to the lat. across the isobars. The surface wind is affected considerably by friction and the configuration of the land, especially in hilly regions where it tends to blow along the valleys; the speed is usually less than the gradient wind, and the direction at an angle (often 20–30°) across the isobars from high pressure to low. The effects neglected by the gradient-wind equation are important, for it is these that lead to inflow of surface air into regions of low or falling pressure and, conversely, of outflow from regions of high and rising pressure. If the surface air is flowing into a region then the air must escape by rising and spreading out aloft; this leads to adiabatic cooling and instability, cloud and unsettled weather; conversely diverging air leads to subsidence, adiabatic warming, stability, clear skies and settled weather. These theories are, in general, confirmed by the observation of unsettled weather in cyclones and quiet weather in anticyclones. When air blows over hills and mts it is forced to rise and, if it contains enough moisture, cloud is formed; if the process continues long enough, or the air is very moist or unstable, rain falls. This type of rain is called orographic rain, and is very prevalent on coasts exposed to frequent winds from the sea. Even if rain is not formed (if, for instance, the moist layer is only shallow) drizzle sometimes occurs, and even very low hills may be shrouded in cloud; these are the conditions of a 'scotch mist' in the W. Isles or the 'crachin' of S. China. Areas sheltered from these winds, which have lost some of their moisture on the hills, are likely to have finer and drier weather.

During the First World War Norwegian meteorologists, notably V. and J. Bjerknes, using a very close network of reporting stations, discovered that the change from one relatively homogenous type of air—air mass as it is called—to another was often very rapid and usually along a clearly marked line. These lines were called fronts. Near fronts are regions of widespread cloud rain, or snow, as will be shown later; the air masses, however, also exhibit many different weather characteristics according to whether they are moving from colder to warmer regions or vice versa, and whether they contain much or little moisture. If they move to warmer regions the lower atmosphere becomes warm and the air becomes unstable, leading to cumulus cloud and showers (*see further* TEPHIGRAM); if they move to colder regions the lower air becomes colder, and may therefore develop fog or a very low cloud sheet known as stratus. At first the air masses were called polar or tropical, but present practice is to classify the air masses broadly according to where they originate as a more or less homogenous mass, laying stress on both humidity and temp. They are:

Arctic or antarctic air, which originates over the polar ice-caps, Greenland and Antarctica, and on reaching low lats. is very cold and unstable; it carries little moisture even if saturated. As it passes over unfrozen seas, cumulus, cumulonimbus and showers develop; the showers are very frequent on exposed coasts.

Polar continental air, which may be even colder than arctic air at low levels; it is not so cold aloft, is stable and very dry, having its origin in winter anticyclones that persist over Russia, Siberia and Canada. When passing over the sea convection clouds develop more slowly than with arctic air; stratus or stratocumulus appear first, shower cloud develops after a comparatively long sea track. The lowest temps. in England are recorded when this air mass comes from the E., since it has only a very short sea track.

Polar maritime air, which is formed when arctic air has been for some time over the ocean or may form in both anticyclones and stationary depressions over the oceans in high lats. It is moist and unstable, and very prolific of cumulus, cumulonimbus and showers. It is the commonest air mass over the Brit. Isles.

Tropical maritime air. This forms in sub-tropical anticyclones (such as the semi-permanent Azores anticyclone), and is moist and stable. It brings muggy conditions to Britain with SW. winds. It is moist and stable with sea fog or very low stratus cloud very prevalent over the S. and W. coasts of Britain. The top of the cloud is rarely above 5000 ft, often only about 2000 ft, with clear blue skies above.

Tropical continental air, which accumulates over the hot continents in summer, mainly central Asia, Africa, mid U.S.A. and Australia. It is very unstable, but dry, so rarely contains any cloud. It is hazy, and, with rising winds, picks up sand from the deserts to form sand-storms, such as the khamsin or ghibli in Egypt. When tropical continental air from the Sahara crosses the cooler Mediterranean Sea it picks up moisture and brings hot, oppressive, damp conditions; it is known as the sirocco.

Equatorial air. This exists in a wide semi-stagnant belt near the equator; it is hot, moist and unstable, with cumulus cloud, which develops into cumulonimbus and heavy showers or thunderstorms when it passes over the land in the afternoon. Because of the high moisture content it is very uncomfortable, and the very dry tropical continental air, which sometimes replaces it in W. Africa, is therefore known as the harmattan or 'doctor'.

Fronts. At the transition zone between 2 air masses the warmer air, being lighter, rides over the colder, so that, providing the following air is moving the faster relative to the front, when warm air replaces cold (a warm front) the warm air slides above the cold, and when cold air replaces warm (a cold front) the cold air undercuts the warm air and pushes it upwards. This is not a convective process, although latent instability (*see* TEPHIGRAM) may become active after some lifting has taken place, and produce convection. Sheet clouds are therefore formed, and steady rain falls. Generally rain begins to reach the ground when the cloud base comes below about 10,000 ft; since the warm front slopes at about 1 : 100, the rain belt at a warm front is about 200 m. wide, following a 'prefrontal' cloud belt 400 m. wide. The haloes which can be seen through the cirrostratus of a warm front are therefore usually a sign of coming rain. The cold front normally has a slope twice as steep as that of the warm front, so that the rain belt is not so wide; further, the warm air high up at the rear of the cold front often travels faster than the cold air beneath, so that it slides down the cold front, which, in that part, is therefore free from cloud. Instability often develops at a cold front, and then the frontal cloud no longer remains in sheet form, but develops into cumulonimbus with heavy rain or even thunder. If, owing to friction, the warm surface air is held back, it gets trapped by overrunning cold air, which causes violent turbulence leading to a line-squall with a typical roll cloud. When a cold front overtakes a warm front the cold air meets cold again, and the warm air is lifted entirely off the surface. This combined front is called an occlusion. If the cold air ahead is warmer than that behind, it too is lifted, the cold occlusion; if the cold air behind is warmer, it slides up above the former as at a warm front, the warm occlusion. When equatorial air replaces tropical continental air, as in

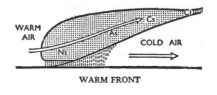

WARM FRONT

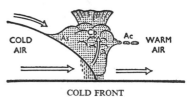

COLD FRONT

For the meaning of abbreviations of cloud types *see* CLOUD.

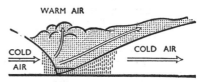

BEGINNING OF AN OCCLUSION

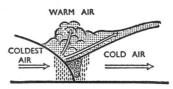

COLD OCCLUSION

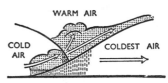

WARM OCCLUSION

the beginning of the SW. monsoon in India, a monsoon front is formed which is a cold front below and a warm front above. This system has a very high latent instability, so that monsoon rains often break with a violent thunderstorm.

Formation of depressions in the temperate zone. The present theory of the formation of depressions, first stated by the Norwegian school of meteorologists, is that they start as small bends or waves in a more or less stationary front, with warm air inside the bend, which is convex towards the cold air. In favourable circumstances the depth of the waves increases, and the wave itself moves along the front, the first part of

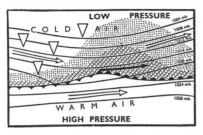

1. Wave develops on an almost stationary front.

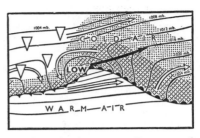

2. Wave develops a small centre of low pressure, the wind beginning to circulate round it.

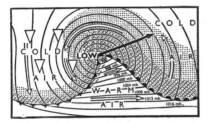

3. The fully developed depression; the occlusion is beginning to form. The rain is a little in front of the cold front in some places.

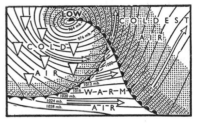

4. The occlusion is now well developed (here a warm occlusion); the end of the cold front is becoming more parallel with the isobars and moves very slowly.

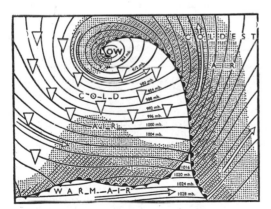

5. The occlusion has begun to curl around the centre of the depression, which is now moving quite slowly. A new wave has begun to develop on the almost stationary part of the cold front.

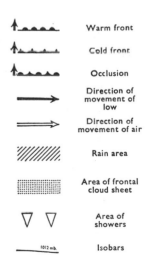

STAGES IN THE LIFE OF A DEPRESSION

the wave acting as a warm front (warm air overtaking cold), and the rear part as a cold front. As the depth of the wave increases the air pressure falls inside and around it, and the winds in the neighbourhood increase. The cold front moves faster than the warm, begins to overtake it, and an occlusion is formed; eventually the cold air lifts all the warm air out of the circulation of the low or pushes it well away from the centre where the front then tends to become quasi-stationary; a new low may then develop. The process is illustrated on p. 387, with shaded areas representing the rain, dotted areas where the sheet cloud persists, and the international shower symbols where showers are most predominant.

Forecasting. When once a synoptic chart has been analysed and the causes of the different weather phenomena in the different parts understood, it is possible to 'move' the different weather conditions along from one place to another by measuring the gradient wind and making due allowance for such effects as large pressure tendencies, vertical motion, etc. Making allowance also for the different terrain which the new air masses and fronts would now occupy or have passed over, and for the different time of day, the weather a few hours hence may be described with a fair degree of accuracy. This is short-term forecasting; it is reasonably dependable for as much as 24 hrs ahead. For longer periods the number of interdependent factors becomes so large that the task, except in a few typical and well-estab. situations, is far too complex for any real accuracy today. Recently mathematical methods have been introduced for the prediction of the pressure patterns (*see* WEATHER FORECAST).

The upper air is now becoming a familiar region; it has long been known that the air temp. decreases from the ground upwards, except for certain levels known as inversions (associated with anticyclones or frontal surfaces) where the temp. may increase temporarily with height, and to an upper region called the stratosphere, where the temp. usually remains constant or with little change for sev. miles upwards. The level where the stratosphere begins is called the tropopause; below is known as the troposphere. The tropopause is at varying heights, being highest in equatorial air at about 50,000 ft, and lowest in arctic air at about 16,000 ft. Since the temp. decreases at high levels in the troposphere at about 4° F. or 5° F. in every 1000 ft the coldest air temp. is found, not at the poles, but in equatorial lats. at the tropopause where it is highest. In the stratosphere, as has already been stated, the temp. remains fairly constant for some 20 m., but at a height of about 25–30 m. it has been found to increase again, reaching, at a height of some 40 m., temps. higher than any experienced on the earth's surface; it drops to a minimum again at about 50 m. up, and then increases to very high temps. These temps., which were originally estimated from the propagation of sound, and have been measured in America, using rockets, are still a little

problematical, for the air is so thin at these great heights that it is doubtful what is meant by temp. Upper air charts, which are now drawn regularly, suffer from 2 great difficulties: the comparatively small number of observations, at best some 300 m. apart, except in the U.K., and the difficulty of knowing the height of the observation with any degree of accuracy. The height of the observation is, in fact, except when modern radar methods are used, calculated from the measured temps. and pressures up to that height. The gradient wind equation still applies at the higher levels, but, because of the decrease in air density, the wind speeds are much greater for the same pressure gradient than they are at the surface. However, by using in the gradient wind equation the change in height for constant pressure instead of the change in pressure for constant height, this difficulty is overcome. Consequently upper air charts are now drawn with contour heights of the 700 mb., 500 mb. or 300 mb. pressure surfaces, taking the place of isobars (as in the *Daily Aerological Record*). Further charts are now drawn showing the difference in height (thickness) between the 1000 mb., 500 mb. and 300 mb. pressure surfaces; the winds calculated from these charts represent not an actual wind, but the wind difference between the air near the earth's surface and the wind in the upper air, i.e. they illustrate the relative motion of the air at the 2 levels. Attempts are being made to extend the period of short-term forecasts by study of these charts, for the patterns have been found to change comparatively slowly. Additionally circulation indices (single figures expressing the total westerly wind current in a zone round the world) and other regional 'means', as well as short-period mean pressure and temp. maps, are being studied.

Since the Second World War there has been a very rapid development of M. which properly includes the whole of atmospheric physics. In weather forecasting, the greatest progress is in the calculation of future weather maps up to a few days ahead by solving the basic equations of fluid dynamics, using the most advanced electronic computers. The U.S.A. has introduced weather satellites which circle the earth at heights of a few hundred miles and transmit to ground stations photographs of the clouds taken by television cameras. The World Meteorological Organisation, in collaboration with the International Union of Geodesy and Geophysics, is planning a comprehensive attack on the study of the world's weather with the concept of a World Weather Watch. Automatic reporting stations, including floating buoys over the oceans, freely floating balloons, possibly sev. thousands at any one time, and a communication system based on special satellites capable of collecting and relaying observations entirely automatically are among the new ideas which are expected to bear fruit towards 1970. See D. Brunt, *Physical and Dynamical Meteorology*, 1939; O. G. Sutton, *Micrometeorology*, 1953; S. Petterssen, *Weather Analysis and Forecasting*. vol. i. and vol. ii., 1956; H. C. Willett and F.

Sanders, *Descriptive Meteorology*, 2nd ed., 1959; P. D. Thompson, *Numerical Weather Analysis and Prediction*, 1961; and many other text-books. A recent book for the general reader is R. C. Sutcliffe, *Weather and Climate*, 1965. *See* CLIMATOLOGY; CLOUD; FOG; HYGROMETER; RAIN AND RAINFALL; THUNDERSTORM; WAVE; WIND.

Meter, Electric, *see* ELECTRIC METERS.

Meter, Gas, *see* GAS METER.

Methane, or **Marsh Gas,** CH_4, the simplest hydrocarbon of the paraffin series. It is produced in nature by the decay of vegetable matter under water, and thus rises in bubbles from marshes and swamps. It also occurs in the natural gas of petroleum dists, is set free from fissures in coal as 'fire damp', and is one of the chief constituents of coal gas. It is prepared by heating a mixture of sodium acetate and soda lime, according to the equation: $C_2H_3O_2Na + NaOH = CH_4 + Na_2CO_3$. Better methods of obtaining the pure gas are (i) the action of water on aluminium carbide: $Al_4C_3 + 12H_2O = 4Al(OH)_3 + 3CH_4$, and (ii) the action of dilute hydrochloric acid upon methyl magnesium iodide: $2CH_3 \cdot MgI + 2HCl = 2CH_4 + MgI_2 + MgCl_2$.

M. is a colourless, tasteless gas, which is liquefied at $-11°$ C. under a pressure of 180 atmospheres. It burns with a pale blue flame and forms a highly explosive mixture with certain proportions of air or oxygen, the explosions in coal-mines being largely due to the ignition of such a mixture. It is almost insoluble in water, more soluble in alcohol, and is a very stable gas, resisting the action of a large number of reagents. When mixed with chlorine in the dark, no action occurs, but on exposure to sunlight an explosion occurs and carbon is deposited. In diffused sunlight no explosion occurs, but the hydrogen atoms are displaced by equivalent quantities of chlorine, with the formation of substitution products; the most important is chloroform, $CHCl_3$.

Methanol, *see* METHYL ALCOHOL.

Metheglin, *see* MEAD.

Methil, *see* BUCKHAVEN.

Methley, *see* ROTHWELL.

Method, Scientific, *see* SCIENTIFIC METHOD.

Methodism (Gk *methodos*, rule), name of a Christian organisation which originated with John and Charles Wesley. The term was first applied to a group of Oxford students who, led by the brothers Wesley, sought to acquire regular habits of religious study and prayer. In 1735 the Wesleys went out to Georgia in the hope of missionary work, but were not successful. On their return to England they both experienced, in May 1738, a spiritual transformation, which changed them and particularly John Wesley from scrupulous high churchmanship to itinerant, though disciplined, evangelism. The movement, which resulted from Wesley's organisation of his converts, did not easily fit into the Eng. Church system. In the early years there was much persecution and Wesley, debarred from many church pulpits,

took to preaching in the open air. When in 1784, Wesley laid hands on Thomas Coke to set him apart as superintendent of the rapidly growing work in America, he accelerated the gradual drift from the Church of England, which resulted soon after Wesley's death in the Methodists becoming a separate body.

Wesley preached the Arminian doctrine of universal salvation, which caused bitter controversies with the Calvinists, both inside and outside the Eng. Church. He laid great emphasis on the effects of Christian faith upon Christian character and believed that perfection in love was attainable in this life. He gathered his converts into societies, each member of which had to attend a weekly class meeting. His rules are still the basis of modern M.

During the 19th cent. there were many secessions from the Wesleyan Church—the Methodist New Connexion (1797), led by Alexander Kilham, who in his pamphlet *The Progress of Liberty*, 1795, asked for more power for laymen; the Primitive Methodists (1812), a revivalist body founded by Hugh Bourne and Wm Clowes and influential among the working class movements; the Bible Christians (1815) originating in the W. country; the Protestant Methodists (1828); the United Methodist Free Churches (1857).

In 1907, the New Connexion, the Bible Christians and the United Methodist Free Churches joined to form the United Methodist Church. In 1932, Wesleyans, Primitives and United Methodists became 1 organisation. Two small groups, the Wesleyan Reform Union and the Independent Methodist Churches, remained in separation.

Methodist organisation is 'connexional', The supreme governing body is a conference, which meets annually. In Wesley's lifetime this was a select ministerial council presided over by John Wesley himself. In the Wesleyan Connexion, lay representatives were not introduced until 1878 (women in 1911). Today it consists of ministers and lay representatives in equal numbers. Under Conference are the Dist Synod which includes all the ministers and elected laymen in each dist of England, Scotland and Wales, the chairman being a minister set apart for the responsibility by Conference. Each dist is composed of circuits—groups of societies, which share a staff of ministers. The chief court of the circuit is the Quarterly Meeting.

The work of the Methodist Conference devolves upon sev. large administrative depts, notably those for Overseas and Home Missions, Christian Citizenship and Youth Work. There are 7 theological colleges in England and sev. residential schools, notably Kingswood, Bath, which is the successor to the school founded by Wesley himself in Bristol. The *National Children's Home* is a Methodist organisation responsible to the Conference. The *Epworth Press* is the Methodist publishing house, which issues religious and general books and periodicals, the chief of which are *The London Quarterly and Holborn Review*, *The Preacher's Quarterly* and *The Methodist Magazine*. *The Methodist Recorder* is an independent newspaper.

John Wesley said in 1739, 'The world is my parish', and there are Methodist churches in the U.S.A., many of the countries of Europe, Africa and Asia, in Australasia, Lat. America and the W. Indies. There is a World Methodist Council, which, dating from 1881, seeks to implement another saying of Wesley's: 'The Methodists are one people in all the world, and it is their full determination so to continue.' But Methodism is fully committed to the Ecumenical Movement. Since 1925 Canadian Methodists have belonged, with the Congregationalists and Presbyterians, to the United Church of Canada. Since 1947 Methodists have participated in the Church of S. India, and, since 1964, in a United Church of Zambia. In most countries unity negotiations are proceeding, and, in England, reunion with the Anglicans seems the likely outcome of conversations which began in 1955.

In the U.S.A., where the work derives directly from Wesley's own preachers there are, in all, 7 Methodist Churches affiliated to the World Methodist Council, and innumerable smaller bodies. The Methodist Church in America is the second largest Protestant Communion with 24,000 pastoral charges, 40,000 churches, 27,000 ministers and over 11,000,000 members. The Church is episcopally governed, and is divided into 6 jurisdictions, with 103 Conferences and about 600 Dists.

In 1964, in association with the Conference in Great Britain and Ireland, there were 4500 ministers, 21,217 local preachers, 701,306 members and 495,696 Sunday school scholars. There are 19,272,185 members throughout the world. *See further under* BOURNE, HUGH; CLOWES, WILLIAM; COKE, THOMAS; WESLEY, JOHN and CHARLES; WHITEFIELD, GEORGE. *See* J. Wesley, *Journal*, *Works*, and *Letters* (various eds.); R. E. Davies, *Methodism*, 1963; E. S. Bucke (editor), *The History of American Methodism*, 3 vols, 1964; H. D. Rack, *The Future of John Wesley's Methodism*, 1965; J. H. S. Kent, *The Age of Disunity*, 1966; E. G. Rupp and R. E. Davies (editor), *The History of the Methodist Church in Great Britain*, vol. i, 1966.

Methodius, *see* CYRIL AND METHODIUS.

Methuen, Algernon, Sir (1856–1924), full name **Algernon Methuen Marshall Stedman**, founder (1889) of the publishing firm which still flourishes under his name. He was knighted in 1916.

Methuen, Paul Sanford, 3rd **Baron** (1845–1932), field-marshal, *b*. Minehead, Somerset, succeeded Frederick Henry Paul M., the 2nd baron (1818–91). He was descended from the lord chancellor of Ireland, John M. (*d*. 1706). Educ. at Eton, he joined the Scots Guards in 1864. He took part in the Ashanti war of 1874 and in the Egyptian war of 1882. He commanded 'Methuen's Horse' in the Bechuanaland expedition of 1884–5. During the Boer War of 1899–1902 he was in command of the 1st Div. of the First Army Corps. After defeating the Boers at Belmont, Enslin and the Modder R., he was

taken prisoner in 1902 by Delarey, but released. He was appointed commander-in-chief of the E. command in 1903, and was general officer commanding-in-chief of S. Africa, 1908–12. From 1909 to 1915 he was governor of Natal, and from 1915 to 1919 of Malta. He was made field-marshal in 1911.

Methuen Treaty, commercial treaty arranged between England and Portugal in 1703. It was negotiated by Sir Paul Methuen, and by it Portugal was to provide 28,000 troops for the war of the Sp. Succession (q.v.), Britain to maintain half of them; Portuguese wines were received at a lower duty than those imported from France; and a similar advantage given to Eng. wool in Portugal. It was abandoned in 1836. The popular consumption of port wine in England dates from the M. T.

Methuselah, according to Gen. v. 25–7, the son of Enoch and grandfather of Noah, of the family of Seth. He is the oldest man mentioned in the Bible, dying at the age of 969 years. This is, however, mere infancy compared with ages of the 10 antediluvian kings listed in the Babylonian tablets—e.g. Alulim 67,200 years, Alagar 72,000 (*see* B. Meissner, *Babylonien und Assyrien*, 2 vols., 1925). There is an obvious analogy between the Mesopotamian and the biblical lists. It is impossible to regard Gen. v as preserving a genuine historical tradition concerning the ages of the antediluvians.

Methven, vil. and par. in Perthshire, Scotland, 6 m. WNW. of Perth. The English defeated Bruce near here in 1306. Pop. (vil). 700; (par). 1670.

Methyl (CH_3), compound radical, i.e. a collection of atoms which can enter into the composition of a series of compounds and retain its identity. It functions in the role of a positive radical, and in this respect has something in common with the positive radical ammonium, NH_4. It has no stable separate existence, though it can be isolated for a very brief period (*see* RADICAL).

Methyl hydride or methane	.	$CH_3 \cdot H$
Dimethyl or ethane	.	$CH_3 \cdot CH_3$
Methyl chloride	. .	$CH_3 \cdot Cl$
Methyl alcohol	. .	CH_3OH
Methyl sulphate	. .	$(CH_3)_2SO_4$
Methyl cyanide	. .	CH_3CN
Methylamine	. .	CH_3NH_2
Methyl acetate	. .	CH_3COOCH_3
Dimethyl ether	. .	$(CH_3)_2O$
Nitromethane	. .	CH_3NO_2

Methyl Alcohol (CH_3OH), **Methanol** or **Carbinol**, the simplest of the monohydric alcohols, occurs combined in sev. natural substances, e.g. methyl salicylate, oil of winter-green. On distilling this oil with dilute potash an aqueous solution of pure M. A. is obtained. It was chiefly prepared from the products of the destructive distillation of seasoned hard wood, such as oak, thorn, birch and beech, from which the bark had been removed. The operation is performed in iron retorts at 200–260° C. The alcohol is obtained by redistilling the crude distillate over lime, finally purifying by the formation of the crystalline calcium chloride compound or of the oxalic ester, from which it is obtained by distillation with water or with potash. One hundred parts of dry wood produce about 50 parts of 'pyroligneous acid' containing 4 per cent of M. A., together with acetic acid, acetone, tar water, etc. M. A. is a colourless liquid (sp. gr. 0·814 at 20° C.); it boils at 64·7° C., and has a vinous odour and burning taste. It mixes with water in all proportions. When passed over a copper or nickel catalyst at 240° C. it decomposes into hydrogen and formaldehyde. This has important applications. It is largely used in the preparation of organic dyes and varnishes, and for the preparation of methylated spirit and perfumes.

Synthetic methanol. Methods have been perfected for the synthetic production of methanol. It had been known for some time that carbon monoxide could be made to combine with hydrogen, $CO + 2H_2 = CH_3OH$, with the aid of catalysts. Many of these have been investigated on the large scale, but the most efficient appears to be a mixture of zinc oxide and chromium sesquioxide obtained from basic zinc chromate. In presence of this water gas alone, or a mixture of hydrogen and carbon monoxide in the ratio $CO : H_2 = 1 : 2$, gives methanol at 350–400° C. under pressures of about 200 atmospheres. This is condensed and redistilled.

Methyl Benzene, see TOLUENE.

Methyl-Butadiene, see ISOPRENE.

Methyl-Glycine, see SARCOSINE.

Methyl Methacrylate, see PLASTICS.

Methylaniline, colourless liquid, smelling like aniline; chemical formula, $C_6H_5NH\cdot Ch_3$; sp. gr. 0·976 at 15 °; boiling point, 192°. It is is readily oxidised in air, when it becomes brownish in colour. It is obtained by heating aniline hydrochloride and methyl alcohol under pressure at 180°; the base is separated by adding an alkali and distilling in steam and, after separation, drying over caustic soda, and distilling. It can also be obtained by reducing methylene-aniline by zinc and sodium hydroxide. M. has been used as a drug under the name 'exalgin'.

Methylated Spirit. In order to meet the large demand for alcohol destined to be used for purposes other than for drinking, there are 2 alcohol mixtures which can be obtained duty free.

Mineralised methylated spirit. This is obtained by mixing 9 volumes of ordinary 'plain' spirit (which shall be not less than 50° under proof, and is usually more) with 1 volume of wood naphtha or wood spirit, and a small amount of mineral naphtha. The last ingredient serves the purposes of making the liquid unfit to drink. Since 1918 colouring material in the form of methyl violet has also been included. Such a spirit contains methyl alcohol (7·7 per cent), ethyl alcohol (83 per cent), water (9·21 per cent), as well as small amounts of acetone and other ketones, esters, unsaturated compounds and substances of a basic nature. This spirit finds wide application in everyday life. It gives a white opalescence when added to water. By law it may not be purified.

Industrial methylated spirit. This is meant to meet the need of an alcohol which contains a higher percentage of ethyl alcohol, and which can be employed for the many industrial operations in which this compound is required, particularly as a solvent for varnishes, drugs, perfumes, etc. It contains 95 per cent of ethyl alcohol and 5 per cent of crude naphtha, without the addition of any mineral naphtha. There is no colouring material added and no turbidity is given when mixed with water. Numerous restrictions are placed on the proper use of this form of spirit. It can only be obtained direct from the methylators in quantities of 5 gallons or over, and it must not be used for drinking purposes or left in any final product which can be taken internally.

Methylphenobarbitone, see BARBITURATES.

Metis, in Gk mythology, the personification of counsel, daughter of Oceanus and Tethys. Another legend makes her the first wife of Zeus, who, fearing she might bear a child more powerful than himself, devoured her in the 1st month of her pregnancy. Later there sprang from his head, full grown, Athena.

Metius, Adriaan (1571–1635), Dutch geometrician, b. Alkmaar. Among his works are *Doctrinae sphericae libri v., Calendarium perpetuum,* 1591, and *Praxis nova geometrica Problemata astronomica,* 1623 or 1625.

Metius, James (fl. 16th–17th cents.), brother of Adriaan, also a native of Alkmaar. He disputed with Lippershey (q.v.) the claim to have invented the refracting telescope in 1609.

Metohija, see KOSOVO-METOHIJA.

Metol, white, crystalline sulphate of para-methylaminophenol $C_6H_4(OH)$ $(NH.CH_3.$ $\frac{1}{2}H_2SO_4)$ made by heating *para*-chlorophenol with aqueous methylamine and copper sulphate. M. is used as a developer (see PHOTOGRAPHY), particularly for under-exposed plates. It darkens in light, and has the drawback of often producing skin trouble. See also PHENIDONE.

Meton (fl. 432 BC), Athenian astronomer. He is famous for having introduced, in collaboration with Euctemon, the metonic cycle, a period of 19 solar years used to determine eccles. feasts, since after this period the phases of the moon recur on the same dates. See GOLDEN NUMBER.

Metonymy (Gk *meta,* change; *onoma,* name), a figure of speech in which one word is used for another that it suggests, such as 'the bottle' for strong drink, 'Milton' for the writings of Milton, 'Stilton' for cheese originally made in Stilton. Typical examples are 'The pen is mightier than the sword', 'Trade follows the flag'. *See also* FIGURE OF SPEECH.

Metope (Gk *metopé,* a middle space), in architecture, the square space between each pair of triglyphs in the frieze of the Gk Doric Order.

See COLUMN.

Metre, measurement, *see* METROLOGY.

Metre, in poetry, is an arrangement of

syllables in an orderly succession so as to constitute verse. The syllables are divided into a number of similar or dissimilar groups, each of which constitutes a line or verse, and in modern languages the end syllables of these lines are often related by rhyme. The lines themselves can be subdivided into feet, each line normally consisting of a certain number of these feet regularly repeated. In Gk and Lat. verse, M. consisted of a regular succession of long and short syllables, and the verse accent did not usually coincide with the ordinary accent of each word. In England, however, quantity has ceased to be definite, and it is upon the accent or stress that M. depends. It is therefore with the alternation of accented and unaccented syllables that the laws of M. deal.

In English each foot is supposed to consist of an accented syllable combined with either 1 or 2 unaccented syllables or with another accented syllable. In this way 6 kinds of foot are available: (1) the *iambus*, of an unaccented followed by an accented syllable; (2) the *trochee*, of an accented followed by an unaccented syllable; (3) the *dactyl*, of an accented followed by 2 unaccented syllables; (4) the *anapaest*, of 2 unaccented syllables followed by 1 accented; (5) the *amphibrach*, of an accented syllable between 2 unaccented; (6) the *spondee*, of 2 accented syllables. These different feet are well illustrated in the lines written for the purpose by Coleridge, using the classical reckoning by long and short syllables:

'Trochee trips from long to short:
From long to long in solemn sort
Slow Spondee stalks; strong foot! yet ill able
Ever to come up with Dactyl trisyllable.
Iambics march from short to long;
With a leap and a bound the swift Anapaests throng;
One syllable long, with one short at each side,
Amphibrachys hastes with a stately stride.'

These different feet may be arranged so as to form various kinds of lines. Theoretically each line should consist of a certain number of similar feet, but in practice there is not often this regularity. Freedom in the use of syllabic equivalents makes the verse supple instead of stiff, and its value was clearly understood by so early a poet as Chaucer. The principle of syllabic equivalents is, briefly, that 2 unaccented syllables are equivalent to 1 accented. Hence, in spite of the normal demand for an accented syllable in each foot, many really consist of 3 unaccented syllables. This great freedom, which is characteristic of the best Eng. verse, makes it difficult to measure this verse by precise rules. Much of it could be scanned in many different ways.

It is possible, however, to speak of certain types of verse, and to show the normal construction of each. Perhaps the best-known verse is the *iambic pentameter*, known as the *heroic couplet* when each pair of lines is connected by rhyme, and as *blank verse* when unrhymed. The elegiac is a similar measure, but here the rhymes are

alternate and the poem is commonly divided into stanzas of 4 lines. *Rhyme royal*, used by Chaucer in sev. of his minor poems, is written in stanzas of 7 iambic pentameter lines rhyming *ababbcc*. *Octosyllabics*, consisting generally of 4 iambic feet, are useful for rapid narrative, and were commonly used by Scott and Byron for this. The M. known as *ballad M.*, also common in hymn tunes, consists of lines of 8 and 6 syllables alternately, rhyming alternately. The *Spenserian stanza*, used throughout Spenser's *Faerie Queene*, is made up of eight 5-foot iambic lines, followed by an iambic line of 6 feet, rhyming *ababbcbcc*. See AMPHIBRACH; ANAPAEST; DACTYL; IAMBUS; SPONDEE; TROCHEE.

See G. Saintsbury, *A History of English Prosody*, 3 vols. 1906–21; L. Abercrombie, *Principles of English Prosody*, 1923; T. Taig, *Rhythm and Metre*, 1929; S. O. Andrew, *The Old English Alliterative Measure*, 1931; C. M. Ing, *Elizabethan Lyrics: English Metres and their Relation to Poetic Effect*, 1951; D. Davie, *Purity of Diction in English Verse*, 1952; S. E. Sprott, *Milton's Art of Prosody*, 1953.

Metre Bridge, *see* WHEATSTONE BRIDGE.

Metric System, *see* METROLOGY.

Metrology. *See also* PHYSICAL CONSTANTS. The following symbols and abbreviations are used in the tables, which include the metric equivalents of imperial units and the imperial equivalents of metric units:

Av = averdepois (spelling, *see* O.E.D.); c = cubic; cc = cubic centimetre; ch = chain; cm = centimetre; ct = carat; cwt = hundredweight; dr = drachm; dwt = pennyweight; fl. oz = fluid ounce; ft = foot; fur = furlong; gal = gallon; gm = gram; gt = grain (troy, av); hr = hour; in = inch; kg = kilogram; km = kilometre; lb = pound av; m = metre; mg = milligram; mm = millimetre; oz = ounce av; p = pole; pt = pint; qt = quart; sec = second; sq = square; st = stone; yd = yard.

I. WEIGHTS AND MEASURES

British Legislation. The legal basis of the existing system of weights and measures in the U.K. is the Weights and Measures Act, 1963. Metric measures have been legal for trade since 1864 but it was not until 1897 that the Board of Trade was legally required to include metric weights and measures among its standards. Both the yard-pound-gallon system and the metric system are now legal in the U.K. for use in trade, and the President of the Board of Trade announced in May 1965 that it is hoped that this country will reckon substantially in metric units by 1975. Indeed the 1963 Weights and Measures Act defines the yard and pound, and effectively the gallon also, in metric terms.

Administration. Although the central authority for weights and measures administration is the Board of Trade (acting through its Standard Weights and Measures Dept) the executive work is carried out by inspectors appointed independently by the local authorities: these appointments, however, can be given only to candidates who have passed the qualifying examination of the central authority. Those so appointed then generally become members of the Institute of Weights and Measures Administration. The net cost of the local service (after allowing for the statutory fees charged for verification) is a charge on the local rates.

Formerly the routine verification and stamping of traders' weights was the prin. function of the local inspectorate, but the trend of legislation has so widened their duties that they are now in constant contact with every phase of local trading practice relating to the sale of goods by weight or measure. It is the responsibility of the Standard Weights and Measures Dept of the Board of Trade to draft regulations for the instruction and guidance of inspectors, to design apparatus for their use and to do such other central administrative work as may be required to give effect to the law.

The units and standards. The yard is defined in the Weights and Measures Act, 1963, as equal to 0·9144 metre exactly and 'metre' is there defined as having the meaning appearing to the Board of Trade to reproduce in English the meaning assigned to it by the General Conference of Weights and Measures (CGPM). As the metre is defined by the CGPM as 1 650 763·73 wavelengths in vacuum of the radiation corresponding to the transition between the energy levels $2p_{10}$ and $5d_5$ of the krypton-86 atom (XI CGPM 1960), the yard is also effectively defined in terms of these standard optical wavelengths. Though the 1963 Act lays it down that the 'United Kingdom Primary Standard' of the yard is the former Imperial Standard Yard, a bronze bar dating from 1845 which was the ultimate standard until 1964, it is clear in the 1963 Act that the length of this standard has to be ascertained in terms of the defined yard equal to 0·9144 metre.

Similarly the pound unit is now defined as 0·453 592 37 kilogramme exactly, and 'kilogramme' is defined as having the meaning appearing to the Board of Trade as reproducing in English the definition currently assigned to it by the CGPM. Both the pound and the kilogramme are units of mass, or quantity of matter, not of weight in the sense of a force; owing to the variation of gravity over the earth's surface the latter meaning would be unacceptably vague. The 'United Kingdom Primary Standard' of the pound is the former Imperial Standard Pound, a platinum billet also dating from 1845; this also must now be checked by reference to the international metric standard. For a brief summary of the historical background up to the middle of this cent. *see* A. E. Berriman, *Historical Metrology*, 1953. More recent information can be found in the 2 following papers: 'The yard unit of length', *Nature*, vol. 200, page 730, 1963, and 'The United Kingdom standards of the yard in terms of the metre', *Brit. Jour. of Applied Physics*, vol. 15, page 291, 1964. There are 5 copies of the yard standard and 5 of the pound, kept in places of safety; this arrangement is a relic of the need, when the yard and pound were independent of

other standards, to provide reliable means of replacing them accurately in the event of their loss or damage. The former national copy of the metre, which until 1960 was defined by the international prototype metre in the custody of the International Bureau of Weights and measures (B.I.P.M.) near Paris, and the national copy of the international kilogramme, are in the custody of the National Physical Laboratory (N.P.L.), Teddington. The N.P.L. has the duty, when necessary for the maintenance of an accurate standard, of referring the national kilogramme to the B.I.P.M. It realises the metre on a routine basis by direct reference to optical wavelengths. To enable the Standard Weights and Measures Dept to fulfil its obligations to local weights and measures authorities the N.P.L. calibrates the dept's most important standards to specially high accuracy according to an agreed schedule complying with the Weights and Measures Act, 1963.

The gallon is defined as the weight in air of density 0·001 217 g/ml of 10 lb. of water of density 0·998 859 g/ml weighed against weights of density 8·136 g/ml. The litre (abbreviation l), until 1964 equal to its 1901 value i.e. that vol. of water which at its temp. of maximum density has a mass of 1 kilogramme, was redefined by XII CGPM 1964 as equal to 1 cub. decimetre (dm³) i.e. 0·001 cub. metre. This is 28 parts per million smaller than the 1901 litre, but the Board of Trade takes the view that although the definition of the gallon involves the litre, the content of the gallon is unchanged, the board not having issued an order giving a trans. of the CGPM 1964 definition. This metric equivalent of the gallon is accordingly 4·546 09 cub. decimetres (dm³) *see* 'SI', below).

The only other basic unit in the Brit. system of measurement is the sec. of time interval, which is common to Brit. and metric systems. Formerly defined by astronomers in terms of the rotation of the earth, in 1960 (XI CGPM) it was re-defined as the fraction (1/31 556 925·9747) of the tropical year for 1900 Jan. 0 at 12h ephemeris time—the tropical year is the time interval between consecutive passages, in the same direction, of the sun through the earth's equatorial plane, and the date mentioned is the astronomers' way of referring to what is generally understood as 31 Dec. 1899, at Greenwich mean noon. Further, in 1964 XII CGPM in effect adopted the definition 1 sec. of time-interval in the interval occupied by 9 192 631 770 cycles of the radiation corresponding to the $(F = 4, M_F = 0) - (F = 3, M_F = 0)$ transition of the atom caesium–133 when unperturbed by exterior fields. This sec. was defined so as to have the same value within the limits ± 2 parts in 10^9 set by astronomical measurements, as the sec. adopted by XI CGPM (*see* above). It can, if required, be converted to Universal Time from the known but variable relationship between them.

Whereas in the Brit. system 'reckless impartiality' has been shown in the relationships between units of a kind (e.g. 2 pints = 1 quart, 3 feet = 1 yard, 5½ yards = 1 rod, 6 feet = 1 fathom, etc.), in the metric system multiples and submultiples of units are all in powers of 10 and are indicated by prefixes attached to the names of the main units (*see* 'SI' below). The following are some of the relationships between Brit. units and between Brit. and metric units.

LINEAR UNITS

in		ft		yd		chain		links
792	=	66	=	22	=	1	=	100
36	=	3	=	1	=	0·9144 metre exactly		
12	=	1			=	30·48 cm exactly		
1					=	25·4 mm exactly		

pole		chain		furlong		
40	=	10	=	1	=	201·168 metre approx.

ft		yd		furlong	mile		
5280	=	1760	=	8	=	1	=	1·6093 km approx.

Under the 1963 Act the rod, pole or perch (5½ yd) is no longer lawful in trade. The surveyor's chain of 100 links (also not lawful for trade) was invented by Gunter (q.v.) to decimalise the acre.

1 engineers' chain = 100 ft
1 sea mile (British) = 6080 ft
1 international sea mile used by all other countries = 1852 metres
1 cable = 100 fathoms = 600 ft

Apart from the sea mile the U.S. measures of length (except for surveying) are the same as the British.

AREA

in²		ft²		yd²		
1296	=	9	=	1	=	0·836 13 m² approx.
144	=	1			=	929·03 cm² approx.
					=	6·451 6 cm² approx.

yd²		poles²		roods		acre	
4840	=	160	=	4	=	1
1210	=	40	=	1		
30·25	=	1				

1 acre = 10 chain² = 100,000 links² = 4046·9 m² approx.
1 mile² = 640 acres = 259 hectares approx.

The U.S. units of area are the same as the British.

VOLUME

in.³		ft³		yd³		
46·656	=	27	=	1	=	0·764 55 m³ approx.
1·728	=	1			=	283·17 dm³
1					=	16·387 cm³

UNITS OF CAPACITY

British

pints		quarts		gallon		
8	=	4	=	1	=	4·546 09 dm³ approx.
2	=	1	=		=	1·136 5 dm³ approx.
1	=	4 gills	=	20 fl. oz	=	568·26 cm³ approx.
1 gallon	=	277·420 in³ (calculated)				

U.S. UNITS OF CAPACITY

(*a*) Liquid measure

pints		quarts		gallon		
8	=	4	=	1	=	231 in³
					=	3·785 41 dm³
2	=	1			=	0·946 35 dm³
1	=	4 gills	=	16 fl. oz	=	0·473 176 dm³
1 fl. oz	=	4 fl. drams	=	480 minims	=	29·573 5 cm³
1 U.S. gallon	=	0·832 67 U.K. gallon				

(*b*) Dry measure

bushel		pecks		quarts		pints		
1	=	4	=	32	=	64	=	35·239 1 dm³
1	=							2 150·42 in³

APOTHECARIES' MEASURE

$$
\begin{array}{llll}
& minim & fl.\ oz. & cm^2 \\
\text{British} & 480 = 8 \text{ fl. drachm} = 1 \text{ (U.K.)} = 28 \cdot 413 \\
\text{U.S.A.} & 480 = 8 \text{ fl. dram} \;\;= 1 \text{ (U.S.)} = 29 \cdot 574
\end{array}
$$

BRITISH AND U.S. WEIGHT UNITS

Avoirdupois units

grain	ounces	pound	
7000	= 16	= 1	= 453·592 37 gramme exactly
437·5	= 1		= 28·35 gramme

pounds	stones	quarters	hundredweight
112	8	4	1
14	1		

$$
\begin{array}{ll}
1 \text{ long ton (U.K.)} & = \quad 2{,}240 \text{ lb.} \\
1 \text{ short ton (U.S.)} & = \quad 2{,}000 \text{ lb.}
\end{array}
$$

Apothecaries' units

grains	scruples		ounce	
480	= 24	= $\begin{cases} 8 \text{ drachm (U.K.)} \\ 8 \text{ dram (U.S.)} \end{cases}$ = 1	= 31·1035 gramme	

Troy units

grains	ounce	
480	= 1	= 31·1035 grammes

Note: 1 troy ounce = 1 apothecaries' ounce.

OBSOLETE AND MISCELLANEOUS UNITS

M = Mercantile lb.; li = Roman libra;

$$
\begin{array}{lllllll}
\text{Fotmal} & & = & 70\ M & = & 72\ lb & = & 100\ li \\
\text{Sack} & = 5 \text{ fot} & = & 350\ M & = & 360\ lb & = & 500\ li \\
& \text{Load of lead} & = & 6 \text{ sacks} & = & 30 \text{ fotmals}
\end{array}
$$

The tradition of this load of 6 sacks is reflected in the avoirdupois scale by:

$$
\begin{array}{lllll}
\text{Fodder (lead)} & = & 6 \times 26 \text{ st} & = & 19 \cdot 5 \text{ cwt} \\
\text{Sack (wool)} & = & 26 \text{ st} & = & 364 \text{ lb} \\
& = & 13 \text{ tods} & = & 2 \text{ weys} \\
\text{Last} & = & 2 \text{ loads} & = & 12 \text{ sacks}
\end{array}
$$

Tun of wine = 252 Exchequer gal = 2 pipes = 3 puncheons = 4 hogsheads. The tradition of this tun is reflected in the 210-gal unit used by the Port of London Authority as the basis of certain charges, but the quantities implied by the name pipe, etc., vary widely. For example, (in gal); pipe (Port) = 115; (Madeira) = 92; Butt (Sherry, Whisky) = 108; Hogshead (Claret, Burgundy) = 48; Aum (Hock) = 30; Puncheon (Brandy) = 120.
Barrel (beer) — 36 gal; (U.S. oil) 42 gal (U.S.)
Shipping ton = 40 c. ft merchandise
Rod (brickwork) = sq pole (272 sq ft) × 1·5 bricks thick
Paper (writing) 1 quire = 24 sheets; 1 ream = 20 quires.

$$
\begin{array}{lll}
\text{Type height: 1 point} & = & \tfrac{1}{72} \text{ in.} \\
\qquad\qquad\quad 1 \text{ em} & = & \tfrac{1}{6} \text{ in.}
\end{array}
$$

Ell = 45 in
Score = 20. Long 100 = 120. Gross = 12 doz
Penny (new) = $\tfrac{1}{3}$ oz; 240 pence = 5 lb
1 oz = 3 pennies = 5 halfpence
Halfpenny (diameter) = 1 in
Carat rating for gold. This carat is not a specific weight, although divided into 4 carat grains. In this scale pure gold (1000 fine) is rated 24 carat. The standard fineness for Eng. gold coin is 22 ct = 961·67 fine. Sterling silver is 11 oz 2 dwt = 925 fine; it contains 18 dwt of alloy in the pound of 12 troy oz.

Metric system. The metre and the kilogramme have already been defined incidentally to the definitions of the yard and pound. The metric and Brit. second are identical (*see* earlier).

The metric system as known by most physicists has been based on the centimetre, gramme and sec. (cgs system), but as the outcome of a suggestion in 1901 by Giorgi the modern basis is the metre, kilogramme and sec. (MKS) system expanded into the Système International d'Unités (SI) in 1954 (X CGPM), formalised in 1960 (XI CGPM) and slightly extended in 1964

(XII CGPM). The CGPM resolutions have been endorsed by the International Organisation for Standardisation (ISO). SI is a coherent system of units, i.e. the quotient or product of any 2 unit quantities is the unit of the resultant quantity. Thus the sq. ft and sq. metre are units in coherent systems in which the ft and the metre are the units of length, but the ac. is not a coherent unit in the ft system and the hectare (10 000 m²) is not a coherent unit in the metric system.

The SI is based on the following 6 units:

Metre (m)—unit of length (defined above).

Kilogramme (kg)—unit of mass (defined above).

Second (s)—unit of time interval (defined above).

Ampere (A)—unit of electric current; it is that constant current which if maintained in 2 parallel rectilinear conductors of infinite length, of negligible circular cross section, and placed at a distance of 1 metre apart in a vacuum, would produce between these conductors a force equal to 2×10^{-7} newton per metre length (IX CGPM, 1948). *See* below for the definition of the newton unit of force.

Degree Kelvin (°K)—unit of thermodynamic temp.; this is the degree interval of the thermodynamic scale on which the temp. of the triple point of water is 273·16 degrees exactly (X CGPM, 1954).

Candela (cd)—unit of luminous intensity; it is such that the luminance of a full radiator at the temp. of solidification of platinum is 60 units of luminous intensity per sq. cm. (IX CGPM, 1948).

In chemistry the use of the mole (mol) has been recommended as a further basic unit, corresponding to 'amount of substance', by the ISO.

Another unit was adopted by the XII CGPM, 1964, namely the unit for activity of radio nucleides; while it was affirmed that the appropriate SI unit for this phenomenon is the reciprocal sec. (s^{-1}), the curie was adopted on account of its estab. position, and defined as $3·7 \times 10^{10} s^{-1}$. The curie is not a part of SI.

Derived from the 6 basic SI units listed above, and the 2 supplementary units of plane angle (radian, rad) and solid angle (steradian, st), the following units have been given special names. These are the only units which are so treated; all other SI units (with the exception of 1 dm³—*see* above) can only be expressed in terms of the fundamental and supplementary units, or the following named units. (Temp. difference is usually expressed in degrees Celsius (centigrade) instead of degrees Kelvin, but the unit for the 2 scales is the same: 1 degree C = 1 degree K.)

force	newton	N = kg m/s²
work, energy, quantity of heat }	joule	J = Nm
power	watt	W = J/s
electric charge	coulomb	C = As
electric potential	volt	V = W/A
electric capacitance	farad	F = As/V
electric resistance	ohm	Ω = V/A
magnetic flux	weber	Wb = Vs
inductance	henry	H = Vs/A
luminous flux	lumen	lm = cd sr
illumination	lux	lx = lm/m²

By way of illustration some derived SI units with complex names now follow:

area	square metre	m²
volume	cubic metre *	m³
frequency	cycle per second	Hz
density	kilogramme per cubic metre	kg/m³
velocity	metre per second	m/s
angular velocity	radian per second	rad/s
acceleration	metre per second squared	m/s²
pressure	newton per square metre	N/m²
surface tension	newton per metre	N/m
dynamic viscosity	newton second per metre squared	Ns/m²
thermal conductivity	watt per meter degree Kelvin	W/(m°K)
magnetic flux density	weber per square metre	Wb/m²
luminance	candela per square metre	cd/m²

*The XII CGPM 1964 resolved that the word 'litre', formerly meaning the volume occupied by 1 kilogramme of water at the temperature of its maximum density and under standard atmospheric pressure, should no longer have this meaning but should henceforward be used to indicate 1 cubic decimetre (1 decimetre = 0·1 metre, 1 cubic decimetre = 0·001 cubic metre—*see* below) which is 28 parts per million smaller, except that the term litre should not be used for precise measurement. As the object of this last decision was to avoid confusion between the old and new meanings of the term litre, and the 2 meanings differ by closely 1 in 36 000, it is reasonable to restrict the term litre to the expression of measurements not more closely than 1 part in 20 000. In Fr. law the word litre has always meant 1 cub. decimetre, and in France and in some other countries the restriction on its use is not being applied.

In the metric system the names of multiples and submultiples of the units are formed by adding prefixes to the basic units, as follows.

Factor			Example
1 thousand million	$= 10^9$	giga (G)	GHz
1 million	$= 10^6$	mega (M)	MW
1 thousand	$= 10^3$	kilo (k)	kg
1 hundredth	$= 10^{-2}$	centi (c)	cm
1 thousandth	$= 10^{-3}$	milli (m)	mg
1 millionth	$= 10^{-6}$	micro (μ)	μm *
1 thousand millionth	$= 10^{-9}$	nano (n)	nm
1 million millionth	$= 10^{-12}$	pico (p)	pF

*The prefix μ, meaning micro or one millionth, has sometimes been loosely used in the past to indicate one millionth of a metre (10^{-6}m), and called 'micron'. The correct abbreviation for 10^{-6}m is μm, pronounced micro-metre.

Other prefixes are: 10^{12}, tera, T; 10^2, hecto, h; 10^1, deca, da; 0·1, deci, d; 10^{-15}, femto, f; and 10^{-18}, atto, a.

SOME EQUIVALENT VALUES

Linear unit	1 metre	1·093 61 yard
Mass unit (weight)	1 kilogramme	2·204 62 pound
Time unit	1 second	1 second
Area unit	1 metre^2	1·195 99 yard^2
Volume unit	1 metre^3	{ 1·307 95 yard^3 { 219·969 gallon (U.K.)
Speed unit	1 metre per second	{ 3·280 84 foot/second { 2·236 94 mile/hour
Density unit	1 kilogramme per cubic metre	{ 0·062 428 pound/foot^3 { 0·010 022 pound/gal (U.K.)
Force unit	1 newton	0·224 809 pound-force
Pressure unit	1 newton per square metre	1·450 38 $\times 10^{-4}$ pound-force per square inch
Energy (work heat) unit	1 joule	{ 0·737 562 ft pound-force, { 9·478 17 $\times 10^{-4}$ Btu
Power unit	1 watt	1·341 02 $\times 10^{-3}$ hp

More information on the modern metric system (SI) can be found in Brit. Standard 3763 : 1964, *The International System (SI) Units*, Brit. Standards Institution, 2 Park Street, London, W.1., and many equivalent Brit. metric values are given in Brit. Standard 350 : 1963, *Conversion Factors and Tables*. Comprehensive conversion factors and information on the metric system will be found in a booklet entitled *Changing to the Metric System : Conversion Factors, Symbols and Definitions*, H.M.S.O., 1965.

II. HISTORICAL

There have been 4 pounds in English measures:

(1) Tower lb.	= 5400 gr = 12 tw. oz
(2) Troy lb.	= 5750 gr = 12 tr. oz
(3) Mercantile lb.	= 7200 gr = 16 tw. oz
	= 15 tr. oz
(4) Averdepois lb.	= 7000 gr = 16 oz

The tower and troy pounds reflect the monetary pound of account (£ = 20*s* = 240*d*), for there was a time when the penny was made of sterling silver and weighed a pennyweight (dwt) tower; the weight of the penny, however, was progressively reduced and the poundweight of such coin contained more than 240 pence.

The tower lb was the standard at the Royal Mint in the Tower of London until the end of 1526 when Henry VIII estab. the troy lb, then in more general use elsewhere. The troy penny-weight is rated 24 grains (gr), and it is in terms of this grain (now regarded as the averdepois grain) that the 4 pounds are compared. The troy lb became obsolete by the Act of 1878, but the troy ounce retains limited legality (*see* WEIGHTS).

The mercantile lb of 16 tower oz = 360 tower dwt was the tower doublemark, for the mark = 8 oz = 160 dwt where the pound = 12 oz = 240 dwt. It was also equal to 15 troy oz = 300 troy dwt and sometimes called the pound of 25 shillingsweight (troy). It was liable to confusion with the pound averdepois.

The averdepois lb of 16 oz was a commercial pound and had a particular association with the medieval wool trade through the stone of 14 lb and the sack of 26 such stones = 364 lb which was an approximation to another sack of 360 lb = 350 mercantile lb = 5 fotmals = 500 Rom. librae.

III. TECHNICAL METROLOGY
Time Measurement

1 hr = 60 min = 3600 sec
Mean solar day = 24 hrs = 86,400 sec = return of sun to meridian
Solar (tropical) year = 365·2422 days
Average civil year = 365·2425 days
= Julian sequence of 3 years of 365 days, followed by a leap year of 366 days (in years whose number is divisible by 4) subject to the Gregorian correction that cent. years are not leap years unless divisible by 400.
Sidereal day = 86164·09 sec
Sidereal year = 366·2564 sidereal days
= 365·2564 mean solar days
= Circuit of the earth round the sun with reference to a fixed star. The difference between the sidereal and solar years is due to precession of the earth's axis. It was the invention of the pendulum clock (Huygens, 1657) and its regulation by reference to star observations that enabled the sec. to become an accurately measurable time interval. *See also* ATOMIC CLOCK; HOROLOGY.

CIRCULAR MEASURE

Circle = 360° = 21 600′ = 1 296 000″
1° = 60′; 1′ = 60″; Quadrant = 90°
 = 5400′
Radian = 57·295 78° = angle subtended at centre by arc = radius
Circumference = $2\pi r$ (r = radius)
 ,, = 360° of arc = 1·296 million s
π = 3·14159 = (22/7) approx; Area = πr^2
Radius subtends 206 265 s of arc
If quadrant arc = 1 m; rad = 0·636 62 m

THE EARTH

Radii: sphere of equal volume, 6371 km
 polar, 6356·6 km; equatorial, 6378·1 km
Quadrant: meridian; 10 002 km actual
 10 000 km nominal
 equator; 10 019 km nominal
Surface area, 5.101 × 10^{14} m²
Land area, 1·49 × 10^{14} m²
Ocean area, 3·61 × 10^{14} m²
Volume, 1·083 × 10^{21} m³
Mass, 5·976 × 10^{24} kg
Mean density, 5517 kg/m³
Density at 5000 km, 11 500 kg/m³

Atmosphere

On weather charts atmospheric pressure is recorded in millibars (mb).
 1000 mb = 1 bar
 = 1 000 000 dyn/cm²
 = 750·062 standard millimetre of mercury (mm Hg)
 = 29·530 standard inches of mercury (in Hg)
 = 100 000 N/m²
The standard millimetre and inch of mercury are based on mercury density 13·5951 g/cm³, g = 980·665 cm/s² and 1 inch = 25·4 mm (*see* BS 2520 : 1954). Standard atmospheric pressure (1 atm) = 1 013 250 dyn/cm² 6 101 325 N/m². Density of half-saturated air at 20°C and 760 mm Hg = 1·199 g/dm³. The density increases in proportion to increased pressure and decreases in inverse proportion to (the temperature plus 273·15°C); at 20°C it decreases with humidity roughly by 0·000 1 g/dm³ for each 1 per cent increase in relative humidity, and decreases with altitude roughly as follows:

Altitude (thousands of feet)	3	6	10	14	18
Relative density	0·9	0·8	0·7	0·6	0·5

Beaufort wind scale: 0 = calm, 5 = fresh breeze, 10 = whole gale, 12 = hurricane.
Velocity of sound in air = 1100 ft/s approx. = 34 km/s approx.

Gravity

Gravity varies with latitude, and (slightly) with altitude; equator, 9·78 m/s²; London, 9·81 m/s²; poles, 9·83 m/s². These values are due to both the Earth's attraction (due to G, the gravitational constant equal to $(6\cdot670 \pm 0\cdot006) \times 10^{-11}$ m³/kg s²) and the centrifugal force due to the Earth's rotation (equivalent to about $0\cdot03$ m/s² at the equator). Standard acceleration (standard gravity) $= 9\cdot816\ 65$ m/s², by convention; rounded equivalent $= 32\cdot1740$ ft/s².

Some measured values

Velocity of light 299 792·5 $\pm$ 0·4 km/s (URSI 1957, IUGG 1957); 299 792·50 $\pm$ 0·10 km/s (Froome, *Nature*, 1958).
Density of mercury at 20°C and 1 atm $= 13\cdot545\ 88$ g/cm³.
Density of water at 20°C and 1 atm $= 0\cdot998\ 206$ g/cm³.

Thermometry

C = Celsius, which has superseded the name Centigrade.
F = Fahrenheit
°F to °C, subtract 32 then multiply by $\frac{5}{9}$
°C to °F, multiply by $\frac{9}{5}$ then add 32.
Colours of hot bodies: red, 550 to 700°C; cherry, 900°C; orange, 1100°C; white, 1400°C+.
Blood heat (normal) 98·4°F $= 36\cdot9$°C, 10°C = 50°F, 15°C = 59°F, 20°C = 68°F, 25°C = 77°F.
The thermometer scales are based on the Kelvin thermodynamic scale of Temp. which is hard to realise so that in practice the International Practical Scale of Temp. 1948 (IPST) is used; this more easily realised scale approximates as closely as possible to the IPST. It is based on various fixed points, viz., boiling point (b.p.) of oxygen, $-182\cdot970$°C; melting point (m.p.) of ice, 0°C; b.p. water, 100°C; b.p. sulphur, 444·600°C; freezing point (f.p.) of silver, 960·8°C; f.p. gold, 1063·0°C. Interpolation between these fixed points is by defined instruments and formulae, and above 1063·0°C temps. are defined in terms of Planck's law of radiation.

On the thermodynamic scale of temp. which starts from 0°K at absolute zero of temp., m.p. ice, 0°C, $= 273\cdot15$°K and triple point of water (ice, water and water vapour all in equilibrium) $= 273\cdot16$°K.

Some general physical constants

Volume per mole of ideal gas (0° C, $9\cdot806\ 65$ m/s²) $= 22\ 420\cdot7$ cm³ atm
Unit of heat, work, energy; 1 joule (J) $= 10^7$ erg
International calorie $= 4\cdot1868$ J; international joule $= 1\cdot000\ 19$ J (obsolete)
Avogadro number (N) $= 6\cdot024\ 97 \times 10^{23}$ atoms/mole
Electronic charge (e) $= 1\cdot602\ 02 \times 10^{-19}$ coulomb
Planck's constant (h) $= 6\cdot6249 \times 10^{-34}$ Js
Electron mass (m) $= 9\cdot1083 \times 10^{-28}$ g
Gas constant $= 8\cdot316\ 95$ J/deg K mole.

New Elizabethan standards proclaimed in 1587 included only averdepois weights (based on a 4-stone weight of Edward III) and troy weights based on the pile in Goldsmiths Hall. These remained the standards until the (first) Weights and Measures Act (1824) estab. a new troy weight, but this was lost in the fire that destroyed the Houses of Parliament in 1834. A new averdepois lb became the sole legal standard under the Act of 1878.

There have been 2 prin. gallons in Eng. measures; the Exchequer ale gallon, which is perpetuated in the present standard gallon holding 10 lb of water, and the Excise wine gallon, which is the prototype of the present standard gallon of the U.S.A. In a statute *c.* 1300 this wine gallon is defined by its capacity for 8 troy pounds of wheat, but it was standardised on a cylindrical basis at 231 cub. in in 1706 (when the Act of Union required the Eng. weights and measures to be used in Scotland) and discarded in favour of the 10-lb ale gallon by the Act of 1824.

The bushel is defined as 8 gallons but prior to the Act of 1824 the standard dry measure was the Winchester bushel (explicitly abolished in 1835 by 5 and 6 W. IV. C. 63) and 3 bronze examples of this are extant from the reign of Henry VII. Probably its intended capacity was 4·5 stones = 63 lb of wheat, but it was standardised on a cylindrical basis (2150·42 cub. in) in the reign of Wm III, and this is the prototype of the standard bushel of the U.S.A.

Metronome, instrument used for determining and securing the movement of musical compositions. It was invented by Maelzel about 1814, and consists essentially of a pendulum of which the point of suspension is between the extremities. The pendulum is driven by a spring and wheel which ticks the oscillations. A movable weight is attached to the pendulum and an upright scale graduated to correspond with marks on the rod is placed behind. The period of the pendulum's vibration can thus be varied to any required time by adjusting the weight until it is opposite one of these lines, the mark near the line giving the number of oscillations per minute.

Metropolitan Magistrates' Courts, petty sessional courts in inner London presided over by a paid professional magistracy, generally called stipendiaries. Bow Street M. Court has the distinction of being the only court having jurisdiction in extradition cases. Everything which can be said to relate to public order or the prevention of nuisances comes within the general jurisdiction of the M. M. C.; serious crimes are remitted to the London sessions or criminal sessions at the Central Criminal Court.

Metropolitan Museum of Art, see AMERICAN ART MUSEUMS.

Metropolitan Opera House, New York, U.S.A., was first built on 39th Street in 1883. In 1892 it was closed as the result of a fire but reopened the following year. It was famous for the high standard of its productions, and an appearance there was a prize coveted by the greatest singers from all over the world. A new M. O. H. in the Lincoln Center was opened in 1966. See I. Kolodin, *The Story of the Metropolitan Opera, 1833–1950,* 1953.

Metropolitan Police. The M. P. came into being as the result of Peel's Police Bill of 1829, in the form of the 'New Police' experiment of that year. After a period of struggle for existence in the face of fierce hostility, they succeeded in securing public approval and respect, and they were in general outline the model on which all the prov. forces were allowed to develop. The area under supervision of the Metropolitan Police includes the whole of Greater London, excluding the City of London, which comprises its 32 boroughs. Additionally, the area also includes parts of the administrative councils of Surrey, Essex and Herts (roughly speaking, the area within a 16 m. radius of Charing Cross). As with other police their primary duties are the prevention and detection of crime and the preservation of order. They are the authority for regulating the street traffic, and they license the drivers and conductors in the Metropolitan Traffic Area in respect of buses and coaches. Similarly they license cab drivers and proprietors in the M. P. dist. They make regulations for cabs to stand and ply for hire, but do not regulate the conduct of proprietors of other vehicles. The M. P. are the only force for which the home secretary is responsible to Parliament. The force is administered by a commissioner from the M. P. office at 10 Broadway, Westminster, SW.1. The M.P. mounted branch is under the control of an assistant commissioner and in the charge of a chief superintendent; it consists of about 200 horses and 210 men. It is directly descended from the Bow Street Horse Patrol and was incorporated in the M. P., 1836. A new police college for members of all police forces was opened at Ryton-on-Dunsmore, Warwickshire, in Oct. 1948. At the M. P. training school at Hendon, and at Peel House, a 13 weeks' recruits' course is given. See also METROPOLITAN MAGISTRATES' COURTS; POLICE; SCOTLAND YARD.

Metropolitan Water Board, body responsible for the water supply to much of Greater London and parts of the administrative cos. of Essex, Herts, Kent and Surrey. The Board was constituted by the Metropolis Water Act, 1902, and is now composed of 39 members, 6 of whom are appointed by the Greater London Council,

one each by 26 of the London bor. councils, one by the Common Council of the City of London and one each by the Essex, Herts, Kent and Surrey Co. Councils. The Thames Conservancy and the Lee Conservancy Catchment Board appoint 1 member each. M.W.B. supply services cover an area of some 540 sq. m., comprising a pop. of 6,258,000. The average daily supply in 1964–5 was 381 million gallons. The chief sources of supply are the Rivs. Thames and Lee and a number of wells and springs in the Lee Valley and the Kent area. The total available storage capacity of reservoirs is 29,952 million gallons. Charges are levied on the net ann. value of the premises supplied with appropriate charges for metered and non-domestic supplies. The capital debt of the Board is about £66,785,000 (1965) and the net water rental approximately £14,854,000 (1965).

Metrorrhagia, see MENSTRUATION.

Metsada (Heb. a fortress), flat-topped rock formation in the Wilderness of Judea rising to almost 1400 ft from the W. shore of the Dead Sea. Its boat-shaped top, the longer axis lying roughly N.–S., was fortified by Jonathan Maccabaeus and later by Herod the Great. During the 1st cent. AD Palestine Jewry revolted against its Rom. overlords and a long and bitter siege resulted in the fall of M. During the mid-1960s interesting and valuable archaeological discoveries resulted in M. being made more accessible to the tourist.

Metsu, or **Metzu, Gabriel** (1629–67), Dutch painter, b. Leyden. He studied under Gerard Dou, and in 1648 was admitted into the Painters' Guild at Leyden, Amsterdam, where he settled as a painter of *genre* pictures, his interior scenes almost challenging Vermeer (q.v.). His chief works are 'The Market-place of Amsterdam', at the Louvre; 'The Sportsman', at The Hague; 'The Game-dealer's Shop', at Dresden; 'The Repast', at the Hermitage, Leningrad; and 'The Duet' and 'The Music Lesson' in the National Gallery, London. See R. H. Wilenski, *Introduction to Dutch Art,* 1927.

Metternich-Winneburg, Clemens Wenzel Nepomuk Lothar, Duke of Portella, and later **Prince von Metternich** (1773–1859), Austrian statesman, b. Koblenz. In 1795 he married the grand-daughter of Kaunitz, thus assuring himself a prominent position at court. He became minister at Dresden in 1801, and 2 years later was transferred to Berlin. During the years 1806–7 he represented Austria at Paris, where, in spite of his anti-Napoleonic policy, he managed to keep on good terms with Napoleon, whom he tried to bring into an alliance with Austria. The war which followed was terminated by Napoleon's victory at Wagram and the treaty of Vienna (1809). After this M. became chancellor and foreign minister. For some time he veiled his enmity against Napoleon, and succeeded in negotiating the marriage between Napoleon and Marie Louise in 1810. But during the next 2 years the attitude and the successes of Napoleon led to the formation of the great alliance between Russia, Austria and Prussia, in which, M.

secured for Austria the leading position (Töplitz, 1813). The victory of Leipzig enabled him to dicate terms to Napoleon, and he took a leading part in the negotiations which followed this.

From this date M. figures as the champion of reaction throughout Europe. By his diplomacy he again managed to secure the leading position in the Holy Alliance, which he used quite cynically as an instrument for repressing the nascent forces of liberalism inside and outside the Austrian Empire. The revolution of 1848 came as a great shock to him, and its results were seen in Austria in the fall of his gov. He left Austria with an armed escort and took refuge in England. In 1851 he returned to his castle on the Rhine, but took no further part in politics.

For a generation M. was the mainstay of a federal Europe which at least preserved a species of European peace by the negative method of ruthlessly crushing any force, however progressive or justified, which tended towards separatism. In the last resort he was unalterably opposed to popular sovereignty, yet too cynical and too humane to believe in blind repression even while he practised it. He believed in a philosophy of equilibrium, in relation both to the classes and powers within a state and to the interrelations of the European powers. Since both had been disturbed by the Fr. Revolution and Napoleon, M. conceived it essential to restore the balance and to maintain it. In that he realised that paternal gov. must justify itself by its wisdom, popularity and efficiency, M. was a reformer. But he was the servant of an autocrat who disliked change, and nothing came of his suggested internal reforms; his reputation sank to its lowest point in the generation following his death but has since been partially restored. His memoirs were pub. at Vienna (1878–84), and were trans. into English in 1880. *See* E. L. Woodward, *Three Studies in European Conservatism*, 1929. *See also* P. Quennell (ed., with biographical foreword), *The Private Letters of Princess Lieven to Prince Metternich, 1820–6*, 1948, and life by A. Cecil, 1948.

Metz, Fr. tn, cap. of the dept of Moselle, on the Moselle. The chief tn of the Gallic Mediomatrici, it was known to the Romans as Divodurum, and was later called Mediomatrica and Mettis. Under the Merovingians (q.v.) it was the cap. of Austrasia (q.v.), and passed to the empire in 870. Taken by the French in 1552, it was ceded to France formally in 1648. By the treaty of Frankfurt in 1871 (*see* FRANCO-PRUSSIAN WAR) it was annexed to Germany, and by the treaty of Versailles (q.v.) was restored to France. M. is the seat of a bishop. It is a spacious city with many fine, anct buildings, including the cathedral of St-Étienne, which is partly 13th cent. Verlaine (q.v.) was *b*. here. The tn has metal foundries, and is the centre of a coal-mining dist. It has textile and leather manufs., and a large trade in agric. produce. Pop. 103,000. *See* ALSACE-LORRAINE; WESTPHALIA, TREATY OF.

Metzu, Gabriel, *see* METSU.

Meudon, Fr. tn in the dept of Seine-et-Oise, a SW. suburb of Paris. Situated near the M. Forest, it has long been a popular holiday resort. Ronsard (q.v.) lived here, and Rabelais (q.v.) was a curé here. There is a famous royal château, now an observatory, and a military air station. Motor-cars and chemicals are manuf. Pop. 34,900. *See also* BELLEVUE.

Meulebeke, industrial tn in the prov. of W. Flanders, Belgium, 8 m. N. of Courtrai. There are manufs. of lace and textiles, and bleaching works. Pop. 10,400.

Meulen, Adam François van der (1632–90), Flem. painter, *b*. Brussels, worked mainly in France. Colbert appointed him battle-painter to Louis XIV. He painted the prin. battles and sieges in Flanders for the Château of Marly. In 1673 he was made a member of the academy. Many of his pictures are at the Louvre and Versailles.

Meum, genus of umbelliferous plants. *M. athamanticum* is the Spignel, Meu or Baldmoney of Scotland and N. England. The leaves are bipinnate, with crowded, bristle-like segments, and the umbels of flowers are yellow, perennial.

Meung, Jean de (Jean Clopinel) (*c*. 1240–1305), Fr. poet, scholar and satirist living in Paris and best known for his remarkable 18,000-line continuation, *c*. 1277, of the *Roman de la Rose* begun by Guillaume de Lorris (q.v.). With him the allegory becomes a vehicle for forthright views on such topics as gov., monasticism and women, allowing him to display his encyclopaedic scholarship. Other works include translations from Vegetius and Boethius.

Meunier, Constantin (1831–1905), Belgian sculptor and painter, *b*. near Brussels. Among his best-known pictures are 'The Salle St Roch', 1857, 'A Trappist Funeral', 1860, and the notable series depicting the miners and factory hands in Lemonnier's *Le Tour du monde*. He was an innovator, in a time of polite classicism, in representing the workman in rough working clothes. His best statues are 'Miner', 'Puddler', 1885, and 'Mower', 1892, and a series of bas-reliefs which he called a 'Monument to Labour', *See* lives by G. Treu, 1898; C. Lemonnier, 1903.

Meurice, François Paul (1818–1905), Fr. dramatist, studied law and literature. He joined the romantic school, and (in collaboration with others) adapted Shakespeare to the Fr. stage with *Falstaff*, 1842, and *Hamlet*, 1847. He was made chief editor of Victor Hugo's *Événement*. In 1878 he dramatised *Les Misérables*, and afterwards *Notre-Dame de Paris* and *Quatrevingt-treize*, and also adapted (with A. Vecquerie) Sophocles' *Antigone*. Among his original plays were *Benvenuto Cellini*, 1852, *Fanfan la Tulipe*, 1858, and *Struensée*, 1893.

Meursius, Johannes (properly **Jan de Meurs**) (1579–1639), Dutch classical scholar, became prof. of hist. and afterwards of Greek at Leyden Univ. (1610 and 1611). In 1625 he accepted the chair of hist. at Sorö in Denmark, as the execution of Barneveldt, whose children he taught, had exposed him to ceaseless persecution. Among many other works he wrote *Res Belgicae*, 1612, a *Glossarium Graeco-Barbarum*, 1614, and *Historia Danica*, 1630. *See also* J. Gronovius, *Thesaurus Graecarum Antiquitatum*, 1697–1702.

Meurthe et Moselle, dept in the NE. of France, being formed, after the treaty with Germany in 1871 (*see* FRANCO-PRUSSIAN WAR), out of the remnants of the old depts of Meurthe and Moselle. The prov. is drained by the Moselle, and its tribs., and by the Chiers, a trib. of the Meuse. Grand Rougimont (2041 ft) in the Vosges is the highest peak. The manufs. of cast and sheet iron, of iron and steel goods and of earthenware and glass are very considerable. Rock-salt is found in abundance. Viticulture flourishes, and cereals, potatoes and hops are widely grown. The prin. tns are Nancy (the cap.), Briey, Lunéville and Toul (qq.v.). Area 2036 sq. m.; pop. 678,000.

Meuse: 1. Dept of NE. France, composed of parts of the anct provs. of Champagne and Lorraine. It is watered by the Meuse, the Orne and the Chiers. The main ridge of highlands, which sinks from the S. northwards, forms the watershed between the Seine and the Rhine. The hills of the Argonne (q.v.) are clothed with magnificent oak forests. Cereals, potatoes, beets and vines are raised, and there is livestock breeding. The prin. industries are brewing and glass- and tile-making. The chief tns are Bar-le-Duc (the cap.), Commercy and Verdun (q.v.). Area 2408 sq. m.; pop. 218,000.

2. (Flem. **Maas**) Riv. over 550 m. long, rising in the dept of Haute-Marne, France. Passing Verdun and Sedan in a northerly direction it enters Belgium, and after bending E. beyond Namur flows N. again past Liège in Belgium and Maastricht in the Netherlands. After a curve W. it enters the Waal, the left arm of the Rhine, at Woudrichem. It now divides, the N. branch, called the Merwede, proceeding to Dordrecht, whence it eventually reaches the sea through 2 channels, the Oude and the Nieuwe-Mass, which, after entering the Hollandsch Diep, flows into the sea through the New Waterway. The former outlets, Haringvleit and Krammer, are in the course of being dammed, as part of the new delta plan, which will be completed in about 1980. The M.'s main affluents are the Sambre, the Ourthe, the Geer and the Roer. For the military operations in the dept and in the M. valley in the First World War *see* FRANCE AND FLANDERS, FIRST WORLD WAR CAMPAIGN IN and WORLD WAR, FIRST, under various sub-headings relating to the W. front. The M. to the S. of Namur was part of the main line of defence of Belgium, in the Second World War, stretching N. over Wavre and Koningshooikt to Antwerp. The crossing of the M. was forced in the sector defended by the Fr. Ninth Army at Houx, 4 m. N. of Dinant, on 13 May 1940. For operations of the First and Third Amer. Armies on the M. around Namur, Dinant, and Commercy, and St Michiel, in Sept. 1944; for details of von Runstedt's Ardennes counter offensive (17 Dec. 1944) and plan to break through the Allies' line

to the M. in the Liège-Namur area; and for the operations in the Netherlands at Nijmegen and Arnhem over the M. in the autumn of 1944, *see* WESTERN FRONT IN SECOND WORLD WAR.

Meux (formerly **Lambton**), **Sir Medworth** (1856–1929), admiral of the fleet. 3rd son of the 2nd Earl of Durham. Entered the navy in 1870 and was present at the bombardment of Alexandria and the battle of Tel-el-Kebir, 1882. Commanded the naval brigade during the Boer War (q.v.) and the Royal Yacht 1901–3. In 1908 he was appointed Commander-in-Chief, China, and from 1912–16 he was Commander-in-Chief, Portsmouth. In 1911 he assumed the name of Meux. He was an M.P. from 1916–18.

Mevagissey, picturesque fishing port and health resort, 6 m. S. of St Austell (q.v.), Cornwall, England. Pop. 2050.

Mevis, *see* NEVIS.

Mew, Charlotte Mary (1869–1928), poetess, *b.* Bloomsbury, daughter of an architect. Although she pub. only 2 books of verse, *The Farmer's Bride*, 1915, and *The Rambling Sailor*, 1929, Thomas Hardy thought her the best woman poet of her time. Reserved, secretive, over-restrained, she has been compared with Emily Dickinson (q.v.).

Mewès, Charles, *see* DAVIS, A. J.

Mews, row of stables and coach-houses with living-quarters above, built in a paved yard behind large London houses of the 18th–19th cents. Most M. stables are now garages.

Mexborough, urb. dist and tn of the W. Riding of Yorks, England, 5½ m. NE. by N. of Rotherham, on the R. Don, a railway depot with printing works, foundries, glass works and collieries near by. Pop. 17,053.

Mexicali, cap. of the state of Baja California (Norte), Mexico. Situated close to the U.S.A. border in the Valley of M., it is the economic centre of a rich agric. area which owes its fertility to irrigation made possible by the construction of the Morelos dam on the R. Colorado. This development has taken place over the last 50 years, its pop. in 1910 being 410 inhabs. and 281,333 in 1960. The climate is hot and very dry. The main crops in the area are cotton, wheat, vegetables (for the U.S. market) and barley.

Mexican and Central American Native Languages. Unlike N. America (*see* NORTH AMERICAN NATIVE LANGUAGES), in Mexico and a great part of Central and S. America (*see* SOUTH AMERICAN NATIVE LANGUAGES) the native pop. still flourishes. Of the 17 reps. of Lat America, only 3 (Costa Rica, Argentina and Uruguay) are mainly white; 9 (Mexico, Salvador, Honduras, Nicaragua, Panama, Venezuela, Colombia, Chile and Paraguay) are mainly *mestizo*, i.e. of mixed descent; 4 are mainly Indian (Guatemala, Ecuador, Peru and Bolivia); and the vast rep. of Brazil is about half white.

The native language of Mexico is Aztec, a Nahuatl language, i.e. belonging to the Nahoa linguistic family. It is spoken by some 715,000 people in N. and central Mexico. The great state of Oaxaca in S. Mexico offers the most complex linguistic situation existing in that country. There are a large number of tribal and linguistic groups which differ greatly in culture, speaking about 50 different languages. Nowadays, however, the most important native languages are Mixtec and, especially, Zapotec, which is spoken by sev. thousand people in S. Oaxaca; a Zapotec dialect, called Villa Alta, is spoken in NE. Oaxaca.

The Mayas, one of the most important and most civilised peoples of native America, still form the bulk of the pop. of Yucatán. They may be divided into 3 main groups, speaking allied languages: (1) the Mayas proper, subdivided into many tribes speaking various dialects, and numbering about 300,000, in Yucatán and the neighbouring states of Mexico and Guatemala; (2) the Quiché (some 500,000), between Lake Atitlan and the Pacific, S. Guatemala; and (3) the Huasteka (about 50,000) in San Luis Potosi, already separated from the main stock in anct times. *See also* LANGUAGES, CLASSIFICATION OF; LINGUISTIC FAMILIES; NORTH AMERICAN NATIVE LANGUAGES; SOUTH AMERICAN NATIVE LANGUAGES.

Mexico (Los Estados Unidos Mexicanos), country lying in the southern part of the N. Amer. continent. Bordered in the N. by the U.S.A., in the W. and S. by the Pacific, it has frontiers in the SE. with Guatemala and Brit. Honduras and on its eastern seaboard are the Gulf of M. and the Caribbean Sea. With a total area of 760,337 sq. m. it is the 3rd largest country in Lat. America, with which, geography apart, it has more in common than with the N. Amer. countries. The frontier with the U.S.A. is about 1600 m. long and southwards the country narrows until at the Isthmus of Tehuantepec there is only 140 m. between the Pacific and the Gulf of M. It has a lengthy coastline, with 3000 m. on the Pacific (excluding the peninsula of Lower California) and 1100 m. on the Gulf. With a pop. estimated in 1964 at 39,500,000 (the 1960 census recorded 34,923,129) it is the 2nd most populous country in Lat. America and the biggest Sp. speaking nation in the world.

Physical features and climate. Mts are the dominating physical feature of nearly all M. Essentially the country consists of a central plateau flanked on either side by mt ranges—in the E. the Sierra Madre Oriental and in the W. and S. the Sierra Madre Occidental—with coastal plains between the mt ranges and the seas. Two areas outside this general pattern are the peninsula of Lower California in the W. and the peninsula of Yucatán in the E. The 2 N.–S. running Sierras gradually come together to meet at about 19° N., thus enclosing the southern end of the central plateau, but the mt range continues southward as the Sierra Madre del Sur. At the lat. where the 2 Sierras meet the country is crossed E. to W. by a belt of volcanic mts reaching from Veracruz in the Gulf of M. to Colima on the Pacific. The central plateau which comprises the economic heartland of M. has an average altitude of about 6000 ft; rising from about 3000 ft on the U.S. border in the N. where

the plateau is at its widest, to about 8000 ft in its southern part where it has narrowed considerably and is bordered in the S. by the transverse volcanic belt. In this belt are the great volcanoes Orizaba (18,851 ft), Popocatêpetl (17,716 ft), Ixtaccíhuatl (17,341 ft) together with many others, some extinct and some active. The E. and W. Sierras are both formidable mt ranges rising to heights of 18,000 ft and averaging in width about 100 m.; but the E. area presents fewer obstacles to transverse communications than that of the W. Within the central plateau there are further mt ranges forming intermontane basins which in the S. are as high as 8000 ft whilst in the N. as its altitude declines the plateau becomes a semi-arid plain. The peninsula of Lower California is a narrow strip of semi-arid and arid mountainous land running southward 760 m. from the W. coast of the U.S.A. The peninsula of Yucatán in the E. mainly consists of low-lying, jungle-covered plain separated from the rest of the country by a nearly impenetrable belt of tropical forest. Many other regions of M. are forested with tree types ranging from pine and oak to other valuable hardwoods and dyewoods. Rivs. are numerous and are important for irrigation purposes and sources of electric power.

The climate varies with altitude from the hot coastal lowlands to the high areas too cold for vegetation to grow. Three zones or *tierras* of climate can be broadly distinguished, relating to altitude: the tierra caliente (hot land) generally lying below 2000 ft with mean temps. of about 80° F.; the tierra templada (temperate land) between 2000 and 6000 ft with a mean ann. temp. of about 73° F. (though with considerably varying ranges of temp. depending on lat.); and the tierra fria (cold land) above 6000 ft to the permanent snow line of about 14,000 ft, with average temps. of around 60° F. and sharp and considerable changes in range. Inadequate rainfall constitutes M.'s major climatic problem, nearly half the country (roughly the northern half) being arid or semi-arid with desert or near-desert conditions. In the S. part of the central plateau the rainfall when it comes is adequate but it periodically fails. The Gulf coastland and extreme S. receive abundant rainfall.

Population and People. The 1960 census recorded a total pop. of 34,923,129, there being 17,415,320 males and 17,507,807 females. The 1964 estimate of pop. is about 39,500,000, representing an ann. rate of increase of $3\frac{1}{2}$ per cent. In 1950 there were less than 26 million inhab. Whilst the pop. is geographically reasonably well-distributed, over half live in the S. part of the central plateau—a region called the 'Core' of M. and comprising the Federal Dist and 11 states covering about 17 per cent of the country's area. In the W. region, comprising 4 states covering about 10 per cent of the land area, live about 10 per cent of the pop., and in the S. comprising 7 states and 20 per cent of the area live about 15 per cent of the people. However, the N. region comprising 8 states and Lower

California S. accounts for over 50 per cent of the land area but contains only 22 per cent of the pop. The pop. density for M. as a whole is 45 people to the sq. m. whilst in the Core the density is 99·5 and in the N. only 18. According to the 1960 census 50·7 per cent of the pop. live in tns of over 2500 inhab. compared with 46·1 per cent in 1950. This faster rate of pop. increase in urb. centres than in rural dists is the main element in the socio-economic changes in recent years. In 1960 there were 15 cities with pops. of over 100,000, of which 5 exceeded 200,000, namely, M. City (2,832,133), Guadalajara (740,390), Monterrey (801,085), Puebla (297,257) and Ciudad Juárez (240,583). As regards ethnic characteristics, the vast majority of the people are mestizo—a mixture from Indian and Sp. forbears; about 15 per cent are white; about 2 per cent of Afro-Asian origin; and just over 10 per cent, on the basis of language and cultural differences, are Indian. Whilst Spanish is the language of M., about ¼ of the 3½ million Indians speak only their own Indian language, and whilst the language of the Aztecs—Nahuatl—is the most common there are a number of others. Geographically, the Indians tend to be concentrated in the S. parts of M. though about one-third live in the Core region. In 1963 the crude birth rate for the country as a whole was 45·0 per 1000; the crude death rate 10·4 per 1000; and the infant mortality 69·5 per 1000 live births.

The Economy. Traditionally M.'s economy has been based on agriculture and mining, but during the past 15 years there have been important advances in industrialisation. This period has also been characterised by substantial overall economic development which is indicated by the nearly 6 per cent ann. rise in the real gross national product between 1950 and 1963, accompanied by a 35 per cent rise during that period in real per capita income. Already one of the leading Lat. Amer. countries, M., as distinct from many of them, has a well-balanced diversified economy, being free from dependence on the exploitation of one particular commodity. Of the economically active pop. of 12,500,000 (1961), about 54 per cent are employed in agriculture (including forestry and fishing) and 13 per cent in manufacturing industries; however, the contributions of these economic sectors to the gross national product in 1963 were agriculture 18 per cent and manufacturing 24 per cent, whilst the contributions of other sectors were—mining 2·5 per cent, petroleum 3·5, construction 5, transport 5, commerce 22, public administration and defence 2·5, and other services 17·5 per cent. The Central Gov. takes an active part in the direction or guidance of many sectors and aspects of the economy, doing so through a series of semi-autonomous economic organisations of which the Nacional Financiera (somewhat akin to a development bank) is the most important.

Agriculture. With agriculture employing over half the working pop., M. is still essentially an agric. country. Whilst not developing as fast as industry, agriculture has managed despite the rapidly rising pop. both to obtain self-sufficiency in food production and to increase production of export crops. Two great obstacles in the way of further development are the shortage of cultivable land and the system of land tenure. Various estimates exist as to the amount of land that is potentially cultivable, the most typical being about 20 million hectares or only a little more than 10 per cent of the total land area. Today about 14 million hectares are under cultivation out of an estimated 89 million hectares of farm land. About half of M.'s farmers belong to an ejido—an institution of collective land tenure through which land redistribution has taken place since 1915 although each farmer cultivates his own land—which altogether account for 44 per cent of the total crop land. This leaves 56 per cent of the land in the hands of 1,365,000 private farm owners, of whom 1 million are small farmers with an average holding of 1·3 hectares, whilst the remainder (365,000) control nearly 50 per cent of the total cropland. The shortage and maldistribution of land are aggravated by the need for irrigation and the shortage of financial credit for farmers.

A wide variation of soil and climate enables diversification of crops, and there is some specialisation by region, for example, corn, wheat and other cereals in the central states and N. highlands; cotton in the NE.; coffee in the highlands of Veracruz and Chiapas; citrus fruits and sugarcane in tropical and semi-tropical areas; sisal in Yucatán; and cattle raising in the N. Maize is the staple food and leading crop and is grown throughout the country; during recent years there has been an export surplus, a significant reversal of the traditional imports. Wheat is also a staple food and is following the same trend as maize, whilst other important foods crops are rice, chick-peas, beans, oats and barley. Cotton, coffee and sugarcane are the 3 leading export crops, M. being the world's chief cotton exporter after the U.S.A. and only behind Brazil and Colombia as regards coffee exports. The 1964 cotton crop was about 2,500,000 bales and the 1963–4 sugar cane crop about 1,175,000 tons. M. produces nearly half the world's supply of sisal, grown almost exclusively in the states of Yucatán and Campeche. Market-garden vegetables, grown mainly on the W. coast, and many varieties of fruits are exported mainly to the U.S.A. Other significant crops are tobacco, potatoes, sesame, alfalfa and cacao. Cattle-raising is a traditional Mexican farming activity and tends to be concentrated in the N. In 1963 there were about 36,000,000 head of cattle and exports reached a total of ¾ million head, thus ranking among the leading export items. There are also about 12 million hogs, 6 million sheep, 4 million horses, 3 million donkeys and 2 million mules.

Minerals. Traditionally a rich source of precious metals, today M.'s vast mineral wealth puts her among the world's leading producers. Whilst still the world's leading producer of

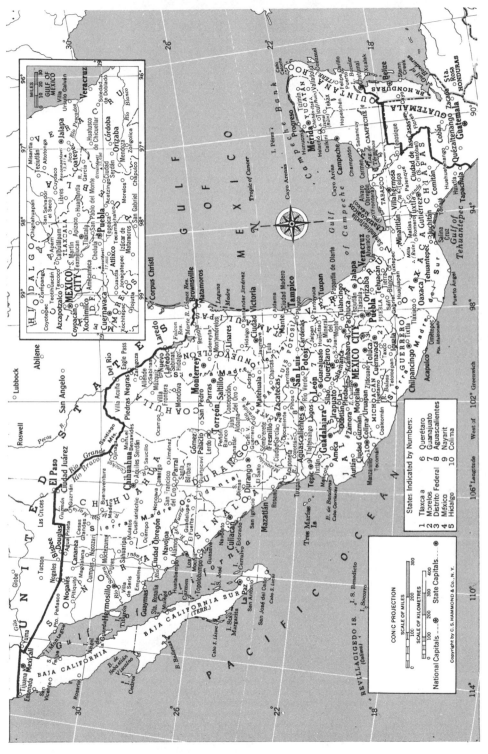

Mexico

Type of Education	Nos. of Schools	Nos. of Teaching Staff	Nos. of Students
Pre-school	1,852	6,675	230,164
Primary	34,240	117,348	5,368,247
Secondary	1,218	24,334	267,736
Technical	646	7,815	111,910
Teacher training	165	—	52,624
Higher	325	17,342	94,073

silver, M. is the second largest producer of sulphur, third of antimony, mercury and graphite, fourth of lead, fifth of zinc and eighth of copper and gold. Other metallic minerals are tin, tungsten, molybdenum and cadmium. In addition M. has great resources of both iron and coal and these are being rapidly exploited for the development of her basic industries. For many years M. has been an important oil producer; but despite massive proved resources the industry has not developed in line with the rest of the economy, substantial quantities of oil having to be imported. The chief zone of metallic mineral products runs along the Sierra Madre Occidental from the U.S.A. border 1600 m. S. to the State of Oaxaca, though every state has some mining and the chief silver mines are the Pachuca dist 60 m. NE. of M. City. The large coalfields are in the NE. state of Coahuila near Savinas and produce a good quality coking coal. The iron ore deposits occur in various parts of the country, but the richest is Cerro del Mercado in the state of Durango. The sulphur deposits are mainly located in the Isthmus of Tehuantepec. The main oilfields are situated near the coast round the Gulf of M. and most of the refineries are in the same area: total production during recent years has averaged over 100,000,000 barrels a year, making M. the 4th largest producer in the W. hemisphere.

Traditionally both oil and metallic mineral production has been controlled by foreign companies. However, in 1938 foreign-owned oil companies were expropriated by the tate and put under the control of a gov.-controlled body Pemex (Petroleos Mexicanos), and in 1960 a law was passed with the object of Mexicanising the mining industry, which required foreign companies to sell 51 per cent of the interest in their companies to Mexican nationals.

Communications. In general, M.'s system of transport and communication cannot satisfactorily supply the services demanded of it by the current pace of economic and social development. A major cause of this situation is the mountainous character of the country which has made and makes the construction of railways and roads a costly business. The Federal Gov., mainly through the agency of the Nacional Financiera, is actively intervening to stimulate an improvement. There are about 15,000 m. of railways running mainly N.–S. and connecting the major urb. and industrial centres, but there is only 1 cross-country line, namely that across the Tehuantepec Isthmus, a distance of only 150 m. A number of short auxiliary and branch lines

have been built to connect agric. and mining areas with the main trunk lines, and there are through routes to M.'s international neighbours. 98·6 per cent of the railways are state or partly state-owned and are operated by 13 different organisations. The 2 main companies are Nacionales de M. with 10,500 m. and Del Pacifico with 1580 m. Important improvements have been made to M.'s road system during the past decade in terms of both quality and quantity, between 1955 and 1965 the total mileage increasing from 15,000 miles to 30,000 miles.

Civil aviation has been expanded rapidly and there are about 900 airports and landing fields in the country used by approximately 60 airlines carrying passengers and freight. Three Mexican and 16 foreign airlines provide international services. M. has 15 ports on the Pacific, the main ones being Salina Cruz, Mazatlán, Guaymas and Ensenada; and 19 ports on the Gulf, of which the chief are Tampico, Veracruz, Coatzacoalcos, Tuxpán and Progreso. In 1960 the national merchant fleet, Transportación Maritime Mexicana, was inaugurated and there are regular services between the Mexican Gulf ports and the Atlantic and Gulf ports of the U.S.A.

The telephone system is centralised under state supervision; there are about 400 radio broadcasting stations; and M., having been the first Lat. Amer. nation to operate television, now has over 20 broadcasting stations.

Education. Education is compulsory, free and secular for children between 6 and 14 years of age. Responsibility for public education is shared jointly between the Federal and State govs., the prin. Federal authority being the Ministry of Education whilst other depts have jurisdiction over special types of education. However, the illiteracy rate is still 34 per cent, having been reduced from 58 per cent in 1944. The rapidly increasing pop., the number of low income families and wide geographical dispersion present considerable problems to the education authorities, but under its Eleven-Year Educational Plan for 1959–70 the gov. is aiming to achieve universal education. As recently as 1959 3 million children or 40 per cent of those eligible were unable to attend primary school. The number receiving secondary education in 1961 was only just over 250,000, but a high proportion do not complete the course. M. has over 20 univs., the most famous being the National Autonomous Univ. of M. located in M. City. Here also is the National Polytechnic Institute. The states of Jalisco and Nuevo León each have 2 univs. and 17 other states have 1 each.

The number of estabs., teachers and students in different types of education are shown in the 1961 U.N. figures on page 405.

Government. The present constitution of M. dates from 1917 and whilst basically similar to that of 1857 it contains important provisions and guarantees concerning land, labour and social welfare. It declares M. to be a Federal Republic consisting of free and sovereign states to which are reserved all powers not granted to the Federal Gov. Executive power is vested in the President elected by direct popular vote for a term of 6 years and without the right to re-election. There is no Vice-President. The President's cabinet is appointed by and is responsible to him. Legislative power is vested in a bicameral Congress consisting of a Chamber of Deputies (178 members) and a Senate (58 members). Deputies are elected for a 3-year term by direct popular vote on the basis of 1 deputy representing 170,000 people and each state having at least 2 deputies. Senators are elected in the same way for 6-year terms with 2 Senators per state. Congress has regular sessions during only 4 months of the year (Sept.–Dec.) but a Permanent Committee composed of 15 deputies and 15 Senators is in permanent session the rest of the year to transact routine business.

Judicial power is vested in the Supreme Court of 21 members appointed by the President after senatorial approval. The Supreme Court appoints members of the rest of the judiciary. There are 29 states, 2 ters. and a Federal Dist. Each state has its own Governor and legislative assembly, both elected by popular vote. The Chief of the Federal Dist and Governors of Ters. are appointed by the President.

Currency. The unit of currency is the peso ($) divided into 100 centavos. Notes are issued in denominations of 1, 5, 10, 20, 50, 100, 500 and 1000 pesos; and coins in 1, 5, 20, 25 and 50 centavos and 1 and 5 pesos.

Foreign Trade. Traditionally M.'s foreign trade has consisted of exporting raw and semi-processed materials and importing capital and consumer goods including foodstuffs. Over the past 2 decades the pattern has been changing owing to her industrial development and M. is exporting an ever-increasing vol. of finished and semi-finished products: in 1964 manuf. goods accounted for 18 per cent of total exports by value, and consumer goods accounted for only 20 per cent of total imports. In general the trend has been towards diversification of exports and limitation of imports other than capital goods and necessary raw materials for industrial use. In 1964 total exports by value amounted to U.S. $1,045,000,000 and total imports to U.S. $1,492,000,000. The principal export items were raw cotton accounting for 16 per cent of the total; coffee beans 8·5 per cent; refined sugar 7·3 per cent; shrimps 5 per cent; petroleum and derivatives 3·7 per cent. As regards exports of metals and metallic minerals, silver accounted for about 4·5 per cent of the total, zinc for 3·4;

iron and steel for 2·3; and lead for 2·1 per cent. Sulphur, a developing commodity, accounted for 3·6 per cent of total exports. Other important export items are wheat, fresh and preserved fruits, fresh vegetables, fresh and frozen meat, live cattle, salt and textile yarns. M.'s chief customers in 1964 were the U.S.A., taking over 60 per cent of her exports, followed by Japan, taking about 7 per cent, and W. Germany about 2 per cent; other important customers were Italy, Switzerland, Brazil, France, U.K., Canada and the Netherlands. Of the total imports of U.S. $1492 million in 1964, the prin. items were private automobiles accounting for 7 per cent of total value; machinery installations 5 per cent; trucks 4 per cent; metal spare parts for machinery 2·8 per cent; automobile parts 2·8; tractors 2·4 per cent; and machine tools 2·4 per cent. M.'s chief sources of imports were the U.S.A. accounting for nearly 70 per cent, followed by W. Germany with 7 per cent and the U.K. with 3·5 per cent; other important sources were Canada, France, Italy, Switzerland, Japan and Sweden. In 1964 Mexican exports to the U.K. amounted to £8,315,000 and total imports to £18,357,000; the prin. export items being crude fertilisers and crude minerals, sugar and non-ferrous metals; whilst the chief import items were electrical and other machinery, transport equipment, chemicals and pharmaceuticals. Although not a member of the Central Amer. Common Market, M. is favourably concerned in its development. Normally M. has an unfavourable balance of trade, but these deficits are usually compensated for by invisible earnings, particularly from tourism and also remittances from Mexican workers in the U.S.A. and exports of gold and silver.

Industry. Industry has developed substantially since 1940. Initially the impetus came from the Second World War when M. was able easily and profitably to export manuf. goods, particularly textiles, whilst after the war industrial development became one of the gov.'s major objectives in its economic policy.

The chief characteristic of the progress during the past 15 years has been the continuous and rapid growth of producer-goods industries compared with slower rate of increase in production in the non-durable consumer goods industries. M. is now self-sufficient so far as both non-durable and durable consumer goods are concerned and exports them in significant quantities; she produces a wide variety of producer goods including electrical equipment, vehicle components, engineering machinery such as lathes and boilers; in addition motor vehicles, railway rolling stock, diesel engines, radio and television sets are assembled using either imported or locally produced parts. Gov. policy is to encourage home industry and does so by tariff protection, by the encouragement of foreign investment so long as it does not develop the controlling interest in an enterprise, and by limiting in various ways the import of the goods it wishes to develop at home.

However, textiles, food and beverages are still

the most important manufs. in terms of value, with textiles as the largest Mexican industry. The main centres of the textile industry, based on cotton, wool, silk and man-made fibres, are in the Federal Dist and in the tns of Puebla, Monterrey, Guadalajara and Torreón. The second largest industry is iron and steel with the state-owned Altos Hornos steel mill producing over 40 per cent of M.'s ann. output; in 1964 it produced some 1,200,000 tons of steel ingots. Other important iron and steel mills are located in M. City, Cannaanea, Monterrey, Torreón and Clihuahua. Sugar is the third major industry with over 70 sugar mills in various parts of the country. The food-processing industry is developing rapidly, particularly as regards fruit and vegetable canning and the processing of seafoods. Tourism is important both as a home industry and in respect of foreign exchange earnings, and the gov. participates actively in it. Electrical power production has been rapidly increased from 1,235,000 kW installed capacity in 1950 to over 5,000,000 kW in 1964, with further expansion in progress. Under the gov.'s economic plan, emphasis is being put on industrial chemicals, petro-chemicals, man-made fibres, industrial machinery, components and spare parts. Around 40 per cent of M.'s industry is concentrated in the Federal Dist, which is well served with transport and power. The next 2 major industrial concentrations are at Monterrey and Guadalajara, but efforts are being made to achieve a better distribution throughout the country.

Foreign Investment. Foreign investment plays a significant part in the Mexican economy, it having been estimated that during the past 5 years foreign investment has accounted for just over 14 per cent of M.'s total investment. It has been estimated that in 1963 the U.S.A. accounted for 85 per cent of the U.S. $1500 million of foreign investment. The next largest foreign investor is Canada with about 13 per cent, followed by the U.K. with around 4 per cent. Traditionally, mining was the main field of foreign investment (and oil until the expropriation in 1938) and in 1940 accounted for nearly 50 per cent of foreign investment. There has since been a relative decline in favour of manufacturing which is today the major field.

Social Welfare. The Constitution and other legislative measures provide the Mexican people with considerable social and economic protection. Working hrs are limited by law to a maximum of 8 hrs a day or 7 hrs a night, with a guaranteed rest day every 6 days. There is equal pay for equal work, regardless of sex, and overtime is paid at double rates. The right to organise in trade unions is estab. by law. Minimum wages and compensation are covered by legislation. In 1963 an old law was resuscitated requiring employers to operate profit-sharing schemes with their employees. The Social Insurance Law of 1942 covers the provision on a compulsory basis of financial and medical protection of many kinds to employees, including peasants and domestic workers.

Workers are covered by social insurance, the payment of premiums being divided between the employer, employee and the State; benefits are paid for industrial injuries, occupational diseases, sickness, maternity and old age. The gov. depts responsible for social welfare are the Ministry of Labour and Public Welfare and the Ministry of Health and Welfare, the latter being responsible for the Public Health Service.

Armed Forces. The president is the supreme commander of the armed forces. The country is divided into 32 military dists. In 1963 the regular army consisted of 50 infantry battalions, 2 infantry brigades, 21 cavalry regiments, 1 mechanised cavalry regiment, 3 regiments of artillery and 2 coastal batteries, with a total strength of about 51,000. There is also a conscript army of about 250,000 officers and men organised into National Service Divs. each about 6000 to 7000 strong. The air force has 8 squadrons, and the navy 4 frigates, 3 gunboats, 25 escort vessels and some patrol craft.

History. It is impossible to fix with certainty the earlier events in Mexican hist. About the 7th cent. AD the Nahua nations began to settle in the valley of M., and a leading tribe, the Toltecs (probably meaning artificers), founded a city named Tollan on the site of the present vil. of Tula, about 30 m. NW. of M. city. This kingdom was a centre of civilisation, but in the 11th cent. it fell before the assaults of another Nahua tribe, the Chichimecs, who adopted the arts and culture of the race they had overthrown. The various subdivs. of this family founded cities throughout a tract of ter. commensurate with modern M. Of them the Aztecs (q.v.) were the chief, and they founded the city of Anahuac or M., and at the time of the Sp. conquest had attained a widespread suzerainty. On the coming of the Spaniards under Cortés in 1519, Aztec rule was finally overthrown, chiefly by means of the assistance the Spaniards received from the peoples who had been subjugated by the Aztecs. After the disgrace of Cortés M. was governed by a viceroy and council for nearly 300 years.

In 1821, after a prolonged revolutionary campaign, the independence of M. was secured, and an emperor, Agustin de Iturbide, seated on the throne. He abdicated in 1823 and, attempting to return, was shot in the following year. M. was proclaimed a rep. in 1824. In 1846 there was war with the U.S.A., which ended in the defeat of M. New M. and Upper California were ceded to the conquerors, who, however, paid compensation of $15,000,000. In 1863, through the intervention of Napoleon III of France, the unfortunate Maximilian, an Austrian archduke, was created Emperor of M. His reign was brief, and despite Fr. assistance he was deposed and executed. After a long period of anarchy Porfirio Díaz obtained the presidency (1876). He did far more to bring the rep. into line with other civilised communities than any of his predecessors. After a long and prosperous term of office a series of revolutionary movements destroyed his power and in 1911 he was forced into exile. His successor was Madero, but complete anarchy had set in, and in 1913 he was murdered. The next president, Huerta, incurred the hostility of the U.S.A., who favoured his rival Carranza, and in 1914 he was forced to flee the country; thus the last prospect of order in M. vanished. Carranza retained power for 6 stormy years, but in 1920 he was assassinated. Obregón and Calles, who were the next presidents, effected some improvements. Calles, who was president from 1924 to 1928, carried out various reforms, but his administration was marked by a bitter struggle between Church and State. From 1929–31 churches in M. were closed by gov. order. Eventually an understanding was reached: public worship was restored but any Church intervention in public affairs was strictly prohibited. There was an abortive revolution in the spring of 1930, when many army units mutinied under the leadership of Gen. Aguirre. The U.S.A. actively supported the federal gov. of M. and after the capture and execution of Aguirre the revolt collapsed. The remainder of the year saw peaceful conditions under the administration of Portes Gil, who succeeded Calles. In the ensuing elections, Pascual Ortiz Rubio, a candidate of the so-called Revolutionary party, was elected by practically 100 per cent of the votes cast, but he soon resigned and was succeeded in 1934 by Gen. Cárdenas.

A question which agitated M. for 5 years (1937–41) was that of the ownership and control of the oil resources. In 1937 Cárdenas promulgated a decree which aimed at bringing all these resources under national control. The foreign oil companies, sceptical of the Mexican offer of indemnification, appealed to their respective govs. The dispute was eventually settled by negotiation, the last foreign oil concession in M. being bought out by the Mexican gov. in 1950.

M. is today preponderantly a democratic nation. Its democratic sympathies were shown during the Sp. Civil War, when M. exported considerable supplies of arms and ammunition to the Sp. Rep. Gov. The Camacho Gov., which took office in 1940, realised the danger to M. implicit in the aggressive designs of the Axis powers, and readily responded to the various proposals made by the U.S.A. in 1941 for closer co-operation and settlement of outstanding differences. The murder in M. in 1940 of Leon Trotsky, who had been granted asylum there some years previously, involved the gov. in difficulties with the Communists, who were assumed to be responsible for the outrage. In June 1942 M. formally declared war on the Axis powers, as a response to Axis sinkings of Mexican ships, her contribution being almost wholly represented by the supply of strategic materials. On 27 Jan. 1945 the final report of the Mexican-Amer. commission for economic co-operation was issued: it dealt with industrial development, agriculture, aviation, highway transport, and tourism. It was on the initiative of M. that a conference of foreign ministers of all the member states (excepting Argentina) of the Pan-Amer. Union was opened at M. city (Feb. 1945). The succeeding year was marked by the

drawing closer of the ties of friendship with the U.S.A. In Mar. 1947 President Truman paid a visit of goodwill to M. city and emphasised America's adherence to the principles laid down by Roosevelt regarding relations with the other Amer. reps. During the Second World War M. had been in a seller's market and had experienced boom conditions. With the end of the war her trade balances became adverse, draining the country of dollar credits. Under presidents Alemán Valdés, Ruiz Cortines and López Mateos, the country was put on a sound economic basis, and much progress made in the field of social reform. President Kennedy visited M. in 1962; and U.S.-M. friendship survived certain differences resulting from political developments in Cuba and the Dominican Rep. (qq.v.).

Archaeological research. The anct monuments and other traces of their life and art executed by the aborigines give a high estimation of the degree of civilisation to which they had attained. In many parts of the country, especially at Cholula, Papantla, Tula and Xochiacalco, are found graduated pyramids known as Teocalli, or 'Houses of the Gods', constructed of mounds of earth faced with masonry, in some instances elaborately carved. The fearful rite of human sacrifice was common; some authorities consider that 20,000 victims were destroyed annually in the cap. alone. On the summit of these pyramids the sacrifices took place to the god Tezcatlipoca, 'the soul of the world', or to Huitzilopochtli, the god of war, or to Tlaloc, the rain god. Few traces of domestic architecture remain.

The form of gov. was elective monarchy, which was almost absolute, though the king was expected to confer with his council before deciding upon any important step. There was a well-defined code of laws, and the standard of morals was high. Wars were frequent, and the arms and armour of the Aztecs, though inadequate to oppose the Spaniards, were elaborate. The Mexican rank and file wore no armour; the chiefs had quilted cotton tunics and some reinforced them by thin plates of gold or silver. Their missile weapons were slings, bows and arrows, and javelins, pointed with bone or copper. Their warfare with the Spaniards resembled that of the Persians against the Greeks. Prisoners of war were usually reserved for sacrifice.

The Aztecs were highly cultured, and, besides possessing a rudimentary system of picture writing, they were extraordinarily gifted in the pictorial and minor graphic arts, especially in feather work of which the garments of the upper classes principally consisted. Prescott remarks that the Aztecs and the Incas far surpassed all other races on the Amer. continents in civilisation. The Mexican civilisation, though inferior to that of Peru in political capacity and most of the arts, was sufficiently imposing, and its ruthless destruction was a loss to the world. As will be seen in the article MAYA, notable stone carvings have been found at Tenayuca, a site which has, in the opinion of experts, been continuously occupied since the Archaic period. *Art and culture.* Not only did the Aztecs produce a massive, well-proportioned architectural style, the remains of which still survive: they also cut many delicate miniature figures from crystal and jade, and showed a high degree of skill in fashioning copper and gold ornaments. Their craftsmanship is at its finest in the sacred masks used in religious celebrations; many of these are extant, and are encrusted with elaborate and fanciful patterns of pearls, turquoise and other jewels, in which a feather motif predominates. The Aztecs' unusual and effective colour combinations are still favoured by the Mexican peasant. The Sp. conquerors introduced renaissance and baroque styles. But Sp.-Mexican architecture shows marked signs of Mexican-Indian influence, even at the time when every effort was being made to eradicate all traces of the Indian civilisation. This is particularly noticeable in church architecture; baroque is often simply a basis on to which Indian masons and artists have moulded their traditional patterns. Churches are frequently decorated with multicoloured, polished glass, wood, or stone ornamentation; beaten metal-work is worked in Indian designs. Examples of this fusion in M. city include the churches of St Fernando and St Francisco, and the façade of the cathedral. Prov. architecture bears still stronger traces of Indian style, as at Pueblo and Morelia. Both Sp. and Indian strains in art survive today, together with an abundant oral literature of myth and legend, which is being consciously invoked by modern Mexican artists in their determination to create a truly Mexican culture, while at the same time absorbing the artistic influences of Europe and N. America. Diego Rivera (q.v.) shows this in his paintings of peasant life and in the propagandist character of many of his wall paintings. Mural painting has been a main development in which Jose Clemente Orozco, David Alfaro Siqueiros and Juan O'Gorman have also been eminent.

See H. B. Parkes, *A History of Mexico* (revised ed.), 1950; F. Cline, *Mexico: Revolution to Evolution, 1940–60*, 1962; G. J. Butland, *Latin America*, 1965; H. Davies (editor), *The South American Handbook*, 1965; Inter-Amer. Development Bank, *Annual Reports*. (*See Plate*.)

México, state of central Mexico, containing within its borders the Federal Dist of which the cap. is Mexico City. Situated in the S. part of the Central Mexican plateau and enclosed by mts in the E., S. and W., its general elevation is about 7000 ft. Across the S. of the state runs the Cordillera Neovolcánica with such peaks as Popocatêpetl (17,880 ft) and Iztaccihuatl (17,340 ft). The climate is temperate with an adequate rainfall. Economically it is one of the leading states of the country. Agriculturally very fertile, the main crops are maize, alfalfa, wheat, beans, magney, potatoes, peppers, fruit, sugarcane and coffee. The chief minerals are gold, silver, iron ore, copper, sulphur and marble. Quite apart from the Federal Dist, there is considerable industrial activity in various parts of the state. The centre of the Aztec Kingdom and with a long hist. before that, the state owes its importance not only to its climate but also to its geographical position in relation to the Atlantic and Pacific. The cap. is Toluca (q.v.); other important tns are Naucalpan de Juarez, Tenanciugo, Texcoco and Chaleo. Area 8268 sq. m. Pop. 1,897,851 (1960).

Mexico, Gulf of, great inlet situated between the U.S.A. on the N. and M. on the W. and S. It has an area of some 800,000 sq. m., and is entered by a section of the Equatorial Current, thus initiating the Gulf Stream which sweeps its shores clockwise in a semicircle. It is subject to sharp wind-storms and hurricanes.

Mexico City, cap. of the United States of Mexico. It is one of the oldest and greatest cities of the Americas, and is situated in a fine valley, the valley of Mexico, on the Anahuac plateau, well above sea level, at the S. extremity of the Mesa tableland and near the former lake of Texcuco. Its high elevation (7350 ft) ensures an equable climate. The range of temp. is 20°–85° F. with 58° as a mean; the nights are always cool; normal ann. rainfall is 26 in. No other city in the new world is richer in historical tradition or romantic lore. It was the heart of the Aztec (q.v.) culture, and on its broad plaza stood the great Teocalli or sacrificial pyramid, Tenochtitlán, the veritable Mecca of Mexico. When Cortés first saw the city it was built on an is. in a large lake, with causeways to the shores. After the conquest the city became the cap. of 'New Spain' and, even though the rule of Iturbide, its first national emperor, was short, the city could boast of being the cap. of the third largest empire of the world, ranking only after China and Russia. The greatest names in its hist. are those of Juárez, the lawyer-president who is commemorated in the avenue named after him, Hidalgo, the priest liberator, and Morelos, another champion of popular liberties. Generally speaking, the city is spacious and pleasing. The main plaza, Zócalo, is over 300 yds long and is overlooked by the splendid cathedral whose 2 towers rise to over 200 ft and are a conspicuous landmark. The cathedral (the foundations of which were laid in 1573 and the whole building completed in 1811) stands upon the site of the Teocalli: it is 400 ft long by 200 ft wide, and is in the form of a Gk cross; it has 22 side chapels, an altar of marble columns, a balustrade with 62 statues, a giant candelabrum of precious metals, and some 20 Doric columns support the vaulted roof. This cathedral is probably the finest eccles. building on the Amer. continent. The city is laid out with geometric exactness; the streets are wide and handsome, though the chief business thoroughfare, the Plateros, is narrow. This street, is, however, lined with many magnificent shops. Near the plaza is the Palacio Nacional, containing the gov. depts., the museum, observatory, the senate and other important institutions. Over the portals of the Palacio hangs the 'liberty bell' of Hidalgo, which is rung by the president at midnight on the anniversary of Mexican independence. The present Palacio replaces another which was destroyed in 1689. It was built in 1691, but the top floor was added by President Calles. The museum contains among other interesting objects the Calendar Stone, assigned to Toltec culture, and the Sacrificial Stone which was found in the ruins of the great Teocalli. Among other important buildings are the national library, the Minería or school of mining engineering (one of the oldest buildings), the new legislative house, the new Communications building, palace of justice, univ. and the Monte de Piedad or state pawnshop (this latter founded in 1775). A beautiful example of Churrigueresque architecture survives in La Merced Monastery, in the N. quarter of Merced Market. Two notable modern buildings are the post office and the Palace of Fine Arts Theatre. From the city the Paseo de la Reforma, a broad boulevard, extends in a S.-westerly direction for some 3 m. to the castle of Chapultepec, one of the residences of the presidents. The Univ. City on the outskirts is an important modern experiment in both education and architecture.

The city is a general clearing-house for the transit trade of the country and its industries comprise the greatest industrial complex in the country. The climate is dry, healthy and temperate, but the altitude causes a rarification of the air which is detrimental to certain subjects. From M. C. the snow-covered peaks of the volcanoes Popocatepétl and Ixtaccíhuatl can be clearly distinguished. In 1960 the pop. of the city was 2,832,133 and of the Federal Dist 4,870,876. (*See Plate: Mexico.*)

Meyer, Adolf (1866–1950), Swiss-American psychiatrist, *b.* Niederweiningen. He studied medicine at Zürich and qualified in 1890. He was early attracted to specialise in neurology and psychiatry. In 1892 he went to Chicago; from 1895 to 1902 he taught at Clark University, Worcester, Massachusetts, and from 1902 to 1909 was director of the pathological institute of the State hospitals for the insane, New York. During part of this time (1904–9) he was also prof. of psychiatry at Cornell Univ. medical school. In 1910 he was appointed prof. of psychiatry at Johns Hopkins Univ. and chief psychiatrist at Johns Hopkins hospital, Baltimore; he retired in 1941. From 1913 he also directed the Henry Phipps Psychiatric Clinic. M. exerted a far-reaching influence on many fields of medical work; both as teacher and research worker he had a profound effect on Amer. psychiatry.

Meyer, Conrad Ferdinand (1825–98), Swiss poet and novelist, *b.* Zürich. Being bilingual, he only decided in favour of German after the war of 1870. His first work, written when he was 39, was the verse collection *Zwanzig Balladen von einem Schweizer*, 1864, followed in 1871 by *Romanzen und Bilder*. His prose works show the same desire for absolute perfection. His 2 best-known novels, *Jürg Jenatsch*, 1874, and *Der Heilige*, 1880, are full of life and action, blended with the cool observation of the realist. His historical *Novellen*, such as *Das Amulett*,

1873, Die *Hochzeit des Mönchs*, 1884, and *Die Richterin*, 1885, reveal the same creative power. See A. Burkhard, *C. F. Meyer, the Style and the Man*, 1932; W. D. Williams, *The Stories of C. F. Meyer*, 1962.

Meyer, Hans (1858–1929), Ger. explorer, *b.* Hildburghausen. He was director of the Bibliographisches Institut, 1885–1914. After exploring Ger. E. Africa he ascended Kilimanjaro; in 1889 he reached the summit of Kibo and found the crater, and studied the volcanoes and glaciation of Ecuadorian Cordilleras in 1903. In 1911 he made another long expedition in E. Africa. From 1915 to 1928 he was prof. of colonial geography and colonial politics in the univ. of Leipzig.

Meyer, Heinrich (1759–1832), Ger. painter and art critic, made the acquaintance of Goethe in Rome (1786) and in 1797 settled down in Weimar, where he enjoyed the great poet's friendship and inspired him, it seems, with many of those opinions on art and aesthetics which appeared in *Kunst und Alterthum; Winckelmann und sein Jahrhundert*, 1805 (with Goethe), etc. He ed. Winckelmann's works (1808–20).

Meyer, Julius Lothar (1830–95), Ger. chemist, *b.* Varel, Oldenburg, studied medicine at Zürich, chem. under Bunsen at Heidelberg, and physics at Königsberg under Neumann. Virchow was his teacher in pathology, but under the influence of K. F. W. Ludwig and Kirchhoff he turned his attention to physiological chem. and mathematical physics. During the Franco-Prussian war he tended the sick and wounded at Karlsruhe Polytechnic. From 1876 onward he held the chair of chem. at Tübingen. In his *Die modernen Theorien der Chemie*, 1864, he helped to develop the startling theory of the periodic classification of elements and recalculated the atomic weights.

Meyer, Victor (1848–97), Ger. chemist, *b.* Berlin. He became prof. of chem. at Zürich in 1872, at Göttingen in 1885, and 4 years later succeeded Bunsen, his old master, at his own univ. of Heidelberg. He discovered the aliphatic nitro and related compounds, thiophen and a convenient method of ascertaining the density of vapours. *See* life by R. Meyer, 1917.

Meyer-Lübke, Wilhelm (1861–1936), *b.* Dubendorf, Switzerland. Prof. at Jena Univ. (1887), Vienna (1890), Bonn (1915). Pub. many important works on the Romance languages, including *Die lateinische Sprache in den romanischen Ländern*, 1888, *Einführung in das Studium der romanischen Sprachwissenschaft*, 1901 (3rd ed., 1921), *Grammatik der romanischen* 1890–1902, *Romanisches etymologisches Wörterbuch*, 1911 (3rd ed., 1935) and historical grammars of Italian, Sardinian, Portuguese, French, Catalan and Rumanian.

Meyerbeer, Giacomo, really **Jakob Beer** (1791–1864), Ger. composer of Jewish extraction, *b.* Berlin, son of Herz Beer, a banker. He appeared as a prodigy pianist at the age of 6, and studied under Clementi, Zelter and the Abbé Vogler. Abandoning his early intention of being a pianist, he went to Venice to study composition (1815) where he composed sev. It. operas in the style of Rossini, successful but none of them important except the last, *Il Crociato in Egitto*, 1824. In 1826 M. took up his abode in Paris, where his chief operas were produced: *Robert le Diable*, 1831, *Les Huguenots*, 1836, and *Le Prophète*, 1849. Meanwhile he received the appointment of *Kapellmeister* to the King of Prussia, and in Berlin produced a Ger. opera entitled *Ein Feldlager in Schlesien*, 1844, in which Jenny Lind (q.v.) made her first appearance in Prussia. He procured the acceptance of Wagner's *Rienzi* and *Der fliegende Holländer*. In 1854 he produced *L'Étoile du nord* at the Opéra Comique, and in 1859 *Le Pardon de Ploërmel*. His last major work was *L'Africaine*, a revision of which was in preparation at the Paris Opéra when he *d*. M. is one of the most important figures in the hist of Fr. opera, but his work is now all but forgotten so far as performance goes. It is remarkable for its brilliant effects and powerful climaxes, rather than for any mastery of form or coherence, and its melodic invention is artificial. He wrote much instrumental and choral music of a less ambitious nature, and about 40 songs. (*See Plate: German Music.*)

Meyerhof, Otto Fritz (1884–1951), Ger. physiologist, *b*. Berlin, educated at Königliche Wilhelms Gymnasium, Berlin. Prof. at Keil, 1918–24, he was a member of the Kaiser Institute for Biology, Berlin-Dahlem, 1924–9, and director of research at the Institute of Biology, Paris, 1938–40. He investigated oxidation and utilisation of lactic acid in muscle, publishing *Energy Transformation and Chemistry of Muscle*, 1922, and shared the Nobel prize for physiology and medicine with A. V. Hill in 1923. Other pubs., on respiration and fermentation of cells and enzymes (in English): *Chemical Dynamics of Life Phenomena*, 1924, and 'Chemical Studies on Muscle' in *Journal of General Physiology*, 1926.

Meynell, Alice Christiana Gertrude (1847–1922), poet and essayist, *b*. Barnes, near London, daughter of T. J. Thompson. She spent most of her young days in Italy. Her first vol. of verse, *Preludes*, 1875, was illustrated by her sister, Lady Butler, painter of 'The Roll Call', and won warm praise from Ruskin. Then, for nearly 20 years, poetry was left aside for marriage to Wilfrid M. (q.v.) and journalism. Her *Poems*, pub. in 1893, definitely estab. her fame, while her *Rhythm of Life*, pub. at the same date, placed her in the front rank of living writers in prose. This was followed by *The Colour of Life and other Essays*, 1896, *The Children*, 1896, *The Flower of the Mind*, 1897 (an anthology of Eng. verse), and *The Spirit of Peace*, 1898. She also ed. the *Selected Poems* of Hake and the *Poetry of Pathos and Delight* of Patmore, and contributed to various periodicals. Among later works are *London Impressions*, 1898, *John Ruskin*, 1900, *Later Poems*, 1902, *Children of the Old Masters, Italian School*, 1903, *Ceres' Runaway*, 1910, *Mary, the Mother of Jesus*, 1912, *Collected Poems*, 1913, *Essays*, 1914, and *Last Poems*, 1923. Her writing is akin to that of Christina

Rossetti in fine and delicate craftsmanship. *See* A. K. Tuell, *Mrs Meynell and her Literary Generation*, 1925, and life by Viola Meynell, 1929.

Meynell, Sir Francis (1891–), English book designer and typographer, younger son of Wilfrid and Alice M. (q.v.); educ. at Downside and Trinity College, Dublin. In 1923, with Vera M. and David Garnett, founded the Nonesuch Press, which became known for many well-produced and scholarly eds. of standard authors, all of which are designed by M. In 1945 M. became typographic adviser to H.M.S.O. He was knighted in 1946. Pubs.: *The Typography of Newspaper Advertisements*, 1929; *Seventeen Poems*, 1945; *English Printed Books*, 1946; *Poems and Pieces*, 1961.

Meynell, Wilfrid (1852–1948), journalist, poet and essayist, *b*. Newcastle upon Tyne, husband of Alice M. (q.v.). In their early married days M. and his wife pub. the *Pen*, a short-lived critical monthly review. A more significant joint venture was *Merry England*, a monthly of 12 years' duration, the contributions to which were largely their own work. M., who left the Society of Friends for the Rom. Catholic Church at 18, ed., for Cardinal Manning, his great friend, the *Register*, which he conducted according to a home rule and 'Young England' policy, in contrast with that of the *Tablet*, which was the paper of Rom. Catholic Toryism. Meanwhile M. was writing stories, verse and articles, sometimes under his own name and sometimes as 'John Oldcastle' (e.g. in his practical handbook, *Journals and Journalism*, 1880), as 'Francis Phillimore' or anonymously. Throughout the 45 years of their married life M. and his wife collaborated in numerous literary projects of one kind or another. Perhaps M.'s greatest service to literature was his discovery of Francis Thompson (q.v.), who for 19 years was an adopted son in the M. household. M.'s works include *The Man Disraeli*, 1903, *Verses and Reverses*, 1912, *Aunt Sarah and the War*, 1914, *Rhymes With Reasons*, 1918, and *Come and See*, 1919. In 1934 he was awarded the C.B.E.

Mezereon, or *Daphne mezereum*, Small fragrant shrub (family Thymelaeaceae) indigenous to Britain, with fragrant red or white flowers borne in Feb. and followed by red berries. It is poisonous, but has medicinal uses.

Mézières, Fr. tn, cap. of the dept of Ardennes, on a bend of the Meuse, opposite Charleville. It was defended by Bayard (q.v.) in 1521, was invested in 1815, and again in 1870 during the Franco-Ger. war (q.v.). During the First World War, N. was for a time the seat of the Ger. G.H.Q. Machinery, hardware and nails are manuf. Pop. 11,800. (*See also* MANGIN.)

Mezöberény, tn of Hungary, in Békés co., 10 m. NW. of Békéscsaba (q.v.). It has manufs. of pottery and bricks, and a trade in agric. produce, flax and tobacco. Pop. 10,900.

Mezöhegyés, tn of Hungary, in Békés co., 28 m. SSW. of Békéscsaba (q.v.). It has a state stud farm (founded 1785) and manufs. of agric. tools. Pop. 8200.

Mezőkövesd, tn of Hungary, in Borsodbauj-Zemplén co., 23 m. SSW. of Miskolc (q.v.). It is the chief tn of the Matyó dist, which is known for its embroidery. It has a large trade in tobacco, and there are mineral springs. Pop. 18,800.

Mezőtúr, tn of Hungary, in Szolnok co., on the R. Berettyo, 24 m. SE. of Szolnok (q.v.). It is in a dist producing cereals, hemp, tobacco and livestock, and was one of the first centres of the co-operative farm movement under the Communist regime. Pop. 18,400.

Mezuzah, narrow hollow strip of wood or other substance, with a piece cut out near the top and containing a scroll of parchment on which are written the *Shema* (Deut. vi. 4–9, and xi. 13–21). On the back of the scroll is written the Heb. word 'Almighty', and this is left exposed when the scroll is fixed in the case. The M. is affixed to the exterior and interior doorposts of Jewish homes and public buildings.

Mezzanine, *see* ENTRESOL.

Mezzo-soprano, species of voice which has a somewhat lower range than a soprano, but is higher than a contralto. It is the voice most normal to women, and has a varying compass generally from A beneath the treble stave to A 2 octaves above.

Mezzotint, method of engraving invented about the middle of the 17th cent. and known on the Continent as 'la manière anglaise'. M.s are engraved on copper, which, in the early part of the 19th cent., was sometimes steeled. The method of mezzotinting is to cover the surface of the plate, in all directions, uniformly with fine dots, sometimes as many as 100 to the inch, by means of a rocker or a roulette. The former is a chisel-shaped instrument with a slightly curved edge, serrated with fine teeth. A print from the plate so prepared, in consequence of the number of cavities and the burr (q.v.) raised round them, would appear a deep uniform black. The plate is then worked on with a 'scraper' to obtain the high lights, and the burnisher is finally used to obtain the highest lights, the artist working from dark to light. Mezzotinting was introduced about the reign of Charles I by Prince Rupert, the inventor being L. von Siegen. Among the great exponents of the method are John Smith (1625–1742), James MacArdell (1729–65), Valentine Green (1739–1813), John Raphael Smith (1752–1812) and David Lucas (1802–81). *See also* COLOUR PRINTING and ENGRAVING. *See* C. Davenport, *Mezzotints*, 1904; and M. C. Salaman, *Old English Mezzotints*, 1910.

Mfumbiro, chain of volcanic mts near the boundary of SW. Uganda and Congo. It consists of 2 groups: the W., which lies directly N. of Lake Kivu and contains 2 active volcanoes; and the E., where is the loftiest peak, Karissimbi (14,780 ft).

M.G.B. (Russian abbreviation for **Ministry of State Security**), name of the Soviet security service, 1946–53. Its functions, methods and position in the state were essentially the same as those of its predecessors N.K.V.D. (q.v.) and N.K.G.B. (q.v.), and it was likewise under Stalin's direct orders. Among its main opera-

tions were those directed against the 'cosmopolitans' (mostly Jewish intellectuals) in 1949 and against the former supporters of Zhdanov (mostly Leningrad party leaders). These were forebodings of the new wave of mass terror, similar to the Great Purge (q.v.), which began in 1952 with the discovery of the so-called 'Doctors' Plot' but came to an end at Stalin's death.

Mho (the reciprocal of the ohm), practical unit of electric conductivity or admittance. *See* UNITS, ELECTRICAL.

Miagao, trading and manufacturing tn on the S. coast of Panay Is. in the Philippines. Hemp, rice and sugar are produced. Pop. *c.* 30,000.

Miami, tribe of N. Amer. Indians belonging to the Algonquian family. They originally inhabited Wisconsin. They offered steady resistance to the white colonists throughout the 18th cent. Today there are under 300, mostly in Oklahoma.

Miami: 1. City and co. seat of Dade co. Florida, U.S.A., on M.R. and Biscayne Bay. It is in an area famous for the production of citrus fruit and winter vegetables, and there is a considerable amount of fishing, both sporting and the sponge fisheries in Biscayne Bay. M. is just N. of the tropic, and is a flourishing winter resort. Its sea frontage is studded with skyscrapers. Though it is essentially a resort, it manufs. concrete, meat and bakery products; novelties, clothing, beverages; and is also a fashion centre. It has important air services to the W. Indies and S. America and is a port of entry. M. is subject to hurricanes, which have done great damage. Pop. 291,690.

2. (Great M.), Riv. in Ohio, 160 m. long, joining Ohio Riv, near the Indiana border, partly canalised.

Miao, Chinese national minority inhabiting the mt dists. of Hunan and Kweichow, SW. China. In 1954 they numbered 2½ million.

Miaskovsky, Nikolai Yokovlevich (1881–1950), Russian composer, *b.* near Warsaw, son of a Russian military engineer stationed in Poland. M. joined the army, but resigned his commission in 1907, already having composed sev. pianoforte preludes, studied with Gliere and Krizhanovsky, and entered the St Petersburg Conservatory in 1906 to study under Liadov. He was badly wounded in the First World War. In 1921 he became prof. of composition at the Moscow Conservatory. His works include the oratorio *Kirov is with us*, 27 symphonies, the symphonic poems *Nevermore* (after Poe) and *Alastor* (after Shelley), 9 string quartets and numerous piano pieces and songs. *See* G. Abraham, *Eight Soviet Composers*, 1943; A. Ikonnikov, *Miaskovsky*, 1946.

Miasma (Gk *miainein*, to corrupt or pollute), term formerly used to denote poisonous particles, smells or emanations, which, by entering the body, were supposed to cause disease. Until the discovery of the microbic origin of infections in the latter half of the 19th cent., M. were universally held to be the cause of infectious diseases. Since offensive emanations frequently occur in environmental conditions which favour the transmission of infectious disease, the old idea that M. caused these diseases was based on shrewd observation, although scientifically wide of the mark (*see* EPIDEMIOLOGY).

Miass, tn in the Chelyabinsk Oblast of the Urals, 46 m. WSW. of Chelyabinsk on the Trans-Siberian railway. Centre of a gold-mining area. Automobile industry (lorries) since 1944. Pop. (1965) 117,000 (1933, 22,000). Founded in 1773 as copper-smelting works.

Mica, group of minerals which are distinguished by their very perfect basal cleavage, causing them to split readily into thin flakes, and by their vitreous, pearly lustre. The M.s are complex silicates of aluminium and either alkali metals or iron and magnesium, together with water and occasionally fluorine. Average hardness 2·5. Sp. gr. about 3. They are frequently found in schists, gneisses and granites. Muscovite or white potash M. is clear and colourless, and may be obtained in large, flexible and elastic plates. It was formerly used for glazing windows under the name of Muscovy glass, and is still in use for lamp chimneys. Lepidolite, or lithia M., is generally rose-red or violet in colour, while biotite, magnesia M., is black or dark brown. Other types of M. are phlogopite, lepidomelane, paragonite and Zinnwaldite. The minerals of the M. group are alike in having a prism angle of nearly 60°, thus simulating hexagonal structure, perfect basal cleavage, and in crystallising in the monoclinic (or oblique) system. Potash M. on weathering forms clay and potassium salts, the latter being retained by the soil.

Mica Schist, schistose or fine-grained foliated rock, rich in biotite or muscovite or both. It is a typical metamorphic rock, and occurs very largely in the Highlands, where the older strata outcrop (q.v.). It generally contains quartz and felspar, and garnet, kyanite, schorl, chlorite, etc.. are common accessory minerals.

Micah, the Morashtite (i.e. native of Moresheth, a vil. near Gath, on the confines of Judah), one of the 12 minor Heb. prophets, a younger contemporary of Isaiah, referred to in Jer. xxvi. 18 as having prophesied in the days of Hezekiah and Ahaz, kings of Judah. Only a part of the book is generally thought to come from M. himself. Interpolations, generally post-exilic, are frequent and continually break the chain of thought. *See* commentaries by Wade, 1925; *also* Findlay, *The Books of the Prophets*, 1913, and Robinson, *Prophecy and Prophets in Ancient Israel*, 1923.

Michael (Who like God?), the archangel spoken of in Dan. (x. 13, 21; xii. 1) as chief of the heavenly host and as the guardian of Israel. He appears in Jude ix, and in Rev. xii. 7 he is the leader of the Heavenly Hosts against Satan and the Hosts of Evil. In Christian tradition he expelled Satan and his angels from Heaven after the primeval rebellion against God (*see* DEVIL). His festival day is 29 Sept. (*see* MICHAELMAS DAY).

Michael, name of a succession of 8 emperors who, at different periods, occupied the throne of the E. from 811 to 1282, the last being Michael

VIII, the founder of the Palaeologic dynasty.

Michael (1596–1645), first tsar of Muscovy and Russia of the house of Romanov. He was elected tsar by the Assembly of the Land, 1613, after the Time of Troubles. A weak and inconspicuous person, he had the hard task of re-establishing order in the country and defending it against external enemies (Poland and Sweden), in which he relied upon his father, Patriarch Philaret of Moscow, sev. favourites and the Assembly of the Land, which met 16 times in his reign.

Michael I (1921–), ex-King of Rumania, only son of Carol (Charles) II and Helen of Greece. He succeeded his grandfather, King Ferdinand, in 1927, his father having formally renounced the succession; in 1930, however, Carol claimed the throne and was proclaimed king, his deposed son being given the title of crown prince and Prince of Alba Julia. In 1940 Carol abdicated and M. succeeded him. His reign was marked by the Ger. domination of Rumania during the Second World War, and later by the rapid growth of Soviet influence in the country. In Dec. 1947 M. abdicated, but in Mar. 1948 renounced his abdication, alleging it had been forced on him by the Communist dominated gov. In June 1948 he married Princess Anne of Bourbon-Parma, by whom he has 3 daughters. M. and his family now live in Britain.

Michael, 'the Brave' (1558–1601), voivode of Wallachia from 1593, secured for Wallachia during his reign a place in world hist. He invaded Turkish ter. and took by storm Rustchuk, Silistria and other places on the Danube, and also defeated a large Turkish and Tartar army which invaded Wallachia. In 1595 he defeated Sinan Pasha, who had invaded Wallachia, but only drove him out with the help of Sigismund Báthory of Transylvania. His independence was acknowledged by the sultan in 1597. In 1599 he invaded Transylvania, defeated Andreas Báthory (Sigismund's successor), was proclaimed prince and, having expelled (1600) the voivode of Moldavia, united under his sceptre 3 principalities and all Rumanians. He was, however, driven out of Transylvania by a revolt, but returned, and with the imperial Gen. Basta defeated the Transylvanian forces at Goroszló, expelling Sigismund Báthory, who had returned to power after the murder of his cousin Andreas. M. was murdered in 1601 on Basta's orders.

Michael, St, and St George, Order of, *see* ORDERS OF KNIGHTHOOD, GREAT BRITAIN AND IRELAND (5).

Michaelis, John Benjamin (1746–72), Ger. writer, *b.* Tittau. He studied medicine at Leipzig, but being attracted by poetry pub., with Gellert and Weisse, a collection of fables, and soon after gave up his profession of a doctor. His works, which consist of odes, satires, lyrics, comic operas, etc., were pub. in 4 vols., 1791.

Michaelis, Karin (1872–1950), Dan. novelist, *b.* Randers, wife of Sophus M. (1865–1932), also a writer. She wrote romantic novels displaying an intimate knowledge of female psychology, and her novel *Den Farlige Alder*, 1910, created the phrase 'the dangerous age'. She is also well known for her children's books centring round the little girl Bibi.

Michaelmas Daisy, *see* ASTER.

Michaelmas Day, festival of St Michael and All Angels, celebrated in the W. Church on 29 Sept. M. is frequently used for dating terms, etc. The traditional food for the day is the Michaelmas goose, and the flower the Michaelmas daisy.

Michaud, Joseph François (1767–1839), Fr. historian and publicist, *b.* Albens, Savoy. He went to Paris in 1791, where he became editor of *La Quotidienne*, in which he espoused the royalist cause. He narrowly escaped death during the Reign of Terror. His *Biographie Moderne*, 1806, was the earliest work of its kind. He also pub. *Histoire des croisades* (7 vols.), 1812–22, his prin. work, and *Correspondance d'orient*, 1833–5, and ed. (with Poujoulat) the series *Nouvelle collection des Mémoires pour servir à l'histoire de France*, 32 vols. 1836–54.

Michaux, André (1746–1803), Fr. botanist and traveller, *b.* Sartory. He travelled first to England (1779), whence he introduced into France sev. new varieties of trees and shrubs; second, to the Auvergne and the Pyrenees (1780), bringing back sev. sorts of grain; third, to Persia (1782), whence he brought back a fine herbarium and valuable seeds; fourth, in N. America (1785), from Hudson Bay to Florida and the Mississippi.

Michel, Clémence Louise (1830–1905), Fr. anarchist, *b.* Vroncourt in Haute-Saône. She became a teacher but soon gave this up for social and political work. She joined the Communists in their rising of 1871 and was transported to New Caledonia. On her release (1880) she returned to Paris and joined another anarchist rising, for which she was sentenced to 6 years' imprisonment. She was, however, released after 3 years, in 1886, and soon afterwards went to London. She returned to Paris in 1895. Her works include *La Misère*, *Mémoires*, 1886, *Les Microbes humains*, 1886, *Le Monde nouveau*, 1888, *Les Crimes de l'époque*, and *La Commune*, 1898. *See* E. Giraut, *La Bonne Louise*, 1906.

Michel de Notredame, *see* NOSTRADAMUS.

Michelangelo, (Michelagniolo di Lodovico), Buonarroti (1475–1564), It. sculptor, painter, architect and poet, *b.* Caprese; great representative of the It. Renaissance at its height. He was the second son of an impoverished Florentine gentleman given the temporary post of local magistrate at Caprese by the Medici. The family moved to Florence soon after M. was *b.* When 13, after some parental objection, he was allowed to become apprentice in the workshop of the painter Ghirlandaio (q.v.). He studied the frescoes of Masaccio (q.v.) in the Brancacci Chapel, where it is said, his nose was broken in a quarrel with his fellow pupil, Torrigiano. After a year he was accepted (1489) as one of the promising youths whom Lorenzo the Magnificent admitted to work in the school in the Medici gardens under the sculptor Bertoldo. In the spirit of the classical sculpture collected there

he executed the 'Faun's Head' which so pleased Lorenzo that he took M. into his household. The classical study encouraged by this milieu is also evident in his 'Battle of Centaurs and Lapiths' (Casa Buonarroti, Florence) in the style of an anct bas-relief. M. stayed in the Medici palace until his patron's death in 1492. He had further encouragement from Lorenzo's heir, Piero de' Medici, but a presentiment of the latter's fall caused him to flee to Bologna, 1494. Befriended by Gianfrancesco Aldovrandi he executed 3 statuettes for the Basilica of San Domenico. He returned to Florence after a year, to find it under the anti-Medicean sway of Savonarola (q.v.). In 1496 he went to Rome. A 'Cupid' by him (now lost), sold there as a genuine antique, had gained him notice. In a 5 years' stay he produced 2 works in strong contrast, 'Bacchus' (National Museum, Florence) and the beautiful 'Pietà' (St Peter's, Rome). Returning to Florence by his family's wish, 1501, he was next engaged on the colossal 'David' (Accademia, Florence) for the Signoria, carved from an imperfect block of marble other artists could do nothing with. M. had not given up painting. His 'Holy Family' (Uffizi) was executed in 1503 for Angelo Doni. In 1504 he and Leonardo da Vinci were making drawings for frescoes of battle scenes in the Council Hall. The work of both remained unfinished. M. was summoned to Rome in 1505 by Pope Julius II to design his sepulchral monument, the much-thwarted venture on which he was to toil at intervals for 40 years. He came back from Carrara, where he superintended the quarrying of marble for the task, to find the Pope had turned against him. They were reconciled at Bologna, where M. executed a statue of Julius (later destroyed in the city's revolt) for the façade of San Petronio. The Pope now had a new project. At the suggestion of the architect Bramante, who is supposed to have wished M. to fail, Julius asked him to paint the ceiling of the Sistine Chapel. Reluctantly accepting, M. in 20 months completed that masterpiece with its great interpretations of Genesis, the whole conception being conveyed by the human figure and gesture alone.

On the death of Julius in 1513, his heirs made a fresh contract for the tomb; but many setbacks followed and it was not finished, and then on a much reduced scale, until 1545, the great figure of Moses (San Pietro in Vincoli, Rome) being its main feature. The supporting 'Slaves' dispersed in the Louvre, Paris, and Accademia, Florence, show M.'s roughened treatment of surface, also deliberately used in the 'Pitti Madonna' (1504–5), National Museum, Florence, and the 'Taddei Madonna' (1505–6), Royal Academy. In 1520 he was commissioned to design the Medici sepulchral chapel in San Lorenzo, Florence, another work of giant and much interrupted labour, completed in 1535. It has the 2 superb groups of Lorenzo de' Medici above the figures of 'Dawn' and 'Dusk' and Giuliano de' Medici above 'Night' and 'Day'.

In an Italy invaded and torn by dissensions, 1527–30, M. was engineer-in-chief of fortifications at Florence. Required in 1534 to paint the altar wall of the Sistine Chapel he produced a second mural masterpiece in the 'Last Judgment', its violence reflecting a more tragic spirit than the ceiling. His later works included the design of the dome of St Peter's, for which he was made chief architect in 1547, and frescoes for the Capella Paolina of the Martyrdom of St Peter and the Conversion of St Paul. His last work of sculpture was the moving 'Rondanini Pietà' 1564 (Castello Sforzesco, Milan). He *d.* in Rome in that year but was reburied with ceremony in Santa Croce, Florence.

M.'s manysidedness is completed by his sonnets, the best of them addressed to Vittoria Colonna, widow of the Marquis of Pescara, to whom he was deeply attached. As a sculptor and painter he was a giant among artists, and had enormous influence on those who followed him. An Eng. trans. of M.'s *Complete Poems* was pub. in 1961; his *Letters*, in 2 vols., ed. and trans. by E. H. Ramsden, appeared in 1963. *See* G. Vasari, *Lives of the Painters*, 1550, Everyman's Library, new ed., 1963; *also* lives and studies by C. H. Morgan, 1960; C. de Tolnay, 1960; G. Brandes (trans.), 1963; R. J. Clements, 1963; R. Schott (trans.), 1963. (*See Plates: Art, Sculpture.*)

Michelet, Jules (1798–1874), Fr. historian, *b.* Paris. In 1831 he pub. the *Introduction à l'histoire universelle* and his *Histoire romaine*, and soon afterwards began his chief work, the *Histoire de France* (from early times to the outbreak of the revolution, 17 vols, 1833–67). In 1838 he was appointed to the chair of hist. at the Collège de France. His later works include *Le Prêtre, la femme et la famille*, 1845, *Le Peuple*, 1846, and *Histoire de la revolution française*, 1847–53, which is still a standard work. Because of his liberal political views, he was forbidden to lecture in 1851, and subsequently lived in retirement. Among his non-historical works are *L'Oiseau*, 1856, *L'Insecte*, 1858, *La Mer*, 1861, *La Montagne*, 1868, his memoirs, *Ma Jeunesse*, 1884, and his *Journal*, 1888.

Michelson, Albert Abraham (1852–1931), Polish-Amer. physicist, *b.* Srelno, near Poznan; lived in the U.S.A. from 1854 until his death. A distinguished prof. at the univ. of Chicago, M. was the first Amer. scientist to win the Nobel prize; in the same year (1907) he was awarded the Copley medal of the Royal Society. His greatest achievement was the construction of the interferometer (q.v.) that bears his name, and its applications to the determination of the standard metre in Paris, to the measurement of the angular diameter of a star (Betelgeuse) for the first time (1920), and to an attempt, made in collaboration with Morley, to detect the motion of the earth through the ether. The negative result of this experiment was the prelude to Einstein's theory of relativity. Other notable achievements were the determination of the velocity of light and the construction of the échelon diffraction grating for the examination of the fine structure of spectral lines. His pubs. include *Velocity of Light*, 1902, *Light Waves and*

their Uses, 1903, and *Studies in Optics*, 1927. *See also* MICHELSON-MORLEY EXPERIMENT.

Michelson-Morley Experiment. In the 19th cent. light was believed to travel through a medium called the ether (*see* AETHER), which was supposed to permeate all space and all bodies. It was further supposed that all bodies, including planets and celestial objects, moved through this absolute ether without disturbing it. If these suppositions were correct, then it would be possible to refer the motions of all celestial bodies to axes fixed in this absolute ether. Such motions would be absolute in the real sense that they were measured relative to these axes.

In order to test these hypotheses Michelson and Morley in 1887 performed an experiment to determine the velocity with which the earth moved through the ether. The idea that prompted the experiment can be best understood by considering the following problem. Suppose a man can row a boat in still water with a velocity of *c* m.p.h. If he now rows the boat in a riv. that is running with a velocity of *v* m.p.h., a distance of *l* m. upstream and then back *l* m. to his starting point, what is the time he takes for this double journey? The first half of the trip takes him $\frac{l}{c - v}$ hrs, the return $\frac{l}{c + v}$ hrs, so that the time for the whole journey is $\frac{l}{c - v} + \frac{l}{c + v}$, which is equal to $\frac{2l}{c^2 - v^2}$ hrs. If he rows *across* the stream for a distance *l* m. and back again, a simple calculation shows that the time taken is $\frac{2l}{\sqrt{c^2 - v^2}}$ hrs. This is easily found by using the principle of the parallelogram of velocities. The rower will set his boat upstream at such an angle that the resultant of the velocity of the boat and that of the riv. will be in a direction straight across the riv. In other words, the experiment demonstrates that the riv. is *actually running*, and it enables the man to *determine the velocity v* m.p.h. with which it is running. This idea may be applied to the problem of the earth's velocity through the ether. Michelson and Morley's apparatus (essentially Michelson's interferometer) is represented in the figure. Light from a source S strikes a half-silvered mirror M, so that part of the light is reflected to the mirror at B, while part is transmitted and later reflected at the mirror A. The 2 trains of light return to M and are there superposed to form interference fringes seen by an observer at O. The experimenters arranged that MA, for example, was parallel to the direction in which the earth was moving, so that the light that travels with velocity *c* m.p.h. relative to the still ether would travel upstream from M to A with a velocity $(c - v)$ m.p.h. relative to the mirrors, and back downstream with a velocity $(c + v)$ m.p.h. to the mirrors. At the same time the light travelling along MB and back again moves with a velocity $\sqrt{c^2 - v^2}$ m.p.h. relative to the mirrors for MB is perpendicular to the direction in which the earth is moving. Hence this journey would take less time than the other, and the difference between the 2 times could be detected and measured by observing the displacement of the interference fringes that would take place on rotating the whole apparatus through 90°, so that the positions of MA and MB were interchanged. The measurement would be one of extreme delicacy, because c is so very much greater than v that the difference between the 2 journeys is exceedingly small. Nevertheless the apparatus was capable of performing this measurement, but the result of the experiment was *negative*; subsequent attempts confirmed this. It was not possible to detect or measure the velocity with which the earth moved through the ether. This surprising result was at first thought to deny the existence of such an ether, but Lorentz and Fitzgerald pointed out that the result of the experiment could be explained by the hypothesis that the length of a measuring rod laid parallel to MA is different from its length when laid parallel to MB, and that this difference is of the exact amount to make the times for the journeys MA and MB the same. The Lorentz-Fitzgerald hypothesis of the contraction of the measuring rod was the beginning of the theory of relativity, and the hypothesis was inspired by the necessity for an explanation of the M.-M. E. *See* INTERFEROMETER; RELATIVITY.

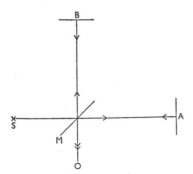

THE MICHELSON-MORLEY EXPERIMENT

Michigan, N. central state of the U.S.A., with an area of 96,716 sq. m. including 38,500 sq. m. of Great Lakes (over 3000 m. of shore) and 1194 sq. m. of inland water. M. consists of 2 peninsulas: the 'Upper' between Lakes Superior and M., bordering on Wisconsin; and the 'Lower' between Lakes Erie, M. and Superior, with a boundary against Ohio and Indiana. The latter is much the most populous and has a far richer agriculture and the bulk of M.'s industry. The Upper peninsula is important largely for its (depleted) timber reserves and its iron and limestone deposits. The Lower peninsula is a structural basin containing coal and petroleum reserves, now largely exhausted. Pop. 7,823,200. *See* G. N. Fuller (ed.), *Michigan: A Centennial History of the State and Its People* (5 vols.), 1939,

and Federal Writers' Project, *Michigan: A Guide to the Wolverine State,* 1941; F. C. Bald, *Michigan in Four Centuries,* 1961. (*See Plate.*)

Michigan City, city, yachting port and summer resort, with fisheries, in dunes area of Indiana, U.S.A., 30 m. E. of Chicago. It manufs. railway cars, furniture, catalysts, etc. Pop. 36,650.

Michigan, Lake, one of the Great Lakes of N. America, emptying at the N. through the Straits of Mackinac into Lake Huron. Area 22,400 sq. m. Length 307 m.; greatest width 118 m.; greatest depth 923 ft; shore line 1304 m.

Michoacán, state of Mexico with a coastline of 105 m. on the Pacific. The Sierra Madre Occidental traverses the state W.–E. under various local names, as does the Cordillera Neovolcánica. The highest peaks are Tancítaro (12,620 ft), Patamban (12,300 ft) and de Quinceo (11,000 ft). The volcano Paricutín (8450 ft) started activity in 1943, and the state falls in the seismic zone of Mexico. The climate varies from tropical and humid on the coast to the extreme cold of the mts, simply depending on altitude. There are innumerable rivs., the chief being the Lerma and Babas, in addition to sev. lakes including Lake Chapala which lies between the state and Jalisco state. Essentially an agric. region, its soil is the most fertile in Mexico with its evergreen fields. The main crops are maize, wheat, beans, fruit, coffee, sugarcane and cotton. Many irrigation schemes have been developed in recent years. Cattle-raising, timber production and agric. are all important activities. There are a number of important mining centres, the chief minerals extracted being silver, gold, lead and zinc. Most of the industry is related to the state's agric. output, namely, cotton textile manuf., sugar refining, flour-milling and other foodstuff processing. The cap. is Morelia, and there are about 15 urb. centres with pops. of over 10,000 inhab., the main ones being Uruapan (pop. 46,000), Zamora (32,000), La Piedad (42,000) and Zitácuaro (24,000). Area 23,202 sq. m. Pop. 1,851,876 (1960).

Michurinsk (until 1932 **Kozlov**), tn in the Tambov oblast (prov.) of central Russia, 45 m. NW. of Tambov. It has engineering, food and textile industries, and is a major railway junction. It is an important centre of horticulture with sev. research institutions. M. was founded in 1636 as a fort. tn in the Muscovite S. defence line. Pop (1965) 89,000 (1910, 50,000).

Micipsa, king of Numidia, 148–118 BC, eldest son and successor of Masinissa (q.v.). Afraid of his nephew Jugurtha (q.v.), he sent him in 134 BC to Spain, to serve under Scipio.

Mickiewicz, Adam (1798–1855), Polish poet, *b.* Zaosie, near Nowogrodek in Lithuania. He was educ. at Nowogrodek until 1814, when he entered the univ. of Vilna. He was for a time a schoolmaster at Kowno. In 1824 on the condemnation of the members of the Philoretian societies M., after imprisonment, was banished to Russia. He had already pub. 2 vols of miscellaneous verse, and on his arrival at St Petersburg was at once received in literary circles with open arms. In 1840 he was appointed to a newly founded professorship of Slavonic literature in the Collège de France, but was expelled from his chair by the Fr. Gov. in 1844, and was without employment until 1852, when the post of librarian at the Arsenal was obtained for him by Prince Napoleon. He *d.* of cholera at Constantinople while engaged in forming a Polish legion against Russia and was buried at Montmorency in France. His body was in 1890 removed to the cathedral at Cracow. M. is the most inspired poet of Poland, and the flaming ardour of his poems, allied with their national melancholy, causes him to be the most popular in his own country, although, unfortunately, but little known in England. His chief works are *Konrad Wallenrod*, 1828, and *Pan Tadeusz*, 1834, trans. in Everyman's Library, and his numerous sonnets, *Ode to Youth*, etc. *See* L. Mickiewicz (his son), *Adam Mickiewicz, sa vie et son œuvre*, 1888, and M. M. Gardner, *Adam Mickiewicz*, 1911. (*See Plate: Poland.*)

Mickle Fell (2591 ft), highest point of Yorks, England, a peak of the Pennines (q.v.) near the co. boundary with Westmorland and Durham.

Micmacs, tribe of N. Amer. Indians of Algonquian stock who formerly roamed Nova Scotia, New Brunswick and Newfoundland. They may have been encountered by Norse travellers, and after Cabot's voyage in 1497 acted as middlemen between Whites and Indians of the interior. They were largely converted by Fr. missionaries and have lived peacefully in their ters. There are about 4000.

Micon (fl. 5th cent. BC), Gk painter and sculptor, a contemporary of Pheidias and also of Polygnotus (q.v.), with whom he worked on the Painted Porch at Athens. He was renowed for his skill in drawing horses and for his battle scenes, e.g. between the Amazons and Athenians and of the battle of Marathon.

Microbe, *see* BACTERIA.

Microchemical Analysis, term used to include the methods employed for the recognition and determination of minute quantities of substances. For the *Qualitative* tests special reagents are often used. Thus for example, sodium-bismuth thiosulphate will detect the presence of potassium (1 part in 57,000); alkaline phenol-phthalein, decolorised by boiling with zinc powder, gives a red colour with water containing 1 part of copper per 100,000,000; potassium thiocyanate gives a blue colour with osmium compounds (1 part per 1,000,000) when shaken with ether. The *Spot* or *Drop Tests* are invaluable in this connection. They are carried out by allowing a drop of solution under test to react with a chosen reagent on filter-paper, when characteristic colours or stains appear. To quote 2 examples: (*a*) If a drop of a solution of a soluble lead salt is placed on a spot of ammoniacal hydrogen peroxide on filter-paper and allowed to stand, a blue coloration is observed when the spot is treated with a drop of benzidine dissolved in acetic acid (detects lead, 1 part in 33,000); (*b*) a drop of stannous chloride added to a spot of ammonium molybdate

reagent on filter-paper gives an intense blue colour. On warming (unless arsenic is present as well) the colour disappears.

Quantitative microanalysis has made rapid strides, and it is now possible to perform a quantitative analysis of an organic body, using as little as 2 mg. of the substance. This is invaluable, especially as many newly discovered bodies involve difficult and laborious methods even to obtain small yields. Pregl was the pioneer of the new methods. Sensitive balances—e.g. the Kuhlmann (weighing to 0·002 mg.)—are used, and minute attention to detail is insisted on. *See* F. Pregl, *Quantitative Microanalysis* (revised by J. Grant, 4th Eng. ed.), 1951.

Microcline, species of felspar, the crystallisation of which is triclinic, with polysynthetic twinning. A section cut parallel to the base reveals a reticulated structure, this being due to the regular intergrowth of twin lamellae. Composition is silica 64·30, alumina 19·70, ferric oxide 0·74, potash 15·69, soda 0·48. Chemical formula $K_2(Al_2)Si_6O_{16}$. Some felspars, once regarded as orthoclase, are included in the M. species, as also are part of the chesterlite and amazonstone.

Microcosm and Macrocosm. Arising from the belief of the ancts. that the cosmos has a soul, the idea followed that the vital movements of man, the microcosm or little world, corresponded to those of the universe, the macrocosm or great world. From this astrology followed, or the belief in the idea that the movements of the heavenly bodies affect human lives. Pythagoras, Plato, the Stoics and Paracelsus were exponents of the doctrine, as were the mystics of the 17th cent. *See* ASTROLOGY.

Microcosmic Salt ($NaNH_4HPO_4$, $4H_2O$), sodium ammonium phosphate, is so called because it is formed in the evaporation of human urine and was regarded by the alchemists as an extract of the human microcosm. It is obtained by adding a strong solution of di-sodium phosphate to ammonium chloride and filtering the sodium chloride. The salt is used in blowpipe experiments, since it decomposes on heating, to give a glassy bead of sodium metaphosphate.

Microfilm, *see* COPYING.

Microliths. Vitreous rocks are not altogether void of crystalline material. Under the microscope numerous small crystallites are to be seen which may be drop-like (globulites), rod-shaped (belonites) or like coiled and twisted hairs (trichites). Besides these crystallites exist needle- and rod-shaped bodies called M., which are distinguished from the above by the fact that they react on polarised light (q.v.), and can be generally referred to some mineral species, felspar, augite, hornblende, olivine, etc. Combinations of simple M. occur presenting a curious forked appearance (skeleton crystals), and their linear arrangement indicates the fluxion structure of the rock. M. are also small points of flint used to tip arrows in prehistoric times (*see* STONE AGE).

Micrometeorology, that branch of meteorology (q.v.) which deals in great detail with the physics of the atmosphere very near the surface of the earth. The treatment is usually highly mathematical. It is of importance in the study of evaporation, of heat transfer and of the diffusion of smoke and gases by the wind. *See* R. Geiger, *Das Klima der bodennahen Luftschicht*, 1950; O. G. Sutton, *Micrometeorology*, 1953.

Micrometer, instrument for determining the size of components to within $\frac{1}{1000}$ in. or less. The measurement is made between a fixed abutment and the end of a spindle which has an accurately machined thread and screws into the body of the instrument. Each complete turn of the spindle causes it to advance through a distance equal to the pitch of the thread, which in Brit. micrometers is 0·025 in. A sleeve attached to the spindle has its circumference graduated in 25 equal parts so that a rotation through 1 div. corresponds to an axial movement of $\frac{1}{1000}$ in. The total movement of the spindle is just over 1 in. and separate instruments are made to cover the ranges 0–1 in., 1–2 in., 2–3 in., etc.

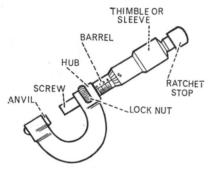

THIMBLE OR SLEEVE

BARREL

HUB

SCREW

ANVIL

RATCHET STOP

LOCK NUT

MICROMETER

Micron, *see* METROLOGY.

Micronesia (from Gk *mikros*, small; *nēsos*, is.), name of that part of the Pacific Ocean between long. 130° and 180° E. and between lat. 20° N. and the equator, which embraces the Ladrone, Palau, Caroline, Marshall and Gilbert archipelagos. Except for the Gilbert Is., which are British, and Guam in the Ladrone Is. (American), the is. of M., formerly German, were, between the two world wars, under Jap. mandate. The S. Sea Is. form a complex geographical, political and racial patchwork, without any clear principles of order. But M. is the conventional name of the groups mentioned in this article as distinguished from the much more populous groups compendiously designated Melanesia and Polynesia. The Micronesians show resemblances variously to the other 2 groupings, but are also marked by later overlays of race and custom from Malaysian sources. Yet all scientific evidence points to the certainty that the local peoples of all 3 groups are traceable back to SE. Asia by way of the Malaysian is. The oceanic pops. are believed to have numbered about 3,500,000 when the whites first arrived, and of these the Micronesians numbered only

some 200,000. At the lowest point the Micronesians fell to a little over 80,000; in 1921 the total was 90,000, and today is about 105,000. The pop. of the Jap. mandate, taken as a whole, grew steadily in numbers after Japan took control, but if the is. are considered separately quite marked differences appear. The W. groups show 2 clearly distinguishable pop. elements, the so-called Chamorros, who show greater racial and ethnic affiliation with the Malaysian peoples, and the Kanakas, who, like the rest of the Micronesians, are linked more with the Polynesians and, to some extent, the Melanesians. The Amer. is. of Guam is unique in M., and indeed in the oceanic region as a whole, for here contact with whites goes back to the 16th cent., when the is. was a port of call for Sp. ships, and was a place of exile for lawbreakers and political prisoners from the Philippines. M. shows varied social systems, and totemic clans were a widespread feature. Where peoples in M., as also in Melanesia, have been christianised, the formal change to a family organisation based on biblical standards is accomplished as part of the process of conversion. The groups are described under their separate titles. *See* F. M. Keesing, *The South Seas in the Modern World*, 1942; R. Linton, *Ethnology of Polynesia and Micronesia*, 1928. (*See Plate.*)

Micro-palaeontology, aspect of Palaeontology (q.v.) concerned with the study of microscopic fossils such as foraminifera, radiolaria, ostracods, bryozoa, spores and pollen. *See* M. F. Glaessner, *Principles of Micro-palaeontology*, 1947.

Microphone, piece of apparatus by which sound waves are converted into voice frequency electric currents which can be transmitted or recorded as such. The simplest type is the standard G.P.O. telephone instrument, which consists of a diaphragm behind which are packed granules of carbon backed by a solid surface. Sound waves make the diaphragm vibrate, so that the granules are alternately compressed and released at the same frequency as the sound reaching the M. The resulting variations in resistance cause fluctuations in a current through the M., passed to the telephone circuit via a suitable transformer. The quality is poor, but satisfactory for telephone communication.

The moving-coil M. is similar to the moving-coil loudspeaker (q.v.), where the process is reversed. It is capable of good quality output. The ribbon M. consists of a very light ribbon of aluminium foil suspended at its ends between the poles of a permanent magnet. The sound waves vibrate the foil and, as it moves between the magnet poles, voice frequency currents are induced in it. The crystal M. depends for its action upon the piezo-electric effect encountered in certain crystals such as Rochelle salt, when subjected to mechanical stress. The stress is produced by the sound waves striking a diaphragm to which the crystal is joined, when the electric impulses appearing across the crystal can be amplified. In the better type, no diaphragm is used, but a number of crystal elements are connected so that their outputs combine. The sound impinges directly on the crystals and this results in a very even frequency response free from objectionable diaphragm resonances. The output voltage is low, and considerable amplification is necessary.

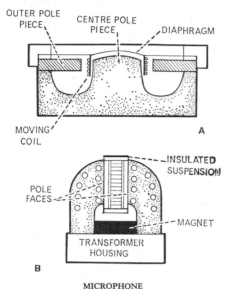

A, moving coil microphone; B, ribbon microphone.

Microphotography, production of very much reduced images on photographic film usually of printed or MS. documents. Not to be confused with photomicrography (q.v.). M. has been gaining ground in the last few decades as a means of solving the problem of storing large and bulky newspapers, drawings or little used archives. It has been claimed that microfilmed newspaper can be stored with a 95 per cent saving of space. M. also serves as a cheap intermediary in the process of reprinting. Equipment exists to enlarge microfilm and to take a print of the enlargement, which may be of any readable size, below, at or above that of the original. Lithographic plates can be made from the print and a new edition printed with better reproduction quality than if the photograph had been same size. Microfilm, or microtext as it is often called, is made in 3 main forms: roll film (35mm. wide) with the image black on transparent; microfiche (any rectangular size, although standardisation is being introduced gradually), with the image similarly shown; and microcard (with the image in black on opaque white). In research publishing the microfilm has an important place, since single copies can be produced at a moderate cost and shipped long distances at low freight charges. They can then be either read or printed out at the other end of their journey. Most research and univs. libararies, and all the larger public libraries in Britain, now have microfilm readers, and a few have printers. There are also possibilities for microfilm in such developments as automated library systems, using aperture cards or roll film with coded magnetic signals. See INFORMATION STORAGE AND RETRIEVAL.

Micropyle, pore in seed coat, or testa. Before maturation of the ovule, it serves as a passage for entry of the pollen tube. At germination of the seed it is the only place through which water can enter.

Microscope and Microscopy. The *microscope* is an instrument designed to produce a magnified image of an illuminated object, with the detailed appearance faithfully preserved. The technique of preparing and exhibiting objects so that these conditions are fulfilled constitutes *microscopy*. The requisite magnification is attained by the use of lenses or mirrors (*see* LENS and LIGHT), singly or in combination, the primary distinction being between *simple M.s*, in which the image is erect and virtual, and *compound M.s*, in which a real and inverted image is projected into the focal plane of an auxiliary lens system or on to a screen or photographic plate.

The following account is concerned solely with the compound M., which is to be preferred to the simple in all cases where manipulation of the specimen or extreme portability is not the primary consideration, owing to its greater power of resolving fine detail and its practical convenience. The real image, moreover, can be subjected to measurement or optical analysis in a manner impossible with a virtual one. Compound M.s may be divided into various types according to their action, which may be by refraction or reflection, and also according to the system of image formation employed, which may be *conventional* or by *phase difference*. The term *conventional* is here used to designate all systems which fulfil the classical requirement of equality between all light paths from a point in the object to the corresponding point in the image; in the phase difference system this condition is deliberately violated in order to secure interference effects that would not otherwise occur.

Image formation. An object is rendered visible by virtue of the disturbance which it causes to light or other waves which it intercepts. The disturbance may be analysed into sev. distinct components, viz. absorption, reflection, refraction, diffraction, polarisation and fluorescence, and these are used singly or in combination to secure the visibility of the magnified image of the object. The classical theory of M. image formation, due to Abbe, may be generally summarised in the statement that a ray of light impinging on an object is modified by diffraction into an assembly consisting of an undeviated ray and a set of others diverging from it at angles dependent on the magnitude of the diffracting structure relative to the wave-length of the light. Ideally all of these should be reunited in their original phase relationships in the image, which is formed by their mutual interference (*see* LIGHT). In practice, however, this is not completely possible, and the image differs from the object according to the extent to which the ideal relationship is unfulfilled. Experiments and calculations made in the 19th cent. proved that the direct and the diffracted rays arising from objects having the nature of a periodically opaque grating were either co-phasal or in reversed phase, so that when reunited in the image they interfered to produce a pattern of varying intensities. It was not, however, until 1932 that it was discovered by Zernike that this is not the case if the object is completely transparent, and varies in thickness or refractive index; it then yields diffracted rays which are substantially a quarter of a wave-length out of phase with the direct rays, and so do not interfere to produce a pattern of varying intensities, but one of varying phases, to which the eye is not sensitive. In the phase difference (or phase contrast) system these rays are artificially brought into a relationship in which interference produces an image of varying intensities.

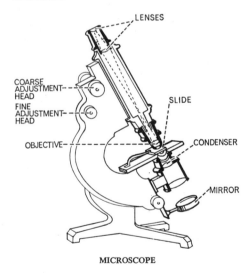

MICROSCOPE

Components of the microscope. Apart from the specimen, the essential optical elements of a M. are the projecting lens (objective, object glass) and the illuminating system, whilst in common use the real image projected by the objective is received by a lens system (eye-piece, ocular) which presents to the observer's eye a virtual image further amplified, and which thus functions as a simple M. The most important of these optical elements is the *objective*, upon which the resolving power and magnification depend. This normally consists of a system of lenses of glass, quartz or fluorite, in suitable combination, designed to project an image having a minimum degree of aberration (*see* LENS) when the object

and image lie in predetermined planes. As it is only possible to correct the lens for one such pair of planes, the image deteriorates if this condition is violated, and any divergence from the preselected conditions of observation must be compensated by a corresponding adjustment in the location of the image plane to restore equilibrium. The optical properties of the glasses used in construction do not permit all the spectral colours (*see* SPECTRUM) to be united in a perfectly corrected image; the common achromatic objectives are chromatically correct for 2 colours, but spherically for only one, whilst more complex *apochromats* are chromatically corrected for 3 colours, and spherically for 2, thus producing a more brilliant and sharper image than the former. Restriction of the illumination to approximately monochromatic conditions therefore improves the definition of the achromat, and for use in the ultra-violet region (*see* ULTRA-VIOLET LIGHT), where isolated spectral lines are used for illumination, objectives are spherically corrected for 1 wave-length only. The great advantage of the *reflecting* objective is that ideally it is free from chromatic aberration through the entire range of the ultra-violet, visual and infra-red spectra, and its spherical correction is equally independent of wave-length. In the past the difficulties of shaping the non-spherical surfaces necessary have resulted in indifferent quality, but a new pattern constructed by Burch is found to compare favourably with the best refracting objectives. Its unique qualities lend themselves particularly to researches in microspectrometry.

The resolving power of an objective depends both on the wave-length of the illumination and the obliquity at which the objective can accept the rays diffracted by the object. This feature is governed by the focal length and diameter of the lenses, and is measured by a factor known as the *numerical aperture* (N.A.), which in combination with the wave-length of the illumination defines the resolution possible; the minimum interval between separable points is commonly obtained from the formula

$$\text{Resolving Power} = \frac{\text{Wave-length}}{2 \times \text{N.A.}}$$

The N.A. of the system is limited in value to that of the lowest refractive index between the objective and the specimen, as the more oblique rays are lost by internal reflection. To avoid this the *homogeneous immersion* system is employed, which, by the use of a suitable fluid filling the space between the objective and specimen, minimises discrepancies of refractive index, and thus increases the possible resolving power of the system by 50 per cent; the need for tube-length variation to adjust the working conditions is also automatically obviated.

It is clearly important that the detail resolved should also be visible. To permit this it is generally stated that adjacent elements should subtend an angle of 2 minutes of arc at the eye, but this may be considered as a theoretical minimum based on the ultimate effort of a perfect eye. To ensure that this separation is attained, it is customary to recommend a magnification of about 500 times the N.A., but in practice a great subtense is more convenient, and this figure can be increased by 100 per cent, or more in suitable circumstances, without deterioration of the image.

The influence of illumination on the image is profound, and a thorough appreciation of what it can be made to do is perhaps the most useful lesson that a microscopist can learn, as he will thereafter analyse the image in terms of his experience instead of regarding it as an immutable representation of the object. The illuminating system consists essentially of a suitable light source, preferably of small area and high intensity, a lens or reflecting system (*substage condenser*) to produce an image of the light source in the plane of the object, and a diaphragm to regulate the obliquity and conformation of the illuminating rays. By the employment of a diaphragm of suitable aperture and shape the rays converging in the specimen may be made to utilise only selected portions of the objective aperture, with consequent modification of the image, and by the use of very oblique illumination the image may be constituted by diffracted rays alone, appearing luminous against a dark background. Substage condensers are usually of 2 patterns, one conforming to the general plan of an objective, and ideally, but very seldom, as well corrected, working either dry or in immersion contact with the specimen, and the other a reflecting system invariably immersed and furnishing extremely oblique annular illumination. The first is employed at a suitably regulated aperture to provide direct illumination of the specimen, and may be used for oblique or darkground lighting effects with objective of medium power; the second furnishes darkground illumination for objectives of high aperture. Attainment of the full resolving power of the objective depends almost as much on the condenser as upon the objective itself, and it is extremely important that both components should be co-axial; it should therefore be possible to centre the condenser to the M. axis.

In visual use the image furnished by the objective is further amplified by an eye-piece, the two being mounted in a tube the length of which is adjustable to secure the optimum circumstances for image formation. The entire tube, and the condenser independently, can be moved axially, to focus the image and illuminant; the tube is usually, and the condenser occasionally, provided with a second extremely sensitive focusing action termed the *fine adjustment*, which is perhaps the most important mechanical feature of the instrument, and which is commonly graduated for use as a micrometer.

Eye-pieces vary in construction according to their purpose, and sev. differing systems are employed. For normal visual use Huygens' form is general, but many modern eye-pieces are based on other formulae, and for use with apochromatic objectives special correction is necessary.

For photography the eye-piece is computed to project a real image, although negative lens systems unsuitable for direct vision can be employed for this purpose, or the eye-piece may be omitted.

It is no longer possible to give any general description of the M. as an instrument, as specialised patterns differing widely in form and function are constructed for research in distinct fields. The ultimate resolution at present available is provided by the electron M. (q.v.) in which magnetic fields focus beams of electrons *in vacuo*; the visible image is produced by fluorescence or photography, and the object is often prepared by the deposition of metallic vapour on to it. Resolution so far obtained is of the order of 0·001 microns (1 micron = 0·001 mm.), but the instrument is limited in application by the slight penetrating power of the radiation involved and by technical considerations that enforce a magnification measured in thousands of diameters. Protein molecules, virus and bacteriophage particles were seen for the first time by the use of this instrument, which can also be used to measure them. The ultra-violet M. likewise yields a photographic image, although in favourable cases a fluorescent eyepiece may be used with it. The resolving power is about 0·14 microns at a wavelength of 2753 Angstrom units, compared with a resolving power of 0·27 microns attainable by the visual spectrum. A special technique as well as special apparatus is required for work in the extreme ultra-violet, but useful results are attained with the longer wave-lengths, owing to selective absorption by specific substances in the specimen, which enhance visibility. Fluorescence microscopy employs ultra-violet illumination of the object, visual light emanating from which forms a visible image; it can be used in the identification of certain bacteria. Differential absorption is a marked feature of microscopy in the infra-red region, many substances having characteristic absorption spectra in that zone; as remarked earlier, the reflecting M. is particularly adapted to this work, which is of profound value in biochemistry and physiology.

Visual microscopy has lately been advanced by the phase contrast technique, which by the use of an interferometer arrangement renders slight differences of refractive index in the specimen as differences of brightness in the image. This has the result of allowing fresh unstained material to be examined living, and can reproduce in the image many of the effects hitherto attained only by staining. In conjunction with cinéphotography this permits the phenomena of growth, mitosis, etc., to be recorded and studied at more convenient speeds. The phase contrast system is still capable of great development, but is clearly an advance in microscopy comparable with any of the classic advances of the past.

Bibliography. There is no completely up-to-date book on microscopy: L. C. Martin and B. K. Johnson, *Practical Microscopy*, 1949, is recommended for general guidance, and C.

Beck, *The Microscope*, 1924, for critical study. E. M. Chamot and C. W. Mason, *Handbook of Chemical Microscopy*, 1930, vol. i, is a most valuable book on the practical side, whilst among the older authors Dallinger, C. Beck and E. J. Spitta will remain outstanding. For photomicrography (q.v.) J. E. Barnard and F. V. Welch, *Practical Photomicrography*, 1925, 1936, is valuable. *See also* B. Lee, *The Microtomist's Vade-Mecum*, 1950, and B. O. Payne, *Microscope Design and Construction*, 1954.

Microscopical Society, The Royal, was estab. in 1839 for the promotion of microscopical and biological science by the communication, discussion and pub. of (1) improvements in the construction and mode of application of the microscope and (2) biological and other subjects of microscopical research. It consists of ordinary, honorary and ex-officio fellows of either sex and section members. The jour. of the society is pub. every 2 months from the offices of the society at Tavistock House, Tavistock Square, London, WC.1. The *Proceedings* of the society is pub. annually.

Microscopium (the Microscope), S. constellation named in 1752 by Lacaille, situated N. of Grus and Indus at the junction of Capricornus and Sagittarius.

Microstylis, genus of terrestrial orchids, with handsome leaves and small greenish-yellow or purple flowers.

Microtome, instrument adapted for cutting thin sections, particularly of biological material, preparatory to observation under the microscope. There are many varieties, but the essential part of the instrument is a device for leading the material, embedded in a suitable block, to a cutting instrument, or for leading the cutting instrument to the block by mechanical motion, or by thermal expansion of the holder. A section of thickness less than ·0001 mm. can be cut. Traditionally steel razors are used, with the material embedded in paraffin wax, or temporarily frozen, and this especially for electron-microscope work, where the naturally broken edge of plate glass is the best cutting edge. The thickness of the material governs the degree of resolution obtained by the electron microscope.

Microtus, *see* ARVICOLA.

Midas, legendary king of Phrygia, son of Gordius (q.v.). Dionysus promised to fulfil any one favour he chose to ask, and M. requested that all he touched might turn to gold; and so it did—even his food. Praying for relief, he was ordered by Dionysus to bathe in the sources of the R. Pactolus (q.v.). M. was saved, but the sands of Pactolus became gold-bearing. The story is clearly aetiological.

Another story related that M., chosen to umpire a musical contest between Apollo and Pan, decided in favour of the latter. Apollo thereupon changed his ears into those of an ass. M. contrived to hide the disfigurement beneath his tall Phrygian cap; not however from his barber. The secret weighed so heavy on the man's mind that he dug a hole and whispered

into it 'King M. has ass's ears', and then filled up the hole. But a reed grew on the spot and whispered the secret.

Middelburg: 1. Cap. of the prov. of Zeeland, Netherlands, on the is. of Walcheren, 4 m. N. of Flushing. It has an old abbey dating from the 12th cent. M. was a Hanseatic tn. Pop. 23,200.

2. Tn and dist of W. Transvaal, S. Africa, on a trib. of R. Klein Olifant, 95 m. E. of Pretoria. There are extensive coalfields in dist, where there also exist iron, copper and cobalt. Pop. (1960) Whites, 4886; all other races, 12,907.

3. Cap. of a div. of the same name, Cape Prov., S. Africa, 232 m. NW. of Port Elizabeth (q.v.), in a fertile agric. dist. Pop. (1960) Whites, 3984; Bantu, 10,817; Coloureds, 6320.

Middens, Kitchen, *see* KITCHEN MIDDENS.

Middle Ages, The. Period known as the M. A. covers the thousand years from the death of Constantine I (q.v.) to the birth of the modern nation-state, AD 337 to AD 1500, and is the intermediate period between the culture of classical antiquity and the Renaissance. It was not, however, a homogeneous period. Until the 11th cent there was a formative age, often described as the Dark Ages. Much of Rom. civilisation was lost under the surge of Germanic invaders in N. Europe, Germany and Italy, and the Moorish domination in Spain. One link, a tradition of order, remained as an ideal in a welter of disorganisation and invasion, and Christianity survived the barbarian invasions, to be ultimately adopted by the invaders themselves. By the end of the 11th cent. the ideal came nearer to practice as political organisation in W. Europe achieved a degree of stability sufficient to allow the growth of a civilisation which may be called medieval.

Medieval knowledge of physical science was negligible, and education was conservative, but there was, in this civilisation, much of significance and outstanding moral value. Latin was the international language, and it enabled the growth of cosmopolitan univs. and of a common fund of knowledge. The estab. of papal authority over the churches of the W. world created an international organisation more efficient than any which has appeared since the dissolution of the Rom. Empire. In political affairs the theory was held that Europe formed a super-national state, a Holy Rom. empire. Though never of any great significance in the ultimate political development of Europe, this ideal could be used as a rallying-point on occasions of general European concern; by it was raised the greatest of the crusades, in 1188, under the Emperor Frederick I. Throughout the M. A. the search for European unity was a recurrent theme. The 20th cent. has seen a renewal of this theme, and with it a fuller recognition of the brilliance of the contributions of such men as Thomas Aquinas, Dante, Chaucer, Giotto and Fra Lippo Lippi in the fields of philosophy, literature and art, and of the enduring value of the architecture of the M. A., of which many examples are extant today. *See* F. Funck-Brentano, *The Middle Ages* (trans.), 1922; J. Huizinga, *The Waning of the*

Middle Ages, 1924; Margaret Deanesly, *A History of the Medieval Church*, 1925, and *A History of Early Medieval Europe*, 1955; C. G. Crump and E. F. Jacob (ed.), *The Legacy of the Middle Ages*, 1926; C. Dawson, *The Making of Europe*, 1932; *Cambridge Medieval History* (12 vols.), 1923–39; *Cambridge Economic History of Europe from the Decline of the Roman Empire*, vol. i, 1941; W. R. Lethaby (revised D. T. Rice), *Medieval Art*, 1949; C. W. Previté Orton, *The Shorter Cambridge Medieval History*, 1952; R. W. Southern, *The Making of the Middle Ages*, 1953; F. B. Artz, *The Mind of the Middle Ages*, 1954.

Middle Congo, until Aug. 1960, one of the 4 ters of Fr. Equatorial Africa (q.v.), since then the republic of Congo (Brazzaville) (q.v.).

Middle East, term loosely used to embrace the various countries in N. and NE. Africa, countries and is. in the E. Mediterranean, and the various Arab states, together with Persia and E. Turkey. Strictly the term includes only the Turkish succession states or countries, i.e. the countries over which the Turks were suzerains before the First World War, viz. Palestine, Syria, Transjordan, Hejaz, Nejd and Egypt, all of which countries, together with the Balkans, were previously comprised under the term 'Near E.' The term 'M. E.' was coined by the Cairo Conference in 1921 to differentiate the political questions involved in these Arab states and Egypt from the quite unrelated questions such as the Dardanelles problems and the conflicting views of Turkey and the other Balkan States concerning the Balkans generally, and thus the term 'Near E.' became restricted to the Balkans. During the Second World War, however, the term 'M. E.' soon took on a much wider significance both politically and in a military sense. All the countries included in the M. E., whether actually involved in campaigns or not, were of great strategic importance to the Allies in the Second World War, but above all to Britain in the protection of India and the Persian oilfields from attack from the W. A minister of state in the M. E. was appointed in June 1941, to represent the War Cabinet, charged with the duty of concerting measures necessary for the prosecution of the war in that part of the world, other than the conduct of military operations. A M. E. supply centre was set up in Cairo in April 1941. Later this body served a pop. of some 80,000,000, including in its scope Egypt, the Sudan, Palestine, Transjordan, Saudi Arabia, Eritrea, Brit. Somaliland, Syria and Lebanon, Iraq, Persia and, for certain purposes, Turkey and Malta. The centre carried out its administrative work under the direction of the minister of state. Originally a purely Brit. agency, the centre later developed into an Anglo-Amer. body. There were many notable campaigns in M. E. countries, particularly the Ger. conquest of Crete (May–June 1941); the battle of the W. Desert (Nov. 1940–Feb. 1941), in which Wavell routed Graziani's forces; the conquest of It. E. Africa, including Ethiopia (Feb.–Nov. 1941), by Gens. Cunningham and Platt; the Axis (q.v.)

offensive under Rommel in 1942 which was eventually stopped on the line El Alamein–Quattaro; and Alexander and Montgomery's victory over Rommel in Oct.–Nov. 1942. Syria was conquered by Brit. forces in June 1941. Axis plotting in Iraq was checked by the Brit. counter measures in April–May 1941, and Persia was occupied in Aug. 1941. *See also* AFRICA, NORTH, SECOND WORLD WAR CAMPAIGNS IN; CRETE, BATTLE OF (1941); IRAQ, *Revolt in Iraq*; ITALIAN EAST AFRICA, SECOND WORLD WAR CAMPAIGN IN (1941); PERSIA, *Anglo-Soviet Invasion* (1941); SYRIA, *British Invasion* (1941).

The H.Q. of Middle E. Command in Aden, and of U.S.S.R. bases in the Caucasus and Turkestan, the oilfields and pipe-lines in Iraq and Persia and the shipping routes to the M. E. all combine to give that region its vital importance in world strategy. The unsettled conflict between the Arab states and Israel, particularly over the Arab refugee question, the growing disunity among the Arab states themselves, and the unsatisfactory state of Brit. relations with many M. E. countries had, by 1949, severely upset the stability and security of the M. E. The negotiations of June 1949 of the Conciliation Commission of the U.N. reached deadlock largely because of the refusal of Israel to take back any Arab refugees until Palestinian frontiers had been settled. At present there are about 900,000 Arabs in receipt of relief, 800,000 being refugees; and of these refugees 600,000 come from within Israel and 200,000 from outside that state.

In 1956, after the final withdrawal of Brit. forces from the Suez Canal (q.v.) zone, the Egyptian Gov. announced the nationalisation of the canal. This resulted in a further deterioration of the M. E. situation. In Nov. 1956 Israel attacked Egypt, Brit. and Fr. forces occupied part of the Suez Canal zone, and the canal was blocked by the Egyptians. In Dec. U.N. forces replaced Brit. and Fr. forces and an uneasy peace ensued. Since then Egypt has intervened, with varying success, in the affair of sev. M. E. states, notably Syria, Iraq and the Yemen; and Russia has exerted influence through the economic and technical aid she has provided. However, the separatist tendencies of the Arab states have so far prevented the growth of any constant power bloc in the area, and W. influence remains strong in such countries as Libya, Jordan, Israel and Persia.

Middle English, *see* ENGLISH LANGUAGE and ENGLISH LITERATURE.

Middle Latitude, in navigation, the mean of 2 lats. It is the distinctive name of a method called in navigation (q.v.) M. L. sailing, by which, using plane sailing to find the departure and M. L., the difference of long. can be found from the formula D. long. = Dep. × secant M. L. Most books of nautical tables include one from which the answer to this can be obtained by inspection.

Middle Oil, name given to one of the fractions obtained by the distillation of coal tar in pot-stills. The products obtained from it are naphthalene, phenol, cresols and xylenols.

4923

Middle Park Stakes, see HORSE-RACING.

Middle Temple, see INNS OF COURT.

Middle West, The, term rather loosely applied in the U.S.A., as much to an attitude of mind in politics and economics as to a geographical section. At various times the states of Ohio, Indiana, Illinois, Michigan, Iowa, Wisconsin, Minnesota, N. and S. Dakota, Kansas and Nebraska have been termed M. W. states. Though most of these, especially those of the E., have considerable industrial cities, in the main they are all alike in being principally agric. states, with flat plains of prairie soil. The characteristic frame of mind of the farmers, who make up the bulk of the pop., is explained by the fact that, while they raise most of the food of the nation, the money control lies principally in New York, Boston and Philadelphia. In hard times the farmers are compelled to file mortgages on their farms. These mortgages find their way to the banks, and the banks are controlled in the E. Hence the bitter hatred often manifested towards Wall Street, the financial section of New York city. Politically most of these states are nominally Republican, but actually they have often inclined strongly to that type of Republicanism which is termed progressive. With the great growth of industrial-urb. pops., the strength of the democratic vote has increased markedly. As a revolt against Wall Street control, the farmers and small tn folk of many of the M. W. states in the famous campaign of 1896 followed W. J. Bryan (q.v.), Democratic nominee for president on a free silver platform. In later days their prophet was R. M. La Follette (q.v.), governor of, and senator from, Wisconsin and a progressive and radical Republican. Political isolationism has always been a midwestern attitude. The type of mind so often satirised in the novels of Sinclair Lewis is primarily the M. W. mind. The people are ardently American, very much averse from mixing in European affairs, intensely religious, and suspicious of anything that has to do with high finance and big business. It was the M. W. which largely opposed America's entry into the League of Nations and which later opposed cancellation of war debts. It is the M. W., too, which has most persistently demanded relief for the farmers in every crisis brought about by low world prices. A typical M. W. tn has been described under the pseudonym of Middletown by R. S. and H. M. Lynd. See Middletown (1929) and Middletown in Transition (1937 and 1947). But today the M. W. has a far more mixed pop., less dominated by the farmer, and these old attitudes are breaking down.

Middleham, small tn and par. in the N. Riding of Yorks, England, on the R. Ure, a racehorse training centre. There are ruins of a castle, home of the Nevilles and of Richard III. Pop. 663.

Middlesboro, or **Middlesborough,** city in Bell co., Kentucky, U.S.A., 64 m. NNE. of Knoxville, Tennessee. It has coal- and iron-mining, and manufs. of steel and bricks. It was a strategic point in the civil war, near Cumberland Gap through which passed the old Wilderness Road by which Kentucky was settled. Pop. 12,610.

Middlesbrough, co. bor. and manufacturing tn, situated at the mouth of the R. Tees in the N. Riding of Yorks, England, 238 m. from London; seat of a Rom. Catholic bishop. The tn has parks, recreation grounds and a flourishing Little Theatre catering for amateur dramatic talent. There are Colleges of Technology, Further Education and Art, and grammar and secondary modern schools, public baths, libraries, a museum, an art gallery, hospitals, a mental hospital and sanatorium, and the cheapest public omnibus transport system in the country. Large-scale industrial developments have taken place immediately to the E. of the tn, consisting of the construction of a huge steel processing plant and chemical works. At the Port of M. the Tees Conservancy Commissioners are providing considerable dock and riv. improvements to supplement the deep-water wharves and the Brit. Railways docks which cope with ships of up to 13,000 tons. The port is an ocean terminal for world-wide cargo sailings, and there is considerable tramp traffic and coastwise trade.

The corporation has erected nearly 10,000 houses on various housing estates. A development plan for M. was approved in May 1953, and work is continuing on the new residential estates already estab. The plan includes the development of industrial and commercial sites, and locations are available for firms wishing to settle in the tn. The heavy industries, shipyards, docks and wharves are on the banks of the riv., and the tn, which is of comparatively recent growth, spreads southwards towards the Cleveland Hills. Transport facilities are good, and there is ready access to National Parkland, sea, moor and country, which are all within a radius of 10 m. The R. Tees at M. is spanned by a transporter bridge and a vertical lift bridge, both of which are almost unique in the U.K., but necessitated by the low-lying nature of the land on either bank.

The highly industrialised Tees-side area of which M. is the centre is one of the biggest producers of pig-iron in the country. Within the tn there are constructional works, chemical plants and numerous engineering and allied industries. Pop. 157,395. See Ruth Glass (editor), The Social Background of a Plan: a Study of Middlesbrough, new ed., 1962.

Middlesex (A.-S. Middelseaxan), former co. of England, bounded on the W. by Bucks, on the NW. by Herts, on the E. by the R. Lea and Essex, on the SE. by London and on the S. by the R. Thames and by Surrey. The earliest recorded event in its hist. is Caesar's crossing of the Thames (54 BC) probably at Brentford (q.v.), into the kingdom of the Catuvellauni, who occupied M., Herts and Essex. The most substantial remains from the Rom. period are at Brentford, Staines and Sulloniacae (Brockley Hill), a settlement of Watling Street where a pottery works fl. Three major Rom. roads crossed M., Watling Street, Ermine Street and the London-Silchester road through Staines.

The Rom. order in M. finally collapsed in the early part of the 5th cent. The considerable number of Saxon place names in M. indicates early Saxon settlement though Saxon remains are few. The first recorded use of the name M. is in a charter of AD 704. Because M. provided a good vantage point for an attack on London, it became royal policy in later Saxon and Norman times to make large grants of lands to the Church, thus keeping the area in friendly or militarily weak hands. In succeeding cents. M. experienced the barons' rebellion against King John (1215) and the Peasants' Revolt (1381). The battle of Barnet (1471), in which Warwick the kingmaker was killed, was fought mostly on M. soil. In the Tudor period M. became a favourite place for royal residences, the prin. one being Hampton Court (q.v.). During the Civil wars (1642–9) Hounslow Heath, Colnbrook and Uxbridge provided camping grounds for the opposing armies. In 1642 royalist forces marched on London after the battle of Edgehill, but after capturing Brentford found the way barred by superior parl. forces at Turnham Green. The M. elections of 1769 were important in constitutional hist. (see WILKES, JOHN).

The local Gov. Act of 1888 transferred 50 sq. m. of 'metropolitan' M., with 2½ million inhab., to the newly created co. of London; the remainder (apart from Monken Hadley transferred to Herts) being formed into a new administrative co. of M. with a pop. of only 390,000.

Owing to extensive urb. development the rural areas of the co. are chiefly confined to the N. and the W. Until the 20th cent. M. was not industrial, though brick and tile making and market gardening were important. Since the First World War the co. has developed into an important manufacturing dist. The industries now represented cover a very wide field, including electrical products, food-stuffs, motor vehicles and musical instruments.

The Government of London Act, 1963, abolished the administrative co. of M. as from 1 April 1965 and placed the greater part of it within the jurisdiction of the new Greater London Council. Sunbury-on-Thames and Staines were transferred to Surrey and Potters Bar to Herts. By the Administration of Justice Act, 1964, M., less Staines, Sunbury-on-Thames, Twickenham and Potters Bar, but with the addition of Barnet and E. Barnet, became one of 5 separate areas of Greater London for the purposes of administration of justice, with its own commission of the peace and a separate court of quarter sessions. M. had no co. tn, though Brentford, where co. elections were often held, was an important local centre before 1889. Prior to its abolition the co. council met at the Guildhall, Westminster, where M. quarter sessions were also held. The area of the administrative co. was 148,687 ac. and the pop. 2,239,770. It comprised 18 bors. and 8 urb. dists. See W. Jerrold, *Highways and Byways in Middlesex*, 1909; *Victoria County History of Middlesex*, 1911– ; Report on Royal Commis-

sion on Historical Monuments (*Middlesex* vol.), 1937; J. E. B. Gover, A. Mawer and F. M. Stenton, *The Place-Names of Middlesex* (Eng. Place-Name Society, vol. xviii, 1942); Sir C. Radcliffe, *Middlesex*, 1954. (*See Plate.*)

Middlesex Regiment, The (The Duke of Cambridge's Own), traces its hist. to the 59th and 77th regiments of foot. The 59th Foot was raised in the W. country by Col. Arabin in 1755 for service in the Seven Years War and, 2 years later, it was renumbered the 57th Foot, and then, during the Amer. war, 1775, it received its second title, the W. M. R., though most of its personnel were men of Scots birth. The 77th Foot was raised by Col. James Marsh in 1787, and in 1807 was given the title of E. M. R. Formed to augment the army in India, the cost being borne by the E. India Co., it took part in the siege and capture of Seringapatam, then reputed the strongest fortress in India. In a later assault on the same fortress Lt. John Lawrence, of the regiment, was wounded and left for dead, but survived to become the father of Sir Harry Lawrence and Lord Lawrence, two of India's most distinguished soldiers. In the Peninsular war the 57th's first experience of a great battle with Napoleon's veterans was at Albuera, where they earned the sobriquet of 'the Diehards' from the fact that their commanding officer, Col. Inglis, though terribly wounded, continued till the end of the fight to rally his men with the repeated call 'Die hard, my men, die hard!' In the siege and capture of Badajoz, in which Picton's div. was so prominent, the 77th, which was part of that div., was reduced to 100 men in all. Subsequently both the 57th and 77th regiments were sent to the Crimea and fought under the Duke of Cambridge. The 77th received the surrender of Balaclava, and both regiments fought at Inkerman and took part in the siege of Sevastopol. Later, in New Zealand, the 59th gained distinction for the courageous way in which it attacked the Maori stockades in the Maori war of 1860. In 1881 the 2 regiments, 57th and 77th, which had for some time been linked for the purpose of providing drafts, became permanently incorporated as the 1st and 2nd battalions of the Duke of Cambridge's Own (M. R.). In the S. African war the 2nd Battalion fought at Spion Kop, Vaal Krantz, Colenso and Pieter's Hill. The 3rd and 4th regular battalions were raised early in this war. In the First World War the M. R. raised 46 battalions and fought in all the great battles in NW. Europe and in Gallipoli, Egypt, Palestine, Macedonia and Mesopotamia. Soon after the war ended the 3rd and 4th regular battalions were disbanded. In the Second World War units of the regiment served in NW. Europe, N. Africa, Sicily, Italy and SE. Asia. In the Korean War (1950–3) the 1st Battalion was one of the 2 leading Brit. battalions to join the U.N. force.

Middleton, Richard Barham (1882–1911), poet, *b.* Staines, Middlesex, descended from Richard Barham (q.v.). Educ. at St Paul's and Merchant Taylors', he was for 6 years an insurance clerk. After trying unsuccessfully to make a living by his pen he poisoned himself while in Brussels. As a writer he belongs to the school of the nineties. In 1912, after his death, there appeared his *Poems and Songs* (2 series), *The Ghost Ship*, a collection of stories, and *The Day Before Yesterday*, a book of essays containing delightful child studies after the manner of Kenneth Grahame. M.'s *Letters to Henry Savage* were pub. in 1929, and *The Pantomime Man*, a book of prose pieces, in 1933. *See* life by H. Savage, 1922.

Middleton, Thomas (1580–1627), dramatist, *b.* London. Educ. at Queen's College, Oxford, he was entered a student at Gray's Inn, and evidently used his legal knowledge in *The Old Law*, a play written about 1599 in collaboration with Wm Rowley, and in *Michaelmas Term*. He wrote plays by himself and also in collaboration with Drayton, Webster, Munday, Dekker and Rowley, and, besides plays, composed many pageants and masques. The first play written by himself was *The Chester Tragedy*, 1602, from which year he wrote regularly for the theatre. He was at his best when writing comedies of manners, his satire being keen and his dialogue excellent. One of his plays, *A Game at Chess*, 1624, achieved the distinction of being objected to by the Sp. ambas. on political grounds, as leading politicians of England and Spain appeared under the names and guises of chequers. He was appointed city chronologer in 1620, in which capacity he composed a chronicle of the city, now lost. His chief plays, many posthumously produced, are *A Trick to Catch the Old One*, 1608, *The Familie of Love*, 1608, *A Mad World, my Masters*, 1608, one of his best plays, *A Faire Quarrel*, 1617, *A Chaste Maid in Cheapside*, 1630, *Women beware Women*, 1657; *No Wit, No Help like a Woman*, 1657, *More Dissemblers besides Women*, 1657, and *The Witch*, 1778. In collaboration with other playwrights he wrote: with Dekker, *The Roaring Girl*, 1611; with Ben Jonson, *The Widow*, 1652; with Rowley, *The Spanish Gipsy*, 1653, and *The Changeling*, 1653.

The outstanding characteristics of his comedies, some of which are highly praised by Lamb, are the wide observation of men and manners and the boldness of treatment. His tragedies rival those of Webster in scenes of strong passion. He is, however, uneven as a dramatist, and repeats himself. M. obviously knew the life of the people, and was a good 'mixer'. This is manifest his pamphlets *The Black Book*, 1604, and *Father Hubbard's Tales*, 1604, which show no small acquaintance with the haunts and habits of pimps, bullies, Cyprians and thieves. Among his pageants and masques are *The Triumphs of Truth*, 1613, *The Triumphs of Honour and Industry*, 1617, and *The Inner Temple Masque*, 1619. His works were collected by Dyce in 1840 and by A. H. Bullen, 1885–6. *See* R. Withington, *English Pageantry*, 1918–20; W. D. Dunkel, *The Dramatic Technique of Thomas Middleton in his Comedies of London Life*, 1925; M. C. Bradbrook, *Themes and Conventions of Elizabethan Tragedy*, 1935; S.

Schoenbaum, *Middleton's Tragedies*, 1955.

Middleton, muncipal bor. of Lancs, England, 5 m. NNE. from Manchester. It is an important seat of the cotton trade, and calico printing is carried on. There are also iron works. Pop. 56,674.

Middleton-in-Teesdale, town of Durham, England, 22 m. SW. of Durham city, on the R. Tees. It has a quarrying industry. Pop. 1700.

Middletown: 1. City, co. seat of Middlesex co., Connecticut, U.S.A., on the Connecticut R., 14 m. S. of Hartford. It is the seat of Wesleyan Univ., and manufs. textiles, elastic webbing, metal products, automobile parts, clothing, rubber goods, chemicals, machinery, cigars and asbestos. It produces tobacco, apples and dairy products. Pop. 29,700.

2. City in Orange co., New York, U.S.A., 57 m. NNW. of New York City, in a rich agric. dist. Manufs. include straw hats, hardware, cigars, machine tools and fur and leather goods. Pop. 22,580.

3. City in Butler co., Ohio, U.S.A., on the Miami R., 35 m. N. of Cincinnati, with manufs. of tobacco, paper, aircraft, steel and industrial machinery. Pop. 33,700.

Middlewich, tn in Cheshire, England, 21 m. E. of Chester. There are salt works, manufs. of silk thrusters, earthenware and joinery works. Pop. 5833.

Midgard, Scandinavian name for the earth as intermediate between the Asgard (q.v.) of the gods and Utgard of the Jötuns (q.v.).

Midges are small dipterous insects (family Chironomidae). They differ from the gnats cr mosquitoes in the absence of the long, slender, horny proboscis. Most of them are quite harmless, but the females of some minute species of the genus *Ceratopogon* have the mouth highly developed, and with pointed lancet-like organs are able to draw blood. A typical M. is *Chironomus plumosus*, the aquatic larva of which is the blood worm. Many of the gall M. (Cecidomyidae), including the Hessian fly and the wheat M., are serious plant pests.

Midhurst, tn, par. and rural dist on the R. Rother in the Sussex Weald, 12 m. NNE. of Chichester, England. It has a grammar school, 1672, many buildings of architectural and historical interest, and the King Edward VII sanatorium. The ruins of Cowdray House, destroyed by fire (1793), stand in Cowdray Park where polo matches are played. Pop. of rural dist 17,370.

Midi, region of France, comprising broadly the area between the Bay of Biscay and the Mediterranean, with Toulouse as the chief tn. Its name is due to the fact that it was once a middle land between France and Spain.

Midi, Canal du, or **Canal de Languedoc,** canal of France, connecting the Garonne with the Mediterranean. Length 150 m.

Midi, Dent du, mt of the Alps, SE. of Lake Geneva, between the Swiss valleys of Chambéry (NW.) and Salvan (SE.). It was first ascended in 1784 by Clément, curé of Chambéry. Height, 10,696 ft.

Midi-de-Bigorre, Pic du, peak of the Pyrenees, S. France, 6 m. S. of Bagnères-de-Bigorre, almost on the Sp. frontier. The solar corona was first photographed in full sunlight from the observatory near its summit, in 1931. Altitude 9465 ft.

Midianites, nomadic race, descended (Gen. xxv. 2) from Midian, the son of Abraham and Keturah. They occupied the land to the S. of Moab and Edom. Joseph was sold to Midianite merchants (Gen. xxvii). The M. frequently united with Moab against Israel (Num. xxii). They were crushed by Gideon (Judges vi–viii). Their national god was Baal-Peor. *See also* KENITES.

Midland Bank, The, one of the 'big five' joint-stock banks, founded in Birmingham in 1836. The original title was the Birmingham and M. B., and the paid-up capital was £28,000. The bank followed the traditional lines of Brit. banking throughout the first half-cent. of its career, but from 1888 onwards the policies of amalgamation and branch extensions were adopted and vigorously pursued. In 1891 the Central Bank of London was absorbed, and this provided an estab. in the metropolis with a seat in the London Bankers' Clearing-House. The City Bank was absorbed in 1898, and in 1918 the largest amalgamation, that with the London Joint Stock Bank, took place. Besides the smaller banks in England and Wales which the M. B. had taken over, it acquired in 1917 the capital of the Belfast Banking, with its branches and agencies throughout N. Ireland. Similarly the capitals of the Clydesdale (1920) and N. of Scotland (1924) Banks were acquired, while in 1965 the Northern Bank was taken over with its branches in N. Ireland and the Rep. of Ireland. M. B. also acquired in 1958 with the Clydesdale Bank the capital of Forward Trust, a hire purchase finance company. Each of these institutions, however, preserves its autonomy. M. B. has its own Executor and Trustee Company founded in 1909, and it holds 45 per cent of the capital of Midland and International Banks. The total number of branches of the M. B. Group exceeds 3350.

Midland Dialect, *see* ENGLISH LANGUAGE.

Midland Railway of England, The, *see* RAIL-WAYS.

Midlands, name denoting the central cos. of England, lying between the Thames and the Trent and between E. Anglia and the cos. on the Welsh border. The area includes the cos. of Derby, Leicester, Northampton, Nottingham, Rutland, Stafford, Warwick and Worcester (qq.v.). The region is part of the lowland zone of Britain. *See also* ENGLAND, the subheadings INDUSTRY, RURAL ENGLAND and URBAN ENGLAND.

Midleton, William St John Fremantle Brodrick (1856–1942), 1st **Earl** and 9th **Viscount,** statesman, educ. at Eton and Balliol College, Oxford. He was secretary of state for war, 1900–3; secretary of state for India, 1903–5. He was prominent in Unionist politics in S. Ireland and succeeded his father in the viscounty, 1907; was

a member of the Irish Convention, 1917–18; and was created Earl of Midleton and Viscount Dunsford, 1920. He became a senator of the Irish Free State in 1921. His book, *Ireland, Dupe or Heroine,* appeared in 1932. His autobiography, *Records and Reactions, 1856–1939,* was pub. in 1939.

Midleton, mrkt tn, 13 m. E. of Cork, Rep. of Ireland. It has a whisky distillery, woolcombing and worsted mills, a gas bottling factory and 3 secondary schools. 5 m. to the E. lies the Carmelite College at Castlemartyr and 9 m. to the SE. the oil refinery at Whitegate. Pop. 2770.

Midlothian, or **Edinburghshire,** co. of Scotland, bounded on the N. by the Firth of Forth, on the W. by W. Lothian, on the E. by the cos. of Lanark, Peebles and Selkirk. The co. is now administratively separate from the city of Edinburgh (q.v.). The Moorfoot Hills lie in the SE. of the co., with Blackhope Scar (2136 ft) their highest point. The Pentland Hills (q.v.) cross from Peebleshire into Edinburgh. The rift valley between these 2 hill ranges is drained by the R.s N. and S. Esk (q.v.), which reach the Firth of Forth at Musselburgh, and by the R. Tyne, which passes into E. Lothian. The plain to the W. of the Pentland Hills is drained by the Water of Leith and the R. Almond. The Moorfoot Hills are drained by the Gala Water to the R. Tweed. Agriculture ranges from market gardening on the rich land near the coast to sheep farming in the hills. The chief crops are oats, barley, potatoes, swedes and wheat. Pig, cattle and poultry farming are prominent. Coal-mining is the prin. industry; coal is found in the Esk valley and in a small field in the SW. of the co. where oil shale is also extracted and processed. Paper is the chief manuf., and textiles (carpets and nets), wire and food-stuffs are important. There are 5 small burghs in the administrative co.: Musselburgh, Dalkieth, Bonnyrigg, Penicuik and Loanhead (qq.v.). The administrative co. is a single parl. constituency, with the exception of Musselburgh burgh which is included in E. Edinburgh constituency. Area 201,046 ac.; pop. 115,323 (both figures refer to the administrative co. only).

Midnight Sun. At the summer solstice, about 21 June, the sun does not set, but sinks to the N. point of the horizon at midnight at the Arctic circle. At N. Cape in Norway it is visible at midnight from about 12 May to the end of July. This phenomenon is called the M. S. Owing to the inclination of the rotational axis of the earth from the normal to its orbit, the sun is constantly visible during the summer at and within the Arctic and Antarctic circles for a period of 48 hrs to 6 months, according to distance from the poles.

Midrash, oldest Heb. exposition of the O.T., which accumulated after the exile from the explanations of scriptural passages and is the basis of rabbinical teaching. It was divided into the *Halachah,* which interpreted, applied and extended the precepts of the Law into a detailed code of conduct, and the *Haggadah,* which amplified and illustrated the O.T. narrative and teaching by legendary, speculative or imaginative additions; to this latter part the term M. is usually confined. *See* S. M. Lehrhman, *World of the Midrash*, 1962.

Midriff, *see* DIAPHRAGM.

Midshipmen. The name originally given to the ratings quartered amidships whose duties included boarding and entering enemy ships and taking charge of prizes. Pepys was responsible for changes which altered the status of M. to that of trainee officers, which has continued to the present day except for a brief period between 1956 and 1961 when the rank was temporarily abolished. Naval cadets (q.v.) are promoted M. after 1 year at the R.N. College, Dartmouth, and spend 1 year with the fleet, on conclusion of which they are promoted Acting Sub-lieutenant. *See* NAVAL CADET; NAVAL EDUCATION.

Midsomer Norton, par. of Somerset, England, 9 m. SW. of Bath. Near by is the Benedictine abbey of St Gregory and Downside School (q.v.), at Stratton-on-the-Fosse. In the tower of the church at M. N., dedicated to St John the Baptist, are 3 bells presented by Charles II. There is a trade in coal from the small Somerset coal-field. Pop. 6000.

Midsummer Day, 24 June, and one of the 4 Eng. term or quarter days. The summer solstice is, however, on 21 June. On Midsummer Eve, the night before, fairies and spirits were thought to be abroad. Revels were held and bonfires lit in honour of St John the Baptist, whose feast-day is on the 24th.
See ST JOHN'S, EVE OF.

Midsummer Eve, *see* ST JOHN'S, EVE OF.

Midway Island, Battle of, *see* PACIFIC, NAVAL OPERATIONS.

Midway Islands, group of small is. in lat. 28° 15′ N., and long. 177° 20′ W., lying NW. of the Sandwich group and forming the W. is. of the Amer. Hawaiian group. They consist of an atoll on which are 2 small is., Sand Is. and Eastern Is., and a number of islets. They were discovered by Capt. Brooks of the *Gambia* in 1859, who took possession of them in the name of the U.S.A. The barrier reef here is almost continuous except for a 3-m. gap on the W. side. In the S. part of the gap is Seward Roads, opposite the passage into Welles Harbour inside the lagoon. With a smooth sea there is a boat passage through the reef westward of Eastern Is. Sand Is. is of white coral sand; on its N. side are cable and wireless station buildings and a lighthouse, air-line hotel and U.S. naval base. Eastern Is. is covered with trees, shrubs and coarse grass, and has a sand beach of dazzling whiteness, except in its E. point, which is coral rock. The is. were made an Amer. reservation in 1903. An Amer. naval victory was fought off here in June 1942. *See* PACIFIC, NAVAL OPERATIONS. *See* T. V. Tuleja, *Climax at Midway*, 1961.

Midwifery (O.E. *mid*, with; *wif*, woman, properly the woman with or attendant upon a woman in childbirth), *see* OBSTETRICS; PUBLIC HEALTH.

Mieres, Sp. tn in the prov. of Oviedo. It has steel works and chemical factories, and there are

coal, iron, sulphur and cinnabar mines near by. Pop. 17,100.

Mierevelt, or **Miereveld, Michiel Janszoon van** (1567–1641), Dutch painter, *b.* Delft. He studied under Willemsz and became court painter to the House of Orange. He produced an enormous number of careful portraits, among them 'Lord Vere of Tilbury' and 'Elizabeth, Queen of Bohemia' in the National Portrait Gallery.

Mieris, Frans van (1635–81), called the elder, Dutch painter, *b.* Delft. He studied under Gerard Dou. His works are mainly portraits and domestic scenes, and he especially favoured the portrayal of the life of the wealthy. One of his best pictures is 'The Cavalier and Lacemaker', 1656, in the Vienna gallery.

Mieris, Frans von (1689–1763), the younger, son of Willem and also a *genre* painter; but he is better known as an antiquary and historian. He pub. *Historie der nederlandsche Vorsten*, 1732–5, and *Groot charterboek der graven van Holland*, *van Zeeland en heren van Vriesland*, 1753–6.

Mieris, Willem van (1662–1747), *b.* Leyden, son of Frans the elder, was a *genre* painter like his father, whose pupil he was, but his work is inferior.

Miers, Sir Henry Alexander (1858–1942), Brit. mineralogist. *B.* Rio de Janeiro, he was educ. at Eton and Trinity College, Oxford. In Brit. Museum (1882–95) he was engaged in research in crystal morphology. Appointed first Waynflete prof. of mineralogy at Oxford (1895); in 1908 he became principal of the univ. of London, and in 1915 vice-chancellor of Manchester Univ., and prof. of crystallography there. He was chairman of the Brit. Educational Mission to U.S.A. (1918) and the first president of the Gemmological Association of Great Britain. His writings include a text-book on *Mineralogy*, 1902, and articles on the same subject. The mineral miersite, a silver-copper oxide, was named after him in 1898.

Mierzeja Wiślana, *see* FRISCHES HAFF.

Mies, Van der Rohe, *see* VAN DER ROHE.

Migmatite, mixed rock (Gk *migma*) consisting partly of metamorphic and partly of igneous material, the 2 components being intimately mixed as a rule. M. forms as the result of the partial melting of solid rock.

Mignard, Pierre (1612–95), Fr. portrait painter, brother of Nicolas M., the engraver (1606–68), *b.* Troyes, and studied under Vouet at Paris, and later at Rome. He painted portraits of Pope Alexander VII and many It. princes. In 1657 he was summoned to Paris by Louis XIV, and on the death of his enemy, Le Brun, succeeded to all that artist's official posts.

Migne, Jacques Paul (1800–75), Fr. author and theologian, *b.* St Flour, Auvergne; ordained in 1824. He is famous chiefly as editor and publisher of the *Patrologia* (221 vols.), 1844–55, an exhaustive library of the Gk and Lat. fathers of the Church; and *Scripturae sacrae cursus completus* (28 vols.), 1840–5.

Mignet, François Auguste Marie (1796–1884), Fr. historian, *b.* Aix-en-Provence. In 1882 he went to Paris and pub. his *Histoire de la*

Révolution française, 1824, which has a vividness and accuracy which have made it a standard work on the subject. In 1830, in conjuction with Thiers, M. founded the Liberal jour. *Le National*. He also pub. *Notices et Mémoires historiques*, 1843, *Histoire de Marie Stuart*, 1851, *Charles Quint*, 1854, *Rivalité de François I et de Charles Quint*, 1875, and the romantic drama *Antonia Perez et Philippe II*, 1845.

Mignonette, genus *Reseda*, of ann. herbs of the family Resedaceae, indigenous to the S. countries of Europe and the Mediterranean generally. The fragrant *R. odorata* was introduced into Britain from Egypt in the middle of the 18th cent. It is a favourite garden plant, with large pyramidal white and red heads; there are dwarf and double-flowered varieties. The stem branches from the base, and the plant grows as a rather diffuse clump, bearing alternate lance-shaped leaves, simple or 3-lobed.

Migraine, or **Hemicrania**, paroxysmal headaches, usually on one side, and often associated with nausea, vomiting, vertigo and visual disturbances. The attacks are apt to start early in the morning and to last up to 24 hrs. They recur at more or less regular intervals and as a rule there are no premonitory signs. Any form of headache may be labelled by its owner as M., and as often as not the diagnosis is self-adopted because in the popular mind M. and martyrdom are inextricably linked. However, anybody who boasts of their attacks of M. may safely be said not to suffer from it. Genuine sufferers are far too afraid of the attacks to be proud of them. Macdonald Critchley has defined M. as 'constitutional in nature, inherited and bearing a vague association with personal or family "allergic" tendencies and a still vaguer one with epilepsy'. This definition is sufficient to indicate that the exact aetiology of M. is not known. M. usually starts in adolescence and often tends to become less severe after middle age. M. that comes on for the first time in middle life should be regarded with suspicion as being due to some intracranial lesion. Like all complaints M. varies in its severity, but patients with the lesser degrees of the complaint are in a minority. Treatment is unsatisfactory because the cause is not fully known. Analgesics help the milder attacks, but the most efficacious treatment is an injection of ergotamine tartrate. If given early enough it may abort an attack. The antihistamine drugs have been used with success in some cases. Regular courses of phenobarbitone may reduce the frequency and severity of the attacks.

Migration of Animals, periodical movement from one dist to another, mainly regulated by the food supply, though it is concerned also with breeding. It occurs in a large variety of animals, but most consistently among birds; in fact, it is believed that nearly every bird migrates in some part of its range. Much valuable information has been collected in recent years by the work of bird marking and observation stations; mention should be made particularly of Gatke's pioneer work on Heligoland and the more recent investigations on wildfowl by Peter Scott, as well as the schemes originated by the Brit. Museum (Natural Hist.). Large numbers of birds are caught and liberated after metal rings have been fixed on their legs, the return of which with particulars and date of capture is invited. Fish, such as salmon and cod, can be marked similarly, using metal tags attached to the gill cover. Apart from the enormous distances which many birds have been proved to travel, one of the most remarkable facts elucidated is that birds of a species (e.g. skylark) sometimes cross in their line of migration, some settling in dists which others have just left. The regularity of migratory movements is remarkable in such birds as the puffin or the swift, but spasmodic or irregular migrations have occurred on various occasions, as notably in 1863 and 1888, when Pallas's sand grouse, a native of the plains of Tartary, invaded Britain in great numbers. Similarly, the crossbill and the waxwing make occasional incursions. More than one species of Lepidoptera (butterflies) annually migrate over the N. Sea. Crabs and lobsters and some molluscs are known to move considerable distances to fresh feeding-grounds. A number of fish (e.g. the salmon) are anadromous in habit; that is, they live in the sea, but enter fresh water to spawn and afterwards again descend to the sea; while, on the other hand, the eel spawns in the deep sea off Bermuda, and does not return, the young entering the rivs. of Great Britain as elvers. In the search for breeding-grounds, some of the aquatic mammals migrate long distances from their usual haunts. Many other mammals make fairly regular migrations, their movements being regulated primarily by the changes of the seasons. The routes followed by birds and other migrating animals have probably remained unchanged since prehistoric times. There is good evidence that day flying migrant birds fly by sun navigation, and that night fliers make use of star-patterns. This ability is inherited, not learned. It must be remembered that the young individuals of such species as the cuckoo follow their parents after a lapse of sev. weeks. The considerable distance travelled by the Arctic tern is referred to in the article on terns. The New Zealand mutton bird, one of the shearwaters, migrates to that country from Siberia, near the Arctic Circle, and the godwit or kuaka of the same country comes down from still farther N., in Alaska. On the last part of their journey to New Zealand, both these birds fly across the open ocean from New Caledonia Is., whereas most birds keep close to the coast lines. The departure of the kuaka from Spirits' Bay at the extreme N. of New Zealand is one of the wonders of bird life, and is described as follows by Mona K. Gordon in *Children of Tane*, 1938: 'Here at the end of March and on into April the kuaka gather by companies, pouring into the bay from all parts of the country in contingents fifty to a thousand strong. They alight on the beach until there is hardly standing-room for all; every hour of the day brings more and more armies to swell the vast assemblage. Towards evening they show signs of restlessness and agitation until the sky is stained with the rose and gold of sunset. Then, as with one accord, the godwits, crowded almost inextricably on the sands, mount into the air and take a course due north in trailing, wedge-shaped formation.' See A. Meek, *The Migration of Fishes*, 1916; C. B. Williams, *The Migration of Butterflies*, 1930; G. V. T. Matthews, *Bird Navigation*, 1955; J. Dorst, *The Migration of Birds* (trans.), 1962.

Migration of People, see COMMONWEALTH AND EMPIRE SETTLEMENT ACTS; EMIGRATION; IMMIGRATION.

Miguel, Maria Evarist, known as **Dom Miguel** (1802–66), third son of John VI of Portugal. In 1822 his mother, Carlota Joaquina, plotted to overthrow her husband and estab. M. upon the throne. The attempt failed, and M. consequently spent some years in exile. In 1826, however, John VI *d*. and his eldest son, Pedro of Brazil, renounced his right to the succession in favour of his daughter, Maria da Gloria, it being arranged that she should marry M. Although he had sworn allegiance to the new queen and to the constitution, and in 1827 had been appointed regent, M. ignored his oath, procured his recognition as sole king and opposed all forms of liberalism in his dominions. In 1834, faced with growing hostility by England, France and Spain, he renounced his pretence to the throne and retired to Rome, later going to Baden, where he *d. See* PORTUGAL, *History*.

Mihailovich, Draza (1893–1946), Yugoslav soldier, *b*. Shumadiza, served with the Serbian Army in the Balkan wars, 1912–13, and in the First World War. In the Second World War, when Yugoslavia was overrun by the Germans in 1941, he took refuge, with his troops, in the forests and hills, being recognised by the exiled Yugoslav Gov. of King Peter as commander-in-chief and war minister. He was also recognised by the Brit. military authorities in the middle E., who attached liaison officers to his forces. This was the origin of the Chetnik movement. Meanwhile, however, a Communist resistance movement was developed under Tito. M. tried to combine the 2 resistance movements, but, eventually, his monarchist views led him to collaborate with the Germans and Italians against the Communist partisan forces. Allied support was transferred to Tito, and M. was also repudiated by the Yugoslav exiled gov. M. fell into Tito's hands in Mar. 1946, and 3 months later he was tried, convicted of treason, and shot in Belgrade. *See also* YUGOSLAVIA, *History*.

Mihrab (Arabic), in Muslim architecture, a niche indicating the direction of Mecca, towards which worshippers incline when praying (*see* MOSQUE).

Mikado, former title of the emperors of Japan, for which Tenno has recently been substituted in general use. The present M. succeeded his father, Taisho, in 1926, and is the 124th of the imperial line going back to the 1st cent. BC. In 1945 the Emperor Hirohito repudiated his divinity; the constitution of 1946 made the emperor a constitutional monarch.

Mikania, large genus of evergreen climbing plants (family Compositae), natives of tropical America. *M. scandens* will grow on a trellis in the open in summer.

Mikes, Kelemen (1690–1761), retainer of Ferenc Rákóczi II of Transylvania, whom he followed into exile. He was *b.* at Zágon. His *Turkish Letters* is the best Hungarian prose work of the period.

Mikhaël, Éphraïm (1866–90), pseudonym of **Georges-Éphraïm Michel**, Fr. Symbolist poet, *b.* Toulouse. His most important works are *L'Automne* (poems), 1886, and the lyrical drama, *Briséis* (with Catulle Mendès), 1892.

Mikhaylovskiy, Nikolay Konstantinovich (1842–1904), Russian literary critic, publicist and sociologist, a leading theorist of Populism (q.v.).

Mikkeli, inland tn and co. of S. Finland, the wartime H.Q. of Mannerheim (q.v.). More than one-third of the area is covered by lakes, with over 1000 is. Area 8819 sq. m.; pop. 235,200. Its cap. is also called M. (pop. 19,900).

Mikkelsen, Ejnar (1880–), Dan. polar explorer. He took part in many expeditions of exploration to the N. Atlantic, Greenland, Franz Joseph's Land and Alaska. In 1907 he was instrumental in helping to disprove the polar land theory, as in 72° N. lat. and 150° W. long. a sounding 339 fathoms failed to reach the bottom. In 1909 M. and Iversen explored Greenland in search of Mylius Erichsen's records, the main body of the expedition returning without them. Their safety was despaired of but they reached Europe in 1912, after spending the previous winter on Bass Rock, near Shannon Is. M. commanded the colonising expeditions to Scoresby Sund in 1924 and SE. Greenland in 1932. He was inspector of E. Greenland from 1933–9 and 1945–50. He has pub. *Conquering the Arctic Ice*, 1909; *Lost in the Arctic*, 1913; the novel *John Dale*, 1921; *Norden for Lov og Ret* (trans. *Frozen Justice, a Story of Alaska*, 1922); *Mirage on the Arctic* (trans. 1955). Other works include *Med 'Gronland' til Scoresbysund*, 1925, a hist. of the E. Greenland Eskimos, 1935, and his autobiography, of which 5 vols. have appeared in Danish, 1953 to 1960. The second volume has been trans. as *Two Against the Ice*, 1957. M. was awarded the Patron's medal in gold by the Royal Geographical Society in 1934.

Mikolajczyk, Stanislaw, Polish statesman, see POLAND, *History*.

Mikoyan, Anastas Ivanovich (1895–), Armenian Communist, educ. at a theological seminary. He joined the Communist party in 1915, and worked in Tiflis and Baku. In 1921 he became head of the party organisation in Nizhniy-Novgorod, and 1922–6 in N. Caucasus. Since 1926 he has been in charge of trade, both foreign and internal, and since 1930 also of food industries. He has been a deputy prime minister since 1937 and a member of the party's Central Committee since 1923. M. supported Stalin in the inner-party struggle after Lenin's death and was made candidate member of the Politburo (q.v.) in 1926 and a full member in 1935. During the Second World War he was one of only 9 men who served for various periods on the State Defence Committee, the country's supreme body at that time. After Malenkov's resignation as Prime Minister (1955) M. became one of the most prominent members of the 'collective leadership'. He supported Khrushchev as the latter built up his personal dominance, and was frequently used for important missions abroad. He was a First Deputy Prime Minister from 1955 to 1964, when he became Chairman of the Presidium of the U.S.S.R. Supreme Soviet (i.e. President of the U.S.S.R.). He retired from this post in Dec. 1965, on grounds of health. His survival through every purge which threatened him is testimony both to his political intuition and to his valued political and economic judgment.

Mikoyan-Shakhar, see KARACHAYEVSK.

Mikszáth, Kálmán (1847–1910), Hungarian author and politician, b. Szklabonya, married Ilona Mauks in 1873. In numerous novels and short stories M. satirised contemporary society with much good humour and some cruelty. His work is, unfortunately, often marred by poor construction. Eng. trans. are *The Good People of Palócz*, 1893, and *St Peter's Umbrella*, 1900. See study by A. Schöpflin, 1941.

Mikulov (Ger. Nicolsburg), Czechoslovak tn in the region of Tihomoravský, on the Austrian border. In 1866 a preliminary peace treaty was signed here after Austria's defeat by Prussia (see PRUSSIA, *History*). Pop. 5300.

Milá y Fontanals, Manuel (1818–84), Sp. scholar and author. Amongst his pubs. are his treatise, *De los trovadores en España* and *De la poesía heróico-popular castellana*. He was one of the first to fight for the revival of Catalan literature.

Milan I (1854–1901), Prince of Serbia from 1868 to 1882, and King of Serbia from 1882 to 1889, was b. at Jassy, Rumania. On the assassination of his cousin, Michael Obrenovič (1868), M. was proclaimed prince and ruled under a regent till he came of age in 1872. In 1876 he allied himself with Russia, and declared war against Turkey, winning the independence of Serbia and the kingship for himself in 1882. His pro-Austrian policy made him unpopular and in 1889 he abdicated in favour of his son, Alexander, and retired to Paris. In 1894 he served as commander-in-chief of the Serbian Army for a short time, but was banished as a result of a quarrel over Alexander's marriage.

Milan (It. **Milano**): 1. Prov. of Italy in W. Lombardy (q.v.). It lies generally in the fertile plain of Lombardy, but has foothills of the Alps in the N. The SE. boundary is formed by the R. Po, and the prov. is watered on the W. by the Ticino and on the E. by the Adda. Rice, cereals, livestock, fruit, wine and silk are produced, and there are important industrial centres. The prin. tns include M., Monza, Lodi, Melegnano, Desio and Magenta (qq.v.). Area 1065 sq. m.; pop. 2,800,000.

2. (anct **Mediolanum**). Second city of Italy, cap. of the prov. of M., and chief tn of Lombardy, 290 m. NW. by N. of Rome. It stands in the W. of the great plain of Lombardy, on the R. Olona, at the convergence of important It. and trans-Alpine road and rail routes. The city is of Celtic (see CELT) origin, and was taken by the Romans in 222 BC. In the Middle Ages it was a place of great consequence (see next article). Napoleon I made it the cap. of the Cisalpine Rep. (q.v.) in 1799, and subsequently of the short-lived It. Rep. and Kingdom of Italy. In 1814 it reverted to the Austrians. The city rebelled against Austria—the 'Five Days of Milan'—in 1848 (18–22 Mar.), and after the battle of Magenta (q.v.) in 1859 it was joined to Piedmont (q.v.). During the Second World War widespread damage to the city was caused by air-raids. The city is of modern appearance, despite its antiquity, and the best streets are wide, well laid out and kept with scrupulous care. It is roughly circular, and many of the prin. thoroughfares radiate from the city's centre, the *Piazza del Duomo*. The *Piazza* is dominated by the wonderful Gothic archiepiscopal cathedral, which, with the exception of St Peter's (q.v.) in Rome, is the most magnificent eccles. structure of Italy. It was begun in the 14th cent. on a site previously occupied by 2 earlier cathedrals, and since then has been subject to constant addition and alteration; one of its bronze portals was completed as recently as 1951. The building is adorned with over 2000 statues, and has 135 pinnacles, on the highest of which is the gilded statue of the *Madonnina*. Napoleon—by whose orders the upper part of the façade was added—was crowned King of Italy in the cathedral in 1805. The see of M. is usually occupied by a cardinal of great prestige in both Church and State, and in most of the churches of the archdiocese (and in a few elsewhere), instead of the Rom. liturgy, the Ambrosian liturgy is celebrated—an interesting relic of an otherwise obsolete rite (see AMBROSE, ST, and LITURGY). M. has many other anct churches, among them the splendid basilica of S. Ambrogio (Ambrose), founded by the saint in the 4th cent., but in its present Lombard Romanesque form dating from the 12th cent. Another notable church is the Dominican church of Sta Maria delle Grazie (damaged during the war, but largely reconstructed), in the old convent adjoining which is the famous painting 'The Last Supper' by Leonardo da Vinci (q.v.). This is painted on one of the end walls of the refectory. Among the notable secular buildings of M. is the Brera Palace, which contains an academy of fine arts, an observatory, a library (660,000 vols.) and a picture gallery containing Raphael's *Sposalizio* and works by Tintoretto, Giovanni Bellini, Veronese, Tiepolo, Luini, Lotto, Crivelli (qq.v.) and other masters. It is one of the two great art collections of M., the other, the Ambrosiana, being made glorious by its Leonardo drawings and Raphael's cartoon for the 'School of Athens' fresco in the Vatican. The great 15th cent. Sforza (q.v.) castle has many medieval and Renaissance works of art, in addition to its collection of antiquities, and there are other

masterpieces in the Poldi Pezzoli museum. Other celebrated institutions of M. are the opera house of La Scala (q.v.) and the *Ospedale Maggiore* (Great Hospital), a magnificent structure begun in 1457; it was grievously damaged during the Second World War, and when reconstructed will be the seat of the univ. The univ. was formed in 1925 by the amalgamation of a number of institutions, and there is also a non-State (Catholic) univ. (1920) and a school of economics. M. is the chief commercial centre of Italy, with a large trade in silk, cotton, cereals and rice. There are textile, chemical, automobile, precision engineering, glass, confectionery, leather, rubber, porcelain, tobacco and foodstuff industries. The city is also an important publishing centre. Pop. 1,581,000. (*See Plate: Italian Architecture.*)

Milan, Bishopric and Duchy of. The position of M. in the Middle Ages may be traced to the influence of her bishops. St Ambrose, who occupied the see from 374 until 397, rebuked the Emperor Theodosius I and denied him entry to the cathedral after the massacre of Thessalonica (AD 390). The emperor did public penance and was immediately absolved. After the estab. of the Lombard kingdom in 569 the bishops of M. became the rallying point of opposition both to Arianism and to foreign rule; and their temporal authority was further increased by Charlemagne's defeat of the Lombards in 774. In the confusion which followed their emperor's death the archbishops became the only real centre of authority in M. During the next 200 years the tyranny of the nobles drove the common people to seek the protection and authority of the Church, under whom the city increased in numbers and independence, and learned the art of self-gov. It was Archbishop Aribert (1018–45) who invited Conrad to Italy and crowned him King of Germany with the iron crown of Lombardy. In the 13th cent. Archbishop Ottone Visconti, as leader of the nobles, defeated the Torriani at Desio (1277), and from that time until 1447 the Visconti ruled the city. Following the death of Filippo Visconti in that year a rep. was proclaimed. It lasted for only 3 years. In 1450 Francesco Sforza (1401–66) (*see* SFORZA) became Duke of M. by right of conquest. He had married Bianca, Filippo's heiress. The dukedom continued in the line of Francesco's eldest son, Galeazzo, until 1481, when it was seized by Galeazzo's brother Lodovico, Il Moro (1451–1508), the patron of Leonardo da Vinci. On the death of his son Francesco in 1535 M. became a dependency of Spain under Charles V. *See* D. Muir, *A History of Milan under the Visconti*, 1924; L. Collison-Morley, *The Story of the Sforza*, 1933.

Milan, Edict of, decree of Constantine the Great (AD 313) securing toleration for Christianity throughout the Rom. empire.

Milan Decree, promulgated by Napoleon, 1807. It declared the whole Brit. empire to be in a state of blockade, and forbade all countries to trade with Great Britain or to use any article of Brit. manuf. It was never effective, owing to

European dependence on Brit. trade and manufs.

Milanion, *see* ATALANTA.

Milano Marittima, *see* CÉRVIA.

Milazzo (anct. **Mylae**), seaport in Sicily, 17 m. W. of Messina. It was originally a Gk colony, and stands, partly on a hill, on the W. promontory of the Bay of M. (q.v.). Here in 1861 Garibaldi (q.v.) defeated the Neapolitans. There is a boat service to the Lipari Is. (q.v.), and there is a trade in tunny fish, fruit, silk, olive oil and wine. Pop. 13,500.

Milazzo, Bay of, inlet of the Tyrrhenian Sea (q.v.), on the NE. coast of Sicily. It is about 16 m. wide and is bounded on the W. by a narrow peninsula which ends in Cape M. It has been the scene of many naval engagements, including the first Rom. naval success over the Carthaginians in 260 BC (*see* CARTHAGE).

Mildenhall, mrkt tn of Suffolk, England, 12 m. from Bury St Edmunds and 76 m. from London, and situated on the R. Lark. In and before the Second World War it had an important RAF aerodrome, now used by the U.S. Air Force and as an Air Ministry meteorological station. In 1934 it was the starting point of the Britain to Australia air-race. It has a typical E. Anglian market cross. Near M., at W. Row, in 1942–3, was found a hoard of Rom. silver tableware, now in the Brit. Museum, known as the M. treasure and said to be the finest of its kind to come into the keeping of the nation as treasure trove. It consists of bowls, dishes, spoons, platters and goblets, ornamented with foreign hunting scenes, embossed figures of fine quality and classical design, and niello work. Similar hoards, but not in such perfect condition, were found near Coleraine, Londonderry, in 1854 and, in 1919, during excavations on Traprain Law, E. Lothian. It is assumed that these and other hoards were buried by their owners to save them from falling into the hands of marauders. (*See also* TREASURE TROVE). *See* J. W. Brailsford, *The Mildenhall Treasure* (Brit. Museum), 1947. Wamil Hall, ½ m. W., is Elizabethan. Pop. (including military personnel at M. base) 8500.

Mildew, description of a fungus infection of the surface of a plant host; Powdery M. is caused by fungi of the Erysiphaceae (e.g. Apple M., *Podosphaera leucotricha*); Downy or False M. by fungi of the Peronosporaceae (e.g. Grape Downy M., *Plasmopara viticola*); Dark M. by fungi of the Melioaceae. M. is also descriptive of the rotting of cloth, fabric, etc., by fungi or moulds.

Mildmay, Sir Walter (*c.* 1520–89), statesman, *b.* Chelmsford. He became chancellor of the exchequer in 1566. A convinced Protestant, M. founded Emmanuel College, Cambridge, and gave generously to sev. other educational estabs.

Mildura, city of Victoria, Australia, in a fruit-growing dist under irrigation, 351 m. from Melbourne. A bridge spans the R. Murray. Its industries are cordial factories, olive oil factory, saw- and planing-mills. Pop. 12,279.

Mile, *see* METROLOGY.

Mile End, dist of E. London. Once a hamlet of

Stepney par. with historical associations, it now forms the central and NE. parts of the bor. of Stepney (q.v.).

Miles, Bernard (1907–), actor and theatre director, founder of the Mermaid Theatre at Blackfriars, *b.* Uxbridge, educ. there and at Oxford. After some years as a schoolmaster he made his first appearance on the stage in 1930, and spent sev. years acting and working backstage in provincial repertory companies. He has appeared in revue and music-hall and in Shakespeare with the Old Vic company. In 1951 he built the first Mermaid Theatre in the garden of his house at St John's Wood, reconstructing it at the Royal Exchange for a 3 month season in the summer of 1953. The present Mermaid Theatre, built inside the shell of a bombed warehouse at Puddle Dock, opened in May 1959. M., who appeared frequently in his own productions, was awarded a C.B.E. in 1953. He has made many appearances in films and on television. He pub. *The British Theatre*, 1948.

Miles, Nelson Appleton (1839–1925), Amer. soldier, *b.* Westminster, Massachusetts. He entered the army in 1861 and served with the Federals in the Civil war. He became brigadier-general of volunteers in 1864, 3 years later holding the same position in the regular army. In 1895 he became commanding general of the U.S.A., successfully dealing with the Indian outbreaks of the Cheyennes and Comanches, the Sioux in Montana, the Nez Percés and the Apaches. In 1898 he directed the military operations of the war with Spain. He pub. *Personal Recollections*, 1896, *Military Europe*, 1898, *Observations Abroad*, 1899, *Serving the Republic*, 1911.

Mileto, It. tn in Calabria (q.v.), 36 m. SW. of Catanzaro. It was razed in an earthquake in 1908, when 2300 lives were lost. The fine cathedral dates from 1930. M. has an observatory. Pop. 8700.

Miletus, once of the greatest cities of Asia Minor, belonged territorially to Caria and politically to Ionia, being the southernmost of the 12 cities of the Ionian confederacy. Its ter. was rich in flocks, and the city was celebrated for its woollen fabrics, the *Milesia vellera*. At a very early period it became a great maritime state, and by the mid 7th cent. BC had founded or helped to found more than 60 colonies. It was the bp. of the philosophers Thales, Anaximander and Anaximenes, and of the historians Cadmus and Hecataeus. It was the centre of the great Ionian revolt during the suppression of which it was sacked by Persian forces (494 BC). In 334 BC it was besieged and almost destroyed by Alexander the Great, but recovered and retained some commercial importance. During the Hellenistic and Rom. periods its 4 harbours were gradually silted up by the Maeander, and it yielded pride of place as a maritime city to Ephesus (q.v.). There are considerable remains. Its site is occupied by Palatia.

Milfoil, or **Yarrow** (*Achillea millefolium*), plant with thrice-pinnatifid leaves and white, pink or purple flowers (family Compositae). It is common on pastures.

Milford, Sir Humphrey Sumner (1877–1952), Brit. publisher; publisher to the univ. of Oxford, 1913–45. From 1919 to 1921 M. was president of the Publishers' Association of Great Britain and N. Ireland. He was knighted in 1936. He ed. the *Oxford Book of English Verse of the Romantic Period, 1798–1837*, 1928, and also the poems of Cowper, 1905, Clough, 1910, Leigh Hunt, 1923, and Robert Browning, 1949.

Milford, *see* MILFORD HAVEN.

Milford Haven, 1st Marquess of (Prince Louis Alexander Battenberg, later Mountbatten, Earl of Medina and Viscount Alderney) (1854–1921), *b.* Gratz. He entered the Brit. Navy at 14 years of age, becoming midshipman in 1869. In the Egyptian war he received the Egyptian medal and Khedive's Bronze Star for distinguished services. In 1884 he married his cousin Victoria, eldest daughter of Princess Alice and grandchild of Queen Victoria. A widely experienced authority on naval affairs, he served on many naval committees before his appointment as director of naval intelligence at the Admiralty, 1902. Rear-admiral, 1904, he became First Sea Lord, 1912. The perfect state of the navy on the outbreak of the First World War in its readiness for immediate mobilisation was largely due to his forethought and general ability. But, by reason of his Ger. origin, suspicion fell on him, and in Oct. 1914 he voluntarily resigned in favour of Lord Fisher. By royal request he gave up his foreign titles in 1917, assuming the surname Mountbatten and entering the peerage as M. of M.H. Pubs.: *Men-of-War Names*, 1897, 1908, and *British Naval Medals*, 1919. *See* life by M. Kerr, 1934.

Milford Haven, seaport of Pembrokeshire, Wales, 8 m. SSW. of Haverfordwest, founded by a colony of Quaker whalers from Nantucket, Massachusetts, as a whaling centre. Later it became a naval dockyard (afterwards moved to Pembroke Dock) and was used as a naval base in both world wars. It is engaged in fishing and shipbuilding. The natural harbour, one of the finest in the world, runs inland for some 20 m. and varies in breadth from 1 to 2 m. with a depth of 15–19 fathoms. The docks are being extended to give all the repair, supply and personal services essential for a major port. A proposal announced in 1957 to develop M. H. as a major oil port is under way. Two tanker terminals and a refinery have been built, and a second refinery and third tanker terminal are now under construction. The M. H. Conservancy Board has been set up to control navigation in the harbour. Pop. 12,802. *See* Sir J. F. Rees, *The Story of Milford*, 1954.

Milford Sound, fjord on the SW. coast of S. Is., New Zealand, extending for 10 m. and about 1 m. in breadth. It has numerous waterfalls. One means of access is by Milford Track, passing by Clinton R., which runs into Lake Te Anau. There is also a motor route through the Homer Tunnel.

Milhaud, Darius (1892–), Fr. composer, *b.* Aix-en-Provence, studied at the Paris Conservatoire. Attached to the Fr. legation at Rio de Janeiro in 1917–18, he was secretary to Paul Claudel (q.v.), who was to become his librettist for *Christophe Colomb*, and for sev. of whose plays he wrote incidental music. Back in Paris, he came under the influence of Satie (q.v.) and at the instigation of Jean Cocteau (q.v.) joined the group of young composers who became known as 'Les Six'. He soon seceded, however, and made his way independently with a large number and great variety of works, being first represented at the festivals of the International Society for Contemporary Music in 1922 and 1924. Meanwhile his first opera, *La Brebis égarée*, written in 1910–15, was produced by the Paris Opéra-Comique in 1923. His 2 most ambitious operas, *Christophe Colomb* and *Maximilien*, were produced in Berlin (1930) and Paris (1932) respectively. In 1940 M. was driven by the war to the U.S.A., with his wife and son, and he held a professorship at Mills College, Oakland, California, until 1947, when he returned to Paris and became prof. of composition at the Conservatoire. M.'s catalogue of works in almost every category of music is enormous, including 14 operas (3 for children), 13 ballets, incidental music for over 30 classical and modern plays, much film and radio music, many choral and orchestral works (9 symphonies, etc.), music for military and jazz bands, for instruments and voice with orchestra, chamber music (18 string quartets, etc.), many piano works and about 200 songs.

Miliaria Populosa, *see* PRICKLY HEAT.

Militant Athiests, League of, in Soviet Russia. It was formed by the Communist party in 1925 for anti-religious propaganda, which it carried out in the most violent manner, denouncing priests to the G.P.U. (q.v.), interfering in church services and bringing about the destruction of many church buildings. It was abolished in 1943.

Military Academies, *see* MILITARY EDUCATION.

Military Cross, instituted by royal warrant, 28 Dec. 1914, for award to Brit. officers of the substantive rank of captain or of lower commissioned rank, and to warrant officers (Indian and colonial forces included), in recognition of distinguished and meritorious services in time of war. It consists of a silver cross, having on each arm a crown, and bearing in the centre the royal cipher. The ribbon is white with a broad mauve stripe down the middle.

The cross confers no precedence, but entitles the recipient to the addition after his name of the letters 'M.C.' Between Aug. 1914 and 31 Jan. 1920, 36,824 awards of the M.C. were made to personnel of the Brit. forces for services in the field. In addition to these, 2939 first, 167 second and 4 third M.C. bars were conferred. During the Second World War a grand total of 10,892 M.C.s was awarded. Of this number 10,784 were awarded to the army, being 10,280 crosses plus 480 first bars plus 24 second bars; 38 to the navy and royal marines, being 37 crosses plus 1 first bar; and 70 to the RAF, being 69 crosses plus 1 first bar. The M.C. is an army decoration, and the awards to members of the other services are for good work done while attached to the army.

Military Education and Military Schools. The purpose of education in the armed forces is to improve general education so that the serviceman can learn and perform his military duties more efficiently, and to equip him more adequately for a return to civil life; and to services officers and other ranks in their professional duties. In the Brit. Army much is done within units, but the more technical and advanced instruction is given at military schools, such as the Staff Colleges, School of Artillery, School of Infantry, etc.

Officers. Most Brit. officers begin their studies at the Royal Military Academy, Sandhurst. Thereafter they spend a substantial part of their careers attending courses of instruction, which vary according to their arm of the Service—Armoured Corps, Infantry, Artillery, Engineers, Signals, Medical, etc., each having its own Schools. Advanced instruction—in the higher direction of war—is given at the Imperial Defence College, London; the Joint Services Staff College, Latimer; the Staff College, Camberley; and the Royal Military College of Science, Shrivenham. A few Brit. officers attend courses at the Staff Colleges of other Commonwealth countries—Australia, Canada, India and Pakistan—under a reciprocal exchange agreement. Similar exchange arrangements exist with the Royal Naval Staff College, Greenwich; the RAF Staff College, Bracknell, and the staff and war colleges of some of our Allies. Vacancies are also allotted to Brit. officers at the NATO Defence College.

Other ranks. The soldier's general education aims at equipping him to perform his military duties efficiently, to qualify for promotion to the higher non-commissioned ranks and in a few cases to commissioned rank and to improve his chances of well paid employment when he returns to civil life. Every soldier is expected to obtain a 2nd Class Certificate, and those seeking higher promotion a 1st Class or Special Certificate. Most of the instruction is done within units under the supervision of officers of the Royal Army Education Corps attached to the H.Q. of Higher Formations. Courses and special classes are also held under arrangements made by the R.A.E.C.

The soldier also receives most of his military instruction within his unit; but Warrant Officers and N.C.O.s are frequently sent on courses at Military Schools. These vary according to their rank and arm of the Service, but are mostly for the purpose of fitting them to become leaders and instructors within their units.

Note. Although the above deals mainly with the Army, the policy and general methods of instruction are similar in the RN and RAF. The same principles are also followed in the fighting services of other Commonwealth countries and in those of our NATO allies. The Brit. defence service's policy of increasing integration is likely to result in many more schools of instruction becoming common to all

3 services—as is the case already with the Imperial Defence College and the Joint Services Staff College.

Military Graves, see WAR GRAVES.

Military Intelligence, see INTELLIGENCE, MILITARY, AND SECURITY.

Military Knights of Windsor, body of retired officers attached to the Order of the Garter (see ORDERS OF KNIGHTHOOD, GREAT BRITAIN AND IRELAND (1)). They were formerly known as Poor Knights, ranking below the ordinary knights. The institution originated in 1349, when it consisted of 26 veterans. Members are now appointed by the sovereign from officers who have rendered meritorious service. They are granted a small stipend together with quarters in Windsor Castle, whence their designation. Until 1906 the institution was part of an eccles. college under the dean of Windsor, but was then transferred to the governor of Windsor Castle. Stipends are derived from the college revenues, and every Knight of the Garter on appointment to that order contributes a sum for apportionment among the knights. The uniform is that of the early 19th cent. and was assigned by William IV, who prefixed the word 'Military' to the name of the institution. The number was fixed at 13 in 1919.

Military Law is laid down in the *Manual of Military Law*, issued by command of the Army Council, as being 'the law which governs the soldier in peace and in war, at home and abroad'. M. L. is contained in the Army Act (see also under ARMY), the Acts relating to the Reserve and Auxiliary Forces, and certain other Acts applied to the army, such as the Cheap Trains Act, 1883, relating to conveyance of troops; the Regimental Debt Act, 1893, relating to the effects of deceased officers and men; and the Emergency Powers Act, 1920, which makes special provision for the protection of the community in cases of emergency; supplemented by the Queen's Regulations for the Army and the Army Reserve, by other regulations, e.g. those for the Territorial Army, by Royal Warrant, e.g. those relating to pay, promotion, etc. and by Army Orders and Army Council instructions. The Army Act is an Act of Parliament dealing with discipline, courts-martial, enlistment and allied subjects, and has in itself no permanent operation, for it continues in force only so long as Parliament from time to time decides. It is annually brought into operation by the Army and Air Force Act, which must become law by 30 April, and it is by this system of ann. Acts that Parliament retains control over the land forces of the Crown. The Army Act is part of the statute law of England, and though that part of it which relates to discipline is administered by army tribunals and not by the civil courts, it is construed in the same manner, and carried into effect under the same conditions as to evidence and otherwise, as the ordinary criminal law of the country. Though the object of this special code of law is twofold, namely to provide for the maintenance of discipline and for administrative matters, in practice the term is more often used with reference to the disciplinary provisions alone. There is not in England, as in many foreign countries, a special law defining the relations between the military and civil powers in cases of riot and insurrection or the intermediate state known as an *état de siège*. Troops when called out to assist the civil power in these cases in Great Britain are under M. L. as soldiers, but they are also as citizens subject to the ordinary civil law to the same extent as if they were not soldiers. Their military character is superimposed on their civil character and does not obliterate it (see A. V. Dicey, *Introduction to the Study of the Law of the Constitution*, 1855). M. L. must not be confused with martial law, which latter means the suspension of the ordinary law and the gov. of a country or parts of it by M. tribunals of its own army. See also ARMY, under various subheads; COURTS-MARTIAL (showing the changes made since the First World War); ENLISTMENT; IMPRESSMENT; OFFICIAL SECRETS.

In the U.S.A. the first articles of war were drawn up in 1775; in 1806 the present code was estab., which is practically the same as the Eng. code. In 1864 the first M. L. estab. was made with the name of Bureau of Military Justice. In 1883 this bureau was consolidated with the judge-advocate's dept. There is a judge-advocate for each military div., who is responsible for the whole machinery of court-martial.

Military Medal, instituted by royal warrant in Mar. 1916 for award to warrant officers, non-commissioned officers and men of the Brit. forces for bravery in the field. Women (whether subjects or foreign persons) were made eligible by a later warrant, but only on the special recommendation of a commander-in-chief, for bravery and devotion under fire. The M. M. is a silver medal, bearing the royal effigy on the obverse and, on the reverse, the words 'For Bravery in the Field', encircled by a wreath surmounted by the royal cipher and a crown. The ribbon has dark blue stripes on either side and 3 white and 2 red stripes in the centre. Some 11,000 M.M.s were awarded in the Second World War.

Military Nursing Service (Queen Alexandra's Royal Army Nursing Corps). Nursing in the army was originally performed by soldiers' wives, and it was not until Florence Nightingale went to the Crimea in 1854 with 38 nurses that a proper service was inaugurated. From that beginning sprang the army nursing service, and at that time also began the slow advance towards official recognition, legal professional status not being conferred until the passing of the Nurses' Registration Act in 1919. Provision was made for the appointment of nurses to all military general hospitals in 1866, but it was not until 1881 that an army nursing service was formed. The Egyptian campaign of 1882 accelerated the organisation of the nursing service for overseas work, and sisters were sent to military hospitals at Gibraltar and Malta. The H.Q. of the service were fixed at the Royal Victoria Hospital, Netley. The reserve service came into being in

1897. During the S. African War (1899–1902) the nursing service greatly expanded, and the experiences of that campaign led, in 1902, to the appointment of a committee, under the presidency of St John Brodrick (later Earl Midleton), to inquire into the situation. The outcome was the estab. in 1902 of the Queen Alexandra's Imperial Military Nursing Service (Q.A.I.M.N.S.), Queen Alexandra being its first president. In 1926 the service in India was amalgamated with the Q.A.I.M.N.S. In 1914 the actual service was only 300 strong, but in that same year 2223 trained nurses were enrolled with the reserve and 1803 were sent abroad. By 1919 the service and its reserve had a membership of 10,404. During the First World War the service did excellent work, and many of its members gained distinction (for a brief official account see War Office, Nursing in the Army, 1930). At the outbreak of the Second World War, the total peace estab. of Q.A.I.M.N.S. in the various military hospitals at home and abroad was 624. On 10 Sept. 1939 the first 6 army sisters landed in France; 1300 were evacuated with the Brit. expeditionary force at Dunkirk. Army sisters sailed with the army to every war area, and shared its fortunes. In Florence Nightingale's day it was specifically stated that the nurses were for the base hospitals in the war area. In the Second World War, however, they shared the hazards of total warfare. In Singapore the sisters worked in a hospital between the Brit. fire and the Jap.; they learned that the Japanese were at their gate, and fully expected to be taken prisoner. Much the same conditions obtained in Greece. No army sisters fell into the enemy's hands in France or in Greece, but from Singapore some were lost in the evacuation, and many were missing, while in Hong Kong 14 sisters remained in enemy hands, and underwent terrible hardships, some being murdered. On 1 Feb. 1949 the Q.A.I.M.N.S. gained full military recognition and was renamed 'Queen Alexandra's Royal Army Nursing Corps'. See Ada Harrison (editor), Grey and Scarlet, 1944, and Ian Hay, One Hundred Years of Army Nursing, 1953.

Military Police, Corps of Royal, branch of the military forces which maintains law and order amongst soldiers, controls military traffic, guards military installations and participates in anti-espionage work. A body of mounted M. P. was formed in 1855, which became a distinct corps in 1877. The Military Foot Police came into being in 1885. These two were amalgamated in 1926 to form the C.M.P. Three new branches were formed in 1940: C.M.P. (V.P.) ('Blue Caps') for the security of vulnerable points; C.M.P. (T.C.) ('White Caps') for traffic control, including the organisation of traffic through minefield gaps; and C.M.P. (S.I.B.) for special investigation work equivalent to that carried out by the civil C.I.D. In the Second World War heavy casualties were suffered by the corps, which at the end of the war had a strength of 35,000. The title 'Royal' was granted in 1946 in recognition of the corps' wartime service. The branch is commanded by the provost-marshal under the adjutant-general, who is responsible for the discipline of the army. In the Brit. service M. P. wear red tops to their hats, and 'Red Caps' are famous the world over. See S. F. Crozier, History of the Corps of Royal Military Police, 1954.

Military Security, see INTELLIGENCE, MILITARY, AND SECURITY.

Military Stars, see STARS, MILITARY.

Military Transport, see MILITARY VEHICLES; TRANSPORT, MILITARY.

Military Vehicles. Up to 1914 practically all M. V. were horse (or mule) drawn. Since then the motor vehicle, both wheeled and tracked, has gradually replaced the horse. Today all modern armies are almost completely mechanised. Tracked vehicles—in the form of tanks, tracked supply vehicles and armoured personnel carriers—are normally employed in the combat areas; wheeled vehicles being used for moving troops, equipment and supplies; and sometimes in the form of armoured cars for long-range reconnaissance work. The development of helicopters and vertical take-off (q.v.) aircraft is likely to revolutionise the future means of transport in land warfare.

Militia (Lat. *miles*, a soldier) had the acquired meaning of the domestic force for the defence of a nation, as distinguished from the regular army. The M. was a constitutional force raised under the sanction of Parliament. Organised by cos. and cities, it was essentially a local force; the property qualification for its officers connected it with the land, while the command of the sovereign effectually combined in it the interests of the 3 estates. Among the Anglo-Saxons, no special organisation being adopted, efficiency was rarely attained. This the nation found to its cost when the Danes overran it during Alfred's reign. Alfred, to prevent a similar occurrence, reorganised the M. or *fyrd*, dividing it into 2 parts to ensure continuity of service, making land the basis of numbers, but the family system that of discipline. Each shire had not only to furnish its quota in time of war, but also to provide arms, keep them in repair and to undergo so many days' training every year. When the Crown began to contend with the Norman barons it found an effective weapon in the revival of the Saxon M., and the Eng. yeomanry became thenceforth the fear of England's enemies. The shire contingent was commanded in pre-Conquest times by the ealdorman, later by the sheriff and lastly by the (lord) lieutenant, until 1871.

In 1604 James I abolished the *fyrd*, and expanded and reorganised 'Trained (commonly called Train) Bands' (q.v.). The first stage of the civil war of 1642 was a series of isolated struggles to secure the allegiance of the local M. and seize their magazines. An Act of 1662 reorganised the M., and this formed the basis of the M. law until 1908. Monmouth's infantry in 1685 consisted substantially of the M. of the W. cos. The M. was neglected until 1757, when, a large portion of the regular army being absent in the Seven Years

War, it was organised for home defence. Sev. M. Acts were subsequently passed, notably those of 1761, 1768 and 1802. In practice M. were raised by voluntary recruitment, but if volunteering failed a levy by ballot could be made upon all the inhab. of the locality between the ages of 18 and 50. The power of making this ballot always existed, and would have by law to be enforced by Parliament but for the Militia Ballot Suspension Act, which, when the measure was unnecessary, was passed from year to year. Many classes were exempt from the ballot, as peers, soldiers, volunteers, yeomanry, resident members of univs., clergymen, par. schoolmasters, articled clerks, apprentices, seafaring men, Crown employees, free watermen of the Thames; in England any poor man with more than one lawful child; in Scotland any man with more than 2 lawful children, and not possessed of property to the value of £50; in Ireland any poor man not worth £10, or who did not pay £5 per annum for rent, and had more than 3 lawful children under the age of 14. The effect of this legislation was to transform the M. from a local police and national defence force into a reserve for the regular army. These early military functions were now fulfilled by the volunteers (q.v.), but against the wishes of the gov.; and from 1808 to 1812 a series of local Militia Acts was passed to create a new compulsory home service force of men from 18 to 30. Like the general M., this force was recruited by M. authorities (in practice by par. officers); officers were required to be men of landed property, not necessarily an efficient method of selection.

To enable the maximum number of line regiments to proceed to the Crimean War and Indian mutiny, practically every M. regiment was embodied for home defence. In 1908, under the Territorial and Reserve Forces Act, a special reserve was formed into which the M. was absorbed. The M. in Bermuda, Channel Is. and Malta were not affected by this change. In 1921 the Special Reserve was renamed the M., but all the units comprised in it with one exception were allowed to go into suspended animation. The exception, the Royal Monmouth Royal Engineers (q.v.), was continued as a Supplementary Reserve unit. It became part of the Territorial Army in 1953 but was still allowed to retain the word M. in its title. The rest of the M., which for many years had had only a purely nominal existence, was formally disbanded in that year. The term 'militia' was applied quite inappropriately to men called up under the Military Training Act passed early in 1939. See Col. J. G. Hay, *History of the Militia*, 1906.

The M. of the U.S.A. is essentially a state and not a federal body. M. service was a feature of colonial life, and the same categories were liable to M. service in the 'plantations' as at home. The war with France in the New World was largely waged by the M. of the New England states and Virginia and New York. According to the M. law of 1903 the M. consists of every able-bodied male citizen of the respective states, and every able-bodied man of foreign birth who has declared his intention of becoming a citizen, who is more than 18 and less than 45 years of age. It is divided into 2 classes; the National Guard, which is the organised M., and the rest, which is called the Reserve M. The National Guard consists of men who voluntarily enlist for military training and for peace-time service when called upon by the governor of their state to preserve order in case of strikes, riots, etc. In other words, the National Guard of each state is its own army, including an air component. The largest is that of New York State. The guard is organised on the same lines as the regular U.S. Army, and may also be called into service by the President of the U.S.A. Federal supervision is maintained by the National Guard Bureau. *See also* NATIONAL GUARD; UNITED STATES ARMY.

Milk is secreted by the mammary glands of the female animal and is a complete food for young and growing animals. It is a complex mixture of substances which varies with the species and with the breed. The M. of the domestic cow is of more economic significance than that of any other species and with its derivatives forms an important part of the human diet particularly on the continents of Europe, America and Australasia. In 1964 the consumption of M. and its derivatives in the U.K. was equivalent to 5,197,000,000 gallons of which 2,339,000,000 gallons were produced in the U.K. The consumption of liquid M. in the U.K. is about 254 pints per head per annum.

In the U.K. cow's M. has a total solids content of about 12·5 per cent including about 3·8 per cent fat. The solids-not-fat and fat contents vary considerably from cow to cow from day to day, and depend on such factors as breed, season, feeding, age, number of previous lactations, stage of lactation and herd management. The Food and Drugs Act prohibits the adulteration of M. sold for human consumption, but there is no legal standard for composition. There are, however, presumptive standards, and if on analysis M. is found to contain less than 8·5 per cent solids-not-fat or less than 3 per cent M. fat, it rests with the seller to prove than the M. was as yielded by the cow and was not adulterated.

M. is the only food which contains some elements of all the nutrients which are necessary to maintain life and promote body growth— proteins, fats, carbohydrates, mineral matter and vitamins. The protein content of M. is about 3·3 per cent. The most important M. protein is casein; other proteins present in much smaller quantities are albumin and globulin. The carbohydrate content of M. is about 4·5 per cent in the form of lactose. M. is a source of calcium and phosphorus, and of Vitamins A, B_1, $B+$, C, D and E. The importance of M. in the diet is due mainly to its contribution of high quality animal protein, its high calcium content and to the presence of the Vitamins A, riboflavin and other members of the B_2 complex. The energy value o M. is about 390 Calories per pint.

There are 4,250,000 milking cows in the U.K. including 3,250,000 in the dairy herd, the predominant breed in the dairy herd being the

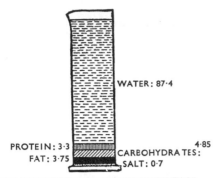

WATER: 87·4

PROTEIN: 3·3

FAT: 3·75

4·85
CARBOHYDRATES:

SALT: 0·7

THE COMPOSITION OF MILK BY PERCENTAGE

Friesian; other breeds include the Ayrshire, which is predominant in Scotland, the Dairy Shorthorn, Guernsey, Jersey and S. Devon. The ann. average yields of M. per dairy cow was about 775 gallons in 1964, in contrast to 680 gallons in 1954. The production of M. on farms in England and Wales is subject to the M. and Dairies (General) Regulations 1959 which are principally concerned with the protection of M. against infection and contamination on the farm and between farm and consumer, and lay down regulations concerning buildings, water supplies, methods of production, etc. Similar provisions are included in regulations covering Scotland and N. Ireland. Although some cows are still handmilked, the majority are milked by machine, particularly in the U.K., where the M. is transferred, either manually or by pipeline, from the milking machine receptacle, is cooled and is usually transported in cans. There is, however, an increase in direct transfer to refrigerated bulk tanks (100–500 gallon capacity) where the M. is cooled to 40° F. and is then collected by road bulk tankers.

Bovine tuberculosis was eradicated from herds in the U.K. by the end of 1960 and T.T. licensing was discontinued in England and Wales in 1964, and in Scotland in 1965. The Grade A (T.T.) licensing system was discontinued in N. Ireland in April 1963, but producers holding the Ministry's Certificate of Superior Hygienic Quality receive a price premium. A farmer in the U.K. intending to produce M. or M. products for sale must obtain gov. authority to do so and then apply to his area M. Marketing Board (q.v.) to be registered as a producer. Apart from producer-retailers who bottle or carton on the farm about 3·5 per cent of the total M. produced, producers sell M. to the boards who pay for the M. on the basis of records of tests for compositional and hygienic quality; in some boards there are price reductions if the M. contains antibiotic residues which are usually derived from the treatment of cows with anti-mastitis preparations. Special premiums may be payable for M. produced by Channel Is. and S. Devon cows and retailed as such because of the higher solids and fat contents.

All liquid M. sold by retail in England and

Wales must, except with the consent of the Ministry of Agriculture, Fisheries and Food, be specially designated according to the degree of heat-treatment given to destroy or inhibit the growth of micro-organisms. Since Oct. 1965 there have been 4 special designations, namely: 'untreated', raw M. bottled or cartoned on the farm or at the dairy; 'pasteurised', M. retained at a temp. of not less than 145° F. and not more than 150° F. for at least 30 min. and immediately cooled to a temp. of not more than 50° F., or M. retained at a temp. of not less than 161 ° F. for at least 15 secs. and immediately cooled to a temp. of not more than 50° F.; 'sterilised', M. homogenised and then heated to at least 212° F. in sealed bottles (usually 220°–230° F. for 20–30 min.). 'Ultra-Heat-Treated' (U.H.T.) M. heated (in a continuous manner) to a temp. of not less than 270° F. for not less than 1 sec. and packed under sterile conditions.

All M. on retail sale is subject to testing by Local Authorities and must pass tests prescribed in the M. (Special Designation) Regulations 1963, and as amended in 1965, to determine the efficacy of the heat-treatment. There are similar designations which vary in detail in Scotland and N. Ireland. Approximately 6 per cent of the M. retailed as liquid in the U.K. is untreated. The majority of liquid M. retailed is pasteurised and is distributed in bottles or cartons, but M. which is sterilised in bottles is popular in some areas. Sterilised M. has a longer shelf-life than pasteurised M., but has a slightly cooked flavour. The sale of U.H.T. M. became legally permissible in the U.K. in Oct. 1965. This M. has a shelf-life of about a month while retaining a flavour similar to that of pasteurised M.; the flavour gradually deteriorates, but the M. remains wholesome for sev. months. In general, heat-treatment leads to some reduction in the Vitamin B_1 and Vitamin C content of the M., and under sterilising conditions the nutritive value of the protein is slightly impaired; however, these losses have no marked effect on the nutritional value of M. as a food.

M. is used directly or indirectly for the manuf. of a number of important products, principally cream, butter, cheese, condensed and evaporated M.s, M. powders, whey, casein, yoghurt, ice-cream and chocolate. Cream and skimmed M. are produced by the centrifugal separation of M. The cream may be retailed, or may be converted into butter by churning, when the oil-in-water emulsion is inverted to a water-in-oil emulsion. The skimmed M. may be used for stock feeding, may be dried, or alternatively may be treated to precipitate the casein which is then washed and dried in a tray drier. M. powders, either from skimmed M. or whole M. are prepared by heat-treating the M., concentrating under vacuum and either spray or roller drying. In some cases, roller drying is carried out without pre-concentration. 'Instant' M. powders, so-called because they can be more readily wetted and dispersed in water, are prepared by partially spray-drying and then tray-drying the agglomerates, or by re-wetting spray-dried

powder and then tray-drying. Cheese is manuf.
by adding to M. cultures of lactic streptococci to
develop acidity and then rennet to clot the M.
The protein and fat are precipitated as a curd
which is then cut and the whey, consisting
primarily of lactose in solution, is run off. The
curd may then be treated in a variety of ways
depending on the type of cheese being made. The
whey may be used for stock feeding. Yoghurt is a
fermented M. which is becoming increasingly
popular in Europe. It is prepared by inoculating
M. with a mixed culture of *L. bulgaricus* and *Str.
thermophilus* and incubating at a temp. of 40° C.
for about 2½ hrs. *See* V. C. Fishwick, *Dairy
Farming*, 1952; J. G. Davis, *Dictionary of
Dairying*, 2nd ed., 1955; E. R. Ling, *A Textbook
of Dairy Chemistry*, 1956; Federation of U.K.
M. Marketing Boards, *United Kingdom Dairy
Facts and Figures*, 1965. (*See Plate: Dairy
Farming*.)

milk may be sold are prescribed by the gov.
The Boards are responsible for organising the
flow of milk from farms to tn dairies, country
depots and creameries; for the collection of milk
from farms either by the Boards' transport fleets
or by hauliers operating under contract; for
administering the system of gov. fixed margins
and allowances relating to liquid milk movements and processing. The Boards advertise and
promote the sale of milk and milk products.
The Boards offer differing varieties of services
to milk producers such as the Artificial Insem-
ination and Milk Recording Services to improve
cattle breeding, and the Low Cost Production
Service to assist producers to become more
efficient. The Boards also own manufacturing
creameries and retail dairies.
The number of registered producers and total
sales of milk off farms in each Board area in the
year 1964/5 is shown below:

Milk Marketing Board	Established	Registered Producers	Sales of Milk off Farms Million Gallons
England and Wales	1933	100,449	1,990
Scottish	1933	6,022	206
Aberdeen and District	1934	529	23
North of Scotland	1934	323	10
Northern Ireland	1955	17,365	127
United Kingdom (total)		124,688	2,356

See Federation of United Kingdom Milk Marketing Boards, *United Kingdom Dairy Facts and Figures*, 1965.

Milk Chocolate, *see* COCOA AND CHOCOLATE.

Milk Marketing Boards. There are 5 Milk
Marketing Schemes in the U.K., 1 for England
and Wales, 3 for Scotland and 1 for N. Ireland,
which were estab. under the Agric. Marketing
Acts. The Schemes must be approved by
Parliament, but are self-governed and are
administered by Boards consisting principally of
members elected by milk producers.
The Schemes possess the force of statutory
authority and all milk sold off farms in the U.K.
must be sold through the appropriate Scheme.
About 96 per cent of the milk is sold wholesale
either to the Board (in England and Wales, and
in N. Ireland), or (in Scotland) to a buyer under
an arrangement to which the Board is a third
party. The remainder is sold under licence,
issued by a Board, by producer-retailers direct to
consumers or distributors.
The prices at which the Boards or producers
sell milk for liquid consumption are subject to
gov. approval and in practice are determined by
the gov. Milk surplus to the requirements of the
liquid market is sold by the Boards for manuf. at
considerably lower prices negotiated by the
Boards with the manufacturers. Accordingly,
the prices producers as a group receive for the
milk depend on the pooled realisations from the
different markets within the framework of the
guaranteed price structure, but the price received by an individual producer depends on the
compositional and hygienic quality of his milk,
and is independent of the market in which it is
sold. The maximum retail prices at which liquid

Milk River, in the U.S.A., a trib. of the
Missouri, rising in the Rocky Mts, in NW. of
Montana, and draining part of Canada where
it is used for irrigation. Total length about
730 m.

Milk Sugar, *see* LACTOSE.

Milkwort (*Polygala*), or **Rogation Flower,**
genus of hardy annuals and perennials and
hardy and tender evergreen shrubs. The common M., *P. vulgaris*, occurs on chalky heaths
and bears terminal racemes of white, pink or
blue flowers. Other Brit. species include the
large-flowered chalk M. (*P. calcarea*), *P. amara*,
with small blue flowers and fleshy leaves in a
rosette, and *P. austriaca*, with large pink flowers.
Some of the hardy species are grown on sunny
borders or rockeries. Sea M. is *Glaux maritima*,
and belongs to the primrose family.

Milky Way, *see* GALAXY.

Mill, Hugh Robert (1861–1950), chemist and
geographer. He was vice-president of the Royal
Geographical Society from 1927 to 1931, and
president of the Geographical Association in
1932. His pubs. include *Life of Sir Ernest
Shackleton*, 1923, *History of the Royal Geographical Society*, 1930; and *Life Interests of a
Geographer* (autobiography), 1945.

Mill, James (1773–1836), philosopher and
historian, *b.* near Montrose. Educ. at Edinburgh
Univ., he went to London in 1802, and in that
year became editor of the *Literary Journal*, and
later of the *St James's Chronicle*. From 1808 he
earned his living as a contributor to the
Edinburgh and other reviews, and by his *History*

of India, 1818. He was an enthusiastic supporter of Bentham and a friend of Ricardo and other political economists. In 1821 he pub. his famous *Elements of Political Economy*, in 1829 his *Analysis of the Human Mind* and in 1835 a *Fragment on Mackintosh*, a bitter attack upon his fellow philosopher. His writings belong to the utilitarian school.

Mill, John (*c.* 1645–1707), Eng. theologian, *b.* Hardendale, Westmorland. In 1681 he became rector of Bletchington, Oxon., and was made chaplain to Charles II. Four years later he became principal of St Edmund's Hall, a position he retained till his death, and in 1704 was made a prebendary of Canterbury. His famous *Greek Testament* was pub. in 1707.

Mill, John Stuart (1806–73), philosopher and economist. Educ. by his father, his studies embraced a range unusually wide. In 1823 he became a clerk in the India House, and was promoted until in 1856 he became the head of his dept, and 2 years later, when the gov. of India was transferred from the E. India Co. to the Crown, he declined a pension of £1500 a year.

He founded the Utilitarian Society (1823), from which developed the utilitarian movement; and also the Speculative Society (1826). In 1825 he ed. Bentham's *Rationale of Judicial Evidence*. His *Logic* was pub. in 1843, and in 1848 his *Principles of Political Economy*. Between 1858 and 1865 he wrote his treatises on *Liberty*, *Utilitarianism*, *Representative Government* and his *Examination of Sir W. Hamilton's Philosophy*. M.'s conception of physical objects as 'permanent possibilities of sensation' has had great influence on the development of the theory of knowledge. In 1865 he entered the House of Commons as a member for Westminster, where he made no great mark. After this political experiment he returned to literary pursuits, and wrote *The Subjection of Women*, 1869, *The Irish Land Question*, 1870, and an *Autobiography*. His *Autobiography* gives a singular, and in some respects painful, account of the methods and opinions of his father in his education. Though remaining all his life an adherent of the utilitarian philosophy, M. infused into it a certain element of idealism. M. typifies the philosophic radicalism of the Victorian era. He held that systems of laws and morals should promote 'the greatest happiness of the greatest number', that education is the cure for all social evils, and that rational argument can ultimately convince humanity of what is good. Freedom of thought, of speech and of the individual has found few stronger supporters; the theme of his *Liberty* is that 'If all mankind minus one were of one opinion, and only one person were of the contrary opinion, mankind would be no more justified in silencing that one person than he, if he had the power, would be justified in silencing mankind'. His *System of Logic* is of great philosophic importance; it revives the question, which Hume had raised, of the validity of scientific method. His *Letters*, ed. H. S. R. Elliot, were pub. in 2 vols., 1910. *See also* CLASSICAL ECONOMISTS. See G. J. Holyoake, *John Stuart*

Mill, as some of the Working Classes knew him, 1873; W. L. Courtney, *The Metaphysics of J. S. Mill*, 1879; A. Bain, *A Criticism* (with personal recollections), 1882; C. M. Couglas, *John Stuart Mill: a Study of his Philosophy* (a most important work), 1895; M. St J.. Packe, *The Life of John Stuart Mill*, 1954; M. Cowling (ed.), *Mill and Liberalism*, 1963; Shirley Letwin, *The Pursuit of Certainty*, 1965. (*See Plate: Economic Thought, History of*.)

Mill, *see* COTTON; FLOUR-MILLING; WOOL.

Mill, in law. The owner of a M. is entitled to the use of a stream undiminished in volume; if owners above interfere, he can sue them.

Mill Hill, residential dist in the N. of Hendon, in the London Bor. of Barnet, noted for the public school founded in 1807 mainly for the sons of nonconformists, but reorganised on broader lines in 1869. St Joseph's College at M. H. is a Rom. Catholic foundation for training missionaries.

Mill Springs, vil. of Wayne co., Kentucky, U.S.A., 80 m. S. of Lexington. Here the Confederates under Cittenden were defeated by the Union forces under Thomas in 1862, opening the way for the advance into E. Tennessee. Prehistoric remains have been found in nearby caves.

Millais, Sir John Everett (1829–96), painter, *b.* Southampton. He showed an early aptitude for art. He won a silver medal from the Society of Arts in 1839 and in 1840 he passed on to the Academy schools, where he was awarded all the prizes. Ambitious of lifting native art from its conventional mediocrity, he joined the Pre-Raphaelite Brotherhood with his friend Holman Hunt. The banquet scene from Keats's *Isabella*, 1849, was his first painting on Pre-Raphaelite principles, and the close imitation of the smallest details of nature also appear in his naturalistic representation of the child Christ in 'Christ in the House of his Parents', better known as 'The Carpenter's Shop', 1850 (in the Tate Gallery). His unconventionality in this work provoked much abuse, and even called forth an unmerited rebuke from Dickens. Ruskin, meanwhile, was championing M. with the rest of the Pre-Raphaelite band. With strict adherence to the Pre-Raphaelite style M. then produced 'The Return of the Dove to the Ark', 1851; 'Mariana of the Moated Grange', 1851; 'The Huguenot', 1852; the universally admired 'Ophelia', 1852 (in the National Gallery), for which Mrs Rossetti was the model; 'The Proscribed Royalist', 1853; 'The Order of Release', 1853. Mrs Ruskin, whom M. afterwards married, sat for this last-named picture. The afterglow in 'Autumn Leaves', 1856, and the moonlight in 'The Eve of St Agnes' (exhibited in 1863) are two of his most splendid atmospheric effects. Meanwhile he illustrated Trollope's novels and Tennyson's poems (1860–9). He abandoned the Pre-Raphaelite manner in the 1860s, forsook imaginative themes and developed a popular manner of his own in which dramatic force and expression of sentiment play a leading part, as in 'The Boyhood of Raleigh', 1870. In his latter days he turned to portraits, landscapes, like the 'Chill October' of 1871, and single figures, as in child portraits such as 'Cherry Ripe', 'Little Miss Muffet' and the well-advertised 'Bubbles', for which Adm. Sir Wm James was the model; also a few figure pieces such as 'The North-West Passage', 1874, sometimes considered his masterpiece; it represents an old sailor, painted from Edward John Trelawny, the friend of Byron, listening to a tale of Arctic exploration. His portraits include those of W. E. Gladstone, Tennyson, Cardinal Newman, Lord Beaconsfield and Wilkie Collins. He married the former Mrs Ruskin in 1855. In 1885 he was created a baronet and in 1896 he became president of the Royal Academy. While he may not have possessed the imagination of an idealist, his ability to depict what he saw produced pictures of great brilliance, and his early work survives all criticism. See *Life and Letters* by J. G. Millais, 1899; lives by J. E. Reid, 1909, and A. Fish, 1923; Sir W. James, *The Order of Release*, 1949.

Millar, Gertie (1879–1952), actress, *b.* Bradford, Yorks. Daughter of a mill-hand, she first appeared in a Manchester pantomime in 1892. She toured in musical comedy and was brought to the notice of George Edwardes by the composer Lionel Monckton, whom she married. She was a great success, first at the old Gaiety Theatre, where she made her London debut in 1901, and then as leading lady at the second Gaiety Theatre, where she reigned for 7 years. Later she starred in the Adelphi in *The Quaker Girl*, at Daly's Theatre in *Gypsy Love* and also in variety at the Coliseum and the Palace Theatre. She retired from the stage in 1918. After the death of her husband in 1924, she married the second Earl of Dudley, who *d.* in 1931. She was one of the most popular of the many brilliant musical comedy leading ladies of the Edwardian era.

Millau, Fr. tn, in the dept of Aveyron, on the Tarn. In the 16th–17th cents. it was a Huguenot (q.v.) stronghold. It is in a coal-field and has manufs. of gloves and furniture. Pop. 21,300.

Millay, Edna St Vincent (1892–1950), Amer. poet and playwright, *b.* Rockland, Maine, graduated from Vassar in 1917. She first won distinction with 'Renascence', 1912, a poem in octosyllabic couplets, the title of which was used for her first vol. of verse in 1917. While living in Greenwich village, she wrote plays for the Provincetown Players: *Aria da Capo*, 1921, *Two Slatterns and a King*, 1921, and *The Lamp and the Bell*, 1921. The first 2 are satirical fantasies, the last-named is a 5-act drama on the theme of the strong mutual affection of 2 girls of the Middle Ages. For *The Harp-Weaver* she won the Pulitzer Prize in 1923. This vol. is notable for its sonnets of disillusionment. Other writings include *The Buck in the Snow*, 1928, *Fatal Interview* (sonnet sequence), 1931, *Wine from these Grapes*, 1934, *Conversation at Midnight*, 1937, *Hunstman, What Quarry?*, 1939, *There are no Islands any more*, 1940, *Make Bright the Arrows*, 1941, and *Mine the Harvest*, 1954. *See* study by E. Atkins, 1936.

Millbank Prison, London, originally called the Penitentiary, was erected (1813–6) on a site now occupied by the Tate Gallery, as a direct result of the philanthropic teaching of John Howard (q.v.). The old vindictive or retributive theories of punishment found expression in prisons that were dens of wildness and squalor; the schemes of Howard, and later of Jeremy Bentham (q.v.), advocated the erection of penitentiaries for the reformation and not merely the incarceration of prisoners. The gov. of the early 19th cent., impressed by prison reform arguments, purchased land at Millbank and at great cost erected the M. Penitentiary on the system advocated by Bentham in his *Panopticon*, 1791. The system failed dismally, and in 1843 there was a partial reversion to older methods. M. was a military prison from 1870 until closed in 1890, and the building was demolished in 1903. *See* A. G. F. Griffiths, *Memorials of Millbank*, 1875.

Mille, Cecil Blount de (1881–1959), Amer. film producer, *b.* Ashfield, Massachusetts. His biblical epics were noted for their lavish and spectacular scenes. Silent films included *The Ten Commandments* and *King of Kings*. His prin. sound films were *The Sign of the Cross*, *The Crusades*, *The Plainsman*, *Union Pacific*, *North-West Mounted Police*, *Reap the Wild Wind*, *Samson and Delilah*, *The Greatest Show on Earth* (Academy Award film, 1952) and *The Ten Commandments* (remake). In 1927 he was decorated with the Order of the Holy Sepulchre, and in 1944 with the Order of Orange-Nassau. He received a special Academy Award for 35 years of pioneering leadership in motion pictures, 1949, and the Irving G. Thalberg Award in 1952. (*See Plate: Cinematograph.*)

Milledgeville, city of Baldwin co., Georgia, U.S.A. A trade and processing centre for the cotton and clay area, it manufs. tiles, bricks, clothing and candy. Named after John Milledge, one-time governor of Georgia, and was once the cap. of that state. Here is the Georgia state college for women, the state lunatic asylum and penitentiary. Pop. 11,120.

Millennium, period of 1000 years during which it was believed the kingdom of Christ would be estab. on earth after His second Advent (q.v.). The idea originated in Judaism; but it was also common among the early Christians, who looked forward to the *Parousia*, or second coming of Christ. Indeed, in the post-Apostolic age, *chiliasm* (from Gk for 'thousand') was a widespread belief, especially in Asia Minor, based on a literal interpretation of Daniel, and on the Apocalypse, the only N.T. book in which the 1000 years is mentioned. In spite of its many adherents, however, millenarianism never was part of the apostolic tradition (cf. the primitive creeds) or universally taught in the Church; and when the Alexandrian philosophers, especially Origen, introduced their spiritual-allegorical interpretation of scripture and the idea that there would be no final conflict between Paganism and Christianity, but a gradual spread of truth throughout the world, chiliasm died out. Millenarianism had some revival at the period of the Reformation, being adopted by the Anabaptists, who regarded the Pope as Antichrist; in Cromwell's time the Fifth Monarchy Men (q.v.) were millenarians. It flourished, moreover, during the Thirty Years War, and still persists in various forms among some sects. *See also* ADVENTISTS. *See* articles on M. in *The Catholic Encyclopaedia* (ed. C. G. Herbermann), 1907–12, and J. Hastings's *Encyclopaedia of Religion and Ethics*, 1912; *also* E. J. Hodous, 'The New Testament teaching on the Second Coming', in *A Catholic Commentary on Holy Scripture*, 1952.

Miller, Arthur (1915–), Amer. playwright, *b.* New York, and educ. at the univ. of Michigan. His first Broadway play, *The Man who had all the Luck*, 1944, was a failure, but his second, *All My Sons*, 1947, won the Drama Critics' Award. This was followed by *Death of a Salesman*, 1949, which won the Pulitzer Prize and the Drama Critics' Award, *The Crucible*, 1953, and *A View from the Bridge*, 1955. He has also written a novel, *Focus*, 1945, and *Situation Normal*, 1944, an account of army life. In 1956 he married, as his second wife, Marilyn Monroe (q.v.). After her death he wrote *After the Fall*, which dramatised their life together, following it with *Incident at Vichy*. These were both acted by the newly formed repertory company of the Lincoln Center for the Performing Arts.

Miller, Henry (1891–), Amer. writer, *b.* Manhattan, educ. Brooklyn. He went to France in 1930 and pub. his first book, *Tropic of Cancer*, in Paris in 1934; when pub. in England, 1963, it was widely condemned as obscene. His novels and essays are largely autobiographical; he writes of Greece in *The Colossus of Maroussi*, 1941, and of the U.S.A., to which he returned at the beginning of the Second World War, in *The Air-Conditioned Nightmare* and *Remember to Remember*.

Miller, Hugh (1802–56), writer and geologist, *b.* Cromarty. By trade M. was a stonemason, and it was only by being a stern 'taskmaster of his own energies' that he acquired that literary style and scientific learning which won him renown. After publishing *Poems*, 1829, and *Scenes and Legends of the North of Scotland*, 1835, he became in 1839 editor of the bi-weekly *Witness*, and in its columns appeared a series of strikingly original geological essays, afterwards embodied in *The Old Red Sandstone*, 1841. His autobiography, *My Schools and Schoolmasters*, was pub. in 1852. *See* life by P. Bayne, 1871.

Miller, Joaquin, pseudonym of **Cincinnatus Hiner Miller** (1839–1913), Amer. poet, *b.* Liberty, Indiana. He wrote *Songs of the Sierras*, 1871, a melodrama of Mormonism, *The Danites*, 1880, *History of Montana*, 1886, and *The Building of the City Beautiful*, 1887, some ideas from which he attempted to put into practice in a social community on his estate. *See* life by M. S. Peterson, 1937.

Miller, William (1782–1849), *see* ADVENTISTS.
Miller, William (1810–72), poet, *b.* Glasgow. He is remembered for his poem 'Wee Willie

Winkie' which, with others of his *Scottish Nursery Songs*, 1863, caused him to be styled the laureate of the nursery.

Millerand, Alexandre (1859–1943), French statesman, *b.* Paris. He became a journalist, later working under Clemenceau on *Justice*. He was minister of commerce in Waldeck-Rousseau's cabinet (1899–1902), and expelled from his party, 1904. In 1920 he became Prime Minister, and 8 months later president of the Fr. Rep. But he was soon at loggerheads with the Radical and Socialist majority, which, under Herriot, had triumphed in the 1924 elections, and shortly afterwards resigned.

Miller's Thumb, *see* BULLHEAD.

Milles, Vilhelm Carl Emil (1875–1955), Swedish sculptor, *b.* near Upsala, and studied in Paris. His best work consists of portrait busts, animal groups, fountains and monuments. His open-air sculpture in Stockholm exemplified the part sculpture can play in the modern city. Examples of his work are also to be found at Chicago and other cities. The Tate Gallery has his 'Europa'. *See* monograph by P. Verneuil, 1929.

Millet, Aimé (1819–91), Fr. sculptor, *b.* Paris, achieved fame in 1857 with his statue of 'Ariadne', which was bought for the Luxembourg. This was followed by 'Mercury', now standing in the court of the Louvre, and the famous 'Vercingétorix', a colossal statue in beaten copper at Alise-Ste-Reine in Côte-d'Or (1865). He executed the 'Apollo' surmounting the Grand Opéra.

Millet, Jean François (1814–75), Fr. painter, was the son of a peasant of Gruchy, near Gréville (La Manche). Like Burns, he turned to hs art after toiling in the fields. He first studied art at Cherbourg and in 1838 entered the studio of Delaroche in Paris. In 1848 he settled in Barbizon, a vil. he rarely left afterwards, where he had the companionship of Diaz, Rousseau, Dupré and Troyon (Barbizon school). After many vicissitudes he secured a notable success with 'The Winnower', exhibited at the Salon in 1848. 'Sowers and Binders', 1850, 'The Reapers', 1854, 'The Gleaners', 1857 (now in the Louvre), 'The Angelus', 1859, and 'Death and the Woodcutter', 1859, are among his finest works. M. was a master in depicting the sombre melancholy of work and rustic peasant life, a melancholy often emphasised by a twilight atmosphere most sensitively expressed. Some of his best work is to be found in his drawings, pastels and etchings. *See* lives by A. Sensier (Eng. trans.), 1881; J. Cartwright (2nd ed.), 1896 (with letters); J. C. Ady, 1910; P. Gsell, 1928; *also* Moreau-Nélaton, *Millet raconté par lui-même*, 1921.

Millet, seed of some species of *Panicum*, which are extensively cultivated in India and Africa, and also in S. Europe, being especially well suited to growth in a dry, sandy soil. The common M. is *P. miliaceum*; the little M. *P. miliare*; the It. M. comes from *Setaria* or *Chaetochlea italica* and has been generally cultivated in Asia from remote times. Pearl M.,

Minnesota

Above: Some of the many thousands of lakes which enhance the scenery of Minnesota.

Above right: Part of the University of Minnesota (opened 1869) in Minneapolis.

Right: A dairy farm in the south-eastern part of the state; more butter is produced in Minnesota than in any other state.
Photos: U.S. Information Service

Mississippi

Wood-pulp vats at Natchez; the state is a leading hardwood producer.

Mechanical cotton-pickers are estimated as being capable of doing the work of from fifty to eighty hand labourers.

The State Capitol building at Jackson was modelled on the National Capitol in Washington, D.C.
Photos: U.S. Information Service

Missouri

Above: The municipal auditorium (right) overlooking a landscaped plaza in a redeveloped area of Kansas City; beneath the plaza is a large three-level car park.

Below left: In the hilly regions of this rich agricultural state, terrace farming is practised to prevent the heavy rainfall from washing away the topsoil.

Below right: Hunters and hounds in the Ozark Mountains, an area popular with sportsmen and holiday makers.
Photos: U.S. Information Service

Montana

Above: The mountains of the Lewis Range in the Rockies, reflected in the waters of Lake McDonald in Glacier National Park.

Right: Most of the irrigated regions are dependent on melted snow for their water supply.

Below right: The state supports large herds of cattle on its rich grasslands.
Photos: U.S. Information Service

Morocco

The Oudaïa kasbah in old part of Rabat, the capital, dates from the time of the Almohad sultans (12th–13th cent.).

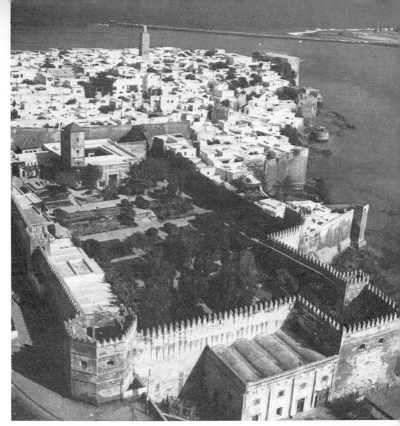

The fortified kasbah and oasis of Tinerhir, on the edge of the Great Atlas Mountains.
Moroccan Tourist Office

Morocco

Top: The Avenue Forces Armées Royales in Casablanca, the economic centre of Morocco.

Above: A troop of camels on a high plateau in the interior desert region.

Left: One of the fourteen entrances to the mosque of Karueen, Fez, the largest mosque in North Africa and centre of an Islamic university.
All photos: Moroccan Tourist Office

Pennisetum glaucum, grows in tropical Africa and India. Indian M., Kaffir or Guinea corn, is *Sorghum vulgare*, whose grain is known as durra. M. seeds are round, and vary in size and in colour from yellow to white, grey, brown, red and black. M. is much used in food for poultry, pigeons and cage birds. M.s are grown largely where conditions are unfavourable for maize and M. flour provides a staple food for large sections of the pops. in S. Africa, Zambia and Rhodesia, E. Africa and in the interior of W. Africa. Production is almost entirely in the hands of Africans. The great M. or sorghum is the most important M. crop, but in drier areas the lesser M.s, such as pennisetum, the bulrush M. and eleusine are widely grown, both as pure and mixed crops. Sorghum is an important crop in S. Africa and in Botswana, Lesotho and Swaziland, Lesotho alone producing nearly 30,000 tons; Malawi and Zambia also depend very largely on M.s for food. In Tanzania they are the staples for food and brewing of beer. Sorghum is also grown extensively for food in Kenya, and in parts of Uganda eleusine is the staple cereal. In N. Nigeria the prin. grain crops are bulrush M. (or gero) and sorghum. In Mali and Guinea M.s are the staple food throughout the N. areas, and also in the palm belt in Dahomey.

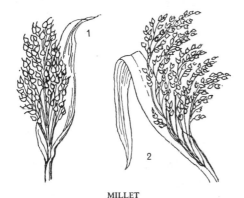

MILLET

1, *Sorghum vulgare;* 2, *Panicum miliaceum.*

Milletia, tropical genus of climbing trees and shrubs (family Leguminosae) with pink and purple flowers. The M.s are used for poisoning fish.

Millibar (abbreviation mb.), unit of atmospheric pressure used in meteorology. It is defined as one-thousandth part of a bar, which is equal to 1,000,000 dynes/sq. cm. (a dyne is the absolute unit of force in the centimetre-gramme-second system of units). The mean atmospheric pressure at sea level over the whole globe is about 1013 mb. At 0° C., in lat. 45°, 1000 mb. is equivalent to a height of 750·1 mm. or 29·531 in. of mercury.

Millikan, Robert Andrews (1868–1953), Amer. physicist, *b.* Morrison, Illinois. Graduating at Oberlin, 1891, he gained a Ph.D. at Columbia, 1895, and then studied at Berlin and Göttingen, 1895-6, returning to Chicago Univ. as an assistant to Michelson (q.v.). He was prof. of physics at the univ. of Chicago, 1907-21. He was vice-chairman, National Research Council, Washington, from 1917, and in 1918 was a lieutenant-colonel in the U.S. Signal Corps. He became famous as a result of his ingenious researches that led to an evaluation of the charge of the electron (*see* OIL-DROP EXPERIMENT), and to the view that the electron is the fundamental unit of negative electricity (*see* his *The Electron*, Chicago Univ. Press, 1917). He was early recognised as an inspiring teacher and showed a keen interest in the philosophy of science. M. was awarded the Nobel prize for physics in 1923 for his work on electrons. His pubs. include *Mechanics, Molecular Physics and Heat*, 1902, *The Electron: its Isolation and Measurement, and the Determination of some of its Properties*, 1921, *Evolution in Science and Religion*, 1928, *Science and the New Civilisation*, 1930, *Time, Matter, and Values*, 1932, *Cosmic Rays*, revised ed. 1946, and *Electrons, Protons, Neutrons, and Cosmic Rays*, revised ed. 1946.

Millin, Sarah Gertrude, *née* **Liebson** (1889–), S. African author, *b.* near Kimberley. She has written biographies of Rhodes, 1933, and Smuts (2 vols.), 1936, and her own autobiography, *The Night is Long*, 1941, and *Measure of My Days*, 1955. Her numerous novels of S. African life include *The Dark River*, 1920, *Adam's Rest*, 1922, *The Jordans*, 1923, *Mary Glenn*, 1925, *The Coming of the Lord*, 1928, *Three Men Die*, 1934, *What Hath a Man?*, 1938, *The Herr Witchdoctor*, 1941, *World Blackout*, 1944, *King of the Bastards*, 1950, and *The Burning Man*, 1952. Other works include *The South Africans*, 1926, *South Africa*, 1941, and a *War Diary* in 6 vols., 1944–8.

Millinery. This term is generally used to designate women's hats and their trimmings (ribbons, lace, feathers, artificial flowers, etc.), and is also applied to the art of making and trimming hats and bonnets. Originally the word meant 'Milan goods', such as textile fabrics, gloves, ribbons, 'Milan bonnets', needles and cutlery. Many articles of M. are sold by haberdashers and drapers. Milliners are those who make and trim hats and headgear of all descriptions for women and children (as opposed to 'hatters', who make head-gear for men), and are nearly always women; designers of millinery include members of both sexes. *See also* HAT.

Milling Machine, machine for removing metal by means of a multi-toothed cutter which rotates about either a horizontal or a vertical axis while the workpiece, clamped to a horizontal table, is traversed past it. The table can be raised and lowered and also moved horizontally at right angles to the feed motion so that the relative positions of the cutter and workpiece may be adjusted before starting and the depth of cut controlled. The cutter may be made in one piece from alloy steel or may consist of a steel holder

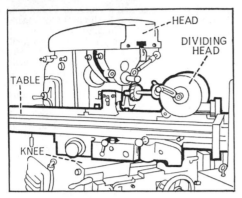

UNIVERSAL MILLING MACHINE

carrying inserted teeth of tungsten carbide. It is usually driven by an electric motor through a gearbox so that the speed or rotation may be varied to suit the type of cutter and the material being machined. The rate of feed is also variable.

Millipedes, or **Millepedes** (order Chilognatha), small, active animals forming with the centipedes the class Myriapoda (many-footed). They are vegetarian in habit, and though they consume much decaying matter, they also damage and destroy cultivated plants. Common species are *Julus guttatus*, *J. terrestris* (sometimes called wire-worm) and *J. pulchellus*. Trapping by means of buried roots and dressing the ground with lime or soot are methods of keeping M. in check.

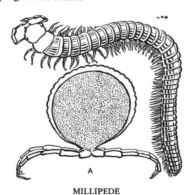

MILLIPEDE

A, single segment; transverse section, highly magnified.

Millom, tn of Cumberland, England, 23 m. from Barrow, with smelters, red hematite and iron ore mines, blast furnaces, chrome, tanning and nylon stocking factories and light clothing manufs. Pop. 8500.

Millport, burgh and watering-place on Great Cumbrae Is., Bute, Scotland, has a good sandy beach and fine harbour in safe S.-facing bay. There is a marine research station with museum

and modern aquarium (open to the public) where oyster breeding is carried on. Pop. 1592.

Mills, Bertram, *see* CIRCUS.

Mills, Percy (Herbert), 1st **Viscount** (1890–), Brit. industrialist, educ. at NE. Co. School, Barnard Castle. He became a prominent industrialist in the Midlands. He was minister of power, 1957–9; paymaster-general, 1959–61; minister without portfolio, 1961–2. Created baron, 1957; viscount, 1962.

Mills Bomb, *see* BOMB; GRENADE.

Millstätter, Lake, *see* CARINTHIA.

Millstones, *see* BREAD.

Milltown, tn in New Brunswick, Canada, on the St Croix R., 62 m. W. of St John. The chief industry is a textile mill. Pop. 1892.

Millwall, riverside dist, on the W. side of the Isle of Dogs (*see* DOGS, ISLE OF), in Poplar (bor. of Tower Hamlets). It contains the M. Docks, opened 1868, centre of the London grain trade. The name derived from windmills on the riv. bank in the early 18th cent. *Great Eastern* was built and launched here in 1858.

Milman, Henry Hart (1791–1868), Eng. cleric and historian. He was educ. at Eton and Brasenose College, Oxford. He took holy orders, and was prof. of poetry at Oxford from 1821 for 10 years, and in 1827 was appointed Bampton lecturer. Rector of St Margaret's, Westminster, and canon of Westminster from 1835, in 1849 he became dean of St Paul's. In 1838 he ed. Gibbon, and in the following year pub. a life of the historian. The works upon which his fame rests are his *History of the Jews*, 1830, *History of Christianity under the Empire*, 1840, and *The History of Latin Christianity down to the death of Pope Nicholas V*, 1855. *See* life by A. Milman, 1900.

Milne, Alan Alexander (1882–1956), author, journalist and playwright, *b*. London. Educ. at Westminster and Cambridge, where he ed. *Granta*, he began journalism in London in 1903, and was assistant editor of *Punch* from 1909 to 1914, contributing a number of pleasing articles in a light bantering vein. He pub. *The Day's Play*, 1910, *Once a Week*, 1914, *If I May*, 1920, *Four Days' Wonder*, 1933, *Peace with Honour*, 1934, *Behind the Lines*, 1940, *Once on a Time*, 1943, *Chloe Marr*, 1946, and *The Norman Church* (poem, 1948). His most successful work was in his tales and poems for children, *Winnie the Pooh*, 1926, *Now We Are Six*, 1927, and others enjoying great popularity. One of his best plays is *Mr Pim Passes By*, 1919; others are *Wurzel-Flummery*, 1917, *The Romantic Age*, 1920, *The Truth about Blayds*, 1921, *The Dover Road*, 1923, *The Ivory Door*, 1927, *Other People's Lives*, 1932, *Sarah Simple*, 1937, and *Gentleman Unknown*, 1938; *Toad of Toad Hall*, 1929, is a play based on Kenneth Grahame's *Wind in the Willows*. *It's Too Late Now*, 1939, is an autobiography.

Milne, Edward Arthur (1896–1950), scientist, *b*. Hull; educ. at Hymers College, Hull and Trinity College, Cambridge. He was successively assistant director of the Solar Physics Observatory, Cambridge, 1920–4; lecturer in mathematics, Trinity College, 1924–5; Rouse Ball prof. of mathematics, Oxford, and fellow of Wadham College, 1928. Noted for his researches in astrophysics, he wrote *Equilibrium of the Chromosphere*, 1924, *Thermodynamics of the Stars*, 1930, *The White Dwarf Stars*, 1932, *Relativity, Gravitation, and World Structure*, 1935, a new theory of the universe, for which he was awarded the Royal Astronomical Society's Gold medal; *Foundations of Dynamics*, 1936, *Electromagnetism*, 1938, *Kinematic Relativity*, 1948, *Modern Cosmology and the Christian Idea of God* (pub. posthumously), 1951. He was president of the London Mathematical Society, 1937–9, and of the Royal Astronomical Society, 1943–5, and gained many academic distinctions in Britain and the U.S.A.

Milne, George Francis, 1st Baron (1866–1948), field-marshal. Joining the army in 1885, he served in the Sudan, 1898, and S. Africa, 1899–1902. When the First World War began he served in France, became major-general, 1915 and commanded 27th Div. and 16th Army Corps. At the end of 1915 he was with the Brit. forces at Salonika; and from the following May commanded the whole Brit. contingent in Macedonia. He served under various Fr. commanders-in-chief in the Near E. till the Ger. surrender, remaining with the command until 1920. At home he held the E. command, 1923–6, and became field-marshal, 1928, and chief of imperial general staff, 1926–33, being raised to the peerage, 1933.

Milne, John (1850–1913), seismologist and mining engineer, educ. in Rochdale, Liverpool and London. He was employed as geologist in Dr Beke's expedition to NW. Arabia, 1874. He then served the Jap. Gov. for 20 years, establishing the seismic survey of Japan (968 stations). M. travelled widely in Russia, China, Borneo, Australasia, U.S.A. and elsewhere. For the Brit. Association he estab. a seismic survey of the world. His works include *Earthquakes*, 1883, *Seismology*, 1888, and *The Miner's Handbook*, 1894.

Milner, Alfred, 1st Viscount (1854–1925), colonial administrator; *b.* of Eng. parents at Giessen, Germany. He was educ. at Tübingen Univ., King's College, London and Balliol College, Oxford. For 4 years, 1881–5, he devoted himself to journalism, writing chiefly for the *Pall Mall Gazette* under John Morley and W. T. Stead. He owed his appointment as undersecretary for finance in Egypt, where he remained for 4 years, 1889–92, to G. J. Goschen, chancellor of the exchequer, whom he had already served as private secretary, 1887–9. His statesmanship was first put to a serious test when he was made governor of Cape Colony and high commissioner for S. Africa in 1897. His policy helped to precipitate the war which broke out between the British and the Boers in 1899; and this, combined with the disasters that overtook Brit. troops, accounts for the organised opposition with which he met on his return home in 1901, when he was made Baron M. He was then made governor of the Transvaal and Orange R. colonies. This post he retained till 1905. He was

made viscount in 1902. He was generally reactionary in his views, though a brilliant administrator, and was strongly opposed to the granting of self-government to the new colonies. He took a leading part in the rejection of the 1909 budget. At the formation of the Coalition gov., in the spring of 1915, he became chairman of the committee on agriculture. Member of war cabinet without portfolio, 1916–18. Secretary for the colonies, 1919–21, he visited Egypt and reported on necessary changes; his report being neglected he resigned. He pub. *Questions of the Hour* in 1925. *See* C. Headlam (ed.), *The Milner Papers, 1897–1905*, 1931–3; E. A. Walker, *Lord Milner in South Africa*, 1942; A. M. Gollin, *Proconsul in Politics: Lord Milner*, 1964.

Milner, Sir Frederick George, 7th Baron (1849–1931), politician and reformer, educ. at Eton and Christ Church, Oxford. He is remembered as the champion of the ordinary soldier in and after the First World War. Chiefly through his efforts the administration of pensions was transferred from the commissioners of Chelsea Hospital to a specially created ministry. He founded the first recuperative hospital for the shell-shocked at Hampstead. When this was no longer necessary its funds were transferred to Enham vil. settlement, afterwards united with Papworth (q.v.) settlement, M. identifying himself with this movement for the benefit of tuberculosis patients from army and navy.

Milnes, Richard Monckton, *see* HOUGHTON, 1st BARON.

Milngavie, police burgh of Dunbartonshire, Scotland, 6 m. NNW. of Glasgow, mainly residential with a few light industries. Pop. 8894.

Milnrow, tn of Lancs, England, 1½ m. SE. of Rochdale, with cotton spinning and light engineering industries. Pop. 7819.

Milo (Titus Annius Milo Papinianus), Rom. politician and agitator, *b.* Lanuvium. As tribune of the plebs in 57 BC he took an active part in obtaining Cicero's recall from exile. In 53 M. was candidate for the consulship, and P. Clodius (q.v.) for the praetorship. Each kept a gang of gladiators who fought each other in the streets of Rome. On 20 Jan 52 BC M. and Clodius encountered one another by accident at Bovillae. A brawl ensued, in which Clodius was slain. The riots which followed led to Pompey's appointment as sole consul to restore order. M. was brought to trial; he was defended by Cicero (*Pro Milone*), but was convicted and went into exile at Massilia. Returning in 48, he supported the revolutionary schemes of the praetor M. Caelius, but was taken and put to death at Cosa.

Milo, is. in the Aegean Sea, *see* MELOS.

Milon (6th cent. BC), Gk athlete, *b.* Croton. Famous for his enormous strength, he was 6 times victor in wrestling at the Olympic games, and as often at the Pythian. Other exploits and the peculiarly horrible manner of his death are probably legendary. It was said that in his old age he was passing one day through a forest when he saw a tree whose trunk was split. Wishing to try his strength, he attempted to force the two prongs apart; but they closed on his hands, and he was eaten by wild beasts. The death of M. is the subject of a remarkable statue by Pierre Puget in the Louvre, Paris.

Miloš Obrenović (1780–1860), Serbian prince, founder of the Obrenović dynasty (q.v.). He played a leading role in Czerny Djordje's (q.v.) rising against the Turks in 1804. When Czerny Djordje had to escape to Austria, 1813, M. came to terms with the Turks. In 1815 he succeeded in establishing himself as ruler of Serbia, and in 1817 was elected prince, acknowledging Turkish suzerainty. Czerny Djordje was murdered at M.'s instigation: in 1830 the sultan recognised M.'s title as hereditary, but in 1839 Russian intrigues forced M.'s abdication. In 1858 M. returned as prince on Alexander Karageorgević's deposition.

Milreis, former name of the Brazilian currency unit. From 1 Nov. 1942 the currency unit was renamed the cruzeiro (Cr $), composed of 100 centavos.

Milt, see PISCICULTURE.

Miltiades (*c.* 540–*c.* 489 BC), Athenian general and victor of Marathon; son of Cimon, and nephew of another M. who had made himself tyrant of the Thracian Chersonnese (mod. Gallipoli). When the tyranny became vacant, M. was sent out to take possession of the ter. on behalf of Athens. He joined Darius on the Scythian expedition (513 BC), was left with other Greeks in charge of the bridge over the Danube, and afterwards claimed to have advocated its destruction before the Persians could return (*see* HISTIAEUS). After the suppression of the Ionian revolt M. fled to Athens (*c.* 493). When Attica was invaded by the Persians he was chosen one of the 10 generals, and in that capacity induced the polemarch Callimachus to give a casting vote in favour of immediate battle. M. thus crowned his career with the victory at Marathon (490). He then persuaded the Athenians to entrust him with 70 ships for an unspecified purpose, and proceeded to attack the is. of Paros in order to satisfy a private grudge. Being wounded in the leg, he was compelled to raise the siege and return to Athens, where he was impeached by Xanthippus, father of Pericles, for having deceived the people. He was found guilty; but because of his service to the state the death penalty was commuted to a fine of 50 talents (1843 kgs of silver). Unable to pay, he was thrown into prison, and there *d.* of his wound which had turned gangrenous. The fine was subsequently paid by his son-in-law Callias. See H. Berve, *Miltiades,* 1937.

Milton, John (1608–74), poet, *b.* in Bread Street, London. His father, a scrivener, was the son of a yeoman of Oxfordshire, who cast him off on his becoming a Protestant. From him the poet inherited his lofty integrity, and his love of, and proficiency in, music. M. received his first education from a Scottish friend of his father's, Thomas Young, a Puritan of some note, one of the writers of *Smectymnuus* (q.v.). He was at St Paul's School, and in 1625 went to Christ's College, Cambridge. His sister Anne had married Edward Phillips, and the death of her

first child in infancy gave to him the subject of his earliest poem, 'On the Death of a Fair Infant', 1626. It was followed during his 7 years at Cambridge by the poems, 'On the Morning of Christ's Nativity', 1629, 'On the Circumcision'. 'The Passion', 'At a Solemn Music', 'On May Morning' and 'On Shakespeare', all in 1630; and 2 sonnets, 'To the Nightingale' and 'On Arriving at the Age of Twenty-three', in 1631. In 1632, having given up the idea of taking holy orders, for which his father had intended him, he lived for 6 years at Horton, near Windsor, devoted to further study. Here he wrote *L'Allegro* and *Il Penseroso* in 1632, *Arcades* in 1633, *Comus* in 1634 and *Lycidas* in 1637. The first celebrates the pleasures of a life of cheerful innocence, and the second of contemplative, though not gloomy, retirement, and the last is a lament for a lost friend. *Arcades* and *Comus* are masques set to music by Henry Lawes, having for their motives respectively family affection and maiden purity. In 1638 he completed his education by a period of travel in France and Italy, where he visited Grotius at Paris and Galileo at Florence. The news of impending troubles in Church and State brought him home the following year, and with his return may be said to close the first of 3 well-marked divs. into which his life falls. These may be called, first, the period of preparation and of the early poems; second, the period of controversy and of the prose writings; and third, the period of retirement and of the later poems.

Soon after his return M. settled in London, and employed himself in teaching his nephews, Edward and John Phillips, turning over in his mind at the same time various subjects as the possible theme for the great poem which, as the chief object of his life, he looked forward to writing. But he was soon to be plunged into the controversies and practical business which were to absorb his energies for the next 20 years. The works of this period fall into three classes—those directed against Episcopacy, including *Reformation of Church Discipline in England,* 1641, and his answers to the writings of Bishop Hall (q.v.), and in defence of *Smectymnuus;* those relating to divorce, including *The Doctrine and Discipline of Divorce,* 1643, and *The Four Chief Places of Scripture which treat Marriage,* 1645; and those on political and miscellaneous questions, including the *Tractate on Education, Areopagitica, A Speech for the Liberty of Unlicensed Printing,* 1644, his greatest prose work, *Eikonoklastes,* 1649, an answer to the *Eikon Basilike* of Dr Gauden (q.v.), *The Tenure of Kings and magistrates,* 1649, in defence of the execution of Charles I, which led to the furious controversy with Salmasius and M.'s *Pro Populo Anglicano Defensio,* 1650, the second *Defensio,* 1654, which carried his name over Europe, and *The Ready and Easy Way to Establish a Free Commonwealth,* written on the eve of the Restoration.

In 1643 M. had married Mary Powell, the daughter of an Oxfordshire cavalier, a girl of 17, who soon found her new life as the companion of an austere poet, absorbed in severe study, too abrupt a change from the gay society to which she had been accustomed, and in a month returned to her father's house on a visit. When the time fixed for rejoining her husband arrived, she showed no disposition to do so, upon which he began to aim at a divorce, and to advocate in the works above mentioned 'unfitness and contrariety of mind' as a valid ground for it, views which incurred for him much notoriety and unpopularity. A reconciliation, however, followed in 1645, and 3 daughters were *b*. of the marriage. In 1649 the reputation of Milton as a Latinist led to his appointment as Lat. or Foreign Secretary to the Council of State, in which duties he was, after his sight began to fail, assisted by A. Marvell (q.v.) and others. In 1652 his wife *d*. and 4 years later he married Katherine Woodcock, who *d*. in childbirth in the following year. To her memory he dedicated one of the most touching of his sonnets. At the Restoration he was, of course, deprived of his office, and had to go into hiding; but on the intercession of Marvell, and perhaps Davenant (q.v.), his name was included in the amnesty. In 1663, being now totally blind and somewhat helpless, he asked his friend Dr Paget to recommend a wife for him. The lady chosen was Elizabeth Minshull, aged 25, who appears to have given him domestic happiness in his last years. She survived him for 53 years.

The Restoration closed his second and introduced his third, and, for his fame, most productive period. He was now free to devote his whole powers to the great work which he had so long contemplated. For some time he had been in doubt as to the subject, he had considered the Arthurian legends, but had decided upon the Fall of Man. The result was *Paradise Lost*, which was begun in 1658, finished in 1664 and pub. in 1667. A remark of his friend Thomas Ellwood (q.v.) suggested to him the writing of *Paradise Regained*, which, along with *Samson Agonistes*, was pub. in 1671. Two years before he had printed a *History of Britain*, written long before, which, however, is of little value. The work of Milton was now done. In addition to his blindness he suffered from gout, to which it was partly attributable, and, his strength gradually failing, he died 'of the gout struck in', and was buried in the chancel of St Giles, Cripplegate.

In M. the influences of the Renaissance and of Puritanism met. To the former he owed his wide culture and his profound love of everything noble and beautiful, to the latter his lofty and austere character, and both these elements meet in his writings. Leaving Shakespeare out of account, he holds an indisputable place at the head of Eng. poets. For strength of imagination, delicate accuracy and harmony of versification, he is unrivalled and almost unapproached. In his use of blank verse, he has, for majesty, variety and music never been approached by any of his successors. He had no dramatic power and no humour. In everything he wrote, a proud and commanding genius manifests itself, and he is one of those writers who inspire reverence rather than affection. The standard life of Milton is by

David Masson, *see also* D. Saurat, *Milton, Man and Thinker*, 1944; E. M. W. Tillyard, *Studies in Milton*, 1951, and D. Daiches, *Milton*, 1957; D. Bush, *John Milton*, 1966. (*See Plate: English Literature.*)

Milton: 1. **Milton Regis,** *see* SITTINGBOURNE.

2. **Milton Abbas,** model vil. in Dorset, England, 7 m. from Blandford. There was formerly an abbey here; Abbey House is now a school and the fine abbey church is in use. Pop. 550.

3. **New Milton,** *see* LYMINGTON.

4. Tn of Norfolk co., Massachusetts, U.S.A., on the Neponset R., 7 m. S. of Boston. The U.S. Meteorological Bureau has an observatory on the Blue Hills near by, and M. Academy is here. Granite is quarried, and there are manufs. of crackers, chocolate, metal products; engraving is carried on. Pop. *c*. 25,000.

Miltonia, genus of epiphytal orchids, with large, flat, brilliantly coloured flowers resembling pansies in shape.

Milwaukee, lake-port, city and rail centre, co. seat of M. co., Wisconsin, U.S.A., on W. shore of Lake Michigan at the mouth of the M. R., 80 m. N. of Chicago. It serves a grain and beef producing region and has milling, brewing and meat-packing industries, also manufs. of machinery, turbines, diesel engines, car bodies, knitted and leather goods and general engineering. Downer Coll., M. School of Engineering, Wisconsin State College, St Mary College, M. Art Institution and School of Art are sited here. Pop. 741,324. (*See Plate: Wisconsin.*)

Milyukov, Pavel Nikolaevich (1859–1943), Russian historian and politician. He was leader of the Constitutional Democratic party (*see* CONSTITUTIONAL DEMOCRATS), and 1907–17 a member of the state Duma (*see* DUMA). After the Feb. revolution (q.v.) he was foreign minister in the Provisional Gov. (q.v.). Later he lived in Paris, and *d*. in London. *See* G. Fischer, *Russian Liberalism*, Cambridge, Mass., 1958.

Milyutin, name of 2 Russian statesmen:

1. **Dmitry Alekseevich, Count** (1816–1912), minister of war 1861–81, reorganised the military administration and introduced (1874) universal military service; resigned with Loris-Melikov (q.v.).

2. **Nikolai Alekseevich** (1818–72), brother of the above. As deputy minister of the interior he was an active participant in the Great Reforms (q.v.), particularly in the preparation for the emancipation of the serfs. As state secretary in Poland after the 1862 uprising he carried out the same reform there, giving it a particularly liberal interpretation.

Mimamsa (Sanskrit 'investigation'), 2 divs. of the orthodox Hindu philosophy, comprising a series of commentaries on the *Vedas*, the sacred books of India. The first div. is the *Purva-mimamsa* ('Prior Inquiry'), called also the *Karma-mimamsa* ('Investigation concerning Works'). The second is the *Uttara-mimamsa* ('Latter Inquiry') or *Brahma-mimamsa* ('Investigation as to the Supreme Spirit'). The principles of the M. are given in a series of *sutras*, or aphorisms, which are themselves so obscure as to need elaborate commentaries. The philosophy of the *Uttara-mimamsa* is that of Vedanta (q.v.). *See* R. K. Garbe, *Philosophy of Ancient India*, 1897.

Mimbar (Arabic), in Muslim architecture, a pulpit in a mosque (q.v.).

Mime, word sometimes used for an actor (Lat. *mimus*), now obsolete in that sense and used of wordless sketches in which the meaning is conveyed only by gesture. Gk M.s, however, played by men only, were spoken; the popular mime was a crudely realistic farce, the literary M. of Sophron (*c.* 440 BC) was a mythological burlesque and had some influence on Aristophanes. The semi-dramatic dialogues of Plato are a form of M., as are some of the works of Theocritus and Herondas (*c.* 250 BC). The It. M. was a simple, often vulgar, farce played by strolling actors, men and women, and became popular in Rome where it assumed some importance when written (and not improvised) by Decimus Laberius (106–43 BC). His younger rival was Publilius Syrus, who arrived in Rome in 46–5 BC. Under the Rom. Empire the acted M. (others were written for reading only) was incredibly indecent, dealing mainly with adultery or blasphemy. This roused the hostility of the Christian Church, and in the 6th cent. all theatres were closed and actors excommunicated. They then appeared only in private houses. The traditions of the mime lived on, and again reached a great height of popularity with the 16th cent. *commedia dell'arte*. During the 19th cent., M. plays, like *L'Enfant prodigue*, were popular. In recent times Jean-Louis Barrault and Marcel Marceau have brought mime to the attention of audiences all over the world, and it also plays an important role in ballet. It should be an essential part of every actor's training.

Mimicry, evolutionary process by selection, which occurs both in animals and plants, giving them in the simplest way the equivalent of some advantage possessed by the object imitated. Sometimes the mimic assumes the appearance of a harmless creature so as to come within easy reach of its unsuspecting prey; an instance of this is the caracara, or curassow hawk, of Central America, which very closely resembles the gallinaceous curassow, and the hawk's victim, confusing them, allows it to approach within striking distance. More commonly M. is protective and instances of this occur in many branches of the animal kingdom, such as the stick insects (Phasmidae), which assume a marvellously twig-like appearance on the shrubs or trees where they feed; or stingless insects which bear a sufficiently close resemblance to wasps and bees to be avoided by birds and other insectivorous enemies. A striking example of M. is the angler fish, which dangles small fleshy lumps at the end of long filaments over its large mouth. The small fish that nibble at the 'bait' fall an easy prey. M. occurs most frequently in plants, where the object is to attract insect pollinators. 'Müllerian M.' occurs when sev. species of animals (e.g. butterflies) all mimic one another and in this way

reduce the mortality involved in the 'education' of their predators. *See* G. D. H. Carpenter and E. B. Ford, *Mimicry*, 1933, and H. B. Cott, *Adaptive Coloration in Animals*, 1940. *See also* ANIMALS, *Colours of*.

Mimir, Scandinavian water-giant who owned the fountain of wisdom beneath the world-ash Yggdrasil which was the source of memory and wisdom, and known as M.'s Well. *See also* ODIN.

Mimnermus (7th cent. BC), Gk elegaic poet, a native of Colophon in Ionia. He was the first to use elegaic verse as a vehicle of mourning and erotic feeling. Only a few fragments survive. *See* C. M. Bowra, *Early Greek Elegists*, 1938.

Mimosa, large genus of leguminous plants with feather-shaped leaves which in some species are sensitive to the touch, particularly *M. pudica* and *M. sensitiva*, both natives of Brazil, one bearing rose and the other purple flowers. The plant wrongly known as M. by florists is *Acacia*, a member of the same family, Mimosoideae.

MIMOSA PUDICA
A, the leaf closed after stimulation;
B, the expanded leaf.

Mimulus, or **Monkey Flower,** genus of fragrant anns. and perennials of the family Scrophulariaceae. *M. moschatus* is the common musk. *M. cardinalis*, cardinal flower, is a popular garden plant bearing blooms which vary from scarlet to pale yellow. *M. cupreus* is orange and crimson. *M. glutinosus* is a valuable shrub which bears orange or scarlet flowers almost all the year round. *M. luteus* is a NW. Amer. plant, now naturalised in Britain; it has showy yellow flowers and is common by the sides of streams.

Min, early Egyptian deity of fertility, of ithyphallic human form, with right arm raised holding whip. At Koptos, centre of his worship, Petrie (q.v.) found 3 primitive colossal statues of M.; 2 are now at Oxford. His most important festival was at the beginning of harvest. The lettuce was sacred to him.

Min River, riv. of China in the prov. of Fukien. It flows in a SE. direction after leaving Yenping, and enters the sea about 30 m. below Foochow. It is navigable by small boats for most of its course. Length *c.* 360 m.

Mina, sum of money equal to the sixtieth part of a talent, never minted as a coin but only employed for purposes of account.

Minab, or **Minau,** dist and tn of Persia, in the prov. of Kerman, 52 m. SE. of Bandar Abbas. It is noted for dates. Pop. of tn about 7000.

Minaret (from Arabic *manarah*), in Muslim architecture, a tower from the top of which the muezzin chants the call to prayer (*see* MOSQUE).

Minas, tn of Uruguay, cap. of the SE. dept of

Lavalleja, 80 m. by rail from Montevideo. M. is one of the most picturesque tns in the country. The neighbouring forested hills supply fine granite and marble. It was the bp. of U.'s national hero Juan Antonio Lavalleja. Pop. 38,000.

Minas de Rio Tinto, see Rio Tinto.

Minas Gerais, inland state of Brazil with its E. border only 60–65 m. from the sea from which it is separated by minor ranges of mts. Most of M. G. lies on the Brazilian plateau and whilst it is mountainous in the S. and SW., the remainder consists of hilly uplands on which over 15 million head of cattle are grazed. The climate is good, with hot summers and warm winters; the rainfall is adequate and reliable. M. G. was famous in the 18th cent. for its great production of gold and diamonds and whilst both are still mined in fair quantities, its present chief mineral production comprises iron ore—its resources having been estimated at $\frac{1}{5}$ of the world's total resources—and manganese. Other important minerals are bauxite, nickel, amiantus, chrome, graphite, mica and quartz crystal. Traditional industries have been stimulated and new ones developed, particularly in the metallurgical field, due to the recent easy availability of electric power, from hydro-electric projects on sev. of the many rivs. that flow through the state. Despite the importance of its minerals and industry, M. G. remains essentially agricultural, having about $\frac{1}{4}$ of Brazil's cattle and being a leading producer of beans, maize, fruit, coffee, sugar and dairy products. It is well served by railways and roads, and uses for its external trade the ports of Rio de Janeiro and Santos to the S. and Vitória in the E. Belo Horizonte is the cap. and other important tns are Diamantina, Ouro Preto, Juiz de Flora. Area 226,656 sq. m. Pop. 9,798,000.

Minch, or Minsh (stormy sea), arm of the Atlantic Ocean which separates the NW. mainland of Scotland from the is. of Lewis (q.v.), belonging to the Hebrides (q.v.). It is from 20 to 46 m. in width, and about 60 m. from NNE. to SSW., and has a rapid current. A portion of it, called the Little M., is a passage separating the is. of Skye (q.v.), in the Inner Hebrides, from the middle part of the Outer Hebrides, S. Harris, N. Uist and Benbecula (q.v.). This is from 14 m. to 20 m. in width.

Minchinhampton, tn of Glos, England, 4 m. SE. of Stroud. M. Common is a noted beauty spot of the Cotswolds. Once a centre of the woollen industry, M. now has only one mill. Pop. 3500.

Mincio (anct **Mincius**), riv. of N. Italy, which rises (as the Sarca) in the W. of Trento prov., flows E. and S. to the N. end of the Lake of Garda from which it emerges at the SE. end as the M., and after passing Mantua (where it forms 3 lakes) enters the Po, 10 m. SE. of Mantua. Length 120 m.

Mind, seat of consciousness, thought, volition and feeling; soul (q.v.) as opposed to body. St Thomas Aquinas defines M. (*mens*, from *mensurare*, to measure) as those faculties of the soul which in their operation dispense entirely with matter. Primitive man is not conscious of a material body and an immaterial M., but rather an acting, feeling and thinking body—the unit of himself, or of the material conscious self; and if such phenomena as dreams and ghost-seeing may have made him conceive the possibility of a separation of himself from his earthly body, yet this conception never takes the form of anything we should call immaterial. The inner self, the soul or ghost, remains for him merely a more tenuous body. Gk philosophers were not pre-occupied with the question of M. and matter; their chief problem was the question rather of idea and matter, or the conceptual world as separated off from the world of the sense. To behold the idea, said Plato, man must get rid, so far as he can, of eyes and ears, and the whole body, and rely solely upon the pure light of the M.; for to the body are due only our aberrations and failures to see the truth. The problem of the relation of M. and body becomes an insistent one only from the time of Descartes (q.v.). The basis on which Descartes builds is the undeniableness of consciousness, from which he proceeds to establish the existence of God and of the world and, through the medium of the principle of causality (*see* Cause), assumes that he has bridged the gulf between himself and external reality. The main point on which this development centres is the sharp distinction which Descartes draws between M. and matter—the 2 substances into which the world of experience is divided. With him M. is a thing which thinks, and 'however we may regard the adequacy of this term to express the essential character of the soul, at least it emphasises the entirely immaterial nature of consciousness, and makes it possible for exact thinking to avoid that confusion of the conscious life with the outer world, which lies at the bottom of the obscure hylozoism of earlier philosophers, and the conscious materialism of more modern times' (A. K. Rogers, *History of Philosophy*, 1901). If M. and matter are so absolutely and totally different in their nature, how can they come together to form a single world, or react upon and affect each other, as apparently they do? In his *Tract on Man* Descartes undertakes to show how, assuming the body to be nothing but a machine of clay, the mere mechanical motion of parts is enough to account for what we call life; but 'clearly when the *reasonable soul* shall be in this machine, it will have its principal seat in the brain'. Descartes, however, was not prepared to carry his conception to its final consequences, for that would have been to deny altogether the influence of the will, i.e. of ourselves, upon our actions. Accordingly he admits that while our more habitual and reflex actions are due to mechanism alone, yet it also is possible for the M. to interfere and alter the motions of the body. The seat of this interaction he supposed to be a part of the brain known as the pineal gland; but how this conjecture could conceivably be tested he did not explain. In short, he admitted the fact of a mutual influence between the soul and the body, but did not attempt to explain its possibility. Whence the doctrine of Occasionalism (*see* MALEBRANCHE), which admitted the difficulty of an interaction but 'solves' it by falling back on the omnipotence of God: i.e. it is no power of the human M. that effects an alteration in the physical world, but a direct act of God.

Descartes had seen that strictly there is only a single substance: matter and M. are not conceivable in themselves, but can only be understood by reference to God; and Spinoza (q.v.) therefore is entirely consistent in reducing them from substances to mere attributes of the one substance, God (*see* SUBSTANCE). Spinoza's doctrine of substance leads the way to a different solution of the problem of the Cartesians concerning the relation of M. and body or, in other words, the problem of explaining how one substance can act upon another of a wholly different nature and how to avoid the apparent automatism which man seems to share with brutes and even inanimate things—difficulties not really obviated by Occasionalism. According to Spinoza, if the attributes of thought and extension (the only two *known* attributes of an infinite number belonging to the nature of God) are not two separate things, but only aspects of one and the same thing, they cannot interfere or interact on each other. But as they are both attributes of the same substance, that which in one light appears as a mode of extension or physical fact, will be, in another light, a mode of thought or fact of consciousness; and therefore the two modes will correspond. In this way Spinoza purports to justify the claim of science to explain all physical events, including the movements of the body, in purely physical terms. Leibniz (q.v.) put forward a reconstruction of the idea of substance, both mental and material. Descartes had defined matter as *extended* substance, passive, inert and able to receive motion only from outside. Leibniz substituted power of resistance for extension as the essential quality of matter, and from that new standpoint there was opened up the possibility of removing the absoluteness of that distinction between matter and M. upon which Descartes was so insistent. With Leibniz reality is made up of an infinite host of individual beings, or monads (*see* MONAD AND MONADISM) representing an infinite number of different grades of development, and what we call a body is, for him, not an actual material thing, but a group of monads of the less developed sort; and every soul or higher monad has such a group of interior associates with which it stands in a specially close connection. In this way Leibniz attempts to establish a real unity in the world.

In the 19th cent. the scientific doctrine, or law of the conservation of energy (*see under* ENERGY), gave a new unity to the mechanical interpretation of the universe, together with a new emphasis to the feeling, on the part of scientists, that it is impossible to make consciousness serve in any sense as an explanation of bodily acts. Consequently there has been a

widespread disposition to accept the old Cartesian doctrine of the automatism of the physical body, and to regard the psychical processes as simply running alongside the physical movements, without exerting any influence upon them (the doctrine of psycho-physical parallelism). Modern science, however, is recognising increasingly the importance of the mental factor both in health and disease (*see* PSYCHIATRY; PSYCHOLOGY), and from the opposite approach it is significant that such concepts as 'the free-will of the atom' have been introduced into the latest theories of matter. *See* W. M. Kyle, *Mind and Experience*, 1957; E. Schroedinger, *Mind and Matter*, 1958; E. Weiss, *The Structure and Dynamics of the Human Mind*, 1960; J. Wisdom, *Problems of Mind and Matter*, 1963; G. Ryle, *The Concept of Mind*, 1964.

Mindanao, second largest and most southerly of the Philippine Is., covering an area of 36,537 sq. m. Three or four ridges cross the is., with intermediate depressions and many rivs. and lakes. It has the volcanoes of Apo (9690 ft), Macaturing and Sanguil in the N., and in the SW. stretches a long, narrow peninsula continuing in the Basilian Is. and Sulu group. The prin. bays are Butnan on the N., Davao on the SE., Savangani, Sibuley and Illana on the S. The chief rivs. are the Rio Grande de M., rising in the N. and flowing into Illana Bay, and navigable for 70 m. from its mouth, and the Pulangi. The interior of the is. is wild, and covered for the most part with unexplored forests. Copra and pineapples are important exports, and coconuts, corn, rice and rubber are grown. Coal, copper, gold and iron are found. Pop. 1,828,071. To the E. is M. Trench, a narrow trough in the Pacific, running *c*. 15 m. from N. to S., where in 1962 the record depth sounding of 6297 fathoms was made. *See* PACIFIC OCEAN, *Depth*.

In the Second World War Jap. forces landed on M. at Davao (20 Dec. 1941) and the is. fell in April 1942. Amer. forces landed on 11 May 1945, and on the 13th captured the largest aerodrome and the rest of the is. *See* PHILIPPINE ISLANDS.

Minden, Ger. tn in the *Land* of N. Rhine-Westphalia (q.v.), on the Weser, 115 m. NE of Düsseldorf. It once belonged to the Hanseatic League (q.v.). In 1759 it was the scene of an Eng., Hanoverian and Brunswick defeat of the Fr. There is a fine 11th–13th cent. cathedral. Iron, glass and chemicals are manuf. Pop. 48,800.

Mindererus Spirit, known in the *Pharmacopoeia* as *Liquor ammonii acetatis*, the dose being 2 to 6 fluid drachms, is a solution of ammonium acetate, prepared by neutralising ammonium bicarbonate with acetic acid. It is used as a diaphoretic in febrile diseases, as an eyewash and also on hot flannels in the case of mumps.

Mindoro, one of the Philippine Is., lying SW. of Luzon, 90 m. long, 60 m. broad and covering an area of 3759 sq. m. The highest point of the is. is Mt Halcon (8484 ft). Calapan, in the NE., is the cap. Rice, cocoa, tobacco, hemp, cotton, etc., are grown, and various kinds of timber are exported and coal and sulphur are worked. It was captured by the Jap. forces early in 1942, and occupied until Dec. 1944. Pop. *c.* 120,000.

Mindszenty, Jozsef (1892–), primate of Hungary. He openly defied the Nazis and was imprisoned by the Germans until his release by the Red Army. He was made cardinal in 1946. The advent of a Communist regime brought him into conflict with the State. He refused to compromise on Christian principles, especially in regard to education, or to leave the country, and in 1948 was arrested on charges of offences against the State, having previously warned his people against any confessions that might be extracted from him. He was sentenced to life imprisonment. After the Oct. rising in 1956 M. was set free and returned to Budapest; but he was soon obliged to take refuge in the U.S. embassy, where he has since remained. *See also* HUNGARY, *History.*

Minehead, mrkt tn and seaside resort of Somerset, England, 2½ m. NW. of Dunster and 25 m. from Taunton. It is close to the moors and woods and has a harbour used for boating and sailing. It is within the Exmoor National Park, and is its main tourist centre. Pop. 7674.

Mineral Dressing, purification of ores, coal, oil, etc. *See also* METALS.

Mineral Oil, *see* PETROLEUM.

Mineral Phosphates, mineral deposits containing phosphoric acid in combination. Some occur in coprolites as calcium phosphate. These are stony deposits found in conjunction with Jurassic rocks. They represent the fossilised excrements of animals. Other M. P. are apatite, $3Ca_3(PO_4)_2.CaF_2$; wavellite, $2Al(OH)_3$. $2AL.PO_4.9H_2O$; turquoise, $Al_2(OH)_3PO_4.H_2O$; monazite, $(Ce,La,Di)PO_4$, and pyromorphite, $Pb (CbCl)(PO_4)_3$. The most important deposits of M. P. occur in N. Africa and Florida. *See* PHOSPHATES.

Mineral Rights, Taxation of, *see* LAND TAXES.

Mineral Waters, so called owing to the presence in them of mineral constituents derived from the rocks over which they flow. The waters are sometimes cold, or may be warm or even boiling. As a general rule the thermal waters are more mineral than cold waters, although there is no relation between the temp. and the chemical composition. M. W. may be classified according to the prevailing mineral substance contained in them. Earthy M. W. generally contain carbonate or sulphate of calcium, and occur abundantly in limestone dists. Such are the hot springs of Bath. The waters of Baden and Contrexéville are also of this type, the waters generally being imbibed. Ferruginous or chalybeate waters contain a large proportion of ferrous carbonate, and are known by their 'inky' taste. Brine springs contain sodium chloride or salt. The brines worked as sources of salt are derived from borings into saliferous beds; such are the springs of Cheshire, Salzkammergut (Austria) and Bex (Switzerland). These springs also contain the chlorides of potassium, magnesium and calcium, sulphates of calcium and other metals, silica, phosphates, nitrates and gases such as

carbon dioxide, sulphuretted hydrogen, etc. The hot springs of volcanic dists usually contain dissolved mineral matter, chiefly silica, with sulphates, carbonates, chlorides, etc. The oil springs of America are typical mineral springs. Medicinal springs are M. W. which are believed to have a curative effect on diseases. These medicinal waters may be (1) Alkaline, containing lime or soda and carbonic acid, as at Vichy and Saratoga. Some alkaline M. W. contain lithium carbonate (e.g. at Bilin and Karlsbad). (2) Bitter waters with sulphates of magnesia and soda, as at Sedlitz and Kissingen and Epsom. These waters have aperient properties. (3) Salt, as at Wiesbaden, Cheltenham, Droitwich and Homburg. (4) Earthy, as at Bath and Lucca. (5) Sulphurous, containing sulphur in the form of sulphides and sulphuretted hydrogen, as at Aachen, Harrogate and Aix-les-Bains. (6) Special varieties. Thus arsenical waters are found in the S. Tyrol and in France, whilst barium-containing M. W. are represented in some places (e.g. Harrogate). The waters of these springs may be warm and acquire their medicinal reputation from their thermal qualities. In sulphurous waters the sulphuretted hydrogen and sulphurous acid are sometimes oxidised into sulphuric acid which remains free in the water. Waters containing carbon dioxide are used as table waters (e.g. Apollinaris). Helium is occasionally found in M. W., and also disintegration products from radium. The spa waters code of practice lists (1) natural spa water, from a natural spring—no processing except filtration or CO_2 addition; (2) manuf. spa waters, (*a*) as (1) but with salts added or (*b*) salts dissolved in other than a spa water. Either may be artificially carbonated. All waters may be 'still' or 'sparkling' and labelled accordingly. In class (2) (*b*), potass, lithia, etc., waters must contain at least 5 gn bicarbonate per pint. Seltzer water may be compounded to the producer's own formula. (*See also* BALNEOLOGY; HYDROTHERAPY.)

Artificial Mineral Waters were prepared in still form, 1697, by N. Grew, in a variety by Lemery, 1720, and in sparkling form from 1750 to 1775 by Venel, Shaw, Bewley, Cavendish, Bergman and notably Joseph Priestley (q.v.). Struve later copied many spa waters exactly, but after Dakewell's 1932 invention of flavoured saccharine waters, the name 'mineral waters' was bestowed on all artificially carbonated soft drinks. Unsweetened artificial M. W. usually have CO_2 contents of 4 to 6 vols. Bunsen.

Mineralogy. The study of M. is of great antiquity; the first systematic descriptive work appeared in 1747, and the principles of crystallography (q.v.) were first applied to it in 1772. M. is concerned with the chemical and physical characteristics of minerals, discusses their modes of occurrence, whether original or secondary, and their modes of origin, whether aqueous, igneous, or organic (*see also* CRYSTALLOGRAPHY and GEOLOGY). Qualitative and quantitative analysis determines the chemical formula of a mineral, and methods involving the principles of crystallography reveal the crystal system. Cleavage, or the facility of a crystal for breaking regularly along well defined planes, sometimes indicates the crystal symmetry. Etch figures, caused by the action of various reagents, and surface markings are often of great use in determining the crystal class of a mineral. Thus iron pyrites is found in cubes, but striations on adjacent faces are so disposed that the full amount of cubic symmetry is impossible, in spite of the fact that the cubes are otherwise perfect. Twinning, or the conjunction of more than one individual according to a definite plan, as in diamond (q.v.) is an important characteristic of some minerals, Many physical characteristics are of utmost use to the mineralogist, including hardness, elasticity, cohesion, pyro-electric effects, sp. gr., specific heat, structure, colour, tenacity, lustre, fusibility, electric and magnetic properties. Minerals do not always show perfect crystalline form; some appear in crystalline conglomerations with no perfect units, whilst many minerals are not even crystalline at all. Minerals in most close-grained rocks can be determined by microscopic examination (see PETROLOGY). X-ray diffraction methods (q.v.) often reveal the nature of the building groups and their relative positions in the crystal. Colour effects produced by the impingement of ultra-violet light on crystal specimens often show up the presence of a particular mineral. The electron microscope (q.v.) has also been used in mineral identification.

Minerals are generally classified into groups, the members of which have a certain unity chemically, physically and crystallographically.

1. Native elements—including metals and non-metals, e.g. gold, silver, copper, sulphur, etc.

2. Halides—including fluorides (fluorspar, CaF_2), chlorides (salt, $NaCl$), more complicated bodies like cryolite ($3NaF, AlF_3$).

3. Sulphides—galena (PbS), blende (ZnS), greenockite, cinnabar (HgS), pyrites (FeS_2), marcasite (FeS_2).

4. Oxides—cuprite (Cu_2O), cassiterite (SnO_2), corundum (Al_2O_3), rock crystal (SiO_2).

5. Sulpharsenites, etc.—tetrahedrite ($3Cu_2S \cdot Sb_2S_3$); tennantite ($3Cu_2S \cdot As_2S_3$); pyrargyrite ($3Ag_2S \cdot Sb_2S_3$); proustite ($3Ag_2S \cdot As_2S_3$).

6. Carbonates—the calcite class, e.g. calcite ($CaCO_3$), rhombohedral. The aragonite class, rhombic.

7. The sulphates—the rhombic sulphates, e.g. barytes ($BaSO_4$). Others such as gypsum ($CaSO_4, 2H_2O$).

8. The aluminates—spinel, $MgAl_2O_4$.

9. Borates—borax ($Na_2B_4O_7, 10H_2O$).

10. Phosphates—apatite, $Ca_5(PO_4)_3F$ or $3Ca_3(PO_4)_2.CaF_2$.

11. The tungstates and molybdates.

12. Niobates and tantalates.

13. The uranates.

14. The silicates—perhaps the most important group of all. This includes amphiboles (hornblende); pyroxenes (augite, monoclinic; enstatite, rhombic); the felspar group (ortho-clase, anorthite); mica; topaz; tourmaline; the zeolites; the garnets; and many others.

Minerals of analogous constitution often have the same crystalline form. This isomorphism is well shown by the carbonates; calcite ($CaCO_3$); magnesite ($MgCO_3$); calamine ($ZnCO_3$); chaly-bite ($FeCO_3$); rhodochrosite ($MnCO_3$), which are similar in form, occurring in rhombohedral crystals, and show the same cleavage and optical properties. Substances having the same chemical composition may crystallise in two forms, i.e. they are dimorphous. Thus calcium carbonate occurs in the rhombohedral system as calcite and in the rhombic system as aragonite. The silicates, which form the largest class of all minerals, exhibit fully these phenomena of isomorphism, dimorphism and polymorphism. Titanium dioxide is found in the forms rutile and anatase (which are both tetragonal, but differ in characteristic angles) and brookite, which is rhombic. A few minerals show the phenomenon of enantiomorphism, owing to peculiar structure of the particles building up the whole. Thus right- and left-handed quartz are so related that one is the mirror-image of the other. Many minerals, when found in good specimens, are utilised for the fashioning of gem stones. Amongst these a few may be quoted: diamond, ruby, sapphire, spinel, beryl and emerald, zircon, sphene, garnet, etc.

To the class of silicates belong the majority of rock-forming minerals, which are classified into families or groups, such as the amphiboles, pyroxenes, felspars, micas, zeolites, etc., according to their similarity of chemical composition and crystalline properties. In their modes of occurrence minerals are essential or accessory, according as their absence would either alter the rock and make it fundamentally different or would not affect its petrographical species. Thus quartz is an essential constituent of granite, its removal altering the petrographic species to syenite. All essential minerals are original, but the converse is not true. Thus topaz and sphene may be original constituents of granite, but are yet accessory minerals in that their absence does not alter the rock fundamentally. Accessory minerals frequently occur in cavities where they had room to crystallise out from the general mass, as, for example, the crystals which line the 'drusy' cavities in granite. Secondary minerals, the result of subsequent changes in rocks, are generally due to the chemical action of percolating waters and gases, either from above (as in the formation of kaolin) or from below (as in the formation of gneisson and tourmaline). Groups of minerals are found associated, indicating a significant paragenesis. It is observable that basic minerals tend to separate out together from rock magmas by the process of magmatic differentiation. In saline deposits calcite, gypsum, rock salt, carnallite, etc., are frequently found associated. The decomposition of minerals by the action of percolating waters frequently gives rise to pseudomorphs, i.e. the external form of a mineral is retained while being replaced by other minerals. Thus calcite organ-

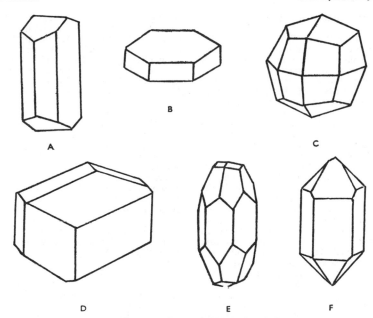

CRYSTALS OF SOME TYPICAL MINERALS

A, Orthoclase felspar (monoclinic). Crystals common. Prismatic, made up of pinacoid, prism and basal faces. Twinning very common on three laws: (1) Carlsbad, (2) Manebach, and (3) Baveno.

B, Mica (monoclinic). Usually in six-sided tabular crystals.

C, Garnet (cubic). Rhombohedra or trapezohedra, or as combinations of these forms.

D, Hornblende (monoclinic). Crystals common. Prismatic, combination of clinopinacoid, prism, clinodome and hemiorthodome.

E, Calcite (hexagonal, rhombohedral, calcite type). Three main types: (1) dog-tooth type, combination of prism and scalenohedron; (2) nail-head type, combination of prism and flat rhombohedron and (3) prismatic crystals.

F, Quartz (hexagonal). Hexagonal prism bounded above and below by hexagonal pyramids.

isms may become silicified, due to the interchange of silica for calcite, thus giving pseudomorphs of silica after calcite. As well as occurring in the crystalline form minerals assume a concretionary form, some being particularly prone to assume this form. Siderite is generally nodular, while calcite is often found in concretionary form. *See also* CLEAVAGE; CRYSTALLOGRAPHY; ISOMORPHISM; PETROLOGY; and individual articles under the names of metals and mineral compounds. *See* E. S. Dana, *System of Mineralogy*, 1837 (ed. C. Palache, H. Berman, and C. Frondel, 1944), and *Text-book of Mineralogy*, 1926; W. R. Jones and D. Williams, *Minerals and Mineral Deposits*, 1948; H. H. Read, *Rutley's Elements of Mineralogy*, 1948; Chambers's *Mineralogical Dictionary*, 1948.

Miner's Anaemia, *see* ANKYLOSTOMIASIS.

Minerva, Rom. goddess of wisdom and good counsel, identified with the Gk Pallas Athena, worshipped with Jupiter and Juno in the Capitol (q.v.). Her festival, *quinquatrus*, on 19 Mar., lasted 5 days. A carved image of her, called the 'Palladium' (q.v.), supposed to have been brought from Troy by Aeneas, was preserved in the temple of Vesta.

Mines, Military and Naval. Military mining belongs to the oldest application of engineering to the art of war. At least four cents. before the Christian era such warfare was known. Long before gunpowder was used places were captured by gaining access through mine galleries. Gunpowder was first used in mine warfare in 1487, after which mining became more common. At the siege of Sevastopol in the Crimean War over 5 m. of galleries were driven by the opposing armies. The First World War produced conditions similar to those of siege warfare, and special troops had to be trained for this. The Germans were the first to use mines in Flanders in Dec. 1914. The great mining feat of the First World War was the blowing up of the Messines Ridge on 7 June 1917 by the British, who used 1,000,000 lb. of explosives on a 10-m. front. The effect of this attack was to put a stop to Ger. aggressive mining. With the improvements in the range and weight of field artillery and bombing aircraft, the need for underground protection in future wars brought into being methods of mining to cope with these improvements.

In the Second World War, owing to the generally more fluid nature of operations, mining in the old sense (i.e. tunnelling) was little practised. The term 'mine' came to mean containers of explosives, or 'bombs'—placed on the ground or just beneath the surface—which exploded under pressure, or were occasionally controlled electrically or by other means. The Germans produced 2 models of remote-controlled tank, loaded with explosive and detonated by radio; these were intended to destroy enemy field-works, and were used against the Anzio bridgehead, without much success, in the role of the old siege mine. Defensive mining, on the other hand, increased in importance. In the W. desert, owing to the general absence of natural obstacles, minefields became the prin. feature of defensive positions, such as the perimeter of Tobruk and the Tel-el-Iessa–Qatara line. The mines used were of 2 types, anti-tank and anti-personnel. The former depended for their effect on blast alone, and required generally speaking a larger explosive charge (usually amatol) to break the tracks or damage the suspension of the tank. The Ger. *Teller*-mine can be taken as the type of anti-tank mine as developed up to 1945. Anti-personnel M. can be either blast or fragmentation. Both were denotated by pressure on the cover, like the anti-tank M., or by means of a trip-wire. Fragmentation M. caused damage either by the simple splintering of a metal container similar to the projectile casing of an H.E. shell, or by a shrapnel effect, as in the Ger. *S*-mine. This was in effect a short mortar buried upright in the ground with a very weak propelling charge. When detonated it projected a container into the air about the height of a man's waist; it then burst, scattering laterally a quantity of shrapnel bullets. The development of mine-detectors, which depended for the efficacy on 'echoes' rebounding from metal objects, caused a revolution in the design of land M. These now tended more to rely on blast effect as the charge had to be housed in a non-metallic container such as wood, plastic, or even papier-mâché (*Papp*-mine). Non-metallic fragmentation M. were, however, made with glass and pottery casings.

Naval M. were first used during the Amer. Civil War; some were controlled from the shore by electrical means, while others were operated automatically. During the Russo-Jap. war an improved mine was used which could be arranged to take any depth of water between 50 and 70 fathoms. This was a 'non-controlled' type and was the type generally in use throughout the First World War. These M., which have positive buoyancy, remain at a pre-determined depth beneath the surface and are attached by a length of wire cable to a sinker which rests on the sea-bed. The mine explodes when hit by a ship. Controlled mines are used primarily for harbour defence. They are fired by the completion of a circuit in a controlling station ashore to which they are connected by an electric cable. A mine

barrage consists of M. laid at staggered depths to catch both surface ships and submarines. It is now possible to lay M.s in depths of 1,000 fathoms set to watch 300 ft below the surface. Such a barrage was designed in the First World War to catch capital ships on the surface and submarines down to a depth of 100 ft. Contact M. are laid from many kinds of vessels, including submarines. Widespread minelaying by Germany in the First World War at first increased Brit. antipathy to this form of warfare, but later it was estab. as an important factor in naval operations. The Germans introduced a 'magnetic mine' in the Second World War, but one was washed up intact on the Brit. coast, and its secrets soon learned, with the result that all vessels were protected by a 'de-gaussing' girdle, which had the effect of de-magnetising or de-polarising the ship. Acoustic M. were also developed and used by both sides. Detonation was effected by the vibrations of a ship's propeller oscillating a contact arm within the mine. 'Oyster' M., operated by the change in pressure of water when a ship passes overhead, were also used. These last 3 types of mine are called 'ground' M., as they have negative buoyancy and lie on the sea-bed. They are used in shallow waters and are laid by both submarines and aircraft: in the latter case they are dropped by parachute. If not observed when dropped, ground M. provide a very serious threat to shipping and were the cause of many sinkings in the last war.

One of the most important and hazardous operations of war is that of mine-sweeping. Moored M. are swept by vessels towing a wire fitted with cutters which sever the mine cable. The mine then rises to the surface and can be exploded or sunk by rifle fire. Magnetic M. are swept by vessels towing electrically charged cables which create a magnetic field, thereby activating the needle of the mine. Aircraft were also used in exploding magnetic M. To sweep acoustic M., an electrically driven hammer in a box was fitted ahead of the bows of a ship and the vibrations set off the mine. No description has yet been pub. of the method of sweeping pressure M. The R.N. has built many small minesweepers since the war to deal with the threat of the ground mine, the latest device being a highly sensitive type of sonar (q.v.) apparatus capable of locating and classifying an object on the sea-bed with remarkable accuracy. These vessels are built largely of non-magnetic materials such as wood and aluminium. *See* Royal Naval Minewatching Service. *See* A. M. Low, *Mine and Countermine*, 1940, and J. Cowie, *Mines, Minelayers, and Minelaying*, 1949.

Mines Rescue, see Rescue.

Ming, dynasty of China which reigned from 1368, after the Mongols were expelled, until 1644. Its founder was Chu Yuan-chang, who estab. the cap. at Nanking, but his son, the Emperor Yung-lo, moved the cap. to Peking, in 1421. The M. period was notable, not so much for creative work in letters and art, as for interest in and preservation of the work of the past. During this period the earliest contacts of the modern W. world with China were made by the Portuguese mariners, and by the Jesuit missionaries who followed them. The M. dynasty was eventually overthrown by the Manchu dynasty. See CHINA, *Chinese Art*, on M. porcelain.

Mingechaur, tn (pop. 32,000 in 1964), reservoir (240 sq. m.) and hydro-electric station (357,000 Kw) on the R. Kura in Azerbaijan in Transcaucasia. The tn was founded in 1948, the power station constructed between 1953–5. The scheme also provides for the irrigation of over 2 million ac. of the Kura lowland.

Minghetti, Marco (1818–86), It. statesman and economist, *b.* Bologna. He entered the service of Pope Pius IX after his election (1844), and was appointed member of the Consulta della Finanze. When Pius yielded to the demands of Austria, he resigned office and fought in the Sardinian Army in Lombardy. In 1859 Cavour appointed him secretary-general to the foreign office and subsequently minister of the interior (1861). After Cavour's death (1861) he became premier (1863), and concluded with Napoleon III the Sept. Convention (1864). He was later ambas. to London (1868) and premier (1873–6).

Minho: 1. Sp. **Miño,** riv. of Spain and Portugal, which rises in the Cantabrian Mts and flows S. through Lugo, SW. through Orense and between Pontevedra and the Portuguese prov. of M. to the Atlantic. Its chief trib. is the Sil. Length 210 m.

2. Prov. of N. Portugal, containing the dists of Braga and Viana do Castelo (qq.v.). It has a coastline on the Atlantic in the W., is mountainous in the N. and E. and is watered by the Lima. The chief tn is Braga. Area 1868 sq. m.; pop. 875,000.

Minhou, see FOOCHOW.

Miniature Dachshund, see DACHSHUND.

Miniature-painting, usually applied to portraits painted on a very small scale. M. is generally executed on ivory and is, as to composition, drawing and finishing, subject to the same process as any other kind of painting, but the colouring, at all events of the face, is dotted or stippled on. The term miniature (from Lat. *miniare*, to colour with red ochre) was originally applied not to a small portrait, but to the highly specialised art of illustrating MSS. Each of the 250 miniatures in illustration of the celebrated Cottonian Genesis was about 4 in. square. Later the miniature became merely a large initial letter containing on or around it a pictorial representation on a small scale of some incident or person spoken of in the text. From this fact it is possible that the term miniature when it became exclusively applied to small portrait-painting on enamel, ivory, or any other material had become erroneously associated with Lat. *minuere*, to diminish. Ivory is commonly selected for M., because the peculiar hue of the better kinds presents great facilities for the imitation of human skin, Eng. artists have been conspicuous in the past as miniature painters,

among the most notable being N. Hilliard and Isaac Oliver (qq.v.). Others of importance include Peter Oliver, Isaac's son, whose celebrated miniature, 'The Entombment of Christ', was begun by the father and finished by the son; Samuel Cooper (1609–72), a 'miniature Van Dyck'; Richard Cosway (1740–1821), whose miniatures for snuff-box lids were famous; and Sir Wm Ross (1794–1860). *See also* PERSIAN ART. See J. L. Propert, *History of Miniature Art*, 1887; J. J. Foster, *Chats on Old Miniatures*, 1908; F. R. Martin, *The Miniature Painting and Painters of Persia, India, and Turkey*, 1912; O. E. Saunders, *English Illumination*, 1928; R. Lister, *British Miniatures*, 1951; G. Reynolds, *English Portrait Miniatures*, 1952.

Miniature Poodle, see POODLE.

Minié, Claude Étienne (1814–79), Fr. inventor of the M. rifle, *b.* Paris. He entered the army as private and rose to the rank of colonel (1858), having seen active service in Africa. The rifle bearing his name was invented in 1849. *See also* FIREARMS. *The Detonating System*.

Minim, fluid measure, see METROLOGY.

Minim, character or note in music, equal in duration to one-fourth of a breve, or 2 crotchets. Its name is derived from the fact that in the 14th cent. it was the shortest note (*nota minima*). Amer. terminology, following German instead of English, uses 'half-note' for M.

Minima, see MAXIMA AND MINIMA.

Minims, or **Minimi,** friars of the religious order founded in 1444 by St Francis of Paola. There is also a 2nd and a 3rd order.

Minimum Wage, rate of pay below which wages may not fall. It is fixed either by legislation or as a result of collective bargaining. Until the Second World War agitation to secure a M. W. was said to arise principally from the worker who sought protection from employers with greater bargaining power. In the Middle Ages employers sought protection from the excessive charges of craftsmen. Full employment after World War II increased the bargaining power of trade unions. Throughout the hist. of trade unions many disputes have had a M. W. as their main object (*see* LABOUR DISPUTES), and trade boards (q.v.) have secured adjustments favourable to the worker. In 1524 there was municipal regulation of wages in large Eng. tns and an Act of Elizabeth I marked a definite step in the progress of the movement. Under the Trade Boards Act of 1918 a large number of trades were included in M. W. decisions, and hitherto sweated labour was placed on a more favourable footing. The U.N., through the International Labour Organisation, has a special dept which considers the question, and in practically every part of the world there is a movement in favour of a M. W. In conditions of labour scarcity such as those since the end of the Second World War employers often have to pay more than the statutory M. W. In some trades the M. W. fluctuates according to the rise or fall in the cost of living.

See LABOUR DISPUTES; TRADE BOARDS; WAGES COUNCILS.

Minin, Kuz'ma (*d.* 1616), Russian patriot, a butcher from Nizhny-Novgorod. A volunteer army organised by M. and commanded by Prince Pozharsky expelled the Poles from Moscow in 1612 (*see* TROUBLES, TIME OF).

Mining. The term M., in its broadest sense, is the art of extracting useful minerals from the crust of the earth. It embraces (*a*) prospecting, locating minerals underground by drilling, by seismic, electrical or magnetic methods, or by radioactive counting methods (uranium); (*b*) exploration, which determines the extent of mineral deposit; and (*c*) development or exploitation, which deals with the method of working the deposit. The prin. products mined include the metalliferous ores of gold, silver, zinc, copper, lead, tin, uranium, etc. and the non-metalliferous minerals such as coal, peat, gypsum, limestone, kaolin, marble, granite, asbestos, precious stones, mineral oil and oil shales. These deposits may form (1) tabular or sheet-like deposits or (2) non-tabular or irregular masses. Further, a tabular deposit may occur as (*a*) a bed or layer, or (*b*) a vein or lode. Many of the most important mineral deposits occur as beds containing a valuable metal such as gold, copper, iron, or lead. The non-tabular deposits include the diamond-bearing 'necks' of old volcanoes: large 'bosses' of granite or masses of haematite.

The prin. methods of working mineral deposits are (1) open-cast or surface workings; (2) open and underground workings combined; (3) alluvial or placer M.; (4) wells and boreholes; and (5) underground workings.

Open-cast M. is only possible where the mineral lies at or near the surface and is relatively flat. Among the minerals often worked by this method are coal, lignite and the ores of gold, copper, iron, lead and tin. Under favourable conditions the method is economical and reasonably safe. The first process is the removal of the overburden or rock covering the valuable bed of mineral. After this the mineral itself is excavated and removed. If the mineral is hard it will require blasting or breaking by machinery. Nowadays the overburden and mineral ore are worked by mechanical methods. Large power shovels, mounted on tractors and driven by electric motors or steam, excavate the material and load it into lorries, trucks or conveyors. Dragline and bucket excavators are used for loose rock and alluvial, and these can dig under water. The locomotive crane and bucket is also used for gravels and muds, the bulldozer for clearing surface rubbish and for excavating earth. The removal of both overburden and mineral begins from the top downwards in successive horizontal slices, benches or terraces, until the bottom is reached. In some cases the overburden is deposited in the trench previously occupied by the mineral. This is known as back-filling. In open-cast M. the ratio of overburden tonnage to mineral tonnage is a deciding factor in economical working.

A combination of open and underground workings is employed when the ore deposit is thick and pitches steeply from the surface. The actual workings are open, but the ore is removed by underground levels and shafts. The so-called milling process is often adopted for working iron-ore deposits. While the overburden is being removed by shovels, etc., a shaft is sunk and cross-cuts driven into the deposit. At short distances along these levels small puts or rises are put up to the surface in the ore body. Workmen then excavate the ore around the top of each rise and shoot the ore into it. A door at the bottom of each rise enables large wagons to be loaded rapidly. These are then hoisted up the shaft. As the ore is worked each small pit takes the form of a funnel.

Alluvial or placer deposits are those filling up the floor of rivs., and consist of the sediment carried down by the water and deposited along parts where the current became sluggish. The material consists of layers of gravel, sand and clay containing, perhaps, small quantities of gold, tin or other metal. Practically all these are heavier than the sand and clay and can be separated by washing in sluices or by the more primitive methods of pan and rocker. The M. methods commonly used are dredging, sluicing or hydraulicking. The dredger is mounted on a float or barge and brings up the alluvial from the riv. bed. Tin-dredging is carried out on a large scale in Malaya. Shovels, grabs, scrapers or dragline excavators are used when the deposit is thick. These machines deliver the material to the sluices or other appliances for separating the valuable metal from waste material. Dredging operations can now be carried down to depths of 130 ft below pond level.

Another method is to divert the course of the riv. and work the alluvial by streaming. Riv. alluvial containing valuable metal is often treated in long inclined troughs or sluices in which a stream of water is kept flowing. The lighter particles of waste sediment are carried away while the heavier and valuable metal settles to the bottom. Wood, stone or iron riffles are fixed in the bottom of the sluices to collect the particles of metal. In the case of gold, mercury is added to assist in trapping it. Washing tables are sometimes used instead of sluices. When a collection or clean-up is due the water is diverted into a parallel series of sluices, then the metal is collected and the mercury recovered and used again.

Hydraulic M. is used when the deposit is soft and lies under a loose overburden. In this method, known as hydraulicking, strong jets of water are projected against the bank of gravels and overburden, which are loosened and washed away by the action of the water. Beds of gold or tin-bearing gravels are often hydraulicked. The method requires an ample supply of water at a high pressure. Huge reservoirs are often constructed for storing water. When the fall of ground is not sufficient the washings of gravel are forced up to an elevated tank connected to sluices supported on trestles. Liquid, soluble or gaseous minerals are often extracted from the ground by means of wells or boreholes. The prin.

minerals obtained in this way are natural inflammable gas, petroleum, salt and carbonic acid. When under pressure mineral oil will rise to the surface, or it may have to be sucked up by means of pumps. Natural accumulations of saline water or brine can be tapped by wells or boreholes. A borehole has been put down to a depth of over 3 m. in search of oil.

In underground M. the method of working depends on whether the deposit occurs as a bed, vein or an irregular mass. A steep bed is generally worked on the same lines as a vein. In the case of a thin vein dipping steeply the deposit is generally reached by a vertical shaft. In hilly country an adit or horizontal tunnel may be used. From the shaft level cross-cuts are drawn to the vein, usually about 100 ft apart, vertically. From these cross-cuts drives or levels are made along the vein in both directions. Each level is provided with facilities for loading and transporting ore. 'Winzes' are tunnels to the dip of the vein, and 'raises' to the rise. These are driven to prove the vein, for ventilation and for working purposes. A raise is driven to meet or 'hole through' to a winze from the level above, thus forming a connection between the two levels. The levels, winzes and raises cut the mineral vein into a series of rectangular blocks or pillars, each of which forms a unit that is afterwards completely or partly removed by M. operations. If the deposit is thick it is divided into a number of horizontal slices, each slice being in turn divided into rectangular blocks. The miner tries to locate his drivages in the valuable portions of the vein, leaving the barren rock as buttresses or pillars to support the sides or roof.

When removing the blocks of ore there are 2 typical methods, i.e. working downwards or underhand stoping, or upwards known as overhand stoping. The term stoping means working away any deposit in a series of steps. In underhand stoping the miner begins at the floor of the level. Any waste rock is deposited upon platforms of timber (stulls) and the metal is drawn up into the level by a windlass. The chief disadvantage of this method is the cost of winding up the metal and water. A cheaper way of underhand stoping is to start from the upper end of a winze in a series of steps as before, but the ore is allowed to roll down the winze into wagons in the level below. In overhand stoping work is commenced from a raise or from 2 ends of a winze. When a sufficient height has been excavated timber supports (stemples, stull-pieces) are fixed from wall to wall and covered with boards on which the dirt is thrown.

In filling-up methods the mineral is removed completely and its place filled with waste rock.

In top slicing and caving a section of ore is undermined by cutting a horizontal slice and then allowing the overlying material to collapse. The process is repeated slice by slice throughout the deposit. When working hard sections of ore, sub-drift caving may be used; in this method the ore is removed in vertical slices.

Mechanisation. In more recent years, great advances have been made in the use of mach-

inery in underground coal mining. Cutting machines have a horizontal jib about 5 ft long which carries an endless chain to which a number of pick cutters are attached. As the chain revolves the machine cuts a horizontal slice about 6 in. thick and of any depth up to the length of the jib. When the coal has been cut the overlying material can be removed by shot firing. The loose coal is usually loaded by hand on to conveyors which transport it away from the working face. Mechanical loaders are sometimes used but at present they suffer from the twin disadvantages of causing excessive dust and of producing an undesirably large proportion of small pieces.

See R. Peele, *Mining Engineers' Handbook,* 1942; T. Bryson and A. Harvey, *Science for Miners,* 1946; Truscott, *Mine Economics,* 1947; W. W. Staley, *Mine Plant Design* and *Mine Surveying,* 1949; J. Spalding, *Deep Mining,* 1949; F. Winiberg, *Metalliferous Mine Surveying,* 1950; T. Bryson, *Mining Machinery,* 1953. *See also* COAL: COAL MINING: LIGNITE. (*See Plates: Mining*; *Brazil, Zambia, Ontario, Yukon.*)

Ministry (Church), *see* BENEFICE; BISHOP; CLERGY; DEACON; EPISCOPACY; ORDERS, HOLY; PRIEST. (Political), *see* CABINET; GOVERNMENT; and under names of M.s, e.g. AGRICULTURE AND FISHERIES.

Minius, *see* MINHO.

Mink, name given to some species of the weasel family. The Amer. M., *Putorius vison,* is larger than a stoat, and the fur varies from light to dark brown in colour. It is aquatic in habit, feeding on fish and small mammals. When attacked it produces a very offensive secretion. The European M., or marsh otter (*P. lutreola*), closely resembles the other species, its white upper lip being its chief distinction. If taken young M.s are easily tamed, and have been used as ferrets. For the manuf. of fur coats, ties and trimmings, the most desirable types of wild M. are found in Canada and N. America. M.s are also raised in captivity, and compare very favourably with the wild types. In recent years some varieties have been developed. They are known collectively as mutation M., of which the most valuable are silver blue, pastel and white. *See* FUR.

Minneapolis, city, co. seat of Hennepin co., Minnesota, U.S.A., adjoining St Paul on W., on the Mississippi R. at the Falls of St Anthony 350 m. NW. of Chicago. It is the commercial, financial and industrial centre of a large agric. area. It manufs. flour, dairy products, farm and electrical equipment and construction machinery. Educational institutions include the Univ. of Minnesota, Augsburg College and Theological Seminary, School of Art, M. College of Music, the MacPhail College of Music and the Dunwoody Industrial Institute. The M. Symphony Orchestra is well known. The city contains 147 parks with an area of 6000 ac. and 6 large natural lakes, Minnehaha Falls, Wold Chamberlain Field (airport), M. Institute of Arts, Amer. Swedish Institute, Walker Art

Center, the Federal Reserve Bank, Northrop Memorial Auditorium, Fort Snelling (just outside), Lake Minnetonka. M. lies at the head of navigation of the Mississippi, an important factor in its early growth, though the riv. is not now used commercially. Pop. 482,870. (See *Plate: Minnesota*.)

Minnesingers (Ger. *Minnesänger*, lovesingers), Ger. lyric poets who fl. *c.* 1150 to *c.* 1350. Their lays dealt mainly with love, which was generally treated from the conventional medieval *amour courtois* standpoint, especially by the earlier M.; later examples are on topics such as country life, military adventure and politics. The earliest M. were chiefly Austrian or Bavarian. The art spread rapidly throughout Germany, and in 1207 the famous *Sängerkrieg*, or 'Battle of the Bards' (celebrated in *Tannhäuser*), was held at the Wartburg in Thuringia, where the Landgrave, Hermann I, held open court for all minstrel folk. Among the most famous M. were Friedrich von Hausen, Heinrich von Ofterdingen, Otto von Botenlaube, Heinrich von Morungen (the noble Morringer of the ballad), and above all Walter von der Vogelweide, whose songs were not only skilfully wrought but also imbued with strong national and political feeling. M. were generally of noble, sometimes princely, rank, but some were mere wandering minstrels. Ruediger von Manesse, burgomaster of Zürich (*d.* 1304), collected nearly 1500 *Minnelieder* (see MANESSE). The best modern selection is by F. H. von der Hagen (4 vols.), 1838. *See* H. Brinkmann, *Enstehungsgeschichte*, 1926, and J. Siebert, *Dichter Tannhäuser: Leben-Gedichte-Sage*, 1934. *See* GERMAN (AND AUSTRIAN) MUSIC.

Minnesota: 1. N. central state of the U.S.A., the 'Gopher State', bounded N. by Ontario and Manitoba, E. by Ontario, Lake Superior, and Wisconsin, S. by Iowa and W. by N. Dakota and S. Dakota. With an extreme length N. to S. of 405 m., it varies in width E. to W. from 180 m. to 350 m. and has an area of 84,068 sq. m., including 4059 sq. m. of inland waters. From the Height of Land in the N. centre waters flow N. to Hudson Bay, E. to the Atlantic and S. to the Gulf of Mexico. The SW. of M. is level prairie at an average height of 1200 ft, intensively cultivated. The N. and NE. are the crystalline hills of the Superior Highlands, forested and rich in iron. The largest of the '10,000 lakes' is Lake of the Woods at the N., shared with Canada, 70 m. long N. to S. and 10 to 50 m. across E. to W., with thousands of is. and an area of 1500 sq. m. The former dense forests of the N. have been greatly reduced. The prin. rivs. are the Mississippi, which rises in the N. lake region and becomes part of the Wisconsin boundary; the St Croix, along the Wisconsin boundary through most of its southward course to the Mississippi 15 m. SE. of St Paul; the Red R. of the N., which flows N. along the N. Dakota border into Canada; and the M. R., 332 m. long from the S. Dakota border to the Mississippi near St Paul. Agriculture is the prin. industry and is very

varied. The W. borders on the wheatlands of the Dakotas, the SE. on the corn and cattle belt, while the E. and N. (where not forested) produce dairy stuffs. By far the most important mineral product is the iron ore, partly haematite and partly taconite, of the Vermilion, Mesabi, and Cuyuna ranges, richest in the U.S.A. In manufs, food products are far ahead, followed by machinery. Minneapolis, the chief city, is a major grain and flour centre. Other major cities: St Paul (the State cap.) and Duluth. The univ. of M. opened in 1869. The state has 8300 m. of railways, 108,500 m. of roads and 177 airports. It has 2 U.S. senators and 9 congressmen. The governor and 131 state representatives are elected for 2 years, the 67 state senators for 4 years.

History. Fr. explorers and fur traders were in M. as early as 1660, and it was claimed by France in 1671. The part E. of the Mississippi R. passed to England in 1763 and to the U.S.A. in 1783. France ceded the part W. of the Mississippi to Spain in 1762, but received it again in 1800 and sold it in 1803 to the U.S.A. as part of the Louisiana Purchase. M. became a state in 1858. A flood of Scandinavian and Ger. immigrants entered after the civil war. The first iron ore from the Mesabi Range was shipped in 1892. *See* W. W. Folwell, *A History of Minnesota* (4 vols.), 1921–30; T C. Blegen, *Minnesota: its History and its People*, 1937, *and Minnesota: A History of the State*, 1963.

2. Riv. of U.S.A., a trib. of the Mississippi, which it joins after a course of 330 m. across the state of M. (*See Plate*.)

Minnow (*Phoxinus phoxinus*), small cyprinid fish common in most parts of Britain and throughout Europe. It is distinguished from other species of its genus by its small size and by its brown and green colouring.

Miño, *see* MINHO.

Minoa, *see* HERACLEIA.

Minoan Scripts, name given by Sir Arthur Evans to the prehistoric scripts of Crete. At the beginning of the Middle Minoan period (*c.* 2000 BC) a pictographic script was in use, principally on seal stones. It was soon displaced by a simplified version in which the pictograms were reduced to formal outline patterns; this was named Linear script A. It appears to have been in use all over Crete, and possibly in Minoan colonies overseas, for a long time, lasting into the first part of the late Minoan period. It was replaced about the 14th cent. BC by a modified version, known as Linear script B, which so far has been found in Crete only at Knossos, but at many sites in the southern Gk mainland.

The Linear A inscriptions are of 2 main types: clay tablets and short inscriptions on stone or metal objects. The largest archive of clay tablets is that from Hagia Triada in the S. of the is. close to Phaistos. The tablets are clearly, from the presence of numerals, accounting documents. The inscribed objects seem to be of a religious nature (offering-tables, double axes, etc.). The script runs from left to right, and may be presumed to be organised like the closely related

Linear B; but in default of sufficient material it remains undeciphered and the claims that have been made must be treated with reserve.

The Linear B system is much better known. The accident of its first discovery in Crete made it appear simply a reformed version of Linear A; but it is now known to have been used on clay tablets at 3 sites on the Gk mainland (Mycenae, Pylos in Messenia and Thebes in Boeotia), and inscribed earthenware jars have been found elsewhere. The date of the Knossos tablets is generally believed to be the 14th cent. BC; those from the mainland date from the 13th cent., and it seems to have gone out of use with the collapse of the Mycenaean kingdoms in the 12th cent. The script consists of about 90 signs used to spell words phonetically; a number of commodity signs or ideograms, used to denote the object being counted; and a simple numerical system on a decimal base. The signs are written from left to right. The tablets do not seem to have been deliberately baked to preserve them, but owe their survival to the fortunate accident of a fire which destroyed the buildings containing them. Many of the commodity signs are recognisable pictures of persons, animals, chariots, weapons, vessels, etc. Thus the approximate content of many tablets was clear from the start. Work by Sir Arthur Evans and many scholars, of whom the Americans Dr Alice Kober and Dr E. L. Bennett Junior deserve special mention, opened the way to the decipherment which was achieved by Michael Ventris (q.v.) in 1952. The syllabic nature of the script was evident both from the number of signs and the related Cypriot script (*see* below) which had already been deciphered. Ventris's chief contribution was the observation of the alternation of signs in repeated words and the classification of these in a table, the so-called grid, to represent the relationship between them. Thus he was able to group together most of the more frequent signs which shared the consonanted or vocalic elements of their values, so that by identifying a few signs the values of the remainder could be read off. The discovery of sign-groups which he believed to denote Cretan place-names enabled him to solve the grid; and this permitted the transcription into syllabic form of a few words whose meanings were clear from their usage. The words thus revealed showed an astonishing resemblance to their Gk equivalents. Further investigation showed that the language was undoubtedly Greek, but that it was far more archaic than any hitherto known dialect. The writing system also proved to be an incomplete and ambiguous notation, leaving the reader to supply a number of sounds to complete the word.

The first results were pub. by Ventris in collaboration with John Chadwick (q.v.), in the *Journal of Hellenic Studies* 73 (1953), pp. 84–103. The same 2 authors collaborated in a large vol., *Documents in Mycenaean Greek*, pub. in 1956. Despite some initial scepticism Ventris's theory was rapidly accepted by Gk scholars throughout the world. The story of the decipherment has been told by John Chadwick in *The*

Decipherment of Linear B, pub. in 1958. The results of the decipherment have been to add 500 years to the hist. of the Gk language, and to present a picture of some details of the civilisation known previously only through archaeology and Homer. The most remarkable discovery is the complexity of organisation and the concentration of production under the supervision of royal palaces.

The Phaistos Disk is a circular flat disk of baked clay, about $6\frac{1}{2}$ in. across, inscribed on both sides in spiral fashion in a script which remains without exact parallel. It was discovered in the Middle Minoan palace at Phaistos in southern Crete in 1908, and appears to date to about 1600 BC. The chief feature of note is that each of the 45 different characters was impressed upon the wet clay by means of a punch or stamp cut for the purpose. Its decipherment is a favourite amusement of amateurs, but the brevity of the inscription prevents any real progress until more examples of the script are found.

The Cypriot syllabic script was in use from at least the 6th to the 3rd cent. BC, and was used to write the Cypriot dialect of Greek until the Gk alphabet was adopted in Hellenistic times. It appears to be a modified survival of some kind of Minoan script, though not a direct descendant of Linear B, for a special Linear script, known as Cypro-Minoan, was in use in the is. during the Mycenaean period. It was deciphered with the aid of inscriptions with the same text in both syllabic and alphabetic form. It distinguishes 5 vowels and 11 consonants and although as simple in construction gives a rather more accurate notation of Gk words than Linear B.

Minoans, *see* CRETE.

Minopolis, *see* MONOPOLI.

Minor, in music, lesser. A M. third extends to 2 semitones, e.g. A–C, a major third of 4, e.g. A–C♯. A M. tone has the ratio 9 : 10, e.g. in the scale of C major the interval D–E. A major tone has the ratio 8 : 9, e.g. in the same scale the interval C–D. A M. scale may be represented by the white keys of the piano from A (but with G sharpened to form a leading-note). All other M. scales are successions of whole tones and semitones in the same order.

Minor, in Scots law a person under lawful age or majority. In Eng. law the term generally used is infant. As opposed to pupil it means a male over 14, or a female over 12, and under 21. M.s in this restricted sense are capable of consent, but are treated as persons of such inferior discretion and judgment as to require legal protection. Pupillarity, on the other hand, is a state of total incapacity. A M. who has no curator (guardian) may validly enter into a contract to marry, or any other contract, lease his heritable lands and give his movables to whom he will. But the acts of a M. who has a curator are, generally speaking, invalid without the latter's consent. Nevertheless he may, without such consent, do any act which does not affect the property under his curator's control. In all cases, whether he has a curator or not, a M.'s contracts may be voidable during his minority and for a period of 4 years after he attains majority. This period is known as the *quadriennium utile*.

Minor Planet, *see* ASTEROID.

Minorca (Sp. **Menorca**), second largest of the Balearic Isles (q.v.), lying NE. of Majorca (q.v.). It was in Brit. hands 1713–56, 1763–81 and 1798–1802. Its loss to the French in 1756 was the reason for the execution of Adm. Byng (q.v.). It is generally low, but has some hills in the centre. It is wind-swept and deficient in rainfall, but stock is raised and there is some agric. produce. Copper, lead, iron, marble, alabaster and slate are found, and shoes are manuf. The is. abounds in antiquities, and has become a popular tourist resort. The cap. is Mahón (q.v.). Area 258 sq. m.; pop. 43,000.

Minos, in Gk legend, king of Crete (q.v.); the name may have been an official title of Cretan rulers at Knossos. M. was son of Zeus by Europa and brother of Rhadamanthus and Sarpedon. On account of his wisdom and justice he was appointed after death one of the judges in Hades (*Odyssey* xi, 568), together with Rhadamanthus and Aeacus, king of the Myrmidons. Only in Attic legend is he of evil repute (*see* THESEUS), due perhaps to an old feud with Crete. M. was husband of Pasiphae (q.v.) and father of Androgeos, Ariadne and Phaedra (qq.v.). When Daedalus (q.v.) fled from Crete he was pursued by M., who, on reaching Sicily, was drowned in boiling water by the daughters of King Cocalus. *See* Sir A. Evans, *The Palace of Minos*, 5 vols, 1921–36; L. Cottrell, *The Bull of Minos*, 1955.

Minot, George Richards (1885–1950), Amer. physician, *b*. Boston and educ. at Harvard. Prof. of medicine at Harvard, 1928–50; before this he was physician-in-chief at the C. P. Huntington Memorial Hospital, Harvard, 1922–8; he was also director of the Thorndike Memorial Laboratory. He was awarded, jointly with Wm P. Murphy and George H. Whipple, the Nobel prize in medicine (1934) for researches on the liver treatment of pernicious anaemia. He pub. sev. works on the blood and its disorders, and dietary deficiency.

See F. M. Rackemann, *The Inquisitive Physician*, 1956.

Minot, Lawrence (*c*. 1300–52). Brit. poet. He wrote 11 songs celebrating the triumphs of Edward III. They are written in the Northumbrian dialect, with a sprinkling of Midland forms, and were first pub. by Joseph Ritson in 1795 under the title *Poems on Interesting Events in the Reign of King Edward III. See* ed. by J. Hall (3rd ed.), 1914, and T. Wright, *Political Poems and Songs*, 1859.

Minot, city of N. Dakota, U.S.A., in Ward Co., 100 m. NW. of Bismarck. It is a collecting centre for grain. Poultry, wheat, sausages and building materials are produced, and dairy produce is processed. It has a state teachers' college. Pop. 30,600.

Minotaur, fabulous monster, half bull, half man, *b*. to Pasiphaë, wife of Minos (q.v.), and kept by him in the labyrinth at Knossos, and fed

upon young men and maidens sent as yearly tribute from Athens (*see* THESEUS). Among the labyrinthine ruins of Knossos have been found Minoan wall-paintings of public acrobatics performed on bulls by young men and women. *See* L. Cottrell, *The Bull of Minos*, 1955.

Minsk (Belorussian **Mensk**): 1. Oblast (prov.) in central Belorussia, hilly in the NW., but largely lowland, and 38 per cent covered with pine and birch forests; there are large peat deposits. It has engineering, wood-working, food and light industries; coarse grain and potatoes are grown, and hogs and cattle are raised. The prin. tns are M., Borisov and Moladechno. Area 15,600 sq. m.; pop. (1965, excluding M. tn) 1,509,000 (24 per cent urb.), mostly Belorussian (before the Second World War many Jews).

2. Cap., economic and cultural centre of the above and of the Belorussian Rep. It has large and varied engineering (lorries, tractors, bicycles, machine tools, instruments), light and food industries. It is an important transportation centre (Moscow–Warsaw and Kharkov –Liepaja railways, airport). The Belorussian Academy of Sciences (founded in 1922 as the Institute of Belorussian Culture, transformed in 1929), a univ. (1921) and sev. other higher educational estabs. are situated here. Pop. *c*. 500,000 (1917, 153,000; 1920, 104,000; 1939, 239,000; 1948, 231,000), mostly Belorussians and Russians (before 1930's half Jewish). M. has been known since 1067, and belonged to Polotsk (q.v.); it became cap. of M. principality in 1101, and Lithuanian in 1326. Magdeburg Law (q.v.) was introduced in 1499. It was an important commercial and cultural centre of Lithuania, became Russian in 1793 (prov. cap.), and cap. of Belorussia in 1918. It was occupied by the Germans in 1918 and 1941–4, by Poles in 1920, and was largely destroyed during the Second World War. Industrial development began in the 1870's; it received new impetus in the 1930's and after 1945.

Minster (Lat. *monasterium*; Ger. *münster*), church attached to a monastery or forming part of it. The name is now applied in England to certain large churches or cathedrals, such as Westminster, Beverley and York.

Minster in Sheppey, tn and resort of Kent, England, in the is. of Sheppey, near the N. shore, an agric. area, and a residental dist. The anct abbey church was founded in 660 and dates from the 12th cent. Pop. 7,800.

Minster in Thanet, vil. of Kent, England, on the R. Stour, 6 m. W. of Ramsgate. It derives its name from the nunnery founded in the 7th cent. by King Egbert. There is a 12th cent. monastic grange, occupied since 1937 by Bavarian nuns; the par. church is Norman, with a dressed chalk vault. Agriculture is the chief occupation, cherries and lavender being especially cultivated. Pop. 2710.

Minstrels, itinerant musicians and poets akin to the Fr. *jongleurs*, fl. from the 10th to the 14th cents. The term was derived from the Lat. *minister*, a servant, since minstrels were employed as such by the troubadours and minne-singers, many of whom were of noble birth. Their duties consisted chiefly in playing accompaniments for their masters. The original word seems to have been *ménestrier*, a term introduced in the 14th cent. to denote a higher class of musical entertainer than the old *jongleur*, and out of this word grew the word *ménestrel* for a profession which had wide differences of social importance, ranging from humble wanderers to well-paid permanent servants of great nobles or of royalty. Both in England and on the Continent M.s formed themselves into guilds to protect their professional interests. Some of these guilds were still in existence in the 17th cent. *See* JONGLEURS; MEISTERSINGER; MUSIC; TROUBADOURS.

Mint (*Mentha*), large genus of aromatic plants (family Labiatae). Spearmint (*M. spicata*) is grown for its shoots and leaves which are utilised for culinary purposes. It can either be grown in the open garden in a moist rich soil and dried and stored for use, or it can be forced by placing the roots in boxes of rich soil in a temp. of about 60° F., and keeping moist. The Brit. species are variable, and hybridise with one another rather freely. Among those with the whorls crowded into terminal spikes are round-leaved M. with sessile wrinkled leaves; horse M., which is much more agreeably scented and has ovate leaves; and the very common hairy M. Corn M. and the marsh-whorled M. have the whorls of flowers separate and occurring in the axils of leafy bracts. The catmints form the genus *Nepeta*. *See* PEPPERMINT.

Mint. The twin pillars of the Brit. monetary system are the Bank of England and the Royal M. The bank furnishes the bank-notes and governs the quantity of bank-money; and M. manufs. and supplies the metal coin. About AD 1000 there were some 70 Eng. M.s, but following the Norman Conquest and the improvement of communications their number dwindled. M.s at Canterbury, Durham and York survived into Tudor times; and during the Civil war Charles I set up his own M.s at Oxford and elsewhere, while Parliament continued in London to manuf. and issue coin impressed with the royal head.

There were M.s in Britain before the Romans came, and from Rom. times onwards there was always a M. on Tower Hill. In the 10th cent. King Athelstan made this his prin. M. In 1811, in order to enjoy the advantages of steam-power, the M. was removed from the Tower to its present home on Tower Hill. Boulton, of the engineering firm of Boulton & Watt, was responsible for the installation. The building, on the site of a Cistercian abbey, was designed by John Johnson and erected by Sir Robert Smirke. The Tower M. had, in the 17th cent., installed screw-presses and other machinery like that already in use in France. The new equipment enabled the M. to give the now familiar milled edge which was to prove an effective handicap to the coin clipper. The 19th cent. saw the introduction of modern weighing machines and,

in the eighties, a large building extension and the installation of modern presses. In 1850 the M. was 'nationalised', and 1870 brought further changes; the Coinage Act of that year, besides consolidating the law regarding coinage, gave the title of Master of the M. to the chancellor of the exchequer and charge at the M. to a deputy-master and comptroller. Before nationalisation the work had been done under contract, with severe penalties for the issue of coin that failed to meet statutory requirements. Contracting was profitable, Sir Isaac Newton, who was master of the M. from 1699 to 1727, amassing a considerable fortune. Sir John Herschel was another famous master.

The prin. operations of coining are: (1) melting the assayed metal into a prescribed composition and casting it into bars of suitable size for making the particular coin; (2) rolling the bars into 'fillets' of coin thickness; although the rollers exert a pressure of many tons they have an accuracy of 1/10,000 in.; (3) cutting blank disks of due diameter and weight for the coin required; (4) annealing the blanks in gas furnaces; (5) blanching them in dilute acid to remove the oxide acquired in the furnace; (6) impressing the (cold) blanks with the authorised designs (and milled edge) in 70-ton presses capable of stamping upwards of 100 coins a min. The final process is 'telling' (counting) and packing for distribution to the banks. In 1947 the composition of the higher denomination coins was changed from silver to cupro-nickel and the processes of individually weighing and ringing the coins were discontinued. The silver coins minted before this date are being systematically withdrawn and replaced by cupro-nickel ones. Distribution for all coins is carried out by the Royal Mint direct to all banks. Up to the First World War the right of individuals to bring gold to the M. to be coined into sovereigns was, though little exercised, a notable feature of the gold standard. The restored gold standard (1925–31) did not restore gold coin. The M. supplies coin to the Commonwealth as well as to foreign countries. Medals, seals of State and revenue stamp plates are also made at the M. *See also* PYX, TRIAL OF THE; SOVEREIGN.

Minto, Gilbert Elliot, 1st Earl of (1751–1814), administrator, *b.* Edinburgh and educ. in Paris, Edinburgh and Oxford. He was called to the Bar in 1774, and entered Parliament in 1776 as a Whig. He was an associate of Burke, and took part in the impeachment of Warren Hastings (q.v.). In 1777 he succeeded to his father's baronetcy, and in 1798 was created Baron M.; he became Governor-General of India in 1807 and held that post with great ability. Returning home in 1813 he received an earldom.

Minto, Gilbert John Elliot-Murray-Kynyn-Mound, 4th Earl of (1847–1914), administrator. Educ. at Eton and Trinity College, Cambridge, he served 3 years in the Scots Guards. He was with the Turkish Army fighting Russia, 1877; with the British in Afghanistan, 1879; and a volunteer, 1882, at Tel-el-Kebir. Military secretary to Lord Lansdowne, Canada, 1883–5, he succeeded to the earldom, 1891. Governor-General, Canada, 1898–1904; he was Viceroy of India, 1905–10, his viceroyalty being notable for the Morley-Minto reforms (q.v.). *See* memoir by J. Buchan, 1924.

Mintoff, Dominic (1916–), Maltese politician, educ. at Malta and Oxford Univs. After working in England as a civil engineer, he returned to Malta in 1943 and from 1944 helped to reorganise the Maltese Labour party. From 1947 he was a member of the Legislative Assembly, deputy Prime Minister, and minister of works and reconstruction. In 1949 he resigned from the gov. In the same year he was elected Labour party leader. When his party won the general election in 1955, M. became Prime Minister. He approved the Brit. proposals for the integration of Malta into the U.K. (Dec. 1955), and in 1956 campaigned for the proposals in the national referendum. Subsequently M. bitterly criticised the Brit. gov.'s attitude towards Malta's economic problems and resigned the premiership in April 1958, since when he has led the prin. opposition.

Minton, Thomas (1765–1836), founded a pottery factory in 1796 at Stoke-on-Trent, after being apprenticed as an engraver for transfer-printing at Caughley (*see* WILLOW PATTERN), and working for Spode (q.v.). In 1798 he began making porcelain, but between 1811 and 1821 none was made. China-ware (q.v.) became the chief production under Herbert M., the founder's son (1792–1858), and a high standard has been maintained to the present day.

Minuet, one of the most widely known social dances throughout Europe during the later 17th and the 18th cents. Originating in France, said to have developed from the *branles* of Poitou and Anjou, the M. became a supremely elegant dance for a single couple. The *branle de Poitou*, or *de Mener*, from which it may have arisen, was one of the short dances in a set, or suite, of *branles* often used in the opening dances of a ball. The origin of the name is obscure, for the theory that it derives from the smallness of the steps is not borne out by the technical treatises of the 18th cent. Two features of the M. helped to popularise the dance; one being the characteristic step, which used 2 bars of moderate 3/4 time, the first, termed the 'cadence', being given greater stress than the second bar; the other feature being the uniform ground pattern used by the dances, known as the reversed S, or Z. This uniformity of step and figure made the M. simpler than most dances then in fashion, though its very simplicity necessitated great elegance of bearing and grace of movement. Towards the end of the 18th cent. its vogue declined, and the spurious M.s introduced to the stage and state balls by dancing masters of the late 19th cent. were based on forms of social dances then in use, and were totally unlike the true M. Many M. airs of the early 18th cent. were in 6/4 time, which enabled the complete M. step to be performed to 1 bar instead of 2.

The name M. is also applied to the musical composition written to the time and rhythm of the dance, introduced into their suites by Handel and Bach. Haydn regularly and Mozart usually had M.s in their symphonies and string quartets; other works in sonata form by them and by their contemporaries also frequently contained M.s. All these instrumental M.s are as a rule faster than those intended for dancing and thus point forward towards the scherzo (a term already used by Haydn in his Op. 33 string quartets) into which Beethoven developed the M.

Minuscules, small letters developed from anct uncial and cursive alphabets. Writing being used for business as well as literary purposes (apart from the monumental or lapidary character), 2 styles become distinct, the rapid cursive and the formal book-hand. In the 9th cent. the M. which had been gradually evolved during previous ages, practically superseded the uncial lettering for general use, though in scholastic and religious books much of the latter was retained. As time went on both Lat. and Gk M. became still smaller and more flowing. The blending of the Lat. majuscules and M. into combined service is due mainly to the Caroline or Carolingian script. Our present Eng. hand-writing is mainly founded on the It. 15th cent. style.

Minusinsk, tn in S. Siberia, in the Krasnoyarsk Kray, 170 m. S. of Krasnoyarsk, centre of the Minusinsk basin (q.v.). It is a riv. port on the Yenisey, with varied food industries. There is a rich local museum (founded 1877). M. was founded in 1822. Lenin spent 3 years of banishment in the nearby vil. of Shushenskoye. Pop. (1964) 40,000 (1926, 20,000).

Minusinsk Basin, triangular mt basin in S. Siberia, in the Krasnoyarsk Kray, S. of Krasnoyarsk. It lies at 750–2000 ft, the Kuznetsk Alatau and Sayan mt. ranges rising a further 4000 ft all round, and is traversed by the Yenisey. The climate is extremely continental and fairly dry; the vegetation W. of the Yenisey is steppe, E. of it wooded steppe. The M. B. is one of the main agric. areas of central and E. Siberia; grain is grown and cattle, sheep and horses raised. The Yenisey was virtually the only link with the outside world until 1927 when a railway was built from Achinsk on the Trans-Siberian line, and coal, gold-mining and forestry developed; in 1959, another railway connected M. B. with the Kuzbass, and iron-mining began; now, with the completion of the Abakan-Tayshet line, the area is on a major trunk route (the S. Siberian railway), and is expected to develop industrially. Many anct barrows are to be seen. Pop. Russian (since 18th cent.) and Khakas (q.v.).

Minute (Lat. *minutus*, small): 1. Of the time, being the sixtieth part of an hour.

2. Of an arc, being the sixtieth part of a degree in the measurement of a circle.

Minute Men, popular title for the soldiers of the militia during the Amer. War of Independence, and refers to their hasty preparation for war (at a minute's notice). The first contest of the war was between M. M. and Brit. troops, at Lexington. A modern adaptation of the term is

'Minuteman', the name given to an Amer. type intercontinental ballistic missile (long-range rocket)—indicating its instant readiness for action.

Minya, Al, administrative div. of Upper Egypt, with an area of 782 sq. m., drained by the Nile, A. M. is the cap., situated on the Nile midway between Siut and Beni-Suef. It has manufs. of earthenware and a gov. cotton factory. Pop. of div. 1,061,500; of tn 93,000 (1965).

Minyae, legendary Gk people originating in Thessaly, whence their eponymous ancestor Minyas migrated to Boeotia and founded the empire of the M. with its cap. at Orchomenus (q.v.). They were also believed to have settled in the is. of Lemnos and Thera, as well as in the S. of Elis. The legend may be an echo of the Dorian invasions (*see* DORIANS).

Miocene (Gk, 'less recent'), geological name for the middle div. of the Tertiary strata lying between the Oligocene and the Pliocene, and the geological period it represents. It contains fossils of living species in intermediate ratio (25 per cent., Lyell). There are no large deposits of this age in the Brit. Isles, but small beds are found at Bovey Tracey and in the Is. of Mull. Elsewhere they are widely distributed over the world. They consist of sandstones, gravels, clays; limestones, marls, clays and sands; and contain marine shells, mastodons, rhinoceroses, lions, apes, deinotheria, 3-toed horses, camels, beavers, tapirs, etc., conifers, beeches, oaks, maples, walnuts, poplars, magnolias, etc. The Oeningen beds in Switzerland have contributed largely to our knowledge. In 1948, on Rusinga Is. in Lake Victoria, part of the fossilised skull of a M. ape was found, the study of which suggested that apes developed from the monkey group. Limb bones found in the same region point to the fact that apes of the early M. had not an arboreal life. The period of formation, the *M. epoch,* was that of the final uplifting of the present great mt chains. The great earth movements which took place in S. Europe during the M. period were responsible for much of the elevation of the Alpine and Apennine mts. In Europe the formation is estuarine and lacustrine mainly, and indicates a configuration of shallow seas and large inlets very different from the present. The climate resembled that of India and Australia. Palms, magnolias, acacias, figs, evergreen oaks, were among the typical vegetation; insect life was larger and more varied. During this epoch Britain remained land subject to denudation, and the evidence of the removal of hundreds of feet of solid rock by this slow process gives some idea of the duration of the period. There are signs of a gradual cooling of the climate towards the present conditions, but the more tropical times are represented by beds of coal in Greenland and Spitsbergen. In Britain the chalk hills remain as evidence of the earth movements of the time.

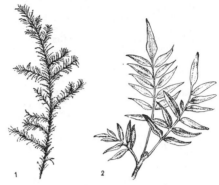

MIOCENE PLANT FOSSILS

1, *Sequoia haydeni*; 2, *Sapindus stellari folius* (soap-berry).

MIOCENE
Skull of an ape
(*Proconsul
africanus*).

Miquelon, is. off the S. coast of Newfoundland, forming with the adjacent is. of St Pierre (*see* ST PIERRE: 3) a Fr. ter with a total area of 93 sq. m. M. is divided into 2 parts, Grande M. and Petite M., connected by a narrow isthmus of sand. The inhab. are almost entirely occupied with fisheries since the is. is barren and rocky with only a little sparse vegetation. The cap. is the tn of St Pierre, on the is. of that name. The is. were ceded to Britain under the Treaty of Utrecht (1713), returned to France in 1763, captured by the British again in 1794, but given back to France under the Treaty of Ghent (1814). In the days of Amer. prohibition, they were used as a base by rum-runners. Pop. 550.

Mir, one of the names for the vil. com. in Russia before 1917. Existing at least since the 16th cent., the M. was a form of peasant self-gov. with considerable power over individual peasant households (e.g. collecting taxes and redistributing the land). Slavophiles (q.v.) and Populists (*see* POPULISM) considered M. a peculiarly Russian institution and wanted to perpetuate it. But the M. was a hindrance to the development of agriculture and Stolypin's (q.v.) reform enabling peasants to leave it (1906) was a boon.

Mir Turab Ali, *see* SALAR JUNG, SIR.

Mira (*o* Ceti), first variable star discovered (*see* CETUS).

Mirabaud, Jean Baptiste (1675–1760), Fr. writer *b.* Paris. He wrote *Alphabet de la fée gratieuse,* 1734, and various treatises, including *Le Monde, son origine et son antiquité* and *Opinions des ancients sur les Juifs* and trans. Ariosto's *Orlando furioso* and Tasso's *Gerusalemme liberata.*

Mirabeau, André Boniface Louis Riqueti, Vicomte de (1754–92), Fr. politician, brother of Honoré Gabriel M. (q.v.), joined the Fr. Army. He took part in the expedition which assisted the

Amer. revolution in 1781. In 1789 he became a deputy to the States-General, where as a reactionary he bitterly opposed his brother. His corpulence and drunken habits won him the name of Mirabeau Tonneau (the Barrel). He emigrated to Germany in 1790.

Mirabeau, Honoré Gabriel, Comte de Riqueti (1749–91), Fr statesman, *b.* Bignon, was a son of Victor, Marquis de M. (q.v.). After a stormy youth, during which his father sev. times procured *lettres de cachet* for his imprisonment, he eloped with Mme de Monnier, he himself being already married. After a brief stay in Switzerland the two went to Holland, where M. earned a living by literary work. Having replied to his father's denunciations with some violent libels, he was arrested and imprisoned at Vincennes for over 3 years. Here he wrote his famous *Letters to Sophie*. Later he visited England and Prussia. When the States-General were convened (1789), being rejected as a representative by the Provençal noblesse, he appealed to the people, and became a third estate deputy of Aix. Then came the great period of his career. His power with the people was immense, yet he sought to use it not to overthrow but to remodel the monarchy somewhat on Eng. lines. But his health was already failing, and he could not win the confidence of the king he was trying to save. When he *d.* his position was already being threatened by the extremists.

A collection of his *œuvres oratoires* was pub. in 1819. Besides these there are many letters, among them *Lettres originales écrites du donjon de Vincennes* and the *Lettre de Mirabeau à un de ses amis en Allemagne, See* C. W. Warwick, *Mirabeau and the French Revolution*; 1905, and Antonina Vallentin, *Mirabeau: Voice of the Revolution*, 1949; *also* lives by H. de Jouvenel, 1930, and P. Nezelof, 1937.

Mirabeau, Victor Riqueti, Marquis de (1715–89), Fr. political economist, *b.* Pertuis in Provence. As an author his *Théorie de l'impôt* brought him a term of imprisonment, and afterwards seclusion on his estate, but continuing to write he founded a school of political economy. His health and fortune were finally ruined by constant family quarrels and lawsuits.

Mirabilis, genus of perennial plants (family Nyctaginaceae). *M. jalapa* is the Marvel of Peru, a fragrant garden plant with flowers of various colours, grown like dahlias.

Miracle Play, term used in England for the plays dealing with scriptural and sacred subjects from about the 13th cent. to the end of the 16th cent. In France the term miracle was restricted to dramas dealing with the lives of the saints, while the scriptural plays were known as 'mysteries'. The origin of the M. P. must be sought in the dramatic representations of the great events of the Christian year rendered liturgically in churches, especially at Christmas and Easter. The earliest example we have of such a liturgical drama dates from the year 967 (*see* J. M. Manly, *Specimens of pre-Shakespearian Drama*, 1900–3), and from this time the development is steady, blending both Norman and Saxon lines of growth. The stagecraft of the church dialogues became more and more elaborate, until they had to pass into the open. Here the clerical element diminished, and lay actors took the place of priests and cantors. During the 11th and 12th cents. the M. P.s passed into the monastery schools for teaching purposes. Originally all these plays were in Latin, and were dedicated to St Nicholas, the patron of youth, but in the 12th cent. they were interspersed with French. The institution of the festival of Corpus Christi in 1264, though not commonly observed in England till a good many years later, gave a great impulse to pageantry, and the great 'cycles' of plays are nearly all connected with this feast. The 'cycle' consisted of a series of plays dealing with events from the Creation onwards, and each play was acted on a 'pageant' or stage of 2 storeys on wheels, which was dragged from place to place for the repetition of the drama. There are 4 main cycles extant, all showing traces of continuous reaction. The York cycle (15th-cent. MS.) consists of 49 plays, the Wakefield or Townley plays (MS. 1450) are 32 in number, the Chester cycle (MS. 1475) has 25, to be acted not at Corpus Christi but at Whitsuntide. The Coventry cycle (with 42 plays) dates from the latter half of the 15th cent. The plays were acted by the city companies, each company or guild being responsible for the production and acting of 1 play. The miracles are marked by considerable dramatic skill, and show in a somewhat undeveloped form the treatment of all the main dramatic motives. A particular feature is their realism. *See* A. W. Pollard, *English Miracle Plays, Moralities and Interludes*, 1895; E. K. Chambers, *The Medieval Stage*, 1903; E. H. Moore, *English Miracle Plays*, 1907; A. C. Cawley (ed.), *Everyman and Medieval Miracle Plays*, 1956.

Miracles. (Lat. *miraculum*, object of wonder. Gk *thauma*; whence 'thaumaturge', wonderworker). St Thomas Aquinas defines a miracle as 'a happening outside the order of all created nature; therefore', he says, 'God alone can work miracles by His own proper power, since He alone is not a creature'. In the early and Middle Ages M. were considered as the most cogent proof possible of the truth of Christianity. More recently, however, what used to be a strong argument for Christian faith became one of the chief obstacles to its acceptance, and there came into being a school of apologists who tried to remove the element of mystery and the miraculous from religion. Spinoza (q.v.) was the first in modern times to make a vigorous attack on the credibility of M. He states that 'nothing happens in nature which is in contradiction with its universal laws', and thence, since M. *are* a violation of the laws of nature, he argues that they cannot happen. The logical force of this argument is vitiated by the initial presupposition that 'nature' does not include non-material agencies and entities, which is really the point at issue. The Eng. deists (q.v.) also denied the possibility of M. Hume appeals to the 'firm and unalterable experience' which has estab. the laws of nature, and goes on: 'The consequence is that no testimony is sufficient to establish a miracle, unless the testimony be of such a kind that its falsehood would be more miraculous than the fact which it endeavours to establish'. Here again the point in question is taken for granted. Strauss attempted to explain the N.T. M. as myths growing up in the minds of the disciples in accordance with their preconceived notions of the Messiah. Modern science, however, is no longer as deterministic as it was. A principle of indeterminism has been discovered in minute particles. The literature of the subject is enormous. *See* especially writings of Hume, Pascal, Butler, Paley, Trench, Newman and Illingworth. *See also* J. M. Thompson, *Miracles in the New Testament*, 1911; E. O. Davies, *The Miracles of Jesus*, 1913; A. Richardson, *Miracle Stories of the Bible*, 1943; C. S. Lewis, *Miracles*, 1947.

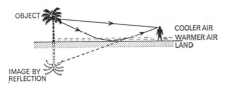

FIG. 1. COMMON MIRAGE

Mirage, name given to various phenomena due to reflection and refraction of light in unusual states of the atmosphere; commonest and most striking in regions of calm subjected to great heat or cold e.g. hot and cold deserts and polar regions. Generally speaking, 2 strata of different densities lying steadily one over the other give rise to 2 images, one direct and usual, the other an inverted reflection from the surface of contact. Thus clouds may be reflected from a thin stratum of dense air on the sand of deserts at sunset and after, giving the appearance of water; the convectional currents of air give a shimmering or wavy appearance, thus adding to the illusion. At the sea the layer of air on the water may in calm weather remain warmer for some height, giving an inverted reflection from above of ships below the horizon. In the early morning the latter effect occurs over deserts, the former at sea. It is quite possible to find M.s over roads in England by placing the eye a few inches above the ground, e.g. in calm, hot weather, when the air is quivering. *Looming* is a form of M.; the object appears nearer and larger; it is well known at sea, when objects below the horizon are yet visible. Special instances are the 'Spectre of the Brocken' and the 'Fata Morgana' (q.v.). Owing to the rays of light coming over great distances, and the variation in density being gradual, they are curved, and the image will be seen along the tangent of the ray at the eye; this accounts for the displacement.

Miramichi, riv. of Canada, rising in New Brunswick. Its course of 220 m. is generally NE. It discharges into Miramichi Bay in the Gulf of St Lawrence. The port of Chatham (q.v.) stands

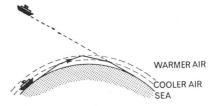

FIG. 2. EXAGGERATED DIAGRAM OF LOOMING

at its mouth, and in the upper part of the riv. much salmon and trout fishing is carried on.

Miranda or **Sá de Miranda, Francisco de** (*c.* 1490–1558), one of the earliest Portuguese poets, studied law at Lisbon. He wrote in the 'It. style' (using the metres of Dante and Petrarch), but mainly in Castilian. His poetical epistles and eclogues are his most noted works. He upholds the poetical ideal of an old and feudal Portugal before the rising of the mercantile society of the Discoveries. He also wrote lyrics, sonnets and 2 comedies.

Miranda, Sebastián Francisco de (1750–1816), Venezuelan patriot and general, b. Caracas. He accompanied Bernado Gálvez, Sp. governor of Louisiana, in the expedition against the English in Pensacola. When the Fr. Revolution broke out he became a general in the Fr. Army and, under Dumouriez, fought in the campaign against the Prussians which culminated in the battle of Valmy (1792). He besieged and captured Antwerp and, in the absence of Dumouriez, acted as commander-in-chief of the Fr. armies. At Neerwinden he was forced to retire, was arrested and tried before a revolutionary tribunal in Paris, but was absolved and later fled to England, where he resumed his activities on behalf of the independence of Lat. America. In 1805 he fitted out a ship, the *Leander*, and in 1806 set sail for the Caribbean in the hope of founding an independent state to be called Colombia. But he failed to gain expected support from Jefferson, who, having just purchased the Louisiana Ter., had no wish to quarrel with Spain. When the *Leander* and its crew reached Venezuela M. found the coast-guards ready with cannon to resist him and he was obliged to return to London. M. later sailed to Caracas, where he was met by Bolívar, and marched against the Spaniards. He was defeated at Puerto Cabello and forced to sign a treaty yielding the country to the Sp. royalists (1812). M. himself was finally taken to Cádiz, where he d. after more than 3 years' incarceration in the Caracas prison. Though he failed in his life's purpose, he was the intellectual father of the revolution which was eventually undertaken successfully by Bolívar. *See* W. S. Robertson, *Francisco de Miranda and the Revolutionizing of Spanish America*, 1908, and *The Life of Miranda*, 1930; *Archivo del General Miranda* (Caracas) (15 vols.), 1929–38; J. N. Sardi, *Aventura y tragedia de Don Francisco Miranda*, 1935.

Miranda, maritime state of N. Venezuela, on

the Caribbean. Coffee is extensively grown, and minerals await development. Los Teques is the cap. Area 3070 sq. m.; pop. 492,349.

Mirandola, Giovanni Pico, Count Della, *see* PICO DELLA MIRANDOLA.

Mirbeau, Octave Henri Marie (1850–1917), Fr. writer, *b.* Trevières (Calvados). Among his better known novels, naturalistic in style, are *Le Calvaire*, 1886, *L'Abbé*, 1888, *Le Jardin des supplices*, 1899, *Le Journal d'une femme de chambre*, 1900, *Les Vingt-et-un Jours d'un neurasthénique*, 1901, *Dans l'Antichambre*, 1905, and *Dingo*, 1913. Plays: *Les Mauvais Bergers* (depicting the struggle between capital and labour), 1897, and *Les Affaires sont les affaires* (a vigorous social play), 1903. *See* life by M. Renon, 1924.

Mircea (1386–1418), Prince of Wallachia. He was defeated in 1390 by invading Turks. He defeated the next invasion, 1394, but had to flee the country. He returned with Sigismund of Hungary and in spite of the defeat of the crusade (Nicopolis, 1396) regained his throne. In 1417 he was finally forced to acknowledge Turkish suzerainty and surrender the Dobrudja.

Mirfield, urb. dist of W. Riding of Yorks, England, on the R. Calder, 4½ m. NE. of Huddersfield. James Montgomery worked at M. as a boy, and the Brontë sisters were at school here. There are malting works and the chief manufs. are blankets, carpets and cloth. The Community of the Resurrection, an Anglican theological college, founded in 1892 at Pusey House by Charles Gore, was moved to M. in 1898. St Peter's College, Roe Head, is a junior seminary for the Verona Fathers, a missionary order founded 1872. Pop. 12,294.

Miri, seaport of Sarawak, with an open-sea anchorage. The area is an important oilfield, and there are exports of petroleum. Pop. 13,500.

Mirnyy, tn (unt'. 1959 a vil.) in the Vilyui R. basin, in the Yakut Autonomous Rep. of E. Siberia (lat. 62° 30′ N., 113° 50′ E.). It has grown up since 1956 as the centre of newly-discovered diamond fields. Pop. (1964) 17,000 (1959, 5700).

Miro, Joan (1899–), Sp. painter, *b.* Montroig, Barcelona. He settled in Paris, 1919, attracted by the Cubism of his compatriot Picasso. Later, influenced by Surrealism, he developed a gaily coloured 'sign language'. *See* C. Greenberg, *Joan Miro*, 1948.

Mirror (Fr. *miroir*), optical instrument of glass or metal, having a polished surface to reflect images. The use of M.s is very anct; they were known in the Early Iron Age, being then mostly thin plates of polished metal. Under the Caesars silver M.s were common. The back of the M. was often handsomely adorned with chasing or repoussé. In the Middle Ages steel, silver and glass M.s were much used, the glass being backed with metal, especially lead. Modern silvered M.s were first known as *Venetian*, having been first made on a large scale at Murano. They were first manuf. in England in the 17th cent.

Mirs Bay, opening on the S. coast of China, E. of Hong Kong. Length 140 m., breadth 60 m.

Great Britain leased the S. shore in 1898 for 99 years.

Mirzapur, tn of Uttar Pradesh state, India, on the r. b. of the Ganges, 30 m. from Benares. The tn is noted for its carpets, rugs and brassware. It is also a centre for the preparation of shellac.

Mis Tor, Great and **Little,** are 2 hills of Devon, England, in Dartmoor (q.v.) forest, 16 m. ESE. of Launceston. The former reaches a height of 1767 ft, and the latter 1600 ft. Here is the 'Devil's Frying Pan'.

Misamis: 1. Misamis Occidental, prov. in W. Mindanao, Philippine Is. The terrain is mountainous. Coco-nuts and corn are grown along the coast. Pop. *c.* 209,000.

2. Misamis Oriental, prov. of the N. coast of Mindanao, Philippine Is., including Camiguin Is. Its irregular coastline contains Ilgán Bay. There is much mt and forest land. Coco-nuts and corn are grown and fishing is carried on. Chromite is found here. The population is *c.* 370,000.

Misappropriation. The M. of property by any person who has been entrusted (solely or jointly with another) with or has received such property either for safe custody, or that he may apply, pay, or deliver the property or its proceeds for a particular purpose, or to a particular person, is a misdemeanour, punishable with imprisonment up to 7 years (Larceny Act 1901, replacing analogous sections in the Act of 1861). Bankers, merchants, brokers and agents guilty of M. are affected by this Act, while M. by trustees on an express trust created by deed or will, or by mortgages, or by factors or agents generally, is similarly punishable under the Larceny Act of 1861 (*see also* LARCENY). It is difficult to see on what principle M. by the above kinds of bailees should be only a misdemeanour, while embezzlement by clerks or servants, i.e. persons usually much lower in the social scale, should be a felony, punishable with imprisonment up to 14 years. *See* EMBEZZLEMENT.

Miscarriage, *see* ABORTION.

Misdemeanour, *see* CRIMINAL LAW.

Miseno, Capo (anct **Misenum Promontorium**), promontory of Campania (q.v.), Italy, at the NW. extremity of the Bay of Naples. Under the Rom. republic M. was a villa resort; but in 31 BC it became the chief station of the Mediterranean fleet and remained so under the empire. The Saracens destroyed the tn in 890.

Miserere, (Lat. *misericordia*, mercy), name under which Psalm li. (Vulg. l) is commonly known. Four psalms commence with the words *M. mei Deus*, but the pre-eminence of this psalm has led to the name being appropriated to it. M. is the greatest of the penitential psalms, and tradition states that it was called forth by the prophet Nathan's announcement to David of his sin.

Misericord (or **Miserere**), term applied to various relaxations of strict monastic rule. It is used particularly of a small ledge under the seats in the choir, which, when the seat was turned up, formed a projection on which the monk could rest when standing. The underside of this ledge is

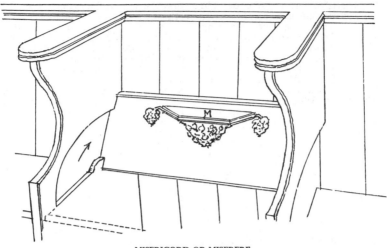

MISERICORD OR MISERERE
One seat is tipped back to expose the misericord (M) beneath.

often richly covered with grotesque or humorous subjects.

Misericordia, or **Brethren of Mercy,** most famous of the confraternities formed in Florence in 1244 for the seemly burial of the destitute. During the plague of 1348–9 they performed valuable work. The members, when on duty, wear a dress covering all but the eyes. Their work now embraces the duties of an ambulance corps.

Mishawaka, city in Indiana, U.S.A., on St Joseph R. near S. Bend. It manufs. clothing, rubber and plastic goods, metal products, power transmission units, etc. Pop. c. 35,000.

Mishna, traditional commentary on the written Heb. Law, handed down orally until about the beginning of the third cent. AD, when it was committed to writing. The M. consists chiefly of the discussions and decisions of the scribes and rabbis between c. 200 BC and the above date. After AD 200 discussion of the Law and the M. continued in the schools both of Babylon and of Palestine. These further discussions constitute the *Gemara*, which, with the M., form the Talmud (q.v.). *See* P. Blackman (editor), *Mishna: In Hebrew and English,* 7 vols., 1964.

Misiones, prov. of NE. Argentina, bordered by Paraguay in the W. and Brazil in the E. It also lies between 2 major rivs. the Alto Paraná in the W. and the Uruguay in the E. (the rivs. in fact being national frontiers). Most of the prov. is on fairly high ground (maximum about 2000 ft) and is densely forested. The rainfall is plentiful with no dry season, and the climate is hot and humid. About 90 per cent of Argentina's yerba maté (Paraguayan tea) is grown in M. Timber and tung oil are important products, together with tobacco, citrus fruits, rice and sugarcane. M. derives its name from its settlement in 17th cent. by Jesuit missionaries. Posadas is the cap. Area 11,506 sq. m.; pop. 391,000.

Misiones, Las, dept in S. Paraguay bordering the R. Paraná. The low-lying country is best-suited to cattle raising, though maize, sugar and rice are also grown. Some yerba maté is also produced. As the name implies the area was settled by Jesuit missionaries in the 17th and 18th cents. San Juan Bautista is the cap. Area 3024 sq. m.; pop. about 60,000.

Miskolc (formerly **Miskolcz**), city of NE. Hungary, cap. of the co. of Borsod-Abauj-Zemplén, on the Sajó, 90 m. NE. of Budapest (q.v.). It is the second city of the country, and stands in a valley at the E. foot of the Bükk hills. There is a notable 15th cent. church (restored 16th cent.). In the heart of the tn is the Avas hill (770 ft), which is honeycombed with wine-cellars. M. has a large technical college (1949), and has metallurgical, chemical, cement and other industries. It has an airfield. Pop. 159,800. *See* DIÓSGYÖR.

Mispickel, obsolete name for the mineral **Arsenopyrite,** from which arsenic is prepared by roasting, air being excluded; it is crystalline, orthorhombic, steel-grey and hard; chemically, FeSAs. M. is chiefly obtained commercially from U.S.A. and Germany.

Misprision (literally, neglect or contempt) means concealment of a crime in the sense of keeping one's knowledge of its commission to oneself without participation in it as principal or accessory. M. of treason was formerly, but is not now, regarded as equivalent to the full offence. *See* CRIMINAL LAW.

Misrepresentation, *see* CONTRACT.

Misrule, Abbot or **Lord of,** *see* LORD OF MISRULE and REVELS, MASTER OF THE.

Missal, book containing the prayers and rubrics for the celebration of mass (q.v.) throughout the year. The text of the mass consists of an invariable framework known as the Ordinary, and a large number of prayers, etc., which change throughout the year.

Formerly these variable portions were found in separate vols., e.g. the *Antiphonarium, Graduale, Epistolarium*, etc. The process of combining them into one vol. became general probably *c.* AD 900. At the Reformation the Anglican Prayer Book, 1549, superseded the old Sarum M. The Rom. M., revised in 1884, is universal in W. Catholicism, save for local Ambrosian, Mozarabic and various monastic rites.

Missel Thrush, Mistletoe Thrush, or **Holm Thrush** (*Turdus viscivorus*), common bird throughout England and most European countries. The male is 11 in. long, and is the largest of Brit. thrushes and also of Brit. song-birds. Its colour is greyer than the song-thrush, and in flight a white tail feather is shown upon each thigh. The song is not so varied and melodious as that of the song-thrush. The eggs are bluish-white, spotted with purplish-brown. The food consists principally of berries (particularly those of the mistletoe) and insects. It is sometimes called the storm cock.

Missenden, Great, vil. of Buckinghamshire, England, 31 m. from London, and a popular residential dist. Here is M. Abbey, founded 1133 by Sir Wm de Missenden, dissolved in 1538. The building, restored in 19th cent. Gothic, is now a college for adult education. The par. church is 13th cent. Pop. 5737.

Missi Dominici, supreme court of the Frankish kings. The system of M. D. is said to have been introduced by Charlemagne who appointed them to act as a court of appeal from the courts of the Crown vassals. The M. D. were also sent round the kingdom in Charlemagne's time in order to report on the state of the various dists, to investigate grievances and to proclaim the emperor's decrees.

Missiles, *see* ROCKETS; SPACE TRAVEL.

Missing Link, *see* DARWINISM; EVOLUTION; MAN.

Mission, foreign legation, or, collectively, the members of an embassy. Secretaries and attachés are not, as a rule, employed in the same M. or embassy for more than 2 years. The duration of the appointments of heads of M.s at foreign courts may not exceed 5 years, at the end of which the appointment may be renewed by the foreign secretary. Members of M.s retire at 70 years of age. The chief of a M. is styled in the Foreign Office regulations 'minister', whether his official title be that of ambas., minister or *chargé d'affaires.*

Missions: 1. *Roman Catholic.* The command laid by Jesus Christ on His Apostles to 'go and teach all nations' was carried out by them first of all among the Jews of the Diaspora. The outstanding name in this work is St Paul, whose travels through Asia Minor to Rome, and whose projected journey into Spain, are described in the Acts of the Apostles and in his own Epistles. Without citing any authority other than the N.T., we can record missionary work in the 1st cent. in Palestine, Syria, Asia Minor, Greece, Macedonia, Italy and Spain. Britain received the missionaries in the 2nd or 3rd cent., but Christianity did not survive the Rom. with-

drawal except in Wales and the W. The 4th and 5th cents. saw a flourishing Church estab. along the N. coast of Africa, with the great Athanasius as Bishop of Alexandria in the 4th, and the even greater Augustine as Bishop of Hippo in the 5th cent. This same 5th cent. was signalised by the name of St Patrick, whose contest with Druidism before he estab. the faith in Ireland is well known. The end of the 6th cent. saw the dispatch by Pope Gregory the Great of St Augustine to England, where the sees of Canterbury, York, Rochester, and London were estab. About 100 years later, so firmly had the faith taken root in England that the English started themselves to take up missionary work. It was St Willibrord who opened the campaign with an expedition, in which he was the leader of 11 other missionaries, to evangelise Holland in the year 691; Willibrord estab. his see at Utrecht as Archbishop of the Frisians. Following on the heels of Willibrord came Winfrid of Devon, or, as he was later called, Boniface. St Boniface has been called by some the greatest missionary after St Paul; the field of his labour was Germany. He was murdered by pagans in 754, and buried in his own monastery at Fulda. The Ger. bishops still hold their ann. meeting at the tomb of their great Eng. apostle. Both Willibrord and Boniface were Benedictine monks. So also was St Ansgar of Picardy, who, in the 9th cent., set out to work in Scandinavia; for 40 years he preached and taught in Denmark and Sweden, with his see at Hamburg. The same cent. saw the work of the 2 Gk brothers, Cyril and Methodius, amongst the Slavs of Bohemia, Moravia and Pannonia. The same cent., yet again, seems to have marked the beginnings of widespread Christian missionary work in Russia; this was carried out not by W. missionaries but from the E. This first great wave of missionary activity had largely spent itself by the end of the 11th cent. The friars were busy in the E. during the 13th and 14th cents., with the name of John of Montecorvino, a Franciscan, outstanding. John, accompanied by the Dominican Nicholas of Pistoia, travelled to Persia and thence to India; when Nicholas *d.* John pushed on alone and reached Peking, where he *d.* in 1328.

The second great missionary impetus coincided with the voyages of discovery made by the Portuguese and Spanish in the 16th and 17th cents. As the Benedictines were outstanding in the 8th and 9th cents., so now the Jesuits take the centre of the stage. St Francis Xavier, in 11 years, converted thousands to Christianity in India, Ceylon, Malaya and Japan; he *d.* in 1552. Matteo Ricci, another Jesuit, is famous for his work in China, where he understood better than any the importance of adapting his W. outlook to his E. environment; the Chinese gave him a state funeral in 1610. Yet another Jesuit priest was John Brebeuf, who worked among the Hurons of N. America and was put to death by the Iroquois in 1649. In S. America, in the same cent., the name of the Franciscan St Francis Solano is the most illustrious missionary name, though any account of S. America would be utterly incomplete without the story of the Jesuits' work in Paraguay, which started in 1582 and was continued till 1767 and, in 1955, was the subject of Fritz Hochwalder's play *The Strong are Lonely*. The 17th cent., again, which saw the beginning of the first purely missionary societies in the Church with the foundation of the *Missions Étrangères de Paris*, saw also the foundation in Rome of the Congregation *de Propaganda Fide*, commonly called simply *Propaganda*, which was to be the Church's foreign missionary H.Q. From now on these missionary societies will multiply, with women forming their own societies to work alongside the men. The *Holy Ghost Fathers* go back to 1703, owing their first beginning to a Frenchman and their present formation to a convert Jew, Francis Libermann; their H.Q. are in Paris and they work mainly in Africa. England's *St Joseph's Missionary Society* was started by Father Herbert Vaughan, later Cardinal Archbishop, in 1866, with H.Q. at Mill Hill; Africa, India, Borneo and the Philippines are their field. The following year, 1867, brought to birth the Italian foundation, by Bishop Comboni, of the *Verona Fathers* who (until the expulsion of foreign missionaries in 1964) worked largely in the Sudan; the year after, 1868, found Cardinal Lavigerie, a Frenchman, setting up the supranational society known as the *White Fathers* for work in Africa. Seven years later, in 1875, Arnold Janssen founded at Steyl, in S. Holland, the *Society of the Divine Word*, which inside 4 years was sending missionaries to China; Belgium has its powerful organisation in the *Scheut Fathers*, with H.Q. in Brussels and heavy commitments in the Far E.; America has the *Maryknoll Fathers*, founded in New York in the present cent., and likewise at work in the Far E. In Ireland we have the famous *Maynooth Mission to China*. The *Marist Fathers* have done great work in Oceania and the *Missionaries of the Sacred Heart* (French foundation) in Australia. There are numerous societies of nuns, chief of whom are the *Franciscan Missionaries of Mary*, and the *Medical Mission Sisters*. The position in the middle of the 20th cent. is that there are, in the Rom. Catholic foreign missionary countries, approximately 45 million Rom. Catholics, 22,000 missionary and 9000 native priests, some 16,000 brothers and 83,000 sisters all told. A detailed conspectus of the work can be seen at the Eng. H.Q. of the *Papal Mission-Aid Societies* at 23 Eccleston Square, London, S.W.1.

(2) *Anglican and Free Church*. The reformation and post-reformation period was also one of exploration and colonialisation. Some of the first Anglican communities abroad were those served by chaplaincies from England. America was thus one of the first places where Protestant mission work began. The first missionary society was the Corporation for the Propagation of the Gospel in New England founded by the Long Parliament in 1649. John Eliot, translator of the Bible into the Red Indian language, was its first missionary. William Penn

took the Society of Friends (q.v.) to America as well. At the turn of the 17th cent. came the foundation, under the inspiration of the Rev. Thomas Bray, of the Society for Promoting Christian Knowledge (1698) and the Society for the Propagation of the Gospel in Foreign Parts (1701). The Moravian Movement founded in 1772 has always played a great part in world evangelism. John Wesley, who went to America as an Anglican missionary, was profoundly influenced by the Moravians and out of this sprang the great Evangelical Revival of the 18th cent. This revival inspired many people to offer themselves as missionaries and led to the founding of many missionary societies. The most notable of these were: the Baptist Missionary Society (1792); the London Missionary Society (1795)—a pioneer in inter-denominational work; the Church Missionary Society 1799—Anglican, though some of its first missionaries were Ger. Lutherans; the Methodist Missionary Society (1813); and the Brit. and Foreign Bible Society (1804)—another interdenominational society whose work was, and still is, the supplying of the Scriptures in many languages.

In the 19th cent. missionary expansion from Britain grew fast, partly as a result of Brit. colonial policy: the Churches in Britain estab. themselves in many parts of the world, but notably, during this cent., in Africa and Asia. To the societies already at work were added those which specialised in a certain class of people (e.g. seamen, Jews, lepers) or in a geographical area (e.g. China Inland Mission, Ruanda Mission, Univ. Mission to Central Africa). A great deal of mission work has been conducted through medical work and education: this has been a major factor in helping the peoples of Africa and Asia to gain their own independence.

One major difficulty of the Protestant missions has been the conflict caused by the divs. of Christendom. To discuss this problem a Missionary Conference was convened at Edinburgh in 1910, which is now regarded as the first significant step in the modern ecumenical movement. The immediate results were the formation of the Conference of the Brit. Missionary Societies and the International Missionary Council (I.M.C.). The pressure for united Churches followed on from this. The first united Church involving Churches from the Brit. Isles was the Church of S. India (1947), and other united Churches will be inaugurated in the next few years. The World Council of Churches came into existence in 1948 and in 1961 united with the I.M.C., forming a strong body concerned with the mission and unity of the Churches throughout the world.

The various Churches founded from Britain have now in most cases become independent and autonomous, while still receiving help from the Churches in these is. The leadership of the Churches is also mainly in the hands of nationals. Another major development is the changing methods of mission now being developed to help to face a new situation; industrial missions, the use of radio, the development of agric. work, lay training colleges and study centres for the study of and encounter with other religions are the most notable of these. While the Church does not claim the majority of the world pop. as members it is estab. in most places and playing a great part in the life of new nations, and adapting itself to new situations. *See* N. Goodall, *The Ecumenical Movement*, 1964; S. Neill, *A History of Christian Missions*, 1964; M. Warren, *The Missionary Movement from Britain in Modern History*, 1965. Most missionary societies pub. magazines and information about their own work.

Mississippi, the Magnolia State, S. central state of the U.S.A., bounded on the N. by Tennessee, on the S. by the Gulf of Mexico and Louisiana, on the E. by Alabama, and on the W. by the Riv. M. The surface is one of low plains, but varied in type. The alluvial slot of the M. valley (the 'bottomlands') is liable to flood but is immensely rich in cotton production. The delta coast of the SW. is swampy but produces rice and sugar. Away from the riv., in the E. and NE. of the state are low, dissected hills, largely a poor and sterile region of low standards of living. Here cotton cultivation is giving way to a more varied agriculture. On the uplands and bluffs, pine, oak, walnut and magnolia trees abound, but in the sandy S. dists pine trees alone are plentiful. In fact one-third of the state is forest, chiefly yellow pine, on which large lumber and paper manufs. depend. The chief rivs. are the M, the Yazoo, the Big Black, the Pearl and the Pascagoula. The climate is nearly subtropical, though frosts occur in severe winters even in the S. The soil is, on the whole, extremely fertile, and agriculture is a very important industry; the state is among the first 4 cotton-growing states in the Union. Maize, rice, wheat, rye and oats are also grown in large quantities, and the sugar-cane is cultivated in the S. part of the state. The prin. vegetable is the sweet potato, but the common potato, peas and beans, and most of the vegetables known to European countries, are also grown. Plums, peaches, figs and oranges are abundant. Agric. in M. is now passing through a revolution with the mechanisation of cotton farming and the replacement of the Negro share-cropper by a 'neo-plantation' worked mechanically. Manufs. now equal in value the agric. products, and among the chief are lumber and timber, turpentine and resin, cotton-seed oil and cake, cotton goods and fertilisers.

M. was settled in 1716, and ceded by the Fr. to Great Britain in 1763; in 1798 it was organised as the ter. of the M. In 1817 the ter. of Alabama was organised from the M. ter., and in the same year M. was admitted to the Union. There is a Senate of 49 members, and a House of Representatives of 140. M. sends 2 senators and 7 representatives to Congress. Area 47,716 sq. m. Pop. 2,178,140 of whom 49 per cent are Negroes. Chief cities: Jackson (cap.), 144,420; Meridian, 49,370; Biloxi, 44,050. *See* pub. of the M. Historical Society (19 vols.); *Encyclopaedia of Mississippi History, 1540–1907*, 1907; D. Rowland, *History*

of Mississippi, 1925; Federal Writers' Project. *Mississippi: Guide to the Magnolia State*, 1938; J. K. Bettersworth, *Mississippi, A History*, 1959. (*See Plate*.)

Mississippi River, most important riv. of N. America, rises in the state of Minnesota in the basin of Lake Itasca, and flows into the Gulf of Mexico. It is, with the Missouri, its chief trib., the longest riv. in the world (4818 m.) and drains an area of about 1,250,000 sq. m. Some authorities derive the name from the Chippe-wayan (q.v.) *missi*, big; *sipi*, riv. Altogether the M. has 42 trib. streams, and the navigable mileage is 12,798. Its chief tribs. are, on the E., the Wisconsin, Illinois, Ohio and Yazoo; and on the W. the Minnesota, Des Moines, Missouri, St Francis, White, Arkansas and Red R.s. It is still important commercially for coal and oil trans-port, although a good deal of its traffic has been diverted to the railways, and has on its banks many important tns: St Paul, La Crosse, Prairie du Chien, Dubuque, Burlington, Quincey on the upper riv., i.e. above the mouth of the Missouri; and St Louis, Cairo, Memphis, Vicksburg, Natchez, Baton-Rouge and New Orleans on the main riv. A great disadvantage is the frequent occurrence of floods. Great damage was done by floods in 1927, and 10 years later almost the worst floods in the hist. of the continent occurred through the overflowing of the M. and the Ohio. A million persons were made homeless, and the entire pop. of the M. valley between Cairo and New Orleans had to be evacuated. But the floods of 1947 broke every flood record since 1844. The course is contained within artificial banks or levees. Many of them were raised by the Federal Gov. in 1936 as part of the New Deal (q.v.); but there are some sections protected by smaller, weaker dykes, and it was these that gave trouble in 1947. Over 100,000 ac. were flooded, and the damage was estimated at more than £3,000,000. Now 'flood-ways' (broad channels kept free of settlement) have been built to take peak flow.

The actual discovery of the M. was made by a Fr. missionary, Jacques Marquette. The Comte de Frontenac, then governing Canada in the name of Louis XIV, sent out Marquette to ascertain whether the riv. really existed. Early in 1673 Marquette, with a few men, proceeded westward from Quebec along the Great Lakes, made his way SW. and S., and discovered the M. on 17 May. Robert Cavelier de La Salle (q.v.) sought permission of Frontenac to undertake the conquest of the riv. and its region. Frontenac sent La Salle to France where the king gave full authorisation to carry out the expedition. With Father Marquette and an Italian named Tonti and a party of 23 Frenchmen, 20 Indians and 10 Indian women, La Salle travelled across the lakes and began the descent of the riv. The party reached the point where in the 16th cent. Hernando de Soto had abandoned the attempt to explore the riv. Eventually the party reached the Gulf of Mexico. La Salle took possession of the riv. and its region for France. Back in France La Salle was honoured by the king, and a second expedition was fitted out. On the return trip, however, La Salle tried to enter through the Gulf of Mexico, but was unable to find the riv.'s mouth. The captain of the fleet, growing impatient, sailed away without its leader. La Salle advanced into Texas, a small group accompanying him, and there he fell victim to an assassin's dagger. It was the destiny of the 3 discoverers, de Soto, Marquette and La Salle, to die obscure deaths just as they had the prize within their grasp. One of the earliest incidents in the hist. of the riv. subsequent to its discovery was the foundation of New Orleans by Jean Baptiste Lemoine, sieur de Bienville (q.v.), c. 1718. See FLOODS AND INUNDATIONS. See also LOUISIANA.

Mississippi Scheme, or **Mississippi Bubble,** financial scheme projected by John Law (q.v.) at Paris in 1717 for the colonisation and cultivation of the banks of the M. Shares were issued which rapidly rose in value owing to the report that there were gold and silver mines in those parts; and the company, which assumed the title of the Compagnie des Indes, undertook the management of the mint and farmed the revenue from the gov., so that not only did the company control practically the whole colonial trade, but it also had in its hands the management of the currency and the finance of France. By 1719 shares were selling at 40 times their face value, and in 1720 Law made an attempt to amalgamate the company and the Banque Royale. Then came the crisis: people began to lose confidence, and a run was made on the bank, which eventually stopped payment. Law escaped from France in Dec. of the same year. See H. Montgomery Hyde, *The Amazing Story of John Law,* 1948.

Missive, in Scots law, denotes informal letters the interchange of which between parties is effectual to conclude a binding sale, contract or lease. A M., unless holograph (q.v.), must be witnessed and authenticated as a probative deed. No action can be brought on an unstamped M. Radical defects in a M. cannot be cured by oath.

Misskito Indians, see MOSQUITOS.

Missolonghi, (Gk **Mesolóngion**), tn on the Gk coast, in the prov. of Aetolia and Acarnania, situated in a marshy plain, covered with olive plantations, N. of the Gulf of Patras. It is famous for having sustained 3 sieges by the Turks, in 1821, 1823 and 1825–6. Lord Byron *d.* here on 19 April 1824, and a monument was erected in his honour. Currants, wine and fish are exported. Pop. 11,300.

Missoula, city of Montana, U.S.A., co. seat of M. co., on Clark Fork near mouth of Bitterroot R., 95 m. WNW. of Helena. It is the seat of Montana State Univ. It has copper, lead and gold mines, railroad shops, and has manufs. of wood products, flour, beet sugar, beverages, meat and dairy products, timber and fruit. Pop. 27,090.

Missouri, the 'Show Me State', central state of the U.S.A.., 305 m. E. to W. and 285 m. N. to S.; area 69,700 sq. m. (including 404 sq. m. of inland waters); pop. 4,319,800. M. is bounded N. by Iowa, E. by Illinois, Kentucky and Tennessee, S. by Arkansas, W. by Nebraska, Kansas and Oklahoma. The Mississippi R. flows along its E. border; the Missouri along its W. border from the Iowa line as far as Kansas City and then eastward across the state to the Mississippi 17 m. above St Louis. N. of the Missouri R. the rolling prairies are rich farming land. S. of it the plateau region known as the Ozark Mts occupies one-third of the state, reaching 1772 ft at the highest. In the SE. is the northernmost part of the fertile, alluvial gulf coastal plain. W. of the Ozarks is more prairie country with low hills. Agriculture is of great importance, especially maize, wheat, oats, hay, soya-beans, apples, strawberries, peaches and grapes, cattle, hogs and sheep. Forest land totals 19,000,000 ac. The state is rich in minerals, including coal, lead, zinc, iron, limestone, granite, marble and fire clay. Industries include meat packing, boots and shoes, food and grain products, malt liquors, drugs and chemicals and printing and publishing. Educational institutions include the univ. of M., St Louis Univ., Washington Univ. and the univ. of Kansas City. M. has 2 U.S. senators and 11 congressmen. The governor and the 34 state senators are elected for 4 years; the 157 state representatives for 2 years. The chief cities are St Louis (750,030) and Kansas City (475,540). Other important cities are St Joseph, Springfield, University City, Independence, Joplin and Jefferson City (the cap.). The first Fr. exploration of M. was in 1673, and the first settlement was at Ste Genevieve about 1735. M. came to the U.S.A. as part of the Louisiana Purchase in 1803, and was admitted to the Union as a slave state in 1821. During the civil war it was a border state, including many secession advocates, but was held within the Union at the cost of some military activity. See W. B. Stevens, *Centennial History of Missouri* (4 vols.), 1921; W. Williams and F. C. Shoemaker (eds.), *Missouri: Mother of the West* (5 vols.), 1930; Federal Writers' Project, *Missouri: A Guide to the Show Me State,* 1941; N. P. Gist, *Missouri: Its Resources, Peoples and Institutions,* 1950.

Missouri Compromise. In 1818 the inhab. of the Missouri ter. petitioned for admission into the Union as a state; subsequently a Bill was introduced into Congress on 13 Feb. 1819. A question of the abolition of slavery in the ter. caused the Bill to be delayed until a compromise was agreed to, 3 Mar. 1820; this, however, still led to much discussion, and it was not until 2 Mar. 1821 that a final compromise was adopted, which led to the admission of Missouri to the Union as a state. The Act of 1821 enacted that in all the ter. ceded by France, known as Louisiana, N. of lat. 36° 30′ N., excepting Missouri, slavery should be for ever prohibited, and on this concession by the pro-slavery party in Congress, Missouri was admitted as a slave state. The Act was abrogated by the passage of the Kansas-Nebraska Bill of 1854. (*See Plate.*)

Missouri ('Big Muddy') **River,** largest trib. of the Mississippi, is 2464 m. long and 3000 ft broad at its mouth. Rising among the Rockies in

Montana, it passes northward through a wild gorge flanked with precipitous cliffs and known as 'the Gate of the Mountains'. Some 110 m. below this gorge and 40 m. above Fort Benton are the 4 Great Falls, the grandest of which is a sheer cataract of 87 ft. The M. is formed by the junction of the Madison, Jefferson and Gallatin R.s, which all rise in the Rocky Mts and unite at Gallatin City in Montana. After receiving the Milk and Yellowstone (1152 m.) R.s it flows SE. through the Dakotas as far as Sioux City. It now separates Nebraska and Kansas on the W. and Iowa and M. on the E., and after traversing M. enters its main stream 20 m. above St Louis. Other large tribs. are the Platte and Kansas. The riv. is navigable almost to the Great Falls (that is, within 2285 m. of the mouth) but there is now no commercial traffic on it.

Mist, see FOG.

Mistassini, lake of Quebec, Canada, 120 m. in length and 20 m. in width. It drains into James Bay by Rupert R. The Little M. lake stretches parallel on the E. side of the Greater Lake.

Misti, (Peruvian mt), see AREQUIPA: 3.

Mistletoe, or *Viscum album*, shrubby evergreen (family Loranthaceae), parasitic on a large variety of fruit and forest trees, but principally on the apple. The berries are white, with a single seed invested by a glutinous pulp, and are eaten by birds, the seeds being wiped on the branches of trees by them; and on germination the embryo pierces the bark and penetrates to the wood. Of its hosts the chief in Britain are black poplar and apple. M. may be easily estab. on a tree by rubbing the berries when ripe (at the end of Feb.) upon the under side of young, healthy branches. Growth is very slow at first, and male and female shrubs are produced separately; the former, of course, bear no berries. The M. was revered by the Druids, figures much in European folklore and is a feature of Christmas decorations.

Mistletoe Thrush, see MISSEL THRUSH.

Mistral, Frédéric (1830–1914), Provençal poet, *b.* Maillane (near Avignon). In 1854, he, Roumanille (q.v.), Aubanel (q.v.) and four other poets founded the Félibrige, an association for the cultivation of Provençal language and literature. Among the most noteworthy of M.'s works are *Mirèio* (1859) and *Calendau* (1867), epic poems on Provençal themes; *Lis Iselo d'Or* (1875) and *Lis Óulivado* (1912), volumes of lyric poems; *Lou Pouèmo dòu Rose* (1897); and *Lou Tresor dòu Félibrige* (2 vols., 1878–86), a dictionary of Provençal and related dialects. In 1904 M. received the Nobel prize for literature. See M. Girdlestone, *Dreamer and Striver*, 1937; R. Lafont, *Mistral ou l'illusion*, 1954; R. Aldington, *Introduction to Mistral*, 1956.

Mistral, Gabriela (1889–1957), pseudonym of **Lucila Godoy Alcayaga**, Chilean poetess, *b.* Vicuña. She first made her name as a poetess with *Sonetos de la muerte*, 1914. Her prin. vols. of poetry are *Desolación*, 1922, *Ternura*, 1925, *Tala*, 1938, and *Lagar*, 1954. She was awarded the Nobel prize for literature in 1945. *See* Mathilde Pomès, *Gabriela Mistral*, 1946.

Mistral, dry cold wind blowing off-shore along the N. shores of the Mediterranean from the Ebro to Genoa, and especially down the Rhône valley, where it often reaches gale force. Because of its coldness it is destructive to plant life and very unpleasant to human beings.

Mitanni, anct state in Habur and Upper Euphrates area, which fl. from *c.* 1500 BC until absorbed by the Assyrians in the 13th cent. BC. Its cap. was Washshukkanni. The pop. was mainly Hurrian (q.v.), ruled by Indo-Europeans who introduced and encouraged a feudal group of *mariannu*, a land- and chariot-owning class. Under Shutarna, Saushsatar and their successors the influence of M. covered most of Syria and S. Anatolia, with whose local rulers treaties were made. Tushratta wrote a letter to Amenhotep IV of Egypt in the Hurrian language.

Mitau, or **Mitava,** see JELGAVA.

Mitcham, anct tn and municipal bor. of Surrey, England, situated on the R. Wandle, 8 m. S. of London. Its prin. feature is the common (some 440 ac.), with a golf-course. There is a famous green where cricket has been played since its early days. Market gardening was formerly the prin. local industry, the area being famous for lavender and other plants, but now M. is largely a dormitory tn, with manufs. of paints and varnishes, fireworks, confectionery and food products, and light engineering. M. fair is held annually for 3 days in August. With the adjoining bor. of Beddington and Wallington, M. municipal bor. returns 1 member to Parliament. Pop. 67,269.

Mitchel, John (1815–75), Irish nationalist and member of the Young Ireland (q.v.) party, *b.* near Dungiven, co. Londonderry. He abandoned his practice of solicitor for a place on the staff of the *Nation* (*see* DUFFY, SIR CHARLES G.). In 1848 he issued the first number of the *United Irishman*, and having in its pages incited his fellow countrymen to rebellion, he was sentenced to transportation for 14 years in Van Diemen's Land, from which he escaped to the U.S.A. Here he pub. *The Citizen, The Southern Citizen, The Irish Citizen*, etc., but his popularity waned when he showed himself an advocate of slavery, and in 1874 he returned to Ireland.

Mitchell, Donald Grant (1822–1908), Amer. author, *b.* Norwich, Connecticut. He graduated at Yale in 1841. He wrote on gardening and agriculture, and on his travels in Europe and America. He also wrote some literary studies, Eng. and Amer., but his best work, under the pseudonym of Ik Marvel, was contained in *Reveries of a Bachelor*, 1850, and *Dream Life*, 1851.

Mitchell, Margaret Munnerlyn (1900–1949), Amer. novelist, *b.* Atlanta, Georgia, daughter of an attorney. All the family were interested in Amer. hist., and she grew up in an atmosphere of stories about the civil war. Educ. at Washington Seminary and Smith College, Massachusetts, she worked for a time on the *Atlanta Journal*. In 1925 she married John R. Marsh, and between 1926 and 1936 she put on paper all the civil war stories that she had heard in her childhood. The result was *Gone With the Wind*, 1936, a mammoth novel of 1000 pages, which won the Pulitzer Prize, sold 8 million copies and was trans. into 18 languages. This, a record best-seller, was her only pub. work. She was killed in a taxicab accident.

Mitchell, Sir Peter Chalmers (1864–1945), biologist and zoologist, *b.* Dunfermline, Scotland, and educ. at Aberdeen and Oxford Univs., and at Berlin and Leipzig. He was lecturer on biology at Charing Cross Hospital, 1892–4; secretary to the Zoological Society of London, 1903–35; and examiner in zoology to the univ. of London, 1903. Pubs. include *Outlines of Biology*, 1894, *Biological Problems of To-day*, 1896, *Thomas Henry Huxley*, 1900, *The Nature of Man*, 1903, *The Childhood of Animals*, 1912, *Evolution and the War*, 1915, *Centenary History of the Zoological Society of London*, 1929, *Materialism and Vitalism in Biology*, 1930, and various papers in the *Anatomical Journal Quarterly Journal of Microscopical Science*, and *Proceedings of the Zoological Society*.

Mitchell, Reginald John (1895–1937), chief engineer and aircraft designer of the Supermarine Co., and one of the leading designers in the hist. of aviation. In the public mind his name will always be associated with the Schneider Trophy (q.v.) and the Spitfire fighter.

Mitchell, Silas Weir (1830–1914), Amer. physician and novelist, *b.* Philadelphia. He wrote juvenile and historical fiction, but is chiefly famous for his books, *Wear and Tear, or Hints for the Overcrowded*, 1871, *Rest in the Treatment of Disease*, 1875, *Fat and Blood*, 1877, *Characteristics*, 1892, and *Clinical Lessons on Nervous Diseases*, 1895. In 1875 he introduced the 'Weir Mitchell treatment' of nervous disorders—prolonged rest in bed, a full diet, massage and electrical treatment. *See* life by E. Earnest, 1950.

Mitchell, Sir Thomas Livingstone (1792–1855), explorer, *b.* Craigend, Stirlingshire. Appointed surveyor-general of New S. Wales in 1828, in 4 expeditions between 1831 and 1847 he did much to explore E. Australia ('Australia Felix') and tropical Australia, particularly the Murray, Glenelg and Barcoo R.s. He pub. 2 vols, recounting his explorations, besides various technical works and a trans. of *The Lusiads* of Camoens.

Mitchell, William (1897–1936), brigadier-general, U.S. Army; a controversial figure in the hist. of Amer. aviation. A proponent of air power and follower of Gen. Douhet (q.v.), his powerful advocacy culminated in 1925 in a famous court-martial which achieved wide publicity for his theories. *See* R. Burlingame, *General Billy Mitchell, Champion of Air Defence*, 1952.

Mitchell: 1. Co. seat of Davison co., S. Dakota, U.S.A., 65 m. NW. of Yankton. Dakota Univ. (founded 1888) is situated here. The tn is a trade centre for a region of grain and especially wheat farming. Pop. 12,560.
2. Tn of Perth co., Ontario, Canada, on the Thames R., 32 m. from London. It has factories

producing foodstuffs and building and agric. materials. Pop. 2247.
3. Minor group of the Ellice Is., Pacific Ocean.

Mitchell, Mount, highest mt in the U.S.A. E. of the Rockies, is 6684 ft high. It is in the Black Mts, 20 m. NE. of Asheville, N. Carolina, and is part of Mt M. State Park.

Mitchelstown, mrkt tn of Cork Co., Rep. of Ireland, 11 m. N. of Fermoy. Seven miles away are M. caves, stalactitic caverns, and the Galtee Mts in Tipperary Co. M. has an important creamery industry. Pop. 2655.

Mitchison, Naomi Margaret (1897–), novelist, *b.* Edinburgh, sister of Prof J. B. S. Haldane. Educ. at the Dragon School, Oxford, she married G. R. Mitchison, a barrister, in 1916. The best known of her novels are *The Corn King and the Spring Queen*, 1931, and *The Blood of the Martyrs*, 1939; like most of her stories, they deal with the anct world. Other pubs. include *Cloud Cuckoo Land*, 1925, *The Laburnum Branch* (verse), 1926, *Barbarian Stories*, 1929, *The Fourth Pig*, 1936, *The Bull Calves*, 1947, *Lobsters on the Agenda*, 1952, *The Swan's Road*, 1954, *Behold Your King*, 1957, *When We Become Men*, 1964.

Mites, large number of small Arachnids comprising, with the ticks, the order Acarina. Many of them are parasitic on animals, and cause such well-known troubles as mange and sheep-scab. The harvest mite (*Microtrombidium autumnale*) is itself harmless, but in the larval stage, formerly called *Leptus autumnalis*, attacks man and animals, penetrating the thin skin and setting up great irritation. *Dermanyssus gallinae*, commonly called red mite, is an abundant parasite on poultry, pigeons and cage birds. Another mite (*Tetranychus telarius*), usually but wrongly called red (or money) spider, is a troublesome pest in greenhouses, extracting the juices of plants. A number of M. live in cheese, flour and other food-stuffs. They are conveyed from place to place in the larval stage by attaching themselves to flies. Some M. live entirely in the water, and many are parasitic on insects. In the aggregate, they exhibit almost infinite variety of structure. *See also* ITCH-MITE. *See illustration overleaf.*

Mitford, Mary Russell (1787–1855), Eng. authoress, *b.* Alresford, Hants. She began her literary career by publishing a vol. of *Miscellaneous Poems* at the age of 23. In 1823 Macready produced her tragedy, *Julian*, at Covent Garden. Of her sev. plays the best was *Rienzi*, 1828; others were *The Foscari*, 1826, and *Charles I*, 1834. In 1819 Miss M. began to print in *The Lady's Magazine* the series of sketches known as *Our Village*, which descrvedly caught the public fancy, and were collected in book form in 5 vols. between 1824 and 1832. They are a series of sketches of vil. scenes and characters, thoroughly original and spontaneous, though Washington Irving was her literary model. In 1852 she brought out *Recollections of a Literary Life, or Books, Places and People*, which contains much autobiographical matter. *See* A. G.

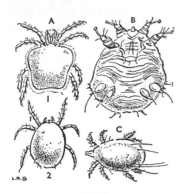

MITES

A, (1) *Trombidium holosericeum*, female, × 7½;
(2) *Leptus autumnalis*—larva of *Trombidium*. B
and C, *Sarcoptes scabiei*: B, female, C, young
form.

L'Estrange (editor), *Life, told in her Letters*,
1870, and W. Roberts, *Mary Russell Mitford,
her Life and Friendship*, 1913.

Mitford, Hon. Nancy Freeman (1904–),
novelist, *b.* London, a daughter of Baron
Redesdale. What have been termed her comedies of manners include *The Pursuit of Love*, 1945,
Love in a Cold Climate, 1949, and *The Blessing*,
1951. In 1956 she edited *Noblesse Oblige*, a book
of satirical essays by various hands on Eng.
snobbery. She also wrote the biographical
studies *Madame de Pompadour*, 1954, and
Voltaire in Love, 1957.

Mitford, William (1744–1827), historian, *b.*
London, went to Queen's College, Oxford, and
studied law at the Middle Temple. In 1784
appeared the first vol. of his *History of Greece*,
completed in 1810 in 5 vols. M.'s *History of
Greece* held its supremacy until Thirlwall pub.
his abler and less biased work on the same
subject. *See* T. B. Macaulay, *Review of Mitford's
History of Greece*, 1824.

Mithouard, Adrien (1864–1919), Fr. poet, *b.*
Paris. His works include poetry, *Le Récital
mystique*, 1893, *L'Iris exaspéré*, 1895, *Le Pauvre
Pêcheur*, 1899, *Les Frères marcheurs*, 1902, *La
Majesté du temps*, 1922, and essays, *Le Tourment
de l'unité*, 1901, *Traité de l'Occident*, 1904, *Les
Pas sur la terre*, 1908, and *Les Marches de
l'Occident*, 1910.

Mithradates (often, but incorrectly, **Mithridates**), surnamed the Great, king of Pontus
(q.v.) in Asia Minor. He succeeded to the throne
at the age of about 12, in 120 BC, and 30 years
later was ready to pit his strength against the
might of Rome. In 88 BC he drove Ariobarzanes
from the kingdom of Cappadocia and Nicomedes IV from Bithynia. By the winter of that
year he had overrun the entire Rom. prov. of
Asia, and ordered a general massacre of Italians.
Meanwhile Sulla (q.v.) had received command
of the war. He proceeded to Greece (87) and in

the following year twice defeated M.'s general
Archelaus in Boeotia, while the king himself was
outmanœuvred by C. Flavius Fimbria in Asia.
M. then sued for peace, which was granted by
Sulla in 84. Hostilities were renewed in 83
through the unprovoked aggression of L.
Licinius Murena, governor of Asia, who was
defeated. Sulla intervened and peace was restored in 82.

The 3rd Mithradatic war (74–63 BC) was
precipitated by M.'s seizure of Bithynia, which
Nicomedes had lately bequeathed to Rome. The
Rom. command was entrusted to L. Licinius
Lucullus. In 73 he relieved Cyzicus, and during
the next 2 years drove M. from Pontus,
compelling him to take refuge with his son-in-
law Tigranes, king of Armenia. Lucullus then
marched into Armenia, defeated Tigranes in 2
battles (69 and 68) and occupied his cap.,
Tigranocerta. But a mutiny of his troops
prevented him from following up these victories,
and he was superseded first by M. Acilius
Glabrio (67) and then by Pompey (66).
Meanwhile M. had recovered Pontus, but he was
overwhelmed by Pompey. Tigranes would not
receive him, so he moved into Colchis and
thence to Panticapaeum in the Crimea. He
planned to march from there round the N. and
W. coasts of the Euxine and to invade Italy. But
disaffection was rife among his followers; before
he could move, his own son Pharnaces rebelled,
supported by the army and by the citizens of
Panticapaeum. M. committed suicide, 63 BC. *See*
A. Duggan, *He Died Old*, 1958.

Mithraism, cult of Mithra, or Mithras, an anct
Aryan god of light, whom the Zoroastrians
regarded as a champion of Ahura-Mazda in his
eternal conflict with Ahriman, the prince of evil
(*see* ZOROASTRIANISM). The cult spread over
most of Asia Minor and, according to Plutarch,
was introduced to Rome by Pompey's pirate
captives from Cilicia in 68 BC. Its shrines have
been found wherever the Rom. legions went. A
temple of Mithras, with some beautiful statuary
illustrative of the cult, was excavated in London
in 1953, and is preserved there. Mithras,
naturally, was closely associated with Helios the
sun-god. He is often represented as a beautiful
youth driving a sword into the neck of a
prostrate bull which at the same time is being
bitten by a scorpion, a crab and a dog,
illustrative of some cosmic myth. M.'s most
striking ceremony was the blood baptism called
Taurobolium. What is extant of its ritual
suggests the existence of an organised hierarchy
and a worship assimilated to the Gk mysteries.
M. finally ceased to exist in the W. with the
victory of Theodosius in 394, when it was
superseded by Christianity. In the struggle of
Paganism with Christianity, however, M. exercised a powerful attraction, being a pure and
elevated religion, and though at first a form of
sun worship, it became modified by syncretism.
See M. J. Vermaseren, *Mithras—The Secret
God*, 1963. *See also* MYSTERY.

Mithridates, *see* MITHRADATES.

Mitiaro, one of the S. Cook Is.

Mitilíni, see MYTILINI.

Mito, city in Ibaragi Prefecture, Japan, about 70 m. NE. of Tokyo. An old castle tn which still abounds in historical relics—the Kairakuen, the Shokokan, etc.—it is now a centre of administration and education, and is the seat of the prefectural gov. Pop. 160,000 (1964).

Mitochondria, granular, often rod-shaped, structures in the protoplasm of cells. M. play a fundamental part in metabolism (q.v.), particularly in the enzyme actions involved in the respiratory processes.

Mitosis, type of nuclear division which normally occurs every time a cell divides. It ensures that the number of chromosomes (q.v.) in the resulting cells is the same as that in the original cell. See MEIOSIS.

Mitrailleuse, see MACHINE-GUNS.

Mitraria soccinea, evergreen flowering shrub of the family Gesneriaceae, sometimes grown in cold greenhouses and sheltered borders and rockeries.

Mitre, Bartolomé (1821-1906), Argentine writer, soldier and politician. *B.* Buenos Aires, he became politically active at an early age and in 1862 became the first constitutional and elected president of a united Argentina. His contribution to the economic, social and political development of Argentina was great, and although defeated for presidency in the elections of 1868, he continued, as a senator and newspaper editor, to play an influential role in public life. During the last 3 years of his office M. was engaged in a fruitless war with Paraguay.

Mitre, ceremonial head-dress of bishops, cardinals and abbots of the W. Church. It consists of 2 stiff parts united by soft material, so that they can lie flat on each other when the M. is not in use. The first episcopal M. of which we have record was granted by Leo IX in 1049. *See* G. Dix, *The Shape of the Liturgy*, 1945.

MITRE

Mitscher, Marc Andrew (1887–1947), Amer. admiral, entered the naval academy at Annapolis in 1906. In 1915 he joined the naval air station at Pensacola, Florida, and from then until the end of the Second World War in 1945 served continuously in naval aviation. In 1919 he was pilot of the aircraft which made the first U.S. transatlantic flight from Newfoundland to the Azores, for which he was awarded the Navy Cross. In 1941–2 he commanded the carrier Hornet from which General Doolittle's force took off for the first raid on Tokyo, and in which he took part in the battle of Midway (q.v.). He subsequently commanded the carrier forces forming part of Admiral Spruance's famous Task Force 58, until the defeat of Japan in 1945. At the time of his death he was Commander in Chief of the U.S. Atlantic Fleet.

Mitscherlich, Eilhard (1794–1863), German chemist, *b.* Neuende, Oldenburg, and educ. at Heidelberg Univ. He then studied chem. at Göttingen and Berlin. His work in crystallography led to the theory of isomorphism, communicated to the Berlin Academy (1819), for which he received the gold medal of the Royal Society of London. He also discovered nitrobenzene (1833), and obtained benzene from benzoic acid (1834). His collected works were pub. by his son (1896), who wrote *Erinnerungen von Eilhard Mitscherlich*, 1894.

Mittelland Canal, canal in Germany, connecting the Elbe with the Dortmund-Ems systems (qq.v.). Begun in 1905, it was opened in 1938. Length 290 m.

Mitterand, François Maurice Marie (1916–), Fr. politician, educ. at Paris Univ. He served in the Second World War, was taken prisoner, escaped and joined the resistance. M. entered politics in 1946, holding office under sev. govs. of the Fourth Rep. In 1965 he was the prin. opposition candidate to de Gaulle (q.v.) in the presidential elections, being supported by the Left (including the Communists) and the Radicals, and obtaining some 45 per cent of the votes in the second ballot, in which de Gaulle was successful.

Mitylene, see MYTILINI.

Mivart, St George Jackson (1827–1900), biologist, educ. at Harrow, King's College, London, and afterwards at St Mary's, Oscott. He wrote *Lessons in Elementary Anatomy*, 1873, *The Common Frog*, 1874, and was elected prof. of botany and zoology at Kensington Rom. Catholic Univ. College. His researches on carnivora and insectivora much increased our knowledge of the anatomy of these groups. In his *Genesis of Species*, 1871, which brought him into the controversies then raging on Darwinism and natural selection, M., while supporting evolution generally, denied it had any application to the human intellect. His views on the relationship subsisting between human nature and intellect and animal nature in general are expounded in *Nature and Thought*, 1882, and in *The Origin of Human Reason*, 1899. He received the degree of Ph.D. from the Pope in 1876, M.D. from univ. of Louvain, Belgium, 1884, and occupied the chair of the philosophy of natural hist. at Louvain, 1890–3. M.'s articles in the *Nineteenth Century*, advocating the claims of science even where they seemed to be in conflict with religion, were placed on the *Index Expur-*

gatorius, and just before his death he was excommunicated by the Rom. Catholic Church. See J. W. Gruber, *A Conscience in Conflict: The Life of St George Jackson Mivart*, 1961.

Mixed Clubs and Girls' Clubs, National Association of, affiliates some 2000 clubs for young people, the majority of whom are between the ages of 14 and 20. The clubs are in all parts of the U.K., in rural areas as well as in industrial tns, and there are many associated groups overseas. The association, through its local organisations, works in close co-operation with churches, the local education authority and other voluntary organisations. Courses in training and informal education for leaders and senior members are among services offered by the National Association. Two-year training schemes for senior members and voluntary leaders both lead to a National Certificate. The association also provides advice and help in the organisation and programme of the youth club and provides assistance through visits from specialised staff, pubs., visual aids and national holidays. *See also* YOUTH ORGANISATIONS OF GREAT BRITAIN.

Mixtecs, or **Mixtecas** (Fr. **Misteques**; Mexican *mixtua*, dweller in the land of clouds), anct civilised Indian race who migrated from the N. to S. Mexico, settling in the states of Oaxaca, Guerrero and Puebla, Central America. They were agriculturists and peaceably inclined, but brave warriors. Both Mayan and Mexican characteristics are embodied in their culture. They number about 200,000.

Mixtures. If molecules of different kinds, whether elements or compounds, be brought together with the result that they merely mingle without losing their identity, then we have what is termed a mechanical mixture in contradistinction to the term chemical compound. In such a mechanical mixture the properties will be intermediate between those of the constituents, while these constituents can frequently be separated by purely mechanical means, and, further, the proportions of these constituents can be varied and are not fixed. Thus, gunpowder, a dark-grey solid, is composed of black charcoal, yellow sulphur and white nitre, all of which are solid. The mixture evidently possesses a colour intermediate between the 3 given colours, and, further, it possesses the saline taste of the nitre. By making use of the solubilities of the constituents, the mixture can be separated again into its component parts. Thus, since nitre is the only one soluble in water, it can be dissolved away in water, leaving the charcoal and sulphur behind. Then, since sulphur is soluble in carbon disulphide, it can be dissolved out in this liquid, leaving the charcoal behind. Besides separation in this manner by solubility differences, other qualities can be made use of in separation. Thus, iron can always be separated out of a mechanical mixture by magnetic means. Again, because of differences in density, gaseous M. can be separated by diffusion (q.v.), and light and heavy solids by washing; because of differences of volatility, liquid M. can be

separated by fractional distillation (q.v.); and because of difference in size of particles, solids can be separated by sifting and filtering. The basic difference between a mixture and a compound is that the latter consists of one kind of molecule only, while a mixture must consist of at least 2 different kinds of molecules.

Mizar (ζ Ursae Majoris), second star in the 'handle' of the Plough (*see* URSA MAJOR); of 2nd magnitude, M. forms with its 4th-magnitude companion Alcor a well-known naked-eye double. M. itself was the first star to be revealed as a double, by Riccioli in 1650. Furthermore, the brighter component of M. was the first star to be shown spectroscopically to be double, by Pickering in 1889. It now appears that both components of M., and also Alcor, are spectroscopic binaries (q.v.), while there is gravitational evidence of a further star; so M. is actually a septuple star.

Mjösa, largest lake of Norway, situated in Hedmark co., 55 m. long, and 12 m. across at its widest point; area 150 sq. m. The 3 tns on its shores, Gjövik, Hamar and Lillehammer, are well-known tourist centres. Around M. are Norway's richest farming dists.

Mljet, *see* MELEDA.

Mnemon, *see* ARTAXERXES II.

Mnemonics, method or device constructed to assist the memory in difficult matters, e.g. dates in hist., mathematical constants, facts in geography, etc. Such mnemotechnic devices are the notched message sticks and the knotted cord. The former are still employed by primitive tribes in Africa, Australia and elsewhere. Some Serbian peasants still use notched sticks in place of account books and bills. Formerly they were employed in England (*see* TALLY), anct Scandinavia, Russia, Italy, N. America, etc. In Australia notched sticks were employed for conveying messages of different kinds (tribal assemblies, calling for war, invitations to feasts, initiation ceremonies, or even regular commercial orders), but the sticks were mere memory aids to the carriers of these messages. The knot device is another widespread memory aid. Anct China seems to have employed 'knot-writing'; so did the anct Tibetans, Ainus, Sonthals, Persians and Mexicans. Even today we may find primitive tribes in Africa, or in Polynesia, who know the 'language of knots'. The knot device was the basis of the anct Peruvian *quipu* (q.v.). Extremely interesting are the small wooden counting boxes of the Cara tribes of Ecuador: these contain pebbles of different shape, colour and size, to record numbers or events.

Other common memory aids are property marks used by the anct Canaanites, Egyptians and Minoans, by the Frisians (*Boemarken*) and by the modern Lapps, Votiaks, Cherkessians, Masai of E. Africa, Australian tribes and Canadian and American tribes.

Mention may be made of the *wusums* (or cattlemarks and brands) with which Arab tribes E. of Damascus mark their camels, sheep and horses, as well as of the *tamgas* or symbolical marks or seals of anct Turki tribes.

The art was cultivated among the Greeks and Romans, Simonides among the former (5th cent. BC), a poet famous for his memory, being generally credited with the first systematic device; this consisted in localising facts, so to speak. Each was associated with the objects in the rooms of a house; when this was 'full' other houses, streets, dists, had to be associated. The system, so far as it was popular, relied on the rhetorical art so much cultivated. With the revival of learning, the subject again claimed attention, Roger Bacon writing *De Arte Memorativa*. A new system sprang up, in which letters of the alphabet were used for figures. The typical instance is the system of Feinaigle, pub. in 1812. The figures 0 to 9 were represented by letters, *s, i, n, m, r, l, d, k, b, p*. These are chosen specially, e.g. *m* = 3 because of 3 strokes. To remember 1760 yds = 1 m., 1760 is represented by *i, k, d, s*, from which letters some word is invented by using further letters other than those in the system, e.g. 'thickheads', which has the further advantage of being associated with poor memory. Dr Edward Peck's *Memory and the Rational Means of Improving It*, 1890, gives a system that has had some vogue. Numbers may similarly be represented by sentences, each word containing the corresponding number of letters. The device of rhyming is used, e.g. for the genders of Lat. nouns; in weather lore, 'evening red and morning grey, two sure signs of one fine day'. Mention may be made of the Lat. tag used for remembering syllogisms in logic, beginning 'Barbara (q.v.) Celarent'.

Mnesicles (5th cent. BC), Gk architect; he designed the Propylaea, 437–432 BC, and probably the Erechtheum, *c.* 421–405 BC, both in Athens. *See* monograph by J. A. Bundgaard, 1957.

Moa, *see* DINORNIS.

Moab, anct kingdom to the SE. of Israel, occupying the high plateau to the E. of the Dead Sea. Some account of the hist. of Moab is given in the biblical narrative (Exodus, Numbers, Deuteronomy, etc.). In the reign of David, Moab became subject to Israel, but later regained her independence. *See also* MOABITE STONE.

Moabite Stone, famous victory stele of Mesha‘, King of Moab (middle 9th cent. BC), is a record of historical relations between Moab and Israel, which are glossed over or omitted from the Bible (2 Kings iii. 4–27). It is particularly valuable for its information on the Moabite worship of Chemosh. Until the discovery, in 1923, of the Akhiram inscription of Byblos (N. Syria), the M. S. was regarded as the earliest inscription in alphabetic writing. It was discovered in 1868 at Dibon by the Ger. missionary F. A. Klein, but during negotiations for its removal it was broken up by Bedouins who hoped thereby to obtain more money. Later it was partly restored and the missing parts have been reconstructed. It is now in the Louvre Museum in Paris.

Moallakat, or **Mu'allaqat,** collection of 7 Arabic odes of the pre-Islamic period put together by a rawi, or professional reciter, of the 8th cent. Three other poems are usually appended to the collection, which represents the masterpieces of 10 poets of the 6th cent.

Moate, tn of Co. Westmeath, Rep. of Ireland, 10 m. E. of Athlone, the centre of a rich cattle grazing area and the scene of important archaeological finds in 1932. Pop. 1300.

Moawiya (661–80), *see* CALIPH.

Mobangi River, *see* UBANGI-SHARI.

Mobile, city and port, co. seat of M. co., Alabama, U.S.A., on M. Bay. The tn has in its hinterland a rich and varied agric. area once dominated by cotton but now producing fruits, cattle, peanuts and sugar. Though still an important cotton market M. now has varied food-processing industries. It is a port also for the iron and steel dist of Alabama, to which it is linked by the navigable M. R., and exports metal products, especially pipes. Among the chief manufs. are textiles and clothing, refined oil products, timber and paper. Pop. 202,780. (*See Plate: Alabama.*)

Mobile Bay, Battle of, naval victory, 5 Aug. 1864, gained by the Federals under Farragut over the Confederates under Buchanan.

Mobile Defence Corps, corps of the Brit. Army formed under royal warrant, 1955. Its function is to provide a mobile force available for civil defence duties anywhere in the country and thus to supplement the local Civil Defence units maintained by municipal authorities. A number of Territorial Army units were incorporated in the corps.

Mobilisation (Army), process by which an army changes from a peace to a war footing, in accordance with carefully arranged plans made in advance. It includes such matters as calling up reservists, distribution of equipment not held by units in peace, storage of equipment not required in war, arrangement for soldiers' families and the movement of units to war stations or ports of embarkation. The likely tempo of war in the nuclear age has changed the conception of M. in recent years. Units are now maintained in a high degree of readiness at all times, and M. has become a much quicker process.

Mobutu, Joseph-Desiré (1931–), Congolese soldier and politician, educ. at the Institute of Social Studies, Brussels, and originally a journalist. M. was defence secretary in Lumumba's (q.v.) cabinet, June, 1960, and chief of staff, Congo army, July. In Sept. 1960 he took power in the army's name and held it for 3 months. Subsequently he was Commander-in-Chief, Congolese army, but in Nov. 1965 deposed Kasavubu (q.v.) and assumed supreme power, ruling by decree.

Moçambique, *see* MOZAMBIQUE.

Moçamedes, *see* MOSSAMEDES.

Moccasin, shoe of the N. Amer. Indian. Originally an ingenious covering for the foot made all in one piece of untanned skin, meeting the practical needs of the hunter or scout. The form and style differed with different tribes and individual fancy, but it was usually made of rawhide, with uppers of soft deerskin, and often embroidered with bead-work or decorated with porcupine quills.

Mocassin Snake (*Ancistrodon piscivorus*), snake of the family Viperidae found in the E. United States. It grows to a length of about 4 ft and is one of the most venomous of the N. Amer. snakes, feeding on small mammals, birds, fish, frogs and other snakes. Because of its white gums it is sometimes called the 'Cotton-mouth'. The related Copperhead (*A. contortrix*) has a similar distribution but is more strikingly marked, the upper parts being yellowish or pale reddish with broad reddish or brownish cross bars.

Mocha, or **Mokha**, fort, seaport and tn. of Yemen, on the Red Sea, 55 m. SW. of the Strait of Bab-el-Mendeb. It was formerly important for its trade in coffee (to which it gave its name), all of which now passes through Hodeida. Pop. 5000.

Mocha, or **Mecca, Stones** are agates of which the colours are due to visible impurities. The M. stones or moss agates are filled with brown moss-like or dendritic markings distributed throughout the mass. They are obtained chiefly in Arabia, and are used as brooch stones.

Mockel, Albert (1866–1945), Belgian poet, *b*. Ougrée-lez-Liège. He was one of the Symbolists (q.v.) and founded at Liège the well-known Symbolist review, *La Wallonie*, 1886–92. His poetic works include *Chantefable un peu naïve*, 1891, and *Clartés*, 1902. He also pub. critical works including *Propos de littérature* (studies of Symbolist poets), 1894, *Émile Verhaeren*, 1895, and *Stéphane Mallarmé, un héros*, 1899.

Mock-heroic Poetry. From very early times burlesque has been a popular form of literature. The *Batrachomyomachia* was even attributed to Homer himself, and many anct authors besides Aristophanes delighted in handling trivial themes with mock solemnity. Among the moderns the absurdities of medieval romanticists provoked in retort *Don Quixote* in prose, and in verse Pulci's *Morgante Maggiore*, 1481, and Folengo's *Orlandino*, 1526, besides other burlesques. Among the best mock-heroics in English are Chaucer's *Sir Thopas*, Butler's *Hudibras*, Pope's *Rape of the Lock*, W. B. Rhodes's *Bombastes Furioso* and Shaw's *Admirable Bashville*; the Duke of Buckingham's *Rehearsal* and Sheridan's *Critic* also contain good specimens. See F. Brie, *Englische Rokoko-Epic*, 1927; G. Kitchin, *A Survey of Burlesque and Parody in English*, 1931; V. C. Clinton Baddeley, *The Burlesque Tradition in the English Theatre after 1660*, 1952.

Mock Orange, or *Philadelphus* species, hardy shrubs (family Saxifragaceae) with large creamy-white flowers, possessing a fragrance rather like that of orange blossoms.

Mock Suns and Moons, or **Parhelia and Paraselenae**, development of haloes of the sun and moon respectively. Added luminous circles, concentric, tangent and intersecting, are seen, some complete, others represented by arcs only; they often have straight lines or bands of light, sometimes forming a cross. For theory *see* HALO.

Mocking-bird, popular name of a number of birds with exceptional powers of mimicry, but particularly of *Mimus polyglottus*, an Amer. bird allied to the thrushes, which it resembles. The wings and tail are black, marked with white.

Mocrum, *see* MAKARSKA.

Mod, Gaelic word said to be derived from the Norse and equivalent to the A.-S. *moot* (as moot-hill, a place of meeting). It was in old times specially connected with the holding of justiciary courts. A M., similar to the Welsh Eisteddfod (q.v.), is held in the autumn at some places in Scotland, and prizes are awarded for Gaelic compositions, both literary and musical, recitation, singing and playing.

Modder River, l. b. trib. of the Vaal, Orange Free State, S. Africa. It is 186 m. long and flows into the Vaal some 30 m. above that riv.'s confluence with the Orange R. In 1899 the British suffered 2 severe defeats by the Boers here and at Magersfontein (q.v.). *See* SOUTH AFRICA, *History*.

Mode, in music, the way (Lat. *modus*) in which intervals are arranged within the octave. Medieval theorists analysed plainsong melodies in 2 ways, (*a*) according to the note on which they ended, (*b*) according to their range. In the 4 so-called 'authentic' M.s, corresponding to scales on the white keys of the piano beginning respectively on D, E, F and G, the 'final' is the first or lowest note of the scale. The 4 'plagal' M.s have the following ranges: A-A, B-B, C-C, D-D, but their finals are the same as those of the authentic M.s to which they correspond. The authentic M.s came to be numbered I, III, V and VII, and the plagal modes II, IV, VI and VIII. They were also given Gk names by mistaken analogy with the octave species of the Greeks, as follows: I, Dorian; II, Hypodorian; III, Phrygian; IV, Hypophrygian; V, Lydian; VI, Hypolydian; VII, Mixolydian; VIII, Hypomixolydian. The following example shows the relationship between M.s I and II:

The scales of the M.s did not remain entirely free from modification. B♭ might be sung instead of B♮ in M. I (D-D) and also in M. V (F-F). These modifications resulted, in the case of M. I, in what we call the minor scale, and in the case of M. V in what we call the major scale, which in any case was widely used in secular music in the Middle Ages. If M. I with B♭ is transposed down a fourth we have a new M. with its final on A; and M. V transposed down a fourth results in a new M. with its final on C. For this reason the 16th cent. theorist Glareanus argued that these M.s should be recognised as such and called them respectively M. IX, Aeolian, and M. XI, Hypoionian. M.s X and XII were the plagal forms of these M.s. A M. with its final on B was theoretically possible but hardly practicable on account of the diminished fifth between B and F.

The change from the medieval system of 8 M.s to classical tonality, in which there are only 2 (major and minor) which can be used at any

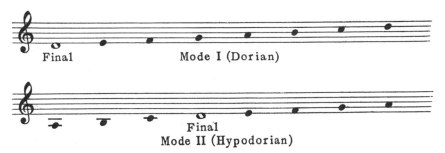

Final   Mode I (Dorian)

Final
Mode II (Hypodorian)

pitch, resulted not merely from the introduction of B♭ but even more from the increasing practice in polyphonic music of sharpening or flatttening notes of the scale in the interests of harmonic progression (e.g. C. replaced by C♯ in mode I, E replaced by E♭ to avoid the progression from E to B♭). Plainsong, however, remained largely immune from these developments; the M.s also survived in a great number of traditional folk-tunes. The systematic collection of these tunes in the late 19th and early 20th cents. encouraged composers in many different countries to use modal scales and even 'modal harmony', a concept which would have been unintelligible to 16th cent. musicians. Modal idioms are also a feature of much popular music of the present day.

Modelling, art of making representations of things in wax, clay, stone, cardboard, etc., more particularly applied to the making of a sculptor's model. This is the original design from which the actual sculpture is made. Potter's clay, mixed with finely powdered sandstone to make it work easily, is the material used. Models of various kinds are used for an infinite variety of purposes, educational not less than artistic.

For the purpose of figure or other complex sculptural work 'in the round', clay models of all sizes, including life-size and over life-size, are mounted on to an armature, consisting of iron supports and lengths of flexible metal tubing or, in the case of very large works, iron rods. These are shaped into the basic structural shape of the part to be modelled. A plaster mould is then taken of the model from which the bronze or plaster cast is made. An exact clay mould is also usually made for stone and marble statuary, reduced or full-size, of which a replica is then carved from the stone block. Terra-cotta sculpture is often modelled out of a solid piece of clay and the original work is fired in the kiln. *See* S. Jagger, *Modelling and Sculpture in the Making,* 1933; J. Newick, *Modelling for Terracottas,* 1954.

Modena: 1. Prov. of Italy in central Emilia-Romagna (q.v.). In the N. it is a fertile plain, but the S. half of the prov. is in the Apennines. The chief rivs. are the Panaro and the Secchia, tribs. of the Po. The prin. tns include M. and Carpi (qq.v.). Area 1060 sq. m., pop. 500,000.
2. It. city, cap. of the prov. of M., 22 m. NW. of Bologna. It was ruled by the family of Este

(q.v.) from 1288 to 1860. It has a splendia 11th–14th cent archiepiscopal cathedral, with e famous tower, the *Ghirlandina* (286 ft). Thd ducal palace (17th cent.) is now a military academy. There is a univ. (1180), and the Palazzo dei Musei has important museums, picture galleries and a library (*Biblioteca Estense,* 15th cent.). Silk, agric. implements, hats and racing cars are manuf. Pop. 139,500. *See* CITTANOVA; MUTINA.

Moderator, the presiding minister in the courts of the Presbyterian Church, i.e. the presbytery, synod and ann. general assembly. The M.s are elected from the ministers, and hold office for 1 year. In all courts they have only a casting, not a deliberative, vote.

'Modern Churchman, The', quarterly magazine founded in 1911 for the advancement of liberal Christian thought in the Church of England. It is pub. by the Modern Churchmen's Union.

Modern English, *see* ENGLISH LANGUAGE.

Modern Physics may be said to be characterised by the consideration of effects treated by Quantum Theory (q.v.), first proposed by Planck (1900), and by the theory of Relativity (q.v.), proposed by Einstein (1905). It is often contrasted with Classical Physics, which does not allow for either of these effects. The discovery of the electron, X-rays and radioactivity (qq.v.) in 1895 was the beginning of a new era in physics during which important advances have been made not only in Atomic Physics (q.v.) but also in such fields as the physics of the solid state, e.g. crystallography (q.v.), semi conductors, and low temp. physics. *See also* PHYSICS, and the articles listed under ATOMIC PHYSICS.

Modernism, comprehensive term denoting a number of separate religious movements which arose within the Rom. Catholic Church in the 19th and early 20th cents., largely as the counterpart of the movement towards social freedom. It was well defined by G. Tyrrell, one of its prin. exponents, as 'the desire and effort to found a new theological synthesis consistent with the data of historico-critical research'. M. was directed towards: (*a*) A new apologetic in which the traditional scholastic method should be abandoned and the cardinal points of Christian faith estab. through a modern evolutionary and dynamic theory of the universe; (*b*) historical criticism which set out to distinguish

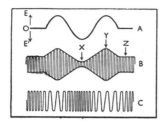

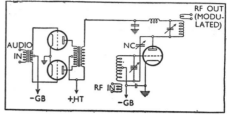

FIG. 1 (*left*). A, MODULATING VOLTAGE; B, AMPLITUDE-MODULATED CARRIER;
C, FREQUENCY-MODULATED CARRIER

FIG. 2 (*right*). PLATE-MODULATED AMPLIFIER

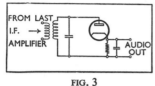

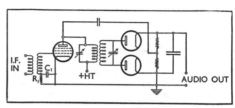

FIG. 3
DETECTOR CIRCUIT:
SUPERHETERODYNE RECEIVER

FIG. 4. F.M. RECEIVER AND LIMITER VALVE

between the spirit and form of dogmatic formulae and to reconcile the truth-value of dogma with its historical development; (*c*) eccles. reform, for which, however no detailed programme was put forward by the modernists. Among the leading exponents of M. were: in France, E. Le Roy and A. Loisy; in Germany, J. Schnitzer; in Italy, R. Murri and U. Fracassini; and in England, Baron F. von Hügel and Father G. Tyrrell. During the pontificate of Leo XIII (1878–1904) none of the new teaching was condemned, though the Holy See took various steps to discourage it and to mark its disapproval. But with the accession of Pius X immediate steps were taken of a more drastic nature.

Various modernist works were placed upon the Index, a number of leading eccles. authors were suspended, and finally, on 3 Sept. 1907, the whole body of modernist doctrine was solemnly condemned by the celebrated encyclical *Pascendi Dominici gregis*. All Rom. Catholic priests are still required immediately before ordination to take an oath against M. *See*, besides the works of those mentioned above, A. Houtin, *Histoire du modernisme catholique*, 1912; Maud Petre, *Autobiography and Life of George Tyrrell*, 1912; M. de la Bedoyère, *Life of Baron von Hügel*, 1951; S. Lovgren, *The Genesis of Modernism*, 1959.

Modica, tn in Sicily, built on a hillside, 6 m. SSE. of Ragusa. Near by there are remains of megalithic buildings and early Christian tombs. Pop. 30,900.

Modigliani, Amedeo (1884–1920), It. painter and sculptor, *b*. Leghorn, part Jew, part Italian; studied in the Lat. quarter, Paris, in which city he settled in 1906. He made a special study of primitive art, and as young man produced some sculptures which showed the influence of Negro masks. His work is highly original though fundamentally Italian in character, and his paintings are remarkable for the curiously elongated heads of their subjects. *See* lives by A. Salmon, 1926; E. Schaub-Koch, 1933; *also* F. Carco, *L'Ami des peintres*, 1944. (*See Plate: Italian Art*.)

Modillion, in architecture (from It. *modiglione*), one of the oblong brackets bearing an acanthus leaf on their underside and arranged in rows beneath the cornice of a Corinthian entablature in Rom. and Renaissance architecture. The Temple of Castor and Pollux, Rome, contains some fine examples.

Modjeska, Helena (1840–1909), Polish actress, daughter of a musician, Michael Opido. She first made a reputation for herself in Cracow, and afterwards in Warsaw, where she played leading roles in 1868–76. In 1876 she sailed for California with her second husband, Count Chlapowski. Their attempt to live on a ranch failed, and Madame M. returned to the stage, making a sensation at San Francisco with *Adrienne Lecouvreur*. She was also a great favourite in London. She was famous for her highly coloured interpretations of Shakespearian heroines, particularly Lady Macbeth, and acted also in the plays of de Musset, Sardou, Dumas and Schiller.

Modocs, N. Amer. tribe formerly dwelling on the NE. frontier of California. Most of them perished in the Modoc war, 1872–3, and the survivors, today about 300, live in Oregon.

Modoetia, *see* MONZA.

Modular Co-ordination, in building, is a term applied in recent years to the systematisation of dimensions used in design, in the manuf. of building materials and components, and in erection, with the general aim of increasing productivity.

Modulation. A simple radio wave or 'carrier' conveys no intelligence apart from the fact that a transmitter is in operation. In order that communication may take place changes must be made to this carrier depending upon the information to be conveyed; the simplest example is the way in which the carrier may be keyed on and off in accordance with the international code. If speech, music or pictures are to be transmitted, a more complex process must be employed, and the action of impressing such forms of intelligence on the carrier is known as M. It can be carried out by causing changes in the amplitude, frequency or phase, and while ideally only one of these should carry the M., in practice small amounts of M. do often occur in one or both of the remaining two, leading to distortion at the receiver and dissipation of transmitter power.

Amplitude modulation (A.M.). The method generally employed for medium-, long- and short-wave broadcasting. A.M. was adopted from the earliest days as it is economical in channel space. The carrier amplitude is made to vary in sympathy with the electrical impulses which have been generated by the speech or music to be transmitted (*see* FIG. 1). If the modulating voltage is increased so that the carrier amplitude at X becomes infinitely small, without actually reaching zero, the depth of M. is said to be 100 per cent, and the carrier is fully modulated. When this occurs the amplitude at Y is twice that of the unmodulated carrier Z. The production of an A.M. carrier at high efficiency involves the use of considerable modulating power, and the modulator must be designed to deliver an output equal to half the input power to the amplifier to be modulated. Fig. 2 shows an arrangement for a plate-modulated amplifier. Receivers for A.M. are simpler than those required for other systems since it is only necessary to convert the amplitude-modulated carrier into the audio-frequency voltage, which also varies in amplitude. Fig. 3 shows a typical detector circuit as used in a superheterodyne receiver.

Frequency modulation (F.M.) has only come into prominence since 1939, largely owing to the work of E. H. Armstrong and to the development of very-high-frequency (V.H.F.) broadcasting. Transmitters for F.M. are simpler than their A.M. counterparts, and the modulating power required is in all cases small, use often being made of a reactance valve in conjunction with the oscillator controlling the transmitter frequency. The modulating voltage is applied to this first valve in such a way as to vary its reactance so that the oscillator frequency is made to swing about a mean value at a rate corresponding to the audio-frequency being transmitted and by an amount proportional to this voltage. This deviation, as it is called, is expressed in kilocycles per second. An F.M. receiver is more complex than that for A.M., and the process of detection is carried out by means

of a 'discriminator', whose output voltage is, within limits, linear for a given deviation of radio-frequency input. A typical circuit is illustrated in Fig. 4, which also shows the limiter valve which precedes it. The latter is most important if the full advantages of F.M. are to be realised, for it limits the A.M. components which may result from natural or man-made interference, and prevents them reaching the discriminator. The limiter acts similarly to a 'leaky-grid' detector so that, if the receiver is to be used both for F.M. and A.M., the A.M. output is obtained across C_1 and R_1.

Phase modulation (P.M.), whilst different in principle from F.M., is similar when the resulting carrier and sidebands are examined and the receiver is on the same lines as that for F.M. M. is effected by causing the speech wave to shift the phase of carrier to its sidebands.

The advantages of F.M., and to a certain extent P.M., over A.M. are: (1) Improved signal to noise ratio for a given field strength, as it discriminates against noise which is A.M. in character. (2) Simplicity of M. equipment at the transmitter and low modulator power. (3) Better intelligibility at the edge of the service area by virtue of an inherent 'capture' effect which tends to make the receiver hold the wanted signal. (4) Greater volume range for music which obviates much volume compression. The disadvantages are: (1) F.M. and P.M. require a wide band of frequencies for their transmission, thus restricting their use to the V.H.F. region of the radio spectrum. (2) The receivers are more complex than those required for A.M. (3) F.M. is more susceptible to selective fading than A.M.

Modulation, in music, is an incidental change of key in the course of a composition, one of the most powerful means in any music conforming to the diatonic major and minor system of obtaining contrast, formal balance and dramatic effect. The most usual procedure in getting from one key to another is to do so by way of a chord which is related to both, either (*a*) diatonically, with all the notes of the pivot chord forming part of the scales of each key, (*b*) chromatically, with some of its notes foreign to either or both keys, or (*c*) enharmonically, with one or more notes of the pivot chord changing its identity, e.g. G♯ becoming A♭. But the pivot chord may itself be in no key at all, e.g. a chord of the diminished seventh, or there may be an unprepared plunge from one key into another. M., to near or remote keys, is capable of being effected in an endless variety of ways. See C. Zoeller, *The Art o Modulation*, 1930.

Modulus: 1. In physics, a coefficient characterising a material in terms of the effect produced in it by an external agent. *See* ELASTICITY for Young's M., Bulk M. and Rigidity M.

2. In mathematics, (i) the positive square root of the sum of the squares of the real and imaginary parts of a complex number (q.v.); (ii) the number by which the logarithm (q.v.) of a number to a given base must be multiplied in order to convert it into its logarithm to a

different base; (iii) the symbol $|\sqrt{x}|$, read as Modulus $\sqrt{x}$ or simply Mod $\sqrt{x}$, indicates that the magnitude is to be used without regard to the sign $+$ or $-$.

Moe, Jörgen Ingebrektsen (1813–82), Norwegian poet and folklorist, *b.* Ringerike, of peasant parents. He studied theology at Christiania, and became a clergyman in 1853. He was ultimately appointed Bishop of Kristiansand (1875), where he *d.* M.'s first pub. was *Samling af Sange, Folkeviser og Stevi Norske Almuedialecter*, a collection of folk-songs, 1840. Two years later, in collaboration with Asbjörnsen, he pub. Norwegian folk-tales, *Norske Folkeeventyr* (2 series, 1842–4 and 1871). As a poet, M. is best known by his *At Laenge paajuletraeet*, 1855. His *Samlede Skrifter* appeared in 2 vols., 1924. *See* F. Grimmer, *Dikteren J. Moe*, 1929.

Moehringia, family Caryophyllaceae, genus of minute creeping plants, allied to Arenaria, natives of N. temperate and arctic regions. *M. pendula, M. dasyphylla* and *M. muscosa* are useful rock garden plants.

Møen, is. of Denmark, lying between Zealand and Falster. It is divided from the former by Ulv Sound and from the latter by Grøn Sound; length 20 m., area 86 sq. m. It is the highest is. of Denmark after Bornholm, with precipitous limestone cliffs (500 ft high) on its E. extremity. The soil is chalky and fertile. Its chief tn is Stege. It has a lighthouse visible for 14 m. Pop 13,800.

Moeran, Ernest John (1894–1950), Eng. composer, *b.* Heston, Middx, of Irish descent. He was educ. at Uppingham School and afterwards studied at the Royal College of Music in London. His studies were continued with John Ireland, after service in the First World War. He first came to public notice in 1923 with a London concert. His works include 2 sets of choral songs with old Eng. words, 2 Rhapsodies, a Symphony and other orchestral works, chamber and piano music, many songs, folksong arrangements, etc.

Moeris, Lake, 35 m. long and 4½ m. broad, situated in the prov. of Fayum, central Egypt. It is now known as Birket-el-Karun. Once much larger, on its banks was the labyrinth (q.v.) described by Herodotus; Amenemhat III was responsible for the embankment of the lake, in which sacred crocodiles were kept. *See* R. H. Brown, *The Fayûm and Lake Moeris*, 1892.

Moeritherium, extinct mammal found in the Eocene and Oligocene beds of Egypt, not larger than a tapir, and the earliest member of the proboscideans. Tusk formation had begun and the second pair of incisors in each jaw were much enlarged. M. displays the beginning of specialisations which led to the later mastodons and elephants.

Moesia, anct name of a dist. in E. Europe, bounded S. by Thrace and Macedonia, W. by Illyricum and Pannonia, N. by the Danube, E. by the Euxine, thus corresponding roughly to mod. Serbia and Bulgaria. The inhab. were a Thracian people, who were finally subdued *c.* 25 BC by Rom. forces under M. Licinius Crassus,

MOERITHERIUM: RECONSTRUCTION BASED ON REMAINS

grandson of the triumvir. M. was organised as a prov. of the empire shortly before the death of Augustus. Domitian (AD 81–96) divided it into M. Superior and M. Inferior, being the W. and E. halves respectively, divided by the R. Cebrus. These 2 provs. were invaded by the Goths (*see* MOESO-GOTHS) in 250, and when Aurelian surrendered Dacia (q.v.) to the barbarians and moved its inhab. S. of the Danube, the central region of M. was called Dacia Aureliani.

Moeskroen, *see* MOUSCRON.

Moeso-Goths, name given to certain Visigoths who settled in Lower Moesia (q.v.), at the mouth of the Danube, in the 3rd and 5th cents. They were converted to Christianity by Wulfilas, who trans. the Bible for them.

Moffat, James (1870–1944), Scottish theologian and translator of the Bible, educ. at Glasgow Academy and Univ. Ordained in 1896, he was Yates prof. of Gk and the N.T. at Mansfield College, Oxford, 1911–15. He will be chiefly remembered for his trans. of the Bible. In 1924 he revised an earlier version of the N.T. which he had pub. in 1899, and in this new version he used modern and colloquial phraseology. He subsequently made a similar version of the O.T., publishing Genesis and Esther in 1924, and the remainder in 1925. M. was prof. in the college of the United Free Church of Scotland for some years, and was prof. of church hist. in the United Theological Seminary, New York, where he *d.* His pubs. also include *Introduction to the Literature of the New Testament*, 1911. *Hebrews—International Critical Commentary*, 1924, and *Everyman's Life of Jesus*, 1924.

Moffat, Robert (1795–1883), one of the pioneers of missionary work in Africa and father-in-law of David Livingstone, *b.* in E. Lothian. In 1814 he offered his services to the London Missionary Society, and in 1816 he was sent out to S. Africa, where he worked with great success in Namaqual. Afterwards, having married (1819), he and his wife spent nearly 50 years mainly among the Griquas and Bechuanas. His *Missionary Labours and Scenes in South Africa* appeared in 1842. *See* J. S. Moffat, *Lives of Robert and Mary Moffat*, 1885.

Moffat, police burgh, burgh of barony (1635)

and par. of Dumfriesshire, Scotland, on the Annan, 20 m. NE. of Dumfries. It is noted as a health resort. Pop. 1916.

Mogadishu, or **Mogadiscio,** cap. of Somalia (formerly It. Somaliland). The old tn is interesting and the modern tn is well laid out, the main street being particularly fine. M. is the permanent seat of a U.N. consultative mission and centre of Somali political activity in relation to Fr. Somaliland. Ships anchor in an open roadstead. Pop. Italians, 3000; Somalis and Africans, 70,000. (*See Plate: Somali Republic.*)

Mogila, Peter (*c.* 1596–1647), Russian Orthodox prelate, of a noble Wallachian family, became metropolitan of Kiev, 1632, and drew up a *Catechism,* 1645, and the *Confession of Faith,* 1643, accepted by the synod of Jerusalem, 1672.

Mogilëv (Belorussian **Mohilëv**): 1. Oblast (prov.) in E. Belorussia, in the Dnieper lowland, traversed by the Dnieper and partly covered with mixed forests. It has large peat deposits. There are varied industries, grain-, potato- and flax-growing, hog-raising and dairy farming. The prin. tns are M. and Bobruysk. Area 11,000 sq. m.; pop. (1965) 1,207,000 (38 per cent urb.), mostly Belorussians (before 1939 many Jews).
2. Cap., economic and cultural centre of the above, on the Dnieper. It is an important industrial and transportation centre (engineering, chemical, light and food industries). There is a cathedral (1780) and a local museum (1867). Founded *c.* 1267 as a castle, by 1341 M. was Lithuanian. In 1569 it became Polish and in 1772 Russian; it became a tn in 1526 and prov. cap. in 1778. From the 14th cent. it has been a notable commercial centre. It was the site of the Russian Supreme H.Q. in 1914–17, and the scene of much fighting in 1943–4. Pop. (1965) 156,000 (1913, 70,000; 1926, 50,000; 1939, 99,000).

Mogul, Moghal or **Mughal,** Arabic and Persian forms of Mongol, is usually applied to the Mohammedan empire in India founded by Baber, a descendant of Tamerlane, in 1526. The emperors of Delhi were usually styled the Great Moguls. The M. Empire crumbled after the death of Aurungzebe (1707), and the rule of the M.s came to an end after the Indian Mutiny in 1858, the last of the line dying in prison at Rangoon in 1862. *See also* AKBAR and INDIA, *History.*

Mogul Painting, see INDIAN ART.

Moguntiacum, *see* MAINZ.

Mohács, tn and riv. port of Hungary, in Baranya co., on the Danube, 23 m. ESE. of Pécs. Two famous battles were fought here: on 29 Aug. 1526, when Solyman II (q.v.) defeated and killed Louis II of Hungary; and on 12 Aug, 1687, when the Turks (*see* TURKEY, *History*) were routed by Charles of Lorraine. M. is in a coal-mining dist. Pop. 15,900.

Mohair, *see* WOOL.

Mohammad, Mohammed or **Mahomet** (properly **Muhammad,** 'praised' or 'praiseworthy'), the founder of the religion of Islam (*d.* 632). He was *b.* into a good though impoverished family of the tribe Kuraish in Mecca. He was early orphaned, and first his grandfather and

then an uncle took charge of him. As an infant he was given to a Bedouin foster-mother, and as a boy acted as shepherd, and later, living in a trading centre, had some training in business ways. It is said that the Kuraish had great respect for M., so that when the Kaaba had to be rebuilt, and rival clans disputed the honour of replacing the Black Stone, he was made the arbiter, and the compromise which he suggested was approved by all. He married a well-to-do widow, Khadija (q.v.), 15 years his senior and 40 years old at the time of the marriage. The gross idolatry and the evil ways of Arabs pressed heavily on M.'s heart. He spent hours of solitude in a cave at the foot of Mt Hira where divine light shone on him at the age of 40. He called his people to the worship of one God and to abandon their life of vice and sin. M.'s preaching seems to have lasted some 10 years and to have had little success; at first opposition was slight, but as the Kuraish recognised the implications for their sanctuary and trade, hostility was intensified. Stories tell of persecution, and about 80 men and women fled to Ethiopia, where they stayed for some years. Despairing of Mecca M. went to the neighbouring tn of Taif to find support, but failed dismally. For a time the Kuraish boycotted the clan to which M. belonged and finally conspired to murder him. In the meanwhile Islam took root in Medina (q.v.). Three years later, when some Muslims from there promised to defend M. as they would defend their own families, the exodus to Medina commenced. The Muslims slipped away from Mecca in small groups to form a solid core of zealous believers in the new home. M. and Abu Bekr (q.v.) were almost the last to leave in 622. M. was in a dangerous situation: few of the townsfolk were sincere converts, old hatreds persisted, tribal chiefs were jealous of the upstart, and the local Jews were wealthy and strong. The Koran (q.v.) is full of references to 'hypocrites', those who put their own interests before those of M. and the new religion. The position of the emigrants was precarious: some lived on the charity of the Helpers (the Muslims of Medina) and most were poor. From this time M.'s activities changed; he became less of a preacher, more of a law-giver and a politician, and the change is reflected in the Koran. The agreement which regulated his relations with Medina survives in part; it sets religion above the interests of the tribes and aims at welding them into a unit with the Jews in amiable neutrality. An attempt to seize a rich caravan on its way to Mecca led to the battle of Badr in which the Meccans were defeated; they had their revenge the next year but did not follow up their success. In 627 Mecca made a grand attempt to crush the small community of Muslims by forming a big alliance of tribes to besiege Medina. They were foiled by the simple expedient of a big ditch across the open side of the tn. and M. worked on the mutual suspicions of the allies. In 628 M. led an army against Mecca, but retired without fighting after getting permission to enter the tn in the following year to perform the pilgrimage. In 630 Mecca was captured almost without bloodshed, and a big confederation of tribes was defeated. M. declared a general amnesty which won the hearts of all his opponents.

M. was now the first man in Arabia; his triumph did not go to his head. The victory in this year was almost the last fighting in Arabia. In 632 M. *d.* without having made any arrangements about the succession. At that date Arabia might have been divided into zones; the tribes near Mecca and Medina had a high percentage of Muslims, but the percentage grew less as the distance from the centre increased till, on the outskirts, the only bond might be a treaty or agreement between M. and the local chief. Indeed, in places there were rival prophets.

There can be no doubt that M. was sincere in his belief that he had a message from God, and his personality must have been attractive for him to win the devotion that was given to him. Humanly speaking, one reason for his success was that he had an object in view, the conquest of Mecca, and never lost sight of it, while his opponents had no fixed policy. He could neither read nor write, nor could he, as many Arabs could, make verses. As long as Khadija was alive he took no other wife, but after her death he married sev.; some of these marriages had a political aim, as he chose daughters of his closest adherents, others were to provide for destitute widows. He married only one virgin, Ayesha (q.v.). No son by a wife survived. At first in Medina the Muslims looked towards Jerusalem in their worship; later the order was given to face Mecca. Arabia was cursed by the blood feud; M. condemned extravagant acts of vengeance and promised God's blessing to those who accepted blood money in place of blood. He did not forbid polygamy but regulated it, and did something to stop it by ruling that the bride price must be paid up in full when a wife was divorced, and making the husband maintain her for some months. He made women masters of their own property and forbade the killing of unwanted female babies. In Islam woman is not held responsible for bringing sin and death to the world. M. also forbade the drinking of wine, gambling as it was practised in Arabia, and interest on loans. The Koran calls him a man of 'sublime morals'. Muslims regard him as the ideal man, the supreme example of all virtues. *See also* ISLAM. See Tor Andrae, *Muhammad, the Man and his Faith*, 1936; Muhammad 'Ali, *Living Thoughts of the Prophet Muhammad*, 1947; Kwajah Kamal-ud-Din, *The Ideal Prophet*, 1956, W. M. Watt, *Muhammad in Mecca*, 1953, and *Muhammad in Medina*, 1956.

Mohammad II (1430–81), Sultan of Turkey, called the Conqueror, *b.* Adrianople, succeeded his father, Amurath II, in 1451. Taking Constantinople in 1453, he next fortified the Dardanelles, conquered Greece and most of the Balkan ters., while at sea he became the terror of S. Europe.

Mohammad V (1844–1918), penultimate sultan of Turkey, *b.* Constantinople. When the

Turkish revolution occurred in 1909 at the instigation of the 'Young Turks' committee, the army under Shevket Pasha (assassinated 1913) took possession of Constantinople, deposed and exiled the Sultan Abdul Hamid, and replaced him by his brother, M. Reshid. M. V. *d.* in 1918 and was succeeded by his brother Vahid-ed-Din, who was deposed in 1922 and was the last Turkish sultan.

Mohammad Reza Shah Pahlavi (1919–), Shah of Persia. He succeeded to the throne in 1941 upon the abdication of his father, Reza Shah Pahlavi. He has been m. 3 times, his first wife being the sister of Farouk of Egypt (divorced, 1948). He m. thirdly Farah Diba in 1959, and a son and heir, Prince Reza, was *b.* in 1960. M. has survived a number of attempts to oust him from the throne, and has proved a progressive and capable ruler.

Mohammed Ahmed, *see* MAHDI.

Mohammed Zahir Shah (1914–), King of Afghanistan. Succeeded his father, Mohammed Nadir, in Nov. 1933, on the latter's assassination.

Mohammedan, Mahometan or **Muhammadan Archecture and Art,** *see* MUSLIM ARCHITECTURE AND ART.

Mohammedanism, *see* ISLAM; Muslims object to this name because they explain it as meaning worship of Mohammad.

Mohammerah, *see* KHORARRAMSHAHR.

Mohave, Amer. tribe of the Yuman linguistic stock. In the 18th cent. they were 3000 or 4000. The 900 or so still in existence live on the Colorado R. Reservation, Arizona.

Mohawk, largest trib. of the Hudson R. in New York, U.S.A.; it rises in the co. of Oneida and joins the Hudson at Cohoes. Length 140 m.

Mohawks, tribe of Amer. Indians which belonged to the Iroquois (q.v.) Confederacy. Today there are about 400 in New York state.

Mohawks, or **Mohocks,** lawless band who infested London about 1711 and 1712. They wandered the streets of London at night, and under cover of the darkness attacked harmless citizens.

Mohenjo-daro, anct city of Sind, India, *see* INDUS VALLEY CULTURE.

Mohicans, branch of the Algonquian stock, who originally inhab. the Hudson valley, but gradually withdrew to Connecticut. Today they number under 1000. They are known by James Fenimore Cooper's novel, *The Last of the Mohicans.*

Mohilёv, *see* MOGILЁV.

Mohl, Hugo von (1805–72), Ger. botanist, *b.* Stuttgart. He studied at Tübingen, where he became prof. of botany (1835). It was M. who suggested the name protoplasm for the vegetable cell, the conception of which he clearly defined in 1846, showing the true relationship between the nucleus and the rest of the cellular system (*see* CELL). His prin. work is *Grundzüge der Anatomie und Physiologie der vegetablischen Zelle*, 1851 (Eng. trans., 1852).

Möhler, Johann Adam (1796–1838), Ger. Roman Catholic theologian, *b.* Igersheim,

Württemberg. In 1821, as a young priest working among peasants, he was discovered by Johann Sailer and called to Tübingen Univ. Wishing, however, to lead a spiritual life in accordance with a theology other than the formalist system then in vogue, he left and travelled through Germany, attending various courses, including that of the Protestant Neander (q.v.), who revealed to him the supernatural in hist. After resuming work as a prof. at Tübingen, M. set himself to show Catholics the true nature of the Church, as one, dynamic, ever youthful and enlivened by the Holy Spirit. The result was 2 books: *The Unity of the Church*, 1824, and *Symbolism*, 1832. Leo XIII's Encyclical *Immortale Dei*, on the idea of the Church, borrowed much of M.'s thought, which is apparent also in the teaching of Pius XI and Pius XII on the Mystical Body. M.'s miscellaneous works were ed. by Döllinger (2 vols) 1839–40. See K. Eschweiler, *Möhlers Kirchenbegriff*, 1930.

Mohmand, warlike Pathan tribe inhabiting the mountainous dist of the NW. frontier of Pakistan. Many are now engaged in trade in the Peshawar valley. *See* W. S. Churchill, *The Malakand Campaign*, 1898.

Möhne, riv. of Germany in the *Land* of N. Rhine-Westphalia (q.v.). It rises near Brilon and joins the Ruhr near Neheim. It is dammed for a reservoir at Günne; the dam was breached by mines dropped by R.A.F. aircraft during the Second World War (18 May 1943). Length 43 m.

Mohocks, *see* MOHAWKS.

Mohole Project, project to investigate the mantle of the earth by drilling through the crust to obtain samples of the underlying mantle. The crust is thinner below the oceans than below the continents and this project, planned and executed by Amer. scientists, involves drilling at sea from a specially equipped vessel.

Mohorovicic Discontinuity, boundary or discontinuity between the crust and mantle (q.v.) of the earth discovered in 1909 by the Yugoslav seismologist A. Mohorovicic, also known as the M. discontinuity or Moho. Attempts are now under way to drill to the Moho, which lies at depths of 10–75 kms., being shallowest below oceans.

Mohr, Karl Friedrich (1806–79), German physicist, son of a chemist, *b.* Koblenz, educ. at Heidelberg, Berlin and Bonn Univs. It is claimed by some that he was the first to enunciate the principle of what is now called the conservation of energy in his paper *Über die Natur der Wärme*, 1837.

Mohs's Scale, graduated scale of hardness of minerals, based on a classification of 10 minerals arranged in such an order that each of them scratches all those below it, but cannot scratch any of those above it. The order is (10) diamond; (9) corundum and sapphire; (8) topaz; (7) quartz; (6) orthoclase; (5) apatite; (4) fluorite; (3) calcite; (2) gypsum; (1) talc.

Mohun, Charles, 4th Baron (*c.* 1675–1712), duellist, notorious for his violent temper and wild behaviour. He was twice charged with murder, but was acquitted each time. His last duel was with the Duke of Hamilton in which both men were killed. (The duel is described in Thackeray's *Henry Esmond*.)

Mohur (Persian *muhr*, seal, seal ring), gold coin, originally Persian, used in India from the 16th cent. It was introduced in that country by Akbar, being at first a stamped gold token rather than a coin. The M. was legal tender in Brit. India up to about 1860, its nominal value being 16 rupees in Calcutta, and 15 rupees in Bombay and Madras, where it was minted. Its weight was 180 grammes (troy) and it contained 165 grammes of pure gold. There were also half and quarter gold M.s of proportionate nominal value. In 1899, when a gold standard was estab. in India, the Brit. sovereign was declared legal tender and the M. was accordingly superseded.

Moidore, Moyodore, Moedor or **Lisbonine,** former gold coin of Portugal (*moeda d'ouro*, gold coin), worth 4000 reis; current in England in the early 18th cent. Later it was the name used for 27s., its approximate value.

Moine Schists, or **Granulites,** or **Moine Series,** name of the thick series of flaggy quartz granulites and micaschists, formed by the metamorphism of sandstones and shales, which outcrops in N. Scotland and in W. Ireland. The prin. outcrop forms much of the Scottish Highlands. The M. S. overlie the Lewisian rocks; they are Pre-Cambrian, and were folded and metamorphosed during the Caledonian earth movements which affected NW. Europe in early Palaeozoic times and which may have begun as early as the late Pre-Cambrian. In the Grampian mts the M. S. is known as the central Highland Granulites and passes upwards into the Dalradian Series.

Moir, David Macbeth (1798–1851), physician and writer, *b.* Musselburgh. He early contributed to Constable's and Blackwood's magazines, often under the pseudonym of Δ (Delta). His works include, besides poems, the *Autobiography of Mansie Wauch*, 1828, 1839, and *Outlines of the Ancient History of Medicine*, 1831. The authorship of the *Canadian Boat Song* is attributed by some to M. *See* Sir G. Douglas, *The Blackwood Group*, 1897.

Moirae (Lat. *Furiae*), the Fates They were 3 in number. Sometimes they appear as goddesses of fate in the strict sense; more often, however, they are conceived as deities allegorical of the duration of human life. In this second capacity Lachesis assigns to man his term, Clotho spins the thread of his existence, and Atropos breaks that thread.

See W. C. Greene, *Moira*, 1944.

Moiré (Fr. *moiré*, watered silk), now used exclusively to denote watered or clouded silk, though the actual process of calendering can be applied to any material, whether woollen and silk stuffs or linen. Formerly the term was interchangeable with mohair (*see* WOOL). The calendering process, whatever the particular fabric used, consists in wetting and folding in a particular manner and then subjecting it to hydraulic pressure of about 100 tons between cylinders or rollers. This removes the nap, makes the material smooth, and imparts a wavy appearance.

Mois, name given by the Annamites to the uncivilised peoples dwelling in the Indo-Chinese mts. They are called Khâs by the Thai and Penongs by the Cambodians.

Moiseiwitsch, Benno (1890–1963), pianist, *b.* Odessa. He was at the Imperial School of Music there and at the age of 9 won the Rubinstein prize. In England since 1908, he was granted his certificate of naturalisation in 1937. He made his début at Queen's Hall, London, in 1909, and gained immediate success. He travelled extensively, giving recitals and appearing with all the important orchestras in concerts.

Moissan, Henri (1852–1907), Fr. chemist, *b.* Paris. He became a doctor of science in 1885, prof. of toxicology at the École de Pharmacie in 1886, and prof. at the Sorbonne in 1900. He is celebrated for his valuable experiments with fluorine, being the first to isolate and liquefy it. He also made some interesting experiments in diamonds, and succeeded in manufacturing them artificially. He likewise simplified the production of acetylene gas. His pubs. include *L'Isolement du fluor, Réproduction du diamant, Carbure de calcium, Le Four électrique,* 1897, *Le Fluor et ses composés,* 1900, and articles on manganese, iron, chrome, etc.

Moivre, Abraham de, see DEMOIVRE.

Mojaisk, see MOZHAYSK.

Mojave, or **Mohave, Desert,** area of desert and semi-desert, part of the Basin and Range region of about 15,000 sq. m. in S. California, U.S.A.

Moji, one of 5 tns forming the area known as Kitakyushu (q.v.) which was estab. in 1963 at the N. end of Kyushu, Japan. M., an important commercial port facing Shimonoseki across the Shimonoseki Strait, is linked with the is. of Honshu with a railway tunnel and a road tunnel under the sea. M. was badly bombed in the Second World War.

Mokaddasi, Shams ed-Din al (*Mukaddasi,* from Jerusalem), *b.* AD 946, an Arab (Mohammedan) geographer. He travelled widely, and wrote an account of various countries under Muslim rule. See *Descriptio Imperii Moslemici* (de Goeje's ed. in *Bibliotheca Geographorum Arabicorum,* iii), 1877, and *Syria and Palestine* (Le Strange's ed., Palestine Pilgrims' Text Society, iii), 1886.

See also A. Kremer, *Kulturgeschichte des Orients,* II, 1877, and G. Le Strange, *Palestine under the Moslems,* 1890.

Mokha, see MOCHA.

Mola di Gaeta, see FORMIA.

Molasse, group of sediments of Tertiary age occupying the Swiss Plain. The material making up these sediments was derived from the Alpine mts which during much of the Tertiary were being elevated by earth movements and were thus exposed to rapid erosion. The M. consists largely of sandstones and conglomerates.

Molasses, or **Treacle,** by-product of sugar manuf. M. from cane sugar is utilised as human food; M. from beet sugar is bitter and unpleasantly flavoured, though much is used in Germany for mixing with dry food for livestock as a substitute for roots. In France M. is employed in the production of alcohol. See J. G. Davies, *The Principles of Cane Sugar Manufacture,* 1938.

Molassians, see EPIRUS.

Molay (Molai), Jacques de (1228–1314), last of the grand masters of the Templars (q.v.). Descended from the lords of Longwy and Raon, he joined the order of the Templars and was sent to the chapel at Beaune. Later he distinguished himself in Palestine against the infidels. When in Cyprus he was summoned by Pope Clement V to Paris when all the Templars there were arrested. De M. was imprisoned and put on trial, but refused to save his own life by admitting any charges against the order. For this he was burned at the stake.

Molbech, Christian Knud Frederick (1821–88), Dan. poet, *b.* Copenhagen. He was prof. of Dan. at Kiel from 1853 to 1864, and dramatic censor at Copenhagen from 1871 to 1881. His chief poems are *Digtninger,* 1845, *Fra Danäidernes Kar,* 1873, and *Efterladte digte,* 1888. Among his plays *Ambrosius,* 1878, and *Dante* are the best. He also produced an excellent trans. of the Divina Commedia.

Mold, mrkt tn, assize and administrative co. tn of Flints, Wales, 12 m. SW. of Chester, with limestone quarries and coal and lead mines near. Pop. 6857.

Moldau, see VLTAVA.

Moldavia, NE. portion of Rumania formerly one of the Danubian principalities. *See* RUMANIA.

Moldavian Republic, union rep. of the U.S.S.R. (formed in 1940), comprising the central part of Bessarabia and a strip along the l. b. of the Dniester; largely hilly, with black earth soils. It is one of the most productive agric. regions of the U.S.S.R. Winter wheat, maize, sunflowers, sugarbeet and tobacco are grown; but viniculture and horticulture are even more important economically. There are food and light industries. The prin. tns are Kishinev (cap.), Tiraspol' and Bendery. Area 13,000 sq. m.; pop. (1965) 3,303,000 (26 per cent urb.), mostly Moldavians (Rumanians), Ukrainians and Russians. For hist. see BESSARABIA. The M. Autonomous Rep. was created within the Ukraine in 1921 (cap. Tiraspol').

Moldavians, branch of the Rumanian people living in N. Rumania, also in the Moldavian Rep. (q.v.) and adjacent parts of Bessarabia where they number (1962) 2,380,000. They are the only Romance-speaking people in the U.S.S.R., though nearly half their vocabulary is of Ukrainian origin. They are mostly peasants, since 1947 collectivised, and Orthodox Christians. Their origins are not entirely clear, though they are doubtless the product of a mixture between the Romanised original Thracian inhab. of the area and the Slavs. They came under Slav and Byzantine cultural influences, and until the 17th cent. Church Slavonic was their literary and official language; the first works in Moldavian (using the Cyrillic alphabet) date from the 16th cent. *See also* BESSARABIA.

Molé, Mathieu (1584–1656), Fr. magistrate, *b.* Paris. He became attorney-general in 1614, and was appointed by Richelieu first president of the parlement (1641–53), becoming keeper of the Great Seal (1651). His *Mémoires* were pub. in 1855–7.

Mole, *see* NAEVUS.

Mole, species of insectivore of the family Talpidae. *Talpa europaea*, common Brit. burrowing mammal, is about 6 in. in length, with a cylindrical body, long pointed muzzle, short tail, broad, powerful 5-clawed fore-limbs and long, narrow hind-limbs. The fur is soft and velvety, and usually greyish black, but occasionally of other colours. Although one of the Insectivora, the M.'s food is chiefly earthworms, but insects are eaten in large numbers, and evidence goes to show that a proportion of vegetation forms part of the dietary. M.s are very voracious and cannot live more than a few hours without food. The nest, with its system of galleries and approaches, is a wonderful work, made usually under banks or among the roots of trees. The M. hills are formed as the animal excavates, and on lawns and pastures they cause disfigurement and inconvenience, but the soil is always rich, for the animal avoids poor land where food is likely to be scarce. M.s are usually caught by means of spring traps or by nooses fixed on bent twigs and placed in the runs. N. Amer moles differ from those of the Old World in having tusk-like front upper incisors. *See also* FUR; SHREW MOLE. (*See Plate*: Mammals.)

Mole (Lat. *moles*, a mass), large structure, usually of stone, serving as a pier or breakwater, or joining 2 places separated by water. Hadrian's M. is his mausoleum, now the castle of St Angelo at Rome.

Mole Cricket, orthopterous insect, highly elaborated for a burrowing life in the ground, where, like the mole, it lives on worms and insects. It is from 1½ to 2 in. long, dark brown and covered with soft hair. The tibiae of the forelegs are flattened and terminated much like the forelegs of the mole. The M. C. retains its power of flight, though it goes above ground only at night. The larvae are white; they mature very slowly.

Mole-rat, blind burrowing rodent of the family Spalacidae, having teeth almost like those of rats but in many respects resembling moles. One species inhabits the S. of Russia. Another, found in the Malayan Archipelago, is as large as a rabbit.

Molech, or **Moloch**, originally **Melek** (king), but given the vowel points of *bosheth* (abomination) in Hebrew to discredit it. The title is found widely among Semitic races as a divine name, but in the O.T. it is especially connected with the religion of Ammon, e.g. 1 Kings xii. 7, 'the abomination of the children of Ammon'. M., or Milcom (1 Kings xi. 5; 2 Kings xxiii. 13, etc.), was the special tribal god of the Ammonites, as was Chemosh of the Moabites. The distinctive feature of his worship was the sacrifice of children by fire, and this, though vigorously opposed by the prophets, was introduced into Judah during the last period of the kingdom (Isa. lvii. 5; Jer. xix. 5). Solomon built a sanctuary to M. at Tophet. *See* GEHENNA.

Molecule, denotes in chem. the smallest particle of an element or compound exhibiting the chemical properties of the individual; any further div. completely alters its properties, so that it gives rise to new products. Most M.s are ultra-microscopic and are investigated by the indirect methods of physics and chem. It was the study of gases in which M.s are most free to move that gave rise to the molecular theory. The physical laws common to all gases are Boyle's, Charles's and Dalton's, whilst Avogadro's hypothesis has been particularly useful in the study of gases (*see* GAS AND GASES). Based on these is the kinetic theory of gases (q.v.), which, briefly, asserts the laws to be due to kinetic energy of M.s rather than to any potential forces acting between them. The further study of the physical nature of M.s proceeds in general in the direction of diffusion, viscosity and internal friction of gases.

It is in chem. that success has been most attained. Analysis determines the elements of which any substance is composed, and which must be present in the M. All the M.s are found to be similarly constituted, and the atomic proportions of elements present are generally easily determined. Thus, analysis shows that methane contains the elements carbon and hydrogen in the proportion of 12 to 4 by weight. Now, if we divide each of these numbers by the atomic weights of carbon and hydrogen respectively (12 and 1), we find that the ratio of the number of atoms of carbon to the number of atoms of hydrogen present in methane is 1 : 4, giving as the simplest or empirical formula CH_4. Moreover, the hydrogen in methane can be replaced in 4 stages by the action of chlorine to give the products methyl chloride (CH_3Cl), methylene chloride (CH_2Cl_2), chloroform ($CHCl_3$), and finally carbon tetrachloride (CCl_4), indicating that the formula is probably CH_4 and not C_2H_8, C_3H_{12}, etc. The chemist may then proceed to assign proportional molecular weights to substances. These determinations depend on the hypothesis of Avogadro that equal volumes of gases at the same temp. and pressure contain an equal number of M.s, an hypothesis steadily confirmed in the kinetic theory. The chemist adopts the simple formula, or the simplest multiple which allows his reactions. In a very large number of cases the methods of physics corroborate the simple chemical formula. The molecular weight in grammes of any gas occupies a volume of 22·4 litres at 0° C. and 760 mm. pressure. To return to methane, 1 litre of the gas at 0° C. and 760 mm. weighs 0·717 gm. Thus 22·4 litres would weigh 22·4 × 0·717 or 16·06 gms. This settles the formula for methane, CH_4 (C = 12, H = 1). The other formulae mentioned, e.g. C_2H_8 (12 × 2 + 8 × 1 = 32), would not fit in at all.

It must be remembered that for computing accurate M. weights, the standard taken is $O = 16$ or $H = 1\cdot0076$, and that the density determinations merely serve to fix the approximate value. The accurate result is then obtained from analytical data. (In the case of the rare gases, however, density has to be obtained accurately, as analytical data are impossible.) So far the method is limited to gases. Van't Hoff showed that Avogadro's hypothesis may be applied to substances in dilute solution; results may thus be obtained from consideration of osmotic pressure, and its effect on vapour pressure, boiling and freezing point of the solvent. These methods are useful for non-electrolytes like cane-sugar, but for electrolytes ionisation complicates matters.

Information as to molecular weight in the liquid state can be obtained from surface tension methods (see PARACHOR; SURFACE TENSION, etc.); the most direct, accurate and recent method for determination of molecular weight is by means of a mass spectrometer.

A further study by chemists reveals the structure or architecture of the M. itself. Groups of the constituents of M.s may be removed and tend to remain associated, indicating possibly a closer or stronger structure of those constituents within the M. Substances show the same elements united to form M.s of different substances, yet in the same proportion, the M.s not only presenting different properties but splitting into different groups of atoms in the course of chemical reactions. This, with the aid of the theory of valency (q.v.), enables the chemist to picture the probable architecture of the M.s. These and allied cases occur under the form of isomerism and polymerism (qq.v.). For example, the M. of caffeine is represented thus:

$$
\begin{array}{ccc}
CH_3N\!\!-\!\!CO & & \\
| & | & \\
CO & C\!\!-\!\!NCH_3 & \\
| & \| & \\
CH_3N\!\!-\!\!C\!\!-\!\!N & \!\!\!\!>\!\!CH &
\end{array}
$$

Van't Hoff examined these structures and propounded geometrical theories. For example, fumaric and maleic acid are both represented by:

$$
\begin{array}{c}
HC\!\!-\!\!COOH \\
\| \\
HC\!\!-\!\!COOH
\end{array}
$$

Wislicenus explained this difference in properties by geometrical formulae thus:

Fumaric Acid　　　Maleic Acid

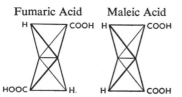

The presence in the M. of an asymmetric carbon atom gives rise to the possibility of optical activity, where 2 M.s related to each other as the right hand is to the left are able in solution to rotate the plane of polarisation of light in opposite directions. Many instances of this activity are known, not confined to the carbon atom (see STEREOCHEMISTRY). The actual size of an average M. is of less interest than its physical structure and chemical properties. It was investigated by Lord Kelvin, who expressed it by stating that if a drop of water were magnified to the size of the earth, its M.s would be somewhere in size between those of a small shot and a cricket ball. In recent years, however, the study of giant or 'macro' M.s has made great advances, and is a specialised subject, polymer science. Among substances with macro-M.s may be mentioned rubber, proteins, natural and artificial fibres, various plastics and antibodies—possibly also viruses.

Molecular Biology, see BIOPHYSICS.

Molenaer, name of 2 Dutch painters, husband and wife, Jan-Mienze M. (c. 1606–68) genre painter and Judith (née Leyster) (c. 1600–60) whom he married in 1636. Both followed Hals (q.v.) in the style and spirit of his more Bohemian subjects, though Jan M. was influenced by Rembrandt in his later work. (See Plate: Dutch Art.)

Molenbeek-Saint-Jean (Flem. **Sint-Jans-Molenbeek**), manufacturing suburb of Brussels, Belgium, just NW. of the city. It makes textiles, carpets, oil, margarine, soap, tinned foods, mirrors, and has foundries of iron, copper and bronze. Pop. 62,600.

Moleschott, Jakob (1822–93), Dutch physiologist and metaphysician, b. s'Hertogenbosch. He held the chair of physiology successively at Zürich, Turin and Rome. In metaphysics he denied any vital principle, regarded life as metabolism between the organic and inorganic worlds, and enclosed his materialism in the formula 'Without matter no force; without force no matter'. His views were developed in Der Kreislauf des Lebens, 1852. Among his numerous scientific treatises was a Natural History of Man and Animals, 1855. He wrote a biography of J. G. Forster.

Molesey, East and **West,** 2 adjacent pars. of Surrey, England, on the r. b. of the Thames, within the urb. dist of Esher (q.v.). Combined pop. 15,100.

Moleskin, kind of silk fabric having a thick soft shag similar to the fur of a mole; also a kind of shaggy cotton fabric which is used for workmen's trousers by reason of its good wearing qualities.

Molesworth, Mary Louisa (1839–1921), writer of children's books, b. Rotterdam, of Scottish descent, her maiden name being Stewart. Educ. in Switzerland, in 1861 she married Major R. M., nephew of Viscount M. She wrote sev. adult novels signed with the pseudonym Ennis Graham, but found her real province in children's books. She wrote delightful fairy stories, of which the best known are The Cuckoo Clock, 1877, The Tapestry Room, 1879, Four Winds Farm, 1887, and Fairies Afield, 1911. She also excelled in stories about real children, among which are *Carrots—Just a Little Boy*, 1876, *The Adventures of Herr Baby*, 1881, *Two Little Waifs*, 1883, *Us*, 1885, *Silverthorns*, 1887, *The Old Pincushion*, 1889, *The Red Grange*, 1891, and *The Carved Lions*, 1895. She wrote over a hundred books in all.

Molesworth, Sir William (1810–55), politician, *b*. London. He entered Parliament in 1832 and was a prominent radical. For many years he controlled the *Westminster Review* with John Stuart Mill. He held the office of secretary of state for the colonies for a few months before his death. It was he more than any other who exposed the evils associated with the transportation of convicts, and he did much to arouse interest in colonial problems generally, placing his wealth and capacity for hard work at the disposal of the colonial reform movement.

Molfetta, It. fishing port in Apulia (q.v.), on the Adriatic, 15 m. WSW. of Bari. It has an 18th cent. baroque cathedral, as well as a Romanesque cathedral of the 13th–14th cents. Pop. 60,000.

Molière (1622–73), name assumed by Jean-Baptiste Poquelin, the greatest comic dramatist of France. He was *b*. Paris, the son of a rich upholsterer, who was also *valet de chambre du roi*. He studied law at the univ. of Orléans. But the career of lawyer was not congenial to Poquelin, while the theatre attracted him irresistibly. He got together a little troupe, founded the 'Illustre Théâtre' and took the name of Molière. The company ended in bankruptcy, and M. was jailed for debt, but his father bailed him out. M. and his troupe left Paris for the provs., and for the next 12 or 13 years they went from tn to tn playing. M. was not only the manager of the troupe, and an actor, but the adapter of the plays they presented and, soon, an author himself. At first he wrote farces after the orthodox It. type, with its stock characters. Some of these he afterwards recast, and developed into real comedies, as, for instance, *Le Fagotier*, which became *Le Médecin malgré lui*; *Gorgibus dans le sac*, which became *Les Fourberies de Scapin*: and *La Jalousie du Barbouillé*, the later *George Dandin*. Two works of comedy proper mark this period, *L'Étourdi* and *Le Dépit amoureux*. With the help of a reputation won in the provs., and the patronage of the Prince de Conti, who introduced him through Monsieur, the king's brother, to the king and queen, M. launched his troupe in Paris under the title 'Troupe de Monsieur'.

In 1658 his company acted Corneille's tragedy *Nicomède* before Louis XIV, but the reception was tepid, largely because M. thought that the characters should use the diction of people in real life. But M. saved the situation with his now vanished farce, *Le Docteur amoureux*. As *pièce de début* before the Parisian public he gave *Les Précieuses ridicules*, 1659, the first satire on Fr. would-be cultivated society, especially as seen in the provs. Its truthfulness to life, its gaiety and good humour, secured for M. the public favour for ever. M.'s troupe then moved to Richelieu's

theatre in the Palais Royal, where they remained until his death. They subsequently amalgamated with their rivals, the Hôtel de Bourgogne, and so formed a company which, housed in various premises, has preserved throughout the historic name of the Comédie Française.

Comedy after comedy followed with remarkable rapidity for 13 years. M. endeavoured to bring comedy up to the standard of tragedy, even to surpass it if possible, but he was obliged for financial reasons to provide also conventional farces and, to satisfy the taste of the court, operatic comedies or comedy-ballets, such as *Les Fâcheux*, in which the words are only a pretext for music and dancing. *Sganarelle, ou le Cocu imaginaire*, was produced in 1660; *Don Garcie de Navarre*, *L'École des maris* and *Les Fâcheux*, in 1661. *L'École des femmes*, in which, as in *L'École des maris*, M. shows what happens when people's natural tendencies are ignored, was a brilliant success, but it brought upon its author those jealousies and bitter attacks which were to pursue him to the end of his life. To these attacks he replied (1663) in the mordant *Critique de l'École des femmes* and *L'Impromptu de Versailles*. The first-named of these pieces is important as an expression of M.'s own views on the true use of rules and the whole duty of a dramatist.

In 1664 *Le Mariage forcé*, *La Princesse d'Élide* and the first 3 acts of *Tartuffe* were performed. *Tartuffe* was an attack upon hypocrisy in religion, as it may come to flourish in the house of a *bourgeois dévot*. But the religious community, Jesuits and Jansenists alike, feared the satire was, or would be thought to be, of more general application, and they prevailed upon Louis XIV to suppress it. Only after 5 years was the whole play authorised and played with extraordinary success, 1669. *Don Juan*, 1665, was another play in which hypocrisy was attacked; in *L'Amour médecin*, *Le Médecin malgré lui* and *Le Malade imaginaire* the doctors of the day are pilloried and quackery exposed; sincerity and coquetry come to close quarters in *Le Misanthrope*; the mortifications of the man who marries into a superior social rank are depicted in *George Dandin*; *L'Avare* shows that distrust comes to be the essential characteristic of the miser, and the immortal *Bourgeois Gentilhomme* makes fun of the *bourgeois* who would quit his native sphere and become a *gentilhomme*.

M.'s art marked an epoch in the development of the Fr. drama; it brought about a new dramatic ideal. The ideal hero of classic tragedy gave place in M.'s comedies to the real man with all his foibles and his duality of character—'On peut être intelligent en son entendement et sot en son caractère'. M. shows the man in his surroundings, not more or less detached from them as was the classic hero, and thus incidentally throws a clear light on the whole group to which he belongs. His chief aim seems to have been to amuse by depicting things as they actually were, in strict truthfulness to life. Whether he had the deliberate moral aim to cure men of their foibles and vices is a moot point. The many opinions expressed by M. which seem to show that he had this aim should, according to Faguet, be looked upon as constituting his *apologia* rather than his set purpose. There is little room for sympathy in the amusement evoked by M.'s characters; the laughter they cause is the critical laughter of the intelligence. M. set the fashion for comic writers after him. See D. Mornet, *Molière*, 1943; W. G. Moore, *Molière: A New Criticism*, 1949; D. B. W. Lewis, *Molière: The Comic Mask*, 1959; L. Gossman, *Men and Masks*, 1946.

Molina, Luis (1535–1600), Sp. Jesuit whom Pascal's *Lettres provinciales* have rendered memorable, *b.* Cuenca, in New Castile. He entered the Society of Jesus at an early age, and for some time taught theology at the college of Coimbra in Portugal. Later he was appointed prof. of theology at Evora, returning to Spain at the end of 20 years. Shortly before his death he was appointed prof. of theology in Madrid. His chief work is *Concordia Liberi Arbitrii cum Gratiae Donis*, 1588. He also wrote commentaries on the first part of the *Summa* of Aquinas, and *De Justitia et Jure*. M.'s doctrine is an attempt to reconcile the free will of man with predestination, and gave rise to protracted disputes with the Thomist school of theology, headed by the Dominicans. Today Molinism is either abandoned or much modified by the chief Jesuit theologians. See F. Stegmüller, *Geschichte des Molinismus*, 1935.

Molina, Tirso de, see TIRSO DE MOLINA.

Molinae, see MOULINS.

Molinari, Stefano, see MULINARI.

Moline, city in Illinois, U.S.A., on the Mississippi R. (with bridges and a power dam) at the mouth of Rock R., opposite Davenport, Iowa, and adjoining Rock Is. and E. Moline. A railway, highway and air centre for a grain-growing and stock-fattening area, M. has extensive farm equipment and machinery manufs. Pop. 42,700.

Molinia, genus of grasses common on damp moors. The long stiff stems of *M. caerulea* are gathered and sold for cleaning tobacco pipes. A variegated form is grown in the garden as an edging plant.

Molinier, Guilhem, 14th cent. Occitan (or 'Provençal', q.v.), writer, *b.* Toulouse. He was one of the founders (1353) of the Toulouse literary academy, the Consistori del Gay Saber, of which he became Chancellor. On behalf of the academy he composed a lengthy grammatical and poetical treatise, *Las Leys d'Amor*, 1356, for the guidance of those entering the academy's poetical competitions.

Molinos, Miguel de (1640–*c.* 1696), Sp. mystic and ascetic, *b.* Patacina, Aragon. He was ordained priest, and in 1669 went to Rome, where he became acquainted with many distinguished people. In 1675 he pub. his *Spiritual Guide*, an ascetical treatise which roused the antagonism of the Jesuits. His system of Quietism (q.v.) taught absolute neutrality of the will after a single act of self-consecration, thus

opening the door to acquiescence in moral evil of any form. It was finally condemned by Pope Innocent XI in 1667, and M. was sentenced to life imprisonment. He *d.* in communion with the Church. See J. Bigelow, *Molinos the Quietist*, 1882.

Molise, see CAMPOBASSO.

Mollah, see MULLAH.

Mollendo, port and beach resort of S. Peru, in the dept of Arequipa. It is the terminus of the S. Railway running 107 m. from Arequipa. The railway is linked with Bolivia via Puno, a small tn on shore of Lake Titicaca, where steamers cross to Guaqui, Bolivia. Its roadstead is an open one and exposed to storms. The prin. export is wool. Pop. 15,000.

Møller, Poul Martin (1794–1838), Dan. writer, *b.* near Veile, son of a par. priest who subsequently became a bishop. After studying theology and being ordained he visited China as a ship's chaplain (1819), during the voyage writing his poem *Glaede over Danmark*. In 1826 he became prof. of philosophy at Christiania; prof. extraordinary at Copenhagen (1830). His works include the romance, *En dansk Students Eventyr*, 1824; the play, *Eyvind Skaldaspiller:* a book of aphorisms, and a trans. of the *Odyssey*. His *Efterladte Skrifter* appeared in 1839–56. See V. Andersen, *P. Møller. Hans liv og skrifter* (3rd ed.), 1944.

Mollet, Guy (1905–), Fr. politician. After the liberation of France he became prominent in political affairs, being a member of the constituent assemblies, 1945 and 1946, and Socialist deputy for Arras since 1946. He was premier from Jan. 1956 to May 1957, and minister of state under de Gaulle, 1958–9.

Mollison, James Allan (1905–60), Brit. airman who made a number of long-distance record flights in the 1930's, including Newfoundland to Croydon in 13 hrs 16 min. in Oct. 1936.

Molluscs (*Mollusca*), or **Shell Fish,** constitute one of the chief divs. (phyla) of the animal kingdom, and were evolved at a very remote period in its hist. The great majority live in the sea, some of them at very low depths (a few below 2900 fathoms); others occur in shallow water, and many above low-tide mark. A considerable proportion inhabit rivs. and lakes, and very large numbers have adapted themselves to a terrestrial life, some even contriving to live in deserts, though most terrestrial M. are very dependent on moisture. The diet is much varied; carnivorous M. prey chiefly upon other members of the phylum. Many feed exclusvely, on minute lowly organisms, and others are entirely vegetarian. A few M. have long been valued as food, or as bait for other animals, some yield dyes (e.g. *Murex*, formerly used as a source of Tyrian purple), and others secrete pearls and pearly shells which have been and are employed for great diversity of ornament. The modern systematic arrangement of M. is in 5 classes, as follows: Class 1, Amphineura, comprises 2 orders. The first, Polyplacophora or Isopleura, includes the coat-of-mail shells, or sea woodlice (*Chiton*). These differ in many respects from other M., having points in common with crustaceans and annelids, but after investigation of their life hist. there is no doubt as to their association with M. The other order, Aplacophora or Solenogastres, includes a few worm-like creatures which, instead of a shell, bear on the dorsal surface minute calcareous spines. Class 2, Gastropoda, is divided into 2 sections: Streptoneura (with a twisted nerve loop), the members of which are bisexual, furnished with a shell and generally with an operculum, and Euthyneura (in which the visceral loop is untwisted), which are hermaphrodite M., scarcely any with an operculum

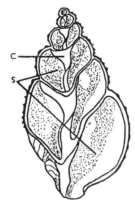

HALF SHELL OF WHELK

c. columella; s, spiral cavity inhabited by whelk.

in the adult state. The first section contains 2 orders, Aspidobranchia or Diotocardia, of which the limpets, top-shells and ear-shells are typical, and Pectinibranchia, typified by rock snails, whelks, harp shells, cones, wing shells and periwinkles. The first order (Opisthobranchia) of the other section are all marine, e.g. bubble shells, sea hares and umbrella shells. The second order (Pulmonata) comprises the true snails and slugs and the false limpets. Class 3, Scaphopoda, includes only the tooth shells (Dentaliidae), which are a very distinct group of sand burrowers; tubular shells resembling the tubes constructed by some marine worms. Class 4, Lamellibranchia or Pelecypoda, comprises the bivalves. All the members of this class, unlike other M., have no head, nor cephalic eyes, nor jaws nor tongue. All are aquatic and most of them marine. They are classified in 4 orders: (i) Protobranchia (e.g. *Nucula*), (ii) Filibranchia (e.g. common mussel, pearl oyster, scallops), (iii) Eulamellibranchia (e.g. freshwater mussel, cockle, razor shell, oyster, shipworms), (iv) Septibranchia (e.g. *Poromya*). Class 5, Cephalopoda, is arranged in 2 subclasses: Tetrabranchia and Dibranchia. Of the former, the pearly nautilus is the solitary living example, but with it have been classified all the oldest fossil

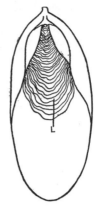

INTERNAL SHELL OF CUTTLEFISH
(Sepia)
L, laminae.

forms (the Ammonoids). *Nautilus* itself has been found in the oldest Palaeozoic formations. It differs from all other cephalopods in having 4 instead of 2 gills, and a number of small retractile feelers instead of 8 or 10 arms with suckers or hooks. The sub-class Dibranchia consists of 2 orders: (i) the Octopoda, in which are the octopus, the argonaut and other forms with 8 similar arms; (ii) the Decapoda, including the squids, cuttlefish and other M. with 8 similar arms and 2 longer ones that can be retracted. In all cases M. reproduce by means of eggs. but in the freshwater snails (Vivipara) and other instances the young are hatched within the parent's oviduct. Some bivalves produce eggs in enormous numbers, e.g. the common oyster, a million or more, and the Amer. oyster, 10 or 50 times as many. Terrestrial M., on the other hand, deposit very few eggs, and these are enveloped, in some cases, in a gelatinous mass, in others, in a thin soft skin, and in a few are protected by a hardened calcareous shell. Many M. deposit their ova in capsules (e.g. common whelk), others produce them in spiral ribbon-like structures. The ova of most marine M. develop into free-swimming larvae (Trochophore and Veliger), but in a few cases there is no metamorphosis. No mollusc has an internal body skeleton, and hence their name, from the Lat. *mollis*, soft. In most of them the external shell, which is secreted by the mantle or outer covering, affords adequate protection. In the shell a vast variety of structures and arrangement occurs, but it is of no more importance to systematic zoologists than the structural features of the animal. The shell may be single as in the limpet and snail, or be formed of 2 valves as in the mussel or oyster, or it may consist of a series of plates as in the Chitons. In the squid it is wholly internal, and from a number of M. it is altogether absent. The foot is a modification of the ventral surface, and in the Cephalopods part

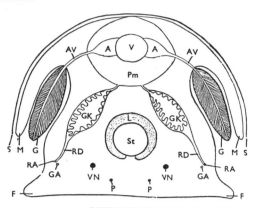

A, A. Auricles ⎫ of heart.
V.   Ventricle ⎭
Pm. Pericardium.
AV. Afferent blood vessels leading to 'gills'.
G.   Ctenidia or 'gills'.
S.   Shell.
M.   Mantle.
GK. Glandular part of kidneys.
RD. Renal duct.
RA.   Renal aperture.
GA. Genital aperture.
VN. Visceral nerves.
P.   Pedal nerves.
St.   Stomach.
L.   Liver.
F.   Foot.

SCHEMATIC TRANSVERSE SECTION OF A BILATERAL MOLLUSC
The structure of all molluscs may be considered as derived by modification of such an arrangement.

of it is elaborated into the so-called arms, the other part forming a funnel through which water is ejected to cause the animal to move in the opposite direction. In the cockles it is adapted for leaping, in the limpet for clinging, in the razor shells for burrowing and in the pond snails for gliding. The operculum is the flat hard structure with which the whelk closes its shell. It also is subject to much elaboration. Breathing is accomplished in aquatic forms by means of gills, the ctenidia, which show a variety of form and arrangement in the different orders. In most M. the mantle, which secretes and lines the shell, is folded in such a way that it encloses part of the vascular system, and in aquatic forms the gills also are enclosed within the mantle cavity. In land M. the cavity forms an air chamber, sometimes termed a lung, with an opening through which air is inhaled and exhaled at very irregular intervals. This arrangement facilitates the interchange of gases between the vascular system and the air. *Eustace*, a Brazilian mollusc, has a gill and a respiratory chamber, and is thus intermediate between wholly aquatic and terrestrial M. Some M. have paired gills; others have a single gill. The octopus and cuttlefish have 1 pair, *Nautilus* 2 pairs and *Chiton* many pairs of gills. Considerable variation occurs in the form of the gills; some are filamentous, others are formed of a series of thin, overlapping plates or leaves, others are reduced to a single septum. In the Scaphopoda there are no special breathing organs, but exchange of gases takes place over the whole surface.

The vascular system, too, shows great differences in development in various M. In some, the heart is very reduced; in others, a single auricle and ventricle are present, whereas in others there are 2 auricles and a ventricle. Forms with the best developed vascular systems have occasional sinuses or spaces into which the walls of the blood vessels do not extend. Blood flows

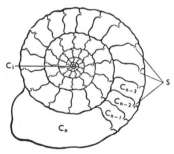

SURFACE OF SECTION OF AMMONITE (FOSSIL SHELL)
c_1—c_{n-3}—c_n. Chambers successively occupied as growth proceeded.
s, siphuncle; through this passed an organic cord connecting the first chamber, c_1, with the visceral hump in the last chamber, c_n.

through the sinuses and into other vessels. In poorly developed vascular systems of certain M. the actual vessels are comparatively short, and the blood passes into an extensive haemocoel. The odontophore or radula, which occurs in all M. except the Lamellibranchs, is a remarkable structure; its upper surface is covered with spiny outgrowths, and with this the limpet rasps the rocks for food, and carnivorous M. penetrate the shells of other M. From complete absence in some species to the wonderful eye of the cuttles, organs of vision are to be found in all stages of development. A sense of hearing, and also a sense of smell, are undoubtedly present in the more highly specialised M. As an instance of the tenacity of life in many M., a desert snail in the Brit. Museum was found to be alive after having been fixed to a tablet for 4 years, where, of course, it could not obtain food or water. *See*

The Cambridge Natural History, vol. iii, 1895–1909; A. H. Cooke, *Molluscs, Brachiopoda*, 1895; Sir E. R. Lankester, *Mollusca*, 1906; E. A. Ellis, *British Snails*, 1926; O. B. Böggild, *Shell Structure*, 1930; A. H. Verrill, *Strange Sea Shells*, 1936; Ida Colthurst, *Shells of the Tropical Seas*, 1938; F. M. Duncan, *British Shells*, 1943; J. T. Nichols and P. Bartsch, *Fishes and Shells of the Pacific World*, 1946; J. Allan, *Australian Shells*, 1950; J. E. Rogers, *The Shell Book*, 1952; A. W. B. Powell, *Antarctic and Subantarctic Mollusca*, 1953; A. Mozley, *An Introduction to Molluscan Ecology*, 1954; R. T. Abbott, *American Seashells*, 1954.

Mollwitz (Polish **Malujowice**), vil. of Lower Silesia, now in Opole prov., Poland, about 5 m. W. of Brieg. Frederick the Great routed the Austrians under Neipperg here in 1741. Frederick's own share in the victory was negligible, for when his cavalry, under Schülenburg, were hurled from the field by Römer, the Austrian cavalry leader, Frederick, who was involved in their rout, fled from the field of battle. It was the Prussian infantry under Schwerin who won the victory by their steadiness and rapid fire.

Molly Maguires, name of a Ribbon society which flourished in Ireland between 1835 and 1855, and harassed the landlords and their supporters. It was also the name of a more notorious secret society which terrorised the coal dists of Pennsylvania, U.S.A., for some 15 years before 1877. In that year many of the ringleaders were convicted and hanged, and the society was broken up. *See also* WHITEBOYS.

Molnár, Ferenc (1878–1952), Hungarian playwright and novelist, *b.* Budapest, studied at Geneva Univ. His plays have always had a higher reputation in England and the U.S.A. than in Hungary, where his novel *The Paul Street Boys*, a sensitive study of childhood, is considered his best work. His autobiography, *Companion in Exile*, appeared in 1951. He *d.* in New York. See *Plays of Molnar*, trans. B. F. Glazer, 1927, and in J. Gassner's *Masters of Drama* (3rd ed.), 1954.

Moloch, *see* MOLECH.

Molotov (real name **Skryabin**), **Vyacheslav Mikhaylovich** (1890–), Russian Communist. He joined the party in 1906. After the Feb. revolution (q.v.) in 1917, as a member of the Russian Bureau of the party's Central Committee, M. represented, against Kamenev and Stalin, an irreconcilable attitude towards the Provisional Gov. (q.v.), thus anticipating Lenin's position. After the Oct. revolution (q.v.) he specialised in the organisational work of the party, soon rising to important positions. From 1920 to 1925 he was head of the party organisation in the Ukraine, and from 1921 to 1930 second secretary (after Stalin) of the party's Central Committee; from 1926 he was a member of the Politburo (q.v.) and of the Presidium of the Executive Committee of the Communist International. He was chairman of the Council of People's Commissars (prime minister), 1930–40; a deputy chairman, 1940–53 (of the Council of Ministers from 1946); and a first

deputy-chairman, 1953–7. From 1941 to 1945 he was deputy-chairman of the State Defence Committee (q.v.) and from 1939 to 1949 and again 1953 to 1956 he was Commissar for Foreign Affairs (from 1946 Minister). From the early 1920's M. was a faithful lieutenant of Stalin and was rewarded by a position in the party second only to his. After Stalin's death his influence declined. He was appointed ambas. to the Mongolian People's Rep., and later, 1960–1, the U.S.S.R.'s permanent delegate to the International Atomic Energy Agency in Vienna. As a diplomat he earned a reputation for extreme stubbornness, and this quality quite often brought him success. He has remained a Stalinist out of conviction, and wrote a memorandum, evidently on Stalinist lines, to the Party Central Committee before the 22nd Congress in 1961. After this Congress, according to a statement by Suslov in 1964, he was expelled from the party.

Molotov, *see* PERM.

Molteno, Sir John Charles (1814–86), S. African statesman, of Milanese extraction, *b.* London. In 1831 he sailed for S. Africa, in 1854 became first member for Beaufort in the legislative assembly, and in 1872 was appointed first Cape Premier. In 1878 he retired from public life, being opposed in every respect to Sir Bartle Frere's policy. *The Life and Times of Sir J. C. Molteno* by his son, Percy A. M., gives an account of the Cape colonists' struggle to obtain a liberal and workable constitution.

Moltke, Helmuth Carl Bernhard, Baron von (1800–91), Prussian soldier and statesman, *b.* Parchim, son of a Dan. general. In 1822 he left the Danish for the Prussian military service, becoming staff major in 1832. In 1839 he took part in the Syrian campaign as adviser to the Turkish commander-in-chief. Becoming chief of the general staff in 1849, he took an important part in the conduct of operations in the Dan. war (1864) and in the subsequent peace negotiations. He was sent to Florence in Feb. 1866 to negotiate an alliance with Italy against Austria. With the Prussian king he defeated the Austrians at Sadowa (1866). His foresight had much to do with the success of Germany in the Franco-Ger. war of 1871, the details of the plan of campaign being prepared by him as early as 1867. On his return to Prussia M. was created field marshal. M. pub. many works, among which were *The Italian Campaign of 1859*, *The German Army*, 1871, and *The Franco-German War*, 1872. See life by F. E. Whitton, 1921.

Moluccas, or **Spice Islands**, sev. groups of is. lying between New Guinea and Sulawesi, Indonesia. They include Ternate and Halmahera; Buru and Seram (in the Ambon group); the Banda Is.; Timor-Laut, Larat and others of the SE. is.; and the Bachian, Obi, Kei, Aru, Babar, Leti and Wetar groups. The M. are mountainous and volcanic, and the soil is very fertile; the chief products are all kinds of spices, copra, forest products, rice and coffee. The climate is fairly healthy, though hot and moist. Ambon is the chief tn and most important commercial centre.

The English were in possession of the M. in the early 17th cent., when there were frequent battles with the Dutch; but later in that cent. the Dutch, by securing their base in Java, became masters of the archipelago. Van Diemen, having conquered Ceylon, isolated Malacca, with the result that the M. fell to the Dutch in 1642. According to Raffles (q.v.) desolation and ruin tracked the steps of the Dutch power, and in the outer is., especially in the M. and Sulawesi, his summary condemnation was not unmerited. Ambon was occupied by the Japanese in Feb. 1942, but the is. reverted to the Dutch in 1945. In 1950 they were recognised as part of the Rep. of Indonesia. The area of Ambon is 75,000 sq. m., pop. 401,000; Ternate 115,900 sq. m., pop. 494,000. See H. M. Tomlinson, *Tidemarks*, 1924; J. Verken, *Moluccas—Reise, 1607–12*, 1930; J. J. Saar, *Reise an Banda, 1644–60*, 1930; R. H. Gofton, *Pageant of the Spice Islands*, 1936.

Moluccella, genus of hardy and half-hardy anns. (family Labiatae), with flowers in axillary whorls. *M. laevis*, Molucca balm, is grown in the garden.

Molybdenum (symbol Mo, atomic number 42, atomic weight 95·95, first obtained in the metallic state by Hjelm, 1782), a silvery-white, brittle metal, occurs in the mineral molybdenite, MoS_2, the disulphide of Mo, which resembles graphite in appearance, but which can be distinguished from it by the green tinge which it gives to the Bunsen flame. It also occurs in wulfenite, $PbMoO_4$, or lead molybdate, and in a rare form as Mo ochre, MoO_3, the most important of the 3 oxides of Mo. The metal is obtained by heating the oxide with charcoal, or in a current of hydrogen, or by heating with aluminium. Molybdenite when roasted oxidises to form the oxide, which is soluble in ammonia, forming ammonium molybdate, a reagent used to test for phosphates. Mo is used in the production of high-speed steels; 90 per cent of the global production of Mo comes from the U.S.A.

Molyneux, William (1656–98), mathematician and philosophical writer, b. Dublin. A fellow of the Royal Society and at one time president of the Dublin Philosophical Society, he was returned to the Irish Parliament in 1692, and created a stir by his plea for the legislative independence of his country in *The Case for Ireland*, 1698. He wrote the first Eng. treatise on optics, *Dioptrica Nova*, 1692, a subject suggested, perhaps, by his wife's tragic loss of sight.

Molza, Francesco Maria (1489–1544), It. poet, b. Modena. His *Ninfa Tiberina*, 1538, has been described as a glowing pastoral mosaic, but most of his poetry seems but a frigid, if finished, paraphrase of Gk and Lat. verse.

Mombasa, seaport and tn of Kenya (q.v.), on the E. coast of M. Is. The is. of M. is 3 m. long and 2 m. wide (area $5\frac{1}{2}$ sq. m.); it is separated from the mainland by a narrow channel, the N. part of which leads from the Indian Ocean to M. Old Port, while the S. part leads to Kilindini Quay and railhead. Kilindini, the chief port of the is.,

is thoroughly modern, with spacious sheds along the quay, and is the finest harbour on the E. African coast. It is a railway terminus some 330 m. from Nairobi. M. Old Port is situated on the N. side of the is., where it is dominated by the old Arab tn; it is now used exclusively for dhows. At Mbaraki, on the is. of M., there is a slipway and anchorage for yachts.

The Portuguese sailed into M. in 1498, when Vasco da Gama had an unfriendly reception. The tn was sacked by Pedro Cabral in 1500 and in 1505 by Francesco de Almeida, the first Portuguese viceroy of India. In 1698 the Arabs entered the port after the garrison had held out until only 11 men and 2 women were left, these being murdered by the Arabs before the Portuguese fleet could reach M. A detailed account of early settlements by the Arabs will be found in *The History of the Imams and Seyyids of Oman* by Salil-ibn-Razik, which has been trans. into English. M. has grown rapidly with the development of Kenya and is thriving and prosperous. Pop. European, 2000; Indian, 28,850; Goan, 1750; Arab, 13,500; African, 42,850.

Mombert, Alfred (1872–1942), Ger. poet and critic, trained as a barrister, wrote many lyrics, mostly in a symbolistic vein. Early conventional verses were collected in *Tag und Nacht*, 1894; those which followed became more experimental, as *Der Glühende*, 1896; *Die Blüte des Chaos*, 1905; *Ataïr*, 1925. In 1919 he wrote an allegory on the Great War in terms of mythology, a favourite vehicle of his which he had used previously in a trilogy of what he called 'symphonic dramas', written between 1907 and 1911, having as their central figure 'Aeon', who symbolises mankind. *Sfaira der Alte*, 1936, was the last work he wrote before falling foul of the Nazis. The concentration camp to which they sent him hastened his death, but in the few months which remained to him after his release he wrote a second part to *Sfaira* embodying his experiences. It was pub. posthumously. The best selection of his works is his own, *Der himmlische Zecher*, 1952. See studies by R. Benz, 1942 and H. Hennecke, 1952.

Moments. The moment of a force about a given point is the product of the force and the length of the perpendicular drawn from the given point upon the line of action of the force. M. may be represented graphically by the area of a triangle. If P (Fig. 1) is the given point, AB represents the force in magnitude and direction, and PN is drawn perpendicularly to AB, then the moment of the force about $P = AB \times PN$ which is equal to twice the area of the triangle PAB. The common convention of signs is that the moment is positive if the force tends to turn the body about the point in a counter-clockwise direction, negative when the body tends to turn in the opposite direction.

Moment of inertia. A constant of a body which is most important in the mathematics of the rotation of a rigid body. Consider a rigid body divided up into very small particles; the moment of inertia of the body about a given axis is defined as the sum of the terms obtained by multiplying the mass of each element by the square of its perpendicular distance from the given axis. A few simple cases are noticed here. The easiest method of calculating the moment of inertia is by means of the integral calculus. A uniform rod of length $2l$ and line density ρ rotates about an axis perpendicular to it through its centre C (Fig. 2). Take an element δx at distance x from C. Its mass $= \rho\delta x$, its moment

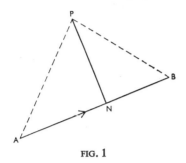

FIG. 1

of inertia $= \rho x^2 \delta x$, therefore total moment of inertia of the rod $= 2\int_0^l \rho x^2 \delta x = 2\rho.\dfrac{l^2}{3} = M\dfrac{l^3}{3}$ where M = total mass = $2l\rho$. The moment of inertia of a rectangle, sides $2a$ and $2b$, is found by dividing it up into thin rods parallel to one side, e.g. side of length $2b$. Then the moment of inertia of the rectangle about a line through its centre parallel to the side $2a = M\dfrac{b^2}{3}$, where M is the total mass of the rectangle. A circular plate (Fig. 3) is divided up into annular rings. If O is

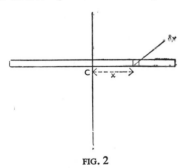

FIG. 2

the centre, consider the ring, the radii of whose boundaries are r and $r + \delta r$. Its mass $= 2\pi r.\rho.\delta r$, where ρ = area density. Its moment of inertia about an axis through O perpendicular to the plane of the plate $= 2\pi r\rho\delta r \times r^2$. Total moment of inertia of the plate $= \int_0^a 2\pi\rho r^3 \delta r$, where a is the radius.

Therefore moment of inertia $= \dfrac{Ma^2}{2}$, where M = mass of the plate. Two very important

theorems in connection with the theory are the following: (1) If we take 3 perpendicular axes OX, OY, OZ (Fig. 4), and consider the moment of inertia of a particle of mass m about these axes, the position of the particle being in the XY plane and having co-ordinates (x, y), i.e. OM $= x$, MP $= y$, then $I_x = my^2$, $I_y = mx^2$, $I_z = mr^2$, where I denotes the moment of

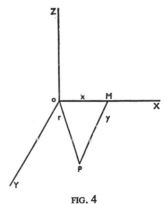

FIG. 3

inertia, and the suffix the axis about which the moment of inertia is taken. Then $I_x + I_y = m(x^2 \times y^2) = mr^2 = I_z$. (2) Again, if I_1 = moment of the body about an axis through the centre of gravity and I_2 = moment of inertia about a parallel axis at a distance h from the first axis, then $I_2 = I_1 + Mh^2$, where M = mass of the body. Thus the moment of

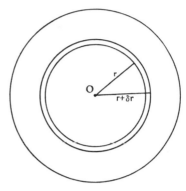

FIG. 4

inertia of a circular plate about an axis perpendicular to its plane $= \dfrac{Ma^2}{2}$, and the moment of inertia about a diameter $= \dfrac{Ma^2}{4}$, since the first axis is perpendicular to the diameter and, from the symmetry of the figure, the moment of inertia about any diameter is the same. Any 2 perpendicular diameters may be taken, the result following by the first theorem.

The moment of inertia about a tangent $= \dfrac{Ma^2}{4} + Ma^2$ by the second theorem.

Bending moment. Consider a beam fixed at one end and caused to bend by a load applied to the free end. When the beam bends, the upper surface is elongated and the lower surface is compressed, and the stresses generated are

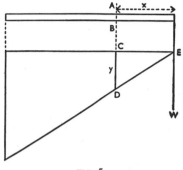

FIG. 5

obviously equal and opposite in direction, thus constituting a couple. This couple resists the bending which must necessarily be caused by an external couple, which is called the B.M. at the section of the beam under consideration, and is equal to the M. about the section of the external forces on the part of the beam on one side of the section.

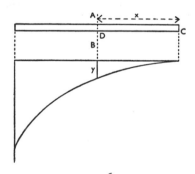

FIG. 6

Examples: (1) *Cantilever with a load at the free end* (Fig. 5). Take section AB, whose distance from the free end $= x$. Then the bending moment at this section $= Wx$. If the weight W is represented graphically by y, then the bending moment is represented by xy, which is twice the area of the triangle CDE. (2) *Cantilever with uniformly distributed load* (Fig. 6). let $w = \dfrac{W}{l} = $ weight per unit length. Then load on part DC is considered as acting at its centre of gravity. Bending moment at $AB = \frac{1}{2}wx^2$. The B.M. diagram in this case is a parabola and the

4996

bending moment is represented by y. (3) *Beam uniformly loaded and supported at both ends* (Fig. 7). Let R_1 be the reactions, $w = $ weight per unit length. Then bending moment at $AB = R_1x - \frac{1}{2}wx^2 = \frac{1}{2}wx$ $(L - x)$ where $L = $ length of the beam. The B.M. diagram is a parabola. The B.M. is clearly greatest at the middle point $= \frac{1}{2}w.\dfrac{L}{2}\left(\dfrac{L}{2}\right) = \dfrac{wL^2}{8}$. The more complicated questions of rolling loads, and loads unevenly distributed, admit of similar solutions.

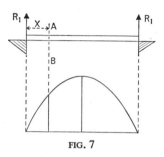

FIG. 7

Momentum: 1. *Linear Momentum*, classically defined as the product of the mass of a body and its velocity, v, is a vector (q.v.) with its direction along that of the velocity. For velocities approaching that of light the relativistic definition of linear M. (p) must be used, $p = mv = m_0v/(1 - v^2/c^2)^{\frac{1}{2}}$, or alternatively, $E^2 = p^2c^2 + (m_0c^2)^2$, where E is the total energy, i.e. kinetic energy plus rest mass energy, m_0 is the rest mass, m is the inertial or relativistic mass and c is the velocity of light. For a photon, or neutrino, with zero rest mass this reduces to $p = E/c$. The total linear M. of a system, resolved in any given direction is conserved. Within the system the linear M. of one part can be changed at the expense of another or the rest of the system. The force acting on a particle is equal to the rate of change of linear momentum of that particle.

2. *Angular Momentum.* The angular equivalent of linear velocity is angular velocity, $W = u/r$, and relates to an axis perpendicular to the velocity and distant r from the body. Its direction is along this axis, the axis of rotation. In rotation the moment of inertia (*see* MOMENTS) is the analogue of mass in linear motion. For a mass m the moment of inertia about an axis d distance r away is mr^2. The angular M. may now be expressed as the product of moment of inertia and angular velocity, $IW = mr^2.u/r = mvr$ and in general m is the inertial mass, $m = m_0/(1 - v^2/c^2)^{\frac{1}{2}}$. For any closed system, angular M. is conserved, but whereas linear M. appears to be able to assume any value, the quantum hypothesis suggests that angular M. related to a preferred direction is quantised (rather like electric charge), and occurs only in multiples of a very small unit $h/2\pi$ where h is Planck's Constant. The magnitude of $h/2\pi$,

sometimes written **h**, is 1.054×10^{-27} gm cm² sec⁻¹, or 6.6×10^{-15} eV.sec (eV = Electron Volt, q.v.). This hypothesis is the foundation of the explanation of many atomic and nuclear phenomena, and no exception has so far been found.

Mommsen, Theodor (1817–1903), Ger. classical scholar and historian, *b*. Garding in Schleswig-Holstein. His detailed knowledge of Rom. hist. and critical methods of procedure attracted the attention of the Berlin Academy, who commissioned him to examine Rom. inscriptions in France and Italy. In 1848 M. became prof. of jurisprudence at Leipzig, but he was compelled to retire from this office in 1850 owing to his revolutionary tendencies in politics. In 1852 he was appointed to the chair of Rom. law at Zürich, and in 1854 at Breslau. In 1858 he became prof. of anct hist. at Berlin, and during his professorship he compiled the famous *Corpus Inscriptionum Latinarum* and assisted in the compilation of the *Monumenta Germaniae Historica*. From 1873 to 1895 he held the position of secretary to the Berlin Academy of Sciences. From 1873 to 1882 he was a member of the Prussian House of Representatives, and was consistently democratic in his views. His chief works besides those mentioned are *Oskische Studien*, 1845, *Die Unter-italischen Dialekte*, 1850, *Corpus Inscriptionum Neapolitanarum*, 1851, *Die Rechtsfrage zwischen Cäsar und dem Senat*, 1857, *Geschichte des römischen Münzwesens*, 1860, and an ed. of the famous *Monumentum Ancyranum*. But it is for his *History of Rome*, 1853–6, that the name of M. will chiefly be remembered. His extensive knowledge and critical insight place the work in the forefront of Rom. hist. *See* studies by C. Bardt, 1903; L. M. Hartmann, 1908; U. von Wilamowitz-Moellendorff, 1918; W. Weber, 1929. (*See Plate: History*.)

Momordica, genus of tropical climbing plants (family Cucurbitaceae), with white or yellow flowers and ornamental gourds of various shapes, sometimes called balsam apples. *M. balsamina* is the balsam apple, *M. charantia* the balsam pear.

Momper, Joos (Jodocus) de, the Younger (1564–1635), Flemish landscape and marine painter, *b*. Antwerp. He was the prin. member of an artist family and son-in-law of Joos de Momper (1500–59). His landscapes are a link between those of Pieter Brueghel and Elsheimer (qq.v.). He employed other Antwerp painters to put in incidental figures.

'Mona (Monna) Lisa', *see* 'GIOCONDA, LA'.

Monaco, independent principality on the Mediterranean, forming an enclave in the Fr. dept of Alpes-Maritimes (q.v.). Founded from Massalia, it was called by later Lat. writers *Monoeci Portus* (sometimes *Herculis Portus*) after a Gk temple of Heracles Monoikos on the adjacent promontory. It became a Genoese stronghold in 1215, and has been ruled by the Genoese family of Grimaldi since 1297. In 1731 it passed into the female line; Jacques de Goyon Matignon, Count of Torigni, took the name and

arms of Grimaldi on his marriage to Louise Hippolyte, daughter of Antoine I, heiress of M. It was annexed by France in 1793, and was placed under the protection of the Kingdom of Sardinia by the Congress of Vienna (q.v.). In 1848 Menton (q.v.) and Roquebrune, until then in M., became free cities, electing to be incorporated in France in 1860. In 1861 M. came under Fr. protection, and by a treaty of 1918 succession to the throne must be approved by the Fr. Gov. In 1911 a constitution was promulgated, providing for a national council (of 18 members elected for 4 years) elected by universal suffrage. Women were given the vote in 1945. The gov. consists of the Prince of M., a minister of state and 3 gov. counsellors. The code of justice (the Code Louis, adopted in 1919) is based upon the Fr. code. There is a semimilitary police force. M. has a customs union with France (since 1865), issues its own postage stamps, is a Rom. Catholic bishopric and has a national flag (red and white, horizontally). There is a harbour, with an area of 47 ac. and a minimum depth of 25 ft. The ter. of the principality is divided into 3 sections. They are, from S. to N.: Monaco-Ville (the cap., on a rocky headland 200 ft high, with a 15th–16th cent. palace, a 19th cent. cathedral and an oceanographical museum; pop. 2000); La Condamine, the business dist; and Monte Carlo (q.v.). There is no income tax, and the prin. source of revenue is the Casino at Monte Carlo. The official language is French. The reigning prince is H.S.H. Rainier III (1923–), who succeeded his grandfather in 1949; his consort, the Princess Grace, was formerly Miss Grace Kelly, the film actress. A son and heir was *b*. in 1958. A dispute with France, 1962, was settled, 1963. Citizens of M. are called Monégasques. Area 0.6 sq. m.; pop. 20,500. (*See Plate*.)

Monad and Monadism. The philosophy of Leibniz (q.v.), which is included in these terms, is intermediary between that of Spinoza (q.v.) or monism, and that of Descartes (q.v.) or dualism. A monad may be said to be the ultimate constituent of all substance; monads are simple and similar in constitution; they differ only qualitatively; each is a self-contained individuality; and a monad has 2 qualities: perception, or capacity to mirror the universe, and appetite, or striving. From the highest monad, which is God, to the very lowest all are constituted so that at all moments they are all in harmony, although each works out its own development under its own laws independently of all the others. Man is built up of a complexity of monads, while his soul is a single monad, the centre of his being. *See* G. W. Leibniz, *Nouveaux Essais* (trans. A. G. Langley), 1896, and *Monadologie* (trans. R. Latta), 1898.

Monadhliath Mountains, mt mass of Inverness-shire, Scotland, lying between Loch Ness and Badenoch (q.v.) dist.

Monadnock, Mount, or **Grand Monadnock**, isolated mt in Cheshire co., SW. of New Hampshire, U.S.A. It has given its name to a type of residual mt left standing above an erosional plain. Altitude 3165 ft.

Monagas, state of NE. Venezuela, with the gulf of Paria on the E., Sucre to the N., Anzoátegui to the W. and having the R. Orinoco as its S. boundary. As with other parts of the llanos (plains) region of Venezuela, cattle raising is important in M. but it also contains important oil-fields which together with others in NE. Venezuela produce ⅓ of the nation's oil output. The cap. is Maturín. Area 11,160 sq. m. Pop. 246,000.

Monaghan: 1. Inland co. in the prov. of Ulster, Rep. of Ireland. The N. is watered by the Blackwater (q.v.), the S. by the Fane and Glyde, and the W. by the Erne (q.v.). The surface generally is hilly, the Slieve Beagh range, 1250 ft at its highest point, extending along the whole NW. boundary into Fermanagh. None of the rivs. is navigable. The Ulster Canal, which unites loughs Neagh (q.v.) and Erne, traverses the co. near M. and Clones but is now disused. The S. contains rich and productive land, but the most fertile part is the central, including the baronies of M., Cremorne and Dartree. Agriculture is the main occupation, and cattle and pigs are raised and oats and potatoes grown. Leather, footwear, furniture and knitwear form the chief manufs. Area 500 sq. m.; pop. 47,088.

2. Co. tn of M. and a thriving agric. centre. St Macartan's cathedral is in Fr. Gothic style, and St Macartan's College, the seminary of the Clogher diocese, is 1½ m. N. Charles Gavan Duffy (q.v.) was *b.* in M. Pop. 4013.

Monapia, *see* MAN, ISLE OF.

Monarchianism, term applied derisively by Tertullian to those heretics of the 2nd and 3rd cents. who denied the doctrine of the Trinity and constituted themselves the defenders of the monarchy of God or Christian unitarianism. Latter-day historians classify monarchians into the Adoptionist (from the view that Christ was the Son of God by adoption only) or Dynamistic sect, who held Christ to be a human being endowed with divine powers, and the Modalistic sect, who regarded Him as the incarnation of God the Father, and maintained generally that the Trinity was really reducible to different conceptions under which the One Divine Being might be viewed. It seems that one Theodotus, a shoemaker, was the first to teach that Jesus was a mere man, and incurred excommunication for his views. Artemon, who belonged to the ante-Nicene Monarchians (or Adoptionists), declared the doctrine of the Trinity to be an innovation dating from Zephyrinus and a relapse into heathen polytheism. He asserted also that Christ was a mere man, but born of a virgin and superior in virtue to the prophets. His views, for which he too incurred excommunication, were developed by Paul of Samosata (q.v.). The Dynamistic heretics are largely associated with the Alogians, or deriders of the Logos (q.v.). The name mainly associated with the Modalistic M. is that of Praxeas, against whom especially Tertullian hurled his fulminations. Praxeas was both Monarchian and Patripassian (the W. name for the heresy of Sabellius, viz. that God the Father became incarnate and suffered (*passus est*), the Son being only a form or modality of the same Person). They were more widely spread than the Adoptionists, but both sects belong only to the early cents. *See* L. J. Tixeront, *Histoire des dogmes,* i, Paris, 1905; L. Duchesne, *Early Historians of the Christian Church,* i, 1909; P. Hughes, *History of the Church,* i, 1934.

Monarchy, *see* SOVEREIGNTY.

Monarda, genus of N. Amer. perennials (family Labiatae). *M. didyma,* the sweet bergamot, or Oswego tea, bears whorls of fragrant scarlet flowers from June to Aug. *M. fistulosa* is the Wild Bergamot.

Monash, Sir John (1865–1931), Australian soldier, *b.* Melbourne, of Jewish descent and educ. at the Scotch College and Melbourne Univ. M. has been styled the greatest Jewish soldier since Masséna; he reached higher rank as an officer in the Brit. Army than any previous Jewish soldier. In Gallipoli he showed tactical perception and powers of organisation, which he exhibited to an even greater degree when in 1918 he succeeded Birdwood (q.v.) in charge of the Australian Corps. After the armistice he organised the repatriation of the Australians. He pub. *War Letters,* 1935, and *The Australian Victories in France in 1918,* 1936.

Monasterboice, anct monastic settlement, 6 m. NW. of Drogheda (q.v.), co. Louth, Rep. of Ireland. (*See Plate: Ireland.*)

Monastery, abbey, priory or convent for monks, friars or nuns. An abbey (as the name implies) is under the rule of an abbot or abbess; similarly a priory is ruled by a prior or prioress. In cathedral M.s the bishop was the abbot, and the superior of the estab. was a cathedral prior. In its early stages, when monasticism was practised in the eremitical form, the M.s were merely groups of cells or huts. St Pachomius, the founder of coenobite M.s, built his first M. in the form of a vil., with rows of huts large enough to accommodate 3 monks in each, and with a common refectory and a church. Under his rule the monks worked at different trades such as tailoring, carpentering, etc., so that workshops formed part of the buildings, the produce being shipped to Alexandria and sold to support the community. As time went on and the number of convents grew, experience led to the formation of a regular plan; the estabs. were made more compact, which also helped to guard them from outside attack, and were encompassed with means of defence, the monks erecting massive buildings containing all the necessary accommodation and surrounded with high walls as a protection against a possible enemy.

The E. or oriental M.s differed in their architectural plan from those of the W. That of Santa Laura (i.e. Holy M.), Mt Athos, may be taken as a typical E. M. It is enclosed with high stone walls, and occupies between 3 and 4 ac. of ground. The main entrance, which is composed of 3 iron doors, is on the N. side, and is guarded by a tower, the only other entrance being a small

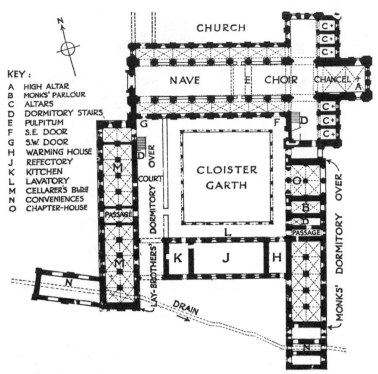

KEY:
A HIGH ALTAR
B MONKS' PARLOUR
C ALTARS
D DORMITORY STAIRS
E PULPITUM
F S.E. DOOR
G S.W. DOOR
H WARMING HOUSE
J REFECTORY
K KITCHEN
L LAVATORY
M CELLARER'S BLDG
N CONVENIENCES
O CHAPTER-HOUSE

PLAN OF A TYPICAL ENGLISH MONASTRY: KIRKSTALL ABBEY, *c*. AD 1180

postern on the S. side. On entering there is an outer courtyard with a chapel immediately facing, and to the left the guest-house with a cloister running along the front. The refectory, kitchens, storehouses, etc., are also in this courtyard, which thus becomes the centre of the material life of the community, while the inner courtyard forms the centre of the religious life. As one enters, the church at once arrests attention as the chief feature of the whole building. It is placed almost in the middle of the courtyard, which is surrounded by cloisters on to which open the cells of the monks, and in front of it there is a marble fountain. Although the refectory stands in the outer courtyard, the entrance is effected from the inner courtyard; it is a large cruciform building, and is decorated with frescoes representing various saints. In the E. M.s this building is usually found sited near the church, in the place of a chapter-house; meals are often taken in solitude in the cells.

The Coptic M.s adopted a different plan of architecture, the courtyards being absent. The church occupies the N. side of the building, and alongside it runs an immense gallery with the cells opening out on either side.

During the great monastic epoch in the W. that followed St Benedict a large number of beautiful M.s were built. The Benedictine M.s all followed one architectural plan, which was modified according to the site. The buildings were erected in a series of groups; the church, as the centre of the religious life of the community, formed one side of a square cloister, round the other sides of which were other buildings forming a necessary part of the monastic life: the chapter-house, the dormitory, the common room and the refectory. Another group was formed by the infirmary, with its garden and the school for the novices, while beyond the M. enclosure lay the abbot's house and the outer school, with the guest-house for distinguished visitors not far distant. In large M.s there were sometimes 3 guest-houses: the one already mentioned, the other two being for monks and poor travellers and placed on either side of the main entrance. The buildings connected with the material wants of the community lay to the S. and W. of the church, the kitchen, buttery, bakehouse, brewhouse, etc., the refectory being reached by a passage from the kitchen, and beyond these again were ranged the workshop, stables and farm buildings. The great Swiss M. of St Gall (AD 820) was a typical Benedictine M., and the same plan is followed out more or less faithfully in most of their buildings, with slight variations due to the locality. So, for instance, at Canterbury the cloister and monastic buildings

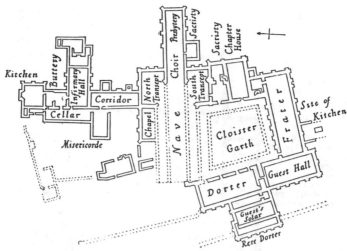

Marie Hartley

PLAN OF EASBY ABBEY
The above sketch plan is reproduced, by permission of the Ministry of Works, from a measured plan.

are situated to the N. of the church instead of the S. as is usual, and at Worcester and Durham the dormitories show a slight difference in the arrangement. At Westminster Abbey and St Mary's Abbey, York, the normal Benedictine plan is adhered to. Buckfast Abbey, a pre-Reformation Cistercian house restored since 1882 by Benedictines of the Cassinese congregation, is another example of the Benedictine style.

The Cluniacs grouped their buildings somewhat differently, and in the plan of the abbey of Cluny, founded by Wm, Duke of Aquitaine, the cloister is placed considerably farther W. than is usual, and the monastic buildings do not open out of it, but are placed in a separate group. Moreover Cluniac M.s, except Cluny itself, were ruled by priors, not abbots, so that the abbot's estab. is lacking. There were not a great number of Cluniac houses in England; the one at Lewes was the first, but the best preserved are at Castle Acre and Wenlock.

Following on the Cluniac M.s came those of the Cistercians, the chief characteristic of which was their plainness and simplicity, the outward expression of the rigid rule they adopted. Unnecessary decoration of any sort was forbidden, such as turrets, pinnacles or stained glass, and the sites chosen were usually wild and desolate. The effect of these regulations was the production of a definite Cistercian style in which the buildings were divided into 2 wards, separated by a wall. In the outer were the barns, granaries, stables, workshops, etc., and in the inner the monastic buildings proper, with the church occupying the central position. At

Clairvaux (AD 1116) there were 2 cloisters, and on the E. side beyond the monastic buildings there were gardens, orchards and fishponds placed outside the M. walls. The church was also built on a slightly different plan from those of other communities, with a very short E. limb, which was, as a rule, square. It also invariably had 2 small chapels on the E. side of the transepts, which were divided off with solid walls, and at Clairvaux there were 9 chapels radiating round the apse, also divided by solid walls. The chapter-house was always quadrangular, and was divided into 2 or 3 aisles by pillars or arches. The position of the refectory is also a characteristic; in the Benedictine houses it was placed parallel to the nave of the church on the side of the cloister farthest removed from it, and it ran E. and W., but in the Cistercian it was placed at right angles to the church, and ran N. and S. The buildings may be placed in 5 groups: (1) The outer ward containing all the buildings connected with labour of all kinds. (2) Those connected with hospitality and the material requirements of the community placed just within the inner ward. (3) The church and monastic buildings. (4) The inner cloister, with the library, lecture-hall and literary requirements. (5) The infirmary and novices' quarters. The first Cistercian house to be founded in England was Waverley Abbey, near Farnham, of which little now remains. That of Fountains Abbey, Yorks, is the best preserved, others being at Rievaulx, Kirkstall, Tintern, Netley, etc.

The Augustinian (or Austin) canons followed the Benedictine plan more of less, but a leading characteristic of their buildings is the immense length of their churches, which were devised to accommodate large congregations. At Llanthony and Christ Church (Twynham) the choir is shut off from the aisles. Sometimes there are no aisles at all, as at Bolton and Kirkham, while at Brinkburn and Lanercost there are only N. aisles. The abbey of St Augustine at Bristol was typical of the Austin canons, their church now being used as the cathedral.

The Premonstratensians (so called from their first abbey at Prémontré in France) followed the building plan of the Austin canons. The first English estab. was at Newhouse in Lincs (AD 1140), but the best preserved are those of Easby, Yorks, and Bayham, Sussex.

The Carthusian plan was distinct from all others, adapted to the quasi-eremitical life of the order. The M. (called in English charterhouse) was arranged in a series of detached cells or small cottages, each containing a living-room, work-room, etc., with a small garden surrounded by a wall, and opening on to a corridor, which in its turn opened on to a cloister connecting the whole. These cells occupied 3 sides of the cloister, and on the W. lay the church, the chapter-house and refectory, with the other necessary offices. The best preserved of Eng. medieval charterhouses is that of Mt Grace in Yorks, though that of Witham in Somerset is the earliest. Others were at Sheen, Richmond and the famous Charter House in London. The modern charterhouse at Parkminster, Sussex, is built according to the old plan.

A medieval experiment which has never been revived is that of double M.s, the first examples of which occur in Gaul in the 7th cent. In these, 2 separate communities of monks and nuns occupied adjacent buildings and often worshipped in the same church. Eng. examples were Whitby and Ely in A. S. times (*see also* GILBERT OF SEMPRINGHAM, ST).

The monastic buildings of the Mendicant orders formed a distinct class. They were usually planted in large tns, and were of necessity adapted to the sites chosen, so that there was seldom any regularity in the buildings, and their best efforts were concentrated on their churches, which were built with a view to accommodating large congregations. These were generally long-shaped buildings without any transepts, the nave being divided into 2 parts, one for the community and the other for the congregation. The E. end was, as a rule, square. The destruction of the beautiful M.s in Britain was the work of Henry VIII and his adviser, Thomas Cromwell. They saw in the monastic property vast possibilities of wealth. The Act of Dissolution passed in 1536 suppressed all M.s with an income of less than £200 a year, but though this still left the larger M.s free, they fell into the king's hands in 1539 through the Act of Suppression and the attainder of individual abbots. The properties were acquired by nobles who often used them as quarries for materials for building their own houses. The prin. mod. M.s in Britain and the Rep. of Ireland, estab. since the end of the 18th cent. are as follows: *Benedictine:* Downside,

Ampleforth, Douai, Buckfast, Prinknash, Ealing and Quarr. *Cistercian (Trappist):* Mount Melleray, Roscrea (both in Ireland), Mount St Bernard, Nunraw. *Carthusian:* Parkminster. See A. H. Thompson, *English Monasteries*, 1913; M. R. James and A. H. Thompson, *Abbeys*, 1925; F. H. Crossley, *The English Abbey*, 1935, 1945; C. Baskerville, *English Monks and the Suppression of the Monasteries*, 1947. For a list of Eng. houses see Dom David Knowles, *The Religious Houses of Medieval England*, 1940. For the geographical distribution and detailed character of the monastic houses of Great Britain between the Norman Conquest and the Dissolution, *see* the Ordnance Survey Map of Monastic Britain, 1950, which contains most useful letterpress. The best introduction to monastic studies is that by Dom David Knowles in *Monastic Sites from the Air*, Cambridge, 1952.

Monasticism (Gk *monachos*, solitary) originates in the urge to lead a life of perfection in greater security than is normally possible in the world. Hence the monk's prin. goal is personal sanctification through observance of the 3 religious vows: poverty, chastity and obedience. The monk spends his day in the two-fold activity of prayer and work; the Divine Office is the centre and source from which both his private prayer and his work derive their inspiration. That work originally consisted of manual labour, but in the Middle Ages it rapidly extended to include educational and artistic tasks. Christian M. began in Egypt (*see also* HERMIT), where St Anthony (q.v.) is usually considered as its founder. It was introduced in the W. during the 4th cent. The earliest monks in Gaul, Italy, Ireland and elsewhere followed the well-estab. E. pattern as represented especially by the rules of Ss Pachomius and Basil. The first fundamental departure from that model was made by St Benedict (q.v.), whose Holy Rule was the earliest piece of monastic legislation adapted to European needs. It quickly superseded all other systems, and Benedictine M. was the sole form of religious life known to the W. from the 8th to the 12th cent. See BENEDICTINES; CAMALDOLESE; CARTHUSIANS; CISTERCIANS. M. in the strict sense declined with the emergence of the Mendicant Orders (q.v.), but shared in the great spiritual revival that accompanied and followed the Counter-Reformation (q.v.).

The learned work of the Maurist Benedictine Congregation in France is famous, as is also the Cistercian reform of La Trappe (*see* TRAPPISTS). The 19th cent. was characterised by a notable revival of M. in Europe and its spread to America. After the Fr. Revolution Eng. monks returned from abroad and re-estab. themselves in England. Dom Guéranger in France and the brothers Wolter in Germany refounded M. in their respective countries. It. M. revived especially through the efforts of Abbot Casaretto of Genoa and Subiaco; the Austrian monastic orders flourished anew, relieved of the old imperial despotism of the 18th cent., while Swiss and Bavarian monasteries were able to send out missionaries to the U.S.A. and elsewhere to set up M. in countries which hitherto had not known it. See F. Gasquet, *English Monastic Life*, 1904; C. Butler, *Benedictine Monachism*, 1919; G. Morin, *L'Idéal monastique* (4th ed.), 1929; D. Knowles, *The Monastic Order in England*, 1940, and *The Religious Orders in England*, 3 vols., 1948–59; H. U. von Balthasar, *Die grossen Ordensregeln*, 1947; M. Wolter, *The Principles of Monasticism*, 1962; H. Van Zeler, *Approach to Monasticism*, 1963. See also LAMAISM; MONASTERY; and articles on the various monastic orders.

Buddhist M. goes back to the Founder (*c.* 563–483 BC), who estab. the *Sangha* or order of monks. The earliest Buddhist monks were wandering mendicants (Pali *bhikkhu*, Sanskrit *bhikshu*), and the custom of the begging round is still maintained in Buddhist countries, especially in SE. Asia, though monks now usually live in fixed monasteries (*Vihāra*). By the lower ordination (*Pabbajjā*) a candidate becomes a novice (*sāmanera*) who, though still technically a layman, wears the yellow robes and observes the ten major precepts which include strict celibacy, not eating after midday and not handling money. Full monkish status is gained by the higher ordination (*upasampadā*), for which a minimum of 5 members of the order is required. The *bhikkhu* must observe 227 rules. Breach of the 4 prin. prohibitions (against sexual intercourse, murder, theft and laying false claim to higher spiritual attainments) is termed defeat (*pārājika*) and entails permanent expulsion from the order. Lesser offences are purged by confession and penance. A *bhikkhu* may revert to the lay life at any time. One who has had the higher ordination for 10 years is termed a *thera* (Sanskrit *sthavira*) or 'elder'; one of 20 years' standing is a *mahā thera*: 'great elder'. The monastic life is for the gaining of enlightenment. *Bhikkhus* can guide and instruct the laity, but are not bound to do so. They may not exercise any secular calling, especially for gain. The parallel order of nuns (*bhikkhūnī*) has *d.* out, at least in SE. Asia. The above applies chiefly to the Theravada school. In Mahāyāna Buddhism, monasticism has developed different outward forms and in some schools has been abandoned. Monastic vows are often replaced by the *bodhisattva* vow to save all beings; this may be taken by laymen. Buddhist monks are not 'priests' if by this is meant mediators between God and man (since Buddhism is non-theistic). But some such term as 'priest' seems necessary to describe Buddhist clerics or ordained teachers in, e.g. Japan, who do not follow the monastic way. Likewise not all Tibetan *lamas* are monks. See BUDDHA AND BUDDHISM.

Monastir, see BITOLA.

Monazite, the orthophosphate of cerium, $Ce(PO_4)$, which is found naturally as a crystalline mineral. It contains, in addition to cerium, lanthanum, didymium, other rare earths and a little thorium. M. crystallises in the monoclinic system, and its colour is from red to brown; hardness about 5, and density 5·2. It gives a characteristic absorption spectrum, and is radioactive because of the contained thorium. It is found in India, Indonesia, Norway (Arendal), Ceylon, Brazil and U.S.A., usually associated with granites, gneisses and pegmatites. Good crystals of the mineral in bulk are rare, but M. is widely distributed in M. sand, found largely in Brazil. M. is an important source of thorium and cerium. The mineral contains enough thorium to make it worth while to obtain thoria, which is the main basis of gas mantles. The percentage of thoria in M. may be as much as 10, but it is usually less.

Monboddo, James Burnett, Lord (1714–99), Scottish judge and metaphysician practised as an advocate till 1767, when he was made judge in the court of session. Among his contemporaries he had the reputation of an eccentric because he gave learned suppers, rode on horseback after the manner of the ancients and because of his *Origin and Progress of Language*, 1773, and his *Ancient Metaphysics*, 1779–99, he exposed man's affinity to the orang-outang, thus in a measure anticipating the Darwinian theory. See T. L. Peacock, *Melincourt*, 1856, where the idea is ludicrously developed. Boswell describes, in his *Tour of the Hebrides*, an interview between Lord M. and Dr Johnson.

Moncayo, mt in Spain, on the border between the provs. of Soria and Zaragoza, near Tarazona (q.v.). Height 7600 ft.

Monceau-sur-Sambre, tn in the prov. of Hainaut, Belgium, 3 m. W. of Charleroi, on the R. Sambre. It has coal-mines and iron foundries. Pop. 11,400.

Mönch, peak in the Bernese Alps, Switzerland, 3 m. NE. of the Jungfrau (q.v.). Altitude 13,468 ft.

Mönchen-Gladbach, see MÜNCHENGLADBACH.

Monck, Sir Charles Stanley, 4th **Viscount** (1819–94), first Governor-General of Canada, *b.* Templemore, Tipperary. He entered Parliament in 1852 as member for Portsmouth. He was appointed captain-general and governor of Canada and Brit. N. America in 1861. M. was the chief promoter of the federal constitution of Canada (1867).

Monck, George, 1st Duke of Albemarle (1608–70), general and admiral, *b.* Potheridge, Devon. He fought at Cádiz (1625) and Rhé (1627). He was a colonel under Charles I in the Scottish war (1639). In 1644 he was taken prisoner by Fairfax at Nantwich, and was then imprisoned for 2 years in the Tower (1644–6). He became lieutenant-general of the ordnance under Cromwell, and fought with distinction at Dunbar (1650). In 1654 he became commander-in-chief in Scotland. In 1659 he supported the recalled Rump parliament when it came into conflict with the army leaders. In 1660 the Rump made him captain-general and commander-in-chief. Convinced that the only solution to the existing state of political confusion was the recall of the Stuarts, he took a leading part in the restoration of Charles II. He continued to command the army until his death. As admiral of the fleet in 1666 he won a decisive victory over the Dutch. Lives of M. have been written by

J. D. G. Davies, 1936, and O. Warner, 1936.

Monckton, Walter Turner, 1st **Viscount** (1891–1965), Brit. lawyer and politician, *b.* Plaxtol, Kent, and educ. at Harrow and Balliol College, Oxford. He was called to the Bar, 1919; K.C., 1930. M. was Edward VIII's adviser during the abdication crisis of 1936. He was solicitor-general, 1945. From 1951 to 1957 he was Conservative M.P. for Bristol W., and minister of labour, 1951–5. He was minister of defence, 1955–6, and paymaster-general, 1956–7. He was created a viscount, 1957.

Monclova, tn in Coahuila state, Mexico, situated at an altitude of 1920 ft. The climate is hot and dry with great seasonal variations. M. is 100 m. N. of Saltillo and an important railway junction. Essentially an industrial tn, it is the site of Altos Hornos, Mexico's largest steel mill producing over 40 per cent of the country's steel output. It is also the commercial centre of an agric. dist producing wheat and maize.

Moncrieff, Sir Alexander (1829–1906), soldier and inventor, *b.* Perthshire. He invented in 1868 the 'M. pit,' or 'disappearing system', a method of mounting the heavy ordnance in coast batteries. A shelter receives the gun after firing, the energy of the recoil being stored and subsequently utilised to carry the gun into firing position when required.

Moncton, city and port of entry, Westmorland co., New Brunswick, Canada, on the Petitcodiac R. and on the Trans-Canada Highway, 89 m. NE. of St John. It is the regional H.Q. of the Canadian National Railways (including Newfoundland railways) with large and well-equipped locomotive and car shops; it has a well-developed airport, sited in an area possessing highly favourable atmospheric conditions, used regularly by Trans-Canada Airlines and Maritime Central Airways, and as an alternative airport by overseas airlines flying the N. route. Possessing ideal transportation facilities M. has become a preferred distribution centre for the Maritime Provs. and Newfoundland. It is the seat of a new Fr.-speaking Univ. Manufs. include woollens, cotton goods, castings, woodwork, biscuits. Water supply is plentiful, electricity ample. Natural gas and oil wells are located within 14 m. Pop. 43,840.

Mond, Sir Alfred, *see* MELCHETT.

Mond, Ludwig (1839–1909), chemist, *b.* Kassel, Germany. Educ. at the univs. of Marburg and Heidelberg, where he studied under Bunsen (q.v.). He came to England in 1862, and introduced the process of recovering sulphur from waste products of the Leblanc soda process. In partnership with J. T. Brunner (1873) he estab. the ammonia-soda process (Solvay) at works in Cheshire, now the largest alkali works in the world. He manuf. chlorine as a by-product, and produced gas from waste products, recovering ammonia. He evolved a new process for the manuf. of pure nickel, in conjunction with Lange and Quincke, from nickel carbonyl, also his own discovery. In 1906 he founded and endowed the Davy-Faraday Research Laboratory of the Royal Institution. A

portion of his collection of early It. paintings, etc., he left to the nation. Pub. papers in *Transactions* and *Proceedings* of the Royal Society, Royal Institution, Brit. Association, Chemical Society and Society of Chemical Industry.

Mond, Sir Robert Ludwig (1867–1938), chemist and archaeologist, *b.* Farnworth, Lancs, son of the preceding. He was educ. at Cheltenham College, Cambridge Univ., Zürich Polytechnicum and Edinburgh and Glasgow Univs. He collaborated with his father in the discovery of the gaseous compound, nickel carbonyl. He perfected the industrial production of iron carbonyl, and discovered the first derivative of a metallic carbonyl (cobalt nitroso-carbonyl) and a new ruthenium carbonyl. His 30 years of archaeological work were carried out in Egypt, Palestine and Brittany.

Monday, second day of the week. The word is derived from the O.E. *Monandæg* (Moonday).

'Monde, Le', Paris daily newspaper, founded in 1944. It is one of the leading Fr. papers of independent outlook.

Mondino de' Luzzi (Mundinus), (*c.* 1270–1326), It. anatomist, *b.* Bologna. He graduated about 1290 and in 1306 began teaching anatomy at Bologna. In 1316 he wrote his *Anathomia,* the first book devoted solely to anatomy. It was first printed at Padua, 1478 (facsimile reproduction, 1930; Eng. trans. by C. Singer, 1925). M. reintroduced human dissection and taught with the dissected body directly in front of him.

Mondovi, It. tn in Piedmont (q.v.), 13 m. E. of Cuneo. Napoleon defeated an Austrian army here in 1796. The tn is built partly on a hill. It has an 18th cent. cathedral, and had a univ. (1560–1719). Pottery is manuf. Pop. 13,900.

Mondrian, Piet (1872–1944), Dutch abstract painter, *b.* Amersfoort. He studied art at Amsterdam and in 1911 went to Paris, where he was strongly influenced by Cubism (q.v.). Returning to Holland, he was prominent in the formation of the *de Stijl* group which cultivated a non-figurative form of art related to architecture. His paintings based on the rectangle were severely mathematical. He worked in America from 1940. (*See Plate: Dutch Art.*)

Mondsee, *see* SALZKAMMERGUT.

Monel Metal, one of the prin. alloys of nickel; contains 65 per cent of nickel, 32 per cent of copper, with small amounts of manganese, iron, carbon, sulphur and silicon. It is essentially a solid solution of copper in nickel, has great tensile strength, is not seriously weakened even at 400° C., can be cold-worked without becoming brittle, is not appreciably corroded by the air, and withstands the action of sea-water, alkalis and ammonia. It is therefore used in a great variety of industries, for castings, chemical, textile and laundry equipment, and for power plant components such as turbine-blading, valves, pumps, etc.

Monera, classification of atoms of protoplasm destitute of any structural features. *See* PROTOZOA.

Monet, Claude (1840–1926), Fr. artist, *b.*

Paris. M. was of great importance as a leader of the Impressionists. Essentially he was a painter of light (and shadow) by means of pure colour rather than the old chiaroscuro, but aesthetic values and poetic feeling, as well as the scientific realisation of light, inspired him. In youth he worked at Le Havre with Boudin, who taught him to work in the open air. In 1862, at Gleyre's studio, he met Renoir and Sisley and together they painted landscape. He visited England in 1870–1, during the siege of Paris, and may have been encouraged to pursue atmospheric colour by the works of Turner he then saw; and by the city itself as is shown by his 'Westminster' 1871, and the 37 views of the Thames resulting (1904) from his sev. visits. From 1872 his work became typically 'impressionist', his title for a picture 'Impression' giving rise to the name in 1874. Notable pictures of his in England are the 'Plage de Trouville', painted in 1870, and 'Poplars on the Epte', both in the Tate Gallery. Series paintings include cathedrals, railway stations and Venetian scenes. 'View of Argenteuil', 1872, 'Les Meules', 1891, and the series of 'Nymphéas', 1900, are some of his most famous works. *See* G. Geffroy, *Claude Monet*, 1922; S. Gwynn, *Claude Monet and his Garden*, 1934; C. Roger-Marx, *Monet*, 1949; *also* study by C. P. Weekes, 1962. (*See Plate: French Art*.)

Monetary Policy. The objectives of economic policy as stated in 1959 by the *Report of the Committee on the Working of the Monetary System* (better known as the Radcliffe Report) are the maintenance of a high and stable level of employment, reasonable stability in the purchasing power of money, steady economic growth and improvement in the standard of living, a margin on the balance of payments sufficient to make some contribution to the economic development of the outside world and to provide for a strengthening of London's international reserves. These objectives may conflict. We may, for instance, be able to maintain a stable price level only at the cost of reducing the level of demand which itself causes an increase in unemployment. Or we may be able to achieve a relatively high rate of growth but only at the cost of a high rate of inflation (q.v.). Economic policy therefore normally involves making decisions as to which of these objectives are the more important.

There are sev. methods by which these goals of economic policy can be pursued and M. P., by which the level of activity in an economy is controlled by regulating the money supply and the rate of interest, is one of them. Alternative and sometimes complementary policies are fiscal policy, incomes policy, the operation of the nationalised industries and other public agencies, import regulations, the maintenance of competition and so on.

The 4 main instruments of M. P. are open market operations by the central bank, bank rate (q.v.) and the control of deposit ratios (*see* BANK OF ENGLAND) and requests, backed by the threat of action, from the Chancellor or Governor of the Bank of England to the commercial banking system.

Before the end of the Second World War the main instruments of M. P. were bank rate and open market operations. Formerly bank rate alone had been regarded as the most important, but economists and bankers then came to think that open market operations, which can force the commercial banking system to borrow from the Bank of England at high rates of interest, were necessary to make alterations in bank rate effective. In recent years control of deposit ratios and official requests have been used to notable effect. (Bank rate had fallen into disuse between 1932 and 1951.) See *Report of the Committee on the Working of the Monetary System*, 1959; E. V. Morgan, *Monetary Policy for Stable Growth*, 1964; R. S. Sayers, *Modern Banking*, 1964. *See also* BANKS AND BANKING; BANK RATE; BALANCE OF PAYMENTS; INCOMES POLICY; ECONOMICS; FISCAL POLICY; ECONOMICS OF EMPLOYMENT.

Money. Under a barter (q.v.) system goods can only be exchanged for other goods, but since the introduction of M. this is no longer the case. Many commodities have been used as M., including cowrie shells, tobacco and cattle. The invention of M. has been attributed to the Lydians in the 7th cent. BC and since then it has increasingly acted as the medium of exchange without which great expansions of trade would be impossible. Besides being a medium of exchange, M. is a means of credit and a measure of value. It may also be regarded as a store of value, or liquid asset. M. is a claim on goods and services which will be promptly honoured. Legal tender M. is by definition a means of settling debts. The legal tender currency of the U.K. consists of Bank of England notes of 10s. and £1, together with subsidiary token metal coins which are legal tender for limited amounts. Paper notes are of limited durability and fail entirely to meet the intrinsic value requirement, but are honoured promptly as a claim to goods and services. Gov. paper M. is at once a mere auxiliary of bank-M. and the base upon which bank-M. is built. Bank of England notes represent a claim on the community; bank-M., now the prin. M., represents a claim on a bank.

The nature of bank-money. If a man opens his first banking account by placing M. (say £100) on current account with a banker he exchanges one kind of M. for another, notes and coin for bank-M. (an entry in his favour in the bank's books). Bank-M. may be transferred from account to account by cheque, or withdrawn as notes and coin 'on demand'. The banker, then, takes the customer's £100 notes and coin and gives him £100 bank-M. He keeps 8 per cent of the notes and coin in his till, leaving £92 free for lending (or the purchase of securities). When this is lent out a part will return to the banking system (the customer's bank or another) and permit further loans; and so on. Ultimately the greater part of the customer's original £100 notes and coin will be outside the banking system, the £8 will (still) be in his bank supporting his £100 bank-M.; the remainder will also be inside the banking system supporting further deposits some 12 times their value. It is in this sense that banks are said to create money.

The Bank of England note is 'a claim on the community'. In the days of gold coin the holder of a £5 note had a claim on the Bank of England for 5 golden sovereigns, which when new contained £5 worth of metal. Today the holder can no longer get gold for his note. How much each note will buy depends on how many there are, exactly as in the case of golden sovereigns. *See* QUANTITY; THEORY OF MONEY. The idea of the limitation in the amount of M. is of the first importance. There is a limited amount of gold in the world, and the rate of increase is limited by the number and size of mines and the profitability of working them. There is no such limit on paper M. and its proper limitation must be sought elsewhere. Meantime 'how much . . . depends on . . . how many' (the Quantity Theory in its crudest form) needs qualification. Faster spending will heighten the effect of more M. and slower spending offset or reverse it. The expectation of (still) more M. (or less) will also heighten the effect. More goods and services on the other hand, or the expectation of them, allow more spending without increase of price.

Exchange rates. M. is not international. Despite exceptions M. should be regarded as stopping at frontiers. In the absence of special arrangements, if country A wants to buy goods in country B, and conversely, then M. of country A can be bartered for M. of country B and a rate of exchange estab. What country A exports will exchange for what country B exports and there will be a running balance of payments, and no 'gap'. Any currency unit, e.g. the £, will with such a free exchange establish an open market price in terms of any other unit, a price which will reflect the relative demands of the countries concerned. If of course country A for any reason doubles its M. without increasing its production, then its M. will tend to lose half its exchange value. There will at all times be a 'natural' rate and no room for a black market.

See also BALANCE OF TRADE; BANK RATE; BANKS AND BANKING; BILL OF EXCHANGE; BIMETALLISM; CURRENCY; ECONOMICS; EXCHANGE; EXCHANGE, FOREIGN; EXCHANGE CONTROL; EXCHANGE EQUALISATION ACCOUNT; HAVANA CHARTER; INFLATION; INTERNATIONAL MONETARY FUND; MERCANTILE SYSTEM; METROLOGY; MONEY MARKET; MONETARY POLICY; PAPER MONEY; PRICE.

See D. H. Robertson, *Money*, 1928; J. M. Keynes, *A Treatise on Money*, 1930, and *The General Theory of Employment, Interest and Money*, 1936; *Report of the Macmillan Committee on Finance and Industry*, 1931; G. Crowther, *An Outline of Money*, 1949; F. W. Mueller, *Money and Banking*, 1951; F. Benham, *Economics*, 1955; A. Day, *An Outline of Monetary Economics*, 1958; E. V. Morgan, *A History of Money*, 1965; G. Hobeder, *Money and the International Economy*, 1965; P. Samuelson, *An Introduction to Economics*, 1965.

Money Market. If a bank is to be always in a position to meet its depositors' demands for notes and coin with a cash reserve of 8 per cent or so, it must be able to lend a good part of its money where it can get it back at very short notice. The bill of exchange, maturing for settlement within a few months, and saleable at a discount at any time, has long met this requirement of the commercial banks: directly by the banks themselves buying bills of exchange, and indirectly by the banks lending their money in the M. M., the short-term market for money which comprises, besides the banks, the bill brokers and discount houses, together with the accepting houses or merchant bankers. The M. M. buys and sells money tomorrow for money today, the price being interest or discount. With the assistance of the M. M. a bank endeavours to arrange its portfolio of bills so that dates of maturity are suitably spaced. Short money is also lent to the Stock Exchange. The bill of exchange finances overseas trade. By buying (discounting) bills of exchange the bill brokers, discount houses, etc., lend the money which enables the exporter to obtain payment for his goods without waiting for the date when the foreign buyer has to settle the bill (*see* ACCEPTING HOUSE).

Besides borrowing from the commercial banks, M. M. funds are derived from direct deposits and from London branches of foreign and colonial banks, which often have considerable sums to spare for short periods. When the commercial banks are short of funds they obtain money from the Bank of England not by direct borrowing but by calling in loans to the M. M. and so forcing the market to borrow from the bank, at a higher rate.

Two wars have left their mark on the great London M. M., on 'Lombard Street', to use the name by which it is known the world over. The scarcity of commercial bills of exchange made the market operators ready buyers not only of the Treasury bill (a three-month bill, now the chief instrument of gov. short-term borrowing) but also of gov. securities nearing their dates of maturity.

The commercial banks' loan to the M. M. (money at call and short notice) may amount to some 7 per cent of their deposits, bills discounted (including Treasury bills) to say 20 per cent; a total of 'quick assets' amounting, with cash and balances with other banks, to about 30 per cent of deposits. The greater part of these 'quick assets' bring the banks little more than $\frac{1}{2}$ per cent interest.

The M. M. has been criticised for preserving outdated practices which might elsewhere be considered restrictive; the least desirable features of its operations being the privileged access to the Governor of the Bank of England of the 12 members of the discount houses syndicate and the syndicated tender for Treasury bills whereby they agree the price at which they will tender.

Moneylender. With certain exceptions, anyone who acts as a M. must (*a*) register his name and address or addresses; (*b*) carry on his business only in his registered name and at his registered address or addresses; and (c) supply the borrower on request and on tender of expenses copies of all documents relating to the loan. Non-compliance with these statutory requirements (Moneylenders Act, 1900) renders a M. liable to fine, and, on a second conviction, to imprisonment. The exceptions are banks, registered friendly societies (q.v.), pawnbrokers, building societies, insurance offices and indeed any business the prin. object of which is not the lending of money. A borrower who, not being an infant (see INFANT), enters into a moneylending transaction must not expect that he will necessarily get the sympathy of a court of law. The Act of 1900 merely provides that a court may reopen a transaction and relieve the borrower from the necessity of paying more than a certain sum of interest, fines, expenses, premiums, renewals or other incidental items, where the transaction is 'harsh and unconscionable' or the interest, etc., excessive, having regard to the M.'s risk and all the circumstances of the case. The Moneylenders Act, 1927, prohibits the exaction of compound interest on loans by M.s and any increase of the rate of interest by reason of any default on the part of the borrower (see also INTEREST). This Act also provides that a M. shall take out an ann. licence—called 'a M.'s excise licence'—in respect of every address at which he carries on business, the duty on such a licence being £15. Penalties are provided for taking out a licence in any name other than his true name or for other infringements of the statute. A licence will be granted only to a person who holds the necessary certificate from the petty sessional court of the div. in which the M.'s business is carried on, and the grounds on which a certificate may be refused are specified in the Act. They relate chiefly to character. Conviction for any offence under the Betting and Loans (Infants) Act, 1892, or the Moneylenders Act, 1900, may entail suspension or forfeiture of a certificate. This Act also imposes various restrictions on moneylending advertisements, the chief of these being that circulars may be sent only to persons in response to a written request for the same, and that newspaper advertisements or posters, etc., containing invitations to do business with a M. may be pub. only under the conditions prescribed in the Act. Legal proceedings in respect of money lent by M.s may not be brought after the expiration of 12 months from the date on which the cause of action accrued. The Act exempts pawnbrokers' loans from the provisions as to certificates and limitation of actions. The Companies Act, 1929, provides that every company licensed under the Act of 1927, whenever it was registered or estab. as a place of business, must, in all its trade catalogues, circulars, showcards or business letters, give specified particulars as to the names and nationalities of the directors. A borrower could, however, always count on getting relief or avoiding a transaction altogether if induced to enter into it by a false or fraudulent misstatement, and indeed a M. so acting is liable also to criminal proceedings. In the U.S.A. the law relating to the lending of money varies in the different states. All states have a legal rate and a rate allowed by contract: the first varies from 5 per cent to 8 per cent; and the second from 6 per cent to 12 per cent, while in this second case some states allow any rate. The penalty for usury varies also from fines to loss of principal, and in some cases imprisonment.

Moneywort, name given to 2 distinct plants: (1) family Primulaceae, creeping jenny or loosestrife (*Lysimachia nummularia*), it has a creeping stem, heart-shaped leaves, short one-flowered stalks and bright yellow flowers; (2) Cornish M. (*Sibthorpia europaea*) is a hardy perennial, with minute pink and yellowish flowers of W. England and Ireland and S. Europe.

Monferrato, former marquisate and duchy in Italy, the ter. of which is now mainly in the prov. of Alessandria, in Piedmont (q.v.). The marquisate was founded in the 11th cent., and in 1536 came into the possession of the Gonzaga (q.v.) family, under whom it became a duchy. Part of the duchy passed to the House of Savoy (q.v.) in 1631 and the remainder in 1703. The cap. was Casale M. (q.v.).

Monge, Gaspard (1746–1818), Fr. mathematician, prof. of mathematics in the École Polytechnique, Paris. He laid the foundation of descriptive geometry, i.e. the representation of solids by 2-dimensional drawings.

Mongolia (the country of the Mongols) embraces a vast and indefinite extent of country in E. Asia between 43° and 53° N. lat., 88° and 119° E. long. Its length from E. to W. exceeds 1700 m. and its width from N. to S. 750 m. Area about 850,000 sq. m. Bounded N and W. by Siberia, E. by Manchuria, S. by China proper and Sinkiang. It is divided into 2 parts, Outer M. in the N., now a rep. under Soviet domination, and Inner M. in the S. and E. Inner M., which was divided in the 1920s into 4 Chinese provs., Jehol, Chahar, Suiyuan and Ninghsia, now enjoys the status of an Autonomous Region (excluding Ninghsia) within the Chinese People's Rep. Pop. 10,000,000 (1964 estimated). Its cap. is Huhehot, formerly Kweisui, cap. of Suiyuan Prov. By the 1945 Sino-Russian treaty, which was a replica of the secret wartime Yalta Agreement, the Chinese Gov. under Chiang Kai-shek officially granted Outer M. independence. The central portion of M. comprises the Great Gobi, a vast tract of sand, small stones and sparse vegetation. The country to the SE. of the Gobi is more elevated and terminates in a high mt range (the Alashan), which, beginning near the Huang-Ho, runs N. for 150 m., then turns at right angles to the E., whence under the name of the Inshan Mts it extends for sev. hundred m. until it turns N. again. The dist S. of the Inshan Mts contains fertile valleys, but farther W., where it is surrounded by the great N. bend of the Huang-Ho, it is again either arid like the Gobi or only fit for pasture ground. The E. part, bordering on Manchuria, contains rich meadow-land. The slopes of the Khingan mts are well watered and in the S. part overgrown

Motor-cars

Left: 1888 Benz, with the hood down (restored).

Below left: Lanchester (back view).

Below: Coventry Daimler. *All photos: Crown copyright: Science Museum, London*

Motor-cars

1906 Model 'N' Ford.
Lent to Science Museum, London, by Ford Motor Co., Dagenham

1908 Rolls-Royce 'Silver Ghost' (40–50 h.p.).

1922 prototype Austin 7.
Rolls and Austin, Crown copyright: Science Museum, London

Motor-cars

Left: 1933 Daimler. *Crown copyright: Science Museum, London*

Below: A 1965 Jaguar: the 4·2 litre Mark 10 saloon. *Jaguar Cars Ltd*

Bottom: A 1965 Morris Mini-Minor De Luxe. *B.M.C. Ltd*

Motor Transport, Commercial

Model of L.G.O.C. 'B'-type motor
omnibus of 1910.
*Crown copyright: Science Museum,
London*

A London 'Routemaster' bus, seating
64 passengers.
London Transport

13·9 h.p. Unic taxicab of 1922.
*Crown copyright: Science Museum,
London*

Motor Transport, Commercial

A 7-ton tipper.
Vauxhall Motors Ltd

A light van.
Vauxhall Motors Ltd

A petrol tanker.
Shell-Mex and BP Ltd

Mountaineering

Above left: Gustave Doré's reconstruction of the accident during the first ascent of the Matterhorn (1865) in which four lost their lives.
The Times

Above right: View of Mont Blanc (A) from the Tour Ronde. B, Col Major; C, Mont Blanc de Courmayeur; S, Red Sentinel Rock; N, outward end of Brenva snow *arête*; Y, bay of Brenva glacier. Four routes marked are: *left:* Via della Pera (Pear Route); *left centre:* Route Major; *right centre:* Sentinel Route; *right:* Brenva Route.

Below: A bivouac on the central pillar of Freney, Mont Blanc; the climber on the left has his feet in his rucksack for warmth.
Chris Bonington

Mountaineering

Above: Mt Eiger (Switzerland), whose north wall (*left*) presents formidable problems to the mountaineer.
Swiss National Tourist Office

Far left: Scaling a rock-face in Grisons canton in the Swiss Alps.
Swiss National Tourist Office

Left: Climbers on Medusa Wall, Esk Buttress, in the Lake District; the lower climber has belayed a rope round a firm rock, and both are wearing rubbers, suitable footwear for dry weather.
Chris Bonington

Mozambique

Above: The fortress of San Sebastian, Mozambique Island, founded by Albuquerque in 1508.
J. Allan Cash

Right: Picking tea near Gurue in the north-central mountains; 'black tea' is one of the country's exports.
Portuguese State Office

Right: Barrage across the 1,000-mile-long Limpopo River, source of extensive irrigation schemes.
Portuguese State Office

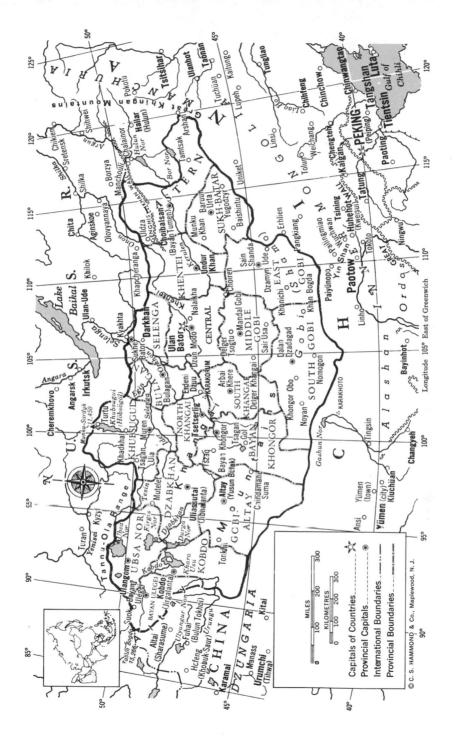

Mongolia

© C. S. HAMMOND & Co., Maplewood, N.J.

Capitals of Countries .... ⭐
Provincial Capitals .... ◉
International Boundaries ....
Provincial Boundaries ....

MILES
0   100   200   300

KILOMETRES
0   100   200   300

with pine, fir, oak, lime and walnut trees. NW. M. is also well watered but poorly wooded; near the boundary between M. and Siberia the country rises into the Altai Mt chain. Rain is rare except near the great mt ranges. The wealth of the Mongols consists in their great herds of horses and sheep, and, in the hilly tracts, of cattle. Inner M. became part of the Manchu Chinese empire in 1644. Outer and W. M. submitted to Chinese control during the reign of Kang Hsi emperor (1662–1722), which cession has resulted in some development of resources and a transport trade with China and Siberia along the great caravan routes, the chief of which run from Kalgan and Kweihwa Cheng to Kiakhta, via Urga (Ulan Bator), and from Kalgan through Kobdo to W. Siberia. The Trans-Mongolian railway opened in 1956. It passes through Urga and links M. with China and Russia. Since 1917 motor-car services have been running across the Gobi during the summer, from Urga to Kalgan.

Under the provisional republican gov. of China (1912) a separate dept was formed for the administration of M. and Tibet. The Russo-Mongolian agreement of 1912 resulted from a series of revolutions consequent on excessive Chinese interference. In 1915 the treaty of Kiakhta between China, Russia and M. was signed, by which the Kutukhta Lama was recognised as the ruler of Outer M., under Chinese suzerainty; in 1924, however, it became an independent rep. in alliance with the Soviet Federation. Chinese immigration has recently greatly increased in Inner M., resulting in a much greater degree of productivity; by means of irrigation even the fringe of the Gobi desert has been made to yield crops. So great was this immigration that when in 1924 Outer M. became a rep., Inner M. became a part of China. In that year, on the death of the last theocratic ruler of outer M., there was a revolution, as a result of which the Mongolian People's Revolutionary Gov., organised on Soviet lines, was estab. The highest power is vested in a parliament (the Great Huruldan) which is elected by universal suffrage. The pop, is estimated at 900,000. In 1937 the Japanese set up a new autonomous gov. of Inner M., with its seat at Kalgan. The area dominated by this gov. is estimated to be 304,510 sq. km. and the pop. 2,136,000, of whom some 60 per cent are Chinese and the remainder Mongols. Japan secured exclusive mining rights in E. M., and rights to build railways in M. and Manchuria. Of Outer M. Urga (pop. 100,000), known since 1924 as Ulan Bator, is the chief centre of pop. and commerce, and here dwells the Kutukhta Lama, the third highest pontiff of the Buddhists. Other tns are Uliassutai and Kobdo. The Mongols do not practise agriculture, but rear great herds of horses, cattle, sheep and camels; hides, furs, wool and horns are the chief exports. The country is rich in minerals, including gold and silver, but they are little exploited. In 1960 a new industrial centre was founded at Darkhan, N. of Ulan Bator, close to the Siberian frontier. This was developed under the third 5-year plan (1960–65). The fourth 5-year plan calls for the estab. of the industrial tn. of Choibalsan in the E.

M. has long been considered the world's chief theatre of evolution, and recent discoveries, especially those made in 1922, 1923 and 1925 by the Central Asiatic Expeditions, under Roy Chapman Andrews, have confirmed this opinion. These expeditions, sent by the Amer. Museum of Natural Hist., travelled over the Gobi desert in cars supported by camel caravan. Important discoveries in the W. Gobi included the fossil remains of various species of dinosaur, e.g. the small Protoceratops, a 9-ft species which is considered to be the ancestor of the giant Triceratops of Montana; nests of fossilised eggs of this dinosaur were also found. In the same strata, Lower Cretaceous or Upper Jurassic, were found skulls of a tiny mammal, the earliest mammal known. Other finds included fossil bones of the Baluchitherium, a giant rhinoceros of the Miocene period, when M. was probably fertile grassland with a clement climate, the mastodon, amblypod, titanothere, etc. Evidence was also found of late palaeolithic man, in the shape of chipped flints, egg-shell ornaments, etc. In the E. Gobi, in Inner M., fossils of mammals of the Upper Eocene period were discovered, also graves and worked copper mines of early historical times. Another expedition found, in 1923, Mousterian implements in the Ordos desert of Inner M. Discoveries made in N. M. by a mining engineer, 1912, led to a Russian expedition under P. K. Kozlov, 1924–5, which excavated burial mounds about 70 m. N. of Urga. The tombs showed Hellenic, Hanian, Scythian, Chinese, Siberian and Sarmatian influences. Skulls found seemed Aryan rather than Mongolian in shape. The tombs are believed to date from the Tang dynasty (AD 618–907).

See J. Gilmour, *Among the Mongols*, 1888; V. Obrutschew, *Report of Journeys, 1892–1894, in Central Mongolia*, 1901; C. W. Campbell, 'Journey to Mongolia' (in *Geographical Journal*, Nov. 1903); K. Kozloff, *Works of the Expedition of the Imperial Russian Geographical Society in Mongolia and Khan (Tibet) during 1889–1901* (Eng. trans. in *Geographical Journal*, April, May and June 1908); J. Hedley, *Tramps in Dark Mongolia*, 1910; R. C. Andrews, *Across Mongolian Plains*, 1921; A. S. Kent, *Old Tartar Trails*, 1925; R. Chapman Andrews, *The New Conquest of Central Asia*, 1933; H. Haslund, *Tents in Mongolia: Adventures and Experiences among the Nomads of Central Asia*, 1934, and *Men and Gods in Mongolia*, 1935; L. Forbath, *The New Mongolia*, 1936; O. Lattimore, *Mongol Journeys*, 1941; H. Haslund-Christensen, *Mongolian Journey*, 1949; S. V. Cammann, *The Land of the Camel*, 1951. *See also* MONGOLS. (*See Plate.*)

Mongolian Languages, *see* URAL-ALTAIC LINGUISTIC FAMILY.

Mongolism, *see* MENTAL DISORDERS (MEDICAL).

Mongols, people of Central Asia, living chiefly

in Mongolia (q.v.), and also in Sinkiang and Manchuria. They may be divided into the W. M. or Kalmucks and the E. M., and are a sturdy people with high cheek-bones, flat faces, straight black hair and a characteristic 'mongolian fold' of skin over the inner angle of the eye. They are nomad herdsmen and dwell in tents, or *yurts*, taking unkindly to any other way of life. Formerly an energetic and warlike people, their acceptance of Lamaism has been largely responsible for their present pacific torpor. They emerge into hist. with the coming of Genghis Khan. He was occupied in conquests in the E. from 1206 to 1226, and it was his genius which for a time built up the fabric of a great Mongolian empire. At his death he divided his ters. between his sons; Ogotai received the country between the Irtish and Lake Baikal; Jagatai the country between Bokhara, the Irtish and Gobi; Tuli the land S. of the Baikal; and his grandsons Orda and Batu, Khwarezm, the region drained by the Jaxartes, Ural and Oxus. Ogotai, with the help of Tuli, became emperor of China and put an end to the Chin and Sung dynasties (1234). Batu, after occupying Russia, seized the Hungarian cities of Pesth and Gran (1241), and in 1236 Mongolian troops overran Georgia and Armenia. Hulagu (Hulagoo, Hulaku), Tuli's son, defeated the Persian Assassins, crushed the caliphate of Bagdad and took possession of Syria, together with Aleppo and Damascus, while the great Kublai Khan, another of Tuli's sons, estab. a line of emperors in China which lasted from 1277 to the final expulsion of his race in 1367. Meanwhile the M., or, to give them a more generic name, the Tatars, were establishing (about the year 1224) the Kipchak empire in SE. Russia under Batu. The khanates of Astrakhan, the Crimea and Kazan, and in Turkestan the khanates of Bokhara and Samarkand, were all held by M. Though the power of the Golden Horde or W. Kipchaks waned, that of the White Horde or E. Kipchaks—the inheritance of Orda, Batu's brother—grew apace, and in 1378 Toktamish, an E. Kipchak, became ruler of both hordes. But he had no sooner completed his Russian conquests than he was plunged into a bitter struggle with Timur, or Tamerlane, a Mongol chieftain who had estab. a supremacy in Samarkand (1369). A wider meaning is sometimes given to the word when the term Mongolian or Mongoloid is used to include the whole yellow race, the N. M. including the Koreans, Japanese, Finno-Ugrians, E. Siberian Eskimos, and even the Amer. Indians, while the S. M. include the Chinese and Indo-Chinese, Tibetans and Malays, all of which races are believed to have had a common derivation. For bibliography *see* MONGOLIA. (*See Plate: Race.*)

Mongoose, or **Mungoose** (from native *mangus*) (*Herpestes griseus*), genus of small weasel-like animals, common in many parts of Asia, especially India, and in Africa. They form a sub-family of the civet tribe. The largest species is the Egyptian Ichneumon. The common Indian M. is tawny or grey in colour, and about 17 in.

long, excluding the tail, which is about 14 in. long. It is very voracious, and fights and kills even large and poisonous snakes with the utmost agility and daring, and for this service has been introduced into the W. Indies and other countries. It is readily tamed and makes a delightful though mischievous pet. Observers do not confirm the popular notion that the M. visits certain plants to counteract the effects of poisonous snake bites, which are as fatal to it as to other animals. (*See Plate: Mammals.*)

Monica, St (332–87), mother of St Augustine of Hippo. She was the wife of Patricius, a pagan citizen of Tagaste, and converted both her husband and indirectly her son to Christianity.

Monier-Williams, Sir Monier (1819–99), Eng. Sanskritist, b. Bombay. He was educ. at King's College, London, and Balliol College, Oxford. Prof. of Sanskrit at Oxford, he was chiefly responsible for the foundation of the Indian Institute. His pubs. include a *Sanskrit-English Dictionary*, 1899.

Monifieth, burgh of Angus, Scotland, on the N. side of the Firth of Tay. There are machinery and carpet works. Pop. 3494.

Monism, the philosophic system which attempts to reduce the universe to a single principle. It is thus directly opposed to dualism, between which and M. stands the monadism (*see* MONAD AND MONADISM) of Leibniz (q.v.). M. tends to reduce the universe either to a material principle, thus developing into a form of materialism, or into a mental principle leading to idealism and pantheism. The early Gk philosophers were monists of the materialist school, postulating the sev. elements as the material cause of all things. Thus Thales took moisture as the first principle and Heracleitus fire. An important advance was made by the Eleatic philosopher Parmenides, who invented the epigrammatic formula, 'the ent (*on*) is, the nonent (*mē on*) is not', thus distinguishing the one which is from the many which become and are not. This theory was supported by Zeno, who sought to disprove plurality by his paradoxes of space, time and number. In the stoic philosophy M. was a fundamental doctrine.

M. has been conspicuous in the thought of sev. modern philosophers, most of whom tend to the idealistic school. Spinoza, 'the classic type of pantheist', attempted to reconcile the dualism of Descartes by relating mind and matter to one infinite, all-embracing substance, God, and by regarding all else as but modes of that infinity. Hegel is perhaps the most distinguished of the idealistic school. Proceeding from the idealism of Kant, Fichte and Schelling, he arrived at an explanation of matter, individuality, sensation and will as forms of thought. Hegel's teaching was developed into positivism and the atheism of Strauss, Feuerbach and Bruno Baur. Schopenhauer and von Hartmann merge all finite existence in the cosmic will. *See also* MATERIALISM. See A. Schopenhauer, *The World as Will and Idea*, 1844; K. R. E. von Hartmann, *The Philosophy of the Unconscious*, 1869; G. W. F. Hegel, *Philosophy of Mind* (trans.), 1894; T.

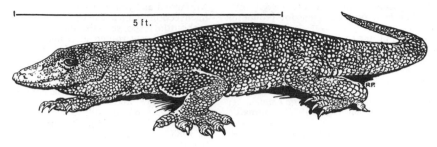

5 ft.

MONITOR
The Komodo Dragon with scale.

Gompertz, *History of Ancient Philosophy* (trans.), 1901–12; R. McKeon, *The Philosophy of Spinoza*, 1928; G. V. Plekhanov, *Development of the Monist View of History* (new ed.), 1956.

Monitor, name for a number of lizards (family Varanidae) which include some of the largest forms. They are widely distributed throughout the E. hemisphere, and their habitat varies from dry sandy spots far away from the water to the marshy banks of rivs. The Nile M. (*Varanus niloticus*) is about 6 ft long, with a long head and small rounded nostrils. An even larger species is the Ocellated M. of China and Siam. It preys on birds and smaller lizards, and, if attacked, defends itself fiercely. The largest species is the Komodo Dragon (*V. komodoensis*) from the Is. of Komodo. It grows to 12 ft.

'Monitor', a type of warship named after the famous Amer. warship M. which on 9 March 1862 fought an indecisive action with the *Merrimac*, a vessel of a similar type, in Hampton Roads. The essential features of these ships were shallow draught, a low freeboard, and an armoured revolving turret. The M. herself was lost in a gale off Cape Hatteras, but the principle of the revolving turret was later adopted in all navies, the *Royal Sovereign* being the first Brit. warship to be so fitted. It was not until 1882, however, that the fixed broadside was finally discarded. During the First World War a number of Brit. M.s were employed off the coast of Belgium. These did great damage to Ger. shipping and largely rendered Ostend and Zeebrugge ineffective for offensive work. They mounted one twin turret of 12 in. or 15 in. guns and one was equipped with a single 18 in. gun which had been removed from the *Furious* on the latter's conversion to aircraft carrier. In the Second World War Brit. M.s were used against enemy forces in Libya, supported the invasion of the Normandy coast, and took part in the capture of Walcheren.

Moniuszko, Stanislaw (1819–72), Polish composer, the founder of a national Polish school of opera in many respects comparable to that of Glinka (q.v.) in Russia. He was *b*. at Ubiel (Minsk) and after some local teaching sent to Berlin, where he studied with Rungenhagen in 1837. He then became an organist at Wilno, where he taught, conducted and produced a one-act operetta in 1839. After sev. more works that remained unperformed he produced *The Lottery* at Warsaw in 1846. His next stage work, *Halka*, though followed by 11 others, became his most famous, in fact the classical Polish folk opera. A first version was produced at Wilno in 1848 and a definitive one at Warsaw on 1 Jan. 1858. M. also wrote 6 Masses, a Requiem, secular choral works, a concert overture, 2 string quartets and nearly 300 songs.

Monk, George, see MONCK.

Monk, Maria (*c*. 1817–50), Amer. authoress. She pub. *The Awful Disclosures of Maria Monk*, 1836, in which she alleged that she had escaped from the Montreal nunnery of the Hôtel Dieu. The book, containing tales of misconduct in Catholic convents, had a huge sale. She was eventually exposed and her story proved to be false.

Monk, see MONASTERY; MONASTICISM.

Monk-fish, see ANGEL-FISH.

Monk-seal (*Monachus monachus*), true seal, common in the Mediterranean, and on account of its tractability easily trained to perform tricks.

Monkey, name, usually applied to anthropoid primates, excluding man. M.s are arboreal in habit, and are rarely found away from the warmer parts of Africa, Asia and America. It is usual to classify the M.s into 2 great divs., the Catarrhini (q.v.) of the old world and the Platyrrhini of the new. There are many points of difference between those of the old world and those of the new. An important distinction is in the div. between the nostrils, which is invariably broad in new-world M.s, while the nostrils open almost sideways. In the old-world M.s the div. is thin and the openings of the nostrils tend downwards. No new-world M.s have cheek-pouches, and the thumbs differ less from the other fingers; but of old-world M.s some have cheek-pouches and others are without them. Most have a laryngeal or air pouch, and these are rare in the Amer. genera. But in many of these, prehensile tails are highly specialised, though in some the tails are short or feeble. Some old-world M.s have ischial callosities or pads, where the animal sits; these are always absent from the new-world M.s. *See also* CHIMPANZEE; ENTELLUS MONKEY, etc. (*See Plate: Mammals.*)

Monkey Flower, *see* MIMULUS.

Monkey Nut, popular name for groundnut (q.v.).

Monkey Pot, *see* LECYTHIS.

Monkey Puzzle (*Araucaria araucana*), hardy evergreen conifer, native of Chile, and varying from a few feet to 150 ft in height. There is a variety with golden-tinted foliage.

Mon-Khmer Language, *see* LINGUISTIC FAMILIES, *Austro-Asiatic Linguistic Family.*

Monkhouse, Allan (1858–1936), journalist, dramatist and novelist, *b.* Bishop Auckland, Durham. He became a dramatic critic and leader writer for the *Manchester Guardian*, and later contributed to that jour. a weekly article, 'A Bookman's Notes'. He wrote a number of plays, most of which were produced at the repertory theatres in Manchester, Liverpool and Birmingham. The two best were *Reaping the Whirlwind*, 1908, and *The Conquering Hero*, 1924—this latter being a pacifist study. His novels, which included *My Daughter Helen*, 1922, and *Farewell, Manchester*, 1931, reflected the conflict between belief in business and sentimental Socialism.

Monkhouse, William Cosmo (1840–1901), poet and art critic, *b.* London. His working life was spent in the offices of the Board of Trade, where he rose to assistant secretary in the financial dept. His poems include *Corn and Poppies*, 1890, the *Dead March*, and *The Christ upon the Hill*, 1895. As an art critic he is remembered by his *Life of Turner*, 1879, *The Italian Pre-Raphaelites*, 1887, and a number of studies of contemporary artists.

Monkland, New and **Old,** adjoining pars. in NE. Lanarkshire, Scotland. Old M. (pop. 77,000) includes Coatbridge (q.v.) and New M. (pop. 44,000) includes Airdrie (q.v.).

Monkshood, *see* ACONITUM.

Monkton, vil. of Ayrshire, Scotland, 1 m. N. of Prestwick at the junction of the main roads from Ayr to Irvien and Kilmarnock. Here are the ruins of Old St Cuthbert Church, which had associations with Wm Wallace. Aircraft and other engineering work is carried on at Prestwick Airport, the second U.K. international airport, which adjoins the vil. Pop. *c.* 1000.

Monkwearmouth, *see* SUNDERLAND.

Monluc, Blaise de, *see* MONTLUC.

Monmouth, James Scott, Duke of (1649–1685), prince, the son of Charles II by Lucy Walters, *b.* Rotterdam during his father's exile. The king was extremely fond of him; in 1663 he was made Duke of M., and 2 years later on his marriage with the wealthy Scottish heiress, Anne of Buccleuch, was granted the dukedom also of Buccleuch. In 1670 he became captain-general of the forces. His personal charm, his clemency towards the Covenanters at Bothwell Bridge (1679), his almost royal progresses through the W. and NW. of England, and above all his Protestantism, a point in his favour of which Shaftesbury made full use, brought him a popularity which his indifferent talents hardly merited. When, yielding to Argyll's persuasion,

M. landed at Lyme Regis to raise a Protestant insurrection against James II, his appeal met with little response. His undisciplined forces were hopelessly routed at Sedgemoor (1685), and 9 days later he was beheaded on Tower Hill. *See* E. D'Oyley, *James, Duke of Monmouth*, 1938.

Monmouth, municipal bor. and parl. div. of Monmouthshire, England, at the confluence of the R.s Wye and Monnow, 16 m. N. of Chepstow. There are still some remains of the castle (built before 1070), where Henry V was *b.* in 1388. A picturesque bridge, unique in its two-storeyed fortified gatehouse, crosses the R. Monnow. M. is a good tourist and fishing centre, and has flourishing markets. M. School (q.v.) is well known. Pop. 5505.

Monmouth, Battle of, victory gained in 1778 at M. Court House by the Americans under Washington over the British under Clinton.

Monmouth Royal Engineers (Militia), Royal, the only representative in the Brit. Army today of the historic militia force (*see* MILITIA). Originally an infantry regiment, it became an engineer unit in 1877. It was one of the 4 co. militia regiments which maintained a separate existence when the Militia was absorbed in the Special Reserve in 1908. When the rest of the Special Reserve was discontinued after 1921 it survived as a Supplementary Reserve unit. It was incorporated in the Territorial Army in 1953, but was allowed to retain the word Militia in its title. *See* hist. by B. E. Sargeaunt, 1910.

Monmouth School, public school for boys, founded at Monmouth (1615) by Wm Jones of the Haberdashers' Company. Today the Worshipful Company of Haberdashers (q.v.) is represented on the board of governors. There are some 450 pupils.

Monmouthshire, maritime co. lying on the Eng.-Welsh border, with a coastline of 22 m. along the estuary of the Severn (q.v.) and that part of the Bristol Channel that lies between the Wye and the Rhymney (qq.v.). During the Rom. occupation an important camp was estab. at Caerleon (q.v.), and the only Rom. tn in Wales was built at Caerwent (q.v.). There are also ruins of feudal strongholds at Chepstow, Caldecot (qq.v.), Raglan and elsewhere, and the impressive remains of Tintern Abbey (q.v.) and the Cistercian abbey of Llanthony are in the co. Medieval M. (formerly called Gwent) was undoubtedly Welsh. The Act of Union of 1536 created the present co. out of 'divers Lordships Marchers within the said Country or Dominion of Wales'. Later in the Tudor period it was brought under the jurisdiction of the courts of Westminster in certain matters, while separate courts were provided for the rest of Wales. The coast of M. is exposed to remarkably high spring tides, which rush up the seven in a 'bore' from the Bristol Channel, rising at Chepstow sometimes to 60 ft. The S. part, E. and W. of the Usk (q.v.), comprises the Caldecot and Wentloog levels, which are protected from the sea by sea-walls. N. of the Caldecot level, between the Usk and the Wye, the surface is undulating, rising here and there into bold bluffs and varied by knolls and dells. The N. and W. of the co. are mountainous. About 4 m. from Abergavenny (q.v.) is the remarkable peaked mt called Pen-y-Val or Sugar Loaf (1955 ft). Between Abergavenny and Usk is the wooded hill-fort of Coed-y-Bonedd, one of sev. M. camps. Skirrid Fawr (1596 ft), known locally as the Holy Mt, has fine views of the Black Mts, the Usk valley and the Sugar Loaf; over 2000 ac. of the latter have been presented to the National Trust. Chief rivs. are the Wye, Usk, Rhymney, Sirhowy, Ebbw, Avon-Llwyd and Monnow, the first two being famous for salmon and trout fishing. The co. is rich in coal and mining is a major industry. There are numerous iron works, and limestone is burnt extensively, both for building purposes and for use in the iron works. There is an aluminium factory at Rogerstone and nylon-spinning at Mamhilad near Pontypool. Wheat is plentiful in the vales of the Usk and Wye and in the N. and E. Newport (q.v.) is the chief port and serves the mining and industrial area of M. Monmouth (q.v.) is the co. tn. M. is in practice legislatively included in Wales for almost every purpose, from education to coal-mining. The recent report of the Local Gov. Boundary Commission proposes that M. be extended to include the W. side of the Rhymney valley, in the co. of Glamorgan, and S. Breconshire, and should be renamed 'Gwent'. M. is divided into 6 hundreds and 5 parl. divs. (Abertillery, Bedwellty, Ebbw Vale, Monmouth and Pontypool), each returning one member; the bor. of Newport also returns one member. Area 346,781 ac.; pop. 443,689. *See* T. Richards, *South Wales and Monmouthshire*, 1949; C. J. O. Evans, *Monmouthshire*, 1954.

Monna Lisa, *see* GIOCONDA, LA.

Monnet, Jean (1888–), French economist, worked for de Gaulle throughout the Second World War after the fall of France. Immediately after the war he played a leading part in measures aimed at reviving the Fr. economy. The European Coal and Steel Community grew from his ideas, and he was its chairman 1952-55; in the sense that E.E.C. developed from this, M. can be said to be its originator. Since 1961 he has been chairman of an Action Committee for a United States of Europe.

Monnikendam, fishing vil. in the prov. of N. Holland, Netherlands, on the IJsselmeer, 12 m. NE. of Amsterdam. Its old bell-tower, weigh-house and the 15th cent. Great Church are notable. Pop. 3100.

Monnoyer, Jean Baptiste (1635–99), French painter, *b.* Lille, who specialised in the painting of fruit and flowers. He was employed by Le Brun to decorate the palace of Versailles, and invited to England by the Duke of Montague to adorn his house (the former Brit. Museum) with examples of his art. M. also decorated sev. other historic mansions of England. There are sev. of his flower pieces in Hampton Court Palace. He etched a collection of his own designs which was pub. in a folio vol.

Monoceros, 'The Unicorn', equatorial con-

stellation between Orion and Canis Major, probably named by Bartsch (1624). Contains no bright stars, but lies in the Milky Way and is rich in faint stars, clusters and nebulae.

Monochaetum, genus of the evergreen flowering shrubs (family Melastomataceae) bearing large panicles of rose, red, mauve or purple flowers. *M. alpestre*, of Mexico, with purple-rose flowers; *M. hartwigianum* and *M. humboldtianum*, purple, of S. America are grown in heated greenhouses in Britain.

Monochord, appliance invented by Pythagoras for studying musical intervals by means of a movable bridge under a single string stretched over a sound-board by a weight. From it the musical instrument of the same name, a sort of one-stringed guitar, was evolved, and also the trumpet marine (q.v.). The clavichord was an application of the same principle, manipulated by a keyboard.

Monochrome, painting executed in imitation of bas-reliefs, in tints of one colour only, relieved by light and shade. In photography panchromatic plates and, exceptionally, isochromatic plates are used for the correct rendering of colours in M.

Monocotyledon, plant with one cotyledon (q.v.) or seed leaf (e.g. wheat, tulip), as distinguished from a Dicotyledon (q.v.) (e.g. bean, carrot, dandelion). This distinction is the main basis of 2 great divs. of the Angiosperms, the group which comprises all flowering plants. In the M. the radicle or rudimentary root usually remains undeveloped, but throws out roots from its crown. In the Dicotyledon it usually elongates and forms a primary, or tap, root. The stem of M.s has no central pith or separate bark, and the whorls of the perianth occur in threes. But, as a rule, the most visible and easily recognised distinction is that the leaves are parallel veined except in a very few cases, notably the black bryony, arum and herb-Paris. M.s are separated into 3 main divs.: (1) Spadiciflorae, flowers arranged on a spadix and frequently enclosed by a large spathe (e.g. arum); (2) Petaloidae, with petaloid perianth (e.g. lily or daffodil); (3) Glumiferae, perianth absent and flowers borne in spikelets in the axils of scales or glumes (e.g. sedges and grasses).

Monodon monoceros, *see* NARWHAL.

Monoecious, botanical term used of a plant which bears distinct male and female flowers on a single individual. If male and female flowers are borne on separate individuals, the plants are said to be dioecious.

Monogenitism, *see* LANGUAGE, ORIGIN OF.

Monogram (Gk *monos*, sole; *gramma*, a letter), cipher or character formed by an interlacing of letters and intended as an abbreviation of a word, particularly of a name. M.s were not uncommon on Gk and Rom. coins from the 5th cent. BC onwards, and in various sepulchral texts and manuf. objects from the 1st cent. BC. In the 5th and 6th cents. AD M.s became very fashionable. Most famous is the M. of Christ (☧, formed from *chi* and *rho*, the first 2 letters of the Gk word *Christos*), which Constantine the Great (q.v.) adopted to symbolise the triumph of Christianity (*see also* LABARUM). M.s also appear on the A.-S. coins, especially those of King Alfred, and on seals. In later times they were often used by printers and engravers on the title-pages of books, as well as by artists (Rembrandt, Dürer, F. Hals, S. van Ruisdael and others) on their works.

Monohydroxysuccinic Acid, *see* MALIC.

Monolith (Gk *monos*, sole; *lithos*, stone), stone block or column, usually of great size and monumental in purpose. Some are natural stones, e.g. the Buck Stone, Staunton, in the Forest of Dean. Single standing stones are prehistoric monuments, and many occur in the W. and N. of Britain, their precise age being unknown. Some are the sole remaining stones of circles or avenues; others, sometimes of dressed stone, in Wales are inscribed in Ogam or even Lat. characters, while yet others are hewn obelisks, such as may be seen in Egypt. Those in Egypt are dated approximately to 3000 years BC, or like those of Peru are of the 12th cent. or even later. Certain M.s are boundary marks. In Baalbek (q.v.), an anct Syrian city, is the largest cut stone in the world, weighing 1500 tons. The great statues of Akhenaton at Karnak may be regarded as M.s. M.s of considerable size were common to both the Inca and pre-Inca architecture of Peru (*see also* PERU, *Ancient Civilisation of the Incas*). One of those at Cuzco is 27 ft long, 15 ft wide and 12 ft thick. The stones in Peru vary as to their geological composition, according to the region. Among the ruins of Mitla (q.v.), Mexico, are some great monolithic columns. Prin. among the sculptured stone objects preserved in the national museum of the city of Mexico is a famous calendar stone of the Aztecs, or sun-stone, a beautiful and massive M. of carved basalt, circular in form and 12 ft in diameter. The stone was both a sun-dial and a calendar, such as the Egyptians and the Chaldeans used, and the cyclical animals carved on it have given rise to the supposition that the chronological system which produced the stone may have had some connection with Chinese and Indian astronomical systems. Often the worship of stones persisted in Europe into the Christian period. (*See* MENHIRS.) *See also* MEGALITH CULTURE.

Monongahela, riv. of U.S.A. in W. Virginia and Pennsylvania, formed by the junction (S. of Fairmont, W. Virginia) of Tygart R. and W. Fork R. It flows 128 m. NNE. to the Allegheny, which it joins at Pittsburgh to form the Ohio R. Entirely navigable by means of locks, it is an important coal artery. It is joined at McKeesport, Pennsylvania, by the Youghiogheny R.

Monophysitism, heresy which arose in the 5th century as a reaction against Nestorianism. Teaching that in Christ there was but one nature, its effect was to deny the humanity of Jesus. It was anathematised at the Council of Chalcedon (451), but the decision caused a great schism. Nearly all Egypt refused to accept the decisions of Chalcedon, and the Coptic Church has remained Monophysite to the present time. So

have the Armenian, Jacobite and Ethiopian Churches. *See* EUTYCHES; EASTERN ORTHODOX CHURCH.

Monopodium, botanical term for a branching system in which there is a single main or primary axis which continues growth, and which gives rise to subsidiary lateral branches. A M. is contrasted with a sympodium, in which the growth of the main axis is limited, and further growth is brought about by successive lateral branches.

Monopoli (anct **Minopolis**), It. seaport and bathing resort in Apulia (q.v.), on the Adriatic, 31 m. SE. of Bari. It has a cathedral (12th cent.; restored 18th cent.), and a fortress of the Emperor Frederick II. There are boat-building and cement industries, and a trade in agric. produce, olive oil and wine. Pop. 24,300.

Monopoly, literally means single or sole selling. This is the root principle of all M.s at all periods. Most anct and civilised legal systems have endeavoured in one way or another, however ineffectually, to put some kind of a veto on M.s. In England legislation against M.s goes back to the reign of Elizabeth I, and so great was the abuse of the royal power of granting M.s that in 1639 they were finally abolished by statute. The problem in England was always aggravated by the conflict between public utility and the anct prerogative of the Crown (q.v.) to regulate trade. The privileges and exclusive rights of trade granted for a pecuniary consideration to merchants by the Norman kings, and abused by later monarchs (especially the Stuarts, who used them as convenient levers of political favouritism), furnish the most obvious example of the artificial or legal M.s, or M.s which do not arise from the free play of economic forces.

It was against artificial M.s that past legislation in England was always directed; though it has become evident that 'natural' M.s—i.e. where natural circumstances nullify competition—are an additional problem. Modern legislation has attempted to secure M. values to the community, partly by facilitating the municipalisation of certain utility services (*see* MUNICIPAL TRADING) and partly by nationalisation of industries such as coal, gas and electricity, and to outlaw monopolistic practices themselves. Elizabeth I frequently granted M.s to her favourites and it was not till the last year of her reign that a Bill, introduced by Lawrence Hyde, received such great support from an otherwise pusillanimous House that the queen was obliged to yield. Before these concessions the matter came before the courts, which were disposed to declare M.s void on the common law ground that they were in restraint of trade, for in the case of the royal grant of sole right to sell playing cards it was said that every M. had 3 inseparable incidents: raising the price, deterioration of the commodity and impoverishment of workers and others. The only exception the courts were inclined to make was in favour of the royal grant of letters patent for the exclusive privilege of trading in things introduced or invented by the grantee himself, or where the grant was apparently beneficial to the community. An Act of 1622, however, declared all M.s void except those granted by letters patent for the sole working, for 14 years, of any new manuf. to the 'true and first inventor thereof', and this statutory provision is still the foundation of the present law as to patents for inventions. Finally, in 1639, as a result of the ineffectiveness of the above Act to check the royal grant of M.s to corporations, all legal M.s (except patents for inventions) were abolished. Analogous to patents for inventions is the M. conferred by copyright, a right which has recently been considerably strengthened (*see* COPYRIGHT) in favour of authors.

Natural M.s are divided into 3 classes: (1) land M.s; (2) M.s valued from industries in which competition is inapplicable, e.g. gas (which is now a M. of the state) and water supply, tramway service, etc.; and (3) state M.s, e.g. the licence to deal in intoxicating liquors (*see* LICENSING LAWS). To this classification might be added partial M.s where a kind of M. price in the shape of 'superiority of reward' is obtained by workers in trades or professions where an uncommon degree of integrity is required, or a high degree of confidence reposed in the workers, e.g. goldsmiths, physicians, lawyers, etc.

M. has flourished more consciously in the U.S.A. than in most other countries; but even Amer. experience of control is inconclusive. In spite of the Sherman (q.v.) and Clayton anti-trust laws M.s continued to spread, and the sphere of 'free competition' to narrow. The Acts almost fell into disuse or were revived to check some especially large and menacing combine. Roosevelt's 'New Deal' (q.v.) ended this nerveless 'trust-busting' by creating a permanent machinery for the regulation of industry by the administration. But the National Industrial Recovery Administration (N.I.R.A.) lasted only 2 years, during which time there was a distinct increase in monopolistic practices and restraint of trade. Almost all the N.I.R.A. codes provided for the control of prices, and generally such provisions were evaded. The increase of prices and the hostility of consumers would probably have brought N.I.R.A. to an end even had it not been declared unconstitutional by the court Criticism of the Act emphasised the antithesis between the desire for 'free enterprise' professed by the manufacturers, and the enormous pressure towards restrictive regulation exerted when they acted as a group. If all industries pursue restrictive policies all suffer in the long run; and the advantage derived if a single industry pursues a monopolistic restrictive policy is lost if all do so. Even while N.I.R.A. was in operation other Acts were being passed to give the administration greater power to intervene in the internal affairs of companies. The Public Utility Holding Company Act was carried against strenuous opposition in 1935. By that Act all companies in the public utility and steel industries had to register with the Securities and Exchange Committee, which was empowered to simplify their structure so as to restrict each to a single integrated process. This Act was followed by an experiment in an entirely different method of state control—gov. ownership and public corporations in competition with private enterprise. With the Tennessee Valley Authority, and similar hydro-electric schemes, the gov. entered the industrial field proper in a big way, one of the main reasons advanced being that such schemes would promote employment. The reaction from N.I.R.A. was shown by a campaign for a new trial of the old anti-trust laws. The Temporary National Economic Committee in 1938 revealed the widespread growth of combination in the U.S.A. The view was taken that a less corrupt application of the existing anti-trust laws might provide a solution. Little, however, was done up to the entry of the U.S.A. into the Second World War. The Amer. type of war control was developed from the industrial and political experience of the preceding decade. In Britain the war controls were largely in the hands of former directors of the largest firms, and little was done to limit the power of the larger combines. In the U.S.A., on the other hand, a direct attack was made on various trusts, and war-time controls were used to reduce M. rather than to strengthen it. But the development of control in America was not founded on any clear theory. The solutions formulated and the measures adopted were empirical, even opportunist, though the broad line of development from the attempted distant control by the early anti-trust laws to the direct participation by the administration in the industrial field is clear enough.

Monopolies and Restrictive Practices (Inquiry and Control) Act, 1948. The Brit. gov. introduced legislation in 1948 to set up an independent M. commission to determine whether monopolistic conditions existed in particular industries referred to it for investigation by the Board of Trade and, if asked to do so, to decide whether the conditions investigated were against the public interest. The industries so referred were those in which there were restrictive agreements over prices or other conditions of business or in which 'at least one-third of the goods of that description which are supplied in the United Kingdom or any substantial part thereof' was under one control. This latter definition of a firm with M. powers raised—or begged—3 fundamental questions: first, whether one-third was too large or too small a proportion to yield M. powers (*see* COMPETITION); second, the meaning of 'goods of that description' (goods technically different may nevertheless be close substitutes for one another and may therefore constitute 'one' commodity); third, the size of a 'substantial part' of the U.K. (some firms may have a local but not a national M., e.g. newspaper companies owning the only morning newspaper in a tn or area).

Between 1948 and 1955 the Monopolies and Restrictive Practices Commission reported on a wide variety of industries, from tinned goods to electric lamps and from linoleum to matches. In some cases it found monopolistic and restrictive practices. But the gov. tended to rely more on publicity than on legislation to remove them from the economy. In 1955 the commission reported adversely on 6 groups of collective agreements—exclusive dealing, resale price maintenance, exclusive buying, aggregated rebates, discrimination in price and exclusive selling. The majority found that all 6 kinds of agreements were contrary to the public interest and recommended that (subject to a few exceptions) all should be prohibited. The minority recommended that all the practices should be compulsorily registered and prohibited if found (on investigation of each practice) to be against the public interest. The gov. responded to this report by the Restrictive Trade Practices Act, 1956. In some respects it was a compromise between the majority and minority recommendations of the commission. But the gov. also claimed that it went considerably beyond both recommendations because, first, it applied to all known restrictive practices affecting the production, processing and supply of goods, and thus included not only the 6 categories examined by the commission but also the practices of common prices and of level tendering; and, second, it put the onus of showing that the agreements were in the public interest on those who wished to continue them. The Act contained 5 major provisions: (1) It provided for the registration of a wide range of restrictive agreements and arrangements (excluding services and labour) with a new body, the Restrictive Trading Practices Register. (2) The Registrar of Restrictive Trading Practices was empowered to take proceedings before the Restrictive Practices Court in the case of a practice he considered might be contrary to the public interest; the court was to decide whether or not the practice was contrary to the public interest. (3) The criteria on which the court was to act were that all practices were to be found contrary to the public interest unless the restriction was not detrimental to persons not parties to it (such as consumers or would-be entrants to the trade), *and also* was necessary (i) for the protection of the public; (ii) as a defence against a large firm itself resorting to restrictive practices; (iii) to enable the parties to negotiate 'fair' terms with persons controlling a large part of the trade; (iv) for a certified redundancy scheme; (v) to avoid unemployment or a substantial reduction in exports; (vi) for the maintenance of another restriction already found not contrary to the public interest. (4) The Monopolies and Restrictive Practices Commission was to be changed to the Monopolies Commission; It was not to be concerned with agreements liable to be registered and examined by the new court, but was to continue to inquire into 'single firm' M.s (and into agreements relating wholly to exports). (5) The Act outlawed the collective enforcement of resale price maintenance, but gave individual manufacturers and others who fixed resale prices power to enforce them in the courts, even when there was

no contractual relationship between the supplier and the distributor. The Act did not implement the recommendations of the 1949 Lloyd Jacob Committee (*see* RESALE PRICE MAINTENANCE) that enforcement of resale price maintenance by individual firms should not be permitted to restrict the development of newer methods of retailing or prevent costs or prices from being reduced. The implementation of that recommendation had to await the Resale Prices Act, 1964. The prohibition of individual resale price maintenance came into effect 30 April 1965.

By the end of 1963 the public section of the register estab. under the Restrictive Trade Practices Act, 1956, contained particulars of 2430 agreements and nearly 1000 of these had been discontinued by the parties to the agreements. 525 had so altered the terms of their agreements as to put an end to the restrictive aspects. If an agreement is to continue it has to be justified before the court. So far only 9 of the agreements contested before the court have had the main restrictions upheld. One of the most notable cases was that of the Galvanised Tank Manufacturers' Association. In 1959 a price fixing agreement had been held to be against the public interest. In June 1964 they were found to have been in breach of their undertaking not to enforce or give effect to their agreement in future. The significance of the case is that it marked the extension of the court's interest to information agreements which are not registrable under the act.

Under the 1956 Act the Monopolies Commission has pub. 6 reports (imported timber, chemical fertilisers, the supply of cigarettes and tobacco and of cigarette and tobacco machinery, electrical equipment for mechanically propelled land vehicles, wallpaper and the solus sites system of retail petrol sales). Three further references have been outstanding for some time (household detergents, colour film and cinema films).

Proposals for strengthening existing legislation on monopolies and mergers were outlined in White Paper, *Monopolies, Mergers and Restrictive Practices* (Cmnd 2299, Mar. 1964). Legislation on monopolies and mergers was introduced under the *Monopolies and Mergers Act*, 1965, though legislation on restrictive practices was deferred. Under this act the Monopolies Commission on a reference by the Board of Trade may enquire into the supply of all types of services, including professional services. In any M. situations which have been the subject of an adverse report the Board of Trade may require the pub. of price lists, regulate prices, prohibit acquisitions or impose conditions upon acquisition. The Board of Trade may also dissolve mergers or monopolies. After a reference to the commission the gov. is empowered to halt or regulate the progress of a merger. A special procedure for the regulation of newspaper mergers is instituted which is very close to that recommended by the Royal Commission on the Press (*see* NEWSPAPERS).

Under the new Act the Board of Trade referred

the proposed acquisition of Pressed Steel by the Brit. Motor Corporation and, while the Board of Trade decided not to use its powers to hold up the merger, the companies went ahead despite the reference. In Oct. 1965, however, the intervention of the board persuaded the Imperial Tobacco Company not to proceed with its proposed acquisition of Smith's Potato Crisps. *See* J. Downie, *The Competitive Process*, 1958; J. B. Heath, 'Still not enough Competition', in *Ancient or Modern?*, 1964; Midland Bank Review, *Monopoly Legislation in Britain*, 1965. *See also* ECONOMICS; FORECASTING, ECONOMIC; LAISSEZ FAIRE; PLANNING, ECONOMIC; RESALE PRICE MAINTENANCE.

Monorail, name given to a device which has wheels running upon a single rail and is used to carry relatively light loads, generally about a warehouse or the depts of a factory. Often a lifting tackle is incorporated. In some instances the wheels run on an ordinary type of light, bulb-headed rail, and in others they are arranged to travel on both sides of the bottom flange of an I-section beam, the rail in each case being overhead. When the machine is operated by electricity it is known as a telpher, a name devised by the inventor, Prof. Fleeming Jenkin, in 1882, from the Gk words *tele*, far, and *fereim*, to carry. An up-to-date model consists of a bogie, running on an overhead rail, and driven by an electric motor which takes its current from a live rail running alongside the track. Attached to the trolley is a receptacle to carry the load, which may be as much as 5 tons. Telphers can be controlled by an attendant, or they may be entirely automatic; their operating costs per ton mile are extremely low. *See also* RAILWAYS (MONO-RAILWAYS). (*See Plate*: *Railway*.)

Monotheism (Gk *monos*, sole; *theos*, God), belief in one only God as the ruler of the universe; opposed to polytheism, which worships many gods, and to all systems of moral dualism, asserting the ultimate supremacy of good over evil. It differs from deism (q.v.) in asserting the fact of divine revelation. Many hold that primitive man was monotheistic. The Jewish and Mohammedan and Christian religions are strictly so. *See* N. Soderblöm, *Das Werden des Götterglaubens* (2nd ed.), 1926; W. Schmidt, *Origin and Growth of Religion* (Eng. trans.), 1931; W. F. Albright, *From the Stone Age to Christianity* (2nd ed.), 1946; H. R. Niebuhr, *Radical Monotheism and Western Culture*, 1961.

Monothelitism (Gk, 'having one will'), heresy which arose in the 7th cent. M. taught that Christ had but one will, whereas the Catholics held that though Christ's personality was one, yet He had two wills (according with His twofold nature, human and divine), which were, however, always in perfect harmony. The hist. of this heresy shows that it arose out of Monophysitism (q.v.). For when the Emperor Heraclius asked Sergius, the Monophysite patriarch of Constantinople, how that sect could be reconciled to the Church, Sergius said it could be held, without prejudice to the authority of the council

of Chalcedon, which had condemned the Monophysites, that, after the union of the two natures in Christ, there was but one will and one operation of will. In 630 Heraclius accordingly issued an edict requiring acceptance of this tenet; but in 636 Sophronius, patriarch of Jerusalem, assembled a council and condemned M. Sergius adhered to his old opinion, and in 639 drew up a formula of faith. The same year Pope John IV, in a council at Rome, rejected the formula, and condemned M. M. was again condemned in the Sixth General Council, at Constantinople (680). The Lebanese Maronites embraced M., but were reconciled to the Church in the late 12th cent. For full particulars of the conflicts of the 7th cent, *see* article 'Monothelitism' in *The Catholic Encyclopaedia*.

Monotremata, order of mammals, containing only 3 species: *Ornithorhynchus paradoxus*, *Echidna aculeata* and *Proechidna bruijnii*, spiny ant-eaters. The young are hatched from eggs and are fed on milk secreted not by mammae, but on a bare patch of the mother's skin. They have features which seem to make them intermediate between reptiles and the higher mammals. They have only one aperture for the urinary, genital and intestinal canals. Teeth, if present, consist of 4 horny plates. In various respects they approach birds and to a certain extent connect mammals with reptiles. Darwin thought that the earliest mammals in some respects resembled M, *See* MAMMALS.

Monreale, tn in Sicily, built on a hill 1200 ft above sea level, 5 m. SW. of Palermo. It has a magnificent archiepiscopal cathedral, founded in 1174, which is Norman in style but has Byzantine decorations and very fine golden mosaics. The 13th cent. massacre known as the 'Sicilian Vespers' began on the road between M. and Palermo (*see* SICILY, *History*). Pop. 18,200. (*See Plate: Italy*.)

Monro, Alexander, *primus* (1697–1767), anatomist, *b*. London, son of a Scottish army surgeon. He was educ. at Edinburgh Univ., acted as apprentice to his father, and studied surgery in London and medicine at Paris and Leyden. At the early age of 22 he was appointed prof. of anatomy at Edinburgh. He was a gifted teacher and a skilful anatomist. His chief writing was *Anatomy of the Human Bones*, 1726. His collected works were pub. by his son, 1781. In 1756 he was given the degree of M.D. Edinburgh and was made a fellow of the Royal College of Surgeons there. *See* life by A. Duncan, 1780.

He was succeeded as prof. by his son Alexander *secundus* (1733–1817), who was *b*. in Edinburgh, studied medicine there (M.D., 1755) and at Berlin and Leyden. He was elected fellow of the Royal College of Physicians of Edinburgh in 1759. Both as teacher and investigator he was greater than his father. His prin. works were *Observations on the Structure and Functions of the Nervous System*, 1783, *Structure and Physiology of Fishes*, 1785, *Description of the Bursae Mucosae*, 1788, and *Three Treatises on the Brain, the Eye, and the Ear*, 1797. In the first he described the 'foramen of Monro' in the brain.

He also did valuable work on the lymphatic vessels. *See* life by A. Duncan, 1818.

His eldest son, Alexander *tertius* (1773–1859), *b.* in Edinburgh, was conjoined with him in the professorship from 1798 to 1808 and then continued alone in that office until 1846, without distinction as a teacher. Between them the 3 Monros held the chair of anatomy at Edinburgh for 126 years. *See* J. A. Inglis, *The Monros of Auchinbowie*, 1911; R. E. Wright-St Clair, *Doctors Monro: a medical saga*, 1964.

Monro, Sir Charles Carmichael (1860–1929), soldier. In 1879 he joined 2nd Foot (The Queen's). Lieutenant-general, 1915. In 1915 he was given command of the First Corps, and when the Third Army was formed he was its commander. Soon after this he succeeded Sir Ian Hamilton as commander-in-chief in Gallipoli and conducted the evacuation with outstanding success. From 1916 to 1920 he commanded the Indian Army, being made a general in 1917. He became a baronet in 1921, and was governor of Gibraltar from 1923 to 1928.

Monro, Harold (1879–1932), Brit. poet, *b.* Brussels. Educ. at Radley and Cambridge, he settled in London in 1911 and became known as the founder of the *Poetry Review*. From 1919 to 1925 he ed. *The Monthly Chapbook*, which he had founded. Vols. of his verse include *Poems*, 1906, *Judas*, 1908, *Before Dawn*, 1911, *Children of Love*, 1914, *Trees*, 1916, *Strange Meetings*, 1917, *Real Property*, 1922, *The Earth for Sale*, 1928, and *Elm Angel*, 1930. He also pub. a book of criticism, *Some Contemporary Poets*, 1920, and an anthology, *Twentieth Century Poetry*, 1929.

Monro, Thomas (1759–1833), physician and connoisseur, educ. under Dr Samuel Parr and at Oriel College, Oxford. He was physician at Bethlehem Hospital, London, 1792–1816, and was a patron of artists, notably J. M. W. Turner (q.v.), Young and Thomas Girton (q.v.).

Monroe, Harriet (1860–1936), Amer. poetess and critic, *b.* Chicago. Educ. at the Academy of the Visitation, Georgetown, she pub. sev. vols. of verse, including *Valeria*, 1891, *The Dance of the Seasons*, 1911, *You and I*, 1914, and *The Difference*, 1924. She was better known, however, as the founder and editor of *Poetry*, the first Amer. periodical devoted exclusively to verse. She also collaborated in compiling *The New Poetry*, 1932, an anthology of 20th-cent. verse. *Poets and their Art*, 1932, is a book of essays, and *A Poet's Life*, 1937, her autobiography.

Monroe, James (1758–1831), fifth president of the U.S.A., was *b.* Westmoreland co., Virginia. He was educ. at William and Mary College, but, in 1776, entered the army. Soon afterwards he joined Washington's army as lieutenant, taking part in the engagements at Harlem Heights, White Plains and the attack on Trenton. He then became a major under the Earl of Stirling (1777–8), fighting at Brandywine, Germantown and Monmouth. He temporarily abandoned a military career for law studies under the direction of Jefferson. In 1780 he was nominated military commissioner for Virginia, in 1782

elected to the Virginia Legislative Assembly, and in 1788 became a member of the state constitutional convention. In 1790 he became a senator of the U.S.A., and 4 years later was sent by Washington to Paris as Amer. plenipotentiary. President Washington recalled him in 1796, as a result of his observations on the Jay Treaty negotiations over Amer. vessels. In 1799 he was made governor of Virginia. In 1802 he was sent by Jefferson as envoy-extraordinary to negotiate the purchase of Louisiana. The next 4 years he was at London and in Spain. In 1811 he became secretary of state, secretary of war 1814–15, and on 4 Mar. 1817 president in place of Madison. The chief event of his administration was the controversy over the admission of Missouri (q.v.) to the states at a time when the question of slavery agitated the whole country. In 1823 M. declared in his ann. message that the independence of the Hispano-Amer. reps., which for sev. years had been endeavouring to shake off the European yoke, must be maintained at any price, a declaration which has since become celebrated as the 'M. Doctrine' (q.v.). He retired into private life in 1825, but subsequently served as a member of the Virginia Constitutional Convention until ill health compelled him to retire in 1829. *See* S. M. Hamilton, (ed.), *The Writings of James Monroe*, 1898–1903, and life by W. P. Cresson, 1946.

Monroe, Marilyn (real name **Norma Jean Mortenson**) (1928–62), Amer. actress, *b.* Los Angeles; married (1956) Arthur Miller (q.v.); marriage dissolved, 1960. She began as a photographer's model. Her first star role came in *Don't Bother to Knock*, 1952. Others were *Niagara*, *Gentlemen Prefer Blondes*, *How to Marry a Millionaire*, *There's No Business Like Show Business*, *The Seven Year Itch*, *Bus Stop*, *The Princess and the Showgirl*, in which she played opposite Sir Laurence Olivier (q.v.), *Some Like It Hot*, *Let's Make Love* and *The Misfits*, written for her by Arthur Miller.

Monroe: 1. Co. seat of Ouachita par., Louisiana, U.S.A., on the Ouachita R., 76 m. W. of Vicksburg, Missouri. It is a cotton market with processing industries. Pop. 52,220.

2. City, co. seat of M. co., Michigan, U.S.A., on the Raisin R. near Lake Erie and 35 m. SW. of Detroit. It has limestone quarries, fisheries and nurseries, and manufs. sheet steel, paper and food products and furniture. Pop. *c.* 22,000.

Monroe Doctrine, one of the most important political declarations in modern times, is remarkable in that it is not embodied in an Act of the U.S. Congress, is not part of the U.S. Constitution, and is not part of the body of international law. President Wilson epitomised it thus: 'The Monroe Doctrine was proclaimed by the U.S.A. on her own authority. It always has been maintained, and always will be maintained, upon her own responsibility.' In brief, the M. D., backed by all the resources of the U.S.A., says to all the rest of the world: 'Hands off the Amer. hemisphere.' It was adumbrated in the farewell speech of George Washington, the first President of the U.S.A., and by Thomas Jefferson, the third, but found expression during the administration of President James Monroe (q.v.). The young rep. had always feared that powerful European nations might establish colonies in the W. hemisphere, and so prove dangerous neighbours. This was especially marked during Monroe's presidency, when the rebellions against Spain and Portugal by the Sp. and Portuguese colonies in S. and Central America raised the threat of repressive European intervention on a large scale in the New World. There was also the possibility that Russia might try to extend her Alaskan ters. In Dec. 1823, therefore, Monroe signed a message, which, though largely written by John Quincy Adams (q.v.), then his secretary of state, has become known as the M. D. In it he declared that the U.S.A. had no interest in European wars, but warned European powers that any attempt on their part to extend their system to any portion of the W. hemisphere would be considered as dangerous to the peace and safety of the U.S.A. His gov. would not seek to interfere with any existing colonies or dependencies of European countries now held in the W. continent, but could not allow any interposition of European powers for the purpose of oppressing or controlling any of the newly set-up Lat.-Amer. govs. This plainly told the members of the Holy Alliance that they would not be allowed to make war on Spain's lost colonies, and, further, that no Euoropean or extra-Amer. power would be allowed to secure Amer. ter. in the future, either by conquest, purchase or treaty. This doctrine has been reiterated in set or implicit terms by nearly every president who has succeeded Monroe.

It was invoked against France in 1865. Taking advantage of the Amer. Civil War the Emperor Napoleon III sent Fr. troops to Mexico and set up a Mexican empire, with Prince Maximilian of Austria as ruler. As soon as the civil war was ended the U.S. Gov. sent a sharp message to France, and was prepared to use its armies and navy to enforce it. But the French withdrew their troops, the people revolted, Maximilian was shot, and the Mexicans once more ruled Mexico. In 1895 it was again invoked in the boundary dispute between Venezuela and Great Britain. The general respect for the M. D. in the 19th cent. was due less to fear of offending the U.S.A. than from the realisation that Great Britain, with its immense naval strength, was a powerful if silent supporter of the Monroe principles as being largely in her own interests. The doctrine underwent a marked extension in the first quarter-cent. preceding the First World War, a period which seemed to indicate the development of Amer. imperialism through intervention in the internal affairs of the Lat.-Amer. states. The so-called Theodore Roosevelt corollary to the M. D. was first enunciated in 1904 and was exemplified by that president's action against Colombia over the Panama Canal and his intervention in Cuba to keep internal order. This expanded interpretation of the M. D. was not repudiated by Taft or Wilson, as was shown by Amer. intervention in Haiti. However, to reassure the Lat.-Amer. states that the U.S.A. did not intend to use their powers so as in effect to create any kind of hemispheric protectorate, during the centenary of the Monroe message secretary of state Hughes formally stated that the U.S.A. had no such intention and that it was 'part of our policy to respect the territorial integrity of the Latin-American republics'. President Franklin Roosevelt withdrew the last detachment of marines from Haiti, abrogated the Platt Amendment—which purported to legalise the right of intervention in that state—by mutual agreement with Cuba, and entered into a new treaty with Panama, relinquishing the right of intervention in that state. In his 'good neighbour' policy, Franklin Roosevelt's course of action was a radical departure from the 'big stick' policy of Theodore Roosevelt, and at the Buenos Aires inter-Amer. Conference in 1936 a declaration was drawn up prescribing the principles which were thenceforth to govern the relations of all the states of the Amer. continents. These principles proscribed all territorial conquest, or intervention in each other's affairs, internal or external; and provided for the peaceful settlement of debt collection or of other disputes.

Despite the U.S.A.'s policy of generous economic aid to Central and S. America, suspicion of U.S. motives remains a powerful force in Lat. America. The growth of leftist nationalism in many of these states since the Second World War has actually tended to increase this suspicion, despite various U.S. moves to counter it, e.g. the U.S.A.'s announcement of her intention to withdraw from the Panama Zone (1965). Both Cuba and the Dominican Rep. (qq.v.) offer recent examples of the U.S.A.'s continued practical application of the M. D. Her decisive action regarding the Cuban missile build-up in 1962 won general approval from Lat.-Amer. govs., as the Russian threat the build-up contained was obvious. But the U.S.A.'s previous decision, 1961, to allow and encourage Cuban exiles to invade Cuba from Amer. soil, and her efforts since 1962 to interfere with Cuba's trade, are more hostilely regarded. Amer. armed intervention in the Dominican Rep. in 1965 caused considerable criticism in Lat. America, where some have considered it a return to the Theodore Roosevelt interpretation of the M. D. *See* D. Perkins, *The Monroe Doctrine*, 1960.

Monrovia, chief port, commercial centre and cap. of the Republic of Liberia, W. Africa. M. was founded in 1822 as a settlement for freed slaves from America. It is connected to the hinterland by the St Paul R. (on whose mouth it stands) and by a railway linking it to the iron ore deposits in the Bomi Hills. A modern, deep-water harbour was completed in 1948. Pop. 80,000.

Mons (Flem. **Bergen**), cap. of the prov. of Hainaut, Belgium, 32 m. SW. of Brussels. The city is situated between 2 important coal-mining dists, the Borinage to the W. and the Centre to the E. Its importance is mainly commercial. It has manufs. of cotton goods, paper, porcelain, oil, chocolate, soap and tobacco, and is the most important coal market of Belgium. M. stands on the site of a Rom. camp, and has sev. interesting buildings, including the tn hall (1443–67) and the collegiate church of Ste-Waudru (1450–1621), with its belfry. There are also 3 museums. Pop. 27,000.

Mons, Battle of. At the outbreak of the First World War the small Brit. expeditionary force, under Field-Marshal Sir John French (later Lord Ypres), was rushed across to France and took up a position to the left of the Fr. line about M., a small Belgian tn near the Fr. border, 32 m. SW. of Brussels. On 22 Aug. 1914, the Germans gained a victory over the French at Namur, and threw them back, thus making a breach in the Entente line with the British isolated on the left. The Germans under von Kluck and von Bülow (total 4 corps) now attacked the 2 Brit. corps on 23 Aug. A frontal attack was launched and the Brit. infantry poured in a sustained, well-aimed rapid fire with rifles and machine-guns. This Ger. attack failed, and von Bülow now made a flank attack on the right of the British, who had not been informed of the full details of the Fr. withdrawal. When Sir John French learnt of the vastly numerically superior forces to which he was opposed, he gave orders for a withdrawal in order to escape complete envelopment and annihilation. *See also* WESTERN FRONT IN FIRST WORLD WAR.

Mons Capitolinus, *see* CAPITOL.

Mons Palatinus, *see* PALATINE HILL.

Mons Star, *see* STARS, MILITARY.

Mons Summanus, *see* VESUVIUS.

Monsarrat, Nicholas John Turney (1910–), novelist, *b.* Liverpool. Educ. at Winchester and Cambridge, where he studied law, he turned instead to writing. His early novels were followed by a series of non-fiction vols. beginning with *H. M. Corvette*, 1942, and relating his experiences as a naval officer in the Second World War. But his greatest success was a novel, *The Cruel Sea*, 1951, which was awarded the Heinemann Prize. *The Story of Esther Costello*, 1953, is a work of sordid realism. *A Fair Day's Work*, 1964, is a novel set on an ocean liner.

Monserrat, *See* MONTSERRAT.

Monsignore, title of honour given to prelates in the Rom. Catholic Church and to certain officers of the papal court.

Monsoon (from the Arabic *mawsim*, a season), term used generally for any wind which blows regularly at fixed seasons, but especially applied to those winds which blow over the Indian Ocean to India. From April till Oct. they blow from the SW. (NE. in Bengal), from Oct. to April they blow from the NE. Their regularity is caused by the regular change of the seasons. During the winter the cold air from the interior of Asia flows outward in a general S.-westerly direction towards the warmer sea; when the land, on the contrary, becomes more heated than the sea the direction of the current of air

changes and flows inwards in a N.-easterly direction. The change to the SW. M. is accompanied in parts of India by violent thunderstorms and torrential rains. It sometimes happens that the M. fails to bring the expected rains, and the result is such a famine as occurred in 1895 and again in 1899. The SW. M. is deflected to the S. and SE. in the equatorial belt, and accompanied by violent typhoons in the neighbourhood of the E. Indies and Madagascar. The M. is best known where contrast of air is very great—between air from the Sahara and the Gulf of Guinea in W. Africa, between air from the Sudan and the Indian Ocean in E. Africa, as well as the classical Indian case. The term M. was originally brought to England from the E. Indies by Portuguese traders in Elizabethan times, but accounts of the winds were chronicled by Aristotle and Pliny, as well as by the Arab historian, Sidi Ali in 1554. *See also* METEOROLOGY; WIND.

Monstrance (Lat. *monstrare*, to show), or **Ostensory,** vessel used in the Rom. Catholic Church for holding the Sacred Host in benedictions, processions and expositions of the Blessed Sacrament. It stands on a circular base, and the upper part is now usually circular with rays extending on all sides from the centre. The host is itself held in a small crescent-shaped *lunula*, or *lunette*, kept (with the host) in a special pyx in the tabernacle, but fitted for the purpose of exposition into the central glass frame of the M. M.s of a similar kind are also used for the exposition of relics.

MONSTRANCE

Monstrelet, Enguerrand de (1390–1453), Fr. chronicler, probably *b.* Ponthieu. He was attached to the service of John of Luxembourg, and was at Compiègne when Joan of Arc was captured by the Burgundians. His *Chronique*, covering the years 1400–44, continued Froissart's *Chronicle*, and is a clear and reasonably accurate account of current events.

Monstrosity, see TERATOLOGY.

Mont, or **Menthu,** hawk-headed god of Hermonthis (Armant), became important when the princes of Hermonthis reunited Egypt as the 11th dynasty, and his worship spread to Thebes. As the reunion was achieved by force of arms, M. was regarded as a god of war. Believed to appear as the Sacred Buchis bull.

Mont Blanc, see BLANC, MONT.

Mont Cenis, see CENIS, MONT.

Mont-de-Marsan, Fr. tn, cap. of the dept of Landes, on the Midouze. It has nursery gardens, and oil, wood and resin industries. Pop 20,200.

Mont-de-Piété (It. *Monte di Pietà*), estab. where money is lent to the poor at a moderate rate of interest, was founded, to combat the evils of usury, about the middle of the 15th cent. at Orvieto (1463) and Perugia (1467). The first estab. in Paris was opened in 1777, suppressed during the revolution, but later restored as a national undertaking with the right to charge 9 per cent on all loans to pay working expenses; any surplus gain goes to public charities. While the estab. at Paris is the largest in the world there are also similar centres of municipal pawn-broking in many European countries. In England the system appeared for a time during the 18th cent., being abandoned as a non-practical idea after some 70 years. See also PAWNBROKER.

Mont Pelée, see MARTINIQUE.

Mont-St Jean, vil. in the prov. of S. Brabant, Belgium, 11 m. SE. of Brussels, and just NE. of the scene of Waterloo (q.v.).

Mont St Michel, granite islet in the Bay of St Michel, near the mouth of the Couesnon, 15 m. SSE. of Granville, in the dept of La Manche, France. It is connected to the mainland by a causeway 1 m. long. The is. rises to a height of 240 ft, and is crowned by a Benedictine abbey, estab. in the 10th cent. in the place of an 8th cent. oratory. The vil. (pop. 250) on the S. and E. sides of the is. is protected by ramparts. The fortress-abbey withstood the English in the Hundred Years War and the Huguenots in the religious wars. The Order of St Michel, founded by Louis XI, used to meet in the splendid Knights' Hall. After the Fr. Revolution the abbey was used as a political prison.

Montacute, Thomas de, see CECIL, ROBERT.

Montacute House, mansion situated 4 m. from Yeovil, Somerset, England; begun in 1588 by Thomas Phelips, and completed c. 1601 by his son, Sir Edward Phelips, Speaker of the House of Commons and master of the rolls under James I. It has curvilinear and finialled gables, open balustraded parapet, carved statues of the 9 worthies standing in niches in the E. front, and fluted angle columns. The property, including St Michael's Hill (the Mons Acutus), was presented to the National Trust through the Society for the Protection of Anct Buildings in 1931. A collection of fine period furniture, pictures and tapestries has been formed in the house.

Montagna, Bartolommeo (1450–1523), It. painter, *b.* Orzinuovi, near Brescia. According to Vasari he was a pupil of Andrea Mantegna.

He is regarded as the most eminent master of the school of Vicenza. His masterpiece is the altarpiece of San Michele at Vicenza (1499), later removed to Milan.

Montagnards, see MOUNTAIN, THE.

Montagu, Charles and **George,** see HALIFAX, EARL OF.

Montagu, Edward see MANCHESTER, EARL OF.

Montagu, Edward and **John,** see SANDWICH, 1st and 4th EARLS.

Montagu, Edwin Samuel (1879–1924), statesman, second son of 1st Baron Swaythling. He was educ. at City of London School and Trinity College, Cambridge. Elected M.P. in 1906, he became financial secretary to the Treasury in 1914, and in 1915 privy councillor and chancellor of the Duchy of Lancaster. On the formation of the coalition he became financial secretary to the Treasury once more, and from the summer of 1916 minister of munitions until the end of Asquith's premiership. Secretary of state for India in 1917, he collaborated in the M.-Chelmsford report, but in 1922 was obliged to resign for publishing a dispatch from the India Gov. without cabinet authority.

Montagu, Elizabeth, *née* **Robinson** (1720–1800), authoress and social leader, *b.* York. In 1742 she married Edward M., grandson of the first Earl of Sandwich. She was one of the best-known and most popular of the 'blue-stocking' (q.v.) coterie, and entertained largely at Sandleford and at M. House, London. Among her writings was an *Essay on the Writings and Genius of Shakespeare*, 1769, being a spirited reply to Voltaire. She was a voluminous correspondent and her *Letters* were collected and pub. (1809–13) by her nephew, Matthew M. There is a biography by Mrs E. J. Climenson, 1906.

Montagu, George (1751–1815), writer on natural hist., *b.* Lackham, Wilt s. He served in the war with the Amer. colonies. He was one of the earliest members of the Linnean Society, for which he wrote papers on the birds and shells of S. England. He had a splendid collection of birds and other animals, which was purchased by the Brit. Museum. He pub. an *Ornithological Dictionary of British Birds*, 1802, and *Testacea Britannica*, 1893, on Brit. shells.

Montagu, Lady Mary Wortley (1689–1762), authoress, *b.* Thoresby, Notts, daughter of Evelyn Pierrepont, later 1st Duke of Kingston-upon-Hull. In 1712, after a lengthy and quarrelsome courtship by illicit correspondence, she married Edward Wortley M., who seems, once married, to have devoted little attention to his wife. In 1716 he was sent as ambas. to the Porte. Lady Mary accompanied her husband through Europe to the E., at that time almost unknown to Europeans. In Turkey she learned of the practice of inoculation (q.v.) for smallpox, which on her return in 1718 she made known in this country, having it performed on both her own children. Pope's quarrel with her is historic; he passed rapidly from fulsome admiration of her to scurrilous attack, but his reasons for doing so remain obscure. In his satires he accused her of malice, miserliness and disreputable disease; she expressed scorn for his low birth, physical deformity and crooked mind. In 1739 Lady Mary left her husband and family to go abroad again, urged by her passion for travelling, and partly by a desire to see again Francesco Algarotti (q.v.), then a promising young man whom she had met and admired in England. They did not meet until 1741, and then only briefly. Lady Mary, however, remained in self-imposed exile in Italy and elsewhere until her husband's death in 1761, when she returned to England. Her *Town Eclogues* were first pub. in 1716 under the title of *Court Poems*. Her *letters* were pub. in 1763. and her *Works* (far from complete) in 1803. Her reputation has been marred by Pope's largely unfounded accusations, and by the equally unflattering view of Horace Walpole, who met her in Florence in 1740. Her letters are remarkable for their wit, their vivid descriptions and their revelation of a woman both intellectual and worldly, full of courage, gaiety, curiosity and underlying pessimism. *See* G. Paston, *Lady Mary Wortley Montagu and her Times*, 1907; Violet Stuart Wortley, *Magic in the Distance*, 1948; L. Gibbs, *The Admirable Lady Mary*, 1949; R. Halsband, *Life of Mary Wortley Montagu*, 1956; *The Complete Letters of Lady Mary Wortley Montagu, 1708–1720*, vol. i, ed. R. Halsband, 1966.

Montague, Charles Edward (1867–1928), journalist and novelist, *b.* Twickenham, Middx. He was educ. at City of London School and Oxford Univ. He was for many years chief leader-writer on the *Manchester Guardian*, and in 1898 married the daughter of its editor. C. P. Scott (q.v.). His novels are of considerable merit, and among his other writings *Dramatic Values*, 1911, contains excellent comments on the tendencies of 19th cent. drama. His works include *A Hind Let Loose*, 1910, *Disenchantment*, 1922, *The Morning's War*, 1923, *Fiery Particles*, 1923, *Rough Justice*, 1926, and *Right off the Map*, 1927. Some of these are based on his experiences in the First World War. M. was a governor of the Manchester Univ. *See* O. Elton, *C. E. Montague*, 1929.

Montaigne, Michel Eyquem, Seigneur de (1533–92), Fr. writer, *b.* at the château of St Michel de M., in Périgord. At the age of 6 he entered the Collège de Guienne, Bordeaux, where one of his 'familiar tutors' was George Buchanan (q.v.) and another Marc-Antoine Muret. M. does not hide the fact that he was lazy and read merely as his fancy suggested. At 21 he became a member of the Cour des Aides at Périgueux, and 3 years later a councillor of the Parlement at Bordeaux. In 1570 he resigned his post and retired to his château de M., where he lived with his books for the remainder of his life. He had already (1569) pub. his trans. of the *Theologia naturalis* of Raymond Sebond (a 15th cent. prof. of Toulouse), and in the same year he also ed. the works of his deceased friend La Boétie. In 1572 he began to write his *Essais*, and pub. the first 2 books in 1580. In the latter year he travelled in Switzerland, S. Germany,

Italy and the Tyrol, and on his return was elected mayor of Bordeaux; though at first he declined the dignity he gave way on receiving a letter from Henry III commanding him to accept. Generally speaking, he seems to have fulfilled his duties with much tact, in spite of a somewhat hasty departure when the plague broke out with renewed vigour. The 5th ed. of his *Essais*, to which a third book was added, appeared in 1588. At his death he left to his wife and Mlle de Gournay, his adopted daughter, the task of issuing a definitive ed., which appeared in 1595.

Few books have exercised a greater and more enduring influence on the literature and thought of the world than M.'s *Essais*. His criticism is analytical, sceptical and inconclusive; there is a continual weighing of evidence, and nothing certain emerges save his uncertainty. The titles of the essays frequently afford no indication whatever of their contents, and are but suggestions to prompt ideas. He talks in a disconnected way on innumerable topics, often completely losing sight of his original theme, yet always with a clear object in view. The essays seem unduly egoistic, but this was M.'s method of arriving at general rules of conduct. In the search after self-knowledge he lays bare his own moral and psychological outlook, caring as little for the exposure of his own weaknesses as for the revelation of those things upon which he prided himself. The foundation and essence of his ideas are contained in the ironical *Apologie de Raymond Sebond*, being an eloquent diatribe against the value of human reason so far as metaphysic and science are concerned. M. had no sympathy with innovation. He was born in a disillusioned age when the splendid dawn of the Renaissance had faded into the light of common day. M. takes himself as a representative of 'la moyenne humanité'. Nature, while remaining our guide, must be submitted to discipline; for the human mind is a 'dangerous vagabond', in whose footsteps misfortune is sure to follow if it is not held in check and prevented from forming personal opinions dangerous to tradition. With M. indeed begins the reaction of the 17th cent. as represented by the *opinions générales*, i.e. by authority, and for the same reason, and because he hated all innovations, he condemned the reformation as an arrogant revolution. All his attention is given to points of practical morals, in the constant discussion of which he ranges himself on the side of antiquity as opposed to medievalism. In this connection his views on education are of great interest. M. recommends the learning of foreign languages, but deprecates the wasting of so much time on Latin and Greek; he also thinks that the master should not confine himself to books. *See* A. Gide, *Montaigne*, 1929; J. Plattard, *Montaigne et son temps*, 1933; P. Moreau, *Montaigne, l'homme et l'œuvre*, 1939; C. Dédéyan, *Montaigne chez ses amis anglo-saxons*, 1948.

Montalbán, Juan Pérez de, *see* PÉREZ.

Montale, Eugenio (1896–). It. poet, *b.* Genoa. He is one of the chief exponents of the *poesia pura*, of which school the leading poet was

Giuseppe Ungaretti (q.v.). His best-known works are *Ossi di Sepia*, 1925, *La Casa dei Doganieri*, 1932, and *Le Occasioni*, 1939.

Montalembert, Charles Forbes de Tryon, Comte de (1810–70), Fr. politician and historian, *b*. London, the son of a Fr. *émigré* and his Scots wife. In 1830 he joined Lamennais on the staff of *L'Avenir*, but later severed his connection with this and became a devout Catholic. In 1836 he pub his *Histoire de Ste Elisabeth d'Hongroie*, which was followed by *Du vandalisme et du catholicisme* in 1839. His great work was *Les Moines d'occident depuis St Benoît jusqu'à St Bernard*, 1860–1877.

Montana, NW. state of the U.S.A., bounded on the N. by Canada, E. by N. and S. Dakota and S. by Wyoming and Idaho, the latter also bounding it on the W. It is the third largest Amer. state, with a total area of 147,138 sq. m. There are Indian settlements, with a total Indian pop. 16,800. The E. part consists of the almost level surface of the Great Plains, rising gently from 1800 ft in the E. to 5000 ft in the W. against the abruptly rising front ranges of the Rocky mts, which occupy the rest of the state and through which the boundary with Idaho runs. The Great Plains are a Tertiary sediment sheet, the 'Rockies' mostly linear ranges running along denuded anticlines. In the N. is Glacier National Park. The Missouri R. rises in Yellowstone park to the S. of the state line; the Yellow-stone, Flathead, Bitteroo and Milk R.s drain the greater part of the state, while the Misoula and Kootenarri drain the NW. corner. In the riv. valleys and where irrigation has been extensively introduced the soil is very productive, and wheat and other cereals, flax-seed, potatoes, corn, hay, sugar-beet and fruit are grown. But M. is chiefly a pastoral state: sheep and beef cattle are reared in large numbers, and there are wide areas of forest. Total farm and range acreage is *c*. 64,181,000. The state has over 20,000,000 ac. of forest land.

Of the immense potential water power, only about a third has been developed. The great industry of the state is mining, the total value of the mineral products amounting in 1962 to $184,400,000. Coal, copper, manganese, zinc, petroleum, gold, silver and sapphires are found. Other industries include smelting and flour-milling. The cap. is Helena, 21,800. Butte (27,500) and Great Falls (58,000) are the largest tns. Other tns: Billings, Missoula, Anaconda. M. was organised as a ter. in 1864 and admitted to the Union in 1889. It has a senate of 56 members, and a house of representatives of 94; it sends 2 senators and 2 representatives to Congress. Pop. 674,770. *See Montana*, issued by the Dept of Agriculture, Labor, and Industry; *Montana's Production, 1930–46*, by the Bureau of Business Research, Montana State Univ.; J. K. Howard, *Montana: High, Wide, and Handsome*, 1943; J. McL. Hamilton, *From Wilderness to Statehood: Montana 1805–1900*, 1957. (*See Plate*.)

Montanism, heretical movement of the 2nd cent., originating in Phrygia. Montanus, a native of Mysia, was its leader. He believed he had a mission to restore the Church to its pristine purity, but his chief claim was to be the Paraclete promised by Jesus to his disciples. He taught that revelation to man still continued, and this was frequently delivered by himself and by his female companions, Prisca and Maximilla. He proclaimed that the end of the world was at hand, and that then Christ would reappear at the tn of Pepuza in Syria. No forgiveness was possible after mortal sin; the sacraments were therefore unnecessary, and marriage was discouraged as an inferior state. At first the sect spread rapidly and made its most famous convert in Africa, where Tertullian (q.v.) joined its ranks. M. was condemned unhesitatingly in sev. local councils, and finally in the Council of Constantinople (381). It died out in the W. about the 4th cent., and did not survive much longer in the E.

Montargis, Fr. tn in the dept of Loiret on the Loing. There is a 12th cent. church and an anct château. Mme Guyon (q.v.) was *b*. here. It is a railway junction and has paper-mills and tanneries. Pop. 17,700.

Montauban, see COUSIN-MONTAUBAN.

Montauban, Fr. tn, cap. of the dept of Tarn-et-Garonne, on the Tarn. It was a Huguenot (q.v.) centre, and was frequently besieged. It successfully resisted de Luynes (q.v.) in 1621, but surrendered to Louis XIII in 1629 after the fall of La Rochelle (q.v.). Ingres and Bourdelle (qq.v.) were *b*. here. Textiles and porcelain are manuf., and there is a trade in agric. produce. Pop. 30,300.

Montbard, Fr. tn, in the dept of Côte-d'Or, on the Burgundy canal. It has the ruins of a 14th cent. castle. Buffon and Daubenton (qq.v) were *b*. here. There are steel works. Pop. 6400.

Montbéliard, Fr. tn, in the dept of Doubs, on the Rhine and Rhône canal. The anct castle of the counts of M. is now a museum. Cuvier (q.v.) was *b*. here. M. is the centre of a region which manufs. watches, textiles, furniture and metal goods. Pop. 21,700.

Montbretia, family Iridaceae, genus of S. African herbs, akin to Tritonia; *M. flava* and *M. laxiflora* are grown in greenhouses for their spikes of lovely yellow or cream flowers. The M.s of gardens are hybrids of *Crocosmia aurea* × *C. ponsii*.
See over.

Montcalm, Louis Joseph, Marquis de (1712–1759), Fr. soldier, *b*. Candiac, near Nîmes. In 1727 he entered the army, becoming a captain at the age of 18. He served in Italy and Germany, being wounded at Piacenza (1746). In 1756 he was placed in command of the Fr. troops in Canada, captured Fort Ontario and Fort William Henry from the English (1757), and repulsed Gen. Abercrombie's attack at Ticonderoga (1758). Lack of reinforcements and provisions forced him to retire to Quebec, where he was besieged in 1759 by Wolfe, both falling mortally wounded in the battle of the Heights of Abraham. In 1827 a monument to the joint honour of Wolfe and M. was erected in Quebec.

MONTBRETIA LAXIFLORA

See F. Parkman, *Montcalm and Wolfe*, 1884 (revised ed. 1964); H. R. Casgrain, *Wolfe and Montcalm*, 1906. (*See Plate: Canada*.)

Montcorbier, *see* VILLON, FRANÇOIS.

Monte, Giovanni Maria del, *see* JULIUS (popes), *Julius III*.

Monte Carlo, resort in the principality of Monaco (q.v.), on the Riviera (q.v.), 10 m. ENE. of Nice. The centre of the tn stands on a rocky escarpment to the N. of Monaco harbour. During the summer months it is a popular watering place, and in winter it is much frequented because of its artistic and sporting events; the ann. motor-car rally is famous. M. is best known, however, for its gambling casino, built in 1879 and later enlarged. The concessionaire of the casino (the Société Anonyme des Bains de Mer et Cercle des Étrangers) pays a yearly grant to the principality. The first gaming estab. at M. was opened by 2 Frenchmen named Langlois and Aubert; they were unsuccessful, and they were followed by other unsuccessful adventurers. The present flourishing casino owes its foundation to François Blanc (q.v.), who obtained a gambling concession from Charles III in 1861 (the price being about £70,000). Pop. 11,000. (*See Plate: Monaco*.)

Monte Cassino, Abbey of, famous Benedictine monastery standing on a hill 1700 ft high above the tn of Cassino (q.v.) in Italy. It was founded by St Benedict (q.v.) in 529, the site being chosen with a view to defence against barbarian assault. The monastery, one of the great centres of faith and learning in the Middle Ages, was destroyed in 589 by the Longobards (q.v.), in 884 by the Saracens (q.v.), in 1030 by the Normans and in 1349 by an earthquake. In the Second World War it was devastated by bombing and shellfire, 15 Feb. to 18 May 1944 (*see* CASSINO, BATTLE OF). Except for remains of piers, the basilica (1649), which included among its treasures splendid frescoes and mosaics, was demolished, as were the 3 beautiful cloisters and the great stairway. The crypt and the tombs of St Benedict and St Scholastica remained intact, and a portion of the W. end of the buildings survived.

The valuable archives and the library (40,000 vols.) had been sent to Rome for safety, and these, together with some paintings, were preserved. The work of reconstruction was begun as soon as practicable after the end of the war, and in 1956 the monstery was formally reopened. It was reconsecrated by Pope Paul VI in Oct. 1964.

Monte Cinto, mt, the highest point in Corsica, 34 m. NNE. of Ajaccio. Height 8890 ft.

Monte Cristo, rocky islet in the Tyrrhenian Sea (q.v.), 28 m. S. of Elba. It belongs to Italy, and was made a penal settlement in 1874. The is. was made famous by the novel by A. Dumas, *père* (q.v.), *The Count of Monte Cristo*.

Monte Rosa, *see* ROSA, MONTE.

Monte San Giuliano, *see* ERYX.

Monte Sant' Angelo, It. tn in Apulia (q.v.), 27 m. NE. of Foggia. It is in the Gargano peninsula and stands 2765 ft above sea level. The church of S. Michele is frequented by pilgrims. Pop. 23,500.

Monte Viso, *see* VISO, MONTE.

Montebello, It. vil. in Veneto (q.v.), 10 m. SW. of Vicenza. It was the scene of 2 Austrian defeats: by Napoleon in 1796, and by the Italians under Eugène de Beauharnais in 1805.

Montebello Casteggio, It. vil. in Lombardy (q.v.), 14 m. SSW. of Pavia. It was the scene of 2 Austrian defeats: by the French under Marshal Lannes in 1800, and by the French and Piedmontese in 1859. Pop. 3000.

Montecatini Terme, It. watering place in Tuscany (q.v.), 8 m. WSW. of Pistoia. It is a modern tn, with wide avenues, and is the best-known spa in Italy. Its warm springs have been used since Rom. times. Pop. 16,200.

Montecuculi, Raimondo, Count (1609–80), Austrian general, *b.* Modena. In 1625 he entered the Austrian Army as a volunteer, serving through the Thirty Years War. In 1657 he fought against the Swedes, and in 1660–4 against the Turks who had invaded Transylvania. In 1672, when Austria supported Holland against France, M. was in command of the imperial army and opposed Turenne on the banks of the Rhine (1672–5). The Emperor Leopold made him a prince of the empire and Duke of Melfi. *See* his *Mémoires*, 1703.

Montefiascone, It. tn in Lazio (q.v.), 9 m. NNW. of Viterbo. It occupies the site of the Etruscan Fanum Voltumnae, has a 16th cent. cathedral and a fortress, and produces a well-known muscatel wine. Pop. 5000.

Montefiore, Sir Moses Hayim (1784–1885), Jewish philanthropist, *b.* Leghorn, Italy. He became a member of the London Stock Exchange and made a large fortune. In 1818 he became president of the Sp. and Portuguese community, and worked to remove the civil disabilities of the Jews in England. He did much to assist Jewish settlement in Palestine in the 19th cent. *See* L. Loewe (ed.), *Diaries of Sir Moses and Lady Montefiore*, 1890.

Montego Bay, tn on the N. coast of Jamaica, and the second tn of the is., 113 m. from Kingston by rail. It is an attractive and historically interesting resort. It was a large Indian vil. when Columbus visited it (1494). There are traces of Arawak life in the sea caves. Lard was an export in the time of the Sp. occupation—whence its name, from *manteca* (hog's butter). St James's Church was built 1775–82. In the bay is a cluster of coral atolls, known as the Bogue Islets. There is an international airport near the tn. Pop. 23,610.

Monteith, *see* MENTEITH.

Monteleone di Calabria, *see* VIBO VALENTIA.

Montélimar, Fr. tn in the dept of Drôme, on the Roubion, a trib. of the Rhône, 27 m. SSW. of Valence. It is famous for its nougat, and there are textile and chocolate industries. Pop. 16,900.

Montelius, Gustaf Oscar Augustin (1843–1921), Swedish archaeologist, great exponent of typology, *b.* Stockholm. He became a prof. and director at the Hist. Museum, Stockholm, in 1888. Some of his books are *Ancient Dwellings in Europe*, 1895, *The Prehistoric Age in Sweden*, 1895, *Primitive Civilisation in Italy*, 1895–1910, *The Bronze Age in North Germany and Scandinavia*, 1900, and *The Bronze Age in Sweden*, 1900. All are now superseded by more modern works.

Montello, *see* MONTEBELLUNA.

Montem, custom formerly practised by Etonians, who went in fancy costume to 'Salt Hill', a mound near Slough, and there collected money from bystanders, to support the senior colleger of the school at King's College, Cambridge. It was abolished in 1846.

Montemayor, Jorge de (1520–61), Sp. poet, *b.* Montemor-o-Velho, Portugal. His fame rests on his pastoral romance, *Diana*, 1558, the first pastoral novel in Spain.

Montenegro (Serbo-Croatian **Crnagora**; Turkish, **Karadagh**), constituent rep. of Yugoslavia. With a coastline on the Adriatic, it is bounded on the NE. by Serbia, on the NW. by Croatia and Bosnia-Hercegovina, and on the S. by Albania.

M. belonged in the Middle Ages to the Serbian kingdom. After the battle of Kosovo in 1389 (*see* BLACKBIRDS, FIELD OF THE and SERBIA) the Montenegrins were able to remain independent of the Turks, though eventually obliged to confine themselves to the mts. In 1516 the secular prince resigned and transferred the gov. to a prince-bishop (*vladika*), an office which became hereditary (*see* DANILO, PETROVIĆ NIEGOŠ). In 1851 Danilo I (q.v.), on succeeding to the throne, declared the line of prince-bishops at an end and ruled as a secular prince (*gospodar*). A Turkish invasion in 1853 was halted by the intervention of the great powers, and in 1910 the prince of M. assumed the title of king. The Montenegrins took part in the Balkan war (q.v.) of 1912, and in 1913 they captured Scutari, but were compelled to abandon it. During the First World War the Austrians entered Cetinje (then the cap.) in 1916, and the king, Nicholas I, fled. One of his sons declared himself king, but abdicated after a short period. In 1919 the Grand Assembly of M. decided that the country should join the new kingdom of the

Serbs, Croats and Slovenes—Yugoslavia (q.v.).

M. is everywhere mountainous, the mts being for the most part heavily forested. In the N., Mt Durmitor rises to 9146 ft; in the E., Mt Komovi rises to 9300 ft. The S. of the country is in general rocky and arid. There are some fertile riv. valleys running into the Adriatic and the great lake of Scutari (q.v.); the prin. rivs. are the Morača, Piva, Tara and Lim. Some grain, tobacco, mulberries and vines are grown, but the chief occupation is the raising of swine, sheep and goats. The climate is severe in the mts, but Mediterranean on the coast and in the valleys. The majority of the inhab. belong to the Orthodox church. The prin. tns are Titograd (the cap.) and Cetinje (qq.v.). Area 5341 sq. m.; pop. 471,500. *See* F. Stevenson, *A History of Montenegro*, 1913; P. Edmonds, *To the Land of the Eagle*, 1927.

Montenotte, *see* CAIRO MONTENOTTE.

Montepeloso, *see* IRSINA.

Montepulciano, It. tn in Tuscany (q.v.), 28 m. SE. of Siena. It stands on a hill and has beautiful medieval and Renaissance buildings, including a 16th–17th cent. cathedral and sev. palaces. Its wine is well known. Politian (q.v.) was *b.* here. Pop. 3,300.

Montereau (-faut-Yonne), Fr. tn in the dept of Seine-et-Marne, at the confluence of the Seine and the Yonne. John the Fearless was murdered here in 1419 (*see under* CHARLES VI OF FRANCE). Porcelain and machinery are manuf. Pop. 14,200.

Monterrey, cap. of state of Nuevo León and 3rd largest city of Mexico. It is the chief city in the N. and is the country's leading industrial centre. Situated at an altitude of 1765 ft on the banks of the R. Santa Caterina, M. is surrounded by mts and has a temperate climate, being hot and dry in summer and cool and wet in winter. An important communications centre, it lies on the Mexico City-Nuevo Laredo railway, and is connected by rail with its nearest port Tampico on the Gulf of Mexico. Metallurgical industries are predominant, M. producing 75 per cent of Mexico's iron and steel output; after that the range of industry is very considerable. Important to its industrial development have been the coalfields of Coahuila (q.v.) and the Falcon Dam on the R. Salado built jointly by the Mexican and U.S. Govs. Although today a fine modern city, the imprint of the Sp. period remains and there are many attractive period buildings. In addition to the fine cathedral, there is the red granite State Capitol, which housed the first printing press in Mexico; the Bishop's Palace (1782) now a museum; and La Purisima, an interesting contemporary church. The pop. of M. has quadrupled since 1950 and is still growing rapidly. M. has a univ. and also the famous Technological Institute. Pop. 596,993 (1960).

Montesi Scandal, see ITALY, *History*.

Montespan, Françoise Athenaïs de Rochechouart, Marquise de (1641–1707), mistress of Louis XIV, *B.* Tonnay-Charente, was the daughter of the Duc de Mortemart. In 1663 she married Louis, Marquis de M. Having become maid of honour to the queen she attracted the attention of Louis XIV, who made her his mistress, 1667. She was both beautiful and witty, and remained for many years the favourite of the king, to whom she bore 7 children. She was popularly supposed to be a believer in black magic. She was supplanted by Mme de Maintenon in 1691, left Versailles and retired into a convent. Her *Mémoires*, 1829, have been trans. into English, 1895. *See* life by H. Carré, 1939.

Montesquieu, Charles de Secondat, Baron de la Brède (1689–1755), Fr. philosophical historian, *b.* near Bordeaux. In 1714 he was appointed councillor of the Parlement of Bordeaux, and 2 years later on the death of his uncle, Jean Baptiste de Secondat, he succeeded to his title and fortune as well as to his judicial office as president of the Parlement of Bordeaux. In 1721 he pub. anonymously his *Lettres persanes*, a subtle satire on contemporary Fr. institutions and manners, written in the guise of a correspondence between 2 Persian noblemen travelling through Europe. This book achieved an immediate and resounding success, and determined him to continue a literary career. In the wide social and political satire and reflections on gov. and jurisprudence in this work we can already see the beginnings of *L'Esprit des lois*. After travelling for 3 years in foreign countries in order to gain the knowledge necessary for the ambitious work on jurisprudence which he already contemplated, he wrote *Considérations sur les causes de la grandeur des Romains et leur décadence*, 1734, a most able study of anct Rome. In 1748 appeared *L'Esprit des lois* in 31 books. This work, which took 20 years in compilation, and which is one of the most important works of the 18th cent. judged from its influence on jurisprudence, is in effect the sum of M.'s observations and reflections, with the deductions he had drawn from the social and political phenomena of many states. It is to be observed that M. here uses the word *loi* not in the narrow technical sense, save in the last 6 books, which are purely legal hist., but as connoting 'the necessary relations existing between different things resulting from the nature of the things themselves'. The work is stupendous in range, but lacking in uniformity of plan; M. had no definite design for the whole, but included in the 31 books all the thoughts, deductions and reflections accumulated over many years without regard for systematic arrangement or even logical sequence. M.'s admiration for the free Eng. constitution, which is to be inferred from book xi of his work, had much influence on the earlier course of the Fr. Revolution, as well as having its effect on his discussion of the various types of gov. and of liberty in relation to gov. *See* J. Dudieu, *Montesquieu, l'homme et l'œuvre*, 1943; R. Shackleton, *Montesquieu: A Critical Biography*, 1961.

Montesquiou, Comte Robert de (1855–1921), Fr. writer, *b.* Paris. Although M. wrote many books of criticism, he devoted himself mainly to poetry, full of artifices and preciosities. His vols.

of poetry include *Les Chauves-Souris*, 1893, *Le Chef des odeurs suaves*, 1893, *Les Hortensias bleus*, 1896, *Perles rouges*, 1899, and *Les Paons*, 1900. He will probably be best remembered as J. K. Huysmans's model for the sinister character of des Esseintes in *À Rebours*. Marcel Proust is also supposed to have used him in part as model for one of the figures in *À la Recherche du temps perdu*.

M.'s essays include *Roseaux pensants*, 1897, and *Autels privilégiés*, 1898.

Montessori, Maria (1870–1952), It. educationist and doctor, *b.* Ancona. She was educ. at the univ. of Rome where she was the first woman to receive the degree of Doctor of Medicine. In 1904 she became an instructor in the psychiatric clinic of the univ., and took a special interest in pedagogical anthropology and the training of mentally deficient children. Her interest was aroused in the work of Édouard Séguin some 50 years previously in France. Her conclusion was that the pedagogical treatment of mental illnesses was more important than the medical. Her practical work at the clinic was the basis of the whole of her future educational activities. In 1898 she became directress of the Scuola Ortofrenica (mind-straightening school) at Rome, for feeble-minded children, and achieved such startling results that the so-called 'idiots' were able to compete with normal children of their own age. She then began to suspect that if her scientific method was applied to normal children it would bring about a radical reform of education. Her first experiment in this direction took place in 1906. It was attended with such success that she gave up her medical practice and her 2 chairs at the univ., and confined her future field of research to the education of normal children. The Rom. slum dist of San Lorenzo was notoriously filthy and overcrowded. The Instituto Romano di Beni Stabili attached to each block a *Casa dei Bambini*—a kind of crèche. Under Dr M.'s direction the children responded wonderfully to her system of free discipline. By 1909 the M method was estab. Her 'children's houses', built in proportion to the size of the children themselves, and designed to correspond to their psychological needs, appeared in all parts of the world. The M. system (*see* EDUCATION) rapidly became world famous, and was introduced into Swiss state schools and in schools in England and the U.S.A. as well as in Italy. A series of international courses for training M. directresses began in Rome in 1913 and 1914, were transferred to the U.S.A. and Spain during the First World War, and have continued ever since, either yearly or biennially, in different countries of Europe, particularly in Holland. Thirteen of these were held in London in the inter-war years, and another in 1946. During the Second World War Dr M. resided in India, holding courses in Madras, Karachi, Ceylon and Poona. Her teachings there found special favour among all castes, the students working harmoniously together. Her method was essentially empirical, based on the principles of non-interference with the child's freedom and individuality, and the use of sensory training during the earliest stages of education. She believed that the best kind of education is provided by learning for oneself. The stress on manual training might be criticised, but there is no doubt that she proposed through her method to develop the imagination and intelligence. Her pubs. include *The Method of Scientific Pedagogy as applied to Infant Education in the Children's Houses* (translated into 14 languages), which appeared in English entitled *The Montessori Method*, 1912, *Pedagogical Anthropology*, 1913, *The Advanced Montessori Method*, vols. i and ii, 1918, *The Secret of Childhood*, 1936, *Education for a New World*, 1946, 1948, and *To Educate the Human Potential*, 1948. The following were pub. in English in 1965: *The Montessori Method, Spontaneous Activity in Education* and *The Montessori Elementary Material*. Permanent institutions for the training of M. teachers, either directly or indirectly associated with Dr M.: the M. Training College, Cranleigh, Surrey; The Child Education Foundation, 535 E. 84th Street, New York; Arundale M. Centre, Adyar, Madras; The Municipality of Amsterdam; The M. Centre, 68 St Mark's Road, London, W. 10. There are M. societies in London (68 St Mark's Road); in Edinburgh (63 Merchiston Crescent); in Holland (Amsterdam, Olympiaplein 59); in Italy (Via Nicotera 29, Rome); in France (22 Rue Eugène Flachat, Paris). See E. M. Standing, *Maria Montessori*, 1958. *See also* INFANT SCHOOLS. (*See Plate: Education*.)

Monteverdi, Claudio (1567–1643), It. composer, *b.* Cremona, where he studied music under the cathedral *maestro di cappella*, Ingegneri. About 1591 he became attached to the ducal court of Mantua, where he remained until 1612, producing his first 2 operas, *La favola d'Orfeo*, 1607, and *Arianna*, 1608, besides 2 smaller stage works. *Arianna* is lost except for the famous Lament, but *Orfeo* remains as a monument: the first opera of real importance, though it was preceded by the stimulating experiments of Peri and Caccini (qq.v.). Meanwhile M. had written the first 5 books of his madrigals, which are scarcely less important as 'modern' developments of their species. The Duke, Vincenzo Gonzaga, appointed M. his *maestro di cappella* in 1602, but on his death in 1612 his successor, Francesco, abruptly dismissed him from Mantua, and he returned to Cremona to spend a year in poverty. In Aug. 1613, however, he was appointed *maestro* to St Mark's in Venice, the most coveted church appointment in N. Italy, and he remained there until his death, adding church music of great splendour to his previous output. Two further operas survive from this period: *Il ritorno d'Ulisse in patria*, 1641, and *L'incoronazione di Poppea*, 1642, both of which show a great development in the lyrical treatment of the text. *See* studies by L. Schrade, 1950; H. F. Redlich, 1952; D. Arnold, 1963. (*See Plate: Music*.)

Montevideo: 1. Cap. of the republic of Uruguay, situated on the N. shore of the estuary of the Río de la Plata (which is here 60 m. wide)

and 132 m. E. from Buenos Aires. It is one of the great cities of the continent with a pop. of 1,075,000; nearly 42 per cent of U.'s total pop. The public buildings worthy of notice are the cathedral, the univ., the tn hall, the tall Palacio Salvo and the Solis theatre. The climate is temperate, though inclined to be windy and damp. There are many plazas, notably the Independencia, and public parks, and generally M. is an attractive, spacious city. The trade of M. is extensive and it handles 90 per cent of Uruguay's imports and exports. Wool, hides, meat and meat products and cereals, together with other agric. products, are the main exports. M. is U.'s chief port catering for both local and international traffic. M. is the anchorage during the winter months of Antarctic whaling flotillas. M. is an important resort and the tourist industry is a significant foreign-exchange earner. Many of the hotels and casinos are state-owned. The pleasure beaches to the E. of M. are internationally famous. All Uruguayan railways converge on M. There is a modern airport at Carrazco, 12 m. from the port. The city was founded by the Sp. governor of Buenos Aires in 1726; it became free in 1814, and in 1828 was made the cap. of the republic.

2. Dept of Uruguay, comprising the small area around the city of M. Area 208 sq. m. (*See Plate: Uruguay*.)

Montezuma I (*c.* 1390–1464), Emperor of anct Mexico, succeeding his brother in 1436. He extended the Mexican conquest, rebuilt Tenochtitlán, the chief Aztec city, erecting houses of lime and stone on the site of modern Mexico, and developed the ceremonial of the tribal religion.

Montezuma II (1466–1520), Emperor of Mexico, succeeding his uncle in 1502. He was a great warrior and legislator, but his arrogance alienated the people, and when Cortés landed at Veracruz in 1519 and attempted to march on Tenochtitlán, he was well received by the inhab. and made M. his prisoner. M. was restored to his throne as a vassal of Spain, but his subjects revolted and killed him.

Montfaucon, Bernard de (1655–1741), Fr. scholar, *b.* at the château of Soulage, Aude. He was at first a soldier, and served in Germany under Marshal Turenne, but in 1675 he entered the Benedictine congregation of St Maur. His ed. of Athanasius, 3 vols., 1698, estab. his reputation as a profound scholar. He made a journey to Italy for the purpose of consulting MSS. in the It. libraries. In this pursuit he passed 3 years, and upon his return in 1702 pub. an account of his journey and researches in his *Diarium italicum*. His greatest and best-known work is *L'Antiquité expliquée et représentée en figures*, Paris (5 vols., 1719), to which, in 1724, was added a supplement in 5 vols.

Montferrand, *see* CLERMONT-FERRAND.

Montferrat, *see* MONFERRATO.

Montfleury, Antoine Jacob (1640–85), Fr. dramatist, *b.* Paris. He wrote numerous dramatic works which are characterised by their originality and licentiousness. Some of them are

Le Mari sans femme, Trasibule, L'Impromptu de l'hôtel de Condé, L'École des jaloux, L'Escolle des filles, Crispin gentilhomme, La Dame médecin and *La Femme juge et partie*.

Montfort, name of an anct Fr. family, which is taken from the castle of M. or M. l'Amaury, near Paris. It was founded by Wm, son of Amaury, Count of Hainault, who married the heiress of M. about 952. Some members of the family are *Simon IV de M*. (*c*. 1160–1218), who took a prominent part in the crusade against the Albigenses; *Amaury de M*. (1192–1241), who was made Constable of France in 1230; *Guy de M*. (*d*. 1228), brother of Simon IV, whom he accompanied on his military exploits; *Yolande* (*d*. 1265), who married Arthur II of Brittany; and *Simon de M., Earl of Leicester* (*d*. 1265), a younger son of Simon IV de M. (*see* separate article).

Montfort, Simon de, Earl of Leicester (*c*. 1206–65), Eng. statesman, *b*. in France, son of Simon IV of Montfort l'Amaury. M. came to England in 1229 and successfully claimed the earldom of Leicester, 1231 (formally invested, 1239). He became one of Henry III's favourites and married Henry's sister, Eleanor. For 20 years M. assisted in royal ceremonial and administration, being governor of Gascony, 1248–52, where he ruled with extreme rigour. Later he acted as the king's ambas. on sev. occasions. It is not known when and how M. developed his ideas on administrative reform which led eventually to his becoming the leader of a rebellion against the king. He was a friend of Grosseteste (q.v.), a man of strong religious principles, and, as his Gascon administration showed, one with an almost fanatical respect for efficiency and orderly gov. He had many of the qualities of leadership, but seems to have given the impression of arrogance and was unwilling to delegate authority. Probably the inefficiency and resultant injustices of Henry's administration finally drove M. to the side of the dissident magnates, and his power, ability and liking for authority made him the obvious leader.

In 1258 M. and his baronial followers forced Henry to accept the Provisions of Oxford by which the king's powers were in effect transferred to a committee of barons. After St Louis' decision in favour of the king (1264) on the subject of the Provisions, open war broke out between M. and the king's followers. On 14 May 1264 M. won a great victory at Lewes, capturing the king. By the Mise of Lewes Henry acceded to all M.'s demands and for a year M. was the effective ruler of England. But power was slowly slipping from him. Many of his baronial followers were deserting him; the queen was in France, collecting an army to fight him; and Henry's son Edward was now old enough to take part in gov. and was proving himself a far stronger character than his father. Possibly it was in the hope of getting support from the commons to counter the growing defection of the nobility that M. summoned representatives from some of the tns to his 'parliament' (Jan. 1265), a decision of importance in the future hist.

of Eng. representative institutions, though its direct influence on the development of the House of Commons has probably been exaggerated. But M. was doomed to failure. When the Earl of Gloucester deserted him (1265) his chances of military victory against the royalists became negligible, and at Evesham, in Aug., M. was defeated and killed by a vastly superior force commanded by Prince Edward, his body mutilated and the limbs distributed as a warning to various tns. *See also* HENRY III. *See* lives by C. Bément (Eng. trans. 1930) and B. C. Boulter, 1939. *See also* E. Jacob, *Studies in the Period of Baronial Reform*, 1925; Sir F. M. Powicke, *Henry III and the Lord Edward*, 1947; and life by M. W. Labarge, 1962. (*See Plate: Parliament.*)

Montgolfier, Joseph (1740–1810) and **Étienne** (1745–99), Fr. papermakers of Annonay, near Lyons, who invented the first practical man-carrying balloon in 1783. They used hot air as a lifting gas, and the first aerial journey was made at Paris on 21 Nov. 1783 after previous tethered ascents and one free ascent with animals. The brothers seldom went up in their balloons and did not even make the first voyage (*see* BALLOON).

Montgomerie, Alexander (*c*. 1556–*c*. 1610), poet, *b*. Ayrshire. He held office in the Scottish court in 1577 and became court laureate. His chief poem is *The Cherrie and the Slae*, 1597, written in a 14-line stanza (of which M. was the greatest master, if not the inventor), which contains many beautiful passages. Other works are *The Flyting betwixt Montgomery and Polwart*, 1621, and *The Mindes Melodie*, 1605, a version of 15 of the Psalms, with other pieces. His poems were ed. by J. Cranstown, 1887.

Montgomery, Gabriel, Comte de (*c*. 1530–1574), Fr. soldier and officer in the Scottish lifeguard of the King of France. At a tournament given by Henry II in honour of his daughter's marriage with Philip of Spain, M., at the Henry's command, entered the lists against him unwillingly and accidentally killed him. He took refuge in England and became a Protestant. On the outbreak of the religious wars in 1562 he returned to France and defended Rouen. Later he invaded Béarn. In the third religious war M. escaped from the massacre of St Bartholomew and fled to England. Next year he returned to Normandy, but he was captured at Domfront, taken to Paris and beheaded.

Montgomery, James (1771–1854), poet and hymn-writer, *b*. Irvine, Ayrshire. He took up journalism, editing the *Sheffield Iris*. In 1806 he produced his *Wanderer of Switzerland*, and in 1810 pub. another vol. of verse entitled *The West Indies*, in which he appeals for the abolition of the slave trade. These were followed by *The World Before the Flood*, 1812, *Greenland*, 1819, a poem founded on the Moravian missions to Greenland, *Songs of Zion*, 1822, and *The Pelican Island*, 1826, written in imitation of Shelley, which is generally considered his best work. He also wrote *Lectures on Poetry and General Literature*, 1833. His many hymns include the well-known 'For ever with the Lord', *See* W,

Odem, *The Sheffield Poets*, 1929.

Montgomery, Lucy Maude (1874–1942), Canadian novelist, *b.* Clifton, Prince Edward Is., of Scottish descent. Educ. at Dalhousie Univ., Nova Scotia, she was a teacher for 3 years. In 1911 she married Ewan MacDonald, a Presbyterian minister. Her first novel, *Anne of Green Gables*, 1908, was meant as a book for children, but delighted readers of all ages. Others are *Anne of Avonlea*, 1909, *Kilmeny of the Orchard*, 1910, *The Story Girl*, 1911, *Chronicles of Avonlea*, 1912, *Rainbow Valley*, 1919, and *Anne of Ingleside*, 1939. She was awarded the O.B.E. (*See Plate: Canadian Literature.*)

Montgomery, Robert (1807–55), poetaster, *b.* Bath. In 1828 he pub. *The Omnipresence of the Deity, Death, A Vision of Death, A Vision of Hell*, and in 1830 *Satan*, which was scathingly reviewed in an article by Macaulay. This classic castigation, which has perpetuated the memory of its victim from the oblivion it would have earned, appeared in the *Edinburgh Review*, April 1830. With an unfortunate facility in florid versification, combined with muddled metaphor, M. had no genuinely poetic gift. Educ. at Lincoln College, Oxford, he was ordained in 1835, and devoted himself zealously to his duties as curate at Whittington in Shropshire. In 1836 he came to London, and then went to St Jude's Chapel, Glasgow, in 1838, and back to London again in 1843 to the Percy Street Chapel, St Pancras. At all these places he drew very large audiences, though his style of preaching is said to have resembled that of his poetical effusions.

Montgomery of Alamein, 1st Viscount of Hindhead; Field-Marshal Bernard Law Montgomery (1887–), *b.* Kennington, London, son of the Rt Rev. H. H. M., Bishop of Tasmania; educ. at St Paul's School. Entering the army in 1908, he became lieutenant-colonel in 1931, colonel in 1934. He served in the First World War, 1914–18, being mentioned in dispatches. He commanded 1st Batt. Royal Warwickshire Regiment, 1931–4; was G.S.O. 1, Staff College, Quetta, 1934–7; commander of the 9th Infantry Brigade, Portsmouth, 1937–8. He commanded the 3rd Div., 1938–9, participating with it in the Dunkirk evacuation; corps commander, 1940–1941. In Aug. 1942, with the rank of lieutenant-general, he succeeded Gen. Ritchie as commander of the Brit. Eighth Army under Gen. Sir Harold Alexander, Commander-in-Chief, Middle E. Under his command the Eighth Army won one of the most brilliant victories in the hist. of the Brit. Army, when, between 23rd Oct. and 7th Nov., the Brit. forces at El Alamein, after repelling all the assaults of Marshal Rommel's mixed Axis forces, turned to the offensive and completely routed the Ger. marshal. M. was knighted in Nov. 1942. In the winter of 1943, after a brilliant pursuit of Rommel's army across Libya and Tripolitania, he entered Tripoli and thereby completed the conquest of all Italy's African empire. In Mar. 1943 he again defeated Rommel's reinforced army at the battle of the El Mareth line and followed this with another defeat at Akarit and

the capture of the Tunisian ports of Gabes, Sfax and Sousse. In the summer of 1944 he led the allied armies in the great victory of the battle of Normandy and led the 21st Army Group to the Rhine and across that riv. to the Elbe. After the war he was appointed chief of the Imperial General Staff. He was created a Knight of the Garter and also raised to the peerage in 1946. In 1948 he became chairman of the commanders-in-chief of the W. Alliance, formed for the defence of W. Europe, and Deputy Supreme Commander, SHAPE, 1951–8. The N. African campaign (*see* AFRICA, NORTH, SECOND WORLD WAR CAMPAIGNS IN), which first revealed his 3 characteristics, tactical skill, confident resolution and the intuitive power to use opportunity, showed also how spiritual and intellectual resources could be used to restore and maintain indispensable morale. It was his outstanding campaign, but the battle of Normandy (*see* WESTERN FRONT IN SECOND WORLD WAR) was the greater. The battle plan here was his; the relentless execution secured him a great victory. In recent years he has interested himself in world diplomacy, and has had informal talks with Mao Tse-tung and other leaders. *See* his *From Normandy to the Baltic*, 1947, *From El Alamein to the River Sangro*, 1948, *Forward from Victory*, 1948, *Memoirs*, 1958, *An Approach to Sanity: a study of East-West Relations*, 1959, *The Path to Leadership*, 1961. *See* A. Moorehead, *Montgomery*, 1946, and Sir F. de Guingand, *Operation Victory*, 1947. (*See Plates: World War, Second; British Army; Alabama.*)

Montgomery: 1. Municipal bor. of Wales and co. tn of Montgomeryshire, stands at the foot of a high and well-wooded eminence, about 1½ m. from the Severn and 168 m. NW. by N. of London. The anct castle of M., of which some ruins still remain, was founded by Henry III in 1223 and supplanted an earlier fortification 1 mile N. Pop. 972.

2. Tn of W. Pakistan, 100 m. SW. of Lahore. M. was founded by the Brit. in 1865 and is a centre of fruit growing.

3. State cap. of Alabama, U.S.A., and seat of M. co. It is situated on the Alabama R. at the head of navigation for larger vessels. It is one of the prin. cotton centres of the U.S.A. There are manufs. of fertilisers, syrups and cotton goods. Its chief buildings are the Capitol and the city hall. It was the seat of the Confederate Gov. in the first part of 1861. Pop. (tn) 134,390.

Montgomery, inland co. of N. Wales, between Shropshire on the E. and the Welsh cos. Merioneth and Cardigan on the W. Area 510,110 ac. The surface is almost wholly mountainous (Plynlimmon 2468 ft, q.v.), a large portion consisting of bleak elevated moorlands, but towards the Eng. border there are sev. warm, fertile and well-wooded valleys. The Severn (q.v.), the Vrynwy (Liverpool's main water supply) and the Dovey (q.v.) are the prin. rivs. The co. belongs almost entirely to the basin of the Severn. The mineral wealth of M. is not great, but copper, lead and zinc are present, and millstones, slates and limestone can be quarried.

Cattle and sheep, and the pure breed of Welsh ponies called 'Merlins', are reared. The Welsh flannel manuf. was extensively carried on in the co. The cap. is Montgomery and the co. council offices are distributed between Welshpool and Newtown (qq.v.). Other tns are Llanidloes, Llanfyllin and Machynlleth (q.v.). The co. sends one member to the House of Commons. Pop. 44,165.

Month (interval of time) is the time which elapses between one new moon and the next. This interval is not constant owing to the movements of the moon's orbit relative to the earth. Its length is 29·530588 days. There are 5 classes of M.: the 'sidereal M.', or the time of the circuit of the stars, 27·321661 days; the 'anomalistic M.', or the time of revolution from perigee to perigee, 27·554550 days; the 'tropical M.', or the time of passing from any point of the ecliptic to the same again, 27·321582 days. The 'nodical M.', or interval from a node to a similar node, is 27·212220 days; the 'common or synodic M.' is the interval 29·530588 days noticed above. These values are correct for the present cent.

Montherlant, Henry de (1896–), Fr. novelist. A Catholic by inheritance, he early asserted that the evangelical spirit lacked virility and in his early works he celebrated the glories of athletics and the prowess of the human body. Much of his best work is partly autobiographical. *La Relève du matin*, 1920, is a story of college days. *Le Songe*, 1922, one of the best Fr. stories of the war, is largely his own story. *Les Bestiaires*, 1926, is a Proust-like book filled with the colour and thrill of bull-fighting—M. was himself an amateur bull-fighter. Other novels are *Les Jeunes Filles*, 1936–9, and *Le Chaos et la nuit*, 1942. His plays include *La Reine morte*, 1942, *Fils de personne*, 1943, *Malatesta*, 1946, *Le Maître de Santiago*, 1947, *Port Royal*, 1954, *La Guerre civile*, 1962. See J. de Laprade, *Le Théâtre de Montherlant*, 1950.

Montholon, Charles Tristan, Comte de (1783–1853), Fr. soldier and writer, *b*. Paris. He first entered the navy, but later joined the army and served in many campaigns with Napoleon. In 1809 Napoleon made M. chamberlain; and in 1815 he accompanied Napoleon to St Helena, and remained with him till his death. With Gen. Gourgaud he pub. *Mémoires pour servir à l'histoire de France sous Napoléon, écrits à Ste Hélène sous la dictée*, 1822–5.

Monthyon, *see* MONTYON.

Monti, Vincenzo (1754–1828), It. poet, *b*. Alfonsine, near Ravenna. At the beginning of his career he was a violent enemy of the French, but in later life he became a Republican, next a panegyrist of Napoleon, and lastly a eulogist of the Emperor of Austria. He was prof. of eloquence at Pavia during the Fr. rep., and during the empire historiographer for Italy at Milan. Most of his poems deal with current political events. His *Bassvilliana*, 1793, written on the murder of Hugo Basseville, the Fr. ambas. at Rome, is a wonderful imitation of Dante and gained him a high reputation. His other chief works were *Il Bardo della Selva Nera*,

1806, a eulogy of Napoleon; a masterly trans. of Homer's *Iliad*, 1807; *Proposta di alcune correzioni ed aggiunte al vocabolario della Crusca*, 1817–26, an attack on the pedantry of the Cruscan dictionary. He also wrote the tragedies *Aristodemo*, 1786, *Galeotti Manfredi*, 1788, and *Caio Gracco*, 1800, and various odes and other poems.

Monticelli, Adolphe Joseph Thomas (1824–1886), Fr. painter, *b*. Marseilles, of It. descent. He studied the work of Watteau (q.v.) and the Venetians in the Louvre, becoming successful in Paris for his richly coloured compositions. In 1870 he returned to Marseilles and led a solitary and eccentric life. He combined romantic memories of the *fête galante* and old Provence into the brilliant colour that has caused him to be known as 'the first Fauve'.

Montilla, Sp. tn in the prov. of Córdoba. It gives its name (*Amontillado*) to a type of pale, dry sherry (q.v.), and manufs. coarse linen and earthenware. Pop. 19,800.

Montluc, or **Monluc, Blaisse de Lasseran** (1502–77), marshal of France, *b*. St Gemmes, Gers. After a brilliant military career he became lieutenant-general of the gov. of Guienne (1564) and executed Protestants 'with a ferocious gaiety'. His last military act was the siege of La Rochelle (1573), after which he devoted himself to compiling his *Commentaires*, printed 1592, memoirs of his military life.

Montluçon, Fr. tn in the dept of Allier, on the Cher. On a hill above the tn is a Bourbon castle, and there are many other interesting old buildings. M. is near a coalfield, and has metallurgical, chemical and rubber manufs. Pop. 55,200.

Montmartre, N. dist of Paris on the hill of M., which is surmounted by the great white basilica of the Sacré-Cœur. It is by traditional repute the Bohemian quarter of Paris, and a haunt of artists and writers, both French and foreign. It is celebrated for its cafés and places of amusement. There is a cemetery where many famous people are buried.

Montmédy, Fr. tn in the dept of Meuse, on the Chiers. It is partly on a cliff 330 ft high, and was fortified by Vauban (q.v.). There are hosiery and leather manufs. Pop. 1800.

Montmorency, Anne Pierre Adrien, 1st Duc de (1492–1567), marshal and constable of France, *b*. Chantilly. He distinguished himself in the wars between Francis I and the Emperor Charles V, and was taken prisoner with his sovereign after the battle of Pavia (1525). He was made constable of France in 1538; he was suddenly banished from court in 1541, but returned on the accession of Henry II and again controlled affairs.

In 1557 he was in command at the battle of St Quentin, in which he was taken prisoner. During the minority of Charles IX, M., with the Duke of Guise and the Marshal St André, composed the triumvirate which resisted the influence of Catherine de' Medici. In 1562 and 1567 he commanded the royal army against the Huguenots, and in both wars gained victories over them, but was fatally wounded at St Denis, 1567.

Montmorency, Henri, Duc de (1595–1632), Fr. soldier, son of Duke Henry I and grandson of Anne, constable of France. He took part in the religious wars (1621–30), took Rhé and Oléron in 1625, and defeated the Piedmontese in 1630. He was made marshal the same year, but then rebelled against Richelieu, joined the party of Gaston, Duc d'Orléans, and put himself at the head of the insurgent army. He was, however, defeated at Castelnaudary in 1632, taken prisoner and beheaded as a traitor at Toulouse.

Montmorency, riv. of Quebec, Canada, rising in Snow Lake and entering the St Lawrence 6 m. NE. of Quebec. The falls at its mouth, 150 ft wide and 274 ft high, supply electric power to Quebec.

Montorsoli, Fra Giovanni Angelo da (c. 1507–63), It. sculptor, b. Montorsoli, near Florence. He studied under Andrea Ferrucci at Fiesole, and worked for Michelangelo at San Lorenzo, Florence. In about 1527 he became a friar and in 1530 was invited to Rome by Pope Clement VII, who employed him to restore some statues. Some of his works are the tomb of the poet Sannazzaro, at Naples; the statue of Andrea Doria, at Genoa; the fountain in the piazza and the façade of the cathedral at Messina; and various statues in the church of the Servites at Bologna.

Montparnasse, dist of Paris, on the l. b. of the Seine, a haunt of artists and writers. There is an observatory, and Cité Universitaire, a residential centre for univ. students. Many famous people are buried in the M. cemetery.

Montpelier, city, cap. of Vermont, U.S.A., co. seat of Washington co., on the Winooski R. The State Capitol (1836, rebuilt 1857) is one of the most magnificent buildings in the U.S.A. In the vicinity are large granite quarries. M. manufs. textiles, wood and concrete products and machinery. It also has printing works, and there is a junior college. Pop. 8780. (*See Plate: Vermont.*)

Montpellier, Fr. tn. cap. of the dept of Hérault, on the Lez, 80 m. WNW. of Marseilles. A possession of the counts of Toulouse, M. passed in the 13th cent. to the kingdom of Majorca, and in 1349 to France. At the time of the Reformation many of the inhab. became Protestants, and the tn was besieged for 8 months by Louis XIII in 1622 during the revolt of the Duc de Rohan (q.v.). M. is irregularly built, with narrow, steep streets and some fine 17th–18th cent. houses. There is a cathedral, begun in the 14th cent., a univ. (1289) and a botanic garden estab. in the reign of Henry IV. The terraced Promenade du Peyrou has a triumphal arch and a notable fountain. The Musée contains a very fine collection of paintings. There are chemical, foodstuff, textile and engineering industries, and there is a large trade in wines and spirits. Auguste Comte (q.v.) was a native of M. Pop. 119,000.

Montpensier, Anne Marie Louise d'Orleans, Duchesse de (1627–93), known as 'La Grande Mademoiselle', b. Paris. She was the daughter of Gaston, brother of Louis XIII. She was an ambitious woman, aiming at one time at marriage with Louis XIV, but was defeated in this by Cardinal Mazarin (q.v.). As a result of this slight, she sided with the Frondeurs against the court, and later retired to her estates for sev. years. In 1681 she married the Duc de Lauzun, but the marriage was unhappy. Her memoirs, first pub. 1729, cover the years 1630–88.

Montreal, commercial metropolis of Canada, holds a commanding position relative both to ocean and to riv. navigation. Situated on the l. b. of the St Lawrence R., 1000 m. inland from the Atlantic, it is the second largest E. coast port on the N. Amer. continent, being exceeded only by New York. The city is built on M. Is., a triangular-shaped is. 32 m. long by 7 to 9 m. wide, at the confluence of the St Lawrence and Ottawa R.s. M. proper has an area of 50 sq. m. Its built-up areas spread out in all directions from the lower slopes of beautiful Mount Royal, from which the city takes its name. Mount Royal, visible for many miles by air, land and riv. routes, presents a pleasing spectacle to visitors approaching the city. M.'s beginnings go back to 1535 when Jacques Cartier, sailing up the St Lawrence, came upon a large fortified Indian vil., Hochelaga. Seventy-six years later, in 1611, Champlain estab. a trading post on the is., and in 1642 Paul de Chomedy, Sieur de Maisonneuve, founded Ville Marie, subsequently renamed M. The place remained under Fr. rule until 1763, when Canada became a Brit. possession under the treaty of Paris. It was formerly the federal seat of gov., but this was removed to Quebec in 1847 and later to Ottawa. The Ottawa R., which joins the St Lawrence both above and below the city, drains an area of about 80,000 sq. m., being on the St Lawrence–Great Lakes waterway, which allows passage of vessels of up to 25 ft draught, may be considered, in addition to its pre-eminence as an ocean port, as the chief port of the Great Lakes and St Lawrence R. system.

The pop. of M. (1961) was 1,191,062, with a further pop. of 918,447 in the surrounding suburbs, making a total of 2,109,509. About 68 per cent of the inhab. are of Fr. origin, some 20 per cent are of Brit. origin, the balance being made up of important groupings of other nationalities, thus making M. one of the most cosmopolitan cities in N. America. It is a bilingual city: French and English. M. is the largest city in Canada, the farthest inland ocean port in the world and one of the greatest centres of electrical power resources in the W. hemisphere. It is also a terminus of the Trans-Canada internal gas pipeline. From its beginnings as a Fr. colonial settlement, M. has been the cradle of Canadian financial, transportation and industrial development. Canada's prin. banking and investment institutions are located here. It is the H.Q. of the Canadian Pacific Railway and of the Canadian National Railways, and the world H.Q. of the International Civil Aviation Organisation. As such it is the terminal for Amer., Canadian and overseas air routes. Ocean, lake and riv. transportation also converge at M., which is on the St Lawrence Seaway, allowing ships of up to 35 ft draught to pass up to the Great Lakes. The port is served by both Canadian railways, connected to the harbour front by 62 m. of terminal line operated by the National Harbours Board. Navigation opens about mid-April and goes on until the beginning of Dec. The main piers, wharves and jetties give about 10 m. of berthing accommodation, with up-to-date ancillary equipment in the form of cold-storage, grain elevators, advanced types of crane, etc. Nearly 20 million tons of cargo are handled yearly, the chief commodities being grain, petroleum and meat. The main products of M.'s factories are clothing, tobacco and electrical equipment.

The civic gov. of M. differs from that of most Amer. and Canadian cities. Known as a Metropolitan Municipality, in some ways it resembles the local gov. of the larger U.K. cities and in other respects it is similar to that of continental cities. For electoral purposes it is divided into 11 dists, each of which sends 6 members to the city hall. Of these 3 are elected by property owners and 3 by the electors at large. In addition 13 public bodies appoint 33 representatives to the city council. The total membership of the council is, therefore, 99 councillors, plus the mayor of the city, who is elected by majority vote of the electors at large.

M. is noted for its many beautiful public buildings. Some of the more imposing are Notre Dame Church (Rom. Catholic), Christ Church Cathedral (Church of England), St James Cathedral (Rom. Catholic), Church of St Andrew and St Paul (Presbyterian), Sun Life building, Royal Bank, Bell Telephone, Civic Library and M. Art Association. McGill Univ. (q.v.) and the univ. of M. (founded 1878) are located in the city, as are a number of other educational institutions. St Joseph's Oratory, internationally famed shrine which annually attracts thousands of visitors, is located in M. An is. city, there are numerous bridges connecting it to the mainland. Victoria bridge, completed in 1859, marked one of the great engineering achievements of the 19th cent. Originally a tubular bridge, its total length of 9184 ft has been replaced by one of cantilever design. Jacques Cartier bridge, completed in 1930, of cantilever design, is 8670 ft in length, constructed in 3 sections, the central span of which rests on St Helen's Is. It was on this is., a legend says, that Chevalier de Lévis burned his flags so as not to surrender them to the Brit. in 1760. To diminish traffic congestion, the Metropolitan Boulevard, a limited access throughway, has been constructed, running E.–W. across M. Is. M. still retains much of its old-world atmosphere. After Paris it is the largest Fr.-speaking city in the world. See S. Leacock, *Montreal: Seaport and City*, 1942; V. Morin, *The Historical Records of Old Montreal*, 1944; W. P. Percival, *The Lure of Montreal*, 1945; M. Gibbons, *Old Montreal*, 1948. (*See Plates:*

5030

Quebec; Canadian Architecture; Canada.)

'**Montreal Star, The**', estab. 1869 and pub. in Montreal. It is noted for coverage of national and international news; associated pubs. include the *Family Herald*, a leading farm fortnightly; *Weekend Magazine*, which appears in each Saturday's *Star* and in 37 other newspapers; and *Perspectives*, a weekend supplement which appears in 6 Fr.-speaking newspapers.

Montreuil (-sous-Bois), Fr. tn in the dept of Seine, an E. suburb of Paris. It is famous for its peach orchards, and has gypsum quarries and textile manufs. Pop. 92,300.

Montreuil (-sur-Mer), Fr. tn in the dept of Pas-de-Calais, overlooking the Canche. The church of St-Saulve dates from the 12th cent. The château of Beaurepaire was the Brit. G.H.Q. in the First World War. Pop. 3500.

Montreux, resort at the E. end of Lake Geneva in the canton of Vaud, Switzerland, which includes the vils. of Clarens, Vernex, Territet, Glion and Veytaux. It is popular for winter sports. Near Veytaux is the castle of Chillon (q.v.). Total pop. 18,500, chiefly Fr.-speaking.

Montrose, James Graham, 5th **Earl** and 1st **Marquess of** (1612–50), Scottish soldier and statesman, educ. at the univ. of St Andrews. He was a Presbyterian and, disgusted by Charles I's high-handed policy towards the Scottish Church, joined the national movement, assisted at the signing of the covenant (1638), 3 times occupied Aberdeen for the Covenanters and finally overthrew Viscount Aboyne, Charles's lieutenant in the North, at the bridge of Dee (1639). But the excesses of the extreme Covenanters sickened M., and after vainly attempting to persuade the Covenanters to moderation, he went over to the king in 1641 and was imprisoned the same year for 6 months in consequence of a supposed conspiracy against Argyll. In 1644, with the rank of lieutenant-general and the title of marquess, he rallied the loyalist Highland clans to Charles, defeated the covenanting forces at Tippermuir and Aberdeen, and in the following year won 4 other pitched battles at Inverlochy, Auldearn, Alford and Kilsyth. His subsequent attempt to raise the royalist standard in the lowlands was an utter failure, and in Sept. 1645 he suffered a crushing defeat at Philiphaugh. M. escaped and took refuge in Norway. The responsibility for this sudden and disastrous reversal of fortune rests in part on M. himself. He had been blind to the fact that, while Highland troops might perform unheard-of deeds of daring to defend their clannish honour, they were incapable of disinterested combination to further a national cause. M. was in the Low Countries when he heard of the king's execution. He is said to have sworn an oath to avenge Charles's death. In 1650 he landed in Caithness with only a remnant of the little army that he had originally collected, for he had been shipwrecked on the way, and was easily defeated by Leslie at Carbisdale. M. escaped from the battlefield, but was betrayed to the Covenant by Macleod of Assynt, with whom he had sought refuge. The same year he was hanged in the Grassmarket, Edinburgh, Argyll, his life-long enemy, looking on. M. was one of Scotland's greatest men; he was a fine soldier and a man whose ideas of tolerance were far in advance of his time. The title Earl of M. dates from 1505, when Wm, Lord Graham, a title dating from 1445, was made Earl of M. John, 3rd earl, was regent of Scotland and chancellor (1603–8). James, 4th marquess and a supporter of the union of 1707, was created duke in that year. The 7th duke, James Angus Graham (b. 1907), emigrated to Rhodesia and became a member of the Smith gov. For the 1st marquess see lives by G. Wishart, 1903; J. Buchan, 1928. See also Margaret Irwin, The Proud Servant (novel), 1934, and Agnes Mure Mackenzie, The Passing of the Stewarts, 1937.

Montrose, royal burgh, holiday resort and seaport of Angus, Scotland, 39 m. SSW. of Aberdeen. It stands at the mouth of the S. Esk, where it forms the M. basin. The tn received its charter from David I, and became a royal burgh in 1352. It is rich in historic memories. Industries include canning of fruit and vegetables, pharmaceutical products, timber, flax spinning and shipbuilding. Pop. 10,800.

Montserrat, or Monserrat, mt mass in the prov. of, and 23 m. NW. of the city of, Barcelona, Spain, on the r. b. of the Llobregat. Its highest point is 4070 ft. At a height of 2910 ft on the E. side is a Benedictine monastery, dating from the 9th cent. and containing a famous wooden image of the Blessed Virgin.

Montserrat, is. of Brit. W. indies, southern-most of the Leeward Is. (q.v.); it lies in lat. 16° 45' N. and long. 61° W., and has an area of 38 sq. m. and a pop. of 13,000. It is entirely volcanic, having sev. groups of mts, the highest, Chance Mt in the S., reaching 3002 ft. The mt summits are forested and streams are plentiful, but the hills in the N. are treeless and dry. The climate is comparatively cool and healthy; the mean ann. temp. is 78° F. and rainfall from 40 in. to 70 in. The main occupation is the cultivation of sea-is. cotton, bananas, limes, sugarcane and vegetables. M. has an executive council of 4 ministers and 2 officials and a mainly elected legislative council. The Queen is represented by an Administrator. Plymouth, the cap., is on the 3W. coast and has an open roadstead. There are 118 m. of roads of which 60 m. are motorable, the small airport is on the E. coast. The is. was once fortified and the ruins of many forts and batteries survive.

History. M. was discovered by Columbus in 1493 and named M. from a fancied resemblance to a mt of that name near Barcelona. It was first colonised by the British under Sir Thomas Warner in 1632, the colonists including a body of Irish transferred from St Kitts. To this day the people of M., though mainly of African descent, speak with an Irish brogue. In 1667 the is. was attacked by a powerful Fr. force and was captured when most of the Irish went over to the enemy. Restored to Britain in 1668, it remained Brit. until 1782, when, with a number of other is., it was taken by the French under the Marquis

de Bouillé. Under the Treaty of Versailles in the following year it was again restored, and it has remained British ever since. See A. M. Alareda, Histoire de Montserrat, 1931; Sir A. Burns, History of the Brit. West Indies, 1954; official reports pub. biennially by H.M.S.O.

Montucla, Jean Étienne (1725–99), French mathematician, b. Lyons; studied classics and mathematics at the Jesuits' college in his native tn, and in 1758 he began pub. of his great Histoire des mathématique, afterwards completed by Lalande (q.v.).

Monument, The, London, stone column commemorating the Great Fire of London (q.v.), situated near the N. approach to London Bridge and Pudding Lane, where the fire started. Designed by Sir Christopher Wren and erected, 1671–7, by the city surveyor, Robert Hooke, it is a gigantic fluted Doric column, 202 ft high. Three sides of the base are covered with allegorical reliefs and appropriate inscriptions. Steps lead to the top, which is surmounted by a finial simulating a ball of fire.

Monumental Brasses are plates of metal alloy engraved with an inscription, figure or symbol and let into a slab of stone to form a memorial to a deceased person. They are most valuable records of civil, military and eccles. costume, and of much interest to the student of heraldry and genealogy. The metal, although widely known as brass, is in fact a composition of copper, lead, zinc and tin more properly known as latten. Brasses appear to have originated on the Continent, the earliest known being of 1231 at Verden, Hanover, and first appeared in England towards the end of the 13th cent. It was not until the reign of Edward II that they became common; the earliest brass remaining is that to Sir John Daubernoun (1277) in the church of Stoke D'Abernon, Surrey. There were declines and subsequent revivals until the time of James I, when the art rapidly declined, almost disappearing in the 18th cent. A very few later brasses are known; those of 1773 and 1747 in the church of St Mary Cray, Kent, depict a man and wife in Georgian dress, and there are one or two notable modern examples. Brasses which have been re-engraved on the reverse side and later re-used are known as palimpsests. See particularly the Transactions and Portfolios of the Monumental Brass Society (in progress); M. Stephenson, Monumental Brasses in the British Isles, 1926, with a later Appendix; Notes on Brass-rubbing, Oxford, Ashmolean Museum, 1952; H. W. Macklin (revised by Charles Oman), Monumental Brasses, 1953.

Monuments, Ancient. The Ministry of Public Building and Works is empowered under the Anct Monuments Act, 1931, the Consolidation and Amendment Act, 1913, and the Historic Buildings and Anct Monuments Act, 1953, to grant state protection to such historic buildings and anct M. as are considered to be of national importance. Lists of the M., ranging from pre-historic camps, megaliths and tumuli to the remains of castles, monastic houses, bridges and even relatively modern buildings, are pub. from time to time by H.M. Stationery Office. The Acts also lessen the risk of unsuitable treatment and of exploration by unqualified persons. The ministry, through its inspectorate of anct M., is able to give expert advice on treatment, and in certain cases guardianship is accepted and preservation work carried out by the State. A few M. are in the custody of the ministry by deed of gift, while others are the property of the Crown. Some occupied buildings are also in charge of the ministry, e.g. the Tower of London; the Banqueting Hall and the Horse Guards, Whitehall; the Royal Hospital, Chelsea; the Royal Naval College, Greenwich; Hampton Court Palace; Holyroodhouse, Edinburgh; Dunblane and Glasgow Cathedrals. It should be noted that a structure occupied as a dwelling other than by a caretaker cannot in general receive protection under the Acts. The Ministry publishes authoritative guides to anct M. and historic buildings.

For more than 30 years royal commissions on anct and historical M. have been engaged in making an exhaustive first-hand survey of the anct and historical M. to be found in Great Britain. The scope of the survey extends from prehistoric times down to the beginning of the 18th cent., and it embraces as far as is possible every object that may throw light on the past life of the country. In addition to castles, churches, monastic buildings, manor houses and cottages, a description is given of prehistoric antiquities. The inventories, pub. by H.M. Stationery Office, are magnificently illustrated by photographs and plans.

Since its inception in 1900 the *Victoria County History*, a large series of vols. in which one or more deal with each co., has pub. information about anct M. While the earlier vols. are not altogether satisfactory, the most recent, pub. under the auspices of the Institute of Historical Research, include period studies and detailed topographical records.

Anct M. are recorded on Ordnance Survey maps. There are special period maps, e.g. *Ancient Britain*, *Rom. Britain*, *Britain in the Dark Ages*, *Monastic Britain*, *Neolithic Wessex*, *Trent Basin*, *Celtic earthworks of Salisbury Plain*, which show the distribution and geographical setting of various classes of M. On the general Ordnance Survey maps M. may be recognised by the lettering used to describe them: all prehistoric remains (i.e. before AD 43) are lettered in O.E.; Rom. remains (AD 43 to AD 420) are in Egyptian characters; while Ger. text is used for Saxon and medieval remains down to AD 1700. The following are the most common terms used on the maps to denote archaeological remains: long barrow; long cairn; horned cairn; burial chamber; standing stone; stone circle; stone avenue; camp; earthwork; Rom. road; castle mound. Where possible the age is indicated and in cases of doubt the term 'ancient' is used. *See* ARCHAEOLOGY; HADRIAN'S WALL; MEGALITH; MENHIRS; PREHISTORY; ROMAN REMAINS IN BRITAIN; STONEHENGE; etc.

Monza (anct **Modoetia**), It. tn in Lombardy

(q.v.), 8 m. NNE. of Milan. It was once the cap. of the Longobards (q.v.), and in the Middle Ages was an important commercial city. King Humbert I (q.v.) was assassinated here in 1900. In M.'s Gothic cathedral, partly 13th cent., is preserved the famous iron crown of Lombardy. Textiles, hats and carpets are manuf., and there are dyeing and engineering industries. Horse and motor races are held. Pop. 81,400. (*See Plate: Crown.*)

Moody, Dwight Lyman (1837–99), Amer. evangelist, *b.* Northfield, Massachusetts, U.S.A.; opened a Sunday school in Chicago in 1858, which subsequently developed into the Chicago Avenue Church. After directing the Young Men's Christian Association there for 4 years (1865–9) he was joined by Ira David Sankey (q.v.). Together they wrote the M. and Sankey 'gospel hymns', which were so characteristic a feature of their revivalist meetings both in England (1873, 1881 and 1882) and America. *See* life by W. R. Moody, 1930.

Moody, William Vaughn (1869–1910), Amer. poet and playwright, *b.* Spencer, Indiana. Educ. at Harvard, he was for some time assistant prof. of rhetoric at the univ. of Chicago. Among his works are *The Masque of Judgment*, 1900, *Poems*, 1901, *History of English Literature*, 1907, *The Great Divide*, 1909, a play which caused a great sensation, and *The Faith Healer*, 1909. *See* study by D. D. Henry, 1934.

Mooltan, *see* MULTAN.

Moon, William (1818–94), inventor of M.'s embossed type for the blind, *b.* Kent. Becoming totally blind in 1840 he set about producing an embossed type for those so afflicted, and in 1845 brought out his system, which differed from former systems in almost totally discarding contractions. His first pub. in M. type, *The Last Days of Polycarp*, appeared in 1847, followed by *The Last Hours of Cranmer* and other books of devotion. He issued an ed. of the Bible, and extended his system to foreign languages, beginning with Irish and Chinese. He was made a fellow of the Royal Geographical Society in 1852 and of the Society of Arts in 1859. *See* BLINDNESS AND THE BLIND. *See* his *Light for the Blind: a History . . . of Moon's System of Reading for the Blind*, 1873.

Moon, Mountains of the. From classical times Africa, with its geography hidden beyond the Sahara, has been a source of myth and legend, some based on truth. The sources of the Nile remained undiscovered until 1861, when Capt. Speke explored the region S. of Victoria Nyanza. Ptolemy and all other geographers had placed the source in the 'mts of the M.', and these were mapped E. and W. in equatorial Africa. There was nothing but rumour and legend, based probably on information 'passed down' among African tribes to Egypt. Capt. Speke considered the crescent of mts explored by him N. of Lake Tanganyika to be part of them. Dr Beke considered them to be a N. and S. extension of the Ethiopian plateau. They are now generally identified with the group round Ruwenzori farther W. on the Congo and Uganda border.

Moon, satellite of the earth, is one of the many satellites of planets in the solar system, but is unique in one respect: its mass, 1/81 of the earth's, is by far the largest in relation to the planet that it orbits. The only comparable bodies are the 4 inner satellites of Jupiter, Saturn's satellite Titan and Neptune's satellite Triton; but these 6 have much more massive parent planets. The apparent magnitude (q.v.) of the full M. is $-12 \cdot 7$, or about 1/470,000 of the sun's brightness. The M.'s diameter is 2160 m., its mass $7 \cdot 23 \times 10^{19}$ tons. The mean density is $3 \cdot 35$, or 3/5 of the earth's, while the surface gravity is 1/6 of the earth's. On account of its low gravitational attraction the M. has lost any atmosphere it may once have possessed, and all the evidence shows it to be a changeless, airless, waterless, lifeless world.

Apparent motions. The M. completes its westward circuit in a month (q.v.) which on account of the irregularities of its motion may be defined in various ways. The interval between successive full M.s is the *synodical month* of $29 \cdot 530588$ days. The M.'s orbit is inclined to the ecliptic at an average angle of $5° 8' 43''$, varying between the extremes of $4° 59'$ and $5° 19'$ in a period of 173 days. Since the angle between the ecliptic and the equator is $23° 27'$, the M.'s declination or distance from the equator may lie anywhere between $28° 46'$ and $-28° 46'$. Thus the M. tends to be highest when the sun is lowest, *i.e.* in winter. On account of the variation in declination, the interval between moonrise on successive nights is not constant, but has the average value of 50 min. The *harvest moon* is the full M. nearest the autumnal equinox, September 21, when the nearly full M. rises after sunset and only 18 min. later each night; the next full M. is the *hunter's moon.* Corresponding phenomena in the S. hemisphere occur about the spring equinox, March 21.

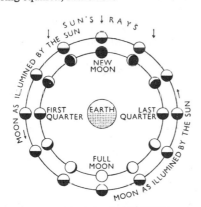

THE PHASES OF THE MOON
The inner circle shows the moon as seen from the earth.

Phases. These are due to the varying angular distance from the sun. Between new M. (con-

junction) and half M. (quadrature) the appearance is crescent, between half M. and full M. (opposition) it is gibbous. These positions are shown in the accompanying diagram. The 'horns' are always turned from the sun, and hence point to the left for the young M. after sunset, and to the right for the old M. before sunrise. The 'old M. in the new M.'s arms', or *earth-shine,* is the disk of the young M. faintly illuminated by sunlight reflected from the earth.

True motions. The M.'s orbit around the earth is an ellipse; the mean distance from earth's centre to M.'s centre, found from radar measurements, is 238,855 m., with an uncertainty of less than 1 m. The mean eccentricity of the orbit is 0·0549, varying between 0·044 and 0·067 in a period of 173 days; thus the M.'s distance can vary between the extremes of 221,460 m. and 252,740 m. The M.'s average speed in its orbit is nearly 2300 m.p.h. The point of closest *approach,* or *perigee,* moves E. around the orbit every 8·85 years; while the points of crossing the ecliptic, or *nodes,* move westward around the ecliptic every 18·61 years. The changes mentioned are among the simpler of the many perturbations affecting the M.'s orbit, owing to the complicated dynamics of the earth-moon-sun system; lunar theory being one of the most intricate branches of celestial mechanics. The tables of the M.'s motion by E. W. Brown (q.v.) contain 1500 separate variable terms. An apparent secular acceleration of the M.'s motion is in fact due to the slowing-down of the earth's rotation by tidal friction; see TIME AND TIME MEASUREMENT.

Appearance and physical conditions. The M.'s rotation is 'captured', so that it always turns the same face to the earth; on account of librations (q.v.) we can see 59 per cent of the surface at one time or other. The most remarkable features are the mt ranges and craters, noted by Galileo in 1610 when he first turned a telescope on to the M. Scheiner drew the first recognisable map in 1619, many features were named on the 1647 map of Hevelius (q.v.) and the 1651 map of Riccioli (q.v.), and during the 18th and 19th cents. increasingly accurate maps were drawn from visual observations. The M. was first photographed in 1840, and photography has enabled the intricate detail of the M.'s surface to be permanently recorded and mapped, culminating with the U.S. Air Force charts (1962) on a scale of 1:1,000,000 or approximately 16 m. to 1 in. The surface features include great smooth areas, the *maria* or 'seas', as well as mt ranges and craters. Heights of mts are measured from the shadows they cast; the Leibnitz mts near the S. pole rise to 26,000 ft. Over 30,000 craters can be counted, ranging from 1,000 ft craterlets to giants like Tycho (54 m.), Copernicus (56 m.) and the walled plain Clavius (150 m.). Bright streaks or *rays,* up to 1500 m. long, radiate from Tycho and some other craters. Clefts or *rills* about $\frac{1}{2}$ m. wide are less easily seen features. Whether volcanic action or the impact of meteorites formed the craters is still disputed; the shapes of the craters resemble explosion craters on earth, rather than volcanic cones and most astronomers have favoured the impact theory (but *see Exploring the moon*, below). The major meteoric bombardment may have occurred in the early hist. of the solar system, thousands of millions of years ago; meteorite craters on earth are rapidly eroded, but they would be preserved in the airless M. Close-up photographs by American *Ranger* and Russian *Luna* spacecraft have not finally settled the question. The M.'s surface reflects only 7 per cent of sunlight at full M., and much less at quarter phases, suggesting dark, rough texture; radar reflections show the surface to be rather smooth at cm wavelengths. The surface temp. is nearly 120° C. at 'midday' or full M., and − 150° C. at 'midnight' or new M., and falls as low as − 100° C. during the brief period of a lunar eclipse; thus the surface has very poor heat conductivity and must be porous or dusty. Radio emission from a few in. below the surface shows a much smaller temp. range, again indicating low conductivity.

Exploring the moon. The first man-made object to reach the M. was the Russian space-probe *Lunik* 2, which crashed upon the M.'s surface on 13 Sept. 1959; its instruments recorded no measurable magnetic field. The hidden reverse side of the M. was revealed on 7 Oct. 1959 by *Lunik* 3, and nearly 500 new features were mapped. Further attempts to reach the M. were unsuccessful until the American *Ranger* 7 (31 July 1964) televised over 4000 close-up pictures before crashing; the last picture, transmitted 1000 ft above the M.'s surface, showed craters only 3 ft in diameter. *Ranger* 8 (20 Feb. 1965) similarly transmitted 7500 pictures, and *Ranger* 9 (25 March 1965) transmitted 5800. The Russian *Luna* 9 made the first 'soft' landing (3 Feb. 1966) and transmitted pictures of surface structure. The Americans made the second soft landing in *Surveyor* 1 on 2 June 1966. It appears from close-ups that the lunar topography was shaped both by meteorite impact and by lava flows; that craters with ray systems may have been formed by the impact of comets; that the surface is porous and unable to support very large boulders, but can apparently support a spacecraft; that any dust layer is thin; and that small dimple craters are due to collapse of underlying structure. The Russian space-probe *Zonn* 3 (20 July 1965) photographed the reverse side in detail, showing it to have fewer *maria* and to be lighter and more mountainous than the visible side.

Origin and future of the moon. The idea that the M. was pulled from the earth by tidal action is untenable in detail, and modern theories consider the origin of the earth-moon system as a double planet. The difference in density between the earth (5·52) and the M. (3·35) is difficult to account for if they were formed together, and one theory supposes the M. to have been captured by the earth. Concerning the future of the earth-moon system, Sir George Darwin (q.v.) predicted that, as tidal friction has reduced the rotation of the M. and is reducing that of the earth (*see* TIME AND TIME MEAS-

UREMENT), the day and the month will both lengthen until they become equal to 50 of our present days. At that time the M. will be much more distant than it is now, but ultimately solar tides will bring it close again, until perhaps it is disrupted. But the time-scale of these dynamic processes is much longer than that of the physical evolution of the sun (q.v.). (*See Plate*: *Space Travel*.)

Moon-worship and myths. The worship of the M., as of other heavenly bodies, was one of the earliest forms of polytheism. It prevailed widely among the E. nations and under many aspects. In Egypt Isis was identified with the M. In Phoenicia Ashtoreth, as the feminine equivalent of Baal, was the M.-goddess. In Assyria Sin was the M.-god. Mt Sinai is supposed to have derived its name from this god, to whom worship was paid there. A number of names, however, manifest the prevalence of his worship, e.g. Sennacherib (meaning 'the M.-god has increased brothers'), Jericho, by its name, would seem to have been the seat of M.-worship in times before the Israelite conquest. Cautions against the worship of the M. and punishment by death for the convicted worshipper are to be found in Deut. iv and xvii; whilst a superstitious salutation of the M. by kissing the hand is mentioned in Job xxxi. 26–7. In the O.T. we meet more than once with crescent-shaped ornaments (Judges viii. 21 and Isa. iii. 18), but whether these are an indication of the worship of the M. is uncertain. Language which was probably derived from the appearance of the M. during eclipses is used by the prophets—the M. is to be darkened or turned into blood before the 'terrible day of the Lord' (Joel ii. 10 and 31). In the figurative language of Scripture the M. is frequently noticed as presaging events of the greatest importance through the temporary or permanent withdrawal of its light. Even in the 14th cent. in England the moon was supposed by the common people to have much influence over human affairs. Various activities such as gathering herbs, slaughtering animals for food or taking particular medicines were regulated by the 'age' of the M., and these set periods were thought to be a necessary part of practical knowledge, ignorance of which infallibly entailed loss. Some of these superstitions prevailed even later, especially in the Scottish highlands, and throughout Scotland the waning M. was believed to have an evil influence, while full M. was thought to be the most favourable season for initiating an enterprise. The belief that the changes of the M. influence the weather is really little better than a superstition, for the only actual influence is a slight tendency to dispersion of cloud shortly after full M. If this occurs, it may be due to the effect of the sun's heat reflected from the M. and falling on the earth's atmosphere. There are numerous lunar myths from very early times and among many widely different races and countries. In Gk myths the M. loved Endymion (q.v.) and was bribed to be the mistress of Pan by the present of a fleece, like the Dawn in Australia, whose unchastity was rewarded by a gift of a red cloak of opossum skin. Both solar and lunar myths usually account for the observed phenomena of eclipse, waning and waxing, spots on the M., and so on, by various mythical adventures of the animated heavenly beings. Thus in the Andaman Is. the sun was held to be the wife of the M., and among aboriginal tribes in India the M. was the sun's unfaithful bride whom he cut in two but occasionally allows her to shine in full beauty. In late modern folk-lore the M. is a place to which the wicked are consigned, rather than the impersonation of a man or a woman. The mark of the hare on the M. has impressed the imagination of Mexicans, Bantus, Sinhalese and others in bygone times and evoked myths among all of them.

See G. P. Kuiper (ed.), *Photographic Lunar Atlas*, 1960; Z. Kopal, *The Moon*, 1960; G. Fielder, *Structure of the Moon's Surface*, 1961; Z. Kopal, *Physics and Astronomy of the Moon*, 1961; N. P. Barabashov *et al.*, *An Atlas of the Moon's Far Side*, 1961; R. B. Baldwin, *The Measure of the Moon*, 1963; B. M. Middlehurst and G. P. Kuiper (eds.), *The Moon, Meteorites, and Comets*, 1963; Z. Kopal *et al.*, *Photographic Atlas of the Moon*, 1965.

Moonstone, variety of orthoclase, yielding moon-like white reflections. The best specimens, which are used in jewellery, are found in Ceylon.

Moor Park, Herts, England, near Rickmansworth, on the Metropolitan Railway. The house, built about 1727, was the seat of Lord Ebury but is now the club-house of the adjoining golf-course. Near by is the Merchant Taylors' School (q.v.), moved from Charterhouse Square in 1933. There is another M. P. on the Wey, 2 m. from Farnham, (q.v.), Surrey. It was the residence of Sir Wm Temple and here Swift first met 'Stella' (Esther Johnson), and wrote *The Tale of a Tub* and *The Battle of the Books*.

Moore, Albert Joseph (1841–93), painter, b. York, youngest son of Wm M., of York, a painter and brother of Henry Moore (1831–95), marine painter. He is noted for decorative compositions which obviously belong to the same period as those of Leighton and Watts, but make no attempt to tell a story. The special merit of such pictures as 'Blossoms' (Tate Gallery), 1881, and 'Dreamers' (Birmingham), 1882, is the harmonious blend of colour combined with graceful posture and charming lines of drapery.

Moore, Edward (1712–57), dramatist and author, b. Abingdon, Berks. Garrick played the part of Beverley, the gambler, in M.'s once popular tragedy, *The Gamester*, 1753, and Horace Walpole and the Lords Chesterfield and Lyttelton contributed to his weekly jour., *The World*, 1753–7. His *Fables for the Female Sex*, 1744, were much admired.

Moore, Francis (1657–1715?), astrologer and almanac maker, b. Bridgnorth, Shropshire. Moving to London, he practised there as a doctor. His *Vox Stellarum* (Voice of the Stars), an almanac containing forecasts based on astrology, first appeared in 1700 and is still pub. yearly as *Old Moore's Almanac*. See ALMANAC.

Moore, George Augustus (1852–1933), novelist, b. Moore Hall, Mayo. Educ. at Oscott he was intended for the army, but his own inclination was towards painting, though he began by writing poetry: his *Flowers of Passion* appeared in 1878. As a young man he studied painting in Paris, and *Modern Painting*, 1893, displays his intimate knowledge of the w ork o contemporary artists. He remained in Paris for 10 years, but was recalled to London as a result of the Land League agitation; he had already decided that he was not a painter. His first book, *A Modern Lover*, 1883, appeared while he was living in lodgings in impoverished circumstances. This and other books earned him the heated opposition of librarians and others, but his success gradually enabled him to ignore the Puritans and Philistines. *Confessions of a Young Man*, 1888 (revised 1904 and 1916), is a record of his early life; by its frankness and unconventionality it aroused much discussion. His lively interest in the Irish movement is shown by his comedy, *The Bending of the Bough*, 1900, and *Hail and Farewell*, comprising *Ave*, 1911, *Salve*, 1912, and *Vale*, 1914, a trilogy of candid autobiographical revelations. M.'s early novels, *A Mummer's Wife*, 1885, *Esther Waters*, a masterpiece of realism recounting the life of a domestic servant, 1894, *Evelyn Innes*, 1898, and *Sister Theresa*, 1901, are an imitation of the Fr. philosophical novel, besides restoring in England the Fielding tradition and introducing an element of the realism usually associated with Zola. But if his later work, which with the chief exception of *In Single Strictness*, 1922 (reissued in 1927 as *Celibate Lives*), is concerned with historical themes, he developed a form of 'prose narrative' which is entirely individual. *The Brook Kerith*, 1916 (revised 1927), which retells the story of Jesus, and *Heloïse and Abelard*, 1921, are the best examples of this. By their grandeur of conception, their wealth of incident and descriptive detail, and their melodious, highly finished style, they have estab. M. as one of the most accomplished literary craftsmen of the cent. Other later works are *Avowals*, 1919, and *Conversations in Ebury Street*, 1924, which are chiefly criticism; *A Storyteller's Holiday*, 1918 (revised 1928), *Ulick and Soracha*, 1926, and *Aphrodite in Aulis*, 1931, which are fiction; *The Coming of Gabrielle*, 1920, a comedy, *The Making of an Immortal*, a play about Shakespeare, 1927, and *The Passing of the Essenes*, 1930, a play giving a new historical version of the life of Jesus. M. is unique amongst modern writers in that he revised and largely rewrote almost all his chief works. M. was entirely identified with his art; he never married. His Irish home, which remained empty for many years, was burned by the Republicans in 1923. If he was no real painter, at least his reactions to the fine arts made him a champion of the Fr. Impressionist school of painting in England. See studies by Susan L. Mitchell, 1916; J. Freeman, 1922; H. Wolfe, 1931; J. Hone, 1936; C. Morgan, 1938; and his *Letters*, ed. J. Eglinton, 1942.

Moore, Henry (1898–), sculptor and painter, *b.* Castleford, Yorks, son of a coal miner. He studied at Leeds College of Art and the Royal College of Art, London, proving to be a brilliant pupil. He first gained insight into the real nature of sculpture from geological specimens on which he studied the effect of natural forces on stone, wood, etc.; and at the British Museum from primitive art, and particularly Egyptian, Mexican, early Gk, Etruscan and Negro sculpture. His first commissioned work was 'North Wind', for the underground railway H.Q. in London. As official war artist, 1940–2, he produced the famous series of drawings of shelterers in the London tube stations. Other famous works include 'Madonna and Child' (St Matthew's Church, Northampton), 'Reclining Figure' (Tate Gallery), 'Three Standing Draped Figures' (Battersea Park, London) and 'Family Group' for Stevenage New Tn, and Figure for the UNESCO building, Paris. Other works have been widely exhibited and admired in both hemispheres.

Out of widely differing influences, M. evolved a style which in individuality and innovation of form has often been compared to Picasso's. His work, which consists chiefly of stone and wood carving, makes truth to material rather than verisimilitude its first aim. It has a monumental power and a vitality of expression which have commanded the attention of a wide public and ranked M. amongst the most notable sculptors since Rodin. M. was made a Companion of Honour, 1955, and awarded the Order of Merit in 1963. *See* J. P. Hodin, *Henry Moore*, 1958; E. Neumann, *The Archetypal World of Henry Moore* (trans.), 1959. (*See Plates: Art*; *Sculpture*.)

Moore, John (1729–1802), novelist, *b.* Stirling. He attended Glasgow Univ. and was a doctor by profession. As he was attached to the Brit. Army in Flanders in a medical capacity (1747–8), was for a time surgeon to the Eng. ambas. at Versailles and travelled for 5 years (1772–7) on the Continent as tutor to the young Duke of Hamilton, he had ample opportunities for observing the social manners of his time. Carlyle availed himself of M.'s *Journal of a Residence in France*, 1793, whilst Byron modelled his Childe Harold on Zeluco, a selfish libertine, whose name supplies the title to the most popular of M.'s novels, 1789.

Moore, Sir John (1761–1809), general, *b.* Glasgow, the son of John M. (q.v.), He entered the army as ensign in 1776. During the descent on Corsica he was wounded at the capture of Calvi (1794); in the W. Indies he distinguished himself at the taking of the Vigie and Morne Fortuné (1796), and 2 years later he was engaged in quelling the Irish insurrection. In 1799, during the Dutch campaign, he was wounded at the engagement of Egmont-op-Zee, and he was again disabled at the battle of Alexandria during the expedition to Egypt (1801). At the camp at Shorncliffe in England, where a memorial to him now stands, M. evolved a system of training for light infantry, as an answer to the Fr. use of *tirailleurs*. From this nucleus developed the light div., which took a prominent part in Wellington's operations in Spain. In Oct. 1808 M. took command of the Brit. forces in Portugal. He left Lisbon, advanced over the border, and arrived at Salamanca on 23 Nov. There he learned of Napoleon's victories over the Sp. forces at Gamenal and Tudela, near the Ebro, and, fearing attack by greatly superior forces, determined to withdraw. On 3 Dec., however, he learned that Napoleon was moving southward to Madrid and not westward against the Brit. forces, and seized the opportunity to strike at Napoleon's line of communication in Old Castile, distract his attention, and give the Spaniards a breathing space. M. knew the dangers he faced, and knew that a rapid retreat to Corunna would be inevitable as soon as Napoleon turned northwards in answer to the threat to his rear. M. hoped to fall upon an isolated Fr. body under Soult, but on the 23rd received the expected news of Napoleon's advance against him, and immediately turned for Corunna. The pursuit was pressed through the wilderness of Galicia, with great suffering to the Brit. troops and a noticeable deterioration in discipline, for both of which M.'s refusal to stand and fight, though probably correct, was largely responsible. Arriving at Corunna M. found the transports delayed and turned to give battle. He was killed at the height of the action. Though errors of detail were committed, the campaign as a whole was a sound strategic concept, disrupting Napoleon's plans, and giving a much-needed respite to the hard-pressed Spaniards. *See* lives by J. C. Moore, 1834; J. F. Maurice, 1897; C. Oman, 1953. Also *Diary*, ed. by J. F. Maurice, 1904; C. W. C. Oman, *History of the Peninsular War*, 1902–11; J. F. C. Fuller, *Sir John Moore's System of Training, 1794–1823*, 1925.

Moore, Marianne Craig (1887–), Amer. poetess, *b.* St Louis, Missouri. Educ. at Bryn Mawr, she was from 1921 to 1925 an assistant in New York public library. She contributed poems to the *Egoist*, the organ of the Imagist group, but they did not appear in book form until her friends had them pub. in London in 1921. A second collection of verse, *Observations*, 1925, obtained the Dial award, and later she won 2 more poetry prizes. Subsequent vols. are *The Pangolin*, 1936, *What Are Years*, 1941, and *Nevertheless*, 1944; her *Collected Poems* appeared in 1951. Her work consists of free verse in disciplined but unconventional metrical patterns. Witty and ironical, she has a vein of dry humour. *Predilections*, 1955, is a book of essays. *See* R. P. Blackmur, *The Double Agent*, 1935.

Moore, Mary (Lady Wyndham) (1862–1931), actress, *b.* London. After the death of her first husband, James Albery, she married Sir Charles Wyndham, 1916. Her association with the latter began in 1885; she acted in numerous plays with him, and became a partner with him in the proprietorship of the Criterion, Wyndham's and the New Theatres. Her earliest big success was as Ada Ingot in *David Garrick*. Her son Bronson

Caroline Moral Theology, 1949; K. Hormann, *An Introduction to Moral Theology*, 1961.

Moral Welfare, *see* JOSEPHINE BUTLER SOCIETY; PROSTITUTION; VIGILANCE ASSOCIATIONS. As to moral welfare of children and young persons, *see* CHILDREN AND YOUNG PERSONS, WELFARE OF; JUVENILE OFFENDERS; PROBATION; TREATMENT OF YOUNG ADULT OFFENDERS.

Morales, Cristóbal (*c.* 1500–53), Sp. composer, *b.* Seville, where he studied; was chapel master at Avila cathedral, 1526–30, and became a singer in the papal choir in Rome, 1535. While there he wrote many masses and motets which rank him among the finest contrapuntists of his time. He had a long holiday in Spain in 1540–1 and returned there for good in 1545, being chapel master at Toledo cathedral until 1547. In 1549 he became chapel master to the Duke of Arcos at Marchena, where he probably *d.*, although he was chapel master at Málaga cathedral in 1551–3. Apart from some It. and Sp. madrigals M.'s work consists exclusively of church music.

Morales, Luis (*c.* 1509–86), Sp. painter, *b.* Badajoz, referred to as 'El Divino' from the idealism of his sacred subjects in the Prado, Madrid. A typical work is the 'Virgin and Child'. *See* life by Berjano Escobar, 1921.

Morality, term commonly used to describe the plays also known as moral plays or moral interludes. These plays, though developed out of the miracle plays (q.v.), are still more closely related to a Lat. origin. Their real source is Prudentius (*c.* 400), who in his *Psychomachia* had the same subjects as did all the moralites, namely, 'personified abstractions fighting for the human soul'. A brief outline of one of the earliest extant moralities, *The Castle of Perseverance* (*c.* 1450), will give some idea of the *dramatis personae*. It tells the hist. of Humanum Genus tempted by Luxuria. When about to be lost entirely he is saved by Poenitentia, who brings him to the castle of Perseverance. Here he remains until his old age, when he is tempted by Avarice. Then follows a swift descent towards Hell, whence he is saved by Pity and Mercy. The latest development of the M. was to make it convey some special lesson, theological or educational. In Bale's *King Johan* it became the medium of hist., and hence led to the historical drama. For *Everyman*, the most famous of the M.s, *see* ed. by A. C. Cawley, 1956; *see also* A. W. Pollard, *English Miracle Plays, Moralities and Interludes*, 1895, and E. K. Chambers, *The Medieval Stage*, 1903.

Morand, Paul (1888–), Fr. diplomat (ambas. at Berne, 1944) and writer, *b.* Paris. He began in literature as one of the most determined exponents of modernity. His poems in free verse had affinities with the Dadaists. His books of short stories, *Ouvert la nuit*, 1922, and *Fermé la nuit*, 1923, dealt with various parts of the world seen through the lives of women. His chronicle of the 20th cent., *L'Europe galante*, 1925, is a daring series of stories about women, in his earlier manner. Other works are *Bouddha vivant*,

1927, *Magie noire*, 1928, *Champions du monde*, 1930, *Flèche d'orient*, 1932, *Londres*, 1933, *Rond-Point des Champs Élysées*, 1935, *Les Extravagants*, 1937, and *Isabeau de Bavière*, 1938.

Morandi, Giorgio (1890–1964), It. painter, *b.* Bologna, noted for a personal style of still-life. Early influences on his work were the paintings of Cézanne, Chirico and Carrà (qq.v.). With a narrow range of subjects he achieved many subtle variations of design and arrangement. He also produced numerous etchings.

Morar, dist and loch of W. Inverness-shire, Scotland. The loch, 12 m. long, is noted as being the deepest in the Brit. Isles, its maximum depth being 1017 ft.

Morata, Olimpia (1526–55), It. scholar and poet, *b.* Ferrara. Her works include many Lat. and Gk poems, mostly religious, and commentaries on Homer, and Cicero.

Moravia, Alberto (1907–), It. novelist, *b.* Rome. He is a relentless realist in his unflattering representation of human nature, but his objectivity is impaired by his preoccupation with sex. His first novel *Gli Indifferenti*, 1929, won him inter-European recognition. Other important works are *Agostino*, 1944; *La Romana*, 1947; *L'Amore congiugale*, 1949, and *Il Conformista*, 1951.

Moravia (Ger. **Mähren**), ter. of Czechoslovakia, bounded on the W. by Bohemia (q.v.) and on the E. by Slovakia (q.v.). Together with the former Austrian Silesia (*see* SILESIA), it formed until 1948 a prov. (area 10,324 sq. m.; cap. Brno), but it is now divided into the administrative regions (*kraju*) of Severomoravský (N. Moravia) and Jihomoravský (S. Moravia). M. lies mainly in the basin of the Morava, which divides the Moravian plateau in the W. from the Carpathians (q.v.) in the E. In the N. the Sudetic Mts (q.v.) form the boundary with Poland. Sheep and horses are reared, and agriculture and forestry are well developed. There are deposits of iron (Olomouc), coal and lignite (Ostrava) and other minerals. The woollen industry is important (Olomouc).

The earliest known inhabitants may have included the Boii (q.v.), among other tribes. In the 6th cent. M. became part of the Avar (*see* AVARS) dominions, and in the 8th cent. was settled by Slavs (q.v.). On the destruction of the Avar empire, M. became subject to the Holy Rom. Empire. Christianity was introduced into M. in the 9th cent. by Cyril (q.v.) and Methodius, and in the same cent. the Moravian ruler, Sviatopluk, asserted his independence of the king of the E. Franks (*see* GERMANY, *History*) and founded the Great Moravian kingdom, which included Bohemia. Sviatopluk was killed in 894, and his kingdom was overrun by the Magyars (q.v.). In 1029 M. became a fief of Bohemia, and a Bohemian margravate in 1182. In 1849 it was declared a separate Austrian crownland, and it became a prov. of Czechoslovakia in 1918. *See also* AUSTRIA, *History*; BOHEMIA, *History*; CZECHOSLOVAKIA.

Moravian Gap, *see* OSTRAVA.

Moravians, the The Moravian Brethren, the Bohemian Brethren or the Unity of the Brethren (*Unitas Fratrum*), small Protestant sect who claim to trace their origin to the 15th cent. In 1467 some of the people known as Taborites gathered round the Calixtine Bishop of Prague and formally constituted themselves a sect. At the Reformation they had friendly intercourse with Luther (q.v.), though their sympathies were, on the whole, more with the other reformed churches. At this time there were some 400 churches of the sect. During the 16th cent. persecutions many of the brethren fled to Poland, where they were gradually absorbed into other Protestant bodies. The Bohemians and M., being implicated in the revolution which came to an untimely end in 1620, were almost completely exterminated. No more is heard of them until under Christian David, a carpenter, certain M. emigrated to Saxony, where they were well received by Count Zinzendorf (1700–60), who became their leader. Here they lived at first as ordinary Lutherans, but later erected a church of their own. They lived a strict life, with daily prayers, a community of interests, stern exclusiveness and a form of episcopacy. Branches now exist elsewhere, and they have 4 provs., German, British, N. American and S. American, each managing its own affairs. Once in 10 years a general synod meets, representing all the provs. The Moravian Church has always been characterised by missionary vigour. *See* hist. of the brethren by J. Müller, 1922–30; *also* B. T. Jenkins, *Moravian Brethren in North Wales*, 1938.

Moravská Ostrava, *see* OSTRAVA.

Moray, Earl of, *see* RANDOLPH, THOMAS.

Moray, James Stuart, Earl of, *see* MURRAY.

Moray (formerly **Elgin**), N. Scottish co., fronting the M. Firth and lying between Banff and Nairn, mountainous in the S., but flat in the N. and sandy on the coast (Culbin sandhills, now afforested, lie to the extreme NW. of the co.). M. is watered by the R.s Spey (q.v.), Lossie and Findhorn (q.v.). The anct prov. of M. embraced a large part of N. Scotland. Today Elgin is the co. tn. and other centres include Lossiemouth and Forres (qq.v.). The chief industries are agriculture, cattle and sheep grazing, stone quarrying, distilling and fishing. M. and the adjoining co. of Nairn together return 1 member to Parliament. Area 305,000 ac.; pop. 49,170.

Moray, eel of the family Muraenidae. The strong jaws are armed with dagger-like teeth. The large species that hide in the crevices of coral reefs can inflict savage bites. The species known to the Romans (*Muraena helena*) is occasionally found in the Eng. Channel. Most species of M.s are found in tropical seas.

Moray Firth, arm of the N. Sea. It is about 18 m. across the entrance from Tarbat Ness to Burghead (q.v.), and about 30 m. long from there to the entry to the Caledonian Canal. The Spey, Findhorn (qq.v.) and Nairn are the chief rivs. draining into the M. F.

Morbihan, dept of W. France, named after the

Gulf of M. (Inner Sea). It was formed in 1790 from part of Lower Brittany. Its Atlantic coastline has many inlets. The Vilaine and the Blavet, into which flow the Auray and the Scorff, are both canalised. The highest land (975 ft.) is in the Montagnes Noires of the N. Barren heath covers a quarter of the prov., whilst a third part produces good crops of wheat, rye, buckwheat and mangels. Fisheries and oyster culture are important. The prin. tns are Vannes (the cap.), Lorient and Pontivy. M. is noted for its prehistoric remains, especially megaliths. Area 2738 sq. m.; pop. 530,800.

Morcar (fl. 1065–87), Earl of Northumbria, brother of Edwin, Earl of Mercia. He became Earl of Northumbria in 1065, on the expulsion of Tostig (q.v.) and was recognised by Edward the Confessor and Harold. When Tostig invaded England (1066) Edwin and M. resisted him. Though defeated at Fulford they inflicted heavy losses on the invaders, which almost certainly helped to decide Harold's subsequent victory at Stamford Bridge. M. swore fealty to William the Conqueror (1066), but in 1071 joined Hereward at Ely. He was later captured and *d.* in prison. *See* F. M. Stenton, *Anglo-Saxon England*, 1943.

Morchella, *see* MOREL.

Mordant, *see* DYE.

Mordaunt, Charles, *see* PETERBOROUGH AND MONMOUTH, EARL OF.

Mordecai, Benjamite exile in Persia, cousin and foster-father of Esther (q.v.). With the elevation of Hadassah as queen under the new name of Esther, M. joined the Persian court and so learned of a conspiracy against King Ahasuerus (Xerxes, 486–465 BC) which he frustrated. When the king raised Haman to be vizier, M. refused to salaam to him, thinking that every Jew should show enmity to an Amalekite; Haman then determined to destroy not only M. but the whole Jewish race. For the service M. had earlier rendered the king the latter ordered Haman to show honour to M. The Jews were delivered through the intervention of Esther, and M. became vizier instead of Haman, who was hanged.

Morden, *see* MERTON.

Mordva, people in the U.S.S.R., living in small groups among the Russians in the large area between Gor'kiy and Rayazan' in the W. and the Urals in the E. Total number (1962) 1,300,000 (1939, 1,750,000). The M. speak 2 different languages, Erzya and Moksha, which belong to the Finnish family. They have been known since the 6th cent., were Christianised in the 18th cent., and to a considerable degree are Russianised. *See* W. Kolarz, *Russia and Her Colonies*, 1952.

Mordva Autonomous Republic lies in central European U.S.S.R., SE. of Moscow, in the Volga upland in the E. and the Oka-Don lowland in the W., and is partly covered by oak forests. Area 10,100 sq. m.; pop. (1965) 1,011,000 (28 per cent urb.), Russians (since the 12th cent.), Mordva and Tatars. Grain, hemp and potatoes are grown, and there are saw-milling and food industries. The prin. tns are

Saransk (cap.) and Ruzayevka (important railway junction). The famous former monastery of Sarov is located in the rep., as was the Pot'ma concentration camp until the mid-1950s.

More, Sir Anthony, *see* MORO, ANTONIO.

More, Hannah (1745–1833), authoress, *b.* Stapleton, Glos. She came to London in 1774 and made the acquaintance of Dr Johnson (whom she flattered unduly) of Burke and the leaders of the 'blue-stocking' (q.v.) coterie. Garrick produced her play, *Percy,* 1777, an artificial and introspective play which finds an outlet for emotional intensity in tragic action. After the death of Garrick, however, she came to the conclusion that play-going was immoral, and she henceforth led a retired life. She consorted chiefly with the clergy and philanthropists, started Sunday schools in Cheddar and organised a movement that led to the formation of the Religious Tract Society, 1799. She wrote *Coelebs in Search of a Wife,* 1809, and a tract, *The Shepherd of Salisbury Plain,* and also many other religious works. She left her fortune to charities and religious institutions. Her *Letters* were ed. by R. B. Johnson, 1925. *See* life by M. G. Jones, 1952; *also* M. A. Hopkins, *Hannah More and her Circle,* 1947.

More, Henry (1614–87), philosopher, *b.* Grantham, Lincs. At Christ College, Cambridge, from which he took his M.A. degree in 1639, he lost himself in the delights of philosophical, and especially Platonic, studies. His *Philosophical Poems,* 1647, *Divine Dialogues,* 1668 ('containing Disquisitions and Instructions concerning the Attributes of God and the Providence in the World'), and *Enchiridion Metaphysicum,* 1673, are all penetrated with Neoplatonic mysticism and spiritualistic phantasies, which he owed in part, it seems, to his intimacy with Lady Conway, the Quaker. M. represents more than any other member of the school the mystical and theosophic side of the Cambridge Platonists (q.v.).

More, Paul Elmer (1864–1937), Amer. author and editor, *b.* St Louis, Missouri. He was educ. at Washington Univ. and Harvard. He taught Sanskrit and classical literature at Harvard and Bryn Mawr College, 1895–7. He lectured on Plato at Princeton Univ. and was literary editor of the *Independent,* 1901–3, and of the *New York Evening Post,* 1903–9, and editor of the *Nation,* 1909–14. His pubs. include *Shelburne Essays,* 11 series, 1904–28, *Life of Benjamin Franklin,* 1908, *Platonism,* 1917, *The Religion of Plato,* 1921, *Hellenistic Philosophie,* 1923, *The Demon of the Absolute,* 1928, *and The Sceptical Approach to Religion,* 1934. *Pages from an Oxford Diary,* 1937, is autobiographical. *See* study by R. Shafer, 1935.

More, Sir Thomas (1478–1535), lawyer, statesman and saint, *b.* Milk Street, Cheapside, London. He received the rudiments of education at St Anthony's School, Threadneedle Street, at that time said to be the best in the city. In about 1489 he was placed in the household of Cardinal Morton, Archbishop of Canterbuty, a high privilege which he owed to the influence of his father, Sir John M., later a justice of the court of king's bench. He was at Oxford, 1492–4, where he studied with Grocyn and Linacre. There he acquired his interest in the New Learning. He became a friend of Colet (q.v.), and on his return to London struck up a lasting friendship with Erasmus (q.v.). M. soon made a name for himself as a lawyer. He entered Parliament in 1504, first attracting public notice by his bold opposition to Henry VII's demand for a grant on the occasion of his daughter's marriage, as a result of which the Commons reduced the subsidy considerably. On Henry VIII's accession, M. soon attracted the attention of the young king and Wolsey. In 1518 M. was appointed master of requests and made a privy councillor. He had already been sent on embassies to the Low Countries. While on a mission to Flanders he began to write his most famous work, *Utopia,* which was first pub. in Latin in 1515. It had immediate popularity and was trans. into German 1524, French 1530, Italian 1548, English 1551 and Spanish 1790. It gives an account of an imaginary ideal is. and people, but the opinions on religion and politics are not always those by which he himself was later guided. M. accompanied the king to the Field of the Cloth of Gold in 1520, and in 1521 he was knighted and made treasurer of the exchequer. In the Parliament of 1523 he was elected Speaker of the House of Commons, being in effect put into that office by the court in order to make use of his popularity in the Commons to carry the money grant which Wolsey required. But instead M. effectively defended the Commons' privileges against Wolsey, and in 1529 he succeeded Wolsey as lord chancellor of England, in which capacity he showed great ability.

In his *Utopia* M. had declared for tolerance of religious creed in his ideal state with a liberality of philosophical detachment to which there is no parallel in any Englishman of that period. But at the same time he was not in sympathy with Protestantism in the world as he knew it, and he opposed a Bill designed to relax the severity of the heresy laws. Above all, the royal divorce was a matter on which he refused to give way, and when he realised that the marriage with Anne Boleyn was settled he petitioned the king to be allowed to resign the great seal, alleging indifferent health. The resignation was reluctantly accepted. For a while M. lived in retirement, devoting his energies to a controversy on religious subjects with Tyndale and others. But he was too conspicuous a figure to be allowed long to enjoy the happiness of a retired life. In 1534 M. refused to take the oath of supremacy, though he expressed himself willing to pledge political loyalty to the king. He was indicted for high treason in Westminster Hall, found guilty and sentenced to be hanged, drawn and quartered. The king commuted the sentence to beheading. At the block he protested that he *d.* for his religious opinions. He was canonised in 1935, together with Bishop Fisher (q.v.) of Rochester. Among his works, apart from

Utopia, are a life of Pico della Mirandola, 1510, and a *History of Richard III*, written about 1513. He wrote many controversial works, as well as epigrams and dialogues in Latin. He wrote his *Dialogue of Comfort* in the Tower. His austere yet happy religious character, his constancy and fortitude under misfortune, combine to make him one of the most attractive figures in Eng. hist.

M.'s early ideas of celibacy were dispelled after he had become acquainted with the family of John Colte of New Hall, Essex, for the 'honest and sweet conversation' of the daughters attracted him and he married the eldest. After her death he married Alice Middleton, a widow, about 1511. Erasmus has left a vivid and touching picture of his happy life in his Chelsea home. After the execution of M., the vindictive king expelled Lady M. from the Chelsea house and set aside the assignments which had been validly executed by M., and settled his property on Princess Elizabeth. M.'s eldest daughter, Margaret, married to his biographer, Wm Roper, was remarkable for her wide accomplishments—Latin and Greek, music and the sciences so far as they were accessible—and also for her great devotion to her father. *See* lives by R. W. Chambers, 1935; D. Sargent, 1936, A.Cecil, 1937; *also* Elizabeth F. Rogers (ed.), *The Correspondence of Sir Thomas More*, 1947.

Möre and Romsdal, co. of W. Norway. It has a long coastline on the Atlantic with many fjords. The prin. industry is fishing. The chief tns are Kristiansund, Ålesund and Molde the cap. At Sunndalsöra is Norway's biggest aluminium plant. Area 5811 sq. m.; pop. 213,500.

Morea, *see* PELOPONNESE.

Moréas, Jean (1856–1910), Fr. poet and novelist, *b*. Athens. His real name was Joannis Papadiamontopoulos. His acquaintance with Verlaine inclined him in such earlier work as *Pèlerin passionné*, 1891, to the symbolist school; but, believing symbolism to have no enduring literary quality, he became the founder and leader of the 'École Romane', whose ambition it was to rival the Pléiade (q.v.), and turned to the old medieval-romantic style, producing in that vein his *Contes de la vieille France*, 1904. But his best work is a reversion to the classical precision of Malherbe and Corneille, and includes *Iphigénie*, 1903, a tragedy, and *Les Stances*, 1899–1927. *See* R. Niklaus, *J. Moréas, poète lyrique*, 1936.

Moreau, Gustave (1826–98), Fr. painter, *b*. Paris. He studied with Picot and exhibited regularly at the Salon, but later became something of a hermit in his Paris house (since converted into a museum). Towards the end of his life he was an influential art teacher. At his death he left 8000 pictures, water-colours and drawings to the nation, this fine collection being housed in the Moreau Gallery. His subjects were chiefly taken from classical or religious story; among his best-known works are the 'Athenians with the Minotaur', 1855, 'Oedipus and the Sphinx', 1864, 'Galatea', 1880, and 'Moses on the Nile', 1878. A passionate and 'decadent'

quality in his 'Salome' led Huysmans to admire and describe it in his novel *A Rebours*. *See* study by L. Bénédite, 1922.

Moreau, Hégésippe (1810–38), Fr. poet, whose sad death in a refuge heightened interest in a posthumously pub. collection of his poems entitled *Le Myosotis*. Some of his best pieces are his *Ode à la faim* and the elegy *La Voulzie*. His *Contes à ma sœur* (prose) were pub. in 1851. *See* G. Benoît-Guyod, *La Vie maudite d'H. Moreau*, 1945.

Moreau, Jean Victor (1761–1813), Fr. general, *b*. Morlaix, in Britanny. He took the side of the revolution, and in 1794 he was made general of a div. When Pichegru fell under suspicion the Directory appointed M., in 1796, to the chief command on the Rhine and Moselle. He defeated Latour at Rastadt and the Archduke Charles at Ettlingen, and drove the Austrians back to the Danube; but the final victory was gained by the archduke, thanks to brilliant manoeuvring which compelled a Fr. retreat to the Rhine. A suspicion of participation in the plots of Pichegru led to M. being deprived of his command. In the following year he succeeded Schérer in the command of the army in Italy. By a skilful retreat he saved the Fr. army from destruction. The Directory, nevertheless, deprived him of the chief command, and gave it to Joubert. After Joubert's death M. again assumed the command, and conducted the defeated troops to France. M.'s character, military talent and political moderation induced the party which overthrew the Directory to offer him the dictatorship of France. He declined this, and helped Bonaparte on 18th Brumaire. M. gained victory after victory over the Austrians in the campaign of 1800, and won the battle of Hohenlinden. A strong feeling of mutual distrust then arose between M. and Bonaparte. The latter surrounded him with spies, and he was accused of participation in the plot of Cadoudal and Pichegru against the life of the first consul. He was arrested, sentenced to 2 years' imprisonment, which was commuted into banishment, and went to America. He landed at Gothenburg (1813), however, and accompanied the Emperor of Russia and the King of Prussia in the march against Dresden, where a Fr. cannonball broke both his legs and he *d*. soon afterwards.

Morecambe and Heysham, municipal bor. and seaside resort on the NW. coast of Lancs, England, 3½ m. WNW. of Lancaster. The Lakeland mts are nearby. There are 6 m. of promenade, two piers, five theatres, gardens and parks. The 'Miss Great Britain' National Bathing Beauty competition is held annually in the swimming stadium. The autumn illuminations are famous. Heysham harbour, in the bor., is a terminus for the Royal Mail boat service to Belfast. Pop. 40,950.

Morel, or **Morchella**, genus of fungi, of which the common M. (*M. esculenta*) is one of the most delicate edible Brit. fungi (q.v.). The cap is much wrinkled and ridged, and is attached to the stem from centre to edge. It is yellowish or buff in colour, and somewhat resembles a mass of honeycomb. M.s are often dried for seasoning soups, sauces and gravies, and are commonly used fresh in ragouts.

Morelia, cap. of state of Michoacán, Mexico. Situated in the NE. of the state at an altitude of 6200 ft on the R. Grande de M. which flows into Lake Cuitzeo a few miles to the N. Founded in 1540, with the name of Valladolid, there are many fine colonial period churches and buildings, some of great historical interest. The revolutionary Morelos was born and lived in the tn. It is the centre of a rich cattle-raising and agric. region, and its industries are based on this and on forest products. An oil pipeline brings oil from the refinery at Salamanca in the neighbouring state of Guanajuato. The Univ. of M. (late Colegio de San Nicholás) is one of the oldest seats of learning in Mexico. Population 100,000.

Morellet, L'Abbé André (1727–1819), Fr. writer, b. Lyons. Many of the articles on theology and metaphysics in the great *Encyclopédie*, 1751 onwards, were from his pen. Some of his writings were collected together in his *Mélanges de littérature et de philosophie au XVIIIᵉ siècle*, 4 vols., 1818, and the posthumous *Mémoires sur le XVIIIᵉ siècle et la Révolution*, 1821. Among his other works are *Petit écrit sur une matière intéréssante: la tolérance*, 1756, and a *Manuel des inquisiteurs*, 1762, based on the *Directorium Inquisitorum* of a 14th cent. Aragonese inquisitor, a work that horrified him.

Morelos, state of central Mexico, adjoining in the N. of the Federal Dist and the state of Mexico. Mostly very mountainous apart from the coastal region, it is traversed E.–W. in the N. by the Cordillera Neovolcanica and lies in the seismic zone of Mexico. Altitudes in the state range from about 2600 ft to over 17,500 ft, thus producing great varieties of climate, the N. tending to be cold and dry and the S. hot and humid. There are numerous rivs. and sev. lakes, some of which have thermal waters. M. is an agric. state, the main crops being rice, sugarcane, beans, wheat, coffee and fruits. Cattle-raising is also important. Mining goes on but is not of great economic significance. There has been some industrial development but this is mainly related to processing agric. products and textile manuf. Tourism is an important industry. The cap. is Cuernavaca (q.v.) (pop. 36,000), and other sizeable tns are Zacatepec (14,000), Cuantla (12,000) and Yautepec (9000). Area 1,917 sq. m.; pop. (1960) 386,264.

Morena, Sierra, *see* SIERRA MORENA.

Moreri, Louis (1643–80), Fr. encyclopaedist, b. Provence. In 1674 he pub. his *Grand Dictionnaire historique*, which, after much expansion and revision at the hands of various editors, reached its twentieth ed. in 1759.

Moresnet, part of Eupen (q.v.), 5 m. SW. of Aachen. Before the First World War it was a com. and neutral ter. with joint Belgian and Ger. administration from 1816. In 1919 the allied powers assigned it to Belgium as compensation for damage done by the Germans to their forests. It now forms part of the prov. of Liège (q.v.).

Moreto y Cabaña, Agustin (1618–69), Sp. dramatist, b. Madrid. His finest comedy is *El Desdén con el Desdén*, but his fund of humour and his excellent characterisation are also apparent in *El lindo Don Diego* and the farcical *Trampa Adelante*. He ended his life as a priest.

Moreton Bay, on the E. coast of Queensland, Australia, 40 m. by 17 m., formed inside the is. of M. and Stradbroke. It was discovered by Capt. Cook in 1770. The Brisbane R. flows into M. B.; Brisbane, the cap. of Queensland, is situated 14 m. from its mouth.

Moretto, Il (Alessandro Bonvicino) (1498–1554), It. oil, fresco and portrait painter, b. Rovato, Brescia. He studied under Ferramola, and in Venice under Giovanni Bellini and Titian; eventually he became a devoted admirer of Raphael. Moroni (q.v.) was a pupil of M. There are examples of M.'s work in the galleries of Brescia, Florence, Venice, Verona, Berlin, Paris and Vienna, and in the National Gallery which possesses a fine altar-piece.

Morgagni, Giovanni Battista (1682–1771), It. anatomist, b. Forli. In 1715 he became prof. of anatomy at Padua, a position he retained till his death. His anatomical reputation was made by his *Adversaria anatomica*, 1706–17, and he may be considered the founder of pathological anatomy, his great work *De Sedibus et causis morborum per anatomem indagatis*, pub. in 1761, establishing pathological anatomy as a science.

Morgain, or **Morgue le Fay**, witch of Arthurian legend and sister of King Arthur. In the romance of *Morte d'Arthur* she revealed to Arthur the intrigue of Guinevere with Lancelot.

Morgan, Augustus de, *see* DE MORGAN.

Morgan, Charles Langbridge (1894–1958), novelist and playwright, b. Kent. He studied at the naval colleges of Osborne and Dartmouth, and from 1911 to 1913 served on the Atlantic and China stations. In the First World War he was made prisoner during the Naval Brigade's defence of Antwerp, but allowed on parole in Holland, where he spent 4 years. From 1919 to 1921 he was at Brasenose College, Oxford. Joining the staff of *The Times*, he was dramatic critic, and in 1923 he married the novelist Hilda Vaughan. In the Second World War he served at the Admiralty with Naval Intelligence. His first novel *The Gun-room*, 1919, was based on his early naval experiences. *Portrait in a Mirror*, 1929, won the Femina Vie Heureuse Prize and gained him popularity in France; *The Fountain*, 1932, won the Hawthornden Prize; and *The Voyage*, 1940, was awarded the Tait Black Prize. Others of his novels are *The Judge's Story*, 1947, *Breeze of Morning*, 1951, and *Challenge to Venus*, 1957. His essays were pub. as *Reflections in a Mirror*, 2 series, 1944, 1946, and *The Writer and his World*, 1960. His plays include *The Flashing Stream*, 1938, *The River Line*, 1952, and *The Burning Glass*, 1954. He was a close friend of George Moore (q.v.), who made M. his literary executor. Among other distinctions he was an officer of the Legion of Honour and a member of the French Academy.

Morgan, Sir Henry (c. 1635–88), buccaneer and colonial governor, b. Glamorganshire. According to tradition he was kidnapped at Bristol and shipped to Barbados as a slave. M. however, joined the buccaneers (q.v.) soon became their leader, and ravaged the Sp. colonies, his justification and that of the governor of Jamaica (Modyford), who gave him his privateering commission, being that the Sp. claimed exclusive possession of the Caribbean. It was only after M.'s victories that the Sp. king at length acknowledged England's title to Jamaica. His most extraordinary feats were those of Puerto Bello (1668), Fort Chagres and his sea-fight near Maracaibo. After taking the city of Panama he was ordered to return to England (1672) to answer charges brought against him by the Spanish. He was sent to the Tower, but was soon afterwards released and was knighted by Charles II in 1674, receiving the commission of lieutenant-general of Jamaica. He returned to Jamaica in that capacity and as senior member of the council and commander-in-chief. For a few months he was acting governor. He d. in Jamaica. See A. O. Exquemeling, *Buccaneers of America*, 1684 (a contemporary account of M., the source for the stories of M.'s great cruelty, which may possibly be exaggerated). See also W. A. Roberts, *Sir Henry Morgan, Buccaneer and Governor*, 1933; E. H. Cruikshank, *The Life of Sir Henry Morgan, with an Account of the English Settlement of Jamaica*, 1935; R. T. Forbes, *Henry Morgan, Pirate*, 1946.

Morgan, John Pierpont (1837–1913), Amer. financier, b. Hartford, Connecticut, U.S.A. In 1857 he entered the Bank of Duncan, Sherman & Co., and in 1871 became a member of the firm of Drexel, now M. & Co., the great bankers of the U.S.A. In 1901 he formed the Steel Trust with a capital of $1,400,000,000, and he was controller of railways and ocean transportation lines. He had a vast collection of pictures and art treasures, and was a yachtsman.

Morgan, John Pierpont, junior (1867–1943), Amer. banker, b. Irvington, New York, son of the preceding. He graduated at Harvard, 1889, and became a member of J. P. M. & Co., New York, and of M., Grenfell & Co., London. Chief legatee under his father's will, he inherited the art collections. On his father's death he succeeded to the directorship of New York Central and Hudson R. Railroad. Early in the First World War M. organised a New York bankers' syndicate with $100 million in gold. He acted for the Brit. and Fr. Govs. as agent for purchase of supplies in America; also for the Amer. Gov. when it entered the war in 1917. In 1920 he gave his London house at Princes Gate for an Amer. embassy. M. left a gross estate of $16 million and a net estate of $4·6 million, most of the difference being accounted for by federal and state taxes. In his lifetime M. gave $36 million to charitable and public institutions, including $15 million to the Pierpont M. Library, $9 million to the Metropolitan Museum of Art, and $4 million to New York hospital. In 1933 he made

over to trustees, as an institution to be used for research by the world's scholars, the magnificent library, valued at $8·5 million, which had been collected by his father and himself in a superb marble building near the family residence in E. 36th Street. It contained about 25,000 vols. of illuminated MSS., early printed books and examples of the work of famous presses.

Morgan, Lewis Henry (1818–81), Amer. ethnologist, b. near Aurora, New York. He practised as a lawyer at Rochester, New York, and made a study of the Iroquois, living amongst them to learn their customs. He pub. in 1851 *The League of the Iroquois*. In 1871 he pub. *Systems of Consanguinity and Affinity*, a massive attempt to classify kinship systems; all later work on this subject is indebted to his work. In 1877 came *Ancient Society*, in which he traced the development of social institutions through savagery and barbarism to civilisation. His scheme is now somewhat discredited, but was taken over completely by Engels (q.v.) in his *Origin of the Family*.

Morgan, Sydney, Lady (c. 1783–1859), authoress, b. Dublin, daughter of Robert Owenson, an actor. She began her literary career with a vol. of poems, which she set to Irish tunes. She then wrote the novels *St Clair*, 1804, and *The Novice of St Dominick*, 1805, followed by *The Wild Irish Girl*, 1806, which last estab. her reputation. In 1812 she married Charles M., a surgeon, whom the lord-lieutenant knighted. Two years later appeared her best novel, *O'Donnell*. During the later years of her life she pub. *Dramatic Scenes from Real Life*, 1833, *Woman and her Master*, 1840, *The Book without a Name*, 1841, and *Passages from my Autobiography*, 1859. See life by W. Fitzpatrick, 1860; also L. Stevenson, *The Wild Irish Girl*, 1936.

Morgan, Thomas Hunt (1866–1945), Amer. zoologist, b. Lexington, Kentucky, son of Charlton H. M. He graduated at the State College of Kentucky, 1886, and became Ph.D. at Johns Hopkins Univ., 1890. He was prof. of biology at Bryn Mawr College, 1891–1904, and prof. of experimental zoology at Columbia Univ. His pubs. include *The Development of the Frog's Egg*, 1897, *Regeneration*, 1901, *Evolution and Adaptation*, 1903, *Experimental Zoology*, 1907, *Heredity and Sex*, 1913, *Mechanism of Mendelian Heredity*, 1915, *Critique of the Theory of Evolution*, 1916, *The Physical Bases of Heredity*, 1919, *The Theory of the Gene*, 1926, *Experimental Embryology*, 1927, *The Scientific Basis of Evolution*, 1932, *Embryology and Genetics*, 1933; and monographs and papers on biological and embryological subjects.

Morgan, William Frend De, see DE MORGAN, WILLIAM FREND.

Morgan Combine, see ATLANTIC SHIPPING TRUST.

Morganatic Marriage, name given to a marriage union, otherwise perfectly regular, between a man of the blood of a reigning royal family and a woman of lower social rank, e.g. the marriage of George IV of England, when Prince of Wales, with Mrs Fitzherbert. The issue of a

M. M. are legitimate, though they are debarred from inheriting the rank and property of the father.

Morgantown, city of W. Virginia, U.S.A., in Monongalia co., 55 m. S. of Pittsburg. The W. Virginia state univ. was founded here in 1867. M. is the centre of a bituminous coal-mining, limestone and glass-sand area. Pop. 22,560.

Morgarten, locality on the SE. shore of Lake Aegeri, Switzerland. In 1315 the Swiss defeated a large Austrian army under Leopold of Austria at M., and thus laid the foundations of Swiss liberty.

Morgat, popular seaside resort on Brittany. *See* CROZON.

Morgenstern, Christian (1871–1914), Ger. poet, *b.* Munich, son of a painter. His poetry was deeply influenced by his tubercular condition, which gave him the certainty of an early death. He gained great popularity by his grotesque poems *Galgenlieder*, 1905, and *Palmström*, 1910, where he shows himself a master of words and sounds. In his later years he wrote mainly serious poetry; his religious verse *Einkehr*, 1910, and *Wir fanden einen Pfad*, 1914, as well as the love lyrics *Ich und Du*, 1911, are among the most beautiful and most moving poems in Ger. literature. *See* M. Bauer, *Christian Morgensterns Leben und Werk*, 1933; F. Hiebel, *Christian Morgenstern, Wende und Aufbruch unseres Jahrhunderts*, 1957.

Morgue, name given to a building in which the bodies of people found dead are exposed for identification. The name is, more particularly, that of a building in Paris, behind the cathedral of Notre-Dame, used for this purpose and dating from the 5th cent. *See* MORTUARY.

Morgue le Fay, *see* MORGAIN.

Morhange, Charles Henri Valentin, *see* ALKAN.

Morhof, Daniel Georg (1639–91), Ger. author, *b.* Wismar. In 1665 he became prof. of eloquence and poetry at Kiel, and in 1673 prof. of hist. there. His most famous works are *Unterricht von der deutschen Sprache und Poesie*, 1682, a systematic hist. of European literature, and *Polyhistor*, 1688, an encyclopaedia of general knowledge and science. His *Opera poetica*, 1697, is insignificant. *See* life by R. von Liliencron, 1885.

Moricz, Zsigmond (1879–1942), Hungarian novelist, *b.* Csécse, son of a peasant farmer. He studied theology at Debrecen, and then went to Budapest to study law and literature. He began as a journalist in the cap., but soon branched out as a naturalist novelist. He first became famous for 'Seven Farthings', which appeared in *Nyugat* in 1908. His novel, *Raw Gold*, 1910, destroys the Hungarian illusion of the moral purity and idyllic happiness of the people of the vils. and farms. One of his most successful works was *Behind the Back of God*, 1911, in which he painted a sombre image of the middle class, stifled by the narrow life of a prov. tn. In 1922 he pub. *The Fairy Garden*, a novel the scene of which is laid in Transylvania in the 17th cent. One of his greatest

works, *Transylvania*, is available in German, Vienna, 1936.

Morier, James Justinian (*c.* 1780–1849), Brit. traveller and novelist, *b.* Smyrna. Educ. at Harrow, he was secretary of legation in Persia from 1809, and during the 6 years of his residence he became thoroughly acquainted with the character of the people. He pub. *Journey through Persia, 1808–9*, in 1812. The best of his E. novels, entitled *The Adventures of Hajji Baba of Ispahan*, appeared in 1824 and was followed by *Hajji Baba in England*, 1828, *Zohrab the Hostage*, 1832, *Ayesha*, 1834, and *The Mirza*, 1841.

Mörike, Eduard (1804–75), Ger. poet, *b.* Ludwigsburg. He studied theology, and from 1834 was a Protestant pastor, but he retired in 1843. He was appointed prof. of literature at the Katharinenstift, Stuttgart, an office he held for 16 years. He belonged to the Swabian school of Uhland, and his *Gedichte* are, for the most part, simple lyrics, graceful in style and original in conception. He is at his best in love or nature poems, based on his inner experiences. He also wrote short stories, the most famous being *Idylle vom Bodensee*, 1846, and *Mozart auf der Reise nach Prag*, 1856, as well as an autobiographical novel *Maler Nolton*, 1832. His complete works were ed. by H. Maync, 1914, and letters by K. Fischer and R. Kraus, 1903. *See* B. von Wiese, *Mörike*, 1950; M. Mare, *Eduard Möricke*, 1957.

Morin, or **Morinus, Jean** (1591–1650), Fr. writer and theologian, *b.* Blois. A Protestant clergyman at Leyden, he was converted to Catholicism and became a priest of the Oratory at Paris in 1618. He ed. the Paris *Polyglot*, 1645, which includes the Samaritan Pentateuch and the Targum. M. claimed the superiority of the Samaritan over the Heb. version. He also wrote a Samaritan grammar and *Exercitationes* on the Heb. and Gk texts of the Bible.

Morioka, city of Iwateken, Japan, 85 m. SE. of Aomori. The seat of the prefectural gov., it is the centre of commerce and industry of the dist. Long noted for its excellent cast-iron kettles, it also produces dairy products, iron, steel, sulphur and furniture. Pop. 168,000.

Morioris, *see* MAORIS.

Morison, Stanley (1889–), typographical expert and bibliographer, *b.* London. As adviser to the Monotype Corporation, where he initiated a programme in type design, and in similar positions at the Cambridge Univ. Press and *The Times* (whose official hist. he also ed.), he has transformed the appearance of printed matter. His pub. works include *The Fleuron* (editor), 1923–30, *Four Centuries of Fine Printing*, 1924, *Memoir of John Bell*, 1930, *Ichabod Dawks and His News-Letter*, 1931, *The English Newspaper, 1622–1932*, 1932, *First Principles of Typography*, 1936, *The Art of Printing*, 1938. *Black Letter*, 1941, *English Liturgical Books* (3rd ed.), 1946, and *The Typographic Book, 1450–1935*, 1963.

Morisonians, *see* EVANGELICAL UNION.

Morisot, Berthe Marie Pauline (1841–95), Fr. painter, *b.* Bourges. One of the most distinguished of women painters. She profited by early guidance from Corot (q.v.) and in turn influenced Manet (q.v.), whose brother Eugène she married, towards Impressionism (q.v.). She exhibited in most of the Impressionist exhibitions and Renoir, Degas and Mallarmé were among the admirers of her sensitive studies of women and children. *See The Correspondence of Berthe Morisot*, ed. Denis Rouart, Eng. trans., 1957.

Moriston, glen and riv. of Ross and Cromarty and Inverness cos., Scotland. R. M.'s source is near Loch Cluny, and it flows into Loch Ness at Invermoriston. Glen M. forms one of the major schemes of the N. of Scotland Hydro-electric Board.

Moritz, Gustav, *see* ARMFELT, COUNT OF.

Morlaix, port of France, on the R. Morlaix in Brittany, cap. of the dept of Finistère, 33 m. ENE. of Brest. Many of the houses date from the 15th cent. It was pillaged by the English during the Hundred Years War. The chief manufs. are tobacco and paper. Gen. Moreau (q.v.) was a native of the tn. Pop. 18,900.

Morland, George (1763–1804), painter, *b.* London. He left his home in 1782 and abandoned himself to a bohemian and irresponsible mode of life, which renders his artistic achievement all the more remarkable. Indeed debt seems to have been his greatest incentive to work. His pictures deal with the mellower aspect of domestic and rustic life, and reveal great beauty of conception and harmony of execution. His animal studies inspired his brother-in-law, J. Ward. Of his many fine pictures 'The Gypsies', 1790, and 'Inside of a Stable' are representative. *See* F. W. Blagdon, *Memoirs of George Morland*, 1806. There are lives by G. C. Williamson, 1904; W. Sibey, 1907; B. Henderson, 1923.

Morley, Christopher Darlington (1890–1957), Amer. novelist, poet and essayist, *b.* Haverford, Pennsylvania. Educ. at Haverford College, he went to Oxford as Rhodes Scholar. He worked as a columnist on various periodicals and in 1937 ed. a new edition of *Bartlett's Familiar Quotations*. The best known of his novels are *Where the Blue Begins*, 1922, and *Thunder on the Left*, 1925; others are *Parnassus on Wheels*, 1917, *The Haunted Bookshop*, 1919, *Swiss Family Manhattan*, 1932, and *The Man who Made Friends with Himself*, 1949. He also pub. many books of essays, while *The Rocking Horse*, 1919, *Chimney-smoke*, 1921, *Parson's Pleasure*, 1923, and *The Middle Kingdom*, 1944, are vols. of verse. *John Mistletoe*, 1931, is an early autobiography.

Morley, Edward Williams (1838–1923), Amer. chemist, prof. of chem. at W. Univ., U.S.A. He carried out accurate determinations of the atomic weights of hydrogen and oxygen, and was associated with the Michelson-M. experiment (q.v.).

Morley, Thomas (1557–1602), musical theorist, organist and composer who studied under Byrd. After being organist at St Giles, Cripplegate, he was appointed to St Paul's, and in 1592 he became a gentleman of the Chapel Royal. Six years later he was granted a 21 years' monopoly in music printing, in succession to Byrd. He excelled as a composer in canzonets and madrigals; but he also devoted considerable attention to church music and wrote some songs for the lute and instrumental compositions. Some of his work appears in the Fitzwilliam Virginal Book, and he wrote some of the original music for the productions of Shakespeare, with whom he was almost certainly personally acquainted. His theoretical treatise, *Plaine and Easie Introduction to Practicall Musicke*, 1597, was popular for 2 cents. and is one of the best sources of information on 16th cent. methods of composition and musical life in general (a facsimile appeared in 1937 and a modern reprint, ed. by A. Harman, in 1952).

Morley of Blackburn, John Morley, 1st Viscount (1838–1923), statesman and man of letters, *b.* Blackburn, and educ. at Cheltenham and Lincoln College, Oxford. He became editor of the *Literary Gazette* and the daily *Morning Star*; and in 1867 he succeeded G. H. Lewes in the editorship of the *Fortnightly Review*. In 1878 he ed. for Macmillan the Eng. Men of Letters series, his own vol. on Edmund Burke being most masterly. In 1880 he became editor of the *Pall Mall Gazette*. In 1833 he was elected as Liberal M.P. for Newcastle upon Tyne, and in 1886 he became Irish secretary in Gladstone's cabinet, an office he occupied again in 1892, after the defeat on Home Rule in the general election of 1886. In 1895 he was defeated as an anti-imperialist at Newcastle, but was returned for Montrose Burghs. He stood somewhat apart from politics during the Unionist administration of 1895–1906, being engaged on his *Life of Gladstone*, 1903, but he was a strong opponent of the Boer War policy. In Campbell-Bannerman's cabinet (1906) M. became secretary of state for India. In Asquith's first cabinet (1908) he was raised to the peerage, still retaining the India Office; but in 1910 his age and health forced him to hand that office to Lord Crewe, while remaining in the cabinet as lord president of the Council. Being a pacifist, he retired from public life on the declaration of war in Aug. 1914. M. was one of the original recipients of the Order of Merit at the coronation of Edward VII, 1902. Besides the works mentioned above he wrote *Voltaire*, 1872, *Rousseau*, 1873, *On Compromise*, 1874, *Diderot and the Encyclopaedists*, 1878, *The Life of Richard Cobden*, 1881, *Walpole*, 1889, *Oliver Cromwell*, 1900, *Recollections*, 1917, etc. *See* life by F. W. Hirst (with letters), 1927; *also* F. W. Knickerbocker, *John Morley and his Friends*, 1945.

Morley, municipal bor. in the W. Riding of Yorks, England, 5 m. SSW. of Leeds. M. is mentioned in the Domesday survey, but its development as a large manufacturing tn. producing machinery and woollen goods, dates from only a cent. ago. Pop. 40,338.

Morley College, institution for adult education founded in 1889 in London and named after Samuel M., who supplied a large measure of financial assistance. Its object was to interest working men and women in subjects not directly vocational. It now receives a grant from the

G.L.C. and provides evening classes covering a wide range of subjects. There are some 4000 students.

Morley-Minto Reforms, constitutional reforms introduced in India in 1909 by Lord Morley, as secretary of state for India, and the Earl of Minto, as viceroy.

Mormon Church, called by its adherents 'the Church of Jesus Christ of Latter-Day Saints', or shortly 'Latter-Day Saints'. In the spring of 1820, during a time of religious revival in Manchester, New York, U.S.A., Joseph Smith (1805–44) told of visions which he had had of God the Father and God the Son, and proclaimed the Gospel of Jesus Christ restored to earth. After a series of other visions he claimed in 1827 to have been given the golden plates which had been written in 'reformed Egyptian' by the prophet M. and hidden by his son Moroni, and which gave a hist. of religion in the Amer. continent from the time of Babel down to the 5th cent. AD. Joseph Smith was able to translate this work with the aid of the anct stones of divination, Urim and Thummim, which were also given him. The trans. is known as the *Book of M.*, and after it had been made the plates, etc., were returned to an angel. In 1829 Smith and his associate Oliver Cowdery claimed to have received divine baptism, with the authority of the office of priesthood, lost to the world since early New Testament times. In 1830 they founded the M. sect, and began at once the business of making converts. In 1831 they moved to Kirtland, Ohio; in 1833 Smith became first president, and in 1835 twelve apostles were appointed. In 1837 a bank founded by Smith at Kirtland failed, and the sect was forced to move on to Jackson Co., Missouri, where a branch had already been estab. and where Zion, the new Jerusalem', was now founded. Again, however, the M.s came into conflict with the local inhab., and during the winter of 1839 were driven away to found a new settlement in Illinois which they called Nauvoo. Here in 1843 Smith is said to have received a revelation about 'plural marriages', which he and other leading elders began to act upon without making it public. Some M.s left the church and began to pub. an anti-M. journal called the *Expositor*. The offices of the paper were destroyed, rioting broke out, and Joseph and his brother Hyrum Smith were imprisoned in Carthage where they were shot by a mob while awaiting trial. Among the M.s dissension caused some to break away; they founded the Reorganised M. Church in 1852, with H.Q. today at Independence, Missouri. Brigham Young (q.v.) succeeded as president, and led the main body westward to found Salt Lake City in 1847. The M.s' wish to join the Union as the State of Deseret was overruled, but when the State of Utah was founded after the Mexican war, Young became its first governor. A new temple was estab. at Salt Lake City. Polygamy was officially practised, 1852-90, when it was forbidden by President Wilford Woodruff, and gradually *d.* out.

The M. church, still predominant in Utah, has made many converts in the U.S.A. and Europe. It has 2 orders of priesthood, that of Melchisedek (the president, patriarch, apostles, seventies, high priests and elders; concerned with preaching and spiritual gov.) and that of Aaron (bishops, priests, deacons and teachers; concerned with tithes and administration). M.s believe in the authority of the scriptures (the Bible, *Book of M.* and other writings of Joseph Smith) and in the supreme value of personal revelation, especially that received by the president of the sect. The millenium is expected, and baptism by proxy is practised on behalf of the dead. Strict tithing is observed, and alcohol, nicotine and other stimulants forbidden. There is tolerance for all other churches, but proselytising is carried out with the greatest vigour. The M. temple at Newchapel, Surrey, was opened in 1958 and the H.Q. of the M. C. in Britain is at Leatherhead, Surrey. See J. E. Talmage, *Articles of Faith*, 1899; W. A. Linn, *The Story of the Mormons*, 1901, 1923; W. W. La Rue, *The Foundations of Mormonism*, 1919; E. E. Ericksen, *The Psychological and Ethical Aspects of Mormon Group Life*, 1922; H. Standage, *March of the Mormon Battalion from Council Bluffs to California*, 1928; J. A. Gove, *The Utah Expedition*, New Hampshire Hist. Society Collections, vol. xii, 1928; S. Y. Gates, *The Life Story of Brigham Young*, 1930; N. Anderson, *Desert Saints: The Mormon Frontier in Utah*, 1942; S. W. Taylor, *Family Kingdom*, 1951.

Morning Glory, popular name of tropical climbing plants of the genus *Pharbitis*, family Convolvulaceae. *P. purpurea* (synonym *Ipomoea purpurea*) is the ann. M. G. of tropical America, with funnel-shaped flowers of various colours; *P.* × *imperialis* is the Jap. M. G., and *P. learii*, the Blue Dawn Flower, with bright blue blooms. The seeds of certain varieties induce hallucinatory effects. See CONVOLVULUS.

'Morning Post', prominent Conservative penny daily, founded 1772 as the rival of the celebrated *Morning Chronicle* (*see under* NEWSPAPERS). It was notable for court news and social gossip. Charles Lamb, Samuel Taylor Coleridge, Robert Southey, Wordsworth and Sir James Mackintosh were famous contributors. During the Boer War it gained a tremendous vogue from the messages of its war correspondent, Winston Churchill. Later, however, the social and political outlook of the *M. P.* was shared only by a rapidly declining section of newspaper readers and the paper appeared for the last time on 30 Sept 1937. It was amalgamated with the *Daily Telegraph* (q.v.) the following day.

'Morning Star', until 1966 called the *Daily Worker*, newspaper founded by the Communist Party in 1930. In 1945 it was taken over by a co-operative society specially formed for this purpose: the People's Press Printing Society Ltd, which has a membership of about 30,000 individual members and 900 trade union, Co-operative and Communist Party organisations. Since 1952 it has been pub. by the People's Press Printing Society Ltd.

Morny, Charles Auguste Louis Joseph, Duc de (1811–65), Fr. politician, *b.* Paris, the illegitimate son of Hortense Bonaparte. He was a staunch supporter of Napoleon III, co-operated in the *coup d'état* and became minister of the interior. He was president of the *Corps législatif* (1854–65) and ambas. to Russia (1856–7).

Moro, Aldo (1916–), It. politician, educ. at Bari Univ. He entered politics after the Second World War as a Christian Democrat. He was minister of justice 1955–7, minister of education 1957–9, and has been prime minister since Dec. 1963.

Moro (van Dashorst), Antonio, or **Sir Anthony More** (*c..* 1519–75), Dutch painter, *b.* Utrecht. He studied under Titian in Italy during 1550–1, and in 1552 visited Spain. In 1553 he came to England as painter to Queen Mary, remaining till her death in 1558, when he entered the service of Philip II of Spain at Madrid. In 1568 he returned to the Netherlands and settled at Antwerp. He was a popular and internationally successful painter of portraits, whence the varied forms of his name. *See* lives by H. Hymans, 1910, and G. Marlier, 1934; *also* M. J. Friedländer, *Altnederlandische Malerei*, 1936.

Morocco, (*El Maghreb el Aksa,* the farthest W.), largest of Barbary states, with a total area, according to current estimates, of about 172,000 sq. m. M. is a sovereign independent state, the head of which is King Hassan II. A constitutional monarchy with a parl. and cabinet system of gov. was estab. by 1957. But in 1965 the King proclaimed a state of emergency. He dissolved parliament and assumed the office of prime minister himself. Older estimates gave the area as 219,000-220,000 sq. m., the difference being explained by the uncertain S. boundary. M. is situated in the NW. corner of Africa, its N. coast being washed by the Mediterranean, and the W. by the Atlantic; the E. boundary faces Algeria, while the S. borders Sp. W. Africa, The country is traversed by sev. parallel ranges of the Atlas Mts, the highest point being Tizi-n-Tagharet (15,400 ft) in the Great Atlas. The main range is constituted by the Great Atlas; roughly parallel to but farther S. of it is the Anti-Atlas, or Saharan Atlas, following the general trend of the whole Atlas complex to the NE. From the S. flanks of the Anti-Atlas run torrents that irrigate long oases before losing themselves as wadis in the desert sands. N. of the Great Atlas is the Middle Atlas, which, in some parts, is well wooded, and is the haunt of the small lions of Barbary. The N. slopes of the ranges are for the most part well wooded, and between them lie well-watered and fertile plains, while the S. slopes are exposed to the dry winds of the desert, and are generally arid and desolate. Beyond the Atlas lies the desert, scored by the oasis valleys of the Draa and Sus. On the mts may be seen huge *kasbahs* or feudal strongholds, looking rather like the tall Arab buildings of San'a in the Yemen or other similar buildings in S. Arabia, and comparatively modern. They serve as outposts of imperial authority, and were built by Mulay Ismail, the most famous monarch of the present dynasty; later they became centres of resistance of local rulers. The rivs. flowing from the N. slopes of the Atlas are perennial and of great commercial value; the Muluya, with its trib. the Sharef, drains the NE. of the country and enters the Mediterranean after a course of 400 m.; the Sebou, by removal of a sandbank at its mouth in 1905, was found to be navigable as far as Fez (125 m.). Other rivs. are the Um-er-Rebiah (230 m.), the Tensift (190 m.), the Sus, the Ghir and the Draa, all flowing into the Atlantic. The other rivs. are lost in the sands of the desert. The Mediterranean coast is rocky, and contains many bays and inlets, including the bays of Allucemas, Tetuan and Tangier, the last-named containing the best harbour in M. The most northerly point is the peninsula of Ceuta, dominated by the Jeb-el-Musa and separated from Europe by the straits of Gibraltar. The Atlantic coast is low and sandy for the most part, the trade of the ports of Larache (El Arish), Rabat (with Salli), Casablanca, Mazagan, Safi and Mogador being greatly hampered by the lack of safe harbours. Casablanca is the chief port; Rabat has a good riv. harbour, but it is obstructed by a bar; Safi has only an open roadstead. The harbour of Tetuan on a riv. entering the Mediterranean requires to be cleared of sand; the Jeb-el-Musa or Ape's Hill dominates the promontory, and, with the rock of Gibraltar, was known to the ancients as the Pillars of Hercules, the W. gateway of the Mediterranean. Between 37° N. and 30° N. is the headland of Ghir, enclosing a bay and the port of Agadir, once known as the 'gate of the Sudan'. The climate of M. is generally good and healthy, especially on the W. coast, the country being sheltered there by the Atlas Mts from the hot winds of the desert. The extremes of temp. in Tangier and Mogador are, in the summer, 92°, in the winter, 37° (the temp. at Mogador generally ranges from 60° in Jan. to 75° in Aug.), with a rainy season between Nov and April; but the summer heat at the intermediate ports, Casablanca, Larache, Safi and others, is appreciably greater. The winter Mediterranean coast is drier and less temperate, while in the interior it is intensely hot in summer.

Population and towns. The native pop. consists mainly of Islamite Berbers, known locally as Amazigh, who live mainly in the mts, and Arabs dating from the invasions of 700 years ago, who now inhabit the plains. These stocks have to some extent intermingled with each other and with people of Negroid descent. Moors, or mixed Berber-Arab descent, inhabit the tns. In the mountainous regions of the S., as in the N. Rif, the people are pure Berbers and follow their own laws and customs. The S. Berbers are pastoralists. The Arabic-speaking people of the plains are fairly homogeneous, rather similar to the 'Arab' pop of E. Barbary. The Negroid admixture is palpable everywhere in M. except in the mountainous regions. Some of the Sherifian families (i.e. those claiming descent from the prophet) are almost blond. N. Africa contains nearly two-thirds or nearly 34,000,000 of the speakers of the Arabic language, and of these some 7,000,000 are in M.; but a considerable proportion of the pop. is bilingual in Arabic and Berber, though some Moroccans know no Arabic. Berber or Shilkah is the language of the mt dists; but Arabic of the tns and plains. From 1912 the European element greatly increased owing to the influx of French settlers, and a further marked increase occurred in the early years of the Second World War owing to the influx of refugees from France, whilst M. was in effect also used as the camp for as large a number of Fr. troops as could be transported there.

Following the recognition of M. as a sovereign state during the early months of 1956 (by France on 2 Mar. and by the U.K. on 10 May), the former Fr., Sp. and international zones (Tangier) ceased to exist. However, in both the former Fr. and Sp. zones large numbers of European nationals continue to live. In 1964 the total pop. was estimated at 13,100,000. About 40 per cent are Arabs, 25 per cent are Berbers and 20 per cent are Moors. There are about 400,000 Europeans. The pop. of the prin. tns in 1963 were: Casablanca, 682,388 (Europeans 134,690); Marrakesh, 215,312. (12,316); Fez 174,392 (15,758); Rabat, 156,209 (40,747); Meknès, 140,380 (21,283); Oujia, 80,456 (27,202); Safi, 56,751 (3876); Port Lyautey, 55,905 (8868); Sale, 46,582 (2230); Mazagan, 34,871 (2583); Mogador, 22,291 (1277).

Casablanca was transformed in 2 years from a collection of hovels into a great modern tn with a splendid port; Meknès is also a relatively modern city situated around the remains of a large flimsy imperial palace built to rival Versailles by an 18th cent. sultan. Fez, Marrakesh and Rabat are also fine tns. The reason why the former Fr. zone of M. can boast such fine modern cities is that Lyautey (q.v.), when virtually dictator of M., used large credits drawn on the military budget for development, unhampered by parl. control, though these achievements were purchased at the price of much indebtedness and the domination of such great financial concerns as the Banque de Paris et des Pays Bas, which once directly or indirectly controlled much of the economic life of the protectorate. The prin. tns of the former Sp. zone (with their pop. figures in 1950) are Tetuán (80,732), Larache (41,917), Alcazarquivir (31,919), Arcila (13,763), Villa Nador (23,817), Villa Sanjuro (10,725).

Production and industry. Before the advent of Fr. influence the gov. of M. was fanatical, holding all Christian nations in contempt and aversion. Foreign commerce was, therefore, unsought and the exportation of valuable commodities, e.g. esparto grass and grain, was discouraged by high export duties, thereby preventing the fertility of the soil from being greatly utilised. There were no railways, no wheeled transport and no internal navigation. All goods were borne by camels or other beasts of burden, and the only ports open to European commerce were Tangier and Mogador. But great changes followed on European interven-

tion, coupled with the natural fertility of the soil, and a great many farms have been sold to European settlers who are developing agriculture by modern methods. In the former Fr. zone agriculture is the leading industry, producing wheat, barley, maize and other cereals, linseed, beans, chick-peas, esparto grass, cumin, coriander, birdseed and hemp. The fruit-bearing trees of the N. slopes of the Atlas produce many fruits, particularly almonds, grapes and olives, and also figs, walnuts, oranges, lemons, plums, apricots and dates. The 'citrus' or gum sandarach-tree and the argan-tree are found near Mogador. Other trees grown are cork, cedar and oak. The palmetto is widely grown for its vegetable fibre, and the tizra-tree for its tanning bark. Millions of gallons of wine are produced. Wheat, barley and chick-peas are grown in the Tangier area. The mineral resources of M. are known to be great, the chief mineral exploited being phosphates, the output of which is under a state monopoly. More than 10 million tons of phosphates were exported in 1964. There are deposits of coal, iron ore, lead, zinc and, in smaller quantities, copper, antimony, manganese, gypsum, cobalt, zinc, petroleum and beryl. Iron ore mined in the Rif is exported from Melilla in the former Sp. zone.

The fauna of M. includes the leopard, bear, hyaena and wild pig; the bustard, partridge and water-fowl abound; the dromedary and horse are bred extensively, as also are cattle, sheep, mules, asses and goats. There are abundant fish off the coasts, and the fishing centres near Casablanca and at Fedhala have a preserving industry. The manufs. include leather, pottery, textiles, carpets, embroideries, copper and brass goods, silver filigree, slippers and shawls. Various miscellaneous industries have grown up in recent years for local consumption, including flour-mills, cement factories, soap and candle factories, and breweries. The trade of M. is now chiefly with France, Great Britain, the U.S.A. and Spain. The chief exports are phosphates, manganese ore, lead, zinc, citrus fruits, wheat, fish, wool, palmetto fibre, hides, skins, eggs, cattle, sheep, pigs, barley, almonds, linseed, gums and Tafilet dates. Some native manufs., such as fez caps and leather, are exported to various parts of Africa. The chief imports are cotton, chemical products, building materials, sugar, tea, hardware, petrol, motor vehicles, coal, edible oils, flour, semolina and wine. In the former Sp. zone iron ore, lead, cork, skins and vegetable fibre are produced; the chief exports from Tangier are preserved fish, skins, M. leather and eggs. Total exports in 1964 amounted to £156,800,900; imports totalled £166,400,000.

Communications. There are about 1100 m. of normal-gauge railways in operation. The Tangier–Fez full-gauge line affords through service between Tangier and the chief tns of the former Fr. zone, and a normal-gauge line connects Fez with the Algerian frontier at Oujda. Casablanca is joined by rail with the Algerian border and Tunisia, and with Marrakesh by 2 branch lines, 1 eastward via the Khouribga phosphate mines, the other to Safi and Oujda. The existing railways in the former Sp. zone are Ceuta to Tetuán, Larache to Alcazar, and Nador to Tistutin. There are about 10,000 m. of first-class roads and about 20,000 m. of second class. There are submarine telegraph cables from Tangier to Cadiz, Tarifa and Oran, and wireless stations at Tangier, Rabat, Casablanca and Mogador. Telephones are in use in all the prin. tns, which are connected with the European systems through Ceuta. There are regular air services, through Tangier and Gibraltar, between M. and tns in France, Spain and other European and Arabian countries.

Religion, education and justice. The religion of the country is a strict form of Mohammedanism, much purer than that practised in Turkey and Persia. The bulk of the native pop. is illiterate. There are numerous Koranic schools which give a very elementary education, and a number of higher schools attached to mosques. The most notable is the Kairoween Univ. at Fez, which has high repute in the Islamic world. In the former Fr. zone education on European lines was given in the Fr. schools, and schools were provided by the protectorate gov. for Muslim natives. There are state schools in the chief tns of the former Sp. zone and certain Hispano-Arabic schools for natives. Native justice is administered by religious courts, and the pashas or *caidis* (q.v.) also have a wide jurisdiction in both civil and criminal cases. Courts of appeal have been set up at Rabat corresponding to these jurisdictions. Rabbinical courts have jurisdiction in cases on the personal status of Jews.

Armed Forces. The army strength is about 35,000 organised into 18 infantry battalions, 1 paratroop battalion, an air-portable light motorised group (equivalent to 2 or 3 battalions), a composite armoured battalion (with about 100 tanks) and about 5 batteries of artillery. There is a small air force equipped with Russian MiG 15 and 17 fighters.

History. The recorded hist. of M. begins in the 8th cent. with the introduction of Islam and the estab. of the dynasty of a branch of Mohammed's family, the Idrîsîs, contemporary with Haroun al-Raschid. A succession of dynasties, of which the most famous were the Almoravides (q.v.) and Almohades (q.v.), ended in that of Filali, originally Sherifs of Tafilet, which reigned from 1546 to the present day. What brought the Sherifs to power as rulers of M. was their fight against Portugal, which ended in 1578 with their conquest of all M. except Mazagan. During the Fr. conquest of Algeria M. adopted an anti-Fr. policy by helping and, later, sheltering the formidable Abd-el-Kadir; but with his defeat and capture at Isly (1843) Franco-Moroccan relations were peaceful during the second half of the 19th cent. In 1878, despite Brit. objections, a Fr. military mission was stationed at Fez. England gave France a free hand in M., and a few months later France signed an agreement with Spain, which defined their respective

spheres of influence. In 1906 an international conference was convened at Algeciras to define the interests of the various powers, and to establish order in M. by means of an organised police force. This conference laid down the principle of the 'open door' in M. In July 1911 the Ger. gunboat *Panther* anchored in Agadir harbour ostensibly to protect Ger. interests. After protracted negotiations between France and Germany the latter left Agadir and relinquished all claims to the country in return for compensation in the Congo. In 1912 the Franco-Sp. treaty of Fez divided the country into Fr. and Sp. spheres of influence or protectorates; but the arrangement was not accepted by the various tribes, and the Sp. zone became an arena of contention and guerrilla warfare, which quickly involved the Fr. area as well.

The Fr. protectorate was eventually pacified due to the efforts of Lyautey, who also reorganised the country on more modern lines and developed its resources. Oil was discovered at Jebel Tselfat in 1934. An Anglo-Sp.-Fr. Convention of Dec. 1923 defined the status of Tangier. (For the hist. of the former international zone, *see* TANGIER.) There was a rebellion under Abd-el-Krim in the Sp. zone, 1923–6. The Sp. zone was the base of Franco's military rising against the Sp. rep. in 1935, and Moroccan troops, known as *Moros*, played a great part on the nationalist side.

In Nov. 1942 a large Anglo-Amer. force occupied Fr. M. and Algiers and thereby began the first phase of the N. African campaign for the control of the Mediterranean. At Casabalanca, 14–24 Jan. 1943, Roosevelt and Churchill arrived at general agreement on broad strategic plans for the conduct of the war against the Axis (*see* CASABLANCA CONFERENCE).

In Mar. 1956 France and the Sultan of M. terminated the treaty of Fez; the Sp. protectorate ended, 7 April, and on 29 Oct. the international status of Tangier was abolished. Thus by the end of 1956 M. was a united and independent state, though her economic and cultural ties with France and Spain remained close. In Aug. 1957 the Sultan changed his title to that of king. Mohammed V *d.* in 1961 and was succeeded by his son, Hassan II (q.v.), who has played a prominent part in his country's politics. A new constitution, in 1962, made M. a constitutional monarchy, though the king still retained the final word on all decisions. The last Amer. bases in M., estab. at the end of the Second World War, were withdrawn in 1963. Modernisation and industrialisation have proceeded rapidly since independence and M. plays a significant and moderating part in pan-Arab and pan-African affairs. In June 1965 Hassan II declared a state of emergency and appointed himself premier. This followed prolonged left-wing agitation and disturbances. The disappearance in France and presumed death of Ben Barka, the Moroccan left-wing leader, in 1965, in which some Moroccan ministers were alleged to be implicated, led to strained relations

between M. and France.
See D. E. Ashford, *Political Change in Morocco*, 1961; R. Landau, *Morocco Independent*, 1961; C. F. Stewart, *The Economy of Morocco 1912-62*, 1965. (*See Plate*.)

Morocco, see MARRAKESH.

Moron (Gk *mōros*, stupid), term applied to the highest grade of mentally defective person, those whose 'mental age' is somewhere between 7 and 12 years. The M. is able to transact work requiring rational judgment, but in social matters he is largely dependent on the help or guidance of other people. Such mental defectives may often be educ. in special schools for simple employment, where they can be kept under observation with respect to their social and moral qualities. See MENTAL DEFICIENCY ACTS; MENTAL TESTS.

Morón de la Frontera (anct **Arumi**), Sp. tn in the prov. of Sevilla, with a ruined Moorish castle and a fine Gothic church. There are marble quarries, mines and mineral springs near by, and the tn is known for its cakes. Pop. 25,800.

Moroni, Giambattista (1510–78), It. painter, b. Bondo, Bergamo; studied under Moretto (q.v.). He was especially successful in portrait-painting, and was praised by Titian. Five of his works are in the National Gallery, London, including the incomparable 'Tailor'.

Morosini, famous Venetian family. Among the most famous members were *Domenico M.* (doge, 1148–56), who recaptured Pola and other Istrian tns from the Dalmatian corsairs; *Marino M.* (doge, 1249–52), who introduced the Inquisition into Venice; *Michele M.* (doge, 1382), a celebrated financier; *Andrea M.* (1558–1618), who became histriographer to the rep. (1598), was one of the Council of Ten, continued Paolo Paruta's *Annali Veneti* and wrote a hist. of Venice (1521–1615, pub. 1623) and other works; and *Francesco M.* (1618–94), a great sea captain, who defended Candia against the Turks, 1667–8, and took Athens in 1684. He became doge in 1688.

Morpeth, municipal bor. and mrkt tn of Northumberland, England, 14 m. N. of Newcastle. There are remains of a medieval castle and an anct chantry and clock tower. Newminster Abbey is 12th cent. and the par. church of St Mary is 14th cent. The chief occupation is market gardening, and M. has an iron foundry and a thriving cattle market. Pop. 12,430.

Morphia, popular name for the alkaloid morphine, $C_{17}H_{19}O_3N$. Morphine is contained in opium or the juice of poppyheads (*Papaver somniferum*). The opium extract is boiled with milk of lime and the product filtered. Morphine is contained in the filtrate, all other alkaloids being precipitated. After digesting the filtrate with ammonium chloride to remove all trace of lime, the separate morphine is collected and recrystallised from boiling alcohol. Morphine forms colourless prisms with 1 molecule of water of crystallisation; it is only slightly soluble in water and in cold alcohol, and on this account is used in medicine in the form of its salts, particularly the hydrochloride. Morphine is the most effective anodyne known to science, relieving pain and producing sleep either when administered by the mouth or injected hypodermically. One grain of the hydrochloride may be a fatal dose, but persons habituated to its use are capable of taking more than 15 grains a day. The effects of the M. habit are moral degeneration, disturbance of secretions, lowering of physical and mental powers. The habit is most difficult to break, owing to the moral weakness of the victim; the sudden withdrawal of the drug is highly dangerous, and the only cure is the gradual diminution of the dose under circumstances which render it impossible for the patient to obtain more than his allowance. Various derivatives of morphine also find application in medicine, particularly diacetylmorphine hydrochloride (heroin, q.v.), which acts as a depressant to the respiratory centres and is used to relieve cough; but as an analgesic it is slightly inferior to morphine. The chief uses of M. are for relief of pain, the procuring of sleep (when sleeplessness is caused by pain), the checking of intestinal peristalsis, the arrest of haemorrhage and the relief of muscular spasm. M. is invaluable in the treatment of shock and is extensively used in this condition as it relieves pain, if present, calms the patient and arrests haemorrhage. Side effects of M. are nausea, vomiting and constipation. Two other related alkaloids occur in opium: codeine (*see* CODEIA or CODEINE) and thebaine, the former being a mild narcotic, the latter a violent tetanising poison. The chemical constitution of M. was finally estimated in 1925 by Sir Robert Robinson.

Morphology concerns itself only with the analysis of any organism into its parts, and is not directly concerned with the life which produced, or is possessed by, that organism. Thus M. is that sub-science of biology which deals with the study of form or structure, as opposed to physiology, which is concerned with the functioning of those parts. Expressed in another way, M. is the 'statics' and physiology the 'dynamics' of the organism. The scientific study of the form of an organism cannot be completed merely by description. Such phenomena as those of the development of form in the individual, and the presence of similar forms in different individuals, must be considered before the M. of an organism can be elucidated. Nor in fact can structure be fully interpreted without reference to function, for all aspects of biology are inextricably interrelated; in particular M. merges into comparative anatomy.

Corresponding parts developing in similar ways may have very different ultimate forms and functions. It is this aspect of M. which involves the recognition of homology as distinct from analogy. Petals and foliage leaves of delphinium, the human arm and the wing of a bird are examples of homologous organs. The leaf-like stem of *Ruscus aculeatus* and the leaf of smilax, insects' and birds' wings, are merely analogous, for their modes of development and the relation they bear to associated parts are entirely different. Although homology does not necessarily imply relationship, Haeckel and Gegenhaur regarded it as indicating common descent, and this view is held by most biologists. That branch of M. which traces descent by means of homologous characters Haeckel distinguished as phylogeny. As a result of embryological homologies, discovered by von Baer, Haeckel formulated his 'Biogenetic Law of Descent', generally spoken of as the 'Recapitulation Theory', which states that the development of the individual organism recapitulates the course of its evolution. This theory is now accepted with considerable reservation since many features of an embryo obviously have no evolutionary significance. Thus M., from its apparently insignificant beginnings, has developed into the keystone of evolutionary biology. The analysis of structure into its finest limits is included in histology (q.v.). For a brief hist. of M. and its relation to other sciences, see BIOLOGY. See also ANATOMY; CELL; CLASSIFICATION, PLANT; EMBRYOLOGY; FISH; HOMOLOGY; INVERTEBRATES; MAMMALS; PHYSIOLOGY; REPTILES; TAXONOMY; VERTEBRATES. See E. S. Russell, Form and Function: a Contribution to the History of Animal Morphology, 1916; D'Arcy W. Thompson, On Growth and Form, 1917, 1942; J. T. Saunders and S. M. Manton, A Manual of Practical Vertebrate Morphology, 1931; G. Müller, Die Gestaltfrage in der Literaturwissenschaft und Goethes Morphologie, 1944; Sir A. Keith, Human Embryology and Morphology, 1949; A. Portman, Animal Forms and Patterns, 1952.

Morphy, Paul (1837–84), Amer. chess player. See CHESS.

Morris, Sir Edward Patrick (1859–1935), 1st Baron, Newfoundland statesman, b. St John's; educ. at Bonaventure College, St John's, and univ. of Ottawa. He sat in Parliament for St John's, 1885–1919. In 1905 he became leader of the People's party. Attorney-general and administrator of justice, 1902–7. Premier of Newfoundland, 1909–18. P.C., 1911. He was a member of the Brit. War Cabinet, Feb.–June 1917. He ed. the Newfoundland law reports, 1830–1905, which are cited as Morris's Reports.

Morris, Gouverneur (1752–1816), Amer. diplomat and statesman, b. New York. Admitted to the Bar in 1771. He had joined the patriotic party by 1775, and sat in the Continental Congress, 1778–9. He became assistant financier to Robert Morris (1781–5) after publishing a series of essays on Amer. finances in the Pennsylvania Packet, 1780, and practically founded the national coinage. M. helped to draw up and revise the document setting forth the U.S. Constitution (1787). He then travelled in France, England and Germany, becoming minister to France from 1792 to 1794. He was elected U.S. senator for New York (1800–3) and chairman of the Erie Canal Commission (1810). See Anne Cowley Morris (ed.), The Diary and Letters of Gouverneur Morris, 1888. See also life by T. Roosevelt, 1888, and H. Swiggett, Extraordinary Mr Morris, 1952.

Morris, Sir Lewis (1833–1907), poet, b. Carmarthen, great-grandson of the Welsh poet, Lewis M. (d. 1765). He graduated from Oxford in 1855, and was called to the Bar at Lincoln's Inn in 1861, practising till 1881. Always interested in higher education in Wales, he became deputy-chancellor of the univ. of Wales, and served on the governing bodies of the 3 Welsh colleges. His works include Songs of Two Worlds, 1871–5, The Epic of Hades, 1876–7 (which went through numerous eds.), Gwen, a Drama in Monologue, 1879, The Ode of Life, 1880, Songs Unsung, 1883, Songs of Britain, 1887 (containing odes on the queen's jubilee and the foundation of the Imperial Institute), Idylls and Lyrics, 1896, The Harvest-tide, 1901, and The New Rambler: from Desk to Platform, 1905. M. was made a knight of the order of the Saviour (of Greece) in 1879, and awarded a jubilee medal in 1887.

Morris, William (1834–1896), poet, artist and Socialist, b. Walthamstow and educ. Marlborough and at Exeter College, Oxford. After being articled as an architect he was for some years a painter, and then joined in founding the decorating firm in which Rossetti, Burne-Jones and other artists were partners. He was one of the originators of the Oxford and Cambridge Magazine, to which he contributed poems, tales and essays, and in 1858 he pub. The Defence of Guenevere and other Poems. The Life and Death of Jason followed in 1867, The Earthly Paradise in 1868–70 and Love is Enough in 1875. In the last mentioned year he made a trans. in verse of Virgil's Aeneid. Travels in Iceland led to the writing of Three Northern Love Stories and the epic of Sigurd the Volsung, 1876. His trans. of the Odyssey in verse appeared in 1887. A series of prose romances include the House of Wolfings, 1889, and The Well at the World's End, 1896. A leader of the Socialist movement, he wrote The Dream of John Ball, 1888, and the utopian News from Nowhere, 1891, as Socialist propaganda. In 1890 M. started the Kelmscott Press, for which he designed type and decorations. For his subjects as a writer he drew upon classic and Gothic models alike. A lifelong crusader against ugliness, he was inspired by the love of beauty for its own sake; his poetry is rich and musical, and he has a power of description which makes his pictures live and glow, but his narratives sometimes suffer from length and slowness of movement. See B. I. Evans, William Morris and his Poetry, 1925; F. L. Lucas, Eight Victorian Poets, 1930; E. and Stephanie Godwin, Warrior Bard, 1948; R. P. Arnot, William Morris, the Man and the Myth, 1964.

Morris, William Richard, see NUFFIELD, 1ST VISCOUNT.

Morris (Morrice, Mourice, Mores) Dance, O.E. dance probably of Moorish origin and most likely introduced into England by Eleanor of Castile, queen of Edward I. In Henry VIII's reign it formed an essential part of most rustic and parochial festivities. When later it was associated with the May games, the dancers frequently represented characters of the Robin Hood legend, especially Maid Marian and Friar

Tuck. The hobby-horse was at one time a prominent figure in this dance. It was suppressed by the Puritans and never generally revived. *See* C. Sharp and H. MacIlwaine, *The Morris Book*, 1907; J. H. Crampton, *Folk Dance Book*, 1940; V. Alford, *Peeps at English Folk Dances*, 1940; D. Kennedy, *England's Dances: Folk Dancing Today and Yesterday*, 1948; and also *The Journal of the English Folk Dance Society. See* DANCING. (*See Plate: Dancing.*)

Morris Motors Limited, important motor-car manufacturing company, which was registered 29 June 1926 as having acquired the businesses of previous companies of the name of Hollick & Pratt Ltd and Osberton Radiators Ltd. The business is the outcome of the remarkable capacity, inventiveness and organising skill of its chairman, Lord Nuffield (q.v.) who, from small beginnings at a little workshop he started at the age of 17, developed the great factory at Cowley, Oxon. The company controls Morris Commercial Cars Ltd, Nuffield Exports Ltd, Nuffield Metal Products Ltd, Nuffield Tools and Gauges Ltd, Riley Motors Ltd, the M.G. Car Co. Ltd, The Nuffield Press Ltd, the S.U. Carburettor Co. Ltd and Wolseley Motors Ltd. Merged in 1952 with Austin Motor Co., forming the Brit. Motor Corporation (q.v.). *See* AUSTIN, HERBERT. (*See Plate: Motor Cars.*)

Morrison, Arthur (1863–1945), novelist and writer on art, *b.* Kent. His best stories are *Tales of Mean Streets*, 1894, *A Child of the Jago*, 1896, *The Dorrington Deed-box*, 1897, *The Hole in the Wall*, 1902, *Green Eye of Goona*, 1904, *Green Ginger*, 1909, *Fiddle o' Dreams*, 1933, and a series of detective stories centred on the fictional character, Martin Hewitt, investigator. He wrote also *The Painters of Japan*, 1911, and other books on oriental art. He collaborated in the plays *That Brute Simmons*, 1904, *The Dumb Cake*, 1907, and *A Stroke of Business*, 1907.

Morrison, Robert (1782–1834), Brit. missionary, founder of Protestant missions in China, *b.* Morpeth. He studied in England from 1801 to 1807, when he was sent to Canton by the London Missionary Society. In 1809 he became translator to the E. India Co. He estab. an Anglo-Chinese college at Malacca in 1818. He trans. the Bible into Chinese (1809–19) and compiled a *Dictionary of the Chinese Language*, 1915–23, *Chinese Grammar*, 1815, and *Chinese Miscellany*, 1825.

Morrison, William Shepherd, *see* DUNROSSIL, 1ST VISCOUNT.

Morrison of Lambeth, Herbert Stanley, Baron, (1888–1965), politician, *b.* Brixton. He was educ. at an elementary school in London, and in 1915 he became secretary of the London Labour party, holding office until 1940. Entering local gov. M. was mayor of Hackney, 1919-20, and, in 1922, became Socialist leader in the L.C.C.; an alderman from 1931, he was leader of the council from 1939 to 1940. His first appearance in national politics was in 1923, when he became Labour M.P. for S. Hackney. He lost this seat in 1924, but regained it 5 years later, becoming minister of transport in Macdonald's minority

gov. until the Labour defeat of 1931. Concentrating upon local gov. M. was responsible for the legislation setting up the London Passenger Transport Board. Returning to Parliament in 1935 he became minister of supply in the wartime Coalition Gov. in 1940, but soon exchanged that post for the Home Office and the Ministry of Home Security. From 1942 to 1945 he was a member of the War Cabinet. In the third Labour gov. of 1945 M. became leader of the House of Commons and lord president of the council; from Mar. to Oct. 1951 he was foreign secretary. From 1951 to 1955 M. was deputy leader of the Opposition; he resigned from this position after standing unsuccessfully for the post of leader of the parl. Labour party after Attlee's resignation. He was created a life peer, 1959. His pubs. include *Looking Ahead*, 1943. *The Peaceful Revolution*, 1949, a collection of speeches, *Government and Parliament*, 1954; *Herbert Morrison, An Autobiography*, 1960. *See* life by M. Edelman, 1948.

Morrow, Dwight Whitney (1873–1931), Amer. diplomat and banker. He was a member of J. P. Morgan & Co. from 1914 to 1927. He was ambas. to Mexico from 1927 to 1930 and was successful in bringing to an end the tension between Mexico and the U.S.A. He was one of the U.S. delegates to the London Naval Conference in 1930 and, later, was elected to the U.S. Senate as a Republican from New Jersey. *See* life by H. Nicolson, 1935.

Mors, is. of Denmark, off the W. coast of Jutland, in the Lim Fjord. Chief tn is Nykøbing. Length 22m.; area 140 sq. m.; the population is 27,000.

Morse, Samuel Finley Breese (1791–1872), Amer. inventor of telegraphic system, *b.* Charlestown, Massachusetts. In 1811 he came to England to study art under West. He returned to America in 1815, and was first president of the National Academy of Design, New York, 1826–1842. He also studied chem. and electricity, and in 1832 conceived the idea of a magnetic telegraph. The original M. code (*see* TELEGRAPHY) was devised in 1837 with Alfred Vail and introduced by M. for use with a self-recording telegraph. In 1843 Congress granted $30,000 for an experimental telegraph line between Washington and Baltimore, and M.'s system was soon widely adopted.

Morse, *see* WALRUS.

Morse Code, *see* TELEGRAPHY.

Mortality. *The law of mortality.* In actuarial calculations the law which, founded on the average M. for any given number of years, determines the proportion of persons who die in any assigned period of life or interval of age out of a given number who enter upon the same interval.

Bills of mortality. Abstracts from par. registers giving the number of persons that have died in any par. during certain periods of time, and denominated (according to the period taken) weekly, monthly or yearly bills. They originated in London in the 16th cent., in a time of plague, and have been pub. regularly from shortly after that year till the present time. *See also* BILL OF MORTALITY.

Mortar, material used for jointing bricks. Originally bricks were laid dry; later they were laid in mud slurry. Eventually M. was made of lime putty and sand. Lime putty was made by slaking lime, that is placing hydraulic lime in water and continuously agitating it until a white putty is formed. This is then mixed with sand to form a M. With the production of cement, a stronger M. was produced by mixing cement, lime and sand in given proportions.

As lime is susceptible to damp it often causes staining, efflorescence and free lime, that is natural lime containing a high proportion of magnesium oxide, which can expand thus causing the wall to disintegrate.

Lime used for M. today should be non-hydraulic—i.e. well burnt or complying to B.S. 890. As lime is very bulky and a messy material, materials have been developed to obviate the use of lime. These materials usually take the form of liquid additives which when mixed with water, sand and cement still give M. its workability. These additives are basically common soap. In addition to additives, most cement companies produce a cement which has a plasticiser incorporated during manuf.

Lime M. should never be used externally or below ground level. Lime sand M.s are suitable for external use above ground, providing the lime is slaked and the atmosphere does not contain too much sulphur. Cement M.s are used for underground work in exposed conditions and on walls where high load bearing capacity is required. The method of finishing the M. to provide a presentable finish is called pointing (q.v.). Additives may be made to make the M. more workable, completely frost resistant or coloured.

Mortar, short piece of ordnance with a very wide smooth bore, the width of which in early pieces equalled the length of the M. It was formerly employed against forts during sieges owing to its power to develop high angle fire. Before the First World War M.s were heavily constructed and unsuitable for field work, but during the war a light portable pattern was invented (the Stokes M.) which could develop an accurate destructive fire at short range. In modern warfare such a weapon is invaluable against hostile machine-gun emplacements, snipers' posts or any construction in the front line which cannot be destroyed by rifle fire. As M.s must be well to the front to be of service, their ammunition supply created some difficulty. In the Second World War they were extensively used as an infantry support weapon. Besides the 2-in M., throwing a bomb about the size of a hand-grenade, Brit. battalions in the Second World War included in their support company a M. platoon armed with 3-in. M.s which were carried in Bren-carriers. As pieces of this calibre could conveniently be broken down into loads for one pack animal, they were extensively used in mt warfare. Their high trajectory permitted their use in wooded country where the problem of crest clearance could not be surmounted by light artillery at short range, and on the N. sectors of the Russian front they tended to replace the light field gun as a close-support weapon. As a result of experience by both sides in this theatre heavier models were developed, of which the Finnish Tampela (120 mm.) M. was one of the first. This and similar weapons up to 150 mm. had a round instead of a square baseplate, with detachable wheels, and could be towed like a field-gun, but muzzle foremost. Owing to their smooth bore and less complicated recoil mechanism, M.s could be more speedily and cheaply manuf. than field guns, and were also well suited for transport by air. In the Ger. Army, handicapped by its insufficient estab. of artillery, M.s tended more and more to replace the infantry support gun, especially in airborne divs.

Mortar and Pestle. Mortars are vessels in which substances are ground to fragments or pulverised by beating with an instrument called the pestle. They are made of various substances according to their use. Glass, agate, flint, porphyry, stoneware or cast iron is generally used. Glass and stoneware mortars are used in the laboratory for analytical work, agate is used when the substance is to be reduced to a very fine powder, whereas iron mortars are employed for crushing coarser substances.

Mortara, It tn in Lombardy (q.v.), 20 m. WNW. of Pavia. The Austrians gained a victory over the Sardinians here in 1849 (*see* ITALY, *History*). Pop. 10,900.

Mortehoe, see WOOLACOMBE.

Mortenson, Norma Jean, see MONROE, MARILYN.

Mortgage, transfer of land or other property as security for the repayment of a loan. It is to be distinguished both from a hypothecation and a pawn or pledge. In hypothecation the creditor has rights over but does not take possession of the hypothecated property of his debtor. This latter term in Eng. law is practically confined to a master's (q.v.) power to raise money on his ship or cargo for necessary purposes (*see also* BOTTOMRY), but is a common form of security in Scots law (*see* HYPOTHEC). In the case of a pledge of goods, possession is given to the pawnee, and herein it differs from a true M. of chattels by bill of sale (q.v.). Under a bill of sale to secure a debt, the property in, but not the possession of, the scheduled goods and chattels passes to the grantee, subject either to a condition cancelling the transfer on performance of the condition to repay the loan with interest, or to a proviso enabling the grantor (debtor) to redeem his property by such payment and at once to have it reconveyed to him.

Mortgage of land. A *legal* as distinct from an *equitable* M. is created by a deed (q.v.) charging the land comprised in it to the mortgagee (i.e. the borrower) subject to the mortgagor's 'equity of redemption', a right to have his land back again on payment of the principal money and interest. Most M.s include an express covenant (q.v.) on the part of the mortgagor personally to repay the loan, but such covenant is obviously only useful where the mortgagor has money with which to repay, and, generally speaking, the mortgagee sues on it only if the land becomes less valuable and insufficient to secure the loan. The rights of the mortgagee are: (1) To demand repayment in accordance with the terms of the M. If the mortgagee gains no satisfaction he may sue the mortgagor for any principal and/or interest monies which may be outstanding. The mortgagee sues on the covenant to pay, if there is one, otherwise he sues as if in an action of debt. (2) To enter into possession of the land at any time; though usually the mortgagor is left in possession pending the necessity of realising the security. In any case, if the mortgagee goes into possession he will be called upon to account strictly not only for the rents and profits received by him, but for all he might have received if he had exercised the utmost care. When in possession he may make building leases for 999 years and agric. or occupational leases for 50 years. If he remain in possession for 12 years without acknowledging the title of the mortgagor, he becomes absolutely entitled to the land (*see* LIMITATIONS, STATUTES OF). (3) To apply, after the expiration of the term for repayment, to the court for a *foreclosure* order, i.e. an order fixing a further period (generally 6 months) within which the mortgagor must pay the principal, interest and costs, or be for ever foreclosed of his equity of redemption. (4) To sell the land and out of the proceeds to recoup himself the costs of the sale, the M. debt and interest, which right is less stringent than a foreclosure because the mortgagor is entitled to the surplus proceeds. But there is no right to sell unless *either* (*a*) the mortgagee has given 3 months' notice in writing demanding payment and stating his intention to sell if the money be not paid; or (*b*) some interest is 2 months in arrear; or (*c*) there has been some breach of the covenants in the deed other than that for the repayment of the loan, e.g. to repair or insure the M. property. A right to sell is implied in a M. deed, and therefore no order of court is required. (5) To appoint a receiver of the rents and profits to apply the same in payment of debt and interest. The mortgagor's rights are: (1) If in possession to make building and occupation leases for 999 and 50 years respectively. (2) If he redeems, to get his land back free from all restrictions whatever. (3) If he remains in possession for 12 years without paying any part of the principal or interest, to ignore the mortgagee's rights. Any provision inserted in the M. to prevent redemption on payment or performance of the debt or obligation for which the security was given is termed a 'clog' or 'fetter' on the equity of redemption and is void. No agreement between mortgagor and mortgagee contained in the M. can make the M. irredeemable, and no contract at the time of the M. and as part of the M. transaction, or as one of the terms of the loan, can be valid if it provides that the mortgaged property shall become the absolute property of the mortgagee upon any event whatsoever. But an option of this kind is valid if

granted by an independent transaction after the date of the M. Redemption may, however, be postponed for a reasonable time where there is a corresponding provision for the continuance of the loan, and no circumstances exist which make the clause oppressive or unreasonable. The right of redemption continues unless and until by judgment for foreclosure, or the operation of the Limitation Act, 1939, the character of the creditor is changed for that of owner, or the mortgagor's interest is destroyed by the mortgagee exercising the power of sale. Thereupon, however, his equitable right to redeem arises, and foreclosure is the remedy by which that right is terminated. The right of a mortgagor to redeem on payment of principal and interest and costs was, until the changes made by the Law of Property Act, 1925, not a mere right, but an equitable *estate* or *interest* in the property. But his right or equity of redemption is no longer an equitable estate or interest. Under the present (i.e. since 1925) system of creating legal M.s the mortgagee takes only a term of years, leaving the legal freehold reversion expectant on the M. term in the mortgagor. Thus the mortgagor retains his legal freehold estate and he cannot at the same time have an equitable estate co-extensive with it. Hence instead of his equity of redemption constituting an equitable estate, it subsists only as a right in equity to redeem the property, this right being attached to his legal freehold estate (and similarly in the case of a M. of chattels).

Equitable Mortgages may be created by a demand that is not a deed or by word of mouth or by the conduct of the parties if that was their intention. Although there may have been no actual transfer of the M. a person who advances money for the purpose of paying it off, and whose money is thus applied, becomes an equitable assignee of the M. and is entitled to have it kept alive for his benefit. M.s of houses to which the Rent Acts apply are subject to restrictions under those Acts on the rate of interest and on the exercise of their remedies, including going into possession.

Attornment clauses are sometimes inserted in M.s. The mortgagor attorns or acknowledges himself to be a tenant from year to year of the mortgagee, usually at a nominal rent such as a peppercorn or sixpence. Formerly this was inserted because a speedy procedure was available to enable landlords to recover possession of the property from their tenants, and no such procedure was available for mere mortgagees. The attornment clauses enabled mortgagees to sue for possession as landlords. For many years it was considered that attornment clauses were an anachronism and served no useful purpose. But they were pronounced valid by the court of appeal in 1965, the court deciding that an attornment clause in a M. does create a tenancy although it does not create a relationship of landlord and tenant such as to attract the operation of the Agricultural Holdings Acts or those of the new Rent Restriction Acts. An attornment clause may assist the mortgagor as well as the mortgagee, e.g. where a M. contains covenants by a borrower for the benefit of the lender to use the mortgaged premises in a perpetual way (e.g. as a tied public house). An attornment clause will assist a lender to enforce restrictive covenants, as far as these are reasonable, against a successor in title of the original borrower. The doctrine of restraint of trade applies to an attornment clause contained in a M. See H. G. Hanbury and C. H. M. Waldock, *Law of Mortgages*, 1954.

Mortification (physiology), see GANGRENE.

Mortification, Scots legal term applied to lands given for charitable or public uses. In pre-Reformation times the term denoted land held by the Church in consideration of prayers and masses for the soul of the granter. M.s are now practically obsolete but still competent. The Court of Session has jurisdiction to control the management of the administration of M.s. M. is practically synonymous with Eng. Mortmain (q.v.).

Mortimer, Roger, 1st **Earl of March** (c. 1287–1330). In 1304 he succeeded his father, Edmund M., as lord of Wigmore, and in 1306 was knighted. In 1316 he was appointed lieutenant of Ireland, and in 1317 drove Bruce to Carrickfergus and defeated the Lacys. He became justiciar of Ireland in 1319, fought for his uncle, Roger M. of Chirk, to establish the independent power of the M.s, in Wales in 1320, and in 1322 was captured and sent to the Tower. He escaped to Paris in 1324, and became the lover and chief adviser of Queen Isabella. In 1327 he became justiciar of Wales. Later, in 1330, he was accused of treason and complicity in the death of Edward II, and other charges, and executed at Tyburn.

Mortlake, par. of the London borough of Richmond-upon-Thames, England, 6½ m. from central London. The church of St Mary the Virgin, founded 1348, rebuilt 1543, and often enlarged, contains memorials to Sir Philip Francis and Sir John Temple, besides many tombs of celebrities, notably of Dr John Dee, philosopher and astrologer. M. is the finishing point of the ann. boat race between Cambridge and Oxford Univs. Malting is the local industry.

Mortmain. An alienation of land in M. or *in mortua manu* denotes the transfer of land into the dead hand either of the Church or any other corporation (q.v.), and was so called from the fact that the immortality and other non-human attributes of corporations necessarily prevented the lands in their possession from ever being profitable either to the king or to the immediate feudal lords of those who had alienated them, because there was no possibility of escheat (q.v.), reliefs, wardships, marriages or any other feudal aids. The Statute of Mortmain, 1279, prohibited the transfer of lands or tenements 'in such a way that such lands or tenements should come into mortmain'. The learning on the subject of M. is almost as purely antiquarian as that of feudal aids, but is still of some practical importance from the fact that though the same

reasons do not now exist for prohibiting the conveyance of land to a corporation, and though there are numerous statutory provisions by which almost any corporation can hold land with or without a royal licence, the Mortmain Acts of 1279, 1391, 1888, are still in force. Early in the hist. of Eng. real property law, the conveyance of land was next to impossible, but even when most of the feudal restrictions on alienation had been abolished it still remained, and in the theory of the common law still remains, impossible for a corporation to purchase land without a licence. The only justification for such a prohibition at the present day is the objection to perpetuities, or, in other words, virtual withholding of land from the open market. But at the present day numerous corporations can hold lands in M. without either a licence from the Crown or the authorisation of a public or private Act of Parliament. Every registered joint-stock company (incorporated under the Companies Act, 1948) formed for the acquisition of gain may hold lands for the purposes of the business of the company; but no company formed to promote art, religion, science or charity, or for a non-lucrative purpose, can hold more than 2 ac. of land without the sanction of the Board of Trade. Charity trustees may be incorporated under the Charitable Trusts Acts, and may then hold lands without further licence. Under the Public Health Act, 1875, the Municipal Corporation Act, 1882, and the Local Government Acts, 1888 and 1894, municipal corporations, co. councils and other local authorities are empowered to hold lands for the purposes of those acts. Any assurance of land, or personal estate to be laid out as land, for educational purposes is exempted from restrictions under the Mortmain Acts. A local authority may accept land, money or other property for the purposes of the Housing Act, 1936, and it is unnecessary to enrol any assurance of it under the Mortmain and Charitable Uses Act. A joint board for the purposes of the Public Health Act, 1936, is empowered to hold land for the purposes of its constitution without licence in M. Railway, gas, water and tramway companies could also hold land under their respective private Acts.

Under the Mortmain and Charitable Uses Act, 1888, every conveyance of land, or grant of money to be laid out in land, for charitable uses (q.v.) is forbidden, unless (1) made by deed executed in the presence of 2 witnesses and enrolled in the central office of the supreme court within 6 months after execution, except in the case of copyhold land or stock in the public funds; (2) made at least 12 months, or, if stock in the public funds, 6 months before the death of the grantor; (3) the assurance takes effect in possession without power of revocation or condition in favour of the grantor except a reservation of mines, easements, nominal rent and repairing covenants. If, however, the assurance is made *bona fide* and for valuable consideration (q.v.), (1) and (2) do not apply. There are exemptions from the above restrictions in the case of Oxford, Cambridge, London, Durham and Victoria Univs., and in favour of gifts not exceeding 20 ac. to public parks, 2 ac. to museums, and 1 ac. to elementary schools. By the Mortmain Act, 1891, *any devise* to a charity is good, but the land must be sold within a year after the death of the testator unless the court otherwise orders. *See* Sir W. Holdsworth, *History of English Law*, 1922–38, and *Historical Introduction to Land Law*, 1927; H. M. Chew, *English Ecclesiastical Tenants-in-chief and Knight-service*, 1932 (13th–14th cents.); G. C. Cheshire, *The Modern Law of Real Property*, 1954.

Morton, Henry Canova Vollam (1892–), journalist and author, *b*. Birmingham. He began as a journalist in 1910, and has since been connected with leading London daily newspapers in an editorial capacity and as a contributor. He made his reputation as an author with a number of books about London and the Brit. Isles, based on a close knowledge and regard for present customs, traditions and hist. *The Heart of London* appeared in 1925 and *In Search of England* in 1927, followed by similar books on Scotland (1929), Ireland (1930) and Wales (1932). His travels in the Holy Land were recounted in the successful *In the Steps of The Master*, 1934, *In the Steps of St Paul*, 1936, and *Through Lands of the Bible*, 1938. He has also written *In Search of South Africa*, 1948.

Morton, James Douglas, 4th Earl of (*c*. 1525–81), regent of Scotland. In 1557 he subscribed the first bond of the Scottish reformers, but withdrew his support in 1559. When Mary Queen of Scots arrived in Scotland he became privy councillor. He was instrumental in suppressing Huntly's conspiracy in 1562, and was made lord chancellor in 1563. He offered no opposition to the marriage of Mary with Darnley, instigated the murder of Rizzio, and joined Ruthven and Hamilton in settling the crown matrimonial upon Darnley. In 1566 Darnley denounced him and he was obliged to flee, but later in the same year was pardoned through the influence of Bothwell, for whose marriage with Mary he signed a bond in 1567. He then roused the citizens of Edinburgh against Bothwell, but allowed him to escape and brought about the queen's imprisonment at Lochleven. He became lord chancellor and a member of the Council of Regency, in which capacity he acted as adviser to Murray and practically ruled the country during Lennox's regency. He gained the favour of Elizabeth and induced many prominent men to desert Mary's cause. In 1578 James VI assumed the gov., but a Parliament held at Stirling Castle re-estab. M. at the head of affairs. He was executed in 1581, having been convicted of the charge of sharing in Darnley's murder.

Morton, John (*c*. 1420–1500), archbishop, *b*. in Dorset, and educ. at Balliol College, Oxford. M. first supported the Lancastrians, but submitted to Edward IV after Tewkesbury, and was made master of the rolls, 1473, and bishop of Ely, 1479. He was imprisoned by Richard III,

but escaped and joined the future Henry VII in Flanders. Henry made M. Archbishop of Canterbury in 1486 and lord chancellor in 1487. M.'s ingenuity in extracting money from both the ostentatiously wealthy and the parsimonious originated the proverbial phrase of 'M.'s fork'. He was made a cardinal in 1493.

Morton, John Cameron Andrieu Bingham Michael (1893–), Brit. journalist and author. Educ. at Harrow and Worcester College, Oxford, he became a journalist and has been a contributor to the *Daily Express* since 1924 under the pseudonym 'Beachcomber'. He has pub. a number of books of fantasy, satire, humour and parody, including *Morton's Folly*, 1933, *Gallimaufry*, 1936, *Sideways through Borneo*, 1937, and *Fool's Paradise*, 1941. His historical writings include *Sobieski, King of Poland*, 1932, *The Bastille Falls, and other Studies of the French Revolution*, 1936, *The Dauphin*, 1937, *Saint-Just*, 1939, *Brumaire: Rise of Napoleon*, 1948.

Morton, Thomas (*c*. 1764–1838), dramatist, *b*. Durham. Of his plays, the best known are *The Way to Get Married*, 1796, and *Speed the Plough*, 1798, which contains the famous character Mrs Grundy.

Morton, William Thomas Green (1819–1868), Amer. dentist, *b*. Charlton, Massachusetts. He began the practice of dentistry with Horace Wells, who attempted unsuccessfully to produce anaesthesia with nitrous oxide. M. then thought that the inhalation of ether might prove successful. He used it to extract a tooth without pain and was convinced that he had made a great discovery. He obtained permission to use it at a surgical operation and on 16 Oct. 1846 he administered it at the Massachusetts General Hospital, Boston, to a patient who was made insensible in 3 min. and who felt no pain when a tumour was removed from his jaw. Ether anaesthesia was immediately accepted and a new era in surgery began. On 21 Dec. 1846 Robert Liston (q.v.) amputated a thigh in London, using ether as anaesthetic. M. spent over £20,000 in furthering the use of ether, and a national subscription was raised on his behalf in the U.S.A. He wrote *Remarks on the Proper Mode of Administering Sulphuric Ether by Inhalation*, 1847. *See* life by G. S. Woodward, 1962.

Mortuary. A local authority may provide and fit up a proper place for the reception of dead bodies, make by-laws with respect to the management and charges for the use of the same, and provide for the decent and economical interment of the dead bodies received into any such M. If a local authority does not provide a M. voluntarily, the Ministry of Health has power to require them to do so. The local authority may also provide a post-mortem examination chamber, which, however, must not be at a M. Co. councils have concurrent powers to establish M.s for the reception of unidentified dead bodies, and to require bor. councils to provide post-mortem chambers. Any local authority having power to provide a M. may purchase by agreement, or by compulsion, or take on lease, any land or buildings they may require for a M. *See* BURIAL ACTS; CREMATION.

Moryson, or Morison, Fynes (1566–*c*. 1630), Eng. traveller. He visited Germany, the Low Countries, Poland, Italy, Switzerland and France (1591–5), and Palestine, Constantinople and Scotland (1598). In 1600 he went to Ireland, became secretary to Sir Charles Blount and helped to suppress Tyrone's rebellion. *See* his hist. of Tyrone's rebellion and account of his travels, pub. 1617.

Mosaic, a form of surface decoration used on floors, vaults and walls. In M. work variously coloured fragments of marble, glass, ceramic or other substances are arranged in a cement or mastic bed so as to produce an artistic or geometrical design. The art goes back to a very remote origin, but it reached its highest development in anct times among the Romans. Very few old Rom. villas remain in which there is not some M. work of a greater or lesser degree of elaboration. The best-known example is that of Hadrian's villa at Tivoli, where Pliny's doves are represented with wonderful delicacy of colouring. M. work became a special feature of Christian churches under the Byzantine empire, and E. influence is clearly to be seen in the Rom. work. In the E. the art continued down to the 13th cent. In the W. it declined in the 7th cent., revived again in the 8th for about a cent., but then fell away again until the 14th cent. In modern times the art seems to have been well preserved only at Venice, though Eng. examples exist in Westminster Cathedral and St Paul's Cathedral. See E. A. Anthony, *A History of Mosaics*, 1935; J. Young, *Mosaics*, 1963. (*See Plates: Art: Byzantine Empire, Vol. 3.*)

Mosaic Gold consists of stannic sulphide (SnS_2). It is prepared by heating together a mixture of very finely divided tin with sulphur and ammonium chloride. It is obtained in golden spangles, and it is used extensively for imitation gilding.

Mosaylima, or Moseilema, contemporary and rival of Mohammed (q.v.), claiming to have equal rights with him to the title of 'Messenger of God'. He stated that Mohammed had nominated him his successor, but his claim was not acknowledged by the Muslims. He was killed in 634 by Khalid, a general of Abu Bekr.

Moscheles, Ignaz (1794–1870), Bohemian pianist and composer, *b*. Prague, of Jewish parents. In 1820 he toured Germany, Holland, France and England, giving concerts, and in 1826 settled in London as teacher and soloist, and became one of the directors of the Philharmonic Society. He gave lessons to Mendelssohn in Berlin in 1824 and became his life-long friend. In 1846 he became professor of the Leipzig conservatory. He composed about 140 opus numbers, including piano concertos, sonatas, chamber music and studies for the pianoforte. He was a gifted improviser and introduced some innovations in piano playing later developed by the Liszt school. *See* life by his wife (Eng. trans., 1873) and his correspondence with Mendelssohn, pub. 1888.

Moschus (fl. *c*. 150 BC), Gk bucolic poet, *b*. Syracuse. Some of his pieces have survived, notably a short epic *Europa* and an epigram on *Love, the Runaway*. *See* text and trans. in The Greek Bucolic Poets (Loeb Library), 1912; verse trans. by A. S. Way, 1913.

Moscow (Russian **Moskva**): 1. Oblast (prov.) in Central Russia between the upper Volga and the Oka, lying on the Smolensk–M. morainic ridge in the NW., and the Meshchera (q.v.) lowland in the SE. It is 40 per cent covered with mixed forests and has a moderately continental climate. There are lignite (*see* MOSCOW COAL BASIN), phosphorite and peat deposits. Area 18,100 sq. m.; pop. (1965, without Moscow city) 5,287,000 (64 per cent urb.), almost exclusively Russian. The main features of the economy are a large engineering industry (locomotives and rolling stock, machine tools, agric. machinery), textile and chemical industries, grain, vegetable. potato and flax growing, and dairy farming. There is a dense rail and road network, and the M.–Volga Canal (q.v.). The prin. tns are M., Podol'sk, Elektrostal', Orehkovo-Zuyevo, Serpukhov, Noginsk, Kolomna, Mytishchi and Lyubertsy. The famous St Sergius Trinity monastery (*see* TROITSE-SERGIYEVA LAVRA) is in this oblast. The area belonged to the medieval Kievan State, then in parts to the Rostov-Suzdal' (later Vladimir), Ryazan' and Smolensk principalities. A separate M. principality existed from 1283 which became the core of Muscovy (q.v.) and thus of modern Russia. The battle of Borodino (q.v.) was fought here in 1812. Almost half of M. oblast was occupied by the Germans in 1941-2 and suffered greatly from military operations. In 1960 M. city absorbed sev. suburbs (including Babushkin, Kuntsevo, Lyubluno, Perovo and Tushino).

2. Cap. of the above, of the Russian Federal Rep. (to whose gov. it is directly subordinated) and of the U.S.S.R., situated in the centre of European Russia, on both banks of the Moskva R. M. is the largest city and the main economic and cultural, as well as political, centre of the Soviet Union. Pop. (1965, with suburbs) 6,443,000. In the 16th cent. it was about 100,000; 1790, 175,000; 1830, 305,000; 1871, 602,000; 1897, 1,039,000; 1912, 1,618,000. There was a significant fall from 1917 (the year of revolutions), when it was 1,701,000, to 1,028,000 in 1920. Since then there has been a large and steady increase: 2,020,000 in 1926 and 4,137,000 in 1939.

M. has large engineering, textile, electrical, chemical and food industries. Apart from local power stations, electricity is supplied to M. from the Kuybyshev hydro-electric station through a direct high-voltage line (as well as from local power stations); natural gas is supplied through pipelines from Saratov and Stavropol'. M. is the hub of the Russian railway system, with 11 trunk lines radiating in all directions—connected inside the city by a circular line— and 9 passenger stations. There are 3 riv. ports with passenger services to Gor'kiy, Ufa and Rostov-on-Don via Moskva R.—Oka and via the

Moscow–Volga Canal (q.v.); and 4 airports (Sheremet'yevo, Vnukovo, Bykovo and, opened 1965, Domodedovo). The internal passenger transport system of M. is notable by comparison with that of most Western cities, for the continuing use of sev. different media. Trams have been removed from the central areas, but they, trolley buses and petrol buses are still prominent over much of the city, while the underground railway, started in 1932, now has over 70 stations and a track length of 67 m.

In addition to the U.S.S.R. Academy of Sciences (founded in 1725 in St Petersburg and transferred to M. in 1934) there are many research institutes and specialised academies—medical, agric., pedagogical, etc., the Academy of Arts. M. has 79 higher educational estabs. (including those for correspondence courses, but excluding military) with 477,000 students (excluding correspondence students) as compared with 20 estabs. and 34,000 students in 1915. The most outstanding among them are the univ. founded in 1755 (the oldest Russian univ.), the Higher Technical School (1832), the Agric. Academy (1865), the Railway Transport Institute (1896), the Institute of Chemical Technology (1898), the Conservatoire (1866), the Institute of Architecture, founded in 1789 as the Architectural School. There are 116 museums and permanent exhibitions in M., including the Tret'yakov Gallery of Russian Art (opened to the public in the 1880s), the Museum of Visual Arts, Museum of Oriental Cultures (1918), the State Historical Museum (1873), the Polytechnic Museum, the Lenin Museum and the Agric. Exhibition. There are 3200 libraries, including the Lenin Library (founded 1862) with 19 million vols. Among M.'s theatres are the Bolshoy Theatre of Opera and Ballet (founded in 1780), the Maeyy Theatre of Drama (1806) and the Arts Theatre (1898). M. is the seat of the Patriarch and the spiritual centre of the Russian Orthodox Church. M. Theological Academy (founded 1685, abolished after the revolution, but re-estab. after the Second World War) is in the Troitse-Sergiyeva Lavra (q.v.).

M. has a radial-circular system of main streets. The Kremlin (q.v.), situated on the N. bank of the riv., forms the centre of the tn, and around it, with a radius of about 1 m., is a line of boulevards, extending, however, only on the N. side of the riv. Outside this line, and concentric with it, is another line of boulevards, with a radius of 1½ m.; while beyond all, and forming a girdle round the city, is the outer rampart, with a circumference of 26 m. Farther out lies the Circular Railway, and approximately marking the new (1960) city border is a ring road 68 m. long. There are few old buildings preserved in M., as most of them were built of wood and were burned in the many fires the city has suffered. The most outstanding architectural monuments, apart from the Kremlin, are the Cathedral of the New Convent of the Virgin (1525), the Intercession Cathedral, commonly known as Vasiliy Blazhenyy Church, in the Red Square (1560), the Nativity Church in Putinki (17th cent.), the old Printing House (1679); the 18th–early 19th-cent. buildings in the neo-classical style include the Assembly of the Nobility (1771; now the House of Unions), the old building of the Lenin Library (1786), the old univ. building (1793), and the Bolshoy Theatre (1824). The late 19th–early 20th cent. buildings are mostly eclectic, often imitating the earlier Russian styles. Among these are the Town Hall (1892; now the Lenin Museum), the Polytechnic Museum, the History Museum (1874), the Museum of Visual Arts (1912) and the Kazan' railway station, which was begun in 1914. During the 1920s and early 1930s Constructivism was the dominant style of M. architecture, while since the 1930s to the early 1950s 'Soviet Classicism' was developed. Pre-war examples include the Moskva Hotel, Gor'kiy Street and the underground stations; and other post-war examples include the 'tall buildings', among them the new univ. The post-Stalin period has seen the emergence of simpler—and sometimes painfully uninspired—forms, mainly in order to facilitate rapid mechanised construction; the U.S.S.R has been among the pioneers of large-scale production techniques for urban housing. The results may be seen in the hundreds of 9–12-storey blocks of flats in the new suburbs. More attractive are recent 'prestige' buildings such as the Kremlin Palace of Congresses and the cinema 'Rossiya'; they approach current Western taste in their severity of styling, with large areas of glass. Some of the architectural monuments were destroyed in the 1930s, such as the famous Chapel of the Iberian Virgin (1669), one of the most revered churches in Russia, and the Church of the Redeemer, the most richly decorated church in M., built in 1839–83 in commemoration of the patriotic war of 1812 against Napoleon.

History. M. was first mentioned in the chronicles in 1147 as a settlement near the S. frontier of the Rostov-Suzdal' principality. In the 13th cent. it became the cap. of a separate principality, in the 14th cent. of the grand principality of Vladimir, and later of the state of Muscovy (q.v.). From the early 14th cent. it was the seat of the metropolitans (later patriarchs) and the centre of the Russian Orthodox Church. Peter the Great transferred the cap. to St Petersburg in 1712, but M. retained the status of a second cap. during the imperial period, and again became cap. of the country in 1918. Since the Middle Ages it has been an important commercial centre, and since the 16th cent. the centre of many crafts, attracting a large artisan pop. Large manufs. have developed since the mid 17th cent., and modern industry (at first textiles, then metal-working) since the 1830s. The first M. water-works were built in 1779–1805, the sewerage system in 1874–98; electric light was introduced in 1883, the tramway in 1899, and the underground has been built since 1932.

In the 19th and early 20th cents. M. was the centre of the Slavophile (*see* SLAVOPHILES), Zemstvo (q.v.) and co-operative movements, and one of the main centres of the labour movement and of Social Democracy. The Bolsheviks had a limited influence on the M. proletariat. During the 1920s M. was often the centre of the inner-party opposition to the official leadership. Since Stalin's death it has been the centre of intellectual opposition (particularly the M. writers' organisation) and of student unrest (Nov.–Dec. 1956). (*See Plates: Russian Architecture; Union of Soviet Socialist Republics*.)

Moscow Coal Basin, lignite deposits in Central and NW. Russia, stretching in an arch-shaped strip through Ryazan', Moscow, Tula, Kaluga, Smolensk, Kalinin, Novgorod and Leningrad oblasts. Coal was found here in 1722, and has been mined since the 1850s; extraction was greatly expanded after the 1930s, and the M. C. B. now takes third place in Russia (after the Donets and Kuznetsk basins) in terms of tons produced. However, the calorific value is low and the coal unsuitable for coking, and production has declined since 1958 (1958, 47·25 million tons; 1961, 36·84 m. t.). The chief industrial centres are Tula and Novomoskovsk.

Moscow–Volga Canal, artificial waterway connecting the R. Moskva with the upper Volga. Total length 80 m. Built 1932–7, largely by forced labour.

Moseilema, *see* MOSAYLIMA.

Moselekatse, or **Moselikatse** (*d.* 1870), Zulu chieftain who fled from Zululand after his defeat by the Voortrekkers and estab. the Matabele kingdom N. of the Vaal R. In 1827 M. led the Amangwate Zulus against Mosesh, chief of the Basutos, and was defeated at the battle of Thaba Bosigo (*see* BASUTOLAND, *History*).

Moseley, Henry Gwyn-Jeffreys (1887–1915), physicist, *b.* Weymouth, killed at Gallipoli. A scientist of brilliant promise, he carried out much work on the structure of the atom and showed that the atomic number of an element may be deduced from its X-ray spectrum.

Moselle: 1. (Ger. **Mosel**). Riv. of France and Germany, a trib. of the Rhine. It rises in the SE. of the dept of Vosges, in 2 head streams uniting near St Maurice and flowing N. through the depts of Meurthe-et-Moselle and Moselle, past Metz to the Ger.-Luxembourg border and NE. to the Rhine at Koblenz. Its prin. tribs. are the Meurthe in France and the Saar in Germany. It is navigable from Frouard, near Toul. The M. Valley is one of the great wine-producing areas of Germany. Length 320 m.; area of basin 10,950 sq. m. (*See Plate: Luxembourg*.)

2. Dept of NE. France, formed of part of the anct prov. of Lorraine. It has a boundary with Germany to the E., and with Luxembourg to the N. and NE. It consists largely of a plateau drained by the Riv. M. Coal-and iron-mines are of great importance, and its manufs. include machinery, chemicals and textiles. The prin. tns are Metz (the cap.), Boulay, Château-Salins, Forbach, Sarrebourg, Sarreguemines, Thionville (qq.v.). Area 2403 sq. m.; pop. 920,000. *See also* ALSACE-LORRAINE.

Moselle Wine, from the Moselle valley, is still as it was when Ausonius (q.v.) celebrated it in verse as one of the most beautiful of all wine regions. It is made from the great Ger. grape, the Riesling, and is distinguished by its elegance and clean dry quality which is emphasised by its pleasant tendency to the hint of a sparkle (*spritzig*). The best M. W.s are grown in the middle Moselle between Trèves and Enkirch and in the trib. valleys of the Saar and Ruwer. Berncastel, Brauneberg, Graach, Piesport, Avelsbach, Zeltingen and Wiltingen are among the best-known M. W.s. *See* H. Warner Allen, *White Wines and Cognac*, 1952; A. L. Simon and S. F. Hallgarten, *The Great Wines of Germany*, 1963.

Moser, George Michael (1704–83), Swiss chaser and enameller, *b.* Schaffhausen, but spent most of his life in England, where his watches and bracelets were in great request. He was drawing-master to George III, and assisted in establishing the Royal Academy, of which he was elected the first keeper in 1767. His daughter, Mary M. (q.v.), was a painter.

Moser, Mary (1774–1819), daughter of George Michael M. (q.v.), and Mrs Lloyd after her marriage to Capt. Hugh Lloyd in 1793; she was a flower painter and founder member of the Royal Academy, 1768. She and Angelica Kauffmann (q.v.) were the only women to receive academic honours until Mrs Swynnerton was made A.R.A. in 1933.

Moses (an Egyptian name, cf. Tutmosis), the great Jewish lawgiver, prophet and judge, son of Amram (1 Chron. vi. 3) and Jochebed, both of the tribe of Levi, and brother of Aaron and Miriam (*see* DEUTERONOMY; EXODUS; HEXATEUCH; NUMBERS). Born in Egypt when the Pharaoh, probably Rameses II (*c.* 1298–1232), had decreed that every male child of the Hebrews should be destroyed, he was placed by his mother in an ark upon the Nile, where he was found by Pharaoh's daughter and adopted by her. Brought up as an Egyptian prince, his heart was yet with his own people, and, finding an Egyptian oppressing a Hebrew, he slew the Egyptian and fled to Midian near Sinai, where he received a divine revelation and mission to lead the chosen people out of Egypt. (For the plagues, the crossing of the Red Sea, etc., *see* EXODUS.) At Mt Sinai he communed with God face to face and received the 10 commandments, and through him God made a covenant with Israel. He was the inspired founder of the Jewish institutional religion. The Jews called themselves the disciples of M. (John ix. 29). For 40 years he was military leader, social and religious organiser and lawgiver to the turbulent tribes in the desert wanderings, finally dying on Pisgah, or Mt Nebo, to the NE. of the Dead Sea. *See* J. Hastings, *Dictionary of the Bible* (under M.), 1908; C. L. Woolley and T. E. Lawrence, *The Wilderness of Zin*, 1915; S. Freud, *Moses and Monotheism*, 1939.

Moses (Grandma), Anna Mary (1860–1961), Amer. 'modern primitive' painter, *b.* Washington Co., New York. As a widow, late in life, she took to painting and her exhibition 'What a

Farmwife Painted' made an instant impression in 1940. Her work was subsequently seen in more than 200 exhibitions in the U.S.A., Canada and Europe. *See* O. Kallir, *Grandma Moses: American Primitive*, 1946, and her autobiography *My Life's History*, 1952.

Moshavim, *see* COMMUNITY VILLAGES IN ISRAEL.

Moshavot, *see* COMMUNITY VILLAGES IN ISRAEL.

Moshesh (1785–1870), Basuto paramount chief and founder of the Basuto nation. He defeated the Zulu and other invaders and twice inflicted defeats on European commandos from the Orange Free State (1851, 1852), while in 1858 the Free State again felt the weight of M.'s hand, peace being eventually made through the mediation of Sir George Grey. In 1865 war again broke out between M. and the Free State, M., then 80, being at length defeated, with the loss of the coveted land S. of the Caledon R. The stipulations which M. made in 1862 when first discussing terms under which Brit. protection might be extended to Basutoland contemplated only political control: 'The queen rules my people only through me. The man whom I ask from the queen to live with me will guide and direct me.' M. asked that no magistrates should be sent, and that native law should prevail, save with the consent of the Basuto. The proclamation of 1868 annexing Basutoland declared that the Basuto should be taken to be Brit. subjects; but at the outset relations were guided by the spirit of the discussions of 1862 rather than any assumption that the British had acquired sovereign rights, and indeed the spirit of these stipulations of M. is still the interpretation put by the Basuto on the terms of protection. *See* Sir A. Pim, *Report on Basutoland*, 1935, Cmd. 4907. *See also* LESOTHO.

Mosley, Sir Oswald Ernald, 6th Bart. (1896–), politician, educ. at Winchester and the Royal Military College, Sandhurst. He sat as Conservative M.P. for Harrow (1918–22), as Independent (1922–4) and as Labour (1924–30). He was chancellor of the duchy of Lancaster in the Labour gov. (1929–30). In Dec. 1930 he issued a manifesto, in which he warned the gov. of the need to develop a policy for dealing with the economic crisis, and in the early part of 1931 he and a band of followers seceded and formed a new party, which, however, failed to win a single seat at the election of 1931. His party was known as the Brit. Union of Fascists; their activities were the occasion of some violent mob riots in the years preceding the Second World War. At the end of May 1940 M. was arrested under the Defence Regulations, and a number of his adherents were also interned. After the war he founded a new Union movement (1948). He wrote *My Answer*, 1946, and *Mosley—Right or Wrong?*, 1961.

Mosque (from Arabic *masjid*), a building for Muslim worship. The first M., built at Medina in Arabia by Mohammad in AD 622, was merely a square enclosure surrounded by a wall. On one side of the enclosure was a roughly built shed or shelter giving some protection from the sun. Here Mohammad led the prayers.

At first the worshippers faced N., towards Jerusalem, but in 624 the direction was changed towards Mecca. Even today, wherever the M. may be, whether in England or Cape Town or Singapore or Samarkand, it is orientated towards Mecca, the direction of which is indicated by a niche in the wall—the *mihrab* (q.v.). Before the end of the 7th cent. a minaret (q.v.) was added, from which the call to prayer was chanted, and also a pulpit, the *mimbar* (q.v.). In all large M.s used for congregational worship the *sahn* (open court) was retained, usually with an arcaded *liwan* or cloister on all 4 sides; but the *liwan* on the Mecca side was generally wider than the others; it formed the sanctuary.

In many M.s a portion is railed off, originally for the caliph or his representative. The ruler's commands were pub. in the M.; it was a place for teaching, for listening to literature and for public meetings (which might start revolutions, when the rebels against authority acted in the name of religion). Each country has developed its own style for big M.s and the shapes of domes and minarets differ widely.

See also MUSLIM ARCHITECTURE. (*See Plate: Muslim Architecture.*)

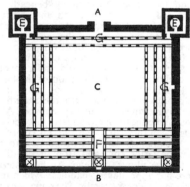

MOSQUE

Plan of the congregational mosque of Al Hakim at Cairo. A, entrance; B, mihrab (prayer niche pointing to Mecca); C, sahn (open courtyard); EE, minarets; F, sanctuary; GG, liwans (covered arcades); xx, small domes.

Mosquito, dipterous (2-winged) insects which form the family Culcidae. Culcidae is divided into 3 subfamilies: the Culcinae, Dixinae and Chaoborinae. M.s may be recognised by their wing venation, which is characteristic, their long legs, of which there are 3 on each side of the body, and their long, slender, horny proboscis, which is carried projecting forwards. The antennae are long and adorned with plumes or whorls of hair. Of the 3 subfamilies, only the Culcinae are of medical importance. There are 3 tribes of Culcinae, the Anophelini, Culcini and

Megarhinini, and, of these, the first 2 contain species that have been incriminated as vectors of disease. Species of Culcini of importance are *Culex fatigans, Aëdes aegypti, Aëdes albopictus* and *Aëdes scutellaris. C. fatigans* is the chief vector of filariasis (q.v.) and occurs throughout tropical and subtropical regions. *A. scutellaris*, found chiefly in Malaya and the Pacific Is., also transmits filariasis. *A. aegypti*, found in tropical and subtropical regions, including the Mediterranean, and *A. albopictus*, found in the oriental region, Australia and Madagascar, transmit yellow fever (q.v.) and dengue fever (q.v.). There is one medically important species of Anophelini, known as *Anopheles*, which is responsible for transmitting malaria (q.v.). Distinguishing one species of M. from another is a matter for specialised study and there is a voluminous literature on the subject. The life cycle of all M.s, however, follows a general pattern, and knowledge of it is of epidemiological importance in devising means for the eradication of these insects (*see under* MALARIA). The eggs of most species are laid on the surface of water or on water plants. The minute larva emerges and suspends itself beneath the surface of the water. The habit of the larva varies according to the species of M., but nearly all have to rise to the surface to breathe. Some suspend themselves horizontally beneath the surface and breathe through an air-tube projected just above the water. Others spend considerable time on the bed of the river or pond, and wriggle to the surface to breathe. One Brit. and a few foreign species obtain air from roots of aquatic plants. Growth is rapid under favourable conditions, and the duration of the larval period varies considerably. Food consists of minute organisms waved into the mouth by constantly moving brush-like appendages. After the fourth moult, the larva pupates just beneath the surface of the water. The anterior end of the pupa is extremely large in proportion to the narrow posterior end, and from it breathing tubes rise just above the water. At the posterior end are flat appendages, 'paddles', which may propel the pupa or act as gills. The pupa does not feed, and after a few days its skin splits and the adult M. liberates itself. The *Anopheles* and other species of M. are native to Britain, but, except for the discomfort of their bite, are as a rule of no medical importance. However, after both world wars, and particularly the first, owing to the return of large numbers of men infected with malaria from service abroad, there was some danger of the Brit. *Anopheles* carrying the disease. Cases were reported of primary malaria contracted in this country (*see* ENTOMOLOGY; EPIDEMIOLOGY; INSECT BITES AND STINGS; MALARIA; PARASITES. *See* J. Smart, *Insects of Medical Importance*, 1945, and R. C. M. Thompson, *Mosquito Behaviour in Relation to Malaria Transmission and Control in the Tropics*, 1951.

Moss, maritime tn in Östfold co., S. Norway, on Oslo Fjord (E.). It has considerable and varied industry, trade and shipping. The conven-

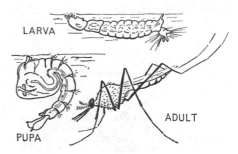

MOSQUITO (*Anopheles maculipennis*)

tion between Norway and Sweden, signed here in 1814 and uniting the 2 states under one king, was annulled in 1905. Pop. 20,600.

Moss-banker, *see* MENHADEN.

Mossamedes, or **Moçamedes,** seaport of Angola. It is a railway terminus with a line recently (1955) built to connect with the S. African system.

Mössbauer Effect. When a gamma ray (q.v.) is emitted by a nucleus, conservation of momentum requires the nucleus to recoil. The energy of the transition, commonly between 2 very precisely defined (i.e. relatively long-lived) energy states in the nucleus, is therefore shared between the gamma photon and the nucleus. E.g., the Iridium isotope of mass 191 is produced by beta emission from Osmium 191 and may be formed in a state of excitation energy 129keV, and half-life $1·3 \times 10^{-10}$ sec. The recoil energy of the free nucleus would then be 0·047eV. This is sufficient reduction of gamma energy to prevent the absorption of the gamma ray by an unexcited Iridium 191 nucleus. However, Mössbauer discovered in 1958 that at 80° K about 1 per cent of the transitions were 'recoilless', or to be more accurate, were accompanied by recoil of the whole crystal in which the nucleus is bound. The explanation is that for certain crystals at low temps. the nucleus can take up only those energies corresponding to fairly well defined states of the crystal lattice. When the recoil energy for a 'free' nucleus is less than the minimum required to excite the nucleus to its next higher bound state in the crystal lattice, the recoil momentum is taken up by the crystal as a whole and the corresponding recoil energy is then extremely small. The resulting gamma photon then has sufficient energy to excite an Iridium 191 nucleus in an absorber at the same low temp. The best example is the 14·4 keV γ from Iron 57, with 70 per cent recoilless transitions at room temp. The precision of the method opens up useful fields of investigation in solid state physics. It has also been applied to the testing of Einstein's General Theory of Relativity, by finding the increase in energy of a gamma photon falling under gravity through a distance of a few metres.

Mossel Bay (formerly **Aliwal South**), municipality of the Cape Prov., S. Africa, 34° 11′ S.

lat., 22° 9' E. long. M. B. has a small but efficient harbour and a submarine oil pipe line to receive oil from tankers. Noted for its fishing and oysters. Fruit and vegetable canning industries are located in the tn. Out in the bay lies Seal Is., about 1 ac. in extent and inhabited by thousands of seals. M. B. is the terminus of a railway from Cape Tn through Caledon and Swellendam. Mail steamer services from Table Bay to Natal call at M. B. It was one of the first bays known in S. Africa to the old Portuguese navigators, and in about 1500 Pedro d'Ataide found refuge in what is today known as Munro's Bay from the storm which wrecked most of his fleet. A year later João da Nova settled there and built a hermitage, which is claimed to have been the first Christian place of worship in S. Africa. Pop. (1960) Whites, 8032; Coloureds, 14,606; Bantu, 2304.

Mossend, see BELLSHILL.

Mosses (musci), a class of plants which, with one other class, the liverworts (Hepaticae), forms one of the large divs. of the vegetable kingdom, the Bryophyta. M. are plants consisting entirely of cells, with distinct stems and leaves and, usually, absorptive rhizoids, but no true roots, and are green in colour. The leaves are one-cell thick, normally, absorbing and parting with water easily, and the plants are small, though often of considerable length. Of

MOSSES

1, *Sphagnum squarrosum*; B, detail of leaves; 2, *Andreaea repestris*; 3, *Buxbaumia aphylla*; 4, *Funaria hygometrica*. A, capsules.

the 3 orders, Sphagnales and Andreaeales are each represented by a single genus (*Sphagnum* and *Andreaea* respectively) and Bryales comprises many genera and species. M. may be propagated by broken-off parts; by gemmae, minute detachable buds; or by one-celled microscopic spores. In suitable conditions the spores germinate and grow by forming a fine thread which branches and multiplies into a green web of interlacing threads, the protonema, on which buds form that grow into moss plants. In most M. the protonema disappears with their growth; in some, notably *Buxbaumia*, it persists and is a source of nourishment. M. produce at the tips of the stems organs of reproduction similar to those of ferns: archegonia, each containing an egg cell, and antheridia, each containing sperm cells or antherozoids, which make their way to the egg cells and fertilise them. The fertilised egg cell develops into a capsule in which spores are produced and matured. When ripe the spores are released to be distributed by wind and other agencies. The capsule and attachment form a different generation from the moss plant, and there is an alternation of gametophyte and sporophyte generations, as shown in the accompanying diagram; the gametophyte is the moss plant; the sporophyte the stalked sporogonium or capsule. See H. N. Dixon and H. G. Jameson, *The Student's Handbook of British Mosses* (3rd ed.), 1924; P. W. Richards, *Book of Mosses*, 1950.

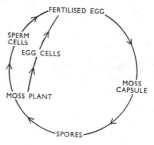

DIAGRAM OF LIFE-CYCLE OF MOSS

Mossley, municipal bor. of Lancs, England, on the Yorks-Cheshire border, 3 m. from Oldham. It is on the R. Tame and has woollen and cotton mills, and iron foundries. Pop. 9795.

Most (Ger. Brüx), Czechoslovak town in Severoteský, (q.v.), on the Bida. It has a 16th cent. Gothic church. There are chemical and metallurgical works, and the dist has lignite mines. The Seidlitz mineral springs are near. Pop. 44,500.

Most Favoured Nation Clause, clause often inserted in commercial treaties, the effect of which is that the one contracting nation guarantees to extend to the other the benefits conceded to any third nation or nations. Generally speaking, a treaty concerns none but the contracting states, and neither rights nor duties arise for states which are not parties to it. But treaties necessarily affect third states when they touch the previous treaty rights of such third states, and the most obvious instance of such an effect is in the case of a commercial treaty between A and B relating to matters which are already the subject of previous treaties between A and C, or B and C, containing the M. F. N. C. Brit. Imperial Preference is exempted from the M. F. N. C. See R. C. Snyder, *The Most Favoured Nation Clause*, 1948.

Mostaganem, fortified seaport of Algeria, 45 m. NE. of Oran. It has a pier available for small vessels, and trades in alfalfa, cereals and leather. Pop. 60,170.

Mostaert, Jan (*c.* 1475–*c.* 1556), Dutch

painter of religious subjects and portraits. He is noted for portraits of richly dressed sitters with elaborate backgrounds and was one of the first to introduce a Renaissance element of style into Netherlandish painting.

Mostar ('old bridge'), tn in Bosnia-Hercegovina, Yugoslavia, on the Neretva. It was the anct cap. of Hercegovina. It is an episcopal tn, has sev. fine mosques and is the centre of a wine-, tobacco- and fruit-producing dist. Pop. 32,300.

Mosul, tn (pop. about 350,000) of Iraq, on R. Tigris, 220 m. NW. of Bagdad in the prov. of the same name (pop. 756,625). Formerly it had large manufs. of cotton cloths named muslin after it; it is still a big trading centre with traffic in gallnuts, cotton, wool, hides, wax and gum. The pop. includes Muslims and Christians of several denominations. M. is on the standard gauge railway from Bagdad to the Syrian frontier and Europe. Oil was found in 1927 at Ain Zalah near by, and in 1934 a pipeline was built to Baiji. During the 18th cent. M. was governed by a local aristocracy, and when the Ottoman Empire broke up both Iraq and Turkey claimed M., which was adjudged to Iraq by the Permanent Court of International Justice. Seat of an appeal court. *See* H. C. Lukach (Luke), *Mosul and its Minorities,* 1925.

Moszkowski, Moritz (1854–1925), German pianist and composer of Polish descent, *b.* Breslau (Wrocław). Taught pianoforte in Berlin and afterwards in Paris where he lived for 30 years. He had a great reputation as a solo pianist and wrote much pleasing music, e.g. overtures, concert suites, a piano concerto, a violin concerto, an opera, *Boabdil* (performed in Berlin in 1892), *Laurin,* a ballet, 1896, and *Jeanne d'Arc,* a symphonic poem.

Motala, tn of Östergötland co., Sweden, on Lake Wetter, 42 m. WSW. of Nörrkoping. It has engineering industries. Pop. 27,000.

Motel (originally Amer.), roadside inn providing transient and very simple accommodation for passing motorists. *See* monographs by J. S. Hornbeck, 1953; G. Baker and B. Furano, 1955.

Motet, polyphonic vocal form of church music. It originated in the 13th cent. through the addition of new words to the metrical sections of *organs* (hence the name, from the Fr. *mot,* the part immediately above the plainsong being called *motetus*). Such compositions soon came to be written separately but were still constructed on a fragment of plainsong arranged in accordance with a metrical scheme. The words were Latin or French, or French in one voice and Latin in another. For this reason a certain number of M.s were obviously intended for secular use. In the course of the 15th cent. the plainsong (or *canto fermo*) came to be a middle part, with a bass part below it. Secular melodies were also used as *canti fermi* instead of plainsong. By the 16th cent. the use of a *canto fermo* had been largely abandoned and the M. was an example of free composition. A notable exception was the Lutheran M., where the use of a *canto fermo* was kept alive in a new form by

using the successive lines of a chorale melody. The increased use of instrumental ensembles with voices in the late 16th and early 17th cents. inevitably changed the character of the M., so that it became virtually indistinguishable from the choral cantata. The 19th cent. revival of interest in 16th cent. music, however, encouraged composers to revert to the older practice of writing M.s either for unaccompanied voices or for voices merely doubled by the organ.

Mother, *see* FAMILY; MATERNITY; MATRIARCHY.

Mother Carey's Chicken, *see* PETRELS.

Mother of Pearl, *see* PEARL.

Mother-of-Pearl Clouds, *see* NOCTILUCENT CLOUDS.

Mother of Thousands, popular name applied to 2 different flowering herbs, the *Linaria cymbalaria* and *Saxifraga sarmentosa.* The first-named is the European ivy-leaved toad-flax (q.v.). The second, also called creeping sailor, strawberry geranium and wandering Jew, a native of China and Japan, has roundish lobed leaves.

Mothercraft, *see* CHILD.

Motherwell, William (1797–1835), poet, *b.* Glasgow. He had antiquarian tastes and a deep knowledge of the early hist. of Scottish ballad literature, which he turned to account in *Minstrelsy, Ancient and Modern,* 1827, a collection of Scottish ballads with an historical introduction. In 1832 he collected and pub. his *Poems, Narrative and Lyrical.* He also joined Hogg in editing the works of Burns. *See* memoir prefixed to his *Poetical Remains,* 1848.

Motherwell, municipal and police burgh and tn of NE. Lanarkshire, Scotland, 1 m. from the r. b. of the R. Clyde, has iron and steel, engineering, wagon building and electrical works, and manufs. various products. It is named from an old well dedicated to the Blessed Virgin. M. was united with Wishaw (q.v.) in 1920. It returns 1 member to Parliament, the constituency including the burgh and a small part of the surrounding dist. Pop. (with Wishaw) 73,400.

Motherwort (*Leonurus cardiaca*), erect perennial plant, Labiatae family, with deeply lobed radical leaves and dense axillary whorls of small pink flowers.

Moths are classed in the Lepidoptera, and are distinguished broadly from the other section, the butterflies, by some variable distinctions which suggest that the div. is somewhat artificial, for there is greater diversity of form and structure between some of the groups of M. than between them and butterflies. Contrasted with the knobbed or club-shaped antennae of butterflies, the antennae of M. are usually spindle-shaped, thread-like or comb-like. The wings are generally held flat when at rest, not vertical. M. generally have a connecting hook for fastening the wings together; this is absent in butterflies. M. vary greatly in size from a wing expanse of 7 to 8 in. to the almost invisible microlepidoptera. The large Nigerian moth measures about 8 in. from wing tip to wing tip when fully expanded. It belongs to the family Saturniidae, and an Indian member of this family is probably the largest moth known. Though many exhibit no special beauty of colouring, others have a wealth of tint that is, perhaps, unique in nature, the colours occurring, as in all Lepidoptera, in the scales on the wings. The 2 uncoloured, transparent spots, one on each of the upper wings, are a characteristic feature of the Saturniidae; they are due to the absence of scales at these places. The females of some species are wingless, as in the mottled umber, or are rudimentary, as in the winter moth, 2 common M. caught on the grease-bands of fruit trees. The china-mark M. (Pyraustidae) are peculiar in the possession of aquatic larvae. The silkworm, the caterpillar of *Bombyx mori*, is the only member of the section of economic value, but, on the other hand, great numbers are serious pests of cultivated crops, the damage in all cases being done in the larval stage. Among the most harmful of them are the goat, vapourer, lackey, cabbage, winter and codlin M., and everyone is familiar with the mischievous work of the larvae of the clothes moth. Hawk M. are important as pollinating agents. *See* R. A. Ferchault de Réaumur, *Mémoires pour servir à l'histoire des insectes*, 1734–42; W. Buckler, *Larvae of British Butterflies and Moths*, 1885–95; R. Meyrick, *Revised Handbook of British Lepidoptera*, 1938; R. South, *Moths of the British Isles*, 1939; W. J. Stokoe and G. H. T. Stovin (editors), *The Caterpillars of British Moths*, 1949; E. B. Ford, *Moths*, 1955.

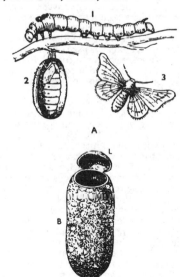

LIFE HISTORY OF A MOTH
A. 1, Caterpillar, × ⅔; 2, cocoon cut open to show pupa lying within, × ½; 3, imago, × ½. B. Cocoon of silk moth; L, lid.

Mo Ti, or **Mo Tzu**, Chinese philosopher; fl. 5th and 4th cents. BC, teaching in the period between Mencius and Confucius. According to

his sytem, Moism, Heaven (*T'ien*) loved man, and universal love was the foundation of society. Hence he taught pacifism coupled with utilitarianism, and believed that all institutions should stand or fall by their ability to further human welfare. His doctrine of universal love or the brotherhood of man as the basis of ethics was strongly controverted by Mencius's dialectic, and his doctrines, which were influential in his own time, had largely died out by the 1st cent. BC. His religious zeal had little appeal under the settled empire. There is a trans. of the *Ethical and Political Works of Motse*, by Y-pao Mei, 1929. *See also* Y-pao Mei, *Motse, the Neglected Rival of Confucius*, 1934; Burton Watson, *Book of Mo Tzu.*

Motif (in music), *see* LEITMOTIF; WAGNER.

Motion, Laws of, are 3 laws on which the whole system of classical dynamics is based. They were formulated by Newton in his *Principia.* In part they act as definitions of concepts rather than the summation of experimental observations. The first law states that 'every body will maintain its state of rest, or of uniform motion in a straight line, unless compelled by some external force to change that state'. The second law states that the 'rate of change of momentum is directly proportional to the force and takes place in the direction of the force'. The third law states that 'to every action there is an equal and opposite reaction', or to put it more simply, if a body A exerts a force on a body B then simultaneously the body B exerts an exactly equal and opposite force on A. Einstein's theory necessitated slight modifications in Newton's views. *See also* DYNAMICS; KINETICS; RELATIVITY.

Motion Pictures, *see* CINEMATOGRAPH; PHOTO-MICROGRAPHY.

Motley, John Lothrop (1814–77), Amer. historian, *b.* Dorchester, Boston. After graduating from Harvard he went to Europe, studied at Göttingen and Berlin, and visited Italy. He worked at the Amer. legation in St Petersburg (1840–2). Having pub. 2 novels, *Morton's Hope, or the Memoirs of a Provincial*, 1839, and *Merry Mount: a Romance of the Massachusetts Colony*, 1849, which had little success, he turned to hist. He decided to write a historical work on the Netherlands, and came to Europe in 1851 to collect material. In 1856 he pub. *The Rise of the Dutch Republic.* It at once became a standard work; it has been trans. into sev. languages. It was followed in 1860 by the first 2 vols. (concluding vols., 1867) of *The United Netherlands, from the Death of William the Silent to the Synod of Dort.* In 1861 M. was appointed U.S. minister at Vienna, and in 1869 at London. His final work was *The Life and Death of John of Barneveld, with a View of the Causes of the Thirty Years War*, 1874. M. still holds a high place among historical writers on account of his research and accuracy and his vivid and dramatic style, which shows the influence of Carlyle. An ed. of his works was pub. in 9 vols., 1904. *See* his correspondence, ed. by G. W. Curtis, 1889, and life by S. St J. Mildmay, 1910.

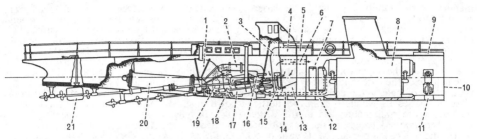

'TURBINIA' MOTOR BOAT WITH AXIAL-FLOW TURBINES

1 and 2, exhaust steam pipe; 3, fan casing; 4, air inlet; 5, hatch; 6, air delivery pipes; 7, feed-water tanks; 8, boiler; 9, hatch; 10, coal door; 11, forward stoke hold; 12, after stoke hold; 13, coal bunker; 14, main steam pipe; 15, fan; 16, reversing motor; 17, high-pressure motor; 18, steam pipe; 19, low-pressure motor; 20, condenser; 21, rudder.

Motley, cloth or clothing of mixed colours, later applied to the parti-coloured dress of the court fool or jester, and to the jester himself. *See* JESTER.

Motmot, or **Houtou** (*Momotus*), genus of birds which inhabit dense forests in tropical America. The plumage is brilliant, green and blue predominating; the tail is long. No nest is made, the eggs being laid in holes in trees or banks. Their food is mainly insects and fruit.

Motor Aphasia, *see* APHEMIA.

Motor Boats, small craft powered by internal-combustion engines, which are used in riv., lake or coastal traffic, or for fishing. Larger ocean-going vessels are called motor ships (q.v.). Open launches are usually 15–35 ft in overall length, with a motor of from 5 to 30 h.p., doing up to 30 or in some cases up to 55 knots; cabin cruisers, of 20–30 ft overall length, usually have a 10–20 h.p. motor, doing about 8–10 knots. Speed-boats are built on the hydroplane principle: at high speed the bow rises up over the water and the boat skims along the surface, thereby reducing resistance. This is achieved by a deeply submerged propeller on a slanting shaft, and by making the stern of shallow, almost rectangular, cross-section cutting out all superfluous wood. One of the earliest hydroplanes was in fact completely box-shaped. It was found, however, that this shape was liable to excessive vibrations at speed, and greater stability was obtained by confining the shallow box shape to one-third to a half of the hull length at the stern, and then lowering the bottom a step of a few inches. Sometimes more steps are provided. The *Miss England III*, which gained the world record (119·81 m.p.h.) in 1932, had a single step in the hull bottom and 2 deeply submerged propellers, which gave increased directional stability. The record was beaten later in the year by *Miss America X* (124·91 m.p.h.). The record stood until 1939 when Sir Malcolm Campbell (q.v.) attained a speed of 141·74 m.p.h. in his *Bluebird* on Coniston Water. This record was broken on 4 occasions by his son Donald Campbell (q.v.) with speeds up to 276·33 m.p.h. (Dec. 1964). Donald Campbell, however, was killed in Jan. 1967 while trying to beat his own record on Coniston Water.

M. B. are usually built of wood, either mahogany, oak, teak, pitch-pine, larch or Brazilian cedar. Different kinds of wood are often used for the different parts of hull and superstructure. The hull may be clinker-built, each plank overlapping the edge of the one below it, or carvel-built, the planed edges of the planks butting together to form a smooth surface. The latter method gives a better appearance and less resistance. Where a very light hull is required, 2 or more skins of thin wood are nailed, screwed or sewn together with a layer of oiled calico, silk or canvas between.

In recent years laminated plywood and glass fibres have become widely used. Glass fibre is particularly suitable for quantity production of hulls; for small boats it is used on its own but for larger ones it is generally reinforced. Light alloys are frequently employed for masts but are not popular for hulls because of the possibility of electrolytic corrosion.

Engines. The petrol engines used in M. B. are generally of the same design as those used in motor cars (q.v.), incorporating change-speed and reversing gear. The latter is sometimes dispensed with, and a mechanism for reversing the pitch of the propeller blades is introduced. As the most efficient propeller speed is about 1000 r.p.m. the marine engine is usually slower than the car engine, and therefore heavier per h.p. developed. This is generally of no great importance, but in cases where weight must be reduced, propeller efficiency is sacrificed. Recently the compression-ignition engine has been steadily gaining in favour, partly because of its higher thermal efficiency and cheaper fuel, partly because of the lesser fire risk; in this connection the Napier Deltic engine (*see* MOTOR SHIPS) has been highly successful, and has been used to power the 'Dark'-class fast patrol boats (40 knots). Further advantages of the compression-ignition engine are its reliability during manoeuvring, since there is no tendency to stalling, and the absence of the magneto, which is liable to damage from dampness and water. The Admiralty has sev. fast patrol boats powered by various gas turbine installations, which after exhaustive trials have proved highly satisfactory. The first application of the gas turbine to a small boat is in the Parsons Turbinia II which uses a 150 h.p. Rover gas turbine. *See* HYDROFOIL.

Motor Cars. *Historical.* Just as it has always been the aim of man to fly, so he has endeavoured to produce a horseless vehicle. In the 16th cent. Johann Hautach produced a vehicle propelled by coiled springs; the Dutch attempted the use of sails, while even steam carriages are recorded. Ramsay and Wildgoose patented in England, in 1619, a horseless carriage. Cugnot, a Frenchman, is, however, entitled to the credit of constructing a vehicle in 1770 which contained the germs of the modern car. His steam carriage on 3 wheels carried 2 passengers at 2 m.p.h., a speed he afterwards increased to 4 m.p.h. Dallery in 1780 ran a steam car in Amiens. Murdock in 1784, and Symington at about the same time experimented in the same direction. In France the Revolution appears to have postponed further effort, but in England Richard Trevithick attained success in 1801. His steam motor in 1802 covered the distance of 90 m. from Camborne to Plymouth. In 1803 his carriage with wheels of 10 ft diameter, and a horizontal instead of a vertical engine, ran at 10 m.p.h., but his further efforts were confined to locomotives for railroads. The curiously mistaken notions as to smooth wheels (one mathematician tried to prove that they would merely revolve on the spot under weight), which led to Stephenson's ratchet-rails, led also to curious attempts on the part of Brunton (1813), Gordon and Gurney to succeed with foot-and-leg propellers. Gurney, who spent large sums of money in experiment, built a coach in 1826 which ascended Highgate Hill. In 1828 he accomplished the journey from London to Bath, and in 1829 a trip through Reading, Devizes and Melksham at such a pace that the horses of a mail cart were 'hard put to it' to keep up. Meanwhile James in 1823 had succeeded with the first tubular boiler, and in 1829 carried 15 passengers at 12 m.p.h. In 1831 Dance ran Gurney's steam carriage regularly between Cheltenham and Gloucester at 12 m.p.h., his coke bill being 4*d*. per hr. In 4 months it ran 3500 m. and carried 3000 passengers. Messrs Ogle & Summers in 1830 built a car which underwent trials before a select commission of the House of Commons; it worked at 250 lb./sq. in. boiler pressure, attained a speed of 35 m.p.h., climbed a hill at 24½ m.p.h., and ran 800 m. without a breakdown. This was a great achievement for a car which was unsprung, running on poor roads, and the speed exceeded that of Stephenson's 'Rocket' (running on rails) the year before. The select commission reported in extremely favourable terms, and in particular recommended a lowering of tolls, which were then often 20 times those for horse vehicles. Largely as a consequence of this, many other motor vehicles were introduced; Hancock's 'Infant' ran from London to Bristol twice; his 'Autopsy' in 1833 plied regularly between Finsbury Square and Pentonville. In this he adopted direct drive by the crankshaft, but later changed to a primitive chain drive. Other services plied between Paddington and the Bank, London and Greenwich, London and Windsor, London and Stratford. More ambitious still was Dr Church's service between London and Birmingham, 1833. All this remarkable success, so little known to the modern motorist, experienced much opposition. Gurney had been stoned by a crowd egged on by irate postillions; coach proprietors and landowners were hostile; and the growing interest of railway companies led to repressive legislation. In spite of this, we hear of Hill's steam coach in 1843 running regularly between Deptford and Hastings, negotiating hills 1 in 12 and 1 in 13, performing the return journey in one day. This coach is interesting as being fitted with a differential gear. In 1862 Patterson ran a steam coach, and Yarrow had one in the exhibition. In 1871 Thompson's road steamers adopted rubber tyres on the driving wheel for the first time; the 'Ravee' performed the record-length journey from Ipswich to Edinburgh and back, a set of 3 rubber tyres costing £241. The modern motor car industry dates from the perfection of the internal combustion engine (q.v.) by Otto, 1876, and the patenting in 1885 by Daimler of a single-cylinder high-speed engine. Messrs. Panhard and Levassor acquired the Fr. and Belgian rights to use the engine, and constructed a car in 1894. In the meanwhile Benz, in 1885, had produced a motor tricycle, also using a petrol engine. Daimler produced the first double-cylinder V-type engine in 1889, while in 1893–4 Serpollet succeeded with his steam carriage. Press enterprise on the part of Giffard, editor of *Le Petit Journal*, was responsible for the Paris–Rouen race in 1894, won by the de Dion Bouton steam tractor. The next year saw the Paris–Bordeaux race won by Levassor driving a Daimler motor 735 m. at 14·9 m.p.h. This led to the founding of the Automobile Club of France by the Comte de Dion. Onward from this clubs were formed, races arranged, and the system of definite trials started. In 1899 the Automobile Club of Great Britain held its first trials, and included heavy vehicles. In the previous year trials had been held for electric vehicles in France, following on those for heavy vehicles in 1897. In the early days of the Brit. motor industry, from 1895 when the restrictions on road traffic were lifted, the only outstanding achievement was F. W. Lanchester's design of a car which was the first to embody all essential features of the modern car. Otherwise the main occupation of the industry was the assembling of motors designed abroad, while the U.S.A. and France made strides in development. Progress has been rapid, especially since 1918. In the first 6 months of 1948 Great Britain took the lead as an exporting country, with 115,980 cars. The total number of cars produced in 1955 was 897,560. But whereas the early years saw a large number of small producers (96 in 1922) making a great variety of specialised cars, the market is now supplied by about 20 manufacturers, of

FIG. 1. THE 1966 MODEL OF THE FORD CORSAIR (V4)

whom the 'Big Five' account for an overwhelming proportion of the output. At the same time the number of models has been greatly reduced. Apart from the possible development of the gas turbine and the compression-ignition engine, no drastic change in design of cars is likely in the near future, but improvements in transmission, including clutch and gearbox, in fuel injection and in design of electrical equipment are to be expected.

Engines. The steam engine, although attractive in theory because the high torque produced at all speeds down to a standstill enables clutch and gearbox to be dispensed with, is no longer used, mainly because of the time required to raise steam in the boiler before starting. Similarly the series wound electric motor, which also has excellent torque characteristics, suffers from the disadvantage of requiring a heavy battery and is used only for delivery vehicles where frequent starting and stopping are necessary but the daily mileage is not great; recharging is carried out during the night. However, recent concern over air pollution caused by petrol and diesel engines has led to a revival of interest in a small electric car which would be suitable for local journeys in large cities. At present private motor cars are almost invariably powered by 4-stroke petrol engines; the disadvantages of the diesel engine, namely its higher initial cost, greater weight and greater noise especially when running at light load, are considered in this application to outweigh its advantages of lower running costs and greater reliability (*see* INTERNAL COMBUSTION ENGINES). Two-stroke engines are rarely used; although simpler mechanically than the 4-stroke they use more petrol and tend to run irregularly at light load. Engines below 2 litres capacity usually have 4 cylinders; the most popular arrangement is to have the cylinders in line, with the crankshaft parallel to the length of the car. Some manufacturers use other, more compact arrangements in an effort to increase the space available for the occupants without adding to the overall length of the car. The in-line engine may be mounted transversely in the chassis; alternatively the cylinders may be arranged in vee form or may be horizontally opposed. Engines above 2 litres capacity often have 6 cylinders, usually arranged in line, and some of the largest engines have 8. Although the Daimler Co. favoured the in-line 8 cylinder for many years, modern 8-cylinder engines have the cylinders arranged in a vee. The 6-cylinder engine runs more smoothly than the 4-cylinder because it is fundamentally a better balanced unit and in addition there are shorter intervals between the firings of successive cylinders. The side valve engine has been almost completely superseded by the more efficient overhead valve engine, with the valves operated either by push-rods and rockers from a camshaft in the crankcase or, in the case of high performance engines, by an overhead camshaft. Sev. manufacturers are experimenting with gas turbines for use in cars. The main advantages of the gas turbine are the ability to run on low grade fuels and freedom from vibration; the main disadvantages at present are high fuel consumption especially at light loads, the absence of engine braking and a rather slow response to the accelerator. However, progress is being made in overcoming these defects and the Rover Co. have for sev. years entered an experimental gas turbine car in the ann. Le Mans 24 hr race with very encouraging results. Another possible rival to the reciprocating petrol engine is the Wankel rotary engine; this is still in the development stage and a number of practical difficulties, notably sealing and cooling of the combustion

FIG. 2. ARRANGEMENT OF ENGINE AND TRANSMISSION IN B.M.C. 1100 MODELS.

chambers, have still to be overcome.

Fuel is supplied to the engine from the petrol tank, which is usually at the rear of the car, by means of a pump of the diaphragm type. Fuel passes through a one-way valve into a shallow chamber of which the diaphragm forms the floor. In operation the diaphragm is depressed against the force of a spring, allowing fuel to enter the chamber, and then released, causing fuel to leave the chamber through another 1-way valve on its way to the carburettor. The diaphragm may be operated through a push rod for the engine camshaft or may be operated by an electro-magnet, in which case it has an armature attached to it. Electric pumps are mounted either behind the dashboard or the scuttle or close to the tank. The level of petrol in the tank is shown on a gauge which is simply an ammeter which measures the current through a variable resistance controlled by a float.

In the carburettor (q.v.), petrol is mixed with the right proportion of air before being drawn into the cylinders. Theoretically the correct ratio of petrol to air for complete combustion is 1 to 15 by weight, but in practice the mixture is made slightly richer than this and during acceleration and for starting a considerably richer mixture is supplied. The carburettor incorporates a main jet, a slow running jet and various auxiliary jets and air passages whose function it is to correct the proportion of petrol where necessary so as to ensure that the ratio is correct at all engine speeds and loads. The mixture flows from the carburettor to the inlet manifold, a short pipe with branches to the individual cylinders or to pairs of cylinders; often the inlet and exhaust manifolds are placed in close contact so that heat from the exhaust gases assists in vaporising the fresh mixture. In some high performance engines the petrol is injected through a nozzle into the inlet manifold or directly into the cylinder, but for general use the advantages of fuel injection over the carburettor are not sufficient to justify its extra cost.

Ignition. The ignition system provides the spark which starts combustion in the cylinder; it comprises a coil, contact-breaker, distributor and sparking plug. The sparking plug screws into the cylinder head and incorporates a central electrode which is insulated from the body of the plug by a thick ceramic covering and is separated by an air gap of about 0·020 in. from a second electrode attached to the body. To produce a spark across this gap requires a voltage of 5 to 10 kV; this is generated in the ignition coil which has 2 windings, a primary winding of a few turns of thick wire and a secondary winding consisting of many turns of very fine wire. The primary winding is supplied with current from the car battery through the contact breaker, which is a rotary switch driven by the engine. Normally the contacts are closed; when they open, interrupting the primary current, a high voltage is induced in the secondary coil and is fed via the distributor to the sparking plugs. The purpose of the distributor is to ensure that successive sparks occur in rotation at the different cylinders of the engine. The contact breaker incorporates a means for adjusting the timing of the spark when the engine is stationary and as the timing which gives the best performance varies somewhat with engine speed and load, early cars were fitted with hand controls so that the driver could vary the ignition timing as he drove along. Modern distributors have automatic advance and retard mechanisms which respond to changes in engine speed and often, by sensing the depression in the inlet manifold, to changes in load as well. An alternative form of ignition, magneto ignition, is little used today except for racing cars and motor cycles. The magneto consists of an iron armature which carries both primary and secondary windings and rotates inside the gap of a permanent magnet. The armature shaft also carries the contact breaker; the magneto generates its own primary voltage so that it is independent of a battery. Magneto ignition is more expensive than coil ignition and produces less powerful sparks at low speeds (a disadvantage when starting the engine), though at high speeds its performance is generally better. One limitation to the performance of conventional ignition systems at high engine speeds is set by the contact breaker which has to interrupt the comparatively heavy primary current every time one of the cylinders fires. With engines having 8 or more cylinders the problem becomes particularly serious. Recently ignition systems incorporating transistors have been used in racing cars; the transistor acts as the main contact breaker carrying the heavy current and the mechanical contact breaker triggers the transistor and carries a small current only.

Transmission. Motor-car engines develop their maximum power at a speed of about 5000 r.p.m. and when the average car is travelling at top speed its wheels are turning at about 1000 r.p.m.; hence some speed reduction between the engine and the wheels is necessary. Moreover the petrol engine (in contrast to the steam engine for example) produces very little torque at low speeds although considerable power is often needed when the car is travelling slowly—for instance when climbing a steep hill. It is necessary therefore to provide a number of alternative speed ratios by transmitting the drive through a gearbox which enables any one of 3 or 4 different ratios to be selected. Top gear is usually a direct drive through the gearbox, the necessary speed reduction being obtained at the axle. The gearbox also provides a means of reversing the direction of the drive so that the car can be driven backwards. Another necessary unit in the transmission is a clutch which can be gradually engaged when the car moves off from rest, so that the wheels of the car are slowly coupled to the engine without allowing its speed to fall too low. The clutch is fitted between the engine and gearbox and is also used to disconnect the two momentarily while changing gear. It embodies a circular plate coupled to the gearbox and faced with friction material, which is clamped between a spring-loaded presser plate and the outer face of the engine flywheel. To disengage the drive the presser plate is withdrawn, against the spring force, by a linkage operated by the clutch pedal.

The traditional position of the engine has always been at the front of the car with the gearbox behind it, driving the rear wheels through a long propeller shaft. This arrangement has the disadvantage that a tunnel is required in the floor of the car body to make room for the propeller shaft, the rear end of which rises and falls with the axle. A few manufacturers have always taken the logical view that the engine and gearbox should be grouped next to the wheels being driven, using either a rear mounted engine driving the rear wheels or a forward engine driving the front wheels. Until recently both these arrangements had disadvantages which prevented their wide acceptance. The rear engined car tended to be tail-heavy and this often resulted in indifferent roadholding. The front engined car required that the driven wheels should also be the steerable wheels (it is impracticable to steer a motor car by its rear wheels) so that the drive had to be transmitted through universal joints

and these were often unsatisfactory. However, in recent years the advances in suspension systems, the development of improved universal joints and the wider use of light alloys in engine manuf. have enabled many of the problems associated with front wheel drive and rear engined layouts to be overcome and more manufacturers are adopting one or other of these arrangements.

In the gearbox the input and output shafts are usually in line, and in top gear are coupled directly. Parallel to these shafts is a third, the layshaft, permanently geared to the input shaft and carrying, in the case of the 4-speed gearbox, 3 gear wheels of different sizes which mesh with corresponding wheels on the output shaft. The output shaft is splined and the wheels which it carries can normally rotate freely on it. In the simplest form of gearbox (the 'crash' gearbox) any one of the wheels may be locked to the shaft by means of dog clutches which slide along the splines and are moved by the gear lever. Thus in 1st, 2nd or 3rd gear the drive is from the input shaft to the layshaft and then through the appropriate pair of gears to the output shaft. In this type of gearbox, smooth engagement of the dog clutches requires some skill and usually involves the process of 'double-declutching' to bring the 2 members to about the same speed before attempting to engage them. In modern synchromesh gearboxes the first part of the gear lever movement causes small cone clutches to engage, so equalising the speeds of the 2 members before the final part of the movement brings them into positive engagement. Additional ratios are often obtained by fitting an auxiliary 'overdrive' gearbox in series with the main gearbox. This usually provides 2 ratios, one a direct drive and the other a step-up to enable the engine speed to be reduced during long periods of fast driving. The overdrive gearbox uses an epicyclic gear train so that the ratio can be changed without disengaging the clutch; overdrive can only be brought into operation when either top gear or the next lowest gear in the main gearbox is engaged.

In the past few years the general increase in traffic congestion has led to a growing interest in automatic transmissions whereby the responsibility for gear changing is taken away from the driver and changes are made automatically in accordance with the position of the accelerator pedal and the speed of the car. Either an automatic clutch or a fluid flywheel is used so that the clutch pedal is dispensed with altogether and the driver has only the brake and accelerator pedals to operate. Various forms of automatic transmissions are in use, some utilising a fluid flywheel and an epicyclic gearbox and others a hydraulic torque converter with a simpler gearbox. Until very recently, automatic transmissions have been fitted only to the larger cars. The main reason for this is that the smaller the engine and the less the reserve of power, the more elaborate the automatic transmission required; yet for small cars the extra cost involved represents a much larger proportion of the total cost of the car, so that the purchaser is

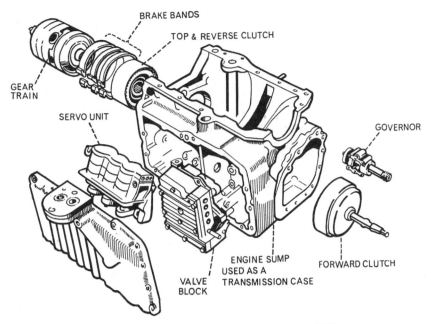

BRAKE BANDS
TOP & REVERSE CLUTCH
GEAR TRAIN
SERVO UNIT
GOVERNOR
VALVE BLOCK
ENGINE SUMP USED AS A TRANSMISSION CASE
FORWARD CLUTCH

FIG. 3. AUTOMATIC TRANSMISSION FOR B.M.C. MINI AND 1100 CARS.

likely to opt for the conventional gearbox. However, the automatic transmission now available on the B.M.C. small cars is a great step forward; although still expensive it could probably be made much cheaper if produced in sufficient quantity. It comprises a hydraulic torque converter together with a 4-speed gearbox; there is no clutch pedal but the driver can override the automatic mechanism and change gear manually if he wishes.

The remainder of the transmission comprises the propeller shaft (where required) and the driving axle. Except where the engine is mounted transversely in the car the drive has to be turned through a right angle at the axle; at the same time the speed is reduced in the ratio corresponding to top gear. The drive is taken to the centre of the axle which is split into 2 halves coupled by the differential. This allows the speed of the 2 road wheels to differ slightly from each other when the car is rounding a corner; the outer wheel, which has to travel a greater distance, rotating faster than the inner.

Braking. Most car braking systems employ internally expanding brake shoes operating in pairs in drums which rotate with the road wheels. Nowadays hydraulic operation is almost universal; the shoes are forced against the inside of the drum by the pressure of hydraulic fluid acting on a piston fitted between the ends of a pair of shoes. The fluid pressure is controlled by the motion, in a master cylinder, of a piston linked to the brake pedal. A hand lever provides an independent means of operating the

brakes on the rear wheels, using cables; it incorporates a ratchet so that it can be set to hold the car stationary. One disadvantage of drum brakes is that they tend to overheat during periods of prolonged use (as in descending long hills) and then lose much of their efficiency. The disc brake comprises a disc attached to the axle and a number of friction pads which are mounted in a stationary caliper and grip the 2 faces of the disc; the pads are operated hydraulically. As the disc is directly exposed to the air stream it is much more effectively cooled than a brake drum. A recent development which has not yet come into general use is an anti-locking device which senses the point at which the wheel is just about to lock and immediately reduces the pressure in the hydraulic system.

Lubrication. In order to minimise the friction between components which move relative to one another, adequate lubrication is necessary. In the engine this is almost invariably by the wet sump method; the bottom of the crankcase is closed by a light metal tray (the sump) which contains a reserve of oil. From the sump, oil is pumped to the main bearings and then by oilways drilled in the crankshaft to the big end bearings; oil is also pumped to lubricate the valve gear. The small end bearings and the cylinder walls are lubricated by splash and surplus oil falls back to the sump. The gearbox and differential casings are partly filled with oil and are topped up when necessary. Joints in the steering and suspension mechanisms are lubri-

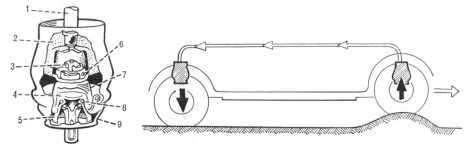

FIG. 4. HYDROLASTIC SUSPENSION

Cross-section of the displacer unit, with a diagram showing how the tail rises in response to upward motion of the front wheel. 1, interconnecting pipe; 2, rubber spring; 3, damper bleed; 4, butyl liner; 5, tapered piston; 6, damper valve; 7, fluid separating member; 8, rubber diaphragm; 9, tapered cylinder.

cated by grease, although the modern tendency is to use rubber bushes or bearings prepacked with lubricant which require no attention.

Electrical Equipment. Much of the auxiliary equipment on a motor car is electrically operated. The lights include headlamps, sidelamps, rear lamps, brake lights, direction indicators, interior and dashboard lights. The ignition system depends upon electricity, as do the starter, horn and windscreen wipers and, in many cases, the petrol pump. The necessary power is provided by a generator, usually a direct current dynamo, which is driven by a belt from the engine crankshaft. Since the starter and many of the other accessories are needed when the engine is not running, a battery is essential. The dynamo charges the battery through an automatic control unit which performs 2 functions: it breaks the circuit when the battery is fully charged, so preventing overcharging, and it also breaks the circuit when the engine stops or runs very slowly, so preventing the battery from discharging through the dynamo and trying to run it as a motor. In recent years the demands made on the battery have increased considerably and some manufacturers of expensive cars have replaced the dynamo by an alternating current generator which charges the battery through a rectifier and has the advantage that it continues to charge at much lower speeds than does the conventional dynamo.

Steering. Steering geometry is based on the Ackerman system, i.e. when the front wheels are turned they do not remain parallel (this would result in scuffing of the tyres) but their axes intersect somewhere along a line passing through the centres of the rear wheels. Various mechanisms are used for transforming rotation of the steering wheel into movement of the front wheels. In the simplest, a pinion on the ends of the steering column engages with a rack (a steel bar having gear teeth cut along one side) which extends across the car. When the steering wheel is turned the rack moves sideways and this motion is transmitted to the front wheels by a system of links. In large cars, power-assisted

steering is quite common.

Suspension. In early motor cars the front and rear axles were each suspended as a single unit, but during the 1930s most manufacturers adopted independent front wheel suspension, in which the 2 wheels were able to rise and fall separately. This had 2 advantages: it enabled the engine to be moved farther forward, so making more room for the passengers, and it improved the roadholding. More recently, independent suspension of the rear wheels has become more popular, although most manufacturers still use the cheaper beam axle. The de Dion rear suspension is a compromise between the beam axle and independent suspension. For many years leaf springs, similar to those used on horse-drawn vehicles, were almost universal; nowadays coil springs are more common. The leaf spring not only acts as a spring but also helps to restrain the wheel or axle from moving forwards, backwards or sideways. With the coil spring this is not so and the wheels must be guided by links which pivot on the car body. A third form of spring is the torsion bar; vertical movement of the wheel twists a long bar of spring steel. In order to prevent prolonged oscillations of the suspension after one of the wheels has hit a bump in the road, dampers or 'shock absorbers' are necessary. Metal springs have many limitations and recently some car makers have turned to rubber springs. In the hydrolastic suspension used on recent B.M.C. cars, fluid is used to transfer the weight of the car to rubber spring units which provide increased stiffness as the load increases; the fluid also acts as a damping medium. Fluid can pass between the front and rear units on the same side of the car; this interconnection results in a steadier ride and better wheel adhesion during cornering.

Starting. It is necessary to fill the cylinders with a charge and to compress it before ignition can take place. This is sometimes done by hand, using a starting-handle mounted in front of the engine, and which, by means of 'dogs', engages with the engine shaft and gives it the necessary amount of rotation. When the engine starts the dogs are thrown out of mesh and are held clear by means of a spring.

An electric starter is fitted to all modern cars. It consists of a small series-wound motor which operates a pinion which meshes with a toothed ring fixed round the flywheel. The electric current is supplied from the car batteries to the field magnets, and then through the armature coils, which has the effect of causing a repelling force between the armature coils and the field magnets, thus producing rotation of the armature. The small pinion is mounted on a sharp spiral on the motor shaft, and, when the latter rotates, the pinion, owing to its inertia, does not at first rotate with it. This causes the pinion to move along the shaft and to mesh with the teeth round the edge of the flywheel. When the engine starts the pinion flies out of gear, owing to the fact that the flywheel drives it faster than the motor. Sometimes the dynamo is made to act as the starting motor. In this case the dynamo-motor shaft is permanently geared to the engine shaft by a chain, so that when the engine has started it drives the motor, which then acts as a dynamo.

See also BUSES AND COACHES; CARBURETTOR; DRIVING LICENCES; INTERNAL-COMBUSTION ENGINE; MOTOR LAW; MOTOR TRANSPORT, COMMERCIAL; MOTOR VEHICLE LICENCES; MOTORING; ROAD SAFETY; TRAFFIC REGULATIONS AND SIGNS; TRANSPORT, MILITARY.

See M. Platt, *Automobile Brakes and Brake Testing*, 1939; H. K. Thomas, *Automobile Engineering* (vols. i–vii), 1939; A. P. Young and L. Griffiths, *Automobile Electrical Equipment*, 1944; S. M. Hills, *Battery Electric Vehicles*, 1944; K. Newton and W. Steads, *The Motor Vehicle*, 1945; R. Dean-Averns, *Automobile Chassis Design*, 1948; E. P. Willoughby, *Motor Manual*, 1948; F. J. Camm, *Motor Car Principles and Practice*, 1948, and *Diesel Vehicles: Operation, Maintenance and Repair* (5th ed.), 1949; *The Autocar Handbook* (20th ed.), 1949; S. P. Smith, *The Electrical Equipment of Automobiles*, 1949; Heldt, *The Automotive Chassis*, 1952, and *Torque Convertors or Transmissions*, 1955; H. E. Milburn, *Motor Cars To-day*, 1956; K. Newton and W. Steads, *The Motor Vehicle*, 1958; J. G. Giles, *Auto and Fluid Transmissions*, 1961; *also* the jours. *Autocar* and *Motor* (weekly). (*See Plates: Motor Cars*; *United States*.)

Motor Cycles. For touring and personal transport the motor cycle was at one time a serious competitor to the motor car because of its low first cost and considerably lower running costs; but in recent years, as society has become more affluent, it has rather declined in popularity. As a vehicle of sport, for races, rough-track riding and hill-climbing, the motor cycle makes a special appeal, and the simplicity and small size of the engine enable the owner to carry out repairs and to satisfy his interest in things mechanical by daily attention to the vehicle. The astounding performance of the dispatch riders at the Royal Tournament is an exhilarating exhibition of the possibilities of a motor cycle when perfectly mastered.

M. C. vary in size from the smallest with engines of about 100 c.c. capacity and having a fuel consumption of 120 or more miles to the gallon to machines with engines of up to 1000 c.c., as large as the engine in a small car; these larger machines are often used with a sidecar. Petrol engines are universal; the smaller M. C. are often powered by 2-stroke engines but for the larger machines efficiency is usually considered more important than simplicity and 4-stroke engines are almost always used (*see* INTERNAL COMBUSTION ENGINES). As in the case of motor cars side valve engines have largely given way to overhead valve. Single cylinder, twin cylinder and even 4-cylinder engines are used. Single cylinder engines are usually mounted upright in the frame. Twin cylinder engines may have the 2 cylinders upright and side by side with both pistons moving up and down together or the cylinders may be arranged in vee formation or horizontally opposed across the frame. The 4-cylinder in-line engine placed longitudinally is impracticable because of its length; one 4-cylinder engine has the cylinders at the corners of a square, in a compact block, and another engine used for racing has the cylinders mounted in line across the frame. Engines are usually air cooled, though water cooling is used in some cases and has the advantage of reducing noise. To assist cooling the exhaust side of the engine is always located towards the front of the machine and in the case of air cooling the cylinder and cylinder head are finned.

Carburettors (q.v.) are similar in principle to those used in motor cars and consist of a float-chamber, which may be top- or bottom-fed, and a mixing chamber which contains the jet or jets, air inlet, and the throttle adjusting the rate of delivery of the air-petrol mixture to the cylinder, and controlled from the handlebars. As the fuel tank is always uppermost on the frame, the carburettor is gravity fed. The Amal carburettor has a main jet and a pilot jet which comes into action at small throttle openings. In the larger types the mixing chamber is vertical and the float-chamber is fitted with a small plunger ('tickler'), which is used for depressing the float and thus flooding the chamber when starting from cold. An air slide controls the amount of air admitted.

Ignition of the fuel is by an electric spark produced either by a high-tension magneto or by a coil. The latter is the cheaper arrangement, requires less attention and gives easier starting (*see* MOTOR CARS).

Transmission. In top gear the engine is required to revolve at about 5 times the speed of the rear wheel and the speed reduction is usually achieved by means of a 2-stage chain drive, the first stage coupling the engine to the clutch and gearbox and the second stage linking the gearbox to the rear wheel. Occasionally shaft drive is used for the second stage; it is particularly suitable for the horizontally opposed twin cylinder engine which has its crankshaft lengthways in the frame. Chain drive is cheaper

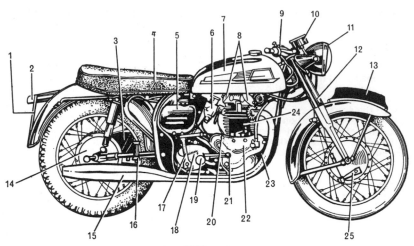

NORTON 650/SS MOTOR CYCLE

1, rear number plate; 2, rear light; 3, rear chain guard; 4, saddle; 5, oil tank; 6, carburettor; 7, petrol tank; 8, valves; 9, instrument panel; 10, speedometer; 11, headlamp; 12, telescopic forks; 13, front number plate; 14, spring wheel hub; 15, exhaust, incorporating silencer; 16, rear step; 17, kick starter (folded); 18, gear-box; 19, foot rest; 20, magneto; 21, gear-change lever; 22, timing case; 23, dynamo; 24, cylinder; 25, front brake.

and theoretically provides a higher efficiency of transmission, though in this application the conditions of operation are far from ideal. In recent years some attempts have been made to improve this by enclosing the rear chain. The gearbox provides 3 or 4 speeds; the various pairs of gears are constantly in mesh and are engaged as required by means of dog clutches. Gear selection is generally by means of a pedal and is of the positive stop type; depression of the pedal to its full extent causes (usually) the next highest gear to be engaged and raising the pedal engages the next lowest gear. With this arrangement it is not possible to change directly from say first gear to third or top gear. As the gearbox runs at a considerably lower speed than the engine, gear changing is a simple operation and no synchromesh is required. The diameter of the clutch is limited by space restrictions so that, unlike the motor car, the motor cycle usually has a multi-plate clutch, operated by a lever on the handlebar.

Electrical Equipment. A generator with automatic voltage control, driven by chain or gearing from the engine, charges a 6-volt accumulator which supplies the lights, horn and, in the case of coil ignition machines, the ignition system. Nowadays the a.c. generator with rectifier is preferred to the d.c. generator because of its ability to provide a high charging current even at low engine speeds.

Lubrication. In early motor cycles oil was supplied to the engine by a hand pump which was operated by the rider every few miles but nowadays engine driven oil pumps, of either the plunger or gear type, are universal. Most engines use the dry sump system in which the oil is contained not in the engine sump but in a separate tank from which it is pumped under pressure to the crankshaft bearings and the valve gear. It eventually drains to the bottom of the crankcase and from there is pumped back to the tank. Two-stroke engines rarely have a separate lubrication system; a certain proportion of oil is mixed with the petrol and since the petrol-air mixture is partly compressed in the crankcase before being introduced into the cylinder, the oil mist reaches all the vital parts of the engine.

Brakes. Brakes are always of the internal expanding type, the rear brake being foot operated and the front controlled by a lever on the handlebar.

Frames are usually made of pressed steel or built up of steel tubes joined by brazed steel lugs, and so shaped as to house the tank and engine and provide adequate lateral stiffness to keep the various parts, especially of the transmission, in true alignment. The rear wheel is usually spring-suspended and the front fork is always fitted with some spring device, either compression springs or rubber suspension. The modern telescopic front fork uses hydraulic or air-oil cushioning. *See also* MOTOR SCOOTER; SPEEDWAY RACING.

See Iliffe & Sons Ltd, *Motor Cycles and how to manage them*, *The Motor Cyclist's Workshop* and *Two-stroke Motor Cycles*; Temple Press Ltd, *Tuning for Speed* ('Slide Rule'); and *Modern Motor Cycle Maintenance* (B. Osborne). *Motor Cycling* and *The Motor Cycle* (weekly) contain information on modern developments.

Motor Generator, combination of a d.c.

motor and an a.c. generator or, more often, an a.c. motor with a d.c. generator on the same shaft for converting the a.c. mains supply to d.c., e.g. for the use of arc-lamps in cinemas. The motor is usually a synchronous motor, the field being excited from the generator. The M.-G. is simple and robust, but not highly efficient.

Motor Launch, *see* MOTOR BOATS.

Motor Law. The purpose of Brit. statute law affecting motorists is to secure safety on the roads. The law prescribes the conditions under which motor vehicles may be constructed and used. The word 'road' refers to any highway and any other road to which the public has access, and includes footways and grass verges as well as the carriage-way itself. The expression 'public road' is used in the legislation relating to vehicle registration and licensing and means a road which is reparable at the public expense.

It is an offence, subject to a fine not exceeding £50, for a person to drive a motor vehicle on a road, or for a person to employ another to drive, unless the driver holds a driving licence (q.v.). The minimum age for obtaining a licence for a motor cycle (a mechanically propelled vehicle with less than 4 wheels, the weight of which unladen does not exceed 8 cwt) is 16 years; for a motor car, 17 years, and for passenger or goods vehicle weighing more than 3 tons unladen, 21 years.

Motor vehicles used or kept on a public road must be registered and licensed with the co. or co. bor. council in whose area the vehicle is ordinarily kept. The council will issue a registration book containing particulars of the vehicle and a licence disc which must be exhibited on the vehicle. If either of these is lost or defaced a duplicate must be obtained for a fee of 5s., which is waived in the case of illegibility where this has not been caused by neglect. The original, if found, must be returned to the council. On renewing a licence it is necessary to produce a current test certificate for a vehicle of the age and type subject to compulsory vehicle inspection. On first registration of a vehicle a registration mark is assigned to it which must be displayed on the front and rear on flat rectangular plates or on flat unbroken rectangular surfaces of the vehicle. (*See* MOTOR VEHICLE LICENCES.)

Insurance. It is unlawful to use, or permit any other person to use, a motor vehicle on a road unless a policy of insurance covering liability in respect of the death or bodily injury of a third party is in force in relation to the user. Penalty: fine not exceeding £50 or imprisonment not exceeding 3 months or both. This policy need not cover liability in respect of the death or bodily injury of a person employed by the insured arising out of and in the course of his employment, or the death or bodily injury of a passenger except where being carried for hire or reward. A person charged with using a vehicle uninsured shall not be convicted if he proves that it was not his or hired or lent to him, that he was using it in the course of his employment, and that he neither knew nor had reason to believe there was no insurance in force. The certificate of insurance must be produced to a constable on demand or within 5 days at the police station specified. Where an accident occurs involving personal injury to another person and the driver does not at the time produce his certificate of insurance to a constable or some person who on reasonable grounds has called for its production, the driver shall report the accident at a police station or to a constable as soon as possible, and in any case within 24 hrs, and produce his certificate. Failure to report is an offence, but if the certificate is not available the driver may produce it in person within 5 days at the police station specified at the time the report was made.

Construction and Use Regulations. These regulations govern the construction, weight, equipment and use of motor vehicles and trailers. Among the items covered are springs, parking brake, brakes, tyres, wings, steering gear, silencer, distribution of weight, mirrors, safety glass, windscreen wiper, horn, speedometer, excessive noise, stopping of engine when stationary, view to front, opening of doors, width of load, footrests for motor cycle passenger, trailer plate and mascots. Direction indicators and stop lights are not compulsory, but if fitted must comply with the regulations. Every motor vehicle and trailer with its accessories shall at all times be in such condition, and the number of passengers carried and the manner of their carriage, and the weight, distribution, packing and adjustment of the load be such that no danger is caused or likely to be caused to any person on the vehicle, trailer or on a road. No person in charge of a motor vehicle or trailer shall cause or permit the motor vehicle or trailer to stand on a road so as to cause any unnecessary obstruction thereof. Evidence of unreasonable use of the highway or the likelihood of obstruction would be sufficient to substantiate the charge; the prosecution would not have to prove actual obstruction. Penalty for infringement of these regulations: fine not exceeding £50.

Vehicle Lighting. The requirements of the law are principally contained in the Road Transport Lighting Acts, 1957/8, and the regulations made under them. During the hours of darkness (between half-an-hr after sunset and half-an-hr before sunrise) a vehicle must show white lights to the front and red lights to the rear (in general 2 of each) visible from a reasonable distance, and 2 red rear reflectors. Vehicles, other than trailers and caravans, must now carry during daytime the lights and reflectors which are obligatory during the hrs of darkness, unless the vehicle has no front or rear lamp or it is masked over or has no wiring. The rear registration mark must be illuminated during the hrs of darkness. Other than goods vehicles exceeding 2 tons unladen and vehicles attached to trailers or having a projecting load which is required to have an additional light, a parked vehicle may be left unlit and without the registration mark illuminated on roads subject to a 30 m.p.h. limit or less. This is provided that in the Metropolitan

WARNING SIGNS

Roundabout   Staggered junction   Series of bends   Two-way traffic straight ahead   Road narrows on both sides   Dual carriageway ends

Uneven road   Level crossing with gate or barrier ahead   Level crossing without gate or barrier ahead   Height limit (e.g. low bridge)   **Accident**   Sharp deviation of route to left (or right if chevrons reversed)

Other danger; plate indicates nature of danger

SIGNS GIVING ORDERS

Stop and give way   Give way to traffic on major road   Pass either side   No entry   No right turn   No U turns

No waiting   No stopping (clearway)   No overtaking   Except for access   No cycling or moped riding   Route for cyclists and moped riders (compulsory)

All motor vehicles prohibited (plate may qualify)

DIRECTION AND INFORMATION SIGNS

Direction to a motorway

One-way traffic

"Count-down" markers at exit from motorway or primary route (each bar represents 100 yards to the exit)

Appropriate traffic lanes at junction ahead

ROAD MARKINGS

No waiting (except for loading and unloading) during:

(a)   (b)   (c)

No loading or unloading during:

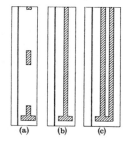

(a)   (b)   (c)

(a) less than the working day   (b) the working day

(c) more than the working day

COLOUR KEY

RED   BLUE   YELLOW   BLACK   WHITE

TRAFFIC REGULATIONS

Some of the road signs introduced to bring the British system more into line with that of the Continent.

Police Dist and City of London there is no regular bus service, or elsewhere that the road is marked by square signs with a horizontal black band on a white background. Further the vehicle must be as close as possible to its correct side of the road, not within 15 yards of a road junction on either side and not more than 25 yards from an illuminated street lamp. Note that these provisions do *not* relax the general law as to parking and obstruction. (See also *Construction and Use Regulations*.)

Traffic Signs. The Traffic Signs Regulations and General Directions of 1964 authorise a new range of signs based on the continental system of symbols. Warning signs are enclosed within a red triangle, while regulatory signs are mainly within a red circle. Informatory signs follow a more logical form of lettering and colour than in the past. A system of lines at the edge of the carriageway, accompanied by a sign indicating the hrs of restriction, indicates a prohibition or restriction on waiting. Markings on the kerb, again accompanied by a sign, indicate a prohibition or restriction on waiting for the purposes of loading or unloading. Non-compliance with coloured light signals, double white line markings, 'Halt at Major Road Ahead' signs (until 1 Jan. 1967, unless their authority is continued owing to the 'Credit Squeeze') and the new 'Stop' signs may involve a maximum penalty of £50, with endorsement of licence and possible disqualification. In the case of other traffic sign offences the maximum penalty is also £50, but neither endorsement nor disqualification is involved.

Road Safety. A Highway Code is issued with the authority of Parliament as a guide to all road users. Although non-observance of the code is not an offence, nevertheless a failure to conform to its provisions may in proceedings, whether civil or criminal, tend to establish or to negative any liability in question in the proceedings. The Pedestrian Crossings Regulations, 1954, provide precedence for a pedestrian who is on a crossing before a vehicle, where traffic is not for the time being controlled by a police officer. Where there is a street refuge or is. there are deemed to be 2 separate crossings. A uniformed school crossing patrol may by exhibiting a 'Stop—Children' sign stop traffic between 8 a.m. and 5.30 p.m. to allow children to cross the road to and from school. Non-compliance with pedestrian or school crossings can lead to a fine not exceeding £50, endorsement and possible disqualification. With certain restricted exceptions motor vehicles first registered 5 or more years ago may not be used on a road unless there is in force a test certificate issued within the last 12 months. This certificate indicates that at the date of examination the vehicle complied with prescribed statutory requirements as to braking, steering and lighting. With the intention of easing the flow of traffic by selective parking only, parking meters have been installed in various parts of the country. As the regulations vary reference should be made to an attendant or to the instructions on the meter itself. Parking in a meter zone is only authorised within a meter bay for payment. No period of grace is allowed for getting change. After 1 Mar. 1966 any person who promotes or takes part in an unauthorised motor competition or trial on a public highway in England or Wales commits an offence. Penalty: fine not exceeding £50. Certain minor events, such as those involving not more than 12 competing vehicles and road safety rallies, are automatically authorised by the Regulations. Most events, dependent on their nature, require specific authorisation from either the appropriate Chief Constable or the Royal Automobile Club. *See also* ROAD SAFETY.

OFFENCES UNDER THE ROAD TRAFFIC ACTS. The Road Traffic Acts, 1960 and 1962, and the regulations made under their authority, form the bulk of motoring statute law. Many of these requirements have been considered within M. L., but certain important matters, particularly the prin. driving offences, remain to be discussed.

It is an offence, subject to a fine not exceeding £100, to sell or supply a motor vehicle or trailer for delivery in such a condition that its use on a road would be unlawful on account of non-compliance with the law as to construction, weight, equipment, brakes, steering gear, tyres or obligatory lamps and reflectors. A person shall not be convicted if he proves that the vehicle was sold for export or that he had reasonable cause to believe that it would not be used on Brit. roads in its unlawful condition. None of these provisions affects the validity of a contract or any rights arising under a contract.

Speed Limits. The Road Traffic Acts prescribe a general speed limit of 30 m.p.h. on restricted roads. A road is restricted if it has a system of street lighting furnished by lamps placed not more than 200 yds apart or is subject to an order imposing a speed limit. On trunk and classified roads the installation of such lighting on or after 1 July 1957 does not automatically result in the road being restricted. Local authorities, with the consent of the Minister of Transport, may make orders de-restricting roads or imposing limits on roads which would not otherwise be subject to a limit. The power lies with the Minister to make orders relating to trunk roads. A person shall not be convicted of exceeding 30 m.p.h. on a restricted road where there is no system of street lighting with lamps 200 yards or less apart unless 'repeater' 30 m.p.h. signs are erected at appropriate intervals. There are also 40 m.p.h. and 50 m.p.h. speed limits. An 'advisory' speed limit of 30 m.p.h. has been introduced for temporary application on motorways where there are serious hazards. Further, at the time of writing (1966), an experimental speed limit of 70 m.p.h. is in operation on all roads, including motorways, not subject to a lower limit.

The only vehicles free of speed limitations on roads other than motorways, are those weighing not more than 3 tons unladen and constructed solely for the carriage of not more than 7 passengers exclusive of the driver and their effects (i.e. cars) and dual-purpose vehicles. Vehicles with seating for more than 7 passengers and goods vehicles are restricted to 40 m.p.h., invalid carriages to 20 m.p.h. On motorways there is a limit of 40 m.p.h. for vehicles towing a trailer with less than 4 wheels or a close-coupled 4-wheel trailer. Penalty: fine not exceeding £50.

Principal Offences. Driving a motor vehicle on a road recklessly or at a speed or in a manner which is dangerous to the public having regard to all the circumstances including the nature, condition and use of the road is punishable by fine not exceeding £100 or imprisonment not exceeding 4 months (second or subsequent conviction, 6 months) or both; on conviction on indictment, a fine or imprisonment not exceeding 2 years or both. Causing death by driving recklessly or at a speed or in a manner which is dangerous to the public having regard to all the circumstances including the nature, condition and use of the road is punishable on conviction on indictment by imprisonment not exceeding 5 years (in Scotland only the High Court of Justiciary may sentence for more than 2 years). On a trial for manslaughter or causing death by dangerous driving the jury may convict for dangerous driving if satisfied that this offence has been committed. Driving without due care and attention or without reasonable consideration for other persons using the road is punishable by a fine not exceeding £100, on the second or subsequent conviction also by imprisonment not exceeding 3 months or both. Leaving a vehicle on a road in such a position, condition or circumstances as to be likely to cause danger to others is punishable by a fine not exceeding £50 or alternatively, on second or subsequent conviction, by imprisonment not exceeding 3 months. Promoting or taking part in a race or trial of speed between motor vehicles on a public highway is punishable by a fine not exceeding £100 or imprisonment not exceeding 3 months or both. Driving or attempting to drive on a road or public place while unfit to drive through drink or drugs is punishable by a fine not exceeding £100 or by imprisonment not exceeding 4 months (second or subsequent conviction, 6 months) or both; on conviction on indictment, a fine or imprisonment not exceeding 2 years or both. Being in charge of a vehicle on a road or public place (but not driving) while unfit to drive through drink or drugs is punishable by a fine not exceeding £100 or imprisonment not exceeding 4 months or both; on conviction on indictment, a fine or imprisonment not exceeding 12 months or both. It is a defence to being in charge to prove (i) that the circumstances were such that there was no likelihood of driving while unfit and (ii) that the defendant had not driven after becoming unfit. A person shall be taken to be unfit to drive if his ability to drive properly is for the time being impaired. A police constable may arrest, without warrant, a person either driving or in charge of a vehicle while unfit through drink or drugs. No person shall be convicted for reckless, dangerous or careless driving, for speeding or for leaving a vehicle in a dangerous position or for failing to comply with a traffic direction

unless: (a) he was warned at the time the offence was committed that the question of prosecuting him would be taken into consideration; (b) within 14 days of the commission of the offence a summons for the offence was served on him; (c) within the 14 days a notice of the intended prosecution specifying the nature of the alleged offence and the time and place where it is alleged to have been committed was served on him or on the registered owner. The notice is deemed to have been served if sent by registered post or recorded delivery to last known address, even if it is returned or is for any other reason not received.

Disqualification and Endorsement. The Road Traffic Act, 1962, introduces new provisions the effect of which is dependent on whether conviction is for an offence under A, B or C: A.1. Manslaughter (Scotland, culpable homicide); 2. Causing death by reckless or dangerous driving; 3. Reckless and dangerous driving committed within 3 years of conviction for these offences or for causing death by reckless or dangerous driving; 4. Driving or attempting to drive while unfit through drink or drugs; 5. Racing on the highway; 6. Driving while disqualified. B. A list of 20 less serious offences including reckless and dangerous driving (other than in A), careless and inconsiderate driving, speeding, driving (or permitting to drive) under age, being in charge while unfit through drink or drugs, leaving in a dangerous position, failing to stop and give particulars after accident, failing to comply with provisional licence conditions, using (or permitting to use) uninsured. C. Conviction for offence under A or B where within the 3 years preceding the commission of the offence and since 29 May 1963 defendant has been convicted with endorsement on not less than 2 previous occasions under A or B. Effect of conviction for offence under: A. Obligatory disqualification for not less than 12 months unless for special reasons, relating to offence only, the Court orders less or none. The minimum disqualification is 3 years where a second conviction within 10 years occurs under A.4. The disqualification period under A.6 is additional to any previous period imposed. Aiding, abetting, counselling or procuring, or inciting the commission of an offence under A leads to disqualification as in B (below). The Court may order disqualification until a driving test has been passed. Endorsement is obligatory if disqualification is ordered; if not conviction must be endorsed unless the Court finds special reasons to the contrary. B. Discretionary disqualification for such period as the Court thinks fit. Driving test and endorsement as in A (above). C. Obligatory disqualification for not less than 6 months unless owing to special circumstances the Court orders less or none. This disqualification period is additional to any imposed on conviction of the third offence.

Application for removal of disqualification where imposed under Road Traffic Act, 1962, can be made after 2 years or half the period of disqualification, whichever is the longer, or where the period is 10 years or more after 5 years. For removal of endorsement, see DRIVING LICENCES. *See Royal Automobile Club Guide and Handbook* (ann.); *Halsbury's Statutes of England and Statutory Instruments*, 1959; G. S. Wilkinson, *Road Traffic Offences*, 1960; L. D. Kitchin and E. K. Wenlock, *Road Transport Law*, 1961; *Stone's Justices' Manual*, 1962.

Motor Licensing, see DRIVING LICENCES; MOTOR LAW; MOTOR VEHICLE LICENCES.

Motor Racing, see MOTORING.

Motor Scooter. Developed from a wartime invention carried by paratroops, the M. S. has now been adapted to suit the needs of the civilian. It is light, compact, easy and safe to ride, and cheap to buy and to run. Credit for the development of M. S.s must go to Italy, where their manufacture has become a major industry.

Motor Ships, ocean-going craft, usually of over 100 tons, powered by internal combustion engines. The total tonnage of M. S. in use today exceeds that of steam vessels. In 1963 the Lloyds register of U.K. shipping listed steam ships totalling 10·6 million tons gross and M. S. totalling 10·9 million tons; in the same year the figures for ships launched in the U.K. were 315,000 tons gross for steamships and 612,000 tons gross for M. S. The advantages of the i.c. engine over the steam engine for marine propulsion are (1) high thermal efficiency, resulting in a low fuel consumption, (2) a saving of space due to the absence of a boiler and its ancillary equipment and (3) (in comparison with coal-burning vessels) easy bunkering. The first ocean-going motor ship in the world was the Dan. *Selandia* of 1912 which was fitted with twin Burmeister and Wain 4-stroke engines, together developing 2400 h.p. The most powerful diesel cargo liner in use today is the *Southampton Castle* (*see* illustration under MERCANTILE MARINE), powered by 2 Sulzer 8-cylinder engines each producing 17,000 b.h.p. and running at a speed of 119 r.p.m.

The engines used in modern M. S. are nearly always vertical compression ignition engines of either the 2-stroke or the 4-stroke type. The 2-stroke engines may be either single-acting or double-acting; the 4-stroke engines are invariably single-acting (*see* INTERNAL COMBUSTION ENGINES). Four-stroke double-acting engines are used in some early M. S. but their inherent complication did not make for reliability or ease of maintenance—both essential factors in marine operation. Almost all the larger M. S. are fitted with 2-stroke engines, often with turbo-chargers (superchargers which are driven by turbines operated by the exhaust gases). By means of turbo-charging, the power of an engine can be increased by about a third with negligible addition to the weight. The biggest engines are coupled directly to the propellers and run at speeds of 100–120 r.p.m. with cylinders up to 3 ft in diameter. Engines of this type include the Doxford, the Harland and Wolff and the Sulzer. The Doxford engine has opposed pistons, each cylinder having a 3-throw crankshaft with the outer cranks at 180° to the inner. The inner crank is coupled by a connecting rod to the lower piston in the usual way and the outer cranks are coupled through sidelinks and connecting rods to the ends of a cross beam which is attached to the upper piston. The 2 pistons and their linkages have different masses, so to correct the balance of the engine the stroke of the lower piston is made greater than that of the upper piston. The latest turbo-charged Doxford engine produces 20,000 h.p. in its 9 cylinder form and weighs nearly 600 tons. Each cylinder is 760 mm. in diameter and the engine speed is 115 r.p.m. Arrangements have been made for complete remote control of the engine from the bridge of the ship.

In the medium-speed field the 4-stroke engine is much more in evidence, and a large number of Brit. designs are current. Medium-speed engines have a shorter stroke than slow-speed engines and require less head room, but it is usually necessary to effect speed reduction in the connection to the propeller by means of gearing. In Germany the M.A.N. concern has produced a highly supercharged 4-stroke engine yielding a power increase of about 87 per cent over the normally aspirated version.

The high-speed lightweight diesel has not until recently been given serious consideration for the propulsion of ocean-going vessels, but since its appearance in 1952 the Napier Deltic engine, primarily intended for high-speed coastal forces craft, has been proposed as a possible prime mover for a multi-engine geared-drive installation, in which engine repair would be effected by means of complete replacement; and in 1956 a Napier Deltic set of this kind was ordered for a bulk cargo carrier (the *Mano*). Working on the 2-stroke cycle, the Deltic has 3 banks of 6 cylinders aligned at 60 degrees to form a triangle (hence Deltic from delta) with crankshafts at each apex, and in each cylinder opposed pistons are connected to their respective crankshafts at the adjacent apices. This engine, capable of 1875 b.h.p. at 1700 r.p.m., weighs only 10,500 lb., and is the first to challenge the performance of the Mercedes-Benz E-boat engine.

Drive. As the most efficient speed of a propeller is below 100 r.p.m., direct coupling of the internal-combustion engine to the propeller shaft implies a long-stroke engine occupying a large space vertically. This is not important in a cargo vessel, but in passenger ships the deck space is needed for accommodation, and in any case the internal-combustion engine is most efficient at high speeds; a high-speed engine develops more power than a slow engine of the same size and, for a given power required, costs less.

It is common practice, therefore, to drive the propeller through reduction gearing from an engine running at 2 or 3 times the propeller speed. The engine is connected to the gearbox through an electromagnetic or hydraulic coupling; often 2 or 4 engines are coupled to the same propeller. The use of couplings provides some cushioning between the engines and the gearbox

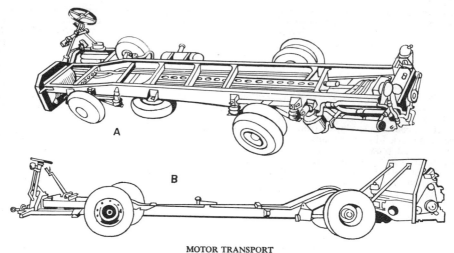

MOTOR TRANSPORT
A, rear-engine coach chassis; B, rear-engine bus chassis.

and also allows one engine to be stopped if necessary, so that repairs can be carried out at sea without reducing the speed of the vessel very much. When manœuvring, some of the engines may be run continuously in the forward direction and others in reverse so that to change the direction of motion of the vessel it is only necessary to uncouple one set and couple the other; there is no need to waste time stopping the engines and restarting them in reverse. In diesel-electric ships the engines are coupled to generators supplying electric motors which drive the propellers. As there is no mechanical coupling between the engines and propellers this arrangement allows great freedom in positioning the engines.

Until 1946 all marine compression ignition engines ran on diesel oil, a refined oil of comparatively low viscosity and considerably more expensive than the heavier oils used in oil fired boilers. Then the engines of the Shell tanker *Auricula* were adapted to run on boiler oil which was preheated to reduce its viscosity and centrifuged to remove impurities. The experiment was successful and nowadays many marine diesel engines, particularly the larger ones, use boiler oil with a resultant saving of up to 25 per cent in fuel costs.

Some M.S. powered by gas turbines have been built, but experience so far has been that the running costs are considerably higher than for diesel propulsion. Free piston engines (q.v.) have also been installed in sev. ships.

Auxiliaries. For driving the deck machinery and other auxiliaries steam is often used; it is generated either in oil fired boilers or in boilers which make use of the waste heat of the exhaust gases from the main engines. The steam may also be used to drive auxiliary turbines coupled to generators for supplying electric power

throughout the ship. *See* G. S. Baker, *The Merchant Ship*, 1949; *The Motor Ship Reference Book*, 1950; D. W. Rudorff, *Modern Marine Engineering*, 1952; *The Motor Ship* (monthly jour.).

Motor Spirit, *see* PETROL.

Motor Transport, Commercial. The term covers the conveyance of goods or passengers by mechanically driven trucks, tractors or hackneys (buses or cabs plying for hire) on the public road (not on rails). As early as 1833 Walter Hancock operated steam buses on regular services in London (*see* MOTOR CARS: *Historical*), but his and similar experiments were brought to an end by the opposition of the turnpike trusts and the success of the steam railway. In 1865 an Act was passed with the intention of protecting horses and cattle on the roads by prescribing that road locomotives, such as were used for hauling threshing machines and rollers, should be preceded by a man carrying a red flag and should not exceed a speed of 4 m.p.h. As the term 'road locomotives' was found to apply to any mechanically propelled vehicle, the Act was practically a ban on motor traffic, although the law was often broken in the early days of motoring; restrictions were eased in 1878, but the hampering rules were not finally removed until 1896. The steam lorry made its appearance in the nineties, but the petrol-engined vehicle was well estab. by 1902. The steam lorry disappeared owing to taxation on its relatively great unladen weight after 1930. Some steam buses operated in London and elsewhere from 1904 to 1919. Meanwhile the internal combustion engine had been developed to a stage where its application to large vehicles became practicable, and in 1904 Thomas Tilling Limited introduced the motor bus to replace a horse bus service in London. Though the earliest of these buses had some foreign components, the Eng. firms, Daimler, Dennis, Guy, Leyland, Crossley, Maudslay and others, soon entered and finally conquered the market.

Passenger Vehicles. Engines have generally been moved away from their traditional position at the front of the bus to locations where they intrude less upon the space available for passengers. It is common practice to place the engine on its side under the floor of the bus and one manufacturer makes a double decker with the engine mounted upright and transversely at the rear of the bus. The maximum dimensions and weights of both goods and passenger vehicles are controlled by law and in 1964 the limits were raised so as to bring the Brit. requirements more into line with Continental practice. Vehicle manufacturers have taken advantage of these changes and in the case of buses the extra length permits the engine to be mounted on its side behind the rear axle with the crankshaft parallel to the length of the bus. In this position it lies largely behind and underneath the rear passenger seat so that the floor level can be lower than with the conventional underfloor engine. Diesel engines are used in almost all buses because of their relatively low fuel consumption and their reliability. Gearboxes have 4 or 5 ratios, often with pneumatic selection to reduce the efforts required from the driver. The latest London Transport Routemaster bus has a fluid flywheel coupled to an automatic gearbox. The Green Line coach version retains manual selection of the gear ratios as it is considered that the lower frequency of gear changing on the coach routes does not justify the extra expense of the automatic transmission. Both vehicles have independent front wheel suspension.

The development of the network of bus routes which now covers nearly the whole country has had a marked effect on the distribution of pop. City workers have been enabled to live on the outskirts of large tns, travelling to and from their office or other place of work in comfort, and to benefit from the better housing conditions available, and the tns have been relieved of some of the overcrowding. At the same time, the replacement of horse-drawn vans by motor vans and lorries of vastly increased load and range of operation has had repercussions on business organisation and the distribution of goods. Direct delivery from the factory, in a single journey without reloading on to trains, has become possible over long distances and has led to estab. of branch factories and distribution centres. As far as passenger transport is concerned, the modern tendency is to use doubledeck buses with up to 78 seats for local traffic, with frequent stops and change of passengers, and single-deck buses for 20 to 45 passengers for routes with low bridges and long-distance express journeys with less frequent stops. The wheelbase is about 14–20 ft, and box dimensions in Britain are 8 ft wide by 30 ft long by 15 ft high. After 6-wheeled vehicles became popular before 1935, they were dropped in favour of the 4-wheeler. Although smaller vehicles can be obtained with petrol engines, the compressionignition oil engine has become almost universal in larger vehicles, and there are several units down to just over 2-litres capacity for small vans, and buses and taxicabs. The underfloor engined coach was initiated in London in 1937 and was developed by B.M.M.O. (Midland 'Red') in vehicles of its own design from 1942 onwards. Most of the leading manufacturers use this lay-out for maximum capacity for singledeck buses and coaches. A 4- or 5-speed gear-box, a 24-volt generator and starter motor and a 185 Ah battery are usual. The fluid flywheel and epicyclic gear-box are standard in London and trends are towards the automatic gear-box, but some operators specify clutch and synchromesh transmission. For delivery of goods of small bulk the cycle-and-sidecar outfit is sometimes used. The electric van, with battery-driven series motor, is ideal for tn deliveries; it has excellent starting and control characteristics, a speed of about 16–20 m.p.h. and a range of 40–60 m. before recharging the battery.

Goods Vehicles were for years divided into 2 categories according to whether they were subject to the 20 m.p.h. limit or not. Those authorised to operate at 30 m.p.h. with an unladen weight under 3 tons included the smallest load carriers, usually based on private car chassis and components, but often of independent design, as in the case of the Trojan (models range from a 1-ton unit to a 33-cwt. articulated type and a 13-passenger bus, with diesel engines as alternative motor units). Loads of up to 6 tons were the usual limit of the 30 m.p.h. class. Above that the maximum capacity 4-wheeler is rated at about 8 tons load or more, depending on the tare weight of the machine; the use of 6 or 8 wheels enables the load capacity to be taken up to about 14 tons or 16 tons respectively inside Brit. load and dimension limits, apart from special type machinery carriers or dump trucks allowed on public highways only under special regulations. Since 1957 the 20 m.p.h. limit on heavy goods vehicles has been lifted to 30 m.p.h.

There are sev. methods of increasing the load of the unit under control of one crew; the attachment of a trailer to a 4-wheeler can almost double the payload, although there is no prospect of lorries hauling trailers being allowed to exceed 20 m.p.h.

The articulated vehicle consists of a tractor towing a trailer which has a rear axle or axles and has its front end supported on a turntable at the rear of the tractor. A pair of light wheels supports the front of the trailer when it is uncoupled from the tractor. This arrangement is more controllable than a separate trailer and the maximum length allowed by law is greater than for a rigid vehicle. The tractor can be used to full advantage as it does not have to remain with a trailer during loading and unloading. The railways have used a light form of articulated vehicle for local delivery for many years. Known as the mechanical horse, it employs a 3-wheeled tractor and is extremely manœuvrable.

As with buses, nearly all heavy goods vehicles are powered by diesel engines though small vans with engines below 2 litres capacity use petrol engines. The heaviest vehicles tend to have a lower power to weight ratio and so need to have a very low first gear. Frequently the rear axle incorporates a 2-stage speed reduction with a pair of bevel gears to change the direction of the drive and a pair of spur gears to transmit the drive from the intermediate shaft to the axle itself. Alternatively the reduction may be made in one step by using a worm and wormwheel instead of bevel gears, but this is expensive. Nowadays lorries frequently use high speed motorways so that a wider range of gear ratios altogether is required. This may be achieved by employing an auxiliary 2-speed gearbox in series with the main gearbox or by using a 2-speed rear axle with alternative ratios. The axles of heavy lorries often carry 4 wheels each, mounted in pairs, since the legally allowed loads are greater than can be carried safely by a single tyre. Front axles invariably carry 2 wheels only, since they must be used for steering. Military vehicles and others which may be required to travel across rough ground often have the drive taken to the front wheels as well as the rear, though provision is made for disconnecting the front wheel drive when it is not required. In recent years considerable attention has been given to making the driver's cab more comfortable with improved visibility, heating and sound-proofing. In many designs the whole of the cab tilts forward to provide access to the engine.

Specialised vehicles include tankers for all types of liquid from milk and beer to petrol and acids; bulk powder carriers for flour and cement; tippers with a hydraulic mechanism to shoot their load on to the ground; dustcarts, ambulances and breakdown vehicles.

In 1963 the total number of goods vehicles licensed in Great Britain was 1,529,000 and the number of public passenger vehicles (motor hackneys) was 96,000.

See J. H. Clapham, *The Economic History of England*, 1926; E. Molloy, *Modern Oil Engine Practice*, 1942; S. M. Hills, *Battery Electric Vehicles*, 1943; M. M. and G. W. Williamson, *The Commercial Motor Vehicle*, 1948; L. D. Kitchin, *Bus Operation*, 1949, (*See Plate*.)

Motor Vehicle Insurance, *see* INSURANCE (ACCIDENT INSURANCE, *Motor*).

Motor Vehicle Licences. These licences are issued for a calendar year or for any period of 12 months or, where the ann. duty is more than £4, for any period of 4 months. Motor vehicles are divided into categories the ann. rates of duty for which are as follows. Bicycle, electrically propelled, or not exceeding 150 c.c., £2; bicycle not exceeding 8 cwt unladen, £8. Hackney carriage, £12 plus 10*s*. for each passenger seat over 20; tramcar, 15*s*. Agric. and certain contractor's machines, £3.15*s*; showman's haulage vehicle, £37.10*s*. upwards; other haulage vehicles, £45 upwards. Farmer's and showman's goods

vehicle, including electrically propelled, £15 upwards; other electrically propelled goods vehicles and tower wagons, £18 upwards; other goods vehicles, £18 upwards. Vehicle not exceeding 7 h.p. if first registered before 1 Jan 1947, other electrically propelled vehicles, £12.10*s*.; vehicles not otherwise included (i.e. cars), £17.19*s*. Additional duty is payable in respect of trailers drawn by the following goods vehicles and is based on the unladen weight of the drawing vehicle: showman's goods vehicle, £15 any weight; electrically propelled goods vehicles, other than farmer's and showman's goods, and tower wagons, not exceeding 1½ tons unladen, £12, greater weight, £18; other goods vehicles, not exceeding 1½ tons unladen, £12, not exceeding 2½ tons, £18, not exceeding 4 tons, £27, exceeding 4 tons, £36. Where 'upwards' is stated above this indicates that duty is based on unladen weight and lowest rate is quoted. The vehicle licence may be surrendered to the registration authority and a rebate obtained for each complete month unexpired at the date of surrender. *See also* DRIVING LICENCES; MOTOR LAW.

Motoring. The first exhibition of motor cars was held in England at Tunbridge Wells, Kent, in 1895, organised by Sir David Salomons. The following year brought the introduction, through the efforts of early Brit. M. pioneers, of the Emancipation Act (1896), abolishing the necessity for cars to be preceded by a man on foot. At the same time the speed limit was raised to 12 mph.

The Emancipation Act is still commemorated annually by the Royal Automobile Club's London–Brighton veteran car run, held on the first Sunday in Nov., which each year attracts 250 cars (the maximum allowed on the run) all built before 1905. Since 1932 'the Motor Show'—the manufacturers' ann. exhibition of the coming year's models—has been held at Olympia and later Earl's Court, London, in Sept. or Oct.

The oldest motor club in the world, the Automobile Club de France, founded in 1896 (a year before the R.A.C.), was formerly the chief controlling force in international motor sport and touring matters. Today the international controlling body is the Fédération Internationale de l'Automobile, with its H.Q. in Paris.

The F.I.A. is made up of delegates from member countries throughout the world, each country being represented by its recognised national automobile club—the R.A.C., for example, in the case of Great Britain and the Commonwealth.

The 'Automobile Club National' is the governing body as far as its own country is concerned, subject to any international regulations made by the F.I.A. and a few additional regulations to suit national conditions.

Ever since the first motor car appeared on our roads, man has been attracted by speed and 1907 saw the completion of the famous Brooklands circuit at Weybridge, Surrey, the scene of many accepted pre-war world records.

WORLD'S LAND SPEED RECORDS
(Flying-Kilometre or Flying-Mile)

Date	Driver	Car	Speed mph	Place	Distance
*1898	Chasseloup-Laubat	Jeantaud (elec.)	39·24	Achères	km.
*1899	Jenatzy	Jenatzy (elec.)	65·82	Achères	km.
*1902	Serpollet	Serpollet (steam)	75·06	Nice	km.
*1903	Augières	Mors (int. comb.)	77·13	Dourdan	km.
*1904	Baras	Darracq (i.c.)	104·53	Ostend	km.
*1909	Hemery	Benz (i.c.)	125·09	Brooklands	km.
*1922	Guinness	Sunbeam (i.c.)	129·17	Brooklands	km.
*1924	Campbell, M.	Sunbeam (i.c.)	146·16	Pendine	km.
*1925	Campbell, M.	Sunbeam (i.c.)	150·86	Pendine	km.
*1926	Segrave	Sunbeam (i.c.)	152·33	Southport	km.
*1926	Thomas	Higham (i.c.)	171·09	Pendine	km.
1927	Campbell, M.	Napier-Campbell (i.c.)	174·88	Pendine	km.
1927	Segrave	Sunbeam (i.c.)	203·79	Daytona	m.
1928	Keech	White Triplex (i.c.)	207·55	Daytona	m.
1929	Segrave	Irving Special (i.c.)	231·44	Daytona	km.
1931	Campbell, M.	Napier-Campbell (i.c.)	246·09	Daytona	km.
1932	Campbell, M.	Napier-Campbell (i.c.)	253·97	Daytona	m.
1933	Campbell, M.	Rolls-Royce-Campbell (i.c.)	272·46	Daytona	km.
1935	Campbell, M.	Rolls-Royce-Campbell (i.c.)	276·82	Daytona	m.
1935	Campbell, M.	Campbell Special (i.c.)	301·13	Utah	m.
1937	Eyston	Thunderbolt No. 1 (i.c.)	312·00	Utah	km.
1938	Cobb	Railton (i.c.)	350·20	Utah	m.
1938	Eyston	Thunderbolt No. 1 (i.c.)	357·50	Utah	m.
1939	Cobb	Railton Special (i.c.)	369·70	Utah	km.
1947	Cobb	Railton Special (i.c.)	394·20	Utah	m.
1964	Campbell, D.	Bristol-Siddeley (gas turbine)	403·10	Utah	m.
1964	Arfons	Green Monster (jet)	544·13	Utah	m.

* Excluding speeds reached in U.S.A.

Brooklands was last used in 1939, but a crop of new circuits grew in its place and today Britain is probably better off in this respect than any other country.

Most notable of these are Silverstone (2·927 m.) run by the Brit. Racing Drivers' Club near Towcester, Northants; Brands Hatch (2·65 m.) on the London–Maidstone road; and Goodwood (2·4 m.) near Chichester, Sussex,

The chief Continental race circuits are at Nurburgring (Germany), Monza (Italy), Monte Carlo (Monaco), Spa (Belgium), Zandvoort (Holland) and Clermont-Ferrand (France), scenes of the respective countries' Grands Prix.

The chief tracks in the U.S.A. are the Watkin's Glen GP circuit near New York and the Indianapolis race-track, scene of the spectacular 500 m. race The earliest competitive event for motor vehicles is commonly held to have been the concours des Voitures sans Chevaux (horseless carriages) organised by Le Petit Journal in France in 1894. The fastest time was that of a M. Lemaître in a Peugot averaging 11·5 mph. Then came the famous race from Paris to Bordeaux and back, 1895, Levassor being the first winner (in 2 days and 48 min. at an average

speed of 15 mph); from Paris to Marseilles and back in 1896, organised by the A.C. de France, an average speed of 15½ mph being attained; many road racing events, such as the Tour de France, over a distance of 1350 m. at an average speed of 35 mph; the Gordon-Bennett race, first held in 1899, over a course of 353¾ m. and first won by Charron in a Panhard at 36·6 mph.

In 1898 came the first of a series of attempts to estab. records over a flying kilometre. In the next few years manufacturers, generally, subordinated racing to the production of reliable cars for sale to the public, but sev. notable records were set up, including the now classic Indianapolis 500 m. record (almost doubled today) by Thomas in a Delage at 82·47 mph., and the R.A.C. Tourist Trophy, 600 m. by K. Lee Guinness in a Sunbeam at 56·4 mph.

But after 1918 numerous important road races were held annually and many record-breaking races were accomplished over distances up to 1500 m.

These were run in the earlier years over closed circuits, and later over newly constructed concrete racing tracks on the Continent. From 1924 came a series of flying-mile attempts at

Pendine Sands and Florida Beach, and in the same period board-track racing, a favourite form of motor sport in America, the greatest event being the 500 m. race at Indianapolis.

It was not until 1926, however, that Amer. speed records were recognised by the F.I.A., so that many performances before that date in Europe were held as official world records irrespective of higher speeds reached in America.

Although it had for many years been an accepted term, an official world land speed record did not exist until the autumn of 1964. Until then, the 'targets' had been the international speed records of the Fédération Internationale de l'Automobile (for 4-wheeled vehicles) and the Fédération Internationale Motorcycliste (for 2- or 3-wheeled vehicles). Although theoretically of no greater importance, the Automobile record had been considered the world land speed record.

In 1964, however, a joint committee was set up between the F.I.A. and the F.I.M. to observe record attempts by all types of vehicles, whether 2, 3 or 4 wheeled, and whether driven through their wheels or jet-propelled. The existing record of the late Donald Campbell (403·1 mph) was soon bettered by Art Arfons, of America, who drove his 4-wheeled jet powered car at 544·13 mph on the Bonneville Salt Flats, Utah.

On page 583 is a short list of world land speed records, officially the international Automobile record until 1964, for the flying kilometre or flying mile, giving an impressive picture of the development of racing cars in 65 years. Since 1922 figures are averages for 2-way runs. These, and other data, are courteously supplied by the Royal Automobile Club.

The outstanding foreign events on the international calendar, apart from the World Championship Grands Prix, are the Indianapolis 500-m. race, U.S.A., and the Targa Florio road-race, Italy, in May, and the Le Mans 24-hr race, France, in June. The world's oldest motor race still being regularly run is the R.A.C. Tourist Trophy.

Motril (anct **Firmium Julium**), Sp. tn in the prov. of Granada, situated in a valley where sugarcane, bananas and flowers are grown. Lead, iron, zinc and copper are found near by. M. has a port on the Mediterranean at Calahonda, 6 m. SE. Pop. 19,200.

Mott, Valentine (1785–1865), Amer. surgeon, b. Glen Cove, Long Island, and educ. at Columbia College, New York; M.D., 1806. He then studied in London and Edinburgh before being appointed prof. of surgery first at Columbia (afterwards combined with the College of Physicians and Surgeons), Rutgers Medical School, 1826–31, the univ. of New York, 1840, and again at the College of Physicians and Surgeons. He became the leader of Amer. surgery. He was the first to ligate the innominate artery (1818) and successfully tied a number of other arteries. He performed a number of bold and successful operations on the bones and joints, including removal of the lower jaw, excision of the collar bone and amputation at the hip-joint. *See* memoir by S. D. Gross, 1868.

Motte, Jean-Marie Bouvier de la, *see* GUYON, MME.

Motteux, Peter Anthony (Pierre Antoine) (1663–1718), Fr. playwright and translator, b. Rouen. He settled in London as a Huguenot merchant on the revocation of the Edict of Nantes in 1685. He wrote dramas, including *Love's Jest*, 1696, *The Loves of Mars and Venus*, 1696, and *Novelty*, 1697. He also trans. *Don Quixote* into English, and Rabelais's works in collaboration with Urquhart and Ozell. *See* life by R. N. Cunningham, 1933.

Mottistone, John Edward Bernard Seely, 1st Baron (1868–1947), politician. Educ. at Harrow and Trinity College, Cambridge; called to the Bar in 1897. After service in the S. African war he entered Parliament. By 1912 he was secretary of state for war, losing the post in 1914 over the 'Curragh incident' (q.v.). During the First World War he reached the rank of major-general. Under-secretary for air in 1919, he resigned over the gov. refusal to separate the air service from the War Office, a step taken later. His pubs. include *Adventure*, 1930.

Mottram, Ralph Hale (1883–), novelist, b. Norwich. He was educ. in Norwich and London, became a bank clerk, and then served as an interpreter in the First World War. His war experiences in Belgium inspired the admirable novel or quasi-novel entitled *The Spanish Farm*, 1924, which was awarded the Hawthornden Prize. In this work M. may be said to have set the standard for war books of a pseudo-fictional type as literature. *Sixty-four, Ninety-four*, 1925, and *The Crime at Vanderlynden's*, 1926, combine with *The Spanish Farm* to form a trilogy. Other books include *Our Mr Dormer*, 1927, *The English Miss*, 1928, *Ten Years Ago*, 1928, *The Boroughmonger*, 1929, *Europa's Beast*, 1930, *Poems Old and New*, 1930, *Castle Island*, 1931, *The Headless Hound*, 1931, *Home for the Holidays*, 1932, *Old England*, 1937, *Trader's Dream*, 1939, *The World turns Slowly Round*, 1942, *The Gentleman of Leisure*, 1947, *Over the Wall*, 1955, *Another Window Seat*, 1957, *Time's Increase*, 1961, *Happy Birds*, 1963. *Autobiography with a Difference* appeared in 1939.

Moúdhros, *see* MUDROS.

Moufflon, species of wild sheep (*Ovis musimon*), formerly common in Spain but now restricted to Corsica and Sardinia. It is some 28 in. high at the withers, or about the size of a common sheep, and the wool of the upper parts is brownish-grey with a dark dorsal streak and white on the legs and face. Horns are present in the males only and the tail is very short. The ram's curved horns are sometimes as much as 3 ft in length. The M. breeds freely with the domestic species. *See also* SHEEP.

Moukden, *see* MUKDEN.

Mould, *see* SOIL.

Mould, general unscientific name for a variety of thread-like fungi, which in the presence of damp attack many kinds of animal and vegetable substances. *Penicillium digitatum* and *italicum*, the blue, green or brown M.s of oranges and other fruit, can only gain a hold when the skin or rind of the fruit has been slightly damaged. *See* ASPERGILLUS; BOTRYTIS; MILDEW; MYXOGASTRES; SAPROPHYTES.

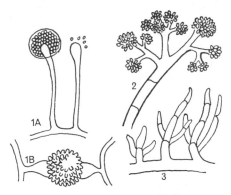

HIGHLY MAGNIFIED MOULDS

1, *Mucor*; A, asexual, and B, sexual sporangia.
2, *Botrytis cirerea*. 3, Fusarium.

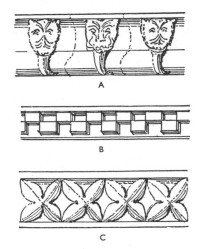

MOULDINGS

(*top*) Romanesque: A, Beak-head and B, Billet (square)
(*bottom*) Gothic: C, Dog-tooth.

Moulding, or Die-casting. Die-casting may be applied to any casting produced from a metal mould or die. 'Pressure' die-casting is employed to advantage when the component to be manuf. is in large quantities and of a thin wall section. It consists chiefly of pumping molten metal into a steel die or mould under carefully regulated conditions. There are 2 types of pressure die-casting machines, i.e. hot chamber and cold chamber. The former has an integral furnace, and the metal is injected automatically, usually by air pressure. This method is generally used for zinc and other low-temp. melting metals. In the cold chamber machine the molten metal is ladled from a separate furnace into the machine, which injects it into the dies at great pressure. This process is repeated approximately every minute. The castings produced by this method are of such accuracy as to require little further treatment prior to being finished before final assembly. This method is generally used for aluminium, brass and other high-temp. melting metals. Gravity die-casting is employed if the casting is large and beyond the range of the die-casting machines; in this method the metal is poured into the mould, and not injected under pressure. Practically all types of non-ferrous metals can be die-cast, the 4 main metals in use today, in order of castability, being zinc, magnesium, brass and aluminium. The die-casting industry, rapidly expanding, is widely used in the motor, radio and electrical trades, and more recently in the manuf. of furniture components. *See* METALLURGY.

Mouldings, in architecture, ornamental and continuous lines of grooving or projections, worked respectively below or above the face of any part of a building. They may be either plain or carved. Any individual part of a moulding is called a 'member', and any member which is ornamentally carved is said to be 'enriched'. In each period of architecture, M. were so distinctive in design that it is possible to estimate the date of a building from the character of its M. alone. The illustration (p. 586) shows a parallel of the prin. Gk and Rom. M. It will be noticed that the Gk examples, where curved, follow conic sections; whereas the Rom. curved M. are all segments of a circle. The most characteristic enrichments of Gk and Rom. M. are the 'egg and tongue' or 'egg and dart', and the 'bead and reel'.

Romanesque M. were based upon Rom. prototypes, but were more clumsy in design and execution. The doorways of Norman churches of this period in England often display M. enriched with grotesque representations of animal or human heads, or with billets (q.v.), or chevrons (i.e. zigzags). Gothic M. were bold in design, and often deeply undercut. Renaissance M., based upon Rom. types, are seen at their best in the work of Peruzzi (q.v.) in Italy, and of Wren (q.v.) and his followers and craftsmen in England. *See also* BOLECTION MOULDING: DRIPSTONE; GUILLOCHE. (*See illustration overleaf*.)

Moulin Rouge, famous Parisian place of entertainment. It received its name from the windmill over the entrance.

Moulins (anct **Molinae**), Fr. tn, cap. of the dept of Allier, on the Allier. It was the anct. cap of Bourbonnais (q.v.). Its many fine old buildings include the remains of a Bourbon castle. Villars and the Duke of Berwick (qq.v.) were *b*. here, and Clarendon (q.v.) wrote some of the *History of the Rebellion* here. There are leather and textile manufs. Pop. 23,900.

Moulins, Giants' Kettles, or **Cauldrons,**

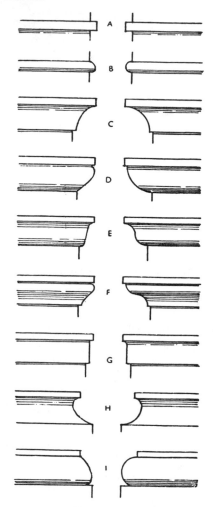

CLASSICAL MOULDINGS
(Greek on left, Roman on right)
A, Fillet; B, Astragal; C, Cavetto; D, Ovolo;
E, Cyma Recta; F, Cyma Reversa; G, Fascia;
H, Scotia; I, Torus.

popular name for hollows worn by melt-water flowing below glaciers.

Moulmein, port, cap. of Amherst dist and of Tenasserim div., Lower Burma, on the E. bank of the Salween R. near its mouth. It is connected by ferry with Martaban on the opposite side of the estuary. The former shipbuilding industry has declined, but rice and timber are exported. An important centre of the teak trade, it has many sawmills. There is a univ. and a training institute for teachers. It was captured by the Japanese on 31 Jan. 1942. Pop. 116,000.

Moulting, general term for the habit in a large variety of animal types of shedding, periodically, the outer covering of feathers, hair, skin, cuticle, etc. In common usage it refers to the ann. renewal of birds' feathers, which usually follows the completion of parental duties.

Moulton of Bank, John Fletcher Moulton, Baron (1844–1921), lawyer, b. Madeley, Salop. He was called to the Bar in 1874, establishing the leading practice in patent law, on which he was recognised as a supreme authority. He took silk in 1885 and sat as a Liberal member of Parliament for Clapham, 1885–6, S. Hackney, 1894–5, then Launceston until 1906, when he became a lord justice of appeal. In 1912 he became one of the lords of appeal in ordinary and received a life peerage. During the First World War he was director-general of explosive supplies to the Ministry of Munitions.

Moultrie, John (1799–1874), clergyman and poet, b. London. Educ. at Eton and Cambridge, he took orders and was rector of Rugby from 1825 until his death. In 1864 he became canon of Worcester. His collected works were pub. in 2 vols. in 1876. His best poems were 'My Brother's Grave' and 'Godiva', both printed in 1820. Vols. of his verse include *The Dream of Life*, 1843, *The Black Fence*, 1850, *St Mary*, 1850, and *Altars, Hearths and Graves*, 1854. His works were ed. in 1876 with a memoir by D. Coleridge.

Mound Birds, or **Mound Builders** (Megapodiidae), remarkable family of gallinaceous birds, which are so called on account of their habit of throwing up large mounds of vegetable matter, earth and sand in which they deposit their eggs, which they cover up and then leave to be incubated by the heat produced by fermentation. In some cases the mounds are co-operative. The species number only about 20, and are characterised by very large feet, short tail and crested head. They are found in the Malay Archipelago and Australia. A familiar example is the brush-turkey (q.v.).

Mound Builders, prehistoric inhab. of N. America, who lived mainly in the valleys of the Mississippi and Ohio. There are various opinions about their identity, but the generally accepted view now is that the Indians are their descendants, and that they belong to the Stone Age. They appear to have surpassed the Indians (when first met by the whites) in civilisation, and made very beautiful objects of stone, shell, bone and beaten metals. But the most wonderful works of their hands were the earth mounds from which they receive their name. These vary in shape, being round, conical or in the shape of animals, and are scattered all over the country between the Allegheny and Rocky Mts, but chiefly in Ohio, Illinois, Indiana and Missouri. The most famous mound in Ohio is the Great Serpent in Adams co., near Bush Creek. This, a gigantic serpent made in earth, measures 1348 ft in length and is 5 ft high. Wisconsin too contains some mounds in the shape of animals, some of which are of gigantic size. These, generally known as effigy mounds, were possibly objects of worship as guardians of the vils. Other famous mounds are: Cahokia, near St Louis, Missouri; Etowah, Bartow City, Georgia; Elephant Mound, near Wyalusing, Wisconsin; and Grave Creek Mound, near Moundsville, W. Virginia.

Mound Dwellings, underground or semi-underground dwellings, which were at one time very widespread. Certain M. D. are of prehistoric date, while others were occupied even in recent times. In Scotland there are many varieties, numerous instances being found on the coasts of almost all the Orkney Is. On the Arctic shores of NE. Siberia, the hyperborean race of the Onkilon dwelt in earth huts, half sunk into the ground, in the form of small mounds covered with a thick layer of earth. Similar dwellings were used by the former natives of Kamchatka and the Aleutian Is., and by the Greenland Eskimoes for winter dwellings. M. D. were usually circular or oblong in shape, had the appearance of a large rounded hillock, and were entered by a low narrow passage. *See* SOUTERRAINS.

Moundsville, co. seat of Marshall co., W. Virginia, U.S.A., on the Ohio R., 11 m. S. of Wheeling. Manufactures include glass, bricks, enamelware and cigars; and coalmining, zinc smelting and refining are carried on. Pop. 15,160.

Mount Athos, *see* ATHOS.

Mount Carmel: 1. Israel, *see* CARMEL, MOUNT; CARMELITES.

2. Bor. of Northumberland co., Pennsylvania, U.S.A., 6 m. from Shamokin. Coal is mined, and mining machinery and miners' supplies are manuf. Pop. 10,760.

Mount Eden, bor. and a suburb of the city of Auckland, N. Is., New Zealand, dominated by M. E. (Maori name *Maungawhau*), a volcanic cone with a large crater from which a fine view can be obtained of the city and harbour and of the ocean on both coasts. The bor., which is a separate municipal entity from Auckland, is primarily a residential suburb of Auckland; it was formerly a fortified Maori vil. Pop. 18,300.

Mount Gambier, tn of S, Australia, near the Victorian border. It is the centre of a grain-growing dist. Pop 15,388.

Mount Isa, tn of NW. Queensland, Australia, 1435 m. by rail from Brisbane via Townsville, and a prosperous, fast-growing silver-lead-zinc mining centre. The discovery in 1954 of uranium ore at Mary Kathleen some 40 m. distant and the proposed development of the mine are expected to make an important contribution to the development of the area. Pop 13,358.

Mount Palomar Observatory, *see* PALOMAR, MOUNT.

Mount Sarmiento, *see* TIERRA DEL FUEGO.

Mount School, The, public boarding school for girls, founded at York in 1785 by members of the Society of Friends, the sister-school to Bootham (q.v.). There are some 250 pupils.

Mount Stephen, George Stephen, Baron (1829–1921), Canadian financier, *b.* Dufftown, Banffshire, Scotland. He emigrated to Canada in 1850, and went into business in Montreal, where he became president of the Bank of Montreal. In partnership with his cousin, Donald Smith (later Lord Strathcona), he purchased the St Paul and Pacific Railway, and they then started the construction of the Canadian Pacific Railway, which was completed in 1885. The following year he was made a baronet, and raised to the peerage in 1891, taking his title from a peak in the Rocky Mts, named after him while the railway was in course of construction. He left Canada in 1888, and lived in Scotland and England, chiefly at Brocket Hall, Herts. A great philanthropist, he gave generously to hospitals in London, Montreal and Aberdeen, leaving the residue of his estate to the King Edward Hospital Fund. *See* K. Morris, *The Story of Lord Mount Stephen*, 1922.

Mount Vernon: 1. City of Westchester co., New York, U.S.A., on the Bronx R., 18 m. NNE. of New York. It manufs. dies, machinery, silverware, radio and electronics equipment, chemicals, rubber goods and vitamin and food products. Pop. 71,900.

2. Amer. national shrine, the former home of George Washington, on the Potomac R., in Fairfax co., Virginia, and 15 m. S. of Washington. It was built in 1743, and purchased for the nation in 1860. The remains of Washington and his wife lie in the estate.

Mount Wilson Observatory, at a height of 5700 ft above sea-level near Pasadena, California, U.S.A., was founded by George Ellery Hale (q.v.) in 1904, as a branch of the Carnegie Institution of Washington. The site enjoys over 300 cloudless nights per year. There are 5 prin. instruments. Three of these are used for observing the sun: the original horizontal solar telescope, a 60 ft tower telescope and a 150 ft tower. These have made important studies of the sun's activity and of its magnetism. The two stellar telescopes are the 60 in. reflector (1909) and the 100 in. Hooker reflector (1917). The latter remained for 30 years the world's most powerful telescope and was used for major astronomical discoveries, revolutionising our concepts of the scale of the universe. With it E. P. Hubble (q.v.), about 1925, ended the long debate concerning the nature of the spiral nebulae (*see* GALAXIES), showing that they are gigantic star systems like our own galaxy, at distances of millions of light-years. Hubble and Humason studied the red-shifts in the spectra of distant galaxies, finding that their speeds of recession are proportional to their distances. W. Baade, using the war-time blackout of the Los Angeles dist, discovered evidence for 2 distinct 'populations' of stars in galaxies. It was the 100 in. telescope's revelation of the vast scale of the universe that led Hale, as early as 1928, to propose the construction of a 200 in. telescope (*see* PALOMAR, MOUNT).

Mountain, The, or **Montagnards,** name given to the extreme Democratic party in the Fr. Revolution. They were so called because they occupied the highest benches in the National Convention, while their opponents, the Girondists, sat on the floor of the house. The party was divided into Jacobins and Cordeliers, and its prin. members were Danton, Desmoulins, Marat, Robespierre, St Just and Collot d'Herbois, the men of the 'Reign of Terror'. *See* J. M. Thompson, *The French Revolution*, 1943.

Mountain Ash, urb. dist of Glamorgan, Wales, 4 m. SE. of Aberdare, forming part of Aberdare parl. bor. The area is highly industrialised, with water works and important factories and collieries. Pop. 29,590.

Mountain Ash, or **Rowan** (*Sorbus,* syn. *Pyrus aucuparia*), handsome flowering tree of the family Rosaceae, with pinnate leaves and large corymbose cymes (*see* INFLORESCENCE) of small cream flowers, which are followed by small fleshy scarlet berries with yellow flesh; these have a bitter acid flavour, and are much eaten by birds. They have been dried and ground into a kind of flour. The tree reaches a height of from 10 to 30 ft, and its tough wood has numerous uses.

MOUNTAIN ASH, OR ROWAN

Mountain Building Period, or **Orogeny.** The major mt chains of the world such as the Alps, Andes, or Himalayas consist of intensely folded or overthrust strata. The periods of geological time in which earth movements producing such structures were especially marked in the geological record are known as orogenic periods or periods of M. B., and may be distinguished from much longer quiescent or non-orogenic periods. In pre-Cambrian times more than 10 orogenic periods have been identified. These very old mt chains have, however, been deeply eroded. The relief of the earth at the present day is largely governed by forms developed in 4 periods of M. B. which have occurred since the Cambrian. These are the Caledonian, the Hercynian or Armorican, the Laramide and the Alpine M. B. periods, which occurred in early Palaeozoic, late Mesozoic and late Tertiary times respectively. The mt chains along the Amer. coast of the Pacific date largely from the Laramide orogeny, while the Alps and the Himalayas are the prin. ranges formed during the Alpine period of mt formation. Isolated mts form in other ways, principally through volcanic action, block

faulting, or erosion; virtually all the extensive ranges of the world, however, originated through orogenic movements which crumpled the pre-existing rocks and uplifted them to form a mt chain.

Mountain Laurel, *see* KALMIA.

Mountain Limestone, obsolete geological name for the Lower Carboniferous rocks known as the Carboniferous Limestone which form a cover, often sev. thousand feet thick, over parts of N. and W. England, Wales and much of central Ireland.

Mountain People's (Russian **Gorskaya**) **Autonomous Republic,** ephemeral administrative-political div. in N. Caucasus (1921–4) with Vladikavkaz (now named Ordzhonikidze) as cap., gradually broken up into separate national units.

Mountain Railways, *see* RAILWAYS.

Mountain Sheep, *see* SHEEP.

Mountain Warfare. Although the technique is quickly acquired by good troops, M. W. requires special training, particularly in snow mts where the use of skis is often necessary. Special light guns and other equipment are also required, which, together with supplies, have to be transported by pack-animals or, more recently, in light tracked vehicles such as the 'Weasel', and in certain circumstances by helicopter or by means of air drops.

For many decades prior to 1947 the Brit., Indian and Gurkha troops of the army of India waged almost continuous warfare against the Pathan tribes of the NW. Frontier of India. They developed a specialised system of tactics, and a very high standard of efficiency in this type of warfare.

In the Second World War the troops in sev. campaigns—notably in Italy and Abyssinia —had to adapt themselves to mt conditions. In the U.K. troops, including the whole of the 52nd (Lowland) Div., were specially trained in M.W. in Scotland and Wales. One unit, Lovat Scouts, underwent mt training in the Canadian Rockies and subsequently fought in Italy. In the Korean campaign (1950–53) the U.N. troops had to fight almost entirely in mt terrain.

Mountain Wine, 18th cent. name for wine from Malaga (q.v.).

Mountaineering. The awe and inspiration associated with mts are well illustrated in the O.T. and in the Gk classics; men feared them and generally avoided them. M. in the modern sense means the ascent of high mts for sport and adventure. It is a product of the 19th cent.; its possibilities were discovered and developed mainly by men in sedentary occupations to whom it offered refreshment of mind and body, an escape from the social duties and restrictions and the monotony of urbanised life. Ascents of high mts previous to the 18th cent. were rare and made by exceptional men. Trajan viewed the sunrise from Etna, Petrarch found more inspiration on at Ventoux near Avignon, Bonifacio de' Rotari climbed the Roccia Melone (11,600 ft) in 1358 Leonardo da Vinci made scientific observations on a snowfield below

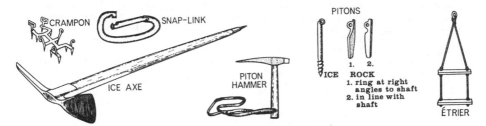

CRAMPON SNAP-LINK

ICE AXE

PITON HAMMER

PITONS

ICE ROCK
1. 2.
1. ring at right angles to shaft
2. in line with shaft

ÉTRIER

SOME OF THE EQUIPMENT USED IN MOUNTAINEERING (NOT TO SCALE)

Monte Rosa, the Mont Aiguille in Dauphiné was climbed with ladders in 1492 at the request of Charles VIII of France; Conrad Gesner, Josiah Simler and some others wrote enthusiastically in the 16th cent. of the pleasures of walking on the mts round Zürich. The exploring spirit of the 18th cent. and the advance of scientific knowledge began to remove the fear and reveal the attractions of mts as a new field of inquiry. The great figure in M. hist. of the 18th cent. is H. B. de Saussure. In 1760 he offered a reward for the ascent of Mont Blanc. After sev. attempts the summit was reached by a young doctor, M. G. Paccard, accompanied by the guide Jacques Balmat, in 1786. Saussure himself, with his valet and 18 guides, made the third ascent in 1787. Col. Beaufoy made the first ascent by an Englishman a few days later. For more than 50 years Mont Blanc monopolised the attention of the adventurous; those who climbed it rarely climbed other high mts and all tried to give some scientific justification. Meanwhile occasional ascents of an exploratory character had been made in other parts of the Alps. For many years a monk, Placidus à Spescha, had been exploring the peaks round Disentis and almost reached the summit of the Tödi in 1824. The Gross Glockner was climbed in 1800 by a party including Horrasch, a priest, the Ortler in 1804 (Joseph Pichler), the Jungfrau (the brothers Meyer) in 1811, the Finsteraarhorn (Leuthold) in 1829. Among early Eng. explorers J. D. Forbes and John Ball (the first president of the Alpine Club) did notable work in the decade 1840–50. M. as a sport is generally dated from the ascent of the Wetterhorn from Grindelwald by Alfred Wills in 1854. In the decade 1855–65 almost all the great peaks of the Alps were climbed. The Matterhorn defeated many attempts before its ascent by Edward Whymper in 1865; 4 of the party were killed on the descent, and this tragic event gave a temporary check to adventurous M. in the Alps. The Eng. Alpine Club was inaugurated in 1857, and under the editorship of John Ball pub. *Peaks, Passes and Glaciers* in 1859. The first number of the *Alpine Journal*, with accounts of climbs and explorations by members of the club, appeared in 1863. The Austrian Alpine Club was founded in 1862, the Swiss and It. in 1863, the Ger. in 1869, the Fr. in 1874. All these early ascents of the great Alpine peaks were led by Swiss guides, many

of whom found guiding a lucrative addition to chamois-hunting. Melchior Anderegg and Christian Almer were the 2 greatest of many fine Oberland guides of this early period; Auguste Balmat, Michel Croz and François Dévouassoud 3 of the best Chamonix men. The conquest of the main peaks left only minor peaks or new and more difficult routes for those who wished to combine exploration with adventure in the Alps. Equipment improved; even for the amateur the short ice-axe replaced the alpenstock. Climbs showing the advance in M. were: in 1876 the Matterhorn, in 1879 the Meije, both by parties of 3 Englishmen without guides; in 1885 the traverse of the Meije by the brothers Zsigmondy and Purtscheller; the Dru in 1878 by C. T. Dent; the Zmutt and Furggen ridges of the Matterhorn, and the Grépon by A. F. Mummery, all 3 with the famous guide Alexander Burgener; the traverse of Mont Blanc via the Aiguille Blanche de Peuteret by Dr P. Güssfeldt with Emil Rey and Christian Klücker. Men of means began the exploration of other great ranges. In 1868 D. W. Freshfield, A. W. Moore and C. C. Tucker went to the Caucasus with François Dévouassoud and climbed Elbruz (18,500 ft) and Kasbek (16,500 ft). E. Whymper in 1879–80 climbed Chimborazo (20,700 ft) and other mts of Ecuador. W. S. Green visited the New Zealand Alps in 1882, the Selkirks in 1888. In 1883 W. W. Graham with 2 Swiss reached a height of nearly 24,000 ft on Kabru in Sikkim. Aconcagua (23,000 ft) was climbed by Zurbriggen in 1897; Illimani (22,000 ft) by Conway in 1898; Kilimanjaro (19,600 ft) by Meyer and Purtscheller in 1889, Kenya by Mackinder in 1899; Mt St Elias (18,200 ft) in Alaska by the Duke of the Abruzzi in 1897; Pioneer Peak (22,500) in the Karakoram by Conway in 1892. By the end of the 19th cent. nearly every great range in the world had its M. hist. In the early years of the present cent. amateurs and guides continued to push up the standards of technique to the limits of what was possible without the artificial aid of hammer and pitons, prominently Joseph Knübel, G. W. Young and Franz Lochmatter. Guideless climbing, especially among the Australians, Germans and Swiss, reached the standards of all but the very best guides. Fifty years after the formation of the Alpine Club there were more than 120 M. clubs in all parts of the world. In ranges outside

Europe the climbing of Mt Robson (12,900 ft) by Mac Carthy in 1913, and of Trisul (23,350 ft) by Longstaff in 1907, are landmarks in the exploration of the Rockies and the Himalaya. The peaks of Ruwenzori were climbed by the Duke of the Abruzzi in 1906. The first years of the period between the wars of 1914–18 and 1939–45 saw a great revival of Fr. M. activity. J. and T. de Lépiney and others made new and difficult ascents in the Mont Blanc dist and inaugurated the Groupe de Haute Montagne. In 1927–8 T. Graham Brown and F. S. Smythe began the series of new climbs on the Brenva face of Mont Blanc. Teutonic climbers made increasing use of pitons, snap-links and rope stirrups to ascend rock faces impossible without them; the Zdarsky sack and the igloo could make a night out at high altitude harmless. International rivalries and encouragement by the Ger. and It. govs. of very daring feats to bolster national prestige led sometimes to a disregard of unavoidable risk from stonefall or bad weather, notably on long face climbs such as the E. and S. faces of the Matterhorn (1931), the N. faces of the Eiger (q.v.) and Grandes Jorasses (1938), climbed only after sev. attempts ending in tragedy.

The Himalayas were the scene of greatest Brit. effort in the period 1920–40. Eight expeditions attacked the Tibetan side of Everest (q.v.), 29,028 ft, all of which met defeat, while H. W. Tilman and E. Shipton showed how much could be achieved by small parties on lesser peaks at low cost. F. S. Smythe led the successful ascent of Kamet, 25,443 ft, in 1931. In 1936 H. W. Tilman and N. E. Odell climbed Nanda Devi, 25,645 ft. But thus far not one of the world's 14,800-metre peaks had fallen despite vast effort expended and sacrifice of life by Ger. expeditions on Kanchenjunga and Nanga Parbat.

At the end of the Second World War the attacks on the world's greatest peaks were for the first time mounted on a military scale with corresponding logistic efficiency and ruthlessness, in which cost was disregarded. This was a new kind of M., not hitherto seen in the world. A feature of the Brit. participation was the use of oxygen in bulk. Govs. or national organisations supplied the money (in England, *The Times*, London). The international record of ascents fell out thus: 1950 Annapurna (Nepal), 26,493 ft, Fr. expedition; 1953 Nanga Parbat (Karakoram), 26,620 ft, Ger. expedition; Everest (Nepal), 29,028 ft, Brit. expedition; 1954 Cho Oyu (Nepal), 26,750 ft, Austrian expedition; K2 (Karakoram), 28,250 ft, It. expedition; 1955 Makalu (Nepal), 27,937 ft, Fr. expedition; Kangchenjunga (Sikkim), 28,146 ft, Brit. expedition; 1956 Manaslu (Nepal), 26,658 ft, Jap. expedition; Lhotse (Nepal), 27,890 ft, Swiss expedition; Gasherbrum II (Karakoram), 26,360 ft, Austrian expedition; 1957 Broad Peak (Karakoram), 26,414 ft, Austrian expedition; 1958 Hidden Peak (Karakoram), 26,470 ft, Amer. expedition; 1960 Dhaulagiri (Nepal), 26,811 ft, Swiss expedition; 1964 Gosainthan (Tibet), 26,291 ft, Chinese expedition.

The 14 highest mts of the world had thus been climbed in 14 years. The highest unclimbed mt is now Gasherbrum III, 26,090 ft, in the Karakoram. Since the ascent of the great peaks the tendency in M. is now towards the attempts on smaller mts offering much higher technical difficulties, such as the Muztagh Tower, 23,860 ft, in the Karakoram, climbed in 1957 by John Hartog's party. Political difficulties on the Himalayan frontier with Tibet have persuaded many expeditions to climb instead on the Peruvian Andes, the Coastal Range of Brit. Columbia and the Alps, where standards of Brit. performance steeply rise.

M. has developed in the 20th cent. the organisation of a popular sport. The prin. clubs in the U.K. comprise some 12,000 members (the host of smaller clubs must double the number), who learn modern technique on the cliffs of Wales, Scotland and the Lake dist, and snow and ice craft in Scotland. In the Alps, Brit. climbers since 1950 have shown equality in skill and audacity with their continental fellows. Outstanding Brit. mountaineers of the present day are C. J. S. Bonington and Ian Clough, who made the first Brit. ascent of the Eigerwand, Joe Brown and Don Whillans who are unequalled on rock, and Dr Tom Patey, who is without rival on ice. Among the foremost pioneers in continental climbing have been Bonatti of Italy, and Lionel Terray and Gaston Rebuffat of France. Since the Second World War, nylon rope has replaced manilla, moulded rubber soles have replaced nailed soles, eiderdown suits are used as bivouac equipment, and as ever freer use is made of pitons, snap-links, 'rope-stirrups and crampons, the limits of the 'impossible' ever recede.

See J. Tyndall, *Glaciers of the Alps*, 1860; L. Stephen, *The Playground of Europe*, 1871; E. Whymper, *Scrambles Among the Alps in the Years 1860 to 1869*, 1871, and *Great Andes of the Equator*, 1892; D. Freshfield, *Italian Alps*, 1875, and *Exploration of the Caucasus*, 1902; Sir M. Conway, *The Alps from End to End*, 1895; A. F. Mummery, *My Climbs in the Alps and Caucasus*, 1895; E. A. Fitzgerald, *New Zealand Alps*, 1896; O. G. Jones, *Rock Climbing in the English Lake District*, 1900; A. W. Moore, *The Alps in 1864*, 1902, 1939; G. W. Young, *Mountain Craft*, 1920, and *On High Hills*, 1927; G. Finch, *The Making of a Mountaineer*, 1924; A. Lunn, *The Mountains of Youth*, 1925, and *Switzerland in Prose and Verse*, 1947; F. S. Smythe, *Climbs and Ski Runs*, 1929, *The Kanchenjunga Adventure*, 1931, and *Kamet Conquered*, 1932; R. L. G. Irving, *The Romance of Mountaineering*, 1935, and *The Mountain Way*, 1938; E. Shipton, *Nanda Devi*, 1936, *Blank on the Map*, 1938, and *Upon that Mountain*, 1943; H. W. Tilman, *The Ascent of Nanda Devi*, 1937; T. Graham Brown, *Brenva*, 1944; W. H. Murray, *Mountaineering in Scotland*, 1947, and *Undiscovered Scotland*, 1951; *Nanga Parbat Adventure* (Bechtold), 1935; R. Clark, *The Early Alpine Guides*, 1949, (with E. Pyatt) *Mountaineering in Britain*, 1957, and *The Day the Rope Broke* (Matterhorn), 1965; M. Herzog, *Annapurna*, 1952; John Hunt, *The*

Ascent of Everest, 1953; W. Noyce, *South Col*, 1954; S. Clark, *The Puma's Claw* (Peru), 1959; H. Harrer, *The White Spider*, 1959; T. Hagen, G. O. Dyhrenfurth, Ch. von Fürer and E. Schneider, *Mount Everest: Structure, Exploration, and Population of the Massif*, 1959; F. Maraini, *Karakoram*, 1961; L. Terray, *Conquistadors of the Useless*, 1963; G. Rebuffat, *On Snow and Rock*, 1963; M. Slesser, *Red Peak*, 1964; W. Bonatti, *On the Heights*, 1964; Swiss Foundation for Alpine Research, *The Mountain World* (ann.). *See also* MOUNTAIN WARFARE; ROCK CLIMBING. See the *Alpine Journal* and jours. and guides of the Scottish M., Climbers' and Fell and Rock Clubs. (*See Plates: Mountaineering*.)

Mountainous (Russian **Nagorno-**) **Karabakh Autonomous Oblast**, *see* NAGORNO-KARABAKH.

Mountains. The M. of the world occur chiefly in great systems made up of more or less parallel ranges; the ranges may widen or narrow, make sudden changes of direction or diverge from one another over part of their course. Despite these fluctuations it remains true that any mt system traces out a long path across the crust of the earth which is very narrow in relation to its length. Mt chains or orogenic belts are the result of the deformation of linear welts in the crust. Mt chains consist largely of intensely folded sedimentary rocks which were originally deposited below the sea. The sequence of the sedimentary rocks is usually sev. tens of thousands of feet thick and was laid down in a series of elongated troughs in the sea bed. Most mt chains in consequence actually occupy rather unstable belts in the crust which have first been depressed as the sediments accumulated during the geosynclinal phase and later elevated during the mt building phase. It was formerly thought that periods of orogeny or mt building were world wide in their extent and short in duration compared with the intervals that separated one period from another in geological time. It is now generally believed that vertical and horizontal movements of the crust are proceeding and have been proceeding during the greater part of geological time more or less continuously, though at an exceedingly slow rate. At any one time, however, large parts of the crust are virtually unaffected by these mt building movements, the effects of which are concentrated in certain active unstable belts. The continents preserve traces of mountain chains as much as 3000 million years old. The youngest mt chains, which are the most spectacular, for they have been exposed to erosion for the shortest period, are those dating from the Alpine orogeny of Tertiary times. Mt building is accompanied by the formation of large granite masses which form in the deeper lying parts of the mt chain. Many of these granites have been dated by the radioactive minerals they contain. It would appear that granite formation becomes especially widespread at intervals of 200 to 600 million years, and it seems likely that at such times mt formation may proceed more rapidly than is usually the rule. To this extent it is possible to speak of periods of mt building or orogeny. Some 15 such periods have now been recognised. The last 3 periods which affected Europe and Asia are the Caledonian orogeny and the Hercynian or Armorican orogeny, dating from early and late Palaeozoic times respectively, and the Alpine orogeny which reached its climax in the Tertiary but whose latest movements continue to the present time. W. America was affected by the Laramide orogeny which gave rise to the M. bordering the Pacific in late Mesozoic and early Tertiary times. The Alpine chain includes the Pyrenees, the M. of N. Africa and the Mediterranean, the Alps, the Caucasus, the M. of the near E. and Persia, of Baluchistan, the Himalayas, the Malay peninsula and the Indonesian is.

The latter, which are often separated by deep sea basins, are of especial interest as representing an embryonic mt chain which has only in part been raised above the sea. The Alpine orogeny hardly affected Britain, though many of the folded structures in S. England formed at the time of the major Alpine movements on the European continent. The results of the Hercynian orogeny are well seen in S. Ireland, in Cornwall and Devon, in S. Wales and the Pennines. The movements are of considerable economic importance since they largely determine the extent of the coal-fields of Britain. The M. of NW. Britain and Scandinavia date from the Caledonian orogeny, though there has been further uplift much more recently in Tertiary times (*see* HIGHLANDS). Volcanoes make some of the highest M. within certain mt chains: Mt Shasta, 14,162 ft, in N. California; Mt Hood, 11,225 ft, and Mt Rainier, 14,208 ft, in the Cascade Range are examples. Many of the Andean peaks in S. America are volcanic in origin. The vulcanicity in these instances was associated with the development of a mt fold belt. There are, however, certain M. which are not the result of folding and orogeny. In E. Africa the peaks Kilimanjaro and Mt Kenya are volcanic cones rising to 19,000 and 17,000 ft respectively which consist of lavas and volcanic ash poured out during the Rift valley movements. These M. are simply the result of the accumulation of a great thickness of volcanic material. M. may result when great thicknesses of beds are removed by erosion to leave a residual mt carved out by the erosion of the surrounding strata. Table Mt in S. Africa is such a mt. Mt chains exert a considerable influence on human activity. Through their rugged nature they act as a barrier to commerce and invasion and have thus come to separate different races from one another, while mt dwellers tend to be independent peoples following different pursuits from their more numerous neighbours on nearby plains. Mt chains divide the prin. riv. basins from each other and thus demarcate the important trade routes which follow these rivs. Today mt chains are increasingly important as sources of hydro-electric power derived from the rapidly flowing mt rivs. Mineral deposits are associated with certain of the granites and volcanic rocks in mt chains and oilfields have been located in folded sedimentary rocks in the foothills of other ranges. The rainfall of any dist is largely controlled by its topographic relief and thus by the location of the M. *See also* GLACIERS; OROGENY; RIVER; VALLEY, etc., and GEOLOGY and its bibliography. *See* Lord Avebury's *Scenery of Switzerland*, 1896; J. Geikie, *Earth Sculpture*, 1898; J. E. Marr, *Scientific Study of Scenery*, 1900; Sir A. Geikie, *Scenery of Scotland* (3rd ed.), 1901; E. Suess, *The Face of the Earth*, 1906; J. W.Gregory, *The Making of the Earth*, 1912; J. H. Fabre, *This Earth of Ours* (trans.), 1923; L. W. Collett, *The Structure of the Alps*, 1936; C. A. Cotton, *Volcanoes as Landscape Forms*, 1944; A. Holmes, *Principles of Physical Geology*, 2nd ed., 1965. *See* MOUNTAINEERING.

Mountbatten of Burma, Admiral of the Fleet Louis (Francis Albert Victor Nicholas), 1st Earl (1900–), younger son of Admiral of the Fleet the first Marquess of Milford Haven and Princess Victoria, daughter of Louis IV, Grand Duke of Hesse. He was known as Prince Louis Francis of Battenberg until, in 1917, his father relinquished the title and took the surname of M. He entered the RN as a cadet in 1913 and reached flag rank in 1946. Appointed chief of combined operations in 1942 and supreme commander SE. Asia in 1943 with the acting rank of admiral, a post which he held until the defeat of Japan in 1945. In 1946, on appointment to command the 1st Cruiser squadron, he reverted to his proper naval rank of rear admiral, but in 1947 he succeeded Lord Wavell as Viceroy of India in which capacity he played a prominent part in the transfer of power to India and Pakistan. In Aug. 1947 he became the first governor-general of India, an office which he held until 1948, when he returned once more to the RN on appointment as Commander-in-chief, Mediterranean, 1952–4. Was First Sea Lord, 1955–9, and subsequently became Chief of Staff to the Minister (later Secretary of State) for Defence, and Chairman of the Chiefs of Staff Committee, a post which he relinquished in 1965. M. became governor of the Isle of Wight, 1965. He was made a viscount in 1946, and an earl in 1947. *See* R. Murphy, *The Last Viceroy. The Life and Times of His Excellency Rear-Admiral the Earl Mountbatten of Burma*, 1948.

Mountevans, Baron, *see* EVANS, RUSSELL, FIRST BARON MOUNTEVANS.

'Mounties', *see* ROYAL CANADIAN MOUNTED POLICE.

Mountmellick, mrkt tn of Laoighis co., Rep. of Ireland, 6 m. NW. of Portlaoise (q.v.). Pop. 2436.

Mountrath, mrkt tn of co. Laoighis, Rep. of Ireland, at the foot of the Slieve Bloom mts. Pop. 1051

Mountsorrel, tn of Leics, England, on the Soar, 7 m. from Leicester. Industries include quarrying, engineering and manufs. of boots and shoes, elastic web, cardboard boxes and hosiery. Pop. 3756.

Mourne Mountains, range in the S. of co. Down, N. Ireland, extending from above Newcastle to Carlingford (q.v.) Lough. The highest summit is Slieve Donard (q.v.) (2796 ft).

Mouscron (Flem. **Moeskroen**), tn in the prov. of W. Flanders, Belgium, 7 m. SSW. of Courtrai, near the Fr. border. Manufs. include woollens, cottons, tobacco and soap. At the hamlet of Risquons-Tout in 1848 the Belgian Army repulsed the Fr. revolutionists, who tried to enter Belgium. Pop. 36,600.

Mouse, name popularly applied to a great number of small rodents of various genera, but correctly only to the smaller species of the genera *Mus, Micromys* and *Apodemus*. The 3 Brit. species are the house M. (*Mus musculus*), the harvest M. (*Micromys minutus*) and the long-tailed field M. (*Apodemus sylvaticus*). The M., whatever its origin, is now common in every continent, and takes serious toll of man's food stores and causes no little damage to architecture. The fur varies greatly in tint and markings when the animals are bred in captivity. The whistling bird-like song of certain mice at dusk is an estab. fact. The harvest M. is unique among Brit. mammals in having a prehensile tail. Its spherical breeding nest, built on cornstalks used as scaffolding, is an exquisite structure. The long-tailed field M. is a handsome, bold creature, and does much damage to field and garden crops, hunting for food at night. It is one of the most prolific of mammals. For the short-tailed field M., which is not really a M., *see* VOLE.

Mouse-deer, *see* CHEVROTAIN.

Mouse-hare, *see* PIKA.

Moussorgsky, Modest Petrovich, *see* MUSSORGSKY.

Mousterian, name given to a flakepoint culture of the Middle Palaeolithic in Europe, W. Asia and N. Africa, derived from the rock-shelter of Le Moustier in Dordogne. Here were found flint implements as well as bones of the mammoth, woolly-haired rhinoceros (*Rhinoceros mercki*), musk-ox and cave-bear. During the end of the last interglacial period and the last or Würm glaciation, Europe was peopled by men of the Neanderthal type, when the Mousterian was his material culture, the earliest which can be associated with a human type; the succeeding culture of the Palaeolithic came into Europe with *Homo sapiens*, man of the modern type, who was still a nomadic food-gatherer and buried his dead with some care.

Mouth, entrance to any cavity or canal; in particular, the entrance to the alimentary canal between the lips, including the cavity in which mastication takes place. The lips are folds of flesh composed of skin, areolar tissue, or superficial fascia, the orbicularis oris muscle, submucous tissue and mucuous membrane. The cheeks are similar in structure, except that they are actuated by the buccinator muscle, which compresses the cheeks and retracts the angle of the lips. The opening of the duct from the parotid gland is situated on the M. side of the cheek opposite the second upper molar tooth, while other salivary ducts are situated on the same surface. The ducts of the sublingual salivary glands open into the floor of the mouth beneath the tongue. The saliva functions as a lubricant and also contains a digestive juice, ptyalin in a few animals, including man, which converts starch in the food into dextrin and sugar. The gums are composed of mucous membrane superposed upon fibrous tissue connecting with the periosteum of the jaw-bone. The teeth are fixed in the gum and jaw-bone, and the mucous membrane of the gum rises up round each tooth. The roof of the M. is formed by the hard and soft palate. The hard palate consists of mucous membrane and fibrous tissue connecting with the superior maxillary and palatal bones; the soft palate is composed of an aggregation of muscles. Diseases of the M. include caries and other infections of the teeth; stomatitis, or inflammation of the M., characterised by swelling, salivation, pain and ulceration; salivary calculus, or stony concretions in the salivary ducts; and mumps, a highly infectious disease of the parotid gland, characterised by swelling and difficulty in swallowing.

Mouvement Républicain Populaire (M.R.P.), *see* FRANCE, *History*.

Mowing Machines. The usual agric. mower is used for cutting fodder crops and has a long cutting bar in which a series of knives work in reciprocating motion, i.e. rather like scissors. The mower may be 'mounted' on the tractor's hydraulic lift and driven from the power take-off shaft or merely trailed and driven from heavy land wheels. Cylindrical mowers are more commonly used on ornamental lawns. These employ high speed horizontally rotating knives which leave the grass cut close in a neat fashion. In recent years rotary mowers have been developed for cutting both lawns and longer grass. The cutting blades rotate about a vertical axis. *See also* REAPING.

Moyen-Congo, *see* MIDDLE CONGO.

Moyne, Charles Le, *see* LE MOYNE.

Moynihan, Berkeley George Andrew, 1st **Baron** (1865–1936), surgeon, *b*. Malta, son of Capt. A. Moynihan, V.C. Educ. at Leeds, London and Berlin, he qualified in medicine in 1887. From 1896 to 1926 he was prof. of clinical surgery at Leeds Univ. He won international fame as an abdominal surgeon, particularly in the treatment of duodenal ulcer. He became a fellow of the Royal College of Surgeons in 1890 and was president from 1926 to 1932. His writings include *Abdominal Operations*, 1905 (4th ed., 1925), and *Duodenal Ulcer*, 1910. He was a founder of the *British Journal of Surgery*, 1913. He was knighted in 1912, created a baronet in 1922, and raised to the peerage in 1929. *See* life by D. S. Bateman, 1940.

Mozambique, or **Moçambique: 1.** Prov. of Portugal in E. Africa, lying between 11° and 27° S. lat., bounded on the N. by the Rovuma R., S. by Natal, E. by the Indian Ocean and W. by Lake Malawi, Rhodesia, Malawi, Rep. of S. Africa and Swaziland. The prin. rivs. are the Rovuma, Pungwe, Busi, Sabi and Limpopo. The flora is rich, there being forests of valuable timber and coco-nut palms, oranges, lemons,

pepper, bananas, cashew nuts, rice, cotton and tobacco. The fauna includes all the wild and domestic species of the African continent, elephants being plentiful. There are coal deposits in the Tete Region, and some gold in the Upper Zambesi. Exports are sugar, cotton, cashew nuts, tea, copra, sisal and timber; total value of exports in 1962 was £2,615,832. Imports are textiles, coal, railway equipment, iron and steel, motor vehicles, agric. machinery, oil and petrol, rice, wines, hardware, clothing and footwear; total value in 1962 was £3,908,125. There are some 1200 m. of railways, and 16,000 m. of roads, of which 2700 are first class. There is an agreement between M. and S. Africa regarding the ann. recruiting of M. labourers for employment in the Witwatersrand mines. The chief tns are Lourenço Marques (cap.), Beira, M., Inhambane, Quelimane and Tete. The Companhia de Moçambique was wound up in 1942, on the expiration of its charter, and divided into 4 dists: Sul do Save; Manica and Sofala; Zambesia; Niasa. Area 297,731 sq. m.; pop. 5,732,317.

2. Once the chief tn of M., situated on a coral is. It has considerable shipping trade.

3. Channel between the E. coast of Africa and Madagascar, length about 1000 m., breadth from 260 to 600 m. At the N. entrance lie the Comoro Is. *See also* PORTUGUESE EAST AFRICA. *See* E. Axelson, *SE. Africa, 1488–1530*, 1940. (*See Plate*.)

Mozarabes, Christians who lived under Moorish rule in Spain, being allowed at the same time to retain their religion. They conformed almost entirely to the customs of their conquerors, even to the extent of using Arabic characters in the writing of Spanish. They were well treated and retained the Mozarabic liturgy, which is still used in a chapel of Toledo cathedral and at Salamanca.

Mozart, Wolfgang Amadeus (1756–91), Austrian composer, *b*. Salzburg, son of Leopold M. (1719–87), violinist and minor composer, was attached to the archiepiscopal court there. M. was very precocious, played and composed at the age of 5, and was taken to the courts of Munich and Vienna in 1762 to appear with his gifted sister Maria Anna (1751–1829). A tour through S. Germany took the family to Paris in 1763 and to London the next year, where they stayed until July 1765. After visits to Holland, Paris again and Switzerland, they returned home in Nov. 1766. M. had learnt much from J. C. Bach in London and was quick to pick up what he heard anywhere; he now composed symphonies and stage music, another visit to Vienna in 1768 resulting in the It. comic opera *La finta semplice* and the Ger. operetta *Bastien und Bastienne*. Three visits to Italy (Dec. 1769–Mar. 1771, Aug.–Dec. 1771, Oct. 1772–Mar. 1773) brought commissions for 3 operas for Milan, and M. learnt much from Padre Martini of Bologna, where he was elected to the Philharmonic Society, although under age. In 1773, aged 17, he settled at the Salzburg court, for which he wrote mainly church and entertainment music, but in Jan. 1775 he produced the opera *La finta giardiniera* at Munich with great success. He felt constrained in the Salzburg service, where he was not appreciated by the tyrannical archbishop, and obtained leave to go on a long tour with his mother in 1777, Leopold being compelled to stay at home. During a long stay at Mannheim he fell in love with a singer, Aloysia Weber, aged 16, whom he wished to marry; but was peremptorily sent to Paris by his father. There his mother *d.* in July 1778, and his success was not great, though his gifts had now fully matured. When he returned to Mannheim in Nov. he found the court removed to Munich and Aloysia engaged for the opera there, no doubt regarding herself as superior to him and jilting him. After the production of his first great opera, *Idomeneo*, in Munich (1781) he accompanied the archbishop of Salzburg to Vienna. There he was dismissed from his employment after a quarrel, but decided to stay in the city. Ger. opera was just then being estab. there, and he abandoned Italian for a time by producing *Die Entführung aus dem Serail* in July 1782, which enchanted the public but yielded him little financial reward. He nevertheless took the risk of marrying, in Aug., Constanze Weber, Aloysia's younger sister, aged 19, who made him a thriftless wife but retained his love to the end. The final period of his greatest work had now begun; he gave concerts for which he wrote superb concertos, started the set of string quartets dedicated to Haydn and produced a great variety of other works in rapid succession, but never showing a trace of haste in their masterly finish and depth of expression. A visit to Salzburg in 1783, to present Constanze to his father and sister, produced the unfinished C minor Mass, almost his last church work, and, on the return journey, at Linz, the symphony called after that tn. In 1786, reverting to It. opera, he produced *Le nozze di Figaro* in Vienna, in 1787 *Don Giovanni* in Prague, and in 1790 *Così fan tutte* in Vienna again, a trilogy of incomparable masterpieces. But these and his countless instrumental works yielded him no material prosperity; he was obliged to give ill-paid lessons and was so much in debt and so greatly harassed during his last years that, having become a Freemason, he was obliged to beg a fellow Mason for assistance again and again. Two journeys to Germany, the second of which brought him a commission for 6 quartets from the King of Prussia, offered him some distraction but little alleviation. In 1791 the production of *Die Zauberflöte* was an immense success, but again financially unrewarding, and the commission of *La clemenza di Tito* for Prague served only to tire him out. He was already ill when he received an anonymous order for the Requiem, which was left unfinished at his death on 5 Dec. 1791. His works number 626 in Köchel's catalogue, but there are many unfinished compositions which bring the number to some 700, an enormous output for an artist who *d.* in his 36th year and who never wrote without the utmost care or failed to exercise his miraculous

skill. See *The Letters of Mozart and His Family*, trans. Emily Anderson (3 vols.), 1938; E. J. Dent, *Mozart's Operas*, 2nd ed., 1947; C. M. Girdlestone, *Mozart's Piano Concertos*, 1948; studies by D. Hussey, 1928; E. Blom, Master Musicians series, 1935; W. J. Turner, 1938; A. Einstein, 1947; A. H. King, 1955; Köchel's Catalogue, 6th ed., 1964. (*See Plate: German Music.*)

Mozdok, tn in N. Caucasus, since 1944 in N.-Ossetian Autonomous Rep., on R. Terek, 59 m. N. of Ordzhonikidze. M. was founded in 1763 as a Russian fort. First Ossetian school, 1766. Until the 1870's the tn was a notable commercial and industrial centre (oil refinery, 1823). The Bolsheviks were overthrown here in 1918. It marked the limit of the Ger. advance in the Caucasus in 1943, and bitter fighting took place. Pop. (1964) 29,000 (1926, 14,000), Russians and Armenians.

Mozhaysk, tn in the Moscow oblast of central Russia, 69 m. W. of Moscow. It has been known since 1231, and was a Muscovite W. frontier fortress from 1303. The battle of Borodino (q.v.) took place near by in 1812 and it was the scene of much fighting in the winter of 1941–2. Pop. (1964) 20,000 (1926, 5500).

M.T.S. (Russian abbreviation for **Machine and Tractor Stations),** state enterprises in the U.S.S.R. which until their abolition in 1958 carried out all machine work in the *kolkhozes* (q.v.) and generally supervised them. During the collectivisation of agriculture (q.v.) political depts of the M.T.S. were the Communist party's strongholds in the countryside. A Secretary of the Dist Party Committee was attached to each M.T.S. and supervised the surrounding group of kolkhozes. In 1955 there were 9000 M.T.S. In 1958 they sold their machinery to the kolkhozes, and were replaced as agric. service points by about 4000 Technical Repair Stations. The aim, little achieved in fact, was to give the kolkhozes a modicum of independence. See R. D. Laird and others, *The Rise and Fall of the M.T.S. as an Instrument of Soviet Rule*, Kansas, 1960.

Mtskheta, small tn in Georgia, 13 m. N. of Tiflis. It has been known since the early 4th cent., and was cap. of Iberia (E. Georgia) until superseded by Tiflis in the mid 6th cent., after which it remained the religious centre of Georgia. It is a treasury of Georgian architecture of the 6th–11th cents., and the ruins of still older buildings (from the 4th cent. BC) have been excavated near by. Pop. (1959) 7100.

Mtwara, recently constructed port in Tanzania where 2 deep water berths have been constructed in a landlocked bay in which there is sufficient water for the largest ships. The port was constructed to handle exports such as cashew nuts, timber, sisal, cassava root, coffee and groundnuts. Inland from M. large areas are capable of cultivation and irrigation schemes are in hand. M. is the H.Q. of the Southern Prov. and is well served by air routes linking it with other tns in E. Africa.

Much Wenlock, *see* WENLOCK.

Mucilage, aqueous solution of a gum; some

gums form a clear solution in water, while others well up to form a sticky viscous liquid, more properly called M. *Mucilago tragacanthae* is prepared from the gum which exudes from the stem of *Astragalus gummifer*. Cherry-tree gum also forms a thick M. Gum kuteera and gum of Bussorah are often imported as adulterants of gum tragacanth; their properties are somewhat similar to those of gum tragacanth. *Mucilago acaciae* is formed by adding 34 parts of acacia to water to make 100 parts; it is used as a substitute for *M. tragacanthae*. *M. amyli*, or starch M., is used for making enemas. A M. formed from the pith of sassafras is used as a soothing application for inflamed eyes, and also as a demulcent drink for inflammation of the mucous membranes and of the kidneys. *M. Ulmi* is formed from elm gum; other M. s are produced by infusing seeds, roots, etc., in boiling water.

Mucin, viscid substance, capable of being split up into a proteid and a carbohydrate (i.e. a muco-polysaccharide), found in the secretions of the mucous membranes of the body and also found in intercellular fluids. One of its main functions is that of a lubricant. M. is insoluble in water but soluble in dilute alkali, and is precipitated by alcohol and acetic acid. M. is very important in the feeding mechanism of many invertebrates.

Mucoid, substance resembling mucin (q.v.) in many ways, but differing from it in some chemical reactions. M. is not precipitated from solution by acetic acid. Sometimes it precipitates slightly, but is then soluble in excess of acid. It is thus distinguishable from mucin.

Mucous Membrane, *see* EPITHELIUM.

Mud, term employed for the impalpable argillaceous matter which settles in quiet waters. When consolidated and devoid of lamination it is known as mudstone. The dark blue M.s of the sea bottom derive their colour from decomposing organic matter and sulphide of iron, while the green M.s are so coloured from the glauconite grains which they contain. Near coral reefs the sea floor is covered with white M. due to the abrasion of coral, while round volcanic is. a grey M. formed from degraded volcanic rocks is found.

Mud Devil, *see* MENOPOME.

Mud Volcanoes are of 2 kinds: (1) where the source of movement is the escape of gases; (2) where the active agent is steam. The former are conical hills formed by the accumulation of fine saline mud which is given out with various gases (marsh-gas, carbon dioxide, etc.) from an orifice or crater in the centre. The latter occur in volcanic regions, and are due to the escape of water and steam through beds of friable rock.

Mudar, *see* CALOTROPIS.

Mudfish, or **Bowfin** (*Amia calva*), fish occurring in the N. Amer. lakes and rivs. which has the air-bladder highly developed as a lung sac so that it can breathe atmospheric air. It is about 30 in. long, and a dark mottled green. It feeds voraciously upon crustaceans and insects, and its flesh is soft and ill-flavoured. The M. belongs to the Holostei, a group of bony fishes well represented in Mesozoic times.

Mudge, Thomas (1715–94), horologist, *b.* Exeter, son of a clergyman-schoolmaster. As a youth he showed so great a taste for mechanics, especially in the field of horology (q.v.), that his father apprenticed him to George Graham (q.v.). Here he made rapid progress in his art, and, on the completion of his indentures, took a leading position in Graham's estab. Admitted to the freedom of the Clockmakers Co. in 1738, he was called to the Livery in 1766. M. is best remembered for having invented the detached lever escapement, which is now found in all good quality watches. *See* WATCH.

Mudgee, tn on the R. Cudgeogong in New S. Wales, Australia, 191 m. SW. of Sydney, altitude 1600 ft. M. is situated in an agric. and grazing area and is noted for the quality of its lucerne. Pop. 5312.

Mudie, Charles Edward (1818–90), founder of M.'s Library. *B.* Chelsea, he began as bookseller in 1840, started his library in 1842 at 1 guinea per annum subscription. He moved from Bloomsbury to Oxford Street in 1852, and opened branches in Bristol and Manchester. At its peak (1888) the library had 40,000 subscribers, but it declined and was closed in 1937. M. was a religious and philanthropic man, but had to defend himself against charges of priggishness in his book selection. Pub. *Stray Leaves* (collection of hymns) in 1872.

Mudros (modern Gk, **Moúdhros**), tn and fine natural harbour on the S. coast of Lemnos, in the Aegean Sea. It was a Brit. base of operations against the Turks in the Gallipoli campaign, 1915. The armistice between Turkey and the Allies was signed here in 1918.

Muezzin, or **Mueddin**, Muslim official whose duty it is to announce the hours of prayer; this he does from the minaret or from the roof or side of the mosque in a chant. The call is as follows: 'Allah is very great; I testify that there is no god but Allah; I testify that Mohammad is the apostle of Allah; come to prayer. There is no god but Allah' The first phrase is repeated 4 times, the others, except the last, twice. There are ritual differences. To the call before dawn is added 'Prayer is better than sleep', and the Shiites (q.v.) add 'Come to the best of work'. The interval between the call and the prayer may be as much as half an hour.

Mufti (Arabic 'expounder of the law'). The Turkish Grand M. was the supreme head of the Ulemas (servants of religion and laws), and with the grand vizier had the supreme guidance of the state. The Turkish laws being based on the Koran, the M. was head of the judges, the chief spiritual authority, and therefore sometimes known as Sheikh-al-Islam (Lord of the Faith). The office was abolished by the Turkish Rep. in 1924. At an election of the president and members of the Supreme Muslim Council in Jerusalem in 1922 Haj Amin El Husseini, an ex-officer of the Turkish Army, was chosen president and combined that office with the office of M. of Jerusalem. Bitterly anti-Brit. on account of the Balfour Declaration (q.v.), he headed the revolt of the Higher Arab Committee in 1936, and when the revolt was ended fled the country. When the Second World War broke out he eventually found his way to Iraq and thence to Italy.

Muggletonians, Eng. sect founded 1651 by John Reeve and Ludovic Muggleton (1607–97), who claimed the gift of prophecy, Muggleton, a journeyman tailor, being the 'mouth' of Reeve as Aaron was of Moses. They further claimed to be the 2 witnesses of Rev. xi and empowered to curse their opponents. Their very unorthodox doctrines were pub. in *The Divine Looking-Glass*, 1656. Wm Penn's book, *The New Witnesses proved Old Heretics*, 1672, was directed against the M., and in 1676 Muggleton was convicted of blasphemy at the Old Bailey in London and fined £500.

See *Complete Collections of the Works of Reeve and Muggleton*, 1756, reprinted 1832.

Mughal, *see* MOGUL.

Mugwort, or *Artemisia vulgaris*, tall bushy plant (family Compositae) with pinnatifid leaves, green above and white and woolly beneath, and red and brownish-yellow flower heads. Unlike wormwood (*A. absinthium*) M. is odourless, but it was formerly infused to make a remedy for rheumatism.

Mugwump, originally an Amer. political slang word (from the Algonquin word meaning 'big men') applied in 1889 to those of the Republicans who would not vote for the candidature of J. G. Blaine for the presidency. It was used in Massachusetts of those who considered themselves great and independent and above mere party politics. It now signifies an independent voter, or one who will not attach himself to any party.

Muhammera, Muhammerah, *see* KHORRAM-SHAHR.

Mühlberg, Ger. tn in the dist of Kottbus, near the Elbe, 52 m. WSW. of Kottbus (q.v.). Near by the Protestant Elector of Saxony was defeated by the Emperor Charles V (q.v.) in 1547. Pop. 4000.

Muhlenberg, John Peter Gabriel (1746–1807), American preacher and soldier, *b.* Trappe, Pennsylvania, son of the Ger.-born Henry Melchior M. (1711–87), a clergyman who in 1748 organised the Lutheran synod in America. M. entered the Lutheran ministry, but gave up his clerical career when the War of Independence broke out. He raised the 8th Virginia regiment (Ger.), and became brigadier-general in the continental army, 1777. He became vice-president of the Supreme Council in 1789, and was elected as a Democratic-Republican to the U.S. Senate in 1801, but resigned to become supervisor of revenues for the dist of Pennsylvania.

Mühlhausen, Ger. tn in the dist of Erfurt, on the Unstrut, 30 m. NW. of Erfurt (q.v.). It belonged to the Teutonic Knights (q.v.) in the 13th cent., and was a member of the Hanseatic League (q.v.). In the Peasants' war it was the H.Q. of Thomas Münzer (q.v.), who was executed here in 1525. There are engineering and textile industries. Pop. 45,200.

Muine Beag, formerly **Bagenalstown,** tn of co. Carlow, Rep. of Ireland. Pop. 1984.

Muir, Edwin (1887–1959), poet and novelist, *b.* Deerness, Orkney Is. His autobiographical *The Story and the Fable*, 1940, revised 1954, which describes his early life, was very successful. In his poetry he represents a significant trend in modern verse, the return to contemplation of the primitive facts of humanity on earth: death, time and love. His poetic works include *First Poems*, 1925, *Chorus of the Newly Dead*, 1926, *Six Poems*, 1932, *Variations on a Time Theme*, 1934, *Journeys and Places*, 1937, and *The Narrow Place*, 1943. His *Collected Poems, 1921–51*, were pub. in 1952 and *One Foot in Eden*, 1956. He is also well known as a translator of Kafka, whose *The Trial* he trans., with his wife Willa M., in 1937. His prose includes a trans. of Herman Broch's *Transition*, 1926, *The Structure of the Novel* (a work of criticism), 1928, *John Knox*, 1929, *The Sleepwalkers*, 1932, *Scottish Journey*, 1935, *Scott and Scotland*, 1936, *The Present Age*, 1939, *and Essays on Literature and Society*, 1949. His novels include *The Marion-ette*, 1927, *The Three Brothers*, 1931, and *Poor Tom*, 1932. *See* study by J. C. Hall, 1956; P. H. Butter, *Edwin Muir*, 1962.

Muir, John Ramsay Brice (1872–1941), historian and Liberal politician. He was educ. at Univ. College, Oxford. From 1913 to 1921 he was prof. of modern hist. at Manchester Univ. His chief work is his *Short History of the British Commonwealth* (vol. i, *The Islands of the First Empire: to 1763*; vol. ii, *The Modern Commonwealth: 1763 to 1919*), 1922, a work which does not treat the overseas empire in isolation but in which such major topics as the gov. of India, the race for colonial possessions, the birth and development of imperialism, and of autonomy in what now are the dominions, take their due place in the vast setting of Brit. hist. His other works include *The Expansion of Europe*, 1917, *British History: a Survey of the History of all the British Peoples*, 1936, *The Record of the National Government*, 1936, *Future for Democracy*, 1939, and *The British Empire: How it Grew and how it Works*, 1940. M. was also a distinguished Liberal politician, and was Liberal M.P. for Rochdale, 1923–4.

Muir, Sir William (1819–1905), Scottish orientalist, entered the Bengal civil service in 1837, was appointed secretary to the governor of the NW. Provs., and was in charge of the Intelligence dept during the mutiny. In 1868 he became lieutenant-governor of the NW. Provs. In 1874 he was appointed financial minister for India. He retired in 1876 and was elected a member of the Council of India in London. He was also elected prin. of Edinburgh Univ. Through his influence the M. College at Allahabad was built and endowed. He was a keen student of Arabic. He wrote *Life of Mahomet and History of Islam*, 1858–61, *Annals of the Early Caliphates*, 1883, and *The Koran: its Composition and Teaching*, 1885–7, etc.

Muir Glacier, large ice-sheet of SE. Alaska, N.

America, with 350 sq. m. of surface area, discharging into Glacier Bay. It was explored by John Muir in 1880. The trunk is formed of about 9 main streams of ice. Earthquake disturbances dislodged part of it (1899). Its most rapid summer movement is about 7 ft per day, and some 200,000,000 cu. ft of ice are daily thrown off into the bay. Since 1794 it has receded about 25 m.

Muirkirk, tn and par. of Ayrshire, Scotland, on R. Ayr. It was associated with the Covenanters. There are coal-mines, and sheep farming is carried on in the neighbourhood. Pop. 3652.

Mui Tsai, Cantonese system of domestic servitude, the M. T. being little girls sold, either directly or through middlemen, to their employers. The system is now illegal in Hong Kong: registration of M. T. under an Act of 1923 ceased in 1930, and all M. T. then registered had attained the age of 18 by June 1936. The 1936 M. T. Commission recommended the extension of the law respecting women and girls, and the 1938 Women and Girls' Ordinance included additional safeguards. This Ordinance was replaced in 1951 by the more comprehensive Protection of Women and Juveniles Ordinance now current. M. T. is now thought to be entirely defunct.

Mukachevo (Hungarian **Muncacs,** Czech **Mukaceyo),** tn in the Transcarpathian oblast (*see* TRANSCARPATHIA) of the Ukraine. It is a light industry centre (food, tobacco, woodworking, textiles), and there is a 14th cent. castle. Pop. (1964) 54,000, Ukrainian, Jewish, Hungarian. M. has been known since the 12th cent. and has been a tn since 1445.

Mukalla, Makalla or **Mokalla,** port 300 m. NE. of Aden, the prin. port of Hadhramaut and seat of gov. of the Qu'aiti State. M., together with Shihr and dependencies, is under one sultan, who is in treaty relations with Britain, his tribesmen being part of the Aden protectorate. Pop. 20,000.

Mukden, or **Moukden** (Chinese **Shenyang),** largest city of Manchuria, cap. of Liaoning, the S. prov. of Manchuria, and the main railway junction for S. Manchuria. The old city was walled around, with an inner wall enclosing the former Imperial City, but now M. has outlying and commercial and industrial dists. N. of the city is Peiling, the burial ground for Ch'ing emperors. Already highly developed by the Japanese before the Second World War, it has now become the most important machine-building centre of the heavily industrialised NE., besides being the prin. trading tn in the whole of that area. It is the hub of 6 important railways and many airlines. Most of the univs. and colleges of the NE. are also at M. The growth of the city can be seen from the following pop. figures: 1946, 863,500; 1948, 1,200,000; 1951, 1,551,000; 1958, 2,411,000.

Mulatto (Sp. and Portuguese *mulato*, a dimin. of *mulo*; Lat. *mulus*, a mule), the offspring of a white person and a Negro. The true M. is characterised by woolly black hair and flat features, and is more usually the child of a black mother and white father. The degrees of Negro

blood are, or were, indicated by *quadroon*, three-fourths white and one-fourth black, and *octoroon*, seven-eighths white and one-eighth black, etc. But special countries have different terms for M.s. In Lat. America they are sometimes called *mestizos*, and in Brazil a M. is a *pardo*.

Mulberry (*Morus*), genus of fruit-bearing trees of which the best known is the black M. (*M. nigra*), a native of Persia, introduced to Britain in the 16th cent. It is hardy only in the S. of England; elsewhere it needs to have the shelter of a high sunny wall. The subacid characteristically flavoured fruit, though it resembles a blackberry or raspberry, is of quite different structure, corresponding rather to a bunch of currants. The leaves are used as food for silkworms, but those of the white M. (*M. alba*), which is not so hardy, make the finest silk.

MULBERRY
A, female flower; B, male flower.

'Mulberry' Harbour, name for the prefabricated harbour used for the Anglo–Amer. invasion of Normandy, 1944. *See* ARROMANCHES.

Mule (spinning machine), *see* COTTON.

Mule, name given to any hybrid, but commonly the offspring of the male ass and the mare. The produce of a stallion with a female ass is called a 'hinny'; it is smaller and weaker than the M., and therefore less valuable. M.s have the general shape of the horse, and sometimes measure as much as 16 hands high, but from the ass they get its obstinate disposition, the head features and the less sensitive, weatherproof coat. As a rule they are extremely hardy and practically free from disease. They are as sure-footed as a goat, and almost invariably possess great intelligence. They are bred in large numbers for use in countries where roads are bad and extremes of weather have to be survived. They are useful as pack animals.

Mulford, Clarence Edward (1883–1956), Amer. writer of W. stories, b. Streator, Illinois. He did newspaper work for a time, then worked in the civil service. His first book, *Bar 20*, 1907, was followed by some 30 others, all about cowboys and W. life, of which he made a careful study. Later books are *Hopalong Cassidy*, 1910, *Bar 20 Days*, 1911, *Buck Peters, Ranchman*, 1912, *The Coming of Cassidy*, 1913, *The Man from Bar 20*, 1918, *The Bar 20 Three*, 1921, *Hopalong Cassidy Returns*, 1924, *The Bar 20 Rides Again*, 1926, *Mesquite Jenkins*, 1928, and *Hopalong Cassidy Serves a Writ*, 1941. M.'s lame, intrepid, 2-gun hero Hopalong Cassidy became so famous that he appeared extensively on both films and television.

Mulgrave, Earl of, *see* BUCKINGHAM AND NORMANBY, DUKE OF.

Mülhausen, *see* MULHOUSE.

Mülheim (an der Ruhr), Ger. tn in the *Land* of N. Rhine-Westphalia (q.v.), on the Ruhr, 16 m. N. by E. of Düsseldorf. It is a well-laid-out tn, with an 11th cent. fortress, an 11th cent. church and many other medieval buildings. Coal and iron are mined in the dist, there is an institute for coal research, and there are steel, machinery, textile and other industries. The tn is an important centre of road and rail communications. Its outskirts are now practically a continuation of those of Duisburg (q.v.). Pop. 166,300.

Mulhouse (Ger. Mülhausen), Fr. tn in the dept of Haut-Rhin, on the Ill and the Rhine–Rhône canal. Made a free city in the 13th cent., M. joined the Swiss confederation in 1515, and voluntarily became Fr. in 1798. There is a workers' garden colony, founded by Mayor Dolfus in 1853. SE. of the tn is an extensive zoological garden. M. is a textile centre, and also manufs. machinery and chemicals. Pop. 109,000.

Mull, largest is. of the Inner Hebrides, off Argyll, Scotland, washed on the W. and S. by the Atlantic. M. is 7 m. W. of Oban and is separated from the mainland by the firth of Lorne and the sound of M. Its coast is indented by numerous sea lochs, of which the prin. are Loch-na-Keal and Loch Scridain, and the surface is mountainous, rising in Ben More to 3185 ft. Tobermory is the chief tn. The inhab. are engaged in agriculture, forestry and tourism. Area 351 sq. m.; pop. 2343.

Mullah, or **Mollah** (Arabic *mawla* from a root meaning 'to be near'), originally meant master, servant, cousin and freedman; then it denoted any Muslim who was not an Arab. *Mawlana*, 'our master', is a polite form of address or mention. In Turkey the Arabic was corrupted to *mulla* and meant learned man (also in Persia and India) and a senior judge.

Mullein, genus *Verbascum*, family Scrophulariaceae. *V. thapsus* is the great or common M., also Aaron's Rod, a biennial herb, with a cluster of large woolly leaves 12 to 18 in. long in its first year. In the second year's growth it has a stout woolly leafy stem, 3 ft high and terminating in a spike of yellow flowers. The wool from stem and leaves was at one time used for lamp-wicks. *V. lychnitis* is the white M., *V. pulverulentum* the yellow hoary M., and *V. nigrum* the dark M. All grow wild in Britain.

Müller, Sir Ferdinand von (1825–96), Ger. botanist and explorer, *b.* Rostock. From 1846 to 1857 he studied at Kiel Univ., and then emigrated to Australia through ill health. From 1848 to 1852 he travelled some 4000 m. botanising, in 1952 was appointed chief botanist to Victoria, and in 1855–6 was botanist in A. C. Gregory's scientific expedition to N. and central Australia. On his return he was made director of the botanical gardens in Melbourne. He introduced and exchanged plants with countries all over the world, and will be chiefly remembered for introducing the eucalyptus-tree into different countries, especially Algeria; he also raised the famous Victoria Regia water-lily. M. wrote valuable works on the eucalyptus and *Fragmenta phytographica Australiae* (11 vols.), 1862–81, also *Flora Australiensis* (with G. Bentham), 1860–5, and *The Plants Indigenous to the Colony or Victoria*, 1860.

Müller, Friedrich Max (1823–1900), orientalist, philologist and mythologist, *b.* Dessau, Germany; a prof. at Oxford from 1950. He pub. the *Rig-Vega*, 1848–74, and was general ed. (1875 onwards) of a series of trans. (by various scholars) of Sacred Books of the E. He also wrote widely on Sanskrit language and literature, general linguistics, mythology, religion, Indian philosophy.

Müller, Hermann (1876–1931), Ger. Socialist statesman, *b.* Mannheim. He was foreign minister in the Bauer Cabinet, 1919, and signed the treaty of Versailles. On the failure of the Kapp *putsch* he became chancellor for a few months, 1920. In June 1928 he was chancellor again, and formed a Grand Coalition which lasted till Mar. 1930.

Muller, Hermann Joseph (1890–), Amer. geneticist, *b.* New York city. He was prof. at the univ. of Texas, 1925–36; on the staff of the Institute of Genetics and of the Medicobiological Institute, Moscow, 1933–7; and of the Institute of Animal Genetics, univ. of Edinburgh, 1938–40; and prof. of zoology, Indiana Univ., 1945–53. He was prominent in experimental work in mutation and radiation genetics, and a strong supporter of the neo-Darwinian theory. His chief experimental work has been carried out with the Mediterranean fruit-fly, *Drosophila*, the standard 'guinea pig' of geneticists. M. discovered the action of X-rays on chromosomes and genes (1927), giving proof that the rays cause mutations. Others had worked on similar lines before 1927, though without definite success, and in 1928 Stadler announced positive results of independent X-ray experiments with plants. Hence it was not the mere discovery of mutagenic action of X-rays which revolutionised genetics, but the manner in which M.'s previous labours had prepared the way for the use of it, and the skill with which he exploited it. He was awarded the Nobel prize for physiology and medicine in 1946. His pubs. include *Studies in Genetics*, 1962, and numerous contributions to scientific jours.

Müller, Johann (1801–58), Ger. physiologist, *b.* Koblenz. He began to study with a view to orders in the Rom. Catholic Church; but in 1819 he abandoned his theological studies and devoted himself to medicine. Whilst yet a student he wrote for a prize the treatise *De Respiratione Foetus*, 1823. He became in 1830 prof. of anatomy and physiology at Bonn. He wrote over 200 articles and monographs, the most important being his monumental *Handbuch der Physiologie* (2 vols.), 1833–40. He made numerous anatomical and physiological discoveries, and to physiology he brought 2 new elements—the comparative and the psychological. M. was an inspiring teacher whose pupils brought honour to their master and to themselves; he was the pioneer responsible for the rise of Ger. medicine to its pre-eminent position in the 19th cent.

Müller, Johann, *see* REGIOMONTANUS.

Müller, Johannes von (1752–1809), Swiss historian, *b.* Neukirch, near Schaffhausen. In 1772 he became prof. of Greek at the Collegium Humanitatis at Schaffhausen. In 1780 he pub. the first vol. of his *Geschichten der Schweizer*, and the following year his *Essais historiques* appeared. In 1786 he became librarian to the elector-archbishop of Mainz, and the definitive ed. of the 1st vol. of his hist. appeared. Further vols. appeared, 1788–1808, based largely on the chronicles of Tschudi (q.v.). Napoleon made him secretary of state for Westphalia, and later a privy councillor and director of public instruction. His *Universal History* was trans. into English 1818. *See* life by W. Stokar, 1938.

Müller, Wilhelm (1794–1827), Ger. lyric poet, *b.* Dessau. In 1817 he went to Italy and his first pub. work was *Rom, Römer und Römerinnen*, 1820, which gave his impressions of his visits. The same year he was made librarian of the ducal library. His best work is contained in the vols. entitled *Gedichte aus den hinterlassenen Papieren eines reisenden Waldhornisten* (2 vols.), 1821–4, and *Lieder der Griechen*, 1821–4. his other works are *Homerische Vorschule*, 1824, *Neugriechische Volkslieder* (2 vols.), 1825, and *Lyrische Reisen und epigrammatische Spaziergänge*, 1827. He also trans. Marlowe's *Faustus*, and ed. *Bibliothek der Dichtungen des 17. Jahrhunderts* (10 vols.), 1822–7. Many of his poems were set to music by Schubert, and have become extremely popular (*Die schöne Müllerin* and *Winterreise*). *See* A. Wirth, *Studien zu Wilhelm Müller*, 1928.

Mullet, term for 2 distinct fish types: (1) The grey M. (*Mugilidae*) comprises about 70 species, of which 3 are found off the Brit. coast. They are valued as food, especially when taken from fresh water, and they are cultivated in M. ponds in Italy and also in Honolulu. (2) The red M. (*Mullidae*) comprises about 40 species, many of which are tropical. The common red M. (*M. surmuletus*) has been famed since classical times for its delicately flavoured flesh. Its average length is about 15 in., and weight 2¼ lb. Its skin is a brilliant red. Red M.s have a pair of erectile barbels which project downwards and forwards when the fish is feeding on the sea bottom and which lie back in grooves at other times.

Mullingar, co. tn of Westmeath, Rep. of Ireland, on the R. Brosna, an important road

MULLET
Above, grey mullet; *below,* red mullet.

and rail junction and a harbour on the Royal Canal between Dublin and the Shannon. The Catholic cathedral of Christ the King was dedicated in 1939. The modern Franciscan college occupies the site of the anct Multyfarnham Abbey near Lough Derrevaragh. Industries include furniture and pencils, and livestock sales are held at the new yard. Pop. 5889.

Mullion, vil. of the Lizard dist, Cornwall, England, 9½ m. S. of Helston. Its church is dedicated to St Melan; the interior has some very fine carved bench-ends, perhaps the best in the whole co. There are splendid views across Mount's Bay to Penzance. The scenery of M. Cove, which is about 1 m. from the vil., rivals that of any cove in Cornwall. The lichen-covered cliffs, rocks piled on rocks, vaulted and ribbed, with chasms and natural arches, rise above the caves on all sides. The cove or harbour, with its jetties and fish cellars and the nearby M. is., were presented to the nation in 1945. About 1 m. W. of M. is the Marconi memorial, set up in 1937 to commemorate the fact that on 12 Dec. 1901 at 12.30 p.m., Marconi, in Newfoundland, received a morse signal sent from this spot, the first ever heard across the ocean. Here also, 22 years later, the short-wave beam system, which revolutionised long-distance communications, was successfully tested. Pop. 1200.

Mullion, in Gothic architecture, one of the upright stone shafts dividing the general aperture of a window into secondary openings, which are again frequently subdivided horizontally by similar shafts crossing the M.s and therefore called 'transomes'.

Mulock, Dinah Maria, *see* CRAIK.

Mulready, William (1786–1963), Irish painter, *b.* Ennis, in co. Clare. His father removed to London soon after M. was born, and here M. had the help of Banks, the sculptor. In 1800 he was admitted as a student of the Royal Academy, and in 1816 elected R.A. He is noted for *genre* paintings, a number of which are in the Victoria and Albert Museum and the Tate

Gallery, London, e.g. 'Choosing the Wedding Gown', 'Crossing the Ford', 'A Roadside Inn', 'The Barber's Shop' and 'Punch'.

Mulso, Hester, *see* CHAPONE.

Multan, or **Mooltan,** tn of W. Pakistan, 180 m. SW. of Lahore. M. is an anct city, thought to have been in existence in the time of Alexander the Great. It is mentioned by the Chinese traveller Hsüan Tsang, in AD 641. There is an old fort and some fine Muslim tombs. A large new medical college was begun in 1952. M. is notorious for great heat and an exiguous rainfall.

'Multatuli', *see* DEKKER, EDUARD DOUWES.

Multiple Proportions, *see* CHEMISTRY.

Multiple Stars, *see* STARS.

Multiplepoinding, in Scots law, an action whereby any number of different claimants to the same money, effects or property (referred to as 'the fund *in medio*') can obtain the decision of the court on the question of which is entitled, or, if more than one, in what proportions they are entitled. The subject-matter, however, is generally a sum of money, and must be such as the holder may be obliged to pay; hence rents to become due cannot be the subject of M. Usually M. is competent only where *conflicting* claims have been made, or where conflicting interests exist which may mature into claims. See *Green's Encyclopaedia of Scots Law*.

Multituberculates, early herbivorous mammals of Mesozoic age possessing dentition of a specialised type.

Multscher, Hans (*c.* 1400–67), Ger. painter and sculptor, *b.* Reichenhofen. He worked at Ulm producing carved and painted altar-pieces. His painting shows a dramatic realism in a style influenced by Netherlandish art. A prin. work is the Wurzach altar, 1437 (Berlin).

Multures. In Scots law M. were the payments in kind exacted under the obligation of thirlage (q.v.).

Mumbij, *see* HIERAPOLIS.

Mumbles, or **Oystermouth,** popular seaside and residential resort on Swansea Bay, forming part of Swansea (q.v.) bor. Here are the ruins of Oystermouth Castle.

Mumford, Lewis (1895–), Amer. critic, *b.* Flushing, Long Is. Educ. at New York Univ., he served in the navy during the First World War, visited London in 1920, and then worked as a freelance writer. His first book, *The Story of Utopias*, 1922, was followed by *Sticks and Stones*, 1924, *The Golden Day*, 1926, *The Brown Decades*, 1932, *Men Must Act*, 1939, and *Faith for Living*, 1940. Much of his work is an analysis of Amer. culture and a plea for moral regeneration. *The Conduct of Life*, 1952, which discusses man's nature and destiny, completes a series of which the earlier vols. are *Technics and Civilisation*, 1934, *The Culture of Cities*, 1938, and *The Condition of Man*, 1944. M. also wrote a study of Herman Melville, 1929, and lectured on education at sev. univs.

Mummius, Lucius (2nd cent. BC), Rom. general. As consul in 146 he ended the war with the Achaean League (q.v.) by the capture and destruction of Corinth, for which he received the surname Achaicus. It has been claimed that this monstrous hooliganism was foreign to M.'s nature and was due to pressure from a commercial group in the senate. Whatever the truth, M. was a social upstart whose plebeian origins are shown by his remark when ordering the removal of the Corinthian art treasures to Rome: 'If they are lost or damaged, you'll have to replace them.'

Mummy (Persian *mummia*, bitumen), term applied at a late date in Egypt to an embalmed body, from an erroneous idea that the blackened condition of embalmed bodies was due to bitumen (as it rarely was). Anct Egyptian religious belief in life after death demanded that the body should last for ever, and in as lifelike a condition as possible, because the soul which left the body at death was expected to return to it. In the dry climate of Upper Egypt the body lasts indefinitely in shallow burials in sand, as were usual in predynastic times. But in the Archaic Period deeper graves with chambers lined with brick or masonry, and a wooden coffin, with the rather later addition of a stone sarcophagus, all delayed the desiccation of the body, and so led to attempts to preserve the body by embalming. The development of the full method of mummification usual in the New Kingdom arose gradually. Details varied from time to time, but the prin. feature was always deliberate drying (removal of the water, which forms 75 per cent of the weight of the human body) by packing in dry natron as the dehydrating agent for 2 to 3 months—*not* steeping in a solution of natron (as usually stated), which could only have resulted in hastening decomposition. In the Old Kingdom evisceration and the modelling of the features in linen soaked in resin were practised. In Dynasty XI the abdomen was not opened to remove the viscera, but this was done again in Dynasty XII. From the time of the Old Kingdom the viscera were placed in a stone box with 4 compartments, or in 4 stone jars. By Dynasty XII these jars were associated with the 4 sons of Horus (q.v.), and had at first 4 human heads, though by the time of the New Kingdom they had 2 human and 2 animal heads. Such jars are erroneously called Canopic jars. By the New Kingdom the brain was usually extracted, and the abdomen filled with linen impregnated with resin. In Dynasty XXI there was a marked change; the organs were wrapped in linen and returned to the body, being packed in sawdust with wax figures of the 4 sons of Horus. Mud or sand was forced beneath the skin to restore the form of the body or limbs. Later there was considerable degeneration in the art of mummification, with often no attempt to preserve the body, this being disguised by extra elaborate bandaging. It was the spread of the practice of mummification to ordinary people that led to the introduction of cheaper methods. For further details *see* A. Lucas, *Ancient Egyptian Materials and Industries* (3rd ed.), 1948. (*See Plate: Burial Customs.*)

Mumps, infectious disease characterised by

inflammation of the parotid glands, and at times of the other salivary glands. Other names for the disease are *epidemic parotitis*, and, in Scotland, the 'branks'. The infection is caused by a virus. After a period of incubation of about 2 to 3 weeks, the disease shows itself by a swelling in the region of the parotid gland, which is situated in front of and below the external ear. There is usually some degree of catarrh, with slight febrile symptoms, but these are seldom pronounced enough to occasion discomfort. As the disease proceeds the swelling becomes increased in size and spreads downwards to the neck and round the angle of the jaw, causing pain when masticating. The patient is otherwise quite well, except for some amount of discomfort attached to the actions of masticating and swallowing. It takes about 4 or 5 days for the swelling to reach its height, after which it gradually abates to a normal condition. Suppuration of the gland is a very uncommon occurrence. The disease does not call for much treatment. The diet should be that proper to a febrile condition, and the food should be soft enough to avoid painful mastication. The disease is highly infectious, and sometimes spreads with great rapidity among young children. Affected persons rarely take it a second time. It occasionally happens that other glands are similarly affected, particularly the testicles in males, and more rarely the ovaries in females, sometimes also the pancreas. An epididymo-orchitis due to mumps may cause sterility.

Mun, Thomas (1571–1641), writer on political economy. He was a member of the committee of the E. India Co. In 1621 he wrote and pub. *A Discourse of Trade from England unto the West Indies*; and about 1630 wrote *England's Treasure by Forraign Trade*, a statement of the Mercantilist doctrine of economic self-sufficiency by the creation of favourable trade balance. This latter was pub. by his son, John M., in 1664.

Muncács, *see* MUKACHEVO.

Munch, Edvard (1863–1944), Norwegian painter, *b*. Löten, studied at Oslo under Krohg; spent many years abroad, 1889–92 in Paris, 1892–8 in Germany. He developed a personal style in the nineties, and on his return to Norway became celebrated for his murals for Oslo Univ., completed in 1913. He exercised a great influence on art, especially in Germany, and his interpretation of the 'melancholy and pessimism of his age' was a force in the growth of Expressionism, no less than that of Vincent van Gogh. He used many great graphic media, woodcut, lithograph, etching, etc., with great originality. He bequeathed an immense collection of his work to the city of Oslo. *See* monograph of J. P. Hodin, 1948. (*See Plate: Norway*.)

München-Gladbach, Ger. tn in the *Land* of N. Rhine-Westphalia (q.v.), 16 m. W. of Düsseldorf. It grew up around a Benedictine abbey founded in the 8th cent. and dissolved in 1802. Its minster dates from the 8th cent., and there is a baroque tn hall (formerly the abbey) and a Romanesque nunnery. It is well known for its choral societies, and it has sev. technical schools. M.-G. is the centre of the Ger. spinning and weaving industry, and has also iron foundries and manufs. of electrical equipment, oil, foodstuffs and chemicals. Pop. 152,300.

Münchhausen, Karl Friedrich Hieronymous, Baron (1720–97), *b*. Hanover, famous for narrating marvellous stories. He served in the Russian Army against the Turks, and on his retiring to his estate of Bodenwerder, amused and astounded his friends and relations by the extraordinary tales of his adventures during the war. A man named Rudolf Erich Raspe (q.v.) collected these tales and pub. a book in English called *Baron Münchhausen's Narrative of his Marvellous Travels and Campaigns in Russia*, 1785. It was pub. in German by Bürger, with many additions. A. Cruikshank illustrated one ed., 1869, and Gustave Doré, 1862, another. The book has been enlarged by the insertion of stories culled from various sources. The text of *Münchhausen's Travels*, as usually reprinted, is, as shown by John Carswell, 'the product of a long tradition of revision and improvisation' and Raspe himself was the author of less than a sixth part of what is printed in Carswell's text. Raspe had some hand in the authorship of the second instalment, *The Sea Adventures*, produced by a London publisher named Smith. In this account another baron, de Tott, founded on a well-known Fr. Hussar, is introduced, partly as a foil to M., partly as a convenient medium for attacking the Catholic Church. In Carswell's ed. the first and second sections, Raspe's original text, and the Raspe-Smith second instalment, *The Sea Adventures*, appeared in 1948, uncorrupted for the first time in England since their original pub. in 1785. *See* R. E. Raspe and others, *Singular Travels, Campaigns and Adventures of Baron Münchhausen* (ed. by J. Carswell), 1948.

Muncie, city, co. seat of Delaware co., Indiana, U.S.A., 54 m. NE. of Indianapolis. A railway centre in an agric. area, it manufs. glass, steel and wire products, etc., and is the seat of a state teachers' college. Pop. 68,600.

Munday, or **Mundy**, **Anthony** (1553–1633), dramatist and miscellaneous writer, *b*. London. He went to Rome, 1578, probably as a spy to report on the Eng. Jesuit College there. On his return to England, 1579, he became an actor, and later a member of the Earl of Oxford's company. He wrote anti-Catholic pamphlets and trans. romances. In 1605 he was appointed chief pageant writer for the City, and by these entertainments he won his greatest fame. There are 18 plays ascribed to M., among them *The Downfall of Robert Earl of Huntingdon*, 1601, *The Death of Robert of Huntingdon*, in which he collaborated with Henry Chettle (q.v.), and *John a Kent and John a Cumber*. He contributed sev. lyrics, some under the name of 'Shepherd Tony', to *England's Helicon*, 1600. He also wrote under the name of 'Lazarus Piot'. M. pub. an enlarged ed. of Stow's *Survey of London* in 1618. Ben Jonson nicknamed him 'Antonio Balladino, the pageant poet'. *See* life by C. Turner, 1928.

Munden, Joseph Shepherd (1758–1832), actor, b. London. After playing in strolling companies he made his mark at Canterbury under Hurst. In 1790 he came to London, where, until about 1811, he was the leading comedian. He had a great gift for facial expression. *See* Charles Lamb, *Essays of Elia*.

Münden, Ger. tn in the *Land* of Lower Saxony (q.v.), on the Weser at the confluence of the Fulda and the Werra, 67 m. S. of Hanover. It belonged to the Hanseatic League (q.v.). There are engineering and other industries. Pop. 20,200.

Mundesley, vil. and seaside resort of Norfolk, England, 7 m. from Cromer. About 2 m. to the S. is Paston, noted for the 15th cent. family of that name (*see* PASTON LETTERS). Close by is Trimingham, said to be the highest point in Norfolk. Pop. 1227.

Mundinus, *see* MONDINO DE' LUZZI.

Mundurucus, tribe of Brazilian Indians, S. of the Amazon, on the R. Tapajós, generally classified with the Tupí stock.

Mungo, St, *see* KENTIGERN.

Mungoose, *see* MONGOOSE.

Mungret, vil., 3 m. W. of Limerick, Rep. of Ireland, with 7th cent. monastic ruin. There is a large cement factory. Pop. 241.

Muni River Settlements, *see* SPANISH GUINEA.

Munich (Ger. **München**), city of Germany, the next in size to Berlin and Hamburg. It is in the SE. of the country, is cap. of the *Land* of Bavaria (q.v.), and stands on the Isar in an elevated plain about 1700 ft above sea-level. The name 'Munichen' appears in monastic records of the early 12th cent.; in the middle of the cent. Henry the Lion (q.v.) made M. the chief market for the salt obtained from the Reichenhall (q.v.) dist. In 1253 it was made a city and became a residence of the dukes of the Wittelsbach dynasty. The old tn was nearly destroyed by fire in 1327, and it was rebuilt by the emperor Louis V (q.v.) very much on the plan which it still exhibits; but it was not until the 18th cent., when the fortifications were razed, that the limits of the tn were enlarged to any extent. The city suffered during the Thirty Years War (q.v.); it was taken by the Swedes under Gustavus II (q.v.) in 1632 and shortly afterwards it was ravaged by plague. In 1742 it fell into the hands of the Austrians. In the 19th cent. the city flourished and expanded, and many institutions were founded in it for the encouragement of art and science. It was in M., after the First World War, that the Nazi movement (*see* NATIONAL SOCIALISM) began, and it was here that Hitler (q.v.) led the abortive *putsch* of Nov. 1923. It was in M., also, that the 'appeasement' meeting of Sept. 1938 took place (*see* MUNICH PACT). During the Second World War the city suffered severely in bombing attacks. The archiepiscopal cathedral of M., the *Frauenkirche*, 1468–88, is one of the largest Gothic churches in Germany; its 2 towers, capped with cupolas, are 320 ft high. The former royal palace, the *Residenz*, was almost completely destroyed in the war, but its contents were saved and the reconstruction of the buildings follows the original design. Opposite the palace is the *Feldherrnhalle* (a copy of the *Loggia dei Lanzi* at Florence), outside which the Bavarian police fired on the Nazis in 1923. Among the other well-known buildings which suffered in the war were the old and new tn halls; the façade of the latter, however, was preserved, as was the famous mechanical clock. The old part of the city still has many picturesque baroque and rococo buildings. Of the numerous parks and gardens the best known are the *Englischer Garten* (600 ac.) and, on the NW. side of the city, the beautiful grounds surrounding the *Nymphenburg* palace, the 17th–18th cent. baroque summer residence of the electors and kings. M. has a univ., with which Liebig and Röntgen (qq.v.) were connected, an important library and renowned scientific and technological museums. It has the celebrated art collections of the *Glyptothek* and of the *Alte* and *Neue Pinakothek*. The city is a centre of road, rail and air communications. It has long been famous for printing and publishing, and for the manuf. of lager beer. Other industries are the manuf. of textiles, optical and precision instruments, electrical goods, motor-cycles, rolling stock and trucks. Pop. 1,085,000.

Munich Pact, agreement made at Munich between Hitler, Neville Chamberlain, Mussolini and Daladier on 30 Sept. 1938, providing for the cession of the Sudetenland to Germany. War was imminent owing to Fr. guarantees of Czech independence and Chamberlain flew to Berchtesgaden, Hitler's residence, to dissuade Hitler from war. As a result he agreed with Daladier to recommend the Czech Gov. to surrender all dists containing more than fifty Germans. This did not satisfy Hitler, and Chamberlain flew a second time to Germany, meeting Hitler at Godesberg. Hitler now increased his demands for the surrender of a much larger zone, with the result that France and Britain mobilised and recommended Czechoslovakia to do the same. At this point Mussolini suggested that another conference should be held, and Chamberlain and Daladier accordingly met him and Hitler at Munich on 28 Sept. 1938. Although Hitler's terms were only slightly modified, they were accepted, Chamberlain returning to London with the worthless agreement in his pocket and the belief that he had brought back 'peace in our time'. The pact provided for a guarantee of the new frontiers created after the Ger. Army had marched into Czechoslovakia (1 Oct.) by all the signatories. Chamberlain and Hitler also signed a joint declaration ruling out war between their two nations. In France as well as in Britain the agreement was welcomed with popular relief; but it gradually became totally discredited as the last stage of the futile policy of 'appeasement', being conclusively proved worthless after the total Ger. occupation of Czechoslovakia, Mar. 1939. *See further under* CZECHOSLOVAKIA and EUROPE, *History. See* R. W. Seton-Watson, *Munich and the Dictators*, 1939, and *Documents on British Foreign Policy: 3rd series, vol. i., 1938* (ed. by E. L. Woodward and R. Butler), 1949.

Municipal Corporations, see LOCAL GOVERN-MENT.

Municipal Trading, see LOCAL GOVERNMENT.

Municipality (derived from Lat. *municipium*), term which came subsequently to denote the duties (*munus*, duty or privilege) undertaken, and the privileges accepted, by the various It. tns and other communities which stood in dependence on the city of Rome. Later the term *municipia* was applied to all urb. communities of Rom. citizens in Italy with a definite organisation and a more or less complete system of self-government. The term M. thus became the appropriate generic name both for cities or tns which enjoyed a measure of local autonomy and for the conventional governing body of such cities or tns. In England the most anct. M.s are those bors. which can show an unbroken hist. back to the Middle Ages or earlier, when, in consideration of certain payments (like the *firma burgi*) they received royal charters of self-taxation and self-government. Other and later municipal corporations include principally large manufacturing tns, which have acquired the status of co. or non-co. bors. by charter or private Act of Parliament. (*See* BOROUGH; BURGESS; CORPORATION; LOCAL GOVERNMENT.) In most cases of anct bors., hist. justifies the assumption that the municipal corporation of mayor, aldermen and burgesses, or at least the common council, arose out of the Merchant and Craft Guilds, for these latter possessed a common stock and corporate trading ventures which gave them both the wealth and the local organisation essential to the conduct of corporate affairs. M.s not dissimilar in some of their essentials from Eng. municipal corporations exist in many countries; but those in the U.S.A. differ in one important respect in that the various grades of members of the commonalty form distinct chambers under a bicameral system which reveals, as it were, the microcosm of a national or state legislature. In Germany tn constitutions varied very considerably. In Prussia the executive council (*magistrat*) of a municipal com. was elected by the representative assembly of the citizens out of their own body; but in other parts of Germany the executive was elected by the entire body of municipal electors.

Hist. shows that the M., com. or other urb. corporate entity endowed with local autonomous privileges has at various times arrogated to itself such formidable political ascendancy as to render itself practically independent. N. Italy, at the time of the Lombard kings, and long before the hegemony of the last cent., was essentially a region of independent city reps., each with an organisation not markedly dissimilar from that of the city state of anct Greece, and owing its anomalous position to the opportunities for the local tyranny of dukes and counts afforded by the feudal system. This aristocratic or caste tyranny was undermined only by the rival spiritual power set up under the aegis of the Christian empire by the grant of episcopal immunities, with the result that the It. city republics presented the curious political phenomenon of a dual system of control, the religious and democratic acting as a counterpoise to the temporal and ducal. By much the same process of evolution rose and waned the free tns of Germany (*see* FREE IMPERIAL CITIES) and the cities of the Swiss cantons. The Eng. bors. or chartered tns had a different hist. As the natural centres of trade they were early in a position to exact from necessitous overlords or needy monarchs fiscal and judicial immunities which soon enabled them to develop themselves into compact strongholds, with resources that in times of civil war or social upheaval were enough of themselves to decide the fate of contending factions in the state. The municipal corporation of England during the 19th cent. acquired by legislation and custom wide powers of self-government, but as the power of the central gov. increased and the services undertaken by the municipal corporations became of increased national importance their powers were curtailed so that now there is extensive control, especially from the financial aspect, of their powers by the central gov. See H. J. Laski (ed.), *A Century of Municipal Progress*, 1935; J. Tait, *The Medieval English Borough*, 1936; G. M. Harris, *Municipal Self-Government in Britain*, 1939; Helen Camm, *Liberties and Communities in Medieval England*, 1944; Lord MacMillan (ed.), *Local Government Law and Administration*, 1945; J. H. Warren, *Municipal Administration*, 1948; J. J. Clarke, *Local Government of the United Kingdom*, 1955.

The Eng. system of municipal administration was the model on which the early cities and tns of the U.S.A. were formed, but the system has now little in common with that of the U.S.A. Few or none of the M.s in the U.S.A. are created by charter. A municipal body in the U.S.A. is a corporation created by the state for state purposes as well as for local administration. This involves a certain distinction between M.s created at the request of the people and those created for the convenience of state administration. M.s come into being under general laws, and are not created by special act. *See* CITY.

Muniong Range, mts of New S. Wales and Victoria, Australia, forming a part of the Great Dividing Chain. Mt Kosciusko (7328 ft) is the highest point in the Australian continent.

Munitions, Ministry of. Following the Fr. example the Brit. Gov., in June 1915, set up a M. of M. by Act of Parliament, with the object of coping with the requirements of the First World War. The ministry was abolished in 1920. There was no M. of M., as such, in the Second World War, the analogous dept being designated Ministry of Supply.

Munk, Kaj (1898–1944), Dan. priest and dramatist, *b.* Maribo as Kaj Harald Leininger Petersen; Munk was the name of the foster parents who adopted him after the early deaths of his own parents. He studied theology at Copenhagen Univ., and wrote there his first extant play, *Pilatus*, at the age of 19, as well as the major part of *En Idealist*, a forceful play depicting Herod's obsession with power in defiance of God, which was finished in 1924 after he had become pastor of Vedersø in W. Jutland. This was followed in 1925 by *Ordet* (The Word), which gives a realistic, rural setting to a theme involving the performance of a miracle; dramatically it is probably his greatest achievement. It was not performed until after the production in 1931 of *Cant*, a verse drama about Anne Boleyn which was largely responsible for establishing his fame. Other plays include *Han sidder ved Smeltediglen* (He sits at the Melting Pot), 1938, an anti-Nazi piece; *Niels Ebbesen*, 1940, a patriotic piece written in protest against, and circulated in defiance of, the Ger. occupying forces; and *Før Cannae*, 1943, an allegorical duologue between Hannibal and Fabius Cunctator, in whom are to be recognised Hitler and Churchill respectively. Originally pro-Mussolini, as in *Sejren* (The Victory), 1936, and pro-Hitler, M. later became violently anti-Nazi after the occupation of Denmark and denounced the Germans whenever possible; he was shot by them shortly after the pub. of *Før Cannae*. See R. P. Keigwin, *Kaj Munk, Some Examples of his Work*, 1944.

Munnings, Sir Alfred (1878–1959), painter, was educ. at Framlingham, and studied art at Norwich and Paris. He first exhibited at the Royal Academy in 1898, specialising in Turf and horse pictures. His 'Epsom Downs' is his best-known work. During the First World War he painted a series of war pictures for the Canadian Gov. A.R.A. in 1919, R.A. in 1925, and president of the Royal Academy from 1944 to 1951. An uncompromising critic of certain tendencies in modern art, he pub. reminiscences, 1950–2, *An Artist's Life—The Second Burst —The Finish*.

Munorisa, *see* MANRESA.

Munro, C. K., pen-name of **Charles Walden Kirkpatrick McMullan** (1889–), playwright, *b.* Portrush, co. Antrim. Educ. at Harrow and Cambridge, he entered the civil service and rose to be under-secretary at the Ministry of Labour. His plays include *At Mrs Beam's*, 1922, *The Rumour*, 1923, *Storm*, 1924, *The Mountain*, 1926, *Bluestone Quarry*, 1931, *Ding and Co.*, 1934, and *Coronation Time at Mrs Beam's*, 1937. *The True Woman*, 1932, is styled 'a handbook for husbands'. In 1947 he was awarded the C.B.E.

Munro, Hector Hugh (1870–1916), Brit. short story writer, *b.* Akyab, Burma. He spent his early years in Devon, and was educ. at Exmouth and Bedford Grammar School, afterwards travelling with his father on the Continent. After serving for a time in the police service in Burma he returned to England, and from 1902 to 1908 was a foreign correspondent of the *Morning Post*. In the First World War he served as a private in the Royal Fusiliers and was killed at Beaumont-Hamel. His books of humorous short stories include *Reginald*, 1904, *Reginald in Russia*, 1910, *The Chronicles of Clovis*, 1912, *Beasts and Super-Beasts*, 1914, and *The Square Egg*, 1924. *The Unbearable Bassington*, 1912, and *When William Came*, 1914, are novels. M.'s pseudonym 'Saki' is the name of the cup-bearer in *The Ruba'iyát of Omar Khayyám*.

Munro, Neil (1864–1930), novelist and poet, *b.* Inveraray, Argyllshire. For a time he worked in a law office, then went into journalism, and after working on various papers was editor of the *Glasgow Evening News* from 1918 to 1927. Latterly he lived at Craigendoran on the Firth of Clyde. His first book, *The Lost Pibroch*, 1896, a collection of Celtic tales, was followed by a number of historical novels, including *John Splendid*, 1898, *Gilian the Dreamer*, 1899, *Doom Castle*, 1901, and *Children of the Tempest*, 1903. Of his humorous dialect stories the 'Para Handy' series, beginning with *The 'Vital Spark'*, 1906, were the most famous; others are *Erchie*, 1904, *The Daft Days*, 1907, *Fancy Farm*, 1910, *Ayrshire Idylls*, 1912, and *Jaunty Jock*, 1918. Books of verse are *Bagpipe Ballads*, 1917, and *The Poetry of Neil Munro*, 1931. *The Clyde: River and Firth*, 1907, is descriptive. In 1908 he was made an honorary LL.D. of Glasgow.

Munro, Sir Thomas (1761–1827), soldier and governor, *b.* and educ. at Glasgow. He was appointed infantry cadet at Madras, 1779, served in the war against Hyder Ali, 1780–4, and was then promoted to lieutenant-colonel and rendered great services to General Wellesley (afterwards Duke of Wellington) during the war with Scindia and the rajah of Berar. He returned to India in 1814 on a commission to reorganise the judicial and police depts. During the Mahratta war he was brigadier-general. He then returned to England, but soon after his arrival he was nominated to the governorship of Madras, and re-embarked for India in 1819. He held the post for 7 years with marked success.

Munshi, *see* TIV.

Münster, Sebastian (1489–1552), Ger. orientalist, humanist, cosmographer, astronomer and cartographer, *b.* Ingelheim. He joined the Franciscans but subsequently adopted the opinions of Luther and apostatised (1524). He taught Hebrew at Heidelberg, but was soon afterwards appointed to the new chair of Hebrew at Basel, where he moved in 1528. The most important of M.'s works are *Grammatica chaldaica*, 1527, *Dictionarium chaldaicum*, 1527, *Dictionarium trilingue, in quo Latinis vocabulis, Graeca et Hebraica respondent*, 1530, *Germaniae descriptio*, 1530, *Novus Orbis*, 1532, *Horologiographia*, 1533, *Biblia hebraica* (2 vols.), 1534–5 and 1546, *Mappa Europae*, 1536, *Organum Uranicum*, 1536, *Cosmographia universalis*, 1544 (at least 46 eds. appeared in the following 100 years), and *Rudimenta mathematica*, 1551.

Münster, Ger. city in the *Land* of N. Rhine-Westphalia (q.v.), on the Dortmund–Ems canal, 62 m. NE. by N. of Düsseldorf. It became a bishopric in the 9th cent. and its prince-bishops came to rule extensive ter. until the secularisation of the principality in 1803. The position of the city on the trade routes made it an important member of the Hanseatic League (q.v.). In 1533 it became the centre of the Anabaptist (q.v.) disturbances. It was neutralised during the discussions which led up to the Treaty of Westphalia (q.v.), and some of the provisions of the Treaty were signed in its Rathaus. In 1814 it passed to Prussia, and in 1816 it became the cap. of Westphalia (q.v.). M. was severely damaged by bombing during the Second World War. The city fell to Brit. troops, after an artillery bombardment, on 2 April 1945. Among the anct structures which remain are the 12th–13th cent. cathedral (much restored), which has fine Romanesque and Gothic sculpture; the 14th cent. church of Our Lady, with its beautiful Gothic tower; the 14th cent. chapel of the Knights of St John; the splendid baroque episcopal palace (now the univ.); and the 13th cent. Buddenturm. The famous Gothic façade of the Rathaus (the original dating from 1335) has been copied. A univ. of M., founded in 1773, was converted in 1818 into faculties of philosophy and theology for Bonn (q.v.). The present univ. (the univ. of Westphalia) was constituted in 1902. M. has busy harbours on the Dortmund–Ems canal, and has an airport. There is a large trade in timber and foodstuffs, and there are engineering, paper, porcelain, brewing and distilling industries. Pop. 182,700.

Munster, SW. prov. of Rep. of Ireland (q.v.), comprising the cos. of Cork, Waterford, Kerry, Limerick, Tipperary and Clare. It was originally, i.e. before Henry II's reign, divided into 2 kingdoms, Desmond and Thomond, and the title and rank of King of M. were borne by the rulers of the respective kingdoms alternately. Area 9314 sq. m. Pop. 849,203. *See* articles on individual cos. for pop. and topography.

Munster Fusiliers, The Royal, famous Irish regiment, descended from the Bengal Fusiliers raised in Charles II's reign, when they were part of the small detachment sent to the E. Indies to protect the factories of the E. India Co. Robert Clive was their first recorded colonel and Plassey their first battle honour. Their familiar sobriquet 'Dirty Shirts' was 'conferred' on the regiment in allusion to their bravery at the siege of Bhurtpore (1805), where they discarded their tunics and fought in their shirts. The 104th Bengal Fusiliers, destined later to become the 2nd Battalion of the Munsters (the old 104th Foot), was embodied in 1839, and won its first great action at Chillianwallah. It was amalgamated with the 101st Foot as the R. M. F. The regiment also rendered great service in the Indian mutiny and in S. Africa. Units of the regiment fought with distinction in the First World War in NW. Europe, at Gallipoli and in the Middle E. The regiment was disbanded in 1922. *See* S. McCance, *The History of the Royal Munster Fusiliers,* 1928.

Münsterberg, Hugo (1863–1916), Ger.-Amer. psychologist, *b.* Danzig. His work in psychology at Freiburg Univ. came to the notice of Wm James, who invited him to Harvard as the first director of its laboratory of psychology. President Amer. Psychological Association, 1898. He pub. works in German on psychology, and in English on the popular applications of psychology. When the First World War broke out, he was an untiring propagandist of Ger. culture. In this connection he pub. *The Peace and America,* 1915, and even attempted by letter to influence the president. To intellectualism he opposed a theory of voluntaristic idealism, which regards the will as the essential principle. *See* J. H. Wigmore, *Münsterberg and the Psychology of Evidence,* 1909.

Muntafiq, *see* NASIRIYAH.

Munthe, Axel (1857–1949), Swedish medical practitioner and author, *b.* Oskarshamn. He was educ. at Uppsala Univ., and worked under Charcot at the Salpêtrière, but, disagreeing with the latter's theories on hypnotism, left him. For 12 years he was gynaecologist in Paris and in *The Story of San Michele,* written during periods of insomnia, he told how he adopted the term 'colitis' as a reassuring name for the imaginary ailments of his fashionable patients of the Faubourg Saint-Germain. In Rome, where he lived in Keats's house, he enjoyed an equally lucrative and fashionable practice and eventually made enough money to realise his ambition to build the villa, with bird sanctuary, of San Michele on the highest point of the is. of Capri. *The Story of San Michele,* 1929, one of the most remarkable 'best selling' vols. of memoirs of recent times, was originally written in English and trans. into 44 languages. M. was for some years physician to Queen Victoria of Sweden. *See* life by G. Munthe and G. Üxköll, 1953.

Muntjac, or **Barking Deer** (*Muntiacus*), species of small deer which range throughout SE. Asia. The hair is short and smooth, and bright rufus bay in colour, with a patch of white on the throat and beneath the tail. The buck's head has the V-shaped frontal bone greatly prolonged into 2 pedicles covered with skin and hair; short antlers grow from the tips. In the upper jaw are 2 sharp canine teeth which often extend below the lower lip.

Muntz's Metal, or **Yellow Metal,** is an alloy of 60 per cent of copper and 40 per cent of zinc. It is called after the name of its Birmingham inventor. Unlike brass it is malleable when hot, and can be more easily rolled than copper. *See* ALLOY.

Münzer, or **Müntzer, Thomas** (1490–1525), leader of the Anabaptists (q.v.), *b.* Stolberg, Harz Mts. He preached exaggerated Christian liberty, opposing civil gov., religious rites, etc. (1521). He headed the Thuringian peasant revolt in 1524, but was defeated by the Elector John and Duke George of Saxony, the Landgrave of Hesse, and the Duke of Brunswick. He was beheaded at Mühlhausen with Pfeifer and others.

Mura, *see* SLOVENIA.

Murad, *see* AMURATH.

Mural Decoration (Lat. *murus,* wall), art of adorning walls with painting in fresco, oils or encaustic, with mosaic compositions or with carving in wood, terra-cotta, stone or marble. The term is also extended to the decorative treatment of vaults and ceilings. In early Egyptian art interior walls were covered with figure and other designs in low relief, or deeply incised, and were gaily coloured. Wonderful examples of M. D. of the Mycenaean Age have been discovered at Knossos. In Assyria walls were decorated with sculptured dadoes and coloured friezes, representing groups of figures. The sculptured friezes and metopes of anct Greece, used as decorations for temples and public buildings, are of incomparable beauty. The Romans employed 3 prin. methods of M. D.: painting in fresco, mosaics and marble incrustations. Some remains of mural paintings have been preserved at Pompeii. In later cents. It. artists painted in oils on plaster. Cimabue and Giotto painted in fresco, leading the way in a form of M. D. which superseded all others. During the Middle Ages mural painting was used extensively in churches until the introduction of large areas of stained glass. In modern times the art of M. D. has declined, save in special cases such as saloons of great liners, restaurants and schoolrooms. *See also* FRESCO PAINTING; MOSAIC; TAPESTRY. *See* H. Feibusch, *Mural Painting*, 2nd ed., 1947.

Murano, suburb of Venice, in Veneto (q.v.), Italy. It is built on sev. is. in the lagoon, and has been famous for its decorative glass since medieval times (*see* GLASS). Optical glass is also now made. The Byzantine church of S. Maria e Donato has fine 12th cent. mosaics.

Murat, Joachim (1767–1815), Fr. soldier and King of Naples, son of an innkeeper, *b.* La Bastide-Fortunière, near Cahors, France. He entered the Fr. Army, in which he served under Napoleon in Italy and Egypt, distinguishing himself at the battle of the Pyramids (1798). For his part in the 13th Vendémiaire he was made a lieutenant-colonel and first aide-de-camp to Napoleon, and after Aboukir was made a general of div. He dispersed the Council of Five Hundred at St Cloud in 1799, and in the following year married Napoleon's youngest sister, Marie Armonciade Caroline. He was made governor of the Cisalpine rep. in 1801, and after taking part in the battles of Jena, Eylau, Austerlitz, etc., was made Grand Duke of Berg and Cleves. In the invasion of Spain in 1808 he commanded the Fr. armies, but shortly afterwards Napoleon gave him the crown of Naples, and he was proclaimed King of the Two Sicilies. He styled himself King Joachim-Napoleon and his rule was generally liberal in character. In 1812 he commanded the cavalry of the grand army which invaded Russia; but after the battle of Leipzig he hurried back to his kingdom and, having broken with Napoleon, made overtures to Austria and Great Britain. When Napoleon escaped from Elba M. thought he could himself win all Italy and then treat with Napoleon as an equal, but he was checked at Ferrara and routed at Tolentino. He then organised an expedition to Calabria against the restored Bourbons, but was captured and shot at Pizzo. *See* lives by H. Weil, 1909–10; A. de Tarle, 1914; *also* L. Monnier, *Murat et le Congrès de Vienne,* 1937.

Muratori, Lodovico Antonio (1672–1750), It. scholar, antiquary and historian, *b.* Vignola, near Modena. In 1694 he became director of the Ambrosian College and Library at Milan, and while there pub. *Anecdota Graeca* and *Anecdota*

Latina, previously unedited fragments. Recalled to Modena (1700), he became librarian and archivist to Duke Rinaldo I. His 3 chief works are *Rerum italicarum scriptores,* 1723–51, dealing with the sources of medieval It. hist.; *Antiquitates italicae medii aevi* (1738–43), describing the constitution, customs and thought of the Middle Ages; and *Annali d'Italia,* 1744–9, first complete ed. 1753–6, a critical hist. of Italy from the birth of Christ down to 1750. His collected works were pub. 1767–80 and 1790–1810, and his letters, ed. by M. Cámporí, 1901–22. *See* life by G. Bertoni, 1926.

Muratorian Canon, MS. fragment of 85 lines discovered in 1740 by L. A. Muratori (q.v.). Dating from *c.* 190 it is the earliest known document listing the books of the New Testament.

Murav'ëv, Count Mikhail Nikolaevich (1796–1866), Russian administrator, strong opponent of Alexander II's reforms. In 1863–9 he was Governor-General in Vilna; he ruthlessly suppressed the Polish rising of 1863.

Murchison, Sir Roderick Impey (1792–1871), geologist, *b.* Tarradale, Ross-shire, Scotland. He studied the older rocks of large parts of England and Scotland, and later the geological structure of the Alps. He advised the Russian Gov. on geological matters and succeeded de la Beche as director general of the Geological Survey of the U.K., 1856. M.'s chief title to fame was the estab. of the Silurian system and his exposition of the Permian, Devonian and Laurentian systems. Amongst other works he pub. *The Silurian System,* 1838, and *The Geology of Russia in Europe and the Urals,* 1845.

Murchison Falls, in Uganda on the Victoria Nile about 20 m. from its exit from Lake Albert. At these falls there is a drop of the riv. of about 130 ft, the whole volume of the Nile passing through a rock-cleft only 19 ft wide in the elevated scarp at its narrowest point and then thundering down 401 ft in a series of splendid cascades. In the pool below are many fish, hippopotami and crocodiles. M. F. is easily reached by road or by steamer from Butiaba. The surrounding dist is immensely rich in the characteristic fauna of E. Africa, including elephants, lions, rhinoceros, buffaloes, monkeys and an infinite variety of antelope. During the winter season the Kenya and Uganda Railways and Harbours organises special excursions. *See* H. B. Thomas and Robert Scott, *Uganda,* 1935.

Murcia: 1. Region of SE. Spain, comprising the provs. of M. and Albacete (qq.v.). It was once a kingdom, which arose after the defeat of the last Visigoth king, Roderic (q.v.), and which, although Christian, was trib. to the Moors. The Moors later absorbed it, and in 1242 it was taken by Ferdinand III and joined to Castile (q.v.). Area 10,109 sq. m.; pop. 1,172,000.

2. Sp. prov. in the region of M., with a coastline on the Mediterranean. It is watered by the Segura and its tribs., the Sangonera and Quipar, and is very mountainous in the S. and E. Oranges, olives, palms, mulberry-trees and vines are grown, and there are large deposits of salt

and minerals, especially lead and zinc. Area 4370 sq. m.; pop. 802,000.

3. Sp. city, cap. of the prov. of M., on the Segura, in a celebrated *huerta* (garden country). It has a 14th–16th cent. cathedral, with an 18th cent. baroque façade, and other old churches. There is a univ., 1915. Textiles, iron, copper and gunpowder are manuf. Pop. 126,000.

Murder, the unlawful killing with malice aforethought (*see* MALICE) of a human being under the queen's peace. Children and idiots, or lunatics, cannot be guilty of M. But a lunatic who kills another person may be confined in Broadmoor or some other criminal lunatic asylum during the royal pleasure (*see also* INFANT and CRIMINAL LAW). The mere killing of another by whatsoever means, whether by an act or omission likely to result in death, raises a presumption of felonious homicide which the accused must rebut by showing some justification (*see* HOMICIDE) or excuse (as, for example, self-defence). It is not M. to kill an infant in the womb, though such act of procuring abortion may be punishable as a felony with imprisonment. But where a child born alive (in Scots law this is proved by anyone who heard the child cry; in Eng. law by medical testimony that it breathed) afterwards dies by reason of drugs or wounds received while in the womb (*a fortiori* afterwards), and those who administered such drugs or wounds are, according to the better opinion, guilty of M. It is not M. to kill an alien enemy actually participating in warfare against the state, but M. committed by a Brit. subject upon a foreigner (not an enemy) abroad is an extraditable crime, and the murderer can be punished by an Eng. court. The guilty state of mind essential to M., though generally one of sedate and deliberate intention to kill, may be inferred from any wanton or cruel act against another likely to result in death (*see also* MANSLAUGHTER and MALICE). 'Constructive' M. means the killing of a person while engaged in committing another felony; for example, if a burglar fearing capture rushes so violently past an inmate of the house as to cause his death, that will be M. however unintentional the killing. But in practice the death penalty was never inflicted in a clear case of merely 'constructive' M. There is no *crime passionnelle* in Eng. law, for no provocation, however great, will justify killing; but if there be no *express* malice (q.v.) the charge will be reduced to manslaughter.

Although suicide is no longer a crime, anyone guilty of complicity in another's suicide is criminally responsible. Accessories before the fact to M. are equally guilty and punishable with the prin. offender; and an attempt to commit M. is punishable with life imprisonment. The punishment for M. is life imprisonment, except in certain cases called 'capital' M. (*see* CAPITAL PUNISHMENT). In A.-S. times it was redeemable by payment of *wergild* (q.v.), or blood money, to relatives of the murdered man. In some of the United States M. is classified into degrees. For example, M. by poison or by any premeditated design is M. in the first degree and punishable

with death; all other kinds of M. are said to be in the second degree, punishable with imprisonment. *See* CAPITAL PUNISHMENT; CRIMINAL LAW.

Murdoch, Jean Iris (1919–), Brit. novelist, *b.* Dublin, educ. Badminton School and Somerville College, Oxford. She worked at the Treasury during the Second World War, then at refugee camps in Europe. In 1948 she became a fellow of St Anne's College, Oxford, and in 1956 married J. O. Bayley of New College. Her first novel, *Under the Net*, 1954, was awarded a prize at the Cheltenham Festival of Literature and Art. *Flight from the Enchanter*, 1956, further develops the fantastic vein of the earlier work. *The Sandcastle*, 1957, is more naturalistic; but this and other works, which include *A Severed Head*, 1961 (dramatised, 1963), *An Unofficial Rose*, 1962, *The Unicorn*, 1963, and *The Red and the Green*, 1965, each make use of a complex pattern of symbols.

Murdock, William (1754–1839), engineer and inventor, *b.* Auchinleck, Ayrshire. In 1792 he used coal gas as an illuminant in his own house, and 10 years later it was used at Soho Foundry. He experimented on a high-pressure locomotive, and in 1784 made a small locomotive steam engine. He also improved on Watt's steam engine, and invented apparatus by which it was possible to use compressed air, devising the first oscillating steam engine.

Mures River, riv. in Rumania and Hungary, a trib. of the R. Tisza, which it joins at Szeged. It rises in the Carpathians and is 450 m. long.

Muret, Fr. tn, in the dept of Haute-Garonne, at the confluence of the Garonne and the Louge. In 1213 the Albigenses (q.v.), supported by the Catalans, were defeated here by the Crusaders of Simon IV de Montfort (*see under* MONTFORT). M. produces a white wine. Pop. 6800.

Murfreesboro, city and co. seat of Rutherford co., Tennessee, U.S.A., 29 m. SE. of Nashville. It is a market centre for an agric. dist, and handles cotton, grain, livestock, timber, etc. It is the seat of Middle Tennessee State College. Near by was fought the battle of Stones R. in 1862. Pop. *c.* 15,000.

Murger, Henri (1822–61), Fr. novelist, *b.* Paris. His most popular work is *Scènes de la vie de Bohème*, 1848, which is the basis of Puccini's opera, *La Bohème*, 1898. Other works are *Scènes de la vie de jeunesse*, 1851, *Le Pays Latin*, 1852, *Adeline Protat*, 1853, *Les Buveurs d'eau*, 1855, *Le Sabot rouge*, 1860, *Madame Olympe*, 1860, and other prose tales and a collection of poems entitled *Les Nuits d'hiver*, 1861.

Murillo, Bartolomé Esteban (1617–82), Sp. painter, was *b.* Seville, where he studied painting under Juan del Castillo. Having saved a little money, which he made by hawking pictures at fairs and painting religious pictures for export to S. America, he went to Madrid in 1641, was encouraged by Velazquez and influenced by the Van Dycks he saw there. In 1645 he returned to Seville, received numerous important commissions and was soon acknowledged as head of the school. In 1645 M. married a lady of fortune and maintained a handsome estab. The Academy of Seville was founded by him in 1660. In early days he painted many pictures illustrative of peasant life; but his early realism gave way to a softness of manner in his later prolific output of religious paintings. In the Louvre and in England there are about 40 of his works. The most celebrated of M.'s pictures are 'Moses striking the Rock', 'Christ feeding the Five Thousand', 'St Anthony of Padua', 'The Prodigal's Return' and 'St Elizabeth of Hungary' (Prado). The picture M. preferred to all his other works was that of 'St Thomas de Villaneuva distributing Alms to the Sick and Poor'. His 'Immaculate Conception' was purchased for the Louvre at the sale of Marshal Soult's collection in 1852 for £23,612. *See* monographs by S. Montoto, 1923, and A. Munoz, 1943. *See also* A. Calvert, *Murillo: Biography and Appreciation*, 1907.

Murmansk: 1. Oblast (prov.) in NW. Russian S.F.S.R. situated largely on the Kola peninsula. It has a cool maritime climate, and is mostly covered with coniferous forests. There are vast aluminium, nickel, copper, iron, rare metals and phosphate deposits. The prin. tns are M., Monchegorsk and Kirovsk. Area 55,900 sq. m.; pop. (1965) 696,000 (95 per cent urb.), Russians, some Lapps.
2. Cap., economic and cultural centre of the above, an ice-free port on the Barents Sea. It has a large fishing industry and is one of the biggest Russian seaports, being the terminus of the N. Sea route. M. was founded in 1915 (Kola near by founded 1264) and used for allied supplies in both wars; it suffered greatly from German bombing 1941–4. It became prov. cap. in 1938. Pop. (1965) 272,000 (1926, 9000; 1939, 117,000).

Murner, Thomas (1475–1536), Ger. satirist and opponent of the Reformation. He was *b.* Oberehnheim, Alsace. In 1505 he was made poet laureate by Maximilian, and in 1513 became guardian of the Franciscan monastery at Strasburg. His satirical works, directed against the Reformation and Luther, include *Die Narrenbeschworung*, 1512, *Die Gäuchmatt*, 1519, and *Von dem grossen lutherischen Narren*, 1522. *See* W. Kawerau, *Murner und die deutsche Reformation*, 1891, and *Murner und die Kirche des Mittelalters*, 1890; W. Pfeiffer-Belli, *Thomas Murner im Schweizer Glaubenskampf*, 1939.

Murom, tn in Vladimir oblast of central Russia, on R. Oka. It has engineering, textile and woodworking industries, also market gardening (M. cucumbers). There are many architectural monuments of the 16th–19th cents. M. has been known since the 10th cent., became cap. of M. principality in the 12th cent. and Muscovite in 1393. Pop. (1965) 91,000.

Muroran, port in the prov. of Iburi, Hokkaido, Japan; has large steel works and exports food, timber and coal. Pop. 165,000.

Murrain, term formerly used to denote severe contagious diseases in cattle such as foot-and-mouth disease (q.v.).

Murray, Charles (1864–1941), poet, *b.* Alford, Aberdeenshire. Most of his life was spent in S. Africa, where he was manager of a mining

company, and became Secretary for Public Works in the Union, retiring in 1924 with a C.M.G. Returning to Scotland, he settled at Banchory. Vols. of his verse, in the Buchan dialect, include *Hamewith*, 1900, *A Sough o' War*, 1917, and *In the Country Places*, 1920.

Murray, Sir David (1849–1933), artist, *b.* Glasgow, gave up a commercial career to study painting. Elected A.R.A. in 1891 and R.A. in 1905. He produced many water-colour landscapes. His 'In the Country of Constable' is in the Tate Gallery.

Murray, George Gilbert Aimé (1866–1957), scholar, poet and author, *b.* Sydney, New S. Wales, son of Sir Terence Aubrey M., president of the Legislative Council, New S. Wales. Educ. at Merchant Taylors' School and St John's College, Oxford. A fellow of New College, Oxford, in 1889, he became prof. of Greek at Glasgow Univ., and from 1908 to 1936 was regius prof. of Greek at Oxford. In 1889 he married Lady Mary Howard, daughter of the ninth Earl of Carlisle. He became prof. of poetry at Harvard Univ. in 1926, and from 1914 was a trustee of the Brit. Museum. From 1923 to 1938 he was chairman of the League of Nations Union (co-president from 1938), and president of the International Committee of Intellectual Co-operation from 1928. O.M., 1941. M. ed. and made brilliant verse trans. of most of the surviving Gk tragedies, and was the author of numerous works on Gk literature and other classical subjects, including *The Rise of the Greek Epic*, 1904, *Five Stages of Greek Religion*, 1913, *Stoic Philosophy*, 1915, *Aristophanes*, 1933, and *Aeschylus, Creator of Tragedy*, 1940. *An Unfinished Autobiography* was pub. in 1960.

Murray, Sir James Augustus Henry (1837–1915), philologist and lexicographer, *b.* Denholm, near Hawick, Roxburghshire. He graduated at London and Oxford, and received the degree of LL.D (Edin.) in 1874. He began teaching at Hawick Grammar School in 1855; became master at Mill Hill School, 1870; assistant examiner in English to the univ. of London, 1875–9; and in 1885 went to Oxford. For many years he was engaged in editing the *New Oxford English Dictionary*, pub. 1884–1933, of which he was the chief creator, though his editorial responsibility covered only A–D, H–K, O, P and T. In 1878 he was appointed president of the Philological Society, London, for which he wrote various papers. He was also the author of articles on *The History and Language of the Border Counties* and *The Dialect of the Southern Counties of Scotland*. *See* memoir by H. Bradley in *Proceedings of the British Academy* (vol. viii), 1919; life by C. T. Onions in the *Dictionary of National Biography*; S. Baldwin, *The Oxford English Dictionary, 1884–1928. An Address*, 1928.

Murray, or Moray, James Stuart, 1st Earl of (*c.* 1531–70), regent of Scotland, was the natural son of James V of Scotland by Lady Margaret Erskine, daughter of the fourth Earl of Mar. On hearing John Knox at Calder, he joined the lords of the congregation (1559) in opposition to the queen regent's party. In 1561 he escorted his half-sister, Queen Mary, from Paris to Scotland, and became her chief adviser. He was created Earl of M. in 1564, but lost the queen's favour when he opposed her marriage to Darnley (1565). After the murder of Rizzio he was restored to favour, but escaped to France at the time of Darnley's assassination and Mary's marriage to Bothwell. After the abdication of Mary at Lochleven, he was summoned to Scotland to take up the duties of regent, and after her escape defeated the queen's forces at Langside in 1568. He came to England to bring accusations against Mary at her trial. He was murdered at Linlithgow by James Hamilton of Bothwellhaugh, and was buried in St Giles's Cathedral, Edinburgh.

Murray, John, name of sev. generations of Eng. publishers. J. M. (1745–93), the founder, *b.* Edinburgh, first served as an officer in the Royal Marines. In 1768 he purchased the book-selling business of Wm Sandby, and thenceforth became a bookseller and publisher at 32 Fleet Street. His son J. M. II (1778–1843), Byron's publisher, founded, 1808, the *Quarterly Review,* and moved the firm to Albemarle Street, where they operate today. J. M. III (1808–92) founded the M. *Handbooks* for travellers. J. M. IV (1851–1928) pub. *Queen Victoria's Letters.*

Murray, Sir John (1841–1914), Canadian naturalist and geographer, *b.* Coburg, Ontario, and educ. in Ontario, the High School, Stirling, Scotland, and at Edinburgh Univ. He was one of the naturalists who made the famous voyage in the *Challenger,* and was appointed editor of the reports of the expedition. He also took part in the explorations in the *Triton* and *Knight Errant* to the Faröe Channel. He wrote books and articles on geographical and marine subjects.

Murray, William, see MANSFIELD, W.

Murray, riv. of Australia, rising in the Australian Alps and flowing W. to the sea through the shallow Lake Alexandrina. For the greater part of its course it forms the boundary between New S. Wales and Victoria. In conjunction with the Darling it drains almost the entire SE. quarter of the continent. Its total length is about 1600 m. Owing to sandbars at its mouth it is inaccessible for large vessels but navigable for small steamers. Its chief tribs. are the Murrumbidgee, Lachlan and Darling. The water of the M. is used for irrigation purposes being dammed at the Hume Reservoir, where the Mitta Mitta joins it, so that it is available in the dry season. The Hume Reservoir stores 1,382,000 ac. ft of water (to be enlarged to 2,500,000 ac. ft), which runs off a catchment area of about 6000 sq. m. of mountainous country on the border of Victoria and New S. Wales. It is composed of an earthen embankment 411 ft long and a massive concrete wall, forming the spillway and outlet works, across the riv. for 1042 ft on the New S. Wales side. On the Victorian side an earthen embankment 3827 ft long brings the total length to 1 m. The reservoir forms a vast inland lake of 33,000 ac.—3 times the size of Sydney Harbour. The large volume of

water stored in it ensures an adequate flow of water in the irrigated areas in the lower reaches of the M. R. In 1949 the govs. of New S. Wales and Victoria agreed on a scheme for the diversion of the headwaters of the Snowy R. (q.v.) across the Australian Alps into the Upper M. and Tumut R.s in connection with a vast hydro-electric irrigation project now in course of construction by the Snowy Mts Hydro-electric Authority (q.v.). *See* J. M. Holmes, *The Murray Valley,* 1948.

Murray Bridge, tn of S. Australia, on the R. Murray, 50 m. SE. of Adelaide, on the Adelaide–Melbourne road and railway line. Centre of an extensive dairying industry, its other pursuits are agricultural and pastoral. It is a popular tourist resort. Pop. 5404.

Murraysburg, vil. and div. of Cape Prov., S. Africa. The vil. is 50 m. WNW. of Graaf Reinet (q.v.). Important wool-producing centre. Pop. (1960) Whites, 992; Coloured, 3654; Bantu, 87,821.

Mürren, vil. of the Bernese Oberland, Switzerland, above Lauterbrunnen, from where it is reached by a funicular railway. It is situated at an altitude of 5415 ft and affords a fine view of the Jungfrau. M. is a popular resort and winter sport centre.

Murrhine, or **Myrrhine, Vases,** celebrated vessels of antiquity, brought from Asia to Rome by Pompey after his victory over Mithradates.

Murrow, Ed(ward) R. (1908–65), Amer. journalist, *b.* Greensboro, N. Carolina; educ. at Washington State College. As European Director of the Columbia Broadcasting System, 1937–45, M. became famous for his broadcasts from London during the critical 1940–1 period. He was Vice-President of the Columbia Broadcasting System, 1945–7, and, under Kennedy, Director of the United States Information Agency, 1961–4, resigning for health reasons. Britain awarded him an honorary O.B.E., 1947, and an honorary K.B.E. in 1965, just before his death. He pub. *This is London,* 1941.

Murrumbidgee, riv. of New S. Wales, rising on the NE. of the Australian Alps and flowing 1000 m. westwards to join the Murray, 90 m. SE. of the mouth of the Darling. It is navigable for 500 m. during the wet season.

Murry, John Middleton (1889–1957), critic, *b.* Peckham, London. He was educ. at Christ's Hospital and Brasenose College, Oxford, and was on the staff of the *Westminster Gazette,* 1912–14, the last 2 years as art critic. During the First World War he served in the political intelligence div. of the War Office and was awarded the O.B.E. Editor of the *Athenaeum,* 1919–21, and of the *Adelphi,* 1923–30, he became Clark lecturer at Cambridge Univ. in 1924. His writings largely consist of literary criticism and criticism of existing social institutions. Among his many works are *Aspects of Literature,* 1920, *The Things We Are,* 1922, *Things to Come,* 1928, *God,* 1929, *Son of Woman* (a study of D. H. Lawrence), 1931, *The Necessity of Communism,* 1932, *Between Two Worlds* (an autobiography), 1934, *The Defence of Democracy,* 1939, *The*

Betrayal of Christ by the Churches, 1940, *Christocracy*, 1942, *Adam and Eve*, 1944, and *The Free Society*, 1947. In 1919 he pub. a collection of *Poems*. He collaborated with Ruth E. Mantz in a biography of his wife, Katherine Mansfield (q.v.), in 1933, and also wrote studies of Blake, 1933, Shakespeare, 1936, Keats, 1949, and Swift, 1954. It is said that the character of Denis Burlap in Aldous Huxley's *Point Counter Point* is founded on M.'s personality. *See* study by R. Heppenstall, 1934; *see also* Katherine Mansfield, *Letters to John Middleton Murry*, 1951.

Mursa, *see* OSIJEK.

Murshidabad, city of W. Bengal state, India. The city lies 115 m. N. of Calcutta and extends along both sides of the sacred R. Bhagirathi. M. was the residence of the Nawab Nazims of Bengal, of whom Suraj-ud-Daula, whose name is connected with the Black Hole of Calcutta, was one. M. was formerly a great centre for ivory carving and embroidery, but few craftsmen remain. Both Clive and Warren Hastings stayed here, and the pleasure garden near the Pearl Lake is still known as the Company Bagh.

Murviedro, *see* SAGUNTO.

Murwillumbah, tn on Tweed R., 581 m. N. of Sydney, close to the New S. Wales-Queensland border in Australia. M. is 20 m. from the coast and the main rural pursuits are banana-growing and dairying. Pop. 7151.

Musa, Abu Abdallah Mohammed Ben, Arabian mathematician, the first of his countrymen to write on the science of algebra, to whom Europe is indebted for its introduction.

Musa, Antonius, *see* ANTONIUS MUSA.

Musa, Ibn Nusair, or **Noseir** (AD 640–715), was appointed Governor of Ifriqiya (Rom. Africa) in 698 or 699 by the brother of the caliph, who was Governor of Egypt; and from this base conquered N. Africa. He left as his deputy in the extreme W. his freedman Tariq, who began in 710 a successful invasion of Spain. M. was jealous, followed him in 712 and conquered most of the country up to Saragossa, leaving Spain in 714.

Musäus, Johann Karl August (1735–87), Ger. novelist, *b.* Jena. His first work, entitled *Grandison der Zweite*, was pub. in 1762 and rewritten about 20 years later under the title of *Der deutsche Grandison*, its object being to satirise the Eng. novelist Richardson's hero. Another victim was Lavater, whom he caricatured in *Physiognomische Reisen*, 1778. His most important work was *Volksmärchen der Deutschen*, a series of satirical tales, 1782–6.

Musca, 'the fly', small constellation between the S. Cross (Crux) and Chamaeleon, probably named by Lacaille *c.* 1752; an older name was Apis, 'the Bee'.

Muscadet Wine is made from the M. grape grown largely in the Nantes dist of the Lower Loire. The M., which gives a sound ordinary wine, must not be confused with the muscat (q.v.); it is the *gamay blanc* or melon of Burgundy.

Muscardine, or **Silkworm Rot**, disease which causes much loss among silkworms. It is caused by a fungus, many allied species of which are parasites on Lepidoptera, both in the caterpillars and in the perfect insects.

Muscat, name of the most highly scented genus of *Vitis Vinifera*, the European vine. Well known as a dessert grape, it yields in Portugal, the Moscatel de Setubal, one of the finest of all sweet white wines, and its flavour is conspicuous in the Fr. M. de Frontignan. Its flavour is sometimes imitated in cheap sparkling wines by elder-flower essence. *See* H. Warner Allen, *The Wines of Portugal*, 1962.

Muscat and Oman, independent sultanate in the SE. corner of the Arabian peninsula, bounded on the N. by the Gulf of Oman, on the W. by Trucial Oman and the Rub' al-Khali desert, and on the S. and E. by the Arabian Sea. In the extreme SW. it has a short border with the Aden Protectorate. Area 82,000 sq. m.; pop. 750,000. A small enclave at the tip of the Masandam peninsula also belongs to M. and O.

Physical features. The country is largely barren except for the Batina plain N. of Muscat and small areas around oases. Behind a narrow coastal plain lies a mt range reaching 10,000 ft at its highest point and descending steeply to the sea in the vicinity of Muscat the cap. W. of the range is the quicksand Umm al-Samim, perhaps 95 m. by 40 m., a sump which collects any drainage there may be.

Economy. Dates are grown, those of Batina being well known. Other crops are pomegranates and limes. In the prov. of Dhofar in the extreme S. sugarcane is grown and cattle are reared. Camels bred by tribes in the interior are famous. Oil has been discovered near the Trucial Oman border and is being exploited. Efforts are being made to improve agriculture by modern irrigation techniques etc., and research stations have been set up at Nizwa and Sohar. The chief tns are Muscat (6208 pop.) and Matrah (14,119 pop.) which is the main commercial centre. Most external trade is with India and Pakistan.

Communications. There are no railways and roads are few, apart from a motor road from Muscat to Khor Fakkan and thence to Sharjah. There are a few motorable tracks laid down by the oil-drilling companies.

Government. The country is ruled by a sultan of the Taimur dynasty, which has provided 13 successive rulers. A long-standing treaty of friendship, commerce and navigation with Britain was renewed in 1951.

History. The caliphs found it hard to rule M. effectively; the name of Mohammad ibn Thaur, who led a punitive expedition in AD 894, is still execrated for the atrocities he committed. From 1009 M. was independent, and Persians devastated much of it in 1265. In 1508 the Portuguese seized the ports, but by 1644 only Muscat, Matrah and the citadel of Sohar remained in their hands. In 1698 M. seized Mombasa and other places on the E. coast of Africa. From 1711 to 1742 there was anarchy, one party calling in the Persians who stayed from 1737 to 1741; one result was the rise of the present reigning family. In 1798 the first treaty with Britain was made and shortly after tribute was paid to the Wahhabis. In 1854 M. was driven out of Bunder Abbas and some other places on the Persian coast, and 2 years later Zanzibar broke away and became an independent state under a member of the reigning family. At the present time, a man who calls himself the Imam rules the interior, ignoring the Sultan in Muscat. This summary gives only a faint idea of the ceaseless strife which makes up the hist. of M. The pop. is believed to consist of both S. and N. Arabs who are at daggers drawn; for cents. the parties have been called Hinawi and Ghafiri and a vil. may contain both parties. In addition, the N. is orthodox Sunnite and the S. Ibadhi, i.e. heretical. The chief products are dates, sugarcane and fruit; the pearl fishery is not so important as it was. Trade is mostly in the hands of Indians, the chief imports being rice, sugar and coffee; there are no industries of any importance. The chief tns are Muscat and Matrah. A new treaty of commerce and navigation was made with Britain in 1939. The interior tribes are ruled by an Imam, who since 1920 has been allowed official sovereign status while owing a quasi-feudal type of allegiance to the Sultan. In 1952 he helped the Sultan to repel infiltrators from Saudi Arabia during the Buraimi Oasis dispute (*see* SAUDI ARABIA). *See* B. Thomas, *Arabia Felix*, 1932; J. Morris, *Sultan in Oman*, 1957; Institute of International Affairs, *Sultanate and Imamate in Oman*, 1959.

Muscatine, city, cap. of Muscatine co., Iowa, U.S.A., and rail centre, on the Mississippi R. (bridged), 25 m. WSW. of Davenport. It manufs. pearl buttons (from riv. mussel shells), steel pulleys, pumps and castings. Pop. 21,000.

Musci, *see* MOSSES.

Muscle, structure of the body capable of causing motion by the contraction of its fibres. Muscular tissue consists of elongated cells and fibres. The fibres making up some of the M.s consist of protoplasmic material with transverse stripes; these are called striped or striated fibres. Others possess no transverse markings, and are therefore known as non-striated or plain muscular fibres. Every muscular fibre has the property of contracting, that is, on the receipt of a certain stimulus a chemical change is brought about, resulting in a change in the elastic tension of the cell. An increase of tension occurs in the points of attachment of the cell to neighbouring tissues, which ordinarily move under the strain, so that the length of the fibre decreases while its diameter becomes proportionally bigger. In some M.s this contraction is voluntary; that is, it is the result of an act of will. This modification of consciousness is accompanied by a certain mode of activity in some of the cells of the large brain, or cerebrum. By this means an impulse is communicated to the nerve-fibres supplying the M.s and is conveyed to the M. by end-plates or expansions of the nerve-fibres situated on the surface of the muscular fibres. Other M.s are not under the control of the will. Such are the M.s causing the movements of the stomach and other

parts of the alimentary canal. They are called involuntary M.s, and are made up of non-striated fibres, except the cardiac M., which

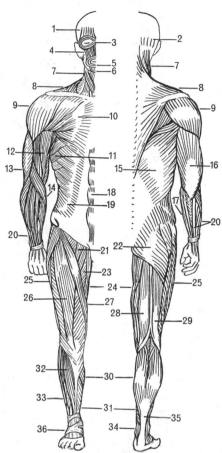

MUSCLES OF THE HUMAN BODY SHOWING FRONT AND BACK VIEWS

1, frontalis; 2, occipitalis; 3, orbicular of eye; 4, levators; 5, orbicular of mouth; 6, depressors; 7, sternomastoid; 8, trapezius; 9, deltoid; 10, pectoral; 11, serratus anterior; 12, biceps; 13, brachialis; 14, brachioradialis; 15, latissimus dorsi; 16, triceps; 17, flexors of hand; 18, rectus abdominis; 19, external oblique; 20, extensors of hand; 21, psoas; 22, gluteus; 23, adductors; 24, gracilis; 25, tensor of fascia lata; 26, rectus femoris; 27, sartorius; 28, semitendinosus; 29, biceps femoris; 30, gastrocnemius; 31, soleus; 32, tibialis anterior; 33, extensors of foot; 34, flexors of foot; 35, Achilles tendon; 36, fascial band.

resembles voluntary M.s in being striated. It is, however, not always possible to classify M.s as voluntary and involuntary, for some of them, such as those of the tongue, larnyx and eyeballs

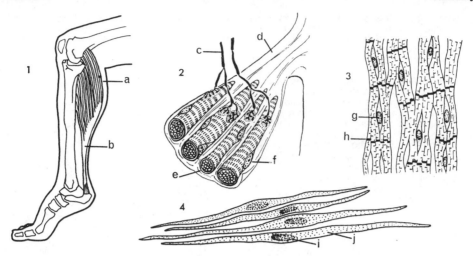

TYPES OF MUSCLE

1, calf muscle: a, gastrocnemius and soleus muscles; b, Achilles tendon attached to tuberosity of calcaneum. 2, skeletal (striped) muscle ends set in white fibrous tissue for attachment: c, nerves ending in motor end-plates; d, white fibres; e, cut ends showing fibre bundles and sheath; f, nucleus. 3, typical cardiac muscle: g, nucleus; h, fibre junctions (intercalated discs). 4, visceral or smooth muscle fibres teased out: i, nucleus; j, cytoplasm.

of the Vertebrata, and certain muscles of Arthropoda, are intermediate in type. The capacity of a M. for responding to a stimulus is termed its excitability. In cardiac M.s the extent of contraction does not depend upon the intensity of the stimulus, but in M.s attached to the bones a relation is maintained between contraction and stimulus. If, however, a M. has been repeatedly contracted without much intermission, a stimulus does not evoke the usual degree of contraction. This condition is called muscular fatigue, and further evidence of it is afforded by the increasingly long period of relaxation. Eventually the M. will fail to respond at all to the stimulus. Muscular fatigue is due to the formation of lactic acid from the glycogen in the M. cells. This glycogen is produced by the action of insulin (q.v.) on the sugar dissolved in the blood, and, apparently by an internal rearrangement of the molecule, glycogen is converted into lactic acid. This change accompanies the contraction of the M., and heat is produced during the process. A young athlete, running as fast as he can, produces about 4 grammes of lactic acid per sec.

During relaxation some of the protein in the M. cell combines with and neutralises the lactic acid, and recovery from fatigue is effected by oxidation of the product. This process results in the re-formation of protein, the conversion of some of the lactic acid into glycogen, and the complete oxidation of the remainder with the elimination of carbon dioxide and the production of heat.

When exercise is moderate the amount of

lactic acid in the blood reaches its maximum after a few minutes and is quickly removed by the increase of the oxygen supply by deep and rapid breathing. If exercise be very strenuous the lactic acid increases until there are symptoms of distress, and eventually a type of *rigor mortis* may be caused. The fleshy part of a M. is usually attached at each end to bands, or tendons, of white fibrous tissue, which is itself non-contractile, but in Vertebrata serves to join the M. to some bone. The attachment which is more fixed is called the origin; that which is more movable is called the insertion. Thus the biceps has 2 origins, in the coracoid process and the glenoid cavity; its insertion is in the tuberosity of the radius, or the outer bone of the forearm. Every M. is supplied with blood-vessels, and lymphatics to carry the substances for repair of tissue, for the combustion which liberates the energy resulting in contraction and for the removal of waste products. For details of mechanism of contraction *see* H. E. Huxley, 'The Contraction of Muscle', in *Scientific America*, Dec. 1965.

See also CLONUS; REFLEX; TENDON OF ACHILLES.

Muscovy, Russian 14th–18th cent. state. Princes of Moscow first appeared as vassals of the Grand Princes of Vladimir (q.v.) in the 13th cent. after the Mongol-Tatar conquest (*see* BATU and GOLDEN HORDE). Thanks to its advantageous geographical position in the centre of the then NE. (now central) Russia (which facilitated commercial development and sheltered it from Tatar raids) and to the consistent and tenacious policy of its princes,

Moscow in the 14th cent. gradually achieved supremacy over neighbouring principalities and replaced Vladimir as the cap. of the Grand Principality. The most outstanding rulers of this period were Ivan the Money-bag (q.v.) and Dmitriy Donskoy (q.v.), who achieved the first victory over the Tatars in 1380. The struggle against the Tatar overlordship continued until it was finally abolished in 1480 by Ivan III (q.v.). The territorial expansion of M. continued until it absorbed all Russian lands (including the reps. of Novgorod in 1478, Vyatka in 1489, and Pskov in 1510, and the Grand Principalities of Tver' (q.v.) in 1485 and Ryazan' (q.v.) in 1521 which had not been annexed by Lithuania (q.v.). In 1547 Ivan the Terrible (q.v.) assumed the title Tsar (q.v.) of All Russia. During his reign the Tatar Khanates of Kazan', Astrakhan' and Siberia were conquered, and M. became a multi-national state. Soon afterwards the house of Rurikidae (q.v.) died out, and the country went through the Time of Troubles. The new house of Romanov (q.v.) continued the policies of their predecessors (conquest of the rest of Siberia, incorporation of the Ukraine). Peter the Great (q.v.), the last tsar of M. and the first Russian emperor (from 1721), inaugurated a new epoch of Russian hist. M. was the cradle of the Great Russian people (*see* GREAT RUSSIANS). Politically it was an autocracy limited by the Boyars' Duma (*see* BOYARS and DUMA) and the Zemskiy Sobor (q.v.). Its legal system was successively developed in the Codes of 1497, 1550 and 1649, which gradually centralised administration and introduced peasant serfdom. Culturally M. was isolated from the rest of Europe, first through Tatar domination, and after the Florentine Union (*see* EASTERN ORTHODOX CHURCH) in 1439 and the fall of Constantinople in 1453 by antagonism between the Orthodox and the Rom. Catholic Churches. The political ideology of the Muscovite state rested on the conceptions of 'gathering the Russian land' (*see* KIEVAN RUSSIA) and 'Moscow—the third Rome'.

Muscovy, or **Musk, Duck** (*Cairina moschata*), species of wild duck native to central and S. America, where it nests in the trees of forest swamps. It is often reared in poultry yards of European countries as an ornamental bird for lakes and parks. It is also called Barbary duck.

Musel, El, *see* GIJÓN.

Muselier, Émile Henri (1882–1965), Fr. admiral, *b.* Marseilles and educ. at the Brest naval school. In 1939 he was a Vice-Admiral and on the collapse of France in 1940 joined de Gaulle (July 1940), who made him commander-in-chief of the Free Fr. naval forces (1940–2), and of the Free Fr. air forces (1940–1). M. led the Free Fr. naval forces in the occupation of Saint-Pierre and Miquelon Is. against the representatives of the Vichy Gov. there. He was made national commissioner of navy and merchant navy in the Fr. National Committee, but resigned in Mar. 1942 and in the following year became assistant to Giraud (q.v.) in Algiers. After the war he was chief of the Fr.

naval delegation of the military mission for Ger. affairs.

Museo di San Marco (Florence), *see* UFFIZI AND PITTI GALLERIES.

Muses, in mythology, the inspiring deities of poetry, daughters of Zeus and Mnemosyne, *b.* in Pieria at the foot of Mt Olympus. They appear to have been originally 3 in number, but from Hesiod onwards are always represented as 9. The assignment of a sphere of literature or science to each, with their respective symbols, dates from the late Rom. period as follows: (1) *Clio*: History; open scroll or chest of scrolls. (2) *Euterpe*: Lyric poetry; flute. (3) *Thalia*: Comedy and idyllic poetry; comic mask, shepherd's staff or ivy-wreath. (4) *Melpomene*: Tragedy; tragic mask, staff of Heracles or sword. (5) *Terpsichore*: Choral dance and song; lyre and plectrum. (6) *Erato*: Erotic poetry and mime; lyre. (7) *Polyhymnia*: Hymn; no symbol, but pensive attitude. (8) *Urania*: Astronomy; staff pointing to globe. (9) *Calliope*: Epic; tablet and stylus.

Cult of the M. was introduced from Thrace, first into Pieria and thence to Parnassus (q.v.) and Helicon (q.v.). Sacrifices offered to them included honey and libations of water or milk.

Museum, name now given to buildings where collections of scientific and natural curiosities and works of artistic and literary merit are maintained for the benefit of the public. The word originally denoted a temple of the Muses (q.v.), and at Athens a small hill sacred to them immediately SW. of the city wall. Later it was used more generally of a literary or educational foundation, and particularly of that part of the palace at Alexandria (q.v.) where Ptolemy I estab. the most eminent scholars of the age (*c.* 280 BC). *See also* LIBRARIES; NATIONAL GALLERY; and IMPERIAL INSTITUTE; IMPERIAL WAR MUSEUM; LONDON MUSEUM; SCIENCE MUSEUM; AMERICAN ART MUSEUMS; ART MUSEUMS; BELGIAN ART MUSEUMS; DOMINIONS (COMMONWEALTH) ART GALLERIES; DUTCH ART MUSEUMS; FRENCH ART; GERMAN ART MUSEUMS; ITALIAN ART; SPANISH ART; RUSSIAN ART; VIENNA ART MUSEUMS. *See* A. S. Wittlin, *The Museum*, 1949, and journal of the Museums Association.

Mushroom, name commonly given to the larger capped fungi, but chiefly to edible fruit bodies of the Agaricaceae, of which *Psalliota* (*Agaricus*) *campestris* is the common Field M., and *P.* (*Agaricus*) *hortensis* the cultivated M. of commerce, of which there are 2 distinct forms, a white and a brown. In appearance the cap is rounded when young, then convex, and finally flat, white and smooth, or brownish with darker scales; the stem is white with a torn volva girdling it; the gills are free, turning from white to pink, and then blackish brown on ageing. Field M.s appear in damp, warm weather, summer and autumn. Cultivated M.s are grown all the year round in prepared beds, which may be housed in dark sheds, cellars, caves or buildings; requiring a temp. of about 60° F., reasonable humidity and good ventilation, plus a good compost. Compost in the past has been preferably of stable manure from grain-fed healthy horses, carefully pre-rotted before use. In the face of increasing scarcity of stable manure, a synthetic compost of straw and chemicals has been evolved by the M. Research Association Ltd, Peterborough, England, and is in commercial use. Pure cultures have now replaced the old Brick spawn for inoculating M. beds. In Britain, most of the 40 million pounds produced commercially each year are grown in specially designed M. houses or glasshouses. *See* A. L. Kligman, *Handbook of Mushroom Culture*, U.S.A., 1950; Ministry of Agriculture Bulletin 34: *Mushroom Growing*, 1950; F. C. Atkins, *Mushroom Growing Today*, 1952; J. Ramsbottom, *Toadstools and Mushrooms*, 1954; *The Mushroom Grower's Bulletin*, monthly jour. *See also* AGARICUS; CHANTERELLE; FUNGI.

Music, although in its modern form the most artificial of the arts, is primarily the most universal and spontaneous. It differs from the other arts in that 'time', both in the rhythmic basis of M. and also in the definite duration of any musical phrase or performance, is an essential factor. In this it contrasts sharply with painting and architecture, which depend on spatial values, and it lacks the representational element of poetry, although poetry, M. and the dance probably had a common origin in ritual. They still share the vital element of rhythm. Physically M. is allied to mathematical science, the 2 fundamental concords, the octave and the perfect fifth, being built up from the frequency-ratios 2 : 1 and 3 : 2 respectively. These facts were known in the 6th cent. BC to Pythagoras, who also defined the tonal position of the fourth.

M. in some form is found among all primitive societies at the present day, but even in its most elementary state it clearly represents a later stage of development from an unknown original. In more advanced tribes it often includes features familiar in European M., such as harmony and imitation. It seems probable that practices of this kind existed in popular M.-making in Europe long before the Christian Church sanctioned the use of harmony. Rhythm, often extremely subtle, plays an important part in primitive M., as it does in Eastern civilisations at the present time. Varieties of scales, including notes smaller than a semitone, also occur. Our modern scale system is derived from the Greeks, though they, under Asian influence, also recognised smaller intervals. Our knowledge of Gk M., however, is limited to a very few actual examples, of different dates, pictorial representation of instruments, a mass of conflicting theory spread over sev. cents. and the opinions of philosophers about the moral and ethical effects of different scales.

The M. of the Christian Church shows marked traces of Jewish influence but it was also affected by the practice of Gk communities in Asia Minor, where Christianity first became firmly estab. Gk influence persisted when Christianity gained a foothold in the W.: for sev. cents. alternate singing in Greek and Latin was practised for the benefit of mixed communities, and as late as the 6th cent. Pope Gregory I introduced to Rome the singing of *Kyrie eleison*, which the Eastern Christians had adopted from pagan ceremonies. The standardisation of Western M. in the Church and the systematic organisation of musical education for singers is associated with the name of Gregory (hence Gregorian chant), though he is not known to have been particularly musical. For some time, however, varieties of chant persisted outside Rome—in Milan, for example, where what is known as 'Ambrosian' chant (after St Ambrose) is still sung, in France (Gallican chant) and in Spain (Visigothic or Mozarabic chant). Gallican chant was suppressed by Charlemagne in the late 8th cent.; Visigothic chant survived in Spain till the 11th cent. Meanwhile the Eastern Church, with its centre at Byzantium, developed its own forms of chant, which have survived till the present day.

The early Christian fathers were strongly opposed to the use of instruments in church, on account of their secular associations. To what extent this opposition was ignored in early cents. is uncertain. By the 8th cent. the Western Church had accepted the organ as a useful support to the singers in large cathedrals. By this time also the theorists had begun to classify the melodic material used in Christian chant (*see* MODES). The rhythmical interpretation of the chant seems to have differed at different periods, though there was always a distinction between long and short notes and it seems reasonable to suppose that metrical pieces such as hymns were sung in a regular rhythm. The repertory of church M. during the early cents. was enormously increased by the composition of new melodies and the extension of older ones. There is no indication that harmonised M. was used before the 9th cent.: the objection to it may very well have been based, like the objection to instruments, on its secular associations. When it was introduced into the Church it took the form of an enrichment of the chant by the simple addition of one or more extra parts; but a natural desire for elaboration soon led to a more florid type of M. in which the notes of the chant had to be sung slowly to allow the singer or singers of other parts to develop an independent melodic line. M. of this kind was known traditionally as *organum*, obviously in origin a popular and not a scientific term. The most flourishing period of *organum*, not only at Notre Dame in Paris but elsewhere in Europe, was in the late 12th and early 13th cents. Its function was not only to enrich the chant but also to alternate with purely melodic sections; and for further contrast it included sections in which both the chant and the added melody or melodies moved forward in a regular rhythm. Contemporary with *organum* was the *conductus*, which was normally a form of free composition, not based on existing material.

Little is known of secular M. before the end of the 11th cent., so that there is no obvious explanation for the emergence of the highly sophisticated art of song-writing practised by the troubadours in S. France, the trouvères in N. France and their counterparts the Minnesinger in Germany and Austria. The influence of these lyrical melodies is clearly marked in the 13th cent. polyphonic Motet (q.v.), which was written both for use in church and for secular occasions. The increasing subtlety of polyphonic M. is noticeable in the 14th cent. M., known as *ars nova* after the title of a treatise by Philippe de Vitry. The same period also saw a great development of the art of writing solo songs with instrumental accompaniment. The leading composers of this period were, in France, Guillaume de Machaut (*d.* 1377)—the first composer known to have written a complete setting of the mass—and, in Italy, Francesco Landini (1325-97).

The 15th cent. was remarkable for an increase in technical resources, especially in imitative counterpoint, and the rise of national schools. In England Dunstable (*d.* 1453) and his contemporaries practised a characteristic smoothness of texture. The great Netherlands school, headed by Binchois (*d.* 1460), Dufay (*d.* 1474) and Okeghem (*d. c.* 1495), reached its height in Josquin des Prés (*d.* 1521). Later Netherlands composers founded schools in other countries, e.g. Willaert (*d.* 1562) and Cyprien de Rore (*d.* 1565) in Venice and Arcadelt (*d. c.* 1567) in Rome, where the tradition of polyphonic church M. reached its apex in the work of Palestrina (*d.* 1594) and the Spaniard Victoria (*d.* 1611). The greatest of the later Flemings, Lassus (*d.* 1594), was a prolific composer in all styles, sacred and secular. This period was marked by the gradual decline of the modal system and a much greater interest in the emotional use of harmony as against polyphonic devices for their own sake. A stimulus was also given to Ger. church M. by the Lutheran Reformation, which encouraged congregational singing and popularised the chorale. Eng. church composers of the period were Tye (*d.* 1573), Tallis (*d.* 1585), Byrd (*d.* 1623) and Gibbons (*d.* 1625). Meanwhile secular music, aided by the Renaissance and the discovery of printing, fl. in the form of Fr. *chanson* and the It. madrigal. Marenzio (*d.* 1599), Gesualdo (*d.* 1614) and Monteverdi (1567-1643) introduced new freedom and expressiveness into the madrigal, which was perfected in England in the works of Morley (*d.* ?1603), Weelkes (*d.* 1623), Wilbye (*d.* 1638) and Tomkins (*d.* 1656).

Instrumental M. of the period, whether for solo instruments or a chamber ensemble, included dance movements and imitations of vocal forms which rapidly acquired a purely instrumental idiom. In addition to dance movements the repertory of the lute and harpsichord included transcriptions of vocal works, in which the opportunity was taken to embroider the original, variations on popular tunes and pieces designed to exhibit virtuosity. Organ M. had a tradition going back to the middle of the 15th cent. Here too the repertory included arrangements, as well as pieces based on Catholic hymn-tunes or Protestant chorales,

various forms of polyphonic composition, and toccatas intended to display the power of the instrument and the player's skill: the outstanding composers in this field were Antonio de Cabezon (1500-66) in Spain and Andrea Gabrieli (*c.* 1520-86) in Italy.

The next new forms, both originating in Italy about 1600, were opera and oratorio. Opera was an attempt to revive the Gk combination of M. and drama, and was also influenced by the madrigal; its first exponents were the Florentines Peri (*d.* 1633) and Caccini (*d.* 1618), but Monteverdi was the first master (*see* OPERA). The first opera house was opened at Venice in 1637, and a thriving tradition began. Oratorio, in part evolved from the incidental M. of the early miracle and morality plays, began in Rome with Cavalieri (*d.* 1602). At first it was staged like opera, but Carissimi (*d.* 1674) endeavoured to separate it by strengthening the choral element. In Germany Schütz (*d.* 1672) produced a new type by combining Venetian influence with old Ger. Passion M., while a flourishing school of keyboard composers arose in Froberger (*d.* 1667), Buxtehude (*d.* 1707), Reinken (*d.* 1722) and Pachelbel (*d.* 1706) for the organ, and Kuhnau (*d.* 1722) for the harpsichord. All these traditions were consummated in the work of J. S. Bach. Italy still led the field in other instrumental forms, especially for strings, thanks to the perfection of the violin by the craftsmen of N. Italy. The trio-sonata and concerto were developed by Corelli (*d.* 1713) and Vivaldi (*d.* 1741), and the harpsichord sonata by Domenico Scarlatti (*d.* 1757). Meanwhile It. opera had overrun Europe, but only in France, where Lully (*d.* 1687) combined it with the ballet, was a national style founded. In England Purcell (*d.* 1695) showed high dramatic genius but estab. no tradition. It. opera was standardised by Alessandro Scarlatti (*d.* 1725), after whom it became too obedient, up to the time of Rossini at least, to the demands of singers, except in the hands of foreigners like Handel, Gluck and Mozart (*see* OPERA).

The first half of the 18th cent. is dominated by the figures of Handel (1685-1759) and J. S. Bach (1685-1750). Handel's style was compounded of It. and Eng. elements, and his genius essentially dramatic, as shown in his Jewish oratorios even more than in his 40 It. operas, although he used all the known forms. He combined unsurpassed lyric sweetness with massive choral effects on a greater scale than ever before. Bach's genius was religious and contemplative, introvert rather than extrovert; his Passions, church cantatas and organ works are the summit of their kind. He was also the composer of much excellent violin and clavier M., and carried the new tonal polyphony to its utmost limits. But his full influence was delayed, since his greatest M. remained unknown for nearly a cent. In France his most important contemporaries were François Couperin (*d.* 1733) in keyboard M. and Rameau (*d.* 1764) in grand opera and ballet. It was in France too that Gluck (1714-87) completed his memorable reform of opera, designed to end the tyranny of singers, emphasise dramatic expression and so return to something like the principles of Monteverdi. The middle years of the cent. saw the rise of an important movement led by Johann Stamitz (*d.* 1757) at Mannheim, where the modern orchestra and the symphony were developed from beginnings in Italy, and sonata form, based on key contrast and a reaction from polyphony, began to come into its own. It was derived partly from the binary form of the old dance movements and partly from the operatic aria of Scarlatti and Handel. C. P. E. Bach (*d.* 1788) advanced the modern piano sonata by applying sonata form to the colour possibilities of the new instrument. Symphony, sonata and string quartet were all perfected by Haydn (1732–1809), the first of the great Viennese classical composers, and further extended by Mozart (1756–91), whose use of chromaticism introduced an almost romantic expressiveness, but who was also a master of counterpoint. He was the one composer to reach the highest rank in every musical form; his operas, remarkable for their subtle characterisation, both summed up the whole It. tradition and led by way of Ger. *Singspiel* to romantic opera. Judging by his experiments in harmony and 'colour', and by the perfection to which he developed the new forms (including the concerto, which he made particularly his own), it has been suggested that, but for his premature death, he would have done much that Beethoven (1770–1827) was left to accomplish. But however much Beethoven's earliest M. may resemble Mozart's latest, his second and third period works, his sonatas, concertos and chamber M., no less than his wonderful symphonies and overtures, opened up vast new ters. in the realm of individual and subjective expression. His last works, long misunderstood, looked far into the future.

If Beethoven is the point of transition from 'classical' to 'romantic' (the terms are unsatisfactory, but have a generally accepted significance) in instrumental M., the same must be said of Schubert (1797–1828) in song, and of C. M. von Weber (1786–1826) in opera. The Romantic Movement (q.v.) of the early 19th cent. was a general artistic reaction against 'academism' and formalistic narrowness; it appealed to the remote, violent and mysterious, became connected with political and social ideals, and ended as a cult of the excessive. Romantic M. soon developed a strong literary content, and sought to express alien ideas of all kinds, often at the expense of formal balance. Beethoven influenced the whole of 19th cent. M., but in many different ways. The classical tradition of sonata and symphony was followed (with deviations) by Mendelsshon (1809–47) and Brahms (1833–97). The leaders in piano M. were Chopin (1810–47) and Schumann (1810–56), whose attempts at the larger forms were less successful. The mantle of song passed from Schubert to Schumann, Brahms and Wolf (1860–1903). The first great exponent of programme M. was Berlioz (1803–69), whose remarkably original

powers of melody, drama and orchestration were not at first recognised. Liszt (1811–86), besides exploiting the virtuoso powers of the piano and making important harmonic innovations, evolved from the symphonic form of Beethoven, the colour of Berlioz and certain elements in Schubert's instrumental works a new form, the 'symphonic poem', in which he practised an elaborate method of theme transformation. This form has been cultivated by many later composers, most successfully by Richard Strauss (1864–1949). The central figures of the period in opera were Wagner (1813–83) and Verdi (1813–1901). Wagner, beginning as a composer of grand opera in the Meyerbeer manner, combined Beethoven's method of symphonic development, Liszt's theme transformation and certain of Gluck's ideals in a vast new stage form, the M. drama, which he described and justified in numerous prose writings. It is peculiar to Wagner and has defied would-be successors, although the operas of Strauss approach it at some points. It is closer to the symphonic poem than to true opera, which it did not supersede. Indeed opera flourished throughout the cent., particularly in Italy and France, where the spectacular methods of Meyerbeer (1791–1864) were succeeded by the more lyrical style of Gounod (1818–93), Massenet (1842–1912) and others and the revitalised *opéra-comique* of Bizet (1838–75). In Italy the traditional line led through Rossini (1792–1868), Donizetti (1797–1848) and Bellini (1801–35) to Verdi, in whom it reached the height of musical and dramatic expressiveness. It then declined into crudity and shallowness in the hands of too many composers, but Puccini (1858–1924) showed a strong lyrical and dramatic gift.

Related to the Romantic Movement are the nationalist movements, which drew much of their strength from folksong. In Russia the movement began with Glinka (1803–57) and reached great distinction in the instrumental works of Balakirev (1837–1910) and Borodin (1833–87) and the operas of Mussorgsky (1839–81) and Rimsky-Korsakov (1844–1908). Tchaikovsky (1840–93), who used all forms, was more influenced by the W. romantic tradition; his symphonies have a strong subjective element. In Scandinavia Grieg (1843–1907) showed a genius for the song and short piano piece, and Sibelius (1865–1957) for the symphony. In Bohemia Smetana (1824–84) founded a national opera, later enriched by Janáček (1854–1928) and Dvořák (1841–1904) enriched the classical forms. Later a lively Sp. school grew up under Albéniz (1860–1909), Granados (1867–1916) and Falla (1876–1946). The end of the cent. saw Austria upholding the symphonic tradition, with more dignity in Bruckner (1824–96) than in Mahler (1860–1911), and the rise of important new movements in France and England. Franck (1822–90) late in life popularised cyclic form by applying Liszt's methods to the sonata, and the far-ranging harmonic experiments of Debussy (1862–1918) bore fruit in 'impressionism'. Ravel

(1875–1937) developed on similar lines with a personal harmonic idiom, and the exuberance of Chabrier (1841–94) and the harmonic subtlety of Fauré (1845–1924) also left their mark. In England Elgar (1857–1934) added a personal and national flavour to the classical tradition in large-scale choral and instrumental works, and Delius (1862–1934) adopted an intensely individual harmonic style. Holst (1874–1934) and Vaughan Williams (1872–1958) returned to folk M. and built up a style capable of mastering both traditional and modern forms on the largest scale.

The 20th cent. has seen a development in M. of revolutionary rapidity to which there have been 2 main contributing factors: first the break-up of the key system, largely due to the influence of Wagner and Debussy, and the search for freer forms, new rhythmic patterns, 'atonality' (the abolition of 'key'), polytonality and harmonic systems built on the whole-tone, 12-note and many other more intricate scales; secondly the rapid perfection of mechanised M., notably wireless, record-player and cinematograph reproduction. Two of the biggest influences in modern M. are Stravinsky (b. 1882), who has formed no definite 'style', but has experimented in many new and daring rhythmic forms and 'tone-colours', and Schoenberg (1874–1951), whose 12-note system, first adopted by Webern (1883–1945) and Berg (1885–1935), has formed a large school in many countries. Other important modern composers, apart from those mentioned above, are Hindemith (1895–1963) in Germany; Bartók (1881–1945) and Kodály (b. 1882) in Hungary; Honegger (1892–1955) and Milhaud (b. 1892) in France; Pizzetti (b. 1880) and Malipiero (b. 1882) in Italy; and in England and America Bax (1883–1953), Ireland (1879–1962), Bloch (1880–1959), Bliss (b. 1891), Copland (b. 1900), Rubbra (b. 1901), Walton (b. 1902), Berkeley (b. 1903), Barber (b. 1910) and Britten (b. 1913). In the period after the First World War the reaction against the excesses of romanticism took an extreme form, resulting (as in the other arts) in various forms of selfconsciousness and exhibitionism, whereas after the Second World War new tendencies have been taken up with an earnestness which suggests that too many composers are taking themselves only too seriously. But it is too early as yet to assess them An important present-day factor, the mechanisation of M., has brought knowledge and appreciation of M., especially classical M., to a vast hitherto uninterested public, and splendid performances of all important works can be heard through the media of wireless and the record-player. The standard of criticism, and thus of performance, is rising, and the demand for new M., for instance in the cinema, can hardly fail to encourage the composer. Jazz (q.v.) M. is a conspicuous contemporary phenomenon throughout the U.S.A. and Europe, as a dance-form and for mechanical transmission. Primarily it is an exploitation of syncopated rhythm, usually at the expense of other musical qualities, and it owes much to primitive Negro M. It is largely ephemeral, but may leave its mark on a few surviving works. A more significant phase of the popularisation of M. is the revival both in Europe and America of musical festivals and societies and the high standard of performance that distinguishes their concerts. See also articles on BRITISH, FRENCH, GERMAN, ITALIAN, and RUSSIAN MUSIC; HARMONY; OPERA; ROMANTIC MOVEMENT; SONG; SYMPHONY; etc.; and on the various composers.

See P. H. Lang, Music in Western Civilisation, 1941; O. Strunk, Source Readings in Music History, 1952; New Oxford History of Music (1954–); D. J. Grout, A History of Western Music, 1960; A. Harman and W. Mellers, Man and his Music, 1965.

Music, Schools of, see ROYAL ACADEMY OF MUSIC; ROYAL COLLEGE OF MUSIC; SCHOOL OF MUSIC.

Music and Dancing Licences. Within the area of Greater London, every house, room, garden or other place used for public music or dancing must be licensed for that purpose by the Greater London Council. There is a right of appeal against the Council's decision to a petty sessional magistrates' court, and then to a court of quarter sessions. Elsewhere licences are required only in those tns where section 51 of the Public Health Act 1890 has been adopted, in which cases the licences are granted by the magistrates. The mere occasional use of a room for music and dancing, or a temporary use for dancing on the occasion of a festival, does not, but a skating rink where music is played does, require a licence. The decided cases show that to require a licence there must be something habitual about the use of the place for public music or dancing, though using the place once a month only would probably be regarded as 'habitual'. The licensing authority, where it is not the Greater London Council, have an absolute discretion to grant or refuse a licence, subject to the obligation to exercise the discretion in a judicial manner.

Music Halls. The 'music hall', or 'variety theatre', was a development of the 'saloon theatres' which existed in London in 1830–40. These were attached to taverns, and were very popular among the middle and lower classes who liked to mix their dramatic amusements with smoking and light refreshments. They gave dramatic performances as well as variety entertainments, but were restricted by the 'patent rights', which were ultimately abolished through the efforts of a number of distinguished literary men, among whom were Charles Dickens, Sir Edward Bulwer-Lytton and Sir Thomas Noon Talfourd. After this the saloons gradually improved in character, and the true M. H. began to appear, the first being the Canterbury in Lambeth, which, under the direction of Charles Morton, provided good music; indeed 'An Operatic Selection' of Gounod's Faust had its first Eng. performance there. Morton also opened the Oxford, and other halls soon followed, their popularity being assured by the cheap prices and physical comforts which they afforded. But the advance in the M. H. excited the jealousy of the theatre, and matters came to a crisis in 1865 when an ambitious ballet was produced at the Alhambra in Leicester Square. The Alhambra was prosecuted for infringing the Stage-play Act, and a long, unsatisfactory trial followed, with the result that the matter was taken up by Parliament and the M. H. were granted the privilege of producing ballets, vaudevilles, pantomimes and other light pieces. Some of the chief in the list of M. H. are the Coliseum, the London Hippodrome, the Pavilion and the Palladium, and associated with them and older halls are the names of George Leybourne, Bessie Bellmore, Harry Champion, the Great Vance, Charles Coborn, Chirgwin the White-eyed Kaffir, Gus Elen and Marie Lloyd. The advent of the cinema, and especially its development throughout the U.S.A. affected the prosperity of M. H., and many were converted into cinema houses, the Empire and the Tivoli in London being notable examples. At the present time the term 'music hall' is giving place to the more applicable name of 'variety theatre', the programme of entertainment often taking the form of 'revue'. *See* M. W. Disher, *Winkles and Champagne*, 1938; H. Scott, *The Early Doors*, 1947; C. D. Pulling, *They Were Singing*, 1952; R. Mander and J. Mitchenson, *British Music Hall*, 1965.

Musical Box, instrument for producing music by mechanical means, little more than a toy with no great artistic scope or value. It was invented in the middle of the 18th cent. by the Swiss, who fitted minute plugs on a metal cylinder so arranged that they would strike separate bars of steel and set them vibrating, and so produce different tones.

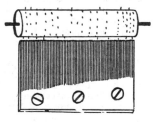

MUSICAL BOX

Musical Comedy, form of theatrical entertainment, developed from *opéra-bouffe*. It usually consists of a slight story interspersed at appropriate points by songs and dances. Musical plays of this type first found their outstanding popularity with the London productions of George Edwardes (1852–1915) at Daly's Theatre and the Gaiety. Notable M. C.s include *The Shop Girl* (Ivan Caryll), which was produced in 1894 and ran for 2 years, *The Geisha*, *A Country Girl* (both by Lionel Monckton), *San Toy* (Sidney Jones), *The Belle of New York* (Gustav Kerker), *The Maid of the Mountains* (Harold Fraser-Simson), *Floradora*

(Leslie Stuart), *Chu Chin Chow* (Frederic Norton), which had the second longest run in the hist. of the Brit. theatre, *The Chocolate Soldier* (Oscar Straus) and *The Merry Widow* (Franz Lehár). Outstanding names of the 1920s were Rudolf Friml (*Rose Marie* and *The Vagabond King*), Sigmund Romberg (*New Moon, The Student Prince* and *The Desert Song*), Vincent Youmans (*No! No! Nanette!*), Jerome Kern (*Sally, Sunny, Show Boat* and *Roberta*) and George Gershwin (*Lady, Be Good*), all American; and Noël Coward (*Bitter Sweet*). The thirties saw *White Horse Inn* (Robert Stolz), the musicals of Ivor Novello (*Glamorous Night, Careless Rapture* and *The Dancing Years*), and in America the rise of Cole Porter (*The Gay Divorcee, Anything Goes* and, more recently, *Kiss Me Kate*). Outstanding names in the presentation of M. C. include C. B. Cochran (1872–1951) in London, and Florenz Ziegfeld (1867–1932) and Earl Carroll (1893–1948) in New York. After the Second World War a new school of Amer. musicals brought a freshness and vitality to M. C. Among its features were revolutionary, inventive choreography and more realistic characterisation. The first musical of this type was Rodgers' and Hammerstein's *Oklahoma!* Subsequent productions included *Carousel, South Pacific, The King and I* (all by Rodgers and Hammerstein), *Annie Get Your Gun* (Irving Berlin) and *Guys and Dolls* (Frank Loesser). The enormously successful Amer. M. C. *My Fair Lady* (Frederick Loewe) was based on G. B. Shaw's *Pygmalion*. Brit. musicals of this period have generally aimed at a more ingenuous appeal (e.g.) Julian Slade's *Salad Days* and *Free as Air*); *The Boy Friend* (Sandy Wilson) was a gentle satire on the M. C.s of the 1920s.

Musical Glasses, *see* ARMONICA.

Musil, Robert (1880–1942), Austrian writer, *b.* Klagenfurt. Having studied both engineering and philosophy he wrote a thesis on Ernst Mach the philosopher-physicist for his doctorate, and his literary inclinations led him eventually to abandon his career as a civil servant in 1922 and seek his fortune as a full-time writer in Berlin. He returned to Austria to live in Vienna in 1933 but withdrew to Switzerland at the *Anschluss* in 1938. From the outset his novels bear witness to his philosophical background, as in *Die verirrungen des Zöglings Törless*, 1906; *Vereinigung*, 1911, and *Die Frauen*, 1924, but his masterpiece, which took him 20 years to complete, is *Der Mann ohne Eigenschaften*, which appeared in 3 vols., the first in 1931 and the last (a mere fragment) after his death. Its analytic exploration of the motivation and the subconscious mind of his characters is reminiscent of James Joyce, though in no way derivative. It was trans. into English as *The Man without Qualities*, 1960. M. also wrote two not very successful plays and some essays.

Musk (*Mimulus moschatus*): 1. Strong-smelling substance secreted in a gland by the musk deer (q.v.).

2. Small perennial plant of the family Scrophulariaceae, with hairy leaves and bright

yellow flowers. Some fine horticult. varieties have been introduced. These are best grown in pots trained on wire frames or in hanging baskets.

Musk, Artificial, substances known chemically as trinitro - dimethyl - tertiary - butyl-benzene (*Musk Xylol*), dinitro - methyl - tertiary - butyl - anisole (*M. Ambrette*), tertiary - butyl dinitro - dimethyl - acetophenone (*M. Ketone*), dinitro - tertiary - butyl - isopropyl - toluene (*Moskene*), Heptamethyl - Indene - Ketone (*Phantolid*). They are used in perfumery as cheap substitutes for natural M., which they closely resemble in odour. They have remarkable fixing and blending properties. Synthetic reproductions of the odorous principle of natural M. are *Exaltolide* (pentadecanolide) and *Ambrettolide* (lactone of hydroxy - hexadecenoic acid), possessing a strong and persistent M. odour. When used in traces as 'exalting' agents both render excellent services in finest perfumes and ambergris colognes. *See also* PERFUMERY.

MUSK

Musk Deer (*Moschus moschiferus*), native of the mountainous parts of central Asia, which yields the musk of commerce. It is a small animal about the size of a roe deer, 20 in. in height, with large ears, long legs and coarse, goat-like hair, which varies from a pale grey to a dark brown, spotted with tints of a lighter colour. It is of special interest to zoologists in that it possesses certain intermediate characteristics between the antelope and the deer, and it is now placed in a special subfamily, Moschinae, of the order Cervidae (q.v.). It is unique among deer in possessing a gall bladder, which is found in most of the antelopes. Antlers and horns are absent in both sexes, but, like the muntjac, the male has the upper canine teeth developed into projecting tusks 3 in. or more long. It is a solitary animal, feeding on leaves and flowers of forest shrubs. It is abnormally hardy and sure-footed on the most dangerous ground, being much assisted by the specialised development of the hoofs. Musk occurs as an unctuous secretion in a gland

beneath the skin of the abdomen of the adult male, the animals being captured and mercilessly killed by hunters. The freshly removed gland has a prevailing odour of uncured hide and the characteristic powerful and most tenacious musk odour develops on drying. The dried glands are known as 'pods' from which the dried secretion of reddish-brown to black colour is carefully removed and as 'musk grains' is one of the most indispensable raw materials used in luxury perfumes in form of alcoholic tincture, traces of which fortify and fix the basic odour, giving it a wonderfully diffusive and subtle 'animal note'. The finest quality of musk pods in commerce is known as 'Tonquin Musk' coming from Tibet and the high mts of the adjoining Chinese provs. The odorous product in musk (1 to 2 per cent) is known as Muscone; it was first isolated in 1906 by Walbaum and identified in 1926 by Ruzicka as being 3-methyl-cyclopentadecanone.

MUSK DEER

Musk Ox, or **Musk Sheep** (*Ovibos moschatus*), animal which, as the generic name implies, has features in common with the sheep and the ox. It is about the size of domestic cattle, and is covered with a dense coat of very long brown hair. The horns of the bulls meet in the middle line of the forehead. The legs are short, but the feet have a large spread, with a footprint much like a reindeer's, and the animals are capable of some speed. They are social in habit, and are now confined to NE. Canada, Greenland and some of the neighbouring is., though, at a remote period, they have had a very extensive range, which included Britain. At some seasons of the year they exhale a strong odour of musk, and this pervades the flesh, although it is well flavoured.

Musk Plants. The odour of musk occurs in a number of plants, besides the common musk. The musk mallow (*Malva moschata*) emits the odour when rubbed, especially in hot weather. The musk stork's bill (*Erodium moschatum*) smells strongly of it if handled; but the moschatel (*Adoxa moschatellina*) diffuses it from all parts of the plant except when bruised. The musk thistle (*Cardinus nutans*) has a powerful musky scent. The musk orchis (*Herminium monorchis*) smells like musk at night. A melon (*Cucurbita moschata*), the musk rose and the muskwood (*Olearia argophylla*) are among many other plants, etc., which give rise to the odour.

Musk Rat, name given to a number of rodents, and also to one insectivore, which diffuse a musky odour. It most commonly indicates the musquash (*Fiber zibethicus*). Allied to the voles and beavers, the musquash is found in Alaska and Canada. It is specialised for an aquatic life, the toes being webbed, and the long, almost naked tail being scaly and flattened laterally. The head and body together measure about 12 in. Though inclined to be omnivorous, it is chiefly vegetarian, and stores up food for the winter by plastering it with mud into curious structures like haycocks. The musk is secreted by both sexes in a large gland in the groin.

Musk Sheep, *see* MUSK OX.

Muskegon, city, co. seat of M. co., Michigan, U.S.A., on Lake Michigan at mouth of M. Riv., in resort area 35 m. NW. of Grand Rapids. It has oil wells and refineries and manufs. paper and leather products, aeroplanes, automobile and marine engines, billiard and pool tables and tools. Pop. 46,480.

Musket, *see* FIREARMS.

Musketry, military term applied to that branch of work which deals with the theory and practice and regulations concerning small arms, the rifle, carbine and revolver, and machine-guns (*see* FIRE-ARMS). The training in the use of weapons is graded from recruit drill, through various range and field practices, to special competitions. In view of recent large increases in the variety of infantry weapons the term 'weapon training' is now often substituted for 'musketry'.

Musketry, School of, *see* SMALL ARMS SCHOOL.

Muskhogean Language, division of American Indian languages, including Alibamu, Chickasaw, Choctaw, Creek, Natchez and Seminole. *See* NORTH AMERICAN NATIVE LANGUAGES.

Muskogee, city and the co. seat of M. co., Oklahoma, U.S.A., 45 m. SE. of Tulsa. It is the centre of an agric. and stock-raising region, and yields natural gas and oil. Its manufs. include road machinery, oil-well equipment, food products, vehicles, furniture, textiles and clothing. Pop. 38,060.

Muskoka, dist, riv. and lake of Ontario, Canada, on the E. of Georgian Bay. The first named has numerous lakes interlaced by streams, and is a popular resort for holiday-makers, summer cottagers and anglers. Bracebridge is the cap. The riv. rises in the Nipissing dist of Ontario and flows in a south-westerly direction, through the lake, into Georgian Bay. The lake is situated in the middle of the dist and communicates in the N. with Lake Rosseau. (*See Plate: Ontario.*)

Muslim Architecture and Art (otherwise known as Arab, Arabian, Islamic, Mahometan, Mohammedan, Moslem, Muhammadan, or Saracenic Art). 'Muslim', an Arabic word, is the term now usually adopted by scholars to describe the architecture produced by the Arab followers of the religion of Islam—i.e. Muslims—in many parts of the E. hemisphere after the prophet Mohammed estab. Islam in Arabia in the year AD 622, which is the first year of the Muslim calendar. This brief statement explains all the alternative names mentioned above, except 'Saracenic' which is really a nickname, like 'Whig' or 'Tory' or 'Quaker', and was introduced into English during the Middle Ages to describe the wild Arab warriors—'Saracens'—encountered by the Crusaders. 'Saracenic' was also applied by Wren (q.v.) to Gothic architecture; and modern scholarship recognises that his use of the term in that connection was not so absurd as it seemed to critics of a cent. ago, for many features of Gothic architecture (q.v.) are now attributed to the contacts made by the Crusaders with 'Saracenic' architecture, though the term is now discarded. Muslim architecture has therefore some significance in the hist. of European Gothic, but is even more important because it has been practised for 13 cents. by a large part of the human race as far N. as Turkestan and Yugoslavia, as far W. as Spain and Morocco, as far E. as China and Indonesia, as far S. as Zanzibar and Nigeria. There is a mosque for Malayan Muslims in Cape Town, and one for Eng. Muslims at Woking.

When the Arab armies, composed of uneduc. and uncultured soldiers, swept westwards from Arabia to Spain and even into central France within a cent. from the foundation of Islam, and eastwards as far as the frontiers of India and China, they had no domestic architecture of their own, for they were nomads, and their only dwellings were black camel-hair tents such as the modern Bedouin still use. Their first mosques (*see* MOSQUE) were rude enclosures for prayer. In each country that they captured, they utilised the services of local architects and craftsmen to build their mosques and—as they became settled and prosperous—their palaces and tombs. Thus distinctive regional schools of M. A. and A. grew up, each influenced by the local tradition. Existing buildings were often despoiled to provide material for mosques, and occasionally old buildings were incorporated in their structure. The following are the 5 chief regions: (i) *Syro-Egyptian*, including Syria and Egypt. The finest mosques, etc., all in stone, are to be seen in Cairo. Many Rom. columns and capitals were used in the earliest mosques there. At Jerusalem the famous 'Dome of the Rock' shows Byzantine influence. In 1517 the Turks conquered Egypt and interrupted the magnificent sequence of building which had continued uninterrupted in Cairo since the 9th cent. (ii) *Turkish*, in which the great Byzantine church of S. Sophia at Constantinople influenced the design of all the large mosques subsequently built there. (iii) *North African* or 'Moorish', comprising the modern countries of Tunis, Algeria, Morocco and most of Spain (*see* SPANISH ARCHITECTURE). (iv) *Persian*, including modern Iraq, where the earlier brick-vaulted buildings of the Sassanids influenced mosque construction. (v) *Indian* (*see* INDIAN ARCHITECTURE). India was invaded from Persia by the Muslims in 1193, when the city of Delhi was founded. Some of the earlier mosques closely resemble Persian examples; but as Hindu craftsmen were employed, a curious medley of design resulted, culminating in the splendid mosques, tombs and palaces built by the Mogul emperors during the 16th–17th cents., and constituting the 'Mogul' or 'Mughal' style. The mosque plan, with certain variations, was common to all the 5 regions, with its distinctive minarets. Domes were largely used, and the horse-shoe arch (*see* ARCH) became a distinctive feature everywhere. Ornamental lattices of stone, marble, wood and stucco were also used in window openings in all these countries, where the glare of the sun discouraged the use of ordinary glazed windows. Marble inlay and paving were also freely employed; and in Persia, where bare brick walls were considered unsightly, the anct craft of glazed tiling was revived, and spread into Syria and India.

All Muslim art is conventional in design, as the Muslim religion forbade the representation of animal or plant life or human portraiture. Some Muslim artists, however, broke away from this tradition, for leaves and flowers are to be found in Persian designs. In miniature painting also and in illuminated MSS. plant, animal and human forms appear, but never with the same freedom as, for instance, in Chinese paintings. The portrait in Muslim art is also conventionalised. Persian paintings are most notable for their combination of line and colour, while in the paintings of India it was as colourists that the Muslim artists most excelled. The flower design in Muslim ceramics derives from the early Persian period; the colours, design and glaze of this pottery are extremely harmonious. Examples of Muslim art as applied to weapons and armour are found especially in Turkey and Persia. The Turkish helmets were cone-shaped and beautifully engraved with arabesque designs with gold and silver decorations. Owing to the religious restrictions laid upon the arts, calligraphy was always a great source of design.

See H. Saladin and G. Migeon, *Manuel d'Art Musulmane*, 1907; P. Brown, *Indian Painting under the Moguls*, 1924; M. S. Briggs, *Muhammadan Architecture in Egypt and Palestine*, 1924; F Diez and II. Gluck, *Die Kunst des Islams*, 1925; T. W. Arnold, *Painting in Islam*, 1928; M. S. Dimand, *Handbook of Mohammedan Decorative Art*, 1930; V. Smith, *History of Fine Art in India and Ceylon*, 1930; K. A. C. Creswell, *Early Islamic Architecture*, 1932, *A Short Account of Early Muslim Architecture*, 1958; M. S. Briggs, chapters on Muslim architecture in T. W. Arnold, *The Legacy of Islam*, 1931, and in G. Garratt, *The Legacy of India*, 1937. (*See Plates*: *Muslim Architecture*; *Jerusalem*.)

Muslin, fine cotton cloth, said to have been first made at Mosul (q.v.), a city of Mesopotamia. It resembles gauze in appearance, except that it is woven plain without any twisting of the warp threads on the weft. Some very fine specimens have been produced in India, the Arni M. of the Madras prov. and the Dacca M., made at Dacca in Bengal, being especially famous. The material is now made in Europe and numerous varieties are produced. It is used for dresses, curtains, blinds, cushion-covers,, etc.

Musorgski, M. P., *see* MUSSORGSKY.

Muspratt, James (1793–1886), Irish manufacturing chemist and founder of the Brit. alkali industry, *b.* Dublin. After service in the Peninsular war and in the navy he began the manuf. of chemical products for commercial purposes. Starting in Ireland with the production of potassium ferrocyanide, he moved to Liverpool, setting up a plant to produce sulphuric acid and later sodium carbonate. Hydrochloric acid was recovered from the fumes by a process evolved by Wm Gossage. This was the beginning of the Brit. heavy chemical industry. His son. James Sheridan M. (1821–71), was also a distinguished chemist.

Musquash, *see* MUSK RAT.

Mussavat, Muslim democratic party in Russian Azerbaijan (*see* AZERBAIJAN), formed 1911–12 in Baku by a group of young intellectuals, many of whom had been closely associated with the local Bolshevik organisation during the revolution of 1905 (q.v.). It was at first pan-Islamic and advanced no specific demands for the Azerbaijani people. As a pro-Turkish party M. had to suspend open political activity during the First World War. After the Feb. revolution (q.v.) in 1917 it was the dominant party among the Muslims in Transcaucasia (q.v.) and later in the Azerbaijani Rep.

Mussel, name for various forms of mollusc, but most commonly applied to the numerous widely distributed Mytilidae. The common M. (*Mytilus edulis*), which forms the familiar wedge-shaped shell, is very abundant in Brit. estuaries. While young the M.s are capable of moving about with the aid of the small brown foot, but later they attach themselves to rocks and to one another by spinning a bundle of tough threads (*byssus*). Though they are even more liable than oysters to pollution, they are important articles of diet in many dists, but they are utilised in greater numbers as bait in deep-sea fisheries. The fresh-water mussels (Unionidae) are also numerous and widely distributed. The pearl M. occurs chiefly in Scottish rivs.

(*See illustration overleaf.*)

Mussel-picker, *see* OYSTER-CATCHER.

Musselburgh, tn and parl. burgh of Midlothian, Scotland, on the Firth of Forth, at the mouth of the Esk, 5 m. E. of Edinburgh, of which it has become practically a suburb. M. has extensive market gardens and manufs. nets, twine, paper, wire, etc. Here is Loretto School (q.v.). The tn is celebrated for its golf links. Pop. 17,592.

Musset, Louis Charles Alfred de (1810–57), Fr. poet, novelist and playwright, *b.* Paris. In 1829 he pub. his *Contes d'Espagne et d'Italie*. In 1830 his play *La nuit vénitienne* was produced but was

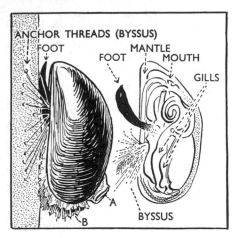

MUSSEL
A, exhalant siphon; B, inhalant siphon.

a failure. In 1833–4 appeared 2 series of dramatic comedies and poems for reading rather than acting, entitled *Un spectacle dans un fauteuil*. His poem *Rolla* was also written in 1833, at the beginning of his liaison with George Sand, whom he had met in the summer of that year. Later in the year he left with her for Italy, and returned alone shortly afterwards broken in health and spirit. The worst side of his moral character was brought out by his sufferings. George Sand gave her account of the catastrophe in a novel, *Elle et lui* (1859), to which M.'s brother, Paul, replied in his *Lui et elle*. The four *Nuits*—*de mai, de decembre, d'août* and *d'octobre* (poems)—reflect the bitterness of soul and disillusionment which ensued on the breach with George Sand and the ending of the romantic dreams of ideal love which they had founded on that relationship. In 1836 he produced an autobiographical novel *Confession d'un enfant du siècle*, which is of great interest in revealing the poet's complex character. During the next 5 years he pub. *Lettre à Lamartine*, the comedy *Il ne faut jurer de rien, Un Caprice*, some of the *Nouvelles*, the fragment *Le Poète déchu, A trente ans*, and the spirited poem *Le Rhin allemand*. His latter years were comparatively unproductive, his works including *Il faut qu'une porte soit ouverte ou fermée*; *Bettine* and *Carmosine*. Alfred de M. was, above all, a lyricist, whose one dominant theme was love in its varied manifestations. His later work is characterised by a melancholy which is preoccupied with the darker problems of life and ends by wooing a despair which sees in its bitter-sweet memories only the thing worth having experienced. *See* P. Gastinel, *Le Romantisme de Musset*, 1933; P. van Tieghem, *Musset, l'homme et l'œuvre*, 1945.

Mussolini, Benito Amilcare Andrea (1883–1945), 'Duce' or dictator of Italy; *b.* Varano di

Costa, by Dovia, com. of Predappio, prov. of Forli; elder son of Alessandro Gaspare M., a blacksmith and Socialist agitator, and a devoutly Catholic mother. M. attended an elementary school at Predappio, and, later, the Salesian school at Faenza. He completed his education at the Royal Normal School of Forlimpopoli, and was for a year a teacher at Gualteri, Reggio nel' Emilia. In 1902 he went to Switzerland and worked as a mason, translated, made revolutionary speeches and was arrested at Lausanne for vagrancy, but was befriended by Socialist organisations. In June 1903 he was expelled from the canton of Berne for revolutionary activities. He returned to Italy and served in a Bersaglieri regiment in 1905–6. At the end of his military service he took a post as a teacher of Fr. at Oneglia, near Genoa, and at the same time conducted atheistic propaganda in the local Socialist newspaper. In 1910 he founded *La lotta di classe* ('The Class Struggle'), a weekly paper, at Forli, using it as a vehicle for extreme Socialist and anti-clerical views. He suffered imprisonment for his articles, but at the end of 1910 he became secretary to the Socialist Society at Trent, then an Austrian possession. He voiced his inherent irredentism in the Socialist paper *Il Popolo* and was banished by the Austrian authorities (Oct. 1911). He then ed. the Socialist paper of Milan, *Avanti!* At the outbreak of the First World War he advocated neutrality, and his sudden conversion to intervention on the Allies' side resulted in his expulsion from the Socialist party at a congress in Milan (Nov. 1914).

This was the turning-point in his career. His old associates abandoned him; but M. was now the powerful owner and editor of a paper, for on 15 Nov. he had founded *Il Popolo d'Italia*, and through this he vehemently advocated It. participation in the fighting. When Italy declared war (May 1915) M. volunteered as a private soldier in the 11th Bersaglieri regiment. His service ended in 1917 when he was severely injured in a firing exercise. In Sept 1917 he resumed editorship of his paper, its chief use now being to combat pacifism, and for this he collaborated with the Fasci di Resistenza, or 'Unions of Resistance', organised for that purpose. With the war ended, the disorder in Italy favoured the growth of the strong counter-revolution M. had been preparing. He had decided to form his own political group and this subsequently adopted the name Fasci Italiani di Combattimento, the term 'Fasci' being already in familiar use. Thus on 23 Mar. 1919 the Fascismo institution was founded; its activities, which were directed by M., are recorded under FASCISM. By playing on the dangers of communism, M. soon acquired considerable passive, and some vital active, support from the It. industrialist class and from the self-employed middle classes. In spite of this his party only secured some 30 seats at the elections in 1921; but by Oct. 1922 his propaganda and shock tactics had reduced the country to such a state of tension that he felt ready to attempt his *coup d'état.* On 30 Oct. 1922 came the 'March on Rome', though M. himself took care to be ready to flee to Switzerland if it failed, and the march itself was a poorly-supported affair. But the bluff succeeded. Had the king agreed, the regular troops under Badoglio (q.v.) could have dispersed the Fascist march in a few minutes. In the result, however, the premier, Facta, resigned and M. formed a coalition ministry with himself as Prime Minister, foreign secretary and minister of the interior. The murder of Matteotti (q.v.), the Fascist gov.'s ablest critic, a few days after he had launched a brilliant attack in the Chamber on the Fascist chiefs, temporarily threatened M.'s political future; but the danger passed, and subsequent events were to show that his party secretary Farinacci was quite prepared to continue gangster methods on a still more thorough scale. M. himself escaped 3 attempts at assassination about this time (1925), but gradually he succeeded in transforming Italy into a totalitarian state with himself as dictator. The chief instruments in this process were the secret police and propaganda. M.'s remedy for Italy's unstable economic condition was to follow the path of economic self-sufficiency which inevitably led him to seek colonial expansion and eventually to embark on his aggressive policy against Ethiopia. In the first years of his regime, however, the majority of the It. people were probably satisfied with him. Administration was more efficient, industry apparently prospered, an ambitious and ostentatious programme of public works was begun, and Italy began to be regarded as a great power abroad.

M. soon deemed it politic to forget his atheism and to follow a policy of conciliation towards the Church. He even submitted privately to having his own marriage blessed by the Church. M. then embarked on a solution of the 50-year-old problem, the Rom. question, i.e. the problem of the relations between the State and the Vatican. The ensuing negotiation resulted in the Lateran Treaty and Concordat (Feb. 1929), by which the papacy gave up its claim to the former papal dominions, retaining unrestricted sovereignty over a small area of Rome thenceforth known as the Vatican City and receiving substantial compensation in cash and securities. M.'s dominant motive in concluding these accords with Pius XI was to bring the Church within the orbit and, as far as possible, the control of the totalitarian state, to enlist the support of the strongest and oldest force in the country, and to win the applause of Catholics all over the world.

To further his aggressive designs on Ethiopia, he replaced Grandi by his son-in-law, Count Ciano. He had gradually relegated his other rivals to obscurity. Thus de Vecchi was sent to the Dodecanese as governor. Balbo (q.v.) was conveniently removed before he could bring to maturity his project of granting Libya independence, and Badoglio was deprived of all influence in Fascist circles. M., always contemptuous of legislative assemblies and cabinet gov., not only assumed office as Prime Minister, but took over the 3 service ministries and the Ministry of the Interior, while putting the Foreign Office under the puppet Ciano.

Thus Italy's policy became essentially that of M. himself; but, with the rise of Hitler in Germany, he faced ever-increasing difficulties. Confronted with the alternative of giving up his aggressive dreams or supporting Hitler, he paid the heavy price involved in the latter choice. This included the abandonment of It. influence in Austria. By 1935 M.'s diplomatic position had weakened as a result of his Ethiopian policy, which had estranged both Great Britain and France. He had, however, successfully conquered Ethiopia for Italy, and so, in the eyes of his fellow countrymen, avenged the humiliation of Adowa 40 years earlier. M. now joined Hitler in supplying Franco with arms and men against the Sp. Republicans and so became a member of the Axis (q.v.) and a partner in the anti-Comintern Pact (q.v.). When therefore in 1938 Hitler actually marched into Austria, M. held aloof and, in the following year, the Berlin-Rome Axis became the so-called 'pact of steel'. In June 1940, with France approaching military collapse and the prospect of Great Britain's isolation, he declared war against both, hoping to secure a cheap reward in the appropriation of Tunis, Cannes and other portions of Fr. ter. However, in the course of the next 2 years he found himself at war with both Russia and the U.S.A. as well as with Britain, while the jealousy and ambition of Hitler, who soon became master of Italy after the It. debacle in Libya and Greece, precluded any possibility of Fr. spoils for Italy.

With the loss of It. E. Africa M.'s prestige began to wane even more sharply than before his visit to Salzburg, which involved sending It. troops to uphold Hitler in his anti-Communist crusade. The plight of Italy became aggravated in early 1943 with the threat of invasion. But with the fall of Tunisia the situation grew steadily worse. In Mar. Hitler demanded the aid of It. troops to relieve Ger. garrisons in France and the Balkans; but M. needed all his military strength at home now that he had lost one army in Africa, besides the better part of 10 divs. roughly handled on the Russian front. In July, with the allied invasion of Italy well under way, the It. military authorities called for massive Ger. aid as the only hope of saving the country. This new request drove Hitler to extreme recriminations against his fellow dictator, and the only course left to M. was to concentrate on defending the Po valley and to leave the rest of Italy to its fate. Soon after M.'s report to the Fascist Grand Council of the outcome of his meeting with Hitler, Grandi, with the support of Ciano, led a revolt against him, and a demand for M.'s resignation, expressed in Grandi's motion that the king be invited to assume command, was carried by 19 votes to 7. On 25 July M. was summoned to the royal palace, informed of his dismissal, and taken into custody as he left. His fall meant the end of the Fascist regime. The king took command of the army, Badoglio was entrusted with the formation of a new gov., and there was spontaneous rejoicing throughout Italy. M. was transferred eventually to a clinic on the Campo Imperatore, near Aquila, in the Abruzzi Mts. It was from here that he was carried off in a daring raid by a strong Ger. parachute force. M. in Nazi hands became, as was no doubt intended by Hitler, a potential rallying point for the endangered Fascists, who had everything to lose from a change of regime or an allied victory. M. set up a Fascist rep. in the N. of Italy and early in the ensuing year (1944) Ciano was tried by a Fascist tribunal for his part in the overthrow of his father-in-law and shot. But gradually, with the defeat of the Ger. armies in Italy, the partisans in the N. of Italy secured almost complete control of the situation, and M., now a sick man, tried to escape across the frontier into Switzerland. But he was betrayed to the partisans and arrested on 28 April 1945, and, together with some 12 members of his ex-Fascist Cabinet and his mistress, Clara Petacci, was executed by partisans, who carried the bodies of their victims to Milan for public display.

Though neither a deep nor original thinker, M. acquired a hold over the It. people by the guns of his illegal bodyguard, by the support of the army chiefs, big industrialists and land-owners, by the most unscrupulous propaganda, and by flamboyant oratory. As a political showman his only rival was Hitler. His personal vanity was almost boundless, yet he had intelligence and powers of leadership and could, on occasions, show streaks of unexpected sensitivity. Though in the first years of his dictatorship he appeared to confer many material benefits on Italy, his policy, from about 1935 onwards, in foreign affairs was disastrous and left his country materially devastated and spiritually exhausted.

There is a copious bibliography on M. and Fascism, and most books, being written either to extol or to condemn, must be read with reserve. *See* his *My Autobiography* (trans. by R. W. Child), 1928; G. Megaro, *Mussolini in the Making* (to 1914), 1928; H. Finer, *Mussolini's Italy*, 1935; Margherita Sarfatti, *The Life of Benito Mussolini* (with a preface by him; trans. by F. Whyte), 1936; J. A. R. Marriott, *Makers of Modern Italy*, 1937; G. Pini, *Official Life of Benito Mussolini* (trans. by L. Villari), 1939; I. Thomas, *Who Mussolini Is* (Oxford Pamphlets on World Affairs, No. 59), 1942; M. H. Macartney, *One Man Alone*, 1944, and *Memoirs of Mussolini, 1942–3*, 1946; P. Saperito (Eng. trans.), *The Fall of Mussolini*, 1948; M. Muggeridge (ed.), *Ciano's Diary*, 1947, and *Ciano's Diplomatic Papers*, 1948; R. Dombrowski, *Mussolini: Twilight and Fall*, 1956; C. Hibbert, *Benito Mussolini*, 1962. (*See Plate: Italy*.)

Mussooree, tn of Uttar Pradesh state, India, 130 m. NNW. of Rampur. Lying on the foothills below the Himalaya at about 6500 ft, M. is a very popular hot-weather resort. It is directly above Dehra Dun.

Mussorgsky, Modest Petrovich (1839–81),

Russian composer, *b*. Karevo, Pskov, was at first a guards officer. In 1857 he began to study music under Balakirev (q.v.) and in 1858 resigned his commission, becoming a civil servant. A sympathy with common folk led him to write realistic songs, following the inflections of their speech, and he endeavoured to do the same with his operatic characters, succeeding in completing one great operatic masterpiece, *Boris Godunov*, produced in 1874 and subsequently revised. All the others remained incomplete, but *The Marriage*, *Khovanshchina* and *Sorochintsy Fair* are performable in ed. versions. His life became more and more poverty-stricken; he took to drink, and *d*. from a spinal disease. The influence of folk-music upon his work was strong, especially in about 70 songs, the best of which are works of genius for character and atmosphere. His other best-known works are *Night on the Bare Mountain*, for orchestra, and the piano suite, *Pictures at an Exhibition*. See M. D. Calvocoressi (ed. by G. Abraham), *Mussorgsky* (Master Musicians), 1946. (*See Plate: Russian Music*.)

Mustapha Kemal, *see* ATATÜRK.

Mustard. The 2 M.s of importance are black M. (*Brassica* (*Sinapis*) *nigra*) and white M. (*B. (S.) alba*). The former is grown in Cambs and adjoining cos. for the production of seeds, which are ground, and after removal of the dark-coloured testas are used as a condiment or are converted into M. oil. The brown or Indian M. (which is not cultivated in Britain) may be used for the same purpose. White M. is one of the quickest maturing crops grown in Great Britain and is commonly grown as a forage crop or green manure. The white M. seedlings are commonly used in salads, and for the purpose should be sown 3 days after cress, with which M. is usually eaten.

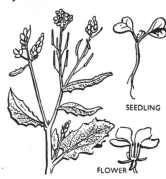

MUSTARD

Mustard Gas (dichloroethyl sulphide, $(CH_2Cl \cdot CH_2)_2S$, **Yperite, Yellow Cross**) was obtained by Richie, 1854, by the action of chlorine on ethyl sulphide. It was described by Guthrie, 1860, and prepared pure by Victor Meyer, 1886, by the action of ethylene chlorohydrin on sodium sulphide, followed by the action of hydrochloric acid. It was first used as a poison gas in the First World War by the Germans at Ypres, 12 July 1917. It was manuf. by the action of sulphur chloride, S_2Cl_2, on ethylene at 30° C. It is a light-yellow oily liquid boiling at 215° C. and solidifying at 14° C. It is a powerful vesicant (blister producer), and affects the eyes and respiratory tract after a period during which the effects are not obvious.

Mustique Island, see ST VINCENT.

Muswellbrook, tn on Hunter R., in New S. Wales, Australia, 179 m. NNW. of Sydney. There are good coal deposits; industries include dairying, sheep and cattle. Pop. 5717.

Mut. Egyptian mother goddess *par excellence*, represented as a vulture, and spouse of Amen-Ra of Thebes. She perhaps derived from Nekhbet, the vulture goddess of el Kab and guardian deity of a prehistoric kingdom of Upper Egypt.

Mutanabbi, Al-, Abu-'l-Tayyib Ahmed-ibn-Hosain (915–65), Arabic poet. He was the leading figure in a galaxy of Arabic men of letters who gathered at the court of Sayf ad-Dawla, at Aleppo, the N. Syrian school of poets. He developed the *qasida* form of poetry to its fullest, and had a great influence on the early development of Persian poetry as well. In the Arabic world he is regarded as one of the greatest poets. His name (Al-M. = 'would-be prophet') recalls an early escapade when he claimed to be a prophet.

Mutation, inheritable change in a characteristic of a plant or animal, by means of which evolution and the formation of new species are considered to take place. New species may arise through a large M. changing the characters very considerably, or through a succession of smaller M.s. M. is considered to be due to changes in the *genes* (q.v.); it has been produced artificially by the action of X-rays and other radiations, and by the chemicals colchicine and mustard oils. It is believed that in nature cosmic rays (q.v.) are important agents. See EVOLUTION; GENETICS; HEREDITY; VARIATION.

Mutator, mercury-vapour convector, which can be used as rectifier (q.v.) or for converting d.c. into single- or 3-phase a.c., or single- into 3- or 6-phase a.c.

Mutesa II, Sir Edward Frederick William Wulugembe Mutebi Luwangula (1924–), Ugandan ruler, educ. in Uganda and at Magdalene College, Cambridge. He became Kabaka of Buganda in 1939 and was crowned in 1942. In a dispute with the Brit. gov. M. was deposed, 1953, but reinstated 2 years later. In 1963 he became commander-in-chief and president of Uganda, duties taken over by Obote (q.v.) Feb. 1966. In May 1966 the Kabaka's palace at Kampala was stormed by Obote's troops. Kabaka was arrested and there was rioting throughout Buganda.

Mutina, anct tn of Gallia Cisalpina (*see* GALLIA), on a site adjacent to but not coincident with mod. Modena (q.v.). Originally a tn of the Boii, it became subject to Rome c. 212 BC and was made a colony. D. Brutus held it against Mark Antony in 44 BC. In the following year Octavian defeated Antony before M.

Mutiny, Indian, see INDIAN SUB-CONTINENT.

Mutiny Act. The first Mutiny Act, that of 1689, made it possible to keep a standing army in time of peace, not only by sanctioning its existence for the first time in England, but also by providing for the punishment of mutiny and desertion with death, and empowering the Crown to commission courts-martial to deal with those offences in time of peace. From 1689 Parliament passed the Mutiny Act annually until 1881, when it was finally superseded and merged in the Army Act of that year, an Act which is also annually renewed. The Jacobite Rebellion of 1715 made it necessary to increase the stringency of the Crown's disciplinary powers, and accordingly the Mutiny Act of 1715 authorised the Crown to formulate Articles of War to regulate generally the forces in the U.K. in time of peace. Prior to that year the Crown could issue such articles only in times of war or rebellion. Among other things, the later Mutiny Acts provided for the punishment by courts-martial of persons guilty of embezzling military or naval stores. See Sir C. G. Robertson, *Select Statutes, Cases and Documents illustrating English Constitutional History, 1660–1832* (7th ed.), 1936.

Mutsuhito (1852–1912), known as **Meiji Tenno,** 122nd Emperor of Japan, b. Kyoto. He succeeded his father Komei in Jan. 1867. The modernisation of Japan was his ruling ambition, and he travelled widely to convince his people of its necessity. He was an extremely popular emperor, whose death was regarded as the end of the Grand Era.

Mutton-bird, Australasian name for a shearwater or petrel used for food and valued for its oil and feathers. The sooty shearwater (*Puffinus griseus*) is the common M. of New Zealand and the short-tailed shearwater (*P. tennuirostris* or *brevicaudus*) that of Australia and Tasmania. The great-winged (*Pterodroma macroptera*), white-headed (*P. lessoni*), and Kermadec (*P. neglecta* or *phillipii*) petrels are also known as M.s. The origin of the name is uncertain. See W. B. Alexander, *Birds of the Ocean*, 1955, and W. R. B. Oliver, *New Zealand Birds*, 1955.

Muttra, see MATHURA.

Mutual Inductance, see COUPLED CIRCUITS.

Muyrca Language, see SOUTH AMERICAN NATIVE LANGUAGES.

Muziano, Girolamo (1528–92), It. painter, b. Aquafredda. He worked in Rome and his most famous picture, 'The Raising of Lazarus', was placed in the Quirinal Palace. The large fortune which he left was used to aid in founding the Academy of St Luke at Rome, where he *d*.

Muztagh, see KARAKORAM.

M.V.D., Russian abbreviation for Ministry of Internal Affairs, formed in 1946 by renaming the N.K.V.D. (q.v.). For a short period in 1953 the Ministry acquired great importance in the Soviet Union when it was fused after Stalin's death with the Ministry of State Security (*see* M.G.B.). In the struggle among Stalin's successors, Beria (q.v.), who was the head of the M.V.D., used its apparatus to strengthen his own position. Soon after his downfall the security service was again, in 1954, separated from the M.V.D. and placed under the K.G.B. (q.v.). The M.V.D. existed until 1960 at both union and rep. levels, and was mainly responsible for the militia, or ordinary police. From 1960 to 1962 it existed only at the republican level, and in 1962 it was renamed the Ministry for the Preservation of Public Order (M.O.O.P. in Russian abbreviation).

Mycelium, see FUNGI.

Mycenae, one of the oldest cities of anct Greece, dating from at least the third millennium BC, was situated in a very strong position on the hill overlooking the N. extremity of the Argive plain. In 468 BC M. was dismantled by the people of Argos, and never rebuilt. In the time of Pausanias the ruins consisted of a great part of the walls, with the so-called Lion Gate, the fountain called Perseia and the 'beehive' tombs. The discoveries which have been made here between 1876 and the present day have greatly increased the knowledge of Aegean culture (q.v.). See H. Schliemann, *Mycenae*, 1878; M. P. Nilsson, *Homer and Mycenae*, 1933, and *Minoan-Mycenaean Religion*, 1950; A. J. B. Wace, *Mycenae*, 1949; for an account of the language of the anct Mycenaeans, see M. Ventris and J. Chadwick, *Documents in Mycenaean Greek*, 1956. See also MINOAN SCRIPTS. (*See Plate: Mycenae.*)

Mycenaean Civilisation, see AEGEAN CULTURE.

Mycetozoa, see MYXOGASTRES.

Mycoderma, genus of fungi, some causing fermentation, such as *M. vini* in wines and *M. cerevisiae* in beer, forming a skin on the liquids. *M. aceti* of vinegar is now *Acetobacter aceti*.

Mycological Institute, see COMMONWEALTH MYCOLOGICAL INSTITUTE.

Mycology, branch of science dealing with fungi. The Commonwealth Mycological Institute (q.v.) at Kew co-ordinates information on plant diseases with the work on insect pests of the Commonwealth Institute of Entomology (q.v.) and that of the various imperial agric. bureaux located at research stations. The Mycological Institute is now under the control of the executive council of the Commonwealth Agric. Bureaux.

Mycorrhiza, association or symbiosis between the root-cells of a plant and the mycelium of a soil fungus by which both are benefited. It is important in many plants, including orchids, heaths, conifers, and many other trees and plants. See M. C. Rayner, *Tree and Toadstools*, 1946; M. C. Rayner and W. Neilson-Jones, *Problems of Tree Nutrition*, 1947.

Myelitis, inflammation of the spinal cord. The nature of the infection causing M. is not known, but it is probably most often due to a virus. There are 3 recognised forms: (1) *acute ascending M.*, rapidly progressive, febrile and causing ascending paralysis and anaesthesia; (2) *disseminated M.*, widespread and affecting the nerve tissue of the brain in addition to that of the spinal cord; and (3) *transverse M.*, a lesion right across the spinal cord at a certain level cha-

racterised by paralysis and anaesthesia below the level of the lesion and loss of control of the sphincters.

Myers, Frederic William Henry (1843–1901), Eng. essayist, poet and author, b. Keswick. M. was the leading spirit, with H. Sidgwick, R. Hodgson, R. Gurney and F. Podmore, in founding the Society for Psychical Research in 1882. His main works include *Catholic Thoughts*, 1873, *Essays Classical and Modern*, 1883, *Phantasms of the Living*, 1886, *Science and a Future Life*, 1893 and the posthumous *Human Personality and its Survival of Bodily Death* (2 vols.), 1903. His best-known poem is 'St Paul', 1867.

Myitkyina: 1. Most N. dist of Upper Burma, in Mandalay div. Indawgyi Lake is in the SW. Rice, timber and sugar are produced. Sparsely populated, it has an area of 10,640 sq. m. 2. Cap. of the dist and of the Kachin State, on the upper Irrawaddy at the limit of navigation. Terminus of the railway to Mandalay, it is also on the highway from NE. India into China and has a civil airport. There is an Intermediate Technical Institute. Lost to the Jap. invaders early in 1942, it became a main objective of the Allied counter-offensive and was finally recaptured in Aug. 1944. The pop. of 70,000 includes a number of Gurkhas. *See further under* BURMA, SECOND WORLD WAR, CAMPAIGNS IN.

Mykolayiv, see NICOLAYEV.

Mylae, see MILAZZO.

Mylitta, Babylonian goddess in Babylon, mentioned only by Herodotus and probably a reference to Ishtar or Astarte, goddess of love.

Mylonite, rock formed by the grinding and shearing of the rocks of the earth's crust under the forces of intense earth movements. The term M. was first introduced by Charles Lapworth to describe rocks ground down by movements in NW. Scotland.

Myna, or **Grackle,** genus of birds of the starling tribe, having dark-brown plumage with white markings on tail and wings. They are excellent mimics.

Mynyddislwyn, urb. dist of Monmouthshire, England, 13 m. from Newport and 7 m. from Pontypool. It is on the S. Wales coal-field, and has manufs. of switchgear, corsets and furniture. Pop. 15,433.

Myogen, see MYOSIN.

Myopia, or **Short-sight,** defect in vision due to a faulty structure of the eye. Parallel rays of light are brought to a focus in front of the retina owing to excessive length of the eye from the surface or the cornea and a too great convexity of the crystalline lens. Thus an indistinct image is thrown on the retina. This defect is corrected by the use of spectacles with concave lenses. The concavity of the lenses is adjusted so that parallel rays are focused on the retina as in ordinary vision. M. often has hereditary connections, and children of myopic parents should have regular examination of their eyes. *See under* REFRACTION, ERRORS OF.

Myosin. M. and Actin are the 2 prin. proteins of muscle. They may be readily coagulated by heat. They may form a reversible complex together known as actomyosin, which makes the muscle rigid. This is the cause of *rigor mortis*. In life, a substance, adenosinetriphosphate is present which acts as a plasticiser, but this will break down after death. *See* H. E. Huxley, 'The Contraction of Muscle' in *Scientific America*, Dec. 1965. *See also* MUSCLE.

Myosis, condition of the eye in which the pupil is abnormally contracted and lacks its power of accommodation. It may be produced by use of certain drugs, e.g. opium.

Myosotis, *see* FORGET-ME-NOT.

Myriapoda, class of arthropods which comprises the Chilopoda or centipedes and the Chilognatha (Diplopoda) or millipedes. The body is long and flattened or cylindrical, and the legs are numerous, though not so numerous as the popular names suggest. In their internal anatomy they resemble the Insecta, with which they have such other features in common as respiration by tracheal tubes and the possession of 2 antennae on the head, but the segmented body exhibits no distinction between the thorax and the abdomen, while wings are always absent. Their range is very extensive, and they live in dark places, as under stones, heaps of leaves, masonry and the bark of trees. Some possess powers of luminosity. The centipedes are always flattened and are characterised by a single pair of legs to each segment, the first pair being capable of inflicting poisonous wounds; they are all carnivorous. Millipedes live on vegetation, and apparently have 2 pairs of legs attached to each segment, but the segments are not perfectly separated; the bodies are round. Some foreign species attain a length of sev. inches. *See also* ARTHROPODA.

Myrica, family Myricaceae, genus of shrubs or trees of temperate or sub-tropical regions; often fragrant, with unisexual flowers. *M. gale* is the Bog Myrtle of Britain; *M. cerifera*, the Wax M., *M. california* and *m. pensylvanica*, bay-berries of N. America.

Myristica, tropical trees of the family Myristicaceae, yielding the nutmegs and mace of commerce, and oils and fats. *M. fragrans* yields the best nutmegs and mace, as well as an essential oil used in soap-making and perfumery. *M. officinalis,* of Java, Sumatra and Celebes, yields nutmeg or mace butter, used in pharmacy. *M. ocuba* of S. America is used for candleway.

Myrmidon, member of a legendary or semi-legendary race, originally inhabiting Aegina (*see* AEACUS). Many of the M.s followed Peleus (q.v.), father of Achilles to Phthiotis in Thessaly. In the *Iliad* Achilles himself is king of the M.s and their leader before Troy. Since the 17th cent. the word M. has been used in Eng. to denote a faithful follower; sometimes in the derogatory sense of a hired ruffian.

Myron, Gk sculptor of the 5th cent. BC, *b.* Eleutherae, on the borders of Boeotia and Attica. He worked almost exclusively in bronze, and was a late contemporary of Pheidias (q.v.); he made statues of the athletes Timanthes (456)

and Lycinus (448), excelling in the representation of movement. The 'Discobolus' at Rome is one of that city's most important statues because it is not, like so many others, a Rom. copy of a Gk original: if not the original work of M., it is at least a very early Gk copy. *See* P. E. Arias, *Mirone*, 1940.

Myrrh, the aromatic gum-resin of *Canarium* (*Balsamodendron*) *myrrha*, tree of Arabia and Ethiopia; used in incense, for perfumery and at one time in embalming.

Myrrhine Vases, *see* MURRHINE.

Myrrhis, Myrrh, or **Sweet Cicely,** small genus of umbelliferous perennial plants. *M. odorata*, a tall, aromatic plant with large tripinnate leaves and umbels of white flowers, is British, and was formerly much used as a pot herb and in salads. *See* MYRRH.

Myrtle, or *Myrtus*, genus of shrubs or trees with white fragrant axillary flowers and ornamental leaves, which are also fragrant. The common M. (*M. communis*) and its numerous varieties are hardy in mild sheltered positions. Its leaves are distilled to yield the perfume Eau d'ange.

Mysia, in anct geography, dist of NW. Asia Minor containing the Bronze-Age city of Troy (q.v.), as allies of which the Mysians occur in the *Iliad*. In historical times the prin. tns were Pergamum, Lampsacus, Abydos and Assos. M. was subject to the Lydian empire of Croesus, then to Persia, then to Alexander and the Seleucids until 190 BC, when the Romans added it to the kingdom of Pergamum. Finally, in 133 BC, with the rest of that kingdom, it was included in the Rom. prov. of Asia.

Mysore: 1. State of India, enlarged since 1956 to include the whole of the Kanara country and covering the former princely state of M. lying in the S. part of the Deccan plateau and along part of the W. Ghats, the Kanarese dists of Bombay and Madras lying along the W. coast, the Kanarese dists of the old state of Hyderabad in the Deccan and the hill state of Coorg. Most of the state is hilly or highland with an agreeable climate, save in the more arid regions obtained from Hyderabad; the coastal belt gets the full force of the SW. monsoon and a heavy rainfall.

History. In anct times M. was ruled by the Kadamba dynasty mentioned by Ptolemy. It was part of the great empire of Vijayanagar through the Middle Ages. In 1610 the Wadiya (chieftain) of Mysore seized Seringapatam and estab. the Hindu dynasty of Mysore. Haidar Ali usurped the throne in the mid 18th cent., his son Tipu Sultan was defeated in the last M. war, and Purnaiya, the Brahmin minister of the usurpers, reorganised the state for the old Hindu dynasty till the heir came of age. He did this very ably, but misrule by Krishnaraja Wadiyar led to Brit. intervention in 1831. M. was restored to a new representative of the Wadiyars in 1881 and developed under able diwans (ministers) to become India's model state, in many respects ahead even of the Brit. provs. M. had a form of representative gov. even before 1947. After Indian independence, M. became a member state of the union with the maharaja as rajpramukh (governor of princely rank). In the reorganisation of 1956 the state was enlarged to meet the demand of the Kanarese-speaking peoples for their own state, the maharaja becoming its governor.

Development. State and private enterprise had done much for M. in the past. It produced rice and ragi, oilseeds, cotton and other food crops; it had tea and coffee estates; and it was developing its quite considerable forest resources. It had a varied industrial development—textile works, silk filatures, tobacco factories, the main gold-field of India, engineering works, the first aircraft plant in India, iron and steel works at Bhadravati, manganese mines and a promising electrical industry. It had pioneered hydro-electric development in India, especially rural electrification, by means of big schemes like Sivasamudram and the Jog Falls. Four further big projects including 2 on the Tunga Bhadra R. are now operating. M. and Bangalore were models of city planning and improvement. Independence has seen progress maintained. India's state telephone works are at Bangalore. The new dists bring in wheat- and jowar-growing areas, a new gold industry from Hyderabad and most important, for the first time in modern times, a stretch of sea coast with promising ports at Karwar, Bhatkal, Mangalore and Malpe, and good fisheries.

Culture. Kanarese is the language of the great mass of the people. There are 3 univs. at M., Bangalore and Dharwar and the Indian Institute of Science at Bangalore.

Government. The governor acts through ministers responsible to an elected assembly of 208. There is also an upper house, the Legislative Council of 63 members. M. has 12 representatives in the Upper and 26 in the Lower House of India's parliament. The cap. is Bangalore (pop. 905,000). Other big tns are M. (pop. 254,000, *see* below), Hubli (pop. 171,000), Kolar Gold Fields (pop. 147,000) and Mangalore (pop. 143,000). Area 74,210 sq. m.; pop. 23,500,000.

2. Former cap. of the above state, situated 10 m. SW. of Seringapatam. It is a city of no particular architectural distinction, but graciously laid out with wide streets and spacious buildings. Situated at 2500 ft, M. is dominated by a long, precipitous hill, Chamundi, rising to 3500 ft, the top being reached by a good motor road. Part way up is a colossal figure, hewn out of the solid rock, of Nandi, the sacred bull of Shiva, *d.* 1659. M. being well lit by electricity, the view of it from the top by night is striking. It has long been known for its magnificent processions and festivities at the ann. Dasara festival. In the maharaja's palace is a fine throne of figwood overlaid with ivory, gold and silver in Hindu designs. Its origin is uncertain.

Mysore Thorn, *see* CAESALPINIA.

Mystagogue, person who in the Gk mystery religions supervised the preparation and instruction of those seeking initiation.

Mystery (Gk 'a secret'): 1. In Christian theology a truth which cannot be known by the human reason unaided by revelation, and which even when revealed transcends human comprehension, e.g. the Trinity, the Incarnation. The great M. of which St Paul speaks in Eph. i was the admission of the Gentiles to God's Israel, the Church—a divine purpose kept secret until Pentecost, though foretold in prophecy and in the teaching of Christ. The Christian Eucharist (q.v.) is frequently called the Holy Mysteries, partly because of its sacramental character and partly because in the early Church the unbaptised were not admitted to the whole of it. This is a sense of the word M. akin to the second meaning.

2. A doctrine and its accompanying rites kept secret from all but the initiates and having a saving if not immortalising effect upon them.

3. It is necessary to distinguish M. in these 2 senses from that derived from Lat. *ministerium*, It. *mestiere*, a trade or craft, and more properly spelled 'mistery' (whence M. plays (q.v.), those acted by trade guilds).

Among the Babylonians scholars detect a M. rite in the second sense in the pantomimes which illustrated the myth of Tammuz and Ishtar. It is, however, doubtful whether we have here a true M., since the doctrines inculcated by these rites were not themselves secret, and the rites purported to do no more than to solace the dead. The earliest M.s of which we have certain evidence, at least as early as 1875 BC, are those connected with the legend of Osiris in Egypt. In Greece certain public cults had secret rites attached to them, such as the Arrephoric and Thesmophoric festivals at Athens. But the prin. Gk M.s were the Eleusinian (*see* ELEUSINIA) and Adanian and those of the originally non-Hellenic Kabeiroi of Samothrace. These were local, whereas the more emotional and licentious Dionysiac and Orphic M.s were practised by societies which sprang up in various parts of the Hellenic world. In the 2nd cent. BC, on the break up of the Alexandrian Empire and the beginning of the Graeco-Rom. period, there was a revival of M. religions which exerted mutual influence upon one another. To this period belongs the cult of Mithras (*see* MITHRAISM) which appears to have made a particular appeal to the Rom. legions, who carried it with them wherever they went. The M. religions offered to their initiates salvation through communion with some saving deity. In Mithraism the initiate passed under a blood bath, streaming from a bull sacrificed overhead. Naturally little is known of initiatory rites; they included sacred lustrations and meals, but the attempt to detect any influence of them on Christian teaching or sacraments has failed. If there was influence, it seems to have been in the other direction. The initiation of a 'mystic' was followed by the enlightenment (*epopteia*) in which the doctrine was revealed by a solemn ritual which seems always to have included dancing. *See* F. Cumont, *Textes et monuments figurés relatifs aux mystères de Mithra*, 1896–9; R. Reitzenstein, *Die hellenischen Mysterien-religionen*,

1910; H. A. A. Kennedy, *St Paul and the Mystery Religions*, 1913; J. Leipolat, *Die Religion in der Umwelt der Urchristentums*, 1926; A. E. J. Rawlinson, *Essays Catholic and Critical*, 1926; O. Bauhofer, *Das Geheimnis der Zeiten*, 1935.

Mysticism (Gk *mustērion*, secret or hidden), belief in spiritual apprehension of truths beyond the understanding, can hardly be said to be either a philosophy or a doctrine. It may be said to be a tendency in religious feeling, a temper or an atmosphere. The starting point of M., and its goal, is that unity underlies diversity. So M. has been defined as an 'attitude of mind founded upon an intuitive or experienced conviction of unity, of oneness, of alikeness in all things'. M. leads to a belief that all things are manifestations of the divine life, and that the spirit is the only eternal thing, and, further, since unity underlies all, man has some share of the nature of God, and through this God-like part of him can apprehend God; for as through the intellect we apprehend material things, so through the soul can we apprehend the spiritual. Reason is not a part of M. According to M.we can only know a thing spiritually by *being* it, and therefore the aim of a mystic is to attain union with the divine, and life becomes one long aspiration, and reality or truth ever and ever deepens and expands. M. appears in Buddhism and Hinduism, and may be said to have arisen in Europe with Plato, although Plotinus, founder of Neo-Platonism, was the first great European mystic. Then came the Christian mystics of the Middle Ages, headed by St Augustine and the Syrian monk who ascribed his work to Dionysius the Areopagite, and the great Irish philosopher Scotus Erigena, who trans. Dionysius into Latin from the Greek. In the 12th and 13th cents. may be mentioned St Bernard of Clairvaux, Richard of St Victor and St Bonaventura and in the 14th cent. Richard Rolle, Walter Hilton, Julian of Norwich. John of Chur and Thomas à Kempis. The Christian M. evolved by these was based on the adoptive sonship of God attained by man through Christ the God-man. Christian M. is thus a deeper realisation of this supernatural unity of man with God through Christ which is finally consummated in the beatific vision. Later we find Paracelsus, Bruno, Campanella, Boehme, Schelling and Swedenborg. In England we have the Cambridge Platonists, including Henry More and John Smith, and later Will Law and Blake. *See also* CABBALA; QUIETISM; ROSICRUCIANS; THEOSOPHY; and the articles on the various religions and persons mentioned above. *See* W. R. Inge, *Christian Mysticism*, 1899, 1948, *Studies of English Mystics*, 1906, and *Mysticism in Religion*, 1947; C. F. E. Spurgeon, *Mysticism in English Literature*, 1913; R. Nicholson, *Mysticism in Islam*, 1921; E. C. Butler, *Western Mysticism*, 1922; F. von Hügel, *The Mystical Element of Religion*, 1923; Evelyn Underhill, *Mysticism*, 1924, 1952, and *The Mystic Way*, 1930; E. Brunner, *Die Mystik und das Wort*, 1924; J. H. Leuba, *Psychology of Religious Mysticism*, 1935; A. Hopkinson,

Mysticism Old and New, 1946; T. Merton, *Ascent of Truth*, 1951; J. H. M. Whiteman, *The Mystical Life*, 1961; D. Knowles, *The English Mystical Tradition*, 1961; Sister Sylvia Mary, *Pauline and Johannine Mysticism*, 1964.

Mytens, or **Meytens, Daniel** (1590–1642), Dutch portrait painter, *b*. The Hague, came to England and became portrait painter to Charles I. When Van Dyck was made the king's prin. portrait painter M. wished to go, but was prevailed upon by the king to stay until about 1635, when he returned to Holland. He painted portraits of many notable persons, including Charles I. (in Buckingham Palace), the Duke of Portland, the Earl of Craven, etc.

My-tho, cap. of M. prov., and a port, situated on l. b. of the N. branch of the R. Mekong (q.v.) delta in S. Vietnam (q.v.), 35 m. SSW. of Saigon. The prov. produces rice, coco-nuts, areca-nuts, betel, oranges, bananas, maize, tobacco and sugarcane.

Mythology (Gk *mythos, logos*, story-telling, or a rationale of stories): (1) imaginative traditions concerning the gods and other supernatural beings; (2) the study of these myths. M. is sometimes distinguished from legend as being entirely fictitious and imaginary, whereas legend is woven around an historical figure or nucleus: e.g. the tale of Troy and the Arthurian romances are legend, not M. The dividing line, however, is hard to draw, for myth and legend are often closely interwoven (cf. Santa Claus), and behind the purest myth there often lurks prehistoric truth. Indeed to become estab. a myth must first be widely accepted as true. The great myths are all deserving of respect if not reverence. They are poetic expressions of early man's profoundest intuitions about the universe and life. A M. indeed is to some extent a necessity as the background to a culture, and even to a reasonably satisfactory human life. Plato, while critically demolishing the anct Hellenic M., declared that the philosopher would have to invent other truer myths to take its place, and himself essayed the task, e.g. in *Timaeus, Phaedo* and the *Symposium*. Christianity (with Judaism), being an 'historical' religion, uniquely offers a *mythos* consisting of historical facts and events: but it too has its inspired M. of the poetic and theological and non-historical, non-factual kind, the stories of Creation, of Eden, of the Serpent, of the Trees of Knowledge and of Life, of the Rainbow, etc., M. then is not (as commonly supposed) confined to an early stage of society, for it still permeates our own, even in the form of non-Christian folklore, e.g. concerning fairies.

Plato was not the only one in anct times to criticise the M. of his day. The theories of Euhemerus (q.v.) on the subject were radically destructive and are still influential today, cf. Sykes, *Dictionary of Non-Classical Mythology*, 1952. In 1825 K. O. Muller (in *Prolegomena zu einer wissenschaftlichen Mythologie*) explained M. as a disease of language, the names of the gods merely expressing natural phenomena. It was not until the late 19th cent. that serious and respectful attention began to be paid to the comparison and elucidation of the world's mythological riches; Land and Frazer alike interpreted M. in terms of savage life and experience. W. Schmidt in his *Ursprung der Gottesidee*, 'Origin and Growth of Religion', 1931, admirably reviews the various theories advanced to account for the origin of religion and its M.

Myth in primitive societies. Much anthropological work has been done on M. among primitive peoples, where it is clear that myths have an important social function as providing a *raison d'être* for the society and its institutions (e.g. the distinction between chiefs and commoners, or the possession of land or magical powers by certain families, etc.). In this light the historical truth or otherwise of a myth is irrelevant, and questions about such matters are based on a misconception of the true nature of M. Indeed modern myths in W. societies have had the same function, as can be seen in the case of racialist M. in Nazi Germany and in S. Africa about the inferiority of Semitic or Negro peoples: M. provides a rationale for social behaviour without any necessary basis in scientific fact.

Classification of deities. The dieties of various M.s fall into well-defined classes. In all systems we have war-gods, water-gods, wind-gods, thunder- and lightning-gods, gods of agriculture and the chase, gods of death, and many other mythic conceptions. Many of the deities of certain systems combine 2 or more of these. We find war-gods who are also gods of agriculture, and wind-gods or thunder-gods who are gods of the chase. Deities of death often preside over agriculture; the seed arises from their subterranean domain.

Cosmogony. An important dept of M. deals with the primitive notion of the world and its creation, and the origin of man. The likeness between cosmological myths in all parts of the world is extraordinary, and cannot be accounted for by the theory of circulated or borrowed conceptions. *See also* COSMOGONY.

Celtic mythology can be gleaned from the remains of altars and images in France and England, and from the mythological tales of Wales and Ireland. Most of its gods, however, were tribal or local in character. In anct Gaul we find Ogmios equated by the Romans with Mercury; Borvo, Bellenos, Grannos and many more—all local gods—with Apollo. The martial Gauls had many warlike deities: Camulos, Albiorix, Caturix. Animal and nature gods abounded, e.g. Mullo, a mule-god, Vintius, a wind-god. 'Corn-mothers' were numerous and local, e.g. Berecyntia of Autun. In myths of Ireland we find supernatural races, such as the Fomorians, Firbolgs and Tuatha Dé Danann, which probably represent the pantheons of emigrant races. The most prominent Fomorians were Balor, a personification of the evil eye; Bres, the god of night, or perhaps of growth; and Domnan, a goddess of the depths of the earth. Of the Tuatha Dé Danann, 'the folk of the

goddess Danu', the prin. deities are Dagda, the most important of all Irish gods, probably an earth or agric. deity; Oengus, son of Dagda, a god of growth; Nuada 'of the Silver Hand', perhaps a harvest god; Manannan, god of the seas; and Lug, the sun-god. The prin. Brit. Celtic gods found in the Welsh *Mabinogi* and other myths were Llyr, god of the sea, and his sons, Bran and Manawyddan; Dôn, the equivalent of the Irish Danu; Gwydion, a Celtic Proteus; Arianrhod, an earth-goddess; and Govannon, a sort of Vulcan. In the Arthurian romances we find many mythological characters disguised.

Egyptian mythology shows up the primitive conceptions of totemism, animism and the like still surviving but with, superimposed upon them, the philosophical beliefs of a priestly class which has arrived at a higher theological capacity. Unable to impart their abstract beliefs to the ignorant, the priestly caste retained such of the early popular beliefs as seemed good to it, and employed them symbolically to inculcate higher religious thought. Herodotus explains that the apes and other animals kept in captivity by the Egyptian priests were in no wise regarded as idols, but as typifying the multifarious attributes of deity. The gods of Egypt were arranged in triads. Egypt was subdivided into nomes or provs., each of which possessed its triad of gods. Thus Osiris, Isis and Horus (qq.v.) at one time presided over a nome, but later, because of their popularity, became national gods. The myth of Osiris, his birth, reign and death, typifies the daily journey of the sun. His wife Isis and their son Horus lost all their original characteristics when interwoven with the Osiris myth. Nephthys (q.v.), sister to Isis, probably represents the sunset. She was wife to Set (q.v.), brother to Osiris and god of darkness, who finally triumphed over him. Wisdom was personified in the god Thoth (q.v.), called by the Greeks Hermes Trismegistos. Anubis (q.v.), or Anpu, god of the lower regions and patron of embalming, was figured with the head of a jackal. Bubastis (q.v.), the cat-headed, represented the heat of the sun. Besides these a large number of the kings of Egypt were deified. A vast and cumbrous ritual crystallised round this M., represented in the *Book of the Coming Forth by Day*, which deals with funerary practices. It is, in fact, a guide to the soul after death through Amenti, the sad underworld of the dead.

Myths of Greece and Rome may be considered together, as in many cases their deities are interchangeable. There is a well-defined pantheon ruled over by the sky-god, Zeus or Jupiter, who has supplanted an older generation of divine beings, and wields thunder and lightning. With his wife, Hera or Juno, he rules the other gods, many of whom are related to him. Hephaestus, the god of smiths, and Vulcan, the Rom. god of devouring flames, are the craftsmen or artificers—though Vulcan's surname Mulciber indicates rather a power of quelling conflagrations. Pallas Athene or Minerva presides over wisdom, but has also something of a martial character. Ares or Mars is the god of war. Aphrodite or Venus presides over love, and Hermes or Mercury acts as messenger between gods and men. Apollo is the god of song and art. Innumerable tales circle around these beings, tales which for beauty have never been equalled in any M. But the Greek mind speedily discerned the insubstantial nature of the system it had evolved, and early doubts were expressed concerning the existence of the gods. No M. ever reached such perfection or underwent such rapid collapse as that of Hellas. The M. of Rome, built by sterner and more conservative folk, held its own for a little longer, buttressed by the power of the state, but it too crumbled speedily before the advance of monotheism (q.v.). See individual articles on gods and myths.

Hindu mythology. The M. of the Aryan conquerors of India is polytheistic. The head of their pantheon is Brahma, whose leadership is frequently threatened by other powerful gods. The fullest account of the Hindu M. is to be found in the Vedic hymns. See HINDUISM.

Semitic mythology. In early Semitic M. polytheism displayed many of the features of totemism and animism. There was also a widely distributed system of pillar worship, and each 'high place' and mt possessed its special deity or ba'al. The religions of Babylonia and Assyria were wildly polytheistic, including gods which represented every attribute and phase of deity. In Babylonian myth we find a great triad, Anu, En-lil and Ea, at strife with darker deities, Apsu, Tiamat and Marduk. The title Bêl was given to all gods alike. Dagon was probably a corn god. One of the prin. Assyrian deities was Ishtar, wife of Marduk and goddess of love and fruitfulness. Ashur, the local god of the city of that name, became the head of the Assyrian pantheon and the national god of war. There were many smaller gods of only local significance. See also ASTARTE; COSMOGONY; ISRAEL; TAMMUZ; and individual names.

Teutonic mythology placed at the head of its pantheon Odin, or Wotan, the All-Father, who presided over the destinies of both gods and men. He possessed all the characteristics of a sun and sky god. His consort, Frigga, typified the Scandinavian matron and housewife. Thor was god of thunder, the Scandinavian Vulcan. Tyr was the sword-god and god of war, Loki the mischievous god of evil, Balder the graceful god of light and summer, whose myth typified the death of that season. The Scandinavians imagined that the *aesir*, or gods, dwelt in Asgard, at the top of the world-tree, Yggdrasil. Round this tree coiled the great world-snake. At its roots dwelt Hel, the dark goddess of death. In Midgard dwelt the race of men. But in the Norse conception even Asgard and its deities would not endure for ever. On the contrary, before the eyes of the gods there ever loomed a day of doom, when after the battle of Ragnarök they and the powers of evil would mutually destroy each other, darkness and chaos prevail, and a new heaven and earth be restored from the few human and divine survivors of the catastrophe.

See ASES or AESIR; BRAGI; BRUNHILDA; FREYJA; FRIGGA; LOKI; NIBELUNGS; VALKYRIES.

See F. M. Müller, *Contributions to the Science of Mythology*, 1897; E. A. W. Budge, *The Gods of the Egyptians*, 1904; Sir J. G. Frazer, *The Golden Bough*, 1907–15; L. H. Gray, J. Mac-Culloch and G. F. Moore (ed.), *Mythology of All Races*, 1916–32; E. Cassirer, *Sprache und Mythos*, 1925; J. E. Harrison, *Mythology*, 1925; B. Malinowski, *Myth in Primitive Psychology*, 1925; H. J. Rose, *Handbook of Greek Mythology*, 1928; W. Schmidt, *Ursprung der Gottesidee*, 1926–35; T. W. Rolleston, *Myths and Legends of the Celtic Race*, 1929; E. O. James, *Comparative Religion*, 1938; C. G. Jung and K. Kerény, *Einführung in das Wesen der Mythos*, 1941; E. Sykes, *Dictionary of Non-Classical Mythology*, 1952; T. A. Sebeok, *Myth*, 1955; J. Campbell, *The Masks of God*, 1959; E. Eliade, *The Myth of the Eternal Return*, 1955, and *Myths, Dreams and Mysteries*, 1960; H. A. Murray, *Myths and Mythmaking*, 1960; C. Levi-Strauss, *Structural Anthropology*, 1963; C. H. Long, *Alpha, the Myths of Creation*, 1963.

Mytilene (modern **Mytilini** or **Kastro**), in anct times, prin. city of Lesbos (q.v.), on the E. side of the is. An Aeolian settlement, M. became a great naval power and founded colonies on the coasts of Mysia and Thrace. Early in the 7th cent. BC a dispute as to possession of one such colony, Sigeum at the mouth of the Hellespont, led to war with Athens and weakened M. The is. became a member of the Delian League (q.v.) after the Persian wars (479 BC), but in 428 M. led the Lesbian revolt. Athens condemned the entire male pop. to death, but immediately reprieved them. Nevertheless more than 1000 prisoners were killed, the walls of M. were demolished and her fleet confiscated (427 BC). See Thucydides, iii. 1–50. M. was made a free city by Pompey at the request of his friend Theophanes, a native of the place. Mytilini is also the name of one of the 3 dists of Lesbos. Pop. 25,800.

Mytishchi, tn in the Moscow oblast of central Russia, industrial and residential suburb 12 m. N. of Moscow, with large engineering industry (lorries, underground coaches, laboratory equipment). The Moscow water works (built 1779) are here. Pop. (1965) 111,000 (17,000 in 1926).

Mytton Flags, series of rocks of Lower Ordovician age, occuring in Salop, England. They consist of thick shales or flags made of ashy material, with a few fossils, including trilobites. They are remarkable for their copious supply of zinc, lead and barytes, and some of the mines were worked by the Romans in Britain.

Myxoedema, metabolic disease caused by a decrease in function of the thyroid gland. This gland, which lies in front of the windpipe, is one of the ductless glands. Its function is the secretion of the hormone thyroxin, which speeds up metabolism, growth and mental activity. If the gland degenerates or is removed by operation a state of sluggish metabolism sets in, with depression of mental function. The body increases in bulk, and the subcutaneous tissue of the face and hands becomes infiltrated with a mucin-like substance, causing a swelling which does not pit on pressure. The mental processes become sluggish, the speech becomes halting, and there is marked loss of mental and physical energy. One of the characteristic symptoms is a total absence of sweating. M. is more common in women than men. The disease may run its course for many years with gradually increasing intellectual and physical incapacity. The connection of the disease with the loss of activity of the thyroid gland is demonstrated by the similarity of the symptoms to those of operative M., by the existence of cases in which the thyroid gland is shown to be atrophied and by the fact that administration of thyroid extract causes a marked improvement.

Myxogastres, Myxomycetes or **Mycetozoa,** class of widely distributed organisms numbering some 400 species. Some of them were known by the middle of the 19th cent. and were understood to be fungi. But the spores on germination, instead of producing germ tubes, give rise to amoeboid bodies; these have the power of spontaneous movement, and combine in a solid mass or plasmodium or vegetative condition which remains buried in the matrix or host until it creeps to the surface and produces its spores in a position whence the wind will disperse them. Most M. are saprophytes, and some creep over and suffocate seedlings, but a few are parasitic on cultivated plants and trees, causing such destructive diseases as finger-and-toe, corky scab of potato and crown gall. *See* FUNGI.

Myxomatosis, virus disease of rabbits, first known in 1898 when it almost wiped out the rabbits in a Montevideo laboratory. The symptoms are distinct, with marked swelling of the face and complete lethargy terminating in death. Early attempts to use M. as a method of eliminating rabbits were only partially successful, but one introduction in SE. Australia spread rapidly, killing four-fifths of the rabbit pop. and, it is estimated, increasing rural production by £50,000,000. In 1952 a Fr. doctor introduced the disease to his estate, but it spread beyond these confines and by 1954 had covered most of France. M. first occurred in Britain in 1953, but whether this was owing to a deliberate or accidental introduction is not known. The disease spread rapidly and this was facilitated by farmers releasing infected rabbits on their own properties. In Australia and France mosquitoes spread the disease, but in Great Britain the rabbit flea is the only likely vector. Although most rabbits are killed, those which escape become immune and breed freely; evidence of this is clear in Great Britain at the present time (1966), where, after an initial rapid fall in numbers, the rabbit pop. is steadily increasing again. The pop. of hares is also increasing owing to reduced competition from rabbits. Hares are little affected by the disease as they live above ground and are on the whole solitary, thus not catching fleas from rabbits or other hares to a great extent.

Myxomycetes. *see* MYXOGASTRES.